YALE LINGUISTIC SERIES

JAVANESE-ENGLISH DICTIONARY

Elinor Clark Horne

NEW HAVEN AND LONDON, YALE UNIVERSITY PRESS, 1974

Library of Congress catalog card number: 73–86900
International standard book number: 0–300–01689–1

Printed in the United States of America by
The Murray Printing Company, Forge Village, Massachusetts.

Published in Great Britain, Europe, and Africa by
Yale University Press, Ltd., London.
Distributed in Latin America by Kaiman & Polon,
Inc., New York City; in Australasia and Southeast
Asia by John Wiley & Sons Australasia Pty. Ltd.,
Sydney; in India by UBS Publishers' Distributors Pvt.,
Ltd., Delhi; in Japan by John Weatherhill, Inc., Tokyo.

This work was developed under a contract with the
U.S. Office of Education, Department of Health, Education,
and Welfare. However, the content does not necessarily
reflect the position or policy of that Agency, and no
official endorsement of these materials should be inferred.

CONTENTS

ACKNOWLEDGMENTS

This project was begun at Yale University under the Department of East and South Asian Languages and Literatures and concluded at Harvard University, Department of Linguistics. The research was pursuant to a contract with the U.S. Office of Education, Department of Health, Education, and Welfare, Institute of International Studies, under the provisions of Title VI, Section 602, NDEA. I wish to express my gratitude to the language specialists at the Office of Education for their interest and support throughout the project; to the administering officials at Yale and at Harvard; and to Karl Teeter, Calvert Watkins, and Einar Haugen of Harvard for their interest and help.

My debt to the earlier Javanese lexicographers is very great. E. M. Uhlenbeck's comprehensive bibliographical essay and bibliography of Javanese studies (in his *Critical Survey of Studies on the Languages of Java and Madura,* 's-Gravenhage, 1964, pp. 42–107) surveys the history of Javanese lexicography (as well as studies in language and literature). Of most immediate help in the present project were Th. Pigeaud's Javanese-Dutch dictionary (*Javaans-Nederlands Handwoordenboek,* Groningen-Batavia, 1938) and W. J. S. Poerwadarminta's monolingual Javanese dictionary (*Baoesastra Djawa,* Groningen-Batavia, 1939).

The Javanese grammatical terminology appearing among the dictionary entries comes from the two Javanese grammars Poerwadarminta, *Sarining Paramasastra Djawa* (Djakarta, 1953), and Antunsuhono, *Paramasastra Djawa,* vols. I and II (Djogjakarta, 1956).

As world interest in Southeast Asia grows, publications concerning the area proliferate. The bibliographies published by the Association for Asian Studies, listing books, articles, and theses and dissertations, grow bulkier with each issue. Scholarly studies on aspects of Javanese culture—works of the stature of Clifford Geertz's *The Religion of Java* (Glencoe, Illinois, The Free Press, 1960) and James R. Brandon's *On Thrones of Gold* (Cambridge, Massachusetts, Harvard University Press, 1970) provide deep insights into Javanese ways of thinking and feeling, without which it is not really possible to convey meanings of Javanese words adequately. Jeffrey Crockett has compiled a 144-page list, *Indonesia: Abbreviations and Acronyms Used in Indonesian Publications,* copyrighted in 1969 (in mimeographed form; the title page states that copies may be obtained from the author, 3750 Northampton Street, N.W., Washington, D.C. 20015, $5.00 postpaid). The items of this voluminous list are not duplicated by the dictionary entries herein.

The present project, from its conception, was strongly encouraged by Isidore Dyen of Yale University. Professor Dyen expended a great deal of time and effort helping to obtain funding for the project. He arranged for the assistance of the first two Javanese informants, who enabled the work to proceed through the initial two years, and later made further efforts to find others. It was he who suggested using computer assistance and, along with Fred Damerau, he consulted with me at length about use of the computer for lexicographical purposes and suggested the methods that were followed in compiling materials. He was unfailingly gracious in making his time, his resources, and his erudition available to me. Without his help, this dictionary would never have come into existence.

Rufus Hendon of Yale University generously made available the Javanese publications he had brought back from Java. At that time, up-to-date materials were difficult to find in this country. Clifford and Hildred Geertz permitted the use of oral materials (transcribed) that they had gathered in Java in connection with Thematic Apperception Tests administered there; this help is gratefully acknowledged. The computer programs used for processing the Javanese materials were Sydney Lamb's UNICON, for making concordances; UNICOUNT, for making word lists and frequency counts; and DISCIN, for indexing. It was my good fortune that Professor Lamb came to Yale about the time I began to process my Javanese materials and was willing to give me his personal help during my initiation into the exciting, exacting, and exasperating world of the computer user. Thomas V. O'Neill of the Yale Computer Center, with his considerable expertise, rendered help far beyond the mere call of duty when help was needed, and with unfailing good humor. John Echols of Cornell University was a friend in need whenever called upon: always encouraging and always helpful. I am particularly grateful to him for bringing me together with Mimi and Pandam Guritno during the final portion of the work. To Susan Horne I express my appreciation for loyal service to the project far beyond the scope of her duties as staff assistant. David Horne of the University Press of New England has made his professional assistance and advice (along with his encouragement and patience) available at all times.

Many Javanese consultants have set their mark upon the definitions. Each offered his or her unique contribution, and it is a great pity that it was necessary to limit the work of each group to the duration of their tenure in the United States. Sumitro L. S. Danuredjo and his wife Koos got the work under way at Yale and stayed with it through its transfer to Harvard. Siswojo Hardjodipuro and his wife Irmani and Muljanto Sumardi and his wife Sutji contributed their help while they were at Columbia University Teachers College; later on, Muljanto read and commented upon the entire manuscript. Throughout, the dictionary profited from Muljanto's and Siswojo's observations as students of linguistics. Harsono Ronohadiwidjojo, of Jogjakarta, did much valuable work while a student at the Harvard Business School and later. Harijono Djojodihardjo, while he was a student at M.I.T., and Mochtar Buchori and his wife Manah, while at Harvard, worked on the dictionary for a period that was all too brief, as did Dadang Sukandar. Sentanoe Kertanegara and Sukanto Reksohadiprodjo, of Jogjakarta, put in many hours of thorough and conscientious work while students at the Harvard Business School and later, and, between them, gave the entire manuscript a scrupulous final reading. During the final year of preparing the dictionary entries, I had the privilege of working with Mimi Guritno and, for the last few months, with her husband Pandam Guritno, during their most recent teaching and lecturing visit to the United States. Between them they read the entire manuscript in its final form and, in many hours of consultation, contributed numerous valuable clarifications, recommendations, and new information. To each of these friends and colleagues I express my humble thanks for their devotion to the project and their special contribution to the dictionary.

Necessarily, I myself made all final judgments on the content of the dictionary entries, after obtaining all the data I could gather, and I accept full responsibility for errors, inconsistencies, and other shortcomings. The compiler of a dictionary has many specific decisions to make regarding the content and format of the material; having chosen one alternative, he must reject conflicting ones. When a reader's judgment differs from the compiler's, it may well be that neither is faulty. It is my wish and hope that readers will communicate their comments and suggestions on the material and/or its presentation; for this I thank them in advance. *Panjaruwé saking para maos badé katampi kalijan senenging manah.*

E. C. H.

Hanover, New Hampshire
May 1973

INTRODUCTION

1. BACKGROUND

1.1. Purposes and Scope of the Dictionary

This work is intended to be a general-purpose dictionary of Javanese as it is now used by educated urban speakers from Central Java, the area of the standard language.

In Indonesia, these are transitional times. The birth dates of the Javanese who worked on the dictionary represent a span of less than a quarter of a century: the older among them, born during the long Dutch occupation, spent their early years under colonial rule and witnessed and participated in the struggle for independence, while the youngest were born into the atomic age and have known only the Java which is part of the Republic of Indonesia—a quite different environment. To speakers in the latter group, Javanese books published during the 1940's and even the early 1950's seem archaic in flavor and are peppered with words that are to them unfamiliar or obsolescent.

The changes in Indonesia are reflected linguistically in the daily juxtaposition of Javanese and Indonesian. Educated urban speakers use Indonesian alongside of Javanese as required by the occasion—mainly, in all official situations, or in social situations where non-Javanese Indonesians are present, or even with other Javanese whom they do not know well and hesitate to address in the socially stratified lexicon of Javanese. Nearly half (around 47 percent) of Indonesia's estimated 125 million population is Javanese; each language exerts continual influence on the other, and each inevitably infiltrates the other. Indonesian words appear in Javanese published materials. Any foreigner using a Javanese dictionary these days will also need to keep an Indonesian dictionary handy.

My practice here has been, in general, to include only a few commonly used Indonesian words which have largely replaced the corresponding Javanese word (also listed) or for which there is no separate Javanese lexical item, or which the Javanese use with Javanese affixation rather than Indonesian (*e.g.* **lengkap**). Conversely, an occasional Javanese word is shown with Indonesian affixation alongside its Javanese affixation (*e.g.* **pertimbangan** among the other forms of the root **timbang**). Technological and academic terminology is Indonesian, borrowed from Western languages for the most part, and I make no effort to duplicate the work of Indonesian lexicographers in that area, though strictly speaking such words are also Javanese. Higher education became available to Indonesians in their own languages only after their nation became politically independent in 1945, and the terminology borrowed into Indonesian—the language of secondary and higher education—has also become a part of each separate Indonesian language.

I have not endeavored to include more than a sprinkling of technical terms from such highly specialized fields as wayang, batik-making, and agriculture, nor esoteric and mystic terms used in astrological and chronogrammatic reckonings. English words whose meanings are obvious (*e.g.* **hèlikopter**) are also not included except in a few cases as examples of the Javanese tendency to assimilate new words into their morphological patterns (*e.g.* from **propaganda, mropaganda** *or* **mropagandakaké** to propagandize; from **aksi** action, **ngaksèkaké** to activate something). English-speaking readers quickly become accustomed to such equations as *Eng. -sion, -tion = Jav. -si* (*e.g.* **komposisi** composition) or *Eng. -tive = Jav. -tip, -tif* (*e.g.* **kréatip** creative).

"Regional" vocabulary—defined as words spoken outside the Central Javanese area—is represented by only a few items which are considered to be generally well known in Central Java. Research into the Javanese dialects is urgently needed, and it is hoped that reports on such work will soon become available. Such large-scale investigation has obviously been beyond the scope of the present project.

I have *not* intentionally omitted commonly used meanings of the lexical items in the dictionary, and I will be grateful to readers who point out meanings that I have overlooked.

1.2. Methods

Source materials for the dictionary consisted of two lists, representing the pre-Revolution and the post-Revolution lexicon. The first of these consisted of all entries contained in the two most recent Javanese dictionaries, those of Pigeaud and Poerwadarminta, published in 1938 and 1939 respectively. The second list came from a group of materials none of which came into existence earlier than the 1950's and the bulk of which originated during the 1960's. Consisting of (a) oral materials (monologues and dialogues) tape-recorded by Javanese speakers and (b) books and periodicals published in Java for the Javanese on a wide variety of subjects, these materials—totaling nearly a million words of running text—were processed by computer into concordances, and a master index to all of the concordances comprised the final list. At a rough estimate, the overlap of the two lists was perhaps around eighty-five percent.

Every word on both lists was examined by at least three Javanese speakers. Words no longer in common use—based on the evidence of the second (post-Revolution) list and the speakers' personal knowledge—were often dropped; and the second list and the live speakers have provided new words and new usages for old words. When differences of opinion arose, the word or meaning in question was generally accepted (after consultation with other speakers), since obviously one does not expect that every speaker will know every word and every meaning.

The audience one is addressing when compiling a dictionary of this sort is nebulous indeed in the view of the compiler. But my intention has been to include a broad enough lexical range to satisfy the needs of those requiring a non-specialized dictionary, and I have made the lexicon as up to date as I could manage.

2. PHONOLOGY AND SPELLING

2.1. Alphabetization

The Javanese material in this dictionary is spelled in the conventional Roman orthography.[1] The following alphabetical order is observed for the listing of citations:

a b c d/ḍ é/è/e f g h i j k l m n o p q r s t/ṭ u v w x y z

Entries are alphabetized without regard to marks or blank spaces intervening between letters within a citation: the circumfix **k(a)...(e)n**, for example, falls between **kaèk** and **kafir.** Digraphs and trigraphs are alphabetized according to their individual letters, without regard to their status as unit phonemes (2.2. below): for example, *tj* follows *ti*, initially or medially. Hyphenated entries and two-word entries are treated as single words. Diacritical marks (accents and subdots) are also disregarded except where citations are otherwise identical, and in such cases the order is as shown above. For example:

adeg *precedes* **aḍèg**
éntar *precedes* **enṭar**
gèḍèg *precedes* **geḍèg** *precedes* **geḍeg**
pèṭèk *precedes* **petèk** *precedes* **petek** *precedes* **peṭèk**
teng *precedes* **ṭèng**
tjèprèt *precedes* **tjèpret** *precedes* **tjeprèt**

1. On 17 August 1972—after the completion of this dictionary—the Indonesian government announced a new spelling system, to be adopted over a five-year transition period. The chief features affecting conventional Javanese orthography are that *dj* becomes *j*, *j* becomes *y*, and *tj* becomes *c*. (Also, *ch*—rarely used in Javanese—becomes *kh*.) Some examples:

Old	New	
djaran	*jaran*	horse
toja	*toya*	water (*Krama*)
njoba	*nyoba*	to try
tjukup	*cukup*	adequate
betjik	*becik*	good

The reason for this practice (rather, for example, than listing all *t*-initials together, separate from the *ṭ*-initials, thus observing both a phonemic grouping and the Javanese-script grouping) is the reader's convenience in interpreting written materials from which the Javanese tend to omit the accents and subdots: they know, after all, which sound to pronounce. The foreign reader coming across an unfamiliar word that begins with unmarked *d, e,* or *t* will not have to guess which kind of *d, e,* or *t* to look under first if they are all grouped together.

2.2. *Spelling and Pronunciation*

Conventional Javanese spelling, on the whole, reflects pronunciation accurately. The following list gives the nearest English equivalents to the sounds represented by the letters. (Phonemes are shown between slashes.)

	Approximate English equivalent	*Example*
/a/	(1) in non-final position: as in *father*	*bakal* material
	(2) in final position: as *aw* in *law*	*pira* how many?
/b/	as in *bay*	*bobot* weight
c	[*varies: individually marked in citations*]	
/d/	[dental *d: d* pronounced with tongue-tip touching inside of upper teeth]	*dadi* to be(come)
/ḍ/	as in *day*	*ḍaḍa* chest
/dj/	as *dz* in *adze* (but dental)	*djadjan* snack
/é/	as *a* in *date*	*mépé* to sun-dry
/è/	as in *set*	*djèdjèr* beside
/e/	as *u* in *cut*	*bener* correct
/f/	as in *fate* (or Javanized to *p* as in *pet*)	*fiksir* fixative
/g/	as in *get*	*geger* back
/h/	as in *hot*	*hawa* air
/i/	(1) as in *bit* in closed syllables[2]	*pait* bitter
	(2) as in *police* in open syllables[2]	*pari* rice plant
/j/	as *y* in *yet* (except in the digraphs *dj* and *tj*)	*jèn* if
/k/	(1) as in *hiker* (except when morpheme-final)	*kaku* stiff
	(2) [glottal stop[3] when morpheme-final]	*anak* offspring
/l/	as in *let*	*lali* to forget
/m/	as in *met*	*malem* night
/mb/	[as *b* with a quick *m* before it]	*mbajar* to pay
/n/	as in *net*	*nanas* pineapple
/nd/	[as Javanese *d* with a quick *n* before it]	*ndeleng* to see
/nḍ/	[as Javanese *ḍ* with a quick *n* before it]	*nḍas* head
/ndj/	[as *dz* with a quick *n* before it]	*ndjaluk* to ask for
/ng/	as in *hang*	*nganti* until
/ngg/	[as *g* in *get* with a quick *ng* before it]	*nggawa* to carry
/nj/	as *ny* in *canyon*	*menjanji* to sing
/o/	(1) as in *zero* in open syllables and in contiguous syllables the last of which is open	*karo* with; *loro* two
	(2) as in *bore* (ô)[4] in closed syllables and in contiguous syllables the last of which is closed	*lakôn* plot; *sôrôt* beam

---

2. A closed syllable ends in vowel-plus-consonant; an open syllable ends in a vowel.

3. *I.e.* closure of the glottis: the sound represented by a hyphen in the exclamation 'oh-oh!' and in 'huh-uh' (informal variant of 'no').

4. This symbol ô—which we use only in the Introduction—represents the same pronunciation as our symbol â (2.5 below); it enables us to retain the spelling *o* for purposes of the discussion.

/p/	as in *open*	*pupu* thigh
q	as Javanese *k*	*Quran* the Koran
/r/	rolled *r* (no English equivalent)	*rolikur* twenty-two
/s/	as in *set*	*usus* intestine
/t/	as in *later* (but dental: see *d* above)	*tutup* closed
/ṭ/	as in *later*	*ṭoṭolan* chicken feed
/tj/	as *ts* in *its* (but dental)	*tjatjah* number
/u/	(1) as in *blue* in open syllables	*guru* teacher
	(2) as in *put* in closed syllables	*bésuk* future
v	as *f* in *fate*; or Javanized to *p*	*vak* vocation
/w/	as in *wet* but with a *v*-ish spirantal quality	*wajang* puppet
x	as in *box, i.e.* as *ks*	*tèxtil* textile
/y/	(1) like a quick pronunciation of *i* in *audio*	*madya* middle
	(2) like Javanese *j* (spelling variant of *j*)	*kyai* [title]
z	[a breathy *s* sound]	*zèt* line of type

Phonemes not occurring initially: *k* as glottal stop, *y*.

Phonemes not occurring finally: *ḍ, dj, è,*[5] *j, mb, nd, nḍ, ndj, ngg, ṭ, tj, w, y.*

Final *e* is limited to foreign borrowings, *e.g. nasionalisme* nationalism, *voltase* voltage.

Final *ek* (*e* plus glottal stop), as in *plek* just like, *utek* brain, is extremely rare in standard Javanese, though common in regional speech.

2.3. Light and Heavy Consonants

Consonants *p, t, ṭ, tj, k̄* (not glottal stop) are LIGHT: sharp and clear, and without the strong aspiration of the English sounds. The corresponding phonemes *b, d, ḍ, dj, g* are HEAVY and have a murmured, breathy quality. *B, d, g* change to *p, t, k̄* in absolute final position. See also 2.9.1 below.

L also has a corresponding heavy variety, conventionally spelled either *l, lh,* or *hl. Z* is the heavy variety of *s;* it occurs in foreign borrowings and is sometimes spelled *s.* See also the symbol °, 2.5.

All vowel phonemes (*a, é, è, e, i, o, u*) after a heavy consonant have the characteristic breathy quality of the heavy consonants and are lowered in pitch.

2.4. Optional Sounds

Words having two forms, one with and one without an optional sound (parenthesized in the citation form), may have different pronunciations when the optional sound is present and absent, according to the pronunciation values listed in 2.2 above. For example, in final *-a(h), e.g.* in *gotra(h)*, the *a* is *â* when the *h* is absent and *ā* when the *h* is present. The pronunciation of *u* in *sekidu(l)* is different depending on whether or not the *l* is pronounced, *i.e.* whether the syllable is open or closed. In *senapan(g)*, final *n* alternates with final *ng.* And so on.

2.5. Pronunciation-Showing Diacritics

In cases where the conventional spelling is ambiguous or misleading with respect to the pronunciation as shown in 2.2 above, we show the word (in the citation form only) with certain diacritical marks which are not part of the conventional system but are unique to this dictionary. These devices serve to retain the conventional spelling for the citation. For some words even these markings are inadequate and the word is rewritten, *e.g.*: **punika** (*prn* **menika**); **teka 3** (*prn* **kok**).

	Approximate English equivalent or Description	*Example*
ā	as in *father* in final position, as contrasted with the normal *aw* pronunciation in this position	*orā* not

5. Though *è* sometimes appears in print for *é* at the end of a word.

â	as *aw* in non-final position, where *a* is normally *ah* (ā). Note that in words where we mark *any* non-final *a* as *â*, we also mark *all other â's* in the word, even the final one; unmarked *a*'s are then to be pronounced *ah* (ā)[6]	*lârâ* ill *danâwâ* ogre *kulâwargâ* family
ǵ	heavy velar spirant, like a murmured variety of *ch* in German *ach*	*antropologi̇́* anthropology
i:	as in *police* in closed syllables, where *i* is normally as in *bit*	*pri:t* tweet!
ḱ	as glottal stop elsewhere than in final position, *i.e.* where *k* is normally pronounced *k̄*	*mbaḱju* older sister
k̄	as Javanese *k, i.e.* as *k* in *hiker,* in morpheme-final position, where *k* is normally glottal stop	*batjek̄* soggy
u:	as in *salute* in closed syllables, where *u* is normally as in *put*	*bju:r* splash!
ʻ	represents a glottal stop where no symbol is conventionally used[7]	*saʻiki* now
˚	above a consonant makes a normally light consonant heavy	*s̊èt* chess move

2.5.1. Pronunciation of Final K

A morpheme-final *k* retains its isolated pronunciation regardless of what affixes follow it:

anaḱ offspring	*anaḱ·ku* my child
	anaḱ·é his/her child
	anaḱ·an interest on money
batjek̄	*ke·batjek̄·en* waterlogged

A morpheme-final *g* which is neutralized to *k̄* (see 2.9.1 below) likewise is *k̄* throughout.

2.5.2. Pronunciation Variations for I, U

Since the pronunciation of *i* and *u* depends on their position in a word, they are often pronounced differently within the same word, and since these pronunciations are automatic and regular, we do not mark them with the pronunciation-showing devices in citation forms:

miring (*mi:/ring*) slanting
timbil (*ti:/mbil*) sty
[contrast *ḍiri* (*ḍi:/ri:*) oneself]
durung (*du:/rung*) not yet
lungguh (*lu:/ngguh*) to sit
[contrast *guru* (*gu:/ru:*) teacher]

See also 3.1.6.1 for pronunciation changes in *i* and *u* before certain suffixes.

2.5.3. Pronunciation Changes for A

According to the regular rules, *a* in various positions may be pronounced differently within the

---

6. I am not sure that the occurrence of non-final â in the syllable preceding final open â is predictable in phonological terms, even given a detailed set of rules (compare *tjāhja* and *tjâkrâ*, for example). A single consonant intervening between penultimate *a* and final open *a* has *â* for both of these, *e.g. bâsâ, sângâ*; this is generally also the case with *a* in a penultimate syllable closed with a nasal consonant followed by a consonant-initial syllable ending in *a, e.g. nângkâ, tâmpâ,* unless the consonant after the nasal is not homorganic with it, *e.g. djānmâ, tānpâ.*

7. The Javanese use this symbol in written materials once in a while.

same word. Since these pronunciations are normal and automatic, we do not mark them in our citation forms:

warna (pronounced *wārnâ*) variety; color
nalika (pronounced *nālikâ*) when (something happened)

We mark final *â* only when some other non-final *a* or *a*'s in the word are pronounced *â:*

kâlâmânggâ spider
kulâwargâ family
upâdjiwâ livelihood

See also 3.1.6.1 below for changes of *â* to *ā* when suffixation changes final *a*'s to non-final *a*'s.

2.6. Spellings in Borrowed Words

In conventional Javanese usage, modern borrowed words are usually spelled as in the language from which they were borrowed. Older borrowings have been adapted to Javanese pronunciation in varying degrees. In our dictionary citations, the pronunciation of *c* is marked individually, since it varies according to the loan language. Most Arabic *ch*'s have been altered to *h* or *k* herein, in keeping with the most prevalent practice, and most Arabic *z*'s to *dj*. Other *z*'s may become *s* or *d* in Javanese. In words borrowed from Indonesian and from modern Western languages, we mark the *d*'s and *t*'s as *ḍ* and *ṭ*, and the *e*'s as *é* or *è*, in the citation forms to show how the Javanese pronounce them, but the words are not conventionally spelled with these markings. We regularize Dutch *oe* to *u*, in keeping with modern practice,[8] and similarly we represent Dutch *oo* as *u* (*e.g. setum,* from *setoom*) except in *oom* 'uncle,' which is apparently the only spelling used for this word.

2.7. Initial Clusters

The following consonant clusters occur initially in present-day Javanese:

b, g, h, k, ng, p plus *j* (or *y* as a variant of *j*);
b, d, dj, g, k, m, n, ng, nj, p, s, t, tj, w plus *l*;
b, d, ḍ, dj, g, k, m, n, ng, nj, p, s, t, ṭ, tj, w plus *r*.

The clusters *st* and *str* occur initially in the spellings of some borrowed words.

Consonant-plus-*w* clusters are formed when an initial consonant plus *uw* exercises its option of dropping the *u:*

b(u)wang, k(u)wasa, s(u)wara and its nasalized form *nj(u)wara.*

Clusters having *l* or *r* as the second member have free variants with *a* (informally, *e*) intervening:

nlangsa has variants *nalangsa, nelangsa;*
printah has variants *parintah, perintah.*

See also 2.9.3 below.

2.8. Syllables

A word has as many syllables as it has vowels. The minimum syllable is vowel (V) alone; the maximum is consonant (C)-C-V-C. (In loan words spelled with initial *str-*, three-consonant syllable initials occur.) The following syllable types occur, both in isolation and as parts of longer words:

Open	*Closed*
V *é* hey!	VC *ing* in, at, on
CV *si* [title]	CVC *nggon* place
CCV *dwi* two	CCVC *djrèng* cash

2.9. Variations in Spelling and in Pronunciation; Formality and Informality

The conventional orthography of Javanese is not standardized and seems to be becoming less so. Spelling is still taught in Javanese elementary schools, especially in Central and East Java, but

8. The spelling *oe* is still commonly retained in some personal names, especially of people born before the 1945 Revolution.

strict standards are not always adhered to. School reading materials in Javanese are in short supply. Javanese magazines–*Panjebar Semangat, Djajabaja, Kunthi* (= *Kunṭi*), and, in Jogjakarta, *Mekar Sari*–exercise a wide influence among adult readers, and these publications appear increasingly inclined to spell words as they are pronounced informally.

In our citation forms and subentries we generally show the more formal variant (when there is a choice): these fluctuate less. In examples we often use less formal variants.

Certain affixes have formal and informal variants. The former are often written but never spoken except in the most formal or literary usage:

Written form; formal spoken form	*Informal conversational form*
ka-	ke- (*except for the passive prefix* ka-, *which is always* ka-)
pa-	pe-
-(k̔)aké	-(k̔)ké
-um-	-em-

In *-an*-suffixed roots with an optionally reduplicated first syllable, the variant with the reduplicated syllable is more formal:

(*te*)·*ṭukul·an* vegetation — *ṭukulan* (less formal); *teṭukulan* (more formal)

In general, the Javanese informalize words by shortening them from the beginning. This is seen *e.g.* in personal nicknames (*Di* from *Pardi*), in forms of address (*Tjan* Tiger! from *matjan*), and in shortened compounds (*bulik* from *ibu tjilik* aunt; *ḍégus* from *geḍé bagus* tall and handsome).

Any word having the infix *-in-* is formal, and is usually confined to literary contexts; the corresponding informal (ordinary) form has the passive prefix *di-* instead of the infix.

Certain trisyllabic words begin with consonant-plus-*e*-plus-optional-*r*. The form without the *r* is less formal:

be(*r*)*kongkong* to stay put; to loaf
dje(*r*)*babah* extending sideways

When *a* varies with *e* in the first syllable, as it often does, the *e* is less formal (see also 2.9.2 below).

Punctuation, like spelling, in current Javanese practice is not altogether regular, *e.g.* in numbers with decimal points (the point is often a comma). The handling of compounds varies considerably: they are spelled sometimes as one word, sometimes as two, sometimes hyphenated.[9] Capitalization is generally as for Western usage (though not always followed consistently in some nonpersonal names). In this dictionary we observe the common practice of capitalizing the second or third member of the nasal cluster-phonemes of words coming first in a sentence: *mB, nD, nḌ, nDj, ngG.*

Commonly occurring spelling variations in modern use are shown below, along with explanations of which type of variation the user of this dictionary should expect to find words listed under. In this complex situation it is not easy to follow consistent principles. We have tried to straddle the fence between adhering too closely to older "correct" spellings (representing overliterary forms and pronunciations which some younger Javanese describe impatiently as old-fashioned) and choosing only the current spoken variations, a practice which would be difficult to maintain consistently. We regret having to complicate the task of a reader searching for a word among the entries; but once he has become used to the kinds of things he can expect, he should have little difficulty.

2.9.1. Heavy vs. Light Consonants

B, d, and *g* are pronounced as the corresponding light consonants *p, t,* and *k̄* respectively in final position and medially before another consonant:

9. This absence of clear borders is occasionally reflected in dual morphology. *Sur-tanah*, for example, has the nasalized active forms *nge·sur-tanah* (like a monosyllable compounded to another word) and *n̈j·sur-tanah* (*njur-tanah*) (as for a monomorphemic polysyllabic root).

absah *is pronounced* apsah;
padmi *is pronounced* patmi;
digdaja *is pronounced* dik̄daja.
sebab *is pronounced* sebap;
djogèd *is pronounced* djogèt;
ma·ṇḍeg *is pronounced* manḍek̄.

The current trend is for the heavy consonants to change to light in all contexts, even before vowels, so that the following forms are now the more common ones:

di·sebap·aké 'caused by' (*replacing* di·sebab·aké);
djogèt·é 'the dance' (*replacing* djogèd·é);
nge·ṇḍek̄·i 'to stop at' (*replacing* nge·ṇḍeg·i).

The modern practice leads in some cases to homonymy: *larab* and *larap*, for example, are falling together phonologically.

In this dictionary, we retain the heavy consonants in this type of word, since they still occur (though more often in writing than in speech). The change from heavy to light, as described above, is always predictable; but one could not predict which light consonants have recently become neutralized from heavy ones.

2.9.2. A vs. E

In the first syllable of polysyllabic words, *a* often varies with *e*: *e.g. kaṭoprak/keṭoprak, sangkala/sengkala, watara/wetara,* and *ka-/ke-* and *pa-/pe-* (prefixes). The form with *a* is more formal, being used in literary and official speech, lecture style, and so on.

When the *a–e* variation occurs in two-syllable words, we cite both forms as main entries, cross-referencing one to the other (*e.g.* **sabab** is listed as a formal variant of **sebab**, **pasṭi** of **pesṭi**). In longer words, we choose one form or the other, generally the more common spoken form *e* (but *a* in special circumstances, *e.g.* if the *a* belongs to a prefix, since we show affixes in the formal form in citations; or *a* if the word is one which occurs most often in literary or formal contexts, *e.g. baṭara* deity).

2.9.3. Initial Cluster vs. Initial Split Cluster

In words where variation occurs between initial cluster of consonant-plus-*l*/*r* and initial cluster split by *a* or *e* (*e.g. bl-* vs. *bal-, bel-*: see also 2.7 above), we spell the word with the cluster: *e.g.* we cite only **mlaṭi** (not the variant *malaṭi*). The reader should be on the lookout for this variation when he comes across words beginning with *bal-, ger-, sal-, tar-,* or any other such combination: if he fails to find his word in the dictionary, he should try again with the *a* or *e* deleted. (For example, *nalangsa* is a common spelling of the word we cite as **nlangsa**). The picture is further complicated by the fact that the first consonant of the cluster may be a nasal prefix either added to a root or replacing another consonant, *e.g.*:

malumpat (for *mlumpat,* from root *lumpat*);
mariksa (for *mriksa,* from root *priksa*);
nalutuh (for *nlutuh*, from root *tlutuh*);
ngalumpukaké (for *nglumpukaké,* from root *klumpuk*).

Once in a while, a word is treated phonologically as having a cluster but morphologically like a split-cluster form; this occurs with some loan words. For example, *klir* 'color' has the active form *ngelir* (rather than **ngeklir,* the expected form for monosyllables); *stabil* has the split-cluster active form *njetabil* 'to stabilize.'

And, an occasional split-cluster form is infixed (but these are usually literary usages only):

p·in·ariksa (from *pariksa,* from *priksa*);
s·in·arantèkaké (from *saranti,* from *sranti*).

2.9.4. Initial (W)l- and (W)r-

The modern trend is to drop the *w* from the initial clusters *wl-* and *wr-*, and so we cite such words most often under L and R (giving the *w*- form as a variant). In special cases, both are cited as main entries—the *w* form is listed when it remains in current use as the basis for derived forms, *e.g.* *(w)ragad* 'expense' has the locative form *mragadi* (from *wragad*) alongside of *ngragadi* (from *ragad*).

The *w* clusters, when they occur, are also subject to cluster-splitting, alone or affixed:

waringin is a common spelling for *(w)ringin;*
w·in·arangka is derived from *(w)rangka.*

2.9.5. *Addition of Vowel to Monosyllabic Root*

Consonant-initial roots which we cite as monosyllabic have disyllabic variants starting with *e*, in isolation or in affixed forms (the symbol * stands for a cited root: see below, 4.2, p. xxviii):

let has the variant *elet;*
mas[10] has the variant *emas;*
nom has the variant *enom* (or, more formally, *anom*);
ngrem has the variant *engrem;*
gèt has the variant *egèt:* in **nge/di*-*i**, read (*active*) *ngegèt-gèti* or *ngegèt-egèti;* (*passive*) *digèt-gèti* or *digèt-egèti* or *diegèt-gèti* or *diegèt-egèti*).

We make an exception and show initial *e* before the complex nasal phonemes or nasal clusters of a type which appear nowhere initially in the dictionary, *e.g.:*

embuh has the variant *mbuh;*
empun has the variant *mpun;*
endi has the variant *ndi;*
enḍas has the variant *nḍas;*
enggon has the variant *nggon.*

The *e*'s preceding this latter type of monosyllable are just as optional as the others described above, and the reader should keep in mind that under **enḍeg**, for example, **di*** stands for either *dienḍeg* or *dinḍeg;* that *dinggo* is a common passive form from **enggo**; that *nggon* will be cited as **enggon**; and so on. We help the reader along with this by including examples showing the form in the variation from the cited form.

Roots beginning with *uw-* often have a disyllabic variant with *uw-* and a monosyllabic variant with *w-*: *e.g.* *(u)wan, (u)wi, (u)wong.* We cite these usually under U, except in cases (like **wong** person) where the *w* variant is by far the more common one.

2.9.6. *Variation between -ER- and -RE-*

In many words, non-final syllables of the type consonant-plus-*er*-plus-consonant have a free variant with the *e* and the *r* reversed,[11] *e.g.:* *perlu* = *prelu;* *ngerti* = *ngreti;* *per-*, *mer-* (prefixes) = *pre-*, *mre-* (or, more formally, *pra-*, *mra-;* when the *pra-*, *mra-* forms occur, we cite them explicitly).

Our citation form for these words is the *ER* order: that is, we cite *e.g.* **perlu, ngerti.**

2.9.7. *Intervocalic J and W (or H)*

There is considerable variation between the presence or absence of an intervocalic *j* between a high front vowel and a lower and/or farther back vowel (see 3.1.8 below, *fn.* 10)—*e.g.* *pi(j)é, mi(j)arsa, si(j)ung*—and in the presence or absence of an intervocalic *w* between a high back vowel and a lower or farther-front vowel—*e.g.* *tu(w)a, djero(w)an.* A variation on this theme consists of dropping the first vowel and leaving the *j* or *w*, *e.g.* *p(i)jaji, b(u)wang.*

The general practice in citation forms in this dictionary is to include both of the vowels together with the intervocalic *j* or *w*—*e.g.* **pijon, guwa**—but we make exceptions to this when individual

---

10. *I.e.* *mas* meaning 'gold'—not *mas* which is the short form of *kamas.*

11. Not all words of this type are subject to the variation. *Sregep*, for example, is always *sregep.* When the *r* in this pattern represents the *-r-* infix, also, there is no reversed variant: *e.g.* *dj·r·eṭut* is always *djreṭut.* Infixed forms of this type are cited only as cross-references to the root form.

words are statistically far more commonly spelled in a particular way: for example, we list **buah** as the citation form rather than *buwah* or *bwah,* and **swara** in preference to *suara* and *suwara.*

The reader should also be on the lookout for the spelling *h* alternating with *w*, which occurs not infrequently in this type of word: *e.g. djohar/djowar, keduwung/keduhung, sinuhun/sinuwun.* See also 3.1.6.2 below for this type of spelling complication with the suffixes *-a* and *-an.*

2.9.8. O vs. A

When the letter *a* is pronounced *â*, it is often spelled with an *o* nowadays (we retain the *a* spellings here): *soko* (our *saka*), *tuwo* (our *tuwa*), *bongso* or *bongsa* (our *bangsa*), *tanpo* (our *tanpa*), and regularly in proper names (see the next-to-last paragraph on page vi above). Notice especially these *o* spellings before suffix *-a* following a word with final *â* where two *â*'s are pronounced in a row, *e.g. bisoa* (our *bisa·a*), *piroa* (our *pira·a*).

2.9.9. Doubled Consonants

Many Javanese nowadays write a doubled final consonant before suffix *-é, e.g. dolananné* (our *dolan·an·é*), *ḍèwèkké* (informal, *ḍèkké*) (our *ḍèwèké, ḍèké*).

Certain foreign borrowings are conventionally spelled with double consonants (as in the original language) where only one consonant is pronounced: *Allah* God; *massa* the masses. We retain some of these spellings (it would be odd to spell Allah with only one *l,* for example) but where both the doubled and the single consonant are in common use we cite the single-consonant form. *Ummat,* for example, will be found cited as **umat.**

2.9.10. K for Glottal Stop

There is a trend toward writing glottal stop as *k* in positions other than final (again, following the pronunciation), particularly with prefix *sa-*: *sak iki* (our *saiki,* cited as **sa'iki**); *sak durungé* (our *sadurungé*).

2.9.11. Ṭ and Ḍ

The sounds *ṭ* and *ḍ* are sometimes spelled *th* and *dh.* We always represent these sounds with the symbols *ṭ* and *ḍ.*

2.9.12. Optional Initial H

H is common initially in personal names but less common at the beginning of other words. When it does occur, it often has a more usual variant lacking the *h.* We cite under H some words which have common variants both with and without the *h.* If a word cannot be found under H, try again with the *h* removed.

2.9.13. OE.

The spelling *oe* is replaced by *u* herein, following modern usage; the older *oe* form is now seen mainly in personal names and in older and literary writings.

2.9.14. Diacritics

The Javanese know automatically how to pronounce an *e, t,* or *d* in a given word whether or not it has an accent mark or subdot; and so there is no point in their wasting time and ink putting them all in, except in formal or literary writings or for educational purposes. For the benefit of the foreigner, we cite words with their diacritics in place, but alphabetize them in with the unaccented and undotted words. (Users of Poerwadarminta's monolingual Javanese dictionary soon find that words there are alphabetized according to the system of the Javanese script, which separates accented *e*'s from unaccented ones, *ṭ*'s from *t*'s, and *ḍ*'s from *d*'s, along with various other differences.)

2.10. Conclusion

The foregoing sections deal with various ways in which Javanese words conceal their dictionary-citation forms through spelling practices. For a summary of the morphophonemic disguises words can assume, see 3.1.3–3.1.8 below.

3. SUMMARY OF JAVANESE MORPHOLOGY

Javanese words are either roots or derived forms. Derived forms are roots with affixes, or doubled or reduplicated roots with or without affixes. Affixed forms are prefixed, infixed, suffixed, or circumfixed. Sometimes an affix produces a derived root which is subject to further affixation, *e.g.* **piring** from **iring, panèn** from **ani, pinarak** from **parak.**

The grammatical terminology throughout is as used in Horne, *Beginning Javanese* (New Haven, Yale University Press, 1961).

3.1. Morphological Processes

1. Doubling;
2. Doubling with vowel change;
3. Reduplication;

Doubled and reduplicated roots, as well as plain roots, undergo processes 4–7:

4. Prefixation;
5. Circumfixation (simultaneous prefixing and suffixing);
6. Suffixation;
7. Infixation (insertion of an affix into a root);

A process unique to adjectives is:

8. Intensification.

These processes are described below. Since the affixes are all defined in the dictionary, they are not detailed here.

3.1.1. Doubled Roots

The symbol ² is conventionally used to show doublings. This symbol as used herein extends its range back to the nearest space or hyphen:

loro² is to be read *loro-loro;*
bal²an is to be read *bal-balan;*
di-entèn²i is to be read *dientèn-entèni.*

A raised dot, used herein to show morphological division, does not interrupt the range of the symbol ²:

m·uni² is to be read *muni-muni;*
ñj·sidji² is to be read *njidji-njidji* [for *ñj* see p. xxiii, *fn.* 7].

Nearly any root can be doubled, and doubling changes the meaning of a form in a great variety of ways. It would be wasteful indeed to list every possible doubled form of every root in a dictionary; doubling is a productive process and ought to have its own definition, as the affixes have, in this dictionary. Being a process rather than a word, it cannot be alphabetized among the other entries, and so it is comprehensively defined here. The reader will find specific meanings which apply to specific roots listed in the individual dictionary entries, and should infer the general meanings from the definition below.

DEFINITION OF DOUBLED FORMS:

- [= *doubled root*] **1** more than one [noun]; various kinds of [nouns]. *Anak^{2}é tansah diawat-awati.* She kept a constant eye on her children. *manuk^2 kang sabané ing banju* all kinds of water birds. *goḍong^{2}an* foliage. **2** [of adjectives] *referring to more than one noun. kéwan tjilik^2* small animals. **3** sth which is [adjective]. *Weruh jèn ana ireng^2 ana ing kamar.* He saw something black in the room. **4** even though (it is...). *Awan^2 kok turu!* You're sleeping in the daytime—!? *La wong ala^2 ija isih sedulurmu kok.* He may be no good but he's still your relative. *ketjut^2 seger* sour but refreshing. *Panas^2 ngéné arep lunga ngendi?* Where are you going on such a hot day (*i.e.* even though it's so hot)? *Golèkna pring aku, tjenḍak^{2}an ora dadi apa.* Get me a bamboo stalk—a short one will be all right. **5** excessively [adjective]. *Ngelak^2 tak ombéné banjuné.* I'm so thirsty! I'll have a drink of water. *Sambelé adja peḍes^2.* Don't make the sauce too hot! *Adja adoh^2.* Don't wander too far. **6** emphatically [so]. *Sing tjekak^2 baé.* Keep it brief! *Adja manèh^2 kanḍa ngono.* Never say that again. *Adja kanḍa^2 sapa^2 lho.* Don't tell anyone! *Malingé tjegat, lor^2 kono.* Catch the thief—there, to the *north! jèn ana wong kang wani^2 njeḍaki* if anyone *dares* come near it. **7** when, as soon as. *Tangi^2 nggolèki ibu.* When he woke up he looked around for his mother. *Panas^2 énaké ngombé ès.* When it's hot, iced drinks taste good. **8** [*or doubled affixed form*] let's. *Mangan^2.* Let's eat. *Mengko ḍisik lèrèn^2.* Let's take a break first. **9** [*or doubled affixed form*] to [do] only when...; to not [do] until... *Tangi^2 bareng ésuk.* He didn't get up till morning. *Metu^2 kuwi mbok mengko jèn wis mangan.* You can't go out till you've eaten. **10** [*or doubled affixed form*] (*with negative*) to not [do] within the expected time. *Wis suwé anggonku ngentèni, ning ḍèké ora teka^2.* I've waited a long time but he hasn't showed up. **11** [*or doubled affixed form*] to [do] repeatedly *or* at length; [plural subjects] do. *A lan B mèsem^2.* A and B smiled. *ngalok-aloki* to keep calling to smn. *Di-entèn^{2}i ora teka^2.* He waited and waited but she never showed up. *Tikus kuwi sing nalar^{2}aké lara pès.* RATS transmit plague. ***-*an** **1** object resembling [noun]; artificial *or* toy [noun]. *beḍil^{2}an* toy gun. *wong^{2}an* dummy; mannequin; scarecrow. *goḍong^{2}an* artificial leaves. *montor-mabur-montor-mabur* model airplane. **2** in [noun]s, by the [noun]. *rokok bos-bosan* cigarettes in cartons; cigarettes by the carton. **3** to use only [noun] as one's regular habit. *Aku nèk lunga mesṭi montor^{2}an.* Wherever I go, I go by car. *Wah, buku^{2}an terus ja kowé!* You're always studying! *Aku mangan daging^{2}an terus.* I eat meat regularly. *Aku nèk lunga mesṭi djas^{2}an.* I always wear a jacket when I go out. **4** to compare for [a quality]. *ḍuwur^{2}an* comparing them for height... *Étungé bener^{2}an.* Let's compare our arithmetic to see if we got it right. **5** to try to out[do] each other. *akèh^{2}an mangan* to see who can eat the most. *étung^{2}an* to try to outperform each other in arithmetic. *Ora ana gunané bener^{2}an, bareng^2 digarap.* There's no point in competing to see who is better—let's do it together. **6** in a certain manner. *Tjritakna tjenḍak^{2}an baé.* Make your story brief! **7** to [do] reciprocally. *antem^{2}an* to hit each other. *omong^{2}an* to converse. ***-*é** *or* ***-*ing** the [adjective]-est. *abot^{2}ing abot* the hardest thing of all. *Menawi tijang saweg nesu^{2}nipun...* When he was at his angriest... **ᵐng/di*-*(aké)**[1] to do one's best to [do]. *Ḍèké di-ḍongkèl^2 karo anḍahané.* His subordinates tried to oust him. *Opahané di-tjukup^2-aké kanggo urip wong loro.* He did all he could to make his earnings cover their living expenses. *See also 8, 9, 10, and 11 above.* **sa*-*é** **1** no matter [who, what, *etc.*]. *Sa-akèh^{2}é ḍuwité, isih akèh ḍuwitku.* However much money he has, I've got more. *Dolen sa-paju^{2}né waé.* Sell it for whatever you can get. **2** as [adjective] as possible. *sa-adil^{2}é* as fair(ly) as possible. *Diupakara sa-betjik^{2}é.* He was given the best possible care. *sa-bisa^{2}mu* to your utmost ability

A few roots occur *only* in doubled form: for example, *kiwir-kiwir* 'nearly severed'; *wéla-wéla* 'clear, distinct.'

When doubled roots are affixed, their vowels undergo the same regular sound changes as when single roots have the same affixes. These changes are described below in 3.1.5.4 (*Notes on the Chart, 5*), 3.1.6.1, and 3.1.6.2.

---

1. **ᵐng-** is the active morpheme, occurring phonologically as *nga-* (*nge-*, *ngu-*), *m*, *n*, *ng*, *nj*, or *φ* (zero). The active prefix is pronounced with both members of the doubled form (a) optionally if it is attached by adding and (b) necessarily if it is attached by replacing (see 3.1.5.4 below). It is pronounced only once in the form *nge- etc.* with monosyllabic roots. The passive prefix is pronounced only once, before the first member. *E.g.:*

under **ḍongkèl**: **n/di*-*** *would be* **nḍongkèl-(n)ḍongkèl** *acv*, **diḍongkèl-ḍongkèl** *psv;*
under **wegah**: **m̈/di*-*aké** *would be* **megah-megahaké** *acv*, **diwegah-wegahaké** *psv;*
under **kres**: **nge/di*-*** *would be* **ngekres-kres** *acv*, **dikres-kres** *psv*.

3.1.2. Vowel-Change Doubled Roots

Vowel-change doublings are doubled roots with the vowel(s) of the first member altered.[2] The last vowel becomes *a* and the next-to-last vowel becomes *o* (except that if the next-to-last vowel is *i, e,* or *u,* it does not change):

walik → *wolak-walik;*
bul → *bal-bul;*
bengok → *bengak-bengok.*

Open final *a* in the first member is pronounced *ā:*

n̈·tudju → *nudjā-nudju* [for *n̈* see p. xxiii, *fn.* 7];
wiri → *wirā-wiri;*
bali → *bolā-bali.*

Vowel-change doubled forms mean 'to [do] repeatedly, to keep [do]ing.'

3.1.3. Reduplicated Roots (Pseudo-Prefixation, Pseudo-Circumfixation)

A reduplicated root is a consonant-initial root prefixed with its own initial consonant plus *e: be·basa, n·dje·djaluk.* Some reduplicated roots simultaneously take a suffix *-an: te·tembung·an, le·laku·n̂ (lelakon).*

In literary, formal, or official style, the reduplicating syllable often has the first vowel of the root rather than *e: pa·prang·an, li·lipur, su·sutji.*

Reduplicated roots with the nasal prefix *ᵐng-* (below, 3.1.5.4) take the prefix only at the beginning if the prefix is added (*e.g. n·dje·djaluk*) and at the beginning of both syllables if it replaces (*e.g. m̈·pe·pudji*, pronounced *memudji*).

3.1.4. Prefixation

The following prefixes occur:

a-
ber-
m·bok- (variant of *kok-*)
dak- (variant of *tak-*)
di-
ka-
k(a)-, k(e)-
kok-
m- (form of *ᵐng-*)
ma-
m(e)-
me(r)-
n- (form of *ᵐng-*)
ng- (form of *ᵐng-*)
ᵐng- (with various phonological forms)
nga-, nge-, ngu- (forms of *ᵐng-*)
nj- (form of *ᵐng-*)
p(a)-, p(e)-
pe(r)-
pi-
pra-
sa-, sak-
tak-

These are grouped in the following sections according to their usage.

3.1.4.1. Prefixes Not Entering into Circumfixation

The following prefixes do not act as first members of circumfixes:

a-
ber-
ka- (number prefix)
ma-
m(e)- (root-activating prefix: pronounced *m* before *l, r,* or vowel; pronounced *me-* before consonant or monosyllabic root)

---

2. In this dictionary, all vowel-change doublings are listed under the second member, which in nearly every case is the root. **Kampul**, for example, is the root of **kompal-kampul**; **aṭik** is the root of **pangoṭak-aṭik**. In a handful of cases with root vowels *a*, it is the second member whose vowels change, *e.g.* **salah** is the root of **salah-sèlèh**; with these the second member is cross-referenced to the first.

me(r)-

ᵐng- in meanings other than active (see definition of the affix, page 393): the pronunciation is adjusted according to the root as described below (3.1.5.4)

pe(r)-

pi-

pra-

3.1.5. Remaining Prefixes

The remaining prefixes occur either alone or in combination with suffixes, forming circumfixation.

3.1.5.1. Prefixes Which Occur Alone or Form Circumfixes with Suffix -an

The prefixes in this category are:

k(a)-, informally *k(e)-*. The *a* (or *e*) of the suffix is pronounced before consonants and optionally before *l* and *r*: *ke·temu, k(e)laku·n̂, k·rungu, k·obong.* Variant in certain *w*-initial roots is *ku-*: *ku·wadjib·an.*

ᵐng- active prefix (see 3.1.5.4 below): *n·djaluk·an* 'always asking for things'; *n̈·trima·n* (*nriman*) 'tending to accept things as they come.'

p(a)-, informally *p(e)-*. The *a* (or *e*) is pronounced before consonants and optionally before *l* and *r*: *pa·nggon·an, p(a)·latar·an, p(a)radja, p·adat·an.*

3.1.5.2. Prefix Which Occurs Alone or Forms Circumfixes with Suffixes -an and -en:[3]

k(e)-. The *e* is pronounced as for *k(a)-*, *k(e)-* just above.[4]

3.1.5.3. Prefix Which Occurs Alone or Forms Circumfixes with Suffix -é:

sa- (pronounced *sa'* and often spelled *sak-* nowadays).

3.1.5.4. Prefixes Which Occur Alone or Form Causative and Locative Circumfixes: the Active and Passive Prefixes

The passive prefixes are:[5]

di- ng, dipun- kr [done] by him/her; [done] by someone.

ka- (formal and literary variant of *di-*, *dipun-*; added to roots without change, regardless of initial sound).

k(e)- (inadvertent passive prefix: see 3.1.5.2 above) accidentally [done] by someone *or* something.

tak- or *dak- ng, kula- kr* [done] by me.

kok- or *mbok- ng, sampéjan- kr, pandjenengan- ki* [done] by you.

The active prefix, morpheme *ᵐng-*, is pronounced variously according to the root it is used with.

1. *Nga-* or *nge-* before monosyllabic roots, or *ngu-* before *w*-initial monosyllabic roots (rarely and irregularly elsewhere[6]):

---

3. *K(e)-* alone is a passive prefix meaning '[done] inadvertently'; *k(e)-...an* circumfixation is the inadvertent variant of the *di...i* locative passive forms. *K(e)...en* circumfixation with adjectives means 'excessively [adjective].'

4. Before *w-*, *ke-* has the variant *ku-*, *e.g. ku·walik; ku·walah·an, ku·walah·en.* After *k-*, initial *i* and *u* in some roots change (sometimes optionally) to *é*/*è* and *o* respectively (indicated individually in the entries where the change takes place), *e.g.:*

ili → *kèli* to get carried on the current;
isis → *kisisan* or *késisan* to get blown by breezes;
udan → *kodanan* to get rained on (but *cf. ujuh* → *kujuhan* to get urinated on).

5. When we list a *di-* passive form in an entry, we imply that any other passive prefix would be used under appropriate circumstances.

6. *E.g. nge·wènèh·i* or *ng(u)·wènèh·i*, rare variants of *m̈·wènèh·i* (*mènèhi*). A *nga-* variant in a polysyllabic word is listed separately within the entry, *e.g. nga·botoh·an, nga·urip, nga·wonten·aken.*

nge·lih to move
nga·lor northward
ngu·wot to cross a narrow bridge

2. *M* before *b; m* replacing *f, p, w:*[7]
m·bajar to pay
m̈·foto (*moto*) to take a picture
m̈·pangan (*mangan*) to eat
m̈·watja (*matja*) to read

3. *N* before *d, ḍ, dj; n-* replacing *t, ṭ:*
n·deleng to see
n·ḍelik to hide
n·djarag to do unintentionally
n̈·tulis (*nulis*) to write
n̈·ṭoṭok (*noṭok*) to knock

4. *Ng* before *g, j, l, r,* and vowels; *ng* replacing *h, k:*
ng·gresah to complain
ng·jasa·kaké to build for someone
ng·liwet to boil rice
ng·rèwès to heed
ng·obong to burn
n̈g·hanḍuk·i (*nganḍuki*) to dry with a towel
n̈g·klotjop (*nglotjop*) to peel

5. *Nj* replacing *s, tj:*
n̈j·suda (*njuda*) to decrease
n̈j·tjaṭet (*njaṭet*) to take notes

6. *ϕ*, *i.e.* zero (no overt pronunciation) before *m, n, ng,* and *nj* and with a few roots having a *di-* passive form alongside an unprefixed active form:
ϕ/di·maling·i (*malingi* active, *dimalingi* passive) to rob someone
ϕ/di·nunut·i (*nunuti* active, *dinunuti* passive) to accompany someone as a passenger
ϕ/di·ngendika·k'aké (*ngendikakaké* active, *dingendikakaké* passive) to tell something
ϕ/di·njata·k'aké (*njatakaké* active, *dinjatakaké* passive) to verify
ϕ/di·pertjaja (*pertjaja* active, *dipertjaja* passive) to believe

The active and passive prefixes can be used with roots alone, *i.e.* without simultaneous suffixation; but the causative and locative suffixes occur only in conjunction with an active or passive prefix. Not all roots, by any means, take any of this affixation. Some roots take only the active prefix; of these, some have no other active or passive forms and others take causative and/or locative affixation in both active and passive forms. Other roots have both active and passive forms and may in addition have causative and/or locative forms. Only a small percentage of roots have all the possible forms.

The prefixed and circumfixed active and passive combinations are shown in the chart on the following page.[9]

---

7. In references we mark with an umlaut (¨) a nasal prefix that *replaces* the root-initial consonant.

8. This *nj* is nearly always in free variation with the older form *n* in roots containing a medial palatal sound (*dj, j, nj, s, tj*): *e.g.* from *tjatjah, n̈j·tjatjah·aké* (*njatjahaké*) or *n̈·tjatjah·aké* (*natjahaké*) 'to count up.' Where the older form is still the only common usage, it is spelled out in the entry, *e.g.* under **sanga**[b]: **pa·n̈∗n (panangan).**

9. In our dictionary entries we do not list all of these forms as subentries for roots. If a root has plain indicative active and passive forms, we list only these (in the format **^{m}ng/di∗**) as a subentry and imply by this listing that the root also has imperative, subjunctive, and optative indicatives. Similarly, an *-aké* or *-i* causative or locative subentry implies the other causative and locative forms as well. These implied forms, though not shown explicitly, sometimes appear in the examples.

	PLAIN	CAUSATIVE	LOCATIVE
INDICATIVE	^{m}ng/di*	^{m}ng/di*(k)aké _ng_, ^{m}ng/di*(k)aken _kr_	^{m}ng/di*(n)i. _Inadvertent psv:_ k(a)...(a)n
IMPERATIVE	^{m}ng/di*a; _or ng psv_ φ*(n)en	^{m}ng/φ*(k)na (_ng only_)	^{m}ng/φ*(n)ana (_ng only_)
SUBJUNCTIVE	^{m}ng/di*a	^{m}ng/φ*(k)na	^{m}ng/φ*(n)ana
OPTATIVE	(aku tak) ^{m}ng* _ng_, kula ^{m}ng*(n)ipun _kr_ (_acv_), tak *(n)é _ng_, kula *(n)ipun _kr_ (_psv_)	^{m}ng/tak*(k)né _ng_, ^{m}ng/kula*(k)aken _kr_	^{m}ng/tak*(n)ané _ng_, ^{m}ng/kula*(n)anipun _kr_

Notes on the Chart.

1. **^{m}ng/di...** indicates that *either* **^{m}ng-** *or* **di-** (or some other passive prefix) is used in a given form; with **^{m}ng-** the form is active, with **di-** passive.

2. φ here means a zero variant of **di-**, *i.e.* no prefix appears overtly.

3. Parenthesized *k* (= glottal stop) and *n* are inserted between root-final vowel and suffix: *e.g.* from *rasa, ng·rasa·k'·aké* and *ng·rasa·n·i.* Compare consonant-final roots, *e.g.* from *djupuk, n·djupuk'·aké* and *n·djupuk'·i.* Our symbolic notations *k̀, k̂, ǹ, n̂* (*i.e.* accents marked over the inserted *k*'s and *n*s) indicate a simultaneous change in the final vowel of the root, as described below (note 5 to the chart, pp. xxiv–xxv; 3.1.6.2, p. xxvi; and see also p. xxviii, 4.2 and *fn.* 7; 4.4, p. xxix).

4. Literary causatives and locatives can have the passive infix *-in-* in lieu of a passive prefix; in this case the locative suffix is -*(a)n*, as in the inadvertent passive locatives in *k(e)...(a)n* (above, 3.1.5.2). For example:

	Literary variant
di·djaluk·aké	dj·in·aluk·aké
di·lahir·aké	l·in·ahir·aké
di·djaluk·i	dj·in·aluk·an
di·tutup·i	t·in·utup·an

5. Before the causative and locative suffixes the following vowel changes take place.

Final *i* or *é* changes to *è:*

pati dead	*m̀·pati·k̀·aké* (*matèkaké*)
	m̀·pati·ǹ·i (*matèni*)
geḍé large	*ng·geḍé·k̀·aké* (*nggeḍèkaké*)
	ng·geḍé·ǹ·i (*nggeḍèni*)

Consecutive *é*'s both change:

kéré beggar	*-kèrè·k·aké*
lénḍé [root] *to lean*	*-lènḍè·n·i*

If the root is doubled, the changes occur in both members and the *k* or *n* is inserted after both members:

uni sound	*ng/di·uni·k̀-uni·k̀·aké* (*ng/di·unèk-unèkaké*)
	ng/di·uni·ǹ-uni·ǹ·i (*ng/di·unèn-unèni*)
kéné here	*di·kènè·k-kènè·k·aké*

Final *u* changes to *o* (pronounced *ô:* see p. xi, *fn.* 4, above) and—although the spelling does not reveal this—final *o* changes its pronunciation to *ô*, and final *â* (or two contiguous final *â*'s) change to *ā:*

laku action	*ng/di·laku·k̂ʻ·aké* (*ng/di·lakokaké*)
lebu to enter	*ng/di·lebu·n̂·i* (*ng/di·leboni*)
ngono like that	*ϕ/di·ngonô·kʻ·aké* (*ngonokaké, dingonokaké*)
pinḍo twice	*m̈/di·pinḍô·n·i* (*minḍoni, dipinḍoni*)
tekâ to come	*n̈/di·tekā·kʻ·aké* (*nekakaké, ditekakaké*)
kânḍâ to say	*n̈g/di·kānḍā·kʻ·aké* (*nganḍakaké, dikanḍakaké*)
râsâ to feel	*ng/di·rāsā·n·i* (*ngrasani, dirasani*)

In our subentry citations, the symbols *k̀ and ǹ* remind the reader of a spelled vowel change to *è*, and the symbols *k̂* and *n̂* act as reminders of a spelled vowel change to *o* (pronounced *ô*), as shown in the examples above.

3.1.6. Suffixation

The suffixes are as follows. Those marked with an asterisk are used only in circumfixes and are given in the chart on page xxiv.

* *-a* (imperative and subjunctive suffix)
* *-aké ng, -aken kr* (*-k̀aké, -k̀aken* after vowel) (causative suffix)
-an (*-n* or *-an* or *-nan* after vowel) (noun-forming, verb-forming, *etc.* suffix)
* *-ana* (*-nana* after vowel) (imperative and subjunctive locative suffix)
* *-ané ng, -anipun kr* (*-nané, -nanipun* after vowel) (optative locative suffix)
-é ng, -ipun kr (*-né, -nipun* after vowel) (possessive *etc.* suffix)
* *-é ng, -ipun kr* (*-né, -nipun* after vowel) (optative suffix)
-en (*-nen* after vowel) (suffix for physiological processes)
* *-en* (*-nen* after vowel) (passive imperative suffix)
* *-i* (*-ni* after vowel) (locative suffix)
-ing (*-ning* after vowel) (possessive *etc.* suffix)
-ku (first-person possessive suffix)
-mu (second-person possessive suffix)
* *-na* (*-k̀na* after vowel) (imperative and subjunctive causative suffix)
* *-né* (*k̀né* after vowel) (optative causative suffix)

3.1.6.1. Root Changes before Suffixes

Certain pronunciation changes which are not revealed by the conventional spelling result from the normal sound patterns of Javanese (as described above, pp. xi–xii) when suffixes are added to roots, as follows.

1. An *a* (pronounced *â*) at the end of a root, along with any contiguous preceding *â*, is pronounced *ā* when it is no longer final:

tekâ to come	*tekā·ku* my arrival
bâsâ language	*bāsā·mu* your language
médjâ table	*médjā·né* the table
lârâ ill	*lārā·nen* sickly
wâtjâ to read	*wātjā·nen* read it!
ânâ there is/are	*ng·ānā·kʻ·aké* to bring into being
tâmpâ to receive	*n̈·tāmpā·n·i* (*nampani*) to receive, accept

The exception is the suffix *-a*, which does not affect preceding *a*'s:

bisâ can	*bisâ·â* if one could
âdjâ don't!	*âdjâ·â* if it were not so
orā not	*orā·â* if not

2. An *i* or *u* in a final closed syllable (normally pronounced as in *bit* and *put* respectively) are pronounced *i:* and *u:* (as in *police* and *salute* respectively) before suffixes *-a*, *-an* (see 3.1.6.2 below), *-é, -en, -i* and the other locative suffixes, and *-ing*:

suffix -a	*ulih* → *m·uli:h·a* go home!
	atjung → *ng·atju:ng·a* raise your hand!

suffix -an	*éling* → *k·éli:ng·an* to remember
	wangsul → *wangsu:l·an* a reply
suffix -é	*pait* → *pai:t·é* the bitterness
	lawuh → *lawu:h·é* the rice-accompanying dishes
suffix -en	*pikir* → *piki:r·en* think about it!
	djupuk → *djupu:k·en* take it!
suffix -i	*salin* → *ñj·sali:n·i* (*njalini*) to change them
	→ *sali:n·ana* change it!
	tutup → *ñ·tutu:p·i* (*nutupi*) to close them
	→ *tutu:p·ana* close it!
suffix -ing	*kulit* → *kuli:t·ing djaran* horsehide
	ḍuwur → *sa·ḍuwu:r·ing médja* on the table

3.1.6.2. Root Changes with Suffix -an

When the post-vowel form *-n* or *-nan* of the suffix *-an* is attached to vowel-final roots, the same changes take place in the root as with suffixes *-k̒·aké* and *-n·i* (described on page xxiv, *Notes on the Chart, 5*):

legi sweet	*legi·ǹ* (*legèn*) sweet nectar
suwé long (in time)	*ke·suwé·ǹ* (*kesuwèn*) too long
gugu to believe	*gugu·n̂* (*gugon*) belief
pinḍo twice	*pinḍô·n* (*pinḍon*) redone
begdjâ luck	*ka·begdjā·n* (*kabegdjan*) luck
wâtjâ to read	*wātjā·n* (*watjan*) reading matter

In subentry citations we use the symbols *ǹ* and *n̂* to remind the reader that an *è* or *ô* (respectively) precedes the suffix in those cases where the conventional spelling shows the change.

In a final closed syllable, or in contiguous final syllables the second of which is closed, *è* optionally becomes *é:*

gonḍèl earrings	*gonḍél·an* to grip firmly
dlèwèr flowing	*dléwér·an* to flow

The intervocalic *j* and *w* described above (2.9.7, pp. xvii–xviii) often crop up in the conventional spelling of Javanese when suffix *-an* (and also suffix *-a*) combine with roots, as follows:

-i plus *-a* is often spelled *-ija: pati* → *ora patija* not especially
-i plus *-an* is often spelled *-ijan,* or esp. *-éjan: dadi* → *kedadéjan* consequence
-o plus *-an* is often spelled *-owan: djoḍo* → *djedjoḍowan* married
-u plus *-an* is often spelled *-uwan: tudju* → *tudjuwané* his destination

Moreover, when root-final *h* comes before suffix *-a* or *-an,* the *h* (which tends not to be pronounced between vowels in normal speech) is very often replaced in writing–following the pronunciation–by the same *j* or *w:*

karuh → *ora karu-karuwan* unimaginably

In this position, *-èh* often changes to *-é:*

akèh → *kakéjan* too much/many

By a reverse process, vowel-final roots may even insert an *h* before *-a* or *-an:*

bisa → *bisa·ha* if one were able
dadi → *kedadèhan, kedadéhan* consequence

3.1.7. Infixation

Infixes are inserted after the initial consonant, *e.g. gantung* → *g·um·antung.*
Javanese has the following infixes:

-em- (informal variant of *-um-*)
-in-
-l- (substituted for *-r-* infix in roots containing an *r, e.g.* from *gereng* → *g·l·ereng*
-r-

-u-
-um-
-w- (variant of *-u-*)

We list *-l-* and *-r-* infixed forms as main entries, cross-referenced to their root forms, since they are difficult to spot as infixed forms.

We do not list other infixed forms as main entries, but include them only as subentries under their roots, since one quickly becomes able to identify the infix in words that begin *bin-*, *gum-*, *etc.*: *e.g.* *t·in·imbang* from *timbang*, *s·em·ampir* from *sampir*, *d·um·egan* from *degan*, and so on.

-U- infixed forms are not even listed as subentries, since they are applicable to any adjective: see the definition of the infix.

3.1.8. Adjective Intensification

Any adjective can be made to mean 'extremely [so]' in informal speech by considerably lengthening the vowel of its last syllable and raising the pitch by perhaps half an octave or so (feminine voices may go higher). Adjectives are also intensified by lengthening (shown in the examples by a dash) plus changing the last vowel to a phonetically higher vowel:[10]

geḍé large	*geḍi–* huge, enormous
tjilik small	*tjili:–k* tiny
abang red	*abi:–ng* intensely red
dawa long	*dôwu–* extremely long

Adjectives ending in *k'* often change this to *k̄* when they are intensified:

kebak' full	*kebe–k̄* jammed full
meḍok' softened	*meḍu:–k̄* softened to a mush

The *-u-* infix (see definition, page 678) is a form of adjective intensification.

Intensification is in certain instances by specific vocabulary item:

putih white	*putih memplak* pure white
tjeṭa clear	*tjeṭa wéla*[2] crystal clear

We list as main entries (cross-referenced to their roots) only such intensified adjective forms as do not follow this pattern regularly, *e.g.* *sudi:k* from *sudi* 'willing and eager.'

4. THE DICTIONARY ENTRIES

4.1. Organization of the Entries

Each dictionary entry (other than cross-references) consists of a root[1] as citation form (whether or not it occurs as a free form) followed by its various derived forms and phrases, if any.[2] Roots having more than one social variant (below, 5, pp. xxxi–xxxiii) have multiple citations:

---

10. The following scheme shows relative heights of the vowel sounds, shown marked with our pronunciation-showing diacritics (2.5 above):

Front		*Back*
i:		u:
i		u
é		o
è	e	
		â = ô
	ā	

1. Many Javanese words that one hears and reads and wants to look up in the dictionary, however, appear in some form other than the root: the chief disguising elements are prefixes and infixes. Section 7 below has an alphabetic guide to such disguised forms, showing how to break down affixed words and giving references to the sections where the processes are described from the opposite point of view, namely how affixed forms are built up from roots. Each prefix, infix, and suffix is defined in the dictionary.

2. Derived roots (above, 3) are cited as main entries when they are subject to affixation in their derived form, *e.g.* **pinarak** from **parak**. In the case of a few very long and complicated words, a derived form is cited as a main entry, with a cross-reference to its root entry: see *e.g.* **mati**.

rasa *ng,* **raos** *kr*
irung *ng kr,* **grana** *ki*
djaluk *ng,* **teḍa** *kr,* **punḍut** *ki,* **suwun** *ka*

Krama (*kr*), Krama Inggil (*ki*), and Krama Anḍap (*ka*) variants appear also as separate main entries but only with short glosses. The Ngoko (*ng*) entry is the main one, the full definition; what is said there applies to all variants unless specifically excluded. For example, the definition for **abang** (p. 1) first shows all social variants (**abang** *ng,* **abrit** *kr*) and gives the shared glosses; it then shows the shared derived forms and special phrases. The separate definition for **abrit** (p. 2) simply reads **abrit** red, ripe (*kr for* ABANG), implying that full information is to be found at the **abang** definition. (This practice avoids unnecessary duplication of material. When, on the other hand, a non-Ngoko word is not adaptable to such handling, complete entries are provided: see, for example, the definitions of **kula**, p. 312, and **suwun**, p. 581). Similarly, **raos** feel; taste (*kr for* RASA) gives quick-reference glosses showing that in both the meanings 'feel' and 'taste' **raos** is Krama for **rasa**. In the infrequent cases where there are different meanings in different social styles for the same word, these are separated into numbered glosses: *e.g.* **malih 1** to change.... [unmarked, hence neutral]. 2 again, more (*kr for* MANÈH). When part of an entry has a different distribution of social variants than as cited, this is specified at that point.[3]

Each entry is organized as follows (not all forms occur for all roots):

1. Root;
2. Suffixed root (alphabetized by suffix);
3. Doubled root (unsuffixed; suffixed; with second member affixed, alphabetically by affix);
4. Doubled root with vowel change;
5. Reduplicated root[4] (unsuffixed; suffixed);
6. Prefixed root, alphabetized by prefix:[5] for each prefix, single root, then doubled root, then reduplicated root, then circumfixed forms alphabetized by suffix;
7. Infixed root;
8. Phrases containing the root form as first member;[6]
9. Cross-references, alphabetized by root.

Homonyms are grouped as single entries unless it is preferable to separate them for clarity or for simplicity of listing, as for example with **aku**[a] and **aku**[b], which have different Krama equivalents, or with **ing**[a], **ing-**[b], and **-ing**[c], which are preposition, prefix, and suffix respectively.

*4.2. The Symbol **

The symbol * in a subentry stands for the citation form as it appears at the beginning of the

3. For example, see **tutug**, which has different Krama equivalents in different subentries; see also the *ki* forms listed here and there under **adeg**. Within an entry that has Ngoko and Krama citation forms, the notation *ng kr* with a subentry citation shows that the Ngoko word is socially neutral, *i.e.* the Krama word is not used in that meaning. For example, under **ujah** *ng,* **sarem** *kr* –

***-*an 1** salted... 2 *ng kr* a certain leaf used medicinally

means that in the sense 'salted' the form ***-*an** is to be interpreted as **ujah-ujahan** *ng,* **sarem-sareman** *kr,* whereas in the meaning 'a certain leaf used medicinally' the form **ujah-ujahan** serves as both Ngoko and Krama. Under **urip**, which has the Krama equivalent **gesang** in some forms, the notation *ng kr* shows which forms **gesang** is NOT the Krama for. (Also under **urip**, only two of the five meanings have a Krama Inggil form to correspond, and this is marked individually for each.)

4. Note that whereas all other subentries within an entry appear in a fixed alphabetical order according to the affixed form, a reduplication subentry—which has the appearance of a prefixed form—looks out of alphabetical order in all cases where the initial (reduplicating) consonant of the root happens to come later in the alphabet than the initial letter of the first prefixed form listed. For example, under **wudjud**, the reduplicated form **we*an** precedes the prefixed form **a***.

5. Passive forms (listed as **di***, which stands for the root preceded by *any* passive prefix) are alphabetized under **di-** only when they have no corresponding active form or when the passive meaning is not predictable from the active glossing (see, *e.g.*, under **weḍi**, the separate subentries **di*** and **m̃***). Other than these, passives are grouped with their corresponding actives in the **ᵐng/di*** format. See also 4.9 below for interpretation of the glossings.

6. Or as second member when the first word is a function word like *ora* 'not,' or when the root form occurs unaffixed only in phrases (as with **tulis**, for example). Phrases using an affixed form rather than the bare root are listed under that affixed form.

entry.[7] When there is more than one citation form, * stands for both (all) of them unless specifically excluded. (Within example phrases and sentences, * stands for the Ngoko citation only; in non-Ngoko examples, the citation form is spelled out.)

4.3. Active-Passive subentries

A subentry in the form **^{m}ng/di***[8] (with or without suffixes at the end) means that the root has both active and passive varieties of the form. **ϕ/di*** means the same thing except that the active prefix is not overt:

under **deleng, n/di*** means *ndeleng* active, *dideleng* passive;
under **karang, n̈g/di*aké** means *ngarangaké* active, *dikarangaké* passive;
under **tuku, ϕ/di*** means *tuku* active, *dituku* passive.

The nasal prefix marked with an umlaut to show that it replaces the initial consonant of the root makes this replacement with *both* elements of a reduplicated or doubled root:

under **tjingak, n̈j·tje*** means *njenjingak;*
under **tangi, n̈/di·te*** means *nenangi* active, *ditetangi* passive;
under **kemah, n̈g/di*-*** means *ngemah-ngemah* active, *dikemah-kemah* passive;
under **tjukup, n̈j/di*-*aké** means *njukup-njukupaké* active, *ditjukup-tjukupaké* passive;
under **kajuh, n̈g/di·kojah-*** means *ngojah-ngajuh* active, *dikojah-kajuh* passive.

4.4. Implied Non-Ngoko Subentry Forms

Affixes and reduplicating syllables are shown in the subentries *only* as for Ngoko, and it is up to the reader to adjust these for non-Ngoko forms. Some examples:

under **karang, n̈g/di*** implies **n̈g/dipun*** *kr;*
under **râwâ** *ng,* **rawi** *kr,* ***n** implies *rāwān ng, rawi·ǹ* (*rawèn*) *kr;*
under **lara^{a}** *ng,* **sakit** *kr,* **le*** (*lelara ng*) implies *se·sakit kr;*
under **dol** *ng,* **sadé** *kr,* **nge/di*aké** (*ngedolaké* active *ng, didolaké* passive *ng*) implies **n̈j/dipun·sadé·k̀aken** *kr* (*njadèkaken* active, *dipun-sadèkaken* passive);
under **uni^{a}** *ng,* **ungel** *kr,* **ng/di*ǹ(-*)i** [*ngunèn(-unèn)i* active *ng, diunèn(-unèn)i* passive *ng*] implies **ng/dipun·ungel(-ungel)i** *kr;*
under **djamu** *ng,* **djampi** *kr,* ***n̂-*n̂an** (*djamon-djamonan ng*) implies ***ǹ-*ǹan** (*djampèn-djampènan*) *kr;*
under **djaluk** *ng,* **teḍa** *kr,* **punḍut** *ki,* **suwun** *ka,* **pa·n*** (*pandjaluk ng*) implies **pa·n̈·teḍa** (*paneḍa*) *kr,* **pa·m̈·punḍut** (*pamunḍut*) *ki,* **pa·n̈j·suwun** (*panjuwun*) *ka.*

Forms susceptible of ambiguous or faulty interpretation are spelled out. For example, under **anggo** *ng,* **anggé** *kr,* **agem** *ki,* the notation ***n** is readily interpreted as *anggon ng, anggèn kr, ageman ki;* but for ***n-*nan,** the *ki* form *agem-ageman* is written out.

4.5. Causative and Locative Subentries

When the causative suffix *-aké* is marked optional with parentheses—**^{m}ng/di*(aké)**—the form means the same thing with or without the suffix *-aké.*

When the locative suffix is marked optional, however—**^{m}ng/di*(i)**—the implication is that the root is used either with or without the suffix with no change in the English gloss but with differing implications. *With* the suffix, the form implies that (a) the action is done to a direct object, or (b) the action is done repetitively—many times, habitually, and/or by more than one subject (*cf.* the first two meanings in the definition of the suffix **-i**, page 229).[9]

---

7. Morphologically adjusted if necessary. See the explanation of the symbols **m̈, n̈, n̈g, n̈j** (3.1.5.4, *fn.* 7), of the symbols **k̀, ǹ, k̂, n̂** (3.1.5.4, *Notes on the Chart,* 5), and of the symbols **ǹ, n̂** (3.1.6.2). Social variants often must have affixes adjusted in addition: see 4.4 below.

8. **^{m}ng-** stands for the active nasal prefix (above, 3.1.5.4), adjusted to the pronunciation of the specific root.

9. Alphabetical order of suffixes, when both optional and non-optional ones appear in the same entry, is as follows: **^{m}ng/di*, ^{m}ng/di(aké)** *or* **^{m}ng/di*aké, ^{m}ng/di*(i), ^{m}ng/di*i.**

Both *-aké* and *-i* are productive suffixes, and we do not claim to have listed every single possible *-aké* and *-i* form in the dictionary entries. The meaning of a new one can be figured out easily by referring to the definitions of these suffixes, meanings 1 and 2 in each case.

4.6. Phrases

The phrases listed at the ends of entries are shown only for Ngoko, and it is up to the reader to translate them into Krama when Krama words exist for the phrasal words:

under **setengah**, *** tuwa** implies a Krama equivalent *** sepuh**;
under **amba**, *** tjijut·é** implies a Krama equivalent **wijar tjijut·ipun**;
under **banju**, **kaja * karo lenga** implies a Krama equivalent **kados toja kalijan lisah.**

4.7. Cross-References

Cross-references to another entry in its entirety are to the root (citation) form. Cross-references to a derived form of a root are shown by setting off the root from its affixed portion(s) with raised dots:

under **wajang**[a], *see also* P(A)·RINGGIT·AN means: *see* **ringgit**, subentry **p(a)*an;**
under **sumbrubud**, *see* S·UM·RUBUD means: *see* **srubud**, infixed subentry **s·um·rubud.**

Reference to a phrase is to the appropriate part of the first member, *e.g.:*

under **nun**, *shf of* KULA NUWUN is a reference to **kula**, phrase section at the end of the definition, *** nuwun;**
under **ngarsadji**, *contracted form of* NG·ARSA ADJI is a reference to **arsa**, subentry **ng***, phrase.

Cross-reference entries saying that the word is a variant of some other word should be assumed to have the same forms (morphophonemically adjusted if necessary) and meanings as the word they are referred to. For example, the material under **wales** applies also to **bales** as a variant of it; the prefixes will be attached differently with **bales. Basèh**, as a variant of **basik**, has the form *m·bosah-basèh.*

4.8. Examples

Many glossed forms in the dictionary are followed by examples, which are designed to serve a variety of purposes. For one thing, they provide an opportunity to show the spelled-out versions of the subentry shorthand notations (described in the foregoing sections) which we have adopted for the dual purpose of saving space and revealing the structure of derived forms clearly.

For another thing, examples show words in their natural setting, *i.e.* a context, and hence broaden or clarify the semantic range of a form in a way that a bare glossing cannot do. Further, examples can show other words that are commonly used in conjunction with the word under definition–a feature that many students of languages find helpful. (In Javanese, these other words are often Indonesian!) We have attempted as often as possible to provide examples which give glimpses into Javanese life and ways of thinking.

The fact is, truly helpful examples are hard to find. Linguistic contexts extend far beyond the brief phrase or sentence. Many examples that are short enough for the space available in a dictionary are unnatural, simple-minded, or textbook-like, or else they are parts of larger contexts in which they function smoothly but, once excised, become meaningless or alter their meaning or sound incomplete or puzzling. Elicited examples, on the other hand, generally provide less insight than examples in which the speaker or writer was not aware that he was making an example of the word.

4.9. Glossings and Translations

As a general principle we give literal glossings of cited forms for the sake of precision, and free translations of examples for the sake of naturalness. Javanese and English often use quite different grammatical structures to express more or less the same thing, and free translations give the reader the chance to examine the Javanese structure for himself—a practice that ought (incidentally) to help along his spoken Javanese.

Passive glosses are not given specifically in citations in the ^{m}**ng/di-** form. Under **deleng**, for example, **n/di*** 'to look at' implies both the active form *ndeleng* 'to look at' and the passive form *dideleng* 'to be looked at by someone.' Once in a while a passive form has an unpredictable meaning, different from a simple rewording of the active gloss, and then it is listed and glossed separately (and alphabetized under **di-**).

Passive forms in example sentences are most often translated as actives, *e.g.*: *Aku diantem Slamet* 'Slamet hit me' (rather than 'I was hit by Slamet'). English and Javanese passives operate on different principles, and the English active is the more literal rendering in nearly all cases.

We gloss Javanese adjectives with English adjectives, though in sentences English structure often calls for flexibility in translation:

wit ḌUWUR a TALL tree

Botjahé PINTER. The child IS SMART.

SREGEP njambut-gawé. He works INDUSTRIOUSLY.

Sepira SUWÉ·NÉ? How long does it take (*literally*, How much is ITS LENGTH OF TIME)?

TJEKAK·É, akèh banget. TO PUT IT BRIEFLY, there were a great many of them.

BETJIK·É dibalèkaké baé. You'd better give it back (*literally*, THE GOOD THING [is that] it be given back).

There are untranslatable words in any language, denoting things and concepts that are unique to the culture or deeply a part of the national ethos. When words like this appear in dictionary examples, they have to be translated; but the reader is alerted to the inadequacy of such glossings as 'ceremony' for *slamet·an*, 'veranda' or 'hall' for *penḍapa,* and so on, and we apologize for clumsy phrases like 'rice-accompanying dishes' for *lawuh*.

5. SOCIAL STYLES

5.1. Social Implications

The vast majority of Javanese words are neutral with respect to social connotation. But a thousand or so of the most commonly used words in the language are restricted to particular situations defined by the relationship between speakers and the people they are talking about. For each item with built-in social limitations there is at least one other item with the same denotative meaning but complementary social implications. Thus *aku* 'I' and *kowé* 'you,' which are neutral (*Ngoko*) words, have the formal (*Krama*) counterparts *kula* and *pendjenengan. Aku* and *kowé* denote 'I' and 'you' and connote informality; *kula* and *pendjenengan* mean 'I' and 'you' while implying a formal or somewhat distant relationship between the speakers.[1]

5.2. Basic Categories

The basic style is Ngoko (abbreviated here as *ng*): there is a Ngoko word for everything, and the Ngoko lexicon is numbered in the tens of thousands. The formal style, Krama (*kr*), is the

---

1. See Soepomo Poedjosoedarmo, "Javanese Speech Levels," in *Indonesia* (Cornell University, Modern Indonesia Project, Ithaca, N.Y.), No. 6, October 1968, for a detailed treatment of the speech levels, including concrete illustrations of their use and a discussion of current trends and changes in usage and attitudes; also his "Wordlist of Javanese Non-Ngoko Vocabularies" in the subsequent issue (No. 7, April 1969). The figures on the size of the subvocabularies given here are Soepomo's. See also Clifford Geertz's excellent discussion of linguistic etiquette in *The Religion of Java* (Glencoe, Illinois, The Free Press, 1960), pp. 248-60.

second largest category, having around 850 lexical items. In a Krama-speaking situation, one replaces the neutral (Ngoko) lexicon with Krama vocabulary items when they are available.[2] Between Ngoko and Krama is a middle style, Madya (*md*), with about 35 items of its own and characterized otherwise by the use of Krama words (where available) and Ngoko affixes.

5.3. High Krama and Humble Krama

Regardless of which basic style one is using, he draws on a small (around 260-item) Krama Inggil (*ki*) or High Krama vocabulary to show special honor to the person he applies them to. Two schoolboys jabbering in Ngoko about a classmate getting mad would say *nesu* 'angry,' but of the (respected) teacher losing his temper, they would use the *ki* word *duka* 'angry' (while still speaking in Ngoko); two ladies conversing in Krama and wondering to each other what a certain (esteemed) high official is angry about, would also use the *ki* word *duka* 'angry' while keeping the rest of their speech Krama. Krama Inggil words denote mostly body parts and everyday actions. The feature that distinguishes their usage is that one does not apply them to oneself.[3]

A small subdivision of *ki* vocabulary is Krama Anḍap (*ka*), humble Krama Inggil, used when speaking "upward" to an exalted person. The *ka* vocabulary consists mainly of verbs that take indirect objects (give, say, *etc.*): thus one gives (with the *ka* word) "upward" to one's father, a high official, or other social superior, while the father, official, *etc.* gives (expressed by the *ki* word) "downward" to someone lower in the social scheme. As contrasted with *ki* (High Krama), one may—and very often does—apply *ka* (Humble Krama) words to oneself; expression of self-abnegation is deeply characteristic of the Javanese.

5.4. Usage

In general, the use of Ngoko between Javanese speakers implies absence of formality and absence of need to show special respect, while Krama implies reserve and formality, or, in more intimate usage, respectful regard. Madya is used in situations where Ngoko would be disrespectful or humiliating and Krama would be inappropriately exalted.

5.5. Subdivisions of the Three Basic Categories

Further refinements are possible through subdivisions of each major category, as follows.

NGOKO

Ngoko Lugu: ordinary Ngoko, using Ngoko vocabulary throughout except for Krama Inggil reference terms where appropriate.

Ngoko Anḍap: humble Ngoko, used for addressing a highly respected person with whom one is on close terms. There are two varieties:

Antya Basa: Ngoko throughout except that the speaker applies Krama Inggil terms to the person he is addressing.

Basa Antya: the same as Antya Basa except a little humbler, having a few Krama words sprinkled in (more or fewer depending on the degree of respect being shown).

MADYA

Madya Krama: middle Krama, using Madya words where they are available, otherwise Krama; Ngoko affixation; and Krama Inggil references where appropriate.

Madya (A)ntara: the same as Madya Krama except that no Krama Inggil references are used.

Madya Ngoko: the same as Madyantara except that a few Ngoko words are sprinkled in—more or fewer depending on how "downward" the person is speaking.

---

2. Three of these differentiated lexical items are affixes: the passive prefix **di-** *ng,* **dipun-** *kr;* the suffix **-é** *ng,* **-ipun** *kr;* and the causative suffix **-aké** *ng,* **-aken** *kr.*

3. There are three exceptions. One is the humble words described below. Second, a king may apply exalted terms to himself. Finally, there is an oblique usage in which one speaks as his listener would address him: *e.g.* to a servant one might say *Aku ḍahar.* 'I eat,' using the Krama Inggil word for 'eat' which the servant would apply to the master. Other than these, the use of Krama Inggil applied to oneself is arrogant and non-Javanese.

KRAMA

Muḍa Krama: the most refined style of Krama, in which Krama vocabulary is employed throughout (where available) with Krama Inggil references to the addressee.

Krama (A)ntara or *Krama Lumrah:* ordinary Krama, *i.e.* the same as Muḍa Krama but without the Krama Inggil references.

Wreḍa Krama: A slightly less formal variety of Kramantara, using an occasional Ngoko affix and less exalted pronouns for 'you'—a style used when speaking to someone socially lower but with whom Ngoko would be awkward.

5.6. *Irregularities of Correspondence*

There is not an altogether one-to-one correspondence of the lexical items that comprise this system. Some Krama words do double duty, corresponding to more than one Ngoko word. There are certain things which, though they have Ngoko equivalents, are used only in Krama: an example is the phrase *Kula nuwun,* spoken in lieu of knocking when coming to someone's home. Some expressions (*e.g.* coarse, abusive terms) are specifically Ngoko rather than neutral. The Krama Inggil vocabulary corresponds even less precisely to the basic vocabulary. Some, like Krama words, do multiple duty. Others shift about: the *ki* word for 'hand' (Ngoko *tangan*), for example, gets affixed and serves as the *ki* equivalent of four or five Ngoko verbs (none related to *tangan*) referring to various ways of using the hands. *Ki* references are sometimes oblique, so that they are actually substitutions for Ngoko words rather than equivalents of them.

The Krama equivalents for certain Ngoko words are optional. In present-day usage, for example, *lan* 'and' is used in both Ngoko and Krama, but *kalijan* is a specific Krama equivalent of it.

5.7. *Shifting Usage*

To complicate an already complex system, the categories are not rigidly fixed. Words shift from substandard to standard usage, or move (usually downward) from one level to another.[4] Informants nowadays do not always agree on the social status of words. In the dictionary entries, we use a question mark (?) as a symbol (to be interpreted as "for some speakers") to mark instances of changing usage as evidenced by conflicting statements from Javanese speakers. For example, **djarum** *kr?* 'needle' means that to some informants *djarum* is Krama and to some it is neutral; **goḍong (ron** *opt? kr*) 'leaf' means that some speakers say either *goḍong* or *ron* to express 'leaf' in Krama and others use only *ron;* a word marked *sbst? kr* is substandard Krama to some speakers and normal Krama to others.

6. DEGREE WORDS

Degree words show relative nearness or remoteness:

Degree I refers to things, space, or time close to the speaker and/or hearer;

Degree II refers to things, space, or time not remote from the speaker and/or hearer but especially things in the immediate context, for example a visual or auditory experience, or something aforementioned;

Degree III refers to remote things, space, or time.

Most of the degree words are formed by combining various initial segments with the following bases:

---

4. This may portend a relaxation of the rigid Javanese social stratification, resulting at least in part from the establishment of the Indonesian Republic in 1945 with its emphasis on equality. Also, specific changes may rise from specific motivations: for example, Javanese **tandur** *ng,* **tanem** *ng? kr* alongside of Indonesian **tandur,** meaning 'to plant,' may account for the growing use of the originally Krama *tanem* as Ngoko, or socially neutral.

	NGOKO	KRAMA
I	*-éné*	*-iki*
II	*-ono*	*-iku*
III	*-ana*	*-ika*

Note that the Ngoko words for 'this' (I), 'that' (II), and 'that' (III) resemble the Krama base forms shown above (*ika* is an old variant of *kaé*). Note also that the Krama forms that are not formed from the bases are undifferentiated with respect to degree.

1. this, that.			
I	this	*iki*	*punika*
II	that	*iku, kuwi*	"
III	that	*kaé*	"
2. (in) place: *k-* plus base (Ngoko), *ngr-* plus base (Krama).			
I	here	*kéné*	*ngriki*
II	there	*kono*	*ngriku*
III	there	*kana*	*ngrika*
3. unit of scope: *m-* plus base (Ngoko).			
I	unit of this scope	*méné*	*manten*
II	unit of that scope	*mono*	"
III	unit of that scope	*mana*	"
4. in way/manner: *mengk-* plus base (Ngoko).			
I	like this	*mengkéné*	*mekaten*
II	like that	*mengkono*	"
III	like that	*mengkana*	"
5. to place: *mr-* plus base (Ngoko, Krama).			
I	(to) here	*mréné*	*mriki*
II	(to) there	*mrono*	*mriku*
III	(to) there	*mrana*	*mrika*
6. in way/manner: *ng-* plus base (Ngoko).			
I	like this	*ngéné*	*ngaten*
II	like that	*ngono*	"
III	like that	*ngana*	"
7. to place: *r-* plus base (Ngoko, Krama).			
I	(to) here	*réné*	*riki*
II	(to) there	*rono*	*riku*
III	(to) there	*rana*	*rika*
8. one unit of scope: *sem-* plus base (Ngoko).			
I	to this extent	*seméné*	*semanten*
II	to that extent	*semono*	"
III	to that extent	*semana*	"
9. to/from time: *sepr-* plus base (Ngoko, Krama).			
I	to this time	*sepréné*	*sepriki*
II	to/from that time	*seprono*	*sepriku*
III	from that time	*seprana*	*seprika*

7. GUIDE TO LOCATION OF VARIANTS

A great many of the words a reader comes across in his Javanese materials and wants to look up in this dictionary will be disguised in various ways, especially by having prefixes attached to them, as described in sections 3 and 4 above. Here, we summarize these processes from the opposite point of view: instead of showing how Javanese roots are built up by adding various affixes, we list possible ways of tearing down finished words into their component parts—the process to which the reader will need to subject his Javanese words. Below is an alphabetical index to the beginning portions of roots as they appear in their disguised forms, with clues to guide the reader until he gets into the habit of penetrating disguises automatically.

Some forms may need to be looked up in this list twice. With *memedi,* for example, after removing the reduplicating syllable *me-*, a prefixed form remains—an *m* that has replaced the *w*-initial of the root. For *pangedol,* after removing the *pa-* prefix, we must determine that the *ngedol* portion is *nge·dol* (rather than **ng̃·kedol* or *ng·edol*). With words like *amangsuli, anjawang, anudju, etc.*, after stripping off the *a-* prefix we still have a nasal-prefixed form. For *pinariksa,* after reading *pin-* as *p-* according to the guide list, we must reduce *pariksa* to *priksa.*

Some roots are subject to disguise at both ends: *e.g. mrèèkaké* from *prèi, mironi* from *wiru.* To cover these, a summary of final-sound disguising elements appears after the guide list to initial-sound alterations.

Traps and pitfalls remain. There are cases of homonymy brought about by affixation. For example, *meksa* is both a commonly occurring root by itself and the active form of *peksa,* also very common. The root *lésan* is homonymous with *lès* plus suffix *-an.* Some ambiguities of interpretation (is *gegeman* to be interpreted as *ge·geman* or *gegem·an?*) can be resolved by trial and error, but others (is *keboné* 'the garden' or 'the kerbau'?) are determined only by context.

A word of caution: after a certain amount of de-affixing, one gets to the point where he sees affixes everywhere, overlooking the fact that some *di-*'s, *ke-*'s, *pa-*'s, *-in-*'s, nasal consonants, *-um-*'s, *etc.* are not affixes but part of a root, as with *diwasa, gineman, kepala, kumiḍi, mamah, ngerti, njata, peniti.*

If you still don't find your word after exhausting the possibilities of this list, keep in mind—

1. that *l*'s, *r*'s, and *u*'s (*w*'s) might be infixes (3.1.7);
2. that some reduplication syllables have a vowel other than *e* (3.1.3);
3. that contiguous vowels may have *h* spelled between them, or *h* may drop out between vowels, as in *pa(h)it, ta(h)un* (2.9.7);
4. that *j*'s, *w*'s, and *h*'s are spelling variants in certain positions (2.9.7);
5. that *a* may be spelled *o* (2.9.8);
6. that intensified forms of adjectives may change vowels (3.1.8);
7. that the spelling *oe* (and usually *oo*) are modern *u* (2.9.13, 2.6);
8. that *y* is a spelling variant of *j* (2.2);
9. that the Javanese do not always divide compounds into words according to a standardized principle (2.9);
10. that the word may be Indonesian (or Dutch, or from some other language);
11. that the author welcomes comments about lexical items that do not appear in this dictionary!

Alphabetical Guide List to Initial Disguising Elements

A word beginning with–	*May be listed as a root beginning with–*
a-	(1) what remains after deleting the *a-* (3.1.4) (2) ha- (2.9.12)
ba-	be- (2.9.2)
bal-	bl- (2.9.3)
bar-	br- (2.9.3)
be-	ba- (2.9.2)
beb-	b- (3.1.3)
bel-	bl- (2.9.3)
bem-	b- (3.1.7)
ber-	(a) br- (2.9.3) (b) what remains after deleting the *ber-* (3.1.4)
bin-	b- (3.1.7)
bok-	what remains after deleting the *bok* (3.1.5.4)
bre-	ber- (2.9.6)
bu- + vowel	buw-, bw- + the vowel (2.9.7)
bum-	b- (3.1.7)
buw-	bu-, bw- (2.9.7)
bw-	bu(w)- (2.9.7)
ch-	h-, k- (2.6)
da-, ḍa-	de-, ḍe- (2.9.2)
dak-	what remains after deleting the *dak* (3.1.5.4)
dal-	dl- (2.9.3)

A word beginning with–	*May be listed as a root beginning with–*
dar-, ḍar-	dr-, ḍr- (2.9.3)
de-, ḍe-	da-, ḍa- (2.9.2)
ded-, ḍeḍ-	d-, ḍ- (3.1.3)
del-	dl- (2.9.3)
dem-, ḍem-	d-, ḍ- (3.1.7)
der-, ḍer-	dr-, ḍr- (2.9.3)
di-	what remains after deleting the *di* (3.1.5.4)
din-, ḍin-	d-, ḍ- (3.1.7)
dipun-	what remains after deleting the *dipun* (3.1.5.4)
djal-	djl- (2.9.3)
djar-	djr- (2.9.3)
djel-	djl- (2.9.3)
djem-	dj- (3.1.7)
djer-	djr- (2.9.3)
djin-	dj- (3.1.7)
dju- + vowel	djuw- + the vowel (2.9.7)
djum-	dj- (3.1.7)
dre-, ḍre-	der-, ḍer- (2.9.6)
du- + vowel	duw-, dw- + the vowel (2.9.7)
dum-, ḍum-	d-, ḍ- (3.1.7)
duw-, ḍuw-	du-, dw-; ḍu-, ḍuw- (2.9.7)
dw-, ḍw-	du(w)-, ḍu(w)- (2.9.7)
é-, è-, e-	hé-, hè-, he- (2.9.12)
eb-	b- (2.9.5)
ed-, eḍ-	d-, ḍ- (2.9.5)
edj-	dj- (2.9.5)
eg-	g- (2.9.5)
ek-	k- (2.9.5)
el-	l- (2.9.5)
em-	m- (2.9.5)
en-	n- (2.9.5)
eng-	ng- (2.9.5)
enj-	nj- (2.9.5)
ep-	p- (2.9.5)
er-	r- (2.9.5)
es-	s- (2.9.5)
et-, eṭ-	t-, ṭ- (2.9.5)
etj-	tj- (2.9.5)
ga-	ge- (2.9.2)
gal-	gl- (2.9.3)
gar-	gr- (2.9.3)
ge-	ga- (2.9.2)
geg-	g- (3.1.3)
gel-	gl- (2.9.3)
gem-	g- (3.1.7)
ger-	gr- (2.9.3)
gin-	g- (3.1.7)
gre-	ger- (2.9.6)
gu- + vowel	guw-, gw- + the vowel (2.9.7)
gum-	g- (3.1.7)
guw-	gu-, gw- (2.9.7)
gw-	gu(w)- (2.9.7)
h + vowel	what remains after deleting the *h* (2.9.12)
i-	hi- (2.9.12)
jej-	j- (3.1.3)
ju- + vowel	juw- (2.9.7)
k-	what remains after deleting the *k*- (3.1.4, 3.1.5.1, 3.1.5.2, 3.1.5.4)

A word beginning with–	*May be listed as a root beginning with–*
ka-	(1) what remains after deleting the *ka-* (3.1.4.1, 3.1.5.1, 3.1.5.4) (2) ke- (2.9.2)
kal-	kl- (2.9.3)
kar-	kr- (2.9.3)
ké-, kè-	i- (3.1.5.2)
ke-	(1) what remains after deleting the *ke-* (3.1.5.1, 3.1.5.2, 3.1.5.4) (2) ka- (2.9.2)
kek-	k- (3.1.3)
kel-	kl- (2.9.3)
kem-	k- (3.1.7)
ker-	kr- (2.9.3)
kin-	k- (3.1.7)
ko-	(1) what remains after deleting the *ko-* (3.1.5.4: variant spelling of *kok-*) (2) u- (3.1.5.2)
kok-	what remains after deleting the *kok* (3.1.5.4)
kre-	ker- (2.9.6)
ku- + w-	what remains after deleting the *ku* (3.1.5.2, *fn.* 4)
ku- + vowel	kuw-, kw- + the vowel (2.9.7)
kum-	k- (3.1.7)
kuw-	ku-, kw- (2.9.7)
kw-	ku(w)- (2.9.7)
la-	le- (2.9.2)
le-	la- (2.9.2)
lel-	l- (3.1.3)
lem-	l- (3.1.7)
lin-	l- (3.1.7)
lu- + vowel	luw- + the vowel (2.9.7)
lum-	l- (3.1.7)
luw-	lu- (2.9.7)
lw-	lu(w)- (2.9.7)
m-	(1) what remains after deleting the *m* (3.1.4.1) (2) what results from changing the *m* to *p* (most likely), *w*, or *f* (least likely) (3.1.5.4)
ma-	(1) what remains after deleting the *ma* (3.1.4.1) (2) me- (2.9.2)
mal-	ml- (2.9.3)
mar-	mr- (2.9.3)
mb-	(1) b- (2) emb- (2.9.5)
mbok-	what remains after deleting the *mbok* (3.1.5.4)
me-	(1) what remains after deleting the *me* (3.1.4.1) (2) ma- (2.9.2)
mel-	ml- (2.9.3)
mem-	(1) m- (3.1.3) (2) *p* or *w* which has been reduplicated and replaced by nasal prefix (3.1.3, 3.1.5.4)
mer-	(1) what remains after deleting the *mer-* (3.1.4.1) (2) mr- (2.9.3)

A word beginning with–	*May be listed as a root beginning with–*
min-	m- (3.1.7)
mp-	emp- (2.9.5)
mre-	mer- (2.9.6)
mu- + vowel	muw- + the vowel (2.9.7)
muw-	mu- (2.9.7)
mw-	mu(w)- (2.9.7)
n-	(1) what results from changing the *n* to *t* (most likely) or *ṭ* (3.1.5.4) (2) what results from changing the *n* to *s* or *tj* (3.1.5.4, *fn.* 8)
na-	ne- (2.9.2)
nal-	nl- (2.9.3)
nar-	nr- (2.9.3)
nd-, nḍ-	(1) d-, ḍ- (2) end-, enḍ- (2.9.5)
ndj-	(1) dj- (2) endj- (2.9.5)
ne-	na- (2.9.2)
nel-	nl- (2.9.3)
nen-	n- (3.1.3) *or* t, ṭ (3.1.3 + 3.1.5.4)
ner-	nr- (2.9.3)
ng-	(1) what remains after deleting the *ng* (most likely) (3.1.5.4) (2) what results from changing the *ng* to *k* or (least likely) *h* (3.1.5.4)
nga-	(1) what remains after deleting the *nga-* (3.1.4.1, 3.1.5.4) (2) nge- (2.9.2)
ngal-	ngl- (2.9.3)
ngar-	ngr- (2.9.3)
nge-	(1) what remains after deleting the *nge-* (3.1.4.1, 3.1.5.4) (2) nga- (2.9.2)
ngel-	ngl- (2.9.3)
ngeng-	ng- (3.1.3) *or* k (3.1.3 + 3.1.5.4)
nger-	ngr- (2.9.3)
ngg-	(1) g- (2) engg- (2.9.5)
ngre-	nger- (2.9.6)
ngu- + w-	what remains after deleting the *ngu* (3.1.5.4, 1)
ngu- + vowel	nguw- (2.9.7)
ngw-	w- (after deleting the *ng*) (3.1.5.4, *fn.* 6)
nj-	what results from changing the *nj* to *s* (more likely) or *tj* (3.1.5.4)
nja-	nje- (2.9.2)
njal-	njl- (2.9.3)
njar-	njr- (2.9.3)
nje-	nja- (2.9.2)
njel-	njl- (2.9.3)
njenj-	nj- (3.1.3) *or* s, t (3.1.3 + 3.1.5.4)
njer-	njr- (2.9.3)
njre-	njer- (2.9.6)
nju(w)-, njw-	s- or tj- (which has been replaced by nasal prefix) + uw, w (3.1.5.4)
nre-	ner- (2.9.6)
nt-	ent- (2.9.5)
nu(w)-, nw-	t- or ṭ- (which has been replaced by nasal prefix) + uw, w (3.1.5.4)

A word beginning with–	*May be listed as a root beginning with–*
o-	ho- (2.9.12)
p-	what remains after deleting the *p* (3.1.5.1)
pa-	(1) what remains after deleting the *pa-* (3.1.5.1) (2) pe- (2.9.2)
pal-	pl- (2.9.3)
par-	pr- (2.9.3)
pe-	(1) what remains after deleting the *pe-* (3.1.4.1, 3.1.5.1) (2) pa- (2.9.2)
pel-	pl- (2.9.3)
pem-	p- (3.1.7)
pep-	p- (3.1.3)
per-	(1) what remains after deleting the *per-* (3.1.4.1) (2) pr- (2.9.3)
pi-	what remains after deleting the *pi-* (3.1.4.1)
pin-	p- (3.1.7)
pra-	what remains after deleting the *pra-* (3.1.4.1)
pre-	(1) what remains after deleting the *pre-* (2.9.6, 3.1.4.1) (2) per- (2.9.6)
pu- + vowel	puw- + the vowel (2.9.7)
pum-	p- (3.1.7)
puw-	pu- (2.9.7)
pw-	pu(w)- (2.9.7)
ra-	re- (2.9.2)
re-	ra- (2.9.2)
rem-	r- (3.1.7)
rer-	r- (3.1.3)
rin-	r- (3.1.7)
ru- + vowel	ruw- + the vowel (2.9.7)
rum-	r- (3.1.7)
ruw-	ru- (2.9.7)
rw-	ruw- (2.9.7)
s-	(1) what remains after deleting the *s-* (see definition of *sa'* prefix, page 514) (2) z (variant spelling in loan words)
sa-	(1) what remains after deleting the *sa-* (3.1.5.3) (2) se- (2.9.2)
sak-	what remains after deleting the *sak* (3.1.5.3)
sal-	sl- (2.9.3)
sar-	sr- (2.9.3)
se-	(1) what remains after deleting the *se-* (see definition of *sa'* prefix, page 514) (2) sa- (2.9.2)
sel-	sl- (2.9.3)
sem-	s- (3.1.7)
ser-	sr- (2.9.3)
ses-	s- (3.1.3)
sin-	s- (3.1.7)
sre-	ser- (2.9.6)
su- + vowel	suw-, sw- + the vowel (2.9.7)

A word beginning with–	*May be listed as a root beginning with–*
sum-	s- (3.1.7)
suw-	su-, sw- (2.9.7)
sw-	su(w)- (2.9.7)
ta-, ṭa-	te-, ṭe- (2.9.2)
tak-	what remains after deleting the *tak* (3.1.5.4)
tal-	tl- (2.9.3)
tar-, ṭar-	tr-, ṭr- (2.9.3)
te-, ṭe-	ta-, ṭa- (2.9.2)
tel-	tl- (2.9.3)
tem-, ṭem-	t-, ṭ- (3.1.7)
ter-, ṭer-	tr-, ṭr- (2.9.3)
tet-, ṭeṭ-	t-, ṭ- (3.1.3)
tin-, ṭin-	t-, ṭ- (3.1.7)
tja-	tje- (2.9.2)
tjal-	tjl- (2.9.3)
tjar-	tjr- (2.9.3)
tje-	tja- (2.9.2)
tjel-	tjl- (2.9.3)
tjem-	tj- (3.1.7)
tjer-	tjr- (2.9.3)
tjetj-	tj- (3.1.3)
tjin-	tj- (3.1.7)
tjre-	tjer- (2.9.6)
tju- + vowel	tjuw- + the vowel (2.9.7)
tjum-	tj- (3.1.7)
tjuw-	tju- (2.9.7)
tjw-	tju(w)- (2.9.7)
tre-	ter- (2.9.6)
tu-, ṭu-	tuw-, ṭuw- (2.9.7)
tum-, ṭum-	t-, ṭ- (3.1.7)
tuw-	tu- (2.9.7)
tw-	tu(w)- (2.9.7)
u-	hu- (2.9.12)
uw-	w- (2.9.5)
w-	uw- (2.9.5)
wa-	we- (2.9.2)
wal-	(1) wl- (2.9.3) (2) l- (2.9.4)
war-	(1) wr- (2.9.3) (2) r- (2.9.4)
we-	wa- (2.9.2)
wel-	(1) wl- (2.9.3) (2) l- (2.9.4)
wer-	(1) wr- (2.9.3) (2) r- (2.9.4)
wew-	w- (3.1.3)
win-	w- (3.1.7)
wre-	wer- (2.9.6)
z-	dj-, s- (2.6)

The list below shows portions which often appear at the ends of Javanese words and thus may obscure the root form. The suffix *-é* (*-né* after vowels), for example, is extremely common (so frequent that it is possible to lose sight of the fact that in some words a *-n(é)* is not the suffix but part of the root).

As with the initial disguising elements in the foregoing list, a word may end with a combination of elements, so that two portions must be removed to reach the root-final sound. Very commonly, for example, *-ané* is suffix *-an* plus suffix *-é* (though it is sometimes suffix *-ané*).

The morphophonemically altered portions *-èkaké, -èni, -okaké,* and *-oni* occur with high frequency. Now and then, though, a root ends in *-èk, -èn, -ok,* or *-on,* and the suffixes attach without alteration. For example, *ngentèkaké* (*ng·entèk·aké*) comes from root *entèk*—compare *ngentèni* (*ng·enti·ṅi*) from root *enti.*

Alphabetical Guide List to Final Disguising Elements

A word ending with–	*May come from a root ending with–*
-a	(1) the word minus the *-a* (3.1.5.4, Chart) (2) -u (3.1.8)
-aké	the word minus the *-aké* (3.1.5.4, Chart)
-aken	the word minus the *-aken* (3.1.5.4, Chart)
-an	the word minus the *-an* (3.1.5.4, Chart; 3.1.6)
-ana	the word minus the *-ana* (3.1.5.4, Chart)
-ané	the word minus the *-ané* (3.1.5.4, Chart)
-anipun	the word minus the *-anipun* (3.1.5.4, Chart)
-b	-p (2.9.1)
-d	-t (2.9.1)
-é	the word minus the *-é* (3.1.5.4, Chart; 3.1.6)
-èhan, -éhan	-i (3.1.6.2)
-éjan	-èh; -i (3.1.6.2)
-èkaké	-i, -é (p. xxiv, Note 4)
-èn	-i, -é (3.1.6.2)
-en	the word minus the *-en* (3.1.5.4, Chart; 3.1.6)
-ènan	-i (3.1.6.2)

A word ending with–	*May come from a root ending with–*
-ènan	-i (3.1.6.2)
-èni	-i, -é (p. xxiv, Note 4)
-g	-k (2.9.1)
-ha	-a (3.1.6.2)
-han	the same word minus the *-han* (3.1.6.2)
-i	(1) the same word minus the *-i* (3.1.5.4, Chart) (2) -é (3.1.8)
-ija	-i (3.1.6.2)
-ijan	-i (3.1.6.2)
-ing	the same word minus the *-ing* (3.1.6)
-ipun	the same word minus the *-ipun* (3.1.5.4, Chart; 3.1.6)
-k	(1) -g (2.9.1) (2) the same word minus the *-k* (2.9.10)
-kaké	the same word minus the *-kaké* (3.1.5.4, Chart)
-kaken	the same word minus the *-kaken* (3.1.5.4, Chart)
-ké	the same word minus the *-ké* (2.9)
-kké	the same word minus the *-kké* (2.9)
-kna	the same word minus the *-kna* (3.1.5.4, Chart)
-ku	the same word minus the *-ku* (3.1.6)
-mu	the same word minus the *-mu* (3.1.6)
-n	the same word minus the *-n* (3.1.5.4, Chart; 3.1.6)
-na	the same word minus the *-na* (3.1.5.4, Chart)
-nan	the same word minus the *-nan* (3.1.6)
-nana	the same word minus the *-nana* (3.1.5.4, Chart)
-nané	the same word minus the *-nané* (3.1.5.4, Chart)
-nanipun	the same word minus the *-nanipun* (3.1.5.4, Chart)
-né	the same word minus the *-né* (3.1.5.4, Chart; 3.1.6)
-nen	the same word minus the *-nen* (3.1.5.4, Chart; 3.1.6)
-ni	the same word minus the *-ni* (3.1.5.4, Chart)
-ning	the same word minus the *-ning* (3.1.6)
-nipun	the same word minus the *-nipun* (3.1.5.4, Chart; 3.1.6)
-o	-a (2.9.8)
-oa	-a (2.9.8)
-okaké	-u (pp. xxiv–xxv, Note 4)
-on	-u (3.1.6.2)
-onan	-u (3.1.6.2)
-oni	-u (pp. xxiv–xxv, Note 4)
-owan	-o (3.1.6.2)
-p	-b (2.9.1)
-t	-d (2.9.1)
-uwan	-u, -uh (3.1.6.2)
-wan	the same word minus the *-wan* (3.1.6.2)

8. SYMBOLS

/	or
2	indicates that the foregoing (to nearest space or hyphen) is doubled (3.1.1)
*	represents the root(s) as cited at the beginning of an entry (4.2)
¨	above a letter (*m̈, n̈, n̈g, n̈j*) marks a nasal prefix that replaces the first consonant of a root (3.1.5.4)
`	marks a *k* or *n* before which *i* or *é* changes to *è* (3.1.5.4, Notes on the Chart, 5, pages xxxiv–xxxv; 3.1.6.2)
ˆ	marks a *k* or *n* before which *u* changes to *o* (3.1.5.4, Notes on the Chart, 5, pages xxxiv–xxxv; 3.1.6.2)
.	separates off affixes and reduplicated syllables (4.7)
?	social variant in flux (5.7)
( )	enclose optional portions of citation forms

See also the table of pronunciation-showing diacritics, 2.5, pp. xii–xiii.

9. ABBREVIATIONS

abbr	abbreviation
acv	active
adr	term of address: word used as, or in lieu of, a title
cr	crude, coarse (*kasar*)
esp	especially
euph	euphemism (specifically, an oblique reference to a superstitiously avoided term); euphemistic
excl	exclamation
fig	figurative
gram	grammatical term
inf	informal (used in relaxed, friendly speech)
intsfr	intensifier of the qualitative meaning of another word
ka	Krama Anḍap (humble Krama Inggil) (5.3)
ki	Krama Inggil (high Krama) (5.3)
kr	Krama (5.2)
lit	literal
ltry	literary (word used in literature or in formal speech)
md	Madya (5.2)
ng	Ngoko (5.2)
ng kr	Ngoko and Krama (4.1, *fn.* 3)
oj	Old Javanese (*Kawi*)
opt kr	optional Krama (5.7)
pl	plural (referring to a subject or object and/or a repeated or habitual action)
prn	pronounced; pronunciation
psv	passive
ptg	*pating* (see definition, page 434)
rg	regional, *i.e.* used mainly outside the Central Java area
rpr	representing
sbst	substandard
sg	singular (used to differentiate an otherwise identically glossed form from *pl*[*ural*])
shc	shortened compound (a compound of monosyllabic shortened forms)
shf	shortened form, usually a final syllable used informally in lieu of the entire word
smn	someone
sms	same as
smw	somewhere
sp	spelling(s); spelled
sth	something
usu	usually
var	variant(s)
wj	term or expression used in or in connection with the classical drama (*wajang*)

A

ā 1 *alphabetic letter.* 2 *theoretical person.* 3 apiece. *à Rp. limalas* 15 rupiahs each

ā- *prefix.* 1 *adjective and verb formative* (**a-doh, a-dol,** *etc.: see under both root and* **a-** *form*). 2 *ltry* having, characterized by. *kéwan a·sikil papat* 4-legged animals. 3 to put forth. *a·woh* to bear fruit. 4 *ltry* and *(between adjectives). gèpèng a·tipis* flat and thin. 5 upon [do]ing. *Wong mau bungah banget a·tampa ḍuwit.* He was delighted to receive the money. 6 *gives ltry formal flavor. a·marga* because. *a·nanging* but. *Ḍèwèké a·mangsuli...* He replied... *A·nudju sawidji dina...* It happened that one day...

-âª *imperative suffix. Réné·a.* Come here! *Kowé ana·a ngomah baé.* You stay home.

-âᵇ *subjunctive suffix.* 1 may [it happen]. *Bisa·a énggal dadi.* I hope it will be ready soon. 2 (in order) to; so that. *Betjiké ditutupi bisa·a adja nganti dirubung laler.* It should be covered so flies can't get into it. 3 even though; (even) if. *senadjan mengkono·a* even so. *Mangsa bisa·a.* As if you could do it! *Nakal·a kaé wong iku anakku.* He may be bad but he's my son. *Olèh·a ḍuwit kena dianggo tuku montor.* If I had the money I'd buy a car. 4 *with doubled adjective* far more so. *Geḍé²·a iki.* This one is much bigger. 5 *with doubled word* [not] even. *Aku ora éntuk lajang sidji²·a.* I didn't get a single letter. 6 *with doubled question word* [what]ever. *Sapa²·a sing arep mlebu kudu wisuh ḍisik.* Anyone who wants to come in has to wash his hands first. *Pijé²·a kaé kowé kudu lunga.* No matter what, you have to go.

âbâ 1 signal, command. 2 to order (at a certain price). *Aku mau * bakmi gorèng.* I ordered fried noodles. *Ora susah takon regané, terus * waé.* You don't need to ask the price, just order so-much-money's worth. 3 spoken word; to say, speak. ***né** judging by the sound. ***n-*n** *rg* loud noise. **ng/di*ni** 1 to give a signal/command to. 2 to quote [a price]. *Aku di*ni pira séwané.* She told me how much the rent was.

abab breath from the mouth; *fig* empty talk. **k*an** to get blown on; to feel a rush of air, *e.g.* from a passing vehicle. **ng/di*i** to blow on sth. *** baja** halitosis

abad 1 century. * *kapisan* 1st century. *wiwit *-* kepungkur* for centuries now. 2 *ltry* unchanging, eternal

abadi(jah) eternal; eternity

abah ***-*** *ng kr,* **kambil** *ki* saddle

abang *ng,* **abrit** *kr* 1 red. 2 ripe [of red produce]. ***-* lambé** 1 what the listener wants to hear. *Mung dianggo *-* lambé.* He just said that to be nice. 2 small talk; gossip. *tjatjran sing ora² kanggo *-* lambé* passing the time of day. **ng/di*aké** to cause sth to be red. **ng*aké kuping** to make smn angry. **ng/di*(i)** to redden sth. *Kukuné di*i.* She painted her nails. **ng*i** to become red; to ripen. ***-biru** *ng kr* 1 purplish [of bruised or flushing skin]. 2 circumstances; fate. *Ora ngerti *-biruné, kok ngamuk².* You don't even know what it's all about, but you're all hot under the collar! *Guruné bisa gawé *-biruné botjah sekolah.* The teacher can direct the future course of a child's life. **ng*-biru·ni** 1 to turn purple, *e.g.* with effort, anger. 2 at a loss, unable to make a decision. *** dluwang** pale, ashen. *** mangar²** flushed, unnaturally red [of face, lips]. *** manrang, * (m)branang** bright red. *** mèngèr²** *sms* *** mangar².** *See also* BANG, DJRABANG, KRABANG

abangan one who does not adhere strictly to the precepts of his religion

abdas to clean oneself ritually before prayer

abdi 1 servant (*ki for* BATUR, RÉWANG). 2 I,

me [when addressing royalty]. **ng*** to live in smn's home as a servant (*ki for* NGÈNGÈR). **pa·ng*(an)** *or* **pa·ng*ǹ** service, *e.g.* to a cause

abdi-dalem 1 one in service at the royal court. 2 I, me [when addressing royalty]. *** djaba** palace officials under the vice regent. *** pa·n·djaba** person in charge of outdoor activities. *** djuru** palace soothsayer. *** emban** royal nursemaid. *** empu** royal kris-maker. *** garap** clerk in a Solonese regent's office. *** nijaga** court gamelan player(s). *** pawaka** guard at the gates. *** pradjurit** palace guard. *** silir** one in charge of lamps and electricity

abdjad alphabet

aben 1 each, every (*inf var of* SABEN). 2 confrontation, contact (*kr for* ADU). ***é** 1 usually. 2 judging by the sound (*rg var of* ABA·NÉ). ***-*** from time to time, every so often

aber no longer effective/potent. ***-*an** birds of the air; flying creatures. **k*** having lost effectiveness. **ng*** 1 to lose effectiveness. *Djopa-djapuné wis ng**. The magic formula no longer works. 2 to default on an obligation. **ng*aké** to lose effectiveness; (*psv* **di*aké**) to cause sth to lose its potency. *Ombèn^2 sing waḍahé menga ng*aké rasané.* Drinks left uncovered lose flavor. **pa·ng*an** magical power over enemies. *See also* BER

abis *see* HABIS

abiséka *oj* 1 to succeed to the throne. 2 (a king's) name

abit **m·obat-m*** to wave, flutter. **ng/di*aké** to shake *or* swing sth. *ng*aké buntuté* wagging its tail. *Matjané di*aké kebo.* The kerbau shook off the tiger. **ng/di·obat-*aké** to swing sth back and forth. *ngobat-ng*aké péḍangé* flourishing his sword

abjantârâ 1 *oj* sky, heavens. 2 *ltry* before, in the presence of [a monarch]

abjor to twinkle. *Lintang^2 * ing langit.* Stars twinkled all over the sky. *See also* BJOR

ablah **ng*-*** 1 wide open. 2 to sleep sprawled on one's back

ablak **ng*** 1 *cr* to open the mouth wide; to talk incessantly. 2 (*or* **ng*-***) wide open. 3 (*or* **ng*-***) to flap the wings

Abogé first day in the Alip *windu* (*shc from* ALIP REBO WAGÉ), used as the basis for calculating the date on which Lebaran will fall in any given year

abon deep-fried strips of spiced boiled beef

abonemèn to have a subscription, season ticket, *etc.* for. *Aku * trèm.* I have a streetcar commuter ticket.

abot *ng,* **awrat** *kr* heavy, hard, weighty. *grobag sing ** a heavy wagon. *njambut-gawé ** to do hard *or* heavy work. *Djogèd mau * banget.* This dance is very difficult. ** rasané ninggal kulawarga.* It is hard to leave one's family. **-* ja dilakoni.* No matter how uphill it is, he keeps at it. ** sanggané dadi sedulur tuwa.* An older sibling's obligations weigh heavily. *ukuman ** severe punishment. *mbako ** strong tobacco. *drama sing ** a profound drama. ***é** the weight (of). **é pira?* How much does it weigh? ***ing *** the hardest thing of all. **k*an** 1 excessively heavy *etc.* 2 to find sth too difficult. *Pijé rasamu, rumangsa k*an apa ora?* How do you feel about it—would you mind? **k*en** excessively heavy *etc.* **ng/di*aké** to consider (more) important. *Ng*aké turu apa mangan.* Which is more important, eating or sleeping? **ng/di*i** to add weight, importance, *etc.* to. *Barangé ng*i gawanku.* His things made my load heavier. *Pantjèn pantes di*i lahir batin.* It certainly deserves your complete devotion. **ng/di*-bot·i** to make sth (more) difficult. *** marang** to give weight to, consider important. ** marang kasenenganė.* He puts his own pleasure first. *** telak karo anak** to think more of oneself than of one's children. *See also* BOBOT, BOT

abrag (*or* ***-***) household equipment

abrat **ng*-*** to become scattered/spilled. *Katjangé ng*-* saka karung.* The peanuts spilled out of the bag. **ng/di*aké** to spill *or* scatter sth

abreg *var of* AMBREG

abrik **m·obrak-m*** disarranged, in utter disorder. *Kamaré mobrak-m*.* The room is a shambles. **ng/di·obrak-*** to demolish

abrit red; ripe (*kr for* ABANG)

abrul **ng/di*** 1 to bluff, fake. 2 to acquire dishonestly. *Anggoné djadjan nang warung ng* tahu loro.* He sneaked 2 free beancakes at the snack shop.

abrut **ng/di*-*** to tear apart, scatter

absah 1 valid. ** ditjaṭet* validated. 2 paid up. *Utangku saiki wis *.* My debt is paid. **ng/di*aké** 1 to validate, certify. 2 to pay up. *See also* ABSJAH, SAH

absârâ *see* HABSARA

absari *see* HABSARI

absèn to be absent (from). *Ḍèwèké ora naté * ing gerak^{2}an sosial.* She never passes up social activities.

absès abscess

absjah 1 legal [by Moslem law]. 2 paid up. *See also* ABSAH

abuh swollen. **ng*-*i** bloated, decomposed [of corpses]

abuk powder (*rg var of* BUBUK). **ng/di*** 1 to claim possession of sth one does not own. 2 to obtain merchandise without paying (in full) for it

abul **m*(-m*)** scattered about, in disorder. *Wuluné mabul²*. The feathers were all over the place. *Rambuté mabul²*. Her hair is a mess. **ng/di*-*** *or* **ng/di·obal-*** 1 to scatter, put into disorder. 2 to squander

abunemèn *var of* ABONEMÈN

abur flight through the air. **é menjang endi?* Where's it flying to? **k*** 1 to get blown away. 2 gone, vanished. **k* k·angin·an** 1 to get blown on the wind. 2 without home or possessions. *Kula punika tijang k* kanginan.* I drift with the wind; [when humbly presenting oneself as a bridegroom] I have little to commend me. **m*** 1 to fly. *montor m** airplane. 2 to vanish. *Isiné wis m*.* The contents had disappeared. **m* bleber** to take off (in flight). **ng/di*aké** 1 to fly [a plane]; to have/let [*e.g.* a bird] fly. 2 to let [a pawned item] go unredeemed. 3 to give willingly and generously. *See also* BUR

ach oh!

ach- *see under* AK-

âdâ 1 time, season. **né udan.* It's the rainy season. 2 in command. *Sapa sing * ngarepé kéné?* Who's in command here at the front? ***-*** 1 to initiate. *Sapa sing *-* dolanan iki?* Who started this game? 2 a support, prop. *Jèn tanpa ada² bisa ambruk.* If it isn't propped up, it may collapse. 3 a command, an order. 4 a certain Javanese-script punctuation mark used at the beginning of a sentence. 5 central vein of a leaf or feather. **mang*-*** [of eyelashes] curling upward. **ng/di*ni** 1 to originate, initiate. *ng*ni pilot projèk* to launch a pilot project. 2 to order, direct

âḍâ a small dam

adab refined, well-mannered behavior

adabijah *var of* ADANGIJAH

aḍag **ng*-*** to lie on one's back (face up)

aḍah *var of* WAḌAH

âdâini a major artery or vein in arms or legs. *ngetokaké ** *or* **ng*** to exert oneself physically

aḍak (*or esp.* ***an**) convenient, within easy reach, close to things. *Omahku *an.* Our house is centrally located. ***an(é)** usually

adan (to issue) the call to public prayer. **ng/di*i** to ask God's blessing for [a ceremony]. *See also* KAMAT

adang 1 to cook by steaming. 2 to do the cooking (for) [an occasion]. ***an** act/way of cooking *or* steaming. **ané A ora betjik katimbang B.* A's cooking isn't as good as B's. **ng/di*** to cook sth by steaming. *Berasé di* dadi sega.* She steamed the rice. **ng/di*aké** to cook/steam for smn. *See also* DANG

aḍang ***-*** to wait smw for people/things to go past. **ng/di*** to wait for. *ng* bis* to wait for a bus. *mbégal ng* wong liwat* to waylay and rob passersby. **ng*-* tètès·ing bun** to anxiously await an uncertain outcome. **ng/di*i** to block the passage of. *Tesmak kena kanggo ng*i bledug.* Glasses can keep dust out of your eyes. *Banjuné kali di*i tanggul.* The river is kept to its course by dikes. *ng*-*i wong liwat* to block passersby. **p*** act of lying in wait. **p*an** place where smn lies in ambush. *See also* ḌANG

adangijah *opening salutation of a letter*

adas fennel. *lenga ** aromatic oil taken for stomach ache

adat 1 custom, socialized habit. ** gotong-rojong* the customary practice of mutual help. 2 (*or* ***é**) usually, customarily. **ng*** to make it a habit to [do]; to [do] customarily. *Aku ng* teka djam telu.* I always get here at 3 o'clock. **p*an** habit; (by) custom *or* customary practice. *ngowahi p*an* to change one's habits. *P*an ibu rawuh djam telu.* Mother generally gets home at 3. *** pa·kulina·n** custom, usage. *** saben** the usual practice; **kaja * saben(é)** as usual, as is customary. *** tjara** customs and manners, social norms. *** waton** ancient or traditional custom. *See also* OWAH

adawijah *var of* ADANGIJAH

adeg 1 act of setting up. **é geḍong* the erection of a building. **é jajasan* the establishment of an organization. 2 (**djumeneng** *ki*) act of standing. *djedjeg manut *ing uwit* standing straight as a tree. ***an** 1 *pl* to stand around casually. 2 (**djumeneng·an** *ki*) (day of) ascension to a high position. 3 scene *or* division of a shadow play. ***-*** 1 supporting prop. 2 Javanese punctuation mark used at the beginning of a sentence. 3 paragraph of a handwritten letter. *-* (k)anteb [of babies] to keep falling when trying to stand. *-* saka 1 to stand motionless as a pillar. 2 [of tops] to spin on one spot. 3 sentence-initial Javanese punctuation mark. *-*an *sms* *an. **-*ané Sinuhun Hamengku Buwana* the inauguration of Hamengku Buwana as Sultan. **m*, ng*** 1 (**djumeneng** *ki*) to stand (up). *Kita arep m* ḍéwé.* We want to stand on our own feet. *ng* djedjeg* to stand (up) straight. 2 set up. *Omahé wis m*.* The house is all built. *Geḍungé wis ng*.* The building is completed. 3 (**djumeneng** *ki*) to be elevated to the position of. *m* ratu* to become king. *Surapati ng* sénapati.* Surapati was made field commander. **ng/di*aké** 1 to set up. *ng*aké sekolahan* to establish a school. *ng*aké geḍung* to build a building. 2 (**n/di·djumeneng·aké** *ki*) to raise smn to the position of. *didjumenengaké ratu* to be made king. **ng/di*i** (**n/di·djumeneng·aké** *ki*) 1 to set up. *ng*i omah* to build a house. 2 to be present at. *ng*i wong mati* to attend a funeral. **pa·ng*, pi*** 1 height, stature (*see also* DEDEG). *Ḍuḍukanku wis sapeng* djeroné.* I dug to a depth of a man's height. 2 a complete outfit of clothing: shirt and pants *or* shirt and batik wraparound. *See also* DEG

aḍèg courtship [of animals; *cr* of people]

aḍèh ***an** act of galloping; a gallop. **ng/di*aké** to make [a horse] gallop

aḍèk *rg var of* AḌI

aḍem *ng,* **asrep** *kr* 1 cold, cool; having cooled. *hawa ** cold weather; a cool climate. perang * cold war. 2 secure, untroubled. *gawé *ing panguripan* to make life comfortable. 3 short in weight. *Olèhmu nempur wingi * timbanganė.* The rice you bought yesterday weighed short. **k*-katis** to have chills and fever. **k*en** 1 excessively cold/cool. 2 to have/get a chill. **ng*** to cool oneself. *Wong Djakarta paḍa ng* ana ing Tugu.* Djakarta people go to Tugu to escape from the heat. **ng/di*aké, ng/di*-(-*)i** to make sth cool(er)/cold(er). *** ajem** at peace, calm; indifferent, apathetic. *** anjep** uninterested, aloof. *Jèn krungu tembung politik, gagasané *-anjep baé.* Talk about politics leaves him cold. *** n·djekut** intensely cold. *** tis** to suffer from (being) cold. *See also* ḌEM

aḍèng to recover (from). *Laranė wis * saiki.* He's all well now.

aḍep *ng,* **adjeng** *kr* ***-*an** face to face, opposite each other. **m*** 1 to face (toward). *m* ngalor* to face north. *m* menḍuwur* to look up. *Raimu m*a menjang blabag.* Face the blackboard! 2 to make an appearance. *m* nang pengaḍilan* to appear before the court. 3 steadfast. *m* marang tapa-bratané* to devote oneself to meditation. *manungsa sing wis m** true loyal followers. **m* m·anteb** fixed, determined. *M* mantep pikiré.* He has made up his mind. **ng*** 1 in front of, facing. 2 (*psv* **di***) to visit, appear before [a social superior]; to sit humbly at the feet of [an exalted person]. *mBok Ranu sédané di* putrané.* Mrs. Ranu's sons were present at her death. *Ratu ingaḍep para najaka.* The king received his ministers. **ng* tjèlèng bolot·en** to hang around with undesirable people. **ng/di*aké** 1 to face sth. *Omahé ng*aké pasar.* His house is across from the market. 2 to make sth face. *Di*aké ngalor.* He turned it toward the north. 3 to put in front of. *Sega sak piring wis di*aké marang Slamet.* She set a dish of rice before Slamet. **ng*i** (**ng·adjeng·aken** *kr*) before. *ng*i pemilihan umum* prior to the general election. **ng/di*i** 1 to visit *or* appear before [a social superior]. *Aku wedi banget anggonku bakal ng*i guru.* I'm scared to face the teacher. 2 to face (up to), confront. *ng*i pakéwuh* to be up against difficulties. 3 to place in front of. *Slamet wis di*i sega sak piring.* She set a dish of rice before Slamet. *See also* AREP[b], ḌEP

adha (*prn* **âdâ**) *See* IDUL

adi 1 fine, beautiful. 2 name of the 1st *windu.* ***ǹ** to serve, wait on, make things pleasant for. ***ǹ-*ǹ** 1 spoiled, overindulged. 2 that which is fine, beautiful, highly prized. **ng*** to beautify, make fine. *ng* busana* to dress beautifully. *ng* sarira* to beautify one's appearance. **ng*-*** 1 overindulged, spoiled, demanding. 2 (*psv* **di***) to make beautiful; to value highly. **ng/di*kaké** 1 to revere. 2 to have [clothing] made to order. *ngadèkaké klambi* to have a dress made. **ng/di*ǹ-*ǹi** to make sth beautiful/fine. *** aèng** valuable and rare. *** éndah** beautiful, splendid. *** luhung** of outstanding quality, highly esteemed. **-luhungé laki-rabi* the sacred nature of marriage. *∗-luhunging djogèd* the exquisiteness of the dance. *wulang ∗-luhung* revered teachings. ∗ **luwih** fine, sublime, exalted. *kagunan sing ∗-luwih* the fine arts

aḍi *ng kr,* **raji** *ki* younger sibling. ∗ *lanang (wédok)* younger brother (sister). *kakang ∗ku* my brothers and sisters. **ng∗** to call smn, or regard smn as, one's own younger sibling. ∗ **ipé** younger sibling-in-law. *See also* ḌI

adigang (to make) an arrogant display of one's superior power

adiguna (to make) an arrogant display of one's superior knowledge

adigung (to make) an arrogant display of one's superior status. *Ḍèké isih enom, mulané bandjur adigang ∗ adiguna.* He's young so he tries to impress people.

aḍik *var of* AḌI

adil just, impartial, equitable. *angger² sing ∗* fair regulations. *∗ing hjang* divine justice. **ke∗an** justice. *keadilan sosial* social justice. **ng/di∗i** 1 to judge; to act as judge. 2 to put smn on trial. **pa·ng∗an** law court. **pa·ng∗an adat** court of customary (rather than codified) law. ∗ **makmur** characterized by justice and prosperity

aḍil **m·oḍal-m∗** messy, untidy. **ng/di·oḍal-∗** 1 to scatter things about. 2 to uncover, disclose. *Ḍèké pinter nèk kon ngoḍal-∗ rahasiané wong.* She's good at worming people's secrets out of them.

adilâgâ *oj* war, battle

adiningrat *honorific particle used after the city names Surakarta and Jogjakarta (sites of royal courts)*

adipati *see* HADIPATI

âdjâ[a] *ng,* **sampun** *kr* 1 don't! *Adja.* Don't (do that)! Hands off! You can't have it! *Sampun ngantos itjal.* Try not to lose it. ∗ *mengkono.* Not like that! 2 may [it] not. ∗ *ana kang paḍa djahil.* I hope none of them bears a grudge. 3 *with doubled adjective* not too...! ∗ *adoh².* Don't go too far off. ∗ *suwé² anggonmu lunga.* Don't be gone too long. *Sambelé ∗ peḍes².* Don't make the sauce too spicy. 4 *with doubled word* don't by any means...! ∗ *menèh² kanḍa ngono.* Never say that again! ∗ *kanḍa² sapa² lho.* Don't tell *anybody!* **∗a** if it were not for the fact that... *Adjaa adoh mono, bukuné rak wis tak parani.* If it weren't so far, I'd have gone for the book by now. **∗-∗** I'm afraid (that...). *Bapakmu kok ora kundur², adja² kepantjal sepur.* Dad isn't home yet–I'm afraid he missed his train. ∗ **ana kang/sing** don't let it happen that... *Adja ana kang kèri barang² sing dipinḍah kuwi.* Be sure not to leave anything behind that's to be moved. ∗ *ana sing buḍal jèn durung ana tengara.* No one is to leave before the signal is given. ∗ **(ḍi)sik** not too soon! ∗ *ḍisik, mengko² baé jèn udané wis terang.* Not now! wait till it stops raining. ∗ **dupèh** don't rely too heavily on a superficial asset. ∗ *dupèh rupané bagus tanpa tanḍing.* Don't put too much stock in your good looks. ∗ *dupèh sugih mbandjur tetuku tanpa nganjang.* Just because you're rich doesn't mean you shouldn't haggle over prices. ∗ **éntuk** *sms* ∗ OLÈH *below.* ∗ **kongsi** *sms* ∗ NGANTI *below.* ∗ **manèh** *sms* ∗ SING *below.* ∗ **manèh²** don't ever [do] again! ∗ **nganti** 1 don't let it happen that... ∗ *nganti tiba.* Don't fall! 2 [to tell smn] not to... *Ali nuturi aḍiné adja nganti mangan pelem mentah.* Ali told his sister not to eat unripe mangoes. 3 [in order] not to, [in order that] not. *Ḍèwèké nduduti goprak supaja krambilé ∗ dipangan badjing.* He rattled the noisemaker so the squirrels wouldn't eat the coconuts. ∗ **olèh** don't give permission! *Botjah² ∗ olèh dolanan ana ing djaba, jèn isih udan.* Don't let the children play out in the rain. ∗ **pisan(2)** don't by any means... ∗ *pisan² nerak wewalering para tuwa.* Never disobey your parents! ∗ **sing** let alone; much less. ∗ *sing mangan, njeḍak baé wedi.* He was afraid to come near it, much less eat it. ∗ *sing mlaju, mlaku waé ora bisa.* Run? he can't even walk. ∗ **sok** don't ever... *Kowé ∗ sok njatur lijan.* Never gossip. ∗ **tan ora** don't fail to... *Jèn kebeneran rawuh Ngajodja, ∗ tan ora tindak kampir.* If you're ever in Jogja, be sure to drop in!

âdjâ[b] **ng/di∗ni** to urge *or* persuade smn to do wrong. **pa·ng∗n** persuasion, urgings. *Kowé adja pisan² kèlu pang∗n ala.* Don't ever go along with smn who tries to get you to do wrong.

adjab **∗-∗an** to wish sth for/on each other. *∗-∗an runtuhé sidji lan sidjiné.* Each hopes the other will collapse. **∗-ing∗** *ltry var of* **∗-∗an.** **ng/di∗** to hope/wish (for). *ng∗ dadi pradjurit* hoped to become a soldier. *Ora betjik ng∗ tjilakaning lijan.* You shouldn't wish bad luck on other people.

ng/di*(-*) to hope (for), look forward to, anticipate

adjag plants set in among other plants of a different kind. ***an** planted among other plants. **ané winih térong* interspersed eggplant seedlings. **ng/di*** to intersperse. *Witē djati di* nganggo tanduran kopi.* Coffee is grown among the teak trees. **ng/di*i** to plant [an area] with additional plants. *ng*i kebonē klapa* to plant things among the coconut palms. *See also* ASU

adjah ***an** (a) trained (animal). *Gadjahé ana ing sirkus iki kabèh *an.* The elephants in this circus are all performing elephants. **ng/di*aké** to train for smn; to have trained. *A ng*aké asuné.* A had his dog trained. **ng/di*(i)** to train [animals]

adjaib (*or* **ng***) astounding, marvelous, wonderful. *karja sing ** an astounding piece of work

adjak ***an** a suggestion to join in smn's activity. *Adja nurut *an sing ala.* Don't let yourself be persuaded to do wrong. ***-*** to ask smn to [do] with oneself. *Ḍèwèké *-* bal²an kantjané.* He asked his friends to play soccer with him. ***-*an** to ask each other to join in activities. **ng/di*(i)** to ask smn to [do] with one. *A ng* B nonton wajang.* A asked B to see a shadow play with him. *Aku diundang arep di* mangan énak.* I was invited to join them in a delicious meal. **pa·ng*** a suggestion (as above). *Pang*é kasil.* His urgings were successful. *See also* DJAK

adjal[a] ***é** have a try! let's try (and see). **é, aku sing mbukak.* Let me see if I can open it. ***-*** to try, make an effort. *See also* DJADJAL, DJAL

adjal[b] 1 origin, source. *Apa sing dadi * kobongan?* What caused the fire? 2 limit, boundary; dividing line; *fig* death. ** antaraning negara* boundaries between nations. *Apa kang dumadi ing donja iku mawa *.* Every creature on earth has a finite life. ***an** dividing line; time limit. ***-*** *or* **ng*(-mulih·an), ng*(-pulih·an), ng*(-ulih·an)** to return to where one came from; *fig* to die. *Wis ng*-ulihan ing Indonesia.* He's back in Indonesia now. *Durung lawas nggoné pegatan, wis ng*-ulihan.* They haven't been divorced long and now they're remarrying. *Embokné wis ng*.* His mother is dead. **ng/di*i** 1 to form a boundary *or* dividing line for. *Indonesia di*i segara ing sisih kidul.* Indonesia is bounded on the south by ocean. 2 to set a time limit (on). *Garapané di*i nganti sésuk.* The assignment has to be handed in tomorrow. *** ka·mula·n** origin, source. *wong * kamulaning tanah ing Indonesia* a native of Indonesia. *See also* PADJAL

adjan *var of* ADAN

adjang 1 a dish from which food is eaten. 2 site of an activity. **é olah-raga* a place for athletics. *Ḍémokrasi dadi *ing rakjat kanggo kiprah bebarengan.* A democracy is an area for people to pool their efforts. 3 line of work. *kantjané sa** colleague, co-worker. *tunggal ** (to work as) colleagues, co-workers. ***an** a helping of food. **ng/di*i** 1 to dish up smn's food. *Sing ng*i mbakju.* My sister served. 2 to prepare a setting for. *ng*i rembug politik* to clear the way for political talks. 3 to serve as a(n adequate) site for. *Omahmu tjukup kanggo ng*i tamu limang atus.* Your house will hold 500 guests. *Garapané di*i sa*-*é.* He devotes his best efforts to his work. **sa*-*(ing *)** to one's utmost. *Tamuné disuguh sa-adjang²ing *.* The guests were treated royally.

adjar 1 to learn, receive training (in). ** basa* to study a language. ** nembang* to learn to sing. 2 teacher of spiritual knowledge. *Ki * adr* teacher. 3 section(s) of a citrus fruit. *djeruk bali sa** a grapefruit section. ***an** 1 teaching(s); a lesson. **an Sing Kaping Sidji* Lesson One. *Kuwi *ané sapa?* Who taught you that? 2 in the learning stage. *Lagi *an durung isa tenan.* I'm just learning, I can't really do it yet. 3 divided into sections [of fruit]. ***-*an** 1 teaching(s); act of teaching. *angèl *-*ané* hard to teach. 2 to teach each other. **ng/di*** to teach, train; to discipline; to punish. *ng* tatakrama* to teach proper behavior. *Wis di* sakajangé.* He's been severely punished. **ng/di*aké** 1 to teach [a subject]. *ng*aké djogèd* to teach a dance. 2 to have smn trained/disciplined. **ng/di*i** 1 to teach smn to [do]. *ng*i ndjogèd* to teach smn to dance. *Keṭèké di*i sila.* The monkey was trained to sit cross-legged. 2 to divide [fruit] into sections. **pa·ng*an** instruction, training, education. *See also* KURANG

adjat *ltry* 1 a need. ** sing djasmani (rohani)* a physical (spiritual) need. 2 extra Islamic prayer said at midnight. 3 religious offering *or* sacrifice. 4 public prayer meeting.

5 *var of* KADJAT. **ng/di*aké** to wish for [an objective]. **ng/di*(i)** to wish for, plan, intend. *Aku ng* dadi ḍokter.* I hope to become a doctor.

adjeg constant, steady, fixed. *Hawa ing tanah Djawa kuwi * panas kok.* It's always warm in Java. *Reregan *.* Prices are steady. *Djam iki lakuné *.* This watch keeps good time. *Lampu sanḍuwuring menara kaé bjarpeté *.* The tower light flashes on and off at regular intervals. *Buruh kuwi ana sing * ana sing lepas.* There are permanent workers and casual workers. **ng/di*aké** to have/make smn [do] steadily; to accustom smn to [do]-ing. *Anaké di*aké linggih djedjeg.* She always makes her son sit up straight. **ng/di*i** to [do] steadily *or* as a regular practice. *A ng*i teka mruput.* A always shows up early. *See also* DJEDJEG, DJEG

adjeng 1 younger sister; younger female friend. 2 facing (*root form: kr for* AḌEP). 3 progress, forward movement (*kr for* ADJU). 4 front *etc.* (*root form: kr for* AREP[b]). 5 will, want (*md for* AREP[a]). ***a, *ipun** even though (*md for* AREP[a]·A). *See also* DJENG

adjèr to melt, dissolve; *fig* to relent. **ng/di*aké** to melt for smn; to have sth melted. **ng/di*(i)** to melt/dissolve sth. **pa·ng*an** act of melting. *See also* DJÈR

adji[a] *ng,* **aos** *sbst? kr* (to have) value; (to be) worth. *banḍa kang ora seṭiṭik *né* property of no small value. *pitik * wolulas rupiah* an 18-rupiah chicken. ***ǹ-*ǹan (aos-aosan** *kr; ltry var* ***ǹ-ing*ǹan)** to show respect for each other. *Ing sesrawungan adjèn-ingadjènan iku perlu banget.* In social interaction, mutual respect is essential. **k*ǹ** respectable. *Djeneng ora kadjèn jèn guru djadjan ana ing pinggir ndalan.* It isn't considered proper for teachers to eat in public. **k*ǹ-k·éring·an** widely respected (*see also* ÉRING). **ng/di*-*** to esteem, value highly. *di*-* ing wong akèh* respected by many people. *Ṭeṭukulané di*-*.* They pamper the seedlings. **ng/di*ǹi 1 (ǹj/di·suhun[2]** *ki*) to respect, honor, esteem. *ngadjèni wong sing luwih tuwa* to respect one's elders. 2 to assign a value to. *Jèn topi mau reganè mung rong rupiah, rak prasasat bauné ora diadjèni.* If the hats only cost 2 rupiahs, the labor couldn't have been taken into account. **pa·ng*(an)** *sms* ADJI. *** goḍong djati aking** worthless. *See also* BEDJADJI

adji[b] 1 *oj* king. 2 incantation, magic spell. 3 to want, desire. ***-*** 1 spell, incantation. 2 amulet. **(k)* pumpung** to avail oneself of an opportunity to enjoy oneself. *See also* ADJISAKA

adji[c] 1 recitation of the Koran. 2 *var of* KADJI. 3 the month (*Besar*) during which the Mecca mosque is open to pilgrims. **ng*** 1 to learn to read, interpret, and recite from the Koran. 2 to live in the home of highly placed persons in order to learn their ways. **ng/di*kaké** to have smn read aloud from the Koran, or receive instruction in such reading. **pa·ng*ǹ** place where Koran-reading is learned

adjiḍan *var of* ADJUḌAN

adjir *rg var of* ANDJIR

Adjisâkâ King Saka (*ancient monarch alleged to have invented the Javanese calendar and alphabet*). *taun Adji(saka)* year of the Javanese calendar. *taun sèwu limang atus sèket lima (adji)* the Javanese year 1555. *See also* ADJI[b], SAKA[c]

adjrih fear; afraid; awe, respect (*kr for* WEDI). **ng*-*i** awesome. *Pasinḍèné ng*-*i, mula laris banget.* She has a fine singing voice, so she is much in demand. *kekijatan ingkang ng*-*i* fearsome strength

adju *ng,* **adjeng** *kr* forward movement; progress. **ning ékonomi* economic progress. ***n̂** confrontation. **ng/di*k̂aké** 1 to put forward; to (cause to) move forward. *Sapa sing ngadjokaké kursi mau?* Who moved those chairs up front? *ngadjokaké agama Islam* to promote the Moslem religion. *ngadjokaké rantjangan* to submit a plan *or* program. 2 to (have smn) come forward on smn's behalf. *A ora wani omong ḍéwé ndjur wong lija sing diadjokaké.* A didn't dare speak up, so he had smn speak for him. **ng/di*n̂i** to take part in. *Sing ngadjoni sajembara wong akèh.* Many people entered the prize contest. **ng/di*n̂-*n̂i** to accept [a bet] (and raise the stakes). *** undur** ups and downs. ** unduring ékonomi* economic vicissitudes. *See also* MADJU

adjuḍan adjutant (military rank)

adjug ***-*** 1 tray *or* pedestal for an oil lamp. 2 guiding mechanism of a harrow

adjun(g) assistant, lieutenant. ** komisaris (pulisi)* deputy (police) commissioner

adjur 1 severely damaged, crushed. ** dadi awu* reduced to ashes. *Montoré tabrakan nganti dadi *.* The car was badly damaged in a collision. 2 to dissolve, disintegrate, digest. *Pangan ora bisa ndang ∗.* Food doesn't digest right away. *Gula ditjampur banju dadi ∗.* Sugar dissolves in water. ∗ **ati·né** griefstricken. ∗ **kumur²** smashed, wrecked. *Omahé ketiban bom sanalika ∗ kumur².* The house was hit by a bomb and destroyed. ∗ **luluh** completely dissolved. ∗ **memet,** ∗ **mumur** pulverized. *Watuné ∗ mumur.* The stone was crushed to a powder. *Omahé digempur ∗ mumur.* The house was demolished. ∗ **wor kisma** *wj* utterly crushed; [of dead people] (having turned to) dust. *See also* DJUR[a]

aḍo *var of* AḌUH

adoh *ng,* **tebih** *kr* far, distant. *Sekolah ∗ saka omahku.* The school is a long way from my house. *Adja ∗.* Don't go far. *Pantjèn isih sedulur, nanging rada ∗.* We're related, but rather distantly. **∗é** distance (to, between). *Sepira ∗é?* How far (off) is it? **∗-∗an** to compare *or* compete for distance. **∗-∗é** 1 distance apart. 2 not farther than. *Saka Djakarta nang Bogor adoh²é sèket kilomèter.* It's 50 kilometers at the most from Djakarta to Bogor. **k∗an** 1 afar; the far distance. *Anggonku ngrungokaké saka kadohan.* I heard it from a long way off. 2 (*or* **k∗en**) excessively far. *Adja kadohen olèhmu lingguh munḍak ora weruh.* Don't sit too far away or you won't be able to see. **ng∗** to get far(ther) away. **ng/di∗aké** to keep sth at a distance. *Omah sing resik bisa ng∗aké laler.* A clean house keeps flies away. **ng/di∗i** to keep at a distance from; to move away from. ∗ **ng·aluk-aluk** at a great distance. *Kétoké ∗ ngaluk-aluk, djebul tjeḍak baé.* It looks as if it's miles off, but it's actually quite close. **∗-tjeḍak·é** distance (to, between). *Montor bisa ngretèni ∗-tjeḍaké dalan sing diliwati.* Cars show the distance you travel. *See also* DOH

adol 1 (**sadé** *kr*) to sell. *sing ∗* seller, clerk. *Wong dagang jèn kulak murah jèn ∗ larang.* Businessmen buy cheap and sell expensive. 2 to lease out a rice paddy on certain terms. 3 to act vain/boastful about. ∗ **abab** 1 to persuade smn to buy merchandise one cannot deliver. 2 to brag, boast. ∗ **aju/bagus** to show off one's good looks. ∗ **awak** to engage in prostitution. ∗ **awèh tuku arep/gelem** to deal justly/impartially with (*see also* TUKU). *Guru tumraping murid kudu tumindak sarwa ∗ awèh tuku arep.* Teachers must treat all pupils the same. ∗ **bau** to offer one's services for hire. ∗ **bokong** to get paid for occupying smn's seat as a way of holding it in a crowded place. ∗ **gawé** to hire oneself out. ∗ **gembès** *sms* ∗ AWAK. ∗ **karja** to serve for pay. ∗ **kuning** to sell ripened rice before it is harvested. ∗ **plaju·ñ** to sell in haste. ∗ **sanggup** to make empty promises. ∗ **sénḍé** to sell [a paddy] temporarily. ∗ **supata** to disavow with an oath. ∗ **swara** 1 to show off one's singing. 2 to cheat people by lying. ∗ **tuwa** to sell one's ripened rice before it is harvested. ∗ **umuk** to boast. *See also* DODOL, DOL

ados 1 misshapen [of fruits]. 2 fine (*sbst kr for* ADI). **ng∗i** to grow misshapen

adpertènsi (*abbr:* **adv.**) advertisement. *masang ∗* to advertise

adpis advice, counsel. **ng/di∗i** to advise

adpokat 1 avocado. 2 lawyer, defense counselor

adreng strong, firm, eager. ∗ *(ing) tékad* strongly determined. *A ∗ olèhé arep njambut gawé nang Djakarta.* A is most eager to work in Djakarta.

adrès address on a letter. **ng/di∗aké** to address sth. *Lajangé di∗aké marang panggeḍéné.* The letter is addressed to the boss. **ng/di∗i** to write an address on. *amplop sing wis di∗i lan sing ana prangkoné* a stamped self-addressed envelope

adres hard, heavy (*var of* DERES)

adu *ng,* **aben** *kr* 1 in contact; in confrontation. ∗ *arep* face to face. ∗ *geger* back to back. ∗ *tungkak* heels together. 2 to bring into contact/confrontation. *Wong main iku ∗ begdja.* Gamblers put their luck on the line. ∗ *kesèd* to try to outloaf each other. 3 ingredient; compatible accompaniment. *Suruh sa∗né djenengé kinang.* Betel with other ingredients is a betel chew. **∗ñ** 1 contestant. *djago adon* game cock. 2 advocate (of). *adon kemardikan* freedom fighter. 3 ingredient; accompaniment. *tèh nganggo adon gula batu* tea with sugar lumps. **∗ñ-∗ñ** 1 contest, tournament. 2 to set [opponents] on each other. 3 (mixed) ingredients. *adon²é roti* cake ingredients; cake batter. **∗ñ-∗ñan** (mixed) ingredients. *adon²an tjampuran semèn nganggo gamping* a mixture of cement and lime. **ng/di∗(-∗)** to pit against. *ng∗ karosan* to have a confrontation of strength. *Anak²é sing gelut di∗ bapaké.* The boys' fathers let them fight it out. **ng∗ kumba** to knock together the heads of [two combatants]. * **prakara** to bring a case to court; to face up to the facts of a matter; to bring face-to-face. **ng/di*ni** 1 to confront; to face up to. *ngadoni prang* to go to war. *ngadoni pituturing wong tuwa* to go against one's parents' advice. 2 to incite. *Jèn ora ana sing ngadon-adoni, wong tjilik ora bakal brontak.* If no one rouses the people, they won't rebel. 3 to mix; to combine/accompany with. *ngadoni djamu* to mix up a batch of medicine. *Wédangé diadoni patjitan.* Snacks were served with the tea. **pa·ng*an** (*or* **pa·ng*nan** *ng*) 1 fighting area. *pangadonan djago* cock-fighting arena. 2 court for litigation. * **djago** a cock fight; to pit game cocks against each other. * **gambar umbul** a children's picture-card game. * **ketjik (kemiri,** *lsp.*) (to play) a game of matching *sawo*-fruit pits (*kemiri* fruits, *etc.*). * **manis** 1 in a neat or pleasing arrangement. 2 in a friendly manner. * **rasa** compatibility, sympathy; compatible. * **semu** in mutual understanding. * **sèrèt** 1 [of floor tiles *etc.*] fitted together checkerboard style. 2 [of stripes] set in a zigzag herringbone pattern. * **sungut** a clash, conflict; to clash. * **swara** to quarrel. * **ka·tjipta** 1 with centers together. 2 ideal, just right. 3 sadness, grief, heartbreak. *See also* DU

aḍu *rg var of* **gaḍu.** **ng/di*** to sue, bring legal action against. **pa·ng*an** lawsuit

aḍuh *excl of pain, sorrow, joy.* *, *lara wetengku.* Ooo, my stomach hurts! * *aḍemé.* My but it's cold! * *lega rasané atiku.* What a relief! **ng*** to exclaim in pain *etc.* *Ora di-kapak²aké ng*-*.* Nobody did anything to him but he kept yelling ouch! * **bijung** (*or* * **mbok)** *excl of pain.* * *bijung, wetengku lara.* Oo, I have a stomach ache. * **laé** my goodness! oh dear! why...!

aḍuk ***an** 1 [of soil] loosened for planting. 2 stirred from the bottom. **m*** [of soil] dry and dusty. **ng/di*** to bring what is underneath to the surface. *Sawah anggoné ng* nganggo luku.* Soil in a paddy is turned over with a plow. *Djangané adja di*.* Don't stir up the solids in the soup. *Koperé di*-* pegawé ḍuane.* The customs official plowed through my suitcase. **pa·ng*** act/way of bringing things to the surface from underneath

adul ***-*** to carry tales (to). *wong sing ḍemen *-** tale-bearer, tattletale. *Ḍèkè adul² bapakné menawa mentas dipojoki kantjané.* He told his father his friend had teased him. ***-*en** to carry tales habitually. **ng/di*aké** to tell tales about sth. **ng/di*(-*)i** to tell tales to. *Bapak-ibuné anggeré di*-*i mesṭi pertjaja.* Whenever he tells his parents bad things about smn, they believe him. **pa·ng*-*** tale-bearing. *See also* WADUL

aḍul **m*-m*** *or* **m·oḍal-m*** 1 unkempt, disheveled; scattered about untidily. 2 to spend [money] foolishly. **ng/di*-*** *or* **ng/di·oḍal-*** 1 to mess things up, scatter things about. 2 to unravel a mystery, disclose a secret

aḍum *var of* ÉDUM. ***-*an** to discuss (*esp.* private matters)

adus *ng kr,* **siram** *ki* 1 to take a bath. 2 to go swimming. **p*an** 1 place for bathing. 2 the day before the beginning of the fasting month, when people cleanse themselves ritually. * **getih** bleeding from wounds all over the body. * **grudjug** to bathe by pouring water over the head with a dipper. * **kringet** to labor physically. *Wis diréwangi * kringet anggoné gliḍig.* He works himself to the bone. * **kungkum** to take a tub bath. * **nipas** ritual bath 40 days after giving birth. * **sibin(g)** to take a quick bath. *See also* DUS

adv. *See* ADPERTÈNSI

advis *var of* ADPIS

adzan *var of* ADAN

aem *var of* MAEM

aèn (*or* **ng*)** bound to happen, beyond any doubt. **ng/di*aké** to prove sth is real

aèng out of the ordinary. *Tumindaké *.* He acts odd. *Aku mau weruh pit *.* I just saw a funny-looking bike. **ng/di*aké** to regard sth as odd. *Slamet ng*aké kanḍaku.* Slamet thought what I said was peculiar. **ng*-*i** to behave in an odd *or* unusual way

aèr *oj* water. *djambu ** a juicy guava. * **blanḍa** soda water, fizz water

afdrek *var of* APDREK

Ag. *See* AGUSTUS

âgâ *rg var of* SAGA. ***n** that which is saved *or* laid aside. **ϕ/di*** to save up, lay aside. *Ḍuwité di* kanggo tuku omah mbésuk.* He's saving up for a house.

agahan eager. *Saking luwéné anggoné mangan *.* He was so hungry he wolfed his food.

agak 1 thought, opinion, guess. *Jèn *é abot, koperé adja mbok gawa ḍéwé.* If you think the trunk is too heavy, don't carry it by yourself. 2 leader, moving force. *∗é dé-monstrasiné ditjekel pulisi.* The leader of the demonstration was arrested. 3 to threaten (*root form: var of* AGAR). 4 *var of* ANGGAK. **ng/di∗** to think, form an opinion (about). *Di∗ sugih, djebul mlarat.* They thought he was rich, but he was poor. **ng∗-∗** 1 to fake, simulate. *Dak kira botjah mau mung ng∗-∗ waé anggoné lara karebèn ora sekolah.* I think he's just pretending to be sick, to get out of going to school. 2 unable to sleep. *obat sing bisa njegah ng∗-∗* a drug to counteract insomnia. 3 to resist cure. *Lelara sing awèt iku ng∗-∗.* Chronic diseases hang on and on.

agal 1 large. *Iwaké dipilihi ∗ paḍa ∗, lembut paḍa lembut.* He sorted the fish by size. 2 rough, coarse, crude. *watu ∗* coarse stones. *nam²an ∗* rough wickerwork. *Wong iku ∗.* He's a boor. 3 physical *(as contrasted with spiritual);* corporeal; visible. **m∗** large, gross. *Télané m∗, mulané ora bisa mateng.* The cassava is so big it won't cook through. **ng/di∗aké** to make sth coarse(r)/rough(er). **ng/di∗(i)** to treat roughly/crudely. *Jèn ora kena dialusi, di∗ baé.* If you can't persuade him, get tough with him. **∗ alus** coarse and refined; physical and mental/spiritual. *kawruh ∗ alus* worldly and spiritual knowledge. *njambut gawé ∗-alus* any kind of work. **∗ ḍemit, ∗ repit** secret sin

agâmâ *ng,* **agami** *kr* religion. *∗ Buḍa* Buddhism. *∗ Islam* Islam. *∗ Kristen* Christianity. *sekolah guru agama* theological seminary. **ke∗n** religious matters; connected with religion. *buku² keagaman* religious books

agami *kr for* AGAMA

agar **∗an** act/way of rubbing. *∗ané ora rata.* It wasn't rubbed smooth. **∗-∗** 1 a certain seaweed; jelly processed from this. 2 a threat(ening gesture). *Gamané kanggo ∗-∗ baé.* The weapon is just a deterrent. **∗-∗an** to threaten each other. **ng/di∗** to smooth, rub. *Ḍekik² di∗ rata nganggo ḍempul.* He smoothed over the dents with putty. **ng∗ geni** to make fire by rubbing wood against wood. **ng∗ metu kawul** to fail in an attempt to stir smn up. **ng/di∗-∗** 1 to threaten physically. 2 to brandish [a weapon]. **ng/di∗aké** to brandish [a weapon]. **ng/di∗(-∗)i** *sms* **ng/di∗-∗.** *Kètjuné ng∗-∗i nganggo gegaman api.* The bandit held a gun on him.

agé *or* **∗-∗** (**énggal⁽²⁾** *kr?*) quick; right away. *Adja ∗, sésuk waé.* Not so fast–tomorrow is soon enough.

agèk 1 *var of* LAGI. 2 *rg var of* AGLIK

agem 1 measuring unit for rice: [of plants] the number one can hold between thumb and forefinger; [of raw grains] an amount weighing *ca.* 375 *kati* (231 kilograms = 509 lbs.). 2 to use; to wear *(root form: ki for* ANGGO). **ng/di∗** to measure [rice] in the above units. **ng/di∗i** to hold sth between thumb and forefinger. **∗ rasuk·an** *ki* custom-made clothing

agèn 1 neighborhood dealer in periodicals. 2 agent, representative. *∗ pulisi* policeman

ageng large, great (*kr for* GEḌÉ)

ager **∗-∗** seaweed (jelly) (*var of* AGAR.²)

agik *var of* AGLIK

agil **ogal-∗** to teeter, sway precariously. *botjah ogal-∗* an only child. *See also* WOT

aglag **ng∗-∗** *rg* to eat

aglèg *rg var of* AGLIG

aglig **oglag-∗** unstable, wobbly. **m·oglag-m∗** (coming) loose. *Untuné wis moglak-m∗ arep tjopot.* His tooth is so loose it's about to come out. **ng/di·oglag-∗** to move sth back and forth to loosen it

agni *oj* fire

agor **ng∗-∗i** [of adolescent boys' voices] beginning to change

agra *oj* top, peak, point

agrariā agriculture. *kantor ∗* agricultural office

agrèh **ng·ograh-∗** to disturb, irritate. *See also* OGRÈH

agrèk **ng/di·ogrèk-∗** 1 to prod (at) with a stick *or* pole. 2 to disturb, shake up

agrong steep(ly rising, falling). *djurang ∗* a precipitous canyon. *See also* MAGRONG

agul **∗-∗** bulwark. *Pistul iki dak dadèkaké agul²ing atiku.* I put my trust in this pistol. **ng/di∗-∗aké** to use as one's bulwark. *Ḍèké mung ng∗-∗ké oomé sing dadi menteri.* He rides on the coattails of his uncle, a cabinet minister. **ng/di∗-∗i** to bolster, rally. *ng∗-∗i wadyabalané* to rally the spirits of one's troops. *See also* NGE·GUL·AKÉ

agung 1 high, exalted; great, large. *Sultan ∗* (His Majesty) the Sultan. 2 high [of water level]. *See also* MAGUNG

agus *rg var of* GUS

Agustus (*abbr:* **Ag.**) August

ah *excl of protest, disagreement, displeasure. Wis ∗.* That's enough now! Stop it!

*Durung wantjiné *!* It's not time yet! **, kok memelas temen.* My, what a pity!

Ahad *var sp of* ACHAD

ahah *rg var of* AḌUH

ahjun *var of* AJUN[b]

ahli specialist, expert. *ḍokter * urat saraf* neurologist. *ḍokter * penjakit kulit* dermatologist. *wong * budi* a person of intelligence. **ke*an** expertise, specialized knowledge. **ng/di*kaké** to convey expert knowledge to, to train as an expert. *** waris** heir

ai *excl of incredulity or deprecation*

aib var of GAIB

ai:l weary [of the mouth]. *Tjangkemku *.* My mouth needs a rest (from talking, eating).

ain *var of* AÈN

air *see* TANAH

âjâ 1 (to have) trouble, difficulty. 2 *ltry var of* ADJA[a]. **ng*(-*)** to struggle against odds. *Olèhku ngepit wis ng* tekan sekolahan djebul prèi.* I went to all the trouble of riding my bike to school only to find there was no class. *Miturut kekuwatané ṭok, ora ng*-*.* Just do what you can without straining yourself. **ng* laku** to shorten the time of a journey by redoubling one's effort. *See also* ÉWUH

ajab a large long-handled fish net. **ng/di*(i)** to catch [fish] with such a net

ajah 1 time *(inf var of* WAJAH*)*. ** ésuk* in the morning. ** ngéné* at a time like this. 2 *excl of incredulity. *, kowé kuwi bandjur arep anggelar wulang.* Don't tell me you're going to teach! ***an** (community) task. *gotong-rojong kanggo nindakaké *ané kampung²* mutual assistance for carrying out community work. **ng*** to act in one's own way *or* on one's own responsibility. *Jèn ora ngerti takon, adja ng*.* If you don't know how, ask; don't go ahead on your own. **ng/di*i** to do, perform, carry out (esp. community obligations). *ng*i kuwadjibané* to do one's duty. *ng*i ḍawuhing pukulun* to carry out the chief's orders. **pa·ng*** one who does community service

ajak ***an** strainer, sieve; screen. ***(n)é (m·bok menawi** *kr***)** probably, perhaps. ** ija* maybe so. ** ora* probably not. **di*i** 1 to be summoned officially to perform a task. 2 *(acv* **ng*i***)* to strain *or* screen sth

ajam 1 chicken *(kr for* PITIK*)*. 2 hen. ***-*** fitful [of sleep]. ***-*an** 1 waterfowl. 2 a certain grass. *** alas** woodcock, woodhen; **ng*-alas** resembling a woodcock/woodhen

ajan epilepsy. ***an** to have/get epilepsy

ajang ***-*an** shadow *(see also* WAJANG[a]*)*. **di*** to be aided. *Arepa di* kaja ngapa wis ora bisa ketulungan.* No matter how much we help, nothing can be done for her any more.

ajar small bundle of harvested rice ready to spread for sun-drying. **ng/di*i** to prepare [rice plants] for sun-drying

ajat verses in the Koran. **ng/di*i** 1 to carry out, perform. *ng*i ndjogèd* to perform a dance. *Gawéané di*i bebarengan.* They did the job together. 2 to bend [a bow, before releasing the arrow]

ajeg **m*-m*** *or* **ng*-*** 1 unsteady, threatening to topple. *Gawané ng*-*.* He's carrying too big a load. *Wit kaé majeg² jèn kena angin.* The tree shuddered in the wind. 2 far in the distance. *Désa sing ditudju isih ng*-*.* The village they're heading for is a long way off.

ajem untroubled, comfortable. *Lakuné *.* His pace was leisurely. *Mangsuli karo *.* He replied calmly. **-*ing ati* feelings of inner peace. ***(-*)an** free of cares or troubles. *botjah sing *an* a happy-go-lucky boy. **ng/di*** to keep sth [*e.g.* tobacco] moist. **ng/di*-*(i)** to make smn calm/comfortable. *Atiné paḍa di*-*i.* They set his mind at rest. *Jèn minggon paḍa ng*-* ana ing Puntjak.* They spend leisurely Sundays in Puntjak. *See also* JEM

ajer overseer, supervisor. ***an** 1 one's responsibility; a dependent. 2 security, *e.g.* for a loan

ajid 1 *(prn* **aji:d***)* sticky, gooey. 2 rancid, spoiled

ajig **ojag-*** unsteady; to shake, wobble. *Kretegé wis ojag-*.* The bridge sways. **m*-m*** *or* **m·ojag-m*** to shake, wobble. *See also* OJAG

ajo *ng,* **mangga** *kr,* **sumangga** *ki* come on! let's...! ** ta mlebua ḍisik.* Come on in! *Wis *.* OK, let's go! ***n̂** *ng kr* to collaborate in a scheme. *Botjah loro paḍa ajon arep njolong pelem.* The two boys decided to swipe some mangoes.

ajom shaded, protected, sheltered. *panggonan sing ** a shady spot. ***(-*)an** that which is sheltered. *Ajo linggih nang *an kana.* Let's sit over there in the shade. **k*an** protected, sheltered. **k*en** too heavily shaded; overprotected. **ng*** 1 to cast shade; to create shelter. 2 to take shelter (from sun, rain). **ng/di*i** to shade/shelter/protect sth.

*Wit gedé kaé ng*i omahé.* That large tree shades the house. *Sadjroning prang Pangéran tansah ng*i.* God kept him safe throughout the war. **pa·ng*** protection, shelter. **pa·ng*an** 1 a shaded place. 2 patron, protector. 3 act of sheltering/protecting. *Garwané wis kondur ing pang*ané sing Maha Kuwasa.* Her husband has died. *See also* JOM

ajon ***-*** comedian. **ng/di*** 1 to challenge, rebel against. 2 to check the weight *or* measure of [raw rice]

aju 1 beautiful, pretty. *Wah *né!* How beautiful she is! 2 peaceful and prosperous. **ning negara* the national welfare. *** éndah** beautiful, splendid. *See also* KUMAJU

ajub 1 pale. 2 (*prn* **aju:b**) spoiled, rotten. ***-*en** still half asleep. **ng*-*** to seek shelter from sun or rain

ajuh *inf var of* AJO

ajun[a] ***-*** children's swing. ***-*an** to swing (on a swing, hanging tree roots, *etc.*) **ng/di*** to swing smn. **p*an** baby's swing. *See also* JUN

ajun[b] *ltry var of* AREP. ***-*an** facing each other. **k*** a wish, hope, desire. **ng*** in the presence of [smn exalted]. **ng/di*-*** to want, wish (for). **ng/di*aké** to want as one's wife. **ng*an** in the presence of [smn exalted]. *sowan ng*aning Pangéran* to appear before God. **pa·ng*an** *ki* realm, presence. *ing pang*aning Pangéran* in the presence of God; dead, death. *See also* PAMBAJUN

ajur **ng*-*** tall and thin

Akad Sunday. *See also* NGAHAD

akaḍemikus a graduate, an alumnus/alumna

akaḍemisi the alumni

akal idea, scheme. *golèk ** to try to think of a way/solution. *nemu ** to get an idea, hit on a solution. *sugih ** full of ideas. ***-*** to seek a solution. *akal² metjahaké soal akèhing penḍuḍuk* trying to solve the overpopulation problem. **ng*(i)** 1 to seek/find [a solution]. *ng* rékadaja rupa²* to try all kinds of tricks. *A ng*i njilih anḍa.* A hit on the idea of borrowing a ladder. 2 (*psv* **di*-[i]**) to take advantage of smn. *Aku arep kok *i ja.* You're out to cheat me! *** budi** common sense; **ng* budi** to use common sense. *** bulus** an inept *or* transparent lie/trick. *** kodja** a convincing lie; skilled at deception

akar root. *** bahar** a certain seaweed used for bracelets: believed to cure rheumatism

akârâ 1 capital *a* in Javanese script. 2 *oj* shape, form, appearance

akas 1 hard and dry, crusty. *Segané * mulané njereti.* The rice is so hard it sticks in your throat. *Wis tuwa ning awaké isih katon *.* He's old but wiry. 2 nimble. **ng/di*i** to make sth hard/crusty

Akbar the Almighty

-aké *ng,* **-aken** *kr* (**-k̍aké, -k̍aken** *after vowel*) *(causative suffix)* 1 to [do] on smn's behalf. *Aku ditukokaké buku.* He bought me a book. 2 to have smn [do]; to have sth [done]. *ndandakaké pit* to have a bicycle repaired. 3 to use [noun]. *m·beḍil·aké* to shoot a gun. 4 to bring about [an act, a condition]. *ng·gampang·aké* to make sth easy. *m·betjik·aké* to improve sth. *ñ·turu·k̍aké* to put smn to sleep. *di·tjara-Djawa·kaké* to be Javanized. 5 to [do] by accident. *m̈·petjah·aké gelas* to break a glass unintentionally. 6 (I guess) I'll [do] (*see also* TAK-). *Aku dak ng·golèk·aké tamba kowé menjang ḍokteran.* I'll go to the hospital and get you some medicine. *See also individual entries for applicable meanings*

akèh *ng,* **kaṭah** *kr* (there is) much, (there are) many. *wong ** many people. *Gawéané *.* He has a lot to do. ** sing rusak.* Many of them were ruined. *Ḍuwitku kurang *.* I haven't enough money. *Bédané * banget.* They're very different. *disengiti ing ** disliked by many. ***é** amount. *buku seméné *é* this many books. ***-*an** to compare *or* compete for most. *akèh²an olèhé mangan* seeing who could eat most. ***-*é** 1 the number *or* amount of. *Akèh²é sing teka nèng rapat wong sèket.* There will be 50 people coming to the meeting. 2 at most. **-*é éntuk Rp 100,- sedina.* He makes a maximum of 100 rupiahs a day. **k*an, k*en** *(or* **kakéjan** *ng)* excessively much/many. *Momotané k*an.* He has too much to carry. *Ḍèké kakéjan mangan pelem mentah.* He ate too many raw mangoes. **k*an tjangkem** *ng only* 1 (to engage in) too much talk (and too little action). 2 (to do) too much grumbling. **ng/di*(-*)i** to increase the number/amount of. *ng*i gawéjan* to give smn (even) more work. **sa*-*é** no matter how much/many. ***-(se)ṭiṭik** number, amount. **-ṭiṭiké murid gumantung nèng bajaran sekolah.* The number of students depends on the tuition. *See also* KÈH

akèn to tell smn to do sth (*kr for* AKON)
aken 1 to acknowledge (*root form: kr for* AKUb). 2 *causative suffix* (*kr for* -AKÉ)
akep **ng/di*** 1 to put/hold between the lips. *Rokoké di* waé, ora disumet.* He held the cigarette in his mouth without lighting it. 2 to draw on [a cigarette *etc.*]
akérat the hereafter, the next life. *donja ** our world and what is beyond. *ing ng** in the next world
aki storage battery. *-* very old (*rg var of* KAKI2)
akibat result, effect. *sebab lan ** cause and effect. **ng/di*aké** to have a certain effect. *Jèn akèh turuné bisa ng*aké lemu.* Too much sleep can make you fat.
akik agate. ***-*an** uncut unpolished agates. **ng*** hard-hearted, insensitive. *** lojang** yellowish-white agate
akil ***-balèg** *or* ***-balig** to become an adult
aking dry, dried out. *kaju ** dry wood. *sega ** 'dried-up (cooked) rice
akir (at) the end. **ing djaman* the future. ** taun iki* at the end of this year. ***-* iki** lately, recently. ***(-*)é** ultimately. **é diangkat dadi ḍuta geḍé.* He was finally given the post of ambassador. **ng/di*aké** to postpone; to put at the end. *Aku ng*aké bab iki.* I'm putting this chapter at the end. *** tembé** the future
akirat *var of* AKÉRAT
aklak morals, ethics. *pengrusak ** a moral offender. *** bedjad** bad/immoral conduct
aklik **oklak-*** loose in its socket. *garan patjul sing oklak-** a loose hoe handle. **m·oklak-m*** to wobble in place. **ng/di·oklak-*aké** to move [sth loose] for smn. **ng/di·oklak-*(i)** to move sth back and forth in its socket. *Untuné dioklak-*.* He's trying to get his tooth out.
akon *ng,* **akèn** *kr,* **ḍawuh** *ki,* **atur** *ka* to tell smn to do sth. **ng/di*aké** to have sth done; to pass along smn's orders. *Pira ongkosé ng*aké gawé médja?* How much did it cost to have the table made? **ng/di*(i)** to tell smn to do sth. *Pakné (ng)* Ali ngunḍuh pelem.* Ali's father told him to pick some mangoes. *Kabèh penḍuḍuk di*i ngili sumingkir saka kuṭa.* The inhabitants were ordered out of the city. *See also* KON, KONGKON
akrab close relationship, interconnection
akrak *-* a bamboo barricade
akral strong, robust
akrobat acrobat. *See also* MAIN
aksâmâ (*or* **pa·ng***) forgiveness, pardon (*ki for* APURA). *Kula njuwun pang* bapak.* I beg your pardon, Father. *Njuwun gunging pang*.* Please accept my humble apologies.
aksami *var of* AKSAMA
aksârâ 1 letter of an alphabet, written character. 2 belles-lettres, literature. *** Djawa** Javanese-script character. *** ḍojong** italic letter. *** geḍé** capital letter. *** latin** Roman letter *or* type; Roman cursive script. *** murda** capital letter. *** m̀·piring** italic letter. *** réka·n** Javanese letter to accommodate foreign sounds. *** swara** vowel letter; Javanese-script diacritic denoting a vowel. *** tjilik** lower-case letter
aksèp *var of* ASÈP
aksi 1 action; act of aggression. 2 arrogant, overbearing. 3 personal style. *Ḍèké ngguju kélingan *né kantjané.* He laughed when he thought back on his friend's ways. 4 *oj* eye (*var of* ÈKSI). **ng/di*(kaké)** to activate sth
aktipir **ng/di*(aké)** to activate sth
akua *ng,* **kula** *kr* 1 I, me. 2 my (*var of* -KU). ***né** I, me (*contrastive*). **né kang bakal ngrampungaké. I'll* finish it. **sa*** on a par with me. *wong2 sa*-kowé* people like you and me. *** (i)ki** I, me (*showing special concern for oneself*). *O * iki kesel banget.* Oh, I'm so *tired!* *** kabèh** *or* *** paḍa** we, us. *** tak** (*optative prefixation: see also* TAK-). ** tak ndjaluk tulung wong kaé.* I'll ask that man for help.
akub *ng,* **aken** *kr* ***n̂** legally adopted as a member of the family. *anak akon* an adopted child. ***n̂-*n̂** (**aken-aken[an]** *kr*) (one who is) passed off as a relative. *aḍi akon2* a "temporary" younger sibling. **ng/di*** 1 to acknowledge. *Aku ng* jèn salah.* I admitted I was wrong. *Ditakoni ng*.* Under questioning he confessed. 2 to claim *or* acknowledge as one's own. *Iki tak *.* This is mine. *Lungaa, ora tak * anak.* Go–you are not my child. 3 (*or* **ng/di*-***) to claim falsely. *Ḍèké ng* banget karo aku, kaja karo seduluré ḍéwé waé.* He regards me as his own brother. *Ḍèké seneng ng* barangé lijan.* He's always claiming other people's things. *Ḍèké ng*-* kaptèn.* He tells people he's a captain! *A ng* ora tepung B, mangka B iku kantjané ngangsir.* A said he didn't know B, though they robbed together. **ng/di*aké** 1 to adopt smn legally

as a member of the family. 2 to pass smn off as a relative. *Aku diakokaké pamané Pardi.* I was introduced as Pardi's uncle. **pa·ng*** confession, acknowledgment, verification. *peng*ning dosa* confession of sin. *See also* ḌAKU

akum softened from soaking. *See also* KUM

akur harmonious, congenial. *Kétoké kok * olèhé sesrawungan.* They certainly seem to get along well together. *Aku * jèn saiki mangan.* I'm agreeable to eating now. **ng/di*aké** to reconcile [disputants]

âlâ *ng,* **awon** *kr* bad. *wong ** bad person. *Ali olèh bidji *.* Ali gets bad grades. *Garapané tansah *.* His work is always unsatisfactory. *Jèn nandur * mesṭi ngunḍuh *.* If you sow evil, you'll reap evil. *Rupané *.* His face is ugly. *gawé * marang* to do harm to. ***-* sanak.** He may be no good but he's still a relative. ***n(-*n) (awon² *kr*)** scapegoat. *Jèn ana apa² sing ilang, mesṭi aku sing diengggo alan².* Whenever sth is missing, I get the blame. ***n-*nan (awon²an *kr*)** of inferior quality. ***né** 1 what is bad. **né ḍèké ora gelem blaka.* What's bad about it is that he won't tell the truth. 2 rather than. **né ora ana sing teka, mbok ja kowé waé mangkat.* Rather than having nobody show up, shouldn't you go? **k*nen** excessively bad. **ng/di*-*** *or* **ng/di*aké** to speak ill of smn behind his back. **ng/di*ni** to bring harm to; to make sth bad. *Jèn ora gelem di*ni, adja ng*ni lijan.* If you don't want others to harm you, don't harm them. *Gambar kaé ngalan-alani kamar tamu.* That picture makes the living room look awful. **pa·ng*-*** disagreeable sentiments. **pi*** bad, evil. *gawé pi** to do smn harm. *** ng·anggur** to pass the time idly. *Apa muni * nganggur?* Is he just talking to hear himself talk? *Mung * nganggur ḍuḍuk² djugangan djebul nemu peṭi isi mas²an.* He was just digging for want of anything better to do, and he found a box of gold. *** ati·né** wicked. *** belo betjik djaran** a bad child of good parents. *** betjik** 1 good and/or bad. ** betjik gawéanku ḍéwé.* Good or bad, I did it myself. *Di-timbang² ḍisik *-betjiké.* First consider its merits and drawbacks. 2 quality. ** betjiking swarané manuk* the quality of the bird's singing. *** ketara betjik ke·titik** evil will out and good deeds will make themselves known. *** tanpa rupa** unattractive looking. *See also* ÈLÈK

alad **m*-m*** *or* **ng*-*** to flare up; *fig* to burn with desire

alah oh! hey! **! Kuwi rak ora larang.* Oh, come on now! that's not expensive. ** ora!* No, no! *** déné** in vain. ** déné sinau basa Inggris jèn ora wani omong.* It's no use studying English if you don't dare use it. *** ng·anggur** (just) for fun

Alahu *see* ALLAHU

alal *see* HALAL

alam 1 world; universe. *angger² ** natural laws. *Wong lanang ana ing ng* ndonja iki rak akèh ta!* There are plenty of [other] men available, you know! *ngèlmu ** physics. 2 realm, scope. *Sipating * pikirané tjupet banget.* The scope of his intellect is very narrow. **ing Indonesia* things Indonesian. **ng/di*i** to undergo, experience. *Awaké ḍéwé saiki ng*i ungsum panas sing hawané panas banget.* We're having a very hot summer. **pa·ng*an** (an) experience. *peng*an anèh* a strange experience. *para pemuḍa kang durung peng*an* inexperienced young people. *** akir** the next world, life after death. *** arwah** the spirit world. *** donja** world; universe. **ora *** unnatural, out of the ordinary

alamat 1 sign, symbol. ** ala* a bad omen. 2 address on a letter. *aran lan ** name and address. **ng*** 1 address. 2 to symbolize. *Menawa mbulané miring ngiwa, ng* arep larang beras.* When a crescent moon leans to the left, it means the price of rice is going up. **ng/di*aké** to address [a letter] for smn. **ng/di*i** to write an address on. *ng*i lajang* to address a letter

alamun **ng*** to daydream, let one's thoughts wander. **p*an** *or* **pa·ng*** daydream, fantasy

alang[a] ***-*** jungle grass (a tall coarse sharp-leafed weed). ***-*an** place where such grass grows in abundance. *Ḍèké nḍelik nèng *-*an.* He hid in the tall grass.

alang[b] crosswise dimension. *Ing udjuré koṭakané wolu lan ing *é ija wolu.* There are 8 squares up and down [on a chessboard] and 8 across. ***an** 1 hindrance, obstacle. *Jèn ora ana *an apa², kiraku ja sida.* If nothing comes up, I think we can go. **an iku ora kena didjagakaké.* Expect the unexpected. 2 accidental damage, mishap. **an perang* a war casualty; handicapped by war. *Tangané kena *an.* His arm sustained an injury. **k*(-*)an** blocked, impeded; to run into obstacles. **m*** in a crosswise position;

fig unlucky. *Dlamakan loro²né m∗.* His feet are sideways (*i.e.* heels together, toes out). *diuntal m∗* swallowed alive. **m∗ mudjur** *or* **m∗ m·égung** placed randomly this way and that. *Endjeté olèhé ngusar kudu sing paḍa neré, ora kena m∗-mégung.* Your whitewash strokes must all go in the same direction, not every which way. **ng/di∗aké** to place sth crosswise *or* in such a way as to be an obstacle. **ng/di∗(-∗)** to impede, obstruct. *ng∗-∗i kemadjuwan* to impede progress. *Aku di∗-∗i udan.* I was held up by rain. **∗ udjur** 1 dimensions (length and width). 2 location, position. *Aku ora ngerti ∗-udjuré omahé.* I don't know where his house is. *ora weruh ∗-udjuré* to shift locations constantly, not have a definite place. 3 the real facts. *Jèn ora ngerti ∗-udjuré perkara mau ora susah omong.* If you don't know what it's all about, don't speak up.

alap a variety of hawk. **∗-ing∗** to cross-marry: one's sibling marries the sibling of one's spouse. **k∗** 1 useful, applicable to some purpose. 2 possessed, not oneself. **ng/di∗** 1 to put to use, take advantage of. *di∗ gawéné* made useful. 2 to seize possession of. **ng∗ berkah** to seek smn's blessing. **ng∗ menang** to win out, gain victory. **ng∗ njaur** 1 to sell [merchandise] on consignment. 2 pale and wan from malnutrition. **ng∗ opah** [to work] only for the money. **pa·ng∗an** a bewitched place

alas *ng,* **wânâ** *kr* 1 forest; jungle. 2 non-irrigated agricultural land. **∗an** uncultivated; uncivilized. *wong ∗an* forest dweller; boor. *pitik ∗an* wild chicken. *lemah ∗an* uncultivated land. **∗-∗an (wanan-wananan** *or* **wawanan** *kr*) replica of, or that which resembles, forest *or* jungle. **ng/di∗aké** 1 to allow [land] to revert to jungle. 2 to exile smn into the jungle

alasan 1 reason; logic. *∗é ora maton.* His reasoning is specious. 2 excuse, alibi

alat (*or* **∗-∗**) equipment for a specific function. *∗-∗ installasi listrik* equipment for electrical installations. *∗ ḍapur* kitchen equipment. *∗ tjukur* hair clippers

aldjabar algebra

aleb **k∗an** to get flooded/inundated. **ng/di∗i** to flood sth. *See also* LEB

alem **∗an** to expect praise; spoiled, pampered. **ng/di∗** to praise, compliment; to admire, think highly of. **pa·ng∗** public commendation, high praise. **pa·ng∗an** a public figure of great stature. *See also* LEM

alembânâ *ltry var of* ALEM

alesan *var of* ALASAN

alfatékah a paragraph *or* section in the Koran devoted to prayers

algodjo executioner

alhamdulil(l)ah 1 God bless you! *(when smn sneezes).* 2 thank God!

ali *inf var of* AHLI. **∗-∗ (sesupé** *kr*) ring for the finger. **∗ǹ-∗ǹ** a small bracelet. **ng/di∗ǹ-∗ǹi** to encircle with a ring. *Slamet ngalèn-alèni pitiké.* Slamet put a ring on his chicken('s leg).

alib 1 1st year in the *windu* cycle. 2 *var of* ALIF

alif *first Arabic letter.* **∗-∗an** 1 the Arabic alphabet. 2 the ABC's, elementary principles. **ora ngerti ∗ bèngkong** illiterate

alih **∗an** 1 act of moving (changing residence). 2 (having been) moved from one place to another. *lintang ∗an* shooting star. **ng∗** 1 to move, change residence. 2 (*psv* **di∗**) to move sth. *Nggoné bal²an ng∗ enggon.* They went smw else to play soccer. **ng/di∗-∗** *or* **ng/di·olah-∗** to keep moving around. **ng/di∗aké** to move sth from one place to another. **∗-lintang** to change places. *See also* LIH, PINḌAH

alijas or; also known as. *gawéjan mantja, ∗ barang import* foreign-made things, also called imported goods

alik *var of* GALIK. **ng·olak-∗** to turn sth repeatedly (*e.g.* a frying egg). *Ḍèké ngolak-∗ madjalah.* He leafed through (the pages of) a magazine. *See also* WALIK

alim well behaved, always attentive to one's duty. *Embuh bangsané crossboy apa botjah ∗.* I don't know if he's a delinquent or a goody-goody. **∗an** forgive me [for not giving you anything: *said when refusing a beggar*]. **ng/di∗aké** to pursue knowledge. **ng/di∗i** to forgive smn. **p∗an** forgiveness. **∗ ulama** religious scholar

aliminium aluminum

aling **∗-∗** cover, concealment, protective shield. *Kamaré ora ana ∗-∗é.* The room has no screens (for privacy). *Lha wong ana sing kok enggo ∗-∗ baé kok.* There's smn to look after you, isn't there? *tanpa ∗-∗* unprotected, uncovered; candid, forthright. *kréta kang tanpa ∗-∗* railroad flatcar. *Ijah, kowé kuwi jèn guneman anggonmu tanpa* *aling*[2]. When you talk, you don't hold anything back! ***-*an** shielded; concealed from view. **-*an wit gedé kaé, bèn ora kétok.* Get behind that big tree so you won't be seen. ***-*an katon** to reveal sth inadvertently. **ng·olang-*** to toss and turn while trying to sleep. **ng/di*(-*)** to cover up, conceal; to shield, protect

alinia 1 line of writing. 2 paragraph

aliran 1 current. ** listrik* electric current. 2 ideology. ** kiri* the (political) left

alis *ng kr,* **imba** *ki* eyebrow(s). ** nanggal sapisan* eyebrows shaped like the new moon. **sa*** a hair's-breadth

alit small, little (*kr for* TJILIK)

aljas *var of* ALIJAS

alkali alkali; alkaline

alkamdulil(l)ah *var of* ALHAMDULIL(L)AH

Allah God. *Gusti ** God [*in direct address*]. **ka*an** godlike. **Ng*** God [*in phrases*]. *kersané Ng** God's will. *pasrah Ng** to submit to God's will. **ja * ja robbi(l)** *excl of surprise. See also* ALLAHU

Al(l)ahu God [*in special phrases*]. ** (a)kbar* God Almighty. ** alam* God knows. *See also* ALLAH

almarhum *ltry* the late..., the deceased...

almasih messiah, deliverer

almenak almanac

alod tough, hard to chew; *slang* difficult. *See also* KUMALOD

alok 1 a yell, shout. 2 (*or* ***-***) to call out, shout; to cheer. **ng/di*i** to shout a warning (to). *See also* LOK

alon slow. *Jèn tabuhané *, nggoné ndjogèd ija *.* When the music was slow, he danced slowly. ***-* 1** slow and careful. *mlaku *-** to walk cautiously. **-* watoné angger kelakon* slow but sure; easy does it. 2 soft [of speaking voice]. *Olèhé ngomong mbok sing *-*.* Please speak softly. ***-*an** taking one's time. *Lakuné *-*an.* He went at a leisurely pace. **ng/di*-*i** to make sth slow; to slow things down. *See also* LON

along *var of* A·LUWUNG

alpabèt alphabet

alpokat *var of* ADPOKAT

altar church altar

alu pestle for pounding things in a mortar. *See also* LUMPANG

alub **ng/di*** to bring about [sth unfortunate] by mentioning it. *Adja ng* waé.* Don't talk about it–you might make it happen! **ng/di*-*** to parboil [vegetables] by placing them in hot water briefly. *See also* KULUB

aluk **ng*-*** *intsfr* far. *Kétoké adoh ng*-*, nanging djebul tjedak baé.* It looked a long long way off, but it turned out to be close.

alum 1 withered, limp, drooping. 2 in the process of healing. *Gudigé wis *, adja dikukur.* The wound is on the mend; don't scratch it. **ng*-*i** to droop, begin to wither. *See also* LUM

alun 1 wave. ** segara* ocean waves. 2 *ltry* I, me. ***-*** broad grassy area in front (north) and back (south) of a palace or regent's residence. **-* lor (kidul)* grassy area in the front (back). **ng*** wave-like

alung *var of* A·LUWUNG

alup **ng/di*** to bark (at). *Mau bengi asuku ng* terus.* My dog barked all night last night.

alur course, pace, progress. *Kabèh wis kagulang *ing perang.* Everything had been geared to conducting war. ***an** traces, that which tells a tale. **ng/di*aké** to recount events

alus 1 refined; fine, smooth. *barang gegawéan sing *-** beautifully crafted items. *Wuluné * banget.* The feathers are very smooth. *Olèhé ngendika nganggo basa *.* His speech was very refined. *mritja ** finely ground pepper. *tjara Djawané sing * déwé* the very nicest variety of Javanese. 2 incorporeal, invisible. *Memedi kuwi klebu sing diarani badan *.* Ghosts are invisible. **ng/di*aké** to refine, make fine/smooth. *Aku arep ng*aké lakuné mesin sarana dak lengani.* I'll oil the machine to make it run smooth. **ng/di*i** to treat courteously. *Wong di*i kok wangsulané kasar ngono.* I was nice to him and see how rudely he answers! *See also* LUS

aluwung *see* LUWUNG

âmâ insect pest, plant disease; *fig* public nuisance. *kena ** damaged by pests. **ning bebrajan* a detriment to society

amal charity; charitable donation. **k*an** to get a lucky break. **ng*** to give to charity. **ng/di*aké** to give sth. *ng*aké omahé* to donate one's house. *Dèké ng*aké uripé marang kasusastran Djawa.* He devoted his life to Javanese literature. **ng/di*i** to give to [a charitable cause]. *** ka·donja·n** worldly goods donated for charitable purposes. *** karun** hidden (buried) treasure

aman at peace, secure. **ng/di*aké** to protect from threatened danger; to maintain security in [a place]

amanat a speech conveying a message to the people
amanḍel 1 tonsil. 2 almond. * *kagawé lembut* finely chopped almonds; cheese tidbits
amarga *ng* because (*formal var of* MARGA, MERGA)
amargi *kr* because (*formal var of* MARGI, MERGI)
amat **ng/di*-*i** to supervise, watch over, keep a sharp eye on
amatir amateur. *raḍio ** ham radio. *pemain ** nonprofessional player
âmbâ *ng*, **wijar** *kr* 1 large, broad, roomy, spacious. *Kamaré * apa tjijut?* Is the room large or cramped? *Klambiku suwèk *.* My shirt has a big tear in it. ***né** 1 size, bigness. **né kuṭa lan ḍuwuré omah²é* the expanse of the city and the height of the buildings. 2 width. **né telung mèter.* It's 3 meters wide. **k*nen** (*or* **k*n** *ng*) excessively large. *Lengen klambiné k*n.* The sleeves of the shirt are too big. *Kertas iki k*n kanggo mbuntel barang tjiliké seméné.* This paper is too big to wrap such a small thing. **ng*** to spread out laterally. *Djakarta kuṭané ng*.* Djakarta is growing. **ng/di*aké** to make larger/broader. *ng*kaké mripat* to widen one's eyes. *ng*kaké djangkah* to lengthen one's stride. *Saka akèhé tjatjahdjiwané nganti kuṭané prelu di*kaké.* The city has to be expanded because of the population explosion. **sa*né** the same size as. *lemah sa*né iketku iki* a tiny plot of land. * **tjijut·é** size; width. * *tjijuté kuṭa mau wara² paḍa karo Jogja.* That city is about the size of Jogja.
ambah *-* an epidemic. ***-*an** 1 act of traversing. *Angèl *ané.* It's hard to get across (through, over, *etc.*) it. 2 place frequently traversed. *Dalan kuwi *-*anku.* I take that street (habitually, *e.g.* on my way to work). 3 epidemic. *Désa kono lagi ketradjang *-*an, mula ora kena di*.* That village is having an epidemic, so you can't go that way. **k*** to get traversed (by). *Tahun 1930 désa kuwi k* ing lelara tjatjar.* The village was swept by a smallpox epidemic in 1930. **ng/di*** 1 to traverse. *ng* lemah* to move on land (on the ground). *ng* ing awang²* to fly (through the air). *ng* segara weḍi* to cross the desert. *ng* alas* to go through the woods. *Segara mau ora kena di*.* That ocean is not navigable. 2 to get involved in, to handle. *bebadan kang ng* leladan basa lan kasusastran* an organization that deals with language and literature. **ng* agal** to make oneself visible
ambak[a] (*or* ***na** *or* ***-*** *or* ***-ambing**) even though. *Ḍèké kuwi * wong désa nanging sugih banget.* He may be a rustic but he's wealthy.
ambak[b] **ng*-*** to spread widely. *Pariné ng*-* ing bulak kana.* Rice plants cover that whole field.
ambal 1 (number of) times. *Watjanen * ping telu.* Read it 3 times. 2 one stair in a flight. * *sing ngisor ḍéwé* the bottom step. ***-*an** 1 (to do) repeatedly. *Ḍèwèké ngundang *-*an, meksa ora ana sing njambungi.* He called and called but nobody answered. *Mengkono mau *-*an ping telu.* The process is repeated 3 times. 2 a flight of stairs. **ma(ng)*-*(an)** to [do] again and again. *Ḍèwèké matja ma-ambal²an.* He read it several times. *Suraké mang*-*.* They kept cheering. **ng/di*i** to [do] again; to repeat. *Pitakoné ng*i pandjaluké.* He repeated his request. *Dikon ng*i kaping pinḍo manèh.* He told me to do it twice more.
ambar fragrance. **ng*** to give off fragrance; *fig* famous, renowned
ambârâ *oj* sky. **ng*** 1 to fly. 2 to wander from place to place
ambaro breakwater in a harbor
ambat **ng/di*(i)** to pull, tug
ambeg assumption, opinion, feeling. **é isih paḍa baé karo ḍèk bijèn.* He still felt the same as before. ***an** breath, breathing; to breathe. **ané krenggosan.* He was out of breath. *ngampet *an* to hold one's breath. **an gawéan* artificial respiration. *(ng)undjal *an* to take a deep breath; to sigh
ambèien (to have/get) hemorrhoids
ambèjen *var sp of* AMBÈIEN
ambek 1 (having) a character trait. *satrija kang * sija* a nobleman of cruel character. * *darma (wani, welas, lsp.)* of helpful (bold, compassionate, *etc.*) character. 2 forceful nature/character. *Adjrih *ing Sinuwun.* He was in awe of the King's powerful presence. 3 (*or* **m***) conceited, arrogant. **p*an** 1 character(istics), nature. *Ngono mau pantjèn wis p*ané.* That's the way he is. 2 *rg* arrogant. * **gumeḍé** arrogant, high-handed. * **paramarta** in order of importance; (to put) first things first. **ng/di*-paramarta·kaké** to give priority to. *ngambek-paramartakaké*

ékonomi to give top priority to the economy. * **pati** not afraid to die. * **suma(ng)-kéjan** *sms* * GUMEḌÉ

ambèn low wooden or bamboo bench, for sitting or sleeping. ***-*an** bamboo coffin

amben 1 sash worn with batik wraparounds. 2 belly band for a draft animal. 3 *inf var of* SABEN. **ng/di*i** to equip with a sash *or* belly band

ambeng various foods. ***an 1** a variety of foods. 2 dish, plate (*kr for* PIRING)

ambèr *rg var of* LUBÈR

ambet odor (*kr for* AMBU). ***an** durian fruit *nickname:* (*kr for* AMBON)

ambi(k) (together) with; and

ambil **ng/di*** *oj* to (go) get, pick up, take. **ng/di*-*** to try to win over *or* reconcile. *Botjah kaé ng*-* atiné ibu.* The child is trying to make his mother feel sorry for him. **ng/di·ombal-*** *rg* to rake up the past

ambjah **ng*-*** commonplace, present in large quantities. *See also* BJAH

ambjak ***-*an** to move in great numbers. *Wong² paḍa mulih *-*an.* People thronged homeward.

ambjang **ng*-*** to wander restlessly. *Pikirané saja nglantur ng*-* tekan ngendi-endi.* His thoughts went farther and farther afield.

ambjar to burst into fragments. *See also* BJAR

ambjog *see* NGAMBJOG

ambjuk to move in a swarm. *Wong sepirang-pirang * menjang alun².* People flocked to the town square. *See also* BJUK

ambjur to plunge into water. ***-*an** to keep jumping into water, *e.g.* as recreation. **ng/di*i** to plunge for sth. *Ali ng*i djam tangané sing ketjemplung nèng banju.* Ali jumped into the water to retrieve his watch. *See also* BJUR

amblah *var of* ABLAH

amblas lost, gone, vanished. *Ḍuwité entèk * dienggo main.* He gambled away all his money. *Gagasanku *.* I was lost in thought. *Sega sapiring wis *.* He's eaten all his rice already.

ambleg to give way. *Ana linḍu geḍungé *.* The building collapsed in the earthquake. **ng/di*aké** to cause to collapse. *ng*aké omah² sing tuwa* to demolish old houses. *See also* BLEG

ambles 1 to sink below the surface. *Sikilé * ana ing weḍèn.* His feet sank into the sand. *Kambangé obah² bandjur *.* The [fishing-rod] float bobbed and then went under. 2 recessed, set in(ward). *Irungé *.* His nose is flat.

amblong to give way, cave in

ambo **ng/di*** to hoist [sail]

ambok *var of* AMBAK[a], M·BOK

ambon *ng,* **ambetan** *kr* nickname for the (strong-smelling) durian fruit. *See also* AMBU

âmbrâ **ng*-*** 1 widespread, commonplace. 2 (*psv* **di*-***) to scatter, strew

ambrah *var of* AMBRA

ambreg **ng*-*** scattered *or* heaped untidily. *Kumbahané ng*-*.* The laundry lay around in a mess.

ambrih *rg var of* AMRIH

ambrik *var of* AMRIK

ambril *var of* AMRIL

ambring *var of* AMRING

ambrol in a state of collapse. *Bendunganè *.* The dam gave way.

ambruk (*or* **ng***) to drop, collapse. *Djarané *.* The horse fell in his tracks. *Kabinèt krisis, kabinèt *.* Cabinet crisis! cabinet falls! **ng/di*aké** to cause to collapse. *Omahé di*aké linḍu.* The house was leveled by the earthquake. **ng/di*i** to fall on(to). *Montor maburé tiba ng*i omah.* The plane crashed on a house. *See also* BRUK, KABRUK

ambu *ng,* **ambet** *kr* odor. *Ora ana rupané nanging ana *né.* It's colorless but has an odor. **né ora énak.* It doesn't smell good. ***n̂-*n̂** (**ambet-ambetan** *kr*) odor. *ngetokaké ambon² sing ora énak* to smell disagreeable. **k*n̂** 1 to get a whiff of. 2 to get touched lightly by. *Buku mau adja nganti kambon banju.* Don't let water get on the book. *Sekésuk wetengku ija durung kambon apa².* I haven't eaten since morning. *Jèn kambon angin, ḍèké mesṭi lara.* A touch of wind makes him ill. **m*** 1 to have an odor. *Ḍèwèké m* bawang.* He smells of garlic. 2 to perceive an odor, get a whiff of. *Bareng m* bantal, mak sek terus turu.* As soon as he hit the pillow, he dropped off to sleep. 3 spoiled, decaying; to spoil. *sega m** spoiled rice. *barang² ora m** nonperishable goods. 4 to resemble; to suggest, smack of. **m* ati** one who has been loved. **m* ḍem** no longer warm/fresh, having a stale odor. **m* ilu** to have learned one's lesson. **m* kulit daging** a relative, one's flesh and blood. **m* walang** 1 [of rice plants] half eaten by ladybugs. 2 half crazy. **ora m* botjah** [of a child] old beyond one's years. **ora m* éntong-irus** *or* **ora m* sega-djangan** not a blood relation. **ora m* wong Djawa** [a Javanese who is] lacking the essential Javaneseness. **ora m* wong lanang** 1 unmanly. 2 a female virgin. **ora m* wong wadon** 1 unwomanly. 2 a male virgin. **ng/di*** to smell sth. *Semuné arep ng* apa ta apa.* He seems to be trying to get a whiff of sth. **nen sikutmu, m* apa?* Look to your own faults! **ng* tanpa irung** to sense sth. **ng/di*kaké** to cause to smell. *Lengané diambokaké irungé.* They had her take a whiff of the oil. **ng/di*ni** to offer sth for smelling. *Bareng ḍèké semaput, irungé diamboni lenga.* When she fainted, they gave her a whiff of oil. **pa·ng*** sense of smell. **pa·ng*-*** a light fragrance. *See also* AMBON

ambulans ambulance

ambung *ng kr,* **aras** *ki* a kiss (Javanese style: place nose on cheek and inhale). **ng/di*** 1 to touch with the nose. 2 to kiss. **ng* pada** to kiss smn's foot as a gesture of obeisance. **ng/di*i** to kiss smn. **pa·ng*** act of kissing

ambur *var of* AMBUS

ambus **ng/di*** to sniff (at). *Térongé di*-* Kantjil.* Mouse-Deer kept sniffing at the eggplant.

amed *rg var of* KLAMED

amèk **ϕ/di*** to (go) get, pick (up). * *iwak* to catch a fish. * *pelem* to pick mangoes. *See also* MÈMÈK

amel **ng*-*** very fond of [*esp.* a food]

amèn always, constantly. ***-*** to perform [a show] publicly

ameng to have a foul odor. ***-*** to engage in recreation *(ki for* DOLAN(2))

Amérikā America; the United States. *** Kidul** South America. *** Serikat** (*abbr:* **A.S.**) the U.S.

amet *measuring unit for rice plants: 25 gèḍèng's, or ca. 154 kilograms = 340 lbs.*

amik 1 *var of* AMÈK. 2 only (*rg var of* MUNG)

amin, ami:n amen. ***-*** religious ceremony at which food blessed by the religious man is served. **ng/di*i** to say amen (to)

aming only (*rg var of* MUNG)

amis to smell disagreeable (*usu.* fishy). **ng/di*-*i** to make sth smell bad (*esp.* fishy). *** batjin** sth wrong. *Jèn ana * batjiné adja kagèt.* Don't be dismayed if sth goes wrong.

amit 1 to ask permission to leave (*see also* PAMIT). *Kula *.* Please excuse me. 2 (*or* ***-***) I beg your pardon! * *sèwu.* Please excuse me.

amleng to go away without explanation. *Keprijé ta iki, wong wis rong minggu kok amleng waé.* What could be wrong–he's been gone for 2 weeks and there's no word of him!

amoh in rags, worn out. ***-*an** old ragged things, *esp.* clothing. **ng/di*aké** to wear out, make ragged

among 1 to take care of, handle, protect. * *geni* to tend the fire. * *beksa* an organization that maintains Javanese classical dances. * *tamu* to receive (*or* those who receive) guests at a gathering. 2 to engage in, handle. *lelungan prelu * suka* to travel in quest of pleasure. *para * dagang* businessmen, merchants. *Paḍa * asmara.* They're in love. * *karsa* to follow one's own wishes. * *pradja* to have (*or* one who has) jurisdiction over a region. * *tani* to engage (*or* those who engage) in agriculture. ***-*** ritual ceremony held for a child to ensure his safety. **ng/di*i** to hold such a ceremony for. **p*** 1 public official. *pamong pradja* civil servant; person in charge of a certain territory. *para p* désané* village officials. 2 guardian. *** raga, * slira** to talk about oneself. *See also* MOMONG, MONG

amonia(k) ammonia

amonium *var of* AMONIA(K)

amor 1 in the company of [smn else]; to mingle [with others]. *Aku arep nunggang * sopiré.* I want to ride with the driver. *Adja * karo wong lija.* Don't mix with others. 2 mixed/combined with. *Banjuné asin * enḍut.* The salt water was mixed with mud. *** turu** 1 to sleep (in the same bed) [with]. 2 (to have) sexual intercourse. 3 person slept with. *See also* AWOR, MOR

amot *ng,* **awrat** *kr* to hold, accommodate; loaded with. *Prauné * wong.* The boat was filled with people. *Montor iki * wong pira?* How many people will this car hold? **k*** 1 to get loaded [into]. *Beras sakarung k* ing bontjèngan pit.* He loaded the bag of rice on the back of his bike. *Apa bab opahé wis k* ing kontrak?* Are the wages mentioned in the contract? 2 to hold, accommodate. *Wong seméné akèhé otoné mèh ora k*.* The car will barely hold this many people. *Mau mentas ngorèdi petis, saiki isih k* semono.* You finished up the meat sauce and you're still loading up! **ng/di*** 1 to hold, contain. *Koran iki ng* kabar sing wigati.* This newspaper has a lot of important news in it. 2 to load sth into/onto. *Gawané di* ing* *gegeré unta mau.* He loaded his things onto the camel's back. **ng/di*aké** to load sth. *ng*aké barang²* to load goods. **p*an 1** loading place. *Podjok kono kanggo p*an, mula ora éntuk parkir.* That corner is a loading zone—you can't park there. 2 a load. *See also* MOMOT, MOT

ampah valley (*rg var of* ARÉ). **ng/di*** to restrain, hold in check

ampak *-* mountain mist. *-*an in clusters. *Bareng tontonané wis rampung, wong² bubar *-*an.* After the show, the people dispersed in groups. **ng*-*** to form large groups. *Ing sisih kulon menḍung ng*-*.* Heavy clouds gathered in the west.

ampal beetle

ampang 1 dull, tedious. 2 light, without body. *mbako ** light tobacco. *swara ** a light (singing) voice; *gram* light consonant sound (*see also* ANTEB). **ng/di*aké** to cause to be dull/light

ampar floor. ***an** 1 a kind of chair. 2 a mat to sit on. **ng/di*** to hit. *Bleḍèg njamber ng*-*.* Lightning struck all around.

ampas 1 residue after the essence has been removed. **é tebu* sugar cane from which the juice has been pressed. ** tala* honeycomb (wax) with the honey gone. **é krambil* shredded coconut from which the milk has been pressed. 2 fruit or coconut slices in sweet iced drinks

ampeg 1 strong. *mbako ** strong tobacco. 2 oppressed, constricted. *Ḍaḍaku *.* I can hardly breathe.

ampéjan any wife other than the queen (*ki for* SELIR)

ampèl a variety of bamboo

ampel **ng/di*i** to place [kindling] under wood in preparation for making charcoal

amper **ng/di*** to throw at/to. *See also* UJAH

amperu pancreas

ampet **ng/di*** to check, restrain. *Ambekané di** He held his breath. *Ḍèké ora kena di* gujuné.* He couldn't help laughing.

ampil 1 any wife other than the queen (*ki for* SELIR). 2 to carry, bring, take (*root form: ki for* GAWA). 3 to borrow (*root form: ki for* SILIH)

amping *-* *or* *(-*)an blocked by, concealed from view by. *Aku *-*an wit geḍang.* I was hidden behind a banana tree. *Ana tjah wadon kang ngadeg *-* Si A.* There was a girl standing behind A. *plataran *-*an témbok* a walled-in yard. **ng/di*(-*)i** to hem in, block, flank. *Baja mau ng*-*i.* The crocodile blocked his way. *Ḍèwèké mlaku di*i aḍiné loro.* He walked between his two brothers.

ampir *rg var of* ÈMPÈR. ***an** stopping-off place. *Omahé tetep mung kanggo *an baé.* Everyone drops in at his house. **k*** *or* **m*** to drop in, stop off. *Mangga k*.* Do drop in! *Jèn kowé menjang pasar, m*a apotik aku tukokna djamu.* When you go to the market, stop by the drugstore and get me some medicine. **ng/di*aké** to ask smn to stop by. **ng/di*i** to call for smn. *Dak *i ja, terus lunga omahé A.* I'll pick you up on the way to A's house. *See also* KAMPIR

ampjak *-*an to walk together as a group. **ng/di*** *ltry* to surround

ampjang praline-like confection made with peanuts and coconut sugar

amplèk a certain style of short jacket or shirt. **ng*** [of clothing] too small

amplik (*or* *-* *or* **ng***) balanced precariously near the edge of sth

amplok **ng/di*(i)** to cling to sth with arms and legs. *Botjahé ng* guluné kebo.* The boy clung to the kerbau's neck. *Aku mènèk ng* wit pelem.* I shinnied up a mango tree.

amplop envelope. ***an** placed in an envelope. *lajang *an* a letter in an envelope. **ng/di*i** to put into an envelope. *Lajangé dilempit bandjur di*i.* She folded the letter and put it in an envelope.

ampo high-calcium baked-clay tablet eaten *esp.* by pregnant women. **ng*** 1 resembling such a tablet. 2 (*psv* **di***) to make [ingredients] into calcium tablets

ampok roofed veranda-like extension to a house

ampuh endowed with supernatural powers

ampun 1 don't! (*md for* ADJA[a]). 2 to have [done] (*md for* WIS)

amput **di*** darn! (*excl of mild disgust or displeasure).* **ng/di*** *cr* to copulate with [a female]. **dudu *-*é** far below, no match for. *Jèn tinimbang karo botjah kuṭa, duḍu *-*é.* Compared with city boys, he just wasn't in the same class.

amral admiral

amrèh *rg var of* AMRIH

amrih so that, in order that/to. *Tangaré disak * ora krasa aḍem.* He put his hands in his pockets so they wouldn't be cold. *** adja** don't (let it happen that...); so as not to... ** adja dadi regedjegan* in order to avoid a dispute. * **apik·é** *or* * **betjik·é** it would be good/nice if...; one ought to... * *apiké kowé kudu sowan embahmu.* You really ought to go see your grandmother. *See also* PAMRIH

amrik to give off an odor. *Gandané * awangi.* The perfume is fragrant.

amril sandpaper

amring 1 quiet. *Djam rolasan wis * ora ana wong.* By 12 o'clock it had quieted down and there was no one around. 2 sparse. *Wit pelem kuwi goḍongé *.* The mango tree doesn't have many leaves. **m*** *intsfr* quiet. *sepi m** intensely still

amtenar official, civil servant. *pegawé² ** government officials

-amu *formal var of* -MU

amuk fury, violence. **ing linḍu* the violence of the earthquake. ***-*an** to attack each other violently. **k*** to be the object of an irrational *or* frenzied attack. **ng*(-*)** 1 (to go) on the rampage. *gadjah ng** a rampaging elephant. *Kok ng*.* Have you gone crazy? *Lelara pès ng*.* Plague ran wild. 2 (*psv* **di***) to attack furiously. *Jèn gadjahé ng*, wongé rak di*.* When the elephant went berserk it turned on its master. **ng* punggung** *wj* to attack with great fury. **ng* kaja banṭèng ke·tatu·n̂** to attack with great violence. **pa·ng*** (**p*** *rg*) act of raging *or* behaving violently. *munḍak dina pang*é lelara pès ing kuṭa* the increasing virulence of the plague in the city with each passing day. *pang*é penḍuḍuk* the fury of the populace

amun *-* fog

amung only (*rg var of* MUNG)

amut **ng/di*(i)** to hold in the mouth; to suck on. *ng*i ès lilin* to suck a popsicle. *See also* MUT

-an (*or* **-n** *or* **-nan** *after vowel*) *(suffix)* 1 act *or* way of [do]ing. *dina kanggo suntik·an* the day we get our injections. *Dus·an·é angèl.* It's hard to bathe him. *djaran tunggang·an* a riding horse. 2 place where [noun] is found *or* where [verb] is done. *ḍokter·an* hospital. *kaum·an* section where devout Moslems live. *Hardjita·n* Mr. Hardjita's house. *lèrèn·an* stopping/resting place. *lungguh·an* seat, place to sit. *ke·kembang·-an* place where flowers grow *or* are placed. 3 that which is used for [do]ing. *balèn (bali·n̂)* a ride home/back. *bukak·an blèg* can opener. *saring·an* strainer. *sekolah·an* a school. *timbang·an* scales (for weighing). *tukon (tuku·n̂)* purchase price; money for buying. 4 that which resembles [noun] but is smaller; an artificial *or* toy [noun]. *djaran·an* rocking horse. *gunung·an* hill. *koḍok·an* small frog. 5 many [doubled nouns]; various kinds of [reduplicated nouns]. *goḍong²-·an* many leaves; foliage. *ge·goḍong·an* all kinds of leaves, any kind of leaf. *woh²·an* fruits. 6 that which does, is characterized by, or undergoes [root]. *apik(-apik)·an* sth nice, *esp.* a surprise. *Banjumas·an* Banjumas-style speech. *djero·an* intestines, insides. *murah·an* junk, cheap stuff. *ré-wang·an* helper. *wong sabrang·an* foreigner, outsider. *sak angkat·an* one load. *ḍun²-·an* things that have been unloaded. 7 performance, ceremony, *etc.* in which [noun] is centrally involved. *manton (mantu·n̂)* wedding ceremony. *wajang·an* shadow-play performance. 8 *n*th (fraction formative). *sapratelon (sa·pra·telu·n̂)* 1/3. 9 having been [done]. *gawé·an Sala* made in Solo. *lajang amplop·an* a letter (which had been put) in an envelope. 10 to [do, as a group] in a leisurely way with enjoyment. *gegujon (ge·guju·n̂)* to laugh and joke. *langèn (langi·n̂)* to go swimming. *lungguh(-lungguh)·an* to sit around talking and relaxing. 11 prone to [root]. *wedèn (wedi·n̂)* timid. *bisa·n* competent, handy. *bungah·an* happy-go-lucky. *matèn (mati·n̂)* hard to keep alive. *n̈g·kandel·an* trusting, gullible. *bosen·an* easily bored. 12 to put on *or* wear [root]. *sepaton (sepatu·n̂)* to put/have on shoes. *gelung·an* to do one's hair in a bun. 13 to imitate/simulate [root]. *djaran·an* to trot like a horse. *pintjang·an* to limp like a cripple. *sinau-sinau·an* to try to look as if one is studying. 14 to take turns [do]ing, [do] one after the other. *Tilpuné mung sidji, dadi mung gentèn·an.* There's only one phone so we share it. *Ing kuṭa kéné uripé lampu listrik gilir·an.* In this city, the residence blocks take turns having the lights on. *Pulpèn apik ngono kok mung kanggo tjepak·an silih²·an.* How come you keep such a nice fountain pen just for lending people? *Pamplèt² kuwi pantjèn mligi seḍijan djupuk-djupuk·an para tamu.* Those pamphlets are for the audience to help themselves to. 15 approximately *n*. *limang djam·an* about 5 hours. *djam lima·nan* about 5 o'clock. *Omahé nomer telu·nan.* His house number is 3 or sth like that. *ngaso seminggu·an* to take about a week off. *taun sèket·an nem*

or *taun sèket nem·an* around [19]56. **16**
an unspecified number of *n*'s. *Lungané se-
sasèn (se·sasi·ǹ).* He was gone for months.
Éwon (èwu·ǹ) sing paḍa mati. Thousands
died. **17** generalized state of [adjective].
manis djangan sing wutuh·an a stick of
whole cinnamon. *Legèn mau didol men-
tah·an baé.* He sold the sugar-palm sap unprocessed. **18** *var of suffix* -I *when prefixed with* KA- . *See also* KA...AN, PA...AN
under PA-^b; *also definition of doubled
forms (Introduction, 3.1.1); also Introduction, 3.1.6.2. See also individual entries
for applicable meanings*

ânâ^a *ng,* **wonten** *kr* **1** to exist, be; there is/
are. **∗,** *nanging ora akèh.* There are some,
but not many. *Mèh ora* **∗.** There are hardly
any. **∗** *apa?* How come? What's going on?
What's the matter? *pulo kang ora* **∗** *wongé*
an uninhabited island. **∗** *sambungé.* To be
continued. **∗** *sing abang,* **∗** *sing biru.* Some
of them are red and some are blue. *Botjah²
ora* **∗** *sing weruh.* None of the children
knew it. *Ora* **∗** *owahé.* There was no change
in it. *Ora* **∗** *manèh sing dirembug.* Nothing
else was discussed. **2** (*or* **∗ ing**) (to be) in,
at, on, to; to be/stay in [a place]. **∗** *ndjero
(ng)omah* in(side) the house. *mati* **∗** *prang*
to die in war. *tiba* **∗** *lemah* to fall to the
ground. *Tak terangké tekaku* **∗** *kéné.* I'll
explain why I came here. *Kowé* **∗***a ngomah
waé.* You stay home. *urip* **∗** *ing djaman pendjadjahan* to live in colonial times. *Wis* **∗**
kono waé. Stay where you are. **3** there
is/are *n*; to be (equal to) *n. Seduluré* **∗** *pitu.*
He has 7 brothers and sisters. *Adohé* **∗** *setengah kilomèter.* It's 1/2 kilometer away.
Loro lan telu ana lima. Two and 3 are 5.
Wis **∗** *patang taunan aku ora weruh Semarang.* I haven't been to Semarang for about
4 years now. *wong kang umuré wis* **∗** *rong
puluhan tahun* people in their twenties. **4**
to have. *Botjah² lagi* **∗** *liburan sekolahé.*
The young people are having vacation. *Anak
kudu* **∗** *bapaké.* A child needs a father. **5**
(*ng only*) *excl of scorn or disparagement.
Apa ḍokteré gawéné njakot? — Ija ora,* **∗**
ḍokter kok njakot. Do doctors bite you? —
Of course not, as if a doctor would bite.
Kok kodjur temen dina iki, **∗** *adol pitik kok
mung paju sangalas baé.* No luck today—I've
only sold 19 chickens. **∗a (kaé)** even if
there were... **∗***a sega kaé ja kowé ora arep
dak wènèhi.* Even if I had some rice, I

wouldn't give you any. **∗né** the existence
(of). **∗***né mung kuwi.* That's all there is.
djalaran **∗***né perang* because of the war.
Bléntjongé marakaké **∗***né ajang²aning wajang ing kelir.* The oil lamp throws the puppets' shadows on the screen. **∗-∗ waé** *excl
suggesting that words fail one.* **∗-∗** *waé.*
There's always something! **∗-∗** *waé djaman
saiki.* Really, the times we live in...! *Wong
iki* **∗-∗** *waé.* This guy is just too much. *Bar
bandjir terus patjeklik, kok* **∗-∗** *waé kesusah-
ané.* In the wake of the flood came famine,
with dreadful suffering. **ka∗n** (*or* **kah∗n** *ng*)
conditions, circumstances. *kaanan hawa*
weather conditions. *Wis rada tentrem kahanan kantor.* Things are quiet at the office.
Pak pengulu takon² bab kahanan pribadi.
The minister asked me a lot of questions
about myself. *Saiki kahanané wis béda.*
Things are different now. *tembung kahanan
(gram)* adjective, adverb. **ng/di∗aké, ng/di∗i**
(**nga·wonten·aken, nga-wonten·i** *kr acv*) to
create, establish, bring about. *ng∗kaké udjian* to hold an examination. *ng∗kaké pamulangan* to establish a school. *Jèn ora nduwé
apa² ora susah di-anak²aké.* If you haven't
got anything on hand, don't go to a lot of
bother fixing sth. **sa∗né (waé)** whatever
there is. *Ḍaharé sa∗né.* They ate whatever
was available. *Ora susah matjak, nganggo
sa∗né waé.* Don't dress up—wear anything
you have. **∗ dina ∗ upa** another day another meal—*i.e.* come what may, we'll eat, so
why worry? **∗ (u)wisé** an end (to it). *Perangé tanpa* **∗** *uwisé.* The war is endless. **∗
waé sing** there's always one who..., there
are always some who... *Mesṭi* **∗** *waé sing
gelem dadi sukarélawan.* There are always
bound to be volunteers. *See also* ANADÉNÉ

-ânâ^b (**-nânâ** *after vowel*) (*suffix*) **1** *imperative form of suffix* -I. *Ng·réwang·ana ba-
pakmu.* Help your father! *Wong ngemis
kaé wènèh·ana sega.* Give that beggar some
rice. *Anakmu ombè·nana djamu iki.* Have
your child take this medicine. **2** *subjunctive form of suffix* -I*: see* -A^b *for subjunctive meanings. di·tamba·nana dikaja-ngapa*
no matter how much medicine you give
him. *Wong ala di·betjik·ana ija bakal males
ala.* Treat a bad person kindly and he'll repay you with evil. *Kowé manèh dak·wènèh-
·ana, sing anakku ḍéwé ora dak wènèhi.* As
if I'd give you any—I didn't even give any to
my own child! *Ḍokteré atur·ana mréné*

supaja wong lara iki di·priksa·nana. Send for the doctor so he can examine this sick man. *Sanadjan tak wènèh·ana satus rupiah meksa durung tjukup!* I gave him 100 rupiahs and it still wasn't enough!

ânâdéné *ng,* **wondéné** *or* **wondéning** *kr* now, while, and. *Ana botjah loro: * sing sidji djenengé Ali...* Now, there were 2 boys: one one was named Ali...

âna-ini *syllables chanted to coordinate an effort. * ajo hing, * ajo breng: saben muni "hing" karo "breng" tiba satarikan bebarengan.* [chant]: with each "hing" and "breng" they all pulled together.

anak[a] **1** **(putra** *ki)* offspring. ** lanang* son. ** wédok* daughter. *dipèk ** to be adopted as one's own child. **2** nephew, niece. **3** young plant sprout. ***an** **1** the young of an animal. **2** doll. **3** small [of natural phenomena]. *segara *an* small sea; bay. *gunung *an* hill. **4** a copy, duplicate. **an kuntji* a duplicate key. **5** drawer; section, compartment. **an boṭékan* small drawer of a medicine chest or box. ***-*** **(pe·putra** *ki)* to have children. *ora *-** childless. ***-*an** doll, puppet. **-*an kaju* wooden doll. **-*an timun* cucumber used as a doll; adopted child who later marries the adoptive parent. **m*** to reproduce [of animals; *cr* of people: **ma·putra** *ki, ltry*]. *Kutjingku mentas m*.* Our cat has just had kittens. **ng/di*** to call smn, *or* regard smn as, one's own child. **ng/di*aké** **1** to give birth (to). *Anggoné ng*aké kangélan.* She had a difficult labor. **2** to be the parent (of). *Sing ng*aké kowé Pak A, dudu Pak B.* A is your father–not B. **ng/di*-*aké** to raise [a child] from birth to adulthood. **ng/di*i** **1** to father [an illegitimate child]. **2** to provide for [one's children]. **3** to produce a copy *or* imitation of. *** angkat** adopted child. *** anung** outstanding *or* superior child. *** bapa bandara·ku** *ltry* master [term used by servants]. *** bodjo** wife and child(ren). *Ali sa* bodjoné* Ali and his wife and child. *** buah** crew; group under the command of an officer *or* employees under a boss. *** djadah** illegitimate child. *** k·um·anak** to multiply, flourish [of people, animals, plants]. *** kumpeni** soldier. *** kuwalon** stepchild. *** mas** **1** *respectful adr* son-in-law. **2** favorite child; teacher's pet. **3** favored person. *** panḍawa** sibling combination consisting of 5 boys. *** prabu** *title by which a king is addressed by his father(-in-law) or uncle.* *** pudja·n** *wj* a child created magically. *** pupu·n̂** a child adopted in babyhood. *** putu** descendants; **sa*-putu·né** (together) with all his descendants. *** rakjat** child of common people

anak[b] *ng,* **sarem** *sbst? kr* ***an** interest on borrowed money. **ng/di*aké** to lend *or* invest [money] for interest. **ng/di*i** to pay *or* charge interest. *Kowé ng*i pira sesasiné?* How much is your monthly interest? ***-k·um·anak** *ng kr* (to draw) compound interest

anam ***an** woven, braided. **an gedèg* a braided-bamboo wall panel. **ng/di*** to weave, braid. *pring sing di** woven bamboo. **ng/di*-*** to weave in and out. *Perkara mau tansah ng*-* pikiranku.* It keeps coming into my thoughts. **ng/di*i** to weave *or* braid sth into [an article]. *See also* NAM

ananging *formal var of* NANGING

anantâkusumâ *see* ANTRAKUSUMA

anasir element, factor

ânâtjarâkâ *see* HANATJARAKA

ândâ **1** *oj* dark. **2** *oj* blind. **ng*-*** to spread evenly

ânḍâ ladder; ladder-like steps. ***n-*n** **1** a short flight of ladder-like wooden steps. **2** drying rack of bamboo poles. **ng*n-*n** falling in loose waves. *Rambuté ngandan-anḍan.* She has wavy hair. **ng/di*ni** to lean a ladder against. *Témboké wis di*ni.* He put a ladder against the wall. *** djagang** *or* *** djagrag** stepladder with steps on both sides. *** djundjang** latticed bamboo poles forming a trellis for vines. *** lanang** ladder consisting of a pole with rungs projecting on either side. *** pengantèn** stepladder. *** widadari** rainbow

anḍah ***an** **1** subordinate, underling. *Sang Nata sa*ané* the King with his courtiers. **2** *gram* affixed. *tembung *an* derived word, affixed form. **k*** to lose, be defeated. **ng/di*aké** to supervise [one's subordinates]. **ng/di*i** to subordinate *or* subjugate oneself (to). *Sarèhning ḍèwèké botjah tjilik, ja mung tak *i waé.* Since he was just a child, I did whatever he asked.

andak *excl of disbelief.* ** kowé wani?* Would you *dare?* *** ja** *or* *** ora** oh no! ** ja djarané kok bisa omong?* I don't believe it–a talking horse!

andâkâ *ltry* bull; wild boar

andam a variety of fern

andânâ *oj* clear

andang *formal var of* ENDANG

anḍap 1 below, under (*root form: kr for* ISOR). 2 short, low (*kr for* TJENḌÈK). 3 to descend (*root form: kr for* ḌUN). * **asor** humble, self-effacing. *See also* KRAMA

anḍapan wild boar (*kr for* TJÈLÈNG)

anḍar ***an** 1 speech, account, narration. 2 a long-winded account. 3 *gram* declarative, narrative. **ka*an** a long-winded narration. **ng*-*** excessively long. *Tjritané ng*-*.* His story went on and on. **ng/di*aké** to tell, explain

andaru *oj* falling star bearing an omen

anḍé (*or* *[-*]né *or* s[a]*né) 1 in case. *Sa*né kowé lunga pasar, aku tukokna mbako.* If you go the marketplace, buy me some tobacco. 2 and yet, even so. *Ta, rak ora lidok kanḍaku, anḍèkna ora, bijèn kowé léngkak-kéngkok!* You see, I was right —but you wouldn't believe me.

anḍeg *ng,* **èndel** *kr* act of stopping. **é** *motor mau ora krasa.* I didn't feel the car stop. **k*** *ng kr* to get stopped. *Olèhku omong*[2] *k*.* They made us stop talking. **k*-k·ampir·an** to stay *or* stop over at smn's home. **m*** (**kèndel** *kr*) to come to a stop. *Sepuré m* greg.* The train stopped suddenly. *Ḍèké m* olèhé mlaku.* He stopped walking. **m*-majong** (*ltry*) *or* **m*-mangu** to hesitate between alternatives; to [do] in fits and starts. *Ajo ndang mangkat, kok m*-mangu.* Let's go–quit stalling. **m*-t·um·olih** 1 to hesitate from fear. 2 *ltry* to stop and turn the head. **ng/di*** (**ng/di-pun·èndel·aken** *kr*) to stop sth. *Sepuré di* geriljawan.* The train was stopped by guerrillas. **ng/di*aké** to stop sth. **ng*i** to stop (in) at. **ng/di*-*i** to slow sth down. *Adja ng*-*i lakuku.* Don't hinder me. *See also* ENḌEG

anḍèk ***ané** *or* ***na** *or* ***né** *rg var of* ANḌÉ. ***puna** *ltry var of* ANḌÉ

andel 1 believer, one who trusts. 2 Javanese army general [*obsolete rank*]. ***an** 1 gullible, over-trusting. 2 one who can be depended upon. *A dadi *ané sekolahané.* A is the pride of his school. 3 security for a loan. ***-*** (one who is) trustworthy, reliable. **ng/di*** to believe (in), trust. *Aku ora ng* marang kanḍané botjah mau.* I don't have much faith in what the child said. *Ng*a, aku wis weruh.* Believe me, I've seen it. **ng/di*aké** 1 to rely on. *A bisa di*aké dadi wakiling sekolahan iki.* A can be depended on to represent this school well. *Kowé kuwi wis di*aké ora teka.* We were depending on you but you didn't show up. 2 to leave it to smn else to [do], to trust that smn else will [do]. *saling ng*aké* to leave it to each other (with the result that neither does it). **ng/di*-*aké** to depend too heavily on [the wrong values]. *Ḍèké ng*-*aké kesugihané bapaké.* He thinks he's great because of his father's money. **ng*an** (too) trusting. *wong ng*an* a gullible person. *Kowé iku pantjèn wong ora ng*an banget.* You're really hard to convince, aren't you! **pi*** 1 belief, superstition. *miturut pijandel...* according to popular belief... 2 one in whom one puts one's faith/trust. *See also* ENDEL

anḍel *var of* ANDEL

anḍem ***an** indentation in an animal's chest (where the heart is). **ng/di*i** 1 to commit oneself to. *ng*i pati* to pledge oneself to another for eternity. 2 to acknowledge freely. *ng*i kaluputan* to admit one's fault

anḍeng ***-*** skin blemish, mole

ander upright roof-supporting beam in a house frame

anḍèr to gather, form a crowd

anderpati willing to die. *kerengan ** to fight to the death

andèwi endive

anḍih *var of* ENḌIH

andik 1 *ltry* severe, harsh. 2 *rg* somewhat, rather

andika you (*oj, ltry*). ***n** *ki* to talk, converse. **ng*** *ki* to say; to tell. *See also* NGENDIKA

anḍil 1 a share of ownership. 2 scale for weighing opium

andir road worker (*var of* ANDJIR)

ândjâ ***-*nen** *or* ***n-*nan** to avoid, steer clear of. **ng*-*** 1 a variety of spider. 2 to walk on one's hands. 3 to have a good time, enjoy oneself. 4 to become emotional. *Ḍèké sangsaja ng*-* atiné.* He got more and more excited.

andjali *oj* a *sembah* (gesture of obeisance). **(ma)ng*** to make this gesture. **pa·ng*** the above gesture

andjang ***-*** bamboo latticework used as a support for climbing vines

andjat **m*** sloping steeply. **ng/di*i** to labor at an uphill task. *Siti lagi ng*i sinau, wong sésuk arep udjian.* Siti is cramming; she has a test tomorrow.

andjer *var of* ANDJIR
andji ***-*nen** *or* **k*** to avoid, steer clear of
andjing ***-*an** mortise joint, dovetailed joint. **m*** to enter into and become one with. *Jèn pakuné wis m* ngéné, ja ora bisa didudut manèh.* If a nail gets wedged in this tight you'll never get it out again. *Wulangané pak guru tibané wis m* ana ing pikirané botjah²*. The students have a full grasp of what the teacher is teaching. *Warnané wis m*.* The dye has taken. *Sendjata Nanggala wis m* ana ngèpèk-èpèké kiwa.* The weapon disappeared into his left palm. *Djaréné suksmané Pak A m* ana putrané.* They say that A is reincarnated in his son. 2 to be(come) the right time (for). *Aku arep buka, wis m* apa durung?* I want to break my fast; is it time yet? **m* adjur-adjèr** having the (magical) power to penetrate any substance. **ng/di*aké** to fit sth [into]. *Pantèk bandjur di*aké ana ing bolongan.* He fitted the wedge into the opening. *** laut** walrus
andjir 1 stake *or* pole used as a marker; a sign(post). 2 road repair worker. **ng/di*** to repair roads. **ng/di*i** to put up signs *or* markers
andjleg to live *or* be located in/at
andjlog 1 to jump down. 2 to descend sharply. **ng/di*aké** to cause to descend. *ng*aké reregan* to lower prices. **ng/di*i** to jump down onto, pounce on. *See also* DJLOG, ENDJLOG
andjog (having arrived) at, (leading) to/into. *Kali² iku mili * ing segara.* Rivers flow to the sea. *Dalané * menjang ing tengahing kuṭa.* The street leads to the heart of the city. **ng/di*aké** to deliver sth to, cause to arrive at. *See also* DJOG
andjrah (*or* **p***) ubiquitous, present everywhere
andjrak to stay smw permanently. *See also* DJRAK
andjreg *var of* ANDJLEG
andjrit *ltry* to scream, cry out
andjuk **ng/di*** to buy on credit
andjum tangan to extend both hands in a greeting, Arabic or Moslem style
andjun *see* TUKANG
andjur ***(-*)an** advice, suggestion(s). **ng/di*aké** to suggest, advise. *Aku ng*aké marang kowé, éling.* I suggest that you keep it in mind.
anḍok (*or* **m*** *or* **ng***) located smw; to be *or* stay smw. *Enggoné * ana ing kono ora lunga²*. He stayed right there and didn't go out at all. *Kupuné ng* ana ing pupus geḍang.* The butterflies hang around the young banana leaves. *See also* ḌOK, ENḌOK
andon to carry on, engage in. ** djurit* to fight a war. ** ngaso* to take a rest. *** tuwa** older brother-/sister-in-law
andong a certain plant. ***an** *see* BAṬIK
anḍong horse-drawn cab. ***an 1** acting as, or connected with, a horse cab. *kréta *an* a carriage used as a cab. *Iki djaran tunggangan apa *an?* Is this a riding horse or a cab horse? 2 (amount collected as) cab fare. **ané pira?* How much is the fare? *Dina iki *ané Rp. 20.* Today's fares amounted to 20 rupiahs. ***-*an** act of replacing *or* substituting. *Buruh kasar gampang *-*ané.* It's easy to replace laborers. **ng*** 1 to ride in a cab, go by cab. 2 to transport passengers as one's job. 3 (*psv* **di***) to transport [passengers]. **ng/di*aké** 1 to use [a vehicle], or have it used, for profit. *Aku ng*aké mobilku, éntuk²ané ja lumajan kena kanggo tambah butuh.* I transport passengers in my car to supplement my income. 2 to have smn act as one's substitute *or* replacement. **ng/di*i** to change places with, replace, substitute for. *Buruh kasar gampang di*i, buruh alus angèl.* It's easy to replace a laborer but hard to replace an artisan.
ândrâwinâ *ltry* feast, banquet
anḍuk *see* HANḌUK
anduka *var of* ATUKA
andul **ng/di*** to bounce [a child] on one's knee
andum to divide up, distribute, share. ** pegawéan* to assign each person a task. *** laku** *or* *** paran** to part company. *Bareng tekan désa X, paḍa * laku.* When they reached X village, they went their separate ways. *** slamet** 1 farewell party. 2 *farewell expression upon parting or at the close of a letter.* *See also* DUM
anḍung **sa*-*** available, at hand. *Adja kuwatir kaliren, marga aku isih duwé pangan sa*-*.* Don't worry about going hungry—we have plenty of food on hand. *See also* MANḌUNG
anéa how...! what (a)...! *Kodjur *, ora ana angin.* What bad luck! there's no wind. *Pinter temenan *!* How smart he is!
-anéb *ng*, **-anipun** *kr* (**-nané, -nanipun** *after vowel*) *optative form of suffix* -I. *Anggoné*

nggawa wanguné rekasa, dak réwang·ané. What he's carrying looks heavy; I'll help him. *Kutjingmu lara, dak pati·ṅana baé.* Your cat is sick–let me put him out of his misery. *See also* TAK-

anèh strange. *Kok * kowé kuwi!* You're an odd one! *Wah ambuné *.* What a funny smell! *Wé *-*, ana unta kok pangané tikus.* Here's sth strange: a camel that eats mice! **ng/di*aké** 1 to cause sth to be strange. 2 to regard sth as odd. **ng*-*i** very much out of the ordinary. *wong sing duwé pengira sing ng*-*i* a person with wierd ideas

anéka *oj* kind, variety; color. *See also* MANÉKA

anèmer, anémer building contractor

angabèhi *see* NGABÈH

angad *var of* ONGOD

angah **ng*-*** to have an appetite (for). *mBasan weruh bestik Slamet terus ng*-*.* When Slamet saw the steak, his mouth watered.

angap **m*** open(ed) [of the mouth]. *Ana sing m*, ana sing matané mlolo.* Some gaped, some stared. **ng/di*aké** to open [one's, smn's] mouth

angas **ng/di*i** to speak loudly to. *Botjah mau tak *i bandjur mlaju.* I yelled at the boy and he ran off.

angèl hard, difficult. *Garapan iki kétoké *, nanging sakdjané gampang.* This work looks hard, but it's really easy. ***-*an** to seem difficult. *Udjiané kena diarani *-*an waé.* The test just *looks* hard. **k*an** 1 excessively difficult. 2 difficulty. *tanpa k*an* with no trouble. **ng/di*-*** to make sth unnecessarily difficult. **ng/di*aké** to make difficult. *Udjiané di*aké baé ja!* Let's make the exam hard! **ng/di*(-*)i** *sms* **ng/di*-*.** *See also* NGÈL

angèn to herd, tend (*kr for* ANGON)

angen thought, idea. **ng/di*-*** to keep thinking about sth, always have sth in one's mind. *Adja tansah ng*-* sing wis ora ana.* Stop dwelling on what is over and done with. *See also* KANGEN, NGEN

anget 1 warm, hot, not yet cool(ed); lukewarm. *Hawané krasa *.* The air feels warm. *banju ** (luke)warm water. *sega ** warmed rice. *sanḍangan sing ** warm clothing. *kabar ** hot news. 2 short in measure. *Olèhmu nempur wingi takerané kurang *.* The rice you bought yesterday was short. 3 an additional amount. *Siti tuku wekasané embokné, timbangané olèh *.* Siti bought what her mother needed, and they weighed out a little extra for her. 4 safe, secure, cozy. **m*-m*** (luke)warm. *pangundjukan ingkang manget²* a warm drink. **ng/di*aké** to make warm. *pangan sing ng*aké awak* food that warms you up. *See also* NGET

ânggâ body *(oj).* ***-*** water spider

anggâdâ bracelet

anggak boastful, conceited. *Ḍèké mari *.* He was cured of his bragging. ***-*an** to show off, boast, brag

ânggâkârâ *oj* brave

anggal light (not heavy). **ng/di*aké** to make light(er)

anggânâ *oj* 1 alone, by oneself. 2 woman, girl. *** raras** beautiful girl

anggang ***-*** 1 water spider (*rg var of* ANGGA²). 2 with slow easy motions. **ng/di*-*** to [do] with slow easy motions. *Olèhmu ngelus-elus matjan di*-*.* Pat the tiger cautiously!

anggar 1 sheath *or* scabbard worn at the side. 2 the sport of fencing. *main ** to fence. ***an** 1 sheath, scabbard. 2 a loan. 3 committed *or* earmarked funds. ***an blandja** budget. ***-*an** fencing (sport). **ng/di*** 1 to borrow [money]. 2 to buy on credit. 3 to carry [a weapon] in a scabbard. **ng/di*i** to lend [money]. *Jèn ḍuwitmu entèk aku bisa ng*i.* If you're out of money I can lend you some.

Anggârâ *oj* Tuesday. *** Kasih** *alternate name for* SLASA KLIWON

anggauta *var of* ANGGOTA

anggé to use; to wear (*root form: kr for* ANGGO). ***-*** mole cricket found in rice paddies

anggel ***an** *or* ***-*** small wooden dam used to control the flow of water in rice paddies. **m*** dammed up. **ng/di*** to dam up, hold back

anggèn smn's act of [do]ing; customary place (*kr for* ANGGON)

anggep opinion, assumption. **é pinter ḍéwé.* He thinks he's the smartest one of all. **mu apa, teka² kok ndjaluk mangan!* What do you think you are, asking for food the minute you walk in! ***-*an** to consider unworthy, look down on (things, people). **k(a)*** to be considered/regarded (as). *Keris kuwi ka* geḍé kasijaté.* Krises are believed to have magical powers. **ng/di*** 1 to consider, regard. *di* mungsuh* regarded as an enemy. *Duwit di∗ kaja krikil baé.* He values money no more than pebbles. 2 to regard highly. *Ing pasrawungan ḍèké wis di-∗.* He's held in high regard in the community. *Sanadjan A mèlu ana pesamuan mau, nanging ḍèké ora di∗.* A took part in the meeting but nobody paid much attention to him. **pa·ng∗** *or* **pi∗** opinion, thought, attitude. *Pang∗mu kowé kuwi sapa ta?* Who do you think you are?

anggèr *adr* young man!

angger 1 each, every. *∗ wong* or *∗ irung* everyone, every person. *dudu ∗ wong ning wong*[2] *tjenḍekiawan* not just anybody–only intellectuals. 2 every (time); whenever. *∗ bubar panèn* every year after the harvest. *∗ ana bleḍèg muni* with each thunderclap. **∗é** 1 every (time); whenever. 2 if, provided that. *Kena kok gawa menjang pamulangan, ∗é ora kok ilangaké baé.* You can take it to school, so long as you don't lose it. **∗-∗** 1 every time. *∗-∗ ḍèké mesṭi telat.* He's late every time. 2 law; rules. *nglanggar ∗-∗* to violate the law, break the rules. **ng/di∗-∗i** to apply rules (to), furnish regulations (for). *Sing ng∗-∗i malah nglanggar ḍéwé.* The very person who established the rules has broken them. **∗ anu** every time. *∗ anu ḍèké mesṭi telat.* She's always late. *See also* UGER

anggi ∗-∗ a certain medicinal herb

anggit thought, feeling. *∗é apa lo, la wong ésuk*[2] *kok wis nesu.* What's he thinking of, getting mad first thing in the morning! **∗an** 1 composition, invention. *∗an tjekak* a brief article. *∗ané Pak X* written by Mr. X. 2 quick to grasp ideas. **ng/di∗** 1 to invent, think up. *Ng∗a tjangkriman.* Make up a riddle! *Sapa sing ng∗ ora ana sing ngerti.* The author is unknown. 2 to arrange [*e.g.* flowers]

angglong nearly gone, reduced to a small amount [of the contents of a container]. **∗ ati·né** disappointed

anggo *ng,* **anggé** *kr,* **agem** *ki* **∗n** (for) casual (wear). *klambi anggon* a dress for sitting around in. **∗n-∗nan (agem-ageman** *ki)* 1 sth to be worn. 2 act *or* way of dressing. **k∗** for (*see also* KANGGO). **ng/di∗** 1 to use; using, by means of. *ng∗ mesin tulis* with a typewriter; to use a typewriter. *Kajuné dipetjèli ng∗ waḍung.* He chopped the wood with an axe. *Apa kursi iki wis di∗?* Is this seat reserved? *Ora ng∗ tak pikir menèh.* I didn't give it another thought. *Matiné ora ng∗ disuduk, nanging ng∗ dipenṭung.* He wasn't stabbed to death, he was beaten to death. 2 to have sth attached or accompanying it. *Ora susah ng∗ kontrak.* It isn't necessary to have a contract. *Nganggé serat mboten?–Nganggé.* Have you got the letter with you?–Yes. *padusan sing ora ng∗ mbajar* a public bath that doesn't charge a fee. *Kok ng∗ ndjlimet*[2] *barang, mbok ja terus terang waé.* You don't have to do all that arguing–just tell the truth. *Républik Indonesia kuwi ng∗ ḍasar Pantja Sila.* The Republic of Indonesia is based on the Five Principles. 3 to consider, regard as. *Djago A di∗ unggulan, déné djago B di∗ asoran.* Fighting cock A is considered the favorite, while B is the under dog. 4 to misuse, misappropriate [funds]. 5 to wear, *i.e.* use [apparel]. *Ḍèké mlaku ora ng∗ sepatu.* He's walking barefoot. *ng∗ pajung* to carry an umbrella. *Hawané aḍem, mula kudu ng∗-∗ sing rada kandel.* It's cold; you should be wearing sth warm. **ng/di∗kaké** to help smn dress, dress smn; to let *or* have smn wear. *Apa kowé gelem nganggokaké sepatuné aḍimu?* Will you help your little sister put on her shoes? **ng/di∗n(-∗n)i** 1 to dress smn (in), have smn wear. 2 to put/try on [many items]. *See also* ENGGO, KANGGO, PANGANGGO

anggon *ng,* **anggèn** *kr* 1 smn's act of [do]-ing. *Wis tekan ndi ∗mu matja?* How far have you read? 2 **(lenggah** *ki*) place where one lives *or* usually is. **k∗an** to get sth put at one's place. *Apa kowé gelem k∗an barang*[2] *iki?* Can I leave these things at your place? *Aku arep k∗an ponakan*[2]*ku.* My nephews will be staying with me. **m∗** 1 to live, reside. *Aku m∗ ing Djakarta.* I live in Djakarta. 2 placed, located. *Anakku m∗ ana ing pangkat sidji.* My child is in first grade. **ng/di∗i** to occupy [a place]. **p∗an** place. *p∗an dolanan* a place to play. *mesen p∗an* to make a reservation. *See also* ENGGON

anggota 1 a body part. *salah sawidjiné ∗ badan* some part of the body. 2 member of a group *or* body. *∗ partai* political party member. *∗ tentara* soldier

anggrah ∗-∗ brush, twigs, leaves; *fig* sth worthless

anggrak **ng/di∗** to stop smn *esp.* by brandishing a weapon

anggrang **ng*** **1** leaning against sth. **2** left unfinished. *Olèhé gawé omah ng*.* He's never finished building the house. **ng/di*-aké** to lean sth against (sth). *Anḍané di*-aké nuli dipènèk.* He put up the ladder and climbed it.

anggreg ***-*** *or* **onggrag-*** to proceed haltingly rather than smoothly

anggrèk orchid (flower)

anggrem *rg var of* ANGREM

anggreng *ltry* **1** to roar. **2** to groan in pain

anggrik **ng*-*** *intsfr* thin. *Ḍèké kuru ng*-** He's thin as a rail.

anggris $2^1/_2$ rupiahs' worth in coins or paper money (*var of* RINGGIT)

anggrok **m*** to stay smw, stop (over). **ng/di*aké** *or* **ng/di*i** to stay in [a place], stop (over) at [a place]. *See also* ENGGROK

angguk a children's singing-and-dancing game

anggung **1** cooing sound. **2** *oj* constantly. *si punggung * gumunggung* that showoff who is always boasting. **m*** to coo. *** **gawé** useful

anggur grape; grape wine. ***(-*)an** to take it easy. *mBok inggih sampun *an kémawon.* Please don't go to any trouble! **-*an apiké resik² omah.* It'd be better to clean up the house than just sit idle. *wong *an* the unemployed. **ng*** free, at leisure, not working. *mengko nèk wis nganggur²* if you get some free time. *Ja mung trima lowung katimbang ng*.* It's better than doing nothing. *Anḍongé ng*.* The horse-cart is available for hire. *paring gawéjan marang kang paḍa ng** to give jobs to the jobless. *Aku arep ngengkrengaké kwali, mengko geniné munḍak entèk ng*.* I'm going to put the kettle on so the fire won't go to waste. **pa·ng*** the unemployed. **pa·ng*an** unemployment. *** **poret** *or* *** **puf** champagne

anggut *rg var of* ANṬUK

angi *rg* cooled by fanning [of rice that is too hot to eat]. *sega ** rice that has been fanned cool. ***ǹ** rice fanned cool. **ng/di*** to fan [rice] to cool it

angin **1** wind; breeze, draft. **2** air. *Blègé ora bisa klebon *.* The can is airtight. ***en** flatulent. ***-*(an)** to be/get in a draft; to expose oneself to too much air. *Adja *-*.* Don't expose yourself to drafts. ***-*an** to behave erratically. *Njambut gawé adja *-*an, kudu sing mantep.* Don't work just according to your whim–keep at it steadily. **k*an** exposed to, or affected by, wind. *Rambut alus klitjit jèn k*an maḍul².* Fine hair snarls if it gets blown. *k*an silir²* to be in a nice cool breeze. *Geniné ndadi merga k*an.* The fire was spread by the wind. **ng*-*** to get some fresh air. **ng/di*(-*)aké** to dry sth in the wind. *** **ḍarat** offshore night wind. *** **dombang** south wind common during the dry season. *** **ḍuḍuk** to drop dead; to have a heart attack *(folk usage).* *** **genḍing** strong east wind that brings illness with it. *** **m·idid** breeze. *** **laut** daytime offshore wind. *** **lésus** hurricane, typhoon. *** **p·in·usus** small-scale typhoon. *** **silem ing warih** one who plots evil in secret

ângkâ **1** number, digit. **2** mark, grade. **né sedjarah* his marks in history. **3** grade level, class. *sekolah * sidji* low elementary school (consisting of grades 1–3). **4** number in ordinal series. ** telu saka nḍuwur* 3d from the top. **5** *var of* ANGKAH. **ng/di*ni** to number. *Omah² di*i sidji, loro, lsp.* The houses are numbered 1, 2, etc. *** **gandjil** odd number. *** **ganep** even number. *** **ke·lahir·an** birth rate. *** **ke·mati·an** death rate. *** **petjah·an** fraction. *** **Rum** roman numeral. *** **sijal** unlucky number. *** **taun** year name in digits. *** **urut** consecutive numbers, serial numbers

angkah intention, expectation. **ng/di*** to intend, expect. *Ḍèké ng* dadi ḍokter.* He plans to be a doctor. **pa·ng*** *or* **pi*** intention, expectation, goal

angkârâ selfish, greedy

angkas **ng/di*-*** to look forward to, await eagerly

angkâsâ *ltry* sky, heavens. *Sang Hyang ** God. **ng*** in heaven; up in the air

angkasawan radio announcer

angkat adopted; adoptive. *anak ** adopted child. *wong tuwa ** adoptive parents. ***an** **1** act *or* way of lifting; a load. **2** group of people constituting a movement; a generation (of people). **an empat puluh lima* the freedom generation, *i.e.* the generation of people since the 1945 Indonesian Revolution. **3** class group. *Aku klebu *an 68/69 [sewidak wolu sewidak sanga].* I was in the Class of 1969. ***-*an** beginning of a classical dance movement. **k*** movable, portable. **ng/di*** to promote, elevate. *Di* dadi présiḍèn.* He was appointed president. **ng/di*(i)** to lift, raise. *Ḍèké ng* piranti tilpun karo kanḍa Hallo.* She picked up the phone and said Hello. *Barang²é di*i diunggahké nang sepur.* The baggage was loaded (up) onto the train. **pa·ng*** act *or* way of raising. *Lah keprijé pang*é?* And how do I go about lifting it? * **djundjung** hard physical labor. *See also* PANGKAT

angkeb *-* the last (lowest) rib bone

angker 1 haunted, bewitched. 2 quiet, dignified, held in awe and respect

angkin sash with a money pocket, worn by woman market sellers

angklèk *var of* ÈNGKLÈK

angklek *rg* **ongklak-*** *or* **ng*** to proceed at a slow laborious pace

angklik **m*-m*** balanced precariously. **ng/di*-*** to put sth in a high precarious position

angklung 1 a musical instrument consisting of suspended bamboo tubes which tinkle against each other when shaken. 2 an ensemble of the above instruments. **ng*** to play this instrument

angkrah *-* waste material (brush, cloth bits, *etc.*) in a stream

angkreg *-* *or* **ongkrag-*** to proceed haltingly

angkrèk 1 child's toy: a little wooden man that moves up and down on a stick when the string is pulled. 2 *var of* ANGGRÈK. ***an** a foothold in climbing. **ng/di*** to climb by shinnying

angkrik *-* sitting in a high place. **m*-m*** balanced precariously in a high place. **ng/di*-*** to put sth up high

angkring a pair of cabinet-like containers of food, drink, and utensils, carried at either end of a shoulder pole: used by refreshment peddlers

angkrok *var of* ANGKRÈK

angkruk **(m)*-(m)*** to sit perched in a high place. **ng/di*-*aké** to put [sth large] in a high place. *Beras sagoni di*-*aké ana ṇduwur médja.* He put a gunnysack of rice on the table.

angkud ***an** act *or* way of hauling/transporting. *perusahan *an* movers, moving company. **ng/di*(i)** to transport, haul. *Wong² mau di* nganggo montor mabur.* They were taken there by plane. *Adja pindah omah menèh ṇdak ajang-ojong ng*i barangé.* Let's not move again–it's such a nuisance to move all that stuff. **pa·ng*an** transportation; act *or* way of transporting. *Beras larang merga ongkos peng*ané larang.* Rice is expensive because the cost of transporting it is high.

angkuh arrogant, self-satisfied, complacent. **ng/di*i** to treat arrogantly. **pi*** arrogance, conceit

angkul *-* 1 peg for hanging things on. 2 the portion of an ox yoke that encircles the neck

angkup sheath of an unopened leaf or flower bud

angkur reinforcing corner brace for a wall

anglek̄ cloying. *Rasané gula arèn legi *.* Areca-palm sugar is cloyingly sweet.

anglèng **ng/di*aké** to figure out, comprehend (the meaning of)

angler 1 pleasant, smooth. *Swarané *.* Her voice is pleasing. *Tumpakané *.* It gives a smooth ride. *Lagi *-*é turu kok digugah.* He was sound asleep: why did you wake him? 2 [of kites] holding steady in the flight position. *See also* LER

angles 1 smooth and soundless. *Montoré * banget.* The car runs smoothly and quietly. *Réwangku * tanpa pamit.* Our servant sneaked out without saying goodbye. 2 downhearted, dejected. **ng/di*aké** to make sth smooth/silent; to make smn downcast

angling to say, speak *(oj).* **onglang-*** to converse, chat

anglo charcoal brazier. * **pa·dupa·n** covered incense burner

anglong to recede, ebb. **m*** to dangle, hang. **m*-m*** to keep gazing out of *or* down onto. *Adja manglong² djenḍéla.* Don't keep staring out the window. **ng/di*-*aké** to dangle sth. * **djiwa** to waste away, *e.g.* from sorrow

anglung having the form of certain plant tendrils. **m*** to stoop, lean (toward). *Wité pring m* kali.* The bamboo tree bends toward the river. **ng/di*aké** to bow to smn. *See also* LUNG

angob a yawn; to yawn

angok to recede, ebb

angon *ng,* **angèn** *kr* to herd, tend [livestock]. *botjah * kebo* hired boy who tends the kerbaus. **ng/di*** to tend, herd; *fig* to care for, have regard for. **p*** boy who tends livestock. **p*an** place where animals are taken for grazing and bathing. * **angin** to have a proper regard for time. * **irib·an** to keep an eye open for an opportunity. * **keḍap** to keep an eye on what others are doing. * **mangsa** *sms* * ANGIN. *Bengi²* *mertamu, ora * mangsa.* He came to see me late at night, with no regard for the hour. *** ulat** *sms* * IRIB·AN. *** ulat ng·umbar tangan** on the lookout to steal *or* pick pockets. *See also* LARÉ, NGON

angot to recur; to have a relapse. *Adja udan² munḍak kumat * lelaramu.* Don't go out in the rain or you'll have a relapse. ***-* an** recurrent. *Ngeluné *-*an.* She gets recurrent headaches. *See also* NGOT

angrang a certain red ant. *See also* KEMANGRANG

angrèh *oj* (*or* **m***) to rule, hold sway over. *See also* RÈH

angrem 1 to sit on eggs. *babon ** brood hen. 2 to stay in one place. *Aku wingi * sedina.* I stayed home all day yesterday. *Mimisé * ana ing waḍuké.* The bullet lodged in his stomach. *Lempung sing disawataké ing témbok *.* The clay he threw at the wall stuck there. 3 to rise late. *Jèn wis tanggal tuwa, rembulané *.* The moon rises late during the last half of the month. ***an** 1 place where eggs are being hatched. 2 hideout. **ng/di*aké** to cause [eggs] to be hatched. **ng/di*i** to sit on [eggs] to hatch them. **p*an** *or* **pa·ng·an** *sms* *AN. *See also* NGREM

angrob *oj* to rise [of water level]. *See also* ROB

angrog *var of* ANGRUG

angrong *** pa·sanak·an** to have one's eye on smn else's wife

angrug [to speak, sing] in unison

ângsâ 1 *oj* goose. 2 *oj* ancestor, descendant; dynasty. 3 *oj* share, portion. **ng*(-*)** greedy, covetous; excessively ambitious. *Ng*-* ngentèkaké ḍuwit.* He spent all his money furthering his ambitions.

angsab *var of* ASAB

angsah **m*** 1 to face, confront. *m* juda (djurit)* to go to war (battle). *m* kalangan* to enter the tournament ring. 2 vulnerable. *ora m** invulnerable. **ng/di*aké** to send to war. *Pradjurit di*aké.* The soldiers were sent into battle.

angsal 1 if, provided (*var of* ASAL). 2 to receive, accept (*kr for* OLÈH). 3 smn's act of [do]ing (*kr, md? for* ANGGON, OLÈH)

angsang 1 gill (fish's breathing apparatus). 2 grate for holding coals in a brazier. 3 closet or cupboard shelf. 4 base/foot of a receptacle

angseg **m*** feeling stuffed from overeating. **ng/di*** to press (forward). *A ng* B terus supaja énggal digarap supaja gèk rampung.* A pressed B to hurry and finish the job. **ng/di*aké** to press sth forward. *ng*aké garapan* to quicken the pace of the work

angslah taxation. **ng/di*** to levy taxes (on)

angslep *var of* ANGSLUP

angsli *inf var of* ASLI

angslup to set. *Srengéngéné wis *.* The sun has set. **m*** 1 to set. 2 *rg* to enter. **ng/di*aké, ng/di*i** to insert. *Ḍuwité di*aké ing sak.* He put the money in his pocket.

angsog beached [of small boats]

angsoka *formal var of* SOKA

angsring *var of* ASRING

angsrog **ng/di*aké** 1 to throw sth down. 2 to rake, scrape. *ng*aké goḍong² garing* to rake up dried leaves

angsu ***n̂an** act *or* way of drawing water from a well. *Angsonanmu olèh pirang timba?* How many bucketfuls did you draw? **ng/di*k̂aké** to draw water for smn. **ng*(n̂i)** to draw water for household use; *fig* to acquire [learning]. *ng* kanggo ngasahi piring* to get water for washing dishes. *Sumuré mung sidji, sing ngangsoni wong sadésa.* There's only one well and everyone in the village gets their water there. *Akèh pemuḍa Asia paḍa ng* kapinteran in negara Kulonan.* Many young Asians get an education in Western countries. **ng* banju ing krandjang** to learn sth but fail to apply it. **ng/di*n̂i** to draw water from. *ngangsoni sumur* to get water from a well. **pa·ng*** one who draws water. *ndjuru pang** to draw water for a man to help him out, in the hope of becoming his wife. **pa·ng*n̂** 1 place where household water is obtained; *fig* source of knowledge. 2 container for drawing water

angsuk ***an** a harmonious match. *Klambi biru kuwi *ané tjlana ireng.* Blue shirts go well with black pants. **m*** 1 to match, harmonize. 2 to enter. *Kéné m*, nang ndjaba angin.* Come in; it's windy outside. **m* angin** to have/get a cold. **ng/di*aké** 1 to insert sth. 2 to match/combine [sth harmonious] with

angsul *rg kr for* BALI. ***-*** (**we·wangsul** *kr*) gift to a guest departing from a ceremonial meal

angsung (*or* **m***) *ltry* to proffer sth to a king as a token of loyalty. **ng/di*aké** *ltry* to give. **p∗** gift, offering. ∗ **ḍahar** to offer flowers, burn incense, *etc.* at smn's grave. ∗ **pa·ngabekti** to extend one's respects. *See also* SUNG

angsur ∗**an** installment payment. **ng/di∗** to pay by installments; to make such a payment. *Raḍioné di∗ ping lima.* He paid for the radio in 5 installments. **ng∗-∗** [of breathing] heavy, rapid, coming in gasps. **ng/di∗aké** to sell sth on credit. **ng/di∗i** to sell [merchandise] on credit as one's business. *Aku ng∗i raḍio.* I sell radios on the installment plan.

anguk *var of* ANGUR. **ongak-∗** *or* **m∗-m∗** to keep putting one's head out of [a door, window, *etc.*]

angur it would be better (if..., to...). ∗ *mati tinimbang urip didjadjah.* We'd rather die than be subjugated. *Ḍèké ora gelem njambat, ∗ golèk kuli.* He wouldn't ask for help; he preferred to hire workers.

angus soot. **ng∗ 1** to produce soot. 2 (*psv* **di∗**) to blacken with soot

ani ∗**-∗** (to harvest rice plants with) a large harvesting knife. **ng/di∗** *rg var of* NG/DI∗ÑI. **ng/di∗ǹi** to harvest [rice]. *Pariné dianèni ing wong wadon nganggo ∗-∗.* Women cut the rice with harvesting knives. *See also* PANÈN

aniâjâ *var of* ANINGAJA

animisme animistic religion

aningâjâ **k∗** cruelty. **ng/di∗** to torment. *Adja sok ng∗ kéwan.* Never be cruel to animals. **pa·ng∗** cruel treatment

-anipun *optative suffix: kr for* -ANÉ

anis *oj* begone!

anjag ∗**-∗** to keep walking without stopping. **ng∗** to walk rudely in front of smn without excusing oneself. *See also* ONJOG

anjam *rg var of* ANAM

anjang[a] *ng,* **awis** *kr* ∗**-∗** to bargain, haggle. *pinter ∗-∗* good at bargaining. ∗**-∗an** to haggle (over). *∗-∗an rega, nganti suwé olèhé ∗-∗an.* They haggled over the price for quite some time. **ng/di∗** to bargain for [an item]. *Sapi sing di∗ disik diwènèhaké.* He got the first cow he bid on. *Ḍèké ng∗ bétjak.* He agreed on a price [in advance] with the pedicab driver. **pa·ng∗** act *or* way of bargaining. *Merga akèh sing ḍemen, pang∗ing barang madju.* A lot of people want it so the bidding is going up. *See also* NJANG[a]

anjang[b] dried out [of lime]. *endjet ∗* dried lime. ∗**-∗en** (to have) dysuria

anjar *ng,* **énggal** *kr* new; recent. *klambi ∗* new clothes. *pengantèn ∗* newlyweds. *Kita wiwit kang ∗.* We're beginning anew. *Barang² sing diganti, diganti ∗.* The ones she replaced, she replaced with new ones. *ndjupuk wadon ∗* to remarry; to take another wife. *kaanan ∗* a recent development. *Aku lagi elih²an ∗.* I've just recently moved here. ∗**an** new (at). *bintang pilem sing agèk ∗an* a new movie star. *Prijaji mau sadjaké isih ∗an ana ing Semarang.* He looks as if he's in Semarang for the first time. ∗**(-∗) iki** just recently. ∗**-∗an 1** new (at). *Aku ∗-∗an manggon kéné.* I'm a newcomer here. 2 to compare *or* compete for newness. *Paḍa ∗-∗an tuku prabot omah.* They try to outdo each other in buying the very latest household things. **ng/di∗aké** to make sth, or have sth made, like new. *ng∗aké mesin tik* to have a typewriter reconditioned. **ng/di∗i** to [do] for the first time. *ng∗i kaṭok* to have on new trousers. **ng∗-∗i** strange, unusual. *patrap ng∗-∗i* odd behavior. ∗ **grès** brand new. ∗ **mengko** just recently

anjawar a certain plant

anjèh *var of* ANJIH

anjel annoyed, irritated (at). ∗**an ati·ǹ** easily irritated. **ng∗aké** annoying, irritating; (*psv* **di∗aké**) to annoy, irritate

anjep 1 flat, insipid [of food flavor *or* aroma]. 2 cool(er than normal); cold. **ng∗** to use no salt on one's food, as a form of self-denial. **ng/di∗-∗** to cool sth with water. *See also* NJEP

anjer *var of* ANJUR

anjes damp and chilly. ∗**an** a damp chilly place. *See also* NJES

anji(h) **ng∗-∗** finicky, hard to please

anjir cloyingly rich-tasting

anjleng excessively sweet, cloying

anjles *var of* ANJES

anjling *var of* ANJLENG

anjur **ng∗ 1** to stand (up). 2 (*or* **ng∗-∗** *or* **ng·onjar-∗**) to stand in a disrespectful attitude (rather than showing courteous deference) near smn else

anjut *oj* **ng∗** to get carried away by the current. **ng∗ djiwa** *or* **ng∗ tuwuh** *or* **ng∗ urip** to commit suicide. **ng∗-∗** to remind smn of the past. **ng/di∗aké** to have/let sth get carried with the current *or* tide

anon *oj* to see

anor low, humble, inferior. **ng/di∗aké** to

efface oneself, conduct oneself with modesty. ***-raga** humble, modest

anslah *var of* ANGSLAH

ântâ[a] stale-tasting. **tanpa *-*** unexpectedly, without warning. **ng/di*-*** to long for revenge (against). *** watjana** *wj* characteristic speech melody of a character

-anta[b] (**-nta** *after vowel*) *ltry* your. *raka·nta* your older brother

antah *var of* WANTAH

antâkâ *oj* death; dead; to die. **k*** unconscious. **p*** *var of* *

ântâkusumâ *see* ANTRAKUSUMA

antal (*or* ***-*an**) slow in tempo [of gamelan music]. **ng/di*aké** to slow [the music] down. **ng/di*(-*)i** to allow plenty of time (for). *Senadjan wis tak *-*i kok ja meksa isih ana sing luwih mruput tinimbang aku.* Even though I started early, others were there ahead of me.

antar 1 unhurried, leisurely. 2 clearly audible. 3 long. *Tudingé dikepara * supaja géduk.* Make the stick long enough to reach. **m*** *or* **ng*-*** to glow, burn bright. *See also* KANTAR

antârâ *ng,* **antawis** *kr* 1 between, among, within. ** djam pitu lan wolu ésuk* between 7 and 8 A.M. *(ing) * lija* among other things. *Ana toko*[2] *akèh, *né ana tukang tjukur.* There are lots of stores; one of them is a barber shop. **né kuṭa karo pesisir* between the city and the beach. **né taun sèket telu* during '53. **né kuṭa* within the city. 2 after (an interval of). ** dina* after a day; after several days. 3 some, a certain amount (of time). *let * wektu* after a while, after some time. *wis * suwé* quite a while later. *ora * suwé* not long afterward, pretty soon. 4 (*or* ***né**) approximately. ** limang taun* for about 5 years. **né taun sèket telu* around '53. **ng/di*ni** to come between, separate. *Pawon mau di*ni geḍèg.* The kitchen was divided off by a bamboo wall. **sa*** some (amount/interval of) time. **sa*né** between, among. *sa*né omah loro mau* between the 2 houses. *Ḍèké teka sa*né djam sidji karo djam loro.* He got there between 1 and 2 o'clock.

antariksa *oj* sky, firmament

antariksawan astronaut

antawis between, among (*kr for* ANTARA)

anteb 1 firm, steadfast, loyal. 2 heavy, weighty, considerable. *Barang*[2]*é * banget.* Her luggage is very heavy. *swara ** a deep heavy voice; *gram* heavy consonant sound (*see also* AMPANG). **bantal *an** large decorative bed. **(ka)*an** loyalty; steadfastness. **m*** 1 displaying loyalty/steadfastness. *Asuné m* lan tresna marang ndarané.* 2 fulfilled, gratified. *A wis m* merga wis diunggahaké pangkaté.* A is satisfied now that he's got his promotion. **ng/di*** to ascertain smn's feeling. *Apiké ḍèké di* ḍisik, sadurungé gawé putusan.* We'd better get his opinion before we decide. **ng/di*aké** to make firm/strong; to commit oneself to. **ng/di*i** to be loyal to; to remain steadfast in

anṭèk 1 helper to a tradesman or laborer. 2 sycophant, yes-man. **ng*** to be(come) a helper

antem a blow with the fist. ***-*an** to have a fistfight. **ng/di*(i)** 1 to hit, punch. 2 *slang* to eat hungrily. **pa·ng*** a punch. *** krama** to strike out blindly. *Basan montor maburé dibeḍili saka ngendi-endi terus olèhé ngebom * krama.* When the plane was shot at from all sides, it began dropping bombs recklessly.

anteng steady, tranquil. *A lingguh *.* A sat relaxed. *Wah *é lajanganė.* The kite glided steadily. *Lakuné montor maburé * banget.* The plane trip was smooth. *** kitir·an** *or* *** tlalé** to wriggle, squirm

anṭeng **ng*(-*)** [to wait] for a long time without stirring

antèr 1 quiet, serene. 2 calm and even-tempered

anter *rg var of* BANTER. **ng/di*aké** to take, escort smn (*rg var of* NG·ATER·AKÉ)

antéro around, about. *Kabèh mbèbèr klasané ḍéwé*[2] *ing *né langgar.* They spread their sitting mats around the chapel. **sa*né** one of; a certain kind of. *Sing djeneng cougar ki rak sa*né matjan barang.* A cougar is a variety of tiger, isn't it?

anti *ng,* **antos** *kr* **ng/di*-*** 1 to expect, wait for. 2 to keep reminding smn. *Aku di*-* ora lali tuku tembako.* He kept telling me not to forget to buy tobacco. **ng/di*kaké** to wait (for). *Antèkna.* Be patient! **pa·ng*-*** hope, expectation; that which is awaited. *See also* ENTI, KANTI

antih **k*** thread spun on a spinning wheel. **ng/di*** 1 to spin [thread]. 2 to weave

anṭil flood-control levee

anting 1 sliding weight on a scale beam. 2 metal pieces holding car springs to the frame. ***-*** dangling earring(s) for unpierced ears. **ontang-*** without relatives, alone in the world. *anak ontang-** an only child; a child without relatives. **m·ontang-m*** 1 to sway. 2 to exert oneself. *Wis tak lakoni montang-m*, gadjihku meksa ora tjukup sewulan.* I work myself to the bone and still can't make ends meet. **ng/di·ontang-*aké** to cause sth to move back and forth. *Pulisi jèn mlaku ngontang-*aké penṭung.* Policemen swing their clubs as they walk. *Aku mau diontang-*aké guruku dikongkon mrona-mrana nganti kesel.* My teacher wore me out sending me here and there on errands.

antjab **ng/di*** to make a vicious *or* unprovoked attack (on)

antjak woven-bamboo mat on which offerings to the spirits are placed

antjal the blossom of certain tuberous plants

antjam ***(-*)an** a verbal threat. **ng/di*(-*)** to threaten verbally

antjang ***-*** to get ready. **-* arep mlumpat* all set to jump. **ng/di*-*(i)** to get set for sth *or* to do sth

antjârâ *var of* ATJARA

antjas ideal, goal, ambition. ***an** decision, ruling. **ng*** 1 to strive toward an ideal. *Jèn arep ng* dadi pinter, kudu sregep sinau.* If you intend to get an education, you have to study hard. 2 to take a shortcut; to direct smn to a shortcut. *Jèn ng* mung lakon sadjaman.* If you take the shortcut you'll be there in an hour. *Pulisiné ng* dalan menjang Grobogan.* The policeman told us the shortest way to Grobogan. 3 with a single stroke. *Wité diketọk ng*.* He felled the tree at one stroke. **ng/di*aké** to aim *or* direct sth at/toward. *A tansah ng*aké pikirané menjang kahanan ngomah.* A is always thinking about home. *See also* PANTJAS

antjeb sticking/stuck [into]. **ng/di*aké** to stick/stab sth into. *See also* MANTJEB

antjel ***an** *cr* to copulate (with)

antjer ***-*** 1 mark(er). *Saben sepuluh djangkah botjah mau nibakaké djagung kanggo *-*.* The boy dropped a grain of corn every 10 steps to mark the trail. *tembung *-* (gram)* preposition. 2 the approximate location. **ng/di*aké** to give directions to smw. **ng/di*-*i** 1 to place a mark(er). 2 to give smn directions. *Olèhé ng*-*i ora tjeṭa, mula kesasar.* The directions weren't clear—no wonder he got lost.

antjik ***an** sth stood on to make oneself higher. ***-*** sth stood on; to stand on sth. *Nèk ora tekan, nganggo kursi kuwi kanggo *-*.* If you can't reach it, stand on that chair. **k*an** to get stepped (up) on(to). **m*** *or* **ng*** to reach. *ng* déwasa* to reach adulthood. *Bareng m* pinggiran kuṭa, srengéngéné wis surup.* It was sunset by the time they reached the outskirts of the city. **ng/di*(i)** to stand on sth to extend one's reach. *See also* ENTJIK, PANTJIK

antjo a long-handled net

antjog ***-*en** doubtful about; not quite sure what one wants

antjol ***-*en** unmannerly

antjug ***an** *cr* to copulate (with). ***-*** *or* **ontjag-*** *describing the ungainly gait of a tall thin person.* **ng/di*** *cr* to copulate with

antjul 1 *var of* ANTJUG. 2 (*or* ***an**) equipment for scaring birds away from ripening rice plants

antjur 1 (to get) broken, smashed. 2 powdered glass melted into glue (for coating kite strings). *** lebur** totally destroyed

antob a belch; to belch. **ng/di*aké** to cause smn to belch

anṭok 1 banana-tree pod from which the blossoms and fruit grow. 2 splint for mending. **ng/di*i** to apply a splint to

antol a supporting brace. **ng/di*i** to attach a brace to; to brace *or* support sth

antos to wait for (*root form: kr for* ANTI)

ântrâkusumâ 1 vest. 2 *wj* flowered fabric for certain costumes

antré in a line. *Kabèh paḍa * golèk kartjis.* Everyone lined up to get their tickets.

antri *var of* ANTRÉ

antrog *var of* ENTROG. **k*** to get shaken up. *Bajiné kluron merga k*.* The baby was born prematurely because of the rough ride.

antropologi anthropology

antru 1 wedge used as a lever with a certain prying tool (*songkèl*). 2 fulcrum on which a pole pivots for drawing water from a well (bucket at one end, weight at the other)

antu *var of* ANTI

antuk 1 to get, receive (*kr for* ÉNTUK). 2 return to one's home *or* to one's place of origin (*kr for* ULIH). ***an** 1 person who always longs to go home. 2 one who always gets sleepy (*see also* NGANTUK)

anṭuk **m*(-m*)** to nod the head (again and again). **ng/di*i** to nod to/at. *See also* GÈḌÈG

antyâ-bâsâ a variety of humble Ngoko (*see Introduction, 5.5*)
anu 1 um, uh *(rpr a pause to collect one's thoughts). Sapa sing * nggolèkaké?* Who, er, got it for you? 2 *substitution for a word that has slipped the mind. bapak Anu* Mr. What's-His-Name. *Iki kanggo * ngurus seru karo orané tjaturan.* This is for, what-d'ya-call-it, adjusting the volume of speech. 3 *expressing vagueness rather than definiteness. ḍèk * kaé* some time ago, a while back. *angger ** every time. 4 *euph* sex organ. ***a** otherwise; had sth happened. *Udané kok wis terang ja, *a aku ora sekolah.* It's stopped raining, or I wouldn't be going to school. **ng/di*k̂aké** *or* **ng/di*(n̂i)** to uh..., to you-know... *Ḍèké mau ng*... mangan.* He, uh, ate just now. *Aku arep nganokaké mobil...ndandakaké.* I want to have the car, you-know, fixed. *Ḍèké nganoni aḍiké...ngantemi aḍiké.* He, what-d'ya-call-it, punched his brother. *** apa** why? what's the matter? (*inf var of* ANA APA)
anung *see* ANAK[a]
anurâgâ *var of* ANOR-RAGA: *see* ANOR
anuswârâ *gram* nasal consonant
anut to follow; to imitate. *A mung * grubjuk kantja²né.* A did just as his friends did. **ng/di*** (**n/di·ḍèrèk** *ka*) to follow, act in accordance with, obey, pursue. *Paham ékonomi sing di* Amérika iku djenengé kapitalisme.* America's economic policy is capitalism. **p*an** 1 leader of a religion *or* school of thought. 2 a child adopted in the belief that one will then have children of one's own. **pa·ng*** follower, believer. *See also* NUT, TUT
aolija religious disciple, holy person
aor having a bad taste in the mouth
aos 1 producing well, well filled (*esp.* of rice ears); *fig* cogent. *Piḍatoné tjekak nanging *.* His speech was short but to the point. 2 value, worth (*sbst? kr for* ADJI[a])
âpâ *ng*, **punapa** (*prn* **menâpâ**) *kr* 1 what? what (kind of) thing? to do what? *dina ** what day? *Iki *?* What's this? ** djenengé?* What's it called? *Saben * kowé tuku sanḍangan anjar?* How often do you buy new clothes? ** kanggoné?* What's it used for? *Tanḍané *?* How do you know? *Wong mau njambut-gawé *?* What sort of work does he do? *Kowé lagi *?* What are you doing? *Arep *?* What's he going to do? *or* What does he want? *Keṭèk iku wis bisa *?* What sort of things can monkeys do? *Kowé lara *?* What's wrong with you? *Perluné *?* What do you want? *or* What's it for? 2 or *(interrogative, indefinite). Tjilik * geḍé?* Is it small or large? *Nakal * ora?* Was he naughty? *Ija * ora?* Is it true ('yes or no')? *ḍèk dadi latihan tentara * pijé ngono* when I was a military trainee or sth like that. 3 is it the case that...? [to ask] whether. ** ija?* Is it true? *Tamuné * akèh?* Are there many guests? *Aku ditakoni wis * durung tau rabi.* He asked if I had ever been married. 4 what, that which. *Aku ora ngerti * kuwi djenengé.* I don't know what the name of it is. *Tjoba tjritakna * sing diolah.* Tell me what she cooked. 5 whatever; anything. *Ḍèké kena pesen *.* He can order anything [he wants]. *Ora ana alangan sawidji *.* There was no trouble at all. 6 something; anything, everything. ** waé sing arep dituku* anything he wants to buy. 7 *excl pointing out sth, or holding sth up to derision. Pènku tak golèki nang endi² ora ketemu.–Lha kuwi *, nang ngisor médja.* I've been looking everywhere for my pen but I can't find it.–There it is, under the table! *Rampung *, wiwit baé.* Finished?! he hasn't even started! ***a** why on earth...! how come...! ***né** of what? its what? *Sing muni kuwi *né?* What part of it makes the noise? **né sing dientup tawon?* Where did the bee sting him? ***-*** something; anything; everything. *Wong kowé kuwi *-* wedi.* You're afraid of everything! *Lerak kuwi kena dianggo ngresiki *-*.* The *lerak* fruit is used for cleaning things. *Lara? – Ora *-*.* Does it hurt? – It's nothing. *Adja wedi, ora *-*.* Don't be afraid, it's all right. *ora bisa *-** unable to do anything. ***-*né** everything/anything belonging to *or* connected with sth. *Menawa ana *-*né, aku ora tanggung djawab.* If anything bad comes of it, I'm not responsible. **ng*** *ng only* (*see also* KAJA) 1 to (be) do(ing) what? *Ng* kowé nang kéné?* What are you doing here? 2 why? (*see also* KENA, KENANG). *Ng* kok ora mangkat²?* How come you haven't left yet? 3 *var of *, esp. after vowel*). *Ora dadi ng*.* It's nothing. It doesn't matter. **ng*a** *ng only* how/why on earth...! *Ng*a kok atiné bisa ngéklasaké kang semono.* How could she possibly be so unmoved? **ng/di*kaké** to do what to [smn, sth]: *see also* DI·KAPAK·AKÉ. *Lajangé*

*dikon ng*kaké karo ibuné?* What did his mother tell him to do with the letter? * **(i)ja** *sms* * **1, 3,** *but sharpens the question. Iki * ja?* What IS this? *La sapa ta sing ngumbah, * ja si A ḍéwé?* And who could have washed it: could it have been A herself? * **manèh 1** what else? *Nonton * manèh?* What else did you see? 2 furthermore; especially. ** manèh aku iki wong mlarat.* And on top of that, I'm poor. ** manèh bengi[2] adja kakéhan djadjan.* Above all, don't eat too many snacks at night. 3 to a much greater degree. *Kelakuané ora bisa tak benerké, * manèh tak béla.* I couldn't approve of his behavior, much less defend it. * **waé 1** what (sort of) things? *Sanḍangané wong Inḍu kuwi * baé?* What sort of clothing do Hindus wear? *Aranana * baé sing kena digawé gula.* Tell what things can be made into sugar. 2 whatever; anything (*sms* *-*). *See also* APADÉNÉ

âpâdéné *ng,* **punapadéné** (*prn* **menâpâdéné**) *kr* as well as, in addition to. *Kowé * mbakjumu tunggu omah.* You and your sister stay home. *oto kabilaèn * katjilakan lijané* car crashes and other accidents. *Kabèh kudu disuntik, * sing uwis kena lelara mau.* Everyone has to have a shot, including those who have had the disease.

apal to know by heart. ***(-*)an 1** material to be studied/learned/memorized. 2 to memorize by rote. **di*i** to be learned by heart. **ng/di*aké** to study, learn, memorize

apan *-* wooden blade holder of a rice-harvesting tool (*ani*[2]). **ng*-*** shaped like the above

apdrek print made from a negative. ***an** prints. **ng/di*(aké)** to have prints made

apé *rg var of* AREP[a]

apeg having a soiled *or* musty odor. *mbako* * strong-smelling tobacco. *Ḍengkulmu *.* Nuts to you. The hell with you.

apèk 1 to get, obtain [*esp.* food supplies]. 2 *var of* API·Ǹ

apekir *var of* APKIR

apèl 1 an appeal to a higher court. 2 assembly, gathering

apel apple

apem sweet rice fritter used as a ceremonial food during the month before the fasting month. * **domba** *or* * **dombong** a large rice fritter

apes unlucky; to have bad luck. ***an** prone to bad luck. ***(-*)é** at least. *Suwéné *é seminggu.* **k*an** to have an accident or other misfortune. **pa·ng*an** Achilles heel. * **m·blebes** *or* * **pepes 1** (to have) extremely bad luck. 2 if worse comes to worst

api steam. *gaman ** firearms. ***-* 1** to warm oneself by the fire. 2 (*or* ***ǹ-*ǹ**) to pretend, act as if. *Ḍèké *-* ora ngerti.* He made believe he didn't understand. **ng/di*-*** to supervise, be in charge of. **pi*** pretense. * **unggun** campfire

apik *ng,* **saé** *kr* good, nice, attractive. *klambi* * nice clothes. *Bidjiné *.* He gets good grades. *Rak ja basa sing *.* Speak nice Krama! ** ja nggoné paḍa bal-balan.* They play soccer really well! *Tak tandur lan tak opèni *-*.* I'll tend them carefully. *Nganggo tangan sing *.* Use the proper hand (*i.e.* your right hand). *Ora * dadiné.* It didn't turn out well. ***-*an (saèn-saènan** *kr)* sth good/nice. *Mréné ta, aku duwé *-*an.* Come here–I have a surprise for you. **k(e)*an** good deed, kindness. **k(e)*en** excessively good. *Jèn rok kuwi kok enggo sekolah k*en.* That skirt is too nice to wear to school. **ng/di*aké** to make better, improve. *Jèn prèi aku arep ng*aké garasi.* When I have some time off I'm going to fix up my garage. **ng/di*i** to be nice to smn, *esp.* with an ulterior motive. *Ḍèké ng*i aku merga arep ndjaluk tulung aku.* He buttered me up because he needed my help.

apil *sbst kr? md? for* APAL

apirowang to try to look as if one is pitching in and helping

apit 11th month of the Moslem calendar. ***an** odds. **ané pira?* What are the odds? *ngungguli *an* to increase the odds. ***-*** on both sides. *ing *-** flanking. **-* lawang* wooden door frame. **k*** flanked (by). *botjah pantjuran k* ing senḍang* a girl-boy-girl sibling combination. *botjah senḍang k* pantjuran* a boy-girl-boy sibling combination. **ng/di*(-*) 1** to flank. *Aku di* mbakjuku loro.* My two sisters were on either side of me. 2 to lay odds of 2-to-1 against. *Djagoku di*.* The odds are 2 to 1 against my fighting cock.

apiutang *see* PIUTANG

apjun 1 opium poppy. 2 raw opium

apkir ***an** worthless items that have been sorted out from the good ones. **ng/di*** to weed out [the bad]; to condemn, consider unfit. *Barang² iki wis di* déning sing duwé.* The owner says these items aren't up to standard.

aplos *var of* APLUS

aplus ***an** act of relieving smn, *e.g.* from guard duty. **ng/di*** to relieve [*e.g.* a guard]

apoh *var of* APUH

apokat *var of* ADPOKAT

apor foot-weary, weak with exhaustion

apostulik 1 apostle. 2 pertaining to the Christian apostles

apoték *var sp of* APOTIK

apotéker druggist, pharmacist

apotik drugstore, pharmacy

apotiker *var sp of* APOTÉKER

April April

apsantun *var of* HABSARI

apsekar *var of* HABSARI

apsinom *var of* HABSARI

apuh squeezed out, wrung dry. *See also* PUH

apunten forgiveness (*kr for* APURA). **pa·ng*** I don't know (*oblique ki for* EMBUH)

apura *ng,* **apunten** *kr,* **aksama** *ki* forgiveness. **ng*** pardon, forgiveness; (*psv* **di***) to forgive. *ndjaluk ng** to ask forgiveness. *maringi ng** to forgive; to grant pardon. **pa·ng*** forgiveness, pardon

apuran 1 drainage ditch. 2 rental paid for use of a drainage ditch

apurantjang **ng*** to sit or stand in a humble attitude, with fingers interlaced and thumbs together. **ng/di*i** to express esteem for smn by assuming this attitude

apus 1 deceit. *Ḍèké akèh *é.* He's full of lies. *kena ing ** to be the victim of a swindle. *tukang ** or *djuru ** an expert at cheating people. 2 lame, crippled (in arm or leg). 3 horse's trappings. ***-*an** a fake. *Kuwi ming *-*an ṭok, ora tenanan.* It's only an imitation, it's not genuine. **k*an** to get cheated, taken in. **ng/di*i** to deceive/outwit smn. *** krama** to deceive with smooth talk

ârâ *see* HARA. ***-*** large field, uncultivated grassland; playing field for sports. ***-uru** *see* HARA-HURU *under* HARA

Arab[a] (*or* **ng***) Arabian. *basa ** Arabic. *negara ** Arabia

arab[b] **mang*-*** burning brightly, blazing

arad ***an** 1 one forced into labor; a slave. 2 forced labor; slavery. 3 victim sacrificed to the spirits. **ng/di*** 1 to put into forced labor. 2 to pull, drag

arag **ng/di*(-*)i** 1 to sort [pebbles, gravel] according to size by screening. 2 to clean weeds and debris from [a rice paddy] before planting

arah *ng,* **leres** *kr* direction, aim; *fig* goal. **ng/di*** 1 to aim (toward); to reach to/for; *fig* to intend. *ng* lésan* to aim at a target. *ng* pati* to plan on killing smn. *Ng* apa?* What's the use of anything? 2 to put sth in a certain direction. *Di* supaja tradjangané tudjesan nganakaké podjok lantjip.* Place it in such a way that when it's cut it will make sharp angles. **ng/di*aké** to aim, direct. *ng*aké beḍil* to aim a gun. **pa·ng*** aim; expectation. *See also* RAH

arak 1 alcoholic beverage made by allowing liquid to ferment. ** arèn* drink (as above) made from sugar-palm sap. ** ketan* drink made from glutinous rice. 2 *var of* RAK 1. ***-*** a parade. **ng/di*** to take smn around in public. *Malingé sing ketjekel mau di* mubeng kampung.* The thief who got caught was taken publicly all around the town. *Murid sekolahan lijané wis teka, di* guruné.* Students from another school had been brought by their teacher. **pa·ng*** act of parading *or* forming a procession. *Pang*é wis tekan ngendi?* How far has the procession gone?

aral obstacle. *jèn ora ana ** if nothing goes wrong

aran 1 (**nâmâ** *or* **nami** *kr,* **asma** *ki*) personal name. *botjah * Slamet* a boy by the name of Slamet. 2 name, (what sth is) called *or* known as. **é dina pasaran* the names of the market days. *Njolong mono *(é) tindak kang ala.* Stealing is wrong. *tembung * (gram)* noun. **k*** what sth is called *or* known as. *Sing k* parabané, jaiku Kuntjung.* He's called by his nickname, Kuntjung. **k(a)*an (ka·wasta·nan** *kr*) called (by), known as, regarded as. *Lelembat wau kawastanan baktéri.* Those tiny creatures are called bacteria. **ng/di*i** (**ṅ/dipun·wasta·ni** *or* **ñj/dipun·seta·ni** *kr*) 1 to call, name. *Nèk aku ng*i kabèh kok apik.* I'd say they're *all* nice. *Wong Indonesia ng*i Batavia iku Betawi.* Indonesians called Batavia "Betawi." *Agami wau dipun wastani Buḍa.* This religion is called Buddhism. *udjian sing di*i udjian ḍoktoral* the so-called graduate examination. *Guru ng*i barang² sing kudu dituku.* The teacher called off a list of things we were to buy. 2 to regard, consider. *Dipun wastani étja.* They are considered delicious. *É, djebul Pardi, tak *i ḍajoh ngendi.* Why it's Pardi! I thought it was a guest. 3 to accuse

arang *ng,* **awis** *kr* 1 scarce; infrequent. * *kanggoné.* It's not used much. *Ḍèwèké * gelem awèh keterangan marang pihak umum.* He's seldom willing to issue a statement to the public. 2 widely spaced. *Omahé *-* leté dawa²*. The houses are far apart. *-* seldom, rarely. *Ḍèké *-* ana ngomah.* He's hardly ever home. **k(a)*en** excessively widely spaced. **ng*** to become less numerous/frequent. *Saja tuwa saja ng* rambuté.* The older you get, the more hair you lose. **ng*i** to become less numerous/frequent; (*psv* **di*i**) to make less numerous/frequent. *Jèn wis tjeḍak segara, wit²ané ng*-*i.* As you get close to the sea, trees get fewer and farther between. *Wong arep udjian, anggonmu nonton mbok di*-*i ta.* With the exam coming up, I'd think you'd be going to fewer shows. * **kerep** distance apart. *Pananduré kelarik-larik bisaa paḍa *-kerepé.* The planting was done in rows to space it evenly. * **krandjang** many in number and close together. * **wulu kutjing** abundant

aras 1 seat, place to sit. 2 kiss (*root form: ki for* AMBUNG). ***-*en** enervated. *Aku *-*en njambut gawé.* I'm too listless to work. *Arep bali *-*en.* She wanted to go home but didn't have the energy. **pa·ng*an** cheek (*ki for* PIPI). ***-kembang** a favorite among one's superiors

arbèi strawberry; strawberry plant

arda *see* HARDA

ar̊dâwalépâ impudent, impertinent

ardi(ti) *oj* mountain

ardjâ(jâ) *var of* HARDJA

aré 1 valley, lowland. *ing tanah ng** in the valley. 2 (*or* ***né**) *inf var of* DJARÉ(NÉ)

arèh coconut milk that has been simmered until thick

arèk *rg* 1 a native of. * *Surabaja* [a person] from Surabaja. 2 child

arem **ng/di*-*** to soothe, placate. **pa·ng*-*** [rice paddy] turned over to a retired village official as a pension. *glonḍong pang*-** agricultural products offered to a king as a gift or as a tax or tribute

arèn 1 areca palm tree. *gula ** sugar made from areca-palm sap. 2 plate, dish

areng charcoal. *dat ** carbon (chemical). **ng*** to make charcoal. **pa·ng*-*** *var of* PA·NG·AREM-AREM. * **baṭok** charcoal made from coconut shell. * **stingkul** *or* * **watu** coal

arep^a *ng,* **baḍé** *kr* 1 (**arsa** *or* **karsa** *ki*) to want. * *djadjan ora duwé ḍuwit.* He wanted a snack but he had no money. 2 (**arsa** *or* **karsa** *ki*) to intend to; going to; intending to, in order to. *Aku * mulih.* I'm going home. *sing * tuku* customer, prospective buyer. *saben * ana tamu* every time there are going to be guests. *Aku menjang pasar * tuku beras.* I went to the market to buy some rice. ***a** even if/though. **a nḍelik mesṭi konangan.* You may hide, but you'll be caught anyhow. ***an** characterized by wanting everything one sees. *Botjah kuwi *an, mula lemu.* The child never refuses food–that's why he's so fat. **ng/di*i** 1 to want, covet. *Tanduranmu kembang di*i Siti.* Siti wants your flower plants. 2 to be willing to pay [a certain price] for. *Sindjangipun dipun adjengi pinten?* How much will he pay for the shirt? 3 to confront. *Mungsuhé di*i kanṭi wani.* He faced the enemy bravely. **lagi *** just about to [do]. *Iwak iki lagi * ngenḍog.* This fish is about to lay eggs. **wis *** to have just begun to [do]; on the point of [do]ing. *Wis * udan.* It's about to rain. *Tijang² sampun sami baḍé mlebet nalika dilahipun sirep.* People had just begun to come in when the oil lamp went out. *See also* KAREP, SEKAREP

arep^b *ng,* **adjeng** *kr* ***-*** gambling stakes. ***-*an** opposite, facing. *Omah kuwi *-*an.* The houses are across from each other. *Lungguhé *-*an karo aku.* He sits opposite me. **ing*** *ltry* in front. **ng*** 1 (**ng·arsa** *ki*) (that which is in) front; in front (of). *roḍané ng** the front wheel. *wandané ng** the first syllable. *Ana ing ng*é irungmu.* It's right in front of your nose! *Wong² suk²an rebut ng*.* People elbowed their way to the front. 2 earlier, before. *Ing ng* wis diterangaké.* It has been explained above. 3 the coming [time period]. *(suk) minggu ng** next week. **ng*-(m)buri** in front and back (of). *Sepéḍaku ana berkoné ng*-buri kaé.* My bike has electric lamps front and rear. *Kiwa-tengené ng*-mburi gaḍéjané akèh toko²*. There are stores on all sides of the pawnshop. **ng/di*-*** (**ng/di·arsa-arsa** *ki*) 1 to expect. 2 to look forward to. **ng*aké** 1 before; to precede. *ng*aké bedug* before noon. *ng*aké mungsuhé* *ngrangsang negara kita* before the enemy invaded our country. *wis ng*aké* not long before. 2 (*psv* **di*aké**) to face (toward); to face sth toward. *Negarané ng*aké segara, ngungkuraké gunung.* The country has the sea in front of it and mountains behind it. *Mendem wong di*aké ngalor.* People are buried with their heads toward the north. **ng*an** 1 the front. 2 front section of a Javanese house, where guests are received. *See also* BAREP, PANGAREP

arès 1 confinement, incarceration. 2 stalk of bananas. ***-*en** to have a certain affliction of the fingernails or toenails. **ng/di*** to punish by confining. *See also* RÈS

arga *see* HARGA

ari 1 *oj* day. 2 *oj* if, when(ever). 3 *oj* sun. 4 *oj* enemy. 5 *oj* to (come to a) stop. 6 *ltry* younger sibling. ***an** (*or* ***ǹ** *rg*) (paid) by the day. *kuli arian* day laborer. ***-*** (**réntjang** *kr*, **tuntun·an** *ki*) placenta. ***ǹ-*ǹ** [wages] by the day

arih *var of* ARÈH. **ng/di*-*** 1 to cheer up *or* comfort smn. 2 to coax, wheedle, persuade. **pa·ng*** woman who assists the bride during the wedding ceremony. **pa·ng*-*** comfort, solace. *See also* RIH

arija *var of* ARJA

ariâjâ *var of* RIJAJA

arik **orak-*** *or* **urak-*** a rice-accompanying dish of scrambled egg and/or sautéed vegetables. **m·orak-m*** messed up, in disarray. **ng/di*-*** *or* **ng/di·orak-*** 1 to fabricate stories, start rumors (about). 2 to scratch around (in), *esp.* for food. 3 to disarrange, mess up

aring having recovered (from). *bareng wis sawetara * napasé* when he got his breath back. **orang-*** a certain tree. **ng*** to attend the bride and groom during the ceremony. **ng*-*** to play around happily. **ng/di*aké** to restore sth to calmness, bring about recovery in. **pa·ng*** wedding attendants

arip sleepy. *(tamba) ** sth to keep one awake. **k*an** 1 sleepy from staying up too late. 2 to oversleep. **ng*(-*)aké** *or* **ng*(-*)i** causing drowsiness. *Ḍagelané ora lutju, mung ng*-*i baé.* His jokes aren't funny—they just put you to sleep.

aris 1 boundary line marked with a rope (*see also* RIS). 2 under control, composed. ** tatané.* He arranged them tidily. *Mitrané njauri *...* His friend replied calmly... *Paḍa nungkul *.* They bowed their heads resignedly. 3 chairman of village heads. ***an** weekly or monthly social gathering of neighborhood wives, with a lottery

aristokrasi aristocracy

aristokrat aristocrat

arit sickle. **di*** to be cut or mowed [of growth other than grass]. **ng*** to cut grass with a sickle. **ng/di*aké** to cut grass for smn; to have smn mow grass with a sickle. **pa·ng*** sickle with a sharply angled blade. *See also* RIT

ariwarta *see* HARI

arja *see* HARJA

arka *oj* sun

arlodji 1 clock; watch. 2 (*or* *** tangan**) wrist watch

arnal *see* HARNAL

aron 1 [rice which is] half cooked. 2 boiled corn. ***an** convalescent

arpuwis wood resin

arsa to intend to; willing to, going to (*ki for* AREP[a]). **ng*né** in front of, in the presence of [an exalted person]. *Pendjenenganipun lenggah wonten ing ng*nipun keng ramanipun.* He sat (humbly) before his father. **ng*-(a)dji** in the presence of the King. **ng/di*-*** to expect; to look forward to (*ki for* NG/DI·AREP-AREP[b]). *** pungkur** *ltry* front and back. *See also* KARSA

arsi *ltry var of* ARSA

arsip file, record

arsitèk architect

arsitèktur architecture

arta money (*kr for* ḌUWIT)

artâkâ *see* HARTAKA

artati *see* HARTATI

artawan *see* HARTAWAN

arti *ng,* **artos** *kr* meaning, idea conveyed. *Tetanggan kuwi *né jèn njambut gawé kudu sambat-sinambat.* "Neighbors" means that when there's work to be done, it should be done cooperatively.

artikel article, essay

artjâpâdâ *ltry* (*or* **ng***) world, earth. *tumeḍak mring ng** [of deities] to descend to earth

artos *kr for* ARTI

aruârâ *var of* ARUHARA

arubiru disturbance, commotion. **ng/di*** 1 to upset, disturb. *Kéwan kuwi ora kena di*.* You must not tease animals. 2 to interfere in other people's business

aruh ***-*** to greet in a friendly manner.

Ana botjah wadon aju aruh²: Hé Wid. A pretty girl called "Hi, Wid!" to me. **ng/di*-*** to greet *or* speak with in a friendly way. *See also* RUH

aruhârâ (*or* **ng***) turmoil, agitation, distress. *Wong² sing durung tau pasa, sambaté ng*.* Those who had never fasted before made a big fuss about it.

arum *see* HARUM

arungan busy, preoccupied (with)

arus rank [of odors, *esp.* blood; the seashore]

arwah *var of* RUWAH

as 1 ace (playing card). 2 axle

A.S. *see* AMÉRIKA

asab **ng/di*** to smooth sth by rubbing, *esp.* with sandpaper

asah ***an** whetstone. ***-*** to wash (dishes). ***-*an** dishes to be washed. **ng/di*** 1 to sharpen, hone. **ng/di*aké** 1 to sharpen for smn. 2 to wash dishes for smn. **ng/di*i** to wash [things, *esp.* dishes]

asainering sewer. *tukang ** sewage worker

asal 1 (place of) origin; source. *kuṭa *ku* my home town. ** saka ngendi?* Where's he from? *tembung sing *é saka tembung Sansekerta* a word of Sanskrit origin. 2 if, provided (that). ** kowé gelem kawin karo ḍèké, omah iki pèken.* If you'll marry him, you can have this house. **ng/di*aké** to tell, or clarify, one's place of origin. *** dunung** origin, source. *** usul** ancestral origin. **-usulé bangsa Indonesia* the origins of the Indonesian people

asar 3d daily Moslem prayer; the time (between 3 and 5 P.M.) when this praying takes place. **ng*** 1 to perform the 3d meditation. 2 to fast until 4 P.M. *** ḍuwur** 3–4 P.M. *** èndèk** 4–5 P.M. *See also* SALAT

asas goal, purpose; principle; foundation

asat dried; to become dry. **k*** to get dried up/out. *Arepa mentas udan kaé dalané k*.* Even after a rain the road drains well. **k*an** to have run out of water, be dehydrated. **ng/di*i** to dry sth out, drain the water from. **p*an** loincloth worn while bathing *e.g.* in the river. *** ng·gerèng** *or* *** ng·gering** intensely dry, completely dried up/out. *See also* SAT

asbak ashtray

asèb *rg* a belch; to belch

aseb smoke; steam. *kapal ** steamship

aseli *ltry var of* ASLI

asem 1 tamarind. 2 sour; *(fig) excl expressing a sour reaction. *, kapusan aku mau.* Damn, I've been gypped. **m*** 1 sour, unripe. 2 [of clothing] old and faded but still nice-looking. *** gula** sugar-coated tamarind (eaten as a confection). *See also* UJAH

asèp written acknowledgment of a debt, which is retained by the creditor and is negotiable

asépak *see* BARONG

Asiā Asia. ** Sisih Kidul Wétan* Southeast Asia

asih love; compassion; to feel loving kindness. ** murni* pure love. *Ḍèwèké * marang para mitrané.* She's nice to her friends. **mang*-*** to flatter. **ng*-*** to plead for compassion. *Ḍèké duwé pandjaluk ng*-* marang kantjané nunggang mau, adja kanḍa marang konḍèktur.* He begged his fellow passengers not to tell the conductor. **ng/di*i** to love. *** tresna** love. *See also* KASIH, SIH

asik **m·osak-m*** in disorder, in a mess. **ng/di·osak-*** to put into disarray, mess up

asil 1 income. ** lumajan.* He earned a little something from it. *padjeg ** income tax. 2 product. **é panèn akèh.* The harvest was abundant. 3 results. *pakolèh ** to bring results. **ng/di*aké** to produce. *Pulo Sumatra ng*aké karèt.* Sumatra produces rubber. **ng*i** income-producing. **p*an** *or* **pa·ng*an** income, earnings. *See also* KASIL

asin 1 salty to the taste. 2 prepared by a salting process. *enḍog ** salted egg, *esp.* duck egg. *Gelem mangan iwak, nanging ora *.* He wanted fish but not salt fish. ***an** salted foods. **k*en** excessively salty. **m*** *or* **ng*** to treat [foods] by a salting process. **ng/di*i** to salt [foods]

asing 1 foreign. *pèrs ** the foreign press. *wong ** foreigner. *warga negara ** foreign nationals. 2 unfamiliar. *Bal-balan tjara Amérika isih * nèk nang Indonesia.* American-style football is unknown in Indonesia.

asistèn assistant. ***an** residence of a vice regent. **ng*an** subdistrict. *** ahli** instructor (academic title). *** wedana** vice regent

asja *oj* 1 mouth. 2 to laugh

aslep *var of* ANGSLUP

asli source; origin(al form). *wong *né Djepang* a native of Japan. *Serat mau akèh bédané saka *né.* These writings are very different from the original. *Wajang topèng kuwi *né saka désa.* Masked dramas originated in the villages. **ng/di*kaké** to restore the original form [of]

aslup *var of* ANGSLUP
asma personal name (*ki for* ARAN, DJENENG)
asmârâ romantic love. *tembang* * love song. **k*n** to fall/be in love [with]. * **gama** sexual pleasure; the art of sexual relations. * **tura** head over heels in love with
asmârâdahânâ a traditional tale; a story told in traditional literary language
asmârâdânâ a certain classical verse form
asmarandânâ *var of* ASMARADANA
aso *-* *or* **ng*(-*)** to rest. *Saiki wis djam, ajo paḍa ng*!* Time's up–let's take a break. *Tak *-* ḍisik, la jèn wis, bandjur tak tjrita.* Let me rest up and then I'll tell you about it. **ng/di*kaké** to rest sth; to have/let smn rest
asoh *var of* ASUH
asok 1 to pay to the government (tax, tribute, *etc.*) * *ḍenḍa* to pay a fine. 2 to pour (into, out). * *kaju marang pabrik* to supply wood to a factory. **ng/di*aké** *or* **ng/di*i** to pay out [money] to the government. **p*an** money paid, *e.g.* taxes, fines. *See also* PASOK, SOK[b]
asor 1 low, inferior. *Kwalitèté *.* The quality is poor. 2 humble. 3 to lose (in competition). ***an** underdog; contestant not favored to win. **k*an** to be defeated. **ng/di*aké** 1 to cause to be inferior. 2 to defeat in competition. * **unggul** win or lose
aspal asphalt. ***an** paved with asphalt. **ng/di*** to pave with asphalt. *Dalané ora di*.* The road isn't paved.
aspèk aspect, feature. *-* *kagunan* artistic aspects
asra *oj* thousand
asrāmā (*or* **asrâmâ**) sleeping quarters; dormitory. **p*n** monastery; *oj* hermit shrine. * **(lanang)** boys' dormitory. * **mahasiswa** student dormitory. * **ka·putri·ǹ** girls' dormitory; sorority. * **tentara** army barracks. * **wanita** girls' dormitory. * **wanita p.** house of prostitution
asrep cold, cool (*kr for* AḌEM)
asri beautiful. ***ǹ-*ǹ** *or* **p*ǹ** decorations. *pasrèn témbok* wall decorations
asring often, sometimes (*kr for* KEREP, SOK[a])
asrog *var of* ANGSROG
asru *oj* 1 loud. 2 very
assalam(u)alaikum peace be with you (Moslem greeting)
asta hand (*ki for* TANGAN). **ng*** to work (*ki for* NJAMBUT-GAWÉ). *Pendjenengan ng* wonten pundi?* Where do you work? **ng/di*** 1 to bring, take, carry (*ki for* NG/DI·GAWA). 2 to do (*ki for* Ñ/DI·TANDANG). *Pandjenengan ladjeng ng* punapa?* What did you do then? 3 to hold, grasp; to handle (*ki for* ÑJ/DI·TJEKEL). *Pendjenengan sapunika ng* punapa wonten kantor?* What are you in charge of at the office now? 4 to teach (*ki for* M̈/DI·WULANG). **ng/di*ni** 1 to do (*ki for* Ñ/DI·TANDANG·I, NGE/DI·TJAK·I). *Pegawéjan mau di*ni ḍéwé.* He did the job himself. 2 to do by oneself (*ki for* Ñ/DI·TANGAN·I)
asṭa *see* HASTA
astafirlah supplication to God at cemetery services
astâgâ (*or* * **illah** *or* * **pirullah**) oh God!
astânâ 1 *oj* palace, court. 2 burial place of a revered or high-ranking person
astapirlah *var of* ASTAFIRLAH
astèn *inf var of* ASISTÈN
astra *oj* 1 weapon. 2 arrow
astu *oj* amen. *Aum, aum, awignam *! (incantation to cast out evil)*
asu *ng,* **segawon** *kr* dog. ***ñ-*ñ** to hunt with dogs. * **adjag** 1 wolf. 2 hunting dog. * **belang** 1 spotted dog. 2 mongrel. * **belang kalung wang** 1 a newly rich person. 2 an ugly person who is popular for his riches. * **buntung** 1 *term of abuse.* 2 to control others by virtue of one's wealth or power. * **geḍé menang kerah·é** to pass the buck; to get the credit earned by those below one. * **karo kutjing** incompatible. * **kikik** a small long-haired dog. * **a·rebut balung** to fight over sth trivial. * **ng·ujuh** [of a certain wrapped headdress style] tied in an off-center pattern
asuh *oj* to take a rest
asuk *var of* ANGSUK
asung *var of* ANGSUNG
asup *oj* (*or* **ng***) to set [of sun, moon]
asuransi (life, fire, *etc.*) insurance
asut **ng/di*** to agitate. *Buruh² di* supaja mèlu mogok.* The workers were incited to join the strike. *ng* kertu* to shuffle cards
aswa *oj* horse
âtâ *see* SAPI, TAPUK
atag *-***an** one who does things only when pressured *or* threatened. *Wong ming mangan waé kok dadi *-*an.* You wouldn't even eat if I didn't keep after you! **m*** *ltry var of* **ng***. **ng/di*** to threaten *or* pressure smn. **pa·ng*** a threat; a suggestion made as a threat. *See also* TAG

aṭak *-* barrier, road block. **ng/di*-*i** to block off, barricade
atak̇an 1 tray (*var of* TATAK·AN). 2 roll of wrapped coins
atal a variety of yellow ocher used as pigment in cosmetic lotions. *See also* KUMATAL
aṭang **ng*-*** to lie face up motionless, *esp.* when seriously ill or injured
aṭar **ng*** 1 to scurry off. 2 (*or* **ng*-***) to urinate standing up *or* walking (men)
atas **ing (ng)*é** in spite of the fact that. *Ing *é wong sugih kok mung mènèhi satus rupiah.* Though he's wealthy, he only gave 100 rupiahs. **ng/di*i** to handle, cope with. **sa*é** in spite of the fact that. * **angin** *wj* foreign country. * **ḍawuh dalem ingkang sinuhun** upon the king's order. * **karsaning Allah** God willing. * **nama** in the name [of]; on behalf [of]
atat *oj* a variety of parrot
atèb *var of* ANTOB
atéla(h) men's short buttoned-up jacket
aṭèng var of GAṬÈNG
atep thatched roof. **ng/di*** to equip with a thatched roof
atèr *rg var of* ANTÈR
ater to carry, take. *Ojodé * pangan.* The roots convey nourishment [to the plant]. *-* 1 foods for a ritual meal; to take such foods to neighbors. 2 *gram* prefix. *-* *hanuswara* nasal prefix. **ng/di*aké (n/diḍèrèk·aké** *ka*) to take, accompany. *ng*aké lajang* to deliver a letter. *Slamet nḍèrèkaké ibuné menjang ḍokteran.* Slamet took his mother to the hospital. **ng/di*i** to bring ceremonial food to. **ng/di*-*i** to add a prefix to. * **banju** *or* * **nanah** (to have/get) water-on-the-knee. *See also* TER
ati[a] 1 (**manah** *kr,* [**pang**]**galih**[**an**] *ki*) heart; mind. *Présiḍèn penggalihipun saé.* The President is kind-hearted. *Bungah *né.* He's happy. *Atos *ku.* I'm annoyed. *Entèk *né.* She was scared to death. *nduwèni * marang* to have one's heart set on. *Ḍèké ngandakaké isining *.* He told what he had in mind. *Uniné ora terus ing *.* His words were not taken seriously. *karepé ** wish, heart's desire. *resiking ** good intentions. *geḍé *né* encouraged, happy. *tjilik *né* timid, easily discouraged. *keras ** determined. *Adja dadi *mu.* Don't get upset about it. *madju *né* to work hard [at]. *Wis maḍep/mantep *né.* He's sure of what he wants. *satru ** person one secretly dislikes. *tampa ** to be heartened, take courage. *olèh ** to be received with favor. *atiné pidjer arep...* to have a persistent urge to... *sing klebu *né* what one likes/wants. 2 core, pith. *Pelemé wis mateng *.* The mango is ripe inside [though still green outside]. 3 (**manah** *kr*) liver. *iwak ** animal liver (as food). *dikèki * ngrogoh rempela* never satisfied with what one is given. 4 fleshy part of the hand/foot at the base of the fingers/toes. 5 *oj* very, excessively *(used as the first member in many ltry compounds).* ***ǹ** (**manah** *kr,* **galih** *ki*) (having) a certain temperament. *welasan atèn* of a compassionate nature. *kakon atèn* irascible; rigid, inflexible. ***ǹ-*ǹ** 1 knot in wood. 2 soft inner pith of a stalk. 3 hard core, *e.g.* of a pineapple. **ng/di*ǹ-*ǹi** 1 (**ϕ/dipun-manah**[2]**i** *kr,* **ng/di-galih**[2]**i** *ki*) to hearten smn. *Ali diatèn-atèni kamasé.* Ali's brother cheered him on. 2 to remove the core *or* pith from. **sa*-*né (sa-manah**[2]**ipun** *kr,* **sa-galih**[2]**é** *ki*) one's whole heart and soul. *Durung mesṭi wong ngguju kuwi sa*-*né ja mèlu ngguju.* Laughing (outwardly) doesn't mean the heart is laughing too. * **metu wulu·né** jealous. * **sanubari** inner feelings; the heart as seat of the emotions
ati[b] *ng,* **atos** *kr* (**ng**)***-*** to be careful, watch out (for). *Sing ngati-ati lo.* Look out! Be careful! *Ng*-*né olèhé ngopèni motoré.* He's scrupulously careful with his car. **pa·ng*-*** care, caution. *Saking pang*-*né nang ḍuwité nganti ora blandja.* She's watching her money so closely she doesn't even do any shopping.
aṭi *-* locks of hair worn at the sides of the cheeks (men, women)
aṭik *var of* KAṬIK 3. ***-*(ing dridji)** (finger/toe) joints. **-*ing dridji sikil* toe joints. **oṭak-*** loose but still attached. *Untuku oṭak-* arep tjopot.* My tooth is so loose it's about to come out. *oṭak-* didudut angèl* [to look easy but] actually be difficult. ***-*an** a made-up story. **ng/di·oṭak-*** 1 to move [sth loose] back and forth. 2 to manipulate (the parts of). *Djamé adja kok oṭak-*.* Don't try to fix the watch! *Bareng wis dioṭak-* nganti suwé, kedadéjan rupa*[2] *bisa direngga dadi tjrita.* Arranged and rearranged, the separate events were finally fashioned into a story. **pa·ng·oṭak-*** act of connecting *or* manipulating things. *Saking pangoṭak-*ing manah, kula kinten*

pijambakipun tresna ḍumateng Sri. Putting 2 and 2 together, I surmise that he's in love with Sri.

aṭil **oṭal-*** loose, coming off/apart

aṭing **ng/di*-*aké** to hold sth near the fire, to warm it *or* cook it

atis cold, chilly. **k*an** chilly and uncomfortable; to suffer from cold. **k*en** excessively chilly. *See also* TIS

atjak to try, make an effort

atjan *rg* at all, altogether. *ora ** not at all

atjar pickle(s). **ng/di*** to make (into) pickles. *Timuné di**. She pickled the cucumbers. *** **bening** uncooked pickles. *** **mateng** cooked pickles

atjârâ (item in a) program. ** sing ngisi wektuné botjah* a program of activities to fill a child's time. ** sing pungkasan ḍéwé filem.* The last thing on the program was a film. **ng/di*aké** 1 to offer sth to a guest. *ng*aké pasuguhan* to serve refreshments. 2 to welcome [guests] on smn's behalf. **ng/di*ni** to welcome [guests] (with sth). *Ḍèwèké ng*ni lungguh.* He asked the guest to sit down. *Para tamu di*ni ngundjuk.* The guests were offered sth to drink. **pa·ng*** master of ceremonies

atjeng ***an** lustful, lascivious. **ng*** to have an erection

atji *ltry* cassava

atjir **k*-k*** *or* **k·otjar-k*** scattered/strewn all over; in disarray. **ng*** in disorder. *mlaju ng** to flee in embarrassment *or* confusion. **ng/di*-*** *or* **ng/di·otjar-*** 1 to scatter [small messy things] around untidily. 2 to spend lavishly. *ngotjar-* ḍuwit* to squander money

atjlum pale in the face

atjum *var of* ATJLUM

atjung ***-*** to point at, point out. *Botjah tjilik jèn weruh barang anèh mesṭi *-*.* Children always point to strange things they see. *ḍoḍok *-** to show smn the way [to steal *etc.*]; to act as a confederate in wrongdoing. **otjang-*** to keep raising one's hand. **ng*** to raise the hand. **ng/di*aké** to raise, lift. *Ḍèwèké ng*aké pistulé ing baṭukku.* He raised the pistol to my forehead. **ng/di*i** 1 to point at/to sth. 2 *cr* to offer sth (to smn)

atlétik athletics, sports

atlit athlete

atma soul, spirit

atmâdjâ *see* HATMADJA

atmâkâ *see* HATMADJA

atob *var of* ANTOB

atom atom(ic). *bom ** atom bomb. *tenaga ** atomic power

aton *ltry* ***-*** to keep looking (at). *See also* TON

aṭong *inf var of* AṬUNG

atos 1 hard, firm; tough; harsh. 2 careful (*root form: kr for* ATI[b]). **ng/di*aké** to make sth hard *etc. Lempung sing wis ditjitak di*aké sarana diobong.* The molded clay was baked hard. *ng*aké awak* to toughen one's body; to make oneself (magically) invulnerable. **ng*i** to become hard *etc. Apa ager²é wis ng*i?* Has the jelly set yet?

atrap *ltry var of* NGE·TRAP

atrèt to back up. **ng/di*aké** to back up [a vehicle]

atub lush, luxuriant

aṭu(h) *excl expressing a rush of feeling: var of* AḌUH

aṭuka it would be better (if)...; otherwise, or else. ** aku mangkat ḍéwé jèn ngerti ditinggal.* I would have preferred to go myself if I had known I'd be left behind. *Tudjuné waé bakoh olèhku nggudjengi, * rak ngglunḍung.* Luckily I had a good grip on it, or it would have rolled away.

aṭung **k*-k*** 1 to raise the hand. 2 emptyhanded. **ng/di*aké** to hold [*esp.* the hand] up *or* out. *Botjah kuwi ng*aké tangané ndjaluk roti.* The boy held out his hand for a cookie. **ng/di*i** 1 to raise the hand. *Tangan tengen ng*i biṭi.* He raised his right fist threateningly. 2 to make smn raise his hand(s). *Punggawané bank di*i pistul karo rampoké.* The robber stuck up the bank teller with his pistol. *See also* ṬUNG

atur[a] *ka* 1 what smn says (to an exalted person; to smn higher in the social scale). *Samanten rumijin * dalem.* I'll close [this letter] now. 2 to ask smn to do sth (*ka for* AKON, KON, KONGKON). 3 to invite (*root form: ka for* ULEM). 4 to call (*root form: ka for* UNDANG). ***-*** a gift presented [to a social superior]. **k*** submitted *or* presented to. *Serat punika k* pandjenengan.* This letter is presented to you (*opening phrase of a letter).* **k*an panakrama** to welcome and bestow honor on. **m*** to say, speak (*ka for* KANḌA, TJLAṬU). *Slamet m* marang guruné...* Slamet said to the teacher... *Kula baḍé m* manawi...* I would like to report that... **m∗ nuwun** (to say) thank you. **m∗ prasadja** to tell the truth (to). **ng/di∗** to hold *or* carry [a child of high status: *ka for* M/DI-BOPONG]. **ng/di∗aké** 1 to tell sth. *Lelakoné di∗aké guruné.* He told the teacher what had happened to him. 2 to give sth. *Lajangé di∗aké guruné.* He gave the letter to the teacher. **ng/di∗i** 1 to call, ask, invite. *Betjik ng∗i ḍokter baé.* I'd better send for the doctor. *Pandjenengan dipun aturi ḍahar rumijin.* Please have dinner first. 2 to ask smn to [do]; to ask for sth. *Kula ∗i ngendikan tjara Djawi.* Please speak Javanese. *Ng∗i sugeng tindak.* Have a safe journey! 3 to give to. *Aku ng∗i bapak undjukan.* I offered my father sth to drink. **ng∗i priksa** 1 to tell, inform. *Ng∗i priksa menawi kawontenan putra wiludjeng.* I should like to inform you[, Father,] that I am in good health. 2 to show smn sth (*ka for* Ñ-TUDUH-AKÉ, -I). 3 to advise (*ka for* Ñ-TUTUR-I). **p∗an** 1 letter or report delivered to a superior. 2 batik shawl for carrying a child slung from the shoulder (*ka for* EMBAN[2]). **∗ uninga** to tell, inform

aturb **ng/di∗** to organize, regulate, arrange. *Olèhé ng∗ slametan kurang setiti.* He didn't organize the ceremony very carefully. *Ing tanah Djawa perkawinan iku di∗ déning adat.* Marriages in Java are regulated by tradition. *kursus ng∗ kembang* a course in flower-arranging. **(pa-ng)∗an** *or* **per∗an** 1 manners, etiquette. 2 regulation, rule

atus 1 hundred. *s∗* 100. *rong ∗* 200. *pirang² ∗ buku* hundreds of books. *pirang² ∗ èwu* hundreds of thousands. 2 dried (out). *Kumbahané durung ∗.* The laundry isn't dry yet. **∗an** 1 digit occupying the hundred place (*e.g.* the 9 in 968). 2 (numbering in the) hundreds. *∗an taun kang kepungkur* hundreds of years ago. 3 the hundreds. *ékan, dasan, ∗an, éwon* units, tens, hundreds, thousands. 4 about *n* hundred. *rong ∗an* a couple of hundred. 5 100-rupiah bill. *Ḍuwit ∗ané ana lima.* He has five 100-rupiah bills. **pra∗** -hundredth. *sangang pra∗* 9/100. *pitung pra∗* 0.07. *See also* SATUS, TUS

atut-runtut (to live as husband and wife) in peace and harmony

aub shady, sheltered. **k∗en** excessively shady; overprotected. **ng∗** to take shelter. **ng∗ awar²** 1 to give generously to the poor. 2 to lack authority. **pa-ng∗an** 1 shelter, shade; protection. 2 protector, patron

aut small, narrow (*kr for* TJIJUT?)

âwâ *var of* HAWA

awad pretense. *∗é arep adol ali².* He pretended he wanted to sell the ring. **∗-∗** to pretend, act as if. **p∗an** a pretext

awag **∗an** to act randomly *or* without regard for regulations or propriety. *Nèk ∗an, aku emoh main karo kowé.* If you don't play fair, I won't play with you. **k∗an** to [do] by oneself. **ng∗** random, arbitrary. *Wangsulané ng∗.* He answered whatever came into his head.

awak body (**badan** *kr,* **slira** *or* **srira** *ki*). *∗ku gatelen.* I itch. *Sing nonton njel²an nganti paḍa adu ∗.* The spectators were jammed in body-to-body. **∗é** 1 he, she; his/her body. *∗é kuru banget.* He's very thin. 2 *adr* you *(to smn one speaks Ngoko to but does not know well).* **∗é ḍéwé** we, us. *omahé ∗é ḍéwé* our (own) house. **∗-∗** 1 main part, main body. *∗-∗ing keris* the main part of the kris. 2 to bathe quickly only from the waist up. **∗-∗an** a manufactured body. *∗-∗ané bonéka* doll's body. *∗-∗ané montor* the body of a car. **ng/di∗i** to [do] (by) oneself. *Penggawéjan semono akèhé di∗i ḍéwé nganti rampung.* He did that whole job by himself. *Bapak sing njlirani pijambak tindak nang Djakarta.* Father went to Djakarta alone. **ng/di∗-∗i** to outline the main part(s) of [a projected piece of work]. **p∗an** 1 (*or* **pa-ng∗an**) physique. *P∗ané lemu (kuru).* He's fat (thin). 2 (*or* **pa-ng∗**) character, nature. *Pang∗ dursila.* He has an evil character. *p∗an mlarat* born to be poor. **sa∗ sekodjur** one's whole body. **∗ mami** *ltry* I, me. **∗ pènḍèk budi tjiblèk** physically and mentally (morally) weak

awal beginning(s), initial stage. *wiwit ∗* from the (very) beginning. *Kudu wis rampung ing ∗é sasi.* It should be finished by the first of the month. **ng∗** 1 [of horses] to trot briskly. 2 *(psv* **di∗)** to guard smn. **ng/di∗aké** to put forward [a scheduled time]. *Upatjarané di∗aké saka djam lima nang djam papat.* The ceremony was moved up from 5 o'clock to 4 o'clock. **ng/di∗i** to begin/open sth. *Upatjarané di∗i menjanji Indonesia Raya.* The ceremony was begun with the national anthem. **pa-ng∗** a guard. *See also* KAWAL

awan *ng*, **sijang** *kr* 1 the middle part of the day when the sun is at the zenith: from *ca.* 11 A.M. to 4 P.M. *djam rolas awan* 12 noon. *mangan* * to eat lunch. 2 daytime. *turu* * to take a nap. *Paḍangé kaja* *. It was as bright as day. *-* *lampuné ora susah diurupaké.* You don't need to burn those lights in the daytime. **k*an** *or* **k*en** too late; too early *(depending on the reference point). Tekané k*an.* He got here too late (*i.e.* during midday rather than in the morning). *or* He got here too early (*i.e.* in the midday rather than late afternoon). **sa* n·ḍranḍang** throughout the midday period

awang cloud. *-* the sky; (up in) the air. *Ḍèké nulis ing *-* nganggo dridji.* He wrote in the air with his finger. ***(-*)an** without recourse to written notation. *étung *an* to do arithmetic in one's head. *nggambar *an* to draw freehand. ***-*en** 1 to feel dizzy when looking down from a height. 2 to give sth up, forego an opportunity. *Jèn njepéḍah aku *-*en, trima ora mèlu.* If you're going to bicycle, I'll pass it up. *Bareng ketemu, aku *-*en arep kanḍa.* When I saw him, I just couldn't bring myself to tell him. ***-uwung** *sms* *-*

awar *-* a certain tree, whose ground-up leaves are mixed with opium for smoking

awas 1 sighted, able to see. 2 having sharp eyesight. 3 alert, on the lookout. * *tjopèt!* Beware of pickpockets! * *kowé, jèn wani ngaturké pak guru.* I'm warning you, don't tell the teacher. 4 clairvoyant. **ng/di*aké** to keep a sharp watch on. **ng/di*i** to supervise. *sing ng*i* supervisor. **pa·ng*an** supervision. *See also* KUMAWAS-AWAS, WAWAS

awat **ng/di*-*i** to supervise, keep an eye on. *Pitiké jèn saba *-*ana.* If the chickens wander off, keep track of them! *ng*-*i tindaké botjah*[2] to keep an eye on what the children are doing

awé *-* to wave. *Bener likmu, la kaé *-*!* It *is* your uncle: look, he's waving! *-* *nganggo topi* to wave a hat. **ng/di*(-*)** to wave to/at. *Botjah mau tak awé.* I waved to the boys. **ng/di*k̀-*k̀aké** to wave sth. *ngawèk-awèkaké tangané* to wave the hand. **pa·ng*** holding the hand high above the head. *Ḍuwuré panggungan mung sadedeg sapang*.* The stage was the height of a standing man's upstretched fingertips.

awèh 1 to give. *A * dolanan marang aḍiné.* A gave his brother a toy. 2 to have permission. *B arep mèlu, ora *.* B wanted to go too but wasn't allowed to. **p*** gift, thing given. * **pa·m·bagé** to exchange greetings. * **sanḍang pangan** to supply smn's basic needs. * **slamet** to wish smn well. * **urmat** to salute. * **weruh** to convey information, let smn know. *See also* WÈH, WÈWÈH

awer *-* 1 sth used to cover one's nakedness. 2 string used as a fence *or* border. **ng/di*-(-*)i** to use sth for one of the above purposes

awèt long-lasting; unchanged over a period of time. *Ḍèké * nom.* She remains young. *Wédangé * panasé.* The water stayed hot. *Panganan garingan *.* Fried foods stick to your ribs. *lelara kang ** a chronic disease. **ng/di*-*** to make sth last a long time; to preserve sth. *See also* WÈT

awi 1 let's...! (*md for* AJO). 2 please...; help yourself (*md for* MANGGA)

awig skillfully crafted, finely wrought. **ng*-aké** inspiring admiration [of an artistic creation]

awignam astu (namas siḍem) may it come true! may there be no obstacle!

awijat *oj* sky; (up in) the air. *mumbul ing ng** to rise into the air

awil *owal-** to move aimlessly *or* loosely. *Untuné wis ogak owal-*.* The tooth is very loose. *Dridjiné owal-*.* The [baby's] fingers keep opening and closing.

awin **ng/di*** to hold [a chicken] tightly by the head and feet preparatory to slaughtering it. **pa·ng*** a type of spear

awir (*or* ***an**) river flotsam. **ng*-*** attached loosely so as to move freely. *Keṭokané ng*-* jèn kena angin.* The [tied-on] scrap of cloth fluttered in the wind.

awis 1 sparse (*kr for* ARANG). 2 expensive; scarce (*kr for* LARANG). 3 to bargain, haggle (*root form: kr for* ANJANG[a]). ***an** arsenic (*sbst kr for* WARANG(AN))

awit 1 because. * *saka* because of. * *déné (ltry)* because of. 2 to start. *Dalané * munggah.* The road began to ascend. 3 beginning from; since. * *kapan?* since when? * *bijèn* for a long time; a long time ago *or* earlier. *sedjarah * abad kapisan tekan abad kaping nembelas* history from the 1st to the 16th century. **ng/di*i** to begin sth. *See also* KAWIT, PAWIT, SEKAWIT, WIWIT

awon bad (*kr for* ALA)

awor mixed, combined, mingled. *udan deres * gelap* hard rain with lightning. *Adja nganti * karo pitik sing lelaranen.* Don't let [the healthy chickens] get in with the diseased ones. **k*an** combined (with). *banju sing k*an ujah* water with salt mixed in. *Ḍèké tjlaṭu k*an tangis.* She cried as she talked. **p*** metal alloy. *See also* AMOR, WOR, WOWOR

awrat 1 heavy; weighty (*kr for* ABOT). 2 to hold, accommodate (*kr for* AMOT)

awu 1 ash. *dadi ** reduced to ashes, burned to the ground. ** saka gunung² geni* volcanic ash. *waḍah ** ashtray. 2 family ranking according to the order in which the members of the preceding generations were born. **né tuwa sapa?* Who is the older (according to the age of the parents rather than the actual age)? *A luwih tuwa *né.* A has the older forefather. **ng*-*** to ask about smn's ranking (as above). *A karo B paḍa ng*-* sudarma nang negara Ngamarta.* A and B went to Ngamarta to find out who their fathers were. **ng/di*ni** to scatter ashes onto. **p*n** kitchen

awud ***-*an** blindly, at random. **k*** run together, merged, accidentally mixed with [sth else]. **m*** scattered, dispersed. *Balé omahé m*.* His household has dispersed. *m* sa-paran²* to flee in all directions. **m*-m*** *or* **m·owad-m*** scattered, strewn. *Gulané mowad-m*.* The sugar was all over everything. **ng/di*-*** *or* **ng/di·owad-*** 1 to scatter, strew. 2 to waste, squander. **ng/di*aké** to scatter sth

awug **m*** crumbled fine [of soil, preparatory to planting]. **ng/di*** to crumble [soil]

awul *var of* ABUL

awun ***-*** dew (*var of* BUN)

awur **m*** 1 loose(ned), not sticking together. *Lemahé m*.* The soil is loosened up. *Segané m*.* The rice was cooked so that the grains were separate. 2 scattered. *Weḍiné m*.* The sand was scattered around. **ng/di*** to [do] brainlessly. *Olèhé mangsuli ng*.* He gave a stupid answer. *Adja di* waé ta!* Use your head! **ng/di*-*** to scatter. *Berasé di*-*.* He scattered rice grains about. **ng/di*-*aké** to sprinkle/scatter sth. *ng*-*aké weḍi* to sprinkle sand [on sth]. **ng/di*-*i** to sprinkle sth; to sprinkle onto. *Ḍèké ng*-*i gula.* She sprinkled sugar on it. *See also* WUR

axioma axiom

azan *var of* ADAN

azas *var of* ASAS

B

b (*prn* **bé**) 1 *alphabetic letter.* 2 *theoretical person. A ndjupuk bukuné B.* A took B's book.

ba boo!

ba- *see also under* BE- *(Introduction, 2.9.2)*

baam *var of* BAM

bab 1 about, concerning, on (the subject of). *ngrembug ** to talk about. *buku * wajang* a book about shadow plays. *Tak takoni * werna².* I asked him about all sorts of things. ** mBaṭik* Batik-Making [article title]. 2 subject, matter. *ngrembug *-* kang wigati* to discuss matters of importance. *Ora dadi *.* It doesn't pose a problem. ** alit² ingkang mboten saged dipun sinau saking buku²* details that you can't learn from books. 3 chapter. ** Kapisan* Chapter One. *sa*-sa** chapter by chapter. **nge/di*i** to group into chapters; to mark chapter headings on

babad 1 history; historical account. 2 to clear land by cutting growth; *fig* to clear away [difficulties *etc.*]. ***an** cut, mown. *Pradjurit² paḍa ptg glimpung kaja *an patjing.* The soldiers lay like cut reeds. ***-*** to cut down. ***-*** to mow grass.

m/di*(i) 1 to record the history of. 2 to cut, clear away. *m* alas* to clear forest land. *Bareng reribet mau wis di*, lagi baé aku bisa mikirké garapan lija.* After the trouble is cleared up, I can turn my thoughts to other work.

babag the equal of, a match for. *mungsuh sing ** equally matched opponents. ***an** 1 field, area. *ing *an basa lan kasusastran* in the fields of language and literature. **an Terusan Suez* the Suez Canal area. 2 docking area on a river bank or harbor edge. **m*** to equal, be the match of. **sa* karo** equal to, on a par with. *Si A kuwi gedé-tjiliké sa-* aku.* A is the same height as I am.

babah 1 occasion, opportunity. 2 Indo-Chinese male *(title, reference term)*. ***an** opening; opportunity. **m/di*** to make a hole in. *Malingé m* baturan.* The thief broke through the wall foundation. *** bujud** *adr* elderly Chinese person. *** djengkelit** *or* *** djungkir** to roll head-over-heels with the hands on the head (children's game)

babak 1 skinned, bruised. 2 act or scene from a play, or stanza from a song, performed for hire by traveling entertainers. *Sa* pinten?* How much for performing one scene (stanza)? ***an** piece of skin; shaving, peeling. **an kaju* wood shavings. **m/di*** 1 to peel (the outer layer from). 2 to rub, anoint. *** belur** *or* *** bunḍas** *or* *** bunjak** black-and-blue; skinned and bruised. *** salu** a certain large centipede

babal 1 a very young jackfruit. 2 *var of* BOBOL

babar 1 to proliferate. *Sadjroné sak djam waé kéwan sidji bisa * dadi satus.* Inside of an hour, a single germ can develop into 100. **é widji manungsa* the procreation of the human race. 2 to unfold, open out. **ing lakon* the unfolding of the plot. **é prijaji sing njalawadi* disclosure of the guilty person. 3 to be born *(ki for* LAIR). ***an** 1 product, output. *Bebedé *an Sala.* His batik skirt is from Solo. 2 revelation of the truth at the end of a story. 3 birth (*ki for* KE·LAIR·AN); to give birth (*ki for* NG·LAIR·AKÉ). 4 ritual meal celebrating a birth. 5 dyeing of batik. **ané mantjep.* The dye took. **m/di*** 1 to spread sth. *m* elar* to spread the wings. *m* ganda wangi* to exude a sweet fragrance. 2 to produce, put out. *m* prahoto* to manufacture trucks. *kalawarta kang di* ing Djakarta* a newspaper published in Djakarta. 3 to give birth (*ki for* NG·LAIR·AKÉ). *m* putra lanang* to bear a son. 4 to dye [batik]. 5 to remove the wax from fabric after each dyeing in the batik-making process. **m/di*aké** 1 to spread sth. *m*aké lajar* to spread sails. 2 to proliferate sth. *Manungsa wadjib m*aké tuwuh.* It is man's duty to procreate himself. 3 to disclose, unfold. *m*aké wadi* to let out a secret. **pa·m*** spreading; procreation. *See also* BABAR-PISAN

babar-pisan 1 altogether, completely; [not] at all. *Laranė wis mari *.* He's completely recovered now. *Wekasan ora katon *.* Finally you couldn't see it at all. *Aku ora ngira * jèn...* I had no idea that... 2 all at the same time. *Njauri utang baé di-intjrit², ora dilunasi *.* He repaid the debt little by little, not in a lump sum. **m/di*aké** to do more than one thing at a time. *Kawiné di*aké ing dina Senèn.* They held a double wedding on Monday. **m/di*i** to do sth all at once. *mBajaré di*i waé.* Why not pay it all off at one time?

babat tripe (as food). *soto ** tripe soup. *** galeng, * sumping, * tawon** various portions of the animal intestine, producing various forms of tripe

babi 1 pig. *daging ** pork. 2 name of one of the small playing cards *(kertu tjilik)*

babit ***an** act of swinging sth. **m/di*** to swing/slash at. *Asuné di* nganggo arit.* He took a swipe at the dog with his sickle. **m/di*aké** to swing sth

bablas 1 gone, vanished. *Terus * mabur mengulon.* It flew out of sight to the west. *Ḍèké lunga * adoh banget.* He left and was never heard of again. 2 direct, unswerving. *Lakuné * baé.* He walked straight on. *Degan bandjur diombé *.* He drank off the coconut juice at one draught. *Swarané tuntas mula *.* His voice is so strong it carries a long way. *Banjuné ora manḍeg, nanging *.* The water didn't stop–it kept on running. 3 accomplished, brought to completion. *Pangertèné * banget.* He's very knowledgable. *Bareng pangangkahé wis * dadi kemba.* When he got what he wanted, he didn't exert himself any longer.

babo *excl of anger or defiance. Hi * manas ati.* Oh, he makes me so mad! **, *, kowé wani kari aku.* Oho, so you want to fight me? OK!

babon mother hen (*see* BABU)

babrag ***an** rack for storing earthenware. **m*** [of males] having become mature
babrah **m*** to expand, increase. *Kesugihané saja m*.* He gets richer and richer.
babrak a large infected wound. **m*** to spread, widen. *Tatuné m*.* The wound opened up more.
babral **m/di*** to trim, prune [plants]
babu 1 young female servant to a family. 2 *ltry, formal* mother. *bapa *mu* your parents. ** Hawa* Eve (mother of mankind). ***ñ** 1 female animal mate; animal that has reproduced, *esp.* a hen. *Baboné angrem.* The hen is sitting on her eggs. 2 a source that gives rise to *fig* offspring. *Babon mau baliné nggawa anakan akèh.* The principal drew a large amount in interest. *baboning pasukan* the main body of armed forces (as contrasted with auxiliary troops). *Kabèh tjrita wajang kuwi baboné ming ana loro.* All shadow-play stories come from just two sources. *** dalem** female servant who is responsible for managing the household and also serves as sexual partner to the master. *** koki** household servant, *esp.* one in charge of buying and cooking the food. *** tjutji** servant, *esp.* one in charge of laundry and caring for the small children
babud carpet, rug, mat
babuh *var of* BABO
babuk **m/di*** 1 [of animals] to chase. *Ali mlaju ke-ponṭal² di* kebo.* Ali ran like mad with the kerbau after him. 2 to butt with the horns
bâdâ *var of* BAKDA. **be*** [of babies in the womb] to begin getting born
baḍak rhinoceros
baḍâkâ *oj* impediment; defect
badal 1 one who has made the pilgrimage to Mecca. 2 disciple; religious follower. **m/di*(i)** to disregard orders. *Aku ora wani m* ḍawuhing bapak.* I don't *dare* not do what Father told me to do.
badalah boo!
baḍâmâ 1 *oj* weapon. 2 a type of axe
badan 1 body (*kr for* AWAK). *gerak ** athletics, sports. 2 *var of* BAKDA·N. *** alus** ghost, invisible spirit. *** waḍag** body; physical embodiment
baḍan (*or* **be***) organization, body, institute
baḍar 1 disclosure, revelation. *Sawisé * dadi Pétruk manèh.* Unmasked, he was Pétruk once again. 2 unworkable. *Rentjanané * merga ora ana ḍuwité.* The plan fell through for lack of funds. **ke*an** magically restored to one's original form. **m/di*aké** 1 to reveal, unveil. 2 to render unworkable. *Ḍuwit kuwi bisa m*aké werna².* Money is a stumbling block to all kinds of things.
baḍawangan *oj* large land tortoise
baḍé 1 will, want (to) (*kr for* AREP[a]). 2 material (*kr for* BAKAL). 3 going to [do] (*kr for* BAKAL). ** punika * rok.* This material is for a skirt. 4 *var of* BEḌÈK. ***a** even if, even though (*kr for* AREP·A). ***an** exploitation, first working [of *e.g.* virgin soil, a mine]. ***-*** *rg* bridal chair. **m/di·be*** to work/exploit for the first time. **m/di*ni** to educate, train. **binaḍé** future *x*, prospective *x*. *putra binaḍé radja* crown prince
baḍèg an intoxicating liquor of fermented coconut juice
baḍeg no longer edible; having spoiled, smelling bad. *Segané wis *.* The rice has spoiled. *mambu ** smelling bad
baḍèk *formal var of* BEḌÈK
baḍel **m*** underdone, not cooked through
baḍèr an edible river fish
baḍigal cocoon
baḍigul stupid, ignorant. *** angen·é** to try to act smarter than one is
baḍik *rg* dagger
baḍil **boḍal-*** frayed, fraying (*var of* BRO-ḌAL-BRAḌIL)
badir *inf var of* MUBADIR
badjag pirate. ***an** pirated goods; obtained through piracy. **m/di*** to commit piracy against. *Kapalé di*.* The ship was pirated.
badjang stunted in growth. *botjah ** a stunted child; a child whose hair has never been cut. ***an** 1 child whose hair has never been cut. 2 *rg* young mango. **di*aké** allowed to remain uncut [of the hair of a last surviving boy, in the belief that his feminine appearance will enable him to survive]. *** kerèk** a locust-like insect
badjeng **m*** firstborn (*kr for* M·BAREP)
badjigur 1 *term of abuse.* **, ki!* You rat! 2 a certain coconut drink served hot
badjing 1 squirrel. 2 cotton apron with a tool pocket. 3 bunch of tied grass for roof thatch. ***an** professional thief; crook (*also used as a term of abuse).* **m*** to make one's living as a thief. *** rekta** red squirrel
badjo *oj* pirate
badjong ***an** to chip in to buy sth. **m*** to spatter water, *esp.* by kicking in a puddle.

m/di*i to dampen by sprinkling. *Tandur-ané di*i.* He watered the plants.

bâdjrâ *ltry* 1 jewel. 2 lightning. 3 5-pointed spear

badju shirt, jacket. * **bèbèk** a certain bird with a duck-shaped head

badjug **m*** ill-mannered, badly behaved

badjul young crocodile (young of the BAJA). **m*** to chase after *or* flirt with girls. **m/di*i** to chase after, flirt with. * **buntung** playboy, wolf. * **ḍarat** 1 crook, criminal. 2 wolf, woman-chaser

baḍog **m/di*** *cr* to eat

baḍol a certain edible freshwater fish

baḍong 1 female genitals (*ki for* PA·WADON·AN). 2 wing-like part of a wajang costume (*rg var of* PRABA)

bâdrâ ***n** established as a settlement. *désa *n anjar* a newly opened-up village. **be*** 1 to clear a jungle for settling. 2 to begin life again in a new place

baḍur a certain tuberous plant. ***en** *or* ***-*** 1 [of skin] rough. 2 [of silver coins] tarnished

baḍut 1 clown, comedian, jokester. 2 can *or* bottle opener. 3 a certain kind of pliers. ***an** 1 joking. *Senengané *an.* He's always clowning around. 2 laughingstock; butt of jokes. **m*(i)** to joke, clown around. *Gawéané m*.* He's a comedian.

baduwi a nomad

baé[a] *ng*, **kémawon** *kr* 1 just, only. *Sèlèhna kono *.* Just put it down over there. *Togna *.* Let it go! (Just) leave him alone! *Meneng *.* He (just) kept quiet. *Sawetara djam * kowé bakal tekan ing désa.* You'll get to the village in just a few hours. *Karanganku tak gawéné *.* I guess I'll (just) write my composition. *Mung * nggonku mréné rada wengèn²*. (The) only (thing is,) I'll be a little late getting there. *Lombok mung sauwit *.* There's only one pepper plant. 2 instead [of some alternative]. *Aku wedi; ajo mulih *.* I'm scared; let's go home [instead of going ahead]! *Saiki mulih, sésuk * ditutugaké manèh.* I'm going home now; I'll finish it tomorrow. *Ora susah ditjantjang, diumbar *.* It doesn't need to be tethered–it can go loose. 3 *points up or enlivens the foregoing. Kaja ḍèk bijèn *.* Just like in the old days! *Gampang *.* It's *easy! Ana rumah sakit bandjur * ditambani.* He was cured right away in the hospital. *Ora *.* No! Not so! *Ngéné *.* Like *this!* *Paḍa * karo prau.* It's just exactly like a boat. 4 any *x*, every *x*. *Sapa * sing gelem kena mèlu.* Anyone who wants can go along. *Saben warung * adol.* Every shop sells them. *Sawontenipun kémawon.* Whatever there is [will be all right]. *Tjritakna impènmu, saélingmu *.* Tell me all you can remember of your dream. *apa * ing ndonja iki* anything (*or* everything) in the world. 5 [not] even. *Basa * ora bisa.* He can't even speak Krama. *Ora ana sidji * pesakitan sing ngakoni kaluputané.* Not a single prisoner would acknowledge his guilt. 6 *n* and only *n*. *Ngaranana djenengé iwak sepuluh ** Name 10 kinds of fish.

baé[b] ***ǹ(-*ǹ)** [not] usual. *baṭi kang ora baèn²* an extraordinary profit. **se*** any *x* whatever. *nDjupuka kertu sekarepmu, ja se* waé.* Pick a card–any card. **se*né** *in negative constructions* unheard of, weird, out of this world. *Ati² lo, wong kuwi ora se*né.* Careful–he's no ordinary person. *Wingi ana kedadéjan sing ora sa*né, mosok botjah tjilik menang gelut(é) karo wong tuwa.* Yesterday sth really monstrous happened: a child beat up an adult.

baékot *var of* BOIKOT

baem freshwater clam

baén *rg var of* BAÉ[a]

bag ***-g·in·itik** even, equal. *Jèn bab kapinteran, kiraku botjah loro kuwi *-ginitik.* When it comes to brains, I think the two boys are about even.

bâgâ *oj* share, portion

bagal ear of corn

bagas healthy-looking (*var of* BERGAS). * **(ku)waras(an)** healthy, in good physical condition

bagaskârâ *oj* sun

bagaspat *var of* BAGASKARA

bagawan holy man, hermit. **m*** to live as a religious hermit, *i.e.* to lead an ascetic life in solitude

bagé ***a** *a greeting. Bagéa sak tekamu.* (We) welcome (your arrival)! ***an** part, portion, share. *Montor bagéjan ngarep péjok.* The front part of the car was dented. *se*an wong* a group of people. **dudu *an(é)** not within the scope (of). *Iki dudu *anku. aku ora ketjonggah.* This is beyond my power; I can't cure him. ***ǹ** rice paddy under joint ownership. ***-b·in·agé** to exchange greetings. *Ḍèkè ngatjarani lungguh, bandjur *-binagé, takon keslametané.* He asked [the guest] to sit down, then they asked after each other's health. **ka*an** to receive as one's share *or* allotment. *Aku kebagéjan madjang kamar.* My job is to decorate the room. **m/di*** to distribute. *Wingi rapoté di*.* The report cards were passed out yesterday. **m/di*kaké** to greet, welcome. *mbagèkaké tamu* to welcome guests. *Metu saka ing plabuhan wis dibagèkaké prahara geḍé banget.* Emerging from the harbor, they were greeted by a huge storm. **m/di*ni** to give a portion/part/share. *Iki tak bagèni geḍang sidji.* Here, I'll share: I'll give you a banana. **pa·m*** 1 action of greeting and inquiring about smn's well-being. 2 act of dividing/sharing. *Pam*né keprijé?* How do we split it? *Pam*né ora adil.* It wasn't divided fairly. **pa·m*an** share, ration. *pam*an beras (pakéjan, lenga)* food (clothing, oil) ration

bagèh *var of* BAGÉ

bagel **m/di*** *rg* to throw stones *or* sticks at

bagénḍa *title for addressing a king*

bagi *var of* BAGÉ

bagija (*or* **ke*n**) happiness, well-being. **pa·m*** *var of* PA·M·BAGÉ 1

bago 1 inner bark of the *so* tree. 2 sack *or* sacking material of *so*-tree bark. *pirang m* beras?* how many sacks of rice?

Bagong name of a wajang clown. ***an** speech style used by palace retainers. *See also* WULU-TJUMBU

bagor *var of* BAGO

bagrègan broken-down, not in working order

bagus 1 handsome. 2 *adr* high-ranking boy. **m*i** boastful, conceited. *See also* GUMAGUS

bagya *var sp of* BAGIJA

bah *adr* Indo-Chinese male (*shf of* BABAH)

bahak hawk-like predatory bird. ***an** things seized *or* acquired by looting. **m/di·(be)*** to take possession arbitrarily of others' belongings

bahalal *see* HALAL

bahan 1 materials, supplies, ingredients. * *mentah* raw materials. * *kimia* chemical substance. * *bakar* fuel. 2 subject matter, data. * *kanggo metjahké soal*[2] data for solving problems. * *tetimbangan* food for thought

bahar sea, ocean

bahari maritime

bahni(ng) *oj* fire

bahu *var of* BAU

bain *rg var of* BAÉ[a]

baita boat (*kr for* PRAU)

Baitalmukadas Jerusalem

bâjâ[a] 1 crocodile. 2 dangerous, difficult. * *alas iki marga akèh matjané.* This forest is dangerous: there are many tigers. *tan* * without difficulty. **be*** danger, hazard. **(ke)*n** village official responsible for security. **ke*-*** pursued by bad luck. **m*** crocodile-like. **m·be*ni** hazardous, constituting a threat. **sa* (sa)pati** together through thick and thin. **b·in·aja** surrounded by danger. * **ḍarat** wolf, woman chaser. * **ita** *ltry* soldier

bâjâ[b] 1 perhaps, possibly. * *wis karsaning Pangéran.* Perhaps it is God's will. 2 *ltry* is it so (that...)? * *tan kulak pawarta?* Haven't you heard the news? 3 even if, even though. 4 [not] anything. *Ora dadi* *. It doesn't matter. 5 *shf of* UBAJA. 6 *with interrogative word* how [*etc.*] on earth...! *Sapa * sing kena dak sambat sebuti?* Who *can* I confide in? * *keprijé anggonmu mari njerèt, jèn kowé ḍéwé ora nijat marèni?* How can you ever expect to get over the opium habit if you aren't determined to give it up?

bajah duckling (young of the BÈBÈK). **m*i** in critical condition. *Larané m*i.* He is critically ill.

bajak *inf var of* KEBAJAK. **a*-*** *or* **be*an** crowded, jammed

bajan parrot; parakeet

bajang bamboo bed. ***an** 1 a patient being supported and helped to walk. 2 prey. *nggereng kaja matjan nemu *an* roaring like a tiger seeking its prey. 3 shadow (*var of* WE·WAJANG·AN). **m*** to imagine, visualize. **m/di*(-*)** to support *or* carry [a patient who cannot walk]. **m/di*aké** to imagine, visualize

bajangkârâ 1 palace guards in the Madjapahit era. 2 police

bajar pay, salary, wages. ***an** pay. **anmu* pira?* How much is your salary? **m/di*** to pay (for). *m* padjek* to pay taxes. *Arep di* regané, A ora gelem.* He was willing to pay the price, but A didn't want to sell. *Wong adus waé kok nganggo m*!* You have to pay to go swimming–?! *m* tjrèng* to pay cash (for). **m/di*aké** to pay [a price]. *Ḍuwit Rp. 100. di*aké marang A.* A was paid 100 rupiahs. **m/di*i** to pay smn; to pay for sth. **pa·m*(an)** payment; act of paying. *Pem*é suk Djumuah.* Next

Friday is pay day. *Pam*bajaré saben wulan sepuluh rupiah.* The payments are 10 rupiahs a month.

bajas a certain freshwater fish

bâjâwârâ proclamation. **m/di*kaké** to proclaim. *Sang Prabu m*kaké ḍaupé ingkang raji.* The King announced his son's nuptials. *See also* WARA

bajèk *var of* BAJI

bajem spinach. *djangan ** spinach soup

baji baby. ***ǹ** *or* **be*** to give birth to a baby. **m/di*ǹi** to deliver smn's baby. *** abang** a newborn baby

bajonèt bayonet

bajor a certain fish

baju 1 *ltry* wind. 2 (*or* **be***) blood vessel; *fig* strength. *tanpa ** weak(ened), drained of strength. **be*ǹ** amulet having the power to harm others. *** badjra** wind and thunder storm

bajun firstborn (*ki for* BAREP). **pa·m*** 1 *oj* female firstborn child. 2 firstborn child (*ki for* PA·M·BAREP). 3 breast; milk (*ki for* SUSU[a]). *See also* AJUN[b]

bajung **m*** *shf of* LEMBAJUNG

bak 1 basin, tub. 2 seat in a vehicle. ** mburi* back seat. ** plungguhané supir* driver's seat. 3 Chinese ink. 4 sugar-cane plot. 5 three of a kind (in card games). ***-*an** harried, frantic (*var of* BJAK²AN). **m*** *adr* older sister; lady older than oneself (*shf of* M·BAKJU)

bâkâ 1 (*or* **m***) *n* at a time. *m* loro* 2 by 2. *m* seṭiṭik* little by little. *Dikukup m* sagegem.* He grabbed them a handful at a time. 2 stork

bak'adjeng *opt kr for* BAKJU

bak'aju *var of* BAKJU

bakal *ng,* **baḍé** *kr* 1 (raw) material; item to be made from [a material]. ** klambi* clothing material. *bata * panggung* bricks for making a platform. **é kaju.* It's to be made of wood. *blatjo sa** material for one garment. *Moriné kanggo pirang *?* How many dresses will the linen make? 2 (**karsa** *ki*) will, going to. ** geḍé gandjaranmu.* You're going to get a big reward. *Kowé * tak tjangkrimi.* I'm going to ask you a riddle. ** ora* will not, isn't going to. *ora ** not possible. *Ḍèké * ora nonton.* He's not going to see the show. *Ora * nonton.* He can't possibly have seen the show. 3 future, prospective. ** bodjo* prospective husband/wife. ** ratumu* your future king. 4 prospective outcome. *Keprijé *é?* How will it turn out? **é ja padu.* It'll end up in a quarrel. 5 new at/to. *Botjah² sing ndjogèd iki kabèh isih *.* All the girls dancing here are beginners. ***an** 1 learner, beginner. *manuk *an* a bird that is just learning to sing. 2 prospective spouse. 3 potential for the future. *Jèn ndeleng djaman tjiliké ringkih laranen, ora ngira *an dadi sardjana sing konḍang.* Having known him as a sickly child, we would never have expected him to become a well-known scientist. **be*** new (to, at); in the first stages. *Pelikané isih be*.* They're just beginning to develop the mine. *Aku lagi be* ana ing kéné, mula durung djadjah.* I'm new here, so I don't know my way around yet. **m/di*aké** to bring about. *Wong tuwané m*aké Sri dadi bodjoné Harta.* Sri's parents arranged for her to become Harta's wife. **m*i** 1 useful *or* suitable as material. *Mas kuwi m*i banget.* Gold can be made into many different things. *Mori iki m*i kanggo kemédjan.* This linen is for making shirts. 2 (*psv* **di*i**) to prepare sth for the future. *m*i manuk perkutut* to train turtledoves. *See also* TJAKAL-BAKAL

bakar cooked by roasting. *djagung ** roast corn-on-the-cob. ***an** 1 roasted; burned. *pohung *an* roast (*or* burnt) cassava. 2 roasting equipment. **an pohung* cassava roaster. **ke*an** to get burned accidentally. **m/di*(i)** 1 to roast sth over coals. *Saténé di*.* She broiled the shishkebabs. *Wesi mau bandjur di* nganggo areng.* He set the iron in the burning coals. 2 to burn. *Ḍèké m* lajangé kekasihé.* She burned his love letters. **pa·m*** act of roasting. *Pam*é mbaka seṭiṭik.* They are roasted a few at a time. *See also* BENEM

bakaran baccarat (card game)

bakat 1 natural ability. *Ḍèké kuwi duwé * nggambar.* He has a talent for drawing. 2 *oj* strong

bakda 1 end, conclusion. 2 name of the major Moslem holiday, celebrated at the conclusion of the fasting month. 3 after. ** ngasar* after the 4 P.M. prayers. ***n** to celebrate the above holiday. **ka*n** to have the above holiday creep up on one. *Nganti ka*n garapané durung rampung.* Suddenly it was Bakda and his work wasn't finished. **sa*né** after. *sa*né kuwi* after that. *** ḍeng** the 6 P.M. mosque drum signalizing the end of the fasting time and the beginning of the holiday. * **Mulud** 4th month of the Moslem calendar. * **pasa bada** _var name of the above holiday_

baken main, chief (_opt kr for_ BAKU)

baki serving tray

bakijak wooden sandals with a rubber toe strap

bakjak _var of_ BAKIJAK

bak̒ju m* 1 older sister. 2 _adr_ girl or lady older than oneself

bak̒mi a Chinese dish made with noodles

bak̒moé a Chinese dish made with rice and beancake

bak̒moi _var of_ BAKMOÉ

bako (_or_ **m***) tobacco (_shf of_ TEMBAKO)

bakoh _rg var of_ BAKUH

Bakoksi All-Indonesia Ketoprak Organization (_acronym for_ BADAN KONTAK KETOPRAK SELURUH INDONESIA)

bak̒pao Chinese-style pie: pastry filled with pork or soybean mixture

baksil bacillus

bak̒so a dish consisting of noodles, meatballs, and beancake cooked into a Chinese-style soup

baktéri bacteria

bakti _var of_ BEKTI

baku (**baken** _opt kr_) 1 main, essential, basic. _pangan sing_ * basic foods. _Pegawéané kang * mbatik._ Her main work is making batik. 2 rice paddy given to a village chief in lieu of salary. ***ñ** 1 _sms_ BAKU 2. 2 having the right to own a rice paddy in a village. ***né** normally, basically; the heart of the matter [is...] _Bakuné Sri._ That's just like Sri! **be*** basis, foundation. **m/di*ñi** to supply smn's basic needs. _A dibakoni kamasé._ A is supported by his older brother. * **karang** villager who owns a house and yard but no rice fields. * **omah**[2] home owner. * **padjeg** land tax. * **sawah** 1 one who has part ownership of a rice paddy. 2 portion of a paddy subject to tax. **wong** * home owner; permanent resident

bakuh sturdy, strong, firm; determined

bakul 1 market seller. 2 broker who handles rural agricultural products. 3 _var of_ WAKUL. **(be)*an** 1 act of selling in the marketplace. 2 to play solitaire. **m/di*aké** to have smn sell [goods handled by a middleman] at retail. **m/di*i** to buy [goods] from a middleman to sell at retail. * **odjog·an** itinerant peddler. * **rombèng·an** old-clothes man; second-hand dealer

bakula a certain flower

bakung a certain flower

bak̒wan a corn-fritter-like food (in Jogjakarta style, made with shrimp added)

bal 1 ball. _nampani_ * to catch a ball. 2 roll, bolt [of fabric]; bale [of tobacco _etc._]. 3 railroad warning signal. 4 light bulb. ***-*an** 1 (to play) soccer; a soccer game _or_ match. _nonton *-*an_ to watch a soccer game. _*-*an djeruk_ (to play) soccer using an orange for a ball. 2 in the form of bolts/bales. _mBakoné *-*an._ The tobacco is baled. **nge/di*i** to pack into bolts/bales. _nge*i mbako_ to bale tobacco. * **basket** basketball; _main * basket_ to play basketball. * **bisbal** baseball. * **b(l)èter** a soccer ball. * **kasti** a game resembling baseball. * **krandjang** court-ball (a large-scale version of basketball)

bal- _see also under_ BL- (_Introduction, 2.9.3_)

bâlâ 1 army, troops. * _bantuan_ auxiliary forces. _rajap_ * termites that guard the queen and the colony. 2 teammate; one on the same side. _Sapa *ku?_ Who's on my side? 3 subjects of a monarch. 4 a certain mango-like fruit. **ka*** to be a [monarch's] subject. **m/di*ni** to send troops to. * **(ge)gana** airborne troops. * **Keselamatan** Salvation Army. * **koswa** well equipped troops. * **tentara** fighting force, troops. _See also_ BALA-PETJAH

balak [of fruit] to fall from the tree before ripening. **m/di*** to cancel, countermand. _A m* anggoné pesen kembang._ A canceled his order for flowers. _m* karsané prijaji luhur_ to countermand a high official's orders

balang object thrown. _*mu ngenani katja._ What you threw hit the glass. ***an** flower packets held by bride and groom, tossed down at the moment they meet during the ceremony: whoever throws first will be the boss. ***-*an** to throw at/to each other. **m/di*** to throw sth. **m* tingal** to flirt. **m/di*i** to throw at/to. **pa·m*** act of throwing. _Pem*é ora adoh._ He didn't throw it far. _Adohé sapam*._ It's just a stone's throw away.

balap ***an** a race; to race. _A *an karo B._ A had a race with B. _*an mlaju_ (to have) a running race. **m*** to race, speed. _Olèhé njepédah m* banget._ He rode his bicycle very fast. **m/di*aké** 1 to make sth go fast. _Montoré di*aké._ He speeded his car. 2 to have [_e.g._ horses] race

bâlâ-petjah breakable things: crockery, chinaware

balas a weight for holding *or* steadying sth; ballast

balé 1 hall, public building. 2 front hall of a residence, used for entertaining. * **désa** village administration building. * **kambang** a round artificial island with a pavilion (reached by a bridge or walkway) in the center of a round pool surrounded by gardens. * **kuṭa** city administration building. * **omah** household; house plus land. * **per·temu·an** public meeting hall. * **sigala-gala** firetrap, house like a tinder box *(referring to a wj episode in which the Pendawas were to be burned alive)*

balèg see AKIL

balèk *rg var of* BALI

baléla rebellion. * *ing paréntah* an uprising against the government. **m*** to resist authority, rebel

bales 1 steamroller. 2 to answer [a letter]. 3 *var of* BALAS. 4 *var of* WALES

bali *ng,* **wangsul** *kr* 1 to return. *Aku arep * mrono.* I'm going back there. *Ḍèké * turu manèh.* He went back to sleep. 2 to be *or* go home. *Djam sepuluh bengi mesṭi A wis *.* He's sure to be home by 10 P.M. ***ǹ** 1 a ride home/back. 2 to remarry [a divorced spouse]. **bola-*** **(wongsal-wangsul** *kr***)** 1 to move back and forth. *A bola-* lunga menjang Éropah.* He keeps traveling to Europe and back. 2 to [do] again and again. *Bola-* takon waé.* He asked question after question. ***ǹ-*ǹan** **(wangsul²an** *kr***)** to return to each other [of divorced partners]. *Balèn-balènan kepijé, wong sing wadon isih muring.* How can they be reconciled if the wife is still angry? **m/di*k̀aké** 1 to return sth. *Bukuné dibalèkaké menjang perpustakaan.* He took the book back to the library. *Utangé dibalèkaké.* He repaid the money. 2 to refuse to accept. *Wèh²ané dibalèkaké.* She returned his gifts. *A ora tau mbalèkaké wong kang ngundang.* A never turns down an invitation. **m/di*ǹi** 1 to repeat, do over. *Matjané dibalèni.* He read it again. *mbalèni pitakoné* to repeat one's question. 2 to return to. *Piringé dibalèni manèh.* He went back to his meal. *Bodjoné kang wis dipegat dibalèni.* Her divorced husband came back to her. **m/di·bola·n-*ǹi** to [do] over and over. *Anggoné matja buku kuwi tansah dibolan-balèni.* He keeps reading and rereading that book. *See also* BALISWARA, KOSOK-BALI

balig *see* AKIL

balik 1 on the contrary, on the other hand, the other way around. *Aku A, * kowé sapa?* I'm A; who are *you? Kowé iki umurmu lagi sepuluh taun, * ḍèké mèh limalas.* You're just 10 years old, whereas he's 15. 2 *var of* BALI. ***an** in reverse order. *Aksara iki *an.* These letters are backwards (*i.e.* the word is written in its mirror image). **bolak-*** on both sides. *Kertasé ditulisi bolak-*.* Both sides of the paper had been written on. **ke*** turned the other way around. *Klambimu ke*.* Your shirt is inside out (*or* hind side before). *Olèhmu njeluk aku ke*, ora kepénak aḍi nanging malah mbakju.* You've been calling me *aḍi* [the term for smn younger], but you should call me *mbakju* [because I am older than you]. **m*** to turn this way and that. *Turuné tansah gedabigan, m* ngiwa nengen.* She didn't sleep soundly–kept turning from side to side. **m·bolak-m*** to keep turning one way and the other. *Omongé mbolak-m*.* He keeps reversing himself in what he says. **m/di*i** to turn sth the other way around. *m*i mèmèhan* to keep turning clothing that is drying in the sun. *See also* SUBALIK, WALIK

balila *var of* BALÉLA

baliswârâ 1 a certain technique for producing musical sounds. 2 *gram* compound word or phrase reversed from the normal order. **ka*** *gram* an expression with a reciprocal meaning

balok 1 log; beam. 2 fried cassava pieces. ***an** lumber mill

balon 1 balloon (child's toy; aerial conveyance). 2 light bulb. 3 *rg* prostitute

balong rice paddy that is flooded to capacity without overflowing

balowarti *var of* BALUWARTI

balsem balm, ointment. *See also* PÈRU-BALSEM

baluh 1 ballast. 2 fishing tackle. **be*** person who is on one's side in a dispute. **m/di*i** 1 to weight sth down. 2 *(or* **m/di·be*i)** to band together with smn in stirring up trouble

balung **(tosan** *kr? ki?***)** bone. *Awaké kuru banget, kari * karo kulit.* He's so thin he's nothing but skin and bones. **be*** bones, bone structure. *Be* kaja dilolosi.* She was drained of strength. *be* wesi* very strong.

(be)*an frame, skeleton. **ané kaju tahun.* The [house] frame is ironwood. **aning tjrita* the outline of a story. **m*** resembling bone(s). **m* usus** to waver in one's determination *or* devotion to ideals. *** sungsum** intense physical sensation. *Aḍemé nggares, ana *-sungsum.* It's so cold it chills you to the bone. ***-t·in·umpuk** a double wedding

balur 1 (*or* ***-tengiri**) a certain freshwater fish, sold dried and salted. 2 *var of* BELUR

baluwarti brick wall, *esp.* the one surround-the palace at Surakarta

bam molar. *** wekas(an)** wisdom tooth

bambang 1 crop disease of rice. 2 son of a holy man. ***an** *wj* *title for certain superior characters*

bambet bamboo (*kr for* BAMBU)

bambing (*or* ***an**) an object in a precariously balanced position. **m*** precariously positioned. *Ombaké geḍé² mbanting² ing paḍas² m* pegunungan.* Huge waves pound against the overhanging rocks at the edge of the mountains.

bambon 1 room in the inner part of a Javanese-style house, where the family relaxes and also keeps their everyday articles. 2 opium den

bambu *ng,* **bambet** *kr* bamboo. *** runting** bamboo spear

bambung unwilling to conform to proper behavior standards. ***an** characterized by such behavior. *botjah *an* juvenile delinquent

ban 1 tire. ** kempès* flat tire. ** mati* solid (rather than air-filled) tire. ** ndjero* inner tube. ** pompan* inflated tire. *pompa ** tire pump. ** pulkanisiran* a retread. ** sèrep* spare tire. ** tjubles* tubeless tire. 2 sash, fabric belt. 3 railroad track. **nge/di*(i)** to put a tire (on). *** ḍempo** 1 a ball of earth or clay used as a missile. 2 a certain green dragonfly

bânâ **be*** *ltry* request, demand. **m/di*** to request, demand

banar bright(ly lighted). ***an** place characterized by brightness

bânârâwâ marsh, swamp. *sawah ** low-lying rice paddy that becomes a swamp during the rainy season

banaspati *wj* fire demon

banâwâ *oj* boat

bânâwâsâ *var of* WANAWASA

bândâ 1 cord for tying smn's hands. 2 *oj* body. **be*n** with hands tied. **m/di*** to tie smn's hands, *usu.* behind the back. **m* tangan** to clasp the hands behind the back; *fig* to loaf

bânḍâ 1 wealth, fortune, property. 2 capital investment. ***n** to contribute money to a cause. *Botjah² paḍa *n tuku bal.* The boys chipped in to buy a ball. **m*** wealthy. **m/di*ni** to finance sth. *A nalika bukak toko sepisanan di*ni B.* When A first started his shop, B put up the capital. *** banḍu** to have a wealth of relatives as well as money. *** bau** all brawn and no brains. *** béja** expenses. *** ḍengkul** 1 to engage in business with only one's own labor as capital. 2 gambling stakes borrowed from the opponent

bândâjudâ to fight hand-to-hand

banḍang basket for carrying sugar-cane seedlings. ***an** 1 lured away from where it belongs. *Sing gambir kuwi dara *an.* The red pigeon followed our pigeon home. 2 to do things fast. *Adja *an, isih akèh wektu.* Don't rush–there's plenty of time. **ke*** to get carried away, be lured off. **m*** at high speed. *Sekuteré digas m* mlaju.* He gave his motor bike the gas and zoomed off. **m/di*aké** 1 to make sth go fast. *Kebo²né di*aké.* He drove the kerbaus faster. 2 to take *or* lure sth away. *m*aké ḍuwit* to embezzle money. *m*ké pit* to steal a bicycle

bandar 1 harbor city. 2 person acting as banker at the gambling table. **m*** to act as banker. **pa·m*an** port authority

bândâwâlâ(-pati) a duel to the death

bandel 1 [of children] brave, not prone to crying. 2 bird used as living bait

banḍel stubborn, willful. **m*** to act uncooperative or defiant

banḍem missile, object hurled. **m/di*(i)** to throw sth (at). *** (lem)pung** ball of clay (used in children's games). *** po** 1 ball of clay. 2 large green dragonfly

bandeng an edible fish that is born in the sea and later migrates to rivers

banderol excise tax stamp affixed to a product at the factory. *rega pas ** the exact price shown on the tax stamp

banḍil flexible sling for hurling missiles. ***an** 1 a game played with slings; to play *or* compete using slings. 2 ring with a single stone. **m/di*** to shoot (at) with a sling. *m* matjan* to sling [pebbles] at a tiger. **m/di*aké** to hurl [missiles] at

banḍing **dudu *ané** no match for, not the

equal of. **m/di*(aké)** to compare. *Jèn di*aké karo omah² lijané ora pati apik.* It's not very nice in comparison with the other houses.

bandjang fishing tackle for ocean fish

bandjar 1 [planted] in rows. 2 living and trading in a coastal area. 3 (*or* ***an**) household. **m/di*aké** *or* **m/di*i** to bundle [rice plants] and lay them out for planting. *** dawa** [a village that is] geographically connected with another village. *** pa·karang·an** household and yard

bandjel 1 a temporary replacement worker. 2 substitute food used during a shortage. ***an** act of substituting/replacing. **m/di*i** to act as replacement *or* substitute for

bandjeng **be*an** *or* **m*** in an orderly row, lined up

bandjir *ng,* **bena** *kr* flood. **ke*an** to be struck by *or* caught in a flood. *panggonan sing ke*an* a flooded place. **ke*an segara madu** to receive high honor *or* great good fortune. **m/di*(i)** to pour forth [good things]. *di*i ḍuwit* to receive a lot of money. *** banḍang** large-scale disastrous flood. *** getih** blood bath. *** madu** a stroke of good luck; a high honor

bandjur *ng,* **ladjeng** *kr* 1 (*or* **m*** *ng*) and then, after that. *Sakwisé adus * dandan.* He took a bath and got dressed. *Kowé * ngapa?* What did you do then? 2 continuing in a sequence. *Mengkono iku * baé.* It keeps on like that, over and over. ***é** the sequel; the continuation. *Keprijé *é?* What happened next? **é lajang iki arep tak kirimké minggu ngarep.* I'll send the next installment of this letter next week. **ke*** (having gone) too far; too late (now). *La wis ke*, arep keprijé?* It's over and done with; what can you do about it? *Ora sida mangkat saiki.–Aku wis ke* tuku kartjis.* We're not leaving today.–But I've already bought the tickets! *Olèhé gegujon ke* dadi marahi salah tampa.* His laughing caused an unfortunate misunderstanding. **ke*-*** (to get) increasingly beyond the acceptable range. *Nesuné ke*-*.* He's getting madder and madder. *O saja ke*-* nèk kaja ngono.* Well then, it will just keep getting worse! **m/di*aké** to continue sth; to repeat sth in a sequence. *Wis, tak *né tjritaku.* OK, I'll go on with my story. *m*aké sekolahé* to continue one's formal education. *Tindak kaja mengkono adja di*ké.* Don't keep on acting that way. **sa*é** 1 afterwards; subsequently and as a result of. *Jèn pité wis didandani, sa*é kowé arep dak kongkon tuku mbako.* After your bike is fixed, I'll ask you to go get me some tobacco (on it). 2 and so on, in the same vein

bandjut 1 *var of* BANDJUR. 2 *var of* BENGKUNG 1. **m/di*** *ltry* to drag off and kill

banḍo hair band of cloth or velvet

banḍol 1 unmannerly, insolent. 2 [of horses] wild, untamed. 3 bandit chief. **m*** to behave like a bandit chief; to act unconventional and unmannerly

banḍot 1 ram, male sheep or goat. 2 lascivious old man. ***an** a certain snake

banḍosa a covered wooden or bamboo bier

bandrèk 1 skeleton key, master key. 2 adultery. **m/di*** 1 to open with a skeleton *or* master key. 2 to replace sth with a makeshift substitute

bandring slingshot. ***an** to play *or* compete with slingshots. **m/di*** to shoot (at) with a slingshot. **m/di*aké** to shoot at [sth] with a slingshot

banḍu *see* BANḌA

bandul *rg var of* BANḌUL

banḍul iron ball used as a weight. ***an** 1 children's swing. 2 a hanging swinging baby bed. **m/di*** to swing a weight at sth. *A m* lajangan sing temangsang nèng uwit.* A tried to dislodge his kite from the tree by swinging a rock on a string at it. **m/di*i** to weight sth down. *m*i timba* to attach a weight to a bucket (so that it will tilt and fill when lowered into the well)

banḍung *see* LUMBUNG, SUMUR

bané *var of* BANÈN

banèk *var of* BANÈN

banèn sound; voice. *Ora ana *é.* There's no sound from him. ***-*** to make sounds, use the voice. *Adja *-*.* Don't tell anyone!

bang 1 red (*shf of* ABANG). ** idjo* red and green. *setopan * idjo* traffic light. *wesi ** red-hot iron. 2 reddening of the sky during sunrise or sunset; *fig* eastern *or* western region. *Wétan * sulaké.* The eastern sky is red with the rising sun. *bupati (m)* kulon* regent of the western region. 3 *var sp of* BANK. ***-*an** batik with predominantly red coloration (rather than the preferred blues and browns). **m*** *shf of* KEMBANG; **m*-mbolo** *shc from* KEMBANG GEMBOLO (*see also* KAK). **(m)*-*** reddening of the eastern *or* western sky. *m*-* kulon* red sunset sky.

nge/di* to apply red color (to). **nge/di*aké** 1 to put money in the bank. 2 to put up as security. *Omahé die*aké.* He used his house as collateral for the bank loan.

bangah a certain plant, also its blossom

banger fetid

banget *ng,* **sanget** *kr* 1 very (much), considerable, altogether. *ḍuwur ** very tall. *klèru ** very much mistaken. ** ngarep-arep* to look forward to eagerly. ** ditresnani.* She loves him very much. ** bungahé.* He was delighted. *njengkané ** at the very most. *Kula rudjuk sanget.* I quite agree. *Aku ora njana * jèn arep dadi ketua.* I had no idea I was to be chairman. 2 serious, intense. *lelara ** a severe illness. *Ing mangsa ketiga panasé *.* The heat is terrible in the dry season. ** enggoné gawé rusak.* It did severe damage. *Sangsaja sanget gumunipun.* He became more and more astonished. *Adja *-*.* Don't overdo it. 3 emphatic. *Tak djaluk kanṭi * kowé adja mèlu édan²an.* I beg you not to get involved in that mess. **ke*en** excessive. *Rada ke*en olèhmu sudjanan.* You're being overcautious. *Ke*en banget olèhé ngrugèkaké negara.* The damage caused to the nation was incalculable. **m/di*aké** 1 to make sth worse. 2 to emphasize, exaggerate. **pa·m*** emphasis

bânggâ to resist, struggle. *Sing * dipatèni.* Those who put up a struggle are killed.

banggèl **m*** *var of* M·BANGGEL. **m/di*** 1 to snap at (as though to bite). 2 to give a rebuttal (in debating)

banggel **m*** undercooked, raw inside

banggi 1 to resist (*sbst kr for* BANGGA). 2 (good) luck (*kr for* BARA). 3 *shf of* UBANGGI. *See also* PINTEN

bangir **ke*en** [of nose shape] too long and tapered. **m*** long and tapering [of noses: the most refined shape]. **m*-*** tapering too sharply. **m/di*aké** to make [a nose] taper. *Kanggo m*aké irung, betjiké jèn isih baji irungé diduduti penḍak ésuk.* To give your baby a nicely pointed nose, you should stroke it each morning. **m/di*i** to make [a nose] more pointed. *Jèn ngowahi gambarku mengko rada di*i siṭik panggonan irung.* If you fix up my picture, make the nose taper a little more.

bângkâ 1 coarse or harsh in texture. 2 dead but not yet decomposed. 3 (*or* ***n**) hard [of soil]

bangkak 1 hard [of soil]. 2 crop disease

bangkang a certain hard-shelled snail. **m*** to disobey, defy

bangkat strong

bangké corpse, carcass [of animals; *cr* of people]

bangkèk ***an** (**maḍya** *or* **pa·m̈·pekak** *ki*) waist(line). **m*** narrowed at the midsection

bangkèl 1 quarrelsome person. 2 to sell [*usu.* fabrics] on commission. ***an** 1 to sell as above. 2 [merchandise] sold on commission. 3 one who sells fabrics as above

bangkir banker

bangkjak *var of* BAKIJAK

bangkokan large and old [of animals; *cr* of people]

bangkol (*or* ***an**) a wooden peg fitted onto a shoulder carrying pole to prevent the rope that holds the burden from slipping

bangkong (*or* ***an** *or* *** kongkang**) large old frog. **(turu) m*** to lie around in bed instead of getting up

bangkrèh **bongkrah-*** *or* **bungkrah-*** in disorder, strewn with scattered items

bangkrong *var of* BANGKRUNG

bangkrung (*or* **m***) bent, curved [of the human back]

bangkrut bankrupt. **m/di*aké** to liquidate [a business]

bangku short-legged bench or table. *** ḍépok** *or* *** èndèk** low bench used as a seat

bango 1 a variety of stork. 2 small roadside shop dealing in goods or refreshments. *** ṭonṭong** a certain large stork with a long beak

bângsâ 1 (member of a) category, class. ** iberan* (the class of) flying animals. ** alus* supernatural beings. *Lawa kuwi dudu *né manuk.* Bats are not birds. *Sing ngenggoni padésan mau *né tukang golèk iwak.* Fishermen inhabit the village. **né pari kang ditandur ing papan kono* the variety of rice that is planted there. 2 (member of a) nationality, ethnic group. ** mantja* foreigners. *rasa tresna ** patriotism. **ka*n** 1 group of people or things in the same category. 2 pertaining to a nation *or* group. *lagu ke*n* national anthem. **sa*** belonging to the same group/category/nation. *kita sa** all of us (in the nation). *Sing sa*né kuwi aku ora ngerti.* I don't know anything about that kind of thing.

bangsal large assembly hall. *** pantjaniti** palace conference hall

bangsat 1 outlaw. 2 *profane abusive term*

bangsawan aristocrat

bangsul *kr* *sbst var of* WANGSUL

bangun to wake up, get up *(oj)*. ***an** building, structure. **m/di*** to build (up). **m* anjar** to renovate. **m* tapa** to perform an act of asceticism. **m* tresna** the awakening of love. **m* turut** to obey. **pa·m*** real estate development/developer. *** ésuk** dawn (*see also* GAGAT). *** nikah** ceremony held to bolster a foundering marriage

banjak goose; swan. **(be)*an** restless. *Segarané be*an.* The sea is never still. **m*i** *cr* to act hastily and ineffectually. *** angrem** 1 (a certain nebulous spot in) the Southern Cross. 2 [of lances] long and slender. 3 heaped-up rice with an egg inside (for ritual ceremonies). *** ḍalang** 1 swan-shaped golden seal used in court ceremonies. 2 decorated copper piece on a horse's headgear. *** patra** a certain wild bird resembling a duck or goose

banjar a herring-like fish

banjin **dat *** hydrogen

banjol ***an 1** to make jokes, clown around. 2 a joke. **m*** to joke around

banju *ng,* **toja** *kr* water; fluid. ** asem (djeruk, lsp.)* tamarind (orange, *etc.*) juice. ** djero* deep water. *Ora ana * mili menḍuwur munggah.* Like father, like son. *kaja digebjur * sewindu lawasé* to feel relieved. ***n̂ 1** specially prepared water for blackening the teeth. 2 the bathing of a fighting cock. **lara *nen** to have diarrhea. **m* 1** resembling water. *Tatuné m*.* The wound is watery. *Suguhané m* mili.* The refreshments were abundant. 2 *(psv* **di***)* to bathe, wash down. *Djagoné di*.* The fighting cock was doused with water (between rounds). **(m)be*** *(***te·toja** *kr)* to urinate. **m/di*n̂i** to supply with water. *mbanjoni sawah²* to irrigate rice paddies. *Keḍelénipun dipun tojani toja énggal.* Place the soybeans in fresh water. *** asin** salt water, brackish water. *** daging** meat broth. *** goḍog·an** boiled drinking water. *** karo lenga** incompatible. *** kawah** *or* *** ke·kawah·ing ari²** forewater, amniotic fluid. *** keras** preservative fluid. *** kluwak** liquid (used as a blood tonic) in which *kluwak* spice has been soaked. *** landa** carbonated water. *** lanḍa** water in which burnt rice stalks have been soaked (used as shampoo). *** lèḍèng** running (piped-in) water. *** leri** water in which rice has been washed prior to cooking. *** maṣ** gilding fluid used in embroidery. *** mateng** boiled drinking water. *** mawar** rosewater (for washing the face). *** p·in·erang** inseparable. *** rasa** mercury, quicksilver. *** saring·an** filtered water. *** setaman** a preparation of water and flowers used in the wedding ceremony. *** susu** mother's milk. *** tangi** warm water for bathing children and invalids. *** tawa(r)** fresh (*i.e.* not salt) water. *** t·um·ètès** *wj* sound effect produced by the puppet master tapping with slow steady beats on the box *(koṭak)*. *** ka·urip·an** water having the power to revive the dead. *** waju** water that has been kept overnight. *** wantah** fresh (*i.e.* not salt) water; unboiled drinking water. **(m)* wara** to abstain from using water as a form of asceticism. *** wisuh(an)** water in finger bowls placed on the dining table

bank *(prn* **bang)** bank. ** Indonesia* Bank of Indonesia

banon brick; cube *(kr for* BATA)

bantah *(or* ***an)** argument, quarrel. **(be)*-an** to quarrel with each other. **m/di*(i)** to argue (over)

bantal pillow. ***an 1** to use a pillow. 2 pincushion. 3 railroad tie. 4 dam in a sugar-cane field. *** dawa** Dutch wife (long pillow for snuggling). *** pipi** small pillow for the cheek. *** susun** dam in a sugar-cane field

bantâlâ *oj* earth

bantas 1 [of sounds] clear, carrying. 2 of high quality

bantat [of baked goods] heavy because insufficiently leavened

banten **be* 1** human sacrifice. 2 expendable soldiers

banṭèng 1 wild cow/bull. *Pangamuké kaja * ketaton.* He raged savagely. 2 a variety of palm tree. **be*** fighter; fighter for *or* champion of [a cause]. **m*** obstinate, recalcitrant. *** warèng** small bull; cow

banter 1 fast. *Plajuné *.* He ran fast. *Olèhé ngetokaké ḍuwit *.* Money goes right through his fingers. 2 hard, forceful; loud. *Njambut-gawéné *.* He worked hard. *Olèhé tapa *.* He devoted himself to meditation. *mbengok ** to yell loudly

banting ***an** to hit and throw down. **ke* 1** to get hurled. *Prauné ke* ing watu.* The boat was flung against the rocks. 2 at odds with. *Jèn ditimbang karo gagahé, ke* rupané.*

His face doesn't go with his dashing attitude. **m/di*** to hurl, fling down. *Matjan mau di* kebo.* The kerbau flung the tiger to the ground. *Regané di*.* The price was slashed.

bantjak 1 woven-bamboo food container for ceremonial feasts. 2 name of a white-masked wajang clown. ***an** a ritual feast held to signalize a special event in a child's life. **m/di*i** to honor [a child] with a feast. *** ḍojok** two-man comedy show performed by men wearing white and black masks respectively

bantjânâ obstacle, hazard

bantjar copious and free-flowing. *Ilining legèn *.* The sweet sap poured out [from the tree trunk].

bantjèt a certain small frog

bantji 1 an effeminate man. 2 an asexual person. 3 a plant whose leaves are used in folk medicines. **ke*n̂** [of garments] too small *or* short

bantjik *var of* ANTJIK-AN. **m*** dead person's spirit controlling a medium in trance

bantu 1 help, assistance. 2 auxiliary troops, reinforcements. ***n̂** *or* ***an** help, assistance. *banton ḍuwit* financial aid. *bantuan batin* moral support. ***-b·in·antu** to help each other. **be*n̂** *or* **be*an** 1 help, assistance. 2 to cooperate. *Jèn be*an nggawané dadi ènṭèng.* If we carry it together, it'll be light. **m/di*-*** to lend a hand, pitch in. **m/di*k̂aké** to offer smn else's services; to have smn help. *Pemerintah mbantokaké ahli ékonomi loro marang perusahan mau.* The government had 2 economists assist the company. **m/di*(n̂i)** to help smn. **m/di*n̂i** *gram* to modify. **pa·m*** 1 helper, assistant. 2 help, aid, assistance. 3 *gram* auxiliary. *tembung krija pem** auxiliary verb. **pam* letnan dua** (*abbr:* **Pel. Da.**) warrant officer. **pam* letnan satu** (*abbr:* **Pel. Tu.**) chief warrant officer. *See also* BIJANTU

bâpâ father. **ke*n** resembling one's father in nature. **m/di*** to call smn father; to regard smn as a father. *** bijung** parents. *** ka·sulah anak ka·polah.** A child is responsible for the commitments of his deceased father. *** paman** uncle (parent's younger sibling). *See also* BAPAK

bapak *ng kr,* **râmâ** *ki* 1 father. 2 *adr, title* older and/or higher-ranking male. ***(n)é** *adr* husband (if the couple have children). ***(n)é genḍuk/ṭolé** my husband *(oblique reference term).* **m/di*** to call smn father; to regard smn as a father. *** angkat** foster father. *** geḍé** uncle (parent's older sibling). *** k(u)walon** stepfather. *** maratuwa** father-in-law. *** putjung** a tiny red beetle. *** tjilik** uncle (parent's younger sibling). *See also* BAPA, PAK

bapak̊isme emphasis placed on father-son type relationships in Indonesian bureaucracy

bapang 1 signpost, sign board. 2 a certain classical dance performed by males. ***an** 1 earrings that extend sideways. 2 winged kite. **m*** with arms outstretched sideways

baptis baptism. *djeneng ** Christian name. **m/di*** to baptize

bar 1 after. ** mangan* after he ate. *nèk * saka gambar iḍup* on the way [home] from the movie. 2 finished, over; to finish. *Penggawéjanku wis *.* My work is done. *Adja malang-tanggung jèn njambut-gawé mengko ora *-* lho.* Don't dawdle over the job or you'll never finish it. *** dji * bèh** (*shf of* **bubar sidji bubar kabèh**) if one quits we'll all quit. *See also* BUBAR, LEBAR

bar- *see also under* BR- (*Introduction, 2.9.3*)

bârâ 1 fringe hanging from a military sash on either side of the belt buckle. 2 **(banggi** *kr)* (good) luck. 3 hundred million. *sa** 100,000,000. 4 a certain type of fishing gear. ***-*(né)** by good luck. **m/di*** to attach fringe to. *tjinḍé binara* fringed silken cloth. **m·be*** to travel around in search of a livelihood. *** béré** by good luck. *See also* PIRA, PIRANG

barah leprosy

barak 1 age (group). *wong² lanang sa* karo aku* men about my age. 2 temporary quarters for large numbers of people. 3 a house where ill people are quarantined. ***an** a contemporary. *Slamet kuwi *anku.* Slamet is about my age. ***-*** lined up. ***-* dawa banget** standing in a long line. **m*** 1 to stand in a line/row. 2 (*psv* **di***) to quarantine [people]. **sa*an** the same age group. *wong² sa*anku* all the people my age. *Botjah² kuwi kabèh sa*an.* Those boys are all about the same age.

barang 1 thing, object; stuff, matter; goods. ** werna²* all kinds of things. ** tjuwèr* a liquid. *Ing kana ana * anèh.* There's sth funny over there. ** sing lagi karembug* what is being discussed. ** kesenijan* work of art, art object. ** klonṭong* clothing material, *esp.* cotton or linen. ** pendjenengan* *punapa sampun pendjenengan asta?* Have you picked up your baggage yet? **-* wetonan negara lija* imported goods. 2 basic gamelan scale; certain notes of the 5- and 7-note scales. 3 ...or something; ...or anything; ...and things like that. *Sekolahku arep ana kraméan, nganggo gamelan *.* Our school is having a party, with gamelan music and everything. *Bener wis tau tampa potrèté *, nanging gambar iku sok gèsèh karo wudjudé.* It's true they had received a picture of her and all that, but pictures are sometimes different from the reality. *Adja ndadak isan-isin *.* Don't go feeling embarrassed. *Aku ora krasa sajah ora *.* I wasn't tired or anything. ***an** entertainment performed by traveling players. *nanggap *an* to hire such a performance. **-** *or* ***-bèrèng** [not] anything. *Jèn lagi kalah satus rong atus rupijah baé durung *-*.* If you lose 100 or 200 rupiahs, it doesn't matter. *Botjah ora nakal ora *-* kok diukum.* The boy wasn't naughty or anything but he got punished! **m/di*** to perform as a professional entertainer. *Sabubaré m*, tukangé sulap bandjur mulih.* After the magician did his show, he went home. *tukang m* menjanji ing warung² ing Paris* a Paris café singer. **m* amuk** to go on the rampage. **m* gawé** to hold a party, *usu.* to celebrate a wedding or circumcision. **m/di·be*** to perform professionally. **m·be* wirang** to make a show of being embarrassed. **sa*** whatever; anything. *sregep ing sa* gawé* hard-working in whatever work he does. *Sa* kang diweruhi digatèkaké.* Everything she saw, she took seriously. **sa* kalir** anything; whatever. *** ḍéngah** any object, anything. *** geḍé** gamelan octave. *** m̈·piring** gamelan scale combining the 5- and 7-note scales. *** tandang** any action, whatever one does

barat strong wind occurring *usu.* during the rainy season

barbèh *see* BAR

bardji *see* BAR

barèh **borah-*** in disorder, disarranged, scattered

barèng *rg var of* BENḌÉ

bareng *ng,* **sareng** *kr* 1 when [so-and-so happened]. *Wong². * weruh A paḍa ptg brengok.* When the people saw A, they cheered. ** ngarepaké beḍug* before [a past] noon. ** asuné édan wis digawa lunga* after the mad dog had been taken away. 2 whereas, while. *Kowé anaké mung sidji, * aku anaké papat.* You have only 1 child; I have 4. 3 together. *Ajo *.* Let's go together. *Botjah² ambjur *, bjur.* The boys jumped in at the same time. ***an** 1 together (with), accompanied (by). *Paḍa mangan *an.* They ate together. *Ora bisa *an kantja semono akèhé.* You're not allowed to have that many people with you. 2 a companion. *kantja *anku* the person who was with me. **-** at the very same time. **be*an** together (with). *Agami Hinḍu kalijan agami Buḍa punika saged ngrebda sasarengan ing tanah Djawi.* Hinduism and Buddhism flourished side by side in Java. **ke*an** to come together unintentionally. *Ana ing dalan ke*an karo kantjané.* He ran into a friend of his along the way. **m/di*aké** to cause sth to accompany. *Olèhé ngirim di*aké buku²né.* He sent it along with the books. **m/di*i** 1 to come together with intentionally. *Aku arep m*i Siti njang pasar.* I'm going to meet Siti at the marketplace. 2 to accompany; to coincide with. *Ḍèké ora seneng di*i* He doesn't like to have people with him. *Nalika ḍèké teka m*i aku ndandani pit.* He came as I was fixing my bicycle. *Ali m*i manggon ana omah kono.* Ali moved into the house with us.

barep *ng,* **badjeng** *kr,* **bajun** *ki* **m*** *or* **pa·m*** firstborn child. *Anaké telu, kang pem* wédok.* They had 3 children; the oldest was a girl. *m* urip* oldest living child

barès straightforward, without airs or embellishment. **m/di*i** to make sth plain. *Apa kowé gelem djandji, jèn dak *i kowé ora bakal nesu?* Promise not to get mad if I tell it to you straight? *** kurès** plain and honest, straightforward

barèt beret

bari (*or* **m***) (together) with

baris 1 to march. *ndeleng pradjurit ** to watch soldiers marching. ** penḍem* (to make) a secret march. 2 package to be carried by hand. 3 rooster feather from the neck or tail. ***an** brigade; line of marchers. **an P* a brigade of beggars who fought in the Indonesian war for independence. **an pemaḍam api* fire brigade. **m/di*** to tie up [a bundle to be carried by hand]. **m/di*aké** to have [people] march. *Di*aké papat².* They had them march in ranks of 4. **m/di*i** to march for smn *or* before sth.

barkas *var of* BERKAS
barkat *var of* BERKAT
barléjan diamond. * *sakeret* a 1-carat diamond
barlèn silver-plated metal; chrome
barlijan *var of* BARLÉJAN
barlin *var of* BARLÈN
baro *-* a white rice porridge with coconut sugar and grated coconut: served at ritual ceremonies
barong 1 mane. 2 tassel, fringe. 3 *wj* a giant-king character type. ***an** 1 a show featuring a man dressed as a monster; the feature performer in such a show. **an matjanan* a tiger monster-figure. 2 having a mane. 3 fringed, having tassels. 4 thorny bushes growing around bamboo stalks. **m*** to adorn. *Juju rumpung m* rongé.* [He's] a poor man living in a fine home. * **asépak** 1 a certain batik design. 2 figure painted on a saddle flap. *See also* SINGA
baros a variety of tree
baru new. ***ñ** new plant grown from a cutting. **m/di*** to plant [a field] with a new or unusual type of rice
baruna west wind
barung *wj* in time with *or* simultaneous with [a gamelan beat]. *gendèr* * the leading *gendèr* instrument, which performs functions essential to the shadow play
barus *see* KAPUR
barut a cut, scratch. **ke*** to get a cut *or* scratch. *Sikilku ke* pang pelem.* I scratched my leg on a mango branch.
bas 1 work supervisor, boss. 2 string bass. 3 leaf stalk from a certain palm tree (*gebang*): used for making rope. ***-*an** a children's game played by tossing pebbles onto a marked-out diagram, *or* by moving pieces on a diagram of squares. **nge/di*i** to act as foreman of. *Sapa sing nge*i sumur kuwi?* Who's supervising the work on that well?
bâsâ 1 language. * *Djawa (anjar, kuna)* (modern, old-fashioned) Javanese. *ahli* * language specialist; linguist. *djuru* * translator; interpreter. *keslijo* * (to make) a slip of the tongue. *unggah-ungguhing* * social levels of speech *(see Introduction, 5).* 2 (to speak) Krama. *Aku * karo wong tuwaku.* I speak Krama to my parents. 3 to have [a certain] kinship relationship. *Kowé karo aku * kakang.* You are my younger brother. 4 *rg* only. *Ora * ḍemen, malah tresna banget.* He not only likes it—he loves it. 5 when (*var of* BASAN). ***n** *or* ***n-*nan** to address each other (converse) in Krama. **be*n** a saying, a set expression. *Udjaring be*n...* As the saying goes... **m/di*aké** 1 to put (translate) into Krama. 2 to express in the form of a saying. *Wong tuwa sinau marang anaké iku di*aké "kebo nusu gudèl."* Parents learning from their children is proverbially expressed as "the kerbau takes nourishment from its calf." 3 to speak Krama on smn's behalf, *e.g.* applying Krama Inggil words to oneself when speaking to a servant, using the words the servant would use. **m/di*ni** to speak to [smn; each other] in Krama. * **antya** a variety of humble Ngoko *(see Introduction, 5.5; see also* ANTYA). * **pa·dina·n** ordinary colloquial speech. * **gantjar·an** prose. * **pa·gunem·an** colloquial speech. * **logat** dialect. * **pe·pernès·an** flowery expressions flattering a person of the opposite sex. * **r·in·engga** stereotyped literary expression
basah 1 [of bodies] decomposed. 2 *title prefixed to a warrior's name.* ***an** Javanese royal attire. **m/di*(i)** to sprinkle water on. *Klambi² sing wis di*i bandjur diringkel.* She dampened the clothes [for ironing] and rolled them up.
basan (*or* **m***) 1 when; and then after that. *mBasan ora ana sing mangsuli, ḍèké lunga.* When nobody answered, he left. 2 whereas, while. *Kowé sugih bisa tuku pit, m* aku mlarat.* You're rich, you can afford a bicycle; I'm poor.
basang *var of* BASAN
basèh *var of* BASIK
baseng to have a rotten or putrid odor
basi large serving bowl with a cover
basih *var of* BASIK
basik **m·bosak-*** disorderly. *Kamaré mbosak-*.* His room is a mess.
basin a foul odor
baskârâ *oj* sun
baskom wash basin
basma *oj* to burn
basmi to burn (*root form: kr for* OBONG)
basmibuta *oj* to burn to ashes
basoka bazooka gun
basu(h) *var of* WASUH
basuki to prosper, flourish
basul *kr* *sbst var of* WANGSUL
bâtâ *ng,* **banon** *kr* 1 brick; brick wall. 2 cube, brick-shaped block. *ujah sa** a block

of salt. *n in the shape of a brick *or* block. *ujah *n* salt in blocks. **m*** brick-shaped; brick-like. **m* rubuh** loudly in unison. *Wah suraké wong m* rubuh.* The crowd cheered wildly. *keplok m* rubuh* to applaud in unison. **m* sa·rimbag** squarish [of handwritten Javanese script]. *** bumi** brick wall. *** luluh** bricks being processed. *** mentah** unbaked brick

batal [of religious ritual] annulled by a canceling influence. *Olèhku pasa *, djalaran aku mau lali ngombé.* I broke my fast–I forgot and drank sth. *Ali wuduné * amarga kesénggol botjah wadon.* Ali's ritual cleaning was invalidated when a girl accidentally touched against him. **m/di*aké** to render invalid. *Slamet m*aké nijaté lunga Sala.* Slamet canceled his plan to go to Solo.

batalijon battalion

batang ***an** 1 the answer to sth. 2 a certain pattern of drumbeats. **m/di*** 1 to guess (the answer to). *Tjangkrimanku *en.* Guess my riddle! 2 to beat a certain drum *(kenḍang)*

baṭang 1 *cr* dead body. 2 carrion. **m*** to float on one's back (as a form of swimming). **m* kèli** to be carried along with the current. *** gadjah** one who gains prestige in spite of being in disfavor with those higher up. *** le·laku** person making a solitary journey. *** utjap²** two people journeying together

baṭârâ *wj* male mythological deity. *asotya ** wise; clairvoyant. **b·in·aṭara** god-like. *ratu binaṭara* revered king

baṭari female mythological deity

batas *var of* WATES

batèh *rg var of* BATIH

batek̄ **m/di*(i)** to pull (at), tug (on)

bateré *var of* BATRÉ

bates *var of* WATES

baṭi 1 profit, gain; profitable. **né wong sregep* the profits of a hard worker. *Olèhé dedagangan *.* His business is making money (*i.e.* flourishing). *Pitku tak dol.–* apa ora?* I sold my bicycle.–Did you make anything on it? *tuna satak, * sanak* to lose a little but gain a friend (*or* customer). 2 to produce children. *Apa wis *?* Any children yet [in your marriage]? ***ǹ** amount of profit. *Batèné Rp. 5,000.* He made 5,000 rupiahs on it. **ke*ǹ** profitable. **m/di*** to make [a certain] profit. *Ḍèké m* Rp. 5,000.* He cleaned up 5,000 rupiahs. **m/di*k̀aké** to create a profit for, be beneficial to. *mbaṭèkaké wong dagang* profitable for the businessman. **m/di*ǹi** to make a profit on [a transaction]

batih one's household; one's dependents. *Omah tjilik, * akèh.* The house is small and he has many mouths to feed. **(be)*an** next door; in the neighborhood. *A manggon be*an karo B.* A lives near B.

baṭik *ng,* **serat** *kr* fabric (to be) worked by the batik process, *i.e.* dyed successively with different colors, each dyeing preceded by applying wax patternings to those portions which are not to receive that color. ***an** 1 batik work; batik-making. *seratan Sala* a Solonese batik. **ané misuwur banget.* Her batik work is very famous. 2 pock-marked. **m/di*** 1 to do batik work. 2 (*psv* **di***) to work [fabric] in batik. **m/di*aké** to make batik for smn; to have batik made, have fabric worked in batik. **pa·m*** the working of batik. *Pam* iki tanpa pola.* This batik was made without a pattern. *** andong·an** batik goods given to servants *usu.* as Lebaran gifts. *** tjap-tjapan** printed (*i.e.* low-quality) batik. *** tulis** hand-worked (hence desirable) batik

batin *ng,* **batos** *kr* inward (feeling); one's inner self. *matja ** to read to oneself. *bantuan ** moral support. *Djroning * mikir², golèk réka.* Inwardly, she was trying to think of a plan. *Ing * arep diwènèhaké embokné.* He made up his mind he'd give it to his mother. ***é** 1 inwardly. 2 what one says to oneself. **ku: wong saméné kok ḍa arep lunga kabèh!* I said to myself, what a lot of people are going! **ka*an** 1 pertaining to the inner self. *ahli ke*an* a mystic. *ngèlmu ke*an* mysticism. 2 true Javanese religion (as contrasted with superimposed religions). **m/di*** to ponder inwardly

batir *var of* BATUR

batis *inf var of* BAPTIS

batjek̄ sodden; bogged down. **ke*en** waterlogged

batjem ***an** food partially cooked by steaming, then finished by frying. **m/di*** to cook by this process

batjin foul-smelling, rotten. **-* iwak, ala² sanak.* Even though he's no good, he's still a relative.

batjira 1 open field, plain. 2 housing complex in Jogjakarta (formerly a field)

batjok ∗**an** act of hitting with sth sharp. ∗-∗ to strike *or* chop at repeatedly. ∗-∗**an** to hit each other with sharp objects. **ke**∗ to get hit. **m/di**∗**(i)** to strike, slash. *Matjan di∗ nganggo arité.* He struck the tiger with his sickle.
batjot *cr* mouth
batjuk *var of* BATJOK
batjut 1 *var of* BANDJUR. 2 *var of* BATJOT. **ke**∗ (now that it's) too late; but (on the contrary)
baṭok coconut shell. **m**∗ resembling a coconut shell. ∗ **bolu** half-coconut shell with 3 eyes. ∗ **bolu isi madu** person of low background but high intelligence. ∗ **mengkureb** hemispheric shape (like a face-down half-coconut-shell)
batos inward (feeling), inner self (*kr for* BATIN)
batré 1 flashlight. 2 flashlight battery
batu 1 stone, rock (*see also* WATU). *tukang* ∗ stonemason; bricklayer; builder. 2 flint (for striking fire). ∗ **api** 1 flint. 2 jewelry, watches. ∗ **batré** flashlight battery
baṭu ∗**ñ(an)** to pool capital for a business enterprise. *A baṭon karo B.* A and B started a business together. **m**∗ 1 to contribute to a capital enterprise; to buy a share in an enterprise. 2 to eat together from one large bamboo plate
baṭuk *ng kr,* **(pa)larap·an** *or* **pamiḍangan** *ki* forehead. ∗**an** 1 portion of a hat that covers the forehead. 2 portion of a shoe *or* slipper that covers the toes. ∗ **banjak** *or* ∗ **lengar** or ∗ **nonong** bulging forehead. ∗ **ñj·séla tjenḍani** marble-like forehead (the classic ideal)
batuk‘-kering tuberculosis
batur 1 **(réntjang** *ng,* **abdi** *ki)* servant. 2 (*or* **be**∗) low brick or stone wall which keeps moisture back from the foundation of a house. **m/di**∗**aké** to put smn into smn else's service. *ngabdèkaké empu* to send a kris-maker into apprenticeship. **m/di**∗**i** to act as servant to. *Dipun abdèni tijang kaṭah.* He has a number of servants. **m/di·(be)**∗**(i)** to provide [a house] with a wall as above. ∗ **tuku·ñ** slave
bau 1 upper arm; *fig* labor, manpower; a helping hand. 2 square land measure: *ca.* 1.75 acres. *sawah se∗* a 1-*bau* rice paddy. 3 head of a village area. **be**∗ worker; one who performs a job. *Malingé ditekani para be∗ning pulisi.* The thief was surrounded by policemen. **(be)**∗**ñ** many *bau*'s; by the *bau. Sawahé (be)baon.* He owns acres and acres of paddy. **m/di**∗**ñi** to do [a job]. *Dibaoni ḍéwé.* He did it himself. **pa·m**∗**ñ** 1 supporting pole. 2 ship's mast. ∗ **ḍanjang** supporting beam in a house frame. ∗ **ḍenḍa** very powerful; **(m)**∗ **ḍenḍa ñj·tjakrawati** (to be) a firmly established ruler; one who is powerful, rich, respected. ∗**[né] ḍéwé** one's own relative; one's own servant, waiting on oneself. ∗ **kiwa tengen** one's total strength. ∗ **lawé·jan** 1 person with a dimple on the shoulder. 2 person whose last two (or more) spouses have died. ∗ **reksa** *see* BAUREKSA. ∗ **suku** 1 village worker who works in the paddies given to the village head man. 2 communal work done without pay. ∗ **tengen** trusted person, right-hand man
baud skilled (in), expert (at)
bauksit bauxite
baung 1 dog (children's, old people's word). 2 bear (animal). 3 a certain freshwater fish. **m**∗ [of dogs] to howl, whine
baureksa 1 ghost or spirit that inhabits a certain place. 2 one who has long held sway in a certain place. **sing m**∗ guardian spirit of a house, tree, *etc.*
bausastra dictionary. ∗ *basa Djawa* Javanese dictionary
baut 1 bolt, screw. 2 *inf* nut (onto which a bolt is screwed)
bâwâ 1 vocal musical prelude to a main musical number. 2 situation, circumstances. *∗né isih enom tur sugih pisan.* (His status is that) he's young, and rich too. 3 *gram* affix. ∗**né** it is to be expected (that...). **(m)**∗ **ḍéwé** independent, self-sufficient. **m**∗ **(swara)** to introduce a song *or* prayer with a prelude. **m/di**∗**ni** to hold sway over. ∗ **leksana** to fulfill a promise, put one's words into action. ∗ **rasa** counsel, advice. ∗ **swara** song prelude (*sms* 1 *above*). *See also* SEBAWA
bawah geographically a part of; domain. ∗**an** 1 [person, place] under the authority of. *Désa iki ∗an kuṭa Jogja.* This village is a sub-territory of Jogja. *Bajaré siṭik merga ḍèkè ∗an.* His pay is small–he's only a subordinate. 2 celebration of a family event. *Idjabé ésuk, ∗ané benginé.* The wedding was in the morning and the party was held that evening. **ke**∗ under the jurisdiction of. *ora ke∗ ora kepréntah* under

no authority, independent. **m/di*aké** to administer, have authority over

bawak wooden blade-holder for a certain hoe-like implement (*patjul*)

bawal a certain freshwater fish

bawânâ *var of* BUWANA

bawang 1 garlic. * *sa sijung* 1 clove of garlic. 2 a variety of mango. **m/di*** to season with garlic. * **koṭong** person who cannot contribute a full share of effort (*usu.* referring to a child in a game with older people). * **lanang** a garlic consisting of only one bud

bawasir 1 hemorrhoids. 2 deputy regent

bawat long-handled ceremonial umbrella of palm leaves

bawèl never satisfied, always nagging. **m/di*i** to nag *or* keep after smn

bawéra spacious, broad. *kamar kang* * a spacious room. *sawangan kang* * a sweeping view

bawi ***nipun** *sbst kr for* BAWA·NÉ

bawon 1 a share of a rice harvest received for one's services during the harvesting. *nganggo * talunan* [a field which is] planted on the principle that the harvest will be shared only by those who participate in its cultivation. 2 a certain size bundle of newly harvested rice plants. **m/di*i** to give smn his earned portion of the harvest

bawuk 1 dark gray. 2 [of clothing] faded, worn. 3 *term of endearment applied to little girls*

bawur 1 mixed (together). *kembang tjampur-** a bouquet of mixed flowers. 2 [of vision] blurred, hazy. **m/di*aké** 1 to mix [a variety of thing] together. 2 to cause [vision, view] to be blurred *or* unclear

bé 1 for, in favor of. *Kowé * sapa?* Who are you for? 2 to guess, bet. * *kowé durung mangan.* I bet you haven't had anything to eat. 3 name of the 6th year in the *windu* cycle. 4 to fall through. *Kentjané * amarga udan.* The appointment was canceled because of the rain.

be- *see also under* BA- (*Introduction, 2.9.2*)

béasiswā fellowship grant

beb- *see also under* B- (*Introduction, 3.1.3*)

bebah task, responsibility (*root form: kr for* BUBUH)

bebak **m/di*** to peel the skin or husk from (as the first step in processing rice, coffee)

beban a burden

bébas *var of* BEBAS

bebas 1 free(d). 2 bypass route. **m/di*aké** to set free. *Tawanan² wis paḍa di*aké.* The prisoners have been released. *m*aké negara saka pendjadjahan* to liberate a country from colonialism

bebed *ng kr,* **njamping** *ki* batik wraparound worn by males. ***an** to put on *or* wear the above. **m/di*i** to dress [a boy] in a wraparound. * **sabuk wala** child's wraparound worn with one end wrapped below the waist to form a sash

bebeg 1 clogged, stopped up. 2 overstuffed; overburdened. ***an** a dam. **m/di*** 1 to equip with a dam; to dam up. 2 to hold in/back, check, restrain. 3 to grind [herbs] to a powder

bebeh apathetic, listless

bèbèk duck (water bird). * **di·wuruk·i ng·langi** unnecessary; futile

bebel 1 stopped up, clogged; constipated. 2 dull-witted, mentally sluggish

bebeng **ke*** stillborn; *fig* frustrated

bèbèr spread, opened out. *wajang* * paper-scroll drama (*see also* WAJANG[a]). **m/di*(aké)** to spread, open out, display. *m* dagangané* to spread out one's merchandise. *m*aké pengalamané* to tell of one's experiences. *Ana tukang sulap m*aké kapinteranè njulap ana ing pasar.* A magician was displaying his skill in the marketplace.

bèbèt 1 ancestor; descendant; lineage. 2 unblemished in character and lineage. *See also* BIBIT

bebreg overabundant; burdensome

bèbrèk **m*** to widen, open further [of a torn place, wound, *etc.*]

bèbrèl *var of* BEBREL

bebrel **m*** poorly constructed, flimsy

bèbrèt **m*** to make a tearing sound [*e.g.* cloth ripping; an engine being raced]

bebret **m*** flimsy, easily ripped

bed 1 times around/encircling (*shf of* UBED). *Olèhé setagènan mung telung *.* His sash only goes around him three times. 2 *rpr* a blow or slash. *diantem mak ** to get punched

béda *ng,* **bènten** *kr* different. *Olèhé * nganti kaja bumi karo langit.* They're as different as earth and sky. ***né** (the) difference. **ku karo kowé* the difference between you and me. **m/di*** to irritate; to tease. **m/dibe*** to keep getting on smn's nerves *or* teasing smn. *mBok adja mbebéda aḍiné ta.* Don't pester your brother! **m/di*k(-*k)aké** to discriminate against

beḍad detached, loose

beḍaḍag **m*** fat and spreading [of body parts]

beḍag 1 to go hunting. * *pikat* to hunt game birds. 2 to chase. ***an** game animal. **be*** *or* **m(be)*** to hunt. **pa·m*** hunting ground

beḍagal *cr* *abusive term.* * *ala!* Damned fool! **di*** 1 to be coerced into [do]ing. 2 to be raped

bedah acts that are unethical by Moslem standards

beḍah 1 broken through, ripped open. *Témboké* *. The wall is broken through. * *sikilé* to have a cut on the foot. *Bané* *. The tire is slashed. *ḍokter* * surgeon. 2 to be overcome by force. *Kuṭané apa wis *?* Has the city been conquered? ***an** 1 a ripped place; a ripped-off piece, scrap. 2 small drainage ditch in a rice paddy. **m/di(be)*** to drain [water] from a paddy by runoff ditches. **m/di*aké** 1 to rip *or* break for smn. 2 to break accidentally. *Swarané kaja² m*aké kendangan kuping.* The noise was enough to shatter the ear drums. **m/di*(i)** 1 to cut/slash/break through. *m*i penganggo* to cut out garments. *Kasang *en nganggo blaṭimu.* Slit the bag with your blade. 2 to conquer, overcome. * **bumi** 1 price of a burial plot. 2 gravedigger's fee. 3 wages to one who looks after graves

beḍâjâ a certain court dance performed by females; performer of this dance

beḍal **m*** 1 to break loose from a tether or stall. 2 to leave [companions] against one's will

beḍâmâ 1 a certain weapon. 2 a type of axe

beḍami to enter into an agreement, *esp.* a peace treaty. ***ǹ** cessation of hostilities. *nanḍa-tangani piagem beḍamèn* to sign a cease-fire agreement

bédang **m*** having a flared rim (*shc from* LAMBÉ DANDANG)

beḍati oxcart

beḍawang *oj* land tortoise

beḍé 1 *var of* BAḌÉ. 2 *var of* BEḌÈK

beḍeḍeg **m*** 1 soft, mushy, soggy. 2 full to the brim; *fig* emotion-filled. **m*i ati** to astound

beḍèḍèh **m*** flabby, paunchy

bedèdèng **bedèdang-*** to walk with an arrogant swagger

bededeng ***an** *or* **m*** to become long and hard; *fig* to exert all one's strength

beḍegel **m*** to feel resentful

beḍegud vigorous, energetic

beḍegus *rpr* suddenly popping into view. *Mak * djebul kutjing.* Suddenly a cat appeared.

beḍèk ***an** 1 riddle, guessing game. 2 the answer to sth. **ané tjangkriman* the answer to a riddle. 3 (*or* ***-*an**) to ask each other riddles, play guessing games. **m/di*** to guess (at). *Bener olèhmu m* iku.* You guessed right. *Tak * mesṭi wedi.* I bet you would be afraid! **m/di*i** to have smn guess. *Aku *ana.* Ask me a riddle!

beḍèl **m/di*** 1 to perform surgery (on). *di* * mripaté* to have an eye operation. 2 to provide with an irrigation ditch; to divert [a stream]. 3 to disembowel

beḍel **m*** to crack *or* snap easily

bedèndèng *var of* BEDÈDÈNG

bèḍèng ***an** seed bed consisting of heaped-up soil between irrigation ditches

bèḍeng *var of* BÈḌÈNG

beḍenguk *var of* BEḌENGUS

beḍengul *var of* BEḌENGUS

beḍengus *rpr* a sudden appearance. *Mak * ana sapi mlaju nugel dalan.* Suddenly a cow came running down the middle of the road.

beḍès 1 *friendly and familiar term for addressing smn informally.* 2 *excl of surprise.* 3 *rg* ape, monkey

beḍiḍèt **ora m*** not flourish, not grow well [of plants]

beḍiḍig **m*** to consider oneself too good for manual labor

bediding chilly, chilled. *mangsa* * nighttime or early-morning chill. **m*** frightened

beḍiḍing *var of* BEDIDING

beḍigal **m*** 1 eccentric, strange-acting. 2 ill-mannered

beḍigas *ptg* * *or* ***an** *describing hasty ill-mannered actions.* *Ora aba² ḍisik mlebu omah blusuk *an.* He dashed into the house without even announcing his presence first.

beḍijang 1 a fire built for warmth *or* for keeping insects away. 2 to warm oneself at a fire

beḍil *ng,* **sendjâtâ** *kr* gun, rifle. ***-*an** (**sendjatan²an** *kr*) 1 toy gun. 2 to exchange gunfire. **m/di*(i)** to shoot sth. **pa·m*** 1 act of shooting. *Pam*é kliwat.* He missed. 2 distance traveled by a bullet. *Dohé* *sapam∗.* It's a rifle-shot away. ∗ **angin** air rifle. ∗ **lantak·an** breech loader. ∗ **pantjar wutah** shotgun

bedinan *ng,* **bedintenan** *kr* daily. *bahan ∗* everyday supplies. *klambi ∗* ordinary dress. *See also* PA·DINA·N

bedintenan *kr for* BEDINAN

bedja *var of* BEGDJA

bedjad 1 to fall apart. *tampah ∗* a basket that is coming to pieces. 2 socially unacceptable. *watak ∗* of bad character. *moril ∗* immoral. 3 *slang* [of money] gone, used up. *Duwitku ∗.* I'm broke. **m/di∗i** to wreck, tear to pieces

bedjadji **m∗** of value; to have worth. *Saiki aku ora duwé barang sing m∗.* Right now I have nothing of value. *See also* ADJI[a]

bedjagir toady, yes-man

bedjèr having a discharge from the eyes

bèdji 1 pond, reservoir. 2 large-headed nail. **∗ǹ** jeweled [of button earrings for pierced ears]

bedjigur coffee grounds

bédjog (person who is) lame because of one nonfunctioning leg

bedjos capable; can, be able

bedjud **m∗** stubborn, headstrong

bedjudjag **∗an** to wander around idly, loaf around the house. **m∗** ill-mannered, insolent

beḍo a draw, stalemate

bedodok **m∗** 1 boastful. 2 eager to [do]

beḍoḍok **m∗** 1 [of birds' feathers] ruffled, standing on end, *e.g.* from fear. 2 to swell out [of water-soaked seeds]. **m/di∗aké** to cause [feathers] to stand on end

bedodong **m∗** 1 bloated, stiff and swollen. 2 [of penis] erect. 3 *cr* dead

beḍog 1 short-handled axe *esp.* for digging out tree stumps. 2 theft of stray domestic animals. **∗an** 1 a hacked-out stump; act *or* result of digging out a stump. 2 stolen domestic animal. *Saben dina ∗ané pitik olèh loro.* He steals two chickens every day. **∗-∗an** act of stealing [animals] *or* luring away [women]. ∗ **b·in·eḍog** to steal [poultry] from each other. **m/di∗(i)** 1 to dig out [stumps]. 2 to steal [animals]. 3 to kidnap

beḍogol a stump with plants sprouting from it. **∗an** *cr* children, descendants

beḍol **∗an** *wj* technique of removing puppets from the banana log where they are kept. **m/di∗(i)** to pull out, uproot. **m∗ omah** to move, change one's residence. **pa·m∗an** act of pulling out *or* uprooting. *Pam∗ané winih saka ḍeḍeran ngarah-arah.* The seedlings are taken from the seedbed with great care. ∗ **désa** to move an entire village to a new settlement. ∗ **djangkar** to weigh anchor. ∗ **gendéra** to withdraw a military force. ∗ **songsong** traditional Jogjanese court ceremony held after the rice-mountain ceremony (*grebeg*)

béḍor arrowhead

bedor name of one of the small playing cards (*kertu tjilik*). *main ∗* to play cards

bedud **∗an** (**watang·an** *ki?*) opium pipe. **m∗** headstrong, obstinate

beḍuḍak a certain poisonous snake

beḍuḍug **m∗** billowing out; bloated

bedudung **m∗** stuffed, bloated (from overeating)

beḍug 1 mosque drum; gamelan drum resembling a mosque drum. 2 sounding of the mosque drum at noon, to summon Moslems to prayer. 3 noon. **m∗** [to fast] only until noon (rather than sundown). *pasa m∗* to fast until noon. **sa∗** 1 the same size as a mosque drum. 2 time period from 6 A.M. to 12 noon. *Sa∗ njambut gawé terus.* He worked straight through the morning. ∗ **awan** noon. ∗ **bengi** *or* ∗ **dawa** midnight. ∗ **telu** 3:30 A.M.

beḍugul not dressed properly; not wearing a kris

beḍul *var of* BEḌOL

beḍungul *rpr* a sudden appearance. *Aku kagèt merga mak ∗ ḍèkè wis nang ngarepku.* I was startled when suddenly there he was in front of me.

beḍungus *var of* BEḌUNGUL

bèg 1 *rpr* sth falling. 2 back (soccer player/position)

beg *rpr* a dull plopping sound

bega speech difficulty, aphasia

begadad **m∗** to steal domestic animals

begadag *var of* BEGADAD

begadjagan to exhibit crude behavior, have bad manners

begadjul **∗an** playboy, wolf. **m∗** to chase after women

begagah *var of* BERGAGAH

bégal bandit. **∗an** 1 robbery, holdup. 2 loot. **m/di∗** to hold up, rob

begandjok a building in the style of a mosque

begar pleased, delighted

begasi *var of* BERGASI
begdja (good) luck; fortunate, at peace with one's environment. ***n(-*n)** to try one's luck. *Aku tuku lotré mau ja mung *n²*. I bought a lottery ticket just to see if I could win. ***-*né** at best. *ngGonmu mantjing *-*né olèh kulit durèn.* You go fishing and the best you can get is a fruit peeling! **ka*n** (good) luck. *gawé ka*n* to bring luck. *olèh ** to have a stroke of luck. *** ke·ma·jang·an** great good luck. *** tjilaka** good luck and bad; through thick and thin
begeblug epidemic
begedèl *var of* BERGEDÈL
begèdjègan ill-mannered, insolent
begedjil [of children] obstreperous
begedud **m*** willful, obstinate
begegeg *var of* BERGEGEG
begègèh *var of* BERGÈGÈH
begèr delighted, pleased
begidjig ***an** ill-mannered, badly brought up
begigih *var of* BERGIGIH
beginggèng **m*** to improve one's condition (physically, materially)
begleḍug low rumbling sound of an active volcano
bégod **m*** stubbornly disobedient
begog stupid person. **m*** to act stupid, *i.e.* sit around staring blankly into space
begogok **m*** to sit completely motionless
begok a variety of bird
begonḍal *var of* BEGUNḌAL
begu *var of* BEGA
beguguk **m*** to stand one's ground, refuse to give in. **m* n̈g·kuṭa waton** to defy authority
begunḍal yes-man, sycophant
begupon pigeon house (*var of* PA·GUPU·Ñ)
beguron institution for religious and mystic training (*var of* PA·GURU·Ñ)
bèh all (*shf of* KABÈH). *Bar dji bar *.* If one leaves, we all leave!
bèi *shf of* NGABÈH·I
béja 1 cost, charge. 2 customs duty. **pa*n** customs office. **pra*** *sms* *
bèjès small river crab (young of the JUJU)
béjo mynah bird. **m*** to mimic
béjongan the young of a certain freshwater fish (*kutuk*)
bèk 1 *adr* aunt (*var of* BI). 2 (*prn* **bèk̄**) fullback (soccer player/position). ** kanan* or ** tengen* right fullback. ** kiri* or ** kiwa* left fullback. 3 square land measure: 400 *ru*'s, or *ca.* 1.9 acres. 4 *var of* BÈN. 5 *rg var of* BIBI. ***é** maybe. ** ḍèwèké sing ndjupuk.* I bet *he* took it. **m*** 1 to admit defeat. *Aku trima mbèk nèk dikon balapan karo kowé.* I give up before I start if I have to race with you. 2 possession, belonging (*inf var of* DARBÈK). *Iki m*é sapa?* Whose is this? 3 and, together with. *matja m* mangan* to read while eating. 4 sheep's baa (*see also* EMBÈK). 5 *var of* M·BIK. **nge/di*i** to claim possession of. *Kuwi duwèkku, adja di*i.* That's mine–don't try to get it away from me.
bek̄ 1 *rpr* a thud. *Slamet tiba mak *.* Slamet fell down. 2 full; filled with sorrowful or bewildering thoughts. ***-*an** in great pain/difficulty; with strenuous effort. *Guntingé mau tak golèki bek²an nang kamar.* I looked *everywhere* in my room for my scissors. **nge/di*i** to fill sth (*var of* N̈G/DI·KE·BEK·I)
béka (*or* **m***) (to be) a nuisance/hindrance. **m/di*ni** to bother *or* be a nuisance to
bekakas 1 equipment, necessities. ** mantu* things needed for entertaining wedding guests. ** omah* household furnishings. 2 materials/parts of which sth is made
bekakrah *ptg ** *or* **m*** in disorder, a mess
bekakrak̀an confused *or* disordered actions
bekamal salted (*rg var of* KAMAL)
bekangkang **m*** to stand *or* lie with the legs spread wide apart
bekas mark, trace. ** getih* blood stain. *ilang tanpa ** gone without a trace
bekasak ***an** 1 boorish behavior. 2 jungle demon, evil spirit of the forest. *wong *an* boor. **(m)*** rough, crude
bekatul *var of* KATUL
bekèkèng **m/di*(aké)** 1 to seize and pinion. 2 to rape
bèkèl 1 protrusion of the stomach. 2 a variety of fish
bèkel small metal objects used for playing a girls' game resembling jacks. *bal ** small rubber ball used in this game. ***an** the game played with this equipment
bekel 1 (head) village administrative official. 2 low-ranking official at court. **ka*an** area administered by the above village official
bekem **m/di*** to clutch in the hand
bekèn well known, famous
bekeneng *ptg ** *or* ***an** to engage in heated argument
bekèngkèng *var of* BEKÈKÈNG. *ptg ** having

the legs spread wide apart. **m*** to spread the legs apart. **m/di*aké** to spread [the legs] wide apart

bekengkeng **m*** unyielding. *dandan* * to dress in stiffly ironed clothes. *Ḍèké m* ora gelem lunga.* He stubbornly refused to go.

bèker cup, trophy. *djam* * alarm clock. **m*** [of horses] with head drooping from fatigue

bekèr **m*** to howl , screech, yowl

bekès *var of* BEKÈR

beketjeg **m*** to sputter; *fig* to talk copiously

bekètjot *var of* BEKITJOT

bekètrèk *var of* BLEKÈTRÈK

beki:k̄ **bekak-*** to shriek repeatedly. **m*** *sg* to shriek. *ptg* **b·r·ekik** *pl* to shriek

bekikuk crossbreed between a domestic chicken (*pitik*) and a certain hybrid chicken (*bekisar*)

bekingking a certain small snail. **m*** *intsfr* thin, emaciated

bekis **m*** [of animals] to spit

bekisar crossbreed between a domestic chicken (*pitik*) and a wild chicken (*ajam alas*)

bekisik **m*** [of skin] dried, cracking

bekitjik **m*** 1 to sputter; *fig* talkative. 2 to argue habitually. 3 to cheat at cards.

bekitjot a certain leaf-eating snail

bekitu ***an** *or* **bekita-*** to rant in anger

bekiwit **m*** to cheat at cards

bekok **m*** 1 addicted (to) [*esp.* smoking]. 2 [of tobacco leaves] badly formed. 3 ill-mannered

bekokrok **m*** 1 loose, coming unbound. 2 worthless

bekong measuring device, *esp.* for raw rice *or* oil. **m/di*** to measure out [rice, oil]

bekongkong *var of* BERKONGKONG

bekos **m*** to snort

békot *var of* BOIKOT

beksa the classical dance (*ki for* DJOGÈD)

bekta to carry, bring, take (*root form: kr for* GAWA)

bekti 1 money given to a village head or landowner, as a token of respect *or* in acknowledgment of his kindness. 2 to have great respect/esteem [for]. 3 one's respects, one's best wishes (in opening phrase of letters). **m/di*ǹi** to pay one's respects to. *See also* NGABEKTI

bektos *sbst kr for* BEKTI

bektya *ltry var of* BEKTI

bekuh *ptg* * *or* **bekah-*** to keep complaining

bekuk **m/di*(i)** 1 to bend, break, snap; to break a neck. *Matjané tak *é.* I'll break that tiger's neck. 2 to arrest, capture. *Malingé di* pulisi.* The police apprehended the thief. **m/di*i** to get smn's money/property away from him. *Saiki sengsara uripé sarèhning di*i seduluré.* He lives in poverty now that his relatives have relieved him of his wealth.

bekungkung cage-like tiger trap

bekunung **m*** stubborn; unwilling to defer to others

bekur **m*** to coo

bekusuk **m*** old and faded

bekutjuk **m*** to rinse out one's mouth

bèl bell

bel *rpr* puffing/flaring up. **, sanalika geniné murub.* Poof! it went up in flames.

bel- *see also under* BL- (*Introduction, 2.9.3*)

béla 1 to sacrifice oneself in defense of smn/sth. 2 to have a joint circumcision (with) [another boy] *usu.* as a means of economizing. **m/di*ni** to support, defend. *m* perkara* to defend a case (in court). *A m*ni B.* A stuck up for B. **pa·m*** defender; defense. *** sungkawa** to offer one's condolences. *nḌèrèk * sungkawa.* Please accept my sympathy.

belah 1 split; act of splitting. *Kebo iku atratjak *.* Kerbaus have split hooves. 2 one whose livelihood is fishing. 3 counting unit for rice plants: the number of stalks that can be encircled by the thumb and index finger of one hand, or 1/2 *gèḍèng.* 4 *n* hundreds minus 50. *karo* * 150. *telu* * 250. *kapat* * or *patang* * 350. *Ana reregan karo * rupiah.* It cost Rp. 150. ***an** one whose livelihood is fishing. **m*** *ltry* to split asunder. **m/di*i** to split sth. *m*i kaju* splitting logs. *** adji** half its worth (as redemption or replacement value). *** banten** a certain style of man's shirt. *** èwu** *n* thousand minus 500. *karo * èwu* 1500. *** keḍaton** having widely spaced front teeth

belak disease of the soles of the feet. ***en** to have/get the above condition

belang 1 skin blemish. 2 white spot(s) on an animal's coat. *Si Belang* Spotty (the dog)

belas -teen (*var used with 4, 6: see also* LAS 3). *pat** 14. *nem** 16

belatung *var of* BETATUNG

belèh no; not (*rg*). ***an** slaughtering place. **m/di*(i)** to slaughter, butcher. *m* babi* to

slaughter a pig. **pa·m*an** act of slaughtering. *papan pam*an* slaughtering place
bèlèk conjunctivitis. ***en** to have/get conjunctivitis
belèk *inf var of* WELÈH. ***an** a slit. **m*** 1 *inf var of* TEMBELÈK. 2 (*psv* **di***) to cut (off), make a slit (in)
belem ***an** brazier for roasting foods over coals. **m/di*** to roast [*esp.* cassava, corn] over coals
bèlèng **m*** refractory, hard to handle
beléning bank draft
bèlèr *rg var of* MÈLÈR
belèr **ke*** to get cut by sth other than a cutting implement. **m/di*** to cut. **m*i** able/liable to cut. *Pringé m*i lho.* The bamboo might give you a cut, you know!
beler **m*** persistently annoying; inconsiderate; lazy. *Pitik kuwi m*.* That chicken is always underfoot.
belet 1 mud, muck. 2 indigo leaf (*kr for* NILA). **ke*** to need to go to the toilet
beli(h) *rg* no; not
belik 1 a small natural pool. 2 *inf var of* WELÈH. 3 (*or* **m*i**) to begin bearing fruit in season
beling (broken) glass. *Mripaté ali² rupané kaja *.* The stone in that ring looks like glass. *Sikilé kena *.* He stepped on a piece of glass. **m*** rash, reckless, heedless
belis devil, bad spirit; mischief-maker
belit a card game played with the small cards (*kertu tjilik*). **m*** 1 to be a glib talker. 2 to sneak away from work when the boss is out. 3 [of debts, bills] hard to collect
belo foal, colt (young of the DJARAN). *** mèlu setu·n̂** to follow the crowd
bélok **m/di*** to turn. *m* ngiwa* to turn (to the) left
bélong unevenly pigmented [of skin, hair]
belor *cr?* colored glasses, sunglasses
bélot **m*** to disregard the orders of smn in authority
beluk 1 a certain caterpillar. 1 a variety of owl. 3 smoke, steam. **m/di*** 1 to turn. *m* nengen* to turn (to the) right. 2 to call to, yell at. 3 to bend; to bend out of shape. *** a·n̈·tandjak** to follow one's own inclinations. *See also* KUKUK-BELUK
belung [of soil] soggy, heavily moist
belur black-and-blue (mark). *See also* BABAK
bem (musical) mode (for gamelan ensemble)
bem- *see also under* B- *(Introduction, 3.1.7)*
bembeng **m*** big around, thick [of cylindrical shapes]
bèmbrèng **m/di*** to spread (out), stretch (open)
bémo three-wheeled motor vehicle (*shc from* BÉTJAK BERMOTOR)
bèn 1 (**kadjeng·ipun** *kr*) so as to, for the purpose of. *nDeloka ja, * weruh.* Look at it, so you'll know! *Dipun umbar wonten ing latar kadjengipun njenggut.* She let them loose in the yard to graze. ** apa ta kok kutjingé ditalèni?– * ora utjul.* Why did you tie up the cat?–So it wouldn't get away! 2 let [it go]! ** udan.* Let it rain! **, karepmu ḍéwé.* OK, I leave it to you. 3 *rg* all right then! (word of warning). **, tak aturké bapak nèk nakal.* I warn you, if you're naughty I'll tell Dad. **, suk nèk aku lunga ora tak djak menèh.* All right, I won't take you along next time [if you act that way]. 4 I hope; may [it] happen. *Bapak * nukokaké bal aku.* I hope Dad will buy me a ball. 5 *time word: see* EMBÈN. **ng/di*aké** to leave untended. *Nge*aké tamu iku ora apik.* It's not nice to leave guests to their own devices. *Botjah nangis kok di*ké waé.* The child is crying and you just let him cry! *Saking keselé piringé di*ké nang médja.* She was so tired she just left the dishes on the table. *See also* KAREBÈN, TJIKBÈN
ben 1 to oppose (*root form: kr for* DU). 2 *shf of* SABEN
béna *rg var of* BÉDA
bena flood (*kr for* BANDJIR)
bénah *rg var of* BÉDA
benah **m/di*(i)** to clear the clutter from, clean off
benak **m/di*aké** to fix up, set right. *Pengantèné m*aké paèsé sing rusak.* The bride repaired her rubbed-off makeup. *m*aké sepatuné* to tie one's shoe. *Tumpukan buku kaé mbok di*aké.* Please straighten that pile of books.
benampéjan you (*var of* SAMPÉJAN)
benang thread, string, yarn (*kr for* BOLAH*?*). ** gulung* ball of string; skein of yarn. ** (ke)los* spool of thread. *kelos ** a spool for thread. ** lajangan* kite string. *** sari** flower stamen. *** sutra** silk thread
benangpéjan you (*var of* SAMPÉJAN)
benawi large river (*kr for* BENGAWAN)
bénḍa a certain dark brown hard-shelled fruit
benḍa a certain variety of *kluwih* tree

benḍaharā treasurer (male)
benḍahari treasurer (female)
benḍalit to twist, (inter)twine. ***an** to twist and turn, fidget
bendânâ 1 nervous mannerism. 2 setback, piece of bad luck
bendârâ 1 master, mistress. *Dimin diutus *né.* Dimin's master sent him on an errand. 2 Sir; Ma'am. *** pangéran harja** (*abbr:* **B.P.H.**) *title for brothers of the Sultan of Jogjakarta.* *** radèn adjeng** (*abbr:* **B.R.Adj.**) *title for an unmarried princess.* *** radèn aju** (*abbr:* **B.R.A.**) *title for a married princess.* *** radèn mas** (*abbr:* **B.R.M.**) *title for a young unmarried prince*
benḍé small copper *or* bronze gong of the gamelan ensemble, also used as a public attention-getting device. *See also* SORÉ
benḍéga ship's crew
benḍéjot ***an** *or* **m*** weighted down
bènḍel (*or* ***an**) a bound volume; a file of bound papers. **ke*** to get recorded in a file. **m/di*(i)** 1 to bind [books, papers]. 2 to record sth in a file
benḍèl to talk *or* argue habitually; to nag
benḍel *var of* BÈNḌEL
bènḍeng 1 electric wiring. 2 large heavy rope. **m/di*** 1 to connect up [electrical wiring]. *Wingi listriké wis di*.* The electricity was hooked up yesterday. 2 to tie with rope
benḍèng **m/di*** to stretch [fabric] to its widest dimension by pulling from opposite edges
bènḍer (book)binding. *tukang ** book binder
benḍèt **m/di*** to hold sth open by pressing the edges apart
bèndi two-wheeled passenger cart drawn by a horse
bènḍi *var of* BÈNDI
béndjang-éndjang *kr* *sbst var of* M·BÉNDJING-ÉNDJING
bendjèt *var of* BENḌÈT
béndjing future, next, the coming... (*kr for* BÉSUK, SUK[a]). *M* punapa?* When [will it happen]? **m* embèn** day after tomorrow (*kr for* (M)BÉSUK EMBEN). **m*-éndjing** 1 tomorrow (*kr for* SÉSUK). 2 tomorrow morning (*kr for* SÉSUK ÉSUK)
béndjis can, be able; capable
béndjo oval, elliptical
béndjol misshapen
bèndjrèt **m*** to have diarrhea
béndjuh can; able, capable
bendjut lump on the head resulting from a blow
benḍo large-bladed knife for cutting wood. **m/di*** to cut [wood] with a *benḍo*
bénḍol *var of* BÉNDJOL
benḍol *ptg ** bumpy, knobby. ***an** 1 a knob, bump. 2 arrogant, conceited. 3 kris part between handle and blade. **m*** 1 having a knob *or* bump on it. 2 boastful, arrogant. **m·benḍal-m*** covered with bumps/knobs. *ptg* **b·r·enḍol** full of bumps
bènḍot strong and husky
béndrang 1 shrimp rice-accompanying dish. 2 a certain delicious soup, prepared the night before it is to be eaten (*see also* BLÉNDRANG)
béndrong 1 object used as a kite-string reel. 2 rhythmic beats produced by pounding rice with a mortar and pestle. **m/di*(i)** 1 to reel and unreel kite string. *A sing nguṇḍa lajangan, B sing m*.* A flew the kite while B handled the string. 2 to produce the above pounding beats
bendu (*or* **be***) wrath of God. *kala ** heavenly retribution. **ke*(ñ)** to be condemned *or* made an outcast. **m/di*ñi** to condemn. *dibendoni déning masjarakat* cast out by society
benḍul ***an** *or* **be*** a swelling. **m*** 1 to become swollen. 2 to protrude
bendung ***an** 1 dam. 2 dammed-up water. **m/di*** to dam sth up. *Nesuné di*.* She kept her anger under control.
bèné *var of* BÈN
benem (*sbst kr for* BAKAR?) **m/di*** to roast [foods] in a bed of hot coals and ash
bener (**leres** *opt kr*) 1 (what is) right, true, correct. ** kanḍamu.* What you say is true. *wong désa kluṭuk ** a real country hick. *djam wolu ** 8 o'clock on the dot. *wong kang arep weruh ** one who wants to know the truth. *wong kang weruh *ing laku* one who knows the right way to do things. ** tjilik, ning rosa.* He's small, yes, but he's strong. 2 [of a relationship] full-blooded. ***an** fortunate. *Aku pas ora duwé beras, *an kowé kok nggawa beras.* I'm out of rice; it's lucky you brought some. ***é** it is right/true (that...); actually, in fact. **é mretjoné diumbulaké supaja mbleḍos.* The right way is to toss away the [lighted] firecracker before it goes off. **é, ḍèké iku boḍo.* The fact is, she's stupid. ***-*an** to

compete *or* compare for correctness. *Ora ana gunané *-*an, bareng² digarap waé.* There's no point in trying to outdo each other–let's work together. **be*an** 1 justice. *Jèn kowé nganggo paṭokan be*anmu ḍéwé mesṭi *é.* By your own standards of right and wrong, of course you're right. 2 a decision. **ka*** 1 it happens to be a fact that... *Kula kleres rajinipun Mas Bardja.* I am Bardja's brother. *Mengko soré ke* tingalané bapak.* My father's birthday celebration is this evening. 2 coinciding with. *Ke* ora duwé ḍuwit, ndadak éntuk wèsel saka ngomah.* Just when I was out of money, I got a money order from home. **ka*an** 1 properly done. *Jèn ora ke*an, sok ndjeblos.* If it isn't done right, it might blow up. 2 fortunately; a lucky thing. *Ke*an pinudju libur.* Luckily he had the day off. 3 just right. *Wong mau lagi ke*an.* He's doing it just right. *Aku milih pelem bola-bali terus ora ke*an.* I picked mango after mango but none of them filled the bill. **ka*an urip·é** to lead a lucky life. **m/di*aké** 1 to correct, set to rights. *m*aké djam* to fix a watch so that it keeps correct time. *kesalahan wigati sing kudu di*aké* important mistakes that must be rectified. 2 to condone. *Pemerintah ora m*aké aksi sepihak.* The government didn't approve a unilateral action. **m*i** coinciding with. *Nalika aku teka, ḍèké m*i mangan.* She was eating when I got there. *A tekané Amérika m*i usum aḍem.* A came to America in the winter. **sa*é** actually, in fact; it is only right... *Sa*é ḍèké ora salah.* The fact is, he wasn't at fault. *Wis sa*é jèn ḍèké ra setudju karo aku.* He was quite right not to agree with me. **dudu (sa)*é** wrong, improper. *papan sing dudu sa*é* the wrong place. *Dudu sa*é jèn maling ora diukum.* It is wrong for a thief to go unpunished. *Dudu sa*é jèn loro ping loro iku lima.* Two times 2 is not 5. *** luput·é** right or wrong; the true facts. ** luputé kowé sing tanggung-djawab.* Right or wrong, you're responsible. *Durung mesṭi jèn kena dipertjaja *-luputé.* We're not sure he can be depended on to give the true facts. *See also* PENER

bengah **m*** to moo, low

bengangah **m*** bright and glowing

bengangang var of BERNGANGANG

bengawan *ng,* **benawi** *kr* large river. ** Sala* the Solo River

bengèk asthma. ***-*** *or* **bengak-*** to keep shouting *or* crying out. **m/di·be*** to repeatedly disturb/irritate. *See also* ṬÈṬÈK-BENGÈK

bengel (to have) a runny nose

bengèngèng *var of* BERNGÈNGÈNG

bengengeng **m*** to buzz, whine, hum

bengep swollen in the face

bengèr **(m)*-*** [of babies] to cry long and hard

bèngès red powder sold in paper packets, for coloring the lips. ***an** having reddened lips. **be*an** hypocritical. **m/di*** to redden the lips with the above powder

bènget bewildered (*opt kr for* BINGUNG)

benggâlâ place in India famous for its large livestock. *sapi ** large ox used as a draft animal. *weḍus* large goat

benggang with space(s) between. **m/di*** to make a space between things

benggèl *var of* BENḌOL

bénggol 1 a 2½-cent coin. 2 (*or* ***an**) gang leader

benggol *var of* BENḌOL

bengi *ng,* **dalu** *kr* evening, night. *mau ** last night. *mengko ** tonight, *i.e.* this coming evening. ** iki* tonight, *i.e.* this present evening. ***né** in the evening of the same day. **né ana kembang api.* That evening, there were fireworks. ***-*** in the middle of the night; although it is night. **-* lagi pénak²é wong turu, aku krungu: krengkèt².* One night while everyone was fast asleep I heard a rumbling sound. ***-*an** rather late in the evening. *Lungané bengi²an.* He left pretty late. ***ǹ-*ǹan** to see who can stay awake latest. **ke*ǹ** excessively late at night. *Aku kepeksa nginep merga wis kebengèn.* It was so late I had to stay overnight. **sa*** all night long, one whole night

bengingèh **m*** to neigh, whinny

bengis *var of* WENGIS

bengka [of stomach] hard, bloated

bengkah (having) a crack or cleft. *Témboké omah wis paḍa *.* The house walls are cracking apart.

bengkak 1 a tied bundle of long thin things. *sada sa** a bundle of whittled-bamboo pins. 2 swollen. **m/di*** to tie [things] into a bundle

bengkalahi to quarrel, argue

bengkarokan *see* KEṬÈK

béngkas **m/di*** to complete. *Ananing irigasi bisa m* karja usaha njukupi pangan.* Irrigation will round out the program for increasing the food supply. **pa·m*** messiah, deliverer

béngkat, bèngkat a game played by children with certain fruits (*bénḍa*)

bèngkèk (having) stiffness and pain in the small of the back

bèngkèl 1 a stomach ailment. 2 *var of* BINGKIL

bengkeleng throughout. *sedina* (*sewengi*) * all day (night) long

bengkélot **m*** tough, hard to chew

bengkeluk **m*** bent at the end. *pèn sing m* putjuké* a pen with a bent point. *m* menḍuwur* bending upward. **m/di*aké** to bend sth at the end

bengkelung *var of* BENGKELUK

bengkeng 1 bamboo fish trap with a swinging gate. 2 [of muscles] stiff and sore

bengkerengan to argue heatedly

bengkerok **m*** having acne

bengket a bundle of small things (sticks, plants, *etc.*)

bengkijeng **m*** 1 firm, tightly packed, compactly built. 2 firm, determined

bengkojok a skin disease characterized by running sores. ***en** to have/get this disease

bèngkok bent, curved. ***an** bending, curvature. **ané digeḍèkaké.* Curve it more.

bengkok designated officially. *sawah ** rice paddy assigned to the village head for his own use

béngkong, bèngkong curved, crooked, bent. *Pité roḍané ngarep *.* The front wheel of his bicycle is crooked.

béngkot **m*** 1 to turn aside the face, *e.g.* in disapproval. 2 to disregard smn's wishes. *Wis dikanḍani m* waé.* You were told, but you paid no attention.

bengkowang a certain edible root

bengkrèh mutually hostile. **be*an** to fight each other constantly over a long period of time

bengkrès **m*** 1 finely dressed. 2 vain of one's appearance and finery

bengkrik to have a dispute. ***en** stunted in growth. **be*an** a dispute, disagreement

bengkring undersized, thin and sickly. ***en** stunted

bengkrung *var of* BANGKRUNG

bengkuk *var of* BUNGKUK

bengkung 1 long cotton band worn around the midsection by women after childbirth, to hold the muscles firm. 2 (*or* **m***) bent, twisted. **m/di*aké** to bend/wrench sth

benglé a certain herb used in folk medicines. *See also* DLINGO

bengok ***-*** *or* **bengak-*** to shout repeatedly. *Bengak-* ndjaluk tulung.* He kept calling for help. **m*** to shout, yell. **m/di*i** to shout at, call to. **pa·m*** a shout; shouting, yelling. *ptg* **b·r·engok** *pl* to shout

bengong to let the mouth gape open

béngoren [of lips] sore from too much lime in the betel chew

béngos **béngas-*** having black streaky marks on the face

bèngsèng gangster, crook

benguk a certain variety of bean. *témpé ** beancake made with this bean

bengung **m*** to produce a shrill buzzing or humming sound

bengus **m*** to snort

benik button. **m/di*aké** to button [clothing]. **m/di*i** to sew buttons on [clothing]. *** baṭok** coconut-shell button. *** pèdjèt·an** (*or* *** ṭik**, *** tjeplès**, *** tjeṭit**) snap fastener. *** tjangkol** hook-and-eye fastener

bening 1 clear; pure; white. *Mripaté *.* His eyes are clear. *Swarané *.* She has a clear voice. *Banjuné saking *é, nganti lemahé katon.* The water is so clear you can see the bottom. *pitados ingkang ** pure faith. *Lampunipun satunggil abrit, satunggilipun malih *.* One light was red, the other was white. **di* banjuné dikena iwaké.** Keep the water clear and you'll catch the fish: *i.e.* to solve the problem, don't stir things up. 2 weak [of liquids]. *tèh ** weak tea. **m/di*(aké)** to make sth clear/pure. *** kintjling²** transparent. *** kintjlong²** sparkling, crystal-clear. *** leri** clear as mud

bènjèk [of wounds] watery and infected

benjènjèh ***en** covered with infected sores

benjinjih *ptg ** covered with small infected sores. **m*** having an infected sore

benjunjuk ***an** *or* **benjunjak-*** ill-mannered, boorish

bènsin gasoline. *pompa ** gas pump

bentajang ***an** 1 to writhe in pain. 2 to go out in quest of a livelihood. *Sedina muput *an ora éntuk apa².* He tried all day to find a means of support but came back empty-handed. **m*i** causing agonizing pain

bentar split in two; to crack open

bentèl bundle of seedlings ready for planting. *pari sa** one bundle of rice seedlings

bènten different (*kr for* BÉDA)

bèntèng *rg var of* BÈTÈNG

bentèr hot (*kr for* PANAS). ***an** hot water; a hot drink (*kr for* WÉDANG*?*). ***-manah** envious (*kr for* PANAS-ATI)
benṭer a certain freshwater fish
bentet 1 the exact amount. *selawé ** exactly 25. 2 completely filled
benṭèt cracked but not broken through. *Gelasé botjor la wong **. The glass leaks–it's cracked. *enḍog ** a cracked egg. ***an** act *or* result of cracking. **m/di*aké** to crack sth
bentijet **m*** heavy, burdensome
benṭik 1 to make a tinkling *or* chinking sound. 2 a children's game played by batting away a short stick with a long stick. **ke*** to get knocked against by sth. *Gelasé petjah ke* piring.* The plate hit against the glass and cracked it.
bentil 1 *rg var of* BENTÈL. 2 (*or* *** jutun ***) dedicated, devoted. *tani ** a true dedicated farmer
benting *rg* women's sash
bentjânâ disaster, catastrophe
bentjé the male of a certain quail (*gemak*), who stays passively in the nest while the female does all the work
bèntjèng not well matched, not fitting together properly. *Dondomané **. The line of sewing doesn't run parallel [to the hemline, as it should]. *Wong² loro mau tansah * waé.* Those two are always at each other's throats. *** tjèwèng** always disagreeing, never seeing eye to eye
bentjèt sun dial. **m/di*** to pick on, bully
bentji to despise, loathe. ** aku!* Oh, *no!* How awful!
bentjirih subject to frequent illness
béntjok tree frog
bentjolèng ***an** to act uncouth. **m*** ill-mannered, uncouth, tough
bentojong **m*** 1 [of burdens] many, and heavy to carry. 2 to be a burden *or* extra responsibility (on)
benṭot sturdy, muscular
bentrok to clash. *Wong loro kuwi tansah * waé.* Those two don't get along at all. ***an** clash, confrontation
bentuk form, shape
benṭuk (*or* ***an**) to toss sth back and forth. **ke*** to get tossed (off/away/against)
bentul a certain tuberous plant
benṭung 1 strong, muscular. 2 ape with long black hair
bentur severe, rigorous. **ke*** to get hit. *Sirahku ke* tèmbok.* I hit my head on the wall. **m/di*aké** to strike sth [against]. *Klapané di*-*aké ana ing watu.* He kept banging the coconut on a rock. **m/di*i** to strike sth. *Kajuné di*i nganggo palu wesi.* He hit the wood with a hammer.
bentus **ke*** to get a bump on the head. **m*** to bump one's head
benṭut *var of* BENṬOT
benuwa continent
bèr (*or* ***-budi**) generous. *ratu kang adil lan * budi* a just and generous king. *** budi bawa leksana** generous
ber 1 *oj* to fly. 2 *rpr* flight through the air. *Ḍèwèké mbalang, **. He threw a stone. **bar-*** *rpr* repeated flights. *Dibuwang bar-**. He threw them away right and left. *See also* ABER, ABUR, BUR
ber- 1 *prefix: see under individual entries.* 2 *see also under* BR- *(Introduction, 2.9.3)*
bera fallow. *lemah * lan tjengkar* fallow, unproductive land. **be*** to cultivate fallow land. **(be)*n** fallow field. **m*** empty [of one of the hollows where seeds should be, in the game of *ḍakon*]. **m/di*kaké** to allow [land] to lie fallow. *Lemahé ora kena di*kaké babar pisan.* The field should never be left unplanted.
berah labor(er) (*kr for* BURUH)
bérak *cr* human excrement. **be*** *or* **m*** to defecate
bérang large knife
berangkat to leave, set out. *Kapan * nang Djakarta?* When do you leave for Djakarta? **m/di*aké** to send smn out/forth. *Tentarané di*ké saka bètèng.* The troops were dispatched from the fort. *See also* PANGKAT
beras *ng*, **wos** *kr* husked raw rice. **é diadang dadi sega.* She steamed the (raw) rice (and made it into cooked rice). **m*** resembling rice grains. *** abang** red rice. *** djagung** corn ground to the size of rice grains. *** giling** machine-husked rice. *** kentjur** mixture of powdered raw rice and medicinal roots, used for massaging. *** kuning** rice colored yellow with tumeric. *** menir** broken rice grains. *** setengah mateng** half-cooked rice; *fig* stupid. *** tutu·n̂** hand-husked rice. *** wuluh** unhusked rice grains. *** wutah** 1 scattered in abundance. *Mimis² m* wutah.* The bullets rained down. 2 [of modern furniture] having a multi-colored pebbled effect. 3 a certain batik design: white dots on a dark background
berat difficult, causing trouble for others.

(ora) **ke*an** to have (no) objections to. * **setengah** partial, one-sided, biased
berbah *rg kr for* BRUBUH
bèrbudi *see* BÈR
bèrdji silver leaf-shaped ornament sewn on a lady's dress
berdondi *var of* PERDONDI
berduli *var of* PERDULI
béré **ke*-*** *oj* with difficulty, against obstacles. *Olèhé nggarap ke*-*, ndadak upahé siṭik.* He had to work against great odds and was paid only a pittance. *See also* BARA
bereg **m/di*** 1 to chase (off), shoo. *m* pitik* to shoo chickens. 2 to let [cattle] out to graze
berèk ***-*** *or* **berak-*** to keep calling (out)
berek *rg* [of fish] beginning to spoil
bèrem shoulder/edge of a road
berem soft and squashy
bèrèng skin area chafed from moisture. ***en** to have chafed skin. *See also* BARANG
berentjanā to plan (out). *See also* RENTJANA
bèrès in good order. *ora ** disorganized. *Nèk A wis tandang, kabèh mesṭi *.* When A got through, everything was in good shape. **ke*an** order(liness); satisfactory condition. **m/di*aké** *or* **m/di*i** to put in good order. *m*aké soal* to resolve a problem. *m*aké pegawéjan* to do a job right
berèt scratched. *Montoré anjar *.* His new car has a scratch on it. **ke*** to get scratched
bergâdâ group (of soldiers), brigade
bergadjul *var of* BEGADJUL
bergagah **m*** to stand with the legs wide apart
bergas having a fresh attractive appearance
bergasi 1 freight transported by rail. 2 railway freight office. 3 freight car. 4 car trunk
bergaul to make good friends, establish good relations
bergedèl a croquette-like food of potato and egg. ** daging* meat croquette. ** djagung* corn fritter
bergegeg **m*** to remain motionless. *Dikon lunga m* waé.* They asked her to leave but she didn't budge.
bergègèh **m*** to stand with the legs medium far apart
bergerak to persist. *Ora kalilan * nggajuh program.* They were not allowed to continue carrying out the program.
bergigih **m*** 1 to stand with the legs slightly apart. 2 adamant in one's refusal to help
bergogok *var of* BEGOGOK
bergolak seething, turbulent
berguguk *var of* BEGUGUK
bergundung **m*** obstinate, headstrong
berhaḍiah to give prizes/gifts. *sajembara ** a prize contest
bèri 1 gamelan instrument resembling a *gong* but without knobs. 2 serving tray. ***-*** disease characterized by enlarged limbs
beri a certain bird. **m*** 1 to join in, go along. 2 to toss in one's hand (in a card game)
berik (*or* **m***) to fight by locking horns
béring unbalanced, lopsided; *fig* prejudiced; mentally unbalanced. **ora *-*** nothing at all, of no importance
bering disagreeable odor, *esp.* of a certain fruit (*djéngkol*)
berit a variety of mouse. ***an** a plot of ground behind a house for raising fruits and vegetables
berkah blessings. *njuwun ** to ask for smn's blessing
berkakas *var of* BEKAKAS
berkas (*or* ***an**) wrapped bundle
berkasak *var of* BEKASAK
berkat 1 food, blessed by a religious official, taken home from a ritual ceremony by the guests after they have eaten a portion of it. 2 as a result of. ** penggulawenṭahé apik, anak²é paḍa dadi wong kabèh.* Thanks to their fine upbringing, his children have all become worthwhile people. ***an** act of taking home food; the food taken home (as above). **m/di*** to take home [food] from a ceremony
berkèngkèng *var of* BEKÈNGKÈNG
berketjeg *var of* BEKETJEG
bèrko electric bicycle lamp
berkongkong **m*** to stay in one place, sit idly loafing
berkuh *var of* BEKUH
berkutut *var of* PERKUTUT
berlijan *var of* BARLÉJAN
bèrlin *var of* BARLÈN
berngangang **m*** radiant, glowing
berngangas **m*** *var of* M̆·PERNGANGAS
berngèngèng (*or* **m***) glowing, radiant
berngèngès **m*** *var of* M̆·PERNGÈNGÈS
berngingis **m*** *var of* M·PERNGINGIS
berngongos **m*** *var of* M·PERNGONGOS
berod **m*** to attempt to free oneself from restraint
bérok *see* WEḌUS

berok **berak-*** to keep shouting *or* calling out
berong *rg var of* BERUK
bérongen *rg var of* BÉNGOREN
berorganisasi to organize
bersat *ptg ** spread about untidily. *Pirang² kertas ptg * ing médja.* There are papers all over the table.
berselo **m*** stubborn, unwilling to listen to others
bersenam calisthenics
bersendjatā weapon(ry). *See also* SENDJATA
bersih 1 clean, cleansed. 2 to clean a grave and place offerings of flowers on it. ***an** dressing table with a center mirror. **m/di*i** to cleanse sth; to free sth of. *** désa** traditional annual village event with feasting and a performance of a play from the animistic cycle
bersihang *var of* BERSIH·AN
bersot **m*** to go away in the face of advice, wishes, or warnings to the contrary
bertjak pockmarked
bertji a certain fine gauzy fabric. **kuluk *ǹ** traditional fez made of the above
bertjuh obscene [of speech]
beruh **m*** to not see, not know. *Apa kowé weruh kutjingku?–mBeruh.* Have you seen my cat?–No.
beruk coconut half-shell used as a measure for raw rice
berunḍing to negotiate
berung **m*** obstinate; to disobey. **pa·m*** obstinacy; disobedience
bérut *see* ENTUT
berut *var of* BARUT
bèrwèh generous (*shc from* BÈBÈR WÈWÈH; *see also* BÈR)
besa *var of* BEKSA
besalèn blacksmith's workshop; blacksmith's forge
bésan parent(s)-in-law of one's child. ***an** to become mutual parents-in-law. *mBésuk *an ja mbakju?* Shall we have our children marry each other [as an extension of our own friendship]?
besar 12th month of the Moslem calendar. ***an** feast day occuring during this month
besaran mulberry bush/fruit
besasih *ptg ** in disorder, messy
besasik *var of* BESASIH
besat **m*** to depart suddenly, be off like a shot
bèsèk small covered box of plaited bamboo
besel (*or* ***an** *or* **be***) a bribe. **m/di*(i)** to bribe smn
besélat *var of* BESILAT
besem 1 depressed, gloomy. 2 fading, no longer fresh. 3 to burn (*root form: sbst? kr for* OBONG)
besèn a variety of grass
beseng *rg var of* BÈNGSÈNG
besengèk a certain vegetable dish, to accompany the rice at a meal
besengut **besengat-*** *or* **m*** to frown, scowl
bèsèr 1 pathological compulsion to urinate frequently. 2 *cr* to urinate
beséro *see* SÉRO
beseseg **m*** bloated from overeating
besèt ***an** 1 peeled. 2 peelings, parings. **m/di*(i)** to peel the rind (from)
bèsi 1 bowl (*var of* BASI). 2 iron (*var of* WESI)
besijar out [walking, riding] for pleasure
besik **m/di*i** to remove weeds from [soil]
besilat judo-like system of self-defense (*see also* SILAT)
besisik **m*** dried out, flaking [of skin, from exposure to elements]
besiwit **m*** to cheat at cards
beskab short double-breasted buttoned-up jacket
beskal a certain colonial administrative rank
beskuwit biscuit, cracker
beslah ***an** confiscated; confiscated goods. **m/di*** to confiscate
beslit official document of notification
besmi to burn (*root form: kr for* OBONG)
besol a certain tree
besono **besona-*** acting crude/boorish
besoso **m*** crude, ill-mannered
besot **m/di*** to clean [metal] by blowing flame on it
besta rope for handcuffing (*opt kr for* BANDA). **m*** to tie smn's hands
bestèl 1 (*or* ***an**) merchandise sent by mail or railway. 2 (*psv* **di***) to order by mail. **m/di*aké** to send by mail or railway
bestik beefsteak
bestru name of a tree more commonly called KATJUR; the edible fruits of this tree
bésuk *ng,* **béndjing** *kr* (*or* **m***) 1 at some future time. *mBésuk jèn wis gedé aku arep dadi tani.* I'm going to be a farmer when I grow up. 2 next..., the coming... ** mi-nggu (taun, dina Ngahad, lsp.)* next week (year, Sunday, etc.) ***-*** at some indefinite future time. *** apa** when (in the future)?

mBésuk apa mangkaté? When's he leaving? * **embèn** the day after tomorrow. * **embèn dawa** some (indefinite) day long after tomorrow. * **ésuk** tomorrow morning. * **manèh** hereafter. * *manèh nèk didawuhi bapak adja mbantah.* Next time don't argue when Father tells you to do sth. *See also* SUK[a], SÉSUK

besuk volcanic plain

besur **m*** to do as one pleases without regard for others

besus meticulous about one's personal appearance

besusu a certain edible root

besut chief performer in early folk drama. **m/di*** to refine, smooth out. *m* klambi* to press clothing. *m* karangan* to edit an article

besuwel *rpr* a quick careless tucking-in motion. *Olèhé nglebokaké duwit mak *.* She hastily tucked the money in her sash. **m/di*aké** to tuck sth hastily. *Olèhé nggelung mung di*aké.* She quickly did her hair into a bun.

bet *rpr* a swift motion/action. *A disik sing mbalang, *.* A was the first to throw. *Mau katjangé isih akèh, kok ndjur mak * entèk.* There were plenty of peanuts, but they were all gone in no time.

beta *kr* *sbst? var of* BEKTA

betah 1 to feel comfortable. *Aku * bantah banget dolan ing panggonané.* I feel at home there. 2 to (with)stand, endure. *Aku ora * melèk sewengi muput.* I can't stay awake all night. *Kowé kok ja *-*é panasan ana ing djaba.* How can you stand staying out in the sun so long! 3 need (*kr for* BUTUH). ***-*an** 1 act of persevering. 2 to compare *or* compete for endurance. *Ajo *-*an melèk.* Let's see who can stay awake longer. **m/di*aké** to persist in, persevere at. *Betah[2]na olèhmu ngombé djamu iki, bèn énggal waras.* Take this medicine faithfully so you'll get well fast.

beṭak to boil rice (*root form: kr for* LIWET)

beṭat *var of* BEṬOT

betatung black maggot

bètèh exchange of pleas in a court case. *ngadu ** OR **m*aké** to present arguments and counterarguments in court

bèṭèk baskets hanging at either end of a shoulder pole (*pikul*) for carrying things

betèk sth that has been used for some purpose. *séndok * njiduk lenga* a spoon that was used for ladling oil. *Tjangkir iki * apa?* What did this cup have in it? *Iki *é sapa?* Who's been using this? ***(n)é** because (of). **é saka bungahé* because of her happiness. **ipun dèrèng saged nglangi* since he didn't know how to swim

beṭèk bamboo fence. **m/di*i** to build a fence around sth, to fence sth in

bèṭem **m*** to restrain one's laughter

beṭem seed of the *kluwih* fruit. **m*** having a round fat face

bètèng 1 fort(ification). 2 rook (in chess). * *iku ora kena mlaku mèntjèng.* The rook can't move diagonally. ***-*an** 1 fortress. 2 imitation *or* toy fort. **m/di*i** to fortify

beṭeng **ke*(en)** to be prevented from doing sth, *esp.* by rain. *Aku nginep ing padésan merga ke* udan.* I stayed overnight in the village, stranded by the rain.

bètèr, bèter 1 bitters. 2 *var of* BLÈTER

bèṭer **m*** [of nose] large, broad; [of chin] fat, multiple

bèṭèt parrot-like bird with a long hooked beak. **m*** [of nose] hooked. **m/di*i** to clean by removing the entrails. *m*i iwak* to clean a fish

beṭèṭèr *ptg * or* **m*** to lie around idle or unattended to

beṭeṭet **m*** tight, confining. *Klambiné m*, ketjiliken.* The shirt binds; it's too small. *Olèhé nalèni m* banget.* He tied it up tight. *Mendungé m*.* The clouds were oppressive.

beṭik a certain edible freshwater fish

beṭiṭing small-waisted

beṭiṭit **m*** 1 tight-fitting. 2 all dressed up; dressed like a dandy

bétjak pedicab. ***an** pedicab fare. **m*** 1 to ride in a pedicab. *mulih m** to take a pedicab home. 2 to operate a pedicab as one's livelihood. **m/di*aké** 1 to send smn in a pedicab, pay smn's pedicab fare. 2 to transport sth by pedicab. *Gawané di*ké.* She had her bundles taken by pedicab.

bètjèk 1 muddy. 2 a certain fish stew served at ritual feasts

bètjèr (*or* ***an**) money reserved for day-to-day needs. **m*** to buy one's daily needs

betjètjèr *ptg ** 1 to get dropped and scattered, *e.g.* rice grains from a hole in a bag. 2 [of money] squandered

betjik *ng,* *saé kr* 1 good, of high quality. *dadi ** to turn out well. *tunggangan sing * ḍéwé* the best means of transportation. *Anaké * tur ora nakal.* The child was good, not naughty. *Ora ana sing ilang, saka *ing pandjagané pulisi.* Not one was lost, thanks to the effective police guard. *Baṭikané misuwur *.* Her batiks are famous for their quality. *Ija *, ndelenga.* Very well, you may see it. 2 (*or* ***é**) advisable, better. * *balia, iki dudu ambah²anmu.* You'd better go back–this isn't your territory. **é kowé ora tuku mretjon.* I wouldn't buy fireworks if I were you. ***-*an** 1 to compare *or* compete for quality. **-*an, A atiné luwih *.* Comparing the two, A has a better character. 2 to be/get on good terms. *Saiki *-*an baé.* Let's be friends now. **di·be*** to be treated well. **ka*an** goodness; kindness. **m/di*aké** to improve sth. **m/di*i** 1 to make better. 2 to treat kindly. **sa*-*é** 1 to the best of one's ability. *Wis kuduné latihan migunakaké wektu kanṭi sa*-*é.* They should make the best possible use of their time. 2 no matter how good. * **ke·titik ala ketara** the good will make itself known, along with the bad

betjira raised floor

betjitji wild banana

betjitjing 1 above-ground tuberous root. 2 banana cluster at lower end of stalk

betjokok (*or* ***an**) unruly

bètju **m*** to assume a sour facial expression

betjus capable, competent. *Sekolahé ora *.* He didn't do too well in school.

béṭo **m*** to whistle by blowing on the slit between the two thumbs with palms pressed together

beṭok a certain fish. **m/di*** to take, get. *m* tjèlèngan* to take one's savings out of the piggy bank. *m* lotré* to win in a lottery

beton 1 the pit of certain fruits (*gori, kluwih*). 2 concrete wall

béṭongan shirt resembling a T-shirt

beṭot ***-*an** to pull [sth pliable and resisting] back and forth. *Wong loro mau *-*an klambi.* The two kept snatching the shirt from each other. **m/di*(i)** 1 to pull sth off/up/out. *m*i tanduran* to uproot plants. *Lintahé di*.* He pulled off the leech. 2 to pinch smn in the scrotum

betotong **m*** to have a large bowel movement

beṭu **m*** 1 [of face] fat, moon-shaped. 2 *var of* NG·GETU

beṭur **m*** [of girls, women] lazy, unwilling to work at one's tasks

beṭuṭut **m*** glum, down in the mouth

bewah *var of* WEWAH

bèwèh a certain fruit which is prepared for eating or cooking by burying it for a period of time

bèwèl **m*** numerous, profuse

bèwès **m*** 1 to drool, slobber. 2 burdensome, overabundant. *Utangé m*.* He's up to his ears in debt. *Wis duwé putu, nanging isih m*.* She's a grandmother, but she still goes on having children of her own.

béwok *inf var of* BRÉWOK

bi 1 *adr* aunt. 2 *rg* mother. *See also* BIBI

bib *rpr* the beep of a car horn. *See also* BIBIB

bibar to disperse; finished, over; after (*kr for* BUBAR)

bibas *rg var of* BEBAS

bibèk aunt (*var of* BIBI)

bibi 1 aunt (parent's younger sibling) 2 (*adr*: *Djakarta slang*) young woman. 3 *adr* mother (*term used at court by children of a concubine, the official mother being the No. 1 wife*). *See also* BI

bibib *rpr* repeated beeps, *e.g.* car horn; Morse code. *See also* BIB

bibir *oj* lip(s)

bibis water beetle

bibisan a certain plant

bibit 1 origin, beginning; seed. 2 (*or* ***an**) plant or animal used for breeding. **m/di*aké** 1 to use for breeding. 2 to provide with sth for breeding. *Sing m*aké pelem iki bijèn Pak Naja.* It was Mr. Naja who gave us the seedlings for these mangoes. * **bobot bèbèt** heredity, worldly wealth, moral character (the criteria for evaluating a prospective son-in-law). *Wis njukupi sarat: * bèbèt bobot.* He has fulfilled the [above] requirements. * **kawit** origin; motivation. ** kawité Prang Donja I apa?* What started World War I?

biblak (*or* ***an**) (to have) an open wound *or* skinned place. **(an)é apa wis disalep?* Have you put ointment on your cut?

biblèk *var of* BIBLAK

bibrah out of order, in disrepair (*kr for* BUBRAH)

bibrik ***-*** to start [a job, a business]. **m/di*** to trespass on smn's land

biḍag pawn (in chess). *main ** to play chess. **é kenané mung madju, tur mung sakoṭak² waé.* The pawns can move only forward, and only one square at a time.

biḍal to leave, set out as a group (*kr for* BUḌAL)

biḍan midwife
biḍang field, area, scope
biḍar dugout canoe
biḍeg ordinary foot soldier; advance troops
bidengah acts that are unethical by Moslem standards
bidjaksânâ *oj* endowed with wisdom
bidji mark, grade. ***ǹ** pertaining to marks. **né dilebokaké ing buku bidjèn.* He entered the grades in the grade book. **m/di*-(ǹi)** to mark, grade, judge. *Karangané ora dibidjèni.* The compositions weren't graded. *A bisa m* jèn Warti nduwèni rupa kang tjukupan.* A sized Warti up as a pretty good-looking girl.
bidjig ***an** that which gets butted. ***-*an** to butt each other. **m/di*(i)** to butt. *di* kebo* butted by a kerbau
bidjih ore. ** wesi* iron ore
bidngah *var of* BIDENGAH
biḍo a variety of hawk
bidor name of one of the small playing cards (*kertu tjilik*)
bidug *rg* stupid, ignorant
biḍur skin rash with fever. ***en** to have/get such a rash
bif beef. *kornèt ** canned corned beef
bigar *oj* happy, glad
bih confession (Catholic sacrament). **nge/di*i** to hear smn's confession
bihal mule
bihalal *see* HALAL
bija ***-*** *excl of amazement*
bijâdâ female court servant, who dances behind the King
bijah *excl: var of* JAH
bijaja(h) cost, outlay. **m*** in large numbers *or* amounts. *Jèn ungsum pelem sing adol m* nang endi²*. During the mango season there are people selling mangoes everywhere.
bijajak (*or* ***an**) to keep moving around restlessly/aimlessly in such a way as to disturb others. *ptg * pl as above*
bijang 1 *rg* mother. 2 woman of low status. 3 (*or* ***-***) *excl of dismay, pain, sorrow.* ***ané** *or* ***mu** *term of abuse*
bijantu help, assistance. **(be)*an** *or* **(be)*n̂** help, assistance; act *or* way of helping. **m/di*k̂aké** to offer smn's services. **m/di*-(n̂i)** to help, assist. **pa·m*** 1 help, aid. 2 helper, assistant. *pam* awudjud sanḍangan lan pangan* assistance in the form of food and clothing. **sa* karo** in cooperation *or* agreement with. *Kula sa* kalijan kersa-nipun bapak.* I support my father's wish. *See also* BANTU
bijas to turn pale suddenly, go white
bijâsâ 1 usual, ordinary. *omah * waé* just an ordinary house. *luwih betjik seka *né* better than usual. 2 familiar with, accustomed to. *Ḍèké * turu gasik.* He's used to going to bed early. ***né** usually. **ka*n** hab it, practice. **m/di*kaké** to get (oneself) used to. *m*kaké tangi ésuk* to accustom oneself to getting up early
bijèk *rg var of* BIJÈN
bijèn *ng*, **rumijin** *kr* (*or* **m*** *ng*) (at some time) in the past. *Aku ḍèk bijèn wis tau di-tjakot asu édan.* One time I was bitten by a mad dog. ** omahé nang Jogja.* He used to live in Jogja. *ḍèk djaman ** in the old days; once upon a time. ***-*** (since) a long time ago. **-* aku wis kanḍa jèn ḍèké kuwi ora kena dipertjaja.* I've told you from the beginning that he was not to be trusted. **-* kétok apa saiki kétok apa.* See how he's changed! ***(-*)é** formerly (as contrasted with the present or future). *** mula** from the very beginning. ** mula aku ora nga-ndel.* I've never believed him.
bijet **m*** abundant. *Wohé wis m*.* There were a great many fruits [on the tree].
bijing **m*** incorrigible
bijoskop movie; movie theater. *tontonan ** motion picture (show). ***an** movie theater
bijoskup *var of* BIJOSKOP
bijuh (*or* ***-***) *excl of astonishment*
bijung 1 *rg* mother. 2 *adr: rg* woman of lower status. 3 (*or* ***-***) *excl of pain or strong emotion.* ** larané.* Ow, it hurts! ***en** [of children] always wanting one's mother near. **sa*** born of the same mother
bik **m*** in, at, on. *Wis kok golèki m* kana?* Have you looked over there for it?
bikak open (*kr for* BUKAK)
bikal (*or* ***-***) having an itchy skin condition
bikang (*or* **tjara-***) a rice-flour-and-sugar pastry
bikir coconut-shell spinning top
biksu(ka) Buddhist priest
biku *var of* WIKU
bikut with quick movements. *Botjah² paḍa * nglumpukaké krambil.* The boys deftly gathered up coconuts.
bil half-cent coin (used in colonial times). *See also* BRIBIL
bila(h)i bad luck, mishap. *Blai, blai tenan.* What a tough break! *nemu ** to run into

some bad luck. **ke*ǹ** accident, mishap

bilal person whose task it is to announce the 5 daily Moslem prayer times

bilas to rinse with clean water after washing. **m/di*i** to rinse smn after bathing him

bilih when(ever), if (*opt kr for* JÈN, MENAWA). *See also* BOK

bilik compartment, walled-in space. ***-*** separated into groups

bilis rake

bilo having poor vision

bilug **m*-m*** big, brawny (in physical build)

biluk **m*** to turn, veer. *m* mengiwa* to turn left

bilulung *ptg ** or ***an** *pl* to run around in panic or alarm

bilur *var of* BELUR

bima frightening, awesome

bima-sekti 1 (*prn* **bimâ-sekti**) dark mass in a cloud of stars. 2 (*prn* **bimā-sekti**) the Milky Way

bimbang 1 wavering between alternatives. *Atiné kok ṭok-ṭik **. He can't make up his mind. 2 (*or* **ke***) infatuated. *ke* atiné* distracted with love; to fall madly in love at first sight

bimbing ***an** guidance. **m/di*** to guide, lead

bin son of. *Ali * Kasim* Ali, son of Kasim

bin- *see also under* B- (*Introduction, 3.1.7*)

bina **ke*-*** *oj* to a high degree. *Ajuné ke*-**. She's exquisitely beautiful.

binantang *var of* BINATANG

binatang animal (*pejorative term*)

binḍel *var of* BÈNḌEL

binḍeng to speak nasally

bindi club, cudgel

bindiwâlâ spear, lance

bindjing *rg var of* BÉNDJING

bing **m*** in, at, on. *mBing endi sing lara?* Where does it hurt?

bingah happy (*kr for* BUNGAH)

bingar to look pleased. *Ulaté **. His face lighted up. **m/di*aké** to make one's face appear happy: *Bèn ora ngetarani, polatané di*aké.* He put on a happy face to conceal his sadness.

bingbing **m*** placenta

binggel 1 ankle bracelet. 2 bracelet (*ki for* GELANG). ***an** to wear a bracelet on the ankle. **m/di*i** to put sth around smn's ankle

bingkar *rg? kr for* BUNGKAR

bingkas **m/di*** to do away with, kill

bingkem *rg kr for* BUNGKEM

bingkil repair man; repair shop, workshop. ** sepéḍa* bicycle repair man/shop

bingsrung **m*** to play dumb, pretend not to know

bingung bewildered, confused. *Ḍèké nganti * anggoné nliti lan milih saka atusan warnaning djarik.* She got all mixed up trying to choose from among the hundreds of batiks. *Saanak bodjoné * omahé kobong.* His wife and children were dazed by the burning of their house. **m*aké** 1 confusing. 2 (*psv* **di*aké**) to confuse, bewilder. **m*i** to behave as though perplexed

bintal **ke*** to disappear, get lost. *Embuh ke* ana ngendi, kok tak golèki ora ketemu.* I don't know where it's gone–I can't find it anywhere.

bintang 1 (star-shaped) award medal. 2 star. ** pilem* movie star

bintangur a certain tree

bintarā noncommissioned officer

binté ***ǹ** a kicking contest. **m/di*** to kick smn in the calf of the leg with one's shin

binteng(-djaé) a chewy confection of sticky-rice flour, ginger, and sugar

bintit red and swollen [of eyes]

bintjih castrated, spayed (*kr for* BIRI)

bintjil ***an** reckoning of the propitiousness of certain days for holding important events. **m/di*i** to figure propitiousness for [an event]

bintu a certain chemical used in processing batik. **m/di*ni** to dye [fabric] the basic blue by dipping it in a solution of this substance

bintul a small itchy swelling

bintur pincers for catching crabs. **ke*** to get trapped; *fig* to be led astray, led into bad ways. **m/di*** to catch [crabs] with the above pincers

biologis biology

bipèt 1 cabinet for displaying knick-knacks. 2 snack bar

bir beer

bira(h)i *ltry var of* BRA(H)I

birâmâ attractive, pleasing, harmonious

birat cleansed of one's sins. **m/di*** to wash away smn's sins

biri *ng*, **bintjih** *kr* (*or* ***ǹ**) castrated, spayed. *djaran ** a castrated horse. **m/di*** to castrate, spay. *See also* KEBIRI

biring long straight spearhead

Birmā Burma

biro bureau, department
birokrasi bureaucracy
birokrat bureaucrat
birokratis bureaucratic
biru blue. * *enom (tuwa)* light (dark) blue. * *semu idjo* greenish-blue. ***n̂(an)** dyed batik. **ke*n̂** excessively blue; [of batik] too deeply dyed. **m/di*** to make sth blue. **m/di*k̂aké** to have sth made/dyed blue. **m/di*n̂i** to cover [the dyed portion of batik] with wax to prevent it from taking on the color of the next dyeing. * **barlèn** light blue. * **èrem** (to be/get) black-and-blue. * **(k)etju** deep blue. * **langit** sky blue. * **maja²** pure clear blue
bis 1 bus. 2 mailbox. 3 concrete water pipe. ***-*an** bus station. **nge*** to ride a bus. **nge/di-*aké** 1 to send by bus. 2 to mail a letter (for smn). **nge/di*i** to bus sth. **nge*an** bus station. *nunggangi bétjak menjang nge*an* to take a pedicab to the bus station
bisa *ng,* **saged** *kr* 1 can, be able, know how [to]. *Ḍèké umur papat wis * matja.* He could read when he was four. **a kaé ja emoh aku.* Even if I *could* do it, I wouldn't. *Masa *a.* As if he could do that! 2 to manage to [do], succeed in [do]ing. *Ḍèké * nahan nesuné.* He managed to control his anger. 3 to [do] in accordance with one's nature. *Matjan * nggero.* Tigers roar. ***né** what one is capable of. *Jèn djam nem aku ora *, *ku mung djam rolas awan.* I can't make it at 6 o'clock, I can only make it at noon. **né *, ning ming kesèd.* He *can* do it–he's just lazy. ***-*né** how is it possible! *Aku gumun kok kowé sedina ḍek ora mangan, kok *-*mu.* How on earth can you go all day without eating! **di*k(-*k)-aké** to make sth possible; to do one's best. *Udjiané pantjèn angèl ning di-bisak²aké lo.* The test is hard, but do your best! *Aku ngerti jèn kowé sésuk éwuh ning mbok di*kaké.* I know you're busy tomorrow, but do try to work it in. **ka*n** ability, capability. *Adja sok umuk bab ka*nmu.* Don't brag about what you can do. *Ka*n kaja ngono kuwi ora kabèh wong duwé.* Not everyone has the aptitude for it. **sa*né** according to one's capability. *Ora perlu akèh², sa*mu waé.* It needn't be much–just [give] what you can. *Aku mesṭi mampir, embuh kapan; sa*ku.* I'll drop by, I don't know when–whenever I can. **sa*-*** if possible. *Sa*-* *a dadi ing sadjroné sesasi.* Have it ready in a month, if possible. **sa*-*né** to the best of one's ability. *Uruna sa*-*mu.* Give whatever you can. *Aku wis usaha sa*-*ku.* I've done my best. * **uga** perhaps, possibly. * *uga ḍèké nèng perpustakaan.* He may have gone to the library. *See also* GUMISA
bisaé bad, ugly, inferior
biséka *oj* to assume a noble name *or* title. **di*** to be declared king
bisik (*or* *-* *or* **bisak-*** *or* **be***) to whisper. ***an** a whisper; that which is whispered. **be*é naréndra** His Majesty. **be*é nguwuh-uwuh** to give away one's secret inadvertently. **m/di*i** to whisper to. *Aku *ana.* Whisper it to me!
biskal *var of* BESKAL
biskop 1 Catholic bishop. 2 *var of* BIJOSKOP
biskup *var of* BIJOSKOP
biskutjing touch-me-not (shrub)
biskuwit *var of* BESKUWIT
bislongit may God have mercy on his soul
bismillah in the name of God
bisu dumb (unable to speak). **m*** to act dumb, pretend one cannot speak
bi:t beet. *gula ** beet sugar
biṭet scar from a wound
biṭi fist. **m/di*** to punch
biting 1 coconut-leaf rib sharpened to a point, for pinning leaf-wrapped packets. 2 unit for weighing gold. 3 *ltry* unit of 400. *sa** 400. ***an** pinned with a leaf-rib pin. **m/di*i** to fasten [a parcel] with such a pin
bitjanten *rg var of* WITJANTEN
bitjârâ *rg var of* WITJARA
biṭu *-* having a round full face
biwâdâ *oj* **m/di*** to revere, hold in awe
biwârâ *oj* *see* LAJANG
bjah *rpr* suddenly breaking apart. **, sarungé beḍah.* His sarong suddenly ripped. **nge*** 1 common, general. 2 (*psv* **di***) to generalize. *Jèn ana murid sidji sing kesèd, adja di* jèn sakelas paḍa kesèd kabèh.* If one student is lazy, don't assume the whole class is lazy. *See also* AMBJAH, GEBJAH
bjaja(h) *var of* BIJAJAH
bjajak *var of* BIJAJAK
bjak *rpr* suddenly opening/parting. *Lawang mbukak *.* Suddenly the door burst open. **, soroting rembulan nratas méga.* The moon suddenly broke through the clouds. ***-*an** acting with hurried *or* restless motions. *Bareng udjiané kari seminggu, A lagi*

*-*an sinau.* A week before the exam A began to study frantically. *Ḍèké *-*an nggolèki ḍompèté merga isih ditunggu sopir taksi.* He completed the purchase in great haste–the taxi was waiting outside. **nge/di*-(aké)** to open sth (out) wide

bjang *var of* BIJANG. **(m)*-*an** to wander about habitually, enjoy going places

bjar 1 a flash; to flash. *Dumadakan * dadi paḍang kabèh.* Suddenly a flash lighted up everything. *Mak * lampuné murub manèh.* The lights came on again. 2 to open the eyes. 3 daybreak. *Ngantos * saweg sami wangsul.* They didn't get back till dawn. **nge*** to stay awake all night. *Aku mau bengi nge* sinau.* I studied all night last night. *Olèhé sinau nganti nge*.* He studied all night. *** **klékar** *or* *** **paḍang** to wake up in the morning. *Saben * paḍang wong loro kuwi wiwit padon.* They start quarreling as soon as they get up. *** **pet** to go off and on. *Lampuné kok * pet waé.* How come the lights keeping going on and off! *Tjahjané * pet, gèk katon mangah², gèk katon putjet.* She flushed and paled by turns. *See also* AMBJAR

bjat 1 heavy; weight. 2 habit. **ka*an** excessively heavy

bjor ***-*an** shining, sparkling. *See also* ABJOR

bjuk *rpr* mass movement. *Laron iku tekané mak * bebarengan.* The flying ants came in hordes. ***-*(an)** to go smw in large numbers. *Jèn bar panèn djengglèng, pari bandjur *-*an diujangaké.* Right after the harvest the market is glutted with rice. *Walang sangit *-*an mara geni.* The insects clustered around the fire. **ke*an** to have sth swarming all over it. **nge*** to go smw in large numbers. *Tangga-teparoné paḍa nge* rerèwang ing kono.* The neighbors flocked around to help. **nge/di*i** to heap/pour sth onto. *nge*i ujah* to salt sth copiously. *Geniné di*i kaju.* He heaped wood on the fire. *See also* AMBJUK

bjung *rpr* a swarming movement. *Wong² bandjur lunga mak *.* The people flocked out. ***-*an** to move in large groups. *Ana wong pirang² *-*an ing kono.* There were great crowds there. *manuk mabur *-*an* birds flying in flocks. **ma*an** *ltry var of* *-*AN. **nge*** to move as a group. *Manuké nge* mangétan.* The birds flew eastward in flocks.

bju:r 1 *rpr* a splash. *Mak * njegur ing kali.* He jumped in the river. 2 *rpr* a quick movement. ** paḍa mlaju ngiṭar.* They scurried off. 3 monochromatic. *abang ** plain red. *Témboké putih *.* The wall is solid white. **bjar-*** to splash oneself with water. ***-*an** to jump into water (for fun). **nge*** to splash [water] around; to scatter [small objects] about. **nge/di*aké** to spread, scatter. *nge*aké widji²* to scatter seeds. **nge/di*i** to splash sth [with] *or* scatter [sth] onto. *See also* AMBJUR, GEBJUR

blâbâ generous

blabag 1 board. 2 blackboard. 3 one who is responsible for sth. 4 *var of* BLEBEG. **ke*** to be given a responsibility. *Krama dina iki ke* ngilèni sawahé.* It's Krama's job to let water into the paddies today. **m*** hard, boardlike

blabar **m*** to overflow. *Banjuné m*.* The water overflowed. *Alun² djedjel wadyabala nganti m* menjang pasar.* The square was so jammed with troops they spilled over into the marketplace.

blabuk **m/di*aké** to sell fake articles as genuine

blabur 1 blurred, hazy. 2 *rg* flood. **ke*an** flooded, inundated

blad pattern transferred to another paper underneath by drawing heavily over the lines. **nge/di*** to trace a drawing in this way

blaḍak **m*** badly behaved

blaḍeg ***an** continuous successive occurrences. **an redjeki kok ora entèk².* There's no end to his good fortune. **ke*** to keep having sth happen to one. *Ḍèké lagi ke* redjeki.* He's having a run of luck. **m/di*** to happen continuously (to smn). *Jèn saben dina di* iwak pitik gorèng suwé² ja djelèh.* If you're served fried chicken every day, you'll get tired of it sooner or later.

blader **ke*(-*)** to be inconvenienced, annoyed, *etc.* by untidiness around one. **m*(-*)** cluttered; cluttering. *Médja² paḍa katon m*.* The tables were littered with stuff.

bladjar to teach; to learn, study. ***an** 1 education, teaching, instruction. 2 in the learning stage

blaḍo *see* LINTANG

blaḍog gluttonous. **m/di*** to eat greedily

blaḍu muddy, mucky. **ke*** to get trampled into the mud. **m*** muddy

blaèr (*or* ***an**) to salivate freely when about to vomit
blaès oh dear! (*excl of surprise or concern*)
blai 1 *inf var of* BILAHI. 2 *excl of surprise or concern*
blai:k *excl expressing fear or alarm*
blajang **m*** to go smw for pleasure, engage in pleasurable activity
blak 1 *rpr* opening. *Lawangé mak * mbukak.* Suddenly the door opened. 2 paper pattern. ** klambi* dress pattern. **-*an* wide open; concealing nothing. *Omahé ditinggal *-*an.* He left the house with the doors and windows open. *sorot *-*an* open-air movie. *Olèhé rembugan *-*an.* They discussed it frankly. **nge*** 1 wide open. 2 (*psv* **di***) to open sth. 3 (*psv* **di***) to make a pattern; to use sth as a pattern. *Gawéan omahku di*.* He copied my homework. **nge/di*aké** to open; to disclose. *nge*aké lawang* to open a door. *Wadiné die*aké.* He let out the secret. *See also* ABLAK
blâkâ 1 frank, candid; to tell the truth. ** jèn sing ndjupuk ḍèwèké.* He admitted he had stolen it. *Ditakoni kumpulan apa, ora gelem *.* Asked what groups he belonged to, he wouldn't tell. 2 *rg* plain, unadorned. *tèh ** plain tea (no sugar). **m/di*kaké** to tell frankly, tell the truth about. *Ḍèké ora m*kaké djenengé.* He didn't give his right name. *m*kaké kesalahané* to acknowledge one's mistake. **m/di*ni** to tell the truth (to). *Takon marang bijung ora di*ni.* He asked his mother but she wouldn't tell him. *Aku *nana.* Come clean with me! *** suta** to tell the truth, admit frankly
blaki *rg kr for* BLAKA
blalak **-* or* **m*** [of eyes] beautifully wide and clear. **m/di*-*aké** to try to make [one's eyes] look beautiful by opening them wide
blanak a certain edible fish
blânḍâ *see* AÈR
blanḍang **m*** to run fast. *Djam iki ora m* ora kèṭèr.* This watch doesn't run fast or slow. **m/di*aké** to cause to run fast. *Djarané di*aké.* He spurred on his horse.
blandar roof frame. ***an** main section of a house frame. *** pa·n̈g·keret** ridgepole
blanḍit *ptg ** 1 in disorder; scattered around. 2 inconsistent, specious, untenable
blândjâ 1 to shop (for). ** menjang pasar* to go shopping at the market. ** djarik* to shop for batiks. 2 salary, wages. ** pedinan* daily pay. 3 cost of living. *anggaran ** budget. **be*n** to do shopping. **m/di*** to pay [a worker]. **m/di*kaké** 1 to buy things on smn's behalf. *Aku kudu m*kaké ibu.* I have to do the shopping for Mother. 2 to spend [money]
blanḍong woodcutter. ***an** act *or* way of cutting wood. **m*** to cut wood for a living
blandrang *var of* BLANDRENG
blandreng ***an** *or* **m*** continuous, uninterrupted. *terus m* ping lima* 5 in a row. *Olèhé nggendjot pit m* waé.* He kept right on pedaling his bicycle.
blang **-*an* [of housewives] always out visiting, running errands, *etc.*
blanggem cassava cake
blanggrèng blossom of the coffee plant
blangkem ***en** 1 stunned speechless. 2 [of mouth] not having been used (for talking, eating) for hours on end
blangko 1 form/blank to be filled out. 2 to abstain from voting
blangkok varicolored, multicolored
blangkon *iket*-style headdress permanently sewn in shape. ***an** to wear *or* put on the above
blangkrèh *ptg ** in disorder. *Omahé ptg *.* The house is messy.
blantik (*or* *** radjakaja**) dealer in livestock and birds
blanṭongan ant-like insect
blarah ***an** *or* **m*** pervasive [of a disagreeable odor]
blarak (dried) coconut leaf. ** nam-naman* woven coconut leaves
blarongan to reek, smell foul
blarut a scratch, cut. *ptg ** having many cuts/scratches. **m*** cut, scratched. *See also* BARUT
blas 1 altogether. *waras ** fully recovered. 2 *rpr* a swift motion. *Lagi baé diuntjali bal, * wis diuntjlangaké kantjané.* As soon as he caught the ball he flipped it to his teammate. ***-*an** in great haste. *Olèhé matja *-*an.* He skimmed through it. *See also* GEBLAS, KEBLAS
blasah *ptg ** scattered about. *Kekembangan werna² ptg * ana ratan.* There were flowers strewn on the road. **ke*** to get messed up *or* scattered about. **m*** scattered on the ground; to spread, scatter, strew

blasak *an to stray, wander. **ke*** to get lost. **m*(-*)** to wander here and there. **m*aké** 1 misleading. *Tengeré m*aké.* The label is misleading. 2 (*psv* **di*aké**) to cause smn to go wrong. *Aku di*aké tukang bétjak.* The pedicab driver gypped me by taking me on a long roundabout route.

blasar **m*** astray, on the wrong road (*lit, fig*). *tindak m** aberrant conduct

blaster crossbred bird: a female white dove (*puter*) bred with a different male dove, as: *** dara** white dove crossbred with a dove (*dara*). *** deruk** crossbreed with a male gray dove (*deruk*). *** lumut** crossbreed with a male gray-green dove (*lumut*)

blasuk *var of* BLASAK

blatèr popular; friendly, outgoing

blaṭi dagger

blatjan a certain wild cat

blatjo raw cotton to be woven into white cotton fabric

blatju *var of* BLATJO

blaṭok a type of axe

blatung maggot

blau bluing (used in wash water)

blaudrek̄ blueprint

blaur 1 stubborn, headstrong. 2 *var of* BLAWUR

blawah *an to overflow. **m*** 1 to overflow. 2 wide, gaping

blawan *an to speak street language, talk obscenely or coarsely. **m*** to fight

blawong 1 long and big around. 2 a big eater

blawu cement in the powdered state. *semèn ** powdered cement

blawur blurred, not clearly visible

blawus faded from frequent launderings

blebah [of rain] hard, pouring. *** panèn·an** harvest time, when rice is plentiful and cheap

blebed protective covering/wrapping; bandage. **ke*** to get wrapped/wound. *Sikilé ke* ojot wit wringin.* He got his foot tangled in a banyan root. **m/di*** to apply a wrapping to. *Dridjiné di*.* She bandaged his finger.

blebeg 1 *rpr* sudden submergence. *Slamet mak * terus ora kétok.* Slamet disappeared under water. 2 *rg var of* BREBEG. **ke*** to get submerged. **m/di*aké** to submerge sth. *Gendul² kosong di*aké ing banju umob.* He immersed the empty bottles in boiling water.

blèbèk thick flat piece. *wesi sa** a sheet of iron. ***an** in (the form of) sheets. **an* *emas* sheets of gold. **m*** to flow outward in all directions

blèbèr *var of* BLABAR

bleber to fly. *Matjan mlumpat *.* The tiger took a flying leap. *ptg ** to fly in all directions. *Lawané paḍa ptg * metu saka guwa.* The bats came flying out of the cave. **blebar-*** to fly back and forth

blebes 1 *rpr* sudden submergence. *Ḍèké njilem mak *.* He dove under. 2 ruler used as an aligning tool, *e.g.* by bricklayers, weavers. **m*** 1 downward. *Lajangané njiruké m*.* The kite took a long swooping dive. 2 too wet to burn

bleḍag **m*** to billow *or* shoot out. *Komporé m*.* The stove blew up. *Wetengé m*.* His stomach bulges out.

bleḍèg thunder with lightning

bleḍeg *rg var of* BEḌEḌEG

bleḍèh **m*** partly opened up. *Klambimu m* mbok dibenikké.* Your shirt is coming open: button it!

bleḍeng *rpr* entering. *Bareng Slamet mlebu mak * ana klas, botjah² paḍa surak.* When Slamet popped into the classroom, everybody cheered.

bleder *var of* BLADER

bleḍes *rpr* submerging. *Mak *, ḍèké silem.* She suddenly dived in. **m/di*aké** to submerge sth. *Sirahé di*aké banju.* He ducked.

bledig **m/di*** to chase

blèdjèd **m/di*i** 1 to strip, remove the outer layer *or* clothing from. *Urangé di*i kulité.* She shelled the shrimp. *Pétruk di*i.* They took off Petruk's clothes. 2 to rob smn

bledjed (*or* **m***) *intsfr* naked. *wuda (m)** stark naked. **bledjad-*** to undress. *Olèhmu salin gèk bledjat-*.* Hurry and change!

bledjog *an on an impulse, on the spur of the moment. **m/di*** 1 to [do] on an impulse. *Wingi Slamet m* teka ing omahku.* Slamet dropped in on us yesterday. 2 to fire questions at smn

bleḍog *an large loud firecracker. **m*** to explode noisily

bleḍos **ke*an** to be affected adversely by an explosion. *Kantjaku ke*an mretjon, nganti tjatjad mripaté.* A firecracker went off close to a friend of mine and damaged his eyes. **m*** to explode, erupt. *uniné beḍil m** the sound of a gun going off.

Gunung geniné m∗. The volcano erupted. **m/di∗aké** to cause to explode. *m∗aké ban* to burst a tire (by pumping too much air into it). **m/di∗i** to affect adversely by exploding. *Mertjoné m∗i mripaté.* The firecracker went off in his eyes. **pa·m∗** act of exploding

bleḍu *rg var of* BLEḌUG

bledug 1 dust, *esp.* in the air. ∗ *raḍioaktip* radioactive dust. *Kasurané ana ∗é.* The cushions are dusty. 2 earnings apart from salary (tips, commission, *etc.*). *∗ing negara* travel expenses allowed to government officials. 3 baby elephant (young of the GADJAH). **ke∗an** to get covered with sth from the air. *Pangananė ke∗an awu.* The food got ashes in it. **m∗** dusty. **m/di∗i** to get dust onto

bleḍug 1 mud. 2 *var of* BLEḌOG

blèg metal can; metal of which cans are made. *bukakan ∗* can opener. **∗-∗an** in cans; by the can. *roti ∗-∗an* cookies in tins. **nge/di∗i** to can [foods, *etc.*]

bleg *rpr* a swishing *or* shuffling impact. *Djarané digebug ∗.* He lashed the horse. *tiba mak ∗* to fall with a *splat!* 2 altogether. *Témboké putih ∗.* The wall is all white. *Mas lan aḍiké paḍa ∗.* The brothers look exactly alike. 3 the day smn dies (*rg var of* GEBLAG). **blag-∗** *rpr* repeated impacts as above. *nggebugi blag-∗* to rain blows on. **ke∗an** to get hit from above. *Pawoné ambruk ke∗an wit klapa.* The cooking area was demolished by a falling coconut tree. **nge/di∗aké** to drop [sth heavy]. *Watuné die∗aké.* He let the stone fall with a thud. **nge/di∗i** 1 to resemble closely. *Praupané wis nge∗i simbah kakung.* He looks just like his grandfather. 2 (*psv* **di∗i**) to drop sth onto. *Awaké di∗i beras sekarung.* A sack of rice fell on him. **∗ seg** *rpr* sudden inertness. *Nèk turu ∗ sek.* I dropped right off to sleep. *See also* AMBLEG

blegeḍeg **∗an** *cr* pure, true. *Islam ∗an* a Moslem through and through. *komunis ∗an* a communist to the core. **m∗** to boil with a plopping noise (*e.g.* thick porridge)

blegedjis **m∗** you see! you know! naturally!

blegenek *var of* BLEKENEK

blegèr *var of* BLEGER

bleger figure, shape. *∗ing pawakané kentjeng kijeng.* He has a tight, compact build. *∗é omahé* the style of the house

blegiḍig **m/di∗i** to arouse feelings of disgust/antipathy/revulsion

blegong **∗an** a hole. **ke∗** to fall into a hole by accident; *fig* to get gypped. **m/di∗i** to fall into. *Bolongané tutupen, munḍak m∗i.* Cover the hole, or smn'll fall into it.

blegug **m∗** fat, bulging

blekenek **m∗** nasty-looking, unsavory

bleketeg **m∗** muddy, dirty, unwashed

bleketépé woven coconut leaves (for walls, roofs)

bleketjeg *var of* BLEKEṬEG

blekètrèk **m∗** thin and watery, oozing disagreeably. *Geḍangé kematengen nganti bosok m∗.* The banana is overripe and spoiling.

bleketupuk a variety of owl

blekik **ke∗** to get discovered or trapped (when hiding)

blekok a certain heron

blèkrèk **m/di∗i** to cut off. *m∗i blarak* to lop off coconut leaves (from the branch)

blekuk *ptg ∗* 1 *pl* halting, hesitant, uncertain. 2 rumpled, crumpled. **blekak-∗** *sg* 1 hesitant, unsure. *Gunemané blekak-∗.* He spoke haltingly. 2 rumpled

blekuṭak a certain fish

blekuṭuk *ptg ∗ or ∗-∗ or* **m∗** 1 to bubble, boil. 2 to tell lies

blélu, blèlu *rg var of* BLILU

blemben a certain tall stiff grass

blembeng **m∗** short and squat in shape

blembong *var of* BLEMBUNG

blembung **m∗** large, round-shaped, rotund

blenḍang **m∗** bloated; *cr* pregnant

blèndèr board used for sliding a heavy object to move it. **∗an** joking, punning. *tembung ∗an* word/expression used for word play. **ke∗** to slide accidentally. **m∗** 1 to slip out of position. 2 to engage in banter *or* word play. 3 unreliable about keeping one's word. 4 [of women] promiscuous. **m/di∗aké** to delegate one's authority to smn else

blènder 1 pitcher, *i.e. kasti* player who pitches the ball. 2 food blender. **m∗** fat, roly-poly. **m/di∗i** to pitch to [players]

blenḍer **m∗** fat, bulging

blenḍing **m∗** 1 distended, bloated. 2 *cr* pregnant

bléndja **m/di∗ni** to break one's word. *Wis semajan, adja m∗ni.* You promised; don't go back on it.

blendjat *var of* BLENTJAT

blendjog *var of* BLEDJOG

bléṇdo *rg var of* BLONḌO

blendog reddish tree resin. **ke*** to get overcharged for merchandise. **m*** [of resin] to harden

bléndrang a tasty soup prepared a day ahead of eating (*see also* BÉNDRANG)

bléndré **m*** 1 to slip, slide. 2 untrustworthy, slippery

blèndrèng *rg var of* BLÈNDÈR

blenḍuk **m*** 1 round(ed) in shape. 2 bulging in the middle. 3 *cr* pregnant

blenḍung boiled corn kernels. **m*** swollen, inflated; to swell up

blenek̄ ***-*** *or* **m*** short and fat

blenet *var of* PLENET: *see* PLÈNÈT

bleng 1 throughout. *sedina ** all day long. 2 saliferous, brackish. 3 *rpr* entering. *Dilebokaké tjangkem, **. He popped it in his mouth. ***-*** *or* **blang-*** 1 to go in and out easily. 2 to keep booming. **nge*** 1 to deny oneself sth for the duration of a certain time period, *e.g.* to stay awake for 24 hours, as a form of asceticism. 2 (*psv* **di***) to soak sth in salt water. **nge/di*aké** to stuff/cram sth into

bléngah ***-*** 1 light-skinned. 2 pleasant, friendly-looking

blèngèr **m*** [of lips, face] red, rosy, healthy-looking

blenger ***-*** *or* **m*** repelled by a sight or odor

blenggu handcuffs. **m/di*** to handcuff smn

blengker 1 a frame. 2 a tire on a wheel. 3 *var of* BLUNGKER. **m/di*i** to equip with a frame *or* edging material. *Gambaré di*i kaju.* He put a wooden frame on the picture.

blèngkèt close [of blood or other relationships]

blengkik *ptg ** 1 devious, roundabout. *Omongané ptg **. There's sth below the surface of what he's saying. 2 *var of* BLENGKUK

bléngkrah *ptg ** in disarray, messy. **m/di*i** to disarrange, put into disorder

blengkuk *ptg ** full of dips, curves, furrows *etc.* rather than smooth-surfaced. **m*** 1 bent at the end. 2 [to sit] slumped over. **m/di*aké** to bend sth

blengur small goose (young of the BANJAK)

blenjèk **m*** soft and mushy

blenjik *teri* fish salted and rolled up ready to fry

blentèng ***-*** patterned with dots of another color

blentjat *ptg ** *or* ***an** in random rather than consecutive order. *Olèhé mangsuli pitakonan ptg *, ora urut.* He skipped around instead of answering the questions in order.

bléntjong oil lamp used in shadow-play performances for throwing the puppets' shadows on the screen

blentjung **m*** to walk steadily and purposefully without paying attention to anything else

blentong spot, blemish. *ptg ** spotted, covered with blemishes

blenṭot [of physique] firm, compact

blépot messy, greasy, muddy

blérah ***-*** [of eyes] bright, shining

bléré to have a ready laugh

blèrèk *var of* BLÈKRÈK, BLIRIK

blerek *rg var of* BLERET

blèrèng *rg var of* LÈRÈNG

blereng blinded by glaring light. ***-*** 1 glaring light. 2 blindingly glaring. **ke*en** to have the eyes blinded by glare. **m/di*i** to dazzle with glaring light; *fig* to bedazzle, overawe

bleret (*or* **m***) to dim, become gloomy. *Ulaté rada **. He has a glum expression. *Lampuné kok m*.* I wonder why the light dimmed! *Réputasiné wis m*.* His reputation has lost its glamor. **m/di*aké** to make sth dim/gloomy/darker

bléro 1 dissonant, inharmonious. *Gamelané **. The orchestra is out of tune. *Si A saiki kok * panemuné.* Why is A's opinion always different from everybody else's? 2 to waver between alternatives

bles *rpr* entering. *Wetengé disuduk mak **. He was stabbed in the stomach. *Prauné botjor suwé² bandjur mak * kèrem.* The leaky boat finally sank. **nge/di*aké** to stick/stab sth into. *See also* AMBLES, BLEBES

blesar *ptg ** scattered about. *Buku²né ptg * ana ngendi-endi.* The books were scattered all over.

blesat *ptg ** unbound and coming apart

bleseg *rpr* entering, inserting. *Olèhé nglebokaké sikil gampang mak **. His feet slipped right into [the shoes]. **blesag-*** *rpr* repeated insertions. *Olèhé nglebokaké klambi nèng koper blesak-* waé.* He threw his clothes into a suitcase. **ke*** to get stuck in(to). *Tjikaré ke* ana ing dalan.* The wagon got stuck on the road. **m*** 1 pressed/wedged into. 2 made lopsided, damaged, *etc.* by pressing. *Kerisé m* ing sabuk.* His kris was tucked too far down into his belt. *Krandjangé m* ketinḍihan kursi.* The basket got wedged up into the chair that was set down on top of it. **m/di*aké** to wedge sth into. *Kerisé di*aké ing tengah sabuk.* He tucked his kris in the center of his sash.

blèter inflatable bladder of a leather ball. *bal ** soccer ball

bleṭok mud. ***an** muddy place. **m*** muddy

bléwah 1 a variety of melon. 2 *var of* BLÈWÈH

blèwèh ***an** 1 an opening with the edges turned back. 2 a ditch. **m*** opened out; to come open. *Tatuné sing lagi waé didjahit m* menèh.* His newly sutured wound opened up again.

blèwèk *var of* BLÈWÈH

blibar fruit bud of the mangosteen

bliḍuk *var of* BLIṬUK

bligo a variety of pumpkin

bligung **bligang-*** *or* **m*** undressed; shirtless

blijar ***-*** *var of* BLIJAT-BLIJUT

blijur *var of* BLIJUT

blijut **blijat-*** nodding with drowsiness, so sleepy that things swim before the eyes. **m*** sleepy, drowsy

blila *var of* BALÉLA

blilet *sbst kr for* BLILU

blilu **ka*n̂** untrained, lacking in knowledge or skill. **m*** 1 to act ignorant/unschooled. 2 (*psv* **di***) to cheat, swindle. ***tau** to have acquired a skill through experience rather than formal training

blimbing a tart yellow fruit about the size of a mango. ***an** resembling this fruit. *** lingir** a dessert variety of this fruit. *** wuluh** a small sour *blimbing* used in cooking

blinḍi *ptg ** in the form of small round pellets. **m/di*ǹi** to form sth into pellets

blinḍis 1 bald. 2 bare, naked. 3 bankrupt, broke

blindjo *rg var of* MLINDJO

blinger **ke*** 1 to be taken unawares; to get cheated; to get caught in a mistake. 2 *slang* crazy. *Wis ke* pikirané.* He's off his rocker. *Ke* ajuné bandjur édan.* Her beauty drove him wild. **m/di*aké** to cheat/swindle smn. **m/di*i** to mislead, confuse

blingkrah *var of* BLÉNGKRAH

blirik (*or* ***-***) speckled, flecked with color

blisah restless, uneasy

bliṭuk **ke*** to get swindled. **m/di*(i)** to cheat, gyp, swindle

bliwur (*or* **ke***) lost, bewildered, confused

blobok discharged matter from the eye. **m*** having discharged matter in/around the eye

blobor ***an** 1 liquid absorbed. **ané kertas A ngenani kertas B.* The ink that soaked into paper A got on paper B. 2 having been absorbed; having soaked in. **m*** 1 absorbent. 2 to get absorbed. *Tulisané m*.* The writing soaked in[to the paper]. **m/di*i** to soak into. *Kertas A m*i kertas B.* Paper A soaked through onto paper B.

blobos *var of* BROBOS

blodjod **m/di*i** 1 to remove the clothing from smn. 2 to rob, hold up, clean out

bloḍog a certain fish

blodro **m/di*** to smear sth (onto). *Wong²-ané di* pulut nangka.* He smeared jackfruit resin on the dummy.

blog 1 block or plot of land. 2 *rpr* a thud, slap. 3 roll, bolt [of fabric] (*see also* EMBLOG). ***-*an** 1 *rpr* thudding *or* slapping. 2 [fabric] in rolls/bolts

blok̄ bloc. ** wétan (kulon)* Eastern (Western) bloc

blokèk ***an** *or* **m*** to feel nauseated; to vomit

blokèng *rg var of* BONGKOK

blolok ***en** blinded by glaring light. **m*i** blindingly glaring

blombong ***an** a large opening. **m*** large [of an opening]

blonḍo remains of coconut from which oil has been extracted

blondor *rg var of* BLONDRONG

blonḍos *rg var of* BLINḌIS

blondrok *rg var of* BLONDRONG

blondrong **ke*** 1 to get cheated, *esp.* overcharged. 2 to be misled, be given faulty information. **m/di*aké** to cheat *or* mislead smn

blong 1 *rpr* sudden relief from strain or tension. 2 empty. *kosong ** or *koṭong ** completely empty

blongkèng *rg var of* BONGKOK

blongsong 1 material (paper, bamboo, *etc.*) for wrapping fruits while still on the tree, to hasten the ripening. 2 kris decoration. ***an** protective wrapping for fruit. **m/di*(i)** to wrap [fruit] as above. *Pelem kuwi *en ḍéwé.* Wrap that mango yourself. *Pelemé di*i bèn énggal mateng.* They wrapped the mangoes so they'd ripen quickly.

blonjo(h) ***an** to rub (with). **an tamba saawak sekodjur* to rub medication all over one's body. **m/di∗** to rub sth onto. *m∗ ḍaḍa* to smear the chest with ointment

blonṭang (*or* **∗-∗**) dotted with large spots of color

blonṭèng *var of* BLONṬANG

blopot *rg var of* BLÉPOT

blorok speckled, spotted. *pitik ∗* a speckled hen

blorong black-and-white striped

blorot *rg var of* BLONDRONG

blos *rpr* piercing. *Kertasé ditjoblos mak ∗.* He stabbed a pin into the paper.

blosok *var of* BLUSUK

blosong *var of* BLONGSONG

blosot *var of* BROSOT

blotjok (*or* **∗an**) fuzzily *or* indistinctly patterned [of batik]

bloṭong remains of peanuts after the oil has been extracted

blotrong **m∗** paunchy, sagging in the abdomen

blowok **ke∗** 1 to step into a hole accidentally. 2 to get overcharged for merchandise

blubud **m∗** inconsiderate; brazen

blubuk **∗an** [of soil, ash] soft, crumbling. *geni ∗an* ashes with glowing embers among them. **∗-∗** *rpr* the sound of air bubbles emerging from water. **m∗** soft, crumbling

blubur **m∗** soft, crumbly (*e.g.* chalk)

blubus *var of* BLUBUD

bludag **∗an** 1 overflow, spillage. 2 an outpouring of generosity. **m∗** 1 to overflow, spill out/over. 2 generous to a fault. 3 boastful

bluder Dutch-style vanilla cake with raisins

bludir **∗an** embroidered fabric. **m/di∗** to embroider

bludju 1 (*or* **m∗**) having clean simple lines without ornamentation [of crafted objects]. 2 symmetrically shaped cylindrical object

bludreg high blood pressure

bluḍru velvet

bluḍuk **∗an** soft crumbly substance, *esp.* soil. **m∗** soft and crumbly

bluḍus **m∗** to barge into a party or entertainment without having received an invitation or bought a ticket

blug *rpr* a thud. *Krambil ditibakaké ∗.* He dropped the coconut with a thud. *Bubuk, bubuk, ∗.* Let's lie down and go to sleep! **blag-∗** *rpr* repeated thudding falls. *Klapané paḍa tiba blag-∗.* The coconuts kept dropping.

blui *see* BUWI

bluk̄ *rpr* bursting into flame. *Jèn ditjeḍaki geni gasé mbandjur mak ∗ murub.* If gas gets near fire, it flares up suddenly.

blukang *rg var of* BONGKOK

blukèk *var of* BLOKÈK

blukèr *var of* BLUWÈR

bluluk coconut in its first stage of development on the tree

blulung *ptg ∗ or* **∗an** panic-stricken

blumbang ornamental garden pond with fish. **∗an** 1 bed of a pond. 2 batik-bordered fabric used for headdresses, brassières. **∗an siwak·an** river-fed pond

blundrah spotted, stained

blundrèh *var of* BLUNDRAH

bluṇḍus (*or* **m∗**) *intsfr* naked. *Botjahé m∗ wuda.* The child was stark naked.

blung 1 *rpr* a sudden submerging. *Kantjil ketjemplung ana sumur, mak ∗!* Mouse-Deer fell splash! into the well. 2 *intsfr* empty. *suwung ∗* completely empty

blungka (over)ripe cucumber

blungkak melon

blungkang *rg var of* BONGKOK

blungkèng *rg var of* BONGKOK

blungker *ptg ∗* quaking, cowering (from cold, fear). **m∗** 1 to cower, quake. 2 to hug the knees to the chest

bluntjat **m∗** to jump, leap. **(m)∗-(m)∗** to jump around (physically, *e.g.* a grasshopper; *or* to [do] out of sequence rather than in consecutive order)

bluru *ptg ∗ or* **m∗** to disperse, spread in all directions

blurut **m∗** to commit a burglary in broad daylight

blus 1 shirt; blouse. 2 *rpr* stabbing. *Mak ∗ domé mantjeb.* The (hypodermic) needle stabbed into him. **∗an** to put on *or* wear a shirt/blouse

blusuk *rpr* entering. *Tikus mak ∗ nḍelik ing lèng.* The mouse whisked into its hole. **blusak-∗** to keep entering [places where one does not belong]. **ke∗** to enter by mistake. *Sikilku ke∗ got.* My foot slipped into the ditch. *Si matjan ke∗, ketjemplung ing djugangan djero.* The tiger fell into a deep ravine. **m∗** to enter. *m∗ menjang alas* to go into the forest. **m/di∗aké** 1 to put/push sth (into). *Latjiné di∗aké mlebu.* He pushed the drawer shut. *Ban di∗aké sirah njegur menjang ing kali.* He slipped his head into the inner tube and jumped into the river. 2 to persuade smn to do wrong

bluṭak a certain fish
bluṭèh slushy, oozy; partially melted
bluwek̄ *rpr* slipping easily into sth, *esp.* a hole. *Nèkeré mlebu mak* *. The marble rolled right in[to the hole]. *Glaṭiné mak * temantjep nang wetengé.* The dagger stabbed into his stomach. ***an** a hole in the ground. **bluwak-*** to keep going into holes. **ke*** to slip into a hole by accident
bluwèr ***an** nauseated
bluwer **m*** 1 muddy. 2 to play in mud
bluwi *var of* BUWI
bluwus [of fabric] old and faded. **m*** to wear faded old clothing
bo *adr* kerbau! (*shf of* KEBO)
bobat *var of* BUBAT
bobok 1 healing ointment of powdered herbs mixed with water. 2 to sleep (*child's word: var of* BUBUK). **m/di*** to break. *Témboké di**. He broke through the wall. *m* tjèlèngan* to break open a piggy bank. **m/di*aké** to apply [a powder-and-water mixture]. *Tukang batuné ndjupuk adonan semèn bandjur di*ké nang témbok.* The bricklayer took a trowelful of mortar and slapped it on the wall. **m/di*i** to apply [such a mixture] to. *m*i botjah* to put a poultice on a child
bobol **m/di*(i)** to break through sth. *m* tjangklakané barisané mungsuh* to break through the enemy lines
bobor 1 [of eggs] infertile. 2 a soup of vegetables and coconut milk
bobot *ng,* **wawrat** *kr* 1 weight; a weight. **é pira?* How much does it weigh? 2 (degree of) importance, prestige. *Wong mau dudu *mu.* He's not as important as you are. ***an** to go to the bathroom (*ki for* NG·ISING). *Tamuné wis *an.* The guests have washed up. **m*** 1 (*psv* **di***) to weigh. *m* beras* to weigh rice. 2 (*psv* **di***) to put a price on sth. *Tokoné m* reganing bungkus.* The store charges for wrapping packages. 3 pregnant. **m/di*i** 1 to weight sth down. *Kertasé di*i watu.* He weighted the paper down with a stone. 2 to get advice/opinions from. *Sadurungé mutus, betjiké m*i para sardjana.* Before you decide, you'd better get some scholarly opinions. **pa·m*** *ki* pregnant. **sa*(é)** proportionate. *Paukumané sa* karo salahé.* The punishment fits the crime. *Sikilé walang iku ing sa*é kuwat tur kengkeng.* Locusts' legs are strong and sturdy in proportion to the size of the body. *** timbang** consideration of the alternatives. *Apa anané wis dak terangaké, saiki * timbang ana kowé.* I've told you all the facts; now you'll have to decide. *** watu** counterweight. *See also* ABOT, BIBIT, BOT
bobrak badly damaged, broken apart. **m/di*** to damage, break
bobrok in bad condition. *omah ** a ramshackle house. ***an** damaged, wrecked
bod paid in full. *Utangku wis **. My debt is all paid. ***-*an** money, or a substitute, for paying a debt. *Merga utangé akèh, *-*ané ja ora seṭiṭik.* He has so many debts it'll take a lot to pay them off. **nge/di*aké** 1 to pay smn's debt for him. 2 to use sth to pay off a debt. *Aku nge*aké sawahku.* I paid off my debt with my rice paddy. **nge/di*i** to complete payment on a debt. *Anggonku nge*i lagi wingi baé.* I just made the final payment yesterday.
boḍag broad shallow woven-bamboo basket in which rice is kept
boḍèh wild betel vine
boḍèng busy, pressed for time
bodin cassava
boḍing scythe, grass-cutting knife
bodja *ltry* food. *** krama** a reception party
bodjânâ feast, banquet. *** andrawina** large dinner party
bodjlèng *boastful excl used by wj ogres.* ***-* iblis lanat (begidjigan)** *excl of astonishment*
bodjo *ng kr,* **garwa** *ki* spouse. *ngepèk ** to choose a wife. **né wis mèh teka.* Her husband will be here any minute. ***n** the wife of an official. *bodjon lurah* village head's wife. **be*an** to get married. *** djaka-lara** one's original wife whom he has never divorced
bodjod broken through in such a way that ends stick out, *e.g.* a woven basket with a hole poked through it
bodjog measure for raw rice: *ca.* 7 *kati*'s, or roughly 9 lbs.
boḍo stupid, ignorant. ***n** 1 taking a guess. *Boḍon ḍèké iki murid.* I judge from his general aspect that he's a student. *Jèn kowé ora ngerti senengané, *n tukokna rok.* If you don't know what she likes, just get her a dress. 2 one who is untrained. *manut étungan boḍon* from the layman's point of view. ***-*an** to compare for stupidity. *Boḍo²an, A luwih * tinimbang B.*

When it comes to stupidity, A is dumber than B. **m*** to pretend to be ignorant or indifferent. *Lijané paḍa omong²an bab sekolah, ning Tama m**. The others were chatting about school, but Tomo didn't join in at all. **m/di·be*** to cheat *or* make a fool of smn. **m*k(-*k)aké** 1 to play dumb, pretend not to know or care. 2 (*psv* **di*k⁽²⁾aké**) to consider smn stupid/ignorant. *Adja mboḍok-boḍokaké Ali.* Don't keep telling Ali he's dumb! **m*ni** to act dumb/stupid

boḍol 1 to come out [of feathers, hair, *etc.*] *Elaré * kabèh.* Its feathers all fell out. *Sapuné *.* The broom straws came off. 2 worn out, threadbare. *ban ** a worn-out tire. 3 departure (*var of* BUḌAL). **m/di*aké** 1 to remove the feathers *etc.* from. 2 to send smn off. **m*i** 1 to molt (*var of* M·BRODOL·I). 2 (*psv* **di*i**) to pull sth (out). *Kipasé adja di*i.* Don't pull the fan apart!

bodong 1 [of navel] inverted, protruding. 2 stupid, ignorant

boḍor comedian, joker

bog *rpr* a dull plop. *Pelemé tiba *.* The mango fell with a plop. ***-*an** contracted for on a job basis. **ka*an** saddled with a burden. **nge/di*** to buy up (in large quantities; all that is for sale); to buy the crop of a fruit tree before the fruit is harvested. **nge/di*aké** 1 to let sth fall with a plop. 2 to sell the crop of a fruit tree

boga food. *See also* UPABOGA

bogang [of corn, rice] damaged by crop disease

bogèl (cut) short. *Kaṭokmu *.* Your pants are (too) short. **ka*an** too short [*esp.* of a shadow-play performance which incorrectly ends before dawn]

bogem 1 box where jewelry is kept. 2 a certain fruit. *** mentah** a blow in the face

bogoh a variety of tree

bogor *rg* sugar-palm tree. **m*** to draw the sap from this tree

boikot boycott. **m/di*** to boycott

bojã *wj* (*or* **m***) no; not

bojok the small of the back

bojong (*or* ***an**) to move, change one's location. *Si A *an nang Djakarta sak anak bodjoné.* A moved to Djakarta with his family. *Manuk² mau paḍa * bebarengan, parané mengidul.* These birds migrate to the south. **ke*** to be taken to live elsewhere, *esp.* as a bride. **m/di*** *wj* to take [*esp.* a princess] to one's home as his bride. **m/di*i** to take smn to a different place to live. **pa*an** act of moving

bok (*or* **m***) 1 please; why don't you...? how about...? *mBok aku dikèki pelemé.* Would you give me some mangoes? *mBok kowé waé sing mangkat.* Why don't *you* go? *mBok bèn dolanan ḍéwé.* Just let him play by himself. *mBok ija.* Please do! *mBok mengko².* Wait a while! 2 mother (*see also* EMBOK). 3 *2d-person psv prefix: rg var of* KOK. **(m)*an** 1 *rg* please. *Aku dikèki pelemé, m*an.* Would you give me some mangoes? 2 (*or* **⌊m⌋*ané**) if, when(ever) (*rg slang for* MENAWA). **(m)*-(m)*** *excl of astonishment.* **(m)* bilih** if, when(ever) (*opt kr for* JÈN, MENAWA). **(m)* menawa** 1 perhaps, possibly, probably. *mBokmenawa ḍèké sésuk tekané.* He may get here tomorrow. 2 otherwise; or else. **(m)* mati** may I be struck dead... *mBok mati aku ora ndjupuk ḍuwitmu.* I swear I didn't take your money. **(m)* mula** from the first. *mBok mula aku wis kanḍa jèn pantji kuwi panas.* I told you all along the pan was hot. **(m)* wis (ta)** that's enough now. *mBok wis ta adja tansah dipikir.* Come, don't let it weigh on your mind. *mBok wis lèrèn olèhé matja, wis peteng.* You mustn't read any longer; it's too dark.

bokèt *var of* BUKÈT

bokong 1 (**botjong** *or* **potjong** *ki*) buttocks. 2 (the) bottom (part). ***an** 1 the back (part, *esp.* of a vehicle). 2 bottom (of a container). 3 a small rice paddy located among fields belonging to others. 4 flattened top part of a river dike. **m/di*(i)** 1 to push or maneuver sth with the buttocks. 2 to attack from the rear. 3 to support financially. **m/di*i** to turn one's back to smn. *** bunder** (having) round tray-shaped buttocks. *** n·djeḍit** (having) small pointed buttocks. *** kukus·an** footloose, unable to settle down, restless. *** m̈·pandjang ilang** (having) very shapely buttocks. *** tépos** (having) flat buttocks. *** n̈j·tjenṭing** *sms* * N·DJEḌIT

bokor large bowl, *usu.* of brass

boksen 1 (the sport of) boxing. 2 to box

bol 1 bowl-shaped container (*var of* BUL). 2 rectum. ***mu** *cr* *abusive term*

bolah 1 (sewing) thread; string. ** telung gulung* three spools of thread. **é lajangan* kite string. 2 dance, ball. *kamar ** ballroom; clubhouse for recreation

bolam electric light bulb
bolèd *rg* sweet potato; cassava. **m*** 1 tall and thin. 2 (moving) with wriggling snake-like motions
bolèg *var of* BOLÈD
bolèng (*or* ***en**) [of sugar cane, tuberous roots] hardening from plant disease
bolèr small fruit worm. ***en** rotted, infested with worms
bolo *shf of* GEMBOLO. *See also* M·BANG
bolong having a hole/opening in it. *dom ** sewing needle. *Kanṭongané **. There was a hole in his pocket. *Atiné **. He felt relieved. *Irungé buntet, bareng di-Vicks mbandjur **. His nose was stuffy; when he used Vicks it opened up. ***an** a hole. **an irung* nostril(s). **m/di*aké** to make a hole in sth accidentally. **m/di*i** to make a hole in sth deliberately
bolor respiratory disease of horses
bolos **m*** to sneak away from one's obligations. *Adja sok m**. Never play hooky. *tukang m** a habitual truant *or* work dodger. **pa·m*** act of dodging, *or* one who dodges, one's responsibilities
bolot dirt on the human skin. ***en** [of skin] dirty
bolu 1 crisp vanilla-flavored cookie. 2 cultivated plants/trees together with their fruits. *** rambat·an lemah** a complicated, interminable problem
bom 1 bomb. 2 large firecracker. ***-*an** 1 bombing raid. 2 to bomb each other. *Negara A lan negara B wis wiwit *-*an manèh.* Countries A and B have resumed their bombing attacks on each other. **nge/di*(i)** to bomb, bombard (a target)
boma *wj* sky, heaven
bomantârâ *wj* heaven and earth
bombang **ke*** to get neglected because no help is available. *Bareng Nem lunga, kétok banget jèn dalemé ke**. After Nem (a servant) left, the house went to wrack and ruin.
bombong optimistic, confident. **ke* ati·né** encouraged, bolstered. **m/di*** to encourage, impart confidence
bombrong soup made from young corn, *so* leaves, chili pepper, and coconut milk. **m*** 1 (*psv* **di***) to make [ingredients] into the above. 2 not neatly groomed (*shf of* N·DJEMBOMBRONG)
bon 1 an I.O.U.; a statement of indebtedness for a credit purchase. 2 a team of players chosen to represent a certain city or area in competition. ** Jogja* the team from Jogja. 3 *shf of* KEBON. *Pak ** the gardener. ***-*an** player chosen for the above type of team. *Slamet *-*an Kumpulan A.* Slamet is a member of Team A. **nge/di*** 1 to buy on credit. 2 to select smn for a team
bonang gamelan instrument consisting of a set of tuned inverted bronze bowls arranged horizontally. **m*** to play the *bonang;* (*psv* **di***) to play *bonang* along with *or* accompanying [other instruments]
bonḍan a classical dance of Surakarta, performed solo by a female, depicting a mother caring for her child. **m*** to perform this dance
bondjor a long section of bamboo
bondjrot *cr* to defecate
bonḍol a certain bird
bonḍot a certain climbing vine
bonéka(h) doll. *wajang sing kaja ** three-dimensional shadow-play puppet. *negara ** puppet nation
bong 1 person other than a doctor who performs a circumcision. 2 to lie down, go to bed (*children's word*). ** ja, wis bengi.* Go to sleep, honey, it's late. 3 a certain tree. 4 *shf of* OBONG. *kaju ** firewood. 5 mother (*rg var of* (EM)BOK). **nge/di*aké** to put [a child] to bed. *** supit** man who performs circumcisions. *** Tjina** Chinese cemetery
bongbong *var of* BOMBONG
bonggol the part of a tree trunk or plant stalk where it emerges from the soil
bongkang a certain insect
bongkar *var of* BUNGKAR
bongkèng *var of* BOLÈNG
bongko rice-accompanying dish: beans and grated young coconut steamed in banana-leaf wrappings
bongkok 1 stem of a coconut-palm leaf. 2 (*or* ***an**) a tied bundle. *kaju obong sa** a bundle of firewood. **m/di*(i)** to make into a bundle
bongkor (*or* ***an**) lying fallow. **m/di*aké** to allow [land] to remain fallow
bongkot 1 base of a stem/stalk. 2 the end. **é tjritané* the end of the story. *** putjuk·é** the circumstances/facts of. *Ḍèké ora ngerti * putjuké kok mèlu^2 njambung.* He doesn't know anything about it but he keeps interfering.
bongkrah out of order, in disrepair

bongkrèk remains *esp.* of peanuts after the oil has been extracted. *témpé* * fermented beancake made with peanut residue

bongoh pleased. * **kepleng** delighted

bonjèh ***en** having scabies sores

bonjok 1 overripe, beginning to spoil. 2 severely wounded. ***en** (to have/get) a certain scalp affliction

bontèng *rg* cucumber

bontjèk *var of* BONTJÈNG

bontjèng ***an** 1 carrier *or* seat on the back of a bicycle. 2 to ride double, with one on the back carrier/seat. **m*** to ride on the back of a vehicle, *esp.* a bicycle or motorcycle. *Aku m* Slamet.* Slamet gave me a ride on the back of his bicycle. *m* grobag* to catch a ride on the back of an oxcart. *A m* marang suksèsé Sang Kaisar.* A rode along on the Emperor's successes. **m/di*aké** to give smn a ride. *A m*aké B menjang sekolah.* A took B to school. **m/di*i** to get a ride from. *Aku di*i Slamet.* I gave Slamet a lift on my bicycle.

bontjis green bean(s)

bonto *cr* dumb, stupid

bontot (*or* ***an**) 1 package. 2 youngest in a family. **m/di*** to wrap into a packet. **pa·m*** youngest in a family

boom (*prn* **bum**) breakwater

boorwater (*prn* **burwater**) boric acid

bopati *var of* BUPATI

bopong having a light-colored body and dark legs [of horses]. ***an** position for carrying or holding sth, *esp.* a baby, against the chest. *Anaké turu nang *an.* The child slept in her arms. **m/di*** to pick up *or* hold sth as above

bor 1 blackboard. 2 drill (*var of* BUR)

bora(k) **m*(a)** I don't care! to hell with it!

boran (*or* **m***) *rg* possibly, probably

borang booby trap of sharpened bamboo points stuck in the ground

bor̤dès platform at the ends of a railroad car

bordir ***an** embroidery. **m/di*** to embroider

boreg̓ an asset used to secure a loan. **m/di*i** to put up security for. *m*i utang nganggo emas* to secure a loan with gold

borèh *ng kr,* **konjoh** *ki* a mixture of pounded yellow leaves and flowers, used as a cosmetic application for brides and wajang dancers, also in floral religious offerings. *kembang* * a certain flower used in this mixture; or any flowers so used. **m/di*i** to apply the above to the skin. * **atal** a liquid cosmetic lotion applied to the body

borgol handcuffs

borok sores on the scalp. ***en** to have/get sores on the scalp

borong dumb, stupid. ***an** 1 done on a job basis. *gawéan *an* work contracted for as a job. 2 (by the) wholesale (lot). *Djeruk iki didol *an.* These oranges are sold only wholesale. **m/di*aké** to have [a job] contracted for. *Gawéané tak *ké.* I'm going to have the job done by contract. **m/di*(i)** 1 to do [a job] on a contract basis. *Gawéané di* tukang tjèt.* The job was contracted for by a painter. 2 to buy up [an entire lot; a large quantity]. *Ḍèké m*i klambi.* He bought all the shirts they had. **pa·m*** 1 contractor. 2 one who buys by lots *or* in large quantities

boros 1 extravagant. *wong* * a spendthrift. 2 a certain sprout-like vegetable. **ka*an** heavy expenditures. *djaman ka*an* a time of heavy expense. **m/di(be)*** wasteful; causing high expenditure. *Jèn blandja adja ngètjèr kuwi marakaké m(be)*i.* It's wasteful to buy food a little at a time.

borot to have a leak in it. *Tjarèté *.* The kettle leaks.

bos 1 carton. *rokok sak* * a carton of cigarettes. 2 axle. 3 *rpr* a rush of escaping air. ***-*** *rpr* repeated sounds of air escaping. ***-*an** in cartons; by the carton. **nge*** to deflate suddenly. *Bané nge*.* The air rushed out of the tire. *See also* GEMBOS

bosen tired of; bored (with). *Aku wis * mangan iwak.* I'm tired of eating fish. ***an** easily bored. **m*(-m*)i** 1 tiresome, boring. 2 (*psv* **di*[-*]i)** to bore smn. *dolanan sing mbosen²i* dull pastimes

boso a certain fish

bosok rotted. *woh* * a rotten fruit. *kekajon kang wis* * decayed wood. ***an** in a rotted *or* decayed state. **an kaju* decayed wood. **be*** decayed remains. **m*i** decaying

bot *ng,* **wrat** *kr* ***é** even if; in spite of the fact that. **nge/di*aké** to consider sth (more) important. *Katimbang kantja di*aké sedulur.* He thinks more of his family than of his friends. **nge/di*(-*)i** to make sth heavier *or* more difficult. *Gabusé di*i watu.* He weighted down the cork with a stone. *Aku di*i tanggung-djawab.* I was given heavier responsibilities. **sa*-*é** however hard. *Sa*-*é wong pasa isih abot wong* *kaliren.* Fasting may be hard, but starving is a lot harder. * **répot** troubles, burdens. *Wong mau jèn ana * répot ana ing ngarep.* When there's trouble, he's first on the scene to help. * **sih** heavier on one side than the other; biased, partial. * **sèlèh** difficult, burdensome. *Bot² sèlèh nglabuhi negara kita kudu tahan.* We must endure whatever difficulties are entailed in serving our country. *See also* ABOT, BOBOT

boṭèkan medicine chest with small drawers

boten (*or* **m***) no; not (*kr for* ORA)

boṭi large woven-grass bag

botjah *ng,* **laré** *kr* 1 (**putra** *ki*) child, young person. * *lanang* boy. * *wédok* girl. 2 subject (of a monarch). 3 (**réntjang** *kr*) servant. ***an** *or* ***en** childlike. **ka*an** senile, in one's second childhood. **ka*en** 1 childish. 2 excessively young. **m*i** childish. * **ḍampit slasih** boy-girl twins. * **gantung** twins born several days apart. * **haram** illegitimate child. * **keḍana-keḍini** boy-girl sibling combination. * **kembang se·pasang** two-girl sibling combination. * **kembar** same-sex twins. * **ogal-agil** only child. * **paḍang·an** 5-girl sibling combination. * **panḍawa** 5-boy sibling combination. * **pantjur·an kapit (ing) senḍang** girl-boy-girl sibling combination. * **senḍang kapit (ing) pantjur·an** boy-girl-boy sibling combination. * **sukarta** child born under any of a number of superstitiously unpropitious circumstances, which must be counteracted by a particular ritual ceremony. * **wingi soré** a very young child; naive, inexperienced. *See also* GUMOTJAH, KAMIBOTJAHEN

botjèl chipped

botjok *var of* BONJOK

botjong buttocks (*ki for* BOKONG)

botjor 1 to leak (out). *Èmbèré *.* The bucket leaks. *Lèlèhé lèlèt²na sing *.* Smear tar over the leaky place. *Sakabèhing kang diaturaké *.* Everything that was said leaked out. 2 [of birds] to sing habitually. **m/di*aké** to let sth leak (out). *m*aké rahasia negara* to disclose state secrets. **m/di*i** to leak on(to) sth

botoh gambler. **(be)*an** 1 act of gambling. 2 to gamble. *Aku *an karo ḍèkè kalah.* I gambled with him and lost. **m/di*i** to bet on. *m*i djago* to put money on a gamecock. **nga*an** to gamble. **pa*an** gambling association. * **djago** cock-fight addict. * **kertu** one who plays cards for money

boṭok rice-accompanying dish of steamed shredded coconut, salt fish, and chili. *wungkusan ** the above wrapped in banana leaves. **m/di*** to make [ingredients] into the above. * **kénḍo urang** the above with shrimp instead of fish

botol 1 bottle. 2 having a hole in the bottom; having no bottom. *Tjèrèté *.* The kettle has a hole in the bottom of it.

botor seed of a certain leguminous plant (*tjipir*). *See also* LONDJONG

botrawi ornamental pond or small lake

bowol having a hole in it, *esp.* a filled sack. **m/di*i** to make a hole in [a sack *etc.*]

B.P.H. *see* BENDARA

B.R.A. *see* BENDARA

brabad ***an** cooking seasonings and other kitchen needs; to sell such items in the market

brabah to raise one's voice, speak raucously

brabak **m*** 1 having tears of emotion in the eyes. 2 to flush with anger

brabas **m*** 1 porous. 2 to seep out. *Banjuné m*.* The water seeped out. *Wadi iki adja nganti m*.* Don't let this secret get out!

brabat *rpr* a sudden sprint. *Mak * metu.* He dashed out. **ke*** to be injured by a blow. **m*** to dash, sprint

braḍat *rpr* a sudden dash. **m*** 1 to dash. 2 to steal livestock

braḍil *ptg ** *or* **broḍal-*** *or* **m*** frayed, fraying

B.R.Adj. *see* BENDARA

brâdjâ *oj* 1 weapon other than firearms. 2 windstorm

bradjag 1 person in charge, leader. 2 to sing habitually. *Manuké dipakani sega lombok mbandjur *.* After he put the bird on a rice-and-chili diet, it sang all the time. **m*** to produce a rushing *or* pouring sound. *Banjuné m*.* The water gushed out. **m/di*i** to plant [other growth] among [the main plants of a field]

brah scattered, spread about untidily

brahâlâ animistic idol

braham *var of* BAM

brahat traditional rituals during the month of Ruwah

brahi 1 adolescent. *wis ** to have reached one's teens. *neḍeng²é ** old enough to marry. 2 sexual passion. **(be)*ǹ** to feel passionate. **ka*ǹ** sexual passion

brahmânâ *var of* BRAMANA

brahmani *var of* BRAMANI

brahok *var of* BRAOK

brajan (*or* **be***) to make harmonious; to get along well together. *Wong urip kuwi kudu be*.* People must help each other. **(be)* urip** to live and let live

brajat nuclear family: parents with children. **be*an** as a family group. *lunga be*an* to go places as a family

brajut **m/di*** 1 to tie up into a single bundle. 2 to carry more than one child at a time

brak 1 *rpr* a ripping action. 2 *rpr* a slapping sound. *Médjané digebrag mak *.* He smacked the table. **nge*-*** to make a large tear (in)

brakot **m/di*(i)** to bite [of animals; *cr* of people]. *Si Kantjil m*i timun.* Mouse-Deer bit into the cucumber.

bral **nge/di*aké** 1 to sell out. *Tokoné lagi nge*aké barangé.* The store is having a sale on everything. 2 to spend recklessly. *nge*aké banḍané* to squander one's wealth

brâmâ *rg* fire

bramânâ Hindu priest

bramani Hindu priestess

brama(n)tya *oj* furiously angry

brambang 1 (**brambet** *rg? kr*) red onion. 2 a crop disease that attacks rice plants. **m*(i)** [of eyes] to water from irritation; to shed tears soundlessly

brambet red onion (*rg? kr for* BRAMBANG)

brânâ 1 riches; jewels. *radja * penḍem* buried treasure. 2 *oj* a wound. 3 (*or* **m***) *(Jogja slang) var of* MRANA. **ke*n** wounded. *See also* RADJA

branah **be*an** *or* **m*** to produce many children

branang 1 a shrub whose sweet-tasting leaves are often used as tea. 2 *intsfr* red. *abang (m)** bright red. **ke*** 1 to lose one's temper. 2 to get singed/scorched

branḍal bandit. ***an** to behave like a delinquent. *perang *an* war on organized crime

brandang ***an** *or* **m*** to need urgently

brandjang (*or* ***an**) clay mixed with sand

brandjangan a certain bird

brandkas *var of* BRANKAS

brandon (*or* ***an**) to have a business partnership; to share profits in a business venture

brang on the far side (*shf of* SABRANG). ** lor (wétan, lsp.)* the north (east, *etc.*) side of the river. ***-*an** drumbeats accompanying marchers

brangas ***an** 1 quick-tempered. 2 bestial, brutal. **ke*** 1 too soon. *tuwa ke** old before one's time. 2 to get overcooked, to burn. 3 to lose one's temper. **m*** 1 to heat up [food]. 2 to make smn mad. 3 *intsfr* red. *abang m** bright red

branggah 1 spreading widely [of horns, antlers]. *wong ** farmer who owns cattle. 2 kris with a widely spreading cross piece.

brangkal rubble

brangkang ***an** *or* ***-*** [of people] (moving) on all fours. **m*** to creep, crawl

brangkar stretcher (for carrying patients)

brangsang to feel uncomfortably warm and sweaty

brângtâ in love with, enchanted by

brangti *var of* BRANGTA

brangus muzzle. **m/di*** to muzzle [an animal]; *fig* to prevent freedom of speech

brani magnet

branjak **m*** having an arrogant manner

brankas safe, strongbox

brântâ *var of* BRANGTA

brantas **m/di*** to endeavor to wipe out [sth evil]. **pa·m*** a struggle against sth. *pem*an korupsi* the fight against corruption. *pem*an buta-huruf* the struggle to overcome illiteracy

branti *var of* BRANGTA

brantjah having free-and-easy morals

branwir fire brigade; fire truck; fire extinguisher

braok (*or* **broak-*** *or* **m***) loud, shrill. *Swarané braok-*.* She has a piercing voice. ***an** a shrill-voiced person

brasak 1 coarse sand. 2 coarse, crude, boorish

brasat **ke*** to get routed out. **m/di*aké** to get rid of, eliminate

brasta **m/di*** to wipe out. *m* tikus* to exterminate rats

brâtâ a struggle against forces. **m/di*ni** to do, perform, carry on [a struggle]. **pa*n** 1 battlefield. 2 place where an act of asceticism is performed. *** juda** *wj* war in which the five Pendawa brothers and their allies bring about the final destruction of their enemies. *** semadi** the practice of religious concentration and meditation

brâtâwali a plant whose bitter-tasting leaves are used in folk medicines

brati 1 one who isolates himself and lives ascetically. 2 one who has sworn to do (*or* not to do) sth until his goal is achieved. 3 a crossbred duck

bratjok rope used as a halter
braung *rg* ***an** *or* **m*** to wander about
bre- *see also under* BER- (*Introduction, 2.9.6*)
brebah *sbst kr for* BRUBUH
brebeg assault on the ears by loud sounds. **ke*en** to get assaulted by noise. *Kupingku nganti ke*en.* The noise was deafening. **m/di*i** to assault smn with noise. *Adja m*i aḍimu sing lagi turu.* Don't make a lot of racket and wake up your baby brother. **m*i kuping** deafeningly loud
brebek̄ to weather, deteriorate. ***an** weathered, deteriorating
brèbèl **ke*an** to be given a share. *A ke*an ḍuwit, mangka ora mèlu apa²*. A got a share of the money without doing a thing. **m/di*i** to hand out bit by bit; to hand out a little to each
brebel **m*** to flow out. *Ḍèké ora kuwat ngampet m*ing eluhé.* She couldn't hold back her tears.
brebes **m*** **1** to soak gradually into. **2** to flow freely. **m* meles** *or* **m* m·ili** to shed tears
brèbèt *rpr* a ripping sound. **sa*(an)** at a quick glance. *Sak *an rupané kaja Slamet.* At first glance he looked like Slamet.
brebet 1 *rpr* the sound of ripping. *Djariké dienggo lungguh mak * suwèk.* When she sat down her batik ripped. 2 *rpr* a fleeting sound *or* sensation. *Ana ambu wangi mak *.* There was a whiff of sth sweet. *Ana wong liwat mak *.* Smn whisked past. ***-*** to swish, rustle [*esp.* of batik skirts]
brèḍel ban, prohibition. **m/di*** to ban
brèdjèl **ke*** to come out unintentionally. *Ke* tjelaṭuné, barang wadi kok dianḍaraké.* The secret slipped out as he spoke. **m*** to emerge freely. *Ḍuwité m* waé.* He's a liberal spender.
bredjel *rpr* emerging, *esp.* from a hole; (*cr*) *rpr* a birth. *Tjempéné lair mak *.* The baby lamb was born. **m*** to emerge from a hole. *Djagungé paḍa m* saka bolongan kuwi.* The corn kernels slipped out through the hole.
brèg *rpr* a thump. **brag-*** *rpr* repeated thumps
breg *rpr* sth heavy dropping. **, tiba ana ing ngarepku.* It dropped in front of me with a thud. ***-*an** to keep coming one after the other. *Tamuné *-*an.* Guests kept pouring in. *Berasé *-*an.* The (sacks of) rice kept dropping on the pile. **ke*an** to get fallen on. *Bojokku ke*an deleg.* A log fell on my back. **nge/di*i** to fall/drop onto
bregâdâ brigade
bregadag **m*** **1** yellowish red. **2** a certain skin rash
bregadjag ***an** *or* **m*** ill-mannered, discourteous
bregandjok **m*** hard to get along with
bregedeg **m*** in large quantities. *M* udjug² pradjurit pirang² èwu wis mlebu kuṭa.* Suddenly thousands of soldiers poured into the city. *Anggoné tata ḍahar sak médja m*.* She placed foods all over the table. **sa*an** in one mass movement. *Sa*an dibuḍalaké sepuluh batalijun.* Ten battalions were sent out all at once.
bregedjeg ***an** to have a dispute *or* difference of opinion
bregedud **m*** obstinate, deaf to advice
breginging a whining sound. **m*** to whine
bregundung **m*** obstinate, willful, headstrong
brèh **brah-*** *or* **nge*** extravagant, wasteful. **nge/di*-*** to spend lavishly. *** wèh** overgenerous. *Kebangeten olèhé *-wèh nganti awaké ḍéwé ora kopèn.* He gives so much to others he neglects himself.
bréjo **bréja-*** poorly groomed, sloppy in personal appearance
bréjot **m*** heavy and unwieldy to carry
brèk **1** *rpr* ripping. *Sarungku ketjanṭol pang, mak wèk, rekètèk, *.* My sarong caught on a branch and ripped.**2** *rpr* a slamming sound. **brak-*** to make slamming, banging sounds. **nge/di*aké** to bang, slam. *Lawangé adja di*ké.* Don't slam the door.
brek̄ *rpr* feet marching in unison. *Swarané sepatuné *-*, *-*.* Their shoes marked rhythmic beats. ***-*an** in great volume. *Barang² teka *-*an ana pelabuhan.* Goods poured into the harbor.
brekenengan to argue heatedly
breketépé *rg var of* BLEKETÉPÉ
breki:k̄ *pl for* BEKIK
brem **1** a hard liquor of fermented rice or cassava. **2** cookies made with this liquor. **3** a certain insect
brènḍèl to drop, fall off/out, molt
brenḍil *ptg* ***** **1** full of knots *or* tangles. **2** having many small things to carry
brendjul a bump on a surface. *ptg* ***** full of bumps. **m*** bumpy, uneven

brenḍol *pl of* BENḌOL
brenḍul *var of* BRENḌIL
bréné (*or* **m***) *(Jogja slang) var of* MRÉNÉ
brèng *rpr* a metallic clang. **brang-*** to keep clanging
breng 1 *rpr* perceiving an odor. *Ambuné mak **. I caught a whiff of it. 2 *rpr* a concerted departure. *lunga mak ** to leave all at once. 3 *syllable chanted in making a concerted effort: see* ANA-INI
brengangah **m*** flushed with emotion
brengangang **m*** 1 to buzz, whistle, hum. 2 red with emotion. *Kupingé m**. He got mad.
brengengeng **m*** to buzz, whine, hum; *fig* to complain. *m*é sepéḍa motor* the whine of a motorcycle. *Ana laler idjo sing m* ngrubung uwuh.* Green flies buzzed around the garbage. *mBok uwis adja m* waé.* Stop your eternal grumbling!
brengganu *see* DJERUK
brenggèl **m*** bumpy, uneven
brenginging high-pitched whining sound, *e.g.* of a mosquito. **m*** to whine
bréngkal **m/di*** 1 to raise [sth heavy] at one side/edge. 2 *inf* to wake smn up
brengkélé **m*** selfish, self-centered
brengkelo **m*** stubborn, obstinate, opinionated
brengkerengan *var of* BENGKERENGAN
brèngkès (*or* ***an**) fish or meat baked in a banana-leaf wrapping. **m/di*(i)** to make [ingredients] into the above dish
brengkijeng *var of* BENGKIJENG
brengkunung **m*** stubborn, headstrong
brengkut **m*** 1 to be carrying a number of things all at once. 2 to start in on a task in a brisk businesslike way
brengkutis a certain beetle that feeds on offal
brengok *pl of* BENGOK
bréngos *var of* BRENGOS
brengos *ng kr,* **gumbâlâ** *or* **kumbâlâ** *or* **rawis** *ki* moustache. ***an** *or* ***en** to wear a moustache. **wis *en** to have begun wearing a moustache; to have become a man. *** kèplèh** drooping moustache. *kèplèh *é* embarrassed, ashamed. *** lèmèt (angus)** slim (soot-blackened) moustache. *** ng·laler ṅ·péntjok** Charlie-Chaplin-style moustache. *** sumpel** small close-cropped moustache. *** wulu lutung** false moustache made of long black ape hair
brengungung a deep, far-off roaring *or* rumbling sound. **m*** to produce such a sound
brenjèh ***en** covered with skin infections
brenjih *var of* BRENJÈH
bres 1 *rpr* sudden hard rain. 2 *rpr* the sound of colliding. *tabrakan karo pit lija: ** to run bang! into another bicycle
brèsèt 1 unfair [of cock-fighting tactics]. 2 excessively fond of the opposite sex
brèt *rpr* cloth tearing
bret ***-*** *rpr* the pleasant swishing of a batik skirt (*shf of* SREBED^2). *Lakuné *-**. Her skirt swishes as she walks.
brétjok *ptg ** [of tree trunks] badly scarred with cuts
bréwo **bréwa-*** poorly groomed
bréwok long sideburn hair. ***en** having long sideburn hair merging into the beard
brèwu very wealthy
bribah *sbst kr for* BRUBAH
bribi **ke*ṅan** to be awakened by sounds. **m/di*ṅi** to wake smn up by making too much noise
bribik termite-like wood worm. ***-*** just starting out on a job/career
bribil half-cent coin used during colonial times
brigaḍe brigade
brigaḍir second-in-command. *** pulisi** police lieutenant. *** djéndral** brigadier general
brigi **brigā-*** to scowl
brijeng **m*** (to have) sick headaches
brijut 1 *var of* BIJET. 2 *rg var of* BLIJUT
brikèt small brick-shaped cake. *ujah ** a block of salt
bril glare. *setop ** sunglasses
brinḍil 1 denuded. *Wit djatiné **. The teak tree has lost its leaves. 2 to fall off/out. *Goḍongé paḍa **. The leaves had all dropped off. 3 still too young to have leaves/hair/feathers. **m/di*i** to denude sth
bringas ***an** jumpy, restless (rather than desirably calm and serene)
bringkung *ptg * or* **bringkang-*** to feel aversion to smn, *esp.* because of his undesirable behavior
bringkut *inf var of* BRENGKUT
bringsang unbearably hot; hot and sweaty
brintik curly, kinky
brisat *rg var of* BERSOT
brisik **m*i** producing an irritating rasping noise
B.R.M. *see* BENDARA
brobah *var of* BRUBAH
brobos *var of* BRUBUS. ***an** (sth which is) crawled under/through. **m/di*(i)** to creep

under *or* through. *Médjané di∗i.* He crawled under the table. *m∗ ing tong* to crawl through a barrel

brodjol lower on one side than the other. *Puṇḍaké ∗.* He has lopsided shoulders. **ke∗** to come out accidentally. *Tembungé èlèk ke∗.* The bad word just slipped out. **ke∗an** 1 to be given a share. *Aku mèlu ke∗an én-tuk redjeki.* I shared in his good luck. 2 to give birth unexpectedly. *Nang tengah dalan ke∗an.* The baby came while she was on the way [to the hospital]. **m∗** to slip out from a hole

broḍol 1 to drop off/out. 2 threadbare. **m∗(i)** 1 to lose hair/feathers. *Pitiké m∗i.* The chicken is molting. 2 (*psv* **di∗[i]**) to pluck

brog *rpr* a soft thud

brojot *var of* BRÉJOT

brok 1 "home" (safe place in children's games). 2 *rpr* a sudden fall, *esp.* smn falling on his rear. **nge∗** 1 to stay smw. *Aku nge∗ ing kuṭa Jogja.* I settled in Jogja. 2 [of kites] to fail to get off the ground. 3 *slang* to defecate in one's clothing. **nge/di∗i** to take occupancy. *Bala tentara sekutu nge∗i Djakarta.* The Allied forces occupied Djakarta. *Omahé suwung kuwi di∗i wong.* Smn is occupying that empty house illegally.

brokat brocade(d fabric)

brokoh a basket that stands on 4 short legs. **∗an** 1 ceremony held for a child at birth, when the umbilical cord drops off, and in connection with the naming ceremony. 2 voluntary help offered to the village head by his people. **m/di∗i** to honor [an infant] with the above ceremonies

brokok *rg var of* BROKOH

brol (*or* **bral-∗**) *rpr* copious *or* effortless coming forth. *kaṇḍa bral-∗* to speak freely *or* fluently. **∗-∗an** to emerge in large quantities. *Getihé metu ∗-∗an.* He bled profusely. *Ḍuwité ∗-∗an.* Money was spent freely. **sa∗an** emerging copiously and simultaneously. *Nèk manak sa∗an nenem terkaḍang pitu.* Cats have 6 or even 7 kittens to a litter.

brom bronze metal paint. **∗-∗an** painted with bronze paint. *Wajangé kulit ∗-∗an.* The leather puppets are bronze-painted. **nge/di∗** to paint sth with bronze paint

brombong *var of* BRUMBUNG

bron *var of* BROM

brondjong cylindrical basket for transporting large bulky objects

bronḍol 1 sparse [of hair, feathers]. 2 girls' short haircut. **∗an** stump of a cut sugar-cane plant. **m/di∗** to cut *or* wear one's hair short

brondong popcorn. **be∗an** to keep going "bang-bang." **m/di∗** to fire missiles at

brongkal (*or* **∗an**) (forming) a heap. *∗an watu* a pile of stones. *Watuné isih ∗an nang pinggir dalan.* The rocks are in piles along the road.

brongkos a vegetable dish seasoned with a certain fruit *(kluwak)*. **∗an** *var of* BLONG-SONG-AN. **m/di∗** 1 to make [ingredients] into the above dish. 2 to wrap, make into a bundle

brongos *var of* BRONGOT

brongot **ke∗** to get scorched/singed. **m/di∗** to singe, scorch

brono (*or* **m∗**) *(Jogja slang)* *var of* MRONO

brontak **∗an** a rebellion. **m∗** to rebel; to bring off a coup. **pa·m∗** a rebel

brontok having skin rash or acne

brosot **ke∗** to be given the slip. **m∗** to leave without goodbyes or explanations

brotjèl *var of* BOTJÈL, BRUTJÈL

brotol the part of a bird below the cloacal opening

brubah to change sth from its former condition. **∗an** a change; changed

brubuh **m/di∗(i)** to destroy, wipe out

brubul *ptg* ∗ *or* **∗-∗an** *or* **m∗** to pour in *or* out in large numbers/quantities. *See also* GUMRUBUL

brubus *rpr* smoke puffing out. **m/di∗i** to boil sth to get rid of its bad taste

brubut *rpr* fast running. *Djarané mlaju ∗, banter banget.* The horse ran swiftly. *ptg ∗ pl* running swiftly. **m∗** to break into a fast run

bruder Catholic clergyman

brudjul a certain plow for churning soil. **m/di∗** to work [soil] with the above

brug 1 *rpr* a plopping sound. *Sepéḍané gentawingan, ∗.* The bicycle wobbled out of control and fell over. 2 soil-tamping metal plate attached to a handle. 3 bridge. **nge/di∗** to tamp [soil]

bruk 1 *rpr* sth dropping down. *Bukuné di-tibakaké mak ∗.* He banged down the book. 2 trousers. **brak-∗** *rpr* repeated dropping sounds *or* actions. *mBuwang uwuh mung* *brak-* waé.* They threw out the trash just anywhere. **ka*an** 1 to get fallen on. *Ḍèké ke*an bata.* A brick fell on him. *Aḍuh arak ke*an begdja di-enet² temenan.* What an avalanche of good luck! 2 to fall on each other, *e.g.* when fighting. **nge/di*** to embrace suddenly, in a rush of emotion. **nge/di*aké** 1 to drop sth. 2 to drop things here and there. **nge/di*i** to fall onto. *See also* AMBRUK, KABRUK

brukut 1 tightly wrapped/bundled. 2 well enclosed; tightly constructed

brul ***-*an** to swarm in/out. *Laroné paḍa metu *-*an.* The ants came out in droves.

brumbun [of chicks] covered with down

brumbung (*or* ***an**) water pipe. **m*** to get pregnant again, after giving birth, with no intervening menstrual period

brundjung main roof of a traditional Javanese house. **m*** shaped like this roof

brunḍul *var of* BRINḌIL

brung 1 *rpr* a sudden concerted departure. 2 *intsfr* empty. *suwung ** completely empty

brungkah 1 a cut-off stump plus its roots. 2 to cease one's fasting *or* avoidance of certain foods

brungkut *var of* BRUKUT

bruntjah **m/di*** to pass out [foods] to those partaking of a meal

brus *rpr* a collision. *Montoré natab wit asem, *, grobjak.* The car slammed into a tamarind tree.

brusut *rpr* a smooth easy motion. *Metuné mak * gampang baé.* It came out easily.

brutjèl *ptg ** wounded *or* scarred in many places

brutu tailbone, coccyx [of a bird]

bruwah fast-breaking meal at the end of the fasting period. **m*** to eat one's fill after a fasting period. **m/di*i** to eat [certain foods] at the close of the fast

bruwang bear (animal). ** dolanan* toy bear, teddy bear

bruwet 1 not clearly visible; obscure, hazy. 2 depressed, gloomy

bruwun [of hair] sticking out every which way. **m*** to gather vegetables from garden or field. **m·be*** to use smn else's money in one's own interest

bu 1 mother (*shf of* IBU). 2 *adr* mother; wife; older and/or higher-status woman. *** ḍé** aunt (*shc from* IBU GEḌÉ). *** guru** *adr* [female] teacher! *** lik** aunt (*shc from* IBU TJILIK)

buah fruit. ***-*an** fruits; various kinds of fruit

bubak marriage ceremony held for the first daughter of a family. ***an** opened up for cultivation [of land]. **m/di*** to open up [virgin soil] for cultivation. *** kawah** traditional ceremony performed when bride and groom first meet during the wedding

bubar *ng,* **bibar** *kr* 1 to disperse. **!* Dismissed! *Tawoné *.* The bees swarmed out. 2 finished; to get over. *Pamulangané wis *.* School's out. 3 after. ** nglairaké anaké* after the baby was born. ***an** to disperse. *Patemoné *an.* The meeting broke up. *Kantja²né wis paḍa *an.* All his friends had gone away. **m/di*aké** to disperse [a group]. *Parlemèn di*aké.* The Parliament was dissolved. *Pulisi ditekakké kanggo m*aké wong sing paḍa ḍémonstrasi.* The police were called in to break up the demonstrators. **sa*é** after. *sa*é wong tani paḍa njambutgawé* after the farmers finished their work. *See also* BAR

bubat horsehair

bubrah *ng,* **bibrah** *kr* out of order, in disrepair. *Kretegé *.* The bridge is out. **m/di*(aké)** to damage, wreck. *m* pager* to break through a fence. *m*aké pasamuwan* to disrupt a meeting

bubrak **m/di*** 1 to open sth (up) for use. 2 to demolish [a building]

bubruk 1 overburdened with tasks. 2 overplentiful and hence of little value

bubu fish trap with bamboo bars

bubuh *ng,* **bebah** *kr* ***an** a task assigned to smn. **ke*an** 1 to be assigned *or* saddled with a responsibility. 2 to get sth in it by accident. *Kopiné ke*an ujah.* Salt got in the coffee. **m/di*i** to assign a responsibility to smn

bubuk 1 powder(ed substance). *kopi ** ground coffee. *wédang ** hot coffee. 2 a termite-like worm. 3 a girl that nobody wants to marry. 4 (to go to) sleep (*children's word*). **, *, blug!* Lie down and go to sleep! ***an** in powdered form. *Iki *an kopi, dudu *an tjoklat.* This is powdered coffee, not powdered chocolate. ***en** 1 [girl who is] not wanted as a marriage partner. 2 eaten away by wood worms. **m/di*aké** to put [a child] to bed. **m/di*i** to crush to a powder. * **olèh elèng** to figure out a scheme for doing one's nefarious work

bubul 1 yaws. 2 durian fruit sprout. ***en** to have/get yaws. **m*** to keep pouring out. *Untapipun wadyabala saking kiṭa m* boten wonten peḍotipun.* Troops poured forth from the town incessantly. * **juta** *or* * **wuta** an unburst swelling

bubur a ceremonial porridge. **m/di*(i)** to make [ingredients] into this porridge

bubus rice-accompanying dish prepared from certain leaves (*lumbu*)

bubut a certain bird. *mesin ** lathe. ***an** shaped *or* polished on a lathe. ***-*** to pull up by the roots. **-* suket* to uproot grass. **m/di*(i)** 1 to pull sth out by the roots. 2 to turn sth on a lathe. **m*-* djénggot** to stroke one's beard; *fig* to lead an easy life

Buda *oj* Wednesday

Buḍa 1 Buddha. *agama ** Buddhism. 2 pertaining to the pre-Moslem era. *sastra ** pre-Islamic literature. 3 the planet Mercury. **ka*n** pertaining to Buddhism

budâjâ culture; cultural group. **ka*n** 1 a culture; culture. *ka*n mantja* foreign cultures. *pusating ka*n* cultural center. 2 the humanities

buḍak slave. *kaum ** slaves (as a class)

buḍal *ng,* **biḍal** *kr,* **djengkar** *ki* to leave, set out (as a group). ***an** *pl* act of moving elsewhere. *Djam sanga bengi tamuné paḍa *an.* The party broke up at 9 P.M. **an wadya bala Dwarawati* the movement of Dwarawati's troops. **m/di*aké** to send out [a group]. *m*aké tentara* to dispatch troops

buḍé *see* BU

buḍeg 1 deaf. 2 stupid. 3 counterfeit, fake. **m*** to act as though one were deaf. **m/di*aké** to deafen. *Wah raméné, kaja m*-*aké kuping.* What a deafening racket! **m/di*-*aké** to abusively call smn deaf. *Ali m*-*aké baturé, merga olèhé nukokaké welingané klèru.* Ali angrily accused his servant of being deaf when she bought the wrong thing. * **ǹ·ṭreṭeg** stone deaf

buḍeng 1 dull(-sounding); dull(-witted). 2 black monkey

Budha *var sp of* BUḌA

budi 1 character, temperament. *luhuring ** nobleness of character. *rupak ing ** unforgiving in nature. 2 (to exert) power. *Kretegé durung karuwan kelar njembadani *né banju.* The bridge is not likely to withstand the force of the water. *tuna ing ** deficient in mental powers. **-* meksa ora bisa utjul.* He struggled and struggled but couldn't get loose. 3 a certain tree under which Buddha sits and meditates. **(be)*ǹ** character, temperament. *alusing bebudèn* the gentleness of his nature. **pa·m*** effort, attempt. **sa*né** with all one's strength. *Katogna sa*mu.* Pull with all your might! * **segara** forgiving in nature. *See also* BUDIDAJA, BUDIDARMA

budiarda ambition, greed

budidâjâ **ka*n** a business enterprise based on agricultural production. *ka*n ingkang nanem rosan ageng²an* companies with vast sugar plantations. *ka*n daging* a meat industry. **m*** to exert oneself. **pa·m*** a strong effort. *See also* BUDI, DAJA

budidarma 1 generosity; noble-mindedness. 2 good deeds

budiman *oj* intelligent; skilled (in)

budin *var of* BODIN

budirahaju virtue, virtuousness

budja *oj* arm, hand

budjad *var of* BEDJAD

budjâgâ *oj* snake

budjânâ feast, banquet. * **andrawina** dinner banquet

budjang (*or* ***an**) bachelor. **m*** to live the life of a bachelor

budjânggâ *var of* PUDJANGGA

budjel having a rounded tip. *Potloté *.* The pencil needs sharpening.

budjeng hunt *(root form: kr for* BURU*)*

budjid ***en** stunted in growth

budjil a runt, dwarf

budjug ***-*** *or* ***-besèt** *excl of astonishment or incredulity*

budjuk persuasive talk. *kena ** to be misled; to get talked into sth. ***an** persuasiveness. **ané ora mempan.* Her efforts to persuade him were unsuccessful. **m/di·be*** *or* **m/di*i** to talk smn into sth; to mislead smn with talk

budjul *var of* BRUDJUL

budjung sugar-cane leaf (*kr for* GOḌONG TEBU). **m/di*** to chase, go after. *A mladjar dipun budjung B.* B ran after A. *M* ḍuwit Rp 100 malah kélangan Rp 2000.* He tried for 100 rupiahs and lost 2000.

buḍug leprosy. ***en** to have/get leprosy

buḍur nectar from a coconut bud

bug *rpr* a plop or thud. **bag-*** *rpr* repeated thuds. *Krambil² ditibakaké, swarané bag-*, bag-*.* The coconuts kept thudding down as he dropped them. **nge/di*** to whack with thudding sounds

bugel 1 charred firewood. 2 stupid person. 3 cut off short (*var of* PUGEL)

buger *see* SEGER

Bugong *wj* name of a fat clown. *See also* WULU-TJUMBU

buh ***-*an** a task assigned to smn. *See also* BUBUH

bui *var sp of* BUWI

buja(k) **ke*-*** *oj* subjected to constant pressures or hardships

bujar to disperse in all directions. *Bareng pulisi teka, botjah² pada **. When the police came, the boys scattered in panic. **m/di*aké** to cause to disperse. *Tekamu marakaké m*aké manuk².* You scared off the birds when you came.

bujud 1 third-generation ancestor or descendant. *embah ** great-grandparent. *putu ** great-grandchild. 2 cemetery. ***en** unsteady with old age. **be*an** for generations. *Australi nganggep satru be*an karo trewèlu.* Australia has been the enemy of rabbits from way back. **ka*an** 1 place where a priest lives and works. 2 place considered to be holy in animistic religion

bujuk a variety of palm tree

bujung earthenware container

buk 1 all even; without profit or loss. *Utangé wis **. He's out of debt now. *Tuna pira?–Ja ming **. How much did you lose? –I broke even. *Bal²ané mau * telu².* The soccer game ended in a 3-3 tie. 2 a small bridge over a stream. 3 book; notebook. 4 (*prn* **bu:k̄**) *rpr* a soft thud. ***-*(an)** *or* **bak-*** *or* **bik-*** all tied up. *Bak-buk loro².* It's tied at 2-2. ***-*an** to balance out. *Olèhé ngedol pit ming *-*an karo anggoné tuku bijèn, ora baṭi ora rugi.* He sold the bike for what he had paid for it–no profit, no loss. **nge*** 1 to use a book. *ora nge* ora ngepèn* illiterate. 2 to make soft thuds. *Ḍèké ngebuk² punṭukan kuburé bodjoné.* He kept patting his wife's grave. **nge/di*aké** to repay, pay up. **nge/di*i** 1 to pay up. 2 to enter in a (note)book. *Utangé di*i.* He listed the debt in a ledger. **ora *** unfit, unsuitable

buka 1 (to eat) a meal that breaks one's fast. 2 opening, beginning. **be*** 1 introduction, preface, foreword; salutation of a letter. 2 opening, beginning. *Be*ning Prang Donja II iku apa?* How did World War II start? **(m)/di*** to open (up, out). *m* wewadi* to disclose a secret. **m/di·be*** to disclose, reveal. **m/di(be)*ni** to open sth. *mbe*ni rerembugan* to begin talks. *m*ni genḍing* to start the music. **pa·m*** opening, beginning. *See also* BUKAK

bukak *ng,* **bikak** *kr* open(ed); uncovered. **é kantor djam pira?* What time is the office open? *dina ** opening day. *djas ** (Western-style) open jacket with lapels. ***an** 1 open; uncovered. *Lawangé *an.* The door is open. *Pantjiné *an.* The pan isn't covered. *djas *an* an open jacket. 2 opener. **an blèg* can opener. **m*** open(ed); uncovered. **m/di*aké** to open sth (for smn). *Ali m*aké lawang (aḍiké).* Ali opened the door (for his little sister). **m/di*(i)** 1 to open, uncover, disclose. *m* rapat* to open a meeting. *Lawangé di*.* He opened the door. *Bèsèké di*i kabèh.* He took all the tops off the boxes. *m* toko anjar* to open a new store. *m* dalan* to open up avenues, to pioneer. *Wadiné di*.* He revealed the secret. 2 to remove. *m* prop* to pull a cork. *m* klambi (sepatu, lsp.)* to take off one's shirt (shoes, *etc.*) **pa·m*** opening, aperture. *** kuntji** wages paid to smn for looking after graves. *** topi** 1 hatless. 2 to respect, admire. *Aku * topi karo ḍèwèké.* I take my hat off to him. *See also* BUKA

bukèt bouquet

buket thick [of liquids]

bukti 1 proof, evidence. *Tapak dridjiné wis mudjudaké * kang ora bisa diselaki manèh.* The fingerprints constitute undeniable proof. 2 *oj* food; to eat. **a*** *oj* to eat. **ka*(ǹ)** proven, shown. *A ke* salah.* A was proven guilty. *Wis kebuktèn jèn B sing njolong.* It's been proved that B stole it. **m/di*k̀aké** (*or* **m/di*ǹi** *rg*) to give evidence (of). *Tjritané mbuktèkaké jèn wong sing misuwur iku nglakoni rekasa ḍisik.* The story shows that famous people first undergo hardships.

buku book. **m/di*n̂i** to codify. **pa·m*an** financial accounts. *mriksa pembukuané perusahaan* to examine a company's books

bukuh **m*** cross-legged. *sila m** to sit cross-legged with lowered head before a highly esteemed person, to show respect and humility

bukung 1 [of birds] tailless. 2 (*or* ***an**) cut short. *Saiki rambuté *(an).* She wears her hair short now. **m/di*(i)** to cut off; to cut short. *Rambuté di*(i).* His hair was cut off/short.

bukur a variety of clam

bul 1 large bowl-shaped earthenware container. 2 *rpr* puffing upward. *Jèn ana lésus, weḍiné mumbul *.* During windstorms, sand blows up in the air. **, sanalika geniné murub.* The fire flared up. 3 *Jogja slang var of* DJEBUL. **bal-*** *rpr* repeated puffings. *Ḍèké bal-* ngrokok.* He puffed away at his cigarette.

bulak (*or* **be***) a broad treeless field

bulan (*or* **m***; **tjândrâ** *ki?*) moon. *See also* REMBULAN

bulé albino

bules to feel suffocated. **m*i** suffocating

bulet 1 solid, firm. *kesatuan nasional sing ** solid national unity. 2 oval, elliptical. **be*an** *or* **m*** 1 tangled, snarled. 2 evasive. **m/di*aké** to twist *or* snarl sth. *m*aké rembug* to twist words; to get the conversation off the subject

buli (*or* ***-***) small earthenware container

bulik *see* BU

buljon meat stock

bulu a certain tree. ***-*** 1 feather duster. 2 *wj* decorative feathers on female headdresses. *** bekti** tribute paid to a sovereign power. *** tangkis** badminton

bulud (to the) exact (measure)

bulug 1 short and thick [of cylindrical shapes]. 2 dusty. 3 (*or* ***en**) mildewed

bulung *see* DJERUK

bulus large land tortoise

bum 1 customs office. 2 wagon shaft

bum- *see also under* B- (*Introduction, 3.1.7*)

bumbu 1 seasonings, spices (prepared by grinding with mortar and pestle). 2 *fig* spice, distinctive touch. ***n̂** seasoning in general. *Mritja kuwi kanggo bumbon.* Peppercorns are used for seasoning. ***n̂ tjraki·n̂** dried seasoning; medicinal herbs. ***n̂an** way of seasoning. *Bumbonané ora énak.* It isn't seasoned very tastily. *Bumbonané sapa iki?* Who prepared the seasonings? **m/di*k̂aké** to use as seasoning. ** santenan mau dibumbokaké marang iwak pitik.* She seasoned the chicken with the spiced coconut milk. **m/di*n̂i** to season, flavor. *mbako sing dibumboni menjan* incense-flavored tobacco. *A mbumboni rembugan.* A added spice to the conversation.

bumbung bamboo pipe. ***an** 1 cylindrical bamboo cooking pot. 2 the part of an earring which slips through the pierced ear hole. **m*** to get pregnant again immediately after having a child, *i.e.* with no intervening menstrual period. *** wungwang 1** hollow bamboo section. 2 cone-shaped bamboo utensil used above a steaming pan (*kukus·an*)

bumi earth. *ilmu ** geography. *saindengé ** all over the world. **né loh djinawi.* The soil is fertile. *Olèhé béda nganti kaja * karo langit.* They're as different as earth and sky. ***n̂** *rg* communally owned rice paddy. *** angus** scorched earth; **m/di*-angus** to pursue a scorched-earth policy during war. *** pulih·an** soil consisting of river sediment. **wong *** a native (of). *wong * pulo mau* the natives of the island. *See also* PRIBUMI

buminâtâ *oj* king

bumipâlâ *var of* BUMINATA

bumipati *var of* BUMINATA

bumitâlâ the center of the earth

bumpet *rg var of* BUNTU

bun dew. ***-*an** 1 ([**pa**]**sunḍul·an** *ki*) crown of the head. 2 the topmost part. **ke*an** to get wet with dew. **nge*-*** 1 to put sth out in the dew. 2 to take [a baby] for an early-morning walk. **nge*-* ésuk ngudan-udan soré** to propose marriage to a girl. **nge/di*aké** to let dew get on sth. *Di-e*²aké telung késuk.* She left the batik out to get the dew for three mornings [as part of the processing]. *See also* EMBUN

bunḍas *see* BABAK

bunḍel 1 having a knot in it. 2 linked in mating position [of birds, insects, in midair]. 3 close, intimate. 4 *rg* a batch of 1,000 [*e.g.* corn ears, tobacco cuttings]. 5 (*or* **be***) revered village elder. **(be)*an** 1 a tied knot. 2 money, valuables, wisdom *etc.* kept safe. *be*aning atiné* the treasures of her heart. 3 appointment; promise. **m/di*i** 1 to tie a knot in sth. 2 to knot [valuables; one's belongings] into the corner of a kerchief. 3 to take seriously

bunder 1 round; spherical. 2 firm(ly determined). ***an** 1 circle. 2 traffic rotary. **m/di*i** to make round; to shape into rounds. *** kepleng** *or* *** memet** perfectly round

bunḍet tangled, snarled. **ke*** to get tangled

bunek̄ 1 to feel cramped, claustrophobic. 2 to feel oppressed. **be*an** that which causes the above feelings

bunel depressed; at a loss; bewildered. **m*i** causing the above feelings

bunèn place in a rice paddy for sun-drying rice plants

bung 1 stalk, shoot, tall blade. 2 *title used esp. between people of disparate rank to emphasize equality of status. Bung Karno* (President) Soekarno. * *sopir ngguju.* The driver laughed. **nge*** 1 resembling a tall stalk. 2 to put out a shoot. 3 (*psv* **di***) to call smn *Bung*

bungah *ng,* **bingah** *kr* happy, glad (**rena** *ki*). ***an** carefree, happy-go-lucky. **be*** a pleasant surprise, *usu.* unexpected money. *Lotréné nganggo be* duwit Rp 100.* The lottery carried a 100-rupiah prize. **ka*an** joy, gladness. **m/di·be*** *or* **m/di*aké** to make happy; to cheer smn up. **m/di*-*aké** to force oneself to be happy. *Di*-*aké atiné supaja ora pati kelara-lara.* He tried to cheer himself up so he wouldn't feel so much pain. **m*i** to rejoice unjustifiably; to gloat

bungkah base, lowest part; foot (of a mountain)

bungkak roof peak of a traditional Javanese house

bungkang *see* KEBO

bungkar ***an** 1 disassembled parts. 2 plot of land from which sugar-cane plants have been cut. **m/di*** 1 to unload [things] from a vehicle. 2 to overhaul, put into shape

bungkem to keep the mouth closed. **m/di*** to prevent smn from speaking (*e.g.* with a gag; by bribery)

bungker 1 to shrivel; to remain stunted. 2 not quite right in the head

bungkik stunted in growth

bungkil 1 remains of peanuts after the oil has been pressed out. 2 lower end of a bamboo stalk or banana-tree trunk

bungkrah (*or* ***-bungkrèh**) untidy, in disorder

bungkrèh *see* BUNGKRAH

bungkrèk *var of* BUNGKIL

bungkring *var of* BENGKRING

bungkuk **m*** to bend. *m* kawat* to bend a wire. **m*aké** to bend the back; to bow

bungkul knob; knob-like object/part; counting unit for knob-shaped things. * *pajung* knob on an umbrella handle. *brambang sa** one onion. ***an** knobby shape; knobby part

bungkus 1 wrapped packet; wrapping material. 2 [born] with the caul covering the head. ***an** 1 a wrapped packet. 2 (food) cooked in a leaf wrapping. **m/di*(i)** to wrap. **pa·m*** act *or* way of wrapping. *See also* WUNGKUS

bunglon chameleon. *watak ** changeable; opportunistic

bungur 1 a certain plant, also its blossom. 2 [of livestock] the portion of the nose through which a ring is inserted. 3 *cr* mouth

bunjak scraped, skinned, wounded

bunoh *var of* BUNUH

buntak a certain fish

buntal floral decoration worn by wajang dancers and bridegrooms. * *djanur kuning* crescent-shaped decoration of young coconut leaves. **m/di*** to make [flowers, leaves] into decorative pieces

buntar 1 lower end of a spear handle. 2 lower end of a rooftop. 3 far end of an irrigation ditch. **m/di*** to prod with a spear handle

buntas last part, end

buntek̄ short and thick [of cylindrical objects]

buntel wrapping. *Buntelé sikilé dibuwang.* He discarded the bandage wound around her leg. *kulit * ing awaké uler* membrane wrapping a caterpillar's body. ***an** (that which is) wrapped, swathed. **an punika roti.* This package has bread in it. *Sikilé kok *an nèng apa?* How come your leg is bandaged? **m/di*(i)** to wrap sth. **pa·m*** act *or* way of wrapping. *Pam*ipun boten kénging kentjeng²*. Don't wrap it too tight. *** kadud** wage that includes all living expenses. *** majid** winding sheet

buntet closed at one end. *Irungé *.* His nose is stuffed up. **m/di*i** to close, clog. *rereged sing m*i bolonganing kulit* dirt that clogs the pores. *Aku m*i pring kuwi supaja ora dienggoni tikus.* I plugged the bamboo stalk so mice couldn't nest there.

bunting youngest in a family. **m*** slender-waisted

buntjang **di*** to be blown (away). **ke*** to get blown

buntji a certain card count in the game of *pèi*

buntjik flesh wound. ***en** wounded

buntjis *var of* BONTJIS

buntjit 1 the last to be eliminated in *e.g.* a competition. 2 youngest member of a family

buntjrit ***en** emaciated; stunted in growth

buntjur lump on the head raised by a blow

buntu stopped at one end; clogged; *fig* bogged down. *dalan ** a dead-end road. *Rembugané *.* The talks are deadlocked. **ke*an** stopped up, clogged. **m/di*i** to clog, stop up
buntul youngest in a family
buntung having an arm, leg, or tail missing
buntut 1 tail. 2 the last one in a line *or* series. *lotré ** pool in which one guesses at the final digit of a number. 3 aftermath; follow-up. ***an** last-born child. **m/di*(i)** to follow; to follow smn's example. *Si A m* si B.* A followed B. A did as B did. **pa·m*** last-born child. *** tjolok** white tip on a black tail. *** urang** hair on the back of the neck
bunuh confused, bewildered
bupati top administrative officer of a district. ** sabrang Wétan (Kulon)* regent of the East (West) district. **ka*n̂** 1 district, regency. 2 official residence of a regent
bupatos *sbst kr for* BUPATI
bupèt *var of* BIPÈT
bur 1 *rpr* flight through the air; *fig* gone, vanished. 2 a drill. *sumur ** drilled well. ** untu* dentist's drill. ***-*an** 1 birds of the air. 2 unredeemed pawned item. 3 children's game played with picture cards. **nge/di*** to drill, bore. *nge* minjak* to drill for oil. **nge/di*aké** 1 to fly [a plane]; to have/let [a bird *etc.*] fly. 2 to relinquish possession of; to let [a pawned item] go unredeemed. *** éngkol** brace-and-bit. *** manuk** to depart in haste with only the clothes on one's back. *** matjan** large drill. *** potrèk** drill for making tiny holes. *See also* ABUR
burak 1 out of order, in disrepair. 2 mythological horse with a human face
burak̔rak̔an in disarray, disorganized
buras eczema-like skin disorder; white spot on the skin. ***en** to have/get this disorder
burat *oj* (*or* *** sari** *or* *** wangi**) flower sachet
burdir *var of* BORDIR
burek̄ *var of* BURENG
burem [of the moon] hazy, clouded over
bureng 1 vague, unclear. *Tulisané katon *.* The writing isn't clear. *Perkara iki isih *.* The facts of the case are obscure. *katja ** translucent glass. 2 [of the moon] hazy
buri *ng,* **wingking** *kr* 1 back, rear. *omah sing ** the house in back. *ana ing * omah* in back of the house. *sikil ** hind leg(s). *Surungen saka ing *.* Push it from behind! *Botjah wédok ana ngarep, botjah lanang ana ing *.* The girls were in front and the boys were in back. *Ing *mu kuwi sapa?* Who's that behind you? *sing ana * ḍéwé* the one at the very back. 2 later, after a while. *Anggepé, gampang ketemu *.* His idea was that it would be easy to find again later on. 3 last..., the past... *ḍèk minggu ** last week. **ka*** in the past, over and done with. *Perkara mau wis ke*.* That's water under the bridge. **m*** 1 in/at the back part of the house, *i.e.* the family living quarters. *kantja m** wife. *lunga m** to go to the bathroom. *wong m** servant. *metu m** to do sth extralegally. 2 last... *ḍèk Djemuwah m** last Friday. **mem*** (**ḍateng wingking** *kr*) 1 to *or* toward the back. 2 to the bathroom. **pa·m*** 1 one of lower rank; a subordinate. 2 (in) the future. *Wong kuwi kudu ngélingi pam*né uga.* One must think of the future too. **sa(m)*né** (**sa·wingking·ipun** *kr*) behind, in the back. *Sak mburiné omah ana tamané.* There's a park behind the house. *Ḍèké urut sa*ku.* He's following behind me. *See also* TUT-BURI
burik pock-marked; scarred, blemished
burit *var of* BERIT. ***an** 1 back yard. 2 hind part
burokrasi bureaucracy
burokrat bureaucrat
burokratis bureaucratic
burtjèt a snipe-like bird
buru[a] *ng,* **budjeng** *kr* ***n̂** 1 act of hunting. *panggonan buron* hunting ground. 2 to chase each other. 3 (*or* **be*n̂**) that which is hunted. *buron galak* wild game. *buron pulisi* a fugitive from the law. **ke*-*** 1 pursued by troubles. *Uripé ke*-*.* His life is a series of misfortunes. 2 *rg* in a hurry. *Olèhé mangan ora susah ke*-*.* Don't eat too fast. **m/di(be)*** to hunt, pursue. *di* asu* chased by a dog. *di* ing kasusahan* pursued by sorrows. **m* kalah·é** to try to win back lost money. **m* tjukup** to make a long story short... **m* utjeng kélangan deleg** penny wise and pound foolish. **pa·m*n̂-an** place to hunt
buru[b] to have just finished [do]ing. *Aku * mangan.* I've just eaten.
buruh *ng,* **berah** *kr* wage earner, salaried employee; work force, labor; to work for wages. *para ** the workers. *serikat ** labor union. *A dudu tani nanging * tani.* A isn't

a farmer, he's a farm laborer. ***an** wages, salary. *Larang *ané.* The cost of labor is high. **m*** *or* **(m)be*** to work for wages. *be* negor*[2] *kaju* to earn money chopping wood. **m/di*aké** 1 to hire smn for wages. 2 to hire out [a job]. *Amarga Siti lara, olèhé umbah*[2] *di*aké.* Siti was ill, so she hired smn to do her laundry. **m/di*i** to hire smn. *wong sing di*i saben dina* workers who get paid by the day. *m*i wong sing nggarap sawah* to hire laborers for a rice paddy. **per*an** (the) labor (force). *Kantor ** the Labor Office

buruk a disease of chickens. ***an** prey of predatory animals

burung *see* SARANG

burus flawless, unblemished

bus *rpr* the hissing of air escaping

busak *var of* BUSEK

busânâ 1 raiment. ** èdi*[2] beautiful garments. 2 to get/be dressed (*ki for* DANDAN). **m/di*ni** to decorate; to deck out

busek̄ (*or* ***an**) eraser. **m/di*aké** to erase for smn. **m/di*(i)** to erase

busèt *rg* 1 ape. 2 *excl of surprise*

busi spark plug

busik [of skin] dry and flaking. **ora *** *or* **tan *** unhurt; invulnerable

busuk 1 ignorant; stupid. 2 [of firecrackers] no good, a dud

busung 1 pregnant [of animals; *cr* of people]. 2 disease that causes bloating. ** kèkèt* swelling of the legs. ** weteng* bloating of the stomach (from malnutrition or disease)

busur (*or* **m·be***) to eat greedily, stuff oneself

but (*or* **m***) *rpr* a whisking motion. *Ḍèké lunga mak *.* Off he dashed. *Mak * ḍompèté disawut tukang tjopèt.* His wallet was suddenly snatched by a pickpocket. **bat-*** *rpr* a series of deft motions. *Olèhé njambut gawé bat-* terus.* She works quickly. **nge*** 1 to drive fast. *Adja nge* ing dalan sing ramé.* Don't speed on crowded roads. 2 (*psv* **di***) to [do] quickly. *Garapanku tak *.* I rushed through my homework.

buta *wj* ogre, giant

butadjeng jealous (*root form: kr for* BUTAREP)

buṭak bald; bare

butarep *ng,* **butadjeng** *kr* ***an** excessively jealous of one's spouse. **m/di*aké** to suspect [one's spouse] of infidelity

buṭek̄ [of water] not clear, riled up

buteng short-tempered

butjal to discard (*root form: kr for* BUWANG). **be*** to go to the bathroom (*kr for* NG-ISING)

butjek̄ cracked or broken but still holding together, *e.g.* an eggshell

butjèl *see* TJÈTJÈL

butju hump, hunch (on the back)

butuh *ng,* **betah** *kr* thing needed; to need. **mu ḍuwit pira?* How much money do you need? *tuku ** to buy daily needs. **é rak tekan nang ngomahé ta?* What he wants is to get home, isn't it? *Aku * kertas kanggo nulis.* I need some paper to write on. ***-*** needed articles, daily necessities, food and clothing. **ka*an** needed article; a necessity. *apa ka*anmu* whatever you need. *Ka*ané wong urip kuwi sédjé*[2]. Everyone has his own needs. **m/di*aké** *or* **m/di*i** to need. *m*aké pitulungan* to need help. *Jèn di*aké ḍèké ora ana.* He's never around when you want him.

buṭuk [of fish] beginning to spoil

butul through to the other side. *Domé ditudjesaké ing prop gabus nganti *.* He pushed the needle all the way through the cork. ***an** doorway or entrance to a house or yard. **m/di*** to pierce

butun a certain citrus fruit

buṭung animal's haunch(es)

bu(w)- *see also under* BU-, BW- (*Introduction, 2.9.7*)

buwâjâ *var of* BAJA[a]

buwak *rg var of* BUWANG

buwal **m*** to bubble forth copiously, *e.g.* water from a spring

buwânâ 1 continent. 2 *ltry* world. *saindenging ** all over the world. *gawé * balik* to destroy, plunder

buwang *ng,* **butjal** *kr* ***an** 1 thrown out. *barang*[2] **an* discarded articles. 2 sewer (for refuse disposal). 3 in exile. *wong *an* an exile. **be*** 1 excrement. *lara be* getih umbel* dysentery. 2 (*or* **m·be***) to urinate, defecate. **m/di*(i)** 1 to get rid of. *Larahan kuwi *en ing tong kotoran ing djaba.* Throw the garbage in the trash can outside. *Sipat*[2] *kang ala kuwi kudu di*.* You should eliminate those bad habits. *Aku ora tau m*i ḍuwit kanggo djadjan.* I never waste money on snacks. 2 to let fall; to toss. *Wis, ḍaḍuné énggal di*.* OK, throw the dice. 3 to exile smn. 4 to put sth in an inappropriate place. 5 to place [a child] in an adoptive *or* foster home. **durung bisa m∗ umbel** helpless, unable to cope. **m∗ rai** to turn one's face away as a sign of rejection. **m∗ rasé olèh kuwuk** to discard sth worthless (in one's greed for sth better) and get sth even worse. **m∗ tilas** to alibi oneself; to hide the traces of one's guilty act. **pa∗(an)** (place of) exile

buwârâ **m∗** *rg* to find a livelihood far from one's place of origin

buwel to billow upward in clouds

buwi (*or* **∗ǹ**) jail, prison. **m/di∗** to put smn in jail

buwuh *var of* WUWUH

bw- *see also under* BU(W)- *(Introduction, 2.9.7)*

bwat *var of* BJAT

byuh *var of* BIJUH

C

c (*prn* **sé**) *alphabetic letter*

çaka (*prn* **sâkâ**) *var of* SAKA[c]

cc. (*prn* **sé sé**) cubic centimeter

cèntimèter (*prn* **sèntimèter**) (*abbr:* CM.) centimeter

ch- *see also under* H-, K- *(Introduction, 2.6)*

chalak (*prn* **kalak**) being, creature

chalifah (*prn* **kalifah**) 1 caliph. 2 deputy, second in command. 3 *title for a king*

chamsin (*prn* **hamsin**) day of Pentacost

chas (*prn* **kas**) typical

chianat (*prn* **kianat**) to betray. *wong ∗* traitor. **pa·ng∗** traitor. **pa·ng∗an** treachery, betrayal

chotbah (*prn* **hotbah**) sermon

chotib (*prn* **hotib**) preacher

citrun (*prn* **sitrun**) lemon-like citrus fruit

cm. (*prn* **sé èm**) *see* CÈNTIMÈTER

crossboy, crossgirl (*prn* **krosboi, krosgirel**) juvenile delinquent (boy, girl)

D

d (*prn* **ḍé**) *alphabetic letter*

ḍ (*prn* **ḍé** *or* **ḍé titik**) *alphabetic letter*

da- *see also under* DE- *(Introduction, 2.9.2)*

ḍa *plural marker: inf var of* PAḌA

ḍa- *see also under* ḌE- *(Introduction, 2.9.2)*

dabag woven-bamboo wall *or* fence panel

ḍabjang **n/di∗(-∗)** to support [a patient] and help him walk

ḍablang *var of* ḌAPLANG

dableg **n∗** stubborn, obstinate

ḍabreg a large quantity. *Pegawéjané nganti ∗.* He's swamped with work. **sa∗** a lot, a large amount

ḍâḍâ *ng kr*, **djâdjâ** *or* **pranâdjâ** *ki* chest, breast; *fig* heart, feelings. *lara ∗* tuberculosis. *ngilani ∗* to treat smn with contempt. *Iki ∗ku, endi ∗mu? (a challenge to fight).* **n/di∗** 1 to hit with the chest. *Balé* *di∗ bandjur ditanḍang.* He let the soccer ball bounce off his chest and then kicked it. 2 to get sth off one's chest. *n∗ kaluputané* to admit one's mistakes. 3 to accept with courage. *Jèn ana kesalanahé tak ∗né ḍéwé.* If there's any blame, I'll take it myself. **(anak) pa·n∗** third child in the family. **∗ manuk** barrel-chested. **∗ menṭok** breast of poultry; the white meat

ḍaḍag valiant, intrepid. **n/di∗i** to accept without flinching

dadah *ng kr,* **g(r)inda** *ki* **∗an** ointment/powder for massaging a baby. **ke∗** to be put on the defensive. **n/di∗** 1 to massage [a baby]. 2 to treat [a helpless victim] harshly. *A n∗ B.* A gave B a working-over. *Guru n∗ murid²*. The teacher gave the students a tough exam. **pa·n∗** massaging materials

ḍaḍah a hedge

dadak **∗an** suddenly; immediately. **ke∗** 1 (that which is) sudden. *mati ke∗* sudden death. 2 to be caused to happen suddenly. *Pangkaté nang Djakarta kuwi ke∗ saka larané bapaké.* Her sudden departure for Djakarta was occasioned by her father's illness. **n∗** 1 suddenly, without warning. *Udané n∗.* All at once it began to rain. 2 unexpectedly and/or undesirably. *N∗ isin² barang.* So shy! *N∗ apa?* *Now* what? *Kok n∗ takon barang.* What a thing to ask! *Wis tata² n∗ ora sida.* Everything was all set and then it fell through. *Kowé mau n∗ lunga barang, kantjamu mau mréné dadiné ketjelik.* You shouldn't have gone out; a friend of yours came and didn't find you here. *Jèn anggoné akon ndandani n∗ wongé ora sanggup.* If you hurry the repair man, he can't do a good job. 3 (*psv* **di∗**) to [do] right away, [do] ahead of time. *mBok adja di∗, mengko² waé jèn rada sela.* Never mind doing it right now—wait till you have time. *n∗ mangsa* to force [fruits, flowers], *i.e.* cause them to mature ahead of season. **pa·n∗** behavior. *ndjegur ana pan∗ sing ora betjik* to fall into bad ways. **d·um·adak·an** suddenly, all of a sudden

ḍaḍak a sap that causes skin itch. **∗an** an irritant to a personal relationship

ḍaḍal 1 broken through by flood waters. *Bendungané ∗.* The dam was broken. 2 disarranged, out of order/line. **n/di∗** to repossess one's rice paddy because the lessee failed in his obligations. **n/di∗aké** to break (through) sth. **n/di∗i** to trim, prune

ḍaḍali a swallow-like bird

ḍaḍap 1 a certain shade tree. 2 shield. **n∗** to strike with a shield. **n/di∗aké** to seize smn's possessions in default of a debt. **∗ ajam, ∗ bong** common varieties of *ḍaḍap* trees. **∗ srep** *ḍaḍap* tree whose leaves are used in folk medicines. **si ∗ lan si Waru** *hypothetical people; A and B*

dadar omelet, egg pancake. **∗an** 1 a certain rice-accompanying dish. 2 test, examination. 3 scale for assaying gems or metals. **n/di∗** 1 to make [egg] into omelet. 2 to test, try out. *n∗ kapinteran* to test intelligence. *Saben telung sasi sepisan di∗.* They are tested every three months. **n∗i** [of the moon] to rise. *mbulan n∗i* full moon. **pa·n∗(an)** 1 test. *pen∗an pungkasan* final examination. 2 scale for assaying gems or metals. **∗ lèlèr** reward for services

ḍaḍar **n∗i** to rise (*var of* N·DADAR·I)

ḍaḍat **n/di∗** to tear/break through sth

dadi *ng,* **dados** *kr* 1 to be, become, assume the role of. *Ḍèké ∗ tukang bétjak.* He's (*or* he became) a pedicab driver. *Iki kang tansah ∗ pikirané.* This is what he thinks about constantly. *Sapa sing ∗ Djanaka?* Who played the part of Djanaka? *jèn aku ∗(a) kowé* if I were you. *∗ nesu* to get mad. *∗ peteng* to darken. 2 as, in(to), so as to become. *dipilih ∗ présiḍèn* to be elected president. *kepara ∗ loro* divided in two parts. 3 done, ready, successfully completed. *Potrèké ∗ ora?* Did the picture turn out well? *Tjatjarku ora ∗.* My vaccination didn't take. *Ora apik ∗né.* No good will come of it. *Ana ∗ning rembug antarané A lan B.* An agreement has been reached between A and B. 4 [in games] to be "It"; to be a defender. 5 so, therefore, thus. *Aku wis dudu ketua menèh, ∗ adja takon aku.* I'm not chairman any more, so don't ask me. **∗ǹ** to build a fire. **∗ǹ-∗ǹ(an)** *ng kr* transformed from human shape. *matjan dadèn²an* a ghost tiger, a human being in the form of a tiger. **ke∗an** (*or* **kedadéjan** *ng)* 1 result, consequence. *Olèhé rembugan ke∗ané keprijé?* What came of the discussion? 2 occurrence, eventuality. *Kedadéjan kaja ngono kuwi arang².* Things like that don't happen very often. 3 brought to a (successful) conclusion. *Anggoné ngenjang kedadéan.* He got the merchandise he was bargaining for. 4 (to be) made up of. *Katrangan iku bisa ka∗an* *satembung baé.* (Grammatical) modifiers can consist of a single word. **n∗** 1 to grow rapidly. *Teṭukulané n∗.* The plants flourished. *Sawisé geniné diwènèhi lenga mambu terus n∗.* When he poured kerosene on the fire, it flared up. 2 to increase in intensity. *Larané ora saja mari, ning malah ndjur n∗.* His illness didn't get better: it got worse. 3 transported, possessed. *Djaran képang kuwi olèhé ndjogèd nganggo n∗.* Performers of the bamboo-horse dance move in a state of trance. 4 to let oneself get caught and become "It" in a game. **n/di∗kaké** 1 to cause sth to be/become. *njang²an didadèkaké* to conclude a bargain. *ndadèkaké klambi* to finish (making) a shirt. *ndadèkaké ketua* to appoint a chairman. *Adja ramé² munḍak ndadèkaké lan bingungku.* Don't be boisterous or you'll get me all mixed up. *Kaja ngono waé kok didadèkaké wadi.* Why keep it a secret? 2 to consider sth (as). *didadèkaké tontonan* regarded as a curiosity. **d·um·adi** *ng,* **d·um·ados** *kr* 1 to come into existence. 2 *ltry var of ∗.* **∗ ati** to take sth to heart. *Adja ∗ atimu lo.* Don't feel bad about it. **∗ lan** to be the cause of. *Apa sing ∗ lan matiné?* What caused his death? *Menawa ngenani kulit, bisa ∗ lan larané.* If it comes in contact with your skin, it'll hurt. **∗ wong** to be(come) important/influential

ḍaḍil **ḍoḍal-∗** badly torn

dadjal-laknat *var of* LAKNAT

ḍadjeng *inf var of* ḌI ADJENG: *see* ḌI

ḍaḍo steel-and-flint device for lighting fires

dâdrâ **n∗** to worsen. *Korèngé n∗.* His cut is getting worse.

ḍaḍu dice. **∗n̂** cube-shaped

ḍaḍuk dried-out vegetation

ḍaḍung heavy rope. *∗ tapuk* rope halter. **di∗a m̂·peḍot di·palang·ana m·lumpat** to resist restraint, not want to be fenced in

ḍaḍut chubby

dadya *ltry var of* DADI

daérah territory. *∗ pesisiran* coastal area. *djogèd ∗* a regional (classical) dance. **ke∗an** pertaining to a territory. *rasa ke∗an* provincialism. **∗ pa·dalam·an** hinterland. **∗ inḍustri** industrial area. **∗ istiméwa** (*abbr:* **D.I.**) special administrative region. **∗ minus** low food-producing area. **∗ katulistiwa** equatorial zone. **∗ panas** tropical zone. **∗ swatantra** autonomous territory

ḍaérah *var of* DAÉRAH

ḍaftar *var of* DAPTAR

ḍag 1 out of [supplies *etc.*]. 2 absent, out. **nge∗-∗** out in the open, unprotected. *Pangananané nge∗-∗, dirubung ing laler.* The food was left uncovered and flies got at it. *Tjanḍi mau nge∗-∗ baé.* The temple has no roof. **nge/di∗aké** to leave open/uncovered

dâgâ **∗n** the bottom or foot end (of smn in a lying position: *see also* ULU·N̂²). **n(de)∗n** to lie (for sleep, meditation) at the foot of a sleeping or buried person. **n/di∗aké** to place sth at the foot of [a sleeping or buried person]

dagang to engage in business. *kantor ∗* business office. *prau ∗* merchant ship. *wong ∗* businessman, merchant, trader. *pusaté ∗* commercial center. **∗an (grami·n̂** *kr?)* 1 business, trading. *rembug prekara ∗an* to talk business. 2 merchandise. *barang ∗an saka sabrang* imported goods. **(de)∗an** (**[ge]grami·n̂** *kr?*) (to have) business/commercial dealings with. **mer∗** to deal in merchandise. *mer∗ nang pasar* to buy and sell at the marketplace. **pa∗** businessman. **pa∗an** trade. *kuṭa pe∗an* a trading city. *pa∗an karèt* the rubber trade. **∗ lajar** to do business by sailing from place to place. **∗ tuna andum baṭi** to do good through others

ḍag-ḍig-ḍug *rpr* rapid heartbeats. *Rasané ati ∗ ora kepénak.* My heart was pounding uncomfortably.

ḍag-ḍog *see* ḌOG

ḍag-ḍug *see* ḌUG

dagel *var of* ḌAGEL

ḍagel **∗ Mataram** a radio comedy group. **n∗-Mataram** to make jokes in the style of this group

ḍagi *inf var of* UNDAGI

daging meat, flesh. *kulit ∗* a relative, one's flesh and blood. **∗-∗an** 1 meats. *panggonan ∗-∗an* place where meats are sold. 2 resembling meat. **n∗** [of animals, fruits] fleshy, meaty. **∗ sapi** (uncooked) beef. **∗ tjatjah** (raw) ground beef. **∗ weḍus** mutton

ḍaglig **ḍoglag-∗** shaky. *Méḍjané kok ḍoglag-∗, mbok diganḍjel.* The table wobbles; put sth under one of the legs.

ḍagrèg ragged, worn out

ḍagu *rg* chin

dah boo!

ḍah (*or* **n∗**) word of greeting *or* farewell. **nge/di∗i** to say/wave "hi!" or "'bye!" to

dahânâ *oj* fire
ḍahar 1 to eat (*ki for* M̈-PANGAN). *tjaos* * to offer food to the spirits. 2 to believe (in), follow (*ki for* NG-GUGU). **(ḍe)*an** food, things to eat (*ki for* PANGAN). **ma*an** *formal var of* MAḌARAN. **n/di*** to eat (*ki for* M̈/DI-PANGAN). *** atur** to heed, follow advice (*ki for* NG-GUGU). *** kembul** to eat together; to share a meal from a common plate
ḍahas [of soil] dry, dried out
ḍahjang *var of* ḌANJANG
dahuru *var of* DAURU
dahwèn a busybody, snoop; nosey, inquisitive
dâjâ 1 strength, force, impetus. **ning linḍu* the force of the earthquake. **ning djaman* the trend of the times. ** uwab* steam power. *Atiné isih durung menep *ning panggonan kang anjar.* She had not yet been able to get the feel of the new place. 2 *inf var of* BEḌAJA. ***-*** to exert force. *Olèhé mlaju krenggosan *-* énggala tekan ngomah.* He ran with all his might to get home fast. **ke*(n)** characterized by strength *or* impetus. *Ke* kepéngin ketemu bodjoné nganti lali sarapan.* He was so anxious to see his wife that he forgot about breakfast. **n/di*ni** to give strength *or* impetus to. *Mugi*[2] *buku punika saged n*ni kemadjenganipun wulangan basa Djawi.* We hope this book will stimulate Javanese language teaching. *Hawa ésuk kuwi bisa n*ni rasa seger.* Morning air refreshes you. **sa*-*** with all one's strength; as firmly as possible. *Olèhé njiksa *-*.* They tortured him cruelly. *See also* BUDIDAJA, RÉKADAJA
ḍaja *inf var of* BEḌAJA
ḍajoh guest, visitor. *Pak, ana *.* Dad, there's smn here to see you. *nemoni ** to have guests. ***-*an** to play going visiting (*children's pastime*). **ḍe*** guests, visitors; audience. **ḍe*an** to visit each other. **ke*an** 1 to have a visitor. *Aku ke*an tepunganku.* A friend of mine dropped in. 2 to receive an unwelcome visit, *esp.* to be burgled. *ngGonku ija ke*an bandjir.* The flood waters came to our place too. **n/di*i** to pay smn a visit. **pa*an** 1 place where one visits. 2 place where one receives guests. *See also* MERḌAJOH, M̈-PARA ḌAJOH, TAMU
ḍajum *var of* ḌAJUNG 2
ḍajung 1 oar, paddle. 2 [of soil] loosened and aerated preparatory to planting. *lemah ** soil prepared as above. **n/di*aké** to prepare [soil] as above. **n/di*(i)** to row/paddle [a boat]. *** olèh keḍung** 1 to find a better way of doing sth. 2 to maneuver oneself into a more advantageous position
dak 1 *prefix: var of* TAK-. 2 (*or* **n***) *inf var of* ANDAK
ḍak 1 descend; unload (*root form: kr for* ḌUN). 2 (*or* **n***) or else (*inf var of? md for?* MUNḌAK). 3 (*or* **n***) every (*inf var of* PENḌAK)
ḍakah (*or* ***-srakah**) greedy
ḍakal **ke*al** to climb with difficulty. *Olèhé munggah gunung ke*an.* He struggled up the mountain.
dakar male genitals
ḍakar *var of* ḌAKAL
ḍaken *sbst kr for* ḌAKU
dakik *var of* ḌAKIK
ḍakik **(n)*-*** elaborate, sophisticated, detailed. *kawruh kang *-** intricate knowledge. *Pitakonané ora n*-*.* His questions weren't very detailed.
ḍakir (*or* ***-***) to dig a hole with the hands or forefeet
dakmenang to behave in an overbearing or domineering way
daknang *inf var of* DAKMENANG
ḍakon (to play) a certain game consisting of a shallow oval-shaped wooden board containing rows of round hollowed-out places into which fruit pits (*ketjik*) are placed according to certain rules
ḍaku **n/di*** to claim (ownership of); to acknowledge as one's own
ḍakur *var of* ḌAKIR
dak'wa accusation. **n/di*** to accuse. *A n* B ndjupuk djam tangané.* A accused B of taking his watch. **pa-n*** accusation
ḍak'wa (*or* **n***) of different/disparate lengths (*shc from* TJENḌAK DAWA). *Sikilé *.* One of his legs is shorter than the other.
dal 1 to bring out (*root form: kr for* TU). 2 name of the 5th year in the *windu* cycle
dal- *see also under* DL- (*Introduction, 2.9.3*)
ḍal ***-*an** to wander, leave home frequently; one who wanders
dalah 1 (*or* ***an**) and (also), together with. *A * anak bodjoné* A and his family. *Aku kirim mung Rp pitu *an sokongan.* I only sent 7 rupiahs, including the donation. 2 *rg var of* SÈLÈH
ḍalam internal. *kemantrian * negeri* ministry of internal affairs. **pa*an** 1 interior

area, hinterland. 2 area not occupied by the Dutch during the 1945 Revolution

dalan *ng,* **margi** *kr* 1 road, street, passage. *ndandani* * to repair a road. * *sepur* railroad track. *dalan banju* water trough, pipe, *etc.* * *panganan* digestive tract. *Ḍèké sumingkir mènèhi * botjah²* *kuwi.* He stood aside to let the boys past. 2 way, route. *Apa kowé weruh *é soal iki?* Do you know how to solve this problem? *Apa kowé weruh * menjang pasar?* Do you know the way to the market? * *mlebu (metu)* the way in (out). *mbukak* * to open up avenues, to pioneer. 3 way, means; *slang* person made use of, go-between. *Pijé ja *é supaja gelis sugih?* How does one get rich quick? *Kowé kok bisa olèh gawéan kuwi, sapa *é?* Who got that job for you? ***an** roadways, street areas. *Adja dolan ing *an.* Don't play in the street. **de*** *ltry: sms* *AN. **ke*an** 1 to have a road, passage, *etc.* on/through it. *Kuṭa Tjilatjap ke*an sepur.* The train goes through Tjilatjap. 2 to be passed by a road *etc.* *Ana ngarep omahmu ke*an * gede̩?* Does the highway go past your house? *Ing mangsa panèn akèh wong ke*an redjeki (ora mung wong tani waé).* During the harvesting season many people get windfalls (not only the peasants). **n*** on the way (to, from). *Njang n* sing ati².* Be careful on your trip. **n/di*aké** to handle [merchandise] in the capacity of middleman. **sa*-*** in every road. *Sa*-* A tansah meruhi wong² kang sangsara.* All along the way he saw people suffering. * **buntu** dead end. * **gawat** danger, threat. * **gede̩** highway, main street. * **suṭik ng·ambah** person to be ignored or avoided

ḍalang central performer of a leather-puppet shadow play, who leads the musicians, narrates, sings, and speaks the dialogue while manipulating the puppets. ***an** 1 sawhorse. 2 saw blade. 3 bicycle frame. **n*** to conduct a shadow-play performance. **n/di*aké** to depict in a shadow play. **n/di*i** *slang* to plot sth. *Sapa sing n*i ḍémonstrasi anti-Pemerintah?* Who was the ringleader in the anti-government demonstration? **pa*an** 1 shadow-play performance. 2 shadow-play lore, including knowledge of the tales, the language used, the art of manipulating the puppets. *tembung pe*an* vocabulary associated with shadow-play drama. * **opah²** to do a difficult job and then have to pay smn else for it. * **ora kurang laku·n̂** a smart person can always find a way

dalas *var of* DALAH

dalem 1 (*or* **n***) in(side of), within. *ing * sewulan* within a single month. *Ing * sekiloné pira?* How much is it per kilogram? 2 the inner rooms of a house, *i.e.* the main family section. 3 house, home (*ki for* OMAH). 4 walled-in residence compound of an aristocratic family. 5 (*or* **n***) you, your; he, his (*referring to smn exalted: see also* NANDALEM, PANDJENENGAN DALEM, SAMPÉJAN DALEM). 6 (*or* **a***) *ka* I, me; my (*also, a response when called*). 7 forward (soccer player/position). *kanan/kiri* * right/left forward. **de*** to live in [a place] (*ki for* M·ANGGON). **n* sèwu** I humbly beg your pardon. **pa*an** 1 a building lot (*ki for* POMAH·AN). 2 residence compound of an aristocratic family

dalèr *var of* DALIR

dalir stripe(s) on an animal's coat. **n*** striped; stripe-shaped. *Gambaré n* abang.* It has a red stripe drawn on it. *nandur katjang n*²* to plant peanuts in long rows

dalit ***an** a patched place, *esp.* in earthenware. **n/di*** 1 to patch. 2 to use [food, money] as sparingly as possible

dalon *sbst kr for* TJÈLÈNG

dalu 1 evening, night (*kr for* BENGI, WENGI). 2 overripe. **ke* mangsa** *or* **ke* warsa** to have lapsed/expired. **ke*n̂** overripe

ḍalung large kettle *esp.* for cooking rice

ḍam 1 dam. 2 a turn at night watch in the village watchman's base. ***-*an** a game somewhat like chess

dâmâ ***n** precious because of its scarcity. **ke*(n)-*(n)** spoiled, overindulged. **n/di*-*** to spoil [a child]

ḍamai peace(ful). *poliṭik* * a policy of peace. *dalan* * a peaceful way

ḍamang 1 to understand. *A wis * bab iku.* A has a good grasp of the matter. 2 easily done. **n*aké** understandable; (*psv* **di*aké**) to clarify, make comprehensible

damar 1 hardened tree resin. 2 (**dilah** *kr?*) lamp, lantern. **n* k·angin·an** beautiful [of eyes]. * **séla** hardened tree resin

ḍambul a game played by tossing small balls or pebbles in the hands

damel job, task; celebration; to make, do, cause (*kr for* GAWÉ). ***-*** *or* **de*** weapon (*kr for* [GE]GAMAN)

dami 1 dried rice stalk; a field of dried rice stalks. 2 inner peeling of a ripe breadfruit or jackfruit section. *ǹ 1 dried rice stalk. 2 whistle or bubble pipe made from such a stalk. *nan field of dried rice stalks. n* bosok resembling decaying straw. Pakulitané n*-bosok. Her skin is tannish. * teles reddish yellow. Ulesé djaran mau * teles. The horse is a strawberry roan.

ḍami inf var of BEḌAMI

ḍamis 1 to fit together [2 joined parts]. 2 esthetically harmonious

ḍâmpâ skin disease characterized by a red rash

ḍampak barrel-chested

ḍampar 1 throne. 2 low table (usu. round) where people sit cross-legged to eat, play cards, etc.

ḍampèng n* 1 to hide by crouching behind sth. 2 ltry to plead for sympathy

ḍamping steep wall of a ravine or canyon

ḍampit boy-girl twins

ḍampjak *-* spreading out so as to fill in an area. Lakuné para ḍémonstran *-* ngebaki dalan. The demonstrators marched abreast, blocking the road. de*an forming a group. Manuk^2 mabur de*an. The birds flew in flocks. n/di*-*aké to deploy in a broad array. Opsiré n*-*aké barisan. The officer spread out his troops.

ḍampjang 1 in a bunch/cluster. 2 var of DAMPJAK. *an a bunch, cluster

ḍampjuk 1 to reach the same point from different directions. A lan B * ana pasar. A and B met at the marketplace. 2 to resolve differences and reach an agreement

ḍamplak (or *-*) big around [of long, roughly cylindrical objects]

damu n/di*(ni) to blow (on, out). Wuluné di* nganti kabur. He blew the feather up in the air. n* senṭir to blow out a kerosene lamp. n*i geni to blow on a fire (to encourage it to burn). Segané isih panas, didamoni ḍisik. The rice is hot; blow on it.

dan rg var of ENDANG

dânâ 1 charitable gift. * sokongan peladjar funds for students. 2 regent (inf var of WADANA). de* to offer funds for charitable purposes. ke*n to receive charity. n* excl of surprise, disbelief. n/di*kaké to give, donate. n/di*ni to give to. Botjah jatim piatu di*ni. The orphans were given charitable donations. * bau to offer one's help freely to others. * drijah to give generously to help others. * krama polite, well-bred. * raga to offer one's help generously

ḍânâ var of RANA^a. n* Jogja slang var of MRANA

danar *-* [of female complexions] fair, light

danâwâ wj ogre, giant

dandan ng, **dandos** kr to get/be dressed. Tjag-tjeg terus *. I dressed quickly. * tjara Djawa wearing Javanese-style clothing. lemari * closet with a mirror. *an 1 apparel; way of dressing. Asalé wong kuwi kétok saka *ané. You can tell where a person is from by the way he's dressed. 2 accessories; embellishments. 3 a place to dress. 4 a foregone conclusion. Kuwi wis dadi *an. It was bound to happen. *-* to do repair work. Jèn prèi mbok *-*. When you're free, how about fixing a few things? n/di*aké (prn n/di·dandak·aké ng) 1 to have sth repaired. 2 to have [clothing] made. n/di*i 1 to dress smn. 2 to repair. Tjoba tak *ané. I'll see if I can fix it.

ḍanḍan 1 strong bamboo rope. 2 intermediary who represents a prospective bridegroom in asking the girl's parents for her hand. 3 umbrella handle. n/di* to tie with bamboo rope. n/di*i to ask [a girl's parents] for her hand on smn's behalf

dandang bottom part of a rice steamer: a copper pot for water, over which a woven-bamboo cone (kukus·an) containing the rice is placed. * sablug or * sublug a one-piece rice steamer in which rice rests on a perforated metal sheet above the water

ḍanḍang 1 oj carrion crow. 2 pickaxe. n* 1 to wait for smn to die. 2 intsfr bright; clear (var of N·ḌRANḌANG)

ḍanḍang-gula a certain classical verse form

ḍanḍeng n* to wander, roam

ḍanḍer cassava

ḍanḍing n* slender and graceful

dandos to be/get dressed (kr for DANDAN)

dang (or n*) quick, immediate. *! Hurry up! nDang lunga. Go right now. *an measuring unit for raw rice equivalent to 10 beruk's. *-*an cooked by steaming. sega *-*an steamed rice. nge/di* to cook [esp. rice] by steaming. Berasé die* dadi sega. She steamed the rice. nge/di*aké to steam [rice] for smn. pa* 1 the time required to steam rice. sa·pa* sapanginang a moment, a short while. 2 person who steams rice.

pa*an kitchen. **kaju *** firewood. *See also* ADANG, ENDANG

ḍang *rpr* a musical beat. **nge/di*** to wait for, lie in wait for. *Ibu lagi nge* djanganan.* Mother is waiting for the vegetable man (to come by). **nge/di*-*i** to put sth in the way of. *nge*-*i lakuné* to block smn's way. *Aḍiké di-(e)ḍang²i bantal bèn ora tiba.* Put a pillow beside the baby so he won't fall. *See also* AḌANG

ḍangah ***-*** (to walk) briskly, to stride

dangak **n*** facing upward; craning the neck. **n/di*aké** to face sth upward. *Lampuné di*aké.* He directed the beam upward.

ḍangak *var of* ḌANGAN

ḍangan *ki* 1 willing (to help). *mbokbilih * ing penggalih* if you don't mind. 2 comfortable (*ki for* KEPÉNAK). 3 to recover (from) (*ki for* MARI). 4 relieved (*ki for* LEGA). 5 pleased; to like (*ki for* SENENG). 6 well (*ki for* WARAS). ***an** (one who is) always willing to help as needed

danganan implement handle/holder

ḍangḍeng *var of* ḌANḌENG

ḍangḍer *var of* ḌANḌER

ḍang-ḍing *see* ḌING

ḍanghjang *var of* ḌANJANG

ḍangir weeding and loosening of surface soil with a hoe. **n/di*** to weed and loosen [soil]. *** alis** to shave and shape eyebrows

ḍângkâ 1 location, place; *cr* habitation of an ogre *or* evil spirit. 2 cave where a corpse is kept

ḍangkal 1 dirt on the body. 2 *var of* ḌAKAL. ***en** to have dirt on the body. **n*** 1 *sms* *EN. 2 to remove dirt from the body

ḍangkèl main root of a tree. **n/di*** to remove a tree by the roots

ḍangklèh *var of* ḌÈNGKLÈH

ḍangkrok *var of* ḌANGKRUK

ḍangkruk **n*** to sit with the knees drawn up and the back bowed

ḍangsah *var of* ḌANSAH

ḍangsi *see* ḌANSAH

ḍangsul (*or* **ke***) soybean (*sbst kr for* ḌELÉ)

dangu 1 stem of the sugar-palm blossom. 2 (a) long (time) (*kr for* LAWAS, SUWÉ). 3 to ask (a question) (*ki for* TAKON)

dangur cassava

ḍanjang supernatural guardian of a tree, house, bridge, *etc.* in animistic belief

ḍansah to dance (Occidental style). *** ḍangsi** to keep dancing; to dance and dance

danu *ltry* wild water buffalo

daoké boss (*term for addressing a Chinese foreman*)

ḍaon a plant leaf

ḍâpâ **n*** *inf var of* PENḌAPA

ḍapi **n*** *inf var of* PENḌAPI

ḍaplang **n*** to stretch the arms out to the sides. *See also* KEḌAPLANG

ḍaplok *see* GERANG

ḍaptar list. ** padjeg* tax register. ** sokongan* list of contributions. **n/di*aké** to register oneself/smn. *Aku n*aké kanggo udjian.* I signed up for the exam. **n/di*(i)** to keep a record of. *Sing n* tjatjah djiwa kuwi tjarik.* The census records are kept by the clerk. **pa·n*an** registration; listing

ḍapuk ***an** 1 arrangement(s), formation. **ané wis dadi.* The arrangements are complete. **aning basa* linguistic form(s). 2 role assigned. **ané semuan wajang jaiku...* The cast for the wajang performance is as follows. **n/di*** 1 to arrange, set up. *n* organisasi* to establish an organization. *n* kabinèt* to form a cabinet. 2 to assign a role to. *Aku di* dadi Sentjaki.* I'm to play Sentjaki. *A di* dadi warga organisasi mau.* A has been appointed a member of the organization.

ḍapur 1 (in the) form/shape (of). **é bunder.* It's round. **é kaja timba.* It's shaped like a bucket. ** keris* design of a kris blade. *Tjrita iku gawénen * lajang marang mitramu.* Tell the story in the form of a letter to a friend. *Kowé waé sing isih * tjémpé.* You're very young yet. 2 clump, cluster; group, category. *geḍang sa** a cluster of banana trees. ** kabeneran.* Lucky for us! *Kula menika namung (a)* utusan, dados mboten mangertos isinipun buntelan menika.* I'm only an errand boy; I have no idea what is in the package. 3 *wj* play derived from classical epics and Javanese mythology. 4 kitchen. 5 *cr* face. ***an 1** form, shape. **an basa* linguistic forms. 2 cluster, clump. ***mu** *cr* nuts to you! the hell with you! **a*** in the form of; resembling. *préntah a* pitakonan* a command in the form of a question. **n/di*** 1 to form a group/category. 2 to derive from [classical sources]. *Tjrita iki di* saka Ramayana.* This tale is from the Ramayana.

dar- *see also under* DR- (*Introduction, 2.9.3*)

ḍar **nge/di*aké** to express, explain, expound (*inf var of* M/DI·WEḌAR·AKÉ)

ḍar- *see also under* DR- (*Introduction, 2.9.3*)

dârâ 1 pigeon, dove. 2 a virgin. **n*** Sir, Ma'am; master, mistress (*shf of* BENDARA). *Ḍèké diutus n*né.* His master sent him on an errand. *n* ḍokter* (*adr*) doctor. *Inggih n*.* Yes sir/ma'am. **n* adjeng** daughter of the master. **n* kakung** the master of the house. **n* mas** son of the master. **n* putri** wife of the master. *** banḍang·an** male pigeon being trained by use of a tame female. *** gambir** brown pigeon. *** giring** homing pigeon; pigeon in the mating season. *** kaplak·an** *sms* * BANḌANG·AN. *** kutjir** crested pigeon. *** mégan(-tritis)** gray pigeon. *** pos** carrier pigeon. *** topong** black pigeon with a white head. *See also* KUMANDARA

ḍârâ 1 [of poultry, plants] having reached the reproductive age. 2 medium-sized, not too large. 3 stomach

dârâdasèh *var of* DARADASIH

dârâdasih (*or* **n*i**) to materialize, come about. *Impèné *.* His dream came true. *N*i tenan, lagi dirasani kok teka.* Speak of the devil: we were just talking about you.

dârâgepak a certain style of Javanese house with verandas on all sides

darah 1 descendant, *esp.* of an aristocrat. 2 lineage, descent. **n*aké** to descend from, be a descendant of. *** dalem** close relative of a monarch. *** muḍa** hot-blooded youth

ḍarah *var of* DARAH

darak *var of* DARAN

ḍarak ***-*** 1 in neat rows. 2 [of garments] too long

daran **n/di*i** 1 to name/call sth (*var of* NG/DI·ARAN·I). 2 to accuse

ḍarang **ke*-*** in desperate straits, at the end of one's rope

ḍarat land (as contrasted with water, air). *wong mlaku ** pedestrian. *angkatan ** army, land forces. *Aku muḍun saka bis bandjur mlaku * menjang hotèl.* I got off the bus and walked to the hotel. ***an** 1 land, shore. *kéwan *an* land animals. *pradjurit *an* or *tentara *an* infantry(man); foot soldier(s). *munggah ing *an* to come ashore. 2 inland, away from shore. **men*** to land, come ashore. **n*** 1 to land. *KKOné wis n*.* The Marines have landed. *Montor maburé n* djam sewelas ésuk.* The plane touched down at 11 A.M. 2 (to go) by land. **n/di*aké** to bring to land; to land sth/smn

darbé *ltry* to have, own, possess. **de*an** a possession, belonging. **n/di*ǹi** to have possession of. *See also* DARBÈK

darbèk the possession/belonging of. **ku* mine. **é Ali* Ali's. *See also* DARBÉ

darès a variety of owl

dari **n*** to rise [of the moon] (*var of* N·DADAR·I)

ḍarik ***-*** in orderly rows

daring **(pa)*an** 1 container for storing rice. 2 large flat bamboo surface where hulled rice is spread out to dry before storing

darma 1 (**darmi** *kr*) duty, obligation. 2 donation, contribution; to donate, contribute. 3 close, intimate. *mitra ** a good friend. 4 *ltry* father. **n/di*ni** to contribute to. **sa*** (to do) from a sense of duty *or* as an obligation. *** jasa** a good deed. *** wisata** a group study trip. *See also* BUDIDARMA

darmawan contributor

darmi duty, obligation (*kr for* DARMA)

daru falling star that gives off blue light: an omen of great good fortune. *ketiban ** to receive a propitious omen

darube(k)si misfortune brought about by black magic

Darul Islam (*abbr:* **D.I.**) a certain rebellious Moslem group

darung ***an** and then, after that. **ke*-*** to go astray. *Jèn ngomong sing perlu waé, adja ke*-*.* Talk business–don't get off the subject. **n*** 1 to [do] repeatedly or habitually. 2 and then, after that

darurat emergency. *kahanan ** an emergency. *tindakan ** emergency action. *rumah sakit ** a makeshift hospital

darus **n*** to read aloud from the Koran

das zero

dâsâ (*or* **n***) the 10 place, 10 digit (*kr for* PULUH). *dwi ** (*ltry*) 20. *See also* SEDASA

dâsânâmâ 1 a polysyllabic synonym for another polysyllabic word formed from a string of corresponding synonymous segments of each word: a form of Javanese word play. 2 a book giving an account of such formations

ḍasar 1 bottom. **é ḍus* the bottom of the box. *ana ing * laut* at the bottom of the sea. 2 basis, foundation, principle. ** omah* house foundation. *tjèt ** a foundation coat of paint. *Paḍa déné ngadjèni iku * sesrawungan.* Mutual respect is the basis of cooperation. **-* ḍémokrasi* principles of democracy. 3 basically, by nature. *Botjahé*

∗ *tambeng.* He's an obstinate child. ∗ *wong tuwané mredi banget marang anaké.* In the main, her parents took good care of her. **4** background. ∗ *biru* a blue background. **5** to arrange or display one's merchandise. **∗an** 1 a display of merchandise. 2 place where merchandise is displayed. **∗é** fundamentally, basically. *∗é pantjèn ḍemen gegawéan.* By nature, he enjoys working. **a·ḍe∗** based on. *aḍeḍasar iki* on this principle. **ḍe∗** basis, foundation; on the basis [of]. *ḍe∗ marang rerasan rakjat* on the basis of the people's opinions. **n∗** at/on the bottom. *Prauné kèrem laut n∗.* The boat sank. **n/di∗aké** 1 to place on display. 2 to base sth. *paham sing di∗aké marang adjaran Marx* an ideology based on Marxist teachings. **n/di∗i** to use as a foundation. *Tjèt iki kanggo n∗i tjèt idjo mau.* This paint is to be used as a foundation for the green paint. **pa∗an** 1 place where merchandise is displayed. 2 a display of merchandise

ḍasbor dashboard

ḍasi necktie (Occidental style). **∗n̄** to wear a necktie. ∗ **klawèr** four-in-hand tie. ∗ **kupu** butterfly-shaped tie. ∗ **setrik** bow tie

dasih *ltry* female servant

ḍaster 1 nightgown, sleep wear. 2 protective coat

ḍasul *kr* *sbst var of* ḌANGSUL

dat 1 essential nature. ∗ *ullah* or ∗ *ollah* the essence of God. 2 *shf of* ADAT. ∗ *saben* the usual way. 3 chemical substance. ∗ **alus** soul (*cf.* ∗ KASAR). ∗ **areng** carbon. ∗ **enḍog** protein. ∗ **kasar** body. ∗ **kapur** calcium. ∗ **latu** iron preparation for vitamins. ∗ **njah** chemical salts. ∗ **putih telur** albumen

ḍat **∗-∗an** fitful [of sleep]. ∗ **njeng** fickle, changeable

datan *oj* no; not

ḍateng 1 (to go) to, toward (*kr for* MARANG, [ME]NJANG). 2 concerning (*kr for* MARANG). 3 to come, arrive (*kr for* TEKA). **d·um·ateng** 1 to, toward (*kr for* MARANG). 2 to go to(ward) (*kr for* T·UM·EKA). ∗ **ka·suwun** *ka* thank you. ∗ **sendika** *ka* yes

ḍatjah ubiquitous

ḍatjin unit of weight: *ca.* 61.76 kilograms = 136 lbs. **∗an** 1 balance scale for weighing by *ḍatjin*'s. 2 in *ḍatjin*'s, by the *ḍatjin.* **n/di∗** to weigh sth in *datjin*'s

ḍatu *oj* king. *See also* KEḌATON

datuk **n∗** to form *or* become an addiction

ḍatuk *var of* ḌATU

daugan *rg var of* DEGAN

ḍauk *inf var of* ḌAWUK

daulat blessing bestowed by a dignitary. **n/di∗** to seize control over a superior authority. *Kepala pabriké di∗ punggawané.* The factory boss was ousted by his subordinates. ∗ **betjik** a good omen

ḍaup to be/get married to. **n/di∗aké** to hold a wedding ceremony for [one's child]

dauru turmoil, chaotic situation

daut 1 toothless; to have teeth missing (*ki for* OMPONG). 2 to become detached from the body (*ki for* PUPAK). 3 to come to an end (*ki for* PUPUT). **∗an** 1 ceremony honoring an infant at the time the umbilical cord drops off. 2 the fallen-off umbilical cord

ḍaut *var of* DAUT. **n/di∗** to remove [seedlings] from the seedbed for transplanting to the field

dâwâ *ng,* **pandjang** *kr* long. *Rambuté ∗ apa tjenḍak?* Is her hair long or short? *jèn dipikir ∗* if you give it long thought. *tjrita ∗* a long story. **∗né** the length (of). *Kajuné ∗né sepira?* How long is the stick? **ke∗n** excessively long. **ke∗-∗** long-drawn-out. *Soal tjilik mau wekasané dadi ke∗-∗.* The trivial case dragged on and on. **n/di∗kaké** to make sth longer (than it was). **n/di∗ni** to make sth long. **sa∗-∗ning lurung isih ∗ gurung** rumors reach everywhere. ∗ **ambané** the dimensions/area (of). *∗-ambané 4 M^2* ⟨*patang mèter pesagi*⟩. It's 4 square meters in area. ∗ **ilat·é** to tattle. ∗ **irung·é** embarrassed. ∗ **tangan·é** light-fingered. *Si Tangan ∗* the pickpocket. ∗ **tjenḍak·é** the length (of). *Bukuné kabèh paḍa surasané, mung ∗-tjenḍaké waé béda²*. The books all say the same thing; they differ only in length.

ḍawah 1 to fall, drop (*kr for* TIBA). 2 order, command (*ki; rg var of* ḌAWUH). 3 to say, speak (*rg ki for* TJLAṬU, TUTUR). **∗an** dam. **n/dipun∗** to sow seeds (*kr for* Ñ/DI·SEBAR*?*)

dawâlâ *wj* white silk scarf worn around the neck to hold the batik in place

daweg 1 *var of* SAWEG. 2 *rg var of* DEGAN. 3 *sbst kr for* AJO

ḍawet a drink prepared from coconut milk, coconut syrup, and rice-flour squares (*tjénḍol*). ∗ *tlasih* the above drink flavored with basil

dawir torn, ragged [of human ears]
ḍawoh *rg var of* ḌAWAH
ḍawuh 1 an order, command (*ki for* PA·KON); to tell smn to do sth (*ki for* KON [*root form*]. 2 to say, speak (*ki for* TJLAṬU). 3 advice; to say, tell (*ki for* TUTUR). 4 *rg var of* ḌAWAH. **n/di*aké** to proclaim (*ki for* NG/DI·UMUM·AKÉ). **sa*é** as an exalted person orders. *Sa*ipun bapak temtu kula lampahi.* I'll do whatever you tell me to, Father. *Sa*ipun bapak kula ladjeng terus mangkat.* I left as soon as you told me to, Father. *** dalem** *or* *** pa·ng·andika (dalem)** (to issue) a royal command
ḍawuk 1 dappled, dotted with color. 2 faded from repeated laundering. **wis *** very old (*usu.* of animals)
ḍawul ***-*** untidy, in disarray. *ptg* **ḍ·r·awul** *pl* untidy, disarranged
de- *see also under* DA- (*Introduction, 2.9.2*)
ḍé 1 *shf of* BAḌÉ. 2 *inf var of* BEḌÈK. 3 *shf of* GEḌÉ
ḍe- *see also under* ḌA- (*Introduction, 2.9.2*)
débagan *inf var of* GEDÉBAGAN
ḍébat a debate. ***-*an** to exchange opinions; to discuss a difference of opinion. **n/di*** to debate, argue about. *** kusir** a discussion in which one participant will not listen to any opinion that differs from his own
ḍebat *var of* ḌÉBAT
débèt debit. * *lan krédit* debit and credit
déblag **n*** 1 broad, strong. 2 (*psv* **di***) to slap smn on the back. 3 (*psv* **di***) to repair an eroded earth barrier separating rice paddies. **sa*** a broad section of sth. *Aku olèh kuwih sa*.* I got a big piece of cake.
dèblèg **n*** cluttered; having many objects adhering to it
dèbleg 1 *rg var of* DÉBLAG. 2 *var of* DÈBLÈG
ḍèblèng (*or* ***an**) turning back, upward, and outward, *e.g.* kerbau horns; the tied ends of a headdress (*iket*)
déblo *var of* DÈBLÈG
debog banana-tree log (used *e.g.* as a puppet rack: the puppet sticks are plunged into the soft wood)
ḍebus *see* LENGA
ded-, ḍeḍ- *see also under* D-, Ḍ- (*Introduction, 3.1.3*)
dedah *var of* TEDAH
ḍeḍak rice chaff
dédé no; not (*sbst kr? md? for* DUDU)
ḍéḍé to sun oneself
dedeg height, stature. **n/di*i** to attend, be present at. **sa*** the same height (as). *Ḍuwurku wis sa*é kakangku.* I'm as tall as my older brother now. **sa* pa·ng·adeg** as high as a standing person. **sa* (sa)pa·ng·awé** as high as a person can reach upward. *** pa·ng·adeg** *or* *** pi·adeg** height, stature. * *pangadegé tjukupan.* She's quite tall. *See also* ADEG, DEG
ḍeḍeg **n/di*(i)** 1 to hammer softly. 2 to play [a gamelan percussion instrument] with gentle beats
ḍèḍèk ***an** (thing) set aside for future use. **n/di*i** to set aside for later use
dedel **n*** 1 to ascend quickly. *Montor mabur n* sanalika.* The plane shot upward. *Ḍèké tahun iki lagi n*.* He's come up in the world this year. *Rega beras n*.* The price of rice is skyrocketing. 2 (*psv* **di***) to press. *Lawangé di* menga.* He pushed open the door. **pa·n*** act of pressing. *Saka kuwating pan*ing banju, bendungané ambrol.* The water pressure was so great the dam burst.
ḍèḍèl to rip. *klambi sing ** a torn shirt. **n/di*** to rip sth open. *** ḍuwèl** badly torn, ripped to shreds
ḍeḍel sluggish. *Banjuné *.* The water won't flow readily. *A * atiné.* A is slow to grasp things. **ke*an** 1 stopped up; moving sluggishly. 2 constipated
ḍeḍep **n/di*i** to watch from a concealed place. **pa·n*an** a place of concealment. *** njenjet** *or* *** tiḍem** dead quiet. *** sirep** magic sleeping potion/spell
ḍeḍepa **n*** to plead for mercy or sympathy
deder **n*** steep(ly graded)
ḍeḍer ***an** seedling; seedbed. **n/di*** to sow seeds. *n* pepeteng* to sow the seeds of trouble. **pa·n*an** seed bed; plot where seeds are sown
ḍèḍès disagreeable odor ejected by civet cats
ḍeḍes **n/di*(-*)** to plague smn with questions about what he has been up to. *Ḍèké n*-* aku.* She kept asking me where I'd been. *Bareng di* suwé ngaku.* Under questioning he finally confessed.
ḍèḍèt ***an** tendril of a vine. **n/di*i** to uproot vines
ḍeḍet (*or* **n***) *intsfr* dark and still. *peteng n* (lelimengan)* pitch dark. **n/di*** to tug (at) with jerking motions. **n*i** 1 to tighten when jerked. *Pantjingé n*i.* His fishline

became taut. 2 (*psv* **di∗i**) to jerk sth taut. 3 to trample on [soil *etc.*] to firm it. *See also* ḌET

dedreg to remain adamant

ḍéfinisi definition

deg **∗-∗an** to stand around. **nge/di∗aké** 1 to build, set up. *nge∗aké gedung* to erect a building. *nge∗aké sajembara* to hold a contest. 2 to raise smn to the position of. *di∗aké ratu* to be made king. **nge/di∗i** 1 to build, set up. 2 to be present at. *nge∗i* to attend a wedding. *See also* ADEG, DEDEG

ḍèg 1 ship's deck. 2 blanket

ḍeg 1 *rpr* a sudden start. *Mak ∗ énggal²* *mlaju nang pawon.* She gave a start and dashed to the kitchen. 2 throughout. *sedina ∗* all day long. **∗-∗** *rpr* thumping heartbeats. **∗-∗an** startled, frightened; with heart pounding. *Wah, kowé gawé ∗-∗an waé.* Oh! you scared me. *Saka ∗-∗anku, mèh baé atiku pamitan.* I was so scared I nearly died. **n∗** *see* ENḌEG. **nge/di∗-∗i** to give smn a scare. **sa∗an** at one time. *Kuwih sa loḍong dientèkaké sa∗an.* He ate a whole jar of cookies without stopping.

degan young coconut, with sweet juice and soft meat. **d·um·egan** [of coconuts] to be at the above stage of development

degèg **n∗** to thrust forward the chest

ḍegel mortified, resentful

ḍeglag to sit leaning back so far that one falls. **n/di∗aké** to lean sth way back. *Aku n∗aké kursi.* I tipped the chair back. *Bajiné di∗aké.* She held the baby in a leaning-back position [to feed him].

ḍèglèg **n∗** to sit leaning back

ḍeglèg *var of* ḌEGLIG. **n·ḍeglag-n∗** to fidget, squirm

ḍegleg simple-minded (*var of* ḌÈGLÈNG)

ḍèglèng simple-minded; eccentric. **n∗** to sit leaning back

ḍegleng simple-minded (*var of* ḌÈGLÈNG)

ḍeglig *rpr* a sudden bending. **ke∗** to bend suddenly at the joint. *Sikilé ke∗ mak ∗.* His leg suddenly bent under him. **n∗** 1 [of knee] slightly bent and forward. 2 (*psv* **di∗**) to bend smn's elbow/knee

ḍeglo simple-minded

ḍéglog to limp because of an injured leg *or* because one leg is shorter

ḍeglug **ḍeglag-∗** to limp because one leg is shorter than the other

ḍégol [of arm, leg joints] enlarged, knobby

ḍegol *var of* ḌÉGOL

ḍégus tall and handsome (*shc from* GEḌÉ BAGUS)

ḍèhèm attention-getting cough *or* clearing of the throat; to cough *or* clear the throat for attention. **n/di∗i** to cough *or* clear the throat at [smn, *or* at a falling star when making a wish]. *Lintang alihan di∗i: ehem.* He wished on a star by clearing his throat.

ḍéjal **ke∗an** to make one's way with difficulty. *Malingé mlaju ke∗an.* The thief stumbled off.

déjan (*or* **∗é**) *rg* I guess, I think; quite probably

ḍéjé a certain locust-like insect

ḍèjèk (*or* **∗-∗**) hunched over; greatly burdened. *Tjopèté didjotosi nganti ∗.* They beat the pickpocket till he could hardly stand. *Olèhé nggawa koper nganti ∗-∗.* He staggered under the weight of the suitcase. *Bareng nganggur, uripé ∗-∗ tenan.* When he was out of a job, things were really hard for him.

ḍéjog (to walk) with a limp because one leg is shorter than the other

dèk 1 *inf var of* DUWÈK. 2 (*or* **n∗**) from (*rg var of* SAKA)

ḍèk 1 (**kâlâ** *kr*) last, past; when [past]. *∗ minggu* last week. *∗ anu kaé* some time ago. *∗ aku ana pasar malem* when I was at the fair. *∗ tjilik(an)* when I was a child. 2 belonging, possession. *∗mu* yours. 3 *title* younger person (*var of* ḌI). *∗ Marta agi nang Djakarta.* Marta (younger than me) is in Djakarta. **n∗** 1 last, past; when [past]. 2 possession, belonging. 3 *shf of* TJENḌÈK. **nge/di∗** (*prn* **nge/di·ḍèk**) to block [an opponent, *e.g.* in soccer]. **∗ apa** when [in the past]? **∗ bijèn** in the past, a long time ago; used to [do]. **∗ bijèn²** in the remote past. **∗ embèn** the day before yesterday. **∗ mau** just now, a short while ago. **∗ semana** a long time ago; way back at that time. **∗ wingènané** the day before yesterday. **∗ wingi** yesterday

ḍekah small village (*kr for* ḌUKUH)

ḍékan dean; head of an academic faculty

ḍèké *inf var of* ḌÈWÈKÉ

dèkèk *ng*, **sèlèh** *kr* **∗-∗** *or* **de∗** to put things smw. *Jèn ∗-∗ adja sak enggon².* Don't put things down just any old place. **n/di∗(aké)** (**ṅ/di·paring·aké** *ki*) to put sth smw. *Piring iki di∗ ngendi?* Where should I put this plate? *Ing pawon ∗na pasangan ja.* Set a mousetrap in the kitchen. **n/di∗i** to put

[sth] into/onto. *Montoré di＊i raḍio.* He installed a radio in his car.

ḍekek̄   having a neck so short it seems to be growing out of the shoulders. **n/di＊aké** to retract the head into the shoulders

ḍekekel   **n＊** huddled up with cold

ḍekem   **＊an** 1 *rg* stone-filled basket for reinforcing a dam. 2 *sbst kr for* ḌELÉ. **n＊** 1 [of birds, animals] to sit/lie with legs folded under the body. 2 [of people: *cr*] to sit with knees drawn up; to lie with knees folded under the body. **n/di＊i** 1 to sit/lie protectively over sth. *Kuṭuké di＊i mbokné.* The mother hen sat on her chicks. 2 to refuse to share. *Pité adja kok ＊i waé.* Don't hog the bicycle!

ḍeken   **n/di＊** to block [an opponent, *e.g.* in soccer]

ḍèkèng   **ke＊-＊** in constant difficulty or trouble

dekep   1 to grasp firmly. 2 to trap [*e.g.* an insect] *esp.* with the down-turned palm

ḍekep   *var of* DEKEP

ḍekes   **n＊** to sit cross-legged (*var of* ŊG-KE-ḌEKES)

ḍèk̇i   **di＊** *inf var of* DI-ḌÈḌÈK-I

ḍekik   small indentation. **＊ pipi·né** dimple

ḍekis   *var of* ḌELIK

ḍéklarasi   1 company-reimbursed travel expenses. 2 declaration. **＊ kemerḍékaan** declaration of independence

ḍekluk   **ḍeklak-＊** to keep nodding sleepily

dèk̇na   **n＊** in spite of the fact that; even so

dèk̇né   *var of* DÈKNA

dèk̇né   *var of* ḌÈWÈKÉ

dèk̇nèn(é)   *var of* ḌÈWÈKÉ

dekok   *var of* ḌEKOK

ḍekok   1 (to have) a dent, hollow. *Montorku ＊.* My car has a dent in it. 2 [of eyes] deep-set. **＊an** 1 a dent(ed place). 2 strong tea. **ḍekak-＊** full of dents. **n＊** 1 *cr* to sleep. 2 (*psv* **di＊**) to dent sth. **n/di＊(aké)** to steep [tea] for a long time

ḍékon   *acronym for* ḌÉKLARASI ÉKONOMI economic declaration (concept initiated by Soekarno)

ḍekong   *var of* ḌEKOK

ḍékor   1 décor. 2 stage setting. **n＊** to sit on the bare floor

ḍekos   *shf of* INḌEKOS

dèk̇puna   *var of* DÈKNA

ḍékrit   a decree. *ngetokaké ＊* to issue a decree

dek̇sa   guilt, sin

deksija   cruel; arrogant

deksura   to treat others with contempt, to humiliate people

ḍeku   **n＊** to sit cross-legged before an exalted person in a humble and deferential attitude

ḍekukul   **n＊** with nead bowed

dèk̇wur   **n＊** of various heights [said of things which ought to be the same height, *e.g.* fence posts: *shc from* TJENḌÈK ḌUWUR]. *Sikilé médja n＊.* The table has one leg shorter than the others.

del   *rpr* a sudden motion, *usu.* upward. *Matjané diunḍa ＊.* [The kerbau] tossed the tiger on its horns.

del-   *see also under* DL- (*Introduction, 2.9.3*)

ḍel   1 *rpr* a breaking sound. **＊, benangé peḍot.** The thread snapped. 2 *rpr* an explosion. *Bètèngé dimrijem, ＊.* The fort was hit by cannon fire.

ḍéla   *ng,* keḍap *kr* **＊-＊** every so often, from time to time. **se＊** moment, short interval. *Sekeḍap ndjih.* Just a moment, please. *Ḍèké mikir seḍéla.* He thought for a moment. **se＊ manèh** any moment now

ḍelak   **n＊** [of animals] badly in need of food and drink

ḍelalah   *var of* DILALAH

delap   covetous. **＊-＊é** *slang* what nerve! (as a comment on smn's greed or covetousness)

delas   *var of* DALAH

délé   **＊-＊** *excl of surprise*

delé   (*or* ke＊) soybean. **＊ kaplak** ripe(ned) soybean. **(ke)＊ǹ** resembling a soybean. **n＊** to plant soybeans

deleg   1 the facts of the matter. *Aku ora ngerti ＊é.* I don't know anything about it. 2 a pike-like fish. 3 cross section of a tree trunk. 4 (*or* **＊an**) rolled-up tobacco leaf. **n/di＊i** to roll [tobacco leaves]

ḍeleg   **＊-＊** *or* **ḍelag-＊** stunned with shock or grief

ḍélegasi, ḍelegasi   delegation

dèlèh   *ng,* suka *kr,* paring *ki* **n/di＊(aké)** to put sth smw. *Potloté di＊aké ing médja.* He laid the pencil on the table.

dèlèk   *var of* DÈLÈH

deleleg   **n＊** downcast, gloomy

delem   hollowed-out coconut shell, for holding water

dèlèng   **＊ mripat·é** to have a squint. **n＊aké mripat** to squint up the eyes

deleng   *ng,* tingal *kr* **de＊an** show, display, sight(s) to be seen. **n/di＊ (ǹ/dipun·tingal·i** *kr*) to look at, observe. *∗en ta!* Look! *sing n∗* spectators, audience. *N∗a ing nḍuwur.* See above. *n∗ ngiwa-nengen* to look in both directions. **n∗ tanpa mripat** 1 to sense sth. 2 *Jogja slang* are you blind?! **n∗ usuk** to lie around idly on one's back. **n∗-n∗** to depend [on], be up [to]. *nDeleng²* *marang wong désa kuwi.* It's up to the villagers [to decide, take action, *etc.*] **n·de∗** (**ne·ñ·tingali** *kr*) 1 to see things. *Matané sing kiwa ora kena dianggo nde∗.* He can't see out of his left eye. 2 to look around, see the sights. **n/di∗aké** to see, observe. **d·in·eleng(an)** (**t·in·ingal[an]** *kr*) visible; to appear, be seen. *asri tiningalan* beautiful to see. *Gunung kuwi jèn dineleng saka kadohan kaja buta turu.* (Seen) from a distance, the mountain looks like a sleeping giant. *See also* PANDELENG, PRIKSA

delep **n/di∗aké** to conceal, hide from view. *See also* PANDELEP

dèlèr **n∗** to flow sluggishly [of viscous fluids]

deles 1 pure-bred, of unmixed blood. 2 a cloth strip serving as a wick in an oil lamp

ḍèlèt *var of* ḌÉLA

delik **∗-∗** wide-eyed, staring. *See also* PENDELIK

ḍélik of various sizes (*shc from* GEḌÉ TJILIK)

ḍelik **∗an** 1 hide-and-seek. 2 in secret. *Olèhé mangan pelem ∗an.* She ate the mango where nobody could see her. 3 hiding place. 4 fallout shelter. **n∗** 1 to hide. *Ḍèké n∗ ing ndjero kamar.* She hid in her room. 2 isolated, hidden away. *Papan² sing n∗² saiki wis akèh sing ana sepuré.* Many remote places now have train service. **n∗-n∗** to [do] in secret. **n/di∗aké** to hide sth. **pa·n∗an** *sms* ∗AN

deling 1 clear(ly visible, audible). 2 bamboo (*kr for* PRING). **d·um·eling** [of sounds] clear and sweet

ḍèlit *var of* ḌÉLA

ḍelog earthenware crock. **∗-∗** stunned, motionless with shock or grief

delok *var of* DELENG

ḍélok, ḍèlok *var of* ḌÉLA

ḍèlot *var of* ḌÉLA

ḍèluk *var of* ḌÉLA

delul **n∗** headstrong, self-willed

ḍèlut *var of* ḌÉLA

dem- *see also under* D- (*Introduction, 3.1.7*)

ḍèm **nge/di∗(i)** to claim as one's own. *Potlot kuwi wis di∗i A.* A says that pencil is his.

ḍem *ng,* **srep** *kr* **∗-∗an** to have a grudge (against). **nge∗** to cool oneself/sth. **nge/di∗aké** *or* **nge/di∗i** 1 to cool sth, make cold(er) *or* cool(er). 2 to make comfortable/secure. *Si A ngeḍem-eḍemi atiné.* A set his mind at rest. *See also* AḌEM

ḍem- *see also under* Ḍ- (*Introduction, 3.1.7*)

demang a village administrative position (*now obsolete*)

ḍemarkasi demarcation. *lini ∗* line of demarcation (in battle)

ḍembèl [of unwashed hair] sticky, greasy

ḍembel *var of* ḌEMBÈL

démblo **n∗** thick, many-layered

demblok **n∗** smudged, smeared, messy

demèk **∗an** the feel of sth. *Rainé ∗ané panas.* Her face was hot to the touch. **n/di∗** to touch, feel

ḍemek̄ **∗-∗** (to walk) slowly with short steps. *See also* KEḌEMEK

demèmèl *var of* DERMIMIL

ḍemen *ng,* **remen** *kr* to like, take pleasure in. *∗ tetulung* to enjoy helping others. *Lanang ∗ wadon, wadon ∗ lanang.* Boys like girls and girls like boys. *duwé ∗* to have a desire [to have/do sth]. **∗an** 1 activity (*usu.* improper) which one enjoys. 2 *cr* girl/boy friend. 3 to have an extramarital affair. **ke∗en** to take great pleasure in. **n∗aké** pleasing, appealing. **n/di∗-∗aké** to do one's best to like sth. *Sanadjan omahé tjilik lan lawas, di∗-∗aké anggoné manggon ana kono.* The house is small and old, but he's trying to enjoy living in it. **n/di∗i** 1 to like, have a fondness for. 2 to love illicitly. **∗ njar** to acquire and tire of new things quickly

demenak **n∗aké** 1 pleasant, agreeable, causing delight. 2 appetizing, delicious-looking

demi in the name of. **∗ Allah** in God's name

ḍemi *var of* DEMI

demimil *var of* DERMIMIL

ḍemit 1 spirit that inhabits a particular place. 2 furtive, stealthy. **ḍe∗** spirit. **(ḍe)∗an** furtive, secretive. *Semuné ḍe∗an.* He has a furtive air about him. **∗ ora n·dulit sétan ora dojan** freed from ghosts and spirits

ḍémo three-wheeled motorcycle used *esp.* during colonial times

demok **ke∗** to touch accidentally. **n/di∗** to touch with the hand. **n/di∗-∗** *or* **n/di∗i** to keep touching/handling

ḍémokrasi democracy

ḍémokrat 1 democratic party member. 2 one who holds democratic views
ḍémokratis democratic. *pemerintahan ** a democratic government
ḍémonstran demonstrator, one who conducts *or* participates in a public demonstration
ḍémonstrasi demonstration; to demonstrate *Pemuḍa*² *paḍa * anti pemerintah.* The young people demonstrated against the government.
ḍemonstratip demonstrative; conspicuous. *Olèhé dandan * banget.* She was flashily dressed.
ḍempak [of nose shape] large and thick with a bump at the end
ḍempal strong (of physique)
ḍèmpèl **n*** to stick to, stay close to
ḍempel 1 to stick together. *Kembang gulané *.* The candies are stuck together. 2 close, intimate. 3 door *or* window frame
ḍèmpèt [two separate things] growing as one, *e.g.* Siamese twins. *geḍang ** two bananas growing in one skin
ḍempipit **n*** to keep in the background, remain unobtrusive
ḍèmpjèk ***-*** side by side spreading over a wide area
ḍèmpjèng *var of* ḌÈMPJÈK
ḍemplo ***-*** chubby, plump
ḍempo ball of earth *or* clay
ḍempul putty. ***an** broken. **n/di*** to break. **n/di*(i)** to apply putty (to)
demung large bronze gamelan xylophone. **n*** to play this xylophone
dèn *adr* high-status male (*shf of* RADÈN)
dèn- *prefix: ltry var of* DI-. *Mungsuhé *-usir bubar.* He put the enemy to rout. ** prajitna.* Be cautious!
den **nge*** to exert one's full strength by tightening the abdominal muscles, *esp.* for defecating, giving birth. **nge/di*aké** to concentrate one's strength toward [a goal]
denang **ka*an** to get caught doing sth one does not want noticed. *Ḍèké mlaku alon*² *saka mburi supaja adja ke*an.* He skulked along so as not to be seen. **n/di*i** to see smn doing sth furtively; to observe sth that has gone unnoticed by others
ḍenḍa 1 a fine. *Diukum * Rp 150.* He was fined 150 rupiahs. 2 club, cudgel. 3 a certain group of classical verse forms. ***n** a fine. *mbajar *n* to pay a fine. *ḍuwit *n Rp 300* a 300-rupiah fine. **n/di*** to fine smn. ***ning dosa** good works done in penance for a sin. *See also* BAU, SAPU
ḍénḍang 1 a variety of beetle. 2 a certain poison
ḍènḍèng sliced seasoned dried meat, ready for cooking. **n/di*** to prepare [meat] as above. *** gepuk/gupuk** a dish made from meat prepared as above. *** kenting** meat (prepared as above) with red pepper. *** ragi** the above meat with seasoned grated coconut
ḍenḍeng **n*** stubborn, obstinate
ḍenḍes **n*** *slang* fine, good; tasty
ḍenḍong ***an** to hum
déné 1 that (*relative*). *Aku seneng * kowé lulus.* I'm glad that you passed. *Kuwi diarani anèh, * ana wong wadon kok njambut gawé kanggo penggautan.* It was considered queer that a woman should work for a living. 2 while, whereas. *Sing mluku wong lanang, * sing nandur wong wadon.* The men do the plowing; the women do the planting. *Séwa omah wis tak bajar, * ḍuwit sekolah durung.* I've paid the rent but not the school tuition. 3 now (*narrative device*). ** botjah papat kuwi, lanangé telu, wadoné mung sidji.* Now, of the four children, three were boys and one was a girl. *Tjil, kowé * dikurungi mengkono iku ana apa ta?* Now Mouse-Deer, why are you caged up like that? *See also* ANADÉNÉ, APADÉNÉ, AWIT, ÉWA, PAḌA, SAKA[a]
ḍéné **n*** *Jogja slang: var of* MRÉNÉ
ḍènèh ***-*** *or* **n*** having the chest and belly thrust forward
dènèng ***-*** in plain sight [of sth which ought not to show]. *** kok** *or* *** si** why (is it so)? ** kok lunga.* Why are you going?
ḍèng **nge/di*** to let sth show. *Jèn hawané panas wong*² *wédok awaké die*.* In hot weather the women wear revealing clothing. **nge/di*aké** to reveal, expose. *Bab kuwi wis di*aké marang A.* A has been told about it.
ḍeng 1 *rpr* a loud report, *esp.* a beat of the mosque drum. 2 noon; the noon mosque drum. *wajah beḍug * 12* noon on the dot. **ḍang-*** to keep booming
ḍénga *var of* ḌÉNGAH
ḍéngah **sa*** any...(at all), every... *Sa* kaju jèn diobong adjur dadi awu.* Any wood becomes ash when burned. *Sepur ṭruṭuk kuwi manḍeg ing sa* setasijun.* Slow trains stop at every single station. *sa* wong kang*

gelem mangan anyone who wants to eat. *Iki diwènèhaké sapa?–Sa∗ (wong)!* Who's this to be given to?–Anybody! **barang ∗** any object, anything. **∗ pilih·a** any...at all

dengak, ḍengak *var of* DANGAK

ḍengal **n∗** to emerge (*esp.* upward) from a flat surface. *See also* ḌENGIL

déngan a certain bird

dengangak, ḍengangak *var of* DANGAK

dengangap **n∗** to keep wanting to [do]. *Asuné n∗² ndelokké wong mangan.* When a dog sees smn eating, it wants to eat too.

dengap **∗-∗** to breathe laboriously; *fig* to find life overwhelmingly difficult

dengarèn *inf var of* DINGARÈN

ḍengèl *var of* ḌENGAL

dengèngèk, ḍengèngèk **n∗** to lift the head suddenly. *Slamet n∗ bareng krungu suara mau.* Slamet looked up when he heard the sound.

ḍenger to know. *Aku ora ∗.* I don't know.

ḍenggleng simple-minded

ḍengglong *var of* ḌENGGLENG

dengguk, déngguk to gain weight

ḍenggul *var of* ḌENGGUNG, DJENGGUL

ḍenggung 1 major stone in a certain game played with stones (*gulaganṭi*). 2 leader or most prominent member of a group. 3 one's turn (at sth). *ketiban ∗* to get one's turn; to get the blame for sth

ḍengil **ḍengal-∗** 1 to keep emerging above a surface. 2 alone. *Nang setasiun mau sepi banget, mung aku ḍengal-∗ idjèn.* The station was deserted; I was all alone. **n∗** alone, by oneself

dengingak **n∗** to stare upward

ḍengis *var of* ḌENGUS

dèngkèk 1 (having) a bent *or* hunched back. 2 name of one of the small playing cards (*kertu tjilik*)

dengkèk, ḍengkèk **ke∗** 1 to get bent *or* arched. 2 to be the victim of a misfortune. *Ḍèké ke∗ Rp. 100,000.* He suffered a loss of 100,000 rupiahs. **n/di∗(aké)** to bend sth into an arch. *n∗ rotan* to flex a piece of rattan. *Gegeré di∗aké.* He arched his back.

dengkek, ḍengkek *rg* deaf

ḍèngkèl inability to move the legs. **∗en** unable to move the legs; rooted to the spot

dengkèng **n∗** arc-shaped. *Gegeré n∗.* He's swaybacked. *Peḍangé n∗.* The sword has a curved blade.

ḍengket, ḍengkèt, ḍèngkèt (*or* **n∗**) to adhere [to]; to be right next [to]. *Kajuné ∗ karo wesi.* The wood is stuck fast to the iron. **n/di∗aké** to place [things] in close juxtaposition; to stick [things] together

ḍengklak **ke∗** [of neck] to get bent backward. **n∗** to bend [the neck] back, *i.e.* turn the face upward

ḍèngklang lame; limping

ḍengklang *var of* ḌENGKLING

ḍèngklèh, dengklèh **∗-∗** broken and hanging (from). *Pangé ∗-∗.* The (broken) branch is hanging loose. *ptg* **ke∗** *pl* to swing, hang down

ḍèngklèk **n∗** to hop on one foot

ḍengklèk *var of* ḌENGKLAK

ḍengklik **∗-∗** *or* **ḍengklak-∗** *describing the bone-knocking gait of a very thin animal*

dengkling lame; limping

ḍengkling **n∗** 1 having the arm bent inward at the elbow. 2 (*psv* **di∗**) to bend [smn's knee, elbow]

ḍengklok **ke∗** to bend the knee inadvertently. **n∗** to bend/flex the knee

ḍengklong lame; limping

ḍengkluk *var of* ḌINGKLUK. **ḍengklak-∗** to keep nodding, *e.g.* when drowsy. **n∗** to lower the head

ḍèngkok **n∗** to sit with bowed head

ḍengkuk **ḍengkak-∗** to keep nodding with downturned face

ḍengkul *ng kr,* **djengku** *ki* knee. *ngekeb ∗* to hug the knees; *fig* to loaf on the job. **∗mu** *cr* damn you! **a∗ paron** *wj* strong-kneed. **n/di∗** to hit smn in the knee. **sa∗** knee-high; knee-deep. **wis sa∗** [of girls] old enough to make love. **∗ iket²an** hired through nepotism. *Mulané ora petjus, la wong ∗é iket²an ngono.* No wonder he's incompetent–he only got the job because he's related to the boss.

ḍengleng simple-minded

dengongok **n∗** to look upward, crane the neck

ḍengul *var of* ḌENGUS

ḍengus to appear suddenly. *Diarani ora arep teka, djebul mak ∗.* Just when they thought he wasn't coming, he showed up.

déning 1 [done] by. *kababar ∗ X* published by X. *kabur ∗ angin* blown away by the wind. 2 with respect to, for, because of. *Ana tunggangan sing luwih ∗ rikat tinimbang sepur.* Some forms of transportation are faster than trains. *njrengeni ∗ kliruning tindak* to scold smn for behaving badly

dènira, dénira *ltry* [done] by you, by him/her
dènja *ltry* [done] by him/her
ḍénok, ḍènok 1 young girl. 2 (*or* ***-***) chubby, pleasantly plump
denta *oj* ivory; white as ivory
dènten *sbst kr for* DÉNÉ
ḍèp **nge/di*** 1 to withhold [a document] so that it cannot be acted upon. 2 to claim as one's own
ḍep ***-*an** that which is placed in front (of). **-*ané apa?* What was put in front? **nge/di*aké** 1 to face sth in a certain direction. *Montoré di*aké ngalor.* He headed the car northward. 2 to put sth in front of. *Aku nge*aké téla.* I placed a cassava before him. *Malingé di*aké nang pengadilan.* The thief was brought before the court. **nge/di*i** to have sth in front of it. *Ḍèké lagi nge*(i) sega panas.* The hot rice is in front of him. *Ḍèké di* putuné lanang.* His grandson visited (came before) him. *See also* AḌEP
ḍepa fathom (measure of length, *i.e.* the distance between the fingertips of the outstretched arms. **n/di*ni** to measure in fathoms. **n*ni lemah** to lie face down, unconscious, with arms outstretched
ḍépah (*or* **se***) short but wiry (in physique)
ḍepaplang *var of* DJEPAPLANG
ḍépartemèn, ḍepartemèn (administrative) department
ḍépé ***-*** to plead earnestly and politely. *Slamet *-* ndjaluk pit.* Slamet kept asking for a bicycle.
ḍèpèl ***-*** *or* **n*** to sit huddled close to smn; *fig* to attach oneself to smn with an ulterior motive
ḍepèpèl *var of* ḌÈPÈL
ḍepèpès *var of* ḌEPIS
ḍepès *var of* ḌEPIS
ḍepipil, depipil **n*** to sit lost in thought
depiping *var of* DJEPIPING
ḍepipis *var of* ḌEPIS
ḍepipit *var of* ḌEMPIPIT
ḍepis **n*** to crouch, sit huddled up
ḍeplok (*or* ***an**) reduced to fine particles by pounding. *katjang *(an)* finely pounded peanuts. **n/di*** to pound fine
ḍépo storage area
ḍépok 1 holy man's shrine. 2 [of *e.g.* glassware, lamps] having no base/foot. **n·ḍe*** to reside in one's shrine. *Penḍita mau nḍe* ing Gunung Lawu.* The holy man lives in his shrine at Mount Lawu. **pa*an** 1 a holy man's shrine. 2 a complex, *i.e.* group of associated buildings
ḍépot, ḍepot *var of* ḌÉPO
ḍéprok **n*** 1 to sit down wearily. 2 to stay smw uninvited. *A n* ana omahé B.* A is a self-invited guest in B's house.
ḍepus *see* LENGA
der- *see also under* DR- (*Introduction, 2.9.3*)
ḍèr boom! bang! *Bleḍègé muni "*!"* The thunder boomed. **ḍar-*** *rpr* repeated bangs *or* boomings
ḍer- *see also under* ḌR- (*Introduction, 2.9.3*)
ḍeraḍag *var of* ḌERAḌOG
ḍerâḍog *wj* *rpr* a triple knocking (one short, two longs) on the wooden puppet chest with a rapping instrument, to give signals to the gamelan musicians
derap (*or* **n***) [of horses] to run at a trot
derbé *inf var of* DARBÉ
derbombok a dark gray long-necked long-legged water bird
derdah 1 shoo! scat! 2 a quarrel, dispute
ḍerḍeg **n*** to shake, tremble
ḍéré young female chicken that has reached the age for reproducing
ḍèrèk same-generation relative (*kr for* DULUR). ***an** *rg var of* KEMIRI. ***-*** in rows/ranks. **n*** 1 to accompany [a social superior: *ka for* MÈLU]. *Aku mau n* ibu nang pasar.* I went to the market with Mother. *nḌèrèk béla sungkawa.* I deeply sympathize with you in your bereavement. 2 to obey, follow (*ka for* NG·ANUT, M̆·PITURUT). *Kula namung n* punapa ingkang pandjenengan kersakaken.* I'll do whatever you wish. **n/di*aké** 1 to take, escort [a social superior: *ka for* NG/DI·ÈLU·K̂AKÉ, NG/DI·IRING(AKÉ), NGE/DI·TER·AKÉ, NGE/DI·TUT·AKÉ]. *Djana n*aké ibuné menjang ḍokteran.* Djono took his mother to the hospital. *nḌèrèkaken sugeng.* Goodbye! Have a safe journey! 2 to have [a person] go to live with and be supported by smn (*ka for* NG/DI·ILU·K̂AKÉ). **pa·n*** follower, retainer, attendant
ḍérèksi director
dèrèng not yet (*kr for* DURUNG)
dereng (*or* **ka*** *or* **ka*-***) eager. *See also* KAPIDERENG
derep to offer one's services at the rice harvest. ***an** the harvested crop. **n/di*aké** to have [workers] harvest rice. *ngenèni utawa n*aké pariné* to harvest the rice or else get smn to do it. **n/di*i** to harvest (the product

of). *Sawahé di*i.* They took the harvest from the paddy. *Pariné di*i.* They harvested the rice.

dèrès ***an** sap drawn by tapping a tree. *krambil *an* coconut palm used only for tapping. **n/di*** 1 to strip the bark from [a tree, to process it]. 2 to tap [a tree] for sap. **pa·n*** process of tapping for sap *or* stripping bark. *Pan*é suwéné nganti sesasi.* It took a month to draw the sap (strip the bark). **banju *** sap obtained from tapping

deres 1 hard, forceful [of an outpouring]. *udan ** hard rain. ** pates* intensely hard. *Saja * wetuning eluhé.* She cried harder and harder. *Kusiré * anggoné metjuti djarané.* The driver rained blows on his horse. *Jèn wis nesu, tembungé *.* When he's mad, words stream out of him. 2 *var of* DARUS. **ka*an** to get rained on hard. *Nganggoa pajung kaé jèn ke*an udan, mesti klotjut.* Even with an umbrella, you get soaked in a downpour. **n/di*aké** to persuade smn over his protests. *Kabèh pinuwuné marang bapaké sing n*aké ibuné.* The child's mother talked the father into giving him what he wanted. **sa*é angin**[2] to have no existence in reality

dergil (*or* **n***) enterprising, industrious, resourceful

ḍerik a treeless mountain area

derkuku a variety of turtledove

derma *var of* DARMA

dermâgâ *ng,* **dermagi** *kr* 1 main road, thoroughfare. 2 pier; harbor

dermagi *kr for* DERMAGA

derman (*or* *** anak**) having many children, a mother many times over

dermbombok (*or* **n***) var of DERBOMBOK

dermèmèl *var of* DERMIMIL

dermemeng **n*** to grumble, mutter to oneself

dermèn ***an** child's whistle made from a rice stalk

dermi *var of* DARMI

dermimil **n*** 1 to talk continuously. *Awit awan Ali n* waé.* Ali has been talking ever since noon. 2 to mutter. *mBokné mudji n*: slamet, slamet.* His mother kept uttering prayers for his safety. *Pisuhé saja n*.* He kept muttering curses under his breath.

dermimis *var of* DERMIS

dermis **n*** to ask for things all the time without shame

ḍeroḍug *var of* ḌERAḌOG

ḍerok **n*** to sit doing nothing

dersânâ a variety of guava

deruk a certain variety of dove which is tamed as a pet or used for hunting. **d·um·eruk** [of chickens] the same size as this dove

Ḍés. *see* ḌÉSÈMBER

ḍes 1 *rpr* the sound of a blow. *Ḍèké diantem mak *.* He took a hard punch. 2 *rpr* the hiss of air escaping. **ḍas-*** right on the nose. *Omongané ḍas-*.* He talks straight to the point.

désa *ng,* **ḍusun** *kr* village, rural settlement. *lurah ** chief village administrator. *(se)saka ** village administrators other than the *lurah.* ***n** rural, countrified. *tjara n** village customs/ways. *wong n** village dweller; boor. **n*ni** countrified; boorish. **pa*n** 1 rural area. 2 rural, pertaining to villages. *** mawa tjara, nagara mawa tata** every region has its own ways; village customs are different from city customs. *See also* MERDÉSA

ḍeseg **ke*** to get pushed (aside, around). *Tandurané ke* suket.* The plants were choked out by grass. *Aku ke* memburi.* I got elbowed back. **n*** to push, press. *A n* enggoné lungguh.* A pushed his seat [nearer]. *A n* B supaja mbajar utangé.* A is pressing B to pay up what he owes. **n/di*aké** to help smn push; to push/press on smn's behalf

ḍesel ***-*an** crowded, pressing each other. *Sing nonton pasar malem akèh banget nganti *-*an.* The fairgoers were pressed tightly against each other. **n*** to push (against, into). *Adja n*[2] waé.* Quit shoving! *A n* ana ngarep.* A pushed his way to the front. **n/di*aké** to push sth (into, against). *Ḍèké n*aké anaké ana ngarep.* He pushed his child to the front (of the line).

Ḍésèmber *(abbr: Ḍés.)* December

ḍésèntri, ḍésentré *var of* ḌISÈNTERI

ḍesis whisper

ḍesok having a dent in it. **ḍesak-*** full of dents

desṭa 11th month of the Javanese year (19 April–12 May)

desṭar wrapped headdress (*ki for* IKET)

ḍesuk *var of* ḌESEG

ḍesus **ḍesas-*** gossip, rumors. *Adja ngrasakaké ḍesas-*é tangga teparo.* Don't pay attention to what the neighbors say.

det ***-*** *rpr* normal heartbeats

ḍèt *rpr* a horn honking. * ṭilang *rpr* the cry of a certain bird (*kuṭilang*)

ḍet *rpr* a sudden jerk. *See also* ḌEḌET

ḍétèktip, ḍétèktif detective. *tjrita* * detective story

ḍèṭèng n* (to walk) with chest high and shoulders back

détija *wj* ogre, giant

détya *var of* DÉTIJA

ḍevisa *var of* ḌÉVISEN

ḍévisen, ḍevisen foreign exchange; rate of exchange

déwa *wj, ltry* 1 male deity. 2 *rg var of* DÈRÈS. di*-* revered, esteemed. ka*n 1 realm of the supernatural beings. 2 godlike. * ng-édja wantah a deity on earth (*i.e.* visible to human eyes); *fig* a highly revered person. *See also* DÉWATA, DÈWI

déwâdaru *var of* DÉWANDARU

déwadji *adr* king. *Sendika (kangdjeng)* *. Yes, your Majesty.

ḍéwan council. * Perwakilan Rakjat (*abbr:* D.P.R.) Parliament

déwandaru 1 a certain mythological tree with magical properties. 2 one of two banyan trees in North Square, Jogjakarta (*see also* DJANADARU, RINGIN)

déwangkârâ *ltry* sun

déwâresi mythological deity

déwâsâ *var of* DIWASA

déwâtâ male deities collectively. ka*n 1 realm of supernatural beings. 2 having a deity-like nature. *See also* DÉWA

ḍéwé *ng*, pijambak *kr* 1 alone, by oneself. *Aku arep mulih* *. I'm going home alone. *Montor²an iki mlaku* *. This toy car goes by itself. 2 oneself; one's own. *Aku* * *sing nulis.* I wrote it myself. *Iki bukuku* *. This is my own book. *Dèké ora duwé sapi* *. He has no cattle of his own. 3 separate, apart. *Wohé ana* * *ana ing ḍuwur.* The fruit is by itself at the top [of the tree]. *Mung aku* * *sing ora sekolah.* I'm the only one who doesn't go to school. 4 most, -est. *sing apik* * the best one. *wekasan* * the very last one. *sepur kang ésuk* * the earliest train. *an (prn ḍèwèkan ng)* alone. *Dèwèké lunga menjang negara mantja ḍèwèkan.* He went abroad by himself. *ḍèwèkan karo kowé* alone with you. *-* [each] his own; separately, (by) oneself. *Kakang-aḍi lunga pasar ḍéwé².* The brothers went to the marketplace separately. *Murid² paḍa nulis djenengé *-*.* Each student wrote his own

name. n* by oneself. *Jèn kabèh paḍa kumpul Ali mesṭi n*.* Whenever the boys get together, Ali remains apart. n/di* kaké to isolate. *Wong sing lara kuwi prajoga diḍèwèkna.* A sick person should be kept apart. *Piring² sing reged kudu di-ḍèwèk²aké.* Keep the dirty plates separate. n*i (*prn* nḍèwèk̇i, *rg* nḍèwèni *ng*) 1 to have sth all to oneself. *Ora susah sambat, kowé ora nḍèwèki olèhé susah.* Don't complain; you aren't the only unfortunate one. 2 (*psv* di*i) to separate out from the rest. *Ora ana kang diḍèwèki.* None of them was omitted.

ḍèwèk *var of* ḌÉWÉ

ḍèwèkan *see* ḌÉWÉ-AN

ḍèwèké *ng*, pijambak̇ipun *kr* he, she. * *ḍéwé* he himself (she herself)

ḍèwèk̇i *see* N-DÉWÉ-I

ḍèwèk̇né *var of* ḌÈWÈKÉ

ḍèwèk̇nèn *var of* ḌÈWÈKÉ

dèwi *wj, ltry* female deity. * *Sri* goddess of rice. *See also* DÉWA

ḍéwot *var of* ḌIWUT

ḍéwutan a certain grass

dharma (*prn* darmâ) *var sp of* DARMA

di- *ng*, dipun- *kr* 1 *psv* prefix: 3d person, oblique 2d person. *Anakku arep di-priksa ḍokter.* My child is to be examined by the doctor. *Alun² di-rengga² gendéra.* The square was decorated with flags. *Banjuné apa wis di-ombèni?* Have you drunk the water? *Muga di-paringana kuwat.* Give me strength! 2 oblique imperative pfx. *Dipun isèni panili sak séndok.* Add a teaspoon of vanilla. *Segané adja di-entèkké.* Don't eat all the rice. *Di-waspada anggoné mapag mungsuh.* Be watchful when you face the enemy! *Di-ngati-ati.* Look out! *Di-betjik.* Do it well! *kaja (ng)apa (kados punapa *kr*) decidedly, very much so. *Wong iku nadjan asora dikaja apa, adja diina.* No matter how lowly he is, don't humiliate him. *Arepa mbengok dikaja ngapa, ḍèké ora krungu sebab buḍeg.* You can yell your head off but he won't hear you: he's deaf.

D.I. *see* DAERAH, DARUL ISLAM

ḍi *adr* younger sibling; person younger than oneself (*shf of* AḌI). * adjeng 1 *adr* younger sister; younger female friend. 2 *adr* (one's) wife. * mas *adr* younger brother; younger male friend

ḍialèk dialect, regional speech

ḍialoġ dialogue

dibja magically empowered, supernaturally invulnerable. **ka*n** invulnerability, supernatural power

dibya *var of* DIBJA

ḍiḍal to become detached; to lose the outer layer. *Djempolé *.* The skin peeled off his thumb.

ḍiḍèh *var of* ḌIḌIH

ḍiḍih congealed animal blood (used as a food)

ḍiḍik ***an** 1 formal education. 2 that which has been learned. *Tindak-tanduk kaja ngono kuwi *an ngendi!* Where did you learn to behave like that! 3 to acquire an education (at, from). *A *an Gadjah Mada.* A studied at Gadjah Mada University. **n/di*** to educate, train. **pa·n*** teacher. **pa·n*an** (formal) education

ḍiḍis to remove lice from the hair. **n/di*i** to delouse sth

ḍidjik **ke*-*** to move with slow silent steps; to sneak

Ḍiḍong *see* WLANDA

digdâjâ supernaturally powerful; magically invulnerable. **ka*n** magical power; supernatural invulnerability

digdjâjâ *var of* DIGDAJA

ḍiglug **ḍiglag-*** to walk with a limp because one leg is shorter than the other

digsura ill-mannered, badly behaved

digwidjâjâ *var of* DIGDAJA

ḍihik *var of* ḌIHIN

ḍihin 1 formerly. 2 (at) first

dijan (**dilah** *kr?*) (oil) lamp. *** ḍuḍuk** table lamp. *** gantung** hanging lamp. *** gas** gas lamp. *** lenga pèt** kerosene lamp. *** sorot** searchlight, spotlight. *** teplok** kerosene lamp hung against walls or pillars

diju *wj* ogre, giant

ḍik 1 really, indeed. *Ija *.* Yes indeed! *Ora *.* Not at all. 2 *var of* ḌI. 3 *var of* ḌÈK. ***an** *or* ***é** actually, indeed. **n*** in, at, on. *nḌèk endi?* Where?

dika **n*** you (*md*). *Pit n* napa pun dados?* Is your bicycle fixed yet? **n/di*kaké** to ask/tell smn to do sth. *See also* ANDIKA

ḍiké *var of* ḌÈWÈKÉ

dikep, ḍikep *var of* DEKEP

ḍikir (to recite) a certain chant (*lha-illah-haillalahi*) at the close of an Islamic service. ***an** to hold a ceremony at which the above is chanted. **n/di*i** to chant the above (for) [a religious service]

dikné 1 *var of* ḌÈWÈKÉ. 2 (*or* **n***) if, in case

ḍiktat educational materials (*usu.* mimeographed)

ḍiktator, ḍiktatur (political) dictator

ḍikté dictation (as a school writing exercise). **n/di*** to dictate. *n* lajang* to dictate a letter. *Pitakoné di*.* The questions were dictated to him.

ḍikut in haste. *Lakuné *.* He walked fast.

ḍil *rpr* jerking sth loose. *Untuné ditjopot mak *.* He jerked out the tooth.

dilah lamp, lantern (*kr? for* DAMAR, DIJAN). **d·um·ilah** *oj* light, bright

dilalah (*or* **n***) (but) as luck would have it. *Aku ora duwé ḍuwit, n* kantjaku njilihi Rp 1000.* I had no money; luckily a friend lent me a thousand rupiahs. *Aku wis arep mangkat, n* udan!* Just as I was about to leave, (by bad luck) it had to rain!

dilat **n/di*(i)** to lick. *Tatuné di*i.* He licked his wounds. *Geniné n* mengétan.* The flames licked eastward. **n* idu·né ḍéwé** to go back on one's word

dilem a certain plant with aromatic leaves

ḍileng to have an eye ailment *or* defect

dilep **n*** to stay by oneself, not join in

dilik **n/di*** to see, look at, watch

dilir **n*** copious, abundant. *Suguhané n*.* There were all kinds of refreshments. *Ana wong pirang² n* arep paḍa nonton tanḍingan bal-balan.* Crowds streamed in to see the soccer match. *Pendjaluk wiwit n*.* Requests began to pour in.

ḍili:t **se*** a moment, a short while

ḍilman two-wheeled horse-drawn passenger carriage

ḍilu:k̄ **se*** a moment, a short while

ḍilu:t *var of* ḌILUK

dim measure of length: *ca.* 2.54 centimeters = *ca.* 1 inch

dimar lamp, lantern

dimèk 1 *var of* DEMÈK. 2 so that, in order to

dimèn so that, in order to

dimik sulfur-tipped stick for kindling a fire with flame from another fire

ḍimik **ke*-*** (to walk) slowly and silently; to sneak

ḍimpil 1 chipped at the edge. 2 name of one of the small playing cards (*kertu tjilik*)

din- *see also under* D- (*Introduction, 3.1.7*)

ḍi:n *rpr* a horn honking

ḍin- *see also under* Ḍ- (*Introduction, 3.1.7*)

dina *ng*, **dinten** *kr* (24-hour) day. *** *iki*** today. *saben ** every day. *saben *né* day in and day out. **n*** to [do] all day long. *pasa n** to fast until 6 P.M. **n*-*** to [do] day after day. **pa*n** daily. *blandjané pe*n* the daily shopping. *basa pa*n* everyday speech, ordinary conversation. **sa*** one day. *se* iki* this whole day (just ending). *se* mengko* this whole day (just beginning). *se* bengkeleng* or *se* muput* all day long. *se* kaping telu* three times a day. **sa*né** within a single day. **sa*-*** daily. *barang² keperluan se*-** things needed every day. **sa*-*né** day after day, every single day. *** bengi** night time. *Nalika semana * bengi.* It was night at the time. *** betjik** an auspicious day by astrological reckoning. *** geḍé** important day; holiday. *** mengko** these days, nowadays. *** naas** an inauspicious day. *** tara** the weekdays collectively excepting Friday, the Moslem holy day

ḍinamis dynamic

ḍinamit dynamite. **n/di*** to dynamite sth

ḍinamo dynamo for generating electric power

dinar golden coin

ḍinasṭi dynasty

ḍinḍal **n/di*** to sell sth to raise money

ḍinḍing brick wall; partition

ḍiné dinner party

ḍines employed, working; (connected with) office employment. *A lagi *.* A is at work now. *A * ana Perusahaan X.* A works at the X Company. *lajang ** an official letter. *lunga ** to take a business trip. *menganggo ** dressed in official attire. ** bengi* (to work on) the night shift. *ikatan ** (a contract for) scholarship money given in return for government service. *Jèn *é wis rong puluh taun, biasané mbandjur éntuk pènsiun.* When you've worked for twenty years, you usually get a pension. ***é** it is to be expected that... **é kowé kudu mangan nḍisik.* Of course you'll have dinner first.

ḍing 1 indeed, to be sure. *Ija *.* Yes indeed! *Ora *, aku ming gujon kok.* No no, I was only kidding! *Aku mau mung ngapusi *, sadjané durung teka.* I fooled you! he's really not here yet. 2 *rpr* gamelan drumbeats corresponding to the vowel scheme of a classical verse form. 3 *var of* SING. ***é** the fact is... **ḍang-*** whoever; anybody. *Iki diwènèhaké sapa?–Ḍang-*.* Who'll I give it to?–Anybody! **(sa)*-*(é)** any one (at all). *Sing kanggo aku sing ndi?–Ḍing².* Which one is for me?–Either one. *Iki diwènèhaké sapa?–Sa*-*é.* Who is this one supposed to be given to?–Anyone at all. *See also* ḌONG-ḌING

ḍinga *var of* ḌÉNGAH

dingarèn how strange! it's unusual that... ** wajah méné kok wis kondur.* How come you're home so early? *Elo, kok kowé teka *.* What are *you* doing here? **n/di*aké** to consider sth strange. *Jèn ora mangan sega, mesṭi di*ké karo wong.* People think you're peculiar if you don't eat rice. *See also* KADINGARÈN

ḍingḍong *rpr* the sound of a bell ringing. **n*** to ring

ḍingkel a certain fatal chicken disease. **ke*an** to exert oneself to the utmost. *Njambut gawé nganti ke*an ora ana tandjané.* He worked as hard as he could but nothing came of it. **n*** to hang around the house all the time

dingkik **n*** to keep watch secretly; to lie in wait

ḍingklang (to walk) with a limp. *Wong * kok mlaju banter.* Look how fast that lame man can run! *See also* KEḌINGKLANG

ḍingklik a low wooden stool or bench. ***an** to use sth as a stool. **ḍe*** resembling a wooden stool. *** pa·m̄·wasuh·an** a bench to sit on while beating the wash clean. *** pa·n̄·tulis·an** a bench used as a writing table by village officials

ḍingkluk **n*** with head bowed and shoulders drooping

ḍingkruk *var of* ḌINGKLUK

ḍingkrung *var of* ḌINGKLUK, DJINGKRUNG

ḍingkul **ḍingkal-*** to keep bowing the head. **n*** to bow the head

ḍini **ḍana-*** *inf var of* GEḌANA-GEḌINI

dinten day (*kr for* DINA)

dipa *var of* DWIPA

ḍipan wooden bed; sofa

dipâng̃gâ *oj* elephant

dipati *inf var of* HADIPATI

ḍipet tightly closed [of eyes]. *merem ** having the eyes closed tight. **n/di*** to close smn's eyes

ḍipisi division (military unit)

ḍiplikat *var of* ḌUPLIKAT

ḍiplomā diploma

ḍiplomasi diplomacy

ḍiplomat a diplomat

ḍiplomatik̄ diplomatic

ḍipo *var of* ḌÉPO

dipun- *prefix: kr for* DI-

dir **nge/di*aké** to boast about. *Ḍèwèké*

nge∗*-*∗*aké ajuné.* She's vain of her good looks. **èngsèl** ∗ door hinge

ḍir a marble. **∗-∗an** to play marbles

dirâdâ *oj* elephant

ḍirèksi managing executive, director, member of a board of directors

ḍirèktur director, head of a company

dirgahaju good luck (to...)! long live...!

dirgâmâ *wj* trouble, difficulty. *See also* GAMA

dirgantârâ *wj* the sky; [up in] the air

ḍiri (*or* **∗ pribadi**) oneself; one's identity. *adjining* ∗ self-respect. *pertjaja marang* ∗ *pribadi* to believe in oneself. *A ora njrèmpèt babar pisan ngenani* ∗*né B.* A never let on that he knew who B was. *See also* MANḌIRI

ḍisé in spite of the fact that; not...after all. ∗ *A arep lunga.* A meant to go but didn't.

ḍisènt(e)ri dysentery

ḍisik *ng,* **r(um)ijin** *kr* 1 first; ahead; to proceed. *Kowé apa aku* ∗*?* You first, or me? *Kowé* ∗*a, aku dak nusul.* You go ahead, I'll follow. *Sing diopèni* ∗ *sing ketaton.* The wounded were cared for first. *Ḍèké wis ngerti luwih* ∗. She had found out first. *Sadurungé kowé menjang kantor, mampira* ∗ *menjang toko.* Before you go to the office, stop in at the store. *sepur sing* ∗ *ḍéwé* the very first train. 2 former(ly). *Sing* ∗ *wis mèh ilang, sing kèri isih rada umum.* The former has almost died out; the latter is still popular. **∗é** the first thing; at first. ∗*é tekan ing retja geḍé.* First they came to a large statue. ∗*é mung saplenik, saja suwé saja geḍé.* At first it was tiny, but it kept growing. **∗-∗é** formerly; in the beginning. *Ḍisik²é bangsa Indonesia kuwi agamané agama animisme.* Originally, animism was the religion of the Indonesians. **∗-∗an** to compete for first. *Ora tau* ∗*-*∗*an utawa suk²an.* They never try to get ahead of one another or crowd each other out. *Balapané* ∗*-*∗*an njumed lilin.* They had a race to see who could get the candle lighted first. **ke∗an** to be preceded *or* beaten to the draw. *Wis ke*∗*an Suta.* Suto was here ahead of you. **n∗** 1 to precede. *Kowé n*∗*a menjang sekolahan.* You go on to school ahead of me. 2 former(ly). *Aku n*∗ *arang² banget lara.* I hardly ever used to get sick. **n/di∗aké** 1 to have smn [do] first. *Wong wadon di*∗*aké.* The women were told to go first. 2 to put sth first. *Adja sok n*∗*aké barang sing ora perlu.* Don't give priority to unnecessary things. **n/di∗i** to precede. *Ḍèké mlaku n*∗*i sing wadon.* He walked ahead of his wife. *n*∗*i mlebu* to go in first. *Sa-bisa² n*∗*ana kurmat.* Try to be the first to pay your respects.

ḍisiplin discipline, control

ḍiskriminasi discrimination

ḍiskusi discussion. ∗ *ora resmi* informal discussion

ḍistrik (*or* **ka∗an**) administrative district: subsection of a region (during colonial times)

ḍit *inf var of* ḌUWIT

Dité *oj* Sunday

ḍiting, ḍiṭing **n∗** carefully groomed; finely dressed

ḍito ditto, as above

Ḍitslan Germany

ditya *wj* ogre, giant

ḍivisi *var sp of* ḌIPISI

diwangkârâ *oj* sun

diwâsâ an adult. *Jèn umurmu wis ganep selikur taun kowé dadi* ∗. When you become 21 you're an adult.

diweg *kr* *sbst var of* DAWEG

ḍiwut (*or* **∗-∗**) covered with hair. *uler sing* ∗*-*∗ a hairy caterpillar. *Djènggoté* ∗*-*∗ *ora tau ditjukur.* His beard is full; he never trims it.

dja *inf var of* ADJA[a]

djâbâ *ng,* **djawi** *kr* 1 outside. *Ana ing* ∗ *aḍem.* It's cold outside. 2 outside of, except for (*inf var of* KEDJABA). **∗n** 1 outlying territory. 2 superficial, on the exterior only. **n∗n** (on the) outside. *n*∗*n omah* outside the house. *wong n*∗*n djaman* a man of a different era. **pa·n∗** the outside; outdoors. **sa·(n)∗né** (on the) outside (of). *ing san*∗*ning omah* outside the house. **∗ djero** in(side) and out(side); through and through. *Mori mau ditémbok* ∗*-djero.* The fabric was wax-coated on both sides. *Ḍèké iklas* ∗ *djero.* He's utterly sincere. *See also* KEDJABA

djabal mountain

djabalikat *oj* the world

Djabaltarik Gibraltar

djabang **∗ baji** 1 newborn baby. 2 *excl uttered before killing sth (e.g. snake, insect) to prevent one's unborn baby from being marked by the ugly sight*

djabarail male angel believed by Moslems to withdraw the soul from the body upon death

djabat *an office held temporarily. ***an tangan** to shake hands. **n/di*** to hold [an office] temporarily. *Walikota Jogja saiki di* karo A.* A is the acting mayor of Jogja. **pa·(n)*** (*abbr:* **Pd.**) one who holds office temporarily pending elections. *Pd. Walikota* mayor pro tem

djabel **n*** 1 to pull sth loose from its moorings. 2 to take back, retract

djablas gone, vanished. *Sega sapiring wis *.* He made short work of his plate of rice.

djablog *cr* **n*** to eat

djabon a variety of tree

djabrail *var of* DJABARAIL

djabris ***an** small catfish (young of the LÉLÉ). **n*** to give smn a dirty look

djabud **n/di*(i)** to pull out, draw. *n* untu* to extract a tooth. *n*i djènggot nganggo ḍuwit sèn* to pull hairs from the beard using coins as tweezers. **n* njawa** to kill, murder

djabung a certain resinous substance used as glue. **n/di*** to join, connect (*esp.* with the above substance)

djabur ***an** refreshments served at a collective prayer gathering during the evening of the fasting month, *i.e.* the permissible time for eating and drinking. **n/di*i** to serve [refreshments] as above

djadah 1 a snack made of glutinous rice. 2 child. *karam ** illegitimate child

djaḍam resin, used as glue, produced by a certain broad-leafed aloe plant

djaḍem *var of* DJAḌAM

djaḍi *var of* DJÈḌI

djaḍir **n*** thick-lipped

djâdâ 1 itinerant peddler. 2 chest, breast (*ki for* ḌADA). *** bang ma-winga²** *ltry* furiously angry. *** rumat** to pass along rumors

djadjag ***-*** to size up. *pandeng *-** a calculating look. **n/di*i** to measure, estimate. *n*i djeroning bebudèn* to judge the depth of smn's character. *Katresnan boten saged dipun *i sarana akal.* Love cannot be measured in terms of reason. *Gunemku kanggo n*i atiné.* I spoke in order to assess her state of mind.

djadjah familiar with the environment. *Aku lagi bebakal ana ing kéné, mula durung *.* I'm new here so I don't know my way around yet. ***an** a colony. *pemerintah *an* colonial government. **n/di*** 1 to get to know, become familiar with, explore. 2 to hold sway over. *kaum sing di** a subjugated people. **n* désa m̀·wilang kori** to travel to many places. **pa·n*** colonialist, subjugator. **pa·n*an** colonialism; colonization

djadjal (*or* ***é**) have a try! (let's) see if... **é, aku sing ngétung.* Here, let *me* count them. ** aku djupukna pring.* See if you can get me some bamboo. **, segané ditjulik wis mateng apa durung.* Try the rice and see if it's done. *Ija ta wis * kaja apa pitakonmu.* OK, let's hear your question. ***-*** to try, make an effort. *See also* ADJAL[a], DJAL

djadjan 1 (to eat, buy) sweets, between-meal snacks. 2 to eat out. *Aku diadjak * menjang rèstoran.* He asked me to have lunch with him at a restaurant. ***an** 1 sweets collectively; various sweets. *waḍah *an* container for cookies *etc.* *warung *an* a snack shop. 2 to buy/eat snacks *or* eat out habitually. **n*** to have intercourse with a prostitute. **n/di*aké** (*prn* **n/di·djadjak·aké**) to buy smn a snack *or* a meal out. **n/di*i** to buy/eat snacks regularly. **pa*an** house of prostitution; red-light district. *** pasar** party needs (sweets, flowers, *etc.*) bought at the marketplace

djadjang krawat a certain village official

djadjar 1 having equal rank *or* position. 2 lined up in a row. 3 the lowest rank among the employees at the Sultanate of Jogjakarta. ***an** *rg* net yield of a harvest. **n/di*i** to walk side by side in ranks

djaḍor *var of* DJAḌIR

djaḍul **n*** scowling, gloomy-looking

djadwal schedule, time table

djaé ginger (root). *wédang ** hot ginger drink

djaéton, djaétun olive; olive tree

djag ***-*an** to walk around in a carefree inconsiderate manner, *e.g.* intruding where one does not belong. **n*** it is so, it is true that...

djâgâ *ng*, **djagi** *kr* 1 guard, watch; to guard, keep watch. ** bengi* night watchman. *pikèt ** sentry. *tukang * toko* store attendant. *kantja ** companion of the watch. 2 provisions. *Sega iki *né mangan bengi mengko.* This rice is for tonight's meal. ***n** a precaution(ary measure). *Aku mau tuku lilin kanggo *n jèn se-mangsa² listriké mati.* I bought candles in case the electricity goes off. ***-*** *or* **dje*** (to act as) a precautionary measure. **n/di*** to guard, protect (against). *n* Sang Prabu* to guard the King. *Anakmu *nen.* Keep a close eye on your child! *Kuwadjibané pulisi n∗ supaja wong² manut marang unḍang².* A policeman's job is to see to it that people obey the laws. **n/di∗kaké** to rely on. *Ḍèké bisa di∗kaké.* He's dependable. **n∗kaké enḍog·é si blorok** to await an uncertain outcome. **n/di∗ni** to guard with a precautionary measure; to provide against. *Djupukna bantal, tak nggo n∗ni si bajèk.* Bring me a pillow to protect the baby. *Taliné sing kanggo n∗ni balon mau wis kari loro.* There were still two ropes preventing the balloon from rising. *Aku tuku beras akèh nggo n∗ni mangsa patjeklik.* I've bought a lot of rice for when it's scarce. **pa∗n** guard's post, sentry box. **pa·n∗** 1 guard, watchman. 2 a precaution. ∗ **baja** village constable. ∗ **béla** executioner. ∗ **karja** soldier of the Jogja Sultanate. ∗ **kersa** 1 regent's guardsman. 2 village constable. ∗ **latri** night watchman. ∗ **pradja**, ∗ **pura** Surakarta palace soldier. ∗ **reksa** village constable. ∗ **ripu** a certain river fish. ∗ **runa** preparations against threatened danger *or* food shortage. ∗ **satru** 1 front porch with no supporting columns. 2 garden fence. 3 a certain marching formation. ∗ **sura** soldier. ∗ **tirta** person who oversees irrigation; person who keeps flood watch. ∗ **wèsṭi** village constable

djagad world, earth; universe. *saindenging* ∗ all over the world. ∗ **geḍé** (∗ **[t]raja** *oj*) the cosmos, the universe. ∗ **ka·muksa·n** heaven

djagal butcher. **n/di∗** to butcher, slaughter. **(n)∗an** place where animals are slaughtered

djagang 1 tripod. 2 prop, supporting pole. 3 one of various houses near the great walls of Jogjakarta. **n/di∗i** to support, or be prepared to support, sth that is falling *or* may fall. ∗ **gunting** bamboo trees crossed scissorwise as a supporting prop

djager ∗**an** sawhorse. **n∗** to stand straight up

djagi guard, watch (*kr for* DJAGA)

djago *ng*, **sawung** *kr* 1 rooster, cock. *adu* ∗ cock fight. ∗ *adon* fighting cock. ∗ *belèh-an* rooster raised to be slaughtered. 2 champion, *i.e.* one who fights for a cause *or* on behalf of others. 3 candidate; contestant. ∗ *politik* political candidate. ∗**n** 1 young rooster that has reached the reproductive stage. 2 candidate, contestant. ∗**-∗an** *rg* ceremony held as part of the wedding procedures for a bride who has not yet begun to menstruate. **n/di∗kaké** to put smn up as a candidate. **n/di∗(n)i** 1 to pit [two cocks *or* champions] against each other. 2 to have smn act as one's champion. 3 to back [a contestant/candidate]. ∗ **éntar** a person who cannot stand the sight of blood. ∗ **kapuk** older person who keeps active in his former field(s) of interest. ∗ **katé wani·né ana ing omah·é ḍéwé** a coward. ∗ **kawak·an** former champion gamecock. ∗ **kepruk** bodyguard. ∗ **kluruk** cock's-crow; the crack of dawn. ∗ **mlilé** rooster who is afraid of hens; *fig* man who is shy with women. ∗ **wiring-galih djalu m·ungal** 1 fighting cock that always wins. 2 outstanding person

djagong ∗**an** 1 seat, place to sit. 2 to sit around informally. **dje∗an** *pl* to sit around. **n∗** to attend a ceremony, *esp.* a wedding. *Bapak karo ibu tindak n∗.* Father and Mother have gone to a wedding. **n∗ baji** to attend a ceremony for a newborn baby. **pa∗an** 1 a ceremony. 2 a place where people sit around at such ceremonies. ∗ **baji** ceremony for a newborn child. ∗ **mantèn** wedding celebration

djagrag 1 three-legged supporting stand, tripod. 2 physical stature. **n/di∗(i)** to stand (sth) up straight

djagung corn. ∗ **g·um·arit** young corn. ∗ **tjanṭèl** a variety of corn whose kernels grow at the top of the plant. *See also* ONTONG

djagur fist. **n∗** to punch downward. **n/di∗i** to pound smn gently on the head with the fist

djah *adr* elephant! (*shf of* GADJAH)

djahanam 1 hell. 2 *excl* damn!

djahat a flaw, imperfection

djahé *var of* DJAÉ

djahil *var of* DJAIL

djahit *var of* DJAIT

djaid **n∗** [of eyes] almond-shaped

djail (to have) ill feelings toward smn. *tembung* ∗ spiteful words. **n∗i** 1 (*psv* **di∗i**) to wish smn ill. *Murid n∗i guruné.* The student has it in for the teacher. 2 [of rice] to sprout. ∗ **m̀·pringkil** person with a grudge. ∗ **muṭakil** malicious, spiteful

djais fate, destiny. **ke∗** (pre)destined. *Wis ke∗ jèn manungsa bakal mati.* Man is mortal.

djait pertaining to sewing. *mesin* ∗ sewing machine. *tukang* ∗ tailor, seamstress. **ke∗ ati·né** *ltry* infatuated. **men∗** to make clothing. **n/di*** to sew, stitch; to suture. **pa·n*** tailor, seamstress

djâjâ *oj* 1 victory; victorious. 2 power(ful)

djâjâdaru *var of* DJAJANDARU

djajandaru one of two banyan trees in North Square, Jogjakarta. *See also* DÉWANDARU, RINGIN

djak ***-* hir²** giddiyap! ***-*an** to agree to [do] together. *A karo B *-*an adu djago.* A and B arranged to have their gamecocks do battle. **nge/di*(i)** to ask smn to [do] with one. *Ngundanga kantjamu, *en ngréwangi.* Call your friend over to help you. *A di* mangan, sing ngadjak B.* B asked A to eat with him. *See also* DJAK

djâkâ 1 young unmarried man. *Anaké wis ana sing * ngono.* He has a teenage son. 2 (*or* **dje***) young adult male. **per*** a bachelor. *** k·um·ala-kala** male teen-ager. *** lara** *or* *** rara** one's first spouse. *** ṭingṭing** virgin male

djâkâbèlèk Mars (planet)

djâkâblaro a variety of bird

djâkâbolot a certain variety of rice

djâkâlodrâ wild man in a street show

Djakartā Djakarta, capital city of Indonesia, on the northwest coast of Java

djâkâsawur a certain grass

djakat yearly alms given (in proportion to one's ability to pay) for distribution to the poor. **n/di*i** to give alms to. *** pitrah** annual alms in money, or the equivalent in rice, given at the end of the fasting month, proportionate to the number in the donating family

djâkâtuwâ cockatoo; parrot

djâkâwuru a variety of owl

djakèt waist-length jacket

djaki *sbst kr for* DJAKA

djaksa public prosecutor. **ka*n** 1 public prosecutor's office. 2 judiciary branch. **n/di*ni** to prosecute [a criminal; a case]. **pa*n** prosecutor's office

djal ***é** have a try! **é, iki angkaten.* Here, see if you can lift this. *See also* ADJAL^a, DJADJAL

djal- *see also under* DJL- (*Introduction, 2.9.3*)

djâlâ net for catching birds or fish. **n/di*** to net [birds, fish]

djaladri *oj* sea, ocean

djalak a variety of bird kept as a pet. ** apa sing bisa ngotjèh?* What kinds of *djalak* bird can talk? **n*i** [of unweaned babies] to have diarrhea. *** ampir** to stop off at places frequently when on the way smw; one who does this habitually. *** ḍinḍing** characteristically feminine way of walking. *** djamang** talking mynah bird. *** m·empan** to work a bit at a time. *** ng·oré** a certain shape for kris blades. *** orèn** black mynah bird

djalan gait; to walk, proceed. *Montor²an jèn diputer mengko rak bisa * ḍéwé.* If you wind up the toy car, it runs by itself. ***-*** to take a walk

djalaniḍi *oj* sea, ocean

djalantârâ viaduct for conveying water above a road on an overpass

djalar **(dje)*an** because; cause, reason. *A boḍo *an emoh sinau.* A doesn't know anything because he won't study. *Pijé ta *ané?* What's the reason for it? **an saka polahmu, aku rekasa.* Because of what you did, I'm in trouble. **n*** to become prevalent. *Penjakit mau n* tekan endi².* The disease is everywhere. **n/di*i** to cause. *n*i lara* to cause illness. *Anggoné mbantu bisa n*i menang.* His help gave them the win.

djaler male; manly (*kr for* LANANG). ***-*** streaks of color on the skin, *e.g.* blue where a vein shows; red from whip blows

djali kernel-producing plant. *djagung/ketan ** a plant that produces corn-like (barley-like) kernels. *watu ** plant that produces inedible kernels

djaliger a variety of fish

djaling the portion of the skull above the ears

djalir *see* DJURU

djalisu a variety of tree

djalma 1 human being. *bisa tata ** [of animals] able to speak. 2 reincarnation. **n*** [of animals] tame, friendly with people. **man*** 1 to turn into a human being. 2 to be reincarnated. **pa·n*** 1 transformation of a spirit into human shape. 2 reincarnation; a reincarnated being. *** tan kena ing-ina** unpredictable

djalon bamboo lengths used to hold a straw roof in place

djalu 1 **(djambet** *kr;* **pândjâ** *opt kr?*) spur on a cock's foot. 2 *oj* male. **ke*** injured by a cock's spur. **n/di*** to strike with the spur. *** mampang** a certain parasitic plant

djaluk *ng,* **teḍa** *kr,* **punḍut** *ki,* **suwun** *ka* ***an** a request, sth asked for. *Aku arep menjang toko, apa *anmu?* I'm going to the store; what would you like me to get for you? **n·dje*** *ng kr* to beg. *Kéré kuwi uripé ja mung tansah ndje* baé.* Beggars make their living by begging. **n/di*aké** to ask for sth on smn's behalf. *A n*aké panggawéan kanggo B menjang C.* A asked C to give B a job. **n*an** *ng kr* always asking for things. **n/di*(i)** to ask for. *Aku n* ngombé.* Please give me sth to drink. *Anaké wadon wis di* karo pak lurah.* The village head asked her for her daughter (in marriage). *Adja pidjer nakal baé, apa kowé n* digitik?* Don't keep being naughty! are you asking for a spanking? *Jèn di*i tulung, A mesṭi teka.* If smn asks A for help, he always comes. **n* lawang** to request admittance. **n* pang·apura** to ask smn's pardon. **n/di*-*(i)** to ask for things habitually. **pa·n*** a request. *Pan*é apa?* What did he ask for?

djam 1 timepiece. *gelang ** wrist watch. 2 (**pukul** *opt kr*) o'clock. ** loro* two o'clock. ** pira?* what time? 3 hour. *rong ** two hours. *pirang *?* how many hours? 4 time. ** seméné kok isih sinau!* Still studying at this hour! ***-*an** for hours (on end). *Olèhé djungkatan *-*an.* She spends hours combing her hair. *Jèn tukang, ora *-*an nggaṭukaké bongkaran mesin iku.* It wouldn't take an expert long to put that motor back together again. **nge/di*i** to time sth in hours. *nge*i olèhé njambut gawé* to time one's work. *** bèker** alarm clock. *** gantung** wall clock. *** gémbol·an** pocket watch. *** kalung** pendant watch. *** kanḍut·an** pocket watch. *** kikuk** cuckoo clock. *** lontjèng** striking clock. *** setengah** half-past. ** setengah papat* 3:30, *i.e.* halfway to 4. *** tangan** wrist watch. *** wèker** alarm clock. *** wèsmister** grandfather clock

djamak 1 usual, ordinary. ** lumrahé wong urip kuwi djedjoḍohan.* Most people get married. 2 *excl of frustration.* **, kaṭik mutung pang seméné waé ora bisa.* Son-of-a-gun, I can't even break this little branch! **ora *(-*)** out of the ordinary. *Ḍuwité akèhé ora *.* He's awfully rich. *Lalènmu ora *-*.* You're so *forgetful!*

djaman time period, time span. **é aku isih enom* when I was young. ** wis owah.* Times have changed. *ing * kuna* once upon a time. *bangsa Djawa ing * semana* the Javanese of those remote days. *ḍèk * Djepang* during the Japanese occupation. *ḍèk * kedjawan* in the old days, long ago. **n*(i)** current. *tembung*[2] *sing wis ora n*i* words that are no longer in use. *** akir** 1 the future. 2 life after death. *** aman** peace time. *** édan** transition period; time of turmoil. *** (ka)langgeng(an)** eternity; the life after death. *** ke·mas·an** golden age. *** mengko** nowadays. *** ora énak** former times (referring *esp.* to the colonial period). **ora * ora mamak** 1 not up to date with things. 2 uncertain of one's origins. *** pati** *or* *** ke·pati·ǹ** life after death. *** (ke)ramé(an)** life in this world; the world of the living. *** saiki** nowadays

djamang ornamental leather head piece worn in the classical dance. ***an** 1 to wear *or* put on the above. 2 resembling the above

djamas to shampoo one's hair (*ki for* KRAMAS)

djambak **n/di*** to pull smn's hair. **dj·um·a·mbak** a handful of hair pulled in anger

djambal 1 meat together with its fat. 2 a certain edible freshwater fish. 3 a certain dye used in batik-making. **dianggo *an** to be an object of ridicule. **n/di*** to eat the rice-accompanying dishes without rice. *Enḍogé di*.* He ate just the egg.

djamban *ng kr,* **pa·siram·an** *ki* bathroom (Occidental style, *i.e.* lavatory and bathing place combined)

djambé betel nut. *** aju** betel nut specially prepared for ceremonial offerings rather than for chewing. **kaja * s·in·igar** looking enough alike to be twins. *** suruh** betel nut prepared for chewing; **sedulur * suruh** such close friends they are like relatives

djambéjah knife used as a weapon

djambèt **ke*** involved, associated. *Ḍèké ke* ing bab slunḍupan.* He was mixed up in a smuggling operation.

djambet 1 cock's spur (*kr for* DJALU). 2 guava; heart (playing-card suit) (*kr for* DJAMBU). 3 to join (*root form: sbst kr for* DJABUNG). 4 bird/fish-trapping net (*sbst kr for* DJALA). 5 drill (*sbst kr for* DJARA). 6 castor-oil plant (*sbst kr for* DJARAK). 7 harrow (*sbst kr for* GARU)

djambijah *var of* DJAMBÉJAH

djamblik **n*** close together, not far apart

djambu (**djambet** *kr?*) 1 guava. 2 heart (playing-card suit). ***ǹ** 1 pink. 2 resembling a guava tree. **n*** *ng kr* homosexual. *** aèr**, *** bol**, *** dersana**, *** kagèt**, *** kluṭuk**, *** tlampok** *etc.* common varieties of guava

djambul 1 raised forelock. 2 raised decorative object worn at the front of the head, *e.g.* a feather on a hat. **n/di*** to form [hair] into a raised forelock. **nganti * wan·en** until one is very old

djamdjam *var of* DJANDJAM

djamerut emerald

djamin ***an** 1 a guarantee. **an telung sasi* a three-month guarantee. 2 *inf* food served to a close friend *or* to smn of lower status. *Sopir² sing nḍèrèkké tamu² wis diparingi *an.* The drivers who brought guests have been served. **n/di*** 1 to guarantee. 2 *inf* to serve food to smn (as above)

djampang a certain swamp grass

djampeng stone deaf *(used also as a term of abuse). * kowé ja, dikanḍani bola-bali kok ora krungu.* You stupid, I kept telling you but you wouldn't listen.

djampi medicine (*kr for* DJAMU, TAMBA)

djamprah [of tail hair] long and luxuriant

djamprak *var of* DJAMPRAH

djamprong *wj* my fine-looking lad!

djamrut *var of* DJAMERUT

djamu *ng,* **djampi** *kr* 1 (**loloh** *or* **usada** *ki*) medicine, health potion. ** sing djoḍo* the right medicine for the malady. 2 to dose oneself. *Saben ésuk aku * enḍog.* I eat an egg every morning for my health. ***n̂-*n̂an** act of treating with medication. *Lelara ing sadjroné kuping angèl banget djamon²ané.* Ailments of the ear are very hard to treat. **dje*** to take health potions repeatedly. **mer*** to treat medically; to have medical treatment. *Olèhé mer* wis ngentèkaké ḍuwit.* He's spent a lot of money trying to get cured. **n/di*k̂aké** to treat [a malady] with medicine. *Larané didjamokaké ing ḍokter.* He was treated by a doctor. **n/di*n̂i** to give medicine to. *** kuwat** potion to increase one's sexual potency. *** singset** slenderizing medicine. *** temu-lawak** tonic or physical-fitness preparation from a certain tuberous root

djamur 1 mushroom. 2 fungus growth of any kind. 3 an unexpected piece of luck; an inadvertent side effect. ***an** 1 mushroom-shaped. *keluk atom kaja ** atomic cloud. 2 a children's singing game. ***en** moldy, mildewed. *** brama** a certain edible mushroom, used also as a poultice. *** impes** a large inedible fungus used as a poultice. *** karang** sponge in the growing state. *** kuping** thin ear-shaped tree-bark fungus used for soups. *** trutjuk** mushroom shaped like a broad bamboo hat. *** upas** a destructive plant mold

djan *intsfr for quality words. Jèn mlaku * banter banget.* He walks really fast! ***(-*)é** actually; on the contrary. **é aku ora ngerti.* Actually, I don't know. **-*é kowé arep apa?* What do you *really* want? **nge/di*i** to set a price on [one's merchandise]. **sa*** even though (*shf of* SANADYAN). *Ḍèwèké nékad waé sa* ngerti jèn ora éntuk.* He went right ahead and did it, even though he knew he wasn't supposed to. **sa*é** in truth; on the contrary. *Ḍèké sa*é sengit banget.* The fact is, he hates it.

Djan. *see* DJANUARI

djânâ *shc from* ADJA[a] ANA

djanak a short stick used in a certain children's game (*benṭik*)

djânâprijâ **ka*** famous, renowned

djandika *inf var of* DJENGANDIKA

djandjam 1 (*or* **sumur ***) sacred well in Mecca. 2 (*or* **banju ***) holy water drawn from this well

djandjan [of horses] dun-colored

djandjang 1 a large cluster of coconuts or *salak* fruits. 2 long [of neck]

djandjèhi *inf var of* DJANDJI·ǸI

djandji 1 to have an agreement, make a promise. 2 if, when(ever). *Tikusé * kétok, mesṭi tak penṭung temenan.* If the mouse comes out, I'll give him a good smack. ***an** *or* ***ǹ** to have/make a mutual agreement. *Aku wis djandjèn arep ketemu nang pasar.* We agreed to meet at the marketplace. ***né** on condition that...; provided the agreement is... *Totohan kenèker kena² baé, *né jèn wis, dibalèkaké marang sing duwé manèh.* It's all right to gamble with marbles so long as it's understood you'll give them back afterwards. ***ǹ-*ǹan** to promise each other, make a mutual agreement. **n*** 1 (*psv* **di***) to exact a promise from. 2 as agreed; at the appointed time. *tumeka n** to show up as agreed; *fig* about to die, *i.e.* one's time has come. **n/di*k̀aké** to promise sth. *Buku sing wis didjandjèkaké tak djupuk.* I went and picked up the book he had promised me. **n/di*ǹi** to promise smn; to make a promise. **per*** *or* **pra*** (to have/make) a promise or agreement. **per*an** *or* **pra*an** 1 agreement, understanding. *Betjiké didadèkaké pradjandjian waé.* There ought to be a definite agreement.

2 promissory note. 3 condition, provision. **pra*an lawas (anjar)** Old (New) Testament

djangan a soup-like dish made with vegetables in coconut milk. ***an** vegetables for this dish. **n/di*** to make [ingredients] into the above

djangdji promise, agreement (*var of* DJANDJI)

djanges **n*** *intsfr* black. *ireng n** jet black, pitch black

djanget rawhide rope

djânggâ neck (*ki for* GULU)

djanggal awkward, ill-suited, inharmonious

djanggan **dje*** pupils of a holy man

djanggar rice plants that have sprouted, *i.e.* are too old to harvest

djanggel 1 young corn on the cob. 2 the bones of a horse's tail. ***an** on probation; awaiting a final decision. **n/di*aké** to sell sth on approval (to be returned if unsatisfactory)

djanggélan a certain grass

djanggereng physical appearance

djangget **n*** to adhere to firmly

djanggir male kerbau calf

djanggitan imp, devil

djanggleng fruit of the teak tree. ***an** young teak tree ready for planting. **n*** 1 to stare motionless and absorbed. *Olèhé nonton TV n*.* He was engrossed in watching TV. 2 *rg* to stand

djanggreng **n*** to look big, loom up

djanggrung (*or* ***-***) (standing) erect and firm

djanggut 1 (**keṭekan** *ki*) chin. 2 rounded front section of a kris sheath. **n*** 1 close by; on hand. 2 (*psv* **di***) to stroke the chin in self-admiration. 3 (*psv* **di***) to grasp smn's shoulder with the chin (fighting technique). **dj·um·anggut** nearby; ready at hand. *Wangé djumanggut.* He has plenty of money available. *** ng·golèng** lantern-jawed

djângkâ 1 goal, objective. 2 term, length of time. 3 prediction, prophecy. 4 compass for drawing circles. 5 tool for shredding tobacco leaves. **n/di*** 1 to have an objective for smn. *Ḍèwèké di* dadi ḍokter.* They're hoping he'll become a doctor. 2 to use a compass *or* tobacco shredder. **pa·n*** goal, objective

djangkah 1 step, stride. *ngambakaké *é* to lengthen one's stride. *Tebihipun boten wonten sa*.* It's only a step away. **é sing arep katindakaké déning kabinèt* the steps to be taken by the Cabinet. 2 goal. *Amba *é.* He has a broad range of objectives. ***an** *wj* wide foot stance of large puppets. **n*** 1 to walk, step. *n* pitung djangkah* to take seven steps. 2 (*psv* **di***) to set as a goal. **n/di*aké** to advance [the foot]. *Ḍèwèké n*aké sikilé, rékané arep nḍupak wong tuwa mau.* He raised his foot to kick the old man. **pa·n*** ideal, objective. *kadohan pan** an unrealistic goal. **dj·um·angkah** to step. *A djumangkah mlebu ngomah.* A stepped into the house. *djumangkah unḍak²-an* to go upstairs. *nututi djumangkah kekarepan* to follow smn's wishes step by step

djangkang a certain fruit. *banju lanḍa ** shampoo made from this fruit

djangkar 1 anchor. *buwang ** to drop anchor. 2 anchor-shaped hook on a rope, for retrieving a bucket from the bottom of a well. **n/di*** 1 to retrieve [a bucket] with the above. 2 to address smn improperly (*e.g.* by calling one's elders by name; by omitting a title; by using Ngoko to smn of higher status)

djangkep complete; in full; even (not odd) (*kr for* GANEP)

djangkrik house cricket (often used for gaming). *adu ** cricket fight. *** **(m)bering** flying cricket. **kaja * m·ambu kili** infuriated

djangkung tall and slender

djanglot a certain plant

djanma *var of* DJALMA

djantèn (*or* ***an**) young corn on the cob

djanti a variety of tree

djântrâ 1 wheel, cog, moving part; wheel that operates machinery, *e.g.* water-propelled mill wheel, spinning wheel, windmill. 2 cycle, pattern of behavior *or* events. **ning proḍuksi* production cycles

djantu (*or* ***ñ**) spices or herbs used as ingredients, *esp.* in folk medicines. **n/di*ñi** to add such ingredients to. *Djladrèné apem didjantoni ragi seṭiṭik.* She put a little yeast in the pancake batter.

djantung 1 heart. *lara ** heart disease. 2 hearts (playing-card suit). *as ** the ace of hearts. 3 banana blossom. **dje*** heart. *kaja lading ngiris-iris dje*é* like a knife cutting into her heart. **n*** resembling a banana blossom

djantur magic tricks, sleight-of-hand. *mbarang ** to perform tricks. ***an** 1 sleight-of-hand. 2 *wj* narration introducing a major scene, recited from memory by the puppet-master. **3** poles from which tobacco leaves are suspended in sheds. **n/di*** **1** to perform sleight-of-hand tricks. 2 to hang sth upside down. 3 *wj* to declaim the plot

Djanuari (*abbr:* **Djan.**) January

djanur pale green young coconut leaf, often used for decorations. **n* gunung** *excl of surprise. Kok n* gunung, Minggu² kok teka mréné.* You here on a Sunday! –how unusual.

djâpâ magical incantation. ***n-*nan** the practice of using incantations for curing illness. **n/di*ni** to utter an incantation over smn. *** joga, * semadi** magic formulas used in the practice of yoga. *** mantra** a magical incantation uttered to cure illness

Djapan *var of* DJEPANG

djapi *sbst kr for* DJAPA

djapit *var of* DJEPIT[a]

djaplak *var of* DJIPLAK

djaprut **n*** to assume a scowling or sulking facial expression

djapu **djopa-*** *magic words uttered by a faith healer before he begins his healing procedure, or by smn trying to console an ill or injured person*

djar **nge/di*aké** to leave smn alone. *Akèh wong diedjaraké nglanggar prenatané.* Many people get away with breaking the law. *Di*na waé!* Leave it alone!

djar- *see also under* DJR- (*Introduction, 2.9.3*)

djârâ **1** drill, brace and bit. 2 *ltry* old. ***n** sawdust-like particles made by drilling into sth. **n/di*** to drill, bore. *Kajuné di* supaja bolong.* He drilled a hole in the wood. **n* angin** to do the impossible. *** éngkol** a drill with a handle. **n* langit** to do the impossible

djarag ***an** intended, destined. *Aku mono *an wong mlarat.* I was born to be poor. **ke*** done on purpose. *Ajo salaman, wong ora ke* kok.* Sorry–I didn't mean to do it. **n/di*** to [do] intentionally. *Ḍèwèké ora n*.* He didn't mean to do it. **dj·in·arag·an** done intentionally

djarah ***an** (that which is) obtained by looting. **n/di*** to seize, snatch. **n* rajah** to seize smn's belongings

djarak **1** castor-oil plant. *lenga ** castor oil. 2 *fig* material or spiritual benefits. *Bareng wis entèk *é, kantjané mung sidji loro.* After he lost his money, his friends numbered few indeed. *Pangriptané lagi liburan, merga entèk *é.* The writer is taking some time off: he's run out of ideas. *Bareng ditjekel anaké, tokoné mati *é.* When the son took over the store, business fell off. *Wong geḍé sing kurang anggoné nggulawenṭah anak, bakal mati *é.* When important people fail to rear their children properly, a fine heritage is lost. ***an** color of certain ducks. **n/di*i** **1** to calculate using castor-oil beans as counters. 2 to tell smn's fortune

djaran *ng,* **kapal** *or* **kuda** *kr* **1** (**titih·an** *or* **turangga** *ki*) horse. 2 chess knight. ** iku lakuné nganggo njémplak barang, dadi mèntjèng ḍisik bandjur ngentjeng.* The knight makes jumping moves–first a diagonal then straight. ***an** **1** rocking horse; toy horse; imitation horse. 2 to play horse. **3** on horseback. **dje*** on horseback. **n*** to ride a horse. **n*-n*** to gallop. *** ḍawuk** **1** gray horse. 2 gray. **3** a certain *lurik* fabric pattern. **4** a certain star. *** èbèg²an** woven-bamboo hobbyhorse used in a folk dance. *** gujang** love potion. *** kembang durèn** yellowish horse; **n* kembang durèn** with gaping mouth. *** képang** *sms* * ÈBÈG²-AN. *** koré** a small horse bred in certain islands. *** momot·an** pack horse. *** rakit·an** a team of horses. *** sembrani** legendary flying horse. *** tèdji** thoroughbred horse. *** pa·ñ·tolèh** a magic charm to make one rich. *** topong** white horse with a brown head. *** tunggang·an** riding horse

djarang **1** hot or boiling water. *nggoḍog ** to boil water. 2 *rg* scarce, rare; seldom. **n/di*i** to pour boiling water on

djarapah giraffe

djarat (*or* ***an** *or* **pa***) cemetery. *Matik, wong *an!* Eek, a ghost!

djaré **1** (*or* ***né; tjrijosipun** *kr,* **ngendikanipun** *ki*) it is said... **né Slamet...* according to what Slamet says... ** mas Dikun.* I heard it from Dikun. **(né) kowé arep lunga, kok ora sida.* You said you were going–how come you didn't? *Aku krungu *...* I hear (that...) 2 *excl of incredulity. * apik banget.* You wouldn't believe how beautiful it was. *Ḍokter mung gèḍèg², wong tatu * diwur-wuri weḍi.* The doctor only shook his head that anyone would sprinkle sand on an open cut. **3** *excl expressing repudiation of a circumstance, smn's assumption, etc. Aku wis adus *.* I have too taken my bath [though you think

I haven't]. *É, didol pijé, wong dudu duwèké ∗.* How can we sell it–it doesn't belong to us. *Kowé nggawa ḍuwit ora? Aku ora duwé ḍuwit ∗.* Did you bring any money? *I* haven't got any.

djarem **n∗** bruised, black and blue

djari *oj* finger. **sa∗ m̀·piring** (as thin as) a finger's-breadth

djarik *ng,* **sindjang** *kr,* **njamping** *ki* 1 ankle-length batik wraparound skirt. 2 *ng kr* rag; ragged clothing. 3 *rg var of* SLÉNḌANG. **∗an** to put on *or* wear a wraparound. **∗ kadèn** narrow wraparound for carrying a baby. **∗ lurik** wraparound made of some fabric other than batik. **∗ lungsed ing sampir·an** knowledge that is not being put to use. **∗ tjijut** narrow wraparound used as a shoulder scarf *or* for carrying a baby. **∗ tjuwil·an** adult's wraparound cut down for a child

djaring 1 net for trapping fish, birds; *fig* trick for snaring an unwary person. 2 spider web. **∗an** 1 intestines; internal organs. 2 trick for entrapping smn. **∗-∗** trick question *etc.* for catching smn up. **n/di∗** to trap in a net. *n∗ iwak* to snare a fish. **bisa n∗ angin** able to do the impossible. **∗ tangkeb·an** snaring net assembled from two sections

djarit *var of* DJARIK

djarong a variety of tree

djarot 1 fibers on the outer skin of certain fruits. 2 strong and handsome. **dje∗an** fine manly appearance

djarum 1 (*ng? opt kr for* DOM?) needle. 2 hands of a timepiece. **∗an** sewing, needlework (*kr for* DONDOM·AN?). **n/di∗i** to sew

djarwa (**djarwi** *kr? sbst kr?*) 1 meaning, explanation. *∗ bab lahiré Pantja-Sila* an explanation of the origin of the Five Principles. *∗né pijé ta téori kuwi?* What does the theory mean? *kurang ∗* hard to understand. 2 the modern Javanese equivalent of an Old Javanese expression. *Tembung Kawi mau ∗né lima.* There are five meanings of this OJ word. *or* This OJ word means 'five.' **n/di∗kaké** *or* **n/di∗ni** to give the meaning of; to render OJ in modern Javanese. *n∗kaké sasmitan mripat lan tembung²* to interpret smn's eye signals and words. *Étungé di∗kaké Pak Guru.* The teacher explained the arithmetic. *n∗kaké buku² Sanskerta ing basa Djawa* to explicate Sanskrit books in Javanese. **pa·n∗** act *or* way of explaining/interpreting. *buku sing angèl pa-n∗né* a book that is hard to understand. **sa∗** according to the facts. *matur sa∗* to tell [it] as it is, to give the straight facts

djarwaḍâsâ *or* **djarwaḍosok** 1 modern Javanese equivalent of an OJ saying. 2 folk etymology

djarwâsutâ *sms* DJARWAḌASA

djarwi *kr? sbst kr? for* DJARWA

djas men's Occidental-style jacket. **∗-∗an** to put on *or* wear such a jacket, or a suit. **∗ buka** *or* **∗ bukak·an** blazer-style jacket with lapels. **∗ tutup** jacket that buttons up to the neck and has a Chinese-style collar

djâsâ service rendered, *esp.* to one's country

djasad body, substance. *mupangati marang ∗ing manungsa* beneficial, good for people. **ke∗** 1 to get eaten. 2 to join the family. *Ali kantjaku kenṭel lan wis ke∗.* Ali is such a close friend he's like one of the family. **n∗i** relating to the body. *Jèn lara n∗i waé kena ditambani, ning jèn lara ati tjilaka.* A physical hurt will heal; heartache is hopeless.

djasbèn *var of* DJÈSBÈN

djasem a variety of tree

djasirah peninsula

djasmani physical body. *rohani lan ∗* body and soul

djâṭâ *see* PARIDJAṬA

djatah quota, ration(ed amount). *∗ gula sepuluh kilo* a ten-kilogram ration of sugar. *∗ èkspor kopi taun 1970* the quota for 1970 coffee exports. **n/di∗(i)** to ration; to set quotas (for)

djat-djit *see* DJIT

djati *ng,* **djatos** *kr* teak. *kaju ∗* teakwood. *wit ∗* teak tree. **(pa)∗n̄** place where teak trees grow in abundance. *alas djatèn* teak forest. **∗ ke·tlusub·an rujung** good blemished by bad. *See also* SEDJATI

djaṭil **∗an** a dance performed while astraddle a woven-bamboo horse (*djaran képang*) accompanied by *angklung* music. **n∗** to perform this dance

Djatim East Java (*acronym for* DJAWA TIMUR)

djatingarang *see* NAGA

djatmika (*or* [*ltry*] **a∗**, *or* **n∗ni**) having the characteristics of the ideal nobleman

djatos teak (*kr for* DJATI). **se∗** *see* SEDJATI

djatuh (to go) bankrupt

djatukrâmâ *oj* mate, spouse

djaul **ke∗** to get overcharged. *Aku ke∗ patang rupiah.* They charged me four rupiahs too much.

Djâwâ^a *ng*, Djawi *kr*   pertaining to Java. *ba-ku* * (of) genuine Javanese (origin). *basa* * Javanese language. *tanah* * Java. *wong* * a Javanese. ke*n 1 basically Javanese (*usu.* referring to the Javanese religion, as contrasted with superimposed religions). 2 area where Javanese live. n/di*kaké to translate into Javanese. n*ni having Javanese characteristics. nge* (to go) to Java. * Barat West Java. durung * not know how to behave properly. * Tengah Central Java. * Timur East Java

djâwâ^b 1 native (as contrasted with imported); for everyday use. *dluwang* * common paper. *gula* * brown sugar. *iwak* * beef. *lenga* * coconut oil. *sabun* * laundry soap. *weḍus* * goat. 2 meaning, intention. *né that is...; it means... *Kuwi* *né ndjaluk dipakani.* That [gesture] means he wants to be fed. ke*n land that is not to be leased to outsiders

djawab a reply; to reply. *an 1 a reply. *Durung ana kang awèh* *an.* No one has answered yet. 2 a delicate request. n/di* 1 to reply to. 2 to make a delicate request. *Bapaké botjah wédok wis di*.* He has asked the girl's father for her hand in marriage. pa·n* act of replying/requesting

djawah rain (*kr for* UDAN)

djawat *an office, agency, bureau. *an tangan to extend both hands in a Moslem greeting. n/di·dje* to accost, make advances to. n* tangan *sms* *AN TANGAN. pa·n* 1 wing-tip feather. 2 military flanking forces

djawâtâ mythological deity

djawi 1 pertaining to Java (*kr for* DJAWA^a). 2 (*or* n*) outside (*kr for* DJABA). 3 (*or* dje*) cow, ox. *ǹ young cow *or* bull

djawil *an an informal invitation. djowal-* to keep prodding at smn with the fingers to get his attention. n/di* to prod/jab smn to get his attention. n/di(djowal-)*i to keep poking at smn. *ptg* dj·r·awil *pl* to pluck at smn (as above). *Wong² paḍa ptg greneng, ptg djrawil.* People began to murmur and nudge each other.

djawoh *kr* *sbst var of* DJAWAH

djawuh *kr* *sbst var of* DJAWAH

djé 1 *Jogja slang var of* DJARÉ 3. *Aku *.* (No one else but) I! *Jodja Surabaja kuwi adoh *, lha kok mung diinahi rong djam.* It's a long way from Jogja to Surabaja and you're only giving me two hours to get

there! 2 name of the fourth year in the *windu* cycle. 3 (*or* *né) *inf var of* DJARÉ·NÉ

djebabah extending outward at the sides. *Dèwèké mati n* ing lemah.* He lay spread-eagled on the ground, dead. *Sinṭingané iket n* dawa banget.* The ends of his headdress stick way out sideways. n/di*aké to place sth with the parts extending outward

djebad [of bamboo] coming unwoven

djebebeg n* feeling bloated; *fig* vexed

djebèbèh n* spread wide. *Iwaké n*.* The [split] fish was opened out. *Sinṭingané iket n* dawa banget.* The tied ends of his headdress stick out to the sides. *Tutupé kurang n*.* The cover is too small [for this container]. n/di*aké to spread sth wide

djebèbèr *var of* DJEBÈR

djebeber n* soaking wet

djèbèh congenitally mute (*rg*). *an [of *iket* headdresses] tied with the ends extending outward and turned downward. n* having the headdress tied as above. *Aku mau weruh pak Wangsa iket²an n*, sadjaké arep ndjagong mantèn.* I saw Mr. Wongso with his headdress tied [as above]—he must have been on his way to a wedding.

djeben * bebed a boy who is at the age (8-9 years old) when he enjoys learning to wear batik wraparounds

djebeng fringe, tassel. dj·um·ebeng in the form of fringe; forming a tassel

djebèr n* 1 having a broad flaring rim. 2 treble, tinny, high-pitched. *Raḍioné swarané n* ora kempel, sadjaké batuné lembèk.* The radio has a high crackling tone; the battery must be weak. n/di*aké to flare sth at the edge

djebibir n* blue with cold [of lips]

djebil broken through, penetrated. *Pertahananku seḍéla² pidjer *.* Our defenses were frequently penetrated.

djebir n* full and thick [of lips]

djeblag *an *or* n* (in an) open (condition). *Lawangé menga n* kena angin.* The wind blew the door open. n/di*(aké) *or* n/di*i to open sth

djeblèg *var of* DJEGLÈG

djeblès *rpr* the sound of sth (*esp.* a head) knocking against a hard object. djeblas-* (to make) repeated sounds as above. ke* to get bumped. *Baṭukku ke* lawang.* I banged my forehead on the door. n/di*aké to knock [the head] against sth hard

djebling *rpr* a quick detaching motion. *See also* TJEPLING

djeblis *rpr* the sound of drawing on an opium pipe. **djeblas-*** *rpr* continuous drawing on a pipe while smoking. **n*** to smoke opium. **sa*an** one smoke (pipeful) of opium

djeblog 1 muddy. 2 *rpr* a muffled thud. 3 of inferior quality. 4 unlucky at cards. ***an** 1 mudhole. 2 act of butting. 3 *cr* female genitals; prostitute. **ke*** 1 to fall into *or* get stuck in sth. *Sikilé ke* saḍengkul.* He sank into mud up to his knees. 2 to bump one's head (against). *ke* lawang* to bump the head on a door. 3 to get cheated. **n*** 1 to get muddy. 2 (*psv* **di***) to butt (with head, horns). 3 (*psv* **di***) to chase. **n/di*aké** 1 to cause sth to be muddy. 2 to cheat smn. 3 to cause to get stuck in sth; *fig* to give smn a bad steer *or* incorrect directions

djeblos 1 *rpr* a bursting *or* explosion. 2 *rpr* a feeling of tension. *Nalika diundang supaja madju udjian, atiné mak *.* When he was called in for his oral examination, he tightened up. 3 *rpr* a quick cutting through. *Ngerti² kok mak * tekan alun².* Before I knew it, we had whisked through the outskirts and arrived at the town square. ***an** a connecting way between two points. **ke*** 1 to fall into *or* get stuck in sth. 2 to suffer a financial setback. **n*** 1 to explode, burst. *Anjar² ana gunung geni n*.* A volcano erupted recently. 2 to fail to produce an expected result. *Dikon tuku paṭi n*, merga warungé lagi kentèkan.* He was supposed to get flour but he couldn't: the store was out. 3 to incur a loss. *Sudagar karèt paḍa n* merga regané karèt mlorod akèh banget.* Dealers in rubber suffered losses when the prices dropped way down. 4 to collapse or give way when stepped on. 5 to come true. 6 a fake, imitation

djeblug **ke*** to bump one's head (against). **ke*an** to be adversely affected by a bursting. *Tangané ke*an granat.* A grenade went off in his hand. *Botjahé tjilik nangis ke*an plembungan.* The child cried when his balloon burst. **n*** 1 to burst, go off; *fig* to lose one's temper, blow up. 2 *rpr* a muffled thud. 3 (*psv* **di***) to butt (with head, horns)

djebluk *var of* DJEPLUK

djeblus *var of* DJEBUS

djebobog **n*** ungroomed, tangled [of hair]

djebol worn out, broken through at the bottom. *krandjang sing ** a basket with a hole in the bottom. **n/di*** 1 to press against sth, force sth outward. 2 to uproot

djebomblog *var of* DJEBOMBROT

djebombrot *ptg * or* **n*** untidy in personal appearance

djébor long-handled dipper

djebrèd **n*** *or* **dj·um·ebrèd** flaring outward at the edges

djèbrès unwiped, messy [of the mouth, after eating]

djebrig *var of* DJEGRIG

djébrod **n*** wide-hipped [of girls]

djebrol *rpr* a sudden emergence. **n/di*(i)** to pull sth out. *n* katjang tanah* to uproot peanuts from the soil

djebrot *cr* **n*** 1 to be born. 2 to defecate

djebrul *var of* DJEBROL

djebubug **n*** bunched up. *Olèhé djarikan kok n* ora bisa nrinṭing.* Her wraparound is all bunched up instead of smooth-fitting.

djebug mature betel nut

djebul 1 but, instead; as it turned out. *Hem, * ora apa².* So—it wasn't anything after all. *Sawaté ora ngenani pelem, * kena katjané ting ing dalan geḍé.* The stone he threw didn't hit the mango: it hit the street light. *É, * Pardi, tak darani ḍajoh ngendi.* Why, it's Pardi! I thought a guest had come. 2 passage(way). *Dalan iki *é tekan endi?* Where does this road lead to? ***an** (underground) passage. ***an·é** but as it turned out... ***é** but instead. *Ḍèké njuwun ḍuwit kanggo tuku buku, nanging *é mung kanggo kesenengan lijané.* He asked for money to buy books, but he really spent it on fun. **ora ana *é** without substance or tangible outcome. *Omongé akèh nanging ora ana *é.* He talks a lot but nothing ever comes of it. **n*** to lead to. *Kali iki n* ing segara kidul.* This river empties into the South Sea. **n/di*aké** to put sth through a passageway *etc.* *Sirahé di*aké.* He stuck his head out.

djebur *var of* DJEGUR

djebus *rpr* a quick cutting through. ***an** a connecting way between two points

djeḍag competent; can, able (to). **ka*an** lack, shortage. *ka*an udan* scarcity of rain

djeḍé **n/di*** to guess (the answer to)

djeḍeg **ke*** to get assigned to a responsibility. *Bapak ke* nampa para tamu.* Father is in charge of receiving the guests. **ke*an** at a loss. *Aku ke*an, ora ngerti apa kang kudu tak tindakaké.* I'm at my wits' end: I don't know what to do.

djeḍèk *var of* DJEḌÉ

djeḍèr *rpr* an explosion. **djeḍar-*** to keep making loud noises. *Lawangé djeḍar-* kena angin.* The door kept banging in the wind.

djeḍèt *var of* DJEḌÈR

djèḍi large copper cauldron with a rounded bottom, used *esp.* for processing sugar cane. ** wesi* iron cauldron

djeḍiḍig **n*** [of hair] in need of cutting

djeḍil **n/di*** to pull sth from its moorings. *Untuku di*.* He extracted my tooth.

djeḍinḍil **n*** soaking wet

djeḍing cistern for storing water (piped from the well) for bathing

djeḍir **djeḍar-*** to thrust forward the lips to signalize disgust, disbelief. **n*** thick-lipped. *Lambéné n*.* His lips protrude. **n/di*aké** to thrust [the lips] forward

djeḍit **n*** all dressed up, *usu.* in a tight-fitting skirt

djedjak **n/di*aké** to move [the legs] in a stiff-kneed kicking motion. **n/di*(i)** to push *or* kick with the leg

djedjeg 1 straight, upright. *ngadeg ** to stand (up) straight. *keris ** straight-bladed kris. **é negara* the stability of the nation. 2 regular, not deviating from the standard. *basa Djawa ** standard Javanese. *Sasi Pèbruari ora *, kurang saka telung puluh dina.* February isn't a full month; it has less than 30 days. **n/di*aké** to make sth straight/upright. *n*aké omah dojong* to true up a leaning house. *n*aké adeging negara* to stabilize the nation. **ora * pikir·an·é** mentally defective. *See also* ADJEG, DJEG

djèdjèh **n*** to sit higher up than others (breach of manners)

djedjel to crowd in(to). *Ing dalan geḍé wong² wis *.* Crowds jammed the streets. **n/di*(i)** to force-feed. *** rijel** jam-packed

djedjep **n*** 1 to wait expectantly *or* apprehensively. 2 *var of* N·DJEDJET

djèdjèr near, next to. ** embokné* beside his mother. *Wis, *a.* Come, sit next to me. **-** *pl* side by side. *Paḍa lungguh ana ing bangku *-*.* They sat lined up on a bench. **n/di*** to put next to each other. *Baṭok telu iki tak *.* I'll put these three coconut shells in a row. **n/di*i** to be beside. *Ḍaḍap di*i Waru.* B (Waru) sat next to A (Ḍaḍap). *** wajang** side by side like puppets in a banana log

djedjer 1 existence, fact of being. **ing urip* the existence of life. *ngélingi marang *ing kawanitané* to bear in mind that one is a woman. *enggoné * dadi sastrawan* the fact that he was a literary artist. 2 *wj* (to play) a major court audience scene. *Ora suwé wajangé *.* Soon the court scene began. ** Ngestina* scene at the Ngestina court. 3 *gram* sentence subject. ***an** 1 *wj* portion of a shadow play that opens with a court scene. 2 standing (*i.e.* growing) rice plants. 3 pole, staff. 4 capital, investment money. 5 spear handle (*kr? ki? for* LANḌÉJAN). 6 carved kris handle (*kr for* UKIR·AN). **n*** to stand (up) (straight). *Adja ngadeg n* nèng tengah lawang.* Don't stand right in the doorway. **n/di*i** 1 to dry [rice plants] by standing them in the sun. 2 to apply carvings to [a wall]. *** sabrang·an** *wj* scene set in a foreign court, introducing a second kingdom

djedjet **n*** 1 *intsfr* cold. *Mau ésuk aḍem n*.* It was awfully cold this morning. 2 *intsfr* lacking salt, insipid. *Sopé wis anjeb n* ngono kok.* The soup needs a lot more salt.

djeḍoḍog *cr* **n*** to sit (down)

djéḍor **n*** thick, swollen [of lips]

djeḍor boom! bang! **djeḍar-*** to keep booming. *Botjah² djeḍar-* ngunèkaké mertjon.* The children kept setting off firecrackers.

djeḍot **ke*(an)** to get hurt by contact with sth. *Sirahé ke* tjagak.* He bumped his head against a pole. *Tangané gosong ke*an mertjon.* The firecracker went off in his hand and burned it.

djeḍuḍug *var of* DJEBUBUG

djedu:l *rpr* a sudden appearance. *Mak * pulisi kétok.* Suddenly the police were on the scene. **dj·um·edul** to appear suddenly. *Kok lagèk saiki ḍèwèké djemedul ing atiku.* He just popped into my mind!

djeḍul 1 to join, meet up with. *Dalan tjilik iki jèn ngétan terus * dalan geḍé Malioboro.* This narrow road runs eastward into Malioboro Boulevard. 2 (*prn* **djeḍu:l**) *var of* DJEDUL. **n*** *or* **dj·um·eḍul** to emerge into view. *Bareng wis suwi njilem ḍèké bandjur n*.* He swam under water for a long time and finally surfaced.

djeḍung a certain green hairless caterpillar

djeḍur *var of* DJEḌOR

djèg **ke*an** occupied by force. *Kuṭa mau wis ke*an pradjurit musuh.* Enemy forces have taken over the city. **nge/di*i** to occupy by force

djeg *var of* DJAG. **sa*** throughout (a lifetime). *See also* ADJEG, SADJEG

djegadul **n*** grim-faced, scowling, drawn-looking

djegagig *rpr* a start of surprise. *Malingé mak * kepeṭuk sing duwé omah.* The burglar suddenly came face-to-face with the owner of the house.

djégal **ke*** to get tripped. **n/di*** to trip smn. *A tiba krungkep merga di* sikilé.* Smn tripped A and he fell flat on his face.

djégang (to sit) in a casual pose with one knee drawn up

djegeḍeg (*or* **n***) motionless. *Greg, manḍeg *.* They suddenly came to a standstill.

djegègèng **n*** to withdraw unsociably from a group

djegègès ***an** *or* **n*** to laugh constantly

djegènggèng *var of* DJEGÈGÈNG

djegèr very young. *wiwit lair ** ever since I was born

djegereg *var of* DJEGREG

djegigig **n*** (to laugh) heartily. *Keprungu wong n*.* He could hear smn laughing hard.

djegigis **n*** to laugh constantly

djeginggat **n*** to give a start. *Aku n* tangi saka turuku, krungu swara beḍil.* I was startled awake by a shot.

djeginggis **n*** [of hair] ragged, in need of cutting

djegir **n*** to stand up straight

djeglag *var of* DJEBLAG

djeglèg slam! ***-*** *or* **djeglag-*** *rpr* repeated slamming sounds. *Ḍèké pidjer *-* mbukak nutup lemari.* She keeps slamming the cupboard open and shut. **n/di*aké** *or* **n/di*(i)** to slam sth shut

djegleg **n*** to sit silent and sorrowful

djeglig *rpr* an arm/leg suddenly bending *or* twisting. *Sikilé mak * terus tiba.* His knee gave way and he fell.

djeglong **1** a certain downward movement in the classical dance. **2** (*or* ***an**) hole, depression; *fig* trap. **ke*** to fall into a hole *or (fig)* trap. **n*** having a hole in it. *Dalané n*.* There's a pothole in the road. **n*-n*** full of holes. **n/di*aké** to cause smn to fall into a hole *or (fig)* trap. **n/di*(i)** to make holes in sth

djeglug **ke*** to bump [the head] inadvertently. *Baṭuké ke* lawang.* He bumped his head on the door. **n*** to bump one's head deliberately. **n/di*aké** to bang smn's head against sth

djegog dog's bark. ***-*** to bark repeatedly. **n*** to bark. **n/di*i** to bark at. *Malingé di*i asuné.* The dog barked at the thief.

djegong deep; concave. *Nganggoa piring sing * kuwi, adja sing tjèpèr.* Use a deep dish, not a shallow one. ***an** a dish-shaped depression. *ptg* **dj·l·egong** full of depressions

djégos can, be able; know how (to). *Kowé ora * manah.* You're no good at archery!

djegot **n*** to sulk, be unwilling to do things

djegrag **n*** [of hair, feathers] to stand on end

djégrang (to have become) too short; outgrown [of clothing]

djegrèg slam! *Aku mau krungu mak *.* I just heard a door slam.

djegreg (*or* **n***) motionless, stock-still. *Ḍèwèké manḍeg *.* He stopped in his tracks. *lungguh n** to sit motionless. *A n* kaja dipaku.* A stood nailed to the spot.

djegrig *ptg * or *-* or* **n*** stiffly upright. *Suket Manila kuwi rupané *-*.* Manila grass grows in stiff clumps. *N* wuluku tjumbu matja kabar mau.* I was scared stiff when I read the news.

djegug *var of* DJEGOG

djégung **ke*** to get twisted *or* entangled. **n/di*** to twist/entangle sth

djegunggut ***-*** *or* **n*** to move around *or* back and forth in the same place

djegur *rpr* a splash. *Ḍèké njegur mak *.* He jumped in, splash! **ke*** to fall into [water]. *Pantjiné ke* sumur.* The pan fell in the well. **n*** to plunge into. *Aku n* kali.* I jumped in the river. **n/di*aké** to plunge sth into water. **dj·um·egur** to produce a splashing sound. *See also* DJLEGUR

djekangkang **n*** to lie *or* fall on the back with the legs up

djekat inf var of DJAKAT

djekèk *slang* genuine, pure, (like the) original. *Omongé Djawa *.* He speaks with a Javanese accent. *botjah ndésa ** a country hick, a rustic through and through. *Lumrahé wong ngira jèn Djanaka utawa Ardjuna iku satrija Djawa *.* Most people think Djanaka and Ardjuna are real Javanese heroes.

djekékal ***an** *or* **n*** to have difficulty getting up *or* remaining upright

djekèkèl *var of* DJEKÉKAL
djekengkeng *var of* DJEKANGKANG
djekèṭèt *var of* DJLEKÈṬÈT
djekeṭet **n∗** [of clothing] tight, too small
djekeṭut *ptg* ∗ full of creases *or* wrinkles. **n∗** 1 creased, wrinkled. 2 [of eyebrows] folded into a scowl
djekiṭat **n∗** neatly groomed, trim-looking
djekiṭit *var of* DJEKIṬAT, DJLEKIṬAT
djekiṭut *var of* DJEKEṬUT
djeklèk to break, snap. **∗an** 1 trigger. 2 cigarette lighter. **n/di∗** to break/snap sth
djekluk *rpr* a clicking sound, *esp.* of knuckles. **n/di∗i** to crack smn's joints by flexing the fingers or toes. **dj·um·ekluk** to bend, bow
djekrèk 1 mousetrap. 2 *rpr* sth snapping shut. *Tikusé mlebu ing pasangan, mak ∗, lawangé mineb.* The mouse went in the trap and the door snapped shut. **∗an** mousetrap. **n/di∗i** to punch (a hole in) [a ticket]
djeksa *var of* DJAKSA
djekut **n∗** *intsfr* cold. *aḍem n∗* intensely cold
djekutrut **n∗** downcast, out of sorts
djel- *see also under* DJL- (*Introduction, 2.9.3*)
djelas clear. *Jèn durung ∗ adja wedi takon.* If it's not clear to you, don't be afraid to ask. **n/di∗aké** to explain, clarify
djelèh 1 bored (with), tired of. 2 to shout. **∗an** 1 boring. 2 easily bored. **∗-∗** 1 bored. 2 to shout. **di∗i** to be considered a bore. *Parto kuwi di∗i Siti kok ora rumangsa.* You'd think Parto would realize Siti is sick and tired of him. **n∗i** boring. *Wong mau n∗i.* He's a bore.
djeli:h *intensified form of* DJELÈH. **djelah-∗** to keep shouting. **n∗** to shout, holler. **(n)∗-∗** to keep hollering. **pa·n∗** act of shouting. *Krungu pen∗.* He heard a yell.
djelma *inf var of* DJALMA
djelu **n∗** irritated, annoyed. **n·djela-n∗** to keep feeling exasperated (at, about)
djeluk **∗-∗** to keep calling smn. **n∗** to call smn. *Ḍèké n∗ anaké.* She called her son.
djélung **∗an** *or* **∗ umpet** (to play) hide-and-seek
djem- *see also under* DJ- (*Introduction, 3.1.7*)
Djemahat *var of* DJEMUWAH
djembak a certain vegetable grown in swampy areas
djembangan large earthenware container used for water *or* as a flowerpot
djembar broad, spacious. *Kamaré ∗.* The room is large. *Pandelengané katon ∗.* There's a broad view. *kurang ∗ bebudèné* narrow-minded. *Panjebarané ora ∗.* They are not widely distributed. **∗é** breadth; size. *Tegalané ∗é limang puluh m² ⟨mèter pesagi⟩.* The field is 500 square meters in area. *Alun², samanten ∗ipun, prasasat kebak tijang.* The square, expansive as it is, was filled with people. **n/di∗aké** to make sth broad(er). *n∗aké kawruhé* to broaden one's knowledge. *Kamaré arep di∗aké.* The room is to be made larger. **∗ ati·né** compassionate. **∗ polat·an·é** having broad knowledge. **∗ kubur·é** May you go to heaven! (*said to a dead person*)
djembeg muddy, damp and messy
djèmbèl impoverished, destitute. *kaum ∗* the poor
djembèng **n∗** to open up *or* widen [anus, vaginal opening] with the fingers
djember (*or* **∗-∗**) muddy, mucky. **n∗i** 1 muddy. 2 nauseating. 3 (*psv* **di∗i**) to make sth muddy
djembèwèk **n∗** with lips drawn apart and turned down
djembimblik **n∗** to have the face screwed up to cry
djemblang **n∗** bloated [of the belly]
djèmblèk [of the eyes] to water; to produce matter
djemblèk spotted with absorbed liquid; *fig* spotty in performance, not up to standard. **ke∗an** to get spotted. *Kertasé ke∗an mangsi.* The paper got an ink spot on it. **n∗** 1 *sms* ∗. 2 to absorb [stains]. *Kertasé n∗ kena mangsi.* The paper soaked up the ink spots.
djèmblem **n∗** 1 chubby in the face. 2 to remain silent, contribute nothing to the conversation
djembleng **n∗** speechless, struck dumb
djembling **n∗** bloated [of the belly]
djemblok *var of* DJEMBLÈK. **∗an** *see* SUWENG, TJANṬING
djembluk **n∗** 1 bloated, distended [of the stomach]. 2 ill-formed, clumsy
djemblung *var of* DJEMBLUK
djembombrong **n∗** [of women] untidy, not neatly groomed
djèmbrèng **n/di∗** to spread *or* lay out sth
djembru:ng **n∗** messy, unkempt, littered

djembul decorative plume stuck in a hat
djembut pubic hair
djemèk damp, mushy, gooey
djeminul (*or* **n*)** unsteady; to shake, wobble
djempalik ***an** topsy-turvy. *Atiku *an.* I'm all upset. **n*** to turn upside down. *tiba n** to fall head over heels. *Montoré n* nang sawah.* The car overturned in a rice paddy.
djempânâ palanquin
djemparing arrow (*kr for* PANAH)
djempérok **n*** 1 too heavily made up with cosmetics. 2 nicely groomed
djempina 1 a certain tuberous root. 2 prematurely born child
djempling **n*** to emit a high-pitched sound. *Ḍèké mau kagèt nganti n*.* She was so startled she squealed.
djempo feeble with old age
djempol 1 thumb. 2 the best. *Nèk ura² waé aku *.* When it comes to singing, I'm tops. *Gambarané *.* His picture is great! ***an** the best. *kalebu wong *an* a first-rate person. *** sikil** big toe
djemprit **n*** to squeal
djemrut emerald
djemumut *ptg ** or *-** all dirty, covered with dirt
Djemunten *sbst kr for* DJEMUWAH
djemurut *var of* DJEMRUT
Djemuwah Friday (the Moslem holy day). ***an** Friday worship at the mosque. **sa*** one 7-day week
djèn ***-*an** all by oneself (*inf var of* IDJÈN·²-AN). **nge/di*i** 1 *inf var of* NG/DI-ADJI·ǸI. 2 *inf var of* NG/DI·IDJEǸ·I
djenak deeply absorbed (in the enjoyment of). *Jèn wis sekak * banget nganti lali mangan barang.* When he plays chess, he gets so engrossed he even forgets to eat.
djenang a certain porridge or soft pudding for ritual-meal ceremonies (*slamet·an*). ***an** [of gems] imitation. **n/di*** to make [ingredients] into porridge. **n/di*aké** to hold a ceremony in smn's honor to signalize a significant event. **n*aké abang** to hold a name-changing *or* circumcision ceremony for smn. **n/di*i** to signalize [an event] with a ceremony at which porridge is served. *** abang** a sweet red-colored porridge served at name-changing *or* circumcision ceremonies. *** abang-putih** a half-red, half-white porridge. *** baro²** porridge with grated sugared coconut. *** gaplèk** celluloid. *** gempol** snack consisting of rice balls with coconut milk and thick coconut-sugar syrup. *** karèt** celluloid. *** se·lajah** a group of people having the same opinion. *** ngangrang** rice porridge with coconut milk and syrup. *** palang** red porridge with a decorative white cross on top. *** protjot** porridge served at a ceremony for a seven-months-pregnant woman. *** putih** a salty white porridge
djenar 1 *oj* yellow. 2 a variety of tree with small fragrant blossoms and yellow wood
djenat 1 heaven. 2 **(swargi** *ki***)** deceased. *Wis * lawas.* He's been dead a long time. *bapakmu swargi* your late father. ***é** the late...
djenḍel ***an** gold ore. **ke*en** 1 to get stuck smw. 2 deep in debt. **n*** 1 to become thick/solid. *Kali² n*.* The rivers froze over. 2 to remain stuck smw. *Kuntjiné n* nang lawang.* The key got stuck in the door. **n/di*aké** to thicken *or* solidify sth. *Kandjiné kanggo n*aké duduh.* The flour is for thickening the gravy.
djenḍéla window
djenḍil **n*** to be "It"; to be on the defending side (in games). **n/di*aké** to avoid, shun
djendjem secure, at peace, untroubled
djenḍol **n*** swollen
djéndral general (military rank). ***an** reception held for generals
djenḍul **n*** swollen
djené 1 yellow (*kr for* KUNING). 2 (*or* ***an**) gold (*kr for* MAS^a^). ***-*an** *ng kr* imitation gold
djenèh 1 as you well know; it is plain that... *Adja mangan pelem waé, * mengko lara weteng.* Don't keep eating mangoes–you know they'll give you a stomach ache. *Djarané kok boten purun mlaju, mengké tekan pasar * empun awan.* The horse won't budge; at this rate it'll be noon before we get to the marketplace. **, dudu salahku.* It's obviously not *my* fault. 2 (just) because. ** kowé mau ndadak mèlu omong barang, saiki kowé dadi katut nang perkarané.* Just because you had to open your mouth, you're involved in it now. ** kowé mlérok, ja disangka ora wedi.* You see–when you smile they think you're not afraid!
djeneng *ng*, **nâmâ** *or* **nami** *kr* name; (what sth is) called, known *or* regarded as; **(asma** *ki***)** personal name. **é sapa?* What's his name? *Embuh ja *é.* I don't know what

it's called. *kertu ** name card. *kéwan sing *é unta* an animal known as a camel. *Jèn njambut-gawé alon², kuwi *é kesèd.* If you work slowly, it means you're lazy. *wong * Ali* a man called Ali. ** ora kadjèn jèn guru djadjan ana ing pinggir ndalan.* It's not considered respectable for teachers to eat in public. *Sing * menṭèk kuwi apa kéwan apa bangsané lelembut?* Is the so-called rice pest a germ or an evil spirit? *Apa ora * mentalan, wong mengkono iku?* Isn't he (what you'd call) hard-hearted, a man who would do that? *Iki kok énak temen, *é diolah apa iki?* This tastes really good; how is it cooked? ***é** that which is called; so-called; you might say (that...). *O, iki *é wong kodjur.* Oh, what bad luck! *Ing kono mau *é padusan sing ora bajar.* It was a bathing place where no fee was charged. **é tuku kepeksa.* [In view of what had gone before,] you might say that she *had* to buy it. *Ing tanah mau ora ana sing *é sepur.* There are no such things as trains in that country. **n/di*aké** 1 to name sth. *Lumrahé pasar iku di*aké miturut dina pasarané.* Marketplaces are usually named after the day names. 2 to call sth (by a name). *Kang di*aké dina pasaran, jaiku: Legi, Paing, lsp.* The so-called "market days" are Legi, Paing, *etc.* **n/di*i** 1 to name sth. *Slamet n*i anaké Sariman.* Slamet named his son Sariman. 2 to be present at (*ki for* Ñ/DI·TEKA·NI?). *n*i pengantèné kantjané* to attend a friend's wedding. *** baptis** Christian name. *** pantjer** name assumed as an adult, *usu.* made up from parts of other names in the family. *** samar·an** *or* *** sandi** 1 secret name; name concealed in the words of a verse. 2 pseudonym. *** tjilik** childhood name given by the parents. *** tuwa** name one chooses for oneself, *usu.* at the time of marriage. *See also* DJUMENENG, PANDJENENGAN

djenes damp and dirty

djenèwer gin

djeng 1 *title, adr* younger sister; younger female. ** Pama mbésuk kapan njusul?* When will your wife get here, Pomo? 2 *oj* foot, leg. 3 *inf var of* KANGDJENG. *See also* ADJENG

djengandika *wj* you; your

djengat **n*** in an upright position

djèngèk **n*** to crane the neck

djengèk *rg var of* BÈN. **n*** *var of* N·DJÈNGÈK

djengèn *md for* BÈN

djengèngèk *var of* DENGÈNGÈK. **n*** *var of* N·DJENGÈK

djenger **n*** shocked, stunned, taken aback

djengès **n/di*** to ridicule, jeer at

djenggan **dje*** *var of* DJE·DJANGGAN

djenggar roomy, spacious. **n/di*aké** to give sth plenty of room. *Widjiné téla gantung jèn wis ṭukul bandjur kudu di*aké.* After papaya seeds sprout they must be thinned.

djenggarang **n*** [of buildings] tall, sizable

djenggé *var of* DJENGGLÉ

djenggeleg *ptg ** to loom up, stand out [of separate objects in a group]

djenggèlèk *rpr* a sudden awakening and arising. *ptg * pl* awakening and arising. **n*** to wake up and raise the head or sit up

djenggeneg *var of* DJENGGELEG

djènggèr comb (of a bird, *esp.* chickens). *** sumpel** small comb. *** wilah** large billowing comb

djenggereng magnificent, splendid. **n*** to make a splendid appearance

djènggès a form of black magic

djenggileng wide and staring [of eyes]. **n*** to stare (at) wide-eyed and steadily

djengginggat *var of* DJENGGIRAT

djengginggis *var of* DJEGINGGIS

djenggirat *rpr* a sudden start. *Aku diklakson saka mburi mak * kagèt.* I nearly jumped out of my skin when a horn blew right behind me. **n*** to give a start. *Bareng kèlingan duwé semajan bandjur n* tangi.* He sprang out of bed when he remembered he had an appointment.

djenggiri *wj, ltry* mythical animal like a tiger with horns

djenggit **n/di*** to pull hairs from smn's scalp by the roots

djengglé **n*** to sit idly staring into space

djengglèng *rpr* the clash of metal against metal. *Enḍas²ané sepur digaṭukké karo gerbong mak *.* The locomotive clanged as it was coupled with the cars.

djengglik **n*** to sit by oneself apart from others

djengglung *rpr* a deep ringing sound, *esp.* of a gong

djénggot *ng kr*, **gumbâlâ** *ki* beard; *fig* beard as a symbol of the widom of old age. ***an** to wear a beard. *** ñj·tjanṭuk** beard that juts forward. *** wesi** a certain plant whose bark inhibits fermentation of sugar-palm sap

djenggreng *var of* DJENGGERENG

djenggrik **n*** 1 to teeter, threaten to topple. 2 *intsfr* thin. *kuru n** thin as a rail
djenggruk **n*** to sit concentrating. *Anggoné sinau n**. He's absorbed in his studying.
djenggul (*or* **dje***) the leader, the top man
djengguleng handsome. *ptg* * [of waves] rolling
djenggung 1 *rpr* a stroke of a gamelan *gong. Gongé muni mak* *. The *gong* went bong! 2 one's turn at sth (*var of* ḌENGGUNG). **n*** to pound smn gently on the head with a fist
djenggunuk **n*** to loom, stick up
djenggureng **n*** stern-faced, grim-looking
djengil **djengal-*** *or* **n*** lone, alone. *Untuné mung gari sidji djengal-**. She has only one tooth left. *Aku mau nang Sala nunggang bis mung n* ḍéwé.* I was the only passenger on the bus to Solo.
djenginggis *var of* DJEGINGGIS
djengit **djengat-*** to keep assuming an upright position. *Entupé tawon kétok djengat-* nang bokongé.* The bee's stinger keeps going up and down on its rear end. **n*** in an upright position
djengkang **ke*** to fall over backwards, fall one one's back (face up). **n/di*aké** to push smn over backwards
djengkar 1 to depart, set out (*ki for* BUḌAL, M̈·PANGKAT). 2 to move, change residence (*ki for* PINḌAH)
djèngkèl irritated, frustrated, exasperated
djengkélang **n*** to fall down from a high place; to fall out of a vehicle
djengkelit a somersault. ***an** to turn somersaults for one's own amusement. **ke*** to get thrown head over heels. *Aku tiba ke* saka ngepit.* I tumbled off my bike. **n*** to fall head over heels
djèngkèng to kneel on one knee
djengkerung **n*** rolled into a ball, curled up
djengkerut *ptg* * full of creases/wrinkles. **n*** to fold into creases. *Baṭuké rada n**. His forehead is creased in a frown.
djengking *rpr* falling head-down bottom-up. **djengkang-*** 1 to remain lying in the above position (the Moslem praying attitude). 2 *joking, cr* to pray repeatedly. **n*** to lie prostrated with head down and bottom up. **n/di*aké** to tilt sth (*e.g.* a teapot) bottom upward. *ptg* **dj·r·engking** *sms* DJENGKANG-*
djèngklèk ***-*** *or* **djéngklak-*** to jump with joy
djengklèk **ke*** to get twisted; to give way under one. *Sikilé ke* bandjur tiba.* He turned his ankle and fell.
djengklok *var of* DJENGKLÈK
djéngkol lima-bean-like vegetable eaten (*usu.* raw) as a rice-accompanying dish. ***en** (to have/get) dysuria from the above
djengku knee (*ki for* ḌENGKUL)
djengongok **n*** to crane the neck
djenguk **n*** to sit idly staring into space
djeni *kr* deep golden (*intensified form of* DJENÉ). *Téla gantungipun prajogi dipun unḍuh amargi sampun * sanget.* The papaya should be picked now–it's deep gold.
djenis kind, class, (sub)group. *Kapal mabur mau * Convair.* The planes are Convairs. *Atlétik * olahraga kang apik kanggo iki.* Calisthenics is a good sport for this purpose.
djenitri a certain seed, often used for necklaces and other trinkets
djenṭar **n*** pointing straight up (*esp.* of long tails)
djenṭârâ (*or* **n***) [of young men] handsome and elegant
djenṭat *var of* DJENṬAR
djenten *var of* DJINTEN
djenṭik little finger. *** manis** ring finger, fourth finger
djenṭir **n*** pointing straight up [of small short tails]
djenṭit *var of* DJENṬIR
djéntol, djentol **n*** to become swollen [of insect bites/stings]
djenṭot *var of* DJENṬU. ***an** (to play) a game of marbles. **n*** to shoot a marble by holding it in the crook of the index finger and snapping it with the thumb
djèntrèh **n/di*** to set up [a display]
djèntrèk (*or* ***-***) lined up. *Wong akèh wis *-* nang pinggir dalan.* Crowds lined the edge of the road. **n/di*(i)** to put in a line. *Ḍuwit tjiliké paḍa *-*ana, arep tak étung.* Put the coins in a row; I want to count them.
djenṭu husky and firm [of physique]
djentus **ke*** to get knocked against sth. *Sirahé ke* témbok.* He hit his head on the wall. **n*** to bang one's head (on)
djenu a certain plant that is poisonous to fish. **n/di*** to catch fish by poisoning them with the ground-up root of this plant
Djepan *var of* DJEPANG
Djepang Japan. *ḍèk djaman ** during the Japanese occupation
djepapang *var of* DJEPAPLANG
djepaplang ***an** to keep the arms stretched

out; to extend the arms repeatedly. n* to extend the arms out to the sides

djepat *an act of springing out. ke*an to get hit by sth springing out. n* to emerge suddenly. *Piré n∗.* The spring shot out.

djepèt clip, clamp. * *kertas* paper clip. * rambut hairpin

djepiping n* to cock the ears. *Jèn wong*^{2}-*ané obah, Kantjil n∗.* When the dummy moved, Mouse-Deer's ears shot up.

djepit^{a} (*or* *an) gripping tool, pincers, tongs. * *kertas* paper clip. * *rambut* hairpin. ke* to get pinched/squeezed. n/di* to use a pinching tool; to pinch, grip. *Djupukna tjaṭut kuwi tak nggo n∗ paku iki.* Hand me the pliers, I want to pull out this nail. *n∗ mèmèhan* to pin the clothes up to dry with clothes pins

djepi:t^{b} *an place to squeeze into for concealment *or* to be unobtrusive. ke* situated in an unobtrusive *or* out-of-the-way place; in a difficult *or* undesirable position. *Awaké ke∗ watu tangkeb.* He was squeezed between two rocks. *Ḍèwèké rumangsa ke∗, ora weruh lor kidul.* He was hard-pressed and bewildered. n* in an unobtrusive *or* obscure position. *Olèhé lingguh n∗ nang podjokan mulané aku ora weruh.* He was sitting way back in the corner so I didn't see him. *Omahé n∗.* His house is way off the beaten track. pa·n*an *sms* *AN

djeplak open(ed up). *an 1 mouth of a trap. 2 top-hinged window or door that opens outward. n* 1 to open up/out. *Pajungé ora bisa n∗.* The umbrella won't open. 2 *cr* to speak; to blurt out. n/di*-*aké to open [a hinged-panel door, window]

djepluk n* 1 to explode. 2 to fade, become drab. 3 to fail. *Udjiané n∗.* He failed the test. 4 throughout [the morning]. *sekésuk n∗* all morning

djeprak n* to open up/out, to spread. *Meraké buntuté n∗.* The peacock's tail was spread open.

djeprèt 1 *rpr* a zipping *or* snapping. *Siti dipotrèk mak ∗.* He snapped a picture of Siti. *Manuké diplinṭeng ∗ pas kena sirahé.* He shot the bird in the head with his slingshot. 2 *rpr* the sun shining. *panas n∗* to be *or* become sunny. dj·um·eprèt bright [of sunshine]

djeprik *ptg* * *or* n* standing up/out [of hair, feathers]

djeprot *rpr* stabbing. *Tjèlèngé dipanah kena wetengé mak ∗.* He shot an arrow into the boar's stomach.

djepruk n* 1 piled high, puffed up [of opened-out flower petals, curled or combed-up hair, *etc.*]. 2 throughout [the morning] (*var of* DJEPLUK)

djeprut *rpr* sth breaking with a snap

Djepun *var of* DJEPANG

djepupung n* lying face down humped up and stiff

djeput throughout [the morning] (*var of* DJEPLUK)

djèr a certain diacritical mark in Arabic script. *-*an in a molten *or* dissolved state. *Timbel luwih gelis ∗-∗ané katimbang wesi.* Lead melts faster than iron. *Ketip palsu kuwi ∗-∗an timbel.* Counterfeit dimes are lead alloys. nge/di*aké to melt for smn; to have sth melted. nge/di*(i) to melt/dissolve sth. *nge∗ wesi*^{2} *tuwa sing wis ora kanggo* to melt down scrap iron. *Glepung kandji kaedjèri toja.* The starch is dissolved in water. pa·nge*an act of melting/dissolving. *wadjan pange∗an* skillet for melting things. *See also* ADJÈR

djer why...! after all. *Mèh boten pitados jèn ibu séda, ∗ kula mentas saking Sala tur ibu boten gerah.* I could scarcely believe Mother was dead; why, I had just been to Solo and she wasn't even ill. * basuki mawa béja good things come through hard effort

djer- *see also under* DJR- (*Introduction, 2.9.3*)

djeram citrus fruit (*kr for* DJERUK)

djerbabah *var of* DJEBABAH

djerbèbèh *var of* DJEBÈBÈH

djèrèng n/di* to spread (out), extend. *n∗ méméan sing lagi dipépé* to spread clothes out to air. *Perkarané di∗ karo djaksané.* The prosecutor laid forth the details of the case. *Murid kena n∗*^{2} *pikirané ḍéwé.* The students are encouraged to use their imagination. *Pemetuné semono kuwi wis di∗-∗ meksa ora tjukup kanggo urip sesasi.* He did his best to stretch his income but it still didn't cover his monthly expenses. dj·um·èrèng spread, laid out. *Karté wis djumèrèng nang ngarepé.* The map was spread out in front of him.

djérigèn jerry can. *Sing nang ∗ kuwi ming mligi bènsin.* The stuff in the jerry can is pure gasoline.

djering a certain tart fruit eaten raw as a

rice-accompanying dish: considered beneficial for the kidneys

djerit a high-pitched cry. *Keprungu *é wong "Tulung!"* They heard smn scream "Help!" *-* to utter shriek after shriek. **djerat-*** to utter random *or* meaningless cries. *Si bajèk djerat-*.* The baby is jabbering. **n*** to cry out. **pa·n*(an)** act of screaming *or* (*fig*) complaining. *papan kanggo njebar pan*an* a place for airing complaints. *ptg* **dj·l·erit** *pl* to keep screaming

djerkangkang *var of* DJEKANGKANG

Djerman Germany

djernèh *var of* DJENÈH

djero *ng,* **lebet** *kr* 1 deep. *sumur ** a deep well. *Ḍèké *.* It took her baby a long time to be born ('she is deep'). 2 the interior. *saka n** from the inside. *mlebu menjang * omah* to go in the house. *ana ing * banju* under water. *Ditémbok djaba *.* Exterior and interior walls were installed. **ning batin mikir²* to think over to oneself. 3 the court, the palace. *Iki tulisané djuru tulis saka n*.* This batik was done by a court batik maker. ***an** 1 internal organ(s). 2 the inside. ***n** *var of* *. *nDjron ngomah peteng nḍeḍet.* It was pitch dark in the house. *Ampal kuwi manggon ing *n lemah.* Beetles live underground. ***né** the depth. *Pira *né?* How deep is it? **ke*n** excessively deep. *Olèhé ngeḍuk sumur ke*n nganti banjuné akèh banget.* They dug the well so deep there was water in abundance. **men*** (**mlebet** *kr*) 1 (farther) to the inside. *Men* manèh mantri, ana ing kanan-kèriné patih lan ratu.* Farther in are the (chess) bishops, on either side of the queen and king. 2 *rg* to enter; to go in the house. **n/di*kaké** to make deep(er). *bur kanggo n*kaké sumur* a drill for deepening the well. **sa(n)*né** 1 in(side of). *sa*né kuṭa* inside the city. *sa*ning patang dina* within four days. *nglakoni mati sak*ning urip* to suffer greatly. 2 during; while. *sa*ning mangan* as he ate. *Sa*né iku tukangé sulap muni werna².* All the while, the magician kept up a line of patter. * **tjeṭèk·é** the depth (of). *Aku ora ngerti * tjeṭèké kali mau.* I don't know how deep the river is.

djerpupung *var of* DJEPUPUNG

djerṭot *var of* DJEṬUT

djerṭut *var of* DJEṬUT

djerug *see* TIKUS

djeruk *ng,* **djeram** *kr* citrus fruit. ** saadjar* one section of citrus fruit; a certain necklace style. ** sambel* citrus fruit for making spicy sauce. **n*** 1 resembling a citrus fruit. 2 homosexual. * **bali** large sweet white grapefruit. * **brengganu** a variety of citrus fruit. * **gulung** sweet red grapefruit. * **keprok** orange, tangerine. * **krandjang** a variety of orange. * **krénggot·an,** * **kuwik** common citrus fruits. * **legi** orange. * **leter** a variety of citrus fruit. * **manis** seedless navel orange. * **matjan** grapefruit. * **nipis** sweet lime. * **patjit·an** a variety of citrus fruit. * **petjel** sour lime-like fruit. * **purut** a small fragrant lemon-like fruit; **n*-purut** deeply wrinkled [of human skin]. * **n̈·tambang·an** sweet red grapefruit. * **uwik** a variety of orange. * **wadi** a common variety of citrus fruit

djerum **n*** lying at ease [of cattle, *e.g.* while chewing the cud]

djès 1 *rpr* a locomotive puffing. *Enḍas²ané sepur mlaku *, *, *.* The engine started up. 2 *var of* DJRÈS

djes *rpr* a powerful stabbing. *njrumbat kambil mak ** to open a coconut by ramming it with a sharp tool

djèsbèn jazz band

djèt jet. *montor ** jet engine. *montor mabur ** jet plane

djet *rpr* a jerk, jolt. *Dumadakan montoré dirèm mak *.* He slammed on the brakes and stopped with a jerk.

djeṭaṭus **n*** [of the jaw] undershot, jutting forward

djeṭaṭut **n*** gloomy, depressed

djeṭèt **n/di*** to switch [an appliance] on *or* off

djeṭit *rpr* joints clicking when flexed

djeṭot *var of* DJEṬUT

djeṭoṭot *var of* DJEṬUṬUT

djèṭung home free; on goal (in children's games). *(Aku wis) *!* (I'm) in free! ***an** 1 goal, home, free place. 2 to play tag or the like. ***an ḍelik·an** hide-and-seek. ***an ranté** a game of tag played around a row of pillars

djeṭut *rpr* knuckles cracking. *ptg ** repeated knuckle-cracks. **n/di*** to pull one's fingers or toes to crack the joints. *Djempolé di* muni mak kluk.* He cracked his thumb joint. **n/di*i** to crack smn's joints. *Dridjiné di*i muni ptg djerṭot.* [The masseuse] cracked all his finger and toe joints. *ptg* **dj·r·eṭut** *sms ptg **

djeṭuṭut **n*** 1 feeling chilly. 2 scowling in anger
djew- *inf var of* DJUW- *at the beginning of a word*
djèwèr **n/di*** to tweak [smn's ear]
dji one (*counting form: see also* SIDJI). **, ro, lu* 1, 2, 3. *sepisan * iki* just this once. *** **ro** 2 against 1. *** **lu** 3 against 1. *** **tus** 100 against 1
djiarah to seclude oneself, *esp.* in a cemetery, for holy meditation. **n/di*(i)** to go smw for solitary meditation. *n*i guwa* to seclude oneself in a cave
djibah **ke*** entrusted (with), assigned (to). *kang ke* nata tentremé* the one whose reponsibility it is to maintain the peace **n/di*aké** to assign [a responsibility] to
djibeg overburdened, weighted down with sorrow or care
djibil incompetent; to fail
djibleng *cr* 1 to lose, be defeated. 2 less, inferior
djiblès (a)like, similar (to). *Wernané *.* They are the same color. *** **persis** *or* *** **tjèrles** exactly alike, just the same
djiblok to fall, drop
djibril *var of* DJABARAIL
djibur *splash!* **djibar-*** to make splashing sounds
djideng *cr* 1 to lose, be defeated. 2 less, inferior
djidji:k revolted, disgusted. *ngrasa ** to feel repelled. **n*i** revolting, sickening
djidun **n/di*** to pinch sth between the knuckles of the index and middle fingers
djiḍur (*or* ***an**) drum used in Occidental music. **pa·n*** drummer, drum player
djigang *var of* DJÉGANG
djiglok *var of* DJIBLOK
djigrang too short [of clothing]
djiguh in a difficult position; awkward, uncomfortable. *Jèn nang kéné adja *-* dianggep kaja nang omahmu ḍéwé waé.* Just make yourself right at home here!
djih *inf var of* ISIH. **nge/di*aké** to keep sth aside. *Rotiné di*aké separo kanggo mangan soré.* They left half the cake to eat that evening.
djihadfi sabilullah holy war, war in defense of Moslem principles
djijad **n/di*** to force, compel. *Jèn ora gelem mèlu ja wis adja di*.* Don't make him go along if he doesn't want to.
djijarah *var sp of* DJIARAH
djik *inf var of* ISIH
djikuk *var of* DJUPUK
djil **n*** limited to one. *sidji n** one and only one
djilat **n/di*** to lick. *tukang n** a yes-man
djilid volume in a series. ** Sidji, Loro, lsp.* Volume 1, 2, *etc.* ***an** 1 by the volume; in volumes. 2 book binding. **n/di*** to bind. *Pegawéané n* buku.* He's a bookbinder.
djilih to borrow (*root form: Jogja var of* SILIH)
djiling **n/di*** to hit smn on the head
djilma *var of* DJALMA. **n*** [of animals] resembling *or* having the characteristics of a human being
djim 1 evil spirit, devil. 2 (*prn* **dji:m**) times! time out! (in games: requested by extending the arm(s) with thumb(s) up). **ka*an** 1 realm of the evil spirits. 2 possessed of devils
djimak sexual intercourse
Djimakir name of the eighth (final) year in the *windu* cycle
djimat 1 good luck charm, amulet. 2 *var of* DJIMPIT
Djimawal name of the third year in the *windu* cycle
djimbrang **n*** *intsfr* bright. *paḍang n** intensely bright/light
djimleng *intsfr* quiet. *meneng ** very quiet, not saying a single word
djimpé [of arms, legs] weak, powerless, exhausted
djimpit a small amount; a pinch. *ujah sa** a pinch of salt. *Mèsema se* waé, aku wis lega.* Smile a little and I'll be happy. **n/di*(i)** to take a pinch (of). *n*i gula* to take a pinch of sugar
djimprak *var of* DJINGKLAK
djimprek̄ (*or* **n***) enervated, without strength
djimuk *var of* DJUPUK
djin *var of* DJIM
djin- *see also under* DJ- (*Introduction, 3.1.7*)
djina(h) adultery. **ber*** to commit adultery
djinah 10 (market term). *pelem se** 10 mangoes. *Akèhé ana sepuluh *.* There are 100 of them.
djinântrâ water wheel; windmill
djinasah mortal remains, lifeless body
djinasat *var of* DJINASAH
djinawi *see* LOH
djinḍel *var of* DJENḌEL
djindja to get over sth. *Aku wis *.* Never again! I've learned my lesson.

djindjing ***an** act of carrying sth small. **n/di*aké** to carry [a small object] for smn; to have smn carry, have sth carried. **n/di*(i)** to carry [sth small]

djindjit to stand on tiptoe

djinḍul **n*** to swell up. *Baṭuké kedjeglug lawang nganti n*.* He has a bump on the forehead from hitting it on the door.

djinem **(ka)*an** 1 an errand performed on orders from a government *or* palace official. 2 (*or* **pa*an**) one who performs such an errand

djing (*or* **n***) future; next (*inf kr? md? for* BÉSUK, SUK). **n*-éndjing** *md* tomorrow; tomorrow morning

djingga 1 dark red, maroon. 2 pink *or* orange food coloring. 3 a certain dark-red fabric. *** loka** dark red

djingglang a certain shrub whose sweetish leaves can be used as tea. **n*** *intsfr* bright. *paḍang n** very light/bright

djinggleng **n*** to fix the eyes (on). *Anggoné namatké potrèt nganti n*.* He stared at the picture for a long time.

djinggrang **n*** *intsfr* light, bright. *paḍang n** intensely bright

djinggring **n*** thin-looking, gangly

djinggruk **n*** (to sit) motionless with knees drawn up and head lowered

djingkat **n*** to jump with surprise

djingklak ***an** *or* ***-*** to jump with joy

djingklong a certain large mosquito, the most common variety of which does not bite

djingkol *var of* DJÉNGKOL

djingkrak *var of* DJINGKLAK

djingkrung **n*** to lie curled up; to lie with the knees drawn up to the chest

djinis kind, variety, genus. *saben * sato-kéwan.* ***é** actually, the fact is

djintel **n*** [to sleep] curled up. *Tukang bétjak wis n* turu katekuk ing bétjaké.* The pedicab driver curled up in his cab and took a nap.

djinten cumin seed; caraway seed. *See also* TUMBAR

djintul **n*** a small itchy swelling

dji:p jeep

djipang a prickly-skinned squash-like vegetable used for soup

djiplak ***an** a fake, a copy of the original. **n/di*** to copy, duplicate. *Ḍèké konangan anggoné n* kantjané.* He got caught copying from a classmate.

djipuk *var of* DJUPUK

djipun a variety of tree

djirèh *var of* DJIRIH

djiret, djirèt a lassoing rope. **ke*** to get choked, strangled (not necessarily to death). **n/di*** 1 to rope [an animal]. 2 to kill by strangulation

djirigèn *var of* DJÉRIGÈN

djirih 1 faint-hearted, cowardly. 2 fear; afraid; awe, respect (*kr for* WEDI)

djirit *var of* DJLIRIT

djisim corpse, cadaver

djit **n·djat-*** to wobble, move unsteadily

djiṭet **n/di*** to sew up a torn place. *ptg* **dj·l·iṭet** *or ptg* **dj·r·iṭet** full of mended places

djiṭok *var of* GIṬOK

djitu precise, just right. *wangsulan ** a precise answer

djitun *var of* DJIDUN

djiwa 1 soul, spirit, life. *ngurbanaké *né* to sacrifice one's life. *tanggung ** to risk one's life. ** merdika* the spirit of freedom. *nganjut ** to commit suicide. 2 spirits, state of mind. 3 person (as a statistic). *Keluargamu *né pira?* How many in your family? *tjatjah ** population; census. *Kartjis iki mung kanggo sa*.* This ticket admits one only. ***ku** *term of endearment used by lovers.* **ka*n** pertaining to the mind, spirit, inner life. *ngèlmu kedjiwan* psychology; psychiatry. **n/di*ni** to pervade; to imbue sth with a certain spirit. *Adjarané di*ni Marxisme.* His teachings are Marxist-inspired. *Marxisme n*ni adjarané.* Marxism pervades his teachings. *** angga** *or* *** raga** body and soul; the physical and the spiritual. *pasrah * raga* to put oneself in God's hands. *Kelakon kongsi diréwangi toh * raga.* They risked their lives. *See also* LALI

djiwânggâ *contracted form of* DJIWA ANGGA

djiwir *var of* DJÈWÈR

djiwit **n/di*** to pinch between the thumb and index finger. **dj·in·iwit katut** to share empathetically in a relative's sorrow *or* disgrace

djiwut *var of* ḌIWUT

djladjah **ng/di*i** to travel around (to). *Aku mèlu kantja² n*i désa².* My friends and I went sightseeing from village to village.

djladrèn (*or* ***an**) dough, batter

djlâgrâ phlegm (*ki for* RIJAK)

djlalat *rpr* a quick glance. ***an** *or* ***-*** to glance about

djlamprah **n***spread *or* scattered over a wide area
djlamprong *var of* DJAMPRONG
djlang ***-*an** to wander around, go aimlessly here and there
djlanggrung ***-*** tall and well-built (of physique)
djlantah used cooking oil (for reuse). * *iwak pitik* coconut oil in which chicken has been fried (and which can be used again later). **ke*** having a bad reputation
djlaprat **n*** [of moustaches] thick and curving upward at the ends
djlarang a certain large squirrel
djlarèh streak, stripe. **djlorah-*** striped, full of streaks. **n*** having *or* forming a streak. *Kebulé montor mabur djèt isih n**. The jet plane left a vapor trail.
djlarèt *var of* DJLARÈH
djlarit thin line, narrow strip. *Ḍèké njawang ing tjakrawala bokmenawa katon *é pasisir.* He scanned the horizon in the hope of seeing (a strip of) land. **n*** forming a slim line. *Alisé n* nanggal sepisan.* Her eyebrows are slender crescents.
djlébrah **n*** large, broad
djlebud **n*** unkempt
djleḍor bang! boom! *ptg ** *or* **djleḍar-*** repeated explosions. *Bola-bali keprungu djleḍar-* swarané beḍil.* They kept hearing guns go off. *See also* DJEḌOR
djlèg 1 *rpr* slamming. *Lawangé ditutup mak * terus dikuntjing mak tjeklik.* He banged the door shut and locked it. 2 *var of* DJÈG
djleg 1 *rpr* a quick downward motion. *Sred, sepéḍa dirèm, muḍun *.* He slammed on his bicycle brakes and hopped off. 2 *rpr* a quick change. *Omahé * sanalika dadi keḍaton.* In a flash his house was turned into a palace. **nge/di*i** to drop onto sth
djlegoḍah **n*** big, bulky, taking up lots of space
djlegong *pl form of* DJEGONG
djlégor the (edible) leaves of the sweet-potato plant
djlégrang ***-*** big and tall
djlegur *rpr* a splash (*var of* DJEGUR). *Montor mabur mak * tiba nang laut.* The plane plunged into the sea. **dj·um·legur** to splash
djlegut **n*** absorbed in an activity. *Wiwit mau ésuk ḍèké n* ndandani raḍio.* He's been working at repairing that radio all morning.
djlekèṭèk **n*** commonplace, prevalent
djlekèṭèt **n*** [of moustache, eyebrows] thick and heavy, curving upward
djleketut *ptg ** *or* **n*** wrinkled with age
djlekiṭat **n*** small and slim with pointed ends. *brengos n** a trim moustache
djlekiṭit *var of* DJLEKIṬAT
djlémbrak *ptg ** hanging down untidily [of hair, overlong clothing]
djlemp(r)ah *ptg ** a mess, in disorder
djlémprak *ptg ** scattered about untidily
djlèng *rpr* metal clanking. *Enḍas²ané sepur digaṭukké karo gerbong muni *.* The locomotive is being noisily coupled with the cars.
djlenggur *ptg ** to keep booming
djlenggut *var of* DJLEGUT
djlenṭar **n*** 1 pointing upward [of long objects]. 2 (running) fast
djlenṭir (*or* **n***) to stick up/out [of short objects]
djlèntrèh explanation, clarification. *Aku ndjaluk *é.* I asked him to explain it. **n/di*(aké)** to set forth, lay out. *Bakul mau n* daganganè nang pinggir dalan.* The seller spread her wares on the sidewalk. *Ḍèké n*aké lelakoné nang Djakarta.* He told me about what had happened to him in Djakarta.
djleprak *ptg ** *or* **n*** to point stiffly upward. *Dumadakan buntuté merak bandjur n**. Suddenly the peacock spread its tail.
djleprik *ptg ** *or* **n*** to point stiffly upward [of small objects]. *Manuk kuwi sirahé ana wuluné ptg *.* The bird's crest sticks up.
djlèrèt *var of* DJLARÈH
djlerit *pl form of* DJERIT
djlig *rpr* quick motion. *Jèn nunggang montor mak * waé wis tekan.* If you drive, you will get there in no time. **djlag-*** to move back and forth. *Ḍèké djlag-* mulih nang Magelang saka Jogja.* He makes frequent trips to his home in Magelang from Jogja.
djligut *ptg ** *or* **djligat-*** *pl* to hang around, mill around
djlimet **n*** intricate, detailed. *Wajang iki tatahané n* banget.* This puppet is intricately carved. *Pegawéné padjek anggoné mriksa pembukuané perusahaan nganti n*.* The tax officer went over the company accounts with a fine-tooth comb.
djlimprak *var of* DJLÉMPRAK
djling *intsfr* all gone. *Ketjapé sing nang gendul wis entèk *.* There's not a drop of soy sauce left in the bottle.

djlinggring **n*** [of clothing] short, showing the legs

djlirit **n*** forming a thin line. *Alisé n* nanggal sepisan.* Her eyebrows are slim like crescent moons. *Pasisiré pulo Madura katon lamat² n*.* You can just barely see the shoreline of Madura.

djliṭeng black, dark [of skin]

djliṭet *pl form of* DJIṬET

djlog *rpr* a sudden descent. *Mak * meḍun saka wit.* He came down the tree in a flash. **djlag-*** to keep going up and down. *Kréta iku jèn ditunggangi djlag-*.* You get jounced when you ride in a cart. *See also* ANDJLOG, ENDJLOG

djlomprong **ke*** to get lost; to be misinterpreted. **n*aké** 1 misleading. 2 (*psv* **di*aké**) to mislead, misdirect, misrepresent. *Aku di*aké kon tuku montoré sing mesiné wis bobrok.* He let me buy his car when he knew the engine was no good.

djlonèt (*or* **n***) good-looking, handsome

djlong ***-*** 1 *rpr* a metallic clang. 2 (*or* **djlang-***) (to walk) with long strides

djlonggrong ***-*** tall and well-built (of physique)

djludjur **n*** to glide sinuously

djlu:g *rpr* a thudding, *esp.* of footfalls

djlumat **n/di*(i)** to mend with fine stitching

djlumprit *ptg * pl* to cry out, shriek

djlungup **ke*** to fall forward, fall face down. **n/di*aké** to push smn from behind

djlupak a wick in a saucer serving as an impromptu coconut-oil lamp for a ritual-meal ceremony

djluwog *ptg ** riddled with holes. **ke*** to fall into a hole

djo green (*shf of* IDJO). *setopan bang-** traffic light

djoan meaning (*inf var of* IDJO·AN)

djobin *var of* DJUBIN

djoblos **n/di*** to stab, prick

djoḍang palanquin-like container for transporting foods to be distributed

djoḍèr disclosure. *gawé *é barisan* to reveal the whereabouts of troops. **ke*an** to get caught in the act; to be revealed/unveiled

djodjo a certain climbing vine. ***-*** itinerant peddler

djodjoh **ke*** to get stabbed. **n/di*** to pierce with a sharp object

djoḍo 1 one member of a mated pair. ** kang pinasṭi* predestined husband/wife. *Tjangkir iki dudu *né lèpèkan iki.* This cup doesn't match this saucer. 2 the union of a mated pair. ** iku dudu gawéaning manungsa.* Marriages are made in heaven. 3 well mated, the right match (for). *Aku * karo kowé.* You and I get along well. *Aku dudu *mu.* I'm not well suited to you. *Jèn ora olèh djamu sing *, mesṭi tiwas.* If he doesn't get the right medicine he'll die. ***n** *sms **. *nDuwèni keris ki *n, jèn ora keberan marakaké lara.* The kris you own should suit you: otherwise harm will befall you. **(dje)*an** married; act of marrying. *wong dje*an* married people. *wurungku dje*an karo kowé* my calling off of our marriage. *A dje*an karo B.* A is married to B. **n/di*kaké** to match [people]. *Djaman mbijèn jèn arep omah² mesṭi wong tuwa sing n*kaké.* In the old days, parents arranged their children's marriages. **n/di*ni** to mate [two things]. *Babon iki di*ni djago kaé.* I mated this hen with that rooster. **sa*** a (mated) pair. *dara se** a pair of doves. **dj·in·oḍo** married, mated. *durung djinoḍo* not married yet

djog 1 *rpr* an arrival. *Lagi teka * wis dikongkon menèh.* He no sooner got there than he was sent on another errand. 2 (to add) an additional amount. *Wédang tèh sing nang téko kuwi mengko dienggo * jèn ana sing ndjaluk tambah ngombé.* The tea in the pot is for seconds in case smn wants more. *Iliné kali iki * nang Kali Progo.* This stream flows into the Progo River. **ke*an** to get sth added to it; *fig* to be invaded *or* descended upon. *Wédang tèhku ke*an kopi.* Smn poured coffee in my tea. **nge*** to add. *nge* bènsin* to put in some (more) gas. **nge/di*i** to put (more) into sth. *Montoré arep di*i bènsiné.* He's going to have gas put in the car. *Aku kepeksa nge*i Rp 25 ḍisik.* I have to give them 25 rupiahs more. *See also* ANDJOG

djogan (*or* **ka***) floor

djogèd 1 (**beksa** *ki*) the classical Javanese dance (an art form accompanied by gamelan music). 2 *rg* woman street dancer. ***an** 1 (the performing of) a classical dance. 2 (*or* **dje*an**) to jump around. *Saking bungahé *an.* He danced with joy. **n*** 1 to perform a dance. 2 to hop around. 3 to enliven; to act lively. *Masakané énak banget nganti n* ilatku.* Her cooking is delicious–it's so flavorful.

djoglo steeply pitched top section of the roof of a traditional Javanese house
djoh *inf var of* ADJA[a]
djohar 1 a certain shade tree with tiny luxuriant leaves. **awal* first blooming of the above tree. 2 star. **rina* morning star
djok *inf var of* ADJA[a]. **nge/di*** 1 to prepare [tea] in a teapot. 2 to pour. *Tèhé diedjok.* She poured the tea. **nge/di*aké** 1 to pour for smn; to have smn pour. 2 to move sth forward (*inf var of* NG/DI·ADJU·KA-KÉ). **nge/di*i** to pour [sth] into. *Gelasé diejoki tèh.* She filled the glass with tea.
djoki race-horse jockey
djola **n*** to jump with surprise, give a start
djoli palanquin
djolok within reach, close by
djolor **n*** to sway, move sinuously
djomblah *var of* DJUMLAH
djomblong *var of* DOMBLONG
djombros **n*** unwashed, unkempt [of hair, moustache]
djombrot 1 having the remains of a meal unwiped from the mouth. 2 having business *or* financial troubles
djomplang **n*** to tip over. *Kwaliné n* isiné wutah kabèh.* The kettle turned over and spilled. *Prauné n*.* The canoe capsized.
djompo *var of* DJEMPO
djompong young teak leaf
djonḍang *var of* DJOḌANG
djonḍil *rpr* a jerk *or* jump. **n*** to jump, jerk. *Mak ḍor! aku kagèt nganti n*.* Bang! I nearly jumped out of my skin. **(n)*-*** *or* **n·djonḍal-*** to keep hopping up and down. **n*-n*** to kick up the heels. *Djaran olèhé mlaju ndjonḍil^2.* The horse ran with a sprightly gait.
djondjang ***an** (to walk) with a lopsided gait because the legs are of different lengths. **n*** to limp
djong *var of* DJUNG
djonggol **n*** lumpy(-looking)
djonggrang ***-*** *or* **n*** tall and lean
djonggring *var of* DJUNGGRING
djonggrok *cr* **n*** to sit (down)
djonggrong ***-*** tall and well-built (of physique)
djongkang **n*** to tip over. *Kwaliné n*.* The kettle overturned. **n/di*aké** to tip sth over
djongkèng **n/di*(aké)** to raise sth with a lever
djongkèt *var of* DJONGKÈNG
djongki *var of* DJOKI
djongkit **n·djongkat-*** to move in a series of up-and-down motions
djongkong soft cookie made with coconut milk
djongok **ke*** to fall forward. **n*** to lean forward, crane the neck to see. **n/di*aké** to push smn forward so that he falls
djongor 1 *cr* mouth. 2 *var of* DJONGOK. **n*** *cr* [of lips] thick and protruding
djongos 1 restaurant waiter. 2 houseboy, servant in a foreign household
djontong **n*** to long, yearn. *Atiné wis n* kepingin arep lunga nang Djakarta.* He longs to go to Djakarta.
djontrot a decoy. **n/di*** to capture by decoying
djor ***-*an** to vie with each other. *Wong wédok jèn njanḍang seneng *-*an.* Women try to outdo each other in dress. **ke*an** to be topped, outdone, one-upped. **nge/di*** to let smn have his own way. *nge* anak* to allow one's child to do as he pleases. **nge/di*aké** to outdo on smn's behalf. **nge/di*i** to top sth. *Sing nge*i toh^{2}ané sapa?* Who'll raise the bet?
djorog ***-*an** to keep pushing/shoving each other from behind. *Botjah^2 paḍa ḍisik^{2}an *-*an.* The boys kept trying to push ahead of each other.
djos 1 *rpr* hissing, sizzling. *Sepuré mlaku, *, *, *.* The train, puffing, began to move. 2 *rpr* a sharp weapon piercing flesh
djot *rpr* a start of surprise. **ke*** startled, taken aback
djoṭak ***an** on unfriendly terms. *Ḍaḍap karo Waru *an nganti telung sasi luwih.* A and B weren't speaking for over three months. **n/di*** to be on unfriendly terms with. *Aku wedi nèk kok *.* I'm afraid you'll be mad at me.
djoto **(me)n*** swollen; to swell up. *See also* RIJEK
djotos a punch. *djuru ** boxer, fighter. ***an** to exchange blows, have a fist fight. ***(-*)an** (the sport of) boxing. ***-*an** to punch each other. **n/di*(i)** to hit, punch. **en menèh.* Hit him again!
djowar *var sp of* DJOHAR
djrabang reddish (the color of a certain variety of cricket). *djangkrik ** reddish cricket. *rambut ** reddish hair. *See also* ABANG
djrak **nge*** to stay smw permanently; to settle. *See also* ANDJRAK

djrakah a variety of tree
djrambah 1 low wooden platform used as a seat. 2 floor
djrangkong skeleton. **(dje)*an** having a skeleton; having vertebrae
djranṭal *rpr* quick running. *Botjahé mak * marani mbokné.* The child ran to his mother. **n*** *or* **dj·um·ranṭal** to scurry
djras *rpr* cutting, slashing
djrawil *pl form of* DJAWIL
djrèdjès **n*** to well up (in the eyes); to water. *Eluhé n* terus.* Her eyes filled with tears. *Mripatku n*.* My eyes watered.
djreḍoḍok *var of* ḌROḌOG
djrèg 1 *rpr* the sound of metal against metal *or* wood against wood. *Lawangé montor diinep muni *.* He shut the car door. * *nong, * gung (sounds of gamelan instruments).* 2 *var of* DJÈG
djreg *var of* DJLEG
djrènḍol, djrenḍol *ptg ** full of lumps *or* swellings
djrèng *rpr* coins clinking. *mbajar ** to pay cash
djrèngkang *var of* DJENGKANG
djrengking *pl form of* DJENGKING
djrep *rpr* piercing, stabbing. *Disuduk nganggo keris mak *.* He was stabbed with a kris.
djrès *rpr* a match striking. **nge/di*aké** to strike a match
djrèt 1 *rpr* a whizzing sound. *Manuké dibeḍil mak *.* He shot the bird with an air rifle. 2 *rpr* the sounds of smn having diarrhea
djreṭut *pl form of* DJEṬUT
djrih *oj* fear
djrimet *var of* DJLIMET
djri:ng *var of* DJRÈNG
djriṭet *pl form of* DJIṬET
djro *var of* DJERO
djrodjog *var of* DRODJOG
djrodjos *var of* DRODJOS
djrog *rpr* a heavy thud. *Koperé tiba nang lemah, *.* The suitcase fell to the ground.
djromah 1 inside the house (*contracted from* (ING) DJERO OMAH). 2 (*or* ***an**) inner room of a house serving as the family quarters (as contrasted with the section in front, where guests are entertained)
djromblong *pl form of* DJOMBLONG
djrongkong *var of* DJENGKANG
djronṭol **n*** to run, scurry
djros 1 *rpr* chopping. *Wadungé diangkat, wer, ditibakaké, *.* He raised the axe and brought it down on the log. 2 *var of* DJRUS
djrot *rpr* a spurting sound
djru *inf var of* DJURU
djrug *var of* DJROG
djrumat *var of* DJLUMAT
djrundjung **ke*** to fall, plunge. *Montoré rèmé blong ke* nang sawah.* The brakes failed and the car plunged headlong into a rice paddy. **n/di*aké** to cause sth to plunge
djrungdjung *var of* DJRUNDJUNG
djrungup *var of* DJLUNGUP
djrunṭul **n*** to run, scamper. *mlaju n** to scurry. *Tikusé n* nang kamar ḍahar.* The mouse whisked into the dining room.
djrus *rpr* piercing, stabbing. **nge/di*** to stab, pierce
djrut *var of* DJROT
dju forward (march)! (*shf of* M·ADJU)
djubah tabard, cassock
djubel crowded, jammed
djubin 1 floor tile; tiled floor. 2 diamonds (playing-card suit). * *loro* the 2 of diamonds. ***an** 1 having a tiled floor. 2 forming a diagonal *or* diamond shape. *Anggoné nandur kekembangan *an.* He planted the flowers in a diagonal arrangement. **n/di*** to tile [a floor]. *** adu manis** *or* *** ḍam** tiles laid checkerboard fashion. *** selèk** tiles laid in bricklaying fashion
djubleg **n*** 1 steep, precipitous. 2 silent and motionless. 3 *see* SADJEG
djublus **n/di*** to stab, pierce
djubrija haughty, arrogant
djubur rectum
djuḍag deep ravine; canyon. **n/di*** 1 to push smn off a cliff; *fig* to bring harm to smn. 2 to evict; to ask smn to leave
djuḍas irresolute, easily led; treacherous
djuḍeg in a quandary. *Ḍèké * ngrasakké anaké sing ora gelem sekolah.* He can't handle his dropout son. *Saking * ing ati, aku bandjur lunga idjèn ngumbara menjang ndi².* I was at such a loss I went off by myself and just wandered. **ke*an** unable to cope. *Gawéné lingguh ḍeleg² ke*an anggoné arep njaur utangé.* He just sits, helpless to think of a way to pay what he owes.
djuḍir **n*** having an overhanging upper lip
djudju **n/di*** to have the mouth full of food. *Ḍèké kesusu anggoné mangkat njambut gawé, olèhé mangan di* waé.* He was in such a hurry to get to the office that he

just stuffed some food in his mouth and ran off.

djudjug ***an** 1 destination. **anmu endi?* Where are you headed for? 2 place frequently visited. *Jèn grebegan, omahku dadi *an tumrap sedulur²saka kuṭa lija.* At festival time all the out-of-town relatives come to our house. **n/di*** to go toward, head for. *bareng tekan enggon sing di** when he got to where he was going. **n/di*aké** to take smn smw. *Satekané kéné *na kantoran.* As soon as they get here, bring them to the office. **n/di*i** to go smw frequently. *Omahé sering di*i kantja².* People are always dropping in on him.

djudjul 1 too small for the purpose. *Tempat tiḍur iki jèn dienggo Susila mesṭi *.* This bed is too short for Susila. 2 change. *Aku ngekèki ḍuwit Rp 10, mesṭi olèh * Rp 2.50.* I gave you 10 rupiahs; I get 2.50 rupiahs' change. 3 (*prn* **djudju:l**) unable to stand. *Aku kok * weruh anakku pènèkan uwit.* I can't bear watching my son climb a tree. **ke*** to be overtaken. **n/di*** to (try to) overtake. *Aku n* Bapak djalaran ngomah ana tamu.* I ran after Father to tell him smn had come to the house to see him.

djudjur straight (not crooked); honest, direct. **ke*** always running into bad luck. **n*** (to go) straight across/through, to take a direct route by way of

djuḍul title. **(a)dje*** entitled

djug (*or* *** lap** *or* *** plentjing**) (to stop in) for a moment. *A mau mréné mung * lap ming ngandani jèn bodjoné wis nglairké bandjur lunga.* A dropped in briefly to say his wife had had her baby.

djuga solitary. **mung sa*** the only one

djugag 1 short(ened), abbreviated. 2 *wj* a song with shortened lyrics. **n/di*** to terminate, break off

djugang ***an** a hole dug in the ground. **n/di*i** to dig a hole (in)

djugar to fail to materialize. **n/di*aké** to call off, forestall, prevent

djugil iron crowbar; lever

djugrug to slide down, collapse. *Bètèngé dimrijem sanalika *.* The fort, bombarded by cannon, suddenly collapsed. ***an** (act of) earth sliding; earth that has slid. *Bata tumpukan kaé tilas *an bètèng sing *.* That pile of rubble is all that is left of the fort that collapsed. **ke*an** to get buried. *ke*an gunung kembang* to have a flood of good luck. **n/di*i** to bury under sliding earth. *Nalika bètèng *, lemahé n*i omah² kidulé.* When the fort collapsed, the earth buried the houses to the south of it.

djugug *var of* DJEGOG

djuk (*or* **n***) *var of* BANDJUR. **n*** *inf var of* N·DJALUK

djukuk *var of* DJUPUK

djulalat *var of* DJLALAT

djuleg **n*** sloping steeply

Djuli[a] July

djuli[b] **djula-*** hula-hula dance

djulig cunning, sly. **ka*an** shrewdness, cunning. *Kantjil kuwi ka*ané ora ana sing nandingi.* No one can ever outwit Mouse-Deer.

djuluk **dje*** [of royalty] named, called, having the title (of); nicknamed. **n/di*aké** to move sth upward. *Sarungé mlotrok bandjur di*aké.* His sarong was sliding down and he hiked it back up. **n/di*i** to name *or* nickname smn. *See also* PENDJULUK

djulung destined for unnatural death

djum **nge/di*aké** to put in order (for smn). *Kamaré B di*aké A.* A tidied B's room for him. *Sa-bisa² perkarané di*aké Pak Lurah baé.* Let's see if we can get the village head to resolve the conflict. **nge/di*(i)** to put in good order. *Dolanané di*i ibuné.* His mother put away his toys. *nge* rambut/kuku* to do one's hair/nails. *nge* pasulajan* to patch up a quarrel

djum- *see also under* DJ- (*Introduction, 3.1.7*)

Djumadilakir 6th month of the Moslem calendar

Djumadilawal 5th month of the Moslem calendar

Djumahat *var of* DJEMUWAH

djumantârâ *ltry* the sky; (up) in the air

Djum'at *var of* DJEMUWAH

djumblah *var of* DJUMLAH

djumbleg *see* SADJEG

djumbleng 1 buried toilet tank. 2 primitive toilet consisting of a hole over a buried tank

djumbuh 1 similar, along the same lines. *Penggawéanku * karo penggawéané A.* My work is the same sort of work as A's. *Pinguin iku akèh sing ulesé putih, mesṭiné supaja * karo warnané ès.* Penguins have a lot of white on them, so that they blend in with the color of the ice. 2 in the category [of]. *tembung kang aksara purwané * karo aksara irung* words whose initial letter is a nasal.

***an** similar to each other. **n/di*aké** to accord with. *rasa kang wis di*aké lan kahanan* feelings that are in line with the circumstances

djumbul **n*** to jerk, jump, give a start

djumeneng 1 to be elevated to the position of (*ki for* M·ADEG). ***** *ratu* to become king. 2 standing up (*ki for* ADEG); to stand up (*ki for* NG·ADEG). 3 as, in the capacity of (*ki for* DADI). ***an** (day of) ascension to a high position (*ki for* ADEG(2)AN). **n/di*aké** to elevate to the position of (*ki for* NGE/DI·DEG·AKÉ). *di*aké ratu* to be made king

djumerut[a] emerald

djumeru:t[b] dirty, messy, muddy

djumlah total, sum

djumleg *see* SADJEG

djumpalik *var of* DJEMPALIK

djumput 1 tweezers, small pincers. 2 *var of* DJIMPIT. **ora *** without pay; [to do] for nothing

djumrut[a] *var of* DJUMERUT[a]

djumru:t[b] *var of* DJUMERU:T[b]

djumuk *var of* DJUPUK

djumut *rg var of* DJUPUK. **ke*an** to grope one's way in the dark

Djumuwah *var of* DJEMUWAH

djun large earthenware water crock

djunḍil *var of* DJONḌIL

djundjang *see* ANḌA

djundjung ***an** a burden. ***-*an** lifting, raising. *Kursi iki *-*ané abot banget.* This chair is very heavy to lift. **n/di*** to lift, raise; *fig* to exalt. **n* asma(né...)** to praise the name (of), to speak (of) with esteem. **n* dradjat(é...)** to raise the rank *or* status (of). **n* punḍak** to shrug the shoulders

djung 1 land measure for rice paddies: 4 *bau*'s, or *ca.* 7 acres. 2 junk (Chinese boat)

djunggring selâkâ *wj* heaven; realm of the deities

djungkang **n/di*(aké)** to lift and tilt sth. *Dandangé *na siṭik, dak tjiḍukané banjuné.* Please tip the steaming pan–I want to ladle out the water.

djungkat *ng*, **serat** *kr*, **peṭat** *kr?*, *ki* comb. ***an** to comb one's hair. **n/di*i** to comb smn's hair. *** plengkung** curved comb for holding hair back when worn under a cloth headdress. *** suri** 1 decorative comb. 2 fine-tooth comb for removing lice. *** tjenṭing** comb with a curved rattail, for combing coiffures

djungkel **ke*** to fall head first. *Ḍèké tiba ke*.* He fell headlong. **n*** to turn upside down; to turn a somersault. **n/di*aké** to cause sth to turn over. *Tongé *na bèn garing.* Tip the barrel upside down so it'll dry out.

djungkir **djungkar-*** 1 to remain upside down; to keep turning upside down. 2 *cr* to pray, assuming the Moslem position kneeling with the upper part of the body prostrated on the ground. **n*** 1 upside down; bottom up. 2 to turn a somersault. **n* (m)balik** to turn a somersault. **n* walik** head over heels

djungkit **n*** to rise slightly. **n/di*aké** to raise sth a bit

djungkrah *var of* ḌUNGKRAH

djungkruk **n*** to sit with bowed head

djungkung **n*** to sit with head lowered

djungok *var of* DJONGOK

Djuni June (month)

djunṭit **n*** pointing upward [of short objects]

djupuk *ng*, **penḍet** *kr*, **punḍut** *ki* ***an** things picked up, taken, fetched. *Barang²é toko sing lagi kobong kuwi dadi *ané wong pirang².* The goods in the burned-out store were looted. ***-*an** to take (pick up) each other's things; to take *etc.* things one after the other. *Kabèh paḍa *-*an sepatuné kantjané.* Everybody is taking everyone else's shoes. **n/di*aké** to get/fetch for smn. *Kamasmu *na sanḍangan.* Go get your brother some clothes! **n/di*(i)** to (go) get, pick up, take (away). *n* watu* to pick up a stone. *Buku mau olèhmu n* saka ngendi?* Where'd you get that book? *n* lajang* to get (pick up) the mail. *Bukuné *en.* Go get (pick up, take) the book! *Pistul²ané dipunḍut ibu guru.* The teacher took away his toy gun. *Ngati-ati lo, botjah kuwi seneng n*.* Careful–that boy steals. *Ḍèké kepéngin n* baṭi sing rada akèh.* He wants to make a big profit. *n* bodjo* to marry. *n* ḍuwit ing bang* to withdraw money at the bank. *n* punggawa anjar* to take on a new employee. *Botjah² kuwi paḍa n*i barang² ing toko sing kobong kuwi.* Boys are looting the burned-out store. **pa·n*** act of getting *etc.* *Pan*é sing mangan seṭiṭik² murih adja kuwaregen.* Those who were eating took just a little of each so as not to overeat. *Pamenḍetipun karèt punika saking tlutuhipun wit karèt.* Rubber comes from rubber-tree sap.

djur[a] ***-*an** (that which is) crushed, melted, dissolved. **-*an bata* brick dust, brick powder. *Ketip palsu kuwi *-*an timbel.* That counterfeit dime is a lead alloy. **nge/di*(i)** to reduce to fragments; to melt, liquefy; to digest. *See also* ADJUR

djur[b] (*or* **n***) *inf var of* BANDJUR

djuragan businessman; owner of a business. ** baṭik geḍé* a large-scale dealer in batiks. *Saben dina tukang bétjak mau kudu pasok ḍuwit Rp 50 karo *é.* The pedicab driver has to pay the cab owner 50 rupiahs a day.

djurang ravine, gorge, canyon. **ke*-*** always having bad luck. **n/di*aké** to make trouble for smn, get smn in trouble

djuri *var sp of* JURI

djuring a section of durian fruit. *Pipiné kaja durèn sa*.* Her cheeks are beautifully shaped (*i.e.* like durian sections).

djurit war; battle. *See also* PRADJURIT

djurnal 1 bookkeeping ledger. 2 journal, periodical

djurnalis journalist

djurnalistik journalism

djuru person who performs a certain job. **-*né kliling nitipriksa bagéané ḍéwé*[2]. The officials make inspection rounds of their own sections. ** ngundjuki pamrajoga marang Présiḍèn* presidential advisor. ** paniti sastra* a specialist in the study of literature. *** (a)dang** person who cooks the rice. *** basa** interpreter; translator; **n/di*-basa·ni** to interpret; to translate. *** djalir** head of a house of prostitution. *** gambar** artist, painter. *** geḍong** administrator of the possessions of high officials. *** gusali** head blacksmith. *** kuntji** cemetery caretaker. *** ṅg·karang** writer, author. *** ladi** waiter; one who serves. *** lélang** auctioneer. *** ma(ng)sak** professional cook. *** muḍi** ship's helmsman. *** nudjum** soothsayer, fortune teller. *** pa·ṁ·pisah** referee, arbiter. *** pa·ṁ·prajoga** adviser, consultant. *** ṁ·priksa** inspector. *** raḍio** radio specialist; radio man. *** rawat** nurse. *** sabda** orator. *** sita** process server, bailiff. *** slamet** Saviour (Christian). *** susila** official in charge of dealing with prostitution. *** (ṅ)·tambang** ferry operator. *** terbang** airplane pilot. *** tik** typist. *** tjitra** clerk. *** ng·upakara** nurse. *** warta** reporter. *** witjara** announcer; spokesman

djurug **n/di*(i)** to fill sth in with earth; to level; to bury

djuruh sweet thick syrup or sauce, *usu.* made of coconut sugar

djurung **n/di*aké** *or* **n/di*i** to give one's consent to sth. **dj·um·urung** to agree (to sth). *See also* PANDJURUNG

djurus certain hand movements in the Javanese karate system (*pentjak*)

djurusan 1 academic department. 2 destination, direction. *sepur * Sala* the train for Solo

djus 1 a certain chapter in the Koran. 2 *rpr* bursting into flame. 3 *rpr* a sharp weapon piercing flesh. **djas-*** 1 not well behaved, ill-mannered. 2 in slipshod fashion

djustisi justice

djut 1 *rpr* a jerking stop. 2 *rpr* air flowing under pressure. *Bané dipompa *, *, *.* He pumped air into the tires. 3 (*or* **n***) *inf var of* BANDJUR

djutu **(me)n*** lumpy, swollen

djuwadah glutinous-rice snack (*var of* DJADAH)

djuwal **n/di*** to sell

djuwârâ, djuwārā best known, number one, champion. *tilas * ndonja* former world champion. **ka*** famed, renowned. **ka*an** championship. **n/di*kaké** to bring into prominence

djuwarèh **ka*an** to be inadvertently disclosed. **n*i** 1 boring to listen to. 2 (*psv* **di*i**) to reveal a secret

djuwâtâ *var of* DJAWATA

djuwawah **n*** widely opened. *suwèk n** having a large rip in it, badly torn

djuwawul *ptg ** *or* **n*** messy, unkempt

djuwawut barley. *** p·in·ara sapta** tiny, insignificant

djuwèh tired of saying the same thing over and over. **n/di*i** to keep after smn, keep saying the same thing. *Botjah kuwi kudu di*i dikon sinau.* That boy has to be nagged continually to study.

djuwet **ke*an** always fidgeting, continually fussing with one's clothes *or* hair

djuwèwèh *var of* DJUWAWAH

djuwèwèk having the lips drawn outward and downward (*var of* TJUWÈWÈK)

djuwing **n/di*-*** to mutilate, dismember. *Atiku rasané kaja di*-*.* I felt as if my heart were torn to shreds.

djuwis **n*** thin-lipped

djuwita *oj* girl, lady

djuwiwig thin, fine [of hair]

djuwiwis *var of* DJUWIWIG

djuwog *-* 1 full of holes. *Dalané wis *-*.* The street is riddled with potholes. 2 tangled, unkempt [of hair]. **ke*** to fall into a hole
djuwowog **n*** tangled, messy, unkempt
djuwowol *ptg * or* **n*** untidy, scattered, disarranged
djuwowos *var of* DJUWOWOG
djw- *see under* DJUW-
dladag **n*** swiftly flowing
dladjah **n/di*i** 1 to explore. 2 to wander aimlessly in [a place]
dladjig *ptg * or *-* pl* to move about restlessly, to fidget, lack repose. *-* *or* **dlodjag-*** *sg as above*
dlamak'an palm (of the hand); sole (of the foot)
dlamong **n*** 1 to speak thoughtlessly *or* irresponsibly. 2 *var of* N·DLEMOK
dlanggung street intersection. ** prapatan* crossroads
dlantjang paper (*kr for* DLUWANG)
dlarèh *ptg ** streaked with red, *e.g.* scraped skin
dlarung **ke*(-*)** to stray, wander. *Jèn ngomong sing perlu waé, adja ke*.* Stick to the point: don't get off the subject. **n*** to get (too) far from, to exceed the limits. **n/di*aké** to cause sth to get out of bounds
dlawèr **n*** 1 to hang down too far. *Koloré kétok n* metu.* The string of his underwear is showing. 2 to wander aimlessly. 3 *var of* N·DLÈWÈR
dlèdèk **n*** to flow slowly, ooze. *Laharé n* saka puntjaké gunung.* Lava oozed from the mountain peak.
dledjer *ptg * pl* sticking up/out in plain sight
dléja **n*** to allow one's thoughts to stray from the matter at hand
dléjor *-* *or* **dléjar-*** to walk unsteadily
dleleg **n*** to sit deep in thought
dlemèk *ptg * or *-** covered with spots (of dirt; of color)
dleming **n*** delirious, raving
dlemok spot, mark, blemish. ** mangsi* ink spot. *ptg ** covered with spots, spattered. ***an** *or* **n*** to have/make a spot *or* stain. **n/di*(i)** to spot/stain sth
dlemong *var of* DLEMOK
dlèngèr **n*** careless, inattentive
dlepak *var of* DJLUPAK
dlèrèd **sa*an** (at) a glance. *Sa*an rupané pada.* At first glance they look alike.
dlèrèng *-* marked with reddish streaks. **sa*an** (at) a glance. *Aku mau weruh montoré ning mung sa*an.* I only caught a brief glimpse of the car.
dlèsèr **n*** 1 (moving) at a low altitude. 2 to stray, not keep one's attention focused
dlèwèr *rpr* flowing. *Dridjiné kepèngès, getihé mak *.* He cut his finger and it bled a lot. ***an** to flow, ooze. *Getihé *an.* Blood trickled out. **ke*an** to get dripped on. **n*** to flow, drip. **n/di*i** to drip *or* ooze on(to). *Kringeté n* pipi.* The sweat dripped down his cheeks. **d·um·lèwèr** to flow, drip. *Eluhé dumlèwèr ing pipi.* Tears ran down her cheeks.
dlima pomegranate
dlinges **ke*** to get run over
dlingo (*or* ** benglé*) certain herbs brewed into folk medicines
dlodjor *var of* DLONDJOR. **n/di*aké** to stretch [the legs] out in front of one
dlodog **ke*en** too much, excessive. *Omongé ke*en.* He exaggerates everything. *Anggoné ngekèki kétjap mau ke*en.* She put in too much soy sauce. **n*** 1 to pour out. *Setrupé n* metu.* The syrup spilled. 2 having an informal, fun-loving temperament
dlohok **dlohak-*** to talk boorishly
dlolé *rpr* sth hanging down. *Lintah kabetot, *.* He pulled off the leech and it hung limp. **n*** to hang down
dlolèr **n*** to protrude outward/downward. *Gadjah kaé tlaléné pada n*.* The elephants' trunks hang way down.
dlolo **n*** [of eyes] wide open. *Mripaté nganti n*.* His eyes bugged out.
dlondèng **n*** tall and slender (of physique)
dlondjor **n*** [of long objects] to slide down. *Pringé pada n* medun.* The bamboo stalks came sliding down [off the truck]. **n/di*i** to slide [long objects] down
dlondong *cr* 1 child, offspring. 2 feces. **n*** to give birth
dlongop **dlongap-*** to keep gaping. *Mung dlongap-* ora bisa mangsuli.* He just gaped: he didn't know the answer. **n*** [of the mouth] to hang open
dlonjok **dlonjak-*** to behave in a crude unmannerly way
dlosor **n*** 1 to sprawl on the ground. *turu n** to flop down anywhere to sleep. *Bareng krungu bedil, wong² pada n* sak enggon².* When the people heard gunshots, they threw themselves to the ground wherever they

were. 2 to be too willing to do whatever people ask of one. *Olèhmu n* adja nemen²*. Don't let people walk all over you!

dludag flag-like emblem with a slim vertical shape. **n*** to overflow

dludjur 1 a straight path *or* track. 2 trunk, main stem. ** saka* a direct descendant of. ***an** a basted seam; (act of) basting. **n*** 1 straight. *pring sing n** a straight stalk of bamboo. *Montoré sing rèmé blong mau n* mlaku waé.* The car whose brakes failed kept straight on going. 2 *var of* N·DJLUDJUR. **n* m·bekengkeng** rigid, unyielding. **n/di*i** to baste [a seam]

dluja *var of* DLÉJA

dlundèng *var of* DLONDÈNG

dlupak *var of* DJLUPAK

dlurek̄ **n*** grim-faced, angry-looking

dlurung *var of* DLARUNG

dlusup **n*** to slip into concealment

dlusur *ptg ** swishing. *Swarané ula saba ptg *.* The snake swished along the ground. **n*** to slide along a surface

dluwang *ng,* **dlantjang** *kr* paper, *esp.* for wrapping. ** selembar* a sheet of paper. ** sa glunḍung* a roll of paper. *** djawa** paper of inferior quality. *** merang** rice-straw wrapping paper. *** plui** blotting paper. *** tulis·an** writing paper. *** tutul mangsi** blotting paper

ḍo 1 *oj* two. 2 first and eighth (*i.e.* tonic) notes of the musical scale

ḍobel double(d); duplicated. *mbajar ** to pay double. *Katja wolu iki *.* There are two page 8's here. **n/di*** 1 to double, duplicate. *aksara kang di** doubled letters. 2 to [do] twice as much. *Olèhé djadjan n*.* He took two cookies but only paid for one.

doblé *var of* DOBLÈH

ḍoblé gold plating

doblèh **n*** full and protruding [of the lower lip]

dobol *cr* 1 (to have/get) hemorrhoids. 2 to discharge flatus. 3 to defecate

dobos **n*** to boast, brag, tell tall tales

ḍoctoranḍa (*prn* ḍok...) (*abbr:* **Dra.**) female counterpart of ḌOCTORANḌUS

ḍoctoranḍus (*prn* ḍok...) (*abbr:* **Drs.**) academic degree (equivalent to a Master's degree) preceding candidacy for the doctoral degree; title of a (male) holder of this degree

ḍoḍèl ***-*** *or* **ḍoḍal-*** badly torn

ḍoḍèt *var of* ḌUḌÈT

ḍoḍog ***an** *wj* knocking sounds produced by the puppet master with a rapping instrument (*tjempala*) in various rhythms for various effects. **n/di*(i)** to knock on sth. *Omahmu mau tak *i kok ora ana sing mangsuli.* I knocked at your door but there was no answer.

dodok informer, stool pigeon

ḍoḍok **n*** to sit, squat, crouch. **n/di*aké** to have smn squat. **n/di*i** to sit/squat on. *** atjung²** to point out a house marked for burglarizing. *** érok** large green dragonfly. *** m̄·pungkur** to squat with the back toward an exalted person (a former practice of servants as the King passed by). *** sèlèh** the way things stand. *Diterangaké *-sèlèhé kahananku.* He explained about my situation. *Pikiran mau ndjalari gagasané ora karuwan * sèlèhé.* This thought put him in a very unusual frame of mind.

dodol *ng,* **sadé** *kr* 1 to sell. 2 *ng kr* a confection made of glutinous rice. ***an** 1 act *or* way of selling. *Toko geḍé kaé *ané pepak.* That big store sells everything. 2 to sell as a livelihood; to trade, sell merchandise. *** bokong** to accept pay for occupying smn's seat in order to hold it. *See also* ADOL, DOL

dodor **n/di*(aké)** to poke/prod (at), jab

ḍoḍos ***an** hole, depression. **n*** to make a hole in the ground. **n/di*i** to put a hole through sth. *Tikusé n*i lemari waḍah pangganan.* The mouse gnawed its way into the cookie cupboard.

dodot *ng kr,* **kampuh** *ki* ceremonial batik wraparound with a train. ***an** to put on *or* wear the above

ḍog 1 *rpr* a knock. *Ketua nuṭukké palu nang médja, *!* The chairman rapped the gavel on the table. 2 *rpr* a recent arrival. *Aku lagi baé teka *.* I just now got here. **ḍag-*** 1 irregular, bumpy. 2 *rpr* pounding sounds

ḍogdjer to start up instantly [of a car engine]

ḍogèr a street dance performed to music by one or more females

ḍoglèg ***-*** *rpr* the sound of metal wheels. *Sepur kluṭuk mau swarané *-*.* The slow train lumbered along.

ḍoglèng eccentric, queer

ḍoglig *var of* ḌAGLIG

ḍogling *var of* ḌOGLÈNG

ḍoglong queer, eccentric. ***-*** large and

angular, awkwardly built (of women's physique)

doh *ng,* **tebih** *kr* far-off. *lunga menjang paran* * to go to a distant place. ***é** distance (to smw). ***-*é** distance apart. *Jogja tekan Semarang iku *-*é kurang-luwih suwidak kilomèter.* It's about 60 kilometers from Jogja to Semarang. **nge*** to move far(ther) away from. **nge/di*aké** to keep sth at a distance. **nge/di*i** to keep at a distance (from). *Ḍèké di*i kantja² né.* Her classmates kept away from her. *Jèn tjeḍak di*i, jèn adoh ditjeḍaki.* If you're too close, move away; if you're too far off, move closer. *or (fig)* to keep in the background while keeping watch over smn. **sa*-*é** however far. *Sa*-*é Jogja-Sala isih adoh Jogja-Semarang.* Whatever the distance between Jogja and Solo, it's farther between Jogja and Semarang. **d·um·oh** *ng kr (ltry)* far-off. *wong dumoh (ltry)* a dull-witted person. *** kana * kéné** far from everything, remote. *** tjeḍak·é** the distance (to, between). *See also* ADOH

ḍohan *see* TAWON

doja (*or* **ke***) a variety of tree used as firewood

dojan *ng kr,* **kersa** *ki* to like, have a taste for, enjoy. *Aku lara, ora * mangan.* I'm sick, I have no appetite. ** main* to enjoy playing cards. ***an 1** favorite food. 2 one who will eat anything. **di*i** [food] liked. *sing n*i* food one likes. **n*i** to want smn sexually

dojani *ng,* **setani** *kr* **n/di*** to have an opinion *or* idea about. *Omah mau di* wis paju.* He thinks the house has been sold.

ḍojok a *wj* clown who wears a black mask (*see also* BANTJAK). ***-*** to stagger, have difficulty walking. **n*** to lean, list. *Omahé wis n* ngiwa.* The house leans to the left.

ḍojong 1 slanting. *Jèn * prajogi dipun tjagaki.* If it's leaning, you'd better prop it up. *tulisan ** italic type. 2 deviant, not standard. ** pikirané* to have peculiar ideas. *basa Djawa sing ** dialectal Javanese. **n*** to lean/slant (to). *Ḍèké n* memburi.* He leaned back.

ḍok 1 in, at, on [a place]. ** kana* there, at that place. ** (ng)endi?* where? 2 (*prn* **ḍok̄**) to be in, stay at (a place). *Olèhmu nge* ana ngendi?* Where are you staying? *See also* ANḌOK, ENḌOK

ḍokar two-wheeled horse-drawn cab

ḍokèr any tool used for scratching soil. **(n)*** *or* **(n)*-*** to scratch, claw at. ***-*** *nang lemah* to claw earth

ḍok̓kur to squat facing away from an exalted person (*shc from* ḌOḌOK M̈·PUNGKUR)

ḍoklonjo eau de cologne

ḍokoh 1 greedy; voracious. 2 resolute, diligent

dokok *var of* DÈKÈK

ḍokter (*abbr:* **Dr.**) medical doctor. ***an 1** hospital. 2 place where a doctor practices. 3 area where doctors live and/or practice. **n/di*aké** to take smn to a doctor. **n*an** *sms* *AN. *** ahli** specialist. ** ahli kulit* dermatologist. ** ahli djantung* cardiologist. *** gula** laboratory chemist in a sugar mill. *** kéwan** veterinarian. *** (lelara) djiwa** psychiatrist. *** umum** general practitioner

ḍoktor 1 academic doctor, Ph.D. 2 doctorate, Ph.D. degree

ḍoktrin doctrine, set of theories

ḍokumentasi 1 documentary film. 2 a file documenting a person

ḍokumèntèr documentary (film; photograph)

dol *ng* **sadé** *kr* **nge/di*** 1 to sell. 2 to lease a rice paddy on certain terms (*see under* ADOL). **di* (ngu)wong** to get cheated, be sold a bill of goods. **nge/di*aké** to sell for smn (as middleman). **nge/di*i** to sell sth; to sell to smn. **pa·nge*** trade, selling, merchandising. *Saiki pange* lan panukuning barang sing mubra-mubru ora gampang.* In these times it's not easy to deal in luxury items. **pa·nge*an** place where sth is sold. *** d·in·ol** to sell to each other. *** t·in·uku** to buy and sell, do business. *See also* ADOL, DODOL

ḍol worn out (*shf of* BOḌOL). *ban ** a worn-out tire

dolan (*or* ***-***) (**ameng²** *ki*) to engage in recreation. *kantja ** playmate. *Tindak ameng² ḍateng panggènan kula.* Drop in and see us! *Ajo *.–* menjang endi?* Let's go for a walk (ride, pleasure jaunt).–Where shall we go? *Jèn lara ora kena *-* karo botjah² lija.* When you're ill you can't play with other children. **(de)*an 1** to engage in recreation. **an lajangan* to fly kites. ** ḍomino (bal-balan, lsp.)* to play dominoes (soccer, *etc.*). *mBok rana *an karo kantjamu.* Why don't you run along with your friend! 2 game, pastime, source of amusement. **an tjatur* or ** sekak* a/the game of chess; chess set. *Ameng²ané gadjah* *putih.* Her playmate was a white elephant. **n/di*aké** (*var prn:* **n/di·dolak·aké**) 1 to give smn a good time. *A n*aké B menjang Sala.* A took B to Solo for a pleasure trip. 2 to give smn a plaything. *Ḍèké ora tau n*aké barang lanḍep.* She never gives him anything sharp to play with. **n/di*i** 1 to visit. 2 to amuse/divert smn. **d·um·olan** *ltry* to enjoy recreation. * **ula manḍi** to court danger, play with fire

ḍolar 1 dollar. 2 a variety of cookie sold in the marketplace

dom needle. **nge/di*i** to insert a needle/pin into. *di*i nganggo * bunḍel* fastened with a pin. * **bolong** sewing needle (with an eye). * **bunḍel** straight pin, common pin (with a head). **kaja * sumurup ing banju** stealthy; in secret; in disguise for the purpose of getting information. * **tjanṭèl** safety pin

domba a variety of large goat; *fig* large. **n/di*ni** 1 to keep an eye on. *Prajoga di*ni waé.* We'd better watch him. 2 to lead, be in charge of

dombang *see* ANGIN

domblé **n*** having a flabby protruding lower lip

domblèh *var of* DOMBLÉ

domblo (*or* **ke*** *or* **n***) chubby in the cheeks

domblong *ptg * pl* open-mouthed in wonder, confusion, surprise. **n*** *sg* as above

dombong *see* APEM

domèl **n*** to whine and complain

ḍominasi domination

ḍomino domino. *dolanan ** to play dominoes

ḍompèt wallet, purse

ḍompjok bunch, cluster. *rambutan sak ** a bunch of leechee nuts

ḍompjong *var of* ḌOMPJOK

ḍomplèng **n*** to join smn. *Mengko jèn kowé mulih aku n* montormu ja?* Can you give me a ride when you go home? *Nalika nang Djakarta aku n* omahé kantjaku.* I stayed with a friend of mine in Djakarta.

ḍompo having a poor sense of rhythm or timing, *esp.* for dancing

ḍompol cluster, bunch. *djambu sa** a bunch of guavas. **(ḍe)*an** (forming) a cluster/bunch. *Djambuné ḍe*an nèng uwit.* The guavas are in clusters on the tree. **n*** to form a cluster

ḍonḍang *var of* DJOḌANG

dondom ***an** sewing, needlework; suture. ***-*** to do needlework. **n/di*i** to stitch, sew

ḍonḍong (*or* **ke**) a variety of tree, also its edible fruits

ḍong 1 (to be) smn's turn. **mu.* It's your turn. **é sapa?* whose turn is it? *ketiban ** (*sms* KE*AN *below).* 2 time when [sth happens]; while [sth happens]. *jèn * aḍem* (at times) when it's cold. *Aku * ora ana ngomah.* I wasn't home at the time. *ing dinten *ipun damel* on the day of the celebration. 3 to understand. *Aku ora *.* I don't get it. *Wis *.* Now I get it. 4 *rpr* tapping, pounding. *Swarané paluné panḍéné * ḍèng * ḍèng.* The blacksmith's hammer went tap-tap, tap-tap. ***é** the fact is. **é diwènèhaké A, nanging klèru ditampa B.* It was really given to A, but B got it by mistake. ***-*an** by good luck; if one is in luck. **di*i** to be agreed with, supported *e.g.* in a proposal. **ke*an** 1 to get a turn; to have one's turn. 2 to be accused of sth. **nge*aké** 1 understandable. *Kelakuané kuwi ora nge*aké.* His behavior is incomprehensible. 2 (*psv* **di*aké**) to make understandable. *Aku lagi ngerti ḍoḍok sèlèhé bareng di*aké.* I understand the circumstances now that he's explained. **nge*i** on the point of [do]ing. *Nge*i wong² pada mangan, ḍèké teka.* We were about to eat when he came. *See also* ḌONG-ḌING

donga a prayer. *matja ** to recite a prayer. **né karepé apa?* What did he pray for? ***-d·in·onga** to pray for each other. **n(de)*** to pray; to recite from the Koran. **n/di*-kaké** to pray for sth. **n/di*ni** to bless sth; to ask God's blessing for sth. *Pak kaum n*ni slametané.* The religious official asked God to bless the ceremony. **pa·n*** prayer; act of praying. *Pan*ku.* My prayers go to you *(salutation of a letter).*

ḍongḍang *var of* DJOḌANG

ḍong-ḍing 1 the facts about sth. *Aku ora ngerti *é soal iki.* I don't know the first thing about this problem. 2 to matter. *Ora * kok nangis.* It doesn't matter–you don't need to cry! 3 vowel scheme of a classical verse form. **é tembang kinanṭi jaiku u, i, a, i, a, i.* The vowel scheme of a *kinanṭi* form is u, i, a, i, a, i.

dongèng story. *Kuwi ora temenan, mung * waé.* It didn't really happen, it's just a story. **(de)*an** (various kinds of) stories.

n* to tell a story. **n/di*aké** to tell a story (to). **n/di*i** to tell stories to. *** geḍog** story from the Pandji cycle. *** purwa** story from ancient Javanese mythology

ḍonggl èng *rpr* metal clanging

ḍongkal uprooted, fallen. * *rubuh* or * *rungkat* or * *sol* to have fallen and come out by the roots

ḍongkèl **n/di*** to pry up/out, to uproot; *fig* to oust. **n/di*-*** to make an effort to uproot *or* oust. *A di*-* karo anḍahané.* A's subordinates tried to oust him.

ḍongker *var of* ḌUNGKAR

ḍongklak *var of* ḌUNGKLAK

ḍongklèh broken off, cast down

ḍongkloh ***-*** nearly severed

ḍongkol (*or* ***an**) (having) retired, resigned. *kepala ** the retired boss. **n*** resigned, *e.g.* to the inevitable

ḍongkrah *var of* ḌONGKRAK. **n/di*i** to pry sth out

ḍongkrak jack (lifting tool). **n/di*** to jack sth up

ḍongkrok **n*** to sit idle. *Se-dina²né mung n* ora gelem njambut gawé.* He just sits around all day, he won't work. *Montorku wis mèh telung sasi n* nang garasi.* My [broken-down] car has been sitting in the garage for nearly three months.

ḍongkrong *var of* ḌONGKROK

ḍongok *var of* DJONGOK

dongong **n*** to stare open-mouthed

donja world, earth. *politik ** world politics. *Perang N* Kaping Loro* World War II. *Lakuné ing * iki kudu tulung-tinulung.* We must help each other in this world. **ka*n** worldly goods. *amal ka*n* goods given as charitable donations. *** karun** hidden (buried) treasure

doortrap *see* PIT

ḍop 1 a certain style of hat. 2 wheel cover, hub cap

ḍoprok **n*** to plop down anywhere from exhaustion

ḍor bang! boom!

dora (to tell) a lie (*opt? kr for* GOROH). *** sembada** *or* *** tjara** a cover-up lie

doran handle of a certain agricultural tool (*patjul*)

ḍorèng (*or* ***-***) streaked, spotted. *Tentarané nganggo klambi *-*.* The soldiers wore camouflaged clothing. **n/di*-*** to spot, streak

dos *kr* *shf of* DADOS, KADOS

dosa sin(ful), guilt(y). *ngakoni ** to acknowledge one's faults. *wong ora ** a person without sin. *Adja takon *.* Don't try to deny your guilt! **pi*** *oj* sin(ful), guilt(y)

ḍosèn university faculty member

ḍosin dozen

ḍosok **n/di*** to push (against) sth. **n/di*aké** to push sth in a certain direction. *Koperé kuwi *na mréné.* Push the trunk over here!

ḍot 1 nipple; pacifier. 2 beep! honk! **nge/di*** 1 to give [a baby] a nipple *or* pacifier. 2 to honk (at)

ḍoṭong **di*-*** to be transported by hand by many people together

dowa *var of* DONGA

ḍowah ***-*** 1 opened widely. *Djariké suwèk *-*.* His batik has a big tear in it. 2 to open, pull apart the edges of

ḍowak *var of* ḌOWAH

ḍowal ***-*** badly torn. *See also* ḌÈḌÈL

ḍowèl *var of* ḌOWAL

dowèr **n*** full, prominent [of lower lip]

D.P.R. *see* DÉWAN

Dr. *see* ḌOKTER

Dra. *see* ḌOKTERANḌA

drad round-headed screw; threads matching such a screw. **nge/di*(i)** to screw sth into a threaded hole

ḍraḍil *ptg ** in shreds, ripped to pieces

dradjad 1 status, position. *Saiki *é putri Djawa wis munggah.* The status of Javanese women has risen. *njudakaké *ing pradja* to lower the nation's prestige. 2 degree of temperature. *wolu-likur * Celcius* 28 degrees Centigrade. **ka*an** to be raised, elevated. *wong sing kepéngin ke*an* smn who wants to better himself

dradjag (*or* ***an** *or* ***-***) to behave impolitely, *esp.* to enter smn's house without first announcing one's presence

drah a certain grass with fine leaves

ḍrakalan in great haste

drânâ *oj* patient, calm, strong

ḍranḍang **n*** *intsfr* bright, clear, hot. *paḍang n** very bright/light. *panas n** intensely hot (of noonday sun). *See also* SA·AWAN

drawalan excited, agitated

drawas **ke*an** to have a misfortune *or* accident. **n*i** dangerous, harmful

ḍrawul *pl form of* ḌAWUL

dre-, ḍre- *see also under* DER-, ḌER- (*Introduction, 2.9.6*)

drèdès *var of* DJRÈDJÈS

ḍreḍet *-* *or* **ḍreḍat-*** to keep moving jerkily. **n*** to move with a jerk
drèdjès *var of* DJRÈDJÈS
drèg two-wheeled horse-drawn cart. ***-*an** to behave boisterously
dreg *inf var of* UDREG
drèi screwdriver
ḍrèkèl ***an** *or* ***-*** to have a hard time climbing sth
drèl military salute, salvo. **nge/di*(i) 1** to fire a salute (for). 2 to fire many shots (at); *fig* to fire questions at
dremba greedy
dremolen *var of* DRIMOLEN
ḍrenḍeng, ḍrènḍèng **n*** thundering of drums
dreng *var of* DERENG
ḍrèng *rpr* drumbeats (of an Occidental-style drum). *Tamburé diunèkaké, *, *, *.* The drums went rat-a-tat!
drengki to wish smn ill, bear a grudge
ḍrèngkol *ptg ** drooping, bending downward [of tree branches]
drereg *ptg * pl* to press, shove, jostle
dresel **n*** 1 to sneak into. 2 to push one's way in near the front of a line
drèwès **n*** to drip, flow. *Eluhku n*.* I cried.
ḍriḍil *var of* ḌRINḌIL
dridji *ng kr,* **ratjik·an** *ki* finger; toe. ***ǹ** finger-like. * **manis** ring finger, fourth finger. * **sikil** toe. * **siwil** a sixth finger/toe growing from an outer finger/toe. * **tangan** finger
drig ***-*an 1** printed matter. 2 to behave boisterously. **nge/di*** to print [books *etc.*]. **nge/di*aké** to have sth printed; to have smn print
drija *ltry* heart, feelings
drijah charitable gift. **n/di*aké** to donate sth. **n/di*i** to give charity to. **sa*** donation, contribution
dril drill (heavy cotton fabric)
drimolen ferris wheel
ḍrinḍil **n*** to pour forth; to talk continuously
dringo *var of* DLINGO
drodjog ***-* 1** to show up unexpectedly. 2 to pour forth copiously. **n* 1** steep(ly pitched). 2 *sms* ***-*.** **d·um·rodjog** to show up unexpectedly
drodjos ***an** *or* **n*** to pour forth, flow continuously
ḍroḍog **n*** to tremble, shiver
drodos *var of* DRODJOS
drohun *wj* *swear word; term of abuse*
drom ***-*an** (in the form of) a noisy mob
dromblong *pl form of* DOMBLONG
drondjong ***an** *or* **n*** steep(ly sloping)
ḍronḍong *rpr* a hollow tapping. **ing kenṭong* the sounding of the alarm
drop **nge/di*** to deliver [supplies, reinforcements] to where they are desperately needed. **nge/di*i** to supply [a place] with sth essential. *Daérah² sing minus di*i beras.* Rice was rushed to the areas where there were shortages.
Drs. *see* ḌOCTORANḌUS
drubija bad, wicked. *watak ** evil character
drubiksa *ltry* an evil forest ogre
ḍruḍul **n*** to pour forth. *Sing paḍa metu saka bioskupan isih n* ngono kok.* The moviegoers swarmed out of the theater.
ḍruḍus ***an** *or* **n*** to push one's way through an overgrown area
drug **nge/di*(-*)aké** to stamp [the foot]
drum drum, metal barrel
ḍrusul *var of* DRESEL
du *ng,* **ben** *kr* **nge/di*** to pit [opposing forces] against each other. **pa*-*n̂** to argue. *wong sing ḍemen padudon* one who is always quarreling. *See also* ADU
duane customs office; customs official
dubang saliva reddened by chewing betel (*shc from* IDU ABANG)
dubilah *excl of surprise: inf var of* (NG)·UDUBIL(L)AH(I)
dublag **n/di*** to force-feed
ḍublé *var of* ḌOBLÉ
dubur *var of* DJUBUR
ḍuḍa man left without a wife. * **bantat** childless widower. * **botjah** young man whose fiancée has died. * **kawuk** elderly widower *or* divorcé. * **kembang** young widower *or* divorcé. * **mati** widower. * **urip** divorced man
ḍuḍah ***an** opened up and/or taken out. ***-*** to keep opening things *or* removing the contents of things. **n/di*** to open sth with the intention of removing the contents; to remove, withdraw. *Klambiné di*.* He unpacked his clothing. *Tjèlènganku arep tak *.* I'm going to open my piggy bank. *or* I'm going to withdraw my savings. **pa·n*** (action of) opening/removing
ḍuḍat *var of* ḌUḌÈT
ḍuḍèt **n/di*** to tear sth open and remove its insides

duding *var of* TUDING
dudu *ng,* **sanès** *kr* 1 not (*in equative predicates: cf.* ORA); sth other than. *Iki * pitku.* This is not my bicycle. 2 no (*as an equative reply*). *Iki apa pitmu?—*.* Is this your bicycle?—No, it's not. 3 ...or (is it) not? *Kaé matjan (apa) dudu?* Is that a tiger (or isn't it)? ***n̂** *ng kr* wrong, improper. *Kuwi djeneng dudon jèn mung dirusuhi aḍiné bandjur nabok.* You mustn't hit your brother just because he's annoying you. **ke*n̂** *ng kr* to make a mistake, be wrong. **ke*-*** *ng kr* incredible, extraordinary. *Ambané Samodra Pasifik ke*-* jèn dibanḍing karo Samodra Atlantik.* The Pacific Ocean is far vaster than the Atlantic. *** lan ati·né** not to one's liking. *** rasa** unfeeling, inhumane. *** wong** extraordinary, incredible
duduh 1 juice, sap. ** tapé* fermented cassava juice. 2 sauce, gravy. ** pitik* chicken broth. ** djangan* broth in which vegetables and meat have been cooked. 3 *var of* TUDUH
duduk **n/di*** to push/prod with a stick, *e.g.* to knock fruits from a tree
ḍuḍuk place, position. *Nang ḍasbor ampèr mèter digawèkké *.* He made a place on the dashboard for the ammeter. ***an** 1 act of digging. **anku wis sapengadeg djeroné.* I've dug as deep as a man's height. 2 a dug hole. ***-*** to dig aimlessly. **ke*an** status, circumstances. *Apa ke*ané ranḍa ing sadjroning warisan?* How do things stand with the widow in regard to the inheritance? **n*** 1 to reach [a destination]. 2 (*psv* **di***) to dig (up, out, *etc.*). *n* djugangan* to dig a hole. **n* apus ka·penḍem** to dig into the forgotten past. **n* prakara** to rake up a past matter. *Adja pisan n* prakara asalé.* Don't inquire into his origin. **n/di*i** 1 to occupy. 2 to dig sth up/out. *Ojodé di*i.* He dug up the roots. **pa·n*** 1 act of digging. *Pan*é wis rampung.* He's finished the digging. 2 people, populace; population. **pa·n*an** occupation by military forces. **wis * bodjo** legally married
dudul **n/di*** to push sth into *or* out of. *Gabusé di* mlebu nang gendul.* He pushed the cork into the bottle.
dudut ***an** a pull, tug; that which is pulled. **ke*** to get pulled/yanked. **n/di*(i)** 1 to pull, jerk. *Jèn taliné di*, memedèné bisa manṭuk²*. When you tug on the rope, the scarecrow nods his head. 2 to attract, appeal to. **n*i** growing into adulthood
ḍuèl (to fight) a two-man fight. *Lakoné entèk²ané * karo banḍité nganggo pistul.* In the end, the hero and the bad guy shot it out.
ḍug *rpr* knocking. **ḍag-*** *rpr* knockings, poundings. **nge/di*aké** to knock sth [against sth]. *Sepatuné di*aké nang kèsèd.* He banged his shoes on the mat. *See also* ḌAG-ḌIG-ḌUG
duga *ng,* **dugi** *kr* (*or* ***-*** *or* **de***) judgment, common sense. *ora duwé ** or *ora weruh ** to act impulsively/recklessly. **ke*** 1 capable of [do]ing. *Wong nalika iku ora ke* nggawèkaké kreteg.* People in those days didn't know how to build bridges. 2 to condone, regard as acceptable. **n*-*** to exercise judgment, use one's brains. **pa·n*** assumption, guess. *pan* sing ora ḍedasar kanjatan* assumptions not founded on fact. *** (lan) wetara** common sense. *** pandjenengan** whatever you wish to give/allow; it's up to you. *** prajoga** good judgment. *** r·um·eksa** to look after smn
ḍugal bloating of the stomach. **n*** morally bad, low
dugang ***an** 1 act of kicking (from a sitting position) with the bottom of the heel. 2 thing kicked. **n/di*(i)** to kick (as above)
ḍugḍag *var of* ḌUGḌÈNG
ḍugḍèng magically invulnerable
ḍugḍèr a certain folk festival
dugi 1 judgment, common sense (*kr for* DUGA). 2 (*or* **d·um·ugi**) (up) to, as far as (*kr for* TEKA·N, *rg kr for* TUTUG)
duging small locust (young of the WALANG)
ḍuh *var of* AḌUH
ḍuhur *oj* high-ranking
ḍujung mermaid
duk 1 sugar-palm-tree fiber. *tali ** rope of such fibers. 2 past; when (*ltry var of* ḌÈK). *** ing ng·uni**[b] *ltry* once upon a time. *** sanḍing geni** providing an opportunity for immoral behavior, conducive to wrongdoing
ḍuk to descend (*root form: var of* ḌUN)
duka 1 to be(come) angry (*ki for* MURING, NESU, SRENGEN). 2 passionately angry; lustful (*ki for* NEPSU). 3 to speak angrily (*ki for* M·UNI²). 4 I don't know (*oblique kr?, ki for* EMBUH). *Njuwun *.* (Forgive me,) I don't know. *** jajah s·in·ipi** *oj* furious
dukâtji(p)tâ *oj* grieving, sorrowful
ḍukir **n/di*i** to dig (around in)

duksina *oj* south
ḍuku a certain small round yellowish fruit
ḍukuh *ng,* **ḍekah** *sbst? kr* (*or* **pa*an**) small village under the administration of a different village
ḍukun faith healer; black-magic practitioner. **me(r)*** to undergo treatment by a faith healer. **n/di*aké** to have smn treated by the above. **n/di*i** to deliver [a baby]. **pa*an** medical knowledge. *** baji** village midwife. *** bijasa** general (non-specializing) faith healer. *** djampi** healer who uses herbs and folk medicines. *** djapa** healer who uses incantations. *** patah** chiropractor. *** pétung·an** specialist in astrological reckonings. *** pidjet** masseur. *** préwang-an** female medium. *** sihir** sorcerer. *** si-wir** one who specializes in preventing misfortune. *** sunat** man who performs circumcisions. *** susuk** healers who inserts needles by magic to endow certain qualities, *e.g.* invulnerability. *** (te)mantèn** person who oversees marriage procedures. *** tiba·n** healer whose powers result from being possessed by a spirit. *** tjalak** man who performs circumcisions. *** wiwit** specialist who presides over harvest-initiating rites
ḍul 1 boom! 2 the time (at sunset, 6 P.M.) when people who have fasted during the day are permitted to eat again: signaled by an exploding firecracker. 3 (*prn* **ḍu:l**) *word called out when catching smn in a children's game.* ** Pardi!* One-two-three on Pardi!
dulang **n/di*** to spoon-feed smn
ḍulang round wooden tray
duleg **n*** **1** overpowering [of tastes, odors]. *Leginé n* banget.* It's cloyingly sweet. *Wanginé n*.* The perfume is too strong. 2 (*psv* **di***) to insert a finger into [an opening; sth soft]. *Mripaté A di* karo B rikala gelut.* B stuck his finger in A's eye while they were fighting.
dulit amount taken on the fingertip. *endjet sa** a fingertipful of slaked lime. **n/di*** to take on the fingertip
Dulkadji 12th month of the Moslem calendar
Dulka(ng)idah 11th month of the Moslem calendar
Dulkidjah *var of* DULKADJI
dulu *ltry* **ka*** to be seen; to appear. **n/di*** to look at, see. *kang paḍa n** those who saw it; the spectators. **pa·n*** sight; view. **sa·pa·n*ṅ** (at) a brief glimpse. *Sapandulon rada mèmper masku.* At first glance he looks like my brother.
dulur *ng,* **ḍèrèk** *kr* relative of the same generation. *See also* NAK, SEDULUR
dum ***-*an** portion; (one's) share. *Seka kantor mau aku éntuk *-*an beras.* I got my rice ration from the office. **ka*an** to be apportioned; to receive (as) one's share. **nge/di*** to apportion, distribute. *Olèhmu nge* sing rata.* Divide it evenly! **en karo jumu.* Share them with your sister. **nge/di*-aké** to distribute, hand out. **nge/di*i** to distribute [to, among]. *Murid² anjar paḍa diedumi sabak karo grip.* The new students were given slates and slate pencils. *nge*-*i buku* to hand out the books. **pa·n*** 1 (one's) share. 2 one's lot in life. *See also* ANDUM, PANDUM
dum-, ḍum- *see also under* D-, Ḍ- (*Introduction, 3.1.7*)
dumèh *var of* DUPÈH
dumel **ke*an** to grumble with dissatisfaction within the hearing of the offender
dumil, ḍumil **sa*** a tiny bit, very few
ḍumpjuk the same, indistinguishable. *Keprijé kok * gadjah kabèh!* We all got elephants (in the playing-card deal)! *Warna loro mau kétok * ora bisa kontras.* The two colors look the same–they don't contrast.
dumugi (up) to, as far as, until (*kr for* TEKA·N, TUTUG); to the end (*kr for* TUTUG). **ka*ṅ** to be brought to pass (*kr for* KE·TE-KA·N). **n/dipun*ṅaken** to accomplish, bring about (*kr for* N/DI·TEKA·KAKÉ). **n/dipun*ṅi** to bring about (*kr for* N/DI·TEKA·NI). *See also* DUGI
dumuk a mark *or* touch of the finger. *kena ing ** to have an accusing finger pointed at one. *tjap ** thumbprint (in lieu of signature for an illiterate). **n/di*** to touch with the finger(s). **n* irung** **1** very close to, almost on top of. 2 *intsfr* dark. *Petengé n* irung.* It was pitch dark. *Wengi kuwi n* irung.* The night was dark. **sa* baṭuk sa·njari bumi** willing to lay down one's life for a woman *or* piece of land
dumung a certain black snake
ḍun *ng,* **ḍak** *kr* ***an** a delivery, an unloading. *rong *an* two loads. *Sa*an pirang mbago berasé?* How many bags of rice per load? ***-*an** **1** things unloaded. 2 unloading place. 3 a way down (other than stairs). **ke*an** (**k·anḍap·an** *kr*) to be

affected by the descent of sth. *Bakulé rugi akèh banget sebab ke*an rega.* The market sellers suffered large losses with the drop in prices. **me*** **(m·anḍap** *alternate kr;* **t[um]eḍak** *ki*) to descend; to get off. *Dalané munggah meḍun.* The road went up and down. *me* saka pit* to get off a bicycle. *Reregané wis me*.* Prices have dropped. *Kapalé mabur me* ana ing Djakarta.* The plane landed at Djakarta. *me*é gendéra* flag-lowering. *Aku mau ésuk tangi djam pitu nanging olèhku me* saka peturon djam wolu.* I woke up at 7 this morning but didn't get out of bed till 8. **me* lemah** ceremony in which a baby first touches the ground (*see also* TEḌAK). **nge/di*aké (ng/dipun·anḍap·aken** *kr*) to lower, cause to descend; to help smn descend. *nge*aké pangkat punggawa* to demote an employee. *Koperé di*aké saka sepur.* The trunks were unloaded from the train. *Kutjingé di*aké saka wit.* He got the cat down from the tree. *Bajinipun dipun anḍapaken ing ḍaratan.* The baby was placed on the ground [as part of the ceremony]. **nge/di*i (ng/dipun·anḍap·i** *alternate kr*) **1** to descend from, get off of. 2 to undercut. *Supaja dodolané énggal paju, ḍèké nge*i rega pasar.* To sell his goods fast, he priced them lower than the market price.

ḍung **1** *rpr* a rhythmic sound, *e.g.* of tapping on hollow wood; of syllables chanted to accompany a rhythmic action. ** nong * nong* *rpr* the sound of gamelan instruments. 2 *rpr* an explosion. *Mrijemé diunèkké *!* The cannon boomed. **3** *rg var of* DURUNG

dunga *var of* DONGA

dungkap **n*** nearing, approaching. *Anakku wis rolas tahun n* telulas.* My child is 12 going on 13. *Djam wis mèh n* tekané Djana.* It's almost time for Djono to get here. *Ibuné wis rada n* aturé anaké.* The mother understood what the child was trying to convey. **sa*an** only a short while remaining. *Tempuking gawé isih kurang se*an menèh.* The date of the ceremony is drawing very near.

ḍungkar **n/di*(i)** to dig down to the roots (of)

ḍungkir *var of* ḌUNGKAR

ḍungklak stump, *esp.* of a cut bamboo stalk

ḍungkluk **n*** to bow the head; to look downward

ḍungkrah **n/di*i** to pull out and scatter. *n*i tela* to scatter soil while digging down into furrows; to dig up furrowed soil and scatter it. *Jèn ndjupuk lajang*[2] *saka latji adja di*i.* If you take the letters out of the drawer, don't disarrange them.

ḍungkruk **n*** stooping; with bowed head and shoulders

ḍungkul [of kerbau horns] curving low and downward to the rear (rather than upward, as usual). *kebo ** a kerbau with such horns

ḍungsak **ke*an** to experience great difficulties. *Merga mlarat uripé ke*an.* He's poor, and life is an uphill struggle for him. **n*** to make/push one's way through sth

ḍungsal **n*** to stumble

ḍungsang *var of* ḌUNGSAK

ḍungsir **n/di*i** to dig, root around in [soil]

ḍunuk *term applied as a nickname to a chubby girl.* ***-*** bent, *esp.* with age. **ḍunak-*** unable to see clearly (because of poor vision *or* poor light)

dunung **1** location, where sth is. *Omahku *é ing satjeḍaké segara.* My home is near the ocean. *Sapa sing weruh ngendi *é ḍokter?* Who knows where I can find a doctor? 2 the facts of the matter. *Aku durung ngerti *é iku.* I don't know anything about it. **de*** **1** located, situated. 2 to reside smw. **ke*an** to be the repository of [an emotion, trait, *etc.*]. *Ḍèwèké ke*an sih marang aku.* He is filled with love for me. *Ḍasar pinter, ke*an kesugihan sisan.* He's smart, and rich too. **n/di*aké** **1** to put sth smw. *Para tamu di*aké ing pesanggrahan.* The guests were placed in the guest house. 2 to explain, describe. **n/di*i** to live smw. *Pulo mau ora di*i ing wong.* The island is uninhabited. **pa*an** place where sth is/belongs. *Ing désa kaé dadi papan pe*anku.* That village became my home. *asal pa*ané* one's place of origin. **pa*an peteng** section *or* area where illicit activities take place, *e.g.* gambling, prostitution. **d·um·unung** situated; in, at. *Kamaré klas dumunung sakiwatengené gupitan.* The classrooms are placed on either side of the narrow hall. *désa sing dumunung ing putjuking gunung* a village at the top of a mountain. **durung (n)*** *or* **ora (n)*** to not understand/agree. *Aku kang dianḍaraké isih durung n* kanggoné aku.* I still don't understand (*or* agree with) what he's saying

dupa incense. *ngobong ** to burn incense. **n/di*ni** to burn incense for sth/smn

dupak earthenware lamp
ḍupak ***an** 1 a kick with the bottom of the heel. 2 object kicked. **n/di*(i)** to kick (*esp.* from a sitting position) with the bottom of the heel
dupârâ *see* WAJANG[a]
dupèh just because [of sth irrelevant]. *Djaran sing nomer telu didjagoi * geḍé.* He bet on the third horse just because it was big. ** anaké wong sugih ḍèké umuk banget.* He brags a lot just because he's a rich man's son. ***né** *rg var of *.* ***-*** to consider oneself superior because of a superficial asset. *** apa?** why on earth...?
dupi *ltry* when [sth happened]
ḍuplikat a copy, duplicate
dur *ltry* bad, evil
ḍur 1 continuing, going on through. *sepur ** a through *or* non-stop train. 2 (*prn* ḍu:r) *rpr* a heavy explosion. **ḍar-*** *rpr* repeated explosions. **nge*** to continue on through. *Anggoné main kertu wingi wiwit soré nge* tekan ésuk.* He played cards all night long, from yesterday afternoon to this morning.
durâkâ a sinful *or* treasonable act. *laku ** to sin; to commit treason. **ka*n** sin; treason
duratmâ(kâ) 1 *oj, wj* abductor. 2 thief (*ki for* MALING*?*)
durbiksa *oj* ogre, demon
durdah shoo! scat!
durdjânâ one who commits immoral *or* illicit acts
durèn durian (tree, fruit). ** sa djuring* a durian-fruit section. **n*** resembling a durian fruit. *pipiné n* sadjuring* having beautifully shaped cheeks
durgâmâ *oj* a hazardous *or* difficult circumstance placed deliberately in smn's way
ḍurlop *var of* ḌURLUP
ḍurlup long passageway connecting the main part of a house with the annex
durma a certain classical verse form
durmâlâ *oj* evil-doer, evil genius
dursila *oj* widely reputed as an evil character
durung *ng,* **dèrèng** *kr* 1 not yet. ** mangsané.* It's not time for it yet. *Ḍèké isih * marem.* He still wasn't satisfied. *Lakuné * suwé kepranggul kantjané.* He hadn't been walking long before he met a friend. *Kabèh wis teka, mung kari Slamet sing *.* Everyone is here now except Slamet. *Garapanku * tak garap.* I haven't done my homework. *wong² sing umuré * wolulas taun* people under eighteen. 2 no (*answering a question containing* wis *or* durung). *Apa * mangan?–*.* Haven't you eaten?–No. *Wis teka apa *?–*.* Is he here yet?–No. 3 not to mention... *Mengkono tlitiné wong ngupakara tanduran mbako, * pandjagané murih ora karusak ing ama.* That's how carefully they raise tobacco plants–to say nothing of how they protect them from pests. ***-*** not very long yet. **-* wis tjuṭel lakoné.* His life ended almost before it began. *Gawé siwur mbok sing kukuh, *-* wis poṭèl.* Why don't you make a stronger ladle–this (recently made) one is broken already. **sa* lan sa·uwis·é** in advance. *Wusana sa* lan sauwisé bakal paringmu wangsulan, aku matur nuwun.* Let me close by thanking you in advance for your reply to this letter. **sa*é** before. *sa*é mangkat* before we leave. *sa*é Slamet teka* before Slamet gets here. **jèn *** if not (yet); until. *Apa wis tau dipriksa? Jèn *...* Have you ever been examined? If not... *Aku ora arep mangkat jèn * éntuk kabar saka A.* I'm not leaving till I hear from A. *** nganti** no sooner... ** nganti manjuk² tekan omah wis lunga manèh.* No sooner had he come home than he left again. *** sepira·a** not the whole story by any means. *Iku mau * sepiraa betjiké.* And this is far from being the only good thing about it. *** tau** not yet ever. *Aku * tau weruh segara.* I've never seen the ocean.
durus **ke*an** to come true, be fulfilled
dus bad, evil (*oj*). ***-*an** plated. *Gelang iki dudu emas tenan ning *-*an.* This bracelet isn't solid gold–it's gold-plated. **nge/di*** to plate. *nge* logam* to plate metal. **nge/di*i** to bathe smn (*see also* ADUS)
ḍus carton, cardboard box. *rèk sa eḍus* a box of matches
dusṭa, ḍusṭa evil deed; theft. **n/di*** 1 to abduct. 2 to steal (*ki for* MALING*?*)
dusṭâbudi oj deceitful nature
ḍusun village, rural settlement (*kr for* DÉSA)
dusur **ke*** to lose one's balance and fall forward
duta, ḍuta 1 *oj* messenger, courier. 2 ambassador. **ke*an** embassy. **n/di*** to send smn as a messenger. *** besar** ambassador. *** muḍa** deputy ambassador. *** pa·ng·lawung** messenger bringing word of a death
ḍutjung *see* REBUT

du(w)-, ḍu(w)- *see also under* DU-, DW-; ḌU-, ḌW- (*Introduction, 2.9.7*)

duwa **n/di*** 1 to push (against, off, away). 2 to resist, defy, stand up to

ḍuwak torn (*oj*). ***-*** *intsfr* torn. *suwèk *-** badly torn

duwé *ng,* **gaḍah** *kr* 1 (*or* **n*** *ng;* **kagungan** *ki*) to have, own. *Médja kursi ora *, *né mung ambèn.* They have no chairs or tables, only benches. *Aku * tjangkriman, beḍèken ja.* I have a riddle: guess it! *lagi sepisanan * anak* to have one's first child. 2 to have a certain quality. *wong ora * kesel* a tireless person. ** (ka)luput(an)* guilty, at fault. *Apa mas * luput?* Has my husband done sth wrong? **de*(ǹ)** (**gaḍah·an** *kr*) to own things. *wong deduwèn* a well-to-do person. **de*ǹ(an)** (**ge·gaḍah·an** *kr*) possessions. **ke*ǹ** *ng kr* well off. **n/di*ǹi** 1 to have, get possession of. *Sing kopondoki nduwènana éring.* Have respect for the people you are staying with. *Kantjaku bisa nduwèni omah sing kaja kaḍaton.* A friend of mine has acquired a palatial home. 2 to have charge of [a territory, as governing officer]. **sa*-*né** whatever one has; according to one's possessions. *Ḍèwèké mèlu nguruni sa-duwé²né.* He contributed as much as he could afford. **d·um·uwé** *ng kr* to take good care of one's possessions. *** atur** to contribute to a discussion. *** gawé** to hold a celebration, *esp.* of a marriage or circumcision. **ora *** poor. *wong ora ** poor people. *** perlu** *sms** GAWÉ. *** rembug** to bring sth up for discussion. **sing *** the owner. **sing * omah** home owner; host, hostess. *See also* DUWÈK

duwèk *ng,* **gaḍah·an** *kr,* **kagungan** *ki* the possession [of]; belonging [to]. *Buku iki *ku.* This book is mine. *kagungané pak guru* the teacher's. *Ḍuwèké sapa?* Whose (is it)? *pabrik srutu gaḍahanipun bangsa tijang Indonesia* cigar factories owned by Indonesians. *See also* DUWÉ

ḍuwel 1 a certain small poisonous snake. 2 *var of* ḌUÈL. **n*** to stay at home all the time, remain indoors

ḍuwet blueberry; blueberry plant

ḍuwik *var of* ḌUWIT

ḍuwit *ng,* **(h)arta** *or* (*sbst?*) **jâtrâ** *kr* 1 money. ** selawé rupijah* 25 rupiahs. *sugih ** having plenty of money. 2 having money. *Isih tanggal nom, ning aku wis ora *.* It's still early in the month but I'm out of money. 3 obsolete coin worth a little less than one cent. **mata *en** overfond of money. ***-*an** play money, toy money. **n*** *ng kr* to pay. **ora n*** free of charge. **n/di*i** to pay for sth. *** kertas** paper money, bill(s). *** paju** negotiable currency. *** petjah** coins, change. *** putih** coins, silver money. *** rètjèh** *or* *** tjilik** coins, change

duwung rather than...; it would be better if... (*var of* LUWUNG)

ḍuwung kris (*kr for* KERIS)

ḍuwur *ng,* **inggil** *kr* high; tall. *Ḍèwèké geḍé *.* He's big and tall. *Regané *.* The prices are high. *Aburé * temenan.* It's flying really high! *ing ** above; at the top. *buku ing ** the above(-mentioned) book. *Wohé ana ing *.* The fruits grow at the top. *Disoki santen nganti setengah *.* Fill it half full (halfway to the top) with coconut milk. ***é** the height (of). *Saking *é nganti nèh sunḍul langit.* It was so tall it almost scraped the sky. **mu sepira?* How tall are you? ***-*an** comparative height; to compare *or* compete for height. **-*ané paḍa karo aku.* He's as tall as I am. **(ḍe)*an** *ng kr* high-ranking person. *rakjat golongan ḍe*an* people of high status. **ané tresna, sor²ané asih kabèh.* His superiors loved him, as did his subordinates. **ke*an** excessively tall/high. **n*** at the top; above. *kasebut ing n** mentioned above. *kreteg sing ana n*é kali* a bridge over a river. *Ḍèké bisa weruh motor saka ing n*.* He could see the car from above. *N*mu kuwi apa?* What's that above you? *N*é dluwang mau wur²ana pakan.* Sprinkle some crumbs on top of the paper. **n/di*aké** to make sth higher (than it was). **n/di*i** to make sth high. *Pageré di*i bèn weḍus² mau ora bisa mlebu.* They made the fence high enough to keep the sheep out. **sa·(n)*é** above; at the top of. *Sa*é paturon ana barang rupané anèh.* There was a strange-looking object on (*or* above) the bed. *ing sanginggiling anḍa* at the top of the ladder. *** kukus·é** famous. *** lengkung²** very tall [of people]. *** sisih** higher on one side than the other. *See also* PANḌUWUR

dw-, ḍw- *see also under* DU(W)-, ḌU(W)- (*Introduction, 2.9.7*)

dwâdjâ *oj* flag, emblem

dwârâ *oj* gate, doorway

dwi 1 *oj* two. 2 *oj* bird's wing. *** dasa**

ltry twenty. * **kala** biweekly. * **lingga** *gram* doubled root. * **lingga salin swara** *gram* doubled root with vowel change. * **purwa** *gram* reduplication of first syllable. * **tija** *ltry* twice. * **tunggal** inseparable, two in one. * **wasana** *gram* reduplication of final syllable (*e.g. tjekakak*)

dwidja *oj* guru, spiritual leader

dwidjâwârâ *oj* greatly revered holy man

dwipa *oj* 1 island. *Djawa* * the island of Java. 2 archipelago. * *Nusantara* Indonesia. 3 *oj* elephant

dwipânggâ *oj* elephant. * **kang sarwa retna** golden elephant decorated with diamonds (for court ceremonies)

dwipantârâ Indonesia(n archipelago)

dwirâdâ *oj* elephant

dyah *ltry* noble lady; princess

dyaksa, ḍyaksa *oj* skilled; intelligent

dyatmika *var of* DJATMIKA

E

é[a], **è** (*prn* **é** *or* **é titik**) *alphabetic letters*

é[b] 1 let's see...; h'm! 2 hey! say! *É adja.* Here, don't do that. *É mrénéa!* Hey you, come here!

-é[c] ng, **-ipun** *kr* (**-né, -nipun** *after vowel and with certain kinship terms*) 1 *3d-person possessive suffix. potlod·é* his/her pencil. *buku·né* smn's book. *bapak·(n)é* smn's father. *embah·(n)é* smn's grandparent. *embok·(n)é* smn's mother. *ibu·né, ibu'é* smn's mother. *kakang·(n)é* smn's older brother. *Anak·é papat.* They have four children. *Sepur mau laku·né rikat banget.* The train goes very fast. *Banget kagèt·é.* He was very much taken aback. *Aku arep ngreksa omah·é Jogja.* I'll be looking after his Jogja house. *wong sing djeneng·é Ali* a man named Ali. *Mesṭi kobong·é.* Naturally it will burn (*i.e.* its burning is certain). *Ana kantja·né dolanan.* A friend of hers came to see her. 2 your *(oblique, respectful). Ngendika·nipuṇ basa Djawi kok sampun luwes sanget.* You speak Javanese very fluently. 3 of. *panas·é geni* the heat of the fire. *pit·é kakangku* my brother's bicycle. *Ḍuwit·é A kurang.* A is short of money. 4 the aforementioned. *Loḍong·é dipetjah.* He smashed the jar. *Ḍèké ngulat-ulataké dodolan·é kabèh.* He looked over all the merchandise. *nalika ḍèké teka réné ping pinḍo·né* the second time he came here. 5 the/smn's action of [do]ing. *Mangan·é alon*[2]. He ate slowly. *Mangan orané gumantung marang mateng·é sega.* Whether we eat or not depends on whether the rice is done. *Kuwi kudu·né ora kaja ngono.* You shouldn't do things like that. 6 the/smn's ...ness. *Sepira ḍuwur·é?* How tall is he/it? *Bungah·é ora karuwan.* He was overjoyed. *Olèhmu ngentèni pirang djam suwé·né?* How long did you wait? 7 the/smn's *X* is... *lumrah·é* usually (*i.e.* the usual thing is...). *Tudju·né ora apa*[2]. Luckily it was nothing serious. *Sadjak·é arep udan.* It looks like rain. *Tjekak·é wong mono kudu tulung-tinulung.* In short, people must help each other. *Batin·é karep·é apa.* He wondered what she wanted. *Wangsulan·é sing dodol...* The seller replied... 8 in connection with [sth mentioned earlier]. *Olèhé mangan ora ana swara·né.* They ate soundlessly ('their eating, there was no sound connected with it'). *Jèn ana anaké sing lara, prasasat ora ana ngaso·né.* When one of the children is sick, there's no rest for her. *Ing alas kono ana matjan·é.* That forest has tigers in it. *Aku ndjaluk pangapura·né.* I beg your pardon for it. *Telung dina·né ḍèké mati.* Three days later (*i.e.* after it) he died. *Nanging ana nanging·é manèh.* But there's another "but." 9 another *X*; the other *X* (of a pair *or* series). *Sing sidji biru, sidji·né* *abang.* One is blue, the other is red. *Sing sidji wuta, sing sidji buḍeg, sing sidji·né bisu.* One was blind, another was deaf, the third was mute. *Sing lima matja, papat·é manèh nulis.* Five of them read, the other four wrote. **10** per, each, a(n). *Sedina·né kowé olèh pira?* How much do you earn per day? *Negara mau mbutuhaké daging rong juta kilogram setaun·é.* This nation consumes 2 million kilograms of meat a year. **11** [time] after [time]; each [time] in the continuing series. *Sing mènèhi panganmu saben dina·né sapa?* Who gives you your food day in and day out? *Tanggal limalas saben sasi·né, segara mau angok² mengidul antarané djam rolas awan nganti djam loro.* The 15th of every single month, the tide is out (southward) between 12 noon and 2 P.M. **12** by contrast. *mau·né* as contrasted with formerly. *Wong saomah paḍa bungah, mau·né nangis waé.* The whole family rejoiced; before, there had been nothing but weeping. *Durung pulih kaja mau·né.* He was not yet restored to (his previous condition of) health. *Aku saiki·né lagi njèlèngi.* Now, on the other hand, I'm *saving* my money. **13** of course! by all means! *(between two occurrences of the same verb or adjective). Bisa·né bisa, ning kesèd kok.* Of course he can do it–he's just lazy. *Apa bandjur kena dienggo njèlèngi?–Kena·né kena.* Can it be used as a piggy bank?–By all means. *Apa tjukup dienggo tuku sepéḍa anjar?–Tjukup·é tjukup, nanging aku gemi.* Is there enough to buy a new bicycle?–Oh yes, plenty; but I'm frugal. **14** *second element of psv optative circumfix: see* TAK- 3 *and Introduction, 3.1.5.4, chart*

e 1 (*prn* é) *alphabetic letter.* 2 uh..., er...

eb- *see also under* B- (*Introduction, 2.9.5*)

éba 1 how...! *∗ senengé.* How happy he was! 2 *oj* good, fine. 3 *oj* elephant

ébah to move (*kr for* OBAH)

ébar **ng/di∗aké** to make a display of, bring to people's attention. *ng∗aké kabudajan lan kesenian nasional* to popularize the national culture and art

ébat *see* HÉBAT

èbèg 1 (to dance) a village folk dance using a woven-bamboo hobby horse. *djaran ∗(-∗)-an* horse used for this dance. 2 decorative saddle lining

èbek̄ (*or* **∗an**) 1 *oj* full. 2 filled with sorrowful *or* confusing ideas. **ng/di∗i** to fill

èbèr **∗an** merchandise which the seller has taken on credit from the supplier. **∗-∗** *or* **ng∗** to sell such merchandise. *bakul ∗-∗* one who sells merchandise handled as above. **ng/di∗aké** to sell [goods] as above

èbi tiny shrimp dried and salted

èbjèk *var of* ÈPJÈK

èblèg a folk dance (*var of* ÈBÈG)

éblis *var of* IBLIS

ébor long-handled scoop. **ng/di∗-∗i** to hold a ritual ceremony for [a woman in the third month of pregnancy]

ébra **ng/di∗aké** 1 to allow sth to expire. *Pos wèselé di∗aké.* He let the postal money order lapse. 2 to fail to carry sth out. *Nijaté arep slametan di∗aké.* They canceled the plan to hold a ceremony.

ebré **ng/di∗** to knit

èbrèk **ng/di∗** to rip to pieces

ed-, eḍ- *see also under* D-, Ḍ- (*Introduction, 2.9.5*)

édab **ng∗-∗aké** *or* **ng∗-∗i** amazing; awesome. *Wong kok ḍuwuré ng∗-∗i.* He's so *tall!* *Kekuatané ng∗-∗aké.* His brute strength is terrifying.

édah *var of* IDAH

édan 1 (**éwah** *kr*) crazy. *∗ taun* chronic mental illness. *asu ∗* mad dog. *tijang éwah* madman. 2 *slang* wild, provocative, inspiring strong emotion. **∗-∗an** in a crazy manner. *Olèhé njupir adja ∗-∗an lho.* Don't drive like a madman! **k∗an** crazy [about], infatuated [with]. *Slamet k∗an marang Siti.* Slamet is mad about Siti. **ng∗** to feign madness. **ng/di∗(-∗)aké** to call *or* consider smn crazy. **ng/di∗i** to be madly in love with. *See also* DJAMAN

éḍang *n* apiece. *sidji ∗* one (for) each. *Geḍangé paro ∗ karo aḍiné.* He divided the banana with his brother.

éḍar **∗an** circular. **ng/di∗aké** 1 to circulate [a written message]. 2 to edit; to publish. **ng/di∗i** to circularize. *Aḍiku ng∗i kantja²-ku uleman.* My sister passed the invitation around among my friends. *Aku mau di∗i sirkulèr.* I received a circular. **per∗an** circulation. *per∗an uang* circulation of currency

èḍèr **ng/di∗(-∗)** to leave sth lying around conspicuously. *Ḍuwité mbok dilebokaké ḍompèt, adja di∗-∗ ngono.* Put the money in your wallet, don't leave it in plain sight that way.

èdi *var of* ADI. **∗ pèni** beautiful and valuable

éḍing *var of* ÉḌANG
edj- *see also under* DJ- (*Introduction, 2.9.5*)
édja ***n** spelling. *ngowahi *n* to change the spelling system. **né *n Inggris.* It's English spelling. **ng/di*** to spell
edja **ng/di*** to wish, want. *Sing di* dadi ḍokter.* He wants to be a doctor.
edjag **ng/di*-*** to step on, trample on
édjah *var of* ÉDJA
édjak *var of* ÉDJA
édjâwantah **(ma)ng*** to take form, become visible (*ltry:* of deities)
èdjèg 1 to jog, run with small steps. 2 to keep saying/asking sth. **ng*** 1 to jog. 2 to keep dropping in. *** èlèr** to say/ask again and again
èdjèk *var of* ADJAK
edjib **ng/di*aké** to rely (only) on. *Jèn ana apa², kowé lo sing dak *aké.* If anything goes wrong, I'll rely on you. *Adja ng*aké kasugihanmu waé.* Don't put too much faith in your wealth.
èdjlèg **ng*** to keep moving along without paying attention to distractions. *** èwèr** to keep going back and forth (in and out, up and down)
édong ***-*** *or* **édang-*** to have difficulty walking, *e.g.* after being circumcised
éḍum shady; sheltered. **k*en** excessively shady; overprotected. **ng*** to take shelter from sun, rain. **pa·ng*an** 1 shelter, protection. 2 protector
éfisièn efficient; efficiency
eg- *see also under* G- (*Introduction, 2.9.5*)
egah *var of* WEGAH. ***-*** unhurried, leisurely
egas **ng/di*(i)** to scare smn
ègèng **égang-*** to have difficulty walking. **ng*** to walk with difficulty
égla **m*** *or* **ng*** in plain sight, clearly visible. *Gunung Semèru katon ng*.* You can see Mount Semèru clearly. *Jèn ndèkèkaké ḍuwit adja ng*.* Don't leave money around in plain sight.
églé, èglèg, èglèh, èglèng *var of* ÉGLA
égol **(m)égal-(m)*** to move from side to side. *Kursi iki jèn dilungguhi égal-*.* This chair wobbles when you sit in it. *Jèn mlaku mégal-mégol.* She walks with her hips swaying. **ng/di·(égal-)*aké** to move sth from side to side. *ngégal-*aké bokong* to sway the hips as one walks
égos **m*** to one side; askew. *Olèhé motong m*.* He cut it slantwise (rather than straight across). *Jèn mau lempeng ora m*, mesṭi tekan kantor pos.* If we had gone straight instead of turning aside, we'd have come to the post office. **ng/di*aké** to avoid sth by turning aside
égrang stilts. *nunggang ** to walk on stilts. ***-*an** to use stilts, walk on stilts
ègrèk flimsy (*var of* ÈKRÈK)
éguh *var of* IGUH. **k*** convinced, impressed. *Ḍèké tetep ora k*.* He remained unmoved.
égung **m*** placed randomly this way and that. **ng/di*aké** to place [things] in a disorderly or uneven line
eh, èh, éh 1 *excl of disgust, rejection. *, adja tjeḍak² aku.* Ugh, don't come near me! **, salah manèh.* Damn, another mistake. 2 *excl of awe. E-e-eh. Pantjèn ja tjakrak temenan botjah iki.* My, what a handsome boy!
Éhé second year in the *windu* cycle
ehem, èhem 1 ahem (*self-conscious cough*). 2 *excl of criticism, ridicule. *, ngono waé isin.* Come now, why so bashful?
éjang 1 grandparent (*ki for* EMBAH). ** kakung* grandfather. ** putri* grandmother. 2 grandfather (*ki for* KAKI[a])
èjèg restless. **éjag-*** to keep fidgeting restlessly. **ng*** to move about restlessly
èjèl ***-*an** to argue with each sticking to his own view. **ng*** stubborn, unwilling to yield. **ng/di*(i)** to argue with [smn] from sheer obstinacy
èjèng *var of* ÈJÈL
éjog **éjag-*** to shake. **ng/di·éjag-*** to shake sth. *Wité diéjag-* supaja katèsé tiba.* Shake the papayas down from the tree.
éjong **m*** *or* **ng*** to meow. **m·éjang-m*** *or* **ng·éjang-ng*** to keep meowing
éjub 1 shady; sheltered. 2 dusk. ***-*** a shelter from sun, rain. **k*en** excessively shady; overprotected. **ng*** to take shelter. **pa·ng*an** 1 protection, shelter. 2 protector
èk (*or* ***-***) feces (*children's word: indicates a need to go to the toilet*)
ek- *see also under* K- (*Introduction, 2.9.5*)
éka 1 *oj* one. 2 unity, agreement. ***n** 1 unity, agreement. 2 the unit digit in a number. *Taun 1957 ékané pitu.* The digit in the unit place of year-number 1957 is 7. **n, dasan, atusan, éwon* units, tens, hundreds, thousands. *tembung *n* number, counting word. **ng/di*-*** to think [about], reflect. **sa*** in agreement; **sa*-praja** in cooperation for a common goal. *Wong² sa*-praja arep ndandani sekolah kuwi.* The people are

pooling their efforts to repair the school. *saijeg *praja* a joint effort

ékah *-* *or* *-**èkèh** (to walk) with the legs far apart. **m*-m*** *or* **m*-m·èkèh** to walk as above. *Mlakuné (m)ékah²*. He walks spraddle-legged.

ékâprâjâ *see* ÉKA

ékar (*or* *-*) lopsided; crooked; dishonest. *Lakuné **. He walks with a limp. *or* His conduct is shady.

èkèh *see* ÉKAH

èkèk *var of* KÈK. **ng/di*-*** 1 to saw away at [sth tough, rubbery]. *Olèhé mbelèh pitik di*-* djalaran ladingé keṭul.* He had trouble killing the chicken because the knife was dull. 2 *slang* to play [a stringed instrument]

èkèl *-* short and stocky (of physique)

èkèr 1 impatient for sth. *Wiwit ésuk wis * kepéngin lunga.* She's been anxious to leave all day. 2 to keep trying to provoke smn. *-* to work long and hard. ***-*an** 1 scratch marks. 2 argument; to argue. **ng/di*-*** to scratch *or* claw at

èket ***an** by 50's; 50 at a time. *See also* SÈKET

éklas *var of* IKLAS

ékoh **(m)ékah-(m)*** (to walk) with the legs far apart. *Lakuné ékah-*.* He's walking wide-legged.

ékonomi (*or* **per*an**) 1 economics. *fakultas ** department of economics. 2 the economy

ékonomis economical. *Ngimport beras saka luar negara kuwi ora *.* It's not economical to import rice.

ékrak 1 bamboo dust pan. 2 *slang* stretcher

èkrèk *-* flimsy, poorly constructed. **ng/di*-*** *var of* NG/DI·ÈKÈK-ÈKÈK

ékrok **ékrak-*** unsteady, loose in the joints

ekrok **m*** spread out, unfolded. *Kembangé mawar m*.* The roses are in bloom. *Buntuté merak m*.* The peacock's tail is opened out. **ng/di*aké** to spread sth open. *ng*aké pajung* to open an umbrella. *Pitik mau bandjur ng*aké wuluné.* The chicken ruffled out its feathers.

èksak *var of* IKSAK

èksamen *var of* IKSAMEN

èksetrā(h) et cetera

èksi eye (*oj*). **k(a)*** visible, in sight. **mang*** *ltry* to watch, observe. **ng/di*** *ltry* to look at, see. **(ng)*-ganda** *ltry name of the historic Mataram kingdom.* **pa·ng*** vision, sight

èksim scabies

èkspor(t) export. **ng/di*** to export

èksportir exporter

èkstrā(h) extra

èkstrak̄ flavoring extract

el- *see also under* L- (*Introduction, 2.9.5*)

éla 1 (*or* *-*) to [do] along with others. *Sarèhné kabèh paḍa nonton pilem ja aku *-* nonton.* As long as everyone else was going to the movie, I went too. 2 (*prn* **élā**) *ltry* well! well! (*excl of surprise*). *** dalah** *or* *** keprijé** *(ltry) excl of surprise*

elak place where a small water channel empties

elastis flexible, elastic

èlèd **m*** [of tongue] (sticking) out. *Asu édan kuwi biasané ilaté m*.* Mad dogs usually have their tongues hanging out. **m*-m*** *or* **m·élad-m*** [of the tongue] to keep emerging. **ng/di*aké** to stick out [the tongue]

èlèg **ng/di*** to tease, stir up. **ng/di*-*i** to coax. *Bareng di*-*i ḍuwit, gelem lunga.* When they tried money as a persuader, he went along.

èlèk *ng* bad (*inf var of* ALA). *Padusané kok * ngéné.* How unattractive this swimming pool is! ***-*an** of inferior quality. **k*en** excessively bad. *Bakal iki k*en jèn dinggo tjaosan.* This fabric is too poor to be used as a gift. **ng/di*-*** to talk about smn behind his back

élèktris electric; electricity

élèktro *var of* ÉLÈKTRIS

élèktronik, élèktronis electronic(s)

èlèr (*or* ***an**) sun-dried tobacco leaves. **ng/di*** to spread [tobacco] in the sun to dry

elho *excl* (*var sp of* LO)

élik *-* to warn smn. **ng/di*aké** 1 to warn. *Pramugari kliling ng*-*aké penumpang² sing durung ngentjengaké tali kursiné.* The hostess went around cautioning the passengers who hadn't fastened their seat belts. 2 to forbid. *A di*ké nganggo pité sing nggembos.* A was told not to ride the bike with the flat tire.

éling *ng,* **ènget** *or* **émut** *kr* 1 to remember, bear in mind. *Kowé rak isih * ta?* You remember, don't you? 2 to regain consciousness. ** melèk* to come to and open the eyes. ***an** 1 memory, recollection. 2 to have a good memory. ***-*an** to remember only vaguely. **k*an** to recall, think back on. *O wis k*an aku. Now* I remember. **ng/di*-*** to remember, keep in mind. *Slamet sing ng*-* regané.* Slamet kept track of the prices. *Aku ora *.–Ajo, di*-*!* I don't remember.–Well come on, rack your brain! **ng/di*aké** to remind smn. *Mengko jèn lali, *na.* If he forgets, remind him. **ng*i** to remember, recall; to keep in mind. *Uripé serba méwah, ora ng*i jèn rakjat isih sengsara.* They lived in luxury, disregarding the fact that people were suffering. **pa·ng*-*** 1 a reminder. *Potrèt iki arep tak simpen kanggo peng*-*.* I'll keep this picture as a remembrance. 2 sth that should be kept in mind. *Muga² kedadéjan mau bisa kanggo pang*-* angkatan muḍa.* I hope this will be a lesson to the younger generation. **sa*é** all that one remembers. *Tjritakna impènmu, sa*mu baé.* Tell me everything you remember about your dream. **ora *** 1 to not remember. 2 unconscious; to lose consciousness. *Ḍèwèké semaput ora *.* She fainted. **ora nganggo *-*** without regard for the future *or* for others. *See also* PÉLING

èlmi *sbst? kr for* ÈLMU

èlmu *ng,* **èlmi** *sbst? kr* knowledge; science (*var of* ILMU)

élo ell (measure of length: *ca.* 0.688 meter = *ca.* 45 inches. ***n̂** by the ell. **ng/di*n̂i** to measure [fabric] in ells

elo *excl* (*var sp of* LO)

élok (*or* *-*) out of the ordinary, recherché. **ka*an** a miracle, a wonder. **ng*i** to act strange

èlu to accompany (*childish var of* M* *below*). **éla-*** to do what others are doing, go along with the crowd. ***n̂(-*n̂)en** 1 to tag along with people habitually. 2 to side with smn in an argument. **k*** to be carried along (with). *A tansah dipepéngin si B, bandjur k*.* B kept coaxing A and A finally gave in. *Saka baudé tjaturan nganti wong² akèh sing paḍa k* katut.* He's such a smooth talker that many people fall for it. **m*** (**tumut** *kr,* **n·dèrèk** *ka*) 1 to accompany, join in, [do] with. *Ḍèké m* menjang pasar.* He went with her to the marketplace. *Aku m* kuliah.* I attended the lectures. *m* lotré* to participate in a lottery. *Slamet ora m* mlebu.* Slamet didn't go in with the others. 2 to live with and be supported by. *Wong tuwané m* anaké.* The parents live with their son. **m* grubjug** to jump on the bandwagon. **m*-m*** to butt in; to tag along. *Siti mèlu² tjlaṭu: Ija aku m*.* Siti chimed in: I want to go too. **ng*** to go along with the crowd. **ng/di*k̂aké** (**n̂/dipun·tumut·aken** *kr,* **n/di·ḍèrèk·aké** *ka*) 1 to have smn go along with [a person]. 2 to have smn live with and be supported by [smn, *usu.* a relative]. *Anaké diélokaké bulike.* She sent her son to live with his aunt. **ng/di*n̂i** to go along with smn as a companion *or* servant. *A ora gelem dièloni B.* A didn't want B to go with him as retainer. *See also* ILU

élur, elur worm. **ng*** resembling a worm. *Antriné ng* dawa banget.* The waiting line wound a long way.

em *excl expressing hesitation.* **,* wedi aku.* I'm [too] scared [to go]. **, aku ḍéwé durung ngerti djalarané mati.* Well...I don't know myself what caused her death.

em- *see also under* M- (*Introduction, 2.9.5*)

-em- *inf var of* -UM-

émah *-* to marry, have one's own home (*kr for* OMAH²)

émail 1 tooth enamel. 2 porcelain glaze

emak 1 maidservant who takes care of the children. 2 mother, mom (*var of* EMBOK)

éman unfortunate, regrettable; to regret. ***é** unfortunately. **é ḍèké ora bisa tjara Inggris.* It's too bad he can't speak English. ***-*** regrettable. *Ah *-* temen, bebed suwèk.* Oh, what a pity–the skirt is torn. **ng/di*** to care about, have concern for. *** karo** to care for deeply. *Ḍèké * karo bojoné.* He cherishes his wife.

émansipasi emancipation

emas *var of* MAS[a]

émba **m*** like, resembling. **m*-m*** to pretend (to be); to disguise oneself as. *Radèn Ardjuna m*² pedjah.* Ardjuna played dead. *Malingé m* pulisi.* The thief impersonated a policeman. **ng/di*** to do an imitation of. *ng* tjarané wong lija ngomong* to disguise one's voice. **ng/di*-*** to do one's best to mimic. *Ḍèké ng*-* solah-tingkahku, nanging ora ana sing mèmper.* He tried to act like me, but it wasn't like me at all. **sa*** like, resembling

embag *var of* EMBEG

embah 1 (**éjang** *ki*) grandparent. 2 *adr* old man. **ng*** to call smn, *or* regard smn as, one's own grandparent. *** bibi** great aunt (grandparent's younger sister). *** bujud** great-grandparent. *** lanang** grandfather. * **paman** great uncle (grandparent's younger brother). * **uwa** great aunt/uncle (grandparent's older sibling). * **wédok** grandmother

émbal *var of* ÉPAH

emban nursemaid (*usu.* a woman). *embok* * female nursemaid. *-* (**p·atur**[a]**·an** *ki*) batik shawl for carrying a child slung from the shoulder. ***an** the part of a ring where the stone is set. ***-*an** child being carried in a shawl. **ng/di*** to carry a child in a shawl on one's chest. **ng* ḍawuh** to carry out an order. **ng/di*aké** to carry a child for smn. **ng/di*i** to serve as a nursemaid to/for. * **tjinḍé** a child-carrying shawl of fine soft material; * **tjinḍé * silad·an** to play favorites; biased, partial. *Dadi guru ora kena * tjinḍé * siladan karo murid²é kabèh.* A teacher mustn't treat any pupils differently from others.

embang side, direction. * **kana** (over) there. * **kana·né** 1 beyond, on the other side of. 2 the old days, back when

embat 1 timberwork on *e.g.* a bridge, dam. 2 soft, mushy (*root form: kr for* EMBUT?). ***an** carrying pole. *-* **tjlarat** look before you leap. **m*(-m̄·pentul)** springy; to bounce, spring. **ng/di*** 1 to align [a spear, arrow] with the target before releasing it. 2 to heft [a carrying-pole load] to test whether it is too heavy. 3 to manipulate, wield. *putra kang ing tembé gumanti ng* pusaraning pradja* prince who will eventually come into power

embeg (*or* *-*) swampy land, marshland

embèk 1 sheep's baa. 2 *excl conceding defeat in a contest.* **embak-*** to keep baaing. ***-*an** to wrestle, with the rule that one cedes by saying *embèk.* **ng*** to baa, bleat. *See also* BÈK

èmbèl *-* supplement, postscript. **ng/di*-*i** to add a little something to. *Karanganmu iki wis apik, ora perlu di*-*i manèh.* Your article is just fine now; don't put anything else in.

embel (*or* *-*) swamp, marsh. **k*** to get stuck in a muddy place. **ng*** to be(come) swampy

embèn the day after tomorrow. * **buri** later on; at some future time. ** buri kowé tak tjritani dongèngané.* Some day I'll tell you the whole story.

èmbèr pail, bucket. *banju sa** a pail of water

embes ***-*an** 1 water that has soaked into soil. 2 extra earnings from an unrevealed source. **ng*** 1 to ooze, seep. 2 covered with condensed moisture. 3 soggy, sodden

èmbèt, embèt **k*** to get involved *or* incriminated. **ng/di*(-*)** to involve/incriminate smn

embil **ng/di*** to pick, choose. *Tjup *!* Mine! *(expression with which children lay claim to sth)*

embing side, direction. * *kéné* here. *-* *or* ***-bing** (**tuntun·an** *ki*) placenta

embjah **ng*-*** to try first one then another. *Pilihen salah sidji, adja ng*-*.* Choose one—don't try them all.

embjang *inf var of* AMBJANG

emblèg, èmblèg chunk, wad, mass. *mBakoné sa*é pira?* How much for a wad of tobacco? ***-*an** in the form of chunks *or* lumps. **ng/di*-*** to form into wads. *Lemahé di*-* dadi gunungan tjilik.* The soil was heaped into mounds. *Awaké ptg plenting *-*an.* His body was swollen and lumpy. *Kertasé *-*an.* The papers were wadded in thick layers.

emblog roll, bolt (of fabric). ***-*an** 1 in large quantities; extensive. 2 in rolls; by the roll. *mori *-*an* a bolt of cambric. **ng/di*** to apply thickly. *Gambaré di* tjèt abang.* He plastered red paint on the picture. *See also* BLOG

embok (**ibu** *ki*) mother. *Ija kok mbok.* OK, Mom. *Diwènèhaké *né.* He gave it to his mother. ***-*en** always wanting one's mother near. ***né** 1 smn's mother. 2 *adr* wife (*i.e.* the mother of our children). **ng*** to call smn, or regard smn as, one's mother. **sa*** having the same mother. * **adjeng** *adr* middle-class woman. * **emban** female nursemaid. * **gedé** aunt (parent's elder sister). * **mas** *adr* female of low status. * **ngantèn** *adr* middle-class woman. * **nom** most recent wife in a polygamous household. **si** * *reference term* one's mother; the female servant who takes care of the children and household. *Aku diwènèhi simbok panganan.* Mother (*or* the female servant) gave me some cookies. *Tresnané simbok marang anak iku gedé temenan.* A mother's love for her children is very great. * **tjilik** aunt (parent's younger sister). * **tuwa** wife other than the most recent one in a polygamous household

embong *var of* EMBOK

èmbrèh 1 sweeping the ground [of excessively long clothing]. 2 having a clean *or* neat appearance. 3 not poor and not rich; having enough for one's needs. **ng*** sweeping the ground [of long clothing]

èmbrèt, embrèt worker who is paid by the day. **ng*** to travel at low cost in a carriage hired by a group. **ng/di*aké** to hire work done by the day. *Aku ng*aké kumbahan.* I have smn do my laundry each day.

embuh *ng* 1 (**kilap** *kr,* **duka** *or* **ñj·suwun duka** *oblique ki*) I don't know. ** dadiné.* I don't know what became of it/him. *mBuh apa sebabé.* I don't know why. 2 perhaps; I wonder, I doubt. ** temenan * ora.* Maybe it's true and maybe it isn't. ***-*an** dubious. *Montoré mbuh²an waé bisa tekan Sala apa ora.* I doubt if his car will make it to Solo. *Aku mau bengi ora sinau ning aku arep udjian mengko, mbuh-mbuhan wis.* I didn't study last night but I'm taking the exam anyway—who knows! **embah-*** to keep saying "I don't know." *Kok embah-* waé ditakoni.* I'm asking you, why do you keep saying you don't know? **ng/di*i** to say "I don't know" to. *Ḍèké takon kowé, ning tansah kok *i.* He asked you but you just kept saying you didn't know.

embun dew (*var of* BUN). ***(-*)an** (**[pa]·sunḍul·an** *ki*) crown of the head; highest part of sth. **ng*** 1 to have [sth] on top of the head *or* at the very top. *ng* mas* gold-tipped. 2 (*psv* **di***) to accept with deference. *Anak lumrahé ng* welinging wong tuwané.* Children usually defer to their parents' wishes. **pa·ng*** that which is respectfully accepted. *Pamaréntah ngleksanakaké pang* saka Parlemèn.* The government carried out the Parliament's requests.

embur **ng*-*** soft and spongy

embut (**embat** *kr?*) ***-*an** [of fruits] softened by pounding to release the juices inside. **m*** soft, mushy. **ng/di*-*** to soften [fruit] as above

èmeng 1 bewildered. 2 sad (*ki for* SUSAH). **ng*i** confusing

emi **ng/di*-*** to take solicitous care of

émigrasi emigration. **ng/di*kaké** to cause to emigrate. *Akèh penḍuḍuk diémigrasèkaké ing pulo mau.* Many of the people were sent to that island to live.

émjah *var of* ÈMJÈH

èmjèh insignificant, trivial. **ng/di*aké** to consider inconsequential

émod *var of* ÈMU

emoh unwilling (*see* MOH)

émor *var of* ÈMU

empak sth used for igniting (*var of* EMPAN)

empal slices of spiced meat fried in coconut oil. ***-*an** forming heaps

empan 1 place, function. *Ing endi *é politik ing ulah raga?* Politics has no place in athletics. *Islamé *é kanggo menangi kuwating pambudi mau.* The function of Islam is to strengthen the character. 2 sth used for igniting. *ndjaluk ** to ask for a light. 3 effective for its purpose. *Péso iki ora *.* This knife doesn't cut. ***-*an** wick *or* tinder for igniting. **m*** effective. *Kanḍané m*.* Her advice worked (*i.e.* he took it). *Budjukané ora m*.* Her efforts to persuade him were not successful. *Kaju iki jèn dienggo gegenèn m* banget.* This wood would make excellent kindling. **ng/di*aké** to light [a smoke]. *Rokoké di*aké sentir.* He lighted his cigarette at the kerosene lamp. **ng/di*i** to feed (*rg var of* M/DI·PAKAN·I). *** (lan) papan** the appriate circumstances, the right time and place; **nganggo * papan** to choose the right time and place. *Tjarijos sampéjan niku saleresé, nanging enggih kedah nganggé * papan.* What you say is true, but say it under appropriate circumstances.

émpang ornamental garden pond

empèk **ng*** to ask if one may share. *Mengko bengi aku tak ng* turu kéné ja.* Could I bunk with you tonight? **ng/di*-*** to plead (for). *Ḍèké sa-bisa² kudu ng*-* atiné bodjoné murih rembugé mengko bisa disarudjuki.* He has his work cut out for him trying to get his wife to agree with him.

empel *var of* AMPEL

èmpèng light (not heavy); *fig* untrustworthy

empèng **ng/di*** 1 to nurse, suck. 2 to have one's baby nursed by smn else. **ng/di*i** to nurse smn else's baby

èmpèr porch-like part of a Javanese house

èmper resemblance. *Uripé kéwan iku akèh *é karo manungsa.* Animals' lives resemble those of human beings in many respects. ***é** 1 it seems (as if). **é paḍa memudji.* They seem to be praying. 2 what is appropriate. **é ḍèwèké kuwi dadi ḍokter.* He ought to be a doctor. ***-*an** to resemble each other. *Kakang-aḍi kaé *-*an.* Those brothers look alike. **m*** 1 to resemble. *Ḍèké m* kowé.* He looks like you. 2 appropriate, to be expected. *O ja m* jèn Sri* *sing dadi djuara, wong ḍasar tjah pinter.* It's not surprising that Sri is at the top of the class–she's very bright. *m* waé* of course; it goes without saying. *Polah ngono kuwi ora m*.* Such conduct is improper. **ng/di*-*** to compare for resemblances. **ng/di*aké** to cause to resemble. *Pikiran kawula ka*na kalijan panggalih dalem.* Make my thoughts be like Thy thoughts. **ng/di*i** to resemble sth. *Klambiné ng*i klambiku.* Her dress is just like mine. **sa*** like. *Rupané mblenḍuk sa* kaja djambu.* It's round like a guava. *omah geḍé sa* guḍang* large buildings that look like warehouses

empèt, èmpèt ***-*an** crowded, jammed

empet *var of* AMPET

emping wafer made of thin-sliced sun-dried fruits *or* young rice plants, fried and eaten as snacks. ** mlindjo* the above made of *mlindjo* fruits. ***an** money paid as an advance. **ng/di*** 1 to make [ingredients] into the above wafers. 2 to lease [farm land]. 3 to request payment before the job is completed. **ng* lara ng·géndjah pati** looking for trouble. **ng/di*i** to pay land rental to [smn]. *See also* KUMEMPING

empjak 1 roof frame. 2 sheltering roof for young plants. *** gadjah** center portion of a roof frame

èmplag ***-*** to have difficulty walking because of obesity

emplah **ng*-*** 1 (to have) a large torn place. 2 a broad treeless plain

emplak **ng*-*** large treeless plain with soil too poor to cultivate

emplang **ng/di*** 1 to open sth wide. 2 to fail to pay one's debts. **ng/di*-*aké** *or* **ng/di*-*i** to put sth in the sun to dry *or* air

èmplas trivial, insignificant

emplèk sheet, layer. ***-* ketepu** a children's hand-clapping and singing game. ***-*an** forming sheets/layers. *Guḍigé *-*an.* He's covered with scabies sores. **k*an** layer, sheet. *k*an karèt mentah* a sheet of raw rubber

emplèng *var of* EMPLÈK

emplep **ng/di*** to gain *or* retain possession of sth selfishly *or* dishonestly. *Bukuné olèhé buku tjah loro urunan di* ḍéwé.* We both chipped in to buy the book but he kept it for himself. *Bukuné di* A ḍéwé, ora gelem njilihké B.* A used the book himself–he wouldn't let B use it.

èmplok *var of* AMPLOK

emplok **ng/di*(i)** to put [food] into the mouth. *Saking kentèkan pangan, apa waé sing ketemu paḍa di*i.* There was so little food they ate anything they could get hold of. **sa*an** one mouthful

emplong *var of* EMPLANG

empluk covered earthenware food container

empok **ng*(i)** 1 to discharge stomach gas or flatus. 2 (*psv* **di***) to play a joke on smn. 3 to get a whiff of sth

empot **ng/di*** to draw on [a cigarette]

emprah ***-*(an)** dropped *or* scattered in disarray. **ng*** to [do] in a careless *or* slipshod fashion

émprak certain Arabian music accompanied by dancing

emprak **ng*-*** to shoo, scare off

emprèt **ng*** [of elephants] to trumpet. **ng/di*(i)** to scoff at, look down on

emprit a certain small hummingbird (considered an omen of danger). *** a·buntut beḍug** to make a mountain out of a molehill. *** gantil** 1 a variety of the above bird (the seeing of which is considered a death wish). 2 roof embellishment. *** kadji** a white-headed variety of the above bird. *** tonḍang** a variety of the above bird

emprok **ng*-*** to launder [clothing] by pounding it against sth, *usu.* a rock

empu 1 *ancient title for scholars, poets, outstanding artists, master craftsmen.* 2 large tuberous root used in folk medicines. ***n̂-*n̂** folk medicine brewed from roots and herbs

empuk tender, soft; *fig* unable to say no, a soft touch. **di*(i)** to be spoken to persuasively. *Nèk di*i rak saja suwé diwèwèhaké.* If you keep urging him, sooner or later he'll give in. **k*en** excessively soft. **ng/di*aké** to soften, tenderize. **ng*aké watu item** to work hard at sth difficult, *or* think sth is too easy, and then have to give up in the end

empun (*prn* **mpun** *as inf kr,* **empun** *as md*) 1 don't! (*social var of* ADJA[a]). 2 to have [done] (*social var of* WIS)

empur ***-*** *or* (*esp.*) **m*** pleasantly mealy in the center [of cooked cassava, sweet potato]

empus ***an** bamboo section used for blowing on fire to make it burn hotter. **ng/di*** to blow on. *mBok di* geniné.* Please blow on the fire.

emput *var of* AMPUT

èmu soft, mushy [of fruits, *e.g.* from being handled in the marketplace]

émut to remember (*kr for* ÉLING)

en- *see also under* N- (*Introduction, 2.9.5*)

-en (**-nen** *after vowel*) 1 (*ng*) *psv imperative suffix. Deleng·en.* Look (at it)! *Pring kaé gawa·nen mréné.* Bring that bamboo over here. 2 *suffix for a bodily process or condition. Dridjiné getih·en.* His finger bled. *Matané walang·en.* His eyes bugged out. *aras²·en njambutgawé* lackadaisical toward one's work. *mata ḍuwit·en* money-mad. 3 *second element of* KA...EN *circumfix. k·aḍem·en* too cold

énak *ng,* **étja** *kr* pleasing to the senses, *esp.* taste, smell. * *dipangan* good to eat. *ambu sing ora ** a disagreeable odor. * *ja.* It feels good (*e.g.* stretching the muscles)! *or (sarcastic, to smn who didn't show up for work)* Taking it easy, eh? ***é** it is advisable. *Ora ana bis, *é paḍa mlaku waé.* There's no bus; we'd better walk. ***-*** comfortable; enjoying oneself. *Uripé *-*.* He has a good life. *Lagi *-* olèhé makani manuké.* She was happily feeding her birds. ***-*an** 1 good things to eat. 2 to lead a comfortable life. 3 to see which tastes best; to compete in making sth taste good. **k*en** *ng only* excessively comfortable *or* pleasurable. *K*en turu nganti lali djandji.* He slept so well he forgot his appointment. *K*en mangan nganti bola-bali tanduk.* It was so delicious he ate helping after helping. **ng/di*-*** to take things easy. *urip ng*-** to live comfortably. *Sasuwéné nglakokaké montor, ora kena disambi ng*-*.* While you're at the wheel you can't just sit back and take it easy. **ng/di*aké** 1 to make sth taste good/better. 2 to make smn comfortable. **ng/di*i** *ng only* to give pleasure/comfort to. *Kabar betjik iku ng*i atiné.* Good news makes you feel good. **sa*é** as one pleases. *Pegawéjané ora bakal rampung jèn olèhmu nggarap sa*é.* You'll never finish if you loaf on the job. * **kepénak** pleasure, comfort, ease. *See also* KEPÉNAK

énang *sbst kr for* ONANG

énḍa to elude, dodge. * *mangiwa * menengen kaja prendjak tinadji* (*wj*) clever and agile at eluding one's enemies. **(m)*-(m)*** to disguise oneself. *Ḍèké ménḍa² dadi bakul beras.* He posed as a rice seller.

enḍa **m*** to subside. *Udané rada m*.* The rain let up somewhat. *M*a olèhmu nangis.* Stop crying! **ng/di*aké** to cause sth to subside. *Enḍakna tangismu!* Stop that crying!

éndah fine, beautiful. **ka*an** beauty, loveliness. **ng/di*aké** 1 to accomplish. *Apa kang diḍawuhi tansah di*aké.* He always does whatever he's told to do. 2 to consider seriously. *Kowé kuwi ora tau ng*aké apa kang tak kanḍakaké.* You never pay any attention to my advice.

endak *var of* ANDAK

enḍak ***-* tjatjing** medicine for stomach worms. **m*** 1 to subside. *Nesuné wis m*.* His anger has cooled. *Liweté wis m*.* The rice has almost stopped boiling. 2 to stoop, duck. 3 to walk in a squatting position in the presence of an exalted person, to show humility. **m* m̀·penḍukul** full of ups and downs. *Dalané m*-menḍukul.* The road is hilly (bumpy). **ng/di*aké** to cause to subside. *A bisa ng*aké nesuné B.* A managed to calm B down. **ng/di*i** to bow to smn

énḍang (grand)daughter of a holy man. **ng/di*i** to visit. *Nèk ana wektu kantjaku di*i ja?* If you get any time, go see my friend!

endang (**énggal** *kr?*) (*or* ***-***) quick, soon; immediate. *nDang djupukna gula kana.* Quick, bring me some sugar. *Lagi tanggal limalas kok * éntuk bajar.* It's only the fifteenth: how come you're getting paid so soon? *Gawéané dirampungké (e)ndang nonton bioskup.* Finish the job, and right after that we'll go to a movie.

enḍas 1 (**sirah** *kr*) head (of an animal). 2 *cr* (**sirah** *ng kr,* **mastâkâ** *or* **mustâkâ** *ki*) human head. 3 (**sirah** *kr*) the upper *or* front part of sth. ***mu** *cr* damn you! ***-*an** 1 engine, locomotive. 2 (**sirah²an** *kr*) the upper *or* front part of sth. 3 (**sirah²an** *kr*) digit of a calendar-year number. * **gulu** chicken head and neck. * **gunḍul di·kepet·i** to make smn even more comfortable

endat **m*** to rebound, bounce. **m*-m*** *or* **m*-m̀·pentul** to bounce, spring. **ng*-*** bouncy, resilient. *See also* ENDUT

enḍé **di*-*** to be delayed, put off. *Olèhé mbajar utang tansah di*-* waé.* He always procrastinates when it comes to paying his debts. **ng*-*** to wait for a long time

enḍèg *var of* EMBLÈG

enḍeg *ng,* **kèndel** *kr* ***-*an** (**pa·kèndel·an** *kr*) place where sth stops. *nḍeg²an sepur* *(bis)* train (bus) stop. **m*** **(kèndel** *kr*) to halt, come to a stop. **ng/di*** to stop sth. *Béasiswané dindeg.* His fellowship was cut off. **ng/di*aké** to cause to stop. *Olèhé ng*aké motor dumadakan.* He stopped the car suddenly. **ng/di*i** to stop (in) at. *Warung kaé sering dindegi bakul.* Sellers often stop in at that snack shop. **ng/di*-*i** to slow sth down. *See also* ANDEG

èndèk, endèk 1 low, close to the ground. 2 short in stature (*slang var of* TJENDÈK)

endek *var of* TJENDAK, TJENDÈK. ***-*** lees, dregs. **ng/di*i** to bow to (*var of* NG/DI·ENDAK·I). *** amun²** shimmering heat waves

èndel act of stopping (*kr for* ANDEG). **k*** to (come to a) stop (*kr for* M·ANDEG, M·ENDEG)

èndèl 1 half-grown Manila duckling (young of the ÉNTOG). 2 female servant. 3 child. ***-*** embellishment, accompaniment, supplement. **ng*** to accompany; to supplement

endèl *rg var of* PENDÈL

endel one who can be relied upon; one who is entrusted with sth. **ng/di*** to believe (in), trust. **ng/di*aké** to put too much faith in, rely on too heavily. *Adja sok ng*aké kekuatanmu.* Don't overestimate your strength. *See also* ANDEL

endem stupor caused by liquor or drugs. ***-*an** to get intoxicated deliberately; a party held for this purpose. *Bubar udjian botjah² terus pada *-*an.* After the exam, the boys had a drinking party. **k*an (ke·wuru·n̂** *ki*) under the effect of drink/drugs. **m*** **(wuru** *ki*) 1 intoxicated; drugged. 2 *slang* crazy about smn, sth. *** gendjé** eccentric, queer. **m* segara** seasick(ness). **m*i** intoxicating. **ng*i** 1 intoxicating; having a stupefying effect. 2 (*psv* **di*i**) to get smn drunk/drugged

endem ***-*an** 1 thing concealed. 2 mutual ill feelings. **ng/di*** to conceal, keep hidden. **ng* basa** to hold back one's true feelings. *See also* PENDEM

endeng **ng*(-*)** [people] in large numbers

èndèp, endèp *ng,* **andapan** *kr* wild boar

èndèr **ng/di*aké** 1 to explain (*inf var of* NG/DI·ANDAR·AKÉ). 2 to reveal, disclose. *Adja seneng ng*-*aké wadining wong tuwa.* Don't tell family secrets!

endet **ng/di*** 1 to keep sth to oneself. *A bisa ng* wadi.* A knows how to keep a secret. 2 to take sth for oneself. *Batiné entèk di* réwangé.* The servant helped himself to all the profits.

endi *ng,* **pundi** *kr* 1 where? *nDi kartjismu?* Where's your ticket? *Menjang * ta?* Where are you going? 2 which (one)? ** sing bener?* Which one is right? *Buku ndi sing duwèkmu?* Which book is yours? **ng*** *ng only* where? in what place? *Bapak ng* ta bu?* Where's Dad, Mother? **ng*-*** **(pundi²** *kr*) everywhere, (in) every place; [not] anywhere. *A tak golèki menjang ng*-*.* I've been looking everywhere for A. *Aku arep ora nang ng*-*.* I'm not going anywhere. **ng*-*a (pundi²a** *kr*) everywhere, anywhere. *Pundi²a wonten rumput.* Grass is everywhere. *** ana** as if there could be such a thing as...! *Endi ana gadjah djambon?* Who ever heard of a pink elephant? *** waé** 1 where? *Kowé mentas saka * waé?* Where have you been? *Kowé arep menjang * waé?* Where're you going? 2 everywhere; anywhere (at all). *Lelara mau * waé ana.* That disease is very prevalent.

endih **k*** to lose, get overpowered. **ng/di*** 1 to beat, overcome. 2 to take over, preempt. *ng* panggonan* to take smn else's seat

endik *rg* in, at, on. *Omahé * endi?* Where does he live?

endika *var of* ANDIKA. *See also* NGENDIKA

endil half-cent coin. **ng/di*-*** 1 to take care of, look after. 2 to hand over little by little *or* a few at a time

endip ***-*** *or* **endap-*** frail, sickly. **m·endap-m*** *or* **ng·endap-ng*** 1 nearing death. 2 badly frightened

endjah **ng/di*-*** *slang* to want to have everything available. *Pilihen salah sidji, adja seneng ng*-*.* Pick one—don't try to get them all.

endjak *var of* IDAK

éndjang *kr* *sbst var of* ÉNDJING

èndjep **m*** with lower lip thrust forward as a gesture of dislike or disparagement. **ng/di*aké** to thrust forward [the lower lip]. **ng/di*i** to gesture at [smn, as above]

èndjèr (*or* ***an**) *wj* (to engage in) preliminaries to a fighting scene (depicted in a dance), during which the opponents size up each other's fighting strength

endjet *ng,* **apu** *kr* slaked lime (to be mixed with betel nut, for chewing). **ng/di*(i)** to apply slaked lime to

endjih *Jogja var of* INGGIH

éndjing morning (*kr for* ÉSUK). *See also* BÉNDJING

endjlog **ng/di*aké** to cause *or* assist smn to descend. **ng/di*i** to jump down onto. *See also* ANDJLOG, DJLOG

éndjoh can, be able; capable, competent

éndjor ***-*** swollen

endjot a pedal. ***-*an** to pump, pedal. **ng/di*** to operate sth by a pedal

enḍog *ng,* **tigan** *kr* egg. *kulit(é) ** eggshell. ***é blorok** 1 speckled hen's egg. 2 sth unexpected. *ndjagakaké *é si blorok* to expect the unexpected. ***-*an 1 (tigan·an** *kr)* to produce eggs for eating rather than hatching. 2 *ng kr* (to play) a children's game played by piling fists on one child's back and then withdrawing them by turns. **ng*** to lay egg(s). **pa·ng*** act of laying eggs. *Pang*é ana ing kulité kéwan sing isih urip.* [These flies] lay their eggs in live animals' skins. *** abjor** a nearly rotten egg. *** asin(an)** egg salted in the shell. *** kamal** egg salted (in the shell) with ground-up brick dust. *** kopjor** rotten egg. *** mata sapi** fried egg sunny-side-up. *** pinḍang** egg salted (in the shell) with guava leaves. *** tjeplok** fried egg. *** wok·an** rotten egg. *See also* LONDJONG

enḍok in, at, on. *Sésuk nḍok kana ana wajang.* There's to be a shadow play there tomorrow. **ng*** to be in *or* stay at. *See also* ANḌOK, ḌOK

énḍol ***-*** a waddling gait. **m*-m*** 1 to move with a waddling gait. 2 [of a chicken's crop] stuffed with feed

endon end, goal. *Karepé arep duwé gawé mantu geḍèn²an, tekaning * ḍuwité ora tjukup.* He planned a big wedding, but toward the end he ran out of money. *See also* PANDON

enḍon in, at, on. **ng*** to be/stay smw. *Aku sedina ḍeg kok ng* ana omah waé.* I've been at home all day.

énḍong 1 a small container. 2 a quiver (for arrows). **ng*** to go visiting. **ng/di*i** to visit smn

enḍong **ng/di*aké** to allow [land] to lie fallow. **ng/di*i** to apply [water] to. *ng*i banju sawah* to inundate a rice paddy. *** ka·susah·an** to undergo grief and trouble

éndra *ltry* mythological deity. **ka*n** realm of deities

éndrâdjâlâ *oj* shrewd, crafty. **ma·ng*** to practice trickery

éndrak a gum disease

éndrâsârâ *oj* a ruse; trickery

éndrâtjâpâ *oj* rainbow

éndrâwilâ *oj* blue diamond. **ng* (wilis)** [of hair] black and glossy

éndrin a rat poison. **ng/di*** to poison [rats, mice]

enḍuk *inf var of* GENḌUK. **ng/di*-*i** to try to catch [an animal] by coaxing it closer

endut ***-*** bouncy, springy. **endat-*** to waver indecisively, vacillate between alternatives. **ng/di*-*aké** to make sth springy. *See also* ENDAT, MENDUT

enḍut mud, sediment. **ng*** (to become) muddy *or* covered with sediment

ènèh *var of* WÈNÈH

ènèk *var of* ANA[a]

ènèl ***-*** *or* **ng*(-*)** to hurry along

ènèng *rg var of* ANA[a]. ***-*an** to pull back and forth from opposite directions. *Botjah loro *-*an tampar.* The two boys are having a tug-of-war. **ng/di*-*** to keep pulling sth toward oneself *or* back and forth

enengna *wj* ...so much for that (*marks a transition in the narrative*)

enes **ng*** deeply grieved. **ng/di*-*i** to bring deep sorrow to

ènèt *var of* NJÈT

eng well... um...

eng- *see also under* NG- (*Introduction, 2.9.5*)

èngèh *rg var of* WÈNÈH. *See also* NGÈNGÈH

èngèk *slang* ***-*** *rpr* the playing of a stringed instrument. **ng/di*-*** to play, saw away at [a stringed instrument]

èngès **ng/di*** 1 to sharpen (the end of). 2 to show [the teeth]

ènget to remember; to regain consciousness (*kr for* ÉLING)

éngga *sms* SA* *below.* ***né** if, supposing; when(ever). **né aku ora bisa, sapa sing arep ngganti?* In case I can't do it, who'll take over? **ng/di*-*** to dwell on, conjure up in the imagination. *Ora ana gunané ng*-* barang sing wis ora ana.* It's no use living in the past. **sa*** 1 up to; until. *Sa* sapriki kula mboten naté nampi serat saking pijambakipun.* I haven't heard from him to this day. 2 like; (it seems) as if. *Piwulang² kang samar² sa* arang banget kang bisa nemokaké.* Apparently there are few who can understand his mystic teachings. **sa*né** if, supposing. *sa*né aku ora bisa teka...* in case I can't be there...

engga (*prn* **ngga** *as inf kr,* **engga** *as md*) please (help yourself, *etc.*); here you are (*giving sth*) (*social var of* MANGGA)
énggak to tread water
enggak no; not (*rg var of* ORA). **ng/di*-*** to keep urging smn to do sth
énggal 1 quickly, right away (*kr for* ENDANG?). ** mrénéa.* Come here, quick! 2 new; recent (*kr for* ANJAR). ***ing tjarita** to make a long story short... ***-*** as quickly as possible (*kr for* AGÉ²?). ***-*an** in a great hurry. *Kok *-*an, diundjuk ḍisik kopiné.* What's the hurry?–drink your coffee first! **ng/di*aké** to speed sth up. *** iki** (*** mangké** *kr*) just recently
énggar **ng*-* ati·né** to relax, take it easy
enggé (*prn* **nggé** *as kr,* **enggé** *as md*) to use, wear (*root form: social var of* ANGGO)
enggèh *rg var of* INGGIH
enggèk in, at, on. *Ḍuwité mau kok simpen * endi?* Where did you put the money?
enggel main (essential, central) part
enggèn (*prn* **nggèn** *as kr,* **enggèn** *as md*) place; (act of) doing (*social var of* ENGGON)
enggeng **ng/di*** to leave sth where it is. *Adja di* munḍak gosong.* Don't leave it [on the stove]–it'll burn!
enggèr *var of* ANGGÈR
engget ***-*** line of demarcation, dividing point. *Tatuné ana ing *-*.* The wound is right at the joint. **ng/di*(-*)** to mark with a dividing line. *Saantarané kamar tamu lan kamar makan di*-*i rak buku.* A bookcase acts as a divider between the living and dining rooms.
enggih (*prn* **nggih** *as inf kr,* **enggih** *as md*) yes (*social var of* IJA)
enggik 1 *var of* ENGGÈK. 2 (*prn* [e]nggi:k) *rpr* the chirp of a certain beetle. ***-*an** 1 beetle that chirps as above. 2 narrowed part. ***-*en** sickly, prone to illness. **m*** small at the center, hourglass-shaped. **m* -ṁ·penṭol** irregularly thick and thin in shape. **ng*-*** very slim. **ng/di*aké** to make sth thin
enggo (*usu. prn* **nggo**) *ng,* **enggé** *kr* used as (*shf of* KANGGO). *Kertas kuwi nggo apa?* What's that paper for? **di*** *inf var of* DI·ANGGO. *Papan kuwi dinggo rapat mengko soré.* That place is to be used for a meeting this afternoon. *See also* ANGGO, KANGGO
énggok ***an** pretext, excuse. ***(-*)an** a turn in a road; a branching road. **m*** to turn (in, off, aside). *m* ngalor* to turn north. *Ajo m* kéné ja.* Come on, let's turn off here. *m* saka rembugan wiwitan* to shift away from the original topic. **m·énggak-m*** to turn this way and that. *Lakuné bis tansah ménggak-m*.* The bus kept zigzagging. **ng/di*aké** to turn sth. *ng*aké montor* to swerve the car. *ng*aké rembugan* to change the subject. **ng/di·énggak-*aké** to turn this way and that; to maneuver. *Buntuté iwak kanggo ngénggak-*aké.* The fish's tail is for steering.
enggok 1 in, at, on. *Omahé nggok endi?* Where does he live? 2 throat (*inf var of* GOROK·AN). ***-*** 1 *inf* throat. 2 ointment for the throat and neck. **ng/di*i** to place sth smw. *Médjané dinggoki kembang.* She put flowers on the table. *Anaké dinggoki klambi abang.* She dressed her daughter in red. **ng/di*-*i** to apply medication to the throat and neck. *See also* MANGGOK
enggon *ng,* **enggèn** *kr* 1 (**lenggah** *ki*) place. *ana *é kantjaku* at my friend's place (home). *nggoné bakul² djarik* the place [at the market] where the batik sellers are usually found. *A bisa olèh * kepénak.* A managed to get a good seat. *Jèn sekolah nèng sekolah menengah iku, angèl éntuk nggon.* It's hard to get into high school. 2 smn's act of [do]ing. *ngGoné ḍuḍuk² ditutugaké.* He kept at his digging. *ngGoné bal-balan ngalih *.* They moved (the site of) their soccer game. *Aku bungah, *mu nulis kok apik².* I'm delighted that you write so well. **é mangan kétoké énak.* He seems to be enjoying his food. ***-*an** here and there. *Awakku larané *-*an.* I'm sore in various places. *tembung *-*an* a regional word. **ng/di*i** to occupy [a place]. *Kursi kuwi adja di*i, sebab wis rusak.* Don't sit in that chair, it's broken. **sa*-*** everywhere; anywhere. *Uwuhé dibrukaké sak-enggon².* The trash was strewn all over the place. *Uripé sa-nggon².* He has no home. *See also* ANGGON
enggos **enggas-*** out of breath. *See also* KRENGGOS
enggreg **ng/di*-*i** to slow smn down, interfere with one's pace
enggrik *var of* ENGGÈK
enggrog ***-*** *rpr* a wild boar snorting
enggrok **ng/di*i** to stay at, stop (over) smw. **sa*an** (to stay smw) for a while. *lungguh sa*an* to sit for a while. *See also* ANGGROK

engguh **ng/di*** to consider, think of as. *Kowé kuwi wis tak * sedulur ḍéwé.* I think of you as my own brother.
engis **ng/di*-*** to hurt smn's feelings, offend smn
engkab **m*** to peel off, break off. *Sepatu wis m*² ngono kok dienggo?* Why are you wearing shoes with the soles coming off? **ng/di*** to peel sth off
engkak a variety of small crow
engkas still lacking, yet to come. *mengko sawetara dina ** in a few more days. *Seminggu * netes.* In another week they had hatched. *sepuluh rupiah ** 10 rupiahs more
engké *inf var of* MANGKÉ
èngkèl ***-*an** 1 to argue. 2 immobile. *Krasa lemes lan *-*an.* He froze and remained rooted to the spot. **ng*(-*)** immovable; to have difficulty moving. *Dikanḍani bener² kok tansah ng*.* I told you what was right but you remained unconvinced. *Ḍèké lémpoh, kok ng*-* lakuné.* He's so tired he can hardly walk.
engkèt, èngkèt ***-*** *rpr* creaking sound made by a shoulder carrying pole (*pikul·an*). *See also* KRENGKÈT
èngklèk 1 to hop on one foot. 2 (to play) hopscotch. **(ng)*** to go by foot. *Aku mau mréné (ng)* waé.* I walked here. **ng/di*-*** to wear [a sheathed kris] at the back of the waist
engklèk **ng/di*-*** to carry [*esp.* a baby] against the breast
éngko to plot, scheme
engko *inf var of* MENGKO
engkod ***-*** *rpr* wood creaking
éngkog ***-*** *or* **éngkag-*** to waddle
éngkok ***an** act *or* way of guiding (a discussion). ***-*** rippled, wavy. **ng/di*i** to lead, guide [a discussion]
éngkol 1 wrench; curved wrench handle. 2 strange; roundabout. 3 unit of measurement: the distance from elbow to fingertips. *sa** one such unit. ***-*** *or* **éngkal-*** zigzag. *Dalané éngkal-*.* The road twists and turns. *Taplaké médja dokokana *-*.* Put decorative zigzags on the tablecloth. **ng*** 1 twisting and turning. *Dalané kok ng*.* How the road winds! 2 (*psv* **di***) to measure sth in units as above (3). **ng/di*aké** to turn *or* bend sth. *See also* MÉNGKOL
éngkong **ng/di*aké** to bend [a straight object]
éngkrah **sa*-*é** whatever smn does. *Sa*-*é dideleng waé.* Observe everything he does.
éngkrang a certain style of Jogjanese male classical dancing. **sa*-*é** whatever smn does. *Sa*-*é ndjèngkèlké.* Everything he does is irritating.
èngkrèg ***-*** 1 (too) weak (to). 2 *rpr* creaking sounds. **sa*an** a short while. *Aku silihana sepéḍamu, sa*an waé.* Lend me your bicycle for a few minutes.
engkreng **ng/di*aké** to place sth on a burner. *ng*aké wadjan* to put a pan on the stove. **ng/di*i** to place sth on [a burner, stove]. *Anglonė adja di*i ḍisik.* Don't put it on the brazier yet.
engkuk a certain barbet-like bird. **ng/di*-*** to keep massaging smn, *esp.* in the neck; *fig* to overwork smn. *** kemong** *rg* a gamelan instrument
engkup **ng/di*aké** to close (up). *Pajungé *na.* Close the umbrella.
ènglèng **m*** to tilt the head to one side. **ng/di*aké** to tilt/turn smn's head, *e.g.* a barber giving a haircut
éngos **ng/di*i** to avert the head so as to avoid smn. *See also* PÉNGOS
èngsèl hinge. *** dir** door hinge. *** kenir** folding hinge. *** kupu** flat hinge on a box lid
èngsem *var of* ÈSEM
engu *var of* INGU
enguk ***-*** to sniff
èni **ng/di*-*** to take care of
eni *var of* ANI, ÈNI
ening 1 quiet, hushed. 2 clear, pure (*ltry var of* BENING)
enir **enar-*** *or* ***-*an** uneasy, apprehensive. *See also* NIR
enj- *see also under* NJ- (*Introduction, 2.9.5*)
enja *var of* NJA
enjak *var of* IDAK
enjèk **ng/di*(-*)** to mash, trample; *fig* to take advantage of smn
ènjeng, ènjèng *slang* mentally defective
ènjong, enjong I, me; my (*rg var of* AKU[a], -KU)
enjot *var of* GENDJOT
ènsiklopéḍi encyclopedia
énṭa **ng/di*(-*)** to create an image (of); to depict. *kang di* djogèdé* what the dance symbolizes. *Retja kuwi ng*-* wong sing lagi matja.* It's a statue of a person reading. *Senadjan barang sing arep mbok gambar ora ana, rak bisa di*-*.* If you haven't got the

thing you want to draw a picture of, conjure it up in your imagination! **pa·ng*-*** image created. *Tjrita iki mung fantasi, maudjud saka pang*-*né pangripta.* This story is pure fantasy, drawn from the author's imagination.

enṭak **ng*-*** vast and barren, void of vegetation

enṭang **ng*-*** 1 clear, bright, sunny. 2 left out in the open unprotected. **ng/di*-*aké** to leave sth out in the open. *See also* KENṬANG

éntar 1 metaphor(ical use of words). 2 [of knowledge] vast, far-reaching

enṭar **ng*** to run off. **ng/di*aké** to leave sth unprotected *or* unattended to

entârâ *var of* ANTARA

entas *inf var of* MENTAS. **ng/di*aké** *or* **ng/di*(i)** 1 to take sth off (out of, down). *Méméané wis di*i kabèh.* The clothes have all been taken in from the clothesline. *Wong mau di*ké saka mblumbang.* They pulled the man out of the pond. *Dagingé di*.* She removed the meat from the stove. 2 to marry off [one's child]. **pa·ng*an** edge of a swimming area, where swimmers come out of the water. *See also* PENTAS

entawis *kr* *var of* ANTAWIS

enṭé *intsfr* early [in the late-afternoon period]. *soré *-** first thing in the evening

enteb **ng/di*** to remove [rice] from the stove to cool. **ng/di*aké** 1 to place on the stove. *Wadjané wis di*aké nuli disoki santen.* She put the pan on the stove and poured in some coconut milk. 2 *var of* NG/DI·ANTEB·AKÉ. **ng/di*(i)** to weight sth down

èntèh *var of* ENṬÉ. *Isih soré * wis turu.* It's early in the evening but he's already gone to bed!

entèk *ng,* **telas** *kr* 1 all gone; used up. *Apa bènsiné *?* Are we out of gas? *Kopiné *.* The coffee's all gone. *durung nganti * enggoné mangan* before he finished eating. *Pariné * dipangan tikus.* The rice was all eaten up by mice. *Pariné wis * didoli.* The rice has all been sold. *Pitakoné ora *-*.* He never runs out of questions. 2 to take, require, consume. ** pira anggonmu ngedusaké?* How much did it cost to have it gold-plated? *Gelis banget mubalé geni, tjatjah wuwung * omah telu.* The fire spread quickly; it consumed three houses. 3 end, final part. *Telasipun wulan Sijam dipun muljakaken Lebaran.* The last day of the fasting month is celebrated as Lebaran day. *Pegawéanku ora ana *é.* There's no end to my work. ***-*an** 1 finally; the end. *saben *-*ané sasi* at the end of each month. **-*ané ḍèké bandjur pinḍah menjang Djakarta.* He finally moved to Djakarta. 2 to the last one. *Tanggaku kemalingan nganti *-*an.* My neighbor was robbed of every last thing he owned. 3 to an extreme degree. *Seriké banget, marga diunèk-unèkaké *-*an.* He got mad at them for yelling at him so violently. **k(a)*an** low on, short of; to run out of. *k*an pangan* low on food. *Ḍèké ora k*an akal.* He never runs out of ideas. **ng*** at the outer limit. *wis ng* karosané* to have reached the end of one's strength. **ng/di*aké** to use up completely. to finish. *Undjukanipun dipun telasaken rumijin.* Please finish your drink first. *ng*aké pegawéjan* to finish a job, finish the work. *ng*-*aké ḍuwit* to spend all of one's money. **sa*é** at the end of; after sth is over. *sa*é sulap* after he did his magic tricks. *** ati** 1 frightened. 2 dispirited, discouraged. *** djarak·é** **1** out of money. 2 at the end of one's creative powers. *** enting** *ng only* all used up, completely gone

enṭek̄ full, filled out [of women's breasts]

ènten to exist; there is/are *(md for* ANA[a])

entèn ***-*** brown-sugar-coated peanuts

ènṭèng light (*i.e.* not heavy; not difficult; not serious). *Kupu iku * banget awaké.* Butterflies have light bodies. *Pegawéané *.* The work is light. *Laranè wis *.* His illness has improved. ***an** to enjoy helping others. ***an bau** to enjoy helping others with manual labor. **k*en** excessively light. **ng/di*aké** 1 to make sth light. 2 to make light of, not take seriously. **ng*i** to recover. *Ali wis ng*i.* Ali is getting better. *** lambé** to talk a lot; to engage in gossip

entèng ***-*** *intsfr* all gone (*var of* ENTING)

enṭeng **ng*-*** *intsfr* noontime. *beḍug ng*-** high noon, the hottest part of the day

entes *rg var of* MENTAS

enṭet **ng/di*** to hold back. *Saking nesuné ora bisa ng* tjlaṭuné.* He was so angry he couldn't refrain from speaking out. *Lho sing rong rupiah di* ja?* So—you kept out the other two rupiahs for yourself, did you?

enti *ng*, **entos** *kr* ***n̂-*n̂an** (**entos²an** *kr*) to wait for each other. **ng/di*n̂i** to wait (for). *Aku mèlu, entènana.* I'm going with you: wait! *Dientèn-entèni ora teka².* He waited and waited but she never showed up. **ngentèni k·um·elem·é gabus** *or* **ngentèni timbul·é watu item** to expect the impossible to happen. *See also* ANTI

entih *var of* ANTIH

enṭik 1 the essential growth-producing sprout from a root. 2 small woven-bamboo basket, used sometimes as a measure. ***-*(an)** little finger. **ng*** to develop the growth-producing sprout at maturity

enṭil **ng*** to nurse (*inf var of* M̈·PENṬIL). **ng/di*-*** to give out sparingly, try not to spend. *Bajarané di*-*.* They pay the wages bit by bit. *Duwit seṭiṭik di*-*, malah ditjolong uwong.* I had a little money I was saving, and it got stolen. *See also* KENṬIL

enting *intsfr* all gone. *Ketjapé wis entèk *.* The soy sauce is all used up. ***-*** a confection of cane sugar, coconut sugar, and peanuts

enṭir cricket's chirp. **ng*** 1 to chirp. 2 to waver, oscillate. 3 to give off smoke

enṭit a card game played with Chinese cards (*kertu tjilik*). **ng*** 1 [of animals] to copulate. 2 to lay eggs. **ng/di*-*** to take (pick up, go get) little by little *or* one at a time. **sa*** a tiny bit

entjak-entji to hesitate with indecision. *Adja *, lunga apa ora?* Make up your mind: are you going or not?

entjeb **ng/di*i** 1 to stick sth into [soil *etc.*]. 2 to cling fast to

entjèh glass tube

èntjèng ***-*** a certain plant. ***-*an** facing diagonally. *Omahku *-*an karo omahé.* My house is cater-corner across from his. **ng/di*aké** to place diagonally opposite. *See also* PÈNTJÈNG

èntjep **m*** to twist the lips quickly to one side as a gesture of dislike, contempt. **m·éntjap-m*** to make the above gesture repeatedly. **ng/di*aké** to twist [the lips] in this gesture. *Lambéné di*aké.* She gestured disdainfully. **ng/di*i** to gesture at [smn] as above

èntjèr 1 [of liquids] thin, weak. *susu ** thin (diluted) milk. *tèh ** weak tea. 2 mentally active. ** pikirané.* She has a quick mind. **ng/di*aké** to make [a liquid] thin(ner). *di*aké mawa banju* diluted

entjik 1 *pejorative* a full-blooded Chinese. 2 (*prn* **ntjik**) *adr* Chinese girl/woman. **k*an** 1 to get stood (up) on, to lengthen one's reach. 2 possessed by evil spirits. **ng/di*i** to stand on sth to extend one's upward reach. *ng*i kursi* to stand on a chair. *See also* ANTJIK

entji:m sister. **ng/di*** to long for, have one's eye on

entjit ***-*an** 1 pacifier. 2 squeaky rubber doll. **ng*** to nurse, suck

entjlok *var of* ÉNTJOK

éntjo comfortable, easy, pleasant

entjod up-and-down movement of the feet. ***-*an** to keep moving the feet up and down. **ng/di*** to move the feet up and down on sth. *Uwoté adja di*-*, mengko ambrol.* Don't stamp on the bridge or it'll collapse.

éntjok rheumatism. ***an** a perch; act of perching. **ané papah geḍang.* It perched on a banana leaf. **ng/di*aké** to have/let [a creature] alight on sth. *Manuké di*aké ing punḍaké.* He let the bird light on his shoulder. **ng/di*i** to alight on. *Irungé di*i laler.* A fly lit on his nose. *See also* PÉNTJOK

éntjon teammate, partner

éntjong **ng/di*aké** to cause sth to be off center (*var of* M̈/DI-PÉNTJONG·AKÉ)

éntjos **m*** slantwise, crooked, lopsided. **m·éntjas-m*** *pl as above. Tulisané méntjas-m*.* His handwriting goes every which way. **ng*** slantwise, on the diagonal. *Plajuné ng* ngiwa.* He ran off to the left. *Wité diketok ng*.* He cut the tree off slantwise.

entjret *var of* INTJRIT

entjrit *var of* INTJRIT

entjung eggplant

éntjup, entjup **ng/di*** 1 to catch with thumb and finger. *Kupu kuwi tak *é.* I'm going to catch that butterfly! 2 to guess (the answer to)

énṭog, ènṭog *var of* MÉNṬOG

enṭok-enṭing 1 having a large head and a small body. 2 *Jogja slang* having a small head and a large body. *See also* ṬOK-ṬING

entol ***-*an** to bargain strenuously with a market seller. **ng/di*** 1 to make a show of standing firm on an offer. *Betjiké di* seka seṭiṭik, suwé² rak diwènèhaké.* Just give way little by little and she'll finally let you have it. 2 to jack sth up. 3 to pry

énṭong rice ladle of coconut shell or wood. ***(-*an)** shoulder blade(s). **ng/di*** to ladle out [rice]. *** palwa** paddle, oar

éntos, énṭos able; capable

entos to wait (*root form: kr for* ENTI)

éntra mark, symbol. ***(-*)** scheme, plan. ***n-*n** (that which is) imitation, fake. **ng/di*(-*)** to imitate, do in the same way (as)

éntrah **sa*(-*)é** whatever one does. *Sa*é ora ana sing menging.* No matter what he does, nobody tells him not to.

entrah ***-*an** plan, intention

entrig ***-*an** to proceed by small prancing paces; to jump up and down, hop around

entrog **ng/di*-*** *or* **ng/di·entrag-*** to shake (up). *Aku tau di*-* bis.* I got jounced around on the bus. **ng/di*(aké)** to shake sth; to trample on sth. *See also* ANTROG

éntrok brassière-like item of ladies' under-clothing

enṭu **ng*(-*)** to make one's way smw in the face of difficulties. *Kowé ng*, sadjak ana perlu banget.* You've gone through a lot to get here–it must be urgent.

éntuk *ng,* **(pik)antuk** *kr* 1 to get, obtain. *Kuwi gèk *mu saka ngendi?* Where did you get that? *Aku wis * pegawéjan lija.* I've found another job. ** pènsiun* to receive a pension. 2 to receive permission. *Kowé ora * lunga.* You aren't allowed to go. 3 to receive as spouse. *Entèk²ané Slamet * Siti.* Slamet finally married Siti. ***(-*)an** *ng only* thing(s) obtained, *e.g.* a harvest; the answer to a problem; profits from sales; stolen loot. **ng/di*aké** *ng only* to allow, let

entul **ng*-*** to bounce up and down (on). *See also* PENTUL

entung all gone (*var of* ENTING)

enṭung cocoon. **ng*** in the cocoon stage

entup stinger. ***-*an** stinging creatures. **ng/di*(i)** to sting. *Tawon iku ng* nganggo *.* Bees sting with their stingers.

entut 1 **(sarib** *ki***)** flatus. 2 *slang* baloney! nuts! **ng*** **(sarib** *ki***)** to discharge flatus. *** bérut** stomach gas; flatus. *See also* KEPENTUT

énuk **énak-*** *rg var of* ÉNAK²

enung **di*-*** to be looked after, taken good care of

ep- *see also under* P- (*Introduction, 2.9.5*)

épah compensation for services (*kr for* OPAH)

èpèk 1 leather *or* velvet belt. 2 bunch of bananas coming from a single bud. 3 share of stock. ***-*** palm of the hand

epik **ng/di*-*** to touch, handle

èpjèk (*or* ***-***) 1 noisy [talk]; talkative. 2 very busy, tied up

èplèg ***-*** *rpr* hand-clapping

epoh a variety of mango

er *see* HER

er- *see also under* R- (*Introduction, 2.9.5*)

éra [of eyes] not functioning together, out of focus with each other. *mata ** wall-eyed; cross-eyed. *See also* KÉRA

érak, erak hoarse (of voice); sore (of throat)

éram awesome; awed. ***-*an** that which inspires awe. **k*en** lost in awe of sth. **ng*(-*)aké** *or* **ng*(-*)i** awe-inspiring. **pa·ng*-*** 1 that which inspires awe. 2 a miracle, magic

érang **ng/di*-*** to get mad at, raise one's voice to

érawati loud sounds of the elements, *esp.* wind, thunder

ereb **ng/di*(i)** to cut, slice

èrèd **ng/di*(-*)** to drag smn along; to involve smn else in [a nefarious activity]

èrèg **ng/di*-*** to persuade, talk smn into

èrèk ***-*** *intsfr* short, low. *(tj)enḍèk *-** extremely short/low. ***(-*an)** to circle [*e.g.* an opponent] warily. **ng/di*i** to court [of chickens; *cr* of people]

èrēk *var of* ÉRAK

èrem (to get) a black-and-blue mark. *biru ** (to have) a bruise, black-and-blue place

èrèng ***-*** sloping valley wall *or* hillside. *See also* PÈRÈNG

ereng **(ng)*-*** 1 to keep roaring. 2 to keep moaning with pain

èrep estate, property

èrès 1 to bluff, bluster. *Ḍèké ming * waé, tenanana mengko rak wedi.* He's just bluffing–show him you mean it and he'll be scared off. 2 *var of* IRIS

eres *var of* IRIS

èrgelèk liquor bottle

èrgulo rose (flower). *banju ** rosewater

éring **k*an** held in respect. *wong k*an* a highly respected man. **ng/di*aké** to inspire awe/respect in. *Kepinterané ng*aké aku.* His brilliance overawes me. **ng/di*i** to hold in respect. *Sarèhning tijang sepuh, wadjib dipun *i.* He's old and deserves your respect. **ng*-*aké** *or* **ng*-*i** inspiring awe/respect

èrmawar rose (flower)

èrmil airmail

érok ***-*** a perforated utensil for removing

frying foods from the pan and draining them. 2 bricklayer's trowel. *See also* ḌOḌOK

Éropā(h) Europe

èru **érâ-*** tumult, violent disorder

érut *var of* GAÉRUT

ès 1 ice. *banju ** ice. *udan ** snow; to snow. *lemari ** icebox. 2 iced drink. 3 *cr* female genitals. *** batu** cake of ice, ice block. *** ganḍul** *or* *** gantung** shaved ice on a stick. *** gosok** shaved ice. *** krim** ice cream (Occidental style). *** lilin** popsicle, ice cream on a stick. *** puter** ice cream (Javanese style). *** setrup** cold drink made with syrupy ice. *** soklat** iced chocolate drink

es 1 shoo! scat! 2 *sound of disapproval. Essss, omong kosong iku.* It's a lie! 3 pst! **di*** to be addressed in one of the above ways. *Ḍèké tansah di* ing Sudjana.* Sudjono kept saying "pst! " to her.

es- *see also under* S- (*Introduction, 2.9.5*)

ésa power, authority

èseg hoarse

èsèk ***-*** *rpr* rustling. **-*é kaju djati* the rustling of the teak trees

èsèl 1 railroad switch. *tukang ** switch operator. 2 *var of* ÈNGSÈL

esel *var of* USEL

èsem a smile. *manising ** the sweetness of her smile. *gawé ** to make smn smile. **m*** to smile. *M*a kang pait madu.* Smile sweetly! **m*-m*** *or* **m·ésam-m*** to keep smiling; to grin. **ng/di*i** to smile at. **pa·m*** act *or* way of smiling

èsi **di*-*** to be ridiculed. **ka*-*** to get treated cruelly. **ng*-*** to torment, torture

ésih *var of* ISIH

eslup *var of* ANGSLUP

èsmu 1 a written Arabic phrase used as a magical protection from danger *or* illness. 2 *oj* appearance, aspect

èsprès 1 fast. *Jèn * bajar ḍobel.* If you want it fast, you have to pay double. 2 express train

èsrèg 1 restless, unable to sit without squirming. 2 (*or* *-*) *rpr* the rustling sound of slight movements

èsṭa *var of* ISṬA

èsṭi **ng/di*** to think about, reflect on

esṭi determination, resoluteness. **di*** fixed, set [of will]. **nen murih kelakon. Make it happen!*

èstri female (*kr for* WADON, WÉDOK). **ng/di*ǹi** to attend, be present at (*ki for* Ñ/DI·TEKA·NI?). *para tamu mantja negara sing paḍa ngèstrèni pahargjan* the foreign visitors who attended the reception. *See also* PAWÈSTRI

èstu *sms* SA* *below.* ***nipun** *sms* SA*NIPUN. **ng* pada** to do homage to, show esteem for. **ng/di*k̂aké** 1 to obey. *Èstokna ḍawuhing guru.* Do as the teacher says. 2 to laugh (*oblique ka for* NG(GE)·GUJU). **ng/dipun*k̂aken** to carry out an intention (*kr for* ÑJ/DI·SIDA·KAKÉ). **sa*** 1 really, actually (*kr for* NJATA, TEMEN(AN)). 2 to go through with, succeed in [do]ing (*kr for* SIDA). **sa*nipun** actually, in fact (*kr for* NJATA·NÉ, SA·TEMEN·É)

ésuk *ng,* **éndjing** *kr* 1 morning. 2 early in the morning. *Isih *, srengéngéné durung ḍuwur.* It was early; the sun wasn't high. *sepur kang * ḍéwé* the first train in the morning. ***é** the following day/morning. **é ḍèké bali mrono.* He went back there the next day. ***-*** early in the morning. ***-*an** 1 to compete *or* compare for earliest. **-*an, aku nèk tangi rak * ḍéwé.* I'm the earliest riser! 2 rather late in the morning. **k*en** too early. **ng/di*i** to make sth early, set sth ahead in time. *Tinimbang kasèp, luwih betjik di*i tekané.* It's better to get there ahead of time than too late. **sa*** all morning. *** ḍelé soré témpé** shifty, unreliable. *Omongé * ḍelé soré témpé.* You can't rely on what he says. *** m̀·pruput** early in the morning. *** soré** 1 morning and evening. 2 *ng kr* a certain flower that blooms twice each day–morning and evening. 3 *ng kr* differently batiked on each side. *Iketé * soré.* His headdress has a different batik design on each side. *** umun**² *or* *** uṭuk**² very early in the morning. *See also* BÉSUK, KÉSUK

et *excl expressing surprise, dismay, warning*

et-, eṭ- *see also under* T-, Ṭ- (*Introduction, 2.9.5*)

étak *var of* IDAK

étan east. ***-*an** the eastern part. **ng*** eastward. *mlaku ng** to walk east. **ng*-ǹg·kulon** all over. *Tansah wira-wiri ngalor-ngidul ng*-ngulon.* He wandered far and wide. **sa*(é)** to the east of. *See also* PANGÉTAN, WÉTAN

étang arithmetic; calculation (*kr for* ÉTUNG)

etas *var of* MENTAS. ** waé teka.* He just got here.

été **m*-m*** *or* **ng*-ng*** [of stomach] to stick out. *Olèhé nganggo kaṭok kok m**².

Your pants are too low at the waistline—your stomach hangs out. **ng/di*k-*kaké** to cause sth to stick out; to allow sth to show. *Lagi duwé ḍuwit semono waé kok di*-*aké.* You have all that money and you're leaving it in plain sight—!

èṭèh **ng*-*** to lie sprawled face up. **ng/di*(-*)aké** to allow sth to show; to reveal. *Barang wadi, adja di*aké waé!* It's a secret—don't tell!

èṭèk shallow (*var of* TJEṬÈK). **ng*-*** in plain sight, visible, showing

ètel solid, firm. *** ati·né** calm and courageous

èṭèng 1 a Jogjanese male classical spear dance. 2 obstinate. **m·éṭang-m*** to show, stick out [of stomach]. **ng*-*** in plain sight. **ng/di*-*aké** to disclose, reveal

èter *var sp of* ÈTHER

èṭèr 1 *rpr* rattling. 2 *rpr* water trickling out. **ng*** to trickle continuously. **ng/di*-*** to scatter, strew

eter **ng*-*i** earth-shaking; causing smn to tremble

etes forceful, significant. * *pangandikané.* What he says carries a lot of weight.

èther (*prn* **èter**) ether

étikèt manners, etiquette

etj- *see also under* TJ- (*Introduction, 2.9.5*)

étja pleasing to the senses (*kr for* ÉNAK)

étjak *var of* IDAK

étjé formerly used ten-cent coin. *sa** 10 cents. **ng/di*** to make fun of, jeer at. *Kantjil ngawasaké saka kadohan karo ng*-*.* Mouse-Deer watched from afar, gloating.

etjèh **ng/di*-*** to squander

ètjèk **ng/di*(-*)** to challenge, threaten with words

ètjèr ***an** (traded) at retail, in small amounts. *rega *an* retail price. *pedagang *an* retailer. *Sing ora bisa tuku sagendul ija trima tuku *an.* Those who couldn't afford a whole bottle bought smaller quantities. **k*** 1 scattered. *Berasé k* nang ndjubin.* Rice was strewn on the floor. 2 to get left behind. *Bukuku k* nang nggoné kantjaku.* I left my book at a friend's. **ng/di*** 1 to buy/sell in small amounts. *Jèn ng* regané luwih larang.* It costs more to buy in small quantities. 2 to plant [seeds] in a hole. **ng/di*-*** to scatter, strew. *Mangsiné di*-* ing ndjogan.* He spattered ink on the floor. **ng/di*aké** to sell [merchandise] at retail. **ng/di*i** to give a small amount to. *Apa kowé bisa ng*i aku lenga?* Can you let me have a little oil?

etju *intsfr* blue. *biru ** deep blue

éṭok ***-*** to pretend. *Aku *-* turu.* I pretended I was asleep. ***-*an** make-believe; faked. *Anggoné tarung mung *-*an.* They were only making a pretense of fighting. **m*** to show clearly, be in plain sight

étol ***-*** to waddle

éṭor able; capable. *Ora * waé, ngomongé gedé²*. You can't do anything but you talk big.

éṭos *var of* ÉṬOR

étung *ng*, **étang** *kr* arithmetic; calculation. *djuru ** bookkeeper; specialist at calculations. ***an** 1 arithmetic; arithmetic problem, puzzle. 2 overcareful with money. *Jèn ndjilih ḍuwit nèng Ali kudu dibalèkaké lho, wong ḍèké *an.* If you borrow money from Ali, be sure to pay it back—he keeps track. ***é** although. **é ḍèké kuwi wong mlarat, nanging duwé omah.* He's poor, but he owns a house. ***-*** to count. **-* tekan sepuluh* to count to ten. ***-*an** to settle expenses with each other. **ng/di*aké** to count on smn's behalf. **ng/di*(i)** 1 to count (sth). **en.* Count them! *ng* tekan telu* to count to three. 2 to consider, regard. *Kena di* sidji loro sing nganggo kaja ngono.* You could say that not many people dress that way. 3 to figure, calculate. *ng* petjahan* to compute fractions. **ng* katjang** very easy, nothing to it. *Mungsuh wong adjaran gampang baé ngalahké, kaja ng* katjang.* It's a cinch to beat a beginner. **pa·ng*** enumeration; calculation. *Pang*é ora bener.* The count (*or* calculation) wasn't accurate. *** awang·an** oral arithmetic. *** lésan** oral arithmetic. **ora *** to pay no attention, not stop to think. *Njambut gawé wiwit ésuk nganti bengi, ora * wajah.* He works from morning to night without regard for time. *Nalika aku krungu swarané banju teka, aku ora *, bandjur mènèk ing wit.* When I heard the [flood] water coming, I climbed a tree without stopping to think. *See also* PÉTUNG

évolusi evolution

éwa of an unsympathetic *or* jealous nature. **ng/di*k-*kaké** to act supercilious (toward), treat with disdain. *mèsem ngéwak²aké* to smile in a superior way. *** déné** *or* *** mengkono** *or* *** semono** even so; but still; in spite of [the foregoing]. *Wis diadjar barang, * semono ora kapok.* He's been punished and everything but he still hasn't learned.

éwah 1 to change (*kr for* OWAH). 2 crazy (*kr for* ÉDAN)
éwang *-* to help, lend a hand. **ng/di*i** to help smn, help with sth. *See also* RÉWANG
èwed busy; having difficulty (*kr for* ÉWUH)
èwèg **ng/di*-*** to carry around. *Botjah lagi bisa njusu, adja di*-*.* Don't carry the baby around while he's nursing.
èweg uneasy, uncomfortable. **ng/di*-*** to disturb, trouble
èwèh *rg var of* WÈNÈH
èwèng **ng*** obstinate. **ng/di*-*** *or* **ng·éwang-*** 1 to push at, keep shoving. 2 to carry around. *Saking senengé ḍèké mlaku rana-réné ng*-* idjasahé.* He's so happy he carries his diploma everywhere with him.
èwèr **ng/di*-*** to pull sth out. *Bolahé adja di*-*.* Don't pull the thread out. *Senengé kok ng*-* wadining lijan.* She draws people's secrets out of them.
èwu thousand. *s** 1,000. *rong ** 2,000. ***n̂** 1 digit occupying the thousands place. *ékan, dasan, atusan, éwon* units, tens, hundreds, thousands. 2 thousands; by the thousand. *Èwon kang paḍa mati.* Thousands died. 3 thousand-rupiah bill. *sèwon* one 1,000-rupiah bill. *rong èwon* two 1,000-rupiah bills. ***n̂-*n̂** many thousands. *Sing mati éwon²*. People died by the thousand. ***n̂an** approximately a thousand. *Gadjihé rong èwonan.* His salary is a couple of thousand rupiahs. **ma*-*** many thousands (of). **pra*** -thousandth. *pitung pra** 0.007. *See also* SÈWU
éwuh *ng,* **èwed** *kr* 1 busy (at). *Ḍèké lagi * apa?* What's she working at? 2 uneasiness, reluctance; (to feel) uncomfortable, ill at ease. *Arep mangsuli, ija *.* She wanted to answer but couldn't get the words out. 3 *slang* having a menstrual period. ***-*** 1 *sms * 1, 2 above.* 2 to hold a party/ceremony. **k*an** at a loss; troubled. *Aku k*an anggonku nulungku.* I don't know how I can help. *Ḍèké meneng, semu k*an anggoné arep guneman.* She was silent; she seemed to have trouble finding words. **ng*aké** troublesome, disturbing. *Ng*aké temen kaanan iki.* What a nuisance this is! **ng/di*-*i** to create difficulties for smn. *Jèn lagi sinau adja di*-*.* Don't disturb him while he's studying. *** aja (ing pa·m·budi)** in a dilemma, torn between alternatives. *djaman * aja* troublesome times. *** pakéwuh** uneasiness, awkwardness; (to feel) uncomfortable, ill at ease. *Sampun kagungan èwed-pakèwed.* Make yourself at home! *See also* PAKÉWUH, SEKÉWUH
èxcèm *var sp of* ÈKSIM
èxposisi exhibition

F

f (*prn* **èf**) *alphabetic letter* (*often Javanized to* P *in foreign loan words: see also under* P)
fā fourth note in the musical scale
fadjar dawn
fakir indigent holy man who begs and performs magic for a living. *** miskin** the poor
fakultas academic discipline in a university
fasèh fluent. *Basa Arabé *.* He's fluent in Arabic.
fasih *var of* FASÈH
fasis fascist
Fébruari (*abbr:* **Fébr.**) February
fètsin monosodium glutamate
fiksir solution for fixing photographic reproductions. **di*** to have fixative applied to it
filem film, movie. **m̂/di*** to take motion pictures (of). *turis Amérika sing milem wajang wong* an American tourist taking movies of the dance-drama. **per*an** film production
firullah *see* ASTAGA
firus 1 turquoise. 2 virus
fisikā physics. *ilmu * nuklir* nuclear physics

fitri *see* IDUL
flambojan a tree that bears violet-colored blossoms in profusion
fonetis phonetic
formatir 1 person appointed by the head of a nation to formulate a cabinet of ministers. 2 person(s) appointed by a conference or congress to formulate policy for the group
formulir form, blank. ∗ *pendaftaran* registration form
foto 1 photograph, snapshot. *pas* ∗ passport picture. *tukang* ∗ photographer. 2 to have one's picture taken. **m̃/di∗** to take a picture of. *A moto B.* A took B's picture.
fotografi photography
fraksi splinter group in Parliament
frambusia yaws
fungsi function, position
fusi fusion, union (of groups). ∗ *saka organisasi buruh werna²* a union of various trade organizations

G

g (*prn* **gé**) 1 *alphabetic letter.* 2 *see* GUNUNG
ga 1 *inf var of* GAWA. 2 *shf of* SAGA. 3 *shf of* UGA. *Ḍèké* ∗ *teka.* He came too. ∗ **ja** ∗ **ora** to keep changing one's mind. ∗ **sampéjan** I don't know *(sbst kr for* EMBUH)
ga- *see also under* GE- (*Introduction, 2.9.2*)
gabag measles. **∗en** to have/get measles
gabah rice grain; an ear of rice. **∗an** [of eyes] shaped like a grain of rice, *i.e.* narrow and tapering: very refined. **ge∗** hasty,rash. *tindak kang ge∗* a hasty action. **ng/di∗** to feed rice to. *Darané di∗.* He fed rice grains to his pigeons. **ng/di·ge∗** to encourage, coax. *Bareng dige∗ ḍèké terus madju.* After some urging, he came forward. **kaja ∗ di·inter·i** in a state of confusion *or* chaos. ∗ **s·in·awur** a certain batik design
gabeng dried up/out. *Tebuné ∗.* The sugar cane has no juice.
gaber ∗-∗ *or* **ng∗** to eject [air; food] forcibly through the lips. *Ḍèké ngombé banju mau, djebul tjokak sanalika ḍèké ∗-∗.* He drank the liquid, but when it turned out to be vinegar, he spit it out.
gabès *var of* GABUS
gabes [of fruits] dry and tasteless. **∗an** luckless. **ng∗** to keep nibbling. *Adja ng∗ waé!* Stop eating snacks!
gabig **gobag-∗** 1 to keep shaking the head. 2 to wobble, shake
gabjeg **ng∗** to nag constantly
gabjes *var of* GABJEG
gablag **ng∗** to talk incessantly
gableg to have (*cr var of* DUWÉ)
gablog a certain dish made with mashed glutinous rice. **ng/di∗(i)** to hit smn on the back
gablug 1 *rpr* a thud. *Mak ∗ anakku tiba saka tempat tiḍur.* My son fell off the bed. 2 dull. *Pésoné ∗.* The knife is dull. **g·um·ablug** to fall with a thud
gabrès messy around the mouth after eating. **ora ng∗** unconcerned. *Nèk ana apa² ḍèké ora ng∗.* He doesn't care if things go wrong.
gabrol *var of* GABRUL
gabrug *rpr* a heavy thud. **∗an** to get sth without exertion. *Njambut-gawé ki sing tenanan, adja ∗an kaja ngono.* Put effort into the work–don't expect to just get by.
gabrul **ng/di∗** to acquire dishonestly. *Jèn djadjan adja ng∗ waé.* You have to pay for all the snacks you eat.
gabrus *rpr* a collision. **∗an** a collision; to collide. *Ana montor ménggok ∗an karo anḍong.* A car, turning, collided with a horse carriage. **ng/di∗** to collide with
gabrut smeared with mud
gabu a large whitish banana

gabug [of rice ears] producing no grains; [of people] sterile, unable to reproduce. **ng*i** [of nursing mothers] unable to produce milk. ***aos·é** the facts of the matter. **aosé tjrita mau kudu dinjatakaké ḍisik.* First, the facts should be established.

gabung ***an** joint, cooperative. **ng/di*** to join forces with. **ng/di*aké** to join [two things]. *Irian Barat wis bisa di*aké manèh karo wilajah Indonesia.* West Irian has been reunited with Indonesia. *Olèh²ané bareng di*aké djumlahé ana sepuluh èwu rupiah.* His combined earnings amount to 10,000 rupiahs.

gabus 1 cork; the tree whose bark produces cork. 2 pith of the cassava plant. 3 an eel-like river fish. **ng/di*** 1 to sharpen, hone. 2 to bet on [a racing rooster]. 3 to hold smn's cards for him while he leaves the game temporarily

gada club, bludgeon. *ngikal ** to brandish a club. **ng/di*** to strike with a club. *** gitik** courage; prowess

gadag **ng*** pervasive [of odors]

gaḍag thick rope

gaḍah 1 to have, own (*kr for* DUWÉ). 2 the possession/belonging (of) (*kr for* DUWÈK-). *** laré** to give birth (*kr for* BAJI·Ñ)

gaḍang ***an** 1 candidate, prospect. 2 ready for planting. **ng/di*** to want, wish for. **ng/di*-*** to expect, look forward to. **ng/di*aké** to hope for, expect. *Putrané ḍéwé di*aké nggentèni Sang Prabu.* She intended that her own son should succeed to the throne.

gaḍé *ng*, **gantos** *kr* ***an** (**gantos·an** *kr*) pawnshop. ***n̂** (**gantos·an** *kr*) 1 pawnshop. 2 (an article) in pawn *or* to be pawned. *Djamku isih ana ing gaḍèn.* My watch is pawned. 3 [money] received for a pawned article. *ḍuwit gaḍèn* money raised by pawning sth. **ng/di*** to lend money on articles. *sing ng** pawnbroker. **ng*an** pawnshop; pawnbroker. **ng/di*kaké** 1 to pawn sth. *Aku nggaḍèkaké djamku.* I pawned my watch. *Djamku isih tak gaḍèkaké.* My watch is in pawn. *Ḍèké nggaḍèk-gaḍèkaké utawa utang².* He often pawns things or borrows. 2 to lease [a rice paddy]. **pa*an** pawnbroker; pawnshop. *** peteng** unlicensed pawnshop/pawnbroker. **tukang *** pawnbroker

gaḍel 1 tartar that collects on teeth. 2 a certain poisonous root. **ng*** 1 coated with tartar. 2 to stick to the throat

gaḍil boar's tusk

gaḍing 1 elephant's tusk. 2 ivory. 3 nasal mucous (*ki for* UMBEL). **g·um·aḍing** resembling ivory, *esp.* in color

gadjah (**liman** *kr?*) elephant. **ng*** resembling an elephant. **ng* elar** headstrong. **(ng)*an** elephant compound. *** meta** furious, enraged. *** m̈·paran·i wantil·an** to deliberately subject oneself to risk

gadjeg ***é** I think; (*in questions*) do you think? *Ana pawon *é ana tutup kas.* I think there's a box cover in the kitchen. **godjag-*** hesitant, undecided. *Jèn godjag-* ora susah lunga.* If you're not sure, don't go.

gadjig **godjag-*** shaky, unsteady; *fig* uncertain, wavering. *Atiné godjag-*.* He couldn't make up his mind.

gadjih 1 salary, wages. 2 the fat (of meat, as opposed to the lean). *menangi ** to experience only good things. ***an** 1 payday. 2 to receive one's salary at a fixed time. **ng*** 1 fatty [of meat]. 2 (*psv* **di***) to pay smn a salary *or* wages. **ng/di*i** to oil *or* grease sth. **pa*** dry riverbed (which gets inundated during the rainy season) used as a rice paddy

gadjul a substitute for the real thing. ** pangan* substitute food, *i.e.* sth other than rice. **ng/di*** to kick with the tip of the foot. **ng*i** to act as a substitute for. *Krama dina iki lara, aku ng*i ḍèké.* Krama is sick today; I'm taking his place.

gaḍo ***-*** vegetable salad with peanut-butter sauce. ***n̂** 1 steamed beef-and-egg roll. 2 a music program consisting of a minimum selection of gamelan melodies. **ng*** to eat the accompanying dishes without the rice. *Tak ng* iwak pitik baé ja?* Is it all right if I have just chicken? **ng* ati** to cause constant sorrow for smn. *Botjah iki tansah ng* ati.* I'm always eating my heart out over this child.

gaḍog 1 *rpr* a bumping sound. 2 not (going) through. *Dalan iki *.* This is a dead-end street.

gadri section of a Javanese-style house behind the front part where guests are received *(pendapa)*. ** tengah* central section of a house. ** mburi* rear section adjoining the central part: the opposite number of the *pendapa*. ** wétan (kulon, lor, kidul)* side sections (to the east, west, north, south) surrounding the central part

gadrug *-* corpulent

gaḍu (*or* *n̂) planted during the dry season. *sawah gaḍu/gaḍon* a "dry-planted" paddy. *pari gaḍon* rice grown in such a paddy. **di*** to be planted during the dry season. * **walik·an** paddy that can be planted in either dry or rainy season; **panèn *(n̂) walik·an** (to get) a harvest from such a planting

gadug within reach. *Nèk ora *, munggaha kursi kuwi lho.* If you can't reach it, stand on that chair. **di*(-*)aké** to do one's best to reach/attain sth. *Aku ora isa.–Ajo di*-*aké.* I can't do it.–Try! **sa*-*é** whatever one can attain. *Rampungna gawéjanmu sa-*-*é.* Do as much of the work as you can.

gaḍug a bump, thump; *rpr* the sound of a bump. *Mak * aku nabrak lawang.* I bumped my head on the door. *Aku krasa *ing roḍa montor mabur ana ing lanḍesan.* I felt the wheels touch down on the runway. **ke*** to knock against sth

gaḍuh ***an** that which is given to smn to use but not to own. *Iki dudu montorku ḍéwé, mung *an.* This isn't my car, I just have the use of it. *diparingi *an* to be blessed with (the birth of) a child. **ng*** to have the use of sth. *Montorku iki olèhku ng*.* This car is available for my use. *Kita namung sadremi ng* gesang.* We are only entrusted with our lives temporarily. **ng/di*i** to give sth on the above basis. *A di*i omah pemerintah.* He was given a government house to live in.

gaduk *var prn of* GADUG

gadul *rpr* a rebound. *Mak * balé mentjelat.* The ball bounced off. **godal-*** to bounce back and forth. **g·um·adul** springy, bouncy

gaḍul tartar (*var of* GAḌEL)

gaḍung 1 a variety of turnip that grows on a winding stalk. 2 light green. ***an** not real. *matjan *an* human being in the form of a tiger. **ng/di*** 1 to plant the above turnips in [a plot]. 2 to get smn stupefied by having him eat the above turnips. 3 to dye sth pale greem. 4 to cheat at games. * **mlaṭi** green headdress with a white spot in the center. * **Tjina**, * **tjrobo** names of medicinal plants

gadur **ng*** to prattle on and on, talk nonsense

gaé *inf var of* GAWÉ

gaèk old. *Wis * isih néka²*. You're an old goat and still fooling around! **ng*** to nag

gaèl **ng/di*-*** 1 to snarl (at). 2 to gnaw

gaèng **ng*** to cry, whine

gaérut arrowroot

gâgâ (**gagi** *kr?*) non-irrigated land on which rice is planted. *pari ** rice grown on such land. **ng* (rantjah)** to plant [rice] in a dry field. **pa*n** *sms* *

gagah 1 strong, muscular. 2 manly, courageous. ***an** rough type of male classical dance. ***-*an** to show off one's possessions *or* strength. **ng/di*i** to face up to [danger, difficulty]. **g·um·agah** having an inflated opinion of one's own manliness. * **ke·djibah mingkuh ke·tempuh** to go through with sth because one has promised to do so

gagak crow (bird). **ng/di*(i)** to take away and eat [a sacrificial offering left for the spirits]. * **lintjak** to keep moving from place to place

gagal to fail. *Olèhé usaha tenanan nanging *.* He tried hard but failed. **ng/di*aké** to cause sth to fail. *Gerakan mau bisa di*ké.* They managed to put down the rebellion.

gagan *-* a certain edible plant

gagang 1 central stalk, stem. * *wulu* quill of a feather. *Panggonané kembang krambil nglumpuk dadi sa*-*.* Coconut blossoms cluster on each stem. 2 holder, handle. * *erèk* matchstick. *Geḍéné ukuran beling sa* pèn.* A thermometer is about the size of a pen handle. 3 temple, ear piece (of eyeglasses). **ng*** stalk-like. **ng* aking** very thin

gagap *-* to grope. *Bengi iku peteng banget, aku kepeksa *-*.* The night was so dark I had to feel my way. *Ḍèké isih *-* ngenani bab kuwi.* He's feeling his way in that matter. **ng*(-*)** to grope. *peteng ng** pitch dark. *Aku isih ng*-* apa baja tenané tjritané.* I'm probing for the truth of the story. **ng* tuna ng·gajuh luput** to fall far short of one's aspiration. **ng/di*i** to grope in search of sth. *Ḍèké ng*i kuntjiné sing tiba.* He groped for the fallen key. *ng*i atiné* to explore one's feelings. ***-gugup·an** nervous, edgy

gagar to fail to complete the normal cycle. *Enḍogé *.* The egg didn't hatch. ***an** 1 handle. 2 guide, manual. **an salaki-rabi* marriage manual. **ng*** resembling a funeral bouquet. * **majang** bouquet used traditionally at the funeral of an unmarried person

gagas ***an** idea, thought. *duwé *an* to have an idea. **ng/di*(i)** to think about, think over. *Tjoba ta *en.* Think it over! *Kowé kuwi ora^2 sing di*.* What you're thinking of is impossible. *Ḍèwèké ng*^{2}, keprijé ré-kané supaja tomat iku bisa suda isiné.* He racked his brains over how to make seedless tomatoes.

gagat *** bangun** *or* *** ésuk** *or* *** r(a)ina** daybreak, sunrise

gagé (*or* ***an**) quick, immediate. ***-*** instantly, immediately

gagi non-irrigated field (*kr for* GAGA?)

gaglag **ng/di*** *cr* to eat, devour

gagrag new, up-to-date. ** arsitèktur* modern architecture. *djogèd * anjar* a new style of dancing. ***an** in a new style. *panganggo wanita *an anjar* the latest thing in women's dress. **ng* 1** to create, invent. *ng* djogèd anjar* to create a new dance. 2 damaged, spoiled. *** anjar** in a new style *or* fashion. *omah * anjar* a modern house

gagrak **ng*** 1 dashing, splendid. 2 to laugh happily from time to time

gagu speech defect: substitution of *L* for *R*

gagut **ng/di*** to eat with gusto

gah *slang* no! I don't want it! (*shf of* WEGAH)

gaib 1 secret, esoteric. *kawruh ** mystical knowledge. *daja ** magical powers. 2 [of a child] intelligent and mature beyond one's years. 3 a certain official *(obsolete: colonial).* **ka*an** the realm of the mysterious *or* esoteric. **g·in·aib** having mystical powers. **g·um·aib** 1 haughty, arrogant. 2 knowledgable beyond one's years

gâjâ personal style, way of conducting oneself. **né pantjèn ja ngono kuwi.* That's typical of him! *lagu lawas sing digawé * Pawèstri Telu* an old song adapted to the singing style of the Girls' Trio. ** baru* new style. ** bebas* free style. **mang*** to act arrogant, show off

gajahan bamboo handle of a coconut-shell dipper

gajam a certain tree that bears edible fruits. ***an** a certain style of kris sheath

gajel **ng*** to nibble, eat constantly

gajem ***an** 1 cud. 2 *inf* favorite dish. **ng*(i)** to chew the cud. *Kebo jèn wis mangan ḍèké trima ng*(i).* After the kerbau eats, he's content to just chew his cud. **wis ng*i** [of people] very old. **ng/di*i** *inf* to eat constantly, always be hungry

gajeng 1 pleasant, warm, cordial. 2 (*or* **ng***) in rotation. *Olèhé ndeleng potrèt ng* mubeng giliran.* They tooks turns looking at the picture.

gajer **ng*** on and on without stopping

gajes *var of* GAJEL

gajol 1 trowel. 2 hatchet

gajong water container used for scooping water when bathing

gajor 1 a hook on which a *gong* is hung. 2 [of jaw, chin] prominent, jutting forward. 3 *var of* GAJUR

gajuh **(ge)*an** aspiration, objective, ideal. **ng/di*** to attain; to aspire (to). *Ḍèké ng* dadi ḍokter.* He hopes to become a doctor. *djaman ng* angkasa luar* the era of space conquest. *ng* idam^{2}an utama* to have high ideals. *ora kena di** unattainable. **ng* ing tawang** to set one's goals too high. **pa·ng*** action of achieving *or* aspiring to sth

gajuk within reach

gajung container with a handle, or tin can, holding about 1/5 liter = *ca.* 1/2 pint: used *esp.* for measuring oil

gajur deer tusk

gajut **ge*an** a connection; in connection with. *sinau sing ana ge*ané karo pegawéané* to take courses that are connected with one's job. **ng/di*(aké)** to connect; to take in connection with. *Tjritamu jèn di*aké karo keteranganè ḍèwèké akèh tjotjoké.* Your story, when taken in connection with his statement, shows many points of agreement.

gak no; not (*rg var of* ORA). **nge/di*** 1 to guess (at). 2 to belittle. **nge/di*aké** *inf var of* NG/DI·GAWA·KAKÉ

gal *shf of* ÉNGGAL. ***-énggal·an** in a great hurry. **(ng)* dina** *rg* every day

gal- *see also under* GL- (*Introduction, 2.9.3*)

galah a long pole. *lompat ** pole vault

galak untamed, dangerous, sinister. *kéwan ** wild (fierce) animal. **ng·ge* ratjak** to arouse dangerous wishes *or* stir up bad intentions. **sa*-*é matjan, ora ana matjan mangan anak·é ḍéwé** however cruel smn is, he would never bring disaster to his own relative. *** gaṭung** to rely on one's luck

galang ***an (kapal)** drydock. **ng/di*** 1 to foster, encourage. 2 *rg* to round up stray livestock

galap ***-gangsul** fault, shortcoming. ** gangsulé atur nuwun pangaksama.* I'm sorry if I have said/done sth wrong.

galar a mat made of bamboo pounded flat

galé *rg* (look) over there!

galeng 1 irrigation channel or pathway in a rice paddy. 2 crease mark on the skin, *e.g.* from tight clothing. ***an** irrigation channel. **ng*** [of a channel] to traverse [a paddy]. **ng/di*i** to make irrigation channels in. *Sawahé di*i.* They provided the paddy with irrigation ditches.

galer 1 a line. 2 lines on the palms of the hands. ***an** line *or* pathway in a rice paddy. ***-*** lines of the palm. ***-*an** lines, paths. *menawa katlusur *-*ané sedjarah...* if we trace the path of history... **ng*** to have the appearance of a line. *ptg* **g(l)aler** full of lines; showing lines. *Kali² paḍa ptg * putih².* [From the plane] rivers look like silver lines. *Ototé gulu ptg glaler.* His neck tendons stood out.

gales, galès **ng*** [of colors] deep, intense. *ireng ng** jet black

galib ***é** as a rule. **é sapa sing teka nḍisik mbukak lawang.* Generally whoever gets here first opens the door.

galih 1 hard wood; knot in wood. 2 heart, mind (*ki for* ATI[a]). 3 of a certain nature *or* temperament (*ki for* ATI[a]·Ǹ). 4 thought, feeling, idea (*ki for* PIKIR). 5 to discuss (*ki for* REMBUG). *djamu* ***an** folk medicine for regulating the menstrual cycle. **ng/di*** to think, consider (*ki for* M̈/DI·PIKIR). *Buku punika sampun ka* saé dèning panitija.* This book has been approved by the committee. **pa·ng*** 1 (*or* **pa·ng*an**) heart, feelings (*ki for* ATI[a]). 2 inner feeling (*ki for* BATIN). 3 nature, temperament (*ki for* BUDI). 4 thought, opinion, feeling (*ki for* PA·M̈·PIKIR)

galijeng **ng*** to feel groggy

galijung galleon

galik ***-*** sweet, high-pitched, and melodious. **ng*-*** to produce sweet high tones. *Swarané suling nganti ng*-*.* The flute sounded beautiful.

galing a certain vine. **golang-*** a certain batik design

galnisir **ng/di*** to galvanize

galo *ng,* **punika lo** *kr* (look) over there! * *kaé ḍokaré mréné.* Here comes a horse cart!

galok **ng*-*** to howl/yowl continuously

galon 1 gallon. 2 golden lace. 3 *rg* clay

galu *oj* diamond, precious gem

galuh *ltry* 1 diamond, jewel. 2 girl

galur **ng*** interminable, lengthy. *Olèhé nangis ng*.* She cried for a long long time.

gâmâ *** dirgama** danger; misfortune

gamam to waver, vacillate, hesitate

gaman *or* **ge*** *ng,* **dedamel** *kr* weapon. *** api** firearms

gamar to fear that... *Aku * jèn ḍèké kesasar.* I'm afraid he's lost.

gambak *var of* GAMBÈK

gambang xylophone-like gamelan instrument with wooden keys. ***an** 1 to play the xylophone. 2 (*or* **ge*an**) resembling a xylophone. *Igané ge*an.* His ribs show through his skin. **ng*** to play the xylophone

gambar picture, drawing, illustration, photograph. *djuru ** artist, painter. **(ge)*an** 1 drawing, picture. **ané sapa ja?* Who drew (painted) it? 2 illustration. *Wong mau kena kanggo (ge)*an wong sing ḍemen main.* He can serve as an example to others who gamble. ***-*an** imitation of a picture. *Iki dudu * tenan, ming *-*an.* This isn't the real painting, it's just a copy. **ng/di*** to make a picture (of). *Jèn kowé bisa ng*, djadjal aku *en.* If you can draw, draw me! **ng/di*aké** 1 to make a picture for smn. *Gambaré apik la wong di*aké bapaké.* No wonder his picture is good—his father drew it for him! 2 to create a picture of. *Adja ng*aké kahanané bodjomu sing ora².* Don't get to thinking about your dead husband. *Djogèd kuwi ng*aké wong lagi susah.* The dance depicts a grieving man. **ng/di*i** to make a picture on. *Adja sok ng*i apa² nèng tèmbok lho.* You must *never* draw pictures on the wall! *** iḍup** moving picture

gambas 1 a certain fruit which when young is edible if cooked. 2 dried pod of the above fruit when mature: for household uses

gambèk until, to the point that. *Olèhé nangis * ndjenḍul mripaté.* She cried so hard her eyes were all swollen.

gambèr **ng*** hanging limp (*esp.* penis)

gambir (**santun** *opt kr*) 1 a certain vine; the fragrant white-and-yellow blossom of this vine. 2 a plant whose leaves are used as a betel-chewing ingredient and in tanning hides; the betel-chewing mixture made from this leaf. 3 reddish-brown. *** sawit** 1 a certain gamelan melody. 2 a certain batik pattern; a jacket-skirt combination made of this batik

gambjong a certain classical dance performed by females. ***an** *or* **ng*** to engage in social (rather than classical) dancing

gamblang clear, understandable

gamblèh **gomblah-*** [of one's wearing apparel] drooping untidily. **ng*** 1 [of the

lower lip] drooping; *fig* talkative. 2 *cr* to cry, weep
gamblik **ng*** in a precarious position near the edge of sth
gamblok (*or* ***an**) bunch. *Térongé pira sa*?* How much is a bunch of eggplants? **ng*** to cling to. *Sing ng* nang gegermu kuwi apa?* What's that sticking to your back? *Kowé ora susah bajar, ng* aku waé.* You don't have to pay–just stay close to me.
gamblong *see* LENGA
gambos soft, spongy in texture [of cassava]
gambrèng apt to cry over nothing
gambreng **ng*** 1 thick, bushy. *Brengosé ng*.* He has a bushy moustache. 2 to smell disagreeable. 3 to grumble with dissatisfaction
gambrès **ng*** to harvest [rice] by cutting each stalk individually close to the ear
gambret flirtatious. **ng*** very fragrant
gambuh (to sing, chant) a certain classical verse form. *See also* WALANG
gambul **ng*** [of animals] to rub the horns/antlers against sth
gambus (*or* ***an**) song-and-dance performance with tambourines and six-stringed Arabian lutes
gamel groom (for horses). **é dikon njeḍijakaké djarané.* He told the groom to prepare his horse. ***an** (**gangsa** *kr*) classical Javanese musical instrument; ensemble of such instruments. ***an barut** xylophone with black metal bars (inferior to one with yellow metal bars). ***an tjangkem** Javanese-style music produced by human voices imitating instruments. **ng*** to act as groom. **ng/di*(an)i** (**ng/dipun·gangsa·ni** *kr*) to accompany with classical music. *Ringgit tjutjal punika temtu mawi dipun gangsani, dipun sinḍèni, lan dipun gérongi.* Leather-puppet shadow plays are always accompanied by instrumental music, solo singing, and choral singing. *Ḍèké ndjogèd, di*i tjangkem: tak, ḍing, tak, gung! tak, ḍing, tak, nong!* He danced while the others imitated instrumental music for him.
gameng **ng*** clearly visible from afar (*esp.* clouds, rain)
games **ng/di*** to eat all one can get of [a favorite food]
gamil **ng*** to talk incessantly
gamoh soft, tender. *Iwaké *.* The meat is easy to chew.
gamol [of meat] thick and tender
gampang *ng*, **gampil** *kr* 1 easy. *O * waé.* It's easy! *Dikira * waé nanging satemené angèl.* People think it's easy but it's really hard. *supaja ** in order to facilitate things. 2 (*or* ***an**) easy-going, not demanding. ***-* angèl** unpredictable, *i.e.* sometimes easy to please and sometimes not. **ng/di·ge*** *or* **ng/di*aké** 1 to make sth easy/easier. *Perkakas iki bakal ng*aké gawéanmu.* These tools will make your job easy. 2 to treat lightly rather than seriously. *Kowé kuwi adja ngge* kewadjibanmu.* Don't make light of your responsibilities. **g·um·ampang** *ng*, **g·um·ampil** *kr* irresponsible, apt to take things too lightly
gampar ***an** 1 a game in which a stone is kicked around. 2 wooden sandals. **ng/di*** to kick
gampèng hollow place under an overhanging bank; *fig* unseen danger, a lurking threat. **ng*** to conceal oneself under an overhang
gampil easy (*kr for* GAMPANG)
gamping lime. ** iku dienggo nglabur.* Lime is used for whitewashing.
gampleng *rpr* the sound of a punch landing
gamplong *see* LENGA
gânâ 1 property owned by an individual before marriage, which thus is not divided in the event of divorce. 2 [payment] in the form of. *mbajar * barang/ḍuwit* paid in goods/cash. 3 fetus. 4 figurine of a person *or* animal. 5 *oj* cloud. 6 small bee (young of the TAWON). **ng/di*ni** 1 to make a payment toward. *Kanggo bersih désa tahun iki, wong diparengaké ng*ni beras utawa panganan.* People are asked to contribute either (raw) rice or foods for the harvest party this year. 2 made into a certain shape. *Sadjèné di*ni wong numpak prau.* The offering for the spirits was shaped into a man in a boat. ***-gini** property acquired jointly during marriage and which thus is divided in the event of divorce
ganal 1 strong, robust. 2 (*or* ***an**) crude, boorish
gândâ odor. ** arum* a fragrant scent. **né arum djamban.* It smells awful. ** sing ora énak* a disagreeable odor. **ng*** 1 to have an odor. *Gasé ng*.* Gas smells. *ng* arum* to smell fragrant. 2 (*psv* **di***) to smell, perceive an odor. **ng/di*ni** to make sth smell. **pa·ng*** 1 olfactory sense. 2 the way sth smells. **pa·ng*n** *ltry* strength. **g·um·anda rusa** [of bananas] yellowish, *i.e.*

neither overripe nor underripe. * **kusuma** a certain classical verse form. * **pura** a tree whose fragrant leaves are used medicinally. * **rija** a certain tree, also its fruit. * **rukem** a certain plant resin used in batik-making and soldering. * **rusa** a certain tree whose wood is often used for fences

gandar 1 lower part of a wooden kris sheath. 2 wooden arrow shaft. 3 squared length of wood used in furniture-making. 4 mortal remains. 5 having slender graceful lines. * **iras** kris handle and cover made from separate pieces of wood

gandarwa, gandarwo *ltry* giant, ogre

gandarwi *ltry* female ogre

gandèk *rg* knowledgable, able, competent

gaṇḍèk (*or* **ng***) a certain palace official whose function is to pass along the monarch's orders

gandem good to eat. *Iwaké *.* The meat is delicious.

gaṇḍèng connected, related. *Soal iki lan soal mau *.* This problem and the other one are related. **é pijé?* What's the connection? ** karo dina kamardikan, tokoku tutup.* My shop is closed for Independence Day. **(ge)*an** connected; with joined hands. *Perkara iki *an karo Pardi barang.* This thing concerns Pardi somehow. *Botjah loro mau mlaku *an.* The two young people were walking hand-in-hand. **ng/di*** to connect. *Ana prau sing di* karo kapal keruk.* There was a small boat attached to the dredging ship. *di* nganggo jijid* glued on. *Aku ng* tangané.* I took hold of her hand. **pa·ng*** act *or* way of joining. *tembung peng* (gram)* preposition

gandes, gaṇḍes gracious, charming

gaṇḍi *oj* hammer. ***ǹ** wooden mallet. ***ǹ tjutjud** swordfish with a hammer-shaped head. **ng/di*ǹi** to hit with a mallet. *Gaṇḍènana enḍasé!* Hit it on the head!

gaṇḍik 1 cylindrical mortar for rolling *or* grinding up herbs, spices, *etc.* on a square stone pestle (*pipis*). *tjilik ** small but wiry (of physique). 2 [of animals] to copulate

gaṇḍil ear lobe

gândjâ 1 pointed part of a kris, forged to the blade. 2 top part of a decorative pillar. * **iras** top part of a kris that matches the bottom. * **wulung** top part of a kris that does not match the bottom

gandjah *var of* GÈNDJÈH

gandjar ***an** 1 reward, prize. 2 heaven-sent burden *or* trial. **ng/di*** to reward smn, give a prize to

gandjel (*or* ***an**) prop, support. **ng*** 1 (*psv* **di***) to prop sth up. 2 to have/get sth wrong with the eye *or* stomach. *Mripatku ng*.* I got sth in my eye. *Wetengku ng*.* I have a stomach ache.

gandjil odd (not even). *angka ** odd number. ***an** remainder after an odd number is divided by 2

gandjing ***an** *rg* to mate, copulate. **gondjang-*** to shake, tremble

gandjit **gondjat-*** unsteady. *Kursi kuwi gondjat-*.* The chair wobbles.

gandjras fine, splendid [of attire]

gandjret **ng*** to rotate rapidly. *Ḍèwèké ngadeg sikil sidji bandjur mubeng ng* kaja gangsingan.* She balanced on one leg and spun like a top.

gandjur *oj* spear. **ng/di*** to attack with a spear

gaṇḍok 1 bunch, bundle. 2 front veranda. 3 (*or* ***an**) pavilion, wing (of a house). **ng*** to stick to, hang around. **ng/di*(i)** to tie into a bunch

gaṇḍong **ng/di*(i)** to tie into a bunch

gaṇḍor [of bamboo] softened and hollowed by disease

gaṇḍos rice-flour-and-coconut cookie. * **wingka** one variety of such a cookie

gaṇḍowârâ a certain ear ornament

gândrâ power, strength. *ilang ** drained of strength. **ng*** strong. **ng* (sa)pira?** how strong? **ora ng* sapira** negligible, insignificant

gandri *var of* GADRI

gandrik heavens! my God! **, la kok akèh ja?* Heavens, what a lot of them there are! **, horoh ta, rusak!* *Now* look what you've done–it's broken! * **putra wajah·é Ki Ageng Séla** *phrase uttered in self-protection when one sees lightning striking*

gandrung 1 dragonfly. 2 passionately devoted to. ** révolusi* dedicated to revolution. ***-* kapirangu** lovesick

gaṇḍul 1 *rpr* sth hanging. *Pantjingé disenḍal alon², mak *, olèh klambi amoh rontang-ranting.* He pulled up the fishing rod slowly and lo and behold! there was an old ragged shirt hanging from it. 2 *rg* papaya. **(ge)*an** 1 to hang onto sth for fun. *Botjah² paḍa *an wit.* The children are playing in the tree. 2 dependent on. *Ing Djakarta kéné aku mung *an pamanku.* I depend on my uncle for things here in Djakarta. **3** sth to cling to. *Wong urip mau kudu duwé ge*an.* Man needs faith to live by. ***-*** *or* **goṇḍal-*** to dangle. *Ana glunḍung pringis *-*.* There was a grinning skull hanging there. **ng/di*** to hold onto, cling to; *fig* to depend on. *ng* trèm listrik* to hang onto an electric train (outside, to avoid paying); to depend on electric trains (for transportation). *Rembugan mau isih ng*.* The talks are still pending. **ng/di*aké** to hang sth. *Klambiné di*aké ing tjeḍak tempat tiḍur.* He hung his shirt beside the bed. **ng/di*i 1** to hang sth on(to). 2 to stick to. *Aku ng*i panemuku mau.* I'll stand by my opinion. 3 to hold smn back. *Ḍèké arep lunga, tak *i.* He wanted to leave but I talked him out of it. *ptg* **g·r·anḍul** *pl* hanging. *Pelemé ptg granḍul.* Mangoes are hanging all over [the tree]. **g·um·anḍul** to hang smw. *Djeruk bali gumanḍul ana wit.* An orange hung from the tree.

gandum 1 wheat. 2 *sbst kr for* DJAGUNG?

ganḍung **gonḍang-*** *rg* bicycle

ganep *ng,* **djangkep** *kr* 1 complete(d); (in) full. *Umuré wis * setaun.* He's a full year old now. *Pirantiné durung *.* He hasn't got all his equipment yet. *Olèhé mènèhi ḍuwit wis * ora ana kurangé.* You've given me the money in full now. *jèn wis * patang puluh dina* at the end of the forty days. *Bareng * ping telu meksa ora éntuk, ḍèwèké ora ndjadjal manèh.* When he failed a third time, he didn't try again. *Ḍèké ora gelem mèlu balbalan jèn mung dianggo *-* waé.* He wouldn't play soccer if they only wanted him to fill out the team. 2 even (not odd). *angka ** an even number. *Omah² sing nomeré gandjil sisih kiwa, sing * sisih tengen.* The odd-numbered houses are on the left, the evens are on the right. **(ge)*an** that which makes sth complete. *buku kang minangka ge*ané kanggo suksès kemadjuan* a book which serves as a supplemental aid for successful progress. *Iki *ané kekuranganku mbajar wingi.* This makes up what I couldn't pay in full yesterday. **ng/di*i** to make sth complete. *Ukara ingisor iki *ana.* Complete the following sentences. *Gelas iki kanggo ng*i gelas setèlan sing petjah.* This glass fills out the broken set. **ora *** mentally defective. *Ḍèké ora *.* He's not all there.

ganès **gonas-*** attractive; flirtatious

gang 1 (*abbr:* **Gg.**) alley(way); passage. 2 interstice, fissure. 3 strong. **nge/di*-* 1** to partition up/off [a space]. *Papan mau nuli di*-*.* They divided the place up with partitions. 2 to classify, subdivide. *See also* ADIGANG

ganggam (*or* **ng***) hesitant, reluctant

ganggang separated by [a certain distance]. **ng/di*** to separate, part

ganggeng a certain water weed

ganggu **ng/di* 1** to bother, interfere with, cross. *Aku arep sinau, adja ng*.* I'm trying to study–don't bother me. 2 to cast an evil spell on. **ng/di* gawé** to cast a spell on. *A di* gawé, mung ḍukun bisa nambani ḍèké.* Smn put a spell on A: only a witch doctor can help him. **ng/di* gugat** to disturb, cross. *Ènaké djagongan nang gadri wétan baé ja, ora ana sing ng* gugat.* Let's sit on the east porch–no one will disturb us there. *Présiḍèn ora bisa di* gugat.* The President can do no wrong.

gâNgsâ 1 classical Javanese musical instrument *or* ensemble of instruments (*kr for* GAMEL·AN). 2 bronze. 3 gamelan gong. 4 goose. ***n** (food) fried without oil *or* with a minimum amount of oil. **ng/di* 1** (*psv* **di***) to dry-fry. 2 to gag smn to prevent him from speaking

gangsal 1 five (*kr for* LIMA). 2 pomegranate (*rg kr for* DLIMA)

gangsar to go along smoothly. *Iliné kalèn wis bisa *.* The ditch is flowing freely. *Muga² * ora ana alangan sewidji apa.* I hope everything will go without a hitch.

gangsing ***an** spinning top. **an bumbung* bamboo top. *nggandjret kaja *an* to spin like a top

gangsir (edible) mole cricket. ***an 1** cricket hole/tunnel. 2 hole through which a thief tunnels under a house wall. 3 certain Jogjanese food specialties: (a) a snack of fried *mlindjo* skin; (b) rice-accompanying dish of fried seasoned beef. **ng/di*** to tunnel under a wall

gangsul 1 improperly grouped, out of order. 2 curt. 3 odd (not even). *angka ** an odd number. 4 *var of* GINGSUL

gangsur **ng* 1** to creep, wriggle (on the stomach). 2 to rub, massage

ganitrikunḍa *oj* rosary

ganjang ***an** snack food. **(ng)/di* 1** to crush, stamp out. ** impérialisme* to crush imperialism. 2 to eat [foods] raw

ganjik **ng*** 1 talkative. 2 *var of* NG-GANJUK
ganjong a variety of arrowroot
ganjuk **gonjak-*** improper, unseemly. **ng*** too close (to). *mBok adja ng* ngono, rada rana siṭik.* Don't stand so close to me, move back a little!
ganol *rg* cassava blossom. **ng*** to sit around idly
ganong *var of* GANUNG
gânṭâ idea, notion, concept. ***n** visualization, imaginings. **ng/di*(-*)** *or* **ng/di*kaké** to picture, imagine. *Ḍèwèké njamaraké kedadéjan kang di*-*.* He apprehensively awaited the events he had pictured in his imagination.
gantal future. ***an** time interval; **ora *an** within [a certain] time interval. *Ora *an sasi Siti sida dadi bodjoné pak Sastra.* Inside of a month Siti did become Mr. Sastro's wife.
gantang 1 to pound [rice] to remove the hulls. 2 unit of weight: equivalent to 10 *kati* (*ca.* 6.17 kilograms = *ca.* 13.6 lbs.) in Central Java, half that in East Java
ganṭang *var of* GLANṬANG
gantar *var of* GÈNTÈR
gantas loud. **ng/di*i** to cut off/down [trees, plants]
gantèn betel chew (*kr for* KINANG)
ganṭeng **ng*** 1 straight and strong (*esp.* of rope). 2 handsome, dashing
ganter **ng*** 1 to produce loud steady sounds; *wj* to tap fast and steadily on the puppet chest with a wooden knocker. 2 to remain awake for a long period of time, as a self-imposed ordeal in order to achieve sth
ganṭèt **ng/di*aké** *or* **ng/di*(i)** to fasten things together, *e.g.* by stringing things on a line
ganti *ng,* **gantos** *kr* 1 (to make) a change, replacement. * *sepur* to change trains. *Ḍèké lagi * (klambi).* She's changing clothes. 2 in (one's) turn. *Saiki * aku sing matja.* Now it's my turn to read. *Saben taun kudu *.* They change off every year. * *ngantem* to hit back, return a punch. *Anusapati ḍéwé * dipradjaja déning aḍiké kuwalon.* Anusapati himself was slain in turn by his foster brother. ***ǹ** 1 that which replaces sth. *Saiki bajaren ḍisik, mengko rak bakal éntuk gantèn.* Pay for it now; you'll be reimbursed later. 2 by turns. *Ora suwé djangkriké B gantèn njurung.* Pretty soon B's cricket attacked in its turn. *pari gantèn* rice planted during the dry season. ***-*** to change off. *Botjah loro *-* njupir.* The two boys took turns driving. **gonta-*** to keep changing back and forth. *Sanadjan kahanané gonta-*, nanging reregan kok adjeg.* In spite of the shifting circumstances, prices remain firm. ***-g·um·anti** *sms *-* above.* **ng/di*** to replace. *Gelas sing petjah mau mengko bakal tak *.* I'll replace the broken glass. **ng/di*ǹi** to replace by succession; to take the place of. *Sapa sing bakal ng* Pak Krama?* Who can fill Mr. Krama's shoes? *Radèn Kangsa digaḍangaké ibuné nggantèni Sang Prabu.* Kangsa's mother wanted him to succeed the King. **g·um·anti** to succeed to [a high position]. *gumanti kaprabon* to become king. *See also* GENTI
gantil ***an** object from which sth hangs. **aning ati* one's sweetheart. **ng*** hanging (from). **g·r·antil** [many things] hang. *Tomaté ptg grantil.* There are tomatoes hanging everywhere on the plant.
ganting *var of* GANTIL
gantjang *var of* GANTJAR
gantjar 1 fluent, moving quickly. *mlaku ** to walk swiftly. *Kalèné * iliné.* The ditch flowed rapidly. *Rembugané *.* The talks went smoothly. 2 pace, flow. **ing tjrita* the course of the story. **(ge)*an** 1 with swift movements. *Aku bandjur mulih ge*-an.* I hurried home. 2 to paraphrase. *Tjritané ing nḍuwur iki gawénen *an.* Tell the above story in your own words. **ng/di*aké** 1 to speed the course of. *Lakuné di*aké.* He quickened his pace. *kanggo ng*aké iliné banju* in order to make the water flow faster. 2 to rephrase. *ng*aké tembang* to paraphrase the words of a song
gantjeng **ng*** suspended between two points. *kawat ng* dipasang olèh tjagak loro* a(n electric) wire strung between two [utility] poles. *ptg* **g·r·antjeng** *pl* stretched, suspended
gantjer **ng*** straight, steady. *Swarané mitralijur ng* ora peḍot²*. The sound of machine-gun fire never let up.
gantjèt (*or* **ng***) to copulate [of animals; *cr* of people]
gantjleng 1 *rpr* an axe swinging through its arc. 2 (*or* **ng***) *intsfr* black. *ireng ng** pitch black
gantjo pickaxe
ganṭol hook, barb-shaped piece of wood *or*

wood. **ng/di*(i)** to hook and hoist sth with the above

gantos 1 to pawn (*root form: kr for* GADÉ). 2 change, replacement; by turns (*kr for* GANTI)

gantung hanging, suspended. *djam ** wall clock. *dijan ** hanging lamp. *(pa)ukum-(an) ** death penalty by hanging. ***an** hanger for clothing. **ge*an** guide, guiding force *or* power. **ng*** 1 to hang oneself. 2 (*psv* **di***) to hang sth. *Ali ng* klambi.* Ali hung up his shirt. *Ali di*.* Ali was hanged. **ng* kepuh** to wear the same clothing day after day. **ng* untu** ravenous, famished. **ng/di*aké** 1 to hang sth. *Klambiné di*aké ing tjanṭèlan.* He hung his shirt on a hook. 2 to depend. *Adja ng*aké marang lijan.* Don't rely on others. **ng/di*i** to hang up [clothing]. **pa·ng*** act *or* way of hanging. *dina peng*é* the day he was to be hanged. **pa·ng*an** hangman's noose; gallows. **g·um·antung** 1 to hang (down). *Kurung-ané gumantung wonten ing tritisan.* The cage hung on the porch. *pala gumantung* fruits that grow on trees. *Sumbu mau gu-mantung ing lenga.* The wick remained suspended in the oil. 2 to depend. *Gu-mantung wonten pandjenengan.* It depends on you. *Gumantung saka panasé hawa.* It depends on how hot it is. *Lunga orané gu-mantung marang udan orané.* Whether we go or not depends on whether or not it rains. *** bodja** *or* *** kawin** legally mar-ried but still awaiting the opportunity to celebrate the marriage with the customary festivities. *** siwur** seventh-generation an-cestor *or* descendant

ganu *rg* formerly

ganung inedible hard core of pineapple or breadfruit

gaok 1 the cawing of a crow. 2 *rg* crow. **ng*** to caw. *ptg* **g·r·aok** noisy, boisterous. *Adja ptg graok, bapak lagi saré.* Don't make so much racket–your father is sleep-ing.

gaota **ng*** to work, earn one's living. **pa·ng*n** work, a job, one's livelihood. *nja-mbut-gawé kanggo peng*n* to work for a living

gap ***-*an** to grope around. *Tangané *-*an nggolèki kuntji.* He fumbled for his key.

gapé **ng/di*** to pay attention to. *Kowé adja tansah ng* apa omongé.* Never listen to anything he says!

gapit 1 tongs. 2 stick by which a shadow-play puppet is held. 3 bamboo handle. *ilang *é* to lose one's power *or* authority. **ng*** 1 to equip sth with a stick *or* handle. 2 partial, biased, unjust

gapjak 1 wooden sandals. 2 *Jogja slang* friendly, outgoing

gapjuk *rpr* an embrace. *Mak * ngrangkul anaké.* She threw her arms around her child. **ng/di*aké** to acquaint smn [with]. *A ng*aké B karo C.* A introduced B and C to each other. **g·um·apjuk** friendly

gaplèk dried cassava-root slices. *glepung ** cassava flour, starch. **ng/di*** 1 to make [cassava root] into dried slices. 2 to give smn a spanking

gaplik **ng*** 1 teetering near the edge of sth. 2 in small numbers/quantities. *Olèhé ma-ngan ng*.* She ate very little.

gaplok 1 a worn-out bamboo pole. 2 *rpr* the sound *or* action of spanking. ***an** 1 ex-perienced. *wong *an* one who is worn out but experienced. 2 act of spanking. ***-*** *or* **goplak-*** (to deliver) repeated blows. *Arit kuwi keṭul, jèn dienggo mbatjok mung tiwas goplak-* waé.* That sickle is dull; it'll be a waste of time to cut with it.

gapluk *var of* GAPLOK

gaprek̄ crumbling, decayed, rotting

gapruk *rpr* bodies colliding. *Kepeṭuk * karo kantjané.* He ran into (*i.e.* met; *or* collided with) a friend of his. ***an** act of colliding, *e.g.* in a body-contact sport. **ng/di*aké** to bump into, collide with [another person]

gaprus *rpr* breaking, shattering. *Mak * ka-tjané petjah.* The glass got smashed.

gaprut smeared, spattered. *Klambiné * getih.* His shirt had blood all over it.

gapuk 1 rotting, decayed, crumbling. 2 *cr* old [of people]

gapunten *sbst kr for* GAPURA

gapura (*or* ***n**) gate(way), entrance

gar **me*** to open out, expand. *Kembangé me*.* The flowers are blooming. *me*é in-ḍustri baṭik* the expansion of the batik in-dustry. **me*-m·ingkup** 1 to open and close by turns. 2 [of breathing] constricted. *Ambegané me* mingkup.* He's short of breath (*e.g.* from illness, exertion). **nge/di*aké** to open sth out. *nge*aké pa-jung* to open an umbrella. *Gegemané di*-aké.* He unclenched his fist. *nge*aké peda-gangan* to expand one's business

gar- *see also under* GR- (*Introduction, 2.9.3*)

gârâ ***-*** **1** turbulence in nature; *wj* scene (about halfway through a shadow play) of nature's turbulence followed by a clown scene. **2** commotion. *Angger Ali mulih terus mesṭi ana *-*.* Whenever Ali comes home, there's trouble. **3** *slang* idea, instigation. *Iki *-*né sapa ja?* Whose idea was this? Who's the wise guy? **ng* kasih** alternate name for *Slasa Kliwon* (an auspicious day). *** ita** a variety of banana. *See also* ANGGARA

garam *var of* GAREM

garan handle, *esp.* of a tool. ** arit* sickle handle. ** lading* knife handle. ** wajang* puppet-handling stick. ** petjut* whip handle. ***é** since, because of the fact that. **ge*** instruction book. *ge*ipun para guru* teachers' manual

garang ***an** **1** dried near a fire. *tembako *an* dried (smoked) tobacco. **2** equipment for drying [clothing *etc.*] or broiling [food]. **3** a variety of mongoose. **ng/di*** **1** to roast [food] over coals. **2** to dry sth near a fire. *** gati** *rg* the *kemlanḍingan* plant

garansi a guarantee, warranty

garap ***an** work (to be) done at home. **an ngomah* housework. **an étung* arithmetic homework. **ng/di*** **1** to work (at), do. *ng* sawah* to till a rice paddy. *ngGarap mori ngono mau djenengé mbaṭik.* Working fabric in this way is called making batik. *Sing ng* wong pirang² atus nganti sasèn².* It took hundreds of workers months to do the job. **2** to do sth in fun. *Di* ngono baé kok nangis.* I was only teasing–don't cry! **ng* banju** *or* **ng* gawé** *or* **ng* sari** to menstruate. **pa·ng*** act *or* way of working. *Tjèlènganku kanggo ngragadi peng*é sawah.* My savings savings went for covering the expenses of working the rice paddy.

garasi garage

garba *oj* stomach. ***n** *gram* assimilation of vowel sounds at word boundaries *(e.g. teka + ing = tekèng). tembung *n* word formed by such assimilation. **ng/di*** **1** to summarize the contents (of); to interpret by selecting the essential parts. **2** *gram* to join [words] by vowel assimilation. *See also* GUWA

garbini *oj* **ng*** pregnant

garbis a variety of melon

gardjita (*or* **ng***) *ltry* swept with a strong emotion

garḍu *var of* GERḌU

garebeg religious festival *var of* GREBEG)

garèk *var of* GÈRÈK

garem **1** *rg* salt. **2** a certain salt-like fertilizer. *** Inggris** laxative salts

garèng **1** *wj* clown-servant, the slow-witted eldest son of Semar *see also* WULU-TJUMBU). **2** *or* ***-pung**) a variety of cicada. *** gati** *rg* the *kemlanḍingan* plant

garès shin bone *var of* GARES)

gares **1** shin bone. **2** [of soil] hard, stony. **ng/di*** to kick smn in the shins; *fig* to hurt smn's feelings

garèt *var of* GARIT

garet *var of* GERET

gari to remain, be left over *inf var of* KARI)

garing dry; dried up/out. ***an** rice-accompanying dishes that are "dry," *i.e.* fried (as contrasted with soups or sauced foods). **ng/di*aké** to dry sth. **pa·ng*an** place for drying. *kamar peng*an* drying room. *** kemlingking(en)** bone dry. *** k·um·risik** dried to a crisp. *** mekingking** bone dry

garis **1** line separating one thing from another. **2** fate, destined event. ***an** ruler. **ng/di*(i)** to make a line. *ng*i nganggo *an* to draw lines with a ruler. *** ḍemarkasi** line of demarcation (in battle). *** kèntjong·an** diagonal line. *** kliling** circumference. *** lini** **1** battle line, zone of demarcation. **2** equator. *** sipat gantung** line forming a 90-degree angle with the horizontal. *** srèmpèd·an** tangent to an arc. *** tengah** diameter of a circle

garit scratch mark. **ng/di*** to scratch with sth sharp. *kaja di* atiné* feeling despondent. *djagung* **g·um·arit** young corn

garningson fort, garrison

garong robber. ***-*** [of weeping] loud and long. **ng/di*** to rob, hold up

garot **ng/di*(i)** to gnaw on/at

garpu fork

garu **1** harrow-like farm implement. **2** *rg* comb. **3** sandalwood. **4** a certain star. ***n̂** *sms* ***** 1,2 *above.* **ng/di*k̂aké** to have smn break up soil with a harrow; *fig* to overwork smn. **ng/di*(n̂i)** **1** to loosen soil with a harrow. **2** to comb one's hair

garuḍa eagle. *** jaksa** mythological eagle with a giant's face

garut *var of* GAÉRUT

garwa spouse (*ki for* BODJO). *ingkang ** your (his, her) husband/wife. *** ampéjan** any wife of a king other than the legal queen. *** padmi** the first wife in a polygamous household: the mother of the legal heir(s)

gas 1 gas(oline). 2 aeroform gas. 3 (*prn* **g̒as**) gauze. 4 unit of length: *ca.* 1 meter, a little over a yard. ***-*an** in a great hurry. **nge/di*** to speed up. *Mobilé di**. He stepped on the gas.

gasah **ng/di*** 1 to hone; to polish. 2 (*or* **ng/di·ge***) to stir up, provoke, incite

gasak **ng/di*** 1 to charge, assault, attack. 2 to steal, embezzle. *ng* ḍuwit kantor* to misappropriate official funds

gasèk 1 up to, until. ** saiki ḍèké durung mbajar utangé.* He still hasn't paid his debt. 2 cleaned up (*var of* GASIK)

gasik 1 (*prn* **gasi:k**) early. *Ḍèké tekané *.* He got there early. *Prajoga luwih * nggonmu mapan turu.* You'd better get to bed earlier. 2 (*or* ***-***) cleaned up, drained out [of *e.g.* a garden area]

gasir *var of* GANGSIR

gasolin gasoline

gaṭak bamboo stalks used as a living fence or separation between areas. **ng/di*i** 1 to act as a border for. *Pekarangané di*i pring.* His garden is marked off by a bamboo border. 2 to cheat smn out of [money, property]

gatal a leaf-wrapped packet of coins, rice, and flowers: tossed toward each other by bride and groom upon meeting during the wedding ceremony (whoever throws first will be the boss)

gaṭèk ***an** bright, quick to catch on

gatel an itch; to itch. ***en** 1 to itch from a pathological cause. 2 to have a guilty conscience. **ng*i** to cause itching. **g·um·atel** [of morning sunshine] causing a pleasantly warming sensation. *** tjangkem** *cr* talkative

gaṭèl *cr* penis; glans penis

gateng a certain freshwater fish

gaṭèng a children's game resembling jacks: played with pebbles

gaṭèt odd (not even). *angka ** an odd number

gati *ng*, **gatos** *kr* serious, important. ***-*** hurriedly. *Gati² anggoné mangan.* He ate hastily. **ng/di*k̀aké** to take seriously. *Wong désa umumé ora nggatèkaké tanggalan.* Village people don't usually pay much attention to calendar dates. *See also* GUMATI, WIGATI

gaṭil *var of* GAṬÈL

gatjleng **ng*** *intsfr* black (*var of* GANTJLENG)

gatjlok *rpr* an axe chopping. ***-*** *or* **gotjlak-*** repeated chopping sounds; to keep chopping

gatjo 1 object (marble, picture, *etc.*) used in children's games for winning over the opponent's similar object. 2 boy/girl friend. 3 companion

gatjos *rpr* a sharp implement piercing sth

gatjrok *var of* GATJRUK

gatjruk *rpr* a sharp implement swinging *or* striking

gatjuk *var of* GATJO

gaṭo *rg* penis

gaṭok *see* GUMAṬOK

gatos serious, important (*kr for* GATI)

gaṭot a dessert made of cassava, brown sugar, and coconut

gâtrâ 1 form(ed), shape(d). 2 in the formative stage; embryonic. 3 *gram* clause

gaṭuk 1 to meet, match. *Bareng wis * sida rembug.* When we got together we were able to discuss it. *Persis * ing garis sidji lan sidjiné.* It matches exactly, line for line. *Kotjapan² lan tembang²é ki ḍalang * karo genḍing.* The puppet-master's dialogue and singing go together with the gamelan music. 2 *rpr* an unexpected coming together. *Mak * aku ketemu Siti ing pasar.* I unexpectedly ran into Siti at the marketplace. ***an** 1 matched, joined. **ané ora paḍa.* The things that were put together aren't alike. 2 a harmonious matching. *Sega gorèng kuwi *ané atjar.* Fried rice goes well with pickles. **goṭak-*** 1 in complete agreement *or* harmony. *goṭak-* maṭuk* perfectly matched. 2 to keep meeting accidentally. *Nèng Djakarta aku pidjer goṭak-* karo Tadi.* I kept running into Tadi in Djakarta. **ng/di·(goṭak-)*aké** to match [things] up. *Wong² mau tak *ké.* I introduced them to each other. *Djogèd kang kasebut iki bisa di*aké marang djogèd² daérah.* These dances can be adapted to various folk dances. *dalan geḍé sing ng*aké kuṭa sidji lan sidjiné* a highway that joins one city to another. *Jèn digoṭak-*aké, aku lan kowé kuwi iki isih sedulur.* Piecing together our genealogies, it turns out that you and I are related.

gaṭul *var of* GAṬÈL

gaṭung *see* GALAK

gauk long-drawn-out wailing sound; (*Jogja*

slang) air-raid warning siren. *swara *ing lokomotip* the sound of a locomotive whistle. ** ombak-banju* the rising and falling wail of a siren. **ng*** to wail

gaung howling *or* wailing sound. *ptg* **g·r·aung** *pl* many such sounds from all directions

gauta *var of* GAOTA

gâwâ *ng,* **bekta** *kr* **(ge)*n(an) 1** that which is carried/transported. **n kang abot* a heavy burden. *Lajangé iki gawané wong Indu.* This literature was brought in by the Hindus. *Bebektanipun dipun emot ing grobag.* The freight was loaded into the cart. 2 that which goes along with [sth else]. *anak *n* stepchild, *i.e.* child from a former marriage brought to a new marriage. *Ban iki gawané pit sing tak tuku wingi.* These tires came with the bicycle I bought yesterday. *Tjatjadé kuwi wis *n wiwit lahir.* He's had that defect from birth. **ka*** because [of], resulting [from]. *Ka* saka nesuning ati, gelasé dibanting.* He was so mad he smashed the glass. **ng/di*-*** to bring in, involve. *Jèn kowé ditjekel polisi djenengku adja kok *-* lho.* If you're caught by the police, don't drag my name into it! **ng/di*kaké** to bring/carry/take on smn's behalf. *Aku gawakna mritja kanggo masak.* Bring me some pepper for cooking. **ng/di*(ni) (ng/di·ampil[i]** *or* **ng/di·asta[ni]** *ki*) to bring, carry, take. *Bukuné di* mulih.* He took the book home with him. *Laler kuwi sok ng* lelara rupa².* Flies carry diseases. *Kowé ng* duwit ora?* Did you bring any money? *Botjah² pada ng*ni pelem mulih.* The children took the mangoes home. **ng/di*ni** to give [a wedding gift] to a bride. *Aku arep ng*ni djarik kanggo mantuku.* I'm taking a batik to my son's bride. **ng/di·ge*** *sms* NG/DI*(NI) *above.* **pa·ng*** (act of) transporting. *Abot pang*é.* It's heavy to carry.

gawang 1 two wooden uprights joined by a horizontal piece across the top. **2** goal posts; goalkeeper (in soccer). **3** measuring unit for firewood. ***an** wooden frame shaped as above (1) for making batik. ***-*(an)** *or* **g·um·awang** clear. *kèlingan kanṭi *-** to remember clearly

gawar cord strung between posts to mark off a forbidden area. *nradjang (ing) ** to trespass; *fig* to sin. **ng/di*i** to mark off [an area]. *** kenṭeng** palm-fiber cord used for marking sth off; **ng/di*-kenṭengaké** to mark off [an area] with cord (for smn); **ng/di*-kenṭengi** to furnish [an area] with a boundary marker

gawat serious, tense, fraught with danger. *Djedjoḍoan iku pantjèn *.* Marriage is full of pitfalls. *Kahanan ing negara mau *.* Things are tense in that nation.

gawé *ng,* **damel** *kr* **1** job, task. *Sregep ing sabarang *.* He works hard at every job. *dadi ** to cause (extra) work [for], be a burden [to]. **2** celebration. *duwé ** or *mbarang ** to hold a party/celebration. ***né** one's habit *or* practice. *Djenengé panḍu, *né tetulung.* They're called Boy Scouts; they help people. **mu mangan turu, ora tau njambut-gawé.* All you do is eat and sleep–you never work. **ku saben ésuk ngresiki omah.* I clean the house every morning. **ϕ/di*** *see* (NG)/DI* *below.* **(a)*** to cause [feelings], bring about [a condition]. ** ala* to do harm; to slander. ** serik* to hurt smn's feelings. *Adja sok a* susahing wong tuwamu.* Never bring grief to your parents. *Kowé * ḍeg²an waé.* You scared me! ** gujuné wong sing ndeleng* to make the spectators laugh. **di*** made of. *montor mabur sing di* dluwang* a paper airplane. **ϕ/di*-* 1** to invent tall tales. *Jèn ora meruhi ḍéwé kahanan iku, mbok adja sok *-*.* If you didn't see it yourself, don't make up stories about it. *Keprijé udjiané?–Ah dak *-* waé.* How was the exam?–Oh, I just shot the bull. **2** to [do] in an artificial manner. *Botjah wadon kuwi lakuné di*-* karebèn katon njengsemaké.* She puts on that walk to make herself look attractive. **(ge)*an 1** a product of, made in. *Djam kuwi *an endi?* Where are clocks made? **2** manufactured (not natural). *ambegan *an* artificial respiration. *pupuk *an* chemical fertilizer. **3** a task. *Dak wènèhi ge*an ja!* I'll give you something to do! **4** act of making; to make things. *ge*an tangan* handicraft. *Dasaré pantjèn ḍemen ge*an, mula *né apik.* He really enjoys making things, so they're well made. **me(r)*** to work (at). *Kowé lagi me* apa?* What are you doing? **(ng)/di* 1 (ng/di·asta** *ki*) to make, construct, do. ** apa?* What are you making? ** omah* to build a house. **nen karangan.* Write a composition. **a étungan.* Do the arithmetic. *ng* tjoban² bab nandur wowohan* to conduct fruit-growing experiments. **2 (ng/di·asta** *ki*) to make [materials] into. *Bakal iki* *apiké di* klambi.* This cloth should be made into a shirt. 3 *sms* A* *above.* **ng/di*kaké (ng/di·asta·kaké** *ki*) 1 to make (for smn). *Wangsulan ingisor iki gawèkna pitakoné.* Make up questions to go with the following answers. *Aku nggawèkaké lajangan kanggo kowé.* I made a kite for you. 2 to have sth made. *Klambiné digawèkaké déning gerdji.* He had his shirt made by a tailor. **pa*** employee; official. **pa*an** 1 job, task. 2 *gram* action (as expressed in a verb). **pa·ng*** act *or* way of making; action, deed. *Peng*né apa ana ing pabrik?* Are they made in factories? *ngedohaké pang* nisṭa* to refrain from evil doings. **pa·ng*an** *sms* PA*AN *above.* **sa*-*** whatever one does. *Sa*-*né ora tau bener.* Nothing he does is right. * **parigawé** *ng kr* things to be done. *Wong saomah paḍa tumandang jèn ana * parigawé.* Everybody in the family pitches in when there's a lot to do. *See also* MERGAWÉ, NJAMBUT, PANGGAWÉ

gawèl *see* TJAṬÈK

gaweng **ng*** to become dark. *Langité ng*.* The sky is clouding over.

gawer **ora ng* sapira** to be of little significance. *Gendjik sidji wis tak ganjang, ora ng* sepira.* I've eaten a whole piglet but I'm still just as hungry as I was.

gawil **gowal-*** *pl* loose, coming off. *Sikilé médja wis gowal-*.* The table legs are wobbly. **ng*** *sg* loose. *Pakuné ng*.* The nail is coming out. *ptg* **g·r·awil** *pl* coming loose. *Sekrupé ptg grawil.* The bolts are all coming undone.

gawing **ng*** at the edge, in a precarious position

gawok astounded

gé 1 to be made into sth (*inf var of* DI·GAWÉ). *Pring iki * apa?* What's this bamboo for? 2 quick(ly) (*inf var of* AGÉ, GAGÉ). 3 the fourth market day (*shf of* WAGÉ). ***-ing** combination of the second and fourth market days (unpropitious in numerological reckonings) (*shc from* WAGÉ PAING). *See also* GÉGÉ

ge- *see also under* GA- (*Introduction, 2.9.2*)

gebag 1 at the same age level. *Botjah loro mau katoné *.* The two boys look about the same age. 2 stick, club (*kr for* GEBUG). 3 to win [a lottery] (*root form: kr for* GEBUG). ***an** a batch, group. **ng/dipun** to choose a winner in a game of chance (*kr for* NG/DI·GEBUG)

gebambèr **ng*** hanging down, dangling loosely

gebandjiran *inf var of* KE·BANDJIR·AN

gébang **ng/di*** 1 to make fun of, tease, do in fun. 2 *wj* to court, make love to

gebang a certain palm tree whose bark and leaf fibers are made into sacking material. ***-*an** to fight against each other. **ng/di*** to fight, engage in battle

gèbèg ***-*** to shake one's head

gebeg **ng/di*** to polish, scour

gèbèl *var of* GÈMBÈL

gebeng **ge*an** 1 innermost feelings. 2 guiding principle. 3 classification. *ge*aning paramasastra* grammatical categories

gebentus *inf var of* KE·BENTUS

gèbèr *var of* GÈMBÈL

geber a screen. **ng/di*i** to screen off [an area]; to furnish [a place] with a screen

gèbès to shake one's head in disagreement. ***-*** 1 *sms* *. 2 to refuse, turn down

gebeṭeng (*or* ***en**) to be prevented from going on one's way, *e.g.* to be held up by rain

gebibir **ng*** wet and cold

gebimbir *var of* GEBIBIR

gebing (*or* ***an**) (in) slices, sliced. **ng/di*(i)** to slice

gebintjih *sbst kr for* KEBIRI

gebiri *var of* KEBIRI

gebjag ***an** a performance. **ng*** to fall off/down. *Geḍègé ng*.* The bamboo wall collapsed. **ng/di*aké** to perform. *Beksan Sala arep di*aké sasi ngarep.* A Solonese dance is to be performed next month.

gebjah **ng/di*** 1 to generalize. *Jèn tjaramu ng* ngono kuwi aku ora maṭuk.* I don't agree with your generalization. 2 to work [soil] fine with a hoe-like tool. **ng/di*-ujah** to generalize, make no distinction. *Jèn botjah sidji ing klas ora sinau, sak klas ora bisa di*-ujah ora ana sing sinau.* If one boy in the class doesn't study, you can't say the whole class doesn't study. *Kartjisé ng* kaja ujah paḍa asiné, ora mbédakaké wong duwé lan wong mlarat.* The tickets are all the same—no difference for rich and poor people. *See also* BJAH

gebjar 1 to glitter, sparkle, shine. *Mripaté *-* kaja barlijan.* Her eyes sparkled like diamonds. *sa*ing ṭaṭit* as the lightning flashed. 2 glance, sight. *Ora ketara * ing nétra.* It's not conspicuous. *Ketingal ngléla *ipun.* It's very eye-catching. 3 superficially attractive. *Ḍèwèké kuwi ming *é* *waé.* Her beauty is only skin deep. **sa∗an** at a glance, in a flash. *Sa∗an ing langit katon terang banget.* There was a bright flash in the sky. *ptg* **g·l·ebjar** *or* **g·um·ebjar** *pl* sparkling. *Penganggoné wajang wong ptg glebjar.* The dancers' costumes glitter.

gebjas flask, vial

gebjog wooden exterior house wall. **∗an** coast, shoreline (*var of* GEBJUG·AN)

gebjug similar, almost the same (*Jogja slang*). **∗an** 1 coast, shoreline. 2 to guess at random. *Nèk ∗an, reganė pira?* What would you guess it costs? **ng∗** 1 [of water, waves] to hit, pound, beat. 2 to go along with the crowd, do as others do

gebju:r 1 *rpr* splashing. 2 to take a splash bath. **∗an** coffee or tea with sugar dissolved in it. **ng/di∗** 1 to splash water on one's body. 2 to plunge into. 3 to make [coffee, tea] with sugar in it. **ng/di∗** to splash water onto. *See also* AMBJUR, BJUR

geblag 1 the day smn dies. 2 to lean backward too far (in a standing position). **ke∗** to fall over backwards, fall on one's back. 2 wide open. **ng/di∗aké** to cause smn to lie *or* fall on his back

geblas **ng∗** to depart suddenly without a word. *Bareng aku méngo, ḍèké wis ng∗.* When I turned around, he had gone. **ng/di∗aké** to cause to go (off, away) suddenly. *Ḍèké ng∗aké pit.* He speeded off on his bicycle. *See also* BLAS

geblèg 1 rug *or* mattress beater. 2 a snack made of scraped cassava. **ng/di∗i** to clean [a rug, mattress] by beating it; to beat sth with a wide implement

gebleg 1 certain fabric of inferior quality. 2 stupid, ignorant

geblog 1 palm's-breadth as a measure of width. 2 roll/bolt of fabric

geblug 1 (*prn* **geblu:g**) *rpr* a thud. 2 dull, blunt. **ng/di∗(i)** 1 to hit, land a blow (on). 2 to tread on [soil] to tamp it firm

gébog **ng/di∗** to tie (up) securely

gebog 1 a large wooden container. 2 banana-tree log (*var of* DEBOG). 3 roll/bolt of fabric

gebos *cr* to discharge flatus

gebrag *rpr* sth striking a wooden surface. **ng/di∗** 1 to hit [sth wooden]. *Médjané di∗ mak brak.* He thumped the table. 2 to urge on a horse by pressing the heels to its sides

gebral *rpr* a bursting sound

gebras *var of* GEBLAS, KEPRAS

gebrès 1 *rpr* a sneeze. 2 to sneeze. **∗-∗** 1 to keep sneezing. 2 to eject forcibly from the mouth. *Lomboké ∗-∗ kepeḍesen.* The pepper was so hot he spit it out.

gebru:g *rpr* a heavy thud. **ng/di∗** to drop sth heavily. **g·um·ebrug** to fall heavily. *Tibané matjané gumebrug seru: brug.* The tiger fell with a great thud.

gebug *ng,* **gebag** *kr* club, cudgel. **∗an** act of striking with a club. *Telung ∗an waé wis tjukup.* Three whacks is enough! **∗an (lotré)** the determination of a lottery winner (by drawing). **ng/di∗** to choose the winner in a game of chance. *Lotréné wis di∗ djam wolu mau.* The lottery winner had been chosen by eight o'clock. *di∗ ḍaḍu* to be the winner in a dice game. **ng∗ ratjak** to generalize. **ng/di∗aké** to strike with [a stick]. *Pring mau nuli di∗aké marang gegeré A.* He brought the bamboo stick down on A's back. **ng/di∗(i)** to strike, beat. *Petjuté diwalik dianggo ng∗i djarané.* He beat the horse with his whip handle.

gebuk *var of* KEBUK

gebung roll, bolt. *dluwang sa∗* a roll of paper. **ng/di∗** to roll, make into a roll

gedabag braided-bamboo wall panel of inferior quality

gedabi:g *rpr* a quick movement. **∗an** to keep moving around; to twist, writhe. *Uripé ∗an.* He leads a restless life. *Aku ora bisa turu mau bengi, tansah ∗an waé.* I couldn't get to sleep last night–I kept tossing and turning.

geḍabjah *ptg ∗* dressed in loose, drooping garments. *memedi kang ptg srompal, ptg ∗* a scarecrow of shredded rags dressed in floppy clothing. **∗-∗** *rpr* the visual impact of smn walking in loose floppy clothing. **ng∗** 1 overlarge clothing; too much clothing. *Penganggoné sarwa ng∗.* He's always dressed sloppily. *Mung arep lunga rong dina waé, gawané ng∗.* You'll only be away two days: you're taking too many clothes. 2 careless, absent-minded

gedabrul **ng∗** to play around, fool around

gedabul **ng∗** 1 dirty, muddy. 2 *var of* NG·GEDABRUL

gedabur *var of* GEDABRUL

geḍag **ng∗** to speak to smn angrily. *Bareng ḍèké ng∗, aku ng∗ ganti.* When he snapped at me, I snapped back. **sa∗an** (at) this time [as contrasted with others]

geḍakal ***an** 1 to proceed rapidly on all fours. *Nalika krungu swara beḍil, ḍèké *an nggolèki panggonan kanggo umpetan.* When he heard gunshots he scurried for cover. 2 to greet warmly. *Saka kadohan ḍèké wis *an mapag aku.* He waved me an enthusiastic welcome from afar.

geḍampal ***an** *or* ***-*** to struggle against obstacles

geḍânâ ***-geḍini** boy-girl sibling combination (*var of* KEḌANA-KEḌINI)

gedandap *rpr* a disagreeable surprise. *Ḍèké mak * diaruh-aruhi pulisi.* He was startled when a policeman greeted him. ***an** taken aback, unsettled, disagreeably surprised

geḍanḍul *rpr* a sudden drop into a hanging position when knocked off balance *or* deprived of support. **ng*** to hang onto, cling to (under circumstances as above)

geḍang *ng,* **pisang** *kr* banana. *goḍong ** banana leaf (used for wrapping). *pisang gorèng* fried banana. *keplèsèd kulit ** to slip on a banana peel. *** ambon** dessert banana (the variety familiar in the U.S.A.). *** bjar** banana used for frying. *** gendruwo** large red banana. *** kapok/kepok** banana used for cooking. *** kidang** reddish banana. *** kluṭuk** seed-filled banana whose leaf provides excellent wrappers. *** kodja** sweet dessert banana. *** mas** sweet finger-size banana. *** radja** perfectly formed banana used in ritual meals. *** susu** small plump sweet banana. *See also* RUBUH²

geḍangkal *var of* GEḌAKAL

geḍangklik fitting loosely [of a dovetailed joint]. *ptg * or* **geḍongklak-*** [of loose-fitting joints] to wobble. **ng*** to fit too loosely into its matching part

geḍangkrang **ng*** to sit (discourteously) in a high position

geḍangsang ***an** 1 to try to catch up with *or* overtake. 2 [to do] with great difficulty *or* in the face of obstacles

geḍé *ng,* **ageng** *kr* 1 large, great, imposing. ** ḍuwur* big and tall (of physique). ** tjenḍèk* well built but short (of physique). *omah ** a big house. ** gandjarané.* He got a large reward. ** apa tjilik?* Is it large or small? *dosa ** a great sin. *Swarané *.* He has a deep voice. *aksara ** capital letter. *dina ** a big (special) day. *wong ** an important person. *wis ** grown up. ** nginumé.* He drinks heavily. 2 high [of water level]. *Kaliné *.* The river is up. ***ǹ** (on a) large scale. *tetanèn geḍèn* large-scale farming. ***ǹ-*ǹan** 1 (on a) large scale. *korban geḍèn²an* a vast number of victims. *Anggènipun mantu ageng²an.* They held a huge wedding. 2 to compete for size; to compare for largest. *Negara A lan negara B saiki geḍèn²an roket.* Nations A and B are competing to see who can produce the largest rocket. ***né** 1 (the) size/greatness (of). *Sepira *né?* How big is it? **ning tékad* the strength of his determination. *ḍuwit *né Rp. sepuluh juta* (money in the amount of) 10,000,000 rupiahs. 2 at most, the maximum. *Radjapati *né mung diukum salawasé urip.* The maximum sentence for murder is life imprisonment. ***-*né** at the very most, at the outside. **ge*ǹ** *ng only: var of* KE*Ǹ *below. gegeḍèn rumangsa* a feeling of pride *or* superiority. **ke*ǹ** excessively large/great. *Jèn kegeḍèn banju sawah énggal² dibeḍah.* If the water in the paddy gets too high, it is quickly drained off. *kegeḍèn enḍas* conceited. **ng/di*kaké** 1 to make large(r); to [do] to a large extent. *Menawi kaliten, mboten saged dipun agengaken.* If it's too small, it can't be made larger. *Gambar iki digeḍèkaké.* This picture was enlarged. *Rerusuh ing Indonesia déning pekabaran mantja negara digeḍèk-geḍèkaké.* The unrest in Indonesia was exaggerated by the foreign press. *Ora nggeḍèkaké sinau, nanging nggeḍèkaké turu.* He's not doing much studying, but he's getting a lot of sleep. *nggeḍèkaké ati* encouraging, heartening. 2 to raise [children]. **ng/di*ǹi** to [do] on a large scale. *Pahargjan tahun punika dipun agengi.* The festivities were expanded this year. **g·um·eḍé** *ng kr* conceited, arrogant. *** ati·né** encouraged; proud and happy. *** ḍuwur ora pangur** grown up but still lacking proper manners. *** enḍas·é** obstinate; conceited; inconsiderate. *** lengen·é** strong, powerful; ***ǹ-*ǹan lengen** to compare *or* compete for strength. *** obor ḍuwur kukus·é** famous and influential. *** tjilik** 1 large and small, all sizes. *Saben wong * tjilik paḍa dibutuhaké negara.* Everyone in every age group is needed by the nation. 2 size. *miturut * tjiliké barang* according to the size of the object. *See also* PANGGEḌÉ

gedébag ***an** to roll around in one's sleep. **ng*** 1 to roll in one's sleep. 2 broad, expansive. *Ng* pawakané.* He's powerfully built. *apem ng** a huge pancake

gedebeg (*or ptg* * *or* *-*) (making) the sound of feet walking. *Lakuné kebo mau ptg * karo mangani suket.* The buffalo clumped along grazing. *Aku krungu *ing wong.* I hear smn coming.

geḍébjah **ng*** [of hair] long and unkempt

gedéblag *var of* GEDÉBAG

gedebog *formal var of* DEBOG

gedebug *rpr* a heavy thudding *or* stamping. **gedebag-*** to stomp repeatedly

gedebus **ng*** to babble, talk a lot of nonsense

geḍèḍèr (*or* ***an** *or* **ng***) hanging loosely and sloppily

gèḍèg to shake the head. *-* *or* **géḍag-*** to keep shaking the head. **ng/di*aké** to shake [the head]. *Si A mung ng*aké sirahé.* A just shook his head. **ng/di*i** to shake the head at smn. *** (lan) anṭuk** **1** to merely nod *or* shake the head rather than contributing opinions. *Adja *-(m)anṭuk waé, mbok ja omong.* Don't just sit there agreeing–speak up! **2** to collaborate in a scheme. *Malingé wingi * (karo) anṭuk karo sing djaga malem.* The thief worked hand in glove with the night watchman. *Si * lan Si Anṭuk* those who never voice their own opinions; collaborators in sth nefarious

geḍèg panel of braided *or* woven bamboo. *omah ** a house made of bamboo panels. *pager ** a wall built of such panels. ** atèn*[2] a panel of woven bamboo pith. ** kulitan* a panel of woven bamboo bark. **ng/di*(i)** to provide [a house] with bamboo-panel walls; to enclose [a house] with a woven-bamboo-panel fence. **pa*an** place where the above panels are sold. *** rai·né** thick-skinned, insensitive

geḍeg *-* to shake the head in disbelief. **ng*** to dress elegantly

geḍegel **ng* ati·né** to have hurt feelings

gedegreg sudden [of stopping]. *manḍeg ** to stop dead

geḍem huge, enormous

geḍempal *var of* GEḌAKAL

gèḍèng measuring unit for rice plants: the amount that can be encircled by the thumbs and index fingers of the two hands (*see also* BELAH), *ca.* 6.17 kilograms = 13.6 lbs., or 10 *kati*'s. ***an** a bundle of rice plants formed according to the above measure; act of forming such bundles. **ng/di*i** to bundle [rice plants] as above

geḍengkreng **ng*** (to sit) absolutely still

geḍepes *rpr* the action of seating oneself quietly and properly

gedibagan *var of* GEDÉBAGAN

gedibal **1** dirt adhering to the feet. **2** *cr* a subordinate, servant

gedibel **ng*** to feel heavy and clumsy to the wearer *or* user (*e.g.* feet in oversize shoes)

gedibigan to keep moving restlessly, to fidget

geḍig *-* *or* **geḍag-*** boastful, vainglorious. **ng/di*** to beat [dried soybean pods] with a bamboo stalk in order to open the pods to extract the beans

geḍingkring **ng*** (to sit) in a high position; (to sit) higher than smn else (a breach of etiquette)

geḍini *see* GEḌANA

gedjâbâ *inf var of* KEDJABA

gedjarag done unintentionally (*inf var of* KE·DJARAG)

gedjeblès *inf var of* KE·DJEBLÈS

gedjedjer **ng*** to stand up straight

gedjeg **ng*** to nag

gedjeglug *inf var of* KE·DJEGLUG

gedjegur *inf var of* KE·DJEGUR

gedjig **1** wooden pole or bar for digging or prying. **2** lame because of a short leg. **ng*** to dig or pry with the above

gedjlig **1** sluice, waterway with a valve. **2** *rpr* a leap, bound

gedjlug *var of* GEDJUG. **ng*** to thud downward. *Bané pitku ng*.* My bicycle wheel bumped over a depression. **ng/di*aké** to cause sth to thump down

gedjlungup *inf var of* KE·DJLUNGUP

gedjodjor **ng*** stretched out. *Sikilé ng*.* His legs are stretched out. **ng/di*aké** to stretch out [the legs]

gedjoh *var of* GEDJROH

gedjos *var of* GEDJUS

gedjras *rpr* the sounds made by a hoeing implement as it strikes the earth

gedjroh **ng*** to pierce, stab

gedjru:t *rpr* suddenly bursting out/forth

gedjudjur *var of* GEDJODJOR, KE·DJUDJUR

gedjug crowbar. ***an** a door that is hinged at the top so that it opens upward. **ng/di*** to strike with a crowbar

gedjus **1** *rpr* a sharp weapon piercing flesh. **2** *rpr* the sound of an explosive device fizzling out instead of exploding. **3** *rg* nonsense! ridiculous!

geḍobjah *var of* GEḌABJAH

geḍobjoh **geḍobjah-*** loose, ill-fitting. *Klambiné geḍobjah-* kegeḍèn.* His shirt's too big.

geḍobrag ***an** to clatter, thump. *Adja *an, bapak lagi saré.* Don't bang things around, your father is sleeping.
geḍobrah *var of* GEḌOBROH
geḍobroh [of clothing] too large, loose, ill-fitting
gedobrol **ng*** to boast, tell tall tales
gedobros *var of* GEDOBROL
geḍoḍor ***an** *or* **ng*** to hang loosely [of overlarge garments]
geḍog heavy thumping sound. ***an** horse stable. **geḍag-*** (to make) repeated thumping sounds. **ng/di*** to pound (on). *ng* médja* to pound the table. *See also* WAJANG[a]
gedogrog **ng*** to remain motionless
geḍoh ***an** 1 dregs. 2 *cr* actions, behavior
geḍong 1 building of brick or stone (as contrasted with wood, bamboo). 2 building that houses an organization. ** Wanita* Women's Club. 3 palace outbuilding where food is stored and prepared. 4 cloth wrapped around babies' limbs to ensure straight growth. ***an** 1 a complex of brick houses. 2 sleeping rooms at the back of a Javanese house. 3 cloth wrapping for a baby's limbs. **ng/di*(i)** 1 to build [a modern building]. *Omahé di*.* He built his house of brick/stone. 2 to enclose sth in a building. 3 to wrap [a baby's arms and legs] with cloth. **di* ana di·kuntji·ǹana.** No matter how well protected you are, you must die when your time comes. **pa*an** 1 principles of Javanese philosophic lore. 2 inner thoughts; wisdom. *** pa·m·belèh·an** slaughtering house. *** komiḍi** theater. *** peteng** jail, prison. *** t·in·umpang·an umbul[2]** a person who has had a piece of luck
gedrah (*or* **ng***) usual, commonplace
gedrig 1 printing (as contrasted with handwriting). *tulisan ** printed matter. 2 printed (by hand, rather than written in cursive style)
gedrug young *laos* plant. ***-*** *or* **gedrag-*** to keep stamping the foot. *nesu gedrag-** hopping mad. **ng*** to stamp the foot (on). **ng/di*aké** to stamp [the foot]. *Sikilé bola-bali di*-*aké.* He stamped again and again. *ptg* **g·l·edrug** *pl* stamping the feet
gedubang *var of* DUBANG
gedublong **ng*** 1 to defecate. 2 to prattle, talk nonsense
geḍubrag *var of* GEḌOBRAG
gedug *var of* GADUG
geḍug **ge*** heroic leader in battle. **ng/di*aké** to pound sth (against sth). *Sikilé di*-*aké ing témbok.* He kept knocking his foot against the wall. *See also* ḌUG
geduga *inf var of* KE·DUGA
géduk, geduk *var of* GADUG
geḍumpal *var of* GEḌAMPAL
geḍungsang *var of* GEḌANGSANG
geduwung *inf var of* KEDUWUNG
geg- *see also under* G- *(Introduction, 3.1.3)*
gega to believe; to act according to *(root form: kr for* GUGU)
gegânâ *oj* sky, heaven; [up in] the air
gégé 1 speeding-up process. *banju ** water for bathing a baby to make him grow faster. 2 *var of* GAGA. ***ǹ** in haste. *A gègèn adus.* A took a quick bath. **ng* (mangsa)** to speed up the normal pace, try to force sth before its time. *See also* GÉ
gègèk **ng*** 1 to laugh persistently. 2 to keep asking
gegel (*or* ***an**) a joint(ed place), *esp.* of puppets. *kéwan *an* insect with jointed legs
gegem ***an** to clench the fist. **an tangan* a (clenched) fist. *Sing nang *anmu kuwi apa?* What are you clutching in your hand? **ng/di*** to hold, grip. **en sing kentjeng lo.* Hang on tight! **ng* tangan** 1 to make a fist. 2 lazy. **ng* watu** secretly plotting revenge. **ng/di*aké** to hold for smn. **sa*** a fistful; sth held in the clutched hand
gègèr turbulence, tumult; in chaos. *djaman ** time of war. *Nalika keprungu swara gemleger, wong sak pasar *.* When an explosion was heard, everyone in the marketplace panicked. **ng/di*aké** to cause panic *or* tumult. **(pa)*an** *sms* ***
geger *ng kr,* **pengker·an** *ki* the upper back. *Tak tumpangaké ing *ku.* I'll carry it on my back. **ng*** resembling a back. **ng* sapi** [of roads] high in the middle and sloping off at the sides. *** bungkuk/wungkuk** bent with age *or* deformity. *** butju** hunchbacked
gègès **ng*** 1 to cough persistently. 2 to make merry. 3 *cr* to say, talk
geges **ng*** 1 *intsfr* cold. *aḍem ng** intensely cold. 2 (*psv* **di***) to lop off. *wit sing di* ojodé* a tree whose roots have been severed
geget to laugh heartily. **ng* (untu)** to clench the teeth in anger
gegleg **ng*** to sit silent and sorrowful
gégoh to keep moving around restlessly *or*

noisily. **ng/di*i** to disturb smn. *Aku arep sinau ja, adja ng*i.* I'm trying to study—don't bother me with your fidgeting.

gègrèg [of hair, feathers] to fall *or* drop out. **ng/di*aké** to pluck (out). **ng*i** to molt, shed

gègrèk **ng*** to laugh constantly

gèh *rg var of* INGGIH

Gé-Ing day-name combination (*shc from* WAGÉ PAING

géjan in a hurry. **, selak udan!* Quick—it's about to rain!

géjang *var of* GÉJONG

gèjèt pole for picking fruits high on the tree

géjol tough, rubbery [of *salak* fruit]. **géjal-*** to chew on sth rubbery

géjong ***an** to swing. *Botjah² lagi *an ing mburi.* The children are swinging out back. **géjang-*** to dangle. *Pelemé géjang-*.* The mango hung from the branch. *ptg* **g·r·éjong** *pl* hanging, dangling

géjot **ng*** heavy to lift *or* carry

géjuk *var of* GAJUK

gèk 1 oh my! why! *Turu * tanpa bantal ja sengsara banget.* Sleeping without a pillow—oh, it was miserable. *Senadyan sugih banḍa, aku iki wong mlarat, * ora duwé anak.* I'm rich in worldly goods but I'm a poor man: I have no children. 2 *excl of doubt, misgivings, apprehension.* ** ndilalahé...!* Oh, what bad luck...! *Mengko * ora ketemu.* I doubt if it'll be found. *Ing podjokan kaé ana swara, mengko * memedi.* There's a noise in that corner—what if it's a ghost! 3 now what (why, *etc.*)? *Ing batin ngunandika, "Gèk anaké sapa?"* She said to herself: "Now whose child could it be?" *Nanging * arep lunga menjang endi?* But where on earth are you going? ** sapa ja ḍèwèké iku?* And who might HE be? *Wis ta, * butuh apa?* OK now, what do you need, hm? 4 quick; (and) then (after that). *supaja * rampung* in order to finish quickly. ** turua, sésuk munḍak mangsuk angin.* Go right to bed, or you'll have a cold tomorrow. *Ajo * mangkat.* Come on, let's get going. *mBok ja * ṭak-ṭek tumandang, adja ngalamun waé.* Get ready—don't sit daydreaming! 5 and, moreover. *Rambuté ireng meleng * tambah dawa.* Her hair was jet black, and long. 6 last, past; when (*var of* ḌÈK). 7 *var of* JÈN. 8 *var of* LAGI. **ng*** in, at, on. *Sing geḍé ng* endi?* Where's the big one? **nge/di*aké** *inf var of* NG/DI·GAWÉ·KAKE. *Aḍimu digèkké lajangan kana!* Go make a kite for your little brother! *** gelem * ora** any old way, in slipshod fashion. *** ija * ora** indecisive, undecided. *Olèhé arep menjang Éropa * ija * ora.* He can't make up his mind whether to go to Europe.

gek̄ **(ng)*²** *rpr* swallowing. *Ḍèké ngombé nggek-nggek.* He drank it down.

gekeng **ng*** 1 with concentrated effort. *Olèhé njambut-gawé ng*.* He worked concentratedly. 2 firm, fast. *Gelasé ditjekeli ng*.* He held the glass tight.

gel- *see also under* GL- (*Introduction, 2.9.3*)

gela disappointed, let down. **ke*n** disappointed, hurt. **ng/di*kaké** 1 to disappoint smn. 2 to irritate smn. **ng*ni** disappointing; irritating

gelah ***-*ing djagat/bumi** the dregs of society

gelak ***an** quickly finished. **ng*** to [do] quickly; to quicken one's pace

gélang 1 a variety of purslane. 2 blossom of the areca palm

gelang *ng kr,* **binggel** *kr* bracelet. ***an** 1 ring, hoop. *tudjon *an* ring-toss game. *mlebu *an wesi* to jump through an iron hoop. 2 watch bracelet. 3 gymnastic traveling rings. 4 wrist; ankle. **an sikil* ankle. ** tangan* wrist. **ge*** 1 (various kinds of) bracelets. 2 to wear a bracelet. **ng/di*i** to provide smn with a bracelet. **pa*an** wrist; ankle

gelap 1 dark; undercover; illicit. *upas ** plainclothes detective. *tjandu ** unlicensed opium. 2 lightning that strikes sth. ** padju* lightning bolt that splits sth. ** wédang* lightning bolt that burns living tissue. *Disamber ing *!* May I (you) be struck by lightning! **ng*** 1 to flee. *Maling ng* jèn konangan.* A thief bolts if he is caught in the act. 2 *contraction of* ING *. *Samber ng*.* Damn! **ng/di*aké** 1 to embezzle. *ng*aké ḍuwit kantor* to misappropriate official funds. *Ḍèké ng*aké bolah satus gulung.* He stole 100 spools of thread from where he works. 2 to break through [a roof] on smn's behalf. *Pajoné di*aké tangga²né.* The neighbors pitched in and fixed the roof for him. **ng/di*(i)** to break through [a roof] to repair *or* replace it

gelar 1 array, layout, deployment. 2 title; academic degree. ***an** woven grass mat (*kr for* KLASA). **ng/di*aké** to spread, unfold, reveal (on smn's behalf). *ng*aké kawruh* to spread knowledge. **ng/di*(i)** to reveal, spread, disseminate. *ng* klasa* to spread a mat. *ng* wulang* to teach, dispense learning. **ng/di*i** 1 to spread onto. *Di*i babut.* He covered it with a carpet. 2 to confer a degree/title on. **pa*an** an open hall where a monarch holds audiences and other less formal talks. **pa·ng*** 1 act of spreading, disseminating. 2 education, *i.e.* the dissemination of knowledge. **g·um·elar** spread out, unfolded, revealed. *kabèh kang gumelar* the earth and everything in it, *i.e.* all that is spread out before us

gelas 1 drinking glass; glassful. 2 *rg* glass (the substance). ***an** 1 [of kite strings] coated with bits of ground glass. 2 ground glass for kite strings. **ng/di*** to coat [a kite string] with glue containing sharp glass fragments. **ng/di*aké** to glass smn's kite string for him

gelek̄ *rg* frequently

gelem *ng*, **purun** *kr*, **karsa** *ki* to be willing (to); to accept willingly. *A ora * disekolahaké.* A doesn't want to be entered in school. *Ora ana wong sing * manggon ing kono.* No one is willing to live there. *Boten wonten ingkang purun ngawon.* Neither one would give in. *Jèn butuh mari, * ora * kudu ngombé tamba.* If you expect to get well you have to take medicine, whether you want to or not. *Kudu wani ngrekasa * kepénak.* You have to risk adversity and accept comforts gratefully. *Jèn ditawani mangan adja *.* If you're offered a meal, refuse it. ***an** 1 willing, obedient. 2 promiscuous. 3 covetous; apt to steal. **ng/di*i** to agree (to), express willingness. *Adjak²* *ḍéwé, bareng di*i ora sida.* You asked me to go with you, and now that I've said I would, you change your mind! **sa* ija ora** in slipshod fashion, any old way. **sa*é** whatever one would like (to). *Anggènipun njukani sapurun sampéjan kémawon.* Give just as much as you feel like giving. **sa*-*é** to [do] to one's utmost. *Djarané digebugi sa*-*é.* He beat the horse with all his might. *** ora** 1 (are you) willing (or not)? 2 (*or* ***-* ora**) careless(ly), in slipshod fashion. *Kaju apik kok olèhé nggarap * ora.* It's beautiful wood, but what slovenly work he did on it!

gèlèng **gélang-*** to keep shaking the head

geleng **g·um·eleng** to make up one's mind. *Apa kowé wis gumeleng ing karep menawa kowé arep lunga adoh?* Are you quite certain you want to go so far away? *** pikir·é** *or* *** rembug·é** meeting of the minds

geli 1 annoyed. 2 to have a compulsion to laugh

gelik ***-*** alone in a deserted place

gelis (**énggal** *kr?*) speedy, quick. *Laramu bèn * mari.* I hope you'll get well fast.

gélo rupiah (*Jogja slang*). **géla-*** to move the head back and forth, *e.g.* the motions of watching a badminton game

geluk smoke

gelung *ng kr*, **ukel** *ki* traditional Javanese ladies' hair style: long hair wound into a bun at the back. ***an** to do up *or* wear the hair in this style. **ng/di*** 1 to arrange [the hair] as above. 2 to tie into a bundle. *** bokor** ladies' hair style for a special occasion. *** kaḍal m̄·pènèk** male hair style worn beneath a wraparound headdress: long hair wound on top of head. *** konḍé** everyday ladies' hair style, with the rope of hair wound into a round form. *** s·in·upit**, *** tekuk** ladies' hair styles for special occasions. *See also* KUNTJUNG

gelut (*or* ***an**) to fight, struggle, wrestle

gem- *see also under* G- (*Introduction, 3.1.7*)

gemah prosperous [of a nation]. *** (a)ripah** prosperous and flourishing in wealth and population

gemak *ng*, **pujuh** *opt? kr* a small female quail, formerly used for fighting. ***an** 1 Indian wrestling with thumbs rather than forearms. 2 a striped locust-like insect. *See also* BENTJÉ

gemang unwilling. *Ajo ngunḍuh pelem.–Ah *.* Let's pick mangoes.–No, I don't want to. *Jèn * njambut-gawé, ora bakal bisa tuku sanḍang-pangan.* If you won't work, you can't buy the things you need.

gembâjâ red material for kerchiefs

gembak large braided-bamboo container

gembâlâ beard (*ki for* DJÉNGGOT)

gèmbèl 1 dewlap (of cattle); wattles (of rooster). 2 unkempt, rangled, unruly [of hair]

gembel a short iron-headed club. **ng*** productive, fruitful. *Wit pelem ngarep kuwi ng*.* The mango tree out front is loaded with fruit.

gembèlèng (*or* ***an**) conceited. **gembélang-*** (to walk, conduct oneself) with a superior air. **ng*** haughty

gembélo **ng*** large [of the head]; *fig* vain, conceited

gembèng (*or* ***an**) to cry easily. *botjah *(an)* a crybaby. *** krèwèng** *or* *** tjèng-èng/tjingèng** apt to cry at the slightest provocation

gembès flat(tened), deflated. **ng*** to go flat. **ng/di*aké** to deflate, let the air out of. **ng*an** prone to becoming flat. *Ban iki ng*an.* This tire is always going flat. **ng/di*i** to deflate

gembes *rg var of* NGEMBES

gembil fat, plump [of cheeks]

gembili (a plant which produces) an oval turnip-like fruit with a potato-like flavor

gembira overjoyed. *** laja** an ocean deep

gèmbjok 1 long [of hair]. 2 fringe

gembjong *see* KAṬOK

gémbjor ***-*** *or* **gémbjar-*** thin and run-down after an illness

gemblak 1 tinker; tinsmith, brass worker; person whose trade is making things from odds and ends. 2 small bottle. 3 (*or* ***an**) male performer of classical songs and dances. **ng/di*(i)** to have homosexual relations (with) [other males]

gemblang **ng*** *or* **g·um·emblang** clear and bright [of sky, weather]

gembleb chubby-cheeked

gèmblèh ***-*** *or* **gèmblah-*** hanging down limply [of fleshy parts]

gemblèng ***an** 1 forged iron (bars). 2 blacksmith's hammer used in forging. 3 rigorously trained. *pradjurit *an* a well-disciplined soldier. **ng/di*** 1 to forge [iron]. 2 to train rigorously

gembleng ***é** roughly totaling. **é limang èwu rupiah.* It's about 5,000 rupiahs altogether. **ng/di*aké** to total up, consolidate. *Utangmu di*aké ana pira?* How much do your debts amount to altogether? *ng*aké kakuwatan* to concentrate one's forces

gémblok **ng*** to cling to. *Aku kesel lho, mbok adja ng* baé.* I'm tired–please don't hang onto me. *A ng* ing tjagak lan njoba mènèk.* A clung to the pole and tried to shinny up it.

gemblong a snack made of mashed glutinous rice or cassava

gemblung crazy, maddened. **ng*** 1 to feign madness. 2 to root out [wild tubers]. 3 to plunge *or* roll into

gembok padlock. **ng/di*** to lock with a padlock

gémbol ***an** sth carried on one's person where it is concealed. *blandja minggon kanggo *an* a weekly allowance for pocket money. **an kawruh* knowledge, know-how. *duwé *an* to have a secret talent; to have an ace in the hole. **ng/di*** to carry sth concealed. *Di* mrodjol.* He had it in his pocket but it fell out. *sing di* mrodjol, sing dikanḍut mrutjut* to lose everything one gets his hands on. *ng* wadi* to have a secret. *ng* rasa serik* to harbor ill feelings. *ng* watu* to have it in for smn

gembolo a certain edible tuber

gémbong (*or* **ge***) leader, head. *** *nasionalis*** nationalist leader. *** *rampok*** robber leader

gembor watering can. **gembar-*** *or* **(ng)*-*** 1 to do a lot of loud talking *or* shouting. 2 to cry noisily. *ptg* **g·l·embor** *pl* to carry on noisily as above

gembos (*or* **ng***) to become deflated suddenly. *Bané ng*.* The tire suddenly went flat. *See also* BOS

gembrang *rpr* a metallic clatter

gembrèng 1 tin can used as a noisemaker. 2 oil can. *lampu ** lantern in a tin housing. **ng*i** to beat on a tin can, *esp.* to scare birds away from crops

gembrèt ***-*** to keep making shrill disagreeable sounds. **ng*** 1 off key, out of tune. 2 to scamper, scurry

gembring 1 filmy, gauzy. 2 *rg* fake, counterfeit. **ora * ora waring** destitute

gembro lazy, lackadaisical

gembrong **(ge)*an** to make a lot of noise

gembrot 1 a dish made with shredded coconut with boiled vegetables. 2 bulky, ponderous (of physique)

gembu:k 1 tender, soft. 2 a short round pillow. ***an** a doughnut-like snack. ***-*** very soft/tender

gembuleng **ng*** dark, gloomy, threatening

gembung trunk of the human body. **ora * ora irung** impoverished

gembu:r ***-*** *or* **ng*** soft and spongy

gembus 1 a certain dish (*témpé*) made from leftover beancake. 2 *slang* baloney! *(excl of scorn, disbelief)*

gembut soft, squashy [of fruits]

geméla clear, plain. *** wéla**[2] perfectly plain/obvious

gemes irritated, provoked. **ng*aké** irritating; provocative

gemet all gone. *njirnakaké ama nganti ** to exterminate the pests completely

gemi frugal, thrifty. * *nastiti* thrifty and careful. *ǹ thrifty by nature. **ng/di*ǹi** to use frugally. *Pametuné digemèni.* He makes his earnings go as far as possible.
gemijèn *rg var of* BIJÈN
gempal chipped. **ng/di*aké** to lessen bit by bit. *Tindakané ng*aké kemakmuran negara.* His acts are chipping away at the national prosperity. **ng/di·ge*(i)** to chip away (at). *Sedina muput njambutgawé ng*i watu karang.* All day long he works at chipping rock from the cliffs. *ngge* kaluhuran* to undermine smn's dignity. *ngge* prabon* to chip away at the kingdom. * **ati·né** without hope. * **rusak·ing negara** the gradual destruction of the nation
gempang done away with, cleaned out
gémpar **ng/di*** to kick
gempèl *var of* GEMPIL
gempi soft, requiring little or no chewing
gempil chipped, damaged. *Témboké *.* The wall is nicked. *kekendelan kang ora ** unflinching bravery. **ke*** to get chipped (away at). **ng/di*aké** to chip a piece from
gemplang unbearably hot. **ng/di*** to dry sth in the sun. **g·um·emplang** hot. *Panasé gememplang.* The heat from the sun is insufferable.
gempleng *var of* GEMBLENG
gemplung *intsfr* empty. *suwung ** completely empty
gempol 1 a certain fruit, also its tree. 2 rice balls used in a certain porridge. **g·um·empol** [of veal] very tender
gémpor *var of* GÉMPAR
gemprong ***an** sounds produced by beating a wooden pounder rhythmically against a wooden box. **ng/di*** to shout/yell (at)
gempung 1 annoyed, vexed. 2 *var of* GEMPANG
gempur ***an** act of destroying; destroyed, smashed. **ng/di*** to demolish
gemuh big and fat
gemuk lubricating grease. **ng/di*** to grease sth
genah 1 well behaved, conforming to normal standards. *Anaké wong *.* He comes from a nice family. *Wis *.* Everything is fine now. 2 clear, plain. ***é** the reason for *or* clarification of. **é pijé ta?* How is it to be explained? ***-*an** to clarify mutually. *Wis *-*an bab baṭiné.* They got it straightened out with each other about the profits. **ng*** [of one's behavior] normal, within proper limits. **ng/di*aké** to make clear. *ng*aké pitakon* to clear up a question. *mBok ja bab kuwi di*aké ḍisik.* Make sure you've got it straight. **pa·ng*** act of clarifying. *tembung pang* (gram)* demonstrative word. **ora (ng)*** improper; abnormal. *Ora * kowé kuwi.* Shame on you! *Wong sing ngguju² ḍéwé kaé pantjèn wong ora *.* That man over there who's laughing all by himself must be not quite right in the head. **wis * wis prenah** everything is going along well
genḍajur **ng*** *var of* NGENḌAJUR
genḍak ***an** (a man's) mistress. **ng* sikara** *wj* to disturb, interfere with
genḍalungan to talk impolitely *or* misuse the speech levels, *e.g.* to use Krama improperly
gendam a charm, magic spell. * *pangasihan* a magic spell for making smn fall in love. **ng/di*** 1 to cast a spell (on); to meditate in order to bring about a miracle. 2 *rg* to catch fish. **pa·ng*an** *sms * above*
gendani a tiny bamboo-like plant
genḍek̄ [of neck] short and thick
gènḍèl 1 bunch, bundle. 2 small packet of coconut sugar. ***an** *or* ***en** hanging down and swollen [of a part that has been cut, *e.g.* newly pierced ears]. ***-*** to hang down. **ng/di*** to hang sth. *Klambiné di* ing nḍuwur kono.* He hung up his shirt there.
gènḍel *rpr* sth heavy pulling downward. *Pantjingé krasa mak *.* I felt a tug on my fishing line. **g·um·ènḍel** heavy, pulling downward. *Koper mau tak djundjing rasané gemènḍel.* That trunk is heavy to lift.
genḍel *var of* BÈNḌEL, GÈNḌEL
genḍeleng **genḍelang-*** *or* **ng*** to have a stupid look
gèndèng ***-g·in·èndèng** to pull back and forth. **ke*** to get pulled/dragged. **ng/di*** to pull (at), drag. **ng* gèrèt** *or* **ng* tjènèng** to cooperate, pull together. **pa·ng*** act of pulling. *daja peng** pull; power of attraction
gènḍèng *var of* GÈNDÈNG
genḍèng roofing tile; tiled roof. **ng*** to sing to the accompaniment of gamelan music
genḍeng crazy, idiotic. *Atiku bingung, kaja wong *.* I was all mixed up, as though I were out of my mind. *Par, botjah *.* Par, you idiot! **ng*** to behave witlessly
gendèr xylophone with bronze keys suspended over bamboo sounding tubes. ***an** in evenly spaced rows. **ng*** 1 to play the

above xylophone. 2 arranged in evenly spaced rows. **pa·ng*** player of the above instrument. *** barung** the leading *gendèr,* which has important functions in shadow plays
gendéra flag. *tjagak ** flagpole. *ngèrèk * (setengah tijang)* to fly a flag (at half staff)
genḍèrèh **genḍarah-*** hanging loosely [of overlarge clothing]. **ng*** to hang down and sweep the floor. *Djubahé ng*.* His gown is too long.
genḍéwa bow (for shooting arrows). **ng*** bow-shaped
genḍil **ng/di*** to keep a child too dependent on one by doing things for him
genḍila 1 crude, ill-behaved. 2 eccentric
genḍing music performed by a gamelan ensemble; to perform such music. ***an** 1 Javanese music in general. 2 to produce gamelan music. 3 place where musicians play. **ng*** to perform a gamelan melody. **pa*an** place where musicians play. **sa*mu** though you do your utmost. *Mlajua sa*mu mesṭi ketjekel.* No matter how fast you run, you will get caught. *Sa*mu tak ladèni.* Use all your strength–I'm ready for you.
gendir ***an** 1 to play marbles. 2 *wj* a certain puppet arm movement. **ng/di*** to shoot [a marble]
genḍis sugar (*kr for* GULA)
géndjah 1 early-ripening variety of rice, fruits. 2 different (from), contrary (to). **ng/di*** 1 to plant an early-maturing crop. 2 to hurry sth to a premature result. *** (ing) budi** inconstant; untrustworthy
gendjé a plant whose leaves are intoxicating
gèndjèh easily bored
gendjik piglet; baby boar (young of the BABI, TJÈLÈNG)
gendjit *var of* GENDJIK
gendjlèng *rpr* pounding, hammering
gendjlong *rpr* loud heavy pounding
gendjlung *rpr* heavy pounding
géndjor ***-*** spongy, soft, springy
gendjot 1 to bounce, spring. 2 sheep pen. ***an** a pedal. ***-*** to move up and down; to move restlessly. ***-*an** pedaling action. *Pitku angèl *-*ané.* My bicycle is hard to pedal. **ng/di*** 1 to move sth up and down. *Adja kokèhan di* gasé.* Don't pump the gas pedal too much. *ng* pit* to pedal a bicycle. 2 *slang* to punch, sock, kick. **pa·ng*** act of moving up and down. *pang*ing péḍal pit* motion of bicycle pedals
gendjrèng 1 *rpr* metal clanging. 2 a bell. 3 cash (as opposed to credit)
gendjrèt **ng*** to scamper off, run away
gendjring bell (*var of* GENDJRÈNG)
gendjrit *var of* GENDJRÈT
gendju:k̄ ***-*** soft and spongy
gendju:r ***-*** soft, yielding, not (yet) firm
genḍju:t ***-*** bouncy, springy
genḍok half of a pair of sugar cakes (*see also* TANGKEB). **sa*** one such piece
génḍol ***-*** to keep bouncing/springing. **ng/di*aké** to hang, suspend. *Krandjangé di*aké ing mburi truk.* He hung the basket on the back of the truck. **ng/di*(i)** to hang onto, cling to. **ng/di*i** to hold back, deter. *A arep mulih sésuk ning tak *i.* A wanted to leave for home tomorrow but I talked him out of it. *ptg* **g·r·énḍol** *pl* hanging. *Pelemé ptg grénḍol.* There are mangoes hanging all over the tree.
genḍon edible soft inner skin of the areca palm. *** rukun** [of marriage partners] to get along well together
génḍong 1 piggy-back ride. 2 batik used as as a sling for carrying things. ***an** 1 thing carried on the back. 2 to ride on smn's back. ***(-*)an** to take turns carrying on the back. *Botjah² paḍa dolanan *an.* The boys gave each other piggy-back rides. **ng/di*** 1 to carry on the back. *Dagangané di*.* He carries his wares on his back. *Aku *en.* Carry me! *or* Give me a piggy-back ride! 2 to carry in a sling. *Lengené sing tatu isih di*.* He has his wounded arm in a sling. **ng* ng·arep** to carry [a baby] slung from a batik in front of one. **ng* lali** single-minded, oblivious to everything else. **ng* m̄·pikul** overburdened
génḍor ***-*** soggy, squashy
génḍot **ng/di*i** to hang sth onto. *Wité pelem di*i pépéan.* She hung a clothesline from the mango tree.
gendra turbulent. *Perkara iki marakaké *.* The problem stirred up a lot of trouble.
gendring **ng*** to flee, speed off
gendruwo male malevolent spirit
genḍu a certain insect
genduk **ng*i** near at hand, within touching distance
genḍuk 1 *adr* little girl; unmarried adolescent girl. 2 young female servant
gendul bottle. ***an** by the bottle(ful); in bottles. *ombèn²an *an* bottled drinks
genḍung (*or* ***an** *or* **g·um·enḍung**) to boast

gendu:t 1 *rpr* bouncing, springing. 2 fat, paunchy

géné * **apa** *ng* it is unlikely (that...). * *apa, wong utang kok ora gelem njaur.* Imagine a person borrowing money and not being willing to pay it back! * **ja** *or* **ja** * *ng,* **(kénging) punâpâ(hâ)** *kr* why? how (come)? *Jagéné lampuné saiki mati?* How come the lights went off? *Putrané lanang apa waras? putrané wédok génėja?* Is her son well? and how about her daughter? *Iki mau *ja?* What's the matter with this? *or* What happened about this? * **ki** *or* * **saiki** *ng* it turns out, surprisingly, that... * *saiki bisa, bareng gelem sinau.* See? you *can* do it, if you're willing to study. *Djaré bisé mangkat djam wolu, * ki isih nang kéné mangka wis djam sepuluh saiki.* The bus was supposed to leave at eight, and it's still here at ten! * *ki isih duwé ḍuwit, la kok mau nganggo utang barang.* You have money–why did you borrow?

genem **ng/di*i** to cook [leaf-wrapped foods] by steaming

geneng in a high location. *Pekaranganė *.* The yard is on high ground. *leḍok ** rolling, hilly (of gardens, fields). ***an** high ground, a high location

genep *inf var of* GANEP

gènes, genes reddish-brown. *Soganė *.* The batik dye is reddish-brown.

genet flour

geng *ltry var of* AGENG

genggeng **ng*** to look splendid/majestic

génggong large. *djangkrik ** a certain large cricket

gèngsot leaning, not quite vertical

geni *ng,* **latu** (*or* **grâmâ**?) *kr* fire. **(ge)*** *or* **(ge)*ǹ** to stay near a fire, *esp.* to warm oneself. *Ḍèkė lagi (ge)genèn.* He's warming himself by the fire. **ma*-*** *ltry* to burn brightly. **ng/di*ǹi** to warm sth up, put sth on the stove to heat. **ora ana * tanpa kukus** you can't suppress news; the truth will leak out

geni:t sexy, flirtatious [of girls or effeminate men]

genjal *rpr* the feel of sth soft and yielding. **g·um·enjal** soft and yielding

gènjèh *var of* GONJÈH

genjol *var of* GENJAL

genju:s *rpr* lunging with a sharp object

genṭa 1 large metal bell with a clapper. 2 cowbell. ***n** bell-shaped

gentajang ***an** to sway from side to side; staggering, unsteady. *Lakuné *an, kakèjan ngombé arak.* He walked unsteadily–he'd had too much to drink.

gentang to hull rice by pounding (*root form: kr for* TUTU)

gentawing *var of* GENTAJANG

gentéjong *ptg* * hanging everywhere, *e.g.* fruits from a tree. **gentéjang-*** to hang for a long time

gèntèng *see* GÈRÈNG

genṭèng *var of* GENḌÈNG

gèntèr long bamboo pole, *esp.* for reaching things high up. **ng/di*(aké)** *or* **ng/di*i** to get sth down from a high place with a pole

genter **ng*** to keep making loud noises. *swarané kenṭongan ng** the constant beating of a bamboo drum

gentéwang *rpr* a downward swoop *or* unexpected fall

genti *ng,* **gentos** *kr* 1 a change, replacement; to change, shift. *Jèn dalané muḍun * persnèling.* When there's a downgrade, shift gears. 2 in (one's) turn. *B * nepsu menjang A.* B got mad right back at A. *Ajo tjangkrimana aku, mengko * kowé bakal tak tjangkrimi.* Ask me a riddle, then I'll ask you one. * *tahun * rentjana* a new year, a new plan. ***-*** *or* ***-*ǹ** to change off, take turns. *Olèhé ngombé genti-gentèn.* They took turns drinking. ***ǹ(-*ǹ)** *or* ***ǹ(-*ǹ)an** *ng,* **gentos(-gentos)an** *kr* changing off; in (one's) turn. *Botjah*[2] *ngombé gentèn.* The boys took turns drinking. *Djeḍing lan sumuré mung sidji, dadi mung gentèn*[2]*an.* There was just one well and bathhouse, so they took turns using it. *Ora saben dina pasar bukak, gentèn*[2]*, penḍak limang dina sepisan.* The market wasn't open every day; it was held once every five days in each place. **ng/di*** to replace. *Rèbewèsé wis kadaluwarsa, kudu di* anjar.* His driver's license has expired; it has to be renewed. *Sapa sing bakal ng* Présiḍèn?* Who'll be the next president? **ng/di*kaké** to make sth over to smn, transfer [property] to smn else. **ng/di*ǹi** 1 to take the place of, fill the position of. *Sapa sing bakal nggentèni kepala kantor kéné?* Who's going to be the new head of this office? *nggentèni watang putung* to replace smn in an inferior position. *Sang Buda ora kersa djumeneng nata nggentèni sang rama.* Buddha did not wish to succeed his father as king. 2 to receive [goods] through other than normal retail channels. *Aku ora duwé beras babar pisan, apa aku bisa nggentèni seliter baé, sésuk tak ∗.* I'm out of rice; can you let he have one liter? I'll pay you back tomorrow. ∗ **tapak** to follow in smn's footsteps. *See also* GANTI

genţijeng   ng∗ strong, robust

gentijung   *rpr* a downward swoop

genţileng   ng∗ [of eyes] black and shining

genting (*or* **ng∗**) frayed, broken nearly through. ∗**an** in a frayed *or* nearly broken condition

gènţjeng   *rpr* sth hitting its true mark *or* getting to the appropriate place

gentjer unswerving, right on, continuous. *Sinauné ∗.* He studied straight through. *Swarané beḍil ∗.* There was the incessant sound of gunfire.

genţo   1 robber, bandit. **2** *pejorative term of abuse*

gentojong   ∗an *or* **ng∗ 1** (top)heavy. **2** [of gait] unsteady, lopsided

gènţol   *var of* GANŢOL

genţong earthen pitcher for keeping a supply of water handy. **ng∗** resembling an earthen pitcher. **ng∗umos** unable to keep a secret

gentos a change; by turns (*kr for* GENTI)

gentur with complete devotion. ∗ **tapané.** He devoted himself entirely to his meditations. **ng∗ tapa** to meditate rigorously

genuk small clay container for rice

gepah *sbst kr for* GUPUH

gépak   ng∗ to turn off/away. *Tekan prapatan wongé ng∗ ngulon.* He turned west at the intersection.

gepak flat (as contrasted with rounded or convex)

gèpèng, gepèng flat, two-dimensional. ∗**an** flat(tened). ∗**an wesi** a flat piece of iron. **ng/di∗aké** to make sth flat

gepit   ng/di∗ to squeeze

gepjok   ng/di∗(i) to hit, whack

geplak a sugar-coated snack of glutinous rice and coconut

gepluk   *var of* GEPUK

gepok   ∗an connected with, related to. *Jèn ∗an bab pawulangan, takona S.* If it has anything to do with schools, ask S. **ma∗an** *or* **mang∗an** concerned/connected [with]. *ma∗an karo kabudajan lan kasusastran* relating to culture and literature. *Aku emoh ma∗an karo wong sing gawéné ngapusi.* I won't have anything to do with a cheater.

ng/di∗ 1 to come in contact with; to concern. *Roḍané ng∗ as.* The wheel is resting on the axle. *Konperènsi kasebut ng∗ kepentingan Indonesia.* The above conference dealt with Indonesian interests. **2** to reprimand lightly. ∗ **sénggol** to have a connection (with). *Aku ora wani ∗ sénggol karo pandjenengan.* I don't want to have anything to do with you. *Aku ora ∗ sénggol perkara mau.* That matter doesn't concern me.

geprèt (*or* **g·um·eprèt**) uncomfortably hot

gepruk   *var of* GEPUK

gepuk   ∗an profit; windfall. **ng/di∗(i) 1** to beat, pound; to assault. *Ḍènḍèng wis di∗?* Has the meat been pounded yet (in preparation for a certain dish)? *Tentara Negara A ng∗ tentara B.* The troops of Nation A are attacking the B nation's troops.

ger   1 *rpr* laughing. **2** funny. **gar-∗** *rpr* repeated laughter. **∗-∗an** *pl* to laugh constantly

ger- *see also under* GR- (*Introduction, 2.9.3*)

gerah   1 ill; painful (*ki for* LARA). **2** *oj* thunder. ∗ **ujang** feverish; bewildered; having a compulsive appetite

gerak to move (*oj*). ∗**an** a movement, motion. ∗**an anti korupsi** anti-corruption movement. ∗ **badan** sports, athletics. *See also* GERIK

gerang   1 worn out, of no further use. **2** old enough to know better. *Botjah wis ∗ kok isih durung ngerti tatakrama.* You're old enough by now to know your manners! ∗**an** *cr* old; one who is old enough to know better. ∗ **ḍaplok/gaplok** an old hand; one who is sophisticated, worldly-wise

geras   1 absorbent. **2** generous with one's money

gerba   *var of* GARBA

gerbong railroad car (for freight or passengers)

gerdji tailor, seamstress

gerḍu sentry box, guard's hut. ∗ **listrik** power house, generating plant

geré [of rice paddies] not productive

gèrèd   ng/di∗(i) to drag, tow, pull

gerèd   *rpr* a squeaky door opening. *Lawangé jèn dibukak muni mak ∗.* The door squeaks when you open it. **g·um·erèd** to squeak, squeal. *gumerèting erèm* the screech of brakes

gereg   ng/di∗ to drive [livestock]

gerèh, gèrèh (*or* ∗ **pèṭèk**) a small flat round dried salt fish. ∗ **buntung** the above, headless

gèrèk left (over) (*var of* KARI). *Ḍuwitmu * pira?* How much money have you got left?
gèrèng **ng*-gèntèng** to nag, whine, complain
gerèng *var of* GÈRÈNG. **ng*** *intsfr* dried up/out. *Sumuré asat ng*.* The well has gone bone dry.
gereng (*or* **ng***) 1 to roar. 2 to moan in pain. *ptg* **g·l·ereng** *pl* to roar
geret groove, furrow, trench. ***an** *or* ***-*** 1 grooved, furrowed. 2 marked with scratches. **ng/di*(i)** to make scratch marks (on)
gerik **gerak-*** to move this way and that; to act, behave. *Wong kuwi gerak-*é njalawadi.* That man is acting suspicious. *See also* GERAK
gerilja̅ guerrilla. *perang ** guerrilla warfare. **ng*** to behave in a sneaky way; (*psv* **di***) to sneak sth away from smn. *Panggonané nèng kantor wis di* wong lija.* He was elbowed out of his job by smn else at the office.
geriljawan (the) guerrillas
gering 1 (**kera** *kr*) thin, emaciated. 2 sick [of animals]; *cr* of people. ***en** sickly, frail
gerit **ng/di*** to scratch. *Katjané di* nganggo paku.* He scratched the glass with a nail. *ptg* **g·l·erit** *pl* to scratch. *swarané grip ptg glerit* the (sound of the) scratching of slate pencils. **g·um·erit** to make a scratching sound
germa 1 hunter. 2 pimp, procurer
germemen *var of* GERMEMENG
germemeng **ng*** to grumble, mutter under one's breath
germeng *var of* GERMEMENG
gernat grenade
gero ***-*** to utter a cry/snarl/growl. *nangis *-** to cry with loud wailing. **ng*** to roar. **pa·ng*** act of roaring. *pang*nipun singa* a lion's roar
gerok hoarse
gérong 1 male chorus accompanying gamelan music. 2 a variety of melon. ***an** choral singing. **ng/di*i** to accompany [an instrumental melody] with unison singing
gerong (*or* **ng***) hollow, sunken [of eyes]
gerot *rpr* an abrasive sound. *Aku narik kursi, mak *.* The chair scraped as I pulled it out. ***an** characterized by abrasive sounds. *alas *an* dense forest. ***-*** *or* **g·um·erot** to make abrasive sounds. *Jèn kowé mlaku nèng kreteg pring kuwi mengko rak *-* pringé.* When you walk across a bamboo bridge, the bamboo stalks creak against each other.
gerpu *var of* GARPU
gertak ***an** (act of) bluffing. **ng*** 1 (*psv* **di***) to order around, shout down. 2 [of peppery foods] bitingly hot. *** sambel** a bluff; **ng/di*-sambel** to bluff. *Kowé ora susah wedi karo omongané, mung * sambel.* Don't be afraid of what he says–it's all bluff.
geru ***-*** in haste (*var of* GURU[2])
gerus **ng*** 1 (*psv* **di***) to grind. *di* lembut* ground to a fine powder. 2 in pain. 3 (*psv* **di***) to iron, press
gès *var of* GRÈS
gesah *var of* GUSAH
gesang life; to live; soul; functioning, operating; active (*kr for* URIP)
gèsèh different, varying from. *Omongané * karo tindaké.* His words belie his actions. *Iwaké rupa*[2]*, ḍapuré ija *-*.* There were all kinds of fish, all different shapes. *Gambar iku sok * karo wudjudé.* A picture is often different from what it's a picture of. **ng*i** 1 differing from normal. *Gèk ana kedadéjan apa A iki, kok ng*i temen.* There's sth going on with A–he's not himself at all. *Jèn si Kuntjung mesṭi ng*i.* You're a queer one, Kuntjung! 2 (*psv* **di***) to challenge by offering an alternative. *Usulé di*i.* His proposal was followed by another, of opposite intent.
gèsèk a small edible sea fish
geseng 1 bruised, black-and-blue. 2 burned, scorched
gesik 1 sand; ground brick. 2 toothpaste made of powdered red brick. **ng/di*** to brush the teeth with this powder
gesit *var of* KESIT
gèsper small buckle for adjusting straps at the back of trousers, below the belt
gèsrèk 1 to rub (against). 2 different, at odds. ***an** friction. **ng/di*** 1 to rub sth. 2 [of kite strings] to get tangled
gèt ***-*an** *or* ***-*en** easily surprised/upset. **ka*** startled, taken aback (*see also* KAGÈT). **nge*** 1 startling, surprising. *Tekané banju dadakan nge* banget.* The sudden flood took them by surprise. 2 to make a sudden movement. **nge*aké** startling, surprising; (*psv* **di*aké**) to startle, surprise. **ng/di*-(-*)i** to startle/surprise smn. *Kowé iki mbok adja ngegèt-egèti ta.* Don't scare me like that! *See also* KAGÈT
getah *** pertjah** gutta-percha

getak **ng*** 1 (*psv* **di***) to shout at. 2 [of highly spiced foods] bitingly hot. * **gadjah** a plant whose leaves are used in folk medicines

geṭak earthenware rice-cooking pot

géṭang *var of* GOṬANG

getap ***an** 1 easily shocked. 2 easily annoyed; quick-tempered

getar rancid-tasting

getas 1 to break apart easily. 2 [of the human voice] clear and true

gèṭèk 1 raft operated by poling. 2 litter for carrying a passenger. 3 stick, pole. 4 scar. ***an** to ride on a raft

geṭèk 1 the morning half of a day. *karo ** a day and a half. 2 bamboo fence

geṭek ***an** chin (*sbst kr for* DJANGGUT)

gèṭèl *var of* GRÈṬÈL

getem, geṭem a variety of crab. ***-*** *or* **ng*** to express anger by gestures rather than words. **ng* untu** to show *or* clench the teeth in anger

getèn hard-working, industrious

geter 1 to shake, tremble. 2 *wj* double taps on puppet chest (one of the *ḍoḍog·an* sound effects). ***-*** rapid beating of the heart under emotional stress. **ng*aké** *or* **ng*-*i** *or* **ng·ge*i** to cause trembling. *Udjiané ng*-*i.* The exam is making him nervous. *Sing disawang tangané kang alus, ng*aké atiné.* The sight of her soft hands set his heart to fluttering. **g·um·eter** 1 to shake, tremble. 2 earth-shaking noise. * **pater** turbulence in nature, *esp.* wind and lightning storms

geṭet indignant

getih *ng,* **rah** *kr* blood. * *abang (putih)* red (white) blood cells. *ngemu ** (to have) a blood blister. ***en** to bleed. * **nipas** blood from post-natal bleeding. * **umbel** dysentery

geṭing to have an aversion [to]. **é karo aku setengah mati.* He hates me. *Wong tuwané * banget karo ḍèwèké.* Her parents are dead set against him. **ng*aké** irritating. **ng/di*(i)** to have an aversion to

getir sour, tart

gètjèk *var of* GOTJÈK

getjek̄ **ng/di*(i)** to beat, pound, soften up. *Bawang dipun * lembut.* Pound the garlic fine. *Malingé di* pitakonan*[2] *karo pulisi suwé*[2] *ngaku.* Pressured by the police, the thief finally confessed.

gètjèl (*or* **gétjal-***) asymmetrical (*esp.* of spherical objects). *Balé gétjal-*.* The ball is not perfectly round.

getjel **ng/di*** to massage the neck and head

getjèt inconstant. **ora *** steady, constant, straight

getjit **ng*** to run fast

getjok a dish prepared from ground-up meat. **ng/di*** to tenderize [meat] by pounding. * **gunem** word of mouth. * **mentah** raw ground meat

gétjol *var of* GÈTJÈL

getjos *rpr* a sharp blade striking. **getjas-*** (to make) repeated axe strokes

getjrèk **getjrak-*** to chop (at) with a sharp blade

getjrok **getjrak-*** (to make) repeated axe strokes

géṭok ***an** in fun; in pretense. *Olèhé ngantem *an.* He hit him playfully. *Tangisé mau tangis *an lan mung gawéjan baé.* She wasn't really crying, she was just putting on an act.

geṭok a measure for cloth: the distance between thumb-tip and opposite side of hand when thumb is extended sideways and the four fingers are doubled into a fist. **ng/di*** to hit oneself in the knee. * **gunem** *or* * **tular** word of mouth. *kasagedan ingkang angsalipun saking * tular* know-how acquired by listening to others

getol **ng*** eager, anxious

geṭu **ng*** having one's attention devoted wholly to the task at hand. *Olèhé sinau ng*.* He concentrated on his studying.

geṭuk 1 mashed food, *esp.* cassava. 2 cassava cookie. ***an** small inner room of traditional houses, *usu.* for sleeping. * **lindri** mashed cassava pressed through a grinder so that it resembles hamburger. * **matjan tutul** mashed cassava dotted with syrup

getun remorseful. *Aku * ḍèké ora tak djak.* I feel bad about not asking him to come along. **ng/di*i** to regret, feel remorseful (about)

geṭunu *var of* GEṬU

géwar *var of* GIWAR

gèwel *rpr* biting

géwol inferior. *tembako ** poor-quality tobacco

gezag prestige

Gg. *see* GANG

gibas fat

giber ***-*** *intsfr* fat. *Ḍèké lemu *-*.* He's obese.

giḍal *var of* GAḌEL
gidrah *ptg* * *or* *-* [of huge men] to dance, march, *etc.* in a group. *ratu denawa ptg* * the ogres marching
gidro *-* *or* **gidra-*** to have a tantrum. *nesu gidra-** in a frenzy of anger
giḍuh deluged by immediate and urgent matters. **ng/di*i** to distract smn who is under great pressure
gigah to wake up (*root form: opt? kr for* GUGAH)
gigal to drop (off, out)
gigat to accuse (*root form: kr for* GUGAT)
gigi 1 tooth. *sikat* * toothbrush. *gosok* * toothpaste. *nggosok* * to brush the teeth. 2 tooth-like projection, cog, gear
gigi:h steamed glutinous rice
gigik cog, gear (*var of* GIGI). **ng*** to giggle, chuckle
gigil ***en** to shiver with cold (*see also* KAMIGIGIL). **ng*** 1 incessant. *Watuké ng**. He coughs constantly. 2 to shiver
gigir *var of* GEGER. *-* mountain range
gigis eroded, worn in spots
gigit **ng/di*** to bite (on), bite (down) on. *ng* lambé* to bite the lips. *ng* untu* to clench the teeth
gigrig 1 to fall, drop out. *Wuluné **. He's shedding his feathers. 2 frightened. **ora * wulu·né sa·lamba** undismayed; not the least bit frightened
gigrik **ng*** to keep laughing
gigu revolted, disgusted. **ng*ni** revolting. *Kéwan mau nggigoni.* That creature revolts me.
gih (*or* **ng***) *inf var of* INGGIH
gija turn! (*command to farm animals*)
gijak *ptg* * *or* *-* noisy, clattering
gijanti 1 a certain plant. 2 site of the 1755 peace talks which resulted in the division of the Mataram kingdom into Jogjakarta and Surakarta
gijar ***an** a radio broadcast (*var of* SIJAR). **an ujon²* gamelan music broadcast. **ng/di*aké** to announce; to broadcast. *Bab mau wis di*aké ing surat² kabar.* It's been publicized in the newspapers.
gijat energetic, vigorous. **ka*an** activity. *nindakaké ke*an subvèrsip* to engage in subversive activities. **ng/di*aké** to stimulate, encourage, press for activity
gik *var of* ḌÈK, GÈK. **(ng)*** in, at, on. *Potloté (ng)* nḍuwur médja.* The pencil is on the table.
gila 1 revolted (by); to find loathsome. *Aku * klabang.* Centipedes repel me. 2 (*prn* **gilā**) to long *or* thirst for. ** pangkat* power-hungry. ** hormat* to demand adulation from one's subordinates. **ka*-*** 1 revolting, loathsome. 2 extreme; extremely good-looking. *Ajuné ka*-**. She's very beautiful. *Ampuhé ka*-**. His strength is awesome. **ng(ge)*ni** causing loathing *or* revulsion. *Rupané ng*ni.* He's repulsive-looking. *See also* KAMIGILAN
gilang *-* 1 [of corpses] lying in the open uncovered. 2 (*or* **g·um·ilang**) bright, glittering, shiny
gilap shiny, gleaming. **ng/di*aké** to cause to shine/gleam. *ng*aké montoré* to polish the car. **g·um·ilap** to shine, gleam
gilar *-* 1 broad, vast. 2 immaculate, spick and span. 3 shining, glowing
giles **ng/di*** to mash, flatten. *ke* sepur* run over by a train. *ng* djamu* to mash ingredients for folk medicine
gili *rg* road, street
gilig 1 cylindrical. 2 well developed, well formulated. ***an** 1 formed into a cylinder. *wesi *an* iron ingot. 2 to have formulated an agreement. ***en** eroded, worn down. **ng/di*aké** to form into a cylinder; *fig* to round out *or* formulate. *Rakjaté ng*aké tékad.* The people stiffened their determination. **ng/di*i** to form [things] into cylindrical shapes
giling ***an** 1 mill; millstone. 2 ground, milled. 3 act *or* way of milling. **ané alus.* It was ground fine. **ng/di*** to grind, mill. *tebu sing arep di** sugar-cane to be ground. **sa*** a handful of cooked rice: used as a measuring unit. *See also* PANGGILING
gilir ***an** one's turn; by turns. *Saiki *anku.* It's my turn now. *Lampu nang kampungku *an.* The electricity in my village alternates days (*i.e.* is on one day, off the next). *** g·um·anti** periodically; off and on; by turns
gilo *ng,* **punika** *kr* (see) here! **, tak kèki wungkusan.* Look, I've brought you a snack! **, paturoné kéné.* Here, this is the bedroom.
gilok *-* *Jogja slang* sometimes, from time to time
gilut **ng/di*** to exert, exercise. *ng* kesenengané ing bab seni* to indulge one's enjoyment of art. **ng/dipun*** to chew (*root form: kr for* MAMAH)

gim 1 golden thread *or* braid in decorative applications to clothing. 2 (end of the) game; result of the game (*esp.* tennis). *(Wis)* *. (That's) game! *Tènisé wis* *. The tennis game is over. **é pira?* What's the final score? ***an** group of games, *esp.* those comprising a set in tennis. *Mainé pirang *an?* How many games did the set go?
gimbal 1 unkempt [of hair]. 2 loose skin folds hanging from the neck of certain animals. 3 a dish made with fried rice-flour chips containing peanuts or fish. 4 overhanging eaves of a traditional Javanese house
gimblah *-* *intsfr* fat. *lemu* *-* obese
gimbleg *var of* GIMBLAH
gimi *-* in a hurry. *Adja* *-*. Take your time!
gimik, gimin *rg var of* DISIK
gimnastik gymnastics
gin- *see also under* G- (*Introduction, 3.1.7*)
gina use(fulness), benefit, meaning (*kr for* GUNA)
ginda massage (*root form: ki for* DADAH)
gindjel kidney
gindjlong *var of* KINTJLONG
ginem 1 talk (*kr for* GUNEM). 2 *wj* puppet dialogue (spoken by the puppet-master)
ginggang separated by [a small distance]. *ora* * *sarambut* not a hair's-breadth apart
gingsir to slide (down). *Lemahé* *. The soil slid down. *Atiné* *. His heart sank.
gingsul [of teeth] uneven
gini 1 property acquired jointly during a marriage, which hence is divided in the event of divorce. 2 *oj* woman. *See also* GANA
ginjer **ng*** to press and fondle (in massage)
gintel **ng/di*** to pinch with thumb and forefinger
gintes *var of* GITES
gintju red coloring matter. **ng/di*** to redden the cheeks or lips with cosmetics
gintung a certain tree
ginu:k *-* *or* **ginak-*** very fat
girah[a] to shoo (*root form: kr for* GURAH)
girah[b] (*rg kr for* KUMBAH?) ***an** laundry. **ng/di*aké** to launder for smn. **ng/di*(i)** to launder. *Si gen̩duk lagi ng* klambi.* The servant girl is washing clothes.
girang a certain tree. *-* *or* * **g·um·uju** jubilant, triumphant
girap *-* to feel intense loathing
giras wild, untamed; afraid of human beings
giri 1 *oj* mountain. 2 (*or* *-*) to rush into action. *Adja* *-*. Not so fast! *Adja* * *nangis, ditlusur d̩isik sebabé.* Don't just burst into tears–try to find out why. **ka*-*** breathtaking. *Ajuné ka*-*.* She's exquisitely beautiful. *Rupané ka*-*.* He looks terrifying. **ng/di*-*** to hurry smn
girik identification card
girilâjâ *oj* mountain
giring **ng/di*** to drive [livestock]. *ng* kebo nèng kan̩dang* to drive the kerbaus into the stable. * **ésuk** the time (*ca.* 11 A.M.) when cattle are driven to the river for bathing and watering. * **soré** the time (*ca.* 6 P.M.) when cattle are returned to the stable. *See also* TEMU[b]
giris frightened. **ng·ge*i** frightening
giro *var of* GERO. *See also* KANTOR, KEBO
gisang *rg var of* PISANG
gisik (*or* **ge***) beach, shore
gita 1 song, chant. 2 (*or* *-*) in great haste
git̩ang *var of* GOT̩ANG
gitar guitar. **ng*** to play the guitar. **ng/di*i** to accompany [smn's singing] with guitar
gitaris guitar player
gitel *var of* GINTEL
gites, git̩es **ng/di*(i)** to kill [lice] by pressing with the thumbnail
git̩et *var of* DJIT̩ET
git̩i *-* in haste
gitik stick, club. **ge*** club used for beating. **ng/di*** 1 [of fighting cocks] to beat with the wings and legs. 2 *slang* to draw the winning lottery number. **ng/di*(i)** to beat with a stick
git̩i:r fast (of running pace)
git̩ok *ng kr*, **griwa** *ki* nape of the neck
giwang 1 to yield, give way. 2 (*or* **ge***) earring set with a single jewel. **ke*** to be subjected to temptation. **g·um·iwang** [of sun] to set. * **kara** *oj* sun
giwar **ng*** to swerve, veer. **ng/di*i** to move out of the path of
gja 1 *oj* (and) then, (right) after that. 2 to the left! *(command to a farm animal)*
gjak *var of* GJA 2
glabad thin protective membrane
glabèt ***an** *or* **globat-*** to have the tongue hanging out and moving from side to side
gla̩dag 1 split-bamboo fence support. 2 bamboo ceiling. 3 short hunting spear. 4 porter; janitor. ***an** 1 rack (for keeping spears; for drying). 2 footloose. **ng*** 1

(*psv* **di***) to hunt with a spear. 2 smooth; free of holes. 3 (*or* **g·um·laḍag**) swiftly flowing

glaḍé *var of* GLAḌI

glaḍi drill, training, rehearsal; to practice, rehearse. * *resik* final rehearsal; dress rehearsal. ***n̈** (to engage in) drill, training. *glaḍèn militèr* military training. **ng/di*** to train, drill. *Jèn sirahmu ora kena di*, tanganmu baé *nen.* If you can't train your mind, train your hands! *di* baris* to be drilled in marching. **pa·ng*** act of practicing/drilling

gladrah ***an** neglected. *Beras sepirang-pirang *an ana ndjogan.* There's rice all over the floor and no one picking it up. **ng*** 1 available everywhere, plentiful. 2 disinterested, indifferent

gladri front porch

glagah 1 stalk of the sugar-cane blossom. 2 a variety of sugar cane

glagar lengths of bamboo *or* wood fastened together for fence sections

glagat outward indication. *Wong tuwa mau weruh * sing ora betjik.* The old man saw sth he didn't like the looks of. *Rembug lan *é wong bisa dadi piranti ngrampungaké kuwadjiban.* A person's remarks and general aspect are [a detective's] tools for doing his job. ***é** it seems from appearances... *nDelok *é arep udan.* It looks like rain.

glagep *rpr* gasping for breath. *Ḍèké slulup, *, *, mèh waé klelep.* He sank below the surface, gasped for air, and nearly drowned. ***an** 1 to gasp for air. 2 to stammer under emotional stress. ***-*** *or* **glogap-*** 1 to keep gasping for air. 2 to stammer

glajar ***an** 1 to wander from place to place. 2 (*or* ***-***) to reel, stagger. **ng*** *sms* *AN. *Wis bengi ngéné kok isih ng*.* How come you're still up and around at this time of night?

glajem **glojam-*** *or* **ng*** to flatter, speak hypocritically, tell the listener what he wants to hear

glaler *pl form of* GALER

glali lollipop, or any hard candy

glambèr cow's wattles

glambir *var of* GLAMBÈR

glambjar **ng*** insipid. *Gunemané ng*.* What he said is pointless. *Réntjanganė isih ng*.* His plans are vague. *Sop kuwi rasané ng*.* The soup tastes flat.

glambrèh *ptg* * hanging about in disorder

glanḍang ***an** nomadic. *wong *an* those with no roof over their heads; harmless drifters. **g·um·lanḍang** loud and clear. *Swarané gumlanḍang.* His voice carries well.

glang ***-*an** [of women] to walk the streets

glanggang arena for combat; *fig* field, area. * *politik ndonja* the area of world politics. ***an** rice field planted to sugar cane after the rice has been harvested

glangsar *rpr* a person *or* animal falling. ***an** to lie on the ground taking it easy. **ng*** to fall to the ground

glangsur ***an** to inch forward on the stomach. **ng*** 1 *sms* *AN. 2 (*psv* **di***) to anoint, rub

glanjong ***an** to converse nonsensically *or* inconsequentially

glanṭang ***an** equipment for hanging sth in the sun and air. **ng*** 1 (*psv* **di***) to dry sth in the sun. 2 *intsfr* hot [of sun]. *panas ng** intensely hot

glapé *var of* GAPÉ

glaput covered with a substance. *Awaké * getih.* He had blood all over him.

glasah ***an** *or* **ng*** lying strewn about untidily

glasar *var of* GLANGSAR

glaṭak[a] **ng*** having an all-consuming appetite for both normal and bizarre food items

glaṭak[b] *rg* bamboo fence

glaṭé **gloṭa-*** *or* **ng*** aimless, without purpose

glaṭi knife used as a weapon

glaṭik a small gray bird that frequents rice paddies. **ng*** resembling this bird. **ng* m·ungup** [of fingernails] reddened at the tips. **ng* sa·kurung·an** cooperative; harmonious. * **bélong** black-headed white-cheeked *glaṭik* bird. * **buras** a *glaṭik* bird with a spotted head. * **watu** *or* * **wingka** a pearly-colored *glaṭik* bird

glawat **ng*** to struggle against superior forces

glébag *rpr* a turning motion. *Mak * seḍéla waé wis nang sisihku.* He pivoted and came to my side. ***an** to keep turning. *Olèhé turu *an.* He tossed and turned in his sleep. **ng*** to turn (over, around)

glèbès ***an** to keep shaking the head

glebjar *pl form of* GEBJAR

gléḍah ***an** act of searching. **ané wis bubar.* The search is over. ***-*** to search for. **ng/di*** to search sth. *Omahé di*.* His house was searched.

glèḍèg 1 *rpr* the sound of rolling. *Lha kaé ana* *, *. I hear wheels! 2 swiftly flowing. ***an** 1 anything having wheels. 2 wagon, cart. 3 road leading toward a traditional-style home where an important person resides. **g·um·lèḍèg** 1 to roll. 2 to flow swiftly

gleḍeg *rpr* a heavy rumbling. ***an** [of fire] to flare up *or* spread rapidly. **g·um·leḍeg** producing a heavy rumbling

gledrug *pl form of* GEDRUG

glega trunk of a coconut palm (*sbst? kr for* GLUGU)

glegeg *rpr* gurgling. ***-*** *or* **glegag-*** *rpr* repeated gurgles. *Ḍèké ngombé *-*.* He gulped the drink. **g·um·legeg** to gurgle

glègèk a belch. ***en** to belch. **glégak-*** 1 to belch repeatedly. 2 to keep laughing. **ng/di*aké** to cause smn to belch; to burp [a baby]

gleger *rpr* a sudden heavy sound. *Mrijemé muni *!* The cannon boomed. **glegar-*** to keep booming. **g·um·leger** to boom, crash

glègès *var of* GLEGES[a]

gleges[a] **glegas-*** to keep laughing to oneself. **ng*** to laugh inwardly

gleges[b] sugar-cane blossom

gléjang *rpr* swinging

glèjèh **ng*** to rest, *esp.* lying down

gléjong *var of* GLÉJANG

gléjor string bean. ***-*** *or* **gléjar-*** to walk unsteadily

glèlèng ***an** *or* **glélang-*** *or* **ng*** (to walk) with a swaggering *or* arrogant gait

gleler **ng*** to sneak away/out; to leave without saying goodbye

gleles *var of* GLELER

glélo **ng*** to nod drowsily

glémbjor **glémbjar-*** hanging about in disorder. **ng*** to hang loosely

glémboh ***-*** fat, obese

glémbong *var of* GLÉMBOH

glembor *pl var of* GEMBOR

glembug **ng*** to try to convince *or* persuade smn. **pa·ng*** an attempt at persuasion

glembus **ng*** 1 pale from illness. 2 to fade

glémpang **ng*** to tip over. **ng/di*aké** to tip sth over

glémpo a large handkerchief

gléṇḍang **ng*** 1 empty. 2 to go traveling without money or provisions

glenḍèh young peanut. ***-*** *or* **glenḍah-*** [of walking gait] slow-paced and with arms swinging

glendem **glendam-*** *or* **ng*** 1 to behave quietly. 2 to sneak other people's property

glènḍèng **ng*** 1 speedy. 2 (*psv* **di***) to drag sth

glenḍeng ***an** in the form of long uncut stalks (of bamboo)

glèndèr stick of wood *or* bamboo used as a prop. **ng*** to slope

gléndjor ***-*** swollen and water-filled

gleneng **ng*** to flow smoothly and placidly

glenes **glenas-*** *or* **ng*** to leave without saying goodbye; to sneak away/out

glenggem *var of* GLENDEM

glènggèng **ng*** to sing loudly and continuously

glenggeng *rpr* the sound of rapid drinking. *Mak * banju segelas diombé.* He gulped down a glass of water.

gléngsor ***an** *or* **ng*** to sit on the ground

glenik ***-*** to talk in a low voice

glenjèh **ng*** to chew betel habitually

glepang *sbst kr for* GLEPUNG

glépot soiled, stained

glepuk **ng/di*** to hit, *esp.* with a stone

glepung powdered substance; flour, *esp.* rice flour. **ng/di*** to make [*esp.* rice] into flour. *** djagung** corn flour, cornstarch. *** enḍog** powdered egg. *** gandum** wheat flour. *** gaplèk** powdered dried cassava. *** hunkué** green-bean flour, powdered bean. *** ketan** glutinous-rice flour. *** masina** corn flour, cornstarch. *** terigu** wheat flour

glereng *pl form of* GERENG

glèsèh *var of* GLASAH

gleser *rpr* crawling motions

glésor ***an** to roll around on the ground

gléṭak *ptg * or* **ng*** lying scattered *or* sprawled. **ng/di*aké** to put/leave sth (lying around). **g·um·léṭak** lying sprawled/scattered

glèṭèk **ng*** ubiquitous. *** peṭèl·é** plain, obvious

gleṭek 1 *rpr* the sound of sth falling. 2 *rpr* an unexpected piece of good luck. 3 *rpr* a joint twisting

glétjé **glétja-*** *or* **ng*** to shirk, lie down on the job

gléwang **ng*** 1 to tip over. *Krétané ng*.* The cart overturned. 2 [of sun, moon] to pass the zenith. **ng/di*aké** to tip sth over

gléwo ***-*** chubby, plump

glibed to go past, pass by. ***an** *or* **glibad-*** to keep going past; to walk the floor. **ng***

1 to stick around. *Adja ng∗ waé, dolan kana!* Don't hang around here–go play! 2 to twist/distort smn's words

gliḍig one who helps out at a ceremony. **ng∗** 1 to work as a day laborer. 2 (*prn* **nggliḍi:g**) obnoxious; destructive. **g·um·liḍi:g** swiftly flowing

glidrah *ptg* ∗ moving *or* dancing ponderously (*esp.* of *wj* ogres)

gligap (*or* **∗an**) to start with surprise. *katon ∗an kagèt* to look startled

gligi cylindrical. **∗ǹ** 1 forming a cylinder. *gelang gligèn* arm band. *wesi gligèn* iron bar. 2 to reach an agreement *or* understanding

gligik ∗-∗ *or* **gligak-∗** to chuckle

gligir **∗an** hexagonal. **ng∗** long and smooth. *Tilasé tatu ng∗.* The scar from the wound makes a long smooth mark.

glijak ∗-∗ at a comfortable (rather than hurried) pace

glijek̄ *var of* KLIJEK

glijeng ∗-∗ *or* **ng∗** to feel faint. *Aku* (or *sirahku) ng∗.* My head is swimming.

glijer 1 *rpr* falling asleep. *Let seḍéla mak ∗ turu.* After a while he dozed off. 2 *rpr* a dizzy feeling. 3 *rpr* a bobbing movement. **ng∗** to feel dizzy/faint

glimbung **glimbang-∗** to lie around taking it easy

glimpang *var of* GLÉMPANG

glimpung *rpr* a sudden fall. *ptg ∗* lying strewn about. **ng∗** to lie curled up snugly

glinḍing 1 *rpr* rolling. 2 oxcart with solid wheels. 3 small round pellets. 4 name of one of the small playing cards (*kertu tjilik*). **∗an** 1 in the form of pellets. 2 wheel. **ng∗** to roll. **ng/di∗aké** to roll sth. **ng/di∗i** to make spherical. *Ḍèké ng∗i geṭuk.* She formed the mashed cassava into balls. **g·um·linḍing** to roll

gli:ng *rada* ∗-∗ somewhat deficient mentally

glinggang dead tree/wood

glingseng (*or* **ng∗**) *intsfr* black. *ireng (ng)∗* pitch black; deeply sun-tanned

glinṭeng (*or* **ng∗**) *intsfr* dark. *ireng (ng)∗* intensely dark/black

glinting *rpr* sprawling. *Mak ∗ aku tiba sakpitku nggloso ing aspal.* I sprawled on the pavement along with my bicycle. *ptg ∗ pl* to sprawl. *Wong² ptg ∗ turu ing tritisan setasijun.* People were sprawled in sleep on the station platform. **ng∗** *or* **g·um·linting** to lie sprawled

glintir (*or* **∗an**) small round object; grain. *∗an daging* meat ball. **ng/di∗i** to form into pellets *or* balls

glinuk ∗-∗ *or* **glinak-∗** awkwardly fat

gliput *var of* GLAPUT

glisik **ng/di∗i** to whisper to smn

gliṭi:k̄ *ptg* ∗ producing a tickling sensation. **ng/di∗(i)** to tickle smn

gliṭo **ng∗** to flick the thumb against smn's head as a reprimand. **ng/di∗ni** to reprimand smn as above

globroh [of clothing] too large

gloḍag 1 roomy, spacious. 2 *rpr* a thrown object hitting a hard surface. **ng∗** empty of passengers

gloḍog 1 wooden beehive. 2 *rpr* a deep rumbling. **ng∗(i)** to come peeling off

glogog *rpr* liquid gurgling; smn swallowing. **glogag-∗** to gurgle/swallow repeatedly. **∗ sok** to speak one's mind

glogor wooden *or* bamboo flooring material. ∗-∗ *rpr* the croak of a hoarse voice

glojor **∗an** *or* **ng∗** [of walking gait] unsteady, staggering

glolo [of weeping] weary. *nangis ∗* to cry wearily (as though tired of crying). *Paḍa nangis ptg ∗ ptg slenggruk.* They cried tiredly and with much sniffling.

glombjor (*or* **glombjar-∗**) flabby, loose, without body or stiffness

glombor [of clothing] too large. *Klambiné ∗.* Her dress hangs on her.

glompong *var of* GLUMPANG

glonḍang *rpr* a hollow thud. *Blèk koṭong ketundjang kutjing: ∗!* The cat landed on an empty can. **ng∗** empty. *Akèh bangku sing ng∗.* Many seats were unoccupied.

glonḍong 1 leader of a council of village heads. 2 log; unfinished tree section. **∗an** 1 jurisdiction of the above official. 2 log

glondor *var of* GLONTOR. **ke∗** to slip and fall

glong *rpr* relief. *Bareng krungu ḍèké slamet, rasané atiku mak ∗.* I felt a surge of relief to hear he was safe.

glonggong 1 stem of the papaya leaf. 2 a certain pond reed. **ng∗** to sing/chant loudly. **ng/di∗aké** to sing sth loudly. **g·um·longgong** (to sing, chant) loudly, strongly

glongsor *rpr* flopping down. *monḍok ∗ (slang)* to room and board at smn's house. **∗an** *or* **ng∗** to flop down anywhere

glontor (*or* ∗-∗) *rpr* washing, pouring. **glontar-∗** to keep making washing (pouring, flushing) sounds. **ng/di∗** 1 to wash down [food]. *Jèn kesereden, mbok di* ba-nju.* If it's hard to swallow, wash it down with water. 2 to flush the toilet. **g·um·lon-tor** to flow

glopot *var of* GLUPRUT

gloso *rpr* flopping down, sprawling. **ng*** to flop, sprawl

glosod, glosor *var of* GLOSO

gloṭak *rpr* an impact. ***an** *or* ***-*** to keep making impact sounds. *Adja *an waé, aku arep turu.* Stop banging around–I'm trying to sleep.

glubud **ng*** brash, bold, forward

gluḍug 1 deep far-off thunder. 2 *rpr* a deep thunder-like sound. **g·um·luḍug** producing thunder-like noise

gluga red coloring matter extracted from a certain fruit (*patjar*)

glugu (**glega** *sbst? kr*) trunk of a coconut palm

glugut 1 particle, bit. 2 itchy particles (hairs, powder) clinging to certain plants, *esp.* bamboo. ***an** place on bamboo stalks where itchy particles occur. **ng*** 1 having the above particles. 2 itchy; *fig* irritable, ill-natured

glujur ***an** 1 to stagger. 2 (*or* **ng***) to wander aimlessly

glumpang [of children] fat, overweight

glunḍung 1 a roll; a rolled-up object. *dlu-wang sa** a roll of paper. 2 counting unit for coconuts. *krambil sa** one coconut. 3 *rpr* the sound of rolling. 4 *rpr* plunging into a deep depression. *ptg * pl* to roll (around). ***an** forming a roll. **an dluwang* rolled paper. **ke*** to get rolled; to roll accidentally. *Botjah mau ke* ombak.* The boy was rolled over by the surf. *ke* saka tempat tiḍur* to roll out of bed. **ng*** to roll. *Matjan ng* ana ing lemah.* The tiger rolled on the ground. **ng/di*aké** to roll sth. **ng/di*i** to roll onto. *Adja ng*i baji.* Don't roll over on the baby! **g·um·lunḍung** to roll. *Balé gemlunḍung.* The ball rolled. *** semprong** 1 [of women] to marry without a dowry. 2 to turn sth over to smn in unaltered condition. *Njoh, ḍuwitmu tak balèkaké * semprong.* Here, I'm giving you back your money. *** suling** [of men] to marry without giving a bride-price

glunek̄ *var of* GRUNEK

glungsar, glungsur *var of* GLONGSOR

gluntung *rpr* falling and rolling. *ptg * pl* to roll, writhe. ***an** a roll. **ng*** to roll. **ng/di*aké** to roll sth. **g·um·luntung** to roll (around). *Krambilé gemluntung.* The coconuts rolled on the ground.

glupak **g·um·lupak** on edge, apprehensive. *See also* GLUPUK

gluprut stained, messy. *Badané * bleṭok.* He was covered with mud.

glupuk **glupak-*** apprehensive, nervous

gluput *var of* GLUPRUT

gluṭek̄ *ptg * rpr* light clattering sounds. ***an** to produce such sounds

gluṭi:k̄ *ptg ** patiently absorbed in a complex task. *Botjah loro ptg * nggolèki kantor imigrasi sarana ndelok peṭa kuṭa.* The two of them pored over the city map trying to find the immigration office. **ng*** to devote one's attention to sth intricate

gluṭu:k̄ *var of* GLUṬEK

gluwèh ***an** to fool around. **gluwah-*** *or* **g·um·luwèh** careless, frivolous, inattentive

gobab to lie, cheat, deceive

gobag a children's game played by moonlight, in which the players try to reach the enemy goal. *** bunder** (to play) this game with a round goal. *** sodor** (to play) this game with an oblong-shaped goal

gobang 1 large-bladed knife. 2 obsolete coin worth one *bénggol* = $2^1/_2$ cents. *telung ** $7^1/_2$ cents. *nem ** 15 cents

gobèd 1 slicing knife with a serrated blade. 2 knife for chopping tobacco leaves. ***an** folds in a batik wraparound finger-pressed into place and held with a pin or clip

gobèr 1 flapping loosely. 2 fake-sounding, *e.g.* a voice over a loudspeaker

gobig ***-*** *or* **ng*** to shake from side to side; *fig* to refuse to acknowledge sth

gobjag **ng/di*** to shake sth

gobjog continuous [of sounds]. *Krungu ana kenṭong *.* They heard the insistent sound of the alarm.

gobjos **ng*** to sweat profusely

goblog *cr* stupid

gobog *cr* ear

gobrah (*or* ***-***) smeared, messy, covered with sth

gobrès *var of* GABRÈS, GUBRIS

goḍa temptation; a testing of the character. *kena ** subjected to temptation. **ning urip* life's trials. **ke*** subjected to temptation. *Ranḍa mau gampang ka* déning rangsang asmara.* The widow was an easy prey to the call of love. **ng/di*** to test smn's character; to subject smn to temptation *or* torment.

Tjah lanang mau ng tjah wédok tanggaku.* The boy seduced the girl next door. *Asu kuwi adja di*, mengko njokot.* Don't tease the dog–he'll bite you. **pa·ng*** temptation. *** rentjana** temptation. *nanggulangi * rentjananing alam* to resist worldly temptations; **ng/di*-(ng)rentjana** to plague, torment. *wong di*-rentjana lelembut* a man tormented by spirits

goḍag space, interstice. ***an** a partitioned-off space. **ng/di*** to chase. *di* asu* chased by a dog. **ng/di*i** to divide into separate spaces. *Kamaré di*i.* They partitioned up the room.

goḍang *var of* GUḌANG

goḍèg 1 hair worn at the side of the face: sideburns (men), combed-back part at the temple (ladies). 2 copper decorations for a horse bridle. *** tjambang** long wide sideburns

goḍi cloth strip for wrapping *or* tying

godjag **ng/di*(i)** to wash out [a bottle *etc.*] by shaking water in it

godjèg (*or* [ge]***an**) to fool around, laugh and joke

godjog *var of* GODJAG

godjrèt smeared, stained. ** getih* smeared with blood

goḍog ***an** 1 boiled. 2 equipment for boiling. **ng/di*** 1 to boil. *ng* wédang* to boil water for hot drinks. 2 to train rigorously. **enḍog *** boiled egg

goḍoh ear lobe. *** putih** a coward

goḍong 1 (**ron** *opt? kr;* **undjung·an** *kr?*) plant leaf. 2 leaf of a double door *or* window. 3 the broad part of an oar. 4 spades (playing-card suit). **ge*an** (**ron²an** *opt? kr*) 1 foliage. 2 edible medicinal leaves. **dadi·a * moh ñj·suwèk** I'll never have anything to do with you again.

godor bar; material shaped into a bar

godrag [of girls] restless, unable to settle down

godrah stained, smeared. ** getih* blood-stained

godrèg *var of* GODRAG

godrès *var of* GODRAH

godril a certain classical verse form

godros *var of* GODRAH

gog *rpr* a hen's cackle. ** * petok* [hen cackling]

gogèt [of animals] to fight with the teeth

gogo ***-*** to grope in water with the hand. **ng/di*(ni)** to grope for sth, *e.g.* fish

gogoh ***-*** to feel around with the hand. **ng/di*(i)** to grope around in sth. *Kanṭongé di*i ning ḍuwité ora ana.* He felt in his pocket but his money wasn't there.

gogok **ng/di*** to drink from an earthen water pitcher. **kenḍi *** spoutless earthen pitcher

gogor baby tiger (young of the MATJAN)

gogot *var of* GOGÈT

gogrog to become detached prematurely. *Pelemé paḍa *.* The mangoes fell from the tree before they were ripe. ** olèhé meteng* to have a miscarriage. ***an** prematurely detached. **ng/di*aké** to cause to be detached prematurely. *Kanḍutané di*aké.* She had an abortion. *** asem** [of rain] pouring intermittently

gojang unsteady; to shake *or* swing. *médja ** a wobbly table. **ng/di*** to shake/swing sth. *Sirahé di*.* He shook his head.

gojor [of fabric] lightweight, having little body

gol 1 *var of* GUL. 2 act of [do]ing (*var of* OLÈH). **é mangan kok akèh ja botjah kuwé.* What a lot that boy eats! **nge*-*i** irritating, exasperating

gol. *see* GOLONG·AN

golèk *ng,* **pados** *kr* 1 to get; to seek. *A lunga * tamba.* A went to get some medicine. ** iwak* to catch a fish; to go fishing. ** pangan ḍéwé* to earn one's keep. ** panggonan kang éjub* to look for a shady place. 2 *ng kr* doll; puppet. *wajang ** three-dimensional wooden puppet; the type of drama depicted by such puppets. ***an** 1 thing obtained *or* sought. *Ali²né ilang dadi *an wong saomah.* The whole family looked for the lost ring. 2 *ng kr* doll; wooden puppet. 3 act *or* way of getting/finding. ***-*** to make an effort to get. *Aku tak njoba ** penggawéjan.* I'll try to find a job. ***-*an** *sms* *AN 3. *Kawruh mau gampang waé *-*ané.* Such knowledge is easy to obtain. **ng*** to get, obtain. *ng* ḍuwit* to earn money. **ng/di*aké** to get *or* seek on smn's behalf. *Aku *na degan lo.* Go get me a young coconut. **ng/di*-*aké** to make an effort to get *or* find. *Jèn kanggo mbajari sekolahmu, ḍuwité ija tak *-*aké.* I'll do my very best to get money for your school expenses. **ng/di*i** 1 to look for, try to get. *Di*i mrana² meksa ora ketemu.* He looked for it everywhere but he couldn't find it. *ng*i tembung ing kamus* to look up a word in the dictionary. *Kosok baliné tembung mau ora tak *i.* I can't think of the opposite for that word. **ana galihing kangkung.* Look for the soul that inhabits the body. 2 to find. *ng*i ḍuwit* to find [lost] money. * **menang·i ḍéwé** unwilling to accept defeat. *See also* WAJANG[a]

golèng *var of* GOLING. *-* *intsfr* beautiful. *Ajuné *-*.* She's very beautiful.

golèt *var of* GOLÈK

goling **golang-*** shaky, unsteady. **ng*** 1 to fall (down), drop. 2 to tip over

golok dagger

golong forming a group. *sega ** fist-sized rice ball for ritual meals. ***an** (*abbr:* **gol.**) group, organization; class, subgroup. *Sidji²ning *an ngreti menjang wadjibé ḍéwé².* Each group knows its own duties. **an kiri/kiwa* left-winger, radical. ** kanan/tengen* right-winger, conservative. *prijaji pirang² *an* people from all walks of life. *Maling kuwi klebu *ané wong² kang dadi amaning bebrajan.* Thieves can be classed as a detriment to society. *Pemrintah ora mbédak²aké *an.* The government does not discriminate against any group. **golang-*** to come together, form a group. **ge*an** forming groups. *wilangan ge*an* a grouping number (*e.g. puluh* '-ty,' *atus* 'hundred'). **ka*** 1 to belong to, be a member of. 2 grouped with, considered as. *Negara mau ke* madju.* This nation is considered advanced. **ng*** to gather. *Botjah² ng* dadi rong pérangan.* The boys formed two groups. **ng/di*aké** to group, classify. *di*aké dadi rong pérangan* grouped into two categories. **ng/di*i** to shape [rice] into fist-sized balls. **g·um·olong** (grouped) together; in agreement. *Wedi kuwi tuwuh saka gumolongé sipat² werna².* Fear arises from a composite of factors. *gumolong ing karep* firm in a wish *or* intention

golor leaf stalk. ** geḍang* central stalk of a banana leaf

gom 1 scurvy-like disease of the mouth resulting from a vitamin C deficiency. 2 milky plant resin used as paste. ***en** to have/get the above disease

gombak children's hair style: head shaved everywhere except on the crown. **ora * ora kuntjung ambek·é kaja t·um·enggung** arrogant, haughty

gombal (*or* ***[-*]an**) rag, scrap; ragged clothing. **ng*** to wear ragged clothing; *fig* poor

gombèl rooster's neck wattles

gombjok 1 fringe; tassel. 2 floral design on a kris. ***an** 1 fringed; tasseled. 2 forming a cluster. **ng/di*i** to decorate [a kris] with a floral design

gombloh having a guileless *or* dull-witted look. **ng*i** to assume such a look

gombol grove of trees. ***an** group, gathering, mob. **ng*** to flock together, gather

gombong hollow. **ng/di*** to soak sth in water

gombrang **ng/di*** to cut off, lop off

gompèl *var of* GOPÈL

gonḍang 1 a certain large tree, occurring in many varieties. 2 esophagus (*ki for* GURUNG). **ng*** 1 empty. 2 (*psv* **di***) to butt with the horns. *** kasih** similar things of disparate appearance, *esp.* siblings with different skin coloring

gonḍèl earrings. ***an** to have a firm grip (on). **ng/di*i** 1 to hold onto firmly. *ng*i buntuté matjan* to have a tiger by the tail *(lit, fig).* 2 to dissuade. *A ndjaluk mulih dina iki ning tak *i.* He wanted to go home today but I talked him out of it.

gondjak ***an** (to arouse) sexual desire. **ng/di*** 1 to take too lightly; to make fun of. 2 to attempt to seduce smn

gondjèh *var of* GÉNDJAH

gondjing 1 to slope, tilt. *Ombaké molak-malik, prauné *.* The waves rolled; the boat tipped up. 2 unsteady. *Anggoné njekeli stang *.* He didn't have a firm grip on the handlebars. ** weruh rupa kang aju manis* discomposed by the sight of a pretty face. **ng/di*aké** to unsettle. *A bisa ng*aké pasamuwan.* A disrupted the meeting. *Mripaté jèn njawang banget ng*aké.* The look in her eyes was very disconcerting. **g·in·ondjing** (causing) agitation. *kaja bumi ginondjing* earth-shaking. *Ungeling genḍing ginondjing ngangkang.* The music was stirring.

gondjit *var of* GANDJIT

gondjol calluses on shoulders or neck

gonḍok 1 goiter. 2 short and thick. *gendul ** a squat-shaped bottle. ***en** to have a goiter

gonḍol **ng/di*** 1 [of animals] to snatch *or* carry in the mouth. 2 to pilfer

gonḍong 1 shuttle (part of weaving loom). 2 goiter

gondrong [of hair] long and ill-kempt

gong gamelan instrument, coming in various

sizes, consisting of a set of vertically suspended bronze gongs. ***an** 1 a beat of the *gong.* 2 set of melodies played as a unit. **nge*** to play the *gong.* **nge/di*i** 1 to accompany [a dance] *or* signal [a dance movement] with *gong* beats. 2 to agree with, not contradict. 3 to interrupt; to follow immediately. **pa*an** place occupied by the gamelan instruments, *esp.* the *gong,* during a shadow play. *** bondjor** a blowing instrument made from a large bamboo section. *** geḍé** largest of the *gong*'s. *** l·um·aku t·in·abuh** one with many facts at his command, a walking encyclopedia. *** mung sa·selé** to hear testimony for only one side in a lawsuit

gonggang separated by [a certain distance]. *ora * sekilan* not so much as 1/8 fathom apart

gonggo a certain large spider

gonggong (to play) a certain card game played with Chinese cards (*kertu tjilik*). **ng*** to bark

gonggrong **ng/di*aké** to put sth in/on a high place

gongsèng 1 belled anklets (worn by children). 2 to dry-fry (*root form: var of* GANGSA)

gongsong *var of* GANGSA

gongsor [of earth] to slide down. **ng/di*i** to slide onto. *Lemahé ng*i omah mau.* The landslide covered the house.

goni 1 jute. 2 gunnysack. *beras sa** a sack of rice

gonjèh 1 sensitive, tender. 2 [of undercooked *or* overripe tubers] disagreeably crumbly or mealy

gontèng 1 a certain large-headed termite. 2 *rg* cucumber

gontjang **ng/di*aké** to unsettle. *Kabaré ng*aké donja.* The news shook the world. *Imané di*aké budjuk alusé wong wédok.* His integrity was undermined by a woman's sweet talk.

gontjèng *var of* BONTJÈNG

gontok to punch. ***an** a fist fight

gopèl chipped. *Tjangkiré *.* There's a piece out of the cup. ***an** chip, broken-off piece

gopès chipped at the edge

goprak 1 noisemaker for scaring birds and squirrels away from a crop. 2 of inferior quality

goprèk (*or* ***an**) inferior (*var of* GOPRAK)

goprok *var of* GOPRAK

gor ***-*an** neglected, left uncared for. **nge/di*aké** to neglect. *Wit kembang kuwi mati merga di*aké waé.* The flowering plants died because they weren't tended.

gorḍel leather belt

ǵorḍèn 1 window curtain. 2 folding screen

goreg **ng/di*aké** to jolt, shake up. *Kabaré ng*aké donja.* The news rocked the earth. *See also* OREG

gorèh erratic, uncontrolled. *Pikirku *.* I'm all mixed up. ** atiné* uneasy, troubled. **ng/di*aké** to upset; to agitate. *ng*aké ati* to make smn uneasy

gorèng deep-fried. *katjang ** fried peanuts. *pisang ** fried banana. ***an** 1 deep-fried (foods). 2 pan for deep-frying. **ng/di*(i)** to deep-fry. **ng/di*-sanga·n** to fry with little or no oil. **pa·ng*an** pan for deep-frying

gori jackfruit in its unripe state: used in cooking. *See also* NANGKA

goroh (**dora** *opt? kr*) (to tell) a lie. *watak ** untruthful by nature. ***an** 1 untruthful by nature. 2 to say sth untruthful as a joke. *Aku mung *an.* I'm just kidding. **ge*an** to lie habitually. ***-*apa** I'm telling the truth! (*i.e.* why lie?) **ng/di*aké** to lie about sth. **ng/di*i** to lie to; to cause trouble to smn by lying. *ng*i rakjat* to deceive the public. *Mobilé tansah di*i baé.* He keeps finding his car is not as it was represented to him. *** growah** better not lie!

gorok spade, shovel; claw-shaped rake. ***an** throat. *lara *an* (to have) a sore throat. **ng/di*** 1 to saw [wood *etc.*]. 2 to cut smn's throat. 3 *slang* to overcharge customers. **pa·ng*an** hand saw

gorong ***an** *var of* GURUNG·AN

gosip gossip, talk; to gossip. **ng/di*aké** to gossip about

gosok menthol stick for migraine headache. ***an** 1 act of rubbing/polishing. *Berlian iki apik *ané.* This diamond is beautifully polished. 2 provocation, goading. 3 interchange of knowledge. ***-g·in·osok** to exchange knowledge. *Sarana *-ginosok kita bisa munḍak sesurupan.* By learning from each other we can increase our awareness. **ng/di*** 1 to scrub, polish. *di* nganggo rempelas* rubbed with sandpaper. *ng* sepatu* to polish shoes. *Djogané di* ing malam.* The floor was waxed. *ng* untu* to brush the teeth. *Botjahé di* karo weḍak.* The child was massaged with medicated powder. 2 to incite, egg on. *A ng* B bèn ngantem aku.* A goaded B into hitting me. **ng/di*aké**

to rub sth [into, onto]. *Lisah peṭak wau ka∗aken ḍateng badanipun.* She massaged his body with the cajuput oil. **pa·ng∗** act of rubbing/polishing. *Pang∗é sepatu ora rata.* His shoes aren't polished evenly. ∗ **untu** tooth powder

gosong burnt, scorched. *Iwaké ∗.* The fish burned. *Rainé nganti mangar² ∗.* Her face was flushed and burning.

got gutter; ditch

goṭang 1 incomplete; imperfect. *Uripé ∗ tanpa sisihan.* His life is incomplete without a wife. *Walangé sikilé ∗.* The locust has a leg missing. 2 *rg* empty, unoccupied. **ora ∗** perfect. *Isih sugih trepsila lan ora ∗ kasusilané.* He has fine manners and flawless morals.

gotèk to say, tell, report. *Sapa sing ∗ raḍioné ilang?* Who reported a lost radio? **∗an** to discuss. **∗é** it is said... *∗é A dipilih dadi lurah.* I hear A was appointed village head. **ng∗** to discuss

goṭèk 1 pole for getting fruit from a tree. 2 *rg var of* DUWÈK. **ng/di∗i** to knock [fruit] from a tree with a pole

gotjèk **∗an** 1 to cling to. 2 sth to hold onto. *Pantji kuwi ∗ané wis poṭol.* The handle came off the pan. **ng/di∗i** to take hold of. *∗ana sing kukuh.* Hold onto it tightly!

gotjèl *var of* GOTJÈK

gotji large earthenware jug

gotjo **ng/di∗** to punch smn in the stomach

gotong **ng/di∗** to carry cooperatively. *Koṭak mau di∗ wong lima ganti².* The chest was carried by five men changing off. ∗ **majid** to travel a dangerous route with few companions. ∗ **rojong** (*abbr:* **g.r.**) cooperative community self-help, mutual cooperation; to work together cooperatively. *Tjara G.R. ing padésan² mono sedjatiné pantjèn salah sidjiné sifat sing originil tinemu ing Indonesia.* The tradition of mutual self-help in [Javanese] rural areas is one of the original features of Indonesia. *asil saka ∗ rojongé ahli²* resulting from the cooperative efforts of specialists. *Wong mau ora tau ∗ rojong karo wong lija.* He never pitches in and helps. *Sapa sing nggawa? –Ja ∗ rojong kita kabèh!* Who'll carry it? – We'll all carry it together!

goṭot strong, robust

gotra(h) 1 blood relative(s). 2 social group; society. *kula sa∗* of the same family *or* social group (as)

gotri buckshot

gowang [of blades] nicked

gowèh gumboil. **∗en** to have gumboils

gowèk **∗-∗** *or* **gowak-∗** 1 to feel nauseated; to keep retching. 2 *rpr* the sound of vomiting

gowèng chipped at the edge

gowok 1 a purplish berry; the plant it grows on. 2 hollow(ed out). *kaju ∗* a hollow tree/log. *Untuné ∗.* He has cavities in his teeth. **∗an** a certain children's game

gr *rpr* an animal's growl

gr. *see* GRAM

g.r. *see* GOTONG ROJONG

grabad seasonings; auxiliary cooking needs. **ng/di∗** to deal in the above items at the marketplace

grabah crockery, earthenware

grabjag **∗an** 1 flash flood; flooding wave. 2 sloppy; careless. *Olèhé nggarap gawéjan mau ∗an mula ora apik asilé.* He did a slapdash job, so it didn't turn out well. **∗-∗** *or* **ng∗** to come on strongly and/or suddenly. *Ombaké ng∗.* The waves flooded the area. **sa∗an** instantaneous(ly). *Sega mau dipangan sa∗an entèk.* The rice was all eaten up in no time.

grabjas **sa∗an** instantaneous, (happening) in a flash

gradag *rpr* clatter or tumult caused by people swarming into a place

gradjag **∗-∗** *rpr* water falling. **ng∗** *or* **g·um·radjag** to flow rapidly; to pour (down). *ng∗ getih* to bleed profusely during menstruation or childbirth

gradji (**grantos** *kr?*) saw. **∗n̂** 1 sawdust. 2 place where a saw is operated. *gradjèn apèn* steam-sawmill. **∗n̂an** sawed. *Kajuné delegan apa gradjènan?* Is the wood whole or sawed up? **ng/di∗** to ask for a tip in addition to one's fee for a service. **ng/di∗(n̂i)** to saw. *Pang²é digradjèni, bandjur uwité di∗ ngantjas.* He sawed off the branches, then he sawed down the tree. **pa·ng∗n̂** place where a saw is operated; sawmill. ∗ **api** industrial steam saw. ∗ **balok** pit saw, two-man saw. ∗ **gorok** hand saw. ∗ **gubah·an** fret saw for cutting decorative patterns. ∗ **senṭeng** frame saw for sawing curves

gragal gravel, pebbles. **∗an** a stony *or* gravely area

gragap *rpr* a sudden start, *esp.* from sleep. *Mak ∗ aku tangi.* I sprang up. **∗an** startled, caught unawares, flustered. **ng∗** to act flustered *or* startled. *Aku ng* tangi.* I was startled from sleep. *Olèhé mangsuli ng* djalaran ora sinau.* He got flustered when he answered—he hadn't studied.

gragas **ng*** to eat indiscriminately, *esp.* things that are not good for one

gragèh ***-*** to grope around

grâhâ eclipse. * *(rem)bulan* lunar eclipse. * *srengéngé* solar eclipse

graham molar (*sbst ki for* BAM)

grahânâ *var of* GRAHA

gra(h)ita comprehension, mental grasp. **ng*** to think (about) deeply. **pa·ng*(n)** idea, awareness. *ṭukul pang** the germ of an idea. *A duwé pang*n jèn sing nemu djam mau mesṭi B.* It dawned on A that B must have found the watch.

grajah ***an** to feel around, grope. ***-*** 1 to feel, grope. *Aku krasa tangan sing *-* ana sakku.* I felt a hand groping in my pocket. 2 to try to pick a quarrel. **ng/di*i** to feel around in. *Aku ng*i ḍompètku.* I felt in my wallet. **g·um·rajah** 1 prolific. *Wis gemrajah putuné.* He has many grandchildren. 2 itchy all over

grajak hold-up man. ***an** stolen. *barang *an* stolen goods. **ng/di*** to rob. *Aku di*.* I was held up. *Omahku di*.* My house was robbed.

grajang ***an** *or* ***-*** to feel, touch. *Sikilé *-* ing kono.* He felt around with his foot. **ng/di*** to sense; to perceive with the senses. *swara kang ng* urat sjaraf* a noise that grates on the nerves. *Wis bisa di* lamun rentjananė Inggris iku diterusaké.* It can be observed that the British plan is to be kept in effect. *Jèn duwé kekarepan, adja gampang di* ing lijan.* If you want sth, don't let others sense it. **ng/di*(i)** to feel of, pass the hand over. *Pistul agahan di*.* He fingered the pistol he was leveling at them. *Aku ng* ugel²é, pranjata wis anjep.* I felt his wrist; it was feverish. *Wong wuta iku jèn matja aksarané di*i.* Blind people read by feeling the letters. **pa·ng*** 1 act of touching/feeling. *Adja seru² pang*mu.* Don't press too hard! *Pang*é saja suwé saja nemen.* He intensified his caresses. 2 sense of touch

grajeng *intsfr* dark. *peteng ** pitch dark

gram (*abbr:* **gr.**) gram (unit of weight)

grâmâ fire (*kr for* GENI?)

gramang **ng*** [of insects] to creep, crawl. **semut *** red ant

grambjang **ng*(an)** [of thoughts] to stray, wander. *Pikirané ng*(an).* He's day-dreaming. **g·um·rambjang** [of sounds] shrill, penetrating

gramblèh *ptg ** hanging about in disorder. *Klambiné ptg *.* His clothes are hanging all over the place.

gramèh a freshwater fish often kept as a pet. **ng*** 1 discourteous. 2 to prattle inconsequentially; to speak hypocritically

grami 1 fire (*sbst kr for* GENI). 2 (to engage in) business (*sbst kr for* DAGANG). **(ge)*ǹ** (to engage in) business (*kr for* [DE]DAGANG[AN])

gramjang *var of* GRAMBJANG

grânâ 1 nose (*ki for* IRUNG). *mandeng putjuking ** to stare at the tip of one's nose; to concentrate the mind and will during meditation. 2 *ltry* elephant's trunk

granat grenade

granḍèl a certain long-stemmed papaya

granḍul *pl form of* GANḌUL

granggam *var of* GANGGAM

granggang bamboo spear

grangsang ***an** *or* **ng*** wanting to eat everything one sees; to eat compulsively. **g·um·rangsang** intensely hot. *Hawané gemrangsang.* It's awfully hot out.

grantang a xylophone-like gamelan instrument. **ng*** 1 to play this instrument. 2 resembling the sound of this instrument. *Sambaté ng*.* He complained whiningly.

grantes **ng*** in despair

grantil *pl form of* GANTIL

granting *pl form of* GANTING

grantjeng *pl form of* GANTJENG

grantos saw (*kr for* GRADJI?)

graok *pl form of* GAOK

graong ***an** *or* **ng*** to yelp, howl

grapjak friendly and outgoing; genial; sprightly

grasak coarse sand

grasi grace, pardon

grates **ng*** sorrowful

graṭil **ng*** destructive. *botjah ng** a destructive child

gratis free of charge. **di*aké** offered free. *Wis di*aké, meksa ora ana sing teka.* I'm giving them away, and still there are no takers.

graṭul ***-*** *or* **groṭal-*** *or* **gruṭal-*** *or* **ng*** [of speech] halting, awkward. *See also* GROṬAL

graul *var of* GRAUT

graung *pl form of* GAUNG

graut **ng/di*** to scratch with the nails *or* claws

grawah ***-*** *rpr* the sound of swiftly flowing water, *esp.* in a deep gorge. **g·um·rawah** to flow swiftly. **djurang *** a gorge with a river at the bottom

grawal ***an** in haste. *Ḍèwèké *an meṭukaké aku.* He hurried to meet me.

grawil *pl form of* GAWIL

grawul *ptg ** in coarse grains. *Glepungé ptg *.* The flour is coarsely ground. **growal-*** unsteady. *Kréta mau growal-*.* The cart is rickety.

grawut *var of* GRAUT

gre- *see also under* GER- *(Introduction, 2.9.6)*

gréba **ng/di*** to conjure up in the imagination

grebeg traditional religious festival held three times annually, featuring mountains of rice. ***-*** ear-shattering. *Swarané *-*.* The noise is deafening. **ng/di*** to surround and escort smn. **g·in·(a)rebeg** [of a king] to have the court dignitaries appear before one during the course of the above celebration

gredèb ***-*** to have a tic affecting the eye

gredeg *rpr* a rush of people arriving simultaneously. **g·um·redeg** *rpr* the sound of people walking

grédja Christian church

grédjah **ng/di*** 1 to count, enumerate. 2 to consider; to think about/over

gredjeg ***an** to quarrel. **ng/di*** to force, compel

grèdjèh, gredjèh *var of* GREDJIH

gredjih **ng*** (to rain) continuously. *Udané sedina ng* ora lèrèn²*. It's been raining all day without letup.

greg *rpr* a jolt, *esp.* a sudden stop. *Sepuré manḍeg *.* The train jerked to a stop. *Mak * aku nglilir.* I woke up with a start. **grag-*** to stop and start by turns. **ng·grag-ng*** [of the voice] hoarse

grégah *rpr* a sudden awakening. *Mak * tangi.* She awoke with a start. **g·um·régah** to wake up suddenly; to get up suddenly, to rise up. *A gumrégah nuli njanḍak pistulé.* A got up abruptly and seized his pistol. *Gemrégah tangi ngrebut dradjadé ḍéwé.* They rose up and assumed their rightful ranks.

greged a strong urge; intensity of feeling. ***en** exasperated. ***-*** to feel a surge of emotion. ***-* suruh** fuming with anger. **ng*aké** irritating, exasperating

grègèl *rpr* a loosened grip. **ng*i** to lose hold of. *Senadjan wis ditjekel kentjeng isih ng*i.* He was holding it tight but even so it slipped out of his grasp.

gregel *ptg ** bulging awkwardly in various places. **ng*(i)** to feel sth poking one. *Ḍèké kerep ng*i pangentjoting péḍal sepéḍa.* He kept feeling her knees bang against him as she pedaled the bicycle.

greges pebbly soil; earth mixed with gravel. ***-*** *or* **gregas-*** to have chills (when one is feverish)

gregèt *rpr* a squeaking door

gregut **ng*** *or* **g·um·regut** assiduous, energetic

gréjang *pl form of* GÉJANG

gréjong *pl form of* GÉJONG

grèk *rpr* rasping. *Pageré dikèkrèk mak *.* He sawed through the fence.

grembel **ng* 1** thick. *goḍong ng** dense foliage. 2 to flock to, gather in. *Adja ng* nang kono kabèh.* Don't all crowd into that space!

grémbjang inverted; *rpr* a sudden about-face. *malik ** to turn upside down, turn the other way around; to do an about-face. *Kanḍané wong wadon mau bandjur malik * dadi ngoko.* Suddenly the woman (who had been speaking in Krama) switched to Ngoko.

grembul *var of* GREMBEL

grèmèng ***an** *or* **ng*** to rave deliriously

gremeng *ptg ** *or* ***-*** *or* **gremang-*** *or* **ng* 1** to converse softly, talk in murmurs. 2 to loom up in the dark. **g·um·remeng 1** to talk in murmurs. 2 to mutter, grumble. *gemremeng nesu* to mutter in anger

gremet ***an** characterized by crawling. *ama *an* insect pests. **ge*(an)** to crawl as one's characteristic locomotion. *kéwan ge*an* (the class of) insects. *walang *an* a crawling grasshopper. ***-*** *or* **gremat-*** to move by creeping; to proceed at a crawl. **gremat-* waton·é (angger) slamet** slow and steady gets you there safe and sound. **ng*** to creep; to move at a crawling pace. *Semut ng**. Ants crawl. *Lakumu kok ng* rindik.* How come you're walking so slow?

gremis to drizzle. *udan ** drizzling rain

grénda grindstone. **ng/di*** to sharpen with a grindstone

grènḍèl door *or* window catch

grenḍèl **ng*** to lag behind. *Ora ana sing ng*.* There were no stragglers.

grenḍet **grenḍat-*** to keep getting interrupted. *Krétané lakuné grenḍat-*.* The cart kept having to stop.

grendjak *var of* GRENDJET

grendjel *rpr* the feel of sth hard. *Bandjur krasa mak * kaja ana atos² ing djeroné lumut.* Suddenly he felt a hard object in the soil. *ptg ** repeated sensations of being bumped or pressed against. ***-*** *or* **grendjal-*** to keep feeling sth pressing against one. *Wetengku grendjal-*.* Something kept jabbing me in the stomach. **ng*** to feel sth hard *or* uncomfortable pressing against one

grèndjèng metal foil. ** mas (slaka)* a sheet of gold (silver)

grendjet impulse, urge

grénḍol *pl form of* GÉNḌOL

grendul glutinous-rice balls used as a filling for porridge

greneng a complaint. *ptg * pl* murmuring in complaint. ***an** *or* ***-*** to mutter, grumble. *Wong² paḍa *an dikira kena ing apus.* The people began to mutter, feeling they had been cheated. **ng/di*i** to grumble to/about

greng 1 thicket of thorny bamboo. 2 *rpr* a jerk, jolt. *Aku kontak mak *.* I got a(n electrical) shock. **sa*an** with a sudden quick motion. *Koperé bisa diangkat sa*an.* He swept up the suitcases in one motion.

grenggeng ***-*** *or* **grenggang-*** *or* **g·um·renggeng** (to make) a humming, buzzing, whining

grengseng enthusiasm, urge, desire. *Aku ora duwé * arep nonton sorot.* I don't particularly want to go to the movies. **é pantjèn kaja kagungan perlu.* His urgency indicates he has sth pressing in mind. *Meneng² ana *é.* He's quiet but enthusiastic. **ng*** *or* **g·um·rengseng** (to behave) with enthusiasm

grenjih **ng*** 1 incessant. *nginang ng** to chew betel constantly. 2 to keep whining *or* teasing for sth

grenuk *ptg * pl* sitting around talking

grèpès *var of* GRIPIS

grès 1 *rpr* a knife slashing, *esp.* when performing a circumcision; (to perform) a circumcision. *Apa wis *?* Has the circumcision been done? **é djam pira?* What time is the circumcision? 2 brand new. *Montoré (anjar) *.* His car is brand new.

gres *rpr* cutting, slashing

gresah **ng*** to bemoan one's fate. **pa·ng*** complaint. *pang*é kaum buruh* the complaint of the workingman

grèsèk ***-*** *or* **ng*** to look around (for), try to find

grèṭèl a pole used for getting fruits down from high on the tree

grètjèh, gretjèh *var of* GREDJIH

grètjèk **ng*** talkative. **g·um·rètjèk** [of speech] copious. *Gunemané gemrètjèk.* He talks a lot.

gretjih **ng*** [of rain] incessant

gretjok **ng/di*i** to keep calling smn's attention to his shortcomings

gréwal *rpr* rock breaking. **ng/di*** to break (crack, chip) rock

grèwèng *ptg ** burdensome. *Gawané ptg *.* He has too much to carry.

gribig woven-bamboo panel used as a screen. ***an** screened (off) with the above

gridig ***-*** *or* **g·um·ridig** (walking) grouped, bunched. *Kebo²né digiring gumridig urut pinggiring dalan.* He drove the kerbaus in a cluster along the edge of the road.

gridja *var of* GRÉDJA

grig *rpr* a stab of fear

grigis *var of* GIGIS

griguh **grigah-*** to walk unsteadily with age

griha *var of* GRIJA

grija house (*kr for* OMAH, RUMAH). **pa*n** house lot (*kr for* POMAH·AN)

grijeng *rpr* a quick upward motion. *Koper mau diangkat sepisan mak *.* He lifted the trunk easily. ***-*** *or* **ng*** to wail. *nangis *-** to weep and wail

grijèt *rpr* squawking, screeching. *Mak * lawangé mbukak.* The door creaked open.

grijul **grijal-*** [to chew] laboriously because one has few, or no, teeth. **ke*** to step on sth inadvertently. *Sikilé ke* krikil.* He stepped on a pebble.

griming *ptg * or *-* or* **g·um·riming** 1 to feel itchy *or* irritated. 2 to feel chilly

grimis *var of* GREMIS

grinda *var of* GRÉNDA. **ng/di*** to massage [a baby] (*ki for* N·DADAH). **pa·ng*** massaging materials

gringging ***en** asleep, all pins and needles. *Sikilku *en.* My foot's asleep. *-* 1 to tingle with a pins-and-needles feeling. 2 to hesitate timidly

gringsang unbearably hot

grining **g·um·rining** *intsfr* clear, pure. *Banjuné bening gemrining.* The water is crystal clear. *kuning gumrining* pure clear yellow

grinting a variety of grass

grip slate pencil

gripir clerk in a law court

gripis [of teeth] chipped, broken

grita (*or* ***n**) belly band with strings at either end for tying it in place: worn by babies or by women who have just borne children

griwa nape of the neck (*ki for* GIṬOK, TJENGEL)

grobag 1 two-wheeled roofed oxcart. 2 railroad freight car. ***an** cartload. *beras *an* a cartload of raw rice. **ng*** to drive an oxcart as one's trade. **ng/di*(aké)** to load sth into an oxcart. *** wong** oxcart drawn by manpower

grobjag *rpr* a heavy thump. *Pitku ketjemplung kalèn, *, bjur.* My bicycle bumped down into the ditch and splashed. ***an** 1 to make thumping sounds. 2 to make frantic efforts to raise money. **g·um·robjag** to thump, bang

grobjos **g·um·robjos** (to sweat) profusely. *Kringeté gemrobjos.* He was pouring sweat.

grobog 1 large storage box. 2 food cupboard

groboh rough, crude. *Omongé *.* He talks like a boor. *Gawéané *.* His work is crude (without artistry). **ng/di*** to search sth. *Bareng omahé di* ketemu beḍil sepirang-pirang.* When they searched his house they found a number of rifles.

grodjog *rpr* water falling. ***an (banju)** waterfall. *-* (to make) the sound of water falling. **ng*** 1 to flush the toilet. 2 (*or* **di***) to keep hitting. **ng/di*aké** to cause [water] to fall. *Kaliné dibendung, banjuné di*aké mengisor.* They dammed the river and it created a waterfall. **g·um·rodjog** to fall. *Swarané banjuné gumrodjog tanpa peḍot, * * *.* The water roared down continuously.

grog *-* *rpr* a wild boar snorting. **grag-*** *rpr* a flat sound, *e.g.* the thud of fruit falling; smn coughing

grojok brusque

grok *rpr* seating oneself

grombjang *rpr* metallic clatter

grombol 1 group, gathering. 2 grove of trees. ***an** 1 group, gathering; to gather, form a group. 2 gang, group of terrorists. **ng*** to gather, form a crowd

grondjal *ptg ** characterized by ups and downs. *Dalané ptg *.* The road is bumpy. ***an** *or* **ng*** to jump up and down *or* flail the arms and legs, *esp.* in frustration

gronggang *var of* GRONGGONG

gronggong ***an** a small opening. **ng*** not tightly closed, opened a mere crack. *Tutupé ng*.* The lid isn't on tight.

gronong spoiled, overindulged

grontol salted shredded coconut mixed with cooked corn seeds, eaten as a snack

gropak 1 fried cassava chip. 2 *rpr* a branch snapping. **g·um·ropak** to break with a snap

gropjak *ptg ** to keep banging, thumping

gropjok (to engage in) a hunt, chase. ** tikus* a war on rats. **ng/di*(i)** to hunt down, close in on. *Pulisi lagi njrempeng ng*i pedunungan peteng ing kuṭa.* The police are conducting raids on the illicit areas of the city. **pa·ng*** a hunting down, a concerted closing-in action

grosok coarse in texture

groṭal *-* [of speech] halting, lacking fluency. *Jèn guneman tjara Djawa, aku *-* banget.* When I speak Javanese, I keep getting stuck. *See also* GRAṬUL

growah 1 caved in; lacking support. *Watuné *.* The stones gave way. *Gegeré *.* He's swaybacked. *penggalih kang isih ** an opinion that needs bolstering. 2 [of sun, moon] obscured, clouded over

growak ***an** cave; hole in the ground

growal *ptg * or *-** rough, uneven. *Dalané ptg *.* The road is bumpy.

growong 1 hollow. 2 *rg* solar eclipse. ***an** a hole, a hollow. **ng/di*i** to hollow out; to make holes in

grubjag *rpr* a thudding fall

grubjug 1 (to do) as others are doing. *mèlu **

karo wong akèh to go along with the crowd. 2 *rpr* the sound of feet. *Kebo²né pada dibandangaké, swarané ptg* *. The kerbaus' hooves thundered as they were driven along. 3 *rpr* a thudding fall. ***an** (to do things) with others. *Senengané *an.* He likes doing things in a group. **ng*** to move in a group; to do as others are doing. *Kabèh ng* ing omahku.* They all flocked to my house. **ng/di*i** to do sth along with others. *Aku mèlu ng*i tangga² awèh derma.* I joined with the neighbors in giving a donation. **g·um·rubjug** to make sound with the feet. *Keprungu swaraning wong gumrubjug.* We heard a lot of people tramping along.

grubug *mangsa* ***an** typhoon season. ***-*** roaring sound, *esp.* of wind, fire. **g·um·rubug** (to make) a roaring sound. *Lésusé swarané gemrubug.* The hurricane made a terrific roar.

grudjug to pour [water]. ***an** to bathe by pouring water over the head. ***-*** (*prn* **grudju:g²**) (to make) the sound of water falling. **ng*** 1 to flush the toilet. 2 (*psv* **di***) to hire [underpaid workers] to harvest rice. **ng/di*(i)** to pour (onto). *Awuné di* banju.* He poured water on the ashes. **g·um·rudjug** to run, flow, pour. *swarané banju gemrudjug* the sound of water running. *Banjuné tebu gemrudjug tumiba ing tadah tjèpèr.* The sugar-cane juice flows down into a shallow container.

grudug *rpr* a sudden rush as people converge. *Mak *, rampoké mlebu omah.* The gang of robbers burst into the house. ***an** (act of) going along as one of a group. *Senengé *an.* He likes to go places in a crowd. **grudag-*** to follow the crowd. **ng*** to move in a group. *Wah, wingi kamasku sakuluarga ng* teka omahku.* Yesterday my brother and his entire family came to our house! **ng/di*aké** to blow on [fire] to make it blaze up. **ng/di*i** to go smw in swarms. *Omahé di*i watu.* His house was showered with stones. *Kamaré bandjur di*i wong pirang².* People poured into the room. **g·um·rudug** *pl* (to come) swarming. *Tangga teparoné kang krungu pendjerité iku bandjur gumrudug teka.* The neighbors heard her screams and came running.

grumbul undergrowth, shrubbery. **(ge)*an** area of underbrush *or* thickets. **ng/di*i** to go along with, join

grumpung [of nose] deformed (flat, tipless)

grumuh sturdy, physically sound

grumut ***an** to lurk. *Bengi² *an ana apa?* Why are you hanging around at this time of night? ***-*** *or* **grumat-*** *or* **ng*** to sneak along; to sneak up on smn. **ng/di*i** to approach furtively, sneak up to

grundel *ptg* * *pl* to complain. ***an** *or* **ng*** to grumble with dissatisfaction. **ng/di*i** to grumble at, complain to

grunek̄ a complaint; a grudge. ***an** *or* **grunak̄-*** to complain, grumble

gruneng **ng*** to grumble, complain

grunggung a buzzing, humming, murmuring. **g·um·runggung** to produce such a sound

grup group, gathering

grusu **grusa-*** to act impetuously. *Iki enggon larangan, kowé ora kena grusa-* mlebu mréné.* This is a restricted area: you can't barge in here!

gruwek̄ **ng/di*** to wound by piercing with nails *or* claws

gruwung 1 hollow. 2 *var of* GRUMPUNG

gubah movable screen for creating privacy as desired. ***an** 1 bed concealed by a movable screen. 2 an artistic creation. **ng/di*** to make an artistic creation. *ng* wajang lulang* to make a leather puppet. *ginubah déning S.* drawn (painted, composed, *etc.*) by S. **ng/di*(i)** to conceal sth with a movable screen. **pa*an** *sms* *AN *above*

gubar a certain type of gamelan *gong*

gubed ***an** act *or* way of encircling sth. **ng*** to turn in a certain direction. *ng* mengétan* to turn eastward. **ng/di*(-*)** to wind around, encircle. *Matjan di* ula.* The snake wound itself around the tiger. *Witipun djatos ka*-*.* The teak trees are wrapped round and round (with protective wrappings). **ng/di*aké** to wind sth around. *Taliné di*aké wit.* He wound the rope around the tree.

gubeg (*or* ***an**) to bandage, bind up

gubel **ng/di*** *ltry* to keep after, plague, haunt. *Dèké ng* embokné ndjaluk rabi putra Mesir.* He kept begging his mother for permission to marry the Egyptian girl. *Pikirané di* pitakon rupa².* His thoughts were plagued by many questions.

gubrah *var of* GUBRAS

gubras spattered, smeared. * *getih* blood-stained

gubrat *var of* GUBRAS

gubris **ng/di*** to heed, take note of

gubug thatch-topped wooden watchtower

in a rice paddy, where children operate movable scarecrows to keep birds away from the ripening ears. * **Pèntjèng** the Southern Cross

gudag **ng/di*** to chase

guḍal discharge from the genitals

guḍang **1** storage room *or* building; *fig* center, storehouse. *Berasé disimpen ing **.* The rice is stored in the shed. **é montor mabur* airplane hangar. *Thailand kuwi * beras kanggo Asia Tenggara.* Thailand is the rice bowl of Southeast Asia. *Amérika iku * ilmu pengetahuan.* America is a science center. **2** (*or* ***an**) vegetables mixed with grated coconut and chili peppers. **ng/di*** to make [ingredients] into the above dish

guḍé a tree that produces a certain bean that can be made into fermented beancake *(témpé)*

guḍeg a dish consisting of breadfruit, chicken, and egg cooked in coconut milk. **ng/di*** to make [breadfruit] into the above

gudèl kerbau calf (young of the KEBO). **ng*** resembling a kerbau calf. **ng* bingung** to behave erratically *or* frenziedly. *See also* Ñ·TEMU

guḍig scabies. ***en** to have/get scabies

gudir jelly produced from seaweed. * **sarang·an** a certain porridge made of this seaweed, *or* from a certain fruit

gudjeg **ng/di*** **1** to hold smn tight. *Wis di* meksa bisa utjul.* I had a tight hold on him but he got loose. **2** to nag

gudjeng laughter; to laugh (*kr for* GUJU). **(ge)*an** to hold onto. **ng/di*aké** to hold for smn. *Bungkusanmu dak *aké apa?* Shall I hold your package? **ng/di*i** to hold/grasp sth. *Jèn njabrang dalan ng*i tanganku lo.* Hold my hand when we cross the street.

gudjer *var of* GUDJEG

gudjih talkative

gudrah messy, stained, smeared (with)

gudras *var of* GUDRAH

gugah *ng,* **gigah** *opt? kr,* **wungu** *ki* ***-*** to (try to) wake smn up. **ng/di*aké** to wake a person up on smn else's behalf. **ng/di*(i)** to wake *or* rouse smn. *Ibumu tak *é.* I'll wake up your mother. *Muga² atiné ginugah lan kersa paring sumbangan kanggo rumah sakit iki.* I hope they'll be awakened to the need and will donate to this hospital.

gugat *ng,* **gigat** *kr* ***an** accusation. **ané ora kebukti.* The charges weren't proved. **ng/di*** to accuse; to sue. *Wong mau di* prakara olèhé sa-wenang² marang darbèking lijan.* He was charged with seizing other people's property. **ng/di*aké** to bring a charge *or* suit against. *A di*aké marang Pengadilan Negeri.* A is to be brought before the Civil Court. **pa·ng*** accusation. *See also* GANGGU

gugrug to slide down(ward). *Lemahé *.* There was a landslide.

gugu *ng,* **gega** *kr* ***ñ** belief, faith. ***ñ tuhu·ñ** *ng kr* superstition. **ng/di*(ñi)** **1** to believe in, trust, act according to. *A ora kena di*.* A is not to be trusted. *Aku arep nggugoni karepku ḍéwé.* I'll do as I please. **2** (**ḍahar** *or* **ḍahar atur** *ki*) to take smn's advice

guguh toothless; very old

guguk **ng*** unrestrained, uncontrolled, *esp.* weeping

gugup startled; nervous, jumpy. ***an** nervous by nature. *See also* GAGAP

gugur **1** to fall, drop; *fig* to die. **2** to collapse, cave in. *lemah ** landslide. **3** ineffective. *Sembahjangé *.* His prayers were not answered. **ng/di*** to destroy. *ng* gunung* to level a hill. **ng/di*aké** to interfere with. *ng*aké iman* to cause smn's faith to waver. *ng*aké kanḍutan* to abort a pregnancy. **ng/di*i** **1** to engulf. *Lemahé ng*i omahku.* The landslide buried my house. **2** to render sth ineffectual. * **gunung** (to do) cooperative labor without pay

gugut **ng/di*** to kill [lice] by pressing them against the front teeth

gujang **ng/di*aké** to have smn wash down [livestock] by scooping water and pouring it over them. **ng/di·(ge)*(i)** to wash down [livestock]. **ora bisa ng* lajah** to have nothing to eat. **pa·ng*** act of washing livestock. **pa·ng*an** place where livestock are washed. **djaran *** love potion

gujer **ng/di*** to pet, fondle

guju *ng,* **gudjeng** *kr* a laugh; laughter. *gawé ** to make smn laugh. ***ñ(-*ñ)** to joke. *Ngapuramu lo, iki mung gujon.* I'm sorry–I was just kidding. ***ñ⁽²⁾ parikena** always poking fun at/with others; ostensibly joking but actually in earnest. **ge*ñ** **1** object of laughter; a laughingstock. **2** to kid around. **ng*** to laugh. *ng* gar-ger* or *ng* ger-geran* to laugh intermittently; to keep laughing. **ng* tuwa** to cry. **ng/di·(ge)*** to laugh at, make fun of. **di* pitik** to be laughed at by chickens (alleged to result from violating the behavioral norms of quiet controlled actions and speech. **di·ge*** **ing wong** envied by others. **ng*k̂aké** funny, amusing; (*psv* **di*k̂aké**) to make smn laugh. **ng/di*n̂i** to keep smn amused. **pa*n̂** *or* **pi*n̂** joking around, clowning. **g·um·uju** *ng,* **g·um·u-djeng** to laugh. *Batosipun gumudjeng.* She laughed to herself.

gujub close, friendly, mutually helpful. **ng/di*i** to take a personal interest in. **(pa)*an** a social relationship *or* association based on mutual interests (as contrasted with PA·TEMBAJA·N)

gujur **ng/di*** to splash *or* pour water (onto)

gul a goal, *i.e.* a point-scoring play (in soccer). ***-*an** to take turns being goalkeeper while the other kicks (for soccer practice). **ge*an** *or* **ke*an** to get scored against. *Awaké ḍéwé ge*an loro.* They made two goals against us. **nge/di*aké** **1** to score a goal. **2** to allow [the ball] to enter the goal. *Balé di*ké kiperé mungsuh.* The opposing goalie let us score. **3** to use sth as a bulwark. **nge/di*i** **1** to score a goal against. **2** to bolster (the forces/spirits of). *** kiper** goalie. *** pal** goal posts. *See also* AGUL

gula *ng,* **gen̩dis** *kr* sugar. *** arèn** sugar from the areca palm: made into paired cakes. *** batu** lump sugar; sugar in crystal form. *** djawa** coconut sugar from the areca palm. *** geseng** reddish-brown. *** klapa** **1** sugar made from coconut-palm sap. **2** striped red and white. *** keṭok** waste sugar, *i.e.* sugar that cannot be processed. *** kuntjung** coconut-sugar cake with a peak in the middle. *** mangkok** bowl-shaped cane-sugar patty. *** pasir** granulated cane sugar. *** tandjung** coarse-grained brown sugar

gulâganti a children's game played with pebbles

gulang **ng/di·(ge)*** to teach, train

gulâwenṭah **ng/di*** to bring up [children]. **pa·ng*** upbringing

gulé a stew-like dish with curry and spiced coconut milk. *** *ajam (kambing)*** the above dish made with chicken (mutton)

gulet wrestling (as a sport). **ng*** **1** to wrestle. **2** to tag along, hang around

guli smn's act of [do]ing (*rg var of* OLÈH·É). *** *mangan akèh.*** He eats a lot.

guling **1** pillow. **2** dam-reinforcing material of woven bamboo. **ke*** to roll accidentally. **ng*** **1** to roll; (*psv* **di***) to roll sth. **2** *oj* to sleep. **ng/di*aké** to roll sth. **pa*an** a bed. **g·um·uling** to roll (away, around)

gulma billion. **sa*** one billion

gulo *var of* GILO

gulu neck (**djânggâ** *ki*). *nigas ** or *ngeṭok ** to cut smn's throat. ***n̂** collar *or* neck of a garment. *gulon djedjeg* stand-up collar. *** antjak** **1** lower part of the neck of poultry (prepared as food). **2** tapering end of a knife blade. *** banjak** **1** swan-like neck. **2** long thin object formed like a gooseneck. *** mendjing** Adam's apple. *See also* PANG-GULU

guluh dirt on the skin. ***en** to have/get dirt on the skin

gulung a roll; rolled (up). *benang ** ball of string, spool of thread, skein of yarn. ***an** made into a roll. *** *kertas (bakal)*** a roll of paper (fabric). ***-*** *or* **gulang-*** **1** to roll repeatedly *or* constantly. **2** inseparable. *Botjah² loro mau gulang-* dolanan.* The two boys are always playing together. **ge*an** to roll repeatedly *or* constantly. *ombak ge*an* rolling waves. **ng/di*aké** to roll sth (for smn). **ng/di*(i)** to make into a roll. *ng* babud* to roll up a carpet. *ng* setagèn* to roll up a sash (when not in use). *En̩dogé di*.* She made the egg into egg rolls. *Goḍong mau diradjang di*-*.* The [tobacco] leaves are shredded and made into rolls. **g·um·ulung** rolled; forming a roll. *** koming** **1** to roll (over, around), to writhe. **2** under a strain. *A nganti * koming ngrasakak̨é olèhé kentèkan ḍuwit.* A is at his wits' end–he's run out of money.

gum- *see also under* G- *(Introduction, 3.1.7)*

gumagus [of males] vain of one's looks (whether justified or not). *See also* BAGUS

gumati *ng,* **gumatos** *kr* affectionately attentive. *Sing gemati njang sidji²né.* Look after each other! **ng/di*ǹi** to heap affection on. *Aku digumatèni bodjoku.* My wife pampers me. *See also* GATI

gumaṭok fixed, stable, firm. *Penemuné wis *.* His opinion is unchanged. *Ora ana bukti² kang *.* There's no definite evidence. *pranata kang ** fixed regulations

gumbâlâ **1** moustache (*kr for* BRÉNGOS). **2** beard (*ki for* DJÉNGGOT)

gumbira *var of* GEMBIRA

gumeder noisy

gumisa *ng,* **sumaged** *kr* to try to act competent *or* capable. *See also* BISA

gumjak noisy

gumjeg talkative, fluent. *Kok léné * temen.* How [the ladies] do chatter!

gumjur bewildered; in shock
gumoh [of babies] to spit up while nursing
gumotjah *ng,* **kumlaré** *kr* child-like. *Wong tuwa tindak-tanduké kok* *. He's grown up but he acts so childish. *See also* BOTJAH
gumping a precipitous slope
gumrebeg deafening, ear-shattering. *See also* BREBEG
gumrubul to move in a swarm. *Wong * saka toko mau ora ana kenḍat.* People emerged from the store in a steady stream. *See also* BRUBUL
gumuk small hill, knoll
gumul *oj* to wrestle
gumun (**ngungun** *ki?*) astonishing; astonished; to wonder [what *etc.*]. ** aku!* I'm astounded! *Pitakonku * banget.* My question took him by surprise. *Aku * (déné) ḍèwèké wis ngerti djenengku.* I was surprised that he knew my name. *Aku * kena apa kok olèh tindakan mengkono.* I wondered why he acted that way. *sing gawé *ku* what surprises me (is...). **ng*aké** astonishing; (*psv* **di*aké**) to astonish. **ng/di*i** to find sth astonishing. *sing di*i aku* the thing that surprises me (is...). *Botjah² ng*i tontonan sulapan.* The children were amazed by the magic show.
guna[a] *ng,* **gina** *kr* use(fulness), benefit. *Apa *né lajang iki?* What good is this letter? *barang kang gedé banget *né* a very useful thing. *tanpa ** useless. **ka*n** artistic skill, craftsmanship; art object/form. *ka*n mbaṭik* the craft of batik-making. *aspèk² ka*n* artistic aspects. *ka*n djogèd klasik* the art of the classical dance. *ka*n saka djaman Madjapahit* art objects from the Madjapahit era. **ng/di*kaké** to use, make use of. *See also* PIGUNA
guna[b] *-* a magic spell for doing harm to another. **ng/di*ni** to cast, *or* have smn cast, a spell on another. *** gawé** *sms* *-*; **ng/di*-gawé·ṅi** *sms* NG/DI*NI. *Aku kuwatir mbokmenawa digunagawèni.* I'm afraid she'll put a spell on me. *** piranti** *or* *** sarana** *or* *** sekti** *sms* *-*. *See also* ADIGUNA
gunâkâjâ husband's earnings which are given to the wife
gundam (**ng**)*-* to cry out in fear *or* disgust
gunḍes *intsfr* all gone, used up. *Barangé entèk* *. Every last one of his belongings was gone.
gunḍik 1 common-law wife. 2 female (flying) termite (*see also* LARON, RAJAP). 3 queen ant. **ng/di*** to take as one's common-law wife
gunḍil 1 [of rice plants, coconuts] having no hair *or* fibers. 2 [Javanese which is] written in Arabic characters without vowel-showing diacritics
gunḍul 1 devoid of hair *or* vegetation. *Sirahé* *. His head has been shaved bald. *tanah ** barren land. 2 the part of the head where the hair grows. 3 one of the Chinese playing cards *(kertu tjilik).* ***an** with head uncovered. **ng*** without headgear. **ng/di*i** to give smn a haircut. *** plontos** shaved bald
gunem *ng,* **ginem** *kr* talking, speech. *Ḍèké njelani *é botjah².* He interrupted the boys' conversation. ***an** 1 conversation. 2 (**andika·n** *or* **ngendika** *ki*) to talk, speak. **ng/di*** to discuss. *Apa sing paḍa di*?* What are they talking about? **ng/di*i** to (try to) persuade. **pa*an** conversation
gung 1 large, great. *Kula njuwun * ing pangaksama.* I apologize most humbly. 2 *rg var of* DURUNG. 3 *rpr* the sound of the gamelan *gong.* **nge/di*aké** 1 to increase the supply of [water]. *Banjuné bisa die*aké sarana mbendung kali mau.* We can build up the water level by damming the river. 2 to assess too great a value to. *A nge*aké kapinteranė.* A puts too much stock in his own cleverness. *Apa ta gunané nge*aké wong sing wis mati?* Why glorify a dead man? *See also* ADIGUNG
gungan *inf var of* UGUNG·AN
gunggung sum total. ** karo tengah taun* a year and a half altogether. ***an** 1 sum, total. 2 numbers (to be) totaled. 3 addition (arithmetic process). **ng/di*** to total up, add. **g·um·unggung** 1 added up. 2 conceited, fond of adulation. *** gepuk** *or* *** kepruk** *or* *** kumpul** the sum total; all told. ** kumpul suwéné patang puluh patang dina.* It took 44 days in all.
gungsir **ng/di*(i)** to dig (in). *ng*i lemah* to dig in the soil. *Télaku di* tikus.* My cassavas were dug up by mice.
guni *var of* GONI
gunjer *var of* GINJER
guntang 1 bamboo pot used as a water container. 2 to hull rice by pounding it (*var of* GANTANG). **g·um·untang** clearly audible
gunting scissors, shears. ***an** a piece cut from sth. **an koran* newspaper clipping.

ng/di*aké 1 to cut (out, into) with scissors. 2 to cut for smn. **ng/di*(i)** to cut with scissors. * **blèg** metal shears. *See also* SRIGUNTING

guntur thunder

gunung (*abbr:* **G.**) *ng,* **redi** *kr* 1 mountain. 2 *ng kr* head of an administrative *or* police district in Surakarta. 3 *ng kr* name of one of the Chinese playing cards *(kertu tjilik).* ***an** 1 likeness of a mountain. 2 *wj* mountain-shaped puppet symbolizing great natural forces. 3 (*or* **ge*an**) village administrative head. **ng*i** *ng kr* mountain-bred; boorish, crude. **pa*an** mountainous (terrain). *ḍaérah pa*an* a mountainous region. *wong pe*an* mountain people; boorish, uncultivated people. * **anak·an** hill. * **geni** volcano. * **guntur** striped clothing fabric. * **se·pikul** a small earring with a diamond on each side

gup. *see* GUPERNUR

gupak messy, smeared. * *bleṭok* mud-stained

gupâlâ *see* RETJA

gupenur *var of* GUPERNUR

gupermèn government-owned *or* -controlled (as contrasted with private). ***an** territory owned *or* administered by the government

gupernur (*abbr:* **gup.**) governor. * *djéndral* governor general. ***an** governor's official residence

gupis chipped (of teeth, *esp.* baby teeth)

gupit ***an** alley(way). **ng*** 1 narrow, cramped. 2 (*psv* **di***) to divide up into small spaces

gupjuk lively, animated

guprat smeared, stained (with)

gupruk *var of* GUPJUK

gupu a shelter for people or animals. **(pa)*n̂** dovecote

gupuh eager, quick, in a hurry

gur 1 *rpr* a *gong* beat. 2 (*or* **ng***) only. *Anaké (ng)* sidji.* He has only one child.

gurah[a] to rinse out the mouth (*ki for* KEMU). **(pa)*an** water for rinsing the mouth (*ki for* KEMU·N̂)

gurah[b] *ng,* **girah** *kr* to drive away. *Pitiké di*.* He shooed the chickens.

guramèh *var of* GRAMÈH

gurawal *var of* GRAWAL

gurda *oj* banyan tree

gurdi tool for drilling holes

gurem 1 chicken flea. 2 trivial, insignificant, of little consequence. * **ṭèṭèl**[2] a commonplace person with grandiose ambitions

gurénda *var of* GRÉNDA

guri *rg var of* BURI

gurih pleasantly rich-tasting, *esp.* suggesting the flavor of coconut milk. *sega ** rice cooked in coconut milk

gurinda *var of* GRÉNDA

gurit ***an** 1 back yard. 2 a scratch. 3 (*or* **ge*an**) meaningful verse with philosophical content; nonsense rhyme composed of repetitious-sounding syllables chanted by children

gurita 1 octopus. 2 *var of* GRITA

guru 1 teacher. * *bantu* elementary-school teacher. * *besar* professor. *mantri ** school superintendent. *sekolah ** teacher-training school. * *kena digugu lan ditiru.* Teachers must set an example for others. 2 guide *or* instructor in metaphysical matters. 3 standard, criterion, measuring device. 4 *ltry compounding element for specific poetic devices of meter, sound pattern, mystic meanings.* ***-*** hasty, rash. *Kok *-* ana apa?* What's your hurry? *Adja *-* nesu.* Don't fly off the handle! **ma*** *or* **me(r)*** *or* **ng·ge*** to acquire knowledge. **ng/di*k̂aké** to put smn in the hands of a *guru* for instruction. **ng*n̂i** 1 *guru*-like in one's conduct. 2 (*psv* **di*n̂i**) to instruct, *esp.* in religious or mystic matters. **pa*n̂** institution for metaphysical training. * **alem·an** fond of praise. * **bakal** 1 (raw) material. 2 (*or* * **dadi**) objects for offerings *or* dowries. * **dina** numerological propitiousness of a day one is considering for a certain event. * **lagu** poetic meter; rhyme scheme. * **laki** (one's own) husband. * **nadi** *oj* instructor in metaphysical matters. * **sastra** *ltry* having the same consonants in the same order (complex alliterative device). * **sedjati** teacher who instructs in the perfection of death. * **swara** *sms* * SASTRA but with vowels instead of consonants. * **tjantrik** ancient system of teacher-pupil education. * **wilang·an** *ltry* syllabic scheme, metric scheme. *See also* SAKA[b]

guruh thunder. **g·um·uruh** (to make) loud thundering sounds

gurung 1 (**gonḍang** *ki*) esophagus, windpipe. 2 *rg var of* DURUNG. ***an** water channel

gus *adr* boy of higher status. *Ampun wedi, *.* Never fear, Son. *See also* BAGUS

gusah **ng/di*** to send *or* drive away. *Pitiké di*, "Suh, suh."* He shooed away the chickens.
gusali *see* DJURU
gusar furious
gusek̄ *rg var of* BUSEK
gusi *ng kr,* **wingkis·an** *ki* gums (in the mouth). ***ǹ** gum-shaped. *** papak** the (obsolete) practice of filing the teeth level
gusis used up, all gone. *Banḍané dikampak *.* They were robbed of everything they owned. *Ḍuwité *.* His money is all gone.
gusti lord, master. *** Allah** *adr* God. *** Kangdjeng** your Majesty. *** pangéran angabèhi** oldest son of a monarch but not the crown prince. *** radèn aju** *title applied to a married princess*
guṭang *var of* GOṬANG
guṭek̄ ***an** a room created by partitioning. **ng/di*-*** to divide up into small rooms
guṭeng *intsfr* black. *ireng ** jet black
guṭet *var of* GUṬEK
guṭi small; low, inferior. *tjili-** teeny-tiny
gutjel **ng/di*** to hold tightly
gutji *var of* GOTJI
gutuk 1 a stick for throwing. 2 commensurate [with], balanced [by]. *Njambut gawé abot² kok ora * karo hasilé.* He works hard but doesn't have much to show for it. 3 *(or* *** wadja)** toothless *(ki for* OMPONG). **ng/di*** to throw a stick (at). **ng* lor kena kidul** to criticize A obliquely by directing one's comments to B in A's hearing
gutul *rg* to reach. *Njong ora *.* It's out of reach. ** Banjumas wis peteng.* It was dark by the time he reached Banjumas.
guṭul *cr* penis
gu(w)- *see also under* GU-, GW- *(Introduction, 2.9.7)*
guwa 1 cave, cavern, grotto. 2 *Djakarta dialect* I, me. **ng/di*** to burrow through *or* under; to undermine. *** garba** uterus, womb
guwâjâ facial color; facial expression
guwak **ng/di*** to throw away, discard
guwang, guwat *var of* GUWAK
guwek̄ a certain long-eared owl. **ng/di*** to pierce with claws *or* nails
guwi:k ***-*** [of pigs] to grunt, squeal
guwing having a harelip
gw- *see also under* GU(W)- *(Introduction, 2.9.7)*
gwâjâ *var of* GUWAJA
gyanti *var sp of* GIJANTI

H

h 1 *(prn* **hā***) alphabetic letter.* 2 *see* HADJI. *(for words beginning with* H *see also under the vowel after the* H*: Introduction, 2.9.12)*
hā so! aha!
ha. *see* HÈKTAR
habib Arabian descendant of Mohammed
habis 1 end. ** wulan/taun* at the end of the month/year. 2 well...! why...! **, kana wong loro aku idjèn.* There I was, alone against the two of them. ***-*an** to the utmost. *Ḍèwèké nglawan *-*an.* He struggled with all his might.
habsârâ god, deity, spirit
habsari goddess, deity, spirit
hadi(j)ah award; gift
Hadiningrat *see* SURAKARTA
hadipati 1 regent, ruler, sovereign. 2 *title used before the names of foreign heads of state and officials just below the ruler in Jogjakarta and Surakarta.* **k*ǹ** *(prn* **kadipatèn**) residence of the crown prince in Jogjakarta and Surakarta
hadjat *var of* KADJAT
hadjeng safe and sound
hadji 1 *(abbr:* **H.**) hajj *(title used before the name of a Moslem who has made the pilgrimage to Mecca: see also* KADJI*).* 2

katchoo! *Dèké gebrès mak *.* He sneezed.
- to sneeze repeatedly
hadyan *male nobility title: shf of* RAHADYAN
hagni *oj* fire
hah *excl of surprise*
ha-hak *rpr* laughter
hail(l)olahu *see* LAILLAHA
hajat life. *ilmu * biology
hajo so! aha!
Hajuningrat *see* JOGJAKARTA
hak 1 right, privilege. **é milih* the right to
vote. **é rakjat iku paḍa.* Everyone has
equal rights. 2 open mouth! *(children's
word).* *, ngemut apa ja?* Open your
mouth—what are you chewing? *bu.* Put
some food in my mouth, Mother! 3 *rpr*
laughter
hakékat 1 religious concept of what is true
and real. 2 basically, actually, truly
hakiki (that which is) essential, necessary
hakim 1 arbitrator. 2 judge
hal circumstances, case, matter. *mau wis
gomblang.* The case is cleared up.
halah well...
halal permissible, *i.e.* not taboo in Islam.
bahalal or *bihalal* to ask pardon for
one's sins and mistakes (a Lebaran-day custom)
halat *var of* WALAT
hallo *var sp of* HALO
halo hello! (on the telephone; as a greeting).
*ja * hello (on the telephone, to smn who
has been waiting on the line)
halpbèk halfback (in soccer). *kanan/kiri*
right/left halfback
halte place where a public vehicle stops
ham ham (meat)
hambok even though
Hamengku Buwânâ *name of each Sultan of
Jogjakarta. Hamengku Buwana IX ⟨ingkang
kaping sanga⟩* Hamengku Buwana the
Ninth
hamil pregnant. *pil anti * birth-control pill
hânâtjarâkâ the Javanese alphabet
handpat handle; part by which sth is held.
setang sepéḍa handholds on a bicycle
handlebar
handuk towel. **an* to use a towel. *ñg/di*i*
to dry smn with a towel
hangabèhi *formal var of* NGABÈH-I
hângsâ a certain large goose
hanuswârâ *gram* nasal sound
har *-*an* to live lavishly
hârâ 1 there! see! *ta, kapokmu kapan!*

You see—? when will you learn your lesson! 2 *excl of impatient wonderment.
Apa *...* What on earth...? *Lampuné mati,
pijé nggonku sinau. The lights went out:
how in the world am I going to study?
huru turbulence, upheaval. *See also*
HURU-HARA
harak *excl: var of* RAK 1
harâkâ *oj* 1 betel nut. 2 areca nut. 3 refreshment offered to a guest
haram forbidden, sinful. *Njolong kuwi *.*
Stealing is a sin. *botjah * illegitimate child.
*ñg/di*aké* to prohibit. *Agama Islam nga-
ramaké wong mangan babi.* The Islamic religion forbids its people to eat pork.
djadah illegitimate child
harda 1 covetous. 2 extremely, excessively
hardja comfortable, cozy, pleasant
harga *oj* mountain
hari day *(oj).* **an* daily. *buruh *an* day
laborer. *raja* important day; holiday.
warta/warti newspaper
harja 1 *male nobility title.* 2 *title accorded
Javanese dignitaries visiting from non-central
Java*
harmonika(h) harmonica
harnal hairpin
harnèt hair net
hart heart(ṣ) (playing-card suit)
harta money *kr: (var of* ARTA). *ka*'an*
public finance (in the Jogjanese court).
*menteri ka*an* Jogjanese court minister of
finance
hartâkâ 1 treasurer. 2 *oj* money
hartati sugar; sweet
hartawan wealthy person. *para * the rich
harum 1 fragrant; *fig* favorably known.
*ngGanda *.* It smells nice. 2 [of sounds,
esp. voices] low and pleasant. *(n)dalu* a
certain flower that blooms at night and
scents the night air. *manis* cotton candy
hasareng *var of* SARENG 2
hasih *var of* ASIH
hasil *var of* ASIL
hasta *oj* 1 hand, arm *(see also* ASTA). 2
proboscis; elephant's trunk
hasṭa *oj* 1 eight. 2 thousand. *Brata* the
Eight Precepts [for governing]
hatjing katchoo!
hatjo, hatju *var of* HATJING
hatmâdjâ, hatmâkâ *ltry* child; son
haung *rpr* an animal's growl *or* snarl. *ptg *
repeated snarling/growling
hâwâ 1 air. *segara* sea air. 2 weather;

climate. *kaanan* * weather conditions. *golèk * lija* to get a change of climate. * **nepsu** passion, passionate emotion; appetite. *Ḍèké ngampet * nepsuné.* He controlled his anger. *ngudja * nepsu* to give vent to one's strong feelings. *Adja mangan kakéjan, mung sanuruti * nepsu.* Don't overeat; let your appetite be your guide.

hawani *oj* earth

hé *ng* 1 hey! hey there! 2 eh? huh? *Ngandel apa ora kowé, *?* Do you believe it, hm?

hébat fine, splendid. *Wah * lho.* That's fine! Good for you! ***-*** at a peak *or* climax. **ñg*-*aké** *or* **ñg*-*i** amazing, remarkable

he'eh, he'e m-hm, uh-huh *(informal 'yes')*

hèh 1 *rpr* indrawn breath. 2 hey!

heh 1 *excl of surprise, dismay.* **, kok pirsa?* You mean you *saw* it? 2 *rpr* a sigh

hèk fence, *esp.* of concrete or brick

hek 1 uh; um. 2 *rpr* a grunt (of exertion; of disgust). 3 *rpr* cackling laughter

hèktar(e) (*abbr:* **ha.**) hectare (land measure, equivalent to 2,471 acres)

helang *oj* hawk

hèm man's Occidental-style shirt

hem 1 *excl of pleasure, admiration.* *Wah, *, énaké pelem kuwi nèh.* My, what delicious mangoes! **, apik ja nggoné paḍa bal-balan.* Wow, they play soccer really well! 2 *excl of relief.* **, djebul ora ana apa*². Whew! nothing happened after all. 3 *excl of dismay, annoyance.* ** anjepé.* It's so *cold!* **. Pantjèn botjah rèwèl temen.* What a pest you are. 4 *rpr* clearing the throat. 5 hm'm! hm'm?

hèngsèl *var of* ÈNGSÈL

hening *var of* ENING

her *command to a farm or draft animal*

hèrḍer German shepherd dog

hes *var of* HUS

hevea (*prn* **héféā**) a common variety of rubber tree

héwan(i) pertaining to animals. *ḍokter ** veterinarian. *keḍokteran ** veterinary medicine

hh *var sp of* HEH

hi 1 *excl of revulsion or fear.* *Hiiii, mengkirig aku.* Ugh, it gives me the shivers. 2 *jeering sound.* **, *, hik! ajo matjan, madjua.* Come forward if you dare, Mr. Tiger!

hiḍep *var of* IḌEP

hidjrah 1 Mohammed's flight from Mecca to Medina (*ca.* 622 A.D.), marking the beginning of the Moslem calendar. 2 (to make) the evacuation of Indonesian troops from Dutch-occupied West Java to Indonesian-occupied Central Java (an event of the war for independence)

hidrogèn hydrogen. *bom ** hydrogen bomb

hiḍup *var of* IḌUP

hih *var of* HI

hija *var of* IJA

hijah *var of* JAH

hiju shark

hijung *excl of pain or strong emotion*

hik *var of* HI

hikajat adventure story

hikmah, hikmat supernatural power *or* wisdom

hima cloud, vapor, mist. ***-*** thin fine cloud; cloud covering the moon. **ka*n** mist-covered, cloud-blanketed. **ñg*** cloud-like, mistlike. * **kapura** cloud mass around the sun. * **maja** fine thin cloud mass

himantâkâ mist rising from water

himalajā *oj* mountain

himawan *oj* mountain

himpun small edible fish that collect in huge compact masses in the sea. **ñg/di*(i)** to collect, compile. **ñg* alis** to knit one's brows. **pa*an** association, organization. **pa·ng*** collector; compiler

hina *var of* INA

hinajanā a certain Buddhist sect

Hinḍu 1 culture and religion of India. 2 pertaining to Hinduism. *bangsa ** Indians; Hindus

hing *syllable chanted in making a concerted effort: see* ANA-INI

hinggil *var of* INGGIL. *See also* SITI

hipnotis 1 hypnosis. *kena ** hypnotized. 2 (*psv* **di***) to hypnotize

hipnotisme hypnotism; hypnosis

hir *command to a farm or draft animal*

hirib *ltry var of* IRIB

his 1 *excl of scorn.* 2 *command to a farm or draft animal*

hjang 1 God. 2 mythological deity. *kersaning ** God's will. *Sang ** God. *Sang * Tunggal* God the Almighty. ***-*** the best, the finest. **ka*an** place where the deities reside. **ka*an djunggring-selaka** *wj* heaven; realm of the deities. **nga*an** to go to heaven. * **maha ésa** *or* * **manon** *or* * **suksma** *or* * **widi** God

hjas *see* PAHJAS

hjuh *scornful excl*
hla(h) *excl (var sp of* LA 1*)*
hlo *excl (var sp of* LO*)*
hm *var sp of* HEM
ho 1 *excl of glee.* 2 *rpr* a tiger's roar
h.o. *see* HONGERUDIM
hobi hobby, enjoyable pastime
hoha(h) *var of* HUHAH
hojag *var of* OJAG
holopis to work together cooperatively. * **kuntul baris** *words chanted by a group of workers to keep their concerted motions rhythmic*
hom- *var of* UM- *in* UM-PIM-PAH, UM-PIM-SUT
homa *oj (or* ***n**) sacrifice; victim. **pa*n** 1 place where sacrifices are offered. 2 place for solitary meditation
hongerudim *(abbr:* **h.o.**) severe malnutrition
honorarium 1 honorarium. 2 royalty payment
horé hurray!
horeg *var of* OREG
horoh oh-oh! **, rak lali ta!* You forgot, didn't you? ** ta, rusak!* Oh-oh–it broke.
hosé hurray!
hotèl hotel. *pegawé ** hotel clerk
hret *rpr* stopping. *Mak * krétané mandek.* The cart stopped.
hs *var sp of* HUS
hu 1 *excl of scorn.* **, adja nggugu Sri!* Hmf! don't believe Sri. 2 *rpr* mild laughter used as a conversational device rather than to express amusement. * **Allah** prayerful uttering of God's name during meditation
huh *excl (var of* HU*)*
huha(h) huge object. *iwak gedéné sahuha* an enormous fish
hu:k̄ *-* bow-wow!
hukum *var of* UKUM
hulu head, leader *(var of* ULU)
hulun *var of* ULUN
hum- *var of* UM- *in* UM-PIM-PAH, UM-PIM-SUT
hun unit of weight for opium
hungkué, hungkwé, hunkwé 1 flour made from a certain small green bean. 2 gelatinous pudding made with this flour
huntjuwé pipe for smoking tobacco
hup stop!
hur gidiyap!
hurdah 1 who goes there? 2 shoo! scat! **n̈g/di*** to speak (to) in a harsh strident voice
huré *var of* HORÉ
hurmat *var of* KURMAT, URMAT
huruf letter, character, script. * **gedrig** printed *or* typewritten character. * **latin** 1 character of the Roman alphabet. 2 handwritten (cursive) character
huru-hârâ turmoil, disturbance. *See also* HARA
hurup *var of* HURUF
hus 1 shoo! 2 sh! 3 *excl of disapproval.* ** adja.* Hey, don't do that! **, botjah kok ora genah.* What a bad boy!
husâdâ *var of* USADA
husé hurray!
hutspot [in cookery] mish-mash; stew (Occidental style)
hyang *var sp of* HJANG
hyun *var of* AJUN[b]

I

i 1 *alphabetic letter.* 2 oh! *I babo manas ati.* Oh, he makes me so mad!
-i **(-ni** *after vowel)* *(suffix)* 1 to [do] repeatedly, regularly; to [do] many times *or* to many objects. *ng·unduh·i pelem* to pick mangoes. *m̈·pentung·i asu* to beat a dog. 2 to [do] to [sth, as direct object]. *n̈·tampa·ni tamu* to receive a guest. *n·duwé·n̈i sawah* to own a rice paddy. 3 to direct *or* apply [*root*] to sth. *ng·lungguh·i kursi* to

sit on a chair. *ṅ·tulis·i buku* to write in a book. *ṅg·kirim·i lajang bapakné* to send a letter to one's father. *ng·enggon·i omah* to live in a house. *nge·doh·i piala* to stay away from evil. *ṁ·basa·ni wong tjilik* to speak Krama to the common people. *ṅg·kusir·i anḍong* to drive a horse cab. *ṅ·teges·i tembung* to give the meaning of a word. *Adja n·ḍisik·i kantjané.* Don't get ahead of the others. *di·loro·ni* to be set upon by two attackers. **4** to provide sth with [*root*]. *ṁ·pager·i* to enclose with a fence. *ng·ombé·ṅi wong* to give smn a drink. *m·bumbu·ṅi djangan* to season soup. *ṅj·slamet·i* to hold a ritual feast in honor of. **5** *(acv only)* having the characteristics of [*root*]; to [do] characteristically. *ṁ·wédok·i* womanly. *n·ḍeḍet·i* to tighten, become taut. *m·broḍol·i* to shed, molt. **6** *(with* TAK- *prefix)* I guess I'll... *Tak ng·réwang·i ibu.* I'll go help Mother. *See also* -AN 18*; see also individual entries for applicable meanings*

iba ***-*** *or* **sa*** how...! *Sa* senengku jèn sida lunga menjang Canada.* How pleased I will be, if we really go to Canada!

ibadah 1 religious practices. 2 devoutly religious. **ng*** to practice one's religion in deeds

ibadat *var of* IBADAH

ibarat (*or* **ng***) like, in the manner of. *ng* kutjing karo asu* like cats and dogs. **ng/di*aké** to compare sth to

iben *sbst kr for* IDU

iber pertaining to flight *(sbst kr for* ABER*?).* ***-*an** flying creatures. **m*** to fly. *Manuké m* bablas.* The bird flew away. **ng/di*aké** to fly sth, let sth fly. *ng*ké dara* to release a pigeon. **ng/di*i** to fly over/around sth

ibing *sbst ki for* IDEP. **ng*** to join in a Javanese dance around the lady performer

iblis evil spirit

ibu 1 mother (*ki for* EMBOK). 2 *term for addressing or referring to one's wife, or a woman of higher age or social standing.* ***né genḍuk/ṭolé** my wife, *i.e.* the mother of our little girl/boy. ***-*nen** always wanting one's mother near. **ng*** to call smn mother; to regard smn as one's own mother. **sa*** having the same mother. *A karo B iku sa* ning sédjé bapak.* A and B have the same mother but different fathers. *** geḍé** 1 aunt (parent's older sister). 2 *(misuse?)* grandmother. *** kuṭa** capital city. *** maratuwa** mother-in-law. *** tjilik** aunt (parent's younger sister)

ibut busy (at), involved (in)

ichtijar *var of* ISTIJAR

id. *see* IḌEM

idab *var of* ÉDAB

idah (*or* **ng***) **1** time period (100 days) after divorce or death of husband during which a woman does not remarry; [of this time period] to elapse. *wis (durung) ** the above time period has (has not) elapsed. **2** taboo period for sexual relations: the forty days following childbirth and the time of menstruation

idajat religious guidance

idak **k*an** to get stepped on. **ng*** to (take a) step. **ng/di*(i)** to step on. *Enḍogé di*.* He stepped on the egg. *Karepé kebo matjané arep di*-* pisan.* The kerbau tried to trample the tiger. *Djubiné reged wong di*i sikil reged.* The floor is dirty from being walked on by dirty feet. *See also* KIDAK, PIDAK

iḍam ***-*an** **1** food yearned for during pregnancy. **2** a wish, dream, desire. **ng*** to yearn for certain foods during pregnancy. **ng*(-*) ka·wor·an/ka·wurjan** to look pregnant

idé idea. ** ḍémokrasi* the idea of democracy

iḍem (*abbr:* **id.**) same; as above; as cited

idep eyelash(es). ***-*** the doors on certain fish traps *(itjir, wuwu)*

iḍep **1** to know, see. **2** *oj* thought(s), knowledge. **3** *oj* obedient. ***-*** oh well! (expressing resigned acceptance). **-* mlaku.* Oh well, the walk will do me good. **ng/di*** to consider, take into account

ider to peddle one's wares from place to place. ***an** **1** one who travels about. **2** peddler's wares. **3** passed around. *lajang *an* a letter (to be) circulated. **4** circuit of a rice paddy being plowed. *sa*an* once around the field (plowing). **5** communally owned and worked rice paddy. **k(a)*an** to get sth passed *or* distributed to one. *Omahku mentjil, mula ora k*an bakul roti.* Our house is off the beaten track, so the bread vendor doesn't come around. **m*(-m*)** to go from place to place, to circulate. *mider*[2] *nunggang pit* to ride around on a bicycle. *m*ing rat (ltry)* to go to the four corners of the globe. **m* amèn**[2] to travel around looking for work *or* performing shows for profit. **ng/di∗aké** **1** to peddle [wares] from place to place. **2** to circulate, distribute. *ng∗aké kabar* to spread news. *ng∗aké ḍuwit palsu* to circulate counterfeit money. *ng∗aké sirkulèr* to hand out circulars. **3** to take up a collection. **ng/di∗i** **1** to go all around smw. *ng∗i djagat* to go around the world; to orbit the earth. *ng∗i toko* to go from shop to shop. *Banju ng∗i djagad.* Water encircles the globe. **2** to pass around. *Tamuné di∗i patjitan.* She passed snacks to the guests. *Di∗i sirkulèr.* He passed around a circular among them. **3** to plow around the edges of [a paddy]. **4** to burn incense smw to ward off evil spirits. *ng∗i sawah* to burn incense in a rice paddy

idi permission. **k∗ǹ(an)** to receive permission. **ng/di∗ǹi** to give permission to

iḍi **∗-∗** *excl of disgust, revulsion*

idid **m∗** *or* **ng∗** to blow steadily. *angin m∗* a steady breeze

iḍih *excl of revulsion*

idin *var of* IDI

idjab **1** portion of the marriage ceremony before the bride and groom meet, in which the groom declares his intention to marry the bride and signs the marriage contract in the presence of the religious official. **2** *rg* fine, splendid. **ng/di∗aké** [of the religious official] to administer the above ceremonies to [a bridegroom]. **ng/di∗(i)** to contract oneself in marriage to [one's bride]

idjabah a wish; a prayer. **ng/di∗i** to grant a wish/prayer

idjadjah *var of* IDJASAH

idjak *var of* IDAK

idjasah **1** diploma. **2** certificate of course completion

idjèh, idjèk *var of* ISIH

idjem green (*kr for* IDJO)

idjemak in accordance with the opinions of Moslem specialists

idjèn **1** (**pijambak** *kr*) alone, by oneself. *Aku kari ∗.* I was left by myself. *Ali bisa mbanda maling ∗.* Ali subdued the thief single-handed. **2** (**pijambak** *kr*) single (not married). **3** digit occupying the unit position, *e.g.* the 4 in 354. **∗an (pijambak·an** *kr*) single (not married). **∗-∗ (pijambak²** *kr*) one by one. *Mlebuné idjèn².* They entered single file. **∗-∗an** all alone. **di∗i** unmatched, without equal. *Pinteré di∗i.* She's the smartest one. **k∗an** *or* **k∗en** **1** lonely. **2** to get left by oneself. **ng∗i** **1** unique, in a class by itself. **2** to do by oneself. *Gawéan semono akèhé di∗i.* He did all that work alone! *See also* IDJI

idjengandika *var of* DJENGANDIKA

idjep **∗-∗** fish-trap bars

idji unit, item, piece. *enḍog rolas ∗* a dozen eggs. *widji loro utawa telung ∗* two or three seeds. **∗an** at retail. *Barangé didol ∗an.* The items are sold individually. **di∗-∗** kept separate. *Olèhé nata panganan di∗-∗, adja ditjampur.* Set out each food separately—don't mix them together. **s∗** one unit; one. *See also* IDJÈN, SIDJI

idjih, idjik *var of* ISIH

idjir a bit at a time. **ng/di∗(i)** to deal with [things] little by little *or* one at a time

idjlig **idjlag-∗** to go back and forth repeatedly. *idjlag-∗ Jogja Magelang* to make frequent trips between Jogja and Magelang

idjmak *var of* IDJEMAK

idjo *ng,* **idjem** *kr* green; [of the face] pallid. *∗ enom (tuwa)* light (dark) green. **∗an** **1** an edible green pigeon-like bird. **2** extemporaneous; spontaneous, impulsive. **3** meaning. *"Kebo nusu gudèl" kuwi ∗ané apa?* What does the saying "a kerbau nursed by its calf" mean? **∗n(-∗n)** *or* **∗nan** *ng kr* **1** rice that is sold while still growing in the field. **2** money paid for such a crop. **ng∗** **1** to become green. *Tandurané lagi paḍa ng∗.* The plants are coming into leaf. **2** (*psv* **di∗**) to color sth green. **3** (*psv* **di∗**) to buy [a rice crop] while it is still growing. **ng/di∗kaké** **1** to make sth green; to have sth made green. *Klambiné di∗kaké.* She had her dress dyed green. **2** to sell the crop of [a paddy] in the growing state. **ng/di∗ni** to make sth green. **∗ gaḍung** a medium shade of green. **∗ pupus** the light fresh green of new leaves, *esp.* banana leaves. **∗ rojo²** *or* **∗ rijo²** pure clear green

idjol *ng,* **lintu** *kr* exchange item; replacement. *Pelem iki bosok, kana djalukna ∗.* This mango is spoiled; go ask for another one. **∗(-∗)an** to exchange with each other. *Mantèn loro kuwi ∗an kembar majang.* The bride and groom exchange bouquets. *∗an baé apa keprijé, kowé ana ngomah olah², aku tak matjul.* Let's change off: you stay home and cook, and I'll work in the fields. **∗é** (as) a substitute for, in place of. *Gluguné kena* *kanggo balungan omah *é kaju djati.* You can use coconut wood instead of teak for house frames. **ng/di*aké** to exchange, replace. *Sing biru di*aké sing abang.* The blue one was exchanged for a red one. *ng*aké tjèk* to cash a check. **ng/di*i** to exchange [one thing] for [another]. *Ḍèwèké kuwatir jèn pité di*i wong.* He was afraid smn would switch bicycles on him. *Ḍuwitku sing ilang di*i pamanku.* My uncle gave me some money to replace the money I had lost. *** (a)nggon** to swap temporarily. *Aku *(a)nggon pit karo masku.* My brother and I used each other's bicycles.

idjrah *see* HIDJRAH

idu 1 **(ketjoh** *ki***)** saliva; to salivate. 2 land measure: $1/8$ *bau* = *ca.* $1/4$ acre. **k*n̂** to get spat on. **ng*** to salivate. **ng/di*k̂aké** to spit sth out. **ng/di*n̂i** to spit on sth. **pa*n̂ (ketjoh·an** *ki***)** cuspidor. *** batjin** bad-tasting morning saliva. *** di·dilat manèh** to eat one's words. *** geni** to have everything one says come to pass

idul ***-*** *or* **idal-*** to go around naked. *** adha** *sms* * KORBAN *below.* *** fitri** orthodox Moslem name for the major holiday (*see* LEBAR·AN, RIJAJA). *** korban** day of religious sacrifices, feasting, and distributing food to the poor

iḍum *var of* ÉḌUM

iḍup life; to live. *gambar ** moving picture. **ng/di*i** to bring to life. **pa·ng*an** life, act of living

iga rib. ***-*** split-bamboo crosspieces used as a reinforcing framework for fences. *** lanḍung** longest rib. *** wekas** shortest rib

igar (*or* ***an**) obsolete coin worth $1/2$ *ḍuwit.* **ora sa*-*a** not (so much as) a single cent

igel ***an** [of peacocks] to spread open the tail. **ng*** 1 to spread the tail. 2 to bend the hand (a classical dance movement). **ng/di*aké** to open out [the tail]. **pa·ng*** act of spreading the tail *or* making the above dance movement

igir ***-*** mountain ridge

igit **ng/di*-*** to be exasperated with. *Pandjenengan di*-* tenan.* He's out of patience with you. **pa·ng*** exasperation, resentment

iglag *var of* ÉGLA

iguh 1 *sms* PA·NG* *below.* 2 to move, make motions. **ng/di*aké** to exert one's efforts toward sth. **pa·ng*** effort, exertion. *Présiḍèn ngjakini pang* mau.* The President backed the cause. *Manut pang*é sisihanku, aku bandjur bukak toko.* At my wife's instigation, I opened a shop. *** pertikel** advice. *See also* ÉGUH

igul ***-*** *describing a feminine hip-swaying walk*

ih *excl of disgust or fear*

ihi 1 *excl of disgust.* 2 *(wj) excl of anger*

ihtijar *var of* ISTIJAR

ija *ng,* **inggih** *kr* 1 yes; OK; (it's) so. *Aku njambungi *.* I answered yes. *Kowé adja nakal.–*.* Don't be naughty.–Okay, I won't. *Rasané énak.–Apa *?* It tastes good.–Really? *Tak kira *.* I think so. *Ajaké *.* Probably so. 2 also; both...and... *Ḍèk tjilik aku * ngono.* When I was little, I was that way too. *Sawahé klebu djembar, tegal * duwé.* His rice paddies are large; he has dry fields too. *Kéwan * bisa males kabetjikan.* Animals, too, can return kindness. *Ḍèké * bungah * susah.* She was both happy and sad. *Radèn Djanana * Radèn Ardjuna * Radèn Danandjaja* Djanaka, also called Ardjuna, also called Danandjaja. ** apik atiné * bagus rupané.* He's kindhearted as well as good-looking. 3 well! why! ** kuwi sedulurmu ḍéwé.* Well, he's your own relative! ** sapa sing ora nesu, wong diantem.* Well, who *wouldn't* get mad–he hit me! **4** it is emphatically the case that... *Énggal*[2] *minggir, nanging * meksa kesrèmpèt.* She moved to the side of the road quickly, but she still got hit. *Jèn tlatèn, dadiné * betjik.* If you're careful, it will certainly turn out all right. *Jèn ana wong menjanji ora seneng, jèn tembang Djawa * seneng.* He doesn't like Occidental-style singing; Javanese songs he *does* like. *Entèk pira ja?–Wah, * entèk pirang*[2]. How much does it cost?–It's very expensive. *Dipangan mentahan?–Ah * ora.* Do you eat them raw?–Of course not, stupid. 5 *(at end of predicate: enlivens predicate or invites agreement) Embuh * djenengé.* How should I know what it's called! *Udané kok wis terang *.* Hey, it's stopped raining! *Lajanganė tak ulukné saiki *?* I'll fly the kite now, okay? *Sapa sing mbenṭètaké gelas iki *?* Who chipped this glass, anyway? **6** *(between identical verb forms)* [do] to be sure [, but...]. *Ngadjèni * ngadjèni, ning ora susah minggrang-minggring adol manis.* Show respect by all means, but don't fall all over yourself. ***-*** yes yes, to be sure. *Ija, ja Tjung.* Yes, I know, 'Tjung. *Karepku mono ja-ijaa, nanging lagi ora duwé ḍuwit.* Sure I want it; but I don't have the money for it. ***-*a** [as though] sth were of some consequence. *Bregas kaja ija-ijaa, ning se-djatiné akèh sing kropos.* It looks impressive, but it's basically unsound. *Ali kuwi kaja *-*a.* Ali thinks he's really somebody! **ng/di*ni** to respond to affirmatively. *Wong pitu sing ngorani lima, sing ng*ni loro.* Of the seven, five said no and two said yes. *Sadjané aku ora ngerti pitakonané A ning ming tak *ni waé.* I didn't really understand A's question but I agreed anyway. *** ḍing** emphatically yes; emphatic excl as above (4). ** ḍing.* Yes indeed! *Wong ndjupuk kaja ngono baé * ḍing kok ora olèh.* Shame on you, taking things that way–you can't do that! *** wis** all right *(expressing resignation). Nèk angsal nggih kalih niku.–Inggih sampun mangga, kula tjaosaken.* I'll give you 200 rupiahs for it and that's final. –Very well, you can have it.

ijag ***-*an** *or* **(ng)*-*** to rush about helter-skelter. **ng*-*aké** to hurry smn; to try to speed sth up. *See also* JAG

ijak *var of* IJA

ijan large square tray for spreading rice and cooling it by fanning. **ng*** to spread and cool rice as above

ijat ***an** a deal, *i.e.* a hand of dealt cards. **ng/di*** to deal [cards]

ijeg in agreement. **é wong² anggoné arep milih Pak X* the single-mindedness of the people in their intention to elect Mr. X. **ijag-*** ponderous, swaying clumsily. **ng*-*** **1** to move in a ponderous *or* unwieldy manner. **2** (*psv* **di*-***) to knead, squeeze. **sa*** in agreement. *Loro²né ora sa*.* The two haven't reached an agreement. *Kabèh paḍa sa* arep nonton bioskop.* We all agreed to go to a movie. **sa*-*** heavy, cumbersome. *See also* JEG

ijem **ng/di*** to humidify [tobacco]

ijer **ng*** to blink, wink. **ng/di*aké** to blink [the eyes]

ijik ***-*** (*prn* **iji:k²**) *rpr* a baby bird's cheeping. *tjilik *-** tiny. **ng/di*-*** to make fun of. *See also* TITIK

ijo **1** hurray! **2** oh my! **3** a certain group of playing cards *(kertu tjilik).* **4** come on! (*var of* AJO)

ijok *var of* IJA

ijom *rg var of* AJOM

ijong *excl of pain or strong emotion*

ijub *var of* ÉJUB

ijuh my my!

ijung *var of* IJONG

ijuran dues. ** sesasi* monthly dues

ika *var of* KAÉ. *See also* IKI

ikajat *see* HIKAJAT

ikal ***(-*)an** spool, reel; object used as a reel. **ng/di*** to wind *or* thread sth around *or* through sth. *Benangé di* ana ing blèg.* He wound the string around a can. **ng* basa(-padu)** to twist words in order to win an argument. **ng* gada** to swing a club. **pa·ng*** act of reeling sth. *Apa wis rampung pa·ng*é?* Have you finished winding it?

iker ***-*** border decoration. **ng/di*-*** to decorate the edge (of)

iket a plaited batik head cloth which the wearer dons by winding it around his head (**ḍesṭar** *or* **uḍeng** *ki*). ***an** way of combining *or* joining. **aning ukara (gram)* sentence structure. ***-*an** (**ḍesṭar·an** *or* **uḍeng·an** *ki*) to put on *or* wear the above head cloth. **ng/di*** to tie (together). *Peṭiné di*.* He tied up the box. *ng* ukara* to construct a sentence. **ng/di*(-*)** to put a head cloth on smn. **ng*-*i ḍengkul** to practice nepotism. **pa·ng*** **1** sth which serves as a tie *or* binder. *Ali² iki minangka pang*ing katresnan.* This ring symbolizes the binding of our love. *tembung pang* (gram)* conjunction. *** wulung** blue-black head piece worn by high officials

iki *ng,* **punika** (*usu. prn* **menikâ**) *kr* this; this thing/place/time *(Degree I: Introduction, 6). buku ** this book. *dina ** today. ** apa?* What's this? *wiwit ** from now on. ** lo bukumu.* Here's your book! ** udan, ngati-ati dalané lunju.* It's raining now; careful, the road is slippery. *kaja ing ngisor ** as follows. *gambar ing nḍuwur ** the picture (which appears) above. *kowé (i)ki* you *(joking, familiar; contemptuous). sepréné ** up until now. *saiki ** at the present time. ***-*** stuff like this *(derogatory). La mangané kok *-* waé!* Not this same old stuff for dinner! **ika-*** to hem and haw. *Ḍèké ora ika-*.* He's forthright. *Kepénak banget tanduké, ora ana ika-*né.* She was perfectly poised, speaking with no awkwardness.

iklan advertisement

iklas 1 wholehearted. *Olèhku mènèhi ḍuwit iki kanṭi * (ing ati).* I give this money with all my heart. 2 able to avoid overinvolvement in response to deep emotional experiences. **ng/di*aké** to accept things without too much struggling, resign oneself to the inevitable

ikli:k to keep occupied, busy oneself

iklim climate. *** panas** the tropics. *** seḍang** temperate zone

iklu:k absorbed, engrossed

ikmat *see* HIKMAT

ikrak *var of* ÉKRAK

ikram 1 consecration. 2 special attire worn during a pilgrimage to Mecca

ikrar statement of guiding principles. *nganakaké ** to draw up a platform. **ng/di*aké** to draw up a statement of guiding principles

iksak̄ exact. *ngèlmu ** a natural (physical) science

iksamen (to take) a test/examination. *lulus ** or ** olèh* to pass a test. ** sing pungkasan* final examination. **ng/di*** to give smn a test

iksetrā(h) *var of* ÈKSETRA(H)

ikstrā(h) *var of* ÈKSTRA(H)

iksu *oj* sugar cane

iktidal to stand with hands folded across the stomach while meditating (first Islamic praying position)

iktikad determination, intention

iku *ng* that (thing, time, place) *(Degree II: Introduction, 6)* (*var of* KUWI)

ikut foreskin. **ng/di*(i)** to take; to pick up/out; to choose. *Sing abang adja di*i, kuwi duwèkku.* Don't take the red one—that's mine.

ila (*or* *-*) **1** taboo. *tembung *-** forbidden words. 2 lore handed down from generation to generation. 3 *var of* ÉLA. *-* sth used for [a designated purpose]. *Djenang karo sega golong kuwi mung kanggo *-* sadjèn.* Porridges and rice mounds are used only for ritual offerings. *kanggo *-* supaja ora watuk* as a cough preventive. **-*né wong duwé gawé kuwi kudu tarup, arepa ketemuné mantèn ora nang ngomah.* In accordance with wedding customs you must decorate your house even though the wedding ceremony is not to be held there.

iladuni occult lore. **ng*** versed in mystic lore

ilafat *var of* ILAPAT

ilag *-* charm, prayer, *etc.* to ward off evil

Ilah(i) God (*var of* ALLAH)

ilak **ng*-*** **1** spreading out broad and level. *Sawahé katon ng*-* saka kadohen.* From afar you can see the paddies extending for vast distances. 2 *intsfr* clear, light, bright. *paḍang ng*-** very bright

ilam cervical vertebra

ilang *ng,* **itjal** *kr* 1 lost; gone. *Ḍuwitku *.* My money is gone. *Anaké *.* His child got lost. ** wediné.* He wasn't afraid any longer. *Tembung mau wis mèh *.* This word is virtually obsolete. 2 null and void. *Kupon iki * jèn ora ditebus dina iki.* The ticket cannot be redeemed after today. **k*an** *(prn* **kélangan** *ng,* **kétjalan** *kr) or* **ka*an** **1** to lose (possession of) inadvertently. 2 missing. *Kerep k*an, ditjolong D.* Things were often missing: D had stolen them. **ng*** to disappear; to conceal oneself. **ng/di*aké 1** to cause sth to go away. 2 to lose sth belonging to smn else. *Bukuku disilih Paimin, djebul di*aké.* I lent my book to Paimin and he lost it. 3 to render null and void. **ng*-*aké** remiss; to act is disregard of one's obligations. *Botjah kok ng*-*aké bapakné sing dadi guru.* That boy completely disregards the fact that his father is a teacher [and hence certain standards are expected of him]. *Kowé iki ng*-*aké, saben dina dirumat meksa ora nrima.* You have no gratitude: you are cared for day after day and you simply accept it as your right. **ng/di*i** to do away with. *Apa tamba iki bisa ng*i lelaraku?* Can this medicine cure my illness? **pa·ng*an** a magic charm that makes one invisible. *** gapit·é** to have lost what makes one effective: *kaja Gaṭutkatja (or Baladéwa, or other puppet figure) * gapité* to have lost one's strength *or* effectiveness

ilapat symbol. *Jèn kowé ngimpi weruh matjan, kuwi * kowé arep kabegdjan.* If you dream of a tiger, it's an omen of good luck. **ng*** to symbolize, be an omen (of). *Angin aḍem iki ng* udan.* A cool wind foretells of rain.

ilar **ng*-*** broad, vast. **ng/di*i** to shun, avoid

ilat 1 (**liḍah** *ki*) tongue. **é mlotjot.* It burned his tongue. *tjotjog karo *é wong Amérika* suited to the American taste. *mati *é* having no sense of taste. 2 wooden peg used to regulate the flow of water in a pipe. *-* 1 a certain shrub whose leaves are used medicinally. 2 bamboo bridge.

3 sole (sea fish). ***-*(an)** 1 a variety of fig tree. 2 prong of a buckle *or* clasp. ***-*an** 1 tongue-shaped object. ** sepatu* tongue of a shoe. 2 leather shoulder holster for a kris or saber. *** baja** a plant whose meaty serrated leaves are used for grooming and blackening the hair

ilep **ng/di*aké** to put under water; to soak

ilèr a certain plant whose leaves are used in folk medicines

iler drooling saliva. **di*i** to get drooled on. **ng*** 1 to drool. 2 to drool over sth, have the mouth water (for). *Montor mau gawé ng*é wong kang weruh.* Everyone who sees the car drools over it.

iles **k*** (*prn* **kèles**) to get stepped on. **ng/di*** to step on

ilet flow (*sbst kr for* ILI)

ilham heaven-sent inspiration

ili 1 flow, current. *Mengétan *né.* It flows eastward. 2 money or item given to replace what smn lost. ***n̄** a river-irrigated rice paddy. ***n̄an** replacement of sth lost. **-* sms* 2 *above.* ***n̄-*n̄** 1 stream, flow; *fig* life blood. 2 replacement of sth lost. **k*** to get carried along on the current (*see also* KÈLI). **k*n̄** to get irrigated by flowing water. *Sawah mau kilèn banju kali kuwi.* This paddy is irrigated from the river. **m*** to flow, run. *Banjuné tebu mau m* saka gilingan.* Sugar-cane juice flowed from the mill. *m* lenga* [of fried food] swimming in grease. *Suguhané mbanju m*.* The refreshments kept coming. **ng*** to flee from approaching danger. **ng/di*k̀aké** 1 to cause sth to run/flow. *ngilèkaké banju kanggo ngelebi sawah* creating a flow of water to inundate the paddy. 2 to cause to flee. *Sadurungé kuṭa mau diobong, wong² diilèkaké ḍisik.* Before the town was burned, the people were evacuated. **ng/di*n̄i** 1 to irrigate sth. *ngilèni sawah* to irrigate a paddy. 2 to replace lost money *or* articles for smn. 3 to buy in small quantities, *usu.* fruits while still on the tree. **pa·ng*n̄** 1 act of fleeing a place. 2 place evacuated by fleeing people. *See also* KÈLI

ilik **ng/di*-*** to tickle

iling to step aside, avoid. **m*-m*** *or* **m·ilang-m*** to look this way and that. *Aku miling² suwé² weruh A.* I looked all around and finally spotted A. *Ḍèké milang-m* ndeleng kuṭa.* He went sightseeing all over the city. **ng/di*(i)** to pour sth. *Lenganė di*i ing botol geḍé tjilik.* He poured the oil into bottles of various sizes. **ng/di*-*i** to keep looking for/at. *Ḍèké seḍéla² ng*-*i penganggoné anjar.* She couldn't keep her eyes off her new clothes.

ilir large woven-bamboo fan. **m*** to drift with the current. **ng/di*aké** to allow [a boat] to drift. **ng/di*(i)** to select [a sprout] from which to raise new rice plants. **ng/di*i** to fan sth. *ng*i sega* to fan rice cool. **sa*é** along with the current. *Prauné mlaku sa*é banju.* The boat drifted with the current.

Illah God *(var of* ALLAH *in certain contexts)*

illallah 1 there is no God but Allah. 2 *excl of dismay, despair*

ilmi knowledge; science (*kr for* ILMU*?)*

ilmijah science; scientific knowledge. *karja ** scientific works

ilmu (*or* **ng***) 1 (body of) knowledge; science; a science. 2 mystic philosophical lore. *** alam** physics. *** basa** linguistics. *** ka·batin·an** theosophy. *** ka·budaja·n** anthropology. *** bumi** geography. *** Djawa** Javanese cosmographic mysticism. *** ka·dji·wa·n** psychology. *** étung·an** mathematics. *** falak** astronomy. *** fisika nuklir** nuclear physics. *** hajat** biology. *** hukum** jurisprudence. *** kéwan** zoology. *** kodrat** physics; natural science. *** pa·lintang·an** astronomy. *** pa·m̄·pisah** chemistry. *** tuwa** mystical philosophy. *** te·tuwuh·an** botany. *** wangun** geometry

ilo **ng*** 1 to look at oneself in the mirror; *fig* to introspect. 2 to devote one's attention to. 3 to set an example for others. **ora ng* giṭok·é** to have too high an opinion of oneself in relation to others; the pot calls the kettle black. **ng/di*k̂-*k̂aké** to warn smn. **pa·ng*n̂ (tingal·an** *or* **pa·n̈·tingal·an** *ki*) mirror. *ng* ing pengilon* to look at oneself in the looking-glass

ilok 1 suitable, proper, acceptable. *Adja mangan karo mlaku², ora *.* Don't eat while walking in public: it's in poor taste. *Apa *, mentas mangan mangan manèh.* It's not normal—he's just eaten and now he's eating again. 2 (*or* ***-***) sometimes, occasionally. **ora *** not ever. **ora *-*** extreme. *Ambané ora *-*.* It's enormous!

ilu 1 to accompany (*childish var of* M·ÈLU). 2 mucous, phlegm; discharge from sores. ***n̂** 1 to go along with others characteristically. *Botjah kuwi ilon.* He's always tagging along. 2 teammate. ***-*** *or* **ila-*** *or*

- **kapiluju** to tag along with others, join smn in an activity. *ñ-*ñ to tag along characteristically. *ñ-*ñen to do what others are doing. **ng*** to discharge foul matter; *cr* to talk loquaciously. **ng/di*k̂aké** (**ñ/dipun·tumut·aken** *kr,* **n/di·ḍèrèk·aké** *ka*) 1 to have smn accompany a person. *Satrija mau diḍèrèkaké abdiné.* The nobleman had his servant go with him. 2 to have smn go to live with and be supported by [a relative]. *Anaké diilokaké buliké.* She sent her son to live with his aunt. **ng/di*ñi** to go along with smn as companion or servant. *A ora gelem diiloni B.* A didn't want B's companionship. *See also* ÈLU

ima *see* HIMA

imah *var of* ÉMAH

imalajā *see* HIMALAJA

imam person who leads a prayer in Islamic ritual. **ng/di*i** to lead [prayers]

iman 1 belief, faith; to believe (in), trust. 2 integrity. 3 *inf var of* IMAM. **ng/di*aké** to believe, put one's trust in

imawan *see* HIMAWAN

imba 1 a certain plant with slim shapely leaves. 2 eyebrow(s) (*ki for* ALIS). 3 *var of* ÉMBA

imbah to launder (*root form: sbst kr for* UMBAH)

imbal 1 to repeat a musical theme. 2 wages (*sbst kr for* OPAH). ***an** repetition of a theme. **ng/di*aké** to convey a message. ***pa·ngendika** *or* ***watja·n** to have a conversation/discussion

imbang weight. ***-*an** equal; in balance with each other. **-*an kesugihané* equally prosperous. **ng/di*i** to maintain equality with. *Kowé kudu bisa ng*i kesenenganė bodjomu.* You should try to keep up with your husband's (wife's) interests. **sa*** in balance; of equal weight *or* importance. *Kekuatan negara A lan B se*.* Nations A and B are equally powerful. *See also* TIMBANG

imbar 1 a recess, a break. 2 loose, free (*sbst kr for* UMBAR)

imbet 1 to ripen fruits (*root form: sbst? kr for* IMBU). 2 supplement (*kr for* IMBUH)

imbu ***ñ** fruits (*fig:* matters) that have been set aside to develop. **ng/di*** to allow [fruits] to ripen in a warm, covered place; *fig* to keep sth concealed

imbuh *ng,* **imbet** *kr* (**tanduk** *kr? ki?*) ***-*(an)** sth in addition; a supplement; a second helping. *Aju kaṭik * sugih banḍa pisan.* She is beautiful, and rich to boot. *Pametuné kebonku kanggo *-* tuku butuh.* The proceeds from my garden supplement my pocket money. **-*ané sing Rp 1000. ora sida tak tukokaké buku.* I didn't spend that additional 1,000 rupiahs for books after all. **ng/di*i** to give sth as a supplement(ary amount). *Iki tak *i Rp 1000. kanggo tuku buku.* Here, I'll give you another thousand rupiahs to buy books.

imel ***-*an** 1 snacks; sth to nibble on. 2 (*or* **ng***) to keep nibbling

imet *rg* **sa*** a tiny bit, a very few

imigrasi immigration. *kantor ** immigration office

iming **ng/di*-*** to tantalize. **ng/di*-*i** to tantalize (with). *Bareng di*-*i nganggo suket, djaran mau mbanḍang.* When they dangled grass in front of the horse, he ran fast. *Ḍèwèké di*-*i pangkat ḍuwur.* They tempted him with an offer of high position. **pa·ng*-*** temptation to evil. *Atiné kaṭukulan pang*-* asor.* His heart was sown with the seeds of temptation.

imit **ng/di*-*** to conserve, to consume sparingly. **sa*** bit by bit, a little at a time. *Nèk mangan sa*.* He eats like a bird.

impeng *var of* IMPLENG

imper *oj* resemblance

impéralis imperialist

impéralisme imperialism

impes 1 bladder. 2 cow's bladder used for holding oil. **ng/di*aké** to reduce [a swelling]. *See also* MIMPES

impi *ng,* **su(m)pena** *kr* ***ǹ** (**su[m]pena** *kr*) a dream. ***ǹan** *ng kr* to dream constantly. ***ǹ-*ǹen** *ng kr* to keep seeing in one's dreams. **ng*** (**su[m]pena** *or* **ñj·su[m]pena** *kr*) to dream. *Aku ng* mabur.* I dreamed I was flying. **ng/di*-*** to dream of, long for. **ng/di*k̀aké** to dream of/about. *Ḍèké diimpèkaké dadi ratu.* She dreamed he was king. **pa·ng*ǹ** a dream. *See also* PRIMPI

impleng 1 person in charge of the village irrigation system. 2 (*or* ***-***) water trough *or* channel. **ng/di*** to peek. *ng* saka bolongan kuntji* to peek through a keyhole

implik *var of* IPLIK

impling leaden opium container

impor(t) an import. *barang*[2] *** imported goods. **ng/di*** to import

importir importer

imprih **imprah-*** to move back and forth

impun *see* HIMPUN

-in- *ltry: psv infix* 1 *formal var of* DI-. *t·in·imbang* compared [with]; than. *basa r·in·engga* elegant (fancy) language. *k·in·ubeng ing pager kawat* surrounded by a wire fence. *g·in·awé-gawé* false, assumed [of a misleading mannerism or aspect]. 2 *(in second member of doubled root)* to [do] successively *or* reciprocally. *tulung-t·in·ulung* to help each other. *pati·ṅ-p·in·ati·ṅan (patèn-pinatènan)* to kill each other. *Mengkono saterusé nganti turun ping pitu, wales-w·in·ales.* And so in this way one avenged the next for seven generations.

ina lowly. **ka∗n** deficient, remiss. *Jèn anakmu paḍa bubrah, kowé sing ka∗n.* If your children don't turn out well, it's you who are at fault. *Kaja² olèhku nggarap ora ka∗n.* I don't think I skimped on my work. **ng/di∗** to insult, humiliate. **pa·ng∗.** 1 an insult. 2 *gram* a contrary-to-fact condition. **∗ loka** place where social outcasts live. **∗ papa** inferior, lowly

inah time allotment. *Kula njuwun ∗ wontena saking sewulan.* I asked for at least a month's time. **ng/di∗aké** to allow smn [a certain time]. **ng/di∗i** to allow [a time period]

inak *inf var of* ÉNAK

inalilah(i), inalailah(i) (*or* **∗ wa ∗ rodjiun**) from God, back to God *(excl uttered upon hearing of a death)*

inḍak rise, increase (*kr for* UNḌAK)

inḍekos to take room and board. **∗an** 1 room and board. 2 boarding house. **ng/di∗aké** to board smn; to have smn board. **ng/di∗i** to board smw. *Omahku di∗i botjah loro.* There are two boys taking room and board at our house.

inḍèks index

indel **ng/di∗** to boil sth. *Santené di∗ nganti dadi lenga.* The coconut milk was boiled down to oil. **ng/di∗aké** to give smn free rein

inḍèn to order and pay a deposit on [a piece of merchandise]

indeng, inḍeng **sa∗ing** all over, everywhere in. *sa∗ing pulo² Indonesia* throughout Indonesia

inḍet *var of* ENḌET

inḍik **m∗-m∗** to sneak toward sth in order to seize it. **ng/di∗** to sneak up on. *Matjané ng∗ weḍus mau.* The tiger inched toward the sheep. **ng/di∗-∗i** to eye covetously

inḍil **∗-∗** not fully grown

inḍing cloth used as a sanitary napkin

inḍit **k∗** (*prn* **kènḍit**) to get carried along. **ng/di∗** to carry at the waist or hip. *ng∗ klenṭing* to carry a water jug (encircled by one arm) on the hip

indjak *var of* IDAK

indjen **∗an** peep hole. **∗en** (to have/get) a swelling on the head. **∗-∗** *or* **indjan-∗** to keep peeking. **ng/di∗** to peek/peer (at). *Ng∗ saka djenḍéla.* She peeked out the window. *nDjupuk semprong dienggo ng∗ gebjas mau.* He took a magnifying glass and peered at the flask.

indjih *Jogja var of* INGGIH

Indjil Christian Bible

indjoh *var of* INDJUH

indjuh capable; can; be able

inḍo a Eurasian of mixed Indonesian and European (*usu.* Dutch) blood

inḍoktrinasi indoctrination. **ng/di∗** to indoctrinate

Inḍonési(j)ā pertaining to Indonesia. *Républik ∗* The Republic of Indonesia. *wong ∗* an Indonesian. *basa ∗* Indonesian language. *negara ∗* Indonesia. *∗ Raya* Great Indonesia (name of the national anthem)

indra *see* JAKTI

indrak thrush (gum disease). **∗en** to have/get thrush

indrija 1 the senses. *pantja ∗* the five senses. 2 *oj* heart. 3 *oj* wish, desire

indu *oj* moon

Inḍu *var of* HINḌU

inḍuk *see* KAPAL

inḍul **∗-∗** 1 chubby. 2 *rpr* the motions of a plump person walking

indung *oj* mother

inḍung people who reside in a village but lack the rights of ownership because they are not members of the communal group (according to customary law). **ng∗** 1 to occupy (without owning) a house one has erected—by permission—on smn's property. 2 *var of* NG·ÉNḌANG, NG·ÉNḌONG. **ng∗ tèmpèl** to live in smn else's house, or on another's land in a house one has built there, but lack the rights of ownership. **ng∗ tjangkok** to live on smn's property and have the rights of ownership. **pa·ng∗** one who lives in another's home *or* on another's property. **∗ ganḍok** an inhabitant who has rights of ownership. **∗ tlosor** one who lives in another's home

indupati *oj* moon
ineb ***-*an** window shutters. **k*an** shut in *or* out. *Wah kodjur, k*an lawang aku!* Oh dear, I'm locked out (in)! **m*** closed; to get closed. *Lawangé m*.* The door (is) closed. **ng/di*(aké)** to close. *See also* NEB
inep **k*an** to have a house guest. *Aku wingi k*an kantja.* A friend of mine spent the night last night. **ng*** (**[ñj]·sipeng** *kr,* **lereb** *or* **ñj·saré** *ki*) to stay smw overnight (or longer). *Rong dina ng* ana Sala.* He spent two days in Solo. **pa·ng*an** overnight lodging place
infèksi infection; infected
inflasi (to have) inflation. *Rega² saiki angèl penjandeté amarga lagi *.* Prices are hard to control now—we're in a period of inflation.
ing[a] 1 in, at, on, to. *omah² ing désa* the houses in the village. ** mburi omah* behind the house. *ukara * ḍuwur* the above sentence. *ratu * Mandura* the king of Mandura. *tiba ana * lemah* to fall to the ground. *kesenengané * bab seni* his interest in art. ** ngendi waé* everywhere. *ana * pinggir segara* at the seashore. ** sawidjining dina* one day, *i.e.* on a certain day. ** taun 2001* in the year 2001. ** saiki* at present. ** tembé* later on, in the future. ** sadurungé perang* before the war. ** antarané djam wolu lan djam sanga ésuk* between 8 and 9 A.M. 2 by [smn/sth, as agent of psv verb]. *dibégal * baja* attacked by crocodiles. *digugat * wong sadésa* accused by all the villagers
ing-[b] *ltry* *psv prefix: var of* -IN-. *ing·aran* called, named
-ing[c] (**-ning** *after vowel*) of. *katresna·ning bijung* a mother's love. *keḍèp·ing mripat* the wink of an eye. *lara·ning anaké wédok* his daughter's illness. *putjuk·ing buntut* the tip of its tail. *swara·ning tangisé* the sound of her weeping. *molah-malih·ing kahanan* changing conditions. *ing satengah·ing segara* at sea; in the middle of the ocean. *ana sangisor·ing wit* underneath the tree. *ing sawidji·ning dina* on a certain day
ingah (to keep) domestic animals (*root form: kr for* INGU)
ingak *sbst kr for* UNGAK
ingaluhur a high official
ingas a certain tree with poisonous sap
ingel **k*** (*prn* **kèngel**) sprained neck. **ng/di*-*** 1 to massage the neck at the base of the skull to relieve headache. 2 to tease
inger **k*** (*prn* **kènger**) 1 to get turned to one side inadvertently. 2 (to have/get) a sprained neck resulting from an injury. **m*** to turn, be turned (in a certain direction). *M* maḍep ngidul.* It's turned facing south. *or* He turned south. *ninggal m* sedéla* to leave smn/sth just for a moment. **m*-m*** *or* **m·ingar-m*** 1 to turn this way and that. *Jèn didjungkati adja mingar-m*.* Don't keep turning your head while I'm combing your hair. *Aku m*² ora bisa turu.* I kept tossing and turning—couldn't get to sleep. 2 to talk evasively *or* off the subject. **ng/di*-*** *or* **ng/di·ingar-*** to keep turning sth. *Séndénanipun kénging dipun ingar-* manut sasenengipun ingkang numpak.* The back rest can be adjusted to any position the passenger likes. **ng/di*aké** to turn sth in a different direction (for smn). *Lemariné di*aké mréné.* Turn the cupboard in this direction. *Rembugé di*aké.* He changed the subject. **ng/di*(i)** to turn, change the direction of. **ng/di*i** to renounce. *Anaké ḍéwé kok di*i.* He turned his back on his own son! *See also* UBENG, M·UBENG
inget *var of* ÈNGET. ***-*an** to watch *or* stare at each other. **ng/di*aké** *or* **ng/di*i** to watch fixedly, stare at
ingga *var of* ÉNGGA
inggah rise (*kr for* UNGGAH)
inggar *var of* ÉNGGAR
inggat **m*** (**lolos** *ki?*) to run away, leave with no intention of returning. **ng/di*aké** to abscond with. *Baturku ng*aké pitku.* Our servant ran off with my bicycle. **ng/di*i** to avoid. *Kanggo ng*i padu aku meneng.* In order to avoid an argument, I didn't say anything.
inggih yes, all right; also, too (*kr for* IJA). *Nuwun *.* Yes (, your Majesty). *** ora ke·panggih** *ng kr* to give empty promises. *** punika** that is (*kr for* JAIKU)
inggil high; tall (*kr for* ḌUWUR)
inggit *var of* IGIT
inggita behavior, conduct
Inggris 1 pertaining to England. *wong ** Englishman. *negara ** England. 2 (*or* **basa ***) English language
inggu a certain plant whose disagreeable-smelling sap is used for cough medicines
ingi *inf var of* WINGI
ingih ***-*** disconcerted, caught unawares. **ingah-*** incongruous. *Lumrahé wong ndésa kétok ingah-* jèn pisanan weruh kuṭa*

gedé. Country people usually look out of place when they first go to the city.

ingip **m*-m*** to stick out a little at the tip *or* head. *Djangkriké m*²terus mlebu lèng manèh.* The cricket barely stuck its head out and then went back in the hole. **ng/di*(-*)aké** to show the tip of. *Barang mau di*-*aké marang anaké.* He showed his child the very tip of it. **ng/di*(-*)i** to show the tip of sth to. *Anaké di*-*i barang mau.* He showed his child the very tip of it.

ingkang (one) who, (that) which (*kr for* KANG, SING). *** abdi** I, me (*when addressing royalty*). *** sinuhun** your/his Majesty (*applied to monarchs of Jogjakarta, Surakarta*)

ingkar **m*** to evade, sidestep. **ng/di*i** to repudiate. *Adja ng*i djandji.* Don't go back on a promise. *Ḍèwèké ng*i apa sing tak kanḍakaké.* He refused to accept the advice I offered. *See also* MINGKUR

ingked *var of* INGSED

ingkel **ng/di*-*** to tease, pester

ingkem **m*** to close one's mouth; *fig* to finish speaking *or* refrain from speaking. *A mung m* waé.* A didn't say anything. *Lagi waé m* olèhé omong, kok teka.* She had no sooner finished speaking when in he walked. **ng/di*aké** to close [the mouth]; to refrain from commenting (on)

ingklig **ingklag-*** to move back and forth, keep coming and going. **ng*** to walk steadily forward without heed for one's surroundings

ingklik blossom of the cassava plant. **ng*** resembling this blossom

ingkling *rg var of* ANGKLÈK

ingko *var of* ÉNGKO

ingkrang **ng/di*aké** to elevate [the feet]. *Sikilé di*aké.* He put his feet up (on the table, a footstool, *etc.*).

ingkug ***-*** to waddle. *Saking lemuné jèn mlaku *-*.* She's so fat she waddles when she walks.

ingkul to [do] fast. *Galo, olèhé mlaju *.* Look how fast he's running! *Jèn kon turu *.* When you tell him to go to sleep, he drops right off.

ingkung chicken cooked whole. **ng/di*** to cook a chicken whole

ingkup **m*** closed up, folded. **ng/di*aké** to close by folding. *ng*aké pajung* to close an umbrella. *Djaja ng*aké gaganging katjatingal.* Djaja folded his glasses.

ingkus **m*** drawn in(ward); [of the chest] sunken. **ng/di*aké** to make narrower, draw in. *Pajungé di*aké.* He closed his umbrella part way.

inglar **ng/di*i** 1 to deny, disavow. 2 to avoid sth

inglep *var of* INGSLEP

ingnang *ltry* I, me; my

ingong *var of* INGNANG

ingrat the world. *kaloka ** known the world over

ingsed ***an** act of moving/shifting. *Sri ng*aké lingguhé sawetara *an.* Sri changed seats several times. **m*** to move, shift position. *Ḍèké nékad, ora m*² saka ing omahpekaranganè.* He stubbornly refused to budge from his property. **m·ingsad-m*** to keep moving/shifting. **ng/di*aké** to move *or* shift sth

ingseg **m*-m*** *or* **ng*-*** to sob, cry uncontrollably

ingsep *var of* INGSLEP

ingser **k*** (*prn* **kèngser**) (*see also* KÈNGSER) 1 to have been moved/shifted. *Médjané kèngser siṭik seka panggonané.* The table is a little out of position. 2 [of joints] sprained. **m*** to move, change one's position. **m·ingsar-m*** to move this way and that. *Omongé mingsar-m*.* First he says one thing then another. **ng/di*** to move, shift the position of. **ng/di*aké** to have sth moved; to have smn move sth

ingslep **m*** to enter, slip into. *Bareng wis ambegan aku m* manèh.* I took a breath and dove under again. *Srengéngéné arep m*.* The sun is about to set. **ng/di*aké** to slip sth smw. *Suraté di*aké ing ngisor lawang.* He slipped the letter under the door.

ingsun *ltry* 1 I, me *(used by monarchs).* 1 (**ningsun** *after vowel*) my. *awak ** my body; I. *ati ningsun* my heart

ingu *ng,* **ingah** *kr* ***n̂(-*n̂)** 1 (**ke·langen·an** *ki?*) domestic animal; pet. 2 meal served to neighbors who help one out. **ng/di*** 1 to keep [a domestic animal]. *ng* iwèn* to raise poultry. 2 to groom. *ng* kuku* to do one's nails. **ng* djénggot** to grow a beard. **ng/di*k̂aké** 1 to have smn keep an animal for one; to look after smn's pet. 2 to serve a meal to neighbors who are lending a hand. *Sing diingokaké apa?* What are you serving to the neighbors? **ng/di*n̂i** to serve meals to. *Jèn monḍok ana kana diingoni pira?* How many meals [a day] do you get where you board? **pa·ng*n̂(an) (pa·ng·ingah·an** *kr*) place where domestic animals are kept

inguk ***-*** *or* **ingak-*** to look around, pop up and down to see. **m*-m*** *or* **m·ingak-m*** to look around , to look from side to side. **ng/di*** to look at/toward. *Liwat rèstoran mau ng* ndjero.* As he passed the restaurant, he glanced inside.

ingwang *oj* I, me

ini *see* ANA-INI

inis refreshing, cool, pleasant

inja wet nurse. **pagawéané njusoni.* A wet nurse's job is to nurse babies. **ng/di*ni** to suckle [babies, as a wet nurse]

injak *var of* IDAK

injong *rg* I, me

innalilah(i), innalailah(i) *var sp of* INALILAH(I)

insaf *var of* INSAP

insan *** kamil** soul, spirit

insap 1 aware (of); to realize. 2 to become reformed after acknowledging one's mistaken ways

insiḍèn (a provoking) incident

insinje badge

insinjur (*abbr:* **Ir.**) (civil) engineer

insja(a)llah with/by God's will

insjaf *var of* INSAP

inspèksi 1 inspection. *Bapak tindak *.* Father has gone on a tour of inspection. 2 administrative unit headed by an inspector

inspèktur inspector (police or civilian)

instansi agency, service, office

instruktur (military) instruction

instrumentaliā instrumental (gamelan) music

inṭa *var of* ÉNṬA

intar *oj* metaphor(ic). *See also* ÉNTAR

inṭar (*or* **ng***) (to run) fast

inten (séla *kr?*) diamond; precious jewel. *** barléjan** diamond

intènsip intensive. **ng/di*(aké)** to intensify

inter inter-, among. *pamèr *-djawatan* an inter-service exhibition. **ng/di*i** to whirl [rice grains] on a bamboo tray to separate out the unhulled grains; *fig* to whirl briskly. *Polahé kaja gabah di*i.* They're acting frenzied. *Bisé kok pidjer ménggak-ménggok ngono, kaja di*i.* The bus twisted and turned every which way.

interlokal long-distance telephone (call). **ng/di*aké** to place a long-distance call for smn. **ng/di*(i)** to call long distance

internat dormitory

internir 1 person who is interned. 2 place where *e.g.* enemy aliens are interned. **ng/di*** to intern

interpiu interview

inti essence. **ning rembug* the core of the discussion. **-sarining tjrita* the essence of the story

inṭik **inṭak-*** to keep coming and going, to move back and forth constantly

inṭil 1 sheep/goat dung. 2 steamed cassava-flour-and-brown-sugar dish served with shredded coconut. **ng*** [of sheep, goats] to drop dung

intip scorched rice at the bottom of the pan. **m*-m*** to be in sight just at the top. *Sirahé kétok m*²*. Only the top of his head showed. **ng*** 1 forming a scorched layer of rice at the bottom of the pan. 2 (*psv* **di***) to peek (at). ***ing nraka** the wickedest souls of all

intir **m*(-m*)** low, flickering; on and off. *Digangsa mawa geni kang m*² waé.* Fry it over a very low fire. *lara pilek sing lumintu m** (to have) colds one right after the other. **ng*-*** 1 *intsfr* hungry. *luwé ng*-** famished. 2 (*psv* **di*-***) to hand sth out little by little. **ng/di*(-*)aké** 1 to lower [a cooking fire]. 2 to give [things] out in small amounts

intjak *var of* IDAK

intjat to make one's escape (*sbst kr for* ONTJAT)

intjeng ***-*** to keep peeking. **ng/di*(aké)** 1 to take a look/peek (at). *ng* samburiné témbok* to peek out from behind a wall. 2 to aim, direct. *ng*aké beḍil* to aim a gun

intjer watch wheel. ***an** target. *Sakku tansah dadi *ané tukang tjopèt.* Pickpockets are always going for my pockets. **ng/di*** to go after, try for. *Sing ringkih tansah di* déning péhak² kang mbanḍa.* The weak are always exploited by the wealthy. *Ḍompèté di* tjopèt.* There was a pickpocket after his wallet. **ng/di*aké** to take aim with. *Beḍilé di*aké.* He aimed the gun. **pa·ng*** act of trying for *or* aiming at sth. *Pang*é kentjeng temenan.* He steadied his aim.

intji inch

intjih ***-*an** to covet each other's possessions. **ng/di*i** to want, go after, try to get

intjim ***-*an** to threaten each other. **ng/di*-*** to threaten, intimidate

intjip *var of* ITJIP

intjon *var of* ÉNTJON

intjrit **ng/di*-*** to give out in small amounts.

Njauri utang baé di-*.* He repaid the loan little by little. *A ng*-* olèhé nganggo banjuné supaja awèt.* A uses the water sparingly so as to conserve it.

intjup **ng/di*** to catch [a flying creature] between thumb and forefinger. *Kupuné tak *.* I caught the butterfly.

inum ***(-*)an** intoxicating drink. **m*** to drink, *esp.* liquor. *Wong Amérika iku sing akèh² pada m*.* Most Americans drink. **m*an** intoxicating drink. *minuman keras* hard liquor. **ng/dipun*** to drink (*sbst kr for* NG/DI-OMBÉ). **ng/di*i** to offer/give a drink to

ipah 1 grated coconut mixed into coconut sap during coconut-sugar processing. 2 earnings (*sbst kr for* OPAH)

ipak *ltry* **ng*-*** to move in rolling wave-like motions

ipat ***-*** curse, malediction. **ng/di*-*i** to forbid smn to do sth on pain of invoking a dreadful curse

ipé in-law of the same generation. *kakang ** older-brother-in-law. *mbakju ** older-sister-in-law. *adi ** younger-sibling-in-law. *See also* PRIPÉ

ipel ***-*** short and fat

ipeng *var of* IMPLENG

ipet *var of* IPIT

ipi *var of* IMPI

ipik **ng/di*-*** stingy with [one's possessions]. *Duwité di*-*.* He likes to hang onto his money.

ipil ***-*** to gather bit by bit. *Aku arep *-* golèk kaju menjang alas.* I'm going to the forest to collect firewood. **sa*** a tiny bit

ipit **sa*** a very small amount. **sa*-*a** [not] any at all. *Ora nduwèni rasa seneng sak ipit²a.* He didn't derive the smallest pleasure from it.

iplik (*or* ***-*** *or* **ng***) (to walk, run) with quick short steps

ipret *var of* IPET

iprik ***-*** to gather firewood

ipuk ***an** place where sth is sown. ***-*** dealer in second-hand articles; junk man. **ng/di*** to urge; to persuade. **ng/di*(-*)** 1 to sow; to cultivate. *ng*-* kagunan batik* to cultivate the art of batik-making. 2 to gather, collect. **pa·ng*** place where sth is sown

-ipun (**-nipun** *after vowel*) *suffix: kr for* -É[c]

ir *see* HIR

Ir. *see* INSINJUR

ira[a] **ng*-*** to estimate, guess. **pa·ng*-*** opinion; guess. *See also* KIRA

-ira[b] (**-nira** *after vowel*) *oj* the; his, her (*ltry var of* -É[c])

iradat *var of* WIRADAT

irah ***-*an** 1 theme, basic idea. 2 clarification, analysis. 3 *wj* a certain type of male dancer's headdress. **ng/di*-*i** to take as a theme. *tjrita tjekak sing di*-*i sedjarah* a short story based on history

irâmâ 1 rhythm. 2 regulation of the volume of instrumental music or singing. 3 speech levels (*see also* UNGGUH: UNGGAH-*ING BASA). **ng/di*(ni)** to create rhythm (in), give a rhythm (to); to be in rhythm (with)

iras two things combined into one. **ng/di*** 1 to combine two things. *Kula namung sowan, ng* wonten perlunipun sekedik.* I wanted to see you, and I have a message for you too. *Tjandi punika témbokipun ng* pajon.* The walls of this temple also function as a roof. *Ana sing djaga ng* tukang nglakokaké.* There's a watchman who doubles as a machine operator. 2 to eat from the utensil the food was cooked in *or* at the place where the food was bought. *Aku tuku panganan terus tak * ana warung.* I bought a snack and ate it right there at the shop. *Adja sok ng* saka pantji, ora ilok!* Don't eat out of the pan—it's not the right way to do it. *See also* IRUS

irat ***(-*)an** split piece. **-*an pring* bamboo strips. **ng/di*(i)** to split into thin strips

irèh *var of* IRIH

-iréka, -irèki, -irèku (**-niréka** *etc. after vowel*) *oj* the; his, her (*ltry var of* -É[c])

ireng *ng,* **tjemeng** *kr* 1 black. 2 dark in color. *Pakulitané *.* Her skin is dark. *Lataré *.* It has a dark background color. ***an** 1 land which has not been planted since the last harvest; fallow land. 2 village-owned land. 3 indigo dye; batik that has been dyed indigo. 4 *slang* opium. ***-*** sth black/dark. *Ana ireng² mènèk ing uwit.* There was a black figure climbing the tree. **ng/di*(aké)** *or* **ng/di*i** to blacken; to make dark(er). *** n·djanges** *or* *** (ng)·gantjleng** intensely black. *** manis** dark-skinned and pretty. *** tjemani** *or* *** tunteng** intensely black

iri envious, jealous. ***n̂** 1 to argue about who will do what. *Supaja ora pada irèn, dilotré.* So that nobody would think smn else got an easier task, they drew lots. 2

envious by nature. *ṅ-*ṅan to envy *or* be jealous of each other. *See also* IRIHATI

irib appearance, form. **m**∗ to have the appearance of. **ng/di**∗**(i)** to resemble. **sa**∗ 1 having the same appearance. *Ora paḍa pleg, mung sa∗.* They're not the same, they just look alike. 2 appropriate [to], harmonizing [with]. *See also* ANGON

irid economical, frugal. *Motor iki bènsiné ∗ banget.* This car doesn't use much gas. *kasenengan kang ∗* an inexpensive hobby. *∗an thrifty by nature. *∗-∗an to go one after another. *Wong sepirang-pirang paḍa mlaku ∗-∗an menjang alun².* Large numbers of people thronged to the town square. **k**∗ *(prn* **kèrid)** to get taken to/along inadvertently. **ng/di** 1 to save, economize. *Aku lunga mawa sepéḍa baé supaja ng∗ ragad sawetara.* I went by bicycle to save money. *ng∗ wektu nem sasi* to save six months' time. 2 to escort, accompany, lead. **ng/di**∗-∗ to use as sparingly as possible. *Wis di∗-∗ berasé nanging meksa ora tjukup kanggo urip sesasi.* No matter how carefully I used the rice, it still didn't last all month. **pa·ng∗an** the practice of using sth sparingly

irig large bamboo sieve for sifting sand *or* catching fish. **ng/di**∗ to sift sand *or* catch fish with the above

irigasi irrigation

irih *∗-∗ slowly, cautiously. **ng/di**∗**(i)** 1 to clean sth. 2 to divert the flow of [a watercourse]

irihati envious, jealous. *See also* IRI

irik *∗-∗ intsfr* short, low. *tjenḍi:k ∗-∗* extremely short. **ng/di**∗-∗**i** to have a covetous eye on sth

irim *∗-∗ a certain plant

iring 1 side, flank. 2 fallow land; soil that has not been planted since the last harvest. 3 land measure: ¼ *bau* = not quite half an acre. *∗an side, flank. *ing ∗an omah* beside the house. *saka ng∗an* from the side. *∗-∗(an) side by side. **k**∗ *(prn* **kéring)** accompanied, escorted, flanked. **ng/di**∗ **(n/di·ḍèrèk** *ka)* to escort, accompany. **ng/di**∗**aké** 1 **(n/di·ḍèrèk·aké** *ka)* to escort, accompany. *di∗aké déning kapal* escorted by a ship. *di∗aké asuné* accompanied by his dog. 2 to slant *or* slope sth. *Médjané di∗aké.* He tipped up the table. **ng/di**∗**i** 1 to place sth next to. 2 to accompany. *di∗i obahé tangan* accompanied by an arm

movement. **pa·ng**∗ person *or* thing which accompanies/escorts/leads. *pang∗ djisimé* one who accompanies a body to the grave. *kidung pang∗ kang asung pambagya* a song accompanying a welcoming ceremony. *See also* PIRING[b]

iris *(or* ∗an) slice, cut piece. *∗an téla* a cassava slice. **k**∗ to cut accidentally; to get cut. *Dridjiku k∗.* I cut my finger. *Pekaranganku bakal k∗ sebab arep ketradjang dalan.* My land is to be cut through by a road. **ng/di**∗-∗ *or* **ng/di**∗**(i)** to cut up. *Lomboké di∗-∗.* She diced the peppers. *Ṛedaktur mau ng∗i karjané pengarang.* The editor cut the author's article. *swara sesambaté kang ng∗ ati* the sounds of heart-tearing grief. **pa·ng**∗ act of cutting

irsâjâ *oj* envy; envious

iruh *var of* WERUH

irung *ng kr,* **grânâ** *ki* nose. *∗ mbangir* small pointed (*i.e.* beautifully shaped) nose. *∗ pèsèk* flat nose. *putjuking ∗* the tip of the nose. *bolongan ∗ or* lèng(-lèngan) ∗ nostril. *angger ∗ or* saben ∗ everybody. *Ana ing ngarepé ∗mu.* It's right in front of your nose! *ngambu tanpa ∗* to sense sth. *∗an* pipe linking a blacksmith's bellows to a firebox. *∗-∗an ng kr* nose-shaped latch on a folding door. **ng/di**∗-∗**aké** *or* **ng/di**∗-∗**i** to equip [a folding door] with such a latch

irup **k**∗ *(prn* **kérup)** to get carried off *or* seized. **ng/di**∗**(i)** 1 to take up, draw in. *ng∗ banjuning segara* to suck up sea water. 2 to rabble-rouse

irus vegetable or soup ladle of coconut shell or wood. **ng·iras-ng**∗ to combine two things into one. *Aku arep tuku buku ngiras-ng∗ blandja.* I'm going to buy a book and do my shopping on the same trip. *See also* IRAS

is *jeering exclamation*

isa 1 fifth and final daily ritual meditation in Islam; the time (7:30 P.M.) at which this meditation is performed. 2 *inf var of* BISA. **ng**∗ to perform the fifth daily praying. *See also* SALAT

isab **ng/di**∗-∗**aké** *or* **ng/di**∗-∗**i** embarrassing; to embarrass

isah 1 *var of* ASAH. 2 *inf var of* SISAH 1

isan *var of* SISA·N

isarah *var of* ISARAT

isarat signal, sign

isbat parable. **ng/di**∗**aké** to illustrate with a parable

isèh, isèk *var of* ISIH
isel fleshy, plump
iseng *-* to kill time
isep **ng/di*** **1** to suck (at). 2 to smoke. 3 to absorb; *fig* to learn sth by hearing it from others rather than by studying it out for oneself. *dluwang kanggo ng** blotting paper
isi 1 insides, contents. **né apa?* What's in it? *Apa ana *né?* Is there anything in it? *ḍaftar ** table of contents. *Tjèlènganku wis akèh *né.* My piggy bank has a lot of money in it. ** beḍil iki tjilik.* This gun takes small-caliber bullets. **ning lakoné filem mau* the plot content of the film. 2 full (of), filled (with). *tjangkir * wédang* a cup of tea. *Banjuné ngombé mau * pirang² rereged werna².* The drinking water is teeming with dirt particles. *Beḍil iki *.* This gun is loaded. 3 filled with sth of special quality. *Wong kuwi senadjan tjilik ning *.* He may be small, but he's got brains. *Awaké *.* She's well built. *Keris kuwi ana *né.* That kris is bewitched. ***ǹ(-*ǹ)** the contents. *Isèn èmbèr iku buwaken.* Throw out what's in the bucket. *Médja kursi sing digawé ḍéwé kanggo isèn² omahé.* The house is furnished with tables and chair he made himself. **k(a)*ǹan** to get filled; to get sth put in it. *Blègé kaisénan banju saka kalèn.* The can got ditch water in it. *kisènan krenteging ati* filled with emotion. **ng/di*** *rg var of* NG/DI*ǸI *below.* **ng/di*k̀aké** 1 to put sth into. *Lengané diisèkaké ing lampu.* He filled the lamp with oil. 2 to fill sth in (out). *Tjoba iki isèkna ana ing poswissel.* Enter this on the money order. **ng/di*ǹi** to fill; to put sth into. *Èmbèré isènana banju.* Fill the bucket with water. *Kapuké dienggo ngisèni bantal.* Kapok is used for stuffing pillows. *Jèn baṭikan mau wis rampung olèhé nerusi, bandjur diisèn-isèni.* After applying the outlines to the batik, fill them in. **pa·ng*ǹ(-*ǹ)** that which is used as a filler. *Rebab, tjlempung, lan suling mung kanggo pengisèn-isèn waé.* The music of the strings, zither, and flute is used to fill out the ensemble. **sa*(né)** (together with) the contents. *omahé sa*né* the house and everything in it
isih *ng,* **taksih** *kr* 1 still, (even) now; remaining [in a certain condition]. *Gulané ana loḍong * ana separo.* There's half a jar of sugar. *Embuh wis mati, embuh * urip.* I don't know if he's dead or alive. *Ḍèké * enom.* He's (still) young. *Wohé * mentah.* The fruit is still green. *A * meneng waé.* A said nothing (through it all). *Apa kowé * kélingan tjritané bijèn?* Do you remember that story I told you? *Ḍèké * seḍulurku.* He's related to me. 2 to be *or* keep on [do]ing. *Ḍèké * matja buku.* He's reading a book. *Kilat ṭaṭit * ptg tjlorot.* Lightning keeps flashing. **ng/di*aké** to keep sth in effect. *ng*aké tontonané* to let the show continue. *ng*aké nginep* to keep staying overnight (night after night). *ng*aké pangané* to have leftovers. *ng*aké gawéjané nganti pènsiun* to keep working until retirement. *** wuda** very young [of village children]
isik *var of* ISIH. **k*** to get rubbed/stroked. **ng/di*-*** *or* **ng/di·isak-*** to treat lovingly. *Bonékahé bandjur di*-*.* She caressed her doll. *Klambiné tansah diisak-*.* He treats his shirts with loving care.
isim a written Arabic phrase used for warding off danger or illness
isin (**lingsem** *opt? kr, ki?*) shy, embarrassed, ashamed. *A * digeguju kantjané.* A was embarrassed (ashamed) when his friends laughed at him. ***an** shy by nature. **isan-*** acutely embarrassed *or* self-conscious. *Adja ndadak isan-* barang.* Relax and make yourself at home! **k*an** overcome with embarrassment. *Aku k*an nalika weruh jèn mung nganggo pijama.* I was mortified to realize I was only wearing pajamas. **ng/di*-*** to make fun of, humiliate. **ng/di*-*aké** to subject smn to embarrassment. **ng*-*i** embarrassing, humiliating. *** ora isi** timidity doesn't get you anywhere
ising *-*en (to have) diarrhea. **ng*** (**be·bu·tjal** *or* **wawrat·an** *kr,* **bobot·an** *ki*) to urinate, defecate; to go to the bathroom, wash up. *lara ng* getih-umbel* dysentery. **ng/di*aké** to relieve oneself of [excrement]. **ng/di*i** to get excrement on. *Bajiné ng*i kasur.* The baby wet the mattress. *See also* KEPÉSING
isis refreshing, cool, breezy. **k*an** (*prn* **k*an** *or* **késisan**) 1 to get blown on by breezes. *Klambiné ditokké bèn k*an supaja garing.* He put his shirt out in the breeze to dry. 2 *ltry* bestrewn. *Langit késisan méga.* Clouds dotted the sky. *késisan wadya* strewn with warriors' bodies. **ng*** 1 to go out for some fresh air. 2 [of ghosts *etc.*] to appear; to become visible. **ng/di*(i)** to expose sth to

the breezes. *ng*i klambi* to hang clothing out to air

Islam Islam, the Moslem religion (*acronym for Isa, Subuh, Luhur, Asar, Mahrib: see* SALAT). ***an** circumcision ceremony. **ng/di*aké** 1 to convert smn to Islam. 2 (*or* **ng/di*i**) to circumcise

Islamisme Islam, the Islamic religion

ismu *var of* ÈSMU

iso (*or* * **banḍang**) sinuous portion of animal intestine (used as food)

isoh *rg var of* WISUH

isor *ng,* **anḍap** *kr* **ng*** under, below, at the bottom. *ana ng* wit* under a tree. *nang ng** at the bottom; on the floor. *dalan ng* kaé* that road 'way down there. *kaja (ing) ng* iki* as follows. *Ng*é wit mau kanggo padusan.* The place under the tree is for bathing. **ng* n·ḍuwur** above and below, top and bottom; everywhere, on all sides. **ng*an** a subordinate. *para insinjur punggawa ng*ané* the engineers under his supervision. **sa·ng*é** under, below. *Welut metu saka sa'ng*ing watu.* An eel came out from under a rock. *ana ing sa'ng*é uwit geḍé* under a large tree. *See also* PANGISOR

isṭa *oj* appearance, aspect. **ng/di*** to resemble

Istanā * **Merdékā** Presidential Palace (in Djakarta). * **Negara** State Palace

istidjab 1 effective, efficacious. 2 [of a wish, prayer] granted

istidjrat idol, image

istidrat *var of* ISTIDJRAT

istijar (to exert) effort. *Bisané mung * sabisané.* We can only do our best. **ng/di*aké** to (do one's best to) obtain. *Tamba mau wis di*aké.* He did everything he could to get the medicine. **ng/di*i** to exert great effort to obtain sth

istika *see* SALAT

istilah term; terminology

istiméwa out of the ordinary. *patrap * extraordinary behavior. sidang * parlemèn* a special session of parliament

istingangkah *var of* ISTINGARAH

istingarah without doubt, to be sure

istipar prayer asking for forgiveness

istri *rg var of* ÈSTRI

isu issue, matter of controversy. **ng/di*k̂aké** to make an issue of

isuh *var of* WISUH

isuk *var of* ÉSUK

isun *inf var of* INGSUN

ita *see* BAJA[a], GARA

itang *var of* ÉTANG

iṭar *var of* INṬAR

item *see* WATU

iṭem very black (*intensified form of* IRENG)

iṭeng, iṭes *var of* IṬEM

iṭi **ng/di*-*** to take scrupulous care of

itik 1 tame(d). 2 in the habit (of). *Wis * jèn arep turu kudu ngombé ḍisik.* He always has to have a drink of water before he goes to bed. 3 hair louse (*ki for* TUMA). ***an** *or* ***-*** buttonhole. **ng/di*-*** to bring up [a child]; to raise [an animal] as a pet. **ng/di*-*i** to make buttonholes in [a garment]

iṭik a little bit (*inf var of* ṬIṬIK). **iṭak-*** to keep coming and going. **ng/di*-*** to tickle

itikad *var of* IKTIKAD

itil *ng,* **klentit** *kr,* **prânâ** *ki* clitoris

iṭing **ng/di*** to take good care of

itip **ng/di*** to peep (at)

iṭir ***an** to trickle in a thin stream. **iṭar-*** 1 to [do] little by little rather than all at once. *Jèn kongkonan tetuku adja iṭar-*.* When you send smn on errands, don't let them do just one errand each trip. 2 to trickle. *Kerané kulah isih iṭar-*.* The bathroom faucet is dripping (in a stream). **ng*** to trickle out. *See also* ṬIR

itja *oj* pleasing to the senses (*see also* ÉTJA)

itjak *var of* IDAK. **k*an** (*prn* **kétjakan**) *var of* K·IDAK·AN)

itjal lost; gone; null and void (*kr for* ILANG)

itjer **ng/di*** to go after, try for (*var of* NG/DI·INTJER)

itjik **itjak-*** to play around in the water. **ng/di*-*** to make [coins] jingle. * **iwir** grocery money

itjip ***-*** to taste, sample (*esp.* while cooking food, to test the seasonings). ***-*an** (**keḍap·an** *ki*) a taste, a sample. **ng/di*i** 1 (**n̈g/di·keḍap·i** *ki*) to taste, sample [food]. 2 to test, try out. *A wis ng*i nganggo pitku.* A tried out my bicycle.

itjir a certain type of fish trap with barred doors. **ng/di*-*** to scatter untidily. *Berasé di*-* ing djubin.* The rice was spilled on the floor. **ng/di*(-*)** to sell in small quantities (*rg var of* NG/DI·ÈTJÈR)

itjis *rg var of* ISIS

itjrit *var of* INTJRIT

itjul *var of* UTJUL

iṭu *var of* IṬUK

iṭuk in haste. **iṭak-*** to rush around

itung *var of* ÉTUNG

iwak *ng,* **ulam** *kr* 1 meat for the table. * *babi* pork. * *pitik* chicken. * *sapi* beef. 2 fish. *Dikena *é adja nganti buṭek banjuné.* To catch the fish, don't muddy the water; *fig* To get what you want, don't stir up trouble. ***-*an** toy fish, imitation fish. * **banju** live fish. * **k·lebu ing wuwu** caught in an ambush. * **loh** live freshwater fish

iwel *-* a cake made of glutinous-rice flour, shredded coconut, and brown sugar. **ng/di*-*** to pinch playfully *or* affectionately

iwèn birds; fowl, poultry. *ngingu ** to raise poultry. *See also* SATO

iwi **ng/di*-*** to grimace (at)

iwir **m*** to stretch, become elongated. **ng/di*-*** to stretch sth (bit by bit)

iwit frugal, thrifty. **ng/di*-*** to [do] sparingly. *Lawuhé siṭik, mula di*-* olèhé mangan.* There was only a little food, so he made it last as long as possible.

iwud (*or ptg **) with hasty motions. *-* a certain hawk. **ng*** with quick hurried motions. *Malingé (ng)* olèhé mbunteli barang.* The thief snatched everything he could lay hands on. **ng·iwad-ng*** to keep making frenzied motions

iwuh *oj* having difficulty (*see also* ÉWUH)

iwut *var of* IBUT

J

j (*prn* **jé**) *alphabetic letter*

ja *inf var of* IJA. *See also* GÉNÉ

jab ***-*an** keyed up; to have the jitters; to make hasty nervous gestures

jack (*prn* **djēk**) the jack (playing card)

jadi(n) *oj* if, when(ever)

jadnja an offering to the spirits

jag ***-*an** *or* ***-ijag** to act with unseemly haste, rush around

jah 1 *excl of skepticism, disparagement.* * *mosok, mboten ngandel kula.* Nonsense! I don't believe you. *Ijah, goroh kowé.* Huh, you're lying. 2 time (*shf of* WAJAH). * *apa?* When? * *(m)éné* at such a time as this. * *éné kok wis ngelih?* How could I be hungry this early? * *méné kok durung mangan?* You haven't eaten yet at this late hour?

Jahudi Jewish; a Jew, an Israeli

jâiku *ng,* **inggih punika** *kr* namely. *parabané * Bawuk* her nickname, (which was) Bawuk. *ésuké * Slasa* the next day, which was Tuesday. *Bandjur ngundang kantjané, *: A, B, C, lan isih ana manèh lijané.* He called his friends–A, B, C, and some others. *Aku weruh, * sepet.* I know the answer [to your riddle]–it's coconut fiber. *Anggonku ana Djakarta kono ora suwé, * mung kira² seminggu.* I wasn't in Djakarta long–only about a week.

jâjâ *oj* 1 father. 2 like, as. * **réna** *or* * **wibi** father and mother; **tunggal * réna/wibi** having the same parents

jajah *var of* JAJA

jajeng *inf var of* ḌI ADJENG: *see* ḌI

jaji *oj* 1 younger brother/sister. 2 *adr* wife

jak *var of* JAH. ***(n)a** *or* ***é** *or* ***nan** *or* ***nèn** probably, perhaps. *Ora *é.* I guess not! I don't think so! ***-*an** to keep moving around restlessly; to get in others' way. *See also* AJAK

jakin 1 it is true; in fact, actually; certain. **, aku ora ndjupuk ḍuwitmu.* I swear I didn't take your money. *"Inggih!" wangsulané kanṭi *.* "Yes!" he replied with assurance. 2 to feel sure (of sth one deeply hopes). *Aku * jèn ḍèwèké slamet.* I *know* he must be safe. **ka*an** belief, conviction. *Columbus olèh ke*an jèn bumi iki wanguné bunder.* Columbus was convinced the world was round. **ng/di*aké** 1 to convince.

*tembung² kang ng*aké* convincing words. 2 to determine the facts about. *Aku arep ng*aké apa bener.* I want to find out if it's true. **ng/di*i** to accept the truth of; to find sth convincing. *Penemuné ng*aké, mula wong² ng*i penemu mau.* His views are so convincing that people accept them.

jaksa 1 *oj* **bird.** 2 mythological giant

jaksi mythological giantess

jakti 1 *oj* holy man, pundit. 2 *formal var of* JEKTI. *** indra** *oj* highly esteemed pundit. *** wara** *oj* exalted pundit

jakut crystal used in jewelry settings

jâkuwi *ng var of* JAIKU

jamani *oj* hell

jan *oj* if, when(ever)

jang 1 *var of* HJANG. 2 *var of* JAH. *** mulja** (*abbr:* **J.M.**) your/his excellency

japwan *oj* if, when(ever)

jar 1 yard (measure of length). 2 *oj* if, when(ever)

jâsâ **(je)*n** 1 that which has been made *or* built. *Gambar iki jasané A.* This painting was done by A. 2 organization, foundation. **ϕ/di*** to make, build. **ng/di*kaké** to make/build for smn; to have sth made/built. **ng/di*ni** to build smw. *Pekarangan mau di*ni omah.* He put up a house on the lot. *** kambang** pavilion in the middle of a garden-encircled ornamental lake

jasin *see* SURAH

jati *var of* JAKTI

jatim fatherless; orphaned. *omah ** orphanage. *botjah/anak ** fatherless child; child whose father died before he was born; orphan. *** piatu** orphan, *i.e.* child with neither parent living

jatin *var of* JATIM

jatindra *contracted from* JAKTI INDRA

jatmâ(kâ) *ng,* **jitma** *kr* soul (as contrasted with body)

jatna *var of* JITNA

jâtrâ money (*sbst? kr for* ḌUWIT)

ja'uk **ora *** *slang* no good; unattractive

jâwâ *oj* outside

jé 1 hurray! 2 *teasing excl*

jeg *rpr* a shake. *Wité dijog mak *.* He shook the tree. ***-*** *or* **jag-*** *rpr* swaying unsteadily. *Kursiné jag-*.* The chair wobbles. *Wité dipènèk *-* arep ambruk.* When he climbed up the tree, it swayed as though it was about to collapse. *See also* IJEG

jej- *see also under* J- *(Introduction, 3.1.3)*

jejes **ng*** [of rain] incessant

jèk *rg var of* JÈN

jeksa, jeksi *var of* JAKSA, JAKSI

jekti *ng,* **jektos** *kr* real, actual. **ka*ǹ** proven, shown by the evidence. **ng/di*ǹkaké** to test the truth of. *Aku kepéngin ngjektèkaké apa bener reregan saiki muḍun.* I'd like to see if it's really true that prices are down. **ng/di*ǹi** to notice sth particularly, take special note of. **sa*** real(ly), actual(ly); in fact. *kaja prija sa** like a real person. *Sa*né aku arep lunga nanging aku kentèkan ḍuwit.* I really wanted to go, but I ran out of money.

jektos *kr for* JEKTI

jem **nge/di*** to keep moist, prevent from drying out. **nge/di*-*(i)** to free oneself of troubles. *Atiné di*-*.* He calmed himself down. *See also* AJEM

jèn **(bilih, menawi** *opt? kr*) 1 when(ever), if. ** ana sing ndjaluk, tak wènèhi.* If anyone asks for it, I'll give it to him. *Jèn adus, kosokan, sabunan.* When you take baths, scrub yourself with soap. *Aku arep tuku sepatu sing murah mau, ning * isih.* I want to buy those low-priced shoes–if they still have them. *Sikilku diresiki, * wis disoki tamba.* He cleaned my leg and then put some medicine on it. *Kéné, ḍuwitmu wènèhna aku! – * ora?* Here, hand over your money! –And if I don't? ** adjaa kepingin sekolah* if I hadn't wanted to go to school. 2 [to say *etc.*] that... *Aku ngerti * kowé sing metjahaké ting.* I know that you broke the light. *A weruh * B teka.* A saw that B was coming. 3 if/when it is [*x*] (that we are speaking of). ** iki pijé?* How about this one? ** aku ora.* Not me! ** nglangi pantjèn pinter.* When it comes to swimming, he's good. ** dina Minggu* on Sundays. ** beḍug paḍa lèrèn mangan.* At noon, they take a lunch break. ** apa ḍèké sarapan?* When does he eat breakfast? *Wong² * ngundang, Pak Wangsa.* People call him Mr. Wongso. 4 or else, for fear that. *Linggiha sing anteng, mengko * tiba lo.* Sit still, or you'll fall. 5 what (a)...! *É, botjah ki * nakal!* Hey, what a bad boy! *Wong ki * bedja.* What a lucky guy–how lucky can you get! *** durung** before; until. *Adja kolebokaké ḍisik * aku durung lunga.* Don't put it there before I leave (*or* until I've left). *** ta** if (emphatically). ** ta gelem, mesṭi bali manèh.* If he really wants to, I'm sure he'll come back.

jer ***-*an** dizzy; nauseated

jèt (*prn* **djèt**) jet. *motor mabur ** jet plane

jeti *inf var of* JEKTI
jetos *inf (sbst?) var of* JEKTOS
jijid sticky substance. *Enḍog koḍok digandèng nganggo* *. Frogs' eggs are held in masses by sticky stuff. **ng*** in a sticky condition. *Djangané wis ng**. The vegetables are oozing decayed matter.
jijis **ng*** [of rain] incessant
jitma soul (*kr for* JATMA)
jitna cautious. *** juwana léna kena** better safe than sorry. *See also* PRAJITNA
J.M. *see* JANG
jo *ng* come on! let's...! (*shf of* AJO). *, *ndang ḍahar* *! Come on–let's hurry up and eat!
jod ***-*an** to swing back and forth. **nge/di*-*** to swing sth back and forth
joḍemporem iodoform
joḍium iodine. * *tingtur* tincture of iodine. **ng/di*** to treat with iodine. *Tatuné wis di**. He put iodine on his cut.
jodjânâ measure of distance: *ca.* 1507 meters = *ca.* .93 mile
jog **ng(e)/di*** to shake. *Wité di* mak jeg.* He shook the tree [to bring down the fruit].
joga 1 (to practice) yoga. 2 child, offspring. 3 *oj* appropriate, suitable. **ma*** to practice yoga. **sa*** in a proper way; according to what is appropriate. *** brata** *or* *** semadi** to concentrate and meditate in the practice of yoga
yogi pundit, revered teacher. *** swara** a highly revered pundit
jogja 1 proper, appropriate. *Tindak mengkono mau ora* *. That's no way to act. 2 *inf var of* JOGJAKARTA
Jogjâkartâ central Javanese city, former kingdom and still the site of the court headed by the Sultan, and one of the two major cultural centers (*see also* SURAKARTA). **nga* Hajuningrat** *the complete formal name of this city*
jogjâswârâ *gram* a word with final *a* denoting male, paired with a word with final *i* denoting female (*e.g.* *déwa* male deity, *dèwi* female deity)
Jogyâkartâ *var sp of* JOGJAKARTA
joh 1 *attention-directing excl. Aku arep omong wigati;* *. I have sth important to say: listen! 2 *inf var of* AJO. 3 *inf* yes, yup
jok *** (n)âpâ** *rg* how? how come?
jom ***-*an** that which is shaded *or* sheltered. *turu awan ing *-*an* to take a nap in the shade. **ke*en** overshaded; overprotected. **nge*** 1 to cast shade; to create shelter. 2 to take shelter from sun, rain. **nge/di*i** to shade/shelter/protect sth. **pa*an** protection, shelter. *pa*an kéwan* an animal shelter. **pa·nge*an** 1 a shaded place. 2 protector, patron. 3 act *or* way of protecting/sheltering. *See also* AJOM
ju (*shf of* MBAKJU) 1 older sister. *Dumen karo *mu.* Share them with your sister. 2 young woman of low social status
jud *var of* JOD
juda *ltry* war, battle. **pa*n** *oj* battlefield. *** negara** 1 administration of the country. 2 etiquette
judjânâ *var of* JODJANA
judo judo (system of self-protection). *main* * to engage in judo as a sport. *Tjopèt mau kena * déning kenja mau.* The young lady handled the pickpocket by judo.
juga child (*var of* JOGA)
juju river crab. **ng*** [of livestock] so thin that the ribs show. *** gembur·an** soft-shell crab. *** rumpung** a river crab that has lost a claw. *** rumpung ing djaladri** a certain flat fish. *** rumpung m·barong rong·é** one whose home is luxurious beyond his means
jujun **ka*** 1 attracted (by); madly in love (with). 2 *rg* to grieve for [a dead person]. **ng*aké** attractive. **ng*i** 1 attractive. 2 attracted to
jukti *oj* suitable, appropriate
juman **ka*an** *oj* happiness, well-being
jumani *var of* JAMANI
jun ***-*an** 1 a swing. 2 to play on a swing. **nge/di*** to swing smn. *See also* AJUN[a]
Junani pertaining to Greece. *negara* * Greece. *tembung sing asalé saka tembung* * words of Greek origin
jung *shf of* BIJUNG. *See also* JUNGTA
jungjun *var of* JUJUN
jungta aunt (parent's older sister) (*shc from* BIJUNG ANTA)
jur ***-*an** to sway flexibly. *Wit-witan *-*an ketradjang angin geḍé.* The trees swayed in the high wind.
juri 1 jury. 2 umpire, referee
juris lawyer
jusja *oj* age; (years) old
justisi justice. *pangadilan* * a court of justice
juswa 1 old, elderly (*ki for* TUWA). 2 age (*ki for* UMUR)
juta million. ***n** (numbering in the) millions.

*Ḍuwité *n tjatjahé.* He's worth millions. **pra*** -millionth. *sa pra** .000001

juton *var of* JUTUN

jutun hardworking, dedicated. *tani ** a true dedicated farmer

juwan *var of* JUMAN

juwânâ healthy, well; safe and sound. **(ja)*n** health, well-being, safety

jwa *oj* don't!

jwang *var of* HJANG

K

k (*prn* **kā**) *alphabetic letter*

k- *pre-vowel form of* KE-

ka[a] from *etc.* (*shf of* SAKA[a])

ka-[b] *(see also entries under* KE-: *Introduction, 2.9.2)* 1 *psv prefix: formal, ltry, written var of* DI(PUN)-. *Sabinipun ka·tanem·an pantun.* The field is planted to rice. *Tembung mau kanggoné mung ana ing tulis waé, ora tau ka·utjap·aké.* This word is only written, never spoken. 2 **(kaping** *kr?*) *prefix: ordinal marker. sap sing ka·pitu* the seventh level/floor. *Buku sing ka·telu kuwi duwèkmu.* That third book is yours. ***... belah** *n* hundreds minus 50. *ka·ro belah* 150. *ka·pat belah* 350. *ka·wolu belah* 750. ***... sasur** *n* tens minus 5. *ka·pat sasur* 35. *ka·lima sasur* 45. *ka·wolu sasur* 75. ***... tengah** *n* minus $^1/_2$. *ka·ro tengah* $1^1/_2$. *ka·pat tengah* $3^1/_2$. *ka·wolu tengah* $7^1/_2$. *See also* KA...AN, KA...EN

k(a)...(a)n 1 *(noun-forming circumfix)* condition *or* result connected with [*root*]. *ka·butuh·an* (one's) needs. *ka·tresna·n·ing bijung* mother love. *ka(h)·ana·n* circumstances, situation. *ka·betjik·an* kindness. *ka·pulo·an* archipelago. *ka·Allah·an* godlike quality. 2 *(noun-forming circumfix)* place where [*root*] is to be found. *ka·lurah·an* residence of the top village official. *k(a)·ratu·ñ* palace; court. 3 *inadvertent psv var of* DI...I. 4 *formal var of* K(A)...EN. *k·akèh·an* too many/much

kabajan a village administrative official

kabar 1 news, information. ** angin* rumor. ** kawat* telegram. *lajang ** newspaper. *njebarakė *-* palsu* to spread false tales. ***-*** to notify. *Aku ditutuh ngalor-ngidul déné ora *-*.* Everyone criticized me for not letting them know. **ñg*** 1 to lose effectiveness. *prawan ngabar* a girl who is no longer attractive. *Rasané ngabar.* It's lost its flavor. 2 to evaporate. **ñg/di*aké** to tell, give news of. *Aku arep ngabarakė kahananė waé.* I'm going to tell them about it. **ñg/di*i** to inform. *Jèn ḍuwit wis ko-tampani aku kabarana.* Let me know when you get the money. **pa*an** 1 the news. 2 the press. *See also* K·ABER

kabèh *ng,* **sedâjâ** *kr* (in) all; every one. ** wis teka.* Everybody has arrived. *Toko² wis tutup *.* The stores are all closed. *loro ** both (of them). **ñg/di*aké** to use all of sth. *Ujah sing nèng botol mau di*aké.* She put in all the salt that was in the bottle. **sa*é** **(sedaja·nipun** *kr*) all (of). *Sa*é pitutur betjik.* All of his advice is sound. *Sa*é wong mesṭi mati.* All men are mortal.

kabèl ***an** to crave (*esp.* a certain food). **ñg*i** to cause a craving (for)

kabel cable, wire. ** listrik* electric cable

kabjak **ke*** to dart about hurriedly and nervously

kablak **ke*** to ruffle the feathers. *Pitiké ke*.* The chicken fluffed out its feathers. **ñg/di*aké** *or* **ñg/di*i** to ruffle. *ngablakaké suwiwi* to flap the wings

kablong to lose (*cr var of* KALAH)

kabluk tapioca powder. *See also* MABLUK

kabong fed up (with), sick and tired (of)

kabor gamelan melody played at the beginning of a shadow play

kabruk *rpr* falling. *Ḍèké tiba mak *.* He fell

down. **ñg/di*(i)** [of birds] to fall upon, attack. *See also* AMBRUK, BRUK

kabul 1 to come true. *Wusanané bisa * panuwuné.* His wish has finally been fulfilled. *donga ** a prayer of thanks for a wish granted. 2 to accept one's bride from her father or guardian and declare her his wife (during the marriage ceremony). 3 spoiled [of raw rice that has been stored too long]. **ñg/di*aké** *or* **ñg/di*i** to cause to come true. *Panuwunku di*aké.* He fulfilled my wishes.

kabut *see* KALANG

kaḍak *see* WALANG

kaḍal 1 garden lizard. 2 copper ornament on a riding horse. ***an** 1 a certain fish. 2 a certain bird. 3 a weed with edible roots. 4 (*or* **ka*an**) lizard-like, in a squatting position. **ñg*** resembling a lizard's crawl. **ñg* ñ·weteng** tapering gradually in shape from midsection to ends. *** idjo** 1 chameleon. 2 metal tarnish. *** idjo·nen** tarnished. *** ñ·pènèk** a certain hair style (*see also* GELUNG)

kadang 1 a relative. 2 sibling. ***-* anak·é si X** he's X's child (and so it is to be expected that he would act that way). **ñg/di*** to treat *or* regard smn as one's own relative. *** kadéjan** a relative. *** konang** to acknowledge as relatives only those of one's relatives who are rich or successful. *** ka·tut** a relative by marriage only

kaḍang sometimes, occasionally. ***-*an** sometimes. *** kaḍeng·é** *or* *** kaḍing(an)** *or* **kala(né)** *or* *** k·in·ala·n** (*** kawis** *or* *** kawisipun** *kr*) from time to time, occasionally. *See also* TERKAḌANG

kadar, kaḍar 1 whatever is available. ** mangan* to eat whatever one can find. *turu ** to sleep out in the open. *Apa ana panggonan * kanggo lungguh?* Is there any place where I could sit? 2 fate, destiny. **é èlèk.* He is foredoomed. 3 (*or* ***an**) *excl of wonder.* ** apa/sapa!* What/who on earth–? ** ija?* Is it *true?* **di*** fated. *A di* dadi pemimpin.* A is destined to be a leader. **ke*** to sleep out in the open. **sa*é** whatever one wishes. *mlaku² ing sa*é* to wander at will. *dana sa*é* to donate whatever one wishes

kadarpa 1 love, desire. 2 the god of love

kadas spiritually impure, delinquent in one's prayers *or* prayer preparations

kaḍas a certain skin rash. ***en** to have *or* get this rash. *** kuḍis** ringworm. *See also* KUḌIS

kaḍatun, kaḍatwan, kaḍatyan *oj* palace; court (*ltry var of* KEḌATON)

kaḍâwâ a green dove-like bird

kadé *rg var of* KAJA

kadéjan *see* KADANG

kadèk 1 (*or* ***na** *or* ***néja**) naturally, of course; that is why. 2 like, as (*rg var of* KAJA). 3 from (*rg var of* SAKA[a])

kadèn *see* DJARIK

kaḍeng *** pareng** *rg* perhaps, probably. *See also* KAḌANG

kader *var of* KADAR

kaḍer military cadre. **ñg/di*(i)** to form into a cadre

kaḍèt military cadet

kadi 1 *oj* like, as. 2 from (*rg var of* SAKA[a]). *** paran** *or* *** pundi** *oj* how?

kaḍi from (*rg var of* SAKA[a])

kading *** alem·(an)** to seek out compliments. *Iki mengko bakal ana tamu, kowé adja * alem ja.* We're having guests soon—don't show off for them.

kaḍing *** kala·(né)** *or* *** k·in·ala·n** sometimes, occasionally. *See also* KAḌANG

kadingarèn out of the ordinary, surprising, strange. **ñg/di*aké** to regard sth as strange. *See also* DINGARÈN

kadis history of the life and teachings of the prophet Mohammed

kadjang 1 roof of dried palm leaves. 2 pillow (*ki for* BANTAL). **ñg*** to make a dried-palm-leaf roof. *** sirah** *sms* *2

kadjantâkâ *oj* impoverished, destitute

kadjat (to hold) a party, ceremonial event. ** sunatan* circumcision party. ** kaulan* celebration to fulfill a pledge. ** mantu* wedding party. *Aku duwé * mitoni anakku.* I held a ceremony for my daughter's seventh month of pregnancy. ***an** 1 to hold a celebration. 2 food provided for a celebration. **pa*an** guests attending a celebration

kadjeng 1 wood; tree (*kr for* KAJU). 2 intention; wish (*kr for* KAREP). ***ipun** so that, so as to...; let [sth happen] (*kr for* BÈN, KAREBÈN, TJIKBÈN)

kadji a Moslem who has made the pilgrimage to Mecca; title used before the name of such a person. **ñg*** to read from the Koran. *See also* HADJI

kadjog displeased with the turn of events. *Bareng mèlu pamané Siti *, wong biasané* *ora tau njambut-gawé apa²*. When Siti went to live with her uncle, she didn't like it: she hadn't been accustomed to doing any work.

kados like, as; as if/though (*kr for* KAJA). * **déné** as though; and yet (*kr for* KAJA DÉNÉ). * **pundi** how? (*kr for* KEPRIJÉ)

kadud burlap sack, gunnysack; sacking material

kaduk *var of* KLADUK

kadung never satisfied

kaḍung to have taken an irrevocable step. *Aku wis * pamit ibu bapak.* I've said goodbye to my parents (and so I can't go back now). *Sarèhning wis * kelair, ja kepeksa dilairaké.* Since it slipped out inadvertently, he had to tell the whole thing. *Kuwih ana ing médja adja dipangan.–Wis * bu!* Don't eat the cookies on the table.–Too late, Mother!

kadya(ngga) *oj* like, as

kaé *ng,* **punika** (*usu. prn* **menikâ**) *kr* 1 that, that (remote) thing/place/time *(Degree III: Introduction, 6). Botjah * anaké sapa?* Whose son is that boy over there? ** apa?* What's that over there? *Delengen *.* Look over there! *ḍèk ana pasar malem ** that time (a long time ago) when there was a fair. *Ajo nglangi kana *.* Let's swim 'way over there. 2 *expression of deprecation. Sugiha * ora lumrah wong.* He may be rich but he's not nice. *La kaé ana botjah tjilik ja ora wedi.* Look at that child–*he's* not afraid! *Woh²an isih ketjut * kok larang tenan.* Those fruits are sour–how come they are so expensive!

kaèk ***-*** *or* **koak-*** (to speak) loudly, aggressively, boastfully

k(a)...en (**...n** *or* **...nen** *after vowel*) *excessive circumfix. k·aḍem·en* excessively cold. *ke·geḍé·n̉* excessively large

kafir *var of* KAPIR

kâgâ *oj* bird. * **kresna** crow; blackbird

kagak *rg* no; not. *Ora *!* Certainly not!

kagem for (*ki for* KANGGO)

kagèt 1 startled, taken aback. ** aku, dak arani kowé sapa!* You startled me–I thought you were smn else! *Saking *é tiba klumah.* He was so surprised he fell over backwards. 2 a variety of guava. ***an** nervous, jumpy, easily startled. **n̈g*aké** surprising, startling; (*psv* **di*aké**) to startle, surprise. * **sangkèt·é** 1 stiff. 2 jumpy; jumpy behavior, timidity. *See also* GÈT

kagok 1 (to feel) awkward, disagreeable. 2 [of speech] aberrant, accented, dialectal. 3 *rg var of* KAGÈT

kagol to feel frustrated. ***an** easily upset *or* frustrated. **n̈g/di*aké** to frustrate; to cause smn to feel helpless

kagum amazed, awed, impressed. **n̈g*aké** amazing, awe-inspiring; (*psv* **di*aké**) to astound *or* impress smn. **n̈g/di*** to find sth amazing. *Aku ng*i Borobuḍur.* I was overawed by the Borobudur temple.

kagungan 1 to have, own (*ki for* DUWÉ). 2 the possession/belonging of (*ki for* DUWÈK)

kaim *sbst kr for* KAUM

kain 1 wraparound skirt worn by ladies. 2 fabric, material. ** bambu* olive-drab khaki. ** panas* flannel. ** rami* burlap. ** tjita* textile

kaing ***-*** *rpr* a dog yelping in pain

kaipé *ltry var of* IPÉ

kait connection, link. ***an** interconnection. *Dakwa kuwi *ané karo saksi kepijé?* What is the defendant's connection with the witness? **n̈g/di*(aké)** to form a connection (with, between). *Polisiné ng*aké bukti² radjapati.* The police have linked up the evidence with the murder. **n̈g*(aké) rembug** to have a verbal understanding [with]. *Maling mau ng* rembug karo wong djero.* The thief had lined up a confederate on the inside. **sa*** connected (with); in agreement (with). *Wong loro²né wis se*.* The two of them are in it together.

kâjâ *ng,* **kados** *kr* 1 like, as; as if, as though. ** ngono* like that. ** adat sabené* as usual. *paḍa waé * ana ngomah* just like at home. *Apa * olèhmu ngimpi kaé?* Is it the way you dreamed it? *Ḍèké ngobahaké tangané * arep mbalang.* He cocked his arm as if he were going to throw. 2 *ng kr* income. **né geḍé.* His earnings are sizable. 3 *oj* body. ***-*** (it seems) as if. **-* suwéné seminggu.* I think it takes a week. **di*** to be treated as. *Rengkuhen di* sedulurmu ḍéwé.* Treat him as though he were your own relative. * **déné** 1 (it seems) as though. *Sadjak *déné ora nggapé kahanan kiwa tengené.* He didn't seem to be aware of his surroundings. 2 and yet; while. *Djaré ora arep rabi, *déné weruh wong wédok kok kedandapan.* He says he doesn't want to get married, but whenever he sees a girl he gets all excited. * **ija** * **ora** uncertain. *Kaé rak Santo ta?–* ija * ora.* That's Santo, isn't it?–I can't tell. * **(ng)apa** *ng only* decidedly, very much so (*see also*

DI-). * *ngapa baé raméné!* How crowded it is! * **ta** such as. *manuk*[2] *iberan *ta gagak, ulung, lsp.* flying creatures such as crows, hawks, *etc.*

kajang force, power, energy. *Wis diadjar sak *é.* They beat him with all their might. **ke*** to do a back bend. **n̈g*** 1 to do a back bend. 2 (*psv* **di***) to throw/hurl at. *Ḍèké di* nganggo bal.* He was hit by a thrown ball. *Olèhé sinau di*.* He threw himself into his studies.

kajangan heaven (*var of* KA·HJANG·AN). **mer*** to go to heaven

kajing **kojang-*an** *pl* to scatter in panic

kaju *ng,* **kadjeng** *kr* 1 wood. 2 tree. 3 firewood. *tukang ** carpenter; dealer in (fire)-wood. 4 *ng kr; cr* dead body. ***n̂** 1 *ng kr* tree-of-life puppet, held up to the screen to mark the conclusion of a scene. 2 (*or* **ke*n̂**) trees; wooded area. **n̈g*** 1 resembling wood. 2 to grow into a tree. * **agar·an** *or* * **bakar** firewood. * **daja** wood used for construction. * **dang** firewood. * **glinggang** dead wood; dead tree. * **legi** *or* * **manis(-djangan)** tree whose bark produces cinnamon. * **putih** myrtle tree; **lenga** * **putih** cajuput oil. * **ta(h)un** ironwood. * **tjenḍana** sandalwood. *See also* MAIN

kajuh unit of length (8 *katju*'s) for measuring fabric. ***an** merchandise sold on commission. **n̈g/di*** 1 to sell [merchandise] on commission. 2 to reach for sth high above one's head. 3 to embrace. 4 to row [a boat]. **n̈g/di·kojah-*** to sell [merchandise] on commission

kajun *ltry* 1 a wish (*see also* AJUN[b]). 2 living, alive

kajwan *oj* tree of life (*see also* KAJU-N̂)

kak *rg var of* KAKANG. ***-*** *rpr* a goose honking. * **sukak** *gembolo* blossom; * **sukak mbang mbolo** I'll do as I please!

kâkâ *oj* older brother

kakak 1 a parrot-like bird. 2 *rg var of* KAKANG. **n̈g*** to laugh uproariously

kakang *ng kr,* **râkâ** *ki* 1 older brother. *Ora duwé kakang ora duwé aḍi.* He has no brothers or sisters. 2 *adr; cr* husband. 3 a similar but larger object. *Apa kowé duwé éngkol *é iki?* Have you got a wrench like this only larger? **n̈g*** to treat *or* regard smn as one's own brother; resembling an older brother. *Aku karo ḍèké ngakang.* He and I are like brothers. * **aḍi** older-younger sibling relationship. *Botjah kaé * aḍi.* Those children are brothers (*or* sisters; *or* brother and sister). * **bi** *adr; rg* older sister; an older female. * **embok** *adr; stage usage* older sister; older female. * **ipé** older-brother-in-law. * **kawah aḍi ari**[2] the baby is born and then the placenta. * **mas** *ltry* older brother

kakap an edible sea fish

-ḱaké *ng,* **-ḱaken** *kr* *post-vowel form of suffix* -AKÉ

kakèk *rg var of* KAKI[a]. ***-*** (having become) very old. * **mojang** grandfather

kaken stiff; awkward (*kr for* KAKU)

-ḱaken *kr for* -ḰAKÉ

kaki[a] *ng kr,* **éjang** *ki* 1 grandfather. 2 old man. 3 *adr; affectionate, respectful* young man. ***ǹ** (being) an old man (*see also* NINI). *Muga*[2] *bisaa nganti kakèn*[2] *ninèn*[2] *atut-runtut.* May you have a long and harmonious married life! ***-*** very old. **n̈g/di*** to treat *or* regard smn as one's grandfather. **k·um·aki** cocky, overwise, insolent. * **among** godfather; male good spirit that protects human beings

kaki[b] measure of length: *ca.* 1 foot (1/12 *tjengkal*). ***ǹ** in (denominations of) feet, by the foot. **n̈g/di*ǹi** to measure sth in the above units

kaḱ-kong having a long trunk and short legs (*contracted from* TUNGKAK TJEḌAK BOKONG)

kakrak torn (off). **n̈g/di*kaké** to tear (off)

kakrèk *var of* KAKROK

kakrok *swear word.* * *ané.* Damn it!

kaku *ng,* **kaken** *kr* stiff; awkward; ill at ease. *Guluku *.* I have a stiff neck. *Atiné *.* He is hard-hearted. *Solah tingkahé *.* He acts gauche. ***n̂(an)** (**kaken·an** *kr*) characterized by inflexibility. *kakon atèn* easily offended; unforgiving. **ke*n̂en** excessively stiff. *Olèhé ngandji adja kekakonen.* Don't starch it too stiff. **n̈g*** to stiffen, become rigid. **n̈g/di*k̂aké** to stiffen sth; to offend *or* irritate smn. *See also* KAMIKAKON

kakung male (*ki for* LANANG)

kakus toilet

kal- *see also under* KL- *(Introduction, 2.9.3)*

kâlâ 1 time, season. *Ing *né pinudju nganggur.* She happened to be free at the time. 2 bird-trapping noose on a long handle. 3 stinging animal. 4 wickedness, evil. *baṭara * (wj)* evil ogre: spirit of death. 5 last, past (*kr for* ḌÈK). * *punapa?* when (in the past)? (*kr for* ḌÈK KAPAN). ***-*** from time to time; off and on. **n̈g/di*** to snare an animal. *ngala asu édan* to rope a mad dog. *djaka* **k·um·ala-*** teenage boy. * **bendu** heaven-sent retribution in the form of a large-scale disaster. * **dasa** astrologically propitious time. * **djengking** scorpion. * **mangsa** sometimes, occasionally. * **méndjé** a variety of scorpion. * **mendjing** Adam's-apple. * **mèntèl** scorpion. * **mèntèk** rice pest (believed to be evil spirits). * **warta** magazine, periodical. *See also* TJANDIK

kalah *ng,* **kawon** *kr* 1 to lose, be defeated. *Kowé * apa menang?* Did you lose or win? **é akèh banget.* He lost heavily. *ngojak *é* or *nututi *é* to try to recover one's losses. *trima ** to accept defeat. 2 less; inferior. ** gedé (karo)* not as large (as). *Kaum wanita ora * karo kaum prija.* Women are not inferior to men. ** angka* or ** bidji* to be of lesser value, to count for less. ***an** to lose habitually. **ke*an** loss. *nebus ke*ané* to regain one's losses. **ñg*** to give in/up. *Ora gelem ngalah.* I won't give up. *Wong tuwa kudu ora ngalah karo botjah.* Parents shouldn't give in to their children. **ñg/di*aké** 1 to defeat, overcome. 2 to let/have smn win. **ñg*an** accommodating by nature, willing to yield. **ñg/di*i** to accommodate oneself *or* smn else. *Ngalahana lungguh.* Take your seat! *Aku ngalahi mampir nang ndalem.* I gave in and went to his house. * **ambruk** to collapse in utter defeat. * **atas** to lose (out). * **menang** whether one wins or loses. * **se·paro** not beaten yet. * **sa·usap** off *or* different by only a little bit. *See also* PIKALAH, TJATJAK

kalak a certain flower

kalam 1 the word of God. 2 brush-tipped pen for writing Arabie characters. 3 penis (*ki for* PA·LANANG·AN, PELI)

kâlâmânggâ *inf var of* KEMANGGA

kâlâmentâ a certain kind of grass

kalamun *oj* if, when(ever)

kalandjânâ an alfalfa-like grass used as cattle fodder

kalang gypsy band. ***an** (**kambeng·an** *kr*) arena. **ke*an** to fly around; to hover in the air. **ñg/di*** 1 to surround, encircle. 2 to detour around sth. * **kabut** panicky; in a state of rout

kalas **-** indistinct, hazy; [of handwriting] spidery

kâlâwidjâ the deformed among the palace officials (believed to have mystic powers)

kalbu heart, mind, consciousness

kaldu broth, bouillon

kalem calm, tranquil, at peace

kalèng can. ** susu* milk can. *susu ** canned milk. ***an** canned, in cans

kalèt *var of* KELÈT

kali *ng,* **lèpèn** *kr* river. ***ǹ(an)** (**lèpèn·an** *kr*) ditch, small stream. **ñg/di*ǹi** to furnish with a channel. *Tjedak omah dikalèni nggo dalan banju.* They made a ditch near the house for drainage.

kalih 1 two (*kr for* LORO). 2 second Javanese season (*kr for* KARO 6). 3 and, with, etc. (*md for* KARO 1-5). ***an** *var sp of* KALIJAN. **ñg·kolah-ñg*** 1 to keep moving (*i.e.* changing one's residence). 2 (*psv* **di·kolah-***) to keep changing the position of. *Anggoné nggorèng daging dikolah-*.* She turns the meat again and again as it fries.

kalijan and, with, etc. (*kr for* KARO 1-5*; opt kr for* LAN)

Kalimantan Borneo

kalimâsâdâ *wj* magical book having the power to resurrect a hero whose death was untimely

kaling 1 nose ring for cattle. 2 *var of* KALÈNG. ***an** outcome, upshot. ***ané** it turned out that... **kolang-*** the edible insides of the fruit of the areca sugar palm. ***-*an** concealed; shielded. *mBulané *-*an.* The moon is behind the clouds. *Anginé ora gedé sebab *-*an Pulo Sèwu.* It doesn't get much wind; it's protected by the Thousand Islands. *See also* ALING

kalir wish, want. *sabarang ** anything one wants. **sa*é** according to one's wish. *Njumbanga sa*é, ora ana peksan.* Donate if you wish; it's not compulsory.

kaliren to starve. *botjah sing ** starving children. *mati ** to starve to death

kalis 1 impervious; unreceptive. ** ing sambékala* safe and sound. ** saka sakabèhing pitutur* deaf to all advice. 2 non-cohesive. *Lenga karo banju kuwi *.* Oil and water don't mix. *Digodog nganti *.* Boil it until it doesn't stick to the pan.

kalkir **ñg/di*** to trace sth onto transparent paper placed over the copy

kalkun turkey

kalo bamboo sieve

kalok famed, renowned

kaloka *var of* KALOK

kalong a certain large bat

kaloren feeble, weak

kalori calorie (unit of heat)
kalung *ng kr,* **sangsang·an** *ki* necklace, garland. ***an** *ng kr* to put on *or* wear a necklace. **ñg/di*aké** to place around smn's neck. *Kembangé di*aké anaké.* She placed the flower garland around her child's neck. **ñg/di*i** to place around the neck of. *Anaké di*i kembang.* She placed a flower garland around the child's neck. *** brondong** necklace of small gold balls. *** usus** to look attractive in anything one wears
kâmâ 1 love; sexual passion. 2 male sperm
kâmâdjâjâ the god of love. ** lan ratih* the god and goddess of love: symbol of the perfect marriage
kamajan 1 charm or incantation used for casting a magic spell. 2 magic spell; enchantment
kamal 1 salted [of eggs, *esp.* duck eggs: brine-soaked in the shell and later boiled]. *enḍog ** salted (duck) eggs. 2 *oj* tamarind. **ñg/di*** 1 to salt [eggs]. 2 to apply a poultice to
kamandâkâ *oj* misleading, deceitful
kamanḍalu earthenware jug for carrying water to the home
kamar room. **ñg/di*** to confine, *esp.* in a room. *Kutjingé adja di*.* Don't shut the cat away! *** bodjana** banquet hall. *** bolah** public hall. *** duduk** family sitting room. *** ketjil** bathroom, lavatory. *** manḍi** bathing room. *** obat** dispensary. *** stuḍi** study, den. *** tahan·an** detention room; prison cell. *** tamu** room where guests are entertained
kamas older brother; respected male of equal status. *See also* MAS[b]
kamat call to Moslem worship similar to the *adan*
kambang 1 fishing-rod float. 2 to float. ***an** 1 to float. 2 duck (*opt? kr for* BÈBÈK). **ñg*** 1 to float. *Lenga iku ngambang ing nḍuwur banju.* Oil floats on water. 2 to come to the surface. **ñg/di*(aké)** to cause sth to float. *Botjah² paḍa ngambangaké prau²né.* *ptg* **k·r·ambang** *or* **ñg·k·r·ambang** *pl* to float. *Semuté ngrambang.* The ants are floating on the surface. **k·um·ambang** to float. *balok kumambang* a floating log. *See also* ULER
kambèk and; with
kambeng ***an** 1 arena (*kr for* KALANG·AN). 2 jungle grass (*opt kr for* ALANG²)
kambi *var of* KAMBÈK
kambil 1 saddle (*ki for* ABAH², LAPAK). 2 coconut (*var of* KRAMBIL). **ñg/di*** *ki* to saddle up [a horse]
kambing goat, sheep
kambong a certain ocean fish
kambu swarm. *tawon ** a swarm of bees
kambuh (to have) a relapse *or* recurrence of illness. ***an** (one who is) prone to recurrent illness. **ñg/di*i** to cause a worsening of [an illness that was on the mend]
kamdulilah *see* SOKUR
kami 1 I, me *(regal usage).* 2 *oj* we, us
kamibotjahen (kapilaré *kr?*) childlike. *Bapakné jèn dolanan karo anaké tjilik, dadi *.* When the father plays with his child, he too acts like a child. *See also* BOTJAH
kamigigilen shivering with cold. *See also* GIGIL
kamigilan easily revolted. *Ḍèké * weruh anak tikus mau.* The sight of the baby mice repelled her. *See also* GILA
kamikakon 1 stiff, sore. 2 straitlaced, inflexible, harsh. *See also* KAKU
kamikekelen 1 to laugh hard. 2 chilled to the bone. *See also* KEKEL
kamil *see* INSAN
kamilegan, kamilegen to have overeaten
kamipurun to act daring (*kr for* KUMAWANI; *see also* PURUN)
kamisanḍanen *var of* SANḌA·NEN
kamisasaten staring dazedly, wide-eyed but unseeing
kamisepuh village official (*kr for* KAMITUWA; *see also* SEPUH)
kamisesegen [of breathing] rapid and shallow. *See also* SESEG
kamisèsèten to come/peel off [of skin, *esp.* at the fingertips]. *See also* SÈSÈT
kamisisèten *var of* KAMISÈSÈTEN
kamisosolen to have difficulty speaking because of strong emotion. *See also* SOL
kamisutjèn turning upward and outward [of the tied ends of an *iket* headdress]
kamitenggengen to stare dumbfounded and open-mouthed
kamitigan to ripen too early and hence lack flavor
kamitjutjèn *var of* KAMISUTJÈN
kamitolèhen to think back with fondness on things past. *See also* TOLÈH
kamitolihen *var of* KAMITOLÈHEN
kamitontonen to keep seeing in the mind's eye. *See also* TONTON
kamituwa *ng,* **kamisepuh** *kr* village elder,

village official. *Prijaji sing dadi * mau wus tuwa.* The man who became a village official was quite old. *See also* TUWA

kamiwelasen to become increasingly sorry for *or* sympathetic to. *See also* WELAS[a]

kamli heavy blanket

kampak 1 band of robbers. 2 large axe. **ng/di*** 1 to rob as a gang. 2 to chop with the above axe

kampanje campaign. ** pemilihan umum* election campaign

kampel ***-*an** possessed by a spirit

kampemèn army camp ground

kamper mothballs

kampi *inf var of* KAMPIJUN

kampijun champion, winner, number one

kampil 1 (*or* ***an**) a small purse woven from dried grass. *ḍuwit sak ** a pouch of money. 2 *rg* pillow

kampir ***-*an** possessed by a spirit who happened to be passing through. *See also* AMPIR

kamplèh ***-*** loose and nearly detached

kampleng **ng/di*** to hit smn in the face *or* on the head

kamplung 1 to fall into [water]. 2 all used up. *Sawah lan omah * kabèh kanggo nglunasi utangé.* It took all his fields and house to pay off the debt.

kampong *var of* KAMPUNG

kampot measure for harvested rice plants: 5 sheaves of *ca.* 37 kilograms = *ca.* 81.6 lbs.

kamprèt 1 a certain small bat (flying animal). 2 *var of* NGAMPRET

kampret *var of* NGAMPRET

kampuh ceremonial batik wraparound (*ki for* DODOT). *** djingga** symbol of revolution. *Arep mirong * djingga mbaléla kuwasaning radja.* He planned to take up arms and challenge the authority of the king.

kampul ***-*** *or* **kompal-*** to keep drifting *or* floating. *Widji² enggoné kompal-* nganti pirang² dina.* The seeds drifted on for days. **ng*** *or* **k·um·ampul** to float

kampung 1 slum area in or near a city. 2 yard around one's house. *wong* ***an** person with crude boorish manners. **pa*an** *sms* *. *wong (pa)*(an)* person from a slum area

kamu *oj* you *(plural)*

kamus 1 dictionary. *nggolèki tembung ing ** to look up a word in the dictionary. 2 leather belt worn with a batik wraparound

kan 1 porcelain teapot. 2 covered enamel pitcher for cool boiled drinking water

kânâ *ng,* **ngrika** *or* **mrika** *kr* 1 (over) there, that (remote) place *(Degree III: Introduction, 6).* 2 he, she, they. *Gèk * putrané ḍirèktur.* After all he's the director's son! 3 go on, go ahead. *Wis ta *, adja ndadak isan-isin barang.* Oh, go ahead—don't be embarrassed. ***né** the ones over there. *Kéné ngono ora apa² ning *né kuwi.* For us it's all right, but how about those others? ***-*** everywhere. *Klenṭengé tiba ana *-*.* The cotton seeds fell in all directions. **di*kaké** to be handled in that way (*var of* DI·NGANA·KAKÉ). ***-kéné (ngrika-ngriki** *kr*) here and there; all around. *Kuwi pantjèn regané dadi * kéné ja paḍa'é.* That IS the price; it's the same everywhere.

kanak ***-*** children. *taman *-** kindergarten. ***-k·um·anak** 1 to flourish, proliferate. 2 to bear compound interest. *See also* ANAK[a,b]

kanâkâ *oj* 1 gold. 2 nail, claw (*ki for* KUKU)

kanan *ltry* right (as opposed to left); starboard. *** kéring** left and right; all around. *plataran *-kéringé omah* the yard surrounding the house. *Mantriné ana ing *-kéringé patih lan ratu.* The bishops [in chess] flank the king and queen.

kanang *oj* (one) who, (that) which

kânḍâ *ng,* **tjrijos** *or* **sa(n)djang** *kr,* **andika** *or* **ngendika** *ki,* **m·atur** *ka* 1 to say, tell, talk (to). 2 *ng kr* script, *e.g.* of a play. ***-*** to keep telling sth to smn; to tell sth around, tell to various people. **(ke)*n (witjanten·an** *kr*) to talk; to converse. **ng/di*kaké** to tell (about), report. **ng/di*ni** to say (to smn). *ngGoné nganḍani bisik².* He told it in a whisper.

kanḍang animal pen. ** pitik* chicken coop. *Brandkas iku *ing sétan.* The money box is the devil's home. **ng*** to return to the stable. **ng/di*aké** to put *or* keep [animals] in an enclosure. **ng/di*i** to equip [property] with animal pens. *nganḍangi plataran buri* to build a stable in the back yard. *** langit kemu méga** free as a bird

kanḍap *sbst kr for* KALAH

kanḍas 1 shallow, at a low level. *Sumuré wis *.* The well has almost run dry. 2 to run aground; to go to the bottom *(lit, fig). Prau * ing pasir.* The boat ran aground on a sand bar. *Manisé * ing bebalung.* She is sweet to the very core. *Usahané tansah *.* His efforts always founder. ***an** a shallow place

kanḍèh cured of a bad habit

kandel 1 thick, heavy. *peḍut* * a thick mist. *kemul* * a thick blanket. *Menḍungé* *. The clouds were heavy. 2 *slang* rich. ***an** decorative metal plating on a kris sheath (*kr for* PENḌOK). **ñg/di*aké** to make sth thick (for smn). **ñg/di*i** to make sth thick(er than it was). * **bokong** rich, well off. * **kulit·é** *or* * **kuping·é** 1 stubborn, wilfull. 2 thick-skinned, insensitive. * **tipis** thick and thin; [of script] copperplate style, *i.e.* with slim upward strokes and heavy downward strokes. * **tipis·é** (the) thickness (of). * *tipisé gumantung bukuné.* How thick it is depends on what sort of book it is.

kanḍiḍat candidate

kandjar *ltry* knife used as a weapon

kandjat not too bad, better than nothing. **ora** * not very strong

kandjeng *inf var of* KANGDJENG

kandji 1 powdered starch (for cooking or laundry). 2 cured, reformed. *Aku wis* *. I've learned my lesson! ***ǹ** starched. *klambi kandjèn* a starched shirt. **ñg/di*k̀aké** to starch for smn. **ñg/di*ǹi** to starch [fabric]

kandjo left unfinished. *Sekolahé* *. He dropped out of school. *Masakané* *. She didn't finish preparing the meal.

kanḍung **ñg/di*** to contain, hold. *tablèt sing nganḍung vitamin* A, B pills containing vitamins A and B

kanḍut **ñg/di*** 1 to carry in the pocket. *Di* mrutjut.* He had it in his pocket but it came out. 2 to carry within oneself/itself. *Ḍèwèké nganḍut kesusahan.* She was filled with sadness. *Tembungé nganḍut pangantjam.* His words implied a threat. *Èsemé nganḍut wadi.* She smiled secretively. *nganḍut goḍong ranḍu* to speak evasively; to withhold facts, lack frankness. 3 pregnant. *nganḍut patang sasi* four months pregnant. ***an** 1 what smn carries concealed (*e.g.* in the pocket; in the heart). *ala *ané* shifty, untrustworthy. 2 foetus

kang *ng,* **ingkang** *kr* 1 (one) who, (that) which. *apa²* * *wis tau tak lakoni* everything that has happened to me. 2 your/his/her [relation]. * *garwa* your wife/husband. * *raji* his/her younger sibling. 3 *ng kr* (*or* * **bagus**) *rural var of* KAKANG. * **slira** you. *See also* SING

kangdjeng regent. * **gusti pangéran** (*abbr:* **K.G.P.**) his/your highness the prince. * **gusti pangéran anom** crown prince. * **pangéran arja (angabèhi)** *male nobility title.* * **radèn tumenggang** (*abbr:* **K.R.T.**) *adr* top administrative officer of a district. * **ratu** *adr* 1 queen. 2 daughter of a king by his first queen (who is mother of the legal heirs). * **ratu ajunan** *title for the king's consort of most ancient lineage*

kangèh **kongah-*an** to moan in deep distress

kangen to yearn for, miss. *Aku wis* * *kowé.* I've missed you. *tamba* *, sth to remember smn by. ***-*an** to catch up on things that have happened since last seeing each other. **ñg/di*i** to cause yearning/longing. *Tjritané ngangeni.* His stories make me homesick. *Di*i kok ora ngerti.* You have no idea how I've missed you! *See also* ANGEN

kanggé for (*kr for* KANGGO)

kanggeg to interrupt, discontinue. *Ḍèké rada* * *anggoné arep miwiti guneman.* He changed his mind about saying sth. * **ati·né** let down, disappointed; reluctant to speak out

kanggo *ng,* **kanggé** *kr,* **kagem** *ki* 1 for; for the benefit/purpose of. *Barang² iki* * *kowé.* These are for you. *ḍuwit* * *djadjan* money for snacks. *Kalungé diwènèhaké Siti* * *tanḍa katresnan.* He gave Siti the necklace as a token of his love. *Wong adus* * *ngresiki awak.* People bathe in order to get clean. * *sawetara wektu* for some time, for quite a while. 2 usable; in use; used. *Apa kreteg kuwi isih* *? Can we use the bridge? *Tembung kuwi arang *né.* That word isn't used much. *Kertas iki wis ora* *. This paper is no good any more. *montor sing wis* * a used car. *Kursi kuwi wis* *. That seat is taken. ***né** with respect to. *Dina pasaran iku prelu banget *né wong Djawa.* The market days are of great significance to the Javanese. **né Indonesia Djakarta iku kuṭa sing ramé ḍéwé.* Djakarta is the busiest city in Indonesia. *See also* ANGGO

kangih *var of* KANGÈH

kangkang 1 a certain large crab. 2 to sit with the legs spread apart

kangker cancer

kangkrang *var of* KANGRANG

kangkung 1 a certain vegetable used for soup. 2 *rpr* the croaking of frogs

kangmas *ki? court var of* KAMAS

kangrang large red tree ant

kangsèk *rg var of* KONGSI 2

kangsi to collect, gather, unite (*ki*). ***ǹ(an)** to have/make an agreement. *Aku ora bisa* *netepi kangsèn mau.* I wasn't able to keep the appointment. **ma∗** to band together

kangsrah *var of* KÈNGSRÈH

kangwong *var of* KAWONG

kani *inf var of* KANIL

kaniganten *sbst kr for* KANIGARA

kanigârâ *see* KULUK

kanil coconut cream, *i.e.* the thickened part of pressed coconut milk *(santen)* which rises to the top when the liquid is boiled or allowed to sit

kanin *oj* a wound; wounded

kaning *inf var of* KANIL

kanjel *inf var of* KATJEL

kanjil **konjal-∗** 1 restless, jittery. 2 flirtatious

kanon cannon. **ñg/di∗** to shoot with a cannon

kanstof, kanstop lace

kanṭa **tanpa ∗ tanpa kanṭi** all alone; lonely

kantâkâ *oj* to faint (*ki for* SEMAPUT*?*)

kantar **∗-∗** to blaze up. **ma∗(-∗)** *ltry var of ∗-∗. Kobongané saja ma∗-∗.* The flames burned brighter and brighter. *Semangaté ma∗-∗.* He has a fiery temperament. *See also* NG·ANTAR[2]

kanteb 1 (to fall) backwards. 2 to have a piece of bad luck

kantèk *rg var of* KANTI 2

kanten **ñg/dipun∗aken** to confirm (*kr for* ÑG/DI·KARUH·AKÉ)

kanṭeng **∗an** to wait around doing nothing. **∗-∗** *or* **ñg∗** (to wait) for a long time. *ngentèni ∗-∗* or *ngentèni nganṭeng* to have a long tense wait

kanṭèt *var of* GANṬÈT

kanti *ng,* **kantos** *kr* 1 patient, willing to wait. 2 until, up to (*var of* NGANTI). 3 *oj* ray, beam. **∗ǹ(an)** (**kantos·an** *kr*) patient by nature. *See also* ANTI

kanṭi 1 companion. *tanpa ∗* alone. 2 with, accompanied by; in a certain manner. *∗ sumèh* in a friendly way. *Aku ora bisa sinau ∗ tentrem.* I can't study in peace. *njambutgawé ∗ ora ana lèrèn²é* to work unceasingly. **(ke)∗ǹ** 1 to cooperate. *kekanṭèn karo mungsuh* to collaborate with the enemy. 2 hand in hand. *mlaku kanṭèn* to walk along holding hands. **ñg/di∗** 1 to take along as a companion. 2 to lead by the hand. **ñg/di∗kaké** to have smn take sth along. *Sapa sing dikanṭèkaké?* Who did you assign to go with him? *Barangmu kabèh dikanṭèkké A.* Your things are to be brought to you by A. **ñg/di∗ǹi** 1 to accompany. *Aku kirim lajang dikanṭèni prangko sèket sèn.* I sent a 50-cent stamp with my letter. *Lungané dikanṭèni pulisi.* A policeman went with him. 2 to give sth to be taken along. *A nganṭèni lajang kanggo kowé.* A gave me a letter to bring to you.

kanṭil 1 bamboo bed. 2 coffin. 3 magnolia-like flower. 4 to hang (from), stick (to). *Sepet isih ∗.* The fiber still clung to the coconut. *tansah ∗ karo ibuné* to always hang onto one's mother. **∗an** place to hang sth. *∗an kuntji* a key hook. **∗-∗** *or* **konṭal-∗** to dangle loosely. *Domé ∗-∗ ana ing putjuké wesi brani.* The needle hung from the tip of the magnet. **di∗** to be held back dishonestly. *Aku tuku pelem lima, sing mbok kèkké papat; sing sidji mesṭi kok ∗.* I bought five mangoes but you've only given me four—you must have kept one for yourself. **ñg/di∗aké** 1 to hang sth. *nganṭilaké gambar* to hang a picture. 2 to have smn go along with [smn]. *Anaké jèn sekolah di∗aké tanggané.* She sends her child to school with a neighbor. **ñg/di∗i** to hang sth onto. *Lajangané di∗i buntut.* He put a tail on his kite. *ptg* **k·r·anṭil** *pl* [small things] hang, dangle. **k·um·anṭil** 1 to hang loosely. 2 to cling to; to be devoted to

kantin clubhouse for community use: meetings, performances, social gatherings, *etc.*

kanṭing a certain type of small boat

kântjâ (**réntjang** *sbst? kr*) companion, mate, fellow. *∗né sing tunggal désa* smn from his same village. *Aku sa∗ku mlaju rerikatan.* My friends and I ran off. *∗ saklas* classmate. *∗ dolan* playmate. *∗-∗ tani* fellow farmers. *Kowé kéné waé ja, bèn aku ana ∗né.* Please stay here so I'll have smn to keep me company. **ke∗n** to associate [with]. *Aku seneng ke∗n karo kowé.* I like being with you. **ñg/di∗** to make friends with. **ñg/di∗ni** to keep smn company. *∗* **buri** my wife. *∗* **lanang** my husband. *∗* **ombjok·an** playmate. *∗* **wédok** my wife

kantjil mouse deer (a tiny jungle deer with a short tail, hoofs, and large rolling eyes): hero of many folk tales and specialist in outwitting other animals. **∗en** 1 with eyes rolling in fear. 2 unable to get to sleep

kantjing 1 lock. *∗ lawang* door lock. 2 button. **∗an** closed/locked up. **ke∗an** to get locked out. **ñg/di∗** to lock sth (up). **ñg/di∗aké** to button (up). *ngantjingaké* *klambi* to button one's shirt. **k·um·antjing** locked (up). * **gelung** a piece of sparkling jewelry worn in the hair

kantjleb stuck (in)to; *fig* to be obliged to stay smw

kanṭong name of one of the Chinese playing cards *(kertu tjilik)*. ***an** 1 pocket. 2 cloth sack. **ñg/di*i** to put sth in a pocket *or* sack. *Ḍèké nganṭongi kuntjiné.* He put his keys in his pocket.

kantor 1 office. *A se* karo aku.* A and I work in the same office. 2 office desk. ***an** office. **ñg*** to go to the office (to one's work). **ñg/di*aké** to use as an office; to have smn work in an office. **pa*an** office. * **pos lan giro** combined post office and telegraph office. * **pulisi** police station

kantos until (*kr for* KANTI)

kântrâ *oj* known far and wide

kantring **kontrang-*an** distracted; shattered; to go to pieces

kantru *-* to mope in sorrow

kantuk *rg var of* ANGSAL

kantun remaining, left over (*kr for* KARI)

kaos 1 stocking, sock. 2 knit shirt. 3 oil-lamp wick. 4 *rg var (sbst kr?) of* KADJI. * **béṭongan** athletic shirt, track shirt. * **blong** T-shirt. * **dijan** lamp wick. * **kotang** athletic undershirt. * **sikil** sock, stocking. * **sporet** *sms* * BÉṬONGAN *above.* * **tangan** glove

kaot different (*kr for* BÉDA, KATJÈK)

kâpâ (*or* **ke***) saddle. **ñg/di*ni** to saddle (up) [a horse]

kapak axe without a handle (carpenter's tool). **di*(-*)aké** 1 to have what done to it? ; to have sth done to it. *Sikilku mengko di*kaké ḍokter ja?* What is the doctor going to do to my leg? *Manuk kuwi jèn ora di*-*aké krasan.* If you leave birds alone (*i.e.* don't do anything to them), they'll come to feel at home with you. 2 whatever is done to one. *Senadjan di*-*aké, jèn ḍèké ora gelem adja dipeksa.* Whatever you do to him, if he isn't willing, don't force him. **ñg/di*** to use the above carpenter's tool (for). *See also* NG·APA·KAKÉ

kapal 1 ship. *anak ** ship's crew. 2 callus; callused skin. 3 horse (*kr for* DJARAN). ***en** to have/get calluses. **ñg*** callused. **pa*an** palace stables. * **m·abur** airplane. * **inḍuk** aircraft carrier. * **minjak** tanker. * **momot·an** freighter. * **montor** motor boat. * **silem** submarine

kapan 1 when? *Mulihé *?* When did he go home? When is he going home? 2 white cotton thread. ***(-*) waé** whenever. ** waé jèn aku bisa tak teka nggonmu.* I'll come and see you any time I can. ** aku bisa ketemu kowé?–*-* waé.* When can I see you?–Any time. **ñg/di*i** to wrap [a body] in a shroud. **ḍèk *** (**kala punapa** *kr*) when? *(past). Ḍèk * tekamu?* When did you get here? **suk *** (**m·béndjing punapa** *kr*) when? *(future). Suk * mangkatmu?* When are you leaving?

kapang to want, yearn (for). *Jèn ndika * mandjing suwarga...* If you long to enter heaven... *-* formal walking step by which female dancers enter the performing area at court

kapas cotton; cotton plant. *Lebonana *.* Stuff it with cotton. **ñg*** 1 to grow cotton. 2 (*psv* **di***) to apply cotton to. *Apa tatumu wis di*?* Have you put cotton on your cut?

kapati sound [of sleep] (*kr for* KEPATI)

kaper a certain small butterfly

kapes *-* soft in texture. *Boluné jèn didemèk *-*.* The cake is feathery to the touch.

kapi *oj* monkey

kapiadreng *ltry var of* ADRENG

kapiasem to smile to oneself, laugh inwardly

kapiḍârâ *oj* to faint

kapidereng eager (*ltry var of* DERENG)

kapiḍon(g)ḍong *var of* KEḌON(G)ḌONG

kapidulur *oj* to join, combine (with)

kapieneng *var of* KAPINENG

kapila 1 light red. 2 *var of* KAPILAH

kapilah merchant who travels with a desert caravan

kapilaju to tag along with *or* after habitually. *See also* LAJU

kapilaré childlike (*kr for* KAMIBOTJAHEN?). *Kowé adja *.* Don't act like a child. *See also* LARÉ

kapiluh to have/get tears in the eyes. *See also* LUH

kapiluju enchanted. *Aku * mèlu² seneng wonten wajang.* I was carried away by the shadow-play performance.

kapineng *oj* to be *or* remain quiet. *See also* NENG

kaping 1 (*kr for* PING?) (number of) times. ** pinḍo* twice. ** telu sedina* three times a day. *Papat * telu ana rolas.* Four times three is twelve. 2 (*kr for* KA-^{b} 2?) *ordinal marker.* ** papat Pèbruari* the fourth of

February. *bab * telu* chapter three. *Perang nDonja * Loro* the Second World War. *tjap²an kang * pat* fourth printing. ***-*** time after time; *(with negative)* never. *Olèhku nuturi wis *-*.* I've advised him time and again. *Adja *-* dolan karo ḍèwèké menèh.* You are never to play with him again. **ṅg/di*** 1 to [do] *n* times. *Iki mengko olèhé nggirah ngaping telu.* I'm about to give [the clothes] their third rinse. 2 (*or* **ṅg/di*aké**) to multiply. *Serupiah kuwi jèn di*aké sèwu dadi akèh.* One rupiah multiplied by a thousand is a lot of money! **ṅg/di·***number*·**(n)i** to do to sth *n* times. *Wis dikaping-teloni.* I've [rinsed the clothes] three times. *See also* KA-[b] 2, PING

kapinta *var of* KAPITA

kapinten neglected, abandoned (*kr for* KAPIRAN)

kapipotang *see* POTANG, UTANG

kapir atheist; agnostic

kapiran *ng,* **kapinten** *kr* neglected, abandoned. *Saploké bapakné mati, ḍèwèké *.* Since his father's death, he's had to fend for himself.

kapirangu *oj* to hesitate, waver. *See also* RANGU

kapisa *oj* dark brown

kapit **kopat-*** to wag. *Buntuté kopat-*.* It wagged its tail.

kapita *oj* sad; worried

kapital capital, money

kapitalis capitalist(ic)

kapitalisme capitalism

kapitan captain

kapitenggengen *var of* KAMITENGGENGEN

kapjuk splash! **ṅg/di*aké** to spatter [liquid] onto. **ṅg/di*(i)** to sprinkle sth with [a liquid]

kaplak very old. *dara *an* male pigeon being trained to come to one's hand by use of a female pigeon. **ṅg/di*i** to train [a pigeon] as above

kapling a variety of wood

kapok to have learned one's lesson. *Aku wis *.* Never again! **mu kapan!* When will you learn–? **ṅg/di*aké** *or* **ṅg/di*i** to teach smn a lesson; to cause smn to be wary. *Aku tau di*aké karo ḍèké, mulané aku wegah semajanan menèh.* I don't trust him any more: he has given me reason not to. *Tontonané ngapoki.* The show (was so bad that it) taught me never to go there again. *** kawus** to learn sth the hard way

kaprah usual, ordinary. *ora ** unusual, out of the ordinary. **ṅg*aké** to become usual; (*psv* **di*aké**) to make sth usual/ordinary. *See also* SALAH

kaprès having the remains of food around one's mouth after eating

kapri edible pea pod

kapsel any non-Javanese (*usu.* Occidental) ladies' hair style–*i.e.* any style other than the *gelung.* ***an** to wear the hair as above

kaptèn captain. ** kapal* ship's captain

kapti a wish, desire. *saijeg saéka ** working together with a mutual purpose

kaptin *var sp of* KAPTÈN

kapuk kapok. *** kapas** fluffy kapok used for stuffing. *** ranḍu** the stuff extracted from kapok seeds

kapulâgâ cardamom

kapur 1 whitewash. 2 chalk. ** tulis* blackboard chalk. *dat ** calcium. 3 udder. **ṅg/di*** to whitewash sth. *** barus** mothball

kapura *see* HIMA

kapuranta orange(-colored)

kapurantjang sharpened bamboo sticks arranged in a row atop a wall. **ṅg*** to clasp the hands with fingers intertwined and thumbtips touching

kapurit chlorine

kaput rundown, unkempt-looking

kar *see* KART

kar- *see also under* KR- *(Introduction, 2.9.3)*

kârâ 1 a certain climbing vine; the peanut-like product of this vine (of many varieties). 2 *oj* hand, arm; (elephant's) trunk. *éba ** elephant's trunk. **(se)*-*** (**kawis²** *kr*) hindrance, obstacle. *Muga² ora ana *-*.* I hope nothing will stand in the way. *** kapri** edible pea pod

karâbâ *oj* baby elephant

karabèn, karabin carbine rifle

karag rice scraped from the bottom of the cooking pan, sun dried, and fried into chips

karah metal piece by which a blade is affixed to a handle

karam *var of* HARAM

karânâ *ltry* reason, cause; because

karang 1 coconut plantation. 2 coral; coral reef. 3 vein of ore. 4 why...! well...! it is to be expected that...! ** ditabok kon ora nesu!* He hit me–why *shouldn't* I get mad! 5 *rg* rock. ***an** 1 article, piece of writing. 2 vein of ore. **ṅg/di*** to write, compose, invent stories. *sing ngarang* the author. *djuru ngarang* professional writer.

Adja ngarang lho. Don't fib to me! **ngarang (w)ulu** to marry the spouse of a deceased sibling. **n̈g/di*aké** to write sth for smn. **pa*an** yard surrounding a building. **pa·n̈g*** 1 writer, author. 2 act *or* way of writing. **dadi/di·gawé * abang** to be ravaged, destroyed. *** kirna** *or* *** kitri** fruit-producing trees in a yard. *** melok** decorative flower headdress worn by a bride. *** (w)ulu** pillow

karantèn, karantin quarantine. *Prauné ditahan ing *.* The ship was held in quarantine. **n̈g/di*** to quarantine

karapan calf race (a sport in Madura)

karat carat

karawisṭa *oj* decoration, ornament

karbirator *var sp of* KARBURATOR

karbol carbolic acid

karbon carbon paper

karburator carburetor

karé a curried rice-accompanying dish

karebèn *ng,* **kadjeng·ipun** *kr* 1 so that. *Dikon turu * énggal waras.* He told her to stay in bed so she'd get well quickly. 2 to let sth happen/go. *mBok * nutugaké tjritané.* Let her go on with her story! *Pitulungku ora ditrima, ja *.* They didn't thank me for my help, but–that's all right. *See also* BÈN

karèd **korad-*** to eat the scraps left on people's plates

karèk *rg var of* KARI

karem very fond of (*esp.* food, drink). *Aku * pelem.* I love mangoes. ** main* fond of gambling. **(ke)*an** a food one especially likes. **n̈g/di*i** to have a special fondness for. **pa*an** excessive fondness for sth

karep *ng,* **kadjeng** *kr,* **karsa** *ki* wish, intention, purport. *Ora ngreti *é wong mau.* I don't know what he's going to do. *or* I don't know what he wants/means. **ke*an** thing wanted/intended/meant. *Ḍèké nuruti ke*ané bodjo.* She did as her husband wished. **n̈g/di*aké** 1 to want. *Olèh apa kang di*aké.* He got everything he wanted. 2 to want [a girl] as one's wife. *Wis ana sing ngarepaké.* She's received a proposal. 3 to convey meaning. *Apa sing di*aké tulisan mau?* What has the article got to say? **pi*(an)** *sms* KE*AN. **sa*(-*)é** whatever smn wants. *Sa*mu.* It's up to you. *Ing bebrajan urip wong ora tumindak sa*-*é ḍéwé.* People living in a community can't just do whatever they please. *Jèn sa*mu ḍéwé ngono, adja pisan² ndjaluk naséhat aku manèh.* If you decide to go your own way, don't ever come to me for advice again. **dudu *é ḍéwé** not in command of oneself. *Kuwi dudu *é ḍéwé, marga krandjingan.* He's not himself–he's possessed of a spirit. *See also* AREP[a]

karèt rubber; rubber tree

kari *ng,* **kantun** *kr* left (over); (left) behind, at the end. *Mung * sidji.* There's only one left. *Awaké kuru banget, * balung karo kulit.* He's very thin–nothing but skin and bones. *sing ḍisik...sing ** the former...the latter. **a slamet.* Farewell! *Senadyan tekamu * mesṭi tak ḍisikaké.* Even though you got here last, I'll take care of you first. *** ...é waé** very nearly, all but. *Dridjiné kebatjok * ṭelé waé.* His finger is nearly severed. *Wit mau * bregé waé.* The tree has fallen nearly all the way down. ** seké waé* all but dead. ***n̄** what is left. *Merga tekané telat, mung éntuk karèn.* He got here late, so he only had leftovers. ***-*** to hope sth will not happen. **-* ḍèwèké teka.* If only he wouldn't come! ***n̄-*n̄** the very last one; the end. *Karèn²é lakoné bisa matèni banḍité.* At the end, the hero killed the bandit. **ke*n̄** what is left; the end. **n̈g*** to be at the end, to be the last one. *A nèk mlaku mesṭi ngari.* A always walks in back. **n̈g/di*kaké** to leave sth (behind). *Rotiné dikarèkaké sidji loro nggo aku.* Leave a cookie or two for me. **sa*né** all that remains. *sa*né kang tiwas* the survivors. *** aran** *or* *** djeneng** dead (*i.e.* only the name remains). *** ragas·an** reduced to poverty

karib close, intimate. *mitrané * Pardi* his good friend Pardi *or* a close friend of Pardi's

karit **korat-*** 1 chaotic, in disorder. *Wong² ngungsi korat-*.* They fled in confusion. 2 a drain on the finances

karja work, a job; worker; to do [work]. *wong ** tradesman, laborer. *njambut ** to work, engage in labor. *tjrita basa Djawa *né para pengarang kang wis kondang* Javanese-language stories written by well known authors. **n̈g/di*kaké** to rent out [government-owned property]. **k·in·arja** to be used (as, for). *Kena kinarja wuwuh.* It can be used as supplementary material. *** désa** service donated to the community. *** negara** public works done by the government. *See also* PAKARJA

karjawan worker, employee
karma the religious concept that all human acts receive their just reward or retribution in this life or in future incarnations
karnaval carnival
karo *ng,* **kalijan** *kr* 1 and; with. 2 compared with. *Djagoku * mungsuhé kalah geḍé.* My fighting cock is smaller than its opponent. 3 by [a person]. *Dikanḍani apa * ibuné?* What did his mother say to him? 4 [to say/speak] to. *Apa kowé basa * bapakmu?* Do you speak Krama to your father? 5 to, as, of, from, *etc. (in fixed expressions). paḍa ** the same as, similar to. *seneng ** to like, be fond of. *wedi ** afraid of. *mèmper ** to resemble, be similar to. *béda ** different from. *kosok bali ** the opposite of. *adoh ** a long way from. *gumantung ** to depend on. *tjeḍak * omahku* near my house. *tresna ** to (be in) love (with). 6 (**kalih** *kr*) two. 7 *ng kr; or* **kalih** *kr?* second month of the Javanese year (2-24 August). ***n asmara/djiwa/lulut/sih** *ng kr* to have sexual intercourse with. ***-*né (kalih-kalihipun** *kr*) both of them. **ṅg/di*ni (ṅg/dipun·kalih·i** *kr*) to do by two's. *Mesṭi waé ḍèwèké kalah, wong dikaroni.* Of course he was beaten–he was attacked by two of them. **se*** the two [of you]. *Muga² kowé se* paḍa slamet.* Best wishes to you and your wife. *** belah** 150. *** déné** *or* *** manèh** moreover, furthermore. *Kakéhan ḍuwit, * manèh ora ana bis.* It would cost too much, and besides there *is* no bus. *** tengah** 1½
karoron *ltry var of* KALORON
karsa 1 to want; to intend, be going to [do] (*ki for* AREP[a]). 2 will, be going to [do] (*ki for* BAKAL). 3 to be willing to; would like to (*ki for* GELEM). 4 intention (*ki for* KAREP). ***nan** 1 *ki* characterized by wanting everything one sees. 2 *ng kr* (one's) favorite food. **ṅg/di*kaké** *ki* 1 to like (*esp.* food) (*ki for* DOJAN). 2 to want, desire. 3 in the middle of [do]ing (*ki for* LAGI). *Nalika aku sowan mrana mau, Bu A lagi ngersakaké masak.* When I went to see them, Mrs. A was busy cooking. 4 to have smn [do], tell smn to [do]. **lagi *** on the point of being willing to [do]. **wis *** to capitulate, finally agree to [do]. *See also* ARSA
karsèt jewelry chain
kar(t) map, chart
karta *oj* welfare, well-being
karti **karta-*** *oj* welfare, well-being
kartijâsâ *oj* renowned, widely known
kartiprâdjâ *oj* service to the nation
kartisampéka *oj* military strategy
kartjis ticket. ** sepur* train ticket
karton cardboard
kartu *var of* KERTU
karu ***ñ** rice cooked by steaming it halfway done, removing it to a large bowl and pouring boiling water over it, then–after the water is absorbed–returning it to the steamer to finish cooking. ***-*(w)an** *var sp of* KARUH-KARUHAN. **ṅg/di*** to cook [rice] as above. **ṅg*-ṅ·tapung** to have a million things to do. **pa·ṅg*ñ** wooden *or* earthen container used when cooking rice as above
karuh (*or* **ke***) casual [of a friendship]. *mitra (ke)** a casual friend. ***an** clear, plain. *Ora karuwan djaraké.* His genealogy is obscure. **ora *(-*)an** unimaginable, beyond belief. *Bungahé ora karuwan.* He was ecstatically happy. *Raméné wis ora karu²an.* It was terribly crowded. *Ora *an tjatjahé.* There were millions of them. **ṅg/di*aké (ṅg/dipun·kanten·aken** *kr*) to confirm. *Aku kepingin ngaruhaké apa bener A mati tenan.* I want to find out for sure whether A died.
karuk 1 blossom of the guava. 2 dry cooked rice fried
karun *see* AMAL, DONJA
karuna *oj* to weep
karung jute sack, gunnysack. **ṅg/di*(i)** to put into a sack
karuni(ka) *oj* gift bestowed as a token of favor
karunya *var of* KARUNI
karut young corn
karuwan *var sp of* KARUH·AN
kas 1 wooden crate. 2 cash. ** désa* village cash fund. 3 *inf var of* MENTAS. 4 *rg var of* AKAS
kāsâ seventh month of the Javanese year (22 June-2 August)
kasab 1 a living, a job. 2 merchandise. 3 rough(-surfaced)
kasak *see* KUSUK
kasang pouch, kit
kasap bumpy, rough
kasapah 1 *oj* glans penis. 2 *rg* cassava
kasar coarse, crude, rough, unrefined, vulgar. **ṅg/di*i** to treat roughly/crudely. *** alus** rough and smooth, coarse and refined. *pagawéan *-alus* all types of work

kasat *** mata** visible, in (plain) sight. *Sing djeneng lelembut kuwi badan alus sing ora * mata.* Spirits are disembodied invisible beings.

kasbut *var of* KA·SEBUT

kasdu *var of* KESDU

kasèp too late. **ng/di*aké** to delay, to cause to be late. *** lalu wong m·weteng se·suweng·an** much too late (for sth)

kasih compassion, sympathy. ** marang sapada*[2] compassion for one's fellow beings. **ke*** 1 object of love; fiancé(e). 2 *oj* name. **ng/di·(ke)*i** 1 to love. 2 to show favoritism to. *Siti di*i guruné.* Siti is the teacher's pet. **k·in·asih** beloved. *See also* ASIH

kasijat (power of) good; producing good as contrasted with evil

kasil to succeed; to produce results. *Panèné *.* The harvest was bountiful. *Olèhku njambut gawé sedina muput ora *.* I worked all day long and have nothing to show for it. **ng/di*aké** to produce sth as a result. *Olèhé njéwakaké omah ngasilaké pirang*[2] *èwu rupiah.* Renting out their house netted them thousands. *Mobilé anjar di*aké saka séwan sawah.* He bought his new car with what he got from renting his rice field. *See also* ASIL

kasingi a certain plant

kasir cashier

kaskâjâ *oj* strong, powerful

kasmâlâ *oj* dirt, filth; disease, malady

kaspa cassava

kaspé *var of* KASPA

kaskarat (*or* ***an**) poor, destitute

kasta chaste

kastâwâ *oj* gift *or* honor bestowed on one

kasti (to play) a certain game resembling baseball or softball

kastil castle

kastjarjan *oj* astonished, taken aback

kastroli castor oil

kasturi fragrant oil extracted from flower seeds

kasukan 1 to have fun, enjoy oneself, *esp.* gambling at card-playing (*kr? ki? for* MAIN KERTU, SENENG[2]). 2 a certain dance (*sbst kr for* RONGGÈNG)

kasur mattress. ***an** 1 seat cushion. 2 to use a mattress

kasusra *oj* famous, renowned

kasut name of one of the Chinese playing cards *(kertu tjilik).* **ng/di*** to shuffle cards

kasuwari cassowary (ostrich-like bird)

kasuwur renowned, widely known

kaswârâ *oj* famous

katagori category

kaṭah much, many (*kr for* AKÈH)

katâlâ *** watja(na)** trouble one brings on oneself

katam to have finished one's reading of an assigned book (in a school for religious education). ***an** ceremony marking completion of a book (as above). **ng/di*aké** to complete one's reading of [a book, or section of the Koran]

katar *oj* ***-*** to blaze up, burn brightly

katé bantam chicken

katek̄ *var of* KATOG

katèl 1 teakettle. 2 a certain large spider

katelu **(katiga** *kr?*) 1 third month of the Javanese year (26 August-18 September). 2 the dry season. *See also* KATIGA, TELU

katibabal *ltry var of* BABAL

katèngong, katèngsun, katèngwang *oj* I, me; my

kaṭer ***-*** to hang soft and limp. **ng*** soft, limp

katès papaya

kati *ng,* **katos** *kr* catty: unit of weight equivalent to $^1/_{100}$ *ḍatjin* (*ca.* 0.617 kilograms = *ca.* 1.36 lbs.). ***n** in catties, by the catty. **ng/di*ni** to weigh sth in catties. *ngatèni beras* to weigh rice

katib Islamic minister and mosque official

katiga the third Javanese month; the dry season (*ng kr? kr for* KATELU?)

katigen *sbst kr for* KATIGA

kaṭik 1 an edible green pigeon-like bird. 2 moreover; and at the same time. *Djuru rawat, * biḍan pisan.* She's a nurse and also a midwife. *Luwih betjik jèn sugih * atiné tentrem.* It's better to be rich *and* have an easy conscience. 3 *excl of surprise, esp. at sth contrary to one's expectations or wishes. Blai, dalané tjijut, * peṭukan.* Oh-oh, such a narrow road and now we meet another car. ** turon barang.* Why on earth is he lying down [at a time when he is supposed to be doing sth else]! **4** intimate, trusted. **ng/di*** 1 to consider, or regard smn as, a trusted friend. 2 to look after horses. **k·in·aṭik** intimate, trusted. *mitra kinaṭik* a trusted friend. **djuru *** one who looks after horses. *See also* PAKAṬIK

katimumul 1 maybug, may beetle. 2 a skin disease that attacks the nails

kaṭing *-* to carry in the outstretched hand. *Olèhé nggawa lampu *-*.* He held the lamp out in front of him.

katingal to appear (*kr for* KATON, KÉTOK)

kaṭir *-* to squirm, wriggle [of long thin objects]

kâtjâ 1 glass. * *(pengilon)* looking-glass. *lemari ** wardrobe with a built-in mirror. 2 page. * *telu* page three. *-* to fill with tears. *Mripaté *-*.* Her eyes filled. **ke*** to look at oneself in the mirror. **ñg*** to use a mirror, look at oneself. * **benggala** large decorative wall mirror; *fig* an example held up to smn. * **bureng** translucent glass. * **mata** eyeglasses; * **mata ireng** sunglasses; * **mata pa·ñ·tulak-bledug** protective glasses. * **paès·an** large decorative mirror. * **prak-sana** binoculars; microscope. * **surjakanṭa** magnifying glass

katjak (*or* *an) to get sth on it. **an lenga/ bledug* to get oil/dust on it. *Tatumu adja nganti *an banju.* Don't get water on your cut.

katjang bean; nut (*esp.* peanut). *lenga ** pea-nut oil. *sambel ** bean paste. ***an** 1 a va-riety of goat with a puffed neck. 2 neck meat, *esp.* of cattle. **ñg/di*** to plant [a field] with beans/nuts. **pa*an** land planted to beans/nuts. *kaja weḍus diumbar ing pa*an* subjected to overpowering tempta-tion. * **babi** lima bean. * **dawa** *or* * **dja-ngan** string bean. * **(dje)brol** peanut. * **gorèng** fried peanuts; *fig* available any-where; fast-selling. *Bukuné karangané kaja * gorèng waé.* You can get his book every-where. *or* His book is selling like hotcakes. * **landjar·an** string beans (grown on climb-ing vines; often used as a certain dish, *lalab*). * **ora ñ·tinggal landjar·an·é** like father like son. * **penḍem** peanut. * **polong** kidney bean. * **tanah** *or* * **Tjina** peanut

katjâpâ *oj* tortoise

kâtjâpuri *oj* brick wall

katjar *see* KUTJUR

katjèk *ng,* **kaot** *kr* 1 different, dissimilar. **é aku karo kowé* the difference between you and me. 2 better, improved. **ñg/di*i** 1 to make sth different (from sth else). 2 to treat better. *Ja jèn lengganan aku kudu di*i.* You should make an exception of a good customer like me.

katjel woody-textured: of cassava that does not become tender (as it should) when cooked

katjèlu 1 attraction, appeal. 2 attracted; to long/yearn for. **k·um·atjèlu** attraction, ap-peal

katjer a thrush-like bird

katji 1 a fine white cotton fabric. 2 *var of* KATJÈK. * **aku** I go first! (in children's games)

katjik **kotjak-*** spilling out/over. *See also* KOTJAK

katjip shears for slicing plant leaves. **ñg/di*** to cut up [leaves] with the above

katjir **kotjar-*** in disorder/confusion. *Wong*[2] *ḍa mlaju kotjar-*.* People fled in panic.

katjo unruly, disorganized. *(ng)gawé ** to create confusion *or* disorder. *Rapaté *.* The meeting got out of hand. **ñg/di*** to disrupt. **pa·ñg*** trouble-maker. *Upatjarané di* karo pengatjo saka ndjaba.* The ceremony was disrupted by terrorists from outside.

katjrèt **kotjrat-*** to overflow, spill out

katjrit *var of* KATJRÈT

katju 1 handkerchief. 2 a square of cloth. 3 a measure for cloth: a length of fabric equal to the width, measured on the bolt by folding the fabric up diagonally

katjubung a certain plant; also, its (inedible) fruits

katjuk 1 *adr* young boy. 2 penis (of a boy)

katjung 1 boy used for running errands. 2 *var of* KATJUK. *-* to jut out

katjur a certain tree, also its fruit

katog 1 (to) the utmost; (to) the limit *or* end. *Ḍèké wis * olèhé seneng*[2]. He enjoyed himself to the utmost. *kanṭi * karosané* to the limit of his strength. *Montoré *, djamé *, omahé *.* His car is superior, his watch is superior, his house is superior. 2 to have one's fill. *Aku wis *.* I've had enough. *Olèhku ndeleng durung *.* I haven't seen enough of it yet. **ñg/di*aké** 1 to exert oneself to the limit. **na sabudimu.* Do it with all your strength! 2 to [do] to the point of gratification. *Olèhé urip idjèn wis di*aké.* He enjoys his single life to the full-est. *Ngatogaké olèhku dolanan.* I'll play with him till I've had enough. **sa*é** one's fill. *Jèn ngombé gentènan, mesti kabèh bakal keduman banju sa*é.* If you take turns drinking, everybody will get as much water as he wants. *Ḍèké bisa milih pangané sa*é, sasenengé.* He was privileged to choose all the food he wanted, whatever he liked. *See also* TOG

kaṭok *ng kr* (*or* **sruwal** *kr?*), **lantjing·an** *ki* pants, trousers. **∗an** to put on *or* wear trousers. **ng∗** to flatter, fawn on. **ng/di∗i** to put trousers on smn. ∗ **n·djero** men's undershorts. ∗ **kalèt** athletic supporter. ∗ **kolor** men's briefs. ∗ **monjèt** children's playsuit. ∗ **pènḍèk** *or* ∗ **tjenḍak** short trousers

Katolik Catholic; Catholicism. ∗ *Roma* Roman Catholic(ism)

katon *ng,* **katingal** *kr* to appear, show, seem. ∗ *bungah* to look happy. *Wis ora* ∗. You can't see it any longer. *Mung* ∗ *sirahé.* Only his head was showing. **∗é** it looks as if. *∗é kesusu.* He seems to be in a hurry. *∗é paḍa seneng²*. They look as if they're enjoying themselves. **∗en** to see in the mind's eye. *Durung krasan marga isih ∗en omahé lawas.* He doesn't feel at home yet; he still keeps remembering where he used to live. **ng∗** to put in an appearance. *Suwé ora ngaton merga lara.* He didn't show up for a long time–he was ill. **ng/di∗aké** to show, make a display of. *ngetingalaken panarimah* to show gratitude. *Ḍèké seneng ngaton²aké kapinterané.* He's always showing off his brains. **ng/di∗i** to appear as an apparition. *Memediné jèn ngatoni djam pira?* What time will the ghost appear? *Kantjané sinarawèdi tansah ngaton²i.* He kept seeing his bosom friend in his mind's eye. *See also* TON

katong *oj* king

katos catty (unit of weight) (*kr for* KATI)

katrap frambosia (*opt kr for* PAṬÈK?)

katrem to be very fond of

katrol crane (hoisting equipment). **ng/di∗** to help smn ascend, give smn a boost (*lit, fig*)

katu a certain shrub with edible leaves (used as a vegetable) and with berries (used as pop-gun ammunition). *bumbu* ∗ *raga* a rice-accompanying dish containing spiced beef or shrimp and the above leaves

katul fine flour-like coating on raw rice

Katulik *var of* KATOLIK

katulistiwa the equator

katun cotton (fabric)

katungka suddenly, unexpectedly

katut to get carried along/away; to get included. ∗ *angin* swept away by the wind. *Bukumu* ∗ *aku.* I accidentally walked off with your book. *Slamet* ∗ *munggah.* Slamet was promoted along with the others. *Sepatuku* ∗ *ilang.* My shoes are lost, along with other articles. *Aku* ∗ *diétung apa ora?* Did you include me in the count? **∗an** to carry sth along. *Banju udan bisa ∗an lelara.* Rainwater can carry diseases. **ng∗** to go along with. *Aku tekan kéné ngatut kantja².* I came here with some others. **ng/di∗aké** to cause sth to go along (with sth else); to include sth (with others). *Buku iki adja di∗aké ing lemari buku.* This book is not to go in the bookcase with the others. *Tanduranė kudu disusuk di∗aké lemahé ing sakubenging ojodé.* The plant should be dug out along with the soil around the roots. *See also* TUT

ka'u 1 dowdy, slovenly. 2 quick-tempered

kaul **(punagi** *ki?*) a promise to do a certain act if one's hope is fulfilled. *Ḍèké duwé* ∗, *jèn botjahé bisa waras, arep diadjak ngemis.* He vowed that if his child got well he would have her go begging with him. **∗an** 1 celebration held in fulfillment of a vow. 2 to eat [delicious foods] with great enjoyment. *Wohé djambu ngemohi, botjahé ∗an nggoné mangan.* The guavas were very plentiful and the children gobbled them up. **ng/di∗i** to do sth in fulfillment of one's vow. *Péstané iki ngauli olèhku lulus.* This is the party I said I'd give if I passed the exam. **pa∗an** place where a vow-fulfilling celebration is held

kaum 1 group, class, category (of people). ∗ *buruh* the laborer, the working man. ∗ *wanita ora kalah karo* ∗ *prija.* Women are not inferior to men. 2 Islamic official who advises on religious matters and looks after the mosque. **(pa)∗an** special area in a community inhabited by strict Moslems. *santri ∗an* Moslems living in such an area and forming a particular group in Javanese social stratification. ∗ **krama** the working man, the laboring class

Kâwâ Eve (first woman)

kawah 1 volcanic crater. 2 amniotic fluid. **banju (ke)∗(ing ari²)** amniotic fluid

kawak *cr* antiquated. *Sepéḍa mau* ∗ *nanging sentosa.* The bicycle is old but sturdy. **∗an** past its prime

kawal **ng/di∗** to guard, escort. *Montoré Présidèn di∗ pulisi.* The President's car had a police escort. *See also* AWAL

kawan four (*kr for* PAPAT)

kawaos *kr* *var of* KUWAOS

kawâsâ *var of* KUWASA

kawat 1 wire. *pager* ∗ wire fence. ∗ *tilpun*

telephone wire. * *krawangan* wire netting.
2 telegram. *See also* KRAWAT

kawatir *var of* KUWATIR

kawatos *kr   var of* KUWATOS

kawegan   *rg var of* KAWOGAN

kawèr   *-* *pl* hanging down, dangling. ŋg*
to hang (down) loosely

kawès   a certain freshwater fish

kawet   1 crotch. 2 wire for binding cracked
teapots. ŋg* 1 tight, binding. 2 hanging
down. ŋg*aké lambé·né to bite the lips, *e.g.*
when suppressing emotion

kawi   1 Old Javanese (*oj*): archaic form of
Javanese, now used almost exclusively in wajang drama. 2 *oj* author, writer. ŋg/di* to
compose classical verse in *oj*. k·um·awi-*
to pretend that one is skilled in *oj*

kawin   (to get) married. *A* * *karo B.* A is
married to B. *Ḍèké wis* *. He's married.
Ḍèké arep *. She's going to be married.
mas * dowry. ke* poetic epic written in
Old Javanese (*Kawi*). ŋg/di*aké to marry
[a couple], *i.e.* perform the marriage ceremony. per*an marriage. * gantung married by proxy while apart

kawir   *-* attached only loosely; nearly severed

kawirjawan   courage, bravery. ŋg* having
the bearing of a nobleman. *See also* WIRJA,
WIRJAWAN

kawis   *-* obstacle (*kr for* KARA²). pa*an
yard (*sbst kr for* PA·KARANG·AN)

kawit   1 because. * *saka ora bisa nglangi* because of his inability to swim. 2 since, beginning from. * *bijèn* for a long time; a long
time ago. * *kapan kowé lara?* How long
have you been ill? * *saka Sala dalané lempeng.* From Solo the road is straight. *an
(at) first; (at) the beginning. *anak *an* the
first child. *ing telung wulan *an tahun iki*
during the first three months of this year.
*tanpa kenjana-njana *an* without expecting
much at the start. ŋg/di*i to begin sth. *See
also* AWIT, SAKAWIT, WIWIT

kawogan   in charge (of); authorized. *Sapa
sing * nata kursi?* Who's supposed to set up
the chairs? *Aku * ngrampungaké gawéjan
mau.* I was assigned to complete the job.
Radjapati wis diurus déning sing *. The
homocide is in the hands of the authorities.

kawok   kowak-* to speak loudly and/or
boastfully

kawon   to lose; less, inferior (*kr for* KALAH)

kawong   1 familiar, well known. 2 to feel

at home. *an having taken on certain characteristics. *an goḍong like a leaf

kawruh   (se·serep·an *kr?*) (body of) knowledge; lore. *ngangsu* * to acquire knowledge.
* *tetanèn* agricultural know-how. ŋg/di*i
to know; to see. *Sapa sing ngawruhi lungané
A?* Who knows when A left? *or* Who saw
A leave? *See also* WERUH

kawuk   1 old, decrepit. 2 an old water lizard.
* ora weruh slira·né the pot calls the kettle
black

kawul   sugar-palm fibers used for igniting
fires. * *kaju* wood shavings used as kindling

kawula   1 servitor. 2 I, me (*formal var of*
KULA). *dalem* * I, me (*ka: used when addressing a king*). 3 people, subjects (of a
monarch). ŋg* to serve, be in service (in a
high-status household). ŋg/di*-wisuda to
elevate the dignity and prestige of one's
master by the excellence of one's service to
him. ŋg/di*ni to be a servitor to [a high-
status household]. pa·ŋg* servitude, act *or*
condition of being in service (as above)

kawulâwargâ   family (*opt kr for* KULAWARGA)

kawung   1 sugar-palm leaf: used for cigarette
wrappers. 2 a certain batik pattern

kawuri   *oj*   last, previous

kawus   to learn sth the hard way. ŋg/di*aké
to teach smn a lesson

ké-ᵃ, kè-   *var of* KE- *before* I (*Introduction,
3.1.5.2*)

-kéᵇ   (-k̇ké *after vowel*)   *inf var of* -AKÉ (*suffix*)

ke-   (*see also under* KA-: *Introduction, 2.9.2*)
prefix: k- before vowel. 1 to [do] inadvertently. *Aku ke·temu kantjaku.* I ran into a
friend of mine. *Ḍèké ke·plèsèd kulit geḍang.*
He slipped on a banana peel. *Omahku k·o-
bong.* My house caught fire. 2 to be [done
to] inadvertently. *ke·tjekel pulisi* to get
caught by the police. *Ḍèké ke·peksa njilih
ḍuwit.* He was obliged to borrow money.
*...an to get acted upon (*inadvertent var
of* DI...I). *k·ûdan·an* to get caught in the
rain. *...(n)en 1 *var of* *...AN *above. Sikilku ke·tlusub·en eri.* I got a thorn in my
foot. 2 too, excessively. *Wédangé ke·pa-
nas·en.* The tea is too hot. *ke·botjah·en
childish; callow. *See also individual entries*

keba   woven-straw material. *tas* * bag made
of woven straw. *ḍompèt* * woven-straw
wallet

kebajak   Javanese-style ladies' blouse

kebajan   messenger, errand runner. * **désa**

village official whose job is to carry out errands for his superior
kebak full (of), filled (with). *kanṭong* * *ḍuwit* a pocket full of money. *Gelasé* *. The glass is filled. **ke*en** too full. **ṅg/di*i** to fill. *ngebaki kulah* to fill the bathtub. *Gambaré di-tèmplèk²aké nganti ngebaki témbok.* They filled the entire wall with pictures. * **mentjeb²** completely full
kebar counting unit for flat things; sheet, leaf. *klasa sa** one mat
kebat quick. * *kaja kilat* like lightning. * **k·liwat** hasty and careless
kebaut to spend inadvertently. *Wah tjilaka, ḍuwit iuran katut * dak enggo blandja ḍéwé.* My God, I spent the contribution money along with my own when I did my shopping!
kèbek̄ *oj* ***an** full, filled (with). **ṅg/di*i** to fill
kebek̄ *var of* KEBAK
keben a certain tree, the most famous specimens of which are found at the north gate of the palaces at Jogjakarta and Surakarta
kebes wet. *teles* * soaking wet. **ṅg*** to get soaked. *Kok ngebes waé, apa ora duwé pajung?* You're soaked! haven't you got an umbrella? **ṅg/di*i** to get sth soaking wet
kebèt leaf, sheet (of paper). * *sing kèri ḍéwé* the last page. ***an** (in the form of) sheets. **ané amba²*. The sheets are large.
kebintjih castrated, spayed (*kr for* KEBIRI)
kebiri *ng,* **kebintjih** *kr* (*or* ***ṅ**) (having been) castrated, spayed. **ṅg/di*** to castrate, spay. *See also* BIRI
kebit **kebat-*** worried, apprehensive jittery
kebjok **ṅg/di*** to remove wax from fabric by rinsing it in hot water (a step in the batik-making process)
keblak a certain type of ghost
keblas *rpr* a swift motion. **ing banju* a rush of water. *See also* BLAS
kéblat direction, compass point. *Aku mesṭi ora ngerti* *. I have a poor sense of direction. *ngarepaké * nang Mekah* to face in the direction of Mecca. **ṅg/di*** to face (in) [a certain direction]. *ngéblat Mekah* to face toward Mecca
kebluk lazy, good-for-nothing. ***an** beaten, whipped. *enḍog *an* beaten egg. **ṅg*** 1 lazy, shiftless. 2 (*psv* **di***) to beat, whip. **pa·ṅg*** act *or* way of beating. * **mulur** lazy
kebo *ng,* **maésa** *kr* kerbau, water buffalo. ***an** 1 to give rides to children on the back while crawling on hands and knees. 2 (*or* ***-*an**) to play kerbau; a toy kerbau. **di* ranggah** to be sacrificed to ensure the prosperity of a new venture. **ṅg*** resembling a kerbau (referring *esp.* to sluggish actions and/or constant eating). **ṅg/di*kaké** to treat [*esp.* an unwanted child] like an animal. * **ng·abot·an sungu** unable to care for one's many children. * **bukur** *or* * **bungkang** a roach-like insect that walks backwards. * **djerum** a certain style of Javanese house. * **lawung** kerbau not used for farm work. * **menggah** a certain kind of necklace. * **peli·ṅ** male kerbau; *fig* argumentative person. * **putjung** a tiny red insect. * **ṅ·susu gudèl** 1 the old learn from the young. 2 the children support the parents
kebogiro gamelan melody played to welcome honored guests and to close wajang performances. **ṅg/di*ni** to welcome [guests] with this melody
kebon 1 backyard garden for flowers, vegetables. *tukang* * or *pak* * gardener, yard man; man who lives on school premises and looks after the building and grounds. 2 area planted to a single crop. * *kopi* coffee plantation. ***an** planted area. **ṅg/di*aké** to oust [a wife] without divorcing her. * **binatang** *or* * **radja** zoo(logical gardens)
kebos ***an** to get blown on, *esp.* by exhaust fumes from a running engine. **ṅg/di*i** to blow fumes at/on (from a tailpipe)
kebuk 1 lung. 2 club, rod. **ṅg/di*** 1 to slap [the stomach] lightly. 2 to strike with a club/rod
kebul smoke, steam. ***-*** to give off smoke/steam. **ṅg/di*i** to get smoke/steam on sth. *ptg* **k·r·ebul** *or* **k·um·ebul** to give off smoke/steam
kebuli a method of preparing rice with spices. *sega* * spiced rice
kebur **ṅg/di*** to keep scooping and pouring [liquid, *e.g.* soup] in order to prevent oils from separating out, or to keep the food from sticking or scorching
kebut 1 fan for shooing insects. 2 referee's signal flag. 3 dust cloth. 4 complete(d); altogether. *Mèh * teka kabèh.* Nearly everyone was there. *Aku ngrampungaké*

panggawéjan semana akèhé nganti ∗. I saw all of the work through to completion. *buḍal ∗* to leave all together. **∗-∗** *or* **ke∗** to fan oneself to keep insects away. **n̈g/di∗aké** to wave sth. *Gendérané di∗aké.* He signaled with a flag. *ngebutaké suwiwi* to flap the wings. **n̈g/di∗i** to wave [a cloth, fan] at/on. *Djarané di∗i.* He shooed insects away from the horse. *Lemudé di∗i.* He swished away the mosquitoes. *Médjané kotor, ajo di∗i kana.* The table is dirty—dust it, will you? **k·um·ebut** to swing back and forth. *Mèmèhané paḍa kumebut kena angin.* The drying laundry flutters in the wind.

keda a covered drinking cup *or* glass

keḍabjak *ptg ∗ or ∗-∗* loose, floppy [of an overlarge garment]

kedah ought to, have to (*kr for* KUDU)

kedal way of speaking; enunciation. *∗ing gunem ora tjeṭa.* He doesn't enunciate clearly. *∗ rada mesakaké* a somewhat pitying tone. **n̈g/di∗aké** to utter, pronounce [words]

keḍali a swallow-like bird

keḍampal **∗an** *or* **∗-∗ 1** to move awkwardly *or* laboriously. **2** to scramble, move hastily

keḍana **∗-keḍini** boy-girl sibling combination

kedandapan *var of* GEDANDAP·AN

keḍangklik *ptg ∗* hanging down, dangling. **keḍongklak-∗** hanging down and swaying

keḍangkrang (*or* **n̈g∗**) to sit (improperly) in a place which elevates one above others

keḍangsang *var of* GEḌANGSANG

keḍap moment, interval (*root form: kr for* ḌÉLA). **∗an 1** timid, easily frightened. **2** food sampled (*ki for* ITJIP²AN). **n̈g∗ 1** apprehensive; afraid. **2** [of kites] to take a dive, drop suddenly. **n̈g/di∗i** to take a taste of (*ki for* NG/DI·ITJIP·I). **sa∗** a moment (*kr for* SE·ḌÉLA). **k·um·eḍap** frightened. **∗ kilat** *or* **∗ liring** to wink

keḍaplang *ptg ∗ pl* with outstretched arms. **n̈g∗** to stretch the arms out to the sides. *See also* ḌAPLANG

keḍasih a cuckoo-like bird. *kaja manuk ∗* a woman who is abducted and then abandoned. **n̈g∗** to produce the cry *(kuk-kuk!)* of the above bird

keḍaton palace; court. *basa ∗* court-style Javanese language, characterized mainly by certain vocabulary items. **n̈g∗** to return to the court after a long absence. *See also* ḌATU

kéḍé a left-handed person. **n̈g/di∗ 1** to use the left hand (on, for). **2** to give *or* receive with the left hand (a serious breach of etiquette)

keḍébjah **∗-∗** hanging in loose folds [of overlarge clothing]

keḍèḍèr **∗an** *or* **keḍéḍar-∗** to sweep on the ground [of a batik wraparound that is too long]

keḍekes to assume a cross-legged sitting position. *Mak ∗ terus ora omong babar pisan.* He plunked himself down without a word. **∗an** to humbly approach an exalted person by moving forward in a cross-legged sitting position. **n̈g∗** to sit cross-legged before an exalted person, showing respect and humility

keḍelé soybean (*var of* ḌELÉ). **n̈g∗** soybean-like

keḍemek̄ **∗-∗** *or* **n̈g∗** to tiptoe; to walk slowly with short steps

kèḍeng squint-eyed

kedengkèk to twist backward. *Teka seka ngepit, tangané ∗.* He fell off his bike and bent his hand back.

keḍengklak, keḍengklèk to bend backward

keḍèngkrèng (*or* **n̈g∗**) to sit in a more elevated place than others (breach of etiquette)

keḍèp *ng kr,* **kedjep** *ki* a wink, a blink. *∗ing mripat* a wink (blink) of the eye. *Tanpa ∗ mandeng rupané anaké.* She stared unblinking at her daughter. **∗-∗** to keep winking; to blink continuously. **n̈g∗** to wink/blink as a signal. *Jèn arep mulih ng∗ waé.* When you want to go home, blink your eyes. **n̈g/di∗aké** to blink [the eyes]. *kaja ilang di∗aké* to not dare take one's eyes off sth for fear it will disappear. **n̈g/di∗i** to wink/blink at smn as a signal. *ngeḍèpi bodjoné* to blink a signal to one's husband/wife. **sa∗ nétra** a moment; the twinkling of an eye. **sa∗an** (in) one wink/blink. **k·um·eḍèp** to blink the eyes. **kumeḍèp kasèp** to (be late and) miss sth by an eyelash. **kumeḍèp katja/tesmak** to gaze unblinking, to stare in wide-eyed wonder

keḍep **∗ m·anteb** steadfast, loyal

keḍepek̄ sitting in a slumped position. **n̈g∗** to slump into a seat; to sit slumped

keḍepes seated cross-legged (*see also* KEḌEKES). *Lungguhé wong² ptg ∗.* They were all sitting around cross-legged. **n̈g∗** to seat oneself cross-legged

keḍeprek̄ *var of* KEḌEPEK

kèder **1** to lose one's way. **2** wall-eyed

keḍer to vibrate. **ṅg/di*aké** to cause to vibrate. *Prahoto mau ngeḍeraké katja tjenḍéla.* The truck rattled the windowpanes.

keḍésé overpowered, subdued

keḍik a little, a few (*kr for* ṬIṬIK)

keḍinḍing a variety of bird

keḍingklang (*or* *-*) lame, crippled; to hobble. *See also* ḌINGKLANG

keḍini *see* KEḌANA

kedjâbâ *ng,* **kedjawi** *kr* except (for), aside (from), besides. *Aku éman² ḍuwité, * ngono ora kober.* I'm saving money, and besides I haven't time. *Di-arep² teka djam sanga, * jèn udan.* We're supposed to be there by nine o'clock, unless it rains. *ora ana manèh ** only, exclusively (*i.e.* there is nothing else other than). *Tambané ora ana manèh * mung kinine.* Quinine is the only cure for it. ***n** *inf var of* *. **ṅg/di*kaké** to exclude. *Adja nganti ana sing di*kaké.* Make sure no one is left out. *See also* DJABA

kedjawi *kr for* KEDJABA

kèdjèk **ke*** to writhe, squirm. *Pitiké ke* arep mati.* The chicken writhed in its death throes. *Olèhé nangis nganti ke*.* He threw a tantrum.

kedjèl *-* to have spasms/convulsions

kedjem cruel, pitiless

kedjèn 1 plowshare. 2 three-peaked roof. **ṅg*** resembling one of the above

kedjeng [of arm, leg] stiffened because of damage to the joint

kedjep a wink, blink (*kr for* KEḌÈP)

kedjer *-* *or* **ke*** 1 to flutter. 2 to hover in midair. 3 hard [of laughing, crying]. *A ke* ngguju.* A laughed his head off. **ṅg/di*i** to flutter around *or* hover over sth

kedjèt *-* to twitch in death throes

kèdju cheese

kedju stiff, sore, aching

kedjut *var of* KEDUT

keḍoḍor ***an** *or* *-* *or* **ṅg*** to touch the ground, hang down too low [of clothing]

keḍok mask, front, pretense. ** kanggo nulung lijan* a pretense of helping others. ***an** wet muddy place; rice paddy

keḍon(g)ḍong a certain tree; also, its edible fruit

keḍongkrong to assume a hunched-over sitting position. **ṅg*** to sit hunched over

kedubang *var of* DUBANG

keḍuk ***an** a hole dug in the ground. **ṅg/di*(i)** to dig (into, up); to scoop (out). *ngeḍuk téla* to dig up a cassava. *Kapalé keruk ngeḍuki enḍut.* The dredger is scooping out mud. *Liweté wis mateng, gèk di*.* The rice is done; please dish it out. **pa·ṅg*** act *or* way of digging/scooping

kedumel ***an** *or* **ṅg*** to grumble with dissatisfaction

kedumplag *rpr* drumbeats

keḍung 1 deep pool in a river. 2 pond, small lake. **ṅg*** to form a deep pool

kedut muscular twitch, *esp.* of the eyelid. ***en** *or* **k·um·edut** to twitch

keduwel *-* *or* **keduwal-*** 1 to keep fussing with one's hair *or* clothing. 2 to express displeasure, grumble with dissatisfaction. **ṅg*** 1 to grumble. 2 to flow spirally, *e.g.* water running out of a bathtub

keḍuwel ***an** *or* **ṅg*** to linger, dawdle, hang back. *Olèhé nganggo djarik kok *an.* You're certainly taking a long time to put on your wraparound! *Adja ngeḍuwel waé, énggal omonga.* Don't hold back–speak out!

keḍuwet *var of* KEḌUWEL

keduwul *var of* KEDUWEL

keduwung remorseful. **ṅg/di*i** to regret sth. *Ḍèké ngeduwungi olèhé ora énggal² lunga menjang ḍokter.* He regretted not having gone to the doctor sooner. *** ng·untal weḍung** to cry over spilt milk

kègi stuck-up, conceited

kégok *var of* KAGOK

kèh *ng* *sing *-** most of them. *Wong sing manggon kéné sing *-* sugih.* Most of the people who live around here are rich. ***é** the amount (of). **é lima.* There are five of them. *buku seméné *é* this many books. ***-*é** at the most. *Kèh²é sing teka wong sèket.* Fifty people at the most showed up. **nge/di*(-*)i** to increase the number *or* amount of. **sa*é** many of, most of. *Sakèhing wit²an paḍa garing mekingking.* Most of the trees dried up completely. **sa*-*é** 1 no matter how much/many. 2 as much/many as possible. *Aku mangan sa-kèh²é.* I ate as much (many) as I could. ***-(se)ṭiṭik·é** number *or* amount of. *See also* AKÈH

kéjang name of one of the small playing cards *(kertu tjilik)*

kéjok defeated. *Aku trima * menawa balapan karo kowé.* I accept defeat [before I start] if I race with you. *-* *rpr* chickens squawking. **ṅg*** to give up. *Bareng rumangsa wis arep kalah, A ndjur ngéjok.* Knowing he was going to lose, A quit trying. *ptg* **k·r·éjok** to keep squawking

kéjong   water snail. **en** spavined; having skin lesions [of animals]. * **goṇḍang** a certain large snail. * **goṇḍang djarak sungut·é** a person of humble background becomes a king

kèk   grandfather (*shf of* KAKÈK). **nge/di*i** 1 to give. *Rénéa, lé, tak *i pohung.* Come here, sonny, I'll give you a cassava. 2 to put sth (into). *Sapa sing nge*i ujah nang djangan iki?* Who salted the soup?

kek-   *see also under* K- (*Introduction, 3.1.3*)

kékah   (*or* **an**) ritual meal (at which a sheep is slaughtered) held for the purpose of ensuring a baby's health and well-being. **ng̈/di*i** to hold the above ceremony in honor of [a baby]

kekah   solid, strong (*kr for* KUKUH)

kekeb   1 rice-cooker lid. 2 glass lamp chimney. **ng̈/di*i** to put the lid on [a rice-cooking pot]

kékéjan   spinning top

kekel   1 [of rice] well done and sticky. 2 [of laughing, coughing] hard, convulsive. **ng̈*** to laugh hard. **ng̈*aké** 1 (*psv* **di*aké**) to cook [rice] to the well-done, sticky stage. 2 uproarious. *Olèhé ṇḍagel ngekelaké.* His jokes are very funny. **k·um·ekel·en** (to laugh) hard. *See also* KAMIKEKELEN

kekep   **ng̈/di*** to hug, embrace, clasp. *ngekep ḍengkul* to clasp one's knee; to clasp the knee of smn to whom one is showing humility and respect. **pa·ng̈*** act *or* way of clasping. *Ḍèkè nguwalaké pangekepé ḍengkulé.* He released his hold on his knee.

kèker   binoculars, field glasses. **ng̈/di*** to look at sth with binoculars

keker   solid, firm, strong. **ng̈/di*aké** to make firm/strong. **pa*an** a restricted area

kekes   chilly; chilled with emotion, *esp.* fear. * **miris** shivering with fear/apprehension

kèkèt   1 a soft green hairless caterpillar. 2 well (tightly) constructed. **ng̈*** to stick tight, hold together firmly

kéklak   to come off, become detached *or* separated

kèkrèk   **ng̈*** 1 to make a rasping sound. 2 (*psv* **di***) to cut *or* tear sth apart/off. *ngèkrèk goḍong geḍang* to cut banana leaves from the stalk. * **arèn** to grasp the nettle

kékuk   *var of* KIKUK

kèl *ng kr* (*or* **pambeng** *or* **wulan·an** *kr?*), **tarab·an** *ki* to menstruate

kel-   *see also under* KL- (*Introduction, 2.9.3*)

kela   **n** (to make) vegetable soup. **ng/di*** to make [ingredients] into vegetable soup. *Goḍongé téla di* apa?* What kind of soup are you making with the cassava leaves? *See also* KELAN

kelab   **-*** *or* **ng̈*** *or* **k·um·elab** to move in wave-like motions. *Lajangané *-* kabur ing angin.* The kite undulated with the wind current.

kelaḍ-bau   1 bracelet worn on the upper arm as part of a classical dance costume. 2 cord sash worn by military aides

kelah   1 accusation, charge. **ng̈/di*aké** to bring [a civil case] to court

kelam   *var of* KELÈM

kelamun *oj* if, when(ever)

kelan   (to make) vegetable soup. **ng̈/di*** to make [ingredients] into vegetable soup. *See also* KELA

kélangan   *form of* ILANG

kelap   **-*** to glisten, sparkle. *ptg* **k·r·elap** *pl* glittering, sparkling. **k·um·elap** 1 to glitter. 2 to quake in panic

kelar   1 (**kuwawi** *opt? kr*) able, strong enough. *Apa kowé * nggéṇḍong aku?* Can you carry me on your back? 2 finished. *Merga sregep, gawéané bisa tjepet *.* He works so hard he finishes quickly. **ng̈/di*aké** to finish sth

kelas   *var of* KLAS

kelasi   sailor

kelé   **-*** out of use, lying idle. *Vulpèné *-*.* Nobody's using the pen.

kelèḍ   lazy, lackadaisical

kèlèk   1 armpit. 2 (*or* **an**) underarm of a garment. **ng̈/di*(i)** to bully [a younger boy] by forcing him to smell one's armpits

kèlem   1 to become submerged. *Kapalé *.* The ship sank. 2 [of colors] dull. 3 sticky substance around the body of a newborn baby. **ng̈*** to submerge deliberately. *Aku bisa ngèlem ing banju nganti suwé.* I can stay under water for a long time. **ng̈/di*aké** to cause to submerge. *Kapal mau di*aké mungsuh.* The ship was sunk by the enemy. **ng̈/di*(i)** to submerge, inundate. *Udan deres ngèlemi pesawahan.* Heavy rains flooded the paddies. **k·um·èlem** to sink, go under. *ngentèni kemelemé gabus* to wait for sth highly improbable to happen

kelèm   metal clamp. **ng̈/di*** to clamp, attach *or* fasten with a clamp

kelem   *var of* KÈLEM. ***an** 1 steamed sweet cakes, of various types, made of rice flour, sugar, and coconut milk. 2 sweet potato (*sbst kr for* (KE)TÉLA). 3 crocodile (*sbst kr for* BAJA[a])

keleng *ireng* *-* glossy black. **n̈g/di*** to blacken *(term used in batik-making, kris-making)*

kelèp valve

kelèt 1 too small, tight-fitting. 2 emaciated. 3 firmly attached. * *ing lim* glued on. *Anaké * banget karo bapakné.* The child is deeply attached to his father. **n̈g/di*(i)** to skin, peel. *ngelèti kidang* to skin a deer

kèli to get carried along on a current. **n̈g*** to allow oneself to be carried on a current. **n̈g/di*kaké** to set sth adrift on a current. *Sawisé peṭi mau ditutup rapet, terus dikèlèkaké ing bengawan.* He sealed the box and consigned it to the river. *See also* ILI

kelik *adr* little boy. *É * renéa!* Hey, son, come here!

keling 1 racial stock of India, Pakistan. 2 a rivet. 3 (*or* **kelak-***) brass knuckles. **n̈g/di*** 1 to rivet sth. 2 to hit with brass knuckles

kelip five-cent coin used during colonial times. *-* *or* **kelap-*** 1 to glitter, flicker, gleam. 2 [of eyelids] to flutter. **k·um·elip** to flutter, flicker. *Saka kadohan katon dijan kumelip.* He could see a flicker of light way in the distance.

kelir 1 white screen used as a projector for shadow plays or movies. 2 fence dividing one property from another. 3 color (*var of* KLIR)

kéloh **kélah-*** unsteady, weak and wobbly, without strength

kelon (*or* ***an**) asleep in each other's arms. **n̈g/di*i** to hold in the arms while sleeping

kelop *var of* KLOP. *-* [of eyes] wide open and shining

kélor a certain tree whose leaves are used in folk medicines. *sagoḍong ** small. *djagad sagoḍong ** small world. *ora mung sagoḍong ** huge, vast

kéloren *var of* KALOREN

kelos spool, reel. * *benang* a spool of thread. *benang ** thread wound on a spool

kélot **kélat-*** to hang back, drag one's feet

kelud feather duster; whisk broom. **n̈g/di*i** to clean *or* dust with the above

keluh nose ring for cattle. **n̈g/di*i** to equip [cattle] with a ring; to lead [cattle]. *Kebo-sapi di*i, jèn wong dikanḍani.* Cattle are led by the nose; human beings are guided by advice.

keluk 1 smoke, steam. 2 *rg* dust. 3 *rg* famous. **k·um·eluk** to produce *or* give off smoke/steam; *fig* famous

kelun 1 a rolling, billowing motion. 2 nefarious actions. **n̈g/di*** 1 to make sth into a roll. 2 to round up [a group, for a nefarious purpose]. **n̈g*aké ala** to spread bad stories about smn. *ptg* **k·r·elun** to keep billowing. **k·um·elun** smoky; to smoke profusely; *fig* to reach the sky. *Kukusé dupa kumelun.* The incense smoke rises skyward. *Kukusé kumelun metu saka tjrobong.* The smoke billowed from the chimney in great clouds. *See also* LUN

kélut persuaded, won over, charmed

kelu(w)arga *var of* KULAWARGA

keluwé ***n̈** (to go) hungry. *mBok ranḍa saanaké paḍa keluwèn.* The widow and her children never have enough to eat. *Jèn wis djam sidji mbok mangan, adja nganti kluwèn.* When it's lunchtime, eat; don't wait till you are half starved. **n̈g*** hungry, ready to eat. *See also* LUWÉ

kem- *see also under* K- *(Introduction, 3.1.7)*

kem. *see* MENTRI

kemaḍéjan, kemaḍijan *var of* KEMLAḌÉJAN

kémah tent

kemah **n̈g/di*-*** to keep chewing on sth without swallowing it. *ngemah[2] tebu* to chew sugar cane

kemamang 1 an evil spirit in the form of a giant's head. 2 a painting *or* relief of the above, used for decorating a stage where classical-dance performances are given

kemampo nearly ripe

kemandjon to lie awake unable to get back to sleep

kemânggâ spider

kemanggang suitable for broiling. *pitik ** a broiling chicken

kemangi a certain plant whose leaves are served (raw) at ritual meals

kemangrang [of coconuts] in the mature state when the fibers are reddish brown like the *angrang* ant

kemantèn *rg var of* MANTÈN

kemaron 1 large earthenware water jug (*rg var of* PENGARON). 2 having many things on the mind to distract one

kemaruk happy with and proud of a new acquisition. *Saploké duwé pit anjar, bandjur * ditunggangi terus.* Ever since he got his new bike he's so proud of it he rides it all the time. **n̈g*i** to have a voracious appetite after recovering from illness; *fig* to have an appetite for sth. *Wong² mau paḍa ngemaruki nganakaké konggrès.* They just love to hold meetings.

kemat evil spell, black magic. **ŋg/di∗** to put an evil spell (on)

kémawon just, only (*kr for* BAÉ[a])

kemba insipid; without spirit. *Djangané kurang ujah, rasané ∗.* The soup tastes flat—it doesn't have enough salt. *Bareng pangangkahé wis bablas dadi ∗.* After he got what he wanted, he no longer exerted himself. **tanpa ∗** undiminished. *Adrenging tékat tanpa ∗.* He's as determined as ever.

kembang *ng*, **sekar** *kr* flower, blossom; *fig* symbol of beauty; result produced. *∗-∗ paḍa mekar.* The flowers are in bloom. *Dèké dadi ∗é kuṭa Jogja.* She's the flower of Jogja. *Seḍih kuwi ∗ing lara.* Grief can develop into illness. **∗an** floral decoration. **∗-∗an** 1 various kinds of flowers. 2 flowers used decoratively; *fig* embellishments, flourishes. **a∗** to put forth flowers. *Wit²ané paḍa a∗.* The trees are blossoming. **ke∗an** flowers (of various kinds). *ke∗an mantjawarna* all kinds of flowers. **ŋg∗** resembling a flower. *ngembang wéwéjan* light blue. **ŋg/di∗aké** to develop, bring into flower. *ngembangaké panemu²ning para sardjana* to develop the inventiveness of scholars. **ŋg/di∗(i)** to decorate with flowers. *Baṭiké di∗i.* She did the batik in a flower motif. **pa·ŋg∗** development, flowering. *pangembangé agama Islam* the flourishing of Islam. **∗ api** fireworks. **∗ asem** orange-yellow (like the tamarind blossom). **∗ borèh** a certain flower for religious offerings. **∗ djanti** grayish. **∗ durèn** durian-blossom yellow. **∗ gembolo** *gembolo* blossom (*see also* KAK). **∗ gula** lollipop; hard candy. **∗ gula karèt** chewing gum. **∗ kertas** a zinnia-like flower. **∗ lambé** a common topic of conversation. *Dados sekar laṭining ngakaṭah.* Everybody is talking about her. **∗ lesu·ñ** flower mixture for bathing a convalescent. **∗ mimi** a variety of linen. **∗ paès** flower that produces no subsequent fruit (*e.g.* on a fruit tree in its first blooming); **ŋg∗-paès·i** to produce such blossoms. **∗ pala** mace (the spice). **∗ se·pasang** two-girl sibling combination. **∗ setaman** a bouquet of mixed varicolored flowers for ceremonial use. **∗ telu·ñ** 1 flower with three petals. 2 grave offering of three kinds of flower. **∗ tjampur-bawur** bouquet used

as a religious offering. **∗ waru** final glowing ember of an extinguished oil lamp

kembar of similar or identical appearance; twin(s). **∗an** 1 dressed alike. 2 opposite number, counterpart. **ŋg/di∗** to make [things] alike. *Klambiné anaké di∗.* She dressed her children alike. **ŋg/di∗i** 1 to make sth like [sth else]. *Klambiku di∗i dèké.* She wore the same thing I did. 2 to challenge; to equal. *Ora gelem di∗i pinteré.* He doesn't want there to be anyone else as smart as he is. **∗ ḍampit** boy-girl twins. **∗ gantung** twins born several days apart. **∗ majang** twin bouquets for ceremonies, *esp.* weddings

kemben *ng kr*, **(ka)semekan** *ki* long narrow sash worn at or above the waist as part of the traditional women's dress. **∗an** *ng kr* to wear a batik skirt so high that it covers the breast. **ŋg/di∗i** to put the above on smn

kembeng 1 to rinse out the mouth (*ki for* KEMU). 2 *sbst kr for* SUSUR. **∗-∗** *or* **ŋg∗** [of eyes] to water, fill with tears

kembik **∗-∗** on the verge of tears. *ptg* **k·r·embi:k** trying to hold back one's tears

kembong **∗-∗** *or* **ŋg∗** filled with standing water

kembroh *var of* KEPROH

kembul (*or* **∗an**) (to eat) together; [to eat] from the same plate. **ŋg/di∗i** to join smn at a meal; to eat from smn's plate

kembung 1 a certain freshwater fish. 2 [of stomach] to ache, feel bloated

kemédja shirt (Occidental style). **∗n** (to wear) a shirt

kemel sticky, gluey

kemèng high-pitched (of voice)

kemeng stiff and sore from overexertion. **sa∗é** with all one's strength

kemenjan *var of* MENJAN

keméron, kemeron *var of* KEMARON

kemeruk [of coconuts] in the very young stage

kemiḍi *var of* KUMIḌI

kemil **∗an** 1 food held in the mouth but not swallowed. 2 food, things to eat. **kemal-∗** to keep nibbling, eat all the time. **ŋg/di∗** to hold [food] in the mouth for a long time. **ŋg/di∗(i)** to eat, nibble at. *See also* RIJEK

kemiri 1 candlenut; candlenut tree. 2 ankle bone. **∗ guru** large pecan-like nut. **∗ kopong** 1 to quarrel over sth inconsequential. 2 to long for sth of little value

Kemis 1 Thursday. 2 to beg (*root form: var of* MIS). ***an** to make weekly administrative reports on Thursdays

kemit * **bumi** servant in the Sultan's palace in charge of cleaning up and providing water

kemladéjan a certain parisitic plant. * **ng·adjak sempal** trouble-making relatives

kemlakar *var of* KEMLEKAR

kemlandingan 1 a small shade tree; the edible pods of this tree. 2 a large tree spider

kemlekar ***an** *or* ***en** to overeat; uncomfortably full

kemleker ***an** *or* ***en** unable to emerge. *Sadjaké endogé *en.* It looks as if the egg isn't going to hatch. *Seminggu *en nang omah.* I've been cooped up in the house all week.

kemlija to have an altered attitude (toward smn). *Bareng wis dadi wong gedé, Simin saiki *.* Since Simin became a big shot, he hasn't been friendly any more. *See also* LIJA

kemlingking *intsfr* dry. *garing ** bone dry. ***en** 1 excessively dry. 2 limp, without body *or* crispness

kemlondo gauche, boorish

kemlunggi a certain plant

kemodong 1 a certain type of black magic. 2 gamelan instrument consisting of two metal bars over a sounding box, producing a gong-like sound when struck. **ṅg*** to play the above instrument

kemong *see* ENGKUK, MONG

kempal group, gathering (*kr for* KUMPUL)

kempar a certain edible ocean fish

kempel concentrated; adhering to one another. *Radioné swarané ndjebèr ora *, sadjaké batuné lembèk.* The radio sounds high-pitched and broken up, as though the battery is low. **ṅg*** to become concentrated *or* stuck together. **ṅg/di*aké** to cause to stick together. *Sengara bisa ngempelaké barang garing tanpa lim.* You just can't make dry things stick together without glue.

kempèng **ṅg/di*** to nurse, suck

kempès empty of its normal contents. *Wetengé *.* He's very hungry. *Saké *.* He's broke. *ban ** flat tire

kempis *var of* KEMPÈS, KEPIS. ***-*** *or* **kempas-*** to pant; to exhale heavily. **ṅg*** to exhale *or* blow on

kempit ***an** 1 (that which is) carried under the arm. 2 (that which is) sold on commission. **ṅg/di*** 1 to hold or carry under the arm *or* between the thighs; *fig* to protect, look after solicitously. 2 to sell [merchandise] on commission. **ngempit ng·indit** to have one's hands full, be doing many things at once. **ṅg/di*aké** to sell [batik] on commission. **pa·ṅg*** guidance, protection

kempjang 1 a certain gamelan *gong.* 2 loud, noisy. **ṅg/di*i** to join in [an activity]. *Wiwitané mung tak anggo ngempjangi.* At first I did it just to be sociable. * **duwit** a game played with coins

kemplang a cookie made of glutinous-rice flour. **ṅg/di*** 1 to refuse to pay for sth; to pay less than the asking price for sth; to fail to pay what one owes. 2 to put sth in the sun to dry *or* air

kemplong ***an** act of pounding fabric to make it smooth; (fabric) pounded in this way. **ṅg/di*(i)** to pound [fabric] smooth

kemplung ***-*** containing too much liquid

kémpol calf of the leg

kempong baby's pacifier. * **pérot** sunken-cheeked as a result of being toothless with age

kempor **kempar-*** continuous [of smoking]. *udud kempar-** to chain-smoke. **ṅg*** 1 to chain-smoke. 2 to talk much louder than necessary

kempos to be(come) deflated. *Baloné *.* The balloon lost its air. ***-*** *or* **ṅg*** to exhale forcibly, as when winded; [of cattle] to snort

kempot having sunken cheeks, from excessive thinness *or* from the toothlessness of old age

kemprang *rpr* the sound of sth smashing to bits

kemproh slovenly, unwashed

kempu round covered box for betel-nut chew

kempul gamelan instrument consisting of five or six vertically suspended gongs. **ṅg*** to play the above instrument. * **suwuk·an** the small gongs included in a set of large gongs

kempus 1 an edible ocean fish. 2 to lie habitually. 3 *var of* KEMPIS

kemput finished, completed. *Olèhku mlaku*[2] *nganti *.* I walked around sightseeing until I had seen everything.

kemrampo *var of* KEMAMPO

kemrunggi a certain plant

kemu *ng kr,* **gurah** *or* **kembeng** *ki* to rinse out the mouth. **ṅg/di*k̂aké** to use as a mouthwash. *ngemokaké banju* to rinse out the mouth with water. **ṅg/di*n̂i** to rinse out [the mouth]. *Tjangkemé dikemoni.* He rinsed out his mouth. *See also* NGEMU

kemuḍi 1 rudder, helm. 2 steering wheel. *tukang* *, *djuru* * steersman, helmsman. **ng/di*ni** to steer, guide

kemul 1 (**singeb** *ki*) blanket. 2 using sth as a blanket. *Olèhé turu * sarung.* He slept with his sarong covering him. ***an** *or* **a*** *or* **ke*** to cover oneself with a blanket. **ng/di*i** (**nj/di·singeb·i** *ki*) to cover smn with a blanket

kemumu a variety of tree

kemuning a variety of tree with fragrant yellowish blossoms. *See also* KUNING

kèn 1 to tell smn to do sth (*root form: kr for* KON). 2 *ancient ltry title for male or female nobles*

kena *ng,* **kénging** *kr* 1 can, may. *Apa * dipangan?* Is it edible? *Wong mau ora * diandel.* He's not to be trusted. *Ora * tjeḍak²*. You mustn't get too close to it. 2 to touch, hit. *Tanganku * geni.* My hand touched the flame. *Ḍèké mbalang, bet, *.* He threw; it hit. 3 to be subjected to. ** ḍenḍa* to be fined. ** bandjir* to have a flood. ** ukuman sepuluh taun* sentenced to ten years' imprisonment. *Adjèr jèn * panas.* It melts if it's exposed to heat. ***n-*nan** (**kénging²-an** *kr*) to hit home, score a bull's-eye. **ka*n** to be subjected to sth unpleasant. *kekenan atiné* to get one's feelings hurt. **ng/di*kaké** 1 to permit, allow. *Guru ngenakaké murid² mulih djam sewelas.* The teachers let the students go home at 11 o'clock. 2 to aim at, try to hit. 3 to impose sth on [smn]. *Tahanan omah di*kaké A.* A was placed under house arrest. *ngenakaké padjeg* to levy taxes. **ng*ni** 1 about, connected with. *Wong mau omong² ngenani soal sing wigati.* He spoke about certain important matters. *Ngenani bab masak ḍèwèké ahli banget.* When it comes to cooking, she's an expert. 2 to hit, touch, reach. *Sawaté ngenani katjané ting.* The stone he threw hit the street light. *Si A ora njrèmpèt ngenani ḍiriné B.* A didn't let on that he had identified B. 3 to impose sth. *ngenani padjeg* to levy a tax. **sa*né** whatever is possible. *Jèn ora bisa ngrampungaké kabèh, ja sa*né baé.* If you can't finish it, just do what you can. *** apa** why? what for? (*see also* NANG). ** apa kowé kok ora sekolah?* How come you're not in school? **ora * ora** it is inevitable that..., it cannot be avoided that... *Ora * ora wong salah-sèlèh.* A person's wrongdoing is bound to catch up with him.

kenal *ϕ*/**di*** to know, be acquainted with. *Aku durung tau * wong kaé.* I've never met that man. *Aku wis di* nang kéné.* Everyone here knows me. ***-*an** to get to know each other. *Tamu² paḍa *-*an.* The guests introduced themselves to each other. **ng*** to become acquainted with. *Ḍèké ora gelem ngenal wong.* He doesn't want to make friends. **ng/di*aké** to introduce smn. **ng/di*i** to get acquainted with, introduce oneself to

kenang *rg var of* NANG 1. *** apa** why? what for? (*var of* KENA APA)

kenângâ a certain flower used in grave offerings

kenap a small table

kenâpâ why? (*inf var of* KENA APA)

kenari 1 a certain tree; also, its pecan-like nuts. 2 a certain song bird

kenḍâgâ *ng,* **kenḍagi** *opt? kr* 1 a small box for keeping valuables. 2 barrel

kenḍagi *kr for* KENḌAGA

kenḍal [of fat, grease] thick(ened), solid(ified). **ng*** to become thick/solid. *Lengané ngenḍal.* The grease congealed.

kenḍali horse's bit, bridle. **ng/di*ni** to equip [a horse] with a bit *or* bridle. **pa·ng*an** control. *pengenḍalian harga* price controls. *pengenḍalian bandjir* flood control

kénḍang to float (away). *Ana wong * nang kali.* A man was carried away by the river. **ng/di*aké** 1 to set sth floating on the current. 2 to send smn into exile (*ki for* M/DI·BUWANG·AKÉ)

kenḍang 1 two-headed gamelan drum held horizontally and beaten with the fingers. 2 480-sheet ream (of paper). ***an** 1 drumbeat; drum playing. 2 to drum idly, for one's own amusement. ***an ḍengkul** to sit around taking it easy. ***an kuping** ear drum. **ng/di*(i)** to play a drum. **pa·ng*** 1 gamelan drummer. 2 act *or* way of drumming. *** batang·an** a certain medium-sized gamelan drum

kenḍangsul *sbst kr for* KENḌALI

kenḍarah *ptg * or* **ng*** [of clothing] untidy, sloppy, too large and dragging on the ground

kenḍarak'an a certain small heron

kenḍarat a rope for tying up *or* leading cattle. **ng/di*** to drag, pull. *Malingé di* nang kantor polisi.* They dragged the thief to the police station. ṅg/di*i to tie up *or* lead [cattle] with a rope

kenḍat an end; a break, interruption. *Ora ana *é.* There's no end to it. *Mobil ora ana *é tekan djam sewelas bengi.* Cars go by in a steady stream until 11 P.M. *ngaḍuh-aḍuh tanpa ** moaning continually. **ṅg*** to commit suicide by hanging oneself. **ngenḍat tali murda** *ltry var of* ṄG*

kèndel 1 to stop, halt (*kr for* M·ANḌEG, M·ENḌEG). 2 to stop, discontinue (*kr for* LÈRÈN). 3 to become *or* remain quiet (*kr for* MENENG)

kendel courageous, bold. **ka*an** courage, bravery. **ke*en** overbold. **ṅg/di*aké** to rely on. *ngendelaken rosanipun* to rely on one's brute strength. *ngendelaké kesugihan* to get by on one's money. **ṅg/di*-*aké** to steel oneself. *Ḍèké wedi ning di*-*aké.* He was afraid but he screwed up his courage. **ṅg/di*i** to defy. *Jèn di*i rak ora wani ḍèké.* If you stand up to him, he'll back down.

kenḍela a certain large dragonfly

kenḍelong *rpr* suddenly going slack. **kenḍelang-*** to move loosely. **ṅg*** loose, slack, sagging; *fig* low, dispirited

kenḍeng bowstring. **ṅg*** resembling a mountain range; having a mountainous appearance. **k·um·enḍeng** [of smoke, clouds] billowing

kenḍèrèh *var of* KENḌARAH

kenḍi *ng kr,* **lanting·an** *ki* large earthenware water carafe with a spout. **pa*ṅ** *ng kr* place where crockery is made. *** gerit** striped carafe. *** gogok** earthen pitcher with no spout. *** praṭola** huge decorative carafe

kenḍil earthenware or copper utensil for cooking rice. **ṅg*** resembling such a utensil

kenḍit cloth belt, sash. **ṅg/di*** to carry in one's sash. **ṅg/di*i** to put a sash on smn. *** mimang kadang déwa** person who escapes danger

kéndjing morning's duration (*kr for* KÉSUK)

kénḍo a rice-accompanying dish made with shredded coconut. *** urang** the above dish with shrimp added

kenḍo loose, slack. *Taliné *.* The rope is slack. *Saja tuwa awaké saja *.* The older he grows, the flabbier he gets. *Olèhé njambut-gawé *.* His work has slacked off. **ṅg*** to become loose/slack. **ṅg/di*kaké** *or* **ṅg/di*ni** to make sth loose/slack

kenḍor *var of* KENḌO

kenḍukur *ptg * pl* in heaps, piles. **ṅg*** *sg* piled up. *Barang²é ngenḍukur, durung diḍuḍah.* His stuff is all in a heap: he hasn't unpacked yet.

kenḍurak a certain sea snail

kenḍuri (*or esp.* ***ṅ**, ***ṅan**) a ritual feast given in smn's honor for a special purpose

kenḍuru:k *ptg * or* **kenḍurak-*** *or* **ṅg*** 1 hanging in loose folds. 2 large, looming. *Apa sing ngenḍuruk nang podjok kaé?* What's that huge thing in the corner? *Lakuné gendruwo katon kenḍurak-*.* The ghost loomed up as it stalked along.

kéné *ng,* **ngriki** *kr* 1 here, this place *(Degree I: Introduction, 6). Saka * nunggang bis.* From here we take a bus. *wong ing désa ** the people in this village. 2 I, me; we, us. ** sabangsa* our whole nation. ***an** (*prn* **kènèk'an**) things like this, this sort of thing. **di*kaké** to be handled in this way (*var of* DI·NGÉNÉ·KAKÉ). *Adja dikènèk-kènèkaké munḍak tugel.* Don't keep doing this to it, or it'll break.

kenèk 1 assistant to the driver of a public vehicle. 2 *var of* KENA. ***an** place in the rear of a bus *etc.* where the above assistant sits. **ṅg*** to assist the driver (as one's job)

kenèker *var of* NÈKER

kènel ***-*** soft and springy (*e.g.* like a marshmallow)

kenèng *** apa** why? (*var of* KENA APA)

kenep *var of* KENAP

kenèper hairpin, bobby pin

kenès 1 flirtatious, coquettish. 2 talkative

kenèt *var of* KENÈK

keng *rg var of* KANG

kèngès to get cut off, severed

kénging can, may; to touch, hit (*kr for* KENA). *** punapa(ha)** *kr,* *** napa** *md* why? (*social var of* GÉNÉ JA)

kèngkèn to have smn do sth (*root form: kr for* KONGKON)

kengkeng sturdy; stiff, rigid. *Awaké *.* Its body is shell-like. *Wis * penggalihé.* Her mind is made up. **mer*** having a tight grip. *Olèhé njekeli koperé nganti mer* kuwatir jèn disrobot wong.* He gripped the bag firmly so it couldn't get snatched. **ṅg/di*i** to have/take a firm grasp on

kèngser 1 sand bank. 2 a certain gamelan melody. 3 a certain step in a female classical dance. 4 moved, shifted. **ṅg/di*aké** to shift (the position of). *See also* INGSER

kèngsi until, up to (the point that). *Tasmu adja * kèri lho.* Don't forget your bag! *Malingé diantemi * biru èrem.* The thief was beaten black and blue.

kèngsrèh to touch *or* drag on the ground. **ṅg/di*aké** to drag sth on the ground

kengulu pillow

keni **ṅg/di*-*** to care for, tend. *Tanduranè di*-*.* She takes good care of her plants.

kenikir a certain plant whose leaves are used as a vegetable

kenini *var of* KININE

kenir *see* ÈNGSÈL

kenja an unmarried virgin girl. *Sang * Dèwi Marijah* the virgin Mary. *** puri** palace quarters for the princesses

kenjal *rpr* sth soft and springy to the touch. *Aku midak wetengé Slamet, mak * kagèt aku.* I was startled to find I had stepped on Slamet's stomach! ***-*** *or* **k·um·enjal 1** chubby. 2 tough, hard to chew

kenjam a taste, a sample. **ṅg/di*** to take a taste (of); to have a taste (of), *i.e.* to experience

kenjas *rpr* a burning sensation. *Mak * aku njénggol wadjan panas.* Ow, I touched the hot pan.

kenjèh **sa*(an)** *opt kr for* SA·KENJOH·(AN)

kenjil ***-*** *or* **kenjal-*** tough, rubbery in texture

kenjoh ***-*** to chew on [sth tough]. **ṅg/di*(i)** to chew (*ki for* ϕ/DI·MAMAH(I)). **sa*(an)** (**sa-kenjèh[an]** *opt kr*) one chew of betel

kenjol *var of* KENJUL

kenjul ***-*** bouncy, soft and springy

kenjung 1 baby monkey (young of the KEṬÈK). 2 *slang* (you're) crazy, nuts

kenjus *rpr* a burning sensation. *Mak * tangané kenjunjuk geni.* (It burned as) his hand touched the flame.

kènjut to get carried along/away (*lit, fig*). **ṅg/di*aké** to carry sth away; to charm, enchant smn

kenjut ***-*** a spasm. **ṅg/di*** to nurse, suck. **k·um·enjut ati·né** to feel a surge of emotion

kènol ***-*** flabby, soft and rubbery

kenong 1 gamelan instrument consisting of inverted bronze bowls. 2 a helping of rice. ***an 1** a beat of the above instrument. 2 a helping of rice. **ṅg*** to play the above instrument. **ṅg/di*i** to dish out rice. *** djapan** large gamelan *gong*

kenop switch, button

kenṭang 1 potato. 2 bright [of direct sunlight]. ***-*** to lie neglected in the open. *Duwèké sapa buku iki, *-* ana ndjaba?* Whose book is this lying around outside? **ke*** exposed to the sun. *turu ke** to lie in the sun. **ṅg/di*** to plant [a field] with potatoes. **ṅg/di*-*** or **ṅg/di*aké** to leave sth lying around outdoors. *** kimpul·é** the facts of the matter. *Aku ora ngerti * kimpulé kok mèlu disrengeni.* I don't know what it's all about but he's mad at me. *See also* ENṬANG

kentârâ *var of* KETARA

kéntas 1 to get driven out. 2 *slang* to get finished up/off. **ṅg/di*aké** to drive away, chase out. **ṅg/di*i** to finish sth up

kentawis *var of* KETAWIS

kentèl ***an** act of giving smn a knockout blow. **ṅg/di*** *slang* to punch, sock

kenṭel 1 firm, strong, solidified. *Senengmu wédang tjuwèr apa *?* Do you like your tea weak or strong? *Setrupé *.* The syrup is thick (viscous). *Lengané *.* The oil has frozen. *santen ** the cream of coconut milk that rises to the top. 2 close, intimate. *mitra ** a close friend. ***an** thick part. *Kopiné kari *an.* **ke*an** that which has been made thick *etc.* *ke*an rembug* consensus; agreement reached orally. **ke*en** excessively thick. **ṅg/di*aké** to thicken (strengthen, *etc.*) sth. *Djladrèné di*aké.* She made the dough thick. **ṅg/di*i** to make sth thicker *etc.* *Olèhé gawé kopi di*i ja?* Please make the coffee stronger!

kenṭèng container for catching the blood of slaughtered animals. **ṅg/di*** to hammer [dented metal] back into shape with a wooden mallet. **ṅg/di*aké** to have [dents] fixed as above

kenṭeng 1 strong cord. 2 accurate, exact. *Anggoné netepi djandji *.* He did just as he had promised he would. 3 serious, earnest. ***an** act of marking lines with cord. **ané* *ora lurus.* He didn't lay the cords straight. **ṅg/di*** to set plants in a straight line using a cord. **ṅg/di*i** to mark into sections with cord. *Keboné di*i dadi pirang² pérangan.* They divided the garden plot into sections with cord markings.

kenṭès blackjack. **ṅg/di*(i)** to hit smn with a blackjack

kenṭi a variety of pumpkin

kenṭil **ṅg/di*** to use sparingly. *See also* ENṬIL

kenting *see* ḌÈNḌÈNG

kenṭing *rpr* the *ting!* of metal striking metal.

ng̃/di* to hammer *or* pound producing clinking sounds

kèntir *var of* KÈLI

kentjan to make an appointment *or* date

kentjânâ *oj* gold; golden. ***n** resembling gold. * **wingka** child whose parents regard him as superior

kentjang **ng̃/di*** to stretch and tie [rope *etc.*] between two points

kentjar *-* [of light] bright, intense

kèntjèng a large copper cooking pot for steaming foods

kentjèng cash [as opposed to credit]. *Olèh-mu tuku * apa utang?* Did you buy for cash or on credit?

kentjeng 1 tight, without slack. *Olèhé na-lèni tali sing *.* Stretch the line taut. *Awaké *.* She's compactly built (not flabby). *Ḍawuhé *.* His orders are strict. ** ke-karepané.* He's determined. 2 straight, direct. *Mlakua ngétan bablas *, ora susah mé-nggok²*. Go straight east–don't turn. **ka*en** excessively tight *etc.* **ng̃/di*aké** to make tight *etc.* *Ḍèké ngentjengaké taliné kursi.* He fastened his seat belt. **ng̃/di*i** to tighten, make tight. **pa*** deposit, down payment. **sa*(-*)é** as tight *etc.* as possible

kentjèt 1 Achilles tendon. 2 askew, awry. *Sikilé *.* One of his legs is shorter than the other. *Klambimu * merga anggonmu mbe-nikké klèru.* Your shirt is crooked–you buttoned it wrong. *Djaréné nem gélo, lha kok djebul *, anané mung limang gélo.* He said there were six rupiahs but sth's wrong –there are only five.

kentji name of one of the small playing cards (*kertu tjilik*)

kentjing * **manis** diabetes. *See also* PRAWAN

kentjlèng *-* *rpr* a metallic clink. **k·um·en-tjlèng** to clink

kentjling *var of* KENTJLÈNG

kentjlong *rpr* a deep metallic clanking. *Swaraning peḍang natab tamèng mak *.* The sword clanged against the shield.

kèntjong ***an** *or* **di*** [of a little boy's batik wraparound] worn with the bottom of the fold tucked into the sash

kentjrang *rpr* metal clanking. **k·um·entjrang** to clank

kentjrèng *var of* KENTJRANG, KENTJRENG

kentjreng **ng̃/di*** to buy for cash (rather than on credit)

kentjring *var of* KENTJRENG. *-* *or* **ken-tjrang-*** *rpr* coins jingling. *Kok kentjrang-* sadjaké sugih ḍuwit.* It sounds to me as if you've got a lot of money. **ng̃/di*** 1 to clink [metal objects] (together). 2 to buy for cash. **k·um·entjring** to produce clinking sounds

kentjur a palm-like plant; also, its root (used in cooking and in folk medicines)

kéntol *ng kr,* **wengkelan** *kr* calf of the leg

kenṭong (*or* ***an**) village warning device: a bamboo or wooden tube on which one knocks with a stick to produce signals. **ng̃*** to strike the above. **ng̃/di*(i)** to signalize sth with the above. *ngenṭongi bandjir* to give signals notifying the populace of flood conditions. *Jèn lajon arep mangkat mesṭi di*i ping telu.* Three signal beats are given when the time comes to convey the body to the cemetery. *See also* ṬONG

kenṭos the pit of a coconut or *salak* fruit. **ng̃*** 1 to harden, form a cake. 2 to form a seed. *Krambilé wis ngenṭos.* The coconut seed has formed.

kentrung (*or* ***an**) to sing religious songs to the accompaniment of a small drum

kéntun *kr* *sbst var of* KANTUN

kenṭung *-* *rpr* drumbeats

kenṭus 1 a certain cat-sized wild animal shaped like a kerbau. 2 a certain small frog that inflates itself and raises its forelegs when approached by human beings. **k·um·enṭus** resembling the above frog; *fig* arrogant. *bangga kumenṭus* to have an inflated ego. *A saiki kumenṭus basan sugih.* Now that A is rich, he puts on airs. **kumen-ṭus ora petjus** to talk big but produce little

kenṭut muscular, strong

kenul *rpr* a gentle plop

kenup 1 collar button. 2 *var of* KENUT

kenur 1 heavy-duty cord. 2 fishline for deep-sea fishing

kenut a rubber blackjack

kepah ***an** a chewed piece (of sugar cane). **ng̃/di*** to spit out sth one has chewed, *esp.* sugar cane

kepâlâ 1 chief, head, supervisor. ** kètju* robber chief. ** sekolah* school superintendent. 2 *oj* head. *padjeg ** head tax, per capita tax. **ng̃/di*ni** to have charge of. *Sapa sing ngepalani kantor iki?* Who runs this office? * **daérah** (*abbr:* **kepda**) territorial head

kepâmâ well cared for. *Bapaké sugih mula uripé *.* His father is rich, so he is well looked after.

képang 1 woven bamboo. *djaran* * horse of woven bamboo, used in a certain folk dance. 2 braid, pigtail. 3 woven coconut leaves [for roofs, fences]. **ṅg*** to weave bamboo as one's livelihood. **ṅg/di*i** to furnish sth with woven-bamboo work. *Warungé di*i.* He put bamboo panels on his stall.

kepang surrounded; to surround (*root form: kr for* KEPUNG)

kepârâ (*or* **di***) somewhat, rather. * *ngarep* toward the front. *Durung tau njerikaké marang atiné, malah * akèh lelabuhané.* He had never hurt her feelings–if anything, he was oversolicitous.

keparat 1 (you) villain! (you) scoundrel! 2 damn it!

kepareng 1 to have permission. *Aku ora * bapak lunga*[2]. Father wouldn't let me go out. 2 to ask permission to leave (*kr for* PAMIT). **ṅg/di*aké** to give permission. *Aku mbokmenawa pantjèn durung pinarengaké karo Sing Maha Kuwasa omah*[2]. Perhaps God does not grant me permission to marry. **jèn** * 1 if one is permitted. *Jèn * aku arep njuwun ngampil pité oomku.* If I may, I'd like to borrow my uncle's bicycle. 2 God willing. *See also* PARENG

kepati *see* PATI[a], PATI[b]

kepaung morally bad

kepdā *see* KEPALA

kepéjuh *rg var of* KEPOJUH

kèpèk a young *kemlandingan* fruit

kepèk 1 notes for cheating on an examination. 2 a small flat bag. ***-*an** to consult each other's cheating notes. **ṅg*** to cheat on an examination. **ṅg/di*aké** *or* **ṅg/di*i** to copy from [smn's exam notes]

kèpèl *kr* *sbst var of* KAPAL

kepel 1 fist. 2 the amount of food taken in the cupped hands when eating at a ritual meal. 3 a certain tree, also its (edible) fruits. **ṅg/di*** to make (the hand into) a fist. *Tangané di*-*.* He kept clenching his fists. **ṅg/di*(i)** to take [food] in the cupped hands

kepénak *ng,* **sekétja** *kr* comfortable, pleasant (**ḍangan** *ki*). *Hawané *.* The weather is nice. *turu ** sleeping peacefully. **ke*en** (**ke·kétja·nen** *or* **ke·sekétja·nen** *kr*) to make comfortable/pleasant. *Kepénakna.* Make yourself at home! *Dipun sekétjakaken ḍaharipun.* Enjoy your meal! **ṅg/di*i** to make smn feel good. **sa*é (ḍéwé)** as one pleases. *Nèk omong adja sa*é.* Don't just say out whatever you feel like. *Wong*[2] *njambut-gawé sa*é.* The men work at a comfortable pace. *See also* ÉNAK

kepénakan nephew, niece (*kr for* KEPONAKAN)

kèpèng half-cent coin

kepentut to discharge flatus inadvertently. *See also* ENTUT

kepep covered with an airtight cover

kèper 1 twilled cloth. 2 a certain freshwater fish

kepésing 1 to urinate/defecate inadvertently. 2 to need to go to the bathroom. *See also* ISING

kèpèt 1 caudal fin; tail fin. 2 serrated ridges on a crocodile's tail. ***-*** to wag [the tail]

kepet a hand fan. ***an** 1 to fan oneself. 2 fan-shaped. **ke*** to use a fan. **ṅg/di*i** to fan oneself *or* smn else

kepijé *var of* KEPRIJÉ

kepik 1 a small basket. 2 a certain malodorous flying insect

kepis fishing creel

kepiṭing edible saltwater crab

kepjak set of bronze (or other metal) bars with which a puppet-master produces rapping sound effects. ***an** 1 metallic rapping produced with the above. 2 wedding reception. **ṅg/di*aké** 1 to announce sth, *esp.* at a reception. 2 to hold a bridal reception for smn. **sa*an** quick as a wink. *Sega setjeṭing sa*an entèk dipangan wong loro.* The two of them finished off the rice in no time. *Gawéjan jèn ditandangi wong akèh sa*an rampung.* Work done by many hands is quickly finished. * **pisan** the beginning

kepjar to come apart, come unstuck. ***-*** feeling of relief or refreshment produced by eating hot *or* highly spiced foods. (*ptg*) **k·l·epjar** *pl* to come apart. **k·um·epjar** *sms *-* above*

kepjok *var of* GEPJOK, KEPJUK

kepjuk **ṅg/di*(aké)** to splash (onto). *Banjuné di*aké A marang rainé B.* A splashed water in B's face.

kepjur to emerge/fall in small quantities. *Aku sida lunga sebab udané ming *.* I went after all–it was only drizzling. ***-*** to see stars; to feel the head reeling or throbbing. **ṅg/di*i** to sprinkle lightly. *Tanduranè di*i banju waé.* Put just a little water on the plants. *Ibu ngepjuri ujah nang djangan.* Mother sprinkled a little salt in the soup.

ptg k·l·epjur *or* k·um·epjur to have a throbbing head; to see stars. *kumepjur ati* the heart throbs *or* pounds, *e.g.* with fright

keplak a slap in the face. ŋg/di∗(i) to slap smn's face. k·um·eplak to need a slap. *Botjah kok kumeplak, dikandani mesţi ora manut.* You're asking for a slap—you never do as you're told.

keplas *rpr* a swift motion. ∗*ing panah* the humming flight of an arrow. sa∗an at a glance. *Sa∗an rupané kaja tilas patjanganku.* At first glance she looked like my former fiancée.

képlé 1 *slang* prostitute. 2 *var of* KÈPLÈH. ŋg∗ to engage in prostitution

kèplèh drooping, hanging down limply. *Suwiwiné ∗.* Its [broken] wings are hanging helpless. *∗ brengosé* having a long drooping moustache

keplèh soaking wet

keplèk 1 a card game played for money. 2 *rpr* a slashing. ŋg/di∗aké to slash, smash. *Urèté di∗aké ing doran.* He slashed at the grub with his hoe handle.

keplekiken to choke (on) [food]

kepleng *intsfr* round, full. *Rembulané ∗.* The moon was full. *bongoh ∗* completely happy

keplok 1 in harmony (with). *Panemuné ∗.* They're in agreement. *penganggo sing ∗ karo kapribadèn* clothing which suits the personality. 2 applause; to clap. ŋg/di∗ to beat [clothing] while laundering it. ŋg/di∗i to clap for smn (in applause; to summon them). *∗ bokong* to laugh at smn who is in trouble. *∗ ora tombok* 1 to disparage, belittle. 2 to take part in the fun without sharing the cost

kepluk a slap, *esp.* in the face. ŋg/di∗(i) to crumble [lumpy soil] fine

kepoḍang golden oriole (*var of* POḌANG)

kepojuh 1 to urinate inadvertently. 2 to feel the need to urinate. *See also* UJUH

kepok *see* GEḌANG

keponaǩan *ng*, kepénaǩan *kr* nephew, niece. *∗ lanang* nephew. *∗ wédok* niece. *∗ m̐·pi-san·an* child of one's first cousin. *∗ m̐·pi-ndo·an* child of one's second cousin

keprak 1 small wooden box tapped with a mallet to produce castinet-like beats for sound effects. 2 metal sound-effect bars (*var of* KEPJAK). ŋg∗ to produce sounds with the above

kepras ŋg/di∗(i) to trim, prune, cut back

[shrubbery or other growth]. *tjukur ∗* a short haircut

keprèh *var of* KEPLÈH

kèprèt messy, smeared (with). ŋg/di∗i to get sth messy

keprijé *ng*, kados pundi *kr* how? *Jèn kowé ∗?* How about you? *Rasané ∗?* What does it taste like? *Anèhé ∗?* What's strange about it? *Kok aḍem temen iki ∗?* How come it's so cold? *Aku golèk réka ∗ njirnakaké ama.* I'm trying to find a way to get rid of pests. *di∗a* no matter how it is. *Dikeprijéa, ḍèké isih sedulurmu.* Be that as it may, he IS your brother. *∗ manèh* what else? what can one do? *Dialang-alangana ja ∗ menèh, wong wis paḍa senengé.* We try to keep them apart, but if they love each other what can we do? *∗ waé* any way (at all). *∗ waé kowé kudu mangkat dina iki uga.* One way or another, you've got to leave today.

kepripun *md for* KEPRIJÉ

keproh soaking wet

keprok a tangerine-like fruit

kepruk ∗an act *or* result of breaking sth open. ŋg/di∗aké to break open. *Aku ngeprukaké tjèlèngan marang watu.* I broke open my piggy bank on a rock. ŋg/di∗(i) to break open. *ngepruk(i) klapa* to crack open coconut(s). *ptg* k·l·epruk *pl* to break open. *Wong adol kambil paḍa ptg klepruk ngepruki kambil.* The coconut sellers are breaking open coconuts. k·um·epruk to break, smash. *Ana swara kumepruk.* There was a crashing sound of sth breaking. tukang ∗ bodyguard, hired strong-arm man

kepu (*or* ∗-∗) chubby-cheeked

kepuh *see* NG·GANTUNG

kepung *ng*, kepang *kr* ∗an 1 surrounded, encircled. *Kiwa tengen mung ∗an swaraning gangsir ngentir.* Crickets chirped all around us. 2 the partaking of a ritual meal. ŋg/di∗(i) 1 to be (sit, stand) around sth. *Aku di∗ mungsuh.* I was surrounded by enemies. *Botjah[2] paḍa ngepungi omah sing kobong.* The boys stood around the burning house. 2 to attend a ritual ceremony, *i.e.* sit around a communal meal. *Sing ngepung mung wong sing tunggal saomah baé.* Only family members attended the ceremony.

kepus ŋg/di∗ to blow (on); to exhale strongly

ker *rpr* growling, snarling

ker- *see also under* KR- (*Introduction, 2.9.3*)

kéra 1 cross-eyed; wall-eyed. *Matané* *. His eyes don't focus together. *wong* * person born with the above visual defect. 2 name of one of the small playing cards (*kertu tjilik*). **ng*** 1 to cross the eyes. 2 (*psv* **di***) to look at sth cross-eyed *or* with one non-focusing eye. *See also* ÉRA

kera thin, undernourished (*kr for* GERING, KURU)

kerah (*or* ***an**) a fight (between animals); to fight. **ng/di*** [of animals] to bite, chew

kerak 1 old and dried up. 2 dry crust(y part). **ng*** crusty; very dry. *mangsa ketiga ngerak* the height of the dry season

keramik ceramic ware

keran water faucet. *banju* * running water; tap water

kerang a certain mussel, also its shell

kéras ***an** figure of speech, verbal symbol; ambiguous phraseology. *supaja njingkiri *an* in order to avoid ambiguity. **ng/di*** to speak symbolically or figuratively; to use ambiguous locutions

keras hard, harsh, strong. *obat* * strong medicine. *minuman* * hard liquor. *Wataké* *. He's stubborn. **ng/di*i** 1 to make fast. *ngerasi sekrup* to tighten a screw. 2 to confine, restrain

kérat *inf var of* AKÉRAT

kérâtâ *oj* hunter. * **basa** *(in folk etymology)* a search for underlying or original phrases from which words are derived, *e.g.* PI·RING *from se·*PI *jèn mi·*RING; KO·ḌOK *from te·*KA² *nḍo·*ḌOK

kerdja low-paying blue-collar job; to work at such a job. **ng/di*(kaké)** to get a job done

kerḍus paper box *or* carton

kéré beggar. **ng*** to be(come) a beggar; to resemble *or* act like a beggar. **ng/di*kaké** (*prn* **-kèrèkaké**) to call *or* consider smn a beggar. * **munggah ing balé** from rags to riches

keré roll-up bamboo blind. **ng*** to make bamboo blinds (as one's livelihood). * **wadja** bullet-proof vest

kerèh *-* to shout

kèrèk (*or* ***an**) a pulley. * *kutut* pulley used for raising and lowering a dove cage. * *timba* pulley for hauling up water from a well. **ng/di*** to hoist with a pulley. *ngèrèk gendéra* to run a flag up the mast

kerèk *var of* KERIK

kerek̄ **ng/di*** to chew up, bite to pieces

kèrem *var of* KÈLEM

keren wood-burning brazier

kereng harsh, stern, gruff, easily angered. ***an** to come to blows. **ng/di*i** to restrain, inhibit

kerep (**sering** *kr*?) frequent; at short intervals of space *or* time. **ke*en** excessively often *or* close together. *Jèn nonton sorot adja ke*en.* Don't go to movies too often. **ng/di*aké** *or* **ng/di*i** 1 to place [things] at frequent intervals. 2 to do sth often. *Jèn di*i olèhé nglamar, suwé² rak ja éntuk gawéan.* If you keep applying you're sure to get the job.

kerèt **ng/di*** to get hold of, lay hands on

keret 1 section, joint [of bamboo, sugar cane]. *pring sa** a section of bamboo. 2 carat. *barléjan sa** a one-carat diamond. 3 an *r*-showing diacritic in Javanese script. **ng/di*i** to cut [sugar cane, bamboo] into sections with a knife, using a circular motion around the stalk. **pa·ng*** action of cutting (as above)

kerga satchel

kéri *var of* KÉRING

keri to feel a tickling sensation. * *aku.* It tickles! ***n̂** ticklish. ***(n̂) kuping** irascible. * **ora p·in·etjut** to have a chip on the shoulder

kerig to go forth in a group to do a job. **ng/di*aké** to summon *or* mobilize [a group] to do a job

kerik 1 shaving and shaping of the hair on a bride's forehead. 2 *rpr* a cricket's chirp. ***an** act *or* way of shaping and shaving. **ng*** 1 to chirp. 2 (*psv* **di***) to shave and shape [hair; eyebrows]

kéring *ltry* left. *kanan* * right and left. **k·in·éring·an** *var of* K·ÉRING·AN

kering (*or* ***an**) bakery goods

keris *ng,* **ḍuwung** *kr* kris (ceremonial dagger) (**wangking·an** *ki*). ***an** 1 to wear a kris. 2 imitation kris (*e.g.* a toy; a shadow-play prop). **ng/di*** to stab with a kris. **ng/di*i** to have smn wear a kris

kerkas 1 crankcase. 2 holster

kerkèt *-* *rpr* creaking, *esp.* of bamboo stalks or trees rubbing against each other

kerket *var of* KERKUT

kerki:t *rpr* creaking, *esp.* of bed springs

kerkop, kèrkop cemetery for the burial of Occidentals, Christians

kerkot *rpr* heavy creaking, *e.g.* of bamboo poles swaying against each other

kerkuh *ptg* * unwilling, disinclined
kerkut *-* *rpr* grinding one's teeth
kerl **nge/di*(aké)** to curl [hair]
kerlèp *var of* KERLIP
kerlip *ptg* * to glitter, sparkle. *Kuṭané katon ptg *.* The city lights twinkle. *Langité katon ptg *.* There were flashes of lightning. ***-*an** to be in love with each other
kerlop to glitter, flash
kermah a variety of vegetable
kermi worms (as a disease). ***en** to have/get worms
kermun (*or* ***-*an**) to rain lightly, drizzle
kermus *-* *or* **kermas-*** to make crunching sounds. *kermas-* mangan karag* to eat crunchy rice chips. **ñg/di*** 1 to bite/chew sth crunchy. 2 to devour
kernèt driver's assistant (*var of* KENÈK)
kernuk *ptg* * *pl* to sit around outdoors by moonlight
kerod, kérod **ñg/di*(i)** to clean sth from [a surface etc.] by sweeping it off
kerok 1 scrubbing tool for cleaning a horse. 2 name of one of the Chinese playing cards (*kertu tjilik*). ***an** to have a warming massage by having the body rubbed with oil and scraped with a coin. **ñg/di*(i)** 1 to scrape, rub. *Kajuné di* nganggo beling karebèn alus.* He scraped the wood with a piece of glass to smooth it. *ngerok djaran* to rub down a horse. 2 to massage smn with a coin and oil. 3 to scrub the wax from fabric being worked in batik
kerot *rpr* the upper and lower teeth clicking together. *-* 1 [of teeth] clenched. 2 to make gnawing sounds. **ñg/di*aké** to clench [the teeth] in anger. *** tanpa untu** to have good ideas but no means of carrying them out
kerpek̄ *rpr* shattering. *Katja-matané kepidak sak kal petjah mak *.* He stepped on his glasses and they smashed.
kerpus 1 fez-like hat worn by men and children. 2 roof ridge. 3 cell for incarcerating soldiers. **ñg/di*** to lock up [a soldier] as a disciplinary measure
kersa *inf var of* KARSA
kèrsmis Christmas
kerta prosperity and peace. *tata tentrem * rahardja (wj)* orderly, peaceful, and prosperous [of the condition of a country]. *** adji** value, worth; **di*-adji** to be valued (at). *** kerti** peace and prosperity. *** wadana** leader
kerṭap *ptg* * to glitter, sparkle
kertas (piece of) paper. ** karo potlot* paper and pencil
kertèp *ptg* * to glitter, sparkle
kertep jeweled belt buckle
kerṭip *ptg* * to glitter, twinkle, sparkle, with tiny spots of light
kertjap *pl form of* KETJAP
kertjip *ptg* * making sucking noises
kerṭop *ptg* * to glitter, gleam
kertos *sbst kr for* KERTU
kertu card. *** djeneng** calling card. *** Landa** playing cards, bridge cards. *** Lebar·an** Lebaran greeting card. *** lima** name of a card game. *** penḍuḍuk** identification card. *** pos** post card. *** tjilik** *or* *** Tjina** small playing cards of Chinese origin
kérud to get swept away forcibly. **ñg/di*aké** to sweep/carry sth off
keruk scraping or scooping device. *kapal ** dredger. **ñg/di*(i)** to scoop/scrape out; *fig* to get one's hands on smn's belongings. **k·um·eruk buntut** [of coconut] very young and tender
késah to go; to be away (*kr for* LUNGA)
kesambi ironwood tree. *areng ** ironwood charcoal
kesar *-* *or* **k·um·esar** to throb, pound [of the heart, under emotional stress]
kesat dry, rough-textured, providing traction
kesatuan unit. *negārā ** unitary system of government
kesdu *ltry* willing; to want
kèsèd 1 door mat. 2 (*or* **ke***) to wipe the feet on a door mat. **ñg/di*i** to equip with a door mat
kesèd lazy. ***-*an** 1 to loaf, take it easy. 2 to try to outloaf each other. **di*-*aké** to exert oneself to the minimum. *Wis di*-*aké anggoné sinau, meksa olèh angka seḍeng.* He studied as little as possible and still got by. **ñg*i** to act lazy
kesed 1 dry and hard. 2 dry to the touch rather than oily [of a healthy young person's skin]
kesel physically tired. *ora duwé ** tireless. ***an** to tire easily. **ñg*** to act tired. **ñg/di*aké** to tire smn out
kèsèr ***an** two-wheeled cart pulled by men. *-* to drag [a heavy load]. **ñg/di*** to transport [a load] in a two-wheeled cart drawn by manpower. **ñg/di*aké** to have sth transported as above. **tukang *** a man whose job is to pull a cart

keses **kesas-*** hissing sound. **n̈g*** to make a hissing sound. *esp.* on an indrawn breath after taking a mouthful of sth hot. **n̈g·kesas-n̈g*** to keep making hissing sounds. *ptg* **k·r·eses** *pl* producing the above sound. *Ulané ptg kreses metu saka lèngé.* The snake emerged from its hole hissing steadily.

kesesa in a hurry (*kr for* KE·SUSU)

kesik *var of* GESIK. **n̈g/di*** to scour sth with a gritty substance

kesit quick-moving, nimble, hard to catch

keslijo 1 sprained, out of joint. 2 (to make) a slip of the tongue

késod ***an** to keep moving around aimlessly in a squatting position, *e.g.* a child playing on the ground. ***-*** *or* **ke*** to keep rubbing against sth. *Sapiné *-* nang wit asem.* The cow scratched its back against a tamarind tree. **n̈g*** to move along the ground in a squatting position. **n̈g/di*aké** to move *or* scrape a part of one's body against sth. *Sikilé di*-*aké nang suketan.* He rubbed his foot back and forth on the grass [to remove the sticky stuff].

kèsrèk to scratch, scrape against

kesrèk *var of* KESRIK

kesrik *rpr* a scooping, swooping motion. **n̈g/di*** to uproot [grass] by cutting out a shallow round with a blade

kestiwel *var of* SETIWEL

kestop *var of* KANSTOF

kestul, késtul revolver, pistol

kesud **n̈g/di*** to wipe (up) *or* sponge (off) with a cloth

késuk *ng,* **kénding** *kr* morning's duration. *Kowé sa* mau apa matja?* Have you been reading all morning? *Baṭik mau diebun-ebunaké wetara telung *.* The batik is set out in the dew for three mornings. **sa* n·djepluk/tjepluk (sakéndjing muput** *kr*) all morning long. *See also* ÉSUK

kesusu *see* SUSU[b]

ketab ***-*** to knock dirt *etc.* from sth by hitting it against sth. **n̈g/di*** to urge on a horse by kicking its belly. **n̈g/di*aké** to knock sth against sth. *Blègé nuli di*aké ana ing watu.* He hit the can against a stone [to get the dirt out]. *See also* TAB

keṭak 1 a cookie made of peanuts *or* coconut. 2 *rpr* a knock on the head. **n̈g/di*** to knock smn on the head. **k·um·eṭak** conceited, boastful

keṭakli:k *ptg * or *-* rpr* the weak motions of a thin body running, as though the bones were knocking against each other

keṭamul *var of* KEṬEMUL

ketan *ng,* **ketos** *kr* 1 glutinous rice, sticky rice. *glepung ** sticky-rice flour. ** ireng* black (inferior) glutinous rice. ** srikaja* glutinous rice with sweetened coconut-milk sugar. 2 cake made of glutinous rice with sweetened coconut-milk sugar

kétang **ora *** even if/though one must [undergo sth]. *Jèn kanggo mbajar sekolah, ora * isin, ja tak golèk²aké utangan ḍisik.* For school expenses I'll do my best to get a loan, even though I'm ashamed to do so.

ketanggung traditional soldiers of Jogjakarta

ketantil *var of* KETANTING

ketanting *ptg ** with erratic *or* patternless motions, as when panicky. ***an** erratic, crazy. *Olèhé mlaju *an marga diojak asu.* He ran every which way with the dog chasing him.

keṭap ***-*** far in the distance. *Lha kaé, montoré wis kétok *-*.* Look, here comes the car way off there.

keṭapel **n̈g*** to hold on with the arms and legs. *Slamet ngeṭapel nang wit.* Slamet clung to the tree. **n̈g/di*aké** to wind [the arms and legs] around sth to hold on

ketâra *ng,* **ketawis** *kr* obvious, showing plainly. *Botjah mau olèhé ngomong kok groṭal-graṭul * jèn ngapusi.* From the way he stammered around, it was obvious he was lying. **n̈g/di*kaké** *or* **n̈g/di*ni** to allow sth to be seen/known/obvious. *Adja ngetarani jèn kowé mau ngapusi.* Don't ever let on that you were lying! *Bèn ora ngetarani, polatané dibingaraké.* He put on a happy face so nobody would know how he really felt.

ketat tight, constricting. *rok ** a tight-fitting skirt. *Aturané béja masuk saiki * banget.* The import regulations are very strict now.

keṭaṭar *ptg * pl* lying strewn about. **n̈g*** to lie sprawled. *Kebo mau mati ngeṭaṭar nang ndalan.* The kerbau lay dead in the road.

keṭaṭel *rpr* getting caught. *Kaṭokku ketjantol kawat mak *.* My pants caught on the barbed-wire fence with a jerk.

ketawang 1 a certain group of Javanese musical numbers played by gamelan instruments. 2 a certain court dance performed by nine girls. ***an** annual performance of the above dance

keṭawé *ptg * pl* with outstretched

hands. *an to reach out the hand. ŋg*
as if waving the hand. *See also* ṬAWÉ

keṭawèl   *var of* KEṬAWIL

keṭawil   *ptg* * [of arms, legs] flailing about,
thrashing the air

ketawis   obvious, showing plainly (*kr for*
KETARA)

keteb   thick, dense

ketébang   *-* approaching from a distance.
*Kaé Slamet wis kétok *-*.* Here comes Slamet!

keteblug   *ptg* * *rpr* repeated thuds. *Krambilé ptg *.* The coconuts kept dropping.

keteg   (*or* ke*) heart; heartbeats. *ing djan-
tungé* the beating of his heart. * **tangan**
pulse (rate). *Aku diukur panasku lan *ing
tanganku.* He took my temperature and
felt my pulse.

keṭèk   1 monkey. 2 *rpr* a light brittle thud.
an abacus. ŋg 1 resembling a monkey.
2 (*psv* di*) to expose smn to ridicule by
caging him publicly (a form of punishment
for criminals). * **bengkaroḱan** big old repulsive-looking ape. * **sa·ranggon** a group
of bad people. *kaja* * **di·tulup** confused;
frenzied

keṭeḵ   ŋg/di*(i) to make a tongue-clicking
sound (to) [a person, to express disapproval; an animal, to urge it on]. *See also* ṬEK

keṭekan   chin (*ki for* DJANGGUT)

keṭékar   *var of* KEṬÈKÈR

ketèkèng   *-* always in trouble

keṭèkèr   *an or* ŋg* laborious, difficult.
*Olèhé munggah gunung *an.* They struggled up the mountain.

keṭekli:ḵ   sprained. *-* *rpr* the footsteps of
smn wearing wooden sandals. *Saja suwé
saja tjeṭa suarané ṭèklèk *-*.* The clippity-
clop of sandals got closer and closer.
keṭeklak-* 1 to make repeated clippity-
clop sounds. 2 [of walking gait] slow. *Soré² A keṭeklak-* mlaku ngubengi alun².* In
the evening, A strolled around the square.
See also ṬEKLIK

keṭeklu:ḵ   to nod drowsily. **keṭeklak-*** to
keep nodding

keṭékor   *var of* KEṬÈKÈR

keṭekreḵ   *-* clippity-clop. *Djarané mlaku
-.* The horse clattered along.

keṭekur   *rpr* the cooing of a turtledove (*see
also* WUK). **nganggur *** unemployed; idle.
ŋg* 1 motionless; to loaf, idle. *ṭenguk²
nganggur ngeṭekur* to sit around daydreaming all the time. 2 fast asleep. *Isih djam*

wolu wis ngeṭekur. It's only eight o'clock
and he's asleep already. ŋg/di*i to coo at

kèṭèl   1 steam boiler. 2 large rice kettle
with a handle

ketel   thick, luxuriant. *rambut* * thick hair.
alas * dense jungle

ketéla   *var of* TÉLA

ketelu   (ketiga *kr*?) *var of* KATELU

keṭem   ŋg/di* to grasp in the closed hand

keṭemeḵ   *-* *or* ŋg* 1 to walk with short
careful steps. 2 to tiptoe. 3 to stroll at a
leisurely pace

keṭemil   *-* [to eat] little by little. ŋg* to
nibble constantly. *See also* ṬEMIL

ketemlèk   *var of* KETEMPLÈK

ketemplèk   *-* to clip-clop when walking
in sandals

keṭemul   *ptg* * *pl* to eat with good appetite.
ŋg* *sg* to eat with good appetite. *Sega di-
tampani bandjur mangan ngeṭemul katoné
énak.* He took the rice and ate it with gusto.

kèṭèng   half-cent coin

keṭèngkrang   *var of* KEṬÈNGKRÈNG

keṭèngkrèng   *an to lumber along, move
ponderously. ŋg* to sit (impolitely) in a
more elevated position than others; *fig* to
consider oneself above pitching in and helping. *Kabèh paḍa njambut gawé, Slamet malah ngeṭèngkrèng lingguh kursi énak².* All
the others were working, but Slamet just
sat there taking it easy.

keṭèngkrong   *var of* KEṬÈNGKRÈNG

keṭèp   sequins (*usu.* silver, gold) for clothing
ornamentation. **k·um·etèp** hot to the taste
(in temperature or in spiciness). *Sambelé
kumetèp peḍes banget.* The sauce is terribly peppery.

ketep   1 edge, fringe; fine fringe of tiny
bangs worn on girls' foreheads. 2 (*or* ke*)
troops which bring up the rear. ŋg/di*i
1 to provide with a neat edge. 2 to back
up [the vanguard troops]

keṭepeḵ   *var of* KEṬEPREK

keṭepèl   *var of* KETEPIL

keṭèpèl   *an or* ŋg* to struggle (upward,
onward)

ketepil   slingshot. *an to shoot with a slingshot. ŋg/di* to shoot sth with a slingshot

keṭeplok   *-* [of horses' hoofs] to clatter

keṭèprèh   *ptg* * sloppy in one's dress

keṭepreḵ   *-* *rpr* the clatter of horses' hoofs.
ŋg* to trot along clattering the hoofs

ketepu   *see* EMPLÈK, PLÈK

kèṭèr   slow, behind; to come in last. *Mentas*

lara, sinauné ∗. He's been ill; he's behind in his studies. *Djamku ∗ limang menit.* My watch is five minutes slow.

keter, keṭer *var of* GETER

kètès to drip. ∗-∗ 1 to keep dripping. 2 brand (new). *Montoré anjar ∗-∗.* His car is brand new.

ketès *rpr* a slap

keṭèṭèr *ptg ∗ pl* spread in disorder. *Nganggo klambi adja ptg ∗.* Don't wear your clothes loose and floppy. *Perdjurit paḍa mlaju ptg ∗.* The soldiers fled in panic. ∗an *or* ṅg∗ in disorder. *Sanḍangané ngeṭèṭèr.* His clothes are a mess. *Gawéané isih ∗an.* His work is lying around unfinished.

ketèwèl *var of* TÈWÈL

keṭèwèr *ptg ∗ or* ∗an scattered around

keṭi hundred thousand. *sa∗* 100,000. ∗ṅ (numbering in the) hundred thousands

ketib assistant to a religious official (*pangulu*)

ketiga *var of* KATIGA

ketik ∗-∗ *rpr* the sound of typewriting. ∗an 1 act *or* way of typing. *∗ané kurang betjik.* She doesn't type very well. 2 short period spent in typing. *Ḍèké lagi se∗an waé wis lèrèn ngobrol.* She types a little and then stops to chat. ṅg/di∗ to typewrite. *ngetik lajang* to type a letter. ṅg/di∗aké to have smn type; to have sth typed. pa·ṅg∗ 1 act *or* way of typing. *Pangetiké lajang kuwi adja nganti luput.* The letter is to be typed without errors. 2 typist. pa·ṅg∗an place where typing is done

keṭik tooth file; [of teeth] filed even (*ki for* PASAH). ṅg/di∗ to privately talk smn into (*or* out of) doing sth. *A ngeṭik B bèn adja kanḍa².* A persuaded B not to tell anyone. ∗ **kanaka** to have an easy life, never do any work

keṭilang *var of* KUṬILANG

ketimåhå *var of* TIMAHA

keṭimik ∗-∗ *or* ṅg∗ 1 to take short careful steps. 2 to tiptoe. 3 to stroll. *See also* ṬIMIK

ketimun *var of* TIMUN

keting a certain ocean fish

ketingal *inf var of* KATINGAL

ketinggi *var of* TINGGI

keṭingkrang *var of* KEṬÈNGKRÈNG

keṭinṭal ∗an to plod laboriously. *Olèhé nututi peladjaran ∗an merga suwé ḍèké ora mlebu.* It was uphill work for him to catch up in his studies—he had been absent for a long time.

keṭip ten-cent coin. *se∗* a dime. ∗an ten-cent coin. ∗-∗ 1 far in the distance. *Lajangané muluk ḍuwur banget nganti ∗-∗.* The kite is so far up it's just a speck in the sky. 2 (*or* keṭap-∗) to keep blinking the eyes. *Aku keṭap-∗ nang peturon ora bisa turu.* I couldn't sleep a wink. *See also* SEKEṬIP

keṭipel ∗-∗ *or* keṭipal-∗ *rpr* a clumsy walking gait. ṅg∗ to walk slowly and ponderously

keṭiplek̄ **keṭiplak-∗** *rpr* sandals clopping

keṭipli:k̄ *ptg ∗ pl* sluggish, listless. ṅg∗ to toddle; to walk with short quick steps

ketipung small gamelan drum. ṅg∗ to produce *pang-pung* sounds by beating this drum

ketir ∗-∗ *or* ketar-∗ fearful, apprehensive. *Atimu adja ∗-∗, wong durung karuwan.* Don't worry about it—it's not certain that it will happen. ṅg∗-∗aké *or* ṅg∗-∗i causing apprehension/anxiety

keṭiwul *var of* ṬIWUL

kétja *see* SEKÉTJA

ketjak *rg* smeared, messy

kétjalan *form of* ITJAL: *see* ILANG

ketjam ∗an criticism. ṅg/di∗ to criticize *or* condemn

ketjambah beansprout. ṅg∗ to plant bean sprouts

ketjanḍak to get caught. *Malingé ∗ digawa menjang kantor pulisi.* The thief was apprehended and taken to the police station. sa∗é whatever one can manage. *Garapen sa∗é.* Do as much of the work as you can. *See also* TJANḌAK

kétjap soy sauce. ∗ *asin* salty soy sauce. ∗ *legi/manis* sweet soy sauce. ṅg∗ to brag about oneself *or* a member of one's family. ṅg/di∗i 1 to put soy sauce on. 2 to boast to smn. ∗ **nomer sidji** person who considers himself first-rate

ketjap 1 to say sth. *Iki lho ∗é.* Here's what it says. 2 (*or* ∗-∗) to smack the lips. sa∗ (to utter) a single word. *tanpa tembung sa∗* without saying a word. *ptg* ke·r·tjap *pl* smacking the lips

ketjapi a lute-like stringed instrument of West Java. ṅg∗ to play this instrument

kétjé an oyster- *or* scallop-like shellfish

ketjebu:k̄ ∗-∗ *or* ketjebak-∗ *rpr* splashing sounds. *See also* TJEBUK̄[b]

ketjèh (*or* ∗an *or* ke∗) to splash around in water in one's bare feet. **ketjah-∗** to keep splashing. ∗ **ḍuwit** rich. *Bareng dadi* *pemborong A * duwit.* Since A became a contractor he's been swimming in money.

kètjèk a certain dice game. ***an** small reptiles cooked in coconut oil: a preparation for treating skin rashes. **ng̃/di*** to cook [reptiles] as above

ketjeklik 1 sprained. *Sikilé *.* He sprained his ankle. 2 famine; time (before the rice harvest) of food shortage

ketjembang *var of* KETJEMBONG

ketjembong ***an** having stagnant water here and there. **ng̃*** full of water; filled with stagnant water; stagnant

ketjémé a fruit (*var of* TJÉMÉ)

ketjemil **ketjemal-*** to keep nibbling snacks

ketjemong **ketjemang-*** *or* **ng̃*** to talk nonsense, exaggerate, not stick to the facts

ketjemut ***an** *or* **ng̃*** to smile slightly/secretly

ketjeneng stiff and sore. *Ototku ptg *.* I have sore muscles.

ketjengklak 1 to have a sprained back. 2 to sulk

ketjengklèk *var of* KETJENGKLAK

ketjepik **ketjepak-*** to splash around in water

ketjepuk *var of* KETJEPIK

ketjeput throughout. *sawengi ** all night long

kètjèr 1 to drop off/out. *Berasé *.* A few rice grains fell out [of the sack]. 2 *form of* ÈTJÈR. **ke*** to get dropped. **ng̃/di*(aké, i)** *var of* NG/DI·ÈTJÈR(AKÉ, I)

ketjèr 1 gamelan instrument resembling cymbals. 2 (*or* ***an**) round flat sheath at the base of a growing coconut on the tree. *dijan* ***an** hanging kerosene lamp with a round shade that fits over the chimney. **ng̃*** to play the gamelan cymbals

ketjer **ng̃/di*(i)** to add [a taste-tempting ingredient, *esp.* lemon] to. *Sambelé di*i djeruk.* She put lemon in the sauce. **k·um·e·tjer** to have the appetite roused. *Ḍèkè kemetjer kepéngin djadjan.* His mouth watered for snacks.

ketjetjeng *ptg * pl* stiffened, rigid (*usu.* in death). **ng̃*** *sg* stiff, rigid

ketjètjèr *ptg ** to drop out little by little. *Berasé ptg * sebab karungé bolong.* The rice dribbled out through the hole in the sack.

ketjik *sawo*-fruit pit (often used as counters or men in games)

ketjil *see* KAMAR

ketjing a sharp disagreeable odor

ketjipir *var of* TJIPIR

ketjlap **sa*an** for a brief moment. *njawang sa*an* to catch a glimpse of. *Sa*an langit katon paḍang.* For an instant the sky brightened.

ketjoh saliva (*ki for* IDU). **(ke)*an** *or* **pa*an** cuspidor (*ki for* PA·IDU·Ñ)

ketjomb(l)ang *var of* KETJEMBONG

ketjonggah able to manage sth. *Rong djam ja bisa, mbok telung djam pisan ja *.* I can do it for two–even three–hours. *Adja omah² ḍisik jèn durung rumangsa *.* You shouldn't get married until you feel you're fully ready.

ketjopak *rpr* a splash. ***an** to splash around in water. ***-*** *rpr* repeated splashes. **ng̃*** to splash

ketjras *rpr* a slash with a sharp implement

ketjrèk 1 *wj* a brass sounding implement on which the puppet-master raps *(tjrèk! tjrèk!).* 2 handcuffs. **ng̃/di*** to handcuff smn

ketjrès *rpr* a quick slash with a cutting instrument

kètjrèt (*or* ***-***) to spill out bit by bit from a container

ketjrit *rpr* ejecting a small amount of liquid

ketjrok *rpr* a certain farm tool (*patjul*) striking the soil. **ng̃*** to work the surface of soil with this tool. **ng̃/di*i** to dig out [sth shallow] with this tool

ketjros *rpr* a hard slash with a cutting implement

ketjruk *var of* KETJROK

ketjrus *rpr* a quick slash with a sharp implement

kètju robber gang, band of thieves. *kepala ** robber chief. *punggawa ** member of a robber band. **ng̃/di*** [of a gang] to rob

ketju *intsfr* blue. *biru ** intensely blue; deep blue

ketjubuk **ketjubak-*** to make splashing sounds

ketjubung thorn-apple. **ng̃/di*** to intoxicate *or* drug with thorn-apples

ketjuh *rpr* spitting. **ketjah-*** to drool; to keep salivating

ketjupuk **ketjupak-*** to splash around in water

ketjut sour. *Rasakna, legi apa *?* Taste it: is it sweet or sour? *mèsem ** to smile bitterly. *dat ** oxygen. **ng̃/di*aké** to make sth sour

ketlebug *var of* KETEBLUG
kétok *ng,* **katingal** *kr* to look, appear, show. * *apik.* It looks nice. *Wis adoh, wis ora* *. It's far off, you can't see it any longer. *Tangané ditekuk bèn * kijeng.* He flexed his arm to show his muscle. ***é** it looks (as if). **é énak.* It looks delicious. **é akèh.* There seem to be lots of them. **ñg*** to show oneself. *Nèk awan nḍelik, ngétoké nèk bengi.* They stay concealed during the day and come out at night. **ñg/di*aké** to make a show of, let sth be evident. *Ḍèwèké ngétok²aké jèn sugih.* He always makes sure people see he's rich. **ñg/di*i** to appear to smn (as an apparition). *Anakku kok ngétok²i waé.* I keep seeing my child in my mind's eye. *Aku di*-*i tunanganku.* My fiancée's face keeps appearing before me.
keṭok 1 knocking sound. 2 *rg* small coin. *sa* tjilik* ± five cents. *sa* geḍé* ± seven cents. ***an** 1 act *or* way of cutting. 2 a cut-off piece; a cut place. ***-*** to cut into pieces. **-* lombok* to cut up peppers. **-* kuku* to cut one's nails. **ke*** to get cut (up, off, down). *Dridjiné ke* benḍo.* His finger was severed with a chopping knife. **ñg*-ñg*** 1 to ache with weariness. 2 (*psv* **di*-***) to cut into pieces. *Moriné di*-* dadi klambi.* She cut out the cambric to make a dress. **ñg/di*aké** to cut for smn. **ñg/di*i** to cut (up, down, off). *Di* dadi papat.* He cut it into four pieces. *Sikilé di*.* His leg was amputated. *ngeṭok tjlana* to cut off trousers to shorten them. *ngeṭoki rega²* to slash prices. *Wit mau di*i.* They cut up the tree. **pa·ñg*** act *or* way of cutting
kétol ***-*** having large buttocks
ketombé *var of* TOMBÉ
ketonggèng *var of* KETUNGGÈNG
keṭoprak a type of modern popular play depicting stories mainly from Javanese history plays, with improvised spoken dialogue in modern Javanese, realistic (rather than stylized) acting, and a clown who comments on current public topics. ***an** to make a knocking sound. **ñg*** 1 to perform the above type of play. 2 to knock
keṭoproh *ptg * or* **ñg*** sloppy, slovenly
ketos glutinous rice (*kr for* KETAN)
keṭoṭor *ptg * or* **ñg*** to hang down loose *or* limp
ketriwal lost, mislaid. *Katja-matané * nang sepur.* He left his glasses on the train. ***an** to lose sth. *A *an ḍompèt nang sepur.* A left his wallet on the train. **ñg/di*aké** to lose sth that belongs to smn else
keṭu 1 skull cap, worn optionally with a turban wound around the outside. 2 *rg* hat; headgear in general. ***ñ** to put on *or* wear the above. * **uḍeng** turban sewn in place (*rg var of* BLANGKON)
ketua chairman, head. * *djurusan* department chairman in a university. **ñg/di*ni** to chair, preside over
ketug up to, as far as, having arrived at. *Olèhé njambut-gawé * soré.* He works till evening. * *désa mau aku lèrèn.* When I got to the village, I took a rest.
keṭujuk ***-*** [to walk] bent over from age or illness. **ñg*** hunched over with age; very old. *See also* ṬUJUK
keṭuk 1 gamelan instrument consisting of a single inverted bronze bowl. 2 *rpr* a beat of the above instrument. 3 *rpr* a knocking sound. ***an** knocking sound(s). **ñg*** to play the above instrument. **ñg/di*aké** to join, match, bring together. **ñg/di*i** to agree with. *Omongé ora ana sing di*i.* Nobody agreed with what he said. * **kempjang** gamelan instrument consisting of two inverted bronze bowls. * **kenong** gamelan instrument consisting of two inverted bronze bowls set side by side in a wooden base
ketul small tortoise (young of the BULUS)
keṭul dull [of *e.g.* a blade; of wits]. **ñg/di*aké** to dull sth
ketumbar coriander. **ñg*** round(ed) like a coriander fruit. *See also* TUMBAR
keṭumuk ***an** *or* ***-*** *or* **keṭumak-*** *or* **ñg*** to walk carefully and unsteadily [*e.g.* a toddler]. *See also* ṬUMUK
ketunggèng scorpion. **ñg*** to rise. *Buntuté kutjing sing nesu kuwi ngetunggèng.* When a cat is angry its tail goes up.
ketupat rice cake cooked in a palm leaf
keṭuplak ***-*** *rpr* the clatter of hoofs
kétut *var of* KATUT
keṭuṭur *ptg* * [of birds] shivering with cold or dampness
ketuwa *var sp of* KETUA
keṭuweng *rpr* a turn *or* twist of the body. *See also* ṬUWENG
keṭuwik **keṭuwak-*** [of fingers] to keep moving. *Dridjiné keṭuwak-* nguṭeg-uṭeg sekrup ora bisa tjopot².* His fingers kept working at the bolt but he couldn't loosen it up.
keṭuwil *ptg* * with constant motions of

hands, fingers. *djogèd sing ptg* * a dance done with many hand movements. **keṭuwal-** * [of fingers, hands] in constant motion
kew- *see also under* KU·W- *: Introduction, 3.1.5.2)*
kéwâlâ *ltry* only, nothing but, simply
kéwan animal (including all sub-human forms). * **(dje)djrangkong·an** (the class of) vertebrate animals. * **gegel·an** insect with jointed legs. * **g·um·remet** insect. * **lembut** insect. * **ñ·susu·ñi** mammal. * **radja** livestock
kéwani animal-like; bestial
kéwat *var of* KIWAT
kèwèk flirtatious, coquettish
kèwèr *-* to dangle. *Tali kutangé katon *-*.* Her bra strap is hanging down in plain sight.
kèwes smooth, sophisticated; gracious, elegant, poised. *wong luwes a** a poised and elegant person
kéwran *ltry* to have trouble (with); to find sth difficult. **ñg/di*i** to cause difficulty to, be troublesome for
kg. *see* KILOGRAM
K.G.P. *see* KANGDJENG
ki 1 *male title of respect: shf of* KJAI. *Ki Ḍalang* the (highly esteemed) puppet master. 2 this (*inf var of* KI). * **lurah** *(wj) title applied to clowns.* * **sanak** *adr* person (*usu.* a stranger) of equal status
kibar **ñg/di*aké** to move sth back and forth. *ngibaraké gendéra* to wave a flag
kibir to boast of one's excellence
kidak (*or* **ke***) to get stepped on by accident. *See also* IDAK
kiḍal *oj* left-handed
kidang roe deer. **ñg*** resembling a deer. * **kentjana** golden deer. * **kentjana·n** small bronze-painted puppet. * **l·um·aju** sth that is difficult *or* impossible to get. * **mendjangan** *sms* *
kidjing 1 a certain freshwater mussel. 2 (**sekar·an** *ki*) gravestone. **ñg/di*(i)** (**ñj/di·sekar·[i]** *ki*) to place a gravestone (on)
kidul south. * *kulon* southwest. *Asia Sisih * Wétan* Southeast Asia. ***-*an** the southern part. **ñg*** southward. *mlaku ngidul* to walk south. **sa*(é)** to the south of. *ing sa* wétan kuṭa Jogja* southeast of Jogja. *See also* PANGIDUL
kidung epic narrative to be sung. **ñg*** 1 to compose the above. 2 to chant prayers; to sing Javanese songs, *esp.* as a means of preventing illness *or* driving away evil spirits
kiḍung awkward, inept
kijah *-* having a good time. *Nèk wantji soré aku *-* nèng alun²*. In the afternoon I had an enjoyable stroll in the square.
kijai *var of* KJAI
kijal tough, hard to chew
kijamat the end of the world, Judgment Day
kijambak *var of* PIJAMBAK. **1** alone; oneself (*sbst kr? md? for* ḌÉWÉ). 2 alone (*md for* IDJÈN). ***é** he, she (*md for* ḌÈWÈKÉ). ***ipun** he, she (*sbst var of* PIJAMBAK·IPUN)
kijanat treason; betrayal. *nggawé ** to betray. **ñg/di*i** to betray. *See also* PENGKIJANAT
kijas analogy, comparison. **ñg/di*** to compare; to make an analogy with
kijat strong (*kr for* KUWAT)
kijé this (*var of* IKI, KIJI)
kijeng strong, muscular, tough
kijer *-* to narrow the eyes
kiji this (*var of* IKI)
kiji(h) *-* hot and sweaty-looking
kijip *var of* KRIJIP
kiju stiff, aching [of muscles that have held an uncomfortable position for a long time]
kijuk **(kijak-)*an** act *or* result of hedging a loss. *Wis, djambuné jèn éntuk *an karo pelemé.* All right, you can hedge your loss on the guavas with (your anticipated profit on) the mangoes. **ñg/di*** *or* **ñg/di·kijak-*** to hedge a loss
ki:k̄ 1 *rpr* a hiccup. 2 *rpr* a brief laugh behind the hand
kikajat *var of* HIKAJAT
kikib covert, undisclosed. **ñg/di*** to keep sth concealed. *Ḍèké ngikib wewadi.* She kept the secret.
kikik *see* ASU
kikil leg of lamb, calf, *etc.* as food. **ñg*** 1 incessant [of coughing]. 2 shivering with cold
kikir a file (for smoothing). **ñg/di*** to file. *ngikir keris* to file a kris smooth (while it is being made)
kikis side, edge, border; boundary. **ing alas* the edge of the forest. * *segara* coast(line), seashore
kikrik choosy, hard to please, finicky
kikuk clumsy, inept. *djam ** cuckoo clock
kilak to buy (up) for resale (*kr for* KULAK)
kilan measure of length: $1/8$ fathom, or the distance between the tip of the thumb and little finger. ***an** to measure by the above

hand-spans. **n̈g/di*i** 1 to measure sth in hand-spans. 2 to consider trivial. *Gawéan ngono waé tak *i kanggoné aku.* That kind of work is child's play for me. 3 to challenge, dare

kilang juice taken from sugar cane during its processing. **n̈g/di*** to boil sugar-cane liquid. *** minjak** sugar refinery

kilap 1 *rg* lightning. 2 I don't know (*md for* EMBUH). **ke*an** to forget, overlook; unaware, oblivious

kilat 1 (flash of) lightning. 2 lightning-like, swift. **n̈g*** *or* **k·um·ilat(-*)** resembling lightning. *** ṭaṭit** lightning followed by thunder

kilèn west (*kr for* KULON)

kileng *-* having an oily shiny appearance. *Olèhé dolan pepanas rainé nganti *-*.* He played in the sun so long his face is gleaming.

kili 1 object (feather, blade of grass, *etc.*) used as a goad to fighting crickets, or to scratch an itch. 2 *oj* holy woman, female hermit. **n̈g/di*i** to use sth to goad a cricket *or* scratch an itch; *fig* to egg smn on

kilo(gram) (*abbr:* **kg.**) kilogram

kilomèter (*abbr:* **km.**) kilometer

kilong *-* wide-eyed and innocent-looking

kima an oyster-like shellfish in which pearls are sometimes to be found

kimat to have a relapse (*kr for* KUMAT?)

kimawon *kr* *sbst var of* KÉMAWON

kimbah to launder, wash (*sbst kr for* KUMBAH)

kimiā(wi) chemistry. *tjampuran ** a chemical mixture. *bahan ** chemical substance. *réaksi ** chemical reaction. *prosès ** chemical process

kimlo a spicy meat dish

kimplah (*or* *-*) swelling, billowing. *Segarané *-* banjuné.* There are swells in the ocean. *Awaké *-*.* He's hugely fat.

kimplek̄ *-* chubby

kimpling *-* [of water] sparkling clear

kimpul 1 a plant that produces edible tuberous roots. 2 *rg* purse, money bag

kin- *see also under* K- *(Introduction, 3.1.7)*

kina 1 old-fashioned (*kr for* KUNA). 2 (*prn* **kinā**) quinine; cinchona tree

kinah quinine (*var of* KINA 2)

kinang *ng,* **gantèn** *kr* betel chew (betel nut mixed with leaves and lime). ***an** container for betel chew. **n̈g/di*** to chew betel. *Jèn nginanga durung abang.* It's only been a short while (*i.e.* not long enough for betel being chewed to have turned red). **pa*an** container for betel chew. **pa·n̈g*** act of chewing betel. *sapanginang* a brief time, *i.e.* as long as it takes to chew betel

kinani(ng)âjâ *ltry var of* ANI(NG)AJA

kinanṭi a certain popular classical verse form. **n̈g*** to compose *or* chant such a verse

kindjeng dragonfly. *** dom** slender needle-like dragonfly

kinel *-* soft and jelly-like in texture

king *kr* from (*shf of* SAKING)

kingsèp [of swellings] to go down, be reduced

kinine quinine (prepared as medication). *pil ** or *tablèt ** quinine pill

kinjir *-* [of meat] soft and fatty

kinjis 1 *intsfr* new. *anjar *-** brand new. 2 virgin

kinjit *-* oily-looking, greasy-looking

kintâkâ *oj* letter, document

kintèki *var of* KINTAKA

kintel 1 a certain frog that can inflate itself like a balloon. *kaja ** to talk boastfully but in fact be a coward. 2 carpenter's plane. **n̈g/di*** to plane sth

kinten thought, guess, opinion (*kr for* KIRA). *-* approximately (*kr for* KIRA²)

kinṭil (*or* **ke***) to follow along. **n̈g/di*i** to follow, keep on the trail of

kintjer (*or* ***an**) taking aim with one eye closed. **n̈g/di*** 1 to aim. 2 to keep one's eye on sth one covets. *Tjopèté wis suwé olèhé ngintjer ḍompètmu.* The pickpocket has been eyeing your wallet for quite some time.

kintjlap *-* crystal clear; sparkling clean

kintjling (*or* *-*) clear, sparkling, gleaming. *bening *-** crystal clear. *Montoré *.* The car shone.

kintjlong *-* shining, sparkling. *bening *-** sparkling clear. *gilap *-** gleaming brightly

kintun to send (*kr for* KIRIM)

kipa *-* to reject with embarrassment. *A *-* ora gelem tenan disumbang pit.* A refused to accept the bicycle as a gift.

kipas a hand fan. ***an** to fan oneself. **n̈g/di*aké** to fan sth for smn. **n̈g/di*i** to fan sth. *ngipasi geni* to fan a flame

kipat **n̈g/di*aké** to shake [the hand, arm] to remove sth from it. *ngipataké banju* to shake water from the hands. *Tangané mau di*aké banter, bandjur bisa uwal.* She shook off his hand and broke loose.

kiper 1 goalkeeper. 2 cambric-like fabric

kipit *-* *or* **kipat-*** to wag the tail. **ñg/di*-*aké** to wag [the tail]. *Asuné ngipit²aké buntuté.* The dog wagged its tail.

kiprah (*or* *-*) 1 a certain classical-dance movement. 2 merriment, gaiety; merry; to dance around, *e.g.* with joy. 3 to take part in a communal activity

kipu (*or* **ke***) to take a dust bath. *Pitiké ke* nèng lemah.* The chickens are dusting themselves. **pa*ñ** place where birds take dust baths

kir **nge/di*** to examine smn/sth for ailments *or* defects

kira *ng,* **kinten** *kr* thought, guess, opinion (**pa·ng·galih** *ki*). **ku pada luwé.* I think they're hungry. **ku ora.* I don't think so. ***né** probably. **né ḍèké bisa.* The chances are, he can do it. *-* 1 approximately. **-* sesasi* about a month. 2 very likely; to take a guess. **-* wis mati.* He's probably dead. **-*, rasané keprijé?* How do you think it would feel? **ora (kena)** *-* in the extreme. *Ora *-* bagusé.* He's ever so handsome. **ora nganggo** *-* without giving it a second thought. *Ḍèké jèn nganggo ḍuwit ora nganggo *-*.* She spends money like water. **k·lebu ing** *-* to come under suspicion. **ñg*** 1 (*in questions, negatives*) would have thought. *Sapa sing ngira jèn isih urip!* Who'd have thought he'd still be alive! 2 (*psv* **di***) to think, have an opinion, guess. *Tak kira ija.* I think so. *Di* gampang waé, satemené angèl.* He thought it would be easy, but it was hard. 3 (*psv* **di***) to accuse. *Ḍèké di* njolong djam.* He was accused of stealing the watch. **ñg/di*-*** to take a guess (at), give an opinion. **pa·ñg*** *or* **pa·ñg*-ñg*** thought, guess. *saka pangirané* in his opinion. *Rak bener pangiraku ta!* So—I had the right idea, didn't I? **sa*** 1 in the event that... *Sakira kowé ora bisa teka, aku dikabari.* If you can't come, let me know. 2 even so. *Rada geḍé sa* ora dadi apa.* It's too large but I guess it's all right. 3 (*or* **sa*-***) measured (out); limited. *Nesuné ora se*.* He was furiously angry. *Olèhé mangan ora nganggo sa*-*.* He eats all he wants.

kirab (*or* **ke***) to move about in the course of an activity. *Barisan kaḍèt * nang lija kuṭa.* The cadets marched to various towns. *Sawisé ditemokaké mantèné *.* After the ceremony, the bridal couple moved among the guests.

kirânâ *oj* beam, ray

kirang inadequate, short, lacking; less (*kr for* KURANG). ***an** I don't know (*sbst kr for* EMBUH). *** priksa** I don't know (*kr for* EMBUH)

kirâtâ *oj* hunter

kiri 1 left (*var of* KÉRING). *golongan ** left-wingers. 2 *rg* (a) left-handed (person)

kirig *-* 1 to shudder. 2 to shake oneself

kirik puppy

kirim *ng,* **kintun** *kr* to send. ***an** that which is sent. **anku wis ditampa A.* A has now received what I sent him. *udan *an* heaven-sent rain that relieves a drought condition. ***an lagu** a listener's-request radio program of songs. **kiram-*** (**kintan-kintun** *kr*) to send repeatedly. **ñg/di*** 1 to send [food] to [workers]. 2 to lay [flowers] at a grave. **ñg/di*aké** to send sth. *Klambiné sing lawas di*aké mulih.* He sent home his old shirt. **ñg/di*i** 1 to send to. *Aḍi²né sok di*i dolanan.* He often sent toys to his brothers and sisters. 2 to send [food] to [workers]. *Djam loro lagi di*i tjaḍong.* They weren't served their meal until two o'clock. **pa·ñg*** sender. **pa·ñg*an** thing sent. *** donga** to pray. *** slamet** to send one's greetings

kiring [of coconuts] old and dried-up

kirna trillion. *sa** 1,000,000,000,000

kisa a small temporary cage or carrying case for a fighting cock, of woven young coconut leaves

kisas death by beheading. **ñg/di*** to behead

kisat *var of* KESAT

kisi loom thread

kisik coast, shore, beach

kisma *oj* soil, earth. *ginada adjur wor * (wj)* crushed and ground into the earth

kismis raisin

kisruh to lose track, get things out of order. *Ḍuwité akèh banget olèhé ngétung nganti *.* He had so much money he lost track as he was counting it. *Bèn ora *, olèhmu matja djeneng² mau sing urut.* So as not to get mixed up, read off the names in order. **ñg/di*aké** *or* **ñg/di*i** to disturb, interfere with. *Kowé adja takon waé munḍak ngisruhi olèhku ngétung ḍuwit.* Don't ask questions, or you'll make me lose count of my money. *ngisruhi upatjara* to disrupt a ceremony

kisut wrinkled, shriveled. **ñg*i** to become wrinkled/shriveled

kita 1 we, (all of) us; our. ** sabangsa* we as

a nation; our whole nation. *kamardikan* * our freedom. *ing tengahing masjarakat* * in the midst of our society. 2 editorial 'we' *(i.e. plural in form, singular in denotation). tjrita satjuwil kang * aturaké iki* the selected stories we present herewith. 3 *wj* you, your. ** adja wedi kangélan, ulun sing ndjangkung.* Do not fear; I will protect you.

kiṭa city, town (*kr for* KUṬA)

kitab book. ** ramal* book of magic lore. * *sutji* holy book; bible. ** unḍang*[2] *hukum* code book of law

kiter spin, rotate (*root form: var of* KITIR)

kiṭer *-* slimy and cohesive [*e.g.* jelly; frog eggs]

kiṭik hair louse (*ki for* TUMA)

kiṭing [of fingers, toes] crooked; deformed. *-* to hold gingerly in the fingers. **ṅg*** to hold the fingers in a clawing position

kitir 1 note, brief letter. 2 marker, emblem. 3 hem of a garment. 4 small leaf attached to a fruit stem. 5 last leaf remaining on a banana tree. 6 (*or* **ke***) to run in a circle; to spin, rotate. ***an** 1 propeller. *anteng *an* lively, always on the move. 2 pinwheel; windmill. 3 turtledove. **ṅg/di*aké** to cause sth to rotate. *ngitiraké wilah* to twirl a stick. **ṅg/di*i** 1 to send a note to. 2 to put a marker on. 3 to hem *or* embroider [a garment]. 4 to rotate sth. *ngitiri *an* to spin a propeller. 5 to circle around sth. **k·um·itir** to flutter, quake. *Goḍong*[2] *kemitir kena angin.* The leaves quivered in the breeze. *Kumitiré atiku amor karo wedi.* My heart thumped in fear.

kitjak rice-and-coconut-sugar cookie

kitjat (*or* *-*) uncomfortable feeling in the feet from walking barefoot in hot places

kitjel **ṅg/di*** 1 to massage, rub. 2 to pinch

kitjih **kitjah-*** to play around in water

kitjik 1 (*or* ***an**) meat or fish mixed with coconut milk and baked until the liquid is absorbed. 2 *var of* KITJIH. **ṅg/di*** to prepare [meat, fish] as above

kitjir (*or* **ke***) to flow [of body fluids, *e.g.* tears, blood]

kitrang *-* *or* **ke*** to run around frantically. *ngungsi *-** to flee in panic. *Wong wadon iku ke* nggolèki anaké.* The mother dashed about frenziedly looking for her child.

kitri fruit-producing trees in a yard

kiṭuh awkward, inept

kiwa 1 left. *saka * nengen* from left to right. *ana sisih ** on/to the left. *sing * ḍéwé* the one at the far left. *tangan ** left hand [with which it is taboo to give or receive]. *wajang ** the puppets who oppose the heroic Pendawas and face them from the left side of the screen. 2 immoral; unethical. 3 unstrategically located. *papan sing ** a place off the beaten track; an unpopular place which is not often visited. **ṅg*** to the left (*see also* NGIWA *entry*). **ṅg/di*kaké** 1 to move *or* put sth to the left. *mBok lampuné di*kaké siṭik.* Move the lamp a bit to the left. 2 to put sth aside, give no consideration to. *Prakara iku kiwakna waé.* Don't think anything about it. *Bapak ketua sadjaké ngiwakaké usulku.* The chairman seems to have tabled my proposal. **pa*n** lavatory, washroom. **sa*né** to the left of. *Panahé tjumlorot ing sa*né lésan.* The arrow went to the left of the target. *See also* KIWA-TENGEN, NGIWA

kiwat arrogant

kiwa-tengen on both sides; on all sides, all around. *omah lan *é* the house and its environs. *Jèn nruwong gunung, olèhé miwiti saka *.* When they tunnel through a mountain, they start in from both ends. **ku kabèh ja kantja*[2]. I was surrounded by my teammates. **maṅg*** (*prn* **mangiwa-manengen**) *ltry var of* ṄG*. **ṅg*** (*prn* **ngiwa-nengen**) to right and left; all around. *Si Kantjil ndeleng ngiwa-nengen.* Mouse-Deer peered this way and that. **ṅg/di*aké** (*acv prn* **ngiwa-nengenaké**) to move sth to right and left. *Aku weruh pulisi ngiwa-nengenaké sènter.* I saw a policeman flashing his light back and forth. **sa*é** 1 on all sides of, all around, in every part of. *ing sakiwa-tengening negara*[2] *mau* all over (*i.e.* everywhere in) these countries. 2 approximately. *Regané sa*é suwidak rupijah.* It costs in the neighborhood of sixty rupiahs. *See also* KIWA, TENGEN

kiwé *rg var of* KIWA

kiwil 1 kinky-haired. 2 crotchety, hard to please. *-* nearly severed, hanging by a thread

kiwir *-* cut nearly off (*var of* KIWIL[2])

kja giddiyap!

kjai 1 *title applied to highly respected (educated, eminent) males.* 2 *title applied to a revered heirloom.* ***ku** (*facetious*) my husband. ***né** tiger (*euph reference used when in the forest*). **ṅg*** 1 to apply the above title to smn, sth. 2 to have earned the title *kjai*. **geḍé** *title bestowed on men eminent in religion, philosophy, government*

kjajaban to conduct oneself in a disorderly manner

kjambak *var of* KIJAMBAK

kjèjèt *-* lethargic. *Olèhé njambut gawé kok *-* kaja wong kaliren.* You're working with about as much energy as a starving man. ṅg* frail, weakened. *Merga suwé anggoné lara awaké nganti ngjèjèt.* He's been ill so long he's quite weak.

-ḱké *inf post-vowel var of* -AKÉ

k.l. *see* KURANG: * LUWIH

klabak *an *or* *-* distraught. *A *an golèk utang.* A frantically tried to get a loan. ṅg* to move convulsively, *esp.* of chickens in death throes

klabang a certain small centipede. *an pigtail, braid; to wear the hair braided. ṅg/di* to braid the hair. * ajam a game played with dice. * ṅg·sander long and narrow. * telu a three-braid coiffure worn by bridesmaids at a court wedding

klabèt *var of* KLÈBÈT

kladuk to overdo. *Olèhé nggoḍog adja *, mengko lonjot.* Don't boil the rice too long or it'll be mushy. * wani (kurang de·duga) foolhardy

klafer clubs (playing-card suit)

klajab *an *or* ṅg* *cr* to wander about

klajan and; with (*var of* KARO)

klajar *var of* KLAJAB

klaju 1 a certain fruit, also its tree. 2 always wanting to tag along. ṅg/di*ñi to always tag along with. *Ibu mesṭi diklajoni aḍiku jèn tindakan.* My little brother always wants to go everywhere Mother goes.

klakah a split piece of bamboo used as a trough

klakar *ptg* * creeping everywhere. *Uleré geḍi² ptg * nang ndjubin.* Huge caterpillars swarmed all over the floor.

klakep to stop speaking and close the mouth. *mak * meneng* to fall silent suddenly. *an 1 to be silenced suddenly. 2 to keep yawning

klakson car horn

klalun carried by the current *or* tide

klamar 1 rope marking a boundary that is not to be crossed. 2 thin transparent membrane. * salak transparent inner membrane of the *salak* fruit

klambi *ng*, **rasuk·an** *kr* article of clothing,

esp. for the upper part of the body. *bakal* * clothing material. *ñ (ng·anggé rasuk·an *kr*) to put on *or* wear clothing. ṅg/di*ñi (ng/dipun·rasuk·i *kr*) to dress smn. **k·um·lambi** *ng kr* light, drizzling [of rain]. *Udané kemlambi.* There's hardly enough rain to dampen your shirt. * buntung sleeveless shirt. * kaos knit shirt, sport shirt. * keṭèk 1 simple collarless pullover. 2 long winter underwear. * kokok girls' short dress. * kurung 1 pullover shirt. 2 blouse worn by village ladies

klambrang *an *or* ṅg* wandering far afield. *Pikiranku *an.* I've been daydreaming.

klambu mosquito netting. ṅg/di*ñi to equip [a bed] with mosquito netting

klamed *an *or* *-* to make chewing motions with the lips or tongue. ṅg/di*i to tongue-chew [soft foods]; to move [the lips] in a chewing motion. *nglamedi lambé* to move the lips as if chewing. *nglamedi djenang* to mouthe one's porridge. sa*an one mouthful of food; *fig* a small meal, skimpy refreshments. *Olèhmu nitjipi sa*an waé.* Just take a tiny taste.

klamèh *klomah-** bland, effeminate [of a male's facial aspect]

klamit I ask permission to leave (*contracted form of* KULA AMIT). *, kula wangsul rumijin. Excuse me, I must leave now.

klampet to disappear permanently. *Saploké kisinan Slamet bandjur pet * ora tau ngaton².* Slamet was so embarrassed he never showed his face there again.

klampok a variety of guava

klamprah *an *or* ṅg* 1 to lie around unattended. *Klambiné paḍa *an nang djubin.* His clothes are lying around all over the floor. 2 [of overlong garments] to drag on the ground

klamtârâ *rg var of* KEMLANḌINGAN

klamud ṅg/di*i to suck. *nglamudi ès lilin* to suck on an ice lollipop

klamuk *var of* KLAMUT

klamun 1 *oj* if, when(ever). 2 *var of* KLAMUT

klamut *-* hazy, blurred, indistinct

klânâ ṅg* to perform a certain dance which depicts the act of dressing oneself. * topèng a dance performed by a masked male

klanan and; with (*var of* KARO)

klanangan *rg var of* P(A)·LANANG·AN

klandjir *ptg* * *pl* standing up, standing around

klangkèt thin, emaciated

klangsrah *var of* KÈNGSRÈH

klanṭang **ñg/di*** to dry and bleach [a soaped unrinsed garment] in the direct sun

klanṭung (*or* **klonṭang-***) unemployed and drifting; idle. **ñg*** to drift aimlessly

klâpâ coconut (*kr for* KRAMBIL)

klaper *var of* KLAFER

klaprut *ptg * pl* having messy mouths. **ñg*** *sg* having a messy mouth

klaput *-* (in a) thin (layer). *Olèhé pupuran ming *-*.* She powdered her face thinly.

klarah neglected, uncared for. *Bareng bapaké mati A bandjur * kopèn.* After A's father died there was no one to look after him. *ptg * pl as above. Klambiné ptg * nang djubin.* His clothes just lie around on the floor. ***an** *or* **ñg*** *sg as above*

klarap *rg* a small gliding lizard

klaras 1 dry banana leaf, used for wrapping. 2 *rg* corn bract used as a cigarette wrapper

klarinèt clarinet

klas class, grade, rank. *unggah²an ** to go up a class, get promoted. ** sidji, loro, lsp.* first, second, *etc.* grade. *** gèṭèk** cheapest section at the rear of a shadow-play theater, where the seats consist merely of bamboo stalks. *** kambing** lowest-price class

klâsâ *ng,* **gelar·an** *kr* woven grass mat for sitting. ** bangka* cheap poorly made mat. ** pasir* fine thick mat. ** patjar* patterned mat

klasik̄ classic(al). *musik ** classical music. *tjrita ** a classic tale

klasud *-* to grovel, crawl, writhe

klasutan thin membranous covering. ** uteg* brain membrane

klaṭak 1 fried *mlindjo* seeds eaten as a snack. 2 *rpr* a clattering thud. *Aku mbalang pelem mak * kena genḍèng.* I aimed at a mango but the stone hit the roof tile. ***an** caked soil *or* clay. **k·um·laṭak 1** to make a cracking *or* clattering sound. 2 caked, hardened

klatjap ***an** a peeled-off inner skin. **an katjang* peanut skin. **ñg/di*i** to peel a thin inner layer of skin from sth, *esp.* peanuts

klatjir *pl* sticking up tall and slim. **ñg*** *sg as above. Nang sawah kono mung ana wit krambil sidji nglatjir.* There's just one coconut tree in the paddy, standing tall and thin.

klatjup *rpr* closing. *Kembangé mak * mingkup bareng wis soré.* The flowers closed up when night fell.

klawan and; with (*var of* KARO)

klawé *ptg ** *or* ***an** to wave [hands]. **k·um·lawé** to move in undulating motions. *Tangané kemlawé ngawé-awé.* They kept waving their hands.

klawèr *see* ḌASI

klawer *-* long thin slimy-looking things in liquid. *Wédangé ana *-*é mulané trima ora diombé.* There are unpleasant-looking things in his tea—he'd rather not drink it.

klawu gray, ash-colored

klawung *-* *or* **klowang-*** idle; feeling empty and useless

klawus *-* *pl* ragged and dirty. **ñg*** **1** *sg as above.* 2 to wear old faded clothing

klébat *rpr* a brief glimpse. *Malingé mak * ngumpet.* The thief was seen briefly. **ñg*** to put in a brief appearance; visible for only a moment. *A nglébat saka pasemuan.* A didn't stay long at the party. **sa*an** a glimpse. *Aku mung weruh sa*an rupané si maling.* I only caught a glimpse of the thief's face. *Sa*an rupané kaja bapak.* At a glance, he looks like my father. **k·um·lébat** *sms* NG* *above. Jèn ana prau badjag kemlébat, bandjur dibledig.* Whenever a pirate ship appeared, they chased it.

klèbèk, klebek̄ *ptg ** *or* ***an** *or* *-* to put up a struggle

klebes *var of* KEBES

klèbèt *rpr* a flag fluttering. *-* *or* **klébat-*** to wave, flutter. **ñg/di*aké** to wave [a flag]. *Tukang ril sepur nglèbètaké gendéra abang bèn sepuré manḍeg.* The railroad worker flagged down the train. *Bareng gendérané di*aké, *, djarané mlaju brubut.* When the flag dropped, the [race] horses were off.

klebus *var of* KEBES

klebut wooden head-shaped stand on which wrapped headdresses (*iket, blangkon*) are folded into shape

kléḍang *-* 1 to take a stroll. 2 to approach in the distance. *Lagi waé dirasani, Parta *-*.* We had just been talking about Parto when we saw him coming. **ñg/di*i** to pass the time of day with smn

klèḍèk *rg var of* TLÈḌÈK

kleḍèr *ptg * pl* scattered about in disorder

kledjing **kledjang-*** **1** to barge in. 2 mortified, shamefaced

klédjo name of one of the Chinese cards (*kertu tjilik*)

kléḍung a certain fruit, also its tree

kléjang *rpr* falling gently, swinging downward. *ptg* * *or* *-* *or* **ng*** to flutter gently earthward. *Lajangané tiba ngléjang.* The kite floated to the ground.

klèk *rpr* cracking, snapping. *Tekené tjoklèk mak *.* The stick broke with a snap.

klek *rpr* breaking with a snap. *Kapuré mak * tugel.* The chalk snapped in two. **klak-*** *pl* to break, snap

klékar 1 *rpr* a body falling face up. *Ḍèké dibeḍil sepisan mak * nggléṭak.* Shot once, he fell instantly. 2 *cr* asleep. ***an** 1 to lie (around) [on the ground, floor]. 2 to fall to the ground. **ng/di*aké** to lay smn/sth on the ground face up

klèkèh *rpr* a knife stroke. *Pitiké dibelèh mak *.* He cut off the chicken's head.

klèkèk **ng/di*** to slaughter

klekek̄ *rpr* smn being choked

klekep *var of* KLAKEP

kleker *-* 1 (*or ptg* *) *pl* lying curled up asleep. 2 hoarse, croaking [of the voice]

klèlèd **klélad-*** 1 to move slowly, lackadaisically. *mBok tjékat-tjéket, adja klélat-*.* Hurry up–don't be such a slowpoke! 2 to keep sticking the tongue out. **ng*** to move sluggishly. *Adja nglèlèt, sing tjepet olèhé tangi.* Don't be a lazybones–get up!

kleleg ***en** to have/get sth stuck in the throat. **en eri* to get a fishbone stuck in the throat. **ng*i** to stick in the throat

kleleng *rpr* silent compliance with a request. **ng*** to leave without a word. *Bedjo ngleleng mulih tanpa pamit.* Bedjo left without saying goodbye.

klèlèr ***an** to loaf, take it easy

kleler *rpr* a shudder of revulsion. *Aku krasa mak * ana tjatjing nggremet nang sikilku.* Ugh, I felt a worm crawling on my leg! *ptg* * to have a ticklish *or* irritated sensation. ***an** 1 to have a tickling *or* irritated sensation. 2 to dawdle, poke along. ***é** one's general aspect. *Jèn ndelok *é ḍèké arep njolong.* He looks as if he's about to steal sth. *-* *sms ptg *.* *Kok *-* sadjaké hèm ana semuté.* I feel sth tickling me–it must be an ant inside my shirt. **klelar-*** to dawdle, hang back. **ng*** 1 soothed, lulled; to soothe. *Krungu musik kok terus ngleler aku.* It soothes me to listen to music. 2 to depart unobtrusively. *Ora kanḍa² kok terus ngleler mulih.* He went home without saying a word! 3 to dawdle. *Adja ngleler.* Don't be such a slowpoke!

klèlèt 1 opium for smoking. 2 nicotine. **ng*** to smoke opium

klembak 1 a certain tree. 2 the fragrant root of this tree, used for flavoring tobacco. *rokok ** cigarette containing tobacco blended with *klembak* root

klèmbrèh, klembrèh *ptg* * to hang untidily. *Olèhé djarikan ptg *.* She put on her batik wraparound sloppily. *Klambiné paḍa ptg * nang méméan.* The clothes are hung all over the drying rack. **ng*** to hang down too far. *Rambuté nglèmbrèh nang punḍaké.* Her hair hangs down to her shoulders.

klemed **klemad-*** (to eat) soundlessly savoring every mouthful

klemèh **klemah-*** timid, bashful

klemèk **klemak-*** [to eat, speak] slowly, deliberately, hesitantly

klemèr weak, debilitated

klemer *-* *or* **ng*** sluggish, languid

klempak altogether; as a group (*kr for* KLUMPUK)

klempor *ptg* * aglow; twinkling with many small points of light

klémprak *ptg* * *or* ***an** *pl* sitting around comfortably and informally. **ng*** *sg as above*

klemprang *ptg* * to keep clanging, *e.g.* weapons in a duel

klemprek̄ *rpr* a collapse of strength. *tiba mak ** to crumple and fall. **klemprak-*** to keep falling weakly. **ng*** to lie weakly

klempreng **klemprang-*** 1 to pace back and forth. 2 to walk slowly, sunk in thought

klempuruk *ptg* * *or* **ng*** to form piles, lie in heaps

klempus *ptg* * to sleep soundly. **klempas-*** to breathe noisily; to gasp for breath. **ng*** to sleep soundly

klemun *-* dim, murky. *Gunungé kétok *-* ing kadohan.* The mountain is dimly visible in the distance.

klenḍèh *-* *or* **klenḍah-*** [of walking gait] slow-paced and with the arms swinging

klendjar gland

klendjer *var of* KLENDJAR

klenèngan informal gamelan concert

klenger unconscious. **ng/di*aké** to render unconscious. *Sadurungé dioperasi biasané di*aké ḍisik.* Before you're operated on, you're usually anesthetized. **ng*i** causing unconsciousness. *Antemané nglengeri.* The blow knocked him out.

klèngkèng a certain tiny Indonesian fruit: an

expensive delicacy. ***an** 1 to yelp in pain. 2 to sing in a loud, carrying voice. 3 [of an empty stomach] to rumble

klengkeng *rpr* twitching death throes. *Pitiké dibelèh sanalika mak * mati.* The slaughtered chicken moved convulsively and died.

klèngsrèh *var of* KÈNGSRÈH

klenguk *ptg * pl* sitting around watching the world go by

klenik secret, private. *ḍukun ** faith healer who has developed his own cult of beliefs. *ngèlmu ** superstition, folk belief. *ptg ** 1 in secret. *Olèhé omong paḍa ptg *, sadjak wadi.* They're talking privately, probably telling secrets. 2 laid out, set in place

klénjam *rpr* peeling off. *Kulité mak * tjopot.* The skin comes right off. **ng̃*** 1 to come/peel off. *Kulité nglènjèm.* The skin peeled off. 2 (*psv* **di***) to peel sth. *Kulité kenṭang di*.* She peeled the potatoes.

klènjèm *var of* KLÉNJAM

klenjem fried ground-cassava cookie. **klenjam-*** [to eat] with great enjoyment. **ng̃*** to enjoy sensuously. *Ḍèké dipidjeti nglenjem waé.* He loves to be massaged.

klenjeng ***-*** *or* **ng̃*** 1 to feel dizzy, have a headache. 2 somewhat defective mentally

klenjer *rpr* sensuous pleasure. *Dipidjeti krasa mak *.* It feels so good to be massaged. ***-*** *rpr* the smooth disagreeable feel of mucous in the throat. **ng̃*** *or* **k·um·lenjer** sensually satisfying. *Tangi turu ngulèd, rasané nglenjer.* It feels awfully good to stretch when you wake up.

klenjit *sms* NG̃* *below.* *ptg ** characterized by an elusive disagreeable odor *or* taste. *Kamarmu ambuné kok ptg *.* Something in your room doesn't smell good. ***an** [of gamelan melodies] soft and slow. **ng̃*** 1 spoiled, rancid. 2 somewhat defective mentally

klènṭèk *var of* KLÈṬÈK. ***an** peeled off. **an kertas* paper that has been pulled off from sth. **ng̃*** to come unstuck. *Prangkoné nglènṭèk.* The stamp came off. *Tjèté ng̃*.* The paint peeled. **ng̃/di*(i)** to unstick sth, peel sth off

klènṭèng *ptg * pl* to clang. *Swarané watu tiba ing genḍèng ptg *.* Stones kept clanging down on the roof tiles. **k·um·lènṭèng** to make clear ringing sounds. *guju kemlènṭèng* resounding laughter

klenṭèng Chinese temple

klenṭeng cotton *or* kapok seed

klentik coconut oil. **ng̃/di*** to extract the oil from [coconuts]; *fig* to try to get money out of smn

klenṭing earthenware water jug. *ngindit ** to carry a water jug on the hip (supported by the arm). *** waḍah m·asin** one who is trying to live down his past but is bound to give himself away sooner or later

klentit clitoris (*kr for* ITIL)

klentjar *ptg * pl* gleaming, glowing, shining

klèntjèr ***an** *or* ***-*** *or* **ng̃*** to go out smw for pleasure. **ng̃/di*i** to flirt with

klentjèr *var of* KLENTJAR

klentjrang *ptg ** to produce loud ringing sounds. *Swarané tamèng kena peḍang ptg *.* The swords clanged against the shields.

klentjring *ptg ** to produce light tinkling sounds. *Ḍuwité ptg *.* The coins jingled.

klentreng ***-*** *or* **ng̃*** to walk with a graceful sauntering gait

klèntu wrong, mistaken (*kr for* KLÈRU)

klenṭung ***-*** *or* **ng̃*** 1 to return empty-handed *or* unsuccessful. 2 to roll up. *Kertasé nglenṭung.* The paper curled.

klèp valve

klépat *rpr* a quick departure. *lunga mak ** to leave suddenly. **ng̃*** (to leave) suddenly. *Ḍèké nglépat lunga.* He rushed out.

klèpèk *rpr* a darting motion. *Mak * iwaké mumbul seka mblumbang.* Suddenly the fish leaped from the pond. *ptg ** *or* **klépak-*** *or* **ng̃*** to keep wriggling; [of wings] to keep flapping. **ng̃/di*i** to induce [a bird] to flap its wings

klepek̄ *rpr* sudden inertness. *Mesiné montor mak * mati.* The car engine stalled. *ptg * pl* 1 to become inert. *Pitiké paḍa ptg * mati kena pès.* Chickens keep dropping dead from the epidemic. 2 (*or* **ng̃***) to flutter the wings

kleper *ptg * pl* to flutter, fly about. ***an** *or* ***-*** *or* **klepar-*** *or* **ng̃*** *sg as above*

klépjan to slip smn's mind; to get overlooked

klepjar *pl form of* KEPJAR

klepjur *pl form of* KEPJUR

klepon 1 a glutinous-rice-flour cookie filled with coconut sugar. 2 ovaries and uterus of slaughtered animals

kleproh *var of* KEPROH

klepruk *pl form of* KEPRUK

klepus **klepas-*** *or* **ng̃*** (to talk, smoke) to excess

klérab *ptg ** to sparkle, glitter. *Ṭoṭité ptg *.*

Lightning kept flashing. *Banjuné ptg * kena srengéngé.* The water sparkles in the sunlight. **sa*an** at a brief glance. *See also* LÉRAB

klèrek̄ clerk. **ñg*** to work as a clerk

klerek̄ *-* sore [of the throat]; hoarse [of the voice]

klèru *ng,* **klèntu** *kr* 1 mistaken, wrong; a mistake. *jèn ora *...* if I am not mistaken... ** banget nèk ana wong emoh milih.* It's a big mistake not to vote. *mBokmenawa ana *né.* There may be mistakes in it. *Aku * negesaké.* I explained it wrong. 2 to be mistaken for sth else. *Klambiku mau * karo klambiné.* He took my shirt instead of his. 3 morally wrong. *Jèn wong mati nglalu *.* It is wrong to commit suicide. **kléra-*** (**klénta-klèntu** *kr*) 1 to make mistakes frequently. *Enggoné masang sekrup pidjer kléra-* waé.* He kept putting the bolts in wrong. 2 to be habitually mistaken for sth else. *Tembung* mriku *sok klèra-* karo* ngriku. The word '*to* that place' is often misused for '*in* that place.' **ka*an** a mistake. *Kaklèruan mau ndjalari wirang pendjenengan.* The mistake caused you embarrassment. *** **surup** *or* *** **tampa** to misunderstand, misinterpret

klès one of two Dutch military invasions into the Republic of Indonesia. ** Pisan* the first invasion (1947). ** Pinḍo* the second invasion (1948)

klèsèd ***an** 1 to lie/sit around listlessly *or* wearily. 2 to collapse in agonizing pain. **ñg*** to collapse with fatigue

klesed *rpr* stealthy movements. **ñg*** to sneak, move stealthily. *A nglesed njumingkir.* A stole off to one side.

kleser *-* to crawl on the ground

klesik *ptg * or* ***an** *or* *-* (to talk) in whispers

klésod ***an** to keep moving around aimlessly in a crouching position [*e.g.* a child playing in the dirt]. *-* *or* **ñg*** 1 to sit in a low place. 2 to move along the ground in a squatting position

kleṭak **ñg/di*** to gnaw (on)

kleṭeg *rpr* the sound of light contact. ***an** *or* **kleṭag-*** continuous *or* repeated sounds as above [*e.g.* a mouse gnawing through wood; marbles rolling around in a box]

klèṭèk 1 *rpr* a click. *Swarané lawang mbukak mak *.* The door opens with a click of the latch. 2 dried (up, out). *gerèh ** dried salt fish. 3 *var of* KLÈṆṬÈK. 4 *var of* ṬÈKLÈK.

***an** 1 (that which is) dried up/out. 2 impoverished

kleṭek̄ (*or* *-**) *rpr* light knocking. **ñg*** busy at sth that produces light tapping sounds. *ngleṭek nèng pawon* working in the kitchen

kleṭes *rpr* pressing, squashing. *Pitiké mak * mati ketlinḍes montor.* The chicken was run over by a car and killed.

kletik *var of* KLENTIK

kleṭik *rpr* the sound of eating sth crisp (*prn* **kleṭi:k̄**). *Pèjèké ditjokot mak *.* He bit into a fried peanut chip. ***an** crisp food. **kleṭak-*** repeated sounds as above. **ñg/di*** to bite into *or* chew sth crisp. **k·um·leṭik** to produce the above sound

klétja a certain fruit, also its tree

klètjem *rpr* a sudden smile. *Jèn digoda ḍèké bandjur mak *.* When she's teased, she breaks into a smile. **klétjam-*** to keep smiling happily

klètjèp ***an** a peeled-off outer layer. **ñg*** to come off, peel off. **ñg/di*i** to remove the outer layer from. *Urangé sadurungé digorèng di*i ḍisik.* Shell the shrimp before you fry them.

kletji a potato-like root vegetable

klètjut *var of* KLINTJUT

kleṭuk *rpr* teeth biting down on sth hard (*prn* **kleṭu:k̄**). **ñg/di*** to bite sth hard. *ngleṭuk balung pitik* to gnaw on a chicken bone

kleṭus *rpr* teeth cracking sth hard. **ñg/di*** to crack with the teeth. *ngleṭus kembang gula* to chew hard candy

kléwa *-* unwilling to converse. *Didjak tjaturan kok *-*.* He tried to talk to her, but she pretended not to notice.

kléwah *rpr* splitting, slashing. *Semangkané disigar mak *.* He split the watermelon in two. **ñg*** to break open. *Djariké suwèk ngléwah.* Her batik wraparound split. **k·um·léwah** split wide open

kléwang sword with a broad curved blade. **ñg*** to strike *or* cut with the above

kléwas **ñg*** to turn aside the head. *See also* KLÈWÈS

klèwèr *ptg * or* ***an** *or* *-* *or* **kléwar-*** to wave, flutter, hang down limp. **ñg*** 1 to hang limp/loose. 2 to hang around. *A saba pasar nglèwèr.* A went and hung around the marketplace. 3 (*psv* **di***) to let hang. *Jèn wis ora seneng pegaten waé, adja mung di*.* If you don't like her any more, divorce her: don't leave her dangling. **n̈g/di*aké** to make/let sth hang loose. **k·um·lèwèr** *sms* N̈G* 1, 2 *above*

klèwès *var of* KLÉWAS. **kléwas-*** to turn aside the head

klijek̄ ***an** *or* ***-*** *or* **n̈g*** to stroll, saunter

klijeng ***an** *or* ***-*** headachy, dizzy

klika tree bark

klikik *ptg* * *or* ***an** *or* **klikak-*** [of empty stomachs] to rumble. **n̈g*** [of voice] high-pitched and breaking. **k·um·likik** *sms ptg * etc. above*

kliling to make rounds, go around. *Djuru usada * mriksa.* The health officer made a tour of inspection. *garis ** circumference. **sa*é** around, surrounding. *Kembangé ditandur sa*é taman.* The flowers were planted all around the park. *** sadjroning ati** to keep reliving, keep seeing in the mind's eye

klilip a speck in the eye; *fig* nuisance, pest. ***en** to have/get sth in the eye. **n̈g/di*i** to get into [the eye]. *Weḍiné nglilipi mripat.* He got sand in his eye.

klimah 1 phrase, expression. *Lagi omong sa* wis diselani.* He interrupts as soon as I say one sentence. 2 wedding meal, at which the bride and groom put food in each others' mouths to symbolize their promise to take care of each other. *** loro, * sahadat** the two Arabic phrases basic to Islam: belief in no other God but Allah, and belief in Mohammed as the prophet of Allah

klimis glossy, sleek; [*esp.* of hair] oily. **n̈g/di*aké** to make sth glossy/oily

klingking little finger (*oj*). ***an** *var of* KLÈNGKÈNG·AN. **k·um·lingking** *intsfr* dry. *Mèmèhané wis garing kumlingking.* The laundry is bone dry now.

klinik̄ clinic; hospital

klinjèm *var of* KLÉNJAM

klinjit shiny and oily. *Rambuté *.* His hair is oily-looking.

klinter ***an** *or* **klintar-*** to prowl, lurk. *Ana montor mabur *an mbrengengeng ing nḍuwur kuṭa.* There's been a plane circling over the city. **n̈g/di*i** to prowl around sth. *Malingé nglinteri omah.* The thief lurked in the vicinity of the house.

klinting ***an** *or* **klintang-*** 1 to wander around, pass the time aimlessly. 2 to roll around, writhe

klinṭing 1 edible turnip-like root that grows on top of the ground. 2 bell rung by hand. 3 *rpr* tinkling, ringing. *ptg ** full of wrinkles. **klinṭang-*** to keep ringing. **n̈g/di*(aké)** to ring a hand bell. **n̈g/di*i** 1 to keep ringing a bell. 2 (*psv* **di*i**) to summon smn with a bell. **k·um·linṭing** 1 to ring, tinkle. *Ḍuwité tiba kumlinṭing.* The coin fell with a tinkle. 2 full of creases. *Klambiné kumlinṭing.* His shirt is wrinkled.

klintjur *var of* KLINTJUT

klintjut ***an** acutely embarrassed, mortified

klintong ***an** *or* ***-*** to take a stroll

klintrek̄ ***-*** *or* **n̈g*** thick, viscous

klintu *var of* KLÈNTU

klinṭung ***an** *or* **klinṭang-*** to wander about aimlessly

klir color. **n̈g/di*** to color sth. *nglir gambar djaran* to color a picture of a horse. *See also* KELIR 3

klirik **klirak-*** to look around furtively. *See also* LIRIK

kliru *var of* KLÈRU

klisé 1 photographic negative. 2 plate for making engravings. 3 an imitation of the original. 4 cliché

klisik ***an** to toss and turn. **n̈g*** to move *or* turn over in one's sleep

kliṭer ***-*** soft and jelly-like

kliṭi(h) ***an** *or* ***-*** *or* **n̈g*** to pace back and forth restlessly

kliṭik *rpr* clinking (*prn* **kliṭi:k̄**). *Tutup botol tiba ing ndjogan mak *.* A bottle cap plinked onto the floor. ***an** 1 small second-hand articles sold by peddlers in the marketplace. 2 a small-scale peddler. **k·um·liṭik** 1 to clink, rattle. 2 crisp, crunchy

klitjat ***an** to feel overcome with shame

klitjir *ptg * or *-** to flutter in the breeze

klitjit [of hair] smooth and oily

klitjut *var of* KLINTJUT

kliwer *ptg * or* ***an** *or* ***-*** *or* **kliwar-*** moving about in large numbers. *Iwaké paḍa ptg *.* The fish keep darting about. *Wong² mlaku kliwar-*.* Crowds were milling around. **n̈g*** *or* **k·um·liwer** to appear briefly. *Aku mau weruh Slamet kumliwer nang toko.* I caught sight of Slamet in the store. *See also* LIWER

kliwon 1 the first day of the five-day week. *Slasa *, Djemuwah ** Tuesday Kliwon, Friday Kliwon (still observed by many as sacred days). 2 administrative official below a regent. **n̈g*i** to observe Kliwon as a sacred day

klobak ***an** *or* ***-*** ripply, wavy. *Banjuné *-*.* The surface of the water rippled.

klobot (**wiru** *sbst? kr*) dried corn husk, used as cigarette wrappers. *rokok* * corn-husk-wrapped cigarette. **ñg*** to smoke such cigarettes

klogèt *-* wriggling, writhing. *Ulané mlaku *-* nang lemah.* The snake wriggled along the ground.

klojong ***an** *or* *-* 1 to stagger. 2 (*or* **ñg***) to take a stroll

klojor *-* *or* **ñg*** to walk with a stagger

klokop *ptg* * *pl* to come/peel off. ***(-*)an** peelings, parings. **ñg*** to come/peel off. **ñg/di*i** to peel sth. *Kulité di*i nganggo lading.* He removed the bark with a knife.

klokor *rpr* pouring out. *Keboné dibelèh getihé metu mak *.* When the kerbau was slaughtered, blood gushed out. *-* *or* **ñg*** [of the voice] hoarse, husky

klokro *rpr* a surrender to despair

klolod ***en** to choke; to get sth stuck in the throat. **ñg*i** to cause choking, to get stuck in smn's throat

klolor *ptg* * *or* *-* *rpr* undulating motions. *Ulané ptg * paḍa nggremet nang kurungan.* The snakes slithered around in the cage. **ñg*** *sg as above*

klombjor **klombjar-*** 1 watery. 2 flabby, limp

klombroh (*or* ***an** *or* **ñg***) sloppy-looking, loose and ill-fitting

klombrot *var of* KLOMPROT

klomod *var of* KLOMOH

klomoh wet, soggy, sloppy. **ñg/di*(i)** 1 to moisten sth. 2 to cheat *or* deceive smn. *Ḍèké kena di*i, mulané ḍuwité entèk.* He got cheated out of every cent he was worth.

klomproh *var of* KLOMBROH

klomprot *ptg* * *or* **ñg*** sloppy in personal appearance. *A jèn njanḍang mesṭi nglomprot.* A always dresses sloppily.

klonèng bong! (the sound of a bell *or* gong)

klongkong ***an** *or* **klongkang-*** *or* **ñg*** to sing loudly

klonjo eau de cologne

klonjom *var of* KLUNJUM

klonṭang *rpr* a heavy metallic thud. *ptg* * *or* ***an** *or* *-* (to make) repeated metallic thuds. **ñg*** to make a metallic thud

klonṭèng *rpr* a metallic thud

klontjèr *pl form of* KONTJÈR

klonṭok to peel (*root form: var of* KLOṬOK)

klonṭong 1 a small drum-like implement which one shakes to produce light rat-a-tat sounds; also, the sounds produced in this way. 2 an itinerant peddler who deals *esp.* in clothing fabrics and who attracts customers with the above implement; also, goods peddled in this way. 3 empty, emptied; hollow. ***an** 1 noisemaker (as above). **ané diunèkaké: ṭong, *-*.* He rattled the noisemaker to call his customers. 2 emptied. **an rèk* an empty wooden matchbox. *Kuwi isih isi apa mung kari *an?* Is there anything in it, or has it all been taken out? **ñg*** 1 to rat-a-tat with the above noisemaker. 2 [of itinerant peddlers] to sell one's wares

klontrong *ptg* * slipping repeatedly. *Olèhé meḍun saka gunung paḍa keplèsèt ptg *.* On the way downhill they kept slipping and sliding.

klop just right, a perfect match *or* fit; in balance; to come out even. *Tutupé * karo loḍong.* The jar lid fits perfectly. *Pemetuné bisa * karo blandjané.* His income and expenses balanced exactly.

klopak *ptg* * *or* ***an** *or* **ñg*** [of fish] to splash around in the water

klopod messy with dirt *or* mud

kloprah generous. **k·um·loprah** to make a display of one's generosity

kloprot *ptg* * (*pl*) *or* **ñg*** (*sg*) dirty, messy. *Montir kuwi sanḍangané mesṭi ngloprot.* A garage man's clothes are always soiled. **ñg/di*i** to get sth dirty. *Gemuké nglopro ti sanḍangané.* The grease soiled his clothing.

klosod ***an** *or* **ñg*** 1 to move along the ground. 2 to sit/lie in a low place. *turu nglosod* to sleep on the ground

kloṭak *rpr* a heavy thud. *Watuné tiba *.* The rock fell with a thud.

kloṭèk *rpr* a thud

klotjop **ñg/di*(i)** to peel, skin, remove the outer covering from [sth hard, *e.g.* shellfish]

klotjut *var of* KLUTJUT

kloṭok 1 *rpr* a deep heavy thud. 2 genuine, authentic. *wong Djawa* * a true Javanese. ***an** a peeling. **ñg*** to come peeling off. *Tjèté wis paḍa ngloṭok.* The paint is peeling in places. **ñg/di*i** to remove the outer layer from. *Djagungé di*i.* He husked the corn.

klowoh [of the mouth] gaping open. **ñg*** hollow

klowong 1 *rpr* coming loose suddenly. 2 mellifluous [of a turtledove's singing]. ***an** 1 round hole, empty space, unfilled circle. 2 outlined pattern on fabric. 3 space left blank on a form. **ñg/di*i** 1 to outline a batik pattern on fabric. 2 to supply a blank place on a form to be filled in; to leave such a space blank

kluban a rice-accompanying dish consisting of beansprouts and grated coconut mixed with chili and seasonings

klubuk *ptg* * (*pl*); ***an** *or* ***-*** *or* **ṅg*** (*sg*) to struggle against being held *or* confined

klujur *rpr* acute embarrassment. *Bareng kisinan terus lunga mak *.* Covered with shame, he left mortified. ***an** to wander about aimlessly. **an mrana-mréné* wandering here and there. ***-*** much embarrassed. *klujur² lunga* to leave covered with shame. **klujar-*** *or* **ṅg*** to wander aimlessly; to idle, loaf. *Jèn bengi nglujur waé.* He spends his evenings wasting time.

kluk *rpr* joints cracking. *Djempolé didjeṭut muni mak *.* He bent his thumb back to crack the joint. **klak-*** *rpr* snapping sounds

klukuk **klukak-*** *or* **ṅg*** [of empty stomach] to rumble

klulur *ptg * pl* moving slowly. ***-*** *or* **klular-*** *sg* (to move) slowly, sluggishly. *Ḍèké tjilikané klular-*.* As a child he was a slowpoke.

klumbruk *ptg * pl* heaped about in disorder. **ṅg*** forming a pile. **ṅg/di*aké** to pile things in disorderly heaps

klumpruk *ptg * pl* gathered together randomly. *Botjah² olèhé turu paḍa ptg * nang ambèn dadi sidji.* The children all piled into the same bed to sleep. **klumprak-*** weak, debilitated. **ṅg*** to lie weakly; to slump down

klumpuk *ng,* **klempak** *kr* altogether; as a group. **é wis dadi satus rupiah.* It totals up to 100 rupiahs. ***an** *see* KE*AN *below.* ***-*** *or* **ke*** to accumulate bit by bit. *klumpuk² ḍuwit* to save up money. **(ke)*an** 1 group, collection. **aning wewaton² lan patokan²* a collection of principles and guidelines. 2 to come together. *Wong² sadésa paḍa *an arep ngrembug soal mau.* The villagers held a meeting to discuss the problem. **ṅg*** gathered together, forming a group. *Jèn karangan² wis nglumpuk, bandjur ditik.* When the articles have all been collected, they are typed. *Utangku wis nglumpuk nganti pirang² èwu.* Totaled up, my debts run into the thousands. **ṅg/di*aké** to gather, collect. *nglumpukaké krambil* to gather coconuts. *Ḍuwité sing di*aké ora tjukup.* The money he had scraped together wasn't enough. *See also* LUMPUK

klumud moist and dirty

klumuh **ṅg/di*i** to treat with condescending leniency

klumur ***-*** (to move) slowly and reluctantly. *A *-* bali menjang panggonané.* A dragged himself back to his place.

klungsu tamarind fruit pit

klunjum *rpr* peeling off. *Kulité diontjèki mak * gampang banget.* The skin came right off. **ṅg/di*** to peel sth that peels easily

kluntrung *ptg * (pl) or *-* (sg)* (to walk off) dejectedly, dispiritedly, with one's hopes dashed

kluṇṭuh ***-*** (to walk) with stooped shoulders and bowed head

kluṇṭung *ptg * or *-* rpr* a metallic clanking. **ṅg*** to roll/curl up. **ṅg* ati·né** to give up. *Lagi ketanggor alangan siṭik waé kok ndjur ngluṇṭung waé.* Surely you won't lose heart just because of a little setback! **k·um·luṇṭung** forming a roll. *Goḍongé kumluṇṭung kepanasen.* The leaves curled up in the heat.

kluron *ng kr,* **terag** *ki* 1 premature; stillborn. 2 to give birth to a premature/stillborn child

kluruk 1 rooster's crow; *fig* boastfulness. *ku kuk ** cock-a-doodle doo! **ing djago* cock's crow. 2 [of stomach] to rumble with hunger. **ṅg/di*i** to crow at

klusud *rpr* a quick slip. **klusad-*** to glide about. **ṅg*** to slip away. *Olèhé tjekelan wis kentjeng, meksa isih nglusud.* He held it tight but it still slipped loose.

kluṭak *var of* KLUṬEK

kluṭeg *var of* KLUṬEK

kluṭek *rpr* a clatter. ***an** *or* **kluṭak-*** 1 to make continuous soft sounds. *Tikusé *an ing pawon.* The mouse is gnawing in the kitchen. 2 (*or* **ṅg***) to clatter around. *Ibu *an ing pawon.* Mother is busy in the kitchen. *Wis bengi, adja *an waé.* It's late–don't be noisy.

kluṭik *rpr* a metallic plink. *Penitiné mak * tiba ing djogan.* The pin fell on the floor.

klutjup *rpr* a sudden smooth emergence. *Bareng tak pèdjèt widjiné metu mak *.* When I squeezed [the small ripe mango], out popped the seed.

klutjut soaking wet. **ṅg*** to get oneself wet, *esp.* by going out in the rain. *Motoré ora katon, botjahé ora srantan, nékad nglutjut.* The car didn't show up and the boy, impatient, went ahead and walked in the rain.

kluṭuk 1 characteristic *or* typical of a

particular area. *baṭik Sala* * a genuine Solonese batik. *A bener wong ndésa* *. A is a real country hick. 2 (*prn* **kluṭu:k̄**) *rpr* a small hard object dropping. *-* *or* **kluṭak-*** *or* **k·um·luṭuk** to keep making sharp sounds. *Ḍèké ngrungu kumluṭuking tjangkir.* She heard cups clinking (against saucers).

kluwa candied white melon *or* cassava, eaten as a snack. **ñg/di*** to make [melon, cassava] into candied snacks

kluwak mature seeds of the *putjung* tree, used as a spice

kluwek̄ *var of* KLUWAK

kluweng *rpr* a sudden swerve. *Motoré mak* * *ménggok ngiwa.* The car veered to the left. **ñg/di*aké** to turn to(ward) sth

kluwer *rpr* turning. *Motoré ménggok mak* *. The car turned. *ptg* * all in curls. **ñg*** to turn, curve, curl. *Pité ngluwer nengen.* The bicycle swerved to the right. **ñg/di*aké** to turn sth. *ngluweraké setang nengen* to turn the handlebars to the right

kluwih a certain tree; also, its fruits (used in soups)

kluwuk *var of* KLAWUS

kluwung 1 rainbow. 2 a certain spider. **ñg*** 1 resembling a rainbow. *Tjahjané ngluwung.* The lights are rainbow-colored. 2 having a rainbow. *Langité ngluwung.* There's a rainbow in the sky.

kluwus *var of* KLAWUS

km. *see* KILOMÈTER

-kna *post-vowel form of causative imperative/subjunctive suffix* -NA

knalpot exhaust pipe, tailpipe

-kné *post-vowel form of causative optative suffix* -NÉ

ko 1 later on (*shf of* MENGKO). 2 let me...; come on... *, *ngaliha, dak garapé ḍéwé.* Let me do it myself! * **sik** just a minute! (*shc from* MENGKO ḌISIK). *Kosik ta.* Hold everything!

ko- *var sp of* KOK *as second-person psv prefix. See also under* U-*: Introduction, 3.1.5.2*

koak *see* KAÈK

kober to have (enough) time. *Aku ora* * *matja.* I don't get much time to read. *Ḍèké ora* * *salin.* She didn't have time to change clothes. **ñg/di*aké** to make time for sth. *Tak *aké teka omahmu.* I'll make time to come and visit you.

kobèt to have plenty of room (for). *Penḍapané* * *bisa amot tamu sèwu.* The hall is spacious enough to seat a thousand guests. **ñg/di*aké** to accommodate; to take care of. *Sing ngobètaké mburi ora kurang.* There are plenty of people taking care of the refreshments (*i.e.* working in the kitchen at the back of the house).

kobis cabbage. **ñg*** to plant/raise cabbage

koboi cowboy. **ñg*** to act like *or* pretend to be a cowboy

kobok *ng kr,* **widjik** *ki* ***an** a container of water for cleaning the hands or feet. **ke*** *or* **ñg*** to put the hands/feet into water. **ñg/di*aké** to place [the hands/feet] in a container of water. *ngobokaké nang èmbèr* to put the hands/feet in a bucket of water. **ñg/di*i** to put the hands/feet into [water]. *ngoboki èmbèr* to reach into a pail of water. *Èmbèré di*i karo tangan.* He put his hand in the pail of water.

kobol to have a sizable deficit. *Aku sasi iki* *. I'm running way short of money this month. *-* to lose sizably. *Aku *-* kalah main.* I lost a pile of money gambling.

kobongan 1 central room in a traditional house. *Pusaka² disimpen ing* *. Sacred heirlooms are kept in the central room. 2 tent-like structure in which circumcisions are performed. 3 *form of* OBONG

kobra cobra

koḍak̄ camera

kodal **ora** * indestructable; invulnerable

kodanan *form of* UDAN

koḍeng 1 [of eyeballs] turning outward. *Mripaté* *. He's wall-eyed. 2 bewildered. *gawé *ing akèh* causing confusion for many people. **ñg*aké** bewildering; (*psv* **di*aké**) to confuse, bewilder

koḍi a score [counting term used in the marketplace]. *djarik rong* * 40 batiks. *lawon sa** 20 pieces of white cotton material. ***ǹ** ready-made; mass-produced. *Saking akèhé bandjur dianggep barang koḍèn tanpa adji.* There are so many of them they're a dime a dozen.

koḍifikasi codification

kodja small-scale merchant, *usu.* of Indian or Near Eastern origin. **pa*n** the part of a city where such merchants live or trade

kodjah (to give) a lengthy oral account. **é* *luwih akèh tinimbang rembugé.* His words are more plentiful than the ideas they contain. **ñg/di*aké** to give a lengthy account (of). *Pemimpin partai ngodjahaké bab ékonomi negara.* The party leader gave a long-winded speech about the national economy. **ñg/di*i** to talk at great length to. *Bapak* *ngodjahi Slamet nganti rong djam bab urip.* Dad gave Slamet a two-hour lecture about life.

kodjèl *-* to have death throes. *Pitiké *-* arep mati.* The dying chicken twitched spasmodically.

kodjong mosquito netting for a baby's crib. **n̈g/di*i** to equip [a crib] with mosquito netting

kodjor piled-up bars *or* bar-shaped objects. *sa** a pile of bars

kodjur 1 bad luck. 2 all over [the body]. *sak awak ** or *se* awak* all over the body. **n̈g/di*aké** to bring bad luck to; to jeopardize. *** ke·djudjur** always running into bad luck

kodo, koḍo boorish, gauche

koḍok frog, toad. ***an** 1 resembling a frog. *gelas *an* small drinking glass. *ḍingklik *an* low stool. 2 picked from a tree while standing on the ground. *suruh *an* betel leaves picked within easy reach while standing on the ground. ***-*an** imitation frog, toy frog. **n̈g*** 1 to pick [the betel leaves one can reach] from the ground. 2 [to ride a bicycle] standing on the pedals, sitting on the cross-bar, *or* with one leg under the cross-bar. 3 afoot, on shank's mare. *** sa·djro·ning baṭok** narrow-minded. *** idjo** a certain edible green frog. *** n̈g·korèk** gamelan melody symbolizing war. *** ula** gambling game played with dice on a revolving board. *** ng·untal gadjah** a highly improbable event

koḍol **ke*** to stalk [one's prey]. **n̈g/di*** to follow, shadow, tail

kodrat the way things are destined to be, the universal order. **ing manungsa* the nature of mankind. **ing djagat* the way of the world. **n̈g/di*aké** to determine, preordain

ko'en you (*rg var of* KOWÉ)

kogèl *-* *or* **n̈g*** to wriggle, move spasmodically, writhe. *See also* KROGÈL

kogel 1 to commiserate [with]. *Aku * marang kowé, mulané kowé tak ngèngèhi pananan.* I felt sorry for you, so I saved you some cookies. 2 ill at ease, feeling out of place

kogung *form of* UGUNG

kohen you (*rg var of* KOWÉ)

kohir 1 statement of valuation for tax purposes; tax bill *or* certificate. 2 certificate of title to property

kojah a sourish cookie made from tart fruits

kojan 1 steelyard. 2 unit of weight: 27-30 *ḍatjin*'s = *ca.* 3712-4125 lbs.

kojo *var of* KOJUK

kojok 1 bandit. 2 *var of* KOJUK. **n̈g*** to demand, ask for rudely

kojor tough, firm, resistant. ***an** tough meat

kojuk Chinese-style healing plaster for easing muscular aches

kok 1 *excl of surprise, often combined with irritation or wonderment.* ** udané ora mandeg²*. How come it never stops raining! *Botjah wédok * bal²an.* GIRLS playing SOCCER—!? *Aḍimu * luwih ḍuwur tinimbang kowé.* Why, your younger brother is taller than you! 2 *sentence-final exclamation mark.* *Ora *.* Why, no! Certainly not! *Pantjèn *.* It's true! *Aboté ora djamak *.* It's *heavy!* 3 *second-person psv prefix: (done) by you.* *Apa wis * pangan?* Have you eaten it yet? *Iki adja * kanḍakaké sapa² lho.* Don't tell this to anyone! 4 you (*rg var of* KOWÉ). 5 (*prn* **kok̄**) *rpr* a hen's cackle

kokar pin, badge

koki (*prn* **kâgi**) one who cooks as one's livelihood

kokis a cake-like cookie

koklok broken-down, not functioning

koko at some time in the future (*rg var of* MENGKO). **n̈g*** 1 the speech style used when addressing a social equal *or* inferior, *i.e.* smn one addresses as KOWÉ 'you.' 2 (psv **di***) to speak Ngoko (to). *See also* NGOKO

kokob *cr* to drink; to sip noisily from the container with the lips inside it

kokoh rice mixed into soup at mealtime (rather than eating each separately). ***an** rice-soup mixture. **n̈g/di*** to eat one's meal by mixing the rice into the soup. *Segané di*.* He mixed his rice into the other food. *Mangané ngokoh.* He ate by mixing the rice in with the other dishes.

kokok 1 muscular, sturdy. 2 *rpr* a hen's cackle. **n̈g*** to cackle, cluck. *** beluk** a variety of owl

kokosan a variety of *ḍuku* fruit; also, its tree

kokot *** bisu** speechless with rage. *** bolot** dirt on the human body; ***-bolot·en** dirty

kokrok 1 a plant with orchid-like blossoms and hairy leaves. 2 a variety of broad rattan used for tying things up

kol cabbage (*var of* KUL). *See also* SLAMET·AN

kol. *see* KOLONÈL

kolah bathing room (*var of* KULAH)

kolak fruit cooked with coconut milk and brown sugar: eaten as a midafternoon snack after the siesta. **ṅg/di*** to make [ingredients] into the above
kolam pond, pool
kolèd *-* to writhe in snakelike motions
kolèk 1 small sailing vessel. 2 the part of a horse's harness where the reins join the cheekpiece. ***an** *sms* 1 *above.* **ṅg*** to work for one's living
kolèksi a collection. * *prangkoné* his stamp collection
kolèktip collective. *tetanèn* * collective farming
kolèktur tax collector
kolérā(h) cholera. *ketularan* * contaminated with cholera. *pageblug* * cholera epidemic
kolik female nocturnal cuckoo whose melancholy cry is said to presage thievery. **ṅg*** 1 to eye covetously. 2 to work for one's living. *Mumpung isih ésuk tak ngolik ḍisik.* I'm going to work while it's still early in the morning. * **tuhu** the above bird with her mate
kolom newspaper column
kolonèl (*abbr:* **kol.**) colonel
kolong 1 a measure: the amount that can be grasped in the circle formed by thumb and forefinger with tips touching. *lawé sa** a bundle of yarn measured as above. 2 a rope bird-trapping noose. 3 (*or* ***an**) ring-shaped object; metal ring for holding things together. 4 (*or* ***an**) the space under a bed. **ṅg/di*** to encircle/enclose sth with a ring. *ngolong botol* to toss a ring onto a bottle (game of skill). *Asuné di**. The dog was caught with a noose.
koloni colony
kolonial(is) colonial(ist)
kolonialisme colonialism
kolor string used as a belt for trousers, underwear, *or* pajamas. **ṅg/di*i** to equip [trousers *etc.*] with a string belt
kolot conservative; traditional. *kaum* * the conservatives
kolu 1 to get swallowed accidentally (*form of* ULU). 2 (*or* ***ṅ**) cruel, merciless
koma *-* kind, compassionate, considerate
komā(h) comma. * **titik** semicolon
komanḍan commander, commandant, leader. **ṅg*** to have command of/over. **ṅg/di*i** to be in command of [a battalion *etc.*]
komanḍo 1 command. *awèh* * to give a command. 2 commando. *pradjurit* * ranger
kombang a large black buzzing bee that makes holes in trees in which to nest. **ṅg*** 1 [of the above bee] to buzz. 2 resembling the above bee. **ṅg/di*-*i** to complain (about). *A seneng ngombang²i B sing olèhé njambut gawé sak kepénaké.* A is always grumbling that B works at too leisurely a pace.
kombinasi combination. *Montoré ditjèt * abang ireng.* The car is painted red and black. **ṅg/di*(k̀aké)** to combine. *ngombinasi klir* to combine colors. *ngombinasèkaké pikiran²é awaké ḍéwé karo wong asing* to combine our own ideas with those of foreign peoples. *Ḍèké ngombinasi djas baṭik lan pantalon wol.* He wore a batik jacket (in combination) with woolen pants. **pa·ṅg*** act *or* way of combining. *pangombinasining tembung* the way words are combined
kombong (*or* ***an**) pen, coop. * *pitik* chicken coop
kombor [of pants] short and wide-legged. *kaṭok* * wide shorts. ***an** horse feed: bran mixed with grass. *wédang *an* cold weak tea *or* coffee. **ṅg*** 1 [of horses] to eat bran-grass feed from the pail. 2 to feed [a horse] with the above
kombul *form of* UMBUL
komentar a comment. **ṅg/di*i** to comment on, make a comment about
komet puzzled. **ṅg*aké** puzzling; (*psv* **di*aké**) to puzzle, confuse. *See also* UMET
kometir *var of* KUMETIR
komiḍi *var of* KUMIḌI
koming to struggle to get loose
kominis communist
kominisme communism
komis clerk
komisariat 1 branch of an organization. * *Jogjakarta* the Jogjakarta branch. 2 branch police precinct with its own commissioner
komisaris *var of* KUMISARIS
komisi 1 commission, board of investigators. 2 commission, *i.e.* percentage for selling. 3 (*or* ***ṅ**) to sell on commission. **ṅg/di*(ṅi)** to investigate, inspect. **pa*ṅ** commission (*sms* 1 *above*)
komité committee
komitèr *var of* KUMETIR
komoḍor commodore (in the navy or air force)
kompa a pump. **ṅg/di*** to pump air (into). **ṅg/di*kaké** to pump for smn, have sth pumped

kompak cohesive, harmonious [of a group]. **ṅg/di*aké** to make [a group] cohesive
kompèren loser in competition
kompetisi competition, match. *nganakaké * bal-balan* to hold a soccer match
komplah (torn) wide open. *Djariké ketjangkol paku suwèk *-*.* Her wraparound caught on a nail and got a big tear in it.
komplang vacant, unoccupied. ***an** vacancy. ***-*** 1 vacant, unoccupied. 2 filled to the brim. *Banjuné èmbèr *-* nganti wutah.* The pail of water is spilling over. **ṅg/di*aké** *or* **ṅg/di*i** to vacate, leave unoccupied
komplèks 1 intricate, complex. 2 a group of buildings. ** gedung²* a building complex
komplikasi complication; complicated (by). *Wong mau gerah nir bandjur * bludruk.* He had kidney disease complicated with high blood pressure.
komplit complete. *buku olah² ** a complete cookbook. ***an** a set (of clothing, dinnerware, *etc.*)
komplo stupid, ignorant
komplot friend, pal. ***an** a group of trouble-makers. **ṅg*** to make friends [with], get to be pals [with]
kompor stove
komprèng fawn (young of the KIDANG or MENDJANGAN). **ṅg*** 1 [of clothing] too short. 2 to give smn a ride but make him pay for it
komprèn(g)si a conference
komprès cold compress, ice pack. **ṅg/di*** to apply an ice bag to
kompromis a compromise
komprontasi confrontation
komuni (sutji) (holy) Communion; the blessed bread used in communion
komunikasi communication
komunis communist
komunisme communism
kon *ng,* **kèn** *kr* **nge/di*** (*var ng psv:* **kon**) (**ḍawuh** *or* **karsa** *ki,* **atur** *ka*) to tell smn to do sth. *Ali konen dandan.* Tell Ali to get dressed. *Wong paḍa kon melèk.* They were told to stay awake. *Tambané dikon ngombèkaké.* He told her to have [the child] take the medicine. **pa*** 1 an order, command. *Sapakoné bapaké kudu dilakoni.* Everything Dad told us to do is to be done. 2 *gram* imperative. *ukara pakon* an imperative sentence. *pakon tumandang* active imperative form. *pakon tumanggap* passive imperative form. *See also* AKON, KONGKON
konang firefly. ***(-*)en** (to see) stars/spots before the eyes. **ṅg*** (flashing) like a firefly. **ṅg/di*i** (**ṅg/dipun·kénang·i** *kr*) to see smn doing sth covert, to catch smn in the act. *Aku ngonangi tjopèt sing lagi njeler ḍompèt.* I saw a pickpocket lift smn's wallet. *See also* ONANG
konḍang famous. *wong ** a famous man. *putri kang * aju* a girl who is famous for her beauty. **k·in·onḍang-*** *ltry* famed, notable. *Priagung mau kinonḍang-* luhuring bebudèné.* That great man is known far and wide for his noble character.
kondangan *form of* UNDANG
konḍé ladies' everyday hair style (hair wound into a smooth bun at the back of the head). **ṅg/di*** to do [one's hair] in this style
konḍèktur train conductor. *** bis** ticket collector on a bus
konḍisi 1 a condition. 2 a toast; to toast smn; to propose a toast
kondjem bowing low. *sirah * ing siti* with head bowed to the ground (in profound esteem)
kondjuk *form of* UNDJUK
konḍor 1 stretched flabby [*e.g.* a worn-out rubber band]. 2 rupture of the inguinal gland. ***en** to have such a rupture
kondur to return home *or* to one's original place (*ki for* ULIH). ***an** *ng kr? ki?* 1 time to go home. 2 to be leaving *or* to have left for home. *Tamu²né wis paḍa *an.* The guests have left.
konferènsi conference
konfrontasi a confrontation
kong *shf of* BOKONG. *See also* KAK-KONG
kongas *form of* UNGAS
kong-el having a short trunk and long legs (*shc from* BOKONG TJEḌAK TJENGEL)
konggrès a meeting, a congress. ** sing suwéné sangang dina* a nine-day congress. ***an** to hold a meeting/congress
kongkang a large old frog
kongkih *form of* UNGKIH
kongkirèn competitor, rival. ***an** to compete
kongkon *ng,* **kèngkèn** *kr,* **utus** *ki,* **atur** *ka* ***an** 1 messenger; person sent on an errand. *Kowé *ané sapa?* Who sent you? 2 an errand, message. *Adja lali *anku lho.* Don't forget what I sent you to do! 3 to send smn on an errand. *A *an B nukokaké*

lajangan. A sent B to buy him a kite. **n̈g/di*aké** to have smn do sth; to have sth done. *ngongkonaké klambi* to have a dress made. **n̈g/di*(i)** to have smn do sth; to send smn on an errand. *Aku ngongkon Ali tjukur.* I told Ali to go get his hair cut. *Aku diutus menjang pasar tuku sajuran.* I was sent to the marketplace for vegetables. *See also* AKON, KON

kongkrit *var of* KONKRIT

kongkurèn *var of* KONGKIRÈN

kongkurs a singing competition between human beings *or* birds

kongsèng **n̈g/di*** to turn [food being fried] so that it will be cooked evenly on all sides

kongsèp *var of* KONSÈP

kongsi 1 company, firm; association, group. 2 **(ngantos** *kr*) until, up to, as far as. ***n̈** shared ownership of a business

kongsulèn *var of* KONSULÈN

konjoh flower sachet (*ki for* BORÈH)

konjol 1 useless, a waste. *Wong iku mati *.* He died needlessly. 2 unlucky

konjor ***-*** [of meat] tender, soft

konkrit concrete (not abstract)

kono *ng,* **ngriku** *kr* 1 there, that place (*Degree II: Introduction, 6*). 2 go ahead! *Aku ora arep mangan kok; *jèn arep mangan lo.* I'm not going to eat; you go ahead if you want to. ***'an** that sort of thing. *Konokan kuwi regané larang.* Things like that are expensive. **di*kaké** to be handled in that way (*var of* DI·NGONO·KAKÉ)

konperènsi conference

konpoi convoy

konsekwèn consistent; persistent. *Olèhé berdjuwang * tekan patiné.* He persisted in his struggle for right all his life.

konsèntrasi concentration

konsèp 1 concept. 2 first (rough) draft

konsèrvatip, konserpatip conservative

konsèsi concession. *Pamaréntah mènèhi * karo perusahaan asing.* The government granted concessions to foreign firms.

konstruksi construction

konsul consul, representative. ** djéndral* consul general

konsulat consulate

konsulèn consultant, advisory expert

kontak 1 (to get) an electric shock. *Aku * mak greng.* I got a shock! 2 (to be/get) in contact. *A wis bisa * karo B.* A has been in touch with B. ***an** electric fuse box

kontan cash (as contrasted with credit). *Pit mau dibajar *.* He paid cash for the bicycle. **n̈g*** to pay cash

konten door (*md? kr? for* LAWANG)

kontingèn a group representing the place they are sent from. ** olah raga* sports group, contingent of athletes. ** tentara* military contingent

kontjèr long dangling decorative object [*e.g.* ear ornament; paper streamer]. *ptg* **k·l·ontjèr** hanging down. *Rambuté ptg *.* Her hair hangs untidily.

kontjor *rg var of* KOTJOR

konṭol scrotum; *inf* penis (**p·lanḍung·an** *ki*). ***an** padlock. **n̈g/di*i** to divide and thin out [tuberous root plants]. *** ke·djepit, * sapi** varieties of cookie

kontra 1 *oj* famed, widely known. 2 (*prn* **kontrā**) counter-. ** revolusionèr* counter-revolutionary

kontrag to shake, vibrate. *Ana tèng liwat nang ngarep omah, marakaké mèbelé paḍa *.* A tank passing the house made the furniture rattle. **n̈g/di*aké** to shake/agitate sth

kontrak̄ contract, agreement. ***an** [a job] done on a contract basis. **n̈g/di*** 1 to make a contract with; to contract for. 2 to lease. *Omahé A di* rong tahun karo B.* B took a two-year lease on A's house.

kontras contrast

kontribusi a contribution, *usu.* of money

kontrol(e) supervision. ***an** regulation, supervision. *Pegawai pabéan kontrolané kentjeng banget.* The customs authorities exercise rigid control over things brought into the country. **pa·n̈g*an** a check, an inspection

kontrolir government inspector, supervisor

kontul *var of* KUNTUL

kop ***-*an** mark on the skin resulting from treating a headache by pressing a hollow hemispherical object against the forehead. **nge/di*** 1 to treat [a headache] as above. 2 to hit [a soccer ball] with the head as a playing technique

kop. da. *see* KOPRAL

kopèk [of breasts] flaccid, pendulous. **n̈g*** to nurse, suck

koper bag, suitcase, trunk

koperasi a cooperative

kopèt (to have) feces adhering to the skin after a bowel movement. *Aḍik isih *.* Little brother hasn't cleaned himself. **n̈g*** unbathed; inadequately bathed

kopi 1 coffee (in bean form); coffee tree.

2 coffee (as a prepared drink). *(wédang)* * *satjangkir* a cup of coffee. 3 a copy, duplicate, imitation, simulation. **ñg*** 1 to drink coffee. 2 (*psv* **di***) to make a copy *or* simulation (of). **pa*ǹ** coffee plantation. * **bubuk** ground coffee. * **gabah** unpeeled coffee beans. * **lèlès** *or* * **luwak** coffee beans discharged in the dung of civet cats: considered excellent coffee. * **tubruk** strong coffee made by pouring hot water over coffee grounds in a glass

kopik 1 just a moment! (*shc from* MENGKO ḌIPIK). * *aku tak ngombé.* Wait a minute, I want a drink of water. 2 (to play) a certain game with the Chinese cards (*kertu tjilik*)

kopjah fez-like cap in a low cylindrical shape

kopjok a certain gambling game like crap-shooting. ***an** a beating tool. **an enḍog* egg beater. **ñg/di*** 1 to shuffle [cards *etc.*] 2 to beat [eggs *etc.*] **ñg/di*aké** to beat for smn

kopjor 1 bad, spoiled, imperfect. *Enḍogé wis* *. The egg is rotten. 2 a fibrous tasteless variety of mango. 3 a sweet hybrid coconut. **k·um·opjor** [of fruits] juicy

kop. ka. *see* KOPRAL

koplak to move around inside a container. *Sopé * ing mantji.* The soup sloshed in the pan. **ñg*aké** *cr* to give smn a headache

kopling clutch (in gearshift cars)

koplo 1 (*or* *-*) [of cheeks] fat and sagging. 2 stupid, ignorant

koploh loose, detached. *Bané olèhé mulkanisir ora apik, seḍéla waé wis* *. The tire retreading wasn't done well–it came off very soon.

koplok 1 clapper, made of a bamboo section split lengthwise, for scaring off birds. 2 old, worn-out, ragged. 3 stupid, ignorant. **ñg*** 1 to shiver, tremble. 2 (*psv* **di***) to beat, whip [*e.g.* eggs]

kopoh *-* soggy, damp

kopok 1 pus; matter discharged from an infected ear. 2 *rg* deaf. 3 (*or* ***en**) to have a running ear

kopong empty, emptied of its contents; *fig* empty-headed, ignorant. *See also* KEMIRI

kopos *var of* KOPONG

kopra(h) copra (dried coconut meat)

kopral corporal. * **dua** (*abbr:* **kop. da.**) corporal second-class. * **kepala** (*abbr:* **kop. ka.**) senior corporal. * **satu** (*abbr:* **kop. tu.**) corporal first-class

koprasi *var of* KOPERASI

koprot *-* 1 to spill, spread. *Getihé *-* nang ndalan.* There was blood all over the street. 2 to suffer a serious loss *or* setback

kop. tu. *see* KOPRAL

kor 1 small louse (young of the TUMA). 2 corps

korab a great many, a large amount. *Anaké sa*.* He has a lot of children. *Banḍané sa*.* He's rolling in wealth.

koran newspaper. *mlebu* * to get into the papers. **ñg/di*aké** to put into the newspapers

kor'an *var sp of* KUR'AN

korban *var of* KURBAN

korḍèn curtain, cloth screen, drape

korḍinator co-ordinator

koré *see* DJARAN

korèd (*or* ***an**) that which is left behind *or* last in sequence. *Jèn rada telat olèhé mangan mung éntuk *an.* If you're late to a meal, you only get what's left. *Olèhé balapan mlaju tiba* *. He came in last in the race. *Aku iki (tiba) *an.* I'm the youngest in the family (*i.e.* my inheritance will be whatever is left). **ñg/di*i** to pick at [the remainders of a meal]

korèk 1 a scraping tool. 2 beggar. 3 (*or* ***an**) (to strike) a match. **ñg/di*** 1 to scrape clean; to sweep. 2 to cross out [a mistake]. 3 to clean the ears with an ear pick. 4 to reveal one's secret. **ñg/di*aké** to light [smn's smoke] with a match. * **api** (to strike) a match. * **kuping** ear pick

korèksi correction of an error. **ñg/di*** 1 to correct sth. *ngorèksi penemuné lijan* to set others' ideas straight. 2 to evaluate; to grade, mark. *ngorèksi karangan² tjrita tjekak kang bakal kamot ing kalawarti* to read and edit the articles that are to appear in the magazine

korèng scab over a wound. **ñg*** to form a scab

korèp ringworm. ***en** to have/get ringworm

korep 1 corrupt. 2 military corps

korèsponḍèn correspondent, contributor to a publication

korfbal a game resembling basketball, in which the playing area is divided into three courts and the players must stay within the court to which they are assigned

kori door (*kr for* LAWANG). *See also* Ṁ·WILANG

kornèl (to make) a corner kick (in soccer)

kornèt (bif) canned corned beef

korok long-handled swab for cleaning the inside of cylindrical objects. **n̈g/di*i** to clean sth with the above. **n̈g*i kuping (buḍeg)** *cr* to speak to loudly *or* abusively. *Jèn ana kabar politik sing wigati, kabèn kuping buḍeg di*i.* When there's important political news, it must be shouted to everyone.

korsi *var of* KURSI

korub *form of* URUB

korup corrupt. **n̈g*** **1** to act corruptly. **2** (*psv* **di***) to make dishonest use of. *Ḍuwité Djawatan di* karo kepalané ḍéwé.* The Department funds were misappropriated by the department head himself.

korupsi corrupt; corruption. **n̈g/di*** to seize illegally. *Beras kanggo rakjat di*.* They took over the public rice supplies.

koruptor corruptor; corrupt person

korvèt corvette (war ship)

kosèk to move aimlessly. **n̈g*** **1** to toss in one's sleep. **2** (*psv* **di***) to remove untidiness. *Berasé lagi di*.* She's cleaning out the stray rice grains.

kosèr ***an** lowest leaf on a tobacco plant. ***-*** *or* **n̈g*(-n̈g*)** to propel oneself along the ground. *Ḍèké *-* madju.* He shuffled forward. *Ulané ngosèr².* The snake glided along. **n̈g/di*aké** to propel sth along the ground. *Ulané tjepet banget olèhé ngosèraké awaké.* The snake streaked along.

kosik just a minute! (*shc from* MENGKO ḌISIK). **, dak nganggo sepatu.* Wait a second, I have to put on my shoes!

kosmonot cosmonaut

kosmonoti female cosmonaut

kosmos cosmos

kosok **1** to scrub. **2** the sound *or* playing of a stringed instrument. ***an** to scrub oneself. **n̈g/di*i** to scrub sth

kosok-bali *ng*, **kosok-wangsul** *kr* opposite. ***n̄** opposite (from). *Apik lan ala iku kosokbalèn.* Good and bad are opposites. ***né** the opposite; on the contrary. *Kosok-baliné apik kuwi ala.* The opposite of good is bad. *Ḍèké kuwi satemené ora boḍo, malah *né.* He's not stupid at all–quite the contrary.

kosong *var of* KOṬONG

kosot to rub/brush against sth. ***an** that which is rubbed against. *Tèmbok kuwi adja nggo *an.* Don't brush against that wall. ***-*** *or* **ke*** to keep rubbing the body against sth. **n̈g/di*i** to rub/brush against. *Adja ngosoti tèmbok.* Don't rub against the wall.

kostim *var of* KOSTUM

kostum **1** uniform, dress (for certain civil authorities). **2** costume for formal wear

koṭak **1** box, chest; box-shaped object. **2** wooden chest for storing shadow-play puppets, kept beside the puppet-master during the performance and used for various sound effects. ***an** a marked-off square. *blabag pesagi sing dipérang dadi 64 *an* a square [chess] board marked off into 64 squares. ***an montor** automobile chassis. **n̈g/di*-*** to divide into squares. *Simin lagi ngoṭak² keboné.* Simin is marking his garden plot off into squares.

kotang **1** [of women] long in the torso. **2** vest; sleeveless shirt. **3** brassière-like undergarment. ***an** to wear *or* put on one of the above garments

kotbah *var of* KUTBAH

koṭèh **ke*** to get smeared with dirty substances

koṭèk a warning device consisting of a bamboo length tapped with a stick. ***an** **1** *sms* *. **2** rhythmic sounds produced by striking mortars against wooden rice pestles. **n̈g*i** to produce *ṭèk-ṭèk-ṭèk* sounds by tapping the above device in warning

kotib *var of* KETIB

kotjak **1** to spill out/over. **2** [of eyes] clear, bright. **n̈g/di*** to mix by shaking. **n̈g/di*aké** to spill sth. *Sapa sing ngotjakaké kopiku?* Who spilled my coffee?

kotjap(a) *form of* UTJAP

kotjok **n̈g/di*** to shuffle, shake up. *ngotjok kertu* to shuffle cards. *Sakdurungé diombé obaté kudu di* ḍisik.* Shake the medicine before you take it.

kotjolan **1** baby fish (young of an *iwak*). **2** the young of a certain freshwater fish (KUTUK)

kotjor **n̈g/di*(i)** to water *or* rinse sth. **k·um·otjor** to drip, drool, dribble

koṭok a coconut-milk-and-vegetable soup. **n̈g/di*** to make [ingredients] into the above

kotokajam **1** near-sighted. **2** subject to night blindness

kotol *var of* KÉTOL

koṭong empty; *fig* empty-headed, dull-witted. *gelas ** an empty glass. *kertas ** a blank sheet of paper. *Wetengku *.* My stomach's empty. *hotèl sing ** an empty hotel; a hotel having a vacancy. ***an** (in an) empty (condition). *Bisé mangkat nang Sala *an.* The bus left for Solo with no passengers

in it. **ńg/di∗aké** *or* **ńg/di∗i** to empty sth.
Pemrintahé ngosongaké pulo mau. The government evacuated the island. **∗ blong** *or*
∗ plong completely empty

kotor dirty. **∗an** 1 waste material; excreta.
krandjang ∗an wastebasket. 2 *rg* having a
menstrual period

kotos **∗-∗** *or* **k·um·otos** to keep dripping.
*Olèhé mangan nanas nganti kumotos banju-
né.* The pineapple drips juice as he eats it.
gupak bleṭok lan ∗-∗ covered with mud and
dripping with water

kotrèk corkscrew. **ńg∗** to pull [a cork] with
a corkscrew

koṭung *var of* KUṬUNG

kowah basin, large pan

kowak an open wound. **∗-∗** gaping open.
Djariké suwèk ∗-∗. The batik has a large
tear in it.

kowal **ńg/di∗i** to chop up into smaller
pieces

kowangan water spider

kowar vague, hazy, fuzzy, not in focus

kowé *ng,* **sampéjan** *kr,* **pandjenengan** *or* **nandalem** *ki* 1 you. **∗** *kabèh* you *pl;* all of
you. *wong² sa-aku ∗* ordinary people, people like you and me. 2 *ng kr* small monkey (young of the LUTUNG). **∗né** you yourself. *Lha kowéné keprijé?* And what do
you feel about it yourself? And what about
you? *sa∗* like you; your size. *nalika aku
isih tjilik, sa-∗ mengkono* when I was a child
about your age

kowèk (*or* **∗an**) hole, hollowed-out place.
ńg/di∗i 1 to gouge a hole/hollow in. *Lemahé di∗i leté karo tengah kaki.* He made
holes in the soil 1½ feet apart. 2 to chip
pieces from

kowèn 1 stream where laundry is washed.
2 dung-disposal ditch

kowen you (*rg var of* KOWÉ)

kowèng **∗-∗** to howl/yelp in pain

krabang *ptg ∗* [of skin] having a reddish
irritated appearance. *See also* ABANG

krabat relatives. **∗** *saka bapak* relations on
the father's side of the family

krabjaḱan in great haste. *mBok sing sarèh,
adja ∗.* Take it easy—don't rush so.

kraèk *ptg ∗ cr* to yell noisily, make racket
(*pl form of* KAÈK)

kraèng *title applied to a noble of Bugis (Ma-
kasar)*

krah shirt collar

krai a yellow fruit resembling a cucumber

in shape and an apple in flavor and texture

krakab *var of* KRUKUB

krakal stones, rocks. **∗an** rocky road, stony
path. **ńg/di∗** to cover [a road] with stones

krakot **ńg/di∗(i)** to bite (into), gnaw (on)

kram (to be seized with) a cramp

krâmâ 1 speech style used when addressing
smn of higher social status or smn one does
not know well (*see also Introduction, 5*).
*Tembung ∗ iku ana sing béda banget karo
Ngokoné.* Some Krama words are very different (in form) from the corresponding
Ngoko. 2 manners, etiquette. *murang ∗* or
tanpa ∗ unmannerly. *ngungkak ∗* to violate the rules of etiquette. 3 to get married (*ki for* OMAH², RABI). 4 *oj* spouse.
∗n wedding ceremony. **∗n-∗nan** to speak
Krama to each other. **ńg∗** to speak Krama.
ńg/di∗kaké 1 to say in Krama. *Ukara iki
kramakna.* Put this sentence into Krama. 2
to hold a wedding for [one's child]. **ńg/di∗ni**
to address smn in Krama. *Pak Bupati kok
ngramani aku.* Why, the Regent spoke to
me in Krama! **∗ anḍap** humble Krama
Inggil. **∗ (a)ntara** ordinary Krama. **∗ désa**
rural Krama. **∗ enggon²an** regional Krama.
∗ inggil high Krama; **ńg/di∗kaké-inggil** *or*
ńg/di∗-inggil·aké to say in high Krama. *Sing
dikrama-inggilaké iku tembung sing mratélakaké apa?* What sorts of words are said in
high Krama? **∗ lumrah** ordinary Krama.
∗ wenang optional Krama. *See also* PIKRAMA
and Introduction, 5.5

kraman rebellion, uprising. **ńg∗** to rise up,
revolt. *ngraman marang Pemerintah* to rebel against the Government

kramas *ng kr,* **djamas** *ki* to shampoo one's
hair. **ńg/di∗i** to shampoo smn else's hair

kramat 1 holy; spiritually elevated; supernaturally gifted. 2 public honor bestowed
upon smn. 3 (*or* **∗an**) burial place of a
holy person

krambang *pl form of* KAMBANG

krambil *ng,* **klâpâ** *kr* coconut. *Degané wis
njelaki ∗.* The (young) coconut is almost a
(mature) coconut. *ampas ∗* shredded coconut remaining after the oil has been pressed
out. **∗** *gaḍing* a small yellowish variety of
coconut. *gula ∗* (brown) coconut sugar.
pabrik ∗ coconut-processing factory; copra
plant. *parudan ∗* grated coconut; coconut
grater. **∗** *tjukilan* coconut meat pried from
the shell

krambjang *ptg ∗* to float about. **ńg∗** to

wander at will. *Pikiranku ngrambjang.* My thoughts were wandering. **k·um·rambjang** to float here and there
krami *sbst var of* KRAMA 3
kraminan the wood of a certain tree
kramjas *var of* KRANJAS
krampjang **ke**∗ to get included in a bawling out intended for others. **ng/di**∗ to speak angrily to
krampul *ptg* ∗ *or* ∗-∗ *or* **krompal-**∗ *pl* to float. *Méga ptg* ∗ *ing awang²*. Clouds floated in the sky.
kramun ∗-∗ drizzling (rain)
kran *var sp of* KERAN
krânâ *ltry* reason, cause; because
krandjang round woven-wicker basket. ∗ *pendjalin* rattan basket. ∗ *kotoran* or ∗ *rereged* wastebasket. ∗ *uwuh* trash basket. ∗**an** by the basket(ful); in baskets. *Arengé* ∗*an.* The charcoal is sold by the basket. **ng/di**∗**i** to put sth into a basket
krandji chicken coop
krandjingan 1 *curse word.* ∗! *sapa sing ngrusak pager iki?* Damn! who wrecked this fence? 2 excessively fond of. ∗ *nonton bal²an* addicted to watching soccer games. ∗ **sétan** fiendishly addicted to. *Jèn wis main bandjur* ∗ *sétan.* When he gambles he's like one possessed.
krangkèng barred enclosure; iron cage; jail. ∗ *keṭèk* monkey cage. **ng/di**∗ to put into an enclosure. *Malingé di*∗. The thief was jailed.
krangrang *var of* RANGRANG
krangsang *var of* KRENGSENG
kranguk *ptg* ∗ *pl* heads sticking out [*e.g.* from windows] with necks craned
kranjas *ptg* ∗ *or* ∗-∗ *or* **k·um·ranjas** (to taste) hot, biting; (to feel) stinging, burning. *Tatuné disoki tamba, sur, wah rasané* ∗-∗. He put medicine on the cut that stung fiercely. *Wah sambelé peḍes banget rasané kumranjas nang tjangkem.* What hot sauce! it bites my tongue.
kranju:k *ptg* ∗ to sit idly *or* lethargically
kranten *sbst kr for* KRANA
kranṭeng 1 forming a complicated network. *Kawat listriké akih banget ptg* ∗. There's a huge network of electric wires. 2 to sit around waiting
kranṭil *pl form of* KANṬIL
kranṭu:l *ptg* ∗ *pl* to hang, dangle
kraos to feel at home (*kr for* KRASAN)
krapjak a fenced-in game preserve. **ng/di**∗ to fence in [land] for a game preserve. **k·um·rapjak** [of flowing water] to babble, gurgle
kraras *var of* KLARAS
krasak ∗-∗ *rpr* swishing sounds. **k·um·rasak** to make such sounds. *Aku krungu kumrasaking kali.* I heard the river rushing. *swarané angin kemrasak* the sound of the wind rustling
krasan *ng,* **kraos** *kr* to feel at home, feel comfortable. *Aku ora* ∗ *manggon ing kuṭa iki.* I don't feel at home (living) here in the city. *Manuk kuwi jèn ora di-kapak²aké* ∗. If you leave a bird alone, he'll get used to being around you. **ng/di**∗-∗**aké** to make an effort to feel comfortable (in). *Sanadjan di-krasan²-aké urip ing Amérika, nanging ja meksa ora* ∗. He did his best to adjust to American life but he just didn't feel at home. *See also* RASA
krasikan a certain kind of cookie
kratak ∗-∗ *rpr* crackling sounds, *e.g.* fire; wheels on a stony road
kratjak ∗-∗ *rpr* water pouring. **k·um·ratjak** to make the sounds of water pouring *or* gushing
kratjung *ptg* ∗ *pl* to raise hands
kraton palace; court (*form of* RATU)
kraṭu:ng *ptg* ∗ *pl* hands extending. *Botjah² tangané paḍa ptg* ∗ *ndjaluk kembang gula.* The children held out their hands for candy. *See also* AṬUNG
krawak ∗-∗ *rpr* water pouring. **k·um·rawak** to come pouring out
krawang *var of* TRAWANG
krawat ∗**an** bound with wire. **ng/di**∗ to bind with wire (*kawat*)
krawit ∗**an** 1 fine art(s). 2 a gamelan melody. **ng**∗ fine, refined, delicate
krawu **ng/di**∗ 1 to mix [*esp.* grated coconut] into. *Djagungé di*∗. She mixed grated coconut into the boiled corn. 2 to pull up/out. *ngrawu suket* to pull up a handful of grass. **ng/di**∗**kaké** to mix [grated coconut]. *Parudané klapa dikrawokaké nang grontol.* She mixed the grated coconut into the cooked corn seeds.
krawus **ng/di**∗ to speak abusively to
kre- *see also under* KER- *(Introduction, 2.9.6)*
kréasi creation; that which is created. *baṭik* ∗ *anjar* a newly created batik
kréatip creative. *sipat* ∗ creativity
krebet rustling sound of a skirt. *ptg* ∗ *or* ∗-∗ *or* **krebat-**∗ to keep rustling

krebul *pl form of* KEBUL
kréḍit credit. *dèbet lan ** debit and credit
kredjèt to move convulsively. *Tjatjingé paḍa ptg * kepanasen.* The worms writhed spasmodically in the heat.
kredjet deep feelings. *saka *ing ati* from the bottom of one's heart. *ptg ** to keep having sensations. *Rasané ototku ptg *.* My muscles still feel as if they're working [after long exertion].
kréjab *ptg * pl* [hair] hanging down loose. **ṅg/di*aké** to allow [one's hair] to hang down loose
kréjok *pl form of* KÉJOK
krèk *rpr* a rasping sound
krékalan to struggle to one's feet after a fall
krèkèl to climb *or* descend laboriously
krelek *ptg ** stiff and sore from overexertion
krekep *rpr* covering *or* closing sth. *Djangkriké ditubruk nganggo baṭok mak *.* He trapped the cricket under a coconut shell. **ṅg/di*i** to cover sth. *ngrekepi djangan sing nang kwali* to cover the pot of soup
krekes **-* *or* **ṅg*** to have chills
krelap *pl form of* KELAP
krelun *pl form of* KELUN
krembi:k *pl form of* KEMBIK
krembjah (*or ptg * or *an or *-**) fluttering *or* waving motions. **ing tangan* the fluttering of her hands. *Buntuté iwaké ptg *.* The fish's tail keeps waving. ***-* 1** fringe. **2** things that hang and flutter. **ṅg*** to wave, flutter. *Rambuté ngrembjah.* Her hair is fluttering loosely.
krembjang *var of* KREMBJAH
kremes a cassava-and-brown-sugar dish. **-* *or* **kremas-*** *rpr* chewing sth crisp. **k·um·remes** crisp. *Panganan sing kemremes iku kudu disimpen nèng loḍong.* Crisp food should be kept in a covered jar.
kremja **-** sparse, scanty, widely spaced. *Rambuté *-*.* His hair is thinning. *Sing nonton bioskop *-*.* There weren't many people at the movie.
krempel *ptg * or* **ṅg*** sticking together, clustered. *Bakminé jèn digoḍog ngrempel.* The noodles stuck together when they were cooked. *Saka gegana désan² katon ptg *.* From the air, the villages looked as if they were all clustered together.
krempjag *ptg ** overburdened. *Olèhé nggawa ptg *.* She had way too many things to carry.
krémpjang **1** *rpr* a metallic clang. **2** (*or ptg * or* **ṅg***) loose, disarranged, untidy
krempjeng **-** humming with activity, filled with noisy rushing about
krénah, krenah a piece of deceit. **ṅg/di*** to deceive *or* cheat smn
kreneng basket of woven bamboo, often used for storing wrapped fruits while they ripen. **ṅg/di*i** to put [fruits *etc.*] into a bamboo basket
krengeng *ptg ** to buzz, hum
kréngga to fail to come to completion. *Pelemé *.* The mango fell from the tree before it had ripened.
krenggos *ptg * or *an or* **krenggas-*** out of breath, panting. *Ambekané *an.* He was all out of breath. *See also* ENGGOS
kréngotan *see* DJERUK
krengkab *ptg ** breaking open/apart
krèngkang **-** to have difficulty getting up. *Ḍèké *-* ngadeg.* He struggled to a standing position. ***an** to fall in an awkward position for getting up again. **k·um·rèngkang** *sms *-* above. Aku kudu kumrèngkang njambut gawé sing rada abot.* I have to drag myself out of bed and tackle a hard job.
krengked **-** to squeak, creak
krengkèt *rpr* squeaking, creaking. *ptg * or* **-** to keep creaking. *Tempat tiḍurku njuwara *-*.* My bed creaks. **-* mikul dodolané* to carry one's wares on a creaky shoulder pole. *See also* ENGKÈT
krengkit *rpr* a high-pitched squeak/creak. *ptg * or* **-** to keep making such sounds
krengkot *rpr* a heavy creaking sound. *ptg * or* **-** to make such sounds repeatedly
krèngsèng **ṅg/di*** to fry [a fatty food] without additional oil
krengseng **-* *or* **k·um·rengseng** [of boiling *or* simmering liquid] to make a faint hissing sound
krenjes *rpr* dissolving. *Biskuité diemut waé mak * ndjur adjur.* Hold the biscuit in your mouth and it disintegrates. **-* *or* **k·um·renjes** **1** to melt in the mouth. **2** [of carbonated drinks] to give the tongue a prickling sensation
krenjoh *ptg * or* **krenjah-*** *rpr* chewing, *esp.* gum
krenteg deep feeling. *Aku duwé * arep mulih.* I have a great longing to go home. *Aku njumbang saka *ing atiku ḍéwé.* I contribute with all my heart.
krenṭeng firm, tight, taut

krenṭil *ptg* * [of things being carried] numerous, small, and varied
krèntjèng *-* *rpr* water dripping onto metal. **k·um·rèntjèng** to make such sounds
krentjil *ptg* * separated, not bunched. *Tekané ptg* *. They came one by one.
krepèk cheating notes (*var of* KEPÈK)
krèpès flat rather than tapering elegantly. *Irungé * ora mbangir.* His nose is snubby, not pointed. *Bokongé* *. It has a flat bottom.
krepes *rpr* cracking, crunching. **k·um·repes** crisp
krépjak 1 jalousie-style door or window closing. 2 *rpr* a crashing fall. *Geḍègé tiba mak* *. The bamboo wall panel came crashing down.
krepjak **sa*an** *var of* SA·KEPJAK·AN
krèpjèk *rpr* a crashing fall
krepjek̄ (*or* *-* *or* **krepjak-***) *rpr* joints creaking
krépo *cr* badly done. **, nenḍang bal waé ora bisa.* Clumsy—can't you even kick a ball?
kres *rpr* cutting, slashing. **kras-*** *rpr* repeated cutting. **nge/di*-*** to cut several times
krèsèk, kresek̄ *rpr* rustling, crunching; (*fig*) *rpr* empty talk. *Kakéhan* *. There's too much talk and too little action. *ptg* * *or* *-* to keep making the above sounds. *Gendéra kertas mau ptg* *. The paper flags rustled. **k·um·rèsèk, k·um·resek** 1 to produce the above sounds. *kemrèsèking krikil* gravel crunching. 2 to irritate with the above sounds. *Swarané mesin tik gawé kumrèsèking kuping.* The sound of the typewriter grated on my ears.
kreses *pl form of* KESES
kresna *oj* 1 black. 2 first day of the five-day week
kréta four-wheeled horse-drawn cart. ***n** 1 sth which serves as a cart. 2 to ride in a cart
krété baby crocodile (young of the BAJA)
kreteg 1 bridge. *wong ngisor* * hobo, beggar. 2 *rpr* wood *etc.* splintering and about to break. 3 *var of* KRENTEG. *-* *or* **k·um·reteg** to make repeated splintering sounds. *Ambèné wis kemreteg.* The bed creaks as though it's about to give way.
krètèk [cigarette] made from coarsely cut tobacco mixed with cloves. *rokok* * clove cigarette. *-* (producing) a ripping sound
kretep jeweled buckle on a certain belt (*kamus*)
kretes *ptg* * *rpr* chewing sth crisp
krètjèk crisp beef *or* kerbau rind (used in cooking). **n̈g/di*** to make [hide] into the above
kretjek̄ *-* *rpr* water trickling almost drop by drop. **n̈g*** [of speech] to pour out. *Olèhé paḍa takon ngretjek baé.* They kept firing questions at me. **k·um·retjek** [of speech] to pour forth. *Olèhé omong kemretjek.* He talks non-stop.
kretji:k̄ *var of* KRETJEK
kréwal *ptg* * *or* ***an** to have difficulty holding *or* carrying sth
krèwèk pierced by small holes. *Untuné* *. He has cavities in his teeth. **n̈g/di*i** 1 to make small holes in. 2 to scratch holes in the bark of rubber trees to release the latex
krèwèng fragment of broken tile
krewes *var of* KRUWES
kriḍa activity, action, motion. *olah *ning ajuda* training for military duty. **né satrija* the actions of a nobleman
krija a skill; a skilled worker, an artisan. *sekolah* * technical school, trade school. *tembung* * (*gram*) verb. *tembung * lingga* a verb that is active with no nasal prefix
krijak *-* *rpr* chewing sth fresh and crisp. **k·um·rijak** crisp. *See also* KRIJUK
krijeg *var of* KRIJEK
krijèk *var of* KRIJIK
krijek̄ *rpr* crushing, destroying. *Koṭaké ketlinḍes montor mak* *. The box was run over by a car. **k·um·rijek** crowded and noisy. *Anaké kemrijek.* They have a lot of children.
kriji:k̄ *ptg* * [of baby birds] to cheep
krijin *social var of* RUMIJIN. 1 formerly (*md for* BIJÈN). 2 first, ahead (*sbst kr? md? for* ḌISIK)
krijip *-* 1 [of eyes] half closed; narrowed. 2 (*or* **krijap-***) to keep blinking. *Guwek mau matané krijap-**. The owl blinked and blinked. **n̈g*-n̈g* mata·né** to narrow the eyes seductively
krijuk *-* *or* **krijak-*** *rpr* chewing sth crisp. **n̈g*** to chew sth crisp. *See also* KRIJAK
krijung **n̈g/di*** to win a large pot from smn in a card game. *Aku ping telu di* terus karo A.* I lost three big hands in a row to A.
krik 1 *adr* cricket! (*shf of* DJANGKRIK). 2 *rpr* a cricket's chirp. *Djangkriké paḍa ngerik, * * *!* The crickets were chirping. 3 *rpr* razor strokes of smn shaving
krikil gravel, pebbles. *Ḍuwit dianggep kaja* *

baé. He has little regard for money. **∗an** graveled, pebble-covered. **ng/di∗i** to apply gravel *or* pebbles to

krikit **∗an** crumbs made by gnawing. *∗an tikus* mouse gnawings. **∗-∗** to gnaw (at, on). *Asuné ∗-∗ sikil médja.* The dog chewed the table leg. **ng/di∗i** to nibble sth. *Sepatuku bolong di∗i tikus.* A mouse ate holes in my shoes.

krim cream. *ès ∗* ice cream

kriminil pertaining to criminal matters. *perkara ∗* a criminal case. *tindak ∗* a criminal act

krimpjing **∗-∗** to jingle, tinkle

kring 1 precinct. 2 (*prn* **kri:ng**) *rpr* ringing. **nge/di∗** to ring a bell

kringet *ng kr,* **riwé** *ki* sweat. *∗é dlèwèran.* He was sweating profusely. **∗en** *or* **k·um·ringet** (**riwènan** *ki*) to sweat. **∗ buntet** skin rash; heat rash

kringi:k *ptg ∗ pl* weeping softly. *See also* RINGIK

kringkel to curl up while in a lying position. **ng∗** in a curled-up lying position. *turu ngringkel* to sleep curled up

kringsing **∗-∗** thoroughly dry. *garing* **k·um·ringsing** completely dry

krinjis **∗-∗** *or* **k·um·rinjis** to sizzle. *Dagingé nggadjih digorèng ∗-∗.* The fatty meat sizzles and sputters as it fries.

krintjing *rpr* jingling. *ḍuwit ∗* coins, small change. *Kuntjiné tiba mak ∗.* They keys fell with a jingle. **∗-∗** *or* **k·um·rintjing** to jingle

kripik 1 crisp-fried beancake. 2 (*or* **∗-∗**) a certain crisp cookie. 3 (*or* **ng∗**) crisp, fragile, easily snapped. **k·um·ripik** crisp. *apik kumripik nantjang kirik.* Good on the outside, bad on the inside (*of smn or sth whose appearance deceives*)

kriptografi cryptography

krisik **∗an** unable to sleep. **∗-∗** *rpr* a rustling sound. **k·um·risik** dried to a crisp. *Pariné diepé nganti garingé kemrisik.* The rice plants were dried crisp in the sun. **kumrisik tanpa k·angin·an** bothered by one's conscience

krisis 1 a crisis. 2 short of money. *Wah saiki tanggal tuwa, lagi ∗ aku.* It's late in the month and I'm broke!

kristal crystal

Kristen 1 Christian. 2 (*or* **wong ∗**) a Christian. *agama ∗* Christianity

Kristus Jesus Christ

kritig *ptg ∗ or ∗-∗ rpr* the sound of sth on fire. **k·um·ritig** 1 to make such a sound. 2 to proceed in quick succession. *Botjah² bandjur paḍa muḍun kumritig.* The children came thronging down.

kritik̄ 1 a critic. 2 a critique; criticism. **ng/di∗** to criticize

kriting kinky, tightly curled

kritji:k **∗an** act of trickling *or* tinkling. *∗an dadi grodjogan.* A trickle becomes a waterfall; *fig* a mountain is made of a molehill. **∗-∗** *rpr* trickling *or* tinkling. **ng∗** to trickle. *Tutupen krané, munḍak ngritjik waé banjuné.* Shut off the faucet so the water won't trickle out. **k·um·ritjik** to make trickling *or* tinkling sounds. *kemritjiking banju* the trickling sound of water. *Kanṭongané tansah kemritjik.* His pockets are always full of coins.

kriwed *ptg ∗ pl* moving to and fro, milling around

kriwi:k̄ **∗an** a trickle of water. *∗an dadi grodjogan.* A trivial thing becomes magnified out of all proportion. **∗-∗** *or* **ng∗** *or* **k·um·riwik** to trickle

kriwil 1 kinky, tightly curled. 2 difficult or complicated to handle. *Kowé kok ∗ banget.* You're hard to get along with! 3 English-style bicycle gear which, when backpedaled, does not brake. *pit ∗* bicycle hav- such gears

kriwis **∗-∗** sparse. *Udané ∗-∗.* It's not raining much. *Rambuté ∗-∗.* His hair is thinning.

krobjok **∗-∗** *rpr* walking through water. *Olèhé njabrang kali ∗-∗.* He splashed across the river. **ng∗** to make splashing sounds as one walks

krobok *var of* KOBOK

krobong **∗an** inner room (*var of* KOBONGAN). **ng/di∗i** to place a covering over a bed. *Olèhé turu di∗i klambu.* He slept with mosquito netting draped over his bed.

kroḍa [of a volcano] to erupt; *fig* to blow up, lose one's temper

kroḍèn *var of* KORḌÈN

krodjèl in death throes

krodjong **ng/di∗i** to agree (upon, to)

kroḍong a protective covering. **ng/di∗i** to equip with such a cover. **∗ baji** a small mosquito netting for a baby's bed. **∗ dijan** *or* **∗ lampu** lampshade

krog **∗-∗** *rpr* cutting strokes

krogèl *ptg ∗ or* **krogal-∗** to writhe, move spasmodically. *See also* KOGÈL, OGÈL

krojok ***an** to fight together as a gang. **ṅg/di*** to attack [a weaker force], to outnumber. *di*i loro* to be jumped by two attackers. *Gawéané jèn di* wong okèh mesṭi énggal rampung.* If the job is tackled by a large group, it is soon finished. **k·um·rojok** *var of* K·UM·RUJUK
krokèt fried meat-and-potato croquette
krokos *var of* KROPOS
krokot a certain plant that grows among grasses. **ṅg/di*(i)** to chew on, gnaw at
krompjang crash! **! tjangkiré petjah.* The cup smashed. **k·um·rompjang** to shatter, crash
krompjong *var of* KROMPJANG
krompol *ptg * or *-* or* **ke*an** forming a group *or* cluster. **ṅg*** to form a group; to gather, assemble
krongkongan throat
kronis chronic
kronjos *rpr* the sputtering *or* sizzling of food frying
krontjal *ptg * or* ***an** *or *-** to keep moving, twisting, jerking. *Dalané ora diaspal, jèn kanggo liwat ptg *.* The road isn't paved; it gives you a good jouncing. *Kutjingé *-*.* The cat struggled to get free. *Bajiné *-*.* The baby's arms and legs are in constant motion.
krontjong 1 wrist or ankle bracelet. 2 popular music; an orchestra that plays popular music. ***an** 1 to play popular songs. 2 [of an empty stomach] to rumble
kropak ancient writings on palm leaves
kropjak *rpr* the sound of a wooden or bamboo object falling. **k·um·ropjak** to make such a sound
kropjok *ptg * or* **k·um·ropjok** [of coins] to jingle. *Ḍuwité pepajon kumropjok ing djero kanṭong.* His profits jingled in his pockets. **di·bajar** * paid in cash
kropok rotted at the core. **ṅg*** to rot within. **k·um·ropok** irritated, fed up
kropos empty, hollow; having deteriorated internally. **ṅg*** hollow; having a hollow place in it. *Olèhé nata bata sing rapet, adja nganti ngrokos.* Lay the bricks close together: no hollows between!
krosak *rpr* rustling. **-* rpr* repeated rustlings. *Krungu swara *-* ana ing gegrumbulan.* He heard sth rustling in the underbrush. **k·um·rosak** to rustle. *Wit² kemrosak katijup angin.* The trees swished in the strong wind.
krosboi, krosgirl *see* CROSSBOY
krosi *var of* KURSI
krosok 1 dried tobacco leaves. 2 coarse-grained. *weḍi ** coarse sand. 3 *rpr* a crunching sound. **k·um·rosok** to crunch
krotjo 1 a certain small snail. 2 worthless, having little or no value. 3 rank-and-file soldier, lowest-ranking private
krotjok ***an** a bawling-out; name-calling. **-* rpr* water running *or* pouring. **ṅg*** 1 to go along with the crowd, do as others are doing. 2 (*psv* **di***) [many things] hit; [blows] rain onto. 3 (*psv* **di***) to bawl smn out. **k·um·rotjok** *sms *-* above*
kroto 1 the egg of a certain ant (*ngangrang*). 2 young *mlindjo* blossom. 3 cart for hauling loads
krotog *rpr* a thudding fall. **-* rpr* many thudding falls. *Wité pelem dirog wohé *-* tiba nang nggenḍèng.* He shook the mango tree and the fruits came thudding down on the roof tiles.
krowak having a hole torn (broken, eaten, *etc.*) into it. **ṅg/di*(i)** to tear (break, *etc.*) a hole in sth. *Tjoḍoté paḍa ngrowaki pelem².* The bats ate holes in the mangoes.
krowal *ptg * or *-** showing lumps. *Watuné sing nang kali paḍa ptg *.* The stones in river show as humps here and there.
krowod ***an** vegetables and fruits that are made into soup. **ṅg*** to subsist on a vegetarian diet
krowok pierced by a hole. *Untuné *.* He has a cavity in his tooth. **ṅg/di*(i)** to make a hole in/through. *Tikusé paḍa ngrowoki téla kaspa.* The mice riddled the cassavas with holes. **k·um·rowok** [of a waterfall] to gurgle, roar
K.R.T. *see* KANGDJENG
krubeng *var of* UBENG
krubju:k̄ *rpr* splashing. **ṅg*** to splash through water
krubut (*or ptg * or *-**) *rpr* noisy and/or confused rushing. *Bareng bèlé wis muni botjah² ptg * metu saka klas tjepet²an.* When the bell rang, the children rushed pell-mell out of class. ***an** act of mobbing *or* overwhelming. **ṅg/di*** to crowd around, mob, overwhelm. **k·um·rubut** to come/go with a great rush, to crowd in/out/around
kruḍak unable to move; able to move only with the greatest difficulty
kruḍek̄ *var of* KRUḌAK
kruḍug **-** to move about while covered

with sth. *Rékané arep medèni aḍiké kuḍung djarik mlaku *-*.* He's going to scare his little brother by clumping around with a batik over his head.

kruḍung *var of* KUḌUNG

kruget *ptg * or *-* or* **krugat-*** *or* **k·um·ruget** to move one's body; to wriggle, squirm. *Ora suwé wis *-* lan éling.* Soon she began to move, and regained consciousness. *Tjatjingé paḍa ptg * nang plataran.* Worms are wriggling around in the yard. *See also* UGET

krujel *ptg ** crowded into an inadequate space. *Botjah lima paḍa turu ptg * sak ambèn.* Five children were sleeping in the same bed.

krujuk *ptg * or* ***an** *or *-* or* **k·um·rujuk** to form a group; to act as a group. *Wong ngemisé paḍa teka kemrujuk.* The beggars crowded around me. *Uleré sing nang wit pelem kemrujuk.* The mango tree was swarming with caterpillars.

krukat a crew (hair)cut. *(tjukur) ** (to have) a crew cut

krukub shade, fabric covering. *Kemulé dianggo *.* He covered it with the blanket. **ñg/di*(i)** to cover with a fabric covering

kruma germ; bacteria

krumpjang *rpr* a shattering crash

krumpul round gold earring with jewels set around the edge. *ptg ** to gather, assemble. **-** a gathering, group. *Ana *-* wong nang prapatan.* A crowd gathered at the intersection. *See also* KUMPUL

krun 1 crown. 2 crown-shaped object. *** prins** crown prince

krunḍug *var of* KRUḌUG

krungsung **-* or* **k·um·rungsung** about to come to a boil; producing a boiling sound; *fig* uneasy, restless, under pressure. *Wéḍangé wis *-*.* The water is coming to a boil. *Ora selak kemrungsung kudu mulih.* He felt no particular urge to go home. *Bareng djam udjiané wis mèh bar, olèhé nggarap̓ dadi kemrungsung.* As the examination hour drew to a close, he worked under increasing pressure.

krungu *ng* to hear (*form of* RUNGU). *Saka kadohan wis * suraké.* The cheering could be heard from afar. *Aku wis * jèn A pegatan.* I've heard A is divorced. ***ñ** sense of hearing; having a keen sense of hearing. **ñg/di*ñi** to communicate with supernaturally. *See also* MIRENG, PIRENG, RUNGU

krunjus **-** to fry [fatty meat] in its own oils

krunteg *ptg * or* ***an** forming a wriggling mass. *Pelemé bosok sèté ptg *.* The rotted mango is alive with maggots. *Botjah² paḍa ptg * nang tempat-tiḍur.* The children are all playing on the bed in a wriggling heap.

kruntel *var of* KRUNTEG

krupjuk *rpr* dulled *or* muffled jingling. **k·um·rupjuk** to make such a sound

krupuk crisp fried chips. ** legendar* crisp ground-rice chips. ** terung* rice-flour chips. ** urang* shrimp chips. **ñg*** to fry chips as one's livelihood *or* as a source of income

krus carbonated drink. *oranje/limun ** orange/lemon crush

krusek̄ *ptg * or* ***an** *or *-* or* **krusak-*** to rustle. *Sapa ta sing *an nang grumbul kuwi ja?* Who's that rustling around in the underbrush?

krusuk *ptg * or *-** (to make) swishing sounds. *Botjah² paḍa ptg * dolanan nang grumbulan.* The children are playing around in the bushes. **ñg*** *or* **k·um·rusuk** (to make) a swishing sound. *Udané arep teka saka kadohan swarané kemrusuk.* As the rain approaches from afar is swishes. **ñg/di*aké** to cause sth to make the above sound. *Motoré di*aké nang grumbulan.* The car was (run off the road and) forced to crash into the shrubbery.

krutjil small, undersized. *ptg ** in little pieces. *Ptg * ora bisa didadèkké sidji.* It's in smithereens and can't be put back together again. ***an** small *or* undersized (things). *Jèn tuku pelem limang rupiah mung éntuk *an.* If you only pay five rupiahs for mangoes, you get little ones. *See also* WAJANG[a]

krutjuk **-* or* **k·um·rutjuk** (producing) a rush of water. *Banjuné mili *-*.* The water came spurting out.

krutug (*or* **k·um·rutug**) *rpr* many things dropping more or less simultaneously. *Watuné kemrutug ḍa tiba nang genḍèng.* The stones rained down on the roof. **ñg/di*(i)** to rain [missiles] on. *Bètèngé di* mitralijur.* The fort was bombarded with machine-gun fire. **ngrutugi udjar** to bawl smn out

kruwek̄ **ñg/di*** to scratch with the nails

kruwel *var of* KUWEL

kruwes 1 *rpr* crumpling, folding. *Kertasé diremed mak *.* With a quick motion she crumpled the paper. 2 *rpr* scratching, clawing. *Kutjingku njakar aku mak* *. My cat scratched me. *ptg* * to get a cramp. **n̈g/di*** 1 to crumple. *Kobisé di**. She crumpled the cabbage leaves. 2 to scratch, claw (at)

kruwil *ptg* * *or* **n̈g*** all in pieces. *Piringé tiba petjah nganti ptg* *. The plate fell and smashed to bits.

kruwis *-* thin, meager, sparse

kruwit *var of* KRUWIS

kruwuk *ptg* * *or* *-* *or* **kruwak-*** to rumble, growl. **k·um·ruwuk** to disturb with loud talk or noise

ksb. *see* KA·SEBUT

ku- *var of prefix* K(E)- *with some* W-*initial roots: see Introduction, 3.1.5.2, and individual entries under* W

-ku *ng,* **kula** *kr* my, our. *Omah·ku adoh.* My (our) house is far away. *Olèh·ku njambut gawé tumemen.* I worked really hard. *Iki ḍuwit·ku ḍéwé.* This is my own money.

kubeng **n̈g/di*i** to surround, encircle. *Omahé di*i pager.* The house has a fence around it. **sa*é** around. *segara sa*é tanah Djawa* the sea that surrounds Java. **k·in·u·beng** surrounded/encircled (by). *Geḍong mau kinubeng ing pataman.* The building has gardens all around it. *See also* KRUBENG, UBENG

kubik̄ cubic. *sèntimèter* * cubic centimeter

kubluk to beat, whip (*root form: var of* KEBLUK)

kubur (*or* ***an**; **pa·saré·an** *or* **sekar·an** *ki*) grave, tomb; cemetery. **n̈g/di*** (**m̈/dipun·petak** *kr? ki?*, **n̈j/di·saré·k̂aké** *ki*) to bury. **pa*an** grave, tomb. **pa·n̈g*** act *or* way of burying

kuda horse (*kr, ltry for* DJARAN)

kuḍa *-* 1 trestle. 2 wooden roof support

kudang ***-*an** *or* **(ke)*an** loving and playful words spoken to a child as a means of happy communication: often praising the child and expressing hopes for a shining future. *Sing kanggo ke*an anaké pak Wangsa: "pok bung pok bung pong pok."* Mr. Wongso spoke playfully to his child with merry-sounding nonsense syllables. *Ke*ané anaké pak Wangsa: ing tembé bisaa dadi ḍokter.* Mr. Wongso talks to his child about how he hopes he'll be a doctor when he grows up. **n̈g/di·(ke)*** 1 to speak to [one's child] as above. 2 to express angry and hurt disappointment toward [a child, indicating one had hoped for better things of him]. *Pak guru mau ngudang Sardja sebab rong ndina mbolos.* The teacher rebuked Sardja (as above) for skipping school two days in a row. **pa·n̈g*** act *or* way of speaking to one's child (*as* *-*AN, (KE)*AN *above*)

kuḍas ringworm. ***en** to have/get ringworm. *See also* KUḌIS

kuḍi grass-cutting knife having a curved blade with a bulge in it near the handle. * **patjul sing·a lanḍep·a** *ltry* May the best man [of an evenly-matched pair] win!

kuḍis (*or* **kuḍas-***) scabies. ***en** to have/get scabies. *See also* KAḌAS, KUḌAS

kudu *ng,* **kedah** *kr* 1 ought to, have to, must. *Aku * mulih.* I have to go home. *Olèhmu ngopèni * sing betjik.* You're to take good care of them. 2 to [do sth undesirable] habitually. *Anakku wetengé * ora kepénak waé.* My child has to go and get stomach aches all the time. ***né** what ought to be done. *Kuduné ngono.* That's how it has to be. **né kowé ora gelem.* You should have refused. **n̈g/di*k̂aké** to make sth compulsory; to make smn do. *Sapa sing ngudokaké kowé udud?* Who's making you smoke? (*i.e.* whether you smoke or not is up to you). **k·um·udu-*** to feel strong compulsion *or* longing (to). *Aku kemudu-kudu nglahiraké panguneg-uneging atiku.* I felt I simply had to express my feelings.

kuḍu the bark of a certain tree, used for red dye. **n̈g/di*** to dye sth red with the above

kuḍung 1 cloth worn wound around the head. 2 cover(ing), lid. ***an** to wear on the head. **an anḍuk* to wear a towel on the head. **n̈g/di*aké** to use as a head covering. *Aku nguḍungaké katju marang anakku.* I covered my child's head with a kerchief. **n̈g/di*i** 1 to cover smn's head. *Aku nguḍungi anakku nganggo katju.* I covered my child's head with a kerchief. 2 to cover, conceal. *Kaluputané di*i penggeḍéné.* His boss covered up for his mistake. * **inḍing (tapih)** a henpecked husband. * **lulang matjan** to use smn important's name without permission, in order to get favors

kuḍup 1 flower bud; sheath or covering of a flower bud; in the bud, budding. 2 [of the eyes] slanted. **n̈g*** 1 to put forth a bud. 2 resembling a flower bud. *nguḍup turi* shaped like the *turi*-blossom bud. **n̈g*-turi·n̈i** 1 *describing the position of the hands in making the* sembah *gesture.* 2 (*psv* **di*-turi·n̈i**) to provide [a scabbard] with a bud-shaped copper tip

kudur (*or* **∗an**) moral obligation to work in the village rice paddy with no compensation other than one's meals

kudus holy. *roh ∗* Holy Spirit

kuja **k·in·uja-∗** *ltry* to be treated with contempt/scorn. **ñg/di∗-∗** to look down on, treat with scorn

kuju **∗-∗** to have a flushed, sweaty appearance

kujus *var of* KUJU

kuk **1** cake, cookie. **2** *rpr* a locomotive whistle. *Enḍas²ané sepur mlaku djès-djès-djès ∗ ∗ ∗.* The engine started up, puffing and tooting. **3** *rpr* the cry of the *engkuk* bird

kukila *oj* bird. *saur ∗* (to answer) in unison

kuku (finger-, toe-)nail; claw (**kanâkâ** *ki, oj*). **∗ñ** a scratch; scratch mark, claw mark. **ñg/di∗** to scratch, claw (at). *Aku di∗ Slamet.* Slamet scratched me with his nails. **sa∗ ireng** small, tiny. *Kesalahané ming sa∗ ireng.* His mistake was a very small one. *Katresnané sa∗ ireng.* Her love for him is superficial.

kukub **∗an** domain, territory. **ñg/di∗** to apply scent to. *Djariké di∗ nganggo kembang mlaṭi.* She put jasmine scent on her wraparound. **sa∗an** the whole family. *Aku sa∗an manggon ing omah iki.* Our whole family lives in this house.

kukud to close up shop [for the day; for good]. *Isih djam lima soré, kok wis ∗.* It's only five o'clock—why are you closing? *A wis ∗ sebab rugi terus.* A has gone out of business; he was bankrupt. **ñg/di∗** to cause sth to close up; to put smn out of business. **ñg/di∗i** to pack away [one's wares] and close up

kukuh *ng,* **kekah** *kr* solid, strong, resistant. *Djarané dilapaki ∗.* He saddled up the horse tight. *∗ kekarepané.* He has made up his mind. **ñg/di∗aké** to strengthen, reinforce. **ñg/di∗i** to adhere to; to defend. *Djandjiné di∗i.* He kept his promise. *Haké di∗i.* He stuck up for his rights. **pa·ñg∗** a gift betokening the strength of a relationship, *esp.* engagement or marriage. **pa·ñg∗an** confirmation, acknowledgment. **pi∗** written confirmation, a letter of commitment

kukuk owl. **∗ beluk** a variety of owl. **ñg∗** [of laughter] loud and jeering. *Olèhé ngguju ngukuk.* He hooted.

kukuklúruk cock-a-doodle-doo!

kukul pimple on the face. **∗en** to have/get pimples

kukum *var of* UKUM

kukup *tanpa* **∗an** worthless, without value. **ñg/di∗** **1** to pick up by doubled handfuls, *i.e.* in the cupped hands. **2** to take care of [smn who is alone in the world]. *ora* **ñg∗** of no value. *Motor sing tabrakan wis ora ngukup.* The smashed-up car is a total loss.

kukur **∗an** a scratch(ed place). **∗-∗** to scratch an itch. *Asuné ∗-∗.* The dog scratched himself. **ñg/di∗** to scratch sth

kukus smoke, steam. *Ora ana ∗ tanpa geni.* There's no smoke without fire, *i.e.* there must be some truth to it. *Ora ana geni tanpa ∗.* You can't stifle rumors, *i.e.* There's no fire without smoke. *roti ∗* dumpling. **∗an** cone-shaped utensil of woven bamboo in which rice is steamed over boiling water (*see also* DANDANG). **ñg∗** **1** (*psv* **di∗**) to steam, *i.e.* cook by steaming. **2** to give off smoke/steam. **ñg/di∗i** to get smoke/steam on. *Témboké ireng di∗i lampu.* The wall is blackened from lamp smoke. **pa·ñg∗** act *or* way of smoking/steaming. **k·um·ukus** **1** to give off smoke/steam. **2** a certain peppermint-flavored herb. **3** comet, shooting star. **∗ gantung** cobwebby dust in ceiling corners

kul **1** a variety of snail. **2** cabbage. **∗ banḍang** a kohlrabi-like variety of cabbage. **nge/di∗** to disparage; to treat with contempt

kula **1** I, me (*kr for* AKU). **2** [done] by me (*kr for* TAK-). *Sampun dangu ∗ entosi.* I've waited for him for a long time. **3** my, our (*kr for* -KU). *Anggèn ∗ ningali ngantos sabibaripun.* I watched till the very end. **4** yes? what? [*as a response when called: oblique kr for* APA]. *Djon Djon! —Kula?* John! — Yes? **5** family (*compounding form: see individual entries below*). **∗ aturi** please. *∗ aturi pinarak ing grija ∗.* Please visit us at our home. **∗ nuwun** **1** *phrase for announcing one's presence as a visitor at the door of smn's home.* **2** (*or* **∗ nuwun inggih**) *ltry, formal* yes... yes... (*as a listener, acknowledging the other's words at intervals*)

kulâgotrâ *oj* relatives, family. *See also* GOTRA

kulah **1** outdoor bathing room. **2** stained, messy (with). *Klambiné ∗ getih.* His shirt is blood-stained. **ñg/di∗** to mix [the rice] in with the sauces and soup from the other dishes comprising a meal

kulak *ng,* **kilak** *kr* (*or* **ke∗**) to buy (up) for resale. *Wong dagang jèn ∗ murah adol larang.* Tradesmen buy cheap and sell expensive. **∗an** to buy [a quantity] elsewhere for resale in one's own town. **ng/di∗** to buy at wholesale, buy for resale. *Ana bakul teka ngulak mbakoné.* A trader came and bought up his tobacco crop. **∗ warta adol prungu·n̂** to know what's new, be up on the latest happenings

kulâkuli familiar [with], used [to]. *Durung pati ∗ karo tanggané.* He doesn't know the neighbors very well yet.

kulâmitrâ family and friends. *See also* MITRA

kulâsentânâ family and relatives of aristocrats. *See also* SENTANA

kulâwandâ(wâ) family, relatives; relation, kinsman. *See also* WANDAWA

kulâwângsâ *ltry var of* WANGSA

kulâwargâ 1 family. *∗ X·an* the X family, *i.e.* X and all of his relatives and descendants. *sa∗* the whole family. 2 members of a specific group. *∗ manungsa* mankind. *salah sawidjining ∗ Mekar Sari* one of our [*Mekar Sari* magazine's] readers. **di∗** regarded as a family *or* specific group; joined into a family (or other) group. **ka∗n** 1 (in a) cooperative spirit, (in) the manner of a family group. *Kanṭi ka∗n wong désa paḍa gawé kreteg bebarengan.* The villagers built the bridge as a cooperative effort. 2 (to have) family ties, (to have) a blood relationship. *Saka ibu aku isih sesambungan ka∗n karo kowé.* I'm related to you on my mother's side. **k·in·ulawarga** *ltry var of* DI∗ *above. See also* WARGA

kulâwargi *sbst kr for* KULAWARGA

kulâwisudâ **ng/di∗** 1 to appoint. 2 to inaugurate. *See also* WISUDA

kuldi donkey

kulhu name of the shortest verse in the Koran

kuli laborer. **∗n̂** *sms* PA∗N̂ *below.* **ng∗** to work as a laborer. **ng/di∗kaké** to have work done by paid laborers. *Upama dikulèkna gèk pira buruhané.* If we had hired the work done, it would have cost a lot in wages. **(pa)∗n̂** rice paddy worked by villagers whose pay is a share in the crop. **∗ ng·arep** registered owner of a rice paddy, *i.e.* owner in name only (a technique for circumventing onerous tax burdens and other obligations). **∗ kenḍo** owner of a non-irrigated field plus house and yard. **∗ kentjeng** the actual owner of a paddy plus house and yard (as contrasted with the owner in name only). **∗ pokok** *sms ∗* NG·AREP *above*

kulijah lecture. *ngekèki ∗* to give a lecture. **ng/di∗i** to lecture to smn

kulik *var of* KOLIK

kulina 1 accustomed to. *wong mantja sing durung ∗ ngomong basa Djawa* a foreigner who isn't used to speaking Javanese yet. *Bareng mripatku wis rada ∗ karo pepeteng...* When my eyes got used to the dark... 2 well acquainted with. *Aku menawa karo bapakmu wis ∗ banget wiwit tjilik.* I've known your father since he was a child. 3 usual, ordinary. **ng/di∗kaké** to accustom smn to. *Saiki aku lagi ngulinakaké njetir motor.* I'm getting used to driving a car now. **pa∗n** one's habit, what one is accustomed to. *Pakulinané tangi awan.* He's used to sleeping late. *adat pa∗n* a socialized custom

kulit skin, hide; natural outer covering. *Kari balung karo ∗.* He's nothing but skin and bones. *∗é enḍog* eggshell. *∗é digawé kinine.* Its bark produces quinine. *Kandel ∗é.* He's thick-skinned. *wajang ∗* leather puppet used in shadow plays. **∗an** 1 outer skin, peel. 2 unpeeled. *katjang ∗an* peanuts in the shell. *djagung sing isih ∗an* unhusked corn. **pa∗an** skin color; complexion. *Pa∗ané kuning.* She has fair (light) skin. **∗ ajam** epidermis; film, membrane. **∗ daging** flesh-and-blood relative; **mitra k·in·ulit daging** a bosom friend. **∗ wadja** strong, tough

kulon *ng,* **kilèn** *kr* west. **∗an** western, Occidental. *bangsa ∗an* Occidentals. *negara ∗an* western nation. **∗-∗an** the western part. **ng∗** to(ward) the west. **sa∗(é)** the western part (of)

kuluarga *var of* KULAWARGA

kulub **∗an** briefly boiled vegetables eaten with rice and hot sauce. **ng/di∗** to boil [vegetables] briefly, for the above dish. *See also* NG·ALUB

kuluban *var of* KLUBAN

kuluk 1 (**kuṭa** *or* **makuṭa** *or* **panunggul** *ki*) crown; fez-like headdress worn by palace retainers on formal occasions. 2 a certain form of divorce instigated by the wife. **∗an** to put on *or* wear the above headgear. **∗ kaniraga** high black gold-trimmed cap worn formerly by monarchs, now also by bridegrooms

kulup *ltry adr* young boy

kul(u)warga *var of* KULAWARGA
kum ***-*an** that which is soaked; act of soaking. *Iki *-*an apa ja nèng èmbèr?* What's this soaking in the pail? **nge/di*** to soak sth. **pa·nge*** act *or* way of soaking. *See also* AKUM
kum- *see also under* K- *(Introduction, 3.1.7)*
kum(a)- to try to appear (*as root*) (*compounding element: see individual entries below*)
kumaju 1 [of girls] cute, appealing. 2 to act cute, act as though one thinks one is beautiful. *See also* AJU
kumâlâ *oj* jewel; diamond. **ng*** jewel-like; resembling a diamond
kumâlândâ(-lândâ) 1 to act like a European, *esp.* Dutch. 2 westernized. *See also* WLANDA
kumâlantjang impudent, flippant. *Kula njuwun pangapunten * kula.* Please forgive me for speaking too hastily. *See also* LANTJANG
kumâlâsâ *see* WATU
kumalod excessively tough. *See also* ALOD
kumâlungkung to act superior; arrogant; to enjoy praise
kuman germ, microbe
kumanḍang an echo. **ng*** to echo
kumandârâ to act as though one were the master *or* an aristocrat. *See also* N·DARA
kumâpurun to act daring (*kr for* KUMAWANI). *See also* PURUN
kumâputri to act like a girl *or* a princess. *See also* PUTRI
kumârâ 1 disembodied voice of a deceased mystic person. 2 *var of* KUMALA. ***n** village area over which a certain spirit (*ḍanjang*) holds sway
kumat 1 (**kimat** *kr*?) to have a relapse. 2 [of an illness] to recur. 3 *slang* crazy. ***-*an** 1 to have repeated relapses. 2 to keep recurring. *lelara kang *-*an* a recurrent illness
kumatal dried up/out. *See also* ATAL
kumâtjèlu strongly attracted. *See also* TJÈLU
kumâwani *ng,* **kamipurun** *or* **kumâpurun** *or* **kumâwantun** *kr* to act brave, pretend one is courageous. *See also* WANI
kumâwantun *kr for* KUMAWANI
kumawas-awas intent, watchful, on the alert. *See also* AWAS
kumâwasis to try to appear more intelligent than one is. *See also* WASIS
kumawatir *ng,* **kumawatos** *kr* worried, fearful. *See also* KUWATIR, WATIR
kumawatos *kr for* KUMAWATIR
kumawon *rg var of* KÉMAWON
kumba *oj* head. **di*** *or* **di·edu *** [two people] have their heads knocked together [by a third person]
kumbah to wash, launder. ***an** laundry, clothes to be washed. *banju k*an* used laundry water. **ng/di*aké** to have sth washed/cleaned. *ngumbahaké sanḍangané menjang wasserij* to have one's clothes cleaned at a laundry. **ng/di*(i)** to wash. *Klambimu *en.* Wash your shirt. *Tatuné di* ḍokter.* The doctor bathed his cut. *ngumbahi sajuran* to wash vegetables. *See also* UMBAH
kumbâlâ moustache (*kr for* BRENGOS)
kumbang *var of* KOMBANG
kumbi to deny an allegation which is actually true
kumbu a certain sweet filled cookie
kumed parsimonious
kumel worn-out, ragged, rumpled
kumelèp intensely hot
kumemping nearly ripe, *i.e.* just at the right stage for making a certain snack (EMPING)
kumenḍir commander. **di*i** to be commanded (by), be under the command (of)
kumenḍur *var of* KUMENḌIR
kumenom to behave like a young person. *See also* NOM
kumetir supervisor, foreman
kumetjus to try to act as though one is competent and able, to make a show of (assumed) skill. *See also* PETJUS
kumiḍi stage play (western style). *geḍong ** theater for such plays. *tukang ** stage performer. *** setambul** western-style stage play sometimes depicting tales of the Middle East. *** sorèng** acrobatic act
kumini sutji unleavened sacramental bread (in Christian churches)
kuminter to pretend one is smart; to try to outsmart others. *See also* PINTER
kumis moustache
kumis-kutjing a medicinal plant (*sms* PISKUTJING)
kumisaris 1 supervisor of management policy (in Dutch-style organizational structure of an enterprise). 2 police commissioner
kumisi *var of* KOMISI
kumlândâ *sms* KUMALANDA(-LANDA)
kumlangkung *var of* KUMALANGKUNG
kumlantjang *var of* KUMALANTJANG
kumlantjur *var of* L·UM·ANTJUR
kumlaré child-like (*kr for* GUMOTJAH)
kumlungkung *var of* KUMALUNGKUNG

kumlunṭu(s) to try to act as though one were smart
kumluwih to act superior to one's fellow human beings; to expect and enjoy praise. *See also* LUWIH
kumpa *var of* KOMPA
kumpeni 1 the Dutch East India Company. 2 (a company of) soldiers
kumplang *-* filled to the brim with rippling water
kumplit *var of* KOMPLIT
kumpris *inf var of* KRUN PRINS
kumpul *ng,* **kempal** *kr* 1 group, gathering. *panggonan *é para durdjana* a gathering place for thieves. 2 together, joined (with). *Wis * manèh ana ing klas.* He's back in class. *nalika isih * karo wong tuwaku* while I was still living at home. *Sing lumrah wong geḍé ora * wong tjilik.* Prominent people don't usually associate with commoners. 3 sexual intercourse. ***an** 1 gathering, meeting; association, organization. **an bal²an* soccer team. **an sing nglumpukaké sumbangan kanggo wong² mlarat* an organization that collects donations for the poor. 2 to associate *or* form a group [with]. **an karo wong sing seneng main* to associate with gamblers. *-* to hang around as a group. *Jèn tansah *-* karo kantja sanegara, basa Djawamu ora bakal apik.* If you always stick with your own countrymen, your Javanese won't improve. **ṅg*** to gather, form a group. *Wong papat mau ngumpul ing panggonan sing sepi.* The four of them met in a deserted place. **ṅg/di*aké** to gather, bring together. *ngumpulaké * apisah* to join two relatives in marriage (thus making family ties closer). **ṅg/di*i** 1 to be *or* associate with. *mBok adja ngumpuli tjah²kaé.* Don't have anything to do with those boys. 2 to have sexual intercourse with. **pa*an** 1 association, organization, club, team. 2 meeting, gathering. *See also* KLUMPUK, KRUMPUL
kumrajap to swarm like termites. *See also* RAJAP
kumrambut 1 hairlike. 2 [of boiling syrup] at the fine-thread stage. *See also* RAMBUT
kumratu-ratu self-willed, headstrong. *See also* RATU
kumrawan (*or* ***-prawan**) to behave like a young girl. *See also* PRAWAN
kumribit to be blown (on) by breezes. *Suwèkan kertas² ḍa * kabur.* The torn paper scraps were blown around by the breeze. *See also* RIBIT
kumribut agitation, turmoil. *nDadèkaké rada kemriwuting pikirku.* It put my thoughts all in a whirl. *See also* RIBUT
kumriwut *var of* KUMRIBUT
kumrudjak [of fruits] just at the right stage of ripeness for making a certain dish (RUDJAK)
kumruwed to crowd (into), mill around (in). *Bakul² paḍa kumruwed ngebaki pasar.* The peddlers swarmed to the marketplace. *See also* RUWED
kumud *inf var of* KLUMUD
kumuda 1 *oj* lotus blossom. 2 a certain leaf used in folk medicines
kumur *see* ADJUR
kumutjap to speak. *Saking wediné ora wani *.* She was too frightened to say anything. *See also* UTJAP
kuna *ng,* **kina** *kr* old; old-fashioned. *ḍèk djaman ** in the old days. *wong * sing ora tau nganggo pantalon* a conservative man who never dresses in Occidental style. *Sakané dimoḍèl tjara *.* The pillars were wrought in antique style. *basa Djawa ** Javanese as spoken in the old days. ***-k·um·una** *or* ***-ma*** *or* **ma*-*** in *or* since ancient times. *Tjanḍi Prambanan kuwi wis ma*-* nang kono.* Prambanan Temple has stood for many centuries. *** kawak** *or* *** lawak** ancient; very old-fashioned
kunang *var of* KONANG
kunarpa *oj* corpse
kundjârâ 1 jail, prison. 2 *ltry* elephant. ***n** jail, prison. **ṅg/di*** to imprison, put in jail. **pa*n** jail, prison. **djuru (pa)*(n)** jailer; prison warden
kung [of turtledoves] (to have) a fine singing voice. *manuk perkutut sing wis ** a turtledove with an exquisite voice
kungkang large frog
ku:ngkong *rpr* frogs croaking
kungkum to take a tub bath *or* sit-down bath (rather than the customary pour bath)
kungkung **ṅg/di*** 1 to confine, incarcerate. 2 [in children's games] to make smn be It, or a defender, for a long time
kuning *ng,* **djené** *kr* 1 yellow. *pupur ** yellow powder used as body makeup for brides and wajang performers. *beras ** rice colored yellow (served at ceremonial meals). *(le)lara ** (to have) jaundice/hepatitis. 2 [of skin] light, fair. *Pakulitané *.* She has fair skin. ** langsep* having very fair skin. *wong * term of endearment for one's (fair-skinned) sweetheart.* 3 ripe(ned) [of rice growing in

the field]. *mangsa* * the time during which the ripened crop is still unharvested. 4 egg yolk. 5 [of vision] blurred, hazy. *Pandelengku* *. I can't see clearly. ***an** 1 [of rice plants] ripened and ready for harvesting. *bumi *an* soil of a paddy with ripened plants growing on it. 2 egg yolk. 3 brass; nickel. **ñg/di*(aké)** to color sth yellow. **k·um·uning** *ng kr* a certain tree with small fragrant flowers and yellow wood. * **dadar** bright yellow (like egg yolk). * **g·um·rining** pure clear yellow. * **sumringah** pure fresh yellow. * **(ñ)·temu-giring** 1 fresh clear yellow. 2 (having skin) as fair as the *temu* root

kunir turmeric: used in cooking, also as the symbolic representation of the clitoris in the *sunat* ceremony. **ñg*** resembling turmeric

kunjik *rg var of* UNJIK

kunjuk monkey (*as a pejorative term*)

kunjur *-* soft, tender, easy to chew

kuntan *var of* KONTAN

kunṭârâ name of the second *windu*

kuntau Chinese-style judo

kunṭèt *var of* KUNṬING

kuntilanak a malevolent female spirit

kunṭing stunted; unable to achieve normal growth

kuntja train of a ceremonial batik wraparound (*dodot*). ***nan** having a train

kuntjârâ famous, renowned

kuntji 1 key. 2 padlock. *bukak* * to unlock a padlock. 3 a certain root used as a spice and in folk medicines. **ñg/di*(ni)** to lock. *nguntjèni lawang²* to lock (all) the doors. *Gembok iki ora kena di**. This padlock won't lock. **pa*ǹ** cemetery-keeper's lodge. * **Inggris** stillson wrench, monkey wrench *See also* BUKAK, DJURU, WANG

kuntjlup *var of* KUNTJUP

kuntjung 1 children's hair style: head left unshaved only from crown to forehead. *wiwit * nganti gelung* from childhood until adulthood. 2 covered portico of a Javanese-style house connecting the front veranda (*pendapa*) with the inner hall (*pringgitan*) or else extending out from the front veranda to the street. 3 object worn at the forehead, *esp.* the point of an *iket* headdress. 4 tuft, tassel (of a plant). ***an** *or* **ñg*** to wear the hair as in 1 above. **ñg/di*i** to give smn the above hair style

kuntjup flower bud; in bud, budding. ***ing asta** the placing of the palms in the *sembah* position; **ñg*aké asta** to place the hands in this position

kuntul a certain white heron. *nggolèki tapaking * nglajang* to attempt the impossible. ***an** a dancing game. * **di·uni·kaké ḍanḍang** to call white black; to distort facts, twist the truth

kunut a Moslem prayer

kupat rice boiled in a coconut-leaf wrapping. ***an** shaped like the above, *esp.* jewels. **ñg*** 1 resembling the above food. 2 (*psv* **di***) to make [ingredients] into *kupat*. * **luwar** coconut-leaf bags filled with raw yellow rice, hung in the doorway of one's home in supplication for the granting of a wish

kupeng *var of* KUBENG

kupija 1 copy, duplicate, simulation. 2 example, model. **ñg/di*** to make a copy/imitation of

kuping 1 **(talinga·n** *ki***)** ear. *ngrungokaké tanpa* * to sense. *mbrebegi* * deafening, ear-shattering. *ngabangaké* * to anger smn. *ora ngénak-énaki* * not pleasant to hear. *Mlebu * kiwa bablas * tengen.* It went in one ear and out the other. 2 (*or* ***an**) handle. * *tjangkir* cup handle. **ñg*** 1 resembling an ear; earlike. *Olèhé nggawé panganan nguping tikus.* She made tiny cookies. 2 to overhear. *nguping rembug* to overhear a conversation. * **gadjah** 1 a certain plant with large decorative dark-green leaves. 2 a sweet cookie. *See also* SIPAT

kupjah fez-like headgear

kupling *var of* KOPLING

kupluk fez-like headgear. **ñg/di*** to beat, whip [eggs *etc.*]

kupon 1 coupon, ticket. 2 *form of* KUPU

kupu butterfly. ***ñ** resembling a butterfly. *Penitiné mas kupon.* Her pin is a gold butterfly. *-* prostitute. * **brambang** a certain large butterfly. * **djaran** Atlas moth. * **gadjah** 1 a certain large night moth. 2 a certain small owl. * **malem** prostitute. * **tarung** a set of double doors opening outward, faced by an identical set opening inward, so that they touch when closed

kur 1 only (*rg var of* MUNG). 2 *syllable called to summon chickens to be fed.* ***-*an** in the twenties (*shf of* LIKUR²AN).

nge/di*(-*)i to summon [chickens] at feeding time

kura a certain land tortoise

Kur'an the Koran

kurang *ng,* **kirang** *kr* 1 less. *ora * saka* not less than; at least. *Tangané gawéan ora * prigelé tinimbang tangané sekawit.* His artificial hand is no less skillful than his original hand. 2 inadequate, lacking, short. *Apa ḍuwitmu *?* Haven't you enough money? *penjakit * ḍarah* anemia. *Aku * turu.* I didn't get enough sleep. ** mangan* undernourished. ** asin* insipid, tasteless. *Adja nganti *.* Make sure there's enough! *Botjah kéné kok * sidji.* One of our children is missing! **a ja ora akèh.* It's short, but it isn't short by much. ** seṭiṭik* a little bit short (inadequate). ** seṭiṭik menèh ḍèké ketabrak bis mau.* He narrowly missed being run over by the bus. **é akèh.* There's nowhere near enough. *ora ** in plentiful supply. *Pangané ora *.* Food is abundant. *Ora *-* dalané.* There are plenty of ways to get there. *Omahé durung rampung, isih *.* His house isn't finished–there's more to be done. *Sadjaké kowé * tékad.* You don't seem determined enough. *Lagi telu, dadi * lima.* There are three now, so we're still five short. 3 with [a certain amount of time] still to go. *djam nem * sepuluh menit* 5:50. *Isih * telung minggu menèh.* There are still three weeks to go. **ke*an** (to experience) a shortage. *ke*an vitamin A* a vitamin A deficiency. *Saja lawas saja ke*an sanḍang lan pangan.* Clothing and food got scarcer and scarcer. **ng*** to become scarce. **ng/di*i** to lessen. *Olèhé mangan di*i.* She cut down on her food. *Ḍèké ngurang²i sakabèhé, awaké nganti kuru banget.* He denied himself everything and became very thin. *** adjar** 1 (*or* *** asem**) dammit! 2 ill-mannered. *èsem kang *-adjar* an insolent smile. ** adjar jèn bengok² ing kelas.* It's ill-bred to raise one's voice in class. *** begdja** by bad luck. ** bedjané wisa mau bisa tekan tiwas.* At the worst, the poison can cause death. *** lambé** 1 to lack material for discussion. 2 inadequately discussed *or* considered. *** luwih** (*abbr:* **k.l.**) more or less, approximately. *Umuré * luwih enem tahun.* She's about six years old. *** priksa** I don't know. *** tata** 1 in disarray. 2 ill-mannered

kurap chapping of the skin. ***en** to have/get chapped skin

kuras **ng/di*** to drain and clean. *nguras sumur* to clean a well. *Mauné sugih nanging banḍané bandjur di* sing wédok.* He used to be rich, but his wife cleaned him out.

Kurâwâ *wj* family name of the ninety-nine brothers and one sister (descendants of Kuru) who are the first cousins and enemies of the Penḍawas. *** Ngestina** The Kurawas of Ngestina

kurban a sacrifice; a victim. ** pentjulikan* a kidnap victim. *Wong² njemplungaké * menjang sadjroning kawah mau.* People flung offerings into the crater. **ng/di*aké** to offer as a sacrifice. *ngurbanaké pangrasa* to sacrifice one's own feelings. **pa·ng*** a sacrifice

kurda in a towering rage. *Radèn Werkudara jèn wis * ora ana sing wani njeḍaki.* When Werkudara was angry, no one dared approach him. **né gunung Kelud* the wrath of [the volcano] Mt. Kelud

kureb bottom, under side. **ng/di*aké** to place sth face down *or* under side down. *Di*aké di-penet² wetengé.* They laid [the drowning man] face down and pressed his midsection. *Baṭok telu iki tak *aké.* I'll place these three coconut shells cut side down. **ng/di*i** to lie on smn face down. *Ḍèwèké ngurebi anaké sing mati.* He prostrated himself on his son's body. **sa*ing langit** the whole world; everything under the sun. **k·um·ureb** lying face down *or* with the concave *or* under side down. *Tutupé kuwali kumureb nang médja.* The pan cover lay handle up on the table. **kumureb ing abah·an** to submit utterly; to yield up one's life. *See also* MENGKUREB

Kurès the Quraisi tribe of Arabia

kurimen sickly, ailing

kurir messenger

kurma date (fruit)

kurmat honor, respect, esteem. *awèh ** to salute. ***an** respect, esteem, honor. **ng/di*i** to show honor *or* esteem to/for. *Tamuné di*i gamelan.* The guests were honored with gamelan music. **pa*an** an honor; to honor, respect, esteem. *kanggo pa*an tamu saka mantja negara* in honor of the foreign visitors. *See also* URMAT

kursi 1 chair. ** kain* upholstered chair. ** males* easy chair. 2 seat, position. ** ing pemerintahan anjar* a seat in the new government. ***n̈** seated. *Tamuné kursèn.* The guest sat in a chair.

kursus vocational training course

kuru *ng,* **kera** *kr* thin, undernourished. *Ḍèké lemu apa *?* Is he fat or thin? *Geḍangé *-*.* The bananas are undersized. *** **aking** thin and dried-up. *** **m·bekingking** *or* *** **n·djenggrik** thin as a rail. *** **semangka** very fat

kurung *ng,* **sengker** *kr* ***an** 1 cage, enclosure. **an manuk* bird cage. 2 caged, confined. *pitik *an* cooped-up chickens. **ṅg/di*(i)** 1 to enclose, pen up. 2 to put in parentheses. *tembing sing di** the parenthesized words

kurup worth something; worth the trouble. *Tontonané apik, * olèhku mlaku nang alun*[2]. The show was good; it was worth walking to the square for. *Ampasé krambil kurang *, dibuwang waé.* The coconut residue isn't worth keeping; throw it out. *Olèhé njambut gawé ora *, sak djam mung dibajar Rp sepuluh.* It's not worth the bother of working: he only gets 10 rupiahs an hour.

kus *adr* mouse! rat! (*shf of* TIKUS)

kusâlâ good, charitable, generous. *darma ** a good deed

kusi [of skin] grimy, dirty and dry

kusika *oj* skin, hide

kusir driver of a horse-drawn vehicle. *pak ** the driver. ***an** driver's seat. **ṅg*** to drive (as one's livelihood). **ṅg/di*i** to drive [a horse-drawn vehicle]

kusta leprosy

kusuk deep in prayerful concentration or meditation. **kasak-*** to whisper things around; to get involved in intrigue

kusuma *oj* 1 flower. 2 exquisitely beautiful. 3 aristocracy. *trahing * (rembesing madu)* of noble descent

kusung ***-*** (to act) in great haste and with urgency

kusus specific(ally), particular(ly). *Kamar iki * kanggo rapat.* This room is just for meetings.

kusut distraught, frantic, hard-pressed. **ṅg*aké** in turmoil, in a chaotic state. *Ngusutaké pikiranku.* I don't know which way to turn.

kuswa *oj* **ṅg/di*** to kiss (Javanese style: *see* AMBUNG)

kuṭa *ng,* **kiṭa** *kr* 1 city. ** geḍé (tjilik)* a city of more (less) than 250,000 inhabitants. 2 a brick wall enclosing a city or palace. **ṅg*** resembling a city wall. *mbeguguk nguṭa waton* stubborn as a brick wall

kuṭâgârâ *oj* city gate

kuṭah (*or* **ke***) messy, smeared (with)

kutang *var of* KOTANG

kutbah sermon delivered in a mosque

kutil 1 pickpocket. 2 wart, mole, skin blemish. ***an** 1 yield from picking pockets. **anmu olèhmu pira?* How much did you lift? 2 to pick pockets habitually. *wong *an* pickpocket. ***en** to have/get warts; *euph* to have/get smallpox. **ṅg/di*aké** to pick pockets on smn's behalf. **ṅg/di*(i)** to steal from, pick smn's pocket. *aku di* wong ana pasar malem.* Smn picked my pocket at the fair. *See also* UTIL

kuṭilang a black-headed gray-and-yellow song bird. *See also* ṬILANG

kutis dung beetle (*shf of* BRENGKUTIS)

kutjal leek, green onion

kutjek *rg var of* UTJEK

kutjem drained of one's vitality through grief, shock, *etc.* ** guwajané* pale (as from grief). **ṅg/di*aké** to cause the above condition. *ngutjemaké asmané sing wis kondang apik* to cast aspersions on smn's good name

kutjing 1 cat. *kéwan sa** an animal the size of a cat. 2 name of one of the Chinese playing cards (*kertu tjilik*). ***(-*)an** a certain medicinal plant (*sms* KUMIS-KUTJING). ***-*an** to play hide-and-seek; *fig* to play cat-and-mouse with each other. ***en** 1 to get goose bumps. 2 to get a strained biceps muscle. **k·um·utjing** feather duster shaped like a cat's tail. *** **bunḍel** a variety of cat with a knob of fur at the end of its tail. *** **enḍas·é ireng** thief (*euph remark made when sth is discovered to be missing*). *** **sanḍing ḍènḍèng** subjected to severe temptation

kutjir pigtail or braid worn on the crown of the head, *esp.* by the wajang clown Pétruk. **ṅg/di*i** to braid smn's hair as above

kutjira *oj* disappointed

kutjiwa 1 disappointed, let down. 2 disappointing. *Piranti mau isih *.* The equipment isn't as good as we had hoped. ***né** unfortunately; to one's disappointment. **ṅg*ni** disappointing. *Semuwané ngutjiwani.* The performance didn't come up to our expectations.

kutju **ṅg/di*ni** to rub [a stained portion of] a garment between the hands. *ngutjoni klambi sing kewutahan mangsi* to wash the ink stain out of a shirt. *** **tutup téko** tea cozy

kutjup **ṅg/di*aké** to hold [the hand] in a

position to pick up sth, or to pinch (with thumb and index finger not yet touching)

kutjur a sweet fried snack of rice flour, brown sugar, and coconut milk. **ke*** to wash oneself at a spring *or* water pipe. **katjar-*** *rpr* water pouring out. **k·um·utjur** to pour out in profusion. *Weḍusé dibelèh getihé kumutjur.* The goat bled profusely when it was butchered.

kutu (*or* *-* *or* **ke***) (the class of) small insects. **(sa)*-* walang (ng)·ataga** all animate beings. *** baru** band across the chest of a woman's blouse (*kebajak*)

kutub (North, South) Pole

kutug 1 incense. 2 (*or* **ke***) to burn incense. **ñg/di*i** to burn incense for. *ngutugi para leluhur* to burn incense for one's ancestors. **k·um·utug** (to produce) heavy billowing smoke

kutuk a certain edible freshwater fish. *** ng·génḍong kemiri** to go into a thief-infested area conspicuously decked out in valuables. *** m̃·paran·i sunduk** to walk deliberately into danger

kuṭuk 1 a young chicken. 2 tame; *fig* to feel at home, not want to leave. *Bareng wis * bandjur bisa muni.* When [the bird] got used to its surroundings, it began to sing. *A kok * saiki ora tau lunga²*. How come A always stays home these days and never goes out?

kuṭung severed [of hand, arm]. *Tangané * kena granat.* His hand was blown off by a grenade. ***an** short-sleeved

kutut *inf var of* PERKUTUT

ku(w)- *see also under* KU-, KW- (*Introduction, 2.9.7)*

kuw- *var of* KE·W- *in certain* W-*initial roots: see Introduction, 3.1.5.2, and individual entries under* W

kuwadjib ***an** *var of* KE·WADJIB·AN. **ñg*aké** *var of* M̃·WADJIB·AKÉ

kuwag ***an** to do sth (by) oneself (*var of* K·AWAG·AN)

kuwâgâ having a crooked arm

kuwagang able (*var of* KUWAWA)

kuwah soup, sauce, gravy

kuwâjâ gall, bile

kuwal the inner part of a tree trunk between the bark and the core

kuwali metal *or* earthen cooking pot. **sa*** a potful

kuwalon step[-relation]; adopted [relative]. *anak ** adopted child; stepchild. *aḍi ** younger step-brother *or* -sister. *bapak/ibu ** adoptive father/mother

kuwândâ *oj* 1 body. 2 dead body, corpse

kuwangsul *sbst kr for* KUWALI

kuwangwung a small beetle-like insect that attacks coconuts

kuwaos powerful (*kr for* KUWASA)

kuwas 1 paint brush. 2 a sweet lemon *or* orange drink

kuwâsâ *ng,* **kuwaos** *kr* powerful; in authority. *Kang Maha ** God. *Sapa sing * ngekèki lilin kanggo lelungan?* Who is authorized to issue travel permits? **ñg/di*aké** to empower, give authority to. **ñg/di*ni** to have authority over. *Negara A nguwasani Negara B.* Nation A holds sway over Nation B. **sa*né** anything in one's power. *Jèn ora bisa awèh satus rupiah ja sa*né.* If you can't give 100 rupiahs, give whatever you can. **pa·ñg*** power, authority; one in authority. *panguwasa pelabuhan* port authority. *panguwasa rakjat* sovereignty of the people. *** hakim** person appointed by an Islamic minister to be guardian of a bride

kuwat *ng,* **kijat** *kr* strong (physically); strong enough to [do]. *Taliné *.* The rope is strong. *Larané wis suda mung awaké durung *.* His illness is gone but he hasn't got his strength back. *Aku ora * ngampet gujuku.* I couldn't help laughing. **ka*an** strength. *Saja entèk ke*ané.* He gradually came to the end of his strength. **ñg/di*aké** to hold on tight(er); to put forth effort (toward). *Ngungguhaké pangkat kuwi minangka nguwataké kalenggahané.* Giving people raises in rank is a good way of keeping oneself in office. *Jèn dipeksa di*-*aké bisa ndjalari lara.* Overexertion can cause illness. **ñg/di*i** to strengthen, reinforce. **pa·(ñg)*** reinforcement, supporting strength. **pi*** a support, a strengthening device. **sa*é** with all one's might. *Kowé kena mangan sa*é, ning bajar ḍéwé.* You can eat all you want, but you have to pay for it yourself. **k·um·uwat-*** (**k·um·ijat-kijat** *kr*) to make a show of strength; to brag about how strong one is. *** dradjad** *or* *** pangkat** having the power to elevate one's husband to an exalted position. *Hartinah kuwi * dradjat.* Hartinah [as a wife] is a king-maker.

kuwatir *ng,* **kuwatos** *kr* apprehensive, fearful. *Adja *.* Don't worry. *Aku * jèn étungku ana sing luput.* I'm afraid some of my arithmetic is wrong. **ñg*aké** *or* **ñg*i** 1 causing worry/apprehension. 2 (*psv* **di*aké, di*i**) to worry about. *Di*i jèn gunung mau arep ndjeblug.* It is feared that the volcano will erupt. *Jèn ngliwati segara akèh sing di-*i.* While you're crossing the ocean, there are lots of things to be apprehensive about. *See also* KUMAWATIR

kuwatji salted melon seeds, eaten as snacks

kuwatos apprehensive (*kr for* KUWATIR)

kuwâwâ *ng,* **kuwawi** *sbst? kr* 1 able (to), capable (of), strong enough (to). *Aku kuwatir mengko bisé gèk ora *, bandjur keplorot njemplung ing djurang.* I was afraid the bus wouldn't make it and would slide into the ravine. *Soroté rembulan mèh ora * nradjang menḍung tipis.* The moonbeams were barely able to penetrate the thin clouds. 2 *ng kr* person in charge of village irrigation

kuwawi *sbst? kr for* KUWAWA

kuwawung *var of* KUWANGWUNG

kuwé 1 *var of* KUWIH. 2 *inf var of* KUWI

kuwek̄ **n̈g/di*(i)** 1 to paw, scratch. *nguweki lemah* to scratch the soil; to paw the earth. 2 to pinch and twist [smn's flesh]

kuwel a wad; a crumpled/curled mass. *mbako sa** a wad of tobacco. **n̈g*** crumpled, curled. *Goḍongé dadi kuning, ng(r)uwel.* The leaves turned yellow and crumpled. *Ulané nguwel.* The snake is coiled. *See also* UWEL

kuwèni a variety of mango

kuwi *ng,* **punika** (*usu. prn* **menikâ**) *kr* 1 [*as modifier*] X's in general. *Tikus * mungsuhé wong.* Mice are the enemy of man. *Botjah dolanan bal-balan * metjah²aké barang.* Boys playing soccer break things. 2 that (thing) (not far from speaker *or* hearer: *Degree II: Introduction, 6*). *Aku tukokna bonékah kuwi.* Buy me that doll! ** djenengé apa ta?* What's that called? 3 the aforementioned (one). *awit saka ** because of it. ** djenengé sapa?* What's his name? (*referring to smn previously mentioned*). *Botjah loro * ngati-ati.* The two boys were careful. 4 *expression of disparagement, reproof* [*as modifier*]. *Kowé * lagi apa?* You, there, what are you doing? *É la pinter kowé *.* What a smart guy you are! **-** stuff like that (*disparaging*). *Ah tontonané kok mung *-* baé mboseni.* Oh, those same old shows–they're boring.

kuwih cookie, sweet snack. *** **bolu** a small crisp vanilla-flavored cookie *or* cake. *** **dadar** macaroon-like cookie. *** **lapis** a steamed layered dessert. *** **lumpur** a soft cookie. *** **randjam/randjang** Chinese New-Year specialty cake. *** **sus** cream-filled cookie. *** **tar(tjis)** layer cake

kuwik **n̈g/di*** to scratch sth lightly

kuwil **n̈g/di*** to clean oneself after defecating, using the left hand and water

kuwu village administrative official in charge of water. **pa*n̂** 1 military encampment. 2 home *or* estate of the above official. 3 village

kuwuk 1 wildcat. 2 a certain variety of large seashell. ***an** a children's game. **n̈g/di*** to glaze [fabric] by scraping it with the above shell

kuwung 1 concave. 2 peacock. 3 *var of* KLUWUNG. **ke*** aura. **n̈g·(ke)*** (*prn* **nguwung, nge·nguwung**) to shine, radiate

kuwur dizzy, headachy, groggy

kw- *see also under* KU(W)- *(Introduction, 2.9.7)*

kwalipikasi qualification

kwalitèt quality

kwantitèt quantity

kwartal quarter, three-month period. *Saben * murid² éntuk rapot.* Each quarter, pupils get their grade reports. ***an** 1 quarterly, by the quarter. *Saiki lagi liburan *an.* We're having our quarterly vacation now. 2 to complete a (school) quarter; to issue reports at the completion of a quarter. *Sekolahanku wis *an.* My school has completed the quarter (given out the quarterly reports).

kwèh *oj* all

kwintal unit of weight: = 100 kilograms

kwitan(g)si a receipt

kya *var of* KIJAH

L

l (*prn* **èl**) *alphabetic letter*

-l- *infix inserted after initial consonant of certain words, denoting repeated, continuing, and/or multiple actions or effects. See individual listings*

la 1 (*prn* **l̊ā**) *excl of transition from preceding utterance. Kembang iki mawar; * kaé mlaṭi.* These flowers are roses; and those over there are jasmine. ** mréné!* Well then, come here! ** rak tenan!* So, I was right, wasn't I! ** jèn ngono...* Well, in that case... ** bandjur apa kang kok karepaké?* And then what do you want after that? 2 *shf of* KULA (*in response to a call: see* KULA 4). 3 *adr* snake! (*shf of* ULA). 4 (*prn* **lā**) sixth note of the musical scale. *** (i)ja (ta)** 1 yes... yes... (*as acknowledgment that one is listening*). 2 why yes! of course! naturally! I know that! *** kok** and how come...! *** mbok** and (surprisingly). *Apa manèh dikon nuku, * mbok dikèki waé emoh!* I wouldn't even want it as a gift, and he expects me to buy it! *** mbok ja** why yes (*as an encouraging response*). *Bu, aku tak njapu latar ja?– * mbok ija tjah bagus.* Mother, may I sweep up the yard?– Why certainly, honey! *** wong (ija)** 1 *excl introducing supporting evidence. Mesṭi waé akèh sing wedi, * wong sijungé geḍé.* No wonder so many people are afraid of it–it has huge tusks. 2 *excl of surprise, disbelief. Pijé ta kuwi, * wong koṭak kok bisa muni?* How could that be–a box that can talk! 3 *excl of disgust, resignation. * wong ja wis pikun.* Oh, you're getting absent-minded in your old age!

la- *see also under* LE- *(Introduction, 2.9.2)*

labas to eat up. *Seḍéla baé *.* He finished off his meal in no time.

labet *sbst kr for* LABU. **(le)*an** devoted service, good deeds. *Durung tau njerikaké marang atiné, malah kepara akèh le*ané tumrap ḍèwèké.* He never hurt her feelings; on the contrary, he was very solicitous of her. *Sing duwé le*an iku bodjoné.* It was his wife who had done the good deeds. **ng/dipun*** *sbst kr for* NG/DI-LABUH^{a}?. *** betjik** to serve well/devotedly. *See also* LABUH^{b}

laboratorium laboratory

labrag **ng/di*** to inflict suffering on smn who has caused displeasure *or* done wrong. *Djarané di*, disenḍali kenḍaliné.* He whipped the horse savagely and jerked the reins. *mBok Wangsa ng* bodjoné perkara anggoné sok lunga bengi.* Mrs. Wongso took her husband to task for going out nights.

labu vine-grown melon *or* gourd

labuh^{a} 1 to drop anchor. 2 fall, *i.e.* the brief season between the close of the dry season and the onset of the rains, during which leaves fall. **ng/di*** **(ng/dipun·labet** *sbst kr?*) to fling sth into the sea as appeasement to the deities. **p(a)*an** harbor

labuh^{b} *ng*, **labet** *kr* (*or* **le*an**) dedicated service, selfless devotion. *pemimpin sing geḍé banget le*ané marang negarané* a leader who has rendered great service to his country. *mati * negara* to die for one's country. *ngèngeti le*ané sedulur²é* to recall the sacrifices made by one's family. **ng/di*i** to serve unselfishly; to dedicate oneself (*or* one's time, energy, resources) to. *Anggoné ng*i negarané nganti tekan patiné.* He dedicated his life to his country. *ng*i anaké* to sacrifice oneself for one's children. *Budi ng*i ngeteraké tunanganė nang Surabaja nganti ora mèlu udjian barang.* Budi gave up his chance to take the examination by going to Surabaja with his fiancée. *Mung kélangan djarik sidji waé di*i digolèki tekan Sala.* It's only one batik that you lost, but you're putting yourself to all the trouble of going to Solo to look for it. *** pati** to sacrifice one's life

labur whitewash. ***an** act *or* way of whitewashing. *Lurahé nḍawuhaké *an.* The village head told everyone to do their whitewashing [for the annual cleanup]. **ng/di*aké** 1 to whitewash for smn; to have sth whitewashed. 2 to apply [whitewash]. 3 to apply whitewash with [a brush]. *Ḍèké ng*aké kuwasé nang témbok.* He passed the whitewashing brush over the wall. **ng/di*(i)** to whitewash sth. *ng* omah* to whitewash a house

ladak harsh; overbearing. *Kowé mbok adja *-* karo aḍimu.* Don't be too hard on your little brother. **ng/di*i** to tease/torment [a child] to make him cry

ladal(l)ah my goodness! (*excl of surprise*)

ladi *ng,* **lados** *kr* to serve; to dedicate oneself to. *djuru ** waiter. *Putri²nipun saweg lados wonten ngadjengan.* Her daughters are serving in the front room. ***ǹ** 1 one who serves *or* waits on people. 2 act *or* way of serving. *Baki iki kena dienggo ladèn.* This tray can be used for serving. *Baliné saka ladèn, mesṭi mlaku mundur.* After serving him, she always backed out of the room. 3 to serve. *Apa kowé wis ladèn wédang?* Did you serve the tea? 4 person/thing served *or* waited on. *Aḍiku seminggu wingi lara, ndjur dadi ladèn.* My sister was sick last week and had to be waited on for everything. **le*** *sms* *****. *jajasan sing le* marang bebrajan* an organization that serves the community. **ng/di*ǹkaké** 1 to serve sth. *Warung mau ngladèkaké sega gorèng.* That snack bar serves fried rice. *Rokoké ladèkna.* Pass around the cigarettes. 2 to bring a person before [smn higher]. *Pak Krama ngladèkaké anaké suwita marang ndara Pangéran.* Mr. Kromo brought his son for service to the Prince. *Maling mau mbandjur diladèkaké nang kantor pulisi.* The thief was taken to the police station. **ng/di*ǹi** 1 to serve, be of service to. *Sakarepmu dakladèni.* I'll wait on you hand and foot. *ngladèni umum* to serve the public. *Angger aku blandja ana ing toko iki, sanalika bandjur diladèni.* Whenever I shop here I get waited on right away. *Jèn ḍajoh wis ndjupuk rokok sidji, nuli ladènana geniné.* If a guest takes a cigarette, offer him a light. *ngladèni tamu* to serve the guests. *ngladèni wédang* to serve tea. 2 to return blow for blow (in a fight). **p(a)*ǹ** one who serves. *Aku dadi pladèn.* I waited on the guests. **l·um·adi** (**l·um·ados** *kr*) 1 to be served. *Pangundjukanipun sampun lumados.* Cold drinks were served. 2 to be of service to. *sregep lumadi kanggo betjiké lan sempuluré bebrajan* always available for the good and prosperity of the community

lading (**marisan** *sbst? kr*) sharp-bladed knife. *** gapit** pocket knife

lâdjâ *rg var of* LAOS

ladjar *kr* run (*sbst var of* LADJENG)

ladjeng 1 (and) then, after that (*kr for* BANDJUR, TERUS?). 2 run (*kr for* LAJU). **ng/dipun*** to continue (*kr for* Ñ/DI·TERUS·AKÉ?)

ladjer 1 main root of a plant. 2 main issue, central topic. 3 *wj* a play which dramatizes events as described in the epics and in Javanese mythology

ladjim usual, normal. ***é** normally, the usual thing is (that...)

ladjo **ng/di*** to commute (*var of* NG/DI·LADJU)

ladju 1 *oj* and then, after that. 2 straight (on), forward, continuous. *Ladju tindaké sang Pangéran lan panḍèrèké.* The Prince and his retinue continued on their way. **ng/di*** to commute from [home]; to go back and forth from. *Dalemé Prambanan, jèn mulang di* nunggang pit.* His home is in Prambanan and he rides to school (to teach) on his bicycle. **sa*né** afterwards. *Sa*né ora kotjap manèh.* After that it wasn't mentioned again. **l·um·adu** straight (on)

ladjuk *var of* LADUK

ladjur column; file (as opposed to rank). ***an** 1 stalk [of bamboo, sugar cane]. 2 arranged in columns/files. **ng/di*** to arrange in files. *Anggoné nandur pari di*.* Rice is planted in rows. **sa*** 1 one stalk. 2 in the same column/file (as)

lados to serve (*kr for* LADI)

ladrang (*or* ***an**) 1 a certain style of kris sheath. 2 a certain class of gamelan melodies. *** pangkur, * remeng, * ritjik²** subtypes of the above melodies. *** singa ñ·tebah** name of a gamelan melody

laḍu lava

laduk **ke*** excessive. *Rada ke* nḍugalé iku.* His humor is a little too coarse. *Olèhé ngekèki ujah rada ke*.* She put too much salt in the soup.

laé (*or* ***-***) oh dear! my goodness! why...!

laélatulkadar *var of* LALAÉTULKADAR

lafal *var of* LAPAL

lâgâ war; battle. *Sénapati ing nga** commander-in-chief. **pa*n** battlefield

lagak behavior, conduct, actions

lagang [of a child] growing fast, shooting up

lagéjan (*or* **ke***) mannerism; idiosyncrasy, peculiarity. **é gèdèg.* He has a certain way of tilting his head. *Jèn kowé kepingin digatèkaké kepala kantormu kudu ngerti ke*é.* If you want to be noticed by your boss, you should get to know his ways.

lagèk *var of* LAGI

lagi *ng,* **saweg** *kr* 1 to be [do]ing; to be sth (at the time of the context). *Botjahé * kepati turu.* The child was sleeping soundly. *La kaé, * mréné.* There he is now, coming this way. *Apa * ana sing kok pikir?* Have you got sth on your mind? *Tatuné nganti sesasi * mari.* His wound took a month to heal. *Nalika iku durung turu, * mbaṭik.* She hadn't gone to bed yet; she was doing batik work. *Saiki * usumé watuk karo pileg.* This is the season for coughs and colds. *Prabu A * memungsuhan karo Prabu B.* Kings A and B were enemies at the time. 2 while, when, just as. *Wong² * paḍa wiwit mangan, krungu swara kula nuwun.* Just as they were beginning to eat. smn came to the door. *Jèn * netes, geḍéné mung sakmenir.* When they hatch, they're no bigger than a rice grain. *Jèn * ngrokok, adja turon.* Don't smoke in bed. *Menawa wong mau * nesu²né...* When he was at the peak of his fury... 3 just at a certain stage/point (at the time of the context). ** telu, dadi kurang lima.* There are only three so far, so we're five short. *Iki * seganè baé, durung lawuhé.* This is just the rice–not the other dishes yet. *Kuwi * kabar lho.* That's just a(n unconfirmed) rumor. *Kok kesusu, wong * djam sepuluh.* Don't leave so soon–it's only ten o'clock. *Slamet * umur limang taun.* Slamet was five at the time. *Siti * klas sidji.* Siti is in first grade. ** pirang sasi ta tepungé?* How long had you known him? ** duwé ḍuwit sèwu waé wis rumangsa sugih.* He only has a thousand rupiahs but he feels rich. **4** to have just...; no sooner...(than). *Ḍèwèké * lunga/teka.* He's just left/arrived. *Kapinudjon guruné * metu saka kamar.* The teacher happened to have left the room. **5** to begin [B only after A is over]. *Lebar ungsum rambutan, * durèn.* Right after the *rambutan* fruit season, the durian-fruit season begins. *Bareng ésuké arep udjian, benginé * sinau.* He didn't start studying for the exam until the night before. *Terus bareng wis djam setengah papat kira² * buḍal.* He didn't leave till around 3:30. **6** at, in, during [a past time]. *Anggoné buḍal * ḍèk taun kepungkur.* He only left last year. *Aku wis ngono, * nḍèk mbèn.* I did that once, a few days ago. ***-*** **(saweg** *kr***)** recently; new at. *Kapan tekamu?–Lagi² waé.* When did you arrive?–Just recently. *** **arep** about to [do]. ** arep meṭik pelem, nggoné tjekelan mrutjut.* Just as he was about to pick a mango, he lost his grip on the branch. *** **baé** to have just [done]; no sooner... ** baé arep ngaso...* Just as he was about to rest... ** baé mlebu omah dumadakan udan.* He no sooner got in the house than it began to rain. ** baé tak rasani kok kowé ndjedul.* Just as I was talking about you, you come along! *** **iki** now for the first time. ** iki aku ngrasakaké apa sing diarani pelem.* This is the first time I've ever tasted a mango. *Sadjegé urip * iki tumon botjah nakal banget.* I've never before seen such a naughty child. *** **iku** then for the first time (in the past). *** **(nèng) apa** to be doing what? *Kowé kuwi * apa?– * bal-balan.* What are you doing? –Playing soccer. *** **seḍéla** after a short time. *Ḍèké mèlu ngréwangi, nanging * seḍéla wis lunga.* He helped a little, but after a few minutes he left. *See also* SELAGI

lagja *ltry var of* LAGI

lagu song, melody. **né keṭoprak* a song from a folk drama. **-* populèr* popular songs. ** kebangsa(a)n* national anthem. **(le)*n̂** **1** *sms* *. **2** to sing along. *Botjah kabèh bandjur paḍa lelagon bareng.* The children all joined in the song. **ng/di*k̂aké** to sing non-classical songs. *Jèn kowé ora bisa *né, ija lagokna sagelemmu.* If you don't know the tune, sing it with any tune you like.

lah 1 *adr* God! (*usu. as an expression of frustration, exasperation: shf of* ALLAH). 2 *var sp of* LA 1. *Ja wis * dinengké waé.* Just let him be!

lahan **le*an** gratis, free of charge

lahar (*or* **w***) lava. ***an** bed of lava

lahir *var of* LAIR

lail(l)ah(a) 1 there is no God but Allah. 2 *excl of dismay, despair.* *** **hail(l)olahu** there is no God but Allah

lair 1 outer, external. *Ajuning rupané ora tulus tekan batin, mung aju * baé.* Her beauty doesn't come from within—it's only skin deep. 2 **(babar** *or* **m̈·wijos** *ki*) to be born. **é ḍèk kapan?* When was he born? *Tresna iku * saka tjotjoging ati.* Love has its beginnings in harmony of mind. ***an (wijos·an** *ki*) 1 (*or* **ke*an**) birth. *angka ke*an* birth rate. *dina ke*an* birthday (by the Western calendar). 2 birthday (by the Western calendar). ***é** on the exterior. **é, ḍèké kétok semanak.* Outwardly, he appears friendly. **k(e)*** to be expressed (openly). **ng/di*aké** 1 to express (openly). *ketresnané sing wis di*aké marang ḍèwèké* the love she had expressed for him. *Ana perluné kang durung bisa dak *aké.* There's something I can't tell you yet. 2 **(m̈/di·wijos** *ki*) to give birth (to). *** batin** complete; of body and soul. *tresna *-batin* whole-hearted love. *** bungkus** born with the caul covering the head. *** mula** ever since smn's birth; when smn was born. ** mula wis lemu.* He's been fat all his life.

lâjâ *see* GEMBIRA

lajad 1 to visit a bereaved family; to go to the scene of a death. 2 to attend a funeral. ***an** object of morbid curiosity. *Tanggaku mau mènèk krambil tiba dadi *an wong akèh.* My neighbor fell from a coconut tree and a crowd gathered to look on. *Kaḍang² dadi swara padu ramé, dadi *an tangga.* At times they quarreled so noisily the neighbors came to find out what was going on. **ng*(i)** *sms* *. **pa*an** place where a death occurred; a bereaved home.

lajah mortar: flat stone or clay bowl used for preparing seasonings with a pestle (*munṭu*)

lajak 1 proper, appropriate, suitable. 2 (*or* ***na** *or* *** ta**) so *that's* the reason! ** geḍong-klak-geḍangklik lha wong pantèké ora pas.* No wonder it wobbles! the peg isn't the right size. *O * ḍèké ngguju terus, la wong éntuk ḍuwit. I* know why he keeps laughing: he got some money!

lajan 1 *rg* and. 2 small supplementary cooking stove. **k(a)*** *rg* and. **ng/di*i** to notice, pay attention to. *Supaja adja tambah nesu adja di*i.* Ignore her so she won't get any madder.

lajang *ng,* **serat** *kr* 1 **(nawâlâ** *ki*) letter. ** tutupan* a sealed letter. *Uniné * apa?* What does the letter say? 2 a book of stories. ***an** 1 *ng kr* kite. *ngulukaké *an* to fly a kite. **an peḍotan* a kite that has broken loose from its string. **an sendarèn* kite equipped with a bamboo whistle. 2 shadow (*var of* WAJANG·AN). *ora kena kepidak *ané* hot-tempered, hypersensitive. 3 *sms* LE*AN *below.* ***-*an** 1 to correspond. *Merga prangko larang, saiki ora tau *-*an.* Stamps are so expensive we don't write to each other any more. 2 *ng kr* to glide in the air; *fig* to wander. **le*an** 1 to correspond. 2 *ng kr* to fly a kite. **ng*** *ng kr* to glide in the air; *fig* to wander, drift. **ng/di*i** to send a letter to. *Sampun dangu pijambakipun boten njerati.* He hasn't written me for a long time. **p(a)*an** *ng kr* mailman. *** biwara** official public announcement of a government regulation. *** buḍe(n)g** anonymous crank letter. *** ider·an** round-robin letter. *** kabar** newspaper. *** kawat** telegram. *** sorog·an** letter containing a warning, final notice, threat, *etc.* *** watja·n** book of readings. ** watjan kanggo pamulangan Djawa* a reader for Javanese schools. *** wisuda·n** 1 diploma. 2 letter of recognition

lajap (*or* ***-***) sleepy, drowsy. **ng*** to stroll, ramble. **sa*an** a nap

lajar 1 sail. *prau ** sailboat. 2 projection screen. 3 diacritical mark in Javanese script denoting *r* after a vowel. **4** (*or* **[le]*an**) to set sail. **ng/di*i** to sail to [a place]. **pa*an** pertaining to sailing

lajat **ke*an** (to be) too late. *Adja nganti ke*an.* Don't be late!

lajon corpse (*ki for* MAJID?). *dadi ** to die

laju *ng,* **ladjeng** *kr* 1 running pace. *Djaran kuwi *né banter banget.* Horses can run fast. 2 *oj* to wither, fade. **le*** death. **k*** to feel one has been deserted. **l·um·aju** to run. *See also* KAPILAJU, KLAJU, PLAJU

lajung reddish cloud in the sky at sunset. **ng*** drained of color

lajup ***-*** *describing the sound of a voice heard from afar*

lak sealing wax. ***-*an** 1 sealed with wax. *amplop *-*an* sealed envelopes. 2 the soft palate. **nge/di*(i)** to seal with wax. *Ḍusé isih dielak.* The box is sealed.

lakak ***-*** (to laugh) uproariously, boisterously

lakang (*or* **w***) groin; inner part of the thigh. **ke*** to be struck in the groin. **p*an** *rg var of* *

lak. da. *see* LAKSAMANA

lak. dya. *see* LAKSAMANA

laken velvet

laki 1 sexual intercourse. 2 husband. **a*** to marry. **(le)*ǹ** *cr* 1 copulation. 2 to like to copulate. **ng/di*k̀aké** to mate *or* breed [animals]. **ng/di*ǹi** [of animals, *cr* of people] to copulate with. *** rabi** to get married; **sa*-rabi** married couple

laknat 1 curse, malediction. 2 *wj* evil spirit. *** ullah** God's curse

laksa *formal var of* LEKSA

laksamanā admiral (navy, air force). *** madya** (*abbr:* **lak.dya.**) two-star rear admiral. *** muḍa** (*abbr:* **lak.da.**) vice admiral

laksânâ *oj* actions, conduct. **l·um·aksana** to walk, proceed

laku *ng,* **lampah** *kr* 1 walk, gait; forward motion, progress. ***né rikat.* He walked fast. ***né bis tansah ménggak-ménggok.* The bus zigzagged. ***né tjrita* the progress/course of the story. 2 behavior, conduct; to act, conduct oneself. ** kaja mengkono* such behavior. *Adja sok * sing ala.* Never do wrong things. 3 to sell well. *Jèn mangsa udan pajung kuwi * banget.* Umbrellas sell fast in the rainy season. ***-*** procedure(s) (to be) followed. *Wis diwuruki djenengé wong²ané lan *-*né.* He had been taught the names of the [chess]men and their moves. **-*né atjara mantèn mengko bengi agi diterangké karo Pak Sono.* Mr. Sono is explaining this evening's wedding-ceremony procedures. **le*** in death throes. **(le)*n̂** 1 fate, destiny, the way things are. *Sing sabar waé, wong lagi dadi lakon.* Be patient–that's how it is. 2 plot or scenario of a drama. *Mau bengi wajangé lakon Perang Bratajuda.* Last night's shadow play was the Bratajuda war. *pilem sing lakoné ḍètèktip* a detective movie. 3 hero; leading player. *Lakoné sapa?* Who's playing the lead? **ke*an (tindak-tanduk** *ki?*) conduct, behavior. *Ati² kelakuanmu wong nèng mantja negara.* Act with circumspection: you're in a foreign country. *kelakuwan betjik* good behavior. **ke*n̂** 1 in the past. *Sing wis kelakon ja wis.* Let bygones be bygones. *Ora ana gunané nggetuni sing wis kelakon.* It's no use regretting what is over and done with. 2 *narrational device* and so it happened that... *Kalakon didjupuk, gada diwènèhaké ing Radèn Damarwulan.* And she managed to get the weapon and gave it to Damarwulan. **jèn...k(e)*n̂** if...then sth unfortunate... *Jèn aku mau ngentèni kowé kelakon telat tenan.* If I had waited for you, I would have been late. *Jèn konangan sing duwé, kelakon dipalu tenan kowé mau.* If the owner had caught you, he would have given you a thrashing. **m*** 1 **(tindak** *ki*) to walk; to proceed, move forward. *Aku jèn sekolah mlaku.* I walk to school. *Sepuré m*.* The train began to move. *M*né tjepet.* He walked briskly. *Djamku ora m* wong rusak.* My watch isn't running–it's broken. 2 going on *n* years of age (*slang*). *Ḍèké umuré lagi pitung taun wolu m*.* She's seven going on eight. **m*-m*** **(tindak²** *ki*) to take a walk. **m·loka-m*** **(m·lampah²** *or* **m·lompah-m·lampah** *or* **m·lompah-m·lèmpèh** *kr*; **tindak-tindèk** *ki*) to keep walking back and forth. *Kowé kuwi mbok lungguh, kok mloka-m* waé.* Do sit down–don't keep pacing the floor. **ng/di*k̂aké** 1 to put sth in motion; to make sth move/function. *nglakokaké montor* to drive a car. *Djamku dilakokaké.* He fixed my watch so it would go. 2 to depict; to perform (the role of). *nglakokaké dongèng² saka Serat Ménak* to act out tales from the Ménak literature. **ng*n̂i** 1 to endure difficulties voluntarily. *Jèn arep urip kepénak kudu gelem nglakoni.* If you want to live comfortably, you have to be willing to go through a lot first. *Aku wis suwé ora nonton pilem, wong lagi nglakoni.* I haven't seen a movie for quite a while, since I'm depriving myself of pleasures. 2 (*psv* **di*n̂i**) to undergo, endure. *nglakoni sinau sregep* to subject oneself to hard studying. **l·um·aku (l·um·ampah** *kr*) *ltry var of* M* *above.* *** bokong** to walk in a squatting position when approaching a high-ranking personage, to show humility and esteem. *** djantra** cycle of events; pattern of behavior. *sa*-djantrané* everything he does. *** ḍoḍok** *sms* * BOKONG *above.* *** gawé** to fulfill an obligation to the government by doing public work without pay. *** n̈g·kiwa** (to engage in) bad conduct. *** prau** to go by boat. *Jèn * prau nèng Amérika suwéné rong sasi.* It takes two months to get to America on a ship.

lâlâ **ng/di*** to praise, compliment

lalab (*or* ***an**) raw vegetables dipped into hot sauce individually and eaten with the rice. **ng/di*** 1 to eat as above. 2 to eat in one mouthful. *Roti semana kuwi di* waé.* That size cookie was just one bite for him.

laladan territory, jurisdiction. *isih klebu * Ngestina* under Ngestina jurisdiction

lalaétulkadar a miracle that occurs during the fasting month (*Pasa*) on the eve of the 21st, 23d, 27th, *or* 29th

laler fly (insect). * *idjo* or * *wilis* green fly. **ng*** resembling *or* behaving like a fly. *ng* méntjok* shaped like the wings of an alighting fly. *ng* wilis* resembling the green fly in color, or in actions (*i.e.* shifting position frequently; fickle). * **mengeng 1** a gamelan melody. 2 a certain kris style

lali *ng,* **supé** *kr* to forget. ***ǹ** *or* ***nan** ([**ke**]-**supè·n**[**an**] *kr*) forgetful. *wong lalinan* a forgetful person. *Lalènmu ora djamak.* You are unbelievably forgetful. ***-*** **1** to keep forgetting. **2** *ltry* to try to forget. **k(e)*ǹ** to have sth slip one's mind. *Mak pet bandjur klalèn.* Just like that, I forgot. **ng/di*(-*)** to forget intentionally. *Ora bisa dak *-*.* I just can't get it out of my mind. **ng/di·(le)*** *or* **ng/di*kaké** to put sth out of one's mind. *Apa kowé gelem nglalèkaké kaluputanku?* Are you willing to overlook my mistake? * **djiwa** *ng kr* **1** *ltry* insane. 2 a variety of mango

lalja *ltry var of* LALI

lalos *sbst kr for* LALI

lalu *oj* (and) then, after that. **di* mati** it would be better to die. *Di* mati tinimbang wirang.* He preferred to die rather than lose face. **ng*** to commit suicide

lalulintas traffic. *njalahi aturan ** to violate a traffic regulation

lam ***-*** admiration, awe. *gawé *-*ing ati* awe-inspiring. ***-*en** lost in admiration. **ng(e)*-*i** causing admiration *or* wonderment

lâmâ *kr* *sbst var of* LAMI

lamak a protective pad. **ng/di*(i)** to smooth, polish. **ng/di*i** to furnish with a protective pad

lamar ***an** a proposal; an application. *Tanḍa² lan katrangan² dikanṭèkaké ing lajang *an mau.* He enclosed his credentials and other data with his letter of application. **ng/di* 1** to ask [a girl's parents] for permission to marry their daughter. **2** to propose to [a girl]. **3** to apply for a job. **pa·ng*** a proposal; an application

lamat **1** cobweb. **2** *var of* ALAMAT. ***-* 1** vague, indistinct. **2** (*or* **le*an**) thinly coated. *Gambaré dipulas *-*.* The paint was laid onto the picture thinly. *Ḍèké jèn pupuran mung le*an waé.* She only powders her face lightly.

lâmbâ single, unmixed. *baṭik sangkalan * lan memet* a batik with a single intricate design. *ora gigrig wuluné sa** not a bit ('not a single hair') frightened. ***n** single, unmarried

lambah ***-*** [of water] copious but in the wrong place. *Èmbèré wutah nang kamar, banjuné nganti *-* nang djubin.* The pail spilled in the room, and the water went all over the floor.

lambak *var of* LÉMBAK

lamban **1** slow, sluggish. *Pikirané * banget.* He's dull-witted. **2** *form of* LAMBA

lambang **1** symbol, emblem, sign. **2** wooden house foundation. **3** *sbst kr for* IDJOL? ***an** beam used as a ship's mast. **ng/di*i 1** to symbolize, represent, portend. **2** to replace. *ng*i gelas sing dipetjahké* to replace a glass which one broke. * **djangka** omen, portent. * **gantung** wooden house foundation. * **santun** (*sbst kr?*) *or* * **sari** (*ki?*) *or* * **sekar** to have sexual intercourse. *See also* PERLAMBANG

lambar (*or* ***an**) an underlayer; object for sth to rest on. **ng/di*i** to furnish with an underlayer, put a base under. *Tjawané iki kanggo ng*i tjangkir.* Put the cup on this saucer. *Ora ana djedjoḍoan kang bisa betjik jèn ora linambaran ing blaka.* No marriage can succeed unless it is founded on truth.

lambé **1** (**laṭi** *ki*) lip(s). **2** edge, rim. *pepak ** brimful. ***né** (*word of reproach*) what a thing to say! * **gadjah 1** decorative notch where a kris handle joins the blade. **2** a certain style of kris sheath

lambèh *var of* LÈMBÈH

lambung side, flank; upper side of the human body. **é gunung* mountainside. *prau silem sing ana katjané ing *é* a glass-sided submarine. *tangan ukel ** hand curved toward the side (in the classical dance). **ng/di* 1** to wear at one's side. **2** to attack at the side/flank. * **lengis** waistline

lamèh **lomah-*** pleasant, outgoing, friendly

lami old; (a) long (time) (*kr for* LAWAS)

lamis (*or* **le*an**) to say what is expedient *or* ingratiating

lamong *ltry* delirious, raving

lampah walk; behavior (*kr for* LAKU)

lamping object used as a potholder

lampir enclosure, attachment. **ng/di*i** to enclose, attach. *Keterangan sing dak tik iki arep tak enggo ng*i lajang lamaranku.* I'm going to enclose this data sheet I'm typing with my application form.

lampit rattan seat mat

lampor roaring, howling sound heard on rivers: believed to be malevolent spirits stamping around

lampu lamp, light. **né murub.* The light is on. **né dipatèni.* He turned off the lamp. **ng/di*** to undergo; to subject oneself to. *Di* rekasa, olèh²ané ora sepiraa.* I've worked so hard and having nothing to show for it. *Ḍèké ng* ora turu sewengi tinimbang ora rampung gawéané.* He forewent sleep all night rather than leave the work unfinished. *Jèn babi, sanadjan luwé tak * ora mangan.* If it's pork, I'll go without, even though I'm hungry. *Jèn kepeksa di* mati.* If need be, he'll submit to death. *Wis diséwakaké omah nang kuṭa, kok ng* ngladju saka ndésané.* He was offered a rented house in town, yet he goes to all the bother of commuting from his village! **ng/di*ni** to [do] to no avail. *Wis dilamponi ngetokké ḍuwit tekan Djakarta barang, djebulé olèhé nglamar penggawéan ora ditampa.* He spent all that money going to Djakarta for nothing: his job application was turned down. *** abang** red light (traffic signal). *** ḍuḍuk** table lamp. *** gantung** hanging lamp. *** gas** gas light. *** lenga pèt** kerosene lamp. *** robjong** chandelier; decorative lamp. *** sènter** flashlight. *** téplok** kerosene lamp hung on walls or pillars

lampus *oj* dead; to die. *Wis tumekèng *.* He has reached the end of his life. **ng/di*(i)** to kill

lamtârâ a certain small shade tree; also, its edible seed pods

lamuk 1 mosquito. 2 sooty smoke from a kerosene lamp; lampblack. **ng*** to make soot. *Senṭiré ng* nang ndi².* The oil lamp sent black smoke in all directions. **ng/di*i** to blacken sth with lampblack

lamun 1 *oj* if, when(ever). 2 (*or* **ka***) if (only). ** aku sugih...* if I were rich... *Adja lowong * ora nudju perlu.* Don't be absent unless it's absolutely necessary.

lamur having defective vision. *A rada *.* A is nearsighted. ***en** to have/get a visual defect

lamut **ng/di*** to put *or* hold sth in the mouth. *Séndok iki wis di*.* This spoon has been used.

lan (**kalijan** *opt kr*) 1 and. *aku * kantjaku* my friend and I. *sadurung * sawisé* before and after. *ing antarané telung * patang wong* three or four people. 2 with. *timbang * geḍé-tjiliké keris* proportionate with the size of the kris. *tinimbang * X* compared with X. *Adja raket * wong ala.* Don't associate with bad people. 3 plus. *loro * telu* 2 + 3. 4 *in negative predicate* or. *... * orané* ...or not. *Gumantung ana bisa * orané anggoné lulus.* It depends on whether or not he passes the test. ***-*an** addition (arithmetic process). *** iku** (*with time expression*) or so. *wetara let setaun * iku* a year or so later. *** lija(-lija)né** (*abbr:* **lll.**) *ng,* *** sanès(-sanès)ipun** (*abbr:* **lss.**) *kr* and so on; and others like [the foregoing]. *** sa·panunggal·(an)é** (*abbr:* **lsp.**) and so on, et cetera. *** sa·(pe)·paḍa·né** and the like, and such things. *** sa·piturut·é** and so on as follows; and (all) the rest. *See also* DADI, DUDU

lanang *ng,* **djaler** *kr* 1 (**kakung** *ki*) male. *anak ** son. *botjah ** boy. *wong ** man. *mantèn ** bridegroom. *Anaké loro, * kabèh.* They have two children, both boys. 2 manly, brave. ***an** 1 stud, male breeding animal. 2 *cr* husband. 3 male part of joined pieces, *e.g.* tongued part for a tongue-and-groove join; male portion of a nut-and-bolt combination. *sambungan *-wadon* a male-female join. **le*é djagad** *wj* the bravest man in the world (sobriquet for Ardjuna). **ng(le)*** masculine, man-like (complimentary, of men; derogatory, of women). **p(a)*an** (**kalam** *or* **warastra** *ki*) penis. *** kemangi** coward; cowardice. **sing *** her husband. *Bareng krungu marang sambaté sing * bandjur mèsem lan tjlaṭuné...* When she heard her husband complaining, she smiled and said... *** wadon/wédok** 1 male and female. 2 husband and wife. *Pak Djaja *-wadon paḍa ngguju.* Mr. and Mrs. Djaja laughed.

lanat evil, cursed

lanbau *see* MANTRI

Lândâ *inf var of* WLANDA

lânḍâ lye. ** awu* burnt rice stalks to be soaked in water. *banju ** water in which burnt rice stalks have soaked: used as shampoo and spot remover. **ng/di*** to wash [hair] *or* remove spots from [clothing] with the above

lanḍak porcupine. ***an** tunnel, shaft. **ng*** 1 resembling a porcupine. *Rambuté ng*.* Her hair looks like porcupine quills. 2 (*psv* **di***) to build a tunnel *or* shaft

lanḍéjan *ng,* **djedjer·an** *kr (ki?)* spear handle

landep 1 a grass whose leaves, pounded fine, are used as hair tonic. 2 a certain shrub used for hedges

lanḍep sharp. **le*** sharp weapons; anything sharp. **ng/di*aké** *or* **ng/di*i** to sharpen. *ng*aké péso (pikiran, potlod, lsp.)* to sharpen a knife (one's wits, a pencil, *etc.*). * **ḍengkul** stupid, dull-witted

lanḍes material used to protect a surface. ***an** underlayer, protective cover; *fig* basis, foundation. **ng/di*i** to use sth as a protective backing. *Olèhé ngeṭoki pring di*i kaju.* He cut the bamboo on a wooden block.

Landi *inf var of* WLANDI

landjar 1 young childless widow *or* divorcée. 2 additional merchandise thrown in free. ***an** supporting pole for climbing plants. **ng/di*i** to throw in [additional merchandise] free. *Jèn ditukoni sepuluh mesṭi gelem ng*i loro.* When you buy ten from her, she always gives you two extras. *See also* KATJANG

landjer **ng*** to ache in the joints. * **ésuk** the morning star. * **soré** the evening star

landjuk **ng/di*** to reach for sth with the hand

landrat court of law. **ng/di*** to try [a court case]. **ng/di*aké** to bring smn to court, *esp.* in a civil case

lanḍung 1 excessively large; protracted, long-drawn-out. *ati sing ** tolerant and patient. 2 [of growth] luxuriant. ***an ati·ǹ/usus** patient and forebearing in nature. **ng/di*i** to make larger. *Klambiné perlu di*i seṭiṭik.* The jacket needs to be let out a little. **p(a)*an** scrotum; *inf* penis (*ki for* KONṬOL)

langak (puppet with an) upturned gaze (*wj*). ***an** *or* ***-*** *or* **le*** to keep stretching the neck *or* holding the head up. *Bajiné wis bisa *-*.* The baby can hold his head up now. **ng*** to crane the neck; to hold the head up in a strained position

langat (*or* **w***) *rg* lengths of wood or bamboo placed on top of a coffin before interring, to prevent the soil from resting on it directly

langen (*or* **le***) 1 pleasure, enjoyment. *le* genḍing* music for pleasure. 2 to devote oneself to pleasure (*ki for* SENENG²?). **k(e)*an** 1 concubine. 2 a pet kept for enjoyment (*ki for* INGU·Ǹ?). 3 pleasure (*rg ki for* KA·SENENG·AN). * **djiwa**, * **gita** certain classical verse forms. * **mandra** court drama of Surakarta in which the performers sing and dance simultaneously

langenardjan a coat-like garment with a broad sash, worn by men for ceremonial occasions

langenastra soldier of the Jogjakarta Sultanate

langendrija(n) a Jogjanese court drama in which the performers sing as they dance

langes soot from the smoke of an oil lamp. **ng*** to give off sooty smoke

lânggâ **ng/di*** to drink by sucking

langganan to be a subscriber/customer/consumer. ** banju* or ** air minum* water user. ** listrik* electricity user. *Aku wis * karo warung mau.* I'm a customer of that store.

langgar a small prayer house, *usu.* in a village. **ng/di*** 1 to disobey, violate. *ng* hukum* to break the law. 2 to run into, collide with. 3 to catch up with; to overtake. **p(a)*an** violation of law/regulations. *Ngrokok nèng ndjero toko kuwi pe*an.* It's against the rules to smoke in the store.

langgat **ng/di*i** to encourage, lead on

langgeng eternal, everlasting. *Kabèh sing kumelip nang donja kuwi ora ana sing *.* Nothing in this world is permanent. *djaman* **ka*an** the other world; life after death. **ng/di*aké** to perpetuate

langgi rice-accompanying dishes which are dry, *i.e.* fried *or* without sauce or gravy. *sega ** rice with the above: wrapped in a banana leaf and sold by street vendors

langi ***ǹ** 1 (act of) swimming. *ulah raga kajata bal-balan, langèn...* sports such as soccer, swimming,... 2 to go swimming. **ng*** to swim

langir a fruit producing a soapy substance which is used as shampoo

langit 1 sky. *bisa ndjara ** knowledgable; powerful. *tekan ing * sap pitu* or *tekan ing * biru* having an exalted position *or* rank. 2 ceiling. 3 facial expression. *paḍang/peteng *é* to look happy/gloomy. ***an** 1 ceiling. 2 canopy. 3 *rg* palate. **ng*** [of cream] to rise to the top of the milk. **p(a)*an** 1 ceiling. 2 canopy. 3 attic, loft

lângkâ 1 unlikely. *Utangku akèh banget, * bisané énggal lunas.* I have so many debts I'm not likely to be able to repay them soon. 2 uncommon. *Saiki * banget wong tjinḍèn.* Nowadays people rarely wear silk sashes.

langkah 1 a long step, a stride. 2 too far, beyond the objective, wide of the mark. **m*** to step over sth. *Lagi waé manjuk² m**

lawang ḍèwèké wis undang² bodjoné. No sooner had he crossed the threshold than he was calling his wife. *Malingé mlumpat m* pager.* The thief vaulted over the fence. **ka*an** to get stepped over; to get bypassed. *Ḍèké ke*an aḍiné.* His younger sister married before he did. **ng/di*i 1** to step over sth. *ng*i wong² sing turu* to step over sleeping people. 2 to skip, bypass. *Olèhku matja ng*i bab lima.* I skipped Chapter 5. 3 to marry ahead of [an older sibling]. **ng*i ojod mimang** faced with a complex situation. **p(a)*** gift given to an older sibling by a younger one who is marrying first. **l·um·angkah** *ltry var of* M* *above*

langkep full (*md? sbst kr? var of* DJANGKEP)

langkung 1 unit of 25 (*kr for* LAWÉ[b]). 2 to go past; to go (by way of) (*kr for* LIWAT). 3 more; exceeding (*kr for* LUWIH). (*sa*) ***an** (one) 25-rupiah bill

langlang (*or* **ng***) *var of* NGANGLANG

langsang (*or* **w***) a temporary container, *e.g.* made of banana leaves

langsaran for everyday wear. *Klambi iki *.* This is an everyday shirt.

langsé (*or* ***ǹ**) shroud, winding sheet

langseb a delicious round yellow fruit that grows in clusters on a stalk. *Kulité kuning *.* Her skin is fair (*i.e.* the color of this fruit). **ng*** resembling *langseb* fruit

langseng **ng/di*** to (re)heat by steaming

langsir 1 to shift [of the eyes: *usu.* to look girls over]. 2 to get shunted about. *Sepuré *.* The train was being made up. **ng*** to shunt [railroad cars]. *ng* sepur* to make up a train

langsung straight, direct, undeviating

langsur **ng/di*** to anoint, rub

langu [of odors, taste] strong, acrid, disagreeable, overpowering

lanjah 1 practiced, skillful, fluent. 2 of easy virtue. *wanita ** prostitute. **ng/di*aké** to master by constant practice. **pa*an** prostitute; prostitution

lantak ramrod for cleaning a gun barrel. ***an** ingot. *mas *an* a bar of gold. **ng/di*(i)** to push a ramrod into [a gun barrel]

lantap quick-tempered

lantar ***an 1** because, as a result of. 2 mediator; middleman. 3 spoon (*ki for* SÉNḌOK). 4 banana leaf used as a spoon (*ki for* SURU). 5 walking stick (*ki for* TEKEN). 6 sacrifice offered as a means of achieving sth one wishes for. 7 bamboo bridge railing. 8 bamboo pole used for plucking fruit from a tree. *tembung* ***an** *gram* preposition. **ng/di*aké 1** to convey, transport. 2 to act as mediator *or* middleman. **ng/di*i** to cause, bring about. *Apa sing ng*i kobong?* What caused the fire? **l·um·antar** through, (conveyed) by way of. *Aku olèh keterangan lumantar kepulisian.* I got my information through the police.

lantas high-pitched. *Jèn njanji swarané *.* She has a soprano singing voice.

lantih *var of* LATIH

lanting ***an** earthenware water carafe (*ki for* KENḌI). **ng/di*i 1** to take/hold sth at arm's length. 2 to give smn a helping hand

lantip mentally quick

lantjang 1 ahead of time; premature. *Djam iki lakuné adjeg, ora * ora kèṭèr.* This watch keeps good time–not fast, not slow. 2 impetuous. *Siti pantjèn sok *, angger weruh dluwang nèng médja dibuwang.* Siti acts without thinking: when she sees papers on the table, she just throws them out. 3 impudent, flippant. ***-*an** to compete for the lead. *Bis mau *-*an karo taksi.* The bus and the taxi were trying to get ahead of each other. **ke*en** excessively hasty. **ng/di*i** to overtake and pass; to get in front of. *See also* KUMALANTJANG

lantjap oval [of face shape]

lantjar smooth, fluent, flowing. ***an** plate (*kr for* PIRING). **le*an** moving quickly and smoothly. **ng/di*aké** to cause sth to be smooth/fluent. *A nètèsi lenga ana ing as roda pité, perlu kanggo ng*aké ubengé.* A oiled his bicycle axle so the wheel would rotate smoothly.

lantjeng a small black stingless beelike insect. *malam ** wax produced by these insects

lantjing ***an** pants, trousers (*ki for* KAṬOK, SRUWAL). **lontjang-*** unmarried and childless

lantjip sharp. **ng/di*i** to sharpen sth. **ng*i (e)ri** to infuriate an angry person still further

lantjir *var of* LENTJIR

lantjong **m*** *or* **ng*** to go out for enjoyment; to go visiting

lantjung *var of* LÈNTJUNG

lantjur 1 rooster's tail feather. 2 (*or* ***an**) young rooster that has reached the reproductive age. **le*** an outstanding *or* superior man. *Samba le*é pradja Dwarawati.* Samba is the handsomest man in the Swarawati kingdom. **l·um·antjur** [of young roosters] starting to grow tail feathers

lantrah **ng*** excessively long-drawn-out. *Jèn pidato mesṭi ng* nganti suwi banget.* He makes very long-winded speeches. **ng/di*aké** to explain

lantrang *-* overlong [of garments]

lantung *var of* LATUNG

lanṭung *-* *or* **ng*** empty-handed

lantur **k(e)*(2)** too far afield. *Anggonku mbatin ke* nganti mèh ora bisa mangsuli.* My thoughts had wandered so far I had difficulty answering. **ng/di*(-*)** to stray, get off the track

laos galingale root, used medicinally and as a cooking spice

lap 1 *rpr* whisking, fluttering. *Aku mau weruh potlodku nang médja kono kok bandjur mak * ilang.* I saw my pencil on the table a minute ago and now it's gone. *Aku mau ngepit arep ketumbuk montor, mak * atiku.* I was riding my bike and a car almost hit me: what a scare it gave me! *Mak * ora krasa turu kira[2] setengah djam.* I dozed off without realizing it and slept half an hour. 2 cleaning rag; dishcloth. ***-*an** anxious, uneasy, on edge. **nge*** to wipe clean. **nge/di*aké** 1 to use for wiping. *Elapé dielapaké ing baṭuké.* She wiped her forehead with the dishcloth. 2 to wipe for smn. **nge/di*i** to wipe sth

lapak saddle (**kambil** *ki*). ***-*** metal box with a hinged lid, in which tobacco or betel leaves are kept. **ng/di*i** to saddle (up) [a horse]

lapal pronouncement of a prayer. **ng/di*i** to say prayers over; to bless

lapan 35-day period. *se** one such period, *i.e.* a complete cycle in the system by which the days of the five-day week are combined with those of the seven-day week. ***an** *n*th *lapan*. *pitung *an* ceremony signalizing the seventh *lapan* of a baby's life. *See also* SELAPAN

lapang broad, spacious, roomy. ***an** field, plain

lapat *var of* ILAPAT

lapis 1 layer; outer layer. *motor * wadja* armored car. 2 rice-flour layer cake. **(le)*an** in layer(s). *awudjud *an sing tipis* in thin layers. *Kali ing *an ḍuwur dadi ès.* The upper layer of the river froze over. **ng/di*** to arrange in layers. **ng/di*(i)** to furnish with a(n outer) layer. *Médjané di*i formica.* The table was topped with formica.

lapor *var of* LAPUR

lapur to report, make a report. ***an** a report. **ng/di*aké** to report sth; to report that... **ng/di*i** to report (to smn). **pa*an** a report

lar wing(s). **mang*** [of mature insects] to have grown its wings. **me*** to expand. *Kaos sikilé melar.* His socks stretched. *me* mingkup* to expand and contract by turns. **nge*** resembling wings. **nge/di*(aké)** to expand, broaden, lengthen. *ngelar(aké) djadjahan tekan tanah sabrang* to expand one's empire to foreign countries

lârâ[a] *ng,* **sakit** *kr* ill; painful; to hurt; to have sth wrong with one physically, (to have) a disease (**gerah** *ki*). *wong ** ill person; patient. *Tanganku *.* My arm hurts. *wong * mripat* person who has sth wrong with his eyes. *mari *né* to recover from one's illness. *kena ing ** to fall ill. ***n** 1 prone to illness *or* pain. ** atèn* easily hurt (in feelings). 2 prisoner (*see also* SAKIT). ***nen** sickly, frail. ***ning *** 1 the ultimate in illness/suffering. 2 physical illness brought on by mental anguish. *ora* **lorā-*** (*ora* **sakit[2]** *kr*) not sick at all; just pretending to be sick. **le*** an illness. *le* nular* contagious disease. *le* sing awèt* a chronic illness. **le*n** *sms* *N *above.* **le*nen** 1 diseased. *pitik sing le*nen* diseased chickens. 2 *sms* *NEN *above.* **ke*n** to get hurt; to suffer pain. **ke*-*** *ng kr* sorrowful, grieving, broken-hearted. **ng*** to feign illness. **ng/di*kaké** to inflict pain on. **ng*ni** to have labor pains. **ng/di·(le)*(ni)** to inflict pain *or* suffering on smn. *nglelarani ati* to hurt smn's feelings. *** aju** smallpox. *** ati·né** hurt feelings. *** bojok** backache. *** brangta** (in) mental anguish; lovesick. *** ḍaḍa** tuberculosis. *** djiwa** mentally ill. *** ireng (musibat)** addicted to opium. *** karuna** to cry heart-rendingly. *** kuning·(an)** 1 jaundice. 2 yellow fever. *** ng·lambé** to play sick, feign illness. *** panas** fever(ish). *** tuwa** old age as a pathological condition. *** ujang** fever(ish). *** untu** (to have) a toothache. *** weteng** (to have) a stomach ache. *See also* PILARA, UTANG

lârâ[b] 1 virgin girl. 2 young girl of noble birth. **pa*-*** 1 young girls of the court. 2 a man's mistress. *** mendut** a sweet snack to accompany tea

larab 1 layer; sheet. 2 blanket; horse

blanket. 3 tarpaulin. **ng/di*aké** to place in layers. *ng*aké bata* to lay bricks. **ng/di*i** to place a cover over sth

larag **ng/di*** to charge, advance upon [the enemy]

larah 1 reason, explanation. *Pijé ta *é kok dadi A nesu karo B?* Why did A get mad at B? 2 *rg* trash, rubbish. **ng/di*** to investigate, acquire information about

larak **ng/di*** to take forcibly. *Botjah mau di* mulih karo bapakné.* The child's father dragged him home.

lârâkudan single-barrel shotgun

lârâlâpâ wretched with hunger and illness

larang *ng*, **awis** *kr* 1 high in cost. *Regané *.* It's expensive. *Séwané *.* The rent is high. *Jèn didol mesṭi paju *.* You can always sell it for a big profit. 2 scarce, short. *Nalika * ḍuwit kaé weḍusé didol.* When he was short of money, he sold his sheep. *Beras banget *é.* Rice is in very short supply. *or* Rice is very expensive. *Tahun iki * udan.* We've had little rain this year. ***an** forbidden (thing). *Tjolong djupuk kuwi kegolong *an nang agama Islam.* Stealing is forbidden by the Islamic religion. **ng/di*aké** to make sth (more) expensive. *Jèn sing tuku wong lanang bandjur di*ké.* If the buyer is a man, she raises the price. **ng/di*(i)** to prohibit, forbid. *Di* Masuk.* No Admittance. *Sing lara di*i metu saka ngomah.* The patient was forbidden to leave the house. *Angger² mau ng* ukuman mati.* The law forbids capital punishment.

larap 1 swift forward *or* downward motion; *fig* goal. *kaja *é ṭaṭit* like a flash of lightning. *Apa kowé ngreti *é?* Can you understand what he's driving at? 2 cutting board for slicing tobacco leaves. 3 aspect, appearance. **é mèh paḍa.* They look almost alike. **é kepingin dadi mantuné.* He seems to want to marry into the family. ***an** 1 act of conducting a caller into smn's presence. *tanpa *an* (to enter) without being properly announced *or* escorted. 2 log with holes for puppet sticks, used by the puppet-master to keep the puppets neatly and conveniently at hand. 3 forehead (*ki for* BAṬUK). ***-*** to speed. *Ora weruh panah *-* tjumlorot mréné.* He doesn't see the arrow whizzing this way. **ng*** 1 *sms *-*.* 2 (*psv* **di***) to avoid. *Ḍèké di* kantja²né.* His friends steered clear of him. **ng/di*aké** 1 to set sth in motion at high speed. 2 to direct smn to a destination. *Olèhmu ng*aké salah.* You gave him the directions wrong. 3 to conduct [a caller] into smn's presence. **ng/di*i** to whiz through the air to(ward). *Tumbaké ng*i wit.* The lance struck a tree. **pa*an** 1 one who ushers a caller *or* conveys a message. 2 forehead (*ki for* BAṬUK). **l·um·arap** *sms* NG*

laras suitable, appropriate, harmonious (with), becoming (to). *Guneméora sa* karo tindaké.* His words don't match his actions. *Klambi kuwi * banget.* That dress is very becoming to you. *Ḍèwèké ndjogèd sarwi *.* He dances gracefully. *Gamelané ora *.* The instruments are out of tune. 2 musical tone, note of the scale. *titi * lima* five-tone scale. **é gamelan Djawa* the tones of the Javanese instruments. 3 that which is expressed; aspect *or* meaning conveyed. **é kaja déwa nganglang djagat.* He looks like a god walking the earth. *Tegesé tembung A iku nunggal * karo tembung B.* Word A means the same thing as word B. ***an** a used piece of paper. **ma*an** *ltry var of* PA*AN *below.* **ng*** 1 to sing for one's own enjoyment. 2 to relax, loaf, take it easy. 3 (*psv* **di***) to tune [musical instruments]. **ng/di*(-*)** to think over (the appriateness *or* harmoniousness of). *Bareng di*-* ḍèké mutuské jèn ora sida mèlu lunga.* After considering it in all its aspects, he decided against going. *Ḍèké ng* olèhé arep ngatur kebon kembangé.* He gave a lot of thought to arranging his garden attractively. **ng/di*aké** to bring into accord, make harmonious. *Jèn di*aké karo djaman saiki...* To bring it up to date... *Jèn lunga menjang Indonesia, kudu ng*aké karo tjara Indonesia kono.* When you go to Indonesia, you should do as the Indonesians do. **pa*an** *ltry* 1 to leave without saying goodbye. 2 to go about in search of sth

lârâsetu a certain fragrant grass having sweet-smelling roots

lârâwastu *var of* LARASETU

laré child, young person (*kr for* BOTJAH). *** angon** *ng kr* small harmless blue-and-black snake. *See also* KAPILARÉ

lari trace, remains. *ilang ora ana *né* gone without a trace. **ng/di*** to trace, track down, investigate

larik 1 line, row; rank (as contrasted with file). *omah sa* kuwi* all the houses in the row. 2 soothing ointment (*ki for* PILIS). ***an** line, row, rank. *koṭakan *an katelu* the third row of squares. **a*-*** forming a line/row. *djanggel a*-** corn kernels on the cob. **ng/di*(-*)** 1 to arrange in rows. 2 to make lines of irrigation ditches. **ng/di*i** to furnish with ditches. *ng*i sawah* to make irrigation ditches in a paddy

laris quick-selling. *Enggonku dodolan *.* My wares sell like hotcakes. **ke*an** to be all sold out. **ng/di*aké** *or* **ng/di*i** to make sth sell quickly. *Kanggo ng*i, djeruké didol setali telu.* He priced the tangerines at three for a quarter, for quick sale. **p(a)*an** magical formula to make things sell fast. **pa·ng*an** act *or* technique of selling fast. **l·um·aris** to talk

laron flying termite. *See also* GUNḌIK

laru **ng*** to produce charcoal by permitting wood to smoulder for three days in a covered pit

larud to get washed (swept, blown) away. *Sabarang kang ditradjang bandjir *.* Everything in the path of the flood was washed away. *Saking ḍemené main, nganti banḍa pirang² *.* He loved gambling so much that his fortune all went down the drain. ** kabèh kakuwatané.* The strength all drained from him. ***an** (chemical) solution. **ng/di*(aké)** 1 to wash/sweep sth away. 2 to dissolve sth

larug **ng*** 1 to drag the feet as one walks. 2 (*psv* **di***) to drag sth

laruh **ng/di*i** to tell smn to [do]. *Aku di*i adja mbéda botjah.* He told me not to tease the child.

larung to consign [a body] to the water for burial at sea. **ng/di*** 1 to dispose of [sacrificial offerings] by floating them away on a raft. *Slametané di* nang kali.* They set the ritual foods adrift on the river. 2 to bury [a body] at sea

las 1 counting unit for grains *or* grain-like items. *beras sak elas* a grain of rice. *inten rong ** two jewels. 2 an unhulled rice grain found in cooked rice. 3 -teen (*see also* BELAS, WELAS[b]). *ro** 12. *telu** 13. *lima** 15. *pitu** 17. *wolu** 18. *sanga** 19. ***-*an** 1 (in) the teens. *Umuré *-*an.* He's in his teens. 2 welded. *Knalpoté wis *-*an.* The tailpipe has been welded. **nge/di*** to weld. *See also* NG- (*prefix*) 6, 7

lasem *see* SAMPAK

laskar soldier

lat late, delayed (*inf var of* TELAT). *Sepuré tekané * sedjam.* The train was an hour late.

lâtâ a climbing vine

latah a mental disorder present in certain lower-class women past middle age, characterized by involuntary compulsive utterance of obscenities, parodying of others' actions, or other socially or morally offensive behavior

latak sediment in indigo batik dye

latar (*or* **p[a]*an**) 1 yard *or* grounds around a building. 2 background color, field. ** ireng* dark background (of a batik). ** putih* natural background, *i.e.* not dyed

lateng a certain grass with itchy leaves

laṭi 1 lip(s) (*ki for* LAMBÉ). 2 (*or* **le***) having blackened teeth (*ki for* SISIG). **ng/di*ǹi** *ki* to blacken the teeth

latih ***an** 1 training, teaching, drill. *sekolah *an* school where prospective teachers practice. **an tentara* military drill/training. 2 to undergo training, learn a skill. *Aku *an djogèd.* I'm learning to do the classical dance. **ng/di*** to teach, train, drill. *ng* asu* to train a dog. *Aku arep ng* kowé ngetik.* I'll teach you to type. **ng/di*aké** to have smn trained

latin Latin, Roman. *aksara ** or *huruf ** letter of the Roman alphabet; Roman type/script; handwritten (cursive) character/script

latjak trace, trail, track. *ilang tanpa ** gone without a trace. **ke*** to get tracked down and caught. **ng/di*** to trace, track down

latji drawer in a table *or* desk

latjur to cheat. **pa*an** prostitution

latjut exceeding proper limits. *Sumubing djenèwer *é diarani air kata².* The way gin makes a person forget himself, it could be called tongue-loosening water. **ke*** too late; having gone too far

latri *see* DJAGA

latu 1 fire (*kr for* GENI). 2 *rg, ng kr* spark

latung kerosene; petroleum

laut 1 sea. *iwak ** ocean fish. *angkatan ** navy. *andjing ** walrus. 2 off work (for lunch; for the day: of blue-collar workers). ***an** pertaining to the sea. *pradjurit *an* sailor. 2 sea. *Lautan Djawa* Java sea. **ng/di*aké** to let smn off work. *Aku di*aké pak mandor.* The foreman gave me the day off.

lâwâ a certain bat (flying animal). ***-*** long-handled feather duster for cleaning high places. **ng/di*-*** to clean high walls and ceilings with such a duster

lawak ship's hull. **le*** 1 howdah. 2 covered

chest carried stretcher-like on poles, for carrying food at the palace

lawan 1 enemy, opponent. 2 and (*ltry var of* LAN). ***an** 1 enemy, opponent. 2 to resist, oppose. **an banda* to attack a helpless person. ***-le*an** to compete with each other. *Désa sidji lan sidjiné tansah lawan-lelawanan.* The two villages engage in constant rivalry. **ng/di*** to fight. **l·um·awan** 1 to fight, oppose. 2 opposed, fought against

lawang *ng,* **kori** *kr,* **konten** *kr? md?* door. **é menga/tutupan.* The door is open/closed. *ḍoḍog²* * to knock on a door. *ke·ineb·an * tobat* no longer able to obtain absolution. ***an** 1 doorway. 2 small door. * **butul·an** back door. * **kupu tarung** paired swinging doors with openings above and below, like barroom doors. * **lèrèg·an** sliding door. * **monjèt·an** Dutch door. * **régol** outer gate. * **sekèṭèng** inner gate, gateway leading to the interior portion of a Javanese-style house. * **tangkeb·an** double (paired) doors, French doors

lawar (*or* **[le]*an**) 1 pure, undiluted. *Tèhé *an.* The tea has no sugar in it. 2 without equipment. *Anggoné kerengan mung *an waé.* They fought with their bare hands. *Ḍèwèké ditjekel le*an baé déning pulisi mau.* The policeman arrested him singlehanded.

lawas *ng,* **lami** *kr* 1 old. *Klambimu anjar apa wis *?* Is your shirt new or old? 2 (*or* **dangu** *kr*) (a) long (time). *Mariné *.* It takes a long time to get well. *Mariné wis *.* He's been well for a long time now. *Saja * kekurangan sanḍangan lan pangan.* Food and clothing got scarcer and scarcer. *Aku wis * ora ketemu ḍèké.* I haven't seen him for ages. **ora *** before long. *Ora * bétjak wis teka.* Soon a pedicab came along. ***-*** at last, eventually. ***-* kawong·an goḍong** to grow gray in smn's service. **ke*en** *ng* 1 (**ke·lami·ǹ** *kr*) excessively old. *Sardèn kuwi wis ke*en, adja dipangan.* The sardines have been around too long–don't eat them. 2 (**ke·dangu·ǹ** *kr*) an excessively long time. *Ke*en ora ketemu.* It's been ever so long since I've seen him. **sa*é** 1 for a long time; forever. *Sa*é aku ora bakal lali marang kabetjikanmu.* I'll never forget your kindness. 2 throughout (the duration of). *Sa*é urip A durung tau weruh saldju.* A has never seen snow in his life. 3 while, during. *sa*é aku nang Amérika* during the time I was in America. **sa*-*é** 1 for a long time; forever. 2 as long as one wishes

lawé[a] 1 thread, yarn. * *mateng* thread that has been processed for weaving. * *mentah* unprocessed thread. 2 a certain small round fruit whose juice makes the skin itch. ***an** *see* BAU. **ng/di*** to strangle; to throttle by hanging (ancient form of execution). **pa*an** place where thread is sold. * **wenang** circlet of thread worn on the wrist to protect one against disease

lawé[b] *ng,* **langkung** *kr* unit of 25. *se** 25. *telung ** 75. ***an** *or* ***ǹan** (**langkung·an** *kr*) 25-rupiah bill. *ḍuwit kertas lawènan* (money in the form of) 25-rupiah bills. *See also* NG- (*prefix*) 6, 7; SELAWÉ

lawèh **ng/di*i** to be of assistance to, lend a hand to

lawèt a variety of swallow (bird)

lawon white cotton fabric. * *mentah* unbleached cotton

lawuh foods eaten with rice and which, together with the rice, comprise a meal. *sega sa*é* a meal. *Aku mau mangan *é tahu gorèng karo djangan loḍèh.* I had fried bean curd and vegetable soup with my rice. ***an** (the array of) dishes for a meal. **ng/di*i** to prepare *or* provide [dishes] for. *Bodjoné nriman banget, di*i gerèh waé wis seneng.* Her husband is very easy to please–he's content with just dried fish with his rice.

lawung 1 spear. 2 classical spear dance. **ng/di*** to pierce with a spear. **ng/di*(aké)** to permit [a domestic animal] to go loose. **pa*an** place for keeping weapons

lé 1 *excl of surprise* (*sbst kr? for* LO). *Kok * hébat banget.* How splendid! 2 *affectionate adr* little boy (*shf of* ṬOLÉ). *Adja kuwatir *, ora apa².* Don't be afraid, Son, it's all right. 3 smn's act of [do]ing (*contracted from* OLÈH·É)

le- *see also under* LA- (*Introduction, 2.9.2*)

leb **lab-*** to eat avidly. **ke*an** to get flooded/inundated. **nge/di*i** to flood, inundate. *See also* ALEB

lebar 1 (all) over; to finish, get through. *Mangsané pelem wis *.* The mango season is over. *menawa * panèn* when the harvest is in. *Jèn * njambut-gawé kesel.* He was tired when he got through work. 2 after. * *beḍug* after noon. ***an** the major Moslem holiday, celebrated at the close of the fasting month (*Pasa*). **ng/di*aké** to bring to a close. *Klasé di*aké karo guruné.* The teacher

dismissed the class. **sa∗é** after. *sa∗é sinau* when he had finished studying
lebda *ltry* experienced
lèbèr **∗an** spillage. *Tjangkiré wutah, ∗ané tekan endi²*. The cup spilled all over. **ng/di∗i** to spill onto. *Wédangé wutah ng∗i médja.* The tea spilled on the table. **l·um·è-bèr** to pour forth
lebet 1 deep; inside (*kr for* DJERO). 2 to enter (*root form: kr for* LEBU)
lébrag **ng∗** large, broad. **sa∗** in a large-sized lump; in large quantities
lebu *ng,* **lebet** *kr* 1 act of entering; enrollment in school. *∗né tanggal pira?* When does school start? *∗ning basa Sanskerta marang basa Djawa akèh banget.* Many Sanskrit words have come into the Javanese language. 2 *ng kr* dust, dirt. *mesin panjerot ∗* vacuum cleaner. **∗n̂** cost of production. **k(e)∗** 1 contained [in]; classified as, included (in the category of). *Bibiting lelara k∗ ing ususé laler.* Disease germs are present in flies' intestines. *Menawa monḍok iku pa-ngané wis k∗.* When you rent a room, meals are included. *Ora k∗ mbuku.* It got left out of the book. *Jèn bab étung ka∗ sing asor ḍéwé.* In arithmetic, he's among the lowest [in the class]. *Tanah Djawa kuwi k∗ negara panas.* Java is a tropical country. *Regané k∗né ora larang.* It's relatively inexpensive. 2 to get accepted. *Aku wis k∗ nèng S.M.A.* I've been admitted to high school. **k(e)∗ ing ati** to be an object of interest *or* concern. *Sing k∗ atiné babagan ulah raga.* He takes his athletics seriously. **k(e)∗n̂** to be entered, *esp.* by sth detrimental. *klebon maling* broken into by thieves. *Tudjuné mripaté ora klebon apa².* Luckily none of it got in his eyes. 2 possessed (by). *Ḍèké klebon sétan.* He's possessed by an evil spirit. **m∗** to enter. *M∗ kéné!* Come in here! *Bisané m∗ ing waḍah keprijé?* How did it get in the container? *m∗ sekolah* to enroll in school; to go to school; to enter a school building. *Suwé A ora mlebu.* A was absent for a long time. **m∗-m̂·wetu** *or* **m·leba-m∗** (**m·lebet-m̂·wedal** *or* **m·lebet²** *kr*) to keep going in and out. **ng/di∗k̂aké** to insert sth; to insert [sth] into. *Montoré dilebokké nang garasi.* He put his car in the garage. *Bapakné nglebokaké sekolah anaké.* His father entered him in school. **ng/di∗n̂i** 1 to enter sth. *Sawisé lulus, ḍèké ngleboni universitas.* After passing his exams, he enrolled at the university. *ngleboni sajembara* to enter a contest. 2 to insert sth into. *Bolongan mau lebonana wadja gèpèng.* Insert a flat piece of metal into the opening. **sa∗né** inside of. *sa∗né kuṭa* within the city limits. **l·um·ebu** *ng,* **l·um·ebet** *kr* to enter (*ltry var of* M∗ *above*)
lebur destroyed, leveled, wiped out. *∗ tanpa kukupan* utterly crushed. *Sedaja kalepatan sageda ∗ ing dinten rijadi punika.* I hope all my mistakes will be forgiven and forgotten on this Lebaran day. **ng/di∗** to destroy, wipe out. **ng/di∗aké** to cause to be destroyed. *Ḍuwité emas mau di∗aké.* He had the gold coin melted down. **pa·ng∗an** process of breaking down. *pang∗an wesi-wadja* iron-and-steel mill
lẹḍang (*or* **le∗**) 1 to go (out) for a stroll. 2 annoyance, irritation. **ng/di·le∗** to annoy, pester
lèḍèk a solo dance performed by a woman. **ng∗** 1 to perform this dance. 2 (*psv* **di∗**) to tease. *See also* TLÈḌÈK
lèdèng to melt, *i.e.* become melted. **∗an** melted, dissolved; act of melting/dissolving. **ng/di∗aké** to melt for smn; to have sth melted/dissolved. **ng/di∗(i)** to dissolve, melt (down)
lèḍeng 1 water pipe. *banju ∗* running water. 2 *rg* irrigation ditch
lèḍès 1 [of eyes] to feel irritated. *Mripaté ∗.* His eyes felt as if they were full of sand [after he had stayed awake all night]. 2 to get scratched. *Aku tiba sikutku ∗.* I fell and scratched my elbow.
lèding *var of* LÈḌENG
leḍis 1 to smell unwashed. 2 to finish up. *Sega sepiring kok ∗.* He ate the whole plate of rice.
ledjar to cheer up. *Atiné ∗.* She felt more optimistic. **ng/di∗(aké)** to cheer smn up
ledjer form, shape. *∗ing awaké* his physique
leḍok 1 level part along a riverbank at the foot of a steep valley. 2 (*or* **∗an**) a depression in the ground
lèdrèg (*or* **ng∗**) damp, decaying, moldy
lédré intip a waffle-like wafer made of rice flour and filled with mashed banana
léḍung **léḍang-∗** *words chanted in lullabies.* **ng/di·(le)∗-∗** *or* **ng/di·(le)·léḍang-(le)∗** to sing a lullaby to. *Bonékahé diléḍang-∗.* She sang her doll to sleep.
leḍung **∗-∗** luxuriant. *Tanduranė djagung kétok ∗-∗.* The corn plants are flourishing.

leg *rpr* swallowing. *Tjepet^2 pilé diuntal mak* *. He gulped down the pill. **ke*** to get swallowed. *Widjiné ke**. He accidentally swallowed the seed. **nge/di*** 1 to swallow. 2 *cr* to eat

lega relieved, at ease, free. *Wis * saiki.* Everything's all right now. *Aku durung * atiku.* I was still uneasy. *Jèn * tekaa nggonku.* When you have nothing to do, come on over to my place. ***n** free, at leisure. 2 unmarried. ***n golèk momong·an** a well-off person seeking hardship. **ka*n** content(ed), relieved. **ng*kaké** satisfying; (*psv* **di*kaké**) to satisfy, give pleasure *or* relief. **ng/di*ni** to relieve/gratify smn. *** legawa** pleasure, gratification. *** lila** resigned. *Aku *-lila masrahaké pati-uripku.* I'm content to submit to my fate.

legâwâ gratification, pleasure. *Sembah bektimu tak tampa kanṭi lega *ning atiku.* I accept your tribute with a full heart.

legeg *ltry* (*or* *-*) nonplused, at a loss

legèh *ltry* unburdened, empty-handed. *A * tan nggegawa.* A brought nothing with him.

legèjèh **ng*** to lie down for a rest

legena [of Javanese-script characters] bare, *i.e.* without vowel-showing diacritics. **ng*** nude; bare; without additions

legendar rice-flour cookie. *lèmpèng ** fried chips of sun-dried fried rice

legender 1 *rpr* swallowing. *Panganané diulu waé mak *.* He swallowed the cookie in one gulp. 2 to swallow

legi 1 sweet(-tasting). 2 first day of the five-day week. ***ǹ** sweet nectar from coconut *or* areca-palm blossoms. **le*** candy, sweets. **ke*ǹ** excessively sweet. **ng/di*k̀aké** to make sth sweet(er than it was). *nglegèkaké tèh* to sweeten tea. **ng/di*ǹi** to make sth (in such a way that it is) sweet. *** anglek** cloyingly sweet. *** bratawali** intensely bitter. *** n·duleg** *or* *** tjumles** cloyingly sweet

légijun military legion

legik *-* isolated; apart from others. *Ḍèké *-* idjèn ana ndjaba ora bisa turu.* He went outside by himself, unable to sleep.

légo *slang* **ng/di*** to sell [one's belongings] to raise cash

legok to have/get a shallow hole in it. ***an** dent, hollow, depression. **ng/di*aké** to make a depression/hole in sth belonging to smn else. *Sapa sing nglegokké slébor montorku?* Who dented my fender? **ng/di*i** to make shallow holes in sth. *nglegoki lemah* to make depressions in the soil

legunḍi a certain shrub

lèh 1 *var of* LIH. 2 smn's act of [do]ing (*inf var of* OLÈH). **nge/di*aké** to confront smn with his misdeed; to expose smn's mistake *or* wrongdoing (*var of* M̈/DI·WELÈH·AKÉ). *Siti nge*aké Slamet anggoné ora netepi djandjiné.* Siti took Slamet to task for not keeping his promise. *Bareng di*ké anggoné ngapusi kantjané ḍèké bandjur klutjutan.* He was mortified when it came to light that he had cheated his friend.

léha *-* at leisure, loafing. *Olèhé mlaku *-*.* He strolled. *Udjianku saiki wis rampung mulané aku bisa *-*.* My exams are over now, so I'm free.

lèjèh ***an** *or* *-* *or* **ng*** to lie down, lie back

lejep *-* about to drop off to sleep

léjo lion

léjod *-* *or* **léjad-*** to sway, teeter

léjong Chinese dragon

léjor **léjar-*** infirm; unsteady

lèk to appear, emerge. *Rembulané wis *.* The moon is up. *Nalika *é anakku sing mbarep udan geḍé.* It was raining hard when my first child was born. ***-*an** (**wungu·ñ** *ki*) to remain awake during the night for ritual or ceremonial purposes. **me*** to stay awake (*see also* MELÈK). **nge/di*aké** to open *or* keep open [the eyes]. *Jèn arep rabi, *na mripatmu sing amba; jèn wis rabi, remna mripatmu.* If you're not married, keep your eyes open wide [to look over the girls]; if you are married, keep them closed. **nge/di*i** (**m̈/di·wungu·ñi** *ki*) to stay awake for a certain purpose. *nge*i baji* to stay awake waiting for a baby to be born. *Mengko bengi aku arep nge*i gantining tahun.* I'm staying up tonight to see the new year in. **tjagak *** a means of staying awake. *Kanggo tjagak elèk, ajo paḍa ura^2.* Let's sing to keep ourselves awake.

lek̄ ***-*an** crannies, obscure places. *Jèn ngresiki kamar nggon *-*an adja lali.* When you clean the room, don't overlook the corners. **nge/di*** to swallow. *Adja nganti nge* ri.* Don't swallow the bone!

lekas 1 what smn says/advises/instructs. *kaja *é pengarang* as the author states. **é Pamréntah* a Government directive. 2 to act quickly. **, gèk adus!* Hurry, take your bath! *najogjani *é projèk* to speed up the project. ***an** act of getting started without delay. **ng/di*i** to get at sth quickly. *Gawéané di*i gasik supaja bisa rampung.* He started the job early so as to get it over with.

lèkèk *-* (to laugh) in high-pitched tones

lekek̄ [of neck] short and thick-looking

leker **ng*** curled up, coiled. **ng/di*i** to coil around sth

leket to adhere (to). *Limé * banget, angèl ditèṭèl.* The glue sticks firmly, it's hard to get it off. *A saiki * banget karo B sing marai riset bareng.* A spends a lot of time with B now: they're doing research together.

lekik dent, hollow. *** pipi·né** (to have/show) a dimple

lékok **lékak-*** full of curves. *dalan sing akèh lékak-*é* a winding road

lekotro(k) *rpr* clothing suddenly sliding down on the wearer

leksa 1 unit of 10,000. *Akèhé pirang^2 *.* There were tens of thousands of them. *sa** 10,000. *rong ** 20,000. 2 Chinese vermicelli. ***n** (numbering in the) tens of thousands

leksânâ to make sth come true; to grant [a wish]. **ka*n** to have [one's wishes, hopes] fulfilled. **ng/di*ni** to fulfill [smn's wishes]

leksârâ *rg var of* AKSARA

lèktor assistant professor (academic title). *** kepala** associate professor. *** muḍa** lecturer

lèktur reading matter

lel- *see also under* L- *(Introduction, 3.1.3)*

léla *-* *syllables chanted in lullabies.* **ng*** 1 obvious, apparent. 2 uncovered, bare. *retjana wanita ng** a statue of a nude woman. *Pegunungan paḍa ng*.* The hills are bare. **ng/di*-*** 1 to praise, compliment. 2 to sing a lullaby to. **pa·ng*-*** praise; affection. *tembung pang*-** words of praise *or* endearment. ***-léḍung** *words chanted in lullabies*

lelai *see* TJIRI

lelânâ to wander, ramble. *** brata** to go from place to place seeking inspiration in God's words

lélang an auction; to sell at auction. *tukang ** or *djuru ** auctioneer. ***an** 1 having changed hands at an auction. *kursi *an* a chair bought (*or* sold) at an auction. 2 place where an auction is held. **ng/di*(aké)** to auction sth off

lélé freshwater fish resembling a catfish. *** m̀·paran·i ujah asem** bringing out the best in each other, *i.e.* like catfish and salt pointing up each other's flavor

leled slow-moving, slow-acting. **ng*** to act *or* move sluggishly

lèlèh to melt. *Wesiné dipanasi bandjur *.* The iron ore became molten when it was heated. **ng/di*(aké)** to melt sth

lelep **k(e)*** 1 to sink below the surface. *mati k** to drown. *Nganti pirang^2 djam ora k*.* [The corpse] didn't sink for hours. 2 to get overshadowed, lost, overwhelmed. *Swarané montor k* swarané bis.* The sound of the car was drowned out by the bus. *Ḍalang mau saiki k* marga wis tuwa.* People have forgotten about this [once-famous] puppet-master now that he's old. 3 away too long, overdue. *Kerep waé botjah tjilik k* lali jèn dikongkon.* A child sent on an errand often takes so long he forgets he was sent for sth. **k(e)*an** to fill up and sink. *Prauné botjor bandjur k*an banju.* The leaky boat gradually filled with water and sank. **ng/di*aké** 1 to hold/push sth below the surface. 2 to drown smn

lèlèr *see* DADAR

lèlès *see* KOPI

leles *see* SAMBANG

lèlèt **ng/di*aké** to spread/smear sth. *Gemuké di*aké ing tatu mau.* He smeared the grease on the wound. **ng/di*i** to spread/smear onto. *Omahé di*i tjèt.* He painted the house. *See also* LÈT

lelet *see* SAMBANG

lelur **ng/di*i** to follow, act according to. *Welingé simbah perlu ko*i.* You must do as your grandmother said.

lem **nge/di*** to praise *or* compliment smn. *See also* ALEM

lem- *see also under* L- *(Introduction, 3.1.7)*

lema fat; flourishing (*kr for* LEMU)

lemah *ng,* **siti** *kr* 1 earth, soil, land, ground. *katutupan ** covered with earth. *tiba ana (ng)** to fall to the ground. 2 (*or* **pa*an**) a parcel of land. *** asal** native land. *** lempung** clay. *** teles** reddish-brown, *i.e.* the color of wet earth. *See also* SITI

lemantun cupboard (*kr for* LEMARI)

lemarèng *rg var of* MARÈNG

lemari *ng,* **lemantun** *kr* cupboard, cabinet. ** buku* bookcase. ** ès* ice box, refrigerator. ** katja* wardrobe cupboard with a mirror. ** kawat* food cupboard having a wire-screen back. ** koḍok* a small cylindrical cabinet standing on a single four-footed leg. * **makan** food cupboard. * **wesi** safe (for keeping valuables)

lembâgâ, lembagā institution, association. * **Ludrug** an association of *ludrug*-dance performers. * **Tenaga Atom** Institute of Atomic Energy

lembah 1 valley. 2 (*or* ***-manah**) calm, patient, tolerant in nature

lembajung a certain leafy vegetable

lémbak **-* or* **ng*** *or* **l·um·émbak** [of water] forming waves, swelling

lembânâ *ltry var of* LEM. *See also* ALEMBANA

lémbang *var of* LÉMBAR

lémbar **m*** *or* **l·um·émbar** to leap from one place to another

lembar counting unit for flat things. *dluwang se** a sheet of paper. *godong rong ** two leaves. ***an** 1 sheet; flat object. *duwit *an éwon* a thousand-rupiah bill. **ané buku* the pages of a book. 2 a chicken-and-coconut-milk dish for ritual meals. **le*an** in sheets, consisting of sheets

lémbat ***an** one to whom smn else's work is passed on. *Biasané A kerep dienggo *an gawéan B sing marahi mesti gelem didjaluki tulung.* B often passes on his own work to A, who enjoys helping out. **ng/di*aké** to move sth along, pass sth on. **l·um·émbat** *var of* L·UM·ÉMBAR

lembat fine, thin, small (*kr for* LEMBUT)

lèmbèh ***an** to swing the arms as one walks. **ng/di*aké** to swing [the arms]

lembèk weak, pale, spiritless. *Radioku batréné wis *.* My radio batteries are running down. *gindjel ** weak kidneys. *Rupané *.* She looks pale. ** semangaté.* He lacks the fighting spirit.

lembing spear, lance

lémbong *var of* LUMBU

lembu cow (*kr for* SAPI)

lembut *ng,* **lembat** *kr* fine, thin, small. *wulu *-** fine feathers, down. *radjangan *-** thin slices. *ujah ** fine-grained salt. *budi ** (re)-fine(d) character. *kéwan sing * banget* a microscopic organism. *aksara kang ** letters written with fine lines. *swara kang ** a soft voice. **le*** 1 trouble-making invisible spirit. 2 germ, microbe. **ng/di*aké** to make sth fine (thin, small). *ng*aké ujah* to grind salt fine

lèmèk lining, protective underlayer. ** kursi* seat pad. **ng/di*i** to line sth; to furnish sth with an underlayer. *Lojangé di*i kertas putih.* The tray is lined with white paper.

lèmeng **ke*an** to have sth slip one's mind

lèmèr (*or* ***an** *or* ***en**) weak, vacillating

lemes non-rigid. *Awaké *, arang dahar.* He was weak from lack of food. *Jèn ndjogèd tangané * banget.* Her hand motions in the dance are very gentle. *Mertégané *.* The butter is soft(ened). *kulit ** supple leather. **ke*en** excessively flexible *etc.* (*as above*). *Olèhé ngliwet kakéhan banju segané dadi ke*en.* She put so much water in the rice it was mushy. **ng/di*aké** *or* **ng/di*i** to cause sth to be flexible *etc.* *Aku mudun perlu mlaku*[2] *ng*aké suku.* I got off [the bus] to stretch my legs. *ng*aké otot*[2] to limber up the muscles

lèmèt thin and flat

lemèt a dessert of shredded cassava and coconut with brown sugar, steamed in a banana leaf

lemi seed bed of soil with compost. ***ǹ** soil-and-compost mixture. **ng/di*ǹi** to raise [seedlings] in the above

lempat *rg var of* LUMPUT

lempé ***-*** exhausted, ready to drop

lèmpèng 1 a thin flat object; counting unit for such objects. *wesi sa** a sheet of iron. *blabag sa** a board. 2 sweet pancake. ** legendar* ground-rice pancake. ** téla* cassava pancake. **ng*** resembling a pancake

lempèng the portion of the side above the pelvic bone. **ng/di*** *rg* to nurse, suckle

lempeng (*or* **ng***) straight, unbending, unswerving. **ng/di*aké** to straighten sth out

lèmpèr 1 large flat bowl for cooking. 2 unable to walk because of a physical defect

lemper a banana-leaf wrapped snack consisting of a glutinous-rice patty shell filled with meat

lempèt **ng*** [of the belly] flat; concave. **ng/di*aké** to flatten *or* pull in [the stomach]

lempit ***an** way of folding; folded. *klambi *an* folded clothing. *Gendéra *ané adu padon.* Flags are folded corner-to-corner. **k(e)*** 1 to get folded accidentally. 2 to get forgotten/overlooked. **ng/di*** to fold for smn; to have sth folded. **ng/di*(i)** 1 to fold. *Lajangé di* dilebokaké ing amplop.* She folded the letter and put it in an envelope. 2 *slang* to sell in order to raise cash

lémpoh 1 crippled. 2 too tired to walk. * **ng·ider·i djagat** impossible

lempujang a certain medicinal herb

lempuk an edible freshwater fish

lempung 1 clay. 2 constipation. ***en** constipated

lemu *ng,* **lema** *kr* 1 fat, fleshy, sleek. 2 luxuriant, flourishing. ***n̂** fertilizer. **ke*n̂** excessively fat. **ng/di·le*** to fatten sth (up). **ng/di*k̂aké** to make fat. *nglemokaké awak* to put on weight; *fig* to rest up, take some time off. **ng*n̂i** [of babies, during their first year] to begin to put on flesh. *** ginuk²** immensely fat

lemud mosquito

lèn *sbst kr for* LON

léna 1 off guard. *Bareng tak kira ḍèwèké *, aku bandjur mlebu ing kamar alon².* When I thought she wasn't watching, I sneaked into the room. *Ḍèwèké ora tau *.* She was always on the alert. 2 *ltry* death; dead; to die. *Jitna juwana, * kena.* Be careful and live; be careless and die. **ka*n** 1 to die through lack of alertness. 2 subconscious, unintentional. *See also* PRALÉNA

lénang *rg var of* LANANG

lenḍah valley

lénḍang *var of* SLÉNḌANG

lénḍé ***an** 1 back rest; chair back. 2 to lean against, rest one's back against. *lingguh lénḍéjan wit* to sit leaning against a tree. ***-*** to lean [against]. **-* nang saka* to lean against a pillar. **ng/di*n̂i** to lean against. *Olèhé linggih adja nglènḍèni aku ta.* Don't sit leaning against me!

lènḍèh *var of* LÉNḌÉ

lènḍèt *rg var of* LÉNḌÉ

lèndjèh (*or* ***an**) having flexible standards; undiscriminating; fickle, inconstant

lendjer stem, stalk

lénḍot ***an** *or* **ng*i** to lean (on), hang (onto)

léndra an edible ocean fish (*sms* WÉNDRA)

lenḍut mud, clay, ooze

lèng 1 hole, opening. 2 (*or* ***-***) obscure source of important *or* useful things. *Wong mau baut dedagangan tur wis ngerti *-*é.* He's an astute businessman and knows where the profits lie. ***-*an** 1 nostril; ear opening; eye of a needle. 2 having hole(s). *Koṭaké *-*an.* The box has a hole (*or* holes) in it. **nge*** 1 to live in, *or* enter, a hole, cave, *etc.* 2 to make a hole. 3 in a hole *or* hollow. *Mripaté nge* banget.* Her eyes are deep-set. **nge/di*i** 1 to make a hole in. 2 to hole up in, use as one's hole. *Bolonganė di*i semut.* The hole was occupied by ants.

leng *rpr* a departure. *Kok lunga mak * tanpa pamit.* He up and left without saying goodbye! **nge/di*aké** to concentrate on, focus the attention on. *See also* PELENG

lenga *ng,* **lisah** *kr* oil. **(le)*n** to apply oil to the hair. **ng*** oily. **ng/di*ni** to apply oil *or* grease to. *kaja welut di*ni* untrustworthy. *** m·ambu** kerosene. *** batjin** rancid oil from residue of shredded coconut. *** ḍebus** *rg* kerosene; petroleum. *** ḍempel** castor oil. *** ḍepus** *sms* ***** ḌEBUS. *** djarak** castor oil. *** djawa** coconut oil. *** djlantah** coconut oil reused for frying. *** gamblong/gamplong** coconut oil of inferior quality. *** gas** 1 kerosene. 2 gasoline. *** giling** commercially processed frying oil. *** gurih** homemade frying oil. *** (kaju) putih** cajuput oil. *** kastroli** castor oil. *** kasturi** fragrant oil extracted from flower seeds. *** pabrik** factory-processed frying oil. *** pèt** *or* *** pétroli** kerosene; petroleum. *** putih** cajuput oil. *** tjatjab** hair oil. *** tjèlèng** coconut oil remaining in the bowl of an earthenware lamp that has been used for ritual purposes

lengar *see* BAṬUK

léngé, lengé ***-*** sluggish, torpid

lèngèk ***-*** to hold the head up high

lengen 1 arm (including the hand). *Ulané geḍéné sa*.* The snake was as big around as an arm. 2 sleeve. ***an** 1 sleeve. 2 artificial arm. **ané bonéka* doll's arm. **le*** dependable *or* trusted person

lenger ***-*** 1 motionless; speechless. 2 fed up, disgusted

lenggah 1 to sit (*ki for* LUNGGUH). 2 place where one lives *or* is usually to be found (*ki for* ANGGON, ENGGON)

lenggak ***-*** 1 to turn the face up and down. 2 to sit relaxed and idle. **k(e)*** 1 to fall face up. 2 to have a stiff neck from moving the face up and down. **ng*** 1 to look up. 2 (*psv* **di***) to move [the head] so that the face looks up

lénggang [of walking gait] swaying; swinging the arms

lenggang long and slender and tapering

lenggèk ***-*** to undergo death throes

lénggok **lénggak-*** to wriggle, squirm

lénggot ***-*** *or* ***an** reluctant

lengguk *var of* LENGGUT

lenggut ***-*** *or* **lenggat-*** [of head] to sway rhythmically as the body moves. *Sing nunggang gadjah lingguh *-*.* The elephant rider swayed with the elephant's motions. *ndjogèd *-** to dance with the head moving back and forth on a horizontal plane without turning the face

lengis 1 smooth, slippery. 2 having some

distance between. *Jèn nenandur sarwa *, lumrahé tandurané bakal dadi.* If you don't plant them too close together, chances are they'll flourish. 3 a certain slender hibiscus tree whose wood is used for lances. ***-*** slim, slender

lengkap complete, full. **ng/di*aké** to complete for smn. *A ng*aké lamaranku.* A filled out my application for me. **ng/di*i** to complete, fill out. *Kanggo ng*i lamarané ḍèké kudu nglampiri pas foto loro.* To complete his application, he has to enclose two passport photos.

lèngkèt (*or* **l·um·èngkèt**) stuck (to). ** banget karo ibuné* tied to his mother's apron strings. *Wong² désa isih lumèngkèt gugon tuhon.* Villagers still adhere to superstitions.

léngkok ***-*** *or* **léngkak-*** *or* **ng*** 1 unwilling, reluctant. 2 full of curves. *Dalané *-*.* The road winds.

léngkot *var of* LÉNGKOK

lengkung ***-*** tall and slender. *ḍuwur *-** uncommonly tall

lengong **lengang-*** to gaze vacantly

lèngsèr 1 utensil for holding or carrying dishes (*e.g.* tray, saucer). 2 betel-leaf box lid. 3 hard flat stone. 4 to slide, shift. 5 to withdraw humbly from the presence of a highly esteemed person. **ng* malam** to melt down wax for re-use (in batik-making). **ng* pola** 1 to assume a humble attitude when withdrawing from smn exalted. 2 to slide a pattern under fabric in order to transfer it to the fabric (in batik-making). **ng/di*(i)** to put onto, *or* transport with, a tray. *Piringé bandjur di*.* She cleared the table with a tray. *ng*i wédang* to put the tea on a tray. **ng/di*i** to withdraw from humbly (as above). *ng*i ramané* to leave the presence of one's father. **l·um·èngsèr** to withdraw humbly

lenguk ***-*** (to sit) by oneself taking it easy

lenjap *oj* gone, removed, vanished

lènjèd squashed, flattened. **ng/di*i** to flatten, squash

lènjèh blistered

lenjep *var of* LENJAP

léno *rpr* scooping. *Ḍèké ndjupuk adonan semèn mak * bandjur dibobokké nang témbok.* He took a big scoop of mortar and slapped it on the wall.

lénsā lens. ** tjekung* concave lens. ** tjembung* convex lens

lénṭang *rg var of* LONṬANG

lenṭé ***-*** *or* **ng*** worn out, exhausted

lènṭèng *rg var of* LONṬANG

lentéra lamp, lantern. ** gas/listrik/lisah* gas/electric/oil lamp. ** laut* lighthouse light

lentjânâ emblem, badge; slogan-bearing pin

lentjeng straight, direct, without turnings

lentjer *var of* LENTJENG

lentjir attractively slim and tall. ** kuning* tall and fair-skinned. **ng*** excessively tall and thin

lèntjung soft foul bird *or* chicken dung

lèntrèng **ng/di*** to spread thin, press flat

lentreng ***-*** to saunter, stroll

lentrih ***-*** (to walk) with a plodding, labored gait. **ng*** emaciated; without strength *or* spirit; dreary

lentruk **lentrak-*** *or* **ng*** apathetic, listless

lenṭuk ***-*** to keep nodding *or* rolling the head

lenṭung *var of* LANṬUNG

léo male lion

lep *rpr* submerging. *Ḍèké slulup *.* He dove under. **me*** to overflow

lépa a mixture for filling *or* patching. **ng/di*** to apply such a mixture

lépak ***-*** metal box for storing tobacco or betel

lepas 1 detached, loose(ned); to let go (of). *Roḍané *.* The wheel came loose. *ngepit * setang* to ride a bicycle no-handed. 2 off and on; temporary. *Buruh kuwi ana sing adjeg, ana sing *.* There are permanent laborers and casual laborers. **ka*an** to get hit by [a flying missile]. **ng/di*(aké)** to let loose, release, let fly. *Kok *ké, tak sauté.* You let go of it and I'll grab it. *ng*aké pélor* to shoot a bullet. **ng/di*i** to shoot many missiles *or* shoot missiles repeatedly; to hit smn with a missile. *di*i (ing) panah* struck by an arrow. **l·um·epas** loose; released

lepat wrong; mistaken; to miss (*kr for* LUPUT; *kr for* SALAH?)

lepèh, lèpèh ***an** food that has been chewed and then spit out. **ng/di*** to spit out [sth one has chewed]

lèpèk small saucer

lèpèn river (*kr for* KALI)

lepet a snack made of glutinous rice wrapped in a young coconut leaf

lépja (*or* ***n**) to forget (*rg kr for* LALI). **k(e)*n** 1 to have sth slip one's mind. 2 to get overlooked/forgotten

lépra leprosy. ***nen** to have/get leprosy

lèr north (*kr for* LOR). ***-*an** left exposed *or* untended. **ke*-ke*** to get left exposed. *Semangkané kelèr², dirubung laler.* The watermelon was left out and flies swarmed around it. **nge/di*** to expose, leave out. *Krupuké adja di*, mengko mlempem.* Don't leave the shrimp chips uncovered or they'll get limp. *Djariké *en bèn énggal garing.* Open out the fabric so it'll dry fast. *nge* wadi* to disclose a secret. **p(a)*an 1** a spread-out layer. **2** a rice paddy ready for planting

ler 1 stick, stalk, strand; counting unit for stick-shaped objects; *fig* trace, thread. *wulu sak eler* one feather. *ngrokok rong puluh ** to smoke twenty cigarettes. *Ilang *ing kagunan kang asli.* It has lost all traces of esthetic appeal. **2** *rpr* dozing off. *Lagi waé mak * kok ana tilpun.* I was just dozing off when the phone rang. **3** *rpr* a whisking motion. *Rambuté didudut mak *.* He pulled out one hair. *Botjahé diajun mak *.* She swung the child in a swing. **lar-* 1** to keep dozing off. *Lar-* ngantuk banget.* He was so sleepy he kept dozing. **2** to keep making whisking motions. ***-*an 1** in the form of stalks/strands. *Rokoké *-*an apa bungkusan?* Are the cigarettes loose or in packs? **2** overpoweringly sleepy. **nge/di*** to pull, snatch; *slang* to steal. *nge* rambut (benang, tali, lsp.)* to pull a hair (thread, rope, *etc.*). *nge* ḍompèt* to snatch smn's wallet. *Ḍèké terus ngeler-eler panganan.* He keeps snitching cookies. **sa*an** a nap. *turu sa*an* to catch a nap. *See also* ANGLER

lérab ***-*** *or* **ng*** to sparkle, glitter. **sa*an** (at) a quick glance. **l·um·érab** to sparkle, glitter. *See also* KLÉRAB

lérah ***-*** red, gory. **-* metu getihé* bleeding gorily

lerak a small hard round fruit used to produce suds for washing batik

léré *rpr* slipping, skidding. *Weluté mak * útjul.* The eel slipped free. ***-*** a gamelan melody played during the first part of a shadow play. **léra-*** *syllables chanted in a children's song*

lereb 1 to subside. *Nesuné *.* His anger cooled down. *Ora suwé udané *.* Soon the rain let up. *Geniné saiki wis *.* The fire is going out now. **2** to stay overnight (*ki for* NG·INEP). **3** to stop, take a rest (*ki for* LÈRÈN). **ng/di*aké** to cause to subside. *Dajaning udan bisa ng*aké bledug.* The heavy rain has laid the dust. **pa*an** place to rest; stopover (*ki for* PA·NG·INEP·AN)

lèrèg to turn *or* tend (toward). *Lakuné wis * ngétan.* He turned his steps eastward. *Kang kaja mengkono mau *é bisa ndjalari sengit.* That sort of thing tends to create resentment. ***an 1** a drawer. **2** able to shift. *lawang *an* sliding door. **ng*** to shift position, slide in a certain direction. *ng*ing mripat* the shifting of her eyes. *Olèhé ngadeg kabèh paḍa ng* ngiwa.* Please all stand a bit more to the left. **ng/di*aké** to shift the position/direction of. *Setroliné gantung iki kena di*aké munggah muḍun.* This hanging oil lamp can be moved up and down. *Lemariné di*aké nang podjokan kamar.* They pushed the cupboard to the corner of the room. **l·um·èrèg** *sms* NG* *above*

lèrèh 1 to rest (up). **2** to abdicate; to relinquish [the throne]. ***-*** streaked, *esp.* with blood. **ka*an** [a monarch's] subject; subordinate. **ng/di*i 1** to calm smn down. **2** to discharge smn. *Merga korupsi A di*i.* A was fired for corruption.

lèrèk ***-*** striped, streaked. *klambi putih *-* idjo* a white shirt with green stripes. **ng/di*** to make a slit. *ng* amplop* to slit open an envelope. **ng/di*aké** to make stripes/streaks on sth

lerem having settled down. *Atiné *.* Her heart was at peace now. *Bareng wis bengi lan * kabèh...* When evening came and everything had quieted down.. *Prajoga * ḍisik ana ponḍokku.* You'll be better off rooming with me. **ng/di*aké** to calm smn down; to settle sth

lèrèn *ng,* **kèndel** *kr,* **lereb** *ki* to stop, take a rest, discontinue an activity. *tanpa ** without letup. ** omong* to stop talking. *Perangé *.* The war came to an end. *Ḍèké * setengah gawé.* He quit with the job only half done. *Dikon * seḍéla.* He told them to take a break. ** nang ngisor wit* to rest under a tree. *Ana Singgapur kono * seḍélok.* There was a brief stopover at Singapore. *Bijungé kok ora ana *é ta.* Mothers *never* get any time off. *Pabriké *.* The factory shut down. *Présiḍèn sing wis * kena dipilih manèh.* A former President may be elected again. ***an** stopping place; place to rest. *Ora nganggo *an ing dalan.* He didn't stop to rest along the way. **ng/di*aké 1** to bring to a stop(ping place). *Tunggangané di*aké.*

He parked the car. *Truk mau ng*aké mo-motané.* The truck delivered the goods to their destination. 2 to cause sth to stop *or* rest. *Truk mau manḍeg perlu ng*aké me-siné.* The truck stopped to let the engine cool. **ng/di*i** 1 to stop sth. *ng*i anggoné udud* to quit smoking. 2 to stop at/for. *Rumah makan iki di*i bis² Djakarta.* The Djakarta buses stop at this restaurant. *Mon-toré ng*i wong sing arep nunut.* The car stopped for the hitchhiker. 3 to discharge *or* suspend smn. **p(a)*an** stopping place; place to rest

lèrèng [fabric which is] patterned with diagonal stripes

lèrès **ng/di*** to cut (into) [sth soft]. *Gudiré di*.* She cut the gelatine.

leres 1 direction, aim (*kr for* ARAH, NER). 2 right, correct (*opt kr for* BENER). 3 right at [a place] (*opt kr for* PENER)

lèrèt **(sa)*an** (at) a brief glance

lèri *var of* LORI

leri water in which rice has been washed before cooking. *** bungkak** first rice-washing water (often used medicinally)

léro **léra-*** [of eyes] to shift from side to side

lérob **ng/di*i** to skim sth from the surface (of). *Lengané katon nuli di*i.* The oil rises and is skimmed off.

lérod **ng/di*i** to scrape off one's plate with the hands

lérok ***an** a sidelong glance. **ng/di*i** to steal a look at. *See also* PLÉROK

lérong **lérang-*** streak marks. **ng/di*i** to mark with streaks

lèrwèh careless; forgetful

lès 1 (to take) a training course. *Aku * ba-sa Inggris.* I'm taking English. 2 reins, bridle. ***an** 1 (*or* ***-*an**) target; *fig* scape-goat. *Lésané tak pasang.* I set up the [archery] target. *Ali dadi lésan nang omah, bola-bali disalahké waé.* Ali is the fall guy at home–he gets the blame for everything. 2 (*or* ***-*an**) to take target practice; to use as a target. **-*an djeruk sing gemanḍul nèng uwit* to throw things at a tangerine that is hanging from a tree. 3 *gram* object. *lésan nanḍang/pinurih* direct/indirect object. **nge/di*(i)** 1 to teach, tutor. *nge*i basa Djerman* to give German lessons. 2 to aim (at). 3 to hit, strike

les *rpr* falling asleep. *Olèhku turu mak *.* I went right to sleep. **las-*** to go to sleep easily. *Jèn turu las-* waé.* I always drop right off. ***-*an** to feel oneself losing consciousness, through sleep *or* faintness

lésan 1 mouth (*md for* TJANGKEM). 2 oral. *wangsulan ** an oral reply. *udjian ** oral exmination. 3 *form of* LÈS

lèsèh ***an** to sit on the floor/ground. **ng/di*** to scatter on the ground

lesmèn *var of* LOSMÈN

lestantun *kr for* LESTARI

lestari *ng*, **lestantun** *kr* to keep on, remain, endure. *Olèhmu bebodjoan muga² bisa * te-kan kakèn² ninèn².* May your marriage last through your old age. *Uripku * atut-runtut.* Our life together was always harmonious. *Wong² Tengger isih * dedunung ing Tengger nganti sepréné.* To this day, the Tenggerese people remain in the Tengger area. *isih * urip* still alive. **ning bebrajan lan * djinisé* the perpetuation of society and of the race. **ng/di*kaké** to continue, perpetuate, keep in effect. *Paseduluran antarané kowé lan ḍèké betjik dilestarèkaké.* You ought to maintain friendly relations with him. *ka-nggo nglestarèkaké lelabuhané* in order to perpetuate the memory of his public service

lèstrik *var of* LISTRIK

lèstris *var of* LISTRIK

lesu 1 listless. 2 *rg* hungry. ***n̂** to lie down to rest. **ka*n̂** starved; starving. *wong ka-leson* a starving man. **ng*n̂i** to feel weak during convalescence. **pa*n̂** a place to lie down and rest

lesung a broad shallow wooden bowl in which rice is pounded to separate the hull from the grain

lésus whirlwind; cyclone

lèt *rpr* a brush stroke. **lat-*** (to make) repeated brush strokes. *See also* LÈLÈT

let interval of time *or* space; after (an interval of). ** wetara* or *wetara ** for/after (an interval of). ** rong dina* two days later. *Omahé * patang omah karo omahku.* Her house is four doors away from mine. ***-*** sth used as a partition or separator. **-* ka-mar* room divider. **-* buku* book mark. **ke*an** to get divided/separated (by). *Omah-ku ke*an kali karo omahé.* There's a river between his house and mine. **nge/di*i** to put an interval between. *Apik di*i sedina.* Better let it wait a day. *Pada mau kanggo ngelet-eleti angka Djawa.* This punctuation mark is used for separating off Javanese numerals. **ora * suwé** soon, before long

let. *see* LÉTNAN
let. da. *see* LÉTNAN
let. djen. *see* LÉTNAN
lețek dirty. **le*** dirt, filth. *le*ing djagad* the scum of the earth, the dregs of society
leteng stale, rancid
lètèr flat, smooth, level. **ng*** [of dance movements] graceful, smooth. **ng/di*(aké)** to make level/smooth
lèter 1 letter of the alphabet. 2 large-lettered writing. **ng/di*i** to write letters on
leter **ng*** absorbed, engrossed
lètersèter typesetter
lètjèk loose in its setting. *Sekrupé iki wis *; jèn dikerasi ora gelem kentjeng, mung mubeng waé.* The screw has worked its way loose and can't be tightened–it just goes around.
lètjèt bruised
let. kol. *see* LÉTNAN
létnan, lètnan (*abbr*: **let.**) lieutenant. *** djéndral** (*abbr*: **let. djen.**) lieutenant general. *** dua** (*abbr*: **let. da.**) second lieutenant. *** kolonel** (*abbr*: **let. kol.**) lieutenant colonel. *** tu** (*abbr*: **let. tu.**) first lieutenant
léțo *rpr* scooping up sth soft. *Olèhé ndjupuk sambel lotis mak *.* He took a large helping of the hot sauce.
léțok a large amount of sth soft. *sambel sa** a big helping of hot sauce. **ng/di*i** to smear with sth soft. *Rainé botjah² di*i nganggo bleṭok.* The children's faces were covered with mud.
léțong *inf var of* TLÉṬONG
létré *var of* LÈNTRÈNG
lètrèk *var of* LÈNTRÈNG
let. tu. *see* LÉTNAN
letuh 1 dirty, muddy. 2 obscene; pornographic
leveransir supplier
léwa **le*** 1 coy pretense. 2 to put on a coy act
lèweg *rpr* a sharp object striking a soft object. *Kampaké ngenani tjèlèng mak *.* The axe struck the boar. **léwag-*** to strike [a soft object] *or* scoop up [sth soft] repeatedly
lha *var sp of* LA 1
lhó *var sp of* LO 2
libur (to have) a holiday, time off. *dina ** a holiday. *Sésuk aku *.* I'm off tomorrow. *Sekolahané *.* There's no school. ***an** 1 vacation (time). 2 free, having time off. *dina *an* a day off
lid central idea. **ing dongèng* the theme of the story. **nge/di*aké** to explicate (the theme of)
liḍah 1 animal tongue (as food). *iwak ** beef tongue; sole (sea fish). ** gangsa* baked tongue. *semur ** stewed beef tongue. 2 tongue (*ki for* ILAT). 3 (*or, ltry, *-* or* **le***) (flash of) lightning. *** s·in·ambung** to spread by word of mouth. *Kabaré dadi * sinambung.* The rumor spread like wildfire.
liḍas [of tongue, lips] rough, coarse, chapped
liḍi *oj* coconut-leaf rib
liḍis *rg var of* LEḌIS
lidok (to tell) an untruth
lift (*prn* **lip**) elevator. *tukang ** elevator operator
liga ***n** unsheathed. *pedang *n* a naked sword. **ng*** 1 not wearing a shirt. *Jèn panas pénaké ng*.* It feels good to go without a shirt when it's hot. 2 (*psv* **di***) to unsheathe
lih ***an** to change places. *Saiki lijan, aku linggih kana kowé kéné.* Now let's change places: I'll sit there and you sit here. **nge*** 1 to move, change residence. 2 (*psv* **di***) to move sth from one place to another. *See also* ALIH
lija *ng,* **sanès** *kr* other, different. *wong ** another person; smn else. *ana ing * papan* smw else. *Omongané * karo tumindaké.* His words are at variance with his actions. *Ora mung kuwi baé, nanging akèh *né.* That's not the only one; there are many others. *botjah *né sidji* one of the other boys. *wong telu *né* the other three people. ** saka iku* other than that. *antara ** among others; among other things. ***n** 1 another; others. *Barang iki duwèking *n.* This belongs to somebody else. *Adja sok ngrasani *n.* Never gossip about others. 2 *var sp of* LIH·AN. *lan *-*né* and other similar ones; and so on (*see also* LAN). *médja kursi lan piranti *-*né ing omah* tables, chairs, and other household equipment. **ng*** to have changed one's attitude, *esp.* to have become indifferent *or* hostile. *Kena apa kok A saiki ng*?* How come A isn't friendly any more? **sa*né** besides, other than. *sa*né iki* other than this. **ora * (mung)** none other than, nothing (else) but. *Ora * mung njangoni slamet.* I can only wish you well. *See also* KEMLIJA
lijep ***an** [of refined puppets' eye shape] long and gracefully narrow. ***-*** heavy-lidded.

*Ḍèké *-* arep turu.* He's about to drop off to sleep. **ng*** closing the eyes in sleep. *Ḍèké durung nganti bisa ng* turu.* He hasn't quite dropped off to sleep. **sa*an** (to take) a brief nap

lijer * **1** that which has been seized. *Toko iki *ané para pegawéné.* This store has been taken over by the employees. 2 an exchange item. *barang *an* pawned article. *Beras iki *an saka montor.* I got this rice in exchange for a car. 3 newly assigned tour of duty. ***-*** drowsy. **-* keturon.* He dozed off. **ng*** **1** lulled, stupefied. 2 (*psv* **di***) to seize, take possession of. 3 (*psv* **di***) to oust from a job; to transfer to another job. *A di* merga korupsi.* A was ousted for being corrupt. *A ng* B nang Sumatra.* A transferred B to Sumatra. 3 to exchange; to use as a medium of exchange. **ng/di*aké** to pass along [a task]. *ng*aké gawéjané nang kantjané* to shift one's work over to a co-worker

lijong *var of* LÉJONG

liju:r ***-*** to move (bend, bounce) flexibly; to sway insecurely

liju:t *var of* LIJUR

lik 1 little (*shf of* TJILIK). **2** *adr* little boy (*shf of* KELIK)

likat (*or* **w***) shoulder blade. ***en** (to have *or* get) a muscular cramp

liku ***-*** *or* **lika-*** complex, many-faceted. **-*né persoalan* the various facets of the problem. *Koruptor kuwi pinter lika-*.* Corrupt people are full of schemes. *lika-*né wong urip kuwi* the ways in which people go about getting what they need

likuk **likak-*** winding, full of curves

likur twenty- (*as a digit in numbers*). *s(e)** 21. *ro** 22. *telu** 23. *pat** 24. *nem** 26. *pitu** 27. *wolu** 28. *sanga** 29. ***-*an** in the twenties. *Omahé nomer *-*an.* His house number is in the twenties. *Umuré lagi *-*an.* He's in his twenties. **s(e)*an 1** to hold a celebration on the 21st of the fasting month (*Pasa*). 2 (to play) a certain card game. *See also* NG- (*prefix*) 6, 7

likwiḍasi liquidation of assets

likwiḍir **ng/di*** to liquidate [assets]

lila 1 willing(ness). *Rasané ora *.* She felt reluctant. 2 violet (color). **k(a)*n** to have permission. *Aku wis ka*n.* I've been given permission. **ka*na** allow me; may I have your permission...? *Kawula kalilāna njuwun priksa...* I would like to ask you... *Abdidalem kelilāna mundjuk...* Allow me to call your attention to the fact that... **ng/di*kaké** to accept with resignation. *Pité sing ilang saiki wis di*kaké.* He's given up now on his lost bicycle. **ng/di*ni** to allow, approve. *di*ni sakdurungé* approved in advance. * **legawa** wholehearted gratitude *or* pleasure

lilah permission, approval. *awèh (olèh, diparingi) ** to give (receive, be given) permission. **ng/di*i** to give permission to. **pa*** *sms* *

Lilahi God (*var of* ALLAH). *pepesṭèn ** ordained by God

lilih calmed down. *Wis * atiné.* He's not upset any longer. **ng/di*aké** to calm smn

lilin 1 candle. *njumed ** to light a candle. 2 wax (*kr for* MALAM). **ka*** **1** to be overcome. *Ala mesṭi ka* karo betjik.* Evil always succumbs to good. 2 devoted, attached. **ng/di*** to coat with wax. * **ès 1** paraffin. 2 popsicle. * **pèt** popsicle

liling **ng/di*** to amuse/entertain [a baby]

lilir ***an** to be a light sleeper; to wake up easily *or* often. **ng*** to wake up during the normal sleeping time. *Aku ng* djam loro ésuk bandjur ora bisa turu manèh.* I woke up at 2 A.M. and couldn't get back to sleep. *Ng*² bareng wis awan.* He didn't wake up till afternoon. **ng*an** *sms* *AN

lilis neatly groomed

lilit **ng/di*** to twist, wind around. * **uwi** rope that is twisted like a turnip vine

lim glue, paste. **nge/di*** to glue *or* paste sth

lima *ng*, **gangsal** *kr* five. *sèket ** 35. *djam ** five o'clock. *buku ** five books. ***las** 15. ***n** 5-rupiah bill. ***-*** by fives. *Lungguhé *-*.* They sat in groups of five. ***-*né** all five of them. **le*** **(gangsal** *kr***)** group *or* unit of five. *Wong le* paḍa ngrubung montoré.* The five men surrounded the car. **di*ni** to be set upon by five people. **ka*** **1** (*or* **[ka]ping ***) five times; times five; (for) the fifth time; fifth in a series. *bab kaping ** chapter five. *gambar sing ka** the fifth picture. 2 *ng kr* fifth month of the Javanese year (12 October-9 November). **ka* tengah** $4\frac{1}{2}$. **ka* sasur** 45. **ng/di*ni 1** to form a group of five. *Ḍèké tuku sénḍok sidji nggo ng*ni.* She bought one spoon to complete a set of five. 2 to hold a ceremony for [a woman in the fifth month of pregnancy]. *See also* -AN (*suffix*) 8, 15, 16; -É[c] (*suffix*) 9; LIMANG; NG- (*prefix*) 6, 7; PRA-

liman elephant (*kr?, ltry kr for* GADJAH)

limang *ng* five (*as modifier: see also* LIMA). * *djam* (*minggu, rupiah, lsp.*) five hours (weeks, rupiahs, *etc.*). * *atus* (*èwu, juta*) five hundred (thousand, million). *See also* NG- (*prefix*) 6, 7

limasan upper section of a four-section roof. *omah* * house with a four-sectioned roof

limbak *var of* LÉMBAK

limbang (*or* **le***) mate; marriage partner. **le*an** consideration, reflection. *bahan le*-an* food for thought. **ng/di*** 1 to pour (out). 2 to wash out [the eye] with a medicated solution. 3 to consider, weigh

limeng **(le)*an** *intsfr* dark. *peteng ndedet le*an* pitch dark. *Langit mendung le*an.* The sky was completely overcast. **ke*an** to forget (*ki for* LALI). **pa*an** dark place. *ing pa*an* in the dark

limit worn smooth

limpa spleen. *iwak* * beef spleen (as food)

limpad learned, *esp.* in mystic lore. *pendita sing* * an erudite holy man

limpé **k(e)*** off guard. *ngentèni k*né* waiting to catch them unawares. **ng/di*** to sneak up on, take by surprise. **ng/di*kaké** to do sth to smn stealthily. *Bijungé lagi turu dilimpèkaké.* He sneaked out on his mother while she was asleep.

limpung 1 a short two-headed spear. 2 (*or* **limpang-***) a snack of fried sweet potato

limput **k(e)*** easily tempted. **k(e)*an** to get encompassed *or* surrounded. *Panguripané tansah ka*an ing was²*. They are perpetually plagued with worries. **ng/di*i** to encompass. *Samodra iku ng*i saindenging bawana iku.* The continents are entirely surrounded by water. *Ulahraga anjar mau ng*i wargané negara² Inggris.* The new sport has spread throughout the English-speaking countries. *Rasa sedih ng*i atiné.* Grief filled her heart. *Konperènsi mau muga² ng*i negara² Afrika.* It is hoped that the conference will take in the African countries. *pranatan anjar kang ng*i bangsa Indonesia kabèh* a new regulation that applies to all Indonesians. *Ana mogok gedèn² ng*i buruh rong juta.* There is a vast strike involving two million workers.

limrah usual, ordinary (*kr for* LUMRAH)

limun 1 a citrus-flavored carbonated soft drink. * *krus* lemon crush. 2 fog, mist, haze. ***an** hazy, blurred, misty. **le*an** invisibility. *adji le*an* magical power to become invisible. **ka*an** 1 darkness. *ing ka*an* in the dark. 2 to have sth slip one's mind. **pa-ng*an** *sms* LE*AN

limut **k(e)*an** to have sth slip one's mind

lin 1 line. * *tilpun* telephone line. * *udara* airline. * (*h*)*ubungan* line of communication. 2 ribbon

lin- *see also under* L- (*Introduction, 3.1.7*)

lina *ltry* dead; to die (*var of* LÉNA)

lindes *rg var of* TLINDES

lindi *var of* LINDRI

lindih *oj* **k(e)*** overcome, defeated. **ke* pikir·é** not very intelligent

lindjak ***-*** to move up and down; to bounce

lindjek ***-*** to walk with heavily pounding footsteps

lindri [of eyes] beautifully shaped. *See also* GETUK

lindu earthquake

linduk deserted; haunted. **pa*an** a lonely *or* spooky place

lindung **ng/di*aké** *or* **ng/di*i** to shelter, protect, cover. *Durung ana kang bakal ditudju kanggo ng*aké badané.* She had nowhere to go for shelter. *di*i undang²* protected by the law. **p(a)*an** shelter, protection; a fallout shelter

lindur **(le)*an** to talk in one's sleep. **ng*an** to talk in one's sleep habitually

lingga *gram* root, *i.e.* unaffixed form. *dwi* * doubled root. **ka* dina** with a day's lapse

linggih to sit (*ng-kr var of ng* LUNGGUH)

linggis sharp-bladed iron crowbar, used *esp.* for prying off coconut shells. **ng/di*** to pry *or* dig with the above

lingguh to sit (*ng-kr var of ng* LUNGGUH)

lingi (*or* **w***) a certain grass

lingir edge. * *médja* edge of a table. **ng*** to have edges

lingkungan surroundings, environment

linglap **ke*** to get lost/mislaid

lingling *var of* LILING

linglung absent-minded, mixed up, rushing around confused

lingsa louse egg. *nggolèki * sumlempit* to criticize, carp, find fault. *pada* * comma

lingsang (*or* **w***) a marten-like animal

lingsem ashamed, embarrassed (*opt kr? ki? for* ISIN). **k(e)*** overcome with shame. **ng*aké** embarrassing

lingsir the period around 3 P. M. when the sun is about halfway through its western descent. *ing wajah* * in mid-afternoon.

Srengéngéné wis *. The sun is in mid-descent. **ka*** to reach the above point in the day. *Mangané ḍokoh, merga wis ka**. He ate hungrily; it was way past lunch time. **l·um·ingsir** *ltry var of* *. * **bengi** the period from midnight to pre-dawn. * **kulon** *sms* *. *Wis wajah * kulon.* It's mid-afternoon already. * **wengi** *sms* * BENGI. * **wétan** the period around 9 A.M., when the sun is about halfway through its eastern ascent. *Isih wajah * wétan.* It's only mid-morning. **wis * umur·é** past middle age

linguistik̄ linguistics

linguk **lingak-*** to look to right and left

lini *see* GARIS

lintah leech. * **ḍarat** moneylender

lintang 1 star. 2 *sbst kr for* LIJA. (*ngèlmu*) **pa*an** astronomy. * **alih·(an)** *or* * **ng·alih** falling star, meteor, comet. * **Bima Sekti** the Milky Way. * **blaḍo** morning star. * **Gubug-Pèntjèng** the Southern Cross. * **k·em·ukus** comet. * **landjar-ṅg·kirim** morning star. * **rina** morning star. * **wluku** Orion. * **Wuluh** the Pleiades

linting ***an** rolled up, in the form of a roll. **an iwak* fish rolls. **ng/di*** to roll [tobacco]. *ng* rokok* to roll a cigarette. *See also* LINṬING

linṭing **k(e)*** to get rolled up. **ng*** to form a roll. *Kertasé kuwi jèn kena banju bandjur ng**. If the paper gets wet it curls up. **ng/di*(i)** to roll sth up. *Berasé di*i nganggo goḍong geḍang kluṭuk.* She rolled the rice up in banana leaves. *See also* KLINṬING, LINTING

lintir **ng*** 1 to flow down(ward). 2 to receive a transferred position, *e.g.* through in-inheritance. *Sing ng* pangkaté mau jakuwi mas B.* B came into the position [which *e.g.* his father had held at the time of his death]. **ng/di*aké** to transfer [a position]. **l·um·intir** to flow ceaselessly

lintjak low bamboo bench. ***-*** to jump for joy. * **gagak** to jump in small bounds (as a contest: the winner is the one who advances the shortest distance). *See also* GAGAK

lintjek̄ *var of* LINTJAK. ***-*** *or* **lintjak-*** to jump around

lintji **lintja-*** to keep coming and going, to move to and fro

lintjip *var of* LANTJIP

lintjung soft chicken manure

lintjut embarrassed, humiliated. **k(e)*an** to be embarrassed by smn

lintreg ***-*** quivery, gelatinous

lintrik name of one of the small playing cards (*kertu tjilik*)

lintu 1 (ex)change (*kr for* IDJOL). 2 exchange item (*kr for* LIRU)

linu (to have) shooting pains

lip *var sp of* LIFT

lipenstip *var of* LIPSTIK

lipet to the *n*th power; times *n*. * *loro* times two; twice as much/many. *Rega² né saiki wis * pinḍo tinimbang tahun kepungkur.* Prices are twice as high now as they were a year ago.

lippenstip *var of* LIPSTIK

lipstik̄ lipstick

lipur good spirits. *golèk *ing ati* to try to cheer oneself up. **ng/di·(le)*** to make smn happy. *Atimu *en.* Cheer up! **pa·ng*** cheerfulness

lir 1 essence, meaning. *Aku ora ngerti apa *é sesorahé.* I don't understand what he's driving at in his speech. 2 (*or* **ng***) *ltry* like, as. ***é** in other words; the essential thing is...; what it means [is...]. * **péndah** like, as

lirab *var of* LÉRAB

lirang 1 one half of a paired set. *Jèn rong * didadèkaké sidji, djenengé setangkep.* When two sugar-cake halves are put together [with flat sides together, hamburger-bunwise] they make a paired set. *geḍang se** a bunch of bananas (which matches with a similar one opposite it on the stalk). 2 (*or* **w***) sulfur. ***an** in bunches, in halves of a pair, *etc.* (as above). *Geḍangé didol *an.* The bananas are sold by the bunch.

lirih (*or* ***-***) low, sweet-sounding, gentle. *Swarané* *. His voice was low. *nangis* * to cry softly. *Tanganku keplok²*. I applauded softly. ***-*an** in a soft manner. *Raḍioné disetèl *-*an waé.* Please keep the radio low. **ng/di*aké** to cause to be soft/gentle/sweet. *ng*aké genḍing* to play the music softly (sweetly). *Raḍioné mbok di*aké seṭiṭik.* Please turn the radio down a little. **ng/di*i** to speak softly to; to deal gently with

liri:k ***-*** striped. *djas sing *-** a striped jacket. **lirak-*** to look sideways, to look out of the corners of the eyes. **ng/di*** to see *or* look at sideways; to steal a glance. *See also* KLIRIK, PLIRIK

liring a sidelong glance

liru *ng,* **lintu** *kr* (*or* **le***) an exchange item, *esp.* goods to cancel out indebtedness. *Beras* *iki kanggo * utangku wingi.* This rice pays back what I borrowed yesterday. ***n̂(an)** item given in exchange. **lira-*** **(linta-lintu** *kr*) to (ex)change repeatedly. **k(e)*** to be exchanged inadvertently. *Apa potlodmu ora ke* karo duwèkku?* Didn't you mistake my pencil for yours? **ng/di·lira-*** to interchange. *Tembung loro mau sok dilira-*.* The two words are used interchangeably. **ng/di*k̂aké** to give in exchange for. *Sepatuné sing kegedèn dilirokaké sing luwih tjilik.* He exchanged the shoes that were too big for a smaller pair. **ng/di*(n̂i)** to give sth in exchange for. *Utangé wingi dilironi pitik loro.* She gave two chickens to pay up her indebtedness.

lirwa lack of regard; neglect. *supaja adja * ing kasusilan* in order not to overlook what is proper. **ng/di*kaké** to disregard, neglect. *ng*kaké kuwadjiban* to neglect one's duty. *Sinauné ora tau di*kaké.* He never neglects his school work.

lirwèng *contracted form of* LIRWA ING

lis 1 reins. 2 list. 3 frame, edge. **nge/di*(i)** 1 to equip with reins *or* a frame. 2 to guide [a horse] with reins

lisa *var of* LINGSA

lisah oil (*kr for* LENGA)

lisènsi license

lisir *rg var of* LINGSIR

listrik electric; electricity. *daja ** or *kekuwatan ** electric power. *gerdu ** power house, generating plant

listya *oj* beautiful; handsome

lisus *var of* LÉSUS

liter liter

liṭi **liṭa-*** to keep coming and going, move back and forth

litji:k̄ cowardly, fainthearted

litjin slippery; worn smooth

litjit *var of* KLITJIT

litjut *var of* LINTJUT

litnan *var of* LÉTNAN

liwat *ng,* **langkung** *kr* to go past; to go (by way of) (**wijos** *ki*). *wong (sing) ** a passerby. *Montoré * omah kéné.* The car went past our house. *Ora kena * kono.* You can't go that way. *Mung let seḍéla bis *.* After a short wait a bus came along. *Nalika aku nang Salatiga aku * Sala.* I went to Salatiga by way of Solo. **k(e)*** 1 to pass accidentally *or* unawares. *Olèhé mbanḍem pelem ke* nḍuwur wité.* The stone he threw at the mango went all the way over the tree! 2 [in clock time] plus, past. *djam nem k* limang menit* five minutes past six. *Sok nganti k* djam sidji lagi mulih.* Sometimes she doesn't get home till after one o'clock. **ke*(-*)** exceedingly. *Kuburan kaé angkeré ke*-*.* That cemetery is very spooky! *gawat ka*-** terribly dangerous. *Ke* geḍé (ing) atiné wong tuwa jèn anaké putus sinauné.* Parents feel immensely proud when their children graduate. **k(e)*an** to get bypassed. *Apa ana sing isih k*an olèhku njebutaké?* Is there anything I've forgotten to mention? **ng/di*** 1 to pass, go by way of. *Lakuné ng*i alas geḍé.* His travels took him past a large forest. *Kaé lo, dalan sing di*i mau kétok saka kéné.* Look—you can see the road we came on from here! 2 to exceed. *Ongkos produksiné ng*i kira² rupiah sajuta.* Production costs were over a million rupiahs. **ora *** the only thing left [is...]. *La jèn adreng temenan karepmu, ora * aku ja mung njekarep.* If you're really determined, I have no choice but to agree. *Ora * aku mung nḍèrèkaké sugeng.* I only hope you'll have a safe journey.

liwer **liwar-*** *or* **le*an** to mill around, swarm about in crowds. *Akèh botjah² le*an.* There were children everywhere. *See also* KLIWER

liwet *ng,* **beṭak** *kr* **sega *** 1 rice cooked until it has absorbed all the water placed in the pan with it. 2 *rg* rice boiled in coconut milk. ***an** boiled (as above). **ng/di*aké** to boil rice for smn. **ng/di*(i)** to boil [rice]. **pa·ng*** act of boiling rice. *Beras iki gampang pang*é.* This rice is easy to prepare (as above). **sa*an** *or* **sa·pa·ng*** length of time it takes to boil rice

liwung to drift on an air current. *alas gung* **liwang-*** dense jungle

lll. *ng,* **lss.** *kr* etc. (*see* LAN LIJA²NÉ *under* LAN)

lo 1 a certain kind of banyan tree said to harbor malevolent spirits. 2 (*prn* l̊o) *excl of surprise, warning, disapproval. Iki * delengen.* Here, look at this! *Kaé * ana pelam mateng².* Hey, there are some ripe mangoes! *Adja nesu, *.* Don't get mad! *Wah, bedja * kowé.* Wow, lucky for you! ** kok tangan kiwa!* What, using your left hand [breach of etiquette]—! **, kok kesusu kondur!* Surely you're not going home so early!

lobak white carrot

lobok loose-fitting. *Gabusé ki ketjiliken, *.*

This cork is so small it's loose in the bottle. **ke*en** excessively loose. *Kuplukku jèn di-enggo aḍik ke*en.* My cap is too big for my little brother.

loḍag to have (enough) space. *Koperku isih *.* There's still some room in my suitcase.

lodan a variety of whale

loḍang having space *or* time to spare. *Jèn *, dolana mréné.* When you're free, please visit us. *Apa motormu isih *?* Is there still room in your car? *Saiki aku wis *, udjianku rampung kabèh.* I'm off now—all my exams are finished. **ka*an** elbow room, leeway. *Aku diwènèhi ka*an telung sasi kanggo nglunasi utangku.* He allowed me three more months to pay my debt.

loḍèg *var of* LODJÈG

loḍèh a coconut-milk vegetable soup with red peppers

lodjèg loose, shaky. *Setangé *.* The handlebars are loose.

lodjèh **ng/di*** to stab, pierce

lodji large brick house. *** papak** brick *or* stone house with a flat roof

lodjok *var of* LONDJOK

lodog **ng/di*** to put a finger into a hole, *esp.* down the throat as an emetic technique

loḍoh to get damaged [of plant *or* animal tissue]. *Tangané * kesiram wédang.* His arm was scalded with boiling water.

lodong [of fruits] overripe

loḍong a covered glass jar

lodrog to spoil, rot, go bad

log **nge/di*** to swallow (*inf var of* NGE/DI·LEG)

logam metal

logat 1 speech sound, phonetic sound. 2 dialect

logika logic

logro loose, without strain. *Guluné ditalèni *.* She tied a string loosely around its neck. *Klambiné jèn dak enggo * siṭik.* His shirts are a bit large for me. *Basan wis ngombé obat watuk dadi *.* When he took the medicine, his cough was relieved.

loh fertile and well irrigated. *** djinawi** fertile and prosperous, lush. *See also* IWAK

lohor second daily prayer time (*var of* LUHUR 3)

lojan *var of* LOJANG

lojang 1 cake/cookie mold; baking sheet, shallow baking pan. 2 *rg* copper

lojo exhausted

lojop (*or* **ng***) [of sleepy eyes] nearly closing, hard to keep open

lojor ***an** [of fabric] (having been) dipped in a lye solution before being worked in batik. **ng/di*(i)** to treat [fabric] as above

lok 1 a shout, a cheer; to shout, cheer. 2 utterance. *sembada karo *é* consistent with what he had said earlier. 3 (*or* **ke***) fame, renown; famed, renowned. **é tekan endi²*. He is known far and wide. **nge/di*aké** 1 to warn, remind. *Bandjiré teka bengi, tudjuné ana wong sing nge*aké.* The flood came at night; luckily smn gave warning. *Bareng Ali ngrokok Siti nge*ké ṭoklèh.* When Ali lighted a cigarette, Siti reminded him he shouldn't smoke. 2 to make remarks (about). *A nge*aké rambuté B.* A said sth uncomplimentary about B's hair. **nge/di*i** to shout a warning of [trouble, disaster]. *See also* ALOK

loka *oj* realm

lokak not completely filled

lokânantâ *wj* supernaturally produced gamelan music from heaven

lokèt grilled window. *Kabèh * pos ditutup.* All the post-office windows are closed.

lokomotip train engine

lokro loose, slack. **ng*** despondent, without hope

lola 1 alone in the world; deprived of relatives by death. 2 [of coconut palms] having only one fruit

loli lollipop

loloh 1 to feed [a baby animal]. 2 medicine (*ki for* DJAMU). ***an** 1 food fed to a baby animal. 2 *slang* dependent on one's parents

lolor (*or esp.* **ng***) stretched out long

lolos to escape, break out. ***an** loose. *benang *an* a loose thread. **ng/di*(i)** to pull sth out/off

loma generous

lombo **ng/di*ni** to cheat, deceive smn

lombok chili pepper (of many varieties). ** abang (idjo)* red (green) pepper. ** gaḍing* an ivory-colored pepper. ** rawit* small, intensely hot pepper. *sambel ** hot-pepper sauce. ***en** [of eyes, skin] irritated from handling peppers. *** belis**, *** djempling**, *** djemprit**, *** impling**, *** rawit**, *** senṭit**, *** tjimpling** common varieties of chili peppers

lompat galah pole vault

lompjah fried eggroll filled with beansprouts

lompong leaf stem in a trough shape

lon ***-*an** slowly. *Lakuné *-*an.* Their pace

was leisurely. **nge/di*-*i** to slow sth down. *See also* ALON

londjok **ke*** excessive. *Blandjaku akèh banget nganti ke*.* My expenditures are excessively heavy. **ng*** to exceed. *Blandjaku ng* tinimbang pemetuku.* My expenses are more than my income. *Omahé ng* pinggir segara.* The house juts out over the ocean (*i.e.* exceeds the edge).

londjong oval; egg-shaped. *** botor** *or* *** enḍog** *or* *** mimis** *or* *** widara** *describing the visual effect of smn running very fast*

londjor stalk. *tebu/pring telung ** three stalks of sugar-cane/bamboo

lonḍo ***-*** exhausted, fatigued

lonḍot **1** loose. *Sekrupé kuwi wis *.* The screw has worked loose. **2** wet rot (plant disease)

long large firecracker. ** bumbung* bamboo section used as a firecracker. ***an** space under a bed or other furniture; space under a house that is built on raised piles. *Turuné ng*an.* He slept under the bed [where it was cooler]. ***-*an** things removed. **-*ané mau simpenen ing lemari.* Put back the things you took out of the cupboard. **ka*** reduced. *Sumbangané ka* wragad²*. The contributions were cut into by the expenses. *Olèhé ngabotohan rina-wengi, kasugihané tansah kalong²*. He gambled constantly; his fortune dwindled away. **ka*an** **1** space under sth (*var of* *AN *above*). **2** to suffer a loss. **nge/di*(i)** to decrease sth. *Momotané dielongi.* He lightened his load.

longgar having (enough) room; having leeway. *Koperku isih *.* There's room for more in my suitcase. *Ora perlu kesusu, wektuné isih *.* No need to rush—there's plenty of time. *Sekrupé kuwi wis *.* The bolt is loose in the hole. **ka*an** latitude, leeway. *Dak wènèhi ke*an telung dina.* I'll give you three days—that ought to be enough. *ke*an kanggo nggajuh pepénginané* opportunities for indulging one's desires. **ng/di*aké** to increase the space *or* time for sth. *ng*aké wektuné kanggo mèlu ndjagongi kantja²* to make time for visiting with friends. *Bolongané ketjiliken, perlu di*aké.* The hole is too small, it needs to be enlarged. **ng/di*i** to give room, to provide leeway. *Olèhé pesen panganan di*i lima.* You'd better order five extra cakes to make sure there's enough.

longgor to grow tall fast

longit *see* BIS

longkang (*or* ***an**) exterior passageway; open space between two separately-built sections of a house

longo ***-*** to stare vacantly into space with open mouth. **longa-*** empty-headed, dull-witted

longok (*or* ***-***) to look up, hold up the head, stretch the neck. **ng*** to stretch out the neck. *Ḍèké ng* saka djenḍéla.* He stuck his head out the window.

longsong protective cover for a weapon. **ng/di*aké** to use as a weapon cover. **ng/di*i** to cover [a weapon]

longsor to shift, slide, settle. *lemah ** avalanche. **ng*** to sit with the legs stretched out. **ng/di*i** [of earth] to slide onto. *Dalané ng*i kali.* The road washed into the river. **l·um·ongsor** *sms* NG* *above*

lonjoh soft, tender

lonṭang ***-*** or **ng*** empty-handed. *Kabèhé paḍa nggegawa kok kowé mung *-*.* Everyone else is bring sth—how come you're not?

lontar **1** a palm leaf on which ancient Javanese and Balinese literature was written. **2** letter, book, writings

lonṭé prostitute. **ng*** **1** to be(come) a prostitute. **2** to go to a prostitute. **pa*ǹ** house of prostitution

lonṭèng ***-*** speckled, dappled

lontjèng **1** bell on a clock. **2** clock. **ng*** [of a clock bell] to ring

lontjok *var of* LONDJOK

lontjom *var of* ONTJOM

lontjong *inf var of* LONDJOK, LODJOK

lonṭong **1** rice formed into a roll and cooked in a banana-leaf wrapper, to be served (unwrapped) in slices. **2** a broad cloth sash worn by men around the waist next to the skin, with the (narrow) belt outside of it, centered vertically

lopak ***-*** metal box for keeping betel or tobacco

loper messenger; delivery man. ** kantor* office boy. ** koran* paper boy. ** poang* milkman. ** pos* mailman

lopis a sweet cookie of glutinous rice, grated coconut, and syrup

lor *ng,* **lèr** *kr* north. *ora weruh * kidul* disoriented. ***-*an** the northern part. **-*an ketradjang bandjir.* The northern section was flooded. **nga*** northward. *Aburé nga*.* It flew north. **nga*-ṅg·kidul** **1** here and there, all over. **2** on opposite sides. *Ḍèké karo aku mesṭi nga*-ngidul.* He and I always disagree. **sa∗(é)** to the north of. *Prenahé ing sa∗ing dalan geḍé madju mangidul.* It's north of the east-west highway. *See also* PANGALOR

lorèk *var of* LORÈNG

lorèng (*or* ∗-∗) striped. *klambi ∗ idjo* a green-striped shirt. *matjan ∗* tiger

lori 1 small railroad car. 2 small wooden club used as a weapon

loro *ng,* **kalih** *kr* two. *buku ∗* two books. *∗ telung taun* two or three years. *djam ∗* two o'clock. *∗ kabèh* both of them. *Perang nDonja Kaping Loro* World War II. *∗-∗* by two's. *Botjah² baris ∗-∗.* The children marched in pairs. *∗-∗né* (**kalih²ipun** *or* **kekalih** *kr*) both of them. **di∗ni** to be set upon by two persons. *Aku di∗ni.* The two of them ganged up on me. **ka∗n** *or* **sa∗n** (**sekalijan** *kr*) man and wife, married couple. *aku sakloron* my wife and I. *ndara sekalijan* the master and his wife. *See also* -AN (*suffix*) 8, 15, 16; -É^c (*suffix*) 9; NG- (*prefix*) 6, 7; KARO, KLORON, RO, RONG

lorob **ke∗** to get tricked *or* humiliated. **ng/di∗aké** 1 to trick smn into doing wrong *or* into doing sth to his own disadvantage. 2 to degrade, humiliate

lorod **∗an** 1 food left on smn's plate. 2 a hand-me-down. 3 batik from which the wax has been removed. **ng/di∗aké** 1 to leave [food] on one's plate. 2 to give away, hand down [to a social inferior]. 3 to remove wax from [fabric] between dyeings, in batik-making. **ng/di∗(i)** 1 to get rid of. *Akèh pegawé sing di∗i.* Many employees were laid off. 2 to give away [to a social inferior]. *Merga sesak, klambiné di∗ aḍiké.* The shirt was too tight, so he gave it to his little brother. 3 to eat smn's leftovers. 4 to remove wax from. *ng∗i djarik* to melt the wax from a wraparound. *See also* PLOROD

lorog **∗an** drawer. **l·um·orog** to support, agree to. *Bapak lumorog mangèstoni.* Father gives his blessings and moral support.

lorok **∗-∗** striped with broad stripes

los 1 shed, booth. *∗ pamèran* exhibition booth. 2 off, away, (on the) loose. 3 home free (in children's games). 4 spool, reel (*shf of* KELOS). **las-∗** to keep coming and going. **∗-∗an** 1 holding back nothing, freely giving and taking. *Mainé kasar lan ∗-∗an.* They played rough—no holds barred. 2 to come out even, *i.e.* no profit, no loss.

nge/di∗aké to allow smn to go free *or* unimpeded. *Adja gampang² nge∗aké wong sing njurigani.* Don't let any suspicious characters pass. *Aku ora téga nge∗aké ḍèké.* I can't bear to let her go off all by herself. *Wong botjah wis kaja ngono ngadi-adiné kok isih di∗aké baé.* Such a spoiled child, and they keep letting him have his way! **nge/di∗i** 1 to yield. *Aku aluwung ngalah lan nge∗i waé.* I'd rather just give up and let it go. 2 to make sth all even. *Iki sepéḍaku pèken kanggo nge∗i utangku.* Here, take my bicycle to square my debt.

losin dozen. *tjangkir patang ∗* 4 dozen cups

losmèn lodgings, a place to stay

losoh damaged by burning *or* scalding

losor *var of* LONGSOR

lotèk a snack made from mixed vegetables and fruits with beancake or chips

lot̄ēk *rpr* a scooping action. **ng/di∗** to scoop. *Sambelé di∗ nganggo séndok.* He took a generous spoonful of the hot sauce. **ng/di∗(i)** to feed [a baby] with the finger. **sa∗** a fingerful; amount scooped

lotèng attic, loft. **∗an** small attic/loft

lotis a snack consisting of fruits to be dipped in hot sauce. **ng/di∗** to make [ingredients] into the above dish

lotjânâ 1 eye. 2 inner corner of the eye

lotjita thoughts, musings. *∗ku ora lija mung nang nggonmu.* I think of nothing but you.

lotjut **ng∗** to go out in the rain unprotected

lotré 1 lottery, raffle, pool. 2 lottery ticket. 3 lottery prize. *menang ∗ nomer lima* to win fifth prize in a lottery. **∗nan** participation in a lottery. *Lotrènan olèh ḍuwit pira?* How much money has he won in lotteries? **ke∗** to win a lottery. **ng∗** 1 to take part in a lottery. *Sing ng∗ djarit wong lima.* Five people drew for the batik. 2 (*psv* **di∗**) to raffle off. **ng/di∗kaké** 1 to raffle sth off. 2 to supply a lottery prize. *Sing nglotrèkaké djarit ora mèlu ng∗.* The one who donated the batik didn't enter the lottery himself. **∗ buntut** pool in which people try to guess the final digit of the winning lottery number

lot̩ung *var of* LOWUNG

lowah having (enough) space. *Lemari iki isih ∗ akèh.* There's plenty of room in the cupboard. **∗an** room, space. *mènèhi ∗an* to make room, provide space. **ng/di∗i** to provide room. *Olèhé nata kursi di∗i bèn bisa kanggo dalan.* Leave space between the chairs for a passageway.

lowak second-hand, used. *tukang* * second-hand dealer, junk man. ***an** second-hand goods; junk. **ng/di*aké** to sell at second hand. *ng*aké klambi* to sell used shirts. *Sepatuku di*aké ibu.* Mother sold my old shoes.

lowar *var of* LOWÈR

lowèk *var of* LUWÈK

lowèr loose(ned). *Sekrupé wis* *. The screw is loose.

lowok *var of* LOWONG. ***an** dent; small shallow hole

lowong 1 vacant, blank, empty. *Tasku isih* *. My bag is empty. *Ukara sing * iki isènana.* Fill in the blanks in the sentences. 2 absent. ***an** a space, vacancy. *Ing Nopèmber kalawarti mau ora metu, *an.* The magazine was not issued in November; there's a gap. **an gawéan tukang ngetik* a job opening for a typist. **ng/di*i** to make empty. *Kursiné sing ngarep di*i lima.* Five seats in the front are to be left empty.

lowung a little something; better than nothing. *Éntuk baṭi siṭik ja * waton ora rugi.* A small profit is better than a loss. *Buntelan mau roti, * kanggo sarapan.* The package [he found] had bread in it; it would do for breakfast.

lsp. etc. *See* LAN SAPANUNGGALANÉ *under* LAN; PANUNGGAL

lss. etc. (*kr for* LLL.)

lu *ng* 1 three (*shf of* TELU). *dji, ro, ** 1, 2, 3. 2 eight (*shf of* WOLU). *ṇem, tu, *, nga* 6, 7, 8, 9

luar *var sp of* LUWAR

lub *shf of* KULUB. **k(e)*an** a vegetable dish (*shf of* KULUB·AN)

lubèr to overflow. *Kaliné wis mèh* *. The river is about to overflow its banks. *Njuwun *ing pangèstu pandjenengan.* I ask for (the outpouring of) your blessings. **ng/di*aké** to cause sth to pour out. *Olèh²é di*aké marang sanak-seduluré.* He deluged his family with gifts. **ng/di*i** to pour out onto. *Banjuné ng*i tegalan.* The water inundated the field. *Aku di*i ḍuwité.* He showered me with money.

luḍang *var of* LOḌANG

luḍes all gone; finished up. *Ḍuwitku wis* *. I've run out of money. *Olèhé nggopèki bajem nganti * entèk goḍongé.* She picked all the spinach there was. ** tapis* altogether gone. **ng/di*i** to use all of sth. *Sapa sing ng*i krupuk?* Who ate up the potato chips?

ludira *oj* blood

ludjeng 1 safe, well (*md for* SLAMET; *inf var of* WILUDJENG). 2 (*or* **w***) plow (*kr for* (W)LUKU)

ludrug improvised spoken drama dealing with contemporary subjects and acted by males using contemporary language and wearing modern dress

lugas simple, unadorned. *Ḍèké prijaji geḍé nanging * banget.* He's a high official but he doesn't put on airs. ***an** *or* **ng*** to wear civilian clothes

lugu 1 ordinary, regular. 2 original, free of outside influence. *Gambaré* *. The drawing is original. *Tegesé ana sing * lan ana sing éntar.* Some have their usual meanings and some have figurative meanings. ***né** 1 ordinarily, in the normal course of things. **né ḍèké kuwi ora ngerti, la wong ora ana sing nganḍani.* He couldn't have known–nobody told him. 2 in the beginning; originally. ***-*nan** *or* ***n̂-*n̂an** in the original *or* normal state. *Wong urip srawungan iku kang perlu mung lugon²an.* In dealing with people, the important thing is just to be yourself. **ng/di*k̂aké** to make sth original/natural (rather than affected *or* artificial). *Dilugokaké waé ta!* Just make it natural! **ng/di*n̂i** to [do] in a natural unaffected way. *Jèn dilugoni ḍèwèké malah luwih loma.* If you just talk with him plainly, he'll be more generous. **sa*né** in fact; normally. *Sa*né gugon tuhon iku kerep gawé kapitunané wong akèh.* Superstition actually harms many people. *** mung** *or* **mung *** plain and simple. ** mung kapinudjon.* It was purely accidental.

lugut *var of* GLUGUT

luh (**waspa** *ki?*) tears. *ngetokaké* * to weep. *metu *é* to get tears in the eyes. *Eluhé nganti dlèwèran ing pipi.* Tears ran down her cheeks. *See also* KAPILUH

luhung (*or* **l·in·uhung**) noble, supreme, exquisite, superb. *kagunan djogèd Djawa sing adi* * the fine art of the Javanese classical dance

luhur 1 noble, aristocratic. *satrija* * an aristocratic nobleman. *trahing* * of high descent. *Atiné* *. Her heart is noble. *para* * the nobility. 2 high, exalted. *punggawa negara* * a high government employee. *pamulangan tèhnik* * a school for high technical training. *tjita²* * high ideals. 3 the second daily ritual meditation in Islam; also, the time (1 P.M.) at which this meditation is performed (*see also* SALAT). **le*** revered ancestor(s). *pusaka saka le*ku* a revered heirloom. **ka*an** nobleness. *ka*aning bebudèn* nobility of character. *Ka*an ḍawuh dalem.* Indeed you are right, my lord. **nga*** [on] high. *Mugi linuhurna Allah ing nga*.* Hallowed be the name of God. **ng/di*aké** to revere. *ng*aké asmané wong tuwané* to hold the names of one's parents in high esteem. **l·in·uhur** revered, esteemed, hallowed

lujung outer wood of the sugar-palm tree

luk 1 curved portion of a kris blade. *keris ** kris with a curving blade. 2 *ltry* smoke. *keris kang metu *é* a kris from which vapors rose. **nge/di*** to bend, curve. *Dieluk sepisan baé tugel kawat mau.* The wire snapped when I bent it just once. *** bojok** *or* *** geger** to lie down for a rest. **nge/di*aké** to bring under control, cause to obey

lukak *var of* LOKAK

lukar 1 to undress (*ki for* TJUTJUL, UTJUL). 2 to come loose (*ki for* UḌAR). 3 naked (*ki for* WUDA)

luket close, intimate

lukis ***an** picture, painting. **ng/di*** to draw, paint

lukita *oj* 1 saying, expression, phrase; piece of writing. 2 picture, view. **ning alam* a view of the world, a view of the passing scene

luks de luxe; luxurious

luku plow (*var of* WLUKU). **ng/di*(k̂aké)** to plow

lulang *ng,* **tjutjal** *kr* leather, hide. *wajang ** leather puppet. ** weḍus* sheepskin. ***an** shadow play with leather puppets. **ng/di*i** to skin, remove the hide from. (*var form:* W(A)LULANG *ng,* WATJUTJAL *kr*)

lulu **ng/di*** to respond with sarcastic overgenerosity. *Nalika botjah² ndjaluk pelemé tanggaku ng* ngakon ndjebol sak wité sisan.* When the boys asked my neighbor for some of his mangoes, he told them to go ahead and pull up the whole tree. *Ḍèwèké di* ibuné, "Panganen kabèh, aḍiné ora susah dingèngèhi baé, wong isih tjilik baé kok."* His mother replied, "Eat *all* of it; never mind leaving any for your brother, he's too little."

lulub inner bark of certain trees: used for woven ropes

luluh 1 to melt, become dissolved. 2 *rg* centipede. ***an** melted, dissolved; mixed with *or* adapted to; (*gram*) phonetically assimilated. *adon² *an semèn karo gamping* a mixture of wet cement and lime. **ng/di*** 1 to melt *or* dissolve sth. 2 to blame

lulur 1 a yellow powder used as stage make-up for wajang performers. 2 meat adhering to beef backbone. **ng/di*(i)** to apply yellow powder to the body

lulus to pass; to complete the academic work required. ** udjian* to pass a test. ** saka univèrsitas* to graduate from the university. ** klas sidji* to complete the requirements for grade one. ***an** 1 diploma; certificate of completion. 2 a graduate; to graduate. 3 permission. *lajang *an* a letter of permission; a license. **ng/di*** to unsheathe. *ng* peḍang* to draw a sword. **ng/di*aké** 1 to pass *or* graduate smn. 2 to grant [a request; permission]. **ng/di*i** to give permission. *A di*i mulih.* A was given permission to go home. **pa*an** *or* **pi*an** permission

lulut devoted, deeply attached. *** asih** joined in/by love

lum **nge*-*i** to droop, fade, wither. *See also* ALUM

lum- *see also under* L- (*Introduction, 3.1.7*)

lumah surface; upper side. ***-*** to lie face up, lie on one's back. **k(e)-** to be face up unintentionally. *tiba klumah* to fall over backwards. **m*** 1 to lie on the back. 2 with surface *or* upper side up. *èpèk² m** palms up. *Botolé m*.* The bottle is right side up. **ng/di*aké** 1 to put sth in a face-up *or* surface-up position. *Tangan loro di*aké.* He turned both palms up. 2 to have smn lie on his back. **sa*é** all over (the surface of). *sa*é bumi* the world over. *sa*é bumi sakurebing langit* everywhere. *** tangan** to refrain from meddling

lumajan better than nothing, reasonably satisfactory. *Omahku ora geḍé ning ja *.* My house isn't large but it's adequate. *Sok² disilihi buku watjan, * kena kanggo nguṇḍakaké kawruh.* He sometimes lent them reading books, a little something to use for increasing their knowledge.

lumangjan *rg var of* LUMAJAN

lumba ***n** surrounded by an abundance of sth. **n ing kasugihan* rolling in money. **(le)*n** in the midst of. *le*n nang blumbang* splashing about in the pond. *le*n ing djagading politik* embroiled in politics. **m*-m*** to act skittish. **ng*** to buck, shy. *Djarané krungu klakson montor kagèt bandjur ng*.* The horse, startled by the car horn, shied.

lumbu a tuberous plant with large edible leaves and stalk. *djangan* * soup made from these leaves

lumbung storage shed *esp.* for rice, tobacco. **(le)*an** filling many sheds. *Pariné le*an.* He has barnfuls of rice stored up. * **banḍung** barn for rice storage. * **désa** communal village supply of stored rice for emergencies. * **petjeklik** village rice-storage barn for use during the critical shortage of preharvest times

lumèr melted; to melt, become melted. **ng/di*aké** to melt sth

lumer soft, fine-textured

lumpang mortar, in which things are pounded fine with a pestle (*alu*). ***en** *or* **ng*i** to have/get cold sores inside the lips. * **kenṭèng** *or* * **wesi** small metal mortar for use with a metal pestle

lumpat ***an** 1 a leap, jump. 2 to jump around (*e.g.* children playing). **le*an** act of jumping. *Le*an utawa pénékan ora pati bisa.* They're not very good at jumping and climbing. **m*** to jump (over). *Dipalangana m*.* If you put up a (*lit, fig*) barrier, I'll leap right over it. **ng/di*aké** to cause *or* help to jump. **ng/di*i** to jump over sth. *Asuné ng*i kaju.* The dog jumped over the log. **l·um·umpat** to jump (over). * **kidang** out of sequence, in random order

lumpija(h) egg roll

lumpuh lame; disabled, paralyzed, rendered helpless. * **ing sastra** illiterate

lumpuk *ng,* **lempak** *kr* **m*** to gather, come together. *Aku lan kantjaku m* ana sekolahan.* My friends and I met at the school. **di*aké** to be gathered/collected (*var of* DI·KLUMPUK·AKÉ). *Wong² ngemis paḍa di*aké.* They rounded up all the beggars.

lumpur mud

lumrah *ng,* **limrah** *kr* 1 usual, normal, ordinary; representative of the whole; not unexpected. *Jèn mengkono iku *.* That's the usual way. *Mesiné dirèmplèkaké ing sepéḍa *.* The motor is attached to a regular bike. *Wis * jèn weruh ula wedi banget.* It's normal to be afraid of snakes. *mripat ** the naked (unaided) eye. *Panasé ora *.* It's unusually hot. ** (waé) ḍèké sugih.* No wonder he's rich! *Wis *, lé, dalan ing pagunungan iku ménggak-ménggok.* Don't worry, my boy, mountain roads always twist and turn like this. *wong sing ** most people. *urip kaja *ing akèh* to live like ordinary people. *Ukumané luwih abot tinimbang ing negara *.* The penalty there is more severe than in most countries. 2 *rg* generous. *Ah * temen atiné, ngeteraké njang Kaliurang.* How nice it is of him to take us to Kaliurang this way! ***é** usually. **k(a)*** (to have become) normal, ordinary. *tembung sing durung ke** a word not yet in general use. *Wis ke*.* It's commonplace now. **ka*an** customary practice. **ng/di*aké** to make sth customary. *Tjara mau di*aké dadi tata ngadat.* The custom has come to be considered a communal law practice. **sa*é** (according to what is) usual, normal. *buku sa*é* an ordinary book. *Tjoba guneman sing sa*é baé.* Just talk normally.

lumuh to give in, not be willing to struggle (against). *mburu kepénak, * kangèlan* to do the easy jobs and give up on the hard ones. ** dadi tawanan* to surrender and become a captive. **ng/di*i** to give in to smn, put oneself out on smn's behalf. *Nardi kuwi udan² gelem meṭuk nang bioskupan mung ng*i kantjané.* Even though it was pouring, Nardi went to the movie house just to give his friend a lift.

lumut moss. ***en** *or* **ng*** mossy. *watu² *en* moss-covered rocks

lun **nge/di*** 1 to move with a rolling *or* billowing motion. 2 to round up [a group]. **nge*aké ala** to spread smn's bad name. * **ala·né** notorious. *See also* KELUN

lunas 1 paid in full. 2 ship's keel. **ng/di*i** to pay up, pay in full

lundjak ***-*** to jump up and down. **ng*** to jump up (on, at)

lung 1 stem or tender young top growth of the yam vine, cooked and eaten as a vegetable. 2 *shf of* TULUNG. ***-tinulung** to help each other. 3 *shf of* ULUNG. ***-*an** curling tendril motif used in ornamental designs for batik, furniture, woodwork. **nge*** resembling the above (1). *Gulunè nge* ing gaḍung.* She has a long, gracefully curved neck. **nge/di*aké** to give, hand over to (*inf var of* NG/DI·ULUNG·AKÉ). **nge/di*i** to give, hand over [sth] (*inf var of* NG/DI·ULUNG·I)

lunga *ng,* **késah** *kr,* **tindak** *or* **wijos** *ki* 1 to go (away, out). *Ajo *.* Come on, let's go! *Aku * golèk tamba.* I went to get some medicine. *Ḍèké mèsem karo *.* He left, smiling. 2 to be out, to have gone. *Bapakipun késah.* His father isn't home. *Ḍèk aku dolan menjang nggonmu kaé, kowé lagi *.*

When I went to see you, you were out. *n 1 to travel. *Prijaji putri jèn tindakan adaté njampingan lan ngagem kebajak.* Women of high position usually dress Javanese style for travel. 2 to go out for pleasure. *-* *or* **le*an** to go about, travel. *Kowé adja *-*.* Don't go anywhere. *wong le*n* traveler. **ng/di*kaké** to remove, get rid of. *ng*kaké piring² saka médja* to clear the table. *Réwang mau di*kaké saka ngomah.* He sent the servant packing. **ng/di*ni** to avoid. *ng*ni bebaja* to steer clear of danger. (*ing*) **sa*né** during one's absence

lungguh *ng,* **linggih** *or* **lingguh** *ng kr,* **lenggah** *ki* to sit (down, up). **a kono.* Sit there. **é djèdjèr aku.* He sat next to me. *Kepénakna *mu.* Make yourself comfortable! ***an** 1 a seat, place to sit. 2 to sit around. **lunggah-*** (**lenggah²** *ki*) to keep standing (*or* pacing) and sitting again. **le*an** to sit around. **ka*an** position, situation, office. *kepotjot saka ing ka*ané* fired from his job. *kalenggahan dados anggota D.P.R.* a position as member of the Parliament. **ng/di*aké** to seat smn. **ng/di*i** to sit on sth. **ng*i klasa g·um·elar** to inherit valuables. **ng*i klasa pengulu** to marry the husband of one's dead sister. **pa*an** 1 position, office. 2 seat, place to sit. **pi*an** to sit around informally. *See also* PINARAK

lungka hard clayey earth

lungkrah enervated, weak, tired

lunglit emaciated (*shc from* BALUNG KULIT). *Awaké *.* He's nothing but skin and bones.

lungsé too late. *Jèn wis *, terkaḍang kebandjur wuta.* If they let it go too long, sometimes they go blind.

lungsed wrinkled, messy

lungsi *see* PADA

lungsur ***an** 1 (a) used (article). *sepéḍah *an* a second-hand bicycle. *Klambi iki *an.* This dress is a hand-me-down. 2 retired. **an pradjurit* a retired soldier. **k(e)*** 1 [of cheeks, jowls] drooping. 2 to get demoted. *ka* kapraboné* deposed from his throne. **ng/di*** 1 to use sth that is no longer needed by smn else. 2 to remove wax from fabric being worked in batik. **ng/di*aké** 1 to lower sth. *Taliné di*aké nèng sumur.* He lowered the rope into the well. 2 to give away a used article. **ng/di*(i)** to demote smn. **ng/di*i** to give a used article to. *A ng*i aku sepatu.* A gave me his shoes. **l·in·ungsur** *ltry* [of leftover food] to be served to smn lower. *Segané linungsur marang baturé.* The servants were given the table leavings. **l·um·ungsur** [of a rank *or* position] to be transferred to smn lower. *Kapraboné lumungsur marang Pangéran-pati.* The throne went to the Crown Prince. *Kalungguhané lumungsur marang anaké mbarep.* His position was transferred to his oldest son.

lunju slippery; *fig* evasive. **ke*ñ** 1 excessively slippery. 2 to skid, slide

lunta ***-l·um·unta** to pass along, transmit from one to another. **ke*-*** always in difficulty. **ng/di*kaké** to transmit. *ng*aké kesalahané* to pass on the blame. *ng*aké lajang papréntahan* to transmit a government document. **l·um·unta-*** *sms* *-L·UM·UNTA *above*

luntah trash, garbage

luntak 1 to spill out (*root form: kr for* SUNTAK). 2 to vomit (*ng? kr? ki? for* M̈·WUTAH). ***an** vomitus. ***-*** to vomit repeatedly. **ke*an** to get vomited on

luntas a common plant with edible leaves, grown around the yard and often used as a hedge

luntjup sharp-pointed

luntjur to get launched. *Roketé ng*.* The rocket lifted off. **ng/di*aké** to launch sth. *ng*aké roket* to send up a rocket. *Présiḍèn mimpin upatjara ng*aké kapal.* The President led the ship-launching ceremony. **ng/di*i** 1 to ram. 2 to slide *or* drift into/against

lunṭung ***an** in the form of a roll. **an kertas* rolled-up paper. **ng/di*** to roll (up), make into a roll

luntur 1 to fade. *Klambiné *.* The shirt faded. *Mesṭi bandjur * katresnané.* Her love is bound to abate. 2 to come off. *Malamé *.* The wax came off [from the fabrik being batiked]. 3 to bestow. *Njuwun *ing sih dalem.* I plead for your mercy. **ka*an** to have sth bestowed on one. **ng/di*aké** to bestow on smn. **ng/di*i** to come off onto sth. *Klambiku sing abang ng*i klambiku putih.* My red shirt ran onto my white shirt.

lup 1 rifle barrel. 2 magnifying glass

luput *ng,* **lepat** *kr* 1 wrong, at fault. *Bener apa *?* Is it right or wrong? *jèn ora ** if I am not mistaken. *Sapa sing luput?* Whose fault is it? *duwé ** to do sth wrong. **ku ḍéwé.* It's my own fault. *Apa *é?* What's he done wrong? 2 to miss, escape. *Ḍèké * enggoné manah.* His arrow missed (the target). * *pameḍang* to sidestep a sword-stroke. * *ing sambékala* to escape misfortune. ***é...ija** if not...then. *Sing ngrusak pager iki *é A ja B.* If A wasn't the one who damaged the fence, it must have been B. *-* by bad luck. *Luput² montoré njemplung.* The car, unfortunately, went into the ditch. **lupat-*** (**lepat²** *kr*) to keep making mistakes *or* missing. **ka*an** 1 mistake, fault. *mbenerakė ka*an* to right a wrong, to correct a fault. 2 to get blamed. *Ḍèké ke*an nganggo ḍuwit kantor.* He was accused of misappropriating official funds. **ng/di*aké** 1 to blame, accuse. **na kowé.* You have only yourself to blame. *Kowé adja ng*ké wong tuwa.* Don't put the blame on your parents. 2 to err intentionally. * **tj·in·atur** *ng kr* it goes without saying

lur 1 earthworm. 2 *rpr* sth long and thin being extended

lurah 1 top official in a village. 2 *slang* boss. **le*** 1 top office in a village. 2 leader of a group. **ka*an** domain of the village head. *Tanduran pari sa'ke*an entèk dipangan tikus.* The entire village supply of rice plants was eaten by rats. **ng/di*i** to have charge of [a village] as head. **ki *** (*wj*) *title applied to clowns. Ki * Semar nḍatengaken bajubadjra.* Semar called forth a wind-and-thunder storm.

luri **le*** ancestor, forerunner, predecessor. **ng/di·(le)*kaké** to preserve, maintain. *nglurèkaké padatan kuna* to maintain ancient customs

lurik striped hand-woven clothing fabric. ***(-*)an** material worked in stripes

luru (*or* *-*) to seek out. * *pangan* to go looking for food. **ng/di*** to go in quest of. *Sanḍang lan pangan kudu kok * ḍéwé.* You have to earn your own living. *ng* pegawéan* to look for a job

lurub fabric used as a covering. **ng/di*i** to cover sth. *Médjané di*i taplak putih.* She put a white tablecloth on the table.

lurug ***an** 1 a group sent out for a purpose, *esp.* to fight. 2 (*or* **ng***) to go smw as a group. *ng* perang* to go forth to battle. *ng* bal-balan* to go smw to play a soccer match. *Ponakanku mau paḍa ng* turu mréné.* My nephews came here to sleep. *Jèn adu djago nganti *an nang Semarang.* He'll go all the way to Semarang to enter his cock in a fight. **ng/di*aké** to send [combatants] forth. **ng/di*i** to go forth against [an opponent]. **l·um·urug** to go forth as a group

luruh 1 soft-spoken, unassuming; [of wajang puppets] having a refined, humble mein. *satrija sing ** a nobleman of humble character. *Wangsulané swarané *.* He answered in a calm voice. 2 (having) quieted down. *Geniné mentas mobjar² bandjur *.* The fire flared up, then died down. **ng*** 1 to speak softly. 2 to look up [a relative, *e.g.* when visiting another city]

lurung narrow street; alley(way)

lurus straight, direct, unswerving. * **ati·né** straightforward, honest

lus **nge/di*** to rub sth smooth. *Médja dielus nganggo rempelas.* He sandpapered the table. *Montoré dielus-elus terus.* He's forever polishing his car. **nge* ḍaḍa** to draw the hands downward over the chest (gesture expressing grief, pity). **nge/di*-*** *or* **nge/dilas-*** to stroke, caress. **nge/di*aké** to make sth smooth, fine. *Olèhé nulis dielusaké.* He wrote in beautiful handwriting. **nge/di*i** to treat smn with gentility. *Jèn ora kena di*i, diagal baé.* If he doesn't respond to well-mannered treatment, use force. *See also* ALUS

lusi *var of* LUNGSI

lusmèn *var of* LOSMÈN

lusuh no longer in use. *Mesiné wis *.* The machine is obsolete.

lusut to slip away/out, to elude

luṭeng *-* *intsfr* dark, black. *ireng *-** intensely black. *peteng *-** pitch dark

luṭik *var of* LOṬÈK

lutju funny (*i.e.* amusing, comic; peculiar). **lutja-*** to fool around, joke a lot. **le*n̂** 1 jokes; joking around. 2 to joke with each other. **ng/di*(n̂i)** to act funny; to do funny things to. *Senadjan dilutjoni werna², meksa ora ngguju.* We kidded him a lot but he didn't laugh.

lutjut slippery; to slip from one's grasp. **ng/di*i** to disarm smn

lutung black monkey

luṭung *rg var of* LOWUNG

lu(w)- *see also under* LU-, LW- (*Introduction, 2.9.7*)

luwah *var of* LOWAH

luwak civet cat

luwang ***an** 1 hole, pit. **an kanggo mbuwang runtah* garbage pit. * *kubur* grave. 2 bird-trapping noose. **ng/di*i** to dig a hole in

luwar 1 free, clear of. * *saka pakundjaran* released from prison. *Bajiné wis* *. The baby has been born. * *saka bebaja* out of danger. 2 the outside; the outdoors. 3 wing (soccer player, position). * *kanan/kiri* right/left wing. **k(e)*** to go out, leave. **ng/di*aké** to bring about release; to free smn (from). *ngluwaraké pesakitan* to release a prisoner. *Mugi linuwarna saking piawon.* Deliver us from evil. **ng/di*i** 1 to release smn. 2 to exclude, leave out. 3 to fulfill [a pledge]. *ng*i nadar* or *ng*i udjar* to perform an act in fulfillment of a promise. * **biasa** out of the ordinary, exceptional. * **tanggung·an** outside of one's responsibility. * **udjar** to have fulfilled a pledge

luwas old, worn out, ragged

luwé hungry (*kr for* NGELIH?). **k(e)*ǹ** excessively hungry. *Jèn wis djam sidji mbok mangan, adja nganti kluwèn.* When it's lunchtime, eat; don't wait till you're half starved. *See also* KELUWÉ

luwèh *rural* I don't care!

luwèk ***an** depression, small hole

luweng 1 deep hole, pit, cave. 2 cooking pit

luwer **ng/di*(aké)** to swerve [a vehicle]. *Olèhé ng*aké motoré keseron nganti mlebu kali.* He turned the car too sharply and ended up in the river. *See also* KLUWER

luwes 1 graceful, smooth, fluent. 2 flexible, adaptable to many purposes

luwih *ng,* **langkung** *kr* 1 more (than). *Tjanḍi mau umuré wis * sèwu taun.* The temple is over a thousand years old. *piranti kang * betjik* better equipment. * *betjik mulih waé.* We'd better go home. *Regané pitik kaé limang rupijah* *. That chicken over there costs five rupiahs more [than this one]. 2 (*after number*) *n* or more; more than *n*. *sepuluh dina* * at least ten days. *Tjatjah djiwané ana telung juta* *. The population is over three million. 3 exceeding normal bounds. *ngèlmu kang* * esoteric knowledge. *Ḍèwèké badjang, nanging * déning kuwasa.* He's a dwarf, but he has exceptional strength. 4 (*in clock time*) plus, and. *djam papat * limang menit* 4:05. ***-*** 1 especially. *Wong tuwané banget ing bungahé, *-* ibuné.* His parents were overjoyed, especially his mother. 2 all the more so; to say nothing of. *Para lurah sakiwa-tengené kono paḍa éring, *-* wong tjilik.* He was held in high esteem by all the surrounding village heads and even more so by the common people. *Botjah kelas lima baé wis ngerti ilmu bumi donja, *-* botjah kelas nem.* Even the fifth-grade students know a lot about geography–the sixth-grade students even more so. **k(e)*an** 1 superior quality. *Wong mau wuta nanging duwé ke*an pangrungon sing tjeṭa banget.* He's blind, but he has remarkable powers of hearing. 2 (*or* **k[e]*en**) too many/much. *Sénḍok sing mbok balèkaké mau ke*en loro.* You gave me back two too many spoons. *Adja nganti kurang utawa kluwihen saaksara baé.* Don't write any [Javanese-script] characters with too few or too many strokes. **k(e)*(-*)** (**[sa]k[e]langkung[-langkung]** *kr*) 1 especially. 2 exceedingly, excessively. *Ke* nesuné.* He was infuriated. *Sakalangkung bingah déné sampun gaḍah grija malih.* They were overjoyed to have a home again. *Soal udjiané ḍèk mau kluwih angèl.* The exam problems were terribly hard. **ng/di·(le)*i** 1 to exceed, go beyond. *A kuwi geḍéné ng*i B.* A is bigger than B. *Jèn ng*i wates, kedadéjané ja ora betjik.* If you overstep the boundaries, no good will come of it. *Nakalé ng*-*i.* His bad behavior is beyond all bounds. 2 to increase by adding to. *Ḍèké ng*i loro manèh.* He gave me two extra ones. **sa*é** whatever is in excess. *Duwèkku mung pitu, sak̀luwihé duwèkmu.* Only seven of them are mine; the rest are yours. **l·in·uwih** *ng,* **l·in·angkung** *kr* 1 esteemed, revered, distinguished. *penḍita sing linuwih* a holy man who is held in very high regard. 2 having powers beyond the normal. *ḍukun sing linuwih bisa nambani kabèhing lara* a gifted medicine woman who can cure any illness. * **ḍisik** before, more in advance. *rong taun * ḍisik* two years earlier. *Apa pendjenengan wis tau krama * ḍisik?* Have you ever been married before? * **manèh** especially, even more. *Walang sangit iku gawé kapitunané menungsa, * menèh marang kantja tani.* The *walang sangit* beetle causes losses to human beings, especially farmers. **ora** * there is nothing left [but], all one can do [is]. *Mboten langkung, bapak karsaa maringi pangèstu saha bantuan batin.* All I ask of you, Father, is your blessing and moral support. * **rupa kurang tjandra** so-so; good but not outstanding. *See also* KUMLUWIH

luwing 1 centipede. 2 a certain variety of

banyan tree that produces large fruits. **3** *rg var of* LUWÉ

luwung (*or* **a***) preferable. *A* aku mati tinimbang menangi negaraku dipetjah-petjah.* I'd rather die than see my country divided. *Katimbang ngrasani alaning lijan, * orak-arik gawé dongèng.* Rather than speak ill of others, it's better to make up a story.

luwus old, worn-out, dirty-looking

lw- *see under* LUW- (*Introduction, 2.9.7*)

lyang *oj* hole, burrow

M

m **1** (*prn* **èm**) *alphabetic letter.* **2** *abbr for* MÈTER. m^2 ⟨*mèter pesagi*⟩ square meter. **3** *var of* ME- *before* L, R, *or vowel.* **4** *var of* NG- (*prefix*) (*Introduction, 3.1.5.4*). *See also under* EM- (*Introduction, 2.9.5*) *and under consonant that has been replaced by nasal prefix* (*Introduction, 3.1.5.4*)

ma- *see also under* ME- (*Introduction, 2.9.2*) *or under replaced-consonant plus* E- (*Introduction, 3.1.5.4*)

ma[a] **1** name of the Javanese alphabetic character denoting the consonant *m.* **2** *oj* five (*shf of* LIMA). *dji, ro, lu, pat, ** 1, 2, 3, 4, 5. **las* 15. *** **lima** the five sins (opium-smoking, gambling, drinking, promiscuity, stealing). *** **pitu** the seven sins (the above plus gluttony, bearing false witness)

mā-[b] *prefix* to partake of, bring into play. *ma·guru* to acquire knowledge. *ma·udjud* to take shape. *Bapak lagi ma·gawé ana ing sawah.* Father is working in the rice paddy.

mā-[c] *ltry prefix* **1** many, any number of; to intensify *or* multiply [*root*]. *ma·taun-taun* for many years. *rupijah ma·juta-juta* millions of rupiahs. *kaperluwan sing ma·warna-warna akèhé* necessities of all kinds. *Rikaté tikel ma·tikel-tikel tinimbang kuwi mau.* It goes many times faster than that. *ma·ng·ambal-ambal* or *ma·kaping-kaping* or *ma·rambah-rambah* or *ma·wali-wali* time after time. *ma·geni-geni* to burn brightly. *Kebetjikanmu wis ma·tumpuk-tumpuk.* You have heaped kindness on us. *Djadja bang ma·winga-winga.* (*wj*) He was enraged. **2** *adds formal literary flavor before nasal prefix* (*Introduction, 3.1.5.4*): *ma·ñ·tunggal, ma·ng·udi, etc.*

ma'af, ma'ap sorry! (*word of apology*)

maben honey (*rg kr for* MADU)

mabjor *rg var of* ABJOR

mabluk whitish like tapioca powder (*kabluk*). *Rambuté wis **. His hair is getting white.

mabrut **-** *or* **mobrat-*** snarled. *Rambuté **.* Her hair is tangled. *Ḍuwité **.* His finances are in a mess.

mabuk intoxicated. **ϕ*aké** **1** intoxicating. **2** (*psv* **di*aké**) to get smn drunk

mabul **-** *or* **mobal-*** snarled, tangled

mâdâ to criticize, find fault

maḍaran **1** a cook who works for a high dignitary. **2** *kr* stomach (*var of* PAḌARAN)

madat ***an** opium addict. **ϕ/di*(i)** to smoke [opium]

madé *oj* middle

maḍèh **ϕ*i** boring, irritating; (*psv* **di*i**) to bore, irritate

mâdjâ a certain tree; also, its fruit, whose hard shell is made into containers

madjad proper, suitable, appropriate. *Matané laler iku geḍéné ora * karo awaké.* A fly's eyes are disproportionately large for its body. *Pendjaluké iku ora **. His request is quite unreasonable.

madjalah magazine

Madjapa(h)it ancient Hindu kingdom in Java

madjas efficacious. *Obat iki * banget kanggo nambani lara kulit.* This ointment works well for skin disorders.

madjelis association, group, federation.

* **Dagang Sak Donja** World Council of Trade. * **enḍèk** lower parliamentary house. * **luhur** 1 upper parliamentary house. 2 high council. * *Luhur Taman Siswa* Taman Siswa Supreme Council. * **renḍah** *sms* * ENḌÈK

madjer sterile, unable to reproduce

madjik ***an** boss, employer. *sesambunganè buruh *an* cooperation between labor and management

madjlis *var of* MADJELIS

madju *ng,* **madjeng** *kr* 1 to move forward. **!* Come forward! *negara sing wis ** a progressive nation. *Tulisan Arab saka tengen * mengiwa.* Arabic writing goes from right to left. 2 to face, confront. ** perang* to go to war. ** udjian* to take an exam. *Suk apa nggonmu * ing pengadilan?* When do you go to court? 3 by *n*'s. ** pat* four-sided; four-directional. *Saben dina * pat.* They work in groups of four every day. **ka*an** progress, development, advancement. **ke*ñ** *or* **ke*en** *or* **ke*ñen** too far forward; *fig* too Westernized; brash, pushy. *Olèhmu ndokok mikrofon ke*en.* You put the microphone too far forward. *Tumrap wong Djawa ke*an kuwi perlu banget kanggo para wanita, nanging menawa kemadjon ija ora betjik.* Progress is very important for Javanese women, but they shouldn't get too much like Western women. * **ati·né** to work hard (at). * **éwuh mundur ke·paluh** faced with two disagreeable alternatives; between the devil and the deep blue sea. * **marang/ing** to do well in. *Madju ing ulah raga, nanging kesèd sinau.* He's good at sports but not keen on studying. * **mundur** 1 to go forward and back. *Ratuné kena * mundur ngendi-endi ning ora kena luwih saka sakoṭakan.* The [chess] king can move in any direction but only one square. 2 to vacillate. *Kekarepané *-mundur.* He doesn't know whether he wants it or not. *Aku * mundur nonton biskup.* I'm of two minds about going to the movies. *See also* ADJU

madon underdone [of boiled eggs]

madrasah a Moslem school that offers traditional religious training together with modern lay education

madu (**maben** *rg? kr*) honey; nectar from blossoms. * **mangsa** a sweet snack made of glutinous rice

madya 1 *oj* middle, center. 2 middle speech level (*Introduction, 5.2*). 3 mediocre. *Kapinterané mung * waé.* His intelligence is only average. 4 waist(line) (*kr for* BANGKÈKAN). **pa*** middle, center. **sa*** at a medium *or* average rate/level. *Kapinterané sa* waé.* He's a mediocre student. *Olèhé njambut gawé sa* waé, ora susah kemempengen.* Just work at an average rate; don't overdo it. * **(a)ntara,** * **krama,** * **ngoko** subvarieties of the Madya speech level (*Introduction, 5.5*)

madyâpâdâ *ltry* earth; place of human habitation

maédjan grave marker

maem to eat (*children's word*)

maénd(r)a *rg var of* MÉNDA

maèr *var of* MAIR

maésa kerbau (*kr for* KEBO)

magang candidate for a position; apprentice, on-the-job learner

magep *rg var of* MEGAP

magersantun *kr for* MAGERSARI

magersari *ng,* **magersantun** *kr* one who owns and occupies (by permission) a home on the premises of a wealthy or aristocratic person

magi magical power

magreg **mograg-*** 1 to stop frequently. 2 undecided, vacillating. *Atiné mograg-* waé olèhé arep pinḍah nang luar Djawa.* He's of two minds about moving to outer Java. *See also* GREG

magrib fourth daily meditation of Islam; also, the time (sunset) at which this is performed. *salat ** sunset prayers

magrok to stop, settle, come to rest. *Darané * nang wit.* The pigeon lighted in a tree. *Kuluwarga entèk²ané * nang ndésa.* The family finally settled down in a village.

magrong ***-*** [of buildings] large and tall. *geḍong *-** buildings of impressive size. *See also* AGRONG

magung large, great (*oj*). **ke*an** to act superior. *See also* AGUNG

mah *rg* mother. * **tuwa** grandmother

mâhâ high, superior; extreme. * **agung** the great (ones). * **baja** great danger; very dangerous. ***guru** (*prn* **māhāguru**) university professor. * **Kuwasa** the Almighty. ***luhur** God. * **mantri** prime minister. * **mulja** great wealth; very wealthy. * **prana** capital letter (in Javanese script). * **putri** queen. * **radja** king. * **resi** great holy man. ***siswa** (*prn* **māhāsiswā**) university student. * **sutji** most holy

Mahab(h)aratā *wj* epic narrating the history

of the Pandawas and the Kurawas (adapted from the Sanskrit epic) depicted by leather puppets in shadow plays

mahir *var of* MAIR

mahisa *oj* kerbau

mahnit magnet

mahrib 1 the African countries south of Arabia. 2 *var of* MAGRIB

main 1 to play; to perform in, put on [entertainment]. *sing* * player; performer; actor. *main bal (bolah, tjatur, lsp.)* to play soccer (billiards, chess, *etc.*). * *biola* to play a violin. *main pentjak (judo, djotosan)* to engage in karate (judo, boxing) as a sport. * *kumiḍi* to put on *or* perform in a stage play. * *peḍang* to fence. *Bioskupé * djam pitu.* The movie goes on at seven o'clock. *Tukang sulap mau miwiti *.* The magician began his show. 2 to gamble. * *kertu* to play cards for money. 3 plaything; mascot. 4 to make a practice of [doing sth deplorable]. *Tindaké * kasar.* He acts like a boor. *Koran tansah * utang.* Newspapers are always borrowing money. *Politik ditegasi mung * menang²an omong.* Politics [to a dilettante] is only a matter of winning a war of words. ***an** 1 mascot; plaything, sth not to be taken seriously. *Montoré nganggo *an digandulké nang nggon pengilon.* He has a mascot hanging on his rear-view mirror. 2 to play around/along with. *Adja *an lo.* Please be serious! ***-*** 1 *sms* *AN. *Siti mung kanggo *-* waé karo Slamet.* Slamet is just leading Siti on for his own amusement. 2 to make a practice of [doing sth deplorable]. *Pemerintah *-* kanṭi retja²nan, * kanṭi tugu²nan, * pinḍah²an makam pahlawan.* The government devoted much time and energy to [such non-essential projects as] erecting statues, putting up monuments, and reburying heroes in fine graves. **ϕ/di*aké** 1 to perform, put on [entertainment]. *Lagu² populèr di*aké kanggo umum.* Popular songs are put on for the public. 2 to handle with clever manipulations. *Sok sapaa sing arep mainaké PWI mesṭi gagal.* Anyone who tries to undermine the journalists' association is sure to fail. *Usulé ditampa rapat, sing marahi ḍèwèké pinter mainaké persoalané.* His proposal was passed by the meeting because of his skillful maneuvering in presenting the problem. **pa*** player, performer. **pa*an** game, pastime, amusement (*esp.* involving gambling). *** akrobat** 1 to be an acrobat (as a livelihood). 2 to do odd jobs on the side for extra income. *** api** 1 fireworks. 2 to play with fire, play a dangerous game. *** ḍuwit** 1 excessively fond of money. 2 to bribe; to accept a bribe. 3 to misappropriate official funds. *** gila** to carouse. *** kaju** to play rough/dirty. *Djaman saiki kok akèh wong sing paḍa * kaju rebutan kursi.* People will do anything nowadays to get the position they want. *** mata** to flirt. *** sandiwara** to put on an act. *Aku saiki wis ngerti, ora susah * sandiwara manèh.* I understand now; you don't need to pretend any longer. *** tangan** 1 to engage in arm wrestling. 2 (*or* *** kampleng**) to lash out with the hand. *** wédok** to procure girls (for one's own *or* others' pleasure)

mair skilled, capable

mâjâ 1 blossom of the *blimbing* fruit tree. 2 (*or* ***-***) light [of colors]. *idjo (kuning, lsp.)* * light green (yellow, *etc.*). *Banjuné biru *-*.* The water is bright blue. 3 (*or* ***-***) hazy. *putih *-** hazy white. *hima ** fine thin cloud mass. *Rembulané *-*.* The moon was clouded over.

majag *-* heavy-looking, unwieldy

majang 1 blossom of the areca palm. 2 neck muscles of a horse. **ke*an** *see* BEGDJA

majar *ng kr,* **senggang** *ki* 1 light, easy. *panggarap ** light work. 2 recovery, recuperation. *Larané wis ana *é.* She's getting better. **ka*an** opportunity, facilities (for doing sth). **ϕ/di*aké** to cause sth to be less burdensome. *Èsemé bisa majaraké laraku.* Her smile made me forget my pain. *Perkarané Mardi rada di*aké karo keterangané seksi mau.* The witness' testimony made the case against Mardi look somewhat less black.

majat slanting, sloping

majek̄ **mojak̄-*** unstable, wobbly

majeng *-* *or* **mojang-*** to go from place to place. *mojang-* ngungsi nang endi²* to flee from place to place. *Kowé mau tak golèki mojang-* nang endi².* I've been looking all over for you.

majid (**lajon** *ki?*) corpse

majo *rg var of* AJO

majong *var of* MAJENG

major major (military rank). ***an** feast, banquet

maju (*or* **me***) (to bring about) well-being, absence of conflict *or* strain. *Me* djagad iku pangadjapé Sarékat Bangsa².* The goal of the United Nations is to bring about international harmony.

majuh *rg var of* AJO

majuk̄ unstable, leaning (in a certain direction). *Wité * mréné.* The tree is leaning this way. **mojak̄-*** unsteady, leaning way over

mak 1 *particle signaling that the following word represents the impact* (*usu. sensory*) *of an action.* * *djranṭal mlaju mlebu ing alas.* Like a shot he scurried into the jungle. *Kantjil ketjemplung * blung.* Mouse-Deer plunged in, splash! * *klakep meneng* to stop talking suddenly. * *lap, seḍéla baé wis ora katon.* Swish! it could only be seen for a moment. *Sepuré manḍeg * greg djegeḍeg.* The train stopped with a sudden jerk. *Aku * blong bareng krungu jèn lulus.* I was so relieved to hear I had passed! * *ser, wetengé krasa mules.* He felt a cramp in his stomach. 2 a gum resin used medicinally, also for violin-bow rosin. 3 *rg* elderly female; mother (*shf of* MAMAK, SIMAK). 4 father (*shf of* SEMAK, RAMAK). * **ḍé** grandmother; grandfather. * **gus** uncle (parent's younger brother). * **kjai** grandfather. * **njai** grandmother. * **tjomblang** matchmaker, go-between. * **tuwa** aunt; uncle (parent's older sibling)

makadjangan to relax and take it easy (as a group) on the town square after paying homage to the king or attending a celebration

makajangan to go to heaven, go to the realm of the deities. *See also* KA·HJANG·AN

makak̒na *var of* MANGKA

makam (*or* ***an**) tomb, grave

makaten *formal var of* MEKATEN

makelar broker, middleman. * *omah* dealer in real estate. * *montor* car salesman. ***an** the selling profession; brokerage

makluk all living beings, all creation. *tataran uripé ** levels of animate life

maklum 1 understandable, to be expected. 2 pardon, forgiveness. **di*** to be forgiven. ***é** please forgive me [for not giving you anything: phrase said to beggars or other solicitors]

maklumat proclamation, announcement, declaration

makmur prosperous, wealthy. *Muga² bangsa lan negara kita dadi * lan santosa.* May our nation and people become prosperous and strong.

makna meaning conveyed. *Bareng bisa nampa *né, rainé dadi abang sanalika.* When she grasped what he was driving at, she suddenly flushed. ***né** it means...

makrak *var of* MANGKRAK

makramah *var of* MAKROMAH

makrifat mystically attained religious knowledge

makromah veil worn by Moslem women

makroni macaroni

makruh undesirable, to be avoided (according to Islamic creed)

makruni *var of* MAKRONI

maksih *rg var of* TAKSIH

mak̒sijat (power of) evil. *kuṭa ** a city of evil. *duwé kekuatan ** having the power to do evil. ***an** evil, sin; to do evil. *nglakoni *an* to commit evil acts, to act sinfully

maksud intention, purpose, meaning. *duwé * ala* to have evil intentions. *Pemerintah nduwèni * ngadjokaké inḍustri tjilik.* The government intends to promote small-scale industry. *Rak ija wis ngerti *é ta?* You understand what it means, don't you?

makuna old, ancient. *See also* KUNA

makuṭa 1 crown. 2 fez-like headdress (*ki for* KULUK)

mal- *see also under* ML- (*Introduction, 2.9.3*) *or under replaced-consonant plus* L (*Introduction, 3.1.5.4*)

mâlâ blemish, flaw. ***nen** to have blemishes/flaws (of body *or* character). **me*** 1 skin flaw *or* laceration. 2 unpleasantness. *golèk me** to seek out danger or trouble. **me*nen** *sms* *NEN *above.* **ke*n** blemished in body or spirit. *ke*n enḍas* boastful. *ke*n tjangkem* in trouble/danger through smn's ill-advised words

malaékat male angel

Malagasi Madagascar

malah (*or* ***an** *or* ***-***) 1 contrary to expectation; instead. *Aḍukané kakèhan, mula tanduran é * lanas.* There was so much fertilizer that the plants were actually retarded. *Dikon manḍeg iku ora nurut, * pité dibanteraké.* He was told to stop, but he didn't; he only pedaled faster. 2 even, moreover, beyond that. *Suraké wong ija mbata rubuh, * ana sing keplok².* The crowd cheered; some even applauded.

malaikum salam *reply to the Moslem greeting* ASSALAM(U)ALAIKUM

malak̄(i) greedy, selfish, covetous

malakulmaut male angel who conveys the soul from the body at death

malam *ng,* **lilin** *kr* wax. *ati* * quick to recover from anger. *ϕ*/**di*i** to buy *or* pay for [wax used in batik-making]

malékat *var of* MALAÉKAT

malem 1 night, evening (*in certain compounds*). *djaga* * stationary night watchman. *ronḍa* * circulating night watchman. * *gembira* an evening party. *kupu* * prostitute. *pasar* * fair, bazaar. *sepur* * night train. *nganakaké djam* * to declare a curfew. 2 eve, night before. * *Lebaran* Lebaran Eve. * *angkaté* the night before they left. * *Minggu* Saturday evening. * *lowong* the 22d, 24th, 26th, and 28th of the fasting month (*Pasa*). 3 still damp. *Kumbahané isih* *. The laundry isn't dry yet. ***an** ceremony or fair held on the eve of the above dates during Pasa, also on the 29th. * **Barat** a holy night during the month of Ruwah for giving thanks

males *form of* WALES. *kursi* * easy chair

malih 1 to change in appearance, shape. *Bareng kembang abang mau didumuk, bandjur* * *kuning.* When he touched the red flower, it turned yellow! *Wong kuwi bisa* * *dadi matjan.* He can change himself into a tiger. 2 again; more (*kr for* MANÈH). ***an** in disguise. *matjan *an* a devil in disguise; a man in the form of a tiger. **molah-*** to keep changing. *Bunglon iku molah-* ulesé.* Chameleons change color constantly. *See also* ALIH

malikat *var of* MALAÉKAT

malim *var of* MUALIM

maling *ng,* **pandung** *opt? kr,* **duratmâkâ** *ki?* thief; to steal. ***an** 1 to steal habitually. 2 stolen. *pit *an* a stolen bicycle. ***-*an** stolen goods, loot. **ke*an** to get robbed. *Aku ke*an piring sak setèl.* I was robbed of a set of dishes. **me*** (**me·m̄·pandung** *kr*) to steal. *ϕ*/**di*i** to rob. *malingi omah* to rob a house. * **ḍènḍèng** a secret lover

mamah[a] *ng kr,* **gilut** *or* **kenjoh** *ki* ***an** (having been) chewed. *ϕ*/**di*(i)** 1 to chew. 2 to argue with. 3 to do without difficulty. *Soal sing angèl kanggo aku, karo Slamet mung di* waé.* Slamet breezes right through problems that are hard for me.

mamah[b] *inf* mother, mama

mamak 1 stupid, uncomprehending. 2 to behave incoherently or uncomprehendingly. *Pikirané rusak bandjur* *. She's upset and doesn't know what she's doing. *Marga lampuné mati,* * *anggonku mlebu ing omah.* The lights were out, so I had to grope my way into the house. 2 *rg* mother; father. *See also* MUMUK

mamang uncertain; unable to decide

mambang ghost, spirit

mambeg clogged, choked, stopped up

mambrah *-* lying scattered about

mambrih *rg var of* AMRIH

mami 1 *oj* I, me; my. 2 mommy

mamotan *var of* MOMOT·AN

mampang (*or* *-*) angry, furious

mamprah to spread, extend out(ward)

mamprung to dash/fly off swiftly

mampu well-to-do. **ora** * incompetent, incapable

mampul *-* to float, bob

mampus *cr* dead

mamrèh *rg var of* AMRIH

mamrih *rg var of* AMRIH

mamring rare, scarce. *Dina udan sing nonton bioskup (sepi)* *. Very few people go to the movies when it's raining.

mamuk *oj* to run amuck, go on the rampage

man 1 you (*inf var of* SAMANG). 2 uncle (*shf of* PAMAN). 3 *prefix: var form of* MANG- 2

mânâ 1 (**manten** *kr*) unit of that scope (*Degree III: Introduction, 6*). *sa(k)*, se** one such unit (*see also* SEMANA). 2 (**mekaten** *kr*) *excl for finishing off a deprecatory or contrary-to-fact predicate. Anggepé kaja wong baud manah temenan* *. He really thinks he's good at archery! *Sengguhmu kuwi kaja bagus²a* *. You consider yourself pretty handsome, don't you? *mBok tibaa* * *ta, ja!* I wish he's fall! *Diarani botjah pinter, ija jèn pintera* *. They say he's a smart boy—I only wish he *were* smart. *See also* MONO

manabda *ltry var of* ÑJ·SABDA

manah 1 heart, feelings; mind; liver (*kr for* ATI[a]). 2 *kr for* BUDI 1? 3 thought, feeling, idea (*kr for* PIKIR). 4 *form of* PANAH

manalagi the finest variety of mango

manang 1 (*or* *-*) *intsfr* red. *abang *-** intensely red. 2 *oj* to get angry. 3 *oj* to make a mistake

mânâsukâ optional; voluntary. *Akèhé* *. The amount [one contributes] depends on one's wishes. *réclame kupon* * an advertisement for a lottery ticket that one may optionally purchase

manâwâ *formal var of* MENAWA

manawi *formal var of* MENAWI

mânâwibâwâ *oj* boastful, conceited
mândâ ***n** (*rg*) *or* *-* a little, a few; somewhat. *Sopé asiné mung *-*.* The soup needs just a little more salt. *Srengéngéné *-* anget.* The sun is a bit warm. (*aksara*) * **swara** (*gram*) semi-vowel (Javanese alphabetic character representing *wa, ja*)
mandah (*or* ***ané** *or* ***é**) *rg var of* MÉNDAH
manḍak 1 contrary to expectation; even. 2 mere(ly); trivial. ** kowé waé, masa bisaa!* Just you alone–as if you could do it! ** didemèk waé nesu.* Just being touched and you get mad! *ϕ*/**di*aké** to consider too trivial. *Adja sok manḍakaké wong.* Never underestimate people.
mânḍâkaki a certain tropical flower
manḍâlâ *ltry* world
mandânâ *oj* to give, donate
mandang *inf var of* T·UM·ANDANG
mandar even, moreover, contrary to expectations (*sbst kr for* MALAH?). *Botjah² diélikké ḍa peplajon * pénékan.* The boys were told not to run around and then they [went further and] climbed trees! *-* let's hope; may it turn out (that...)
manḍat mandate
mandéjan quite probably, very likely
manḍèkné *rg var of* ANḌÉ
mandéné *rg var of* MÉNDAH
manḍéné *rg var of* ANḌÉ
mandi (**mandos** *opt? sbst? kr*) 1 efficacious. *Tablèté * banget kanggo lara malaria.* The pills are an effective treatment for malaria. 2 strong, powerful [of poison]; poisonous. *ula ** poisonous snake. *ula sing wisané * banget* a snake whose poison is very potent
manḍi *see* KAMAR
mandir **mondar-*** to flutter, vibrate
mandira *oj* banyan tree
manḍirèng *contraction of* MANḌIRI ING
manḍiri independent, self-sufficient. ** ing pribadi* self-reliant. *Anakku saiki wis *.* Our son is self-supporting now. *ϕ*/**di*kaké** to cause to be self-sufficient. *manḍirèkaké anak²é* to equip one's children to stand on their own feet. *See also* ḌIRI
mandjalma *see* DJALMA
mandjang to sing, chant, recite
mandjur potent, efficacious
mandjurung to stimulate, encourage
manḍo to hold out the hand(s) to receive sth
manḍor foreman, work supervisor
mandos efficacious; potent; poisonous (*opt? sbst? kr for* MANDI)
mândrâgunâ supernaturally powerful
mandrâwâ *oj* (from) afar. *sinawang saking ** seen from a distance
mandul *-* springy, bouncy
manḍung 1 on hand, available. *Ana sing * beras, uga ana sing kurang.* Some have plenty of rice and some haven't enough. *Pananan bosok jèn kesuwèn *.* Food spoils if it's kept around too long. 2 unarmed guard at the second (inner) gate of the pavilion leading to the palaces in Jogjakarta and Surakarta. ***an** second (inner) gate of the palace pavilion. *-* heaped up, forming a pile. **ka*an** *sms* *AN. *See also* ANḌUNG
manèh *ng,* **malih** *kr* 1 again; more. *sidji ** another one, one more. *Adja takon *.* Don't ask any more questions. *La lutju *...* And another funny thing... 2 *excl of incredulity.* *Kowé * kuwata ngangkat koper iku!* As if you're strong enough to lift that trunk! 3 to continue [talking]; [to say] further. *Ḍèwèké takon *, keprijé?* Then he asked, how? *Aku kanḍa *: jèn ngono wis kebeneran.* "In that case," I added, "it's all right." ***é** (and) besides; in addition to that. *Siti pinter, *é sregep pisan.* Siti is smart, and she works hard too. *-* 1 [not ever] again. *Aku wis kapok, ora bakal djadjan *-*.* I've learned my lesson–I'll never buy snacks again. 2 one more time. *Slamet *-* ditutuh.* Once again, Slamet got the blame. *See also* ADJA[a], SE·ḌÉLA, LUWIH
manéka *oj* kind, variety; color. * **werna** (of) various kinds *or* colors. *kembang * werna* all kinds (colors) of flowers. *See also* NÉKA
mang 1 *md* you (*inf var of* SAMANG). *Engga * tampani ḍuwité.* Please take the money. 2 *prefix: ltry and old-fashioned var of* NG-: *pronounced variously according to root, as for* NG- (*Introduction, 3.1.5.4*)
mangah *-* 1 hot. 2 (*or* **mongah-***) red, flushed. *See also* MONGAH
mangalor *ng,* **mangalèr** *kr* northward. **ke*en** too far (to the) north. *See also* LOR, PANGALOR
mangar *-* *intsfr* red, flushed. *abang *-** very red/flushed. *Rainé nganti *-* gosong.* Her face was flushed and burning.
mangerti *ng,* **mangertos** *kr* *ϕ*/**di*** to know, grasp, understand (*ltry var of* NGERTI *ng,* NGERTOS *kr*). *Wulangané wis di* kabèh.* Everybody understands the lesson. *Aku ora mangreti apa sababé.* I don't know why.

***a** know!; you should know; I am informing you. *Mangertia, jèn Mardi kuwi ora kena dipertjaja.* I must tell you that Mardi is not to be trusted. **ϕ/di*kaké** to convey information to. *Bapak mangertèkaké Siti bab isiné lajang.* Father told Siti what was in the letter. **ϕ/di*ni 1** to convey information to. *Siti wis dimangertèni bab sédané bapaké.* Siti has been told of her father's death. 2 to know (about), understand. *Isiné lajang wis dimangertèni.* He knows (*or* understands) what the letter says. *See also* NGERTI

mangertos *kr for* MANGERTI

mangétan eastward. **ke*en** too far (to the) east. *See also* ÉTAN, PANGÉTAN, WÉTAN

mânggâ 1 *kr* please (go ahead and...). ** ta kula aturi nampi.* Please accept it. 2 *kr* Come in! (*response to* KULA NUWUN). 3 come on! (*kr for* AJO). *Engga, pak, kula djak teng omahé botjah niki.* Come on, Mister, I'll take you to the boy's house. 4 here! here you are! (*offering sth*) (*kr for* NJA). 5 *inf var of* KEMANGGA. **ϕ/di*kaké** to let/ask smn to precede one; to ask smn to help himself, come in, *etc.* *See also* SUMANGGA

manggâlâ *oj* 1 commander, commanding general. 2 elephant. **ϕ*ni** to lead one's troops in war

manggar blossom of the coconut palm

manggeng steady, steadfast. ** tanpa kendat* on and on without interruption

manggis mangosteen

manggok to be/stay smw. *See also* ENGGOK

manggrik **monggrak-*** beset with difficulties *or* illness

manggrok (*or* ***-***) to stop *or* stay smw. *A * nèng Djakarta.* A settled in Djakarta. *Montoré * ana ing dalan.* The car just sat there in the middle of the street.

manggrong *var of* MAGRONG

manggul a certain ceremonial porridge. ***an** ritual feast (held on the eve of a circumcision) at which the above porridge is served

manggung 1 one of four groups of female court retainers who accompany the monarch when he makes public appearances and display the court ceremonial objects. 2 [of birds] to sing continuously. *** ketanggung** the four groups of female retainers collectively. ***, tjèṭi, bedaja, srimpi** names of the four groups

manggut ***-*** *or* **monggat-*** to keep nodding the head

mangidul southward. *dalan kang ** the road (that goes) south. **ke*en** too far (to the) south. *See also* KIDUL, PANGIDUL

mângkâ (*or* ***kna** *or* **ka***) 1 but (the fact is); whereas; now (as it happens). *Aku didakwa ndjupuk bukuné, ka* aku weruh waé ora.* He accused me of taking his book, but the fact is I never even saw it. *Ḍokar mau ditunggangi wong menjang pasar gegawané akèh, * djarané tjilik tur kuru.* The carriage was loaded down with people carrying produce to market, but the horse was small and thin. *Bakul pitik mau nganti awan ora pepajon * adaté laris.* The chicken peddler hadn't sold anything all morning—and business was usually brisk. 2 even though, in spite of the fact that. *Olèhé mangan entèk rong piring * mau mentas mangan bakmi sapiring.* He ate two plates of rice, though he had already eaten a helping of noodles. *Diwastani anèh déné ana wong wédok kok njambut gawé kanggo penggautan * tjukup ora kekurangan.* It was considered queer [in those days] for a girl to work for her living when she didn't need to.

mangkak̄ dirty(-looking)

mangké in the future (*kr for* MENGKO)

mangkel resentful. **ϕ*aké** causing resentment; (*psv* **di*aké**) to make smn resentful. *Aku dimangkelaké omongané.* What he said made me seethe. **ϕ/di*i** to resent sth

mangkir to fail to appear. ** sekolah ora pamit* absent without being excused

mangkok 1 a small bowl used for eating. 2 basin used for carrying liquid foods sold by street peddlers

mangkrak *oj* to raise one's voice in anger

mangkring to perch, roost

mangkruk (*or* ***-***) seated on a high perch. **-* nang nduwur wit* perched in a treetop

mangku negaran Solonese court drama in which the performers sing as they dance

manglar *see* LAR

manglih 1 *oj* hungry. 2 *var of* MALIH 1

manglong to trespass, encroach [on]

mangro divided, split two ways. *Pikirané *, ḍèké kudu njambut gawé nang Djakarta nanging bodjoné ana ing Jogja.* He's being pulled two ways: his job is in Djakarta but his wife is in Jogja. *** ati·né/karep·é** of two minds, unable to decide. ** atiné anggoné arep nandjakaké ḍuwité kanggo tuku pit apa radio.* He can't decide whether to spend his money for a bicycle or a radio.

* **tingal** to divide one's loyalties. *See also* M̈·PARO, RO

mangrong to glow

mângsâ 1 (**wantji** *kr?*) time; season. *Durung *né mangan.* It's not time to eat yet. * *giling* sugar-cane-processing time. 2 month according to the Javanese calendar (*Kasa, Karo, etc.*). 3 a two-month period. 4 (*or* ***a**) *excl of skepticism. Jak *, ora ngandel aku.* Go on–I don't believe it. * *bisaa!* As if he could do it! *Jèn guwané mentas dileboni uwong, *a lamaté isih wutuh.* If anyone had just gone in the cave, how could the spiderweb [across the opening] be unbroken! ***n** 1 (to go) according to season. *Awohé ora *n.* It has no special season for giving fruit. 2 (*or* **me***) animal's food, prey. **ke*** 1 premature. *Wit iki kembangé ke*.* This tree is blossoming early. *Anaké olèhé lahir ke*.* The baby was born prematurely. 2 to get devoured. *ka* ing sima* eaten by a tiger. *ϕ*/**di*** to eat [its prey]; to feed on. **sa*** 1 when, at the time [of]. *Sa* ḍèké tekan kéné terus konen mulih.* As soon as he gets here, send him home. *Se* olèh ḍuwit aku silihana.* When you get the money, lend me some. 2 (*or* **sa*-***) at any time, whenever. *Sa*-* perlu pitulungan aku kanḍanana.* Let me know any time you need help. * **apit** the period (mid-April to mid-June) covered by the two final Javanese-calendar months. * **boḍo(a)** to disclaim responsibility. * *boḍo, aku ora ngerti.* I don't know and I don't care. *ϕ*/**di*-boḍo·kaké** to leave sth up to [smn]; to take no responsibility for. *Urusan keluargané di*-boḍokaké marang maratuwané.* He leaves all family matters in the hands of his parents-in-law. * **borong(a)** *sms* * BOḌO(A). *Kasil ora kasil * borong, dudu urusanku.* Whether it succeeds or fails is no concern of mine. *Pijé mangkaté nang Bogor?–* borong.* How shall we get to Bogor?–I leave it to you. *Ḍuwité saméné tjukup, * borong mbokné genḍuk sing nandangi.* This much money is enough; I'll let my wife handle it. * **dadi·a slilit** an inadequate amount of food. *Kanggo Bu Sastra beras limang kilo mono * dadia slilit, wong anaké sepuluh.* Five kilograms of rice doesn't go far with Mrs. Sastro–she has ten children. * **kala** the appropriate time. *Jèn wis teka * kalané...* When the time comes... * **katiga** dry (hot) season. * **kuning** time when ripened rice is ready to harvest. * **labuh** season (September-October) preceding the rainy season. * **marèng** season (March-May) preceding the dry season. * **mengko** nowadays. * **renḍeng** rainy season. * **rontog** fall. * **saldju** winter, snowy season. * **tara** drought during the dry season. *See also* TALIMANGSA, TITIMANGSA

mangsak ***an** 1 cooked food. *resèp *an* recipe. 2 packet of prepared betel. ***-*an** to pretend to cook, play at cooking. *ϕ*/**di*** to cook. *ahli ** chef. *buku ** cookbook. *djuru ** (professional) cook. *ϕ*/**di*aké** to cook for smn. *mangsakaké* (*kinang*) to prepare betel for smn to chew

mangsi 1 ink. *waḍah ** ink-well. 2 *excl of skepticism* (*var of* MANGSA 4). ***ǹ** written in ink. *Tulisané mangsèn.* It's written in ink. *ϕ*/**di*** to write/draw in ink

mangsud *var of* MAKSUD

mangsuh *oj* 1 to go to; to confront. * *ing ngajuda* to go to war. 2 vulnerable

mangsuk 1 to enter (into). *Dilarang *.* No admittance! * *Islam* to become converted to Islam. 2 suitable, becoming. *Ḍèké nganggo klambi kuwi * banget.* That dress looks good on her. * **angin** *or* * **lésus** to have/get a cold. **ora * akal** inconceivable, difficult to imagine

mangsur (*or* ***-***) to have diarrhea

mangu (*or* ***-*** *or* **monga-***) to waver, vacillate. *A isih *-* arep mangkat nang Djakarta apa ora.* A can't decide whether or not to go to Djakarta.

mangulon *ng*, **mangilèn** *kr* westward. **ke*en** too far (to the) west. *See also* KULON, PANGULON

mangun * **brâtâ** to pay a penalty; to do a penance

manguntur *oj* throne (*var of* WANGUNTUR)

mani 1 male sperm. 2 *cr* Adam's-apple. ***-*** coral; coral beads

manifèsto manifesto

manih *oj* again; more

manik 1 jewel, precious stone. 2 Adam's-apple. 3 pupil of the eye. ***-*** coral; coral beads. * **mata** the apple of one's eye

manikel *see* TIKEL

manikem 1 jewel. 2 *ltry* female ovum

maning *rg var of* MANÈH

manira I, me (*wj, court language: used by an exalted person speaking to an inferior*)

manis sweet; appealing. *djeruk ** a certain sweet citrus fruit. *botjah/rupa/swara ** a sweet child/face/voice. *tangan sing ∗* the right (not left) hand, *i.e.* the proper hand for giving and receiving. *kanggo gawé ∗é omah* to beautify the house. *wong sing ∗ rembugé* a persuasive talker. **∗an** fruit in a sugar sauce. *∗an nanas* pineapple in sweet sauce. **me∗ 1** ingratiating behavior. *udan me∗* a shower of sweet talk. 2 a bribe; hush money. **me∗an** *sms* ∗AN. **(me)ϕ/di∗i** to sweeten sth; *fig* to sweet-talk smn. *Pinter banget olèhé memanisi.* She's a very persuasive talker. ∗ **djangan** cinnamon; wood of the tree whose bark produces cinnamon

manj- *prefix: var of* MANG- 2

manjak **∗-∗** to barge in uninvited *or* unexpectedly

manjar a certain song bird

manjawak a certain large lizard

manju:k̄ (*or* **∗-∗**) 1 to arrive hastily. *Lagi waé ∗ tekan omah wis lunga manèh.* No sooner had he rushed into the house than he left again. 2 (*or* **monjak-∗**) to wander around smn's place without announcing one's presence. *See also* NJUK

manjul [of forehead] bulging, protruding

manjura a certain key or mode in which Javanese songs are played. *paṭet ∗* mode of the gamelan music in the third part of a shadow play

manon *ltry* to watch, look (at). *Hjang ∗* God (the All-Seeing). **ma∗** to look here and there, look around. **ϕ/di∗i 1** to appear (to smn, in a dream or vision). 2 to give the appearance that... *See also* TON

manpangat *var of* MUNPANGAT

manrang *oj intsfr* red. *abang ∗* bright red

mantak ∗ **adji** to effect sth through other than natural means. *∗ adji panggandan* a magic incantation for locating lost things. *∗ adji lelimunan* to make oneself vanish

manṭang **∗-∗** *var of* NG-AṬANG-AṬANG

manteb in full agreement, with wholehearted consent. *See also* ANTEB

mantel topcoat; raincoat

mantèn 1 bride; groom. *∗ lanang* groom. *∗ wédok* bride. *∗ anjar* newlyweds. 2 pertaining to weddings. *adat² ∗* wedding customs. *kursi ∗* bridal chair (occupied by the bride and groom during the festivities). *ḍukun ∗* person who applies the bridal cosmetics. **∗an** to play wedding, have a pretend wedding (children). ∗ **pangku·n̂** *rg* a bride who has not yet menstruated, hence the groom may not have intercourse with her. ∗ **pari** *rg* harvest ritual depicting the origin of rice, based on a mythological account of lovers transformed to rice stalks

manten unit of this (*Degree I*) or that (*Degree II, III*) scope (*Introduction, 6*): *kr for* MÉNÉ, MONO, MANA

manṭer straight, undeviating. *Lampuné soklé sumorot ∗ nganti adoh banget.* The searchlight sent its straight beam far into the distance. *ḍawuh ∗* a direct order. *Rupané putih ∗.* It was unrelieved white.

mântjâ foreign, alien. *bangsa (basa, negara, tembung, lsp.) ∗* foreign people (language, country, word, *etc.*). *wong ∗* a foreigner. *ing ∗* abroad. **nga∗** [in, from] a foreign place. *ing tanah nga∗* in a foreign land. *bangsa* (*tembung, lsp.*) *∗* foreign people (words, *etc.*). ∗ **kaki** *rg* the old people in a village. ∗ **pat ∗ lima** one's (village) neighbors. ∗ **rawat** *or* ∗ **udrasa** to weep. ∗ **warna** various kinds (of). *See also* MANTJATALPA

mantjâlâ ∗ **putra ∗ putri** able to assume any form magically. *Prabu Baṭara Kresna bisa ∗ putra ∗ putri.* King Kresna can change himself into anything. ∗ **warna** able to change one's shape/appearance magically

mantjapat *var of* MATJAPAT

mântjâtalpâ foreign; foreign country. *lelungan menjang ∗* to go abroad. *sesambungan karo ∗* foreign relations

mantjeb sticking/stuck [into] (*inf var of* T-UM-ANTJEB). *Wulanganė ∗.* The lesson stuck in their minds. *See also* ANTJEB

mantjung 1 to jut out. *Baṭuké ∗.* He has a bulging forehead. 2 a cluster. *kembang sa∗* a bunch of flowers. 3 coconut-blossom sheath. *∗ iku kena digawé upet.* (Dried) coconut-blossom sheaths can be made into wicks.

mantol *var of* MANTEL

mântrâ magic incantation uttered by a witch doctor. *∗ ruwatan* incantation for protecting an only child. **∗n** incantation for producing magical effects. **∗-∗** vague, hazy. *ora ∗-∗* inconceivable. *Ora ∗-∗ jèn X ki lurah.* It's hard to believe that X is the village head. **ϕ/di∗kaké** to utter [magical incantations]. *Upatjara ngruwat iku akèh banget ∗n²é kang kudu di∗kaké déning Kjai Ḍalang.* In an only-child ceremony, the puppet-master must utter a number of incantations. **ϕ/di∗ni** to use an incantation on smn. *mantrani keris* to cast a spell on a kris. *Djamuné wis di∗ni.* The medicine has been "bewitched."

mantri 1 government official in charge of a certain office *or* activity. 2 palace official; minister of the court. 3 bishop (in chess). * *kuwi mung mèntjèng.* The bishop moves only diagonally. **ka*n̂** office *or* residence of the above official. * **alas** official in charge of forestry. * **aris** assistant district chief. * **ka·bupati·n̂** secretary general of a regional office. * **guru** school superintendent. * **kéwan** official in charge of livestock. * **lanbau** official in charge of agriculture. * **lumbung** village official who supervises the rice supply. * **pamong pradja** head of a local district in a city. * **pulisi** chief of police; police superintendent. * **tani** official in charge of agriculture. * **tjandu** head of the opium control division. * **tjatjar** official who vaccinates for smallpox. * **ukur** land registrar

mantrol *var of* MANTEL

mantrus sailor; ship's crewman

mantu 1 child-in-law. (*anak*) * *lanang/wédok* son/daughter-in-law. *ngepèk* * to choose a marriage partner for one's child. 2 (to hold) a wedding for one's child. *Lurahé *, *né pak djuru tulis.* The village head married his daughter to the district secretary. ***n̂** (to hold) a wedding. **ϕ/di*k̂aké** to hold a wedding for [one's child]. * **m·bata rubuh** (to hold) a multiple wedding ceremony

mantuk to return to one's own place (*kr for* MULIH)

mantun to recover (from) (*kr for* MARI)

manṭur to stream, pour. *Lèḍengé sewengi * terus.* The water faucet ran all night.

manuârâ fascinating, strongly appealing, beautiful. *tembung ** seductive words

manudja *oj* human being

manuhârâ *var of* MANUARA

manuk *ng,* **pe(k)si** *kr* 1 bird. 2 *euph* penis. ***an** 1 place for birds. *pasar *an* market dealing in birds. 2 (*or* *-*an; **peksi²nan** *kr*) imitation bird, toy bird. **(me)ϕ/di*i** *ng kr* to watch from a distance. *Bèn dolan botjahé dak manuki saka kéné.* Let the child play; I'll keep an eye on him. * **djiwa** a certain kind of bird. * **unta** ostrich. *See also* BUR, PASA, SAUR

manungsa human being. *kulawarga ** mankind. **ka*n** 1 humanity; human nature. 2 pertaining to human beings. *adat ka*n* human traditions. 3 to appear human. *peri kang wis ka*n* a spirit in human form. 3 *ltry* to be caught doing wrong in secret

manus *oj* human being

manusa *var of* MANUNGSA

manut (to act) according to, in accordance with. * *kanggoné ḍéwé²* each according to his needs. * *udjaring wong...* according to what people say... **monat-*** to follow/obey habitually. *See also* ANUT, NUT, TUT

maolânâ *title for eminent Moslem scholars*

maos 1 *sbst kr for* MADJA. 2 *form of* WAOS

mapatih *oj* prime minister

maprah (*or* *-*) all over the place, spread wide

maputra to reproduce (*ki for* M·ANAK). *See also* PUTRA

mar (having) fear connected with high places. *Atiku emar jèn weruh kowé pènèkan.* My heart is in my throat when I see you climbing. **nge*-*i** hair-raising

mar- *see also under* MR- (*Introduction, 2.9.3*) *or under replaced-consonant plus* R (*Introduction, 3.1.5.4*)

mârâ 1 *var of* AJO, MANIRA. 2 *form of* PARA

mârâkâtâ *var of* MARKATA

marang *ng,* **ḍ(um)ateng** *kr* 1 to, toward; concerning. *A kanḍa* (*takon*) *marang B...* A said to (asked) B... *sija² * kéwan* cruel to animals. *Golongan A ora ngerti * basané golongan B.* Group A doesn't speak group B's language. *Ḍèké ngelem * swarané.* He spoke highly of her voice. *Adja muring² * ḍèwèké.* Don't be mad at him. *Ḍèké tresna * kowé.* He loves you. *Kuwi gumantung * kowé.* It depends on you. *ḍokter sing ahli * mripat* an eye specialist. *Ḍèké ora pertjaja * wong tuwané.* He doesn't trust his parents. 2 (*ng kr*) *form of* WARANG

maras 1 chicken lung (fried and eaten as a rice-accompanying dish). 2 *rg* organ-like piece clinging to the backbone of a chicken (eaten fried or boiled). 3 *rg* timid, cowardly. 4 *form of* PARAS

mârâsepuh *kr for* MARATUWA

mârâtuwâ *ng,* **mârâsepuh** *kr* parent(s)-in-law. * *lanang* or *bapak ** father-in-law. * *wédok* or *ibu ** mother-in-law

marbuka to open (up, out) (*ltry var of* (M)·BUKA). *Wis * pikiré.* He has opened his mind to new ideas.

mardika free (of). *bangsa kang ** a free people. *Bareng duwé omah ḍéwé saiki * ora diganggu wong lija.* How that he has a house of his own, he's free of interference from others. **ka*n** freedom, liberty, independence. *Tanggal pitulas Agustus iku dina* *ka*n Indonesia.* August 17th is Indonesia's Independence Day. *See also* PARDIKA

marem satisfied, content. *Rembugmu ndadèkaké *ing atiku.* Your words set my mind at rest. **ka*an** gratification. *Tumindak sing betjik kuwi bisa dadi ke*aning wong tuwa.* Fine achievements make parents happy. **ϕ*aké** causing satisfaction. *Bidjiné maremaké.* His grades are quite satisfactory. *ϕ*/**di*i** to satisfy, please, gratify. *See also* AREM

marèng brief interval between the close of the rainy season and the onset of the dry season

mares marching music; [of music] in marching tempo

Maret (month of) March

marga 1 *formal var of* MERGA. 2 *oj* road, way

margi 1 road, way (*kr for* DALAN). 2 *kr* because (*formal var of* MERGI)

marhaèn the proletariat

marhaènis those concerned with uplifting the proletariat

marhaènisme political policy of concern for the proletariat

marhum deceased. **Pak Sastra* the late Mr. Sastro. *Dikanḍakaké jèn * iki sawidjining ḍokter.* The deceased is said to be a doctor.

mari *ng,* **mantun** *kr* 1 (**ḍangan** *ki*) to get over, recover (from). *Laramu bèn gelis *.* I hope you'll get well soon. ** nepsu* to get over being angry. 2 to stop, subside. *Mengko² baé jèn udané wis *.* Wait till it stops raining. *ϕ*/**di*kaké** to cure. *Sapa sing bisa marèkaké watukku?* Who can get me over this cough? *ϕ*/**di*ni** to get over sth. *A wis marèni enggoné sok gumeḍé.* A has cured himself of his constant boasting.

marik *-* lined up. *Tanduranė *-*.* The plants were set in rows. **morak-*** untidy, in disorder

marikelu *oj* to sit silent with bowed head, signalizing esteem and humility

marine navy; navy man; (things) pertaining to naval war

maring (to go) to (*var of* MARANG, MENJANG)

marisan knife (*sbst? kr for* LADING)

marit **morat-*** in disorder, in chaos. *Pradjurité bubar morat-* ora karuwan.* The soldiers fled in utter confusion.

maritim maritime

markas headquarters

markâtâ lively. *abang ** cheerful bright red

markis 1 portico built onto the front of a house. 2 a certain fruit

markisah a fruit (*var of* MARKIS)

markonis navigator

marlupa *oj* physically exhausted

marma *oj* so, therefore; that is why

marmer marble. *watu * kuburan* a marble gravestone

marmot *var of* MARMUT

marmut woodchuck, groundhog; guinea pig

marong (*or* ***-***) to burn hotly. *geni sing ** a hot fire

mars *var of* MARES

marta (*or* **a***) invulnerable

martabak an Indian omelet with meat and vegetable filling

martabat rank, degree; high rank, prestige, status

martil hammer

martyâpâdâ *ltry* earth; place of human habitation

maru any wife after the first in a polygamous household. *ϕ*/**di*** to make [one's only wife] a co-wife by marrying another. *Ju Wangsa di* karo bodjoné.* Mrs. Wongso's husband has taken another wife.

maruk **ke*** *or* **ϕ*i** to have an enormous appetite after recovering from illness (*var of* ÑG·KEMARUK·I)

maruta *oj* wind

mas[a] *ng,* **djené** *kr* (*or* **djené·an** *kr*) gold. ** inten* jewelry; treasure. ** pasir* or ** uré* gold nuggets, gold dust. *iwak ** goldfish. ***-*an** imitation gold. *bakul* ***-*an** retail dealer in gold and jewelry. (*tukang*) **ke*an** *ng kr* goldsmith. *** bandjar** gold-plated. *** (e)nom** gold alloy. *** tuwa** solid gold

mas[b] (*adr; shf of* KAMAS) *title used by males to other males of equal social status; by females to their husbands, to men of status equal to their husbands, to men older than themselves; by servants to the master's male children.* *** adjeng** Miss; *** aju** Madam (*terms for addressing females of lower status, or by servants to the master's female children*). *** agus** *term used by servants to address the master's male children.* *** lara** *or* *** rara** *term used by servants to address the master's female children.* *** mirah** *term of endearment for addressing a girl*

mâsâ *var of* MANGSA. *** Allah** *var of* MASJA ALLAH

masak 1 tip given to a girl for acting as a man's dancing partner. 2 *var of* MANGSAK

masalah problem. **-* donja* world problems. **-* ngenani mantja negara* matters concerning foreign countries
masarakat *var of* MASJARAKAT
masdjid mosque
Masèhi Christian. *taun ** in the year of Our Lord. *taun 1290 taun ** 1290 A.D.
masi *excl of skepticism* (*var of* MANGSA)
masih *rg var of* ISIH
masik **mosak-*** in disorder. *Kamaré mosak-*.* The room is a mess.
masin 1 spoiled fish. 2 to peck the dirt
masina 1 corn. 2 corn flour, cornstarch. 3 corn pudding
masinal mechanical(ly). *Penggawéné *.* The work was done by machine.
masinis 1 person who operates a machine. ** kapal* person who runs a ship. ** pabrik gula* one who runs a sugar-processing plant. 2 railroad engineer
masir 1 to eat sand, brick dust, *etc.* [*usu.* of birds]. 2 pleasantly grainy in texture [of ripe *salak* fruits]
masja Allah *excl appealing to God in surprise or anguish.* **, sega semono kok entèk.* Heavens, what a lot of rice you ate!
masjarakat society, the community. *tunané ** outcasts/dregs of society; doing harm to the community at large. (*rumah*) **pa*an** prison; reformatory
maskapé company, firm, business enterprise
maskawin wedding gift from the prospective husband to the bride's family
maskumambang a certain classical verse form
masnis *var of* MASINIS
masrut *see* SARAT
massa (*prn* **māsā**) the masses, the people
massal (*prn* **masal**) *var of* MASSA
mastâkâ 1 head (*ki for* ENḌAS). 2 (royal) crown. 3 mosque turret
masud *var of* MAKSUD
masuk *var of* MANGSUK
mat 1 exactly, just right. *Wis * olèhé ngintjengaké beḍil.* He took precise aim with the gun. *Deloken sing *, rak ana tjatjadé klambi mau.* Look close: there's a defect in the shirt. *Ngombé kopi karo ngrungokaké gamelan pantjèn * banget.* Drinking coffee and listening to music is supremely pleasant. 2 (check)mate. ***-*an** to enjoy oneself thoroughly. **nge/di*aké 1** to focus the attention on. *Ḍèké nge*aké tulisanku.* He scrutinized my handwriting. 2 to give oneself over to the enjoyment of sth
mâtâ 1 eye (of an animal; *cr* of a human being) (*see also* MRIPAT). 2 eye-like part (*e.g.* knot in wood; center of a pimple; jewel in its setting). 3 spot, pip (on playing-cards, dice). 4 kernel, grain. *peté telung ** three beans. *asem se** a tamarind kernel. 5 a little something extra slipped to the village head when paying one's taxes. ***mu!** (*cr*) *abusive term.* ***-*** spy, secret agent. **-*ning mungsuh* enemy agent. **ke*** conspicuous, eye-catching. **ke*n 1** having excessively large eyes. 2 to be seen doing sth underhanded. **ϕ/di*k-*kaké** *cr* to impugn smn's eyesight. *Ḍèké matak²aké wong sing midak sikilé.* He yelled at the person who had stepped on his foot to watch where he was going. **ϕ/di*ni 1** to equip (*e.g.* a doll) with eyes. 2 to impugn smn's eyesight (*as above*). **sa*-*** striking in appearance; conspicuous. *** deruk** small buttonhole for attaching a pin-on button. *** ḍuwit·en** overfond of money. *** éra** [of wickerwork] loose, open. *krandjang * éra* a loosely woven basket. *** itik** buttonhole. *** iwak 1** scar from a wound. 2 corn on the toe. 3 duckweed. *** juju 1** tending to cry easily. 2 defect on an inflated balloon that might give way at any time. *** k·api·ǹ 1** dimly visible. 2 it appears that... *** krandjang** smn who wants everything he sees; smn with an eye for pretty girls. *** kutjing 1** dammar (resin used in batik work). 2 small light indicating that an electrical appliance has warmed up and is ready for use. *** lélé 1** the first leaf buds of tobacco plants. 2 whitish; light in color. *** loro 1** one who tries to straddle conflicting alternatives. 2 double spy. ***né nganti n·dlolèr** *cr* to stare (at). *** pita(ja)** *ng kr* 1 supervisor. 2 parent entrusted with supervisory work. 3 person who conducts guided tours. *** walang·en** *ng kr* staring fixedly and unseeing. *** walik** a certain pattern in woven work
matak *var of* MANTAK
maṭang ***-*** *rg var of* NG·AṬANG-AṬANG
matânggâ *oj* tiger
Mataram a kingdom in Central Java established in the sixteenth century as a protectorate of Jogjakarta and Surakarta
matarum *oj* magical incantation
matèk aku what have I done! (*var of* MATI AKU)
maṭem to like very much. *Jèn karo katjang * banget.* He's crazy about peanuts.

mateng 1 ready to eat. *pelem* * a ripe mango. *Segané wis* *. The rice is done. 2 *slang* (having been) brought to a head *or* to its conclusion. *Rembugé wis* *. They've reached an agreement. *Persiapané wis* *. The preparations are complete. **ϕ/di*aké** to bring to readiness/completion. *matengaké sega* to cook the rice (until it is done). *matengaké rembug* to bring about agreement by discussion. **ϕ/di*i** to cook until done. * **ati** [of fruit] ripe only on the inside. *See also* SAWO

matengga *var of* MATANGGA

matéri, materi substance, matter

materiil (*prn* **matérijil**) tangible, material. *sumbungan moril lan* * moral and material support

mati *ng,* **pedjah** *kr* 1 (**séda** *ki*, **murud** *or* **surud** *ki for kings*) dead; to die. * *djalaran tjatjar* to die of smallpox. * *klelep* to drown. * *konduran* to die in childbirth. * *ngurag* [of animals] to die of old age. 2 inert; no longer used; not functioning. *Apa radioné wis* *? Is the radio turned off? *Geniné durung* *. The fire isn't out yet. *rega* * fixed prices (not subject to haggling). *Tilpuné* (or *djamku*) *. The telephone (*or* my watch) is out of order. *Sikilku* *. My legs are numbed. *Karangan kuwi* *. The article is dull. *dalan* * an old (formerly used) road. *sumur* * a dried-up well. *aksara* * [in Javanese script] consonant; stroke added to a syllable character to remove the final vowel. *bolongan* * clogged-up opening. *tali* * rope knotted too tightly to be untied. *minggu* (*sasi, taun, lsp.*) * the week (month, year, *etc.*) just past. ***ǹ** hard to keep alive. *Rokoké matèn.* His cigarette keeps going out. *Tanduran kuwi matèn jèn ora tlatèn olèhé njirami.* The plant will die if it isn't watered carefully. ***-*** to malfunction off and on. *Mesin tik iki kok *-* waé.* This typewriter keeps going on the blink. **ka*an** death [*official term*]. *angka ke*an* death rate. *tundjangan ke*an* death benefit paid to the widow of an employee. **sa*né** after *or* since smn's death. *Sa*né bodjoné ḍèké dadi mlarat.* She's been poor ever since her husband died. * **aku** what have I done! oh me oh my! * *aku, tibaké ḍompètku kèri.* Oh dear, I've left my wallet somewhere! * **branggah** *ltry* to die an honorable death. * **djarak·é** to undergo a calamity, *e.g.* to lose one's source of income; to have one's descendants fall in social status. * **garing** to die of thirst. * **raga** deep in meditation. * **sabil** 1 to die in childbirth. 2 (*or* * **sahid**) to die as a religious martyr. * **urip** to share each other's destiny. *See also* PATI[a]

maṭi whorl in a horse's coat, believed to be an indication of the horse's temperament

matik aku oh dear! (*var of* MATI AKU)

matikel *see* TIKEL

maṭil **moṭal-*** coming off/apart. *Tjekelané lawang moṭal-* arep tjoklèk.* The door knob is about to fall off.

maṭis accurate, precise, proper. *Dandana sing* *. Dress with care. *Djawabané * kabèh.* All his answers were exactly right.

matjan *ng,* **sima** *kr* tiger. ***(-*)an** (to play) a certain game resembling Chinese checkers. * **gaḍung·an** human being in the form of a tiger. * **gémbong** Indian tiger. * **kombang** panther. * **lorèng** Indian tiger. * **luwé** [of walking gait] graceful and sinuous. * **malih·an** human being disguised as a tiger. * **tutul** leopard, cheetah

mâtjâpat classical verse form consisting of six-line stanzas, of various types according to the final-vowel scheme

matjari *oj* to (go) get, look for

matjem kind, sort, variety

matjet stuck, jammed, not working properly. *Sekrupé * djalaran nai.* The bolt is rusted fast. *Penḍak djam sidji awan dalan iki mesṭi* *. This road is choked with traffic every day at one P.M. *Lèḍengé * djalaran tuké angok.* There's no water coming through the pipes—the reservoir is too low.

matrik aku oh dear! (*var of* MATI AKU)

matrus *var of* MANTRUS

maṭuk to agree; to go well [with], to suit. *Aku * banget karo penemumu.* I'm in complete agreement with your opinion. *Isènana sing* *. Fill in the blanks with something appropriate.

mau *ng,* **wau** *kr* 1 the (aforesaid). *Swara * meneng.* The noise stopped. *Wong telu * pamit mulih.* The three men said goodbye and left. 2 just now, a moment ago; earlier. *Botjah sing nangis * anakku.* The child who was crying just now is mine. *Aku * weruh wong tuku sapi.* I saw a man buying a cow. *Ḍèk * ésuk ilang.* I lost it this morning. *Aku ḍèk * bengi nonton wajang.* I saw a shadow play last night. ***né** *see* *-*NÉ *below.* ***-*** before, earlier. *mBok *-* kanḍa ngono.* Why didn't you say so in the first place!

***(-*)né** before (as contrasted with now); as previously. **né ana petengan, saiki ana ing paḍangan.* It has been dark; now it was light. **-*né aku durung tau weruh iwak kang kaja mengkono.* I had never seen a fish like that before. *Jèn lakuné kesasar, unta iku gampang nggolèki dalané *né.* If camels lose their way, they can easily find it again. *Tangané bisa pulih kaja *né.* His hand healed up and was as good as ever.

maulânâ *var of* MAOLANA

Maulud birth and death day of Mohammed (*var of* MULUD)

ma'ut *rg* dead; death

mâwâ *ng*, **mawi** *kr* 1 with; having; making use of. *wong * prabawa* a man of prestige. *iwak * wisa* poisoned meat. *Sikilé kéwan mau * kuku lantjip²*. The animal's feet are equipped with sharp claws. *Wangsulané * tembung kasar.* He answered coarsely. *Buku Djawa mau sing akèh * aran² Arab.* Many of these Javanese books have Arabic titles. *Olèhé ndjogèd * ndadi lan * kesurupan.* The dancers enter a trance and become possessed. *ndonga * basa Arab* to pray in Arabic. *Apa kang dumadi ing donja iku * adjal.* Every living creature is mortal. *Negara * tata, désa * tjara.* Different people have different ways. 2 *ng kr* glowing charcoal fire. *-* varying according to the circumstances. *Sekolah mau suwéné *-*.* The length of time varies from school to school. *Barangé paḍa regané ora paḍa, *-* sing tuku.* The goods are the same but the price is not the same, depending on who the customer is.

mawak *-* having a large tear in it. *Djariké suwèk nganti *-*.* The batik is badly torn.

mawar rose. *wit ** rose bush. ** mrambat* climbing rose

mawat *oj* to give

mawèh *oj* to give

mawi with; having; making use of (*kr for* MAWA)

mawon *kr* *inf var of* KÉMAWON

mawur in grains. *geṭuk ** powdered *or* ground-up cassava

mb- *see under* B- *or under* EMB- (*Introduction, 2.9.5*)

mé ***an** 1 things (to be) sun-dried *or* aired. 2 clothesline. **a*** *or* **nge*** to put sth outdoors to sun *or* air. **pa*an** place for sunning things. *See also* PÉ, PÉPÉ

me- *see also under* MA- (*Introduction, 2.9.2*) *or replaced-consonant* + A (*Intro., 3.1.5.4*)

m(e)- *root-activating prefix: prn* ME- *before consonant* (*other than* L, R) *and monosyllabic root.* *m·anak* to give birth to young. *me·ḍun* to descend. *m·èsem* to smile. *m·ili* to flow. *m·laku* to walk. *m·réné* to come here. *m·uni* to say

me- *inf var of* MA-ᵇ. *me·ḍukun* to use the services of a faith healer. *me·gawé* to work

mèbel furniture

mébilèr furniture

mèbrèt (*or* *-*) *rpr* the sound of tearing. *Djariké suwèk *.* Her batik ripped.

meḍâjâ to be(come) a professional female dancer

meḍajoh *var of* MERḌAJOH

medal to emerge; to put forth; to take [a route]; to leave (*kr for* METU). *See also* WEDAL

meḍali medal, medallion

medamel *var of* MERDAMEL

meḍangkrang 1 to stand with the legs apart. 2 unfinished. *Gawéané isih *.* The work hasn't been completed. * **ñj·tjagak talang** to live in luxury

meḍeḍeg *var of* M·BEḌEḌEG

mededeng firm, steadfast, determined

mèdèl *-* 1 [of pants] worn low at the waist. 2 [of fat flesh] to shake, wobble

mèdèng *-* *or* **médang-*** *sms* MÈDÈL²

meḍeng 1 adequate. *Klambiné ora *.* Her dress is too small. *Satus rupijah * ora?* Is 100 rupiahs enough? 2 at the midpoint. ** aku mangan, ḍèké teka.* He came while I was in the middle of eating. **sa*an** at the midpoint. *Aku milih sing semeḍengan.* I took the medium-sized one.

meḍit stingy, close-fisted

médja table, tabletop, counter. **sa*** 1 a tableful. 2 the size of *or* as broad as a table

medjadji *var of* M·BEDJADJI

medjânâ ϕ/**di*ni** to mortify, humiliate; to convey a (*usu.* humiliating) meaning to [smn] indirectly by addressing remarks ostensibly to smn else

medjemuk rural celebration held before or after the rice harvest

medjen 1 dysentery. 2 to fail to explode. *Beḍilé *.* The gun wouldn't go off.

medjenun mentally disturbed (*used also pejoratively*)

medjid *var of* MESDJID

medjudjag *var of* M·BEDJUDJAG

medodong *var of* M·BEDODONG

mẹ́ḍok *-* [of face powder] applied thickly

meḍok to soften (up). *Intipé * bareng dikum nang banju.* The hardened rice at the bottom of the pan came loose when it was soaked. * **ati·né** to calm down

médol *-* *or* **médal-*** (to walk) with swaying hips

méḍol *var of* MÉDOL

médong *-* *or* **médang-*** (to walk) with a waddling *or* spraddling gait

meḍuḍug *var of* M·BEḌUḌUG

medudung *inf var of* M·BEDODONG

meg **mag-*** to keep touching/handling

méga cloud. ***n** grayish-blue; cloud-colored. *dara *n* pale gray-blue pigeon. **ka*n** covered *or* obscured by clouds. * **malang** *ltry* uppermost layer of clouds. * **menḍung** a certain sweet snack

megagah *var of* M·BERGAGAH

megap (*or* *-*) to pant, breathe in gasps

megar *see* GAR

megatruh a certain classical verse form

megawé *var of* MERGAWÉ

mègèg (*or* *-*) motionless. *Djarané dipetjuti malah bandjur *.* He whipped the horse again and again, but it didn't budge.

megeg (*or* *-*) (to sit, stand) stock-still

megegeg motionless, stock-still

megèǵèh [of legs] spread wide apart

megegeh *oj* motionless, stock-still

mègèng weakened by illness

megeng 1 to hold the breath. 2 the beginning of the fasting month (*Pasa*). *Sésuk wis *, mengko bengi kudu saur.* Tomorrow we start fasting, so we'll have to eat in the predawn hours. ***an** *rg* ritual meal held on the eve of the fasting month. * **ng·ampet** *or* * **napas** to hold the breath

meger *-* to survive; to come through in good condition. *Aku isih ana, isih *-*.* I'm alive and kicking. *Retjané isih *-* durung dibubrah.* The statue hasn't been taken down yet.

mèglèng *abusive term addressed to smn.* **méglang-*** to strut, swagger, show off

megogok to sit utterly motionless

megok *var of* MEGUK

mégol *-* *or* **mégal-*** (to walk) with hips swaying provocatively

mégot *-* reluctant

megrak [of hair] to stand straight up, stand on end

megrik **megrak-*** feeble. *Saiki megrak-* kerep lara.* His frequent illnesses have weakened him. *Olèhé gawé bango megrak-* ora kukuh.* The roadside stand is flimsily built.

megrok *var of* MEKROK

megruk *var of* MEKROK

meguguk *var of* M·BEGUGUK

meguk *-* to sit around idle

megung stagnant

mèh almost. *Lakuné * tekan sekolahan.* They walked almost as far as the school. ***an** almost; around about. *nganti tengah wengi *an* until nearly midnight. * **baé** just about, very nearly. *Aku * baé keplinḍes montor.* I came within an inch of being hit by a car. * **ora** almost no/not. ** ora katon.* You can hardly see it. *See also* WIS

Mèi (month of) May

mèjèk 1 heavy, unwieldy. *Olèhé nggawa barang ngasi *-*.* The load he's carrying is almost too much for him. 2 *slang* too old to [do]

mèk *var of* MEK

mek̄ *rpr* a touch of the hand. ***-*an** to grope. **nge/di*(i)** to feel (of), to touch. **nge/di*-*** to keep touching; to make messy by touching. *Aku ngemek-emek kanṭongku ning isiné wis mabur.* I felt in all my pockets, but the money was gone. *Médjané adja di*-*, tjèté isih teles.* Don't make finger marks on the table—the paint is still wet.

mékah *-* to waddle, walk like a duck. *See also* MÈKÈH

Mekah Mecca

mekak a short strapless female wajang costume. ***an** to put on *or* wear the above

mekakah to stand with the legs wide apart

mekakat **ora *** extremely; without equal. *Angkané ora * akèhé.* The interest rate is exorbitant. *Aboté ora *.* It's awfully heavy.

mekangkang to sit with the legs spread apart

mékanik mechanic

mékanisasi mechanization. **ϕ/di*** to mechanize. *Pertanian wis di*.* Farming has become mechanized.

mekao strong natural undyed cotton fabric

mekar to open out, expand. *Kembangé srengéngé wis *.* The sunflowers have bloomed. *Krupuké jèn digorèng bisa *.* When you fry shrimp chips. they expand and puff out.

mekaten 1 like this, in this way (*Degree I: kr for* MENGKÉNÉ). 2 like that, in that way (*Degree II, III: kr for* MENGKONO, MENGKANA). 3 *excl* (*kr for* MANA 2). 3 *a particle* (*kr for* MONO 2, 3, 4)

mèkèh *-* *or* **mékah-*** to walk with a waddle

mekeh *-* constricting. *Djasé ketjiliken, mulané jèn dienggo rasané *-* angèl olèhé ambegan.* The jacket is so small it's hard for him to breathe with it on.
mekèten *rg var of* MEKATEN
mekingking *intsfr* dry. *Sakèhing suket pada garing *.* Most of the grass had dried up.
mekoten *rg var of* MEKATEN
mékrad to ascend to heaven. ***an** the day of Mohammed's ascension; to celebrate this day
mekrok to open out. *Kembangé mawar wis *.* The roses are in bloom.
mekruk *var of* MEKROK
meksa 1 still, even so, in spite of the foregoing. *Ḍuwité diigah-iguhaké ja * ora tjukup.* No matter how carefully he figured, the money still didn't go far enough. 2 *form of* PEKSA
mèl 1 magic incantation. 2 *rg* illegal highway toll. **nge/di*aké** to utter an incantation on smn's behalf. **nge/di*i** 1 to utter an incantation for. 2 to pay [an illegal toll]. *Saben pos para sopir kudu nge*i sèket rupiah.* At each post the drivers are held up for 50 rupiahs.
mel *ϕ*/**di*-*** to mouthe constantly. *Tjripingku di*-* nganti entèk.* She nibbled away at my chips till there were none left.
mel- *see also under* ML- (*Introduction, 2.9.3*) *or under replaced-consonant plus* L (*Introduction, 3.1.5.4*)
méla *rg var of* WÉLA
mélai to begin (*kr for* MULAI)
Melaju Malayan
melak *var of* MELOK
melang *-* uneasy, apprehensive, fearful
mèlek milk
melèk 1 (**wungu** *ki*) to stay awake. *Sing isih * réka² turu.* The ones who were still awake pretended to be asleep. 2 (**wungu** *ki*) to wake up; [of the eyes] to open. *Suwé éling, *.* Soon she regained consciousness and her eyes opened. *Njambut gawé wiwit *.* He works from the time he wakes up. 3 eye-opening. *Rupané rada *.* She's good-looking. *mitjakaké mata ** to think smn doesn't know sth which in fact he does know. ***-*an** brazen. *Rumangsaku *-*an diapusi.* I felt I had been cheated outrageously. *** huruf** illiterate
melèng reckless
meleng *-* dark and shiny and gleaming
mèlèr [of the nose] to keep dripping

meles *intsfr* black. *Manuk gagak kuwi ulesé ireng *.* Crows are jet black. *See also* M·BREBES
mélik 1 possession, belonging. **é sapa?* Whose is it? 2 covetousness; to covet. ** marang gandjaran* hungry for a reward. *Sadjaké kowé ki duwé * marang banḍaku.* You seem anxious to get your hands on my money. 3 to obtain possession of. *Ḍèké tuku lemari kuwi * pengiloné.* He bought the whole cupboard just to get the mirror. 4 so that, in order to. *nunggang sepur * gelis tekan* to take a train so as to get there fast. **(ka)*an** to covet others' belongings. *** ng·génḍong lali** to have an overweening desire to obtain sth by any means whatever. *Kangsa * nggénḍong lali arep dadi ratu ana ing Mandura.* Kangsa was obsessed with the desire to be king of Mandura.
melik *-* *or* **melak-*** 1 to keep opening and closing [of *e.g.* an insomniac's eyes]. 2 nervous and jumpy. *See also* SISIK, TITIK
meling *form of* WELING. *-* light in color and glossy. *Djobiné *-*.* The floor tiles gleam. *ϕ***i** shrill, piercing
melit *rg var of* MEḌIT
mélok *var of* M·ÈLU, MELOK
melok conspicuous. *Sing * jaiku kèhé tunggangan.* The striking thing is the great number of vehicles. *Tanḍané lalulintas * ngana, kok ora weruh.* The traffic signal is in plain sight—how could you fail to see it?
melong *-* to shine, gleam
mélor rickety. **mélar-*** loose, wobbly
mélot 1 to bend, give, yield. 2 reluctant
melung 1 to bend, bow. 2 (*or* ***-***) to wail, howl
melur jasmine
mem- *see also under* M- (*Introduction, 3.1.3*) *or under consonant which has been reduplicated and then replaced* (*Introduction, 3.1.3, 3.1.5.4*)
memak thick and soft [of hair on head]
membek̄ *-* to well up. *Ḍèké *-* nahan nangis.* Her eyes filled with tears but she held them in. *Banjuné segara *-* kaja djenang lemu.* The surface of the ocean looked bubbly like fat porridge.
membeng *var of* MEMBLENG
membi:k *-* *or* **membak-*** with face screwed up ready to cry
membleg *-* thick(ened), viscous
mèmblèh *-* having the lips drawn back ready to cry

mèmblèk *var of* MÈMBLÈH
membleng stagnant
memburi *see* BURI
mèmèk to (go) get, pick (up). * *iwak* to (go fishing and) get some fish
memel meaty without fat; having firm good flesh
memes soft. *Wuluné lawa kuwi alus* *. Bats' fur is fine and soft. *Dagingé* *. The [overcooked] meat is mushy.
mèmèt to fish or hunt with the bare hands. *Pétruk dipurih * golèk welut, lintah karo bulus.* Pétruk was instructed to go find an eel, a leech, and a tortoise. *ϕ*i* [of hens] to run around looking for a place to lay an egg
memet 1 intricate, complicated, difficult to grasp. 2 joined into one; mixed together from separate parts
mempeng to work assiduously (at). **é njambutgawé sok nganti kliwat wantji.* He often works after hours. *A lagi * olèhé sinau.* A is plugging away at his studies now. *See also* NGE·PENG
mempès deflated. *ban* * flat tire
memplak *intsfr* white. *kemédja putih* * a snowy white shirt
mempur pleasantly soft and meaty [of fully ripened cassava]
mèmrèng threadbare
memret old and fragile, falling apart with age
mèn *var of* AMÈN, BÈN
men 1 very, decidedly, really (*shf of* TEMEN). *Kowé kok dahwèn* *. You certainly are nosy! 2 only, just (*md for* BAÉ). **ϕ/di*-*(aké)** to exert effort [to do], to make a point of [do]ing. *Olèhé ngopèni montoré di*-* tenan.* He takes scrupulous care of his car. *Pendjenengan kok ngemenemenaken sanget rawuh mriki.* You've really gone out of your way to come here!
Ménak stories about the Islamic hero Amir Ambjah, depicted in *wajang golèk* dramas
menak *rg* ***an** *or* ***en** if, when(ever)
menang 1 (**sasab** *kr?* **mimpang** *rg? kr?*) to win. *Kowé * apa kalah?* Did you win or lose? **é akèh banget.* His winnings were considerable. 2 to a greater degree. * *rosa* stronger. *Umuré * tuwa karo aku.* He's older than I am. ***an** 1 to win regularly. 2 superior, outstanding. **an ḍéwé* the best. ***-*an** to vie for top position. **ka*an** 1 victory. 2 (margin of) profit. **ϕ/di*aké** to cause *or* allow to win. *Ḍèké ngadjak sekak, dimenangaké baé.* She asked him to play chess with her, and she let him win. *Kapinterané sing marahi Sidin menangaké béasiswa.* It was Sidin's brains that won him the scholarship. **ϕ/di*i** (**ϕ/dipun·mening·i** *kr*) to experience, witness, know at first hand. *Aku bijèn wis tau menangi lindu gedé.* I saw a hurricane once. *Muga*[2] *menangana.* I hope I'll live to see it. *jèn menangi petjeklik* in times of food scarcity. * **akal karo okol** brains win over brawn. * **atas** to win (out). * **gertak** *or* * **tjanḍak** the best bluffers will win out
menangèn(a) *rg* if, when(ever)
menâpâ *pronunciation form of* PUNAPA
menârâ 1 tower. * *aèr* or * *banju* water tower. 2 lighthouse. 3 minaret, mosque tower; church steeple
menâwâ *ng*, **menawi** *kr* 1 if, when(ever). * *udan, dolané ana ngarep.* When it rains, they play in the front room. * *krasa luwé* if you get hungry. 2 [to say *etc.*] that... *Dikanḍani * anaké tiba.* They told him that his child had had a fall. *Kuwatir * matjané mrono manèh.* They were afraid that the tiger would come back. *Wis genah * asilé rembug mau ora ana.* It was obvious that the negotiations were ineffectual. 3 otherwise, or else. *Aku njingkir mbok * tabrakan.* I stepped aside or we would have collided. 4 possibly, probably. * *sésuk tekané.* He may come tomorrow. 5 as for, talking about... * *iki keprijé?* How about this one? * *aku, luwih betjik ora mangkat.* I myself would prefer not to go. *mung *-** not yet certain. *Perkara kapan ḍèké mulih mung *-*.* When he'll come home is still up in the air. * **durung** before; until. * *durung éntuk bajar adja tetuku.* Don't buy anything till you get paid. ***-menawi** *ng kr* not yet certain. * **silih** *rg* possibly, probably. * **wis** after(wards). *menawi sampun let sedinten* after a day('s interval). * *wis rampung, balèkna ing panggonané.* When you've finished with it, put it back. *See also* BOK
menawi if, when(ever) *etc.* (*kr for* MENAWA; *opt? kr for* JÈN, NÈK)
ménda goat; sheep (*kr for* WEḌUS)
ménḍa (*or* *-*) to disguise oneself (as). *Pulisiné *-* dadi wong emis.* The policeman posed as a beggar. *Sukmané ula mau * botjah lanang.* The serpent's spirit took the guise of a boy.
méndah how...! what (a)...! *Ah * seneng-ing atiné.* My, how happy she was! ***a** if

only. *a sugih aku arep tuku omah. If I were rich, I'd buy a house.

menḍak (or **ke***) jeweled band encircling a kris just below the handle

mendal *-* to bounce, spring

mendang broken-up discarded rice husks; *fig* trivial, insignificant

mèndel 1 to refrain from speaking (*rg kr for* MENENG). 2 to stop, cease (*rg kr for* LÈRÈN)

mendelep to enter an opening. *Gabusé* * *nang gendul.* The cork went down into the bottle.

mendelip *var of* MENDLIP

mendèlès to stand one's ground stubbornly

mendelo *var of* MENDOLO

mendem under the influence. *inuman drunk. *mbako groggy from smoking. *durèn head-achy and upset from overeating durian fruit

mending preferable. *Tinimbang tuku weḍus* * *tuku pitik, gelis tambah okèh.* It's better to buy chickens than goats—they multiply faster.

mendi:p *-* to flicker

mendjangan (**sangsam** *opt? kr*) large deer with pronged antlers. *iwak* * venison. * **tutul wulung** a certain deer having blue-black spots. *See also* KIDANG

méndjé young seeds of the *putjung* tree (*cf.* KLUWAK). *See also* KALA

mendjila solitary, isolated; apart, in a class by itself. *Ing kono ana wit geḍé sidji* *. A solitary large tree stands there. *rumah sakit kang* * *sarta geḍé ḍéwé sa-Asia* the largest and most eminent hospital in Asia

mendjing *see* GULU, KALA

mendlip *-* *or* **mendlap-*** 1 to waver, flutter, flicker. 2 to vacillate indecisively

méndol *-* stuffed full. *Pitiké telihé nganti* *-*. The chicken's crop was crammed full of corn.

mendolo bulging [of eyes]; pop-eyed. *Iwak mas kuwi matané* *. Goldfish have bulging eyes. *Olèhé ngingetaké botjah wadon kuwi nganti* *. He watched the girl with his eyes bugging out.

méndong a certain grass used for weaving. *klasa* * a grass mat. *kampil* * money pouch of woven grass

méndra *ltry* to travel, roam

méndring *var of* MINDRING

mendri:p *-* *or* **mendrap-*** 1 to flutter, flicker, waver. 2 to hesitate with indecision

menḍung dark rain cloud

mendut a sweet cookie of glutinous-rice flour. *-* *or* **mendat-*** springy, bouncy.

φ/**di***-***aké** to make sth springy *or* bouncy. *See also* ENDUT

méné 1 (**manten** *kr*) unit of this scope (*Degree I: Introduction, 6*). *sa*(*k*) * *or se** one such unit (*see also* SEMÉNÉ). *rong* * twice as much as this. (*wa*)*jah* * at [so unexpected] a time like this. 2 *rg var of* KÉNÉ

mené 1 *oj* later on, in the future. 2 *rg* now. 3 *rg* tomorrow

menèh *inf var of* MANÈH

menèk *rg* if, when(ever)

mènèng *-* *var of* MANANG[2]

meneng *ng,* **kèndel** *kr* to become *or* remain quiet. **a.* Hush! *Aku* * *waé.* I didn't say/ do anything. *Swara mau* *. The noise stopped. *Prahara mau* *. The storm subsided. *See also* NENG

meng 1 too lazy (to...); not feeling up to [do]ing. *Aku nèk nang Sala kon tulak* * *banget.* I don't feel like making the effort to go to Solo and back. 2 *rg var of* ING[a]

mengastâwâ *oj* to welcome smn

mèngèh *-* 1 *intsfr* red. *abang* *-* intensely red. 2 brand new

mengéné *rg var of* MRÉNÉ

mengènèh *rg var of* MRÉNÉ

mengeng 1 not clear; difficult to ascertain *or* classify. *Ali lagi* *. Ali is acting withdrawn and strange (and the reason for this mood cannot be ascertained). *Akèh rimbag[2] sing* * *enggoné bakal ngarani apa tembung iku kagolong krija utawa tembung kaanan.* With many derived forms, it's hard to say whether the word should be classified as a verb or an adjective. 2 buzzing sound

mengèngèh to laugh *or* grin broadly (often jeeringly), showing the teeth

mengèngès *var of* MENGÈNGÈH

mèngèr *-* *intsfr* red. *abang* *-* very red; heavily reddened

menges (*or* *-*) glossy

menggah (*or* ***a**) in case; in connection with; now (*kr for* MUNGGUH)

menggèh (*or* *-* *or* **menggah-***) to pant, breathe heavily

menggos *-* [of breathing] heavy, panting. *Ambegané* *-*. He's breathing hard.

menggrik *-* *or* **menggrak-*** thin, sickly

mengguk asthma. **menggak-*** 1 to have recurrent attacks of asthma. 2 to keep sobbing

mengi asthma

mengkak *intsfr* old. *kuna* * ancient

mengkânâ *ng,* **mekaten** *kr* like that, in that

way (*Degree III: Introduction, 6*). *Barang² * kaé angèl golèkané.* Things like that are hard to get. **ϕ/di*kaké** to treat in that way; to do that to. *Sapa ta djané sing mengkanakaké?* Who would actually do *that* to it! *** iku** that is (to say)...

mengké in the future, later on (*inf kr? md? for* MENGKO)

mengkelang [of feces] large and hard

mengkéné *ng,* **mekaten** *kr* 1 like this, in this way (*Degree I: Introduction, 6*). ** ija bisa.* You can do this too! 2 as follows. *Uniné *.* Here's what it says. **ϕ/di*kaké** to do like this to; to treat in this way. *Jèn dimengkènèkaké ja gelis rusak.* If you do this to it, it'll soon be out of order. **mengkéna-*** what with this and that; no matter what. *Mengkéna-* sarwa ora kebeneran.* No matter what I do, it never pleases her. *Mengkéna-* aku isih seduluré présidèn.* Come what may, I'm related to the president. *Mengkéna-* iki apa ija bakal olèh pituwas.* After all this trouble, I wonder if I'll get anything out of it!

mengkènèk *rg var of* MENGKÉNÉ. *** ènggrèk** trifling, inconsequential. *Bareng * ènggrèk waé, dienggo rebutan.* Why all this fuss over such a little thing!

mengkènèn *rg var of* MENGKÉNÉ

mengkis ***-*** out of breath

mengko *ng,* **mangké** *kr* 1 in the future. *Olèhku mangan * waé.* I'll eat later on. ** aku arep nang pasar.* I'm going to the market after a while. *Sikilku * dikapakaké ja?* What's going to happen to my [injured] leg? *ing ** hereafter. ** jèn wis korampungaké aku diundang.* Call me when you finish. ** awan* this (coming) afternoon. 2 or (else). ***né 1** nowadays. **né akèh wong sing ora duwé gawéjan.* There's a lot of unemployment now. 2 in the future; thereafter, *i.e.* after some future event. *Sing sapa gawé betjik, *né mesṭi diwales kabetjikan uga.* Those who do good will be repaid with good. **né aku arep nerusaké sinau.* Afterwards I'll resume my studies. *** anjar** just recently. *** ḍisik** just a minute! ** ḍisik, tak pikiré.* Wait–I want to think about it. *** iki** any minute now. *** munḍak** or (else). *Ajo paḍa mapan turu, * munḍak karipan.* Let's get to bed, or we'll be too sleepy [tomorrow]. *** seḍéla** *sms* * ḌISIK. *** selak** *sms* * MUNḌAK. *Ajo ndang mangkat * selak kepantjal sepur.* Hurry, or we'll miss the train.

méngkog ***-*** [to walk] heavily, ponderously

mèngkok ***-*** *or* **mèngkak-*** [to do] grudgingly, against one's will

méngkol to turn (off, aside). **a ngiwa.* Turn left. **méngkal-*** to zigzag. *Dalané méngkal-*.* The road twisted and turned. *Olèhmu ndjahit kok méngkal-*.* Your sewing is crooked. **ke*en** excessively curved. *Olèhmu nekuk kawat adja ke*en.* Don't bend the wire too far. *See also* ÉNGKOL

mengkono *ng,* **mekaten** *kr* 1 like that, in that way, so (*Degree II: Introduction, 6*). *Lagi paḍa ramé² *, guruné teka.* Just while they were making all that racket, the teacher walked in. *Sanadjan *, wewatekané apik banget.* Even so, he's of very good character. *O mekaten.* Oh, really? 2 the foregoing. *ngGoné tjlaṭu * karo gedrag-gedrug.* As he said this, he stamped his feet. 3 if only...! *Jèn aku duwé ḍuwit *, aku ja bisa ngutang.* If only I had some money, I could give you a loan. **ϕ/di*kaké** to do that to; to treat in that way. *Jèn dimengkonokaké pèné, ja gelis rusak.* If you do that to the pen it'll wreck it. *** iku** that is (to say...). *Aku arep ngleboni sekolah ḍokter, * iku jèn aku kuwat ngragadi.* I'm going to medical school–that is, if I can afford it. *** mau** the foregoing. ** mau djaréné pak guru.* That's what the teacher said. *** uga** and so...; and [not] either. *A ana kéné, * uga B.* A is here and so is B. *A ora kéné, * uga B.* A isn't here and neither is B.

mengkonok *var of* MENGKONO

mengkonon *rg var of* MENGKONO

mengkos ***-*** out of breath

mèngkot *var of* MÈNGKOK

mengkrik ***-*** perched precariously in a high place

mengkuk *var of* M·BENGKUK

mengkureb lying face down, or with the concave *or* under side down. *Olèhé turu *.* He sleeps on his stomach. *tiba ** to fall face down. *Tanganè tengen mlumah, tangan kiwa *.* His right hand is palm up, his left hand palm down. *See also* KUREB

mengkus ***-*** out of breath

mènglèng to tip the head sideways, *i.e.* bend the head downward toward the shoulder

méngo to swivel the head; to glance to one side. *Méngoa seḍéla waé, delengen sesawangan iku.* Just turn your head and look at the view! *Diundang bolabali * waé ora!* I called and called, and you never even turned your head! **ménga-*** to keep swiveling the head; to look from side to side. *Ménga-* ḍisik sadurungé njabrang.* Look both ways before you cross the street.

méngos *var of* MLÉNGOS

mengsah opponent; enemy (*kr for* MUNGSUH)

mengung (to make) a shrill buzzing *or* humming sound

menik blossom of the green-pepper plant. ***-*** (*prn* **meni:k²**) cute. *tjilik *-** [of girls] little and cute

menika *pronunciation form of* PUNIKA

mening ***-*** spick-and-span. **ϕ*i 1** to experience, witness (*kr for* ϕMENANG·I). **2** *var of* UNINGA

menir grain kernels pounded fine. *beras/djagung ** crushed rice/corn kernel. *Geḍéné mung sak*.* It's no bigger than a kernel of grain. ***an 1** cake made of the above mixed with coconut milk. **2** a certain plant whose leaves are used in folk medicines. ***en** mouth-weary from too much talking *or* eating

meni:s ***-*** attractive, cute, appealing

menit 1 a minute. *djam sidji luwih sepuluh ** 1:10. *djam sidji kurang sepuluh ** 12:50. **2** tiny, minute. *ϕ*/**di*i** to time sth in minutes

mènjak *rg var of* MINJAK

menjambik *rg var of* MENJAWAK

menjan (*or* **ke***) *ng*, **séla** *kr* incense. *ngobong ** to burn incense. *rokok ** incense-flavored cigarette

menjang *ng*, **ḍateng** *kr* **1** (to go) to, toward. *Kowé arep * endi?* Where are you going? *lunga * pasar* to go to the market. *Anḍané disènḍèkaké * tèmbok.* He leaned the ladder against the wall. *ngaḍep * kulon* to face west. *Sléndangé maṭuk * kebajaké.* Her scarf goes well with her blouse. *Aku sengit * botjah adu djangkrik.* I hate for children to hold cricket fights. ** sinau kenḍo banget.* Toward his studies he had a carefree attitude. **2** [to do] at [a place one has gone to]. *Ḍèwèké blandja * pasar.* She shopped at the market. *Botjahé ditambakaké * ḍokteran.* The child was treated at the hospital.

menjawak a lizard-like animal

menjènjèh covered with infected places

menjir **menjar-*** flexible

ménjor **ménjar-*** flexible

mentah not yet ready, *esp.* for eating. *pelem ** unripe mango. *Segané *.* The rice isn't done. ** mateng klebu weteng.* Raw or cooked, I'll eat it! *lawé ** cotton thread that has not been processed for sewing. *getjok ** ground raw meat. ***an** in the uncooked/unprocessed state. *Pelemé geḍi, mengko dipangan *an.* The mangoes are huge—we'll eat them raw. *Legèn kuwi ana sing diedol *an waé, ana sing digawé gula.* Some sugar-palm sap is sold in the natural state, and some is made into sugar.

méntal mental; intellectual. *kekuwatan ** intellectual prowess

mental to bounce. *Balé kena tèmbok *.* The ball caromed off the wall.

mentâlâ 1 invulnerable; not susceptible. **2** (*or* ***n**) able to bear. *Aku ora * weruh ana manungsa kasangsaran.* I can't bear to see anyone suffer. *Apa ora djeneng *n, wong mengkono iku?* How heartless he is—a person who would do a [cruel] thing like that.

Mentaram, Mentarum *var of* MATARAM

mentas 1 (**nembé** *kr?*) just now, a moment ago. *Ngertiné ja lagi * iki mau.* I didn't find out till just now. **2** *form of* PENTAS

mènṭèh ***-*** [of a fat stomach] bulging, hanging out over the belt

mènṭèk ***-* 1** *intsfr* short. *tjènḍèk *-** extremely short. **2** *describing a dwarf's gait*

menṭèk 1 a disease that attacks rice-plant roots: superstitiously believed to be caused by imps. **2** *var of* MÈNṬÈK 1

menṭek̄ 1 (*or* ***-***) filled (out) [*esp.* of women's breasts]. **2** *var of* MÈNṬÈK 1. *** ati·né** conceited. *See also* RIJEK

mènṭèl *see* KALA

menṭel to scrape together [money]. *Ḍuwité wis * arep ditukokaké motor.* He's scraped up enough money for a car.

menṭélas [of bald heads] shiny, gleaming

menṭélé *var of* MENḌÈLÈS

menṭèlès *var of* MENḌÈLÈS

menṭelos *var of* MENṬÉLAS

mènten unit of this scope (*Degree I: md for* MÉNÉ). *se** this much/many (*md for* SEMÉNÉ)

mèntèng ***-*** [of fat flesh] bulging. *Wetengé *-*.* His stomach sticks out.

menṭeng ***-* 1** swollen to the bursting point. **2** very much in earnest about one's work *or* responsibilities

mentengah (to move) toward the center (*var of* ME·NENGAH: *see also* TENGAH)

mèntèr 1 to feel incensed. *Aku *.* I was outraged. **2** *ltry* to get deflected. ***an** easily exasperated

mentèrèng conspicuous, eye-catching, showy
menteri *var of* MENTRI
mentéring an item of clothing (*usu.* batik) given to a servant by the master
mentes well filled (out); *fig* brainy
menṭik (*opt prn* **menṭi:k**) *intsfr* small. ***an** prematurely ripe. ***-*** *sms* *. *tjilik* *-* tiny
mentjeb (*or* *-*) *intsfr* full. *Prauné kebak **. The boat was jammed [with passengers]. *Kulahé wis tak kebaki *-**. I filled the bathtub to the brim.
mèntjès slantwise, on the diagonal
mentjingis having the very tip showing. *Bungé wis ana sing ṭukul kétok **. Just the very tip of a newly sprouted bamboo tree is visible.
méntjlé **méntjla-*** shifty, unreliable
méntjo mynah bird. ** bisa ngotjèh.* Mynah birds "talk."
mentjolèng *inf var of* M·BENTJOLÈNG
mèntjong, méntjong *var of* Ṁ·PÈNTJÈNG
mentjongat to extend outward [of sth long]. *See also* TJONGAT
mèntjrèt to have diarrhea; *fig* copious. *utang ḍuwit anakan sing * ngetokaké anakan saben minggu* a loan which produces interest every week
mentjungul to come into view. *See also* TJUNGUL
mentjureng to scowl. *See also* TJURENG
ménṭog, mènṭog Manila duck
menṭok *see* ḌAḌA
méntol 1 menthol. 2 [of skin blemishes] slightly swollen
mentri cabinet minister. *Perdana ** Prime Minister. **ke*an** (*abbr*: **kem.**) administrative department
menu:k ***-*** chubby, plump
menul ***-*** soft and flexible
menur jasmine
menus ***-*** attractive. *prawan *-** an attractive young girl. **dudu *** shocking; inhuman. *Dudu * ané, mangan kok entèk sepuluh piring.* Unbelievable–he's had ten helpings! *Dudu * tenan sing tegel matèni wong sakulawarga.* Killing a whole family–it's inhuman.
menut a minute (*var of* MENIT)
meprel to come right off; easily removable
mer- *prefix: var of* MA-^{b}. *mer·gawé* to work. *See also under* MR- (*Introduction, 2.9.3*) *or under replaced-consonant plus* R (*Introduction, 3.1.5.4*)
mérad *var of* KÉKRAD
mérah red. *kaum ** communists. *** putih** the Indonesian flag
merak peacock. *** ke·simpir** 1 a variety of peacock with a particularly large, sweeping tail. 2 a graceful, elegant walking gait (of ladies)
merang 1 dried rice straw. 2 rice chaff; rice husks. **sa*** one rice stalk
mérat to escape. ** saka pakundjaran* to break out of jail
merbot a certain low-ranking Moslem official
merdagang *see* DAGANG
merdâjâ *oj* to deceive, cheat
merḍajoh to visit. **ϕ/di*aké** to send smn on a visit. **ϕ*i** to go visiting. *See also* ḌAJOH, Ṁ·PARA ḌAJOH
merdamel to work (*kr for* MERGAWÉ)
merdésa *ng*, **merḍusun** *kr* to go to the country, to visit a rural area. *See also* DÉSA
merdi désa celebration after the harvest
merdjan 1 red coral. 2 *rg* beads of a necklace *or* rosary
merḍu melodious, sweet
merḍusun *kr for* MERDÉSA
meré [of monkeys] to screech, cry
mèrèh ***-*** blood-red. *Tatuné *-**. His wound was angry red.
mèrek trade mark, brand (name). *sédan biru * Fiat* a blue Fiat sedan
mèrèt nice-looking
merga *ng*, **mergi** *kr* (*or, formal,* **a***) because (of the fact that). ** saka iku* because of it. *mati * malaria* to die of malaria
mergawé *ng*, **merdamel** *kr* to work, do a job. **ϕ/di*kaké** to cause to work. *Keboné wis dimergawèkaké sepasar suwéné.* We've been working the kerbau every day for a week now. *See also* GAWÉ
mergi 1 road, way (*kr for* DALAN). 2 because (*kr for* MERGA)
mergil secluded, isolated
mèri envious; to envy. ***ǹ(an)** envious in nature. *botjah mèrèn(an)* a jealous child. **ka*ǹ** cause for envy. *...munḍak dadi kemèrèning lijan.* ...it might make others envious. **ϕ*kaké** *or* **ϕ*ǹi** 1 to be the envy of [smn]. *Dolanané kantjané mèrèni/mèrèkaké aḍiku.* My brother always wants his friend's toys. 2 (*psv* **di*kaké, di*ǹi**) to covet [smn's possessions]; to envy [smn]. *Aḍiku mèrèkaké/mèrèni dolanané kantjané.* My brother always wants his friend's toys. *Kabegdjané wong ki ora kena dimèrèkaké/dimèrèni.* You mustn't envy him his good luck.

meri duckling (young of the BÈBÈK)
merit narrow in the mid portion. *Sikilé* *. Her foot has a pinched-in instep. *Bangkèkané * banget.* She's slim-waisted.
mèrk *var of* MÈREK
merkah [of soil] dry and cracked
merkakah having the legs spread wide apart
merkèntjo, merkéntjo perverse, contrary, hard to get along with
mèrkurokrom mercurochrome
méro *var of* MÉROK
mérok *-* thickly powdered
merpet clouded over
merpih *-* to coax, plead. **ϕ/di*** to plead with, coax
mertamu **ϕ/di*k̂aké** to have smn visit, send smn visiting. **ϕ/di*(n̂i)** to visit, go to see smn. *See also* TAMU
mertanggung *see* TANGGUNG
mertéga butter. **ϕ/di*ni** to put butter on. *Rotiné dimertégani.* She buttered the bread.
merti désa *var of* MERDI DÉSA
mertindjo *var of* TINDJO
mertjon fireworks. * *rèntèng* little firecrackers on a string. ***an** to set off fireworks
mertuwa *var of* MARATUWA
mertuwi *var of* TUWI
mesa *var of* MEKSA 1
mesah *kr* *var of* MENGSAH
mesak̔·aké *ng,* **mesak̔·aken** *kr* 1 to arouse sympathy *or* pity. *Mesakaké.* You poor thing! *rasa* * feelings of pity. *botjah wédok sing kétoké * banget* a girl of pitiful appearance. *Ora ana sing dipangan, *.* Not one of them was eaten–it's too bad. 2 to feel sorry for. *Prijé ta, apa ora *?* How about it: do you feel sorry for him? *Élinga kowé lagi ngandut, mesakna anakmu.* Remember, you're pregnant; consider your unborn child.
mesdjid mosque
mesin machine, engine; sewing machine. * *(men)djahit* sewing machine. * *tik* or * *tulis* typewriter. * calculating machine. *tukang* * (sewing) machine repair man. *Montor mau rusak *é.* The car engine broke down.
Mesir Egypt
mesoji cinnamon-like bark used as a spice
mestail *var of* MUSTAIL
mestak fly opening (men's trousers)
mèster, méster (*abbr*: **Mr.**) Master of Law (former academic title)
mestèr (*or* ***an**) pavement; concrete flooring
mesṭi inevitable, invariable, predictable. *Loro ping loro * papat.* Two times two is always four. *Ès * aḍem.* Ice is bound to be cold. *Wong * mati.* Man is mortal. *Ali² iki * duwèkè wong sugih.* This ring must belong to smn rich. * *waé bungah, wong diolèh-olèhi.* Of course he was pleased–she brought him a present. *Bésuk jèn didol, * paju larang.* When you sell it, you're sure to get a good price. *Pitutur betjik ora * digugu.* Good advice is not always followed. *Apa kowé bungah?– * waé ta!* Are you pleased? –Of course! ***né** as a natural consequence of [the foregoing]. *Ing dina iku ana bal-balan geḍèn, *né akèh wong sing paḍa nonton.* There was to be a big soccer match that day, so naturally there were a great many spectators. **sa*né** appropriate, as it should be. *mapan ana ing papan kang sa*né* to settle in a suitable place. *See also* PESṬI
met soldier's overseas cap. ***-*an** headachy, dizzy
meta *oj* furious
meṭakil *var of* MUṬAKIL
meṭakol to shinny up; to grasp sth by clasping it with the legs
métal, metal metal
metamu *var of* MERTAMU
mété cashew. *-* [of fat flesh] to shake, quiver
mèṭèh *-* (to walk) with a waddle
meṭekul absorbed, engrossed. *Ḍèké agi mangan *, mulané ana wong teka ora weruh.* He was so busy eating he didn't notice that smn had come in.
meṭèngkrak proud, arrogant
meṭèngkrang to sit with the legs up on sth
meṭengkrus to sit motionless
mèter 1 (*abbr*: **m.**) meter (= 39.37 inches). 2 (*or* ***an**) instrument for measuring and recording. * *listrik* electric meter. ***an** 1 in meters (units of length). 2 measured by a meter. *Olèhé lengganan lèḍeng *an.* He pays for his water by the meter reading.
meṭet tight-fitting
meṭéṭah to sit with the knees apart. *See also* PEṬÈṬÈH
meṭeṭet *inf var of* M·BEṬEṬET
meṭèti to snap [a songbird] lightly with the finger, to induce it to sing
meṭiṭing small-waisted
meṭiṭit *inf var of* M·BEṬIṬIT
metjèḍèl disemboweled
metjèḍèt *var of* METJÈḌÈL

metjèṭèt to emerge suddenly, burst out. *See also* TJÈṬÈT

metjoṭot to emerge suddenly, burst out. *See also* TJOṬOT

metoḍā method, way, means

métralijur machine gun

mètrik according to the metric system. * *ton* metric ton

metu *ng,* **medal** *kr* 1 to emerge, come forth. *Ḍèké * saka ngomah.* He came out of the house. **a mréné.* Come out here! *Olèhé nggoḍog nganti * lenganė.* Boil it until the oil is rendered. *mBok adja mlebu-* waé, kéné linggih!* Don't keep going in and out: sit down! *Madjalah iki * seminggu sepisan.* The magazine comes out once a week. *Bajiné lahir * lanang.* The baby was (born and was) a boy. 2 to put out, put forth. *Sawisé lemah mau dirabuk, tanduranė *.* After the soil was fertilized, the plants produced. *tjaṭetan mlebu-*ning ḍuwit* notations of income and expenses. *Kembangé tiba tanpa * wohé.* The blossom dropped off without producing a fruit. 3 to take [a certain route]. *Ḍèwèké * pinggir kiwa.* He went along the left bank. *Dalané keleban, dikon * dalan sédjé.* The road was under water; they had to take a different road. 4 to quit, leave. *A wis *.* A has quit. *-* kuwi mbok mengko jèn wis mangan.* Don't leave till you've eaten. **ke*ṅ** emerging too far. *Olèhmu muter sumbu kemeton.* You put the lamp wick too far out. **pa*** 1 product, yield. *Anggoné mangan saka wulu pa*né sawah.* He lives on what his paddy produces. 2 income. * **m·buri** to engage in a devious *or* underhanded procedure. *See also* WETU

méwah surrounded by luxuries and extravagances

mèwèh *-* having a large tear in it. *Djariké suwèk amba, *-*.* The batik wraparound is badly torn.

mèwèk 1 (*or* *-*) to cry long and loud. 2 *var of* MÈWÈH

mi 1 noodle. 2 third note in the musical scale. 3 *syllable called for summoning goats, sheep*

midid *see* ANGIN

midjil a certain classical verse form

miḍun *var of* ME·ḌUN

migeg **migag-*** to rock back and forth in place. *A njurung montor ḍéwé, migag-* ora bisa madju².* A had to push the car–it would rock but not go forward.

migug **migag-*** to move slowly and ponderously. *A lemu banget, jèn mlaku migag-*.* A is so fat that he walks with an elaphantine gait.

mihun rice-flour noodle

mijeg *-* heavy and awkward. *mBok bakul mangkat nang pasar nggénḍong sajur²an akèh banget nganti *-*.* The woman set out for the marketplace with an unwieldy load of vegetables on her back to be sold.

mijos (*form of* WIJOS) 1 to be born (*ki for* LAIR). 2 to go (by way of), to pass (*ki for* LIWAT). 3 to go (*ki for* LUNGA). 4 to come (*ki for* TEKA)

mi̊ju:d *-* to sway flexibly. *Wité krambil jèn kena angin *-*.* The coconut palm sways in the wind.

mi̊jů:r *-* *or* **mijar-*** to sway flexibly. *-* **ati·né** *or* **mijar-* ati·né** to vacillate with indecision. *Mijar-* atiné nitipké anaké nang nggoné kantjané.* She hesitated to leave her child with a friend.

mi:k[a] 1 to drink (children's word). 2 (*or* **nge***) to nurse, take milk from [the mother]. **nge/di*i** to suckle [a baby]

mik[b] 1 first, beforehand (*inf var of* ḌISIK). (*Ko*) **, aku dak ngombé.* Just a minute, I want to get sth to drink. 2 *syllable for calling a goat, sheep.* 3 only (*rg var of* MUNG)

mikrad *var of* MÉKRAD

mikropon, mikrofon microphone

mikroskop microscope

mil 1 mile. 2 mail. *èr* * air mail. *si* * surface mail. **mal-*** to eat constantly. *Jèn sinau mesṭi karo mal-*.* He always nibbles while he's studying. ***-*an** snacks to nibble. **nge/di*-*** to nibble (on). *ngemil-emil katjang* to eat peanuts. *See also* KEMIL

mila originally; therefore (*kr for* MULA)

milai to begin (*kr for* MULAI)

milet *rg kr for* M·ÈLU, M·ILI, M̈·PILIH

mili 1 *shf of* MILIMÈTER. 2 *form of* ILI

miligram milligram

milik *var of* MÉLIK

milimèter (*abbr*: **mm.**) millimeter

milisi military service; the draft

militèr militia; military men. *kaum* * the military clique

miljar billion

miljun million. *èwu* * billion

miljunèr millionaire

milug *-* big, beefy, muscular

mimang the (above-ground) roots of the banyan tree

mimbar pulpit
mimb(l)i:k *-* about to cry; (to cry) softly
mimi male sea crab which always stays clasped tightly together with the female (*mintuna*). **kaja * lan mintuna** [of husband and wife] inseparable; having close ties of affection
mimik 1 gnat, fruit fly. 2 (*prn* **mimi:k**) to drink (children's word: *see also* MIK[a])
mimis bullet. *londjong ** (to run) like a speeding bullet. ***en** [of nose] bleeding. *Irungé *en.* She has a nosebleed.
mimpang *kr for* MENANG 'to win'?
mimpes [of swellings] to go down. **ϕ/di*aké** to reduce [a swelling]
mimring gauzy, filmy, transparent
min- *see also under* M- (*Introduction, 3.1.7*)
mina *oj* live freshwater fish
minangsrâjâ *oj* to ask for help
minḍah 1 to change one's form (*rg kr for* MALIH). 2 to move sth (*kr for* NGE·LIH). *See also* PINḌAH
minḍak 1 or (else), otherwise (*kr for* MUNḌAK). 2 to increase; to rise in rank (*kr for* M·UNḌAK)
mindring to buy on credit
mindu disagreeably surprised; unbelieving
ming 1 in, at, on (*rg var of* ING[a]). 2 only (*var of* MUNG). 3 but (*rg var of* NANGING)
minggir (to go) to/toward the edge. **ke*en** too far toward the edge. *See also* PINGGIR
minggring *-* *or* **minggrang-*** to hesitate, dilly-dally. *Olèhé njambut-gawé minggrang-* ora tjak-tjek.* He can't get started on the job—he doesn't know how to go about it.
minggu 1 seven-day week. 2 Sunday. ***n̂** 1 weekly. *Aku dibajar minggon.* I get paid by the week. 2 to spend Sunday. *Minggon ana ing pegunungan* to spend Sunday in the mountains
mingid *-* sharp-edged
mingir *-* red-lipped
mingis *-* razor-sharp
mingkeg *-* (to walk) ponderously and laboriously
mingkli:k *-* 1 (in a) high (place). *Jèn lemahé èndèk, diurug ḍisik nganti *-*.* When there's a low spot in the earth, it is filled in to build it up. 2 in a precarious position
mingkri:k *var of* MINGKLIK
mingkug *var of* MINGKEG
mingkuh to avoid, evade
mingkur **mingkar-*** to dodge, be evasive
mingsel (*or* *-*) fleshy. *-* to snuggle up to
mingsra *var of* MISRA
mingut *-* scowling with anger
minimum minimum; minimal
mining *-* *intsfr* red-toned. *djambon *-** deep pink. *rai *-** sunburned face
minjak 1 oil. *kapal ** oil tanker. 2 perfume
minji:k̄ *-* 1 (to walk) slowly and carefully. 2 at the outset of sth new. *Pak W. lagi *-* miwiti mbukak toko bandjur kemalingan entèk²an.* Mr. W. had hardly opened his store when it was cleaned out by thieves.
minju:k̄ *var of* MINJIK
mintâsrâjâ *oj* to ask for help
minṭel *-* *intsfr* fat
minṭi Manila duckling (young of the ÉNṬOG). *-* 1 [of stomach] round and fat. 2 blistered
minṭi:k̄ **minṭak̄-*** to keep going back and forth *or* from one place to another
mintjek̄ *-* *or* **mintjak̄-*** to jump around
mintjlo **mintjla-*** unreliable
mintjrut *var of* MINTJUK
mintjuk *-* *describing the appearance of smn—esp. a woman—walking in a too-tight wraparound*
minṭu:g *-* grossly fat. **minṭag-*** (to walk) with a fat waddling gait
minṭul *-* *or* **minṭal-*** to go around naked
mintuna female sea crab (*see also* MIMI)
minu:k (*or* *-*) chubby, plump, cute-looking [of babies]
minu:l *var of* MINṬUL, MINUK
minus poverty-stricken. *Ḍaérah² sing * didropi beras.* Rice was sent to the deprived areas.
mir (*or* ***-*an**) worried, apprehensive, on edge
mirah 1 cheap; plentiful (*kr for* MURAH). 2 *oj* red. 3 ruby (gem)
miraos tasty (*kr for* MIRASA)
mirâsâ *ng,* **miraos** *kr* tasty, delicious. *See also* RASA
mireng to hear (*kr for* KRUNGU). ***an** sense of hearing; to have a sharp sense of hearing (*kr for* RUNGU·N̂). ***en** to hear non-existent sounds (*kr for* (RE)·RUNGU·N̂). ***-*en** to keep hearing in the mind's ear (kr for RUNGU·N̂²EN). **ke*an** sense of hearing (*kr for* PA·NG·RUNGU). **ϕ/dipun*aken**

to listen (to) (*kr for* NG/DI·RUNGU·K̂AKÉ). *See also* PIRENG
miri candlenut (tree) (*var of* KEMIRI)
miris to feel insecure *or* imperiled
mirit according to (*inf var of* M̈·PITURUT)
mirong 1 to wear a batik over the shoulder and around the body, denoting mourning. 2 ashamed, wishing to hide. * **kampuh djingga** to rebel against, take up arms against
mirunggan 1 extra, additional. *gandjaran ** an additional prize. *Ḍuwit mau dianggep kajadéné ḍuwit **. The money was a windfall for him. 2 extra special. *Dina iki pantjèn **. Today is a very special day. 3 fulfilling a particular need. *papan kang * kanggo njebar pandjeritan* an ideal place for airing complaints. *Ḍokter mau gawé bebadan kang mligi, kang **. The doctor set up an exclusive agency–just what was needed. **ϕ/di*aké** to regard sth as special. *A mirungganaké barang² sing kuna.* A thinks a great deal of her antiques.
mis *Westernized version of* MISA. **nge*** to beg. *wong nge** beggar. *Malingé ngemis² ndjaluk ngapura.* The thief begged for mercy. **nge/di*aké** to beg on smn's behalf. *Anaké diemis-emisaké penggawéan karo ibuné.* She pleaded for a job for her son. **nge/di*i** to beg from. *Bola-bali kok nge*i aku waé.* You're always asking me for money!
misa * **sutji** a religious sacrifice
misi 1 mission. ** nang bulan* mission to the moon. 2 Catholic mission. *sekolah ** Catholic mission school
misionaris missionary
miskin impoverished. *pekir ** needy and poor. *omah ** almshouse where the poor are looked after until they can take care of themselves
misowa(h) Chinese vermicelli
misra **ora *** of no value. *Anggoné kangélan njambut-gawé ora **. Their efforts were of no avail.
mistar ruler (for ruling lines)
mister *var of* MÈSTER
mistik mystic(al). *wong ** a mystic. *tatatjara ** mystic rites
misuwur famous, widely known
miterang *see* TERANG
mitra close friend. **ku betjik* a good friend of mine. ** darma* a proven friend. ** karib* an intimate friend. ** (ke)karuh* speaking acquaintance, superficial friend. **(me)*n** friendly relationship, state of being friends. *Olèhku *n karo ḍèké wis ana rong taun.* She and I have been friends for two years. **pa*n** *sms* (ME)*N
mitralijur machine gun
miwah (together) with; and (*kr for* MUWAH)
mjang *oj* and; with. *bapak * bijung* parents
mlagrang tall; high up
mlajan *rg var of* LUMAJAN
mlanḍingan *var of* KEMLANḌINGAN
mlangkruk *var of* MANGKRUK
mlantjong to go smw for enjoyment *or* sightseeing
mlarat poor, needy. *kaum ** the poor. *Uripé **. He ekes out an existence. **ka*an** 1 poverty. 2 impoverished, destitute
mlas *oj* mercy, pity. * **asih** *or* * **ajun** *or* * **arsa** pitiful; merciful
mlatah to become known everywhere. *Kabaré wis **. The news has spread everywhere.
mlaṭi jasmine
mlaṭing nicely arranged, neatly laid out
mlèbèr *var of* M·BLÈBÈR
mleḍag *var of* M·BLEḌAG
mleḍèh *var of* M·BLEḌÈH
mleḍos *var of* M·BLEḌOS
mlégrok to alight, settle (on), perch
mléjok bent, dented, caved in
mlekèk opened wide. *Tatuné sikil **. The wound on his leg opened up. **mlekak-*** to keep opening up; to remain opened wide
mlekenuk [of children] cute, appealing
mlekok *var of* MLEKÈK
mlekoṭar to run fast
mlekoṭo *var of* MLEKOṬAR
mlekuṭar *var of* MLEKOṬAR
mléla 1 clearly visible. 2 plain, unornamented; common, ordinary. *para kawula maléla kang paḍa nonton* the commoners who were among the spectators. 3 shiny black
mlélé [of eyes] wide open
mlèlèk *var of* MLÉLÉ
mlempem not up to standard in some respect. *Krupuké adja dilèr, mengko **. Don't leave the chips out–they'll get soggy. *Ḍèwèké **. He's dull-witted. *Nèk diwènèhi sing * adja arep.* If they give you inferior ones, don't accept them.
mlèmpèng air vent
mlempu *rg var of* M̈·PLEMPUNG
mlénas [of forehead] high, broad
mlenḍing *var of* M·BLENḌING
mlengker to roll up, curl up
mlèngkong bent, curving, not straight

mlènjèh to come off. *Kulité* *. His skin peeled.
mlenjok bruised. *Téla gantungé tiba* *. The papaya fell and got a bad spot in it.
mlenos *-* smooth and shiny
mlentjung (to walk around) heedless of one's surroundings
mlenṭo protruding; swollen
mlenṭos *var of* M̈·PENṬOLOS
mlépah *-* pitiful, sorrowful
mlepes 1 sodden, water-logged. 2 limp, dull, drained of one's strength. 3 to sit cross-legged with lowered head, *e.g.* when showing respect and humility before an older relative
mleseg *var of* M·BLESEG
mléwah *var of* M·BLÈWÈH
mliding *intsfr* fair (of skin). *Kulité kuning* *. Her skin is very light.
mligi 1 only, nothing but, exclusively. *A mung * sinau.* A does nothing but study. *rumah-sakit kang * kanggo ngopèni wong lara mripat* a hospital that specializes in eye cases. *warung kang * didol iwak asin* a shop that sells dried fish exclusively. 2 pure; honest; unadulterated. *Ḍèké *, ora gawé*². He's straightforward; he doesn't put on airs. *Sing nang djirigèn kuwi ming * bènsin.* The stuff in the can is pure gasoline. 3 special, specific. *tjara kang* * a special process. *papan kang * ing sawidjining kampung* a designated place in the township. ϕ/**di*kaké** to specialize. *mligèkaké marang basa Inggris* to specialize (major) in English
mlijun(èr) *var of* MILJUN(ÈR)
mlilé of low character
mlindjo a certain tree whose young leaves, blossoms, and fruits are used in vegetable dishes; also, the hard-shelled nut-like fruit of this tree, fried as a snack or made into chips. *kulit* * the rind of the above fruit, cooked as an ingredient of vegetable soup
mlingseng *intsfr* dark (of skin). *Ḍèké ireng* *. He's deeply tanned.
mlingsi hard, glossy, and black. ** kaja ḍelé* [as above] like a soybean
mlinjah, mlinjèh *var of* MLÈNJÈH
mlinṭis bald and shiny
mlintjur to loaf, waste time
mlipis elegant, accomplished, refined. *basa* * able to speak polished Krama. *sila* * to sit (cross-legged) with elegant mein
mliṭit beautifully groomed
mlitjat *var of* MLITJÈT
mlitjèt to have/get a sore place *or* blister. *Aku * tungkak.* I have a blister on my heel.
mliwis wild duck
mlokèk *var of* M·BLOKÈK
mlosoh [of living tissue] damaged by burning *or* scalding. *See also* LOSOH
mlowèh gaping open
mlowoh, mlowok *var of* MLOWÈH
mludag *inf var of* M·BLUDAG
mlunṭuh *intsfr* complete, total
mlunṭus 1 bald. 2 having the hair combed very flat and close to the head
mluwa not in use. *Ing kuṭa² ora ana tanah sing* *. Cities have no vacant land in them.
mm. *see* MILIMÈTER
mobah *var of* MUBAH
mobil automobile, car
mobilèr furniture
mobjar *-* flaming, blazing
mobjor *-* 1 conspicuous. 2 to flourish. *Islam ḍèk *-*é djaman Nabi* Islam during its heyday at the time of the Prophet (Mohammed)
moblah *-* spacious
moblong (*or* *-*) pale and round [of face: the classic ideal of beauty]
mobol *-* to come out, spill out
mobrol *var of* MOBOL
mobrot *-* disarranged, untidy
moḍal capital (to be) invested. **per*an** investment of capital
modang a certain batik design used *esp.* for headdresses
modar 1 down with...! death to...! 2 *cr* dead; to die
moḍe (in) style, (in) fashion. *Saiki wis ora* *. It's not fashionable any more.
moḍèl 1 a model, *i.e.* (a) an example to be followed; (b) a small-scale representation of sth. 2 style, fashion. ** Bali* Balinese style. *djogèd * baru* a newfangled dance. *Saiki * anjar.* There's a new way of doing it now. 3 strange, unaccustomed, new. *Wah, * lho pité setangé setiran mobil.* Gosh, what a funny bike—the handlebar is a steering wheel! ϕ/**di*** to make sth in a certain fashion. *Sakané geḍé di* tjara kuna.* The pillars are large and in an old-fashioned style.
moḍèr(e)n up-to-date. *djogèd* * a contemporary dance. *djaman * kaja saiki iki* these modern times
moḍi ** kèngser* a certain sideways shuffling step in a female classical dance
modin Islamic official whose function is to

summon worshipers to the five daily prayings at the mosque
modjah knitted socks *or* gloves
modjèl in death throes
mod̩ol *-* 1 in disorder, messy. 2 disemboweled
mogog *-* sluggish, inert
mogok 1 to stop, stall. *Lakuné djaran mau sed̩éla² *.* Every so often the horse stopped in his tracks. *Montorku * nang tengah dalan.* My car stalled in the middle of the road. 2 to go on strike. 3 a strike. ***an** apt to stall. *Botjah kuwi *an.* The boy quits at the slightest provocation. ***-*an** a strike; to go on strike. **pa*an** work stoppage. *pe*an pegawé negeri* a civil-service workers' strike
mogol only partly finished; half one way and half the other. *Olèhé nggod̩ok téla *.* The cassava isn't fully cooked. *Rembugan * sebab A bandjur pind̩ah nang negara mantja.* The deal never went through–A moved abroad. *D̩èké botjah *, terangé sekolahan ora jèn ora sekolahan dudu.* He's neither educated nor uneducated: he's enrolled in school but he doesn't attend.
moh *ng* unwilling; not want. *Djarané mbegegeg, emoh mlaku.* The horse stalled and wouldn't budge. *Aku diadjak mbalangi pelem mau, emoh.* He suggested throwing stones at the mangoes, but I didn't want to. **nge/di*i** to surfeit. *Wité pelem jèn wis gelem awoh nganti nge*i.* If the mango tree bears fruit at all, it bears so many that you get tired of them. *Waraké ora apik, mula diemohi tangga teparoné.* He's a bad one, and the neighbors are fed up with him.
Mohamad Mohammed. *** Rasul(l)ol(l)ah** Mohammed the prophet of Allah
mohita *oj* sad, sorrowful, grieving. **ka*n** to suffer sorrow/grief
mojang *see* KAKÈK
mok **di*-*** *inf var of* DI·DEMOK²
mokah to cease fasting *or* avoiding certain foods (*Jogja slang: see also* BRUNGKAH)
mokal impossible, out of the question. *Kok gèk *!* Why, that can't be! *Apa wong mau bisa weruh aku ja?– * bisa weruh.* Can he see me?–He couldn't possibly. *Ora * jèn wong mau nganti kepéntjut marang d̩èwèké.* It's inconceivable that he has fallen in love with her. **ϕ*aké** unlikely. *Mokalaké jèn A nganti lulus.* I doubt very much if A will pass the exam.
moksa *var of* MUKSA
mol *rpr* snatching. *Mak * njuwil roti.* He grabbed a piece of cake. **mal-*** to keep snatching. *Pidjer mal-* mangani roti waé.* He took cookie after cookie. *See also* TJEMOL, TJOG
molai *var of* MULAI
molânâ *var of* MAOLANA
molèr to hang down in droplets. *Umbelé *.* His nose is dripping.
molèt **molat-*** to wriggle, squirm, writhe
molo *-* to stuff one's mouth with food
molor *var of* MOLÈR
momog **ke*en** *var of* KU·WOWOG·EN
momoh ***an** worn out, ragged. *See also* AMOH
momol soft, tender
momong ***an** a child to take care of. *kaparingan *an* to bear (*i.e.* be entrusted with) a child. **ke*** voluntarily possessed of a devil. **ϕ/di*** to take care of *or* bring up [children]. *** sarira** 1 physical culture. 2 not married, still living at home. *See also* AMONG, MONG
momor ***an** ingredient. **ka*an** mixed/combined (with). *** sambu** spy; enemy who works from within. *See also* MOR
momot 1 to have [a certain capacity]. *Montor iki * akèh.* This car holds a lot. *Penggalihé pantjèn *.* He's very understanding. 2 loaded (with). *Truk mau * kapuk.* The truck carried a load of kapok. 3 mushy from overcooking. ***an** 1 having the function of carrying things. *djaran *an* pack horse. *motor *an* truck. 2 a load. *D̩okaré kakèhan *an.* The cart was overloaded. *djaran sa*ané* the horse with its pack. *lajang² pos *an* a load of mail. **ϕ/di*aké** to load sth; to load for smn. **ϕ/di*i** to load sth into/onto. *Jèn momoti montorku sit̩ik waé lho.* Don't load much into my car. **pa*an** 1 place where things are loaded; loading zone. 2 a load. *See also* AMOT, MOT
mompjor to glitter, sparkle
momprot *-* spattered, messy
mond̩ol ***an** cloth knot at the back of a fabric headdress (*blangkon, iket*). *-* crop (pouch in a bird's gullet)
mong tiger (*oj*). *-* to take care of [a child]. *** k·in·emong** to take care of each other. **nge/di*** *sms* *-*. *Ad̩imu emongen.* Keep an eye on your little sister. **nge/di*aké** to look after smn's child for them. *See also* AMONG, MOMONG
mongah (*panas*) *-* red-hot, scorching, scalding

monggang a gamelan melody played to welcome arriving guests, also to greet a bride and groom
mongsok *excl of skepticism* (*var of* MANGSA)
monjèt monkey (*rg*). ***an** *see* LAWANG
monjong 1 [of lips, forehead] protruding. 2 *term of abuse for name-calling*
mono *ng* 1 (**manten** *kr*) unit of that scope (*Degree II: Introduction, 6*). *sa(k)**, *se** one such unit (*see* SEMONO). *Wis diwènèhi ḍuwit sa* akèhé kok isih kurang, ndjaluk rong * manèh, apa?* I've given you all that money and it's still not enough, so you're asking for twice that amount? 2 (**mekaten** *kr*) *X*'s in general (*see also* KUWI 1). *Tomat * akèh pitaminené.* Tomatoes have lots of vitamins. 3 (**mekaten** *kr*) *excl of deprecation* (*see also* MANA). 4 (**mekaten** *kr*) in fact. *Djenengé * Wangsamenggala, wong² jèn ngundang: Pak Wangsa.* His name is really Wangsamenggala, but people call him Mr. Wangsa. *See also* SEMONO
monogami monogamy
monopoli monopoly; monopolistic enterprise
monster sample; example
monté *var of* MOTÉ
monten *md for* MONO 1
montir mechanic. ** mobil* auto mechanic
montjèr 1 good at, skilled; well known for one's ability in a certain area. 2 a certain gamelan melody. 3 a certain hanging ornament. 4 excellent; *slang* conspicuous, showy. *Montoré * banget.* His car is flashy.
montjol to stick way up high
montjong [animal's] mouth
montjrot to squirt/gush out
montok̄ big-bosomed
montor 1 engine. ** listrik, bènsin, lan solar* electric, gas, and solar-powered engines. *kapal ** motor boat. *pit ** or ** keblak* motor bike, motorcycle. ** bot* motor boat. *mesin ** car engine. 2 engine-driven vehicle. ** mabur* airplane. **ku mogok.* My car stalled. ***-*an** 1 imitation car, toy car. 2 to (be lucky enough to) drive a car. *Aku jèn lunga mesṭi *-*an.* I drive to wherever I go. *Sing blandja sasat mung sing *-*an.* Only people with cars can go there to shop.
monumèn monument
mopo to rebel, resist; to refuse [to do sth]. *Djarané * ora gelem ngadeg.* The horse simply would not stand up.
moprok to accumulate, get piled up

mor **ka*an** combined (with). *udan deres ka*an angin* hard rain with wind. **nge/di*** to mix [things] together. *Sawarnaning kekembangan di* dadi sidji.* A variety of flowers formed the mixed bouquet. **φ/di*aké** *or* **nge/di*aké** to make/let [things] mingle *or* mix. *Nge*aké banju lan lenga ora gampang.* It's not easy to mix oil and water. *Anakmu adja di*aké botjah² nakal² kuwi.* Don't let your child hang around with those delinquents. **φ/di*i** *or* **nge/di*i** to mix sth with [sth else]. *Lenga patra di*i lenga klentik.* He mixed coconut oil in with the kerosene. *Tjampuhing pulisi lan durdjana, mula aku mèlu nge*i.* The policeman fought with the thief and I joined in. *nge*i rembug* to take part in a conversation. *See also* AMOR, MOMOR, WOR
moral 1 morals, ethics, standards. ** nasional perlu didandani.* The nation's morals need improving. 2 morale. *sumbungan * lan matériil* moral and material assistance
morèh streaked, *esp.* with blood
mori 1 (**peṭak·an** *rg? kr?*) cotton fabric, cambric. 2 *form of* MOR
moril personal/individual morals *or* ethical standards
mortir mortar, cannon. **ke*** hit by mortar fire. **φ/di*(i)** to bombard with mortars
mosi motion; vote. ** ora pitaja* a vote of no confidence
mosok *excl of skepticism* (*var of* MANGSA)
mostor *var of* MONSTER
mot *ng*, **wrat** *kr* **ka*** held, contained. **nge*** 1 to hold, contain. *nge* pekabaran sing ora bener* to include untrue news [in a publication]. *Botol iki nge* lenga seliter.* This bottle holds one liter of oil. 2 (*psv* **di***) to put sth into/onto. *Wongé diemot brangkar.* The man was loaded onto a stretcher. **nge/di*aké** to load sth. *Ḍèké nge*aké barang²é ana ḍokar.* He loaded his stuff into a carriage. *See also* AMOT, MOMOT
moṭa 1 canvas. 2 tent
moṭah perverse, moody
moté coral bead. ** saombjok* a string of coral beads
motip, motif theme, motif. ** klasik* a classic motif
moto 1 monosodium glutamate. 2 *form of* FOTO. ***-*** bulging, bursting. *Woh ranḍu jèn wis garing kapuké *-*.* When a *ranḍu* fruit is dried up, the kapok bursts right out of it. *Mripaté moto² arep metu.* His

eyes were bulging nearly out of their sockets.

motol *-* filled to the bursting point. *Saké *-* kebak katjang.* His pockets are bulging with peanuts.

motor *var of* MONTOR

mowak *-* large [of a torn opening]

mowal *-* torn, ragged, in shreds

mowol *-* tangled, snarled

mp- *see under* EMP-

mr- *var of* NGR- *in nasalized form of (W)R-initial roots*

Mr. *see* MÈSTER

mradjak [of plants] to flourish, grow vigorously

mraman [of fire] to spread

mrânâ *ng,* **mrika** *kr* (to go) to that place (*Degree III: Introduction, 6*). *Ajo ta, *.* Come on, let's go there! *Apa kowé wis tau nonton *?* Have you ever been to see the show there? *-* here and there, to various places. *ngumbara *-** wandering all over. **ϕ/di*kaké** to put sth (over) there. *Lampuné mbok di*kaké.* How about moving the lamp over there? ***-mréné (mrika-mriki** *kr*) *sms *-* above. Patih kuwi kena *-mréné nganti pirang² koṭakan.* The [chess] queen can move any number of squares in any direction. *See also* RANA[a]

mranggi kris-maker

mrantak 1 to reappear everywhere. *Ḍèké gabagen, wis mari, saiki * manèh.* He got over his measles rash but now it's coming back. *Bareng wis terang srengéngéné *.* Af- the rain, the sun came out again. 2 *var of* MRÈNTÈK

mratah ubiquitous. *Klambi kaja ngono saiki wis *.* That style of dress is everywhere now.

mratak *rg var of* MERKATAK

mratanggung *see* TANGGUNG

mré *var of* MERÉ

mre- *see also under* MER- (*Introduction, 2.9.6*) *or under replaced-consonant plus* ER (*Introduction, 3.1.5.4*)

mrebes *var of* M·BREBES

mregedud *var of* M·BEGEDUD

mrèmèn to spread. *Geniné *.* The fire spread. *Guḍigé saja *.* The scabies kept spreading.

mréné *ng,* **mriki** *kr* (to come) to this place (*Degree I: Introduction, 6*). **a.* Come here! *Tak undangé *.* I'll call him over here. *Barang² dikirim bali *.* The goods were sent back here. **ϕ/di*kaké** to put sth toward this direction. *Gambaré kuwi apiké dimrènèkaké siṭik.* The picture should be moved this way a bit. *See also* MRANA, RÉNÉ

mrenges glossy black

mrenggik tapering hourglass-style at the midpoint

mréngkal to put up an argument, be unwilling to cooperate

mrèngkèl *var of* MRÉNGKAL

mrengkeng obstinate, willful

mrèntèk [of fire] to spread

mrih *oj* so that, in order to

mrijang (to have/get) a cold *or* fever

mrijem (to shoot) a cannon, field gun. ** pranakan* small cannon. ***an** imitation cannon, toy cannon. **ϕ/di*aké** to bombard with artillery

mrik *oj* redolent (of)

mrika 1 (over) there (*kr for* KANA). 2 (to go) to that place (*kr for* MRANA)

mriki (to come) to this place (*kr for* MRÉNÉ)

mriku (to go) to that place (*kr for* MRONO)

mrina to take offense at smn for mistreating one's friend, teammate, *etc.* **ϕ/di*ni** to react against smn—with words or blows—in defense of [smn]. *A mrinani B.* A quarreled (*or* fought) with the one who had abused B. *Slamet mrinani anaké sing dipilara Suta.* Slamet stuck up for his son, who had been harmed by Suta.

mring *oj* to, toward. *teḍak * Ngartjapada* [of deities] to descend to earth

mringin to sleep with the eyes slightly open

mripat *ng kr,* **tingal** *or* **paningal** *or* **sotja (sotya)** *ki* human eye (*see also* MATA). **é katja².* Her eyes filled with tears. ** lumrah* the naked eye. *masang ** to concentrate, devote full attention (to). *ndeleng tanpa ** to sense (with a sixth sense)

mritja 1 pepper (white or black). 2 clubs (playing-card suit)

mrongos [of teeth, lips] protruding. *Untuné *.* He has buck teeth.

mrono *ng,* **mriku** *kr* to that place (*Degree II: Introduction, 6*). *Dikanḍani jèn anaké tiba, énggal² *.* When he heard his boy had fallen, he hurried there. *Aku lagi * sing ping limané.* It was the fifth time I had been there. **ϕ/di*kaké** to put sth in that direction. *Aku arep mronokaké bukumu ning kok udan.* I was going to take your book there, but it was raining. *See also* RONO

mrosot to drop, fall; to become low(er), decrease, decline. *Reganė *.* The prices fell.

Moralé botjah^2 djaman saiki rada *. Young people's standards have fallen somewhat these days.
mrupug dry and brittle
mrutu 1 fruit fly. 2 gnat
mu 1 *suffix* your. *buku·mu* your book. *bapak·mu* your father. 2 *inf var of* MAU
mualim 1 guide, leader, teacher. 2 skipper, navigator
mubadir to waste food by leaving it on one's plate
mubah [activities which are] neutral, *i.e.* neither forbidden nor encouraged by the Moslem religion
mubal to flare up, burst forth. *Gelis banget *é geni.* The fire spread rapidly. *Tawoné *.* The bees swarmed out. *Dolanan plasṭik lagi * nang pasar.* Plastic toys are pouring into the marketplaces. **ϕ/di*aké** 1 to cause sth to flare up *or* burst forth. 2 to stir up, rile
mubalig preacher; religious propagator
mubilèr furniture
mubjar (*or* ***-***) bright, glowing. **ke*en** burning/shining excessively brightly. *Lampuné ke*en.* The lamp is too bright.
mublak ***-*** 1 [of land] spacious and devoid of vegetation. 2 attractively pale facial appearance
mubru **mubra-*** luxurious, extravagant. **mubra-* blabur madu** to live in luxury
Mucharam *var of* MUHARAM
muḍa 1 *oj* young. *para ** young males (*see also* MUḌI). 2 junior in rank. *duṭa ** deputy ambassador. *lèktor ** lecturer (academic title). *Sardjana ** Bachelor of Arts. **pe*** young males; **pe*-pe·muḍi** young people. *** Krama** a subdivision of the Krama speech style (*Introduction, 5.5*)
muḍeng to understand. *Aku ora *.* I don't get it. *Aku kaṭik saja ora *.* I'm getting more and more mixed up. **ϕ*aké** comprehensible; (*psv* **di*aké**) to cause to understand. *Tjritané ora karu^{2}an nganti ora muḍengaké.* His story was so incoherent I couldn't follow it. *Aku wis di*aké déning ketrangané.* His information clarified it for me.
muḍi 1 young [of females: *see also* MUḌA]. 2 *inf var of* KEMUḌI
mudjadid reformist. ** agama* religious reformer
mudjaèr *var of* MUDJAIR
mudjair an edible freshwater fish
mudjarab effective, efficacious
mudjisat *var of* MUKDJIDJAT
mudjung in bed under the covers. *Ḍèké nggloso ing tempat-tiduré lan kemulan *.* She fell into bed and pulled up the blanket. *Njaiku bareng weruh aku isih * bandjur digugah.* When my wife saw I was still in bed, she woke me up.
muḍun *var of* ME·ḌUN
mufakat *var of* MUPAKAT
mufangat *var of* MUNPANGAT
muga *ng,* **mugi** *kr* (*or* ***-***) may it happen that...; I hope, let's hope. **-* ija/ora.* I hope so/not. **-* adja udan waé.* I just hope it doesn't rain! *Mugi Allah ngleksanani kersanipun bendara kula.* May God grant my master's wish.
mugeg **mugag-*** heavy and cumbersome
mugen 1 detached, objective. *Sarèhné ngenani riwajaté ḍéwé mulané ḍèwèké ora bisa * pamatjané.* Since the book concerned her own personal life, she couldn't read it dispassionately. 2 serene, calm. *mBaṭik iku bisa nuwuhaké rasa *.* Batik-making can increase one's tranquillity. 3 to stay around home and apart from social intercourse
muget ***-*** *or* **mugat-*** to keep stretching and contracting [of long thin crawling creatures]
mugi may it happen that...; let's hope (*kr for* MUGA)
Muharam first month of the Moslem calendar
muk ***-*an** to grope. *Aku *-*an nggolèki rèk kanggo njumet lilin.* I felt around for matches to light a candle.
muka *oj* face
mukadin *rg var of* MODIN
mukah to break a fasting period by eating before the time is up
Mukaram *var of* MUHARAM
mukdjidjat miracle. *Kur'an iku *é Kandjeng Nabi.* The Koran is the miracle wrought by the Prophet. ** déné aku ora mati.* It's a miracle I wasn't killed.
mukibat *see* TÉLA
mukim 1 place of residence; location. 2 to live smw. *Olèhé * nang Mekah ana sepuluh tahun.* He lived in Mecca for ten years.
mukir *var of* MUNGKIR
mukmin(in), mukminun a devout Moslem
mukok *var of* MUNGKOK
mukrim a female (*e.g.* a first cousin) who is too closely related to one to permit marriage
muksa to cease living by vanishing in body

and soul rather than by dying. **ka*n** *see* DJAGAD

mukti comfortable, well cared for. **ka*ǹ** the good life; worldly comfort. *Ḍèwèké ninggal kamuktèn kraton perlu dadi panḍita.* He left the comfortable life in the palace to become a holy man. **ϕ/di*k̀aké** to make a a comfortable life for smn, provide security for smn. *Aku arep muktèkaké uripmu.* I want to provide you with all the good things in life. *** wibawa** (having at one's command) the full gamut of worldly pleasures. *** wibawa m·bau·ḍenḍa (njakrawati)** rich and powerful

mul ***-*an** a game resembling checkers

mula *ng,* **mila** *kr* 1 originally; from the beginning. *tjilik ** begun as a child. *Ḍèké * seneng bal-balan.* He's always enjoyed soccer. 2 therefore, so, that is why. **né adja seneng main.* That's why you shouldn't gamble. ** awakmu lemu, lha kowé iki dojanan.* No wonder you're fat–you never refuse food. ***kna** *or* ***kné** therefore, that is why. **ka*n** source, origin. *** ḍasar** it is a fact that... *See also* MULABUKA

mulâbukâ origin, cause, reason. *Saiki wis béda karo *né.* It's different now than it was at the beginning. *Apa kowé ngerti *né perang?* Do you know what started the war? *See also* BUKA, MULA

mulad *ltry* ***-*** to blaze, glow. *Geniné *-*.* The fire is burning brightly.

mulai *ng,* **milai** *kr* to begin, start

mulak ***-*** to boil, bubble up, seethe

mulânâ *var of* MAOLANA

mulé (*or* **me***) to honor [deceased ones]. *slametan me* para empu* a ritual celebration in honor of the revered kris-makers. **ϕ/di·(me)*(k̀aké)** to hold a ceremony in honor of

mulek̄ to pervade. *Ambuné * nang kamar.* The odor hung in the room. *Manisé * ulengulengan.* Her sweetness characterizes everything she does.

mules queasy

mulih *ng,* **mantuk** *kr,* **kondur** *ki* to return to one's own place. *Aku arep *.* I'm going home. **é wis awan.* He didn't get home till afternoon. *ngangkataké ** to send smn home. *Punapa pendjenengan kresa ngasta kondur woh²an punika?* Would you like to take these fruits home with you? **sa*é** as soon as one got back; since one's return. *See also* ULIH

mulja 1 well-to-do. *Bijèn nlangsa, saiki *.* Life used to be hard, but he's well off now. 2 restored. *Omahé sing kobong bijèn saiki wis * manèh.* The burned-out house has now been restored. 3 esteemed, honored. *Jang ** your/his excellency. **ka*n** 1 prosperity. 2 honor, esteem. **ϕ/di*kaké** 1 to celebrate, glorify. *dina geḍé sing dimuljakaké ing tanah Djawa* a holiday that is celebrated in Java. 2 to restore sth. **m·in·ulja** honored, esteemed. *Para rawuh ingkang minulja...* Honored guests...

multi multi-, many-; very. *Révolusi kita pantjèn * komplèks.* Our Revolution has been many-faceted indeed.

Mulud 1 birth and death day of Mohammed, during the third Moslem month. 2 the third Moslem month. ***an** 1 religious festival celebrated on Mohammed's birthday. 2 to play tambourine music to celebrate Mohammed's birthday

mulung to offer one's arm to a person one is escorting

mulur 1 to stretch, expand. *Karèt iku bisa *.* Rubber stretches. 2 to exceed [a limit]. *Jèn semajan adja *.* Don't be late for appointments.

mulus pure, flawless, unadulterated. *putih ** pure white. *tresna ** true love. *Organisasi mau * olah raga.* The organization is solely for sports.

mum- *see also under* M- (*Introduction, 3.1.7*)

mumbluk foamy, frothy

mumbruk ***-*** piled in a disorderly heap

mumbuk *var of* MUMBRUK

mumpangat *var of* MUNPANGAT

mumpjar *var of* MOMPJOR

mumpluk frothy, bubbly, sudsy

mumpuni highly skilled. ** sakabèhing kawruh* thoroughly versed in all kinds of knowledge. *pudjangga kang ** a superior scholar

mumuk stupid, senseless. **mumak-*** *or* **mamak-*** to behave erratically because one has not the full use of the senses. *Lha wong mendem, mula mamak-*.* He's drunk, he doesn't know what he's doing.

mumur *see* ADJUR

munadjim astrologer

munâsikâ **ϕ/di*** to disturb, interfere with. *Lelembut ora wani * wong sutji.* Mischievous spirits don't dare to plague holy people.

munḍak *ng,* **minḍak** *kr* 1 or else, otherwise.

Adja panas², *mripatmu* * *lara.* Don't stay out in the sun, or you'll damage your eyes. 2 *form of* UNḌAK

mundri nipple (*ki for* PENṬIL)

munḍu a certain tree, also its fruit

munḍuk *-* [to walk] in a stooping *or* lowered position, as when passing esteemed persons who are seated so as not to be too elevated

munḍung (*or* **ke***) a certain fruit with a peach-like flavor

mundur to move backward. *Biḍagé kenané mung madju, ora kena* *. The pawns [in chess] can only go forward, not backward. *Bok ranḍa* * *saking ngarsanipun sang nata.* The widow respectfully withdrew from the king's presence. *-* to retreat gradually. **-* ngawasaké mungsuhé.* He backed off, watching his opponent closely. **ke*en** too far back. *Olèhku ngundurké montor ke*en nganti nabrak wit.* I backed the car too far and hit a tree. *See also* UNDUR

muneg *-* *or* **munag-*** queasy, nauseated

munfangat *var of* MUNPANGAT

mung *ng,* **namung** *kr* 1 only, just. * *telung taun* only three years. * *let seḍéla bis liwat.* In just a few moments a bus came along. *Kuwi ora temenan,* * *dongèng waé.* It didn't really happen, it's just a story. 2 *ng kr* a variety of small green bean. 3 *ng kr rpr* gong beats. ***-*an** not more than; not much. *Ḍuwité *-*an.* He has only a little money. **nge*aké** 1 limited to; only. *Ora nge*aké aku sing tansah njawang marang wong mau.* I wasn't the only one who kept looking at him. 2 to think only of. *nge*aké karepé ḍéwé* to think only of one's own wishes

munggèng *oj* (situated, located) in, on, at

mungging *var of* MUNGGÈNG

mungguh *ng,* **menggah** *kr* 1 in case, in the event that; about, as for, in connection with; now (*as a narrational device*). **a aku, aku ora gelem.* If it were me, I wouldn't do it. * *pandjupuké banju kang mengkono iku arané ndèrès.* Now, this way of getting the sap from the tree is called the drip method. * *bab mau wis dudu wadi manèh.* About that, there's no longer any secret. *Rada kélingan manèh *ing djedjering ibu.* Again she thought back on her mother's life. *Ditakoni* * *djalarané nangis.* He asked her why she was crying. 2 *ng kr* appropriate, fitting. *Kuwi kaprijé* * *ing panemumu?* How does that suit you(r opinion)? *Klambi iki* * *banget ing aku.* This dress fits me fine. ***ané** supposing. **ané kowé tak wènèhi ḍuwit akèh, apa sing arep kok tuku?* What if I gave you a lot of money: what would you buy with it? **se*(a)** *sms* * 1. *Se*a aku bisa klakon sugih, kowé mesṭi mèlu.* If I were to become rich, you would share in it.

munggur a certain tree, also its fruit

munggwing *var of* MUNGGÈNG

mungkad causing distress (physical or emotional)

mungkar (*or* *-*) to keep adding to one's possessions

mungkin possible, conceivable. **mungkan-*** it is always possible (that...)

mungkir to deny. *Malingé* * *olèhé njolong.* The thief denied having stolen anything. **mungkar-*** to deny repeatedly

mungkok to regurgitate

mungkug *-* *or* **mungkag-*** nauseated

mungkuk *var of* M·BUNGKUK

mungsuh *ng,* **mengsah** *kr* 1 opponent; enemy. * *main* gambling opponent. *Tikus iku *é menungsa.* Rats are man's enemy. 2 (pitted) against; up against. *perangé Panḍawa* * *Kurawa* the war between the Pendawas and the Kurawas. * *wong bawèl mono, apa² sarwa ora kepeneran.* To smn who is never satisfied, everything is wrong. * *wong pinter garapan semono kuwi isa bar sadjam.* A smart person could do that work in an hour. **(me)*an** 1 in conflict. *Tjita² Indonesia *an karo kolonialisme.* Indonesian ideals clash with colonialism. 2 enmity, hostility. *Me*ané nganti tetaunan.* Their hostility has lasted for years. **φ/di*aké** to set [one force] against [another]. *Jèn di*aké A, mesti B bakal kalah.* B is sure to lose if he's matched against A. **φ/di*i** to attack; to be against. *Tjah saklas paḍa mungsuhi ḍèké, mula ḍèké metu.* The whole class was against him, so he left.

mungur *-* red in the face. *nesu banget *-** furiously angry

mungut *var of* MUNGUR

muni 1 *ltry* an ascetic; a mystic teacher. 2 *form of* UNI

munjer to turn, whirl; to wander around, ramble

munjet *var of* MUNJER

munjuk 1 monkey; (*cr*) *name-calling term.* 2 *form of* UNJUK

munpangat useful, having utility. *Wit krambil*

*iku akèh *é.* Coconut trees are extremely useful. **ϕ/di*aké** to put sth to use. *Tanah kosong iki kudu di*aké.* This empty land ought to be made use of. **ϕ/di*i** wholesome, health-promoting. *Puhung iku ojod kang munpangati.* Cassava is a healthful root. *Puhané dipriksa supaja tansah munpangati tumrap kawarasan umum.* Milk is inspected regularly to make sure it is fit for human consumption.

munté *var of* MOTÉ

muntijârâ *var of* MUTIJARA

munṭil ***-*** small tight knot, *esp.* in a Javanese-style hairdo

munṭit small branch locomotive

muntjar sparkling, glittering

muntjlup **muntjlap-*** to move in and out; to keep starting in *or* out. *Iwaké muntjlap-** Fish keep popping out of the water. *Adja mung muntjlap-* nang lawang, terus mlebu waé.* Don't hesitate at the door—come on in.

muntju *var of* MUTJU

muntjul to emerge. *Wong kang nomer telu * saka gang.* A third man came out of the alleyway.

munṭu small stone tool used for grinding seasonings and spices in a flat stoneware bowl (*lajah*). *** katut·an sambel** to become related by marriage

mupakat to agree. *Ajo pit²an, tjotjok?—*.* Let's go for a bike ride, OK?—OK. *Wong sakampung wis * arep ndandani dalan.* The whole village has agreed to repair the road. **ϕ/di*aké** to bring into agreement. *Pihak² sing kerengen angèl dimupakataké.* It's difficult to reconcile quarreling parties. *Keputusané panitya di*aké rapat pléna.* The committee's decisions were submitted to the plenary session for ratification. **ϕ/di*i** to agree to/on. *Utangé kudu disaur luwih saka sing di*i.* He had to repay more money than had been agreed on.

mupangat *var of* MUNPANGAT

mupruk piled up, in heaps, abundant

mur threaded fastener (nut, screw, bolt)

murah *ng,* **mirah** *kr* 1 low in price. *Bijèn sanḍang-pangan iku *.* The cost of living used to be low. *Kartjis botjah iku regané *.* Children's tickets cost less. 2 plentiful. *Désaku * banju.* My village has a good supply of water. ***an** a cheap low-quality article. ***-*an** at reduced rates. *Pelem mau rasané ketjut, nggoné adol ija *-*an waé.* The mangoes are sour, so they're being sold cheap. **ka*an** mercy, compassion. *Éntuk ke*ané sing Maha Kuasa aku bisa munḍak pangkat.* Thanks to God's good graces, I got a promotion. **ϕ/di*aké** to make cheap. *murahaké pelemé* to sell the mangoes cheap. *Regané tak *aké.* I'll lower the price for you. **ϕ/di*i** to lower the price of (goods). *Aku tuku akèh mulané bandjur di*i.* I bought so much she lowered the price. *** ati** compassionate, considerate; generous

murakabi helpful, constructive. *Muga² uripmu bisa * kanggo nusa lan bangsa.* I hope your life will contribute to the nation and the people.

murang to deviate from the normal way. *Ḍèké * dalan liwat ing petegalan.* She left the road and cut across the fields. *tindak sing * ing kasusilan* conduct which departs from decent standards. *** krama** *or* *** sarak** *or* *** tata** contrary to good manners, rude

murba to have authority. *** ing** to have authority over

murbé mulberry

murbèng *contracted form of* MURBA ING. *Kang * Dumadi/Alam/Gesang/Wisésa* God

murda *oj* head. *aksara ** capital letter

murga (*or* ***n**) to improvise, make shift. *Sopé sing kanggo suguhan kurang, bandjur kepeksa *(n) gawé sop manèh.* We ran short of soup to serve, so we had to make up some more in a hurry with whatever we had on hand.

murid student in primary or secondary school. **ke*en** childish, sophomoric, callow

murina *ltry var of* MRINA

muring 1 (**duka** *ki*) (to get) angry. 2 a variety of gnat. ***-*** furious, enraged

murka greedy, selfish. **ka*n** greed

murni pure, unblemished, unadulterated. *asih ** true love. *mas ** solid gold

mursal disobedient, badly behaved

murtad to renounce one's religion *or* principles

murti *oj* body; entity

murtja *oj* to vanish; lost

murud dead; to die (*ki for* MATI)

murwâkâlâ shadow-play performance held as a daytime exorcism ceremony protecting a child from disaster

murwat appropriate, in keeping with the circumstances. *Blandjanipun para punggawa boten patos *.* The employees' wages are not adequate considering the work they do.

sa*é whatever is appropriate. *Sa*é anggonmu mènèhi tak tampa.* I'll welcome anything you contribute.
musafir *var of* MUSAPIR
musapir traveler, wanderer
musawarat (*or* ***an**) deliberation, negotiation. **ϕ/di*aké** to discuss, negotiate
muséum museum
musibat cursed, damned. *Tjandu iku diarani lara ireng *.* The opium habit is known as the cursed black sickness. *kena ing ** struck by disaster
musik̄ music in non-Javanese style. *Gamelané *.* The music was Occidental. ***an** to play non-Javanese music; a musician of such music. *** ngak ngik ngok** rock-'n-roll
musium *var of* MUSÉUM
musjawarah, musjawarat *var of* MUSAWARAT
Muslim a Moslem
Muslimat a female Moslem
Muslimin a male Moslem
musna *oj* to vanish; lost
muspra wasted; a waste. *Akèh wektu lan tenaga kang *.* A lot of time and energy went to waste.
mustadjab potent, efficacious. *Djopa-djapuné pantjèn * temenan.* His magic incantations are very effective.
mustail inconceivable, out of the question
mustâkâ head (*ki for* ENḌAS)
mustakil *var of* MUSTAIL
mustidjab *var of* MUSTADJAB
mustika a fine jewel. *** retna** jewelry
musuh *var of* MUNGSUH
mut ***-*an** sth one holds in the mouth *or* sucks *or* nibbles on. **nge* dridji** to suck the fingers; *fig* to look longingly at sth one wants. **nge/di*aké** to put sth in smn's mouth to hold *or* suck on. *Ḍoté diemutaké bajiné.* She gave the baby a pacifier. **nge/di*(i)** to hold in the mouth. *nge* permèn* to suck hard candy. *Tèrmomèteré di* nganti telung menit.* He kept the thermometer in his mouth for three minutes. *See also* AMUT
muṭakil to bear a grudge, have a chip on the shoulder
mutasi **ϕ/di*** to rotate *or* transfer [an employee]. *A saiki di* nang Sumatra.* A is being transferred to Sumatra.
mutawatir *ng,* **mutawatos** *kr* fearful, apprehensive. **ϕ*i** provoking fear *or* apprehension; dangerous. *See also* KUWATIR
mutawatos *kr for* MUTAWATIR
mutijârâ pearl
mutju ***-*** to bulge, protrude
mutlak 1 unconditional, absolute, not to be bargained. 2 a necessity. *Sekolah kuwi * kanggo botjah.* Education is a must for young people.
mutmainah [of the soul] at rest, at peace
muts soldier's overseas cap
mutyârâ *var of* MUTIJARA
mu(w)- *see also under* MU-, MW- (*Introduction, 2.9.7*)
muwah (*ltry*) *ng,* **miwah** *kr* (together) with; and
muwak ***-*** badly ripped
muwârâ river mouth that empties into the sea
muwat **ϕ/di*** to put sth in(to). *Peṭiné kegeḍèn, ora bisa di* ing bétjak.* The chest is too big–it won't go in the pedicab. **pa*an** act of putting sth in(to). *Aku dikabari bab pemuatané karanganku.* I have been notified about the inclusion of my article [in a certain collection].
muwer to spin, whirl
muwun weeping (*ki for* TANGIS)
mw- *see under* MU(W)- (*Introduction, 2.9.7*)

N

n (*prn* **èn**) *alphabetic letter. See also under* EN- (*Introduction, 2.9.5*) *or under consonant that has been replaced by nasal prefix* (*Introduction, 3.1.5.4*)
n- *prefix* 1 *var of* NG-. 2 *var of* NJ- *in certain roots. See Introduction, 3.1.5.4*
-n *post-vowel form of suffix* -AN
na[a] *inf var of* ANA[a]. *See also under* NE- (*In-

*troduction, 2.9.2) or under replaced-conson-
ant plus* E *(Introduction, 3.1.5.4)*

-na^b (**-k̂na** *after vowel) imperative and subjunctive form of suffix* -AKÉ: *see chart, Introduction 3.1.5.4). N·djupuk·na sega aḍimu.* Get your brother's rice for him. *Aku
djupuk·na dluwang.* Get me some paper.
*Saridin kaé dak · kanḍa·kna wong tuwané,
mesṭi disrengeni.* Saridin would have been
scolded if I had told his parents. *See* -A 2,
3, 4 *for imperative meanings*

na'as portending evil. *dina* ✳ an unlucky
day. ✳*ing tanggal* a date of evil portent

nabi religious prophet. **ka✳an** (*var sp:* ka-
nabéjan) the time of the prophets. ✳ *Adam*
Adam (first man). ✳ **Isa** Jesus

nâdâ musical key

nadar (punagi *kr?*) a commitment to perform a certain act if one's hopes are fulfilled.
(**pa**)✳**an** act of carrying out such a commitment

naḍi *see* GURU

naḍi main artery of the circulatory system

nadjan *shf of* SANADYAN

nadjin 1 [of banana trees] ready to bear
fruit. 2 *form of* TADJIN

nadjis 1 unclean (in the religious sense); abhorrent. 2 feces. *φ/*di✳aké 1 to regard sth
as unclean *or* abhorrent. 2 to soil sth with
feces

nadyan *shf of* SANADYAN

nâgâ serpent. ✳ **dina** (**wulan, taun**) serpent
governing the propitiousness of directions
taken in journeys on a certain day (month
year). ✳ **taun**, ✳ **djatingarang**, ✳ **dina**, ✳ **ri-
djallullah** dragons which govern the north,
south, east, and west respectively, regarding
propitiousness

nâgâkusumâ, nâgâpuspâ, nâgâpuspitâ *var of*
NAGASARI

nâgâsantun *kr for* NAGASARI

nâgâsari *ng,* **nâgâsantun** *kr* 1 a certain hardwood tree with fragrant yellow blossoms
which are used cosmetically. 2 steamed
rice-flour-and-banana cake. 3 a certain batik design

nâgâsâsrâ a kris blade with 13 curves

nâgâsinom *var of* NAGASARI

nagri *oj* nation, state

nagur imitation diamond

nah 1 *inf var of* NONAH. 2 *excl: var of* LA

nahas *var of* NA'AS

Nahḍatul Ulama (*abbr:* **N.U.**) major Islamic
political party

nahwu teachings concerned with Arabic grammar as presented in Islamic schools

naib a district mosque official. **pa✳an** residence of this official

najab to steal in broad daylight. *Ana wong* ✳
njolong mèmèhan tanggaku. The clothes
were stolen off my neighbor's clothesline.

najâgâ *var of* NIJAGA

najâkâ 1 cabinet minister. 2 high-ranking
official under the Sultan of Jogjakarta. 3
official negotiator. 4 leader

nak *adr* child (*shf of* ANAK^a). ✳ (**a**)**nggèr**
adr man who is lower in age but higher in
social status than speaker. ✳ **k·um·anak** 1
to multiply, flourish. 2 to draw compound
interest. ✳ (**n**)**dulur** *or* ✳ **sanak** *or* ✳ **sedulur**
first cousin

nakal 1 bad, wrong, ill-behaved, morally delinquent. 2 *slang* promiscuous. *wong* ✳
prostitute; promiscuous woman. ✳-✳**an** 1
to compare *or* compete for bad behavior.
✳-✳*an, anakmu luwih* ✳. Your son is worse
than mine. 2 to try to get away with sth.
Kowé ki arep ✳-✳*an ja!* You're trying to
cheat me! **ka✳an** misbehavior

nakoḍa *var of* NANGKOḌA

nal ✳-✳**an** *or* ✳**-nil·an** fidgety, always on the
move. *See also* NIL

nal- *see also under* NL- (*Introduction, 2.9.3)
or under replaced-consonant plus* L (*Introduction, 3.1.5.4*)

nâlâ *ltry* heart, feelings

nalar mind, intellect, reason(ing power).
Tjupet ✳*é.* His outlook is narrow. *Mulur* ✳*é.*
He's a deep thinker. *miturut* ✳ logical(ly
speaking). *Gugon-tuhon kang mengkono
mau ora tinemu ing* ✳. Such a superstition
is preposterous. *φ/*di✳ to think sth over.
*φ/*di✳**aké** to explain (the reason for)

naléndra *var of* NARÉNDRA

nalika (at a past time) when. ✳ *aku isih tjilik*
when I was a child. *Tjritakna bab ḍèk* ✳*né
dina unggah²an.* Tell me about promotion
day [at school]. ✳ **kuwi** (just) at that time.
✳ *kuwi Ali liwat tjeḍak kono.* Just then Ali
came along. ✳ **semana** at that (remotely
past) time. ✳ **semono** *sms* ✳ KUWI. *See also*
SANALIKA

naluri 1 a descendant. 2 a tradition

nam ✳-✳**an** 1 woven. *blarak* ✳-✳*an* woven
coconut leaves. 2 a certain tree; also, its

fruit. **nge/di∗** to weave [vegetable fibers]. *nge∗ pendjalin/sepet* to weave rattan *or* coconut fibers. **nge/di∗i** to make [a woven article]. *Kipasé arep tak enami pring kulitan.* I'm going to weave the fan from bamboo bark. *See also* ANAM

nâmâ name (*kr for* ARAN, DJENENG)

namas *see* AWIGNAM

nambang *ltry* thousand. **sa∗** 1,000

nambong 1 to pretend not to know sth/smn. 2 stubborn, headstrong

nami name (*kr for* ARAN, DJENENG)

naming 1 only (*md for? rg var of?* MUNG). 2 but (*rg var of* NANGING)

namung 1 only, just (*kr for* MUNG). 2 but (*rg var of* NANGING)

-nânâ *suffix* *post-vowel var of* -ANA[b]

nanah pus. **∗en** to have a pus-filled infection

nanangan *var of* SANGAN. **pa∗** pan used for frying without oil

nanas pineapple

nandalem *ki* you [when addressing a highly esteemed person]

nandang *var of* NANḌANG

nanḍang to undergo, experience, endure. *∗ lelara* to have a disease. *∗ keluputan* to have faults. *∗ dosa* to have sins, be sinful. *∗ sangsara* to suffer bad luck, have a setback. *∗ tjilaka* to suffer misfortune. *lésan ∗* (*gram*) direct object of a verb

-nané *suffix* *post-vowel form of* -ANÉ

nang 1 *adr* little boy. 2 in, at, on. 3 *rpr* a note sounded on a gamelan instrument. 4 to (*inf var of* MENJANG). 5 to win (*inf var of* MENANG). **∗-∗an** *slang var of* ϕ-MENANG-I. **∗ apa** why? what for? *∗ apa kok ora dipangan segamu?* How come you didn't eat your rice?

nanging (*or, formal,* **a∗**) but. *akèh ∗ ala* plentiful but inferior. *Ora idjo ∗ biru.* It's not green, it's blue.

nângkâ jackfruit (ripened form of GORI). **∗ blonjo** sticky overripe jackfruit. **∗ sabrang** *or* **∗ Wlanda** soursop

nangkoḍa ship's captain

-nanipun *kr suffix* *post-vowel form of* -ANIPUN: *see* -ANÉ

nâpâ what? (*md for* APA)

napas 1 breath; *fig* soul, life. *∗ tjekak* short(ness) of breath. *megeng ∗* to hold the breath. *ngasokaké ∗* to rest up, catch one's breath. *lara ∗* asthma. *kuwat ∗ lan sarira* strong of wind and body. 2 sorrel, bay. *djaran ∗* a sorrel horse. **∗an** breath group. *Pada lingsa iku kanggo misah gatra, dadi kanggo ∗aning pamatja.* Javanese-script commas mark off clauses showing breath groups for reading.

napi what? (*md for* APA)

napkah money given to one's wife for living expenses. **ϕ/di∗i** to give expense money to

napsu *formal var of* NEPSU

naptu *formal var of* NEPTU

nar **∗-∗an** uneasy, apprehensive. **nge∗-∗i** causing apprehension/anxiety

nar- *see also under* NR- (*Introduction, 2.9.3*) *or under replaced-consonant plus* R (*Introduction, 3.1.5.4*)

nârâdipâ, nârâdipati *ltry* king

naradji *ltry* king

nârâjânâ *ltry* young. *ḍèk djaman ∗ku bijèn* back when I was young

nârâkarjâ *oj* worker, laborer

nârânâtâ *ltry* king

nârâpati *ltry* king

nârâprâdjâ *ltry* dignitary

nârârjâ *ltry* king

naréndra *ltry* king

narèswârâ *ltry* king

narèswari *ltry* queen; king's consort

narja *ltry* king

narmâdâ *ltry* river

narpati *oj* king

nas *excl calling attention to one's mismove in a game (e.g. chess) and entitling one to replay the move.* **nge∗i** to call "*nas!*"

naséhat (words of) advice

nasib luck. **∗ku** *èlèk.* My luck was bad.

nasional national

nasionalisasi nationalization. **di∗i** to be nationalized

nasionalisme nationalism

nationalis(tis) nationalist(ic)

Nasrani Christian. *agama ∗* Christianity. *golongan ∗* Christians

nastâpâ *ltry* sad, sorrowing

nâtâ *ltry* king. *Sang ∗* the king; his majesty

naté ever (*kr for* TAU)

natos *kr* *sbst var of* NATÉ

nâwâ *oj* nine. *babahan ∗ sanga* the nine bodily openings

nawâlâ 1 *oj* a letter (*ki for* LAJANG?). 2 ID card. **∗ patra** a letter

nawi 1 *shf of* MENAWI. 2 (*or* **∗an**) *rg var of* DJER, RAK

nawin *rg var of* DJER, RAK

nd-, nḍ- *see under* D, Ḍ, *or under* END-, ENḌ- (*Introduction, 2.9.5*)

ndj- *see under* NDJ *or under* ENDJ- (*Introduction, 2.9.5*)

-né *ng,* **-nipun** *kr* (*suffix*) 1 (**-k̒né, -k̒nipun** *after vowel*) *causative optative suffix: see chart, Introduction, 3.1.5.4.* 2 *post-vowel form of suffix* -É[c]

ne- *see also under* NA- (*Introduction, 2.9.2*) *or under replaced-consonant plus A* (*Introduction, 3.1.5.4*)

neb ***-*an** window shutters. **me*** 1 to settle at the bottom of liquid. 2 to calm down after strong emotion. **nge/di*(aké)** 1 to allow sth to settle at the bottom. 2 to calm smn. **nge/di*(i)** to close [doors, windows]. *See also* INEB

nebda *see* SINGA

neḍas [of lips, tongue] rough, chapped

neḍeng *acv form of* SEḌENG

Néḍerlan(d) Holland, the Netherlands

nedya *acv form of* SEDYA

neg feeling of revulsion. *Adja tjukil² untu salebaré mangan, supaja ora gawé enekė kang pada lenggah ḍahar.* Don't pick your teeth after you eat: it's disgusting to those who are at the table. **nge*-*i** revolting, sickening

negalé *var of* NEGALO

negalo (look) over there! (*rg kr? md? for* GALO, KAÉ LO)

negârâ *ng,* **negari** *kr* nation, state; the government. *wong sa* lanang wadon* every man and woman in the country. *warga ** citizen. *pabrik ** state-owned (-operated) factory. ** kulonan* Occidental country. ** ngétanan* Oriental country. *bank ** national bank. ** mantja* foreign country. **ka*n** pertaining to the nation. *upatjara ke*n* a state ceremony

negari *kr for* NEGARA

nèger Negro

negilé *var of* NEGILO

negilo (look) here! see here! (*rg kr? md? for* GILO, IKI LO)

negulé *var of* NEGULO

negulo (look) there! (*rg kr? md? for* IKU LO)

nèh *inf var of* ANÈH, DJENÈH, MANÈH, TENÈH, WÈNÈH

nèk 1 *var of* JÈN. 2 *rg var of* ANA[a], NINI. 3 (*or* ***[n]é** *or* ***-*[n]é**) perhaps, probably. *Tjoba asuné pakanana téla, * dojan barang.* Give the dog some cassava, he might like it.

néka **(ma)*-*** various kinds (of things). **ora *** simple, plain, not fancy. *See also* MANÉKA

nékad to persist in a determination. **ka*an** wilfull disregard of consequences; persistence in a course of action. *Ka*ané satemah ndjalari tiwasé.* His recklessness finally resulted in his death. *See also* TÉKAD

nèkel nickel (metal)

nèker marble(s). ***an** to play marbles

nèl ***-*an** to fidget, move about restlessly

nel- *see also under* NL- (*Introduction, 2.9.3*) *or under replaced-consonant plus* L (*Introduction, 3.1.5.4*)

nèm young (*kr for* NOM)

nem six. ** atus* (*èwu, juta*) six hundred (thousand, million). *buku* (*botjah, omah, lsp.*) six books (children, houses, *etc.*). **belas* 16. **likur* 26. *sewidak ** 66. ** wang* 50 cents. *Umuré kurang luwih enem taun.* He's about six years old. ***-*é** all six of them. **ne*** (group *or* unit of) six. *djam setengah ne** 5:30. *pangkat ne** sixth grade. **ka*** 1 (*or* **[ka]ping ***) six times; times six; (for) the sixth time; sixth (in a series). 2 sixth month of the Javanese calendar (9 November–22 December). **ka* tengah** $5^1/_2$. **nge/di*i** to form a set of six. *Kanggo nge*i perlu tuku sidji manèh.* We need one more to make six. *See also* -AN (*suffix*) 8, 15, 16; -É[c] (*suffix*) 9; NG- (*prefix*) 6, 7; PRA-

nem- *see also under* N- (*Introduction, 3.1.7*)

nembah 1 *ltry var of* ÑJ·SEMBAH. 2 to offer one's silent respects to God, or to a high authority, without overt expression

nembé 1 to be [do]ing *etc.* (*kr for* LAGI). 2 the future (*rg var of* TEMBÉ). 3 *kr for* MENTAS?

nèmpol smeared messily [onto]. *Ana bleṭok * nang kaṭok, kok dinengaké.* You have mud all over your pants, how come you don't do anything about it?

nen- *see also under* N- (*Introduction, 3.1.3*) *or under consonant that has been reduplicated then replaced* (*Introduction, 3.1.3, 3.1.5.4*)

-nen *suffix* *post-vowel form of* -EN

néndra *ltry* to sleep

nènèk *inf var of* NINI

nènèm young person (*kr for* NONOM). *See also* NÈM

nenepi to meditate (*var of* NJENJEPI, *form of* SEPI)

nèng in, at, on (*inf equivalent of* ANA ING)

neng 1 *rpr* a jerk. *Mak * tasé ditarik.* He snatched her handbag. 2 *rpr* a stinging pain. ***-*an** not on speaking terms with each other. **me*** to be/remain quiet (*see also* MENENG). **nge/di*aké (ñg/dipun·kèndel·aken *kr*)** 1 to refrain from speaking to.

B saiki lagi dienengké karo A. A isn't speaking to B right now. 2 to ignore. *Botjah aḍuh² wis suwé kok di*aké waé.* The child has been crying out in pain but nobody pays any attention! **ng/di*(-*)i** to (try to) quiet smn. *See also* MENENG

nengah 1 (to move) toward the center. *Slamet *, asu mau mèlu *.* Slamet walked toward the middle of the road; the dog did the same. 2 (to move) away from shore, *i.e.* toward the middle of a body of water. **ke*en** too close to the center. *Lakuné nang ndalan ke*en.* She was walking too near the middle of the road. **me*** *sms *.* *Prauné me*.* The boat went out to sea. **pa*** middle child. *See also* TENGAH

nengen (to move) toward the right. *méng-gok ** to turn right. *saka kiwa ** from left to right. **ke*en** too far to the right. **me*** *sms *.* *See also* TENGEN

nenggih (*or* **a***) this (as follows) is... ** pundi ingkang tjinatira...* This is where it is told... (*common opening phrase in a puppet-master's narration*)

nengsem(aké) *form of* SENGSEM

nènṭèng *-* to act defiant toward, talk back to

néon neon. *lampu ** neon light

nepdal numerology; horoscope(-casting) (*opt? sbst? kr for* NEPTU)

nepsu *ng kr,* **duka** *ki* passionate with anger or lust. ** ditjandet.* He kept his feelings under control. ***ñan** quick to anger. **ka*ñ** 1 anger. 2 to be the object of smn's anger. *Aku ora apa² kok kanepson.* What's he mad at me for? I didn't do anything. **φ/di*ñi** to get mad at smn. *** **birahi** beginnings of interest in the opposite sex, *esp.* during adolescence. *See also* HAWA, NESU

neptu Javanese numerology; horoscope; horoscope-casting

ner *ng,* **leres** *kr* direction; aim. *njimpang saka eneré* to deviate from its course. *Olèhé ngusar-usarakè paḍa eneré.* His brush strokes were all in the same direction. **nge/di*aké** to aim, point, direct sth. *nge*aké beḍil* to aim a gun. **nge/di*i** to head for. *Warti nge* kamar turuné.* Warti went to her room. *Kabèh paḍa nge* menjang panggonan kang ḍuwur.* Everyone headed for high ground. *dalan sing nge* geḍung bioskup* street that goes to the movie theater

ner- *see also under* NR- (*Introduction, 2.9.3*) *or replaced-consonant +* R (*Intro., 3.1.5.4*)

nerâkâ hell. *intiping ** the lowest layer of souls in hell. *** **djahanam** the most disagreeable part of hell

nerâtjâ balance (in balance of payments. ** perdagangan* balance of trade

nestiti careful, accurate, scrupulous. **φ/di*kaké** to examine carefully. *Sadurungé ndakwa wong lija, dinastitèkaké ḍisik.* You should be pretty sure of your ground before you accuse anyone.

nesu *ng kr,* **duka** *ki* to be(come) angry. ** gidra-gidro* hopping mad. *Apa sebabé ibumu duka?* Why is your mother mad? ***ñan** short-tempered. *lagi *-*né* in a fit of temper. **φ/di*ñi** to get mad at. *Aku didukani ibu.* Mother lost patience with me. *See also* NEPSU

nèt 1 *var of* NJÈT. 2 *inf var of* PÈNÈT. **nge/di*** to edit [a draft]. *Aku sing matja, kowé sing nge* tjaṭetan rapat mau.* I'll read the minutes; you write them up from my rough notes.

net **me*** compressed; solid(ly filled). *Isiné menet.* It's tightly packed. **nge/di*-*aké** *or* **nge/di*-*i** to compress, squeeze, pack tight. *Tasé adja di-enet² mengko enḍogé petjah kabèh.* Don't squeeze the bag or the eggs will all break.

nètèr 1 *ltry* to put sth to the test. ** kasudiranmu* to try your courage. 2 sloping, slanting

nètjes *var of* NÈTJIS

nètjis neat and orderly

nétra *ltry* eye. *sakeḍèp ** instantaneous(ly); (in) the wink of an eye. *tuna ** blind

nétral neutral, unaligned

ng- [*see also under* ENG- (*Introduction, 2.9.5*) *or under vowel or under replaced-consonant* (*Introduction, 3.1.5.4*)] *nasal prefix.* 1 *produces acv forms: see under individual roots.* 2 *produces directional forms. ñ·tengen* toward the right. *nga·lor* northward. *ana ng·omah* at home. *mlebu ng·alas* to go into the forest. *Bukuné tiba saka nge·tas.* The book fell out of the briefcase. 3 to assume the characteristics of [*root*]. *m·bodo* to act stupid. *ng·ombak-banju* wavelike. *ñj·sudagar* to be(come) a merchant. *ng·lara* to pretend to be ill. *ñj·supé* to pretend to forget. 4 to regard smn as; to call smn sth. *m·bapak* to think of [smn] as a father. *ngadi* to call smn Di [a nickname]. 5 to make [materials] into sth; to use [*root*].

ñj·sambel to make hot sauce. *m̄·palu* to hammer. *ng·gandjar* to reward smn. **6** *n* apiece; every *n*; *n* at a time. *ng·rong rupiah* two rupiahs each. *Sidjiné m̄·pira?* How much apiece? *ñ·telung dina* every three days. *prangko ñj·seketip loro* two 10-cent stamps. *ñ·sidji*[2] one at a time, single file. **7** [*with doubled number*] *n* at a time, *n* by *n*. *Barisé ng·rolas*[2]. They marched in ranks of twelve. **8** increasingly [*root*]. *Njambut-gawé saja ñj·suwé.* He takes longer and longer to do his work. *A saja ñj·sugih.* A keeps getting richer.

ng. *see* NGABÈH

nga 1 nine (*shf of* SANGA). *nem, tu, lu,* * 6, 7, 8, 9. 2 *var of* NG- *prefix before monosyllable roots and* (*irregularly*) *certain others* (*see e.g. under* BOTOH, URIP, WONTEN). **nge/di*kaké** to open sth (*inf var of* M̈/DI·WENGA·KAKÉ). *Ngakna lawang.* Open the door! **nge/di*ni** to keep opening [things] (*inf var of* M̈/DI·WENGA·NI)

Nga'ad *var sp of* NGAHAD

ngabad *ltry* pervasive [of a pleasant odor]

ngabas to do sth without making a genuine effort. *Mesti waé ora kena olèhmu mbalang pelem mau, lha wong *.* Of course you didn't hit the mango you were aiming at–you weren't really trying.

ngabèh **ϕ*i** (*or* **a*i** *or* **i*i**; *abbr*: **ng.**) an official under the Sultan ranking between a *wadana* and a *lurah*). **(pa)*an** residence of the above official

ngabekti to show respect by kissing the knee of an older person. ***ǹ** occasion for show-one's respect as above, *esp.* Lebaran time. *Dina iki nang kraton ana ngabektèn.* Today at court the Sultan is honored (as above). **ϕ/di*ǹi** to pay one's respects to. **pa*** one's respects. *sembah pa** one's best wishes (*in opening phrase of letter*). *See also* BEKTI

ngabid devout, orthodox

ngabjâgâtâ to begin working, start in on a task

ngabor to talk nonsense

ngabotohan *see under* BOTOH

ngadilâgâ *ltry* battleground

ngadirâgâ to get dressed (*ltry var of* DANDAN)

ngadjeng in front (*kr for* NGAREP)

ngagesang *form of* GESANG

ngagir immobile. *Olèhé matja buku karo *.* He's lying still, reading. *Kok * kaja wong ngemis.* Why do you just stand there (like a beggar waiting for a handout)?

ngagla *rg* empty-handed

ngaglah to sit where one impedes the movement of others. *mBok lingguh nèng kéné, adja *.* Sit here–don't block the passageway.

ngaglik precariously close to an edge

ngah *rpr* the moo of cattle. **nge/di*i** to reserve for smn. *Katjangé adja dientèkaké, adimu di*i.* Don't eat all the peanuts, save some for your brother.

Ngahad Sunday. *See also* AKAD

ngajar 1 to catch a bird in the bare hands. 2 *form of* AJAR

ngâjâwârâ to talk nonsense

ngajuwârâ *var of* NGAJAWARA

ngak *rpr* a goose honking

Ngakad *var sp of* NGAHAD

ngal- *see also under* NGL- (*Introduction, 2.9.3*) *or under replaced-consonant plus* L (*Introduction, 3.1.5.4*)

ngaluamah to give in to an appetite. *Bengi*[2] *kok ndjaluk mangan, mbok adja *.* Eating so late at night!–you shouldn't just eat any time you feel like it.

ngaluhur *form of* LUHUR

ngalup 1 to howl, yelp. 2 *var acv form of* ALUB

ngamântjâ *form of* MANTJA

ngambjog to move in with smn temporarily, stay at smn's place

ngampah *rg var of* NGARÉ

ngampret small, narrow, cramped; [of clothing] tight-fitting, too small

ngamrih *inf var of* AMRIH

ngan *adr* deer! (*shf of* MENDJANGAN)

ngânâ *ng,* **ngaten** *kr* like that, in that way (*inf var of* MENGKANA: *Degree III, Introduction, 6*). *Barang * kaé djenengé apa?* What are things like that called? ** iku* that is (to say...). **ϕ/di*kaké** to treat like that; to do that to. *Sekrupé dinganakaké supaja bisa kentjeng.* You have to do like that to the bolt to tighten it. ***-ngéné** (**ngétan-ngèten** *kr*) in various ways. *Arepa *-ngéné kaé, kowé adja keduwung.* Whatever happens, have no regrets.

ngana(h) *var of* RANA[a]

ngang (*or* *-**) *rpr* the whine of an engine

ngangkang loud [of music]. *Bonangé ditabuh * seru banget.* The *bonang*'s were played forte.

ngangkleng *rg* to have a long tiresome wait

ngangkrang *var of* NGANGRANG

nganglang to travel (wander, fly) around. * **pringga** standing by in case help is needed

ngangluh to complain. **pa*** complaint
ngangrang 1 a large red tree ant. 2 (*or* ***an**) to weave
ngangsi *var of* NGANTI. *Olèhé nggawa barang * mèjèk*[2]. He's carrying a back-breaking load.
nganjer *var of* NGANJUR
nganjur (to stand) straight
ngantèk *var of* NGANTI
ngantèn *var of* MANTÈN. *See also* EMBOK
nganti *ng,* **ngantos** *kr* 1 until, to (the point that). *Aku ana kono * djam loro.* I was there till two o'clock. ** mengko tekané bodjoné* until his wife gets here. *Botjah*[2] *pada mangan * wareg.* The children stuffed themselves. ** sepréné* so far, up till now. 2 for [a time period]. *ora * let suwé* not for (a) long (time). *Aku sinau * kira*[2] *sepuluh taun.* I studied for about ten years. ** pitung turunan* for (the next) seven generations; *fig* all of one's descendants forever. 3 already [a certain time]; [not] yet [a certain time]. *supaja adja * kesorèn* so as not to get there late, *i.e.* when it is already late afternoon. *Ora * wengi Siti wis turu.* Siti went to bed very early, *i.e.* when it was not yet night. 4 [to such an extent] that. *Saking bingungé ḍèwèké * lali djenengé ḍéwé.* He was so mixed up that he forgot his own name. 5 to (do such a [surprising, undesirable] thing as). *Hawané * luwih saka satus dradjat.* The temperature actually went over 100 degrees! *Olèhku ngombé banju * telung gelas.* I drank three whole glasses of water. *Kok guruné * ngerti sapa sing maduli.* How did the teacher find out who tattled?! *Ḍèwèké * ora bisa ngampet wetuning eluh.* She simply couldn't hold back her tears. *Mungsuhé * bisa nrabas Banjumas.* The enemy succeeded in getting through Banjumas. *Jèn wis mabuk ḍèké * lali anak bodjoné.* When he gets drunk, he completely forgets his wife and children.
ngantos *kr for* NGANTI
ngantuk sleepy. ***an** one who is always sleepy
ngaplik small (in size), few (in number)
ngaplo to have no results for one's efforts. *Aku mèlu tandur, bareng panèn aku mung *.* I helped plant along with the others, but at harvest time I didn't get anything.
ngapluk abundant [*referring to one's gray hairs*]
ngapret *var of* NGAMPRET
ngaprit fast. *mlaju ** to run like the wind
ngar- *see also under* NGR- (*Introduction, 2.9.3*) *or under replaced-consonant plus* R (*Introduction, 3.1.5.4*)
ngaré valley, lowland; [of terrain] level, flat. *tanah ** a plain; lowland
ngarep *ng,* **ngadjeng** *kr* in front (*see also* AREP[b]). **sa*** in front of
ngarot *rg* a ceremonial feast held before tilling rice paddies
ngarsa in front (*ki for* NGAREP). *** dalem** your/his majesty (the Sultan of Jogjakarta)
ngarsadji *contracted form of* NG·ARSA ADJI
ngas ***-*an** in a great hurry. *Adja *-*an, linggih!* Don't rush around so: sit down!
ngasi *var of* NGANTI
ngaten 1 like this/that (*kr for* NGÉNÉ, NGONO, NGANA; *md for* NGANA?). 2 *excl: kr for* NGONO
ngatjeng *var of* NGATJUK
ngatjuk erect [of penis]
ngaṭur 1 to spout upward. 2 to stand (up) (straight)
ngaurip *form of* URIP
ngawikani *form of* WIKAN
ngawonten... *see* WONTEN
nge- *var of* NG- *prefix* (*see Introduction, 3.1.5.4*). *See also under* NGA- (*Introduction, 2.9.2*)
ngeḍabjah *inf var of* NG·GEḌABJAH
ngeḍagrah *rpr* the movement of a bulky person seating himself ponderously
ngeḍangkrang *var of* NG·GEḌANGKRANG
ngeḍap afraid; having lost one's nerve
ngedébag *inf var of* NG·GEDÉBAG
ngeḍèbjèh **ngeḍobjah-*** clumsy, awkward. *See also* GEḌOBJAH
ngeḍèbrèl *cr* to jabber, yak
ngeḍebus to babble, talk nonsense
ngèḍèd to hold the back stiff *or* arched while walking
ngeḍèḍèr *var of* NG·GEḌÈḌÈR
ngedèndèng to walk with an affected air, a mincing gait, *etc.*
ngeḍèng, ngèḍèng open, frank, having nothing to hide. *Ora ana kang * ngatonaké rupané.* No one wanted to show his face.
ngeḍengkreng *var of* NG·GEḌENGKRENG
ngeḍingkring *inf var of* NG·GEḌINGKRING
ngedjâwâ *ng,* **ngedjawi** *kr* *see under* DJAWA[a]
ngedjibris to talk at great length
ngedjodjor *inf var of* NG·GEDJODJOR
ngeḍobjah *inf var of* NG·GEḌOBJAH
ngedobrol *var of* NG·GEDOBROL

ngeḍoḍor *var of* NG·GEḌOḌOR
ngedubleg to talk endlessly about inconsequential things
ngeḍungkrung to sit with bowed head
ngeg *rpr a grunt.* **, pantjèn abot tenan.* Oof, it's heavy!
ngèh *rg var of* WÈNÈH
ngèk *rpr* a baby's crying. **-* or* **ngak-*** to keep crying. ***-èngèk** *rpr* the sound of a stringed instrument being played with a bow
ngèkèk (to laugh) hard
ngèkès (to cough) continuously
ngèklèk *var of* NGÈKÈK
ngèl **nge/di*-*(i)** to make sth difficult. *Jèn anaké wong mlarat, mlebu sekolah kuwi mesṭi di*-*.* They always make it hard for poor people's children to get into school. *See also* ANGÈL
ngel- *see also under* NGL- (*Introduction, 2.9.3*) *or under replaced-consonant plus* L (*Introduction, 3.1.5.4*)
ngelak (**salit** *opt kr? ki?*) thirsty. **ϕ*i** causing thirst. *Hawa ngéné iki ngelaki.* This kind of weather makes you thirsty.
ngelih *ng,* **luwé** *kr* hungry. **ϕ/di*aké** to cause to become hungry. *Nang pertjobaan mau, tikusé dingelihaké ḍisik.* In the experiment, the rats were allowed to get hungry first.
ngelik 1 high-pitched and penetrating [of voice quality, in singing classical Javanese songs]. 2 change of mood in gamelan accompaniment to shadow plays. *Genḍingé *.* The music made the transition to the next part of the play.
ngèlmi *sbst? kr for* NGÈLMU
ngèlmu knowledge; (a) science (*var of* ILMU)
ngelu *ng kr,* **pujeng** *ki* (to have/get) a headache
ngemasi *ltry* to die
ngembârâ *var of* NG·AMBARA
ngembek̄ (to have *or* to exist) in abundance
ngembeng moist, soggy. ** banju* watery. ** (e)luh* [eyes] filled with tears
ngember *var of* NGEMBENG
ngembes watery, damp
ngembrah prevalent, widespread, commonplace, usual
ngembreg overabundant. *Suketé * kok ora dibabati.* The grass is overrunning everything–I should think you'd mow it!
ngèmèl very fond of [*esp.* food]. *Kebo kuwi * pari.* Kerbaus love rice plants.
ngemèrè·kaké, ·ni *var of* ϕMERI·K̀AKÉ, ·ǸI
ngempet *var of* NGEMPRET
ngempret to make a run, to dash
ngemu 1 filled (with), containing. ** rasa* filled with emotion. ** getih* forming a blood blister, bleeding subcutaneously. *menḍung * udan* rain-filled clouds. *Menawa mbulané miring ngiwa kuwi * firasat arep larang beras.* When the crescent moon is tipped to the left, it contains an omen that the price of rice is going up. 2 *form of* KEMU
ngen ***-*** thought, idea. **nge/di*-*** to keep thinking about. *Kowé lagi nge*-* apa kok meneng waé.* What are you thinking about, that you're so quiet? *See also* ANGEN, KANGEN
ngenḍajah *var of* NGENḌAJUR
ngenḍajur to hang down ponderously, *e.g.* a laden fruit-tree branch
ngenḍanu *ltry* dark, overcast
ngenḍerek̄ [of chickens] to sit in a hunched-over position
ngenḍih *ltry* to defeat, overcome
ngendika *ki* to say, talk, tell, speak to [a social inferior]. ***n** to converse, talk. **ng/di*kaké** to tell sth. **pa*** what smn says [to a social inferior]. *For corresponding ng usages see* DJARÉ, GUNEM, KANḌA, OMONG, TJLAṬU, TJRITA, TUTUR. *See also* ANDIKA
ngenḍujuk bent low under a heavy burden
ngéné *ng,* **ngaten** *kr* 1 like this, in this way, so; as follows (*Degree I, Introduction, 6: inf var of* MENGKÉNÉ). 2 *var of* RÉNÉ. **ngéna-*** (**ngétan-ngèten** *kr*) like this, in these ways. *Kowé kok ngéna-* guluné nèng apa?* Why do you keep going this way with your neck? *mBok ja ngéna-*a ja ora bisa.* No matter how you try, you won't be able to do it. **ϕ/di*k̀aké** to do this to; to treat in this way. *Jèn dingènèkaké mbokmenawa bisa ditekuk.* If you do this to it, maybe you can bend it.
ngènèh *var of* RÉNÉ
ngeng (*or* *-*) *rpr* buzzing
ngeng- *see also under* NG- (*Introduction, 3.1.3*) *or under consonant that has been reduplicated then nasalized* (*Introduction, 3.1.3, 3.1.5.4*)
ngèngèh ***an** food reserved for smn. **ϕ/di*aké** *or* **ϕ/di*i** 1 to give. 2 to leave food for smn who has not yet appeared at the meal. *See also* ÈNGÈH
ngèngèr 1 (**ng·abdi** *kr*) to live in smn's home as a servant. *A ketampan * ana ing*

karandan. A was taken into the widow's home as a servant. 2 [of a child] to live in the home of a relative, to serve him and to learn proper manners and become educated. **ϕ/di*aké** to have smn taken into a family (as above). *Slamet ngèngèraké anaké marang Pak Geḍéné.* Slamet sent his son to live with his [the son's] uncle. **ϕ/di*i** 1 to be in service to. 2 to serve smn as a protegé. **pa*an** act of going into service. *Pa*anmu dak tampa.* I will receive you into my family (in service).

ngèngkèl argumentative

ngèngkèng 1 to keep crying/howling. 2 stubborn

ngengkrik [of crickets] to chirp. *Djangkriké paḍa * "krik-krik-krik!"* Crickets chirped.

ngengleng eccentric, deranged

ngèngrèng ***an** 1 a rough (first) draft; an outline. 2 (having been) drafted *or* outlined. **ϕ/di*** 1 to draft [a document *etc.*]. 2 to draw a pattern outline onto fabric being worked in batik

ngengreng elegant-looking

ngènjèg to walk rapidly straight ahead looking to neither right nor left

ngènjlèg *var of* NGÈNJÈG

ngenjos to douse a fire

ngentar to run (off) fast

ngenṭiju industrious, diligent

ngenṭir crickets' chirping

ngentjrèt to dash, sprint, run (off) fast

ngéntjutaké appealing-looking, captivating (*var of* M̈·PÉNTJUT·AKÉ)

ngepipir to tremble, shiver

ngèprèt to dash off, run away

nger- *see also under* NGR- *(Introduction, 2.9.3) or under replaced-consonant plus* R *(Introduction, 3.1.5.4)*

ngerak *intsfr* dry [of season]. *ketiga ** a dry season that is exceptionally dry

ngèrèng 1 (to make) a loud chirping *or* humming sound, *e.g.* crickets, locusts. 2 to wail

ngerik to chirp loudly

ngerti *ng,* **ngertos** *kr* to understand, know (**pirsa** *or* **priksa** *or* **uninga** *ki*). *Aku ora * asmané.* I don't know his name. *Bener aku *.* OK, I get it. *Bèna, mengko rak * ḍéwé.* Let him find out for himself. ***a** 1 you should know...; please understand... *Ngertija, tresnaku marang kowé iku lair terusing batin.* I want you to know that my love for you is wholehearted. 2 if [one] had known. **a ngéné, aku ora mangkat.* If I had known this would happen, I wouldn't have gone. ***ǹ** quick to grasp/understand. ***né** what smn knows/understands. **ku ḍèwèké iku sugih.* As far as I know, she's rich. *Kabèh butuhmu *mu mung sibu.* For everything you want, you come to your mother! **mu ora ana lija kedjaba mung bab ḍuwit.* The only thing you understand is money. ***-*** 1 what smn knows. *Kok *-*mu kuwi!* How on earth could you know that! 2 suddenly, unexpectedly. **-* wis lungguh ing papané sakawit.* All at once she was back in the same seat. **ma*** *ltry var of ** (*see also* MANGERTI). **ϕ/di*k̀aké** to cause smn to understand/know. **ϕ/di*ǹi** to make known, to convey information. *Montor bisa ngretèni adoh-tjeḍaké dalan sing diliwati.* Cars indicate the distance you travel. **pa*** comprehension, grasp. **sa*é** to the extent of one's knowledge. *Sa*ku, ḍèké durung kawin.* As far as I know, he's not married.

ngertos to know, understand (*kr for* NGERTI)

nges interesting, significant, having appeal *or* substance. **ing wulangan* the essential part of the lesson. *Karanganmu betjiké diganti supaja luwih *.* You'd better revise your article so it will have more appeal. *Mau bengi lakoné wajang wong * banget.* The plot of last night's drama was very interesting. *Kertas² udjian mau amor lajang² sing *-* kaé.* Mixed in with the test papers were some provocative-looking letters.

ngésuk *rg var of* BÉSUK

nget ***-*an** 1 warmed-over food. 2 to stare at each other. **nge/di*aké** to watch closely, examine carefully. **nge/di*(i)** to warm up [leftovers]. **nge/di*i** to watch intently, stare at. *See also* ANGET, INGET

ngeṭakrah abundant, in large quantities

ngeṭangkrong to sit (impolitely) in a higher position than others. *See also* METANGKRONG

ngetawang obvious; conspicuous

ngeṭaweng [of moustaches] having a fine sweeping curve

ngeṭawit small and finely shaped

ngèṭèg to zigzag

ngetégé to stay quiet, not contribute to the conversation

ngetègèr, ngeteger *var of* NGETÉGÉ

ngetègès able to withstand wear and tear *or* endure physical hardship

ngeṭeker 1 to stay put, stay in one place. 2 to remain off by oneself, sad and withdrawn

ngeṭékor to enjoy one's food, eat with gusto

ngeṭékrak to sit in an unmannerly way, *e.g.* sprawled
ngeṭekrek̄ *var of* NGEṬEKER
ngeṭekul 1 to sit with the knees drawn up and the face buried in the arms. 2 to devote oneself wholly to work
ngeṭèl dirty, greasy
ngèten in this way (*md for* NGATEN). **ngétan-*** like this/that, in these/those ways (*kr: see* NGÉNÉ, NGANA)
ngeṭengkreng to sit motionless
ngeṭengkruk, ngeṭengkrus *var of* NGEṬENGKRENG
ngeṭepes to sit cross-legged in respectful silence
ngetépol covered with dirt, mud, grease
ngeṭéprak [of human excrement] piled high
ngeṭèprès to keep up a steady stream of chatter
ngetepus to babble, talk nonsense
ngeṭeṭer to shiver from cold *or* dampness
ngèṭèti to clean [*e.g.* a chicken] by removing the insides
ngetiging *rg* quick-paced, in a hurry
ngeṭijeng to drive oneself hard on the job. *Adja *, lèrèn ḍisik.* Don't work too hard–take a break.
ngeṭiju *var of* NGEṬIJENG
ngeṭikrak scattered around is disarray; in a mess
ngeṭingkrik 1 to sit higher up than others (a breach of etiquette). 2 to consider oneself too good to pitch in and work with the others
ngeṭingkring *var of* NGEṬINGKRIK
ngeṭipleng (to run) fast
ngeṭiprat to run fast, make a dash
ngeṭiprèt, ngeṭipret *var of* NGEṬIPRAT
ngetjèbrès *var of* NGETJÈPRÈS
ngetjemong to talk aimlessly. *Wiwit mau mung * ora ana putusané.* They've been rambling on and on without coming to a decision.
ngetjentjeng *var of* NGETJETJENG
ngetjepoh soaking wet
ngetjeprèh *var of* NGETJEPOH
ngetjèprès to talk on and on
ngetjeproh *var of* NGETJEPOH
ngetjibris *var of* NGETJIPRIS
ngetjipir (to run) fast
ngetjiprèt *var of* NGEṬIPRAT
ngetjipris to talk continuously
ngetjiput (to run) fast, to scurry
ngetjit *var of* NG-GETJIT
ngetjiwis *var of* NGETJIPRIS
ngetjombar having plenty of sauce, gravy, *etc. Jèn ndjangan bobor kudu *. Bobor* vegetable soup has to be made with lots of liquid.
ngetjomé to talk foolishly, prattle
ngetjomèl to talk all the time
ngetjoprès to talk on and on
ngetjriwis *var of* NGETJIPRIS
ngetjumut all covered (with) [sth messy]
ngetjuprus to talk incessantly, to keep talking
ngetjut to nurse, suck (*children's word*)
ngetjutjung *var of* NGETJETJENG
ngetjuwèh to talk continuously
ngetjuwis *var of* NGETJUWIT
ngetjuwit to twitter, squeak [*e.g.* birds, mice]; *fig* to talk too much (*esp.* girls). *See also* TJUWIT
ngeṭokroh so abuṇdant as to be worthless
ngetol *var of* NG-GETOL
ngeṭongkrong to sit higher up than others (unmannerly). *See also* MEṬONGKRONG
ngetoprès *var of* NGETJOPRÈS
ngeṭopros to boast, tell tall tales of one's experiences *or* accomplishments
ngetugur [to sit, lie, sleep] motionless
ngeṭungkru:k to sit with bowed head; to sit looking down. *See also* ṬUNGKRUK
ngeṭungkrung *var of* NGEṬUNGKRUK
ngeṭupru:k *var of* NGEṬEPRUS
ngeṭupru:s to talk non-stop, to keep jabbering
ngeṭuṭu:r shivering with wet and cold
ngeṭuwik to keep scratching oneself
ngéwas (on/to) the diagonal
ngèwèl to shake, tremble
ngèwès to flow, pour out; *fig* to talk a lot. *Nèk wis *, lali mangan.* Once he gets to talking, he forgets to eat.
ngg- *see under* G; *see also under* ENG- (*Introduction, 2.9.5*)
ngi ***ǹ** rice that has been cooled by fanning so that it is not too hot to eat. **nge/di*** to fan [rice] cool
ngigel [of peacocks] to spread the tail
ngigli:g *describing a firm, steadily paced way of walking, without paying any heed to one's surroundings*
ngigli:ng *rg* to come empty-handed, not bring anything
ngijeng to fuss, whine, cry
ngik (*or* **ngak-***) 1 *rpr* the sound of labored breathing. 2 *rpr* the bowing of a stringed instrument
ngikik to giggle

ngikil (to cough) persistently
ngiklik 1 to make a clicking sound. 2 *var of* NGIKIK
ngilmi knowledge; (a) science (*sbst? kr for* ILMU)
ngimel to nibble constantly
nging *inf var of* NANGING
nginglung disorganized, absent-minded, rushing around confused
nginjig 1 to walk with little trotting steps. 2 to walk straight ahead looking to neither left nor right
nginjlig *var of* NGINJIG
ngințar (to run) fast, to scurry
nginți:k̄ (to run) fast
ngițar *var of* NGINȚAR
ngiwa 1 to(ward) the left; to go left. *ménggok* * to make a left turn. 2 unethical; immoral. *laku* * corrupt practices; [of women] promiscuity; prostitution. **ke*nen** too far to the left. *Siti lungguhé ke*nen mula ora klebu potrèt.* Siti sat so far to the left she didn't get in the picture. **ma*** *ltry var of* *. *Lakuné mengiwa.* He walked to the left. *or* His conduct is unethical. *See also* KIWA
ngiwas *var of* NGÉWAS
ngiwung to lose one's self-control, go berserk
ngj- *see under* J-, KJ- (*Introduction, 3.1.5.4*)
ngl- *see also under* L-, KL- (*Introduction, 3.1.5.4*)
nglajeg to keep busy, always be on the go
nglajub [of eyes] sleepy-looking
nglakani to yield a small crop of fruit or none at all
nglambrang to wander aimlessly *or* restlessly
nglamprah to touch *or* drag on the ground
nglamun hazy, indistinct
nglandeng constant, steady, pervasive
nglandjak to exceed. *Blandjaku * saka pametuku.* My expenses are greater than my income. ** tapel wates mlebu ing negara tangga* to go beyond the boundaries into a neighboring country
nglangkèt excessively thin
nglangkunig crooked, winding
nglangsrah to touch *or* drag on the ground
nglangut far off, remote, desolate. *Lajangané * ḍuwur banget.* The kite was way high in the air. *Pikirané nglambrang *.* Her thoughts strayed far off. *Jèn bengi sepi njenjet, rasané bandjur *.* It was very still at night and I felt lonely.
nglaup to shout *or* sing boisterously
nglébrag large and lumpy-looking
nglegarang to sleep in an unusual place *or* manner. *Ḍèké * ing kursi.* He fell asleep in his chair.
nglègèg to sit up straight
nglegèjèh to lie down; to get into bed
nglegéwa **ora *** to not expect *or* anticipate. *Aku ora * jèn baturku ḍéwé sing njolong djamku.* I never thought my own servant would steal my watch. *Aku ora * udjug² djebul ana wong teka.* Quite unexpectedly, someone came straight toward me.
nglegojor *var of* NGLEGUJUR
nglegorong *var of* NGLEGARANG
nglegujur to stagger, walk unsteadily
nglèjèk to lean, list
ngleker sound asleep
nglélah unsteady; lacking strength *or* sturdiness
nglelèḍèk to tease, annoy, pester
ngleler slow. *Jèn njambut gawé adja *.* Don't slow down on the job.
ngléloh *var of* NGLÉLAH
nglembârâ to wander, roam
nglembèrèh to sag; to lie *or* hang loosely
nglemberek̄ to lie weakly. *Djarané saking keselé bandjur * nang dalan.* The horse was so exhausted it sank down on the street.
nglèmbrèh *var of* NGLEMBÈRÈH
nglembrek̄ *var of* NGLEMBEREK
nglembur to work outside of the usual hours. *Embokné * mbațik.* His mother worked at her batik nights. *Bapak arep * tekan djam wolu bengi.* Father is working (overtime) till eight this evening.
nglemburuk *var of* NGLEMPURUK
nglemek̄ 1 damp; limp from dampness. 2 to fade, lose color
nglemir [of fabric] lightweight, gauzy, without body
nglempérak to sit in an improper *or* unmannerly way
nglemperek *var of* NGLEMPREK
nglempis to pant, breathe heavily
nglèmprèh 1 to fly at a low altitude. 2 to touch *or* drag on the ground
nglemprèh (to walk) straight ahead without looking to either side
nglemprek̄ weak, enervated
nglempreng *var of* NGLEMPRÈH
nglempuruk 1 piled up in disorder. 2 sitting/lying with head bowed in apprehension
nglempus fast asleep; (to sleep) soundly
ngleneng slow, smooth, placid, silent
nglengak to crane the neck

nglengger motionless and unresponding, as though in a coma
nglengguruk to lie weakly (*esp.* of chickens in death throes)
nglengkârâ impossible; improbable, unlikely, uncommon
nglenṭar to go fast, speed up
nglèntjèr to go out; to go smw for pleasure
nglentreng *var of* NGLENENG
nglepis to chain-smoke
nglépos *var of* NGLÉPUS
nglèprèh *var of* NGLÈMPRÈH
nglépus fast asleep
nglepus *var of* NGLEPIS
ngleses taking one's ease. *Bar mangan * lèjèh²*. After he ate, he stretched out comfortably.
nglésus sound asleep
ngléṭak excessively thin
nglèṭèk *var of* NGLÉṬAK
ngleṭek̄ to remain apart from others. *Siti * nang kamar dolanan anak²an.* Siti is playing with her dolls alone in her room.
ngletjis to smoke habitually
ngliker *var of* NGLEKER
nglimprek̄ to lie weak and listless
nglindur to talk in one's sleep
nglipus *var of* NGLÉPUS
nglisik rasping sound. *Ora ana walang *.* It was dead quiet.
ngliṭik *var of* NGLÉṬAK
nglojos to go/stay out in the rain
nglombrot carelessly dressed, sloppy-looking
nglomprot *var of* NGLOMBROT
nglotjo to masturbate
nglotjut to go out in the rain by necessity
nglowèh [of wounds] open; opened up
nglumpruk weak, limp, slumped over
ngobos to talk nonsense, make empty boasts
ngodor persistent, dogged
ngojos 1 to sweat profusely. 2 *rg var of* NGLOJOS
ngoko the speech style used when addressing smn of lower social status, or of equal status with whom one has a close relationship; also, when talking to oneself (*see Introduction, 5*). *tembung ** a Ngoko word. *Apa *né gerah?* What is *gerah* in Ngoko? *Aku jèn guneman krama apa * kepénaké?* Should I speak to him in Krama or in Ngoko? *tembung krama inggil sa*né* a High Krama word with its corresponding Ngoko. ***n-*nan** to speak to each other in Ngoko. **ϕ/di*kaké** to put into Ngoko, say in Ngoko. *Ngokokna.* Say it in Ngoko. *Tembung sing tulisané ḍojong adja dingokokaké.* The italicized words are not to be put into Ngoko. * **anḍap** humble Ngoko. * **lugu** ordinary Ngoko. *See also* KOKO
ngolor to flatter, fawn (on)
ngomplèh [of lips] protruding and pendulous
ngomplo empty-handed. *Wis adoh² tekan réné, ndadak *.* After coming all this way, I end up getting nothing!
ngomplong 1 to have a hole in it. 2 *var of* NGOMPLO
ngon *ng,* **ngèn** *kr* **nge/di*** to tend [livestock]; *fig* to watch over, take care of. *See also* ANGON
ngong *ltry* I, me; my
ngonggor *rg* thirsty
ngongkloh weak, listless
ngongklong *var of* NGONGKLOH
ngongsrong panting; short of breath
ngonjlog to walk along in careless disregard of others
ngonjog *var of* NGONJLOG
ngonò *ng,* **ngaten** *kr* 1 like that, in that way, so (*Degree II, Introduction, 6: inf var of* MENGKONO). *Ḍèk tjilik aku ija *.* I was that way too when I was a child. *Jèn * kuwi, kowé mèmper aku.* If you're like that, you're like me. *Ah! kok *.* That [what you just did] isn't nice! 2 if only. 3 *excl expressing wryness, superciliousness; distress. Bisaa * ḍèké arep tuku montor loro.* Naturally he'd buy two cars if he could. *Gangsir kuwi ko-enggo apa ta?–Ja dipangan *.* What do you do with ground-crickets?–You eat them, of course! *Kesel *.* I'm so *tired! Aḍuh, ḍèwèké rak keplinḍes *.* Oh heavens, she was hit by a car! ***-*** contrary to appearances. **-* ḍèké sugih.* He may not look it, but he's rich. **ngona-*** (**ngétan-ngèten** *kr*) to do all kinds of things. *sanadjana ngona-** no matter what you do... **ϕ/di*kaké** to do that to; to treat in that way. *Jèn kowé dingonokaké apa gelem?* How'd you like it if smn did that to you?
ngono(h) *var of* RONO
ngoprès *rg* to chatter, talk about trivia
ngorèk 1 to croak. *swarané koḍok ** the croaking of the frogs. 2 *form of* KORÈK
ngorok 1 to snore. 2 *cr* to (go to) sleep
ngot ***-*an** recurrent; to recur periodically. *See also* ANGOT
ngoten in that way (*md for* NGATEN)
ngotès *rg* to speak

ngowèh to slobber, drool
ngowok [of eyes] deep-set
ngr- *see also under* R-, KR- (*Introduction, 3.1.5.4*)
ngrambjang to wander restlessly. *Njawané * nang endi²*. The soul [of the dead man] is restless. *Pikirané * nang ndi²*. He's daydreaming.
ngre- *see also under* NGER- (*Introduction, 2.9.6*) *or under replaced-consonant plus* ER (*Introduction, 3.1.5.4*)
ngrebda to grow, make headway. *Agama Hinḍu karo agama Buḍa kuwi bisa * bebarengan ing tanah Djawa.* Hinduism and Buddhism flourished side by side in Java.
ngreda *var of* NGREBDA
ngregantjang tall and dashing
ngregujung *var of* NGREMBAKA
ngrem ***-*an** used for breeding. *Pitik iki kanggo *-*an.* This chicken is a brood hen. **nge/di*aké** to have [eggs] hatched. *Enḍogé sepuluh dingremaké kabèh.* He's having the hen hatch out all ten eggs. **nge/di*i** to sit on [eggs]. *Enḍogé di*i babon.* The hen is hatching the eggs. **babon *** a brood hen. *See also* ANGREM
ngrembâkâ to flourish, grow luxuriantly
ngrembujung thick, dense, luxuriant. *Gegoḍongan katon *.* The foliage is dense. *Tresnaku *.* I love her with all my heart.
ngrenggéto heavy, bulky, unwieldy
ngrenggoto *var of* NGRENGGÉTO
ngrèngkèl argumentative
ngrenṭil to isolate oneself. *Ḍèké mau bareng sagrombolan nanging suwé² bandjur * ḍéwé.* He was with the group but after a while he went off by himself.
ngrerangin *ltry* smooth, gracious, at a leisurely pace
ngretjèh to rain steadily
ngrika (over) there (*kr for* KANA)
ngriki here (*kr for* KÉNÉ)
ngriku there (*kr for* KONO)
ngritjih to rain continuously
ngrobjok 1 to cluster around sth, mob smn. 2 *form of* KROBJOK
ngromèd to rant, rave, speak deliriously
ngromèh *var of* NGROMÈD
ngruwil 1 stingy, close-fisted. 2 *form of* KRUWIL
ngu- *var of* NG-, NGA-, NGE- *before* W: *Introduction, 3.1.5.4*)
ngugung to spoil/overindulge smn
nguk 1 (it is) preferable. ** mati tinimbang didjadjah wong mantja.* Better die than live under foreign subjugation. 2 *rpr* a kiss (in the Javanese style). *Ngerti² mak * Siti diambung embahné.* Siti's grandfather suddenly kissed her. ***-*an** 1 to kiss each other. 2 to keep looking out through a door *or* window. **nge/di*** to kiss smn. *See also* ANGUK
ngukak *var of* NGUNGKAK
ngukud intensely cold, bone-chilling
ngukung *var of* ṄG-KUKUK
ngulandârâ to wander, roam
ngumbârâ to drift around, wander
ngumbreng 1 to make a buzzing *or* humming sound. 2 to flock to. *Wong² * ing ngarep penḍapa.* People crowded around the front of the veranda.
ngumplèh *var of* NGOMPLÈH
ngung (*or* *-*) *rpr* the whine of an engine
ngungkak to disregard. ** krama* to forget one's manners
ngungklu:k preoccupied
ngungkruk to bend, bow; to sit with downcast eyes
ngungrum to court [a girl]. **pa*** seductive utterances
ngungun (*ng kr? ki for* GUMUN?) to wonder; surprised, perplexed. *Aku * banget krungu tembungé.* I was amazed at what he said. *Aku * botjah iki kok glibedan waé.* I wonder why he keeps moving around. **pa*** astonishment, wonderment. *Pa*é ora entèk², ndelok kaéndahan kang ngédab-édabi mau.* He was stunned to see such beauty.
ngunjlug to walk on steadily without looking around
ngunjug *var of* NGUNJLUG
nguntjel *rg* obstinate, contrary
nguntjis thin and wan-looking
nguntug to walk hurriedly with bowed head. *bali ** to hurry home intently
ngunul at a fast pace
ngupret [of clothing] tight, binding
ngur *inf var of* ANGUR
ngurag [*of animals*] very old. *mati ** to die of old age
nguris thin and pale-looking
ngutjir to escape from a humiliating situation. *Sardja kewelèh olèhé goroh bandjur lunga *.* Sardja, caught in his lie, left in mortification.
ngutju 1 to walk fast and steadily and intently. 2 to go berserk
nguṭuh shameless, brazen. *Wong wis ditulak kok meksa *.* He was turned down, but he

just laughed it off. *Wong olèhé *, utang ora njaur.* He has his nerve, not paying up what he owes.

ngu(w)- *see also under* NGU-, NGW-, *or under replaced-consonant plus* U, W (*Introduction, 2.9.7, 3.1.5.4*)

ngw- *old var of* M- *as nasal-prefixed form of* W*-initial root* (*e.g. ng·wènèh·i for m̈·wènèh·i*). *See also under* NGU(W)- *or under replaced-consonant plus* U(W) (*Introduction, 3.1.5.4*)

ngwang *oj* I, me; my (*shf of* INGWANG)

ni *female title of respect corresponding to the male title* KI. *See also* NJAI

-ni *suffix post-vowel form of* -I

niâjâ **di*** to be treated cruelly (*var of* DI·ANI(NG)AJA)

nihan *oj* like that; as aforesaid

nijâgâ musicians of a gamelan ensemble. **pa*n** place where the musicians are arrayed

nija(j)i *var of* NJAI

nijâkâ *var of* NAJAKA

nijat 1 intention. *Aku * arep weruh.* I'm determined to find out. **é arep marèni olèhé ḍemen ngabotohan.* He means to cure himself of his addiction to gambling. 2 expression of one's purpose in saying an Islamic prayer before actually uttering the prayer. **ka*an** plan, intention. **ϕ/di*i** to determine, make up one's mind

nik **nak-*** to devote one's attention to sth. *Adja diganggu jèn lagi enak-enik ngono.* Don't bother him while he's trying to figure it out. *kakéjan nak-** overmeticulous. **nge/di*-*** *or* **nge/di·nak-*** to do/treat meticulously. *Djam anjar mau tansah dinak-*.* He's very careful of his new watch. *Sawisé di*-*, pipa mau nuli digosok.* He made the pipe with painstaking care and then polished it.

nika that (thing, place, time) (*md for* KUWI, KAÉ)

nikah *var of* NINGKAH

nikanang *var of* NIKANG

nikang *honorific title.* ** djabang baji* the honorable infant

nikel 1 (*prn with* I *as in* BIT) nickel (metal alloy). 2 *form of* TIKEL

nikèn *respectful title used before women's names*

niki this (thing, place, time) (*md for* IKI)

nikmat comfortable; pleasurable. ** olèhé turu.* He was sleeping peacefully. *sesuguhan sing *-** delicious refreshments. *Aku krasa kurang *.* I felt uncomfortable.

nikotin nicotine

niku that (thing, time, place) (*md for* KUWI)

nil *rpr* a light accidental touch. *Irungé didumuk mak *.* His hand brushed against her nose. ***-*an** restless, fidgety. **sa*** a mere touch, a tiny amount

nila 1 leaves of the indigo tree (*tom*); indigo dye made from these leaves. 2 sapphire. *** werdi** highest-quality indigo

nimas *respectful title applied to socially high ladies, usu. by their husbands.* *** aju** *respectful title applied to ladies of high standing*

ninèk *inf var of* NINI

ning[a] 1 but (*inf var of* NANGING). 2 *rg* in, at, on, to. 3 bright, clear (*shf of* BENING). 4 yellow, fair (*shf of* KUNING). 5 *rpr* the beat of a gamelan *gong*. **nang-*** to keep saying 'but.' *Kowé ki kok pidjer nang-* waé.* You're always making objections! ***-*en** 1 bright, clear. 2 [of liquid] thin, runny

-ning[b] *suffix post-vowel form of* -ING

ningan *inf var of* NANGING

ningkah formal marriage ceremony. *dina ** wedding day. ***an** marriage ceremony. **ϕ/di*** to perform the marriage ceremony. *Apa wis di*?* Have they been married yet?

ningrat an aristocrat. *para ** the bluebloods

ningsun *post-vowel form of* INGSUN

nini 1 grandmother. 2 *affectionate term for addressing girls.* ***-*** [of women] very old; a very old woman. *** among** godmother; female good spirit that protects human beings. *** blorong** mermaid. *** ṭowok** *or* *** ṭowong** a female figure made of a coconut shell, into which a female spirit is said to enter (children's game). *See also* KAKI[a]

ninis to be put out in the fresh air. **pa*an** a place in the house or yard where one can relax and get some fresh air

ninṭing [of clothing] too tight

nipah swamp palm tree

nipas *see* ADUS, GETIH

nipis *see* DJERUK

-nipun *suffix post-vowel form of* -IPUN

nir 1 kidney. *lara ** (to have) kidney disease. *lara * stin* (to have) kidney stones. 2 *oj* lost, gone. 3 *oj* lacking, without. **nar-*** *or* ***-*an** apprehensive, on edge. *See also* NAR

-nira *suffix post-vowel var of* -IRA[b]

nirdâjâ *oj* powerless, lacking strength

-niréka, -nirèki, -nirèku *suffix post-vowel form of* -IRÉKA *etc.*

nirmâlâ *oj* pure, sacred, flawless
nirwânâ nirvana: the freeing of the spirit with the death of the body
nirwikârâ *oj* brave, stalwart
nisab the portion of one's earnings that is to be donated to charity, in accordance with Islamic principles
niskârâ **sa*** all, everyone, everything
nisṭa low, contemptible, shameful. **ka*n** shame, disrepute. *** dama** *sms* *
nisṭip *ltry var of* NISṬA
nitik 1 a certain batik design. 2 *form of* TITIK
nityâ(sâ) countenance
nj- *var of* NG- *prefix* (*see Introduction, 3.1.5.4*). *See also under* ENJ- (*Introduction, 2.9.5*)
nj. *see* NJONJAH
nja 1 (**mânggâ** *or* **suwawi** *kr*) here! take it! * *iki.* Here you are! Here it is! 2 *oj suffix* his, her, their; the (= *modern* -É[c]). **nge/di*ni** to hand over. *** ḍaḍa·ku, endi rai·mu?** *wj* Come on (out) and fight!
nja- *see also under* NJE- (*Introduction, 2.9.2*) *or under replaced-consonant plus* E (*Introduction, 3.1.5.4*)
njablik [of lips, mouth] small, dainty
njaḍam [of mangoes, guavas] just about ripened
njagir *var of* NGAGIR
njah *inf var of* NJONJAH. *See also* DAT
njai *female title corresponding to* KJAI, *applied to the wife of a man given this title; also, a general esteem-showing title.* *** geḍé** *female title corresponding to* KJAI GEḌÉ. ***ku** my wife (*joking usage*)
njak ***-*an** thoughtless, inconsiderate, lacking manners
njal ***-*an** to fidget, move about restlessly, lack repose
njal- *see also under* NJL- (*Introduction, 2.9.3*) *or under replaced-consonant plus* L (*Introduction, 3.1.5.4*)
njâlâwadi *ng,* **njâlâwados** *kr* mysterious; arousing suspicion. *apa² sing* * suspicious circumstances. *prijaji kang* * a mysterious gentleman
njâlâwados *kr for* NJALAWADI
njam ***an** pleasant; enjoyable. ***-*en** to keep savoring sth. **-*en leginé djuruh.* I can still taste the sweetness of the syrup.
njamat golden tassel on a certain fez (*kuluk*) worn by aristocrats for festive occasions
njambik *rg var of* MENJAWAK
njambut *** gawé** *ng,* *** damel** *kr,* **ng·asta** *ki* to work, do a job. *Sing *-gawé dikon mulih.* The workers were sent home. *Olèhmu * gawé saiki ana ngendi?* Where are you working now? *** karja** to work, engage in labor
njamir **njomar-*** to sneer, curl the lip
njamleng very enjoyable (*esp.* of food)
njamping batik wraparound (*ki for* BEBED, DJARIK, TAPIH). ***an** to put on *or* wear the above
njamplung 1 a lump of ripe fruit, *e.g.* jackfruit, together with the pit. 2 a certain plant from whose seeds oil is extracted
njamut ***-*** far off. *Montor maburé kétok *-*.* The plane is way way off. *Isih *-* nggonku rampung.* I'm still a long way from finishing.
njânâ *ora* **ke*(-*)** unexpected. *Ora ke* jèn Slamet arep teka.* I had no idea Slamet was coming. **ϕ/di*(-*)** to expect. *Tak * mengko soré udan.* I think it's going to rain this afternoon. *ora * ora ngrempelu* entirely unexpected. *Aku ora * jèn wong kuwi gawéné ngapusi.* I never would have thought he'd cheat people. *Tekané Slamet ora tak *-*.* I had had no idea that Slamet would come. **pa*** what smn expects *or* anticipates. *Pa*né klèru.* His expectations of what would happen were way off. *Kok kowé ngerti duwé pa* jèn ḍèké sing njolong djamku?* How could you have known that he was going to steal my watch?
njang[a] *ng,* **awis** *kr* ***-*an** to haggle with each other (over). **-*an karo tukang bétjak* to talk terms with a pedicab driver. *Jèn tabah *-*an, ija ora bisa diapusi bakul.* If you bargain boldly, you won't get cheated. **nge/di*** to bargain, haggle. **nge/di*i** to make a bid to [a seller]. *Ḍèké dienjangi setali baé ora éntuk.* He offered her a quarter for it and she turned it down. *See also* ANJANG[a]
njang[b] *ng,* **ḍateng** *kr* (to go) to (*shf of* MENJANG). *Jèn kowé arep * Jogja, ja *a.* If you want to go to Jogja, go ahead! **di*i** to be visited. *mBok di*i seḍéla.* Please go see him for a while. *Omahé di*i tjah tjilik².* Little children came to his house. *Pijambakipun dipun ḍatengi pulisi.* The police paid him a visit. *See also* NJUNG-NJANG
njangklek̄ close by. *Omahé A * saka omahé B.* A's house is just a stone's throw from B's.
njangkleng (a) very long (time)
njangkrang *var of* NJANGKRENG
njangkreng sitting perched in a high place

njanji ***an** a modern-style song. **me*** to sing (modern style). **ϕ/di*kaké** to sing a song for/to smn. **pa*** singer

njanṭeg (*or* ***-***) close by, very near. *Jèn omong ora susah *-*, aku wis krungu.* Don't come so close, I can hear you from here.

njantug within reach. *Ḍèké tak kon ndjupuk koran nang lemari kuwi, ora *.* I asked him to get the newspaper on top of the cupboard but he couldn't reach it.

njantun finger's breadth (*sbst? kr for* NJARI)

njanuk ***-*** to grope, feel around

njaprang [of moustaches] extending out to the sides

njar- *see also under* NJR- (*Introduction, 2.9.3*) *or under replaced-consonant plus* R (*Introduction, 3.1.5.4*)

njari *ng,* **njantun** *sbst? kr* a finger's breadth (as a unit of measurement: *ca.* 1 centimeter)

njarong *intsfr* clear. *bening ** crystal clear [of water]

njaros *rg kr for* NJARI

njas *rpr* a reflex after touching sth hot

njat *rpr* standing up. *ngadeg ** to stand up suddenly. ***-*an** always on the go. **me*** to stand up from a sitting position. *Ḍèké me* mlaju metu.* He got up and ran out.

njâtâ 1 true. ** tenan lo.* It's true! 2 (*or* ***né**) actually, in fact. **ka*n** reality. *Delengen ka*n, adja seneng urip ing pangimpèn.* See things the way they are; don't live in a dream world. **ϕ/di*kaké** to confirm. *Djaréné ana montor tabrakan, mulané aku njatakaké.* I heard there was a car accident and I went to see if it was true. **ϕ/di*ni** to be *or* become a reality to/for. *Durung dinjatani kok wis sambat.* You haven't even had it happen to you yet, but you're already complaining! **pra*** *ltry* it is true; in fact. *Sang Ardjuna pra* linangkung.* Ardjuna was indeed excellent. **sa*(né) (sa·èstu** *or* **[sa]èstu·nipun** *kr*) in fact; as a matter of fact. *Wis ngerti jèn mentas diimpi, merga sa*né ora ana médja.* He knew he had dreamed it, for there wasn't really a table there.

njaṭis prominent, protruding [*esp.* of chin, jaw]

njaṭus 1 to sit doing nothing, not join in the activity. 2 *var of* NJAṬIS

njâwâ soul, spirit, life; (*fig*) *term of endearment for addressing one's beloved. Ḍèwèké mati, *né ilang.* He died and the soul departed. **né ulet banget.* He's hard to kill.

nje- *see also under* NJA- (*Introduction, 2.9.2*) *or under replaced-consonant plus* A (*Introduction, 3.1.5.4*)

njebablang *var of* N·DJEPAPLANG

njeḍil **ora *** inconsequential, trifling

njeḍis *var of* NJEḌIL

njeḍit *see* BOKONG

njegadul gloomy; grim-faced

njegélé *var of* NJEGIL

njegil off by oneself, apart from others

njeglik *var of* NJEGIL

njèk *rpr* the feel of stepping into sth soft and mushy. **nge/di*(-*)** to squash sth; *fig* to humiliate *or* offend smn

njek̄ ***-*** *rpr* a hushed sound *or* feel, such as when touching sth softly *or* walking softly on wet ground. ***-*an** filled, crowded (*rg var of* SEG·²AN)

njekenek̄ disgusting-looking, nauseating

njekenṭang spreading out broadly

njekenṭik curled slightly at the tip

njekenṭing curved at the end

njekenṭit *var of* NJEKENṬIK

njekenṭung rolled up at the end

njekeṭut to fold up, crease. *Alisé *.* His eyebrows were drawn together in a frown. *Dondomané *.* The sewing is folded.

njekiṭat 1 tapering to a point at the tip. 2 [of dress, grooming] neat, meticulous

njekuṭis *var of* NJLEKUṬIS

njekuṭu to make a fist with the thumb between the index and middle fingers

njel ***-*an** close together, crowding each other

njel- *see also under* NJL- (*Introduction, 2.9.3*) *or under replaced-consonant plus* L (*Introduction, 3.1.5.4*)

njemek̄, njemèk, njèmèk (*or* ***-***) neither too moist nor too dry. *Bakminé *.* The noodles are just right.

njememet (*or* ***an**) to chase after girls

njemèmrèng threadbare

njemlèk muddy, dirty, and moist

njemomong *var of* NJREMOMONG

njemplek̄ *var of* NJEMPLUK

njempli chubby, rounded, cute-looking

njemplu(k) chubby, plump

njemuk [of breasts] small and soft

njendit *intsfr* fat. *lemu ** obese

njeng, njèng (*or* **njang-***) *rpr* an effortless lifting motion. *See also* ḌAT

njengèl conspicuous, eye-catching

njengèngès to laugh without mirth; to jeer, smirk

njenggrak sharply scented; acrid

njengik noticeable, conspicuous

njengingis *var of* NJENGÈNGÈS

njengkanuk close by, right under one's nose

njengkirig [of hair, fur, feathers] standing on end

njengklé conspicuous

njengklik precariously balanced on a high place *or* near an edge

njengkluk to sit working at sth. *Wiwit ésuk * ndondomi klambi.* She's been sitting there sewing all day.

njengkorog *var of* NJENGKIRIG

njengkrèk rising steeply. *Dalané *.* The road is steep. *Rega bahan^2 *.* The price of (dress) goods is skyrocketing.

njengkruk engrossed, bent in concentration. *Olèhé matja *.* He's absorbed in his reading.

njengkuret to change position. *Alisé * munggah.* His eyebrows shot up.

njengkuruk downcast, listless

njengkuwek̄ *var of* NJENGKUWER

njengkuwer curved *or* bent into a hook shape

njengkuwik to form a hole; having a hole in it

njenj- *see also under* NJ- (*Introduction, 3.1.3*) *or under consonant that has been reduplicated then replaced* (*Introduction, 3.1.3, 3.1.5.4*)

njenjeb *var of* NJENJET

njènjèh (*or* ***en** *or* **me***) to fester

njenjet *intsfr* quiet. *ḍeḍep ** or *sepi ** very quiet/lonely. ** ing bengi* the dead of night

njenṭang long and protruding. *Untuné *.* He has buck teeth.

njenṭek̄ a squirrel-like animal

njenṭèng loud, shrill

njenṭèt *-* to yell, shout

njentil to shoot a small missile by holding it between thumb and forefinger and snapping it forward

njenṭil small and round

njep **nge/di*-*** to cool sth with water. *See also* ANJEP

njepaplang extending sideways. *Ana kaju * ing tengah dalan.* There was a log across the road.

njepèpèh *var of* NJERPÈPÈH

njepèpèr turned, bent. *Sikilé * metu kaja ménṭok mlaku.* His feet toe out like a duck walking.

njèprès [of moustaches] long and limp

njeprok broad, spreading

njer- *see also under* NJR- (*Introduction, 2.9.3*) *or under replaced-consonant plus* R (*Introduction, 3.1.5.4*)

njerngongos long and protruding. *Untuné *.* He has buck teeth.

njerpèpèh 1 [of feet] spread wide apart. 2 sitting composed and polite

njerwètèh peculiar, eccentric

njes *rpr* a chilly feeling. *Mak * krasa aḍem.* He suddenly felt cold. **nje*** 1 chilly. 2 *intsfr* quiet, lonely. *sepi nje** very quiet, utterly deserted. *See also* ANJES, TJES

njèt *rpr* squeezing, crushing. *dipidak ** to get crushed underfoot. **nge/di*(-*)** to mash, squash. *Kenṭangé di-enjèt^2.* She mashed the potatoes.

njet *rpr* pressing, squeezing. **nge/di*(-*)** to press, squeeze

njeṭaṭem to remain silent, say nothing

njeṭuṭuk 1 inept, lacking deftness *or* dexterity. 2 trembling with cold. 3 *var of* NJEṬUṬUR

njeṭuṭu:r sitting around doing nothing

nji *var of* NI (*title*)

njiḍam to long for certain foods during pregnancy. **ϕ/di*aké** to long for [a food]

njiglig perched in a high place. *Omahé * ngarepaké sawah.* The house is 'way up high with a rice paddy in front of it.

njihi to love (*ltry var of* NGE·SIH)

njik **sa*** a moment. **sa*an** for a moment

njing *var of* NJENG

njinjih *var of* NJÈNJÈH

njinjir soft; *slang* easy, a cinch

njir 1 *rpr* a pang of uneasiness. *Bareng weruh ing djaba peteng, mak * atiné sumelang.* When she saw it was dark outside, she became apprehensive. 2 *inf var of* ANJIR

njiru piece of coconut shell placed at the bottom of a rice-steaming cone (*kukus·an*) for the rice to rest on while it steams

njiṭes to kill an insect by pressing it between the fingers. ** tuma* to kill a louse

njlekenṭang to protrude way out

njlekenṭik curled, turned. *Aṭi^2 *.* The hair at her temples curled.

njlekop *cr* to speak, say

njlekuṭis having a listless apathetic air

njlenèh peculiar, out of the ordinary. *lelakuan sing ** eccentric behavior. *Omongané * ora teges.* What he says is strange and meaningless.

njlenjer *var of* NLENJER

njles *rpr* a chilly feeling (*var of* NJES)

njlingkring slim; long and thin
njlingup narrow, cramped
njluring [of face] thin, pinched-looking
njluwerakė to distort *or* put a false construction on sth. *Nèk guneman tansah menang merga pinter * tetembungan.* He always comes out on top in a conversation because he knows how to twist words.
njo 1 large teapot. 2 *shf of* SINJO
njoh here! take it! (*var of* NJA). **nge/di*i** to give, hand over
njok *rpr* the sound of sth plopping into mud. ***-*** 1 crowded, full to overflowing. 2 *Jogja slang* sometimes, off and on
njong *rg* I, me; my
njonglong to encroach [on]; to trespass. *Witė pelem * nang kebonku.* His mango tree overhangs my garden.
njonjah 1 married woman. **é wis tindak.* The lady of the house is out. 2 Caucasian woman, *esp.* Dutch. ** Amérika* an American lady. 3 (*abbr*: **nj.**) Mrs.
njonjok **ke*** to get burned or pricked by coming into contact with a hot or sharp object; *fig* to get humiliated. *Klambi nylon ke* geni mak djus ngono waé.* A nylon shirt burns like *that!* if flame touches it. *Wanitané rumangsa ke*.* The ladies felt slighted. **ϕ/di*** to touch with sth hot *or* sharp; to humiliate. *Aku njonjok Ali nganggo rokok.* I touched Ali with a burning cigarette. **ϕ/di*aké** to hurt by holding a hot *or* sharp object to. *Tegesané di*aké tangané.* They pressed the burning cigarette against his hand.
njopros [of moustaches] long and unkempt
njos *rpr* sizzling. **nge/di*** to touch sth with a hot iron; to brand. *See also* TJOS
njre- *see also under* NJER- (*Introduction, 2.9.6*) *or under replaced-consonant plus* ER (*Introduction, 3.1.5.4*)
njremomong to glow, burn red
njremumuh swollen and infected
njrepèpèh to plead, beg
njrungus [of face] thin, narrow
nju:k *rpr* a quick touch *or* connection. *Médjané didumuk mak *.* His hand grazed the table. *Lagi waé A mak * teka ngomah, wis disusul utusané B.* A had hardly reached home when he got a call from B. **njak-*** crude, boorish. **sa*an** a short distance. *Mung kari sak *an.* There's only a little way left to go. *See also* MANJUK
njumlik *var of* NJUMPLIK
njumplik small and dainty
njung-njang defiant, reckless
njunjah **njanjah-*** to speak crudely/boorishly. *See also* TJUTJAH
njunjuk *var of* NJONJOK
njunjur 1 soft and mushy, *esp.* from overcooking. 2 *slang* very easy, a cinch
njus *rpr* a lunge with a sharp *or* hot object
nju:t *rpr* a quick whisk. *Ḍèwèké njekeli ḍompètku mak * ilang.* He snatched my wallet. **njat-*** 1 fickle; vacillating. *Duwé kekarepan kok njat-*.* He keeps changing his mind about what he wants. 2 *rpr* repeated sucking motions. **ke*** to get carried away (*lit, fig*). **nge/di*** 1 to snatch. 2 to suck
nju(w)-, njw- *see under replaced-consonant plus* U(W), W (*Introduction, 2.9.7, 3.1.5.4*)
nlângsâ heartbroken, crushed with grief *or* hardship. *Bijèn *, saiki mulja.* Life used to be hard for him; now he's prosperous. *Atiné * déné mlarat disirik ing lijan.* It caused her anguish to be poor and scorned by others. **pa*n** feelings of grief *or* heartache
nlanjak (*or* ***-***) to transgress the rules of proper behavior with officious or presumptuous actions
nlatjap ill-mannered, boorish
nlendjer to stand solitary. *Ing tengah² sawah ana wit wringin *.* There's a lone banyan tree in the very middle of the paddy.
nlenjer to proceed stealthily
nlimpang *var of* Ñ·SIMPANG
nn. *see* NONAH
no *inf var of* KONO
no. *see* NOMER
nok 1 *adr* young girl (*shf of* ḌÉNOK). 2 in, at, on (*inf var of* ANA ING)
nol zero (*var of* NUL)
nom *ng*, **nèm** *kr* 1 (**timur** *ki*) young. *geḍé tjilik, enom tuwa* large and small, young and old. 2 immature. *Pelem iki isih enom².* These mangoes aren't ready to eat yet. 3 light [of colors]. *biru ** light blue. ***-*an** young person. *para *-*an* the young. **ka*an** 1 youth. 2 young people. 3 the territory under the authority of the crown prince (as contrasted with the king's territory: *see also* KA·SEPUH·AN). **ke*en** excessively young. *See also* ANOM, KUMENOM, NONOM
nomer (*abbr*: **no.**) number in a series. *sing * sidji* the first one. *Bab * Sanga* Chapter Nine. **ϕ/di*i** to assign a number to. *Di*i dji, ro, lu.* They were numbered 1, 2, 3.

nomor *var of* NOMER
nonah (*abbr*: **nn.**) an unmarried girl; Miss
nong 1 in, at, on (*inf var of* ANA ING). 2 *rpr* a gamelan *gong* note
nongkrong to squat, *esp.* while eating in a snack shop; to go to a snack shop. *Adja sok * nèng warung kaé lho.* Don't ever eat anything at that snack shop over there. *Kolonialis British * ing wilajah mau.* British colonists were occupying the area.
nongong to gape in astonishment
noni 1 Caucasian girl. 2 Miss
noni:k *var of* NONI
nonok vagina
nonol a certain caterpillar that feeds on coffee beans
nonom *ng,* **nènèm** *kr* ***an** young person. **an loro* young couple. *sawidjining *an bagus* a handsome young man. *See also* NOM
nonong bulging, protruding
nonṭong to remain silent, not speak
noot *var sp of* NOT
Nop. *see* NOPÈMBER
nopal substance used as a coloring agent
Nopèmber (*abbr*: **Nop.**) November
normā standard, norm
norong to stare with gleaming eyes
nor-râgâ *shf of* ANOR·RAGA
not 1 musical note; note of the scale. 2 note, memorandum; notebook. *blok ** notebook
notā *var of* NOT
notaris notary public
notes notebook
notisi notes, jottings
notjog·(-aké, -i) *var of* ÑJ·TJOTJOG·(-AKÉ, -I)
notulen 1 shorthand notes. 2 minutes of proceedings
nrâkâ *ltry var of* NERAKA
nranjam ill-mannered, unrefined
nrantang threadbare
nratjak similar *or* identical in size, quality, *etc.*
nrawang 1 *intsfr* clear, bright. *paḍang ** very bright. 2 filmy, transparent. **pa*an** that which is beyond the realm of the clearly visible. *ngèlmu pa*an* esoteric lore
nre- *see also under* NER- (*Introduction, 2.9.6*) *or under replaced-consonant plus* ER (*Introduction, 3.1.5.4*)
nrèṭèl [of speech] rapid and copious
nriṭil (coming) one after the other. *Keḍèpé *.* He blinks continuously. **ϕ*aké** to [do] continuously. **aké keḍep* to keep blinking
nrunjam *var of* NRANJAM
nt- *see also under* ENT-
-nta *post-vowel var of* -ANTA^{b}, -TA^{b}
nṭet **di*** *inf var of* DI·UNṬET
N.U. *see* NAHḌATUL ULAMA
nudjum the stars as agents of prophecy. *djuru ** astrologer, soothsayer. **pa*an** astrology
nudur obstacle, hindrance. *Aku ora bisa lunga merga ana *.* I couldn't leave–sth came up.
nugrâhâ (*or* **a***) blessing *or* boon in the form of happiness, safety, security. **ka*n** to receive blessings. *See also* PANGANUGRAHA
nuk *adr* bird! (*shf of* MANUK). ***-*an** to grope one's way. *See also* NUNUK
nuklir nuclear (power). *ilmu fisika ** nuclear physics
nuklun (to walk) with an air of dejection, with bowed head
nul 1 zero. *kelas ** kindergarten, preschool. 2 *rpr* a light touch. *Irungé didumuk mak *.* His finger brushed against her nose. **nge/di*-*** to form into round shapes. *nge*-* geṭuk* to heap mashed cassava into small mounds
nulja (*or* **a***) *ltry var of* Ñ·TULI
nun 1 I, me (*as a response when called*). *Botjah*[2]*, kowé tak undangi djenengmu, botjah wédok mangsulana Kula, jèn botjah lanang *.* Boys and girls, I'll call your names; girls answer *I* (*kula*) and boys say *I* (*nun*). 2 hello! anyone home? (*shf of* KULA NUWUN)
nung *rpr* the sound of a note played by a gamelan instrument
nungsung *** kabar** *or* *** warta** to ask for news
nuninggih *inf var of* NUWUN INGGIH: *see* INGGIH
nunuk **nunak-*** to grope one's way. *kaja wong pitjak nunak-** like a blind man feeling his way. *Olèhé ndjogèd durung bisa apal isih nunak-* nirokaké kantjané.* He couldn't remember the dance, so he did his best to do as they others were doing. *See also* NUK
nunut to occupy space in smn's vehicle (or other accommodation). *Aku mulih * montoré kantjaku.* I got a ride home with a friend of mine. *sing ndjaluk ** hitchhiker. ** turu* to sleep in smn else's bed. ***an** that which is accommodated. *Barang sing nang bagasi montor kuwi *anku.* The stuff (being carried) in the car trunk is mine. **ϕ/di*aké** to get space for smn. *Anaké*

di∗aké bibiné. She got her son a ride with his aunt. **ϕ/di∗i** to accompany smn, *esp.* as a passenger. *Aku di∗i Ali.* I gave Ali a ride.

nur beam, ray

nurâgâ *var of* ANOR·RAGA

nuri a parrot-like bird

nus squid, cuttlefish

nusa island (*oj*). ∗ *lan Bangsa* our [Indonesian] nation and people

nusantârâ 1 archipelago. 2 Indonesia. *masjarakat* ∗ Indonesian society, the Indonesian people. *martjapada* ∗ Indonesian soil

Nusatenggarā the Lesser Sunda Islands

nusja *var of* NUSA

nusjantârâ *var of* NUSANTARA

nuswa *var of* NUSA

nuswantârâ *var of* NUSANTARA

nut 1 (to act) in accordance with (*inf var of* MANUT). 2 *inf var of* NOT. **nat-∗** to follow; to obey habitually. **nge/di∗** to act according to, to follow. *Adjarané ora dienut manèh.* His teachings are no longer followed.

nu(w)- *see also under* NU- (*Introduction, 2.9.7*) *or under replaced-consonant plus* U-, W (*Introduction, 3.1.5.4*)

nuwâlâ *var of* NAWALA

nuwun *var form of* ŇJ·SUWUN *used in certain phrases, as follows.* (*Matur*) ∗. Thank you. *Kula* ∗ – Hello! (*phrase called at the door of smn's home, to announce his presence as a visitor*). ∗ *inggih* (*ka*) yes. ∗ (*sanèsé*) *mawon.* Sorry (*to a beggar, when refusing him*). ∗ *wijosipun.* I greet you (*formal opening phrase of a letter*). ∗ *pangèstunipun sedaja kalepatan kula, lair batin.* I ask your wholehearted forgiveness for all my faults. ∗ *sakersa.* Please excuse me [for leaving this social gathering]. **ne∗** (*psv*: **di-se·suwun**) to pray for *or* humbly request [sth]. **pa∗(an)** *or* **pi∗** 1 a humble request. 2 a prayer. *See also* SUWUN

nw- *see also under* NU(W)- (*Introduction, 2.9.7*) *or under replaced-consonant plus* U(W) (*Introduction, 3.1.5.4*)

O

o 1 *alphabetic letter.* 2 *excl making an utterance livelier. O ija.* Yes! *O wis ngerti aku.* I know that!

obah *ng,* **ébah** *kr* to move. *Wong mati ora* ∗. Dead people don't move. *∗ing prau muwuhi ngelu.* The motion of the boat made his headache worse. *kanggo* **∗-∗ djanggut** (to eat) any food available to assuage one's hunger. **m·obah-m·osik** 1 to move. 2 thought, inclination. **ng/di∗aké** to move sth

obar *rg var of* OBONG

obat 1 gunpowder. ∗ *mimis* bullet, ammunition. 2 chemicals; drugs. ∗ *turu* sleeping pill. ∗ **kramas** powdered shampoo. ∗ **kuwat** a tonic. ∗ **njamuk** mosquito repellent. ∗ **tjatjing** vermifuge

obèl **ng∗** to spin off-center, to wobble. **ng/di∗aké** to spin, set spinning

obèng cranking *or* winding tool, *e.g.* brace and bit, drill, screwdriver, engine crank. **ng/di∗** 1 to make batik for profit. 2 to wobble

obin 1 unit of land measurement: *ca.* 0.56 square rod = 14.19 square meters. 2 floor tile (*var of* DJUBIN). **ng∗** 1 to estimate the total yield of a paddy from the yield of one *obin.* 2 to measure [land] in *obin*'s

objag **ng/di∗-∗** to shake sth

objèk middleman in a sale. **∗an** 1 merchandise one sells as middleman. 2 supplemental earnings, *usu.* from moonlighting as a middleman. **ng∗** to earn extra money by acting as intermediary in selling. **ng/di∗aké** to sell [merchandise] as above. *ng∗aké mobil* to act as agent in selling a car

oblah **ng∗-∗** wide open; widely spaced

oblog *var of* UBLUG

obong *ng*, **besmi** *sbst? kr*, **besem** *rg? kr* *-* to burn rubbish; *fig* to rouse the rabble. *(-*)an 1 act of burning. 2 (having been) burned. **k*** on fire; to get burned; *fig* smouldering with resentment. *Omah k*!* House afire! *Kajuné k* dadi awu.* The wood burned to ashes. *Bareng krungu apa sing dikaṇḍakaké, atiné k*.* When she heard what he'd said, she was burned up. **k*an** 1 conflagration. 2 to catch fire, get burned. 3 to suffer loss through fire. **ng/di*** 1 to burn, set fire to. *ng* menjan* to burn incense. 2 to incite. *Adja ng*.* Don't make me mad! 3 to do away with. *ng* kolonialisme* to put an end to colonialism. **ng/di*aké** to ignite; to enflame. *ng*aké paprangan* to start a war. *ng*aké djiwa nasional* to fire up the national spirit. **ng/di*i** *pl* to burn, set fire to. *Akèh omah² di*i.* Many houses were put to the torch. **pa·ng*** act of burning. **pa·ng*an** incinerator. **kaju *** firewood

obor torch; *fig* enlightenment, guiding light; leader. *geni ** torchlight. *awèh ** to offer guidance. *geḍé *é* (*wj*) (a place where) justice reigns. *kepatèn ** to have lost the trail of sth one is tracking *or* investigating. **ng/di*(i)** 1 to illuminate, shed light on (*lit, fig*). *ng* dalan* to light the way. *ng*i pepeteng* to shed light in the darkness. *Pikir kaja di*i.* I've just had an idea! *Botjah² paḍa ng*i pelem tiba.* The children looked for fallen mangoes by torchlight. 2 *rg* to cook by boiling. *ng* téla* to boil cassavas. *See also* SAMBUNG

obral 1 (to hold) a sale. *Jèn lagi *, toko iki ngeṭoki rega².* When this store has a sale, they slash the prices. 2 copious. *Dina iki * bidji apik.* A lot of people got good marks today. ***-*an** act of selling at bargain prices *or* giving things out lavishly. *Menawa wis dadi ḍuwit, mbandjur kanggo *-*an.* When he has any cash, he spends it all. **ng/di*(-*)** 1 (*or* **ng/di*aké**) to put on sale. 2 to spend lavishly, give out copiously. *Ḍèké ng*-* permèn marang kantja²né.* He gave candy to all his friends.

obrok **ng*** *slang* to defecate in one's clothing

obrol ***an** 1 a chat, a conversation. 2 tall talk. **ng*** 1 to chat, have a talk. 2 to talk big; to exaggerate. **ng/di*-*** to pour out in large quantities. *Ḍuwit sepirang-pirang di*-* nggo main.* He gambles away his money like water. *Sapa sing ng*-* bantal?* Who scattered the pillow stuffing? **ng/di*aké** to talk about, tell about

oḍé *rg* **ng*** to take a job. **ng/di*kaké** to hire smn

oḍèg (*or* ***an**) unsteady, loose, wobbly. ***-*** *rpr* sth loose moving back and forth. *Keprungu swara *-* merga kebaratan.* We heard sth flapping in the wind.

oḍe klonjo eau de cologne

oḍèt **ng/di*-*** to disembowel

odjar *rg var of* UDJAR

odjat topic of conversation, *esp.* gossip. **k*** famous, widely known

odjogan itinerant peddler. **wong *** person who hires himself out as a porter

odjok **ng/di*-*i** *or* **ng/di·odjak-*i** to urge. *ng*-*i ses* to try to persuade smn to smoke

odod **m*** to emerge, rise. *Botjah saiki iki m*é kok rikat banget.* Children grow up so fast nowadays. *Sendjata m* saka tanganè kiwa.* The weapon magically emerged from his left hand. *Wit krambil mau ora bisa m*²* The coconut palm couldn't grow any higher than that. **ng/di*aké** to cause to emerge *or* rise. *Bareng sumbuné ḍi*aké, katon luwih paḍang.* When he raised the wick, it became brighter.

oḍo klonjo eau de cologne

oḍol 1 toothpaste (*originally a brand name*). 2 [of batik work] rough, crude. **m*-m*** [of stuffing, insides, *etc.*] to spill out. *Matjan disunḍang kebo nganti ususé m*².* The kerbau disemboweled the tiger. **ng/di*(-*)** 1 to remove the insides (of). *Sapa sing ng*-* bantal iki?* Who took all the stuffing out of this pillow? 2 to spend wastefully. 3 to shadow. *di* polisi* tailed by the police

odor **ng/di*** to push ahead of [others] without waiting one's turn

ogag loose in its socket. **ng/di*-*** to move sth back and forth to loosen it

ogah *rg var of* WEGAH

ogèg *var of* OGAG

ogèl ***-*** *or* **ogal-*** to keep moving back and forth. *Buntuté *-* terus.* It kept wagging its tail. **m*** to move back and forth. *m* ilat* to lick one's chops, expressing hunger. **ng/di*aké** to move sth back and forth. *See also* KOGÈL, KROGÈL

oglèng **m*-m*** to protrude. *Kerisé m*².* His kris stuck out. **ng/di*(-*aké)** to cause sth to protrude. **keṭèk *** monkey show

ogok **ng/di*(i)** *or* **ng/di*-*(i)** **1** to move sth back and forth in [an opening]. *ng*i pipa* to clean out a pipe by moving a stick around in it. *Slamet ng*-* lèng tikus nganggo wilah.* Slamet pushed a stick back and forth in the mouse hole. 2 to disturb, irritate

ogrèg **ng/di*-*** 1 to poke *or* prod (at). 2 to disturb, unsettle

ogrèh **ng/di*-*** *or* **ng/di·ograh-*** to disturb

ogrok *var of* OGOK

ojag to shake violently. *Lemah * saka dajané lindu.* The earth shook from the force of the quake. **ng/di*-*** to shake sth violently. *See also* AJIG

ojak ***-*an** 1 to engage in a chase (with one after the other). *Ana sak djaman pulisi lan maling *-*an.* The policeman chased the thief for an hour. 2 to chase each other around. **ng/di*(-*)** 1 to chase. *tikusé di* kutjing.* The cat chased the mouse. *ng* kalah* to try to regain one's losses. 2 to keep after smn, keep teasing *or* nagging. **ng* ñj·seneng·i** to try to seduce a woman. **ng*-* turus idjo** 1 to chase young girls *or* married women. 2 to make trouble for an innocent bystander

ojeg *var of* OREG

ojod root (of a plant; *gram* of a word); vine stem, stalk; *euph* snake. ***-*an** various kinds of roots. **ng*** to take root. **sa*** one growing period of a crop

ojog **ng/di*(-*)** to shake sth

ojok ***-*an** to chase after, hunt down. *Saiki para muḍa *-*an pegawéan.* Young people are going after jobs these days. **ng/di*(-*)** to cluster around sth

ojong ***-*** *or* **ojang-*** *or* (*rg*) **ajang-*** to move (change residence) frequently. **ng/di*-*** *or* **ng/di·ojang-*** to move [sth large and unwieldy] often

ojos **ng*** to go out in the rain unprotected

ojot **ng/di*(i)** 1 to smooth [a bamboo stalk] with a knife. 2 to cut [a bamboo stalk] into shorter lengths

okèh *inf var of* AKÈH

okèr **ng/di*(-*)** to scratch [sand, soil]

oknum person connected with a certain activity. ** partai X* an X party member. ** sing agawé rusuh* person who was mixed up in a disturbance. ** kang nedya gawé huru-hara* one bent of stirring up trouble

okol 1 physically sturdy, compactly built. 2 (*or* ***-*an**) to fight; to test each other's strength *or* endurance. **ng/di*i** to overpower [an opponent]

oksigèn oxygen

Okt. *see* OKTOBER

Oktober (*abbr*: **Okt.**) October

okulasi to graft [one plant onto another]

olah 1 (*or* ***-***) to do the cooking. 2 *var of* ULAH 1. ***-*an** things cooked; cuisine. **-*ané Jogja biasané legi.* Jogjanese cooking tends to be sweetish. **ng/di*** 1 to cook. *Sajurané di*.* She cooked the vegetables. 2 to till, cultivate. **ng/di*aké** to cook for smn. **pa·ng*(an)** 1 act *or* way of cooking. *Djantung geḍang peng*é prijé?* How do you prepare banana blossoms? 2 cultivation, tillage. *peng*an sawah teles* wet-rice cultivation

olan ***-*** 1 a variety of caterpillar. 2 (*or* **ng*-***) snake-like, *e.g.* a long graceful neck

olèḍ *var of* OLÈR

olèh *ng*, **angsal** *kr* 1 to get. *Aku ngunḍuh djambu * rong krandjang.* I picked two basketfuls of mangoes. ** panggonan* to get a seat. ** gandjaran* to get a reward. 2 to accept. *Aku tukuné rong sèn, * apa ora?* I'll give you two cents for it: it is a deal? 3 to marry, take in marriage. 4 to receive permission. *Filem² mantja ora * diputer.* Foreign films may not be shown. 5 to reach, attain. *Bareng wis * telung dina, kantjané bali.* Three days later his companion returned. *Sekésuk iki enggoné nulis lajang * papat.* He managed to write four letters this morning. 6 to connect, attach. *kawat dipasang * tjagak loro* a wire strung between two poles. 7 smn's act of [do]ing. *Wis tekan endi *mu matja?* How far have you read? *Weruh *é mangan anaké bungah banget.* It delighted her to see her child eat. **ku njambut-gawé tak sambi tembangan.* I sang as I worked. ***an** lucky in getting what one tries for. ***-*** gifts brought home with one. *Ḍèké ndjaluk *-* lajangan.* He asked her to bring him a kite. ***-*an** what one receives for one's efforts. **é njolong *-*an.* He got (stole) a lot of loot. **-*ané diedum.* They split the proceeds. **ng/di*aké** 1 to obtain for smn. 2 to get smn's hand in marriage. *Anaké wédok di*aké masku.* My brother married their daughter. 3 to attach, connect sth [to]. *Taliné didjiret di*aké wit pelem.* He tied the rope to a mango tree. **ng/di*-*aké** 1 to bring [gifts] to those back home. *Bonékahé di*-*aké anakku.* They brought the doll for our daughter. 2 to do one's best to get/obtain. **ng/di*-*i** to bring sth home as a gift. *Anakku dikon ng*-*i bonékah.* I asked him to bring our daughter a doll. **sa*(-*)é** whatever one can manage. *Jèn ora bisa rampung dina iki, ja sa*é waé.* If you can't finish today, just do as much as you can. *** angin** to get an opportunity. *** angin betjik** to get a lucky break. *** ati** to get preferential treatment. *** gawé** to succeed in an effort. *** kadang (ing) tingal** to marry for love. *See also* PIKOLÈH, SEKOLÈH

olèr **ng/di*aké** to extend sth. *Ilaté di*aké.* She stuck out her tongue.

olèt **ng*** to stretch (the arms, legs). **ng·olat-(ng)*** 1 to keep stretching. 2 flexible, elastic

oli(e) lubricating oil

olih *rg var of* OLÈH

oling *var of* ULING. **ng*-*** to writhe, move spasmodically

ollah *see* DAT

olok ***-*an** recriminations. **ng/di*-*** to keep bringing up the subject of smn's shortcomings. *Slamet di*-* merga ngompol.* She kept scolding Slamet for wetting.

olor 1 animal bone marrow. 2 small stream along the edge of a rice paddy. **ng*** to try to obtain favor through flattery. **ng/di*-*** to drag with the mouth *or* beak. **ng/di*(aké)** *var of* NG/DI-ULUR-(AKÉ)

om *var of* UM *in* UM-PIM-PAH, UM-PIM-SUT

omah *ng,* **grija** *kr* 1 **(dalem** *ki***)** house, home. *nèng ** at home. *mlebu ng** to go in the house. *sing duwé ** host, hostess. *balé ** front section of a house. 2 to live (in a house), make one's home (in). ** ḍéwé* to have a home of one's own. *Aku wis * nèng Djakarta rong tahun.* We've lived in Djakarta for two years now. ***an** *ng kr* 1 tame. 2 familiar to the household. *botjah wadon *an* the girl next door. ***-*** 1 **(ge·grija** *kr,* **de·dalem** *ki***)** to live in (a house), make one's home (in). 2 **(émah²** *kr,* **krâmâ** *ki***)** 1 to marry, set up housekeeping; to run one's home and household. *wong sing durung *-** an unmarried person. ***-*an** 1 tent; playhouse. 2 to play house. **ng/di*aké** *ng kr* to tame, domesticate. **ng/di*-*aké (ng/di-pun·émah²·aken** *kr,* **ng/di·krama·kaké** *ki***)** to marry off, hold a wedding for [one's child]. **ng/di*i** 1 to provide for [one's family]. 2 **(n/di·dalem·i** *ki***)** to provide with a house. *Pekarangan iki arep tak *i.* I want to build a house on this lot. 3 to live smw. *ng*i pondokan* to live in a lodging house. **sa*** the household. *wong sa** the whole family. **sa*-*** the entire household with its belongings. *Ana kang ilang sa*-*é.* Some families were completely wiped out. *** kampung** bamboo house with a saddle-shaped roof. *** kéjong** snail shell. *** lodji** large brick house (European style). *See also* POMAH, SOMAH

oman 1 *rg* rice stalk. 2 *var of* UMAN

ombak a wave. **ng*** to resemble *or* move like waves. *Rambuté ng*-banju.* She has wavy hair. *** banju** *see* TRIM

ombé *ng kr,* **undjuk** *ki* ***ǹ** 1 a drink. 2 used for drinking. *banju ombèn* drinking water. *gelas ombèn* a drinking glass. ***ǹ-*ǹ (undjuk²an** *ki***)** 1 a drink. *Ombèn²é tèh.* There was tea to drink. 2 a card game played with Occidental cards. *main ombèn²* to play this game. **ng/di*** to drink. *Pangan ng*ku ora kurang.* I had plenty to eat and drink. *Ng*a tamba.* Take your medicine! **ng/di*kaké** 1 to have smn drink. *Dikon ngombèkaké anaké.* He told her to have the child drink it. 2 (*or* **ng/di*ǹi**) to offer sth for drinking. *Tambané diombèkaké anaké.* She gave her child the medicine. *Dak ombèni wédang kopi.* I'll give him a drink of coffee. **pa·ng*ǹ** 1 **(undjuk[-undjuk]an** *ki***)** sth to drink. *Pangombèn lan panganè ora tau kurang.* There's always plenty to drink and eat. 2 **(pa·undjuk·an** *ki***)** drinking utensil

ombèr ample; broad. *Isih bisa olèh wektu kang *.* We have plenty of time. **ing pasrawungan* freedom of association. *Madjalah mau tebané *.* The magazine has a wide circulation. *Tanduran mau kudu dipersudi kang *.* This plant needs to be given plenty of room. **k*en** excessively spacious. *Kamar iki k*en jèn kanggo kantor.* This room is too big for an office. **ng/di*aké** to give sth more space. *Kamar ngarep di*aké.* They widened the front room. **ng/di*i** to allow leeway. *Di*i rong dina, mengko rak utangé dibajar.* Give him two more days, he'll pay the debt. **sa*-*é** as broad/free as possible. *Sing utang éntuk kalonggaran sa*-*é.* The debtor was given the most liberal terms.

ombjak trend, current. *njelarasaké marang *ing djaman* to adjust to modern trends. **ing kahanan* the force of circumstances. *manut *é wong akèh* to do as everyone else is doing

ombjok bunch, cluster. *kuntji sa** a bunch

of keys. *moté sa** a string of coral beads. ***(-*)an** in clusters/bunches. *Brambang di-edol *an.* Onions are sold by the bunch. **ng/di*i** to form sth into a bundle *or* cluster

ombjong ***-*** leaves used as decorations. **ng/di*i** to support [an endeavor *etc.*] by joining its proponents. **ng/di*-*i** to decorate sth with leaves

ombol ***-*an** grouped into clusters. **k*en** too closely grouped. *Olèhé nandur k*en.* He planted them too close together. **ng/di*** to plant sth in clusters/groups

ombrok *var of* UMBRUK

omèl **ng*** to grumble at, nag. **ng/di*aké** 1 to grumble about sth. 2 *cr* to talk about sth. **ng/di*i** to grouse at, complain to

omjang **ng*** 1 to talk deliriously, rant and rave. 2 *cr* to talk, speak. **ng/di*aké** to spread the word about sth; to babble about sth

omong to speak (**ngendika·n** *ki*). *nerusaké *é* to go on with what one was saying. *A sugih *.* A talks a lot. ***-*(an)** (**ngendika·n** *ki*) to converse. **ng/di*aké** to discuss. *ng*aké pasar malem* talking about the bazaar. *** ḍéwé** to talk out loud to oneself. *** kosong** to talk of inconsequential things. *** tjlemang-tjlemong** *or* *** tjeblang-tjeblung** to talk nonsense, talk through one's hat. *See also* ANDIKA

ompak *var of* UMPAK

ompol inadvertently discharged urine. *Iki *é sapa nang kasur?* Who wet this mattress? **k*an** to get urinated on. **ng*** to urinate in bed *or* in one's clothing. **ng/di*i** to urinate on sth

ompong *ng kr,* **daut** *ki* toothless; having missing teeth. *** géjong** toothless; very old

omprèng ***an** private car used for transporting passengers. **ng/di*** to transport passengers in a private car. **ng/di*aké** to use [a vehicle] for the above

omprong nest of containers for transporting food which is to be eaten elsewhere

onang **k*an** 1 to get caught doing sth. *Kantjil k*an mangan timuné Pak Tani.* Mouse-Deer got caught in the act of eating the farmer's cucumbers. 2 to get discovered. *Matiné k*an sawisé sawetara wektu.* His death came to light after some delay. *konḍang* **ka*-*** known everywhere. **ng/di*i** 1 to see *or* catch [smn] in the act. 2 to disclose. *Aku gela ng*i polahku.* I was ashamed to reveal what I had done. *See also* KONANG

onar trouble resulting from rumors *or* gossip. *gawé ** to cause trouble by talking about smn. **ng/di*aké** to embarrass *or* harm smn by spreading gossip

onḍan free, off duty for a short period. **ng/di*i** to let smn take a break

onḍé ***-*** a sesame-seed cake with a palm-sugar center

onḍerḍil mechanical part. ** pit* bicycle parts

ondjo superior to one's fellows. *kelas sing ** an outstanding class. *Adjiné ora dianggep *.* It's not valued too highly. *Ḍèké katon olèhé * ing désané.* She's the village belle. ***(n)-*nan** to compete in efforts to outshine each other. **ng/di*ni** 1 to raise the bid (when dickering with a seller). 2 to overshadow [others of the same group]

ondjot time extension. ***an** phase, time period. *mawa *an rong tahun* in two-year phases. **ng/di*aké** to extend the time of [a contract *etc.*]. **ng/di*(i)** to grant a time extension (to). **sa*an** 1 period of time. *wetara sa*an* after a while. 2 throughout a time period. *Sak *an luwih madju ketimbang sing uwis*[2]. There was more progress during that one phase than for the whole time previously.

ondjuk *var of* UNDJUK

onḍok **ng*-*** to have a lump in the throat. *Olèhé tjrita karo ng*-*.* He told the story in a broken voice.

onḍol sloppy, coarse, gross. **ng*** *cr* to chase girls. **ng/di*i** to examine [poultry] to determine whether it can reproduce

oneng *oj* (*or* ***-*an**) captivated, infatuated; pining away

ongak *rg var of* UNGAK

onggo **ng*-*** to weep long and bitterly

onggok 1 heart *or* pith of the sugar-palm tree. *paṭi ** flour/starch made from the above. 2 *var of* ONGGROK

onggrok **ng/di*-*aké** to leave sth unattended to. *Ḍèké ng*-*aké pegawéjané wis ana seminggu.* He's neglected his work for a week now.

onggrong ***an** to enjoy admiration, bask in the spotlight. **ng/di*** 1 to admire covetously. 2 to spoil *or* overindulge [a child]. 3 *rg* to allow space between things. *Krupuké di* supaja ora remuk.* Put the [potato] chips in loosely so they won't crumble.

ongkang ***-*** to sit with the feet dangling; *fig* to loaf, take it easy. *Gawéné mung *-*.* His job consists of sitting and ordering people around. **ng*** **1** *sms* *-*. **2** to occupy space. *omah sing * dalan* a house that sits right on the road. **3** disappointed, crushed

ongkèk *var of* ONGKRÈK

ongkèl *var of* UNGKIL

ongklang *rg var of* ONGKANG

ongkog *-* to teeter on all fours [of babies learning to crawl]. **m*** to feel pleased with oneself. **ng*** **1** *sms* *-*. **2** (*psv* **di***) to flatter smn

ongkos (*or* ***an**) cost, fee, expense(s). ** produksi* cost of production. **ng/di*i** to pay the expenses of. *Sing ng*i pemrintah kuwi wong sing mbajar padjeg.* The taxpayers finance the government.

ongkrag **ng/di*-*** to shake sth

ongkrèk object used as a lever. **ng/di*** to pry with a lever

ongkrong **ng/di*-*aké** to put sth up high. *Pariné di*-*aké ing nḍuwur pager témbok.* He put the rice plants on top of the brick wall.

ongod ***an** sharpening implement. **an potlod* pencil sharpener. **ng/di*-*** *or* **ng/di*i** to sharpen sth

ongol *-* a gelatine-like food eaten with shredded coconut

ongseb *rg var of* UNGSEB

ongsrong **ng*** labored [of breathing]. **ng/di*(aké)** to make [one's breathing] labored. *Ambegané di* karebèn katon kesel.* He forced himself to pant so as to appear exhausted.

oni *var of* UNI[a]

onja *ltry* blank. ** pikiré.* His mind is way off somewhere. *gerah ** senile. **ng/di*ni** to elude

onjog **anjag-*** to walk on and on without stopping. *See also* ANJAG

onjok **ng/di*-*aké** to high-pressure smn. *Aku tuku lenga wangi iki sebabé di*-*aké.* I bought this perfume just to get rid of the pest.

ons unit of weight: *ca.* 3⅓ oz. = *ca.* 0.1 kilogram

onta *var of* UNTA

ontal **k*** to get flung aside. *Sing nunggang pit nganti k* limang mèter.* The bicycle rider was thrown five meters. **ng/di*aké** to knock sth to one side

onté bunch, cluster. *Sajurané pira sa*?* How much for a bunch of the vegetables? ***-*an** bunched together. *Sing nunggang wis djedjel rijel *-*jan.* The passengers were jammed in.

ontèl blossom of the jackfruit tree

onṭèl (*or* *-*) **1** crank(shaft). **2** to crank [an old-style car, to start it]

onten to exist; there is/are (*md for* ANA[a])

ontjat to make one's escape. **k*an** **1** to avoid. *Aku k*an ujah sawetara dina.* I went without salt for several days. **2** to have sth get away from one. *Jèn k*an getih, ora bisa urip.* You can't live if you lose too much blood. **ng/di*i** to avoid, escape from. *ng*i bebaja* to avoid danger

ontjé *var of* RONTJÉ

ontjèk ***an** peeled, pared. *urang *an* shelled shrimp. **ng/di*(i)** **1** to peel, pare. **2** to reveal, disclose. *ng*i wadi* to give away a secret

ontjit **ng/di*-*** to chase

ontjlang *var of* UNTJLANG

ontjom a certain kind of fermented beans

ontjor oil-burning bamboo torch. ***-*an** to try to outshine *or* one-up each other. **ng/di*(aké)** to cause to flow. *Banjuné di*aké nang sawahku.* He ran water into my rice paddy. **ng/di*i** **1** to light up sth with a bamboo torch. **2** to inundate [soil]

ontog **m*** *or* **ng*(-*)** irritated, annoyed

ontong **1** the (single, red) blossom of a banana tree. **2** counting unit for corn. *djagung sa ** one ear of corn. **m*** [of banana trees] to blossom. **ng*** resembling a banana blossom

ontor *var of* ANTAR

ontran (*or* *-*) commotion; rebellion. ***-*** *tjilik-tjilikan* small-scale rioting

ontung *var of* UNTUNG

oom (*prn* **om**, *with* **o** *as in open syllables: Introduction, 2.2*) uncle (*term for addressing or referring to one's own uncle or an adult friend of the family*)

opah *ng*, **épah** *kr* (*or* ***an**) compensation for services. *padjeg *(an)* income tax. ***-*** money paid out for tips. **ng/di*aké** to have smn do sth for pay; to hire sth done. **ng/di*i** to pay smn for his services. *Arep di*i apa?* What will he be paid for doing it?

opak **ng*** to make a certain wafer-like snack food. *** angin** the above snack

opas worker, employee (*var of* UPAS)

opèl **ng/di*i** to remove the humps *or* jagged parts from sth and leave it smooth(er). *ng*i djagung* to pick the kernels off from an ear of corn. *Djènggèré di*i.* He smoothed the cock's comb by removing the jagged edge from it.

opèn 1 careful of one's [*or* smn's] belongings. 2 acquisitive. 3 meddlesome. ***an** characterized by one of the above traits. **k*** well cared for, carefully tended. **ng/di*i** 1 to take good care of. 2 to acquire *or* take possession of [things, habitually]. **pa·ng*** (good) care. *Kutjing kuwi gampang pang*é.* Cats are easy to take care of.

oper ***an** (act of) shifting, passing. **ané bal apik banget.* He passed the ball beautifully. **ng/di*(aké)** 1 to change the position of. *Persnèlengé di* loro.* He shifted into second gear. *Balé di*ké nang kantjané bandjur disekit mlebu gol.* He passed the [soccer] ball to his teammate, who kicked it in for a goal. 2 to take over (the operation *or* management of)

operasi operation, maneuver. ** politik* a political maneuver. ** militèr* a military operation. ** karja* a civil (civic) mission. **ng/di*(kaké)** to remove surgically. *Dokteré ng* usus buntutku.* The doctor took out my appendix. *ngoperasèkaké amandel* to remove tonsils

opjak (*or* ***-***) to demand loudly and persistently. **ng/di*-*** *or* **ng/di*i** to keep after, drive, nag. *Jèn durung di*-* durung gelem adus.* If I don't keep after him, he won't take a bath. *ng*[2] manuk sing mangan pari* to drive off birds that eat rice plants

opjok **ng/di*** to beat, whip [*e.g.* eggs, cream]. **ng/di*-*** to prepare for use by moistening. *Kusiré ng*-* suket.* The driver prepared grass to feed his horse. **ng/di*-*i** to apply moisture to. *Anaké panas, sirahé di*-*i banju.* Her child is feverish; she's putting moist cloths on his forehead.

oplèt antiquated car used as a city taxi with a given route

opor thick chicken *or* duck soup. **ng/di*** to make [ingredients] into this soup. *** ajam** the above with chicken. *** bèbèk** the above with duck. *** bèbèk mentas awak·é ḍèwèk** self-reliant

oprak **ng/di*-*** to drive out, scare off

oprèk *var of* OPRAK

oprok ***an** a disorderly heap. **ng*** 1 piled up. 2 exhausted. 3 to defecate in the wrong place, *e.g.* one's clothing

opsir military officer

orā *ng,* **(m)boten** *kr* 1 not (*in narrative predicates: cf.* DUDU). ** akèh* not many. ** ana sing njauri.* Nobody answered. ** bakal tak edol.* I won't sell it. *bédané wong sekolah karo ** the difference between those who go to school and those who don't. *Aku * kok, mbuh jèn Pardi.* I didn't (do it)–maybe Pardi did. 2 no (*as a reply, contradiction, etc.*). *Apa kowé mulih?–*.* Are you going home?–No. 3 ...or not? *Bener *?* Is it right (or not)? *Kowé nggawa ḍuwit *?* Did you bring any money? 4 ...but not. *Arep mlebu * bisa.* She wanted to go in but she couldn't. 5 oh no! (*as a reprimand*). ** kowé kok dadi klajapan tekan pasar!* What made you go to the marketplace [after I told you not to]! ***a** (*prn* **orāâ** *ng*) if not. *Oraa mangan ja ngombé.* If you can't eat, at least drink something. ***né** [whether] or not. *Gumantung ana bisa lan *né anggoné milih.* It depends on whether or not you can make a choice. **sing *-*** unusual, imaginative; silly, trivial. *gunem sing *-** foolish talk. *pangira sing *-** a bizarre unfounded suspicion. ***-*né** (it is) out of the question [that...]. **-*né jèn ilang.* There's no chance of its getting lost. *Opahé *-*né jèn ngluwihi Rp. 300.* The fee can't possibly be more than 300 rupiahs. **ng/di*kaké** to deny the truth of. *Jèn njatané pantjèn ngono, apa bisa ng*kaké?* If it's really true, how can you say it isn't? **ng/di*ni** to say no (to). *Wong pitu sing ng*ni lima, sing ngijani loro.* Of the seven men, five said no and two said yes. **sa*-*né** at least; well anyway. *Sa*-*né ngerti kenṭang-kimpulé.* At least I understand what it's all about. **apa *** ...or not? *Ija apa *?* Is that right? (*i.e.* Yes or no?)

orag *rg var of* OROG

orah *inf var of* ORA

orak *inf var of* ORA

oranânâ there isn't/aren't (*inf var of* ORA ANA)

orang-utan large anthropoid ape

oranje orange(-colored). ** krus* orange crush (drink)

oré hurray! ***an** [of hair] hanging loose. **ng/di*** to allow [one's hair] to hang down loose

oreg to shake from a mighty force. *Gunung geni mau bandjur *.* The volcano shook violently. *Bareng èsprèsé wis tjeḍak lemahé * kabèh.* As the express train drew near, the whole earth shook. *kabar[2] ** earth-shaking news. *Para anggota anggoné padon nuwuhaké *.* The dispute among the members disrupted everything. ***-*an** large-scale disturbance. *Golongan kiri nganakaké *-*an.* The left-wingers are stirring up trouble. **ng/di*aké** to cause to shake violently. *Swarané sepur ng*aké bumi.* The thunder of the train shook the earth.

orèh a cosmetic flower mixture (*var of* BORÈH). ***an** (*var sp:* **oréjan**) 1 notes, sketches. 2 expression, account, narration. 3 trivial. **ng/di*-*** 1 to apply the above flower mixture to the skin. 2 (*or* **ng/di*aké**) to explain, spell out. *Pak Tjamat ng*aké tegesé Pantjasila.* The subdistrict head elucidated the significance of the Five Principles.

orèk ***-*** (to make) a sketch, draft; (to make) doodlings. *Aku *-* gawé tjrita.* I sketched out a story. ***-*an** 1 scratches, marks. 2 sketched-out drafts. **ng/di*** to make marks *or* scratches (on). **ng/di*-*** *or* **ng/di·orak-*** 1 to doodle; to make marks (on). *Adja ng*-* témbok kuwi ja.* Don't mark up that wall! 2 to scratch out, cross out

orèn *var of* URÈN

organisasi organization. ** mahasiswa* student organization

organisatoris organizational; organization-oriented. *Kita mbutuhaké sékretaris kang luwih *.* We need a secretary who is better organized.

organisir **ng/di*** to organize. *Usaha iki di* kaum tani.* This enterprise was organized by farmers.

orgel organ (musical instrument)

ori thorny bamboo. ***ǹ** thicket of thorny bamboo

orisinil original

orkès orchestra (Occidental style). ***an** to have/make orchestral music. *Sewengi muput dalem mau *an.* The orchestra played at the house all night long.

orod to ebb, recede. **ng/di*aké** to hand down, pass along (*var of* NG/DI·LOROD·AKÉ)

orog **ng/di*-*** to shake sth

orok ***-*** a plant that produces a pea-like vegetable

orong ***-*** a roach-like insect. *kaja *-* kepidak* to stop talking suddenly. *nangis *-** to weep loud and long. ***-* n·djundjung genṭong** to try to attain the impossible. **ng*** parched with thirst

orot **ng/di*-*** to use wastefully. *ng*-* banju* to waste water. *Ngirit-irit malah dadi ng*-*.* I try to save money but it slips right through my fingers.

osé 1 hurray! 2 (*or* ***ǹ**) a certain leguminous plant

osèg to fidget; to move uneasily

osèk *var of* USÈK

osèng a small brush. ***-*** 1 *rpr* the sizzling sound made by spreading cooking oil around in a hot frying pan. 2 a meat-and-vegetable dish cooked in a frying pan prepared as above. **ng/di*-*(i)** 1 to prepare [a frying pan] as above. 2 to fry [foods]

osèr **ng/di*-*i** to spread/smear sth (with). *gombal sing di*-*i lim* a rag with glue all over it. *Wadjané di*-*i lenga.* She greased the frying pan.

osik (*or* **m***) 1 to move. *Meneng waé, ora obah ora *.* He didn't move a muscle. *tanpa mobah m** without the slightest movement. 2 moved emotionally. **ng/di*aké** to give smn the impetus to [do], move smn to [do]; to remind smn of

oso **ng*** to speak in a rough *or* angry tone. **ng/di*-*** to keep pressing smn angrily. *Merga di*-*, malah saja gugup olèhé mangsuli.* Under the pressure, he answered more and more nervously.

osog ***-*** *rpr* a rasping sound. **ng/di*** to rub, polish, scrape

osos **ng/di*aké** to let sth escape through an opening. *ng*aké ban* to let the air out of a tire

ot *excl expressing surprise, dismay, warning*

otah *rg var of* WUTAH

otak *var of* UTAK

oṭak ***-*** cane, walking stick. *kaja *-* méga* very tall. **ng/di*-*** to poke *or* prod at with a pole

otang *var of* UTANG

oté ***-*** undressed, naked

oṭé *rg var of* OTÉ. ***-*** a cricket-like insect

oṭèh **ng/di*-*** to scoop *or* stir up [the vegetables that have sunk to the bottom of the soup pot]

otèk 1 a variety of grain used as bird seed. 2 *rg* a small fish net

oṭèk loose but still attached. ***-*** *rpr* the rattling of a loose object

oṭik *var of* UṬIK

otjak **ng/di*(-*)** *or* **ng/di*aké** to shake. *Tambané di*-* ḍisik sakdurungé diombé.* Shake the medicine before you take it.

otjal to cook; to till (*root form: sbst kr for* OLAH)

otjèh ***-*an** a talking bird. **ng*** 1 to talk mindlessly. *Méntjo bisa ng*.* Mynah birds talk. *Bajiné kok wis pinter ng*.* How the baby babbles! 2 *slang* to talk too much; to gossip

oto 1 auto(mobile). 2 protective cloth placed on a baby's chest for warmth

otobis bus

oṭol *rg var of* OKOL

otomatis automatic. *beḍil ** automatic gun

otomobil automobile

otong **ng/di*-*** to bring, carry, take

otonom having autonomy. *pemerintah ** an autonomous government

otonomi autonomy. *Pemeréntah propinsi duwé *.* The provincial government is autonomous.

oṭor *rpr* water running from a faucet in a good-sized trickle. **ng*** to trickle. *See also* ṬOR

otot 1 muscle. 2 blood vessel. **ng*** 1 muscular, sinewy. 2 obstinate, adamant. 3 to talk so loud that the tendons stand out on the neck. *** baju** tendon, sinew, muscle. ** bajuné kaja dilolosi.* The strength drained from him. *** kawat balung wesi** marvelously strong

oṭot **k*** [of meat] very tough. **ng/di*** to pull sth this way and that in an effort to overcome it *or* break it down

owah *ng,* **éwah** *kr* 1 to change. *Djamané wis *.* Times have changed. 2 (to go) insane. ***-*an** a change. **-*an papréntahan* a change of government. **ng/di*aké** to change for smn. *Siti ng*aké klambiné.* Siti altered his shirt. **ng/di*(i)** to change sth. *ng* teges* to change the meaning. *Klambi iki kegeḍèn, kudu di*i.* This dress is too large–it'll have to be altered. *** adat·é** *or* *** ènget·an·é** crazy. *** gingsir** to change constantly

owak **ng*-*** wide open, gaping

owel reluctant to be separated (from); regretful about an anticipated loss. *Aku kok * jèn Siti éntuk Pak H.* I'd be sorry to see Siti marry Mr. H. *Jèn kowé * karo ḍuwitmu, ja adja tuku apa².* If you're so concerned about your money, don't buy anything. *Marang sisihané ana rasa *.* He doesn't like to be away from his wife. **ng/di*** to treat overprotectively *or* possessively. **pa·ng*** overcautiousness, excessive protectiveness

owol **ng/di*-*** to grab sth and make a mess of it

P

p 1 (*prn* **pé**) *alphabetic letter.* 2 *prefix: var of* PA- *before vowel and optionally before* L, R

pa[a] 1 a Javanese script character. 2 *inf var of* APA. **ora ngerti * bèngkong** 1 illiterate. 2 ignorant of the circumstances. *Ora ngerti * bèngkong kok mèlu².* Don't butt in–you don't know anything about it. *See also under* PE-: *Introduction, 2.9.2*

pa-[b] *prefix* 1 act *or* way of [do]ing. *pa·m̈pangan* (*pamangan*) way of eating. 2 *result produced by root. pa·m·berung* obstinacy. *pa·wèh* gift. *pa·m̈·pirsa* (*pamirsa*) vision; knowledge. *pa·ng·gelar* spread of learning. *pa·kon* a command. *pa·n·djaluk* a request. 3 one who performs [action of root]. *pa·n·djaga* watchman, guard. *pa·dagang* businessman. *pe·gawé* white-collar employee. *pe·n̈g·karang* (*pengarang*) writer, author. 4 the time, distance, *etc.* required to [do]. *pa·dang* the time it takes to cook rice. *sa·pa·n̈g·kinang* one betel-chew('s length of time). ***...an** (*circumfix*) 1 *process or result of root action. pa·dagang·an* trade, business. *pa·djagong·an* ceremony to celebrate a special event. *pe·gawé·an* work, a job. *pa·guju·n̈* (*pagujon*) a laugh. *banju pa·ng·ombé·n̈* (*pangombèn*) drinking water.

pa·gunem·an conversation. 2 group of X's; X's considered collectively. *pa·botoh·an* gambling association. *pa·désa·n* a complex of villages under the same administration. *pa·kabar·an* the press. *pa·sawah·an* land devoted to rice planting. *pa·suket·an* grasses (of various kinds). 3 place where [action of root] is done. *p·adus·an* bathtub. *pa·béja·n* customs office. *pa·ḍajoh·an* place where one visits; place where guests are received. *pa·guru·ǹ* (*paguron*) institution of learning. *pa·djaga·n* place where a guard is posted. *alas pa·djati·ǹ* (*padjatèn*) teak forest. *pa·turu·ǹ* (*paturon*) bed; bedroom. *pa·gelar·an* open hall where a king meets with his subjects. 4 [noun] relating to root. *pa·gunung·an* mountainous terrain. *pa·dina·n* that which happens daily. *pa·ḍukun·an* medicinal knowledge. *pa·lanang·an* penis. *pa·lungguh·an* position, situation, job, office. 5 *circumfixed to nouns, usu. denoting places, without altering the meaning.* *(pa)dalem(an)* family residence compound. *(pa)nggon(an)* place. *(pa)ḍepok(an)* hermit shrine. *(p)rai(ǹ)* [*praèn*] face. *(p)adat(an)* habit, customary practice. *See also listings under individual entries*

paben to quarrel (*kr for* PADU)

pabrik plant, factory. * *gula* sugar-processing plant. *masinis* * plant supervisor

pâdâ 1 Javanese-script punctuation mark. 2 end of a stanza. *Olèhé nembang tekan ing* *. He sang one stanza. 3 punctuating phrase at the close of a personal letter. 4 settled. *Wis* *. It's final. *Djandji durung* *. The agreement isn't final yet. 5 *ltry* foot. **ning ulun* your majesty, your excellency. *ngaras* * to kiss smn's foot to show humble respect. *ngraup* * to bathe smn's feet when asking his pardon. *tjatur* * four-legged; *fig, ltry* whole-hearted. 6 *ltry* place, locality. * *manḍala* world, earth. * *wadana* aspect, appearance. **ṁ/di*** to punctuate. * **adeg²** paragraph-opening punctuation mark. * **geḍé** phrase *or* couplet marking sections of poems. * **guru** chapter-opening punctuation mark. * **lingsa** comma (hook-shaped character in Javanese script). * **loro** *or* * **lu(ng)si** period (double-hook-shaped character). * **watjana** facial expression

pâḍâ *ng,* **sami** *kr* 1 alike; the same. *Kabèh* *. They're all alike. *Duwèkku mèh * karo duwèkmu.* Mine is almost the same as yours. * *geḍéné.* They're the same size. *Ambeké isih * baé karo ḍèk bijèn.* His character is the same as ever. 2 *plural marker.* *Suwé² * turu.* They finally went to sleep. *Para tamu wis * kondur kabèh.* The guests have all gone home. 3 (together) with. *Iwaké dipilihi agal * agal, lembut * lembut.* The fish were sorted by size. * *sanalika(-sakala)* immediately, in the same instant. **-** 1 likewise, alike. *Karo-karoné *-* satrija sing linuhung.* Both were high-ranking noblemen. 2 among, out of the total. *-* *kéwan, gadjah iku sing geḍé ḍéwé.* Among the animals, the elephant is the largest. **(pe)*né** *sms* SA·PE*·NÉ *below.* **ṁ/di*** to resemble; to make (a)like. *Geḍéné mangsa anaa sing maḍa!* As if anything could be that big! *Di*a meksa kalah amba.* They're similar, but one is narrower. *Klambiku maḍa rupa karo klambimu.* My shirt is the same color as yours. **ṁ/di*kaké** to compare. *Jèn di*kaké karo Indonesia...* Compared with Indonesia... *Wit wringin di*kaké wong kumlungkung.* A banyan tree can be compared to a boastful person. **ṁ/di*ni** 1 to equal; to be the same as. *Unta kuwi betahé ngelak ora ana sing maḍani.* The camel has no equal in withstanding thirst. *A arep njoba maḍani kesugihané B.* A is trying to get as rich as B. *Klambiné di*ni.* Someone wore a dress just like hers. **sa*-*** in the same *or* similar circumstances. *welas marang se*-** compassion for others in the same boat. *Matur nuwun.– Sa-sami².* Thank you.–And *I* thank *you.* **(sa)pe*né** (**sa·sami·nipun** *kr*) 1 one's equals, one's fellows. *Sape*né wong urip kudu lung-tinulung.* We must all help each other. 2 and the like. *tembung² kang nélakaké akèh, seṭiṭik, sape*né* words that denote many, few, and the like. * **déné** alike, the same. *A lan B * déné pinteré.* A and B are equally intelligent. *Bapak lan ibu * déné asal Sala.* My father and mother both come from Solo. * **karo** 1 the same as, similar to. 2 equals (in arithmetic). *Loro ping telu * karo nem.* Two times three is six.

padal **ṁ/di*** 1 to press and hold. *Koplingé di* nganggo sikil karebèn ora mlaku.* He kept his foot on the clutch so the car wouldn't move. 2 to reject. *madal tamba* incurable; resistant to cure. *Ḍèwèké tetep gerah bisu, madal sakèhing usada.* He remains unable to speak in spite of all the medicine he has had. **ṁ/di*aké** to press sth against/to

paḍang (**padjar** *kr?*) bright, light, clear. *∗é kaja awan.* It was as bright as day. *∗ mbulan* moonlight. *Rainé ∗.* Her face is radiant. *∗ pikirané.* He thinks clearly. **pe∗** light, brightness. *Kanggo pe∗ listrik kuwi luwih murah tinimbang gas.* Electricity is cheaper for lighting than gas. *Pe∗ jèn pinudju nemahi kesusahan* a source of cheer to smn in sorrow. **m̂/di∗aké** to make sth light/bright. *maḍangaké pepeteng* to light up the darkness. *maḍangaké ati* to cheer smn up. **m̂/di∗i** to give light to. *Urubing kaju kuwi maḍangi ing sakiwa-tengené kono.* The burning trees light everything up. **∗ n·ḍranḍang** *or* **∗ n·djingglang** very bright; brightly lighted. *See also* BJAR, BOTJAH, WERUH

paḍaran stomach, belly (*ki for* WETENG)

paḍas sandstone. **m̂∗** resembling sandstone. **∗ kapur, ∗ krokos, ∗ lempung, ∗ pasir** varieties of soft, crumbling rock. **∗ karang** *or* **∗ tjuri** hardened soil along the shore at the foot of a mountain

padasan a large earthen vessel with a tap, containing well water for ritual cleaning of the face, hands, and teeth

paḍet compact. *Koper kuwi tjilik nanging isiné ∗.* The suitcase is small but it's tightly packed. **m̂∗** tightly compressed. *Olèhé ngurugi lemah maḍet banget mulané sengara amblong.* He tamped the soil firm so it wouldn't cave in. **m̂/di∗aké** to compress tightly

padik **∗an** scrutiny; a close look. *Kowé apa wis olèh ∗an penggawéan?* Have you looked over any jobs yet? **m̂/di∗(-∗)** to scrutinize, inspect

pâdjâ 1 [not] at all. *Ḍèwèké ora ∗-∗ ngerti.* He doesn't understand it at all. 2 [not] impressive. *Asilé durung ∗-∗.* The results don't amount to much yet.

padjal origin, source. **m̂∗-(m)ulih·an** *or* **m̂∗-pulih·an** to return to where one/it came from. *Ali²né madjal-mulihan, sawisé ilang suwé.* The ring is back where it belongs, after having been missing for a long time. *See also* ADJAL[b]

padjang **∗an** 1 decorations. 2 used for breeding purposes. *sapi ∗an* a stud bull. **∗-∗** to put up decorations. **m̂/di∗(i)** 1 to decorate. *Dalan² paḍa di∗i djalaran arep 17 Agustus.* The streets are festooned in preparation for Independence Day. 2 [of animals] to mate with

padjeg *ng,* **paos** *kr* 1 tax. *∗ opah(an)* income tax. *∗ personil* personal property tax. *∗ potong* slaughter tax. *∗ sirah* head tax, per capita tax. *∗ tontonan* entertainment tax. *ḍuwit ∗* tax money. *mbajar ∗* to pay taxes. *ngenani ∗* to levy taxes. *narik ∗* to collect taxes. *panarik ∗* tax collector. *para warga ∗* taxpayers. 2 rental money for land. 3 (*ng kr*) *rg var of* ADJEG. **m̂∗ pangan** (**m̂·paos teḍa** *kr*) to board, *i.e.* take one's meals smw regularly. **m̂/di∗aké** to lease out [land]. **madjegaké bau·né** to hire out one's services. **m̂/di∗i** 1 to pay up [one's taxes *or* lease money]. 2 to levy a tax on sth. 3 to harvest smn's rice in return for part of the crop. **pa·m̂∗** rental terms. *Lemah iku lawasé pamadjeg limang taun.* That field is on a five-year lease. **pa·m̂∗an** leased-out land. *punggawa pamadjegan* land-rent collector

padjeng 1 angle (*opt kr for* PADJU). 2 to get sold (*kr for* PAJU)

padju 1 (**padjeng** *opt kr*) angle, corner. *∗ telu* triangle. *∗ papat* rectangle. 2 metal wedge for splitting wood. **m̂/di∗(k̂aké)** to split [wood] with a wedge

padma *oj* red lotus blossom

padmi the first wife in a polygamous royal marriage: the one who gives birth to the legal successor(s)

padni *oj form of* PADMI

padon 1 corner, angle. *geḍong ∗ lima* a pentagonal building. *Genṭongé ana ing ∗.* The water jug is in the corner. *Gendéra dilempit adu ∗.* Flags are folded with corners matching. *∗ mripat/lambé* the corner of the eye/lips. 2 *form of* PADU. **m̂/di∗i** to plow the corners of [a field]

pados to get; to seek (*kr for* GOLÈK)

Pâdrâwânâ eleventh month of the Javanese calendar (19 April–12 May)

padu *ng,* **paben** *kr* to quarrel. *A ∗ karo B ramé banget.* A and B quarreled noisily. **∗n̂** 1 (to have) a dispute *or* difference of opinion. 2 negotiator. **dudu padon** unbelievable. **∗né** as a matter of fact... *∗né ora bisa mangsuli pitakon mau.* The fact is, he can't answer the question. **pe∗n̂** *sms* ∗N̂ *above.* **m̂/di∗n̂i** to contradict; to talk back to. *Jèn dituturi mesṭi madoni.* Whenever I speak to him, he answers back.

padudon *see under* DU

paduka you, your (*wj and stage usage*)

paédah use(fulness); benefit. *Wit djati kuwi geḍé banget ∗é.* **m̂/di∗aké** to put sth to use, turn sth to a useful purpose. *Omah mau* *di∗aké kanggo asrama.* The house is now being used as a dormitory. **ṁ∗i** useful, beneficial. *baktéri kang maédahi marang manungsa* bacteria that are beneficial to mankind

paéka trick, deceit. *kena ing ∗* to be victimized. **∗n** deceitfulness, cheating. **ṁ/di∗(ni)** to cheat, swindle

paèlu **ṁ/di∗** to do as smn asks. *Ḍèké ora maèlu tembungé sisihané mau.* He didn't give in to his wife.

paès 1 bridal make-up and ornamentation, *esp.* for the forehead. 2 ornamentation, finery. *Gadjah sing dititihi ratu dianggoni ∗.* An elephant to be ridden by a king gets all decked out. **∗an** 1 (wearing) make-up, *esp.* bridal. 2 *ltry* a shining example. **pe∗** 1 *sms* ∗ 2. *pekarangan sing nganggo pe∗* a yard with ornamental plantings. 2 to adorn oneself. **ṁ/di∗i** to deck out, *esp.* a bride. *Aku didandani tjara temantèn, di∗i.* She dressed me in bridal finery and made me up with bridal cosmetics. *Gadjahé di∗i.* The elephant was arrayed in finery.

pag. *see* PAGINA

pâgâ kitchen shelf *or* rack for dishes, glassware, food

pagas **ϕ/di∗** *or* **ṁ/di∗** to cut back [a plant] at the top to stimulate thicker growth

pageblog *var of* PAGEBLUG

pageblug epidemic. *∗ pès* an epidemic of plague. *ditradjang ∗* wracked by an epidemic

pager fence, outside wall. *∗ batu* brick wall. *∗ geḍèg* braided-bamboo wall. *∗ kawat* wire fence. *∗ pring* bamboo hedge. **ṁ/di∗(i)** to surround with a fence. *Omahé di∗ bata mubeng.* The house had a brick wall around it. ∗ **ṁ·pangan tandur·an** to do harm to sth entrusted to one's care

pagina (*abbr*: **pag.**) page

pah dad, pop (*inf var of* BAPAK)

pahâlâ *oj* reward; benefit reaped

paham 1 body of knowledge *or* thought; doctrine, ism. *∗ ilmu sosiologi* sociological view. *∗ Islam* Islamic tenets. *∗ komunis* communism. 2 to understand; knowledgable. *Wis ∗?* Is it clear? *Ḍèwèké salah ∗.* He misunderstood. *Bab mau aku ora pati ∗.* I'm not very well versed in that area. *Aku ora ∗.* I don't get it. **∗an** opinion. **ṁ/di∗aké** *or* **ṁ/di∗i** to understand. *Tulisané angèl di∗aké.* His writing is hard to interpret.

pahargja **∗n** celebration. *∗ pitulas Agustusan* Independence-Day celebration. **ṁ/di∗** to celebrate

paheman *oj* organization, association

Pahing *var of* PAING

pahit *var of* PAIT

pahjas decorative; decoration. **ṁ/di∗** 1 to dress in fine raiment. 2 to decorate. *See also* HJAS

paiben *kr for* PAIDO

paidah *var of* PAÉDAH

paido *ng*, **paiben** *kr* **∗n** 1 one whose word is doubted; one who is disparaged. *Tinimbang dadi paidon waé, luwih apik aku meneng waé.* I'd rather keep quiet than be thought a liar. 2 cuspidor (*form of* IDU). **ṁ/di∗** 1 to express doubt *or* disbelief. *Sanadjan kanḍa temen ija meksa di∗.* He told the truth but they still didn't believe him. 2 to disparage, belittle. *Kok gampang temen kowé maido gawéané wong lija.* It's very easy for you to find fault with other people's work!

pailit bankrupt, out of business. **ṁ/di∗aké** to liquidate [a business]

Paing second day of the five-day week

pait 1 bitter. *Rasané rada ∗.* It tastes bitter. *pengalaman ∗* a bitter experience. 2 *var of* PAWIT. ∗ **djuruh** very sweet. ∗ **getir** sharp and bitter. ∗ **gula** *or* ∗ **kilang** *or* ∗ **madu** very sweet. ∗ **ñj·tjeṭak** intensely bitter

pajah *rg* weary. **ṁ∗aké** tiring, causing weariness

pajang boat used for deep-sea fishing

pajing **pojang-∗(an)** to move this way and that in confusion *or* uncertainty

pajon 1 roof. 2 *form of* PAJU. **ṁ/di∗aké** to repair a roof for smn. **ṁ/di∗i** to equip with a roof. *Gendèng mau kanggo majoni omahé.* The tiles are for the roof of his house.

paju *ng*, **padjeng** *kr* to get sold; *fig* to get accepted. *∗ Rp. 10* sold for ten rupiahs. *Nam²ané agal, mula ora ∗ akèh.* The wickerwork is so crude it doesn't sell well. *Andjurané ∗.* They were sold on his proposal. *botjah wédok sing ora ∗ rabi* a girl nobody wants to marry. **(pe)∗n̂** proceeds from selling. *Pepajoné daganganku luwih Rp. sèwu.* I got over a thousand rupiahs for my goods. **ṁ/di∗k̂aké** 1 to succeed in selling. *Motoré dipajokaké tanggaku.* My neighbor managed to sell his car. 2 to sell for smn else (on commission). 3 [of currency] to put into circulation. *Ḍuwité palsu dipajokaké.* They passed counterfeit money. **sa*-*é** at any price available. *Dolen sa*-*né, aku selak butuh ḍuwit.* Sell it for whatever you can get: I need money badly.

pajudârâ *oj* breast (*ki for* SUSU[a]?)

pajug **m̃*** to lean, list, sag. **m̃*-m̃*** *or* **m̃·pojag-m̃*** to shake, rock. *Tjagaké gendéra mojag-majug arep ambruk.* The flagpole wobbles as though it's about to fall. **m̃/di*aké** to lean sth (on, against, *etc.*)

pajung *ng kr,* **songsong** *kr?, ki* umbrella; sunshade. *tutupan ** covered with an umbrella. ** tutupan* a closed umbrella. ***an** to use an umbrella. **m̃*** directly overhead. **m̃/di*i** to shield smn from sun or rain with an umbrella. **pa*an** to hold an umbrella over the head. *** agung** large red ceremonial umbrella. *** kalong** *or* *** lawa** *or* *** moṭa** black sailcloth umbrella. *** sungsun** ceremonial umbrella. *** Tjina** oiled-paper parasol

pak 1 father (*shf of* BAPAK). 2 *adr, title* father; older *or* higher-status male. 3 bundle, package. 4 (*prn* **pak̄**) pack. *Rokoké pira se*?* How much is a pack of cigarettes? ***-*an** male manager of a house of prostitution. ***né** *term by which a wife addresses her husband, if they have children.* **nge/di*(i)** to pack; to make into a bundle. *** (ge)ḍé** 1 uncle (parent's older brother). 2 grandfather (*usage limited to nobles*). *** guru** teacher! ; the teacher. *** lik** *see* * TJILIK *below.* *** lurah** *term for addressing or referring to the village head.* *** tani** the farmer; a particular farmer. *** (tji)lik** uncle (parent's younger brother)

pakakèn a stand for a lamp *or* candle

pakan (*or* ***an**) animal food. **é ora kurang.* There's plenty of fodder. ** manuk* bird feed. *Sega wingi kuwi kena kanggo *é pitik.* We can feed yesterday's rice to the chickens. **m̃/di*** 1 to take effect. *Rèmé dipriksa ḍisik, makan apa ora.* Check the brakes to make sure they work. *Dongané wis makan.* The prayer was answered. *Naséhat sing kaja ngapa waé wis ora makan.* No advice does him any good. *Lading iki wis ora makan.* This knife won't cut any more. 2 *fig* to eat up. *makan wektu/ḍuwit* to take a lot of time/money. *Botjah nakal kuwi makan ati ibuné.* That no-good boy's mother is eating her heart out over him. *Rènténé makan ḍarah.* The rent is exorbitant. **m̃/di*aké** (*prn* **m̃/di·pakak·aké**) 1 to feed *or* feed sth to [an animal]. *Tikusé tak pakakné kutjing.* I'll let the cat eat the mouse. 2 to cause sth to take effect. *Ḍèké makakaké erèmé.* He slammed on his brakes. **m̃/di*i** to feed [an animal]. *Asuné di*i sega.* He fed rice to the dog.

pakansi vacation, holiday

pakarja ***n** 1 work, job, trade. *A pantjèn ora ngerti marang *né B.* A had no idea what B did for a living. 2 work done. **n baṭik* batik work. **n pérak* silver work. 3 deed, act; *gram* the action expressed in a verb. **m̃*** to work, do a job. **m̃/di*kaké** to have smn work. *Aku makarjakaké wong sepuluh kanggo kuwi.* I put ten people to work on it. *See also* KARJA

pakarti *ltry* behavior, actions. **m̃*** to work at. *Ajo paḍa makarti mbangun negara.* Let us all put our shoulder to the wheel to build up our nation.

pakaṭik horse groom. ** ngarit* man who cuts grass for horse fodder. **m̃*** to be in charge of horses. *See also* KAṬIK

pakèh ***an** (*var sp*: **pakéjan**) special garb. **an djaran* harness(ing equipment) for a horse. **an militèr* military uniform. **an wajang* dance costume. **m̃/di*i** to equip [a horse] with a blanket

pakèkèh **m̃/di*aké** to place [one's feet] with toes outward while in a standing position

pakèl a young mango

pakem an original story on which other stories are based. *Bratajuda karo Ramajana kuwi kanggo * peḍalangan.* Shadow-play stories are derived from the Bratajuda and Ramayana epics. *** balung·an** story in skeletal form. *** pa·ḍalang·an** story in script form showing dialogue, narration, and music for a shadow play. *** gantjar·an** story in scenario form

pakéring *ltry var of* ÉRING. *olèh * saka* to be held in respect by. *awèh * marang* to have respect for

pakèwed *kr for* PAKÉWUH

pakéwuh *ng,* **pakèwed** *kr* (to have) difficulty; (to feel) discomfort. *ketemu ** to encounter difficulties. *Adja *, lungguha ana kono baé.* Make yourself at home; have a seat over there. ***an** shy, timid, uncomfortable around people. **m̃/di*aké** to cause difficulty (for). *Parto golèk gawéan supaja adja mekéwuhaké wong tuwané.* Parto got a job so as not to be a burden on his parents. *A ki mekéwuhké, djaréné kon ngedolké pité,* *mbasan wis kedadéjan ora sida.* A is very difficult: he asked me to sell his bike, and when the deal was all set he changed his mind. **m̀*i** embarrassing, awkward. *See also* ÉWUH, SEKÉWUH

pakir *var of* FAKIR

pakis fern, bracken. * **adji** a variety of fern

pakolèh *ng,* **pikantuk** *kr* accomplishment. *Geḍé *é.* They gained a lot. **m̀*i** productive. *pegawéan sing makolèhi* lucrative work. *Ora makolèhi waé kok dianggo rebutan.* It's not worth wasting any effort on. *See also* OLÈH

pâkrâ **ora *** unseemly in one's conduct

paksa *formal var of* PEKSA

paksi *rg var of* PÈKSI

paktā treaty. * *Warsawa* Warsaw Pact

paku nail. **m̀/di*(ñi)** to nail sth. * **djamur** round-headed nail; thumbtack. * **idep** tiny nail. * **keling** rivet

Paku Buwânâ state name of the Sunan of Surakarta. * *XII* the present (twelfth) Sunan

pal 1 measure of distance: *ca.* 0.93 mile = 1507 meters. 2 marker placed at one-*pal* intervals along a road. **nge/di*** convinced that sth undesirable will take place. *B ngepal jèn aku ora isa lulus udjian.* B was sure I couldn't pass the exam.

pal- *see also under* PL- (*Introduction, 2.9.3*)

pâlâ nutmeg. *kembang ** mace (spice). *watu sa** a stone the size of a nutmeg. **m̀/di*** to beat with a stick. * **g·um·antung** fruits that grow on trees. * **kirna** fruits (cultivated) from long-lived trees. * **kitri** fruits from orchard trees. * **ka·penḍem** edible roots. * **ka·sampar** *or* * **ka·simpar** fruits that grow at ground level

pâlâdjiwâ *var of* PALAWIDJI

palagan *oj* battlefield, battleground

palak 1 celestial sphere. 2 astronomy; astronomical; astrological reckoning of propitious times for significant events

pâlâkrâmâ *ng,* **pâlâkrami** *kr* 1 marriage; married (*see also* KRAMA). 2 *ltry* homage, respect. **m̀/di*kaké** to celebrate one's child's wedding, marry off a child

pâlâkrami *kr for* PALAKRAMA

palang *ng,* **pambeng** *kr* 1 obstacle; object placed crosswise to sth. * *sepur* railway gate. 2 bridge hand rail. ***an** cross piece. **pe*** hindrance, impediment. *Jèn ora ana pe* aku mulih sasi ngarep.* If there's no hitch, I'll be going home next month. **ke*** obstructed, impeded. *Bisé ke*.* The bus is blocked. **ke* tanggung** not worth the trouble. *Ke* tanggung jèn mangkat saiki nang stasiun, sepuré mesṭi wis mangkat.* There's no point in going to the station now —the train must have left. **m̀*** to lie crosswise. *Tibané wit mau malang njegati dalan geḍé.* The tree fell across the highway, blocking it. **m̀*(m̀*) tanggung** to create obstacles. *Adja malang tanggung jèn njambut gawé.* Don't make a job harder than it is. **m̀/di*aké** to use as a barrier. *Aku malangaké médja nèng ngarep lawang.* I barricaded the door with a table. *mBok pité adja di*aké nèng ndalan.* Don't park your bike across the roadway. **m̀/di*i** to impede. *Di*ana mlumpat.* He's not to be deterred! *See also* ALANG[b]

palastra *oj* dead; to die

pâlâwidja(h) *var of* PALAWIDJI

pâlâwidji crop other than rice planted in a dry or wet field

palem palm tree

palih half (*kr for* PARO)

palimarma, palimirma *oj* pity, mercy

paling most, -est. * *tjenḍèk* (*geḍé, panas, lsp.*) the shortest (biggest, hottest, *etc.*) one. ***-*** at the (very) most

palsafah *var of* PILSAPAT

palsu false, fake. *untu ** false teeth. *kemenangan ** a hollow victory. *tangan ** artificial arm. *Ḍuwité kretas rong puluhan mau *,* The twenty-rupiah bill was counterfeit. **m̀/di*** to counterfeit, falsify. *malsu lajang²* to forge *or* falsify documents. *Bier di* banju.* The "beer" was plain water.

palu hammer, mallet. *Ketua nuṭukké * nang médja, ḍog!* The chairman rapped the gavel on the table. **ke* ke·penṭung** to suffer a multiple loss. **m̀/di*** to hammer. * **arit** hammer and sickle

paluh muddy swampy ground. **ke*** stuck in the mud. **m̀*** full of mud

palupi *oj* 1 letter, document. 2 example

palwa *ltry* boat. * *udara* flying machine

palwâgâ *oj* monkey

pâmâ *inf var of* UPAMA

paman 1 uncle. 2 uncle who is a parent's younger brother. 3 *adr* older man of lower status than speaker. **m̀*** to call smn uncle; to regard smn as one's uncle

pambeng 1 obstacle (*kr for* PALANG). 2 *kr?* menstruation. ***an** 1 mishap; damage. 2 having a menstrual period (*rg? kr for* KÈL?)

pamèr to show with pride. * *jèn duwé pit anjar* to show off one's new bicycle.

*Slamet * nggoné pinter matja.* Slamet showed how well he could read. ***an** show, exhibition. **an pakaian* fashion show. **m̃/di*aké** to show sth. *Ḍèké mamèraké pité sing anjar.* He showed us his new bike. *Pusaka² kraton di*aké nang perajaan Sekatèn.* The palace weapons were displayed at the Sekatèn festival. **m̃/di*i** to show to smn. *Aku di*i olèhé nduwé radijo.* He let me see that he had a radio.

pamerintah, pameréntah *var sp of* PEMRINTAH

pami *inf var of* UPAMI

pamiḍangan 1 forehead (*ki for* BAṬUK). 2 shoulder (*ki for* PUNḌAK). 3 place where a vow is fulfilled

pamidjangan shoulder (*ki for* PUNḌAK)

pamili relatives, family

pamit 1 permission to leave *or* be absent. *njuwun ** to say goodbye to one's host(ess). *Ḍèké ora sekolah tanpa *.* He stayed out of school without getting excused. 2 (*or* ***an**) to ask permission to leave; to take one's leave, say goodbye. *A *an mulih.* A said goodbye and went home. *A * guruné.* A said goodbye to the teacher. *Ponakanku mau mréné perlu *an arep lunga nang Djakarta.* My cousin came over to tell us he was leaving for Djakarta. **m̃/di*aké** to have smn say goodbye *or* give notice of one's absence. *A lara, di*aké B nang sekolahan.* B notified the school that A was absent because of illness. *Mardi mau mréné mamitaké bodjoné ora bisa teka.* Mardi came to let us know that his wife wouldn't be able to come. **m̃/di*i** to say goodbye to smn. *mamiti kantja* to say goodbye to a friend

pamor 1 face. **é èlèk.* She's homely. 2 decoration on a kris blade. *** petjah** *describing the fresh beauty of a newly adult girl*

pampet to stop flowing. *Getihé *.* It stopped bleeding. **m̃/di*(i)** to cause to stop flowing. *mampet pipa lèḍeng sing botjor* to plug up a leaky pipe

pamrih intention, expectation (*inf var of* PA·M̈·PURIH)

pan 1 pan; baking pan. 2 *rg* clear. *Wis * olèhé ndelok²?* Have you had a good look at it? 3 *oj* certainly, by all means. 4 *oj* but. **nge/di*** to bake in a pan. *Rotiné diepan.* She baked the bread. **pa·nge*** act of baking. *Pange*ipun, lojang kalèmèki kertas peṭak ingkang resik.* To bake, line a cake mold with clean white paper.

pânâ *oj* to know. *Aku wis * banget sapa kowé kuwi.* I am quite aware of who you are.

panah *ng,* **djemparing** *kr* arrow. ***an** archery. **m̃/di*aké** to shoot an arrow for smn. **m̃/di*(i)** to shoot with a bow and arrow

pânâkawan *wj* clown-servant. **m̃*** to be *or* act as a clown-servant

pânâkrâmâ *word of welcome. Katuran * sarawuh djengandika.* Welcome!

panambang 1 (*or* ***an**) craft used for ferrying. 2 *gram* suffix. **m̃/di*aké** to attach a suffix to. *See also* TAMBANG

panampan brass tray (*ki for* TALAM?)

pananggap 1 gently sloping roof section below the steeply ascending portion (*srotong*) above. *saka ** the pillars which support this section. 2 tax assessor's fee; tax assessor

panas *ng,* **bentèr** *kr* 1 hot. 2 (*or* **lara ***) (to have) a fever. *lara * tis* (to have) malaria. 3 angry. 4 having a curse on it; bringing misfortune. *ḍuwit ** cursed (*i.e.* stolen) money. ***an** 1 to sun oneself. 2 to get on people's nerves. ***-*** 1 to stay in the sun. *É adja *-*, mripatmu munḍak lara.* Now don't stay out in the sun—it'll be bad for your eyes. 2 when sth is hot. **-* énaké ngombé ès.* Iced drinks taste good when it's hot. **pe*** to stay out in the sun. **ke*an** to stay out in the sun too long. **ke*en** excessively hot. **m̃*** to sun-bathe. **m̃/di*aké** to heat sth. *manasaké sega* to heat up rice. **manasaké ati** annoying, exasperating. **manasaké kuping** to anger/offend smn. **m̃*i** 1 to get hot under the collar. 2 (*psv* **di*i**) to heat sth; to anger smn. *** n·ḍranḍang** [of weather] intensely hot; sunny. *** kuping·é** angered by sth one has heard. *** mongah²** hot, feverish. *** pati** fire-breathing ghost. *See also* PANAS-ATI

panasar chewing tobacco; tobacco added to betel-nut chew (*ki for* SUSUR)

panas-ati *ng,* **bentèr-manah** *kr* ***ǹ** envious. **m̃/di*ǹi** 1 to irritate, get on smn's nerves. 2 to envy [smn]; to envy smn [sth]. *Dipanas-atèni kantjané.* His friend envied him. *Ḍèké manastèni begdjané kantjané.* He envied his friend his good luck. *See also* ATI, PANAS

panastèn *inf var of* PANAS-ATI·Ǹ

pandak 1 [not] able to endure. *Ḍèké ora * djoṭakan karo aku sedina waé.* She couldn't bear not speaking to me even for one day. 2 [not] having the nerve (to...)

panḍak short in stature

pandamel magic spell (*kr for* PANGGAWÉ)

paṇḍamèn *var of* PUNḌAMÈN
paṇḍan 1 pandanus tree. 2 (*or* * **wangi**) (fragrant) pandanus leaf as a cooking ingredient. ***an** pandanus thicket. * **eri** pandanus thorn, used for weaving hats, mats. * **rawa** a variety of grass
Paṇḍâwâ *wj* group name of the five brothers of the Mahabharata epic, depicted in classical drama
paṇḍé 1 forge, smithy. 2 blacksmith. *palu* * blacksmith's hammer. 3 intelligent, skilled. 4 an expert, a specialist. ***an** place where a blacksmith works. **m̈*** 1 to be *or* become a blacksmith. 2 (*psv* **di***) to forge [metal]
paṇḍéga **m̈/di*ni** to be the leader of. *manḍégani pradjurit* to lead troops
paṇḍékar *oj* skilled duelist
paṇḍekuk̄ pancake
paṇḍel pennant; banner
pandeleng *ng,* **paningal** *kr* vision, view, observation. *Ora njenengaké temen menjang* *. It was by no means an agreeable sight. *Anglam-lami ing* *. I still see it in my mind's eye. **é kuning.* His vision is blurred. ***an** what is seen; view. **sa*** all that one can see. *Kanan kéringipun ḍusun ngriku ngantos sapaningal tebihipun.* There are villages everywhere as far as the eye can see. *See also* DELENG
pandelep *rpr* a quick disappearance *or* concealment. **m̈*** 1 to disappear, conceal oneself. *mandelep kaja dul diduleg* to vanish like a snail withdrawing into its shell. 2 (*psv* **di***) to cause sth to vanish. *See also* DELEP
pandeng scrutiny. * *djadjag*² an exploratory stare. ***an** 1 to try to outstare. 2 objective. 3 *sms* PAM̈* *below.* ***an karo srengéngé·né** to defy a powerful adversary. ***-*an** to stare at each other. **m̈/di*** to look at directly/fixedly. *Mripaté mandeng putjuking irung.* He stared at the tip of his nose, *i.e.* sat humbly with downcast gaze. *Djaran*² *mau tansah mandeng gendéra.* The [racing] horses kept their eyes glued on the flag. **mandeng k·um·eḍèp tesmak** to stare wide-eyed. **pa·m̈*** way of looking (at). *Pamandengé keḍèp tesmak.* He stared unblinking.
paṇḍes (having been) cut off just above the roots. **m̈/di*** to cut sth as above
paṇḍi an expert (*var of* PAṆḌÉ). **m̈/di*** *ltry* to hold [a weapon] at one's shoulder. *Tangané tengen amaṇḍi waos.* His right hand held a spear.
pandika *oj* what smn says; way of speaking
paṇḍing *var of* TANḌING
paṇḍita 1 holy hermit, great mystic teacher, pundit. 2 (Christian) priest. **ka*n** wisdom; mystic knowledge. **m̈*** to be(come) a holy hermit. **sang** * *or* **sang p·in·aṇḍita** *title for addressing or referring to a holy man*
pândjâ spur on a cock's foot (*opt kr for* DJALU)
pandjalma *form of* DJALMA
pandjang 1 large oval-shaped plate. * *ilang* disposable bowl woven of young coconut leaves. 2 long (*kr for* DAWA). **m̈*-ilang** resembling the above disposable bowl. * **blawong** 1 long and big around. 2 a big eater
pandjat ***an** a slope. **m̈*** to slope, slant
pandjenengan 1 you; your (*ki for* KOWÉ). * *kula-aturi mriksani pijambak.* I ask you to see it for yourself. *penggalih* * your ideas/thoughts. *sekul ingkang sampun * ḍahar* the rice that you have eaten. 2 cane, walking stick. ***é** (***ipun** *kr*) 1 he/him, she/her (*ki for* ḌÈWÈKÉ). *Apa pendjenengané wis ditjaosi pirsa bab kuwi?* Has he been told about it? 2 the honorable... *Pendjenenganipun ndara pengéran sampun miḍanget.* The prince has heard about it. ***ku** I, me (*regal usage*). *putramu pandjenenganku* our son. * **dalem** you [to high officials]. * **sekalijan** the two of you; you and your wife (husband)
pandjer down payment. ***an** flagpole. *dijan *an* night light. **m̈*** 1 a down payment, deposit. 2 (*psv* **di***) to keep [an oil lamp] burning all night. *Dijané adja di*.* Don't keep the light on all night. 3 (*psv* **di***) to keep sth up. *mandjer lajangan* to keep a kite flying. *mandjer pantjing ana ing kali* to let a fishing rod float on the water. **m̈/di*i** to pay [(as) a deposit]. *Ḍèké mandjeri sèwu rupiah kanggo omah mau.* He gave a down payment of 1,000 rupiahs for the house. * **ésuk** *or* * **rina** morning star. * **soré** evening star
pandji 1 a group of stories, depicted in *wajang geḍog* tales, about the Javanese prince Pandji. 2 *oj* flag. * **klanṭung** an unemployed person
pandjurung financial contribution to a bereaved family to help with the expenses. **m̈/di*** to give such a donation (to). *See also* DJURUNG
pandom 1 (*or* ***an**) compass. *Jèn wedi kesasar, nggawaa* *. If you're afraid you'll get lost, bring a compass. 2 hands of a timepiece

pandon goal, end, destination. *tekan ing* * (upon) arriving at one's destination; in the end, finally. *Mati iku *ing ngaurip.* All living things finally die. *See also* ENDON

pandrija the five senses. *See also* PANTJA

panḍu *wj* father of the Panḍawa brothers

panduka *rg var of* PADUKA

pandum destiny, fate. *nrima ing* * to accept one's lot. ***an** a share, one's portion. **an beras* rice ration. **ṁ/di*** to apportion, divide up, distribute. **ṁ/di*i** to distribute *or* apportion among. *See also* DUM

pandung 1 thief, burglar (*opt? kr for* MALING). 2 to fail to recognize (*sbst kr for* PANGLING)

pandurat moment, instant. **sa*** for an instant. *Sa* ora bisa ngendika apa*². He couldn't speak for a moment.

panḍuwur *ng,* **paninggil** *kr* **ṁ*** upward. *Tangan tengen diatjungaké menḍuwur.* He raised his right hand. *Tepining kali ndeder manḍuwur.* The river bank rises steeply. **sa*** 1 a superior. *komanḍan kompi sa** the company commander and his superior officers. *Sa*ku kabèh wis paḍa pènsiun.* Everybody above me has retired. 2 and above. *Kaptèn sa* lungguhé nang larikan kapisan.* Captains and up sat in the front row. *lajang watjan kanggo pangkat telu sa** a reading book for grade three and up. *See also* ḌUWUR

panekuk̄ *var of* PANḌEKUK

panembahan *title for a high esteemed person, usu. a holy hermit*

panembrâmâ a gamelan melody and choral number for welcoming a celebrity

panembung 1 a certain gamelan instrument. 2 *form of* TEMBUNG

panèn harvest. ***an** to take in the harvest. **ṁ/di*i** to take the harvest from [a field]. *See also* ANI

panengeran crown of the head (*ki for* UNJENG²AN)

panèwu administrative officer having authority over village leaders (*esp. Jogjanese term: see also* TJAMAT). **ka*ṅ** 1 territory over which the above officer has jurisdiction. 2 office *or* residence of the above official

pang 1 branch. *Wit klapané * telu.* The coconut tree has three branches. 2 drop leaf for lengthening a table. **nge*** to grow *or* put out branches

pangadjab *ltry* wish, hope; goal, ideal. **ku katrima.* My dreams materialized. **ṁ*** to have [a certain goal] for smn; to have high hopes that smn will achieve a goal. *See also* ADJAB

pangadjeng leader; future (*kr for* PANGAREP)

pangagem clothing; way of dressing (*ki for* PANGANGGO)

pangageng person in authority (*kr for* PANGGEḌÉ)

pangajubagja congratulations. **ṁ*** to offer one's best wishes

pangaksâmâ, pangaksami forgiveness, pardon

pangalèr *kr for* PANGALOR

pangalor *ng,* **pangalèr** *kr* **ṁ*** northward (*see* MANGALOR). **ṁ/di*aké** to move sth to(ward) the north. **sa*(é)** everything to the north (of). *Sa*é désa mau wis klebu désa lija.* Everything north of the village belongs to another village. *See also* LOR

pangan *ng,* **teḍa** *kr* 1 (**ḍahar·an** *ki*) food, sth to eat. *sanḍang ** food and clothing, *i.e.* the basic necessities. *golèk ** to get sth to eat; to earn a living. 2 *ltry* cooked rice. **(pe)*an** (**ḍahar·an** *ki*) 1 things to eat. *Apa *an ana ing asrama kuwi énak?* Is the food good at the dormitory? **an sisa* leftovers. *dat *an* calorie. 2 cookies, refreshments. **ṁ/di*** (*ϕ*/**di·ḍahar** *ki*) to eat; to consume. **en sega iki.* Eat this rice. *mangan awan/bengi* to eat lunch/dinner. *Bajarané wis di* karo séwa omah ṭok.* Just the rent alone used up his whole salary. **mangan ati** to displease, disappoint. **mangan ganti adjang** to eat the food provided for an absent person; *fig* fickle. **mangan ng·ombé** 1 to eat and drink. 2 to enjoy one's meals without working to help provide them. **mangan turu** 1 to eat and sleep. 2 *sms* MANGAN NGOMBÉ 2. **mangan ujah** experienced. *wis akèh anggoné ṁ* ujah* rich in experience. **me·ṁ*** 1 to eat frequently. 2 act(ion) of eating. *Memangan ja kudu nganggo tata-tjara.* When you eat, you must watch your table manners. **ṁ/di*aké** to give [food] to. *Weḍus kuwi arep di*aké matjan kaé.* The lamb is to be fed to the tiger. **ṁ/di*i** 1 to eat constantly. 2 to provide food for. *Jèn ora njambut gawé, anak bodjoné arep di*i apa?* If he doesn't work, how is he going to support his family? *Wong lara bèri² umumé di*i katjang idjo.* People with beriberi are usually fed green nuts. **pa·ṁ*** act *or* way of eating. *Pamangané saka seṭiṭik.* He eats little by little.

pangaṇḍap downward (*root form: kr for* PANGISOR)

panganggé *kr for* PANGANGGO

panganggo *ng,* **panganggé** *kr,* **pangagem** *ki* 1 clothing; sth to wear. *Keris iku diétung sawidjiné * tjara Djawa.* The kris is considered an item of Javanese wearing apparel. 2 way of dressing. *Klambiné apik, ning *né salah.* Her dresses are nice, but she wears them inappropriately. **m̈*** to put on *or* wear [clothing]. **m̈/di*ni** to dress smn (in). *See also* ANGGO

pangantèn *formal var of* MANTÈN

pangantyan *oj* bride, groom; bridal

panganugrâhâ blessing, boon (*ltry var of* NUGRAHA)

pangarep *ng,* **pangadjeng** *kr* 1 leader; one who presides. 2 future. *tembung * (gram)* future word. **m̈*** to move to(ward) the front. *Mangga kula aturi mengadjeng.* Please come forward. **m̈/di*aké** to move sth forward *or* toward the front. *mengarepaké kursi* to move a chair up front. **m̈/di*i** to lead, preside over. ***-arep** a hope, desire, wish; **m̈/di*-arep** *ltry* to expect; to look forward to. *See also* AREP[b]

pangaribâwâ influence. ** kulonan* Western influence. **m̈/di*ni** to influence; to bring about through influence

pangawak physical (tangible) form. ** sétan* a devil in the flesh

pangawikan *oj* knowledge, learning

pangéran 1 God. 2 *title for males of the nobility: all sons of monarchs.* *** adipati anom** crown prince. *** harja (angabèhi)** *title for males of the nobility.* *** pati** *inf* crown prince

pangèstu blessing, good wishes, prayers. *njuwun ** to ask for smn's blessings. ***né** thanks to smn's kindness (in asking *or* showing interest). **nipun bapak, sedaja wiludjeng.* We're all fine, thank you. **mu ija betjik.* Fine, thanks. **m̈* pada** *wj* to make a humble gesture of obeisance. **m̈/di*ǹi** to bestow one's blessings on smn. *See also* ÈSTU

pangétan **m̈*** eastward (*see* MANGÉTAN). *Kali mau mengétan iliné.* The river flows east. **m̈/di*aké** to move sth eastward. **sa*(é)** that which lies to the east (of). *See also* ÉTAN, WÉTAN

panggah strong, enduring, remaining as before. *Éjangku wis juswa wolung puluh nanging isih * waé.* My grandfather is eighty but he's still going strong. *Sanadyan dikrubut Kurawa nanging tetep * waé.* He was rushed by the Kurawas but he stood his ground.

panggang broiled food, food cooked over an open fire *or* charcoal. *pitik ** broiled chicken. *roti ** toast. ***an** 1 broiled; (act of) broiling. 2 equipment for broiling. **m̈/di*** 1 to cook by broiling. 2 to toast at an open fire. *Ḍèwèké ndjupuk geni ing anglo kanggo manggang sikilé.* He got some coals from the brazier to warm his feet. *** pé** roof made of dried coconut leaves. *See also* KEMANGGANG

panggawé *ng,* **pandamel** *kr* magic spell. **m̈/di*** to cast a spell (on). *Laranè kena di* sétan.* His illness was brought about by a devil's spell. *See also* GAWÉ

panggeḍé *ng,* **pangageng** *kr* person in authority; boss. **m̈/di*ǹi** to preside over, be in charge of. *See also* GEḌÉ

panggel goiter

panggih to meet (*kr for* TEMU[a]). **p·in·anggih** to meet (*kr for* KE·PEṬUK)

panggil a request for sth. ***an** notice, document. *lajang *an* a letter of notification. **an pangumuman* a public notice. **pe*** *ltry var of *.* *Pe*é arep ketekan.* Her request will be granted.

panggiling ***an** 1 millstone. 2 act *or* way of proceeding through natural cycles. **an djagad* the earth's rotation. **m̈*an** to proceed through natural cycles. *See also* GILING, TJAKRA

panggul **m̈/di*** to carry on the shoulder. *manggul patjul* to carry a hoeing tool. *Beḍilé didjupuk di*.* He took the rifle and raised it to his shoulder.

panggulu *ng kr,* **panenggak** *ki* second child. *anaké sing ** her second child. *See also* GULU, TENGGAK

panggung (*or* ***an**) 1 attic. 2 platform built on piles above flood level. 3 open-air pavilion for spectators. *See also* SILA

panghulu *var of* PANGULU

pangidul **m̈*** southward (*see* MANGIDUL). **m̈/di*aké** to move sth to(ward) the south. **sa*(é)** that which lies to the south (of). *Sa* duwèkku.* Everything to the south is mine. *sa*é omahku* everything south of my house. *See also* KIDUL

pangilèn westward (*root form: kr for* PANGULON)

panginggil upward (*root form: kr for* PANḌUWUR)

pangisor *ng,* **panganḍap** *kr* **m̈*** downward.

Kantjil njeḍaki sumur ndeleng mengisor. Mouse-Deer approached the well and looked down into it. *Saja mengisor saja aḍem.* The lower you go, the colder it gets. **m̃/di*aké** to cause to go down(ward). *Saben olèh pelem di*aké.* Every mango he picked he tossed down. **sa*** (together with) those below. *Kaptèn sa* ora éntuk kenḍaraan.* No transportation is provided for captains and below. *Sa*ku kabèh wis paḍa pènsiun.* All of my subordinates have already retired. *See also* ISOR

pangkat 1 rank, position, status. *wong * luhur* a high-ranking person. *Pamanku munggah *é.* My uncle has been promoted. 2 departure. **é djam pitu ésuk.* He left at 7 A.M. 3 grade in school. **m̃*** **(djengkar** *ki*) to depart, leave. *Ajo mangkat.* Come on, let's get going! *mangkat numpak kapal* to depart by ship. *wilangan* **pa*an** ordinal number(s)

pangkelung **pangkelang-*** to keep bending *or* swaying

pangku to sit on smn's lap. *Anaké ndjaluk * Slamet.* Slamet's daughter asked if she could sit on his lap. ***n̂** 1 lap. *Anaké mlorod saka pangkoné.* The child slid off her lap. 2 a Javanese-script character written at the end of a word to cut off a syllable. **m̃/di*** 1 to hold smn on the lap; *fig* to have sth close in front of one. *Di* mbokné.* His mother held him on her lap. *Omahku mangku dalan geḍé.* The highway goes smack in front of our house. 2 to carry all the expenses of sth, *esp.* a wedding. 3 to cut off a syllable in Javanese script by writing the above (2) character at the end. **sa*n̂** a complete set of gamelan instruments

pangkur a certain classical verse form. *** lâmbâ** a variation of this form

panglari crossbeam to which roofing tiles are affixed

panglima field commander (military rank)

pangling to fail to recognize. *Saupama kepeṭuk ana ing dalan, kira² *.* If I met him on the street I doubt if I'd know him. *Aku ora *–iku arak omahku ḍéwé!* I recognize it—it's my own house! ***an** not good at remembering faces. **m̃*i** unrecognizable because of looking much better than usual. *Pengantèné wadon manglingi.* The bride looked beautiful.

panglong earlier in the month than full moon. *tanggal kaping sanga wajah ** on the ninth of the month, before the moon was full

pangot a large knife with a broadly curving blade

pang-pung *see* PUNG

pangsit Chinese-style meat ball

pangulon *ng,* **pangilèn** *kr* **m̃*** westward (*see* MANGULON). **m̃/di*aké** to move sth to(ward) the west. **sa*(é)** what lies to the west (of). *See also* KULON

pangulu principal Islamic religious official in the community. ***n̂** place where the above official resides *or* officiates. *** banju** village official in charge of irrigation. *** hakim** religious official who officiates at weddings. *** landrat** official who administers oaths. *See also* ULU

pangur 1 chiseling tool. 2 carpenter's plane. 3 tooth file; evenly filed [of teeth] (obsolete fashion). **m̃/di*** to file [teeth]

panik̄ panic

panili vanilla; the plant from whose blossoms vanilla is extracted. *ès krim ** vanilla ice cream

paningal vision; view (*kr for* PANDELENG)

paningset 1 a gift to one's bride symbolizing the tie between them. 2 sash (*ki for* SABUK). **m̃/di*i** to give [one's bride] such a gift. *See also* SINGSET

panitija committee

panitra secretary

panitya *var sp of* PANITIJA

panon *ng,* **paningal** *kr* (*ltry*) sight, vision, eyes. *anglam-lami ing paningal* very pleasing to the eye. *Sanalika *é peteng.* Immediately his vision became dim. *See also* TON

panongsong *form of* SONGSONG

pânṭâ group, team; portion, share. *Ana rong *, sa*né wong sewelas.* There are two teams, eleven members to a team. **m̃/di*(-*)** to divide into groups/portions. *Ibu lagi manṭa² segané sing arep dibagèkké nang wong ngemis.* Mother is portioning out the rice for the beggars. **ma*-*** *ltry var of* PE*N *below.* **pe*n** (having been) divided into groups/portions. *Wong² mau lungguhé pe*n.* The people were seated in groups. *Segané wis pe*n.* The rice is divided into portions. **sa*** one handful, one lump, one group

pantalon long pants. ***an** to put on *or* wear long pants

pantar ***an** about the same age (as). *Ḍèké *anku.* He's about my age. **m̃*i** *sms* *AN

pantasi fantasy; imaginative tale

pantèk wedge driven into a space to make sth fit tighter. **ṁ/di*** to equip [a loose fitting] with such a wedge; to drive a wedge into

panṭeng **ṁ/di*** **1** to pull sth taut *or* straight. 2 to require a total effort. *Tapané manṭeng.* He devoted himself to his meditations.

pantes appropriate, deserving, suitable, becoming. *Dikritik sing *.* It was criticized justly. *Sapa baé kang * diwènèhi pitulungan.* Help is given to anyone deserving it. *papan konggrès sing ** a suitable place to hold the meeting. ** dadi kawigatèn.* It deserves to be taken seriously. ** ngantuk, lha wong sawengi ora turu.* Of course you're sleepy—you didn't get any sleep all night. *Wong Amérika kaé kok ja * nganggo penganggo tjara Djawa.* Javanese-style dress is very becoming to that American. ***an** characteristically appropriate, suitable, *etc. Wong kuwi *an.* She looks nice in whatever she wears. **(me)ṁ*** *or* **ṁ*i** 1 to make attractive/becoming. *mantesi omah* to fix up a house nicely. *Sing kondang pinter memantes iku wong Sala.* The Solonese are known for their attractive dress. 2 to resolve *or* settle [a dispute, conflict]. **sa*é** what is appropriate. *njuguh mangan sa*é* to serve the best food one can afford. *diupakara ing sa*é* to be taken care of suitably. *See also* PATUT

panti house; place. *** waluja** hospital

pântjâ *oj* five. *** baja** danger. *Pradjurité pada sikep gegaman siaga jèn ana *baja.* The soldiers were armed and ready for any eventuality. *** drija** the five senses. *See also* PANTJA SILA

pantjad ***an** sth to stand/step up on; a steppingstone. *Ana tapak dridji kang kena kanggo *aning pepriksan.* There are fingerprints to act as a starting point for the investigation. **ṁ/di*(i)** to stand/step up onto

pantjah **ṁ/di*(i)** to criticize, find fault (with). **ṁ/di*i** to defy, challenge. *See also* WANTJAH

pantjak ***an** *rg* 1 newly arrived. 2 ritual ceremony in honor of a baby, attended by small children, at which the child's future is foretold symbolically. **ṁ/di*** to catch with both hands. *** sudji** iron fence set in a masonry base

pântjâkârâ *oj* to fight, to battle

pantjal **ke*** 1 to get kicked. *Krikilé ke* sikil.* His feet kicked up pebbles. 2 to get left behind, miss one's transportation. *ke* sepur* to miss the train. **ṁ/di*** 1 to kick accidentally. *Kutjingé mantjal piring.* The cat stepped against the plate. 2 to divorce [one's husband]. **mantjal donja** to die. **mantjal kemul** 1 to fall asleep. 2 late supper, midnight snack. **pa·ṁ*** money received by the wife before she divorces her husband. *** donja** to die

pântjâniti *oj* palace conference hall

pantjar **ṁ*** to shine with radiant beauty. **ṁ/di*aké** to broadcast. **pa·ṁ*** a broadcast; act of broadcasting

pântjârobâ *oj* 1 a great storm. 2 transition period. *mangsa ** change of season. *Saiki lagi djaman *.* These are changing times.

pantjas ***an** cut (off). *londjoran tebu sing wis *an* cut sugar-cane stalks. ***-*an** act of cutting wood. **ṁ/di*aké** to cut [wood] for smn. **ṁ/di*(i)** to cut [wood] through with a single stroke. **ṁ/di*i** to forbid. *Di*i ibuné.* His mother wouldn't let him go. *See also* ANTJAS, TJAS

Pantjā Silā the Five Principles on which the Indonesian Republic is based. *See also* PANTJA

Pantjā Silais one who adheres to the Five Principles (above)

pantjèn *ng,* **pantji** *kr, ltry* certainly, really, for a fact; it is true. *Ḍèké kuwi * botjah lantip.* He's a really smart boy! ** bener.* It *is* true. *Toja punika pantji dèrèng umob.* Sure enough, the water *isn't* boiling yet. ***a** *or* ***é** **(pantjèn·ipun** *kr*) it is (would be, would have been) a fact that... **é arep tilik sapa?* Who is he *really* going to visit? **a tamu saka Sala ija, nanging ora bisa rawuh.* There were to be guests from Solo too, but they couldn't make it. **a ésuk iki aku wis tekan Surabaja.* I could have been in Surabaya this morning [if I had left yesterday].

pantjer 1 related by blood. *putra mantu, dudu putra * kakung* his son by marriage—not his own son. 2 direction, destination. *Dalan iki *é marang kantor pos.* This street goes to the post office. 3 original form. *djeneng ** original childhood name retained after marriage (rather than adopting a new one, as is customary). ** ing tembung sing rinimbag* the original form of the [grammatically] inflected word. **ṁ/di*** to stare (at) mindlessly

pantji 1 cooking pan. *wadjan (lan) ** pots and pans. 2 portion, share. 3 for a fact; it is true (*kr, ltry for* PANTJÈN). **m̃*** **1** pan. *Sopé koplak ing mantji.* The soup sloshed around in the pan. **2** (*psv* **di***; *or* **m̃/di*ǹi**) to give smn his portion. *mantjèni sega* to dish out the rice. *Jèn wis dipantjèni ora bisa ndjupuk ḍéwé.* When you've been given your share, you can't help yourself to more.

pantjik **m̃/di*(i)** to stand on [sth, in order to reach higher]. *mantjiki kursi* to stand on a chair

pantjing fishing equipment (rod, hook). *wilah ** fishing rod. ** rawé* fishing line strung with many hooks. ***an** **1** bait. *Apa suwara sedjati apa mung *an?* Is he telling the truth or is it just a come-on? **2** to fish around. *Ngertèni kareping lijan bisa *an.* You can find out what people want by sounding them out. ***en** (to have) a very painful sore throat. **m̃/di*** to catch fish; *fig* to catch by baiting *or* trapping. *tukang mantjing* fisherman. *Mantjing mantu sarana banḍa.* They hooked their son-in-law with money. *Kabèh wadiné wis ke*.* She wormed all his secrets out of him. **pa·m̃*** bait (*lit, fig*). *See also* ÑJ·SENḌAL, TIGAS

pantjlas *var of* PANTJAS

pantjrut *ptg ** to spatter. **m̃*(-m̃*)** to spurt. *Mangsiné mantjrut.* The ink squirted out [from the pen].

pantjur ***an** faucet; spring; fountain. ***an ka(a)pit senḍang** girl-boy-girl sibling combination. **m̃*** to flow downward, stream out. *Getihé mantjur.* The blood poured out. *See also* TJUR

pantog *var of* PENTOG

pantun rice plant (*kr for* PARI)

pantya *ltry var of* PANTI

panu skin disease causing light-colored blemishes

panudju **1** objective, goal. *Jèn pantjèn wis dadi *né, aku ming manut waé.* If that's really what he wants, I can only go along with it. **2** (heart's) desire. *Ana putri sidji sing dadi *ning galih.* He's got his heart set on a certain girl. **ka*(ñ)** in accordance with smn's wish. *kapanudjoning ati* what makes smn happy. *See also* TUDJU

panukma reincarnation. **m̃*** to be reincarnated, to return in another form. *See also* SUKMA

panuksma *var of* PANUKMA

panunggal *ng,* **panunggil** *kr* ***an** things in the same category. **m̃*** the same; joined. *Tudjuané manunggal lan aku.* His destination was the same as mine. *Loro²né wis manunggal ing tékad.* Both were equally determined. **sa*an** things in the same category; **lan sa*ané** (*abbr:* **lsp.**) and so forth. *gagak, ulung, lsp.* crows, hawks, *etc.* *See also* TUNGGAL

panunggil *kr for* PANUNGGAL

panunggul **1** middle finger. **2** gem set in the center (of a ring, earring, *etc.*). **3** the first *or* most important thing, the foremost consideration. *See also* TUNGGUL

paos tax (*kr for* PADJEG)

pap dad, pop (*inf Westernized var of* BAPAK)

pâpâ **1** misery and suffering; poverty, misfortune. *nanḍang ** to endure privation. *Si A bisa uwal saka *né.* A succeeded in fighting his way up from poverty. **2** *inf var of* APA². **ora *** of little significance, no cause for worry. *Sekuteré ringsek nanging wongé ora *.* The scooter was a wreck, but the rider was all right. *** tjintraka** *sms* * 1

papag ***an** **1** vehicle in which smn is met, *e.g.* upon his arrival smw. **2** to meet from opposite directions. *Sidji saka kidul, sidjiné saka lor, arep *an.* One was coming from the south and the other from the north on a collision course. **ka*an** a meeting (from different directions). **m̃/di*** **1** to pick up, call for. *Aku arep mapag kantjaku ana ing statsiun.* I'm going to pick up a friend of mine at the station. *Ḍèké ora di*.* There was no one there to meet him. **2** to meet and pass [sth which is going in the opposite direction]. **m̃/di*aké** **1** to go to meet. *mapagaké tekané mungsuh* to meet the approaching enemy. **2** to have smn go to meet. *Di*aké perḍana menteri.* He was sent to meet the prime minister.

papah center stalk of a leaf. ***an** kitchen shelf. **m̃*** **1** resembling a leaf stalk. **2** to make use of a leaf stalk. *Ḍèké wis tekan ing ḍuwur, bandjur mapah.* He reached the top [of the coconut tree] and sat on a leaf stalk.

papak **1** blunt (rather than pointed *or* tapering). **2** dull [of objects; of wits]. **3** level, even (with). ** lambé* brimful. *geḍong ** flat-roofed building. *prang ** an evenly-matched war. *Kenja iki ora bakal bisa * karo botjah kaé.* She can never come up to his level. **ke*en** excessively blunt (level, dull). *Anggonmu ngeṭoki kukuku adja ke*en.* Don't trim my nails too short. **m̃*** level, of equal height. *Bareng wis tuwa pariné paḍa mateng mapak.* Mature rice plants are ripe and all the same height. **ṁ/di*i** to make level/even. *Pager pring iku di*i.* He trimmed the bamboo hedge evenly.

papan 1 place, position. * *(kang) ḍuwur* a high place. * *bal²an* a place to play soccer; soccer position. * *patemon* or * *pasamuan* meeting place. * *dolanan* children's play area. 2 board. * *tjatur* chessboard, checkerboard. 3 the appropriate circumstances, the right place and time. * *(lan) empané ḍéwé²* each in its own proper place. **ṁ*** 1 to take one's place, get into position. *mapan turu* to get into bed. *Wong aku durung mapan kok!* I haven't even sat down yet! 2 to settle smw. *Bareng wis omah nèng Djakarta rong tahun ja wis mapan saiki.* Now that we've lived in Djakarta for two years, we're finally settled. 3 apt, to the point. *Bantahané mapan banget.* His argument was cogent. 4 because. *Pantjèn wiwit tjilik uripé nang désa, mapan ḍèwèké kuwi seneng njepi.* He's *always* lived in villages —he likes quiet. **ṁ/di*aké** (*opt prn* **ṁ/di-papak·aké**) to put sth in place. *Dolananmu kuwi mbok dipapanaké.* Put your toys where they belong.

papas *var of* PAPRAS

papat *ng*, **(se)kawan** *kr* four. *telung puluh* * 34. *potlod* * 4 pencils. * *limang taun* 4 or 5 years. *djam* * 4 o'clock. ***an** about four. *Ana wong *an sing kèri.* There were about four people left. ***-*** by fours. *Muridé djèdjèr *-*.* The students sat in rows of four. ***-*é** all four of them. *Anaké *-*é dadi ḍokter.* All four of their children are doctors. **ka*** 1 (*or* **[ka]ping** *) four times; times four; (for) the fourth time; fourth in a series. 2 *ng kr* fourth month of the Javanese year (18 September–25 October). **ṁ/di*i** (**ñj/dipun·sekawan·i** *kr*) to form a group of four. *Ḍèwèké tuku gelas sidji kanggo mapati.* She bought one glass, to fill a set of four. *See also* -AN (*suffix*) 8, 15, 16; -É[c] (*suffix*) 9; NG- (*prefix*) 6, 7; PAT; PATANG; PRA-

papilijun 1 pavilion. 2 annex to a main house, *usu.* a garage rebuilt as living quarters

papon container for slaked lime (*form of* APU)

papral *var of* PAPRAS

papras **ṁ/di*** to cut off, trim. *Pangé di*.* He pruned back the branch.

par- *see also under* PR- (*Introduction, 2.9.3*)

pârâ 1 *person pluralizer.* * *ratu* the kings. *kanggo ngurmati rawuhé * tamu* to honor the guests' arrival. * *kantja paḍa dolan nang plataran.* Let's all play in the yard. 2 those who. * *pinter* the skilled ones; the scholars, the intelligentsia. * *botoh* gamblers. * *maos* our readers. * *pamiarsa* the [radio] listeners. 3 *n*th part. * *telu* -third. *sa* telon* one-third. 4 bamboo rack (*rg var of* PAGA). 5 *oj* you, your. ***n** 1 division (arithmetic process). 2 way, course (*see* PARAN). **di*-*** divided up. *Beras éntuk²ané panèn di*-* nganti rata.* The rice crop was divided equally. **ṁ*** 1 to approach. *Wis mara lungguha kono.* Come and sit down! 2 to have a try (at). *Mara tjritakna saélingmu.* Tell me everything you remember about it. 3 (*psv* **di***) to divide (up). *Nembelas di* papat ana papat.* Sixteen divided by 4 is 4. **mara ḍajoh** *or* **mara tamu** to visit (*see also* MERḌAJOH). **mara séba** to visit [a king]. **mara tangan** to hit with the hand. **mara tjangkem** to quarrel. **mara tuwa** parents-in-law. *bapak (ibu) mara tuwa* father-(mother)in-law. **pa*n** quotient. **pa·ṁ*** 1 act *or* way of dividing. *Pamarané kurang adil.* He didn't divide it fairly. 2 divisor. *Bisané éntuk papat saka rong puluh iku perlu pamara lima.* To get four from twenty, you divide by five. *See also* PARAN

parab ***an** nickname, epithet. *Djenengé Sarijem, nanging kang karan mung *ané jaiku Bawuk.* Her name is Sarijem, but she's called by her nickname, Bawuk. **(a)pe*** by the name of. *panḍita linuwih pe* Durna* a revered holy man named Durna. **ṁ/di*i** to (nick)name smn. *Di*i Si Genḍut.* They call him Fatty.

parag **ke*** to get attacked by a destructive force. *Tebuné ke* ing ama.* The sugar-cane was infested with a disease.

parak **ke*** 1 female palace retainer who sits beside the monarch. *ke* kiwa/tengen* retainer who sits on the king's left/right. 2 to be approached *or* visited. *jèn ke* ing lara mau* if you're exposed to the disease. **ṁ*** [of women] to sit humbly before a king to pay one's respects. *See also* PINARAK

pârâmartâ *oj* good; noble. *See also* AMBEK

parâmâsastrâ grammar; grammatical system of a language. * *Djawa* Javanese grammar. *lajang²* * treatises on grammar

parampârâ spokesman; chairman. *dipilih dadi* * to be chosen as spokesman/chairman

paran *ng,* **purug** *kr* 1 way, course, destination. *ana ing ∗* along the way. *Menjang ngendi baé ∗é kakangné, mesṭi dietut.* Wherever his brother went, he was sure to follow. *Ana latjaké getih, kang nuduhaké ∗é.* A trail of blood showed which way he had gone. 2 (*or* **pe∗**) away from home; abroad. **m̃/di∗aké** (*prn* **m̃/di·parak·aké** *ng*) 1 to cause, bring about. *marakaké mumet* to give smn a headache. 2 to convey, escort. *Banjuné tebu mau diparakaké menjang djembangan.* The sugar-cane juice is conveyed to a large earthen pot. **m̃/di∗i** 1 to approach sth. *Ana swara anèh, bareng di∗i meneng.* There was a funny noise; when he went toward it, it stopped. 2 to go get, pick up. *Aku menjang omahé gredji marani klambi.* I'm going to the tailor's to get my shirt. 3 to walk right into [trouble]. **ula marani gitik** *or* **kutuk marani sunduk** *describing a trouble-prone person.* **sa∗é** *or* **sa∗-∗** anywhere, in any direction. *Ḍèwèké lunga sa∗-∗.* He wandered from place to place. *sapari-polahé lan sa∗-∗é* whatever you do and wherever you go. **∗ djudjug·an** a place *or* person visited frequently. *Jèn grebegan, omahku dadi ∗ djudjugan tumrap sedulur²* *saka kuṭa lija.* At festival time, the out-of-town relatives head for *my* house. **∗ tutuh·(an)** scapegoat. *See also* PARA

parandéné even so, nevertheless

parang 1 basic batik pattern having diagonal S-shaped rows. 2 knife, weapon. 3 cliff. *Pasisiripun aḍapur ∗ tjuri.* The coastline consists of stark cliffs. **m̃∗** to use a knife as a weapon. **∗ barong** batik design reserved for royal families' garments. **∗ kusuma** basic design with S-shaped motif. **∗ rusak** design similar to ∗ BARONG but smaller

parangmuka *oj* disturbance, rebellion, aggression

paranjai maidservant to an aristocratic family

paranpârâ *var of* PARAMPARA

Pararaton The Book of Kings (narration of the historic figures Kèn Arok and his descendants, the kings of Madjapait. *See also* RATU

paras 1 a pinch (unit of measure). *suruh sa∗* a pinch of betel-leaf. 2 (to get) a haircut (*ki for* TJUKUR). **∗an** having the top cut off. *La iki ana degan tur wis ∗an, dak ombéné.* Ah, here's a young coconut and it's cut—I'll drink the liquid. **∗-∗** knife. **m̃/di∗(i)** to cut off [smn's hair; the end of a young coconut]. **∗ Sutji** haircut worn by Catholic priests and nuns

parastra *oj* dead; to die

parat (*or* **ke∗**) damn you!

pardika **∗n** [of land] free, unencumbered by taxes. *Kawula mau dipijagemi tanah perdikan.* A parcel of tax-free land was bestowed on the [loyal] subject. **m̃∗** free (*see* MARDIKA)

paré certain climbing vines; the fruits of such vines

parek̄ *ka* **∗an** an audience with a high-ranking official. **m̃/di∗(i)** to have an audience (with)

parem a mixture of dried ground herbs and water, used as a linament. *djamu ∗* a certain medicinal drink. **m̃/di∗i** to apply the above linament to [smn]

pareng 1 to have *or* be given permission. *Udud sing nganggo tjandu ora ∗.* Opium smoking is not allowed. 2 to say goodbye, to ask permission to leave (*kr for* PAMIT). **m̃/di∗aké** to give permission. *Jèn di∗aké Sing Kuwasa aku arep njambut gawé nang Djakarta.* God willing, I'll work in Djakarta. **jèn ∗** 1 if one is permitted. 2 God willing. *See also* KEPARENG

parepat *var of* PERPAT

parepatan meeting, conference

parfem perfume

pari 1 (**pantun** *kr*) rice plant (growing, or harvested but still unhulled). *Suguhané sega liwet ∗ anjar isih anget.* They were served warm boiled rice made from the newly harvested crop. 2 *compounding element: see* PARI- *entries below.* **∗ dalem** *or* **∗ djero** slow-growing rice, *i.e.* the choicest rice, which takes over six months to mature. *nandur ∗ djero* to cast one's bread upon the waters. **∗ gaḍu·n̂** rice grown in a paddy during the dry season. **∗ gaga** rice grown in a dry field. **∗ géndjah** quick-growing rice: first harvest taken from the paddies cultivated during the dry season. **∗ walik·an** rice grown between the *gaḍon* (above) harvest and the beginning of the wet season. **∗ wuluh** unhusked rice grains

paribâsâ proverb, saying, expression. **∗n** 1 *sms ∗.* 2 practically speaking; it could be said that... *Sawengi ketjeput aku ∗n ora nglèjèh.* All night long I got practically no chance to get to bed. **m̃/di∗kaké** to apply a proverb to. *Jèn A kepéngin njuwun putrané B, kena di∗kaké tjebol nggajuh lintang.*

A wanting to marry B's daughter is like the saying "a dwarf reaching for the stars." **m̄/di*ni** to express sth as a proverb

paridjâṭâ 1 a classical verse form. 2 a certain tree, also its fruit

parigawé a special occasion *or* sth important that requires help from many people. *See also* GAWÉ

parik *rg var of* ṬARIK

parik'an a chanting song, consisting of a senseless string of words containing repetitious syllables, made up by children to ridicule *or* taunt smn. *duwé ** to make demands. *Ḍèké gelem dipèk bodjo nanging duwé **. She was willing for him to marry her, but first he had to do thus-and-so. *sugih ** demanding in nature

parikedah *kr for* PARIKUDU

parikena *see* GUJU·Ñ, SEMBRANA

parikrâmâ having nice manners. *See also* KRAMA

parikudu *ng,* **parikedah** *kr* 1 to have a longing *or* compulsion (to). 2 to force; to rape. *See also* KUDU

parimarma, parimirma pity, compassion

paring (*ki for* WÈNÈH) 1 [of an exalted person] to give. 2 a gift. ***an** *or* **pe*** gift from an exalted person. *njuwun *-** to beg (for food, money). **m̄/di*aké** 1 to give sth. *Ibu maringaké dolanan iki marang aku.* Mother gave me this toy. 2 to put sth smw (*ki for* N/DI·DOKOK·AKÉ). **m̄/di*i** to give to smn. *Ibu maringi aku ḍuwit.* Mother gave me some money. **maringi weruh** to tell, inform. **p·in·aring·an** to be granted God's permission. *Menawa pinaringan slamet tahun ngarep aku arep nang Djakarta.* God willing, I'll be going to Djakarta next year. *** **dalem** a gift from a social superior. ***-priksa** (*root form*) 1 to put sth smw (*ki for* DÈLÈH). 2 to forbid (*ki for* ÉLIK). 3 to show (smn) (sth) (*ki for* TUDUH). 4 to advise (*ki for* TUTUR)

paripaos *sbst kr for* PARIBASA

paripeksa *var of* PARIKUDU. *See also* RUḌA-PARIPEKSA

paripolah actions, behavior. *Sa*ku mung sarwa apik tumrap ḍèwèké.* Whatever I do is all right with him. *See also* POLAH

paripurna 1 finished, over. 2 (*prn* **paripurnā**) complete, plenary. *pasamuan ** or *sidang ** plenary session

parisuka to have fun, enjoy [them]selves. *See also* SUKA

pariwârâ *oj* announcement. *See also* WARA

pariwarta news. *See also* WARTA

pariwisâtâ 1 tourism; (the practice of) touring. *objèk ** a tourist attraction. 2 travel agent *or* agency. *See also* WISATA

pariwisatawan tourist

parkir to park [a vehicle]. *panggonan kanggo ** a parking place. *Mobilé di* tjeḍak grédja.* He parked his car near the church.

parkit parakeet

parlemèn parliament

paro *ng,* **palih** *kr* half. *Geḍangé * éḍing karo aḍiné.* He went halves on the banana with his brother. ***n** 1 half-and-half. *Sega paron iku sega sing digawé djagung se* beras se*.* Half-and-half (cooked) rice is made from half corn and half (raw) rice. 2 (*or* ***n-*n**) to share and share alike. *Jèn kasil, olèh²ané paron.* If it's successful, we'll go halves on the profits. **m̄/di*kaké** 1 to split for smn. 2 to have smn share the work and profits, *esp.* of a rice paddy. *Sawahé diparokaké.* He had smn help with his paddy on a share-the-profits basis. **m̄*n** rice paddy worked by two people who share the crop. **m̄/di*(ni)** to split in half. *maroni téla* to divide the cassavas in half. *Ajo didol wong loro, pepajoné ija di*.* Let's sell it and split the profits. **pa·m̄*** act *or* way of dividing. *Pamaro kudu paḍa bèn ora ana sing tukaran.* It'd better be divided equally so they won't quarrel. **se*** one half. *Awaké mati se*.* He's half paralyzed. *Durung entèk se* olèhé mangan.* He hadn't half finished his meal. *Rembulané kari se*.* The moon is in the third phase. **se*-se*** half-and-half. *èsem sing separo²* a half smile. *See also* MANGRO

paroki church parish

paron 1 anvil. 2 *form of* PARO

Parsi Iran (*var of* PERSI)

partai political party. ** politik* political party

parti désa *var of* BERSIH DÉSA

partikelir private(ly owned, operated). *dagang ** a privately-owned business; private enterprise. *sekolah * lan pemerintah* private and public schools. ***an** in a private capacity. *Pulisi mau menganggo *an.* The policeman is not in uniform. *Ḍines apa *an?* Is [the function] an official or social one?

partisipasi participation

paru *-** human lung. **iwak *** beef lung (fried as chips)

parud grater. ***an** (having been) grated.

*krambil *an* grated coconut. **m̈/di*** to grate. *marud klapa* to grate coconut. **pa·m̈*** 1 grater. 2 act *or* way of grating. *Béda pamaruté jèn arep gawé santen.* It is grated differently for making coconut milk.

paruk *rg* earthenware water container

parwâsâ **m̈/di*** 1 to force to surrender. 2 to rape

pas 1 a pass, *i.e.* document entitling one to sth. 2 just (the) right (amount, number). *Kanggo wong papat *.* It's just right for four people. *Ḍuwité mung epas kanggo tuku beras.* He has just enough money to buy rice with. 3 just about to. *Ḍèké * mangan gèk aku teka.* He was just sitting down to dinner when I got there. **nge*** right on time; just at the right moment. *Tekané nge* banget.* He got here right on the dot. **nge/di*aké** to make sth just right. *Olèhé mbeḍil di*aké nang sirahé matjan.* He shot the tiger right in the head.

pâsâ *ng,* **sijam** *kr* 1 to fast. *Olèhé * kuwat limalas dina.* He fasted rigidly for fifteen days. *Aku dikon * nalika wetengku lara.* He told me not to eat anything when I had a stomach ache. 2 *ng kr* ninth month of the Moslem calendar: the fasting month. **m̈/di*ni** to fast for [a certain objective]. *Ḍèwèké masani kanggo anaké karebèn bisa lulus udjiané.* She fasted [as a form of prayer] so that her son would pass his examinations. * **ng·asar** to fast until 4 P.M. * **m·beḍug** to fast until 12 noon. * **n·dina** to fast until 6 P.M. * **manuk** to have breakfast early rather than fasting (during Pasa month). * **tutup kenḍang** to fast on only the first and last days of the fasting month

pasâdjâ *var of* PERSADJA

pasah 1 carpenter's plane. * *kepel,* * *koḍok* varieties of short planes. 2 **(keṭik** *ki*) tooth file; [of teeth] evenly filed (obsolete fashion). 3 effectual. *Guna-gawéné ora *.* The magic spell didn't work. *ora ** unaffected (by); invulnerable. *Dibeḍil, ora *.* He was shot at but unharmed. **m̈/di*(i)** 1 to smooth with a plane. *masah blabag* to plane a board. 2 to chip [ice] from a large cake by moving it across a stationary plane. **pa·m̈*** action of planing

pasak a certain form of divorce, granted by a judge

pasal paragraph, article (of a document)

pasamuwan party, large social gathering

pasang to put in place, set up. * *geber* to set up a screen. * *gendéra* to raise a flag; *fig* to take up arms. ***an 1** arrangement, placing. **ané bata kuwat banget.* The bricks were laid for maximum strength. 2 trap. **an tikus* mousetrap. 3 ox yoke. 4 gambling stake. 5 certain Javanese script characters used for indicating vowels. 6 brick work for a house foundation. **an koṭongan* bricks laid without mortar. ***é** it seems. **é arep udan.* It looks as if it's getting ready to rain. **m̈/di*(i)** 1 to set sth up (out, forth); to set in place. *masang benik* to sew on a button. *m̈* adpertènsi* to place an advertisement. *m̈* ril dalan sepur* to lay railroad track. *m̈* wong²an* to set up a scarecrow. *Keboné m̈* sungu.* The kerbau lowered its horns [to attack]. *Gendérané di* ing putjuking tijang.* The flag was raised to the top of the pole. *Reḍaksi mau luput m̈* keteranganė.* The editor presented the information incorrectly. *Wongé sing nglalu anggoné m̈* nang ril sepur nganti rong djam ngentèni sepur liwat.* The suicide lay on the rails for two hours waiting for the train to come along. *Watuné tak *é manèh.* I'll put the stone back in place. *Saben dina di* urut²an lelakon iki.* They print an episode of this continued story every day. 2 to place [a bet]. *Aku mau mèlu lotré m̈* Rp. lima menang Rp. sepuluh.* I invested five rupiahs in a lottery and won ten. **masang tadji** to defend oneself by attacking his accuser. **m̈/di*i** 1 to equip sth with. *Peturonmu *ana klambu.* Put mosquito netting on your bed. *Anḍané wis di*i unton²é.* They've put the rungs on the ladder. 2 to catch in a trap. *masangi tikus* to trap mice/rats. **pa·m̈*** (action of) putting sth in place. *Pemasangé ésuk, pengunḍuhé soré.* They put it up in the morning and take it down in the evening. **se*** a pair, a couple. *djaran se** a team of horses. *sepatu se** a pair of shoes. *Kéwan mau sikilé telung *.* This insect has three pairs of legs. * **pariwara** to post an announcement. * **ka·prajitna·n** watchful, on the alert. * **rakit** composition, structure, design. *Unggah²ané ana papat, *-rakité paḍa.* There were four staircases, all of the same design. * **semu** *or* * **ulat** to assume a certain facial expression; to make one's feelings evident. * **walat** to put a curse (on)

pasanggiri 1 a promise to the effect that if one's wish is granted he will hold a celebration. 2 a prize contest

pasanggrah ***an** 1 an out-of-town villa or estate used as a residence for high-ranking people *or* as a stopover point for traveling high officials. 2 camp at a battlefield. **m̃*(an)** 1 to stop *or* stay at a villa (as above). 2 to camp on a battlefield. *See also* SANGGRAH

pasar *ng,* **peken** *kr* 1 market(place). *blandja menjang ** to go to the marketplace to shop. 2 five-day week (consisting of the days Legi, Paing, Pon, Wagé, Kliwon). *se** one five-day week. ***an** 1 (the group of) market days. *dina *an* day of the five-day week. 2 market day (in a particular community). 3 (to have) an imitation market. *Botjah*² *lagi *an.* The children are playing market. 4 customers, demand. **an plastik* the market for plastics. 5 ceremony honoring a child five days after birth. **pe*** to go to the marketplace to shop. **m̃*** to do business at the market as a seller or (*rg*) as a buyer. *** Baru** a large shopping center and marketplace in Djakarta. *** kéwan** livestock market. *** malem** fair, bazaar. *See also* SEPASAR

pasaréan 1 cemetery; grave, burial place (*ki for* KUBUR, (PA)·KUBUR·AN). 2 bed; bedroom (*ki for* PA·TURU·N̂)

pasbreg a game played with dominoes

pasèh [of speech] fluent, eloquent

pasek̄ **m̃/di*** to bury

paser a dart. ***an** dart game. **m̃/di*** to throw a dart (at)

pasièn medical patient

pasip *gram* passive

pasir sand (*kr for* WEḌI). ***an** 1 sea turtle. 2 a plant; a vine (*kr for* GAMBIR). **m̃*** resembling sand in texture. *** a·wukir** [of terrain] characterized by seashore and mountains

Paskah (*or* ***an**) Easter

pasok to hand over a payment; to pay a tribute. *Tukang bétjak kudu * Rp satus saben dina karo sing duwé.* The pedicab driver has to turn over 100 rupiahs a day to the cab owner. **m̃/di*aké** to make a payment for. *masokaké sawah* to pay smn for the use of his rice paddy. **m̃/di*i** 1 to hand over [a payment]. *Saben wulan masoki satus rupiah nggo nitjil utangé.* Every month he pays a 100-rupiah installment on his debt. 2 to supply with merchandise. *Tokoné saben dina di*i krupuk.* The shop gets in a supply of shrimp chips every day. *See also* ASOK

paspor passport. ** foto* passport picture

pasrah to give back, return, yield up. *Aku * karo kowé anggoné arep nḍiḍik anakku.* I am placing my child's education in your hands. **m̃/di*aké** to entrust sth, give over, delegate. *A masrahké putrané nang B.* A put his daughter in B's hands [for education, training]. *Ḍèwèké ora gelem masrahaké bali djam tangan sing ditemu mau.* He didn't want to give back the watch he had found. **m̃/di*i** to entrust to, turn over to. *sing di*i ngopèni omah* the one who was entrusted with the care of the house. *A masrahi B dalemé supaja ditunggu.* A is having B look after his house [while he's away]. *** Ng·alah** to submit to God's will, put oneself in God's hands. *** bongkok·(an)** *or* *** pati-urip** to surrender unconditionally. *See also* SRAH

pastèl 1 pastel, drawing chalk. 2 a meat-filled pastry

pasṭi *formal var of* PESTI

pastil *var of* PASTÈL

pastur Catholic priest. ***an** priest's home

pasu bridge of the nose

pasukan group of soldiers, military unit

pasurjan face (*ki for* RAI)

pat *ng* four (*shf of* PAPAT). *dji, ro, lu, *, ma* 1, 2, 3, 4, 5. ***-*** by fours. *Lakuné *-*.* They walked four by four. **ka*** fourth in a series. *buku sing ka** the fourth book. **ka* tengah** three and a half. *** belas** fourteen. *** likur** twenty-four

patah bridesmaid. **ke*(an)** to be assigned a task. *Sapa sing ke*an nandangi?* Who's supposed to do it? **m̃/di*(i)** to assign a task (to). *Ana prijajiné sing di* pamaréntah ndjaga alas*² *mau.* There's an official assigned by the government to keep watch over the forests.

paṭak head (*cr*). **m̃/di*** to hurl sth at. *maṭak asu nganggo watu* to throw a rock at a dog

patang *ng* four (*as modifier: see also* PAPAT). ** puluh* 40. ** puluh papat* 44. ** atus* (*èwu, juta*) four hundred (thousand, million). ** rupiah* four rupiahs. *telu * taun* three or four years. ***-puluh·an** *or* ***-puluh-dina·né** the 40th day after a death; **m̃/di*-puluh-dina·ni** to honor [the deceased] with a ceremony on the 40th day after his death. *See also* NG- (*prefix*) 6, 7

patarangan nesting place, *esp.* for poultry. **m̃*** to go to the nest in preparation for laying an egg. *See also* TARANG

paṭèk (**katrap** *opt kr?*) frambesia

patékah the first chapter in the Koran

patèn 1 patent(ed). *hak ** patent rights. *tamba ** patent medicine. 2 *form of* PATI[a]

pater *see* GETER

paṭes *intsfr* hard, forceful. *Udané deres **. It rained cats and dogs.

paṭet 1 key *or* mode of gamelan music; that part of a shadow play in which a certain mode of music is played. ** nem (sanga, manjura)* first (second, third) part of a play; music played during the first (second, third) part. 2 (*or* ***an**) mood song for a shadow play. **m̈/di*** 1 to stop the vibrations of a gamelan xylophone with the hand after striking the notes. 2 to tone down, restrain. *Olèhé mangan di* karebèn ora munḍak lemu.* She avoids overeating so she won't get fat.

pati[a] *ng,* **pedjah** *kr* 1 (**séda** *ki*) death. **né iwak*[2] *mau merga keratjunan.* The death of the fish was caused by poisons. *sédané Sultan* the Sultan's death. *diukum ** sentenced to death. *ukuman ** death penalty. 2 dead. 3 unusable. *tali ** rope with knots in it too tight to be untied. ***ǹ** 1 having ceased to function. *Lawang kuwi patèn.* The door has been sealed off. *Sambungané patèn, ora kena ditjopot.* The connection is stuck, it can't be taken apart. 2 Javanese syllabic character with a stroke added to remove the final vowel. 3 a sacrificial offering. ***ǹ-*ǹan** (**pedjah**[2]**an** *kr*) act of causing sth not to function. *Lawang kuwi gampang patèn*[2]*ané.* It would be easy to seal off that door. *Sing njebabaké lara kangker kuwi angèl *ǹ-*ǹané.* It's hard to eliminate the causes of cancer. **pe*** death. **ke*ǹ** to suffer loss through death. *Jèn ana sing kepatèn, wong*[2] *sadésa paḍa mèlu tandang.* When a family is bereaved, the whole village shares in the grief. **kepatèn obor** to lose track of a blood relationship through long separation. **m̈/di*** to make unusable. *Lawangé di*.* The door was nailed up. **m̈/di*k̀aké** 1 to allow to die. *Teṭukulan kaé mbok ja dipatèkaké waé.* You may as well let those plants die. **m̈/di*ǹi** 1 to kill. *dipatèni mungsuh* killed by the enemy. 2 to stop sth from functioning. *matèni geni* to put out a fire. *Lampuné patènana.* Turn off the light. *Tjaṭetan iki wis dipatèni.* This note has been crossed out. **sa*né** after/since one's death. *Sa*né bodjoné, ḍèwèké kudu njambut-gawé.* She's had to work ever since her husband died. *** geni** to fast in isolation as an act of self-denial performed to achieve an objective. *** raga** in a state of meditation, unaware of one's surroundings. *** urip** (in) life and death; come what may; destiny. *Soal iki soal *-urip.* This is a life-and-death matter. **-urip aku arep mèlu kowé.* No matter what happens, I'll be right with you. *masrahaké *-uripé* to put one's fate in [smn's] hands. *** waris** having no heirs. *See also* MATI, PATI-RASA

pati[b] *ng,* **patos** *sbst? kr* [not] very. *Aku ora * luwé.* I'm not very hungry. *ora * kerep* not too often. ***a** *sms **. **ke*** 1 *sms **. 2 [of sleep] deep, sound. **ke*-*** outstanding, unsurpassed

pati[c] 1 king; kingship, throne. *pangéran ** crown prince. 2 military brass

paṭi 1 starch, powder. ** pohung* cassava starch. ** onggok* powdery substance in the soft heart of sugar-palm-tree trunks. 2 essence. ** wulangan* the essence of the lesson. **m̈/di*** to make sth into powder/starch

patigawé money donated in lieu of voluntary help in a communal activity

patih 1 (*or* **pe***) assistant to a regent. 2 (*or* **pe***) grand vizier, king's chief counselor. 3 chess queen. **ka*an** residence of the above officials

patihah *var of* PATÉKAH

patik *rg var of* PATING

patikah *var of* PATÉKAH

patikelir *var of* PARTIKELIR

patil stinger of a fish. ***an** used for breeding purposes. *weḍus *an* a breeding goat. **m̈/di*** 1 to sting. *di* lélé* stung by a catfish. 2 to breed *or* mate [animals]. **m̈/di*aké** to have [an animal] mate with another

pating *particle which precedes a word referring to a visual or auditory or action effect and gives it a plural denotation (the effect is repeated or continuous, the performers are multiple, or both). swarané wong ptg brengok* the sound of people shouting. *ngguju ptg tjekakak* [plural people] roar with laughter. *Matané ali*[2]*ptg gebjar.* The jewel in the ring glittered. *ptg keḍangkrang* to dangle, keep hanging down loosely [of *e.g.* fringe, banners, a lantern]. *Ana tunggangan ptg sliri, ptg sriwet, nganti bingung aku.* Vehicles kept whizzing past, one right after the other, until I was bewildered.

pati-râsâ anesthesia. **m̈/di*** to anesthetize. *mati-rasa gusi* to deaden the gum. *See also* PATI[a]

patirta *n resort for taking restorative baths. **m̀*** to bathe in holy water. *See also* TIRTA

paṭis *rg var of* MAṬIS

patjak formal dress. ***an 1** formal dress. *Klambi sing abang iki kanggo *an.* This red dress is for formal wear. 2 formal decorations. ***é** it seems, it looks as if. **é kok nesu.* He looks mad. **pe*** regulations, laws. *Kabèh hak lan kwadjibané para warga wis diatur ana ing pe* organisasi.* All rights and obligations of the members are stated in the regulations. **di*** *or* **ka*** included, set forth [in a publication]. *di* ing anggaran ḍasar* set forth in the statutes. **m̀*** to dress up, dress in formal style. *matjak arep ndjagong mantèn* to get dressed to attend a wedding. **matjak n̈g·kajang batin** well-dressed. **m̀/di*i** to bedeck for a formal occasion. *Omahé wis di*i nganggo djanur arep ana gawé.* The house is decorated with young coconut leaves for the wedding party. **pa·m̀*** act *or* way of decorating. *** baris** in marching array *or* deployment. *** gulu** a certain neck movement in the classical dance

patjalang *ng*, **patjambeng** *kr* 1 a soldier who leads the march. 2 village police. **m̀*** to be(come) one of the above

patjambeng *kr for* PATJALANG

patjang ***an 1** fiancé(e). 2 engagement, betrothal. **m̀/di*aké** to promise [one's child] in marriage. *Anaké A sing wédok wis di*aké karo B.* A has affianced his daughter to B.

patjar **m̀/di*** to color the fingernails with primrose petals. *** banju**, *** kuku**, *** Tjina** varieties of primroses. *** wutah** shotgun bullets; **m̀/di*-wutah** to shoot with a shotgun

patjas *var of* PANTJAS

patjé a certain fruit, often made into a drink

patjek̄ short spear. **pa·m̀*** male animal for breeding. *sapi pamatjek* stud bull. *djago pam̀** breeding cock

patjel stunted in growth

patjet small leech (young of the LINTAH). **m̀*** at an impasse. *Rembuganè matjet.* The talks are deadlocked. *Mobilku matjet.* My car stalled. *Lalulintasé matjet.* The traffic is at a standstill.

patjing a certain flexible reed

patjit ***an** snacks served with tea. **an omong* to chat while having snacks. **m̀*** to eat snacks with tea

patjok ***-*an** to tease each other about smn of the opposite sex. **m̀/di*aké** to tease smn as above. *Martini isin banget jèn di*aké karo Darno.* It embarrasses Martini to be teased about liking Darno.

patjuh **pe*** infraction. *pe*ing angger²* violation of the rules

patjul a hoe-like farm tool for loosening soil. ***an 1** (having been) worked with the above tool. 2 (*or* **wong *an**) person whose job is to work with the above. ***-*** *or* **m̀*** to do hoeing. **m̀/di*(i)** to work [soil] with a *patjul. Lemahé di*i djero.* He loosened the soil deep down. *** kolong(-slanḍok)** a *patjul* with a square *or* rounded blade

paṭok wooden *or* bamboo boundary marker. **(pe)*an 1** *sms* *. 2 regulations. **m̀*** fixed, immovable. *Regané wis maṭok.* The price is fixed. **m̀/di*(i) 1** to mark sth (off) with stakes. 2 to set up regulations *or* criteria for

paṭola a fine soft silk material

patos 1 [not] very (*sbst? kr for* PATI[b]). 2 chief advisor (*sbst kr for* PATIH)

pâtrâ 1 *oj* leaf. 2 letter, document, contract. *ngréka ** to forge a document. 3 *shf of* PATRALIJUN

pâtrâlijun kerosene; petroleum

patrap behavior; way of doing. **é sédjé.* He acts crazy. *Aku diterangaké *é olèhé nindakaké.* He told me how to do it. ***an** penalty, sentence. *Ing sawenèhing negara *an gantung isih ditindakaké.* Execution by hanging is still practiced in some countries. **ka*an** to have [a penalty] inflicted on one. *Wong mau ka*an ukum mati.* He was sentenced to death. **m̀/di*aké 1** to apply sth (to). *matrapaké téori* to apply a theory. 2 to inflict [a punishment]. *Ukuman gantung di*aké marang Ali.* Ali was sentenced to hang. **m̀/di*i** to inflict [punishment] on. *Ali di*i ukuman gantung.* Ali was sentenced to hang. *See also* TRAP

patrem a small dagger

patri solder. *solèd ** soldering iron. *tukang ** solderer. ***ǹ** soldered. *Kuwali kuwi wis patrèn.* The kettle has been soldered. **m̀/di*(ǹi)** to solder sth. *Pantji² sing bolong dipatrèni.* The pans with holes in them were mended with solder.

patroli patrol. ***an** place for patrolmen; sentry box, station house. **m̀/di*** to patrol [a place]

patros *sbst kr for* PATRI

patrum bullet

pat-tiḍur bed, place to sleep (*inf var of* TEMPAT TIḌUR)

paṭu *n̂ a game in which the contestants try to hit each other's tops as they spin. **m̂*** to play this game

patuh regular assignment. *Jèn ndjogèt mesṭi * dadi Werkudara.* In the dance-drama he always plays Werkudara. **m̂*** to have a regular assignment. *Slamet wis matuh, ora susah dipréntahi.* Slamet has a task of his own–he doesn't need to be told what to do. **m̂/di*aké** to assign smn a regular task

paṭuk 1 promontory. 2 sharp bend in a river

patung ***an** to go into a joint enterprise. *A lan B *an tuku sapi.* A and B bought a cow together. **m̂/di*i** to go along with smn in a business enterprise

patut *ng,* **pantes** *kr* suitable, well-advised, appropriate. *Ora * dipasrahi apa².* He shouldn't be given any responsibilities. *gunem sing ora ** an ill-advised remark. *Ḍèwèké wis * dadi lurah.* He's just the man for village chief. *Tembung klisé * disingkiri.* It's advisable to avoid clichés. *Jèn dodolan * regané.* He sells his merchandise at reasonable prices. *Mantèné wis *.* The couple are well suited to each other. ***an** 1 [a child] who is procreated [by...]. *Anaké *an karo Sri.* His son was born to Sri. *Anaké sing *an karo Ali* the child she had by Ali. 2 to look good in any kind of clothing. ***(-*)é** to judge from appearances; it is appropriate that... **é anaké wong tjukup.* From all appearances, he comes from a wealthy home. *Botjah sing goroh *é dikapakaké?* What's to be done to a child who tells lies? **é tumumpang ing paga.* It belongs on the dinnerware shelf. **é jèn kalah bandjur nesu.* Naturally he gets mad when he loses. **sa*é** in a suitable manner, as is appropriate. *Sedulurmu bantunen sa*é.* Help your relatives as they need it. *See also* PANTES

patya prime minister (*ltry var of* PATIH)

Paus Pope. *Kangdjeng ** the Pope

paviljun *var of* PAPILIJUN

pawâkâ *oj* fire

pawèstri female (*oj*). ***n̂** 1 place reserved for women, *e.g.* in a mosque. 2 female genitalia (*kr for* PA·WADON·AN). *See also* ÈSTRI

pawit ***an** capital (to be) invested. **pawitan ḍengkul** 1 to engage in business with only one's own labor as capital. 2 gambling stakes borrowed from an opponent. **m̂/di*i** to finance, put up capital for. *See also* AWIT

pawon kitchen, cooking room *or* shed (*form of* AWU)

pawong (*or* ***an**) female servant. *** mitra** *or* *** sanak** close friend

P.B.B. *see* PERSATUAN BANGSA²

Pd. *see* DJABAT

pé ray (variety of fish). **nge/di*(n̂i)** to put sth in the sun *or* fresh air. *nge* bantal* to air a pillow. *ngepèni djarik* to dry batiks. *Pari iku diepé nganti garingé kumrisik.* Rice plants are sun-dried until they are crisp. **pa·nge*** act of sunning *or* airing sth. **pa·nge*an** place for drying *or* airing things. *See also* MÉ, PÉPÉ

pe- *inf var of* PA- *prefix. See also under* PA- (*Introduction, 2.9.2*)

Pébruari February

peda dried ground-up small fish (rice-accompanying dish)

péḍal pedal. ** gas* accelerator. ** kopling* clutch. ** rèm* brake pedal

peḍang 1 **(sabet** *ki***)** sword. *ngunus ** to draw a sword. 2 counting unit for long thin objects. *peté telung ** three beanpods. ***-*an** toy sword. **m̂/di*** to cut/stab with a sword. **pa·m̂*** sword stroke

péḍeral federal

peḍes 1 hot, peppery. *enḍog dadar ** omelet with hot sauce. *Sambelé adja *-*.* Don't make the sauce too hot! 2 to sting; to feel a stinging sensation. *Wah méndah *é jèn weḍiné nglilipi mripat.* Oh, how it stings to get sand in your eye! *Tembungé *.* His words had a sting. **pe*** (peppery-)hot food. **ke*en** excessively highly spiced. **m̂/di*aké** *or* **m̂/di*i** to make [food] hot. *** perih** oppressive difficulties. *Apa kowé ngerti *-perihé uripé nèng negara mantja?* Do you understand the great problems of living in a foreign country?

pèḍèt a scar on the upper eyelid. ***en** to have such a scar

peḍèt calf (young of the SAPI)

pediding, pediḍing *var of* BEDIDING

pedjah 1 death; dead (*kr for* PATI[a]). 2 dead; to die (*kr for* MATI)

pèdjèt ***an** pushbutton. *Setèlané radio nganggo *an.* The radio is operated with pushbuttons. *benik *an* snap fastener. **m̂/di*(i)** to press *or* exert pressure *esp.* with the thumb. *Pelemé adja di*i munḍak bosok.* Don't pinch the mangoes–they'll get bad spots.

pedjowang *var of* PEDJUWANG

pedjuh *var of* PETJUH

pedjuwang a fighter, *esp.* for freedom

peḍot broken; interrupted. *Lajanganė* *. The kite broke loose. *Talinė* *-*. The rope is broken into short lengths. * *ambekanė* out of breath. *ora* *(-*) or *tanpa* *(-*) continuous, incessant. *Swaranė grodjogan gumrodjog tanpa* *. The waterfall roared steadily. *Barisanė dawa banget ora* *-*. The line of marchers went on and on. ***an** broken (off), interrupted. *benang *an* a broken-off piece of thread. *bodjo *an* a divorced wife. **m̃/di*akė** 1 to break for smn. 2 to cause to be interrupted *or* discontinued. *Aku meḍotakė lampunė.* I burned out the bulb. **m̃/di*(i)** to break off; to interrupt. *meḍot memitran* to break off a friendship. *meḍot olèhė pasa* to break one's fast. *Wandanė *-*en.* Separate [the words] into syllables. *Diḍaḍunga meḍot.* Don't try to confine me! **meḍot dalan** 1 to leave smn along the way and continue on by oneself. 2 to cross a road

peḍut fog, mist

pega smoke, steam. **m̃*ni** to give off smoke/steam

pegat ***an (pisah·an** *kr?*) divorced. *Durung lawas nggonė *an, wis ngadjak ulihan.* Before they had been divorced long, they reconciled. *-* broken, interrupted. *alas *-** forest interspersed with open country. *alas ora *-** unrelieved forest. **m̃/di*** (**m̃/dipun·pisah** *kr?*) to divorce [one's spouse]. **ora *** *or* **tan *** unceasing. *Ora * anggonė ndjaga.* He is always on the alert.

pegawai (*prn* **pegawė**) civil servant, government employee, clerical worker

pegel stiff and sore from strain *or* exertion. **m̃*akė** exasperating, irritating. *** ati·nė** annoyed, fed up

pegeng *rg var of* MEGENG. **m̃/di*** to wean [a child] (*ki for* ÑJ/DI·SAPIH)

pègès **m̃/di*** to cut *or* slice slantwise

pėgo to speak Javanese with a regional accent. ***n** 1 the form of Javanese spoken in Bagelèn in southwest central Java (*term used in Jogja, Solo*). 2 Javanese written in Arabic script

pegogok to sit around idle

pėgos **m̃*** 1 slantwise, on the diagonal. 2 (*psv* **di***) to cut slantwise

pegot *rg var of* PEḌOT

pèh 1 bladder. 2 *shf of* DUPÈH

pėhak side [*e.g.* of an argument]. **m̃*** to side (with), take smn's part

Pèhtjun Chinese New Year

pèi a game played with the Chinese cards (*kertu tjilik*)

pèjèk fried peanut chip

pejik *var of* PIJIK

pėjog *-* *rpr* the squawking of a chicken

pėjok dented. *Ngarepė montor mau* *. The front of the car is dented in. **m̃/di*akė** to make a dent in. *Sapa sing mėjokkė mobilku?* Who dented my car?

pėjor 1 not strong, wobbly, infirm. 2 tiger cub (young of the MATJAN)

pėjot **pėjat-*** 1 full of dents. 2 [of roads] bumpy

pèk (**penḍet** *kr?*), **punḍut** *ki* ***-*an** 1 [to play] for keeps, *i.e.* with the winner retaining the stakes. 2 adopted. *anak *-*an* an adopted child. **nge/di*(i)** 1 to take possession of. *Pèken.* You can have it! Help yourself! *Potlodė iki dak epèkė ja.* I'll take *this* pencil. *Djaranė sudagar diepèk digawa mulih.* They seized the merchant's horse and took it home with them. *Botjah² kampung jèn aku ora ana paḍa nge*i pelem.* The village boys helped themselves to our mangoes while we were away. 2 to acquire by foul means. *Jèn udjian adja sok nge*.* Never cheat on a test. **nge* anak** to take as an adopted child. *Wiwit tjilik Pardi di* anak oomė.* Pardi was adopted by his uncle in early childhood. **nge* mantu** to choose as a marriage partner for one's child. *Mas A di* mantu karo Pak B.* Mr. B chose A as a prospective son-in-law.

pek̄ *rpr* a slap

pekak **m̃/di*** to check, restrain. *A banget² anggonė mekak B supaja ora ngrokok.* A did her best to stop B from smoking. **pa·m̃*** 1 act of restraining. 2 waist (*ki for* BANGKÈK·AN)

pekakah *var of* PERKAKAH

pekakas *var of* PERKAKAS

pekangkang *ptg* * [of legs] spread apart. *Sikilė ptg *.* His legs are spread wide. **m̃*** having the legs spread. **m̃/di*akė** to spread [the legs] apart

pekârâ *var of* PERKARA

pekawis *var of* PERKAWIS

pekèkèh *var of* PERKÈKÈH

peken market(place) (*kr for* PASAR)

pekeneng *ptg* * 1 *pl* (to argue) heatedly and obstinately. 2 *pl* stiff [of muscles]. ***an** *or* **m̃*** *sg as for* PTG *

pekèngkèng *var of* PEKANGKANG

pekengkeng *ptg* * *pl* lying stiff and dead.

Pitik^{2}ku ḍa mati ptg *. My chickens lay dead. **ṁ*** *sg as above. Pitikku mati mekengkeng.* My chicken lay dead.

pekenira *wj, court speech* you; your

pekih religious duties required by Islamic law

pekik *oj* handsome

peking a variety of finch. * **a·buntut merak** (making) a mountain from a molehill

pekir 1 no good any more; going to waste. 2 *var of* FAKIR. ***an** rejected article; sth wasted. **ṁ/di*** to discard, reject. *mekir barang sing tjatjat* to discard a defective article

peklaring *var of* PERKLARING

pékoh [to walk when in pain] with the legs spread and bent

pékong *var of* TEPÉKONG

pekongkong *ptg* * *pl* sitting (improperly) with the legs spread apart. **ṁ*** *sg as above*

pekonjoh *var of* PERKUNJUH

peksa ***n** 1 coercion, compulsion. 2 (having been) forced. *kawin *n* a forced marriage. **ke*** forced, compelled. *Bareng ḍuwité entèk ḍèwèké ke* utang.* When his money ran out he was compelled to borrow. *Aku ke* mèsem krungu kanḍané ngono kuwi.* I had to smile when I heard him say that. **ṁ/di*** to force, compel. *Jèn botjah kéḍé apa betjik di* bèn migunakaké tangané tengen?* Should a left-handed child be made to use his right hand? *Jèn ora gelem mèlu adja di*.* If he doesn't want to come along, don't force him to. **ṁ/di*kaké** to force sth. *Jèn kuntjiné ora djoḍo adja di*kaké.* If the key doesn't fit the lock, don't force it. (*lajang*) **pa·ṁ*** a warrant for search *or* arrest

peksi bird (*kr for* MANUK)

pekungkung *ptg* * 1 *pl* in hunched *or* curled positions, with bent backs. 2 *pl* lying stiff and dead. **ṁ*** *sg as above. Olèhé turu mekungkung kemul sarung.* He slept curled up with his sarong over him. *Kutjing mbekis karo mekungkung.* The cat spat and arched its back.

pekunjuh *var of* PERKUNJUH

pèl floor-cleaning mop *or* rag. **nge/di*** to clean a floor with the above

pel- *see also under* PL- (*Introduction, 2.9.3*)

pela *rg var of* REMPELA

pélas rice-accompanying dish of soybeans and grated coconut

pélat articulation problem (inability to pronounce certain consonants, *e.g.* substituting *l* or *y* for *r*) in children learning to speak

pelat phonograph

Pel. Da. *see* PA·M·BANTU

pèlek̄ tire rim

pelem mango. * *mateng/mentah* ripe/unripe mango. * **djiwa**, * **gaḍung**, * **(h)arum manis**, * **nanas** *etc.* common varieties of mango

peleng focal point of concentration *or* attention. **ṁ/di*** to concentrate *or* focus the attention on. **meleng pudja** *or* **meleng semadi** to meditate by concentrating. **pa·ṁ*an** a place for meditating. *See also* LENG

pèlèt **ṁ/di*** to put the hex on smn; to bewitch, enchant

peli *ng kr*, **kalam** (*or* **warastra**?) *ki* penis

pèlih *var of* PILIH

pelik spark. ***an** obtained by mining. *Emas lan inten iku *an.* Gold and diamonds are mined. ***-*** that which sparkles. **pe*** jeweled earrings. **ṁ/di*** to mine. **pa·ṁ*an** a mine. **sa*** 1 one spark. 2 a tiny bit. 3 one flower

péling *ng*, **pènget** *kr* ***an** a commemoration; to remember, commemorate. *pèngetan wijosané R. A. Kartini* commemoration of Kartini's birthday. **pe*** a reminder; a warning. *Lelakoné bisa kanggo pe* menawa kabèh barang ala kuwi konangan.* What happened to him is a reminder that evil will out. **ṁ/di*i** to commemorate. ***-di*** let it be a lesson... *Péling-dipéling kowé adja nganti ngebrèh kaja ngono.* Heed the lesson of it: don't *you* be thriftless like that. *See also* ÉLING

pelit stingy, parsimonious

pélo a lisp; to speak with a lisp. **ṁ*ni** to affect a lisp

pélog seven-note gamelan scale. **ṁ*** to play in this scale

péloh **pélah-*** limp, flaccid; flexible, pliant. *Wong kok pélah-* kaja Baladéwa ilang gapité.* You're as weak as Baladéwa [puppet] without the sticks!

pelok mango pit. *djenang* * porridge made of scraped mango pit. **ṁ*-ṁ*** conspicuous, in bad taste. *Olèhé pupuran melok^2.* She powdered her face much too thickly.

pelong ***-*** *or* **ṁ*-ṁ*** [of eyes] wide and black

pélot [of blades] bent, curving

Pel. Tu. *see* PA·M·BANTU

pelus a certain freshwater eel

pem- *see also under* P- (*Introduction, 3.1.7*)

pémah to feel at home; tame (*kr for* POMAH)

pembajun breast (*ki for* SUSU^a)

pemerintah, pemeréntah *var sp of* PEMRINTAH

pèmès folding pocket knife

pemréntah *var of* PEMRINTAH

pemrintah 1 the government, the administration. 2 (*or* ***an**) government (as an institution); governmental system. *See also* PRINTAH

pémut *var of* PÈNGET

pèn pen. **nge*** to use a pen. *ora ngebuk ora nge** illiterate

pénak *inf var of* KEPÉNAK

penak rice wrapped into a packet. **sa*** a rice packet

pénak̂an *inf var of* KEPÉNAKAN

pénal to come off, peel off

penatos *rg kr for* PENATU

penatu 1 laundry man; laundry shop. *tukang ** laundry man/shop. 2 laundry to be washed. **m̃*** 1 laundry to be washed. 2 to do laundry as one's trade. **m̃/di*k̂aké** to have clothes laundered at a shop

péndah how...! what (a)...! (*var of* MÉNDAH)

pen̩dak each, every. ** dina Rebo* every Wednesday. **m̃*** to commemorate a death anniversary. *men̩dak (se)pisan (pin̩do, lsp.)* to commemorate the first (second, *etc.*) anniversary of a death. *** pisan** first anniversary of smn's death

pen̩dalit to twist, twine. ***an** to fidget, keep twisting and turning

pen̩dâpâ *ng,* **pen̩dapi** *kr* large open pavilion-like veranda at the front of a house where guests are entertained and shadow-play performances are held for celebrating family events

pen̩dapi *kr for* PEN̩DAPA

Pen̩dawa *var of* PAN̩DAWA

pèn̩dèk, pen̩dèk short (*var of* TJEN̩DAK, TJEN̩DÈK; *rg var of* TJEKAK)

pen̩dekel *ptg ** having many calluses; bulging with tendons/muscles. **m̃*** painfully swollen. *** ati·né** irritated, provoked

pendèl **m̃/di*(i)** to peck (at)

pendelik *ptg * pl* staring with fixed eyes. *Ming pad̩a ptg * nonton ora gelem ngréwangi.* They just sat and stared without offering to help. ***an** *sg as above.* ***-*an** to stare at each other. **m̃*** *sg* to stare fixedly, *Tanggaku mau bengi nggantung, mripaté mendelik.* My neighbor hanged himself last night; his eyes stared glassily. **m̃/di*i** to stare at fixedly. *See also* DELIK

pen̩delis *ptg * pl* showing as small round smooth surfaces. **m̃*** *sg as above. Wudelé men̩delis.* His navel showed. *Watuné nang banju ming kétok set̩it̩ik, rupané men̩delis.* A little of the rock showed, round and smooth, in the water.

pendelo *ptg * pl* [of eyes] bulging, wide. **m̃*** *sg as above*

pen̩delong to go slack suddenly. *mBareng bundelané utjul taliné bandjur mak *.* When the knot was untied the rope suddenly loosened. **m̃*** loose, slack, sagging

pen̩delus *ptg * pl* showing as round glossy surfaces. *Sirahé ptg *.* Their [bald] heads gleamed. *Watuné kétok ptg * nang kali.* The rocks show shiny and round in the river. **m̃*** *sg as above*

pen̩dem underground. *katjang ** peanut. *téla ** sweet potato. *bètèng ** bunker, underground fortification. *baris ** undercover movement of armed forces. ***an** underground; buried. *Ana pen̩demané pet̩i.* There was a buried chest. **ke*** buried, underground. *ke* ing wed̩èn* buried in the sand. *pala ke** root foods. *d̩uduk apus ke** to rake up the past. **m̃/di*** to bury. *men̩dem balung* to bury a bone. *men̩dem urip²an* to bury alive. *mBok adja men̩dem waé ta!* You shouldn't bury yourself [by staying at home all the time]! **men̩dem djero m̃·pikul d̩uwur** to reflect honor on one's parents. **men̩dem kula** *or* **men̩dem raga** to conceal one's true position; to be incognito. *See also* EN̩DEM

pèndèng pressed flat. *Awaké nganti *.* He was flattened [in the crowd]. **m̃/di*** to flatten sth

pen̩det to (go) get, to take (*root form: kr for* DJUPUK; *kr for* PÈK?)

pen̩dikil *ptg * pl* bumpy, rough-surfaced with many small protuberances. **m̃*** *sg* forming a small bump

pen̩dilis *ptg * pl* lumpy, bumpy (with small bumps). **m̃*** *sg* forming a small lump

pending metal belt, *esp.* of gold or silver

pendirang *ptg * or* ***an** to stare impolitely; to dart glances about nervously

pen̩disil *ptg * pl* forming many small bulges, *e.g.* soybeans floating in a pan of water. **m̃*** 1 *sg as above.* 2 obstinate, headstrong

pen̩dita 1 Protestant clergyman. 2 *var of* PAN̩DITA

pendjalin *ng,* **pendjatos** *sbst? kr* rattan. *krandjang ** rattan basket. ***an** 1 made of rattan. *Kursiku kabèh ora ana sing *an.* Not one of our chairs is rattan. 2 a variety of soapberry tree. **m̀/di*** to apply rattan to. *kursi sing di** a chair made with rattan. *** wakul** a variety of rattan

pendjatos rattan (*sbst? kr for* PENDJALIN)

pendjelut *ptg * or* **m̀*** feeling upset (physically *or* emotionally)

pendjété *ptg * pl* having many small swellings *or* bulges. **m̀*** *sg* forming a bulge *or* a swelling. *Susuré kétok mendjété nang tjangkemé.* The wad of chewing tobacco shows in her mouth.

pèndjol a bump *or* swelling of irregular shape

pendjoto *ptg * pl* having many swellings *or* bulges. **m̀*** *sg as above. Baṭuké mendjoto.* He has a bump on his forehead.

pendjuluk **m̀*** 1 high, raised. *Olèhé nganggo kaṭok mendjuluk banget.* He wears his pants too high. 2 (*psv* **di***) to move sth upward. *Aku di*aké sopir tekan truk.* The driver helped me up into the truck. *See also* DJULUK

pendjutu *ptg * pl* having many bumps *or* bulges. **m̀*** *sg* having a bump *or* swelling

penḍojot *ptg * pl* heavily burdened (physically, emotionally). **m̀*** *sg as above. Slamet menḍojot nggotong kaju.* Slamet is carrying a huge load of wood.

penḍok *ng,* **kandel·an** *kr* decorative metal plating on a kris sheath. *** bléwah** a certain style of plating. **golèk *** to help people in order to get praised for it

penḍokol *ptg * pl* swollen, bumpy. **m̀*** *sg* 1 swollen, bulging. 2 affronted. *Atiku menḍokol diblendjani kantjaku.* It offended me that my friend failed to keep his promise.

penḍosol *ptg * pl* showing good-sized humps *or* bulges. **m̀*** *sg* forming a large hump/bulge

penḍukul *ptg * pl* full of humps. **m̀*** *sg* forming a hump. *Dalané mendak menḍukul.* The road rose and fell. *papan² kang menḍukul* humped-up places

pendul (*or* **m̀***) [of eyes] swollen from crying

penḍulus *ptg * rpr* the sight of many smooth rounded objects, *e.g.* bald heads in a crowd

penḍusul *ptg ** showing many humps *or* bulges. *Punḍaké ptg * kena pikulan.* His shoulders have large calluses on them from his shoulder pole. **m̀*** to bulge out, show as a hump. *Awaké dikrukup kemul, mung sirahé sing menḍusul metu.* He's all covered with a blanket–only his head sticks out. *Ototé menḍusul.* His muscles bulge.

pènèk ***an** 1 to climb habitually. 2 act *or* way of climbing. *Sing disenengi *an.* Climbing trees is what he likes best. **m̀/di*aké** 1 to make *or* help smn climb. 2 to climb a fruit tree and get the fruits for smn. *Aku pènèkna krambil kalima waé.* Climb the coconut tree and pick me about five coconuts. **m̀/di*(i)** 1 to climb. *mènèk wit* to climb a tree. *Wit téla gantung di*i mentelung.* The papaya tree sways when you climb it. *tontonan rebutan mènèk katju* a prize contest in which boys climb greased poles to get the prizes at the top. 2 to climb [a tree] and get the fruits. *Télané gantung sing wis mateng kaé pènèken.* Get the ripe papayas from the tree.

pèneng official sticker (for registration, licensing; as a tax receipt)

pener (**leres** *opt kr*) right on [a certain spot]. *Matjané dibeḍil * sirahé.* He shot the tiger smack in the head. **ka*** related in a certain way. *Ḍèwèké isih ke* kamasku sebab putrané pakḍéku.* He's (related to me as) my "brother" because he's my uncle's son. **m̀*** headed toward [a certain spot]. *Olèhé ngintjeng mener sirah.* He aimed at the head. **m̀/di*aké** to head sth toward. *Olèhé ngintjeng di*ké sirah.* He aimed at the head. **m̀*i** coinciding with, right on/at. *jèn meneri libur* when it's vacation time. *See also* BENER

pènèt, penèt **m̀/di*** to squash, flatten

penet **m̀/di*(aké)** to squeeze, massage, knead

peng *rpr* a rush of air past one. *Mak * raiku kesampluk kangmasku.* I felt the wind from my brother's hand as he accidentally brushed it past my face. ***-*an** highly qualified, topflight. *ḍokter² peng²an* outstanding doctors. **nge/di*** to apply oneself seriously to. *Aku lagi nge* sinau.* I'm studying hard now. *Sing panahan paḍa nge* ngarah lésan.* The contesting archers all tried their best to hit the target. *See also* MEMPENG

pengangah *var of* PERNGANGAH

pengantèn *var of* MANTÈN

pengar a sharp odor, *e.g.* of radishes

pengaribâwâ influence. ** kulonan* Occidental influence

pengaron earthenware tank (*form of* KARU)

pengaruh influence. *Ing Djawa-tengah, *é agama Kristen geḍé banget.* The influence of Christianity in Central Java has been considerable. **m̃/di*i** to influence

pengasih accordion plait formed on a batik wraparound that is on the inside (next to the body) rather than showing at the front (as with *wiru·ñ*)

pengastuti blessing, prayer. **m̃*** to bless; to pray for

pèngès **ke*** to get cut (off). *Ḍèké ke* nalika ngradjang brambang.* She cut herself slicing onions. **m̃/di*** to cut, slash. *Blègé buangen mengko munḍak mèngès wong.* Throw away that can–it might cut smn.

pènget commemoration (*root form: kr for* PÉLING)

penggak **m̃/di*** to restrain. *Bodjoné ngerti apa kang dadi karepé nanging ora wani menggak.* His wife knew what he was up to but didn't dare stop him. *Eluhé ora bisa di-*.* She couldn't hold back her tears. **pa·m̃*** restraint

penggang *rg var of* BENGGANG

penggik (*or* **m̃***) narrowed. *Bangkèkané menggik.* Her waist is slim. *Tamparé nggon tengah wis menggik arep peḍot.* The rope is fraying in the middle–it could break any time.

péngin to want, desire. *Wis suwé olèhé * lunga nang Djakarta.* He's been wanting to go to Djakarta for a long time. ***an** 1 covetous. 2 (*or* **pe*an**) that which is needed *or* desired. *Buḍa kuwi tegesé wong sing wis ora duwé pe*an.* Being a Buddhist means being one who no longer has worldly desires. **ke*** to want, desire. *Kowé apa ora ke* menjang Sala?* Don't you want to go to Solo? **me·m̃*/di·pe*** 1 to make smn want sth. *Aku dipe* kembang gula karo kantjaku.* My friend got me hungry for candy. 2 to coax. *A tansah meméngin B.* A kept urging B [to come along]. **m̃*aké** *or* **m̃*i** 1 tempting, appealing. *Djeruké méngini.* The oranges make my mouth water. 2 (*psv* **di*aké** *or* **di*i**) to want sth. *Barang sing di*i mau sida dituku.* She finally bought what she had been wanting.

penging **m̃/di*** to tell smn not to [do]. *Kepéngin mèlu di* ora kena.* She wanted to come along but he wouldn't let her. *Kangmasku menging ngrokok aku, malah ngletjis ḍéwé.* My brother–a chain smoker himself –tells *me* not to smoke.

péngkal a *j*-showing diacritic in Javanese script. **m̃/di*** [of horses] to kick with the hind legs

pengkarag *rpr* hair rising. *Aku weruh memedi saknalika mak *.* I saw a ghost and it scared me out of my wits. *Kutjingku jèn kepeṭuk asu wuluné bandjur mak *.* Our cat's hair rose when she saw a dog. **m̃*** [of hair] to rise. *Mengkarag aku.* I was scared stiff. *Saben liwat kuburan, mengkarak kabèh wuluku.* When I go past the cemetery my hair stands on end.

pengkeluk *rpr* bending, leaning. *Wit mau dak pènèki bandjur mak *.* When I climbed the tree it bent over. *ptg * pl* to bend. *Kembang²é paḍa alum ptg *.* The withering flowers drooped. **m̃*** to bend. *mengkeluk menḍuwur* to bend upward. **m̃/di*aké** to bend sth. *mengkelukaké pipa* to bend a pipe

pengkelung *var of* PENGKELUK

pengker 1 back, rear (*rg kr for* BURI). 2 last, past, the previous (*kr for* PUNGKUR). ***an** back (*ki for* GEGER)

pengkered *rpr* shrinking. *ptg * pl* feeling cowed. *Botjah² didukani guru bandjur paḍa ptg *.* Scolded by the teacher, the boys shrank back. **m̃*** to shrink; *fig* to shrink in fear

pengkijanat traitor. *See also* KIJANAT

pengkirig *rpr* hair standing on end. *Mak * giṭokku.* The hairs on the back of my neck rose. **m̃*** [of hair] standing on end; *fig* scared stiff

péngkolan a bend in the road

pengkorog *var of* PENGKARAG

pengkuh solid, firm, strong. *Pit iki *.* This bicycle is sturdy. **m̃/di*i** to make sth sturdier. *Tjagaké di*i nganggo kaju.* He supported the pole with a piece of wood.

pengong dull-witted

péngos **m̃/di*** to cut on the diagonal. *Olèhé ngiris roti di*.* Please cut the bread slantwise. *See also* ÉNGOS, PLÉNGOS

penguk fetid

pengur *var of* PENGUK

pèni fine, rare, splendid. ***-*** fine things; valuables. *See also* ÈDI

peniti 1 safety pin. 2 decorative pin, brooch

penjak *var of* PIDAK, PLENJAK

penjanjakan rude boisterous behavior

penjènjèng *ptg * pl* arrogant, defiant, rude. ***an** *or* **m̃*** *sg as above*

pènjèt, penjèt, penjet **m̃/di*** to press,

squeeze. *Tomaté adja di*, mengko mlenjok.* Don't squeeze the tomato or it'll squirt!

penjinjing **penjinjang-*** to act arrogant

pènjok having a dent in it. **pènjak-*** full of dents

penjok *var of* PLENJOK

penjonjo(ng) *ptg ** convered with good-sized bumps. *Baṭuké ptg *.* He has bumps all over his forehead. **m̈*** *sg* forming a swelling, *esp.* on the head. *menjonjo saenḍog pitik* a bump on the head the size of a hen's egg

penju tortoise. **m̈*** tortoise-like (*term of abuse*). *Menju kowé ja!* You stupid!

penjuk *var of* PLENJUK

penjunjang ***an** *or* **m̈*** to act rude, defiant, ill-mannered

penjunju(ng) *ptg * pl* covered with bumps. **m̈*** *sg* swollen, forming a lump

pènsijun 1 pension. 2 (*or* ***an**) having retired on a pension. *Pak X *an guru.* Mr. X is a retired teacher. *Ḍuwité kanggo tuku omah mbésuk jèn wis *(an).* The money is for buying a house after he retires. **m̈/di*** to retire smn on a pension

penṭalèt *var of* PENṬALIT

penṭalit *ptg ** topsy-turvy, every which way. *nDjogèt kok sikilé ptg * ora irama.* You were way out of step in the dance–why didn't you follow the rhythm? ***an** to act boorish *or* disrespectful. **m̈*** to grasp *or* clamp with the legs

péntan (*or* **pe***) a made-up tale, a piece of fiction

penṭang **m̈/di*** 1 to draw a bow(string). *Tangané kaja gendéwa pinenṭang.* His arms are like drawn bows, *i.e.* the classical ideal shape. 2 to crucify. **pa·m̈*** crucifixion. **pa·m̈*an** the Cross

pentas ***an** 1 shore, bank. *nglangi menjang *an* to swim ashore. 2 starting place, *e.g.* in children's games. **m̈*** 1 to come ashore; *fig* to escape. *Ajo mentas, adja kesuwèn langèn.* Let's go in out of the water now–we shouldn't stay in swimming too long. 2 [one's child] is married. *Anak²é wédok wis ḍa mentas.* His daughters have all married. *See also* ENTAS, MENTAS

penṭèjèt ***an** *or* ***-*** 1 labored, difficult [of the stance *or* walking pace of a heavily burdened person]. 2 to croak. *Koḍoké *an mentas udan.* The frogs "sing" after a rain. **m̈*** overburdened. *Olèhku ndjundjung lemari ḍèwèkan nganti menṭèjèt.* I barely managed to carry the cupboard all by myself.

penṭéjot *var of* PENṬÈJÈT

penṭeleng *rpr* widening of the eyes. *Mripaté mak * bareng krungu kabar mau.* His eyes popped when he heard the news. ***an** to glare at each other. ***-*** *or* **penṭelang-*** *or* **m̈*** 1 to stare wide-eyed. 2 to glare in anger. **m̈/di*aké** to cause [the eyes] to stare. *Babon ora mangsuli, matané di*aké.* His wife didn't answer, she just glared. **m̈/di*i** to glower at

penṭelèt **m̈/di*aké** to tighten and pull in [the stomach muscles]

penṭelos *var of* PENṬOLOS

pentelung *rpr* suddenly bending. *ptg * pl* to bend. **m̈*** to bend, *e.g.* of a tree in the wind. **m̈/di*aké** to bend sth, cause to bend. *See also* TELUNG[b]

penṭèng **m̈/di*** to stretch [a limb] out from the body. *Sikilé kebo mau di*.* The [slain] kerbau's legs were pulled outward. **menṭèng kèlèk** with hands on hips in a defiant attitude

penṭèngèl *ptg * pl* with heads stretching up *or* out. **m̈*** *sg as above. Sirahé menṭèngèl metu saka banju.* His head is sticking out of the water.

penṭengèl *var of* PENṬENGIL

penṭengil *rpr* a sudden appearance. *Mak * sirahé tikus mau kétok.* The mouse's head popped into view. *ptg * pl* to pop into view. **m̈*** *sg* showing, in (plain) sight

penṭèr [of sky] cleared up after a rain

penṭijèt *var of* PENṬÈJÈT

pentijung *ptg * pl* to bend, bow, lean. **m̈*** bent downward. *Pangé mentijung.* The [fruit-laden] branch is bent low. **m̈/di*aké** to bend sth, cause to bend. *See also* TIJUNG

pèntil rubber tubing used for inflating sth, *e.g.* a ball, a tire

pentil fruit bud

penṭil *ng kr*, **mundri** *ki* nipple. **m̈*** 1 nipple-shaped. 2 (*psv* **di***) to nurse, give suck

penṭilis *ptg * pl* small, round, and shiny. *Akèh tomaté, nganti katon ptg * pirang².* There are lots of shiny round tomatoes. **m̈*** *sg as above. Baṭoké nganti menṭilis.* The coconut shell [with fibers removed] was smooth and shiny.

penṭingil *ptg * pl* to show, be in view [of small things *or* to a small extent]. *Untuné ptg *.* Its (little) teeth show. **m̈*** *sg as above. Awaké dikrukupi kemul, mung* *sirahé sing kétok menṭingil.* His whole body is covered with a blanket–only a little of his head is showing. *See also* ṬINGIL

pentjak Javanese-style karate: self-defense system and stylized art form. **m̃*** to engage in *pentjak.* **m̃*-m̃*** *inf* furious, enraged

pentjar to spread, get disseminated. *Wit²an iku *é warna².* Plants get sown in a variety of ways. *ṭeṭukulan kang widjiné * déning angin* wind-sown plants. *ptg * sms ptg* PLENTJAR *below.* **m̃*** to go in separate directions. *Wong papat mau paḍa mentjar.* The four people dispersed. **m̃/di*aké** to scatter/disseminate sth. *tanduran kang bisa mentjaraké widjiné ḍéwé* plants that are self-sown. *ptg* **p·l·entjar** *pl* scattering everywhere

pentjas *var of* PANTJAS

pentjelat *ptg * pl* going in all directions. *mBasan waḍahé dibukak, djangkriké ptg * metu.* When he uncovered the can, the crickets came out every which way. *Olèhé nata kaju ptg *.* He dumped the firewood any old way. **m̃*** to bound; to get ejected *or* thrown about. *Balé mentjelat mrana gèk mentjelat mréné.* The ball bounced this way and that. *Uleré tiba nang tangan sanalika dikipataké mentjelat bablas.* A caterpillar fell on my arm; I shook it and it sailed off. *Motor maburé ketémbak nanging piluté bisa mentjelat metu.* The plane was hit but the pilot managed to bail out. *Piré mentjelat metu.* The spring bounced out. **m̃/di*aké** to eject, throw off

pentjelèk **m̃*** [of skin] to retract. *Manuké mentjelèk.* The foreskin draws back. **m̃/di*aké** to retract [the foreskin]. *See also* TJELÈK

pèntjèng **m̃*** 1 crooked, lopsided, off center. *Olèhé masang gambar mèntjèng.* He hung the picture crooked. *Arahé mèntjèng saka kéné.* It's on the diagonal from here. 2 incompatible, inharmonious. **m̃*-m̃*** *or* **méntjang-m̃*** placed every which way. *Aku nggarisi méntjang-mèntjèng.* I scribbled lines in every direction. **p·l·èntjèng** off center, skewed (*root form: see* PLÈNTJÈNG). *See also* ÈNTJÈNG, GUBUG

pentjèngèl, pentjengèl *ptg * pl* standing out prominently. **m̃*** *sg as above. See also* TJÈNGÈL

pentjengès *rpr* a jeering laugh. **m̃*** to jeer, sneer. *See also* TJENGÈS

pentjengis *var of* PENTJENGÈS

pentjereng an intent stare. **é mripaté panggah ora kenḍo.* She stared intently and unwaveringly. *ptg * pl* staring fixedly. **m̃*** *sg* to stare fixedly. *Si matjan matané mentjereng.* The tiger's gaze did not waver. **m̃/di*i** to stare at fixedly. *See also* TJURENG

pentjèrèt *ptg * pl* shiny, gleaming. **m̃*** *sg as above. Tjèrèté digebeg nganti mentjèrèt.* She scrubbed the kettle [with ashes] until it shone.

pentjernaan digestion

pentjèt **m̃/di*** to squeeze

pentjil **m̃*** secluded, isolated. *Omahku mentjil.* Our house is off the beaten path. **m̃/di*(aké)** to isolate. *Mungsuhé nedya mentjilaké kuṭa A.* The enemy intends to cut off the city of A. *Darto saiki di*aké karo kantja²ne.* Darto's friends are avoiding him these days.

pentjilak *ptg * pl* to stare around in an unmannerly way. ***an** *or* **m̃*** 1 *sg as above.* 2 to stare fixedly

pentjingil *ptg * pl* standing out prominently [of small *or* slim things]. **m̃*** *sg as above*

pentjit 1 the very top, the tip *or* peak. 2 *rg* young mango. **m̃*** at the very top; *fig* to the limit. *Ḍèké mentjit meṭangkrong mènèk wit geḍé.* He scrambled all the way to the top of a tall tree. *Wah, tjilaka mentjit aku mau.* I had the worst possible luck.

pèntjlok *var of* PÉNTJOK

pentjlok **m̃/di*** to chop, hack (*var of* PENTJOK)

péntjok ***an** a perch(ing place). **m̃*** to perch, alight. **m̃/di*aké** to cause *or* allow sth to alight. *Manuké di*aké ing punḍaké.* He let the bird perch on his shoulder. **m̃/di*i** to alight on. *See also* ÉNTJOK

pentjok a meat dish to accompany the rice at a meal. **m̃/di*** 1 to make [ingredients] into the above dish. 2 to chop, hack, lop off

pentjolot *rpr* a bounding jump. *Koḍoké mak * utjul.* The frog jumped and got away. ***an** to jump about. *dolanan *an* a jumping game; to jump about in play (children). *Badjingé *an ana ing wit²an.* The squirrel jumped around in the tree. **m̃*** to jump. *Djangkrik mentjolot.* Crickets leap. *See also* TJOLOT

péntjong off center, off target. **m̃*** to go/be off center. *Jèn mbeḍil mesṭi méntjong.* He always misses what he's shooting at. **m̃/di*aké** to cause sth to be off center *or* off target. *Olèhé ngiris roti di*ké.* He cut one piece of cake bigger than the other. *See also* ÉNTJONG

pentjongol *rpr* a sudden appearance. *Aku kagèt nalika kantjaku mak * nang djendéla.* I was startled when my friend suddenly appeared at the window. *ptg * pl* [of large objects] standing out prominently. **m̃*** *sg* to stand out prominently. *Gedung sing duwur kuwi mentjongol.* The tall building stands way out above the others. *See also* TJONGOL

péntjor lame

pentjorong *ptg * pl* shining, sending out beams. *Lampuné montor jèn bengi kétok ptg *.* The car headlights sent their beams into the night. ***an** *or* **m̃* 1** to shine, send out beams. *Matané *an djlalatan nèk weruh barang apik.* Her eyes shone when she saw the beautiful things. *mentjorong kaja mripaté ula naga* gleaming like a dragon's eyes. *Aku nitèni mentjorongé lampu montormu.* I recognized your headlight beams. *Berliané nèng ngisor lampu mentjorong.* The diamond sparkles under the light. 2 *slang* conspicuous, showy, eye-catching. *Jèn metu kétok mentjorong mergané klambiné sédjé karo lijané.* When she goes out she gets noticed—she dresses differently from others. *See also* TJORONG

pentjorot *ptg * pl* glittering. **m̃*** to gleam, shine, radiate

péntjos *var of* PÉNTJONG. *See also* ÉNTJOS

pentjos **m̃/di*** to chop, hack (*var of* PENTJOK)

pentju 1 protruding knob of a gamelan *gong.* 2 roof with a tall leveled-off peak. **m̃*** [of roofs] shaped as above

pentjulat *ptg ** to move about rapidly. *Sèt ing pelem bosok mau ptg *.* The maggots in the rotted mango wriggled all over it. *Djangkriké pada ptg * arep metu.* The crickets kept trying to leap out of the box. **m̃*** to leap. *See also* TJULAT

pentjulik ***an** act of kidnaping. *kurban *an* a kidnap victim. *See also* TJULIK

pentjulut *var of* PENTJOLOT

pentjungul to appear suddenly. *Kantjaku mak * nang ngarep lawang.* All of a sudden my friend was right at the front door. *ptg * pl* showing, appearing; [of good-sized objects] standing out from other similar ones. *See also* TJUNGUL

pentjurat act of spurting out. **é banju lèding* the spurting of the running water. *ptg ** to keep shooting out. *Geniné ptg pletik ptg *.* The fire gives off showers of sparks. **m̃*** to spurt, squirt out. *See also* TJURAT

péntjut **ke*** to be captivated (by) [smn's charms]. **m̃*aké** captivating. *Rupané méntjutaké.* Her face is fascinating. **m̃/di*i** to enchant, appeal strongly to

pentog [to have reached] the end, [to have gone] as far as possible. *Olèhé mlaku nang dalan mau nganti *.* He walked all the way to the end of the road. *Dalan iki * tekan kéné.* The road ends here. *Rumangsa kepinteran lan kawruhé wis *.* He felt his ability and knowledge had developed as far as they could. **m̃*** to reach the end, go as far as possible. *Olèhé nggawé kiosk mentog bèteng.* The kiosk was built right up against the wall. **sa*-*é** as far as ultimately possible. *Piranti² dipigunakaké sa*-*é.* They made the fullest use of the equipment.

pentol (*or* ***an**) knob, handle. **m̃*** knobby

pentolo *ptg * pl* wide-eyed, staring. **m̃*** *sg as above*

pentolos *ptg * pl* round and bald [of heads]. **m̃*** *sg* round and bald

pèntong toeing in. *Sikilé rada *.* He's pigeon-toed. **m̃*** pigeon-toed

pentongol *ptg * pl* to show, be visible *or* in view. **m̃*** to show prominently, stick out. *See also* TONGOL

pentul **m̃*(-m̃*)** to bounce, spring. **m̃/di*aké** to bounce sth; to cause to bounce *or* spring. *See also* ENTUL, M·ENDAT, MEMBAT

pentul 1 a small round protuberance. 2 *wj* a clown. **m̃*** full; puffed, swollen

pentung stick, club, cudgel. **ke*** to get clubbed. **m̃/di*(i)** to whack with a stick *or* club

pentungul *ptg * pl* to emerge, come into view. **m̃*** *sg as above. mBasan wis suwi njilem nang mbanju bandjur lagi mentungul.* He swam under water for a long time and finally came up. *See also* TUNGUL

penuh *oj* full. **m̃/di*i** to fulfill

penunuk *ptg * pl* lying in piles. *Wediné sing arep dienggo ndandani dalan wis ptg * nang pinggir dalan.* The sand for repairing the road is heaped along the curb. **m̃*** lying in a heap

péodal feudal

pep **nge/di*** to protect from drafts by covering *or* wrapping

pep- *see also under* P- (*Introduction, 3.1.3*)

pepak (*or* ***an**) completely stocked, containing everything. *Toko mau dodolané **. That store carries everything. *Kraméané akèh, tontonané **. There were lots of festivals and every kind of amusement. *Pendak Lebaran sedulur²ku mesti **. Every Lebaran day the whole family gets together. **m̈/di*i** to add sth to the contents of. *Kebon binatangé di*i onta saka Mesir.* The zoo has just added a camel from Egypt to its collection.

pépé to lie in the sun. *Ajo **. Let's take a sun bath. *Baja iku * ing pinggir kali.* Crocodiles sun themselves on river banks. ***an** 1 things (to be) dried in the sun. 2 clothesline (of rope, bamboo). **m̈/di*** to put sth out to sun *or* air. **pa·m̈*** (act of) airing *or* sun-drying things. *Pamépéné ora kena diklantang.* It shouldn't be put in the sun with the soap not rinsed out of it. *See also* MÉ, PÉ

pèpèd ***-*an** to push each other. *Sing nonton pasar malem akèh banget nganti *-*an.* The large crowd of fairgoers were pushing and shoving. **ke*** hard pressed. *Merga wis ke* dèkè kepeksa matèni garongé.* With his back to the wall, he was forced to kill the bandit. *Djalaran saking ke*é dèkè nindakké korupsi.* His need was so pressing that he engaged in corruption. **m̈*** pressed/pushed (against, to); *fig* pressed to the limit. *Lemariné mèpèt témbok.* The cupboard was pressed to the wall. *Butuhé mèpèd.* His need is pressing. *Wektuku/duwitku mèpèd.* I have just barely enough time/money. **m̈/di*aké** to push sth against sth; *fig* to put sth under pressure. *Kursiné pèpètna nang sanding lemari.* Move the chair up against the cupboard. *Tikusé di*ké.* The rat was cornered. *Dèwèké mèpèdké aku.* He argued me into a corner. **m̈/di*i** to press against. *Sekuteré di*i truk nganti munggah trotoir.* The truck pushed the scooter right up onto the sidewalk.

pepek̄ *emphatic form of* PEPAK. *Kolèksiné prangko * banget, endi² ana.* He has stamps from *everywhere* in his collection.

pèpèr to clean oneself without water after defecating

pèpès ***an** banana-leaf-wrapped food roasted over hot coals. **m̈/di*** to prepare [food] as above

pepes limp, lacking strength. *Sikilé **. He has no strength in his legs. *ndjalari *ing atiné* causing her heart to quail. **m̈/di*(aké)** *wj* to deprive smn magically of his strength. *See also* APES

pèpèt *var of* PIPIT

pepet 1 stopped up, blocked; clogging, blocking. *Kalèné * uwuh.* The ditch is choked with trash. *Sing nonton * nganti akèh sing ora éntuk enggon.* So many spectators were jammed in that lots of them couldn't get seats. ** atiné* feeling unhappy and oppressed. 2 character of the Javanese script for writing the sound *e* (as the *e*'s in *bener*). **m̈/di*(i)** to block

pèprèl **m̈/di*(i)** to remove the outer part from. *Djagungé di*i seka bonggolé.* She took the corn kernels off the cob. *Ali lagi mèprèli klapa.* Ali is pulling the fibers from the coconuts.

per- *inf var of* PRA-3. *See also under* PR- (*Introduction, 2.9.3*)

pera dry, grainy, gritty

pérak silver. **se*** *rg* one rupiah

perak *ltry* close, near. ** ésuk* approaching dawn. **m̈*** to approach. *Merak réné.* Come here! **merak ati** attractive. *ngguju amerak ati* to smile pleasantly. **m̈/di*i** to approach sth

peran role. **ku dadi Ardjuna.* I played Ardjuna.

pérang ***an** section, part. *Buku mau diprintji dadi telung *an.* The book is divided into three parts. **m̈/di*(-*)** to divide (up). *mérang² negara dadi pirang² propinsi* to divide a nation into provinces. **sa*an geḍé** most, the majority. *Sa*an gedé bangsa Indonesia kuwi agamané Islam.* Most Indonesians are Moslems.

perang battle, combat; to fight. **ke*** to get cut. **m̈/di*(i)** to cut (up, down). *Kajuné di* dadi tjilik².* He cut the wood into small pieces. **m̈/di*i** to resist. *Werkudara merangi buta.* Werkudara fought the ogre. *merangi piandel Katulik* to struggle against Catholicism. *** n·Donja Kapisan (Kaping Loro)** First (Second) World War. *** gagal** *wj* battle scene that customarily closes the first section of a shadow play. *** sabil** holy war. *** sedulur** civil war. *** tanḍing** hand-to-hand combat. *** tjatur** war of words. *See also* PRANG

Perantjis French. *basa ** French language. *negara ** France

perbal a summons, subpoena. **m̈/di*** to investigate officially; to make a report on. *See also* PROSÈS-PERBAL

perban bandage. ***an** bandaged. **m̃/di*** to bandage

perbeng *var of* PREMBENG

perdâtâ civil (as opposed to criminal); civil court. *hukum ** civil law. **ka*n** a civil case at law

perdi **m̃/di*** to supervise closely, take scrupulous care of

perdjâjâ **m̃/di*** to murder, assassinate

perdjurit *inf var of* PRADJURIT

perdondi difference of opinion, dispute

perduli to care, heed, be concerned. *Wis ora **. I don't care any more. *Aku ora * ana udan.* I don't care if it rains. *Ḍèké ora * kanḍané bapak.* He paid no attention to his father's advice. *ora * saka golongané* without regard for their ethnic origin. ***ǹ(an)** (one who is) concerned. *Wongé ora perdulènan.* He doesn't care about anything. **m̃/di*(kaké)** to heed, care about. *Adja di* omongané kuwi.* Don't worry about what he says. *Jèn merdulèkaké omongané wong, mbingungaké.* If you listen to what people say, you get all mixed up.

perdunten *sbst kr for* PERDULI

pered not slippery, providing traction

perèh *rg var of* PERIH

pèrèng a slope, incline. **pe*** a range of sloping hills; a series of slopes *or* inclines. **m̃*** to slope, slant. *See also* ÈRÈNG

pèrès leveled-off containerful. ***an** cylindrical container used as a rice measure. **m̃*** to measure [dry material] by level containerfuls. **sa*** one level containerful. *gula se** a level spoonful of sugar. *Réwangku sedina tjaḍongé beras sak **. My servant's daily rice ration is one containerful.

pères *var of* PÈRS

peres ***an** squeezed, wrung. *banju *an* pressed-out liquid. *sapi *an* a milk cow. **m̃/di*(i)** to squeeze, wring. *Kambilé di* metu lengané.* She pressed the oil out of the coconut. *Klambiné di* bandjur diisis.* He wrung out his shirt and hung it up to dry. *Tansah di* tenagané déning para tuan tanah.* He is continually exploited by the landowners. **meres kringet** to work hard. **pa·m̃*** act of squeezing. *Pameresé klapa iku jèn wis diparud.* Coconut is pressed [to extract the oil] after it has been grated.

pergedèl croquette (*var of* BERGEDÈL)

pergok **ke*** to get caught. **m̃/di*i** to catch smn at sth wrong *or* improper

peri female ghost *or* spirit

perih to hurt, sting. *See also* PEḌES

péring **ke*** to one side (*var of* KE·PIRING[b]). *Omahé ke* lor pasar.* His house is a little north of the market. *Lungguhé rada ke* adoh.* She sat off to one side.

perkakah *ptg ** spreading out wide to the sides

perkakas tool(s), equipment. *** ḍapur** utensils

perkangkang *var of* PEKANGKANG

perkârâ *ng,* **perkawis** *kr* 1 thing, matter; concerning (the matter of). ** sing wigati* an important matter. ** mau aku ora mangerti.* I don't know anything about that. *Jèn * mbaṭik ora akèh sumurupku.* I don't know much about batik-making. ** pangan sa-enggon² ana.* As for food, it was everywhere. ** sing wis adja dipikir menèh.* Don't think about the past any more. 2 trouble, a problem. *Aku duwé * wigati.* I have a serious problem. *gawé ** to make trouble, make a big thing out of sth. 3 legal matter, case. (*ḍo-ḍok-*)*sèlèhé ** the facts of the case. *Pengadilan lagi ngrembug * korupsi.* The court is considering the corruption case. *kena ** to get sued. *ngadu ** to bring suit. 4 cause, motivation. *Kok isin kuwi, isin * apa?* He's embarrassed: I wonder why? *Dipredjaja ing wong, embuh *né apa?* Someone murdered her—what could the motive have been? *tanpa ** without provocation. ***n** involved in litigation. **di*** to be made an issue of. *Apa sing wis kepungkur adja di* manèh.* Don't rake up what is over and done with. **m̃/di*** to bring a case to court. **m̃/di*kaké** to bring legal action against

perkâsâ *var of* PERKOSA

perkatak *ptg ** 1 *describing a crackling or tearing sound.* 2 having a skin rash. **m̃*** 1 to produce crackling *or* tearing sounds. *Djariké merkatak ketjanṭol paku.* The batik skirt caught on a nail and tore. *Uwuhé garing diobong merkatak.* The dry rubbish crackled as it burned. 2 to have a skin rash

perkawis thing, matter, case, cause (*kr for* PERKARA)

perkèkèh *ptg * pl* seated (improperly) with the legs apart. **m̃*** *sg as above*

perkeneng *var of* PEKENENG

perkengkeng *var of* PEKENGKENG

perkètèk *var of* PERKATAK

perketek̄ *rpr* a cracking *or* crackling sound. *Pangé dak entjiki muni mak **. The branch went crack! when I stepped on it. **m̃*** to crack, crackle, snap

perkèwed *var of* PAKÈWED
perkéwuh *var of* PAKÉWUH
perkinding *var of* PERKINTING
perkinting *ptg* * *pl* covered with goose pimples from fear, excitement, or other strong emotion. **m̃*** *sg as above. Merkinting aku weruh uler.* I felt a thrill of revulsion when I saw the caterpillar.
perkiti:k̄ *ptg* * 1 *rpr* the crackling sound of burning. 2 having a minor skin rash. **m̃*** 1 having a skin rash. 2 furious. *Atiné merkitik krungu anaké disenèni wong.* She saw red when she heard smn had abused her son.
perklaring a letter of permission
perkongkong *var of* PEKONGKONG
perkonjoh *var of* PERKUNJUH
perkosa strong, manly; force, strength. **m̃/di*** to rape
perkotok *ptg* * 1 *rpr* a loud crackling sound of sth burning. 2 having a severe skin rash. **m̃*** having a severe skin irritation. *Tanganè merkutuk kena uler.* His hand is all broken out where he touched a caterpillar.
perkungkung *var of* PEKUNGKUNG
perkunjuh *ptg* * *pl* [of skin] burned, blistered. **m̃*** *sg as above*
perkutuk *ptg* * *or* **m̃*** having a severe skin rash
perkutut turtledove
perlâjâ *oj* dead; to die. *sanalika* * drop dead. *dana* * a pecuniary contribution to a family in which a death has occurred
perlak protective rubber pad for a bed
perlambang symbol, symbolic representation. *Warna abang kuwi * kawanèn.* Red symbolizes courage. **m̃/di*i** to represent symbolically. *Impènmu mralambangi jèn arep éntuk ḍuwit.* Your dream means that you're going to come into some money. *See also* LAMBANG
perlèng **m̃/di*** to prolong, extend. *Pakansiné di* seminggu menèh.* He was given a week's additional vacation.
perlik *ptg* * to twinkle far off. **m̃*** *sg as above*
perlip boy friend, girl friend; lover
perlop furlough
perlu 1 (that which is) important, necessary; (that which is) to be done. *kabar sing ** important news. *Aku duwé *.* I have sth to attend to. *Jèn ora *, aku emoh tuku.* If it's not necessary, I don't want to buy it. *Apa ta *mu?* What do you need? What have you come for? *Wis, iku mau sing *-*.* There, that's the crucially important thing. *Sembajang limang wektu iku *.* It is compulsory to pray five times [a day]. *Ḍèwèké lagi *.* He is saying his prayers (*i.e.* engaging in a compulsory act). 2 in order to. *Ḍèké menjang pasar * tuku beras.* She went to the market to get some rice. ***né** in order to, with the purpose of. **apa *né** what's the use of...? *Apa *né nangisi barang sing wis ilang?* What good will it do to cry over sth you've lost? **ka*an** *or* **ka*n̂** a necessity; a purpose. *Ana ke*an apa?–Aku ora duwé ke*an apa².* Why have you come here?–No special purpose. *barang² kaperlon sa-dina²* basic daily needs. **m̃/di*k̂aké** to consider important; to find a way to [do]. *Apa sing diperlokaké?* What did he give priority to? *Mesṭi mrelokaké nonton.* You must be sure to see it. *pembangunan sing mrelok²aké tjutjul wragad akèh* a development which makes it urgent to raise large sums of money. *Sadurungé ḍuwité dienggo tuku sing ora *-*, diperlokaké ḍisik tuku beras.* Before you spend the money on nonessentials, be sure to get rice. **sa*** only for the purpose of; only what is necessary. *Jèn omong mung sa*.* He wastes no words. **sa*né** 1 what is important about sth. *Murid² njaṭet sa*né.* The students took notes on the important things. 2 everything one needs. *Sa*mu tak tjukupi.* I'll supply whatever you need.
perlup 1 engaged to be married. 2 loose, loosened. *Sekrupé *.* The screw has come loose.
permadi the middle sibling
permânâ *ng,* **permanem** *kr* [of vision] sharp, clear. **m̃/di*kaké** to scrutinize. *See also* SIḌEM
permanem *kr for* PERMANA
permati careful, circumspect
permèn 1 mentholated peppermint candy wafers (packaged Lifesaver-style). 2 any kind of candy excluding chocolate
permili *rg var of* PAMILI
permingsi *var of* PERMISI
permisi (to ask for) permission to go away
permumuh *var of* TJERMUMUH
pernah 1 position, location. **é plabuhané ana saloré Djakarta.* The harbor is north of Djakarta. 2 related as [a relative outside of the nuclear family]. *Anaké mbakjuku * keponakan karo aku.* My sister's daughter is my niece. ** nom/tuwa* (related as) a younger/older relative. *Merga ḍèké * tuwa aku kudu basa.* Since he's an older relative, I have

to speak Krama to him. 3 settled, at home. *Wis sewulan manggon omah anjar iki, nanging durung* *. They've been living in their new home for a month now but they're not settled yet. **ka*** 1 located. *Bodjonegoro ka* wétané Semarang.* Bodjonegoro is east of Semarang. 2 related. *Pak Guru isih ke* paman karo aku.* The teacher is my uncle. **m̃/di*aké** to place sth smw. *Dolanané ora tau diprenahaké ing panggonané.* He never puts his toys away.

pernâtâ *n 1 regulation, ordinance, rule. 2 formal reception. **m̃/di*kaké** to put into a suitable arrangement. *Nalika X mantu, aku sing mernatakaké dalemé.* When X held his daughter's wedding, I prepared his house for him. *Sadurungé turu, buku^2 sing kanggo sésuk di*kaké.* Before he went to bed, he laid out his books for tomorrow. **m̃/di*(i)** to regulate; to arrange. *Sapa sing mranata katentremaning pradja?* Who is in charge of national security? *Botjah mau ora kena di*.* That boy can't be controlled. *mranata tamu* to seat guests (in a certain seating arrangement). *** mangsa** astrological calculation according to the Javanese calendar seasons (*see* MANGSA 2). *See also* TATA

pernès (*or* *an) [of a narrative] appealing and light-hearted. *lakon sing akèh *ané* a story full of romance and humor. **pe*an** designed to appeal. *basa pe*an* flattering talk designed to gain favor with smn of the opposite sex

perngangah the red glow of flame. *ptg * pl* to glow. *Kaju^{2}né isih kétok ptg *.* The timbers [of the burned-out house] are still glowing embers. **m̃*** to glow. **m̃/di*aké** to cause to glow. *Merngangahna geniné.* Get the fire going!

perngangas *rpr* a broadly jeering laugh. **m̃*** to laugh as above

perngèngès *rpr* a light jeering laugh. **m̃*** to laugh as above

perngingis *rpr* a very light jeering laugh. **m̃*** to laugh as above

perngongos *rpr* a loud jeering laugh. **m̃*** to laugh as above

pernis varnish. **m̃/di*** to apply varnish to. *kursi sing di** a varnished chair

pernjènjèngan to swagger, boast, behave arrogantly

péron station platform. *kertjis ** a ticket permitting one to enter the platform

pérot [of mouth] awry, twisted to one side. **m̃*** to twist the lips to one side (a gesture showing dislike, contempt, disbelief). **mérat-m̃*** to keep twisting the lips. **m̃/di*aké** to twist [the lips] as a teasing *or* disdainful gesture. *mérotké lambéné* to twist the lips. **m̃*i** to make the above gesture. *Jèn ngétjé mesṭi karo méroti.* When she makes fun of people she twists her lips.

Perpat *wj* group of four clown-servants to the Penḍawa brothers. *See also* WULU-TJUMBU

perpek̄ *oj* **m̃/di*i** to approach, come close(r) to

pèrs the press. ** asing* the foreign press. ** ḍélik* libelous or other actionable matter printed in the public press. ** réaksonèr* reactionary press. *adu swara ing ** to carry on an argument via the newspapers. *nempuh dalan ** to make use of the press as a means to an end, *e.g.* to provide enlightenment

persâdjâ plain, unaffected. *Klambiné *.* Her dress is simple. *Gunemané *.* He spoke in a straightforward manner. **m̃/di*ni** to tell the truth (to)

persâpâ *var of* PRASAPA

persasat *var of* PRASASAT

Persatuan Bangsa-Bangsa (*abbr*: **P.B.B.**) the United Nations

persekot prepayment; down payment, advance, deposit. *Kula punapa kedah njaosi *?* Shall I give you a deposit? **m̃/di*i** to pay (for) in advance

persèn 1 per cent. 2 gift, present. 3 a tip. *Ḍèké éntuk * serupiah.* He got a one-rupiah tip. **m̃/di*i** to give a tip to. *mersèni djongos rèstoran* to tip the waiter

persèntase, persèntasi percentage

Pèrsi Iran

persil 1 bale, bundle. ** mbako* a bale of tobacco. 2 a parcel of agricultural land held by long-lease tenure

persis exactly, precisely; a perfect fit. *Anaké * ibuné.* The child is exactly like her mother. *djam lima ** exactly five o'clock. *Tekan setasiun * sepuré manḍeg.* He got to the station just as the train stopped. *Klambiné *.* The shirt fits perfectly.

perslah result(s); a report of the result(s)

persnèleng gears, transmission. **é dioper loro.* He shifted into second gear.

persoal problem. **m̃/di*aké** to make an issue of. *See also* SOAL

person personal; private. *Djip * apa djip djawatan?* Is it a privately owned jeep or an official jeep?

personil 1 personal. *padjeg* * personal property tax. 2 personnel
persudi **ṁ/di*** to exert one's best efforts toward [a goal]
persun *var of* PERSON
pertal ***an** a translation. **ṁ/di*** to translate
pertâṇḍâ 1 mark, indication. **né jèn atiné bungah.* It showed that he was happy. *Menḍungé peteng * arep udan.* The clouds are dark, indicating that it's going to rain. 2 document bearing an official signature. **ṁ/di*kaké** to show, indicate. **ṁ/di*ni** 1 to mark sth. *Garis kuwi sing mertanḍani bédané wektu.* The [International Date] Line marks the difference in time. 2 to show, indicate. *Hawané saja aḍem, mratanḍani jèn wis ngarepaké bangun ésuk.* It was getting colder, showing that dawn was approaching. *See also* TANḌA
pertâpâ ***n** 1 place where one meditates in solitude. 2 hermitage. **ṁ*** to perform an act of solitary meditation. *See also* TAPA
pertéla to announce, explain. ***n** 1 explanation; announcement. **n ḍapuring ḍuwung* specifications for a kris. *Konperènsi mau gawé *n kang wosé ngetjap Negara A kadidéné "aggressor."* The conference issued a proclamation labeling Nation A as an aggressor. 2 a list, listing. **n ungel²an* a list of sounds. **ṁ/di*kaké** *or* **ṁ/di*ni** to announce, explain sth. *mratélakaké sebab* to explain the reason. *Kluruké djago mratélakaké djam papat ésuk.* The cock's crow proclaimed that it was 4 A.M. *Lajang iki mertélakaké jèn A arep teka réné sésuk.* This letter says that A is coming tomorrow. *mertélani bab keséhatan nganggo basa sing gampang* to explain matters of hygiene in simple language. *See also* TÉLA
pertepèl *var of* PORTEPÈL
perti *rg* **ṁ/di*(ṅi)** to care for. *Tandur²ané dipertèni banget.* He tends his plants with great care. * **désa** *or* **merti désa** *var of* BERSIH DÉSA
pertikel 1 way, means. **é njirnakaké malaria* how to stamp out malaria. *sugih* * full of ideas/schemes. 2 advice. *Aku manut marang iguh lan *é.* I followed his advice. **ṁ/di*aké** to advise. *Apa sing di*aké wong tuwa kudu diturut.* You should do whatever your parents advise.
pertingkah 1 actions, behavior. *Aku njawang *é A.* I watched what A did. **é èlèk.* He does bad things. 2 bad behavior, misconduct. **ṁ*** to engage in bad conduct. *See also* TINGKAH
pertingsing demanding, imperious. *kakèhan* * excessively demanding *or* pretentious; given to caprice *or* whims
pertiwi *oj* earth, soil, ground
pertjados *sbst kr for* PERTJAJA
pertjah *see* GETAH
pertjâjâ *ng,* **pitados** *kr* **ϕ/di*** to believe, rely on, trust. *Aku * karo omongané.* I believe what he says. ** marang ḍiri pribadiné* to have faith in oneself. *Guneme ora kena di*.* His word is not to be trusted. *Tjritané angèl bisa di*.* His story is hard to swallow. **ka*n** faith, belief, confidence. *lajang ke*n* a letter expressing confidence. *ka*né agama Buḍa* Buddhist beliefs. *Aku wis ora duwé ka*n karo ḍèwèké.* I have no faith in him any more. **ṁ/di*kaké** to entrust sth to. *Aku mertjajakaké anakku marang mbakjuku.* I placed the care of my son in my sister's hands.
pertjet *rpr* laying an egg; (*cr*) *rpr* giving birth. *Pitikku mak * ngenḍog.* Plunk! my hen laid an egg.
pertjil a young frog that is no longer a tadpole
pertjit *var of* PERTJET
pertjumah useless, in vain. *Nganḍani *, sengara digugu.* It's a waste of breath to give him advice–he won't listen.
peru *var of* AMPERU
pèrubalsem healing disinfectant used for cuts. **ṁ/di*** to apply the above to. *mèrubalsem tatu* to put disinfectant on a cut. *See also* BALSEM
perung missing an ear. *Kupingé *.* He has only one ear. **ṁ/di*** to cut off smn's ear
perwâsâ **ṁ/di*** 1 to use force against; to torture. 2 to rape. **ṁ*-p·in·erwasa** to use force against each other; to push each other around
perwira 1 mighty, powerful, courageous. 2 (*prn* **perwirā**) military officer from lieutenant up. **ka*n** courage; might. *adu ka*n* pitting their bravery against each other
pès the black plague. **nge/di*** to cook [*e.g.* fish] by wrapping in banana leaves and roasting
pes *rpr* air rushing out. *Mak * plembunganè kempès.* Suddenly the air rushed out of the balloon.
pesa *inf var of* PEKSA
pesâdjâ *var of* PERSADJA
pesagi square; rectangular. *kreḍus * tjilik* a

little square box. *ǹ a square; a rectangle. *pesagèn bunder* a square with rounded corners. * **ng·apan-apan** trapezoid having one pair of identical acute and one pair of identical obtuse angles. * **dawa** rectangle that is not a square. * **kubik** cubic, cube-shaped. * **m̀·piring** parallelogram that is not a rectangle

pesat *var of* PLESAT

pèsèk [of nose] flat (rather than having the ideal tapering form). **m̀/di*aké** to make flat. *Mèsèkaké irung umumé paḍa ora gelem, malah sing * paḍa dibangiraké.* People don't want to flatten their noses; in fact, they try to make flat ones taper.

pesen to order. * *buku* to order a book. **m̀/di*** to put in an order for sth. *mesen panggonan* to make a reservation

pesi bird (*kr for* MANUK)

pesijar *var of* BESIJAR

pesing redolent of urine

pesisir shore, coast; coastal region. ***an** shoreline; coastal territory

pesmèn *inf var of* PA·SEMI·Ǹ

péso table knife. * **blaṭi** dagger. * **raut** small razor-sharp knife

pésok having a dent in it. **pésak-*** full of dents

pésta, pèsta a large dinner party

pesṭi predestined fate. **(pe)*ǹ** that which is predestined *or* inevitable. *Rakjat mbajar padjeg iku pepesṭèn.* Taxation is unavoidable. **di*** predestined. *Wong mau di* dadi pemimpin agung.* He is destined to be a great leader. **m̀*** inevitable (*see* MESṬI). **m̀/di*kaké** to make *or* feel certain of; to fix, set, determine. *Ḍokter nambani, nanging ora mesṭèkaké waras.* Doctors prescribe, but they cannot guarantee recovery. *Aku mesṭèkaké jèn bakal menang.* I feel certain I'm going to win. *Adja dipesṭèkaké djamé.* Don't set a time for it. *Adja sok mesṭèk²aké.* Never be dogmatic. *Wong durung karuwan kok di-pesṭèk²aké.* It's not certain yet, but he's already taking it for granted. *Aku mbokmenawa teka nèng nggonmu sésuk ning ora bisa mesṭèkaké.* I may come to see you tomorrow but I can't say for sure. **p·in·esṭi** *ltry var of* DI*. *djoḍo pinasṭi* predestined mates. *See also* MESṬI

pestul *inf var of* PISTUL

pesu **m̀/di*** to exert one's utmost effort. *Ḍèké mesu budi tapa.* He devoted himself to meditation.

pèt 1 officer's cap, cap with a bill at the front. 2 kerosene (*shf of* PÉTROLI)

pet *rpr* sudden darkness. *Dijané dipatèni, *, *.* They blew out the lamps. *Mak * lampuné listrik mati.* Suddenly the lights went out. *Mak * kesupèn.* Just like that, he forgot it. ***-*an** to have a throbbing headache. *See also* BJAR

peṭa 1 a likeness. 2 a map. **pe*n** a likeness. *pe*ning rembulan tanggal sepisan* a representation of a crescent moon

pétak compartment, partitioned-off space. *omah ** a large house divided into separate apartments. **m̀/di*-*** to divide up into compartments; to partition up

péṭak a hairless spot on the skull resulting from a scar

petak **m̀/di*** to bury (*ki for* Ň G/DI·KUBUR)

peṭak white (*kr for* PUTIH). ***an** cambric for working in batik (*rg? kr for* MORI)

peṭakil ***an** *or* **m̀*** 1 to have the legs wound around sth *or* resting on sth higher than the body (improper). 2 [of girls] (to act) boisterous and unfeminine. **m̀/di*aké** to place [the legs] improperly as above

peṭal severed, separated. *botjah tjilik ** a lost child (*i.e.* separated from the parents). *Sirahé * karo awaké.* The head was severed from the body. *Tunangané wis *.* Their engagement has been broken off. **m̀/di*(i)** to separate, sever. *Aku ora bisa meṭal daging²é sing ndjenḍel dadi sidji.* I couldn't separate the pieces of meat that had frozen together.

pétan *ng kr,* **ulik** *ki* to hunt lice in each other's hair (often done by village women, sitting in a line, with each working on the hair of the lady in front of her). **m̀/di*i** to hunt lice in *or* pick lice from [smn's hair]; *fig* to search out [flaws], engage in nit-picking

pétang calculation (*kr for* PÉTUNG)

petang *inf var of* PATANG

peṭangkrang **m̀/di*aké** to elevate [the feet]

peṭangkrèk *ptg * pl* sitting perched in a high place, *e.g.* on a branch (improper). **m̀*** *sg as above*

peṭangkrik, peṭangkring, peṭangkrok, peṭangkrong, peṭangkruk *var of* PEṬANGKRÈK

peṭanṭang *ptg * pl* seated with the legs apart (improper). **m̀*** *sg as above. Botjah wéḍok jèn lingguh ora kena meṭanṭang mengko nḍak diarani ora susila.* A girl shouldn't sit with her legs spread–she'd be considered ill-bred.

petâpâ *var of* PERTAPA

peṭat comb (*kr for* DJUNGKAT)

peṭaṭak *ptg* ∗ *pl* seated with the legs spread (unmannerly). **m̈∗** *sg as above.* **m̈/di∗aké** to spread [the legs] apart while sitting

peṭaṭus *ptg* ∗ having an undershot jaw and jutting chin

peté a variety of bean

peṭéjot *var of* PLÉTOT

pèṭèk **∗an** monk-style haircut, *i.e.* bald on top with a fringe below. **m̈/di∗** to cut *or* wear [the hair] in this style

petèk *rpr* the cackling of a chicken (*see also* PETOK)

petek̄ to have a massage (*kr?, ki for* PIDJET). **m̈/di∗i** to give a massage to [an esteemed person]. *Bapak lagi di∗i ḍukun.* The faith healer is massaging Father.

peṭèk a guess. *∗ ora.* I would guess not. *djuru ∗* or *tukang ∗* soothsayer; mind reader. **m̈/di∗** to guess (the answer to); to mind-read. **m̈/di∗aké** to tell smn's fortune; to make predictions about sth. *Pantjèn njata, ora susah awak di-peṭèk²aké.* Of course it's true–you don't need to be told that by a fortune-teller. **pa·m̈∗** act *or* way of telling fortunes. *Ḍèké pertjaja menjang pameṭèké tukang ∗.* He believes in soothsayers' predictions. *See also* TJOLONG

peṭekel *ptg* ∗ muscular; bulging with muscles all over the body. **m̈∗** muscular (in general; in a particular part). *Pawakané meṭekel atos.* His body is firm and muscular. *Tangané meṭekel.* He has muscular arms.

peṭékol 1 crooked, bent. 2 *var of* PEṬEKEL

pèṭèl **m̈/di∗i** to break *or* snap sth off with the fingers. *Ḍèwèké ngintjup kindjeng di∗i swiwiné.* He caught a dragonfly and broke off its wings.

petel **m̈/di∗(aké)** to press forcibly

peṭèl 1 carpenter's adze. *Untuné sa∗-∗.* His teeth are the size of adzes. 2 powerful. *sikut ∗* strong arms ('elbows'). **m̈/di∗** to work [wood] with an adze. *See also* GLÈṬÈK

peṭel hard-working, industrious

peteng 1 dark. *Kamaré ∗ apa paḍang?* Was the room dark or lighted? 2 obscure; undercover; gloomy. *∗ing gugon tuhon* the darkness (ignorance) of superstition. *Pulisi durung bisa mènèhi keterangan apa², perkara mau isih ∗.* The police can't give out any information; the facts are still obscure. *barang ∗* illicit goods. *lembu ∗* an illegitimate child. *Atiné ∗.* His spirits are low. *Rainé ∗.* He looks gloomy. **∗an** 1 (in the) darkness. *Aku jèn turu senengé ∗an.* I like to sleep in the dark. 2 the dark of the moon. **pe∗** the dark; darkness (physical, intellectual, spiritual). **ka∗an** 1 to be overtaken by darkness. *Aku baliné mau bengi ke∗an.* I didn't get back till after dark. *Aku kepeksa nginep merga wis ka∗an.* I had to stay over; night had come on. 2 to have one's view obstructed. **ke∗en** excessively dark, *i.e.* not bright, [of colors] not light. *Wernané kuwi apik ning rada ke∗en siṭik.* The color is pretty but it's a bit too dark. **m̈/di∗aké** to make darker. *Lampuné di∗aké.* He turned down the light. **m̈/di∗i** to darken sth; to cut off a view. *Adja metengi, aku lagi matja.* Don't cut off my light, I'm reading. *Lungguhmu rada rana siṭik, aku di∗i.* Sit over that way a bit–you're blocking my view. **∗ n·ḍeḍet** *or* **∗ n·dumuk irung** *or* **∗ gagap** *or* **∗ le·limeng·an** pitch dark. *See also* GEḌONG

peṭèngèl *var of* PENṬÈNGÈL

peṭengil *var of* PENṬÈNGÈL

peṭèngkol *ptg* ∗ *pl* twisted, bent, gnarled (*e.g.* tree branches; muscles). **m̈∗** *sg as above*

peṭèngkrèk *var of* PEṬÈNGKRÈNG

peṭèngkrèng *ptg* ∗ *pl* perched in a high place. *ptg ∗ ana ing anḍa* up on a ladder. **∗an** *or* **m̈∗** *sg as above.* **m̈/di∗aké** to put sth *or* smn in a high place

peṭengkreng *ptg* ∗ *pl* sitting silent and motionless. **m̈∗** *sg as above*

petèntèng *var of* PETÈTÈNG

peṭènṭeng *ptg* ∗ *pl* with hands on hips in a defiant *or* arrogant pose. **∗an** *or* **m̈∗** *sg as above.* *Pak Karta ngadeg tangané meṭènṭèng ngawasi wong sing paḍa njambut gawé.* Mr. Karto stood over the men, hands on hips, watching them work.

peṭenṭeng *ptg* ∗ *pl* 1 tensed with effort or (*esp.*) anger. 2 swollen from infection. **∗an** to argue heatedly. *A lan B paḍa ∗an bab politik.* A and B were hotly debating the political situation. **m̈∗** *sg* tensed with anger or effort. *Ḍèké wis meṭenṭeng, mripaté mloṭot.* His muscles were tensed and his eyes glared. *Olèhé njurung motor wis meṭenṭeng nanging motoré obah waé ora.* He strained every muscle to push the car but it wouldn't budge.

peṭèsèl *ptg* ∗ *pl* small but tough. **m̈∗** *sg as above*

peṭèt **m̈/di∗(i)** 1 to graft a cutting (onto). *meṭèt wit pelem* to graft a branch onto a mango tree. 2 to snap the finger lightly against [a song bird] to induce it to sing

petété *rpr* coming into view suddenly. *mBareng koloré pedot, wetengé mak * kétok.* His underwear string broke and showed his bare stomach. **m̈*** to stick out, show [of a bare midsection]

peṭéṭé **peṭéṭa-*** *or* **m̈*** to swagger, act defiant *or* boastful. *Wongé tjilik nanging meṭéṭé, rumangsané apa² ngerti.* He's small but cocky–thinks he knows it all.

peṭèṭèh *rpr* a wide-legged stance *or* sitting position. **peṭéṭah-*** to walk wide-legged with knees bent, *e.g.* when in pain. **m̈*** 1 to walk as above. 2 *var of* M̈-PETÉTÉ

peṭèṭèk *ptg * pl* sitting (improperly) with the legs apart. **m̈*** *sg as above*

peṭeṭek *ptg * pl* lying in small piles. *Akèh tai asu ptg * nang plataran.* There are dog droppings around the yard. **m̈*** forming a small mound/heap

petètèng ***-*** arrogant, cocksure

peṭi box, trunk, chest. ***n̈** 1 a small box *or* trunk. 2 by the boxful. *Olèhé tuku sabun peṭèn.* He bought some boxes of soap.

petik *ltry* **m̈/di*(aké)** to inform

peṭik ***an** that which is picked; act of picking. **an tèh iku dibédakaké dadi rong werna, *an alus lan *an kasar.* They pick two kinds of tea leaves, fine and coarse. **an saka Kitab Sutji* a selection from the Bible. ***-*** to keep picking. *peṭik² kembang* to pick flower after flower. **ka*** picked (out). *dongèng² sing ka* saka Serat Bratajuda* tales selected from the Bratajuda narratives. **m̈/di*aké** to pick for smn. *Slamet meṭikaké kembang Siti.* Slamet picked Siti a flower. **m̈/di*(i)** to pick (out), to extract. *meṭik woh* to pluck fruit. *Sing tak * iki dongèngé Kantjil.* The one I've picked is a Mouse-Deer story. *Krambil² sing wis tuwa di*i ditibakaké.* He selected the mature coconuts and let them fall [from the tree]. **pa·m̈*** selection; act of picking. *Jèn tanpa eri nggampangaké pameṭiké.* They're easy to pick when they have no thorns. **sa*** a tiny bit. *suruh se** a bit of betel-chew

pètikut petticoat

peṭil 1 to fall off. *Kembangé *.* The flower dropped off the stem. 2 small wooden mallet. ***an** a fragment. **an wajang wong* an episode taken from a classical dance-drama. **m̈/di*(i)** 1 to remove sth from a larger part. *Iki lo, ṭokolan peṭikana.* Here, cut the tips from these beansprouts. *meṭil pelem* to pick a mango from the branch. 2 to hit with a mallet

peṭing **(pe)*an** of the highest quality. *mbako sing *an* carefully selected tobaccos. *ngulama Islam kang *an* top-notch Islamic priests

peṭingil *var of* PENTINGIL

peṭingkrang *var of* PEṬINGKRIK

peṭingkrik *ptg * pl* sitting in a high-up position. **m̈*** *sg as above. Prijaji sepuh² paḍa lenggah nang ngisor kowé kok meṭingkring lingguh kursi.* Elderly people are sitting on the floor and you're occupying a chair–!

peṭingkring *var of* PEṬINGKRIK

peṭingṭing *var of* PEṬINṬING

petinṭing *ptg * pl* tight-fitting. *Sanḍangané botjah² wédok ptg *.* The girls' dresses clung to them. **m̈*** *sg as above*

petis meat *or* shrimp extract. **m̈/di*** to make [meat, shrimp] into extract

peṭisil *ptg * pl* wiry (of physique). **m̈*** *sg as above*

peṭit a tapering point, *esp.* the tail of a snake *or* mouse

peṭiṭi **peṭiṭa-*** arrogant, high-handed

petitis 1 plain, obvious. 2 correct. *wangsulan kang ** the right answer. **m̈/di*aké** to demonstrate beyond doubt. *Menawa tuku mas inten kudu di*aké temenan.* When you buy gold and jewelry you should satisfy yourself that they're genuine.

petjah to break (off, out). *Enḍogé tiba *.* The egg fell and broke. *nalika * perang* at the outbreak of war. ** pasedulurané.* Their friendship broke off. *Kabar mau wis *.* The news broke. *rasa *-belah* feelings of dissension. ***an** 1 a fragment. **an genḍèng* a broken piece of roofing tile. **an beling* a splinter of glass. 2 fraction. **an lumrah* ordinary fraction. **an memet* compound (complex) fraction. **an pradasan* decimal fraction. **an repetèn* repeating fraction. ***-*** breaking here and there. *Geḍang iki kulité *-*.* These bananas have brittle skins. *Lambéné *-* merga kurang vitamin C.* His lips were cracking because of a vitamin C deficiency. **m̈*** 1 to break (open, out). *Wuduné metjah.* The abcess burst. 2 (*psv* **di***) to break (into, through) sth. *metjah katja* to break glass. *Tjèlènganè di*, preg.* He smashed his piggy bank. *metjah petenging gugon tuhon* to break through the darkness of superstition. *Tanah Djawa di* dadi telung* *propinsi.* Java is divided into three provinces. *metjah durèn* (*slang*) to break the hymen of a virgin girl. **m̃/di∗-∗** to break intentionally. *metjah² pring saros* to break off a joint of bamboo. **m̃/di∗aké 1** to break unintentionally. *Botjah² metjahaké ting.* The boys broke a street light. *Dolanan larang² iki di∗-∗aké.* He broke all these expensive toys. 2 to solve. *metjahaké soal* to solve a problem. **∗ nalar·é** to learn to think for oneself. **∗ pamor** to (break open and) reveal the beauty within (*referring esp. to the flowering of a girl's beauty*). *See also* BALA-PETJAH

pétjak *rg var of* PITJAK

petjak 1 a pace. 2 length of the sole of the foot as a unit of measurement. 3 mixture of certain seasonings for salting and drying meat. **m̃/di∗(i) 1** to measure (*esp.* land) by pacing; to pace off [a distance]. 2 to treat [meat] with the above mixture. **sa∗** one pace; (one's) every step. *Menawa wong lagi nasibé tjilaka kuwi, mlaku satindak se∗ kok ja klèru.* When luck is running against you, everything you do is wrong.

petjalang *wj* palace guard

petjat ∗-∗ off and on. *∗-∗ éling* to remember only vaguely *or* spottily. **m̃/di∗(i)** to discharge, dismiss. *Ḍèké di∗ saka kalungguhané.* He got fired. **m̃∗i** moribund

pétjé one-eyed; blind in one eye

petjeklik time of critical food shortage (one or two months before harvest)

petjèl **∗an** cut-up pieces. **m̃/di∗(i)** to cut into small pieces. *metjèli kaju* to cut wood into short lengths. *Télané di∗i tjilik².* She cut the cassava into small pieces.

petjel a cooked vegetable salad with peanut dressing. **m̃/di∗** to make [ingredients] into this dish. **metjel manuk m·abur** to do sth that requires great skill. **∗ ajam** chicken boiled in spiced coconut milk. **∗ enḍog** eggs and mixed vegetables in peanut-butter sauce

petjengès *rpr* a sudden jeering laugh. *ptg ∗ pl* to laugh as above. **m̃∗** *sg* to laugh as above. *Dikanḍani mung metjengès ora nggatèkaké.* He was given a talking to, but he only laughed it off.

petjengis *var of* PETJENGÈS

petjétjé *var of* PEṬÉṬÉ

pètji fez-shaped cap

petjing disagreeable odor. **∗an** commission for goods sold. **m̃∗** to ask for a commission

petjingil *var of* PENTJINGIL

petjitjil *ptg ∗ pl* to gawk, stare about in an unmannerly way. **∗an** *or* **petjitjal-∗** *or* **m̃∗** 1 *sg as above.* 2 to stare fixedly. *Mripaté metjitjil.* His eyes stared glassily. 3 striving without success. *Jèn dadi pegawai negeri bajaré ora sepiraa, nganti metjitjil mesṭi ora bisa tuku motor.* Government employees' salaries are so low they can never afford a car.

petjoh to fight [with another rooster]. **m̃/di∗i** to attack [another chicken]

pétjok sickle. **m̃/di∗** to lop off with a sickle

petjok **m̃/di∗(i)** to cut off. *Blaraké kang wis garing di∗i.* He cut the dried leaves from the coconut.

petjongol *var of* PENTJONGOL

petjotjo *var of* PETJUTJU

petjroh *var of* PETJOH

petjuh male sperm

petjuk *rg var of* PÉTJOK

petjungul *var of* PENTJUNGUL

petjus able to [do], capable of [do]ing. *Ḍèké ora ∗ nunggang pit nanging arep adjar nunggang pit montor.* He couldn't manage a bicycle and now he wants to learn to ride a motorcycle! *See also* KUMETJUS

petjut a whip. **m̃/di∗(i)** to whip; *fig* to inspire, motivate

petjuṭat *rpr* emerging suddenly, *e.g.* a squeezed-out fruit seed. *ptg ∗ pl* to bound/emerge suddenly. *Pelemé sing bosok diontjèki sèté ptg ∗.* When he peeled the rotted mango, out swarmed the maggots. **m̃∗** *sg as above. Walangé arep ditubruk metjuṭat.* The grasshopper sprang off as it was about to be caught.

petjutju **petjutja-∗** to keep pouting. **m̃∗** with lips thrust forward. *Metjutju sebab nesu.* He's pouting because he's mad. *Olèhé mangan kok nganti metjutju.* His mouth is so full his lips stick out. **m̃/di∗k̂aké** to thrust forward [the lips]. *Lambéné dipetjutjokaké.* He stuck his lips out. **m̃/di∗n̂i** to gesture deprecatingly to [smn] with a forward thrust of the lips. *Ḍèké di-aruh²i apik² kok malah metjutjoni.* I greeted him pleasantly and he just stuck out his lips at me!

petok (*or* ∗-∗) to cackle; the sound of a hen's cackle. *See also* GOG

peṭokol *var of* PEṬEKEL, PEṬÉKOL

peṭola a cookie-like snack of rice flour, eaten with brown-sugar syrup and coconut milk

peṭongkrok *var of* PEṬONGKRONG
peṭongkrong *ptg* ∗ *pl* sitting up high with the legs drawn up (improper). **m̈∗** *sg as above*
peṭongol *var of* PENṬONGOL
petontong *ptg* ∗ *pl* protruding outward [of long objects]. **m̈∗** *sg as above*
péṭot curved, bent (rather than straight). *See also* PLÉṬOT
peṭot *var of* BEṬOT
petoto *rpr* a sudden emergence. *Bané ndjero mak ∗ terus ndjebluk.* The inner tube swelled up and blew out. *Mak ∗ wudelé kétok.* His navel popped into view. **m̈∗** to emerge. *Kidangé dibeḍil kena sirahé, mripaté nganti metoto.* The deer was shot in the head; its eyes came out.
peṭoṭok *ptg* ∗ *pl* squatting on the haunches with the legs apart (an unmannerly position). **m̈∗** *sg as above*
petotong *var of* PETONTONG
petri **m̈/di·pe∗** to take scrupulous care of. *memetri pesaréjané éjang* to tend the grave of one's grandfather. *Kagunan sing adi-luwih kudu dipepetri.* The fine arts should be cherished.
pétroli kerosene; petroleum
pétromak(s) pressurized gasoline lamp, Coleman lamp
Pétruk *wj* tall long-nosed mischievous clown who serves the Pendawas. *Irung ∗ popular name of a certain curve in a road near Jogja where the road doubles back on itself. See also* WULU-TJUMBU
peṭuk 1 to agree (on). *Rembugé bisa ∗.* They reached an agreement by discussing it. 2 [an official document] requiring payment (of *e.g.* taxes, school tuition). *lajang ∗* a document as above. **∗an** 1 vehicle sent to pick smn up. *ndjaluk ∗an ambulans* to send for an ambulance for a patient. 2 to meet and pass from opposite directions. *Aku ∗an wong² sing paḍa mulih saka pasar.* I met some people who were coming home from the market. **ke∗ (p·in·anggih** *kr*) to meet, run into, see. *Apa wis tau ke∗ matjan?* Have you ever come face-to-face with a tiger? *Angger ke∗ laler patènana.* Whenever you see a fly, kill it. *Ke∗ montor mlaku banter.* A car was coming toward them going fast. **m̈/di∗aké** to go to meet smn who is arriving. *Botjah² mlaju meṭukaké embokné.* The children ran to meet their mother (coming home). *Tekané di∗aké déning Warsini.* Warsini met him [at the station]. **m̈/di∗(i)** to meet, (go to) see *or* pick up. *Aku bésuk ∗en motor, ja.* Please come and get me in the car, OK? *Apa kowé wis tau meṭuki gendruwo?* Have you ever seen a ghost?
pétung *ng*, **pétang** *kr* (*or* **∗an**) 1 calculation. *Kurang weruh ∗.* He's not very good at figures. *∗an kanggo slametan* calculations for (when to hold) ritual ceremonies. 2 excessively careful with one's money. **∗an** number value of days *etc.* used in numerological calculations. **ke∗** to be considered *or* taken into account. *Wis ke∗ ragad kirim.* Transportation costs are included. *Negari wau kapétang negari ingkang sampun madjeng.* It is considered an advanced nation. **m̈/di∗** to calculate, *esp.* numerologically. *See also* ÉTUNG
petung a variety of large bamboo
peṭungkruk *ptg* ∗ *pl* sitting with hunched backs. **m̈∗** *sg as above*
peṭungkrung *var of* PEṬUNGKRUK
peṭungul *var of* PENṬUNGUL
peṭunṭung *ptg* ∗ swollen in many places. **peṭunṭang-∗** 1 swollen. 2 arrogant, conceited. **m̈∗** *sg* swollen
peṭut *ltry* outlaw leader, head of a gang
peṭuṭuk *ptg* ∗ *pl* forming a series of uniform heaps. *Gunung² paḍa ptg ∗.* Mountain after mountain receded into the distance. *Omah²ané wis dadi, ptg ∗.* The tents had been set up in neat rows. **m̈∗** to accumulate, form a heap. *Pawuhané saben wis meṭuṭuk akèh, diobong.* As the trash accumulates, it is burned. *Murah merga meṭuṭuké produksi.* They're cheap because of overproduction. **m̈/di∗aké** to pile things up, accumulate things. *Olèhé meṭuṭukaké téla sak enggon².* They heaped cassavas everywhere.
pi *adr* cow! (*shf of* SAPI)
pi- *noun-deriving prefix: see entries below, see also under individual roots*
piagem royal decree *or* document conferring land *or* high office upon the recipient. **m̈/di∗i** to bestow [land, high office] on
pialā(h) cup, trophy
piatu motherless. *See also* JATIM
pidak **∗an** pedal; sth to step on. **ke∗** to get stepped on. *Ana botjah tjilik mati ke∗-∗.* A child was trampled to death. **m̈/di∗** to step on sth. *midak telèk pitik* to step in some chicken manure. **∗ pedarakan** of the lowest social stratum. **∗ sikil djawil m̈·pungkur** to harm others with pretending unawareness

pidânâ penalty for a criminal offense. * *pati* death penalty. **ṁ/di*** to inflict a penalty on [a criminal]

piḍanget **ṁ*** to hear (*kr? ki? for* KRUNGU). **ṁ/di*aké** to listen (to) (*kr? ki? for* ṄG/DI-RUNGU·K̂AKÉ). **pa·ṁ*** sense of hearing; what is heard; hearer, listener (*kr? ki? for* PA·NG-RUNGU)

pidek̄ *var of* PIDAK

pideksa well built (of physique)

piḍih *ltry* **ṁ/di*** to blacken, make dark

pidjar constant (*rg var of* PIDJER)

pidjer 1 constant, incessant. *Bok adja * njelani waé.* Don't keep interrupting! *Bajiné bisa turu kepénak, ora * sambat baé.* The baby slept comfortably and didn't whimper constantly. 2 sparks that fly when metal is struck. 3 moth-like flying insect

pidjet (**petek̄** *kr?, ki*) to have a massage. *Aku njuwun pidjet ibu.* I asked Mother to massage me. *ḍukun ** or *tukang ** professional massager. ***an** 1 to have a massage. 2 (*or* ***-*an**) to massage each other by turns. **ṁ/di*** to pinch, squeeze, knead. *suwé midjet wohing ranti* a very brief time. **ṁ/di*aké** to have smn massage one. **ṁ/di*(i)** to massage. *Ḍèké midjet² lengené.* He kept kneading his arm. *Apa during di*i?* Haven't you been massaged yet?

pidjetan 1 a small sweet yellow fruit that grows in clusters. 2 *form of* PIDJET

pidji *oj* to assign smn a task. **ṁ/di*** to summon smn and assign him a task. **ṁ/di*k̀aké** to summon smn into one's presence

pidosa *oj* sin, guilt

piguna use(fulness), utility, benefit. **ṁ/di*kaké** to use; to make useful. *Lapangan mau di*kaké kanggo olah raga botjah.* The field is to be used for young people's sports. *Aku arep migunakaké wektuku kanggo sinau.* I'm going to use my time for studying. **ṁ*ni** useful, beneficial. *Ulah raga kuwi migunani kanggo djiwa lan raga.* Exercise is beneficial to body and spirit. *Kertas kuwi barang kang migunani.* Paper is useful stuff. *See also* GUNA

pigurah picture frame

pihak side, party. **-* sing perkaran* the parties involved in the litigation. *sedulur * bapak* relatives on the father's side. **ṁ*** to take sides. *Dadi wasit kuwi ora kena mihak.* A referee must be impartial.

pijagah *var of* WIJAGAH

pijak *rpr* an opening up *or* breaking apart. *Dibukak mak *.* He jerked it wide open. *Semangkané disigar mak *.* He split the melon in half. *Gelasé tiba lan petjah mak *.* The glass fell and smashed. **ṁ/di*(i)** to open sth out/apart; to push apart. *mijak korḍèn* to part the curtains. *mijak wadi* to reveal a secret

pijambak 1 (by) oneself (*kr for* ḌÉWÉ). 2 alone (*kr for* IDJÈN). ***é** he, she (*md for* ḌÈWÈKÉ). ***ipun** he, she (*kr for* ḌÈWÈKÉ)

pijanten *sbst kr for* PIJARA

pijantun *var of* PRIJANTUN

pijârâ **ṁ/di*** to raise, breed, tend. *mijara pitik* to raise chickens

pijarsa, pijarsi *oj* **ka*** audible. **ṁ*** to hear. **ṁ/di*kaké** to listen to. **pa·ṁ*** listener, hearer

pijas *var of* BIJAS

pijé *inf var of* KEPRIJÉ

pijèk *var of* PIJIK

pijek̄ *var of* PIDAK, PIJIK

pijik baby chick. * *dara* baby dove. ***-*** *rpr* the cheeping of baby chicks

pijon pawn (chess piece)

pijul violin, viola. **ṁ*** to play a violin/viola

pijulis violinist, violist

pik 1 *shf of* KOPIK. 2 *inf var of* ḌISIK. 3 *inf var of* PING

pikalah *ng,* **pikawon** *kr* a defeat; act of being defeated. **ṁ/di*(i)** to lose deliberately, allow oneself to be overcome. *See also* KALAH

pikangsal *rg kr for* PAKOLÈH

pikantuk 1 to receive (*kr for* ÉNTUK). 2 accomplishment, gain (*kr for* PAKOLÈH)

pikat 1 a decoy bird. 2 (*or* **ṁ***; *psv* **di***) to lure, trap. *Siti pinter mikat atining prija.* Siti knows how to ensnare men.

pikawon a defeat (*kr for* PIKALAH)

pikep 1 record player. 2 pickup truck

pikèt the watch, guard duty. *éntuk giliran ** to take one's turn at guard duty

pikir *ng,* **manah** *kr,* **galih** *ki* thought, idea, feeling. *Kowé tansah dadi *ku.* I think of you always. *Ulah raga iku saja adoh saka *é.* He dislikes sports more and more. ***an** thoughts, mind. *Pikiranku kotong kaja ḍompètku.* My mind was as empty as my wallet. **ke*** in one's thoughts. *tanpa ke** unthinkingly, mindlessly. *Sing perlu malah ora ke*.* He forgot what he was supposed to do. **ṁ/di*** to think (about). *Ḍèké tansah mikir omah².* She's always thinking about marriage. *Sing kok * mung butuhmu ḍéwé.* All you think of is your own needs. *Di* disik apa sing kudu ditindakaké.* First think about what has to be done. *Kosik, tak *é.* Just a minute, let me think about it. **m̄/di*-*** to think over; to try to think of sth. *Nalika tak *-* ja bener.* On second thought I realized he was right. *Ḍèwèké mikir² keprijé bisané nulungi kantjané.* He pondered what help he could be to his friend. **m̄/di*aké** to think *or* be concerned about. *Wong kuṭa geḍé iku akèh sing di*-aké.* People in large cities have a lot of worries. **m̄*an** full of ideas, brainy. **m̄/di*i** to give thought/consideration to. *Nèk mikiri aku...* If you'd think about me... **pa·m̄*** thought; object of one's thoughts; result of one's thinking. *miturut pamikirku...* in my opinion... *Aku ora gelem ndadèkaké pamikiring wong tuwaku.* I don't want to be a source of worry to my parents.

piknik picnic

pikolèh *var of* PAKOLÈH

pikrâmâ 1 *oj* to marry. 2 *oj* wedding ceremony. **m̄/di*kaké** to hold a wedding for [one's child]. *See also* KRAMA

pikul *ng,* **rembat** *kr* 1 a long pole carried horizontally on one shoulder with carrying baskets suspended fore and aft. 2 *ng kr* a unit of weight: 100 *kati = ca.* 136 lbs. ***an** *sms* * 1. **m̄/di*** to carry/transport with the above equipment. *Dagangané digénḍong utawa di*.* They carry their merchandise on their backs or with shoulder poles.

pikun absent-minded *or* dull-witted in one's old age

pikut **ke*** to get captured. **m̄/di*** to capture; to captivate

pil pill, tablet. ** kinine* quinine medication. ** anti-hamil* birth-control pill

pilah **m̄/di*** to sort, divide up, classify

pilâlâ **m̄/di*** 1 to treat with solicitous care. 2 to prefer

pilalah **ϕ/di*** *or* **m̄/di*** to choose one alternative over another. *Sawisé tamat saka sekolah guru, * nganggur ana ing ngomah.* After graduating from teacher's college she decided to just stay home.

pilar pillar, pile. ***an** a split length of bamboo. **m̄/di*** to split [a bamboo stalk] lengthwise

pilârâ *ng,* **pisakit** *kr* act of causing *or* inflicting physical pain; physical torture. **m̄/di*** to torture, inflict pain on. *di* nganti mati* tortured to death. *See also* LARA

pileg (to have/get) a cold

pilem *var of* FILEM

piler ***en** having a [chicken] disease. *pitik *en* a diseased chicken

pilih to make a choice. ** endi, mati apa urip?* Which do you choose, to live or die? ***an** 1 (having been) selected. *Kaju iki *anku.* This wood is what I picked out. (*wong²*) **an* selected (*i.e.* outstanding) persons, chosen ones. 2 act *or* way of selecting. **an présiḍèn dianakaké saben limang taun sepisan.* Presidential elections are held every five years. ***-*** to make choices. *Menawa golèk kantja kudu *-*.* You have to pick your friends carefully. **ke*** to get chosen/elected. *Sapa sing ke* dadi kaptèn?* Who was chosen (*or* elected) captain? **m̄/di*aké** to select for smn. **m̄/di*(i)** 1 to select. *Miliha mori sing betjik.* Get high-quality cambric. 2 to elect; to appoint. *di* dadi lurah* to be chosen village chief. 3 to sort out. *Iwaké di*i agal paḍa agal, lembut paḍa lembut.* He sorted the fish according to size. **pa·m̄*an** act *or* way of selecting. *** (k)asih** to play favorites, give preferential treatment (to). *Adja *-kasih marang anak²mu.* Don't treat your children partially. *** tanḍing** outstanding, superior. *See also* ḌÉNGAH

pilingan temple (side portion of forehead)

Pilipinā Philippine. *pulo ** the Philippine Islands. *wong ** a Filipino

pilis *ng kr,* **larik** *ki* a preparation of pounded herbs applied to the forehead to soothe and relieve pain. ***an** to have the above at one's forehead. **m̄/di*i** to apply the above to smn's forehead

pilsapat moral, bit of philosophy. *ahli ** philosopher

pilus 1 a small flour-coated cookie. 2 any food coated with flour. *katjang ** flour-coated peanuts

pilut *var of* PILUTA

piluta **ka*** to succumb, yield. *Ḍèké ka* déning pawèwèh saka wanita mau.* He was won over by the lady's gifts. *Akèh wong sing paḍa ka* tundoné bandjur paḍa tuku obat.* Lots of people fall for [this line of patter] and buy the medicine. **pa·m̄*** a winning *or* captivating action. *tembung pamiluta* winning words

pimpin ***an** director, head. **an reḍaksi* editor-in-chief. **m̄*** 1 leader, director. 2 (*psv* **di***) to lead, guide; to preside (over), to chair. *mimpin gerilja* to lead the guerillas.

pa·m̃* leader. *pemimpin massa* a leader of the people

pin- *see also under* P- (*Introduction, 3.1.7*)

pinalti penalty (in games only, *esp.* soccer)

pinângkâ place of origin. *Sapa djenengmu, ngendi *mu?* What is your name and where are you from? *Wit kinah iku *né saka ing negara mantja.* The quinine tree originated in foreign places. **m̃*** (serving) as, for. *Tlaléné gadjah iku minangka tangané.* An elephant's trunk serves him as hands. *Ḍuwit Rp 100 iki minangka sumbanganku kanggo botjah² lola.* This 100 rupiahs is for my contribution to the orphans. **m̃/di*ni** to serve; to satisfy a need. *Wetuné buku iki minangkani pamunḍuté umum.* This book was published by popular request.

pinarak 1 [of exalted persons] to seat oneself. *Sang Prabu lagi * tjeḍak médja mau.* The King sat near the table. *Mangga *.* Please have a seat. 2 *ki* to be shown respect by people sitting humbly before one. *Ratu * para beḍaja.* The King is being honored by the court dancers. **m̃/di*aké** to ask smn to be seated *or* to drop in for a visit. *Aku dipinarakaké ing penḍapa.* She asked me to come in and sit on the veranda. **m̃/di*i** to sit on. *Nuwun sèwu, pendjenengan minaraki buku kula.* Excuse me, you're sitting on my book. *See also* PARAK

pinḍa *oj* like, as, resembling. *Pradjurit² sing nganggo klambi abang * alas kobong.* The red-garbed soldiers looked like a flaming forest. **m̃/di*(-*)** to imitate; to assume *or* impart the guise of. *Olèhé nggawé retja di*-* bapakné sing wis ora ana.* He made a statue of his dead father. **pe*n** a figure of speech; to represent figuratively. *Uripé pe*n kebo nusu gudèl.* His way of life illustrates the expression "the kerbau calf suckles the parent," *i.e.* the (grown) children look after their parents.

pinḍah 1 (**djengkar** *ki*) to move, change residence (*kr for* NG·ALIH?). *Aku * ana daérah lija.* We moved to another area. 2 to change (place, position). ** panggonan* to move away. ** montor mabur* to change planes. *Mangsa panas * dadi mangsa rontog.* Summer gave way to fall. 3 besides, at once, completely (*kr for* PISAN). ***an** 1 changed, shifted. *Aku *an saka sekolah lija.* I transferred from another school. 2 (**djengkar·an** *ki*) act *or* process of moving. *Bapak djengkaran.* Father is in the process of moving. *Kapan olèhmu *an?* When do you move? 3 divorced (*sbst kr? for* PEGAT·AN). ***-*** to keep moving around, keep shifting one's position. **m̃/di*** 1 to change, shift. *Koper² mau di* ana montor mabur lija.* The luggage was transferred to another plane. *Arané Djakarta tau di* sinebut Batavia.* The name Djakarta was once changed to Batavia. *Ṭukulé di*.* He transplanted the seedlings. 2 to divorce (*sbst kr? for* M̃/DI·PEGAT). **m̃/di*aké** to change/shift [things]. *Wong² di*aké nganggo prau.* The people were transported in boats. **pa·m̃*** act *or* way of shifting. *Pamindahé ora kena dibubut baé.* You don't transplant it by just yanking it out. *See also* ALIH

pinḍang a process for preparing eggs *or* meats using salt and certain spices; a dish prepared in this way. *enḍog ** salted spiced eggs. *iwak ** fish prepared as above. ** lulang* prepared beef rinds. **m̃/di*** to prepare [food] as above

pindjung (*or* ***an**) a certain style in which little girls wear batik wraparounds, *viz.* with with a triangular fold down the front across the chest

pinḍo *ng,* **kaping kalih** *kr* twice; (for) the second time; (the) second (one). ** saben sasi* twice a month. *apesé ping ** at least twice. *Wis * dina kuwi teka mrono.* It was the second time that day I had been there. *Geḍéné tikel *né karo duwèkku.* It's twice as big as mine. ***an** third cousin. ***n** redone. *djarik pinḍon* a touched-up batik. **ka*** *ng* *sms* *. *rombongan ka** the second group. **m̃*** *ng* (to do, to happen) twice *or* for the second time. *Olèhé mangan sega minḍo.* He ate a second meal. **m̃*an** third cousin. **m̃/di*ni** *or* **m̃/di*-gawé·ǹi** to do sth twice *or* for the second time. *Gawéané dipinḍoni.* He did his work over. *Ḍèwèké marahi minḍo nggawèni waé.* He made me do it over.

pinès thumb tack

ping (**kaping** *kr*?) 1 (number of) times. ** (se)pisan* once. ** telu* (*papat, lsp.*) three (four, *etc.*) times. *Loro * telu ana nem.* Two times three is six. 2 *ordinal marker.* ** teluné* (for) the third time. *kang * telu saka kiwa* the third one from the left. *sap kang * lima* the fifth floor (*or* layer). ***-*an** multiplication. **nge/di*** 1 (*or* **m̃/di***) to [do] *n* times. *Olèhé ngepan roti ming pinḍo.* Bake the cake in two batches. 2 to multiply.

Ngeping luwih angèl tinimbang nambah. Multiplying is harder than adding. **nge/di*-aké** to multiply by. *telu di*aké sepuluh* 3 multiplied by 10. *See also* KAPING

pinggah device for stepping up *or* down (*kr for* PUNGGAH)

pinggan bowl or basin used for food preparation

pingget (to have) a mark on the skin where sth pressed against it. ***an ati·ǹ** sensitive, easily hurt. **m̃/di*aké** *or* **m̃/di*i** 1 to leave a mark on the skin. 2 to hurt smn's feelings

pinggir edge, side. * *médja* table edge. **ing* *kali* river bank. *nang * omah* in the corner (inside) *or* at the corner (outside) of the house. *ing * dalan* at the edge of the road. * *kuṭa* outskirts of the city. ***an** at the edge/side. *kuṭa *an* slum area at the city's outskirts. **ke*en** *or* **ke·m̃*en** too far toward the edge. *Olèhé njupir keminggiren nganti nabrak wit.* He drove so close to the edge of the road that he hit a tree. **m̃*** to go to(ward) the edge. *Ḍèwèké énggal² minggir.* She moved quickly to the side [of the road]. **m̃/di*aké** to place sth at/to the side *or* edge. *Watuné di*aké.* He moved the stone to one side. **sa*** at/along the edge. *sa* kali* along the river bank. *Ing sa*ing alun² ana omah geḍong geḍé banget.* There are tall buildings at the edge of the square.

pingin *var of* PÉNGIN

pingit ***an** a girl of marriageable age who is isolated from the world by being kept locked in the house until she has married the husband selected for her (a practice that is becoming obsolete). **m̃/di*** to isolate [a girl] in this way

pingkel **ke*-*** (to laugh) heartily. *Paḍa gumuju nganti ke*-*.* They laughed their heads off.

pingkus *var of* PRINGKUS

pinguin penguin

pinihan *inf var of* PA·WINIH·AN

pinisepuh *see* PINITUWA

pinituwa *ng*, **pinisepuh** *ng kr* one's elders; one's higher-generation relatives. *See also* TUWA

pinjak *var of* PIDAK

pinjet *var of* PÈNJÈT

pinta *oj* **m̃/di·(pe)*** to make a demand *or* request. **pa*n** a request, demand. **pa·m̃*** act of requesting/demanding

pinten how many? what amount? (*kr for* PIRA, PIRANG). *** banggi** luckily (*kr for* PIRA BARA, PIRANG BARA)

pinter smart; educated; skilled. *botjah bagus lan ** a good-looking, bright boy. *Sinaumu bisaa sregep supaja énggal *.* Study hard so you'll learn fast. *Nglangi ora pati *.* He's not very good at swimming. *wong tani sing ** a good farmer. **ka*an** capability, skill. *ka*an basa* speaking ability. **m̃*** to assume a guise of knowledgability. *See also* KUMINTER

pintjang lame, crippled. *mlaku ** to walk with a limp. *Ékonominé negara *.* The national economy is crippled. ***an** to feign lameness

pintjuk container for carrying food, made by folding a banana leaf and pinning it with a sharpened palm-leaf rib. **m̃/di*** to wrap [food] as above

pintu door. *** aèr** sluice gate. *** angin** air hole, vent. *** monjèt(an)** Dutch door

pinudju in the middle of [do]ing; to happen to be [do]ing. * *aku linggih ing ngarepan, A liwat.* A went past while I was sitting in the front room. *Dina iki * libur.* (It happens that) it's a holiday today. **(ka)*n̂** 1 *sms *.* *Kapinudjon mung let seḍéla bis liwat.* After a short while a bus came along. *Kapinudjon nalika semono ora udan.* It wasn't raining just then. 2 (heart's) desire. *Ana iwak kang pinudjon, dadi karepé tyasing wong.* There's a certain delectable dish that is considered a great delicacy. *See also* TUDJU

piol *var of* PIJUL

pionir pioneer

pipa 1 pipe, tube. *ngrokok ** to smoke a pipe. * *karèt* rubber tubing. * *wesi* steel pipe. 2 smokestack, funnel

pipèt pipette

pipi *ng kr*, **pa·ng·aras·an** *ki* cheek. * *kempong-pérot* cheeks wrinkled with age. * *ndurèn sadjuring* having beautifully curved cheeks. *bantal ** small oblong-shaped pillow to rest the cheek on. *ḍekik *né* dimple

pipih (*or* ***an**) cloth used as a sanitary napkin

pipil ***an** things (*e.g.* corn kernels) which have been plucked off. **m̃/di*** to pick [things] off one by one; *fig* to do little by little. *Wiwit saiki kudu mipil tuku keperluan kawin.* You ought to begin gradually getting things you'll need for your marriage.

pipis 1 leaf-wrapped boiled cookie. 2 to (need to) urinate (*children's word*). ***an** square stone pestle on which herbs *etc.* are ground fine by rolling a cylindrical implement (*gandik*) over them. **m̈/di*** to grind with this equipment. *Ibu lagi mipis tjabé lemprijang.* Mother is preparing folk-medicine herbs.

pipit close together with no space intervening. **m̈/di*** to press close together. *Kininené di* didadèkaké tablèt.* The quinine is pressed into pills. *Wironé pinipit tjilik.* Her wraparound was pressed into small close folds. *** **adu tjukit** very close (physically, spiritually)

pir (coiled) spring. * *djam* watch spring. *tjikar ** two-wheeled horse cart. ***-*an** equipped with springs. **nge*** springy, bouncy

pira *ng*, **pinten** *kr* how many? what amount? *Bukumu ana *?* How many books have you? *sedina ping *?* how many times a day? *Ḍuwitmu kari *?* How much money have you got left? *djam *?* what time [by the clock]? *tanggal *?* what date? *taun *?* what year? * *umurmu?* How old are you? ***a** no matter what amount. *Piraa waé regané arep dituku.* No matter what it costs he'll buy it. **ora *a** not (amounting to) much. *Pinteré ora *a, ning omongé akèh.* He's not very bright but he talks a lot. ***-*** 1 no matter how much/many. **-* tampanana waé timbang ora éntuk babar pisan.* Take them, no matter how few there are, rather than not getting any. 2 luckily. **-* aku gelem nang pasar, nèk ora rak ora mangan.* It's lucky I was willing to go to the market, or we wouldn't be eating. **ka*n (ka·pinten·an** *sbst? kr*) to get neglected *or* overlooked. *Saking akèhé tamu nganti anakku ka*n.* There were so many guests that my son got lost in the crowd. **m̈*** how much apiece? *Djeruké sidjiné mira?* How much apiece are the tangerines? **ora m̈*a** not much. *Bajaré ora miraa nanging gawéané njenengké.* The pay wasn't much but the work was enjoyable. *** **bara (pinten banggi** *kr*) happily and unexpectedly. *Adja nganti luwih saka iku, * bara ana turahé siṭik.* Far from extras [being needed], there were actually some left over. * *bara dialem, ora didukani baé wis begdja.* He was lucky not to be bawled out—and then on top of it he was complimented! *See also* PIRANG, SEPIRA

pirang *ng*, **pinten** *kr* how much? how many? (*as modifier*). * *djam* (*taun, lsp.*)*?* how many hours (years, *etc.*)? *Entèk * rupiah ja?* How many rupiahs did you spend? ***-*** 1 a lot (of). *Nganti *-* dina ḍèwèké olèhé lara weteng.* His stomachache lasted for days. 2 fortunately. **se*-*** in large quantities. *Wong se*-* ptg klulur tanpa gawéjan.* Crowds of people were hanging around doing nothing. *** **bara (pinten banggi** *kr*) *var of* PIRA BARA

piranti *ng*, **pirantos** *kr* equipment, instrument, apparatus. * *listrik* electrical equipment. * *nulis* writing materials. * *omah* household furnishings. * *tetanèn* farm tools. * *tilpun* a telephone. *Ora duwé *né mbukak prop.* He didn't have anything to pull the cork with. **ning motor sing rusak* a defective engine part. *mawa * mesin* by machine (rather than by hand). ***né** what is usual/ordinary. *Kuwi wis dadi *né.* That is the usual way. **m̈*** equipped, ready. *bareng wis miranti kabèh* when everything was all set. *omah geḍé tur miranti* a large, well-equipped house. **m̈/di*ǹi** to equip sth; to furnish as equipment. *mirantèni omah* to equip (furnish) a house. *mirantèni ḍaharan sing arep disuguhké* to provide a meal for guests. **sa*né** together with all its equipment. *Omahé geḍé, pepak sa*né.* The house was large and completely equipped.

pirantos *kr for* PIRANTI

pirasat 1 omen; presentiment. *Menawa mbulané miring ngiwa kuwi ngemu * arep larang beras.* When the (crescent) moon is tipped to the left, it's a sign that the price of rice is going up. *Aku éntuk * olèhé lotré.* I have a feeling I'm going to win the lottery. 2 face; character-reading by studying the face

pirdus heaven, paradise

piré **m̈*** to avoid (a meeting with); to sidestep, get out of the way. **m̈/di*ǩaké** to get sth out of the way. *Slamet énggal[2] mirèkaké anaké sing arep ketundjang pit.* Slamet whisked his child out of the way just as he was about to be hit by a bicycle.

pireng **dipun*** to be heard (*kr for* DI·RUNGU). **ka*** to hear (*kr for* KRUNGU). **m̈/dipun*i** to communicate with supernaturally (*kr for* NG/DI·RUNGU·ǸI). **pa·m̈*** sense of hearing; what is heard (*kr for* PA·N̈G·RUNGU). *See also* MIRENG

piring[a] dish, plate. * *baṭok* coconut-shell bowl. * *terbang* flying saucer. ***an** 1 in dishes. *Segané wis *an.* The rice is dished out. 2 plate-shaped. 3 phonograph record

piring[b] **pe*an** hint, oblique allusion. **ke*** placed to one side; *fig* relegated to an unimportant position. *ke* mangiwa/manengen* slanting to the left/right. *Ḍèké metu merga rumangsa ke∗.* He resigned because he felt he had been passed over. **m̃∗** 1 slantwise, diagonal. *garis miring* a slanting line. *rada miring kaja manuk mana* sloping like a bird [on the wing]. *aksara miring* italic letter. 2 not of the highest quality. *Djawa miring* substandard Javanese. *disangga miring* to be held in low esteem. 3 lower than standard. *Jèn tuku nang pasar rada miring regané.* You can get it a little cheaper at the marketplace. **mirang-m̃∗** to keep slanting this way and that. *Linggihmu sing djedjeg, adja mirang-miring.* Sit straight; don't keep shifting from side to side. **m̃/di∗aké** 1 to tip sth over, lay sth on one side. 2 to lower the price *or* quality. *See also* IRING, PÉRING

pirma[a] (*or* **pe∗n**) to beg, be(come) a beggar (*esp.* of elderly impoverished *santri*'s). *Olèhé pe∗n mangkat ésuk, ulihé soré.* They go out begging in the morning and return in the evening. **m̃/di∗** to feel solicitous toward. *Jèn kowé kena dak ∗, adja udan²an.* I'm concerned about you; don't go walking in the rain.

pirmā[b] business partnership. **∗n** business partner(s)

pirmah *var of* PIRMA[b]

pirman the word (command, order) of God

pirsa 1 to see (*ki for* WERUH). 2 to know, understand (*ki for* NGERTI, SUMURUP). *ngaturi ∗ (ka)* to tell, inform. *njuwun ∗ (ka)* to ask (a question). *Botjah mau njuwun ∗ marang guruné.* The boy asked the teacher a question. **m̃∗** to see (*ki for* WERUH). *Bapak bareng mirsa, duka.* When Father saw it he got mad. **m̃/di∗kaké** *ki* to show, let see. *Bareng garapané wis rampung bandjur dipirsakaké Pak Guru.* When he finished his work, he showed it to the teacher. **m̃/di∗ni** to see, watch (*ki for* N/DI·DELENG, N/DI·DELOK, Ñ/DI·SAWANG, N̈/DI·TONTON). *mirsani bioskup* to see a movie. **pa·m̃∗** *ki* vision, *i.e.* ability to see; knowledge

pirullah *see* ASTAGA

pirus turquoise (stone)

pi:s 1 *excl uttered when smn coughs or sneezes* (*"God bless you!"*). 2 *var of* PIPIS 2

pisah apart, separate(d). *Ḍèké ora gelem ∗ karo kakangné.* He didn't want to be separated from his brother. *Adja ∗ karo tanganmu.* Don't let it out of your hands. *Wong iku ora ∗ saka piranti² kang bakalé karèt.* Rubber products are indispensible to man. **(pe)∗an** 1 separation, parting. *patemon pe∗an* farewell meeting/party. 2 separated; divorced (*kr for* PEGAT·AN?). *Wis pe∗an karo bodjoné.* He's divorced from his wife. **m̃/di∗aké** to separate [things]. *di∗aké saka wong tuwané* separated from his parents. *Segara sing misahaké wong loro mau ora bisa misahaké atiné.* The ocean that separates them cannot separate their hearts. **m̃/di∗(i)** 1 to separate (out). *Katjang sing bosok di∗i.* The spoiled nuts are put aside. *Wong² mau mesṭi paḍa kerengan, dadi gawéanku ming misahi terus.* They're always fighting; my job is to keep separating them. *Pada lingsa iku kanggo misah gatra utawa ukara.* The function of commas is to mark off clauses or sentences [in Javanese script]. 2 to divorce smn (*kr for* M̃/DI·PEGAT?). **pa·m̃∗** partition, divider. *djuru pamisah* referee; arbiter. **∗ kebo** [of husband and wife] temporarily separated

pisakit physical torture (*kr for* PILARA)

pisan 1 once; the first one, first time. *∗...pinḍo(né)...* in the first place...in the second place. *∗ pinḍo diapura, ping teluné diukum.* The first and second times he was pardoned; the third time he was sentenced. 2 (**pinḍah** *kr?*) at the same time, as well, on top of it. *Wis ora duwé gawéan, wuwuh² ibuné lara ∗.* He's out of a job, and on top of that his mother is ill. *Keṭèké loro ∗ ndjogèd.* The two monkeys both danced at once. 3 (**pinḍah** *kr?*) altogether; ...and that's all there is to it. *Kowé ṭik pinter mbeḍèk.–Pinter ∗.* You're just smart at guessing riddles.–I guess I am! *Sikilmu nèk ora mari², dikeṭok ∗.* If your leg doesn't get well, they'll cut it right off! *Sanadjan kandelé témbok anaa saélo ∗ meksa tembus bom.* Even if the wall were a whole yard thick a bomb could wreck it. 4 (*or esp.* **∗-∗**) [not] by any means. *Ora ∗ wedi.* He wasn't a bit afraid. *Ora njana ∗-∗.* It was completely unexpected. *Adja ∗-∗ mlebu kamar kuwi lho.* Don't ever go in that room! **∗an** (for) the first time. **∗-∗** *see* ∗ 4 *above.* **ka∗** first; first time. *rombongan ka∗ lan kapinḍo* the first and second groups. *Iki lelunganku njang tanah Djawa sing ka∗.* This is my first trip to Java. **ka∗an** in the same instant. *mati ka∗an* to die instantly. **m̃∗(an)** second cousin, *i.e.* child of one's grandmother's first cousin. **(m̃∗) pernah m̃∗**

related as a second cousin. *Aku jèn karo Darto pernah misan.* Darto and I are second cousins. **m̃/di∗aké** to do at the same time. *Kawiné anaké di∗aké karo perajaan ulang tahunku.* Her wedding and my birthday party were celebrated together. **se∗ 1** one time. *setaun se∗* once a year. *Aku tulungana se∗ manèh.* Please help me once more. 2 (*or* **se∗an**) first one; (for) the first time. *Aku weruh saldju se∗an.* I see snow for the first time. *Lagi se∗ iki ndjaluk.* This is the first time he's asked for anything. *udud sa∗an* to smoke for the first time. *turunku se∗* my first descendant. *Dolanané werna², sa∗é tjatur.* There were all kinds of games; the first was chess. *See also* BABAR-PISAN

pisandjang **m̃/di∗i** to advise (*opt kr for* M̃/DI-PITUTUR-I). *See also* SANDJANG

pisang banana (*kr for* GEḌANG)

pisek̄ [of noses] small and flat

pisik̄ physical. *kekuwatan ∗ lan kekuwatan batin* physical strength and spiritual strength

pisikā (*or* **ilmu ∗**) physics

pisiologi physiology

piskutjing touch-me-not (medicinal plant: *sms* KUMIS-KUTJING)

piso *var of* PÉSO

pispot chamber pot; bed pan

pista *var of* PÉSTA

pistul pistol. *∗ banju* water pistol. **m̃/di∗aké** to fire [a pistol]. **m̃/di∗(i)** to shoot with a pistol

pisuh (*or* **pe∗**) abusive words. **pe∗an** to swear at each other. **m̃∗-m̃∗** to swear; to yell abusively. *Batiné misuh² marang sing nulis.* Inwardly he cursed the person who had written it. *Ḍèwèké nguntir kuping karo misuh².* She twisted his ear and yelled at him. **m̃/di∗i** to swear at, heap abuse on. *Djarané digebug bleg karo di∗-∗i.* He struck the horse and kept cursing it.

pisuna *var of* WISUNA

pisungsung a gift presented to a person socially superior to one, *e.g.* smn in authority; an older person. **m̃/di∗aké** to present a gift to [a social superior]

pi:t bicycle. **∗-∗an** to go for a bicycle ride. **∗ doortrap** bicycle with pedals that move only forward (used in racing; in pedicabs). **∗ keblak** (*old-fashioned*) motor bike, motorcycle. **∗ kriwil** English-style bicycle. **∗ mo(n)tor** motor bike, motorcycle. **∗ terpéḍo** bicycle with coaster brakes

pita ribbon

pitadjeng *sbst kr for* PITAJA

pitados to believe (in), trust (*kr for* PERTJAJA, PITAJA)

pitâjâ *ng,* **pitados** *kr* to believe [in], have confidence [in]. *Kita ∗ marang présiḍèn kita.* We have confidence in our president. *Wong agama ∗ ananing roh.* Religious people believe in the existence of the spirit. *mosi ora ∗* a vote of no confidence. **di∗** to be relied upon; to be believed (in). *Ngendi ana maling kena di∗?* You can't trust a thief! **ka∗n 1** confidence, faith. *Aku wis ora duwé ka∗n karo ḍèwèké.* I've lost confidence in him. 2 belief. *miturut ka∗n agama mau* according to the beliefs of this religion. **m̃∗kaké mata** *cr* to try to put sth over on smn, pull the wool over smn's eyes. **m̃∗ni** trustworthy; worthy of confidence. *Katoné ora mitajani.* His appearance doesn't inspire confidence. *Réwangku sing anjar mitajani.* My new servant is reliable.

pitamin(e) vitamin

pitedah indication; advice (*kr for* PITUDUH)

pitenah slander. **∗-∗an** to slander each other. **m̃/di∗** to slander smn; to accuse smn slanderously

pitepung **∗an** to (get to) know, become acquainted. *Ana ing ndalan aku ∗an karo sawidjining prija.* Along the way I struck up an acquaintance with a gentleman. **m̃/di∗aké** to introduce [people to each other]. *See also* TEPUNG

piṭes **∗an** act *or* way of squeezing. *∗ané rosa banget.* He pinches them very hard. **m̃/di∗aké** to pinch for smn. *Aku miṭesaké tumané nalika simbok métani aḍiku.* I crushed the lice as Mother removed them from my sister's hair. **m̃/di∗(i)** to pinch *or* squeeze between the fingers

piṭet 1 (to have) a scar. 2 *cr* blind. 3 *var of* PIṬES

piṭi 1 one of the small playing cards (*kertu tjilik*). 2 small white mouse

pitik *ng,* **ajam** *kr* chicken. *kanḍang ∗* chicken coop. *∗é mati!* The chickens will die! (*phrase used to urge children to eat*). *∗ saba* a loose (uncooped) chicken. *iwak ∗* chicken meat. *enḍog ∗* hen's egg. *sop ∗* chicken soup. **∗ iwèn** poultry; chickens and other birds. **∗ katé** bantam chicken. *∗ katé waniné nèng omahé* person who dares to fight only when he's near home. **∗ tronḍol** a variety of chicken with sparsely placed feathers;

fig a poor man. * *tronḍol dibubuti wuluné* a poor man who is swamped with expenses *or* who is robbed of all his belongings. * *tronḍol diumbar ing padaringan* or * *tronḍol saba ing lumbung* a poor man entrusted with money. * **walik** a variety of chicken with the feathers "inside out," *i.e.* sticking out at an angle rather than lying smooth

piṭil to have become detached. *Gagang tesmaké* *. The temple came off of his glasses. **m̈/di*aké** to detach accidentally. *Sapa sing miṭilaké garan tjangkir kuwi?* Who broke the handle off the cup? **m̈/di*(i)** to detach, break off. *miṭili kembang seka gagangé* to take flowers off the stalks

piṭing *var of* KEPIṬING. ***an** to wrestle. ***-*an** to wrestle with each other. **m̈/di*** 1 to grip, clasp. *Olèhé miṭing kentjeng.* She hugged him tight. 2 to hold smn's head in the crook of one's arm

pitjak (wuta *kr? ki?*) blind. **m̈*** 1 to feign blindness. 2 *slang* to doze off. **m̈/di*aké** *or* **m̈/di*i** 1 to blind smn. 2 to offend smn by doing an improper thing right in front of him as though he didn't exist. **m̈/di*-*aké** to accuse smn of being blind. *mBok adja mitjak²aké aku, wong aku ora weruh enggoné tenan kok.* Don't tell me that [the reason I can't find it is that] I'm blind–I really don't know where it is. * **n̈·ṭreṭeg** totally blind

pitjé *rg var of* PÉTJÉ

pitjek̄ *cr var of* PITJAK. **m̈*** *cr* to fall asleep

pitjik having a narrow outlook *or* range of knowledge

pitjis 1 an old-time form of torture whereby a wrongdoer was skinned alive, bit by bit, by the public. *ukum* * sentence to death by this form of torture. 2 one of the small playing cards (*kertu tjilik*). 3 ten-cent coin (used in West Java). **pa·m̈*** tax. *mantri pamitjis* tax collector. *tanḍa pamitjis* tax receipt

pitonton **m̈/di*aké** to demonstrate, exhibit. *mitontonaké gambar* to exhibit a painting. *Ing sajembara manah sing di*aké titising manah.* In archery competition they display precision of aim. *See also* TON[a], TONTON

pitrah compulsory gift to the poor (in Islam) given at the close of the fasting month. **m̈/di*i** to give [(as) obligatory alms] at this time

pitri *see* IDUL

pitu seven. **las* 17. **likur* 27. *djam* * 7 o'clock; 7 clocks. *Sedulurku wis* *. I have seven brothers and sisters. ***n̂(an)** the seventh [royal descendant]. *wajah Ngarsa Dalem kaping Piton* the grandson of the Seventh Sultan. ***-*** by sevens. *Kursiné ditata *-*.* The chairs were set out in rows of seven. **pe*** (group *or* unit of) seven. *Oto wis dirubung ing kampak pe*.* The car was surrounded by seven robbers. **ka*** 1 (*or* [**ka**]**ping** *) seven times; times seven; (for) the seventh time; seventh in a series. *Sing ka* bukuku.* The seventh book is mine. *lapis sing ka** the seventh floor (*or* layer). *Telu ping * dadi selikur.* Three times seven is 21. 2 seventh month of the Javanese year (22 December-3 February). **ka* sasur** 75. **ka* tengah** six and a half. **m̈/di*n̂i** to hold a ceremony for a woman in the seventh month of pregnancy. *See also* -AN (*suffix*) 8, 15, 16; -É[c] (*suffix*) 9; NG- (*prefix*) 6, 7; PITUNG; PRA-

pituduh *ng*, **pitedah** *kr* 1 indication, demonstration. * *tjarané mbaṭik* a demonstration of the batik-making method. *A awèh * nganti ketjekelé B.* A supplied the clue that led to the arrest of B. 2 advice. *awèh ** to give advice. **m̈/di*i** to advise. *See also* TUDUH

pituhu ***n̂** obedient, submissive (in character). **m̈/di*(n̂i)** to obey. *Sri kuwi mituhu marang guru laki.* Sri is subservient to her husband. *Negara A mituhoni saran kang wis diadjokaké déning Negara B.* Nation A knuckled under to the suggestion put forward by Nation B. *See also* TUHU

pitulung that which benefits. *Wit arèn kuwi geḍé *é marang menungsa.* The sugar-palm tree is of great benefit to human beings. ***an** assistance. **an Negara* Government aid. **ka*an** help, assistance. *Wit pari bisa urip sarana ka*an lemah, banju lan soroting srengéngé.* Rice thrives with the help of soil, water, and sunshine. **m̈/di*i** to come to smn's help *or* rescue. *pranti kanggo mitulungi wong* equipment for rescuing people. *See also* TULUNG

pituna loss, hardship. *gawé * marang menungsa* to cause people trouble. **ka*n** 1 hardship, loss. *nanḍang ke*n* to suffer a setback. *Éwon ka*né wong tani.* The farmers' losses ran into the thousands. 2 to undergo hardship/loss. **m̈/di*ni** to cause trouble, bring about hardship *or* loss. *Wong kesèd iku mitunani tumraping bebrajan.* Lazy people are a detriment to society. *See also* TUNA

pitung seven (*as modifier: see also* PITU). * *puluh* 70. * *atus* (*èwu, juta*) seven hundred (thousand, million). * *djam* (*dina, lsp.*) seven hours (days, *etc.*). * *dina* or * *bengi* one week. *Pitung mèter dawané.* It's seven meters long. * **dina·né** the seventh day after a death; **m̃/di*-dina·ni** to hold a ceremony in honor of [a deceased person] on the seventh day after his death. **m̃/di*-lapan·i** to honor [a baby] with a ceremony during the seventh *lapan* of his life. *See also* NG- (*prefix*) 6, 7

piturut obedient; to obey. **m̃*** 1 as; (to go) according to, in obedience with. *Miturut gugon-tuhon, impèn sing mengkono kuwi apik banget.* According to superstition, such dreams are propitious. *botjah miturut* an obedient child. *jèn miturut panemuku* in my opinion. 2 (*psv* **di***; **n/di·ḍèrèk** *ka*) to obey. **m̃/di*i** to act in accordance with. *A mituruti pendjaluké B.* A complied with B's request. **sa*é** in the same way as the foregoing; following the above; in the same way; and so on. *sa*é nganti entèk* and so on till they're all gone. *ahli sosiologi, ahli psikologi lan sa*é* sociologists, psychologists, and other such specialists. *See also* TURUT

piṭut *var of* TJIṬUT

pitutur what smn says; (words of) advice. **é rama lan ibuné* her mother and father's advice; what her father and mother said. *ora luntur ing ** impervious to advice. **m̃/di*i** (**m̃/dipun·pisandjang·i** *opt kr*) to advise. *Bapaké mituturi anaké akèh²*. His father made a number of suggestions to him. *See also* TUTUR

pituwa chairman, presiding officer. **m̃/di*ni** to preside over, to chair

pituwah advice

piutang (*or* **a***) loan; debt; moneylender (*var of* POTANG). *See also* UTANG

pjah crash! smash! *nḌogé tiba mak * petjah.* The egg fell and broke.

pjaji *var of* PRIJAJI

pjak *var of* PIJAK

pjambak *var of* PIJAMBAK

pjan ceiling

pjang *-*an** to enjoy going places

pjantun *var of* PRIJANTUN

pjarsa, pjarsi *var of* PIJARSA, PIJARSI

pjek̄ *rpr* the plop of sth soft falling

pjèng **pjang-*** *rpr* metallic clanking

pjoh *rpr* a water-filled object breaking open

pjok *rpr* coins jingling

pjuh crack! *remuk mak ** to break with a cracking sound, to snap

pju:k̄ *rpr* water spilling. *Mak *, aku dikapjuk banju.* He splashed water all over me.

pjung *rpr* a mass departure. *Botjah² mak * lunga.* The children all trooped out. ***-*an** flying around in large numbers. *Lemuté nang kamar *-*an akèh banget.* The room is swarming with mosquitoes.

pjur *rpr* spraying, sprinkling. ***-*an** 1 to pound, throb. *Atiku *-*an arep ketabrak motor.* My heart pounded when a car almost hit me. 2 sprinklings, scatterings. *Sing nang ndjubin kuwi *-*an weḍi.* That's sand that's sprinkled on the floor. **nge/di*(-*)i** to sprinkle, strew. *di*-*i banju* sprinkled with water. *Tatuné epjur²ana bubukan lirang bèn énggal garing.* Shake some powdered sulfur on the cut to dry it quickly.

pladjar running pace (*rg kr for* PLAJU)

pladjeng running pace (*rg kr for* PLAJU)

plag *rpr* drumbeats

plagiat plagiarism. *gawé ** to plagiarize

plagiator plagiarist

plagrang ***an** an obstacle. **ané wis dipasangi polisi.* The police have set up the road block. **m̃/di*aké** to use as a passage-blocker. *Sapa sing mlagrangaké sepéḍahé ngarep lawang?* Who left this bicycle right in front of the door? **m̃/di*i** to block [a passage]. *Lawangé di*i pit.* The door is obstructed by a bicycle.

plaju running pace. *Rikat *é.* He ran like the wind. ***n̂** to run around. **ke*** defeated, put to rout. *ke* saka palagan* driven from the battlefield. **m̃*** to run (off, away). *mlaju sipat kuping* to run like the wind. **m̃*-m̃*** to keep running around; to come running. **m̃/di*k̂aké** to run off with sth belonging to smn else. *Plajokna sipat kuping.* Run off with it as fast as you can. *A minggat mlajokaké dagangané B.* A absconded with B's merchandise. *mlajokaké ḍuwit* to embezzle money. **m̃/di*n̂i** to run to smn. *Ḍèké mlajoni embokné njuwun olèh².* He ran to meet his mother and ask if she had brought him anything. *Ḍèké agi waé metu omah tak plajoni merga ana tilpun.* Just after he left the house I ran after him to call him to the phone.

plak *rpr* the sound of a slap

plaksègel official seal affixed to the bottom of a document to show that a tax/fee has been paid

plandjer 1 gland. 2 (*or* **m̃***) to ache in the joints

planèl, planel flannel

plang sign, signpost, signboard. **nge*** to give a hand signal. **nge/di*i** to signal to. *Motor mburi kaé dieplangi, bèn weruh jèn kéné arep ménggok.* Signal to the car behind us that we're going to turn.

planggrang ***an** a roasting grill. **m̃/di*(aké)** 1 to broil. *Saténé di*aké nang nḍuwur *an.* The meat kebabs are broiled on a grill. 2 to carry, stow. *Prau² tjilik ana ing ḍèg paḍa di*aké urut pinggir.* The lifeboats are stowed along the edge of the deck.

planggrok (*or* ***an**) a place (*esp.* an eating place) to rest along the way

plangi colorful shawl worn with a Javanese-style blouse

plâṅgkâ [of animals' coats] spotted black and white

plangkring ***an** bird's perch. **m̃*** 1 to perch, alight; to sit in a high place. 2 to jack up the price [to a patently interested customer]

plangkrong *ptg * pl* sitting in a high-up place, *e.g.* a tree branch. **m̃*** *sg as above*

planit planet

planṭang ***an** crossbar, horizontally placed pole. **m̃*** to ride [a bicycle] by sitting on the bar rather than back on the seat

plantjong place visited by a traveler. *wong ** tourist, traveler. **m̃*** to travel about

plantrang **ke*** to go farther than one had intended. *Olèhé angon saja adoh nganti ke* tjeḍak alas.* He let [the kerbau] graze farther and farther until they were too close to the forest. *Mèh ke* nggonku tjrita.* I almost got ahead of my story. *Ḍèké dadi ke* sisan ora mangan.* She got carried away and forgot to eat. **m̃*** to go smw other than one's intended destination. *Tekan alun² motoré tetep mlantrang.* The car reached the square and then kept right on going. *Wis sak djam kok durung bali, mlantrang nang endi waé.* It's been an hour and he's not back yet–where could he have wandered to? **m̃/di*aké** to take smn too far. *Wong mantja mau ora ngerti kuṭané di*aké tukang bétjak.* The stranger, unfamiliar with the city, was taken on a roundabout route by the [fare-hungry] pedicab driver.

plas *rpr* a sudden departure. *Ḍèké lunga mak *.* He left precipitously. *Ḍèké mlaju *.* Away he ran! ***-*an** in great haste. *Olèhé nulis *-*an nganti ora kena diwatja tulisané.* He scribbled so fast his handwriting wasn't legible.

plâsâ a variety of tree

plat 1 phonograph record. 2 automobile license plate. 3 zinc plating

platina platinum

plato plateau

plaṭok **m̃/di*** to cut [sth hard]. *Krambilé di*.* He cut the coconut.

platuk, plaṭuk (*or* ***an**) 1 trigger. 2 hammer for cocking a gun. *Ḍèké alon² mbukak *é pistul.* Slowly, he cocked the pistol.

plawongan *var of* PLAWUNGAN

plawungan a rack for storing spears and similar weapons

pleḍing *ptg * rpr* the sight of many rumps. **m̃/di*(i)** to humiliate smn publicly

plédoi statement of the defense counselor in response to the argument of the prosecution

pleguk **plegak-*** (to speak) haltingly, stammeringly, with difficulty. *Malingé plegak-* anggoné ndjawab pitakoné hakim.* The thief stuttered and stammered as he replied to the judge's questions.

plégung ***an** cattle-resting place. **m̃/di*aké** to have/let [cattle] rest in a shady place

plèjèk *ptg * pl* ramshackle. *gubug² sing paḍa ptg ** tumbledown shacks. **m̃*** *sg as above. Gubugé mlèjèk.* The shack is dilapidated.

pléjok **pléjak-*** to wobble unsteadily

pléjot *var of* PLÉJOK

plèk 1 *rpr* coming into, and remaining in, contact. *Mak * lintahé nèmplèk nang sikil.* The leech attached itself to his leg. *Laleré mak * méntjok nang panganan.* The fly lighted on the food. 2 *rpr* a slap *or* blow. *Ditjablèk mak *.* She smacked him. 3 a dirty *or* messy place. *Klambiku ana *é tlutuh geḍang.* There's a spot of banana sap on my shirt. ***-*** *rpr* the clop-clop of smn walking in sandals. ***-* ketepu** a children's hand-clapping game. **ng/di*-*** to slap smn on the back

plek 1 just like, coinciding with. *Rupané * matjan.* It looks just like a tiger. *lebar panèn ** just at the close of the harvest. 2 *rpr* a blow of the hand. *Lemuté ditjablèk mak * mati.* He killed the mosquito by smacking it. **plak-*** *rpr* repeated slaps *or* splatting sounds. **nge*i** looking like; coinciding with. *Gamelané nge*i kaja tjritané ḍalangé.* The music is perfectly coordinated with the puppet-master's narration. *Ora nge*i kaja pangarep-arepku.* It didn't come up to my expectations.

plekah a crack, split. **m̃*** to crack, split. *Lemahé mlekah.* The soil cracked. **m̃/di*i** to crack/split sth. *Bukuré di*i.* She cracked open the clams.

plékat a certain style of sarong

plèkèk **m̃/di*** to slaughter, butcher

plekèk **m̃/di*aké** to open [*e.g.* a durian fruit] by pressing it open with the heels of the hands

pleki:k̄ ***en** 1 to swallow sth the wrong way. 2 to hiccup

plekok *var of* PLEKÈK

plekrok *ptg * rpr* the sight of many flowers in bloom. *See also* MEKROK

pleleng **plelang-*** to stare vacantly. **m̃/di*(i)** to stare (at). *Olèhé mandeng mleleng ora kèḍèp²*. He stared long and unblinking.

plembis **plembas-*** to speak haltingly, to stammer

plembung *ptg * pl* inflated. ***an** 1 balloon. **ané kempès.* The balloon became deflated. *Plembunganė ptg *.* The balloons are blown up. 2 a cloth held at the four corners, used as an air-trapping device to keep a swimmer afloat. *nglangi nganggo *an djarik* to swim with an air-filled batik. **m̃*** inflated; swollen, puffed. **m̃/di*aké** to inflate. *mlembungaké *an* to blow up a balloon

plempung *ptg * pl* having swellings on the skin. **m̃*** *sg* swollen, puffed. *Ojod téla pohung kuwi mlempung isi paṭi.* Cassava roots are bursting with starch.

plempus **plempas-*** to stammer, falter in one's speech

plendèk *rpr* a feeling of revulsion. *Bareng dikèki lagi rong pulukan wis mak * ora diteruské.* After two handfuls of food he suddenly couldn't eat any more. **plendak-*** *or* **m̃*(-m̃*)** (to eat) without enjoyment. *Wetengku rada lara mulané olèhku mangan plendak-*.* My stomach was upset; I didn't feel like eating.

plenḍung *var of* PLEMBUNG

plendus **plendas-*** to speak haltingly. *Jèn nang djaba kelas mbagusi, jèn ditakoni guru plendas-*.* Outside of class he knows it all; when the teacher asks him questions he can't answer.

plenek̄ mound, small heap. *Geṭuké sa* pira regané?* How much is a mound of mashed cassava? *ptg * pl* in mounds, forming small heaps. **m̃*** *sg* rounded, forming a small mound

plènèt, plenèt, plenet *rpr* squirting, squeezing. *Aku nglingguhi geḍang mak * mlenjèk.* I sat on a banana and squashed it. ***an** tool for pressing *or* mashing. **an kenṭang* potato masher. **ke*** to get squeezed. *Botjah² enggoné nunggang sikilé mingsed nḍuwur merga kuwatir menawa ke* ing kebo sing paḍa suk²an.* The boys rode with their legs up in the air for fear they'd get squashed by the crowding kerbaus. **m̃/di*** to press, squeeze, mash. *mlènèt kenṭang* to mash potatoes

pleng 1 *rpr* a blow. *Balé ditenḍang mak *.* He kicked the ball squarely. *Rasané mak * marga dikampleng sirahku.* I was dazed by a blow on the head. 2 *rpr* a sudden departure. *Lagi waé teka, bandjur lunga menèh mak *.* He had barely arrived when he left again. **plang-*** *rpr* repeated blows. *plang-* plang-* njiṭak ḍuwit kertas anjar* printing up batches of new paper currency. *lali* **sa*an** to recall sth one had forgotten. *Wah, aku lali sak *an jèn nduwé djandji saiki iki.* Oh-oh, I've just remembered I have an appointment this very minute! *See also* TJESPLENG

plénge *var of* PLÈNGÈH

plèngèh, plengèh *rpr* a sudden smile. *ngguju mak ** to break into a grin. **pléngah-*** to smile and smile. **m̃*** to smile broadly. *Ḍèké mlèngèh kepranan atiné.* He smiled delightedly. **mléngah-m̃*** to keep grinning

plenggong *ptg * pl* to stare in puzzlement. ***an** gaping with surprise, taken aback. **plenggang-*** to keep staring stupidly *or* vacantly. *Mung plenggang-* ora ngerti apa².* He just sits looking dumb—he doesn't know what's going on. **m̃*** to stare dumbly. *Bareng diblakani mung mlenggong.* When they told him the truth, he could only gape. *Kartjisé entèk mlenggong ḍèwèké.* The tickets are sold out; he's dumbfounded with disappointment.

plengkang **ke*** to inadvertently do a split, *i.e.* sit with the legs stretched straight in opposite directions. **m̃*** to do a split. *Penari balèt ki sikilé mesṭi bisa mlengkang.* Ballet dancers can do splits.

pléngkok *ptg ** full of curves, twisting and turning, winding

pléngkrang **m̃/di*aké** to put [the feet, legs] up high while sitting, *e.g.* on top of one's desk

plengkuk *ptg* ∗ *pl* bent, twisted. *Pakuné paḍa ptg* ∗, *ora ana sing bisa dienggo.* The nails are all bent; not one of them is usable. **m̄/di∗aké** to bend sth (into a different shape). *Kawaté di∗aké kanggo tjanṭèlan.* He bent the wire into a coat hanger.

plengkung 1 short tunnel. 2 arc; arch(way). **∗an** *or* **m̄∗** curved, arc-shaped. **m̄/di∗aké** to shape into an arc

pléngo *rpr* a turn of the head. *Diundang mak* ∗. He turned when he was called. **m̄∗** to turn the head

plengok *var of* PLENGGOK

plengong *var of* PLENGGONG

pléngos *rpr* turning the head aside. *Jèn ketemu aku mesṭi mak* ∗. Whenever he sees me he averts his face. **m̄∗** to turn the head. *Ḍèké mléngos djalaran isin.* He turned aside his head in embarrassment. **mléngas-m̄∗** to keep averting the face

plenguk *ptg* ∗ *pl* standing around, hanging around

plenik dot, speck, fleck. *biru nganggo* ∗-∗ *putih* blue with white dots. **m̄∗** small; few. *Suwengé nganggo mata mlenik tjilik.* Her earrings are set with tiny jewels.

plenjak *rpr* stepping in sth soft and mushy. **m̄/di∗** to step in/on sth

plenjèk *rpr* stepping on sth soft. *Mak* ∗ *aku midak telèk.* I stepped right in some chicken manure. **plenjak-∗** 1 (to eat) without enjoyment. *Olèhé mangan plenjak-∗ bandjur ora entèk.* He ate without appetite and couldn't finish. 2 (*or* **m̄∗**) to step on sth soft

plenjok *rpr* the feel of stepping into sth large and soft. **m̄/di∗** to step on/in [sth as above]. *mlenjok tlétong* to step in some horse dung

plenjuk *var of* PLENJOK

plenok large dot *or* fleck. *putih plenok²* *abang* white with large red dots

plenong *var of* PLENUK

pléṇṭas *var of* PLONṬOS

plenṭèt **m̄/di∗aké** to pull in(ward). *Wetengé di∗aké.* He pulled in his stomach.

plenṭi *rpr* swelling, puffing. **m̄∗** bloated. *Wetengé mlenṭi nanging awaké kuru banget.* He has a bloated stomach and an emaciated body.

plenṭing a small swelling. *Kuman mau nganakaké* ∗-∗ *nanah.* The germs cause puffy infected sores. **∗en** to have pox. **m̄∗** to be(come) swollen

plentjar *pl form of* PENTJAR

plentjat *ptg* ∗ *or* ∗-∗ *or* **m̄∗-m̄∗** out of sequence. *Olèhé nggarap ora urut nanging* ∗-∗. He didn't do the problems in order–he skipped around.

plèntjèng **∗an** in an off-target direction. *Anggonmu ngepit adja* ∗*an.* Don't ride your bicycle in a zigzag path. **pléntjang-∗** to keep missing. *Jèn njurupké bolah pidjer pléntjang-∗ waé.* She can't get the needle threaded. **m̄∗** off the mark. *Olèhé mbeḍil pidjer mlèntjèng waé.* His shots kept missing. *Pikiranku pidjer mlèntjèng.* My thoughts kept straying. **m̄/di∗aké** to miss deliberately. *See also* PÈNTJÈNG

plentjing 1 *rpr* a quick action. *Ali mentas mulih ning kok ndjur mak* ∗ *lunga.* Ali had no sooner got home than he left again. 2 small rhinoceros (young of the WARAK). 3 bloom of the kapok tree. **m̄∗** to dart off, *esp.* because frightened *or* embarrassed

plèntjong *var of* PLÈNTJÈNG

plentjut **plentjat-∗** to keep going places; to be always on the go

plenṭong electric light bulb. **ke∗** to get into a muddy place. *Jèn ke∗ sepatumu rusak.* If you slip into the mud you'll ruin your shoes. **m̄∗** muddy

plenṭu *ptg* ∗ *pl* protruding, *esp.* of the stomach. *Wong² désa kono wetengé ptg* ∗. Those villagers' stomachs are bloated [with disease]. **m̄∗** *sg as above.* *Pipiné nganti mlenṭu.* His cheeks bulge. *Butuhé mung kanggo mlenṭuné wetengé ḍéwé.* He's only thinking of how to fill his own stomach. **m̄/di∗k̂aké** to cause to protrude

plenṭung a large swelling. **m̄∗** swollen. *Sikilé mlenṭung sadjagung-djagung.* His legs are puffed out like ears of corn.

plenṭus *rpr* puffing out suddenly. *Bané mak* ∗ *bandjur ndjebluk.* The tire swelled out and burst. **plenṭas-∗** 1 swelled up with pride *or* self-importance. 2 *rg* choked with emotion. **m̄∗** puffed up, swelling out. *Wetengé mlenṭus kewaregen.* He ate so much his stomach sticks out. **m̄/di∗aké** to cause sth to swell

plenuk a rounded heap *or* mound. *ptg* ∗ *pl* in mounds, in small heaps. *Tumpengé ptg* ∗ *akèh banget.* The rice was formed into small mounds. **m̄∗** mound-shaped. *Pipiné mlenuk.* He has rounded cheeks.

plep **nge/di∗** to get/keep selfishly *or* dishonestly (*var of* NG/DI·EMPLEP)

plèpèd a pair of bamboo *or* wooden strips at the edge of a woven-bamboo panel to prevent the weaving from raveling. **m̃/di*** 1 to attach edging to [a bamboo panel]. *Geḍègé di* nganggo pring.* He edged the panel with bamboo strips. 2 to push, press. *Ibu mlèpèd kenṭang arep kanggo nggawé bergedèl.* Mother mashed potatoes to make croquettes.

plepek̄ *-* *or* **plepak-*** oversupplied with fluid. *Irungku wis *-*.* My nose keeps running. *Aku plepak-* ngombé terus.* I drank glassful after glassful. **ke*(en)** suffocated, stifled. *Djenḍélané pawon ora dibukak, sing olah² nganti ke*en.* The kitchen windows weren't opened and the people cooking were nearly stifled. **m̃*** oversupplied with fluid. *Karburatoré mlepek.* The carburetor is flooded. **m̃/di*aké** to immerse sth in liquid. **m̃/di*i** to oversupply with fluid. *mlepeki karburator* to flood the carburetor

pleper *rpr* sudden flight. *Manuké mak * mabur.* The bird suddenly flew off. *-* *or* **plepar-*** to fly around. *Manuké *-* mabur nang kamar.* The bird flew around the room.

plepuh *ptg * pl* swollen in many places

plepus **plepas-*** to stall, dawdle. *Ditakoni ora bisa mung plepas-* waé.* He couldn't answer the questions, he just hemmed and hawed. *Olèhé njambut-gawé ora rampung², mung plepas-* udud terus.* He never finishes his work, he just sits around smoking.

plérah *var of* PLÈRÈH

plerak *var of* PLERUK

pléré **pléra-*** to keep sliding (down). *Botjah² paḍa dolanan pléra-* nang drondjongan.* The boys are sliding down the steep slope. **ke*** to slide down unintentionally. **m̃*** to slide down

plèrèd (*or* ***an**) children's slide, *usu.* leading to a swimming pool. **m̃*** to slide down a slide. **sa*an** (at) a quick glance. *Sa*an rupané paḍa.* At first glance they look alike.

plèrèh *rpr* the sight of red, *esp.* blood. *Tangané kebarut paku ndjur mak * metu getihé.* He scratched his hand on a nail and it bled. **m̃*** blood red. *Olèhé nganggo lipstik nganti mlèrèh.* She wore bright red lipstick.

plerek̄ *var of* PLERUK

pleret *rpr* a sudden darkening. *Mau ésuk srengéngéné metu, mbasan awan mak * menḍung.* It was sunny this morning, but in the afternoon it clouded over. **m̃*** dim, murky

plérok ***an** a flirtatious sidewise glance. **plérak-*** to cast such glances. **m̃*** to look (at) coyly. **m̃/di*i** to cast flirtatious glances at. *See also* LÉROK

pleruk *rpr* a scowl. *Diétjé bandjur mak * nesu.* He teased her and she got mad. *ptg * pl* grim, angry-looking. *-* *or* **plerak-*** *or* **m̃*** wearing a scowl; looking dark. *Ḍèké *-* mlebu ngomah.* Grim-faced, he went in the house. *Méméhané ora paḍa garing, lha wong plerak-* waé.* It's so cloudy the clothes won't get dry. **m̃/di*i** to scowl at smn

ples *var of* BLES

plesat *ptg ** to shoot out in all directions. *Guḍangé ḍinamit ndjeblug kajuné ptg * nang endi².* The dynamite storehouse blew up and the timbers went flying every which way. **m̃*** to jump out; to be thrown out. *Piluté bisa mlesat metu nunggang parasit.* The pilot managed to bail out and parachute down. *Pité montor numbuk wit, sing nunggang mlesat nganti rong mèter.* The motor bike hit a tree and the rider was thrown two meters.

plèsèd ***an** 1 to slip and slide for fun, *e.g.* when playing in the rain. 2 to be a punster, engage in word-play habitually. **ke*** to skid, slip inadvertently. *ke* tiba* to slip and fall. **m̃*** off target, wide of the mark. *Mlèsèd batanganė.* His guess (at the riddle) was wrong. *Mlèsèd saka kekarepané.* It wasn't what she wanted. *Sing prelu kenané ning sok² mlèsèd.* He's supposed to hit it, but he misses every so often. **m̃*aké** 1 (*psv* **di*aké**) to cause to slip *or* skid. 2 (*psv* **di*aké**) to mislead; to lead astray. *Ḍèké di*ké kantjané ḍéwé.* His own friend talked him into doing wrong. 3 to play with *or* on words, *e.g.* by punning. **m̃*i** slippery

plèsèh *ptg * or* **m̃*** scattered. *Goḍong² mlèsèh nang plataran.* Leaves were strewn all over the yard.

plesir (*or* ***an** *or* ***-***) to go smw for pleasure, *esp.* sightseeing. **-* ana ing mantja negara* to take a pleasure trip abroad

plèster, plèstèr, plestèr 1 adhesive tape. 2 concrete mixture for making floors. ***an** covered with adhesive tape *or* concrete. **m̃/di*** 1 to cover with adhesive tape. 2 to cover [a floor] with concrete

pleṭèk *rpr* breaking open. **m̃*** 1 [of dry skin] cracked, chapped. 2 to break (out into the) open. *Woh ranḍu paḍa mleṭèk, kapuké moto².* The kapok "fruits" burst open and the kapok pokes out. ***ing srengéngé** sunrise. *Srengéngéné wis mleṭèk.* The sun has risen.

pleter **m̈/di*** to train, drill. *mleter ndjogèd* to give training in the classical dance. *mleter murid² sinauné* to drill pupils in their studies

plèṭès, pleṭes **m̈/di*** to roll (sth) over sth. *Watu atosé kaja ngapa jèn di* setum ja remuk.* Even the hardest stones are crushed by the steam roller. *Montoré mau mleṭes pitik.* The car ran over a chicken.

plèṭèt, pleṭet *rpr* pressing, squeezing. **m̈/di*(aké)** to press, squeeze, crush. *mleṭet kenṭang* to mash potatoes. **m̈/di*(i)** to pinch, squeeze. *Kukulé adja di*i.* Don't squeeze the pimple.

pletik 1 a spark; *rpr* a spark shooting. *Geniné mak * ngenani klambiku.* The fire shot a spark onto my shirt. 2 white fleck on the iris of the eye which gradually grows larger until the entire black part is white and the eye loses its sight. ***-*** to shoot sparks. **ke*an** to get a spark on it. *Klambiné bolong ke*an geni rokok.* The cigarette spark made a hole in his shirt. **m̈*** 1 losing the sight of an eye (as above). *Mripaté mletik sidji.* He's going blind in one eye. 2 [of rice] undercooked. **m̈/di*(i)** to shoot a spark (onto)

pleṭi:k̄ *rpr* a small cracking sound. *Gelasé mak * petjah disoki wédang.* The glass cracked apart when hot water was poured into it.

pleṭis *var of* PLETIK

pletjèk **m̈/di*(aké)** to draw back [foreskin]

plètjèt **m̈*** skinned, bruised. **m̈/di*i** to remove the outer layer from. *Urangé di*i.* She shelled the shrimps. *Ḍèwèké dibégal, penganggoné di*i.* He was robbed and stripped of his clothing.

pletjit **m̈/di*** to chase

pletjus *rpr* exposure of a fraud. *Mak*, mung para ahli kang palsu.* So! they're only *fake* experts! *Bareng tekan toko mak* ora sida tuku, djebulé ora duwé ḍuwit.* When he got to the store, [after all his talk about big spending] he didn't buy a thing after all—he had no money.

pleṭok *rpr* cracking *or* bursting open. *Krambilé mak * petjah diidak gadjah.* The coconut cracked open when the elephant stepped on it. *Baturku mbakar beton ptg *.* The seeds cracked open as the servant roasted them. **m̈*** to break with a cracking sound. *Pringé mleṭok.* The bamboo snapped.

pleton 1 platoon. 2 concrete wall (*var of* BETON)

pleṭos *var of* PLEṬUS

pléṭot *ptg * pl* unsteady, crooked. *Olèhé nggaris ptg * ora lempeng.* The lines he drew were all crooked. **m̈*** to bend, not be straight enough. *Ladingé dienggo ngiris daging mléṭot.* The knife bends when you cut meat with it. *Olèhé nggambar wong ora apik, mesṭi mléṭot.* He can't draw people—the lines always go the wrong way.

plétré *rpr* sliding down. *Lagi baé ḍuwuré watara 2 m, bandjur mak * keplorod.* He climbed a couple of meters but slipped back down. **plétra-*** to keep sliding down. **ke*** to slide down inadvertently. **m̈*** 1 to slide down(ward). *Kaṭoké rada lobok pidjer mlètrèk waé.* His pants are too big; they keep sliding down. 2 flabby, flaccid, pendulous (*esp.* of breasts). **m̈/di*kaké** to slide sth down(ward). *mlètrèkaké rok* to slide one's skirt down

plètrèk *var of* PLÉTRÉ

pletuk *ptg * or* **m̈*** flecked with white. *Rambuté ptg *.* His hair is graying. *Médjané kok mletuk.* The table is dusty.

pleṭus *rpr* cracking, crunching. *Kembang gulané dikleṭus mak *.* He crunched the hard candy (as he chewed it). **m̈*** to pop, crack. *Ponggé kuwi jèn dibakar paḍa mleṭos.* When durian seeds are roasted they pop.

plèwèh ***an** an opening made by turning back the edges. *Blusé nganggo *an nggok geger.* Her blouse has an opening at the back. **m̈*** opened out; to come open

plèwèk *var of* PLÈWÈH

plikan *inf var of* PELIK·AN

pliket sticky. **m̈/di*i** to cause to be sticky. *Bukuku di*i kembang gula karèt.* He got his sticky gum on my book.

plilik *var of* PLIRIK

plilit *ptg * rpr* a queasy feeling. ***an** to fidget, squirm. **m̈*** [of stomach] to feel upset, to ache

plimping ***an** 1 a slight opening. **an lawang* a door slightly ajar. 2 a slighting remark delivered obliquely. *Ibu paring *an supaja aku sing matur bapak.* Mother said it to me so that I would say it to Father. **m̈*** slightly open. *Djenḍéla mlimping.* The window was open a little. **m̈/di*aké** to open sth slightly. *mlimpingaké lawang* to open the door a crack. **m̃/di*i** to deliver a slighting remark to smn indirectly. **m̃/di·plimpang-*i** to deliver a number of such allusions

plinder **m̃*** numbed in a part of the body because the circulation is cut off. **m̃/di*** to cause to be numb

plinḍes **ke*** to get struck by a moving vehicle. *ke* sepur* run over by a train. **m̃/di*** to run over. *Aku mlinḍes kutjing.* I ran over a cat.

plinguk **plingak-*** to search this way and that with the eyes; *fig* to look stupid. *Aku plingak-* ora ngerti dalané Jogjakarta.* I was trying to find my way around the streets of Jogjakarta. *plingak-* nggolèki kantja* looking everywhere for a friend. *Nang kelas ming plingak-* ora ngerti apa²*. He just sits in class rolling his eyes around stupidly–he doesn't know anything.

plinṭeng slingshot. ***an** 1 slingshot. 2 shot with a slingshot. *Manuké kataman krikil *an.* The bird was hit by a pebble from a slingshot. **m̃*** rugged, well built (of physique). **m̃/di*(i)** to shoot (at) with a slingshot. *Adja mlinṭengi omah.* Don't shoot at the house!

plintir ***an** spun, twirled. **an mbako* tobacco rolled into a corn leaf for a cigarette. *Sing dawa² putih kuwi *an kapuk.* The long white things are spun kapok. **m̃/di*** to spin, twirl. *mlintir bréngosé* to twirl one's moustache

plintjut ***an** embarrassed, humiliated, mortified

plinṭut *ptg ** devious, not to the point. ***an** *or* **plinṭat-*** lacking firm loyalties, available to the highest bidder

plipid (*or* ***an**) a hem. **m̃/di*(i)** to hem sth

plipir edge, border. **m̃*** 1 (to go) along the edge, *e.g.* on the sidewalk. *Plajuné mlipir turut pinggiré kali.* He ran along the river bank. 2 (*or* **m̃*-m̃***) [of formal-style speech] smooth, fluent. *Panembungé mlipir².* He spoke polished Krama. *Basané mlipir.* His Krama is fluent. **m̃/di*i** to go along the edge of. *mlipiri dalan* to walk at the side of the road. *Keboné di*i wit geḍang.* The garden is bordered with banana trees.

plirik **plirak-*** [of eyes] to shift from side to side. **m̃*** to stare fixedly. *Matané mlirik ngawasaké matjan.* He fixed his eyes on the tiger. *Aku mau bengi ora bisa turu, mung mlirik waé.* I couldn't get to sleep last night–my eyes just wouldn't close. *See also* LIRIK

plisir decorative edging on a fabric. **m̃/di*(i)** to edge sth with trimming

pliṭes *inf var of* PLINḌES

plitur wood varnish. ***an** varnished. **m̃/di*** to apply varnish to

pliṭut *var of* PLINṬUT. *ptg ** full of wrinkles. ***an** 1 wrinkled. **ané disetrika ilang.* She ironed out the wrinkles. 2 plait. **pliṭat-*** *or* **m̃*** 1 wrinkled. *Klambiné mliṭut.* His shirt is wrinkled. 2 plaited. **m̃/di*i** to plait. *Apa moḍèlé lengené di*i?* Are plaited sleeves in style?

plok 1 *rpr* sth light falling. *Tjetjaké tiba nang médja mak *.* The house lizard plopped down onto the table. 2 *inf var of* EMPLOK. **sa*é** 1 (ever) since. *sa*é kuwi* ever since then. *Sa*é dadi mantèn kira² ana selapan dina.* It's been about 35 days since they were married. 2 since, because of the fact that. *Sak *é kisinan Slamet bandjur pet klampet ora tau ngaton².* Slamet was so embarrassed he never showed his face there again.

plolo *ptg * pl* staring wide-eyed. **plola-*** *sg* to stare wide-eyed. *Atiné Kantjil ḍeg-ḍegan, matané plola-*.* Mouse-Deer's heart thumped and his eyes bugged out. **m̃*** [of eyes] wide. *Matané mlolo.* He was wide-eyed. *Kantjil kuwi matané geḍé mlolo.* A mouse-deer has huge bulging eyes.

plolong *rpr* a mouth suddenly gaping. *ptg * pl* with gaping mouths. **plolang-*** to keep gaping

plombir tax sticker for a vehicle. **m̃/di*** to fill [a tooth cavity]

plompong one of the small playing cards (*kertu tjilik*). *ptg * pl* open-mouthed. *Wong² paḍa ptg * ngrungokaké kanṭi telatèn.* They listened attentively, with open mouths. **plompang-*** *or* **m̃*** with mouth gaping. *Mung plompang-* ora ngerti apa².* He just gaped–he didn't understand it at all. *guwa bolong mlompong* an empty cave gaping

plong 1 *rpr* sudden relief from tension. 2 empty. *bolong ** an empty hole. 3 *intsfr* empty; utterly. *koṭong ** completely empty. *pitjak ** totally blind. ***-*an** an opening. **-*ané kurang amba.* The opening isn't big enough. **nge/di*aké** to put [a letter] through a letter slot. *ngeplongaké lajang* to mail a letter

plongo **plonga-∗** to have the mouth hanging open. *Ditakoni guruné plonga-∗.* When the teacher asked him a question he just gaped. **m̈∗** to gape. *Botjah² pada mlongo krungu tjrita.* The children listened to the story open-mouthed.

plongoh *rpr* an open-mouthed laugh. **m̈∗** to laugh/smile with the lips parted stupidly

plongok *var of* PLONGO

plonjo eau de cologne

plonjoh *rpr* burning *or* scalding of the skin. **m̈∗** burned, scalded; [of skin] peeling from a burned place

plonṭang black flecked with white [*esp.* of animals' coats]

plontjo a novice, a neophyte; a prospective university freshman who is undergoing initiation *or* hazing. *Mau ana ∗ telu ngresiki dalan.* Three prospective freshmen were cleaning the street [a task assigned to them by seniors]. **m̈/di∗** to initiate, haze

plontjon 1 a rack for storing lances *or* spears. 2 a wooden form for holding *or* shaping wrapped headdresses (*blangkon*)

plonṭos (*or* **∗an**) [of head] shaved clean. **m̈∗** to shave one's head

plopor a pioneering leader. **m̈/di∗(i)** to lead the way; to pioneer [a movement *etc.*]

plorod **∗an** sth used for sliding; a slide. **ke∗** to slide down accidentally. *Ḍèwèké kuwatir jèn bisé ke∗ njemplung ing djurang.* He was afraid the bus would plunge into the ravine. **ke·plorad-ke∗** to keep slipping down. *Botjah² mau enggoné mènèk tansah keplorad-ke∗.* The two boys, trying to climb up, kept slipping back down. **m̈∗** to slide down. *Ḍèké mlorod saka pangkoné.* He slid off her lap. *Lemahé mlorod menjang djurang.* The soil slid down into the gorge. *Ḍèwèké mlorod dadi wakil ketua.* He was demoted to vice-chairman. *Regané saja mlorod.* The prices slipped lower and lower. **m̈/di∗aké** 1 to shift sth downward. *Regané di∗aké.* She lowered the price. 2 to hand down [a used article]. *Seduluré enom ka∗aké marang raka dalem.* The widowed younger sister was given in marriage to the older brother of her deceased husband. *See also* LOROD

plorok **plorak-∗** [of eyes] wide open and looking this way and that. **m̈∗** opened wide [of eyes]. *Mata mlorok ora ndelok.* You're looking right at it and you can't see it!

plosok (*or* **∗-∗**) outlying part. *Kabar mau wis keprungu tekan ∗ désa.* The news spread to the most remote villages. *Olèhku dolan nang Surabaja mbijèn nganti tekan ∗-∗.* I visited every nook and cranny of Surabaja.

plotjot **m̈∗** [of skin] to get burned *or* scalded. *Ilaté mlotjot.* It burned my tongue. **m̈/di∗(i)** to remove the outer layer from. *Urangé di∗i.* She shelled the shrimp. *Wuduné di∗ metu nanahé.* He took the top off the boil and released the infected matter.

ploto **plota-∗** *or* **m̈∗** to tell tall tales. *wong mloto* a braggart, a windbag

ploṭot **ke∗** to get its insides squeezed out. **m̈/di∗aké** to squeeze out for smn. *Aku di∗aké tanpasta karo A.* A squeezed out my toothpaste for me. **m̈/di∗(i)** to squeeze [insides] out. *mloṭot tanpasta* to squeeze out toothpaste. *Djambuné di∗ ḍisik didelok jèn ana sèté.* Squeeze the guava first, to see if it has maggots in it.

plotro(k) *rpr* sliding down suddenly. *Bareng koloré peḍot kaṭoké mak ∗.* When his underwear string broke, his shorts slid down. **plotra(k)-∗** to keep sliding down. **m̈∗** to slide down

plu:k̄ *rpr* a slap, *esp.* in the face

plukok **∗an** *or* **∗-∗** feeling nauseated; to retch. **m̈∗** to vomit

plu:ng *rpr* sth small entering liquid. *Ujahé ditjemplungké mak ∗ nang djangan.* She sprinkled the salt into the soup. *Kantjil ketjemplung ana sumur, mak ∗!* Mouse-Deer fell splash! into the well.

plungker *rpr* rolling/curling up. *ptg ∗* to shiver, quake, cower. **m̈∗** to form a roll, to be curled. *Olèhé turu mlungker.* He sleeps curled up. **m̈/di∗aké** to roll *or* curl sth

plungsung **∗an** skin shed by a reptile

plunṭer *ptg ∗* curling, in curls (*e.g.* plant tendrils). *Rambuté ptg ∗.* Her hair is curly.

pluntir **m̈/di∗** to twist tight. *mluntir tangan* to twist smn's arm. *Kawaté sing kanggo nalèni di∗.* He twisted the binding wire tight. *See also* PUNTIR

pluntjar *ptg ∗* to glisten, glitter

plupuh 1 split-bamboo section for walls, fences. *Pageré ∗.* The fence was of bamboo panels. 2 bamboo bed *or* floor covering. **m̈/di∗** to make sth from bamboo sections. *Djoganė di∗.* The floor was of split-bamboo pieces.

pluru bullet

plurud **ke∗** to slide down(ward). *See also* PLOROD

plusut *rpr* slipping free. m̐∗ to slip free.
Iwaké jèn ditjekel pidjer mlusut waé. Whenever I get hold of the fish, it slips out of my
grasp.

pluta *gram* reduced form of a word resulting from vowel loss and consequent combining of the first two syllables, *e.g. sarah →
srah. Pra ∗né para. Pra* is the reduced form
of *para.* ∗n first-syllable vowel which is removed. m̐/di∗ to reduce [a word] as above

pluwang noose

pluwèk m̐∗ gaping open. m̐/di∗aké to open
sth (up, out). *Aku di∗aké durèn.* He opened
the durian fruit for me.

pluwer *ptg*∗ 1 in curls. 2 having many
turnings. m̐∗ to turn; to curl. *Wedi nèk tabrakan, mobilé mluwer.* The car swerved to
avoid a head-on collision.

pluwi blotting paper. m̐/di∗ to blot. m̐/di∗-
kaké to blot for smn

pluwit whistle; police whistle. ∗*ing sepur*
train whistle

pluwok *ptg*∗ filled with hollows. *Dalané
èlèk banget, paḍa ptg* ∗. The roads are terrible—full of potholes. m̐∗ concave. *Tatuné
mluwok geḍé banget.* The wound is broad
and deep.

po *see* BANḌEM

pod end, termination. *Ora ana* ∗é. There's
no end to it. *ora* ∗(-∗) unceasing, endless

poḍang (*or* ke∗) a certain green bird

poḍemporem iodoform

poḍeng pudding

podjar what smn says (*old-fashioned form
of* UDJAR). ∗an *or* m̐∗ to say (to); to
speak

podjok (*or* ∗an) corner; angle. ke∗ cornered, backed into a (*lit, fig*) corner. m̐∗
in(to) a corner. *Olèhé lingguh modjok.* He
sat in the corner. *Ḍèké nenḍang bal modjok.* He kicked the ball to the corner [of
the field]. m̐/di∗aké to corner smn; to put
sth in a corner. ∗ djedjeg right angle. ∗ lantjip acute angle. ∗ madjupat square.
∗ m̐-piring non-rectangular parallelogram.
∗ telu triangle

poh *var of* PUH

pohung cassava. *See also* TÉLA

pojah huge firecracker

pojok ∗an a teasing nickname. ∗*ané Babi
sebabé ḍèwèké lemu.* He's called Piggy because he's fat. ∗-∗an to call each other
nicknames. pe∗(an) *sms* ∗AN *above.*
m̐/di·(pe)∗i to apply a nickname to smn.

memojoki kantja-kantjané to call one's
friends by teasing nicknames

pok 1 the very end. *Olèhé negor wit nganti
tekan* ∗ *karebèn ora ṭukul manèh.* He cut
the tree at the very bottom so it wouldn't
grow back. 2 *rpr* sth small dropping. nge∗
(to cut) at the very end. *Pang mau dikeṭok
nge*∗. They cut off the branch right at the
tree trunk.

pokah to cut off, lop off

pokal behavior, actions, conduct. ∗é ora kena ditiru, nḍugal. You mustn't act like him
—he's no good. *Aku wis ngerti kabèh* ∗*mu.*
I know all about what you're up to!

pokang thigh, shank

pokïk (*or, esp.,* m̐∗) *cr* dead; to die

poklèk broken, snapped; to get broken. *Ga-
risané* ∗. His ruler broke. m̐/di∗aké to
break/snap sth unintentionally. m̐/di∗(i) to
break (off), snap (off)

pokok essential, main. *Jèn wajang wong djogèd iku dadi* ∗é. Classical dance is the essential ingredient of the dance-drama. *Dodolan
sing* ∗ *iku tamba.* The main thing they sell
is medicines. ∗é in essence, essentially.
*Ḍèwèké golèk alasan werna², *∗é ora gelem
lunga.* He gives all kinds of reasons, but the
fact is he doesn't *want* to leave. m̐/di∗i 1
to back [a business venture] financially.
2 to be the main *or* responsible person behind [sth]. *Sapa sing mokoki perusahaan
kuwi?* Who's in charge of that company?

pokping *var sp of* POPING

pokrol *var of* POKRUL

pokrul lawyer, attorney. m̐∗ to act in one's
capacity as a lawyer. m̐/di∗aké to have [a
lawyer] act for one. m̐/di∗i to take legal action on behalf of [a client]. ∗ bambu a
lawyer who has not yet received a law degree

pol 1 to the limit. *Anggoné ngisi bènsin
nganti* ∗ *tèng.* He filled the gas tank to the
brim. 2 pole (of the earth). ∗ *Lor/Kidul*
North/South Pole. ∗-∗an as much as [one]
can. *Olèhku turu* ∗-∗an. I got all the sleep I
could. nge/di∗aké to [do] to the limit.
Olèhé ngidak gas di∗aké. He pressed the gas
pedal to the floorboards.

pola design, pattern. ∗ *baṭikan* a batik pattern. m̐/di∗ to work [a batik pattern] into
a fabric. *mola njamping* to apply the design
to a wraparound

polah to move (about). *Katon lemes ora bisa*
∗. He seemed limp and unable to move.
Aku ngulataké ∗é. I watched what he did.

*an way of acting *or* moving. *Ḍèwèké nirokaké *an ḍokteré.* He mimicked the doctor. **m̃*** to move (about). *Anak molah* (or *polah*) *bapa kepraḍah.* The father is held responsible for the child's acts. **molah ambeg·an** to gasp, draw in the breath sharply. **m̃/di*aké** to move *or* handle sth. *Sing nunggangi prigel molahaké setir.* The driver manipulated the steering wheel skillfully. *** tingkah** actions, behavior. *Sa*-tingkahé senadyan nḍugal, diarani lutju.* Everything he does is vulgar, but even so he's funny. *See also* PARIPOLAH

polat *form of* ULAT

polḍan 1 having won at the game of *pasbreg* by virtue of playing all one's pieces. 2 paid up. *Utangku wis *.* My debt is all paid. **m̃/di*aké** to pay up [smn's debt]. *Aku molḍanaké utangé.* I paid his debt for him. **m̃/di*i** to pay off [a debt]

polèng diagonally striped

polentèr a volunteer

poligami polygamy. *nindakké ** to practice polygamy

polikliniḱ medical clinic

polisi *var of* PULISI

polisionil of the police. *aksi ** policing actions (*referring to the 1947 and 1948 acts of Dutch aggression during the Indonesian Revolution*)

politiḱ 1 politics. ** ndonja* world politics. *partai ** political party. 2 policy. ** neluk²-aké* a policy of subjugation

politikus politician

politis political

polo 1 head. *ora * ora utek* without a thought in one's head. 2 *cr* brain. 3 house top, ridgepole; *fig* household, roof. *adu ** roof-to-roof [of houses, *i.e.* built close together]. **m̃*** 1 *cr?* head. 2 *sms* * 3. *Désa kono ana pirang molo?* How many households are there in that village?

polok ankle bone

polong clove

polos 1 [of fabric] plain, unfigured. 2 simple, without guile

poma by all means; (*with negative*) by no means. ** tansah ngati-ati.* You must always watch your step. ** dibisa njimpen wadi.* It is essential that you be able to keep secrets. ** adja diombé.* Don't drink it under any circumstances. ** adja lali memaju rehajuning bawana.* You must never forget to work for the well-being of the world. **m̃/di*-*** to impress it on smn that he must... *Ora kurang² anggoné moma² supaja anaké taberi sinauné.* They have always kept after their children to work hard at their studies. *** di*** by all means. *Olèhmu sinau kudu sing sregep, poma dipoma adja kaja pamanmu sing bebatjut buta huruf.* Study hard; you must by no means be like your illiterate uncle.

pomah *ng,* **pémah** *kr* tame, domesticated; to feel at home. ***an** (**pa·grija·n** *var kr;* **pa·dalem·an** *ki*) a house lot. *padjeg *an* house tax, household tax. *See also* OMAH

pompa a pump. **m̃/di*** to pump (into, out of). ** pit* to pump up a bicycle tire. *Banjuné di*.* They pumped out the water.

pon 1 name of the third day of the five-day week. 2 unit of weight: *ca.* 1 lb. ***-*an** by the pound. *Gulané didol *-*an.* The sugar is sold by the pound.

ponaḱan *var of* KEPONAKAN

ponḍamèn *var of* PUNḌAMÈN

pondji *var of* PUNDJI

ponḍoh pithy edible part at the top of a palm-tree trunk at the base of the leaves. **m̃/di*** to pierce the ears for earrings

ponḍok a small crude hut; *fig* my humble home. *Mangga pinarak ing * kula.* Please visit our home. ***an** 1 a place to stay when away from home; lodgings; rented room(s). **an mahasiswa²* a boardinghouse for university students. *Aku golèk *an.* I'm looking for a place to stay. 2 a boarding school where students study the Koran. **m̃*** to live in a rented room away from home. **monḍok ḍèmpèl/tèmpèl** to make one's home on smn else's property. **m̃/di*aké** to board smn, to have smn live in another's home as a paying guest. *Anaké A sing wédok di*ké nang dalemé B.* A is boarding his daughter in B's home. **m̃/di*i** to rent a room in [smn's house]. *Omahé di*i para mahasiswa.* Students rent rooms in his house. **pa·m̃*an** *sms* *AN *above*

ponḍong ***an** 1 act of carrying sth in the arms against the chest. 2 court ceremony in which one carries his bride on the arm, symbolizing that she is a prize being carried off. **m̃/di*** 1 to carry as above. *monḍong anak/baji/tas* to carry a child/a baby/a bag against the chest. 2 to carry one's bride as above

pong ***-*an** sea snail

ponggé edible durian-fruit pit

pongkrang *intsfr* old. *gerang* ∗ very old, worn out

pongol a large protruding object. m̈∗ to protrude, to loom. *Ana watu mongol nang tengah dalan.* There's a huge rock in the middle of the street.

poni girls' hair style (short, with bangs across the forehead)

ponis sentence, punishment; judge's verdict. m̈/di∗ to pass sentence on. *Malingé di∗ pendjara nem sasi.* The thief was sent to jail for six months.

ponṭal ke∗-∗ to have difficulty keeping pace. *Aku jèn diwulang ilmu kimia mesṭi ke∗-∗.* When I studied chemistry [it was hard for me to understand it so] I couldn't keep up.

ponṭang *see* TAKIR

pontèn (water) fountain

pontjot corner

po'oping *var sp of* POPING

po'ping mentholated stick for use as a nasal decongestant

popoh strong, muscular. ke∗(an) to have a task to perform; to have responsibility fall on one

popok 1 ointment of powder mixed with water (*var of* BOBOK). 2 diaper. m̈/di∗(aké) to apply [a powder-and-water mixture]. *Lemah mau di∗aké ing mobilé nganti ora karuan regedé.* They smeared mud on his car till it was utterly filthy. *mopok beras kentjur* to apply a rice-and-herb mixture. *Témboké di∗ nganggo semèn.* The wall was patched with cement. m̈/di∗i to apply the above (1, 2) to. *mopoki botjah* to place a poultice on a child. *Bajiné di∗i.* She put a diaper on the baby.

popol ∗an broken-down part, caved-in portion. m̈∗ to come apart, break down. *Seloté lawang arep dak bukak mopol.* The door latch came off in my hand as I was about to open it. *Duk iku ora gampang mopolé.* Palm fibers don't break easily. m̈/di∗i to cause sth to weaken and collapse. *Di∗i nganggo apa tjagaké?* How did they bring down the pillars?

popor rifle stock

poprok *slang var of* NG-OPROK

poprol *pl form of* POPOL

populèr popular. *Penjanji Amérika mau ∗ tekan tanah Djawa.* This American singer is popular as far away as Java. m̈/di∗aké to cause sth to be *or* become popular. *mo-*

pulèraké tembang to popularize a classical song

por 1 to the utmost, to the limit. 2 forward (soccer player, position). *sènter* ∗ center forward. ∗-∗an to one's utmost capacity. nge/di∗aké to [do] to the limit. *Enggoné saur dieporaké.* He ate as much as he could manage to at the 2:30 A.M. pre-fasting meal. *Olèhé dandan di∗aké.* He dressed with scrupulous neatness. sa∗é to one's capacity. *Mangana sa∗é, aku sing mbajar.* Eat all you can—I'm paying. *sinau sa∗é* to study as hard as possible

porā or not (*inf var of* APA ORA: *see* ORA). *Kowé wedi ∗?* Are you afraid?

poret *see* ANGGUR

porno dirty, pornographic

porok fork. ∗ pit bicycle fork (metal strips on either side of the front wheel from steering mechanism to hub)

porong burned black. *Téla gosong ∗.* The cassava was burned to a crisp.

porselin chinaware; earthenware; porcelain

Portegis Portuguese. *wong* ∗ a Portuguese. *negara* ∗ Portugal

portepèl portfolio, letter case

Portugis *var of* PORTEGIS

pos 1 mail, post. *kantor* ∗ post office. *kertu* ∗ post card. ∗ *tertjaṭat* registered mail. ∗ *wisel* postal money order. ∗ *pakèt* parcel post. *tjap* ∗ postmark. *djawatan* ∗ *lan télégrap* the mail and telegraph department. ∗ *tèl* mail and telephone [service]. *tukang* ∗ mail man. *dara* ∗ carrier pigeon. 2 post of duty. *Aku dikon ngentèni ana ∗ku.* He told me to wait at my post. 3 a unit of distance: five *pal* = *ca.* 4.67 miles. 4 way station, post house where travelers rest. nge∗ to stop and rest at a post house. nge/di∗aké 1 to mail [a letter]. 2 to send sth through the mail

posing to feel dizzy

pospat phosphate

pot 1 pot. 2 (to play) a certain game of marbles. 3 gambling stakes; a bet. ∗-∗an various kinds of pots

potang 1 a loan. ∗ *bank* a bank loan. 2 moneylender. *tukang* ∗ moneylender. 3 foreclosure on a loan. 4 to put smn in one's debt. *B ∗ kabetjikan marang A.* A owes B a favor, *i.e.* B did a kindness for A. *ana ∗an* borrowed for interest; taken on credit. *barang² sing ana ∗an* borrowed things; things that have been taken on credit. ka∗an to be indebted [to smn]. *Aku wis ka*an budi.* I owe him a favor. *Aku ke*an njawa karo ḍèké.* I owe my life to him. **m̃/di*aké** 1 to lend for interest. *Anggoné motangaké ḍuwit nganti ma-juta²*. He has millions of rupiahs out on loan. 2 to sell on credit. 3 to extend [a favor] to. *Wis motangaké budi marang kita.* We're indebted to them for a favor. **m̃/di*i** to lend. *Wingi aku utang kowé, nanging dina iki aku motangi kowé.* I borrowed from you yesterday and you're borrowing from me today. *** (a)piutang (sambut-s·in·ambut** *kr*) 1 to keep borrowing and lending. 2 to be indebted to each other. *See also* UTANG

potèhi Chinese hand-puppet theater, based on Chinese stories and performed by Chinese Indonesians in Chinese-flavored Javanese *or* Indonesian language

poṭèk *var of* POṬÈL

poṭèl broken, chipped. **m̃/di*** to break off. *Ḍèwèké moṭèl geḍang sing isih mentah mau.* He removed the unripe banana [from the stalk].

potelod *var of* POTLOD

poṭèng **m̃/di*(-*)** to dismember. *moṭèng² iwak pitik sing arep diolah* to cut up a chicken for frying

poṭès *var of* POṬÈL

po-the-hi *var sp of* POTÈHI

potjapan *form of* UTJAP. **sa*an** whatever smn says. *Sasolah sa*ané ngresepaké.* Everything she does and says is kind-hearted.

potji (tea)pot

potjok ***an** temporary fill-in work. **m̃/di*aké** to have smn work by the day. **m̃/di*i** to do smn else's job on a temporary basis. *Aku kepeksa motjoki pegawéané kantjaku sakdjeroné ḍèwèké lara.* I had to do my coworker's job while he was out ill.

potjong 1 harvested rice tied in bundles. 2 unit of weight for raw rice, 15 of which make an *agem.* 3 buttocks (*ki for* BOKONG). ***an** 1 winding sheet. 2 corpse wrapped in a winding sheet. **m̃/di*(i)** 1 to bundle harvested rice *or* sugar cane. 2 to wrap [a corpse, preparatory to burial]

potjot *var of* TJOPOT

potjung *var of* PUTJUNG

potlod pencil. ***an** (written, drawn) in pencil

poto *var of* FOTO

poṭok 1 strong, muscular. 2 *rg* fixed. *Regané wis *.* The price is fixed.

poṭol to break, snap, come off. *Pantèké *.* The peg fell out. **m̃/di*(i)** to break/snap sth. *Di* guluné.* His neck was broken. **m̃*i** *pl* to fall off

potong 1 (to have/get) a haircut. ** baṭok* (to have) a haircut shaped like a half-coconut shell (worn *esp.* by those who wear wrapped headdresses). 2 a cut-off piece. *Klambiné se* pira?* How much for a length of clothing material? *daging se** a slice of meat. 3 style, cut. *Klambiné * Tjina.* His clothing is cut Chinese style. ***an** 1 a cut-off piece; a scrap; a deduction. ** pring* a bamboo chip. **an satus rupiah* a 100-rupiah cut (in price). 2 style, fashion, cut. **an klambiné* the cut of her dress. *Rambuté *an moḍèl anjar.* She has a new hairdo. *Ḍèwèké (duwé) *an maling.* He has the cut of a thief. **m̃/di*** 1 to cut (off, down). *Tebuné di* loro.* He cut the sugar cane in two. *Rambuté di* tjenḍak.* She cut her hair short. *Saben wulané bajarané di* limang persèn.* Every day, 5 percent is deducted from his pay. 2 to slaughter. *motong sapi* to butcher a cow. **m̃/di*i** to cut out [clothing]. *Kowé sing motongi, aku sing ndjahit.* You cut it out and I'll sew it. *** ajam** *Chinese swear word.* *** gurung** slaughter tax. *** mangkok** a certain style of collarless Chinese jacket. *** pulkah** style of haircut for boys *or* men

potrèk̄ 1 camera. *bur ** a drill for making tiny holes. 2 photograph, snapshot. 3 to have one's picture taken. *tukang ** photographer. **m̃/di*(i)** to take a picture (of). *Ḍèké tjekrak-tjekrèk motrèki.* He kept snapping pictures. *Gambar mau di* saka ing montor mabur.* This picture was taken from a plane.

potrèt *var of* POTRÈK

po'uping *var sp of* POPING

powan(g) cow's milk

pra 1 *pluralizer: inf var of* PARA. 2 *fraction-forming prefix: shf of* PARA. *-*pat* -fourth, -quarter. *telung *pat* three-quarters. *limang *nem* five-sixths. *sangang *sepuluh* nine-tenths. **satus* -hundredth. 3 *stem-deriving prefix: see under individual entries.* **...an* *circumfix forming fractions in the counting form.* *sa *telon* one-third. *nja *telon* one-third apiece, one-third to each. *patang *liman* four-fifths. *Sa*pitoné patbelas kuwi loro.* One-seventh of 14 is 2. **m̃*** to divide sth into [fractions]. *mratelu* to divide into three parts, to make into

thirds. *Olèhé mralima adil.* He divided it fairly among the five.
pra- *see also under* PER-, *inf var of* PRA-
prâbâ 1 throne. 2 *wj* throne-shaped wings worn as part of a dancer's costume, signifying kingship
prâbâjeksâ a large hall in the palace at Jogjakarta
prâbâkârâ *var of* PRABANGKARA
prabangkârâ *oj* sun
prabâtâ *oj* mountain
prabâwâ 1 awesomeness, splendor, majesty. **né ratu sekti* the awesome presence of the king. 2 authority. **ning negara* governmental authority. **m̃/di*ni** to exert authority *or* influence (over). *luhur lan merbawani* noble and influential. *See also* BAWA
prabot equipment, supplies, accessories, parts. ** kantor* office supplies and equipment. ** omah* furniture, house furnishings. ** sekolah* school supplies. ** perang* military supplies. ** tukang* workman's tools. **m̃*** fully equipped. **m̃/di*i** to equip smn
prabu king, monarch. *Sang ** the king; his majesty. **ka*n** 1 kingship, the throne. *sèlèh ka*n* to relinquish the throne. *sumilih ka*n* to succeed to the throne. 2 royal trappings. *upatjara ka*n* palace ceremonies where royal ceremonial objects are displayed. **m̃*(ñi)** kingly
prâdâ *ng,* **praos** *sbst? kr* gold plating *or* gold varnish for shadow-play puppets. ** putih* silver plating. ***n** plated with gold *or* silver. **m̃/di*** to plate [puppets]
Pra. Da. *see* PRADJURIT
praḍah generous. **ke*** to have blame fall on one. **m̃/di*** to convict, find guilty. **m̃/di*i** to face [adversity] with a stout heart
pradânggâ (*or* **m̃***) *oj* Javanese musical instruments, gamelan ensemble
pradâtâ *var of* PERDATA
prâdjâ 1 kingdom; court, palace. *wong ** courtier. 2 country, nation. *mantja ** foreign country (*or* kingdom). (*punggawa*) *pamong ** district administrative official. *See also* RADJA
pradjurit soldier. ** anggaran* mercenary soldier. ** gegana* soldier of the air force. **ka*an** military prowess. *** dua** (*abbr*: **Pra. Da.**) private second class. *** kepala** (*abbr*: **Pra. Ka.**) senior private. *** satu** (*abbr*: **Pra. Tu.**) private first class. *See also* DJURIT
pradondi *var of* PERDONDI
praduli *var of* PERDULI
pragad to slaughter (*root form: opt? kr for* SEMBELÈH)
pragalba *oj* tiger
pragas *var of* PAGAS
pragèn kitchen storage bin
prah *rpr* falling. *ambjar saka nḍuwur ** to fall from above in small pieces
prahârâ wind and rain storm. ** mau wis meneng.* The storm has subsided.
prahoto motor truck. **sa*** 1 a truckful. 2 the size of (*i.e.* the same size as) a truck
prahu *var of* PRAU
prâjâ *see* ÉKA
prajang ***an** inhabitants of the spirit world. *djim-peri *an* male and female spirits. **m̃*** to wander; [of spirits] to roam
prajatna *var of* PRAJITNA
prajitna cautious. *Kurang sabar lan *.* He was impatient and careless. **ka*n** care, caution. *pasang ka*n* to keep on the alert. **m̃/di*ni** to watch out for, be careful about. *See also* JITNA
prajoga *ng,* **prajogi** *kr* advisable, recommended. *Adja nganti mambu * tutupana.* You'd better cover it so it won't spoil. ***(né)** it is to be recommended that... **né disinau luwih ḍisik.* You would be well advised to study ahead of time. **m̃/di*kaké** to advise, recommend. *Aku mrajogakaké supaja kowé ndjaluk ngapura marang kantjamu.* I suggest that you apologize to your friend. **pa·m̃*** advice, recommendation. *djuru pamrajoga* adviser, consultant. *pamrajoga sing betjik* good advice. **sa*né** whatever is advisable. *Aku mung manut sa*né Bapak.* I'll do as you think best, Father.
prajogi *kr for* PRAJOGA
prak 1 *rpr* a cracking sound. 2 *var of* PERAK
Pra. Ka. *see* PRADJURIT
prakârâ *var of* PERKARA
prakarsa creativity. *sosiawan kang kebak ** a social worker who is full of ideas. *saka *né* because of his ingenuity. **m̃/di*(ni)** to initiate
prakosa *var of* PERKOSA
praksânâ *see* KATJA
praktèk̄ practice. *Ḍokter A olèhé * djam lima tekan djam pitu soré.* Dr. A's office hours are from 5 to 7 P.M. **m̃/di*aké** to practice sth. *mraktèkaké téori* to apply a theory. *Kepinterané di*aké.* He puts his skill into practice. *mraktèkaké omong Inggris* to practice speaking English
praktik̄ *var of* PRAKTÈK
praktis practical. *tjara² sing ** practical ways

pralâgâ *oj* war

praléna *oj* dead; to die. **∗n** an organization to collect money for assisting a family in which a death has occurred. *See also* LÉNA

prâmasastrâ *var of* PARAMASASTRA

prambajun *var of* PAMBAJUN

pramèswârâ, pramèswari queen

prampang 1 feeling hot. *Awaké krasa ∗.* He is feverish. *Jèn awan nang penḍapa kéné ∗.* In midday it feels hot in the veranda. 2 thin, transparent. *Klambiné ∗ banget.* You can see through her dress.

pramudita *var of* PRAMUNḌITA

pramugârâ, pramugarā male steward

pramugari 1 female guide. 2 stewardess

pramuka, pramukā Boy *or* Girl Scout

pramunḍita *wj* *excl of astonishment*

prânâ 1 attraction. *daja adji ∗* magical power to attract people. 2 clitoris (*ki for* ITIL). 3 *oj* breath, breathing; feeling(s). **di∗kaké (dipun·prika·kaken** *kr***)** *var psv for* DI·MRANA·KAKÉ. **ke∗n** strongly attracted to, enchanted by (*ki for* KE·TARIK?). **m̄∗ni** attractive, charming. *Èsemé mranani banget.* Her smile is appealing. *See also* SEPRANA

pranâdjâ chest, breast (*ki for* ḌAḌA)

pranakan 1 breed, stock, blood. *wong Djawa ∗ Arab* a person of mixed Javanese and Arabic blood. 2 womb. 3 long-sleeved cloth jacket worn by officials at the Jogja court. *See also* ANAK

prandéné *inf var of* SUPRANDÉNÉ

prandjèn chicken-house, henhouse

prang *var of* PERANG. **pa∗an** 1 battlefield. 2 pertaining to war. *sénapati pa∗an* general of the army

pranggul **ke∗** to encounter by chance. *Ora suwé ke∗ wong tani.* Pretty soon he met a farmer. **m̄/di∗i** to encounter sth. *Sapiné nèk mrangguli tanduran mesṭi disenggut.* Whenever the cow came upon a plant, she would eat it. *Aku kerep mrangguli tulisan basa mantja sing nulisé klèru.* I often come across foreign-language scripts that aren't written right.

prangkat set of objects. *gamelané sa∗ sléndro pelog* a set of gamelan instruments for both musical scales

prangko postage stamp. *∗ limang sèn* a five-cent stamp. *∗ njekeṭipan* ten-cent stamp. *∗ njetalènan* 25-cent stamp. *∗ pos tertjaṭat* registered-mail stamp. **m̄/di∗ni** to put a stamp on

prangkul an armful; as much as the arms can clasp. *Wit asemé geḍéné sa∗.* The tamarind tree is as big around as your arms can reach. *See also* RANGKUL

prangwedani a velvet *or* plush rug

pranili *rg var of* PANILI

prantas **m̄/di∗i** to see sth through to the finish. *Jèn dipasrahi gawéan mesṭi bisa mrantasi.* He always completes any job that is assigned to him.

pranti *var of* PIRANTI

Prantjis *var of* PERANTJIS

prantos *var of* PIRANTOS

praos gold plating (*sbst? kr for* PRADA)

praoto *var of* PRAHOTO

prapat *ng,* **prasekawan** *kr* quarter, -fourth. *se∗* one-fourth. *telung ∗* three-quarters. **∗an** crossroads, intersection. **m̄∗** 1 (*psv* **di∗**) to divide into quarters. 2 four-corner intersection; any cross-shaped figure. *See also* PAT

prapèn fireplace; place for an open fire, *e.g.* a blacksmith's forge. *See also* API

prapta *oj* arrival; to arrive. **∗ ing** arrival at; to arrive at

praptèng *contracted form of* PRAPTA ING

prasaben every time. *See also* SABEN

prasâdjâ *var of* PERSADJA

prasâpâ curse, oath. *Panḍitané a∗...* The holy man uttered a curse [as follows]. **m̄/di∗kaké** to wish [sth bad on smn]. *A mrasapakaké laranė B.* A wished an illness on B. **m̄/di∗ni** to put a curse on. *A mrasapani B.* A put a curse on B. *See also* SAPA[b]

prasasat like, as; as if, as though. *∗ ujah katjemplung ing segara* carrying coals to Newcastle ('like salt flung into the sea'). *See also* SASAT

prasasti *oj* ancient inscription. *tetinggalan barang kuna awudjud watu² utawa ∗* relics of olden times in the form of rocks or inscriptions

prasatus -hundredth. *sa* **∗an** 1/100. *rong* **∗an** 0.02. *See also* ATUS

prasekawan quarter, -fourth (*kr for* PRAPAT)

prasetya loyal, faithful, obedient. *See also* SETYA

prasman (*ḍahar*) **∗an** 1 communal ceremony to which the guests bring their own meal. 2 a buffet dinner

prastâwâ 1 wise, alert. 2 happening, event

pratâlâ *oj* soil, earth, ground. *kenḍi ∗* earthenware water pitcher

pratâmâ *oj* the first, number one, the best

pratânḍâ *var of* PERTANḌA

pratânggâ(pati) *oj* sun
pratjihna sign, indication, mark. **m̄/di*ni** to indicate, be a sign of. *See also* TJIHNA
pratjima *oj* west. * **sana** west hall in the palace of Jogjakarta
Pra. Tu. *see* PRADJURIT
prau *ng,* **baita** *kr* boat; canoe, rowboat. * *golèkan* medium-sized sailboat. * *silem* submarine. ***n̂** to go boating for pleasure. ***-*an** *or* ***-*n̂an** toy boat; boat model. **m̄*** to ride in a boat. **m̄/di*k̂aké** to transport by boat. *Aku arep mraokaké barang²ku.* I'm sending my baggage by boat. **m̄/di*n̂i** 1 to use a boat (for). *Jèn dipraoni kira² sa djam.* It takes about an hour by boat. 2 to transport by boat. * **ṭengil** *rg* canoe
prawan 1 young girl of marriageable age. 2 *affectionate adr* (my) daughter. 3 unmarried servant girl. **m̄*i** girlish. * **ganḍor** old maid. * **kentjing** *or* * **kentjur** *or* * **sunṭi** physically immature girl. * **tuwa** spinster. *See also* KUMRAWAN
prawâtâ *oj* mountain. * **suta** large, the size of a hill
pré onion leaf used as food flavoring
pre- *see also under* PER- (*Introduction, 2.9.6*)
prèbijèt railroad pass entitling the holder to ride free
prèdjèl *var of* PRODJOL
préé *var of* PRÉ
prègès [of leaves on plants, trees] eaten up *or* into by pests, *esp.* caterpillars
prèh a variety of banyan tree
prèi 1 free, at leisure. *Aku * seminggu.* I have a week off. *Jèn * mbok dandan².* When you're on vacation, how about doing some repairs around the house? 2 free of restraint *or* constraint; disengaged. *Jèn dolan nang omahku * banget djalaran wis kaja dianggep sedulur ḍéwé.* He feels at home in our house because he's like part of the family. *Persnèlingé wis * apa durung?* Is the gear in neutral? ***n̂** having free time. *Aku lagi prèèn.* I'm on vacation. **m̄*** to absent oneself from the normal activity. *Dina iki aku mrèi merga lara.* I'm staying home today, I'm ill. **m̄/di*k̀aké** 1 to give smn time off. *Sekolahan² diprèèkaké seminggu lawasé.* The schools were let out for a week. 2 to disengage. *mrèèkaké persnèling* to shift into neutral
prek̄ 1 *rpr* a sudden weakening *or* collapse. 2 *rpr* the sound of sth smashing. *Tjéléngané dipetjah, *.* He broke his piggy bank. **prak-*** frail, sickly
prel *rpr* breaking to pieces. *Kajuné dipangan bubuk, diangkat mak *.* The wood, eaten by termites, fell apart when he picked it up.
préma *var of* PIRMA
préman private. *anḍong ** a privately owned carriage. *matjak ** to dress in civilian clothes
prembajun breast (*ki for* SUSU[a])
prembèh *var of* PREMBIK
prembeng *-* red in the face, *e.g.* when on the verge of crying
prembih *var of* PREMBIK
prembi:k *-* *or* **prembak-*** about to cry; beginning to cry softly
prémi bonus. * *bebaja* a premium wage for work done in dangerous areas
prempeng 1 to blush, flush. 2 *rpr* a sudden impact on the senses *or* sensitivities. *Suwarané mertjon mau mak * nang kuping.* The noise of the firecracker hurt my ears. *Mak * kelalèn.* He suddenly forgot. *Mak * kupingé bareng dikanḍani jèn ḍèwèké dipitenah.* He flushed angrily when he heard he had been slandered. **prempang-*** to keep flushing
prempul *rpr* swelling suddenly. *ptg ** full of swellings; bubbling, foamy, frothy. **m̄*** to swell up
prending frayed. *ptg ** *or* **m̄*** badly frayed *Taliné mrending.* The rope is weakened by fraying.
prendjak a variety of warbler
préné *ng,* **priki** *kr* **di*k̀aké** *var psv for* DI·MRÉNÉ·K̀AKÉ. *Énggal prènèkna.* Bring it here quick! **se*** *see* SEPRÉNÉ
prèngès *rpr* a sudden broad smile. *ptg ** *or* **préngas-*** all smiles; to keep grinning. **m̄*** to smile/grin broadly showing the teeth
prengkel *ptg * pl* lumpy; callused. *Tangané paḍa ptg *.* His hands are covered with calluses. **m̄*** *sg* having a lump *or* callus
prengus [of animal odor] strong. *Weḍus iku ambuné *.* Goats smell terrible.
prengut **prengat-*** to keep scowling. **m̄*** to scowl, look sullen. **m̄/di*i** to scowl at
préntah *var of* PRINTAH
prenṭel *ptg ** all in curls. *Rambuté brintik ptg *.* His hair is kinky. **m̄*** 1 [of hair] to curl. *Rambuté mrenṭel.* His hair is curly. 2 to save up [money] little by little
prenṭil *ptg ** in the form of many small knob shapes. *Penṭilé pelem wis paḍa ptg *.* The young mango-fruit buds are now little balls. **m̄*** forming a knobby protuberance

prentja *-* spread over a wide area. **m̃/di*** to spread out, spread apart. *Tandurané di* karebèn ora suk²an.* He thinned the plants so they wouldn't crowd each other. *Tandurané brambang wis di*-*.* He's planted onions over a wide area. **m̃/di*kaké** to thin out, space out

prenṭol *ptg * pl* forming knob-shaped protuberances. **m̃*** *sg as above*

prentul 1 a small swelling. 2 *rpr* welling up/out. *Mak * medal luhipun.* The tears welled up. *ptg * or *-** 1 to swell in many places. *Rainé metu *-*é.* His face broke out. 2 to keep welling up

prenṭul *ptg * pl* forming good-sized knob-shaped protuberances. **m̃*** *sg as above. Aku wingènané tanganku keslomot geni, tilasé bandjur mrenṭil, wingi dadi mrenṭul, saiki kok mrenṭol.* Day before yesterday I burned my hand and it swelled a little; yesterday it was bigger, and now the swelling is quite large.

prepak *var of* PREPEK

prepek̄ *oj* **m̃/di*i** to approach. *Baṭara Narada mrepeki Radèn Djanaka sing lagi tindak wanawasa.* Narada approached Djanaka as he walked in the woods. *Wis mrepeki udjian.* It's almost exam time.

prèpèt *var of* BRÈBÈT

prepet *rpr* a sudden change in aspect. **! ḍèké kagèt.* He flushed with shock. *Mak * menḍung.* Suddenly it clouded over. **m̃*** 1 to change suddenly. 2 urgent. *Butuhku wis mrepet, gèk wis utangana!* I need money badly–please lend me some!

près equipment for pressing sth (the juice from sugar cane; a printing press; *etc.*). **nge/di*** to press with pressing equipment

pres *rpr* an impact, *esp.* with breakage. *Gelasé petjah, *.* The glass smashed. *Ḍèwèké nabrak témbok, *.* He ran smack into a wall.

présiḍèn president. ** ora bisa diganggu gugat.* The President can do no wrong.

prèt 1 *rpr* trumpet tootings. 2 *rpr* discharging flatus. ***-*an** to discharge flatus repeatedly

pret 1 *rpr* ejection of air through the compressed lips with a sharp report: an expression of disdain. 2 *rpr* fabric tearing. *Nalika lungguh mau, mak * djariké suwèk.* As she sat down, her batik ripped. **nge/di*i** to express disdain for smn by making the above sound; *fig* to belittle, look down on

prèṭèl to become detached. **m̃*i 1** *pl* to detach themselves. *Wuluné manukku paḍa mrèṭèli.* My bird molted. 2 (*psv* **di*i**) to break [things] (off). *Dolanané di*i.* He pulled the toy apart. *See also* PÈṬÈL

prètjèl **m̃/di*i** to cut up, cut into pieces

pretjet *rpr* a sudden emergence *or* ejection. *Baboné mak * ngenḍog.* The hen laid an egg.

pretog *rpr* a hen's cackling

préwangan witch. *ḍukun ** a female medium

préwé (*or* **ke*ǹ**) *rg var of* KEPRIJÉ

pribadi concerning one's own self. *soal ** personal matters. *Iki kanggo *né ḍèwèké ḍéwé.* It's his own business. *Wah, kuwi sedjarah *ku ḍéwé.* Well, that's the story of my life. **ka*ǹ** personality; identity. *Aku leladi ing biḍang kang tjotjog karo kapribadènku.* I served in a type of work which was congenial to me. *miturut kepribadèn Indonesia* in accordance with the spirit of Indonesia. *See also* ḌIRI

pribé (*or* **ǹ** *or* **ke*ǹ**) *rg var of* KEPRIJÉ

pribumi land, earth. **wong *** a native (of a place). *See also* BUMI

prigel skillful, dextrous. *Sing njupir * molahaké setir.* The driver steered with great skill. *Olèhé ndjogèd * banget.* He's an accomplished dancer. **ka*an** skill, dexterity

prigi *rg* a small dam made of rocks

prigis bare, denuded. *Pupusé wis *.* The leaves have been eaten off [from the tree].

prihatin *ng,* **prihatos** *kr* saddened, grieving, anxious, prayerful. *Aku mèlu *.* I share in their heartache. *Ibuné * banget merga bajiné lara.* The mother is praying anxiously because her baby is ill. **m̃/di*aké** *or* **m̃/di*i** to wish and pray (for). *mrihatini anaké sing lagi udjian* to pray for one's son who is taking an examination

prihatos *kr for* PRIHATIN

prihpun *var of* PRIPUN

prija a male. ***-(a)gung** great man, hero. *** wanita** man and woman, male and female

prijagung *see* PRIJA

prijaji *ng,* **prijantun** *kr* 1 high official. 2 respected person, member of the upper class. ***ǹ-*ǹan** *ng* to assume the aspect of a *prijaji. mBok adja prijajèn²an.* Don't put on airs as though you belonged to the upper crust. **ka*ǹ** inclusion among the gentry. *ndjaga kaprijajèné* to maintain one's prestige as a *prijaji.* **m̃*(ǹi)** resembling a *prijaji. tata-tjara sing mrijajèni* gentlemanly ways. *** tanggung** low-ranking official

prijang *-* (*or, esp.,* **m̃***) to have *or*

get a fever. *Awaké apa mrijang?* Is he feverish?

prijânggâ *oj* oneself. *Manawa ana kurdané ḍimas Werkudara arep dak tanggung* *. If Werkudara becomes angry, I'll handle him myself.

prijantun 1 high-status person (*kr for* PRIJAJI). 2 person (*kr for* WONG[a])

prijuk rice-cooking pot

prika **dipun*kaken** *kr for* DI·PRANA·KAKÉ. **se*** *kr for* SEPRANA

prikântjâ colleague, co-worker. *See also* KANTJA

priki **dipun*k̀aken** *kr for* DI·PRÉNÉ·K̀AKÉ. **se*** *kr for* SEPRÉNÉ

priksa 1 to examine (*ki for* TITI?). *Sing bisa * mung ḍokter.* Only a doctor may examine him. 2 to know, understand (*ki for* NGERTI). 3 to see; to know (*ki for* WERUH). **pe*n** examination; investigation. *papriksan bab korupsi* an investigation into corruption. **m̀/di*** 1 to examine, investigate. *Ḍokteré mriksa larané.* The doctor examined him ('his illness'). *Bareng di*, njata ḍèké ora salah.* When the case was probed, he was found not to be guilty. *djuru mriksa omah* (*kreteg, lsp.*) a house (bridge, *etc.*) inspector. 2 to see; to know (*ki for* WERUH). 3 to understand (*ki for* SUMURUP). **me·m̀*** 1 to see, have eyesight. 2 to look around, see the sights. **m̀/di*kaké** 1 to have smn examine(d) *or* investigate(d). *Lisènsi mau kudu di*kaké prijaji.* You have to be examined for the license by an official. *Ibu mriksakaké aḍik nèng ḍokteran.* Mother had my brother examined at the hospital. 2 to inform (*ki for* M̈/DI·WERUH·AKÉ). **m̀/di*ni** 1 to see; to know about (*ki for* M̈/DI·WERUH·I). 2 to see, watch (*ki for* N/DI·DELENG, Ñ/DI·TONTON). **pa·m̀*** act *or* way of investigating/examining. *Baktéri iku pamriksané mung nganggo mikroskop.* Bacteria can be examined only through a microscope. *See also* NG·ATUR·I, ÑJ·SUWUN

priku **dipun*k̀aken** *kr for* DI·PRONO·KAKÉ. **se*** *kr for* SEPRONO

pril *rpr* a small piece breaking (off). *Biskuité ditjuwil mak *.* A piece broke off the cookie. *Tjangkiré lagi dak asahi kupingé mak * tjuwil.* The cup handle came off as I was washing it.

primbetan *rg kr for* PRIMBON

primbon Javanese almanac

primé (*or* ***ǹ** *or* **ke*ǹ**) *rg var of* KEPRIJÉ

primpen securely put away. *Barang sing adji kudu disinggahaké sing *.* Valuables should be kept in a safe place.

primpi **m̀/di*ǹi** to appear to smn in a dream. *See also* IMPI

prinding *rpr* a sudden chill *or* thrill. *ptg* * 1 fearful, apprehensive. 2 (*or* **prindang-***) goose-pimply with chills *or* thrills. **m̀*** 1 to feel chilled (with fear; with excitement). 2 frayed to the breaking point (*var of* M̈·PRENDING)

pring *ng*, **deling** *kr* bamboo plant; bamboo stalk. *bumbung* * bamboo pipe; bamboo cooking pot. **pa*an** bamboo grove. *** gaḍing** yellowish decorative bamboo. *** wuluh** a certain slender bamboo plant

pringga *ltry* (causing) difficulty, trouble, danger. **m̀*** to be afraid; to show fear. **m̀/di*kaké** to guard sth against danger. *mringgakaké betjik* to advise smn for his own good. **m̀*ni** 1 frightening; dangerous. 2 (*psv* **di*ni**) to guard against trouble. *Djagabaja mringgani désa.* The village watch is on guard against dangers.

pringgitan *see* RINGGIT

pringis ***an** to bare the teeth. *Ḍèké ora nangis, ja mung *an.* He didn't cry [in his pain], he just clenched his teeth. ***-*** *or* **pringas-*** to keep clenching the teeth. **m̀*** *sms* *AN. *Tjoba mringis, wis sikatan apa durung?* Show me your teeth: have you brushed them?

pringkil small lump. *Djangané mau lagi dak wènèhi ujah sak *.* I've just put a lump of salt in the soup. **m̀*** forming a lump. *Lakangku rada mringkil lara.* I have a small painful swelling in the groin.

pringkus **m̀*** shrunken. **m̀/di*aké** to make sth smaller. *mringkusaké ḍaḍa* to sink one's chest in, narrow the chest

pringsilan scrotum

prins *see* KRUN

printah an order, command; to tell smn to do sth. *Ḍèk bijèn Sala iku di* déning ratu.* Solo used to be ruled by a king. *Kok *-* adus iki arep apa ta?* Why do you keep telling me to take my bath? **m̀/di*(i)** 1 to have authority over; to govern. 2 to give instructions *or* information. *Murid² arep di*i sing munggah lan sing ora.* The students are to be told who passed and who didn't. **p·em·rintah** government (*see* PEMRINTAH)

printis *ptg* * covered with a rash. *Kulité ptg * gatelen.* He has an itchy skin rash. **m̀*** 1 (to have *or* get) a skin rash. 2 to make gains (*e.g.* in weight; in wealth)

prinṭis bare, denuded

printji **pe*ǹ** classification; specifications. **ṁ/di*(-*)** 1 to classify. *Soal² mau kena di* dadi telung pérangan.* The problems can be sorted into three categories. 2 to specify (the details of). *mrintji anggaran belandjané* to detail the budget items

prioritas, prioritèt priority. **ṁ/di*aké** to give priority to. *Projèk² sanḍang-pangan di*aké katimbang projèk² lijané.* Food and clothing programs were given higher priority than the other projects.

pripé (*or* ***an**) in-law(s). *See also* IPÉ

pripun how? (*md for* KEPRIJÉ). ** pak, gawéané pun rampung dèrèng.* How about it, man, have you finished the job?

pris prize, reward

prit 1 *shf of* EMPRIT. 2 (*prn* **pri:t**) tweet! **prat-*** to blow a whistle repeatedly

priṭil to fall off. *Kembangé *.* The flower came off [from its stalk]. **ṁ*i** 1 *pl* to fall off. 2 (*psv* **di*i**) to break [things] off. *Epang² di*i putjuké.* He removed the tips of the branches. *Sapa sing mriṭili mawar² iki?* Who picked these roses? *See also* PIṬIL

priṭut *ptg ** wrinkled, full of creases

privé private. *soal ** a private matter

priwé (*or* ***ǹ** *or* **ke*ǹ**) *rg var of* KEPRIJÉ

prodjol **ṁ*** to slip through an opening. *Digémbol mrodjol.* He put it in his pocket but it fell out. **mrodjol ing a·kerep** outstanding, eminent. **mrodjol sela·ning garu** 1 to successfully complete a difficult *or* dangerous activity. 2 to stand out over others. **ṁ/di*aké** to allow to emerge *or* slip out. *mrodjolaké buntelan saka suwèkan tas* to lose a bundle through a torn place in a bag

proḍuksi production. *ongkos ** cost of production

proḍuktip productive

profèsor, profésor professor (academic rank)

prog *rpr* sth being set *or* dropped heavily. *Saking keselé lungguh mak *.* He was so tired he flopped right down. *Gawané dibrukké nang korsi mak *.* He set his burdens heavily on a chair. **! *! *!* Stomp! stomp! stomp! (*sound of heavy footsteps*)

progèl *ptg ** to keep jerking *or* moving spasmodically. *Weluté paḍa ptg * nang ndjeron kepis.* The eels kept wriggling in the fishing creel.

progoh hand's-length (unit of measure). *Lèngé ula sa* djeroné.* The snake's hole is one hand-length deep. *Dawané wetara sa*.* It's about as long as your hand. *See also* ROGOH

programā a program

projèk project, enterprise

prok *var of* PROG

proklamir **ṁ/di*aké** to proclaim, declare. *mroklamirké kamardikan* to declare independence

prol 1 a variety of cookie. 2 *rpr* sth breaking apart. *Kajuné dipangan rajap, bareng diangkat mak *.* The wood had been eaten by termites; when he lifted it, it fell to pieces.

prombèng *var of* ROMBÈNG

promosi 1 promotion in rank, position. 2 final examination for the doctoral degree: an oral defense of one's thesis

promotor 1 promoter, sponsor. 2 professor who acts as adviser to a doctoral candidate

prongkal large lump. *Djangané diwènèhi ujah sak *.* She put a big lump of salt in the soup. ***an** in lumps. **ṁ*** in (the form of) a large lump. *Ujahé durung diuleg lembut, isih mrongkal.* The salt hasn't been ground—it's still in a lump. *Wetengé mrongkol sisih tengen.* He has a lump on the right side of his stomach.

prongkol *var of* PRONGKAL

prono **di*kaké** *ng*, **dipun·priku·k̂aken** *kr var psv for* DI·MRONO·KAKÉ

prop 1 cork material. *topi ** safari hat. 2 cork, bottle stopper

propaganḍā propaganda. **ṁ/di*(kaké)** to propagandize; to feed propaganda to

propèsor, propèsor *var of* PROFÈSOR

propinsi province

propinsialisme provincialism

propokasi provocation. **ṁ/di*** to provoke, rouse to action

prosa **ṁ/di*** 1 to force. *Anggoné mbukak sekrup di*.* He forced the bolt open. 2 to rape

prosès process. ** kimia* chemical process. ** nggawé gula* the sugar-making process. ** pengadilan* court proceedings. *** perbal** an official report of an infraction; **ṁ/di*-perbal** to write an official report (of). *Aku mau nglanggar lalulintas bandjur di*-perbal polisi.* I violated a traffic regulation and a policeman wrote up a report on it.

prot *rpr* popping, bursting

protès a protest. **ṁ/di*** to protest (against)

Protèstan Protestant. *jajasan Kristen ** a Protestant Christian organization
protjot *rpr* emergence at birth. *Wedusé manak mak **. The sheep dropped a lamb. **m̃*** to slip out (*referring esp. to birth*). *Digawa nang rumah sakit nang ndalan anaké wis mrotjot.* Her baby was born while she was on the way to the hospital.
protol *var of* POTOL
pruk crash! smash! *Krambilé dipetjah mak **. He smashed the coconut.
prunan nephew, niece (*rg var of* KEPONAKAN)
prung *rpr* sudden departure. *Laler kuwi angger arep didekep, *!* Whenever you try to catch a fly, he whisks away. *Wusanané mung ditinggal **. Finally she up and left.
prunggu bronze
prunggul **m̃/di*(i)** to cut, prune, trim
prungu *ng* ***n̂** what is heard. *kulak warta adol prungon* to pass along news. **ke*** to hear. *Aku ora seneng jèn rembugé bisa ke* ing lijan.* I don't like to have my conversation overheard. **ke*n̂** sense of hearing. **m̃/di*n̂i** to communicate with supernaturally. *See also* RUNGU
pruntel *ptg * or *-** in curls, kinky, twisted
pruntul *var of* PRUNTEL
pruntus spot, dot. *Sing *-* putih iku endogé.* Those little white specks are the [insect's] eggs. *ptg * or *-** covered with little bumps. **m̃*** to form small specks *or* dots (*e.g.* goose pimples, skin rash)
pruput **m̃*** 1 early in the morning. *ésuk mruput* bright and early. *Mau ésuk olèhé mangkat sekolah mruput.* He left for school early this morning. 2 (*psv* **di***) to come to sth early in the morning. *Karebèn bisa rampung sedina gawéané di* wiwit djam nem ésuk.* He showed up for work at 6 A.M. so as to finish the job in one day.
prus *rpr* breaking. *Tjangkiré tiba mak * petjah.* The cup fell and smashed.
prusa *var of* PROSA
prusi an ointment for healing scabies sores
prusuh **m̃*** 1 foamy, frothy. 2 [of body] healthily rounded. **m̃/di*(i)** to pound [raw rice] to remove the hulls
prutjul lacking horns. *wedus ** a sheep with no horns
prutjut *rpr* a sudden release from a grasp. *Étok[2] arep dipanah, djebul mak **. He pretended he was going to let the arrow fly, but it dropped from his grip. **prutjat-*** to keep releasing *or* getting released. *Prutjat-* iwaké pada utjul.* The fish kept slipping out [from the net]. **ke*** to lose one's hold. *Olèhé njekeli pang ke**. He lost his grip on the branch. **m̃*** to get loose. *Dikandut mrutjut.* He had it in his pocket but it came out. *Panahé mrutjut ngenani adiné.* The arrow [which he was pretending to shoot] got away from him and struck his brother. *Mak * endogé mrutjut saka tangané.* Suddenly the egg fell from his hand. **m̃/di*aké** to release (one's grasp). *Olèhé tjekelan di*aké bandjur tiba.* His grip loosened and he fell.
prutul *var of* PUTUL
publik̄ the public, the people
pudak 1 a certain glutinous fruit. 2 pandanus blossom. *** s·in·upit** a certain way of folding one's batik wraparound
pudja *var of* PUDJI. **m̃/di*-*** to praise, flatter
pudjâbrâtâ *oj* reverence, worship
pudjânggâ a man of letters; one with high literary skill and inventiveness. **ka*n** literary, concerning letters; literary skill *or* knowledge
pudjastuti *oj* to bless, to say prayers for
pudjer *var of* PUNDJER
pudji 1 prayer, wish, hope. 2 praise, worship. ***n̂** *or* ***an** 1 act of praying. 2 object of worship. *bindi wesi kuning pudjèn* a revered weapon of brass. 3 praise, flattery. **pe*n̂** 1 act of worshiping. *Omah kuwi kanggo pepudjèn.* The house is used for worship. 2 object of worship. *pepudjèn sing dipepundi* an idol that is worshiped. **m̃/di*** 1 to hope, pray. *mudji semadi* to meditate. *Aku mudji bisaa klakon duwé motor.* I hope to have a car some day. 2 (*or* **m̃/di*-***) to worship, praise. **m̃/di·pe*** to pray repeatedly. *Saben dina memudji bisaa pinaringan momongan.* She prays every day that she will have a child. **m̃/di*k̀aké** to wish/pray on smn's behalf. *Dèwèké mudjèkaké aku kasil.* He wished me luck. **m̃/di·pe*k̀aké** to keep wishing/praying on smn's behalf. **pa·m̃*** act of praying/wishing. *Pamudjimu tak arep[2].* I hope to receive your prayers. *Pamudji ardja.* I bid you welcome! **pa·m̃*n̂** place where prayers are conducted. *omah pamudjèn* house of worship
puf *rpr* popping, bursting. *anggur ** champagne
pugag **m̃/di*** to remove the tip (from)
pugal hard to domesticate

pugel **m̃/di*(i)** to cut, sever

puguh strong, sturdy, firm

pugut **m̃/di*** to cut off at the tip

puh ***an** 1 for squeezing, to be squeezed. *sapi *an* milk cow. *djuru mriksa *an* dairy cow inspector. *klapa *an* a certain coconut whose milk (considered a delicacy) is opaque rather than clear. 2 cow's milk (*see also* POWAN). **nge/di*(i)** 1 to squeeze, wring liquid from. *Tatuné diepuh getihé.* He squeezed the blood from his cut. *nge*i klambi²* to wring out clothes. 2 to milk [an animal]. **pa·nge*** act of wringing *or* squeezing. *See also* APUH

pujang a certain tuber used medicinally

pujeng dizzy, groggy, headachy (*kr for* NGE-LU, M·UMET)

pujer medication in powdered form

pujuh 1 female quail (*kr for* GEMAK). 2 rain and wind storm in a mountain area. ***an** bladder. *lara *an* gonorrhea. *See also* ÑJ·SUNḌUL, UJUH

puk 1 *rpr* sth falling. *Bukuné tiba saka nge-tas mak *.* The book plopped out of his bag. 2 a bundle *or* roll of fabric as merchandise (*var of* EMBLOG, GEBLOG). ***-*an** [of fabric] in bundles *or* rolls. **nge/di*** to make [fabric] into a roll. **nge/di*-*** 1 to keep patting. *Pak Guru mau ngepuk-epuk gegerku.* The teacher patted me on the back. 2 to keep thudding/plopping

pukir *var of* PUNGKIR

pukul hour, o'clock (*opt kr for* DJAM). ** ti-ga* three o'clock. **m̃/di*** to strike with a hammering blow. *Pakuné di*.* He hammered in the nail. *Aku mau di* padjek.* My taxes have dealt me a staggering blow. *** besi** hammer

pukul-râtâ average. **m̃/di*** to average (out). *Bidjiné murid² kabèh di* karo guru.* The teacher averaged all the students' grades.

pukulun *wj* your excellency

pul 1 pole (of the earth: *var of* POL). 2 gong stroke (*shf of* KEMPUL)

pulas coloring agent (paint, crayon, *etc.*). ***an** covered with a layer of color. *klambi sing *an* a dyed shirt. *Tjritané kuwi rak mung *an.* His story was only a cover-up.

pulâsârâ **m̃/di*** 1 to look after, care for. *Ḍèké semaput, di* ḍokter.* She fainted and was treated by a doctor. 2 to mistreat, be cruel to

pulâsari an herb used in native medicines

pulâwaras a certain medicinal herb

pulé a certain tree whose bark is used in folk medicines

pulèh *rg var of* PULIH

pulen [of rice] nicely cooked: not mushy, not dry

pules [of sleep] deep, sound. *Olèhé turu *.* He's fast asleep.

pulet **pe*an** intertwined. **m̃/di*** to entwine. *Awaké di* ula.* A snake wound itself around his body.

puli a snack made from mashed rice. *krupuk ** the above in the form of fried chips

pulih to recover, to regain a former condition. *Tangané bisa * kaja mauné.* His arm healed so it was as good as new. *Kahanan ing désa mau wis *.* Things are back to normal now in the village. ***an** in the process of recovering. *awak *an* a convalescent body. **bumi *an** soil consisting of river sediment. **pe*** a measure taken to appease *or* avenge smn. *arep pe** bent on revenge. *Apa pe*é duka?* What can one do to cool his anger? **pe*an** reconciliation, restoration to normal. *Negara loro mau wis pe*an manèh.* The two countries have reconciled their differences. **m̃/di*aké** to restore sth to its original condition. *Keprijé bisané mulihaké sikil kang tugel?* How can you replace an amputated leg? **pa·m̃*an** recovery, restoration to normal. *pusat pemulihan* rehabilitation center. *See also* ULIH

pulisi police; policeman. *agèn ** policeman. *mantri ** head of the local police force. **ka*n̄** police force. **m̃/di*kaké** to notify the police. *Tanggaku mulisèkaké anggoné kemalingan mau bengi.* My neighbor reported last night's robbery to the police.

pulkah *see* POTONG

pulkanisir ***an** a recapped tire. **m̃/di*** to recap, retread. **m̃/di*aké** to have [a tire] recapped. *mulkanisiraké ban* to have a tire retreaded

pulo island. ***n** man-made island. ***-* Maluku** the Molucca Islands. **ka*an** archipelago. *Kapuloan Indonesia* the Indonesian Archipelago

pulpèn fountain pen

pulu safflower (used for yellow dye)

puluh *ng*, **(n)dâsâ** *kr* 1 the ten digit. *se** ten (*see also* SEPULUH). *rong ** twenty. *pirang *?* how many tens? *pirang² * taun* decades and decades. 2 *ng kr* although; otherwise. ** sugih nèk laranen wong ora seneng.* Even though you're rich, if you're not in good health you can't enjoy it. *Abot² ja dilakoni, * wedi jèn dipotjot.* He does the work, no matter how hard, for fear of getting fired if he doesn't. 3 (*or* *-*) *ng kr* now what? * *dikapakaké?* What's to be done about it? *Puluh² wis begdjané awakku.* What do I do now? it's just what I deserve! ***an (dasa·n[an]** *kr*) 1 ten-rupiah bill. *Susuké lawéan lan *an.* He got his change in 25- and 10-rupiah bills. 2 some number of tens. *Satus iku wilangan se* *an.* One hundred is 10 tens. *pegawéné kang *an éwon* tens of thousands of employees. **an taun kepungkur* decades ago. *See also* SEPULUH

puluk a handful of food eaten without utensils, *esp.* at ritual ceremonies (*slametan*). *sa* (*rong, lsp.*) ***an** one (two, *etc.*) handfuls (as above). **m̃/di*** to eat without utensils. *muluk sega* to eat rice with the hands

pulunan (*or* **ka***) nephew, niece (*var of* KEPONAKAN)

pulung 1 mystic aura surrounding a chosen one. 2 falling star (an omen of good fortune). *ketiban ** to receive mystic forewarnings of good fortune. **m̃/di*** 1 to tie harvested rice into bundles. 2 to bring in rice after sun-drying. *** ati** the portion of the body below the heart and ribs; *fig* the heart as the seat of emotions

pulus money (*inf substitute for* DUWIT)

pulut resin from breadfruit *or* papaya (used as glue). **m̃/di*** 1 to smear with resin. 2 to trap [birds, small animals] with resin. 3 *slang* to bribe

pum- *see also under* P- (*Introduction, 3.1.7*)

pumpet clogged, stopped up

pumpung (*or* **m̃***) while one has the opportunity. *Muliha saiki baé, mumpung durung peteng.* Go on home now, before it gets dark. * *kowé isih enom sinaumu pengen.* Study hard now, while you're young. *Anakmu nakal, tuturana, mumpung durung kebatjut.* Your child is badly behaved; correct him now, before it's too late. (*k*)*adji ** to take advantage of an opportunity to enjoy sth. **m̃*(-m̃*)** *or* **mumpang-m̃*** to make the very most of. *mumpung⁽²⁾ sugih* to enjoy one's riches to the fullest

pun 1 *familiar title used before a name or name substitute: kr for* SI. 2 to have [done] *etc.* (*shf of* SAMPUN, *kr for* WIS). 3 *shf of* DIPUN-. 4 *md for* WIS. **m*** *sms* * 2 *above*

punagi (to make) a vow that if one's wish is granted he will hold a feast (*ki for* KAUL, NADAR, UDJAR?). **m̃/di*ǹi** to make such a promise to smn

punah *oj* wiped out, gone, destroyed utterly

punakawan *var of* PANAKAWAN

punâpâ (*usu. prn* **menâpâ**) 1 what? (*kr for* APA). *kala ** when [did]...? *mbéndjing ** when [will]...? 2 ...or anything (*kr for* BARANG). *Sampun mrika, sampun ndadak lingsem² *.* Come, there's no need to be bashful or anything like that. ***a** why? how come? (*kr for* GÉNÉ JA)

punâpâdéné as well as, in addition to (*kr for* APADÉNÉ)

punâpâhâ *var of* PUNAPA·A

punapi *ltry var of* PUNAPA

punar [of cooked rice] colored yellow for ceremonial meals. *sega ** yellow rice

punḍak *ng kr*, **pamiḍangan** *or* **pamidjangan** *ki* shoulder. * *mradju-mas* fine firmly squared shoulders. **m̃/di*** to carry on the shoulder

punḍamèn foundation. * *batur* house foundation of brick

pundat **m̃/di*i** to settle, clear up [problems, debts, *etc.*]

punḍes all gone, cleaned out

pundi where? (*kr for* ENDI)

punḍi **m̃/di*(-*)** to honor, hold in esteem. **(pe)*ǹ** object of esteem and reverence. *Gusti pepunḍèn kula.* Your excellency. *Pesaréané éjang pepunḍèné sedulur² kabèh.* Grandfather's grave is revered by the whole family. *Wit ringin geḍé mau dadi pepunḍèné wong² kono.* The people of the area are in great awe of the large banyan tree.

pundjer center; interior. * *ing manah* deep in one's heart

pundji ***ǹ** act of riding on smn's shoulders. **m̃/di*** to carry smn on the shoulders

pundjul 1 outstanding. *klas sing * ḍéwé* the highest-ranking class. 2 in excess. *Kursiné tjatjahé satus * lima.* There are 100 chairs plus five extras. **m̃/di*i** 1 to exceed, surpass. *mundjuli tinimbang kantja²né* to outperform one's teammates. 2 to add [an amount] to. *Nèk di*i sèket rupiah ja tak kèké barang iki.* If you raise your offer on this article by 50 rupiahs, I'll let you have it. *Aku mau tuku pelem di*i loro karo sing dodol.* I bought some mangoes and the seller threw in two extras free. **p·in·udjul** outstanding. *guru sing pinundjul* a superior teacher. *** ing a·papak** superior, outstanding

pundjung high, honored, noble. ***an** food given to an elder, or superior, as a token of respect and gratitude; food from a sacramental ceremony distributed among neighbors and friends. **m̃*** 1 heaped full. 2 (*psv* **di***) to give food as above

pundoh to feel at home

pundut ***(-*)an** 1 *ki* thing requested. 2 *ki* purchases made. 3 refreshments served to guests. **ka*** to die, *i.e.* be taken by God. **m̃/di*** 1 to ask for, request (*ki for* N/DI·DJALUK). 2 to get, take (possession of) (*ki for* N/DI·DJUPUK, NGE/DI·PÈK). 3 to buy (*ki for* φ/DI·TUKU). *** ng·ampil** to borrow (*root form: ki for* SILIH). *** priksa** to ask (*root form: ki for* TAKON)

pung 1 bong! (*rpr* a note played on a small gong, the *ketipung*). 2 *shf of* LEMPUNG: *see* BANḌEM. **pang-*** *rpr* repeated gong beats

punggah *ng,* **pinggah** *kr* ***an** device for stepping up *or* down between levels. **an méng-gok* ramp; gangplank. **m̃/di*i** 1 to climb sth. 2 to elevate, raise. *See also* UNGGAH

punggâwâ 1 employee, worker, clerk. 2 palace soldier, palace guard

punggel ***an** interruption, cutoff point. **aning rembug* the end of the discussion. **ke*** to get broken off. *Lelakoné ke* seméné.* The story is broken off at this point. **m̃/di*** to cut off, interrupt. *Ḍèké munggel kanṭi swara geḍé.* He interrupted loudly. *Tjritané di* seméné waé.* The story ends here. **pa·m̃*** interruption

pungges **m̃/di*** to cut

punggung *see* NG·AMUK

punggur *var of* PUNGKUR

pungkas the end. *sing * ḍéwé* the last one, the one at the end. ***an** the end; at the end. *Anggonku mulih *an ḍéwé.* I was the last one to go home. *udjian *an* final exam. *saka wiwitan tekan *an* from beginning to end. ***an·é** at last, finally, in the end. **ané sing menang sapa?* Who finally won? **m̃/di*(i)** to bring to an end; to finish up *or* off; to kill. *Tjritané di*i.* She brought the story to a conclusion. *Gawéanmu di*i ḍisik nembé lèrèn.* Finish your work first, then take a rest. *Kanggo mungkasi utangé, pité didol.* He sold his bicycle to pay off his debt. **pa·m̃*** *oj* a device for ending life. *sendjata pamungkas* a lethal weapon

pungkir **m̃/di*(i)** to deny, disavow. *Ḍèké mungkiri sakabèhé sing wis tau ditindakaké.* He denied everything he had done.

pungkur *ng,* **pengker** *kr* last, past, previous; ago. ***an** 1 the back (body part). 2 back yard. **ke*** *sms* *. *ḍèk minggu ke** last week. *telung dina sing ke** three days ago. **m̃*** 1 behind, gone by. *djaman sing wis mungkur* in past times. *Sedjarah tragis kuwi wis mungkur.* The tragic story [of her life] is over now. 2 to turn one's back. *Bareng sing nggawa wis mungkur, bèsèk dibukak.* As soon as the person who brought the basket had left ('turned his back'), they opened it. **mungkur gangsir** to wash one's hands (of), take no responsibility for. **m̃/di*aké** 1 to turn one's back toward, have one's back to. *Olèhé linggih mungkuraké guru.* He sat with his back toward the teacher (*breach of etiquette*). 2 to pass by; to have sth behind one. *Apa sing wis di*aké adja diperkara manèh.* What has passed need not be discussed further. **m̃/di*i** to have the back toward, have behind it. *Omahé mungkuri kali.* There's a river behind the house. **sa*é** since one departed. *Durung ganep seminggu sa*é mbakju tindak Sala.* It's less than a week since my sister left for Solo. *Sa*é swargi bapak uripé ngrekasa.* Life has been hard for him since his father died. *See also* UNGKUR

punglu a small round pellet used as a blown missile

pungser *var of* PUSER

pungun *oj* ***-*** to sigh deeply with sadness *or* grief

pungut **m̃/di*** to levy, assess [a tax *etc.*]

punika (*usu. prn* **menika**) 1 this (thing, place, time) (*kr for* IKI). 2 that (thing, place, time: Degree II) (*kr for* KUWI). 3 that (thing, place, time: Degree III) (*kr for* KAÉ). 4 (*or* *** lo**, *sbst* *** lé**) (see) here! (*kr for* GILO); (look) over there! (*kr for* GALO). *See also* INGGIH

puniku *ltry var of* PUNIKA 2 (*Degree II*)

punten (*or* *** [n]dalem**) I don't know (*oblique ki for* EMBUH)

punṭes all gone. *Goḍongé bajem dipeṭik nganti *.* She picked the last of the spinach. **m̃/di*(i)** to take all of sth. *Kembang apik² kuwi adja di*i ja?* Don't take all of those beautiful flowers, will you?

puntir **m̃*** 1 twisted. 2 *inf* uncooperative, perverse. 3 (*psv* **di***) to hold and twist. *Di* kupingé.* She gave his ear a twist. *See also* PLUNTIR, UNTIR

puntjak top, peak

puntjit top, tip, peak. **é wit* tree-top. **ing gunung* mountain-top. ***an** the banana at the bottom (small) end of the bunch. **m̈*** to move to the top. *Olèhé mènèk wit nganti muntjit.* He climbed to the top of the tree.

puntu **(pe)*n̂** what smn thinks *or* talks about. *pepuntoning pikir lan rasa* the subject of my thoughts and feelings. *Pepuntoning atiku mupus.* I felt resigned to my destiny. **m̈/di*** to think *or* talk about

punṭuk (*or* ***an**) mound; hill; peak. *semut ing ** ants in an anthill. ** ingkang inggil pijambak* the highest peak. **pe*** (series of) hills, peaks, mounds. **m̈*** mound-shaped. *See also* UNṬUK

punuk hump on the back. ** kebo* kerbau's hump. ***en** to have such a hump

pupak *ng kr,* **ḍaut** *ki* to become detached from the body. *Waosé bapak *.* Father has lost his teeth. *** puser** [of the umbilical cord] to drop off; rites marking this event in the life of a newborn infant

pupu thigh **(wentis** *ki***)**. ***n̂** adopted in babyhood. *anak pupon* adopted child. **m̈/di*(n̂i)** to adopt. *muponi anak* to adopt a child. **pa·m̈*** act *or* procedure of adopting. *Ora kabèh wong bisa mupu anak, pamupuné kudu nganggo idin.* Not everyone can adopt a child; the procedure requires permission. **sa*** comparable to a thigh. *Geḍéné sa*.* It's as big around as your thigh. *** genḍing** chicken back including the coccyx. *** tjakar** chicken leg, thigh, and foot

pupuh division of a piece of writing, *e.g.* a paragraph, a stanza

pupuk *ng kr,* **sunḍul** *ki* a poultice of pounded herbs, placed on a child's head above the forehead to ward off illness. *durung ilang * lempujangé* still very young. ***an** to have such a poultice on one's head. **m̈/di*aké** *or* **m̈/di*i** to place a poultice on. *Anaké di*i.* She put a poultice on her child's head. *** bawang** one who cannot contribute a full share to a joint endeavor (*usu.* of a small child in a game with older people)

pupung *var of* PUMPUNG

pupur *ng kr,* **tasik** *ki* powder for face *or* body, used for cosmetic *or* therapeutic purposes. ***an** to have *or* put powder on one's face. **m̈/di*i** to powder smn. *A nasiki B.* A powdered B's face for her. *** sa·durung·é bendjut** look before you leap, *i.e.* take preventive measures. *** kuning** a yellow powder applied to the body for massaging. *** sa·wis·é bendjut** to lock the barn door after the horse has been stolen

pupus 1 young new-grown leaf. *idjo ** fresh light green. 2 end of a fish net. **m̈/di*** 1 to pull in a netful of fish. 2 to resign oneself to the inevitable. *Apa kang wis klakon apiké pinupus waé.* What is over and done with should be accepted with resignation.

puput *ng kr,* **daut** *ki* 1 to come to an end, be over. *Tjritané * tekan djilid telu.* It took three volumes to tell the story. 2 dropping off of an infant's umbilical cord; to have the cord drop off. *Anakku wis *.* My baby has lost the umbilical cord. ***an** ceremony signalizing the dropping of the cord. **m̈*** throughout. *sewengi muput* the whole night. *Olèhé madjang omah nganti sedina muput.* It took all day to decorate the house. **m̈/di*i** to honor [an infant] with a cord-dropping ceremony. *** puser** *sms ** 2. *slametan * puser* cord-dropping ceremony

pur 1 a tie (score); all even. **, paḍadéné bauté.* It's a tie; one's as good as the other. *Wis * ja, aku ora nduwé utang manèh.* Now we're square–I don't owe you anything any more. 2 forward (soccer player, position: *var of* POR). **nge/di*aké** to make even. *nge*aké utang* to square a debt. *Wis tak *ké waé, aku ora golèk baṭi.* I'll sell it to you for what I paid, I won't take a profit.

pura 1 *oj* palace. 2 *var of* APURA

purak ***-*** to pretend. **m̈/di*** to cut [an animal carcass] to pieces

purasani high-quality iron

purba ancient. ** kala* ancient times. *kang m̈** God. *See also* PURBA-WISÉSA

purbâ-wasésâ *var of* PURBA-WISÉSA

purbâ-wisésâ authority, control. *Omah iki * nang aku.* This house is under my authority. **m̈/di*(ni)** (*var prn:* **murbâ-misésa(ni)/di*[ni])** to exercise control over; to place under smn's authority. *Botjah iki di* nang aku.* This child has been given into my care. *See also* WISÉSA

pures all gone, used up

puret dim, gloomy

puri 1 palace. *kenja ** princesses' quarters in the palace. 2 Balinese temple

purih leg of beef *or* mutton. **m̈*** for the purpose of; (*psv* **di***) to use for [a purpose]; to enable, bring about. *Murih gelisé, numpaka sepur waé.* To get there fast, take a train. *Murih betjiké si A djaken rembugan.* In order to improve the discussion, get A into it. *Aku di* tunggu omah.* I was assigned ('used') to look after the house. *Kula dipun utus bapak ka* ngaturaken serat punika.* Father sent me to give you this letter. *Aku duwé sapi merga di* susuné.* I keep cows for their milk. **pa·m̃*** 1 intention, purpose. *Wit mau dipapas pamrihé supaja jèn woh adja ḍuwur²*. The tree was cut back so that when it gave fruits they wouldn't be too high up. 2 nefarious purpose, ulterior motive. *Ḍèké njambut gawé awan bengi tanpa pamrih.* He works day and night without self-interest. *Wong mau ngekèki roti karo kepala padjek amarga duwé pamurih padjeké toko bisa dièṇṭèngaké.* He slips bakery goods to the tax official in an effort to get his taxes lowered. *See also* AMRIH

purik temporarily separated from one's spouse. **m̃/di*(i)** to leave [one's spouse] temporarily

puring a certain ornamental garden plant

purna 1 complete, whole; finished. 2 [of the moon] full. *See also* PARIPURNA

purnâmâ *var of* PURNA 2. *Rembulané neḍengé *.* The moon is full.

purug way, course, *etc.* (*kr for* PARAN)

puru(h)ita a learned holy man. **m̃*** to learn from (*i.e.* be a pupil of) such a man

purun 1 to be willing (to) (*kr for* GELEM). 2 bold (*obsolescent kr for* WANI)

purut a certain small aromatic lemon

puruwita *var of* PURUHITA

purwa 1 *oj* the beginning, the origin. *ing djaman ** in ancient times. *dongèng² ** mythological tales describing the ancient origins of the Javanese people. *wajang ** flat leather puppets used in shadow plays which depict the above stories. 2 *oj* north. 3 *gram* initial (letter, syllable). **ning lingga adjeg.* The initial root sound remains unchanged. *dwi ** reduplication of the first syllable. *a* aksara swara* beginning with a vowel. **m̃/di*(ni)** to begin, initiate, create. *murwani atur* to make introductory remarks. *** duksina** north and south. *ora weruh/éling * duksina* bewildered; unconscious. *** kala** 1 ancient times. 2 a certain shadow-play story. *** madya-wasana** the facts from the beginning (through the middle) to the end, *i.e.* the whole story. *Aku ora ngerti *-madya-wasanané, bandjur katut disalahké ngilangaké ḍuwit.* I didn't know much of anything about it, but I was accused of losing the money along with the others. ***ning d·um·adi** the Creation, the beginning of life in the world

purwâkâ preface, introduction; introductory remarks. **m̃/di*ni** to provide with the above. *buku sing di*ni Pak X* a book with an introduction written by Mr. X

purwâkanṭi repetitious use of syllable(s) as a poetic device

purwares forward (soccer player, position). *sènter ** center forward

pu:s (*or *-**) 1 *rpr* a puff of blown-out breath. 2 here kitty! **pas-*** to chain-smoke

pusâkâ 1 heirloom; revered heritage from one's ancestors. *lajang ** document containing words of wisdom from one's ancestors. 2 inheritance (*ki for* WARIS·AN?). 3 rice paddy owned by one family through the generations rather than becoming communal property. 4 magical weapon (kris, lance). **m̃/di*kaké** to pass along to one's descendants. *musakakaké keris* to hand down a kris. **m̃/di*ni** to pass along to. *Bapak musakani kamas keris paringané pakḍé.* Father passed along to my older brother the kris my uncle had given him.

pusang *oj* dizzy, bewildered, dazed

pusârâ *oj* string, rope, cord. ***ning pradja** reign, sway, rule

pusat center [of activity]. **ing dagang* commercial center. **é kabudajan* cultural center

puseng *var of* PUSANG

puser 1 (**tuntun·an** *ki*) umbilical cord; navel. 2 center. **ing tanah Djawa* the (geographical) center of Java. **ing lésan* bull's-eye. **ing dagang/kabudajan* a commercial/cultural center. ***an** whorl; whirlpool, vortex. **m̃*** to make a 180-degree turn. *See also* PUPUT

puspa *oj* flower. *** warna** 1 various kinds of flowers. 2 a certain classical verse form

puspâkadjang a variety of snake

puspâlémbong a certain plant with an edible tuberous root

puspânjidrâ *var of* PUSPALÉMBONG

puspita *oj* flower

pustâkâ *oj* book, letter, document. **ka*n** literature

pusus ***an** water in which sth (*esp.* rice) has been washed. **m̃/di*** to turn *or* roll between the hands. **m̃/di*aké** to clean raw rice (for smn) by wetting it and rolling it between the palms. **m̀/di*i** to clean [rice] as above. **pa·m̀*** act of cleaning rice in this way. *angin* **p·in·usus** hurricane, typhoon

putat a variety of tree

putbal soccer. * **bon** soccer club

puṭel **m̀/di*** to cut off at the tip

puter 1 to go around; to make rounds. *ès ** ice cream made in a hand-cranked freezer. 2 a variety of dove kept as a pet. ***an** 1 a device for winding *or* reeling. 2 a transplanted plant. ***-*** to go around sightseeing. **m̀/di*** 1 to turn sth. *Djamku tak **. I wound my watch. *Arep di* pilem ḍokumèntèr.* A documentary film will be shown ('reeled'). 2 to go around smw. *muter kuṭa Djakarta* to go all around Djakarta. **muter giling** to pray for smn's return. **muter otak** *or* **muter pikir·an** to think hard. **m̀/di*aké** to lend [money] for interest. * **balik** 1 to make a complete circuit. 2 to behave inconsistently. *Jèn omong *-balik.* He contradicts himself. * **giling** a prayer for smn's safe return

puṭer bent *or* withered at the tip through inhibited growth

putih *ng,* **peṭak** *kr* 1 white. *Rupané *.* It(s color) is white. *dat * telur* albumen. *ḍuwit ** coins, silver. 2 pure. ***an** 1 sth white *or* whitened. **an adja dikumbah bareng karo sing kelir.* Don't wash white things with colored things. 2 egg white. **m̀*** to eat only white foods, as a form of fasting or self-denial. **m̀/di*aké** to have sth made white. **m̀/di*(i)** to whiten; to polish. *mutih sepatu* to polish shoes. *mutihi keris²* to polish krises. **pa·m̀*an** 1 a whitened *or* bleached spot. 2 section where Islamic scholars live. * **n·djaba** not as pure as appearances suggest. * **getih·é** pure in heart. * **memplak** *or* * **mulus** *or* * **tjeblèh** pure white, intensely white

putjet pale, wan

putjuk 1 point, tip. **é ilat* tongue tip. **ing wit krambil* the top of a coconut palm. ** gunung* mountain peak. 2 beginning. *ora ngerti bongkot *é* to not know anything about... ***an** the extreme tip. **pe*** leader; one who initiates. *pe*ing negara* a national leader. *lajang pe** a letter containing a declaration of war. **m̀*** point-shaped. *Dridjiné mutjuk eri.* Her fingers are [beautifully tapering] like thorn points. **m̀/di*i** to begin, initiate

putjung 1 a certain Javanese song form, often beginning with the words *Si ** or *Bapak *.* 2 a certain tree; also, the fruits (*méndjé*) or seeds (*kluwak*) of this tree. 3 a certain tiny red insect. 4 thoroughgoing knowledge of spiritual matters

putra 1 child, offspring (*ki for* ANAK). 2 child, young person (*ki for* BOTJAH). 3 prince. ***n** *wj* human being *or* puppet depicting a prince. **ka*n** prince's residence. **p·in·utra-*** to treat smn as one's own child. * **santana (dalem)** king's children and other close relatives. *See also* MANTJALA

putri 1 female (*ki for* WADON, WÉDOK). 2 princess. ***ǹ** young corn. **ka*ǹ** residence of a king's wives (other than the first) and daughters. **m̀*ǹi** womanly, feminine. * **Tjina** a certain classical dance. *See also* KUMAPUTRI

putu *ng kr,* **wajah** *ki* grandchild. ** lanang* grandson. ** wédok* granddaughter. ** (ke)ponakan* great-nephew, great-niece, *i.e.* grandchild of one's sibling. ***-*** grandchildren; descendants in general

puṭu a confection made of rice, grated coconut, and sugar

puṭul to break off. *Tjangkiré * kupingé.* The cup has lost its handle. *Tangané bonéka *.* The doll's hand came off. **m̀*i** 1 *pl* to fall off. *Goḍong²é paḍa muṭuli.* The leaves all came off. 2 (*psv* **di*i**) to break [things] off

putung broken; to break. *Balungé *.* The bone is broken. *Kitirané ndadak *.* Suddenly the propeller snapped. ***an** a broken-off piece; that which is broken. **ané ranté djam* a broken watch chain. **ke*an** to sulk, become sullen, withdraw (from criticism). *Bareng diwada ibuné Ani bandjur ke*an.* When Ani's mother pointed out her mistakes to her, Ani sulked and wouldn't continue the work. **m̀*** 1 (*psv* **di***) to break sth. *mutung wesi gligèn* to break iron bars. *mutung laku* to break one's journey, *e.g.* with a rest stop. 2 *sms* KE*AN. **m̀/di*aké** to break sth accidentally. **m̀*an** 1 breakable, easily snapped. 2 prone to be resentful of criticism

putus 1 brought to completion. *Olèhé sekolah wis *.* He's finished his schooling. *Rembugané olèhé tuku omah wis *.* The deal on the house has been closed. 2 expert; erudite. *misuwur * ing ngèlmu rupa²* famous for one's knowledge in many fields. 3 to win a prize, *esp.* in a lottery. *Aku tuku* *lotré * nomer telu.* I bought a lottery ticket and won third prize. **4** detached, broken off. **(ka)*an** decision. **an sing tetep* a firm decision. **m̀/di*(aké,-i)** to decide. *mutus sing adil* to make a fair decision. *Wong² mau mutusaké manggon ana ing hotèl.* They decided to live in a hotel.

puṭut pupil *or* disciple of a holy hermit

puw- *see also under* PU- (*Introduction, 2.9.7*)

puwa *-* fond of tormenting *or* humiliating others

puwanten *kr for* PUWARA

puwârâ *ng,* **puwanten** *kr* last, final; in the end

puwas satisfied with one's lot

puwâsâ *var of* PASA

pw- *see also under* PU(W)- (*Introduction, 2.9.7*)

Q

q (*prn* **kü**) *alphabetic letter*

Qur'an (*prn* **Kur'an**) the Koran

R

r (*prn* **èr**) *alphabetic letter*

R. *see* RADÈN

-r- *infix inserted after initial consonant, denoting repeated, continuing, and/or multiple actions or effects: see under individual entries. Botjah² paḍa ptg b·r·engok.* The boys kept shouting. *Manuké ptg tj·r·uwèt.* The bird is twittering.

ra- *see also under* RE- (*Introduction, 2.9.2*)

R.A. *see under* RADÈN

ra'ari *var of* RANTEN

râbâ **(ng)/di*(-*)** to search about; to grope (for) uncertainly. *Jèn isih *-* ja adja dilakoni.* If you're not sure, don't do it. *téori sing *-** tentative theories

rabas **ng/di*** to trim, prune, cut back

rabâsâ **ng/di*** to destroy, crush

rabat marked-down price, discount

rabèk *var of* RAWÈK

rabèt *var of* RAWÈK

rabi to take a wife. *Wis * apa durung?* Is he married? ***ǹ** to marry frequently. **ng/di*-k̀aké** to arrange for [a girl's] marriage. *A arep ngrabèkaké ponakané.* A will arrange for his niece to marry. **ngrabèkaké mata** to look at [a female] with lust. **ng/di*ǹi** to marry smn. *A ngrabèni anaké wédok B.* A married B's daughter.

Rabingulakir fourth month of the Moslem calendar

Rabingulawal third month of the Moslem calendar

rabuk fertilizer. ***an** fertilized. *lemah *an* fertilized soil. **ng/di*(i)** to fertilize, apply fertilizer to

râdâ *ng,* **radi** *kr* **1** somewhat, quite; a little; (quite) a bit. ** geḍé* rather large. ** dawa* pretty long. *Bisa mabur * adoh.* It can fly quite a distance. *Ḍèwèké * ngguju.* He laughed a little. ***-*** yes and no; to a small extent. *Diujahi *-* baé.* Add just a dash of salt. *Apa iki kaja klambimu sing ilang?–Ja *-*.* Does this look like the shirt you lost? –Well...somewhat.

radèn (*abbr*: **R.**) *title applied to male royal descendants.* * **adipati** *title for vice regent of Solo or Jogja.* * **adipati arja** *title for government regent.* * **adjeng** (*abbr*: **R.A.**) *title for an unmarried female aristocrat.* * **aju** (*abbr*: **R.Aj.**) *title for a married female aristocrat.* * **beken** (*abbr*: **R.B.**) *title for a certain low-ranking court official.* * **lara** *sms* * RARA *below.* * **mas** (*abbr*: **R.M.**) *male nobility title.* * **(nga)bèhi** *title for a married male or female aristocrat.* * **ngantèn** *title for a married woman of medium-low status.* * **rara** (*abbr*: **R.R.**) *title for an unmarried high-status girl.* * **rijo** (*abbr*: **R.R.**) *title for a district head under the Sultan of Jogjakarta*

radi somewhat; quite (*kr for* RADA)

raḍiator car radiator

radija *var of* RADYA

radiktya *var of* RADITÉ

radin (*or* **w***) even(ly distributed, spread) (*kr for* RATA)

raḍio radio. *djuru* * radio specialist; radio man

radité, raditya *oj* sun

râdjâ 1 king. 2 a variety of banana. 3 *compounding element: see individual entries below.* **k(e)*n** 1 kingdom. 2 tract of land given to a palace official. **ng*** 1 kingly. 2 (*psv* **di***; *or* **ng/di*-***) to regard *or* treat smn as a king. **r·in·adja(-*)** *or* **r·in·adja-putra** to be treated like a king. * **padni** *oj* queen. * **putra** prince. * **ka·putra·n** attire worn by a bridegroom. * **putri** princess. * **ka·putri·ǹ** attire worn by a bride. * **siwi** *or* * **sunu** prince; princess. *See also* PRADJA

râdjâ(a)mal worldly possessions. *See also* AMAL

Radjab *var of* REDJEB

râdjâbrânâ treasure, jewels. ** penḍem* buried treasure

râdjâdarbé possessions, belongings. *See also* DARBÉ

râdjâduwé possessions, belongings. *See also* DUWÉ

radjag 1 leaky. *Pajoné *.* The roof leaks. 2 filled with seepage. *Jèn udan trotjoh djubiné nganti *.* When it rains, water seeps in all over the floor. ***an** *sms* * 2. **ng/di*i** to get water all over [sth]. *Adja dolanan banju nang kono, mengko ng*i kamar.* Don't play with water there–you'll get it all over the room.

radjah 1 lines on the palm of the hand. 2 *oj* passion, lust. **ng/di*** to interpret palm lines. *ng* tangan* to engage in palmistry

râdjâkâjâ cattle; livestock

radjam **ng/di*** to stone smn to death

râdjâmal *see* RADJAAMAL

râdjâmâlâ a variety of banana

radjang ***an** in slices. *brambang *an* sliced onion. **ng/di*(i)** to slice

râdjâpati a crime carrying a death penalty. *See also* PATI[a]

râdjâpèni treasure, valuables. *See also* PÈNI

râdjâsingâ syphilis

râdjâsuwâlâ 1 astrologically propitious time. 2 [of girls] of marriageable age. 3 king's offspring

râdjâtadi treasure, valuables

râdjâwerdi bluish enamel used for jewelry

radjeg fence; wooden fence. ** wesi* iron fence. **ng/di*i** to fence sth in, enclose with a fence

radjèh **rodjah-*** in shreds. *suwèk rodjah-** torn to ribbons

radjin neat, orderly, tidy. *wong ** an orderly person. *Kamaré ditata *.* He tidied up his room. **ka*an** handicrafts. *inḍustri tjilik lan ke*an* small industry and hand-crafted goods

radjungan a small black crab

radjut 1 net(ting); hair net. 2 knitted material. **ng/di*** 1 to make netting. 2 to knit. * **kawat** wire screen

rados ***an** street, road (*alternate kr? rural var? of* RATA·N)

radya royal. ** pustaka* royal library

radyan *ltry var of* RADÈN

râgâ 1 body. *djiwa ** body and soul. 2 rattan basket. **ng*-suksma** to die leaving no corporeal remains

ragad (*see also* WRAGAD) expense(s), cost. **é akèh.* The expenses are heavy. *Ora *-* apa²*. There's no charge. **ng/di*i** to finance, bear the expenses of

râgâini a certain flower

ragang ***an** frame, skeleton. **an omah* house frame. **ané awak geḍé.* He's big-boned. **r·um·agang** to set about [a task]. *Ḍèwèké arep rumagang njambutgawé.* He's about to begin the job.

ragas 1 reptile skeleton. 2 dead (leafless) tree *or* plant. *pendjalin* * a variety of leafless rattan. ***an** in skeletal form; reduced to a skeleton. *kari *an* (*fig*) reduced to poverty

ragi 1 yeast. 2 seasoned and fried coconut (used also as a base for other dishes). 3 *var* (*sbst kr?*) *of* RADI. ***n̂** made with yeast; fermented. **ng/di*n̂i** to add yeast to

ragil (*or* **w***) last-born, youngest child in a family. *Sing mbarep lanang, sing * wédok.* The oldest child is a boy, the youngest is a girl. *** kuning** *pet name often given to a fair sweet youngest child.* *** urip** youngest living child

rah blood (*kr for* GETIH). **nge/di*** 1 to aim for/at. *Aku mau mbalang arep nge* pelem kena gendèngé.* I aimed at the mango but hit the roof. *Sing di* sing nganggo klambi biru kuwi.* He's after the one in the blue dress. 2 to reach sth from above. *Aku nge* timba sing ketjemplung nang sumur.* I fished up the pail that had fallen into the well. **pa·nge*** goal aimed at; intention; expectation. *See also* ARAH

rahab agreeably disposed (to). **ng*i** to suggest eating together. *Sing kagungan dalem ngaturi para tamu ng*i ḍedaharan sakanané.* The host urged the guests to eat.

rahadèn *var of* RAHADYAN

rahadjeng in good health and spirits (*sbst? kr for* RAHAJU)

rahadyan *oj* *male nobility title*

rahaju *ng*, **rahadjeng** *sbst? kr* in good health and spirits; secure, tranquil. **ka*n̂** good health, freedom from difficulties

rahardja healthy, prosperous. *negara sing titi tata tentrem sarta ** a peaceful and prosperous nation. **ka*n** prosperity, welfare

rahas(i)ja *oj* secret. *mbotjoraké * negara* to leak a state secret. *pulisi ** secret police. **ng/di*kaké** to keep sth secret

rahina *var of* RAINA

rahmat (*or* ***ullah**) God's blessing. *mulih ing ** to die. **ng/di*i** [of God] to bless

rai 1 ([**pa**]·**surja·n** *or* **wadânâ** *ki*) human face. *napuk ** to humiliate *or* insult smn publicly. 2 front, façade, surface. **né banju* the surface of the water. 3 page. * *patang puluh* page 40. *se** one page(ful). ***mu** *insulting term of abuse.* ***n̂** 1 likeness *or* imitation of a human face. 2 (*or* **re*n̂**) surface. (*re*)*raèn médja* the surface of the table. **ng/di*n̂i** to draw a face on sth. **p(a)*n̂(an)** (**pa·surja·n** *ki*) facial expression. *** geḍèg** insensitive; shameless

raina daybreak, sunrise. **k(a)*n** 1 (too) late [in the morning]; past dawn [of improperly timed shadow-play performances]. *tangi karahinan* to oversleep ('to get up too late'). 2 to sleep too late. *Aku krainan.* I overslept.

R. Aj. *see* RADÈN

râjâ great, important. *krisis djagad ** a great world crisis. *Indonesia ** (*name of the Indonesian national anthem*). *Djakarta ** Greater Djakarta. *hari ** an important day; a holiday. **ke*-*** to undergo difficulty *or* hardship. *Udan kaja ngéné kok ija ke*-* réné?* I wonder why he made his way here through such a hard rain. *ke*-* anggoné golèk ḍuwit* to have trouble raising money. **ng/di*kaké** to celebrate. **pa*n** celebration

rajah ***an** loot; sth grabbed (at/up). **ng/di*(i)** to grab at, snatch. *Botjah[2] paḍa ng* lajangan sing tatas.* The boys are trying to retrieve the kite that broke loose. *ng*i désa* to loot a village. *See also* DJARAH

rajap termite (male: *see also* GUNḌIK). ***an** a group that acts like termites. **ng*** to behave like a colony of termites. *** bala** *or* *** saraḍaḍu** termites that guard the queen and the colony. *See also* KUMRAJAP

ra'jat *var sp of* RAKJAT

raji younger sibling (*standard ki, sbst kr for* AḌI). **(ing)kang *** (your, his) wife

rajud **ng/di*** 1 to tie together, tie into a bundle. 2 to gather together with the arms; *fig* to help oneself to others' possessions. **pa·ng*** one who takes over others' belongings

rajuk **ng/di*(i)** to take (away), *esp.* by force *or* without permission

rak 1 *excl inviting agreement or confirmation. Anakmu umuré saiki * wis limang taun.* Your son must be five years old now? **ja seneng ta, kowé?* You like it, don't you? *Kuwi * ija kurang kepénak ta?* That isn't very comfortable, is it? 2 (*prn* **rak'** *or* **rak̄**) shelf, rack. ** buku* bookshelf, bookcase. *** (i)ja** hey! say! **ja kakéhan ḍuwit.* Here, that's too much money! **ja basa sing apik.* Come on now, talk nice Krama.

râkâ older brother (*kr? ki? for* KAKANG). *** dalem** his majesty's older brother; your (royal) older brother. **(ing)kang *** 1 exalted older brother. 2 (your, her) husband

rakangat series of praying positions during Moslem worship, varying for each of the five daily services
rakâṭâ *oj* crab
rakèt bat, racket
raket close, intimate. *sesrawungan* * close interrelationship. * *rukun* congenial. ***an** herbs used as stomach medication (*ki for* TAPEL). **k(e)*** firmly attached. *Kertasé kraket karo médjané.* The paper is stuck to the table. *nganti k* galar* destitute. **ng/di*aké** 1 to settle, resolve. *ng*aké pasulajan* to settle a dispute. 2 to attach firmly. *di*aké nganggo lim* glued on. **ng/di*i** to become close with. *Botjah èlèk ngono adja di*i.* Don't make friends with an unsavory boy like him. **r·um·aket** close, intimate
rakit 1 pair, team, span. *kebo rong* * two pairs of kerbaus. 2 bamboo raft. ***an** 1 yoked. *djaran *an* a pair of yoked horses. 2 layout, arrangement. 3 (forming) a set *or* pair. *Klambi iki arep dak enggo *an katokku sing idjo.* I'm going to wear this shirt (as a set) with my green pants. **ng/di*i** 1 to lay out. 2 to equip [a horse]. *ng* djaran* to harness up a horse. **ng/di*aké** to yoke up [a pair of farm animals]
rakjan, rakjânâ *oj* *title for a Grand Vizier*
rak̕jat the people, the public. *panguwasané* * sovereignty of the people. * *tjilik* the common man, the man in the street
rakrjan *ltry var of* RADÈN
raksa *formal var of* REKSA
rak̕sâsâ, rak̕seksa *oj* male ogre
rak̕sasi, rak̕seksi *oj* female ogre
rakup **ng/di*(i)** to gather *or* rake together with the arms. *ng*i dagangané* to gather up one's merchandise [*e.g.* a peddler caught with his wares spread out in a sudden downpour]
rakus greedy
ralat error, misprint. **ng/di*** to correct; to proofread
ram river flotsam. ***-*an** a makeshift dam made from flotsam
râmâ father; older and/or higher-ranking male (*ki for* BAPAK). * **ibu** parents
Ramadan ninth month of the Moslem calendar: the fasting month
Ramadhan *var sp of* RAMADAN
ramah-tamah friendly, informal
ramak father
ramal prophecy. **ng/di*i** to prophesy
Ramayanā epic recounting the life and adventures of Rama, seventh incarnation of Vishnu: adapted by the Javanese from the Sanskrit epic and depicted by human beings in the classical dance-drama
rambah *n* times; *n* after *n*. * *pindo* twice. *Rembugan mau wis * kaping²*. The discussion was by no means the first one. *Mengkono mau nganti * ping loro utawa telu.* Do the above two or three times. *Saka klas nol kuwi mengko nganti tamat * patang taun.* Elementary school (class zero to the end) is four consecutive years. ***an** *n* times. *nganti pirang² *an* any number of times; again and again. *Lagi rong *an wis kesel.* This is only the second time and he's tired already! ***-*** again and again. *Kertuposé wis *-* pamatjané.* She read his postcard over and over. **ma*-*** to [do] again and again. *Perlu disuntik ma*-*.* I had to have a number of injections.
rambak 1 fried animal rind. 2 tree root growing on the surface of the ground
ramban to pick edible leaves for use in cooking *or* as animal fodder. **(re)*an** picked edible leaves. **an kanggo pakan weḍusé* leaves to feed to the goat
rambang (raised) to the *n*th power. *sepuluh * telu* ten to the third power, ten cubed. **ng/di*** 1 to set sth in a container of water. *Lemariné di* karebèn semuté ora bisa mlebu.* They put the cupboard (legs) in water so the ants couldn't get in. 2 to bathe [the eyes] with an eye cup or substitute. 3 to wash down [a fighting cock *or* cricket] by pouring water over it. **ng/di*aké** to raise [a number] to the *n*th power. *ng*aké tjatjah loro* to square a number. *ng*aké tjatjah sepuluh* to raise a number to the tenth power
rambas to ooze, seep. *Getihé *.* The blood soaked through.
rambat ground vine. *téla* * sweet potato. ***an** 1 in the creeping stage. *Bajiné *an.* The baby is beginning to creep. 2 a support for a climbing plant. ***-*** to keep creeping. *Anakku *-*.* My baby crawls everywhere. **m*** 1 to creep, crawl. *mawar m** a climbing rose. *Bajiné m*.* The baby creeps. *Geniné m* nèng omah tangga.* The fire edged toward the neighboring house. **ng/di*aké** to train [a vine] up a supporting pole. **ng/di*i** to creep *or* climb on(to); to edge toward *or* into. *Épidéminé wis ng*i*

désa kono. The epidemic has spread to that village. **r·um·ambat** to creep. *"Policy" iku rumambaté marang tembung mantja.* The word "policy" is creeping into foreign vocabulary.

rambit (*or* *-*) a thorny shrub

rambon a variety of fine fragrant tobacco

rambut hair on the head (**réma** *or* **rikma** *ki*). ***an** *see* RAMBUTAN. **ng*** resembling hair; hairy. **ng*i** [of glassware] having hairline cracks. **sa*** a hair's-breadth. *Bédané mung se*.* There's only a tiny difference. *Kurang se* waé ḍèwèké ketabrak montor.* He barely missed being hit by a car. **sa* p·in·ara pitu** tiny; trivial (*i.e.* a hair split into seven). **sa* p·in·ara sèwu** tiny, infinitesimal. **r·um·ambat** [of boiling syrup] in the fine-thread stage. *** badjang** baby hair. *** dj·um·ambak m·anak** *or* *** dj·um·ebeng m̀·weteng** to have babies in rapid succession. *See also* KUMRAMBAT

rambutan a small red fuzzy-skinned fruit resembling a leechee nut; the tree that produces this fruit

ramé noisy, bustling, alive with activity, making commotion. *panggonan sing ** a noisy crowded place. *Dalané *né ora djamak.* The streets were jam-packed. *surak ** to cheer boisterously. *Ing pawon * swarané wong kang réwang.* There was a great hubbub from those who were helping in the kitchen. *Mung perkara sepélé waé kok *.* What a commotion over such a trivial matter! *-* (to hold) a celebration, festival, or any noisy gathering. *Nang univèrsitas ana *-* ḍémonstrasi mahasiswa.* There was a tumultuous student demonstration at the university. *Saben taun bubar panèn sok *-*.* Every year after the harvest many festivals are held. **k(a)*an** *or* **k(a)*ǹ** 1 celebration, festival. *Sésuk arep ana kraméjan.* There's to be a celebration tomorrow. *ke*an Sekatèn* court festival held during the month of Mulud. 2 noise, bustle; commotion of normal life and activity. *Panḍita mau milih ninggal donja ke*an perlu tapa ing gunung.* The holy man chose to leave the hustle and bustle of the world and meditate in the mountains. *djaman kramèn* worldly life with all its bustle [as contrasted with the peace of eternal life-after-death]. **ng/di*k̀aké** to enliven, bring action to. *ngramèkaké pésta* to liven up a party. **ng/di*ǹi** to disturb with noise and commotion; to stir up, throw into commotion. *Adja gegujon nang kono munḍak ngramèni bapak sing lagi saré.* Don't fool around there–you'll disturb your father, he's taking a nap. *Anaké mung sidji waé wis ngramèni wong sak omah.* They have only one child but he keeps the whole house in an uproar.

Ramelan *var of* RAMADAN

rames [of food items] mixed together. *sega ** rice mixed in with the accompanying dishes. **ng/di*i** to combine [foods]. *Usus babi dikumbah resik nuli di*i nganggo glepung kandji.* Wash the pork entrails and mix them with cornstarch.

rami hemp. *tali ** hempen rope. *kain ** burlap

ramjang *-* *or* **ng*** *or* **r·um·amjang** filmy, hazy, transparent. *Elaré tipis ng*.* Its wings are thin and gauzy.

rampad **(re)*an** a laid-out meal. *Wis tjumawis ana re*ané énak²*. A delicious repast had been set out. **ng*** to set out a meal

rampag *var of* RAMPAK

rampak all the same, with none differing from the others. *Untuné *.* His teeth are even. *Tanduranè dipaprasi karebèn bisa *.* The plants were trimmed to a uniform height. *Swarané bisa * bareng.* Their voices were together [throughout the song].

rampal to come out/off. *Ḍèké tiba nunggang pit montor untuné nganti * papat.* He fell from his motor bike and lost four teeth. **ng/di*i** to sever, separate

rampas ***an** (having been) seized, cut, picked. *barang² *an saka pelabuhan* goods confiscated at the harbor. **ng/di*(i) 1** to seize. *Kampak mau ng* djam tanganku.* The thief snatched my wristwatch. *Pulisi pelabuhan ng* barang² selunḍupan.* The harbor police seized the smuggled goods. 2 to pick [the topmost leaves from tobacco plants]. *Goḍongé mbako di*i.* She picked the top tobacco leaves.

rampèk a short batik garment worn over the trousers by palace guards. ***-* keṭèk** *or* **ng* keṭèk** to get in trouble by joining smn with a shady reputation. **ng/di*(-*)** to play up to smn in an appeal for sympathy. *Anakku lagi ng* atiku.* My child is trying to make me feel sorry for him. *ng*-* supaja diwènèhi kelonggaran anggoné mbajar padjeg* to plead for a time extension in paying one's taxes

ramping slim, slender. **ng/di*aké** to make slim

rampog robber, bandit, highwayman. ***an** *see* PA*AN *below.* **ng/di*** to rob, hold up. **(pa)*an** *or* **p*an** *wj* a group puppet depicting ranks of troops with cannon and battle flag

rampung over, finished, done with; to finish, complete. *Bareng wis djam rolas *.* By 12 o'clock he was finished. *Bareng wis * olèhé tata²...* When they had completed the arrangements... *Tjanḍi iki durung * kabèh, isih kurang.* The temple has never been finished—there are parts lacking. **ka*an** slain. **ng/di*i** to kill, finish off

ran *adr* horse! (*shf of* DJARAN)

rânâ[a] *ng,* **rika** *kr* to that place (*Degree III: Introduction, 6*). *Olèhé * nunggang montor.* They drove there. *Kowé wis tau * apa?* Have you ever been there? ***-*** *or* ***-réné** (**rika-riki** *kr*) here and there. **ng/di*kaké** to put sth in *or* move sth toward that place. *Kursiné di*kaké.* Move the chair over that way. *See also* MRANA

rânâ[b] (*or* **w***) a wide folding screen used as a room divider *or* for blocking off an open doorway

rânâgânâ *var of* RANANGGANA

ranangganâ *oj* battlefield

rânḍa widow. ** kembang* young childless widow. ** mati* widow by death. ** urip* widow by divorce. **ka*n** widow's residence. *** rojal** a certain kind of cookie

randjam bed. **ng/di*** *var of* NG/DI·RADJAM

randjang bedstead, *esp.* of metal

randjap **ng/di*** to crush, mutilate, destroy

ranḍu kapok tree; kapok seeds, from which kapok is extracted. *** alas** large wild kapok tree. *** kuning** kapok wood (used for kris sheaths)

rang 1 hierarchy, order of ranking. 2 athlete's foot. ***en** to have *or* get athlete's foot

rangah (*or* ***-***) [of teeth] sharply pointed

rangap *var of* RANGAH

rangas (*or* **w***) a certain red termite

ranggah [of horns, antlers] wide, spreading

ranggèh **ng/di*(i)** to reach for sth high (over one's head). *ng*i lintang ing langit* to strive for the impossible. **sa*** as high as one can reach

ranggon hut for refuge against wild-animal attack. **ng*i 1** (*psv* **di*i**) to live in [a house owned by smn else]. 2 incurable; chronic

râṅgkâ 1 (**sarung·an** *kr*) kris sheath; upper section of a kris sheath (*see also* WRANGKA). 2 frame; skeleton. ***n** (**mawi sarung·an** *kr*) sheathed. **ng/di*kaké** (**ñj/dipun·sarung·aken** *kr*) 1 to sheathe [a kris]. 2 to stab smn to death with a kris. **ng/di*ni** (**ñj/dipun·sarung·i** *kr*) to provide [a kris] with a sheath. **ngrangkani kuḍi** to handle a difficult person

rangkang 1 *var of* BRANGKANG. 2 *var of* RAGANG

rangké bundle, bunch. *kembang sa** a bouquet. ***ǹ** made into a bunch. *rangkèn kembang* flowers in a bunch. **ng/di*(ǹi)** to make into a bunch

rangkèl *var of* RANGGÈH

rangkep multiple (rather than single). *Aku wis klambèn * telu, kok isih aḍem waé.* I have on three layers of clothing and I'm *still* cold. *tembung ** (*gram*) doubled *or* reduplicated word. *gawé lajang lamaran penggawéan * loro* to submit a job application in duplicate. ***an 1** [of day names] doubled up, in combination with. *Dina pasaran iku nganggo *an karo dina Senèn, Slasa, lsp.* The [Javanese] market days are used in combination with [Western] Monday, Tuesday, *etc.* 2 (clothing) worn as an additional layer. *Manawa mangsa beḍiḍing kudu *an kaos kandel.* When it's cold, you should wear a warm undershirt. *Jèn lunga bengi kudu nganggo *an.* When you go out at night you should wear an extra layer of clothing. **ng/di* 1** to double, make multiple. *Tembung² iki *en.* Double the following words. 2 to double as; to function in [a second capacity]; to double up. *Wakil Présiḍèn ng* menteri mantja negara.* The Vice President also acts as foreign minister. *A mentas dilèrèni, mulané penggawéané di* karo B.* A just got fired, so B is doing A's work as well as his own. **ng/di*i** to add another one. *Klambiné di*i djakèt.* He put a jacket on over his shirt. *Suhé dak *ané kawat.* I'll reinforce this binding with wire.

rangkèt **ng/di* 1** to beat with a stick as punishment. 2 to handcuff

rangkok hornbill (bird)

rangkud **ng/di*(i)** to gather up and take away. *Dagangané di*i pulisi.* The merchandise was confiscated by the police.

rangkul **re*an** to embrace each other by placing the hands on each other's shoulders. **ng/di*** to embrace smn by placing one's hands on his shoulders. *See also* PRANGKUL

rangrang (*or* **k***) a certain large red tree ant

rangsang desire, drive. * *asmara* sex drive. **ng*** 1 passionate. 2 (*psv* **di***) to try to get hold of. *Tangané terus ng* ḍèwèké.* He kept reaching out his hand for her. *Anggoné nggajuh penggawéan sing lowong kuwi ng*.* He's making a big try for the vacant job. 3 (*psv* **di***) to fight *or* attack ferociously

rangsel knapsack, rucksack

rangsuk *var of* RASUK

rangsum a ration of food. *tukang* * person in charge of handing out the rations. **ng/di*** to give out rations

rangu *-* doubtful, hesitant. *Atiné tansah *-* anggoné arep njambut gawé nang Djakarta.* He can't make up his mind about working in Djakarta. **ng·re*** to yearn. *Simin tansah ngre* bisaa olèh gawéjan ing kuṭa.* Simin longs to get a job in the city. *See also* KAPIRANGU

ransel *var of* RANGSEL

rântâ **ka*-*** to grieve inwardly. *trenjuh lan ke*-** feeling compassion and sharing the grief [of the bereaved]

rantab to flake off. *Tjèté paḍa ṭèṭèl bandjur *.* The paint is coming off in flakes. **ng/di*i** to get flakes on sth

rantak *-* *rg var of* MRANTAK

rantam ***an** planned (for), proposed. **an kawitan* planned expenditure, allotted capital. **ng/di*** to make provisions for. *projèk sing di* lebon ragad kurang-luwih Rp sajuta* a project for which about a million rupiahs has been allotted

rantang a vertical nest of food containers with a top handle, for transporting a variety of foods simultaneously. **ng*** to order a meal from a restaurant (for delivery in the above containers)

rantap *var of* RÈNTÈP

rantas 1 frayed nearly through. 2 broken; badly bent. ***an** having broken (off). **an benang* a broken thread

ranté chain. **ng/di*(ni)** to put chains on; to attach with a chain

ranten *oj* younger sibling

ranti 1 tomato. *suwé midjet wohing ** very easy, a cinch. 2 *var of* ANTI

ranting **rontang-*** tattered, ragged

rantjag 1 quick. *Apa sing marakaké kurang *é gawéjan mau?* What caused the work slowdown on that job? 2 [of horses] lame. ***an** done hastily. *gawéjan *an* hastily done work. **ng/di*** to speed up, expedite

rantjah *see* NG·GAGA

rantjak a stick of wood. ***an** a rack for gamelan *bonang*'s. **ng/di*** to cut *or* break [wood]. **sa*** a set of gamelan instruments

rantjânâ **ng*** to plan out; to design. **goḍa *** trouble, disaster, obstacle

rantjang ***an** plan, proposal, program. *miturut *an* according to plan. **an unḍang²* proposed legislation. **an resolusi* a draft resolution. **ng/di*** to plan. *Wis dak *, lan wis kebatjut.* I had it all planned out, and now it's too late. *Apa bisa nindakaké apa kang wis di*?* Were you able to do as you had planned? *Aku terus ng*² pijé mengko jèn klakon adu arep idjèn karo ḍèké.* I kept trying to figure out a way of being alone with her.

rantjas **ng/di*(i)** to trim, prune

rantos *var? sbst kr? for* RANTI

rantun **ng*** 1 laid out in readiness. *Wajangé sing arep metu wis paḍa ng*.* The puppets that are to appear are all laid out. 2 (*psv* **di***) to lay out, prepare. *ng* panganan kanggo tamu* to fix refreshments for the guests. **p(a)*an** *or* **pa·ng*an** a place for laying out *or* preparing a meal

raos feel; taste (*kr for* RASA). **pisang *** a variety of banana (*kr for* GEḌANG RADJA)

rapah leaves, twigs, brush

rapak 1 a divorce petition originating with the wife. 2 dried-out sugar-cane-plant leaves

rapat a meeting. **ng/di*aké** to bring up *or* discuss at a meeting

rapèk **ng/di*(-*)** to appeal for sympathy (*var of* NG/DI·RAMPÈK⁽²⁾)

rapèl a payment received retroactively. ***an** accumulated retroactive payments received. **ng/di*** to receive such payments

rapet tightly closed (up). *Gendulé ditutup sing *.* She covered the bottle tight. **ng/di*i** to cover sth tight

rapi neat, tidy

rapih no longer angry. **ng/di*** to calm smn down

rapor(t) report card, school report

rapot *var of* RAPORT

rârâ *var of* LARA[b]

raras *oj* pleasant, harmonious, beautiful. **ng/di*(-*)** to think over, consider. *** rum** fine, beautiful. *** ka·wibawa·n** happiness and prosperity

raré *rg var of* LARÉ
rari *var of* RANTEN
rarjwa *oj* child
ras race, ethnic origin
râsâ *ng,* raos *kr* 1 (the) taste (of). * *legi*
(*pahit, asin*). It tastes sweet (bitter, salty).
2 physical feel(ing). **né lara.* It hurts.
**ning awakku ora kepénak.* I don't feel
comfortable. 3 emotional feel(ing), inner
meaning. * *seḍih* feelings of sadness/grief.
**né kok seneng jèn lelungan nggawa ḍuwit
tjukup.* It feels good to travel when you've
brought along enough money. **n(an)* (ra-
os·an *kr*) to talk about, talk over, discuss.
**n-*n* (raos²an *kr*) to think of *or* plan on
[do]ing. *A rasan² arep lunga nang Djakarta
suk liburan iki.* A has in mind to go to Djakarta this vacation. re**n* 1 object of discussion. *Re*né apa?* What are they talking
about? 2 to think of [do]ing. 3 (*or* re-
**nan* ng) to discuss. k* to have [a certain]
taste *or* feeling. *k* pahit* bitter-tasting.
Olèhé mangan k énak banget.* His food
tasted delicious to him. *Aku k* aḍem.* I
feel cold. *Wetengé k* lara.* He has a stomach ache. *k* seneng* to feel happy. *Sanadjan dikampleng rainé nanging meksa ora k*.*
They struck him in the face but he didn't
even feel it. ng/di**kaké* 1 to taste, sample.
*Apa kowé wis tau ng*kaké masakanku?*
Have you ever tasted my cooking? 2 to
feel, experience, take note of. *Aku wis tau
ng*kaké urip ing Éropah.* I've had a taste
of living in Europe. *Rasakna jèn wis wiwit
udan saldju!* (Wait till you) see what it's
like when it begins to snow! *Sanadjan getihé akèh sing metu nanging ora di*kaké.* It
bled a lot but he paid no attention to it. 3
to empathize (with), sense and share the
feelings of. ng/di**k-*kaké* (ng/dipun·raos²·
aken *kr*) 1 to take a taste *or* sample of.
*mBok djadjal di-rasak²aké ḍisik roti iki, rak
kaja ketjampuran obat.* Try these cookies—
they taste as if they have medicine in them.
2 to think over, let sth sink in. *Tak rasak²-
aké kok ja bener kanḍamu.* After I thought
it over, I realized you were right. ng/di**ni*
1 to talk about smn; to gossip (about). 2
to have bad feelings toward smn. pa·ng*
feeling; idea. *Pang*né aku wis buḍal menjang Semarang.* He thought I had left for
Semarang. *Pang*mu kowé kuwi apa ta?*
Who do you think you are, anyway? pe**an*
feeling, sensitivity. *Kowé kuwi ora duwé*

perasaan, njenèni uwong sak gelemmu ḍéwé.
You have no pity, venting your anger on
him like that. sa* having the same tastes *or*
feelings; in agreement, in harmony. *Aku karo mas Mardi sa*.* Mardi and I like the same
things. r·in·asa (r·in·aos *kr*) *ltry* to feel.
Jèn tak pikir², rinasa saja nggrantes ing ati.
If I dwell on it, I get sadder and sadder.
r·um·asa *or* r·um·angsa (r·um·aos *kr*) feeling, thought (*see* RUMANGSA). dudu * unfeeling, inhumane. * mala a certain tree
whose sap is made into incense; the sap of
this tree. * mulja a possession that gives its
owner spiritual powers. * pa·ng* 1 feeling,
interpretation. *Miturut * pang*ning atiku,
apiké perkara iki kudu diterusaké marang
bapakmu.* In my judgment, this should be
passed along to your father [to decide]. 2
to size up each other's feelings, attitudes, inner thoughts. * r·um·angsa the inner feeling of the heart. *Dadi pemimpin mono kudu duwé * rumangsa kang lanḍep.* To be a
leader, you must have keenly attuned inner
feelings. *See also* BANJU, KRASAN, MIRASA,
RUMANGSA, SURASA, WIRASA
rasé civet cat
raseksa *var of* RAKSASA
raseksi *var of* RAKSASI
rasio ratio
rasmi *formal var of* RESMI
rasuk **an* article of clothing for the upper
part of the body (*kr for* KLAMBI). m* to
enter and penetrate. *Bumbuné wis m* nang
nggon daging.* The flavors of the spices have
permeated the meat. *Dèké wis m* marang
agama Katulik.* He's become converted to
Catholicism. *Larané m* ing balung.* My
very bones ache. ng/di* 1 to accept fully.
ng agama Islam* to become a convert to Islam. 2 to marry one's sister-in-law or one's
adopted daughter. ngrasuk busana to get
dressed. ng/di*aké* to cause sth to penetrate. ng/dipun*i* to dress smn in a dress *or*
shirt (*kr for* ŊG/DI·KLAMBI·ŇI). r·um·asuk to
enter and penetrate. *Tambané wis rumasuk.*
The medicine has taken effect.
rasul religious prophet. *Gusti (Kangdjeng
Nabi)* * the prophet of God, *i.e.* Mohammed. **an* a ceremony exalting Mohammed.
ng*aké* to hold such a ceremony. * (l)ul(l)ah
Mohammed
rat *oj* world. *sadjagat* * all over the world
râtâ *ng,* radin *kr* (*or* w*) 1 even(ly distributed *or* spread). *Lemahé wis diaḍuk *.* He

crumbled the soil to uniform particles. *Olèhmu ngedum sing* *. Divide it evenly. *nggawé* * to average sth (out). *Jèn digawé * saben pitik boboté sakilo.* The chickens weigh an average of one kilogram. *Aspalané* *. The pavement is smooth. 2 *oj* carriage. *n (rados·an *alternate kr?*) city street. **né aspalan.* The street is asphalt. *-* 1 comparatively. *Ongkos produksi iki *-* setitik.* These production costs are relatively low. 2 roughly, approximately. *rata² rolas gram saben dinané* about twelve grams daily. **m*** to (get) spread. *Kabar mau wis m* tekan kampung².* The news has spread to the outlying areas. **ng/di*** 1 to smooth; to make even. *Ajo, segané di*.* Come on, let's divide the rice evenly. 2 to spread sth (around). **ng/di*kaké** to cause to be even. *ng*kaké dalan nganggo slènder* to smooth a road with a steamroller. **ng*ni** 1 to reach to all points. *kabungahan kang ng*ni* utter happiness. 2 (*psv* **di*ni**) to treat all the same. *Olèhé ngitjipi di*ni kabèh.* He tasted all the samples. *See also* PUKUL-RATA

ratap cry, complaint, lamentation

rateng cooked, done, ready to eat. **(re)*an** cooked food, *esp.* rice-accompanying dishes sold by street peddlers *or* small food shops. **ng/di*i** to cook/prepare [a meal]

ratih 1 *oj* moon. 2 the goddess of love. *See also* KAMADJAJA

ratjak 1 usual, common(place). 2 equal. *Kabèh tak anggep * apik.* I thought they were all equally nice. 3 *var of* RATJEK. ***an** considering everything. *Nèk *an regané pira?* How much would you estimate they'd cost? ***é** usually, ordinarily. *-* on the whole, by and large. **-* bédané sepuluh dradjat.* There's an average difference of around ten degrees. **ng*** 1 occurring commonly. 2 equally distributed. 3 (*psv* **di***) to judge sth from the available data. *Gedé tjilik dadi sidji, di* ana satus.* Taking size into account, I'd say there were about a hundred of them. 4 (*psv* **di***) to make equal, distribute evenly. **ng/di*aké** *sms* NG/DI* 4. *ng*aké winih* to set seedlings in even rows

ratjek̄ a type of worm that infects the stomach or eyes. ***en** infected with this worm

ratjik medicinal preparation of herbs. *tukang* * one who makes such preparations. ***an** 1 prepared, laid out. *Segané wudjud *an.* The meal has been set out. 2 collection, compilation. *Djamu iki *ané apa?* What ingredients is this medicine a mixture of? 3 finger, toe (*ki for* DRIDJI). **ng*** 1 to mix [medicines]. 2 to lay out [a meal]. *Jèn kowé arep mangan disik, ng*a déwé nang pawon.* If you want to eat first, set yourself a place in the kitchen.

ratjun poison. **ng/di*aké** to poison sth. **ng/di*(i)** to poison smn

ratna *var of* RETNA

raton 1 a children's game. 2 gathered in a flock *or* herd, *esp.* birds. **re*** 1 *sms* * 2. 2 *form of* RATU

ratu 1 king, queen, monarch. ** Madjapait* the king of Madjapait. *tawon* * queen bee. 2 chess king. **né kena madju-mundur menjang ngendi-endi nanging ora kena luwih saka sakotakan.* The king can move in any direction but only one square. 3 one of the small playing cards (*kertu tjilik*). *-*ning** *ltry* most, superlative. *nimas *-*ning memanis!* my sweetest darling! **re*n̂** to become a monarch. *Ana rajap wadon sidji sing reraton déwé.* One of the female termites sets herself up as queen. **k(e)*n̂** palace; court (*see* KRATON). **ng/di*** (*or psv* **di*-***) to regard smn as king. **ng/di*n̂i** to reign over. *ngratoni para déwa* to rule over the deities. **r·in·atu-*** to be treated royally. *Merga anak sidji²né, dèwèké rinaturatu.* He's an only child, so he gets treated like a king. *** alit** *or* *** anggèr** *title of the first son born to a king by his first wife.* *** b·in·aṭara** *term for addressing a king.* ***ning kusuma** *term for addressing a queen.* *** panḍita** *or* *** p·in·anḍita** *title for addressing a king.* *See also* KRATON, KUMRATU-RATU

ratus a mixture of incense and other fragrant substances. **ng/di*** to apply the above to. *ng* rékma* to scent one's hair with the above

ratya *oj* king. **ka*n** palace, court

rauk **ng/di*** 1 to gather up/in with the hands. *A menang anggoné main ng* ḍuwit akèh banget.* A won a large pot at cards and raked in his winnings. 2 *var of* NG/DI-RAWUK

raup 1 (**surja·n** *ki*) to wash one's face. *banju ** water for washing the face. ** getih* with the face dripping with blood. 2 the amount one can hold in the cupped hands. *beras sa** a cupped-handful of rice. *-* to agree to. *Djaman wingi² wong tuwa mutusaké laki-rabining anak, nanging saiki ratjaké mung *-*.* It used to be that parents had the final say on their children's marriages, but now they generally go along with the young people. **ng∗ pada** to kiss the feet (of); *fig* to display respect *or* esteem (for). **ng/di∗aké** (**ñj/di·surja·kaké** *ki*) to wash [one's; smn's] face with. *Banjuné bandjur di∗aké anaké.* She washed her baby's face with the water. **ngraupaké tangan** to pass the palms downward over the face after praying. **ng/di∗i** (**ñj/di·sibing·i** *or* **ñj/di·surja·ni** *ki*) to wash smn's face. **p(a)∗an** (**pa·surja·n** *ki*) **1** basin for face-washing water. **2** facial expression. **r·um·aup pada** *sms* NG∗ PADA *above*

raupa (*or* **p∗**) face. *Praupané putjet.* Her face is pale.

raut *rg* **ng/di∗i** to sharpen, hone. **péso ∗** a razor-sharp knife

râwâ *ng,* **rawi** *sbst? kr* **1** swamp(land). **2** small lake. **∗n 1** small swamp; large pond. **2** artificial lake. **3** swampy area

rawat nurse. **∗-∗** *oj* scarcely audible. *krungu tembang ∗-∗* to hear rumors. **ng/di∗** to take protective care of. *ng∗ wong² kang nanḍang tatu* to nurse the wounded. *Pité di∗ betjik.* He takes good care of his bicycle. *Aku ora weruh anggoné ng∗ kuntjiné.* I don't know where he keeps the key. *ng∗ wadi* to keep a secret. **pa∗an** act of caring for. *pe∗an lan pemulihan penderita tjatjad* the care and rehabilitation of the handicapped

rawé a plant whose hairy leaves cause stinging and skin rash. **∗-∗** to wave, flutter. **∗-∗ rantas, m̃·palang² putung** all obstacles shall be surmounted. **ng/di∗** to touch [the above leaves] to the skin

rawèh prohibited, not allowed (*contracted from* ORA AWÈH)

rawèk **rowak-∗** in tatters, torn to shreds

rawi swamp; lake (*sbst? kr for* RAWA)

rawing **rowang-∗ 1** worn, damaged. **2** chanted syllables in a children's song

rawis moustache (*ki for* BRENGOS). **∗an** sliced, in slices. **ng∗ 1** [of hair] thin, not luxuriant. **2** (*psv* **di∗**) to slice. *ng∗ mbako* to shred tobacco leaves

rawit small, very hot chili pepper

rawon a clear brown beef sauce. *sega ∗* rice eaten with the above, plain or with beansprouts and hot sauce added

rawud **ng/di∗** to mix [things] up, put into disorder

rawuh to come (*ki for* TEKA)

rawuk **ng/di∗** to scratch, claw

raziā a raid. **ng/di∗** to raid; to enter and search

R.B. *see* RADÈN

ré second note in the musical scale

re- *see also under* RA- (*Introduction, 2.9.2*)

réaksi reaction. **∗** *kimia* chemical reaction

réaksionèr reactionary

rebab a two-stringed gamelan cello. **ng∗** to play this instrument. **pa·ng∗ 1** cello player. **2** act *or* way of playing the cello

rébah *kr for* ROBAH?

rebah fallen; to fall (*kr for* RUBUH)

rebat pursuing one's self-interest *etc.* (*kr for* REBUT)

rebda *see* NGREBDA

rèbèl to fall, drop. *Botjah tjilik jèn mangan mesṭi ∗.* When a little child eats, he gets crumbs on the floor. **∗an** crumbs that have fallen. **ng/di∗i** to mess up [a floor] with fallen food particles. *Adja sok ng∗i mestèr karo gula.* Don't get sugar on the floor.

rèbewès driver's license

rèbjèg (to make things) unnecessarily complicated, too difficult to handle. **∗** *kakèhan barang gawan* having trouble carrying so many things. *Akèh temen ∗é tur ija ora saṭiṭik wragadé.* There are many problems in connection with it, and no small expense.

Rebo Wednesday. **∗ pungkas·an** *or* **∗ wekas·an** the last Wednesday in Sapar month

rebon a certain small shrimp

rebut *ng,* **rebat** *kr* to [do] in one's self-interest without regard for others. **∗** *menang* to win any way one can. *Wong² suk²an ∗ ngarep.* People elbowed each other trying to get in front. *Kantja² mung ∗ seneng ḍéwé² ora mikir montoré sing rusak.* The group went off pleasure-seeking, without a thought for the disabled car [which had brought them]. **∗an 1** rivalry. *tontonan ∗an mènèk katju* a contest in which boys climb greased poles. **2** object competed for. *C diénggo ∗an A karo B.* A and B [boys] were fighting over C [a girl]. **3** to struggle for possession *or* control of. *wong tani sing padu ∗an banju* farmers fighting over the [irrigation] water. **ng/di∗(i)** to seize for oneself. *ng∗ keradjan* to seize the throne. *Tunangané kantjané di∗.* He got his friend's fiancée away from him. **ngrebut kemiri kopong 1** to quarrel over sth trivial. **2** to yearn for sth of little value. **∗ ḍutjung** to try to get ahead of each other. **∗ ḍutjung ḍa**

golèk papan. They all scrambled for seats. * **tjukup** to put it briefly... (*phrase explaining one's haste in delivering an urgent message*). *Tekaku mréné mung * tjukup waé arep ngandani...* I've just come by for a moment to tell you... * **unggul** to struggle for topmost position. * **urip** to struggle for survival. * **wani** to behave in a foolhardy and irresponsible manner

reda **ng*** *var of* NGREBDA

redânâ 1 *oj* concerning money. 2 money (*sbst kr for* ḌUWIT)

redatin *inf var of* RUDATIN

redatos *inf var of* RUDATOS

redi mountain (*kr for* GUNUNG)

redja 1 flourishing, prosperous. 2 lively, active, festive. *Dalané wis wiwit katon *.* The streets began to liven up [with the morning traffic]. **ng/di*kaké** 1 to bring prosperity to. *ng*kaké negara kita* to make our nation prosper. 2 to enliven. *Negara arep ngedegaké pasar nèng dalan kéné kanggo ng*kaké.* The government is going to establish a market in this street to stimulate activity.

Redjeb seventh month of the Moslem calendar. ***-*an** rice-harvest festival celebrated during Redjeb in rural areas

rèdjèg *var of* RADJAG

redjeki 1 daily food; necessities of life. *ngedum * bahan pangan* to distribute essential food supplies. 2 good luck. **ka*n̉** to have an unexpected stroke of luck. **ng/di*n̉i** to bring smn luck

réḍuksi discount price. *Menawa nunggang sepur éntuk *.* He gets reduced rates on the train.

redya *oj* mountain

règ ***-*an** to fidget, squirm, move nervously about

reg *rpr* a violent shaking. *Nalika gunung Merapi ngetokké lahar wong² krasa mak * sedilit.* When Mount Merapi emitted lava the people felt a momentary tremor. **rag-*** to keep shaking violently. *Jèn ana sepur liwat mesṭi krasa rag-*.* When a train goes by, you feel a violent shaking.

rega *ng*, **regi** *kr* 1 price, cost. ***né** *setengah rupiah.* It costs half a rupiah. *nganjang-anjang ** to haggle over the price. *dolanan sing larang *né* an expensive toy. *Reganė murah.* It's cheap. 2 (*or* **a***) to cost. *barang sing a* limang rupiah* a five-rupiah item. *Pitik iki mung * sepuluh rupiah.* This chicken only costs ten rupiahs. **(re)*n** prices; price level. *Reregan paḍa munḍak kabèh.* Prices rose on everything. *Ḍèké wis weruh reregan pasar mulané ora bisa diapusi bakul.* She knows the price scales, so the peddlers can't gyp her. **ng/di*ni** to put a price on. *Sekuteré di*ni Rp. 50.000.* The scooter was valued at 50,000 rupiahs. **ana * ana rupa, ana rupa ana *** you get what you pay for. * **pasar** market price, market value

regadag *rpr* a hard *or* quick tug. *Djariké ketjanṭol pager digèrèd mak * suwèk amba banget.* Her skirt caught on the fence and it tore a big hole in it.

régé 1 a low round flat basket woven of palm-leaf ribs. 2 a short coconut-leaf-rib broom. ***n̉** woven-bamboo container. *sa régèn* one such containerful

reged dirty. *Tanganku *.* My hands are dirty. ***an** 1 soiled. 2 waste matter. *Tak tulisé nang *an iki.* I'll write it on this scratch paper. *krandjang *an* wastebasket. **re*** dirt, waste matter. *ngresiki re* nang kalèn* to clean the waste out of the ditch. **ng/di*i** to soil sth, *e.g.* with excreta

regèdèg *rpr* a rasping sound. *Latjiné ditarik mak *.* He pulled the drawer open noisily. *Djariké ditarik mak *.* The batik tore.

regedeg *rpr* a sudden multiple arrival. *Barisan branwér karo pulisi paḍa teka mak * bareng.* The fire brigade and the police all arrived at the scene together.

regedjeg ***an** (to have) a noisy quarrel

regéjong ***an** hanging. **ng*** to hang heavily. *Djeruké paḍa ng* nang wit.* The oranges are hanging from the tree.

regem 1 a small vise. 2 small pliers; tweezers. ***an** a firm hold. *korban *an lintah ḍarat* victim of a loan shark. **ng/di*** to pinch, squeeze, clutch. *di* déning rasa wedi* in the clutches of fear

regemeng vague, not clearly visible. *ptg * or *-* or* **ng*** looming in the dark. *Aku weruh bajangan ng*.* I saw a hulking shadow.

règèng ***-*** convalescent

regeng (*or* ***-***) bustling, astir. *Alun² sing mauné sepi bandjur katon *.* The square, which had been quiet, sprang to life. *Wong mau gawé *-*é omah.* He livens up the house.

règès 1 having no leaves. 2 rusted, corroded

regi price, cost (*kr for* REGA)

regije(n)g *rpr* a quick hoisting motion.

Koper² *mak* ∗ *diangkat kuli.* The porter swept the suitcases off the ground. **ng**∗ to carry [a heavy burden]

régol *ng,* **wijos** *kr* **1** outer gateway of a traditional-style house. **2** *wj* (*ng kr*) clown in tales from the *wajang geḍog* cycle. ∗ **n·djero** inner doorways on either side of a traditional-style house

régu **ng/di**∗**ñi** to hinder, obstruct. *Botjah² tjilik ora ngréwangi nanging malah ngrégoni.* Children don't help, they just get in the way.

regu (*or* **w**∗) **1** a small rattan palm with a slender hardwood trunk. **2** dignified. **3** remaining disdainfully silent

regudug *rpr* stampeding. *Botjah² mak* ∗ *te-ka.* The children rushed in all at once.

regul (*or* **w**∗) a marten-like animal

regunuk ∗**an** *or* **ng**∗ looming ominous and ghostly-looking. *Tumpukan watu kuwi jèn bengi kétok ng*∗ *ireng.* At night an ordinary heap of rock looks black and menacing. ∗-∗ moving in the dark with an ominous *or* ghostly aspect. *Kebo² mau* ∗-∗ *mara.* The kerbaus loomed hugely as they approached.

rèh rule, regulation. *manut-miturut ing* ∗*é* following the regulations. ∗**né** *see* SA∗NÉ *below.* ∗-∗**an** a subordinate (person *or* territory). *ḍeḍuwuran lan* ∗-∗**an** superiors and subordinates. **ke**∗ to be under the authority (of). *Désa iki ke*∗ *kabupatèn Banjumas.* This village is under the Banjumas regency. **nge/di**∗ to command [a specific body]. *Major iku nge*∗ *sabataljon.* A major has charge of one battalion. **nge/di**∗**aké** to govern, hold sway over. *Lurah nge*∗*aké wong sadésa.* The village head rules over all the villagers. (**sa**)∗**né** since, in view of the fact that. *Sa*∗*né wis rada wengi, ajo paḍa mapan turu.* Since it's late, let's go to bed. (*Sa*)*rèhning wis kesel, dadi njéwa djaran.* He was so weary he hired a horse. (**sa**)∗**déné** since, because. **r·in·èh** ruled (by). *See also* RÈRÈH

réhabilitasi rehabilitation. **ng/di**∗ to rehabilitate

réjab ∗-∗ *or* **ng**∗ [of long hair] hanging down loose. *See also* KRÉJAB

réjog a street show featuring a performer wearing an enormous frightening mask with plumes extending high and wide. *Ana* ∗ *sagamelané.* There was a street show complete with gamelan music. **ng**∗ to perform such a show

réjok old, worn out, broken down. **réjak-**∗

1 on the verge of collapse. **2** to keep scooping. *Buruh iku wiwit mau réjak-*∗ *nji-ḍuki rereged sing mbunteti kalèn.* The laborer has been working for some time getting out the refuse that is clogging the ditch. **ng/di**∗ to lift *or* scoop out

réjon rayon

réjot shaky, wobbly, ready to collapse

rèk **1** match; lighter. **2** (*prn* **rèk̄**) *rpr* a rasping sound. *Walang kerèk iku muni* ∗ ∗ ∗. A mantis goes *rèk-rèk-rèk! Gordèné ditarik mak* ∗. He drew the curtains noisily. ∗-∗**an** zipper. **ng**∗ to produce a light. *nge*∗ ∗ to strike a match *or* light a lighter. **nge/di**∗**aké** to light sth. *nge*∗*aké* ∗ to light a match. ∗ **bul** *or* ∗ **djeklèk·an** cigarette lighter. ∗ **djès** *or* ∗ **djrès** a match. ∗ **gerèt·an** cigarette lighter

réka **1** plan, intention. ∗*né arep nglumpukaké krambil.* He intended to gather some coconuts. **2** way, means. *Keprijé* ∗*né bisané rampung babar pisan?* How can I ever get it finished? ∗**n** imitation, fake. ∗-∗ to have a foolish idea. *Kakèhan* ∗-∗ *arep mubeng tanah Djawa nganggo pit.* He got the ridiculous notion of touring Java on a bicycle. **re**∗**n** *sms* ∗N *above.* **re**∗**n** *motor mabur* a toy airplane. *Barong iku re*∗**n** *ké-wan.* A *barong* is a man dressed up as an animal. **ng/di**∗ **1** (*or* **ng/di**∗-∗) to (try to) conjure up an idea *or* picture in the imagination. *Di*∗-∗ *murih adja kebandjur-bandjur.* He racked his brain for an idea before it was too late. *Barang sing arep mbok gambar rak bisa di*∗-∗. You can picture in your mind what you want to draw, can't you? **2** (*or* **ng/di**∗**ni**) to cheat; to plot against. *See also* RÉKADAJA

rékâdâjâ a plan, plot, scheme. *sugih* ∗ full of ideas. **ng/di**∗ to (try to) hit on an idea. *Ajo paḍa ng*∗ *golèk tambahan pemetu.* Let's think of a way to earn some extra money. **pa·ng**∗ act of plotting *or* scheming. *See also* DAJA, RÉKA

rekah **1** cracked. *Témboké omah wis paḍa* ∗. The house walls are full of cracks. **2** ill at ease, awkward (*kr for* RIKUH)

rekaos *kr for* REKASA

rekâsâ *ng,* **rekaos** *kr* filled with obstacles *or* hardships. *Lebuné rada* ∗. It's hard to get in. *Uripé tansah* ∗. His life is a constant struggle. **ng/di**∗**kaké** to cause difficulty *or* hardship (for). *A pidjer ng*∗*kaké wong tuwané.* A always makes trouble for his parents.

rékat *inf var of* RIKAT
rekatak *rpr* a whizzing sound. *Mak* *. Zip! *Pedangé diunus mak* *. He whisked out his sword.
rèken **ng/di*** to set a value (on), reckon sth (at). *Regané Rp 450 nanging di* Rp 400.* It cost 450 rupiahs but she marked it down to 400. *Bareng dak kon ng* Rp 70 diwènèhké.* When I raised my offer to 70 rupiahs, he let me have it.
rékening bill presented for payment. * *listrik* (*tilpun, banju, lsp.*) the electric (telephone, water, *etc.*) bill
rekès a request; a letter of request *or* application. **ng/di*** to put in a request *or* application (for)
rèket *var of* RAKÈT
rekètèk *rpr* a tearing sound. *Sarungku ketjanṭol pang, mak wèk,* *, *brèk.* My sarong caught on a branch and ripped.
reketek̄ *rpr* wood *or* bamboo cracking. * *ambruk pangé.* Crack! the branch broke.
rekitik *rpr* a light crackling sound, *e.g.* of paper burning
rekjânâ patih *title for a prime minister*
réklame sales-promotion gimmick. **ng/di*kaké** to promote with a gimmick. *Gambar iki ngréklamekaké rokok krètèk.* This picture is an advertising stunt for clove cigarettes.
reksa **(re)*n** that which is guarded *or* watched over. *Pité kantjaku kuwi dititipké nang ngomahku kéné malah dadi *n.* The bicycle my friend left here at my house is just one more thing I have to look after. **ng*** to guard, watch over. *Sapa sing arep ng* omahé Jogja?* Who's going to look after his house in Jogja? **r·um·eksa** *ltry var of* NG·REKSA. *Aku iki buta sing rumeksa alas kéné.* I am the ogre who guards this forest. *See also* BAUREKSA
rèkstok horizontal bar (used in gymnastics)
rekta wine-red; maroon
rèktor university president
rekutu:k̄ *rpr* a loud cracking sound. *Krikilé disawataké genḍèng mak* *. He threw pebbles on the tile roof with a clatter.
rèm brakes. *makakaké erèmé* to step on the brake. *tukang* * railroad brakeman. **nge/di*** to brake to a stop. *Pité di*.* He braked his bicycle. **nge/di*aké** to apply [brakes]. **é die*aké.* He put on the brakes. * **tromol** hand brake on an English-style gear bicycle
rem ***-*** with eyes closed but not asleep. ***-* ajam** dozing. **me*** **1** [of eyes] closed. *Mripaté merem.* He had his eyes closed. *Matané ula kuwi ora bisa merem.* Snakes' eyes don't close. **2** with eyes closed to one's obligations. *Mripaté wis merem, ora gelem tetulung ing lijan.* He just isn't interested in helping other people. *Botjah sedina kok merem waé, ora gelem njambut-gawé.* The boy just sits around all day—he won't work. **3** to be(come) illiterate. **merem-ḍipet** with tightly closed eyes. **merem melik** *or* **merem melèk** to toss and turn, be unable to go to sleep. **me*-me*** *or* **meram-me*** **1** to keep blinking the eyes. **2** to pretend to have the eyes closed. **nge/di*aké** to close [the eyes]
rem- *see also under* R- (*Introduction, 3.1.7*)
réma hair on the head (*kr for* RAMBUT)
remâdjâ adolescent. * *putra/putri* teenage boy/girl
remak *var of* REMEK
rémati:k̄, remati:k̄ rheumatism
rembag words, talk (*kr for* REMBUG)
rémbak to demolish (*root form: kr for* ROMBAK)
rembang [of sugar cane] ready to harvest. **ng/di*** to harvest [sugar cane]. **pa·ng*an** time for harvesting sugar cane
rembat shoulder pole (*kr for* PIKUL)
rèmbèl [of debts] multitudinous. *Utangé* *. He's deep in debt.
remben slow, undecided, hesitant
rèmbès bloodshot and irritated. *Mripaté* *. He has conjunctivitis.
rembes (*or* **m*** *or* **ng***) to ooze, seep; *fig* to infiltrate. *Èmbèré isènana banju, delengen isih ng* apa ora.* Fill the pail with water and see if it still leaks. *Banjuné kulahé m* nang kamar sanḍingé.* Water seeps from the bathroom into the next room. *Grombolané ng* nang kuṭa.* The rebels have infiltrated the city. * **ing madu** descended from aristocrats
rèmbèt **m*** to spread. *Geniné m* nang omahé tanggané.* The fire spread to the neighboring house. **ng/di*i** to spread to. *Geniné ng*i geḍèg.* The fire spread to the bamboo wall.
rembet *var of* REMENG. **re*an** old clothes, rags, scraps
rémbjak ***-*** *or* **ng*** [of long hair] hanging down. *Ḍèwèké kuwi saiki tiru² Beatle²an, rambuté diingu ng* tekan punḍak.* He's

trying to look like the Beatles, growing his hair down to his shoulders.

rembug *ng,* **rembag** *kr* 1 words, talk; topic of discussion. *A krungu *é B.* A heard what B said. *awèh ** to give advice. *Bab korupsi dadi * ing D.P.R.* The matter of corruption came up for discussion in Parliament. ** perkara dagangan* a business discussion. *matengaké ** to bring about agreement by discussion. 2 *ng kr* powder puff. ***an** 1 topic of discussion. *Jagéné kok dadi *an bab iki karo njaiku?* Why are you discussing this with my wife? 2 (*or* **re*an**) to engage in discussion. **ng*** *ng kr* to powder one's face. **ng/di*(i)** to talk about. *Tjoba kowé *ana karo B ja.* Why don't you talk it over with B? **ng/di*i** to advise smn. **pa·ng*an** *ng kr* powder puff. **pi*(an)** talk, discussion. *pirembug wigati* a crucial talk. **sa*** in agreement. *Kabèh wis sa* arep mangkat ésuk²*. Everyone agreed to leave early in the morning.

rembujuk *var of* REMPUJUK

rembujut ***an** *or* **ng*** producing large quantities of fruit. *Pelemé ng*.* The mango tree is loaded with fruit.

rembulan **(tjândrâ** *ki?*) moon (*formal var of* (M)BULAN). **é nembé separo.* The moon is in the first phase. ** purnama* full moon

remed **ka*** to get wrung/squeezed. **ng/di*** *or* **ng/di*-*** *or* **ng/di*i** to twist, squeeze, crumple. *Lajangé di*.* She crumpled up the letter. *ng* tangan* to wring the hands

rèmèh insignificant, of little worth, trivial. *Kuwi mung * waé.* It doesn't matter. *Soal sing kanggo aku angèl, kanggo A ming dianggep *.* The problem that was hard for me was nothing for A to solve. **ng/di*aké** to treat with contempt, look down on, consider of no importance

remek̄ broken into pieces. *Tjendélané *.* The window is smashed. *Rasané bojokku kaja *-*a.* My back feels as if it were broken to pieces. ***an** smashed fragments. **ng/di*** to smash sth

remen 1 to take pleasure in (*kr for* DEMEN). 2 pleased; to like (*kr for* SENENG). ***an** to be lovers. ***-*** to enjoy oneself (*ki for* SENENG²)

remeng ***-*** dim, vague, obscure. *Padanging rembulan *-*.* The light of the moon was hazy. *Katrangané *-*.* His explanation was vague. *Pupuré *-* wangi.* The powder gave off an elusive fragrance.

remit 1 intricate, delicate, detailed. *Tatahané wajang ng* banget.* The puppet was intricately chiseled. 2 secret, occult, esoteric. **ng*** *sms* * 1

rémong *var of* RIMONG

rempah 1 fried ground beef (rice-accompanying dish). 2 (*or* *-*: *rg*) spices, seasonings. * **tahu** beancake fried with beef

rempajak ***an** *or* **ng*** luxuriant, flourishing, covered with (large) foliage

rempèjèk fried peanuts covered with spiced rice flour

rempek̄ *var of* RAMPAK

rempela gizzard

rempelas 1 a certain tree having rough-textured leaves. 2 sandpaper. **ng/di*** to sandpaper sth

rempelu pancreas. **ng*** to daydream. **ora duwé *** senseless, inane

rempijeg **rempijag-*** (to walk) slowly and painfully, as when convalescent. **ng*** aching in muscles and joints

rempit hidden, undercover. *pakumpulan ** a secret society

rémpjo *var of* ROMPJO

rempojok ***an** *or* **ng*** producing (large) foliage in great abundance

rempu ***-*** to ache all over; to be at the end of one's strength

rempujuk ***an** *or* **ng*** luxuriant with foliage

remu ***-*** beginning to ripen

remudjung a certain plant whose leaves are used for treating kidney disease

remuk broken to pieces. ***an** broken pieces. **an gelas* broken glass. **ng/di*** to crush, destroy, break to pieces

remus **ng/di*** to eat sth crunchy. *ng* sriping kentang* crunching on potato chips

réna *oj* mother

rena 1 (*or* **w***) a certain small centipede. 2 pleased, happy (*kr for* BUNGAH, SENENG). 3 *inf var of* WARNA. **ka*n** glad, delighted. **ng/di*ni** to please, give joy to. **pi*** joy

rénda lace edging, crocheting. **ng/di*** to crochet, make lace

rendah low; humble. ** bebudèné* of low character. *Madjelis ** the Lower House (of Parliament)

rèndèl abundant and undesired. *Utangé *.* He's deep in debt. *Anaké *.* They have a lot of children!

rendem **ng/di*** to immerse, soak

rèndèng leaves of the peanut plant (used as animal fodder)

renḍeng rainy season. *panèn* ***an** to harvest [a crop] planted during the rainy season

rèṇḍèt **ke*** to get scratched *or* picked. **ng*** to feel scratchy/prickly. *Sikilé ana eriné, ng*²*. His foot had thorns in it and they pricked.

renḍet slow; behind. *Jèn njambut gawé * banget.* He's a slow worker. *Djamku * nganti sepuluh menit.* My watch is ten minutes slow. **ng/di*aké** to cause to be slow *or* behind. *Djamé di*ké sepuluh menit.* He set the clock back ten minutes.

réné *ng,* **riki** *kr* 1 to this place (*Degree I: Introduction, 6*). *Rénéa.* Come here! 2 (*ng*) *inf var of* DJARÉ(NÉ). **rana-*** (**rika-riki** *kr*) (to go) this way and that, all over the place. **ng/di*kaké** to bring here. *Sapa sing ngrènèkaké lajangmu?* Who delivered your letter? *See also* MRÉNÉ

renes [of a wage] sufficiently profitable. *Njambut gawé dadi djongos rèstoran kuwi *.* You can get along all right working as a waiter in a restaurant.

rèng lath used for roof construction. *paku ** roofing nail

reng *rpr* the sound of an engine racing. *Montoré distarter * * *.* He warmed up the engine.

rengat (*or* **re*an**) a break, a crack. *** ing ati** hurt feelings

rengeng ***-*** a soft singing *or* humming voice. **ng/di*-*aké** *or* **ng/di*-*i** to sing to smn softly

renget clothes moth

rengga ***n** person looked after. *Ḍèwèké *nku.* He's my responsibility. **re*n** decorations. **ng/di*(ni)** *or* **ng/di*-*** to decorate. *Omahé di*-* apik.* The house was beautifully decorated. **r·in·engga** decorated; fancy. *Bukuné rinengga ing gambaran potrèt.* The book is illustrated with photographs. *basa rinengga* fancy language: stereotyped literary expressions as speech embellishment

renggang apart, separated. *Kekantjané saiki rada *.* Their friendship is strained. *Wesi lan kajuné rak bisa trep, prasasat ora * sarambut.* The iron and wood fit together perfectly, there's not a hair's-breadth of space between them. *** gula k·um·epjur pulut** [of a friendship] intimate, close. **ng/di*aké** to pull sth apart; to cause sth to be(come) separated. **ng*i** to withdraw from the intimacy of a friendship

renggijek̄ **ng*** heavy, burdensome

rengginang a fried sweet cookie of glutinous rice

renggos ***-*** *or* **(re)*an** [of breath] coming in snorts. *Ambegané djaran anḍong mau *-*.* The carriage horse was panting heavily. *See also* KRENGGOS

renggunuk *var of* REGUNUK

rengka 1 a crack, split, schism. **ning negara* a division in national opinion. *Saka panasé lemahé paḍa *.* The heat was so intense the soil cracked. 2 to split. *Kasantosaning kulawarga wiwit *.* The family solidarity began to weaken. **ng/di*kaké** to cause sth to split. *Getering bom mau ng*kaké omah.* The vibrations from the bomb cracked the house apart. **ng/di*(i)** to split *or* crack sth. *Linḍu mau ng* gunung.* The earthquake split the mountain. *Partai² bisa ng* negara.* Political parties can divide a nation.

rengkah *var of* REKAH

rengkang (*or* **w***) obstinate, self-willed, headstrong

rengked closely spaced. **ke*en** excessively closely spaced. **ng/di*aké** *or* **ng/di*i** to space closely. *Olèhé nandur téla di*aké.* He planted the cassavas close together.

rengkeng (*or* **w***) *var of* RENGKANG. **(ka)*-*** (to get up) with difficulty, *e.g.* because of a debilitating illness; because of sore muscles

rengkèt ***-*** squeaking *or* creaking sounds, *e.g.* of bed springs

rengkik ***-*** thin, slim. *ḍuwur lan kuru *-** tall and very thin

réngkod **réngkad-*** to squeak, creak. *Sing réngkad-* mau swarané wong mikul pengaron.* That creaking sound was a man carrying a clay pot on a shoulder pole.

réngkok **réngkak-*** zigzagging, twisting and turning

réngkol ***-*** full of twistings and turnings

réngkong *var of* KÉNGKOK

rengkuh **ng/di*** 1 to regard, to think of [as]. *ng* kajadéné putrané ḍéwé* to think of smn as one's own daughter. 2 to rule, own, dominate. **pa·ng*** act of performing the above actions. **r·um·engkuh** to be dominated by *or* under the sway of

rengu angry, sullen, resentful

renjah 1 crisp, crunchy. 2 [of voice] soft, sweet, clear

renjep ***-*** *describing the atmosphere of soft music played in darkness or lowered light*

rentah to fall (down, off, apart) (*kr for* RUN-TUH)

rènte *var of* RÈNTEN

rènten interest on money loaned. **ng/di∗aké** to lend money at interest

rèntèng (*or* ∗**an** *or* ∗-∗ *or* **réntang-∗** *or* **re∗an**) strung together, forming a line *or* row. *Wong² paḍa mlaku ∗-∗.* The people walked abreast. *merdjan sing wis ∗an* strung beads. *tong wesi ∗an* metal drums placed side by side. **ng/di∗i** to string together, form into a line. *Ḍèkè ng∗i iwak sing arep didol nang pasar.* He strung together the fish he was going to sell at the market.

renteng *see* RUWED

rèntenir moneylender, loan shark

rèntèp (*or* ∗-∗) lined up close together

rèntèt *var of* RÈNTÈNG

rentet closely spaced

rentjak *cr* **ng/di∗** to split, divide up [*e.g.* loot]

rentjânâ temptation. **ng/di∗kaké** to plan sth. *Pak lurah ng∗kaké gawé bendungan.* The village head made plans for the construction of a dam. **pe∗** planner, planning agent. *Biro Perentjana Geḍung²* Bureau for Planning the Construction of Buildings. *See also* GOḌA

rèntjang 1 friend, companion (*ng; sbst kr for* KANTJA?). 2 (domestic) helper; to help (*kr for* RÉWANG). 3 servant (*kr for* BATUR, BOTJAH). 4 placenta (*kr for* ARI²). ∗ **laré** to give birth (*sbst kr for* BAJI·Ṅ)

rèntjèk twig. ∗**an** twigs for kindling a fire. **ng/di∗i** to snap off twigs from branches

renuk **renak-∗** to discuss in low voices

rep *shf of* SUREP

repa *see* REREPA

repet ∗-∗ the time just before sunrise. ∗-∗ *mau aku wis nunggang sepur.* By dawn I was already on the train.

repetir to repeat. *beḍil* ∗ repeating revolver *or* rifle

repetisi a review; a quiz on review material. *djénéral* ∗ rehearsal of a performance

repi (**re**)∗**ṅ** a serenade; to serenade. **ng/di·(re)∗** to serenade. **ng/di·(re)∗kaké** 1 to serenade smn. 2 to engage singers for a special occasion

repih **ng/di·(re)∗** to calm *or* soothe smn

repit *var of* REMPIT

repolper revolver

répolusi revolution

répolusionèr revolutionary

répormir reformed. *Kristen* ∗ reformed Christianity

réporter journalist, reporter

répot busy, (hard-)pressed. *Ḍèké saiki* ∗, *anaké akèh bajaré mung siṭik.* He has problems: he has a lot of children and only a small salary. *Ibu lagi* ∗ *masak nang ḍapur.* Mother is busy cooking in the kitchen. *Adja* ∗-∗ *ta!* Don't go to a lot of trouble! **ka∗an** trouble, weighty responsibility. *ka∗ané dadi bapak* the burdens of being a father. **ng/di∗i** to be a burden on, cause trouble for. *See also* BOT RÉPOT *under* BOT

repot 1 a report. 2 (*psv* **di∗**; *or* **ng/di∗aké**) to report. *Ḍèké ng∗ké jèn benginé kemalingan.* He reported that there had been a theft during the night. **pa∗an** a report

républik republic

rer- *see also under* R- (*Introduction, 3.1.3*)

rèrèh to become calm; to rest. ∗**an** a subordinate (person *or* territory) under an authority. ∗**ané ratu** the king's subjects *or* realm. *A dadi ∗ané B.* A is B's subordinate. **ng∗** to calm down. **ng/di∗i** to calm smn. *See also* RÈH

rerem *var of* RÈRÈN

rèrèn to rest, take time out. **ng/di∗i** to take time out from; to give smn a rest/break. *Gawéané di∗i disik.* Take a little time out! *Lagi mlaku² aku di∗i Paidjo sing nunggang pit.* As I was out walking, Paidjo came along on his bike and rode alongside me.

rerep *var of* LEREP

rerepa **ng/di∗** to beg *or* plead (for)

rès 1 confinement, incarceration. 2 circumcision (*var of* GRÈS). **nge∗** to keep confined. *Kutjingé adja di∗.* Don't shut the cat away! *Kowé nge∗ aku rong djam.* You've kept me waiting [for my ride home] for two hours!

res (*or* ∗-∗) dirt, grit. **nge∗** gritty to the touch; grating to the ear. *Médjané kok nge∗.* The table is all sandy. *swara nge∗* a heart-rending sound. *nge∗ linu* aches and pains. **nge∗-∗i** causing anguish. *Swara sesambat iku tansah ngeres-eresi ati.* His cries tore my heart.

resa *inf var of* REKSA

resados *rg kr for* RESAJA

resah unruly; untidy (*kr for* RUSUH). **pa-ng∗** *ng kr* complaint. *pang∗é kaum buruh* the workingman's grievance

resájâ ∗**n** a request for help. **ng/di∗** to ask smn for help. **pa·ng∗** a request for help

resban(g) bench for sitting (park-bench style piece of furniture)

résènsi, resènsi critical review (of a book, film, *etc.*)

resèp 1 recipe. 2 medical prescription

resep **ng*aké** *or* **ng*i** pleasing, *esp.* to the eye. *sawangan kang ng*aké* a lovely view. *Djenengmu tjekak nanging ng*aké.* Your name is short but pleasing. *Omahé ng*i mata.* The house looks very attractive. *Wiragané pantjèn ng*aké.* Her actions are appealing/provocative. **r·um·esep** to enter, seep in. *Kedadéjan mau rumesep ing atiné.* She took the occurrence to heart.

résèpsi, resèpsi reception; formal party. * *mantèn* wedding party. * *tamu agung* a formal party for state guests

resèrse *var of* RESÈRSIR

resèrsi(r) police detective. * *ahli tapak dridji* fingerprint expert

resi 1 hermit, ascetic holy man. 2 receipt

résiḍèn governor, resident administrator. **ka*an** residency, territory under the authority of the above administrator

resija secret principle *or* knowledge. *Jèn kowé ngerti *né ja gampang waé anggoné mbukak lemari wesi kuwi.* It's easy to open the iron box if you know the secret.

resik 1 clean, cleaned; pure, without fault *or* flaw. *Pekarangané disaponi karebèn *.* She swept the yard clean. *Sega sapiring kok bisa *.* He cleaned up the whole plate of rice. *banju ombèn sing ** pure drinking water. *Bukti² ngandakaké jèn ḍèké * ora salah apa².* The witnesses testified that he was guiltless. 2 clear, net. *Nalika ngedol montor aku tampa Rp 500.000 *.* I cleared half a million rupiahs when I sold my car. ***an** clean, fastidious (by nature). **ng/di*aké** *or* **ng/di*i** to clean sth (up, out). *ngresiki iwak* to clean a fish. *Uleré di*i.* They cleaned out the caterpillars. *Ḍèké ngombé urus² arep ng*ké wetengé.* He took a laxative to clean out his insides. *Karepé ng*aké agama Islam saka tatatjara Hinḍu.* Their purpose was to purify Islam of Hindu influences.

resisir *var of* RESÈRSIR

resit *var of* RISET

resiwârâ revered holy man

resmi 1 *oj* beauty. 2 official, formal. *diskusi ora ** an informal discussion. *katerangan kang ** official information. *klambi ** formal dress. *njanḍang ** to dress formally, dress for a special occasion. 3 (*or* **re*ǹ**) to have sexual intercourse (*ng? ki for* TJUMBANA?). **ng/di*k̀aké** to conduct formalities in some connection. *Rumah sakit anjar diresmèkaké gupernur.* The governor formally dedicated the new hospital. **ng/di*ǹi** to have intercourse with. **sa*** to have sexual intercourse

résolusi resolution, formal statement. **ng/di*** to try to oust smn by submitting a resolution against him. *Kepala sekolahé di*.* A formal statement was brought against the school superintendent in an effort to oust him.

Respati *oj* Thursday

resres(poh) small worm

rèstan remainders, remnants. * *panganan* leftovers; remains of food

rèstitusi reimbursement to a government employee for travel expenses, medical expenditures, *etc.*

rèstoran restaurant

resu receipt

resula waterpalm tree. **ng*** to complain, object. *Buruh² pabrik paḍa ng* djalaran opahé ora njukupi kanggo urip.* The factory workers complained that their wages were not enough to live on. **ng/di*ni** to complain about. *ng*ni gawéjané* to complain about one's job

resun *oj* 1 I, me. 2 you

rèt diamonds (playing-card suit)

ret *rpr* a zipping *or* tearing sound

réta *inf var of* KRÉTA

retja statue. * **gupala** a statue that guards a gate *or* entrance

retjâpâdâ *ltry* the earth (as contrasted with KA·HYANG·AN, the realm of the deities)

rètjèh 1 coins of small denomination. *ḍuwit ** small change. 2 talkative. 3 wet. 4 [of batik] crudely worked

retna diamond, precious gem. * *mustika* a large jewel. *Sang ** (*name applied to a beautiful girl*)

rètnong a certain locust that makes a loud buzz (*contracted from* TJENGGÈRÈTNONG)

retu chaos, turmoil, rebellion. *dahuru ** uprising, rebellion, war

retul **ng/di*** to replace smn. *Ḍémonstrasi mau nuntut supaja sawenèhing pendjabat di*.* The demonstrators demanded that certain of the officials be replaced.

révolusi revolution

révolusionèr revolutionary

réwândâ *oj* monkey

réwang *ng,* **réntjang** *kr* 1 (**abdi** *ki*) servant, (domestic) helper. 2 companion. 3 (*or* *-*; **abdi** *ki*) to help smn; to help with sth. ***-*an** to help each other. **re*** *sms* * 3. *A ora gelem re* nggarap sawah.* A is not willing to help in the rice paddies. **ng/di*i** 1 to help smn; to help with sth. *Réwangana!* Help him! *Ḍèké ng*i njambutgawé bodjoné ana ing omah.* He helps his wife around the house. 2 to exert oneself. *Wis di*i adus kringet anggoné gliḍig.* He works himself to the bone. *Wis tak *i majeng² nganti seminggu meksa ora ketemu.* I've looked everywhere for a whole week but I still can't find it. 3 to join in prayers for smn's good fortune

rèwed **ng/di*i** to bother, disturb

rèwèl fussy, hard to handle. *Kowé kok * banget.* You're hard to get along with!

rèwèng **ng/di·(re)*** *or* **ng/di·réwang-*** to carry sth around, carry sth back and forth

rèwès regard [for], attention [to]. *Geḍé *é marang sisihané.* He's very considerate of his wife. **ng/di*** to heed, give one's attention to. *Jèn ng* ṭèṭèk-bengèk ngono, mangsa rampunga garapanmu.* If your attention is diverted by every little thing, how are you going to get your work finished?

réwo *-* [of hair] untidy, messy

réwok *-* *or* **ng*** hairy, shaggy. *asu sing nganggo rambut *-** a shaggy dog

ri 1 thorn. *ketjotjog eri* pricked by a thorn. *antjik² ing putjuking ** in constant danger. *Dridjinipun mutjuk *.* Her fingers taper elegantly. *nglantjipi eri* to incite an already angry person. 2 backbone of a fish. 3 counting unit for fish. ***ǹ-*ǹan** thorny; a thorny place. **nge*** 1 threatening, inflammatory. 2 resembling a fishbone. **pa·nge*ǹ** thorny place

riba loan shark. *mangan ** to practice usury

ribed 1 (*kr for* RIBUT?) busy, pressed. 2 in a difficult situation, having one's troubles. 3 (*kr for* RUBED?) disturbance, obstacle. **re*** *sms* * 1. **ng/di*i** to disturb, hamper. *Adja ng*i wong njambut gawé.* Don't get in the way of people who are working.

ribit *see* KUMRIBIT

ribut (**ribed** *kr?*) 1 busy, rushed; creating fuss *or* confusion. *Adja *-*, aku arep turu.* Quiet! I'm trying to sleep. *Ah mbok boten sisah *-*.* Oh, please don't go to all that trouble. 2 angry. *Ḍèké saja *.* He got more and more worked up. **re*** trouble, bother. *Re* mau wis dibabad.* The trouble is cleared up now. **ng/di*i** to disturb smn at work. *See also* KUMRIBUT

ridjal noises heard in the night. *Suwara mau diarani * djatingarang.* That noise is said to be the voice of the wind dragon. *** lullah** *see* NAGA

ridjig neatly arranged, well laid out

riḍu **re*** trouble, disturbance, annoyance. **ng(re)*** troublesome, worrisome

rigal *var of* RIGOL

rigèl *var of* RIGOL

rigèn low round woven-bamboo basket

rigen careful and foresighted in handling one's assets. **ng/di*aké** to advise smn about the prudent disposition of [assets]. *Ḍuwité di*aké dititipaké nang bank.* He advised her to put the money in the bank.

rigi:s *emphatic form of* RÈGÈS

rigol *rg* to fall (down, off)

rih ***-*an** to calm/comfort each other. **nge/di*-*** 1 to calm [an angry person]; to comfort [a sad person]. 2 to persuade, coax. *See also* ARIH

rihadi *var of* RIJADI

rija *a title conferred by the Sultan*

rijadi *kr for* RIJAJA

rijah *-* [of colors] light, pastel

rijâjâ *ng,* **rijadi** *kr* communal feast to celebrate the major Moslem holiday (*Lebaran*) held at the end of the fasting month (*Pasa*). *dina ** the above holiday

rijak *ng kr,* **djlâgrâ** *ki* phlegm in the throat. **ng/di*i** to rid oneself of phlegm

rijek̄ **ng/di*(-*)** to wring, crumple. *** mentek djoto kemil** *words repeated over and over in sequence while counting days ahead —one word per day—to ascertain whether a certain future day bodes good or bad* (*if the day falls on* RIJEK *or* MENTEK *the day is propitious, otherwise unpropitious*)

rijel *intsfr* crowded. *djedjel ** jam-packed

rijep *-* *intsfr* green. *Goḍongé ngrembujung idjo *-*.* The abundant leaves were a fresh, clear green.

rijin *var of* RUMIJIN. 1 formerly (*md for* BIJÈN). 2 first, ahead (*kr?; md for* ḌISIK)

rijo *-* *intsfr* green. *idjo *-** pure clear green

ri:k 1 *rpr* a rasping sound. *Salahku tak tjorèk nganggo potelot mak *.* I crossed out my mistakes with a pencil. *eriking djangkrik* crickets' chirping. 2 [of throat] sore, irritated. **nge*** to produce rasping sounds. *Djangkriké nge**. The cricket chirped.

rika (*Degree III: Introduction, 6*) **1** to that place (*kr for* RANA). 2 (over) there (*md for* KANA). 3 you. **ng*** there (*kr for* KANA)

rikâlâ (at a past time) when (*var of* NALIKA)

rikat fast. * *lakuné.* He walked quickly. * *gèk mangkat mengko telat lho.* Quick, let's go, or we'll be late. **é presasat angin.* It goes like the wind. ***an** in a hurry. ***-*** to pack up [one's merchandise, when through selling for the day]. **re*an** in haste. *Re*an lunga.* He left in a big hurry. **ng/di*aké** to accelerate. *Lakuné di*aké.* He quickened his pace. **ng/di*i** to pack up [merchandise]. **sa*-*é** 1 as fast as possible. 2 no matter how fast. *Sa*-*é plajuné kidang meksa * plajuné matjan.* However fast the deer ran, the tiger ran faster yet.

riki (*Degree I: Introduction, 6*) 1 to this place (*kr for* RÉNÉ). 2 here (*md for* KÉNÉ). **ng*** 1 here (*kr for* KÉNÉ). 2 I; we (*kr for* KÉNÉ)

rikma hair (*ki for* RAMBUT)

riku (*Degree II: Introduction, 6*) 1 to that place (*kr for* RONO). 2 there (*md for* KONO). 3 you. **ng*** there (*kr for* KONO)

rikuh *ng* (*ng kr?*), **rekah** *kr* ill at ease, awkward. *Sampun menggalih rekah.* Make yourself at home! *Wé la rada * aku, marga wis entèk.* I was ashamed–I had eaten them all up. **rikah-*** *ng* to feel intensely uncomfortable. **ng/di*i** to make smn uncomfortable. *Adja sok ng*i kantja²mu anggonmu tjaturan.* Don't talk about things that will embarrass the people around you.

ril rail; railroad track

rila wholeheartedly willing *or* in agreement. *Kowé wis * tenan jèn pitmu tak pèk?* Are you sure you're willing to let me take your bike? **ka*n** wholehearted consent/willingness/agreement. *Aku njuwun ka*nmu supaja gelem ngeteraké.* Please consent to take him with you. **ng/di*kaké** (to give, give up) willingly *or* with all one's heart. *Panahé bandjur di*kaké diwènèhaké marang kantjané.* He willingly gave the arrow to his friend. *** legawa** wholeheartedly willing. *Jèn kowé isih gelem bali mréné ja dak tampa kanṭi *-legawa.* If you want to come back here, I will welcome you with all my heart.

rim 1 ream (500 sheets) of paper. 2 leather belt. **3** *var of* RÈM

rimah house (*old kr for* RUMAH)

rimat to care for (*root form: kr for* RUMAT)

rimba *oj* forest

rimbag *gram* inflection by affixation. ***an** 1 an affix. 2 (*or* **re*an**) process of affixation; (having been) affixed. *tembung² *an tanggap* words with passive affixes. **ng/di*** to affix [a word]. *tjarané enggoné ng* seselan um* how to insert the *um* infix

rimi:s (*udan*) ***-*** to rain lightly, drizzle

rimong long dotted scarf used as a sash

rimpung *see* SAMBANG

rimuk **ng/di*** to persuade, talk smn into. **(*) pa·ng*** persuasion

rin- *see also under* R- (*Introduction, 3.1.7*)

rina *ng,* **rinten** *kr* **1** day (as contrasted with night: *see also* DINA). *Jèn wuta, * utawa wengi ora ana bédané.* If you're blind, there's no difference between day and night. *lintang ** morning star. 2 *var of* RÉNA. **k(e)*n** (excessively) late in the morning; to sleep too late. *Tangiku rada kerinan.* I got up pretty late. **ng*kaké** [the night] preceding sth. *ing wengi ngrinakaké dina pengantèn* on the eve of the wedding. *** wengi** all the time. *Di-impi² * wengi.* He dreams of it night and day. *See also* GAGAT, RAINA

rinḍik 1 slow. 2 [of sound] soft, low. **ng/di*aké 1** to cause to be slow. *Ḍèké ng*aké montoré.* He slowed down the car. 2 to make less loud. *Olèhé njetèl raḍio di*aké.* Turn the radio down. *** asu/kirik di·gitik** quickly, instantly. * *asu digitik enggoné nampani ali².* Quick as a wink he seized the ring. *Jèn didjak nonton prasasat * asu digitik.* When we asked him to come to the show with us, he jumped at the chance.

rinḍil to come pouring out. *Pitakoné *.* He asked one question after another. *Anaké *.* They keep having children.

rinding (*or* ***an**) Jew's-harp. **ng*** to play a Jew's-harp

rindjing large bamboo basket

ringa to judge, weigh

ringan *rg* light in weight

ringen gymnastic rings

ringgit 1 shadow play; shadow-play puppet (*kr for* WAJANG[a]). 2 two and a half rupiahs in coins *or* paper money. **p(a)*an** *ng kr* section of a traditional-style house (between the front veranda [*penḍapa*] and the main family section) where shadow plays are performed for guests

ringih *-* having many sharp points. *Iwak hiu kuwi untuné *-* kaja gradji.* Sharks' teeth are sharp as a saw.

ringik *-* *or* **ng*** to cry in a whining, self-pitying way. *See also* KRINGIK

ringin (*or* **w***) banyan tree. *** kurung** sacred fenced-in banyan trees in front and back of palaces (*see also* DÉWANDARA, DJANADARU)

ringkel time of evil portent reckoned astrologically by the days of the six-day week. ** djalma* (*sato, widji, lsp.*) a day of evil portent for human beings (animals, seeds, *etc.*). **ng*** [to lie, sleep] curled up. **ng/di*(-*)** to roll sth up, *esp.* of dampened clothes to be ironed. **pa*an** astrological system of reckoning by days of the six-day week

ringkes concise, compact. *Tèks pariwara kudu * lan tjeṭa.* The text of an announcement should be brief and clear. ***an** shortened form. *pangétungé *an* a quick way to do the calculation. **ané tjrita* an abridged version of a story. **é* in short; to put it briefly. *-* to make concise/compact. **-* sanḍanganė* to pack up one's clothes. **re*an** *sms* *AN. *re*aning paramasastra Djawa* a concise grammar of Javanese. **ng/di*(i) 1** to make concise/compact. *Tjritaku arep tak * baé.* I'll make my story brief. *Sanḍanganku dak *i.* I packed up my clothes. 2 to murder smn secretly. 3 *slang* to sell. *Montoré arep di*.* He's going to unload his car. 4 *slang* to make a fool *or* laughing-stock of

ringkih weak, lacking strength (firmness, stamina, *etc.*). *sawidjining wong wadon kang * awaké* a woman without much physical strength. *Pit gawéan Surabaja kuwi *.* Bicycles manufactured in Surabaja don't hold up well. **ng/di*aké** to make weak. *ng*aké ékonomi nasional* to weaken the national economy

ringkuk **ng*** bent over. *Olèhé turu ng* nang tjakruk.* He slept slumped in the hut. **ng/di*aké** to bend sth

rintang ***an** blockade, barrier. **ng/di*i** to block off, barricade

rinten day (as contrasted with night) (*kr for* RINA)

rintih *-* *or* **ng(re)*** to moan, groan, weep in pain

ri:nti:k ***-* 1** by infrequent drops. *Udan *-* waé.* It's only drizzling. 2 in neat even rows. *Untuné *-* midji timun.* She has small, uniform-sized teeth ('like cucumber seeds').

rintip (*or* *-*) lined up, in a row

rintis ***an** pioneering action. **ng/di*** to pioneer. *R. A. Kartini ng* kemadjuwané para wanita Indonesia.* Kartini led the way in the emancipation of Indonesian women. **pe*** a pioneer

ripah *see* GEMAH

ripak *kr for* RUPAK?

ripik (*or* *-*) to fetch sticks and twigs, *esp.* for kindling. *kaju* ***an** kindling wood

ripta **ng/di*** to write. *Sapa sing ng* buku iki?* Who is the author of this book? **pa·ng*** author

ripu *see* DJAGA

ririh 1 to calm down, control one's anger. 2 *oj* [of sounds] soft, low

ris rope used as a boundary marker (*see also* ARIS). ***-*an** foundation for a fence *or* boundary marker. **nge/di*i** to mark a boundary line with string. **anjar *** brand new

risak damaged, out of order (*kr for* RUSAK)

risalat letter, document

risang *oj honorific title for an exalted personage*

risḍèn *var of* RÉSIḌÈN

riset (to do) research

risi repelled, uncomfortable, irritated. *rasa ** a repelled *or* irritated feeling. ***ǹ** easily repelled, oversensitive. **ng*ǹi** causing the above feeling; (*psv* **di*ǹi**) to irritate, repel

risiḍèn *var of* RÉSIḌÈN

risig *var of* RIDJIG

risih *var of* RISI

risiko a risk. *Adja nglangi nang kali mau, akèh *né.* Don't swim in that river–it's too risky.

risoles egg roll

risuh **ng/di*i** to trouble, pester, plague. *Kekuwatan militèr mau dienggo ng*i sèlèh-dokoké mungsuh.* The military force was used to harass enemy positions.

rit trip, *i.e.* covering of a distance. *Jèn ngangkaté barang nganggo truk sa* ongkosé Rp 1500.* It costs 1500 rupiahs per trip to haul goods by truck. **nge/di*aké** to cut grass for smn with a sickle. **nge/di*(i)** to cut grass with a sickle. *See also* ARIT

ritslèteng zipper

ritul *var of* RETUL

riwajat personal history, story of smn's life

riwé sweat (*kr for* KRINGET). ***ǹen** to sweat

riwed ***an** pest, nuisance. **ng/di*i** to be a bother to. *Adja ng*i anggoné masak.* Don't hinder the people who are cooking.

riweg *var of* RIWED

riwi **riwa-*** *var of* WIRA-WIRI (*see under* WIRI)

riwil *var of* RÈWÈL

riwi:s a droplet. ***-*** [of rain] light, drizzling

riwit a small green chili pepper

riwug ***-*** [of hair] abundant, luxuriant. *kéwan sing rambuté *-** a thick-haired animal. **ng/di*i** to disturb, interfere with

riwus *oj* ***é** *or* ***ning** *or* ***nja** after

riwut *var of* RIBUT

R.K. *see* RUKUN

R.M. *see* RAḌÈN

ro *ng* two (*shf of* LORO). *dji, *, lu* 1, 2, 3. **di*ni** to be attacked by two attackers. ***las** 12. ***likur** 22

rob to rise [of water level, *e.g.* during a flood; when the tide comes in]. *Segarané *.* The tide is in (high). *Bandjiré *.* The flood waters rose. **ka*an** to get flooded. **nge/di*i** to inundate sth, *e.g.* a rice paddy

roba(h) (**rébah** *kr?*) ***an** a change, a difference. **ng/di*** to change, alter. **pa*an** *sms* *AN. *See also* PANTJAROBA

robâjâ *oj* I, me; my

robbi(l) *see* ALLAH

robjong decorative hanging object. *lampu ** decorative chandelier. **ng/di*(-*)** to decorate with hanging objects

rod *oj* to ebb, recede

roda **ng/di*-(pari)peksa** to force; to rape. **pa·ng*(-peksa)** a means of forcing smn

roḍa wheel. **a*** having wheels. *kréta a* loro* a two-wheeled cart

rodjiun *see* INALILAHI

rodjong **ng/di*(i)** to agree with, side with, take the part of. **pa·ng*** urge, stimulus. *pang* sing ora betjik* a bad impulse

rodra *oj* fierce, wild

rog ***-*an** shivering, shaking. **nge/di*-*** to shake sth. *ngerog-erog wit pelem supaja sing mentah paḍa gogrog* to shake a mango tree so the ripe fruits will fall

rogoh ***-*** to keep putting the hand into sth. **ng/di*** to reach for sth. *Sudagar bandjur ng* pistulé.* The merchant reached in his pocket for his pistol. *See also* PROGOH

rogol *var of* RIGOL

Rogung Djiwan *wj* *nickname for clown Pétruk: shf of* LORO KETANGGUNG SIDJI KEDAWAN ('two is too short, one is too long')

roh soul, spirit. ** Sutji* Holy Spirit, the Holy Ghost (in Christianity)

rohani spiritual; of the mind *or* soul. *djasmani lan ** physical and mental. **ka*an** matters pertaining to the spirit. *Penḍak dina Djum'at murid² diwulang kerohanian.* Every Friday the pupils are instructed in spiritual matters.

rohmat *var of* RAHMAT

rojal 1 generous, extravagant. 2 *slang* sexually promiscuous. ***-*an** wasteful, extravagant; to indulge one's tastes frequently. *Sanadjan pametuné akèh, ora dianggo *-*an.* His income is ample but he doesn't spend it on foolish things. **-*an wédok* to chase after girls all the time. *mangan (nginum, main) *-*an* to eat (drink, gamble) to excess

rojo ***-*** *intsfr* green. *Pariné wis idjo *-*.* The rice plants are rich green now.

rojok **(re)*an** to [do] as a group (*referring esp. to working, fighting*). *See also* KROJOK

rojom *var of* ROJONG *in the phrase* GOTONG-ROJONG

rojong *see* GOTONG

rok ladies' Occidental-style dress. ***-*an** 1 to wear an Occidental-style dress *or* skirt. 2 tag; hide-and-seek (children's games)

rokèt rocket

rokok (**ses** *opt? kr*) cigarette. **(re)*an** to have a casual smoke. **ng*** 1 to smoke a cigarette. 2 to be a cigarette addict. 3 (*psv* **di***) to smoke sth. *ng* pipa/srutu* to smoke a pipe/cigar. **kok ng* tjenḍak!** so inquisitive! (*transferred meaning: see also* Ň·TEGES²). **ng*-ng*** to smoke just to pass the time. **ng*an** addicted to cigarette smoking. *** klembak** cigarette flavored with *klembak* root. *** krètèk** clove cigarette. *** menjan** incense-flavored cigarette. *** putih** ordinary cigarette. *** srutu** cigar. *** tjengkèh** clove cigarette

rol 1 role, function. 2 a roll(ed-up object). *filem sa** a roll of film. **nge/di*** to roll sth (up)

rolade scrambled egg rolled in slices of spiced fried beef

rolas *see* RO

rolikur *see* RO

Roma Rome. *Katolik ** Roman Catholic; Roman Catholicism

roman modern Occidental fiction, dramatized in popular theater. ***-*an** to make romantic love to each other

rombak *ng,* **rémbak** *kr* **ng/di*** to demolish

rombèng second-hand, used. *bakul* * or *tukang* * second-hand dealer. ***an** second-hand (goods); second-hand dealer. *kursi *an* used chairs. **ng/di*(aké)** to sell at second hand (for smn). *Gendul²é tilas waḍah kétjap di*aké.* She sold her empty soy-sauce bottles.

rombong large basket for holding charcoal. ***an** a group of people

rompal mutilated, damaged. *Ḍèké diantem, untuné *.* He got his teeth knocked out. ***an** damage; damaged object. **ng/di*(aké)** to mutilate/damage sth

rompi man's vest (Occidental style)

rompja *var of* ROMPJO

rompjo ***-*** fringe, *e.g.* on cowboy-style suede jackets *or* vests. **ng/di*-*** to edge sth with fringe

rompok a small hut

ron 1 not on good terms (with). 2 leaf (*opt? kr for* GOḌONG)

ronḍa the night watch. **ng/di*ni** to take the night watch smw. *ng*ni omahé tangga* to have the watch over the neighbors' houses. **pa*n** night watchman's post

ronḍé small round glutinous-rice balls, sometimes containing peanuts and/or palm kernels. *wédang* * hot ginger-flavored drink with the above in it

rong 1 *ng* two (*as modifier: see also* LORO, NG- *prefix* 6, 7). ** puluh* 20. ** atus* (*èwu, juta*) two hundred (thousand, million). *sidji * taun* a year or two. ** dina/djam* two days/hours. ** pupuh wiwitan* the first two paragraphs. ** tjangkir* (*krandjang, lsp.*) two cupfuls (basketfuls, *etc.*). 2 hole used as a home. **-* tikus* mouse holes. **nge*** 1 to enter a hole; to live in a hole. 2 (*psv* **di***) to make a hole in sth

rongèh unstable, shaky

rongga body cavity. ** irung* nasal cavity. ** ḍaḍa* chest cavity

ronggèng female song-and-dance performer

rongkong rib cage. **re*an** skeleton

rongsok ***an** junk, second-hand goods

ronjok set with diamonds. *suweng* * diamond earrings. **ng/di*** to set [jewelry] with diamonds

rono *ng,* **riku** *kr* to that place (*Degree II: Introduction, 6*). *Adja *, kuwi nganggo mbajar.* Don't go there–you have to pay to get in. **ng/di*kaké** to move to(ward) that place. *ngronokaké médja* to put a table there. *See also* MRONO

rontèk a small banner affixed to a spear just below the point

rontjé ***ǹ(-*ǹ)** a string (of beads, flowers). **ng/di*(ǹi)** to string. *ngrontjèni kembang* to string flowers

rontog [of growing things] to fall, drop off. *Goḍong²é wit²é wis paḍa *.* The leaves have fallen from the trees. *mangsa* * or *u(ng)sum* * fall, autumn. ***an** fallen. **an roti dipangani kutjing.* The cat ate the fallen cake crumbs. **ng/di*aké** to cause sth to fall. *ng*aké pjan* to knock down the ceiling. **nganti ng·rontog·aké tjinḍil** to the extreme, with all one's might. **ng/di*i** to remove [leaves, fruits]. *Pelemé nuli di*i nganti entèk.* He shook the mango tree until all the fruit had fallen. *** ati·né** depressed, despondent

ropel double(d). **ng/di*** to double [things] up. *Karo bingkilé kuwi pit telu di* didandani bareng.* The repair men are working on all three bicycles at the same time.

ropjan ***-*** extravagant luxuries

roro two (*ltry var of* LORO)

ros section between joints of sugar cane *or* bamboo. *tebu sa** one joint of sugar cane. ***an** sugar cane (*kr for* TEBU). ***-*an** joints on insect legs. *Sikilé ana *-*ané.* It has jointed legs. **nge*** up to *or* at the joint. *Keṭoken pring kuwi nge*.* Cut the bamboo at the joint. **nge*an** to plant sugar cane in [a field] (*kr for* Ǹ·TEBU). **pa*an** land planted with sugar cane (*kr for* [PA]TEBU·Ǹ)

rosa strong; exerting power. *Awaké waras lan *.* He's strong and healthy. *Mangané akèh nanging njambut-gawéné ora *.* He eats a lot but he doesn't work much. **ka*n** strength, prowess. *Wong gelut iku adu ka*n.* The wrestlers are fighting with all their might. *Ka*né ngébat-ébati.* He's amazingly strong. **ng/di*ni** to exert force on sth. *Jèn sekrupé ora bisa dibukak adja di*ni.* If the bolt won't open, don't force it. **sa*né** with all one's strength; to the limit of one's strength. *Anggoné njambut gawé ora dipeksa, mung sa*né waé.* He didn't force himself–he just worked up to his full capacity.

rosan *see under* ROS

rosok run-down, dilapidated. ***an** that which has fallen into poor condition. *wesi *an* scrap iron

roster list, roster, schedule

rota *oj* fierce. ** denawa* a fierce mythological ogre

rotan 1 rattan. 2 walking stick (*ki for* TEKEN)

rotèng 12½ cents (old monetary unit: *shf of* KARO TÈNG)

roti bread, cake (*i.e.* Occidental-style baked goods). * *satangkep* a cut hamburger roll. **pa*ǹ** bakery shop. * **kalung** round cake. * **kismis** raisin cake. * **manis** sweet bread. * **mertéga** bread-and-butter. * **m̀·plenuk** a round loaf of bread. * **ponggé** roll or cookie shaped like a durian-fruit pit. * **tawar** ordinary bread

rowa roomy, spacious, sizable

Rp. *see* RUPIAH

R.R. *see* RADÈN

R.T. *see* RUKUN

ru 1 *oj* to have hurt feelings. 2 *oj* arrow. 3 land measure: 1 sq. rod = *ca.* 14.19 sq. meters

rubed *rg* disturbance, obstacle. **ng/di*i** to hamper, disturb

rubéda obstacle, difficulty, misfortune. *nuwuhaké ** to create obstacles, raise objections

rubrik̄ column *or* section in a periodical. * *wanita* woman's page. * *kaséhatan* health column

rubuh *ng,* **rebah** *kr* fallen; to fall. *wit ** a fallen tree. *Pageré *.* The fence collapsed. ***-* gedang** to observe and imitate others (*esp.* during religious rituals) when one is not familiar with the procedures. **ka*an** to get fallen on. *Omahku ke*an wit.* A tree fell on our house. **ng/di*aké** to cause to collapse. *ng*aké pemerintah* to bring about the fall of the government. **ng/di*i** to fall on. *Wité ng*i omahku.* The tree fell on our house. *See also* M·BATA

rubung gathered, clustered (*prn* **rubu:ng**). *Wong² akèh sing * pada ndeleng.* A crowd stood around watching. ***-*** forming a crowd. *Adja *-* nèng kono!* Don't all stand around there! **ng/di*** (*prn* **-rubu:ng**) to gather around. *Wong sing liwat kono pada ng*.* Passersby collected. *Pangananė di* laler.* The food was swarming with flies.

ruda-paripeksa *oj* **ng/di*** to force, compel. *See also* PARIPEKSA, RODA

rudatin *ng,* **rudatos** *kr* sad(dened), sorrowful; worried. **pa·ng*** sadness, grief; anxiety

rudatos *kr for* RUDATIN

rudira *oj* blood

rudjag (*or* ***an**) worked in batik without use of a pattern, *i.e.* with the wax applied to the fabric freehand. **ng/di*** **1** to work [fabric] as above. *Jèn ora bisa mbatik takon, adja ng*.* If you don't know how to make batik, ask: don't just do it randomly. 2 to rape

rudjak 1 sliced fruits in a peppery sauce. 2 a sweet cold fruit drink. ***an** 1 ingredients for the above fruit dish. 2 to eat *rudjak.* **ng/di*(i)** to make [fruits] into the above. **ngrudjak wuni** to buy *or* sell as a group rather than as individual items. *Anggoné adol omah ng* wuni.* He sold his house together with everything in it. **ng/di*i** to hold a ceremony *or* make an offering for [a three-months' pregnant woman]. **r·um·udjak** [of fruits] just at the right stage (*i.e.* not quite ripe) for the above dish. * **legi** *sms* * 1. * **létok** *or* * **lotèk** fruits dipped into sweet hot sauce as they are eaten. * **sentul** in disagreement. * **tjrobo** *sms* * 1. * **wuni** gifts presented by the groom's family to the bride's family after the formal wedding ceremony is over. *See also* KUMRUDJAK

rudji 1 window bar(s). 2 wheel spoke(s)

rudjit **ng/di*(-*)** to cut, slash (*referring esp. to feelings*). *Atiné kaja di*-*.* He was deeply hurt.

rudjuk 1 to agree, consent. *Kowé apa *?* Is it all right with you? 2 to become reconciled after the first (preliminary) stage of divorce, *i.e.* within 100 days or three menstrual periods of separation. **rudjak-*** to agree wholeheartedly. **ng/di*** to remarry [one's spouse] after the preliminary divorce stage. **ng/di*i** to agree on/to. * **rukun** agreement and harmony in a personal relationship. *See also* SERUDJUK

rugi to suffer a financial loss. *Pabrik mau pirang² taun * terus.* The factory has been losing money for years. **ka*an** a loss, setback. *nempuhi karugian* to recompense smn for his loss. **ng/di*kaké** to cause smn to suffer a loss

ruh to see; to know (*shf of* WERUH). *Embuh ora *.* Never mind! Forget it! **nge/di*-*i** to greet, speak with/to in a friendly way (*var of* NG/DI·ARUH²I)

ruhârâ *var of* ARUHARA

rujung 1 wood of the sugar-palm tree, *i.e.* commonplace wood. 2 booby trap consisting of sharpened bamboo sticks concealed upright on the ground. 3 knobby club used as a weapon

rukem a certain plant that produces edible fruits

ruket to stay close to. *A saiki lagi * karo B.* A is sticking close to B these days. **ng/di*** to hang onto, hug, embrace

rukon to join forces. *A * karo B arep nge-degaké toko.* A and B are going to start a shop together.

rukti to preserve, maintain. **pa·ng*** good care, preservation, maintenance

rukuh prayer clothing worn over the head by women: all white with only the face and palms showing

rukuk to bow with the back horizontal and the hands on the knees (one of the Islamic praying positions)

rukun compatible. *Olèhé bebodjoan * banget.* They have a harmonious marriage. *gendon *** compatible. ***an** in cooperation. *Betjiké olèhé paḍa njambut-gawé, *an waé.* They'd do better if they did their work jointly. ***an buri** an illicit agreement, *esp.* a bribe. **re*an** to cooperate. **ka*an** cooperation. *Ka*an gawé kasantosan.* Cooperation makes for strength. **ng/di*aké** to restore to harmony. **ng*aké A lan B** to restore peace between A and B. **pa*an** consensus. **sa*-*é** in peace and harmony. *Wong² njambut-gawé bebarengan sa*-*é.* They worked together in a spirit of cooperation. *** désa** approved by the village. *** ga-wé** work done without pay for the benefit of the community. *** ing agama** the duty of saying Islamic prayers five times daily. *** kampung** (*abbr:* **R.K.**) social subdivision of a village. *** (te)tangga** (*abbr:* **R.T.**) neighborhood organization for mutual help. *** warga** (*abbr:* **R.W.**) neighborhood association which is a part of the city administration

rum 1 *oj* fragrant (*see also* HARUM). 2 rum. 3 Rome. *angka ** Roman numeral

rum- *see also under* R- (*Introduction, 3.1.7*)

rumah house (**grija** *kr;* **rimah** *old kr*). **pa*an** housing facilities. *** bitjara** meetinghouse, town hall. *** bolah** dance hall. *** gila** insane asylum. *** makan** restaurant. *** monjèt** sentry box. *** obat** pharmacy. *** sakit** (**grija sakit** *kr*) hospital. *** sakit djiwa** mental hospital. *** sétan** haunted house

rumângsâ *ng,* **rumaos** *kr* feeling, thought. *Apa *mu ḍèwèké * seḍih?* Do you think he feels sad? *A tetep ora * salah.* A still didn't think he had done anything wrong. ***n** sensitive; to have feelings *or* thoughts. *mBok adja gegeḍèn *n.* Don't be conceited!

Ḍèké kuwi *n banget. He's very sensitive (shy, withdrawn). **ng/di*ni** to realize; to see in true perspective. *Kok ora ng*ni jèn wis geḍé!* Don't you realize you're grown up now! *Wis ng*ni jèn anaké wong ora du-wé, mulané ja nrima waé.* Aware that he was the son of a poor man, he remained humble. *See also* RASA

rumangsuk to enter and penetrate (*var of* R·UM·ASUK). *See also* MANGSUK

rumanti *ng,* **rumantos** *kr* equipped and ready. **ng/di*kaké** *or* **ng/di*ni** to bring into readiness, to make available

rumantos *kr for* RUMANTI

rumaos feeling, thought (*kr for* RUMANGSA)

rumâsâ *var of* RUMANGSA

rumat *ng,* **rimat** *kr* ***an** 1 care. *Saka betjiking *ané bodjoné, bisa énggal mari.* His wife took such good care of him that he got well fast. 2 (that which is) kept, stored. *Barang ora mbedjadji ngono kok arep dienggo *an.* Why do you want to keep such a worthless thing—? **k(e)*** well cared for, well kept. **ng/di*(i)** to take care of. **ng/di*i** to keep stored. *See also* DJADJA

rumbu ***-*** to improve little by little. *isih* ***-*** on the road to recovery

rumbuk *var of* RUMBUT

rumbut [of shrubbery *etc.*] thick, dense

rumijin 1 (at some time) in the past (*kr for* BIJÈN). 2 first, ahead (*kr for* ḌISIK)

rumpâkâ ***n** a poetic narration. **ng/di*** to describe *or* narrate in song *or* poetry

rumpi *var of* ROMPI

rumpil 1 barely passable. *Dalané * banget, okèh watuné.* You can hardly travel on the street, it's so rocky. 2 delicate, fragile

rumpon fish trap consisting of a small diversion from a river

rumpung noseless. *Retjané irungé *.* The statue's nose is missing.

rumput grass (*kr for* SUKET)

runa *oj* obstacle, difficulty

runḍing ***an** to discuss, deliberate. **ng/di*(aké)** to discuss, negotiate. **pa*an** negotiation(s). **pa*an Potsdam** the Pottsdam talks

rundjak **ng/di*** to jump up in an effort to reach sth

runḍuk **ng/di*** to sneak up on, take off guard

rungih (*or* ***-*** *or* **ng***) pointed tapering nose (the ideal Javanese shape)

rungkad torn out by the roots. *wit ** an

uprooted tree. **ng/di*(i)** to tear out by the roots

rungkeb **k*** to assume a face-down position inadvertently. *Ḍèké kesanḍung watu tiba k*.* He tripped over a stone and fell flat on his face. **ng*** (lying) face down. *Olèhé turu ng*.* He sleeps lying on his stomach. **ng/di*i** 1 to cover sth with one's body; to embrace from above; *fig* to embrace, become converted to. *Kiperé mentjolot tiba ng*i bal.* The goalkeeper leaped and then fell on the ball. *Ḍèké ng*i anaké sing tinggal.* She embraced her dead son. *ng*i agama Islam* to become a Moslem. 2 to obey meekly, knuckle under to

rungkud (*or* ***-***) [of underbrush *etc.*] thick, dense. *Ula iku ngleker ing grumbulan sing *-*.* Snakes coil up in thick undergrowth. **re*(an)** densely thicketed area

rungkuk (*or* ***-*** *or* **ng***) [of the back] bent, bowed

rungrum **ng/di*** to seduce. **pa·ng*** seductive words

rungsek̄ *var of* RUSEK

rungsid *oj* cluttered with obstacles *or* pitfalls

rungu *ng* (*for kr forms see* MIRENG, PIRENG) ***n̂** 1 sense of hearing. *Rungoné wis suda akèh lho.* He's become quite hard of hearing. 2 to have a keen sense of hearing. ***n̂-*n̂en** to keep hearing over and over in the mind. **(re)*n̂en** to hear nonexistent sounds. **k*** (**m̂·piḍanget** *ki*) to hear (*see also* KRUNGU). **ng/di*** to hear sth. *Swarané kepénak temen di*.* Her voice is very pleasant to listen to. **ng/di*k̂aké** (**m̂/di·piḍanget·aké** *ki*) to listen (to). *ngrungokaké raḍio* listening to the radio. *Tjoba rungokna ja, aku dak kanḍa.* Just listen, I'll tell you. **ngrungokaké tanpa kuping** 1 to not pay attention. 2 to sense through a sixth sense. **ng/di*n̂i** to communicate with supernaturally. *Aku mau bengi liwat nang ngisor wit pelem dirungoni karo sing baureksa.* Last night as I walked under the mango tree I was spoken to by its guardian spirit. **pa·ng*** 1 sense of hearing. 2 what is heard. 3 hearer, listener. *See also* KRUNGU, PRUNGU

runtag to shake, quake, falter

runtah trash, garbage

runtjing sharp-pointed. *bambu ** bamboo lance

runtuh *ng,* **rentah** *kr* to fall (down, off, apart). *Adja nganti *.* Don't let it fall! *Wektu setaun baé kulawarga mau *.* Within a year the family fell apart. **ng/di*aké** to cause sth to fall, come apart *etc. Adja ng*aké lampu.* Don't knock the lamp off. *ng*aké ati* to break smn's heart. **ngruntuhaké pangaksama** to bestow forgiveness, take pity on. **ngruntuhaké weteng·an·é** to cause a miscarriage; to have an abortion. **ng/di*i** to drop *or* fall on(to). *Wité ng*i omah.* The tree fell on a house. *** ati·né** brokenhearted. *** talak·é** to fulfill the requirement for Islamic divorce. *** weteng·an·é** to have a miscarriage

runtung ***-*** *or* **runtang-*** *or* **re*an** inseparable, always together

runtut a pair, a match, a perfect fit. *See also* ATUT-RUNTUT

rupa *ng,* **rupi** *kr* 1 appearance. **né mèh kembar.* They look almost like twins. 2 kind, shape. *kembang manéka ** all kinds of flowers. *pusaka a* keris* an heirloom in the form of a kris, *i.e.* a kris which is an heirloom. 3 color. **né montoré apa?* What color is his car? ***mu** *cr term of abuse.* ***-*** all kinds of (things). *pegawéan *-** all kinds of jobs. *Sa-dalan² ndeleng *-*.* They saw all kinds of things along the way. **re*n** 1 a color. *re*n biru* the color blue. 2 form, shape. *re*n memedèni* a spooky-looking figure. **sa*** one kind (of thing). *Sing dipangan mung sa*.* They eat only one kind of food. **sa*né** all kinds of (things). *sa*ning kembang* all kinds of flowers. *** dudu *** a strange-appearing object. *** tjandra** astrology

rupak (**ripak** *kr?*) narrow, restricted, confining. *panggonan kang ** a cramped space. *wong kang * kawruhé* people of limited knowledge. **ng/di*(i)** to limit, restrict. *ng* djadjahané mungsuh* to limit the enemy's territory. *Médja iki ng*i kamar.* This table crowds the room. *** ati·né** *or* *** budi·né** *or* *** segara·né** of limited patience *or* forgivingness. *** djagat·é** to see no way out. *Obat ora ana kang katjèké, nganti * djagaté aku.* No medicine can cure it, so there's no hope for me.

rupek̄ *var of* RUPAK

rupi appearance; form; color (*kr for* RUPA)

rupiah (*abbr*: **Rp**) rupiah (Indonesian unit of currency). ** petjah* a rupiah's-worth of change. ** putih* silver rupiah coin. ***an** 1 in the form of one-rupiah bills. *Ḍuwité disaki kabèh *an.* He put the money in his pocket, all in ones. *Aku emoh jèn diwènèhi ḍuwit *an.* I don't accept one-rupiah bills. 2 bill in a certain denomination of rupiahs. *sa*an* one-rupiah bills. *Ḍuwité sing digémbol slawé *an.* They money she carried was in 25-rupiah bills.

rurah (*or* **pa·ng***) destruction. *pang*ing satru* the wiping out of the enemy. **(ma)ng*** to destroy, wipe out

ruru ***-* widara** *name of a children's game*

ruruh soft-spoken (*var of* LURUH). **ng/di*** to look up [a relative] when away from home (*var of* NG/DI·LURUH)

rus rose (flower)

rusa *see* GANDA, G·UM·ANDA

rusak *ng,* **risak** *kr* damaged, out of order, in bad shape. *Djamku wis *.* My watch isn't working. *Tandurané diidak-idak *.* The plants were trampled on and ruined. *Negarané *.* The country is in bad shape. *wong sing nganti * moralé* a man of questionable morals. **ka*an** 1 to get damaged. *Otoné ke*an ana ing dalan.* His car broke down along the way. 2 damage. *Ora ana ka*an apa² ing omahé.* There was no damage to the house. **ng/di·re*** to lay waste, to destroy and plunder. **ng/di*aké** to damage inadvertently. **ng/di*(i)** to do harm to. *ng* kuwarasaning awak* detrimental to health. *Senengané ng*i dolanané kantjané.* He's always wrecking his friend's toys.

rusek̄ crowded. *Kamaré *.* The room was jammed full. **ng/di*i** to crowd, jam

rusija *var of* RESIJA

Ruslan Russia

rusuh *ng,* **resah** *kr* 1 unruly. *Saiki kampungku *.* My village is in a state of unrest. *Ḍèwèké kuwi omongané *, siṭik misuh.* He talks dirty and swears. 2 untidy. *Jèn mangan *.* He eats sloppily. **re*** troublemaker. **re*(an)** *or* **k(a)*an** unrest, disturbance. *Re*ing Indonesia déning pekabaran mantja negara digeḍèk-geḍèkaké.* The unrest in Indonesia was exaggerated by the foreign press. **ng/di*i** to disturb, bother. *ng*i anggoné matja* to interfere with smn's reading. **pa·ng*** complaint

rut **nge/di*** to tie sth to. *Malingé di* nang wit pelem ḍa didelok wong akèh.* The thief was lashed to a mango tree in full view of the public. *Koperé dierut ing sepéḍa.* He tied his suitcase to his bicycle.

rutjah unimportant, insignificant. *buta ** (*wj*) an ogre who plays a minor role

rutjat 1 to undress. 2 to get demoted *or* dismissed. **ng/di*** 1 to remove [clothing]. 2 to demote *or* discharge [an employee]

rutjuh a refreshing drink, *esp.* grated coconut mixed with coconut milk; a sweet-sour drink

ru(w)- *see also under* RU- (*Introduction, 2.9.7*)

ruwah 1 soul, spirit. 2 eighth month of the Moslem calendar: the time for paying homage to one's deceased ancestors. 3 day of death. **ḍèk *é** (**kala geblag·ipun** *kr*) when smn died. ***an** religious festival held during the month of Ruwah

ruwat freed from. ** sakabèhing durmala* out of the clutches of one's foes. ** saka ing papatjintraka* released from one's misery. ***an** shadow-play performance given as an act of animistic exorcism, to protect a threatened household and *esp.* an only child. **ng/di*** to hold such a ceremony. **pa·ng*** act of casting off/out. *pang* papa* liberation from one's poverty

ruwed tangled, complicated, confused. **ng/di*i** to snarl, complicate. *** renteng** complication, problem, entanglement. **-renteng ing negara* turbulence in the nation. *Sing saiki dadi *-rentengé pikiré jakuwi bab perkara omah.* What is preoccupying him now is a household matter. *See also* KUMRUWED

ruwit delicate, exquisite

ruwog bushy-haired

rw- *see also under* RU(W)- (*Introduction, 2.9.7*)

R.W. *see* RUKUN

rwa *oj* two

S

s 1 (*prn* **ès**) *alphabetic letter.* 2 *pre-vowel var of* SA- 1, 2. 3 *inf var of* WIS

sa' 1 (*or, inf,* SE; *or* s *before vowel*) one (*as modifier: see also* SIDJI, NG- 6, 7). *sa' juta* one million. *se·puluh* ten. *se·welas* eleven. *s·atus* one hundred. *s·èwu* one thousand. *libur se·minggu* a one-week vacation. 2 (*or, inf,* SE; *or* s *before vowel*) a(n); per. *se·dina ping telu* three times a day. *se·ketjap rong ketjap* a word or two of conversation. 3 the same as. *Geḍéné saenḍog.* It's the size of an egg. 4 together with, and. *sega sak lawuhé* rice with the accompanying dishes. *aku sabodjoku* my wife and I. *sak tekané omah* as (soon as) he got home. * *paḍa*² or * *pepaḍané* and the like; together with similar things. *welas asih marang *-paḍa*² sympathy toward one's fellow beings. 5 including all members, embracing the entire scope. *wong *-omah* the whole family. *Udané sasoré ora terang*². The rain didn't stop all afternoon. *ing sa-dalan*² in every street. *Ḍèké kena sa-karep*². He gets to do whatever he pleases. 6 [*with suffix*] (in a position) relative to. *satjeḍaké hotèl* near the hotel. *sadjroné kamar* in(side) the room. *satengenku* to my right. *sakiwamu* on your left. *samburiné omah* behind the house. *sangisoring watu* under a rock. *sanḍuwuré médja* on (*or* above) the table. 7 [*with suffix*] within the scope of, to the extent of. *sadjroné omong*² while they were talking. *sadjroné perang* during the war. *saantarané omahku lan omahmu* between my house and yours. *Aku sarapan sak anané.* We ate whatever there was for breakfast. *Tjritakna saélingmu.* Tell me all you remember. *sabisa*²*mu* to your utmost ability. *saantarané djam telu lan papat* between three and four o'clock. *salungané* while he was out. *salawasé uripé* throughout his life. *saakèhé wong sing nonton* among all the spectators. *saénaké waé* whatever one feels like (doing); any old way. *digebugi sapatiné* beaten to death. *mangan sawaregé* to eat one's fill. *nonton nganti sabubaré* to watch to the very end. 8 [*with suffix*] simultaneous with; (just) after. *Sarampungé njulap bandjur ndjaluk ḍuwit.* As he finished his magic tricks, he passed the hat. *Sasirepé banju, wong*² *bandjur bali manèh menjang désa.* When the waters receded, the people returned to the village. *See also Introduction, 3.1.1, definition of doubled roots*

sa- *see also under* SE- (*Introduction, 2.9.2*)

sa'at the appropriate time for sth. *Marni durung gelem ditari rabi wong pantjèn ja durung *é.* Marni doesn't want to get married, and it *isn't* time yet. *Wis tekan *é dipunḍut sing Maha Kuasa.* The time has come for him to be gathered to God.

sâbâ [of animals; *cr* of people] to stray, wander around. *pitik ** a stray chicken. *Ana ula * mlebu ngomah.* A snake got into the house. *Gawéné * ing pasar.* He's always hanging around the marketplace. *manuk sing * bengi* a nocturnal bird. ***n** place where animals are let loose. **se*** to keep wandering off *or* hanging around smw. **ñj/di*** to visit frequently, hang around. *Désa kono di* matjan.* A tiger has been lurking around the village. *karebèn adja di* ing maling* so that thieves couldn't get in. **pa*n** *sms *N above*

sabab *formal var of* SEBAB

sabak school slate

Sa'ban eighth month of the Moslem calendar, when people pay homage to their deceased ancestors

sabar patient, controlled, unresisting. *Ah *, adja paḍa nesu.* There, there! don't get mad. ***an** patient/forebearing in nature. **ka*an** patience, self-control. **ñj/di*aké** to keep oneself under control. *Wis ta, di*aké baé.* All right, just wait patiently. **ñj/di*i** to be patient with/about. * **subur** all things come to him who waits. * **tawekal** patient and undiscouraged in the face of adversity

Sabat Saturday (the Sabbath)

sabda *oj* what smn says; words, speech. *djuru* * orator. *medar* * to speak. **ñj/di*(kaké)** 1 to speak; to say (to). 2 to transform magically. *di* malih dadi tjèlèng* changed into a wild boar

saben 1 every, each. * *dina* every day. * *telung sasi* every three months. * *wong* everyone. 2 every time. * *tampa lajang* every time he gets a letter. **é* usually. **é jèn awan njambut-gawé.* They ordinarily work during the day. *adat *é* as a usual thing. *kaja *é* as usual. *-* 1 every so often. 2 each by each. *-* *tjotjogna.* Match them up! *See also* PRASABEN

sabet 1 a whip, a lash. 2 sword (*ki for* PEDANG). ***an** manipulation of shadow-play puppets. *Jèn ndalang *ané apik banget.* [The puppet-master] handles the puppets with great skill. **ñj/di*aké** to swing [a whip] at/onto. *Petjuté di*aké nang djaran.* He laid the whip across the horse. **ñj/di*(i)** to whip. *Kusiré njabet djaran.* The driver lashed the horse.

sabil religious martyr. *mati* * to die a martyr's death. *perang* * crusade. **ñj/di*i** 1 to become a martyr to, sacrifice oneself for. 2 to fight down [temptation *etc.*]

sabilullah doing God's will. *See also* DJIHADFI

sabin rice paddy (*kr for* SAWAH)

sabit crescent. *rembulan* * crescent moon

sablog *var of* SABLUG

sablug *see* DANDANG

sabrang 1 the far side; foreign (place, person). *gawéan* * manufactured abroad; imported goods. * *dalan* across the street. *wong* * foreigner; outsider. *tanah* * foreign land. 2 a variety of cassava. 3 *rg* chili pepper. ***an** 1 the other side. *Ajo nunggang gètèk tekan *an kana.* Let's go across on a raft. 2 characterized by being foreign. *djedjer *an* (*wj*) scene in which a second (foreign) kingdom enters the drama. *Perdjurit*[2] **an sing pada nganggo topi lan sepatu.* (*wj*) The foreign soldiers are the ones wearing hats and shoes. *Djogèd *an biasané tanpa sampur.* Non-Javanese dancers don't usually wear long scarves with their classical dance costumes. **ñj*** across from; to go across. *njebrang dalan/kali* to cross a street/river. *ngarep statsiun njabrang dalan* across the street from the railroad station. **ñj/di*aké** to transport across. *Gawéané njabrangaké wong saka kéné mrana.* His job is to ferry people across. **ñj/di*i** to cross sth. *njabrangi kali* to go across the river. **pa*an** place for fording a river. * **gabus** a variety of cassava

Sabtu *var of* SETU

sabuk *ng kr,* **paningset** *ki* cloth sash worn by males as part of their Javanese-style dress, or by market sellers to stow money. * *bara* fringed sash. ***(-*)an** 1 to put on *or* wear a sash. 2 act *or* way of putting/having on a sash. *Sabuk*[2]*ané angèl wong kuwi, lawong lemu banget.* It's hard for him to wear a sash because he's so fat. **ñj/di*i** to put a sash on smn. * **galeng** well supplied with land, *esp.* rice-growing land. * **inten** a style of kris. * **tjoṭa** *sms* * WALA *below.* * **udaraga** multicolored sash. * **ukub** sash used with Javanese dress. * **wala** a style of batik-wrapping worn by little girls, with one end wrapped at the waist as a sash

sabun soap. ***an** to soap oneself. **ñj/di*** to wash smn/sth with soap

sad *oj* six. * **pada** six-legged [insect]

sâdâ main rib of a palm leaf. **né kena digawé sapu.* Palm-leaf ribs are made into brooms. * **lanang** wand

sāḍâ (*or* **ka*** *or* * **asudji**) twelfth month of the Javanese year (12 May–22 June)

sadâjâ all (*kr for* KABÈH)

sadak bridal packet (a betel leaf rolled around betel-making ingredients) thrown down by both bride and groom at the moment they meet at the wedding ceremony: according to tradition, the one who throws first will dominate in the marriage

saḍar to realize, be aware. **ka*an** consciousness, awareness. **ñj/di*aké** 1 to remind, warn. 2 to bring back to consciousness, to revive. **ñj/di*i** to realize, become aware. *Bareng njaḍari kesalahé bandjur nangis.* She cried when she realized the wrong she had done.

sadat *inf var of* SAHADAT

saḍda *var sp of* SAḌA

sadé 1 to sell (*kr for* ADOL, DODOL). 2 *var of* SANDÉ

saḍegan 1 tobacco mixture. 2 chin (*rg ki for* DJANGGUT)

saḍel bicycle seat

saḍénga *var of* SEḌÉNGAH
saḍèrèk sibling; relative (*kr for* SEDULUR)
sadi 1 rather, somewhat. * *rana.* Move that way a bit! 2 where from? where have you been? (*shc from* SAKA (NGE)NDI)
sadjak 1 aspect, demeanor. **mu kok paké-woh.* You seem uneasy. *Ḍèké mangsuli karo * isin.* He replied with an embarrassed air. 2 to seem, look as if. *Ḍèké * wedi.* She seemed afraid. *Tandangé * kaja banṭèng ketaton.* He acted enraged. ***(an)é** it seems; to judge from appearances. **é kok wigati temen.* Apparently it's urgent. **ané gumaib.* He looks arrogant.
sa'djeg the course of life. **é gawé dalan.* He's been building roads all his life. **é urip lagi iki tumon botjah nakal banget.* I've never in my life seen such a naughty child. * **dju(m)bleg** *or* * **djumleg** *or* * **umbleg** all one's life. * *djumbleg ḍèké durung tau nunggang sepur.* He's never ridden on a train.
sadji *ng kr,* **saos** *ki* ***ǹ** an offering set out as appeasement for the spirits. **se*ǹ** to place such an offering. **ñj/di*k̀aké** to place sth as an offering. *Menawa malem Djumuat ibu mesṭi njadjèkaké kembang nang ngisor tumbak.* Every Thursday evening without fail Mother places an offering under the lance for the spirits. **ñj/di*ǹi** to make an offering to. *Tumbaké disadjèni.* An offering is made to the [spirit of the] lance.
saduga *oj* one
saḍo two-wheeled horse-drawn cab
Sadran eighth Javanese month (*var of* SABAN). **ñj*** to make an offering at a family ancestral tomb as a family group during the above month. **pa·ñj*an** burial ground where such offerings are made
sadu virtuous, pure, holy
saḍuk *var sp of* SAKḌUK. **ñj/di*(i)** 1 to kick [a soccer ball]. 2 to slap smn in the stomach
saé 1 good, nice, attractive (*kr for* APIK). 2 good; advisable (*kr for* BETJIK)
sa'èstu to succeed in [do]ing, go through with (*kr for* SIDA). *See also* ÈSTU
sâgâ a certain trailing shrub having small round aromatic leaves (sometimes used as tea) and small red-and-black beans. (*woh*) * the beans produced by this shrub. * **blenḍung,** * **mas,** * **telik** red varieties of the *saga* shrub. * **tunṭeng** a black variety, having sweet leaves and black-and-red beans
sagah willing, able (*kr for* SAGUH)
saged can, be able (*kr for* BISA)
sagon * **lempit** *or* * **rambon** coconut biscuit
sagu sago (tree)
saguh *ng,* **sagah** *kr* to agree to [do sth]. *Ibu *, ija ta?* Mother said she would, didn't she? *Jèn ora * mènèhi ḍuwit, ja ora kena mlebu.* If you won't give any money, you can't come in. **ka*an** an agreement, a promise. **ñj/di*i** to promise; to agree to sth. *Aku wis njaguhi ndandani pité A.* I said I'd fix A's bicycle for him. *Pamunḍuté di*i.* They agreed to his demands.
sagung *oj* all
sah 1 valid, legitimate. *Omah iki wis * dadi duwèké A.* A is the legitimate owner of this house. 2 paid up, paid in full. *Utangku wis *.* My debt is paid. 3 separate (*shf of* PISAH). ***-*an** to make a mutual settlement. *Aku wis *-*an utang karo A.* A and I have paid what we owed each other. **nge/di*** to sharpen, hone. **nge/di*aké** to validate. **nge/di*i** to wash (*esp.* dishes: *var of* NG/DI-ASAH-I). **ora * saka** unable to do without. *Wong iku ora * saka piranti² sing bakalé karèt.* Rubber products are indispensible to man. *See also* ABSAH
sâhâ *ltry* and, with; (and) also, as well as
sahabat a close friend
sahadat confession of religious faith. *See also* KLIMAH
sahbandar harbor master, head of the port authority
sahid religious martyr. *mati ** to die as a martyr. *prang ** religious crusade
sahur *var of* SAUR
sahwat sensual pleasure
sa'iki *ng,* **sa'punika (***prn* **sa'menika)** *kr* now. *wiwit ** from now on. * *iki* right now. *ing wektu ** at the present time, these days. ***né** now (as contrasted with the past *or* future). *Mau²né aku nganggur, *né wis njambutgawé.* I didn't have a job before, but I'm working now.
saing competition. ***an** 1 to go sailing together. 2 competitor; competition. **ñj/di*aké** to have smn/sth compete. *A njaingaké djarané karo djarané B.* A raced his horse against B's. **ñj/di*i** to compete with. *Olèhé menganggo njaingi mbakjuné.* She tries to outdress her sister.
sait *var of* SAUT
sâjâ 1 increasingly, more and more. * *tambah ributé.* The work keeps piling up.

Montoré * *dibanteraké.* He drove faster and faster. * *dudu.* No, it's not that either [after still another wrong guess]. **2** especially, all the more so. *Atiné ḍeg²an,* * *nèk weruh wong nggawa beḍil.* His heart thumped, especially when he saw a man carrying a gun. **3** snare for trapping birds *or* fish (*shf of* WISAJA). *prau* * fishing boat. **4** *shf of* RESAJA, SRAJA. *-* especially. *Siti aju,* *-* *jèn nganggo klambi abang.* Siti is beautiful, especially when she wears red. *... *... the more... the more. * *bengi* * *asri.* The later (at night) it got, the more beautiful it looked. **ňj/di*** to trap [birds, fish] in a net. * **lawas** *sms* * SUWÉ *below.* * **manèh** furthermore, moreover; even more so; especially. *Sing wédok ija wong sabar, sing lanang* * *manèh.* The wife was patient, the husband even more so. * **suwé** * ... more and more. * *suwé larané* * *suda.* Her illness gradually subsided. *See also* SANGSAJA

sâjâbârâ *oj* competition with a princess offered in marriage as the prize

sajah tired, weary. **ňj*** to feign weariness. **sa*****é 1** to the point of exhaustion. *Olèhé njambut gawé diteg nganti sasajahé.* He worked until he was ready to drop. **2** in large numbers. *Sing nonton pasar malem sa***é.* The fair was jammed.

sajak Occidental-style dress for ladies (dress; blouse and skirt). ***an** dressed as above; to put on *or* wear such clothing

sajan *var of* SAJA

sajang 1 a pity; to regret; regrettably. *Ah* * *aku ora ngerti dèk mau.* It's too bad I didn't know earlier. *Gambar mau* ***é kok lé ora tjeṭa.* Unfortunately the picture isn't very clear. **2** coppersmith, tinker. **ňj/di*** to pity smn. *Wong ngemis kuwi wadjib di**. Beggars are to be pitied.

sajembârâ prize contest. *ngleboni* * to enter a contest. *nganakaké* * to hold a contest. * *ngarang* (*nggambar, lsp.*) a prize contest for an essay (painting, *etc.*). **ň(j)/di*** to hold a contest for [a specific purpose]. *Pemerintah njajembarakké enggoné milih lagu kebangsaan.* The government ran a contest to select a national anthem. * **pilih** a contest offering a princess' hand in marriage as the prize

sajèt yarn, knitting wool

sajid *title for descendants of Mohammed*

sajidina *title for Mohammed, also, for saints*

sajoga *var of* SAJOGJA

sajogja suitable, appropriate. *tindak-tanduk kang* * proper behavior. ***né** it would be advisable (to...). ***né kowé mangkat ḍisik.** You'd better start first. **ň(j)/di*****kaké** to recommend. *Ḍèwèké najogjakaké supaja barangé dikirim nganggo pos uḍara.* He suggests sending the parcel by air mail. **ň(j)/di*****ni** to agree to, comply with; to consider proper *or* appropriate. *Jèn pantjèn ngono karepmu, aku ja najogjani.* If that's what you really want, I have no objection. *Karepku disejogjani banget karo Bapak.* Father is quite agreeable to my wishes.

sajuk 1 harmonious, congenial. **2** to have a date with; to go steady with

sajup spoiled, rancid

sajur (*or* ***an**) vegetable(s)

sak 1 pocket. **2** *var sp of* SA. **nge/di*****(i)** to put *or* have sth in the pocket. *Iki ḍuwité,* ***en** (*or* ***ana**). Here's the money for it; put it in your pocket. *Aku nge** *kuntji.* I have the key in my pocket.

sâkâ[a] *ng,* **saking** *kr* **1** from, of. *lajang* * *kantja* a letter from a friend. *luwar* * *satruné* freed of the enemy. * *tjilik* since childhood. *Matjané metu* * *ing alas.* The tiger came out of the forest. *Banḍané dumadi* * *sawah.* His wealth consist of rice paddies. *kedjaba* * *iku* aside from that. **2** because of. * *sembranané* on account of his carelessness. *Olèhé nangis* * *ilanging dolanan.* He was crying because he lost his toy. **3** according to. * *ngendikané ḍokter* according to what the doctor says. **4** to such an extent (that). * *senengé nganti djogèdan.* He was so pleased he danced around. **5** than. *Tjatjahé kuwi kurang apa luwih* * *rong puluh?* Are there less than twenty, or more? **6** *n* at a time. *Olèhé mriksa* * *sidji².* He examined them one by one. * *seṭiṭik* little by little. * **déné** because of. *See also* SAKING, SANGKA

sâkâ[b] pillar supporting a roof. **se*** **désa** member of the village administration below the head man. **ňj/di*****ni** to equip with pillars. *njakani omah* to put in the pillars of a house. * **gotjo** pillars at the outer ends (corners) of an addition to a traditional-style house. * **guru** the four central pillars of a traditional house; *fig* leader. * **prapat** *sms* * GOTJO *above.* * **rawa** *sms* * PANANG-GAP *below.* * **pa·ň·tanggap** smaller pillars surrounding the main pillars of a traditional house

Sâkâ[c] Javanese king whose reign began in

78 A.D. and who invented the Javanese alphabet and introduced the Javanese calendar. * **kala** a year according to the above calendar. * **warsa** a year as used in astrological reckoning. *See also* ADJISAKA

sakabat *var of* SAHABAT

sak̔·aké *inf var of* MESAK·AKÉ

sa'kal all at once, immediately. *Tambané bareng diombé larané * mari.* He got well as soon as he took the medicine. *Akèh wong sing dadi mlarat sak kal.* Many people were impoverished all at one stroke.

sakâlâ *ltry var of* SAKAL

sakamantyan *oj* very

sakang *rg var of* LAKANG

sakantuk lucky (*kr for* SAKOLÈH)

sak̔ḍu:k̄ handkerchief

sakelangkung *see* K(E)·LUWIH

saking 1 from, of; because of; according to; to such an extent that; than; *n* at a time (*kr for* SAKA[a]). 2 to such an extent that... * *kagèté tiba klumah.* He was so startled he fell over backwards.

sakit ill; painful (*kr for* LARA). **pa·ñj*** *ng kr* sickness (physical *or* spiritual). *penjakit masjarakat* social ills. **pe*an** *ng kr* prisoner

saklangkung *see* K(E)·LUWIH

saksânâ *oj* quickly, immediately

saksi *var of* SEKSI

saku 1 pocket (*var of* SAK). 2 *var of* SANTIKU

sakuṭu (*or* ***ñ**) *ltry* to conspire

sal 1 shawl, scarf. 2 hospital ward. 3 large hall for gatherings

sal- *see also under* SL- (*Introduction, 2.9.3*)

Sâlâ *inf var of* SURAKARTA

salad (*or* **se***) [of fire] highly destructive. **ñj/di*(i)** to ignite sth. *Saking geḍéné geni nganti njalad geḍèg pawon.* The fire leaped up so, it caught the kitchen walls on fire.

salah 1 (**lepat** *kr?*) to make a mistake, do sth wrong. *Sapa sing *?* Whose fault was it? **ku ḍéwé.* It's my own fault. *Aku ora * kok dinesoni.* I didn't do anything wrong, how come he got mad at me? *Aku nggarap étung * lima.* I made five mistakes in my arithmetic. 2 [one] of [them]. * *sawidjining pelem* one of the mangoes. *Buku iki tjritakna * sidji.* Tell me about one of these books. ***-*** or else, for fear that. *Jèn udjian kowé adja sok ngepèk, *-* bisa konangan.* Don't cheat on exams–you might get caught. ***-sèlèh** to do wrong repeatedly. **ka*an 1** mistake; guilt. *Maling kuwi ke*ané wis tjeṭa.* The thief was plainly guilty. 2 blame. *nampa ke*an* to get the blame. **ñj*** to act different; to do sth different from what the others are doing. **ñj/di*aké** to blame, find fault with. *njalahké wong lija* to blame it on somebody else. **ñj/di*i** to deviate from [proper *or* expected behavior]. *njalahi aturan lalulintas* to violate a traffic law. * **ke·dadi·ṅ 1** to have a different result from the one hoped for. 2 to change one's shape magically. * **(pa·n)deleng** to see mistakenly/inaccurately. * **gawé** wrongdoing; to do wrong. * **graita** to misjudge, make a false assumption. * **kaprah** to misuse, *i.e.* use for the wrong purpose. * **mangsa** to occur out of season. * **paham** *sms* * TAMPA *below.* * **rupa** *sms* KEDADÈN *above.* * **sawidji** *see* * 2 *above.* * **tampa** to misinterpret, make incorrect inferences. * **tjéṭak** a misprint. * **urat** to have a sprained muscle. * **wèngwèng** to get off the track, not stick to business. * **wisel** to fail to follow *or* understand. *Kowé ora ngrungokaké mulané terus * wisel.* You don't listen–that's why you always make inappropriate remarks.

salak a tropical fruit with white meat and thorny skin. * **géjol** a young *salak* fruit; a small sour variety of *salak*

salalahu *see* SALLALAHU

salam 1 a greeting. *awèh ** to greet. *malesi ** to return a greeting. 2 bay leaf. **(se)*an** to shake hands. * **pa·n·donga**, * **pa·ng·èstu**, * **taklim** *written greetings as conventional openings in social letters. See also* WANGALAIKUM

salang 1 collar bone. 2 ropes by which baskets are attached to a shoulder pole (*pikulan*). *wong ** person who carries things on a shoulder pole. * **sebat** resembling closely. *Rupané * sebat karo bodjoné.* He looks a lot like his wife. * **sengguh** to misunderstand. * **suduk** to stab each other. * **surup** mixed up. *Mahasiswa² paḍa * surup ora mlebu sekolah, didarani prèi.* The students, confused, didn't attend classes: they thought it was a holiday. * **tundjang** to run around in panic

salap *rg kr for* SÈLÈH. *See also* SATUS

sâlâsilah family tree, genealogy

salat ritual Islamic meditation. **é batal.* His prayers were ineffectual [because of a sullying influence before *or* during them]. **ñj/di*aké** to offer ritual incantations on behalf of [smn deceased]. **pa*an 1** place for ritual meditation. 2 knowledge about meditation. * **(ng)asar** third daily meditation (performed between 3 and 5 P.M.). * **(ng)isa** fifth meditation (7:30 P.M.). * **istika** communal prayer for rain. * **lohor** *or* * **luhur** second meditation (1 P.M.). * **magrib** fourth meditation (sunset). * **subuh** first meditation (5 A.M.). * **witir** supplementary prayer offered after the *(ng)isa* meditation

saldju snow; to snow. *mangsa* * winter

salé sun-dried banana slices

salèh 1 wise; holy. *wong* * wise man, seer. 2 *rg var of* SALÉ

salep ointment, salve. **ñj/di*** to apply ointment to

salib a cross. **ñj/di*** to crucify

salin *ng,* **santun** *kr* 1 change, replacement; a change of clothing. 2 to change, replace; to change clothes. *Ḍèké adus* *. He bathed and changed. * *slaga* to alter one's behavior patterns. **solan-*** **(sontan-santun** *kr*) to keep changing, to change often. *Botjah wédok ki jèn nganggo klambi solan-**. Girls are forever changing clothes. ***-s·um·alin** *ng kr* to change off, change around. *Sinaumu lan rékréasi kudu *-sumalin.* You have to intersperse your studying with recreation. **ñj/di*i** to change *or* replace sth; to change smn's clothing. *njalini popoké bajiné* to change the baby's diaper. *Pirantiné sing rusak dibenerakè utawa di*i.* Worn-out equipment was repaired or replaced. **ñj/di·solan-*i** **(ñj/dipun·sontan-santun·i** *kr*) to keep changing *or* replacing sth. *njolan-njalini popoké baji* to keep changing a baby's diaper. *Banjuné ja kerep disolan-*i, preluné bisaa seger uripé.* They change the water often so the fish can live well. **pa*** *or* **pi*** new clothing, a change of wardrobe

salit thirsty (*opt kr? ki? for* NGELAK)

sallahlahu *var sp of* SALLALAHU

sallalahu * **allaihi wassalam** (*abbr*: **S.A.W.**) may God bless him and give him peace (*title used after Mohammed's name*)

saloka simile, metaphor. **ñj/di*kaké** to compare sth by use of a simile. **ñj/di*ni** to apply a simile/metaphor to

salon 1 salon. * *ketjantikan* beauty salon. 2 console. *ṛadio* * radio console

salong some of [it, them]. *Patamanan mau * ditanduri kembang mawar.* A section of the park was planted with roses. ***é** the rest, what remains. *Sing geḍé² kanggo kowé, *é simpenen nang lemari.* The largest ones are for you; put the others in the cupboard.

salu 1 veranda. 2 *rg* bench used on a veranda

salur ***an** 1 a channel. 2 sewage. **ñj/di*aké** to direct *or* channel sth

salut salute

salwir·é all (*ltry var of* SA·KABÈH·É). *salwiring kawruh* all knowledge

sa'm- *place prefixation: see under individual roots; see also* SA 6

sâmâ *kr* *sbst? var of* SAMI

samâdjâ *oj* elephant

samak 1 paper *or* leather cover. *dluwang * buku* a paper book-cover. *gambar* * picture on the cover. 2 leather. 3 *rg* floor mat. **ñj/di*** to process leather. **ñj/di*aké** to cover sth for smn. **ñj/di*i** to equip with a cover. *Bukuné *ana.* Put a cover on the book.

samang you; your (*md; var of* SAMPÉJAN)

samangké now(adays) (*kr for* SAMENGKO)

samapta in readiness. *Kabèh *, ora ana sing kaliwatan.* Everything is all set; nothing has been overlooked. **ñj/di*kaké** to make sth ready

samar 1 worried, apprehensive. 2 vague, obscure, inconspicuous. *gegambaran kang *-** fuzzy pictures. *piwulang²é kang *-** obscure teachings. *Pitakoné semu *.* The question was a bit vague. 3 unknown, unexplained. *Ora * marang pernahé.* She was no stranger to the place. *redjeki* * a piece of unexplained good luck. ***an** concealed. *djeneng *an* secret name; pseudonym. **ka*an** 1 worry, apprehension. *ke*aning wong-tuwané* a worry to one's parents. 2 worried, apprehensive. **ñj*** 1 (*psv* **di***) to hide, keep under wraps. 2 to disguise oneself. *Radja X njamar dadi kéré.* King X was in the guise of a beggar. **ñj/di*aké** to worry about. *njamaraké buḍalé anaké* to worry about one's child going off. **ñj*i** threatening. *dolanan sing njamari* a dangerous pastime. **s·in·amar** *ltry* under cover. *Tindaktanduké sinamar.* His actions were mysterious. **s·um·amar** *ltry* obscure(d). *Ing ndjero omah sumamar.* It was rather dark inside the house.

samasta *oj* all, everything; the universe

sambang 1 a sudden serious illness. *kena ing * srawungan* (*inf*) to fall in love with. 2 (*or* **ñj***) *rg* to visit. * **pa·lamun·an** woolgathering, daydreaming. * **leles** *or* * **lelet**

post-natal hemorrhaging. * **rimpung** beri-beri. * **suwel** highwayman, bandit

sambat 1 complaint, outcry. **é wetengé mules.* He complained of a queasy stomach. 2 to complain, wail. *Ḍèwèké *-* nanging ora dirèwès.* He kept making a fuss but nobody paid any attention. *Ora tau sedih, ora tau *.* She never grieved, she never complained. ***an** to help [one's neighbor with work that he could not do alone]. *Wis lumrah jèn ngedegaké omah pada *an.* It's customary for the neighbors to pitch in when smn is building a house. *wong *an* one who helps (as above). **se*** to cry out, wail loudly. ***-s·in·ambat** to help one another (as neighbors). **ñj/di*aké** to do [a job] with the help of one's neighbors. *Gawéané di*-aké, sedina rampung.* With the help of the neighbors, he got the job finished in a single day. **ñj/di*(i)** to ask [fellow villagers] to help. *A jèn di*i ora tau nolak.* A never says no when asked for help. *Jèn ana wong ngedegaké omah, bandjur njambat marang tangga-teparo.* When smn is building a house, he asks his neighbors to give him a hand with it. **pa*** *ltry* complaint. **s·in·ambat** *ltry* named, called. *Sinten sinambating wangi satrija?* What is your name? * **sebut** troubles, problems; **ñj/di*-sebut·i** to seek help from. *Sapa sing kena tak *-sebuti, bisa ngilangi lelarané bodjoku?* Who can I turn to, to cure my wife?

sambâwâ 1 *oj* true; plausible. 2 *gram* imperative

sambékâlâ hindrance, trouble. *Bareng lajang iki aku ngabari manawa nang ndalan aku ora kena *.* (I inform you with this letter that) I encountered no trouble along the way.

sambel hot spicy sauce *or* paste. **ñj/di*** to make [ingredients] into the above. * **djénggot** hot sauce with shredded young coconut meat. * **tumpang** hot sauce made of fermented beans. * **widji·ǹ** hot sesame-seed sauce; **ñj*-widji·ǹ** 1 to make hot sesame-seed sauce; 2 (*or* **s·um·ambel-widji·ǹ**) [of hair] turning gray, flecked with white. *See also* GERTAK

samber **ñj/di*(i)** to strike swiftly, *esp.* from above. *Bleḍègé njamber omah.* The lightning struck a house. *Pitiké di* wulung.* The chicken was attacked by a hawk. *Ulané njamber.* The snake struck. *ptg* **s·l·amber** *pl* to swoop lightning-like. *Manuk gagak sepirang-pirang ptg slamber.* Ravens swooped everywhere. **s·in·amber** struck from above. * **gelap** (*oath*) may I (he, *etc.*) be struck by lightning if...! * **(l)ilèn** *or* * **(l)ilèr** green scarab: worn as a decorative pin. * **mata** a small nocturnal flying insect that often strikes people in the eyes

samberan chicken (*rg kr for* PITIK)

sambet (to make a) connection, continuation (*kr for* SAMBUNG). ***ipun** the continuation (*kr for* TUTUG·É). **ke*** 1 to be entered by evil spirits. 2 *opt kr for* SEMAPUT? **ñj*** to continue (*kr for* Ñ·TUTUG)

sambéwârâ to engage in trade/business. *bakul ** trader, merchant. **s·in·ambéwara** engaged in trade

sambi a variety of tree, also its wood. *areng ** charcoal made from this wood. ***ǹ** 1 an activity which accompanies another. *Tjarita iki kena kanggo sambèn kalané nganggur.* This story can be used as a leisure-time activity. 2 a moonlighting job. *Ḍèwèké guru nanging duwé sambèn dagang.* He's a teacher, but he sells on the side. **di*** [one action] is accompanied by [another]. *Ajo, di* wédangé diundjuk.* Come, have some tea [as we talk]. *Olèhé njambut gawé di* tembangan.* He sang while he worked. **ke*** *var name of the above tree.* **ñj*** to have a job on the side. *Jèn ésuk mulang, jèn awan njambi dagang.* In the morning he teaches; in the afternoon he sells. **s·in·ambi** *ltry* done simultaneously with. *lelenggahan sinambi ngundjuk wédang* sitting around drinking tea

sambit **ke*** to get struck by a whip *or* missile. **ñj/di*(i)** to strike with a whip *or* missile. *Asuné di* watu.* He threw a rock at the dog.

sambiwârâ *var of* SAMBÉWARA

samblèg **ñj/di*(i)** to slap, spank

sambong *rg* dam. *mantri ** irrigation official

sambu *see* M̃·WOWOR

sambuk a whip. **ñj/di*(i)** to whip

sambung *ng,* **sambet** *kr* (to make a) connection, continuation. *Aku tilpun A bola-bali nanging ora bisa *.* I called A several times but couldn't get through to him. **(se)*an** a connection, continuation, extension. *Aku wis olèh *an karo kantor dagang.* I've got a call through to the business office. *Se*an karo kuṭa mau gampang, wong bisa nunggang sepur.* It's easy to make connections to that city—you can take a train. *Tangané tengen *an.* His right hand is (an) artificial (extension of his arm). *bodjo (se)*an* new wife taken by a widower. **se*an obor** *sms* ÑJ* OBOR *below.* **ñj/di*** to connect, continue. *njambung tjrita* to go on with the story. *njambung tampar sing pedot* to tie together a broken string. *njambung katresnan* to resume a love affair. **njambung obor** to perpetuate a friendship by uniting offspring in marriage. **njambung watang putung** to reconcile people who are fighting. **ñj/di*aké** to make a connection for smn. *Tjoba mengko tak *aké pisan.* I'll try to put the call through for you. **ñj/di*i** to join in a conversation. *A njambungi, Ah, pantjèn ija.* A rejoined: Yes, it's true. **pa·ñj*** a joining. *tembung penjambung (gram) conjunction. ptg* **s·r·ambung** full of connections. *Taliné ptg srambung.* The string is made up of short pieces tied together. **s·um·ambung (s·um·ambet** *kr*) to put in a remark. *** obor** 1 continuation of a friendship through marriage of offspring. 2 (to carry out) without fail. *Dawuh iki tindakna, paribasané kudu dilakoni * obor.* Do as I say if you have to move heaven and earth. ** obor lakonana jèn pantjèn wis mantep.* By all means do it if you are determined.

sambut 1 to borrow (*root form: kr for* SILIH). 2 debt (*kr for* UTANG). **ke*** to get caught *or* grasped. **ke* ing prang** *ltry* to be killed in battle. **ñj/di*** 1 *oj* to take hold of, grasp. 2 *oj* to receive. **njambut sila·ning a·krama** *ltry* to marry

samekta ready and waiting. *Krétané wis * ana ing ngarepan.* The carriage is waiting out front. **ñj/di*ni** to get sth ready

samengké now(adays) (*md for* SAMENGKO)

samengko *ng,* **samangké** *kr* (*var prn*: **sa'mengko, sa'mangké)** at present, nowadays. (*ing*) *djaman ** or *ing dina ** or *ing mangsa ** at the present time, nowadays. ** aku manggon nang omahé pamanku.* I'm staying at my uncle's for the present. *Wektu * botjah² pada lara.* The children have been ill lately.

samépa *var of* SAMIPA

sami alike, the same; *plural marker* (*kr for* PADA). *kula ** (*kr*) we, us

samin cooking oil extracted from goat's milk

samipa *oj* nearby, close

samir 1 a round banana leaf fixed in a shallow inverted cone shape: used for covering foods. 2 a fringed silken scarf worn by palace officials as an emblem of their office

samirânâ *oj* wind

samodra *oj* sea, ocean. ** bawana* land and sea, *i.e.* seas and continents. ** Kidul* the Indian Ocean. ** pasang* ebb tide

sampah garbage, waste matter. *krandjang ** wastebasket, trash bin. **ñj/di·se*** to reject smn from a group. *Nasibé sarwa disesampah.* It is his fate always to be rejected.

sampak *wj* quick-paced gamelan music to accompany marching or battle scenes. *perang ** a battle scene with such music. **ñj/di*i** to meet, confront; to run into unexpectedly. *** lasem** *sms * above*

sampan sampan (boat)

sampanje champagne

sampar broom, brush. ***an** 1 female classical-dance garment that touches the ground. 2 leg, foot (*ki for* SIKIL). 3 broom, brush. **ka*** 1 touching the ground. *pala ka** fruits (*e.g.* melons, squash) that grow on the ground. 2 to get kicked accidentally. **ñj/di*** 1 to shove with the feet. 2 to skim over *or* through. *Olèhé matja njampar waé.* He just skimmed [the book]. *Banjuné di* prau sing lagi lajar.* The sailboat skimmed over the water. **njampar banju** *slang* to lease a planted rice paddy. *** angin** leaf of the *turi* plant

sampé *var of* SAMPÈK. **ñj/di*** to brush against sth accidentally with the hand *or* arm. *Tangané njampé gelas tiba lan petjah.* His hand grazed the glass; it fell and smashed. *Wong ngemis mau mbareng lunga njampé méméjan.* When the beggar left, he stole the laundry off the clothesline (*i.e.* his hand "just happened to touch" it).

sampéjan 1 you; your (*kr for* KOWÉ). 2 leg, foot (*ki for* SIKIL). **di*** to be addressed as *sampéjan.* *** dalem** you (*for addressing God or a king*)

sampèk *rg* until, up to (*see also* NGANTI)

sampéka deceit. **ñj/di*i** to cheat, deceive

sampet adequate. **ñj/di*i** to cover adequately. *Dèwèké njambut gawé golèk buruhan kanggo njampeti kabutuhané.* She worked for wages in order to have enough for their needs.

sampil leg of meat (beef, pork, lamb, mutton). ** babi* ham

sampir 1 scarf-like cloth worn on the shoulder (*var of* SAMIR). ** katju* scarf worn as as an item in a classical-dance costume.

*klambi ** ladies' blouse. 2 shoulder (*ki for* PUNḌAK). ***an** clothesline or other line strung for hanging things. *-* *or* **sompar-*** *pl* hanging about. *Nèng endi² kok **. They're hanging everywhere! **ke*an** to get hung smw by accident. *Kena angin klambiné ke*an wit.* The shirt was caught up by the wind and deposited in a tree. **ñj/di*aké** 1 to hang [clothing] smw; to place [a scarf] over smn's shoulder. 2 to place [a burden] on smn. *Anaké di*aké bibiné.* She left her son in his aunt's care. **ñj/di*i** 1 to hang [clothing] smw. *Kursiné adja di*i klambi.* Don't hang shirts on the chair. 2 to foist sth off on. *Aku di*i anaké.* She left her child in my care. **s·um·ampir** to get hung; to be hanging. *Ana klambi semampir ana ing kawat tlégrap.* There was a shirt hanging from the telegraph wires. *See also* SLAMPIR

sampjan *rg var of* SAMPÉJAN

sampjuh to clash head-on

sampjuk **ñj/di*** to splash, splatter. *Aku mau di* banju blumbang.* He splashed pond water on me.

samplak *var of* SAMPLUK

samplokan *inf var of* SA·EMPLOK·AN

sampluk **ke*** to get knocked (against). *Gelasé tiba petjah ke* tanganku.* I accidentally knocked the glass off and it broke. **ñj/di*(i)** to knock sth (off). *njamplak rai* to hit smn in the face. *Gelasé petjah di*.* He (deliberately) knocked the glass off and broke it.

sampur a long scarf worn as part of a classical dance costume

sampurna 1 complete, finished. *Anggoné sinau wis bisa *.* He has completed his studies. 2 perfect, ideal. *Urip iku *né ing embun²an.* Life reaches its culmination in the top of the head. **ka*an** esoteric *or* mystic lore about life. **ñj/di*kaké** 1 to finish off; to kill. 2 to bring about perfection in sth

samubarang *ng,* **samukawis** *kr* (*ltry*) everything, anything at all, whatever. *See also* BARANG

samudâjâ *oj* everything; whatever

samudânâ having a pleasant friendly expression which conceals contrary inner feelings. **ñj/di*** to dissemble one's inner feelings

samudra *var of* SAMODRA

samukawis everything; whatever (*kr for* SAMUBARANG)

samun camouflage(d appearance). **ñj/di*** to camouflage *or* disguise [one's appearance; one's feelings]. *Bunglon kuwi bisa njamun paḍa karo papan sing diintjoki.* Chameleons take on the coloring of their surroundings. *Atiné trataban, nanging sinamun ing guju tjekakakan.* He was taken aback, but he covered it up with a hearty laugh. **njamun laku** to behave in an underhanded fashion. **pa*an** a lonely, deserted place

sa'n- *place prefixation: see under individual roots; see also* SA- 6

sânâ *oj* place, position, site. *singga ** throne. *seni ** art gallery

sanadyan, sanadjan (sinaos *opt? kr***)** (*or* ***a**) even though; even if it were so. ** anaa* even though there are some; even if there were any. *Senadjana aku wong ora duwé, aku ora gelem tjolong-djupuk.* I may be poor, but I would never steal.

sanak relative, relation. *Ora * wong, *é mung ḍuwit waé.* He cares more about money than people. **(se)*an** 1 related. *Djono karo aku isih *an.* Djono and I are blood relatives. 2 relationship with smn; (one's) associate(s). *golèk *an* to seek relationships. **ané mesṭi wong sugih².* The people he associates with are all rich. 3 to make friends. *Gampang *an.* He makes friends easily. 4 reconciled. *A lan B wis *an.* A and B have made up their differences. **ñj/di*** 1 to accept *or* treat smn as a relative. 2 to be nice to smn with an ulterior motive. **s·um·anak** outgoing, friendly. **dudu * dudu kadang, jèn mati m·èlu kélangan** he's not a relative to me, but his death is a personal loss. *** kadang** a relative. *** ke·temu dalan** a very close friend. *** sedulur** relative, kinsman. *See also* KI, NAK

sa'nalika instantly, suddenly. *mati ** to die instantly

sananta *gram* active optative form (*see Introduction, 3.1.5.4, chart*)

sânâpustâkâ public library

sânḍâ ***nen** having full, sore breasts [of nursing mothers]

sanḍal sandal(s). ***an** to put on *or* wear sandals

sanḍang clothing. **(lan) pangan* food and clothing; the necessities of life. ***an** 1 clothing. **an anjar* new clothes. **an sapangadeg* a complete outfit of traditional Javanese clothing. 2 diacritical mark indicating vowel sounds in Javanese script. ***an wjandjana** one of three diacritical marks indicating certain modifications of consonant sounds (*see* KERET, PÉNGKAL, TJAKRA). **ke*an sétan** possessed by evil spirits. **ñj/di*** 1 to wear [an article of attire]. *Kerisé di* wlikat.* He's wearing his kris under his arm (rather than in the normal position at the back of the waist). 2 to strike more than one target. *Olèhé manah njanḍang manuk lan woh pelem.* His arrow hit a bird and a mango. **ñj/di*i** 1 to dress smn. *njanḍangi pengantèn* to garb the bride. 2 to supply smn with clothing. *Réwang mau nèk wis tak sanḍangi terus minggat.* I had no sooner outfitted my servant than he ran out on me. **pa·ñj*** clothing. *** lawé** a certain black stork

sanḍat string or string-like material used for lashing things together. **ñj/di*(i)** to lash together. *Gagang mbakoné di*i nganggo tutus.* They hold the tobacco-leaf stems together with bamboo strips.

sandé 1 to fail to materialize (*kr for* WURUNG). 2 batik as merchandise (*ng? kr for* WADÉ?). *** kala** dusk

sanḍéné *see* ANḌÉ

sander **ñj/di*** 1 to seize, snatch up. 2 to run after and bark at

sandi secret, concealed. ** asma* secret name; pseudonym. ** sastra* secret alphabet *or* writing system. ** upama* symbolic expression. *djeneng ** secret name; pseudonym. *telik ** spy, secret agent. **ñj/di*** to conceal; to put in secret form. *njandi lajang* to write a letter in code. **s·in·andi** *ltry* concealed; cryptic. *tulisan sinandi* a secret code. *** lata** a variety of climbing vine. *** upaja** underhanded ruse, trick. *** upama** *ltry* like, as (if)

sandika 1 as you order! *Plataran disapu.–*.* Sweep the yard!–Yes sir. 2 to agree (to). **ñj/di*(ni)** to agree to sth. *Pak Krama wingi wis njendikani sowan mréné ndandani djam.* Mr. Krama promised yesterday that he'd come and fix the clock.

sanḍing close by, next to. *A linggih *é B.* A sat next to B. *Keprungu swara alus ana *ku.* I heard a gentle voice at my side. ** pinggiré segara* at the seashore. **ñj/di*** to be close/next to. *B di* A.* A sat next to B. *Sakploké duwé lara bludruk ḍèké mesṭi njanḍing obat terus.* Since he's had high blood pressure, he's kept his medicine close at hand. **s·um·anḍing** to be alongside *or* next to. *gambar kang sumanḍing* the accompanying picture.

*** kebo gupak** to associate with questionable people

sandiwârâ a type of contemporary drama of high literary quality, with Indonesian dialogue and Occidental-style music. *See also* MAIN

sândjâ to visit, drop in (*esp.* at the neighbors'). ***n-*nan** *or* ***n-s·in·andja·n** to visit each other, visit back and forth. **ke* baja** to meet with misfortune while away from home. **ñj/di*ni** to visit smn

sandjang 1 to say, tell (*kr for* KANḌA). 2 advice; to say, tell (*opt kr for* TUTUR). *See also* PISANDJANG

sanḍung **ke*** to get tripped (up). **ke* ing rata ke·bentus ing awang²** to run into uninvited trouble. **ke·sonḍang-(ke)*** 1 to keep stumbling. 2 to encounter a series of difficulties. **ñj/di*** to stumble on, trip over

sanépa figure of speech making a wry contradictory comparison, as: *abang dluwang* very pale ('as red as paper'); *arang wulu kutjing* commonplace ('as rare as cat hairs'); *pait madu* very sweet ('as bitter as honey')

sanès 1 not, other than, not the same thing as (*kr for* DUDU). 2 different; other (*kr for* LIJA). 3 different (*kr for* SÉDJÉ). ***é** *md* sorry (*said when refusing a beggar*)

sang *honorific title applied to exalted persons or weapons.* ** hjang* or ** mahadéwa* the gods. ** prabu* his majesty. ** retna* jewel (*applied to a beautiful girl*). *Sang Pistul ndjaluk kurban.* The pistol demands a victim.

sa'ng- *place prefixation: see under individual roots; see also* SA- 6

sângâ 1 nine. *djam * ésuk* 9 A.M. *Dak bidjèni *.* I gave him a grade of 9. *Hasil pertandingané *-*.* The final score was 9-9. 2 *var of* SANGAN. ***n(an)** by nines. *Olèhé tuku mesṭi *nan.* He always buys nine at a time. ***-*** by nines. *Lungguhé *-*.* They sat in groups of nine. **ka*** 1 (*or* **[ka]ping *)** nine times; times nine; (for) the ninth time; ninth in a series. 2 the ninth month of the Javanese year (1–26 March). *** bang** a playing card (*kertu tjilik*) with red marking. ***las** nineteen. ***likur** twenty-nine. *** setengah** eight and a half. *See also* -AN (*suffix*) 8, 15, 16; -É^{c} (*suffix*) 9; NG- (*prefix*) 6, 7; NGA; PRA-; SANGANG

sângâlas *see* SANGA

sângâlikur *see* SANGA

sangan food fried without oil *or* with only a

small amount of oil. **∗an** dry-fried foods (as above). **ñj/di∗** to fry without oil. *See also* NANANGAN

sangang nine (*as modifier: see also* SANGA). *∗puluh* ninety. *∗atus* (*èwu, juta*) nine hundred (thousand, million). *∗wang* 75 cents. *∗sèn/rupiah* nine cents/rupiahs. *See also* NG- (*prefix*) 6, 7

sangar enchanted, haunted. *lemah ∗* haunted ground

sangat *var of* SA'AT

sanget very (much), considerable, altogether (*kr for* BANGET)

sânggâ[a] *ng,* **sanggi** *kr* **(se)∗ǹ** 1 a support, prop. 2 burden, responsibility. *Pitulungané gawé majaré sa∗nku.* His help lightened my burdens. **ñj/di∗** to support from underneath; *fig* to support, bear. *A di∗ pundaké B.* A leaned on B's shoulder for support. *njangga wit* to prop up a tree. *Susah di∗ ḍéwé.* She bore her sorrows herself. *Jèn ana apa² ∗nen ḍéwé.* If anything goes wrong, you can take the responsibility for it yourself. **njangga bokong** to contribute to the success of one's husband. **njangga èṇṭèng** to treat lightly. **njangga krama** to smooth the way in a discussion by agreeing rather than arguing. **njangga ṁ·piring** *sms* NJANGGA ÈṆṬÈNG *above.* **njangga wragad·é** to bear the expenses of. **ñj/di∗kaké** 1 to use as a support. 2 to have smn support himself. *Manganku di∗kaké nang sawidjining rumah makan.* I'm expected to take my meals at a restaurant. **∗ langit** a certain climbing vine. **∗ wang** to rest the chin in the hand

sânggâ[b] measuring unit for rice plants: five or six double handfuls (*gèḍèng*'s), or *ca.* 50 *kati*'s = *ca.* 30.85 kilograms = *ca.* 68 lbs.

sanggâmâ sexual intercourse (*ki for* TJUMBANA?). **ñj∗** to have intercourse. **ñj/di∗ni** to have intercourse with

sanggami *var of* SANGGAMA

sanggar a place of worship; a chapel for prayer and meditation. **∗ pa·langgat·an** throne

sânggârunggi suspicious, untrustworthy. **ñj/di∗ǹi** to suspect smn of nefarious doings

sanggem **ñj/di∗i** to accept *or* agree to [a responsibility]. *Pradjandjian mau di∗i déning A nganggo diseksèni ing lurah désa.* The agreement was entered into by A and witnessed by the village head. **s·um·anggem** pledged, committed to

sanggi to support (*root form: kr for* SANGGA[a])

sanggrah **ma∗, pa∗** *see* PASANGGRAH. **∗ pa·lerep·an** resort, place for recreation

sanggul 1 traditional ladies' hairdo consisting of a smooth bun at the back of the head (*sms* GELUNG). 2 modern hairdo for long hair (*sms* KAPSEL)

sanggup to promise (to do sth). **ka∗an** a promise. **ñj/di∗i** to promise sth; to make a promise to smn

sangit overcooked, burned. **ñj/di∗aké** to overcook, burn; to give [food] a burned taste. **s·um·angit** having a disagreeable burned taste. *témpé semangit* burnt beancake. *See also* WALANG

sângkâ from *etc.* (*var of* SAKA[a]). **∗n** 1 origin. *Saka ngendi ∗né?* Where's he from? *∗ning* (*wong*) *tjilik* from the lower classes. 2 cause, source. *∗né laramu apa?* What made you ill? *∗ning lelembut* caused by the spirits. 3 trip, journey. **tanpa ∗n** a sudden appearance out of nowhere. **∗n paran** origin and destination. *wong tanpa ∗n paran* one whose background and future are unknown. *∗n-paraning dumadi* life and death; the rise and decline of human existence. **∗n-∗n** trip, journey. **ñj/di∗ni** to start from smw. *Olèhé lunga di∗ni saka Djakarta.* He started his journey from Djakarta.

sangkal the handle of a certain tool (*peṭèl*). **ñj∗ putung** angular

sangkep well equipped. *∗ing perang* equipped for war. **ñj/di∗i** to equip, outfit

sangker *see* WALANG

sangkèt a certain plant whose leaves are used medicinally

sangking *var of* SAKING

sangkut **∗an** (to have) a kite-flying contest. **ke∗** to get caught *or* snagged; *fig* to get involved. *Ḍèké ke∗ soal korupsi.* He was dragged into the corruption case. **ñj/di∗** 1 to catch *or* hook onto. *Lajanganku di∗ A.* A snagged my kite [in a contest]. 2 to involve, drag in. *Soal mau njangkut kesalahané sing nḍisik².* The case in question involved earlier acts of guilt.

sanglé *var of* SANGLI

sangli different, not matching, out of harmony. *Tjèté nggon slébor ∗ sédjé karo lijané.* The paint on the fender doesn't match the rest of the paint.

sangling **ñj/di∗** to polish. **s·in·angling** polished. *kaja mas sinangling* made to shine like gold

sanglir 1 [of one's testicles] different in size.

2 dull, tarnished [of *e.g.* gold of less than 24 carats]

sangsâjâ increasingly. *Saja bengi udané * deres.* The rain got harder and harder as night wore on. *... *... the more... the more... **s·in·angsaja** to undergo suffering. *Jèn ora nggugu pituturé wong tuwa, bakal sinangsaja tembé burimu.* If you don't listen to your parents' advice, you'll regret it in the future. *See also* SAJA

sangsam large deer (*opt? kr for* MENDJANGAN)

sangsang ***an** 1 clothes-drying line. 2 necklace (*kr for* KALUNG). 3 hair ornament (*kr for* TJUNḌUK). **ke*** to fall and catch on sth. *Lajanganė ke* nang wit.* The kite caught in a tree. **ñj/di*aké** to hang sth. **ñj/di*i** to wear [sth decorative] in the hair *or* around the neck. **s·um·angsang** stuck, caught. *Lajangané semangsang.* The kite was caught.

sangsârâ (*or* **ka*n**) sorrow, suffering. **ñj*ni** 1 grief-stricken. 2 causing suffering/misery

Sangsekerta, Sangsekarta Sanskrit

sangu necessities (food, money) taken on a journey. ***n̂** severance pay. **ñj/di*k̂aké** to provide a traveler with [necessities]. *Aku njangokaké Rp. sepuluh nang ḍèké.* I gave him ten rupiahs to take with him on his trip. **ñj/di*n̂i** to provide [smn] with necessities. *Apa kowé arep njangoni aku?* Are you going to give me anything to take along? *Iki tak sangoni Rp. sepuluh.* Here's ten rupiahs for your trip. **njangoni slamet** have a good trip! **pa*n̂** severance pay

sa'niki now (*md for* SAIKI)

saniskârâ *oj* all, everything, every one

sa'nj- *place prefixation: see under individual roots; see also* SA 6

Sanskerta, Sanskarta *var of* SANGSEKERTA

santā(h) saint. ***Maria** Mary (mother of Jesus)

santen coconut milk pressed from shredded coconut meat. ***an** having coconut milk mixed into it. **ñj*** 1 to extract coconut milk by pressing. 2 (*psv* **di***) to press milk from [coconut]. **ñj/di*i** to add coconut milk to. *njanteni djangan* to put coconut milk in the soup. *** kanil** *or* *** kenṭel** coconut cream (the thick part of coconut milk that rises to the top)

santer 1 swift. 2 strong. 3 loud. **ñj/di*aké** to cause to be swift/strong/loud

santèt a type of black magic (a variety of *tenung*)

santi **se*** to ask God's blessing

santika *oj* skilled at handling weapons of war. **ka*n** supernatural invulnerability

santiku *rg* I think, I feel (*var of* RUMANGSAKU). * *ḍèké wis mangan.* I thought he had eaten. * *ḍèké lunga.* I think he's out.

santjâjâ 1 *oj* a gathering of friends *or* acquaintances. 2 the fourth *windu*

santlap ***-*an** to yell at each other abusively. **ñj/di*** to yell at smn

santo (*abbr:* **St.**) saint; sacred (one). * *Bapa* Holy Father (Catholic term)

santog 1 a variety of mango. 2 to the utmost (*var of* KATOG). * *anggoné ndeleng lukisan.* He enjoyed the painting tremendously.

santri 1 one who adheres strictly to Islamic principles. *kauman ** group of the above people living in a certain section and forming a particular stratum of society. 2 pupil of Islam living in a monastery. **ñj*** 1 to be(come) one of the above. 2 to travel to the home of one's bride on the eve of the wedding. *Kapan njantriné?* When does the groom arrive? **ñj/di*k̀aké** to have [a boy] live with a family, with prospects of being chosen as a son-in-law. *Anaké disantrèkaké nang kuluarga S.* He's having his son live in the S. household. **ñj*ǹi** to act and dress like a *santri*. **pa*ǹ** place where one receives instruction in Islam and in Koran reading. *** blatèr** liberal-minded *santri*

santun 1 betel-chewing ingredient (*opt kr for* GAMBIR). 2 change, replacement (*kr for* SALIN). 3 essence (*kr for* SARI)

santya *ltry var of* SANTI

sanubari *see* ATI

saos 1 to visit [an exalted person] (*ka: cf.* SOWAN). 2 to offer (*root form: ka for* SADJI). 3 sauce. 4 only, just (*kr; see also* KÉMAWON). **ñj/di*aké** to serve sth (*ka for* ÑJ/DI·SUGUH·AKÉ). *Olèhé njaosaké undjukan nganggo tangan tengen.* Use your right hand to serve drinks. **ñj/di*i** (*alternate form of* ÑJ/DI·TJAOS·I) 1 *ka* to serve smn. 2 to give to smn (*ka for* M̌/DI·WÈNÈH·I). *** atur** *ka* to inform, tell. *** bekti** *ka* to pay one's respects to. *** undjuk** *ka* to tell, inform

saoto a soup or stew made with beansprouts, cabbage, chicken, and soy sauce

sap a layer in a stack. * *kang kaping lima* the fifth floor. ***-*an** in layers, piled up. *nganggo kemul *-*an* to have more than one blanket covering one. **nge/di*i** to furnish with layers. *Lemariné di*i.* He made shelves for the cupboard. * **tangan** handkerchief (*see also* SAPU)

sâpâ[a] *ng,* **sinten** *kr* 1 who. *Iki omahé *?* Whose house is this? *Ana wong teka, embuh *.* Somebody's coming, I don't know who. ** djenengé?* What's his name? ** manèh?* (And) who else? ** wongé sing ora gemes.* Who *wouldn't* be annoyed? ** ngira/njana...?* Who would have thought/expected...? 2 whoever; anyone who... 3 smn else. *Kagèt aku, dak arani kowé *.* You startled me–I thought you were smn else. ***-*(a)** everyone; [not] anyone. *Sapa²a sing tepung mesṭi tresna.* Everyone who knows her loves her. *Aku sing nemu, dudu *-*.* *I* found it–nobody else. ***-s·in·apa** *or* ***n-s·in·apa·nan** *ng* 1 [of strangers] to strike up a conversation. 2 to ask each other 'who goes there?' **ñj/di*** *ng kr* (**ñj/dipun·sinten** *opt kr*) 1 to ask 'who?' *Bareng di* bandjur mlaju.* When they asked him to identify himself, he ran off. 2 to greet, say 'hi!' to. * **aruh** to speak to. *Wiwit iku A ora gelem * aruh manèh karo B.* Since then, A has never spoken to B. * **baé sing** *or* * **baja** *or* **sing *** whoever; anyone who... *Sapa waé sing weruh mesṭi paḍa ngalem apiké.* Anyone who sees it admires its beauty.

sâpâ[b] curse, oath. **ñj/di*kaké** to utter a curse on sth. **ñj/di*(ni)** to put a curse on smn. *di*ni déning wong tuwané* cursed by one's parents. *See also* PRASAPA

Sapar second month of the Moslem calendar. ***an** religious festival celebrated during Sapar. **ñj*** to celebrate this festival

sapâtâ 1 *oj* oath, curse. 2 alone, lonely. *badan ** alone in the world

sapi *ng,* **lembu** *kr* cow. ** ata* cow with a red nose. ** benggala* draft bull. ** dara* heifer. ** kebiri* steer. ** kerdja* cow used for farm work. ** lanang* bull. ** lanangan* bull used for breeding. ** peresan* or ** powan* milk cow. ** rambon* crossbreed between a wild bull and a domestic cow. * ***ǹ** cow used for transporting freight; *wong sapi sapèn* cattle driver

sapih ***an** (having been) weaned. **ñj/di*** (**m̀/di·pegeng** *ki*) 1 to wean. 2 to separate quarreling people

sapit tongs, pincers. **ñj/di*** to handle with tongs. *njapit mawa* to pick up glowing charcoal with tongs

sapta *oj* seven. * **rengga** hermitage

sapu broom. ***n̂** 1 sweeping (to be) done. 2 tax paid by shopowners and market sellers. **ñj/di*(n̂i)** 1 to sweep. 2 to whack with a broom. **pa*n̂** tax (as above). **pa·ñj*** one who sweeps. * **ḍenḍa** 1 a fine. 2 retribution. * **duk** broom made of palm-tree fibers. * **ilang suh·é** a broom that has come unbound; *fig* a disbanded group. * **kawat (agul²)** sponsor, patron. * **lebu** close to the ground. * **liḍi** long-handled coconut-rib broom. * **sada** broom made of coconut-leaf ribs. * **tangan** (* **asta** *ki*) handkerchief. * **uḍar** *or* * **weḍar** *sms* * ILANG SUH·É *above*

sa'punika (*usu. prn* **sa'menika**) now (*kr for* SAIKI)

saput 1 powder puff. 2 all, complete. *omah kang pepak * pirantiné* a completely equipped house. **ñj/di*aké** to apply [powder]. *Pupuré di*aké.* She powdered her face. **ñj/di*(i)** 1 to apply powder to the face. 2 to strike. *Goḍongé ke* angin dadi lebur.* The leaves were damaged by the wind. * **ḍengkul** knee high. * **ésuk (awan, soré, bengi)** all morning (midday, afternoon, evening). * **lemah** pre-dawn time when the eastern sky shows red

sar *rpr* quick heartbeats. *Mak * atiku mau aku arep ketundjang montor.* My heart thumped when a car almost hit me. ***-*(an)** to thud, pound, go pit-a-pat. **nge/di*-*i** to cause [the heart] to beat rapidly

sar- *see also under* SR- (*Introduction, 2.9.3*)

sârâ *oj* arrow

sarab convulsions (children's illness). **ñj/di*** to snap at and devour

saraḍaḍu soldier

saradan a nervous habit (nail-biting, facial tic, *etc.*)

sârâdulâ *oj* tiger

saraf nerve (*var of* SARAP)

sarâjudâ messenger, errand boy

sarak 1 rules of conduct. *murang ** to behave badly. 2 wicked. *wong wadon sing atiné ** an evil-hearted woman

saran recommendation. **ñj/di*aké** to recommend

sarânâ 1 by means of, by, with. *dikabari * tilgram* notified by telegram. *Penggawéné * digoḍog.* The job [of making sap into sugar] is done by boiling it. *nelesi lambéné * ilaté* to wet the lips with one's tongue. 2 offering *or* sacrifice made in order that a wish may materialize

sarandu all over [the body]. **ning awak* or

ning badan the entire body. * *badané dadi lemes.* He became weak all over.

sarang *an metal filter separating the upper
and lower portions of a certain rice-steaming utensil (*dandang sablug*). gudir *an
seaweed porridge. * **burung** the nest of a
certain sea bird, used for preparing a body-
strengthening soup

saranta *var of* SRANTA

sarap nerve. *an (to eat) breakfast. *Aku diwènèhi *an sega waḍang.* She served me last
night's rice for breakfast. *Sawisé adus bandjur *an.* He bathed and had breakfast.
Sarapānâ ḍisik. Have breakfast first. ñj/di*
(*cr?*) to eat (sth, *esp.* for breakfast). *Pantjingé wis di* iwak.* The fish has taken the
bait. ñj/di*i to provide smn with breakfast.
Sarapânâ. Give him some breakfast.

saras healthy; untilled (*kr [also ng?] for* WA-
RAS)

saraséhan bull session

sârâsilah genealogy, personal history

sarat requirement to be filled; that which is
needed. *ing urip* the necessities of life.
Sarat²é kanggo dadi présiḍèn iku apa?
What are the qualifications for becoming
president? ñj/di*i to fulfill a requirement.
*Lumbungé diresiki lan di*i.* The storage
shed was cleaned and supplied with everything that was needed. * **masrut** 1 medicine, remedy. 2 fee paid to a medicine man
for treatment

sârâwèdi ñj/di* to polish gems. s·in·arawèdi
cherished. *mitraku sinarawèdi Mas Singgih*
my dear friend Singgih. *sedulur sinarawèdi*
a friend so close he is like a relative. **tukang**
* dealer in gems; one who polishes precious
stones

sarḍèn, sardine sardine(s)

sardjânâ, sardjānā scholar, specialist in a
branch of knowledge. ka*n scholarship,
i.e. work done by a scholar. *Ke*né kena di-
endelaké.* You can rely on (the soundness
of) his scholarly work.

sardju to agree, be in accord with, assent to

sardula *oj* tiger

saré to sleep, go to bed (*ki for* TURU). *an
grave, tomb (*ki for* KUBUR·AN). ñj* to
stay smw overnight (*ki for* NG·INEP).
ñj/di*k̇aké 1 to bury (*ki for* ÑG/DI·KUBUR).
Swargi bapak disarèkaké ing kéné. Our father is buried here. 2 to put smn to bed
(*ki for* Ñ/DI·TURU·K̇AKÉ). pa*an grave,
tomb. s·um·aré buried smw. *Sing sumaré*

sisih wétan kuwi swargi bapak. Buried to
the east there is our father.

sarèh calmed down. *Ambekané wus *.* He
got his breath back. *Kanḍaa sing *, adja
kumretjek.* Tell it calmly—don't twitter like
a bird. ñj/di* to keep control of oneself.
ñj/di*aké to calm oneself. *Énggal sarèhna.*
Get hold of yourself! *Di*aké ḍisik atimu,
jèn wis lagi kanḍaa.* Calm down first and
then talk to him. ñj/di*i 1 to calm smn
down. 2 [in card games] to pick up a card
that smn has discarded and add it to one's
own hand

sarem 1 interest on money (*root form:
sbst? kr for* ANAK[b]). 2 salt (*kr for* UJAH)

sareng 1 (in the past) when; whereas; together (*kr for* BARENG). 2 by (means of)
[*formal letter-writing term*]. (*Ha*)*sareng serat punika kula ngaturi priksa...* With this
letter I inform you...

saréngat fulfillment of one's religious duties
according to Moslem law

sari 1 (**santun** *kr*) essence, essential ingredient *or* material. 2 sperm (of animals); pol-
len (of plants). 3 menstrual blood. 4 congealed animal blood: cooked as a rice-accompanying dish, also used for batik dyes.
*ṅ *sms* * 4. ñj/di*ṅi to dip [fabric being
worked in batik] into dye. * **paṭi** essence.
* **warta** the essence of the news; the top
story of the day. * **wos** essence; * **wos·é**
in essence; in short

sariah principles for guidance. * *Islam* moral
principles taught by Islam

sarib (to discharge) flatus (*ki for* ENTUT)

sarik ke* to receive retribution for one's
wrongdoing. **tulak** * malediction

sarimbit (together) as a couple, *i.e.* man and
woman; together with one's spouse. *pamanku* * my uncle and his wife. *Lungguhé djèdjèr *.* [The boy and the girl] sat next to
each other. *an to go out on a date together

saring *an 1 seive, strainer. 2 strained, filtered. *banju *an* filtered water. *an saka
piḍato* condensed from the speech. 3 act
of filtering *or* straining. *pabrik *an lenga
tanah* oil refinery. 4 container for (filtered)
drinking water. ñj* resonant. ñj/di*aké
to strain/filter for smn. ñj/di*(i) to strain
or filter sth

sarira body (*ki for* AWAK)

sarkârâ 1 *oj* sugar. 2 a certain classical verse
form

sarodja water lily, lotus blossom

saron xylophone-like gamelan instrument consisting of six or seven heavy bronze bars above a hollow wooden base. **ñj*** to play the above instrument. * **peking** a small *saron*

sarong 1 a partitioned-off space used *e.g.* as a chicken coop *or* for storage. 2 *rg var of* SARUNG

sarpa *oj* snake, serpent

sarta and; with. * *manèh* moreover. **ke*n** accompanied (by). **ñj/di*ni** to accompany. *Ora ana sing njertani.* Nobody went with him. **s·in·arta·n** *oj* accompanied by. *Rawuhé sinartan adiké.* His younger brother went with him.

saru indecent, obscene (in behavior *or* speech). **ke*** to get interrupted for a trivial matter. **ñj/di*** to address indecent/obscene remarks to. **njaru-wuwus** to interrupt [sth serious] with a trivial matter

sarug **ñj/di*** to scuff the feet, kick up dirt, *etc.* as one walks

sarung men's ankle-length wraparound skirt. ***an** 1 to put on *or* wear the above. 2 kris sheath (*kr for* (W)RANGKA). ***an kenḍali** horse's riding equipment (saddle, bridle, *etc.*). **ñj/di*aké** to wrap *or* sheathe [a weapon]. **ñj/di*i** 1 to dress smn in a *sarung.* 2 to wrap [a weapon] in protective cloth; to sheathe [a weapon]. * **bantal** pillow case. * **kaki** socks, stockings. * **keris** outer part of a wooden kris sheath. * **tangan** gloves

sarwa (**sarwi** *opt? kr*) altogether, in every respect. *Kapalé madju * adjeg.* The ship proceeded perfectly steadily. *Djuru rawat mau penganggoné * putih.* The nurse was dressed all in white. *Apa² * ana lan ora kurang.* Everything was available; nothing was lacking.

sarwi *opt? kr for* SARWA

sasab 1 cover, covering layer. 2 *kr for* MENANG? ('to win'). **ñj/di*** to equip with a cover(ing layer). **ñj*i ḍengkul** to show favoritism to members of one's own family; to practice nepotism

sasadârâ *oj* moon

sasag **ñj/di*** 1 to thread one's way through [traffic; underbrush; *etc.*]. 2 to arrange one's hair in a high fluffy hairdo (modern short-haired style)

sasânâ place, location. * **(h)inggil (dwi abad)** an elevated hall at the south end of the Jogjakarta palace [*see also* SITI] built to commemorate the Jogjakarta bicentennial anniversary

sasângkâ *oj* moon

sasar to get lost, miss one's way; to err, go astray. **ke*** to get lost, miss one's way. *Angger diantjer-antjer mesṭi ora bakal ke*.* So long as it's marked, I won't miss it. **ñ(j)*** to deviate from the expected course. *peluru n(j)asar* a stray bullet. **ñ(j)/di*aké** to misdirect, cause smn to go out of his way. *Wong nunggang bétjak di*ké mubeng kuṭa karebèn kétok adoh bandjur mbajar akèh.* The pedicab driver took the [naive] passenger the long way around so he would get paid more. **pa·ñj*** wrong directions; unreliable information. ***-susur** *sms* *

sasat as if, as though; like, as. *Rikaté * angin.* It goes like the wind. *See also* PRASASAT

sasi 1 (**wulan** *kr*) month. *ḍèk * kepungkur* last month. *se* sepisan* once a month. 2 *oj* moon. ***ǹ** 1 monthly. *Bajaré ditampa sasèn.* He gets paid by the month. 2 (*or* ***ǹ-*ǹ**) month after month. *Olèhé nang Djakarta sasèn.* He stayed in Djakarta for months. *Larané ngot²an, nganti sasèn² ora mari.* His illness hung on; he didn't recover for months on end. * **tara** the calendar months collectively with the exception of Pasa, Besar, and Sawal (times of religious celebration)

sasmita signal, sign. * *gendéra* flag signals. *Botjah ora ngerti *, wis tjeṭa disinḍir-sinḍir karo sing duwé omah dikon lunga.* You don't get the message: your hostess is hinting that you should leave. **ñj/di*ni** to give a signal (to). *Ḍalangé njasmitani nijaga ndjaluk genḍing X.* The puppet-master gave the musicians the signal to play X melody.

sasra *oj* one thousand. *sarambut pinara ** trivial, of no consequence

sasrah ***an** gift given to the bride's parents by the groom's parents. **ñj/di*i** to give a present to one's bride on their wedding day

sastra writings, letters, literature. *djurusan sastrā* department *or* discipline of languages and literature. **ora ngerti *** illiterate

sat **ke*** drained, dried out/up. **nge/di*(aké)** to drain (the water from). *Rawa² sing mambeg kudu diesat.* Stagnant swamps must be drained. *See also* ASAT

sâtâ tobacco (*kr for* (M)BAKO). *See also* SURJA

satak a formerly used currency item equal to

100 *ḍuwit,* or 83½ cents. **tuna * baṭi sanak** to lose a little money but gain a friend

satang oar, paddle. **ñj/di*(i)** to row, paddle [a boat]

saté Javanese-style shishkebabs served with a hot sauce. * *ajam* chicken broiled on skewers. * *weḍus* lamb kebabs. **ñj/di*** to make [meat] into the above

sat-mâtâ visible (*shf of* KASAT MATA)

sato animal. ***n** animal-like creature *or* figure. *Ing pepetengan aku weruh saton.* I saw an animal-like shape in the dark. * **iwèn** poultry, fowl. * **kéwan** (the class of) animals, including birds and insects. *wit²an lan * kéwan* plants and animals. * **kuntjung** peacock

satrija 1 nobleman; a man who devotes himself to the service of his country. 2 [in olden days] an aristocrat who helped rule the country and took responsibility upon himself to deal with dangers, for the sake of his people. **ka*n** place where noblemen are quartered. **ñj*** 1 to live the life of a nobleman. 2 to have the characteristics of a nobleman

satru 1 enemy, foe. *Tikus kuwi *né wong.* Rats are man's enemy. * *karo* at odds with. *A * karo B.* A and B are enemies. 2 *var of* SATU. **se*ñ** hostility, enmity. **ñj/di*ñi** 1 to be hostile toward; to consider as one's enemy. *Aku ora rumangsa salah apa² kok disatroni.* I don't know what I've done, but he's hostile toward me. 2 to go smw for a nefarious purpose. *Omahé A mau bengi disatroni maling.* A's house was entered by a thief last night. * **be·bujut·an/ka·bujut·an** enemies of long standing. * **munggèng tjangklak·an** enemies in spite of being related by blood

satu a cookie made from green-bean flour

satunggal 1 a(n), a certain (*kr for* SAWIDJI). 2 one (*kr for* SIDJI)

satunggil *sbst? var of* SATUNGGAL

satus one hundred. * *taun* 100 years. ***an** 1 approximately 100. 2 a 100-rupiah bill. ***é** the 100th day after smn's death. **ñj*** 1 every one hundred; by the hundred. *Tomaté njatus pira, pak?* How much for 100 tomatoes? *Sak botolé njatus isiné.* There are 100 of them to a bottle. 2 to honor [a deceased person] with a ceremony on the 100th day after his death. * **salap** 99. *See also* ATUS

satwa *oj* 1 animal. 2 holiness, sacredness

sauga if, in case, in the event that

saur 1 (to eat) a meal between 2 and 4 A.M. during the fasting month, *i.e.* at the permitted time for eating. 2 oral reply. **(se)*an** to answer back and forth. *perkutut *an* the cooing "conversation" of turtledoves. *Swarané gong *an karo swarané kenḍang.* The gong beats are answered by drum beats. **ñj/di*** to repay. *njaur utang* to repay a loan. *njaur punagi* to make good on a promise. *njaur pati* to avenge one death with another. *njaur wirang* to be humiliated as one has humiliated others. **ñj/di*aké** to use as repayment. *Jèn kentèkan ḍuwit, klambimu kena di*ké utang.* If you're out of money, you can pay off the debt with your clothes. **ñj/di*i** 1 to repay sth. *njauri utang* to repay a debt. 2 to answer orally. **pa·ñj*** payment of (*or* on) a debt. **s·um·aur** to reply orally. * **manuk** a chorused reply. *Wangsulané * manuk.* They answered in unison.

saus sauce (*var of* SAOS)

saut **ke*** to be pulled (in); to pull in, lay one's hands on. *Njambut gawé ngéna-ngéné meksa ora bisa ke* butuhé.* I work myself to the bone but I still can't manage our needs. **ñj/di*** to snatch (up, away). *Kuṭuké sidji di* wulung.* The hawk snatched one of the chicks. *Tasé di* tjopèt.* A pickpocket snatched her handbag.

S.A.W. *see* SALLALAHU

sâwâ 1 python. 2 corpse

sawab a blessing with magical powers. **ñj/di*i** to put such a blessing on smn

sawah *ng,* **sabin** *kr* rice paddy, wet rice field. **se*** to be a rice farmer. **ñj*** to work rice paddies. **pa*an** rice paddies collectively, *i.e.* land devoted to raising rice. * **adjang·an** community-owned paddy. * **bengkok** *rg var of* * LUNGGUH *below.* * **gaḍu·(ñ)** irrigated field for cultivating rice in the dry season. * **gunḍul** vast area covered with rice paddies without intervening villages. * **lungguh** communal village rice paddy. * **rawa** low-lying paddy that gets inundated during the rainy season. * **sorot·an** a paddy that is irrigated by river water. * **taḍah·an** a paddy in a high elevation that is irrigated only by rainfall. * **titisara** communal paddy whose yield is used to defray village expenses. * **ulu** paddy that is easily flooded during the rainy season. * **walik·an** paddy used for raising a second crop of rice after the first harvest but before the beginning of the rainy season

Sawal tenth month of the Moslem calendar, during which the major religious holiday (*Lebaran*) is celebrated

sawâlâ *var of* SUWALA

sawan convulsions, fits, epilepsy (childhood disease). (*djamu*) ***an** a medicinal herb used for warding off the above. ***en** to have *or* get the above condition

sawang 1 to look like, resemble. ** lajon* or ** kunarpa* having a corpse-like pallor (during or after illness). 2 cobweb. ***an** 1 that which is watched. *Botjah wadon aju kuwi dadi *an wong.* Everyone is looking at that beautiful girl. 2 bamboo whistle attached to a pigeon's tail to give off a humming sound as the bird flies. ***en** 1 covered with cobwebs. 2 with eyes slightly open in death. ***-*** cobweb. **se*an** view, scenery, that which is pleasant to look at. **ñj/di*** to watch, *esp.* with pleasure or enjoyment. *Jèn di* katon asri.* It's beautiful to see. *Ora njawang marang banḍa lan rupa.* He doesn't notice riches or appearances. **pa·ñj*** act of looking at. *Saka penjawangku, kok kaja gambar djingklong ta.* From what I see, it looks like a picture of a mosquito.

sawat stone used as a missile. **é ngenani pelem.* The stone he threw hit a mango. ***-*an** to throw at/toward each other. *Botjah² mau *-*an ḍelé.* The boys were pelting each other with soybeans. *Sadurungé tjeḍak mantèn loro mau paḍa *-*an nganggo sadak.* As they approach each other, the bridal couple throw special packets toward each other. **ñj/di*** to throw at sth. *Asuné di* kena gegeré.* He threw a stone at the dog and hit it on the back. **njawat a·balang woh·é** to work hard to achieve sth: *esp.* to try to get to know a girl by getting friendly with smn related to her. **ñj/di*aké** to throw [a missile] at. *Watuné di*aké asu.* He threw the stone at the dog.

saweg to be [do]ing *etc.* (*kr for* LAGI)

sawer snake (*kr for* ULA)

sawi edible greens. ** idjo* lettuce. ** putih* Chinese cabbage

sa'widji *ng,* **satunggal** *kr* a(n), a certain, one. *anudju * dina* once upon a time; one day. *ing * dina djam nem ésuk* one day at 6 A.M. *ana ing *ning pésta* once at a party. *Anaké mung * kuwi.* He has only that one child. *jèn tanpa alangan * apa* if there's nothing to prevent it. *Ora kekurangan sewidji apa.* Nothing was lacking. **ñj*** to agree, be of one mind. *Paḍa njawidji hadjat bebarengan slametan bersih désa.* They agreed to hold a joint ceremony for village prosperity. **ñj/di*kaké** to unite, bring into agreement. *njawidjèkaké panemu sing werna²* to bring divergent opinions into harmony. **salah *-ning** one (out of them all); a(n). *salah *ning negara kang pawetuné utama saka pertanian* a country with abundant agricultural products. *See also* IDJI, SIDJI, WIDJI

sawijah 1 the young of a certain lizard (*tjetjak*). 2 *ltry* each, every; [not] any. ** dina* every day. ** uwong/barang* anyone/anything (at all). **ñj/di*(-wijah)** to consider inconsequential

sawit batik garment with headdress of matching material. ***an** 1 an outfit *or* combination as above. 2 matching wedding batiks of a special pattern, worn by the bride and groom. *Mantèné *an parang, ibu lan bapaké *an truntum.* The bride and groom wore the *parang* design and the bride's parents wore the *truntum* design. **ñj*** to put on *or* wear the above

sawo a delicious tropical fruit; also, the tree it grows on. ** Djawa* or ** ketjik* small varieties of *sawo* fruit. ** Menila* a large *sawo* fruit. *** mateng** 1 ripe *sawo* fruit. 2 brown. **ñj*-mateng** brown-colored. *Pakulitané njawo mateng.* Her skin is brown.

sawud a cookie made of shredded cassava and sugar

sawung 1 rooster, cock (*kr for* DJAGO). 2 chicken (*rg kr for* PITIK). **ñj/di*** to carry [a child] in one's arms (rather than using a sling: *see* EMBAN²). **s·in·awung** *ltry* expressed in the form of a song or poem. *Rasa katresnané sinawung ing kidung.* He conveyed his love in a song. *** galing** 1 an undefeated fighting cock. 2 rooster-shaped golden seal used in court ceremonies

sawur small objects (coins, rice, *etc.*) scattered before a funeral procession as it makes its way to the cemetery. **ñj/di*(aké)** 1 to strew the above. 2 to plant [rice seeds] by scattering them. **ñj/di*i** to bestrew [sth] with small particles, *e.g.* sand. **s·um·awur** scattered, sprinkled

S.D. *see* SEKOLAH

sdl., sdr. *see* SEDULUR

se- *prefix: inf var of* SA. *See also under* SA- (*Introduction, 2.9.2*)

sèb ***-*an** to keep belching; to keep tasting sth one has eaten

séba to visit [a social superior, *esp.* at court: *ka for* TILIK]. **ñj/di*kaké** to present smn to an exalted person. **ñj/di*ni** to pay a visit to [smn of high standing]. **pa*** a visit. **pa*n** place where visits to high officials take place. **pi*** a visit (to smn high). **s·in·éba** to be paid homage. *Sang Prabu sinéba para kawulané.* The king's subjects showed their esteem for him.

sebab because; reason, cause. *Truké mogok sebab kakèhan momotan.* The truck broke down because it was overloaded. *Apa *é?* Why? What's the reason for it? ** (déné) apa?* Why? *Kowé wedi * apa?* Why are you afraid? *Tjritakna apa *é tekamu kasèp.* Tell me why you're late. ** iku* for that reason; because of that. ** iku aku ora teka.* That's why I didn't come. *tanpa ** for no reason. *Ḍèkè ora ngerti *-*é kok mèlu²*. He butted into [the quarrel] without having any idea what it was all about. **di*** to be asked why. **ñj/di*aké** to cause. *Njamuk iku njebabaké malaria.* Mosquitoes cause malaria. *di*aké kurang penerangan* as a result of inadequate information

sebah to feel queasy; *fig* to feel repelled; to find sth disagreeable. *Aku * ing kéné.* I don't like it here. **ñj*i** causing the above feelings. *Tumindak sing ala iku njebahi banget.* Behaving badly turns people against you.

sebal **ñj*** to differ from the usual *or* normal. *tindak-tanduk kang njebal saka padatan* actions which are outside the normal accepted patterns. *Wataké njebal ḍéwé karo sedulur²é.* His character is quite different from his brothers' and sisters'. *Aku kepeksa njebal saka barisan djalaran kesel banget.* I had to drop out of the parade, I was so exhausted.

sebar ***an** distributed, spread about. *lajang *an* pamphlet, leaflet. **ñj/di*(aké) (n/diḍawah** *kr?*) to spread, scatter; to distribute. *Menawa wajahé njebar ora duwé widji.* When it came time to sow, he had no seeds. *njebar kabar menjang endi²* to spread the news. *Ḍuwitku di* karo anakku.* My daughter spends my money recklessly. *Widjiné di*aké manuk.* The birds disseminated the seeds. **ñj/di*i** to spread [things]. *njebari kembang sing wangi²* to scatter fragrant flowers. 2 to bestrew with. *Peturonku di*i kembang.* She strewed my bed with flowers. **s·um·ebar** spread widely. *Katjangé sumebar nang djubin.* The peanuts spilled all over the floor. *Saiki wis sumebar, saben toko baé wis ana sing adol.* They're everywhere now—the stores all sell them. *Kabaré énggal sumebar.* The news spread quickly.

sebarang *var of* SEMBARANG

sebat 1 essential characteristics. *Masé adoh *é karo aḍiké.* The older brother is very different from the younger brother. 2 to name, mention (*root form: opt? kr for* SEBUT)

sebâwâ sound, noise. *Ora ana * manèh.* There was no other sound. *tembung * (gram)* exclamation. **ñj*** to make a noise. *See also* BAWA

sebda *inf var of* SABDA

sebel 1 bored, fed up. 2 hounded by bad luck. **ñj*i** obnoxious

sèbet quick! right away! *** bjar wauta** *wj* at the moment we begin (*opening phrase uttered by the puppet-master*)

sebit torn (off, apart), dismembered. **ñj/di*** to tear (off, apart), to dismember. *** ron tal** woman's bracelet in the form of a thin flat band

seblak **ñj/di*aké** to open *or* extend sth wide. *njeblakaké buku* to open a book. *Tangané di*aké.* He spread his arms wide. **ñj/di*(i)** to spank smn. **s·um·eblak** 1 wide open. 2 shining, glowing

sébra zebra

sebrak *inf var of* SEBRÈT

sebrang *inf var of* SABRANG

sébrat **ñj/di*aké** to disown [a relative]

sebrèt to get torn *or* pulled out/apart. **ñj/di*** to tear; to pull out/apart

sebring zip! whoosh! zing! (*describing sudden rapid motion*)

sebrot **ñj/di*** to snatch. *Tasé di* tjopèt.* A pickpocket snatched her bag.

sebrung *rpr* flying, swooping. *dibuwang ** to be tossed away, sent flying. **sebrang-*** *pl* to fly away/off

sebul **ñj/di*** to blow with breath from the mouth. *njebul kapuk* to blow kapok puffs. **ñj/di*aké** to blow on. *Sing lara di*aké nang ḍukun karebèn mari.* The witch doctor blew on the patient to cure him.

sebut 1 *rpr* a whisking motion. *Mak * ḍompèté disawut tukang tjopèt.* His wallet was suddenly snatched by a pickpocket. 2 dull (not shiny, not bright). ***é... *é...** *rg* to say first one thing then another. **é ija *é ora, kok ora karu²an Kuntjung kuwi!* Yesterday you said yes, now you say no—what an exasperating boy you are, Kuntjung! ***an** 1 technical term. 2 title; rank. 3 subject talked about. ***-*an** *sms* *AN 3. **se*an** *sms* *AN. *Bab mau wis dadi se*ané wong sakampung.* It has become the talk of the town. **ka*** (*abbr:* **ksb.**) (previously) mentioned. *ka* ing ḍuwur* mentioned above. *Pengendikané saiki biasa ka*-*.* Her words are often quoted nowadays. **ñj/di*** 1 to utter, mention. *Sadurungé mati njebut asmané Gusti Allah.* Before dying, he uttered God's name. 2 to confer a title *or* rank. *Sawisé tamat sekolah ḍokter ḍèwèké di* ḍokter.* After he graduates from medical school he'll have the title doctor. 3 (*or* **ñj/di*-***) to cry out in pain *or* strong emotion. **ora njebut** unwilling to acknowledge one's limitations. **njebat-ñj*** to complain. **ñj/di*(-*)aké** 1 to mention. *di*aké ing katja telu* referred to on page three. 2 to tell, give information. **ora duwé *** inconsiderate, ill-mannered. *See also* SAMBAT

séda 1 death; dead (*ki for* PATI[a]). 2 dead; to die (*ki for* MATI)

seḍah betel leaf (*kr for* SURUH)

sedâjâ (in) all (*kr for* KABÈH)

seḍakep *var of* SIḌAKEP

séḍan sedan (car body style)

Sedânâ spouse of Dèwi Sri, goddess of rice. *See also* SRI

seḍang *see* IKLIM

sedanten (in) all (*md for* KABÈH; *sbst var of* SEDAJA?)

sedâsâ ten (*kr for* SEPULUH). **ka*** tenth month of the Javanese year (26 March–19 April). *See also* DASA

seḍekah charitable gift, alms. **ñj/di*aké** to give gifts *or* alms to the poor. *** bumi** village celebration held annually to honor the guardian spirits of the village (*sms* BERSIH DÉSA)

seḍeku to sit bowing in respectful silence

sèḍèng adultery committed by a wife. *laku ** to commit adultery. **ñj*** [of a woman] to commit adultery

seḍeng (**tjekap** *kr?*) just right, adequate. ** ora, adja luwih saka iki.* Whether it's enough or not, don't take any more than this. *Apa * dienggo tambangan?* Is it all right to use as a raft? *Bajaranmu * nggo urip apa ora?* Is your salary enough to live on? *Klambiné wis ora * manèh.* Her dresses don't fit her any more. ***an** average, medium. **an dohé menawa kanggo mlaku².* It's just the right distance for walking. *Omah iku geḍé-tjiliké *an.* The house is of average size. *Rupané ora aju, *an waé.* She isn't beautiful—just average-looking. **ñ*** at just the right stage. *Kembangé neḍeng megar.* The flower is ready to bloom; *fig* the girl is ready for marriage. **neḍeng bira(h)i** of marriageable age. **ñ*i** to reach a certain stage. *Pari kaé lagi neḍengi idjo rojo².* The rice plants over there are at the bright-green stage. **sa*é** whatever is adequate. *nDjupuka beras sa*é.* Take what rice you need.

seḍéngah any [one], every [one]. *Ora * wong bisa.* Not everybody can do it. *Sepur ṭruṭuk kuwi manḍeg ing * setasiun.* Slow trains stop at every single station. ** kaju jèn diobong adjur dadi awu.* Any kind of wood turns to ash when it's burned.

seḍep pleasurable to the senses, *esp.* smell, taste. **ñj*aké** pleasurable. *Kembang² kuwi marakaké njeḍepaké sesawangan.* Those flowers give a pleasing appearance. *** malem** a certain flower that gives off fragrance *esp.* at night

seḍèrèk sibling; relative (*kr for* SEDULUR)

seḍerhânâ simple, modest. *Uripé * banget.* He lives modestly. **ñj/di*aké** to simplify, make less complicated

sèḍet 1 [of females] shapely, well-proportioned. 2 a certain blossom used medicinally

seḍih sad, sorrowful, grieving. **ñj/di*aké** 1 sorrowful, causing sadness. 2 to sadden, grieve. *njeḍihaké ati* to sadden the heart. **ñj/di*i** to feel saddened by. *Ana sidji sing dak*i, jakuwi nèk weruh botjah nggawa plinṭeng.* One thing that grieves me is to see a boy carrying a slingshot.

sedija *var sp of* SEDYA

seḍija to prepare, have available. *Ibu wis * lilin kanggo djaga² menawa listriké mati.* Mother has some candles ready in case the electricity goes off. ***n** available, ready for. *seḍijan djangan* soup-making materials. *Lilin iki kanggo *n jèn listriké mati.* These candles are in case the electricity goes off. **ñj/di*kaké** to provide, lay out. *Segané gorèng wis di*kaké.* The fried rice is all ready. **ñj/di*ni** to make ready *or* available for smn. *Sing nunggang di*ni paturon.* Beds were prepared for the passengers.

s·um·eḍija in readiness. *Wis ana prau sumeḍija.* A boat was waiting.
seḍil soggy, too moist to smoke [of tobacco]
sediya *var sp of* SEDYA
sedjarah history. **ñj/di*aké** to tell the history of; to narrate [past events]
sedjati *ng,* **sedjatos** *kr* true, pure. *putri ** a genuine princess; a good girl. *guru ** one who instructs on the perfection of death. ***né** in fact. *Réwa² réntjang, sedjatosipun boten.* He pretended to be helping but he really wasn't.
sedjatos *kr for* SEDJATI
sédjé *ng,* **sanès** *kr* different, other. *Klambiné disalini klambi *né.* He changed into the other shirt. *Klambiné * (karo) klambiku.* His shirt is different from mine. **ñj*** differing from. *Panemuné mesṭi njédjé ḍéwé.* His ideas are always so different from everyone else's. **ñj/di*kaké** to treat differently (than the others). *njèdjèkaké putrané menteri* to give the minister's son special treatment
sèdjèn *rg var of* SÉDJÉ
sedjid *rg* mosque
seḍot *rpr* a sucking sound. **ñj/di*** to suck, sip, inhale, siphon (off/out). *Jèn ngrokok di* djero.* When he smokes, he inhales deeply. *njeḍot bènsin montor* to siphon gas from a car. **s·um·eḍot** heartsick, pained, grieved
sedul **ñj/di*** to push with the finger
sedulur (*abbr*: **sdl.**) *ng,* **seḍèrèk** (*abbr*: **sdr.**) *kr* **1** sibling. ** lanang* brother. ** wédok* sister. 2 (**sentânâ** *ki*) blood relative, *esp.* of the same generation. *Aku karo ḍèké isih *.* He and I are related. ** šaka bapa* or ** pantjer lanang* a relative on the father's side. *prang ** civil war. ** kolur sanak énak* to care more for a distant relative than a close one. *nemu ** to become close friends; ** temon* a new-found close friend. ***an** (being) close friends. *Muga² anggoné *an (sing) langgeng.* We hope they'll always stay close friends. **ñj/di*aké** to treat *or* regard smn as a relative. **pa*an** 1 blood relationship. 2 friendship. *ngraketaké pe*an* to strengthen the ties of a friendship. **sa*é** together with one's relatives. *Djaka sa*é atiné sumanak.* Djaka has a good relationship with his family. *** asu** half-brother *or* -sister (having the same mother). *** ng·isor galeng ḍuwur** siblings of the same parents. *** susu·n̂** half-sibling nursed by the same mother. *** tunggal kringkel/welad** children of the same parents. *See also* SANAK
seḍu:t *rpr* vigorous suckings with strong contractions (*emphatic form of* SEḌOT)
seduwa to sit cross-legged with the elbows resting on the knees
sedya intention, plan. **né arep golèk gawéan.* He's going to look for a job. **ñ/di*** to [do] intentionally; to intend to [do]. *Atiné mantep, ora nedya bali.* His mind was made up: he did not mean to come back. *Omahé kuwi pantjèn di* diobong karebèn éntuk asuransi.* He deliberately set fire to his house to collect the insurance. **s·in·edya** *or* **s·um·edya** *ltry* to intend to [do]
sèg ***-*an** in constant motion, unable to remain still
seg **1** *rpr* sudden inertness. *Bareng mambu bantal mak * terus turu.* He went to sleep as soon as he hit the pillow. *mati ** to drop dead. 2 *rpr* a crowded condition. *Mak * udjuk² aku dirubung wong akèh.* Suddenly I was pressed on all sides by the crowd. *mak * kewaregen* feeling stuffed after eating. 3 *inf var* (or *md?*) *for* SAWEG. ***-*** *rpr* a series of quick movements. *Ḍèké jèn njambut-gawé *-*.* He works quickly. ***-*an** crowding each other, filled to overflowing. *Barang rupa² *-*an njeḍihaké ati.* All kinds of things filled and saddened her heart. *mBok lingguh kéné, kok *-*an nèng kono.* Sit here, you're crowding each other over there. **nge/di*-*i** to push, crowd. *Koperé motol² wong di*-*i sepatu²né.* He can hardly shut his suitcase, with all those shoes in it.
sega *ng,* **sekul** *kr* cooked rice. ** salawuhé* Javanese meal: rice together with accompanying dishes (*lawuh*). *** dang** steamed rice. *** djagung** cooked ground corn. *** golong** rice balls for ceremonial meals. *** gorèng** fried rice. *** gurih** rice cooked in coconut milk. *** kuning** rice boiled in coconut milk and colored yellow with tumeric. *** liwet** boiled rice. *** lojang** dried-out cooked rice reboiled with coconut milk, sometimes eaten with shredded coconut. *** mas** *sms* * KUNING *above.* *** penak** cooked rice wrapped in a banana leaf, eaten as a snack. *** ponḍoh** *sms* * DJAGUNG *above.* *** pulen** *sms* * PENAK *above.* *** punar** *sms* * KUNING *above.* *** waḍang** yesterday's rice fried for breakfast. *** (w)uduk** rice boiled in coconut milk
segah refreshments (*kr for* SUGUH)

seganten *kr for* SEGARA
segârâ *ng,* **seganten** *kr* sea, ocean. **né rob/surud.* The sea is at high/low tide. *ing tengah ** on the high seas, out in the ocean. *mendem ** seasick(ness). *** **anak·an** strait, channel. *** **muntjar** a round earring set with a circlet of diamonds. *** **weḍi** desert
segawon dog (*kr for* ASU)
sègel a seal, *esp.* an official government seal. *Lajang mau nganggo *.* The letter was stamped with a seal. **ñj/di*** 1 to affix a seal (on). 2 to seal off. *Omahé sing dienggo perkaran di* pengadilan.* The building involved in the case was sealed by court order.
seger fresh, refreshed, buoyant. *Kembangé wis *.* The flowers have perked up. *Ambuné *.* It smells fresh. ***(-*)an** *or* **se*an** sth refreshing. **ñj/di*aké** *or* **ñj/di*i** to freshen, refresh. *Anginé njegeri awak.* The wind refreshes you. *** **buger** in buoyant health. *** **sumjah** refreshed after having felt weary. *** **ku·waras·an** healthy and strong
segrak sharp, acrid. **ñj*** *or* **s·um·egrak** having an acrid odor. *Pokpingé ambuné sumegrak nang irung.* The odor of menthol is sharp to the nostrils.
segu a hiccup, a belch; to hiccup, belch (*ki for* TJEKIK?). *ora * ora wahing* to remain perfectly motionless and quiet. ***nen** to have the hiccups
sèh *Moslem title of esteem*
séhat healthy, hale. **ka*an** health; physical welfare. *usaha ke*an* a health center. **ñj*aké** healthful, wholesome. *Poang kuwi njéhataké nang awak.* Milk is good for you.
sek̄ *var of* SEG
séka 1 wash cloth, face cloth. 2 hot-water bottle. **ñj/di*** 1 to give smn a sponge bath with a cloth. 2 to apply a hot-water bottle (to)
seka *inf var of* SAKA[a]
sekabat close friend (*var of* SAHABAT)
sekak̄ 1 (to play) chess. 2 check! (called when threatening the opponent's chess king). **ñj/di*** to put [the opposing king] in check. *** **mat** checkmate
sekar 1 flower (*kr for* KEMBANG). 2 gravestone (*ki for* KIDJING). 3 grave, tomb (*ki for* KUBUR·(AN)]. 4 classical verse (*kr for* TEMBANG). **ñj/di*** to place flowers on a grave. *Aku arep njekar ibu.* I'm going to place flowers on my mother's grave. *** **turi** a certain style of jacket (having rounded corners at the bottom of the front opening)
sekarat (to be in) death throes
sekarep *inf var of* SA·KAREP[É]. **ñj*** to act as one pleases. *See also* KAREP
sekati *ng,* **sekatos** *kr* certain songs in the palaces of Jogja and Solo, used *esp.* during the month of Mulud for special ceremonies. ***n̂** *ng kr* 1 important court festival held during Mulud. 2 the *gong* music accompanying the ceremonies. ***ńan** *ng kr* to hold the above festival. *Jèn Muludan nganggo Sekaténan.* During the general Mulud festivities, the Sekatèn ceremonies are held at court.
sekatos *kr for* SEKATI
sekawan four (*kr for* PAPAT)
sekawit 1 because (of). 2 (ever) since. 3 formerly; in the beginning. *wiwit sakawit* from the outset. *See also* AWIT, KAWIT, WIWIT
sekeb **ñj/di*** to put sth into [a container]. *Pelemé di* nang grobog waḍah beras karebèn gelis mateng.* They put the mangoes in a storage chest to ripen them faster.
sekèber *former title applied to a baron*
sekeḍik a little, a few (*kr for* SEṬIṬIK)
sèkèk *rg var of* DÈKÈK
sekel sad, grieving (*oj: var of* SENGKEL; *ki for* SUSAH?)
sèkèng weak, feeble. *wong * memungsuhan karo wong sentosa* a one-sided contest
sèker piston (car engine part)
sekerup *var of* SEKRUP
sèket 1 fifty. 2 drawing, sketch. ***an** 1 approximately fifty. *taun *an nem* around the year '56. 2 fifty-rupiah bill. **ñj/di*** to draw, sketch. *See also* ÈKET, NG- (*prefix*) 6, 7
sekèṭèng doorways to the inner part (living quarters) of a traditional Javanese house
sekeṭip one ten-cent coin (*see also* KEṬIP). **ñj*an** worth ten cents. *prangko njekeṭipan* a ten-cent stamp
sekétja comfortable, pleasant (*kr for* KEPÉNAK)
sekèwed *kr for* SEKÉWUH
sekéwuh *ng,* **sekèwed** *kr* to feel ill at ease. *Adja wedi *, énggal mangkata!* Feel free to leave now! *See also* ÉWUH, PAKÉWUH
seking *inf var of* SAKING
sekodjur all over [one's body]
sekolah 1 to attend school. *Jèn ésuk *.* He goes to school mornings. *Olèhé * wis kelas telu.* He's in third grade. 2 school. *mlebu ** to enroll in school; to go into a school

building. *mulih* * to come home from school. *kepala* * school superintendent. ***an** school. **an tukang* trade school. **ñj/di*aké** to enroll smn in school. *njekolahké anaké* to send one's child to school. **sa*an** 1 a student at the same school [as]. 2 the whole school. *botjah sa*an* all the kids in school. * **ḍasar** (*abbr*: **S.D.**) elementary school

sekolèh (*or* ***an**) to have a piece of luck; lucky by nature. **ñj*i** worth going after (*var of* M̌·PAKOLÈH·I). *See also* OLÈH

sekon a second. *sa menit telung puluh* * a minute and 30 seconds. **ñj/di*i** to time sth in seconds

sekongkel to plot, conspire. ***an** conspiracy

sekop spade(s) (playing-card suit)

sekor score. **é pira²?* What's the score (*i.e.* the score is how much to how much)?

sekor(e)s **ñj/di*** to suspend temporarily. *A di* karo kumpulan bal²ané merga nampa sogokan.* A was suspended by his soccer team for accepting a bribe.

sekoteng a hot ginger-flavored drink

sekotji sloop

sekrip writing book, manual of handwriting

sekrup 1 screw, bolt. 2 *inf* nut (to screw onto a bolt). **ñj/di*** to fasten with a screw. **ñj/di*aké** to screw *or* bolt sth onto. *See also* BAUT, ULIR

sèks sex

seksi a witness. **ñj/di*ǩaké** to cause *or* allow sth to be witnessed. *Aku njeksèkaké perkawinané anakku.* I arranged for witnesses for my daughter's marriage. **ñj/di*ǹi** to witness, observe. *Kawiné diseksèni aku.* I witnessed the marriage. *Aku njeksèni kedadéjan kuwi kabèh.* I saw the whole thing. **pa*ǹ** *or* **pi*ǹ** 1 evidence. 2 fee for acting as a witness. * **ng·iwak-iwak** a hearsay witness

sekti 1 to have magical powers. 2 to have knowledge/education. **ka*ǹ** magical power. **s·in·ekti** endowed with supernatural powers. * **mandraguna** magically invulnerable. *See also* BIMA-SEKTI

sekul cooked rice (*kr for* SEGA)

sekuter motor scooter

sekutu 1 allied. *bala tentara* * The Allied forces. 2 plot, conspiracy. **ñj/di*** to form an alliance

sèl cell; prison cell. **nge/di*** to imprison. *Malingé wis di*.* The thief has been put behind bars.

sel *rpr* inserting. *Klambiné diseselaké nang koper mak *.* He slipped his shirts into the suitcase.

sel- *see also under* SL- (*Introduction, 2.9.3*)

séla 1 incense (*kr for* MENJAN). 2 stone, rock (*kr for* WATU). 3 *ltry* precious gem (*kr for* INTEN?). * **gilang** a flat shiny stone upon which one meditates in the wilderness

sela 1 (to have) a gap, interval. *Antarané lemari kuwi isih ana *né.* There's a little space between the cupboards. *Bisé * dadi aku bisa lingguh.* The bus wasn't full, so I got a seat. *Saiki aku * ora duwé gawéan.* I'm between jobs right now. 2 eleventh month of the Moslem calendar. ***n** a partition. ***-*** gap, interval. *Ḍuwitku mau tiba nang *-*né kursi.* My money dropped between the seats. **ñj*** to interrupt. *Aku arep njela atur sedilit.* I'd like to put in a small remark. **ñj*-ñj*** to annoy with repeated interruptions. **ñj/di*kaké** to give priority to [sth, over another thing which is in progress]. *Aku jèn ndandakaké pit nang nggoné Pak Darmo mesṭi diselakaké.* When I have Mr. Darmo repair my bicycle, he always gives my job priority. **ñj/di*ni** to interrupt, intervene. *njelani olèhé omong²an* to break into the conversation. *njelani sing paḍa padu* to separate people who are quarreling. **sa*né** as one has free time. *ndandani raḍio sak *né* to repair radios in one's spare time

selagi 1 (*or* ***a**) even if it were... *Selagia wong papat, ora bakal kuwat ngangkat peṭi mau.* Even four people together couldn't have lifted the box. 2 (*or* ***né**) at the time when..., at the same time (as). * *bapak isih sugeng, omah kéné ora tau sepi.* When Father was alive, this house was never lonely. *See also* LAGI

sélak to deny. *tembung* * (*gram*) a negative word. **ñj/di*i** to deny sth; to renege, go back on. *bukti kang ora bisa di*i* undeniable proof. *Pemerintah ora bakal njélaki bangsa kita.* The government will never fail the people.

selak in, *or* on the verge of, a condition necessitating urgent action. *Tjepet, * mangkat.* Quick! it's about to leave. *Ḍèké * kepantjal sepur.* He's about to miss the train. *Aku * kepéngin rembugan karo ḍèwèké.* I *have* to talk with him. *Jèn * ngelak ngombéa banju.* If you're too thirsty to wait, drink water. *Ajo ta, mengko * diarep-arep ibu.* Let's go—Mother's expecting us. *Aku mlaju mréné, **

wengi. I ran to get here, with night coming on. *Montor isih terus banḍang * kuwaṭir ketututan udan.* The car sped on, so as not to get caught in the rain. *Aku arep lunga, * ora betah.* I'm leaving–I can't stand it. *Olèhé mlaju ingkul, wedi * apotiké tutup.* He ran, to get to the drugstore before it closed. **ke*** 1 hardly able to wait. *Ḍèké ke* kesusu arep mangan.* He can hardly wait to eat. 2 to choke. *Adja tjaturan jèn lagi ngombé, munḍak ke*.* Don't talk while you drink–it'll go down the wrong way. **ñj/di*(-*)aké** to [do] at one's earliest convenience. *Ditindakaké ing saben dina, di*-*aké.* Do it every day: make time for it. **ñj/di*i** to choke on sth

sélakarang dandruff. ***en** to have *or* get dandruff

Sélan *var of* SÉLON

sélang a variety of rattan; the leaves of this rattan plant

selang 1 by turns, alternating. *Saiki * aku sing matja.* It's my turn to read now. *Bakalé lorèk, (*) abang * putih.* The fabric is red-and-white striped. 2 hose, pipe. **ñj/di*** to borrow. *njelang buku* to borrow a book. **ñj/di*aké** to lend. *Ḍuwité kantjaku di*aké aku.* A friend of mine lent me the money. **ñj/di*i** to lend to. *Aku di*i ḍuwit kantjaku.* A friend of mine lent me some money. **s·um·elang** *see* SUMELANG. *** gumun** dumbfounded. *** sebat** resembling closely. *Mobilku lan mobilmu * sebat.* Our cars are almost the same. *** silih** to borrow habitually. *** surup** a misinterpretation. *Anggoné ngandani kurang tjeṭa, mulané dadi * surup.* He didn't tell it clearly, so I misunderstood. *See also* SELING

selangkung twenty-five (*kr for* SELAWÉ)

selap *var of* SELIP

selapan one 35-day period (*see also* LAPAN). *Senèn Legi penḍak Senèn Legi tjatjahé ana telung puluh limang dina, diarani * dina.* From one Legi Monday to the next there are 35 days; this is called a *lapan.* ***an** a ceremony held in honor of a 35-day-old infant. **ñj/di*i** to honor [an infant] with such a ceremony. *See also* LAPAN

sélat *var of* SILAT

selat 1 salad. 2 strait. ** Bali* the Strait of Bali. 3 south; south wind

selawé *ng,* **selangkung** *kr* twenty-five. ***an** *or* ***ǹ(an)** **(selangkung·an** *kr*) 25-rupiah bill. *selawèn loro* two 25-rupiah bills. ***-*** 25 at a time; (for) every 25. *Botjah² tampa buku paringan, *-*.* Each child was given twenty-five books. *** bentet** exactly 25. *** prah** 24. *See also* LAWÉ[b]; NG- (*prefix*) 6, 7

selé jelly, jam. ** nanas* pineapple jelly. *kuwih * gulung* jelly roll. ***ǹ** odd, not matching, paired wrongly. *Sepatuné selèn.* His shoes don't match each other. *or* His shoes are on the wrong feet. **ñj*** 1 unusual, different from others. *tindak kang rada njelé* erratic behavior. 2 (*psv* **di***) to make [ingredients] into jelly/jam. **sa*** one of a pair. *gong muni sa** to listen to, *or* to present, only one side of an argument

sèlèh 1 to resign. ** saka kelungguhané* to step down from one's position. 2 to put sth smw (*root form: kr for* DÈKÈK). **salah-*** *see* SALAH. **ñj/di*(aké)** to put sth down, lay sth smw. *Aku njèlèhaké djamku nang médja.* I put my watch on the table. *Lokomotip di* ana ing mburi.* They put on a locomotive at the end [of the train]. **s·um·èlèh** 1 lying; having been put (down). *Katjamatamu sumèlèh nang médja.* Your glasses are on the table. 2 settled, relieved of responsibilities and tasks. *Atiné saiki wis sumèlèh bareng kabèh anaké wis bisa mentas.* Now that his children are on their own, he can take it easier. *See also* BOT, ḌOḌOK

selèi jelly, jam (*var of* SELÉ)

selèk *see* DJUBIN

seler **ñj/di*(i)** to steal, commit petty theft; *fig* to lure (away). *Barangé di* ing wong.* Somebody walked off with her things. *Lenggahan pirang² atus èwu di*i mrono, adpertènsi majuta-juta rupiah mrono.* Hundreds of thousands of subscribers have been lured there through their multi-million-rupiah advertising.

selèt *rpr* the crack of a whip. **s·um·elèt** [of sun's rays] beating down. *Panasé sumelèt.* It's unbearably hot.

selikur twenty-one. *See also* SA

seling interspersed. **selang-*** alternating, by turns. *Sing abang karo sing biru ditata selang-*.* Red ones alternated with blue ones. **ñj/di*** to intersperse, change off (with). *Anggoné omong di* basa Indonesia.* His speech was sprinkled with Indonesian words. *Penḍak kursi lima di* médja sidji.* There's one table for every five chairs. **ñj/di*i** to interpose. *Kanggo njelingi pasemuan mengko bengi arep dianakke undian nganggo hadiah.* There will be a prize lottery held this evening during the break in the meeting. * **surup** to misunderstand, misinterpret. *See also* SELANG

selip 1 to slip, slide, skid. 2 to misunderstand, misinterpret. **ñj/di*aké** to insert sth into. *Ḍompèté di*ké nang tjaṭok.* He slipped his wallet into his belt. **ñj/di*i** to insert into [sth]. **s·um·elip** inserted into; stuck in between

selir *ng kr,* **ampil** *ki* any legally married wife after the first one. **ñj/di*** 1 to take an additional wife. 2 *slang* to pick the good seeds from a batch

selira body (*ki for* AWAK)

sélo *intsfr* two. *Tjatjahé mung loro *.* There were two and only two.

Sélon Ceylon. *See also* SÉLONG

sélong **ñj/di*** to send smn into exile (*formerly to Ceylon*)

selop formal high-heeled sandal(s). ***an** to put on *or* wear the above

selot 1 increasingly, more (so). ** suwé * lara* to hurt more and more, to get sicker and sicker. *Anggur kuwi * suwé anggoné njimpen * énak.* The longer you keep wine, the better it is. 2 door latch. **ñj*** 1 to increase, become more (so). *Nakalé njelot ndadi.* He's worse than ever. 2 (*psv* **di***) to latch [a door]. *Lawangé di* waé, adja dikuntjing.* Just latch the door, don't lock it.

séluman *var of* SILUMAN

selur in a row, lined up. *Ing dalan tumpakan * tanpa peḍot.* The traffic was bumper-to-bumper.

sem- *see also under* S- (*Introduction, 3.1.7*)

semadi (*or* * **brata**) the practice of religious concentration and meditation

semados to procrastinate (*kr for* SEMAJA)

sémah spouse; household (*kr for* SOMAH)

semâjâ *ng,* **semados** *kr* to procrastinate. ***n** (to have made) a promise, agreement. *Olèhmu *n djam setengah telu.* Your appointment is for 2:30. *Wis *n, adja mbléndjani.* You promised; don't back out. **ñj/di*kaké** to promise sth [to smn]. *Ḍèké njemajakaké klambiné kanggo aku.* He promised his clothes to me. **ñj/di*ni** to promise smn; to put off with promises. *Aku njemajani ḍèké klambi anjar.* I promised him some new clothes. *Nèk ngarepaké apa², ora kena disemajani.* When he wants something, he wants it now.

semaji a rice-accompanying dish consisting of a coconut-and-chili-pepper mixture wrapped in banana leaves and cooked by steaming and baking

semak **ñj/di*** to follow along in one's own copy what smn else is reading aloud

semakéjan *var of* SEMANGKÉJAN

semânâ *ng,* **semanten** *kr* that much/many; to that extent (*Degree III: Introduction, 6*). *Aku jèn kon mangan * ja ora entèk.* I couldn't possibly eat that much. **ḍèk *** at that (remote past) time. *Ḍèk samana aku lagi umur antarané telung sasi.* At that time I was about three months old. *See also* MANA

semang to go ahead and [do sth one ought not to do]. *Kowé mau * lunga barang, kantjamu mréné.* You went off, knowing that your friend was on his way here! **ora *** not bother to [do], not worry about. *Djeruké wis adjaran, ora * ngontjèki.* The orange is cut into sections–you won't have to bother to peel it.

semangat energy, enthusiasm. *ngilangaké ** to kill smn's enthusiasm, take the energy out of smn

semanggi a certain vegetable. *goḍong ** the leaves of this plant. *dalan goḍong ** cloverleaf highway interchange

semângkâ watermelon. * **djingga** a variety of watermelon with red meat. *See also* SIGAR

semangkéjan boastful, arrogant, stuck-up

semangkin more, increasingly (*rg var of* SAJA)

semântâ 1 *var of* SEMAJA. 2 (*or* ***né**; **semaos[ipun]** *kr*) *var of* SA·MANGSA. **ñj/di*kaké** 1 to allow *or* take sufficient time (for). *Adja kesusu, di*kaké olèhé paḍa tjaturan, wong aku prèi.* There's no hurry, let's just go on talking; I'm free today. 2 to have sth appraised

semanten 1 that much/many (*Degree III: Introduction, 6; kr for* SEMANA). 2 this much/many (*Degree I: kr for* SEMÉNÉ). 3 that much/many (*Degree II: kr for* SEMONO). **kala *** at that time (*kr for* ḌÈK SEMANA). * **rumijin** this much (*kr for* SEMÉNÉ ḌISIK). ** rumijin atur kula.* This (what I have said up to now) is my opinion. * **ugi** and so; and [not] either (*kr for* SEMONO UGA)

semaos when, at the time of (*rg kr for* SA·MANGSA, SEMANTA)

semaput (**ke·sambet** *opt kr?*; **kantâkâ** *ki?*) to lose consciousness. *Ḍèké *, bareng wis éling gumun.* She fainted; when she came to, she was bewildered.

semar 1 (*wj*) *name of one of the clown servants to the Pandawas* (*see also* WULU-TJUMBU). 2 (*or* *-*) prop, support. **ñj*i** 1 resembling Semar, both physically (roly-poly; having characteristic speech and walking style) and in character (tolerant and conciliatory). 2 (*psv* **di*i**) to support with pillars. *** mendem** an omelet-like dish. *** t·in·anḍu** traditional house without the main pillars (*saka guru*)

semârâdânâ, semarandânâ a classical verse form (*var of* ASMARADANA)

semat 1 sharpened coconut-leaf rib, used for fastening leaf-wrapped packages. 2 to recur [of illness]

semâtâ out in the open, disclosed. *Adja * jèn kowé ḍéwé perlu.* When you're hard up, don't let anyone find out. *See also* SA·MATA[2]

semawon *rg var of* (M)BOK MENAWA

sembâdâ capable, able to carry things through to completion. **ka*n** to materialize, get carried through. *Ḍasaré wong sugih, apa sing dipéngini bisa ke*n.* He's rich–he can have anything he wants. *Panuwuné ke*n.* His request was granted. **ñj/di*ni** to carry sth through. *Gawéné adol sanggup nanging ora tau njembadani.* He's always making promises and not carrying them out.

sembagi (*or* ***ǹ**) imported clothing material. *Klambiné sembagèn.* Her dress is made of imported fabric.

sembah 1 a gesture of high esteem made to a superior by holding the hands before the face, palms together, thumbs approaching the nose, and bowing the head slightly. 2 one's respects, one's high regards. **se*an** an object of high esteem. **ñj/di*** to gesture humbly to smn as above. *Saiki wis arang[2] banget ana prijaji sing arep di*.* Nowadays very few higher-ups expect to be greeted with a *sembah.* **njembah nuwun** to express one's thanks. **njembah sukur marang pangéran** to give thanks to God. **pa·ñ(j)*** 1 an object of high esteem *or* worship. 2 the act of making a *sembah.* *** bekti** one's respects. *** ḍoḍok** to make a *sembah* while squatting humbly. *** sukur** a respectful gesture of gratitude. *** sungkem** one's respectful regards. *** ñ·suwun** (expression of) thanks. *See also* NEMBAH

semba(h)jang religious worship. ***an** place of worship. **ñj/di*aké** to say prayers for smn. *Aku disembahjangna ja supaja lulus.* Pray for me so that I'll pass.

sembarang some, any (at all); someone, anyone (at all). *Sing digawé dudu * kaju, kudu milih kaju sing atos.* It can't be made of just any wood–it has to be hard wood. *nDjupuka * kertu, aku mesṭi bisa mbeḍèk.* Pick a card, any card: I'll tell you what it is. ***an** 1 *sms* *. *Pak Singgih ki dudu wong *an.* Mr. Singgih is no ordinary person. 2 (to treat) lightly, not (take) seriously enough. *Jèn ngresiki beḍil adja *an lho.* When you are cleaning a gun you have to handle it with due respect. *Rumangsa dienggo *an déning anak.* She felt that her child had treated her with disrespect.

sembelèh **ñj/di*** to butcher, slaughter. *See also* BELÈH

sembèr high-pitched and shrill. *Swarané raḍioné *.* The radio has a thin crackling tone (full of static).

sembèrèt *ptg* * to flow out in many places, *e.g.* water from a leaky bucket. **ñj*** *sg as above*

sembet (*or* **se*an**) 1 garments. 2 rags; worn-out clothing; cloth scraps

sembir 1 a tree whose wood is suitable for gamelan xylophones. 2 torn slightly at the edge. **ñj*** to strike and glance off; *fig* to criticize obliquely

sembodja a tree with sweet-scented blossoms, often cultivated in cemeteries

sembok *var of* SIMBOK

sembrânâ irresponsible, insufficiently respectful, ill-mannered. *Adja * karo wong tuwa.* Don't be disrespectful to your parents. **(se)*n** as above by nature. **ñj/di*ni** to treat lightly *or* with disrespect. *Ora betjik njembranani wong tuwa.* You mustn't make fun of older people. *** parikena** [to say, criticize] in fun but be taken seriously. *Olèhé nembung barangé mung sarwa * parikena.* He was just joking when he asked for it, but she gave it to him.

sembrani legendary flying horse

sembrèt torn. *Djariké * ketjanṭol paku.* Her batik tore when it caught on a nail. **ñj/di*** to tear [fabric]

sembuh ***an** a batik that has been renewed by being redyed. **ñj/di*aké** to have [batik] redyed; to redye [batik] for smn. **ñj/di*(i)** to renew [batik] by rewaxing and redyeing it

sèmbukan a certain vine-grown vegetable

sembur ***-* adas** with the blessing of many people, one's wish may be fulfilled. **ñj/di*(i)** to spit *or* hiss at. *Jèn ana ula adja tjeḍak[2]* *di**. Don't get too close to snakes–they'll spit at you. **s·um·embur** to spit, hiss

semburat 1 tinged with [another color]. *abang * kuning* yellowish red. 2 tinged with red. *Téla gantung wis *, sésuk bisa dipeṭik.* The papaya is reddish; it can be picked tomorrow.

semèdi *var of* SEMADI

sèmèk protective pad. *Serbèté kanggo * gelas.* The napkin was used as a coaster for the glass. **ñj/di*i** to provide with a protective pad. *Bajiné di*i perlak.* She wrapped the baby in a rubber pad.

semekan (*or* **ka***) ladies' sash worn with batik wraparounds (*ki for* KEMBEN)

semelak a drink made from *patjé* fruit

semèn cement in powdered form. **ñj/di*(i)** to cement sth. *** blawu** *sms **

seméné *ng,* **semanten** *kr* this much/many; to this extent (*Degree I: Introduction, 6*). *Seméné geḍéné.* It's this big. *Beras * iki regané pira?* How much does this amount of rice cost? *Anggonmu njandiwara tekan * waé.* Your fooling around has gone too far this time! **di*kaké** done in this way. *Disemènèkaké nganti sawetara meksa durung kétok ana peṭukan.* He's been waiting around like this for a long time but no one has showed up to meet him. *See also* MÉNÉ

semèni *see* UDAN

semènten this much/many (*md for* SEMÉNÉ)

semi to sprout, put out buds. **pa*ǹ** a plant that springs up spontaneously. *Ing mburi omah ana pasemèn kekembangan.* Flowers grow wild (self-sown) in back of the house.

semir polish. ** sepatu* shoe polish. *lenga ** polishing oil; engine oil, lubricant. **ñj/di*** 1 to spread with a greasing *or* polishing substance. *Rotiné di* nganggo mertéga.* She buttered the bread. 2 to bribe, grease smn's palm

sémog fat, fleshy

semono *ng,* **semanten** *kr* that much/many; to that extent (*Degree II: Introduction, 6*). *Ora mung tjukup samono.* That amount isn't enough. *Lagi mikir tekan *, dumadakan ana motor mlebu.* Just as my thoughts got to that point, a car suddenly drove up. *Aku gumun, botjah * kèhé.* I was surprised that there were so many young people. *Wah la geḍému wis *.* My, how you've grown! *** iku** 1 as much as that; that amount. 2 that is (to say). *Ḍèké bakal dadi mahasiswa, * iku jèn ditampa.* He's going to the university–that is, if he can get in. *** uga** and so...; and [not] either. *Aku kagèt, ḍèké * uga.* I was startled and so was he. *A ora ngguju, * uga B.* A didn't laugh; neither did B. *See also* ÉWA, MONO

semonten that much/many (*md for* SEMONO)

sempal broken off, hanging by a thread. *Pangé *.* The broken branch is held to the tree only by the bark. ***an** 1 a fragment. **an saka tjrita Ramayana* a fragment from the Ramayana epic. 2 *wj* a drama wholly invented as an offshoot of events in epic or mythology. **ñj/di*** to break sth nearly off

sémpar **ñj/di*** to kick (away). *Aku mau mlaku² njimpar tleṭong djaran.* As I walked I accidentally kicked some horse dung. **ñj/di*-*** to toss aside, reject

semparèt *rpr* fast running. ** mlaju mlebu senṭong lan bandjur ungkeb² ing paturon.* She dashed to the bedroom and flung herself face down on the bed.

sèmpèr lame, dragging one foot

sempérat *rpr* a quick dash. **ñj*** to sprint

sempèrèt *var of* SEMPÉRAT

sempet to have time (for). **ka*an** time for doing sth. *Aku isa nduwé ka*an ketemu kantjaku.* I managed to work in a visit with my friend.

sempjok *ptg ** to splash repeatedly. ***an** *or* **ñj*** to splash (against). *Banjuné njempjok.* The water pounds the shore. **ñj/di*aké** to splash [sth] against. **ñj/di*(i)** to splash against [sth]

semplah broken, hanging useless. *ptg* **s·r·emplah** [of clothing] tattered, in rags

sémplak *var of* SAMPLUK

sémplang **ñj/di*** to kick to one side

semplok broken, damaged, not working

sempojongan to stagger, walk unsteadily

sémpol *rg var of* SAMPIL

semprang dragonfly

semprit 1 a confection. 2 to blow one's nose (*ki for* SISI). ***an** police whistle. **ñj/di*(i)** to blow a whistle at smn. *Mau ana montor nglanggar lalulintas di* polisi.* The policeman blew his whistle at the car that violated a traffic regulation. **ñj/di*i** to blow smn's nose (*ki for* ÑJ/DI·SISI·ÑI). *ptg* **s·l·emprit** *pl* blowing whistles

semprong 1 bamboo brazier; bamboo section used to blow on fires to produce flame. 2 glass lamp chimney. 3 binoculars, spy glass, magnifying glass. 4 a crisp cylinder-shaped cookie. ***an** [of mangoes] picked while immature and ripened by keeping warm and draft-free. **ñj/di*** **1** to ripen [mangoes] as above. **2** to make fire in a brazier. **3** to examine through a magnifying instrument or other cylindrical object. *Enḍogé di* ḍisik.* Look at the eggs through a cylinder [of rolled paper] before you buy them [to determine the freshness].

semprot *rpr* a sudden gush. *Bareng dibukak gabus banjuné bandjur mak *.* When the cork was removed, the water gushed out. *ptg* * *pl* gushing. *Saka kadohan katon ana barang ptg * pirang² banget.* In the distance they could see any number of waterspouts. *Èmbèré paḍa bolong, bareng diisèni banju paḍa ptg *.* The leaky pail, when filled with water, shot out streams in all directions. ***an** nozzle, spraying device. **di*** to get scolded. **ñj*** to pour from a hole. *Pipané lèḍeng bolong banjuné bandjur njemprot metu.* Water shot out from the hole in the pipe. **ñj/di*aké** to spray *or* squirt [liquid]. *Nusé njemprotaké mangsiné.* The octopus ejected its ink. *Banju saka kali di*aké menjang omah sing kobong.* They sprayed river water on the burning house. **ñj/di*(i)** to squirt *or* spray onto. *Montoré di*i banju.* He sprayed water on his car.

semprul tobacco of inferior quality

semprung *var of* PRUNG

semprut **semprat-*** to keep sniffing; to have a runny nose

sempulur prosperity, well-being

semrawang *var of* SUMRAWANG

semromong to feel hot *or* overheated, *e.g.* from fever

semu **1** tinged with. *abang * kuning* yellowish red. *Ḍèké mèsem * isin.* She smiled a bit shyly. *Rasané asin * pait.* It tastes salty and somewhat bitter. **2** facial expression. **3** it seems; to judge by appearances. ** durung pertjaja marang pangrunguné.* He looked as if he couldn't believe his ears. ***an** performance of a show. ***né** it seems; it looks (as if). **né ora pati seneng.* They don't look too happy. ***-*** rather, somewhat, on the [x] side. *Botjahé *-* ireng.* The child('s skin) is darkish. **ñj/di*k̂aké** to show, perform. *njemokaké djogèd Sala* to perform Solonese dances. **ñj/di*ñi** to hint, make insinuations about. **pa*ñ** **1** facial expression. *solan-salining pasemon* changes of expression. **2** signal expressed in the face. *gawé pasemon* to wink *etc.* as a signal

semur meat boiled in spiced soy sauce. ** ajam* chicken prepared as above. **ñj/di*** to make [ingredients] into the above dish

semut ant. *Ana gula ana *.* (*fig*) People flock to a good thing. ***en** to have pins and needles, to be "asleep" [of a numbed body part]. *** gatel** ant that causes itching. ***gramang** red ant. *** krija** worker ant. *** ngang(k)rang** large red tarantula-like ant that infests fruit trees. *** puḍak** a certain small white ant

semuwa decked out; prepossessing in one's appearance. ***n** command performance of a dance drama. **ñj/di*kaké** to have smn perform in a dance drama

sèn cent (1/100 rupiah). *sa** one cent

séna *oj* soldiers, troops

senapan(g) rifle

sénapati commanding general. **ñj*** to command, be a commander. **ñj/di*ǹi** to have command over [troops]

senar string for a stringed instrument

senḍal **ñj/di*** to jerk (at), pull (at), tug (on). **ñj/di*-*** *or* **ñj/di*i** to keep jerking *or* tugging at. *Djarané di*i kenḍali.* He kept tugging at the horse's reins. **ñj/di*-pantjing** to jerk on a slack (fish)line

senḍang a natural pool of spring water. *** ka(a)pit pantjur·an** boy-girl-boy sibling combination

sendari (*or* ***ǹ**) bamboo whistle attached to a kite so as to produce sound as the kite flies

senḍâwâ **1** a bird of the swallow family. **2** saltpeter, potassium nitrate. **3** a food ingredient resembling meat tenderizer, used also to tint meat red *e.g.* for corned beef. **4** gunpowder

sénḍé ***an** *or* ***ǹ(an)** to lean against; sth for leaning against. *Aku sènḍèn lawang.* I leaned against the door. *Kursiné sènḍènané* (or *sénḍéané*) *wis suwèk.* The chair back is ripped. **ñj/di*k̀aké** to cause to lean. *Aku njènḍèkaké kursi menjang témbok.* I leaned the chair against the wall. **ñj/di*ǹi** to lean against. *Aku lingguh disènḍèni karo mas Marto.* Marto leaned against me as I sat there. **pa*an** sth to lean against. **s·um·énḍé** leaning [on, against]. *Pringé suménḍé nang pager.* The bamboo is leaning against the wall. **adol *** to sell [a plot of land] temporarily, *i.e.* with the understanding that it will be bought back later

s̊ènḍeng Protestant mission

senḍet sluggish. *Banjuné iliné *.* The flow of water is sluggish. ñj/di*i to block *or* slow down the movement of. *Botjah² wédok ora éntuk mèlu munggah gunung munḍak njenḍeti laku.* No girls allowed on the mountain-climbing trip—they'd hold us up.

s̑èṇḍing *var of* SÈNḌENG

sendjâtâ 1 gun, rifle (*kr for* BEḌIL). 1 weapon (*alternate kr for* GAMAN). *luput ing * uwa* magically immune from maledictions. ber* weapon(ry). *angkatan ber* armed forces. ñj* *kr* to use a weapon. * nuklir nuclear arms. * m̐-pakan tuwan to be a victim of one's own trick. * pa·m̐·pungkas a magical weapon for killing one's enemies. * tjakra *wj* a powerful arrow with a pointed round frame as the head. * pi·tulung aid, assistance

séṇḍok spoon (lantar·an *ki*). ñj/di* to eat, stir, dish up *etc.* with a spoon. * bèbèk an enamel-coated soup spoon

senḍu constant criticism. *ñ-waon always finding fault (with). ñj/di* to nag

sendut muscular tic

sené 1 urine (*kr for* UJUH). 2 to urinate (*kr for* NG·UJUH). ñj/dipun*m̀i *kr* to urinate on sth

seneb uncomfortable from overeating; *fig* bored, fed up. ñj*(-ñj*)i to cause a stomach ache; *fig* boring, tedious

senèl [of trains] fast. *sepur * express train

Senèn Monday. *an to make one's regular Monday oral report to an administrative superior. ñj* to [do] on Monday(s). Njenèn-Kemis to fast on Monday and Thursday (an act of self-abnegation performed in the hope of having a wish fulfilled). ñj/di*i to bawl smn out

senéndjong rice mixed into the accompanying dishes (*lawuh*)

seneng 1 (remen *kr?*; rena *kr? ki?*; ḍangan *ki*) happy, glad, pleased. 2 to like. *mu wédang tjuwèr apa kenṭel.* How do you like your tea, weak or strong? 3 to [do] habitually *or* characteristically. *Dèké * tjolong-djupuk.* He steals. *Banjuké * njosor.* Geese attack with their beaks. *an what smn likes/wants (most). *ané tjangkriman.* He loves telling riddles. *é one's habit *or* customary practice. *é njenjolong.* He steals. *-* (remen² *kr?*) to have a good time, enjoy oneself. *Aku nang Djakarta ora dines nanging mung *-* waé.* I went to Djakarta for pleasure, not business. ka*an 1

fun; (source of) enjoyment *or* entertainment; hobby. 2 what smn likes/wants. *Ke-*ané manggon ana ing kuṭa.* He likes living in the city. ñj*aké 1 easy-going *or* outgoing in nature. 2 (*psv* di*aké) to bring pleasure to. *kanggo njenengaké bodjoné* in order to please his wife. ñj/di*i 1 to like, prefer. 2 to like; to love, be in love with. sa*é whatever one likes/wants. *Kowé bisa milih panganané sa*mu.* You can choose whatever food you want. * karo to be in love with

senèt *rpr* a stab of pain. *Mak * tanganku lara banget dientup tawon.* Ouch! a bee stung me on the hand.

senèwen neurotic, emotionally disturbed

s̑èng zinc. *piring * zinc plate

seng *describing a bad odor. Ambuné mak *.* It smells terrible. sang-* to give off a disagreeable odor

sengadi pretense. *né arep lunga.* He pretended he was leaving.

sengâdjâ on purpose. ñj/di* to [do] on purpose *or* with premeditation. *Olèhé ngrusak lawang di* sebabé kuntjiné ilang.* He *meant* to break down the door: the key was lost. *Abdullah pantjèn njengadja matèni bendarané.* Abdullah murdered his master in cold blood.

sengak sharp, acrid, biting

sengar *var of* SENGAK

sengârâ 1 curse, oath. *nibakaké * to take a vow. 2 an impossibility. * bisa.* It can't be done. 3 name of the third *windu*. ñj/di* 1 to swear, take an oath. *Dèké njengara ora bakal rabi.* He swore he would never marry. di* matjan to be intimidated. 2 (*or* ñj/di*kaké) to regard as an outcast; to reject as a possibility. *Krama di* tanggané kiwa-tengen, marga seneng njolong ndjupuk.* The neighbors steer clear of Krama because he steals. *Di*kaké ing akèh.* Most people say it's impossible.

sengèn *rg var of* BIJÈN. ñj/di*i to scold (*inf var of* ÑJ/DI·SENÈN·I)

sengen *rg var of* SRENGEN

sengéngé *inf var of* SRENGÉNGÉ

séngga until, up to (*kr: rg var of* NGANTOS). *n(an)é *var of* SA·ÉNGGA·NÉ

senggak *an a stanza which is interposed by smn into a classical song (which is being sung by smn else) as a variation *or* addition to the main song. ñj/di*i to interpose a verse into [smn's song] as above

senggang 1 leisure. *wektu makarja lan wektuné* * working hours and leisure time. 2 healthy (*ki for* WARAS). 3 on the road to recovery (*ki for* MAJAR)
senggâtâ *var of* SUGATA
sènggèk *var of* SÈNGGÈT
sénggel single
sènggèt a pole for picking fruits high up on the tree. **ñj/di*aké** to pick [high-up fruits] for smn. **ñj/di*(i)** to get [high-up things] down with the above pole. **njènggèt babal ke·tiba·n nangka·né** to get more than one expected
senggojongan, senggojoran to stagger, walk unsteadily
sénggol ***an** touching, in contact. *A lan B *an.* A and B are touching. **ané wong wadon* a woman's touch. **se*an** to associate with, be near each other. **ke*** to get touched *or* jostled unintentionally. **ñj/di*** 1 to touch, handle. 2 to bump against. *kreteg ** a bridge so narrow that people jostle each other when crossing. **ñj/di·sénggal-*** to keep touching/jostling. *Timuné diséng-gal-* Kantjil nganggo sikilé.* Mouse-Deer touched the cucumber again and again with his foot.
senggor *var of* SENGGUR
sénggot (*or* ***an**) equipment for dipping up water from a well: a bamboo lever weighted at one end and holding the bucket at the other. **ñj*** to dip up water with the above
sènggrèk *var of* SÈNGGÈT
senggring *-* *intsfr* thin. *kuru *-** emaciated, nothing but skin and bones. *ptg* **s·l·enggring** *pl* very thin
senggrok *-* *or* **ñj*** *sg* to snort; to draw in the breath noisily. *ptg* **s·l·enggrok** *pl as above*
senggruk material for inhaling, *e.g.* medication; snuff. ***en** to keep drawing in the breath involuntarily while recovering from a crying spell. *-* *or* **senggrak-*** to cry intermittently with much indrawing of breath. **se*an** (to cry) steadily as above. **ñj/di*** to sniff *or* inhale sth. **s·l·enggruk**[2] *sms *-**. **s·um·enggruk** to sniff, inhale
sengguh 1 role, characterization. *Jèn ndjogèd kudu duwé * kaja apa sing dilakokké.* When you depict a character, you have to actually *become* that person. **é kaja sing duwé kuṭa.* He seems to think he owns the city. 2 arrogant, high-handed. **ñj/di*** to think, assume; to think of, regard (as). *Apa aku iki ko* ora njambut-gawé babar pisan?* Do you think *I* never do any work? *Kowé kuwi wis tak * sedulur ḍéwé.* I've treated you as my own brother. **pa·ñj*** assumption, conclusion. *Panjengguhé ḍèké butuh ndjupuk ḍuwit kanggo tambah pawitan.* She assumed he needed the money as additional capital. **s·um·engguh** haughty, arrogant
senggur *-* *or* **se*an** *rpr* the sound of snoring; (*or* **ñj***) to snore. *turu ngorok *-** sound asleep and snoring
senggut **ñj/di*** 1 to eat, graze (on). 2 to cut grass for fodder. **ñj/di*aké** 1 to have *or* let [an animal] graze. 2 to cut fodder for
sengijèn *rg var of* BIJÈN
sengir a variety of mango
sengit to dislike, hate. **ñj*** *or* **nje·ñj*** irritating, causing dislike. *Ḍèké ki njenjengit banget.* She's very annoying. **ñj/di*(i)** to dislike, to hate. **s·um·engit** *see* SUMENGIT
sengka **ke*** too strenuous. *Ke* anggoné njambut gawé bandjur larané kumat menèh.* He overworked and had a relapse. **ñj*** to the utmost, to the limit. *njengkané banget* at the very most. *Olèhé njambut-gawé njengka banget.* He worked himself to the bone. **ñj/di*kaké** to hasten, give impetus to. *Olèhmu mlaku paḍa sengkakna.* Walk faster! *Kelakuané anaké njengkakaké patiné bapak.* The son's behavior is hastening the father's death. *Larané di*kaké mentas kudanan pisan.* His illness was aggravated by his getting caught in the rain. **s·um·engka pa·ng·awak bradja** *ltry* [to arrive *etc.*] in great haste and without advance notice
sengkajèg, sengkajig *ptg ** *or* **sengkojag-*** on the verge of collapse. *Omahé wis ptg *.* The house is on its last legs. *Anḍongé lakuné sengkojag-*.* The carriage wobbles badly.
sengkâlâ 1 a cryptic means of expressing the digits of calendar years (in reverse order) by the use of four ordinary words which mystically represent those digits: a practice used *esp.* for dating structures. 2 misfortune. ***n** 1 markings denoting years as above. 2 misfortune. **ñj/di*ni** to represent [years] cryptically as above
sengkang earrings for pierced ears (*kr for* SUWENG)
sengkéjangan to stagger, walk unsteadily
sengkèjèg *var of* SENGKAJÈG
sengkèjèngan *var of* SENGKÉJANGAN
sengkek short, thick, stubby

sengkel *oj* sad, grieving, sorrowful

sengkelit *ng kr,* **wangking** *ki* ***an** act *or* way of wearing [a kris, knife, *etc.*] stuck in the belt at the back of the waist. **ñj/di*(aké)** to stick [a kris *etc.*] into the back of the belt

sengker 1 one's deceased ancestors. 2 cage; to enclose (*root form: ki for* KURUNG). **ñj/di*** 1 to hold, fix, establish. *dipun* ḍateng Negari* established by the Government. *Wewenangipun pangarang sinengker ing angger.* Authors' rights are guaranteed by law. 2 to confine [an unmarried girl] to her home until she is safely married (a once traditional practice)

sengkil to cough painfully *or* with difficulty. **ñj*i** to cause painful coughing

sèngklèh, sengklèh broken, hanging loose. **ñj/di*aké** to break sth (off)

sengkojongan *var of* SENGKÉJANGAN

sengkojoran to walk unsteadily, stagger

sèngkong *rg* cassava

sengkrak **ñj/di*** to pull, tug, jerk

sengkrang *rpr* a stab of pain *or* a stinging sensation. **sengkrang-*** [of skin] feeling sensitive, *e.g.* when one is feverish. *ptg* **s·l·engkrang** to feel pains all over. **s·um·engkrang** to feel a stab of pain

sengkrèk **ke*** to get pulled. **ñj/di*** to pull. *Kenḍaliné di*-*.* He kept tugging on the reins.

sengkring *var of* SENGKRANG

sengkud in haste. *Olèhé mangan *.* He rushed through his meal. **ñj/di*** to apply oneself (to) with speed and energy. *Ḍèké njengkud anggoné njambut-gawé.* He threw himself into the work.

senglé odd, paired wrongly (*var of* SELÉ)

séngok *slang* a kiss on the cheek, Javanese style; *rpr* such a kiss. *Mak * ḍèwèké diambung wanita mau.* She kissed him smack on the cheek. ***-*an** to kiss each other (Javanese style). **ñj/di*** to kiss smn. **sa*an** a kiss

séngon a variety of tree

sengsem to like, be attracted to (*oj*). *Patamanan sing katon asri gawé *ing atiku.* Beautiful parks appeal to me. **ka*** engrossed in. *ke* anggoné nonton wajang kulit* absorbed in (watching) a shadow play. **ñ(j)*** to interest, hold the attention (of). **ñ(j)*aké** of deep interest; attracting strongly. *Pekarangané nengsemaké banget.* The yard looks beautiful.

sèngslo *var of* SÈNGSO

sèngso asymmetric, off center, unbalanced

senguk *var of* SÉNGOK

sengur fetid

sèni **di*** to be filled (*inf var of* DI·ISI·ÑI). *Botolé di* banju.* He put water in the bottle.

seni 1 art. *kawruh * mung kanggo ** art for art's sake. 2 *var of* SENÉ. (*barang*) **ka*an** art object, work of art. *** n·djogèd** the classical dance as an art form. *** drama** theatrical arts. *** sastra** literature. *** swara** singing as an art form

senijèn *rg var of* BIJÈN

senik[a] basket of woven bamboo

seni:k[b] **senak-*** worried, apprehensive

senindjong *var of* SENÉNDJONG

seni:t *rpr* a stab of pain. ***-*** *or ptg* **s·r·enit** to throb with pain

sentak (*or* ***an**) angry words. **ñj/di*** to speak to angrily, to yell at

sentânâ 1 family, relatives (*kr for* SEDULUR). 2 a child who is taken into a socially high family to become educated and grow up as one of them. 3 retinue and family of a village head man. 4 cemetery (*rg kr for* PA·KUBUR·AN). **ñj*** to live in the home of a socially high family (as above). **s·um·entana** on friendly terms with aristocrats

sénṭé the tuberous edible roots of a certain plant having itchy leaves

sènteg *rpr* the feel of a sudden heavy burden, physical *or* spiritual. **s·um·ènteg** burdensome

sentèg 1 weaving shuttle. 2 *rpr* snatching. ***an** ring-toss game. **ñj/di*** 1 to operate a weaving shuttle. 2 to play ring-toss. *** sa·pisan a·ñ·tigas·i** to say sth only once but effectively

sentèleng exhibit, exhibition. **ñj/di*** to exhibit, show

senṭeng clothesline

sènter 1 center line in a soccer court. 2 flashlight. **ñj/di*(i)** to shine a flashlight (on). **ñj*i** to play center (in soccer). *** por** *or* *** pur(wares)** center forward (soccer player *or* position)

senṭèt *rpr* sudden heating up. **ñj/di*aké** to put sth in the sun to dry. **s·um·enṭèt** to heat up suddenly [of sun]. *Mau ésuk menḍung, saiki panas semenṭèt.* It was cloudy this morning, but all of a sudden it's turned hot.

sènti *contracted form of* SÈNTIMÈTER. **sa*** one cm.

senṭi:k ***-*** *or* **senṭak-*** [of breath] coming

in puffs. *Ambegané *-* katon saka obahé bauné kang lemu.* He was panting, apparently from the effort of moving his big fat arms.

sentil 1 uvula. 2 a small soft protuberance. **ñj/di*** 1 to shoot [a marble] by flipping it with a finger suddenly released from the thumb. 2 to cast aspersions obliquely. *Gubernur njentil tugasé sing ora bèrès.* The governor made slurring hints about her disorganized work.

sèntimèn (to have) ill will *or* envy

sèntimèter (*abbr*: **cm.**) centimeter

sèntir large shawl worn over one shoulder

senṭir 1 makeshift oil lamp consisting of an oil-filled bottle and a wick. 2 [of children] to urinate slightly by accident. **s·um·enṭir** [of a faucet] to keep trickling *or* dripping

senṭit piercing high-pitched sound. **ñj/di*-aké** to conceal [a small object]

sentlèp *rpr* a sharp stinging sensation. *Aku dientup tawon, *.* A bee stung me! **ñj/di*** to sting, prick

sentlup *var of* SENTRUP

sentolop flashlight

senṭong (*or* ***an** *or* *** tengah**) a small inner room in traditional Javanese houses, used for making offerings to the spirits, for wedding ceremonies, and for other special purposes

sentor **ka*** to be caught and carried away [by flowing water]; to be blown on [by wind]. **ñj/di*(aké)** to flush away, *esp.* with water. *njentor W.C.né* to flush the toilet. **s·um·entor** flowing [of water] *or* blowing [of wind] in large quantities. *Sewengi lèḍengé sumentor terus.* The faucet ran all night. *Anginé saja kentjeng sementor.* The wind blew harder and harder.

sentosa strong, sturdy. **ka*n** courage. **ñj/di*kaké** to make strong. *njentosakaké tjagak* to build strong pillars. **ñj/di*ni** to make stronger. *Tjagaké kudu di*ni.* The pillars need to be strengthened.

séntrā center

sèntrem center

sentrong **ñj/di*aké** to cast [light]. *Mak bjar, lampu sorot di*aké marang arahé kéné.* A beam of light was suddenly flashed in our direction. **ñj/di*(i)** to shed light on (*lit, fig*). *Urip pribadiné lagi di* masjarakat.* The public is seeking out facts about his private life.

sèntrum *var of* SÈNTREM

sentrup **sentrap-*** to keep snuffing; to have a runny nose

sentug *rpr* a whiff. *Mak * ganda arum njogok irung.* He caught a whiff of perfume. **s·um·entug** to smell disagreeable

senṭuk ***-*** *or* **senṭak-*** to keep sobbing softly. **ñj*** to sit concentrating on *or* absorbed in sth

sentul a variety of tree

sentut *var of* SETUT

senuk 1 tapir. 2 *slang* prostitute

senu:t *rpr* a stab of pain. ***-*** to throb with pain

sèp head of an administrative unit

sepa insipid, tasteless

sepah 1 *var of* SEPUH. 2 (*or* ***an**) sth to chew on, *e.g.* betel, sugar cane. 3 (*or* ***an**) what is left after one has chewed *or* sucked the juice from sth (*or*, in a sugar-processing plant, after the machine has pressed out the juice). **ñj/di*** 1 to chew the juice from. 2 to spit out [sth one has chewed the good out of]

sépak ***an** that which is kicked. **ñj/di*** to kick. *Sikilé di* djaran.* He was kicked in the leg by a horse. *** bola** (*** raga** *rg*) soccer game

sepakat in (unanimous) agreement. **ñj/di*i** to agree on/to

sepâlâ trivial, insignificant. *Ing tjrita * iki ngaturaké...* In this little story, we tell you...

sepan tight-fitting. *rok ** a tight skirt

separbang savings bank

sepasar *ng*, **sepeken** *kr* one 5-day week. *Wis * kok ora ana lajang.* It's been a week and still no letter from him. ***an** 1 one 5-day week. 2 a ceremony held on the fifth day after a significant event (*esp.* a wedding or the birth of a child). **ñj*** every (5-day) week; week by week. **ñj/di*i** to honor smn with a fifth-day ceremony (as above). *See also* PASAR

sepat a certain edible freshwater fish

sepâtâ *inf var of* SUPATA

sepatu shoe(s). *ilat ** the tongue of a shoe. ***n̂** to put on *or* wear shoes. **ñj/di*n̂i** to put shoes on smn. *** djindjit** high-heeled shoes. *** sanḍat** laced shoes

sepéḍā(h) bicycle. ** montor* motor bike, motorcycle. *nunggang ** to ride a bicycle. **ñj*** to ride a bicycle. *Aku mulih njepéḍah.* I rode my bicycle home.

sepeken one 5-day week (*kr for* SEPASAR). *See also* PEKEN

sepèksi *rural* inspection
sepèktur *rural* inspector
sepèkuk brown cake
sepèl to practice *or* train for a sport. *Ḍèké lagi * nang lapangan.* He's at soccer practice on the field. ***an** (way of) spelling. **ñj/di*** to spell [words]
sepélé trivial, of little consequence. *Perkara mung * ngono kok dadi padu.* Arguing over such a little thing! *Soal sing kanggo aku angèl kanggo ḍèké dianggep *.* Problems that are difficult for me are nothing for him. **ñj/di*kaké** to consider of little importance; to treat with contempt. *Adja sok njepèlèkaké pituturé wong tuwa.* Don't treat lightly the advice given you by your parents. *Aku rada njepèlèkaké djès.* I don't think much of jazz music.
sepen quiet, lonely, deserted (*kr for* SEPI)
sepèrsi asparagus
sepet 1 outer fiber of coconuts or betel nuts. *babut ** coconut-fiber mat. *sapu ** coconut-fiber brush. 2 tart, sour. 3 disagreeable *or* wearisome to look at. **ñj/di*** to waterproof sth by applying a certain liquid. **ñj/di*-*i** to offend the sight. *Ah tontonané kok mung kuwi[2] baé, mboseni lan njepet[2]i mripat.* The show is tiresome, I don't want to see it. *** gula** *or* *** madu** very sweet-tasting
sepi *ng,* **sepen** *kr* quiet, lonely, deserted. *Saking *né ana dom tiba bisa krungu.* It was so quiet you could hear a pin drop. *Saja wengi saja *.* As the night wore on, it got more and more deserted. ***ǹ** area for dead storage. **sepa-*** very quiet *etc. Menawa ḍong liburan sekolahan sepa-*.* The school is utterly deserted during vacation. **ka*ǹ** excessively quiet *etc. Kanggoku omahmu kesepèn.* Your house is too lonely for me (*i.e.* no children in it)! **ñj*** 1 characterized by quiet *or* desolation; to be in a quiet place. *Aku seneng njepi.* I like isolated places. 2 (*or* **n[j]e-ñ[j]***) to withdraw smw for solitude and meditation. *Sang Prabu nenepi ing Parangtritis.* The King isolated himself at Parangtritis for prayer. **ñj/di*kaké** to cause [a place] to be quiet/lonely/deserted. **pa*ǹ** storage area. **pa·ñj*ǹ** sanctuary, place where one meditates in solitude. *** ing pamrih** with no ill intentions. *** mamring** rare, scarce. *** njenjet** hushed, very quiet, utterly still. **ora tau * ing ḍuwit** never get caught short of money
sepijon *var of* SEPIJUN
sepijun a spy
sepinten *kr for* SEPIRA
sepira *ng,* **sepinten** *kr* how much [of sth not specified in units]? ** dawané?* How long is it? *Suwéné *?* How long does it take? ***-pira** (**sepinten-pinten** *kr*) a large amount. *Diwènèhi sepira-pira tetep ora tjukup.* We gave him more and more but it was never enough. **ora *a** not very (much, many). *Ḍèwèké ora *a geḍé.* He's not very tall. *Tatuné ora *a.* His wound didn't amount to much. **ñj*** how much apiece? *Njepira sabongkoké?* How much per bunch? *Njepira sepuluhé pelem kuwi?* How much for ten of the mangoes? *Olèhmu tuku sabun njepira?* How much did you buy of each kind of soap? *Botjah[2] diwènèhi njepira?* How much should we give to each child? *See also* DURUNG, PIRA
sepiral spiral
sepiritus spirits for lamps *or* for medicinal use. *lampu ** spirit lamp
sepisijal special, out of the ordinary
sepit *var of* SUPIT
sepon household sponge
sepontan spontaneous; spontaneity
sepor(e)t sport(s), athletics; to participate in sports
seprânâ *ng,* **seprika** *kr* since that time (*Degree III: Introduction, 6*); up until now. *Wong kok * durung kawin.* So far, he has never married. ***-sepréné** up to the present time. **-sepréné omahé durung dadi.* After all this time the house still isn't finished.
seprèi bedspread
sepréné *ng,* **sepriki** *kr* until now (*Degree I: Introduction, 6*). *Tekan * iki isih dienggo.* They are still in use today. *Wetara wis ana rong puluh taun sapréné.* It's been twenty years now. *See also* SEPRANA
seprika since that time (*kr for* SEPRANA)
sepriki to this day (*kr for* SEPRÉNÉ)
sepriku since then (*kr for* SEPRONO)
sepritus *var of* SEPIRITUS
seprono *ng,* **sepriku** *kr* from that (recent) time on, since then (*Degree II: Introduction, 6*). ** aku ora tau kepeṭuk manèh.* I haven't seen him from that day to this. ** durung ana sing awèh keterangan.* No one has given out any information since then.
Sept. *see* SÈPTÈMBER
Sèptèmber (*abbr*: **Sept.**) September
Septu *var of* SETU

sepud a rush; rush service. *ndjaluk * sedina rampung* to ask for one-day service. **ñj/di*** to rush through, do on a rush basis. *Gawéané di* bèn gelis rampung.* He rushed through the job so as to get it over with.

sepuh old, mature; ripe (*kr for* TUWA). **se*** chairman. **ka*an** 1 old people, senior citizens. 2 those who belong under the authority of the king's territory (rather than that of the crown prince: *cf.* KA·NOM·AN). **ñj/di·se*i** to preside over. *njenjepuhi rapat* to chair a meeting. **ñj/di*aké** 1 to darken [colors]. 2 to have [gold] burnished

sepuluh *ng,* **sedâsâ** *kr* ten. *buku ** ten books. ** persèn* ten percent. *tikel ** ten times as many. *djam ** ten o'clock. ** djam* ten hours. ***-*** by tens, ten at a time. *Wong² éntuk buku sepuluh².* Each person received ten books. **ka*** ten times; (for) the tenth time; tenth in a series. *Ḍèké takon soal iki sing ka*é.* This is the tenth time he's asked that question. **(ka)* tengah** 9½. *See also* -AN (*suffix*) 8, 15, 16; -É[c] (*suffix*) 9; NG- (*prefix*) 6, 7; PRA-; PULUH

sepur train. *enḍas ** locomotive. *gerbong ** railway coach; car of a train. *kuli ** railroad porter. **ñj*** to go by train. *Mengko njepur djam pira?* What train are you taking? *** è(k)sprès** fast train, express train. *** èmbrèt** *or* *** kluṭuk** *or* *** ṭruṭuk** slow local train

sèr *rpr* water emerging

ser 1 *rpr* spinning, whirling. *Roḍané diubengaké mak *.* He spun the wheel. 2 *rpr* a sharp pain. *Mak * wetengé krasa mules.* He had a stomach cramp. 3 *rpr* a quick shift of position. *Mak * sikilé obah memburi ḍèwèké bisa énḍa.* He quickly moved one foot back and managed to dodge.

ser- *see also under* SR- (*Introduction, 2.9.3*)

serak 1 husky, hoarse [of voice]. 2 cloth *or* fiber used as a filter. **ñj/di*(i)** to make [the voice] husky/hoarse

serang ***an** an attack. **ñj/di*** to attack. *njerang markas mungsuh* to strike the enemy headquarters. **pa·ñj*an** an attack, act of attacking

serap to enter; to set (*kr for* SURUP)

serat 1 grain, tree-ring pattern [of wood]. 2 vein pattern [of leaves]. 3 fiber. 4 (to make) batik (*kr for* BAṬIK). 5 comb (*kr for* DJUNGKAT). 6 a letter (*kr for* LAJANG). ** kawat* telegram. 7 to write (*root form: kr for* TULIS)

serba (of) various (kinds). ** guna* various uses. ***-serbi** all sorts of [things]

serban turban. **ñj/di*i** to put a turban on smn

serbat a hot drink spiced with ginger

serbèt napkin, cloth for cleaning. ***-*** to use a cloth *or* napkin for cleaning. *Kowé njapua, aku tak *-*.* You sweep and I'll dust. **ñj/di*i** to clean sth with a napkin *or* cloth

serbu ***an** an attack. **ñj/di*** to charge, attack

Ser. Da. *see* SERSAN

serḍaḍu *inf var of* SARAḌAḌU

serdju *var of* SARDJU

seré citronella grass. *lenga ** aromatic oil extracted from citronella grass: used in cooking, also applied to the skin as a healing agent or insect repellent. *ron ** citronella leaf, used to flavor curry dishes

sèrèd the narrow undyed strip at the edge of a piece of batik fabric. ***an** wearing the undyed strip at the front of one's batik along the edge of the plait (*wiru·n̂*). **ke*** to get dragged (along). **ñj/di*** 1 to leave [the edge] undyed when making batik. 2 to drag sth (along); *fig* to drag in, involve. *Karung berasé di* merga diangkat ora kuat.* He dragged the sack of rice–it was too heavy to lift. *Adja njèrèd wong lija.* Don't involve anyone else in it.

sereg ***an** hasty, done under pressure. *Gawéan *an biasané ora sampurna.* Work done under pressure is usually not flawless. *iso *an* animal intestines as food. **ñj/di*** to put pressure on smn. *Anggoné ndjaluk bali ḍuwité njereg waé.* He demanded his money back. *Tukang djahit tak * supaja énggal masrahaké gawéané.* I kept after the tailor to hurry with the work I had given him.

sèrèh to resign, retire

serékat organization, association, union. ** buruh* labor union. ** désa* village association. *Amérika ** the United States

serem frightening, terrifying

sèrèn 1 to quit [one's job]. 2 to stop. **ñj/di*i** to fire smn. **tanpa *** without end

sereng 1 stern, harsh; angry, displeased. 2 liquid squeezed from a lemon peel. **ñj/di*(aké)** to squirt smn with lemon-peel juice. *Kulité djeruk di*aké nang mripatku.* He squeezed lemon juice in my eyes.

sèrep a spare [part, *etc.*]. ** ban* spare tire. **ñj/di*i** to substitute (for) [sth] with a spare. *njèrepi jèn ana pemain sing kelaran* to substitute for a [soccer *etc.*] player who gets hurt

serep to enter; twilight; to set (*kr for* SURUP)

sèrèt stripe. * *abang* a red stripe. **ñj/di*i** to make stripes on. *njèrèti klambi* to trim a dress with stripes. *See also* ADU

serèt ***an** opium-smoking equipment. **ñj/di*** (**nge/di·ses** *ki*) to smoke opium. **pa·ñj*** (act of) smoking opium

seret 1 wedged, *esp.* in the throat. *Propé * banget.* The cork was in tight. *Wangsulané *.* She answered with difficulty. 2 *slang* [of money] tight, hard to get. *Ḍuwité * metuné.* Money is hard to come by. **ke*an** *or* **ke*en** [of throat] to get sth stuck in it. *Gorokanku ke*en salak.* I got some *salak* fruit stuck in my throat. **ñj/di*aké** to make tight. *Sekrupé mbok di*aké.* Please tighten the screw. **ñj/di*i** to stick *or* get wedged, *esp.* in the throat. *Wah, segané akas, mulané njereti.* The rice is so dry it's hard to swallow.

serga the late (deceased)... (*slang var of* SWARGA)

sergi the late (deceased)... (*slang var of* SWARGI)

sèri, séri 1 part, volume; series, serial number. *filem * loro* part two of the film. *Lotréné sing putus * nomor 7777.* The winning lottery number is 7777. *njritakaké gambar² ** to narrate a story that is shown in a series of pictures. 2 (*or* **seri**) a tie, a draw. *Entèk²ané * telu-telu.* It ended in a 3–3 tie.

seri *see* SÈRI 2

serik offended; feeling harsh toward smn. *Nadyan *a dikaja ngapa, tetep adjènana.* No matter how galled you are, you must still show respect for him. ***an (ati·ṅ)** touchy, easily offended. **se*an (ati)** to offend each other habitually. **ñj*aké** *or* **ñj*i** offensive; (*psv* **di*aké** *or* **di*i**) to gall smn

serikat *var of* SERÉKAT

sering sometimes, often (*kr for* KEREP?). ***-*** every so often, from time to time

serit 1 lice-removing comb having tiny teeth on both sides. 2 young cucumber. ***an** *or* **se*** to comb oneself with the above. **ñj/di*i** to comb the lice from smn's hair

Ser. Ka. *see* SERSAN

sèrkulèr circular; form letter

séro 1 a certain type of barred fish trap. 2 capital share in an enterprise. **ber*** to operate a business enterprise jointly. *A ber* karo B arep mbukak warung.* A and B are going to open a shop together. **ñj*** to catch fish with the above barred trap

sero *var of* SERU

sérok scooping tool. **ñj*i** to make a swooping *or* scooping motion. *Lajangané njéroki mblebes.* The kite made a long swooping dive. **ñj/di*(i)** 1 to scoop sth (up). 2 to pull [a kite] in a swooping dive

sérong (*or* ***an**) diagonal, slantwise. **ñj/di*** to set sth in a diagonal or catty-corner position. *Omahé ora marep ngalor bener nanging njérong ngétan.* The house faces not straight north but northeast.

sérop **sérap-*** to eat noisily from the surface of an implement. *Olèhé mangan bakso sérap-*.* He slurped his noodles. **ñj/di*(i)** to scoop sth from the surface with a skimming implement. *Ḍèké njéropi kalèné sing membleng.* He skimmed the debris off the choked ditch.

serop *var of* SÉROP

serot ***an** drinking straw. **ñj/di*(i)** 1 to sip, suck. *njerod hawa* to inhale. *njerot banju nganggo *an* to drink water with a straw. *Lemud iku njerot getihé menungsa.* Mosquitoes suck human blood. 2 to absorb. **pa·ñj*** act *or* way of sucking/absorbing. *mesin penjerot lebu* vacuum cleaner

sèrpis a tea service

sèrsan *var of* SERSAN

sersan sergeant. * **dua** (*abbr*: **Ser. Da.**) sergeant second class. * **kepala** (*abbr*: **Ser. Ka.**) senior sergeant. * **major** (*abbr*: **Ser. Ma.**) master sergeant. * **satu** (*abbr*: **Ser. Tu.**) sergeant first class

sèrsi plainclothesman

serta *var of* SARTA

Ser. Tu. *see* SERSAN

seru (**sora** *kr?*) 1 loud. *Anggoné njetèl raḍio *.* He had the radio turned up loud. *Adja *-*.* Not so loud! 2 forceful. *Olèhé nggebug djaran saja *.* He beat the horse harder and harder. **ke*n̂** excessively loud *or* forceful. *Olèhé népang bal keseron.* He kicked the ball too hard. **ñj/di*k̂aké** to make sth loud(er) *or* strong(er). **pa·ñj*** act of doing sth loudly *or* forcibly. *tembung panjeru* (*gram*) exclamation

sérub a blindfold. ***an** blindfolded. **ñj/di*** to blindfold. *Aku mau dikon njérub tukang sulapé nganggo katju.* The magician had me blindfold him with a kerchief.

serudjuk in agreement (about). *Wis sarudjuk regané.* They've agreed on a price. *Wong*[2] *mau* * *mangan ana rèstoran.* They decided to eat at a restaurant. **ñj/di*i** to agree on/to. *A njarudjuki marang rembugé B.* A agreed with what B said. *See also* RUDJUK

sérum serum. **ñj/di*** to inoculate smn with serum

seruni a certain flower

sérup ***an** blind-man's buff. **ñj/di*** to blindfold smn

ses 1 *rpr* a sibilant sound. 2 a smoke; to smoke (*opt? kr for* ROKOK, UDUD). **nge*** 1 to produce a sibilant sound. 2 (*psv* **di***) to smoke opium (*ki for* ÑJ/DI·SERÈT). **nge·sas-nge*** to inhale and exhale audibly through the teeth

ses- *see also under* S- (*Introduction, 3.1.3*)

sésa ***-*** to depend (on), be up (to). **-* *marang wong désa kono.* It's up to the people of the village to decide.

sesa in a hurry (*root form: kr for* SUSU[b])

sesak having too little space. *Sepuré* *. The train is crowded. *Klambiné* *. The dress is too small for her. *Ambekané* *. It's hard for him to breathe because of his asthma.

seseg closely spaced. *Aku kerep krasa* *. I often feel short of breath. * *ing ḍaḍa* short-winded. *Gamelané* *. The music is in quick tempo. *Bisé * banget.* The bus is very crowded. **ke*en** 1 to breathe with quick, shallow breaths. 2 excessively close, cramped. *Klambiné ke*en.* His shirt is too small for him. **ñj*** 1 coming in rapid succession. *Rada njeseg pitakoné marang aku.* He fired questions at me. *Gamelan ditabuh saja njeseg.* The music played faster and faster. 2 (*psv* **di***) to fire questions at. *Malingé di* nganti ngaku.* The thief was interrogated until he confessed. **ñj/di*aké** to place [things] close(r) together. *Gamelané di*aké.* They quickened the tempo of the music. *Senadjan di*aké ora klebu merga wis kebak.* Even if you crowd things, it won't go in–there's no space left. *See also* KAMI-SESEGEN

sèsèk **ñj/di*i** to slice on the diagonal; to cut into flakes. *njèsèki téla gantung* to slice papaya

sesel ***an** 1 that which is pushed/inserted into sth. *Sing kanggo *an pantjuran lèḍeng gabus.* They used a cork to plug the pipe. *Saiki ana *ané mikir lija.* Now something else forced its way into his thoughts. 2 (*gram*) infix. **ñ(j)*** to push in. *Ḍèké nesel nang ngarep.* He pushed into the front of the line. **ñ(j)/di*aké** to insert. *Gabusé di*aké nang nggon pantjuran lèḍeng.* He stuffed the cork into the pipe. **ñ(j)/di*i** to insert into. *Tjangkemku di*i katju.* They stuffed a handkerchief into my mouth.

sesep ***an** an infant who is not yet weaned (*kr for* SUSU·Ñ). **ñ(j)/di*** to suck. *Vampir kuwi nesep getihé wong enom.* Vampires suck the blood of young people. **ñ(j)/di*i** to nurse, suckle. *njesepi baji* to nurse a baby

seser (*or* ***an**) ring for the finger. **ke*** defeated, overcome

sèsèt to come off, peel off. *Kulité tangan* *. He skinned his hand. **ñ(j)/di*(i)** to peel/remove skin (from). *Ḍèké lagi nèsèt kulit trewèlu.* He's skinning the rabbit. *See also* KAMISÈSÈTEN

sesi *inf var of* SEKSI

sèstu *var of* SA·ÈSTU

sesuhunan *full form of* SUNAN

sésuk *ng,* **m·béndjing-éndjing** *kr* tomorrow. ***-*** *ng* at some (indefinite) future time. * **embèn** day after tomorrow. * **ésuk** (**m·béndjing-éndjing** *kr*) tomorrow morning. *See also* BÉSUK

sesuker feces

sèt 1 maggot. 2 (*or* ***en**) infested with maggots

set *rpr* sudden tightening. *Karungé ditalèni mak* *. He tied the bag with a quick jerk.

séta *oj* white

seta to like, want (*kr for* DOJAN). **ñj/di*i** to call, name; to think, consider (*kr for* NG/DI·ARAN·I)

setadjab *inf var of* MUSTADJAB

setagèn ladies' wide wrapped sash worn with traditional Javanese dress

setali *ng,* **setangsul** *kr* 1 25 cents. 2 formerly used unit of weight for gold. ***ṅ** *rg var of* *. ***ṅan** (**setangsul·an** *kr*) 25-cent coin. **ñj*ṅan** (**ñj·setangsul·an** *kr*) worth 25 cents. *prangko njetalènan* a 25-cent stamp. * **telung wang** no different; six of one and half a dozen of the other. *Bapaké ḍemen njolong, anaké satali telung wang.* The father steals and the son is a chip off the old block. *See also* TALI·ṄAN

setalpèn fountain pen

setaman a certain preparation for ceremonial use. *banju* * or *kembang* * water-and-flower mixture used ceremonially

setambu:k book of genealogical notations
setambul stage production somewhat resembling an Occidental-style musical comedy (*see also* KUMIḌI)
sétan devil, evil spirit. *walang* * a black locust that produces a loud noise. ***an** *wj* devil characters. **ñj/di*i** to incite smn to quarrel. * **alas** 1 an evil spirit of the forest. 2 *term of abuse.* * **gunḍul** devil with a shaved head. * **ñ·tunggang gadjah** one who rides roughshod over others
sentânâ cemetery (*rg kr for* PA·KUBUR·AN)
setandar(t) 1 bicycle standard attached at the hub of the rear wheel, for holding the bicycle upright when not in use. 2 standard of quality. **pamulangan* the quality of the education. 3 a stand. *TVné wènèhana* *. Set the television on the stand.
setang bicycle handlebars
setangsul a coin; a measure (*kr for* SETALI)
setanplas, setanplat streetcar *or* bus stop
setap military staff
seṭapruk a large amount. *Ḍuwité* *. He's rolling in money.
setasijun *var of* SETATSIJUN
setatseblad government press release
setatsijun (railroad) station. * **bis** bus station
setatut(en) statute, regulation
setaun one year. ***an** a ceremony celebrating smn's first birthday. **ñj*** per year. *Njetauné ḍèké tampa ḍuwit sepuluh èwu rupijah.* She gets 10,000 rupiahs a year. **ñj/di*i** to honor [a deceased person] with a ceremony on the first anniversary of his death. *See also* TAUN
setèk a cutting from a plant grafted onto another plant. ***an** having a cutting grafted onto it. **ñj/di*** to graft [a cutting]
seṭèkrak *var of* SEṬÉKRUK
seṭékruk a large amount
setèl 1 a matching set. *piring sak* * a set of dishes. *Penganggoné * putih.* He's wearing a white suit. 2 to harmonize, go well [with]. *Kuwi * karo karo kaṭokmu sing soklat.* It goes with your brown trousers. *Mas Ḍokter lan garwané iku lé bisa* *. The doctor and his wife get along well. ***an** 1 a (matched) set. 2 suit (jacket and trousers). 3 act *or* way of turning on. *Setèlané raḍio nganggo pèdjètan.* The radio is operated with a pushbutton. **ñj/di*** to switch on. *Raḍioné di* seru.* He turned on the radio loud. *Bingkilé lagi njetèl mesiné montorku.* The repair man is in the process of adjusting my car engine.
setèling, setéling 1 exposition, exhibition. 2 military emplacement
setèm 1 true [of pitch]; in tune. *Anggoné menjanji* *. They sang on key. 2 to match, harmonize. *Klambi iki * karo kaṭokku.* The shirt goes with my trousers. **ñj/di*** 1 to tune [an instrument]. *Pianoné lagi di* karo tukangé.* The piano tuner is tuning the piano. 2 to decide by majority vote. *Usulé di* karo rapat.* The proposal was passed at the meeting.
setèmpel a stamp; a rubber stamp. **ñj/di*** to stamp
setèn assistant to a district head (*wadana*). ***an** office *or* residence of the above official
setengah 1 a half. **djaman* about half an hour. * *tjangkir* half a cupful. *loro * sasi* two and a half months. *Njambut gawé * mati.* He worked himself half to death. * *anjel lan * seneng* half annoyed and half pleased. 2 partly, somewhat. *Tembung²é * medèni marang bodjoné.* What he said was a bit frightening to his wife. 3 queer, eccentric. *Tak kira kok ja rada* *. I think he's only half there. *wong* * a mentally aberrant person. ***-*** 1 half and half. *Dumen *-**. Give each of them half. 2 without serious attention *or* purpose. *Olèhé njambut-gawé *-**. He's only got half his mind on his work. * **mati** extreme. *Panasé * mati.* The heat is insufferable. * **tuwa** *or* * **tuwuh** *or* * **umur** middle-aged. *See also* DJAM, PARO, TENGAH
s̊èter typesetter
setidjab efficacious
setijar effort, endeavor. **ñj/di*aké** to make an effort. *Ḍèké wis di*aké gawéan nang endi² nanging ora éntuk.* People on all sides have been trying to help him find work, but to no avail.
setik stitched plaits. **ñj/di*** to hem [a garment]. * **balik** a hem
setin 1 satin. 2 a marble
setingkul coal as fuel
setip rubber eraser. **ñj/di*** to erase
setir steering wheel. * *kiri* left-hand drive. **ñj/di*(i)** to drive; to steer
setiti careful, accurate, scrupulous. **ñj/di*kaké** to look into carefully. *njetitèkaké kahanan penḍuḍuké* to investigate the condition of the populace. *Jèn arep tuku mas inten kudu disetitèkaké sing temenan.*

When you're buying valuables, you should examine them thoroughly.

seṭiṭik *ng,* **sekeḍik** *kr* a little (bit); a few. *Weḍus ija akèh, mung djaran sing* *. There were lots of sheep but only a few horses. *Kurang * baé aku olèh puser.* I barely missed a bull's-eye. *saka ** little by little. *Diwulang aksara saka* *. They were taught the letters a few at a time. *-* 1 a very little; very few. **-* rak ja kélingan ta?* You remember a little of it, don't you? 2 little by little; a few at a time. *ora *-*a* not the least bit; not a single one. *Ora ngetokaké wragadé *-*a.* He didn't pay any of his expenses at all. ***-*é** at least. *Sepatuné *-*é regané rupiah rong èwu.* His shoes cost at least 2,000 rupiahs. **ñj*** to become few(er). **ora *** a great many; a good deal. *Ora * botjah wadon sing paḍa dadi guru.* Many girls become teachers.

setiwel boots; high shoes. ***an** to put on *or* wear such footgear. *dongèngé kutjing *an* the story of the cat who wore boots

setlika *var of* SETRIKA

setoker fireman on a steam locomotive

setonten quarrel, dispute (*kr for* SETORI)

setop to come to a stop. ***an 1** stopping place. 2 traffic light. *prapatan *an* intersection with a traffic light. **ke*** to get stopped. **ñj/di*aké** to stop for smn. *Wong tuwa mau di*aké bis déning polisi.* The policeman stopped a bus for the old man. **ñj/di*(i)** to bring to a stop. *Pemréntahé njetop impor beras.* The government put a stop to rice imports. *** bril** sunglasses

setoplès a glass jar with an airtight cover, used for storing cookies and the like

setor to turn over money one has taken in (*e.g.* in pedicab fares, movie-ticket sales) to the owner or proprietor of the business. ***an** fee paid (as above). **ñj/di*** to pay smn such a fee. *Saben dina tukang bétjak kudu njetor taokéné Rp 100.* The pedicab driver has to pay the boss 100 rupiahs a day. **ñj/di*aké** to pay such a fee. *Sapérangan di*aké marang pamréntah.* A percentage is turned over to the government.

setori *ng,* **setonten** *kr* a quarrel, dispute. *A seneng gawé * karo sedulur²é.* A is always picking fights with her family.

setoter playing card(s). ***an** to play cards

sétra *oj* 1 battlefield. 2 place where slain corpses are disposed of. **ñj/di*(kaké)** to dispose of [corpses]. **pa*n** *sms ** 2 *above*

setrap punishment. **ñj/di*** to punish smn

setrèng 1 strict, stern, maintaining firm discipline. 2 fan belt

setri wife (*md for* BODJO)

setrik a bow knot. *ḍasi ** bow tie

setrika pressing iron. **ñj/di*** to iron, press. *njetrika klambi* to iron a shirt. **ñj/di*kaké** to iron for smn; to have sth ironed

setrip 1 dash, hyphen. 2 marking line. *sa** one-millimeter mark. 3 chevron. **ñj/di*** to mark with lines *or* dashes

setriwel *var of* SETIWEL

setroli *rg* kerosene

setrum electric current. **ke*** to get an electric shock. **ñj/di*** to give smn a shock

setrup sweet syrup of sugar and fruit juice. ** ès* or *ès ** a cold drink made with fruit syrup

Setu Saturday

setudju in agreement. *Apa kowé *?* Do you agree? *Présiḍèn mau ora * (marang) sistém tetanèn kolèktip.* The President didn't agree to the system of collective farming. **ñj/di*ñi** to reach an agreement (about). *njetudjoni bab anané organisasi buruh* to reach an agreement on the formation of a labor union. *See also* TUDJU

setum 1 steam. 2 steam engine. 3 steam roller. **ñj/di*** to press flat with a steam roller. *** bot** steamboat. *** wasseri** steam press in a dry-cleaning establishment

setunggal 1 one (*kr for* SIDJI). 2 a(n), a certain (*kr for* SAWIDJI)

setunggil *sbst var of* SETUNGGAL

setup 1 a drink made by boiling fruit with sugar and water. ** nanas* pineapple drink. 2 vegetables in coconut-milk sauce. **ñj/di*** to make [ingredients] into the above

setut belt, sash. **ñj/di*(aké)** to overtake and pass. *Montoré njetut truk.* The car passed a truck.

setya loyal, faithful, obedient. ** kawan* a loyal friend. **ñj/di*ni** to be loyal/obedient to. *** tuhu** faithful and loyal

séwa (*rg; or [standard]* ***n**) 1 rented; for rent. *kréta séwan* a hired carriage. 2 rent money. **ñj/di*** to rent, hire. *njéwa gamelan* to rent gamelan instruments. *njéwa djaran* to hire a horse. **ñj/di*kaké** to rent sth out. *wong sing njéwakaké djaran* a man who has horses for hire. *Sawahé di*kaké.* He rented out his rice paddy.

séwâkâ **pa*n** royal court. **s·in·éwaka** to be granted an audience at court (at which the

retainers and subjects sit abjectly in silence before the monarch)
sèwèk *rg* batik wraparound
sèwèt *var of* SÈWÈK
sewelas eleven (*see also* SA, WELAS[b])
sewidak *see* WIDAK
sewiwi *inf var of* SUWIWI
sèwu one thousand. ***n̂** 1 about a thousand. 2 a thousand-rupiah bill. **ñj*** 1 by the thousand; a thousand at a time. *Genḍèng iki njèwuné pira?* How much are these tiles per thousand? 2 to hold a commemorative ceremony on the thousandth day after smn's death. *** dina·né** the thousandth day after smn's death; **ñj*-dina** to hold a thousandth-day ceremony (as above). *See also* ÈWU
sèx sex (*var sp of* SÈKS)
sh sh! hush!
sholat *var of* SALAT
si 1 (**pun** *kr*) *familiar title used before the name or name substitute of a social equal or inferior. Kowé apa ora kélingan * Teguh?* Don't you remember Teguh? ** A lan * B omahé djèdjèr, tangga.* A and B are next-door neighbors. *Si maling mlaju.* The thief fled. ** Lemu* the Fat One. *Apa * djuru durung kétok?* Hasn't the clerk showed up yet? 2 (*ng*) *particle reinforcing the preceding word(s). Aku * ora pertjaja marang kanḍané.* I, for one, don't believe what he said. *Kowé sing nakal *.* *You're* the one who did wrong! *Tjah wadon sapa *?* Who *is* that girl? *Iki duwèké sapa, *?* Who does this belong to, anyway? 3 seventh note in the musical scale. 4 *ltry: shf of* ISI, KONGSI. **nge/di*** to apply the title *si* to. *Pak guru adja disi.* Don't say *si Guru!* *** aḍi** you [said to a younger social equal]. *** Gèḍèg lan * Anṭuk** the dissenting one and the submissive one; the no-man and the yes-man. *** (ge)nḍuk** little girl who assists the woman household supervisor. *** mbok** [*see also* EMBOK] 1 woman servant who supervises the household duties. 2 *reference term* mother; wife (used among those of low status)
sibar ointment for rubbing on the chest. **ñj/di*i** to apply [ointment] to the chest *or* throat. *** djadja** hair on the chest
sibat *inf var of* MUSIBAT
sibin(g) **ñj/di*i** 1 to give smn a quick bath by splashing the body and then going over it with a cloth. 2 to wash smn's face (*ki for* NG/DI·RAUP·I). **adus *** to give oneself a quick sponge bath
sibu mother (*inf var of* IBU)
sibuk busy. **ka*an** bustle, activity. **ñj/di*aké** to busy oneself. *njibukaké njang perpustakaan* to have things to do at the library. *Siti njubukaké awaké karo njambut gawé nang Palang-Mérah.* Siti occupies herself by working at the Red Cross.
sida 1 (**[sa']èstu** *kr*) to succeed in [do]ing, go through with [a projected activity]. *Apa *?* Is the plan still on? Are we still going to do it? ** lunga apa ora?* Are you really going? *Ésuké * lunga menjang gunung.* The next day they went to the mountain [as originally planned]. ** ora mangkat* [to hold to one's plan and] not go. *ora * mangkat* not go after all [though one had planned to]. *Aku mau wis arep muni, ora *.* I was about to speak but changed my mind. *Ora * dipangan matjan.* The tiger didn't eat him up after all. 2 *compounding element in names of batik designs.* ***né (sijos·ipun** *kr*) the prospects. **né pijé, kok wis suwé ora ana kabaré anakmu kuwi.* How about your son?–it's a long time since I've had news of him. **ka*n (ka·sijos·an** *kr*) to get carried through. *Rantjanganè wis ka*n sarwa slamet.* His plan was brought to a satisfactory conclusion. **ñj/di*kaké** *or* **ñj/di*ni** (**ng/dipun·èstu·k̂aken** *or* **ñj/dipun·sijos·aken** *kr*) to carry out [an intention]. *Sidakna ta anggonmu arep njambut-gawé mèlu aku.* Stick to your plan of working with me. *Adja lali njidani djandji.* Don't forget to do as you promised. *** guri** 1 a small plant whose flowers are used for treating bee stings. 2 a batik design representing this plant. *** luhur (ukel)** a batik design of diagonally placed rows of circles: used for bridal batiks. *** mukti** a bridal batik design. *** mulja** bridal batik design with a white background. *** wurung** to abandon a plan. ** wurung anggoné nijat omah*[2]. He gave up the idea of marrying her.
siḍakep with arms folded across the chest. **ñj/di*aké** to fold the arms as above. *** awé**[2] having the arms crossed on the chest in a sanctimonious pose
siḍang meeting, assembly. **ñj/di*aké** to investigate before an assemblage. *Perkara korupsi kantor keuangan saiki lagi di*ké.* The Finance Department corruption case is now under court investigation. *** umum**

P[ersatuan] B[angsa]-B[angsa] the U.N. General Assembly

siḍat an eel-like freshwater fish. ***an** a short cut, a cut-off. **ñj*** to take a short cut

sidâwajah a small plant whose blossom is used for treating bee stings

sidekah, siḍekah *var of* SEḌEKAH

siḍeku(l), siḍekung *var of* SEḌEKU

siḍem *oj* quiet, silent, withdrawn. **ñj/di*** to keep sth quiet, not discuss *or* give out information about. *** permanem** quiet, soundless; **ñj/di*-permanem** to keep sth absolutely quiet

sidi *oj* perfect, ideal

sidik *oj* to know in advance. **ñj/di*aké** *or* **ñj/di*i** to look into, attempt to confirm. *Omongé arep tak *i.* I'll see if what he said is true.

sidji *ng,* **satunggal** *kr* one. *Mung kari *.* There's only one left. *saben dina ** once a day. *telung puluh ** 31. *Pantjèn * kuwi kebangeten.* That one (*i.e.* he, she) is really too much! *Krikil iki lebokna ana baṭok kéné salah *.* Put the pebble under one of these coconut shells. *Ḍèké ngunèkaké salah sidjiné lagu.* He sang a song. **ñj*** one each, one apiece. **ñj*-ñj*** one by one, one at a time. **dadi *** into one; together. *Ḍèké nggoḍi pring loro telu dadi *.* He tied two or three bamboo sticks together. *Rong lirang didadèkaké *, djenengé tangkep.* Two halves are put together to make a pair. *** loro** one or two, a couple. *buku * loro* a book or two. *** rong taun* a couple of years. *** ṭil** one and only one. *See also* -É[c] (*suffix*) 9, IDJI, SA, SALAH 2

siḍum shaded, shady, sheltered. ***-*** a sheltered place. **ke*en** excessively shady; overprotected. **ñj*** to take shelter. **pa·ñj*an** protection; protector

siduwa *var of* SEDUWA

sigâlâ-gâlâ *see* BALÉ

sigar 1 a cut piece, a slice. 2 part, *i.e.* separation line of combed hair. ** kiwa* a part on the left. ***an** 1 cut open. *semangka sing wis *an* a cut watermelon. 2 a hair part. *Djungkatané *an tengen.* He parts his hair on the right. **ñj/di*(i)** 1 to split, cut open. *njigar dadi loro* to cut in two. *Enḍogé kamal di*i sawetara.* She cut the salted egg into several portions. 2 to part one's hair. *njigar tengah* to part the hair in the middle. *** djambé** [of lips] beautifully proportioned, of equal thickness. *** semangka** cut precisely in half. *Téla gantungé diparo * semangka.* She cut the papaya into two equal pieces.

sigarèt cigarette

sigeg 1 end, conclusion; finished, over. 2 [of streets] not through, (coming to) a dead end. 3 *gram* closed [of syllables], *i.e.* ending in a consonant (*cf.* M̈·WENGA). *wanda ** a closed syllable. *ater[2] pa- * aksara irung* the prefix *pa-* followed ('completed') by a nasal sound. **se*** finished, closed (off). *Aksara mau ora kena dadi se*.* These sounds do not occur in final position. **ñj/di*** to cut off, discontinue. *Tjritané dak * seméné ḍisik.* I'll stop the story for now. **pa·ñj*** act of being ended *or* cut off. *sanḍangan panjigeging wanda* diacritical marks denoting the end of syllables. *** genti kotjap·a** *wj* at this point one story is concluded and we start on another (*phrase from a puppet-master's narration*)

sigid *rg* mosque

sigit *oj* handsome

sigra 1 a sneeze; to sneeze (*ki for* WAHING). 2 *oj* quickly, at once

sigrak bursting with energy and buoyant health

sih 1 love, loving kindness. *males *ing bapa lan bijung* to reciprocate one's parents' love. *simbang ** (*ltry*) loving kindness. *welas ** compassion. 2 shoo! scat! **, *, kana lunga kana!* Shoo! go away! 3 *var of* SI 2. 4 *inf var of* ISIH, SISIH. ***-*en** to play favorites. ***-s·in·ih·an** to love each other. **nge/di*** 1 to love. 2 to shoo [an animal]. **pa*an** 1 in the state of new-found romantic love. 2 loved one. 3 a token of love. *See also* ASIH, BOT

sihir black magic. *tukang ** practitioner of black magic. *ngèlmu ** black-magic lore

sija (*or* ***-***) cruel; overbearing, apt to humiliate others. **-* marang kéwan* cruel to animals. *Dupèh sugih waé ambeg * marang kang ora duwé.* Just because he's rich, he treats poor people like dirt. **ñj/di*-*** to treat cruelly *or* humiliatingly. *njija-njija wong mlarat* to treat poor people with contempt

sijâgâ prepared, equipped. ** gegaman* ready for battle, equipped with weapons. **ñj/di*-kaké** to equip, put into condition for sth. **ñj/di*ni** all ready for sth. *njijagani jèn ana perang* militarily prepared for the eventuality of war. *Wis di*ni apa sapandjaluké.*

Whatever he asks for is in readiness for him.

sijal bad luck; unlucky. *angka* ∗ unlucky number

sijam to fast (*kr for* PASA)

sijang the middle part of the day (*kr for* AWAN)

sijap all set, ready; stand by! stand ready! **ñ(j)/di∗aké** to make ready. *njiapaké ubarampéné* to have all the equipment standing by

sijar ∗**an** a broadcast. *Aku mau mèlu ∗an raḍio.* I appeared on a radio program. **ñ(j)/di∗aké** to broadcast, announce. **pa·ñ(j)∗** broadcaster, announcer. **s·um·ijar** announced; widely known

sijasat strategy; a strategem, plan of action

Sijem Thailand. *kutjing* ∗ Siamese cat. *djeruk* ∗ lemon

sijin *sbst var of* RUMIJIN

sijos *sbst? kr for* SIDA. ∗**ipun** the prospects (*kr for* SIDA·NÉ). **ka∗an** to get carried out (*kr for* KA·SIDA·N). **ñ(j)/dipun∗aken** *or* **ñ(j)/dipun∗i** to carry out, carry through (*kr for* ÑJ/DI·SIDA·KAKÉ, ÑJ/DI·SIDA·NI)

sijung 1 canine tooth; fang, tusk. *ngatonaké ∗é* to make a show of strength. 2 tusk-shaped section of sth, *e.g.* an orange. *bawang sak* ∗ one bud of garlic. 3 *var of* TJI·JUNG. ∗**an** separated into sections. *Djeruké wis ∗an.* The orange has been separated into sections. **ka∗** to get bitten with fangs *or* gored with tusks. **ñj∗** 1 to bare the teeth; *fig* to make a show of force. 2 (*psv* **di∗**) to bite with the canines/fangs

sijut *rpr* a whizzing sound *or* motion. *Mak* ∗ *anginé mlebu.* In rushed the wind! *Mak* ∗ *wulungé njiruk.* The hawk swooped like lightning. **sijat-∗** to whiz repeatedly. *swarané mimis sijat-∗* the sound of bullets whistling past. **s·um·ijut** 1 to produce a whistling sound. *Anginé sumijat.* The wind whistled. 2 to feel a swooping sensation. *Jèn mlaku liwat kretek rasané sumijut.* When you walk across the bridge you can feel it swaying.

sik 1 first, beforehand (*shf of* ḌISIK). *Sik sik sik sik...* Let me see... 2 just a minute! (*shf of* KOSIK = *shc from* MENGKO ḌISIK). *Sik ta.* Wait! ∗, *dak nganggo sepatu.* Wait till I put on my shoes!

sikârâ nuisance, trouble-maker. **ñj/di∗** to interfere with, distract, pester

sikat 1 a brush. 2 agile, quick. ∗**an** 1 (object) used as a brush. 2 to use a brush. *Aku ésuk-soré mesṭi ∗an.* I always brush my teeth morning and night. 3 a small bird of the wagtail family. **ñj/di∗** to brush. *njikat untu* to brush the teeth

sikep attitude, way of thinking. ∗**an** 1 an embrace. 2 a short loose woollen coat for ceremonial occasions, worn *e.g.* by a bridegroom at his wedding. ∗**-∗an** to grapple with each other. *Olèhé gelut ∗-∗an nganti suwi.* They struggled for a long time. **ñj/di∗** to embrace. *Botjah mau wedi, njikep guluné djaran.* He got scared and threw his arms around the horse's neck. **pa·ñj∗** act *or* way of embracing. *Ḍèké uwal saka panjikepé.* She broke loose from his arms. ∗ **gegaman** to carry weapons, bear arms

siki 1 *oj* one. 2 *var of* SAIKI

sikik *var of* ḌISIK

sikil *ng*, **suku** *kr*, **sampéjan** *ki* leg; foot. ∗**é tatu.** He hurt his leg. ∗ *médja* table leg. ∗**ku gringingen.** My foot's asleep. ∗ **di·gawé enḍas, enḍas di·gawé** ∗ describing a task done against odds, uphill work. ∗ (**pa**)**pat** 1 four-legged. 2 whole-hearted. *Dak tampani ∗ papat.* I was delighted to receive it.

sikir *var of* SIHIR

siksa punishment, torture. **ñj/di∗** to torment, maltreat. *Adja sok njiksa kéwan.* Never tease animals.

siku 1 a right angle; to form a right angle [with], be perpendicular [to]. *Lemariné ∗ karo témbok.* The cupboard is at right angles to the wall. *Dalan² ing New York trandjang²an ∗-∗.* The streets of New York intersect at right angles. 2 triangle (implement for checking right angles) 3 *oj* elbow. 4 *oj* curse, malediction. **se∗** notch, cut, gap. *se∗ning gunung* notch in a mountain. **ke∗** to be the victim of a curse. *Adja sok dolanan nang tjeḍak wit ringin kuwi, mengko munḍak ke∗ sing baureksa.* Never play near that banyan tree, or you'll come under the spell of the spirit that inhabits it. **ñj∗** 1 forming a right angle; perpendicular. 2 (*psv* **di∗**) to check a right angle with a try square. 3 (*psv* **di∗**; *or* **ñj/di∗kaké**) to put a curse on smn. **pa∗ñ** a cleaver-like knife (*ki for* WEḌUNG)

sikut elbow. **ñj/di∗** to prod with the elbow; to elbow one's way through. *njikut baṭi* to reject. *Jèn kowé pingin nglamar Narti baṭi di∗.* If you propose to Narti, she'll turn you down.

sil ***-*an** constantly in motion. *Ḍèké *-*an terus.* He's always fidgeting.

sila (to sit) cross-legged. **pa*n** a place to sit (*e.g.* mat, carpet). *** n·ḍeku ng·apurantjang** to sit cross-legged with palms on chest and forearms on thighs. *** ñg·keḍepes** to sit cross-legged on the ground. *** panggung** to sit with ankles crossed and knees drawn up to one side. *** timpuh** to sit with knees drawn up alongside the body; to squat on crossed ankles (one of the Moslem praying positions). *** tumpang** to sit cross-legged with the right leg over the left (puppet-master fashion). *See also* SILANING

silad ***an** slivers resulting from trimming a split length of bamboo to the desired length and width. **ñj/di*** to trim [bamboo] as above

silâdri *oj* mountain

silah (*or* ***-***) separated, sorted. **ñj/di*** to separate, sort out. **pa·ñj*** act *or* way of sorting out. *tembung panjilah* (*gram*) relative pronoun

silak **ñj*** turned back *or* pushed aside by a non-human agent, *e.g.* wind. **ñj/di*aké** to push back/aside. *njilakké rambut* to brush back the hair with the hand. *njilakké korḍèn* to push aside a curtain. *Lengené di*aké.* He rolled up his sleeves. **s·um·ilak** opened out, pushed aside. *Korḍèné semilak kena angin.* The curtain was pushed back by the wind. *Langité sumilak.* The sky has cleared (*i.e.* the wind has blown away the clouds).

silâkrâmâ good manners. **ñj/di*** to address smn courteously, welcome smn

silaning akrâmâ *oj* marriage. *njambut ** to marry, take as one's wife

silat judo-like system of self-defense. *See also* BESILAT

silaturahmi a gathering held at the close of the fasting month as part of the Lebaran celebration, at which people beg one another's pardon for past trespasses and promise to try to do better in the future

silèh *inf var of* SILIH

silem 1 under (water); far up (in the sky). *kapal ** submarine. ** ing méga* lost in the clouds. 2 to become immersed (in water, sky). *Bajané * ing banju.* The crocodile dived into the water. *Wusana * ing langit biru.* At last it vanished into the blue sky. **ñj*** *sms* * 2. **ñj/di*aké** *or* **ñj/di*i** to submerge sth. *Bom kuwi njilemaké kapal.* The bomb sank the ship.

silep 1 banana leaves for covering food, *esp.* cooked rice in the pot. 2 submerged in water. **ke*** to be accidentally submerged in water; *fig* to be overwhelmed. *ke* nang mblumbang* to fall into a pond. *Sadjaké ke* angen²é sing kepungkur.* He seems to have been staggered by his recent experience. **ñj/di*aké** to submerge sth, plunge sth below the surface. **ñj/di*i** to cover [a pot of food] with banana leaves. *njilepi liwet* to cover the boiled rice

silih *ng,* **sambut** *kr,* **ampil** *ki* ***an** borrowed. *barang *an* a borrowed item. **(a)se*** (*no ki*) having the name of. *Sang tapa se* X.* The ascetic's name was X. **ñj/di*** 1 to borrow. *Bukuné tak *.* I borrowed his book. *Punapa kepareng dalem njuwun ngampil...?* May I borrow...? 2 to [do] vicariously. *njilih mata* to know at second hand, not be an eyewitness. *njilih tangan* to hire smn to do one's dirty work. ***-s·in·ilih** to lend to each other, borrow back and forth. **nje·ñj*** to borrow habitually. **ñj/di*-*** *or* **ñj/di·silah-*** *ng* to make an effort to borrow; to borrow constantly. **ñj/di*aké** 1 to lend. *Montoré di*aké menjang kantjané.* He lent his car to a friend. 2 to borrow on smn's behalf. *Iki lo, tak *ké pit.* Here, I borrowed a bike for you. **ñj/di*i** to lend to. *Botjahé di*i sarung.* They lent the child a sarong.

silir 1 [of breezes] cool and soothing. 2 [of balance scales] tilted slightly in one direction or the other. 3 court official in charge of the palace lamps. 4 [of outer skin] thin. **ka*(an)** to get blown on. *ka*an angin* soothed by the breezes. **ñj*-ñj*aké** to get some fresh air. **s·um·ilir** blowing softly. *Anginé semilir.* There's a soft breeze.

silit 1 anus. 2 bottom of a utensil, dish, *etc.* *** koḍok** coccyx

silo blinded by glare

siluk a certain kind of tobacco

siluman devil, imp, evil spirit. **ñj*** resembling such a spirit

sima tiger (*kr for* MATJAN)

simah *var of* SÉMAH

simak *rg* mother

simbah grandparent. *See also* EMBAH, SI

simbar *var of* SIBAR

simbok *see* EMBOK, SI

simbul symbol

simik *var of* ḌISIK

simil surface mail to overseas areas (as contrasted with air mail)

simin *var of* ḌISIK

simpang ***an** crossroads, intersection; fork *or* branch in a road. **ñj*** to be off/aside [from]. *Tindak tanduké njimpang saka hukim.* What he did was against the law. **ñj/di*i** to (move aside and) make way for. *Jèn peṭukan karo ambulans kudu di*i.* If you meet an ambulance, you have to let it through.

simpar *var of* SÉMPAR. **ka*** *see* PALA

simpen ***an** that which has been kept *or* put aside; savings. **an beras* stored-up rice. **anku saiki wis Rp 20.000.* I now have 20,000 rupiahs saved up. **ñj/di*(i)** to keep [sth smw]; to store, set aside, save, put away. *Sanḍangané di* ana ndjero koper.* He keeps his clothes in a suitcase. *Kembang mau kena di* lawas.* These flowers will keep for a long time. *Ḍèké kuwi ora bisa njimpen wadi.* He can't keep a secret. *Lajang saka anaké kabèh di*i embokné.* His mother keeps all his letters. **pa*an** storage. *guḍang pasimpenan barang²* a shed for storing various things

simping mother-of-pearl. ***an** *wj* arrangement of leather puppets in banana logs at either side of the screen ready for the puppet master to use, tapering from tall at the outside to short next to the screen. **ñj/di*** to arrange [puppets] ready for use by sticking them into a banana log on their sticks

simpir *see* MERAK

sin- *see also under* S- (*Introduction, 3.1.7*)

sinaos even if/though (*opt? kr for* SANADYAN)

sinar *var of* SUNAR

sinau to study, learn. *Aku durung *.* I haven't done my studying. ** ilmu bumi* to study geography. **ñj/di*** to study/learn sth. *Ilmu alam kuwi angèl di*.* Physics is hard to learn. *njinau ékonomi* to study economics. **ñj/di*ḱaké** to enroll smn. *Aku disinaokké bapak sekolah guru.* My father sent me to a teacher's college. **pa*ñ** school, institute of learning. *pasinaon wong² wuta* a school for the blind

sindap dandruff

sinḍèn *wj* to sing to the accompaniment of the gamelan music [of female singers]. ***an** song sung by a female vocalist. **ñj/di*i** to accompany [a shadow-play performance] with female solo singing. **pa*** female soloist with gamelan accompaniment

sinḍet (*or* ***an**) knot. **ané utjul.* The knot came untied. **ñj/di*(aké)** to knot sth together. *Ḍèké njinḍet tali kanggo nalèni buntelan.* He tied pieces of string together to wrap the package.

sindik hinge pin. **ñj/di*** to put a pin [into a hinge]. **ñj/di*i** to furnish [a hinge] with a pin. *Ḍèké njindiki èngsèl lawang sing tjopot.* He put a pin in the loose hinge.

sinḍir **ñj/di*(i)** to make oblique allusions *or* drop hints to. *A pidjer njinḍiri B anggoné kerep ora mlebu kantor.* A often makes slurring remarks to B about his frequent absence from work. *Aku njinḍir(i) ḍèwèké supaja mulih.* I kept hinting to him that he should go home.

sindjang ankle-length batik wraparound (*kr for* DJARIK)

sindu *oj* water; river

sinḍung (*or* *** riwut**) windstorm

sindur white-bordered red sash tied at the rear: worn by the mother of the bride (*Jogjanese custom*)

sinèh *inf var of* DJENÈH

sing *ng*, **ingkang** *kr* **1** (the one) which. ** biru* the blue one. *wong * ḍuwur kaé* that tall man over there. *Omahé sapa * kobong?* Whose house burned? ** kok éling² kuwi rak mung liburan.* All you think about is vacation! ** endi * duwèkmu?* Which one is yours? *Aku * tunggu iwaké, kowé * mantjing.* I'll (be the one to) take care of the fish; you (be the one to) catch them. ** nomer sidji* the first one. **2** one who [does sth specific]. ** nonton* the audience. ** duwé* the owner. ** duwé omah* the host *or* hostess. ** dodol* clerk, salesperson. ** arep tuku* customer. ** paḍa bal-balan* the soccer players. **3** *n* of them. ** loro wis mati.* Two of them are dead now. ** sidji biru, sidjiné abang.* One of them is blue, the other is red. **4** *denoting a personal relationship.* ** lanang* (the one who is) her husband. ** wadon* his wife. *ingkang ibu* your mother. *ingkang abdi* your servant. **5** in a certain manner. ** ngati-ati!* Watch out! (*i.e.* act cautiously). *Olèhmu nulis * apik.* Write neatly. ** tjekak² baé.* Make it brief. **6** smn's act of [do]ing. *Tutugna *mu takon.* Go on with your questions. **7** (*ng kr: prn* **s̊ing**) *var of* SÈNG. **8** *var of* SAKA[a]. *** akèh** most (of it, them). *toko²* akèh* most stores. ** akèh reged.* Most of it was dirty. *Bakul djarik * akèh² wong wédok.* Most batik sellers are women. **ana *** some of them. *Ana * mlaju, ana * nḍelik.* Some of them ran, some hid. *Ora ana * ngerti.* Not one of them understood. *** ḍisik... * kèri...** the former... the latter... * **djeneng·é** such a thing as; the so-called. *Ing kéné ora ana * djenengé sepur.* There's no such thing as a train here. ** djenengé Amérika iku adoh saka Indonesia.* America is a long way from Indonesia, you know! * **endi baé** either *or* any one (at all). *nDi * arep tuku?—* ndi waé.* Which one do you want to buy?—Either one. * **sapa** whoever, anyone who. ** sapa bisa nambani Sang Putri bakal éntuk gandjaran.* Whoever can cure the Queen will get a reward. * **se·pisan·an** (for) the first time. *See also* KANG

singa lion. * **barong** 1 male lion. 2 man in a street show dressed as a monster with the head of a lion or bird. * **nada** *or* * **nebda** *wj* lion's roar. * **negara** executioner. * **pati** king of the beasts

singangsânâ *var of* SINGASANA

singantâkâ king of the beasts

singâsânâ throne

singat horn, antler (*kr for* SUNGU)

singeb blanket (*ki for* KEMUL)

singel wrapped batik headdress. ***an** to put on *or* wear this headdress. **ñj/di*i** to put the above headgear on smn; to furnish smn with such a headdress

singgah *-* an incantation *or* prayer to drive away evil spirits. **ñj/di*aké** *or* **ñj/di*i** to put away, keep, save

singgâsânâ *var of* SINGASANA

singgat fruit fly; fruit-fly larva. **ñj/di*i** to shred [coconut] fine. * **betatung** moving about rapidly, hyperactive. *See also* UNGKAT

singgel *var of* SÉNGGEL, SINGEL

singget **ñj/di*(-*)** to divide up with partitions. *Omahé di*-* arep dienggo poṇḍokan.* They partitioned up the house into rooms for rent.

singgih **ka*an** (*or* **mila ***) (yes) it is true that... (*kr for* [MULA] IJA [BENER]). *Mila ka*an manawi kula mentas saking Djakarta.* It's true that I've just come back from Djakarta.

singha *var of* SINGA

singid **(se)*an** to hide, take cover. ***an ñ·temu matjan** to run into a person one is trying to avoid. **ñj/di*** to hide, conceal oneself. **ñj/di*aké** to hide smn. **pa*an** hiding place. *metu saka pa*ané* to emerge from one's concealment

singit 1 inhabited by spirits (according to animistic belief). 2 influential; having a forceful personality

singkab the portion of the human side between armpit and waist. **ñj/di*** to open sth apart, *e.g.* curtains

singkal 1 large plow. 2 the banana at either end of a bunch. **ñj/di*** to plow

singkang **ñj/di*(-*)** to reject, disdain, scorn [a person]

singkat brief. ***an** abbreviation. **ñj/di*** to shorten, abbreviate

singkèk having typically Chinese characteristics. *Wong Tiong Hoa mau katoné * djekèk, ora bisa ngunèkaké* R. He was a typical Chinese: he couldn't pronounce Javanese R.

singkir **ñj*** to step aside; to avoid. *Ḍèké njingkir mengiwa supaja ora ketabrak wong.* He moved to the left so as to avoid bumping into anyone. *Jèn ḍèké teka mréné luwih betjik aku njingkir.* If he's coming here, I'd better leave. **ñj/di*aké** to put away/aside; to remove, get rid of. *Wadjané di*ké.* Set the frying pan to one side. *Wit rubuh mau wis di*aké.* The fallen tree has been taken away. *Panḍawa ka*aken ing wana.* The Pandawas were exiled to the forest. *Ḍèké wis di*aké.* He's been fired. **ñj/di*i** to avoid. *njingkiri bebaja* to steer clear of danger. *njingkiri gunem kang ora bener* to avoid improper talk. **s·um·ingkir** to get out of the way. *Sumingkir, sumingkir, aku arep liwat.* Make way, make way, I'm coming through. *Wong Hinḍu paḍa semingkir menjang pulo Bali.* The Hindus fled to Bali.

singkong *rg* cassava

singkrèh *var of* SINGKIR

singkrih *var of* SINGKIR

singkur **ñj/di*** to ignore, reject, turn one's back on. *Adja sok njingkur pituturé wong tuwa.* Never disregard the advice of your elders. *Aku arep takon, dadak di*.* I was going to ask him something but he suddenly turned his back. **ñj/di*aké** *or* **ñj/di*i** to reject, turn one's back on. **pa·ñj*** act of rejecting *or* avoiding

singlèt T-shirt

singlon (*or* **se***) pseudonym. *asma se** an assumed name. *Ḍèwèké manggon ana ing kuṭa K ase* X.* He lives in K city under the name of X.

singsal (*or* **ke***) 1 to get mixed in [with others]. *Wong² paḍa sarudjuk nggolèki korban² sing ke* lijané.* They agreed to go and get the victims [from their own village] who were among the other victims. *Ana kertas sidji sing ke* nang garapan kelas* *papat.* There's a paper mixed in with the fourth-grade homework that doesn't belong there. 2 to be thrown off. *Ḍèké tiba ke* rada adoh.* He fell out and was thrown quite a distance.

singsèh Chinese medicine man

singsèk *var of* SINGSÈH

singset tight, taut; firm, compact. *Olèhé nalèni bungkusan sing *.* Tie the package up tight. **ñ(j)/di*aké** to make tight. **ñ(j)/di*i** 1 to make tight(er). 2 to give [one's fiancée] a gift symbolizing the tie between them. *See also* PANINGSET

singsot to whistle. **singsat-*** to keep whistling. **ñ(j)/di*i** to whistle at/to smn

singub inhabited by spirits; spooky

sungunen to suffer from fear of heights

siniba *see* SUMUR

siniwâkâ [of kings] to sit on the throne before the court

sinjo Caucasian boy. ** Amérika/Inggris* an American/English boy

sinom 1 a popular classical verse form. 2 a downy fringe worn by girls across the forehead at the hairline. ***an** men *or* boys who help the host serve the guests at a wedding or other party

sinten who?; whoever; smn else (*kr for* SAPA[a])

Sinterklas Santa Claus

sintétis synthetic

sinṭing 1 kite tail. 2 crazed. *Panglamaré ora ditampa mulané ḍèwèké saiki dadi *.* His proposal of marriage was turned down and he went mad. ***an** kite tail. **an iket* the tied ends at the back of an *iket* head covering

sinṭir 1 wall-eyed, having out-turned eyeballs. 2 *var of* SENṬIR

sintru movable decorative screen used as a partition

sinuhun exalted one. **ingkang *** your highness (*title applied to the Sultan of Jogjakarta and the Sunan of Surakarta*)

sinuwun *var sp of* SINUHUN

sipat 1 character, characteristic, nature. **é gampang nesu.* He's hot-tempered by nature. *tembung ** (*gram*) adjective. 2 (forming) a straight line; string used for marking a straight line. 3 ointment applied to the eyelid. ***an** 1 alignment. *Apa *ané X marang Y wis bener?* Is X lined up true with Y? 2 string for making a straight line. **se*an** character. *Se*ané kaja embahé.* He takes after his grandfather. **ñj/di*** 1 to align. *Tjagak²é omah kudu di*.* The house pillars have to be in a straight line. 2 to make a straight line with a string. **ñj/di*aké** 1 to align sth. *njipataké A marang B* to line A up with B. 2 to direct a tongue of flame at [of goldsmiths working gold]. **ñj/di*(i)** to apply eyeliner to the lids. **ñj/di*i** to witness, observe. *Aku njipati ḍéwé.* I saw it with my own eyes. *** banju** level, horizontal. *Médjané rata * banju.* The table is perfectly level. *** gantung** perpendicular, perfectly vertical. *lini * gantung* plumb line. *** kuping** swift. *Plajuné * kuping.* He ran like the wind.

sipeng (*or* **ñj***) to stay smw overnight (*rg kr for* NG·INEP)

sipi *oj* **tan *** *or* **tan s·in·ipi** intense, great (*applied to the anger of exalted persons*). *Tan sinipi dukanipun.* He was in a towering rage.

sipil 1 unimportant, of no consequence. 2 civil. *pegawai ** civil-service employee

sipilis syphilis

sipir (*or* **tukang ***) prison guard

sir a wish, desire; to want. *Ḍèké duwé * arep nang Djakarta.* He wants to go to Djakarta. **ku arep tuku klambi idjo.* I'd like to buy a green shirt. *Aku * karo ḍèwèké.* I have my eye on her! **nge/di*i** to like, love, desire. *B di*i A nanging sadjaké ora gelem.* A loves B but she won't have him. **sa*é** whatever one pleases. *Menawa opahé siṭik olèhé ndandani bandjur sak *é ḍéwé.* If he's not getting paid much for fixing it, he'll take his time about it.

sira *ltry and stage usage* (*or* ***mu**) you. *djeneng ** you. *Adja * ambeg sija.* Don't be cruel. **mu ora perlu kuwatir.* You needn't worry.

sirah 1 head (*social var of* ENḌAS, *q.v.*). *padjeg ** head tax, per capita tax. 2 head of a group of marchers. **se*** 1 first payment on a debt. 2 title. **a·se*** entitled. *buku kang ase* X* a book called X

siram to take a bath (*ki for* ADUS). ***an** 1 swimming pool; bathing place (*ki for* P·ADUS·AN). 2 ritual bathing ceremony following circumcision or first menstruation, or (for a bride) before the wedding. **ke*** 1 to get water poured on it inadvertently. *Tangané mlonjoh ke* wédang.* His hand was scalded by boiling water. 2 to have a windfall *or* a run of good luck. **ñj/di*aké** to pour [sth] onto. *Sebagéjan wong munggah pajon karo njiramké banju.* One group climbed up and poured water on the [burning] roof. **ñj/di*(i)** to pour water on. *njirami kembang* to water the flowers. *Rajapé di* wédang.* He poured boiling water on the termites. *njirami geni* to spray water on a fire. **pa*an 1** *sms* *AN *above.* 2 Occidental-style bathroom (*ki for* DJAMBAN)

sirap wooden roofing tiles. **ñj/di*** to shingle [a roof] with such tiles

sirat ray, beam. ***-* madu** just for (the sake of) formality. ***-*an** to splatter each other. **ñj/di*aké** to sprinkle [liquid]. *Banjuné di*-ké ing weḍèn.* She sprinkled the water on the sand. **ñj/di*i** to sprinkle/splatter onto. *Ḍèké di*i banju.* She splattered him with water. *Weḍiné di*-*i mawa banju.* She kept sprinkling the sand with water. **s·um·irat 1** to shine. *Ing langit sumirat warna biru.* The blue of the sky gleams. 2 to splash. *Banjuné sumirat rana-réné.* The water splashed all around.

sirèki, sirèku *ltry* you, your

sirem *oj* dim, obscure

sirep 1 back to normal, calm once again. *Geniné mèh *.* The fire is almost out. *sa*-ing banju* after the flood waters ebbed. 2 a magic spell. *kena ** to fall under a spell. ***an** *wj* quiet gamelan music played during a certain narration (*djanturan*). **ñj/di*aké 1** to put out [a lamp, fire] by accident. 2 to bury smn. **ñj/di*(i) 1** to put out [fire *etc.*]. *Bareng wis bengi, lampu^2 di*i.* As night fell, lights were turned off. 2 to put smn under a magic spell. *** botjah** the time of night when children quiet down for the night. *** djalma** *or* *** wong** the time when everybody else quiets down for the night

sirig ***-*** *or* **se*** *or* **ñj*** to prance like a horse

sirik to refrain from [do]ing. ** menawa kepotongan marang lijan* to avoid becoming indebted to others. ** jèn nglakoni ngemis* to refrain from begging. ***an 1** thing (to be) avoided. **anku urang.* I don't eat shrimp. 2 unpropitious by astrological reckoning. *Djumuwat kuwi dina *anku.* Friday is my unlucky day. **ñj/di*** to avoid. *Ali di* kantja^{2}né.* Ali's friends avoided him. *Aku njirik lombok sebab aku sok lara weteng.* I don't eat chili peppers—they give me a stomach ache.

siring side, flank

sirip 1 caudal *or* tail fin of fish. 2 serrated ridges on a crocodile's tail

sirkâjâ a certain tart-sweet fruit consisting of many sections and full of seeds

sirna *oj* gone, wiped out. *Ama^2 diloropaké karebèn *.* They lured the insect pests into traps to destroy them. **ñj/di*kaké** *or* **ñj/di*i** to kill; to eliminate. *njirnakaké ama^2* to stamp out insect pests. *Bebosoking uwuh kasirnakna.* Get rid of the rotting garbage.

sirsak soursop (a green prickly-skinned fruit)

sirsat *var of* SIRSAK

siru banana-leaf spoon (*var of* SURU)

siruk **ñj*** to dive, swoop. **ñj/di*aké** to cause to dive/swoop. *njirukké lajangan mengisor* to maneuver a kite in a swooping dive

sirung 1 dark, heavily shaded. *Palemahan sing ana sakubenging wit bandjur *.* The ground under the tree is in deep shade. 2 [of eyes] narrowed to cut down on glare. *Katjané montor marakaké * nang mata.* The windshield glare forces you to close up your eyes partway. **ñj/di*i** to cause [the eyes] to narrow. *Srengéngéné njirungi mata.* The sun's glare makes you squint up your eyes.

s̊is **s̊as-*** *rpr* air blowing through a narrow slit

sisa [food] which has been eaten into/from. *pelem * tjoḍot* a bat-eaten mango. *Ḍèké mbuang panganan *.* She threw away the food that was left on the plates. ***n** remains, what is left. *mBok dirampungné *n.* Please finish up what's left [of your work]. ***ning gurinda** weapons (*see also* TEḌAS). **ñj/di*ni** to eat into/from. *Sopé adja di*ni.* Don't eat out of the soup pot.

sisah 1 [not] need to; [not] necessary (*kr for* SUSAH[b]). 2 sad (*rg? kr for* SUSAH[a])

sisan (**pinḍah** *kr?*) altogether, (in) all; at once, at the same time; once and for all (*see also* PISAN). *Aku tuku buku telu *.* I bought three books altogether (*or* at the same time). *Segané entèkna *.* Finish all the rice. *Gagangé wis kawir^2, mulané dipiṭil *.* The flower stalk is almost broken—may as well detach it. **ñj/di*aké** to [do] all at once. *Berasé kuwi gari turah siṭik, mbok di*ké diliwet.* There's only a little rice left; why not just cook it all? *** gawé** to [do] all at once

sisèt *rg var of* SÈSÈT

sisi *ng kr*, **semprit** *ki* to blow one's nose. **ñ(j)/di*ǹi** to blow smn's nose

sisig 1 (**[le]laṭi** *ki*) having blackened teeth (a

former fashion among women). 2 a quid of tobacco chewed with betel. **ñ(j)/di*i** to blacken one's teeth

sisih side, part, direction. * *tengen/kiwa* the right/left side. * *ngarep/mburi* the front/back. *ing * lor/kidul* to the north/south. * *tengah* the middle. * *djaba/djero* the outside/inside. *Ing * ḍuwur lan ngisoré dilim.* Put glue on the top and bottom. *Asia * Kidul Wétan* Southeast Asia. ***an** spouse. **ñ(j)*** to move to the side. *Njisih lo mengko ketabrak montor.* Get over, or you'll be hit by a car. **ñ(j)/di*aké** to move sth aside. *Watu iki sisihna.* Move this rock to one side. *di*aké polisi* waved aside by a policeman. **ñ(j)/di*i** 1 to avoid by moving aside. *Aku angger weruh A mesṭi njisihi.* I avoid A every time I see him. 2 to stand by smn. *Ḍèké nisihi aku ing sadjroné kesedih-anku.* He helped me through my grief. **sa*** one side; one of a pair. *kupingku sing sa** one of my ears. *Sepatuné sing sa* wis bo-ḍol.* One of my shoes is worn out. **sa*é** beside, at the side of. *sa*é kantor pos* next to the post office. **s·um·isih** to move aside. *Wong² paḍa dikon semisih ngadoh kabèh.* The people were all told to move back. *See also* WURSIH

sisik 1 fish scale(s). 2 discarded snake skin. ***-*** to smooth bamboo with a knife. **ñ(j)/di*i** 1 to remove the scales from [a fish]. 2 to smooth by scraping. ***-melik** evidence, trace. *Ḍèké golèk * melik me-njang ngendi Ali saiki.* He tried to get some indication of where Ali was.

sisil **ñ(j)/di*(i)** to nibble, peck

sisip to miss [one's aim *etc.*]. *Anggoné mbe-ḍil pidjer * terus.* His shots kept missing. **ke*an** to carry along accidentally. *Apa ko-wé mau ke*an bukuku?* Did you happen to pick up my book? **ñ(j)*** to miss [a tar-get]. *mBeḍilé njisip waé.* His shot went astray. * **sembir·é** lest. *Jèn udjian adja sok ngepèk, * sembiré bisa konangan.* Don't cheat on tests–you might get caught.

sisir 1 a bunch of bananas. 2 *rg* a comb. 3 a covered veranda. **ñ(j)/di*(i)** 1 to cut crosswise, to grate. *Gulané djawa di*i arep kanggo djuruh.* She slices the sugar-cakes to make syrup. 2 to plow for the second time

sisrik **ñ(j)/di*** to smooth the ridges of [bamboo] at the joints

siswa *oj* student, pupil. *See also* MAHA

sit *rpr* a swift motion. *Tjopèté tjepet banget mak * anggoné njopèt ḍompèt.* The pick-pocket whisked away the wallet with one deft motion.

sita **ñj/di*** to confiscate. **djuru *** bailiff, process server

sitèn a regional official (*contracted from* ASISTÈN-WADANA). ***an** residence of the above official

siti earth, soil, land (*kr for* LEMAH). * **(h)i-nggil** main audience hall at the north end of the Jogjakarta palace (*see also* SASANA), now used as a lecture hall for Gadjah Mada University

siṭik *ng* a few, a little (*inf var of* SEṬIṬIK)

siṭip [of Chinese, Japanese] almond-eyed

sitok, siṭok *rg var of* SIDJI

sitrun lemon

situ ***-*** in haste. *A *-* mulih.* A hurried home.

siwa *rg var of* SIWAK

Siwah Hindu. *agama ** Hinduism

siwak (*or ** **lanang**) uncle who is a parent's older sibling. * **wédok** aunt, *i.e.* wife of such an uncle

siwal to come off as a result of damage. *Ku-kuné djempol *.* He lost his big toenail [after an injury]. *Kursiné tanganané *.* The arm of the chair came off.

siwar dorsal fin of a fish

siwi *oj* child

siwil *var of* SRIWIL

siwur ladle. * *baṭok* ladle made from a half-coconut shell. *See also* GANTUNG

sjaban *var of* SABAN

sjair modern Indonesian poetry

sjârâ *oj* noise; voice

sjaraf nerve (*var of* SARAP)

sjarap nerve (*var of* SARAP)

sjarat *var of* SARAT

sjariat the Moslem law

sjarif *title for the nine Islamic apostles*

sjumânggâ *var of* SUMANGGA

skak̄ check! (*chess term: var of* SEKAK)

skop *var of* SEKOP

skrip 1 notebook. 2 script

skuter motor bike (*var sp of* SEKUTER)

sl- *see also under* SAL-, SEL- (*Introduction, 2.9.3*)

slabruk sleep wear, night clothing

slaḍa(h) lettuce, salad

slaḍang *ptg * pl* [of long objects] lying every which way. ***an** (that which is) carried crosswise. **an pring mau dipikul.* He

carried his bamboo shoulder pole crosswise.
ñj/di∗ 1 to carry sth crosswise. 2 to shoot
[a marble] with a two-handed technique.
ñj/di∗aké to put [sth long] smw. *Ali njla-
dangaké sepédané nang tengah lawang.* Ali
left his bike right in the doorway. *Pringé
di∗aké ngisor wit.* He laid the bamboo
stalks under the tree.

sladri *var of* SLÈDRI

slagrang **ñj/di∗aké** 1 to put *or* leave sth
where it is in the way and does not belong.
2 to put sth up into a high place

slâkâ silver (metal). *See also* DJUNGGRING

slakang *rg var of* LAKANG

slaman *see* SLUMUN

slamat safe, secure; prosperity. *kirim utjap-
an* ∗ to send words of congratulation *or*
good wishes. *See also* SLAMET

slamber *pl form of* SAMBER

slamet *ng,* **wiludjeng** *kr* well, safe and sound,
secure (**sugeng** *ki*). *Apa kowé* ∗? Are you
all right? *andum* ∗ to wish smn well (at
parting; at the close of a letter). *awèh* ∗ to
wish smn health, safety, absence of difficulties. *Djuru* ∗ Saviour (Christian). ∗**an**
(to hold) a ritualistic ceremony during
which sacred food is given away: held as a
measure for promoting the security of the
host and those close to him. *Ibumu* ∗*an
apa?* What kind of ceremony is your mother having? ∗**an brokoh·an** christening ceremony held at childbirth. ∗**an djenang abang**
ceremony celebrating a circumcision or a
birthday. ∗**an kol** annual ceremony com-
memorating a death anniversary. ∗**an m̃·pe-
ṭik** village harvest ceremony. ∗**an m̃·pitu·ñi**
ceremony held during the seventh month of
pregnancy. ∗**an puput puser** ceremony held
when an infant loses the umbilical cord.
∗**an ñj·sepasar·i** ceremony held on the fifth
day after birth. **ka∗an** well-being, security.
kabar ke∗an good news, *i.e.* news that smn
is well *or* safe and sound. **ñj/di∗aké** 1 to
keep smn safe, well, secure. 2 to save (the
life of). 3 to hold a ceremony on smn
else's behalf. *Ibu njlametaké patang puluh
dinané bapaké Siti.* Mother held a fortieth-
day ceremony for Siti's father [neighbor].
ñj/di∗i to honor smn with a ceremony.
Ibumu njlameti sapa? Who is your mother
holding a ceremony for?

slampir *ptg* ∗ *or* **slompar-∗** *pl* hanging all
over, hanging in various places. **ke∗** to get
hung on sth. *Klambiné ke∗ ing pager.* The

shirt was deposited on the fence [by the
wind]. **ke∗an** hung on sth. *Ke∗an apa pundaké anakmu kaé?* What's that slung over
your child's shoulder? **ñj/di∗aké** 1 to
place [a garment] over smn's shoulders. 2
to hang [garments] on a line. *Kok slompar-∗
ki sing di∗aké apa waé!* You're hanging
things all over the place! *See also* SAMPIR

slamur **ke∗** to get one's thoughts diverted.
*Wong² ilang ḍeg²ané, awit ke∗ nggoné paḍa
seneng².* They were having such a good time
they forgot their fears. **ñj/di∗** 1 to (try to)
take one's mind off sth. *Kanggo njlamur wediné bandjur singsot².* He whistled to chase
away his fear. 2 to change the subject. *Jèn
dipatjokké bandjur njlamur².* When they
teased him, he diverted the conversation.

slanḍok *var of* SLONḌOK

slang rubber tubing; hose

slanggrang *var of* SLAGRANG

slarak̄ *var of* SLOROK

Slâsâ Tuesday

slasih basil (blossom; herb) (*var of* TLASIH).
ptg ∗ scattered, in disorder

slawat money given to those who attend a
funeral and offer prayers. ∗**an** [of men] to
sing informally to the accompaniment of
tambourines or tomtoms. ∗ **kupeng·an**
money given (as above)

slawir *ptg* ∗ *pl* waving loosely (*e.g.* fringe,
streamers, coconut leaves). **ñj∗** *sg as above.*
ñj/di∗-∗aké to keep waving [such things]
back and forth, up and down, *etc.*

slebar *ptg* ∗ scattered about; in random
order

slébor fender, mud guard

slèdèr (*or* ∗**an**) 1 to procrastinate. 2 boastful

slèdri celery (in Java, mostly leaves with very
little stalk)

slégrang ∗-∗ strong, powerful

sléjor ∗**an** *or* **sléjar-∗** weak(ened), infirm

sléjot *var of* SLÉJOR

slelep to dive. **ñj/di∗aké** to cause sth to dive
or submerge

slembrah *ptg* ∗ sloppy or careless in one's
dress and grooming

slembrèh *var of* SLEMBRAH

slemet insect. *Remukan panganan dipangan*
∗. Insects ate up the crumbs. *ptg* ∗ *or* ∗-∗
or **slemat-∗** feeling queasy

slémpang *var of* SRÉMPANG

slempit **ke∗** to get mixed in and concealed
among other things. **ñj∗** to slip into [a

place of concealment]. *Potlodku njlempit nang ndjero buku.* My pencil was in a book [where I couldn't see it]. **ñj/di*aké** to slip sth [out of sight]. *Ḍompèté di*ké nang nggoné tjaṭoké.* He put his wallet in his belt. **s·um·lempit** inserted [into]. *Ana rokok semlempit ing lambéné.* A cigarette was stuck between his lips.

slemprit *pl form of* SEMPRIT

sléndang a scarf-like batik ladies wear over one shoulder for decorative purposes *or* for carrying babies or small bundles; also worn decoratively by *wj* deities. ***an** to put on *or* wear this garment

slendep *ptg* * having many sharp objects sticking into it. **ñj/di*i** to stick [a sharp object] into. *Bokongé di*i suntik.* They gave him the injection in the rump. **ñj/di*aké** to stick sth sharp [into]. *Suntiké di*ké nang bokong.* They gave him the hypodermic needle in the rump.

slènder **1** cylinder (car engine part). **2** steam roller. **ñj/di*** to roll [a road *etc.*] with a steam roller

sléndro five-note gamelan scale (*see also* PÉLOG). **ñj*** to play (a note of) this scale

slenget *rpr* a flash of heat. **s·um·lenget** unnaturally warm. *Awaké semlenget.* He's feverish.

slenggring *pl form of* SENGGRING

slenggrok *pl form of* SENGGROK

slenggruk *pl form of* SENGGRUK

slenggur *var of* SENGGUR

sléngkrah *ptg* * in disorder. *Kamaré mesṭi ptg *.* His room is always a mess.

slèngkrang *rpr* putting the feet up while sitting. ***an** *or* **ñj*** to sit improperly with the feet up, *e.g.* on a table

slengkrang *pl form of* SENGKRANG

slengkring *ptg* * to feel pinpricks of pain

slénsa *var of* SLÉNTJA

slenṭem a xylophone-like gamelan instrument with metal keys. ***an** in a quiet unceremonious way. *Pantjèn aku ora undang*[2] *kok, upatjarané *an waé.* I didn't invite guests–it was just a quiet ceremony. **slenṭam-*** to do sth quietly *or* without anyone's knowledge. **ñj*** to play the *slenṭem*

slenṭer *rpr* a precipitous *or* unannounced departure. *Mak * lunga ora pamit.* He up and left without saying goodbye.

slenṭik **ñj/di*(i)** to snap sth with the finger by bending the finger with nail against thumb and then releasing it suddenly. *Jèn nakal bandjur di* kupingé.* When he's bad, he gets a finger-snap on the ear.

slenṭing *rpr* a disagreeable odor. *Aku mambu mak * ora énak.* I caught a whiff of something bad. **slenṭang-*** rumor. *Aku krungu slenṭang-* djaréné...* I hear rumors to the effect that...

slenṭir *ptg* * *or* **slenṭar-*** to leave one after the other. *Para ḍémonstran ptg * lunga.* The [unenthusiastic] demonstrators drifted away one by one.

sléntja different from usual; different from before. *Saiki Siti kok *.* How Siti has changed! *Kowé kok *.* Why has your mood changed?

slep *rpr* slipping into a place unobtrusively. *Mak * ḍèké umpetan.* He slipped into concealment.

slepag *var of* SLEPEG

slépé a belt of gold or silver links, worn by girls for certain ceremonial occasions *or* for the classical dance

slepeg cramped, pressed. *Omahé * banget, kok ngundang tamu okèh banget.* The house is so small, why did he invite so many guests! **ke*** to be pressed for time. *Arep mlaju nanging wis ke*.* He was going to run, but it was already too late. **ñj/di*** to have too little time (to, for). *Njlepeg olèhé gawé omah.* He didn't have much time to build his house. *Jèn di* tukang djahité ora saguh.* If you try to rush the tailor, he may not finish the job. **ñj/di*i** to crowd (out), press. *Lemariné iki gegeḍèn, marakaké njlepeki kamar.* The cupboard is too big, it crowds the room.

slepi (*or* ***ǹ**) cigarette case of woven material

slèrèk ***an** **1** zipper. **2** sliding door. **ñj*** to move by sliding. *Genḍèngé njlèrèk.* The roof tile slid down. **ñj/di*aké** *or* **ñj/di*i** to slide sth. *Lawangé slèrèkna.* Please slide the door shut. *njlèrèki genḍèng* to slide roof tiles

slesep **ke*** to get slipped in between sth by accident. *Suraté ke* ing buku iki.* The letter got slipped into this book. **ñj*** to slip into. *Malingé njlesep grumbul kono.* The thief slipped into the shrubbery. **ñj/di*aké** to slip sth [into]. *Ḍuwité di*aké ing saké.* She slipped the money in his pocket. **s·um·lesep** to go in, find [its] way into. *Domé sumlesep nang kasur.* The needle worked its way into the mattress.

slesih careful, meticulous

slètel key

sléwah 1 two-toned. *Olèhé ngetjèt lawang* *. He painted the door in two colors. *botjah* * child born with different skin coloring on the left and right sides of the body. 2 different, contrasting. *Panemuné * karo panemuku.* His opinion differs from mine.

sléwar *rpr* a sudden turn. *Montoré terus mak * nengen.* The car swerved to the right.

slèwèng **sléwang-*** to wander here and there, stray from the objective. **ñj*** 1 to stray, wander. 2 to commit adultery. **ñj/di*aké** to cause to go astray, divert from the straight and narrow. *njlèwèngaké ḍuwit* to embezzle money. *njlèwèngaké panguwasa* to misuse power

slèwèr ***an** *or* **sléwar-*** to wave, hang loose, flutter

sliḍik **ñj/di*i** to investigate. **pa·ñj*an** investigation, research. *penjliḍikan tenaga atom* research into atomic power

sliju:t sleepy, drowsy

slilit food caught between the teeth; *fig* sth that is trivial but troublesome. ***-*** to pick the teeth. **(ke)*en** to have food caught between the teeth. **ñj*i** [of food] to catch in the teeth. **ora dadi *** a small and unsatisfying amount of food

slimpé ***an** to sneak up on. **ñj/di*** to sneak up on smn

slimpet *var of* SLIMPÉ

slimut *rg* blanket

slinder *var of* SLÈNDER

slinḍit *ptg* * characterized by labyrinthine twistings and turnings. *Dalan mau ptg *.* The road winds tortuously. ***an** a children's game played by running around in patterned circles

slingker *rpr* a sudden swerve. *Ḍèké mak * ngenḍani wong sing arep ditabrak kuwi.* He veered off and avoided hitting the man. **ñj*** to change direction suddenly. *Lawangé ngarep sadjak tutupan, aku bandjur njlingker menjang buri.* The front door seemed to be closed, so I pivoted around to the back.

slingkuh secret, underhanded. *nindakaké ** to do sth on the sly. ***an** (to do) in a secretive *or* underhanded manner. **ñj/di*aké** to take sth stealthily. *njlingkuhaké ḍuwit kantor* to embezzle official funds

slingkur *var of* SINGKUR

slingsing ***an** to pass unawares from opposite directions. *A mau nggolèki B nanging *an nang dalan.* A went looking for B but went right past him on the street without seeing him.

slintru 1 inhabited by spirits. *Guwané *.* The cave is haunted. 2 *var of* SINTRU

slinṭut ***an** *or* **slinṭat-*** in secret, on the sly. **ñj*** to do sth covertly; to sneak. *Aku njlinṭut^{2} liwat gunung^{2}.* I sneaked [past the sentries] through the mountains. **ñj/di*aké** to conceal temporarily [sth one is planning to carry off later]

slira 1 one hundred minus *n* (for keeping score in card games). ** gangsal* 95. ** tiga* 97. 2 a certain large water lizard. 3 body (*ki for* AWAK). ***mu** *or* ***né** *or* **kang *** *or* **keng *** *adr* you (*to a person one speaks to in Ngoko but does not know very well*). **mu tindak saka ingendi?* Where have you been? *Keng * rak wis priksa ḍéwé ta?* You've seen it yourself, haven't you?

sliri *ptg* * *or* *slira-** to keep going back and forth. *Akèh montor ptg * nang ndalan.* Cars kept whizzing past on the road. *Iwaké nglangi slira-*.* The fish swam back and forth.

sliring *var of* SLINGSING. ***an** varying slightly. *Panemuku mung *an waé karo panemuné.* My findings were just about the same as his. **ke*** to have aspersions cast on one. **sa* bawang** paper-thin

slisib *var of* TLISIB

slisih to differ, vary. *Pétunganku mung * seṭiṭik karo pétungané.* My figures are pretty close to his.

slisik 1 *rpr* a harsh sibilant sound. 2 to preen the feathers with the beak. **ñ(j)/di*(i)** 1 to preen [another bird's feathers]. 2 to investigate, look into

sliṭi **sliṭa-*** to keep wiggling, squirming, fidgeting

sliwer *ptg* * *or* ***an** *or* **sliwar-*** to swerve, weave this way and that. *mabur ptg ** flying around. **ing wong kuṭa* the city people milling around. *Ula katon ptg *.* The snake wriggled along.

slobok **ñj/di*aké** to put [an opening] over *or* around. *Tjarané menganggo di*aké saka nḍuwur (saka sirah).* You get into [the garment] by putting it on over your head. **ñj/di*i** to put [fingers, hands] into [an opening]

sloḍo *rg* *rpr* bursting into a place where one does not belong. **sloḍa-*** to enter smw as above

slogrong *rpr* rapid enlargement. *Anakmu wis*

mak *. Your child is shooting up! *-* to grow up, get taller and taller

slohok **slohak-*** to talk boorishly

sloka *var of* SALOKA

slokan *rg* ditch

sloki small liquor glass

slomod **ke*** to come into accidental contact with a burning object. **ñj/di*** to touch with a burning object

slomprèt 1 trumpet, bugle. 2 reed used as a whistle. *tukang* * trumpeter, bugler. ***an** 1 a trumpet. 2 to keep trumpeting. **ñj*** to play a trumpet

slondjor to stretch one's legs. **ñ(j)/di*aké** to stretch [the legs]

slonḍok metal ring for holding sth: *e.g.* a belt buckle. **ñj/di*aké** to thread sth through an opening

slonong *ptg* * *or* **slonang-*** moving precipitously; shooting forward. **ñj*** *or* **s·um·lonong** to move *or* act precipitously. *Montoré njlonong mlebu kalèn.* The car shot forward into a ditch. *Ḍèké bandjur sumlonong omong...* Then he blurted out...

slonṭong ***an** 1 sth hollow; sth empty *or* emptied of its contents. 2 hollow bamboo water pipe. 3 box *or* bag where incoming mail is kept

slontrot *ptg* * *or* **ñj*** fibrous [of cassava, mango]. *See also* SONTROT

slorok̄ 1 a sliding board for barring a door. 2 sliding door used as a room divider. 3 diamond-studded kris cover. *ptg* * to keep calling out one's wares. ***an** 1 a drawer. 2 kris cover. **ñj/di*** to fasten [a door] shut with a sliding bar. **ñj/di*aké** 1 to close a drawer. 2 to thread sth through an opening. *njlorokaké benang nèng djarum* to thread a needle. **ñj/di*i** to equip [a door] with a sliding bar

slosor *var of* TLOSOR

slot doorknob

sluḍing *var of* SLUNḌING

sluku to sit with the legs stretched straight out before one. *-* **baṭok** opening words of a children's song chanted while sitting as above

slulup to go under water. *Ajo betah²an* *. Let's see who can stay under longest. ***an** to keep diving under as one swims. **ñj*** to submerge oneself; (*psv* **di***) to submerge sth. *Bareng weruh polisi, malingé njlulup nang blumbang.* When the thief saw a policeman, he ducked under water in the pond. **ñj/di*aké** to hold smn's face under water

slumbat a bar with a round-bladed tip for splitting open coconuts. ***an** act *or* result of splitting open coconuts. **ñj/di*(i)** to remove the outer fibrous coat (*sepet*) from a coconut

slumun **sluman-*** *or* **slaman-*** to keep going back and forth. *sluman-* slamet* to go safely back and forth through dangers

slunḍing ***an** a substitute, replacement. **ñj/di*i** to substitute for; to act in the capacity of; to change off with

slundup, slunḍup *ptg* * to go in and out repeatedly. *Klonṭong kuwi ptg * menjang désa².* Peddlers come to the villages frequently. ***an** smuggled. *barang² *an* smuggled goods. **slunḍap-*** *pl* to enter and leave; to enter and leave illicitly. *Daḍi mata² kudu pinter slunḍap-*.* If you're a spy, you have to be adept at crossing borders under cover. **ñj*** to enter *or* leave (illicitly). **ñj/di*aké** 1 to insert. *njlundupaké bolah ing dom* to thread a needle. 2 to smuggle [sth, smn] into. **ñj/di*(i)** 1 to stab sth into. *Bantalané di*i dom akèh banget.* The pincushion has a lot of needles stuck into it. 2 to smuggle sth/smn. **pa·ñj*** smuggler. **pa·ñj*an** 1 smuggled. *barang penjlunḍupan* smuggled goods. 2 illegal entry

slup *rpr* quick immersion. *Iwaké kétok nang nḍuwur bandjur mak * angslup.* The fish appeared at the surface and then slipped back under.

sluru **slura-*** to make frequent mistakes

slusub *rpr* quick concealment. *ptg* * *pl* taking quick cover. *Botjah² nḍelik ptg * nang grumbulan.* The boys quickly hid in the bushes. **ke*en** to get entered by sth sharp. *Dridjiku mau ke*en lugut pring.* I got a bamboo sliver in my finger. **ñ(j)/di*aké** to insert sth. *njlusubaké benang ing dom* to thread a needle. **ñ(j)/di*i** to enter, slip into. *Lugut kuwi nlusubi.* The bamboo pricker went in [my finger].

slusur *var of* TLUSUR

sluṭu **sluṭa-*** to keep entering smn's room without permission *or* forewarning. **ñj*** to enter smn's place as above

sluwat *ptg* * full of sharp spiky projections. **ñj*** [of sth sharp] to project outward and upward. *Eriné njluwat.* The thorn is sticking out.

sluwir *var pl form of* SUWIR

so 1 a certain tree (*sms* MLINDJO) whose bark is made into a burlap-like fabric (*bago*). 2 the edible young leaf of this tree. *djangan* * *so*-leaf soup

so'al problem, matter, question. *njandak* * *lija* to change the subject. *-* *djeron lan mantja negara* domestic and foreign concerns. **ñj/di*aké** to cause problems (for), make sth difficult. *Swara*2 *mau ora njoalaké.* Those opinions didn't raise any problems. * **djawab** question and answer (as a teaching technique). *See also* PERSOAL

sobat close friend. ***an** close friendship. **di*** to be regarded *or* treated as a close friend. **ñj*** to get close to. *Ḍèké seneng njobat botjah sugih.* He hangs around the rich kids. **pa*an** close friendship

sobjung a children's singing game

soḍèr *var of* SOLDIR

soḍog **ñj/di*** to prod. *Aku di* nganggo beḍil saka mburi.* Someone pushed a gun into me from behind. **ñj/di*aké** to move sth by prodding *or* pushing at it

sodok *rg* somewhat, a little. *mBok olèhé lingguh * rana, kéné suk*2*an djé.* Please move over a bit—it's crowded here.

sodor a spear with a round knob at the tip instead of a point. **ñj/di*** to prod with the above

sog **nge/di*** to push, press. *Aku krasa di* wong saka mburi.* I could feel smn pushing me from behind. **nge/di*-*** to give smn a scalp treatment by gently scratching and tugging the hair: *esp.* for relieving a headache. *nge*-* rambut* to treat hair as above. **nge/di*aké** to set sth down. *See also* SOSOG

soga 1 bark of the indigo tree, used in dyeing batik. 2 the reddish-brown dye obtained from this bark. ***n** 1 fabric dyed with the above. 2 reddish-brown in color. **ñj/di*** to dye [batik] with the above. **pa*n** room where batik-dyeing is done. * **genes** *sms* * 2 *above*

sogok 1 long stick used for prodding *or* plucking. 2 key. ***an** a bribe; bribery. **ñj/di*(i)** 1 to prod, poke. *Pelemé di* nganggo gèntèr.* He knocked down the mango with a stick. 2 to unlock a door. 3 to bribe smn. **ñj* irung** to give off a strong odor, to assail the nostrils. * **untu** toothpick

sogrok *var of* SOGOK

sok[a] *ng,* **a(ng)sring** *kr,* **sering** *kr?* 1 sometimes, often. 2 [don't] ever...! *Adja * nganiaja kéwan.* Never tease animals. 3 (even) if. * *mengkonoa* even if that is (*or* were) so. * *anaa regané larang banget.* Even if it were available, it would be very expensive. *-* once in a while, every so often. * **uga** even if it were like that. *Aku ora pati pertjaja karo Siti, * uga malah ḍèwèké kuwi wani maling.* I don't trust Siti: even in a case like that she would steal. * **wong·a** anyone (at all). * *wonga bisa nglakoni ngono.* Anybody could do that.

sok[b] *rpr* pouring, splashing. *Pantjiné tiba, mak * djangané kutah.* The pan fell and the soup spilled out! *-* full to overflowing. **ke*an** to get poured on. *Tjlanané ke*an kopi.* Coffee got spilled on his trousers. **nge/di*(aké)** to pour sth (out). *Lengané adja di* kabèh.* Don't pour out all the oil. *Sekaroné paḍa nge*aké sih katresnané.* They poured forth their love for each other. *Wong sing nonton kaja diesokaké.* Spectators poured in. **nge/di*i** to pour onto sth. *Sokana lenga pèt.* Pour kerosene on it. * **glogok** to speak one's mind. *Ḍèké nèk omong * glogok.* He says exactly what he thinks. *See also* ASOK

soka hibiscus

soklat 1 chocolate. 2 brown. **ñj/di*(aké)** to color/dye sth brown. **ñj/di*aké** to have sth colored/dyed brown

soklé *var of* SUKLÉ

sokong ***an** financial support *or* contribution. **ñj/di*** to support financially, or contribute support

sokur 1 it is good (that...). * *ta jèn pitmu wis ketemu.* Thank goodness you found your bike! * *jèn kowé gelem ngampiri aḍimu.* It'd be nice if you could go pick up your little brother. 2 gratitude. *ngutjap* * to express one's thanks. 3 let it be a lesson. * *kowé!* It serves you right! * *kowé tiba, dipenging pènèkan.* So you fell! you had it coming—you were told not to climb. ***an** celebration of a special event (*sms* SLAMET·AN). **ñj/di*aké** to rub it in, (to say) I told you so! *Pitku ilang malah di*aké karo kangmasku.* My bike is lost and my brother says it serves me right. * **alkamdulil(l)ah** *or* * **lah kamdulil(l)ah** thank God! * **bagé (sèwu)** 1 thank God! 2 may it happen that... * *bagé bisa antuk kauntungan.* I hope I'll be able to make a profit.

sol 1 uprooted. 2 fifth note in the musical scale. ***-*an** 1 to push/elbow each other.

2 to stammer with fear. **ka*** to get uprooted. **nge/di*** 1 to uproot. 2 to push aside. *Adja ngesol waé ta!* Don't push! **nge/di*aké** to uproot

solah actions, motions; behavior, conduct. **ñj/di*aké** to move (around), make motions with. *njolahaké sikil* to move the feet. *** bawa** *or* *** djantra** *or* *** tenaga** *or* *** tingkah** behavior, actions. *Ketara ing sa*-tingkahé.* It's obvious in everything he does.

solar diesel oil

solat *var of* SALAT

soldir solder. **ñj/di*** to solder sth

solèd 1 flat aluminum kitchen tool resembling a pancake turner. 2 *slang* kris. **ñj/di*** to turn *or* manipulate [food] with a pancake turner. *** patri** soldering iron

Solo *var sp of* SALA

solung *var of* SULUNG

Soma *oj* Monday

somah *ng,* **sémah** *kr* 1 spouse. 2 (*or* ***an**) family, household. *kepala ** head of the family. *Ana pirang * ing désa kuwi?* How many families are there in that village? *See also* OMAH

somba a certain leaf used for red dye. **ñj/di*** to dye sth red with this leaf

sombèng *rg* torn, ripped

sombong (*or* **ñj***) snobbish, arrogant. **ñj/di*aké** to boast about sth

sompèl chipped, having a piece missing. *Piringé *.* The plate is chipped.

sona *oj* dog. *** belang mati a·rebut mangsa** misfortune resulting from greed

sonḍèr cloth worn around the waist in the classical dance. **se*an** to put on *or* wear this cloth

sonḍer, sonder without. *Tèhku * gula, lho.* No sugar in my tea!

sonḍol **ke*(-*)** to get pushed from behind *or* one side. *Jèn ndelok keraméjan ja adja wedi ke*-*.* When you go to a fair, you mustn't mind being elbowed around. **ñj/di*-*** to push, press, nudge. *Jèn ndjaluk ḍuwit mesṭi njonḍol.* When he asks for money, he keeps poking at me.

sonebril sunglasses, dark glasses

song cave or other opening in a riverbank, cliffside, valley wall, *etc.* **nge*** forming a hole of this type

songar (*or* **se*an**) boastful. *Tindaké mau mung kanggo se*an.* He just did that to show off.

songkèl crowbar-like prying tool, used with a wedge (*antru*) for leverage. **ñj/di*** to pry, exert leverage, open (with the above equipment)

songkèt embroidery. **ñj/di*** 1 to embroider. 2 to darn, mend

songkil *var of* SONGKÈL

songkok *wj* ornamental wings worn at the back of the headdress and (a larger pair) on the upper back, as part of a warrior costume. ***an** to put on *or* wear such wings

songkop woven-bamboo implement (*var of* SOSOG)

songkro old, worn out, out of date. *Tuku kok pit wis * ngono!* Why did you buy such an old beat-up bike?

songsong umbrella, sunshade (*kr? ki for* PAJUNG). **panongsong** *ng kr* one who has the task of sheltering a dignitary from sun or rain with an umbrella

sonja *var of* SUNJA

sonjaruri *var of* SUNJARURI

sonten late afternoon, early evening (*kr for* SORÉ)

sontèng **ñj/di*** to give sth a hard push

sontlèng *var of* SONTÈNG

sontok **ñj/di*** to push, shove

sontrot fibrous thread running down the center of a cassava root *or* mango. **ñj*** full of fibers. *See also* SLONTROT

sonya *var of* SUNJA

sop 1 at a low level, at ebb tide *or* flow. 2 soup (Occidental style). *** pitik** chicken soup. *** kobis** cabbage soup

sopak ***an** false part added on. *susu *an* brassière padding. *untu *an* false teeth. **ñj/di*** to add [a false piece] (onto)

sopan polite, good manners. *Uṭik² upil nang ngarepé tamu iku ora *.* It's not polite to pick your nose in front of guests.

sopinis chauvinist

sopinisme chauvinism

sopinistis chauvinistic

sopir driver, chauffeur. *** bis** bus driver. ***an** 1 act of driving. **ané montor iki pénak ora alot.* This car handles smoothly. 2 pertaining to driving. *nggon *an* driver's seat. **ñj*** to be(come) a driver. **ñj/di*i** to drive [a vehicle]

sor 1 under; inferior. ** tempat tiḍur* under the bed. *Perangé *.* The battle was lost. 2 *rpr* a rapid flow. *Banjuné metu mak * saka pipané.* The water poured out of the pipe. **sar-*** [of heartbeats] rapid, going pit-a-pat. ***-*an** a subordinate. **-*anku kabèh* *sepuluh.* I have ten people working under me. **nge/di*aké** 1 to look down on. *Aku di*ké.* He treated me with contempt. 2 to pour sth. *Banjuné di*ké nang kulah.* He poured the water into the bathtub. **nge/di*i** to pour into/onto. *See also* ASOR, ISOR, SOSOR

sora loud; forceful (*kr for* SERU?)

sorah (to give) a speech, lecture. **ñj/di·(se)*** to deliver a speech (to). **ñj/di·(se)*aké** to deliver a speech about. *njenjorahaké perkara liwat radio* to discuss the matter in a radio speech

soré *ng,* **sonten** *kr* the late afternoon and early evening period (*ca.* 3–7 P.M.). (*wajah*) *giring ** around 6 P.M. (when the cattle are stabled for the night). ***ǹ-*ǹan** *or* ***-*an** (**sonten²an** *kr*) late in the afternoon-evening period. **ke*ǹ** 1 (too) late, *i.e.* in the *soré* rather than the next earlier time period (*awan*). 2 (too) early, *i.e.* in the *soré* rather than the next later time period (*bengi*). **ñj/di*ǹi** to arrive before dark. *Sarèhné omahé adoh, betjiké njorèni.* The house is a long way off; we'd better get there before sunset. **sa*** throughout the *soré.* *** (m)·bendé** *or* *** enṭé²** early in the *soré*

sorèng *oj* skilled. *** a·laga** skilled in battle

soro *var of* SOROH

sorog a key. ***an** a drawer. **ñj/di*** to lock with a key. *See also* LAJANG

soroh **ñj/di*(-*)aké** to hand over, let smn have. *njorohaké ḍuwit* to give smn some money. *njenjorohaké kuntji* to hand over the keys. *** amuk** in an enraged *or* violent condition

sorok long-handled shovel of wood or bamboo. **ñj/di*** to shovel sth with the above

sorot ray, beam. **ing srengéngé/rembulan* sun/moonbeams. **é listrik* light from an electric light. *dijan ** searchlight, spotlight. ***an** irrigated by river water. *sawah *an* a rice paddy irrigated with water piped in from a river. **ñj/di*aké** to let [irrigation water] into a field. **ñj/di*(i)** to shine light on. *di*i lampu* lighted by a lamp. *Satindak tansah di* masjarakat.* Every move he makes is under public scrutiny. **s·um·orot** 1 to shine, flash. *Intené sumorot.* The diamond sparkles. *Srengéngéné semorot mlebu.* The sun shines in. 2 to flow. *Sawah ngisor nampa banju sing semorot saka sawah nḍuwur.* The lower paddies get water that overflows from the upper paddies.

sos *rpr* a swishing sound. **nge*** to produce such a sound. **nge/di*aké** to discharge [air, gas]

sosi a key

sosial 1 social. *ilmu ** social science(s). *suksès ** social success. 2 having a social conscience

sosiawan male social worker

sosiawati female social worker

sosis sausage. **ñj*** to make sausage

sosog implement of woven bamboo, variously shaped for a variety of uses. *Pelemé olèhé ngunḍuh nganggo *.* She picked mangoes with a long-handled basket-like implement. *kurungan ** bird cage of woven bamboo. **di* ing udjar** to be scolded abusively. **ñ(j)/di*aké** 1 to push, prod. 2 to set sth down. *See also* SOG

sosoh **ñ(j)/di*** to remove the husks from [rice] with a mortar and pestle

sosor *var of* TJOTJOR. ***an** under (the authority of). **ke*** to get pecked by a goose *or* duck. **ñ(j)/di*** to attack with the beak. *See also* SOR

sosot angry words. *Ḍèké wareg *.* He was fed up with being yelled at. **ñ(j)/di*-*aké** to keep pressing smn with angry words. *Jèn kliru anggoné njambut gawé disrengeni di*-*aké.* If she did her work wrong she got yelled at.

sosrob *cr* **ñ(j)/di*** to drink

sosrok a broad short-handled dustpan used *esp.* for scooping up dirt or manure. **ñ(j)/di*** to scoop sth up with the above

sot a curse, malediction. *Sakdurungé mati ninggal esot mengkéné...* Before dying, he uttered this curse... **nge/di*aké** to put a curse on smn

sotah *oj* willing. **ora *** dead set against

sotja *var of* SOTYA

soto *var of* SAOTO

soṭo **ñj/di*** to punch with the fist

sotong octopus; squid

sotya 1 human eye (*ki for* MRIPAT). 2 *oj* jewel. **se*** jewels, gems

so'un 1 shiny bean noodle. 2 rice sticks used in soup

sowak **ñj/di*** to spread sth apart, *esp.* to enlarge the field of vision. *Grumbulané di*.* He parted the bushes [and peeked in].

sowal 1 stripped, peeled. *Wité *.* The tree is stripped of its bark. 2 *var sp of* SOAL

sowan *ka* to visit [one who is socially superior]. *Ana wong *.* There's someone here to see you. **ñj/di*aké** to present smn [to an exalted person]. *njowanaken ingkang putra* to present one's son. **ñj/di*i** to visit [smn high]. **pa*** a visit. **pa*an** place where visits to exalted persons take place. *See also* SAOS, TILIK

sowang ***an** 1 small whistle attached to a pigeon's tail. 2 indentation. ***-*** *or* **se*an** each in his own direction. *Wong² désa paḍa bali *-*.* The villagers returned to their homes.

sowèl stripped (*var of* SOWAL)

sp- *see also under* SEP-

spésial special. *bakmi gorèng ** special fried noodles (*i.e.* with eggs)

spésialis specialist. *ḍokter * mata* ophthalmologist

spesifik specific (to). *Sega guḍeg kuwi panganan * Ngajogja.* Rice with *guḍeg* is unique to Jogja.

spion *var of* SPIUN

spirituil of the spirit. *materiil lan ** material and spiritual

spirtus *var of* SEPIRITUS

spiun spy

spn. etc[etera]. *See also* PANUNGGAL

sporet sports, athletics. *kaos ** athletic shirt, track shirt

sportip sportsmanlike

sr- *see also under* SAR-, SER-

srâbâ *oj* voice. **tanpa *(-*)** without notice; without saying anything

srabi pancake eaten with a coconut-sugar-and-milk syrup. **ñj*** to make pancakes

srabud ***an** having too many irons in the fire. *Olèhé njambut gawé *an, apa² ditandingi mulané malah ora ana sing bisa rampung.* He takes on too much work, so none of it is finished.

srah to return, give back. *Iki lho bukumu, enjoh, wis * lho ja.* Here's your book, I've given it back to you. ***-*an** to give over, present (to), yield up. *Bu A lagi munḍut barang arep kanggo *-*an putrané sing tunangan.* Mrs. A is buying an engagement gift for her son. *Ḍèké *-*an penggawéan karo penggantiné.* He turned over his job to his substitute. **nge/di*aké** *or* **nge/di*i** to turn sth over [to smn]. *A nge*i penggawéan nang anaké.* He turned his work over to his son. *See also* PASRAH

srâjâ (*or* ***n**) help, assistance; a cooperative effort. **ñj/di*kaké** to have smn help with sth

srakah greedy. *See also* ḌAKAH

srakat (*or* **ke**) impoverished. *zakat fitrah kanggo wong² kang ke** obligatory alms for the poor

srèk **srak-*** to scuff, drag the feet

srambah **ke*** accessible, available. *Gunung kuwi ja ora pati adoh nanging ja ora ke* déning wong.* The mountain isn't far, but you can't get to it. *Sadjroning sasi Oktober 1944 ora ke* dina Kemis Pon.* There was no Pon Thursday in October 1944. **ñj/di*(i)** to affect widely. *njrambahi badan sakodjur* to spread all over the body. **s·um·rambah** 1 to spread. *Lelarané semrambah sak anak bodjoné.* His wife and children got the disease from him. 2 friendly, outgoing

srambi front veranda, front porch

srambung *pl form of* SAMBUNG

srampang ***an** careless, haphazard. **ñj/di*** to throw [a missile] at. *Asu mau tak * sepatu.* I threw a shoe at the dog.

srânâ *var of* SARANA

srанḍal *inf var of* SANḌAL

srandu *var of* SARANDU. **ke*** to get interrupted. *Patemon mau ke* tekané polisi.* The meeting was interrupted by the arrival of the police. **ñj/di*** 1 to interrupt. *Ora pareng njrandu, nak!* Don't interrupt the grownups, honey! 2 solitary; individualistic. 3 stingy

sranḍul a certain type of wajang drama performed in East Java

srang *oj for* SERANG. ***-*an** hurried, hasty. *Polahmu kok *-*an mbok ja sing anteng seṭiṭik.* Don't rush so–do be calm.

srani Christian; Occidental. *wong ** a Christian; a westerner. **ñj/di*kaké** to convert smn to Christianity

sranta *var of* SRANTI

sranṭal *rpr* scurrying. *Mak * nang endi plajuné botjah iki?* Where is the boy dashing off to? **ñj*** to dash, sprint. **s·um·ranṭal** fast. *Semranṭal plajuné, awit wedi jèn telat.* He ran fast–he was afraid he'd be late.

sranti *ng*, **srantos** *kr* patient, willing to wait. ***n̈** patient by nature. *Ḍèké kuwi wong ora srantèn, jèn tetuku ora tau ngenjang, terus dibajar waé.* He's so impatient that when he buys things he won't even take the time to haggle over the price. **ñj/di*kaké** to wait for sth in patience; to leave sth alone, allow sth to wait. *Betjiké disrantèkaké sésuk baé, jèn wis teka.* We'd better just wait [to find out] till he gets here tomorrow. *Ḍèké* *njrantèkaké djladrèné ḍisik kira² sepuluh menit.* She let the dough sit for ten minutes.

sranṭil *ptg* * in rags, all worn out. **ñj*** penniless. *Senengané main nganti entèk²an saiki dadi njranṭil.* He gambled away all his money and now he has nothing.

srantos patient, willing to wait (*kr for* SRANTI)

srasah sth used as a cover *or* top. **ñ(j)/di*** to cover with a layer of sth

sraséhan an informal discussion

srati *ng,* **sratos** *kr* 1 mahout. 2 one who handles people. *gampang/angèl* ***ǹ-*ǹan·é*** easy/difficult to please. **ñj/di*ǹi** to wait on smn, do things for smn

sraṭil *var of* SRANṬIL

sratos *kr for* SRATI

srâwâ *var of* SRABA

srawang *see* SUMRAWANG

srawé *ptg* * *pl* to keep waving, fluttering. ***an** *sg* to wave, flutter. *Jèn nunggang montor tanganmu adja srawéan metu.* Don't let your hand hang out of the car window. **ñj*** *sms* *AN

srawung (*or* ***an**) to associate with, become acquainted with. **se*an** 1 *sms* *(AN) *above.* 2 acquaintance, association (with). **ñj/di*i** to associate with. **pa*an** acquaintance, association (with smn)

srawut ***an** *or* **s·um·rawut** to do/act in a hasty disorganized way

sre- *see also under* SER- (*Introduction, 2.9.6*)

srebed *-* agreeable swishing sound *esp.* of a woman's batik skirt as she walks. *Lakuné *-*.* Her batik rustles pleasantly as she walks. **ñj/di*i** to cause to swish. *Anginé njrebedi goḍong².* The wind rustled the leaves. **s·um·rebed** to swish, rustle. *Anginé keprungu semrebed.* You can hear the wind whispering.

sred *rpr* a sudden stop. * *sepéḍané dirèm.* He braked his bicycle to a stop.

srèg *rpr* a rustling sound produced by small movements. *See also* ÈSRÈG

sreg *rpr* the feel of settling into place comfortably. *Bareng wis suwi ngadeg ḍèwèké ndjur lungguh mak *.* After being on his feet for a long time, it felt good to sit down. *Klambiné olèhé ngekèki kangmasku dak enggo *.* The shirt my brother gave me is a perfect fit.

sregep industrious. *sinau sing ** to study hard. ***an** hard-working by nature. ***-*an** to try to outdo each other in industriousness. **ka*an** industriousness. **ñj*** to increase one's industriousness. *Suk minggu aku arep wiwit njregep.* I'm going to begin working harder next week. **ñj/di*aké** to make smn apply himself. *Aku bola-bali njregepaké Ali.* I kept after Ali to work harder. **ñj/di*i** to apply oneself harder to. *Njambut-gawéanku tak *i.* I've buckled down to my work. **s·um·regep** hard-working

srèi maliciously jealous; selfish, possessive

srèjèg **sréjag-*** weak, without energy, near collapse

srèk *rpr* scratching, scraping. *Èsé digosrok mak *.* She grated the ice.

srékal a kind of word play based on puns or over-literal interpretation, *e.g.*: *Ana pulisi satruk teka* = A truckful of policemen came, *also interpretable as:* A policeman the size of a truck came. ***(-*)an** to engage in such word play with each other. **ñj/di*** to talk (to) with the above type of word play

srékat *var of* SERÉKAT

srempal *ptg* * all tattered and torn

srémpang bandolier. *Seragamé nganggo * abang.* His uniform has a red bandolier across the chest.

srèmpèd ***an** act of grazing *or* scraping. *garis *an* tangent. ***-*an** to sideswipe each other; to sideswipe one thing after another. **ke*** to get grazed. **ñj/di*** 1 to graze, sideswipe. 2 to refer to obliquely. *Si A ora njrèmpèt babar pisan ngenani ḍiriné si B.* A never let on that he knew who B was.

srempeng **ñj/di*** to do in earnest. *Menawa di* gawéané ja bisa rampung sedina.* If you keep right at the job, it can be done in a day.

sremplah *pl form of* SEMPLAH

srèng **mak *** *or* **srang-*** *rpr* sizzling. *srang-* nggorèngi* to fry [cassava chips *etc.*]. *mertjon srang-** skyrocket

sréngat *var of* SARÉNGAT

srengen *ng kr,* **duka** *ki* to get mad. * *marang* to get mad at. **ñj/di*i** to speak to angrily. *Ḍèké adja di*i.* Don't yell at him. *A didukani ibuné.* A's mother bawled him out.

srengéngé (**surja** *ki?*) sun. **né panas.* The sun(shine) is hot. *grahana ** eclipse. *kembang ** sunflower

srenggut *var of* SENGGUT

sreni:t *pl form of* SENIT

srenteg straight and proper [of women's stance]

srenut *ptg* * to throb with pain
srep 1 cold (*root form: kr for* DEM). 2 *var of* SEREP
srepegan *wj* a fast-paced gamelan melody depicting a battle
srèpèt *rpr* unsheathing a kris. **ñj*** to draw a kris from its sheath
srepet (*or* **s·um·repet**) *rpr* a quick motion. *Bareng tumenga tenan, *, pjur! pemandengku lan pemandengé tatapan.* When she finally glanced up, her gaze met mine excitingly.
sresep **ñ(j)/di*** to penetrate. *Semriwingé bisa nresep nang kulit.* The vapors penetrate the skin. **s·um·resep** to enter, penetrate
sréwot **sréwat-*** in a rush, in a big hurry
sri *oj* 1 shining ray *or* beam. 2 glorious, resplendent. 3 *title for a royal personage.* * *Sultan* his majesty the Sultan [of Jogjakarta]. * *wandawa* his majesty's royal relatives. 4 goddess of rice. * **Sedana** 1 the goddess Sri and her spouse Sedana. 2 symbol of prosperity
sribid ***-*** *or* **ñj*** *or* **s·um·ribid** to blow gently. *angin *-** gentle breezes. *Anginé njribit.* There's a pleasant breeze. *Pendjerité digawa mlaju angin semribit.* Her scream was carried by the wind.
sribombok a certain long-necked long-legged water bird
srig ***-*an** to fidget, move restlessly (rather than sitting poised and quiet)
srigaḍing a variety of flower
srigunting a black insect-eating song bird with a scissors-shaped tail. *See also* GUNTING
srijawan an herb used in folk medicines. *djamu ** medicine made with this herb
srik *rpr* a scooping motion. *See also* KESRIK
srikâjâ *var of* SIRKAJA
srikat *var of* SERÉKAT
srikut ***an** *or* **s·um·rikut·an** busily engaged (using the hands). *Sisihanku lagi semrikutan enggoné tata ḍahar.* My wife was busily setting out the meal. *Pak masnis *an anggoné ngusapi kringet.* The mechanic hastily wiped away sweat.
srimantanti *var of* SRIPENGANTI
srimbit *var of* SARIMBIT
srimenganti *var of* SRIPENGANTI
srimped **ke*** to get entangled, ensnarled. *Ḍèké ke* tampar bandjur tiba.* He got his foot caught in the rope and fell. **ñj/di*(i)** to entangle *or* entwine sth
srimpi a certain court dance performed by four females. ***ǹ** *or* **ñj*** to perform this dance
srimpung **ke*** to get entangled, tied up. *Pitiké sikilé ke* tali.* The chicken got its foot caught in the rope. *ke* marang pengantènané ḍéwé* ensnarled in his own idea. **ñj/di*** to tie the feet together. *njrimpung pitik sing arep didol nang pasar* to tie the feet of chickens to be sold at the marketplace
srinḍitan a variety of small green parrot
srinṭil *rpr* scurrying. *mlaju mak ** to dash. **ñj*** to run, scurry. **s·um·rinṭil** eager, ready and waiting. *Jèn didjak nonton bioskop semrinṭil.* When they asked him to come along to the movies, he jumped at the chance.
sripah a dead person; a death. *Sadjaké mau ana * sebab mau ana kenṭong.* Someone must have died: the bamboo signal sounded. **ka*an** to suffer loss by death. *Kantjaku ka*an bapakné.* My friend's father died.
sripanganti *var of* SRIPENGANTI
sripenganti a gate in front of the palace where visitors wait before being admitted
sriping *var of* TJRIPING
sripit *rpr* a quick motion. ***-*** *or* **sripat-*** 1 [walking] with short steps while wearing a tight skirt. 2 [drinking] in sips. *ngombé wédang sripat-** to sip tea. **ñj/di*** to sip (*var of* ÑJ/DI·SRUPUT)
srira body (*ki for* AWAK)
sris ***-*** *rpr* sizzling
srisig a certain step in the classical dance used (*esp.* by females) to progress sideways by moving only the feet
sri:t *rpr* a shrill sound. *Mak sriiiiiit rèmé makan.* The brakes screeched.
sriti a variety of swallow (bird)
sriwed to hang around *or* move about smw. *ptg * pl* moving about in large numbers and all directions. **s·um·riwed** to move about in profusion. *Anaké sepuluh tjilik²* *semriwed banget.* They have ten small children, constantly swarming about. *Sumriwed aku mikirké kahananku iki.* My head is all in a whirl thinking about my problems.
sriwil offshoot, protuberance; (*or* **dridji ***) a sixth finger *or* toe growing as an offshoot of the little finger/toe. ***an** 1 offshoot. 2 scraps, parings. **ñj/di*** 1 to touch lightly with the finger. 2 to take [a bit of food] on the fingertip. *Ḍèké njriwil rotiné.* He ate a fingertipful of his cake. * **kutil** a

certain wild tree having leaves with wart-shaped welts

sriwing to move with an air current. *Kertasé * kabur.* The paper was blown up in the air by the breeze. ***-*** 1 to feel a current of air. 2 (it is) rumored. *kabar *-** rumor, word of mouth. *Sriwing² aku krungu kowé arep njang Éropa sasi ngarep.* I hear you're going to Europe next month. **ke*** touched by a flow of air. **ñj*** to blow softly. **s·um·riwing** sharp, cool feel *or* taste. *Permèné semriwing jèn dikleṭus.* Peppermint bites the tongue when it is chewed.

sriwut *ptg * pl* rushing about busily and confusedly. *Wong² paḍa njambut gawé nang pawon ptg *.* The kitchen is a beehive of activity. *See also* IWUT

srobot ***an** (having been) taken. *barang *an²* stolen goods. **ñj/di*** to snatch, steal. *Nijaté arep njrobot banḍané Bu S mau.* He planned to get hold of Mrs. S's wealth.

srodog (*or* **ñj***) stiff, standing out. *Rambuté njrodog.* His hair sticks straight out in all directions. **ñj/di*** to push, butt. *Weḍusé njrodok.* The goat butted. *Jèn nang pasar adja njrodog waé.* Don't push your way through at the marketplace.

srog *rpr* brushing, grazing, friction. **srag-*** *rpr* repeated instances of the above. *mlaku srag-** to scuff the feet as one walks. **nge/di*aké** to put sth [in a place]

srogol **srogal-*** constantly moving about in a fidgety, unpoised way; lacking composure

srok̄ *rpr* the act of seating oneself

srondol *var of* SONḌOL

sronggot snout [of pig]; tusk [of boar]. **ñj/di*** to root with the snout; to gore with the tusk

sropot *var of* SRUPUT

srotong 1 opium pipe. 2 *var of* SOTONG. 3 (*or* ***an**) the upper (steeply vertical) roof section of a Javanese house (*see also* PANANGGAP). *omah *an* house with the above style of roof. *saka ** the four pillars which support the upper roof section

srowod *ptg ** in a mess, in disorder

srowol **srowal-*** ill-mannered, gauche

sru *oj* loud; strong

srubud ***-*** 1 *rpr* the sound of wind blowing. 2 *rpr* a fast long-striding walking pace. **s·um·rubud** in a rush. *Jèn katjané montor dibukak anginé bandjur semrubud mlebu.* When he opened the car window, in rushed the wind. *Mahasiswa² paḍa ptg sumrubud metu saka kelas.* The students poured out of the classroom.

srudug **ñj/di*** to butt with the horns

srumbat *var of* SLUMBAT

srumbung 1 a large woven-bamboo container which attaches to the upper back with a sling, in which one carries bundles *etc.* 2 a large cylindrical tube-shaped bamboo piece for encasing wells and plant tubs. ***an** a woman who offers her services transporting things in the above container. **ñj/di*(i)** to equip sth with the above container *or* casing

srundèng shredded coconut fried either with or without oil. ** ḍènḍèng ragi* a rice-accompanying dish of fried beef and shredded coconut. ** katjang* the above dish made with peanuts added

srunḍul *var of* SUNḌUL

sruni 1 a flute-like gamelan instrument. 2 chrysanthemum

srunṭul *rpr* a quick dash. *mlaju mak ** to make a dash. **ñj*** to dash, sprint. **s·um·runṭul** to run fast. *Jèn lagi butuh waé, olèhé semrunṭul.* If you need sth, run quickly and get it.

sruput **srupat-*** *rpr* sipping *or* sucking sounds. **ñj/di*** to sip *or* suck audibly

srutu cigar. *rokok ** a cigar. *ngrokok ** to smoke a cigar. **ñj*** 1 to smoke a cigar. 2 to act boorish

sruwa 1 palm fibers, used for making a brush-tipped pen (*kalam*). 2 *rg var of* SRÈI

sruwal *ng kr* (*or kr for* KAṬOK?), **lantjing·an** *ki* pants, trousers

sruwé sound; voice. **ñj/di*** 1 to pay attention (to). *Ḍèwèké weruh nanging ora pisan njaruwé.* He saw it but didn't pay any attention to it. 2 to criticize, put the blame on. 3 to interrupt a conversation. **pa·ñj*** critical comment. *Panjaruwé saking para maos baḍé katampi kalijan senenging manah.* Readers' comments will be gratefully accepted.

sruwed *ptg * pl* milling around, moving to and fro with hustle-and-bustle. *Sing paḍa ladèn wira-wiri ptg *.* The waiters moved in and out among the crowd.

sruwèk *pl form of* SUWÈK

sruweng *ptg ** *or* **s·um·ruweng** to make a continuous swishing *or* buzzing sound

sruwi ***-*** *or* **sruwa-*** totally, altogether, in every respect. *Mantèné sruwa-* geḍèn²an.* The wedding festivities were on a grand scale.

sruwil *ptg* * (having been) torn to shreds. *Klambiné ditjatjah tikus nganti paḍa ptg* *. Mice nibbled the shirt to pieces.

sruwing *-* *or* **sruwang-*** (to hear) rumors. *Aku krungu sruwang-* jèn...* I hear it rumored that...

sruwung *var of* SRUWENG

ss *shooing sound for driving away insects, animals, etc.*

st 1 sh! *Sssst, adja ramé.* Shush, don't make so much noise. 2 *see* SANTO

st- *see also under* SET-

stabil stable, steady. *Rega² wis* *. Prices are stable now. **ka*an** stability. **ke*an ékonomi** economic stability. **ñj/di*** (*acv prn* **njetabil**) to stabilize

stagèn long wide ladies' sash wound around the waist to hold the wraparound (*djarik*) in place

stan 1 booth, stand. 2 score. *é loro-sidji.* The score is 2 to 1.

starter ignition. **ñj/di*(aké)** (*acv prn* **njetarter[aké]**) to start [an engine]. *Montoré di*.* He turned on the ignition.

stater *var of* STARTER

status status (symbol)

stèleng *see* TÈNTUN STÈLENG

stèn head of a subdistrict

stènsil mimeograph stencil. *an in mimeographed form. **ñj/di*** (*acv prn* **njetènsil**) to mimeograph. *njetènsil soal² udjian* to mimeograph the exam questions

stèr star(ring performer). *filem* * film star

ster queen (in chess). *Ster!* I threaten your queen! (*comparable to* SKAK! *'check!' when threatening the king*)

stingkul *var sp of* SETINGKUL

stoplès *var sp of* SETOPLÈS

strèng 1 strict, firmly in control. 2 fan belt

strip strip; stripe; striped (*see also* SETRIP)

stuḍi study, den

suba *-* esteem, honor. *aturan *-*** etiquette or protocol for honoring smn. **ñj/di*(-*)** to respect highly, show great esteem for

subakti *oj* loyal, obedient, humble

subal 1 stuffing. * *kapuk luwih mendatmendut katimbang wulu.* Kapok stuffing is springier than feathers. 2 hair piece worn by a short-haired girl to form a Javanese-style hair-do (*gelung*). 3 sth of inferior quality mixed in with high-quality goods. **ñj/di*(i)** ▸o mix lower-quality stuff in with [material of high quality]

subalik on the other hand, on the contrary, by contrast. *Ḍèwèké ora sida ketjemplung ing pasangan, *é malah urip mulja.* She didn't come to a bad end after all—in fact, she led a prosperous life. *See also* BALIK

subâsitâ etiquette, rules of behavior

subja **ñj/di*-*** to respect, honor, esteem

sublug *see* DANDANG

subuh first daily ritual meditation for Moslems; also, the time of day (5 A.M.) at which this meditation takes place. *See also* SALAT

subur prosperous, flourishing. **ñj/di*** to plate. *Kerisé di* emas.* The kris is gold-plated. **ñj/di*aké** to cause sth to flourish. *Rabuk njuburaké tetanduran.* Fertilizer makes plants grow well. *See also* SABAR

suda to decrease, diminish. *Larané saja* *. His illness gradually got better. *n subtraction (arithmetical process). **ke*** to have sth subtracted from it, be reduced by. *Lima ka* loro kari telu.* Five minus two is three. **ñj/di*kaké** to cut down, diminish. *Ḍèké njuda olèhé mangan.* She went on a diet. *Lakuné montor di* rikaté.* He slowed the car.

sudagar businessman, merchant. **ñj*** to engage in business, practice trade

suḍang *var of* SUNḌANG

sudârâ *oj* sibling; kinsman. **ñj*** to treat *or* consider smn as one's relative. * **wèdi** *or* * **werdi** *ltry* sibling, relative; intimate friend

sudarma *oj* father. **ka*n** mutual love

suḍat *var of* SUḌÈT

suḍèt *an 1 an open flesh wound. 2 [of a stream] diverted. **ñj/di*** 1 to rip [flesh, in combat]. 2 to divert [water] to a dry part of a field

sudi willing and eager. **ora** * unwilling, dead set against

suḍi a container for offerings, made of a banana leaf folded paper-hatwise and held with a bamboo pin

sudigawé *see* WURUK

suḍija *ltry var of* SEḌIJA

sudi:k *intensified form of* SUDI

sudira *oj* brave, courageous

sudjalma *oj* human being

sudjânâ suspicious, mistrustful. **(ka)*n** suspicious by nature. **ñj/di*ni** to be suspicious of. *Ana wong telu kang tak *ni.* There are three people I suspect.

sudjanma *var of* SUDJALMA

sudjarah *var of* SEDJARAH

sudji 1 bamboo skewer for roasting kebabs (*saté*). 2 *oj* lance. ***ǹ** skewered. *sudjèn saté* kebabs on skewers. **ñ(j)/di*ǹi** to place [meat chunks] on a skewer

sudjud 1 one of the Moslem praying positions: a prostrated kneeling position. 2 religious worship (*kr for* SEMBAHJANG). ***an** knee (*sbst ki for* ḌENGKUL). **pa*an** praying mat *or* rug

sudra an untouchable (lowest Hidu caste). *** papa** pauper

suduk dagger. ***en** to get a pain (stitch) in the side. ***(-*)an** to stab each other. **ñj/di*** to stab. **ñj/di*aké** to stab with [a weapon]. *Keris mau di*aké marang empu Gandring.* He drove the kris into Master Gandring. *** djiwa** *or* *** slira** to stab oneself to death

sugal stern, harsh. *Rembugé rada *.* He spoke severely.

sugâtâ 1 refreshments served to guests (*ki for* SUGUH?). 2 a formal welcome. **ñj/di*-ni** to serve [guests]. **pa*n** *sms *.* *Kula ngaturaken pa*n.* I bid you welcome.

sugeng 1 well, safe, secure (*ki for* SLAMET). 2 life; to live (*ki for* URIP). 3 fat (*rg ki for* LEMU)

sugih rich; *fig* having a wealth of. *sudagar ** a wealthy businessman. *digandjar ** to be richly rewarded. *upama aku *a* if I were rich. ** pari* to have plenty of rice. *panḍita * ngèlmu* a wise man who is rich in knowledge. ** omong* to do a lot of talking. ** akal* to be full of tricks and schemes. **ka*an** riches, wealth. *Ke*ané wong tani awudjud beras pari.* A farmer's wealth is his rice. **ñj*** to increase in wealth. *Ḍèké saja njugih.* He gets richer and richer. **ñj/di*i** to make smn rich. **pa*an** riches, wealth. *Bisané * kuwi rak duwé pa*an ṭujul.* He got rich through the help of a bad spirit. **sa*-*é** however rich. *Sa*-*é wong tani, ora bakal bisa * kaja wong dagang.* No matter how wealthy a farmer is, he can never make as much money as a businessman. **s·um·ugih(-*)** to act as though one were rich, to try to make oneself appear wealthy. *** mlarat** the rich and the poor. *** pari** sensitive *or* sore to the touch

sugu a stick of wood *or* bamboo. **ñj/di*ǩaké** to feed [sticks] into. *Tebu sing digiling disugokaké sidji²*. The sugar-cane stalks being milled were fed in one by one.

suguh *ng,* **segah** *kr* (*or* ***an** *or* **se***) food and drink offered to a guest. **ñj/di*aké** to serve sth. **ñj/di*(i)** to serve smn. *Aku di* kopi.* She served me some coffee. **pa*an** *or* **pi*** refreshment served to a guest

suh 1 broom binding. 2 shoo! **nge/di*aké** to shoo [animals *etc.*]. **nge/di*i** to bind [broomstraws]

suhun *var of* SUWUN. **ñj/di*-*** to have great respect for. *Sang Prabu di*-* para kawula.* The King is highly esteemed by his subjects.

sujud loyal, obedient. **ñj/di*aké** to cause smn to be loyal. *Para kawula di*aké saka lomané panguwasa²*. The subjects' loyalty springs from the generosity of the authorities. **ñ(j)/di*** to serve [one's monarch] loyally

suk[a] *ng,* **béndjing** *kr* next, the coming. ** dina Senèn* (*ngarep*) next Monday. ** taun* next year. ** kapan² baé* some day. ***-*** at some future time. **-* tak dolan nggonmu.* I'll come to see you some time. *** apa** when (in the future)? ** apa mangkaté?* When's he leaving? *** embèn** the day after tomorrow. *** iki** *rg* 1 at some time in the future. 2 tomorrow. *** kapan** when (in the future)? *See also* BÉSUK

suk[b] ***-*an** pushing/crowding each other. *Sepuré sesak, wong² paḍa *-*an olèhé munggah.* The train was so crowded people had to push their way in. **nge/di*** to push aside, shove around. *Botjah mau diesuk wong sepirang²*. The child was elbowed this way and that by the crowd.

suk[c] *shf of* SUSUK, TUSUK *before* KONḌÉ

suka 1 gay, happy, having pleasure. 2 to put sth smw (*root form: kr for* DÈLÈH). 3 to give (*root form: kr for* WÈH[a], WÈNÈH, WÈWÈH). 4 *rg* advisable, preferable. *Luwih * mlaku alon²an.* Better walk slowly. ***-*** *or* ***n-*n** to enjoy oneself. **ka*n** 1 enjoyment, fun; pleasure, pastime. 2 to play cards for fun. **sa*né** as one likes. *Ḍèké nèk omong sa*né.* He says whatever he pleases. ***-pari-*** *or* ***-(pi)·rena** to have a good time. *** sokur** *or* *** (pa)·ñ·trima** to give thanks. *** wibawa** to have a good time

sukak to enjoy oneself. *See also* KAK

sukâlilâ *kanṭi ** with all one's heart

sukârilâ *var of* SUKALILA

sukarta **ñj/di*** to hold a ceremony with a shadow-play performance (*ruwat·an*) as a protective measure for a child born under ominous circumstances according to animistic principles. *botjah ** a child for whom such a ceremony is held (*see* BOTJAH)

suker se* excrement. * **sakit** plagued by illness and difficulties
sukerta *var of* SUKARTA
suket *ng,* **rumput** *kr* grass. **(pa)*an** grassy place. *mlaku ana ing *an* to walk in (tall) grasses. * **dondom·an** a certain wild grass with long thorny seed pods. * **goḍong** everything, everyone; [*in negative*] [not] anything, [not] anyone. ** goḍong adja ana sing krungu.* Don't let anyone know about this. * **segara** sea grass(es). ***tutu·ñ** a grass that grows among rice plants
suklé searchlight
suklih *var of* SUKLÉ
sukma soul; life. *See also* PANUKMA
sukra *oj* Friday
suksès successful, a success. **ja.* Good luck to you! *Anggoné njoba rokèt ora *.* The rocket launch was unsuccessful.
suksma *var of* SUKMA
suku 1 leg, foot (*kr for* SIKIL). 2 a diacritical mark denoting the vowel *u* in Javanese script. 3 *rg* one-half rupiah. ***ñ** 1 marked with the above diacritic. 2 worth half a rupiah. **ñj/di*** to affix the above diacritic to [a script character]. * **djadja teken djanggut** by dint of great effort
sukun 1 breadfruit. 2 (*prn* **su'un**) Chinese vermicelli
sukur *var of* SOKUR
sul shoe sole
sula *ltry* spear
sulah *oj* sharp-pointed weapon. **ñj/di*** to stab smn with a sharp weapon as a punitive measure
sulâjâ quarrel, disagreement; to quarrel, have conflict. ***n** on hostile terms with each other. **ñj/di*ni** 1 to be at odds with. *Aku di*ni.* She doesn't agree with me. 2 to welsh; to fail to honor one's agreement. **pa*n** conflict, disagreement
sulak 1 chicken-feather duster. 2 tinged with. *idjo * kuning* yellowish green. **ñj/di*i** to dust [furniture] with a feather duster
sulaksânâ a good omen. *tedja*[2] * a sign of good luck to come
sulam material used to repair or replace sth broken. **ñj/di*i** to patch, to mend sth by replacing materials. *Pring mau kanggo njulami pager sing rusak.* That bamboo is for patching the broken fence.
sulap 1 sleight-of-hand. *tukang ** magician, sleight-of-hand artist. 2 *fig* blind to, blinded by; enchanted by. *Ḍèké * marang wewudjudan kang kaja mengkono.* He was enchanted by such beauty. ***an** sleight-of-hand trick *or* performance. *dolanan *an kertu* a card trick. **ñj*** 1 to do magic tricks. 2 (*psv* **di***) to transform by sleight-of-hand. *Katju di* dadi dara.* He changed his handkerchief into a dove. **ñj/di*i** to dazzle *or* blind with glaring light *or* (*fig*) a stunning sight. *Katjané njulapi mata jèn kena srengéngé.* The glass makes a blinding glare when it catches the sun.
suled **ñj/di*** to light, ignite. *njuled lilin* to light candles. *njuled dijan téplok* to light an oil lamp
sulfat sulphate
sulih a representative, substitute, stand-in. *tembung* **se*** *gram* pronoun. **ñj/di*aké** to delegate, to have smn act as representative. **ñj/di*i** to represent, to act in place of *or* on behalf of. *di*i karo pokrol* represented by a lawyer. *Anak lanang sing mbarep kudu bisa njulihi bapa.* The oldest son must be able to take the father's place.
suling a gamelan blowing instrument, *usu.* of bamboo, with a flute-like tone, held vertically like an oboe. *tukang ** player of this instrument. **ñj*** 1 to play the above. 2 (*psv* **di***) to distill. *njuling lenga wangi* to distill perfume. **pa·ñj*** act *or* way of playing the above instrument. *Panjulingé apik.* He plays the *suling* beautifully. **pa·ñj*an** a distillation
sulistya handsome, charming, beautiful. **ka*n** beauty, charm
sulit difficult, full of obstacles. **ñj/di*aké** to cause difficulties for. *Kahanan sosial saiki pantjèn njulitaké pamerintah.* Social problems are giving the government a good many headaches. **ñj*-*(i)** to cause difficulties, to complicate things. *Jèn didjaluki tulung adja sok njulit-njuliti.* When smn asks you to help with sth, don't snarl things up even worse.
sultan monarch of Jogjakarta. **ka*an** 1 sultanate. *ka*an Ngajogjakarta* the Sultanate (principality) of Jogjakarta. 2 Jogjanese court drama in which the performers sing as they dance
suluh 1 torch. 2 firewood. 3 yellow(ed); fair, light in color. *Geḍangé wis *.* The bananas have ripened. 4 *rg* scout, one who reconnoiters. ***an** 1 to use a torch. *Jèn mlebu guwa kudu *an.* You need to use a

torch in a cave. 2 inner corner of the eye.
3 mortar for laying bricks. ñj/di*(i) 1 to
cast light on. *mBok dalan iki di*i seḍélok.*
Light up this path for a minute. *Perkarané
di**.* The case was examined from every
angle. 2 to trap [birds, fish] by attracting
them with torchlight. **pa·ñj*an** illumina-
tion; information. *See also* WAJANG[a]

suluk *wj* mood song chanted by a puppet-
master to set the scene. ñj/di*i to introduce a scene as above

sulung 1 small white flying ant. 2 *rg* firstborn, oldest child

sulur aerial roots hanging down from tree
branches

sum hem of a garment; seam. **nge/di*** to
hem; to seam

sum- *see also under* S- (*Introduction, 3.1.7*)

suma *var of* KUSUMA

sumados *var of* SEMADOS

sumaged to try to act competent (*kr for*
GUMISA). *See also* SAGED

sumâjâ *see also* SEMAJA

sumakéjan boastful

sumâlâ *see* BOTJAH

sumânggâ 1 as you wish. * *ing Rama karsané.* Whatever you wish, Father. 2 please
(go ahead and...). 3 come on! (*ki for* AJO).
ñj/di*kaké to leave sth up to smn; to entrust, put sth in the hands of. *Regané paḍa,
njumanggakaké sing endi arep dituku.* They
cost the same; I leave it you which to buy.
*Anaké disumanggakaké nang ndara Pang-
éran bab sekolah.* He put his son's education in the hands of the Prince.

sumangkéjan *var of* SUMAKÉJAN

sumapta *var of* SAMAPTA

sumaput *var of* SEMAPUT

sumarah obedient; to obey

sumâwânâ *rg* and, furthermore

sumba (*or* ke*) a variety of tree

sumbang (*or* *an) a contribution, donation;
gift, present. *Nalika dadi mantèn bijèn éntuk *an raḍio.* They got a radio for a wedding present. ñj/di* 1 to give a gift (to).
2 to contribute to; to support. *Kali² mèlu
njumbang ngunḍakaké pametuné pertanian.*
Rivers contribute to the increase of agricultural products. ñj/di*aké to contribute sth.
*Aku kepéngin njumbangaké tenaga ing bab
mau.* I'd like to help with that.

sumbar 1 girls' game resembling jacks. 2 to
boast. *an act of boasting *or* swaggering.
- to defy, challenge. **se*** a boast, a jeer.

ñj/di*aké to brag about. *njumbaraké kesugihané* to boast about one's wealth. ñj/di*i
to challenge; to jeer at

sumber spring; source, origin. *an swampy,
soggy. ñj* 1 to produce water; watery,
soggy; to have water in it. 2 spring-like;
forming a spring

sumbrubud *inf var of* S·UM·RUBUD

sumbu wick; fuse. *ñ 1 opening for inserting a fuse (in a firecracker, old-style gun,
etc.). 2 to get a good catch of fish

sumbul *see* WATU

sumbut worthwhile, worth the trouble. *Jèn
mung diopahi Rp 100 gawéan iki ora * karo
olèhé ngrekasa.* If I only get paid 100 rupiahs for the job, it's not worth doing it.

sumed *an a non-electric light. *lampu pit
an bicycle oil lamp. ñj/di*(i) to light, ignite

sumèdi *var of* SEMADI

sumèh friendly, smiling. ñj/di*aké to make
[one's expression] friendly. ñj/di*i to treat
smn pleasantly

sumeksa *oj* still, even so

sumekta *var of* SAMEKTA

sumelang (**kuwatos** *kr?*) worried, uneasy,
apprehensive. *Dèké * jèn dagangané ora bisa paju.* She was afraid her merchandise
wouldn't sell. *an tending to worry too
much *or* be overanxious. *Dasaré atiné *an.*
She's a worrier by nature. ñj/di*aké to
fear, worry about. *Di*aké kabèh mati klelep.* It was feared that they had all drowned.
ñj*i worrisome, causing apprehension; (*psv*
di*i) to worry about, fear. *Jèn njetir montor isih njumelangi.* It's nerve-wracking
when he drives.

sumelèt intensely hot. *Djam loro awan
mangsa ketiga panasé *.* At 2 P.M. in the dry
season the heat is unbearable.

sumené ñj/di*kaké to wait for; to delay,
postpone

sumeng (to have *or* get) a fever

sumengit in one's adolescence. *Dèké ki isih
semengit.* She's a teen-ager.

sumer *var of* SUMENG

sumerap *sbst? var of* SUMEREP

sumerep to see; to know (*kr for* WERUH).
See also SURUP

sumitra a good friend. *See also* MITRA

sumjah fresh *or* refreshed feeling. *seger ** refreshed as by the touch of a light breeze

sumjar 1 scattered evenly. 2 [of the face]
sunny, bright-looking. 3 [of *e.g.* a crowd]

buzzing, murmuring, rumbling with noise. 4 heartbroken

sumjur shattered, smashed

sumlenger ***an** easily astonished *or* taken aback. ***en** astonished; dismayed; dumbfounded. **ñj*i** astounding

sumongah arrogant, boastful

sumpah one's oath; to swear, take one's oath. **ñj/di*** to administer an oath to. *Para najaka di* miturut agamané ḍéwé.* The ministers are sworn in according to their own religion. **ñj/di*i** to put a curse on smn. **pa·ñj*an** an oath sworn by smn; a swearing-in. *Penjumpahan Présiḍèn ditindakaké nang geḍung X.* The President was sworn in at the X building.

sumpek̄ crowded, jammed, stuffed; choked, suffocated. **ñj/di*-*i** to crowd, jam, throng to

sumpel *var of* SUMPET

sumpena *var of* SUPENA

sumpet 1 stopper, cork. 2 [of cocks' combs] small and compact (rather than high: *cf.* WILAH). *djènggèr ** small cock's comb. **ñj/di*i** to stop up, close off. *Lèḍengé botjor bandjur di*i nganggo gombal.* He stuffed a rag into the leaky faucet. **s·um·umpet** stuck *or* caught so as to block sth. *Ḍuwité sumumpet nang sak.* His money is wadded in his pocket.

sumping *wj* ear ornament worn as part of a costume for the classical dance. ***an** to put on *or* wear the above ornament. **ñj/di*aké** *or* **ñj/di*i** to put the above on smn's ear

sumpung lacking a nose/beak/proboscis. *Irungé *.* He has no nose. **ñj/di*aké** to cause the loss of a nose *etc.*

sumrawang transparent

sumrepet to feel faint, on the verge of losing consciousness. *Saking panasé *.* It was so hot I nearly passed out.

sumrikutan *see* SRIKUT

sumringah happy, relaxed, smiling

sumromong hot, burning

sumrowong *var of* SUMROMONG

sumub steam from boiling water. **ke*an** to get scalded by steam

sumuk 1 hot and sultry. *Panas lan *é saja ndadi.* The heat and humidity increased. 2 hot and sweaty. *Saiki aku krasa isis, mauné * banget.* I'm nice and cool now; before, I was sweating. **ke*en** excessively humid; excessively sweaty-feeling. **ñj*i** to make smn feel hot and sweaty

sumungah *ltry var of* SUMONGAH

sumur well. ** bur* a drilled well. ***an** a well-like hole. **ñj*** resembling a well. **njumur g·um·ulung** 1 deep, inscrutable. 2 unable to keep a secret. *** banḍung** a large well. *** g·um·uling** underground waterway, vein of water. *** l·um·aku t·in·imba** one who is willing to share his wealth of knowledge with others. *** mati** 1 an old dry well. 2 one who never refuses anything offered to him. *** siniba** one from whom knowledge can be obtained

sumurup to know (*ng? kr for* WERUH?). **sa*ku** to my knowledge. *Sa*ku ḍèké ora salah.* As far as I know, he's not guilty. *See also* SURUP

sun *inf var of* INGSUN

sunah (*or* **di*aké**) meritorious and recommended but not obligatory according to Moslem law. *Mènèhi zakat karo wong kekurangan kuwi hukumé (di)sunah(aké).* Giving alms to the poor is recommended by religious law. *See also* SUNAT

sunan 1 monarch of Surakarta (*short var of* SUSUHUNAN). 2 *Islamic title for saints.* **ka*an** the kingdom of Surakarta

sunar *oj* light, radiance. **ñj/di*i** to give light to, shine on. **s·um·unar** radiant, shining. *Rembulané sumunar.* The moon is shining.

sunat 1 meritorious but not obligatory by Moslem law (*see also* SUNAH). 2 (**tetes** *ki*) ritual act performed on adolescents: piercing of the clitoris (girls), circumcision (boys). ***an** ceremony held at the time of the above act. **ñj/di*aké** to have [a boy] circumcised; to have [a girl's] ears pierced for earrings. **ñj/di*i** 1 to circumcise. 2 to pierce the clitoris of [a girl, symbolically, using a *kunir* root]. **pa*an** circumcising knife

sunḍang *oj* horn of an animal. **ñj/di*** to butt *or* gore with the horns

sundel prostitute. **ñj*** to engage in prostitution. *** bolong** woman devil with a hole in her back

sundep rice borer. **ñj/di*** to stab, prick, pierce

sunduk skewer. ***an** things strung onto a skewer. **ñj/di*(i)** to string things onto a skewer. *Kolang-kalingé di*i arep didol nang pasar.* He strung the palm-fruit kernels to be sold at the market.

sunḍul to reach *or* come up (to), to touch [sth high]. *Sirahé * ngepjan.* His head touches the ceiling. ***an** 1 poultice (*kr for*

PUPUK). 2 *sms* KE*AN *below.* 3 crown of the head (*ki for* BUN²AN). **ke*** to get pushed upward. **ke*an** 1 to get pushed from below. *Untuku wis ke*an untu manèh.* The other tooth is coming in under my [loose] tooth. 2 to have become pregnant again before the preceding child is weaned. **ñj/di*(i)** 1 to push *or* hit from underneath. 2 to send a second letter which countermands, adds to, *etc.* the message of the first. *Suraté bandjur di*i nganggo surat manèh.* He followed up the first letter with another one. **njunḍul pujuh** to move sth in a high arc, *esp.* to push smn in a swing. **pa*an** crown of the head (*ki for* BUN²AN). *** langit** 1 to reach the sky. 2 a small-leafed ivy with small blossoms. *lenga * langit* oil from these blossoms, used in perfume

sung *oj* to give (*root form: cf. forms of* WÈNÈH). **pa*** a gift, offering. *See also* ANGSUNG

sungapan estuary, river mouth

sungé *oj* river

sunggar ***an** a certain puffed-out hair style for ladies; to wear the hair this way. *Seka *ané aku bisa nitèni wong asal Jogja/Sala apa daérah lija.* From the way a girl wears her hair, I can tell whether she's from the Jogja-Solo area or from some other region. **ñj/di*** to comb [the hair] in the above style

sunggâtâ *var of* SUGATA

sunggi **ñj/di*** to carry on the head. *Baturé njunggi koper.* The servant carried the suitcase on his head.

sungging 1 delicate painting on leather puppets. 2 paint used for the intricate designs on leather puppets. *djuru ** one who does puppet painting. ***an** the painting of puppets (done as above). **ñj/di*** to paint [puppets] intricately and delicately

sungil impassable, difficult *or* hazardous to negotiate (*e.g.* a mountain pass)

sungkan reluctant, unwilling. ***an** habitually unwilling

sungkâwâ grief (*ltry kr for* SUSAH). *nḌèrèk béla *.* I share in your grief (*phrase said conventionally to a bereaved person*).

sungkem ceremonious procedure for showing esteem and humility for smn: one kneels before the (seated) respected one, makes a *sembah,* presses the nose to the person's knee, makes another *sembah.* **ñj/di*aké** to have smn show esteem and humility as above. **ñj/di*i** to pay one's respects to smn in this way. **s·um·ungkem** 1 the above esteem-showing procedure. 2 obedient, humble, respectful. *See also* SEMBAH

sungsang the other way around. *Olèhmu turu * waé.* Sleep with your head where your feet are and vice versa. **ñ(j)*** turned the wrong way around. *Bajiné olèhé metu njungsang.* The baby's head was born last. **njungsang n·djempalik** with all one's might. *Diréwangi nganti njungsang ndjempalik.* They turned themselves inside out to help him. *or* He works himself to the bone.

sungsat (*adoh*) ***é** a far cry, quite different (from). *Adoh banget *é.* Far from it! *Kabèh adoh *é karo kahanan ing sadurungé.* Everything was very different from the way it had been before. *Anggonmu nggulawenṭah murid² adja nganti * saka kapribadèn Indonesia.* Don't train your students to diverge from their Indonesian personality.

sungsum bone marrow; *fig* strength. *Aḍemé nemen tekan balung *.* The cold chilled them to the very marrow. *Awakku lemes kaja dilolosi balung *ku.* I was weak; it was as though my strength were draining away.

sungsun layer; story of a building. *Omah mau *é pira?* How many floors has the house got? **ñ(j)/di*** to make (into) layers. *Olèhé numpuk koṭaké di* telu.* He piled the boxes three deep. *** timbun** lying in piles

sungu *ng,* **singat** *kr* horn, antler. **ñj/di*** to attack with the horns

sungut 1 insect's feeler/antenna. 2 tip of a vegetable pod

sunja *oj* quiet, lonely, deserted

sunjaruri the realm of the spirits

sunjâtâ *oj* true, factual. **ka*n** truth, fact. *See also* NJATA

sunjuk *rg var of* NJUNJUK

suntak *ng,* **tuntak** *or* **luntak** *kr* to spill out. *Tèhé *.* The tea spilled. **ñj/di*** to spill *or* pour sth out. **ñj/di*aké** to convey. *njuntakaké serat² papréntahan* to transmit government documents. *See also* WUTAH

sunṭi *see* PRAWAN

suntik shot, injection. **ñj/di*(i)** to give smn a shot

suntrut (*or* **ñj***) sad; depressed; drooping. *Wit²an akèh sing alum, njuntrut kaja wong seḍih.* Many of the trees drooped, like grieving human beings.

suntuk throughout [the night]. *ndelok wajang kulit semalem ** to watch a shadow-play performance all night long

sunu *oj* 1 child. 2 ray, beam, radiance. **se∗** to give birth

sunya *var of* SUNJA

sup *var of* SOP

supadi *oj* in order to, so that

supados *kr for* SUPAJA

supâjâ *ng,* **supados** *kr* 1 in order to, so that. *Djarané dibanḍangaké ∗ énggala tekan ing omah.* He spurred on his horse so as to reach home quickly. 2 [to wish, urge, *etc.*] that... *Lurah tansah njurup²aké ∗ botjahé ditambakaké menjang rumah sakit.* The village head kept urging that the child be sent to the hospital for treatment. **∗ adja** *or* **∗ ora (supados sampun** *kr*) so as not to... *Ḍèké nduduti goprak ∗ krambilé adja dipangan badjing.* He rattled the clapper so the squirrels wouldn't nibble at the coconuts. *Konen ngombé banju iku ∗ ora bakal kena ing lara.* Have him drink this water so he won't get the disease.

supaos *opt? sbst? kr for* SUPATA

supâtâ a vow, an oath; to swear (to). *adol ∗* to swear for emphasis. *Wis diréwangi adol ∗.* He tried to convince them by swearing to it. **ñj/di∗kaké** 1 to have smn swear (to). 2 to swear on smn's behalf. **ñj/di∗ni** to put a curse on smn (to the effect that...). *Anak putuku tak ∗ni ora slamet jèn njerèt.* I invoked a curse on my descendants that they should not be safe from harm if they smoke opium. **pa∗** an oath; a curse. *pa∗ setya* a loyalty oath

supé to forget (*kr for* LALI). **se∗** ring for the finger (*kr for* ALI²). **ñj∗** to pretend to forget; to try to forget (*kr for* LALI²)

supek̄ *var of* SUMPEK

supeket to have a friendly relationship (with)

supena a dream (*kr for* IMPI·Ṅ). **ñj∗** to dream (*kr for* NG·IMPI)

supijah possessiveness, acquisitiveness

supir *var of* SOPIR

supit 1 pinchers, pinching claws; pincers, tongs. 2 circumcision (*ki for* TETAK). *bong ∗* man who performs circumcisions. **ñj/di∗** to pick up with pincers, tweezers, tongs, *etc.* **ñj/di∗i** to circumcise (*ki for* Ñ/DI·TETAK·I). **∗ urang** 1 shrimp claw. 2 a flanking deployment. *Omahé mawa dalan ∗-urang.* The house has paths going around to the back on both sides. *gelung ∗-urang* ladies' hairdo with the hair wound on both sides in a back bun. 3 *wj* a certain military batik-wearing style

suprandéné even so, in spite of it, however

suprih *rg* in order to, so that

sur *rpr* flowing, pouring. *Sikilé disoki tamba, ∗.* He poured medicine on the leg. *Getihé mak ∗.* Blood flowed out. **sar-∗** [of heartbeats] pit-a-pat. **ke∗** to get pushed aside *or* taken over. **nge/di∗** to push aside; to appropriate by pushing sth aside. *Nggonku nang bioskupan wis diesur wong.* Someone took my seat in the movies [when I left temporarily]. **nge/di∗aké** to pour sth. *Ḍèké nge∗aké lenga ing wadjan.* She poured oil in the frying pan. *Tambané di∗ké nang sikilé.* He poured medicine on his leg. **nge/di∗i** to pour onto. *Banjuné nge∗i klambiku.* The water went all over my shirt. **∗ tanah** a ceremony held upon smn's death. **nge/di∗-tanah** *or* **ñj/di∗-tanah** to hold such a ceremony for smn

sura 1 first month of the Moslem calendar. 2 *oj* courageous. **∗n** religious feast held during Sura

suraḍaḍu *var of* SARAḌAḌU

surah a chapter in the Koran. **∗ jasin** the 37th chapter, chanted as part of Moslem funeral rites

surak to cheer. *∗ horé* to shout hurray! *∗é wong nonton* the spectators' cheering. **ñj/di∗(i)** to jeer at, boo

Surakarta central Javanese city, oldest surviving Javanese kingdom (before the 1945 revolution) and site of the court headed by the Sunan: one of the two major cultural centers (*see also* JOGJAKARTA). **∗ Hadiningrat** *complete formal name of this city. See also* SALA

surâlâjâ *oj* the realm of the deities

surâlokâ *var of* SURALAJA

surambi *var of* SRAMBI

surang **ke∗-∗** beset with troubles. *Uripé tansah ke∗-∗.* His life is a series of misfortunes.

suraos *kr for* SURASA

surâsâ *ng,* **suraos** *kr* contents, meaning, connotation. **ñj/di∗** to get the meaning, sense the connotation. *Aku lagi njurasa lajang iki.* I'm trying to figure out what this letter means. **pa·ñj∗** grasp *or* insight into meanings contained in texts, messages, *etc.*

surat 1 letter (*var of* SERAT). 2 *var of* SURAH

surdjan a Nehru-style jacket worn by Jogjakarta males. **∗an** to put on *or* wear this garment

surem dim, gloomy. **ñj/di*aké** to cause to be dim/gloomy

surèn a certain tree whose wood is used for house frames

surep dusk, twilight. *Montoré dibanterakė supaja adja nganti * anggoné teka kuṭa.* He drove faster so as to reach the city before dark.

suretna an especially fine diamond

suri 1 weaving shuttle. 2 a curved comb worn to hold the hair in place. 3 small comb for removing lice. 4 *sbst kr for* DJUNGKAT = comb*?* 5 horse's mane. **ñj/di*ni** to comb smn's hair. *See also* DJUNGKAT

surja 1 *ltry; ki?* sun. *soroting ** sunbeam. 2 face (*ki for* RAI). 3 to wash the face (*root form: ki for* RAUP). 4 dated (*in a letter-writing phrase*). *Kaserat ing Djakarta, * kaping 21 April 1972.* Djakarta, April 21, 1972. **pa*n** 1 face (*ki for* RAI). 2 facial expression (*ki for* ULAT). *** klalun** the pre-twilight period (*ca.* 3–5 P.M.). *** sata** noon-time; the hour or so preceding 12 M. *** seng-kala** chronogrammatic reckoning according to solar years. *** tjandra** sun and moon; **ka*-tjandra** shone upon by sun and moon

surjâkânṭâ magnifying glass

surtanah *see under* SUR

suru 1 spoon fashioned from a banana leaf. 2 a certain thick shrub used for hedges. 3 porcupine quill. **ñj/di*** to use a banana-leaf spoon

surud 1 to ebb, recede. 2 to die (*ki: applied only to kings*)

suruh *ng,* **seḍah** *kr* the betel plant; betel leaves, used for chewing. *djambé ** betel leaf prepared for chewing. *nginang djambé-** to chew betel nut and leaves. ***an** *ng kr* 1 an invitation. 2 one who is asked to help. *A dadi *ané B nang kantor pos.* B asked A to do an errand for him at the post office. 3 to help out. **an nang nggoné tangga* to help out at the neighbors'. **ñj/di*i** *ng kr* 1 to invite. 2 to ask for help. *Budi njuruhi aku dadi sopir montor sing arep dienggo mantèn.* Budi asked me to drive the bridal car. *** aju** betel-leaf preparation for ceremonial offerings

surung shark. **ñj/di*** to push sth forward from behind. *Pité di* bandjur ditjulakė.* He gave the bicycle a push and then let go.

surup *ng,* **serep** *or* **serap** *kr* 1 to enter. 2 dusk, sunset; [of sun, moon] to set. ** rep* just at twilight. 3 door (*as a counting unit for houses*). *Omahku let lima apa nem *, kaé.* My house is over there, five or six doors down. **se*an** 1 knowledge. 2 financial matters. *Adja takon² se*ané wong tuwa.* Don't pry into your parents' money matters. **ke*an** to be entered (into); to be possessed. *ka*an sétan* possessed by a devil. **ñj/di*aké** 1 to put sth into. *Bolah iku di*aké dom.* She threaded the needle. 2 to tell; to inform. *Ḍèké njurup²aké supaja botjahé ditambakaké menjang ḍokteran.* He kept telling them to have the child treated at the hospital. **ñj/di*i** 1 to insert into. *Domé di*i bolah.* She threaded the needle. 2 to know. *Sapa sing njurupi nang endi anakku?* Does anyone know where my child is? **s·um·urup** to enter. **dom sumuruping banju** virtually impossible to find. *See also* SUMURUP, WERUH

sus cream-puff shell. *djladrèn ** cream-puff batter. *kuwih ** cream puff with filling in it

susah[a] **(sisah** *rg? kr***), èmeng** (*or* **sekel***?*) *ki* sad. *Ana sing seneng, ana sing *.* Some were happy, some sad. *A wis lali *é.* A had forgotten her sorrows. **ka*an** 1 sorrow, grief, trouble. *ngalami ke*an* to undergo sorrow *or* difficulties. 2 to experience sorrow. *mBok Wangsa lagi ke*an.* Mrs. Wongso is in mourning. **ñj/di*aké** *or* **ñj/di*i** to sadden, cause sorrow for

susah[b] *ng,* **sisah** *kr* [not] need to; [not] necessary. *Ora * kuwatir.* No need to worry. *Ora * mbajar.* There's no fee. *Jèn nggawèkakė wédang tèh aku ora * nganggo gula.* If you're making tea, no sugar for me, please.

susila decent, morally *or* socially acceptable. *pulisi ** vice squad. *tuna ** prostitution. *djuru ** official in charge of dealing with prostitution. **ka*n** decency, proper *or* ethical behavior

suster 1 nurse. 2 Catholic nun

susu[a] 1 **(p[r]embajun** *ki***)** breast. 2 milk. ** legi* sweetened condensed milk. ** èntjèr* diluted milk. *banju ** breast milk. ***ñ (se-sep·an** *kr***)** baby who is not yet weaned. *Suson umur limang wulan.* The baby is five months old. **ñ(j)*** to take milk at the breast. **ñ(j)/di*ñi** to nurse [a baby]

susu[b] *ng,* **sesa** *kr* **ke*** in a hurry. *Lakuné ke* waé.* She walked hurriedly. *Mengko ḍisik ta, adja ke*.* Just a minute–not so fast. **ke* selak** *or* **selak ke*** in a great hurry. *Ḍèwèké kuwi rak ke* selak arep olèh ḍuwit.*

He can hardly wait to collect his money. **ñ(j)/di*-*** to hurry smn. *Kowé kuwi kok njusu-njusu aku waé.* Don't keep rushing me! *Olèhé njambut gawé adja di*-*.* Don't hurry him while he's working.

susud to shrink, shrivel, become decreased in size. *Awaké * kétok kuru.* He has an emaciated look. **ñ(j)/di*aké** to decrease the size of

susuh nest; breeding place. ** manuk* bird's nest. *Uwuh iku dadi *ing lelara.* Garbage is a breeding ground for disease germs. **ñ(j)*** 1 to build a nest. 2 to hang onto things, never throw things away. **ñ(j)/di*i** to build a nest in. *Kamarku di*i tikus.* Mice built a nest in my room.

susuhunan *full form of* SUHUN

susuk 1 pancake turner, spatula. 2 change. *Aku ngekèki ḍuwit Rp 25 éntuk * Rp 5.* I paid with a 25-rupiah bill and got five rupiahs change. ***an** canal; artificial channel joining two bodies of water. **ñ(j)/di*i** to give smn change, make change. *** konḍé** a decorative horseshoe-shaped hairpin worn in ladies' coiled hair buns

susul ***an** a follow-up message, letter, *etc.*; a later addition. **ñ(j)/di*(i)** to follow smn later, to catch up with. *Kowé ḍisika, aku tak njusul.* You go ahead, I'll follow you (catch up with you). *Pak Djaja lagi ndjagong mantèn di* putrané.* Mr. Djaja was at a wedding when his son came [to tell him of an emergency]. **ñ(j)/di*i** 1 to send a letter after smn, or after an earlier letter, with additional information. 2 to touch up [a crafted object, *e.g.* with additional pieces *or* color]

susun ***an** arrangement, deployment. **ñ(j)/di*** to arrange and classify, sort out. *Bukuné di*.* He organized the books.

susup **ka*an** to get entered. *ke*an komunis* infiltrated by communists. **ñ(j)/di*** to seep in; to work one's way into/through/under. *Malingé nusup ngisor pager.* The thief squeezed under the fence. **ñ(j)/di*aké** to push sth into/through/under. **ñ(j)/di*i** to insert into; to infiltrate

susur *ng kr,* **panasar** *ki* chewing tobacco; tobacco mixed into betel-chewing preparation. ***an** a chew (as above). *sa (rong, lsp.) *an* one (two, *etc.*) chews. **ñ(j)*** 1 to chew tobacco. 2 *ng kr only* to wax thread to prevent it from snarling. *See also* SASAR

su:t (to use) an informal means of settling things (*see* UM-PING-SUT). *Ajo *, sing menang éntuk.* Let's do *sut* for it–the winner gets it.

suta 1 *oj* child. 2 *theoretical person. Si * lan Si Naja* A and B; John Doe and Richard Roe. **se*** to give birth

suṭang the hind (jumping) legs of jointed-leg insects, *e.g.* locusts, crickets

sutâpâ *oj* holy hermit. **ka*n** knowledge pertaining to priesthood. *See also* TAPA

suṭik unwilling, reluctant. *Jèn kowé * reged tanganmu ja ora kelakon ndandani mesiné.* If you're not willing to get your hands dirty you can't fix the engine.

sutji 1 pure, without moral blemish. 2 holy, sacred. **se*** to cleanse and purify oneself before praying. **ka*an** *or* **ka*ǹ** purity; virginity. **ñ(j)/di*kàké** to purify, make clean/pure. **ñ(j)/di*ǹi** to wash and cleanse [a corpse] before burial. **s·um·utji-*** to engage in *or* commit oneself to holy practices. *** murni** pure, unblemished

sutra silk fabric. *** réjon** rayon

sutresna one who loves. *para ** our readers, *i.e.* those who love to read what we write. *See also* TRESNA

suṭup almond-eyed

suṭur *var of* SUṬUP

su'un *var of* SO'UN

su(w)- *see also under* SU-, SW- (*Introduction, 2.9.7*)

suwab a bribe. ***an** bribery. **ñj/di*i** to bribe

suwadi *ng,* **suwados** *kr* ***né** 1 it is advisable. **né matjan kuwi dipatèni waé.* The tiger had better be killed. 2 the reason why. **né ḍèké kerep nesu iku merga lagi susah.* The reason he is short-tempered just now is that he is grieving. **dudu *né** extraordinary, unusual

suwados *kr for* SUWADI

suwak **ñj/di*** to discontinue, put out of use. *Panggonan adol tjandu akèh sing di*.* Many places that sold opium have closed down. *Bareng kita wis merdika, basa Djepang di*.* After we became a republic, the Japanese language went out of use [in Indonesia].

suwal 1 *var of* SOAL. 2 *rg var of* SRUWAL

suwâlâ 1 to move. *Aku ora bisa *.* I couldn't budge. 2 to argue, disagree. 3 *oj* to disobey. **ñj/di*ni** to disobey *or* defy smn

suwalik on the contrary, on the other hand, in contrast. *Suwaliké aku ḍéwé ngrumangsani jèn luput.* But I felt that *I* was the one who was wrong. *See also* WALIK

suwangan mouth of a river
suwaos a certain alloy (*sbst? kr for* SUWASA)
suwap mouthful. *sa** a mouthful. *Gadjihé mung bisa kanggo tuku sega sa**. His salary is pretty small.
suwari ostrich (*var of* KASWARI)
suwâsâ *ng,* **suwaos** *sbst? kr* a gold-colored copper-zinc alloy. ***n** an imitation of this alloy, used in making cheap jewelry. *** bubul** low-quality *suwasa*
suwau *oj* formerly; before now
suwâwâ **ñj/di*** to treat lightly; to disregard. *Jèn wis ngamuk ora kena di**. When he loses control of himself, he's not to be laughed off.
suwawi 1 come on! let's...! (*kr for* AJO). 2 here! take it! (*kr for* NJA, NJOH)
suwé *ng,* **dangu** *kr* (a) long (time). *Wis * ora ketemu.* I haven't seen you for ages. *Ḍèké lunga rada **. He was gone for quite a while. *ora* (*let*) * pretty soon, before long. ***né** the (length of) time. *Sepira *né?* How long does it take? **né seminggu.* It lasted a week. *bareng wis sawetara *né* after a while. ***ning *** eventually. *Banju sing ana ing tong iku suwéning suwé bisa entèk.* Sooner or later, the water will be all gone from the barrel. **-*** after a while; eventually. **-* désané kétok.* At last they came in sight of the village. **ke*ǹ** (for) an excessively long time. *Rada wis kesuwèn ora sandjan²an kok.* We haven't been to see each other for such a long time! **ñj*** to use up time. *Njambut-gawéné saja njuwé.* He takes longer all the time to do his work. **ñj/di·se*** to make sth last an unnecessarily long time. *njenjuwé olèhé njambut gawé* to dawdle at one's work. *Olèhé guneman marang manḍoré dise**. He prolonged his conversation with the foreman [*e.g.* to annoy smn by keeping him waiting]. **ñj/di*k̀aké** to take a long time at. *Olèhé mangan disuwèkaké.* He took his time about eating. **ñj/di*ǹi** to make sth take long(er). *Adja ngadjak tjah tjilik, nḍak njuwèni laku.* Don't take a child with you, it'll slow you down. *Botjah iki njuwèn²i waé.* This boy delayed me terribly! **sa*né** while. *sa*né ana ing mantja negara* while he was abroad. **saja * saja** [ ] to keep getting [ ]er. *Saja * dalané saja munggah.* The path rose higher and higher. *See also* UWÈN
suwèk 1 ripped. ** rodjah-radjèh* torn to ribbons. *Sarungku * njangkem kodok.* My sarong has a three-cornered tear in it. 2 a torn-off piece. *dluwang sa** a scrap of paper. ***an** torn. **an kertas²* torn scraps of paper. **ñj/di*-*** to tear to pieces. **ñj/di*aké** to tear sth accidentally. **ñj/di*(i)** to tear. *njuwèk goḍong geḍang* to tear (up) banana leaves. *ptg* **s·r·uwèk** torn to shreds. *Sanḍangané ptg sruwèk.* His clothes are in rags.
suwel **ñj/di*aké** to tuck in. *Wironé djarit ditekuk di*aké munggah.* She folded the plaits of her wraparound and tucked them high. *njuwelaké ḍuwit ana ing kanṭongané* to tuck some money into one's pocket
suweng 1 (**sengkang** *kr*) pierced-ear earring. 2 vacant (*kr for* SUWUNG). **(se)*an** (**[se]sengkang·an** *kr*) to wear *or* put on earrings. **ñj/di*i** (**ñj/dipun·sengkang·i** *kr*) to put earrings on smn. *** djemblok·an** earring set with a large diamond
suwèni *form of* SUWÉ. *See also* UDAN
suwidak *var of* SE·WIDAK
suwiké green frog's legs (Chinese delicacy)
suwing (having) a harelip
suwir ripped. *Goḍongé * tjilik²*. The leaf is torn to shreds. **ñj/di*(i)** to tear up. *Iwaké di*i tjilik²*. She tore the meat into fine shreds. **s·um·iwir** in small pieces. *Iwaké empuk semiwir.* The meat is so tender it's falling apart. *ptg* **s·(l)·uwir** all to pieces. *Pengangoné ptg **. His clothes are in rags. *Goḍongé ptg sluwir kena angin.* The wind ripped the leaves to shreds. *Wit tjemara kuwi goḍongé ptg sluwir.* The *tjemara* is an evergreen tree with long needles.
suwi:t tweet! (sound of a whistle)
suwita (*or* **ñj***) to live in the home of a prominent family in order to learn their manners, language, and style of living, and in return to serve them during this period. *Kèn Arok njuwita marang Tunggul Ametung.* Kèn Arok was in the service of Tunggul Ametung (as above). **ñj/di*kaké** to send [one's child] to live in smn's home (as above). *njuwitakaké anaké marang pijaji* to have one's child live in the home of prominent people. **ñj/di*ni** to live with and be in service to; to serve [a prominent person]. *nDara Pangéran Prabu di*ni wong² saka désa.* People from the village serve the Crown Prince. **pa*n** service in smn's home
suwiwi wing
suwuk [of music] to stop. *sa*ing genḍing* at the close of the melody. ***an 1** set of gamelan instruments alongside the *gong.*

*gong *an* set of small gongs within the box holding the large *gong.* 2 beat struck with the large *gong* to stop the music. 3 medical treatment by a medicine man consisting of incantations and blowing on the patient's head. **ñj/di*** 1 to stop [music]. *Sasmita²* *kendang iku kanggo mbukani lan njuwuk gending.* Drum signals are for starting and stopping the music. *njuwuk kempul* to interrupt smn who is talking. 2 to blow on smn's head as treatment of an illness. **ñj/di*aké** to have smn treated (as above) by a medicine man

suwun to ask for (*root form: ka for* DJALUK). *njuwun pangaksama* to apologize. *njuwun pamit* to say goodbye. *njuwun sèwu* I beg your pardon. *njuwun duka* I don't know (*oblique ki for* EMBUH). *Aku njuwun duwit marang ibu.* I asked my mother for some money. *Di*i obor bisaa madangi pepeteng.* They asked him for a torch to light up the darkness; *fig* they asked for advice to guide them. **ke*** thank you. **pa·ñj*an** *or* **pi·ñj*** 1 a request. 2 a prayer. *** ng·ampil** to borrow (*root form: ka for* SILIH). *** priksa/pirsa** to ask (*root form: ka for* TAKON). *See also* NUWUN

suwung *ng,* **suweng** *kr* empty, vacant, unoccupied, uninhabited. *Omahé *.* The house is empty (*i.e.* nobody is at home; *or* there is no tenant at present). *warung * nang alun²* a vacant shop on the square. *Atiné *.* Her heart felt empty. **ñj/di*aké** to vacate, clear out of, evacuate. *Lapangané di*aké mergané arep dienggo latihan mbedil.* They cleared the field for use as a rifle range. *** blung** completely empty, without a soul in it

suwur *see* KASUWUR, MISUWUR

sw- *see also under* SU(W)- (*Introduction, 2.9.7*)

swa- self- (*compounding element: see main entries below*)

swabâwâ *oj* sound, noise

swadajā self-help

swadèsi self-sufficient, self-supporting. *wong ngamantja ** self-supporting foreigners. *Rakjat Indonesia iku wektu iki lagi gandrung *.* The Indonesian people at this time are concerned with becoming self-sufficient.

swah *oj* sky, heavens

swajambârâ *var of* SAJABARA

swanten noise; voice (*kr for* SWARA)

swapradjā autonomy, self-rule

swârâ *ng,* **swanten** *kr* 1 noise, sound. **ning montor mabur* the sound of an airplane. 2 voice. **né pait madu.* She has a melodious voice. **né turut usuk.* His voice carries well. *Gedé *né.* He has a deep voice; *fig* He talks boastfully. *adu ** to argue. *adol ** to show off one's singing voice; to cheat smn with fast talking. *angon ** to sing just for the pleasure of it. *ngumbar ** to say whatever comes into one's head without stopping to think first. 3 a voice in sth; opinion; vote. *Sapa sing éntuk * akèh déwé?* Who got the most votes? *Swara² mau apa njoalaké?* Did these [conflicting] opinions raise any problems? 4 vowel sound *or* letter. *aksara manda-** semivowel (*W, J*). **ñj*** to make a sound; to speak. *Ora ditakoni ora apa kok njwara.* Nobody asked you anything, but you had to put in your two cents' worth! **ñj/di*kaké** to give voice to, express. *** ampang** 1 a light (singing) voice. 2 *gram* light consonant sound (*Introduction, 2.3*). *** anteb** *gram* heavy consonant sound (*Introduction, 2.3*). *** èntèng** *sms ** AMPANG *above.* *** irung** *gram* nasal sound

swarga 1 (**swargi** *rg kr*) heaven; the realm of God. 2 (**swargi** *ki*) the late..., deceased. ** éjang* my late grandfather. ***né wong** one's luck *or* fate, one's ups and downs. **ñj/di*kaké** to take solicitous care of, to pamper. *** nunut neraka katut** to share the good and the bad. *Wong wadon kuwi rak kena diumpamakaké * nunut neraka katut karo bodjoné.* The fortunes of a wife fluctuate with those of her husband.

swargâlokâ heavenly kingdom, the realm of the gods

swargi 1 deceased, the late... (*ki for* DJENAT, SWARGA). 2 heaven (*rg kr for* SWARGA)

swasambadā self-supporting, self-sufficient

swasânâ situation, circumstances. *Wis kétok rada semèlèh *né.* They seem to be pretty well settled in. *Kahanan mau kabèh nuwuhaké *né romantis.* All of the foregoing circumstances pointed to a romantic entanglement.

swastā private(ly owned). *perusahaan ** a privately owned business

swimpak̄ bathing suit, swimsuit

swuh *oj* destroyed, crushed

T

t (*prn* ṭé) *alphabetic letter*

ṭ (*prn* ṭé *or* ṭé *titik*) *alphabetic letter*

ta[a] *excl* 1 *invites agreement or comment. Pijé * kowé kuwi?* What's the matter with you, anyway? *Kaé omahé sapa *?* Whose house is that, hm? *Kowé saiki rak ja ora wedi *?* You're not scared now, are you? *Aku saguh, ija *?* I promised, didn't I? 2 *adds exclamatory emphasis. Mengko ḍisik *, adja kesusu.* Just a minute there! not so fast. *Ajo *, menjang sekolah.* Come *on*, let's go to school. **ora *** don't tell me...! *Ora * jèn semono akèhé.* No! it can't really be that much!

-ta[b] (**-nta** *after vowel*) *ltry* your. *anak·ta* your child. *putra·nta* your child

ta-, **ṭa-** *see also under* TE-, ṬE- (*Introduction, 2.9.2*)

ta'at devout, orthodox. *wong Muslim sing ** a devout Moslem. **ñ/di*(i)** to obey. *Perintahé kudu di*i.* The order must be obeyed.

tab ***-*an** to thump (*of the heart, under emotional stress*). *Aku *-*an krungu suara beḍil mau.* I was scared when I heard the gun go off. **nge/di*** to urge on a horse by kicking it in the belly. **nge/di*aké** to knock sth against sth. *See also* KETAB

tabag bamboo building board. **ñ* 1** to make a bamboo board. 2 (*psv* **di***) to build with bamboo boards. *Omahé di*.* He put bamboo walls on his house.

tabah strong, resolute. **ñ/di*aké** to try to face up to sth with strength/resolution. *Wis di*aké nanging meksa ora kuat.* She's done her best to face it courageously, but it's hard to bear.

tabé *var of* TABIK

tabèl table (*e.g.* of figures, facts)

tabel 1 [of face] puffy, swollen. *Merga biḍuren raiku krasa *.* I have a rash that makes my face feel swollen. 2 headstrong

taberi assiduous, diligent. **ka*ǹ** diligence. **ñ/di*ǹi** to apply oneself to sth with diligence. *Ali neberèni olèhé njambut gawé.* Ali worked hard.

tabet remains, trace mark (*kr for* TAPAK, TILAS?). *Iki * apa?* What was in this [unwashed container], *i.e.* what is this the remains of? ** tatu* scar. *tanpa ** without a trace. *Katresnané wis ora ana *é.* Her love has faded without leaving a trace. **ñ*** to leave traces, make a mark. *Kopiné nabet ana ing gelas.* There are traces of coffee in the glass. **ñ/di*i** to leave traces on sth

tabib healer, one who treats ailments (*usu.* Arabic *or* Indian)

tabik Occidental-style greeting (*e.g.* a wave of the hand, a "hello"). ***an** to shake hands. **ñ/di*i** to greet smn. *A nabiki B.* A said "Hi!" to B.

tabir *var of* TAKBIR

tabit *var of* TABIB

tablag *rg var of* TABAG

tablas 1 [cut *or* pierced] all the way through. 2 all used up. **ñ/di*aké 1** to cut/pierce through. 2 to finish, use all of. *Ḍèké nablasaké tumpukan blabag.* He used the whole pile of lumber.

tablèg *rg var of* TABAG

tableg *rg* dike. **ñ/di* 1** to build a dike of earth. 2 to fill a hole with earth

tablèt pill, capsule

tablig Islamic sermon

tabok width of the palm of the hand (used as a measure). *sa** one palm's-width. **ñ/di*(i)** to slap smn. **nabok ñj·silih tangan** to strike at smn through another person

tabon 1 the oldest. *bodjo ** legal (*i.e.* first) wife. *désa ** village where the head of the village complex resides. 2 coconut-shell fiber

tabrak ***an** involved in a collision. **ke*** to get run into *or* get hit (by). *ketabrak* *montor* to get hit by a car. **ñ/di*** to run into, collide with

tabuh mallet *or* hammer for striking percussion instruments. **(te)*an 1** percussion instrument. 2 the playing of [gamelan music]. **ñ/di* 1** to play [a percussion instrument]. 2 to persuade *or* induce smn to talk. *Ḍèké tansah tjrita bab karangan²é, sanadjan ora di**. He's always talking about his writing, without waiting to be asked. **ñ/di*i** to play music for [sth, as an accompaniment]

tâḍâ iron *or* wooden peg for holding roof sections in place

taḍah 1 container for catching sth from above. ** banju udan* receptacle for catching rain water. 2 capacity, consumption. **é tikel sepuluh karo *mu.* He can eat ten times as much as you can. *Negara mau akèh *é wesi.* This nation consumes large amounts of iron. ***an** act *or* way of catching sth from above. *sawah *an* rice paddy irrigated by rain water. *barang *an* stolen goods. **ñ* 1** [palms] facing up. *Tangané naḍah.* She held her hands palms up. 2 (*psv* **di***) to put into smn's hands. *Aku di* beras sepuluh kilo.* I was given ten kilograms of rice. 3 to become addicted. **ñ/di*aké** to use sth for catching. *Èmbèré di*aké banju udan.* He placed the bucket to catch rain water. **ñ/di*i** to catch from above. *Kowé sing njènggèt, aku sing naḍahi.* You knock the fruits from the tree and I'll catch them. *Arang sing kuwawa naḍahi.* Few could have borne such a blow. **pa*an** receptacle for storing clothes *or* finery. *** amin 1** to say "amen" with the hands before the face in Moslem praying style. 2 to follow the crowd, do sth just because others do. *** duka** to give vent to one's anger. *** kringet** T-shirt. *** sih** a variety of bird. *** sirah** pillow. *** udan 1** rice paddy irrigated by rainfall. 2 top bunch of bananas on the tree

tadjem 1 sharp, cutting. 2 weight for a balance scale. **ñ/di*i** to sharpen, hone

tadji sharp blade attached to the attacking part of a fighting animal for contests, *e.g.* a game cock's spurs. ***ǹ** the sharpened tip of a kite. **ñ/di* 1** to attack with a sharpened part, *e.g.* kite tip (in a contest); game cock's spur blades. 2 to accuse one's accuser

tadjin thickened water in which rice was boiled. **ñ*** to make such liquid into porridge. **ñ/di*i** to skim the liquid from [boiling rice]

tadjug in the shape of a four-sided pyramid with a leveled-off top [of roofs; of polished gems]

taèk 1 feces (*inf var of* TAI). 2 (*cr*) *term of abuse or deprecation. *, nèk kowé bisa ngalahaké Bedja olèhé balapan.* Why, you–! as if you could beat Bedja in a race. **ñ*** *cr* to move the bowels

tafsir *var of* TAPSIR

tag ***-*an** one who does things only when threatened. **nge/di*** to get *or* keep after smn to do sth. *See also* ATAG

tâgâ animal. *walang ** crawling animals as a class. *kutu² walang a** all animate creatures

tagèh a certain freshwater fish

tagih *var of* TAGÈH. ***an** payment on/of a debt. *ḍuwit *an* money paid. *lajang *an* dunning letter. **ka*an** addicted to. *ke*an njerèt* addicted to opium-smoking. **ñ/di*(i)** to demand payment of a debt. *Utangku wis di**. He asked for the money I owe him. *nagih pati* to avenge a death. **ñ*i** habit-forming. *Tjandu kuwi nagihi.* Opium is addictive. **pa*an** written acknowledgment of indebtedness

tah *var of* TA[a], UTAWA

tahadjud to pray at a time other than one of the five daily Islamic prayer times: *usu.* for asking God to grant one sth

tahajul *var of* TAKAJUL

tahan to (with)stand, endure. *Aku * ora mangan telung dina.* I can fast for three days. *Ḍèké ora * weruh getih.* He can't stand the sight of blood. ***an 1** prisoner. 2 prison, jail. *kamar *an* detention room. 3 capable of enduring. *Ḍèké *an banget weruh getih.* She's quite able to stand the sight of blood. ***-*an** to try to out-endure each other. *Ajo, *-*an sapa sing kuat ora mangan telung dina.* Let's see if we can both fast for three days. **ñ/di* 1** to restrain. *Sanadyan mangkel olèhé nesu di**. He was resentful but didn't show it. *Aku di* kantjaku ora éntuk mulih sebab arep dikèki mangan awan.* My friend wouldn't let me go home–he wanted me to have lunch with him. *nahan ora mangan telung dina* to impose a three-day fast on oneself. *Malingé di**. The thief was arrested. **ñ/di*-*(aké)** to force oneself to endure sth. *Olèhé njirik* *ujah di*-*aké supaja mari lelarané.* He had to refrain from eating salt in order to get over his illness.

tahdjud *var of* TAHADJUD

tahjat a prayer; praise to God

tahjul *var of* TAHJAT

tahlil group Islamic prayer uttered in unison. ***an** to utter a prayer in this way. **ṅ/di*aké** to pray for smn in unison. *Wong[2] paḍa nahlilaké pradjurit sing tiwas ana paperangan mau.* People are praying for the soldiers who died in battle.

ṭah-ṭuh *see* ṬUH

tahu bean cake, bean curd. *** sama *** (*abbr:* **T.S.T.**) [to do] for each other's mutual benefit though extralegally, *e.g.* to connive through bribery or kickbacks

tahun *var of* TAUN

tai 1 (**tindja** *ki*) feces. *dibetjiki mbalang ** good is repaid with evil. 2 rust. 3 sawdust. ***ṅ** sawdust. ***nen** 1 to move the bowels. 2 to get rusty. **te*** rust. **ṅ*** 1 (**ṅ·tindja** *kr*) to move the bowels. 2 to rust. 3 to give birth to kittens. *Kutjingé nai lima.* The cat had five kittens. *** manuk** 1 bird lime. 2 lime (*euph var of* ENDJET). *See also* TAÈK

tajub ***an** a Javanese social dance in which professional females dance and from time to time ask spectators to dance with them. **ṅ/di*** to dance with a professional female dancer as above. *Ḍèké lagi di* Ali.* Ali is dancing with her now. **ṅ*an** *sms* *AN

tajum mildew. ***an** *or* ***en** to mildew

tajung ***an** a walking step in the classical dance

tak- *ng,* **kula** *kr* *prefix denoting first person singular.* 1 *psv prefix* [done] by me. *Rotiné * pangan.* I ate the cake. *Ḍuwité arep * tukokaké klambi.* I'm going to buy some clothes with the money. 2 *ng only* (*or* **aku ***) *acv optative prefix* I guess I'll... *Aku * mangan.* I guess I'll eat now. ** ngréwangi kantjaku.* I'll just give my friend a hand there. ** taberi karebèn bisa munggah.* I'll study hard so I'll be promoted. *Aku * nggolèkaké tamba aḍimu menjang ḍokteran.* I'll go get your brother some medicine at the hospital. 3 *first element of psv optative circumfix.* *La iki ana degan, * ombéné.* Here's some coconut juice–I'll just drink it. *Botjah[2] bèn ana kéné, * emongé.* Leave the children here; I'll look after them.

ṭak *rpr* a hard object striking a firm surface. *Watuné diuntjalaké ing bolongan mau, muni: *!* He threw the stone into the hole and it went *ṭak!* ***-*an** to move restlessly about disturbing others. *See also* ṬIK[a], ṬUK

takabur conceited, arrogant

takad able to endure pain and sorrow. **ṅ/di*aké** to steel oneself to endure afflictions

takajul superstition. *miturut ** according to superstitious belief. *kapertjajan marang ** belief in superstitions

takal *rg* hoisting device resembling a block-and-tackle

ṭakal **ke*an** to stumble frequently; *fig* to encounter difficulties. *Olèhku nggarap ja ke*an tenan.* I'm having a lot of trouble with my work.

ṭakar *var of* ṬAKAL

takbir to utter God's name in prayer. ***an** act of praying together communally. **ṅ/di*i** to utter certain Islamic prayers in group worship

takdir *var of* TEKDIR

takèk *var of* TAKÈN

takèn to ask (*kr for* TAKON)

taker ***an** 1 measurer. *Jèn tuku beras sing dienggo *an blèk.* When you buy rice, they measure it with a can. 2 amount measured; a measureful. *Jèn ditambahi sa*an tak kira tjukup.* One more canful [*or* other measure] will be enough. **dudu *(an)é** to not meet the standards of. *A dudu *ané B.* A is no match for B. *Jèn penggawéjan kaja ngono kuwi dudu *ané A.* Work like that is not challenging enough for A. **ṅ/di*** to measure in some kind of unit. *naker beras* to measure out rice with a can or other measure. **sa*** one unit of a measure

takir 1 small shallow banana-leaf container. 2 part of a wooden house frame. **ṅ/di*** to fashion [banana leaves] into a container. *** ponṭang** container made from young coconut leaves

tak̔jin certain, clearly established. *Nèk durung *, mbok adja terus ngarani ala.* Don't say anything bad about anyone unless you are sure of your ground. **ṅ/di*aké** to establish the truth of/about. *Pulisi wis nakjinaké menawa A sing njolong.* The police have established the fact that A is the thief.

ṭaklik **ṭoklak-*** loose-jointed; loosely attached

tak̔lim (to show) respect, honor, esteem. *basa ** respectful speech

takok *var of* TAKON

takon *ng,* **takèn** *kr* 1 (**n·dangu** *or* **m̈·punḍut-priksa** *ki,* **n̈j·suwun-priksa** *ka*) to ask (a question). *Tjoba tak * ḍisik ja.* Just a minute, I'll ask him. 2 to call into question. *Adja * dosa.* Don't deny your guilt! ***an** a question. ***-*an** *or* ***-t·in·akon** to ask each other questions. **n̈/di*aké** 1 to ask (about); to ask smn. *Ḍèké ditakokaké marang anaké.* They asked about her daughter. *nakokaké djenenging wong* to ask what smn's name is. 2 to ask for [smn's] hand in marriage. *A nakokaké anaké B.* A asked to marry B's daughter. **n̈/di*i** to question smn. *Aku nakoni, pijé?* I asked him how. **pi*(an)** (**pa·n·dangu·n̂** *ki*) a question. *tembung pi** (*gram*) interrogative word

taksi taxi

taksih still, even now (*kr for* ISIH)

taksir *var of* TEKSIR

ṭak-ṭek *see* ṬEK

taktik̄ tactic, strategem

ṭak-ṭik *see* ṬIK^{a}

ṭak-ṭik-ṭuk *see* ṬUK

ṭak-ṭuk *see* ṬUK

ṭakur ***-*** to paw; to dig with the hands *or* forefeet. *Djarané mbengingèh karo *-*.* The horse whinnied and pawed the ground. **n̈/di*(i)** to paw *or* claw at. *nakuri lemah* to claw at the earth

ṭakʻuṭak *var of* ṬAKUṬEK

ṭakʻuṭek̄ to keep trying. *Ḍèké * ndandani pit suwi ora dadi^{2}.* He worked at his bicycle for a long time trying to fix it, but he finally had to give it up.

ṭakʻuṭik *var of* ṬAKUṬEK

takwa Javanese-style men's jacket. ***n** to put on *or* wear the above

takwan 1 *oj* to ask. 2 *form of* TAKWA

tal a certain variety of palm tree; also, the fruits it produces

tal- *see also under* TL- (*Introduction, 2.9.3*)

tâlâ honeycomb

talad (there is) plenty of time, no need to hurry

talah a pity, a shame (*contracted from* JA TA ALLAH). *Ja * temen ta botjah apik kok dadi maling.* What a pity that such a fine boy should become a thief. *See also* TALIK

talak a form of divorce in which one spouse renounces the other orally three times before witnesses. **n̈/di*** to divorce [one's spouse] in this way. *See also* RUNTUH

talam *ng kr,* **panampan** *ki* serving tray

talang drainpipe; roof gutter. **n̈/di*(i)** to convey [liquid] through a pipe. *nalangi banju* to drain water off with a pipe. **n̈/di*i** 1 to furnish with a drainpipe. 2 *slang* to advance money. *Aku talangana balur tengiri.* Buy me some salt fish [and I'll pay you back later]. *** djiwa** to risk one's life for a cause. *** lumrah·é teles** a go-between gets a commission, of course. *** pati** *sms* * DJIWA. *** tjatur** an intermediary

ṭalang ***-*** [of long things] sticking out at the ends. *wong nggawa pring *-** a man carrying long bamboo sticks

taler sequence, order. *Tjrita iku tjeṭa *é.* The story has a clear(ly related) sequence of events. **isih ana *é** related by blood

tales taro. **n̈*** having the texture of cooked taro (*said of rice that is gummy from being cooked in too much water*)

tali *ng,* **tangsul** *kr* string, rope. ***n̂(an)** (**tangsul·an** *kr*) 1 act *or* way of tying. *Talènané kurang kentjeng.* It wasn't tied tight enough. *tjagak talénan kebo* a post for tethering kerbaus. 2 a tied bundle, *esp.* of harvested rice. *satalénan* one bundle (of rice plants). 3 twenty-five-cent coin (*see also* SETALI). **ke*** tied up; tethered. **n̈/di*k̀aké** to tie for smn. *A nalèkaké weḍusé B nang wit.* A tied B's goat to a tree for him. **n̈/di*ǹi** to tie sth. *nalèni sada* to bind coconut-leaf ribs into a broom. **se*** *see* SETALI. *** ari-ari** umbilical cord. *** banḍang** cavalryman's strap. *** gotji** balancing strings attached to a kite. *** mati** double knot, square knot. *** murda** suicide by hanging. *** pati** *sms* * MATI. *** puntir** a string wrapping which is wound but not tied. *** rasa** nerve. *** sepatu** shoelace. *** wangsul** bow knot or other easily untied knot

talib *rg* heaped-up sand at a riverbank or seashore. **n̈/di*aké** to fold sth around [an object] to cover *or* conceal it; *fig* to do sth under cover *or* in secret. **n̈/di*(i)** to cover *or* conceal sth by folding sth around it

taʻlik *** talah** a pledge uttered by a bridegroom to the effect that if he does not fulfill his duties his wife may divorce him

talika *oj* **ke*** to be seen; to show, appear

talimângsâ lapsing, expiration. **ka*** (to have gone) out of season; (to have) expired, lapsed. *Saiki wis ka* kanggo pelem, mulané regané larang banget.* The mango season is over, so they're expensive now. *Rèbewèsé wis ka*, kudu diganti anjar.* His driver's license has expired; he'll have to get a new one.

taling Javanese-script diacritical mark indicating the vowel *É*. * **tarung** diacritic indicating the vowel *O*. **ñ/di*(-tarung)** to mark [a character] with the above

talinga *oj* ear. ***n** ear (*ki for* KUPING)

taliwândâ *see* TJANTJUT

tallah *var of* TALAH

talok a certain tree that produces edible cherry-like fruits

talpa *see* MANTJA

talu 1 *wj* musical overture. 2 [of a shadow-play performance] to begin. *Djam setengah sanga wajangé **. The performance began at 8:30. **ma*-*** any number of times. *Beḍug muni ma*-**. The mosque drum sounded again and again.

talub Mongolian fold

talun a field which has no irrigation system and hence is planted only during the wet season. **pa*an** a mountain plain

tâmâ **ke*n** to get struck. *ke*n lara* to get sick, to catch a disease. *ke*n asmara* to fall in love at first sight. **ñ/di*kaké** to strike. *Gamané kanggo agar² baé, adja ditamakaké tenan.* The weapon should be just a deterrent–don't really use it. *See also* TUMAMA

tamah *oj* evil

taman ornamental garden. **(pa)*an** *sms **. * **déwasa** middle school. * **indria** kindergarten. * **madya** high school. * **sari** ornamental flower garden for recreational purposes. * **Siswa** name of a national private-school organization

tamat 1 over, finished; the end. *Jèn bab loro aku wis **. I've finished chapter two. 2 careful, detailed. *Olèhé ndeleng ali² mau * banget.* He examined the ring closely. ***an** to complete one's studies (at). *A *an Gadjah Mada.* A graduated from Gadjah Mada University. **ñ/di*aké** to scrutinize

tâmbâ *ng,* **djampi** *kr* medicine, treatment, remedy. *Tambané diombèkaké anaké.* She had her child take the medicine. *La kaé *né botjah nakal!* That's what you get for being naughty! *madal ** incurable. ***n-*nan** to treat; treatment [of an ailment]. *Lara pès iku angèl banget tamban²ané.* Plague is very difficult to cure. **te*** to take medicine. **mer*** *or* **mra*** to have medical treatment. *mertamba menjang ḍokteran* to go to the hospital for treatment. **ñ/di*kaké 1** to treat [a patient]. 2 to have smn treated. **ñ/di*ni** to treat [an ailment]. ** kanggo nambani mripat* eye medicine. * **arip** sth to keep one awake. * **kangen** sth to remember smn by. * **kepéngin** a cure for an addictive habit. * **teka lara lunga** medicine comes, illness goes! (*phrase chanted to a patient being given medicine*)

tambah increasingly; more and more. *Baṭiné penḍak sasi * terus.* His profits increase every month. ** lemu* to gain weight. *Saja * ributé.* He gets busier and busier. ***an** 1 an addition, a supplement. *Dina iki aku éntuk *an bajar kanggo Lebaran.* I got a Lebaran bonus today. 2 in addition (to the rest). *Dagangané rugi, *an kena perkara.* His business is slacking off, and on top of that he's slapped with a lawsuit. ***-*** *sms **. *Munḍak gedé anakku *-* nakalé.* My son gets naughtier the older he gets. **ka*an** to get sth added [to an existing amount *or* number]. *Aku ke*an tamu sidji manèh.* I've been assigned one more guest. **ñ/di*** to add sth (to) [the others]. *Tambaha.* Have another one! *Blandjaku di* Rp satus.* I got a 100-rupiah raise. **ñ/di*i** to supplement sth with, to add sth to. *Djangané di*i banju.* She put some water in the soup.

tambak 1 a pond near the shore where certain sea fish (*bandeng*) are cultivated. 2 a dike *or* dam for regulating water. **ñ/di*(i)** 1 to regulate the flow of. 2 to tackle a problem; to overcome an obstacle

tambal a mending patch. ** ban* tire patch. ***an** 1 act *or* way of patching. 2 (having been) patched. *klambi *an* a patched shirt. ***-*** 1 to put on a patch. **-* ban* to patch a tire. 2 full of patches. **ñ/di*aké** to have sth patched; to patch for smn. **ñ/di*(i)** to put a patch on. *Klambiku *en.* Patch my shirt! **nambal sulam** 1 to make small repairs. 2 to patch up a quarrel. *ptg* **t·r·ambal** full of patches. * **butuh** to make ends meet. *Kanggo * butuh ḍèké nèk soré dodol koran.* He sells evening papers to supplement his income. * **sulam** to do small repairs. *Dalané didandani * sulam.* They patched up the road. * **tepung** a gift of money *or* goods

tamban (*or* ***-***) (at) a snail's pace

tambang 1 rope. *tarik-tarikan ** or *perang ** (to have) a tug-of-war. *tjatjing ** tapeworm. 2 raft. ***an** boat fare; travel money in general. **ñ/di*** 1 to operate a raft. *Gèṭèké di* Suta.* Suta poled the raft. 2 to leave one's spouse but not divorce him/her. **ñ/di*aké** to take smn in a raft. *Djuru nambang ora* *gelem nambangaké jèn ora mbajar ḍisik.* The boatman wouldn't take them across unless they paid in advance. *See also* PANAMBANG

tambas to seep (through, out)

tambel (*or* ∗**an**) money *or* goods reserved for a rainy day. **ñ/di∗i** to set aside, reserve. ∗ **butuh** *sms* ∗

tambeng headstrong, obstinate. ∗ *kaja kebo* stubborn as an ox. ∗ **ḍenḍeng** *or* ∗ **(m)brengkelo** intensely stubborn

tambi 1 wide, flat tree roots growing above the ground. 2 *sbst kr for* TAMBA

tambir 1 broad shallow woven-bamboo bowl. 2 wooden *or* bamboo extension of the deck space of a barge or sampan. **ñ/di∗i** to provide [a boat] with such an extension

tambleg *var of* TABLEG

tâmbrâ an edible carp-like freshwater fish

tambuh 1 ignorant. 2 feigning ignorance *or* lack of interest. 3 *gram* negative. 4 (*or* ∗-∗) confused (about). ∗ *kantja karo mungsuh* unable to distinguish friend from foe. *∗-∗ solahé.* She acted bewildered. **ñ/di∗(i)** to pretend not to know *or* care about. **t·um·ambuh** feigning ignorance *or* lack of interest

tambur 1 drum (Occidental style). *∗é diunèkaké, ḍrèng ḍrèng ḍrèng.* They beat the drums, rat-a-tat-tat. 2 one of the Chinese playing cards (*kertu tjilik*). ∗**an** to play a drum for one's own amusement. **ñ/di∗** to beat [a drum]. **pa·ñ∗** 1 act of drumming. 2 a drummer. 3 small bullets; buckshot

tamèng shield. **te∗** protector; protection; a shield from harm. **ñ/di∗i** to use sth as a shield. ∗ **mata** eyelid

tami *sbst var of* TAMU

tamjang *oj* shield

tâmpâ *ng,* **tampi** *kr* 1 to receive, accept. *Sudagaré ∗ dagangan.* The dealer accepted the goods. *∗né ḍuwit pira?* How much money did he get? 2 to infer. *Sing diadjak guneman bisa ∗.* The person you're talking with can grasp the [obliquely expressed] meaning. *kliru ∗* or *salah ∗* to misunderstand, misinterpret. 3 (*ng kr*) *inf var of* TANPA. ∗**n(an ati)** touchy, sensitive. **ke∗(n)** to get accepted, taken, received. *Ḍèké nglamar gawéjan mau, ora ke∗.* He applied for the job but wasn't accepted. *Bal sing diuntjalaké ke∗n ing tangané.* He caught the thrown ball in his hands. **ñ/di∗kaké** to give, *i.e.* to cause to receive. *Kartjis ditampakaké, bandjur paḍa mlebu.* They gave him their tickets and went in. **ñ/di∗(ni)** to receive, accept. *Lamarané di∗.* His application was accepted. *nampa tamu* to receive a guest. *nampa tilpun* to get a phone call. *kirim lan nampani kabar kawat* to send and receive telegrams. **ñ/di∗ni** to catch. *nampani bal* to catch a ball. *Ḍèké tiba di∗ni masé.* He fell, and his brother caught him. **pa·ñ∗** understanding, grasp. *Kowé adja klèru panampa.* Don't misunderstand. *Apa panampamu pantjèn mengkono?* Is that really what you think?

tampah a large bamboo plate for serving communal meals, spreading foods for drying, tossing rice to separate the grains from the chaff

tampak ∗**an** seed bed. **ñ/di∗** to plant [seeds] in a seed bed

tampang 1 lead sinker for a fish net. 2 batch of shredded tobacco spread on a flat bamboo board ready to be made into a roll. *sa∗* one such batch of tobacco

tampar rope made of twisted fibers. (*lara*) ∗**en** (to have *or* get) a cramp in the calf muscle. **ñ/di∗** to make [fibers] into rope

tampeg **ke∗** to get a (*lit, fig*) slap in the face. *Aku krasa ke∗ atiku amarga ḍèké mblendjani djandjiné.* It was quite a blow when she didn't keep her promise to marry me. **ñ/di∗** 1 to slap smn in the face. 2 [of wind; *fig* of misfortunes] to buffet

tampèl **ñ/di∗** to slap smn on the hand, thigh, or elsewhere other than in the face or head

tampel **ñ/di∗** [of leeches] to pierce the skin and suck the blood

tamper fine-grained salt

tampi to receive, accept (*kr for* TAMPA)

tampik ∗**an** that which is avoided. *Ḍèké dadi ∗an ana ngendi-endi.* He was shunned wherever he went. *Panganan iki dadi ∗an.* Nobody will eat this food. **ñ/di∗** to avoid, shun, reject. *Ḍèwèké nampik pegawéjan mau.* He refuses to do the job. *Aku jakin jèn ḍèwèké mesṭi ora nampik aku.* I feel sure she won't turn me down.

tamping 1 object(s) used as a windbreak *or* rain shield. 2 boundary of a region. 3 steeply sloping sides (*e.g.* of a valley). 4 dike, dam. 5 (*or* **te∗**) village constable. **ñ/di∗** 1 to lay out [*esp.* rice paddies] at the edge of a slope so that the slope acts as a border. 2 to shape the eyebrows

tamplèk flat object for hitting. **ñ/di*** 1 to hit with such an object. *Laleré di*.* She swatted the fly. *Sapa saiki gilirané namplèk²?* Whose turn at bat is it now? 2 to treat rudely. *namplèk puluk* to act rude to smn who is offering sth; to bite the hand that feeds one

tampong **ñ/di*** to slap smn in the face

tampu 1 spattered with rain water. *Omahé *.* The house is wet with raindrops. 2 *var of* TAMPUH. **ke*n̂** to get spattered with rain water. *Bukuné ketampon.* The book got rained on. **ñ/di*n̂i** to spatter on(to). *Udané namponi buku.* The rain got the book wet.

tampuh *oj* clash, conflict

tampung protective shield, shelter. **ñ/di*** to protect, shelter. *Wong² sing arep ditransmigrasèkké di* nang asrama².* Those who are going to be resettled are being housed in dormitories (barracks).

tamtâmâ buck private

tamtu *formal var of* TEMTU

tamu guest, visitor; spectator. ** agung* important guest. *Dikeploki para *.* The audience applauded him. *nemoni ** to have company, receive guests. *kamar ** room where guests are received and entertained. ***-*an** to play "going visiting" (children). **te*** 1 guests, visitors; spectators. 2 (to pay) a visit. **te*an** to visit back and forth. **ke*an** *or* **ke*ñan** 1 to be visited, to have a guest come. 2 to receive an unwelcome visit. **ñ/di*n̂i** to visit, go to see. *Omahé sing ditamoni tjeḍak.* The house where he was visiting was close by. **pa*an** place where one visits; place where guests are received. **t·in·amu-*** to act formal. *See also* ḌAJOH, MERTAMU, M̈·PARA

tan 1 not; no (*shf of* DATAN). 2 without (*cf.* TANPA). *** ana** (there is/are) none, not any. *** antara** a moment later, soon afterward

tanag *var of* TANEG

tanah 1 land, country. 2 parcel of land. *Aku duwé * pekarangan ing Bantul.* I own a plot in Bantul. *tuan ** landlord. ***(an)é** 1 by nature, in character. *wong sing *ané sumèh* a friendly person. 2 in fact; it is true that... *Tanahé ḍèwèké nggemesaké.* (Yes,) he *is* annoying. *** air** mother country. *** asal** country of origin. *** atas angin** Asia. *** ḍarat·an** continent, mainland. *** Djawa** Java. *** mantja** *or* *** sabrang** foreign land, foreign country. *** wutah getih/rah** fatherland. *See also* SUR

tanapi *ltry* 1 and, also, in addition. 2 but

tânḍâ 1 sign, mark, indication. **né apa?* What does it indicate? *Apa *né jèn ḍèké pinter?* How can you tell he's smart? *Mengko jèn muni kloṭak, * jèn suwung.* If it makes a hollow sound, that'll show that it's empty. *Jèn ana ratjun mesṭi ana *-*né.* If there's any poison, there must be some signs of it. 2 a military rank. 3 village man in charge of the market. ***né** the evidence (of it) is... *Katoné akèh sing dipikir, *né lali nanggali lajangé.* He must have a lot on his mind—he forgot to mail his letter. **ke*** to be indicated. *Ḍèké mesṭi luwé, ke* olèhé nangis ora meneng².* His constant crying makes it look as if he's hungry. **ñ/di*** to signify. *Iki kanggo nanḍa apané?* What's this supposed to mean? **ñ/di*kaké** to show, indicate. *Botjah nangis terus nanḍakaké jèn luwé.* The child's constant crying shows he's hungry. **ñ/di*ni** 1 to mark sth. *Sapa sing nanḍani bukuku nganggo mangsi abang?* Who marked my book with red ink? 2 to be a sign of, to signify. ** abang nanḍani jèn kantja.* A red signal means he's on our side. *** jekti** proof, evidence. *** kurung** parentheses. *** mata** souvenir, memento. *** pa·m̈·pitjis** *or* *** pa·ñ·tanggap** tax receipt. *** pa·ñ·trima** receipt. *See also* PERTANḌA, TANḌA-TANGAN

tanḍak a professional female dancer who performs as an entertainer and can be paid to dance with a man as his partner. ***an** 1 act of dancing (as above). 2 to hold a ceremony *or* gathering where such dancing is performed. **ñ*** to dance with a female dancer (as above)

tandang 1 actions, behavior. **é kasar.* He acts crude. 2 to act. *Nèk ḍèké wis *, kabèh mesṭi bèrès.* When he goes into action, he put everything in good shape. *wong sing * ing filem* a film actor. 3 to come to the aid (of). *Jèn ana omah sing kobong, akèh wong sing *.* When a house catches fire, everyone rallies round to help. 4 *gram* passive optative form (*Introduction, 3.1.5.4*). **ke*an** to get tortured. **ñ/di*i (ng/di·asta·ni** *ki*) to do. *Aku arep nandangi ḍéwé.* I'll do it myself. *nandangi pegawéan* to do some work. *nandangi perang* to engage in war. **t·um·andang** 1 to do, behave, act. *A ora tau temandang kanṭi betjik.* A never behaves properly. 2 to engage in [an activity]. *Tukang potrèk kepulisian wis temandang tjekrak-tjekrèk motrèki.* The police photographer was already snapping pictures. *temandang gawé* to do a job. * **gawé** *or* * **solah** *or* * **tanduk** actions, behavior, conduct. * **tulung** to help people out

tanḍa-tangan *ng kr,* **tanḍa-asma** *or* **tapuk-ata** *ki* handwritten signature. **ñ/di*i** to sign. *Lajangé tak *i.* I signed the document. *See also* TANḌA, TANGAN

tanḍeg **ke*an** to have become amassed in large amounts. *ketanḍegan utang* swamped with debts. **ñ*** 1 to accumulate, pile up. 2 (*psv* **di***) to amass, accumulate [things]

tanḍes 1 deep down, to the bottom. *Keboné mangan tanduran nganti *.* The kerbau ate the plants right down the ground. *Manismu * ing atiku.* Your sweetness fills my heart. *Lemahé * ora ana wit²an.* The land is bare, there is no vegetation. 2 strong, firm. *Dalan mau wis kuwat *.* The road surface is hard. *Kanṭi * ngandika...* She said firmly... **ñ*** to mark deeply. *Olèhé nggaris nanḍes.* He drew a line bearing down heavily. **ñ/di*aké** 1 to make a deep mark with. *nanḍesaké paku sing dienggo nggaris* to scratch a deep line with a nail. 2 to emphasize

tanḍing 1 matched [against]. *A * karo B.* A opposed B. *prang ** hand-to-hand combat. 2 equally matched. *A * jèn perang karo B.* A can hold his own against B in combat. *pilih ** matchless, unequaled. *tan ** unevenly matched. **te*an** 1 match, contest. 2 proportion, ratio. *Te*an pira sidji lan sidjiné?* What is the proportion of each [ingredient *etc.*]? *Nem te*an karo sanga paḍa karo loro te*an telu.* The ratio between 6 and 9 is the same as between 2 and 3. **ñ/di*** to weigh alternatives. *Aku lagi nanḍing arep tuku pit utawa mesin djahit.* I'm trying to decide whether to buy a bicycle or a sewing machine. **ñ/di*aké** 1 to compare; to match one against the other. *Menawa di*aké karo Slamet, Bedja durung apa-apané.* Compared with Slamet, Bedjo isn't much. 2 to rival, compete against. **ñ/di*(i)** to oppose, fight against. **ñ/di*i** to equal, be a match for. *Kabèh adji²né A di*i ampuhé karo B.* B was able to equal all of A's magical powers. **pa*an** *or* **per*an** match, contest

tândjâ 1 sharp-pointed pole for making holes to plant seeds in. 2 having a worthwhile purpose, producing useful results. *Ḍuwit semono akèhé ora ana sing *.* Of all that money, none was spent for anything useful. *Wis dilakoni ngrekasa djebul ora *.* He's been working hard but has nothing to show for it. *Ḍèké lunga tanpa *.* He went off somewhere aimlessly. **ñ/di*** to make a hole with the above (1) tool. **ñ/di*kaké** 1 to use sth for making holes. *A nandjakaké pring mau.* A made a hole in the soil with the bamboo. 2 to put sth to good use. *A nandjakaké ḍuwité kanggo tuku omah.* A spent his money for a house. **t·um·andja** put to good use

tandjak a certain leaping move in the classical dance. ***an** point at which an upgrade levels off. *Manḍega ana *an kono.* Stop at the top of the rise. **ñ*** 1 to perform the above dance movement. 2 to rise sharply. *Dalané nandjak banget.* The road slopes steeply. *Reregan barang² wiwit nandjak.* Prices for goods are beginning to skyrocket.

tandjang **ñ/di*i** to intersperse old *or* existing plants with [newly planted ones]

tandjeb *var of* TANTJEB

tandjem **ñ/di*** to pierce, penetrate. **t·um·andjem** to have penetrated deep. *Péloré temandjem, mula nganti suwé operasiné.* The bullet was so deeply embedded that the operation took a long time.

tandjiḍor *var of* TANDJIḌUR

tandjiḍur 1 band music played to accompany a bridegroom on his way to the wedding ceremony. 2 a musician in such a band

tandjih **ñ/di*aké** to obtain verification *or* clarification *or* instructions regarding religious matters

tandjung 1 a certain large tree that bears small white fragrant blossoms. 2 cape, promontory, peninsula. 3 (*or* ***an**) the part of a man's wrapped headdress where the two folds meet, in the middle of the forehead. **ñ*** scented like the above blossoms

tanḍo to lay in supplies. *Jèn arep * beras kudu tuku saiki.* If you want to keep a supply of rice on hand, you'd better buy it now. ***n** stored supplies. **ñ/di*** to store up [*esp.* food] for future consumption. **pa·ñ*n** place where supplies are stored. **t·um·anḍo** laid away, set aside. *Beras kang temanḍo akèh banget.* Large amounts of rice were stored up.

tândrâ *oj* and then, after that

tanḍu stretcher-like conveyance for transporting things *or* persons. **ñ/di∗ 1** to carry sth on the above. 2 to temporarily transfer ownership of [one's rice paddy] to a debtor with the arrangement that the crop will be figured as payment. **di∗ koṭong** [of brides] to be carried on the arms of two people (as part of the traditional court wedding ceremony). **ñ/di∗k̂aké** to make a temporary transfer (as above) to smn. **pa·ñ∗n̂** one whose job is to carry food at the palace on a special conveyance (*below*). **∗ gantung** *or* **∗ lawak** *or* **∗ tjina** stretcher-like conveyance, carried by two bearers, for transporting food at the palace

tanduk 1 actions, behavior. *∗é alus.* She is very gracious. 2 manners, etiquette. 3 a second (or subsequent) helping (*kr? ki? for* IMBUH). *∗é nganti kaping telu.* He had three helpings of food. 4 *gram* active. *tembung krija ∗* active verb. **ñ/di∗** to try for sth. *Sing di∗ ora klakon.* He didn't succeed in what he tried for. **ñ/di∗aké** to apply, do, practice. *nandukaké piala* to do harm. *Pijé bisaku nandukaké basa Inggrisku?* How can I put my English to use? *nandukaké rasa welas* to experience feelings of pity. **ñ/di∗i 1** to react to. *Guneman kaja ngono kuwi ora perlu di∗i.* You needn't respond to such talk. 2 to give smn another helping. **sa∗é** everything one does. *Sa∗é mesṭi bener.* Everything she does is right. **t·um·anduk** active; in process. *Ana rasa aḍem sing temanduk ing awaké.* A cold feeling pervaded his body. *See also* TINDAK

tandur *ng,* **tanem** *ng? kr* to do the planting. *Olèhé ∗ pari sadurungé mangsa udan.* Rice is planted before the rainy season. **(te)∗an** plant(s), vegetation. *∗ané pari dipangan ama.* His rice plants were destroyed by crop pests. **ke∗an** to get planted by nature. *Lemahé ke∗an suket.* Grass sprang up on the soil. **ñ/di∗** to plant. *nandur sawah* to plant a rice paddy. *nandur wit geḍang* to plant a banana tree. **ñ/di∗i** to plant [a field] with sth. *Sawahé di∗i brambang.* The paddy was planted to onions. **t·in·andur** *ltry* to be planted. *Apa kang tinandur ésuk awoh soré.* What is planted in the morning bears fruit in the evening (*an allusion to the fertility of Javanese soil*).

tandya *var of* TANDRA

taneg left undisturbed for a long time. *ngGoḍogé kudu sing ∗, watara nem djam.* Boil it for a long time–about six hours. *Olèhé turu ∗.* He had a good long sleep.

tanem to plant (*ng? kr for* TANDUR)

tang pliers. **nge/di∗** to use pliers; to hold *or* twist sth with pliers

tangan hand (**asta** *ki*). *tangan tengen* right hand. *Lho kok ∗ kiwa!* What, using your left hand–! (*breach of etiquette for giving, receiving*). **∗an 1** imitation hand/arm. 2 arm rest. **ñ/di∗i 1** to hit smn with the hand. 2 (**ng/di·asta** *ki*) to do, accomplish. *Pegawéjan semana akèhé di∗i ḍéwé.* He did all that work by himself. **∗ dawa** light fingers. *Si ∗ Dawa* the pickpocket. **∗ keṭèk** a hand used readily by its owner for hitting. *See also* LUMAH

tangat *var of* TA'AT

tangawud an abbreviated prayer

tangèh remote from realization. *Jèn di-ḍukun²aké, ∗ warasé.* If you keep having the faith healer treat you, your recovery is a long way off. *∗ bisaku tekan rembulan.* I could *never* go to the moon!

tânggâ (**tanggi** *sbst? kr*) neighbor. *∗ désa* neighboring village. **∗n** neighborhood. *rukun* **(te)∗** neighborhood organization for mutual help. **te∗n 1** neighborhood. 2 to live near to. *Tetanggan karo A njenengaké.* It's nice to have A for a neighbor. **ñ∗** to visit the neighbors. **∗ teparo** (**tanggi tepalih** *sbst? kr*) one's neighbors

tanggah *var of* TANGGUH

tanggal (*abbr:* **tg., tgl.**) 1 date. *Iki ∗ pira?* What's the date today? *Dina iki ∗ pitulas.* Today is the 17th. *mapag ∗* or *meṭuk ∗* to have a monthly menstrual period. 2 beginning of the lunar month. *Wis ∗ kok rembulané durung kétok.* It's time for the new moon but it hasn't appeared yet. **ñ∗ sepisan** crescent-shaped like the new moon. **pa·ñ∗an** calendar; almanac. **t·um·anggal** [of the moon] new, waxing. *rembulan tumanggal* crescent-shaped. **∗ nom** the first third *or* half of the lunar month; the days following payday. *Isih ∗ nom kok wis ora duwé ḍuwit.* How come you're out of money so soon after payday? **∗ tuwa** the days of the waning moon; the time when people are often low on money

tanggap 1 responsive; interested, sympathetic. *Ḍèké ora ∗ ing sasmita.* He didn't respond to the signal. *Aku ∗ ing graita.* 2 *gram* passive. *∗ di-* a *di-* passive form.

(te)*an *wj* a hired performer. **ñ/di*** 1 to
ask for an account of sth. *Nanggapa ta.* Ask
him about it. 2 to ask [entertainers] to
perform. *A nanggap wajang.* A hired a wajang performance. **ñ/di*aké** to perform for
[smn, by request]. *A di*aké wajang.* A wajang performance was given for A. **ñ/di*i**
to respond *or* react (to). *A nanggapi omongané B.* A was very much interested in what
B had to say. *Prawan mau nanggapi karep-
krenteging lijan.* That girl responds to the
interests of others. **t·um·anggap** responsive,
sympathetic. *Aku weruh temanggapé A marang B.* I observed A's reaction to B.
* **sabda** published response to a published
article. * **warsa** a celebration held on the
first day of the new year

tanggel to vouch for; halfway between (*kr
for* TANGGUNG)

tanggem steel vise. **ñ/di*** to hold *or* clamp
in a vise

tanggèn dependable; firm (*kr for* TANGGON)

tanggenah **ñ/di*** to entrust smn with a task.
A di* tuku pari. A was assigned the job of
buying rice.

tanggi neighbor (*sbst? kr for* TANGGA)

tanggok *rg* a small cup-shaped container of
woven bamboo

tanggon *ng*, **tanggèn** *kr* dependable, trustworthy; firm, not yielding to pressure.
ñ/di*i to take it upon oneself (to); to pre-
sume (to)

tanggor **ke*** to meet up with; to collide
with inadvertently. *Roḍané ke* watu.* The
wheel hit a rock. *ke* alangan* to meet with
an obstacle. *Ḍèké ke* wong édan.* He was
face-to-face with a madman. **ñ/di*(i)** to
collide with, come up against. *Balé nanggor
saka gul.* The ball bounced off the goalpost.
nanggor perkara abot facing a hard problem

tanggrok *var of* TANGGOR

tangguh 1 dependable. **é panggarap* the
reliability of his work. *ketuwan ** having
the knowledge and judgment of a more mature person. 2 characteristic form of a kris
according to its period of manufacture.
ñ/di* 1 to postpone. *Adja sok nangguh
gawéjan.* Never put off work. 2 to depend
on. *ora kena di** unreliable. **ñ/di*aké** to
postpone. *Gawéan iki ora bisa di*aké.* This
work can't be put off. *Rapat dina iki di*-
aké nganti minggu ngarep.* Today's meeting has been rescheduled for next week.

ñ*i reliable. **t·um·angguh** postponed, left
undone. *Gawéjan sing temangguh wis di-
rampungaké.* He has now finished the work
he had put off.

tanggul earth dam built in rice paddies to
control the flow of water. **ñ/di*** to dam
up, hold back. **ñ/di*i** to provide [a paddy]
with earth dams

tanggulang wooden sluice gate. **ñ/di*i** to
combat, defend against, ward off, hold back
[an attack; *fig* a problem *or* difficulty]. *nanggulangi bebaja* to combat danger. *Rakjat
nanggulangi patjeklik sarana ngedekake lumbung désa.* The people provide against
famine by building up village rice supplies.

tanggung *ng*, **tanggel** *kr* 1 to vouch (for), accept responsibility (for). *Ora ilang ora, aku
! I won't lose it, I guarantee! 2 halfway
between, neither one nor the other. *Klambi
iki *, tak enggo ketjiliken, dienggo aḍiku kegeḍèn.* This shirt won't fit either of us: it's
too small for me and too big for my little
brother. *randa ** a widow of medium age,
i.e. too old to be likely to remarry but not
yet very old. **an* 1 guarantee, commitment. 2 security, pledge (*e.g.* for a loan).
3 responsibility, obligation. *Ḍèké duwé
an abot. He has heavy responsibilities.
- to hold back. *Adja *-*, aku kanḍakna
kabèh.* Don't keep anything in—tell me everything. *Jèn nulung betjiké ora perlu *-*.*
We should go all out to help them. *ke*an* 1
inadequate. *Adja ke*an anggonmu tetulung
menjang aku.* Be sure to give me all the help
I need. 2 to get interrupted partway
through. *Aku lagi ndandani pitku ke*an
kantjaku teka.* A friend stopped in while I
was in the middle of fixing my bicycle.
mer* *or* **mra*** halfway between; (only)
partway to the goal. *Ambèné mer*, jèn kanggo turu sidji kegeḍèn, jèn kanggo wong loro sesak.* This bed is too big for one person
to sleep in and too small for two. *Panganan
semono iku mer*, ora maregi.* That amount
of food isn't enough to satisfy the appetite.
Projèké mra* mergané ḍuwit wis entèk. The
project was abandoned in the middle because the funds were exhausted. *Aku agi
mer* njambut-gawé.* I'm right in the middle
of my work [and can't be interrupted]. **ñ***
1 to be partway through. *Aku agi nanggung
njambut-gawé, ora bisa nampani tilpun.*
I'm working, I can't talk on the phone now.
2 to stop before completion, not last to the

end. *Lakuné nanggung merga kentèkan ḍuwit.* He never got there; he ran out of money. *Olèhé mènèhi ḍuwit nanggung dienggo nonton bioskup.* He didn't give us enough money for the movie. *Jèn ditjiṭak nanggung ora dadi serai.* When it was printed it didn't even fill one page. **ñ/di*(i)** to take the responsibility for. *Apa² di* bebarengan.* We shared all the duties among ourselves. *Listriké aku sing nanggung.* I furnish the electricity. **nanggung ṁ·plorod·ing wuwung lan owah·ing sirap** to guard against misfortune. **pa·ñ*** sponsor, guarantor. *** djawab** (to take) responsibility. *Kamardikan iku nggawa kuwadjiban lan * djawab.* Freedom carries duties and obligations with it. *Ḍèké ora * djawab babar pisan.* She has no sense of responsibility. *** djiwa** life insurance. *** rènténg** mutual responsibility. *** urip·é** a hand-to-mouth living. *Uripé * mergané blandjané mung bisa kanggo seminggu.* He barely scratches a living; his [monthly] salary only lasts a week.

tanghulun *oj* I, me

tangi *ng kr,* **wungu** *ki* to get up (from a lying *or* sitting position); to wake up. **né rada kerinan.* He overslept. ***ǹ** easily awakened; a light sleeper. **ke*** to get waked up. **ñ*** to get smn up. *Nangi A ki angèl.* It's hard to wake A up. **ñ/di·te*** to awaken; *fig* to arouse. *Ḍèké ditetangi rasa méliké marang banḍané.* He was motivated by a desire to get hold of her money. **ñ/di*kaké** 1 to get smn up. 2 to lift smn from bed, *e.g.* a patient. 3 to arouse. *nangèkaké atiné* to stir smn's emotions

tangis *ng kr,* **muwun** *kr* crying, weeping. *suwarané ** the sound of crying. *udan ** a deluge of tears. ***an** 1 things cried over. *Apa sing dadi *an?* What are you crying about? 2 (*or* **te*an**) to pretend to cry. **ñ*** to cry, weep. **nongas-ñ*** **(muwun²** *ki***)** to keep crying. **ñ*an** to cry easily, be a crybaby. **ñ/di*i** to cry about sth. *Ḍèké nangisi matiné anaké.* He wept over his child's death.

tangkar 1 animal's breastbone. 2 to multiply, proliferate. ***an** 1 multiplication (arithmetic process). 2 product, *i.e.* the result of multiplying two numbers. **ñ/di*** to multiply [numbers]. **ñ/di*aké** 1 to breed [animals]. 2 to multiply [numbers]. **pa·ñ*** multiplier. **t·in·angkar** multiplicand. **(*-)t·um·angkar** to proliferate

tangkas swift-moving. *Ḍèké olèhé énḍa * banget mulané ora kena didjotos.* He dodges like lightning so he can't be hit.

tangkeb 1 a single unit made from two joined parts. ** gula* a pair of sugar cakes (with the flat sides together, rounded sides out); *fig* two things that are so close together they appear to be one. *roti sa** hamburger bun. *geḍang sa** two bunches of bananas: one from each side of the stalk, with complementary curving shapes. 2 overlapping portion of a double-breasted jacket. 3 attitude toward smn. **é marang wong rumaket.* He's friendly toward people. 4 one's grasp. **ing rasukan* a tight hold on smn's clothing. ***an** 1 paired. *gula *an* joined sugar cakes. 2 overlapping part of a double-breasted garment, or other objects that fold over each other. *djaring *an* bird net that folds over. *lawang *an* a set of double doors. **ñ*** [of matching objects] joined. *Tutupé nangkeb ana ing pantji.* The pan is covered (with its own lid). **ñ/di*aké** to join [matching things]. **ñ/di*(i)** to grasp, seize. *Pulisiné nangkep maling.* The police arrested the thief. **t·um·angkeb** joined, paired. *** pélas** a batik wraparound that is so short that its edges barely meet

tangkèk person in charge of a Chinese house of worship

tangki large fuel tank. *mobil ** tank truck. *sepur ** tank car on a railroad

tangkil a certain vine that produces oval-shaped fruits. *pari *an rg* a certain variety of rice plant. **ñ*** to hold a royal audience, to receive one's subjects. **pa·ñ*an** 1 hall where royal audiences are held. 2 *oj* throne. **t·in·angkil** [of a monarch] seated majestically for an audience

tangkis 1 flood-control dike along a riverbank. 2 shield, breastplate. **ñ/di*** to ward off. *nangkis serangan* to hold off an attack. **pa·ñ*** act of holding against attack. *penangkis serangan udara* machine-gun *or* antiaircraft missiles. *See also* BULU

ṭangkrèk *inf var of* PEṬANGKRÈK

ṭangkrik *inf var of* PEṬANGKRIK

ṭangkring *inf var of* PEṬANGKRING

ṭangkrok *inf var of* PEṬANGKROK

ṭangkrong *inf var of* PEṬANGKRONG

ṭangkruk *inf var of* PEṬANGKRUK

tangkur *** djaran** a certain ocean fish

tangled 1 to fight (*kr for* TARUNG). 2 to ask (*sbst kr for* TAKON). 3 *var of* TANGGUH

ṭanglung *-* supple, lithe, pliant
tangsang **ke*** to catch on sth, *esp.* when falling. *Lajangané ke* wit pelem.* The kite fell in a mango tree. **ñ/di*aké** to get sth caught in sth. *Sengadja A nangsangaké lajangan ana ing wit.* A deliberately got his kite lodged in a tree. **t·um·angsang** to catch, get stuck
tangsel carpenter's wedge
tangsi barracks. ***ǹ** **1** the spaces in a honeycomb. **2** a building with rooms for housing workers on a particular project
tangsul string, rope (*kr for* TALI). ***an** twenty-five-cent coin (*kr for* TALI·Ǹ(AN)). **se*** twenty-five cents (*kr for* SETALI)
tangtang *var of* TANTANG
tani **1** pertaining to farming. *wong ** farmer. *among ** (*ltry*) to engage in farming. **2** member of the village community who has the right to own farm land. **3** to engage in farming. *jèn arep ** if you want to be a farmer. **pa*ǹ** agriculture. *** bentil** *or* *** jutun** a true dedicated farmer
taning ***an** a mound made up of small loose objects heaped together. **ñ/di*-*** *or* **ñ/di*i** to gather [things] into little heaps. *A naning^2 sega dadi papat.* A made the rice into four mounds.
tank (*prn* **tèng**) tank
tanpa without, with no... *sega * lawuh* rice without accompanying foods. *Lakuné limang djam * lèrèn.* He walked five hours without stopping to rest. *** duga** [to do] without stopping to consider the consequences. *** gawé** no use, not useful. *Jèn ora dipangan, ja * gawé dimasak.* If it's not eaten, there's no use in having cooked it. *** larap** [to enter as a visitor] without being properly announced *or* escorted. *** tanḍing** *or* *** upama** unparalleled, incomparable, without equal. *Larangé * upama.* It's outrageously expensive. *** wilis** innumerable, countless; and so on and on
tanpasta toothpaste
tansâjâ *rg var of* SANGSAJA
tansah always, constantly. *Tjritané guruné * digagas.* They kept thinking about the story the teacher had told. *Lakuné bis * ménggak-ménggok.* The bus kept twisting and turning.
tantang ***an** dare, challenge. ***-*an** to dare each other. **ñ/di*** to challenge. *A nantang B arep diadjak gelut.* A challenged B to a fist fight. **pa·ñ*** **1** a challenge. **2** ultimatum
tante aunt (either blood aunt *or* courtesy aunt: *term commonly used among city dwellers and the middle and upper class*)
tanting **ñ/di*** **1** to estimate the weight of sth by hefting it in the hand. **2** to ask for a decision. *A nanting B bab gelem orané nglakoni panggawéjan mau.* A asked B whether or not he wanted the job.
tantjeb **1** tip of a pointed object used for piercing. **2** place where sth is stuck or (*fig*) belongs, stays. ***an** placing of puppets in their banana-log holder by their pointed sticks. ***ing langit** horizon. **ke*an** to get stuck accidentally. *Ḍaḍané ke*an péso.* The knife pierced his chest. **ñ*** sticking into, piercing. **ñ/di*aké** to stick/stab sth [into]. *A mantjebaké paku ing blabag.* A pounded a nail in the board. **ñ/di*i** to pierce sth. *Blabagé di*i paku.* They stuck nails in the board. **t·um·antjeb** sticking [into]. *Pakuné temantjeb ing wit.* The nail is sticking into the tree. *** kaju·ñ** *wj* conclusion of a shadow play, signalized by placing the Tree of Life puppet before the screen. *See also* MANTJEB
tantun to ask about smn's preference (*sbst? kr for* TARI)
taogé beansprout
taoké boss (*term for addressing a Chinese foreman*)
taotjo fermented soybean paste with split beans in it: a sauce ingredient
tap neatly arranged. ***-*an** **1** neatly arranged. **2** drained off. *lenga tap^{2}an* used oil. **nge/di*** **1** (*or* **nge/di*aké**) to arrange neatly. **2** to drain off [liquid]
tâpâ to withdraw to a secluded place and live in solitude for holy meditation, in order to purify one's being of all outside matters and concentrate the will toward a goal. ***n** act of meditating as above. **ñ/di*kaké** to meditate on smn's behalf as a means of achieving sth for him. **ñ/di*ni** to meditate for [a specific goal]. *Ardjuna napani ungguling Panḍawa.* Ardjuna devoted himself to solitary meditation so that the Pendawas would be victorious. *** m·bisu** to meditate without ever uttering a word. *** brata** to seclude oneself for meditation. *See also* PERTAPA, SUTAPA
tapak (**tabet** *kr?*) (*or* ***an**) trace, track, remainder. *Kesugihané saiki wis ora ana *é.* There is nothing left now of his wealth. **ñ/di*** to leave a mark. *Sikil sing napak*

mung sidji. There was only one set of footprints. **ň/di*aké** to put [*esp.* the foot] in *or* on. *Jèn napakaké sikil alon² supaja banjuné ora njiprat.* Step slowly so you won't splash. **ň/di*i 1** to leave a mark on. *Wédangé kuwi lambarana, mengko munḍak napaki médja.* Put a saucer under the tea, or it'll spot the table. 2 to track down. **t·um·apak** to start (into), embark upon. *Guru kang mauné paḍa mogok wis temapak gawé manèh.* The teachers who were on strike have gone back to work. *** asma** handwritten signature; **ň/di*-asma·ni** to sign (one's signature to). *** djalak** an *X* used as a signature. *** djempol** thumbprint (used as a signature by illiterates). *** dridji** fingerprint. *** sikil** footprint. *** tangan 1** hand print; 2 signature; **ň/di*-tangan·i** to affix one's signature to. *** tatu** scar. *** tilas** footprint; **ň/di*-tilas** to follow in smn's footsteps; to repeat smn else's experience. *napak tilas tindaké para leluhur* to follow the good example of one's forebears

tapak-dârâ 1 a certain flower. 2 *wj* wooden stand on which the banana-log holding the puppets is placed

tapak-liman a certain plant

tapakur *var of* TEPEKUR

tapang (*or* **ke***) a variety of tree

tapas leaf sheath covering the coconut blossom and young coconut

tapé a sweet food made from fermented sticky rice *or* cassava. *** *kaspa*** this food made with cassava. **ň/di*** to make [ingredients] into *tapé*

tapel 1 metal band for reinforcing box corners. 2 horseshoe. 3 **(raket·an *ki*)** poultice of herbs used for babies. *isih mambu ** very young and inexperienced. ***an** to have a poultice on. **ň/di* 1** to adhere to the body. *Lintah iku kéwan sing napel lan njerot getih.* Leeches attach themselves to the body and suck blood. 2 to solder sth. **ň/di*aké** to apply [external medication]. *Obaté di*aké botjah mau.* She rubbed the child with ointment. **ň/di*i 1** to reinforce with metal bands. 2 to apply a poultice to. 3 to shoe [a horse]. *** tratjak** horseshoe

tapel-wates boundary line. *** *kuṭa*** city limits. *** *Ngajodja lan Surakarta*** The Jogja-Solo boundary. **ň/di*i** to form a boundary (between). *Kali iki napel-watesi kuṭa A lan B.* This river marks the border between Cities A and B. *See also* WATES

tapi ***ǹ** grains (*esp.* rice) from which the chaff has been removed by tossing them in a broad, flat container. *beras tapèn* dechaffed rice. **ň/di*k̀aké** to treat rice as above for smn. **ň/di*ǹi** to de-chaff rice. *Olèhé napèni ana latar dadi ora ngregedi omah.* They do the rice in the yard, so it doesn't get the house dirty.

tapih 1 **(njamping *ki*)** ankle-length batik wraparound skirt worn by ladies. *gonḍèlan pontjoding ** or *kesasaban ** henpecked. 2 protective cover. ***an** to put on *or* wear a wraparound. **ň/di*i** to dress smn in a batik wraparound

tapioka tapioca

tapir tapir (animal)

tapis *nganti ** altogether, thoroughly. *Olèhé métani nganti *.* She did a thorough job of removing the lice. **ň/di*(aké)** to do thoroughly, do a complete job on. *Ḍèké napisaké enggoné métani.* She did a thorough job of picking the lice.

taplak tablecloth. *** *médja*** tablecloth. **ň/di*i** to cover with a tablecloth. *naplaki médja* to put a cloth on the table

tapsila *var of* TRAPSILA

tapsir (*or* ***an**) interpretation *or* commentary of documents, *esp.* the Koran. *** *Qur'an*** exegesis of the Koran. **ň/di*aké** to interpret *or* explicate sth. *nafsiraké Koran* to interpret the Koran. **ň/di*i** to provide commentary for. *Tjrita iki kudu di*i.* This story needs to be explicated.

tapsirih cone-shaped brass *or* silver container for betel leaves

tapuk 1 rope halter. 2 white "star" on a horse's brow. 3 performance of a masked dance. 4 to begin. *Wis * gawé.* The ceremony has started. **ň/di* 1** to put a halter on [an animal]. 2 to set to work on [a task]. **ň/di*aké** to begin sth. **ň/di*i** to slap smn. *napuk rai* to give smn a slap in the face (*lit, fit*); to insult smn publicly.

tapuk-âtâ handwritten signature (*ki for* TANḌA-TANGAN)

tapung to steam partially-cooked rice by placing it in a perforated container over boiling water. **ň*** to put partially cooked rice into such a container

tar *abbreviated form of* TARTJIS

tar- *see also under* TR- (*Introduction, 2.9.3*)

ṭar *rpr* a whip cracking

ṭar- *see also under* ṬR- (*Introduction, 2.9.3*)

târâ 1 between; interval (*shf of* ANTARA).

∗ mangsa or *mangsa ∗* between-season time, interval of change between wet and dry season. *saben ∗ mangsa* every six months. 2 interval between holy times. *dina ∗* the weekdays collectively excepting Friday, the Moslem holy day. *sasi ∗* the months collectively excepting Pasa, Besar, and Sawal

tarab menstruation; to menstruate (*ki for* KÈL). **∗(an)** *ng kr* ritual meal held at the time of a girl's first menstruation. *lemah ∗an* soil formation of sand and clay

tarak [that which is being] given up *or* avoided when subjecting oneself to ascetic conditions in the pursuit of an objective (*tapa*). **n̄/di∗i** to do without sth (as above). *A naraki mangan ujah.* A is giving up salt (as an act of self-abnegation). **∗ brata** to seclude oneself for meditation

tarang **n̄/di∗** to hang sth up to dry. **∗an** nesting place, *esp.* for poultry (*see also* PATARANGAN)

tarap aligned in rows

tarékah principles of behavior. *∗ Islam* behavioral principles taught by Islam

tarékat religious acts that bring one closer to God, according to Islamic principles (*e.g.* meditation, devotion to the ethical principles)

taret *var of* TARTJIS

tari *ng,* **taros** *kr* **∗ǹ** to ask for permission. *A tarèn bapa-bijungé.* A asked his parents if he could go. **∗(-∗)an** *ng kr* modern social dancing. **n̄/di∗(n̄i)** to ask about smn's preferences *or* wishes. *A nari B apa gelem balapan.* A asked B if he'd like to race. *mBok botjah² ditarèni gelem mèlu ora.* Ask the young people if they want to come along. **n̄/di∗-laki** to ask [a girl] if she wants to get married. **pa∗ǹ(an)** negotiator

tarih Islamic history

tarik **∗an** 1 a trailer. 2 contribution, donation. 3 a pull, tug, jerk. *Saben muni "hing" karo "breng" tiba sa∗an bebarengan.* Every time they said the words "*hing*" and "*breng*" [in the chant], they all pulled together. 4 (*or* **∗-∗an**) tug-of-war. **ke∗** 1 to get pulled, drawn. 2 (**ke·prana·n** *ki*) drawn (by), attracted (to), charmed (by). *Ḍèké ke∗ déning kahanan kuṭa.* He was engrossed in the activity of the city. **ke·torak-ke∗** to get pulled this way and that. **n̄/di∗** 1 to pull, draw. *Taliné di∗ sarosané.* He pulled the rope with all his might. *narik pedang* to draw a sword. *narik lotré* to participate in a lottery. 2 to collect [money]. *narik padjeg* to collect taxes. *Tontonané nganggo narik bajaran.* There's an entrance fee for the show. **n̄/di·torak-∗** to pull this way and that. *Sléndangé kok torak-tarik waé si!* Don't keep pulling your scarf around! **n̄/di·te∗** to attract, appeal to. *klambi sing nenarik ati* attractive clothes. *Atiku dite∗ déning sesawangan éndah.* All the beautiful sights enchant me. **pa·n̄∗** 1 act of collecting [money]. 2 one who collects [money]. *penarik padjeg* tax collector; tax collection

ṭarik **∗-∗** set out in neat rows. *Tanduran djagung ∗-∗.* The corn is planted in rows. *Kursiné wis ditata ∗-∗ djebulé ora sida kanggo.* The chairs were all neatly arranged but they weren't used after all.

taring rack for kitchen utensils

tarip rate, fare. *∗ bis* bus fare

tarka an accusation. **n̄/di∗** to accuse. *tinarka maling* (*ltry*) accused of being a thief

taros to ask about smn's preference (*kr for* TARI)

tart *var of* TARTJIS

ṭarṭir a little at a time. *∗ kaja manuk ngundjal* bit by bit, like a bird drinking

tartjis layer cake

ṭar-ṭur *see* ṬUR

tarub 1 decorations, *usu.* for a wedding, of young coconut leaves split lengthwise and hung at the entrance gate. 2 a temporary structure erected onto the front of a house for wedding festivities. **te∗** to put up the above (1, 2). **n̄/di∗i** to decorate as above. *narubi omah* to decorate a house with young coconut leaves

taruna a young adult

tarung *ng,* **tangled** *kr* to fight. *Keboné ∗.* The kerbaus locked horns. **n̄/di∗aké** to pit [one fighter] against [another]. *A narungaké pitiké mungsuh pitiké B.* A is having his fighting cock go against B's. **n̄/di∗i** to fight against [an opponent]. *Pitiké A narungi pitiké B.* A's fighting cock is doing battle with B's.

tarwèh *var of* TRAWÈH

tas 1 bag carried in the hand. 2 just now (*shf of* MENTAS). *Aku ∗ waé mangan.* I've just eaten.

tasak **n̄/di∗(-∗)** to go through [an area] in a courageous *or* heedless *or* foolhardy manner. *Ḍèké nasak kuburan.* He cut right across the graveyard!

tasan *inf var of* PENTAS·AN

tasawuf *var of* TASAWUP

tasawup esoteric knowledge of Islamic religious matters

tasbèh rosary, prayer-counting beads

tasih *inf var of* TAKSIH

tasik 1 powder (*ki for* PUPUR). 2 *oj* ocean

tâtâ 1 manners, good behavior. *weruh* * to mind one's manners. *murang* * or *tinggal* * lacking manners. 2 (to put) in an orderly arrangement. *Bareng kabèh wis* *... When everything was all set... * *ḍahar* to set the table, lay out a meal. * *baris* in marching formation. *Saiki wis bisa* *. Things are under control now. ***n** well-mannered. ***nan** 1 regulations, rules. *tatanan djaman perang* wartime regulations. *urip sarwa* **nan* a well regulated life. 2 protocol, established custom. *Lungguhé para utusan miturut* **nan.* The emissaries were seated in a prescribed arrangement. ***-*** to make preparations/ arrangements. *Ḍèké wiwit* *-* *arep buḍal menjang Djakarta.* He started getting ready to go to Djakarta. **ñ/di*(ni)** to arrange, put in order. *Bukuné di*.* He arranged his books. *Pirantiné wis ka* ana ing médja.* The tools were all laid out on the counter. *Kursi²né di*ni nang penḍapa.* The chairs are all set up in the hall. **ñ/di*ni** to set up/ out sth in [a place]. *Penḍapané di*ni ambengan.* Dishes had been laid out in the reception hall. **pa·ñ*** 1 act *or* way of arranging. *Bareng wis rampung penatané...* When the preparations were all finished... 2 administrator. *penata agama* religious official. *Pangkaté panata tingkat sidji.* His rank is first clerk. **sa*** all in place, all arranged. *Bareng wis sa* lingguh...* When everyone was seated... **t·um·ata** (having been) put in order. *Kahanané rada temata.* Things are pretty well under control. * **basa** grammar; social styles of speech. * **buku** bookkeeping, accounting. * **djalma** to speak like a human being. *Nang dongèng² kéwan² paḍa bisa tatadjalma.* In stories, animals can talk. * **gelar** to spread out, deploy [them]selves; arrangement, deployment. * **krama** (* **krami** *kr*) etiquette, proper social conduct. * **lair** the external aspects. *Manut* * *lair anggoné nemoni Prihati ija lumrah waé.* From what we can see, his meeting Prihati is nothing to fuss about. *Asu mau ngambus-ambus aku,* * *lahiré arep muni matur nuwun.* The dog sniffed at me; apparently he wanted to say thank you. * **pradja** public administration. * **prenah** genealogical relationship. * **rakit** 1 way, manner. *olah² lan* *-*rakit ḍeḍaharan* cooking and ways of serving. 2 team of two draft animals. * *raketing kebo* a pair of yoked kerbaus. 3 arrangement, layout. * *rakité omah* the layout of the house. * **susila** manners, etiquette. * **(titi) tentrem** peace and order. * **tjara** manners and customs. *See also* PERNATA

tatab **ke*** to bump into/against inadvertently. **ñ/di*** 1 to bump into, collide with. *Montoré natab wit.* The car ran into a tree. 2 to play [gamelan music]. *natab genḍing* to play a melody

tatag confident; composed. *Jèn madju udjian kudu* *. You should go to your exams confidently. **ñ/di*-*** to brace oneself for, face confidently. *Sarèhning wis kepèpèt, mula A bandjur natag²aké atiné.* Since there was no avoiding it, A steeled himself to it.

tatah chisel for working with non-metallic materials. ***an** chiseling, chiseled work (*esp.* of puppets). **ñ/di*** to cut *or* work with the above chisel, *esp.* for the delicate work on leather puppets. *ngGoné natah wajang lulang mau titi banget.* The leather puppet is intricately chiseled. **t·in·atah m·endat dj·in·ara mèntèr** supernaturally invulnerable. * **wegang** cutting or shaping tool used in a lathe

tatak ***an** 1 coaster, saucer. 2 concave stone block for cupboard legs, for holding insect repellent

tatal dry wood chip. ***(an)é** the wisdom acquired through experience. **ke*an** to be subjected to [an unpleasant experience]

tatap ***an** to hit against each other. *Pemandengku lan pemandengé* **an.* Our glances met. **ke*** to get bumped against sth. **ñ/di*** to hit (against). *Sirahku natab barang atos.* My head hit something hard.

tatar (*or* ***an**; *or, ltry,* **pa·ñ*an**) footholds *or* stepping places cut into a steep place (*e.g.* a cliff, a coconut-palm trunk) to enable one to climb it; *fig* steps upward (toward a goal)

tatas 1 clear, easily perceived. 2 to break, snap. 3 to break off, break loose. **ñ*** 1 (*psv* **di***) to break/snap sth. *Ḍaḍungé di* nganggo lading.* He slashed through the rope with a knife. 2 throughout. *sawengi natas* all night long. **pa·ñ*** commission on a real-estate transfer. * **ésuk** *or* * **ra(h)ina**

daybreak. *Olèhé nonton wajang nganti * raina.* He watched the shadow play till dawn. * **titis** [to discuss] exhaustively. * *titis pangrembugé.* They went into it from every angle.

taté *see* TAU

ṭaṭit lightning followed by thunder. *kesit kaja ** quick as a flash of lightning

tatu a wound, a cut; wounded. **né ditambani.* He put medicine on his cut. *Kowé * apa ora?* Did you get hurt? * *atiné* to have hurt feelings. **ke*n̂** to get wounded. *Sing diopèni ḍisik sing ketaton.* The wounded were attended to first. *kaja banṭèng ketaton* on the rampage. **n̈/di*n̂i** to injure, wound. *A ditatoni atiné karo B.* B hurt A's feelings.

tatur **n̈/di*** to hold [a child] in a semi-lying-back position, with one arm supporting him around the shoulders and the other under the knees (*usu.* so that he can urinate)

tau *ng,* **naté** *kr* 1 ever, at some time. *Apa kowé wis * weruh gambar iki?* Have you ever seen this picture? *Aku durung * weruh segara.* I've never seen the ocean. *Ḍèké mèh ora * lara.* He's almost never ill. *Guruku * kanḍa (jèn)...* Our teacher once said (that...). *Ora * sija² marang wong.* She's never mean to anyone. 2 (*or* **tau-taté** *ng kr*) to have [done] many times, to be quite used to. *Aku tau-taté njambut gawé.* I'm used to working.

tauchid Islamic theology

taun (*abbr*: **tn., thn.**) year. *Umuré rong *.* He's two years old. *se* sepisan* once a year. * *suwidak sanga* (the year) '69. **(te)*an** year after year. *Aku tampa ḍuwit *an.* I receive the money annually. *Olèhé nggarap nganti te*an.* They worked at it for years. **ke*an** superannuated. *Surat idin mau adja nganti ke*an.* Don't let your (annual) permit lapse. **n̈*** for a year; for years. *Patjeklikė naun.* The famine lasted all year. *Aku manggon nèng kéné wis naun.* I've lived here for years. * **Baru** the New Year. * **Djawa** 210-day year made up of 30 *wuku*'s (*see also* WINDU). * **hidjrah** 1 first year of the Moslem era. 2 year according to the Moslem calendar (= the Western year minus 622). * **Saka** *sms* * DJAWA. * **wastu** 354-day year (of which there are five in one *windu*). * **wuntu** 355-day year (three per *windu*). *See also* SETAUN

tau-rasā *excl of satisfaction at smn's similar discomfiture. Tau-rasa, saiki kowé ngerti ḍéwé pijé rasané wong disiksa.* Now *you* see what it feels like to be tortured!

tautjo *var of* TAOTJO

tâwâ *ng,* **tawi** *kr* 1 to peddle one's wares, calling them out. *Ḍèké *, "Lemper!"* He called, "Meat rolls (for sale)!" 2 to offer sth to smn. *Énak mangan ora *-*.* You're nice—eating and not offering any to us. 3 *ng kr* fresh (as contrasted with salt, brackish). *banju ** fresh water; plain water. **n̈/di*kaké** to offer sth for sale *or* use. *nawakaké dagangané* to peddle one's wares. *Djamé ditawakké pira?* At what price is he offering the watch? *Panggonanmu tawakna.* Offer him your seat. **n̈/di*ni** to offer without charge. *Tawanana lungguh.* Offer him a seat. *Di*ni ngombé, arep.* She offered him a drink and he accepted.

tawakal **ka*an** faith *or* trust in God

tawan ***an** enemy captive. **an perang* prisoner of war. **ke*** to get captured. **n̈/di*** to capture [an enemy]

tawang 1 *oj* sky; (up in) the air. 2 aspect, appearance. **é kok ringkih.* It looks very weak. **n̈/di*** 1 to stare (at). 2 (*or* **n̈/di*aké**) to look at [sth transparent *or* translucent] in a bright light. *nawangaké enḍog* to look at an egg by holding it up to the light to see if it is fresh

tawap a religious ritual performed by Moslem pilgrims

tawar 1 insipid; ineffectual. 2 immune to. * *ing wisa* unaffected by poison. 3 to peddle; to offer (*var of* TAWA). ***en** to have swelling of the legs after giving birth. **n̈/di*** to neutralize, counteract the effects of. *nawa ratjun* to counteract poison. **pa·n̈*** antidote; disinfectant

tawas alum crystals

ṭawé ***-*** to reach out with the hand to grasp sth. *See also* KEṬAWÉ

tawekal undiscouraged in the face of adversity

tawi to peddle; to offer (*kr for* TAWA)

tawing shield, cover, *esp.* as protection against the elements. * *témbok ḍuwur* a high protecting wall. **n̈/di*i** to protect, shield. * **lumah-kureb** (a dance characterized by) wild rolling head motions

tawon bee, wasp. **n̈*** bee-like, wasp-like. *nawon kemit* wasp-waisted. **t·um·awon** humming like a swarm of bees (*said of a busy marketplace*). * **ḍohan** honey bee.

* enḍas large bee that stings humans severely around the head. * gula honey bee. * kemit wasp. * madu honey bee. * suk hornet that builds a mud nest

tawu **ñ/di*** to deplete [water] by removing containerfuls of it. **ñ/di*ñi** to reduce the supply of water in. *Adja nawoni blumbang!* Don't run the fish pond dry!

tawur 1 to engage in a large-scale fight. 2 small coins ceremonially distributed among the poor. ***an** a general fight, a brawl

T.B.C. (*prn* **ṭé bé sé**) tuberculosis

T.C.D. (*prn* **ṭé sé ḍé**) vaccine against typhus-cholera-dysentery (*tipus-koléra-ḍisèntri*). *éntuk suntikan ** to get a TCD shot

té kebabs for sale! (*street peddlers' cry: shf of* SATÉ)

te-, ṭe- *see also under* TA-, ṬA- (*Introduction, 2.9.2*)

teba 1 gathering place for birds, animals. *ana ing ** away from home, going about from place to place, on the road. 2 scope, territory. *Paḍangé maḍangi sa*ning penḍapa.* The light lighted up the whole reception hall. *kurang *ning wawasan* having a limited outlook. *djembar *né* having wide influence; broad in scope. **ñ/di*** 1 to gather in [a place: of birds, animals]. *Sawah iku di* manuk.* Birds flock to rice paddies. 2 to go from place to place (*usu. referring to seasonal workers*)

tebah 1 width of the palm of the hand, as a unit of measurement. *sa** one palm-width. 2 *sbst var of* TEBIH. 3 (*or *-* or* **te***) to make (*i.e.* straighten out the bedding on) a bed. **ñ/di*** *rg* to slap, strike with the palm. **ñ/di*i** to make (up) [a bed]

tebak pair of bamboo sections to be used in building a wall. *sa** one such pair. **ñ/di*** 1 to leap and catch [*e.g.* a butterfly; a rolling coin]. 2 to clear [land] for cultivating, settling

tebal **ñ/di*** to dig out [a plant] together with the soil around its roots

tébang **ke*-*** *rpr* the sight of smn approaching. *Lha kaé si A wis ke*-* katon saka kadohan.* Here comes A, way off there!

tebang ***an** field from which the crop has been harvested. **ñ/di*** to harvest [plants, *esp.* sugar cane]. **pa·ñ*an** *tebu* season for cutting sugar cane

tebas ***an** fruits bought as a quantity lot while they are still on the tree. **ñ/di*** 1 to buy [a fruit crop] as above. 2 to buy in wholesale lots. 3 to contract for an entire job. **ñ/di*aké** to sell [fruits on the tree; wholesale lots]. **pa·ñ*** act of buying (as above). **t·um·ebas** available for purchase as a quantity lot

tebel 1 heavy-lidded. 2 thick

tebela *var of* TERBELA

tèbèng structure acting as a protective shelter against the elements

tebeng overhanging portion of a roof, or built-out part over a door or window, as protection against sun and rain. **ñ/di*i** to equip [a building] with such devices

tebes **ñ/di*** to prune, trim, cut back

tebih far-off (*kr for* ADOH, DOH)

tebijat character, nature, habit. **é èlèk.* He is of questionable character.

tebir *var of* TAKBIR

ṭèblung *see* ṬÉJOT

tébok bowl-shaped container of woven bamboo

tebok wooden *or* bamboo stick set into the ground as a marker or plant support. **ñ/di*** to set such a stick in place

tebon corn plant

tebu sugar cane (**ros·an** *kr*). ** telung londjor* three stalks of sugar cane. *tebu sa(e)ros* one piece (between joints) of sugar cane. *gilingan ** sugar mill. *banjuné ** sugar-cane liquid (for processing into sugar). ***ñ** land planted to sugar cane. **ñ*** (**ng·ros·an** *kr*) to plant sugar cane. **pa*ñ** (**pa·ros·an** *kr*) land planted to sugar cane

tebus **ñ/di*** to redeem [a pledge]; to buy sth back; to pay ransom for. **nebus beras mentah** willing(ness) to pay in money in lieu of fulfilling a promise to do sth. **pa·ñ*** redemption; ransom. *Panebusé ali²mu kapan?* When do you have to redeem your [pawned] ring? *Kanggo panebusé ḍèké kudu mbajar satus èwu rupijah.* He had to pay a ransom of a hundred thousand rupiahs. *panebus dosa* redemption from sin

teḍa 1 to ask for (*root form: kr for* DJALUK). 2 food, sth to eat (*kr for* PANGAN). 3 *ka, ltry* to give (*root form*). **ñ*** to eat (*kr for* M̈·PANGAN)

tedah to show, point (to/out) (*root form: kr for* TUDUH)

teḍak 1 to descend, move downward (*root form: ki for* ḌUN). 2 ancestor; descendant; to descend genealogically (*ki for* TURUN[a]). 3 *ki: applied only to a monarch* to leave court, *e.g.* for travel. 4 to copy (*root form: kr for* TURUN[b]). ∗**an** 1 a descendant (*ki for* TURUN·AN). 2 [of a monarch] to leave court. **ñ/di∗** 1 to cheat on a test. 2 [of crop pests] to destroy plants. **ñ/di∗i** 1 to approach, go to (*ki for* M̈/DI·PARAN·I). 2 to have sexual relations with [smn of lower status]. **t·um·eḍak** to descend, get off (*ki for* ME·DUN). ∗ **siti** to come in contact with the ground for the first time in one's life [of an infant, during a ritual ceremony held for the purpose of bringing about such contact]; ∗ **siti·ǹ** the portion of the ceremony in which the actual ground-touching occurs

teḍas able to pierce, damage; effectual for piercing, cutting. *Kajuné ora ∗ diiris péso.* The wood can't be cut with a knife. *Untuku ora ∗.* I can't chew. *Aku ora ∗ katjang.* I can't chew peanuts. *Panganan kuwi ora ∗ dimamah untuné.* He can't chew the food. *ora ∗ diobong* non-combustible. *Tèmbok iki ora ∗ dipaku.* Nails can't be pounded into this [hard-surfaced] wall. **ñ/di∗** to have a harmful effect on. *Sabuné neḍas tangan.* The soap irritates her hands. **ora ∗ tapak palu·ning panḍé, ora ∗ ing ge·gaman sisa·ning gurénda** magically invulnerable

tèḍèng 1 protective cover/shield. 2 hat brim. *ora/tanpa ∗ aling²* open, frank, candid. **ñ/di∗aké** to use sth as a (protective) cover. *Goḍongé di∗aké.* He covered it with the leaf. **ñ/di∗-∗(aké)** to expose, allow to be seen. *Ḍèwèké nèḍèng²aké klambiné.* He's not wearing anything over his shirt. **ñ/di∗i** to cover, protect. *Kembangé di∗i pepajonan.* The roof shelters the flowers.

teḍi *sbst var of* TEḌA

tédja 1 light beam/ray. 2 aura

tèdji thoroughbred horse

teḍuh *rg* 1 cloudy. 2 [of a storm] to subside

teḍun to go down, descend. **ke∗** 1 to get demoted. 2 to have a ruptured hernia. 3 to need to urinate frequently because of a pathological condition. **t·um·eḍun** *sms ∗*

teg *rg var of* TOG

ṭeg *rpr* a hit, blow. *Tikusé bandjur dipenṭung, ∗, mati sa'ekal.* He killed the mouse with one whack.

téga to be heartless enough (to...); to behave callously (toward). *Ḍèké ∗ weruh anaké lunga ḍéwé.* With an unfeeling heart he watched his son leave all alone. *Anaké katut ing lahar, ora ∗ ndeleng.* His child was swept away by the lava flow—he couldn't bear to look. **ñ/di∗kaké** to leave smn to his fate. *Muliha, aku tégakna baé!* Go on back home, let me struggle along by myself! *négakaké wong tuwa* to turn one's back on his parents in their time of need

tegak straight, upright. **ñ/di∗aké** to uphold; to hold upright. *negakaké hukum* to uphold the law. **pa·ñ∗** act of upholding

tegal *ng,* **tegil** *sbst? kr* dry (*i.e.* non-irrigated, non-terraced) agricultural land, used for crops other than rice. **ñ/di∗** 1 to convert [land] to such fields. 2 to plant [crops] in such fields. **pa∗an** dry farmland (as above)

tegang tight, tense. **ka∗an** tension, strain, strife. **ñ/di∗aké** to cause to be tight/tense. *Tontonané negangaké.* The show is full of suspense.

tegar (*or* ∗**an** *or* **te∗an**) to allow the horse one is riding to gallop as he pleases. **ñ∗** to gallop. **ñ/di∗aké** 1 to take a ride on [a horse]. 2 to have [a horse] trained *or* broken in. **ñ/di∗i** to train [a horse] for riding. **pa·ñ∗** professional horse trainer

tegaron a certain variety of tree

tegas clear, unambiguous, firm. *sikep ∗* an unequivocal attitude. *perkara sing tanpa ∗* a matter which is unsettled *or* up in the air. **ñ/di∗aké** to clarify. *Perkara iku kudi di∗aké.* The case has to be explained. **ñ/di∗i** to act firm toward. *Wis wantjiné negasi mungsuh.* The time has come for standing up the enemy firmly. **pa·ñ∗an** clarification, explanation

tégé deep basket of woven bamboo, used for storing fruits

tègel floor tile. **ñ/di∗** to lay floor tiles

tegel sufficiently insensitive [to...]. *Aku ora ∗ weruh botjah tjilik sing paḍa kaliren.* I can't bear to see children not getting enough to eat. *A ∗ njembelèh pitiké ḍéwé.* A can (bring himself to) slaughter his own chickens. **ñ/di∗i** to persist in [an action, without regard for others' feelings]. *A negeli B supaja mbajar utangé.* A hounded B for the money he owed him [in spite of B's poverty]. *Jèn di∗i ora dikèki mangan pitik kuwi mesṭi mati.* If you persist in not feeding the chickens, they'll die.

tegerang a certain wood from which yellow dye-making matter (used for batik work) is extracted

teges 1 meaning, significance, sense. *Apa ∗é?* What does it mean? *Omongané akèh* *tanpa* *. He talks a lot without making any sense. 2 goldsmith's mallet. ***an** 1 stub. * *rokok* cigarette stub. * *srutu* cigar butt. 2 curious, inquisitive. ***é** it means; that is (to say)... *R.R.I. *é Radio Républik Indonesia* the R.R.I., *i.e.* the national Indonesian radio. *Ukara iki *é mengkéné.* The sentence means the following... ***-*an** to try to convince each other. **a*** *sms* *É. **ñ*** to inquire, ask for information. **ñ*-ñ*** to inquire repeatedly. *Kok neges²*. Don't be so inquisitive! (*see also* NG·ROKOK). **ñ/di*aké** to explain the meaning (of) (to *or* for smn). *neges²aké tjara² Islam* to explain Islamic customs (to smn). **ñ/di*i** 1 to explain the meaning (of). *Tembung² mau di*i sidji².* He explained what the words meant one by one. *Ḍèké negesi sing ditulis ana lajang mau.* He interpreted what the letter said. 2 to convince smn

tegil dry field (*sbst? kr for* TEGAL)

tégong ***an** a winding road. **ñ*** to turn, veer. **négang-ñ*** to wind, to curve this way and that

tegor **ñ/di*** 1 to speak to smn in greeting. 2 to ask smn not to [do]. **ñ/di*aké** to cut down for smn. **ñ/di*(i)** to cut down [a tree] at the base of the trunk

tégos **ñ/di*** to cut sth in a skewed line instead of straight. *Olèhé nggunting négos menengen.* The line of her scissors cut veered way off to the right.

teguh sturdy, tough, determined (physically, morally). *nambahi *ing tékadé* increasing the firmness of his determination. *Jèn ora * atiné, bisa dadi wong mursal.* Without moral strength, you can go astray. **ka*an** supreme invulnerability; superior strength. **ñ/di*aké** to make firm/strong. *Ḍèké neguhaké djandjiné arep tuku omahé.* He stood behind his promise to buy the house. **ñ/di*i** to face sth with physical and moral fortitude. * **timbul** supernaturally invulnerable and highly esteemed

tèh tea. *wédang* * hot tea. *sénḍok* * teaspoon. *wit* * tea plant. *kebon* * tea plantation. **pa*an** 1 tea plantation. 2 place where tea and other drinks are prepared for a special occasion

tèhnik̄ 1 technology. 2 technique. *ahli* * technician. *sekolah* * technical school

tèhnis 1 pertaining to technology. *Soal²* * *ḍèké ora ngerti babar pisan.* He has no technical knowledge at all. 2 technically. * *A sing kuwasa.* Technically, A is the one in authority.

tèhnisi technician

tèjèng *cr* able to..., strong enough to...

ṭéjol exhausted

ṭéjot *-* *rpr* the croaking of frogs; *fig* a worthless opinion, a pointless remark. **ñ/di*** to pinch and twist flesh (punishment for children). * **ṭèblung** *or* * **tjèblung** *sms* *-*

tek̄ *var of* TOG

ṭèk 1 *rpr* the sound produced by striking a bamboo tube (*koṭèk*). 2 *rpr* a tapping *or* light knocking. 3 belonging to (*var of* DUWÈK). *Sing endi *mu?* Which one is yours? 4 *adr* monkey! (*shf of* KEṬÈK). ***-*an** invisible demon that makes a tapping noise. **nge/di*aké** to turn on [an appliance]. *Sapa sing ngeṭèkaké lampu?* Who turned on the light? *See also* ṬÈṬÈK

ṭek̄ 1 *rpr* a tapping sound. *Noṭok djenḍéla,* * * *. He rapped on the window. 2 *rpr* a quick action/motion. *Mak * ḍèké nemu akal.* All of a sudden he got an idea. *Iki kok gampang waé, mak *.* See how easy it is! 3 tsk! tsk! (*expression of disapproval*). 4 *rpr* the sound made with the tongue to urge a horse on. 5 grip, grasp. *Ṭeking ati sida lunga.* I have my heart set on going. ***an** a knock, tap. *Pakuné diṭuṭuk sa*an wis mblesek.* He gave the nail a quick blow and in it went. **ṭak̄-*** 1 (with) quick actions/motions. *Nèk mikir tjepet, ṭak-*.* He thinks fast. 2 to vacillate. *Nèk pantjèn nijat mbok wis mangkat, adja ṭak-*.* Once you've made up your mind to go, go–don't hem and haw. **sa* (kliwer)** one quick look. *Aku mau weruh sa*-kliwer montoré.* I caught a glimpse of his car. * **seg** *rpr* sudden inertness. *Diantem sepisan * sek.* He took one blow and was out cold. *Nèk turu * seg.* I dropped right off to sleep. *See also* KEṬEK

teka 1 (**ḍateng** *kr*, **rawuh** *or* **wijos** *ki*) 1 to come, arrive. **né djam pira?* What time is he coming? *Sugeng rawuhipun.* Welcome! *Apa bajiné wis *?* Has the baby been born yet? *Punapa sampun dangu ḍatengipun?* Have you been here long? 2 to go on, continue. *Perkara mau wis suwé * durung putus.* The case has been pending a long time with no verdict yet. 3 (*prn* **kok**) *excl: formal, written var of* KOK 1. 4 from (*var of* SAKA[a]). ***n** (**dugi, dumugi** *kr*) 1 (up) to, until. *wiwit katja sidji tekan katja limalas* from page 1 to page 15. *tekan djam sepuluh* until ten o'clock. *tekan pabrik* as far as the factory. 2 to get to, reach; upon reaching. *Ora antara suwé tekan ing kali.* Pretty soon he came to a river. *Tekan ngomah disrengeni.* When he reached home, he got bawled out. *-* *formal var of* KOK^b. **ke*n 1 (ke·ḍa-teng·an** *kr*) 1 to be visited. *Kula baḍé keḍatengan mara-sepuh kula.* My parents-in-law are coming to see us. *ketekan koléra* to be struck by a cholera epidemic. 2 **(ka·dumugi·ǹ** *kr*) to be brought to pass. *Muga² kekarepanmu bisa ketekan.* I hope your wish will come true. **(ne)ñ*** to come smw for the first time and remain permanently. *wong neneka* stranger, newly arrived settler. **ñ/di*kaké 1 (n/dipun·ḍateng·aken** *kr*, **ng/di·rawuh·aké** *ki*) to cause smn to come; to cause sth to come about. *nekakaké karahardjan* to bring about prosperity. *ngrawuhaké ḍokter* to send for the doctor. *nekakké bebaja* to invite danger. 2 **(n/dipun·dumugi·ǹkaken** *kr*) to accomplish, complete. *Watjané ditekakaké nganti bab katelu.* He's read up to Chapter 3. *nekakaké piweling* to accomplish one's mission. **ñ/di*ni 1 (n/dipun·ḍateng·i** *kr*) to visit, come to. *Aku ditekani pegawé kantor padjeg.* A tax official came to see me. *Wonten gara² nḍatengi.* A terrible storm came up. 2 **(n/dipun·dumugi·ǹi** *kr*) to bring about, cause to happen. *nekani pandjaluké* to make smn's request a reality. *Mugi kadumugèna ing panuwun.* May your prayers be answered. 3 **(n/di·djeneng·i** *or* **ng/di·rawuh·i** *ki*) to be present at, attend. **sa*né** upon smn's arrival. *saḍatengipun saking Éropah* when he got back from Europe. *Satekané omah bandjur mangan.* He ate as soon as he got home. **t·um·eka (ḍ·um·ateng** *kr*) to go to, head for. *Dalan iki temeka ing alun².* This street leads to the town square. *Lajangmu wis tumeka ibumu.* Your mother has received your letter.

tekabur a braggart; to brag about oneself

tékad determination, resolve. **é mati.* He made up his mind to die. *kurang ** irresolute. **-*an** to persist wilfully. *Arepa sanguné mung seṭiṭik Slamet *-*an lunga nang Djakarta.* Even though Slamet had only a little money, he went right ahead and went to Djakarta. **ñ*** to persist in what one has decided to do. *Sadjaké ḍèwèké wis nékad mati.* He seems determined to die. *Tamuné ditjanḍet ora kersa, nékat arep kondur.* We tried to persuade the guests to stay, but they insisted they must go home. **ñ/di*i** to persist (in); to keep after. *Jèn di*i mbokmenawa ja gelem.* If you keep urging him, maybe he'll give in. *Senadyan adoh, di*i baé olèhé urip nang nggunung.* Even though it was remote, they still wanted to live in the mountains. *See also* NÉKAD

tekak a certain nocturnal bird. **ñ/di*** to strangle smn; *fig* to get a stranglehold (on). *Reregan bandjur munḍak nganti nekak gulu temenan.* Prices rose to the point where everything was prohibitive.

tèkbi trident

tekbir *var of* TAKBIR

tekdir fate, destiny. **ñ/di*(aké)** to determine the course of destiny. *Gusti Allah bisa nakdiraké.* God guides our destiny. **t·in·ekdir** destined. *tinakdir dadi wong sugih* born to be rich

tekebur *var of* TAKABUR

tekèk striped gecko lizard. *Apik temen * iku, uniné *, *.* The gecko is pretty; it goes *tekèk, tekèk!* *** mati ing ulu·ǹ·é** doomed by one's own words

tekek̄ to strangle (*var of* TEKAK)

ṭèkèl *-* *or* **ke*an** to climb with difficulty, to struggle up(ward)

tekem handful. *pari sa** a handful of rice plants. **ke*** held firmly, kept under control. **ñ/di*** to hold tightly in the hand. *Badan kawula punika rak sampun ketekem ing asta paduka.* My fate is in your Highness' hands.

tèken handwritten signature. ***an 1** letters *etc.* to be signed. 2 things (to be) written down. **ñ/di*aké** to have sth signed; to have smn sign. **ñ/di*(i)** to sign. *nèken lajang* to sign a letter

teken *ng kr*, **lantar·an** *or* **pandjenengan** *or* **rotan** *ki* cane, walking stick. **ñ/di*i 1** to use a cane. 2 to give smn a helping hand

tekèng to come to (*ltry var of* TEKA ING)

ṭèkèr *-* to scratch for food [of chickens; *fig* of the poor]. **ke*an** to make one's way upward with difficulty; *fig* to scrape a living. *Uripé ke*an.* He lives from hand to mouth. **ñ*-ñ*** *sms* *-*

tekes wig made of coarse palm fibers, worn in a certain dance

teki a certain grass with an edible tuberous root. *emping ** chips made of this tuber, fried and eaten as snacks

tekik a certain variety of tree

ṭekkliwer 1 all, everything. *Pak lurah ngerti *ing désané.* The head man knows everything that goes on in his village. 2 a sudden swerve. 3 to loiter, hang around. *See also* ṬEK

ṭéklé 1 [of arms] deformed, *i.e.* short and bent. 2 unlucky

ṭèklèh curving downward [of the horns of *e.g.* kerbaus, cows, sheep]

ṭèklèk wooden sandal with a rubber toe strap

ṭekli:k̄ *-* 1 *rpr* a clippity-clop sound. 2 to take a stroll. *See also* KEṬEKLIK

ṭéklok 1 broken but not detached. 2 sagging with weariness

ṭeklu:k **ṭeklak-*** to keep nodding drowsily

tèknik̄ *var of* TÈHNIK

tèknis(i) *var of* TÈHNIS(I)

téko teapot

tekor (to show) a deficit

ṭékor [of feet, hands] crooked, deformed

ṭékruk pile, heap. **sa*** a pile (of); a large amount (of)

tèks text of a piece of writing

tèksih *var of* TAKSIH

teksih *inf var of* TAKSIH

teksir a cost estimate. **ñ/di*** 1 to estimate the cost of. *Gelang emas iki di* Rp.10,000.* He estimated the value of this gold bracelet as 10,000 rupiahs. 2 to look over *or* size up [smn of the opposite sex]. *Ali sadjaké kok neksir Dèwi.* I think Ali is interested in Dèwi.

tèkstil textile, fabric

tekuk ***an** a fold(ed place). **an lengen* the crook of the elbow. **ke*** to get folded by mistake. *Ḍèké tiba tangané ke*.* He fell and sprained his hand. **ñ/di*(i)** to fold, double back. *Tangané di*.* He flexed his hand. *nekuk buku* to turn down a page in a book. *Lengenané di*i.* He rolled up his sleeves. **pa·ñ*** act *or* way of folding. *Panekuké keseron mula tugel.* He bent it so far it broke. *See also* TIKEL

tekung ***an** having the arms folded across the chest while meditating. **ñ*** to meditate as above

tel- *see also under* TL- (*Introduction, 2.9.3*)

tel. *see* TILPUN

ṭel *rpr* breaking, cutting. *tugel ** to break with a snap. *kari *é waé* cut nearly all the way off. **, tugel guluné.* His neck snapped. *See also* ṬOKTEL

téla 1 cassava. 2 sweet potato. **te*** in fact; obviously. *Ḍèwèké te* wis duwé bodjo.* He is married. *Te* ora bisa dibeḍèk.* Obviously he can't guess it. **ñ/di*kaké** to express, declare. *nélakaké setudjuné* to express one's agreement. *Ḍèké nélakaké katresnané marang ḍèwèké.* He revealed that he loved her. *** **badjing·an** a sweet dish consisting of cassava cubes boiled with coconut sugar, coconut milk, and spices. *** **jéndral** a variety of cassava. *** **gantung** papaya, pawpaw. *** **granḍèl** a certain long-stemmed papaya. *** **kaspé** cassava root. *** **mukibat** high-producing cassava named for the East Javanese farmer who developed it. *** **penḍem** sweet potato. *** **pohung** cassava root. *** **rambat** sweet potato. *** **uwi** edible root resembling a sweet potato. *See also* PERTÉLA

tela a crack in dried soil. **ke*** to get caught in a dry-earth crack. **ñ*** to crack, split. *Jèn sawah wis nela, akèh botjah golèk djangkrik.* When the rice paddies are dried up, children hunt for crickets there.

télad **ñ/di*** to emulate

telah **ka*** called, known as. *Djenengé Sariman ke* Kuntjung.* His name is Sariman but everybody calls him Kuntjung. **pa·ñ*** name. *éntuk panelah* to be given a name

telak soft palate. **ke*** to get stuck in the throat

telas all gone, used up (*kr for* ENTÈK)

telat (too) late. *Jèn * ja dientèni waé.* If I'm late, wait for me! *Olèhé teka * mulané ora weruh wiwitané.* He got there late, so he missed the beginning. **ñ*** to be late deliberately. *A arep nelat telung djam.* A is going to get there three hours late. **ñ/di*aké** to make *or* set sth late(r); to delay. *A nelataké djam limang menit.* A set his watch back five minutes.

ṭélé *-* 1 weak, limp. 2 *slang* hopeless, impossible. **ke*-*** in detail. *Olèhé nerangaké ke*-*.* He gave a detailed explanation of it.

telèh *rg var of* TELIH

telèk bird droppings. **ñ*** to excrete droppings. **ñ/di*i** to drop [droppings] onto. *** **lantjung/lèntjung/lintjung** moist, foul-smelling chicken droppings

ṭelek̄ *-* to remain silent and numb as a result of a shattering experience

telenan cutting board for kitchen use

teleng 1 deep; (innermost) depths; heart. *ana *ing Samodra Kidul* in the depths of the Indian Ocean. **ing manah kula* the depths of my heart. **ing atiné* the apple of one's eye; that which is deep in one's heart. *dadi *ing atiné* to touch smn's heart deeply; to mean a lot to smn. **ing bobot* center of gravity. **ing lésan* bull's-eye portion of a target. **ka* ing sih** to be smn's pet *or* favored one. **ñ/di*** 1 to try to fathom smn's innermost feelings, to pry into smn's secrets. 2 to center one's concentration (on), to go into seriously, to probe (the secrets of)

ṭeleng 1 pupil of the eye. 2 playing card spot. ***an** (having) round black eyes: the distinguishing characteristic of wajang clowns. **ṭe*** pupil of the eye. *See also* PENṬELENG

tèlep *rpr* popping sth into the mouth. **télap-*** *repeated action as above. mangan télap-** to eat hungrily, to keep putting food into the mouth

telep **ke*** unrecovered; irrecoverable. *kesenian rakjat sing ke* déning djaman* popular art objects that have been lost through the ages. *Sepatuku disilih Harna, mbandjur ke* nang kana.* I lent my shoes to Harno and they're still at his place.

telepun *var of* TILPUN

tèlèr foul discharge from an infected ear. ***en** to have an infected ear

tèlès *rg* able to, can

teles wet. *setengah ** damp. *urang ** fresh shrimp in the shell. **(pe)*an** clothing worn while bathing in public (a village activity). **ñ/di*i** to wet sth. *** k(l)ebes** soaking wet

télévisi (*abbr*: **t.v.**) television. *digijaraké lumantar raḍio ** broadcast on radio and television

télgram *var of* TILGRAM

télgrap *var of* TILGRAP

telih 1 crop (bird's organ). 2 *cr* stomach. 3 water reservoir

telik spy, secret agent. **ñ/di*** to spy on. *Lunga nang endi waé aku tansah di*.* I'm under observation wherever I go. *** sandi** spy, secret agent. *** sandi upaja** trick, ruse. *** mang·éndradjala** spy who destroys the enemy by trickery

ṭeli:k̄ ***-*** isolated, all alone

tèlkim *rg var of* TELKIM

telkim funeral oration delivered by a religious official speaking directly to the body

telnan *var of* TLENAN

ṭélo chicken disease. ***-*** *or* **ṭéla-*** 1 weak, limp. 2 *slang* hopeless, impossible

telong a variety of tree

ṭelong ***-*** *or* **ṭelang-*** to move the head back and forth while gazing emptily into space

telu *ng,* **tiga** *kr* three. **las* 13. **likur* 23. ** belah* 250. ** belah èwu* 2500. ** tengah* 2½. ***n̂** 1 approximately three. 2 a set of three associated things. *kembang telon* a bouquet of three particular flowers which are strewn on graves. ***n̂an** ceremony held for a woman in the third month of pregnancy. ***-*** by threes. *mlebu telu²* to come in three at a time. **te*** (group *or* unit of) three. *Mesṭi ditut-buri panakawan tetelu.* He is always accompanied by his three retainers. **di*n̂i** to be attacked by three opponents. **ka*** (*or* **[ka]ping ***) three times; times three; (for) the third time; third in a series. *Kaping *né aku ora duwé wektu.* And in the third place, I haven't time. *bab kaping ** chapter three. **ka* tengah** 2½. **ñ/di*n̂i** 1 to form a group of three. *Aku tukokna gelas sidji manèh kanggo neloni.* Buy me one more glass to make a set of three. 2 to hold a ceremonial feast for a woman in the third month of pregnancy. *See also* -AN (*suffix*) 8, 15, 16; -É[c] (*suffix*) 9; KETIGA; NG- (*prefix*) 6, 7; PRA-; TELUNG

teluh black magic, voodoo. **ñ/di*(i)** to cast a spell on, put the hex on. **pa·ñ*an** black-magic spell put upon smn. *** bradja** shooting star, meteorite (omen of disaster)

teluk 1 bay, inlet. 2 to give up, surrender. ***an** conquered, subjugated. **ñ/di*aké** to conquer, overcome. *nindakaké politik neluk²aké* to pursue a policy of subjugation

telulas *ng,* **tigâwelas** *kr* thirteen. *See also* TELU

telulikur *ng,* **tigâlikur** *kr* twenty-three. *See also* TELU

telung[a] *ng,* **tigang** *kr* three (*as modifier*). ** puluh* thirty. ** atus* (*èwu, juta*) three hundred (thousand, million). ** dina* (*taun*) three days (years). **ñ/di*-dina·ni** to honor a deceased person with a ceremony on the third day after his death. *** prapat** 1 three-quarters. 2 a quarter till [the following hour]. *nem telung prapat* 6:45. *** tjèk** fifteen cents (*sèn*). *See also* NG- (*prefix*) 6, 7

telung[b] bent, weighted down. *Pangé *.* The branch is heavy with fruit. **ñ/di*aké** to bend down(ward). **t·um·elung** bent down, weighted down. *See also* PENTELUNG

telur *see* DAT

tem- *see also under* T- (*Introduction, 3.1.7*)

ṭem- *see also under* T- (*Introduction, 3.1.7*)
temah to produce [a result], to end up [in a certain way]. *Sangsara * mulja.* Suffering leads to ultimate well-being. ***an** (as a) result, consequence. *Merga kowé kesèd, *an ditokaké saka penggawéjanmu.* You're lazy and you got fired because of it. **di*** to be obliged to take a risk. *Jèn butuh ḍuwit, senadjan utang nganggo anakan akèh ija di*.* If you need money you risk borrowing, even at high interest. *Matia ja di*.* He'll even risk his life. **ke*an** to undergo. *A wis ka*an nglakoni pasa telung dina ora mangan lan turu.* A endured the experience of fasting for three days—no eating or sleeping. **ñ*i** to meet with [a fate]. *Sang Nata nemahi séda ing paperangan.* The king was killed in battle. **sa*** finally, as the ultimate result. *Jèn njambut gawému apik, sa* bisa dadi pemimpin.* Work hard, and you will eventually become a leader. *Kanékatané sa* ndjalari tiwasé.* His recklessness finally led to his death.
temantèn *var of* MANTÈN
tembâgâ *ng,* **tembagi** *kr* copper; brass. ** gembring* a paper-thin sheet of brass. *Saiki aku bisa ngarani endi sing ala, endi sing betjik, endi sing emas lan endi sing *.* I can now tell the good (gold) from the bad (brass). **ñ*** resembling copper *or* brass
tembagan a variety of grass
tembagi *kr for* TEMBAGA
tembâjâ ***n** *or* **pa*(n)** a business relationship with a profit motive (as contrasted with PA·GUJUB·AN)
tembajatan characterized by mutual help and cooperation. *Urip * perlu diterusaké.* Cooperative living must be preserved.
témbak fire! (*as a command*). *regu ** firing squad. ***an** a shot. *krungu *an* to hear a shot. **ke*** to get shot. **ñ/di*** to shoot (at)
tembako *ng,* **sâtâ** *kr* tobacco
tembalo a variety of tree
tembalong a certain large centipede
tembang *ng,* **sekar** *kr* 1 classical verse (recited, chanted, *or* sung). 2 musical beat. ***an** act *or* way of singing (classical songs). *Olèhé njambut-gawé disambi *an.* He sang as he worked. **te*an** to sing for one's own amusement. *Lumrahé wong jèn ana padusan paḍa te*an.* People like to sing in the bath. **ñ/di*(i)** to sing/chant/recite classical songs. *Jèn ura² utawa nembang pinter.* He can sing both popular and classical songs well. **ñ/di*aké** 1 to sing *etc.* [a classical song]. 2 to sing [to/for smn]. *** ḍagel·an** *wj* group of clown songs, each with its own specific length and metric features. *** geḍé** *or* *** kawi** another such group, with its own special features and specific subtypes. *** matjapat** a third such group, now the most common type. *** rawat²** **(udjar·é bakul s·in·ambiwara)** rumor. *** tengah·an** another group of classical verse forms each having its own number of lines, syllables per line, and line-final vowel scheme. *** tjilik** *sms* * MATJAPAT *above*
tembé the future. ***an** first-born [child]; first [egg] laid. *lagi* **ka*ǹ** (now) for the first time. *Wong ija lagi katembèn aku weruh kapal api.* It was the first time I had ever seen a steamship. **ñ*** the future (*var of* *). *** (m)buri** the future. *Adja dipesṭèkaké * mburiné.* Don't try to read the future. *Ing * mburi bakal wurung.* You'll regret it in days to come.
tèmbèl ***an** 1 patch, mended place. 2 act of patching. **ñ/di*** to patch. *ptg* **t·r·èmbèl** full of patches
tèmbel 1 *rpr* a direct hit. *Panahé ngenani wit geḍang mak *.* The arrow hit the banana tree dead on target. 2 *describing a sudden fortunate event. Wingi Slamet éntuk baṭi mak *.* Slamet made a big profit yesterday.
tembelèk chicken droppings (*rg var of* TELÈK)
tembem *wj* black-masked clown (*another name for* ḌOJOK)
tembing cliff; rim of a ridge
tembir edge, rim (of dishes, trays, *etc.*)
tembirang rope used for hoisting and lowering sails
temblag soil reinforcement added to an existing earth wall *or* dike
temblog *var of* TEMBLAG
témbo a small sampan-like boat
témbok 1 wall, *usu.* brick *or* stone. 2 built of bricks *or* stone. *omah ** a brick house. *pager ** a stone wall. **ñ/di*** 1 to equip with walls. 2 to build with bricks and mortar. 3 to put wax on cloth in batik-making
témbong large, dark skin blemish, *esp.* on the face
témbor 1 serving tray. 2 basin for washing hands
témbré of inferior quality
tembung 1 word(s); what smn says. ** mantja* foreign word. **é, "Sapa kowé?"* He

said, "Who are you?" 2 whip (*ki for* TJEMEṬI). ***-*an** wordy. **te*an** words; expression, phrase. *Te*ané kasar.* He talks crudely. *nganggo te*an sing apik* using nice expressions. **ñ/di*** to say (to), ask, speak (to). *Ḍèké nembung arep lunga.* She said she was going to leave. *nembung sarwa sembrana parikena* to say in fun only. **ñ/di*aké** 1 to say/express sth. *uga kena di*aké* in other words. 2 to say/ask on smn's behalf. *Nèk kowé ora wani nembung ḍéwé, aku sing nembungaké.* If you don't want to ask yourself, I'll ask for you. **pa·ñ*** a request. *lajang penembung* a letter of request. **pi*** a request. **pi*an** words, expressions, talk. **pi·ñ*** a request. **ora * ora lawung** to borrow sth without the owner's permission

tembus to penetrate, perforate, pierce. *Bolongan iki *.* This hole goes all the way through. *Dalan iki * ngendi?* Where does this road come out? *Wadja iki ora * peluru.* Bullets can't pierce this steel. *Ḍèké nganggo klambi *.* He's wearing a see-through shirt. *sinar ** X-ray. ***an** 1 the other opening at the far end. 2 tunnel; channel. 3 act of piercing/penetrating. *lajang *an* a carbon copy. **ñ/di*** to pierce, penetrate. *Trowongané nembus ngisor kali.* The tunnel goes under a river. *Aku arep nembus bolongan iki.* I'm going to drill this hole all the way through. *Mripaté bisa nembus ḍaḍa tekan ndjantung.* His eyes see into your very heart. *Urubé bisa nembus ing pepeteng iku.* The light penetrates the darkness.

ṭèmel **ṭémal-*** [to eat] hungrily and rapidly

ṭemèl *var of* ṬEMEL

ṭemel sticking together [of *e.g.* fibers, unwashed hair]

temen 1 real, true; very, decidedly. *Kok anèh *.* How strange! *Pelem iki pantjèn legi *.* This mango is really sweet. *katrangan * oraning tumindak* information about whether or not it actually happened. 2 honest. *gandjarané wong ** the reward of an honest man. 3 industrious. *Anggoné sinau kanṭi *.* He studied hard. ***an** *see* TEMENAN. **ka*an** to actually happen; to turn out to be true. *Pangadjapé ke*an.* His wish came true. **ñ*(-ñ*)** serious; to take seriously. *Oléhé lara nemen nganti dilebokké rumah-sakit.* His illness was so serious he was taken to the hospital. **ñ/di*i** to take/treat seriously. *Anggoné sinau di*i karebèn bisa lulus.* He studied hard so he's pass. **sa*é** in fact, actually, really. *Pegawéan mau dikira gampang waé, nanging sa*é angèl.* He thinks the job is easy, but it's actually hard. *Rumangsané bali, sa*é ora.* He felt as if he was going back, but he wasn't. **t·um·emen** industrious, serious. *See also* TEMENAN, TENAN

temenan (*or* ***an**) real, true; decidedly. *Ah, kuwi ora *, mung dongèng waé.* It's not true–it's just a story. *upama *a...* if it were true... *ratu ** a real king. **ñ/di*i** to take seriously. *See also* TEMEN

temenḍil dung, *esp.* sheep/goat dung

temenggung *title applied to a regional chief*

ṭemil ***-*** *or* **ṭemal-*** to keep nibbling. *Sesoré kok ming *-* waé.* You've done nothing but eat all evening long. ***an** snacks, nibbles. **ñ/di*i** to eat continuously. *See also* KEṬEMIL

ṭemlang, ṭemlèng, ṭemlong *describing the notes sounded by a certain gamelan instrumeng (bonang)*

temlik, ṭemlik *var of* TEMPLIK, ṬEMPLIK

ṭémol *rpr* pinching, grabbing. *njeṭot mak ** to pinch smn hard. **ṭémal-*** [to eat] voraciously. *mangan ṭémal-** to wolf one's food. **ñ*** to take a pinch of sth. *Ḍèké némol bokongé anaké.* He pinched his son in the behind (as punishment). **sa*** one large handful taken in the fingers *or* hand [*e.g.* of rice, from the serving bowl; of flesh, in pinching]

tempah compensation (*kr for* TEMPUH[b])

tempajan(g) *rg* large earthenware bowl *or* jar

tempak having no sharp angles. *podjok ** angle of more than 90 degrees. **ñ/di*aké** to make sth blunt *or* rounded, *i.e.* without any sharp angles

tempaling net for catching butterflies *or* flying insects

tempaos a variety of tree

tempat a place. *** tiḍur** bed

témpé beancake of whole fermented soybeans. **ñ/di*** to make [ingredients] into beancake. *Ḍeléné di*.* She made beancake from the soybeans. *** benguk** beancake made of *benguk* beans

tèmpèh bamboo tray for separating the chaff from the rice grains by tossing them

tèmpèl ***-*an** various elements (to be) assembled. **ka*an** to get stuck to by sth. *Klambiné ke*an kertas.* A piece of paper stuck to his shirt. *ke*an sétan* possessed of an evil spirit. **ñ/di*aké** to attach, affix. *Prangkoné tèmpèlna ing lajang.* Stick the stamps on the letter. **ñ/di*i** to stick sth with. *nèmpèli lajang nganggo prangko* to stick stamps on a letter. **t·um·èmpèl** to adhere, stick. *Bleṭoké temèmpèl ing sepatu.* The mud clung to his shoes. **ng·inḍung** *, **m̃·ponḍok** * to live on another's property under certain conditions (*see* NG·INḌUNG, M̃·PONḌOK)

tempélang a packet made by wrapping sth (*usu.* with banana leaves) by folding the four corners in and holding them with a sharp bamboo pin. **ñ/di*** to wrap sth as above

tempéling *var of* TEMPILING

tempik female reproductive system

tempil ***an** things bought little by little *or* in small amounts. **ñ/di*** to buy as above. **ñ/di*aké** to buy as above for smn

tempiling **ñ/di*** to slap smn on *or* near the side of the face

tèmplèk **ka*an** to get stuck to by sth. *Klambiku ke*an woh pulutan pirang²*. There are a lot of burs sticking to my shirt. **ñ/di*** to adhere to. *Baṭok seṭiṭik isih nèmplèk ing krambil.* A few bits of shell still clung to the coconut. **ñ/di*aké** to attach sth smw. *Lésané dak *aké ing wit wringin.* I attached the target to a banyan tree. *Polané di*aké sisihé mori.* She attached the pattern at the edge of the fabric. **ñ/di*i** to attach sth on(to); *fig* to live off smn, be a parasite. *Motor² mau ing katjané di*i dluwang.* Notices were stuck in the windshields of the cars. *ptg* **t·r·èmplèk** *pl* adhering to, stuck to. **t·um·èmplèk** to get stuck (onto) inadvertently; to be stuck *or* sticking to, be attached to. *Gambaré temèmplèk ing témbok.* The picture is attached to the wall.

templik, ṭemplik **ñ/di*** to take away *or* break off a small piece. **sa*** a little bit, a small piece *or* part

tèmplok *var of* TÈMPLÈK

témpo (enough) time; (duration of) time. *Punggawané diwènèhi * ngaso.* The employees were given time to rest. *Jèn kowé nduwé *, tekaa mengko soré.* If you have time, come over this evening. *Aku ndjaluk * rong djam.* I asked for two hours(' time). *Jèn arep mangan, tak kira isih *.* If you want to eat, I think there's still time. *Wis *.* Time's up. *ora tau ** always (too) busy (to...). ***né** time for sth. *Témponé mangan malah lunga.* It's time to eat, but he went out.

tempolong 1 a small tin container. 2 cuspidor for the use of betel chewers

tempuh[a] **ke*** to get hit. *ke* musuh* attacked by the enemy. *ka* ing angin* caught by the wind. **ñ/di*** to face up to, confront. *nempuh udjian* to take an examination. *nempuh pasinaon* to take up a study. *nempuh bjat* (*ltry*) to attack in force. *nempuh ing pekéwuh* to face up to one's troubles. *nempuh perang* (*bebaja, pati*) to endure war (danger, death). **pa·ñ*** (head-on) attack; collision. **t·um·empuh** to undergo, be subjected to. *Kaliné santer banget, ora temempuh disabrangi.* The river was so swift you couldn't wade across.

tempuh[b] *ng,* **tempah** *kr* (*or* **te***) compensation for damages. *Iki lho *é.* Here's what I owe you (for the damage I did). **ke*(an)** liable for damages. *Sing ke*an ndandani wong sing njéwa.* The tenant is responsible for the repairs. **ñ/di*** to pay for [merchandise] in advance of delivery. **ñ/di*aké** to have smn pay damages. *Anakku tak *aké piringé sing petjah.* I'll have my child pay for the dish he broke. **ñ/di*i** to compensate, to pay damages. *nempuhi karusakan* to pay for the damage. *nempuhi djenḍéla* to pay for a window [which one broke]

tempuk (*or* ***an**) to flow together, join. *Kali mau * karo tlaga.* The river flows into a lake. **ing nétra karoné* the meeting of their eyes. **ing gawé* at the time of the big celebration

tempur [of bodies of water] to join, merge. ***an** 1 to buy rice for household use. *Aku golèk *an.* I tried to buy some rice. 2 confluence. **ñ/di*aké** to buy rice for smn's household supply. *Aku tempurna beras.* Please buy some rice for me. **dudu beras·é di*aké** 1 [this rice] is not rice which is to be sold. 2 we have misunderstood each other. **ñ/di*(i)** to buy rice for household use

temtu 1 of course, to be sure. *Ing endi² * ana wong ala.* There are bound to be bad people everywhere. 2 fixed, set. *Olèhé lunga durung *.* It isn't certain yet that he's going. 3 to go through with (*rg kr for* SIDA). ***nipun** of course (*kr for* MESṬI·NÉ). **ka*an** stipulation, provision. *manut ke*an unḍang² ḍasar 1945...* as provided in the 1945 constitution... **ñ/di*k̂aké** 1 to decide, settle (on). *Dina mantèn wis ditemtokaké.* The wedding date has been set. 2 to fore-ordain, predict. *Ḍèké ditemtokaké bakal dadi pemimpin geḍé.* He is destined to be a great leader.

temu[a] *ng,* **panggih** *kr* to meet as bride and groom during the marriage ceremony. ***n̂** (having been) found. *Iki barang temon, ora kena didol.* This is something you found; you can't sell it. ***n̂an (panggih·an** *kr*) an encounter. **te*** *sms* *. **te*n̂(an) (pe·pa-nggih·an** *kr*) 1 a meeting. 2 to meet, run into (each other), find (each other). **ke*** 1 to see *or* meet smn; to find sth. *ke* kantja lawas* to see (chat with, *etc.*) an old friend. *Ke*né nang endi?* Where'd you find it? *rékadaja sa·ke*né* whatever means could be found. 2 to go well together. *Dina loro mau ke* apik.* Those two days are a good [numerological] combination. **n̈*** to find, come upon. *Golèk dalan ora nemu²*. He tried to find a way but was unable to. *ne-mu peniti* to find a pin. *nemu akal* to hit upon a plan. *nemu alangan* to meet with a mishap *or* obstacle. *nemu gudèl* to find sth of value. *nemu kabegdjan* to have a stroke of luck. *nemu karahardjan* to prosper. *ne-mu (ke)luput(an)* to do sth wrong; to be found out in a fault. *nemu kuwuk* to make use of, exploit. *nemu pakéwuh* to run into trouble. *nemu rahaju* to find safety. *nemu tjatjad* to have/ get sth wrong with one physically. **n̈/di*k̂aké** 1 to bring together the bride and the groom during the wedding ceremony. 2 to find, discover. *Sing nemo-kké Amérika iku djenengé Columbus.* Co-lumbus discovered America. *nemokaké ba-rang ilang* to find a lost object. **n̈/di*n̂i** 1 to receive [guests]. *Ḍèké lagi nemoni tamu.* He has company. 2 to look for, go to see [a person]. *Arep nemoni sapa?* Who do you want to see? 3 to meet with, come up against. *nemoni susah* to encounter grief. **pa*n̂** a meeting. *patemon pepisahan* a farewell meeting. *Sa·patemonku karo ḍèwèké aku krasa seneng.* I felt happy after meeting her. **pa·n̈*** opinion, point of view. *saka penemuku* in my opinion. *béda²ning penemu* differences of opinion. **per*an** meeting, assembly. **t·in·emu (p·in·anggih** *kr*) 1 to find, run across. *Gugon-tuhon iku tinemu ing negara endi²*. Superstition is encountered in every country. *Wis suwé ora tinemu.* I haven't seen him for a long time. 2 to turn out, end up. *Tinemu be-tjik karepku kang sutji mau.* My pure inten-tion turned out for the best. *tinemu akal* or *tinemu nalar* reasonable, sensible. * **gelang** forming a not-quite-closed circle like a brace-let. * **pèk** finders keepers

temu[b] certain roots used medicinally. **n̈*** resembling one of these roots. * **giring** a yellow tuber used in folk medicines. *kuning * giring* intensely yellow. *kuning nemu gi-ring* fair, light-skinned. * **lawak** medicinal root. * **rosé** 1 a certain betel root. 2 suit-able; harmonious. *A lan B * rosé.* A and B get along well with each other.

temulus a certain fish

ten *inf var of* BOTEN, WONTEN. *Ten wonten.* There aren't any.

tenâgâ 1 power, strength. *nganggo * tangan* by hand. ** listrik* electric power. **né ku-rang.* It lacks strength. 2 worker. *Tenaga² diwènèhi klambi.* The workers were given clothing. ** ahli* expert, specialist. *meres ** to work hard. **n̈/di*ni** to use one's strength. *A sing mawiti, B sing nenagani.* A put up the capital and B did the work.

tenan (*or* ***an**) true, real. *Tjangkrimanku angèl *.* The riddle I asked was really hard. *Adja! * lo.* Don't do that! I mean it. *Pan-tjèn * jèn Slamet kawin karo Siti.* It's true that Slamet married Siti. **n̈/di*i** to take *or* treat seriously. *Sandiwara iku kaja ludrug nanging luwih di*i.* The *sandiwara* art form is like *ludrug* but more serious. *See also* TEMEN

ténḍa tent, sun shade

tenḍag *ora *-** interminable. *Barisané dawa banget nganti ora *-*.* The parade went on and on and on. **ka*an** low (on), having a shortage (of), coming to the end (of). *Aku lagi ke*an gula.* I'm running out of sugar.

tenḍang ***an** 1 act *or* way of kicking. **ané banter.* He kicks hard. 2 thing kicked *or* bumped. 3 to kick back and forth. *Ajo paḍa *an.* Let's kick the ball around. ***-*an** to kick *or* bump into each other. **ke*** to get kicked *or* bumped. *ke* djaran* kicked by a horse. *Aku kuwatir jèn ke* apa²*. I'm afraid sth will bump into me. **n̈/di*aké** to kick for smn. **n̈/di*(i)** to kick, bump against. *Balé di* mak pleng.* He gave the ball a good hard kick.

tènḍèn(si) tendency. *organisasi kang *-* po-litik* an organization with political leanings

tened **n̈/di*** to compress, pack tightly

tenèh likely, probable. ** ja digeguju.* Chances are you'll get laughed at. *Jèn oraa apik * ora ana wong plesir rana.* If it weren't so beautiful, people wouldn't be likely to go there for pleasure.

tènes tennis

tèng 1 storage tank. 2 military tank (armored vehicle). ***-*an** 1 toy tank. 2 having had the sleeves shortened by taking up the armhole seams. *Klambiné *-*an.* The sleeves of his shirt have been taken up. **nge/di*(i)** to shorten [sleeves] as above

teng 1 to, toward (*md for* MARANG, MENJANG). 2 stomach, belly (*shf of* WETENG). 3 *inf var of* WONTEN. ***an** pregnancy; foetus (*shf of* WETENG·AN). **nge/di*aké** to cook sth until it is done (*shf of* ∅/DI·MATENG·AKÉ). **nge/di*i** 1 *sms* NGE/DI*AKÉ. 2 *slang* to get smn pregnant out of wedlock

ṭèng *rpr* a sharp metallic ring

ṭeng *var of* ṬÈNG. **ṭang-*** *var of* SANG-SENG (*see under* SENG)

tenga **ñ*** *or* **t·um·enga** to look up(ward); *fig* to look to smn of power or authority to help

tengah 1 (in the) middle, center; (with)in. *ing ** in the middle. *sing ** the one in the middle. *Omahé * alas.* His house is in the middle of the woods. *adu ** center-to-center. *ana * ndalan* in the middle of the road. *garis ** mid-line; diameter. *ing * segara* at sea, in mid-ocean. *mlaku ing *ing pepeteng* to walk in the dark. *kamar ** inner room used as a family room. ** umur* middle-aged. ** wengi* midnight. 2 center (soccer player, position). 3 (in) half. *se** one-half. *Disigar * bener.* He split it right in half. *Tiba ngliwati garis wates *.* It is bisected by the boundary line. 4 *n* minus one-half. *karo ** 1½. *telu ** 2½. *kapat * taun* 3½ years. ***an** 1 (in the) middle part. **ané saka wulu kéwan.* The middle part is fur. *sekolahan *an* middle school. *pegawé *an* a middle-ranking official. 2 around the middle; about half. *Saiki *an Nopèmber.* It's around the middle of November now. *Se*an mèter dawané.* It's about half a meter long. 3 half (*as a fraction*). *rong *an* two halves. 4 half-rupiah coin. 5 to go halves. *Kowé *an karo aku.* How about sharing 50-50 with me? ***-*** (in) the very middle. *ing *-* kuṭa* right in the center of the city. *Soal kuwi aku nang *-*.* On that question I'm neutral. **ñ*** (to move) toward the center (*see* NENGAH). **ñ/di*aké** to put in *or* move toward the middle. *Montor di*aké.* He drove in the center of the road. **ñ/di*i** to place between *or* in the middle of. *Sarungé di*i kembangan geḍé.* She made a large flower design in the center of the sarong. *Sing padu *ana.* Get between the fighters! **ñ*-ñ*i** in the middle of. *Lagi nengah²i mangan anaké tangi.* She was eating when the baby woke up. **sa*é** in the midst of, surrounded by. *ing sa*ing alas* in the middle of the woods. *ing sa*é wong sepirang-pirang* surrounded by people. *See also* MENTENGAH, NENGAH, SETENGAH

tengârâ a signal given by sound, *e.g.* ringing a bell, pounding on wood. ** buḍal* the signal to leave. **ñ/di*ni** to sound a signal

tengawud a Moslem prayer begging for God's protection. *matja ** to utter such a prayer

ṭèngèl ***-*** *or* **ṭéngal-*** having the head sticking up above sth and moving. **ñ*** to stretch the neck and look around. *ptg* **ṭ·r·èngèl** *pl* showing above the surface of sth

ṭengèl *var of* ṬÈNGÈL

tengèn *ng kr,* **wungu·ñ** *ki* having a keen sense of hearing

tengen right (as opposed to left). *tangan ** right hand; right-hand man, helper. *bau ** right-hand man. *wajang ** (*wj*) puppets of the "good" (ultimately victorious) forces, appearing on the right-hand side of the screen. **ke*** 1 guided. *ka* déning Gusti Allah* guided by God. 2 liked, appreciated. *Rokok iki ke* ḍéwé.* These cigarettes are the most popular ones. **ñ*** toward the right (*see* NENGEN). **ñ/di*aké** 1 to move sth toward the right. *Lampuné adja di*aké.* Don't move the lamp any further toward the right. 2 to consider sth essential, give priority to. *Awaké ḍéwé kudu nengenaké pangan.* We have to make food the first consideration. **sa*é** to the right of. *Omahku sa*é sekolahan.* My house is on the right of the school. *See also* KIWA-TENGEN, NENGEN

tèngèng 1 [of neck] deformed, bent sideways. 2 [of neck] stiff. **ñ*** to tip the neck sideways, *e.g.* so as to permit smn in back to see

tenger mark, sign, label. ** watu* stone marker. ** mrapat* an X mark. ** kaurmatan* mark of honor, token of esteem. **te*(an)** *sms *.* *paring te* kanggo téori²* to attach labels to theories. **te*an** 1 (having) a mark *or* identifying sign. *Kuburané te∗an saleb.* His grave is marked with a cross. 2 gift given to a bride's family by the groom's family as an egagement *or* marriage token. **ke∗** to get noticed. *Ḍèké gampang ke∗.* She stands out in a crowd. **ñ/di∗i** 1 to put a mark(er) on, attach a label to. *di∗i nganggo angka* marked with numbers. *nengeri lajang* to sign and date a letter. 2 to betoken. *Mendung nggameng nengeri udan deres.* Dark clouds portend heavy rain. 3 to take note of. *Guru nengeri madju munduring murid.* Teachers keep track of the progress and regression of their students. **pa·ñ∗an** 1 *sms* TE∗AN *above.* 2 *ltry* crown of the head

ṭenger ∗-∗ to remain utterly motionless (*e.g.* loafing; stunned, shocked)

tengga to wait (for); to watch over (*kr for* TUNGGU)

tenggak throat. **ñ∗** to tilt the head back when drinking. **nenggak waspa** to try to hold back one's tears. **pa·ñ∗** second child (*ki for* PANGGULU)

tenggar broad and open. **∗an** a large open field *or* yard. **ñ/di∗** *rg* to put up [a bird cage] in an open place

tenggârâ southeast. *Asia ∗* Southeast Asia

tenggel **ke∗** to be hit squarely (*lit, fig*). *ke∗ tembung kasar* jarred by a crude word. **ñ∗** to hit squarely. *Olèhé maku nenggel.* He hit the nail right on the head. *Pitakoné nenggel tenan.* His question went right to the heart of the matter.

tenggenah **ñ/di∗** to assign a task to. *A nenggenah B nglakokaké montoré menjang Semarang.* A got B to drive his car to Semarang for him.

tenggiling *var of* TRENGGILING

ténggok, tènggok small deep basket of woven bamboo

tenggok the neck above the Adam's-apple

tenggung having considerable authority but not of the highest rank. **t·um·enggung** a high-ranking official in the Sultan's administration

tengik 1 rancid-smelling. 2 of inferior quality. 3 half-cent coin

ṭengil any small round object. *See also* PENṬENGIL

tengiri a certain ocean fish

tengis a certain grasshopper that chirps at night

tengkar **∗-t·um·engkar** [of animals, plants] to proliferate, multiply. **ñ/di∗aké** to increase the numbers of [plants, animals] by breeding

tèngkèk a certain small bird. **ke∗-∗** always in difficulty, pursued by bad luck

tengkel piece cut from sth. *sa∗* one cut piece. *nDjaluk iwaké sa∗.* Give me a piece of the fish. **∗an** a cut-off piece. **ñ/di∗** to cut a piece from. **ñ/di∗-∗** to cut up

tengkorak skull

ṭéngkrang **ñ∗** having the feet elevated. *lungguh néngkrang* to sit with the feet up, *e.g.* on a desk. **ñ/di∗aké** to elevate [feet]. *néngkrangaké sikil* to raise the foot

ṭèngkrèk *inf var of* M̈·PEṬÈNGKRÈK

ṭèngkrèng *inf var of* M̈·PEṬÈNGKRÈNG. **ñ∗** *var of* Ñ·TENGKRENG

ṭengkreng ∗-∗ *or* **ñ∗** silent and motionless

ṭengkruk to work hard and earnestly. **ke∗an** with hard, patient work. *Paḍa diopèni ke∗-an kok mung dirusak sakepénaké ḍéwé baé.* I took considerable pains raising [those plants] and now they're being wantonly destroyed.

tengkulak 1 one who deals in crops *or* cattle trading. 2 wooden *or* leather quiver for arrows

tengkuwèh a dish made from a sweetened pumpkin-like food

ṭènglèng tipped to one side (*usu.* of the head). **ñ/di∗aké** to cock [the head]

ṭengok *rg var of* ṬENGUK

ṭèngṭèng **∗an** (that which is) earmarked. **di∗i** earmarked (for)

ṭengṭeng **∗an** to reek. *Apa ta sing mambu ∗an iki?* What's making this awful smell?

tengu a tiny red insect that attacks the male genitals. ∗ **m̈·pangan brutu·né** one who is entrusted to guard sth steals it himself

ṭenguk ∗-∗ *or* **ṭe∗** to sit around idly. ∗-∗ **ñ·temu keṭuk** to get a fortune without working to earn it. *ptg* **ṭ·r·enguk** *pl* sitting around loafing

ṭengul 1 small can for measuring oil. 2 rag doll. *See also* WAJANG[a]

tènis tennis. *∗é wis gim.* Game! (*i.e.* the tennis game is now over).

ténjok *rg* to lose, be defeated

ténong, tènong a round covered box of woven bamboo, used *esp.* for keeping pastries

tenta **ke∗** to have fallen into the habit of [do]ing. *Jèn lagi mikir, A ke∗ kukur[2].* While A thinks, he absent-mindedly scratches his head. *Ḍèké wis ke∗ seneng ndjedjaluk.* He's developed a habit of asking for things.

tentamèn university-level test *or* examination

tentang **ñ/di∗** to oppose, fight against. *nentang tank²* *mungsuh* to do battle against enemy tanks

tentârâ soldier. ∗ *ḍarat* army soldier, infantryman. ∗ *pajung* paratrooper. *latihan* ∗ military training

tentrem tranquil, serene; at peace (rather than war). *Saiki uripé wis* ∗. His life is tranquil now. *negara tata* ∗ *kerta rahardja* an orderly, peaceful, and prosperous country. **ka∗an** tranquility, peace, serenity. **ñ/di∗aké** to make tranquil/serene; to bring about peace in/at [a place]

tèntun stèleng exhibition

tenun **∗an** 1 fabric, woven material. 2 weaving equipment, loom. **ñ/di∗** to weave. **pa∗an** place (*esp.* factory) where weaving is done. **pa·ñ∗an** weaving loom. **mesin** ∗ machine-operated loom. **tukang** ∗ professional hand-loom weaver

tenung 1 black magic. 2 *rg* practitioner of black magic. *tukang* ∗ black-magic practitioner. **ñ/di∗** to put the hex on. *Ḍèwèké di∗.* Smn caused him to be ill by casting a spell on him.

téori theory, hypothesis, postulate. **ñ∗** to theorize. *Adja néori sing anèh², munḍak gawé gègèr.* Don't invent weird theories about it–you might stir up trouble.

tepa tact, sensitivity. *wong ora duwé* ∗ a tactless person. *Olèhé mènèhi panggawéjan tanpa* ∗. He assigned jobs to people arbitrarily. **∗-∗** tactful, considerate. **ñ/di∗kaké** to take [others' feelings, points of view] into account. *Jèn kongkonan B, A nepakaké kekuwatané B.* When A asks B to do sth, he takes B's ability into account. *A nepakaké awaké ḍéwé jèn kongkonan.* A puts himself in the other person's shoes when he gives orders. ∗ **palupi** an example to others. ∗ **slira** to put oneself in another's place. ∗ **tulaḍa** an example to others

tépak wooden tray with containers comprising a set of betel-chewing equipment

tepak 1 upper part of the back. 2 fly swatter. 3 a certain insect that infests rice crops. 4 *rg var of* TAPAK. 5 *var of* PAS

tepalih close, immediate (*kr for* TEPARO)

tépang **∗an** a kick; act *or* way of kicking. **ke∗** to get kicked. **ke∗ ng·rangsang gunung** to fail to accomplish an unrealistic goal. **ñ/di∗(i)** to kick with the side of the foot. *Djarané di∗i.* He kept kicking his horse.

tepang to be(come) acquainted (*kr for* TEPUNG)

teparo *ng,* **tepalih** *kr* [of neighbors] close, immediate. *tangga* ∗ the neighbors

tépas bamboo fan. ∗ *angin* electric fan. **∗-∗** to fan a flame. **ñ/di∗i** 1 to fan sth. *Geniné tépasana, bèn murub.* Fan the fire so it will burn brighter. 2 to peel fiber from a coconut

tepas portion of a house (*e.g.* a veranda) that is roofed over but not walled in

tepat on the nose, exactly right. *djam loro* ∗ two o'clock sharp. *Olèhé mbeḍèk* ∗. He guessed it right on the nose.

tepékong Taoist idol in Chinese temples

tepekur meditation and prayer, *e.g.* in commemoration of a dead person; to meditate and pray

tepes *rg* coconut-shell fiber

tepi 1 edge, boundary. *∗ning kali* river bank. *∗ning samodra* seashore. *tanpa* ∗ limitless. 2 decorative edging. **∗ǹ** having a decorative edging

tepis edge, border, boundary. ∗ *(w)iring* border, edge. ∗ *kidul* the southern border

teplak *var of* TEPLÈK

têplek̄ *rpr* sth getting stuck in place. *Kertas nuli ditèmplèkaké mak* ∗. He stuck the piece of paper on it. **téplak-∗** *pl as above. mBok prangko²né kuwi énggal ditèmplèkaké, téplak-∗.* Please stick the stamps on the letter right away! *Ril dalan sepur kuwi ora kena kok bandjur dipasang waé téplak-∗ ana tengah sawah.* You can't just plunk down railway ties in the middle of a rice paddy! **t·um·èplek** [to sit/lie on] comfortably

teplèk fly swatter

téplok object hung on a wall *or* pillar. *dijan* ∗ kerosene lamp hung as above. *djam* ∗ wall clock

tépong hind part (under the tail). **ñ/di∗** to hit [*esp.* a horse] on the above part

tépos [of buttocks] flat, unrounded. **ñ/di∗** to slap smn on the buttocks

tepsir *var of* TAPSIR

tepung *ng,* **tepang** *kr* 1 to (get to) know, be(come) acquainted [with]. *Aku* ∗ *karo Slamet wiwit sekolah rakjat.* I've known Slamet ever since elementary school. 2 to join. *Dalan Malioboro* ∗ *karo dalan Gondolaju nang Tugu.* Malioboro Boulevard connects up with Gondolaju Street in Tugu. **∗an** an acquaintance, a friend. *A ditjritani ∗ané mengkéné.* Here's what a friend of A's told him. *Aku kedajohan *anku.* Someone I know came to see me. **ñ/di*aké** to introduce [people]. *C di*aké B karo A nang setasiun.* A introduced B to C at the station. **ñ/di*i** to introduce oneself to. *Siti di*i karo Bedja ning sadjak ora nggatèkaké.* Bedja tried to get acquainted with Siti, but she wasn't having any. *** alis·é** (having) eyebrows that meet above the nose. *** betjik** well acquainted [with]. *** gelang** forming a nearly-closed circle. *Tongé * gelang.* The barrels are arrayed in a circle. *** kebo** having a speaking acquaintance [with]. *** pager** neighborhood. *** rembug** to have a discussion [with]. *** rukun** to become acquainted with one another [of members of a group]. *** tjukit** very close together; *** tjukit adu tritis** [of houses] crowded together. *** wates** the neighboring border. *See also* PITEPUNG

tepus string used to measure length. **ñ/di*** to measure with a measuring string

ter **nge/di*aké** (**n/di·ḍèrèk·aké** *ki*) to take, escort, accompany. *ngeteraké adiné sekolah* to take one's younger brother to school. *nḍèrèkaké ibuné menjang ḍokteran* to take one's mother to the hospital. **nge/di*i** to bring food from a ritual meal to. *Genḍuk lagi nge*i bantjakané si bajèk.* Our daughter is taking the neighbors some of the foods from our baby's ceremony. *See also* ATER

ter- *see also under* TR- (*Introduction, 2.9.3*)

ṭèr 1 *rpr* a sudden loud report. *Ḍèké metjuti djarané, ṭor, *, ṭor, *.* He beat the horse with loud cracks of the whip. *Mertjoné muni *.* The firecracker went bang! 2 *rpr* water trickling continuously (*see also* ÈṬÈR). **ṭar-*** *rpr* repeated loud reports

ṭer 1 *rpr* a swift motion/action. *Jèn njabrang dalan *, adja ménga-méngo.* Cross the street quickly—don't veer from side to side. *Olèhé ngujuh manṭur mak *.* [The child] suddenly urinated. 2 *rpr* a trill *or* tattoo of sounds. **nge*** to produce a trill *or* tattoo of sounds

ṭer- *see also under* ṬR- (*Introduction, 2.9.3*)

terag premature; stillborn (*ki for* KLURON)

terah *var of* TRAH

terak **ke*** to get struck. *Akèh wit²an ambruk ka* angin.* Many trees were struck down by the wind. *ke* penjakit influènsa* hit by an influenza epidemic. **ñ/di*(i)** to strike, run into; *fig* to buck, fly in the face of. *Walang sangit mau nerak genining obor, mesṭi dadi awu.* The insects came up against the torch flame and were turned to ash. *nerak widi* to disregard established conventions. *Ḍèké nerak selané udan pélor.* He broke through the rain of bullets. **pa·ñ*** misdemeanor, transgression

terang clear; cleared up. ** jèn ḍèké salah.* He is obviously guilty. *Langité *.* The sky is clear. *Udané wis *.* The rain has stopped. *Kurang * arep dikapakaké.* It isn't known what is to be done to him. *Bab iku durung patija *.* The facts are not clear(ly known). *Terus * aku ora duwé ḍuwit.* Quite frankly, I have no money. ***an** a dry spell. *Wiḍji mau ditandur ing mangsa *an.* The seeds were planted during a drought. ***(an)é** 1 plainly, it is clear that... *Teranganė ḍèké wedi.* She was obviously afraid. 2 by way of clarification. *Didjaluki utang meneng waé, *é ora duwé ḍuwit.* When I asked him for a loan, he didn't answer; it turned out he had no money. ***-*an** frank, open. *kanḍa *-*an* to speak candidly. **ka*an** 1 information, explanation. *katrangan satjukupé bab tjanḍi² mau* sufficient information about the temples. 2 *gram* modifier. *tembung ke*an* adjective, adverb. **ñ/di*** 1 to request clarification. *Neranga marang A.* Ask A to explain it to you. 2 to prevent rain magically. *Menḍung nanging kok ora udan.—La wong di*!* It's cloudy but it's not raining.—Someone must have put a spell on it! **ñ/di*aké** 1 to clarify. *Terangna apa kanggoné.* Explain what it's for. *Perkara mau di*-*aké.* He explained the case in detail. 2 *gram* to modify. **ñ/di*i** to shed light on. *Ting mau kanggo nerangi dalan.* That light is for lighting up the road. **pa·ñ*an** information. *djuru penerangan* official who gives out information. **m·pi*** to ask for an explanation, to find out. *Tjoba miteranga sing endi sing dikersakaké.* Please find out which one he wants. *** bulan** moonlight. *** gamblang** crystal clear

terap *var of* TRAP

tèras terrace

teras 1 brand new, never been worn. 2 *sbst kr for* TERUS? **ke*en** to an excessive degree. *Olèhé ngeḍuk bolongan kuwi ke*en.* He dug the hole far too deep. **ñ/di*** 1 to use [sth new] for the first time. 2 to do the first plowing on [a rice paddy]. 3 to peel [fruit] thickly

teratur orderly. *mangsa ora ** chaotic times

terbang tambourine-like musical instrument. **∗an** *or* **ñ∗** to play this instrument

terbela box for transporting a body to the cemetery. **ñ/di∗** to place [a body] in this box

terbis impassable. *djurang ∗* a canyon that cannot be crossed

terbit **∗an** 1 edition. *∗an soré* evening edition. 2 (having been) published. **ñ/di∗aké** to publish. **pa·ñ∗** publisher. **pa·ñ∗an** publication

terbuka **∗ ati·né** to achieve understanding through divine inspiration. **t·in·erbuka** to become instilled with divine understanding

terbumi *rg* traditional ceremony held during the month prior to the fasting month

terdjang *inf var of* TRADJANG

ṭèrèk *var of* ṬARIK

tèrès red dye used as food coloring and for coloring the lips. **ñ/di∗** to redden [food; lips] with the above

tères *var of* TÈRÈS

teres **ñ/di∗** to peel the bark from a tree that is to be cut, in order to season the timber

teri a certain small edible ocean fish. *∗ asin* dried salted *teri* fish

terik 1 dish made with meat, beancake, or other ingredients cooked in coconut milk and spiced. 2 swallow plover

tèritorium territory (a military administrative division)

terka **ñ/di∗** to accuse

terkaḍang sometimes, now and then. *See also* KAḌANG

tèrmos, termos thermos bottle

ṭérok **∗-∗** thick(ly powdered). *Olèhé pupuran ∗-∗.* She powdered her face thickly.

térong eggplant. **∗ glaṭik** small round eggplant. **∗ wuluh** a purple eggplant

ṭerong **∗-∗** well advanced [of morning, with the sun high in the sky]. *Wis ∗-∗ ngéné kok lagi mangkat kantor.* How come you're just starting for the office at this late hour?

terpéḍo *var of* TORPÉḌO. *See also* PIT

tèrras *var sp of* TÈRAS

tersinggung offended, hurt. *gampang ∗* sensitive, easily hurt

tertamtu *var of* TEMTU

tertib meticulous

tertjaṭat registered. *pos ∗* registered mail

tertjeb *ptg ∗* sore *or* sensitive from many hurts. *Rasané awakku ptg ∗.* I feel prickly and sensitive. *Rasaning atiné ptg ∗ ngrasakaké anaké sing nakal.* She was stabbed to the heart by thoughts of her wayward son.

tertjel *ptg ∗ or* **ñ∗** [of children] too many and born too close together. **ñ/di∗aké** to keep having [babies]

tertjes *ptg ∗* to have a shivery, sensitive feeling in the skin

ṭeruk **∗-∗** to idle, loaf

terung *see* KRUPUK

terus 1 **(ladjeng** *kr?*) right away, right after that. *Regané ∗ baé tikel loro.* The price doubled immediately. *Goḍongé garing ∗ mati.* The leaves dried up and died. 2 straight (on, as before). *∗ menjang omah* straight home. *Kowé apa ∗ ngawasaké?* Did you watch it all the time? *wiwit semana ∗ tekan saiki* ever since then. *∗ ngalor* straight north. *Bukuku iki pèken ∗.* You can keep my book. **∗an** 1 continuing in the same way; a continuation. *udan ∗an* a long rain. *∗ané tjrita minggu kepungkur* the continuation of last week's story. 2 full length. *Klambiné ∗an.* It's a one-piece dress. 3 link between two things. *∗an Suez* the Suez Canal. 4 a back *or* side exit through a wall. 5 having a batik pattern applied to both sides of it. *Baṭiké ∗an.* Her wraparound is worked in batik on both sides of the fabric. **∗é** the next thing. *Saiki ∗é keprijé?* What happened after that? **∗-∗an** continuously; again and again. *Tanduranė diopèni ∗-∗an.* He tends his plants all the time. *Ḍèkė alok "linḍu!" ∗-∗an.* He kept shouting, "Earthquake!" **ñ/di∗aké (ng/dipun·ladjeng·aken** *kr?*) 1 to continue, keep on with. *Dongèngané di∗aké.* He went on with the story. 2 to forward [mail]. **ñ/di∗i** to apply [the same batik design] to the other side of the fabric. **pa·ñ∗** beam of a Javanese-style house connecting the upper and lower parts of the roof. **bonang (***lsp.***) panerus** *bonang* (or other gamelan instrument) which carries on the melody introduced by the first *bonang* (or other). **sa∗é** after that. *ésuké lan sa∗é* the next day and from then on. *Mengkono sa∗é.* It kept on like that. *or* And so forth. And so on in the same vein. **∗ ing ati** deep down inside. *Tresnané ∗ ing ati.* He loves her with all his heart. **∗ ing tingal/pa·ñ·tingal** perceptive. **∗ terang** frank, candid. *Sing ∗ terang waé.* Be frank about it. *∗ terang aku ora duwé ḍuwit.* To be perfectly frank, I have no money.

terwâtjâ clear(ly visible, audible, comprehensible). **ň/di∗kaké** to make clear; to explain
terwéla clear(ly visible, audible, comprehensible). **ň/di∗kaké** to explain, to make clear
terwèlu *var of* TRUWÈLU
tès *rpr* a drop falling. *Banjuné nètès, mak ∗.* The drop of water fell, plink! *∗... ∗... ∗... ∗ ...eluhé wiwit metu manèh.* Her tears began to fall once again. **tas-∗** *rpr* slow, continuous dripping. *Ing sak ndjeroning guwa, banjuné nètès, tas-∗.* The water in the cave drips slowly and inexorably. **∗-∗an** to keep dripping. *See also* TÈTÈS
tes *rg var of* TAS
ṭès *rpr* a tiny explosion
ṭes *rpr* a firm striking *or* crushing action
tesbèh *var of* TASBÈH
tèsèk a certain hardwood tree whose wood is often used for walking sticks
tesih *inf var of* (*md for?*) TAKSIH
tesmak *ng kr,* **tingal·an** *or* **pa·ň·tingal·an** *ki* eyeglasses. *∗ biru* or *∗ ireng* dark glasses. *keḍèp ∗* staring wide-eyed and unblinking. **sa∗** like glasses. *Mripaté sa∗.* His eyes are (big and round) like spectacles. *∗* **baṭok** 1 unable to see what is right in front of one. 2 round-eyed. 3 thick-skinned, insensitive. *∗* **ḍingklik** *or ∗* **watu** unable to see what is right in front of one's nose
tèstamèn last will and testament
tèt bang! smack! *Ṭar, ṭar, ∗, ḍung, suwarané beḍil tjeḍak banget.* Bang-bang-boom, the gunshots were very close.
tet- *see also under* T- (*Introduction, 3.1.3*)
ṭèt 1 exactly. *∗ tiba tanggal* on the exact date. *djam lima ∗* five o'clock on the dot. 2 *rpr* the blast of a trumpet *or* whistle. **∗-∗an** 1 *pl* trumpeting, whistling. 2 to jabber, yak
ṭet *rpr* a sharp metallic ring
ṭeṭ- *see also under* Ṭ- (*Introduction, 3.1.3*)
tétah **ň/di∗** to hold a child by the hands to steady him as he learns to walk
tetah to blame; to cut down (*root form: kr for* TUTUH)
tetak *ng kr,* **supit** *ki* circumcision. **∗an** circumcision ceremony. **ň/di∗aké** to have [a boy] circumcised. **ň/di∗i** to circumcise [a boy]
tètèg bar, barrier (*var of* TETEG)
teteg 1 barrier, bar placed across sth. *∗ banju* sluice gate. *∗ sepur* gate at a railroad crossing. 2 stoic. *∗ atiné sanadyan ramané séda.* She acted with fortitude, though her father had just died. **∗an** *wj* slow steady tapping on the puppet chest with a stick, for special effects. **ň/di∗** to bar; to meet with a barrier. *Ḍèké neteg lawang.* He barred the door. *Jèn wis neteg témbok bandjur ménggok ngiwa.* When you come to a wall in front of you, turn left. **ň/di∗aké** to steel oneself to sth, to display fortitude against. **ň/di∗i** to bar sth. *Ḍèké netegi wong mlaku.* He blocked off the pedestrians.
tètèh to enunciate clearly. **ň/di∗aké** to enunciate sth clearly. *nètèhaké tembung* to pronounce a word clearly
tètèk breast. **ň/di∗i** to breast-feed [a baby]
ṭèṭèk **∗an** 1 a hollow bamboo tube which produces a sharp sound when rapped with a stick: used by night patrols to sound an alarm, by peddlers to attract customers. 2 a variety of ghost that makes a tapping sound. **balung ∗an** extremely thin. **ň/di∗(i)** to produce a sharp sound by rapping. **ronḍa ∗** night patrol. *See also* ṬÈK 2
ṭeṭek̄ **ň/di∗** to tap lightly
ṭèṭèk-bengèk odds and ends
tetel a mashed-glutinous-rice dish. **ň/di∗** 1 to make [ingredients] into the above dish. 2 to crowd. *Sing nunggang kaja peda di∗.* The passengers were jammed in like sardines. 3 *slang* to stuff oneself with food. **ň/di∗aké** to press sth [into]. *Sega sanguné di∗ké nang kalèng.* He packed some rice into a can, to eat along the way.
ṭèṭèl to become detached, peel off. *Kulité kaju wis ∗.* The bark has come off. **∗an** peeled-off pieces. **ň/di∗(i)** to peel/strip sth off. *nèṭèli kulit kaju* to peel off bark. *Limé angèl di∗.* The glue is hard to get off.
ṭeṭel *var of* ṬÈṬÈL
tetep 1 steady; unchanging. *padunungan sing ∗* a fixed location. *Uripé ∗ mlarat baé.* They remain poor. *Aku ∗ terus mlaku.* I kept on walking steadily. 2 tight; firm; confirmed. *Pengangkatané wis ∗.* His appointment to the post has been confirmed. *Olèhmu nutup botol mau kurang ∗.* You didn't seal the bottle tight. *unḍang*[2] *ḍasar sing durung ∗* a temporary constitution. **∗an** act of confirming *or* establishing. *lajang ∗an* a letter of authorization, confirmation, etc. *Saiki kari ngentèni ∗an.* We're just waiting now for a decision. **ka∗an** confirmation, authorization. **ň∗** tight, close. *Olèhé nutup lawang sing netep.* Shut the

door tight. *Olèhé nutup kalèng sing netep.* Cover the can closely. **ñ/di*aké** to make sth steady/firm. *Apa sing di*aké?* What have you decided on? *prakara sing di*aké déning unḍang²* matters that are established by law. *Rapat netepaké aku dadi ketua.* The meeting appointed me chairman. *Tutup peṭi mau kudu di*aké.* The chest must be closed tightly. **ñ/di*i** to adhere to firmly. *Wis netepi kuwadjibané.* He has fulfilled his responsibility. *netepi djandji (kangsèn)* to keep a promise (an appointment). **pa·ñ*** act of confirming/establishing. *Kanggo penetep, kowé kudu nanḍa-tangani surat iki.* As confirmation, sign this letter. **durung *** temporary. *pemeréntah durung ** interim government

tètèr termite-like pest. ***en** eaten into *or* destroyed by this pest. **ke*** to get beaten in a fight *or* game. **ke*an** behind schedule

teter ñ/di* to nag smn, keep after smn with questions

ṭèṭèr *var of* TÈTÈR

tètès 1 a drop. *banju sa** a drop of water. 2 to fall in drops. *Eluhé paḍa *.* She wept. 3 molasses. **ñ/di*aké** *or* **ñ/di*i** to sprinkle *or* drip sth. *nètèsaké banju ing tanduran* to water the plants. **ñ/di*i** to materialize, come about. **t·um·ètès** to drip steadily (*see also* BANJU). *See also* TÈS

tetes 1 [of hair] neatly groomed. 2 clitoris-piercing ceremony (*ki for* SUNAT). ***an** what hatches out. **ané enḍog wudjud sèt.* Larvae hatch from the eggs. **ñ/di*** to hatch. *Enḍogé netes dadi uler.* The eggs hatch out caterpillars. **ñ/di*aké** to have *or* allow sth to hatch. **ñ/di*i** to cut, snip. *netesi tali* to snip string

tétoron a widely used synthetic material produced in Japan (originally a brand name)

tewah *sbst kr for* TUWUH

tèwèl (*or* **ke***) unripe jackfruit, eaten as a vegetable *or* salad

ṭèwel *rpr* a large mouthful [of meat] *or* fingerful [of flesh being pinched]. *Dagingé ditjokot mak *.* He bit off a large mouthful of the meat.

ṭèwèr *-** to hang limp

tèxtil *var sp of* TÈKSTIL

tg(l). *see* TANGGAL

th(n). *see* TAUN

ti 1 *excl: shf of* MATI. *Ti aku!* How stupid of me! *Ti kowé!* I hope you die! 2 baked goods (*shf of* ROTI: *street peddlers' cry*)

tiba *ng,* **ḍawah** *kr* 1 to fall, drop. ** ing lemah* to fall to the ground. ** mengkureb/krungkeb* to fall face down. ** mlumah/klumah* to fall face up. 2 to turn (to), go (to). *Mangkeling atiku * menjang bis.* My irritation then turned to the bus. *jèn * ing éngggok²an* when you come to a curve. *Hadiah kepisan * marang A.* A got first prize. 3 to experience, undergo. ** ing kemlaratan* to fall upon hard times. ** lara pati* to experience illness and death. *Ḍèké * nomer telu ing udjian.* He came out third in the exam. 4 to coincide with. *Lahirku * dina Senèn.* My birthday falls on a Monday. ** gong* at the stroke of the *gong.* 5 to fall under the heading of. ** untung* unlucky. *Jèn regané limang rupiah, kuwi * murah.* Only five rupiahs?–that's cheap. ***é** (*prn* **tiba'é**) *rg var of* *NÉ *below.* ***n** 1 (having) fallen; act of falling. *watu *n* a fallen rock. *peḍang sa*n* a swordstroke. 2 scapegoat. *Kanggo nutupi luputé, wong lija dienggo *n.* To cover his own mistake, he blamed it on smn else. ***né** as it happens (turns out). *Tibané ana tamu.* There happened to be guests. **né bener.* It turned out to be true. *Mati aku, *né ḍompètku kèri!* Oh dear, I've left my wallet somewhere! **ka*n** 1 to get fallen on (by). *Aku ketiban krambil.* A coconut fell on me. 2 to have sth happen to one. *ke*n gitik lan srengen* to get beaten and yelled at. *ke*n daru* to have a stroke of good luck. *ke*n ḍenggung* to get the blame for sth. *ke*n ḍong* to be accused of sth. **ketiban tai baja** to be accused of sth. **ñ*** to fall deliberately. *Ḍèwèké niba ing ngarepé Sang Nata.* He prostrated himself before the King. *niba-tangi* to keep falling and picking oneself up; *fig* to do one's utmost. *Olèhé njambut-gawé niba-tangi, gadjihé meksa ora tjukup.* He works to the point of exhaustion but still can't earn enough. **ñ/di*kaké** 1 to let sth fall. *Ḍompèté di*kaké.* He dropped his wallet. 2 to cause sth to fall. *nibakaké ukuman mati* to impose a death sentence. 3 to direct sth to(ward). *Kesalahan mau di*kaké marang aku.* He passed the blame on to me. 4 to order a certain amount of money's worth. *Jèn tuku katjang ora susah takon regané, terus nibakké waé.* When you buy peanuts, you don't need to ask the price, just put down the money. **ñ/di∗ni** to fall *or* drop on(to). *Watuné nibani sirahku.* The stone fell on my head. *di∗ni ukuman abot* to be given a severe punishment. **pa·ñ∗** 1 act of falling/dropping. 2 a payment. *paniba tamba* payment made to smn one has injured. *paniba ules* payment to the survivors of smn killed accidentally. *paniba sampir* down payment. **sa∗né** coinciding with. *sa∗ning beḍil muni* just as the gun went off. **sa∗(-∗)né** at the (very) worst. **t·um·iba** (**ḍ·um·awah** *kr*) *ltry var of* ∗. ∗ **kasur** to tumble into a life of ease through no effort of one's own

tibaké *rg var of* TIBA·NÉ

tibèng to fall on(to) (*contracted from* TIBA ING)

tiḍa ∗-∗ dim, vague, uncertain, obscure

tiḍem *see* ḌEḌEP

tiḍur to sound the mosque drum (*beḍug*) during the fasting month as a signal that it is time for the permissible early-morning meal. *See also* TEMPAT

tiga three (*kr for* TELU)

tigâlikur twenty-three (*kr for* TELULIKUR)

tigan 1 egg (*kr for* ENḌOG). 2 betel chew (*rg kr for* KINANG)

tigang three (*as modifier: kr for* TELUNG[a])

tigas 1 (having been) cut off. 2 brand new, never used; virgin. **∗an** [of fabric] uncut. **ñ/di∗** to cut (off). **nigas gulu** to cut smn's throat. ∗ **gagang** [of rice] sold immediately upon being harvested. ∗ **pantjing** cut off slantwise

tigâwâdjâ a certain freshwater fish

tigâwârnâ 1 three-colored; three-patterned. 2 a certain design for kris blades

tigâwelas thirteen (*kr for* TELULAS)

tija *see* DWI

tijang 1 pole; flagstaff; ship's mast. 2 person; adult; someone (*kr for* WONG[a]). 3 *excl* (*kr for* WONG[b]). **ñ/di∗i** to put a mast on [a ship]

tijâsâ *rg var of* KUWASA

Tijonghoā, Tijonghwā Chinese person

Tijongkok China

tijung **ñ∗** *or* **t·um·ijung** bent over, bowed down. *See also* PENTIJUNG

tijup **ke∗** to get blown. *ke∗ ing angin* blown by the wind. **ñ/di∗** to swoop. *Manuk mau nijup muḍun.* The bird swooped low. *angin nijup saka lor* a gust of wind from the north. **t·um·ijup** to blow, gust

tik typewriting. *kertas* ∗ typing paper. *mesin* ∗ typewriter. *tukang/djuru* ∗ typist. **∗(-∗)an** action of typing; (having been) typed. *lajang ∗-∗an* a typewritten letter. **nge/di∗** to typewrite. *nge∗ lajang* to type a letter. **nge/di∗aké** to type for smn. *Karangané tak ∗aké.* I typed his article for him.

ṭik[a] *var of* KAṬIK. *Lo ∗ bisa ta?* How on earth does he do it? *É, botjah ∗ nganjelaké temen.* What an *irritating* boy you are. **ṭak-∗** to make noise *or* clatter. *Adja ṭak-∗ nang kono, bajiné lagi bubuk.* Quiet! – the baby's sleeping. *See also* TOKṬIK

ṭi:k̄[b] ∗-∗ *slang* a tiny bit/amount; a trivial thing. *Ṭikṭik mesṭi nesu.* He gets mad over little things. **∗-∗an** to keep touching/handling (things)

tiké certain leaves (*awar[2], ujah[2]an*) dried and finely ground, mixed with opium, for smoking. **pa∗ñ** office where opium is sold

tikel many times greater; *n* times as much. *Olèh[2]ané ∗ tinimbang ḍèk ḍéwé[2].* They took in much more [working as a team] than both had taken in alone. *Mangané ∗ sepuluh karo ṭadahmu.* He eats ten times as much as you do. *Ing ndalem setahun baé pitiké wis dadi ∗ loro.* In a year, his chickens have doubled in number. *Wulan ngarep gadjihé ∗ loro.* His salary next month will be twice as much. **∗an** having increased manyfold. ∗ **ma∗** many times as much. *∗ ma∗ seka bijèn* much more than before. *Semut iku bisa ngusung barang sing ∗ ma∗ geḍéné.* Ants can carry things that are many times as big as they are. **te∗an** *sms* ∗AN. **ke∗** to get multiplied/increased. *Baṭiné ke∗.* His profits grew. **ke∗-∗** to increase many times over. **ma·ñ∗-ñ∗** (*psv* **di∗-∗**) to increase manyfold. *Bukuné manikel-nikel.* He has far more books now. **ñ∗** to increase in number. *Gunggungé tabrakan nikel.* The total number of accidents climbed. *nikel alis* to knit the brows. *ñ∗ asta* to fold the hands (in a respectful gesture; [*or* **ñ∗ werti**] as a motion in the classical dance). **ñ/di∗aké** to increase sth manyfold. *mikroskup sing bisa nikelaké kaping rolas atus* a microscope that can magnify 1200 times. *nikelaké produksi* to increase production. **ñ/di∗i** to increase the amount of [sth one does]. *Olèhé njambut gawé di∗i.* He's working harder. *nikeli olèhé mènèhi ḍuwit* to increase the amount of money one gives. ∗ **balung** a certain plant. ∗ **tekuk** manyfold, many times as much. *Jèn dibetjiki pamalesé* ∗

tekuk. If he is treated kindly, he will return the kindness many times over. **ñ∗-ñ·tekuk·i** (*psv* **di∗-tekuk·i**) to cause to mount up *or* multiply. ∗ **wos·en** stiff fingers/toes

ṭiklu *var of* TIKLUK

ṭiklu:k ∗-∗ bent/stooped with age

ṭikruk **(ke)∗an** to proceed *or* make one's way with difficulty

tikung **∗an** a curve, a bend. *∗ané kalèn kang ménggok mangalor* a northward bend in the river. **ñ∗** to curve, bend. *Dalané ni-kung mengiwa.* The road curves to the left.

tikus mouse, rat. **∗an** 1 a kind of firework that moves about on the ground as it goes off. 2 a certain herb used in folk medicines. ∗ **djerug** a certain tiny mouse. ∗ **la-ngu** a small, long-nosed rat. ∗ **mati ing (e)lèng·é** a person whose friends have all gone away or died. ∗ **warok** a certain large rat

ṭi:l 1 *intsfr* one. *Putrané mung sidji ∗.* He has only one child. 2 *rpr* plucking, breaking off. *Mak ∗, aku diwènèhi setjuwil.* He broke off a piece and gave it to me.

tilam thin sleeping mat

ṭilang a certain bird (*var of* KUṬILANG). **ḍèt** ∗ *rpr* the cry of this bird. *See also* ṬI-LENG

tilap **ke∗an** to get left alone by smn who goes off without one's knowledge. *ke∗an karo bapaké* deserted by his father. **ñ/di∗aké** to desert smn (as above)

tilar to leave (behind) (*kr for* TINGGAL). **∗an** inheritance (*kr for* WARIS·AN?)

tilas 1 (**tabet** *kr?*) mark, trace, remains. *mbuwang ∗* to get rid of the traces. *∗ ban* tire marks. *∗ kraton* the ruins of a palace. *Aku tatu ∗é dipenṭungi.* I have wounds where he beat me. 2 former, ex-. *∗ mitra-ku sekolah* an old school friend of mine. *∗ kepala pulisi* former chief of police. *Pa-pan iki ∗ pasar.* This used to be a market-place. *kerḍus ∗ waḍah sabun* a box that used to have soap in it. *satjeḍaking ∗ omah-ku* near where I used to live. **(pa)∗an** remains of the past. *petilasan*² *sing rupa tja-nḍi* relics from the past in the form of temples

ṭilek̄ *var of* ṬELEG

tilem to sleep, go to bed (*kr for* TURU)

ṭileng **ṭilang-∗** 1 having large black eyes. 2 unable to close one's eyes

tilgram (to send) a telegram *or* cable. **ñ/di∗** to send a telegram (to). *Bolak-balik di∗, nanging ora mangsuli.* They wired him again and again, but he didn't answer. **ñ/di∗aké** to send by telegraph. *Kabar*² *mau di∗aké mréné, apa liwat raḍio?* Did the news come by telegraph or over the radio?

tilgrap telegraph. *kantor ∗* telegraph office

ṭili ∗-∗ soaking wet

tilik *ng,* **tuwi** *kr* to pay a friendly visit. *Wis lawas aku ora ∗.* I haven't been to see you in a long time. **ñ/di∗i** 1 to pay a visit to. 2 to approach and scrutinize. *Tak kira ana memedi, bareng tak∗i djebul djeruk bali gu-manḍul ing wit.* I thought it was a ghost, but when I went and took a close look it turned out to be a grapefruit hanging on a tree.

tiling **ñ/di∗aké** to listen attentively (to, for). *Kupingé tansah niling*²*aké.* He kept his ears cocked. **t·um·iling** to pay close attention, *esp.* by listening

tilong *var of* ṬILONG

ṭilong ∗-∗ *or* **ṭilang-∗** ignorant, mindless; taken aback. *Aku ṭilang-∗ ora muḍeng.* I felt dazed–I didn't know what was going on.

tilp. *see* TILPUN

tilpon *var of* TILPUN

tilpun (*abbr*: **tel., tilp., tlp.**) telephone; (to make) a telephone call. *∗é lagi kanggo* or *∗é lagi tjaturan.* The line is busy. *nampa ∗* to get a phone call. *Isih ∗?* Are you still on the phone? **∗(-∗)an** toy telephone. **∗-∗an** to telephone each other. **ñ/di∗** to call smn on the phone. *Tak ∗ soréné ora ana.* I called you that evening but you weren't there.

tim 1 steamed (*compounding form*). *sega ∗* steamed rice-and-chicken dish. 2 (*prn* **ti:m**) team. **nge/di∗** to prepare [foods] by steaming them and adding certain seasonings. **pa∗an** rice-steaming equipment

timah[a] tin. ∗ **buḍeng** lead. ∗ **putih** tin. ∗ **sari** zinc

timah[b] (*or* ∗-∗) healing, becoming well. *wis ∗-∗* on the road to recovery

timâhâ a certain beautifully grained wood, used for making kris sheaths and walking sticks

timang belt buckle. **ñ/di∗i** to put a buckle on [a belt]

timângâ *inf var of* TIMAHA

timba bucket for drawing water from a well. **∗nan** bucketful. **∗n-∗nan** to pretend to draw water, play at drawing water. **ñ/di·te∗**

to draw sth in (*fig*). *Adja nenimba kawruh kang ora betjik.* Don't absorb knowledge that is not worthwhile. **ñ/di*kaké** to draw water for smn. **ñ/di*(ni)** to draw [water]. *nimba banju ing sumur* to draw water from a well

timbal[a] (*ki for* UNDANG) ***an** an invitation; a call, summons. (*dawuh*) **an Dalem* yes, your Majesty. **ñ/di*i** 1 to call (to) [a social inferior]. *Anaké di*i.* She called her child. *Timbalana mréné.* Call him over here. 2 to invite [a social inferior]. *Kula matur nuwun sanget déné dipun *i ing dalem pendjenengan.* Thank you very much for inviting me to your home.

timbal[b] ***-t·um·imbal** *or* **te*an** [of sounds] to occur in rapid succession. *swarané mertjon *-tumimbal* the sound of firecrackers going off one after the other. **ñ/di*aké** to pass the word from one to the other

timbang 1 (rather) than; compared with. *Regané luwih murah * jèn wis ana ing pasar.* It costs less than what they have at the marketplace. *Timbang kowé arep lunga njang Semarang, apa kowé gelem mèlu aku baé?* Rather than going to Semarang, wouldn't you like to come along with me? 2 in equilibrium. *A * main sekak karo B.* A and B are evenly matched in chess. *A * boboté karo B.* A weighs the same as B. *A * menawa kekantjan karo B sebab pada olèhé seneng kesenian.* A and B are congenial because of their love of art. *tanpa ** unequaled. *Jèn main sekak dèwèké tanpa *.* No one plays chess as well as he does. ***an** 1 weight. 2 scale, balance; weight used as a counterbalance. 3 marriage partner; mate. ***an·é** by comparison with; rather than. *mBok njambut-gawé apa waé *ané nganggur.* You should be doing some kind of work instead of loafing. **te*an** mate. *Siti wis pestiné dadi te*ané Slamet.* Siti is destined to be Slamet's wife. **ka*** (rather) than; compared (with). *Ka* tenguk[2] mbok adjar[2] nggitar.* Rather than just sitting around idle, why don't you learn to play the guitar? **ñ/di*** to weigh; to consider alternatives, compare. *nimbang mas* to weigh gold. *Jèn di* karo djaman bijèn...* By comparison with the old days... *Timbangen, lé.* Think about it, son. **ñ/di*aké** to have sth weighed; to have smn weigh. *A nimbangaké beras ing karung iku.* A had the rice in the sack weighed. **ñ/di*i** 1 to be the equal of. *Botjah mengkono iku adja kok *i, mundak kowé mèlu dadi ala.* Don't do as that boy does, or you'll be just as bad. 2 to join in [laughter *etc.*]. **pa·ñ*** *or* **per*an** judgment, consideration. *saka panimbangku* in my opinion. **t·in·imbang** (rather) than; compared with. *Regané luwih murah tinimbang jèn wis ana ing pasar.* It costs less than what they have in the marketplace. *Rikaté prau saiki tikel-matikel tinimbang kuwi mau.* Boats nowadays go many times faster than those. *** sih** equally balanced on both sides; symmetrical

timbel 1 lead (metal). 2 tin. *** putih** tin

timbil a sty on the eyelid. ***en** to have *or* get a sty

timbis *var of* TIMBLIS

timblis wooden mallet for breaking things up. **ke*** to get dropped on. **ñ/di*** to drop on(to), hit from above

timbrah greenish discoloration from copper *or* brass. **ñ*** stained with the above

timbreng overcast, clouded over

timbrung **ñ/di*** 1 to attack, come at suddenly. 2 to interrupt. *mèlu[2] nimbrung rembug* to interrupt a conversation

timbul 1 to emerge, stand out. **é ana ing madyaning seni* his emergence in the field of the arts. **é penjakit* the outcropping of a disease. *teguh ** outstandingly strong. 2 raised, embossed. *tulisan ** embossed lettering. **ñ/di*** to strengthen magically. *Sawisé di*, wong mau bisa ngangkat watu gedé mau.* Imbued with supernatural strength, he was able to lift the great rock. **ñ/di*aké** to cause to emerge; to bring forth. *nimbulaké rasa petjah-belah* to cause dissension. *nimbulaké rasa nasionalisme* to foster nationalism

timbun **ma*-*** heaped up. *Berasé nganti ma*-* ngebaki gudang.* The rice was piled in up to the capacity of the warehouses.

timen *inf var of* TEMEN

timik ***-*** (to walk) slowly and with short steps. *See also* KETIMIK

timlo a soup-like rice-accompanying dish

timpah **ke*** 1 to get pressed down. 2 to be on the losing side. **ñ/di*** to press (down) on with the leg while sleeping

timpal a wound that causes peeling of the skin *or* flesh. **ke*-*** to be in constant difficulty. *Uripé tansah ke*-*.* He leads a hard life. **ñ/di*** 1 to wound as above. 2 to dispose of one's feces with a leaf

timplak **ke*-*** 1 characterized by difficulty and sorrow in one's life. 2 (to walk) with a limping gait

timpuh to sit with the knees drawn up alongside the body. *bakul ** sedentary market seller. **ke*** to drop into the above position. **ñ*** to assume this sitting position. **ñ/di*aké** to place [the legs] alongside the body in the above sitting position. *Siti linggih, sikilé di-*aké.* Siti sat down and tucked up her legs. *** alih·an** 1 to keep shifting the feet from one side to the other while sitting as above. 2 to switch to another job on the condition that one may return to the original job

timun (*or* **ke***) cucumber. **pa*an** cucumber patch. *** dj·in·ara** a job easily done. *** mungsuh durèn** a small *or* weak opponent pitted against a strong, powerful rival

timur 1 eastern, Oriental. *Djawa ** East Java. ** Tengah* the Middle East. 2 east wind. 3 young (*ki for* NOM). ***an** east wind

timus a snack made with fried cassava and flour (or, Jogjanese style, with steamed mashed cassava and coconut sugar)

tin-, ṭin- *see also under* T-, Ṭ- (*Introduction, 3.1.7*)

tindak 1 what smn does; actions, conduct. ** sing betjik/ala* a good/bad way to act. ***-*** the way he used to behave. *Ḍèké gumun weruh *ku.* He was surprised to see what I did. 2 to walk (*ki for* M·LAKU). 3 to go; to be away (*ki for* LUNGA). **ñ/di*-aké** *or* **ñ/di*i** to do, perform, commit [an act]. *nindakaké kuwadjiban* to do one's duty. *nindakaké pepati* to commit murder. *Ḍèké mangerti sing arep tak *i.* He understood what I was going to do. *nindakké pegawéjané ḍéwé* to do one's own work. *nindakké pegawéjan ḍéwé* to do the work by oneself. *nindakaké rantjangan* to carry out a plan. **pa·ñ*** conduct, actions. *Téoriné gampang, ning panindaké sing angèl.* The theory is easy; the doing is difficult. **sa*é** whatever one does. *saka sa*é* judging by all he does. *Sa* lan satanduké mesṭi bener.* Everything he does is always exemplary. **t·um·indak** 1 action, activity. *temindak² sing murakabi* useful activities. 2 to act, do. *Gampang tumindaké.* It's easy to do. *Pepréntahané wis ora bisa tumindak.* The government can no longer function. *Taun anjar wis temindak.* The new year has begun. *** tanduk** actions, conduct, behavior (*ki for* KE·LAKU·AN?). *Tindak-tandukku tansah di-ulat²aké.* She watched everything I did. *Tindak-tanduké kaja satrija.* He conducts himself like a nobleman.

tinḍes a heavy object used to weight sth down. **ñ/di*** to weight sth down; *fig* to oppress. *radja kang ninḍes rakjat* an oppressive ruler. **pa·ñ*** suppression, oppression

tinḍih 1 heavy object used to weight sth down. 2 chief, leader. ***en** *sms* KE*EN *below.* **ke*** weighted down; oppressed. *A mainé apik banget nganti B ke* terus.* A played so well that B was constantly on the defensive. **ke*an** to get sth put on it. *ke*an watu* weighted down with a stone. *Platku petjah ke*an koper.* Someone put a suitcase down on my record and broke it. **ke*en** 1 to mutter in one's sleep during a nightmare. 2 to be disturbed in one's sleep by having cut off the circulation smw, *e.g.* the arm, by lying on it. **ñ/di*i** 1 to be on top of; to put sth on top of. *Jèn omong sing genah, adja ming waton ninḍihi.* Talk reasonably; don't just try to get the better of the other person. *Penganggoku tak *i bantal.* I put my clothes under the pillow. 2 to weight sth down with. *Kurungané di*i watu.* The cage was weighted down with a stone.

tinḍik hole pierced for earrings. ***an** 1 having pierced ears; [of ears] pierced. 2 act *or* way of piercing ears. **ñ/di*** to pierce ears

tindja feces (*kr for* TAI)

tindjo (*or* **mer***) to visit (*ki for* TILIK?). **ñ/di*** to pay an official visit to. *Désané di* pak bupati.* The regent visited the village. **pa·ñ*** official visiting observer. **pa·ñ*(a)n** ceremony following the arrival of the newly married bridal couple at the groom's home

tindju boxing (sport)

ting 1 lantern. 2 *inf var of* PATING

ṭing[a] *rpr* a clear high jingling *or* tinkling. ***-*** to keep jingling/tinkling

ṭing[b] (*or* ***-***) utterly, completely, through and through. *Wis entèk *.* It's all gone! *djaka *-** a confirmed bachelor. *See also* TOKṬING, ṬONG-ṬING

tingal 1 a look, a glance. *masang ** to look meaningfully. *mbalang ** to toss a quick flirtatious glance. *mbuwang ** to look away, look aside. 2 human eye (*ki for* MRIPAT). *katja ** eyeglasses. 3 to look (at) (*root form: kr for* DELENG, DELOK). 4 to watch *etc.* (*root form: kr for* TON[a], TONTON). 5 selfish purpose *or* point of view. *Tingalé* *loro, jakuwi ngepèk bodjo lan ngepèk banḍa.* He had a double purpose: to marry the girl and to marry her money. *malih* * to switch loyalties. ***an** 1 (celebration of a) birthday (or other special event) (*ki for* WETU·Ñ). 2 mirror (*kr for* PA·NG·ILU·Ñ). 3 eyeglasses (*ki for* TESMAK). **ka*** 1 to look, appear, show (*kr for* KATON, KÉTOK). 2 visible, showing (*kr for* KETARA). **ka*en** to see in the mind's eye (*kr for* KATON·EN). **pa·ñ*** 1 human eye (*ki for* MRIPAT). 2 vision (*kr for* PA·N·DELENG). **pa·ñ*an** 1 mirror (*kr for* PA·NG·ILU·Ñ). 2 eyeglasses (*ki for* TESMAK)

tinggal *ng,* **tilar** *kr* (*or* **a***) to leave (behind), abandon, neglect. *Buḍa * kamuktèn sing ana ing kraton bandjur tapa.* Buddha left the good life at court and lived as an ascetic. *atinggal kaprajitnan* to fling aside all caution. * *kokoh(an)* to leave a meal (*or, fig,* a job) partly finished. ***an** sth left behind; an inheritance. *Kebisan *ané embah-bujut mau adja nganti ilang.* Skills passed down to us by our ancestors must not be lost. **ñ*** 1 to leave (behind). *ninggal omah* to leave (abandon) a house. *ninggal mati* to leave survivors (upon one's death). *Gawéané durung rampung wis di*.* He's left the job unfinished. *Bareng sepuré wis arep mangkat A durung teka, kepeksa di* B.* The train was about to leave and A hadn't showed up, so B had to leave without him. 2 different from, departing from. *ninggal kasusilan* unethical. **ninggal botjah ana ing waton** to feel uneasy/apprehensive. **ñ/di*aké** to leave [to *or* for smn, *esp.* as a parting gift]. *Dolanané tjatur di*aké keponakané.* [When he went away,] he left the chess set behind for his nephews. **ñ/di*i** 1 to leave behind, *esp.* as a parting gift. *Ḍèk paman kondur, aku di*i Rp. satus.* When my uncle left, he gave me 100 rupiahs. *Kantjaku ninggali buku.* My friend went off without his book. *Lemut malaria jèn njakot uwong ninggali widjining lelara barang.* When the malaria mosquito bites, it leaves disease germs. *Sang Budha ninggali wedjangan.* Buddha left behind many words of wisdom. 2 to leave to/for. *Anaké di*i keris.* He left his son a kris. *Aku di* bukuné kanggo watjan.* He left his books for me to read. * **donja** to pass away. * **glanggang (a)tjolong plaju** to flee from the battlefield. **(ñ)* tapak djero** to leave a deep mark (*esp. fig*). * **tata-krama** to forget one's manners

tinggi (*or* **ke***) bedbug

tingi a certain bark used for making dyes

ṭingil ***-*** [of small objects] to emerge above the surroundings. *Apa sing katon *-* ing banju kaé?* What's that little thing sticking out of the water? *See also* PENṬINGIL

tingkah what smn does; actions, behavior. **é katon tjeṭa.* We could clearly see what he did. * **laku** actions, behavior. *See also* PERTINGKAH

tingkas 1 [of rain] to stop, subside. 2 clear, clearly understood; to understand clearly

tingkat (*abbr*: **tk.**) 1 floor, story. *Kantoré ana * loro.* The office is on the second floor. 2 rank; grade at the university level. *Ali saiki wis * loro.* Ali is a sophomore now. ***an** of a certain rank, at a certain level. *Paḍa *ané.* They have the same rank. They're in the same class. **ñ/di*aké** to raise the level (of)

tingkeb (*or* ***an**) ceremony held in the seventh month of pregnancy. **ñ/di*i** to hold the above ceremony for smn

tingkem a small woven-bamboo basket with a hinged lid. ***an** that which is sealed *or* closed securely. **ñ/di*** to seal, close securely. **ningkem wadi** to keep a secret

tingkes **ñ/di*(i)** to summarize, bring together, collect in compact form

ṭingkrang sitting improperly in an elevated place higher than others. **ñ/di*aké** to put sth in a high place. *A ningkrangaké sikilé ing nḍuwur médja.* A put his feet on the table.

ṭingkrik *var of* ṬINGKRANG

ṭingkring *var of* ṬINGKRANG

ṭingṭing *see* DJAKA

tingtur tincture. *joḍium* * tincture of iodine

ṭinguk **ṭingak-*** to move the head from side to side, as if searching *or* puzzled

ṭini:k ***-*** [of females] small, slender, and well proportioned. *tjilik *-** teeny-tiny

ṭinṭil bird's heart

tinting **ñ/di*i** to sort [grains] according to size by shaking them on a broad shallow tray

tip tape recorder; tape. *krungu genḍing Djawa saka ** to hear tape-recorded Javanese music. **nge/di*** to record on tape. *Piḍatoné di*.* His speech was tape-recorded.

tipak *var of* TAPAK

tipar *rg* a rice field which is irrigated only by rainfall

tipes *var of* TIPUS

tipis 1 thin (not thick). *Buku mau kandel apa *?* Is the book thick or thin? 2 down to the last of the supply. *Ḍuwité wis *.* We are running low on money. ***an ati·ǹ** timid. **ñ*** decreasing in amount. *Berasé nipis.* The rice is running low. *djeruk nipis* a certain sweet lime-like fruit. **ñ/di*aké** to make thin. *nipisaké kaju nganggo lading* to whittle down a piece of wood with a knife. *** lambé·né** fond of gossiping *or* of bawling people out

tiplak a type of sandal

tiplèk *inf var of* TIPLAK

ṭiplu:k̄ ***-*** chubby

tipu deceit, trickery. **ñ/di*** to trick, deceive

tipung (*or* **ke***) a small drum beaten with the hands

tipus typhus

tir tar. **nge/di*** to tar [a surface]

ṭir 1 *rpr* a ground-cricket's chirp. 2 *rpr* a flash. *Mak * katon sinar ndjlarit abang.* There was a sudden flash of red light. ***-*** *rpr* water trickling in a tiny but steady stream. **ṭar-*** *see* ṬARṬIR. **nge*** to drip. **nge/di*-*** to hand out little by little *or* in small amounts. *See also* IṬIR

tirah 1 to sojourn in the mountains in order to restore one's health. 2 left over, remaining (*kr for* TURAH). **te*** *sms* * 1. **ñ/di*aké** to have smn rest/recuperate in the mountains. **pa*an** health resort

tirakat to deny oneself food and sleep as a self-sacrificial act in order to be granted one's desire. ***an** a group performing such an act of self-denial. **ñ/di*i** to fast *etc.* for [a specific goal]. *A lagi nirakati olèhé kepingin lulus udjiané.* A is denying himself so that he'll pass his exams [as a reward]. *A nirakati B supaja lulus udjiané.* A fasted for B so that B would pass his exams.

tiram *var of* TIREM

tirem oyster

ṭirik *var of* ṬARIK

tiris *oj* coconut. ***an** coconut tree; wood of the coconut tree

tirta *oj* water. *** marta** water that can magically restore life to the dead *or* make one immortal. *See also* PATIRTA

tiru 1 to resemble. *Anaké kabèh * bapakné.* All of his children look like him. 2 to imitate, copy. ** barang betjik* to imitate a good thing. ***n̂** an imitation, fake, copy. *kembang tiron* imitation flowers. *Sesorahé wong mau jèn betjik mung tiron waé.* When his speeches are good, he's copied them from someone else's. ***-*** to copy, mimic. *Aku ora arep *-* wong sing ngono kaé.* I don't want to be like people who act that way. **ñ/di*** to copy, emulate. *Aku emoh niru wong mau ing sakabèhé.* I don't want to do everything he does. *Garapanku di* kantja djèdjèrku.* The classmate next to me copied my work. *Tirunen manuk ja.* Do an imitation of a bird. **ñ/di·te*** *ltry var of* Ñ/DI*. **ñ/di*k̂aké** to imitate/copy sth. *Apa solahé Slamet ditirokaké munjuk.* The monkey did everything Slamet did. *nirokaké pitik* to imitate a chicken. **pa·ñ*** act *or* way of imitating. *Paniruné sempurna.* His imitation was perfect.

tis **ma*-*** cold, chilly. **aḍem *** to feel uncomfortably cold. **panas *** (to have *or* get) chills and fever; to have malaria. *See also* ATIS

ṭi:s ***-*an** having a compulsion to touch everything. *mBok adja *-*an ngono kuwi ta!* Hands off!

tisik a mended place. ***an** 1 mended, darned, patched. 2 act of mending. *Tisikané apik.* The patching is neat(ly done). **ñ/di*** to mend, patch

tismak *var of* TESMAK

tisna *fancy var of* TRESNA

ṭi:t *rpr* a squeak *or* twitter. *** ṭuwit** to produce such a sound. *Endas²ané lèri muni *-ṭuwit.* The locomotive screeched. *See also* ṬIṬIT

tita 1 clear, obvious. ** jèn ora ana wong.* It's obvious there's nobody around. *Ḍèké * durung paḍang pikiré.* He evidently can't think clearly yet. 2 thorough. *Wis * anggonku maspadakaké kahanan omah iku.* I've made a close observation of what's going on in that house.

titah God's creatures. **ñ/di*aké** to create; to bring about. *Gusti Allah nitahaké manungsa ing alam donja.* God created man. **sa*é** 1 as determined by God. *Olèhé njambut gawé mung sa*é baé.* He does the work he was created to do. 2 at one's own pace. *Njambut gawému sa*é waé.* Just work along at your own speed. **pa·ñ*** act of creating *or* of predetermining the course of fate. **t·in·itah** (pre)destined. *tinitah urip ing donja iki* destined to live in this world.

t·um·itah created by God. *Manungsa tumitah ing alam donja.* Human beings are God's creation.

titel academic degree. *A ngaku-aku duwé* *. He claims (falsely) that he has a degree. * **Ḍr** Ph.D. degree

titi 1 careful, scrupulous, precise. *Delengen sing* *. Take a good look at it! *kurang* * careless. *Sing * adja nganti luput.* Be careful not to make a mistake. 2 *compounding element: see individual entries below.* ***ǹ** careful and accurate by nature. *A titèn, ora tau klèru ndjupuk potloté kantjané.* A is careful—he'd never pick up his friend's pencil by mistake. ***ǹ-*ǹan** to observe the details of. *Tukangé sulap muni warna² supaja angèl titèn²ané.* The magician kept up a line of patter so it would be hard to keep track of what he was doing. *Tukang tjopèt iku menganggo kang angèl titèn²ané.* Pickpockets dress in such a way that they're hard to spot. **ñ/di·(te)*** to investigate, examine. *neniti prakara* to investigate a case. *sing niti* investigator, inspector. *Gawéané di* manèh karebèn ora ana salahé.* He checked over his work again to be sure there were no mistakes. *Wong mau lagi niti basa Djawa.* He's making a study of Javanese. **ñ/di·(te)*ǹi** to observe and remember (the details of). *Ḍèwèké nitèni jèn aku mesṭi ngrokok rokok tjap X.* He noticed that I always smoked Brand X cigarettes. *Titènana barangmu sing endi.* See which ones are yours. *Aku nitèni mentjorongé lampu montormu.* I recognized your headlight beams. *Titènana, suk jèn wis geḍé rak dadi maling.* Wait and see—he'll be a thief when he grows up. **pa·ñ*** *or* **pra*** 1 investigation, examination, observation. *miturut paniti mau* according to his research. 2 one who inspects/examines. *See also* NESTITI, SETITI, TITI-PRIKSA

ṭiṭi *see* WAJANG[a]

titih to ride; to be on (top of) (*root form: ki for* TUNGGANG. ***an** horse, mount (*ki for* DJARAN). **pa·ñ*** *ng kr* 1 a rider. 2 that which sits on top

titik 1 dot, point; period (punctuation mark). * *ireng* a black dot. 2 diacritical mark, *e.g.* the Javanese accent marks and subdots. * *koma(h)* semicolon. ***an** distinguishing mark *or* characteristic. **ka*** as shown *or* judged from. *ke* saka ulaté* to judge by her expression. **ñ/di*** 1 to judge from appearances, read the signs, know the identifying factors. *Jèn di* saka rupané, wong kuwi sadjak ora mitajani.* You can tell from his looks that he's not to be trusted. *Prau sing isih adoh wis bisa sumurup sebab nitik gendéra kang dipasang ing putjuking tijang.* You can identify far-off ships by the flag they fly. 2 to hunt for a missing person *or* thing. * **ijik** all one's life. * *ijik simbah dalemé nang kéné.* My grandfather has lived here all his life. * **melik** mark, indication, trace

ṭiṭik[a] *ng*, **keḍik** *kr* a little, a few. * *waé olèhé ngekèki gula.* Just put in a little sugar. **se*** a little, a few. *se* rong* * though it is trivial. *Se* rong * rada bakalé akèh lan akèh gunané.* It's of little significance now, but it will become greater and highly beneficial. *See also* SEṬIṬIK

ṭiṭik[b] ***an** flint-and-steel for starting fires. **ñ*** to strike a light using the above. **ñ/di*i** to hit *or* tap [sth small]. **pa·ñ*an** *sms* *AN *above*

ṭiṭil to have a small bit flaked *or* peeled from it. *Pèjèké* *. A little of the [potato] chip broke off. **ñ/di*** to flake *or* break a small amount from sth

titilaras 1 the tuning of a musical instrument. *Gamelané *é isih apik.* The instrument is still in good tune. 2 musical note. *See also* LARAS

titimângsâ 1 time, season. *Wis * kowé dadi mantèn.* It's high time you got married. 2 date. *Lajangé kok ora nganggo * kapan olèhé nulis.* There's no date on the letter to indicate when it was written. **ñ/di*ni** to date sth. *nitimangsa lajang* to date a letter. *See also* MANGSA

titip to ask [smn] to [do a favor, run an errand]. *A * B tuku rokok.* A asked B to buy him some cigarettes. *Punapa kepareng kula * kitir sekeḍik kagem keng mbakju?* Would you please give your wife this note? *Jèn kopermu isih loḍang * klambiku.* If you have room in your suitcase, could you pack my shirt? ***an** given into smn's care. *Ḍuwit *an wis njeḍaki entèk.* The money he gave me is nearly gone. *panggonan *an anak²* a children's day-care center. **ñ/di*aké** to leave sth for delivery *or* safekeeping. *Betjiké ḍuwitmu di*aké nèng omah waé.* Better leave your money at home. *lajang kang dak*aké kantjaku* the letter that I gave to my friend to deliver. **ñ/di*i** to ask smn to [do a favor]. *B di*i tuku rokok déning A.* A asked B to buy him some cigarettes.

titipati 1 time to die. *Simbah pantjèn wis * sebab juswané wis akèh.* Grandmother's time has almost come; she's very old. 2 a certain gamelan melody. *See also* PATI

titi-priksa **ñ/di*** to inspect, investigate, examine, look into/after, observe. *nitipriksa kahanané ing désa* to make a study of the village conditions. **pa·ñ*** inspection, observation. *tjaraka panitipriksa* inspector. *ḍines panitipriksa* inspection service. *See also* PRIKSA, TITI

titir 1 constantly, without letup. 2 an alarm sounded to warn villagers of danger (fire, flood, *etc.*). ***an** act of sounding the alarm. **ñ/di*(i)** 1 to [do] constantly *or* without letup. *A nitir ngedjak nonton bioskup.* A kept nagging me to go to the movies with him. 2 to sound the alarm

titis 1 a skilled shooter. *Ḍèké *.* He's a crack shot. 2 in human form; incarnate. **ñ*** 1 to enter a human body (*referring to a soul beginning a new incarnation*). 2 to change one's form. *Wong tuwa kuwi nitis dadi manuk.* **pa·ñ*** 1 one's aim (with a gun). 2 knowledge about transference of identities. 3 mold for shaping brown sugar into cakes

titisârâ *see* SAWAH

ṭiṭit *rpr* squeaking, twittering. * **ṭuwit** to produce such sounds. *swarané manuk *-ṭuwit* the twittering of birds. *See also* ṬIT

ṭitjik ***-*** to move with slow, silent steps; to sneak

tiwas 1 dead; to die. 2 to [do] in vain. *Hem, djebul ora apa-apa, * aku ḍeg-ḍegan.* So, nothing happened after all–I worried for nothing. **ka*an** to undergo hardships; to get killed. * **ke·bener·an** a pleasant surprise, a lucky coincidence. * **tiwus** *or* * **tuwas** to [do] in vain. * **wis dadi tjangkem djebul tanpa guna** much talk but no results

ṭiweg ***-*** chubby, *esp.* of a child's cheeks

tiwel ***an** wrapped, wound around. **ñ/di*** to wrap *or* wind sth around [sth, *esp.* the legs]

tiwikrâmâ *wj* to transform oneself into a huge giant

ṭiwul a steamed fluffy porridge of powdered dry cassava with brown sugar and grated coconut. *mangan sega ** to eat cassava as a rice substitute

tiwus *see* TIWAS

tja 1 *adr* friend! mate! (*shf of* KANTJA). 2 (*prn* **tjā**) vegetables as ingredients in Chinese dishes. *ajam ** chicken-and-vegetable dish

tja- *see also under* TJE- (*Introduction, 2.9.2*)

tjabak 1 *rg var of* SABAK. 2 *var of* TEBAK. 3 *var of* TJEBAK

tjabang (*abbr*: **tjb.**) branch, arm (of an organization). *kantor ** branch office

tjabar ineffectual. *Adji²né wis *.* His incantations don't work any more. *Sembajangé *.* His prayers failed [because they were done improperly].

tjabé a certain vine, also its fruits (used in folk medicines). ***an** a certain small bird that feeds on insects. **ñj*** covered with gooseflesh. * **lempujang** a folk medicine brewed from the vine fruits above. * **rawit** 1 red pepper, chili pepper. 2 a person who is physically small but very capable. 3 a small variety of the *tjabé* vine and fruits

tjablèk ***an** a slap. *Sa*an wis tjukup.* One smack is enough. ***-*** to keep slapping. **-* lemud* to keep smacking mosquitoes. **-* pupu* to slap one's thigh (as an emotional reaction). **ñj/di*(i)** to slap smn, *usu.* in a friendly *or* affectionate way

tjabud **ñj/di*** to (with)draw, pull out; to revoke, suspend. *Haké milih di*.* He was disfranchised. **ñj/di*aké** to have sth (with)-drawn. *Betjik tjabutna waé untumu sing lara kuwi.* You'd better have that bad tooth pulled.

tjabuk sesame seeds from which the oil has been extracted

tjabul obscene; engaging in obscene activity. **ñj*** to talk obscenely

tjaḍang ***an** (that which is) held in reserve. *A dadi pemain *an.* A is a reserve player. **ñj/di·tje*** *sms* ÑJ/DI·I *below*. **ñj/di*aké** to hold in reserve. *A njaḍangaké satus rupijah kanggo anaké.* A has 100 rupiahs set aside for his son. **ñj/di*i** to hold out the hands as though preparing to catch sth; *fig* to prepare to receive sth. *Ḍuwit iki kanggo njaḍangi jèn ana tamu.* This money is available in case guests come. **tj·um·aḍang** available, set aside. *Ḍuwit wis tjumaḍang, kari ndjupuk waé!* The money is there waiting–all we have to do is get it!

tjaḍok having defective vision

tjaḍong one's share *or* portion. **ñj/di*** to ask for sth. *A njaḍong ḍuwit.* A asked for

some money. *njaḍong ḍawuh* to ask [a social superior] what one is to do. **ñj/di∗aké**
to ask for sth on smn's behalf. *A njaḍong-
aké beras.* A asked for some rice (to give to
smn else). **ñj/di∗i** to give sth out. *A nja-
ḍongi pangan kanggo wong² sing njambut-
gawé.* A handed out food to the workers.
tj·um·aḍong to ask for [rations, orders, *etc.*]

tjag ∗-∗an to enjoy working

tjagak 1 pole, post. ∗ *gendéra* flagpole.
∗ *tilpun* telephone pole. *lampu* ∗ floor
lamp. ∗ *listrik* utility pole. 2 support,
mainstay. *kanggo* ∗ *uripé* in order to sustain life. *Désa iku* ∗é *negara.* The villages
are the backbone of the nation. **ñ/di∗(i)** to
support. *Wité di∗i.* The tree was propped
up with poles. *njagaki wong tuwa* to support one's parents. ∗ **elèk** a means of staying awake. ∗ **palang** barrier

tjagar alam natural preserve

tjah *adr* child! (*shf of* BOTJAH). ∗ *bagus*
boy! (*affectionate*). ∗ *aju* girl! (*affectionate*)

tjahâjâ *var of* TJAHJA

tjahak **ñj/di∗** to trespass on the rights of
another; to violate smn's authority. *njahak
duwèking lijan* to seize smn's property illegally

tjahja 1 beam, ray. 2 appearance, aspect.
∗*né putjet.* She looks pale.

tjai *var of* KUTJAI

tjâjâ face; facial expression. ∗*né abang dluwang.* His face was drained of color.

tjak man (*rg, inf adr*). ∗-∗an act *or* way of
doing. *Tjak²ané apa apik?* Was it done
well? **ka∗an** 1 to get accomplished. *Penggawéjan iki apa sida ke∗an déning A?*
Has A actually done this work? 2 to get
overwhelmed. *ka∗an ing lahar* engulfed in
lava. **nge/di∗aké** 1 to do, carry out. *Dèké
ngetjakaké ambekan gawéan.* He administered artificial respiration. *Pituduhé guru
di∗aké.* He did as the teacher told him to
do. 2 to put to good use. *Duwité di∗ké
kanggo tuku omah.* He used the money to
buy a house. **nge/di∗i** (**ng/di·asta·ni** *ki*) to
do, accomplish. *Iki di∗i nganggo tangan.* It
was done by hand.

tjakaḍong **ñj/di∗** to open [the hand] so
wide that it bends back in an arc

tjakal-bakal founder of a village *or* settlement. **ñj/di∗i** to open up a region for settlement; to become the founder of a community. *Ḍewèké njakal-bakali désa lan*

bebrajan anjar. He established a village and
founded a new community.

tjakar (animal's) paw; (bird's) foot; *cr* human foot. ∗**an** a scratch made by claws.
∗-∗**an** to scratch *or* claw at each other.
tje∗ 1 to claw at. 2 to work for a living.
ñj/di∗(i) to scratch; to use the claws (for)

tjakarwa *rg* blacksmith's tongs

tjakep ∗**an** act of encompassing *or* embracing. **ñj∗** all-embracing, all-encompassing.
ñj/di∗i to reach all the way around sth

tjaket near, close (to) (*md for* TJEḌAK). **ke∗**
loved (by)

tjakil 1 bamboo peg used to hold bamboo
wall sections in place. 2 *wj* a puppet figure acting as ritual antagonist to the hero in
certain combat scenes. ∗**en** to have insomnia. **ñj∗** resembling the above puppet figure; *njakil tjangkem/djanggot* having an undershot jaw like this figure. **ñj/di∗i** to fasten [bamboo sections] with pins

tjakma a certain plant

tjakoḍong *var of* TJAKAḌONG

tjakot a bite. *sa∗* one bite. ∗**an** a bite; act
of biting. ∗-∗**an** to bite each other. **ke∗** 1
to get bitten. 2 to get drawn into a legal entanglement. **ñj/di∗aké** to have *or* let sth be
bitten. *njakotaké tangané nang kutjingé* to
let the cat bite one's hand (in play). **ñj/di∗(i)**
1 to bite. *di∗ asu édan* bitten by a mad
dog. 2 to involve smn in a lawsuit by accusing him. 3 to become habituated *or* addicted (to). 4 to join, get attached. *Sekrupé njakot.* The bolt took hold (by being
screwed into the nut).

tjâkrâ 1 a round frame. 2 *rg* a mark denoting ownership. 3 *wj* a powerful arrow having a toothed round frame as a head. 4 an
R-showing diacritic in Javanese script.
ñj/di∗ 1 *wj* to shoot the above arrow (at).
2 (*rg; or* **ñj/di∗-bawa**) to suspect smn.
pa·ñj∗-bawa suspicion. *Bener panjakraba-
wané.* His suspicions were well founded.
èsem kang rinengga ing panjakrabawa a sus-
picion-provoking smile. ∗-**ṁ·pa·ng·giling·an**
the cycle of life through reincarnations; the
wheel of fortune. *Élinga lakuné tjakra-ma-
nggilingan.* Bear in mind that things are
bound to change. **ñj∗-manggilingan** to proceed through cycles; things will change

tjakrak (*or* ∗-**tjèkrèk**) handsome, fine-looking

tjâkrâwâlâ *ltry* 1 horizon. 2 sky

tjâkrâwa(r)ti *ltry* one who rules the world.

ñj* to rule the world. *ratu binaṭara anjakrawati* a highly esteemed king who reigns supreme

tjakrik 1 appearance, facial aspect. 2 pattern, design

tjakruk a hut used as a station by night watchmen *or* as a shelter when guarding crops against birds

tjakul a freshwater fish

tjakup **ka*** 1 to get hold of, grasp. *Bisané ke* pepénginané kudu njambut gawé temen²*. To get what you want, you have to work hard. 2 contained, included, covered. *bab² kang ka* ing piḍatoné* matters covered in his speech. **ñj/di*** 1 to grasp between the palms. 2 to cover (in a speech, discussion, *etc.*)

tjakur *var of* ṬAKUR

tjal- *see also under* TJL- (*Introduction, 2.9.3*)

tjâlâ (*or, ltry,* **tje***) 1 a messenger sent around to invite guests to a celebration. 2 opening words; to begin talking. *Ḍèwèké tjetjala luwih ḍisik menawa lulus.* First of all, he announced that he had passed his examinations. *** **ina** partially *or* totally blind

tjalak man who performs circumcisions. ***an** person of many talents, one who learns easily

tjâlâpitâ *oj* a sudden rapid movement

tjalik 1 (to make) a one-day excursion. 2 [of headgear] tipped upward and back. 3 a certain small black bird of the wagtail family. **tjolak-*** to make frequent one-day excursions. *Sudagar mau tjolak-* Surabaja Djakarta.* The businessman often travels between Surabaja and Djakarta. **ñj/di*aké** to wear [a batik wraparound] with the lower end pulled up

tjalo 1 a small edible ocean fish. 2 one who acts as a business agent *esp.* as a moonlighting job *or* as an intermediary. *A saiki dadi * montor.* A is now a private dealer in cars (on the above basis).

tjalon 1 candidate, prospect. ** pulisi* candidate for the police force. ** pengantèn* prospective bride/groom. ** biḍan* student nurse/midwife. *Elo, *é ramé temenan, djago Sala mungsuh Ngajodja.* The prospect is really exciting when Solo plays against Jogja. 2 *slang* fiancé(e). **ñj/di*aké** to appoint smn as a candidate. *A njalonaké B dadi lurah.* A proposed B as a candidate for village leader. *** **ratu** crown prince, heir to the throne

tjalung shank of a horse's leg

tjam appearance. ***(-*)é** it appears. **(*)é arep udan.* It looks like rain. **nge/di*(aké)** to consider advisable; to bear in mind. *Di*-aké apa pituturé wong tuwa.* Keep in mind what your parents advise.

tjamah not respected. *Djenengé wis *.* His name is in disrepute. **ñj*** to show disrespect (for). **ñj/di·tje*** to treat with disrespect. *njenjamah kitab Kur'an* to handle the Koran in a disrespectful way. **ñj*aké** showing disrespect. *tindak-tanduk kang njamahaké* disrespectful actions. **pa*** (act of) showing disrespect. *tembung pa** an insult

tjamat head of a subdistrict, *i.e.* an administrative officer having authority over village leaders. **ka*an** subdistrict, territory under the above official

tjambah *var of* KETJAMBAH

tjambang *see* GOḌÈG

tjambor ***an** 1 a mixture. 2 a compound. *wilangan *an* complex fraction. *tembung *an* (*gram*) compound word (*e.g. saputangan* handkerchief). **an tugel* (*gram*) a shortened compound (*e.g. ḍégus, from geḍé bagus*). **ñj/di*** to mix

tjambuk *rg var of* SAMBUK

tjami:k *rpr* the sound *or* movement of the lips chewing. ***an** *or* **ñj*an** 1 snacks, refreshments. 2 tidbits, *e.g.* of news, information

tjampah **tje*** to jeer (at). *Ḍèwèké seneng tje*.* He is fond of ridiculing others. **pa·ñj*** act of jeering. *Panjampahé nganggo tembung ala.* He used foul language in his ridiculing.

tjampâkâ gardenia

tjamplong a crude ladder consisting of a notched board

tjamprèng **tjomprang-*** habitually short of money

tjampuh 1 fight, duel (*usu. wj*); to fight. 2 to gather. *Wong saka ngendi-endi paḍa * ana ing alun²*. People from all over came together at the square. **pa*an** arena, scene of fighting. *Ḍèwèké ambruk ing tengahing pa*an.* He was killed in action.

tjampur to mix (with); mixed. *logam ** metal alloy. *Adja * botjah nakal.* Don't associate with delinquents. ***an** (a) mixture (of). *Ḍèké *an Landa lan Arab.* He is of mixed Dutch and Arabic blood. *susu *an* adulterated milk. **ka*an** mixed (with). *kegèt ke*an nesu* surprise mingled with anger. **ñj/di*** to mix. *Ḍèwèké lagi njampur adonan.* She's mixing the dough. *Kelasé di* lanang wédok.* The class was coeducational. **ñj/di*aké** to mix sth (up) with [sth else]. *Adja njampuraké soal pribadi karo politik.* Don't mix personal matters in with politics. *Radjangan lombok iku di*aké marang bumbu² iku.* The sliced chili peppers are mixed into the spices. **ñj/di*i** 1 to mix sth in. *Susuné di*i.* The milk was watered down. *Olèhmu njampuri gula sepira?* How much sugar did you put in? 2 to meddle (in). *Adja njampuri urusané wong.* Don't stick your nose into other people's business. *** bawur** 1 mixed up. *Bukuné * bawur.* The books were all mixed in together. *Pikiranku * bawur.* I'm all confused. 2 a mixture of flower fragrance for perfume. *** tangan** to interfere, meddle. *Pemerintah perlu * tangan.* The government ought to step in.

tjamtjao 1 the leaf of a certain climbing vine. 2 a gelatinous substance extracted from this vine, used in a drink (*tjao*) for treating high blood pressure

tjamu unit of ten billion. *sa** 10,000,000,-000. *rong ** twenty billion. ***an** numbering in the ten billions

tjamuk ***-*** to have the mouth full. *Ali *-* mangan katjang.* Ali has his mouth stuffed with peanuts. **ñj*-ñj*** *or* **njomak-ñj*** [to eat] with the mouth stuffed; eating, chewing on. *njomak-njamuk mangan ṭiwul* to keep putting mush in one's mouth. *ptg* **tj·r·amuk** *pl as above. Botjah² ptg tjramuk.* The children stuffed their mouths with food.

tjan *adr* tiger! (*shf of* MATJAN)

tjanang a certain variety of yellow betel leaves

tjanḍak continuation, sequel. **é tjrita wingi* the next episode of yesterday's story. *dina *é* the day after that. ***an** 1 to understand things easily. *A *an.* A catches on fast. 2 solution. *Étungan iku *ané pira?* What's the answer to that arithmetic problem? **ke*** to get caught (*see* KETJANḌAK). **ñj/di*** to catch, seize, grasp. *Ḍèké njanḍak penṭung, asuné dipenṭungi.* He seized a stick and beat the dog with it. *Aku tak mlaju ḍisik, mengko tjanḍaken.* I'll run on ahead; you catch up with me. *A arep njanḍak sepur sing djam papat.* A is going to catch the four o'clock train. *A apa wis njanḍak sing dikanḍakaké B?* Did A understand what B said? *Wong mau wis kira² njanḍak swidakan umuré.* He's reached the age of sixty. **ñj/di*aké** to continue, resume. *Aku arep njanḍakaké tjrita iki sésuk.* I'll continue this story tomorrow. **sa*é** whatever one can grasp/attain. *nggawa barang² sa*é waé* carrying everything they could snatch up. *See also* KETJANḌAK

tjanḍet **ñj/di*** to restrain. *Djarané di*.* He reined in his horse. *Aku di* B mulané tekaku rada kasèp.* B detained me—that's why I'm late. **pa·ñj*** control, restraint. *Rega² saiki angèl penjanḍeté.* Prices are hard to keep in check now.

tjanḍi ancient stone structure used as a temple and/or burying place. ***ǹ** having the appearance of such a structure. **ñj/di*** to bury smn in the above. *** bentar** temple gates having the appearance of a single slab split at the opening

tjanḍik counting unit for the leaves used in betel chew (*suruh*). *sa** one such leaf. **ñj/di*i** to make the above leaves into a betel-chewing packet. *** (k)ala** twilight, dusk (the time when evil spirits emerge); the spirits that emerge at dusk

tjândrâ 1 *oj* moon (*ki for* BULAN?). 2 *oj* month. 3 a description couched in figurative terms. **ñj/di*** to describe sth figuratively. **pa·ñj*** a description couched in beautiful figures of speech. *** sengkala** chronogram used as a cryptic way of expressing dates, *esp.* the year a building was constructed. *** sengkala memet** complex chronogrammatic representation of the year date. *See also* SENGKALA

tjândrâmâwâ a cat with a certain coat and eye coloring, said to have the magical power of dropping a mouse in its tracks by merely staring at it

tjandrâsâ *oj* sword

tjandu opium. ** gelap* black-market opium. **ñj*** 1 [of smoking tobacco] to produce tars. 2 to have become addicted to. *Ali njandu nonton bal-balan.* Ali is crazy about watching soccer games. **pa*ñ** place where opium is sold

tjanḍuk *var of* TJANṬUK

tjanḍung *rg* a certain type of sickle or scythe

tjangak a heron-like bird

tjangap 1 a wide opening. 2 *rg* water channel into a rice paddy. 3 *var of* TJANGAR

tjangar ***an** act of opening smn's mouth. **ñj/di*** to force open the mouth of [*e.g.* a child, an animal]. *Ḍèké njangar pitik arep diombèni obat.* He held open the chicken's mouth so as to dose it with medicine. **ñj/di*aké** to open [a child's, an animal's] mouth

tjanggah 1 fourth-generation ancestor *or* descendant, *i.e.* great-great grandparent *or* great-great grandchild. 2 *rg var of* TJAWANG

tjanggal a dead tree *or* stump

tjangik ***-*** *or* **ñj*(-ñj*)** resembling the female *wj* clown-servant Tjangik, *i.e.* tall, thin, and long of neck

tjangkah 1 a forked branch. 2 a lally post

tjangkang 1 (egg)shell, (nut)shell. 2 seashell

tjangkélak to make a quick motion. *Ḍèké énggal * bali mlaju.* He recoiled and then ran off.

tjangkem 1 (**tutuk** *ki*) mouth. 2 sounds (*esp.* bad words) produced by the mouth. *Wah *é.* What disgraceful talk! *guneman tanpa ** to convey one's meaning without speaking. *ditabuhi ** [gamelan music which is] "played" by human voices imitating instruments. ***an** with the mouth, oral. *digameli *an* accompanied by voices imitating gamelan instruments. *manggung (nggereng, mbengingèh, lsp.) *an* to imitate cooing (roaring, whinnying, *etc.*). ***mu** *cr* how dare you say that! **ñj/di*i** *cr* to speak to angrily *or* accusingly. *** amba** 1 large mouth. 2 a loud-mouth, a person who makes a lot of noise. *** gatel** 1 to gossip habitually. 2 fond of bawling people out. *** karut** having a sweet tooth; to eat compulsively. *** koḍok** frog's mouth; **ñj*-koḍok** (to have *or* get) a three-cornered tear in fabric. *** lunju** unreliable. *** urab²-an** prone to use obscene words

tjangking ***an** sth used to carry things. *krandjang *an* a carrying basket. *Kendilé didokoki *an tali.* The pot had a rope handle to carry it by. **ke*** to get picked up *or* carried off inadvertently. **ñj/di*** to take *or* carry in the hand *or* arm. *njangking kenḍi* carrying a water jug against the hip encircled by one arm. *Djam tanganku di*.* He walked off with my wrist watch. *njangking anḍuk* to carry a towel over the arm. **ñj/di*-*** to involve. *Adja mangsuli pitakonan kang njangking² djenengku.* Don't answer any questions that will drag my name into it.

tjangkir teacup, coffee cup

tjangklak ***an** armpit area. **ñj*** 1 uncomfortable *or* sore in the armpit area. *Klambiné wis ketjiliken, mula njangklak.* His shirt is too small—it binds at the armholes. 2 rebellious, disobedient. 3 *var of* ÑJ-TJANGKLÈK

tjangklèk a certain gamelan melody. ***an** a wooden sickle holder tied to the belt at the hip. **ñj/di*** to carry on the waist *or* hip

tjangklong a long wide band, worn over the shoulder, with pockets at either end for carrying small things. **ñj/di*** to carry sth by hanging it over [the shoulder *or* arm, a bicycle handlebar, *etc.*]. **ñj/di*aké** to hang sth over [sth, as above]

tjangklung one's reach; one's stride. *dawa *é* having long arms and legs. ***-*** long-armed, long-legged. *wong kang lakuné *-** a person who walks with long strides. **ñj*** to extend the arm out frontward

tjangkok 1 outer shell, *esp.* of molluscs. 2 tray of a balance scale. 3 landowner, as contrasted with sharecropper (*inḍung*). 4 basic, fundamental, original. *tjarita ** basic story line. ***an** grown from a cutting. *Wité pelem *an.* The mango tree was raised from a cutting from another tree. **tje*** leader, head. **ñj/di*** to take a cutting from a living plant for starting a new plant

tjangkol ***an** hook, hanger. **an klambi* dress hanger. **ñj/di*aké** to hang up [clothing]. *njangkolaké klambi* to hang up a shirt. **benik *** hook-and-eye fastener

tjangkrak 1 *rpr* a sudden swift movement. 2 (*or* ***an**) to act impulsively *or* irresponsibly

tjangkrâmâ *ltry* to relax and enjoy oneself. **ñj/di*ni** to make love to [a woman]

tjangkrang chickenpox. ***en** to have *or* get chickenpox

tjangkrim ***an** a conundrum. **ñj/di*i** to ask smn a conundrum

tjangkring a certain thorny-trunked tree

tjangkul agricultural hand tool resembling a hoe or pickaxe. ***an** work done with a *tjangkul.* **ñj/di*** to use *or* work with the above tool. **ñj/di*aké** to *njangkul* for smn

tjanglung *var of* TJANGKLUNG

tjangtjang *var of* TJANTJANG

tjanguk a lookout who observes enemy movements from a distance

tjanggungong *describing the cry of a peacock*

tjanṭâkâ boastful, arrogant

tjanṭas intelligent and energetic. *Anggoné guneman * banget.* He spoke dynamically.

tjanṭèk *var of* TJAṬÈK

tjanṭèl 1 hook, clasp. 2 belt with a clasp fastener. 3 a corn-like grain. ***an** 1 a hook; *fig* sth to hold onto, *e.g.* an ideal, a memory. *gumantung tanpa *an* homeless, not belonging anywhere. 2 neighborhood, quarter. **ke*** 1 to get caught. *Kaṭokku ke* paku.* My pants caught on a nail. *Ḍèké ke* wanita mantja.* He got led to the altar by a foreign woman. 2 to acquire, latch onto. *Ḍuwit semono akèhé ora ke* apa²*. He has all that money and nothing to show for it. **ñj*** to be(come) fastened *or* stuck. *Pantjingé njanṭèl angkrah²*. The fishhook caught on some waste material. **ñj/di*aké** to hook sth; to acquire. *njanṭèlaké penganggo* to hang clothing on a hook; to buy some clothes. **pa*an** 1 a small village. 2 head of a neighborhood organization. **tj·um·anṭèl** hooked [onto], hanging [from]. *Klambiné tjumanṭèl ing lawang.* His shirt is hung on the door. *ptg* **tj·r·anṭèl** *pl* hanging (in disorder). *Klambiné ptg tjranṭèl.* His shirts were hanging every which way. *** atur** to pass along a request to smn higher up. ** aturé wadana marang bupati ngliwati patihé.* The *wadana's* proposal to the *bupati* was transmitted by the *patih.* *** batin** to have a secret understanding [with]. *** rembug** to come to an agreement through discussion

tjanten talk, discussion (*kr for* TJATUR)

tjanṭeng whitlow (skin infection). ***en** to have *or* get whitlow

tjanṭik a certain type of small sailboat

tjanṭing 1 a small ladle with a cylindrical bowl and a tiny spout at the bottom, for applying melted wax to fabric being worked in batik. 2 comb with a curved rat tail (*var of* TJENṬING). *** djemblok·an** a large wax-applying ladle (as above)

tjantjang ***an** tethered. *Tudjuné asuné *an.* Luckily the dog was tied up. **ñ(j)/di*** to tether, tie up. **pa·ñ(j)*** act *or* way of tethering

tjantjut with sleeves rolled up, *or* batik wraparound tucked up, in preparation for hard work. **ñ(j)/di*** to gird oneself for work. *** taliwanda** to get set for some hard work. *Wong² kampung paḍa * taliwanda arep ndandani dalan.* The villagers set to work repairing the road. *Pamaréntah bandjur * taliwanda mènèhi bijantuan.* The government took on the task of providing assistance.

tjanṭoka *var of* TJANṬUKA

tjanṭol **ke*** to get caught (on). *Sarungku ke* pang.* My sarong caught on a branch. **ñj/di*** to catch on. *njanṭol pang* to catch on a branch. **ñj/di*aké** to hang sth. *Aku tak njanṭolaké klambi.* I'll hang up my shirt. **ñj/di*i** to cause to catch on it. *Pakuné kok njungat ngono, rak ija bisa njanṭoli.* That nail sticks way out–things will catch on it.

tjantrik pupil who lives in the home of a Hindu *or* Buddhist teacher (*guru*) and does service to him as well as learning from him. **ñj*** to be(come) a pupil as above

tjanṭuk 1 a liquid measure: *ca.* ½ pint = 0.2 liter. *lenga sa** one *tjanṭuk* of oil. 2 curved sharp-pointed object. 3 equipment for cupping, *i.e.* bringing blood to the surface by creating a partial vacuum over the skin. 4 to meet, become acquainted [with]. **ñj/di*** to treat smn medically by cupping. **ora * lawung** to not know at all, not have the slightest acquaintance with

tjanṭuka *oj* frog

tjantula rude, unmannerly

tjao a certain vine whose leaves are used for cool drinks and gelatine-like foods. ***** *tlasih* this drink flavored with *tlasih* seeds. **ñj*** 1 (*psv* **di***) to make [ingredients] into the above. 2 very easy. *Tjangkrimané njao ngono.* The conundrum is easy as pie. *See also* TJAMTJAO

tjaos 1 to prepare and/or serve refreshments (*ki for* TJAWIS). 2 to visit [a social superior] (*ka for* SÉBA). 3 to give *or* offer [to a social superior] (*root form: ka for* WÈNÈH). *Korané tjaosna bapak.* Give Father the newspaper. *Apa kowé wis njaosi lajang ibu?* Have you written to Mother? 4 *rg?* to serve as guard to [smn of high status] (*kr? ka? for* TUNGGUK). *** priksa** 1 to show (*root form: ka for* TUDUH). 2 to advise smn (*root form: ka for* TUTUR). 3 to warn smn not to [do] (*md for* ÉLIK)

tjap 1 brand, make, trademark. 2 stamp (mark), seal (mark). *baṭik ** batik with the design stamped on (rather than being handworked). ***-*an** printing, impression. **-*an kaping kalih* second printing. **nge/di*(i)** 1 to place a stamp *or* mark on. *Adja demèk²*, *mengko nge*.* Don't touch it–you'll leave a mark. *Negara mau di* agrèsor.* The nation was branded an aggressor. *Baṭik mau penggawéné dietjap.* This batik was made by stamping the design on. *nge∗ djempol* to put a thumbprint on. 2 to print. *Bukuné di∗ nang Amérika.* The book was printed in America. **nge/di∗aké** to have sth stamped/printed. *Karangané di∗aké ing Balé Pustaka.* His manuscript was printed by the government printing house. **pa·nge∗** act *or* way of stamping/printing. **pa·nge∗an** printing house. **∗ djempol** *or* **∗ dumuk** thumb print. **∗ gawé** an official village rank. **∗ pos** postmark

tjapâgâ a variety of tree

tjapang [of moustaches] long and extending sideways

tjapdjaé a Chinese meat-and-vegetable dish

tjapé weak, weary. *Tjapé ngrungokké omongmu.* I'm tired of hearing you talk. **∗an** (to play) a guessing game. **ñj/di∗** to guess (the answer to)

tjapet **∗-∗** vague, dim. *Aku mung kèlingan ∗-∗.* I remember it only vaguely. **tjopat-∗** not quite adequate. *Bakal seméné ambané dienggo gawé klambi ja tjopat-∗.* Fabric this width isn't quite big enough to make a shirt.

tjapil a broat hat of cloth *or* velvet

tjaping a broad woven-bamboo hat worn as a sunshade *or* umbrella. **∗an** 1 to put on *or* wear such a hat. 2 act *or* way of wearing this headgear. *Tjapingané tansah dibenak-benakaké.* He's always straightening his hat. **∗ bèbèk** an immensely broad hat of bamboo bracts *or* coconut leaves

tjapit pincers, pinchers, tweezers

tjaplak dog flea

tjaplang [of ears] prominent. *Kupingé ∗.* His ears stick out.

tjaplok **ñj/di∗(i)** 1 to seize one's prey. *Adja nganti di∗ baja.* Don't get caught by a crocodile! *iwak² sing ∗-∗* predatory fish. 2 [in games] to capture. *Patihku di∗.* He took my [chess] queen.

tjapluk *describing a quick biting or snapping action.* **tjoplak-∗** 1 to keep gnashing the teeth. 2 to keep putting food in the mouth

tjaprèt **tjoprat-∗** messily marked, stained. *Tjèté tjoprat-∗ ing endi².* The paint spattered all over everything. **njoprat-ñj∗** spread around untidily, making a mess

tjar- *see also under* TJR- *(Introduction, 2.9.3)*

tjârâ manner, way, custom; done in a certain way. *didandani nganggo ∗ Sala* dressed Solonese style. *Désa mawa ∗ negara mawa tata.* Each place has its own ways. *guneman ∗ Djawa* to speak Javanese *or* in a typically Javanese way. *∗né wong golèk pangan* the way people earn their living. **ñj/di∗** to form, shape. *Wité gedang sing kanggo sadjèn di∗ wong²an.* The banana tree used for the offering had been fashioned into a man-like shape. *njara Inggris* to act English, *i.e.* to speak English; to dress like an English person; *etc.* **ñj/di∗-∗** to visualize *or* approximate the form of. *Jèn ora bisa presis nggambaré, ja di∗-∗.* If you can't draw it just like the original, make it as close to it as you can. **ñj/di∗kaké** to speak, form words. *Sir bandjur njarakaké, tembungé mengkéné.* Sri then spoke as follows. *wong sing njara-Indonesijakaké* a person who translates things into Indonesian. **sa∗** in the same manner (as). *sa∗ njonjah²* just like European women. **∗ bikang** a rice-flour-and-sugar pastry

tjarak a hollow kerbau horn used for rinsing horses' mouths out. **ñj/di∗** to rinse with the above

tjarâkâ courier, messenger

tjarakan Javanese alphabet, *i.e.* sequence of script characters for teaching purposes

tjarang 1 bamboo branch. 2 cylindrical bamboo section. **∗an** *wj* an invented play that departs from the events depicted in epic or mythology

tjarat the pointed tip of a batik-making instrument (*tjanting*)

tjarem [of newlyweds] compatible. **∗an** *rg* durian fruit

tjarijos *var of* TJRIJOS

tjarik 1 secretary, clerk (village administrative position). 2 hand-worked batik. **ñj∗** to do a batik design by hand

tjarita *var of* TJRITA. *See also* ÉNGGAL

tjarub mixed together. **∗an** miscellaneous objects. *Barang² sing nèng kotak kuwi ∗an.* The stuff in that box is odds and ends. **ñj/di∗(i)** to mix together. *Bukuku adja di∗ karo bukumu lo.* Don't mix my books with yours. **∗ banju** a variety of things mixed together *or* taken at random; **njarub banju** to take things at random. *Aku arep njarup banju waé.* I'll just take some of this and some of that.

tjarubuk a certain kris-blade design

tjaruk *slang var of* TJARUB. **ñj/di∗** to pull *or* claw sth toward oneself. **njaruk wongwa** to make friendly overtures to an enemy. **ñj/di·tjorak-∗** *pl as for* ÑJ/DI∗

tjas *rpr* the stroke of a cutting tool. **∗-∗an** 1 ruling, decision. 2 act of cutting [wood]. *Pageré ∗-∗an rampag.* The fence sections were evenly cut. **nge/di∗i** 1 to decide (on), make a ruling (about). *Lenga di∗i ora kena luwih saka limang rupiah saliteré.* It was ruled that oil was not to exceed five rupiahs per liter. 2 to cover the facts precisely. *Apa tjritané ngetjasi tenan?* Did he give an accurate account of it? *See also* ANTJAS

tjat now [one thing] now [another]. *Ing kadohan gamelané ngangkang ∗ tjeṭa ∗ ilang.* The distant gamelan music wafted now clear, now faint.

tjaṭak 1 a certain fly that swarms around livestock. 2 dog flea. **ñj∗** to behave disrespectfully

tjaṭèk ∗ **gawèl** *or* ∗ **tjawèl** a gossip. *Adja digugu, ḍèké pantjèn ∗ tjawèl.* Don't believe a word of it–she's a scandalmonger.

tjaṭek̄ **ñj/di∗** [of dogs] to bite. *Sikilku di∗ asu.* A dog bit me in the leg.

tjaṭem a small clamp. **ñj/di∗aké** to close [smn's mouth, *or* any mouth-like aperture]

tjaṭet **∗an** notes, memoranda. *buku ∗an* notebook. **ñj/di∗(i)** to take notes (on); to note down

tjatjab to become gradually immersed. **ñ(j)/di∗** 1 to cross a watery place. 2 to massage hair oil into the scalp

tjatjad defect, flaw. *tanpa ∗* flawless. *manungsa ∗* an invalid. *wong sing ora ∗* smn who has nothing wrong with him. *Mretjon iku bisa gawé ∗é mripat.* Firecrackers can damage the eyes. **∗an** object of criticism. *dadi ∗an* to get criticized. **∗é** the trouble is... *Mung ∗é rada nakal seṭiṭik.* The only thing wrong with him is that he's a bit naughty. **ñ(j)/di∗** to find fault. *Wong iku emoh di∗.* He doesn't like to be criticized. **pa·ñ(j)∗(an)** 1 criticism, act of finding fault. *Ḍèké kuwi mung tukang penatjat.* He's always criticizing. 2 object of smn's criticism

tjatjah 1 number, amount. *∗é pira?* How many of them are there? *ḍuwit kang ora seṭiṭik ∗é* no small amount of money. 2 reduced to small pieces. *daging ∗* ground meat. **∗-∗** to reduce [many things, much stuff] to small pieces. *∗-∗ daging* to grind meat. **ke∗** to get counted; **ora ke∗** to be excluded, to not count. *Ḍèké ora ke∗.* He got left out. *or* He doesn't count (for anything). **ñ(j)/di∗** 1 to count. *Sapiné di∗.* He counted his cows. 2 to reduce to small pieces. *Klambiku anjar² di∗ tikus nganti adjur.* A mouse chewed up my brand new shirt. **ñ(j)/di∗aké** to count up, make a count of. *natjahaké regané kabèh* to add up all the prices. *Tjatjahna barang² iku ḍèk mau.* Take inventory of those things we were referring to. **pa·ñ(j)∗an** 1 calculation, count. 2 equipment for cutting *or* grinding. ∗ **djiwa** 1 population. *∗ djiwané ora kurang saka sajuta.* The population is at least a million. 2 census. *nḍaftar ∗ djiwa* to keep census records. *njatjah djiwa* to take the census. ∗ **eri** counting unit for fish. ∗ **molo** house count. ∗ **petjah·an** fraction. ∗ **sirah** a nose count of people *or* animals. ∗ **tjambor·an** mixed fraction, compound fraction. ∗ **wutuh** integer. ∗ **wuwung** 1 number of roofs *or* roofed sections to a house. 2 counting unit for households in a village. *See also* TJUTJAH

tjatjak 1 equipment for slicing tobacco leaves. 2 to try, make an effort. **ñ(j)/di∗** to shred [tobacco] with the above equipment. **adja ∗** let alone..., to say nothing of... *Sak sèn waé ora duwé, adja ∗ sak dollar.* He doesn't even have a penny, much less a dollar. **kalah ∗ menang ∗** what have you got to lose by giving it a try?

tjatjal chipped, marred. **ñ(j)/di∗** to peel *or* flake off a small bit (from)

tjatjar 1 pock mark. 2 smallpox. *mantri ∗* official who gives smallpox vaccinations. **∗an** 1 vaccination. 2 to do vaccinating. *Mengko soré arep ana ∗an.* They'll be vaccinating this afternoon. **ñ(j)/di∗** to vaccinate for smallpox. ∗ **banju** chickenpox

tjatjing 1 worm. *pendjalin ∗* vermiform rattan. 2 intestinal worms. **∗an** having worms. *djamu ∗an* worm medicine. **∗en** to have worms. **ñ(j)∗** vermiform. **ñ(j)/di∗i** to treat smn medically for intestinal worms. ∗ **kermi** threadworm. *kaja ∗* **ke·panas·en** to undergo a disaster. ∗ **pita** trichinosis; trichini. ∗ **tambang** noodle-like intestinal worms

tjaṭok 1 belt. 2 buckle of a belt used with men's batik wraparounds. **∗an** 1 metal band *or* rope for binding wood. 2 to put on *or* wear a belt. **ñj/di∗** 1 to attach a rope *or* metal binding to secure a joint where two sections of wood meet. 2 to catch [flying insects] with the bare hand

tjatu 1 a ration(ed amount). *∗ beras* rice

ration. 2 *rg* a share in (the harvest of) a communal rice paddy. 3 the privilege of raising a crop on smn's paddy as payment on a loan. ***n̂** (the practice of) rationing. **n̈j/di*** 1 to ration sth out. 2 (*or* **n̈j/di*n̂i**) to heal by faith *or* magic spells. **pa*n̂** 1 (the practice of) rationing. 2 a rice paddy loaned out as above (3)

tjaṭu:k̄ *rpr* the click of teeth snapping together

tjatur 1 (**tjanten** *or* **witjanten** *kr*) what smn says; talk, discussion. 2 chess. *dolanan ** chess set; a chess game. *papan ** chessboard. 3 *oj* four. **(tje)*an** to converse, chat, talk. *wong² sing wis tau tje*an karo ḍèké* those who have talked with her. *Saiki pantjèn akèh wong sing pinter *an.* Nowadays a great many people are good at talking [and not doing anything]. **ka*** 1 it is told. 2 to be talked about. **n̈j/di*** to talk about. *Sédjé sing tak *.* I'm talking about sth different. *Kowé adja sok njatur lijan.* Don't gossip. **pa·n̈j*** one who talks *or* gossips about people. **tj·in·atur** *ltry* 1 it is said. 2 to be talked about. *Tindaké tjinatur déning tangga²né.* The neighbors talk about what he does. *** pada** 1 four-legged. 2 with wholehearted pleasure. *ana ** **m̀·pungkur** to disregard whisperings. *Sing mantep jèn duwé kekarepan, déné jèn ana * mungkur.* You have to be true to your own will; never mind what people say.

tjaṭut pliers, pincers. *tukang ** middleman who jacks prices way up to retailers. ***an** 1 to pluck the beard with tweezers. 2 profits from reselling goods at a higher price; goods sold in this way. **n̈j/di*** to gouge money from [retail customers]

tjawak to be a habitually loud talker

tjawan saucer

tjawang 1 forked stick *or* branch. 2 having a forked shape. *Ilaté ula kuwi putjuké *.* Snakes have forked tongues. 3 one of the small playing cards (*kertu tjilik*). **n̈j/di*** to make sth in a forked shape. **tj·um·awang** forked

tjawé ***-*** to join in what others are doing. *Ora ana sing *-* tetulung.* No one pitched in and helped. **tjowa-*** to join in excitedly *or* frenziedly

tjawèl **n̈j/di*** 1 [of animals] to bite. 2 to drag smn into court, involve smn in litigation. *See also* TJAṬÈK

tjawet 1 men's brief *or* athletic supporter. 2 cloth worn by women as a sanitary napkin. ***an** to wear *or* put on one of the above. **n̈j*** to wear one of the above. **n̈j/di*aké** to wear [a long garment] pulled up between the legs, *e.g.* for wading across a stream. **n̈j/di*i** to put one of the above garments on smn

tjawik to clean oneself after going to the bathroom (*ki for* TJÉWOK)

tjawis *ng kr*, **tjaos** *ki* 1 ready, prepared. *Bareng titihan wis *, nuli tjinéngklak mak prung.* As soon as the horse was ready, he mounted and galloped off. 2 *rg* to visit a high-status person; to guard the home of a high official. ***an** 1 advance preparations. 2 things provided *or* made available. **tje*** arrangements, advance preparations; provisions, supplies. **tje*an** *sms* *AN. **n̈j/di*aké** to prepare, provide. *Di*aké tanah kanggo omah rakjat.* A piece of land was made available for public housing. *Wis paḍa ribut njawisaké tjalon²é.* They're busy preparing their candidates. **n̈j/di*i** to offer, make available. *rèstoran sing njawisi panganan Tjina* a restaurant that serves Chinese food. **tj·um·awis** prepared, ready. *Rak ija wis tjemawis kabèh ta?* Is everything all set?

tjawuh mixed, blended; not sharply distinct. *Berasé * karo gabah.* The husked rice grains were mixed in with the unhusked ones. *Tembung A mau tegesé mèh * karo tembung B.* Word A means just about the same thing as word B.

tjawuk (*or* ***an**) the amount one can hold in the cupped palm. *sa*(an)* one palmful. **n̈j/di*** to scoop and spatter sth, *e.g.* water

tjb. *see* TJABANG

tje- *see also under* TJA- (*Introduction, 2.9.2*)

tjeb *rpr* stabbing, piercing. **ke*** 1 stuck to *or* into. 2 remaining smw. *Ḍèké golèk gawéan nang Banḍung, djebulé ka* nang Djakarta.* He looked for work in Bandung but finally stuck it out in Djakarta. **nge/di*aké** to stick sth [into]. *ngetjebaké dom ing bantal* to stick a needle into a pillow

tjebak a swallow-like nocturnal bird

tjebelèh *var of* TJEBLÈH

tjeblâkâ straightforward, direct, honest. *See also* BLAKA

tjeblèh 1 *intsfr* white. *putih ** pure white. 2 pallid, wan

tjèblek̄ *rpr* a stab into sth soft. *Domé ditantjebaké ing bantalan mak *.* She stuck the pin into the pincushion. **n̈j/di*aké** to stick sth into [sth soft]. **tj·um·èblek** stuck [into]

tjeblèk *var of* TJABLÈK

tjéblok *var of* TJEBLOK

tjeblok to fall, drop. **ñj/di*aké** 1 to drop sth, make *or* let sth fall. 2 to stick sth into the ground; to plant. *** alu** to change off *or* take turns at a job

tjeblung *rpr* splashing. *ptg * or *-* or* **tjeblang-*** to prattle aimlessly. **ke*** to fall into [liquid]. **ñj*** to plunge into [liquid]. **ñj/di*aké** to plunge sth into [liquid]

tjébol abnormally short *or* low. *wong ** midget. *** ng·gajuh lintang** one who attempts things beyond his ability

tjébong tadpole (young of the KOḌOK)

tjebrik damp and messy. **ñj/di*i** to mess sth up with mud *or* water

tjebuk[a] a certain crop pest that attacks peanut plants

tjebu:k̄[b] ***-*** *rpr* splashing sounds. *See also* KETJEBUK

tjebur *rpr* sth splashing into deep water. **ke*** to fall into [water]. *Ḍèké ke* kali.* He fell in the river. **ñj*** to dive into. **ñj/di*aké** to throw sth into [water]

tjéda *oj* (*or* ***an**) (having a) flaw, blemish, defect. *tanpa ** flawless, unblemished. *Djenengé wis *.* His name is tarnished. **ñj/di*** to criticize, find fault

tjeḍak *ng,* **tjelak** *kr* near, close (to). ** pasar* near the market. *tangga sing ** close neighbors. ** karo* close to, near. *Ora ana sing wani *-*.* No one dares go very close to it. ***-*an** 1 a place close by. *Sabané uga ing *-*an kéné baé.* They stick right close to here. 2 to compare *or* compete for closest. *Ajo *-*an tengahé olèhé manah.* Let's see who can get their arrow closest to the bull's-eye. **ke*en** excessively near. **ñj*** to get near(er). **ñj/di*aké** to put sth close(r). *Jèn gambaré ora tjeṭa, di*aké.* If the picture isn't clear, move it nearer. **ñj/di*i** to approach sth. *Tikusé njeḍaki panganan mau.* The mouse came toward the bait. **sa*é** close to. *Sapa sing lungguh sa*é?* Who sat near him? **sa*-*é** even though near; however near. *Sa*-*é kuṭa A karo kuṭa B ija meksa patang djam numpak montor.* City A is close to City B, but even so it takes four hours to drive there. *** tjèlèng bolot·en** to hang around with undesirable people

tjéḍal *var of* TJÉLAD

tjeḍek *rg var of* TJEḌAK

tjéḍok fishing net on a frame. **ñj/di*** to fish with this net

tjeḍu:t *rpr* a sudden jerk *or* tug

tjeg *rpr* snatching. *Mak * tangané ditjekel.* Suddenly someone grabbed his hand. *Mak * ḍèké nemu akal.* All of a sudden he hit on an idea. **tjag-*** 1 to keep touching *or* handling. 2 to handle [a number of things] deftly. *Para peladi paḍa prigel² tjag-*.* The waitresses whisked things on and off the table with great skill. *Tjag-* terus dandan.* I threw on some clothes.

tjegah **ñj/di*** to prevent, put a stop to. *rékadaja njegah munḍaké rega* a means of forestalling a price rise. *Sesambungan kang kaja sing uwis kudu di*.* Connections of the former sort are to be discontinued. **pa·ñj*** act of forestalling

tjegat ***an** that which is obstructed *or* lain in wait for. ***-*an** 1 act of lying in wait *or* impeding *or* ambushing. *Bis iku tinimbang sepur gampang tjegat²ané.* Buses are more accessible than trains. 2 to lie in wait for each other. **ñj/di*(i)** 1 to block, impede. *Tibané wit njegati dalan geḍé.* The fallen tree blocked the highway. 2 to wait for [sth to come along]. *njegat taksi* to wait for a taxi. *Tentara kita di* mungsuh.* Our army was ambushed by the enemy.

tjegemek̄ *rpr* a sudden movement, *esp.* snatching. *Trewèluné sanalika bisa ditjekel *.* He managed to grab hold of the rabbit. *Aku terus bisa nuding * waé ngendi dunungé.* I was able to point out immediately right where he was.

tjegemok **tjegemak-*** to keep touching *or* handling things

tjèger *rpr* a weapon finding its mark. ***-*** *or* **tjégar-*** [of arrows, spears] to keep hitting a target. **ñj*** *or* **tj·um·èger** to stick, stab, pierce

tjeglung *rpr* sth falling into deep water

tjégrok *rpr* alighting, perching. *méntjok (mak) ** to alight, perch

tjegu ***nen** to hiccup; to swallow the wrong way (*kr for* TJEKIK·EN)

tjegug *rpr* swallowing. ***-*** *or* **tjegag-*** *rpr* swallowing repeatedly. *Ḍèwèké tjegag-*.* He drank it down, glug-glug-glug.

tjeguk ***en** a hiccup; to have the hiccups

tjegur *rpr* a splash. *Ḍèké mak * tiba ing kalèn.* He fell splash! into the stream. **ke*** to fall into water. *Ḍèké nulungi sing ke*.*

He went to the aid of the man overboard. **ñj/di∗** to jump into water. *Mak bjur njegur ing kali.* He jumped in the river. **ñj/di∗aké** to plunge sth into water. *njeguraké watu nèng kali* to throw a stone in the river. **ñj/di∗i** to plunge sth into [water]. *Kaliné di∗i watu.* He threw a stone in the river. **tj·um·egur** to fall into water. *Wong² krungu swara tjemegur.* People heard him fall in.

tjèk **nge/di∗(i)** to check (on). *Polisiné nge∗ laporan pepati.* The police checked out the reported murder. *Sadurungé tetuku, betjik dietjèk ḍisik regané.* Better check the price before you buy.

tjek̄ 1 *rpr* a cricket's chirp. 2 *rpr* seizing. *Bulus mau ditjanḍak ∗, ditalèni set.* He grabbed the turtle and tied him up fast. **tjak-∗** to make swift sure motions. *Ḍokteré ngresiki sikil sing ketaton; tandangé tjak-∗.* The doctor's hands moved deftly as he cleaned the wound. **nge∗** to chirp. *Djangkriké nge∗.* The crickets chirped.

tjekak short, brief. *tjrita ∗* a short story. *Sing ∗-∗ baé.* Make it brief. *Wangsulané ∗: Inggih.* He answered curtly: Yes. **∗an** 1 an abbreviation; abbreviated, cut. *tembung sing ∗an* contracted words. 2 in brief. *Kanḍakna ∗an baé.* Tell in briefly. **∗é** in short; to sum up. *Tjekaké wong mono kudu tulung-tinulung.* So as you see, people should help one another. **∗ing gunem/tjrita** to make a long story short. **ñj/di∗** to shorten. *Wajang kulit kuwi lakoné sok di∗.* Shadow-play stories are sometimes cut. *Wagé-Paing kuwi umumé di∗ Gé-Ing.* Wagé-Paing (*day name*) is usually shortened to Gé-Ing. **ñj/di∗aké** to make sth shorter (than it was). *Ḍèwèké njekakaké kaṭok.* He had his trousers taken up. **ñj/di∗i** to make sth (so that it is) small. *Klambiné di∗i seṭiṭik, saiki aku rada kuru.* Make the dress on the small side; I've lost weight. **∗ aos** short and to the point. **∗ ambek·an·é** short of breath, short-winded. **∗ budi·né** short-tempered. **∗ napas·é** short-winded. **∗ tjukup·é** 1 short but to the point. 2 be that as it may

tjekakah **∗an** [of legs] spread wide apart. **ñj∗** having the legs spread wide apart

tjekakak a kingfisher-like bird. *ptg ∗ or* **∗an** *or* **ñj∗** (to laugh) hard. *Ḍèké ngguju ∗an.* He laughed his head off.

tjekakar **∗an** *or* **ñj∗** lying down with the legs sticking up

tjekangkang [of the body] to stiffen, become rigid. *ptg ∗ pl as above.* **∗an** *or* **ñj∗** to lie *or* fall on the back stiffly. *mati njekangkang* lying stiff and dead

tjekap 1 sufficient (*kr for* TJUKUP). 2 adequate (*kr for* SEḌENG?)

tjekeḍung the cupped palm of the hand. **ñj∗** to form a cupped shape. *Tangané njekeḍung.* His hands were cupped. **ñj/di∗aké** to cup [the hands]

tjèkèh *var of* TJÈNGKÈH

tjekèk pure, true. *santri ∗* an orthodox Moslem. *satrija Djawa ∗* a true Javanese nobleman. *Katon singkèk ∗, ora bisa ngunèkaké R.* He seemed to be a full-blooded Chinese–he couldn't pronounce R. **ñj/di∗** *cr* to eat

tjekékal *rpr* getting right up again. *Mak ∗ terus mlaju.* [After falling] he picked himself up and ran off. **ñj∗** to scramble to one's feet

tjekékar *var of* TJEKAKAR

tjekèkèh **ñj∗** with the legs apart below the knees. **ñj/di∗aké** to place [the lower legs] apart from each other. *Sikilé di∗é.* He moved his feet apart.

tjekèkèr **∗an** lying down with the legs moving in different directions, *e.g.* after a sprawling fall

tjekekrek̄ *ptg ∗ pl* dejected, out of sorts, dispirited. **ñj∗** *sg as above*

tjekel *ng,* **tjepeng** *kr* grasp, grip; way of holding/handling. *Montor iki ∗é kok pénak banget.* This car handles beautifully. **(tje)∗an** 1 hold, grasp; to grasp, catch hold of. *ngGoné ∗an mrutjut.* He lost his hold. *Kéwan mau gampang ∗-∗ané.* These animals are easy to catch. 2 a handle, holder. *∗ané koper* suitcase handle. 3 security held for indebtedness. *Pité dienggo ∗an utangé.* His bicycle is his security for the loan. *lajang ∗an* written acknowledgment of indebtedness. 4 money allotted for smn's use. **ke∗** to get caught/seized. *Wong sing adol tjandu peteng akèh sing ke∗.* Many of the black-market opium dealers were arrested. **ñj/di∗aké** 1 to hold/grasp on smn's behalf. 2 to give sth as security for a loan. *Sepéḍané di∗aké.* He put up his bicycle as security. **ñj/di∗(i)** **(ng/di·asta** *ki*) 1 to hold, take hold of, grasp. *Angèl olèhé njekel.* It's hard to hold onto. *Taliné di∗i ing tangan kiwa.* He held the rope in his left hand. *mBasan wis seminggu di∗-∗ pitiké dadi tutut.* The chicken was tamed after he had been taking it in his hand for a week. 2 to seize, arrest. *Malingé di∗ pulisi.* The police arrested the thief. *Tjandu peteng mau diasta Negara.* The authorities seized the black-market opium. 3 to handle, take/have charge of. *njekel pamrintahan* to handle government business. *Kowé saiki njekel apa nang kantor?* What are you in charge of at the office now? 4 to take in pawn. *Pak X njekel djamku.* Mr. X [a pawnbroker] gave me a loan on my watch. **njekel bang² alum·ing pradja** responsible, as ruler, for a nation's moral conduct. **wis di∗ lambé ati·né** to have learned every quirk of smn's character. **ñj/di∗i** 1 to allot money to smn for his use. *Saben ésuk simbah njekeli ḍuwit serupiah nggo djadjan.* Every morning Grandpa gave me one rupiah for snacks. 2 to give sth as security for a loan. *Ali njekeli aku raḍioné.* Ali had me hold his radio as security. **pa·ñj∗** way of holding/handling; *wj* technique of grasping the puppet. *Panjekelé ora kentjeng, mula mrutjut.* He didn't have a good hold on it so it got loose. **tj·um·ekel (tj·um·epeng** *kr*) [to look] tempting to handle. *Botjah kok tjemekel temen!* How huggable that child is! **∗ gawé (tjepeng damel** *kr*) to have *or* take up a job. *ngGonku ∗ gawé ana ing kantor mau wis suwé.* I've been working at that office for some time. *saploké ∗ gawé pisanan* ever since I first took office

tjekeneng *ptg ∗* [of skin, muscles] feeling taut *or* stretched

tjekéngkang, tjekèngkang *ptg ∗ pl* falling on their backs

tjekengkeng *rpr* stiffening, becoming rigid, *e.g.* during a paralytic stroke. **ñj∗** to stiffen. *mati njekengkeng* to have died and undergone rigor mortis

tjekenik *ptg ∗* many [of small things]. *Olèhé njeḍiani panganan ptg ∗.* She prepared a variety of foods in small amounts. *kakéjan ∗* an excessive amount of small stuff. **ñj∗** small, tiny. *ptg* **tj·l·ekenik** *sms ptg ∗*

tjekenṭing *ptg ∗ pl* curling at the tips. **ñj∗** to curl at the ends. *Gelungané njekenṭing ngebaki gulu.* Her hair bun rolls down covering her neck.

tjekenṭung *var of* TJEKENṬING

tjèkèr 1 chicken's leg. 2 *cr* hand. **∗-∗** *or* **tje∗** [of chickens] to scratch for food; [of people, *fig*] to scratch a living. **ke∗an** *or* **ke∗en** to scrape along, scratch a living. **ñj/di∗i** to scratch sth. *Uwuhé di∗i pitik.* The chickens scratched around in the garbage.

tjèket **tjékat-∗** to move quickly. *mBok tjékat-∗, adja klelar-kleler.* Hurry up! don't dawdle.

tjekèt *rpr* biting, pinching (*e.g.* by a dog, a crab)

tjekeṭek̄ *ptg ∗ pl* messy, dirty, untidy

tjekeṭem **ñj/di∗** to grasp, hold tight. *njekeṭem ḍuwit* to clutch one's money

tjekeṭik *ptg ∗* having an intricate structure. **tjekeṭak-∗** engaged in sth intricate. *Slamet tjekeṭak-∗ ndandani djam.* Slamet is engaged in the complex task of repairing a watch.

tjeki a game played with the Chinese cards (*kertu tjilik*)

tjekiḍing *var of* TJEKIṬING

tjekigrèk *var of* TJEKIKÈR

tjeki:k̄ *cr* dead; on the verge of death. **∗en** (**tjegu·nen** *kr*) to hiccup; to choke on, swallow the wrong way. **ñj/di∗** to strangle *or* choke smn

tjekikèr the crowing of a wild cock. **ñj∗** to crow

tjekikik *ptg ∗ or* **∗an** *or* **ñj∗** to laugh lightly, giggle, chuckle

tjeking *intsfr* thin (*Djakarta slang*)

tjeki:t *rpr* a small bite *or* sting

tjekiṭing **tjekiṭang-∗** *pl* holding *or* carrying things without having a tight grip on them. **ñj/di∗** to carry carelessly in this way

tjekiwing *var of* TJENGKIWING

tjeklèk *var of* TJOKLÈK

tjèkli small and attractive, *usu.* of houses or their furnishings *or* surroundings

tjeklik *var of* TJOKLÈK

tjekluk *rpr* joints cracking. **ñj/di∗i** to crack one's joints by pulling *or* bending them

tjéko having the arm permanently bent at the elbow. **∗ brengkelo** obstinate, opinionated

tjekoḍong *var of* TJEKEḌUNG

tjekoh cough (*ki for* WATUK)

tjekok 1 the hollow in the neck below the Adam's-apple. 2 (*or* **∗an**) a folk medicine given to children. **ñj/di∗aké** to give [such medicine]. *A njekokaké djamu marang anaké.* A had his child take medicine. **ñj/di∗i** to forcefully administer such medicine to

tjékor [of feet] deformed

tjékot *var of* TJÉKO

tjekot *rpr* a stab of pain. ∗-∗ *or* **ñj∗** to throb with pain. *See also* TJLEKOT
tjekoṭong *var of* TJEKEḌUNG
tjekowak *var of* TJENGKOWAK
tjekowèk *var of* TJENGKOWÈK
tjekowok *var of* TJENGKOWOK
tjekrèh **tjekrah-∗** to cough repeatedly
tjèkrèk **ñj∗** to appear handsome. *Soré² wis njèkrèk.* By evening, he looked fine. *See also* TJAKRAK
tjekrèk *rpr* a click. **tjekrak-∗** making repeated clicks. *Tukang potrèk kepulisian wis tumandang tjekrak-∗ motrèki.* The police photographer had begun snapping pictures.
tjekrik *rpr* a small pricking sensation. *Mak ∗ ketjotjog eri.* A thorn pricked me. **ñj∗** to act *or* speak insultingly toward others
tjekroh **tjekrah-∗** to cough continuously
tjekrok *rpr* a pricking sensation. *Mak ∗ aku ketjotjog garpu.* I got stabbed with a fork.
tjèktjok *rg* quarrel, argument
tjekukruk **tjekukrak-∗** [of chickens] having a sickly appearance. **ñj∗** [of chickens] to droop with indrawn neck
tjekung curving, bent. *laṭi lan mripat ∗* curving lips and eyes
tjekunṭeng *var of* TJLEKUNṬENG
tjekut *var of* TJEKOT
tjekuṭik *var of* TJLEKUṬIK
tjekuwek *var of* TJENGKUWEK
tjekuwik *var of* TJENGKUWIK
tjel- *see also under* TJL- (*Introduction, 2.9.3*)
tjélad inability to pronounce the Javanese rolled R (speech defect). **ñj/di∗aké** to fail to roll the R's of words. *Nèk nirokaké Tjina omongé di∗aké.* When you imitate a Chinese, you speak without rolled R's.
tjelak 1 eye shadow. 2 near, close (to) (*kr for* TJEḌAK). 3 short (*kr for* TJENḌAK). **ñj/di∗** to apply *or* wear eye shadow
tjelâkâ *var of* TJILAKA
tjeleb indigo dye (*kr for* WEDEL)
tjelèk penis; glans penis (*cr*). *∗é matamu!* Use your eyes! (*cr*). **ñj/di∗aké** to retract [skin]. *Mripatku mau di∗ké kanggo ngilangi klilip.* She rolled back my eyelid to remove the speck. *See also* PENTJELÈK
tjéléménḍé *var of* TJÉRÉMÉNḌÉ
tjèlèng 1 (**anḍapan** *kr*) wild pig, boar. 2 *term of abuse.* **∗an** 1 piggy bank. 2 savings. 3 a bamboo *or* wooden support. **ñj∗** resembling a wild pig. **ñj/di∗aké** to save [money] (for smn). **ñj/di∗i** to save up [money]. **∗ gontèng** a certain variety of small boar. **∗ mogok** a method of drying rice stalks in the sun
tjeleng black, dark (*sbst kr for* IRENG). **∗an** indigo dye (*sbst kr for* NILA)
tjélik, tjelik (*or* **ke∗**) 1 mistaken in an identification *or* interpretation. *Dudu mbahné, dadi ke∗.* It wasn't his grandmother; he was mistaken. *Ḍèwèké ke∗, djeruk mau dudu djeruk temenan, ning sing digawé malam.* He was fooled: the orange wasn't real, it was made of wax. 2 disappointed in a hope *or* expectation. *Supaja adja ke∗ tilpuna ḍisik.* Call first, so as not to find me not at home.
tjélu **tjéla-∗** easily influenced by others
tjèlu **ke∗** *rg* strongly attracted
tjeluk **∗-∗** *or* **tjelak-∗** to keep calling. *Aku tjelak-∗ Ali kok ḍèké ora krungu.* I called and called to Ali but he didn't hear. **∗(-∗)an** what smn is called. *Djenengé Ali ning ∗-∗ané Li.* His name is Ali but they call him Li. **ke∗** to be called. *Djenengé Sarinah ning ke∗ Bawuk.* Her name is Sarinah but she's called Darling. **ñj/di∗-∗** *or* **ñj/di·tjelak-∗** to keep calling. *Adja njelak-njeluk aku, wong aku lagi njambut gawé.* Don't keep calling to me–I'm working. **ñj/di∗(i)** to call [smn, sth]. *Aku di∗ Li.* I'm called Li. *Ḍèké njeluk bétjak.* He called a pedicab. *Ḍèké njeluki anaké.* She called her children.
tjélung the blossom of the *ḍaḍap* tree
tjelup **tjelap-∗** to go in and out of [liquid]. *Jèn adus, adja mung tjelap-∗ kaja bèbèk.* When you bathe, don't just bob up and down like a duck! **ke∗** to get dipped/soaked inadvertently. **ñj∗** to soak oneself; (*psv* **di∗**) to soak sth. *njelup ḍelé* to soak soybeans. **ñj/di∗aké** to dip/soak sth in liquid
tjem **∗-∗an** coconut-oil hair preparation
tjem- *see also under* TJ- (*Introduction, 3.1.7*)
tjemani 1 dark in skin color. 2 *intsfr* dark, black. *ireng ∗* jet black; pitch dark
tjemârâ 1 a certain evergreen tree. 2 false hair worn by ladies to fluff out a coiffure. 3 a horsehair brush for sweeping. **ñj/di∗** to make [materials] into a *tjemara* (*meanings 2, 3*)
tjèmbèng *var of* TJÈNGBÈNG
tjembung curved. *lénsa ∗* convex lens
tjemburu jealous. **∗an** having a jealous nature
tjémé 1 a game played with the Chinese cards (*kertu tjilik*). 2 (*or* **ke∗**) a certain fruit

tjememek *ptg* ∗ *pl* dirty and watery. **ñj**∗ *sg as above*
tjemenḍil pellet-shaped animal dung
tjemèng kitten (young of the KUTJING)
tjemeng black; dark (*kr for* IRENG)
tjemer soggy, messy, muddy. **ñj**∗**-**∗**i** to cause to be messy. *Banjuné adja dibuang ing kono, munḍak njemer²i.* Don't throw the water there–you'll get it all muddy.
tjemeṭi *ng kr,* **tembung** *ki* whip, riding crop. *pentol* ∗ whip handle. **ñj/di**∗**(ṅi)** to whip with a riding crop
tjemil ∗**an** snacks, nibbles
tjemimik *cr* female genitalia
tjemit **sa**∗ a tiny bit
tjemlik **sa**∗ a tiny bit
tjemok **ñj/di**∗ to touch with the hand
tjemol **tjemal-**∗ to keep nibbling, keep reaching for more food. **ñj/di**∗ to seize [smn] by a pinch of his flesh and hold it tight
tjémot *rpr* snatching. ∗ *anaké dibopong genti.* He swept the child into his arms. ∗-∗ *or* **tjémat-**∗ dirty, messy. **ñj/di**∗ to snatch up. *ptg* **tj·r·émot** all messed up. *Delengen rupané, ptg tjrémot!* Look how dirty your face is!
tjemot *rpr* snatching
Tjempa former kingdom in Indo-China. *basa/tanah* ∗ Indo-Chinese language/territory. *beras* ∗ a short-grained rice; *pari* ∗ the plant that produces this rice. ∗ **rowa** a children's game
tjempâkâ gardenia tree; gardenia. ∗ **sa wakul** 1 a certain large gardenia. 2 a stroke of good luck. *katon* ∗ **sa wakul** popular, well liked
tjempâlâ one of a pair of wooden mallets, used for producing sound effects and music signals during shadow-play performances. **ñj**∗ to rap with the above on the wooden puppet chest *or* on metal plates. **ñj/di**∗**ni** to hit. *Anaké jèn nakal di*∗*ni.* When her child is naughty, she beats him.
tjempaluk young tamarind fruit
tjempé lamb; kid (young of the WEḌUS). **ñj**∗ **kèri** to bleat like a lamb/kid
tjempeḍak a certain variety of jackfruit
tjempirut *ptg* ∗ rumpled, full of creases. **ñj**∗ creased. *Kaṭoké njempirut.* His trousers are creased.
tjémplak **ñj/di**∗ to jump onto [one's mount]. *A njémplak pit.* A hopped on his bike. *Djaran iku lakuné nganggo njémplak barang.* The [chess] knight's move is a bounding one.
tjemplang 1 insipid, tasteless. 2 pointless. *Tjritané* ∗. The story was dull. **tjemplang-**∗ to talk pointless nonsense. **ñj/di**∗**aké** to cause sth to be insipid/pointless
tjémplo *rpr* a leap into the saddle. **ñj/di**∗ to jump onto [a bicycle, horseback, smn's back] for a ride
tjemplon 1 sweet fried cassava balls. 2 a small canoe-like boat. 3 a small earthenware pot
tjemplong **ñj/di**∗ to make a wide deep hole
tjemplung *rpr* a splash. *Aku krungu mak* ∗. I heard a splash. **tjemplang-**∗ to dump things into [liquid]. *Jèn nggawé djangan adja waton tjemplang-*∗. Don't just dump ingredients into the soup [without measuring, discriminating, *etc.*]! **ke**∗ to fall in accidentally. *Kantjil ke*∗ *djugangan.* Mouse-Deer fell in a hole. **ñj**∗ to fall [into]. *Bisé keplorot njemplung ing djurang.* The bus skidded and plunged into the ravine. **ñj/di**∗**aké** to plunge sth [into]. *Ḍèké njemplungaké katjang ṭolo ing kwali.* She put soybeans in the pot. **ñj/di**∗**i** 1 to plunge sth [into sth]. *Botjah njemplungi watu nèng blumbang.* The boy threw stones in the pond. 2 to immerse [sth in] a liquid. *Tèhé di*∗*i gula.* He put sugar in his tea.
tjempol short fibers covering the "eyes" of a coconut
tjempuling a hooked fishing spear. **ñj/di**∗ to catch fish with the above
tjempurit 1 the pulp cavity of teeth, horns, antlers. 2 the main stick for manipulating a puppet plus the puppet's arm to which it is attached. ∗ *wajang iku saka sungu.* Puppet sticks are made of [kerbau] horn. ∗**en** [of plants] sickly
tjempurung woven-bamboo *or* rattan canopy for a bier (*banḍosa*) on which a body is borne to the cemetery
tjemumu:k ∗**an** *or* **tjemumak-**∗ to grope *or* feel one's way
tjemung a round metal bowl
tjémut *rpr* snatching
tjenanal ∗**an** to gesture habitually with the hands and arms (rather than preserving the desirable attitude of repose)
tjenanang *ptg* ∗ *or* ∗**an** to look around wildly as one walks along
tjenanil *var of* TJENANAL
tjenanuk *ptg* ∗ *pl* with heads frozen into

motionlessness through amazement, surprise, shock

tjenanul *var of* TJENANAL

tjenḍak *ng,* **tjelak** *kr* short. *Tjritané * apa dawa?* Was the story short or long? ** umuré* a short life. ***-*an 1** brief(ly). *Tjritakna *-*an waé.* Tell about it briefly. 2 even though short. *Aku golèkna pring, *-*an ora dadi apa.* Get me a piece of bamboo, will you–a short one will be all right. **ke*an** *or* **ke*en** excessively short. **ñj/di*-aké** to shorten sth; to have sth shortened. *njenḍakaké tjlana* to have one's trousers shortened. **ñj/di*i** to make sth (so that it is) short(er). *Tjlana sing anjar iku di*i seṭiṭik.* Make the new trousers a little shorter [than the old, overlarge ones]. *See also* ḌAKWA

tjenḍânâ sandalwood. *lenga ** sandalwood oil

tjenḍani slender Chinese bamboo. *** **raras** couch

tjenḍèk *ng,* **anḍap** *kr* 1 short in stature. *Sing lanang *, sing wédok ḍuwur.* The husband is short and the wife is tall. 2 low (*slang usage*). *Montoré mabur aburé *.* The plane flew low. *Lemahé *.* The land is low-lying. ***é** briefly, in short. ***-*an** to compare *or* compete for lowest/shortest. *Nèk *-*an, Ali sing paling *.* Among all of them, Ali is the shortest. **ke*en** excessively short/low. **ñj/di*aké** to make shorter/lower (than it was). **ñj/di*i** to make sth (so that it is) short/low. *Olèhé nggawé pager di*i siṭik.* Make the fence a little shorter [than was planned]. *** **ḍuwur 1** short and tall, low and high. ** ḍuwur lungguhé nang ngarep.* Both short and tall people sat in the front row. **-ḍuwur mangané sega.* Low-ranking and high-ranking all eat rice. 2 not level. *Olèhmu masang gambar kuwi *-ḍuwur.* You hung the picture with one side higher than the other. *** **menṭèk**^{2} *or* *** **menṭek**^{2} extremely short/low. *See also* ḌÈKWUR

tjenḍe:k̄^{a} *emphatic form of* TJENḌÈK

tjenḍek̄^{b} *var of* TJENḌAK

tjenḍekiawan intellectuals, intelligentsia

tjenḍéla window

tjénḍok *rg var of* SÉNḌOK

tjènḍol, tjénḍol a gelatine-like food made of rice flour, cut up and used as ingredients in dishes *or* drinks. **tj·um·ènḍol-*** newly hatched baby bird (which resembles the above in its soft consistency)

tjènel *rpr* the tightening of a rope with which sth [*e.g.* a lassoed animal] has just been caught

tjenéla sandals, slippers

tjènèng **ke*** to get pulled. **ñj/di*** to pull sth toward oneself

tjèng 1 sugar-cane sap. 2 slanting (*inf var of* M̈·PÈNTJÈNG). ** siṭik* slightly slanted. *Olèhé nggarisi *-*.* He drew a lot of diagonal lines. ***-*** *rpr* water striking metal forcibly (*see also* KRÈNTJÈNG)

tjenganglung *ptg * pl* sticking out over the edge of sth, *e.g.* baby birds in a nest

tjenganguk *rpr* a quick change in facial expression. *ptg * pl* looking out. *Wong*^{2} *ptg * nang tjenḍéla.* People are looking out the window. **ñj*** to change one's facial expression suddenly

tjengap ***-*** 1 to open the mouth again and again, as when gasping for air. 2 having trouble doing sth

tjèngbèng special day of cemetery-cleaning and praying held by the Chinese during April

tjengèk ***-*** *or* **tjengak-*** to keep crying out in pain. **ñj/di·tje*** to torment smn to make him cry *or* moan

tjèngèl **ñj*** to crane the neck. *Bareng njèngèl, bisa weruh kanṭi tjeṭa.* By craning his neck he managed to get a clear view. **ñj/di*aké** to crane [the neck], to stick [the head] up high. *Sirahé di*aké.* He stretched his head up high. *ptg* **tj·r·èngèl** *pl* craning their necks. *See also* PENTJÈNGÈL

tjengel *ng kr,* **griwa** *ki* nape of the neck. *See also* KONG-EL

tjèngèng to cry easily. *Adja *.* Don't be a crybaby!

tjengeng [of neck] stiff

tjengèngès *ptg * pl* with lips drawn back in jeering *or* condescending smiles. ***an** to keep jeering, sneering. **ñj*** to laugh jeeringly, showing the teeth. **ñj/di*i** to jeer at

tjèngèr *inf var of* TJÈNGÈL

tjengèr *rpr* the sudden cry of a newborn baby. *wiwit lair ** ever since I was born. ***-*** to cry loud and long. **tjengar-*** *or* **ñj*** to cry loudly

tjengès **ñj/di·tje*** *or* **ñj/di*(i)** to tease, ridicule. *Senengané njengès kantjané sing lagi seneng jang*^{2}*an.* He's always teasing his friends who are in love. *See also* PENTJENGÈS

tjènggèr *var of* DJÈNGGÈR

tjenggèrèng peanuts covered with spiced rice flour (*Solonese term: see also* REMPÈJÈK)
tjenggèrètnong a certain tree locust that makes a loud buzzing sound
tjengging **ñj/di*** *rg* to seize smn by the nape of the neck
tjenggring **ñj/di*** to insult smn, hurt smn's feelings
tjengil wicked, evil. **ñj/di*(i)** to do harm to smn
tjengingis *rpr* a jeering grin. **tjengingas-*** to keep showing the teeth, *esp.* when laughing jeeringly *or* flirtatiously. **ñj*** to bare the teeth (as above)
tjengir **tjengar-*** to keep grinning foolishly *or* screwing up the face. **ñj*** to gesture with the face as above. *Bareng krasa lara bandjur njengir.* When he felt the pain, he grimaced. **ñj*-ñj*** *or* **njengar-ñj*** to keep grimacing *or* grinning foolishly; *fig* helpless, ineffectual. *Sariman bisané mung tjengar-*.* Sariman can't do *anything.*
tjengis a certain variety of very hot chili pepper (*rg*). **ñj/di*** to show [the teeth] (in pain; when jeering, sneering)
tjengkah a clash, conflict; to conflict, clash. ** ing atiné* inner conflict. **ing karep* clash of wills. ** karo kasusilan* in conflict with moral standards. *Agama Islam iku ora nglarangi tatatjara sing ora * karo agama Islam.* The Islamic religion does not prohibit customs that do not conflict with its principles. *wis * karo kanjatan saiki* not in accordance with the realities of today. ***an** 1 to conflict *or* quarrel with each other. 2 a ceremony for an ill *or* aging person to support him in his frailty. ***-*an** to push (against) *or* conflict with each other. **tje*an** to conflict with each other. **ñj/di*** 1 to push against sth, *e.g.* to support it. 2 to engage in a contest of strength by pushing against each other, sometimes at either end of a pole
tjengkal 1 a protective covering of curved wood *or* pressed coconut fibers for preventing a newly circumcised penis from rubbing against the clothing. 2 (sth used as) a door stop. 3 a unit of length: *ca.* 12.3 feet = 3.75 meters. **ñj*** 1 awkward, ungrammatical, meaningless [of the arrangement of items in a sentence]. *Ukarané njengkal.* The sentence doesn't make sense. 2 (*psv* **di***) to use a *tjengkal* (1 *or* 2 above). **ñj/di*(i)** to measure sth in *tjengkal*'s (3 above)
tjengkang a unit of length: the distance between the tips of thumb and index finger stretched wide apart. *sa** one such length. **ñj/di*i** to measure sth in the above units
tjengkar [of soil] unproductive. *lemah sing ** soil that is not very fertile. **ñj/di*aké** to let [land] lie fallow
tjengkaruk 1 the blossom of the guava tree. 2 dried cooked rice
tjèngkèg, tjengkeg a prop, support. **ñj/di*** to prop sth up. **ñj/di*i** to prop sth up with. *Omahé di*i kaju.* The house is propped up with a tree trunk.
tjèngkèh 1 a bunch of bananas. 2 (to stand) with the feet apart. 3 *rg* forked stick. 4 tripod
tjengkèh 1 clove (tree; fruit). 2 clubs (playing card suit). 3 clove-shaped ear drop
tjengkélak *rpr* heading smw suddenly. *Bareng weruh jèn mendung ḍèké * bali.* When he saw the weather looked threatening, he headed back home.
tjengkerem ***an** grasp, clutches. *bébas saka *an pendjadjah* liberated from the clutches of the subjugators. **ñj/di*** to grasp with claws *or* other piercing objects; *fig* to get [a victim] into one's clutches
tjengkerung *ptg ** [of skin] chafed, chapped
tjengkèwèk *var of* TJENGKIWING
tjengkèwèng *var of* TJENGKIWING
tjengkiḍing *var of* TJEKIṬING
tjengkiling apt to hit when angered
tjengkir a very young coconut (not yet edible). **ñj*** resembling a young coconut. ** gaḍing* a small yellow decorative coconut; **ñj*-gaḍing** ivory-colored [of beautiful breasts]
tjengkiwing ***an** shortened form of a name. **di*** [of names] shortened, abbreviated. **ñj/di*** 1 to hold [a child, an animal] by the midsection. 2 to hold *or* carry sth by holding it at the outer edge with one or two fingers
tjéngklak *rpr* a leap onto one's mount *or* into a vehicle. *A mak * numpaki sepéḍahé.* A jumped onto his bicycle. **ñj/di*** to jump into/onto. *A njéngklak sepéḍahé mulih.* A hopped on his bike and went home.
tjengklèng *rpr* a metallic clang. **ñj*** to turn back on itself, *e.g.* a road in a hairpin turn. **tj·um·engklèng** to clang. *Swarané tjemengklèng.* She has a strident voice.

tjengkling *rpr* a metallic ring. **tj·um·engkling** to ring

tjengklong **ñj/di*** to deduct. *Ḍèwèké njengklong Rp. limang atus.* He held out 500 rupiahs.

tjéngkok, tjèngkok 1 regional variety of a language. **ing basa Djawa kang isih kaanggep murni jaiku: * Surakarta, utawa * Ngajogjakarta.* The Javanese generally considered the purest is that spoken in Surakarta and Jogjakarta. 2 speaking *or* singing style; intonation *or* rhythm of one's speech *or* of a song. 3 change of pitch *or* key in classical songs. **ñj/di*** to change pitch *or* key while singing a classical song. **pa*** act of changing pitch/key

tjengkolak wooden piece on a bow handle as reinforcement at the point where the arrow is aimed

tjengkorong ***an** sketch, outline. **ñj/di*i** to draw up a sketch *or* outline (of)

tjengkowak *ptg * pl* full of good-sized holes *or* dents. **ñj*** having a hole/dent in it

tjengkowèk *ptg * pl* full of holes *or* dents. **ñj*** having a hollow *or* indented place. *Korèngé njengkowèk.* His wound is deep and wide.

tjengkowok *ptg * pl* full of good-sized holes *or* dents. **ñj*** having a large hollowed *or* indented shape

tjéngkrang *var of* ṬÉNGKRANG

tjengkrang *rpr* a pricking sensation. **tj·um·engkrang** to keep feeling a pricking sensation. *See also* TJENGKRING

tjengkring *var of* TJENGKRANG. **tjengkrang-*** to keep feeling a pricking sensation. *Rasané kok tjengkrang-*, mesṭi ana eriné.* I feel sth pricking me–there must be a thorn in my skin.

tjéngkrong [of arms, legs] curved, bent

tjengkung *rpr* the tones of a certain gamelan instrument (*kempul*)

tjengkurek̄ *ptg ** scrawled, messy [of handwriting]

tjengkuwèh *var of* TENGKUWÈH

tjengkuwek̄ *ptg * pl* full of fair-sized holes *or* dents. **ñj*** having a hole/dent in it

tjengkuwik *ptg * pl* full of small holes, dents, hollows. **ñj*** having a little hole/hollow/dent in it

tjengoh **ñj*** in plain sight, right there in view. *Ḍèwèké wis njengoh ana ing sopiran.* He was already right there in the driver's seat. **ñj/di*aké** to allow sth to be seen. *Pistulé di*aké.* He made sure his pistol was visible.

tjengol **ñj/di*-*aké** to keep raising sth above a surface. *Ali njengol²aké sirahé ing nḍuwur banju.* Ali kept sticking his head up out of the water.

tjengonglong *var of* TJENGONGOK

tjengongok *rpr* a sudden thrusting forward of the neck, *esp.* by a goose. *ptg * pl* extending the necks as above

tjéngos *var of* TJRÉNGOS

tjenguk baby monkey (young of the KEṬÈK). **ñj*** flabbergasted, dumbfounded. **ñj*i** [of babies] just learning to talk

tjengungong *rpr* the cry of a peacock

tjengunguk *rpr* popping in *or* showing up suddenly

tjenil 1 any small round springy-textured object. 2 *rpr* pinching, pecking. *Sikilku diṭoṭol mak *.* It pecked me on the leg. ***-*** *or* **tjenal-*** 1 having a tough, rubbery texture. 2 lively, vivacious

tjenining *ptg ** *or* ***an** *or* **pa·ñj*an** defiant, cocksure, inconsiderate

tjènol *rpr* the elastic movement of sth springy being released suddenly

tjénṭang, tjènṭang small platter for vegetables *or* stew. ***an** a check mark. **ñj/di*(i)** to tick off, place a check mark (against)

tjenṭang (*or* ***an**) provision, specification. **ñj*** to bend/curve upward

tjenṭé a small xylophone-like gamelan instrument. ***-*** 1 *rpr* the sound of noisy conversation. 2 [of speaking voice] grating, strident. **ñj*-ñj*** to raise the voice in anger

tjènṭèl *var of* TJANṬÈL

tjènṭeng *rpr* a sharp object striking sth

tjenṭèng guard, watchman. ***-*** *or* **tjenṭang-*** [of speaking voice] loud, harsh

tjenṭèt **ke*** sickly, stunted in growth

tjenṭing 1 any long thin object with a pointed tip. *djungkat ** comb with a curved rat-tail. 2 *rg* a small sash-like garment (*setagèn*). **ñj*** 1 resembling the above sash. 2 having a long thin pointed shape. 3 [of women's buttocks] small and pointed

tjentjang ***an** a tethering rope. ***-*an** act of tethering. *Weḍus mau *-*ané angèl.* It's hard to tie up the goat. **ñj/di*aké** to have sth tethered; to have smn tether [an animal]. **ñj/di*(i)** to tether [animals]

tjentjem coconut oil mixed with flowers and fragrant leaves. ***an** liquid in which sth is soaked. *lenga *an* coconut oil mixed with fragrant flowers and leaves: a ladies' hair dressing. **ñ(j)/di*** to soak sth

tjenṭok **ke*** to sulk. **ñj/di*** to anger *or* hurt smn

tjénṭong 1 rice ladle. 2 shoulder blade(s). **ñj/di*** to ladle out [rice]

tjenunuk *ptg* * *or* ***an** *or* **tjenunak-*** to grope one's way. *See also* NUNUK

tjep 1 *rpr* a sudden silence as smn stops talking *or* singing. 2 hush! [to a crying child]. ***-* meneng** to comfort and quiet a crying child. *** klakep** *sms* * 1

tjepak 1 close to, almost at. *Wis * enggoné arep dadi ngantèn.* Her wedding day is very near now. 2 apt, prone. ** dadi nesu* easily angered. ***an** that which is in readiness. *Roti iki kanggo *an aḍiku jèn mulih sekolah mengko.* This cake is for my brother when he gets home from school. ***-*** *or* **ñj*** ready and waiting. *Nalika tak ampiri nang ngomahé, wis njepak nang ngarepan.* When I went to his house to pick him up, he was waiting out front. **ñj/di*aké** to make/have ready. *Ḍèké wis njepakaké bis kanggo meṭuk awaké ḍéwé.* He had arranged for a bus to meet us. *Tjepak²na pirantimu.* Have your tools ready. **ñj/di*i** to prepare sth for smn. *A njepaki mangan B.* A fixed B something to eat. **tj·um·epak** in readiness. *Kebutuhané wis tjemepak.* Everything we need is all set.

tjepâkâ *var of* TJEMPAKA

tjepeḍak *var of* TJEMPEḌAK

tjepeng grasp, hold (*kr for* TJEKEL)

tjèpèr, tjepèr shallow; saucer-shaped. *Piring * apa piring djegong?* Is it a shallow dish or a deep dish?

tjepèt gripping instrument. ***an** implement for pressing. **ñj/di*** 1 to pinch *or* grip with a tool. 2 to press sth between two things

tjepet quick, fast; with a swift motion. *Ajo, *!* Come on, hurry up! *Tumangkaré trewèlu iku * banget.* Rabbits multiply rapidly. *Kok * temen anggoné njopèt.* With one swift motion he picked the pocket.

tjepit ***an** 1 an implement used for holding *or* pressing things together. **an kertas* paper clip; binder. 2 mouse trap. **ke*** to get squeezed/pressed. *Gilinganė mubeng, tebuné ke*.* The mill wheel, turning, pressed the sugar cane [to extract the liquid]. **ñj/di*** to pinch, squeeze, press sth

tjeplé [of Javanese *A* vowels] pronounced in the Banjumas manner [*e.g. lārā*] rather than in the standard Central Javanese manner [*e.g. lârâ*]

tjèples just right, exact, on the nose. **ñj/di*i** to resemble closely, be just the same as. *Sing digawé njèplesi gawéjané A.* What he made looks just like what A made.

tjeplès *rpr* a loud slap. ***an** act of slapping. *sa *an* one good slap. **ñj/di*** to give smn a resounding slap

tjeplik earring prong that slips through the pierced lobe. *benik ** snap fastener

tjepling *rpr* becoming detached. *Sekrupé ditjopot, mak *.* He loosened the nut and it came off.

tjeplis *rpr* sth small being crushed, *esp.* a hair louse pressed between fingernails

tjeplok a circle-shaped mark. *enḍog ** fried egg. ***-*** covered with round figures. **ñj/di*** to fry an egg. *** piring** a certain round white plate-shaped flower

tjeplong *rpr* a sudden opening. *Kajuné dibur bolong mak *.* He bored a hole right through the wood. **ñj/di*(aké)** to make a hole all the way through sth. **tj·um·eplong** relieved. *Bareng ngerti jèn lulus atiné tjemeplong.* He was relieved when he heard he had passed the exam.

tjeplos 1 *describing direct, unadorned speech. Kowé mau kanḍa * ndjaluk tulung, aku ndang mangkat.* You asked right out for help and I came immediately. 2 *rpr* bursting apart. *Tomaté ditjakot mak *.* He bit into the tomato and it burst. ***é** plainly stated; to put it bluntly. **tjeplas-*** to speak one's mind forthrightly. *Jèn arep tjepet, ja ngomonga tjeplas-*.* If you want it in a hurry, just say so. **ñj/di*(i)** to burst a hole in sth. *njeplosi dluwang nganggo dridjiné* to poke holes in a piece of paper with the finger. **tj·um·eplos** plainly stated. *Bab kuwi wis tjemeplos ing lajang kabar.* There was a straightforward account of it in the newspaper.

tjepluk throughout [the morning]. *sakésuk ** all morning long

tjèplukan 1 a certain bird. 2 a certain wild shrub; also, its edible grape-like fruit

tjeplus 1 *rpr* a small burst. *Djeruké ditjakot mak *.* He bit into the lemon and it squirted. 2 *cr* eye. **ñj/di*(i)** to bite into *or* break apart a whole object (grape, pepper, *etc.*)

tjepol to become detached. *Tjekelané *.* The handle came off. **ñj/di*** to take sth off

tjepon a bamboo basket
tjepot *rg var of* TJOPOT
tjèprèt **ñj/di*i** to splatter onto. *Mangsiné njèprèti klambiku.* The ink spattered my shirt.
tjèpret *rpr* a pointed missile striking its target. **tjèprat-*** to strike repeatedly. *Panah²é tjèprat-* ngenani debog.* The arrows kept zinging into the banana log.
tjeprèt 1 *rpr* the click of a camera shutter. 2 *rpr* sth soft getting squashed. **ñj/di*** to take a picture (of). *Tukang potrèk njeprèt pengantèn.* The photographer snapped a picture of the bridal couple.
tjeprol *rpr* a sudden easy detachment. *Katjangé dibeḍol mak *.* He pulled the peanut plant right out of the soil.
tjeprot 1 *rpr* sth bursting out. *Bareng botolé dibukak, mak * isiné wutah.* When he opened the bottle, out poured the [carbonated] liquid. 2 *rpr* sth sharp stabbing. *Mak *, peḍangé mantjep ing ḍaḍané.* The sword plunged into his chest. **tj·um·eprot** to produce the above effects
tjepuk (*or* ***an**) a small round covered container. **ñj*** having the shape of the above container
tjepuri masonry wall around a house *or* garden. **ñj/di*i** to enclose [an area] with such a wall
tjepurung canopy covering a howdah *or* sampan cabin
tjèr 1 *rpr* metal vibrating, *e.g.* cymbals that have just been struck. 2 *rpr* an engine starting up
tjer 1 sibling relationship: *sedulur ** sibling; *kamas ** next older brother; *mbakju ** next older sister. 2 *var of* TJUR
tjer- *see also under* TJR- (*Introduction, 2.9.3*)
tjerak *var of* TJEḌAK
tjeramah lecture, speech, talk
tjerḍas *** tangkas** a quiz contest
tjeré 1 a variety of long-grained rice. 2 no longer married. **ñj/di*** to divorce one's spouse
tjerek̄ 1 dash, hyphen. 2 an *R*-showing diacritic in Javanese script. **ñj/di*** to write one of the above characters (on)
tjéréménḍé a small oval short-legged roach with white spots
tjèrèt kettle
tjeret a tiny amount of liquid poured out. *sa** a dash/splash of liquid
tjeri **pa*ǹ** ditch and cesspool for household water disposal. **tj·um·eri-*** to hate, despise
tjeri(j)os story (*kr for* TJRITA)
tjérit **ke*** to discharge a small amount of feces inadvertently
tjerkakah *ptg * pl* to spread, open out *or* up. **ñj*** *sg as above. Putjuké kudu diprasi supaja bisa njerkakah.* The tip has to be cut back so the plant can bloom.
tjerkèkèh *var of* TJERKAKAH
tjerkot *ptg ** throbbing with pain
tjèrles *see* DJIBLÈS
tjerma leather, hide
tjermé a certain small edible fruit with a large pit; the tree that produces this fruit
tjermin *oj* mirror, looking-glass
tjermumuh *ptg ** covered with infected sores *or* rash. **ñj*** having an infected sore
tjerngèngès *var of* TJENGÈNGÈS
tjerngingis *var of* TJENGINGIS
tjérong ***an** *or* **tjérang-*** having streak marks on the face. **ñj/di*i** to make streaks on [the face]. *Rainé di*i areng.* His face is streaked with charcoal. *See also* TJLÉRONG
tjerṭil *ptg ** throbbing with pain
tjertjeb *var of* TERTJEB
tjerung [of canyons, gorges] deep and with steep sides
tjès *rpr* saliva dripping. **tjas-*** to drip steadily. *Ileré tjas-* baé.* He drools constantly. ***-*an** to drool habitually. **nge*** 1 to drool. 2 to long to possess sth. *Ali nge* weruh pit kuwi.* Ali is drooling over that bicycle. **nge/di*i** to drool on(to)
tjes 1 *rpr* sudden cooling/chilling *or* (*fig*) an emotional cooling off, *e.g.* relief from anxiety. 2 *rpr* loud sizzling. **nge*** to sizzle loudly. *See also* NJES
tjespleng just right; having the desired result. *Ḍèwèké mangsuli pitakon *.* He answered the question right on the nose. *Durung ana djamu sing *.* There's no medication that will cure it.
tjèt 1 paint. *montor * ireng* a black car. 2 *rpr* monkey chatter. *Keṭèk iku nèk muni swarané *, *, *, tjruwèt-tjruwèt.* Monkeys make chattering sounds. **nge/di*** to paint sth
tjeṭa clear; obvious. ** wéla²* very clear, crystal clear. *keterangan sing ** a clear explanation. *bisa ndeleng ** able to see clearly. *Sing * jèn djalaran ratjun mesṭi ana tanḍa²né.* Clearly if the cause [of death] was poison, there would have to be traces of it.

ka* to be shown. *kaja ke* ing nḍuwur* as set forth above. **ñj/di*kaké** to clarify, show. *Isiné undang² di*kaké déning djuru penerang.* The meaning of the law was clarified by the information officer.

tjéṭak pertaining to printing. *mesin ** printing machine. *tukang ** printer. *salah ** misprint. ***an** act *or* way of printing. **an kaping pinḍo* second printing. **ñj/di*aké** to have sth printed. *njéṭakaké unḍangan kanggo mantèn* to have wedding invitations printed up. **ñj/di*(i)** to print. *njéṭak buku* to print a book. *njeṭaki ḍuwit* to print up money. **pa·ñj*** act of printing. *panjéṭaké bukuné* the printing of his book

tjeṭak palate; roof of the mouth. *aksara ** Javanese alphabetic characters representing the palatal sounds (*DJ, J, TJ*). *pait ** bitter-tasting. **ñj*** 1 to stick to the palate. 2 *intsfr* bitter-tasting. *pait njeṭak* intensely bitter

tjeṭanṭang ***an** to stand in a defiant pose with the legs wide apart. **ñj*** standing in the above attitude

tjeṭèk, tjèṭèk shallow; superficial. *Kaliné * apa djero?* Is the river shallow or deep? ** pikiré.* He has a shallow mind. **ñj/di*aké** to cause to be shallow. *Weḍi iku njeṭèkaké pelabuhan.* The sand made the harbor shallow.

tjeṭek̄ **ñj*** bitter (*intsfr: var of* ÑJ·TJEṬAK)

tjeṭenṭeng *describing stiffness in the finger joints*

tjeṭèr **tjeṭar-*** *or ptg* **tj·l·eṭèr** [of whips] to keep cracking. *Sempritané ptg tjruwit, sambuké ptg tjleṭèr.* Whistles blew; whips cracked.

tjèṭèt *rpr* bursting open. **ñj/di*** 1 to cause to burst open by squeezing *or* pressing. 2 *cr* to give birth (to)

tjeṭèt ***an** 1 a bird that sings only when stimulated as described below. 2 an electric switch. **ñj/di*i** to make a soft sound to [a bird] by snapping the thumb against the middle finger, to encourage it to sing

tjeṭeṭek̄ *ptg * pl* silent and huddled up with cold. **ñj*** *sg as above*

tjeṭeṭeng *ptg * pl* standing around doing nothing rather than working at the job

tjèṭi one type of court retainer (*see* MA-NGGUNG)

tjeṭik 1 hip, pelvic bone. 2 to ignite. *Ali wis * geni.* Ali has the fire going. **ñj/di*aké** to stir up; to incite. *njeṭikaké geni* to get a fire blazing. *geni wis mati di*aké manèh* to stir up sth that had quieted down; to whip a dead horse (*fig*)

tjeṭil 1 stingy, close-fisted. 2 *rpr* a tug, jerk. **ñj/di*(i)** to pull sth out with a sudden jerk

tjeṭing small bowl-shaped basket for serving rice. *sa** a bowl [of rice]. ***an** (placed) in a serving basket. *Segané apa *an?* Is the rice ready to serve? **ñj/di*i** to hold a ceremony for a woman seven months pregnant with her first child

tjeṭit *rpr* a snap, click. *benik ** snap fastener. **ke*** out of joint

tjeṭiṭis *ptg * pl* crouching shivering with cold, *esp.* when wet. **ñj*** *sg as above*

tjetj- *see also under* TJ- (*Introduction, 3.1.3*)

tjetjak 1 small lizard commonly found on interior house walls. 2 dot, point. 3 period (punctuation mark). *kaja ** **tjekik** to pick at one's food, eat almost nothing. *** nguntal empjak** to attempt the impossible

tjetjed *oj* flaw, defect

tjetjeg **ñj/di*** to tamp, tap. *Tegesan rokoké di* ing asbak.* He put out his cigarette in the ashtray.

tjètjèk *rg var of* GORI

tjètjèl having a piece, *or* the outer layer, detached. *Médjané *.* The table is chipped. **ñ(j)/di*(i)** to chip; to detach sth from. *** butjèl** having many chipped *or* skinned places

tjetjep **ñ(j)/di*** to sip; *fig* to absorb knowledge. *netjep ngèlmu kebatinan* to learn mystic lore

tjètjèr *var of* KÈTJÈR

tjèṭèt **ñj/di*(i)** to squeeze the infected matter from. *See also* METJÈṬÈT

tjéṭok, tjèṭok bricklayer's trowel. **ñj/di*** to dip and apply [mortar] with a trowel

tjeṭol *rpr* a bird pecking

tjéṭong rice ladle (*var of* TJÉNṬONG)

tjeṭor *var of* TJEṬÈR

tjeṭot **ñj/di*** to pinch and twist flesh (a punishment for children)

tjeṭut **ñj/di*i** to crack one's joints by pulling the fingers

tjeṭuṭuk ***an** *or* **tjeṭuṭak-*** without energy, lackadaisical

tjeṭuṭur *ptg * pl* remaining silent and motionless

tjeṭuṭut **tjeṭuṭat-*** *or* **ñj*** having a morose expression. *Adja pidjer tjeṭuṭat-* baé.* Don't always look so downcast!

tjèwèng 1 a card game played with the Chinese cards (*kertu tjilik*). 2 *rg var of* TJÈNÈNG)

tjèwèr *rg var of* TJUWÈR

tjèwèt incomplete, lacking *or* missing sth. *Jèn ana *é baé adja kurang ing pamengku.* If I leave out something, don't hold it against me. *ukara * djedjeré* a sentence with no subject. *Lapurané *.* His report is incomplete.

tjewèwèk *inf var of* TJUWÈWÈK

tjéwok *ng kr,* **tjawik** *ki* to clean oneself with the left hand and water after urinating *or* defecating. **ñj/di*i** to clean smn as above

tjéwol, tjèwol *rpr* getting a firm grip on sth

tjiblok *var of* TJEBLOK

tjiblon (*or* **tje***) to make "music" by slapping the surface of water rhythmically in unison (children playing)

tjidra untrue, deceitful, disloyal. *Ḍèké ngrumangsani jèn * ing djandji.* He felt he had gone back on his promise. *nindakaké laku ** to act with disloyalty, to be untrue. **ñj/di*(ni)** 1 to betray, be disloyal to. 2 to kill for revenge. **njidra asmara** to commit adultery with smn else's spouse. **tj·in·idra** (having been) betrayed, deceived

tjiḍuk object used for ladling *or* scooping. **ñj/di*** 1 to ladle *or* scoop [liquid]. 2 to arrest for criminal *or* political causes. *** baṭok** *or* *** siwur** coconut-shell ladle

tjiglok̄ to fall down/out. **ñj/di*aké** to drop sth. **ñj/di*i** to let sth fall on(to)

tjihna sign, indication, evidence (to the effect that...). **ka*** shown, made clear *or* evident. *See also* PRATJIHNA

tjiièt **-** *rpr* squeaking. **ñ(j)/di*** to catch, trap. *njiièt maling* to catch a thief. *ptg* **tj·r·ijèt** *pl* squeaking

tjiji:t cheep! peep! (baby birds' cry)

tjiju a certain kind of brandy

tjijum *rg* **ñ(j)/di*** to kiss (Javanese style: *see* AMBUNG)

tjijung *rpr* the cry of a certain starling. *manuk ** the starling that makes this cry

tjijut (**aut** *kr?*) small, narrow. *Dalané *.* The road was narrow. *Kamaré amba apa *?* Is the room large or small? ** wawasané* having a narrow point of view. **ñ(j)/di*aké** *or* **ñ(j)/di*i** to make narrow(er) *or* small(er). *njijutaké klambi* to make a shirt smaller [than another which is too large]. *Dalané di*aké.* They made the road narrower.

tjik *rg var of* TJIKBÈN

tjikal young coconut. ***an** small piece of coconut left after grating a large piece. **an bakaran* roasted coconut shred. ***en** *rg* stiff(ened) as a result of an ailment. *Tangané *en.* His hands have stiffened.

tjikar open cart pulled by a draft animal. *** kasur** *or* *** pir** two-wheeled horse-drawn cart

tjikat quick, nimble, agile

tjikbèn *ng,* **kadjeng·ipun** *kr* 1 so that [sth] will... 2 to let [sth happen], leave alone, let go. *See also* BÈN, KAREBÈN

tjikrak wastebasket. **-** to romp, cut capers

tjil *adr* mouse-deer! (*shf of* KANTJIL)

tjilâkâ unlucky; at odds with one's environment. *Wah, saiki * aku.* Oh-oh, I'm out of luck now. *Tjilaka ané.* What a tough break! *ndadèkaké *né wong pirang²* to bring misfortune to countless people. ***né** unfortunately; at the worst. **ka*n** 1 bad luck, misfortune, mishap. *gawé (ka)*(n)* to bring bad luck. *nemu (ka)*(n)* to have bad luck. *Kéné mau ana ka*n.* There was an accident here a while ago. 2 to undergo a misfortune. *Bapakné dikanḍani jèn anaké ka*n.* He was told that his child had had an accident. **ñj/di*ni** to cause misfortune (to). *Mretjon kuwi sok njilakani awak.* Fireworks often injure people.

tjilakak *var of* TJILAKA

tjilèmèt what a thing to do! how out-of-place!

tjili small (*rg var of* TJILIK). *** guṭi** teeny-tiny, very small

tjilik *ng,* **alit** *kr* small, little. *Geḍé apa *?* Is it large or small? *woh -** small-sized fruits. *botjah ** a small (young) child. *ḍuwit ** small change. *wiwit ** ever since I was a child. *djeneng ** childhood name (used until marriage). *wong ** a small person; the little man, the ordinary citizen. *Gagangé dawa *.* The stem is long and thin. *Banjuné iliné *.* The water is flowing a mere trickle. *swara ** a thin high-pitched voice. ***an** 1 on a small scale. *perkara sing *an* a minor (court) case. 2 childhood. *ḍèk *anku* when I was a child. 3 small coins. *Duwé *an ora?* Have you got any small change? **-*an** on a small scale. *pésta -*an* a small party. **ke*en** excessively small. *sanḍangané botjah² sing wis paḍa ke*en* children's clothing that is outgrown. **ñj/di*aké** to make sth smaller (than it was). *njilikaké* *lengené* to shorten the sleeves. **ñj/di*-*aké** to consider trivial. *Kowé wis ora matur nuwun, malah njilik²aké pitulungané.* You not only didn't thank him, you belittled his help. **ñj/di*i** to make sth (so that it is) small(er). *Nèk gawé klambi menèh di*i.* Make the next dress smaller. **njiliki ati** to frighten smn. *** ati** 1 timid. 2 discouraged, faint-hearted. *** gaṇḍik** small but wiry in physique. *** melik** since [one] was a child. *** menik²** cute [of little girls]. *** menṭik⁽²⁾** tiny. *** mula** ever since childhood. * *mula ḍèwèké wis dojan nangis.* He's been a crybaby all his life. *See also* ḌÉLIK

tjilili *var of* TJLILI[b]

tjilu(k)bah a game played by hiding the face from a child and then suddenly popping into view with an exclamation

tjim *inf* to lay undisputed claim to sth. *Aku * sing abang.* I have dibs on the red one! **nge/di*** to want for oneself. *Slamet nge* pelemé.* Slamet has his eye on the mango.

tjimik *-* *or* **ñj*-ñj*** to pick at one's food, eat with little appetite

tjimit *var of* TJIMIK

tjimpling 1 coconut half-shell, used as a measuring unit. 2 a small, very hot chili pepper

tjimtjao *var of* TJAMTJAO

tjin- *see also under* TJ- (*Introduction, 3.1.7*)

Tjina (**Tjinten** *kr?*) 1 Chinese. 2 a Chinese person. 3 one of the small playing cards (*kertu tjilik*). **pa*n** Chinese section, Chinatown. **enggon * di·dol·i dom** to carry coals to Newcastle. **ke·lebu·ṅ * gunḍul·an** to get cheated. *** lélé abang buntut·é** miserly, niggardly. *** mindring** Chinese money-lender. *** tjraki** miserly, stingy

tjindé a purple-flecked bean

tjinḍé a fine silken material. ***ǹ** 1 to wear the above fabric. 2 imitation *tjinḍé* material

tjinḍil small mouse/rat (young of the TIKUS). **ñj*** to give birth to young. *** abang** child, young person

tjing *adr* cat! (*shf of* KUTJING). **nge/di*** to pick on smn

tjingak to gaze (at) in astonishment *or* wonder. **ñj·tje*** to have an astonished *or* wondering look on the face. *See also* TJINGUK

tjingbing *var of* TJÈNGBÈNG

tjingèng *var of* TJÈNGÈNG

tjingir animal's snout. *-* [of nose] to twitch. *Saradané *-* irungé.* He has a nervous mannerism of twitching his nose. **ñj/di*aké** to move *or* raise [the nose *or* upper lip]

tjingklok the back (hollow) of the knee

tjingkluk *see* ARIT

tjingkrang [of clothing] too short. **ke*an** to live in poverty

tjingtjinggoling a black wagtail with a scissors-shaped tail

tjingtjong unnecessary talk *or* comments. *kakèhan ** excessive unnecessary talk

tjinguk **tjingak-*** astonished, amazed, dumbfounded. *See also* TJINGAK

tjingur *cr* nose

Tjinten *kr for* TJINA?

tjintjal **ke*an** to [do] laboriously *or* against obstacles

tjintjin 1 ring for the finger. 2 thimble

tjintjing (worn) too high on the body. *Adja sok *.* Don't put on your batik wraparound so that it is too far off the ground. **ñ(j)/di*-(aké)** to raise one's garment at the bottom, *e.g.* when walking

tjintjug **ke*an** to have trouble moving. *Dikon njoba mlaku, bisa, mung rada ke*an.* They told him to walk; he managed to, but with difficulty.

tjintrâkâ destitute, poverty-stricken. *See also* PAPA

tjip **nge/di*i** to taste, sample (*var of* NG/DI-ITJIP-I)

tjipir (*or* **ke***) a leguminous plant that bears a peapod-like vegetable; also, the fruit of the pods

tjiples **ñj/di*** to press [sth small] with the thumbnail. *Tumané di*.* He crushed the hair louse.

tjiplong *cr* blind

tjiplos *cr* eye

tjiplu:k *-* chubby, roly-poly

tjipowah abacus

tjiprat *-* to spatter, splatter. *Banjuné *-*.* The water splattered. *Slamet tjiprat² ana lataran.* Slamet was splattering water out in the yard. **ke*an** to get spattered. **ñj*** to splatter (onto). *Laburé njiprat kabèh.* The whitewash got all over everything. *Banju udan njiprat², aku ke*an teles.* The rain water splashed on me and got me all wet. **ñj/di*aké** to spatter sth [onto]. *Pastur njipratake banju sutji marang botjah sing dibaptis.* The priest sprinkled holy water on the child he was baptizing. **ñj/di*i** to spatter onto. *Jèn malamé panas njiprati mori,* *baṭikané ora betjik.* If the hot wax spatters the cloth, the batik won't turn out well.

tjipta 1 ideas, aspirations. *ngeningaké ∗* to meditate; to purify one's thoughts. *Sa∗né dadi.* All his hopes came true. 2 creation, conception. *Manungsa kuwi ∗ning Pangéran.* Mankind is the creation of God. **ka∗** conceived in the mind, dreamed of (*see also* ADU). *Apa kang ka∗ dadi.* Whatever he wishes comes true. **ñj/di∗** 1 to think (about), aspire to. *Adja sok njipta lelakon sing ora²*. Don't set your heart on the impossible. 2 to conceive, create. *Sapa sing njipta téori kuwi?* Who formulated that theory? **∗ ripta** *ltry var of ∗*

tjipuh **ka∗an** under a strain, feeling uncomfortable *or* awkward

tjipwah *var of* TJIPOWAH

tjir **tjar-∗** bit by bit over a long period of time

tjirak a children's game played with fruit seeds

tjiri sign, identifying mark, scar. *∗né jaiku anḍeng² ing baṭuk.* You can tell him by the mole on his forehead. **ke∗ǹ** to have a bad reputation. *Pardi wis ketjirèn seneng goroh.* Pardi is known as a liar. **ñj/di∗ǹi** to mark sth. *amplop ditjirèni "Èsprès"* an envelope marked "Express". **∗ wantji (lelai g·in·awa mati)** an incurable defect of character

tjirit feces (*oj*). **tjirat-∗** emerging little by little. **ke∗** to discharge feces inadvertently

tjis a short spear for guiding elephants. **nge/di∗** to lead [elephants] with the above

tjit 1 (*prn* **tji:t**) *rpr* a mouse's squeak. 2 fabric (*rg var of* TJITA). **nge∗** to squeak

tjita 1 patterned fabric. 2 *ltry var of* TJIPTA. *tjita² kang luhur* noble ideas

tjiṭak *var of* TJÉṬAK. **∗an** mold, form. **ñj/di∗aké** to have sth molded/formed; to have smn mold/form. **ñj/di∗(i)** to shape sth in a mold. *Poḍengé di∗ nang tjangkir.* She molded the pudding in a cup.

tjiṭes **ñj/di∗** to press sth against the thumbnail. *njiṭes tuma* to kill a hair louse as above

tjitjik to have a small appetite *or* capacity. *Jèn ∗ ngono, ja ora lemu²*. You'll never gain weight if you don't eat more.

tjitjil **∗an** 1 installment loan. *Tuku mawa ∗an krédit kang lumrah regané wis mesṭi tikel.* Buying on credit is usually more expensive than paying the regular price. 2 payment on an installment debt. *∗an sepisanan minggu ngarep.* The first installment is due next week. **ñ(j)/di∗** 1 to buy on credit. *Télévisiné bisa di∗ saben wulan.* The television can be paid for in monthly installments. 2 [to do] (bit by bit) in advance. *Ḍèk ésuk aku wis nitjil sinau kanggo bésuk Senèn.* I did my next Monday's studying this morning. **pa·ñ(j)∗** (act of) paying out in installments. *Panjitjilé sewulan satus rupiah.* He has to pay a 100-rupiah installment every month.

tjitjip **∗-∗** to taste food during its preparation to check the seasonings. **∗-∗an** a taste, a sample. **ñ(j)/di∗i (ñg/di·keḍap·i *ki*)** 1 to taste. *Djangané di∗i.* She sampled the soup (while she was cooking it). 2 to try out, test. *Ḍèké arep nitjipi nganggo montorku.* He wants to try driving my car.

tjitjir missing, lacking. *Ana sing ∗.* There's something missing.

tjitra 1 a prose *or* musical composition; depiction in story *or* song. *djuru ∗* clerk. 2 form, figure. **ñj/di∗** to write, compose; to depict in story *or* song. *tjinitra ing tulis* to be put in writing. **pa·ñj∗** secretary, clerk

tjiṭut almond-eyed

tjiwel **ñj/di∗** to pinch between thumb and index finger

tjlakunṭer ornamentation, *esp.* for a kris. *ptg ∗* ornate, fancy. *Tulisané ptg ∗.* His handwriting is full of flourishes.

tjlânâ trousers, long pants. **∗ pandji²** *or* **∗ pandji·ǹ²** knee-length pants with buttons at the knees (formerly worn by *pandji* noblemen)

tjlanḍak **∗an** *or* **∗-∗** always handling *or* touching things annoyingly

tjlangap a wide aperture. *∗ing tjangkem baja* the wide opening of a crocodile's mouth. **ñj∗** to open (up, out) wide

tjlangkrak **∗an** sitting (impolitely) in a higher position than others. **ñj∗** to seat oneself as above

tjlangkrangan crass, having no regard for proper social conventions

tjlangob **∗an** to keep yawning

tjlap 1 *describing a sudden departure.* 2 panic-stricken. *Mak ∗ atiku weruh botjah mèh ketumbuk montor.* My heart was in my throat when I saw a child almost get hit by a car.

tjlaprèt *ptg ∗* [of face] streaked with dirt

tjlarat winged lizard

tjlarèng **tjlorang-∗** messy, streaked with marks. *See also* TJLORÈNG

tjlaṭu *ng,* **witjanten** *kr,* **ngendika** *ki* to say; to talk, speak (**m·atur** *ka*). **pa*ñ** what smn says; speech, talking. *njinau basa patjelaṭon Inggris* to study spoken English

tjleb *var of* TJLUB

tjlebèk marked-off square in a rice paddy. *sa ** one such square, used as a measuring unit

tjlebung *rpr* plunging into water. *ptg * or* **tjlebang-*** [of talk] random, aimless; impulsive, heedless

tjleg *rpr* a quick hand movement, *or* the sound that such a movement produces

tjlégrok *var of* TJÉGROK

tjleguk *rpr* gulping. ***an** craving food *or* drink. **tjlegak-*** 1 to down sth in a series of gulps. 2 to have the mouth watering for sth. **sa*(an)** one gulp. **tj·um·leguk** to gulp sth down

tjlekanṭang *ptg * pl* [of long things] sticking out. ***an** *or* **ñj*** *sg as above. Djaluné njlekanṭang.* It has long talons.

tjlekanṭuk *ptg * pl* curled at the tips. **ñj*** *sg as above*

tjlekaṭuk ***en** to rattle, clatter. *Tjangkemé *en.* His teeth are chattering. **ñj*** to deliver a slap *or* blow

tjlekenik *pl form of* TJEKENIK

tjlekenṭing *pl form of* TJEKENṬING

tjlekenṭung *pl form of* TJEKENṬUNG

tjlèkèr *ptg ** messy, disorderly. *Tulisané ptg *.* His handwriting goes all higgledy-piggledy.

tjlekeṭik *describing a surprisingly easy outcome. Dak kira angèl banget, djebul mak * baé.* I thought it'd be hard, but there was nothing to it.

tjlekeṭut *ptg ** rumpled, full of creases

tjleki:k ***en** *or* **tjlekak-*** to have hiccups

tjlekit *describing the sting or bite of an insect. ptg ** covered with insect bites *or* stings. **ñj*** *or* **tj·um·lekit** to smart, sting. *Omongané njlekit banget.* His words caused a lot of hurt feelings.

tjlékor *var of* TJLÈKÈR

tjlekot *rpr* a stab of pain. *Sirahé krasa mak *.* A pain shot through his head. ***-*** *or* **ñj*** throbbing with pain. *See also* TJEKOT

tjlekunṭeng **ñj*** curly. *Kawaté njlekunṭeng.* The wire curls. **ñj/di*aké** to curl sth

tjlekut *var of* TJLEKOT

tjlekuṭik intricacy, complication. *Elo, la kok akèh temen *é ki.* How complicated this is! **é wong pinter* the complex workings of an intelligent mind. *ptg * or* ***an** complex, intricate. *Soalé ptg *.* The problem is a many-faceted one. *Aku ora seneng karo wong sing pikirané ptg *.* I don't like devious people.

tjlekuṭikan 1 the hollow in a horse's leg between the hoof and the fetlock. 2 *form of* TJLEKUṬIK

tjlèlèk *ptg * or* **tjlélak-*** open-eyed/dumbfounded with astonishment *or* shock. **ñj*** shocking, ugly, repellent (in appearance, nature, behavior)

tjleleng simple-minded. ***an** *or* **tjlelang-*** to look around vacantly as though dazed. **ñj*** 1 to act as if one is simple-minded. 2 to look around with a vacant expression

tjleler prone to steal. *Ḍèké * lho, awas barang²mu simpenana.* He's light-fingered; better keep your things in a safe place. **tjlelar-*** to steal habitually. **ñj*** stealthy. *njleler lunga* to sneak out

tjlemèk apron

tjlemer prone to steal. *wong ** one who steals; a kleptomaniac. **ñj*** to steal (deliberately *or* compulsively)

tjlèmèt *var of* TJILÈMÈT

tjlemik ***an** *or ptg * pl* talking in quick low voices. **ñj*** *sg as above*

tjlemong *rpr* blurting sth out. *Aku mau mak * kok takon apa Siti pegatan.* Without thinking I asked if Siti was divorced. ***an** *or *-* or* **tjlemang-*** to blurt things out repeatedly *or* habitually. **ñj*** to make an unfortunate remark impulsively

tjlempung a zither-like gamelan instrument with thirteen double strings, played by plucking. **ñj*** to play this instrument

tjlemut *rpr* snatching. *ptg * pl* to snatch

tjlèng *rpr* metal clanking

tjleng *rpr* a stab of severe pain. ***-*an** throbbing with severe pain

tjlengkrang *ptg ** throbbing with mild pain

tjlèngkrèk *rpr* a sudden leap up onto sth

tjlengkring *var of* TJLENGKRANG

tjlèntrèng **ñj*** [to use, give, *etc.*] just a little bit, only a small amount. **sa*an** a little bit, a small amount; a short while

tjlénṭot *var of* TJLÉNṬUT

tjlénṭut ***an** to engage in word play (puns, double meanings, *etc.*). **ke*** to say the wrong word by mistake

tjlèprèt spattered, spread about. *Mangsiné ptg *.* There were inkstains all over it.

tjlepuk a long-eared owl

tjleput *rpr* snatching. **tjlepat-**∗ to keep snatching
tjléram *var of* TLÉRAM
tjlereng *ptg* ∗ staring fixedly
tjlèrèt 1 a flash of light; lightning; *rpr* a flash of light(ning). 2 a dotted line. 3 a gliding lizard. 4 *rpr* a swooping, gliding motion. **sa**∗**an** brief, momentary. *Mengkono sa*∗*an ngenani pribadiné A.* This brief account touches on the personality of A. *Sanadjan mung sa*∗*an wis bisa kepeṭuk Siti.* He was able to be with Siti, though only for a brief moment. **tj·um·lèrèt** to flash. *Kilat katon tjumlèrèt ana sisih wétan.* Lightning flashed in the east. ∗ **gombèl** a variety of gliding lizard; *kaja* ∗ **gombèl** shifty, untrustworthy. ∗ **taun** rain and wind storm
tjleret *rpr* light dimming. *Urubé lampu ditjilikaké mak* ∗. She turned the kerosene lamp low.
tjlérong *ptg* ∗ [of face] all streaked with dirt. **ñj/di**∗**i** to get dirty streaks on [the face]. *See also* TJÉRONG
tjles *rpr* sudden cooling/chilling (*var of* TJES)
tjleṭèr *pl form of* TJEṬÈR
tjlètjèk *var of* TLÈTJÈK
tjleṭor *pl form of* TJEṬOR, *a var of* TJEṬÈR
tjléṭot *var of* TJLÉNṬUT
tjléṭut *var of* TJLÉNṬUT
tjlèwèh ∗**an** a long opening, a slit. **ñj**∗ slit, opened. *Sarungé suwèk njlèwèh.* The sarong has a long tear in it.
tjlèwèk *var of* TJLÈWÈH
tjléwo *ptg* ∗ *pl* speaking one's mind. *Wong² pada guneman ptg* ∗ *tanpa paṭokan.* They said what they thought, with no restraint. **tjléwa-**∗ *or* **tj·um·léwo** to talk baby talk. *Karo setengah taun umuré, mulané isih tjemléwo.* He's only a year and a half old, so he doesn't talk too well yet.
tjlikrak *ptg* ∗ *pl* [of children] skipping about gaily
tjlileng **tjlilang-**∗ to look around searchingly. *A tjlilang-*∗ *nggolèki B.* A is looking all over for B.
tjlili[a] a trap for catching *gemak* birds
tjlili[b] **tjlila-**∗ embarrassed, flustered
tjlimèn on a small scale; with little fanfare
tjlimprit *oj* dart used as a weapon
tjlimut prone to steal
tjling *rpr* a metallic ring. *Swarané pedang kena tameng mak* ∗. The sword clanged against the shield.
tjlingker *rpr* slipping into concealment. **ñj**∗ to keep under cover. *Bu X njlingker ing buri omah.* Mrs. X crouched down behind the house.
tjlingkrik *rpr* a sudden upward motion. *Timbané munggah* ∗. The bucket rose (in the well). *Mak* ∗ *mènèk wit.* He scrambled up a tree. ∗**-**∗ *or* **tjlingkrak-**∗ up and up; to rise steadily. *Olèhé mènèk kaja keṭèk,* ∗*-*∗. He climbs like a monkey. *Tjlingkrak-*∗ *pangkaté tansah munḍak.* He gets promoted to higher and higher ranks.
tjlinguk *ptg* ∗ *pl* bewildered, puzzled. ∗**an** *or* **tjlingak-**∗ *sg as above*
tjlingus 1 bashful about being seen. 2 hairs growing in the nose. ∗**an** shy by nature
tjlinṭis ∗**an** ill-mannered, not well brought up
tjlinṭut ∗**an** secretive, furtive. **ñj**∗ to do secretly; to act furtive. *Ajo adja njlinṭut.* Come on, don't sneak around. **ñj/di**∗**aké** to conceal sth. *njlinṭutaké ḍuwit* to hide smn's money from him
tjlirit *rpr* a streak of light. *Aku weruh lintang alijan mak* ∗. I saw a comet streak across the sky. **ñj**∗ forming a thin line. *Brengosé njlirit.* He wore a thin moustache. *lintang njlirit* shooting star
tjliṭut *var of* TJLINṬUT
tjlob *var of* TJLUB
tjlolo **tjlola-**∗ distraught
tjlolong ∗**-**∗ *or* **tjlolang-**∗ to move the head slowly from side to side as though in a daze
tjlomot ∗ **ané** *slang* what bad luck!
tjlonèh *ptg* ∗ varicolored. **ñj**∗ 1 varicolored. 2 *var of* NJLENÈH. **ñj/di**∗**i** to streak sth. *Klambiné di*∗*i areng.* His shirt was all streaked with charcoal.
tjlonèng *var of* TJLONÈH
tjlong ∗**-**∗**an** (to walk) with a quick striding gait. **tjlang-**∗ to waver between alternatives. *Sikepé tjlang-*∗. He keeps changing his attitude.
tjlongob ∗**an** to keep yawning
tjlorèk *ptg* ∗ covered with scribble marks. *buku sing ptg* ∗ a book with pencil marks scrawled on the pages. **ñj/di**∗**i** to make scribble marks on [sth]
tjlorèng *ptg* ∗ *or* **tjlorang-**∗ streaky. *djarit sing tjorèké ptg* ∗ a batik with sloppily done line designs. **ñj/di**∗**i** to make messy streaks on. *A njlorèngi rainé B nganggo areng.* A streaked B's face with charcoal. *See also* TJORÈNG
tjlorèt *var of* TJLORÈK

tjlorong ray, beam. **tj·um·lorong** to emit beams. *See also* TJORONG

tjlorot *rpr* swooping, streaking. *Ana lintang sing ngalih mak* *. A shooting star streaked across the sky. *ptg* * *pl* swooping/streaking motions. *Kilat ṭaṭit ptg* *. Lightning kept flashing. *Iwak*[2] *ptg* *. Fish darted about. *-* *or* **tjlorat-*** to keep darting/swooping. *Suwé*[2] *lampu kang tjlorat-* iku mati.* At last the sweeping searchlight went out. **ñj*** to swoop, glide, dart. *Klarap njlorot.* Flying lizards swoop through the air. **ñj/di*aké** to cause sth to swoop/dart. *Montor mabur sing digawé dluwang di*aké.* He sailed a paper airplane. **tj·um·lorot** to dart, shoot, swoop. *Panahé tjumlorot ing sakiwané lésan.* The arrow whizzed to the left of the target. *Kiperé tjemlorot nggajuh bal.* The goalkeeper leaped to catch the ball.

tjlowok ***an** a dent *or* hollow place in a surface

tjlub 1 *rpr* a plunge into sth. 2 *rpr* blurting out a (*usu.* shocking) utterance. **tjlab-*** *rpr* repeated actions as above. **ke*** to get plunged into sth. *Klambiku mau ke* banju.* My shirt got dunked in the water. **nge/di*-aké** to plunge sth [into]. *A nge*aké péso ana ing debog.* A rammed a knife into the banana log.

tjlulu *rpr* bursting in. *ptg* * *or* **tjlula-*** *pl as above.* *Wong*[2] *mau wis paḍa ptg* * *ing kéné.* People keep barging in here. *See also* TJULU

tjluluk to say; to give information; to point out. *Saka kadohan ḍèké wis *: Aku lulus.* From a distance he was already shouting: I passed the exam!

tjlumik *ptg* * *pl* speaking low but distinctly. **tjlumak-*** (to speak) as above

tjlumpring 1 leaf growing out from a bamboo-stalk joint. 2 a certain style of ancient earring. ***an** a certain style bracelet

tjlunṭang ***an** badly behaved, ill-mannered

tjlupak earthenware lamp, *usu.* set on a stand (*adjug*[2])

tjluring a xylophone-like gamelan instrument

tjlurut 1 *rpr* swishing. *Kembang api * ḍor!* The skyrocket zoomed up and exploded. *Iwak*[2] *mau nglangi ptg* *. Fish kept darting about. 2 *var of* TJURUT. ***an** to lead a nomadic existence. **ñj*** to swish, zoom. *Montor*[2] *njlurut ana ndalan.* Cars swished past on the road.

tjlus *rpr* stabbing, piercing

tjluṭak [of pets] always getting at the food

tjluwek̄ ***an** small hole, burrow. **ñj/di*** to dig into. *See also* TJUWEK

tjluwik ***an** a small hole in a hard surface. **tjluwak-*** having holes here and there

tjluwok ***an** a large hole in a hard surface

tjoba *ng,* **tjobi** *kr* to have a go at; to [do] and see what happens. *É, * rasakna.* Here, take a taste. ** daktakon ḍisik ja.* Let me just ask him first [and see what he says]. ** jèn wis dandan ngiloa.* When you're all dressed, take a look at yourself in the mirror. ** menawa aku sugih, aku mesṭi bisa tuku apa*[2]. Just think, if we were rich we could buy anything. ** gawénen soal iki!* Come on—solve the problem. ***n** a testing ground; a guinea pig. *Tikusé kanggo tjoban obat sing anjar.* They're using the mice for experimentation with a new medicine. ***-*** to give sth a try. *Ḍèwèké mung *-* ndandani nanging sakdjané ora bisa.* He's doing what he can to repair it, but actually he doesn't know how. ***n-*n** that which is tried; an experiment. **ñj/di*** to try (out), test. *Montoré di* ḍisik.* Test-drive the car first. *Slamet saiki lagi di* karo Sing Maha Kuawa.* God is subjecting Slamet to trials. **pa*n** a trial, tryout, test run. *pepalang lan pa*n* trials and tribulations

tjobak *rg var of* TJOBA

tjobi *kr for* TJOBA

tjoblos ***an** pierced, stabbed. **ke*** to get pierced. *Sikilku ke* dom.* I got a needle stuck in my foot. **ñj/di*** to stab, prick, pierce

tjobolo stupid, ignorant

tjoḍot a certain bat that feeds on fruits. ***an** fruits that have been nibbled at by bats

tjog **nge/di*-mol** to accuse smn of sth embarrassing. *Pardi di*-mol Slamet jèn seneng Siti.* Slamet taunted Pardi with being in love with Siti.

tjogemol *var of* TJOG-MOL: *see* TJOG

tjoglèk joined in such a way that the parts can move, *e.g.* a hinged piece of wood

tjogmol *see* TJOG

tjohung *rpr* a peacock's cry

tjok 1 *rpr* alighting. *Laler bandjur mabur, bur; méntjok ana ing panganan,* *. The fly flew around, then lighted on the food. 2 *rg var of* SOK[b]

tjokak vinegar

tjokèr **ñj/di*** to mess up, scratch around in [sand *etc.*]

tjokik *cr* dead

tjoklat *var of* SOKLAT

tjoklèk broken; to break, snap; *rpr* wood snapping. *Tekené* *. The walking stick broke. ***an** short-tempered. **ñj*** 1 (*psv* **di***) to break sth. 2 to lose patience

tjokol *rg* sugar cane *or* corn foliage used as fodder. **ñj/di*** to force smn to eat

tjokor *cr* foot, leg

tjokot *var of* TJAKOT

tjokrèk **ñj/di*** to prod at [soil *etc.*]

tjolik *var of* TULAK

tjolok 1 torch; light used as a torch. 2 message; messenger. **ke*** to get stuck in the eye. *Mripaté ke**. He got a finger in the eye. **ñj/di*** to stick sth into [*esp.* eyes]; *fig* conspicuous, eye-catching. *Djanganè di* lombok.* Put a dash of chili in the soup. *tulaḍa kang njolok* a conspicuous example. *Dandané njolok mata.* The way she dresses hits you in the eye. **ñj/di*aké** to stick sth [into an eye]. *Dridjiné di*aké nang mripaté.* She stuck her finger in his eye. **ñj/di*i** to light sth up in order to search. *njoloki pepeteng* to cast light into the darkness. *Mripaté di*i, pranjata ora tatu.* He flashed the light into the eye and found it wasn't damaged.

tjolong **ñj·tje*** to steal regularly. *wong njenjolong* one who steals habitually. **ñj/di*(i)** to steal sth. **njolong laku** to do sth stealthily. **ñj* peṭèk** to have a deceptive appearance. *Botjah kok njolong peṭèk, kétoké alim ning kok sok njolong.* He had me fooled: he looks like a nice boy, but he steals things. **njolong ulat** to steal a glance (at). *** djupuk** 1 thievery. 2 to steal habitually. *Ḍèké ora gelem tjolong-djukup.* He wouldn't steal. *** laku** in secret. *Anggoné kawin kanṭi tjolong-laku.* They were married secretly. *** plaju** to sneak away, run off

tjolot ***an** a jump. **ané koḍok kuwi bisa adoh.* Frogs can jump far. ***-*** to keep leaping. *Kantjil *-* ana ing pinggir kali.* Mouse-Deer bounded along the riverbank. **ke*an** to have an unexpected piece of good luck. **ñj*** to jump, leap. **ñj*-ñj*** *or* **njolat-ñj*** to keep bounding. *Olèhé mlaku rikatan karo njolat-njolot.* He ran fast, in leaps and bounds. **ñj/di*i** to jump on(to). *Pangkoné di*i tikus.* A mouse jumped into his lap. *ptg* **tj·r·olot** to keep jumping/bounding. *See also* PENTJOLOT

tjombang **ke*** filled with water, *esp.* rainwater. *Dalan² paḍa ptg ke* kebak banju.* The roads were dotted with rain-filled puddles.

tjombèr **(ka)*an** *or* **pa*an** open sewage ditch *or* basin for household waste water

tjomblang matchmaker *or* go-between for matching marriage partners

tjombor (*or* ***an**) horse feed: grass, rice bran, and rice husks mixed with water. **ñj/di*** to feed [a horse] with the above

tjombrang (*or* **ke***) a plant whose ginger-like root is used as a seasoning

tjomot **ñj/di*** to take up, pick up, hold

tjomplong hole, opening, gap. **ñj/di*i** to make an opening in. *ptg* **tj·r·omplong** riddled with holes

tjomprèng 1 a type of boat. 2 (*or* **ke*an**) short of money. *Uripé tansah *.* or *Uripé ke*an.* They never have enough money.

tjonḍok 1 to agree. *Aku karo ḍèké ora tau *.* He and I never see eye to eye. 2 (*or* **tj·um·onḍok**) to stay smw temporarily. *Sepira lawasé anggoné tjumonḍok ana ing alas?* How long did he remain in the forest?

tjonḍol *rg* a mouse that inhabits rice paddies

tjonḍong in agreement (with). **ing pikiré* the oneness of their ideas. **ñj/di*i** to concur (with); to agree (to)

tjong ***-*an** that which is offered to smn. **nge/di*aké** to offer sth by holding it forth. **nge/di*(i)** to offer sth to [smn]

tjongah **ñj/di·tje*** to tantalize smn

tjongat (*or* ***-***) extending outward [of sth long and spiky]. *Katon *ing sikilé bango nalika mabur mau.* The stork's legs stuck out behind him as he flew. *Pringé katon *-*.* The bamboo stalks stuck out [*e.g.* from the back of a truck]. **ñj*** to extend outward. *Gaḍingé gadjah iku njongat mendjaba.* An elephant's tusks stick way out. *pringé njongat munggah.* The bamboo sticks up. *ptg* **tj·r·ongat** *pl* sticking out. *See also* MENTJONGAT

tjongkèl, tjongkil *rg var of* SONGKÈL

tjongklang 1 galloping pace. 2 [of a garment] too short. **ñj*** to gallop. **ñj/di*aké** to run [a horse] at a gallop

tjongkok 1 a support, prop. 2 intermediary in arranging a marriage. 3 procurer, pimp. **ñj/di*(i)** to support, prop up. **ñj/di*i** to hold a ceremony for [an elderly infirm person] to support and sustain him

tjongkrah in disagreement, disputing. *A lagi*

* *karo B perkara mbagi warisan.* A is at odds with B over the division of the inheritance.

tjongol **ñj*** to appear. *Sirahé njongol nang djenḍéla.* His head came in view at the window. **ñj/di*aké** to allow sth to be seen. *ptg* **tj·r·ongol** *pl* to appear. *Iwaké ptg *.* A number of fish came to the surface.

tjongor 1 animal's snout. 2 *cr* human mouth, human nose and lips. **ñj*** having the lips thrust forward. *Lambéné njongor.* His lips were pushed out.

tjongot *var of* TJONGAT

tjono lump *or* swelling on the head

tjonṭal **ke*an** *or* **ke*-*** in frantic pursuit; following with great difficulty

tjonṭang *var of* TJUNṬANG

tjontjal **ke*an** struggling to get free/loose

tjonto example, model. ***né baé** let's just suppose...; to take an example... **ñj/di*** to use as an example; to imitate, copy. *Ḍèké njonto olèhku mlaku.* He walked the way I walk. *Nalika udjian A njonto garapané B.* During the exam A copied from B's paper. **ñj/di*ni** to give an example of; to set an example (for). *Sing geḍé kuwi lumrahé njontoni aḍiné.* The older children usually set the example for the younger ones. *Sawisé di*ni sepisan, ḍèké bisa nggawé lajangan ḍéwé.* After I showed him once, he was able to make a kite himself.

tjonṭok **ke*an** to get caught in the act

tjonṭong banana leaf twisted into a cone-shaped container. *katjang brul patang ** four cones of peanuts. **ñj*** resembling a banana-leaf cone. **ñj/di*(i)** to put sth into such a cone. *Katjangé dibungkus apa di*?* Did he wrap the peanuts or put them in a cone?

tjopèt a pickpocket. ***an** act of picking pockets. **ke*an** to be the victim of a pickpocket. *Aku ke*an ḍompètku.* My wallet was lifted. **ñj/di·tjopat-*** to pick pockets regularly. *Pagawéjané njopat-njopèt ngalor-ngidul.* He goes around everywhere picking pockets. **ñj·tje*** to make one's living by picking pockets. **ñj/di*(i)** to relieve pockets of [their contents]. *njopèt ḍompèt* to lift smn's wallet. **pa·ñj*an** place where pickpockets abound

tjoplok to come loose. *Beniké *.* The button is loose. **ñj/di*** 1 to detach sth. *Gambar kuwi adja di* lo.* Don't take that picture off the wall. 2 to fire smn

tjopot 1 to come loose; to come off/out. *Roḍané * sidji saka asé.* One of the wheels came loose from the axle. *Tapelé *.* The horseshoe came off. 2 to remove [clothing]. ***an** to come apart easily; detachable. *Bedilé *an, jèn ora dienggo di*.* The rifle is easily dismantled; when not in use it is taken apart. **ñj/di*** 1 to undo, remove, take apart. *Ḍèké njopot sranḍal.* He took off his sandals. *Roḍané di*.* He took the wheel off. 2 to dismiss, discharge. *A di* saka pegawéané.* A got fired.

tjor **tjar-*** to pour repeatedly. ***-*an** 1 that which is poured. 2 molten substance. *Panḍé wesi nge*aké *-*an wesi nang tjiṭakan.* The blacksmith poured the molten iron into molds. **nge/di*** to pour from one container into another. *nge* banju ing èmbèr* to pour water into a bucket. **nge/di*aké** to pour sth into another container. *nge*aké wédang ing gelas* to pour hot water into a glass. **nge/di*i** 1 to pour onto. *Kumbahané di*i wédang.* She poured boiling water over the dirty clothes. 2 to water sth. *Pemerintah bangun ḍam perlu kanggo nge*i sawah nèk mangsa ketiga.* The government built a dam to supply water to the paddies during the dry season.

tjorak fabric design, *esp.* for batik

tjorèk 1 batik design. 2 (*or* ***an**) a drawn *or* written line. *Akèh *ané.* There were a lot of lines drawn on it. ***-*an** to scribble. **tje*an** *sms* *AN *above*. *Alisé ndjalirit ireng tje*an.* Her eyebrows were penciled in black. **ñj*** 1 to draw lines. 2 to show off in front of girls. **ñj/di*(i)** to draw a line on (under, through) sth. *Ora ana sing di*.* None of them was crossed off. *Kertas mau di*i nganggo aksara.* Some letters had been scribbled on the paper. *tembung kang di* ngisoré* the underlined words

tjorèng **tjorang-*** untidily streaked with lines *or* marks. *See also* TJLORÈNG

tjorèt *var of* TJORÈK

tjoro 1 cockroach. 2 a lowly person

tjorong 1 microphone. 2 ray, beam. 3 funnel (*var of* TORONG). **tj·um·orong** to send out light beams. *See also* PENTJORONG, TJLORONG

tjos *rpr* sizzling. ***-*an** *rpr* continuous flowing/dripping, *esp.* of tears. **nge/di*** to touch with a hot iron; to brand

tjoṭa *see* SABUK

tjotjak a thrush-like bird. *** gunung**, *** rawa**

varieties of this thrush. * **ng·untal lo** to chase rainbows, dream an impossible dream

tjotjog 1 to agree (with). *Aku * banget.* I quite agree. *Aku * rembugmu iku.* I agree with what you say. *Panemuku * lan panemumu.* My opinion is the same as yours. *Ajo ndeleng gambar idup, *?* Let's go see a movie, OK? 2 to match, suit. *Piring iki * karo stèlan sing nang omah.* This dish goes with the set I have at home. 3 congenial. *Aku luwih * karo kowé tinimbang karo ḍèwèké.* I feel more at ease with you than with her. *A * karo B paḍa olèhé seneng kesenian.* A and B have in common a taste for art. ***an** to compare, match. *A konangan lagi *an karo B.* A got caught comparing his homework with B's. **an tanggal Masèhi karo tanggal Djawa* to match up the dates on the Christian and Javanese calendars. **ke*** to get pierced *or* poked. *ke* tjarang* to get jabbed with a bamboo stalk. **ñ(j)/di*aké** 1 to check over, verify. *Lotréné di*aké éntuk hadiah nomer sidji.* The lottery was verified for winner of first prize. *Ḍèwèké njotjogaké sing dituku; sawisé digunggung, olèh²ané diwuwuhi kekarèné ḍuwit, *.* He checked over his purchases; when he had totaled them and added what he had brought home with the remaining money, it came out right. 2 to make conform, bring into agreement. *Tembung Junani di*aké karo paketjapan sidji²ning basa mau.* The Greek words are adjusted to fit the pronunciation of each borrowing language. 3 to stick sth sharp [into]. *Sunduké di*aké nang wit geḍang.* He stuck the skewers into the banana tree. **ñ(j)/di*(i)** to pierce with a sharp-pointed object. *Eri notjog sikilku.* The thorn stuck into my foot. *Tukang sulapé di* nganggo dom ora krasa.* The magician didn't feel it when he was stuck with a needle. **ñ(j)/di*i** to suit. *Dikon milih endi sing di*i.* He was told to choose whichever suited him. *Ora ana sing notjogi karsané Sang Ratu.* None of them was just what the King wanted.

tjotjoh a pencil-sized metal rod used for crushing *or* grinding betel nuts for chewing. **ñ(j)/di*(i)** 1 to crush *or* grind [betel]. 2 to press *or* poke [meat] in preparation for cooking it

tjotjor 1 beak, bill. 2 roof-tip point at the end of the ridgepole. 3 bottom part of a kris sheath. **ñ(j)/di*** to peck

tjotjot *cr* mouth. *Adja kakèhan *.* Shut up!

tjoṭo lacking sth necessary to one's work. *Bareng Mar metu, aku dadi *.* After Mar left the job, we felt something essential was missing.

tjotoméjo a boor. *kaja ** boorish

tjoṭot *rpr* bursting forth, *e.g.* the insides of a squeezed tomato. ***an** an implement for forcing sth out. **an nggo nggemuki mobil* car lubricating gun. **ñj/di*(aké)** to press sth to eject the contents. *See also* METJOṬOT

tjowèk 1 small saucer-shaped stone bowl for grinding spices and seasonings. 2 saucer-like earthen platter

tjowès **ke*** to get hurt accidentally

tjowèt *rg var of* TJUWÈT

tjowok **ñj/di*** to decrease [a larger amount] by taking some away. *Di* bajaré.* His pay was docked.

tjowong [of face] wan and pinched-looking

tjrabak **pa*an** *oj* place for learning under the guidance of a holy hermit

tjrah antagonism, discord. ** agawé bubrah.* Disagreement causes disruption.

tjraki *kaja Tjina ** miserly, close-fisted. **pa*ǹ** place where herbs and drugs are stored

tjramuk *pl form of* TJAMUK

tjrang *rpr* a dull metallic thud

tjrangap *ptg * pl* [of mouths] wide open. *Pijiké papat ptg *.* The four baby birds' mouths were wide open.

tjranṭèl *pl form of* TJANṬÈL

tjrapang spreading and pointed. *Brengosé *.* He has a wide moustache pointed at the tips. **ñj*** to spread outward to either side. *Sunguné njrapang kaja eri mawar.* Its antlers branch out like thorns on a rose bush.

tjras *rpr* a slash with a sharp blade. *See also* KETJRAS

tjrawak having a disagreeably loud speaking voice

tjre- *see also under* TJER- *(Introduction, 2.9.6)*

tjreblung *ptg * pl* chattering, jabbering. *Omongé tjah² ptg *.* The children are chattering away. ***an** *sg as above*

tjrèk *rpr* the sound effect produced by a puppet-master tapping his bronze bars (*ketjrèk*)

tjremed ***an** *or* **ñj*** to tell dirty stories; to talk obscenely *or* coarsely

tjremimi(h) *ptg * pl* sad, melancholy. **ñj*** *sg as above*

tjremomong *ptg * pl* [of fires] glowing. **ñj*** *sg as above*

tjrémot *pl form of* TJÉMOT
tjremumuh *ptg* * [of sores] reddish and infected-looking
tjrèng 1 cash (as opposed to credit). *mbajar* * to pay cash. 2 *rpr* a metallic clang. **tjrang-*** repeated clanging, as of cymbals
tjrengèk *ptg* * *pl* [of children] wailing long and loud
tjrèngèl *pl form of* TJÈNGÈL
tjrèngès *ptg* * *pl* showing their teeth (smiling; making a face). **ñj*** *sg as above*
tjrengkling *ptg* * *pl* *rpr* repeated metallic clanking sounds, *e.g.* metal being pounded
tjrengklung *ptg* * *pl* *rpr* repeated deep metallic sounds, *e.g.* from thumping an oil-filled steel drum
tjréngos *ptg* * *or* ***an** [of face] streaked with dirt
tjrenṭèng *ptg* * *rpr* heavy metallic sounds, *e.g.* of steel girders banging together
tjrep *rpr* piercing, stabbing
tjres *rpr* a sharp point spearing sth. *Tibané ditaḍahi gaḍingé: *.* He fell and was impaled on the elephant's tusk.
tjrèt *rpr* the emission of feces in diarrhea. **tjrat-*** 1 repeated acts as above. 2 *cr* to make frequent trips to the bathroom. **nge*** to defecate as above
tjret *rpr* a small drip. **tjrat-*** to dribble in small amounts. *Olèhé ngetjori banju tjrat-*.* He poured the water a little at a time. **nge/di*i** to spatter sth with drops of liquid. **sa*an** a small amount, a mere drop
tjreṭil *ptg* * *rpr* the stinging sensation of an open cut
tjrètjès *ptg* * *or* ***an** *or* **ñ(j)*** to drip copiously [of tears; raindrops]. *Luhé nrètjès.* Her tears poured out.
tjrèwèt 1 to talk too much. 2 to complain constantly
tjrigis talkative by nature
tjrijèt *pl form of* TJIJÈT
tjrijos to say, tell (*kr for* KANḌA; *opt? kr for* TJRITA). ***ipun** they say..., I hear... (*kr for* DJARÉ)
tjring *rpr* loud jingling. *Tjring, ḍuwité ḍa tiba ing djobin.* The coins jangled to the floor.
tjringih *ptg* * having many sharp places. *sing ptg * lanḍep² ing pinggiré blèg* the jagged places at the edge of the can. *wong kang kulité ptg ** a fruit with a prickly skin
tjringis *ptg* * *pl* showing the teeth (smiling, grimacing, *etc.*). **ñj*** *sg as above*

tjriping fried chips made from paper-thin slices, *usu.* of cassava. * *geḍang* fried banana chips. * *kenṭang* potato chips. * *téla* cassava chips
tjripu thong sandal(s)
tjrit *rpr* water squirting. *Banjuné ming metu seṭiṭik seka lèḍeng mak *.* Only a little water came out of the faucet. **tjrat-*** *rpr* repeated squirts. *Seḍéla² tjrat-* ida-idu liwat tjenḍéla.* Every so often he spit out of the window. *See also* KETJRIT
tjrita (**tjrijos** *opt? kr*) story, narration. **ka*** it is told... *Ka* nudju ing sawidji dina...* Now it happened that one day... **ñj/di*kaké** (*ϕ* /**di·ngendika·kaké** *ki*) to tell (about). *njritakaké lelakoné* to tell about one's adventures. *Tjritakna kabèh.* Tell us all about it. **ñj/di*ni** (*ϕ*/**di·ngendika·ni** *ki*) to tell smn [a story; about sth]. *Botjah² di*ni bu.* Mother told the children a story. *Aku di*ni bab uripé tawon.* He told me how bees live. **tj·in·arita** *ltry var of* KA* *above*
tjritjis talkative by nature
tjriwis talkative; to jabber, prattle. * **tjawis** to put up a fuss before doing as requested
tjrobo (*or* **ñj***) unclean, sloppy, careless
tjrobong chimney
tjrog *rpr* a falling object getting impaled on sth sharp
tjrok *-* *rpr* the sloshing of wet fabric against a board *or* stone when being laundered. **nge/di*-*** to launder clothes by pounding them against sth
tjrolot *pl form of* TJOLOT
tjromplong *pl form of* TJOMPLONG
tjronḍolo *var of* TRONḌOLO
tjrongat *pl form of* TJONGAT
tjrongoh promiscuous
tjrongol *pl form of* TJONGOL, *a var of* TJUNGUL
tjrot *rpr* liquid spurting. **nge/di*aké** to squirt sth. *Kétjapé di*aké mak *.* He squirted some soy sauce [from the bottle]. **nge/di*i** to spurt onto sth
tjrotjoh *var of* TROTJOH
tjrotjop **ñ(j)/di*** to sip loudly (uncouth table manners)
tjrotjos *ptg* * *pl* flowing in profusion. ***an** *or* **ñ(j)*** to flow. *Luhé *an.* Tears poured from her eyes.
tjrowal *ptg* * full of dents *or* chipped places. *Kajuné ptg *.* The log bore the marks of many axe blows.
tjrowèt *rg var of* TJUWÈT
tjruk (*or* *-*) *rpr* the sound of an

implement striking earth. **tjrak-∗** (to produce) repeated sounds as above. *Ana swara tjrak-∗.* I hear someone hoeing (*etc.*).

tjrumpleng *pl form of* TJUMPLENG

tjrungul *pl form of* TJUNGUL

tjrut *rpr* a small squirt of liquid. **tjrat-∗** *rpr* repeated squirts. **nge/di∗aké** to squirt sth. *ngetjrutaké lenga wangi* to squirt perfume. **nge/di∗i** to squirt sth onto. *nge∗i katju* to squirt [*e.g.* perfume] onto a handkerchief

tjrutjup *var of* TJUTJUP

tjrutjus **∗an** sizzling. **ñ(j)∗** to sizzle, to make a *tjusss* sound

tjruwèt *var of* TJUWÈT

tjruwil *pl form of* TJUWIL

tjruwit *pl form of* TJUWIT

tjuban *rg* needle for mending fishnets

tjublak 1 small perfume container. 2 hollowed out. **∗-∗ suweng** (to play) hunt the earring (children's game). **ñj/di∗** to hollow sth out

tjublek̄ hollowed out (*var of* TJUBLAK)

tjubles tubeless. *ban ∗* tubeless tire. **ke∗** to get pierced. **ñj/di∗** to pierce with a sharp-pointed object

tjublik oil lamp. **∗an** portion removed from sth. *∗an saka karangané X* an extract from X's article. **ñj/di∗** to vaccinate for smallpox. **sa∗** a small piece taken from sth; an excerpt

tjubluk 1 ignorant, stupid. 2 a pit for trapping animals

tjubung a certain poisonous plant. **ñj/di∗** [of this plant] to poison smn. **∗ kasih·an** a purple gem used for ring settings

tjugag **ñj/di∗** to cut off [a narration] in the middle

tjuget **∗an (ati·ǹ)** quick to take offense; easily put in a bad mood

tjuh *rpr* spitting. *idu mak ∗* to spit, pitoo! *∗-∗, tangané loro diidoni.* He spit on his hands.

tjuk *rg; adr* little boy!

tjukai customs duty. *kantor ∗* customs office

tjukak *var of* TJOKAK

tjukat quick, agile. **∗an** agile in nature

tjuké *var of* TJUKAI

tjukeng obstinate, hard to convince. **ñj/di∗i** to maintain sth obstinately

tjuki **∗ǹ** stitched all the way through from top to bottom. *kasur tjukèn* a stitched-through mattress. **ñj/di∗** to stitch [a mattress] as above

tjukil 1 descendant of an original settler. 2 possessions *or* customs handed down from the original settlers. **∗an** picked/pried from. *Kopra kuwi ∗an klapa kaepé garing.* Copra is sun-dried picked-out coconut meat. **ñj/di∗(i)** to extract sth (from). *njukil krambil* to pick coconut meat from the shell. *Kupingé adja di∗i nganggo barang sing lantjip.* Don't ream your ears with a pointed object. *Tjrita mau di∗ saka buku.* The story was excerpted from a book. **∗ kuping** ear-cleaning pick

tjukimai *cr* damn it!

tjukit 1 chopsticks. 2 bamboo sticks used (in pairs) for mixing tobacco and opium for smoking. **ñj/di∗** to use the above sticks (for)

tjukup *ng,* **tjekap** *kr* 1 enough, sufficient, adequate. *Pametuné kebon wis ∗ dienggo tuku sapi.* He made enough on his garden products to buy a cow. *Berasé ∗ kanggo rong dina.* There's enough rice for two days. *Ḍuwitku ora ∗.* I haven't got enough money. 2 well-to-do. *Pak Wangsa klebu ∗, awit taberi lan gemi.* Mr. Wongso is well off because he's hardworking and thrifty. **∗an** good enough; mediocre. *Klambiné ∗an kanggo aḍikku.* The shirt will do for my little brother. *Udjiané angkané ∗an.* His exam grades are fair. **ka∗an** well off. *Uripé saiki bisa ke∗an sebab usahané madju.* He lives well now; his business has improved. **ñj/di∗aké** to make sth suffice; to be adequate for. *Kekurangané ḍuwit blandjan di∗aké karo Ali.* Ali made up the shortage in the expense money. *Apa kowé bisa njukupaké péstané?* Can you cover the expenses of the party? **ñj/di∗-∗aké** to do one's best to make sth suffice. *Opahané ora akèh nanging di∗-∗aké kanggo urip wong loro.* His wages weren't much but he struggled to make them stretch for the two of them. **ñj/di∗i** to fulfill [requirements; a need]; to supply enough of. *Bapakné di∗i uripé karo anaké.* The father's living was provided by his son. *Bajaré saiki bisa njukupi kanggo urip karo keluargané sesasi.* His salary is now enough for his family to live on for a month. *Pangané di∗i, sanḍangan diwènèhi.* He was given plenty to eat and provided with clothing. **sa∗é** (to an) adequate (degree) for the purpose. *ujah sa∗é* the right amount of salt; salt to taste. *Diwènèhi pangan ∗, disanḍangi sa∗é.* She gave them plenty of food to eat and clothed them adequately.

tjukur *ng kr,* **paras** *ki* (to have/get) a haircut. *panggonan* * barbershop. ***an** 1 a haircut. 2 act of cutting hair *or* having one's hair cut. ***-*an** to cut each other's hair. **ñj/di*** 1 to cut smn's hair. 2 to beat smn in a game with a one-sided score. *A di* lima nul karo B.* The A soccer team was trimmed 5-0 by the B team. **ñj/di*aké** to have smn's hair cut. *Aku njukurakė anakku.* I got my son's hair cut. **ñj/di*i** to cut smn's hair. **pa·ñj*** 1 a haircut. 2 a blade (knife, razor) for cutting hair. *** baṭok** (to have) the hair cut at the sides and bottom, leaving the hair on the crown in a coconut-shell shape. *** gunḍul** (to have) the hair cut completely off; **di*-gunḍul** to be beaten badly in a game. *** kepras** [for boys] (to have) the hair cut close to the head. *** krukat** (to have) a crew cut. *** poni** [for girls] (to have) bangs cut at the forehead

tjŭkuruku:k cock-a-doodle-doo!

tjul *rpr* breaking loose. *Mak * manuké utjul.* Suddenly the bird got loose [from his grasp]. **tjal-*** to pour forth, gush out. *Nèk guneman adja tjal-*.* Don't blurt things out without thinking. ***-*an** 1 running loose. *asu *-*an* a runaway dog. 2 outspoken. *Botjah wédok kok ngomongé *-*an, ora pantes.* A girl ought not to speak out like that. **nge/di*aké** to release. *Aku tjulna.* Let me go! *Aku ora téga nge*aké ḍèkė, isih ketjiliken.* I can't let him to off alone–he's too little. **nge/di*i** to loosen [restraints]. *Bandané di*i.* He loosened the ropes that bound him.

tjula horn on the snout of a rhinoceros

tjulat ***-*** to jump, leap, bound

tjulek̄ **ke*** to get jabbed in the eye. **ñj/di*** to poke smn in the eye

tjulik 1 female nocturnal cuckoo. 2 bogey man who pries people's eyes out to gratify the troll under the bridge. **ñj/di*(i)** 1 to test, try out. *Djadjal segané di*, wis mateng apa durung.* Why don't you taste the rice to see if it's done. *Olèhku takon mau kanggo njuliki kawruhmu.* I asked to find out whether you knew it. 2 to kidnap. **pa·ñj*** act of testing *or* trying out. *** tuhu** female cuckoo (*sms 1 above*). *See also* PENTJULIK

tjulika untrustworthy, dishonest. *botjah ** a dishonest boy. *tindak ** a dishonest act. **ñj/di*ni** to steal sth; to rob smn

tjulu **tjula-*** *or* **tjala-*** *pl* to burst in noisily. *See also* TJLULU

tjum- *see also under* TJ- (*Introduction, 3.1.7*)

tjuma *rg* only, just

tjumbânâ **(resmi** *or* **sa·resmi** *ki?*) (to have) sexual intercourse

tjumbu to feel at home smw, to visit frequently. *A wis * nang omah iki.* A is almost like one of this family now. ***n̂** a domesticated animal. **ñj/di·tje*** to make smn feel at home. *njenjumbu botjah sing mentas dipèk anak* to make a newly adopted child feel like part of the family. **ñj/di*k̂aké** to tame, domesticate. *** laler** 1 to change homes frequently. 2 fickle, unpredictable. *See also* WULU-TJUMBU

tjumengklung *rpr* the sound of gamelan music heard from afar

tjumi ***-*** an octopus-like sea fish that ejects an inky substance in self-protection

tjuming *var of* TJUMA

tjumles overpowering. *legi ** cloyingly sweet

tjumlik ***an** a small bit. **ñj*** small, tiny. **sa*** a tiny amount. *Aku ndjaluk rotiné ning dikèki sak *.* I asked him for some of his bread, but he just gave me a crumb.

tjumpleng hole, cavity, burrow. *ptg* **tj·r·um-pleng** riddled with cavities/burrows

tjumplik *var of* TJUMLIK

tjumplung 1 skull (human *or* animal). 2 head of a dead person. 3 hollowed-out coconut whose meat was eaten by squirrels

tjunḍit a fishing net on a frame

tjundrik a short dagger

tjunḍuk 1 **(sangsang·an** *ki*) hair ornament. 2 in agreement, in harmony. *Panemumu * karo panemuku.* Your opinion agrees with mine. **ñj/di*aké** 1 to use as a haïr ornament. *Kembangé di*aké ing sirahé.* She wore the flowers in her hair. 2 to make harmonious [with]. *Buku mau basané di*-aké karo kaanan samengko.* The language of the book has been brought up to date. **ñj/di*i** to decorate [the hair] with. *Sirahé di*i kembang.* She wore flowers in her hair. **tj·um·unḍuk** in harmony (with). **durung * a·tjanḍak** to enter a conversation without knowing what it is about. *** laris** to lower prices to stimulate sales

tjunéja *rg* small rowboat

tjung errand boy! (*adr; shf of* KATJUNG). **nge/di*i** 1 to point at sth with the index finger. 2 to point an object at smn

tjungir boar's mouth. ***-*** *or* **tjungar-*** to raise the nose, *e.g.* in order to catch a scent; in reaction to a bad odor. **ñj*** to raise [the nose]. **njungar-ñj*** to keep sniffing. *Ḍèké njungar-njungir, sadjaké ana ambu sing ora énak.* He sniffed the air as if he had caught a whiff of something bad.

tjungil *var of* TJUKIL

tjungkir kitchen spatula for turning frying foods

tjungkub a roofed shelter erected over a grave. **ñj/di*** to build the above over [a grave]

tjungul *rpr* coming into view. *Ali slulup nganti suwé, weruh^2 wis mentjungul adoh,* **.* Ali swam under water for a long time and then surfaced a long way off. **ñj*** to put in an appearance, to show (up). *A njungul ing rapat.* A showed up at the meeting. *Domé njungul metu.* The needle stuck out. **ñj/di*aké** to cause sth to come into view. *Domé di*aké.* She pushed the needle up through the cloth. *ptg* **tj·r·ungul** *pl* coming into view. *See also* MENTJUNGUL

tjungur *cr* nose and mouth (*var of* TJONGOR)

tjunija *var of* TJUNÉJA

tjunṭang bamboo container for raw rice as purchased in the market (capacity: *ca.* 5 *kati*'s = 3+ kilograms, or *ca.* 7 lbs.)

tjunṭel *var of* TJUṬEL

tjup 1 mine! (*word by which children lay claim to sth*). 2 hush! (*parent to crying child*). **nge/di*i** 1 to claim sth by calling *tjup!* 2 to quiet a crying child. *** embil** *sms * 1 above*

tjupet inadequate, short. *Taliné *.* The rope isn't long enough. *Tjupet nalaré.* He's short on brains. *Blandjané * kanggo urip.* He doesn't make enough money to live on. *Akèh banget *é.* There's a great shortage of them. *Pambeḍilé *.* His rifle shot fell short of the target. *wong kang isih * kawruhé* a person who doesn't know much. **ka*an** short (on), running out (of). *ke*an ing nalar* short on brains. **ke*en** excessively short/inadequate. *Klambiné ke*en.* Her dress is way too small. **ñj/di*** to cut off, cut short. *Kaja^2 wis tjukup lan di* seméné ḍisik.* There seems to be enough and we'll stop with this. *kanggo njupet rerasan* in order to cut short the gossip

tjuplak a skin disease characterized by small hard blisters. **ñj/di*** 1 [*psv* **di***] to pry out [eyes]. 2 hanging loose. **njuplak puser** to cut the umbilical cord. *** anḍeng^2 jèn ora prenah panggonan·é** a relative who is unwelcome because he makes trouble

tjuplik ***an** a quote. **an saka buku mau* a selection from the foregoing book. **ñj/di*** to quote. **ñj/di*aké** to quote sth. *Aku arep njuplikaké keterangan saka Ékonomische Éncyclopaedia.* I'll take the information from the Encyclopedia of Economics. **sa*** a bit. *Aku djupukna gula Djawa sa*.* Get me a little brown sugar.

tjupu 1 a small cup for perfume *or* cosmetic cream. 2 kneecap of large domesticated animals. **ñj/di*** 1 to put/keep sth in a cosmetic cup. 2 to use a cup to staunch the flow of blood. *** manik** a cup-shaped jewelry box

tjur *rpr* flowing, outpouring. **tjar-*** *rpr* repeated *or* continuous outpouring. *Getihé tjar-* mantjur terus.* The blood kept gushing out. ***-*an** to pour out. *Sikilé tatu, getihé *-*an.* He cut his leg and it bled profusely. **nge/di*aké** to pour sth. *nge*aké wédang ing tjangkir* to pour tea into cups. **nge/di*i** to pour onto. *nge*i* to water plants

tjurah *rg* mountain pass; valley, canyon

tjurak *var of* TJUREK

tjurang *rg* to cheat at cards *or* other games

tjurat **ñj/di*i** to cause *or* allow sth to spring *or* bound. *Olèhmu njirami kembang sing ngati-ati, adja njurati klambiku.* Be careful watering the flowers–don't let it splash on my clothes. *See also* PENTJURAT

tjurek̄ 1 ear wax; ear discharge. 2 *cr* ear. ***en** to have an ear discharge. **ñj/di*i** to clean wax from [the ears]

tjureng **ñj*** to scowl. **ñj/di*i** to scowl at. *See also* MENTJURENG, PEN̄TJERENG

tjures 1 wiped out to the last man. *Wong sadésa * katerak bandjir.* Everyone in the village was left dead by the flood. 2 to be last in a genealogical line, *i.e.* to be an unmarried only child. **ka*an turun** without descendants

tjuri jagged cliff. *Pasisiré aḍapur parang *.* The coastline consists of rugged cliffs.

tjuriga 1 *oj* dagger, kris. 2 suspicious, not trusting. **ñj/di*ni** to suspect smn. *Sapa^2 di*ni.* He's suspicious of everyone.

tjurug a waterfall. **ñj*** forming, *or* in the form of, a waterfall

tjurut a variety of rat with a strong disagreeable odor

tjus *rpr* sizzling, *esp.* as produced by pouring water on flame

tjuṭat **ñj/di∗** 1 to flick away [a small object]. 2 to fire smn. *di∗ kaja tjatjing* dismissed summarily

tjuṭel the end; to come to an end. *Wis ∗.* That's all. *Tjritané ∗.* The story ended. *ora ana ∗* or *tanpa ∗* endless, interminable. **ka∗an** to run out of. *Ḍèké ke∗an tjrita.* He came to the end of his stories. **ñj/di∗(aké)** to finish, bring to an end. *Aku kepeksa njuṭel tjritaku merga wis kewengèn.* I had to bring my story to an end–it was late.

tjuṭes *var of* TJURES

tjuti (time) off. *Aku olèh ∗ seminggu.* I was given a week off.

tjuṭik a stick for prodding. **ñj/di∗** to poke with a stick. *Slamet njuṭik bal sing ana longan ambèn.* Slamet pushed the ball out from under the bed with a pole. *Golèkké ∗ tak nggo njuṭik pelem kuwi.* Get me a stick to knock down that mango with. **∗ untu** toothpick

tjutjah **tjatjah-∗** 1 aimless, pointless. *Gunemané mung tjatjah-∗.* They chattered aimlessly. 2 crude, unmannerly speech. *See also* NJUNJAH

tjutjak *var of* TJOTJAK

tjutjal leather, hide (*kr for* LULANG)

tjutji **∗an** laundry to be washed. **ñ(j)/di∗** to wash, launder. **babu ∗** house servant in charge of laundry. **tukang ∗** launderer, dishwasher (by trade)

tjutjud 1 swordfish. 2 witty; knowledgable. **ñ(j)∗** resembling a swordfish. *Tjangkemé njutjut.* His lips stick way out. **ñ(j)/di∗i** to amuse *or* entertain with one's (witty, knowledgable) conversation. *See also* GANḌI·Ǹ

tjutjuk 1 beak, bill. 2 pouring spout. 3 house fee, *i.e.* a percentage of one's gambling winnings for the host. 4 reasonable, fair; commensurate [with]. *Pametuné ora ∗ karo gawéané.* His salary isn't enough for the work he does. 5 decorative hairpin (*var of* TUSUK). 6 change (*var of* SUSUK). **∗an** 1 food pecked at by birds. 2 having a spearlike point. 3 bamboo pole sharpened at both ends, for carrying on the shoulder with bundles attached. **∗-∗** to peck (at). **ñ(j)/di∗(i)** to peck with the beak. **njutjuk ng·iber·aké** to take home some refreshments from a party. **∗ besi** 1 a certain nocturnal bird. 2 large pliers. **∗ ḍanḍang** pickaxe. **∗ urang** a long-billed fish-eating bird

tjutjul 1 (**lukar** *ki*) to take off [clothing]; to get undressed. *Aku arep ∗ karo adus.* I'm going to undress and bathe. *∗ kemédjané* to remove one's shirt. 2 to pay out. *Ḍèké ∗ ḍéwé.* He pays his own expenses. **∗-∗** to undress completely. *See also* UTJUL

tjutjup **ñ(j)/di∗** to attach the lips to sth, *e.g.* when drinking from a bottle; when kissing. *Pariné di∗, isiné diserot kabèh.* [The locust] applies its mouth to the rice stalk and sucks out the insides.

tjutjur a fried sweet made of rice flour and brown sugar

tjuwa (*or* **ke∗n**) disappointed; regretful. **ñj/di∗ni** to disappoint smn, let smn down

tjuwawak *ptg ∗ pl* talking and/or laughing too loud. **∗an** *or* **ñj∗** *sg as above. Olèhmu ngomong ora perlu njuwawak; aku wis krungu.* You don't have to shout, I can hear you.

tjuwèk *var of* TJOWÈK

tjuwek̄ **ñj/di∗** to dig the nails into sth. *Lengenku lara kok ∗.* My arm hurts where you dug your nails into it!

tjuwèr thin, weak, watery. *Setrupé ∗.* The syrup is too watery. *Senengmu wédang ∗ apa kenṭel?* Do you like your tea weak or strong? **ñj/di∗aké** to make sth thin, weak, watery

tjuwèt (*or* **∗-∗**) *rpr* the animated chatter *or* squealing of children, birds, monkeys. *ptg ∗ or* **tj·um·uwèt** to keep making such sounds. *Botjah²[2] lagi tjemuwèté.* The children are just at the jabbering stage.

tjuwèwèk **tjuwéwak-∗** crying *or* whining with the corners of the mouth drawn downward. **ñj∗** 1 to have [the mouth] in the above position, as a grimace *or* while crying. *Tjangkemé njuwèwèk karo ndjogèd ngétjé kantjané.* He made faces and danced around making fun of his friend. 2 (*psv* **di∗**) to pull [one's lips] to either side so that the mouth spreads open as above. **ñj/di∗aké** to open [the mouth] as above. *Tjangkemé di∗aké.* He drew down the corners of his mouth.

tjuwik **∗an** a mark left where sth was peeled with a fingernail. **ñj/di∗** to pry sth up/off with the nail

tjuwil a torn-off *or* chipped-off fragment. *mori sa∗* a piece of cloth. *trasi sa∗* a bit of shrimp paste. **∗an** taken from [a larger piece *or* amount]. *∗an roti* a broken-off piece of bread. *djarit ∗an* a child's wrap-around cut down from an adult's garment. **ñj/di∗(i)** to tear off a piece (from); to tear to pieces. *njuwil² roti* to keep tearing off pieces of bread. *Kartjisé di∗i.* He tore up his ticket. *ptg* **tj·r·uwil** badly torn. *Klambiné wis ptg tjruwil.* His shirt is in tatters.

tjuwiri a certain batik design characterized by many curlicues

tjuwit *∗-∗ rpr* twittering, squeaking. **ñj∗** to twitter, squeak; [of girls] to talk. *ptg* **tj·r·uwit** *pl* twittering, squeaking. *Manuk² wis wiwit pạda tangi, swarané ptg tjruwit.* The birds had begun to wake up and twitter. **tj·um·uwit** *sms* ÑJ∗ *above. Ora ana wong sing wani tjemuwit.* No one dared let out a peep. *See also* NGETJUWIT

tjuwo a broad shallow earthenware platter

tjuwol **ñj/di∗** to grab in the fingers

tjuwowo **ñj/di∗** to close smn's mouth with thumb and forefinger to silence him. **ñj/di∗-∗** to close smn's lips as above affectionately

tjuwowol *var of* TJUWOL

tk. *see* TINGKAT

tlabung 1 sickle (*sbst kr for* ARIT). 2 *var of* TLAḌUNG

tlaḍa *var of* TULAḌA

tlaḍung striking power of a chicken. *Sing perlu dudu ulesé nanging ∗é.* The important thing is not what color [a fighting cock] is, but how hard it can strike. **ñ/di∗** to strike, attack. *Menawa ana sing njẹdaki anaké, sanalika bandjur arep di∗.* If anyone came near her chicks, the mother hen was ready to strike out at them. *Pitiké nlaḍung² adreng arep ngombé.* The chickens shoved each other trying to get a drink. **pa·ñ∗** act of striking/attacking. *Panlaḍungé kuwat banget.* The cock struck fiercely.

tlâgâ lake

tlagi *sbst? kr for* TLAGA

tlakup 1 covering leaf of a flower *or* bud. 2 (*or* **∗an**) ear flaps; a hat with ear flaps. **ka∗** covered over. *ke∗ ing emas* covered with gold. **ñ/di∗aké** 1 to close tightly, seal. 2 to use as a cover *or* coating. *Mas kena di∗aké ing wesi.* Gold can be used for plating iron. *Tangané di∗aké ing gelas.* He put his hand over the glass. **ñ/di∗(i)** to cover with [sth]

tlalang *ptg ∗ pl* [of long things] sticking out in all directions. **∗an** *sg* sticking out

tlalé elongated proboscis, *esp.* an elephant's trunk. *anteng ∗* to wriggle, squirm

tlampik chicken wing

tlampok a variety of guava (*djambu*)

tlanḍing bamboo container for catching coconut sap as it drips

tlandjur **ke∗** *rg var of* KE·BANDJUR

tlangkup *var of* TLAKUP

tlanjak *var of* NLANJAK

tlapak 1 (*or* **∗an**) palm; sole. *∗(an) tangan* palm of the hand. *∗(an) sikil* sole of the foot. *∗(an) sepatu* sole of a shoe. 2 (**tabet** *kr?*) footprint; tracks

tlapuk (*or* **∗an**) eyelid

tlasak **ñ/di∗** to make one's way across *or* through. *anelasak wana wasa* to push through a haunted forest

tlasar **ñ/di∗i** 1 to supply sth with a base *or* underlayer. *Sedurungé ditjèt di∗i ḍisik.* Apply a base coat before you paint it. 2 to move the hand under sth in search of [an object]. *Jèn di∗i ngisor peṭi kuwi kenèkeré rak ketemu.* You can find the marbles by feeling around under the box.

tlasih basil. **ñ∗** resembling the basil blossom

tlatah area, territory, domain

tlatèn (**tlatos** *opt? kr*) using patience and perseverence in a difficult *or* tedious task. *Kudu ∗, terkaḍang nganti sasèn².* You have to keep at it patiently, sometimes for months on end. *Ḍèké ∗ banget ngetik angka².* She worked painstakingly at typing (the long columns of) numbers. **∗an** characterized by patience (as above). **ñ/di∗i** to stick at sth patiently. *A lagi nlatèni olèhé nggarap dondomané.* A is working tirelessly at her sewing.

tlatjak hoof. *Kebo iku a∗ belah.* Kerbaus have split hooves. *tapel ∗ djaran* metal horseshoe

tlatos *opt? kr for* TLATÈN

tlawah a wooden barrel-shaped container for soaking fabric during batik-making

tlebok *var of* TLEBUK

tlebu:k̄ *rpr* sth heavy and ungainly falling

tlẹdèk female dancer who performs with a group of street musicians door-to-door *or* for hire. **∗an** 1 act of dancing (as above). 2 to hold a gathering with such a dancing performance. **ñ∗** to be(come) a dancer (as above)

tlẹdik *ptg ∗ pl* [of small, hard objects] dropping noisily

tlẹdor careless, inaccurate, inattentive to

detail. *Jèn * anggoné nggawé tamba bisa njilakani wong.* If you mix the medicinal ingredients carelessly you can endanger people.

tleḍuk *var of* TLEḌIK

tléḍung *var of* KLÉḌUNG

tlégram *var of* TILGRAM

tlégrap *var of* TILGRAP

tlekem a container (*usu.* metal) for cigarettes *or* tobacco

tlekim *var of* TELKIM

tlekung veil worn by women when praying

tlembuk *rg* prostitute

tlempak a short spear

tlenan cutting board for kitchen use

tlénḍo *var of* TLONḌO

tlenik *ptg ** covered with small things, *e.g.* dishes on a table; embroidered flowers on a shirt

tlening *ptg * or* **tlenang-*** scattered about, in disorder. **n̈/di*** to dump *or* heap things here and there. **k·akèh·an *** of too many kinds, too miscellaneous

tlèntjèng **tléntjang-*** full of twistings and turnings. *Garisé tléntjang-*.* The line zigzagged. **n̈*** at an angle to, not parallel with. *Garisé nlèntjèng.* The line goes off at a tangent.

tlentjeng the wick of a simple *or* makeshift oil lamp

tlepak *var of* TLAPAK

tlepèk splat! (*rpr* sth wet or soggy dropping, *or* sth dropping onto a soggy surface)

tlepok *rpr* sth soft falling and spreading, *e.g.* a cake; cow dung

tlepong *rg var of* TLÉṬONG

tléram *rpr* a flash of light. **sa*an** instantaneous, momentary. *Saka rikaté motoré mung kétok sa*an.* The car went by so fast I only saw it for an instant. *Sa*an kok kaja A.* At a brief glance, he looks like A.

tlérap *var of* TLÉRAM

tlèrèt a flash (*var of* TJLÈRÈT)

tlesep *rpr* a quick vanishing act. *Truwèluné mak * mlebu ing grumbul.* The rabbit scurried into the brush. **n̈*** to slip quickly into. **n̈/di*aké** to slip sth quickly into [sth, *esp.* for concealment]

tlèsèr **n̈*** 1 (moving) at a low altitude. *Jèn namplèk bal mesṭi nlèsèr.* He always hits the ball in a low arc. *Aku krungu swarané ula nlèsèr.* I heard a snake slithering along the ground. 2 to stray; to not keep one's attention focused

tleser ***-*** at a rapid sliding pace. *Ulané lunga tleser² tjepet banget.* The snake wriggled off like lightning. *Tleser² lingguhé pinḍah menjang mburi.* He moved along the seat to the rear.

tlesih complete, detailed. *Tjritakna sing *.* Give a full account of it. *Pulisi mau olèhé mriksa * banget.* The police made a thorough investigation. **n̈/di*aké** to investigate thoroughly. *Aku arep nlesihaké bener lan luputing kanḍané.* I'm going to find out whether what he said was right or wrong. **sa*-*é** as complete as possible

tlètèk *rpr* the ejection of feces. **n̈*** 1 to eliminate feces. 2 to force material out from a tube, *e.g.* grease from a grease gun

tleṭik 1 *rpr* sth small and compact dropping. *Widjiné ditibakaké mak *.* He dropped a seed, plink! 2 a single *or* separate drop of rain, *usu.* as the forerunner of a downpour

tlètjèk *ptg * or* **n̈*** scattered. *Uwuhé ptg *.* The trash was strewn around.

tletjer tree trunk. *** saka** descended from (in a direct genealogical line)

tleṭok *rpr* clattering (of a hard object falling; of raindrops *or* hailstones spattering)

tléṭong animal dung, manure. **n̈*** [of animals] to drop dung

tlikung **n̈/di*** to shackle, tie up

tlinḍes **ke*** to get knocked down and run over. *ke* ing sepur* run over by a train. **n̈/di*** to knock down and run over sth

tlingsing ***an** to miss connections. *mBokmenawa mung *an baé angkating lajangé kamasmu lan tekané tilgram kang saka kowé.* Probably your brother's letter crossed with your telegram to him.

tlingsut **ke*** to get lost *or* mislaid

tlisib **(ka)*an** to miss each other, *i.e.* fail to meet; to cross in the mail. **n̈*** not on target, not where it was meant to be. *Aku njurubké bolah nlisib terus.* I tried to thread the needle but I kept missing.

tlisik to preen the feathers with the beak. **n̈/di*(i)** 1 to preen [another bird's feathers]. 2 to investigate. *Perkarané di*.* He's looking into the case.

tlisir *var of* PLISIR. ***an** decorative edging for fabric. **n̈/di*** 1 to trace (the thread of). *Bareng di*-* djebul isih sanak ḍewé.* When we traced our genealogies, it turned out we were related. 2 (to turn out) differently than expected *or* hoped. *nlisir saka apa sing tak gagas* different from what I had thought. ñ/di∗(i) to trim with fancy edging

tlisut   *var of* TLINGSUT

tlitik   ∗-∗ *rpr* continuous dripping

tliweng   ke∗ to miss one's way; to take a wrong turning (physically, morally)

tlolé   *rpr* sth long and flexible extending. *Ilat geni mèlèd² mak ∗ paḍang banget.* A bright tongue of flame shot out. *ptg ∗ pl as above. Tlalèné gadjah ptg ∗.* The elephants' trunks were sticking out [from the enclosure]. ñ∗ to extend long and flexibly. *Ulané nlolé meḍun saka wit.* The snake slid down the tree. ñ/di∗kaké to extend [sth long and flexible]

tlolèr   *var of* TLOLÉ

tlolor   *var of* TLOLÉ

tlompak   *rg* a water tank for cattle to drink from

tlompé   slow, plodding, deliberate. *Bareng bodjoné lara, ora ∗ bandjur ngundang ḍokter.* When his wife fell ill, he lost no time in sending for the doctor. ke∗ṅ to let sth go too long. *Olèhé nampani ketlompèn, mula balé mrutjut.* He waited too long so he lost the ball [instead of catching it].

tlonḍo   the young of a certain cricket (*gangsir*) that has no wings yet; *fig* young and inexperienced

tlosor   *ptg ∗ pl* having sinuous configurations. *Ulané ptg ∗.* Snakes slithered along the ground. ∗an lying stretched out straight. *Botjah² paḍa ∗an nang suketan.* The young people are lying around on the grass. ∗-∗ *or* ñ∗ in sinuous motion *or* configuration. *Ula iku nlosor gleser².* Snakes swish along the ground. *Ḍèké nampèl nlosor.* He hit a twisting ground ball. ñ/di∗i to move sinuously in/on. *Kebon kéné iki kerep di∗i ula.* Snakes often crawl around in this garden.

tlp.   *see* TILPUN

tluka   *rg var of* TRUKA

tluki   hibiscus blossom

tlumpah   *var of* TRUMPAH

tlunḍag   wooden block used as a doorstep

tlunjuk   ∗an *or* tlunjak-∗ ill-mannered, not well brought up

tlusub   1 sliver or similar object embedded in the skin. 2 *rpr* quick concealment. *Nèk diojak, ∗ ngelèng.* If you chase it, it whisks into a hole. tlusab-∗ to go into and out of; to make frequent visits to. ka∗an *or* ke∗en to get entered surreptitiously. *ke∗en eri* to

get a thorn stuck in the skin. *ke∗an mungsuh* infiltrated by the enemy. ñ∗ to enter and become concealed (in). *Ḍèké nlusup ing tebonan.* She slipped in among the sugar-cane plants. *Ḍèké mlaku nlusub wengi.* He walked away into the night.

tlusuh   ñ/di∗(i) to remove the hulls from rice grains by pounding them

tlusur   ñ/di∗(i) to search, probe. *Anaké di∗ wetengé.* She felt of her son's [painful] stomach. *Jèn di∗, ḍèké iki isih sedulur karo awaké ḍéwé.* Tracing the genealogical line, we found he was kin to us. *Tlusurana kelakuanmu.* Think over what you've done.

tlutuh   sap, resin. ñ∗ to ooze sap

tn.   *see* TAUN, TUAN

tobat   1 oh my! heavens! shame! ∗, *mesakaké!* My, what a pity! *Wani teka menjang ngarepku, ∗, ∗!* How dare he come to me—what nerve! *∗ ora ilok, wong kok ḍuwuré rong mèter.* Heavens, he's two meters tall! 2 to repent, submit to, be at the mercy of. *∗ marang Pangéran* to repent before God, to submit to God's will. *Pitik iku ∗ karo wolung.* Chickens are at the mercy of hawks. mer∗ to repent. *Saiki mretobat, ora gelem main manèh.* He is mending his ways; he won't gamble any more. ñ∗aké 1 awe-inspiring. 2 (*psv* di∗aké) to cause smn to repent/reform. *nobataké maling* to rehabilitate a thief. 3 (*psv* di∗aké) to make smn a victim, render smn helpless. *Ama mau nobataké wong tani.* Farmers are helpless to cope with this crop pest. *Botjah kuwi nḍugalé nobataké wong tuwané.* The boy's delinquent behavior mortifies his parents. ñ/di∗i to swear off. *nobati ngombé* to give up drinking. pa∗ *or* pi∗ repentance. *pasa minangka pi∗* to fast as a penance. ∗ (m)entjit karo a helpless victim of, at the mercy of

tobil   1 small lizard (young of the KAḌAL). 2 oh my! heavens! ∗, ∗, *intjerané kok titis banget.* My, how accurately he shoots!

toblas   heavens! my, but...! what a shame! ∗ ∗ geḍéné nèh, djaran sing arep dibalapaké. My, look how big those race horses are! ∗, ∗, *panganan semono kok entèk.* Shame on you, gobbling up so much food.

toblos   *rg var of* TJOBLOS

tobong   *var of* TOMBONG

toḍak   a certain ocean fish

todjoh   *var of* DJODJOH

toḍong   ∗an holdup, robbery. ñ/di∗aké to

threaten [smn with] a weapon. *Aḍiku nuḍungaké pistul banju.* My little brother pointed a water pistol at me. **ñ/di*(i)** to hold smn up at gunpoint

tog ***ing** in the end, finally, at last. **nge/di*** to exert all one's strength. *Karosané lan pikirané di*.* He exerted all his brawn and brains. **nge/di*aké** 1 to leave sth alone, let it go. *Togna, adja diganggu.* Leave him alone, don't bother him. *Togna baé.* Let it go. Never mind. *Gula mau jèn dietogaké sawetara suwéné, bandjur atos.* Let the sugar sit a while and it'll harden. 2 to [do] to capacity. *Olèhé ngombé susu di*aké.* He drank all the milk he could hold. *See also* KATOG

togé *var of* TAOGÉ

togog a corner fence post. ***an** a pole *or* stake placed at the corner of a wall to protect it from being bumped into. **ñ*** to sit like a bump on a log (not contributing to the conversation, *etc.*)

toh 1 gambling stake. 2 birthmark. **nge/di*i** to bet sth, *i.e.* use sth as a gambling stake. *A nge*i Rp 5000,-* A bet 5,000 rupiahs. **di*i pati** to risk one's life. *** njawa** *or* *** pati** one's life as stake in a gamble. *Digolèki sarana tohpati.* I searched for her at the risk of my life. *Golèk sarang burung kuwi penggawéan * njawa.* Gathering swallows' nests is extremely risky work. *See also* TOTOH

toja 1 water; fluid (*kr for* BANJU). 2 urine (*kr for* UJUH). ***n** *or* **te*** to urinate (*kr for* BE·BANJU, NG·UJUH)

ṭojung ouch! (*var of* AḌUH BIJUNG)

tok- *var of* KOK-[b]

ṭok 1 only, alone, nothing but. *Kuwi * baé.* That's all. *Ora ana tanggané ja mung awaké ḍéwé *.* There were no neighbors–just us. *suling ** a solo flute. *Klambiné angus *.* Her clothes were all sooty. 2 (*prn* ṭok̄) *rpr* a knock. ***-*** *sms* * 1. *iwak sing mung eri *-* baé* a fish that was nothing but bones. **nge/di*** to knock, rap (on). *See also* KEṬOK

ṭokèr *var of* TJOKÈR

ṭok̀lèh **di*** to be teased about sth embarrassing. *Pardi di* Slamet jèn seneng Siti.* Slamet teased Pardi about liking Siti. **ñ*** to reproach smn. *Ibuné noklèh Slamet anggoné mbolos.* Slamet's mother reproved him for cutting class.

ṭoklo [of kerbau horns] downturned

toko store, shop. *** ider** peddler, itinerant salesman. *** ṅg·kambang** a shop on an ocean liner

tokoh leader, public figure. ***-** *politik* political figures. ** pahlawan nasional* a national hero

ṭokolan beansprout

ṭokor *var of* TJOKOR

ṭok̀ṭel 1 at an agreed price. ** waé regané pira?* How much will it be if we don't haggle over it? 2 *rpr* knocking

ṭok̀ṭik to waver. *Atiné kok * bimbang.* He just can't make up his mind!

ṭok̀-ṭing *Jogja slang* having a small head and a large body (*shc from* BAṬOK KLENṬING). *See also* ENṬOK-ENṬING

ṭoktjèr [of car engines] to start immediately. *Bareng mentas diganti aki, montorku bandjur *.* Now that I've replaced the battery, my car starts instantly.

ṭok̀wèl to interfere. *Kowé ora ngerti kok *.* You don't know what this is all about, how come you're butting it?

tolak **ñ/di*** to refuse. *nolak pandjaluking kantja* to turn down a friend's request. **pa·ñ*** refusal, act of turning down

ṭolang ***-*** sticking out lengthwise (*e.g.* a long bamboo stalk carried on the shoulder). **ñ*-ñ*** to extend outward

ṭolé little boy

tolèh **tolah-*** turning the head constantly. **ñ/di*** to turn the head (to one side; to the rear). *Ḍèké nolèh, weruh Ali.* He glanced over his shoulder and saw Ali. **nolah-ñ*** to keep turning the head. *Linggihé pidjer nolah-nolèh ngandani kantjané.* As he sat there he kept turning to tell things to his friend. *djaran* **pa·ñ*** a magic charm to make one rich. **t·um·olèh** to turn the head. *Wong² paḍa tumolèh marang asal dunungé tangis.* People turned toward where the crying was coming from. *manḍeg tumolèh* (*ltry*) to hesitate from fear *or* doubt. *See also* KAMITOLÈHEN

tolèr a long, thin, flexible object. ***-*** [of such an object] extending (outward)

tolih *var of* TOLÈH

ṭolo brown soybeans. ***-*** devoid of hair on the head

tolok *rg* a small basket of woven bamboo

tolol stupid, ignorant

tom indigo tree whose leaves (*nila*) are used for dye. ***-*en** to keep reliving a nightmarish experience. *Aku *-*en weruh botjah ketumbuk montor.* I keep seeing that child get hit by a car. **nge*** to plant indigo trees. **pa*an** indigo plantation

tomat tomato. *** ranti** a certain small round tomato

tombé (*or* **ke***) *rg* dandruff

tomblok a tightly woven bamboo basket, *esp.* for carrying sand

tombok to add an additional amount to complete the price. *Sapimu tak idjoli kebo-ku, nanging kowé * limang gélo.* I'll trade you my kerbau for your cow plus five rupiahs. *Aku diwènèhi ḍuwit Rp 50, djebulané regané Rp. 75, dadi aku kepeksa * Rp. 25 ḍisik.* She had given me 50 rupiahs, but it turned out to cost 75 rupiahs, so I had to give 25 more. ***an** 1 a payment to make up the full price. 2 supplementary earnings. **ñ/di*i** to put up [an additional amount]. *See also* KEPLOK

tombong 1 a large woven-bamboo basket. 2 a kiln for processing earthenware, bricks, lime

tomis a rice-accompanying dish of chili, onions, and soy sauce. **ñ/di*** to make [ingredients] into the above dish. *Énaké di*.* It's delicious prepared as *tomis.*

tompo a small woven-bamboo basket

tomprang a homing-pigeon competition, on which wagers are sometimes made

ton[a] *ng,* **tingal** *kr* **ka*** to appear, seem, look (*see* KATON). **t·in·on** (**t·in·ingal·an** *kr*) *ltry* to appear, look, be seen. *Asri tiningalan.* It looked beautiful. **t·um·on** (**t·um·ingal** *kr*) to see; to be seen (*see* TUMON). **salah *** to misinterpret *or* be mistaken about [sth one has seen]. *See also* ANON, ATON, KATON, MANON, PANON, PITONTON, TONTON, TUMON

ton[b] 1 metric ton (1,000 kilograms = *ca.* 2200 lbs.). 2 unit of area (1 square meter = *ca.* 0.84 square yard. 3 monetary unit (1,000 rupiahs)

tonang a certain ocean fish

tonangan *var of* TUNANGAN

tonḍang *see* EMPRIT

tondjok ***an** food from a ceremony (*sla-met·an*) in banana-leaf wrappings sent around to neighbors or others who did not attend the proceedings. **ñ/di*(i)** to send ceremonial food as above

tondjol **ñ/di*(aké)** 1 to push sth from underneath *or* behind. 2 to show sth off. *Ali senengané nondjol²ké kepinteranė.* Ali is always showing off how smart he is.

tong barrel, keg. ***-*an** in barrels; by the barrel. *lenga *-*an* barrelfuls of oil; oil by the barrel

ṭong *rpr* knocking sounds, as produced by a peddler's noisemaker (*kloṇṭong*), or by the village alarm signal (*kenṭong*) sounding in groups of three beats to warn of fire, flood, or other danger. ***-*an** *rg var of* KEN-ṬONG·AN

tongkèng a variety of garden ivy

tongki duckling (young of the BRATI)

tongkol a certain freshwater fish of the tuna family

ṭongkrong *inf var of* Ṁ·PEṬONGKRONG

ṭonglang *var of* ṬOLANG

ṭongol ***-*** *or* **ñ*** to appear, come into view. *Saka ngendi kowé, kok lagi nongol baé!* Where've you been, just showing up now? **ñ/di*aké** to show [the face, head]. *Ali nongolaké sirahé.* Ali stuck out his head. *ptg* **ṭ·r·ongol** *pl* coming into view. *See also* PENṬONGOL

tongsèng a rice-accompanying dish prepared with sautéed foods, *usu.* including lamb

ṭong-ṭing exactly right, on the nose. *Ṭong-ṭing, ṭong-ṭing!* That's it! You've hit it! (*e.g.* That's the word I was trying to think of).

ṭongṭong-sot a certain type of ghost

tonil stage play in the Occidental style. *radio ** a radio play

tonjo(k) **ñ/di*** to hit, punch

tonto **ke*** to keep reliving a bad experience. *Mau bengi aku ke* wong sing ketundjang montor.* Last night I couldn't stop thinking about that man who got hit by a car.

tonton *ng,* **tingal** *kr* ***an** (**[te]tingal·an** *kr*) a show, exhibition. **an keṭoprak* a folk-drama performance. **an bal-balan* a soccer exhibition. **an rebutan mènèk katju* a prize contest in which boys climb greased poles. *padjeg *an* entertainment tax. ***en** to keep seeing in the mind's eye. **ñ/di*** (**ñ/dipun·tingal·i** *kr*) to watch, observe. *nonton wajang/bal²an* to watch a shadow play *or* a soccer game. (*wong*) *sing nonton* spectators, audience. **ñ/di*** to show, exhibit, display. *Keṭèké di*aké.* They put on a monkey show. **ñ/di*i** to view one's prospective bride during a visit at her home (in arranged marriages). **pa·ñ*an** place for spectators. *See also* KAMITONTONEN, PITONTON, TON[a]

ṭonṭong *see* BANGO

topan (*or* **pa***) typhoon, cyclone

topèng a face mask; *fig* a camouflage. * *gas* gas mask. *wajang* * classical dance-drama performed by masked dancers. *Olèhé semanak marang A mung kanggo * waé.* His friendly attitude toward A is only put on. ***an** 1 to put on *or* wear a mask. 2 leather blinkers worn by a horse. **ñ*** 1 to perform a classical masked dance. 2 to look at oneself front and back simultaneously, using two mirrors

topi Occidental-style hat *or* cap. * *prop* safari hat, cork helmet. *bukak* * hatless. ***ǹ** to put on *or* wear a hat/cap

toplès *var of* SETOPLÈS

topong 1 *wj* crown ornament worn by certain puppets. 2 *rg* a certain style fez

tor a children's game. **nge/di*** to cut down [trees]; to prune *or* cut branches from [trees]

ṭor 1 *rpr* a loud sharp report, *e.g.* a gunshot. 2 *rpr* water trickling from a faucet in a large stream. *See also* OṬOR

torap *rg* **ñ/di*** to inundate [a rice paddy]

torog a subsidy. **ñ/di*i** to subsidize

torong funnel

toros a sugar container shaped like a bamboo cooking pot (*bumbung·an*)

torpéḍo torpedo. **ñ/di*** to torpedo [a target]

tosan 1 iron (*kr for* WESI). 2 bone (*ki? rg kr? for* BALUNG)

tosé *ng,* **tosipun** *kr* 1 *Jogja slang* they say..., I hear... 2 *emphatic particle: var of* DJÉ 1

ṭot *rpr* a trumpet blast. ***-*** repeated trumpetings

totog **ke*** to get knocked accidentally. **ñ*** to extend oneself to the utmost. *Pikolèhé wis notog temen.* It has taken his best efforts to achieve his accomplishments. **ñ/di*(-*)aké** to knock against, collide with

totoh ***an** 1 act of betting. *Apa arep ana *an?* Will there be gambling? 2 gambling stake. **ané apa?* What are the stakes? *Sing dienggo *an rokok.* They were betting cigarettes. **ñ/di*i** to bet sth, use sth as a gambling stake. *See also* TOH

totok pure-blooded. *Landa* * a full-blooded Dutchman

ṭoṭok 1 the back of the hand; the top of the foot. 2 hard outer shell. **ing penju atos banget.* Tortoise shell is very hard. ***-*** to knock on, rap (repeatedly). **-* ing médja* to keep rapping the table with the knuckles. **ke*** to get knocked by accident. **ñ/di*** to knock, hit. *Sirahku di* kangmasku.* My brother gave me a rap on the head. *noṭok lawang* to knock on the door

totol **ñ*** 1 eager, fervent. *Rasaning atiku notol banget kangené, kepéngin ketemu.* I could hardly wait, I wanted to see her so badly. 2 (*psv* **di***) to push *or* work sth into *or* out of. *Tutupé di* mlebu botol.* He pushed the cork down into the bottle.

ṭoṭol ***an** chicken feed. **ñ/di*(i)** to peck (at); *fig* to peck away at, embezzle

ṭowèl chipped at the edge

towok a certain type of spear

trabas **ñ/di*** 1 to take a short cut. *Jèn mangkat sekolah aku nrabas metu dalan tjilik.* I take a short cut to school by way of a side road. 2 to cut a path through sth. *Pradjurit mungsuh nganti bisa nrabas kuṭa A.* The enemy managed to sweep through the city of A.

traḍisi tradition. *Wis dadi *.* It has become traditional.

tradjang 1 behavior, actions. **mu gawé samaring wong-tuwa.* The things you do make your parents uneasy. 2 attack, charge. ***an** place of intersection; act of intersecting. **ané nganakaké podjok lantjip.* The intersection forms a sharp angle. ***-*an** to intersect. *Dalan² olèhé *-*an paḍa nganakaké podjok djedjeg.* The streets intersect at right angles. **ka*** 1 to get hit by [a damaging force]. *ka* ing lara* afflicted with a disease. *Ke* sepéḍa-motor.* He was struck by a motor bike. 2 to be cut through, penetrated. *Tibané udan ke* iberé manuk.* The bird in flight cut through the falling rain. *Pasar mau tengahé bener ke* ing tapel wates kuṭa.* The city line runs right through the middle of the marketplace. **ñ/di*** 1 to attack, strike. *nradjang mungsuhé* to attack the enemy. *Sabarang kang di* mesṭi larud.* Everything struck [by floods] gets swept away. *Montoré nradjang wit asem.* The car ran into a tamarind tree. 2 to cut across *or* through. *Lakuné nradjang ratan geḍé.* Their route cut across the highway. *Lakuné nradjang wong².* He broke through the crowd. *Soroté rembulan nradjang peḍut tipis.* The moonlight penetrated the thin mist. **nradjang grumbul ana tjèlèng·é** to embark deliberately on a dangerous course. 3 to violate, transgress. *nradjang gawar* to trespass; to sin. **pa·ñ*** violation, transgression

tradju balance-type scale. **ñ/di*** to weigh

sth in a balance scale. **nradju-mas** [of shoulders] firm, square, well set up

tragis sad, tragic

trah lineage, descent. *∗ing luhur/uḍèt* of high-class/low-class descent. *∗ing kusuma rembesing madu* of royal descent. *Putrané ∗ saka Radja X.* Her son is descended from King X. **∗-t·um·(e)rah** from generation to generation; hereditary. *Trah-tumerah manggon ing désa.* They live in the village generation after generation. **ñ(e)/di∗aké** to beget

trâjâ *see* DJAGAD

trajak *var of* TRANJAK

traktir **∗-∗an** to buy treats for each other. **ñ/di∗(i)** to treat, buy a treat for

traktor tractor. **ñ/di∗** to do [farm work] with a tractor

trakum trachoma

ṭral bang! boom!

trambal *pl form of* TAMBAL

trambul **ñ/di∗** to join in [an activity]. *nrambul prang* to join the battle. *njelani nrambul* to interrupt a conversation

trampil quick, deft. *∗ olèhé nḍalang* adroit in manipulating the puppets

tranformator electrical transformer

trang *var of* TERANG. **∗-∗** *rpr* water dropping onto metal forcibly

tranjak **∗an** *sms* Ñ∗ *below.* **∗-∗** boorish, ill-mannered. *Ali ∗-∗ mlebu ing omahku.* Ali came barging into my house. **ñ∗** to act with boorish *or* crude manners. *Diapiki kok malah nranjak.* I was polite to him but he responded insolently. *Hus, nranjak.* That's no way to act.

transisi transition. *mangsa ∗* a transition period

transmigran a relocated resident, *esp.* one who has moved from the island of Java to some other Indonesian island

transmigrasi relocation of families, *esp.* away from the island of Java. **ñ/di∗kaké** to relocate families. *Ana djawatan sing gawéané nransmigrasèkké wong*[2]. There's a government agency whose function is to relocate the population.

trantan **∗an** [of babies] to toddle, take the first steps

trantjag *ptg ∗ pl* ascending rapidly. *Botjah*[2] *paḍa ptg ∗ munggah ing gunung mau.* The boys swarmed up the mountain. **ñ/di∗** to ascend rapidly. *Dalané nratjag.* The road rises steeply.

trantjam raw vegetable salad with hot coconut dressing. *∗ ketimun* the above dish made with cucumbers

traos shrimp *or* fish paste (*kr for* TRASI)

trap arrangement, attitude, action. *∗ sirap* nicely arranged. *∗ kaja ngono kuwi ora kena ditiru.* You shouldn't imitate people who act like that. **∗-∗an** 1 steps, stairs. 2 arrangement, application, way in which things are laid out (put in place, made available, etc.). *Saiki ∗-∗ané téori perlu diterangaké.* The applications of the theory should be made clear now. **a∗** *ltry var of* NGE∗ *below.* **ka∗** provided, furnished. *busana kang ka∗ ing awaké* clothing that had been provided for her. **nge∗** to arrange, put in place. *Tjagak gandérané dietrap ing ngarep omah.* The flagpole was set up in front of the house. **nge/di∗aké** to apply sth [to], put sth [in, on]. *nge∗aké téori* to apply a theory. *nge∗aké tutup kalèng* to put a lid on a can. *Ḍenḍa iki dietrapaké marang sapa waé sing gawé kotor.* This fine will be levied on anyone who litters. **nge/di∗i** to put onto/into. *Untané jèn wis di∗i momotan, bandjur ngadeg alon*[2]. When the camel's load had been placed on his back, he stood up slowly. *nge∗i paukuman* to inflict a punishment on smn. **pa·nge∗** arrangement, layout, application. *Jèn pangetrapé listrik kurang bener, bisa ndjalari kobongan.* If the electricity is not properly installed, it can cause fires. *Pangetrapé watu*[2] *tanpa adon*[2]*an semèn.* The stones were laid without cement. **t·um·rap** regarding, with respect to; placed, arranged. *See also* PATRAP, TUMRAP

trapsila well-mannered; good manners

trasèk *rg var of* TRASI

trasi *ng,* **traos** *kr* a seasoning paste made from ground shrimp *or* fish, used as an ingredient for peppery sauce (*sambel*)

tratab *rpr* a start, shock. *Lawang dibukak bjak, ∗!* The door burst open and startled me. *Mak ∗ atiku.* What a shock it gave me! **∗an** *or* **ñ∗** startled. *Aku jèn mlaku nèng petengan sok nratab.* I'm jumpy when I walk in the dark.

tratag a temporary roof affixed to a house to provide additional space for a special event, *e.g.* a wedding ceremony. **ñ/di∗** to build the above. **∗ rambat** roof sections joined together to form the above extension

ṭraṭak *ptg ∗ pl* making light, hollow tapping sounds. *Swaraning gèntèr*[2] *digèrèd ptg ∗.*

The bamboo poles went *tack-tack-tack* as they were dragged along. **n̈*** to make a light tapping sound

tratas **n̈/di*** to pierce, penetrate. *Soroting rembulan nratas méga.* The moonlight broke through the clouds.

traté red lotus

tratjag *var of* TRANTJAG

tratjak *var of* TLATJAK, TRANJAK

tratjuk tongue of a plow, *i.e.* the part hitched to the ox yoke

trawang ***an** transparent material. *kawat *an* wire netting; chicken wire. **n̈*** transparent

trawèh to participate in evening communal prayers during the Moslem fasting month

tre- *see also under* TER- (*Introduction, 2.9.6*)

trèk (*or *-**) *rpr* crackling, as of dry leaves burning

trek̄ truck

trékah idea, scheme. *Si Matjan kapusan *é Kantjil.* The tiger was fooled by Mouse-Deer's trick. **n̈/di*** to think up an idea (for)

trèkbom land mine

trèm tram, street railway

trembajak seagull

trembajun *inf var of* PAMBAJUN

trèmbèl *pl form of* TÈMBÈL

trèmbèlané *ng* damn it! the hell with it!

trembesi a certain variety of large rain tree

trémos *var of* TÈRMOS

trèmplèk *pl form of* TÈMPLÈK

trèn 1 *rg* space on river banks used for raising crops. 2 trend. **é rega² beras mudun.* There's a downward trend in the price of rice.

trendjang *var of* TRADJANG

trendjel a wedge inserted into a loose connection to tighten the fitting. **ka*an** to get crowded out *or* crowded ahead of in a waiting line. **n̈*** **1** to crowd one's way into a line of waiting people; to go straight to the head of a line without waiting one's turn. 2 (*psv* **di***) to tighten a fitting with a wedge

trendjuh **ke*** to be come across *or* met up with. **n̈/di*i** to come across, stumble on, meet up with

ṭrèngèl *pl form of* ṬÈNGÈL

trenggiling anteater. **n̈*** resembling an anteater. *Nrenggiling api mati.* He played dead like an anteater; *fig* he pretended not to be listening.

trengginas quick(-moving, -acting)

trenggulang *rg var of* TANGGULANG

trengguli a variety of tree

trenggulun a tree that yields edible fruits

ṭrenguk *pl form of* ṬENGUK

trenjuh affected, moved to sympathy. **n̈/di*aké** to move, affect. *nrenjuhaké ati* to move, arouse sympathy

trentjem *ptg ** having prickly skin sensations. *Bareng guḍigé dikumbah rasané ptg *.* It felt prickly to have his scabies sores bathed.

trèntjèng no longer rainy, having cleared up. *mangsa ** time when there are no rains. ***an** a clear spell

trep just exactly, a perfect fit. *Wadja gèpèng iki * bisa mlebu ing bolongan mau.* This piece of metal fits into that hole exactly. **nge/di*i** **1** to fit sth onto [an object that is just the right size]. 2 to build sth on [a plot of land]. **sa*** just right. *Tutupé sa* karo waḍah mau.* The lid fits the container exactly.

trèpès flat, unrounded (*esp.* of buttocks, breasts)

tresna to love, to feel love. ** marang aḍiné* to love one's younger sibling. *Sing duwé * banget marang asuné.* The dog's owner loves him very much. ** sak paḍaning urip* to love all human beings. ** marang kemardikan* to love freedom. **ka*n** love. *ka*né marang bodjoné* her love for her husband. **n̈/di*ni** to love. *Slamet olèhé nresnani Siti temenanan.* Slamet loves Siti with all his heart. *Wit arèn kuwi senadjan ala tanpa rupa, ija meksa di*ni.* The areca palm is ugly and shapeless, but it is much loved. *** asih** *or* **asih *** love; to love

treteg *var of* KRETEG

ṭreṭeg *ptg * pl* trembling, shaking. **n̈*** **1** *sg* to shake, tremble. 2 altogether (*in the following phrases*): *buḍeg nreṭeg* stone deaf. *pitjak nreṭeg* totally blind

ṭrèṭèk ***an** to make door-to-door inquiries. **n̈/di*** to inquire about

tretep *var of* KRETEP

trètès **n̈/di*** to bedeck with precious gems

trètjès *var of* TJRÈTJÈS

tri *oj* three (*also used as a compounding element: see main entries below*). **ka*** third. *** baga** one-third

tribâwânâ, tribuwânâ three worlds

trig ***-*an** in constant motion, lacking the desirable serene repose

trigu wheat. *glepung* * wheat flour
triguna combination of three characteristics *or* character traits, namely sacredness (*satwa*), lust (*radjah*), and evil (*tamah*)
trijânggâ monkey
trikâjâ *oj* threefold strength, *viz.* strength of body, of speech, and of thought
triko a certain kind of striped fabric
trikona *oj* triangle
triloka *oj* threefold world
trilotjânâ *oj* [of mythological characters] three-eyed
trim *var of* TRÈM. * **drimolen** ferris wheel. * **ombak banju** merry-go-round
trima *ng,* **trimah** *kr* to accept without protest, to resign oneself to. *Wesi iku larang banget, mulané aku ming * kaju baé.* Iron is too expensive, so I'll make do with wood. *Sarèhné kursiné kurang, paḍa * ngadeg ing tritisan.* Since there weren't enough chairs, they made the best of it and stood on the porch. *Tono mèlu bapaké, aḍiné * kari njang omah waé.* Tono went with his father; the younger brother had to be content with staying at home. *Senadjan ora genah, ja wis *.* It wasn't very nice, but let it pass. *Jèn mlaku semana adohé aku * ora.* If I'd have to walk that far, I just won't go. *Kebo jèn wis mangan ḍèké * nggajemi.* After the kerbau has eaten, he's content just to chew his cud. ***n** a woman who is given (*esp.* by a monarch) in marriage as a reward. **ka*** 1 to get accepted/received. *Jèn rantjangan kabinèt mau ora ke* déning DPR mbandjur keprijé?* What happens if the parliament doesn't accept the cabinet proposals? 2 to receive with appreciation. *Sarèhning lagi ora duwé ḍuwit, mula A ke* banget diwènèhi ḍuwit.* Since A had no funds at all, he appreciated having the money given to him. **ñ/di*** to accept, to resign oneself to. *Bégal bandjur bali, nrima olèh djarané sudagar.* The bandit came back and [for want of anything else to steal] took the merchant's horse. *Apa mung nrima ngombé waé, ora mangan barang?* Was he content just to drink–didn't he eat anything? *Jèn kalah ja nrima.* If I lose, I lose. **ñ/di*kaké** to resign oneself to sth with an effort. *Aku ora nrimakaké jèn A diala-ala mangkana.* I will not put up with A being mistreated that way. *Bareng wong paḍa krungu jèn sing arep didadèkaké Djuru si A, ana sing ora nrimakaké.* When the people heard that A was to be made Clerk, some of them put up a protest. **ñ*n** inclined by nature *or* disposition to accept what life offers; easy to please. *Ḍèké botjah nriman, mangan * saanané.* He's not fussy–he'll eat whatever there is. **ñ/di*ni** to award a woman in marriage to [a subject, courtier, *etc.*]. **pa·ñ*** (**pa·ñ·suwun** *ki*) gratitude, (a word of) thanks. *Banget panarima(ku).* Thank you very much. *Banget panarimané.* He was very grateful. *awèh panarima* to express gratitude. *Sakwisé ngaturaké panrima, tamuné kondur.* The guests thanked [their host] and went home. * **kasih** thank you; **ñ*-kasih** to say thank you. *Wongé apa kok * kasih?* Did you thank the man?
trimah *kr for* TRIMA
trimurti three in one
trinétra *oj* three-eyed
trini *oj* three
ṭrinṭing *ptg* * *rpr* the visual effect of tight-fitting clothing on slim girls. *Akèh tjah aju² sanḍangané ptg *.* There were many beauties in tight dresses. **ñ*** close-fitting, clinging to the figure
tripang a variety of edible sea cucumber (shellfish)
triprakârâ tripartite
trisig *var of* SRISIG
trisna *var of* TRESNA
trisula trident, three-pronged javelin
triswârâ three sounds; three vowels
tritik 1 (*or* ***an**) a certain pattern printed on fabric, *esp.* for headdresses. 2 *var of* TRITIS
ṭriṭik ***an** act of handling *or* fingering things. **ñ*** 1 to touch, handle. *botjah nriṭik* a child who fingers everything he ought not to touch. 2 close together, touching
ṭriṭil **ñ*** to touch, handle, finger
tritis (*or* ***an**) porch
triwarna tricolor(ed)
triwikrâmâ *wj* to display supernatural powers when angered, *esp.* by transforming oneself into a huge ogre
triwulan quarter, *i.e.* three-month period
trobos ***an** a way through *or* across. *Ajo metu dalan *an.* Let's take a shortcut. **ñ/di*** to cut through. *Soroté srengéngé nrobos saka sela²né genḍèng.* The sun's rays filtered through the slits in the roofing tiles.
trombol **ñ/di*(i)** to interrupt [a group activity] raucously and boisterously

tromel *var of* TROMOL
tromol metal box. *∗pos* mailbox
trompèt trumpet. ∗ **lan tambur** trumpet(s) and drum(s); *fig* fanfare
trondjol *var of* TROMBOL
tronḍol plucked, bare of feathers
tronḍolo *cr mildly profane excl of surprise.* ∗ *ki! djebulané bodjoku ḍéwé.* I'll be damned! it turns out it's my own wife.
ṭrongol *var of* ṬONGOL
trontong ∗-∗ to grow light in the east [of the pre-dawn sky]; *fig* to begin to see the light. *Ali ∗-∗ wiwit mangreti apa sebabé.* The reason for it began to dawn on Ali.
ṭronṭong *ptg* ∗ full of holes. *Geḍègé ptg ∗.* The bamboo wall has holes in it. **ñ∗** 1 having holes in it. 2 (*psv* **di∗**) to make a hole *or* opening (in a bamboo wall)
tropong 1 weaving shuttle. 2 binoculars
trotjoh [of ceilings, roofs] to leak. *Pijané ∗.* The roof leaks. **ka∗an** to get leaked on. **ñ/di∗i** to leak onto
trotjos *var of* TJROTJOS
trotoar sidewalk
trotoir *var sp of* TROTOAR
ṭroṭok *rpr* sharp tapping. *Ngunèkaké kenṭongé, ṭok ṭok ∗.* He sounded his clapper, rat-a-tat-tat. **∗an** woodpecker
trowong **∗an** tunnel. **ñ/di∗** to tunnel through sth
trubuk 1 a shad-like sea fish. 2 salted fried roe of this fish, served as a rice-accompanying dish
trubus to sprout; to put out new shoots *or* buds. **∗an** a sprout; a new shoot/bud. **ñ∗** having sprouted *or* budded, having put out a shoot
truk 1 *var of* TURUK. 2 (*prn* **truk̄**) *var of* TREK. ∗ **bijang·ané** (*cr*) *abusive excl*
truka **∗n** a newly settled place. **te∗** to settle an area by opening up new land
trulèk a variety of plover
trumpah 1 open thong sandal. 2 cross pieces at the top and bottom of a wooden *or* bamboo wall section which holds the wall to the house. 3 threshold, doorstep. 4 sole (fish)
truna *oj* 1 young. 2 a young person
truni *var of* TRUNA
trunjuk ∗-∗ to enter in an unmannerly way, *e.g.* by barging in without first announcing one's presence
truntum a certain batik design
trus *var of* TERUS
trutjuk 1 a group of comparably sized objects. 2 a variety of mushroom; an object shaped like this mushroom. **ñ∗** *or* **t·um·ru-tjuk** [objects] of approximately the same size; [offspring] born in close succession. *Geḍangé tumrutjuk.* The bananas are all the same size. *Anaké lima nrutjuk.* His five children were born one right after the other.
trutjukan a thrush-like song bird
trutjut **ke∗** to let sth slip (in, out). *Olèhku tjaturan ke∗.* I said the wrong thing! **ñ/di∗aké** to slip sth (into, out of). *Katèsé di∗aké mlebu krandjang.* He let the papaya slip into the basket.
ṭruṭuk [of public conveyances] to make frequent stops. *Lift iku ana sing ∗, jakuwi sing lèrèn saben lotèng.* Some of the elevators were locals—that is, they stopped at every floor. *sepur ∗* a local (slow) train. **ñ∗** to tremble all over
trutul *ptg ∗ or ∗-∗* spotted, speckled. *Katjang tjindé ptg ∗ wungu.* *Tjindé* beans are flecked with purple.
ṭruṭus *ptg ∗ pl* swishing past. **∗an** *sg as above. Ḍèké mbeling ∗an mrana² tansah ngrerusak.* He rushes around heedlessly like a bull in a china shop.
truwèlu rabbit
t.s.t. *see* TAHU
tu^a^ seven (*shf of* PITU). *dji ro lu pat ma nem ∗* 1, 2, 3, 4, 5, 6, 7
tu^b^ *ng,* **dal** *kr* **nge/di∗k̂aké** to put *or* bring out, to allow to emerge. *Pak Tani ngetokaké si Kantjil saka kurungan.* The farmer let Mouse-Deer out of the cage. *ngetokaké ḍuwit* to pay out money. *ngetokaké panemu* to express an opinion. *ngetokaké buku* to publish a book. *ḍuwit sing ditokaké déning Pemerintah* money issued by the Government. *Ḍèké ditokaké.* He was fired. *Gunung geniné ngetokaké lahar.* The volcano spewed out lava. *Tokna pikiranmu!* Use your brains! **nge/di∗n̂i** to bring *or* put out. *Sawah iku ngetoni pari ṭok.* Paddies produce only rice. *See also* WETU
tuan (*abbr*: **tn.**) *respectful title applied to non-Javanese men.* ∗ **tanah** landlord
tuba a certain plant that is poisonous to fish. **ñ/di∗** to fish using this plant as bait
tubras **ñ/di∗** to knock against sth forcibly. *Malingé diojak, olèhé mlaju nubras².* The thief, pursued, banged into things as he fled.
tubruk **ñ/di∗** 1 to pounce (on). *Manuké*

di∗ kutjing. A cat pounced on the bird. 2 to bump into, knock against. *lagi mlaku nubruk wong* to bump into people as one walks. **kopi ∗** coffee made by pouring hot water over coffee grounds

tuding 1 that which points (*e.g.* a clock hand); index finger. 2 puppet's arm stick. ∗-∗ *or* **tudang-∗** to keep pointing (at). *Tangané tudang-∗ karo bengak-bengok.* He kept pointing and shouting. **ñ/di∗(i)** 1 to point at/out. *Pistulé nuding marang baṭukku.* His pistol pointed at my forehead. *Aku arep nudingi kembang mawar.* I'll point out a rose. 2 to appoint. *Aku di∗ dadi sekretaris fakultas.* I was appointed faculty secretary. **pa·ñ∗** act *or* way of pointing. *dridji panuding* forefinger, index finger

tudjes **ke∗** to get pricked. **ñ/di∗** to stick/prick with a sharp point

tudju intention, purpose. *∗ku arep nang Djakarta nanging keblasuk nang Krawang.* I meant to go to Djakarta, but I accidentally ended up in Krawang. *Bedja duwé ∗ njilakaké kantjané.* Bedja wants to bring bad luck to his friend. **∗an** *or* **∗n̂** 1 destination, target. *Omahku dadi tudjon botjah²*. The kids always come to my house. 2 by good luck. **∗né** by good luck. *∗né ubeng²-an ana.* Luckily there was a merry-go-round there. **ka∗** 1 directed (toward), intended (for). *Dongaku ka∗ marang sedulur²ku kabèh.* My prayers go to all my relatives. 2 (*or* **ka∗né**) fortunately. **ñ∗** 1 in the act of [do]ing. *Nudju apa kowé saiki?–Aku nudju mangan.* What are you doing?–Eating. 2 to happen to [do, be doing]; once upon a time. *Anudju ing sawidjining dina...* One day (it happened that)... 3 (*psv* **di∗**) to head for, aim toward. *Sing di∗ bis mau Sala.* That bus goes to Solo. *Sing di∗ ḍukun guna² kuwi A nanging sing lara B.* The witch doctor's spell was intended for A, but it was B who fell ill. **nudju ari** *oj* on the (very) day. **nudja-ñ∗** (to happen) now and then. *nudja-nudju jèn ketemu aku sakantja* on the occasions when he happens to see my friends and me. **ñ/di∗k̂aké** to direct sth to(ward). *nudjokaké lajang marang Budi* to address a letter to Budi. **se∗** in accord, in agreement (*see* SETUDJU). **t·um·udju** intended (for), directed (to). *Lajang iki tumudju marang anakku.* This letter is going to my son. *See also* PANUDJU, PINUDJU, SETUDJU

tuduh *ng*, **tedah** *kr* ∗-∗ 1 to point (to). *Adja ∗-∗.* Don't point. 2 to point out, advise. **ñ/di∗aké** to show *or* point out sth. *Ḍèwèké nuduhaké pelem mateng.* She pointed to a ripe mango. *Aku nuduhaké dalan.* I showed him which way to go. *Ana punggawa sing nuduh²aké.* An employee showed them around. **ñ/di∗i** to show *or* point out to [smn]. *Tjoba aku tuduhana.* Let me see it. *Tjoba aku kotuduhi penggawéané.* Please show me the work that's to be done. **nuduhi dalan** to show smn the way (*lit, fig*). **pa·ñ∗** 1 act *or* way of pointing (to/out). (*dridji*) *panuduh* index finger. *tembung panuduh* (*gram*) demonstrative word. 2 advice. *See also* PITUDUH

tuḍung 1 anything used for covering the head as protection against the sun. 2 *var of* TOḌONG. **ñ/di∗i** to cover the head

tug *rg* 1 to arrive at. *∗ alun² ḍèké manḍek.* When he got to the town square, he stopped. 2 when [sth happened]. *∗ aku nèng Amérika, ḍèké mati.* He died when I was in America. **nge/di∗aké** to finish, get to the end of. *Ḍèwèké lagi ngetugna mangan.* He is just finishing his meal. *See also* TUTUG

ṭug *rpr* a knocking beat on a gamelan block (*keprak*)

tugas duty, responsibility. *Désa mau diwènèhi ∗ ngopèni tjanḍi.* The village was assigned the task of caring for the temple. **ñ/di∗aké** to assign a task to. *Aku di∗ké nang Djakarta ngurus ḍuwit anggaran blandja.* I was sent to Djakarta to settle the budget. **pa∗** person assigned to a task

tugel 1 to break, snap. *Ḍel, ∗ guluné.* His neck broke. *Pringé ∗ dadi loro.* The bamboo snapped in two. 2 a broken-off piece. *Aku wènèhana se∗.* Give me a piece. 3 [*n* minus 1] and one-half. *karo ∗* $1\frac{1}{2}$. *telu ∗* $2\frac{1}{2}$. **ñ/di∗aké** to break sth accidentally. *Sapa sing nugelaké potlotku?* Who broke my pencil? **ñ/di∗(i)** 1 to break, split, cut (up, off). *nugeli pring* to cut up a bamboo stalk. *Ḍokter kepeksa nugel tangané pasièn.* The doctor had to amputate the patient's arm. 2 to cut across. *mlaju nugel dalan* to run across the road. **pa·ñ∗** an interruption. *"Dasijun," panugelku.* "Dasijun," I broke in.

tugu a stone pillar-shaped structure, *e.g.* a monument

tugur **∗-∗an** the act of staying awake all night in order to watch over sth *or* be in attendance at sth, all night long. **ñ/di*i** to to watch over *or* be in attendance at throughout the night

ṭuh *var of* AḌUH (*as excl*). **ṭah-*** clumsy, gauche. **nge*** to say "ouch!"

Tuhan God (*as term of direct address, when praying*)

tuhu 1 steadfast, loyal. 2 genuine, authentic. 2 truly, indeed, to be sure. *Buku wau * sakalangkung adji.* That book is truly valuable. 4 male nocturnal cuckoo. ***n̂(an)** credulous, gullible. **te*** *sms* * 4 *above.* **ka*n̂** 1 to materialize. *Sumbaré jèn bakal menang ketuhon.* His boast that he would win came true. 2 by good fortune. *Katuwon temen déné katjilakané ora niwasi.* He was extremely lucky not to be killed in the accident. **ñ/di*(n̂i)** to be faithful/loyal to, to honor. *Ḍawuhé dituhoni klawan betjik.* His orders were carried out to the letter. *Ora nuhoni djandjiné.* He didn't keep his promise. **sa*** genuine; having proven steadfast. *kantja se** a true friend. **sa*né** actually, in fact. *Sa*né wong kuwi kudu ḍemen tetulung.* The fact is, people ought to enjoy helping others. *See also* PITUHU

tuhu-priksa *ltry* to investigate, do research (into)

ṭuju:k ***-*** bent and bowed with age. *See also* KEṬUJUK

ṭujul a dwarf *or* devil conjured up magically to help one gather riches

tuk a spring (of water). **nge*** [of spring water] to emerge from the ground

ṭuk 1 *rpr* a stroke of the *keṭuk* gong. 2 *rpr* a knock. 3 *rpr* a perfect fit. *Bisa gaṭuk, *.* They fit together beautifully. **nge*** to make a knocking sound. *nge* lawang* to knock on the door. **nge/di*aké** to match, join, unit (*inf var of* ÑG/DI·KEṬUK·AKÉ). *Senengané ngeṭuk-eṭukaké kantja²né.* She's a born matchmaker. *Gelangé sing tugel ora bisa dieṭukké menèh.* The broken bracelet won't close any more. **nge/di*i** to agree with (*inf var of* ÑG/DI·KEṬUK·I). **ṭak-ṭik-*** *rpr* knocking, thumping. *Atiné kok ṭak-ṭik-ṭuk.* His heart was pounding. **ṭak-*** to come together, join. *Ṭak-ṭuk ning ora kenal.* We met but didn't recognize each other.

tukang 1 worker. ** kaju, * listrik, lan * lijané pirang²* carpenters, electricians, and many other workers. *sekolahan ** trade school. 2 one who operates *or* works at [equipment, materials]. ** bonang, suling, lsp.* one who plays the *bonang,* the pipe, *etc.* ** djam* watchmaker. ** (ke)mas(an)* goldsmith, jeweler. 3 one who [does]. *Lah iki sing * gawé prakara.* Ah, *here's* the trouble-maker. *Slamet sing dadi * ngéling-éling regané.* Slamet is in charge of keeping track of the prices. ** nglakoké* operator of a mechanical device. 4 sloth (animal). ***an** 1 occupation, craft. 2 section where many workers live. **ñ*** to work, labor; to do a job, work at a craft. *Adja isin nukang.* Don't be ashamed to do manual labor. **ne·ñ*** to do odd jobs. **pa*an** 1 handicraft. *sekolah pe*an* school where crafts are taught. 2 a craft; craftsmanship. *** andjun** potter, maker of earthenware. *** bènḍer** bookbinder. *** gembrèng** announcer. *** glembug** a glib talker. *** glenik** one who tries to persuade others to do sth (*usu.* bad); a gossip. *** kumiḍi** (stage) actor. *** obat** quack doctor. *** ng·omong** chatterbox. *** peṭèk** fortune teller. *** pos** mailman. *** pi(j)utang** *or* *** potang** moneylender. *** samak** saddlemaker; leather worker; bookbinder. *** semprit** umpire, referee. *** ñ·tabuh** gamelan-instrument player. *** ñ·tangis** crybaby. *** tapel** blacksmith (specializing in horseshoes). *** tjatur** chatterbox. *** tjengkal** surveyor. *** tjukur** barber; barbershop. *** ng·ukur** surveyor. *** wajuh** 1 specialist in the ceremonial cleaning of sacred royal objects. 2 one who marries more than once

tukar **ñ/di*(aké)** to exchange [one thing for another]. *Ḍuwitku di*aké dadi rupiah.* I changed my money into rupiahs. **ñ/di*i** to irritate. *A pidjer nukari B waé.* A is always getting on B's nerves. *** padu** to quarrel, fight. *** tjintjin** to exchange rings as a token of becoming engaged

tukarmaru a freshwater fish

tukel skein. *lawé se** a skein of thread

ṭuk-mis always philandering, infatuated with every pretty face (*shc from* BAṬUK KLIMIS)

tukra to settle an area by opening up new land (*cf.* TRUKA)

tuku *ng,* **tumbas** *kr,* **punḍut** *ki* **ϕ/di*** (**m̂/di·punḍut** *ki*) to buy. *sing ** customer. *Tak *né rong sèn.* I'll give you two cents for it. ***n̂** 1 bought. *Djarik iki tukon.* I bought [rather than made] this wraparound. *tukon pasar* purchases made at the marketplace. 2 bridal gift. *Tukoné arupa gelang.* His gift to his bride is a bracelet. ***-*** (**me·m̂·punḍut** *ki*) to buy various things; to buy at various times. **te*** *sms *-*. Apa kowé wis tau te* nèng kuṭa iki?* Have you ever shopped in this city? **te*ñ** bought (rather than *e.g.* home-made). **ñ/di*k̂aké** to buy for smn. *Aku tukokna bal.* Buy me a ball! **ñ/di*ñi** 1 to buy sth; to buy at [a specified price]. 2 to give a wedding gift to one's bride. *Anaké A nukoni anaké B awudjud gelang mas.* A's son gave B's daughter a gold bracelet as his wedding gift to her. **pa*(ñ)** 1 gift given to one's bride. 2 purchase price. *Sing satus iki patukon mbako.* This 100 rupiahs is for buying tobacco. **pa·ñ*** act of buying. *Saiki pangedol lan panukuning barang sing mubra-mubru ora gampang.* It's not easy to deal in luxury items nowadays. **t·in·uku** to be sold (*see also* DOL-TINUKU *under* DOL). *** arep, adol emoh** to deal with unjustly/inequitably (*see also* ADOL). *** séṇḍé** to buy with the understanding that the seller may buy it back

ṭukul 1 to begin to grow; to sprout; to develop. *Widji téla gantung mau wis *.* The papaya seeds have sprouted. *Isiné woh sawo dibuwang, bandjur *.* He threw away the *sawo*-fruit pit and it took root. *Wit kopi *é apik nang pagunungan.* Coffee grows well in mountainous areas. *Suwiwiné durung *.* The [baby bird's] wings haven't developed yet. *Pupuku gatel, mbasan tak kukur ésuké * wudun.* The morning after I scratched my itchy thigh, a boil had developed there. 2 to begin to experience [a feeling]. *Siti wiwit * atiné kepingin omah².* Siti's thoughts turned to marriage. *Ṭukul tjiptané arep dadi ratu.* He began to want to be king. *Bareng anaké wis lahir * redjekiné.* After his first child was born, his luck changed for the better. ***an** 1 growing easily without cultivation. *Wit téla gantung kuwi *an banget, widjiné disebar waé * ḍéwé.* Papaya trees will spring up if you just scatter the seeds. 2 (*or* **ṭe*an**) plants, vegetation; wild vegetation. *Puntjaké gunung mau ora ana *ané.* There is no plant life at the top of that mountain. *Kebonku kaé akèh *an pelem.* Mango trees grow wild in my garden. **ke*an** to support growth from inadvertent origins. *Pulo² mau paḍa ke*an wit krambil.* Coconut trees sprang up on the island [from floating seeds]. *Wité pelem ke*an kemlaḍéan akèh banget.* There's a lot of parasitic growth on the mango tree. **ñ*aké** to give rise to [feelings]. *Njumurupi anak²é sing wis paḍa lola nukulaké welasku.* It breaks my heart to see those orphaned children.

tukung a variety of chicken with no tail

tukup **ñ/di*** to cover sth with a quick movement

tula **ke*-*** ill-starred, besieged by difficulties. *kenja ke*-** a girl who leads a difficult life. *Olèhé ketula-tula kok ora uwis².* There was no end to his troubles.

tulad **te*an** an example to be followed. **ñ/di*** to follow an example. *nulad kaja tjara sing ditindakaké para penggeḍé* to do as the bosses do

tulaḍa (*or* ***n**) example, instance, model. **ñ*** to set an example. **nulaḍa laku utama** to perform good deeds. **ñ/di*ni** to give an example (of)

tulah-sarik curse, malediction

tulak 1 to go and return on the same day. *Bapak tindak Sala *.* Dad made a one-day trip to Solo. 2 a black chicken flecked with white. 3 to prevent magically. *** *udan*** to keep it from raining by an act of magic. ***an** an opening at the edge of a rice paddy for regulating the flow of water. **ñ*** to take preventive measures against sth. *nulak udan* to forestall rain. *nulak penjakit* to ward off illness. **pa·ñ*** act of exorcising. *Sadjèn iki minangka panulak sétan.* This offering will drive the demons away. *** balik** 1 a one-day round trip. 2 a fact which contradicts sth one dreamed. *** bilahi** a magical preventive measure. *** bleḍèg** lightning rod. *** sawan** a potion for warding off illness in a child. *** tanggul** a magical preventive measure

tulang 1 small box used as an arena for a cricket fight. 2 *rg* bone

tular ***an** infectious matter. *Lelaraku iku *an saka Ali.* I got my germs from Ali. ***-t·um·ular** to infect each other. **ke*-*** unpredictable. *Tindaké ke*-*.* You never know what he'll do next. **ka*an** 1 to get infected. *Jèn wis disuntik, ora ke*an tjatjar.* If you've been vaccinated, you can't get smallpox. *Kerep kumpulan karo wong sing seneng main, suwé² ke*an.* He was often around gamblers, and eventually he got hooked himself. 2 [of disease, fire, *etc.*] to get spread. **ñ*** to spread. *lelara sing nular* infectious disease. *Geniné nular nèng omah² lijané.* The fire spread to other houses. **ñ/di*aké** to spread, transmit.

Tikus kuwi nularaké lara pès. Mice carry plague. **ñ/di*i** to infect smn. *Wong lara mau nular²i tanggané.* The sick man spread the disease to the neighbors. **t·um·ular** to spread. *Main tjatur iku saka Indija temular menjang tanah Arab.* The game of chess spread from India to Arabia.

tulban *var of* SERBAN

tulèn original, authentic. *basa Djawa kang ** real Javanese. *Jèn démokrasi kita kuwi rak démokrasi sing *.* Ours is a genuine democracy.

tuli *ng,* **tunten** *kr* **ñ*** and then, (right) after that. *Ḍèké adus nuli dandan.* He took a bath and got dressed. **t·um·uli (t·um·unten** *kr*) *sms* Ñ*. *Lebar mangan tumuli lunga.* He left as soon as he had eaten.

ṭuling *rg* **se*** a little bit, a small amount, a few

tuliring a freshwater fish

tulis *ng,* **serat** *kr* ***an** writing, script. *sinau basa lan *an anjar* to study new languages and new writing systems. **anmu apik.* Your handwriting is beautiful. **an Arab* (*Djawa, Latin, Tjina*) Arabic (Javanese, Roman, Chinese) writing. **di*** foreordained. *Ḍèké wis di* bakal dadi wong gedé.* He is destined to be great. **ñ/di·te*** to write (in general). *Sadjaké jèn perkara nenulis rada dadi sirikanmu.* Apparently you have an aversion to writing. **ñ/di*aké** to write for smn. *A nulisaké lajang B.* A wrote a letter for B. **ñ/di*(i)** to write (down). *Tembung² iki tulisen.* Write the following words. *Apa sing tak kanḍakké ora kok *.* You didn't write down what I told you. **ñ/di*-*** *or* **ñ/di·tolas-* (ñj/dipun·serat-serat** *kr*) to keep writing, to write repeatedly. **ñ/di*i** to write on sth. *Blabagé di*i aksara.* She wrote the letters on the blackboard. **pa·ñ*** 1 act *or* way of writing. *Panulismu wandané pisah-pisahen.* Separate the words you write into syllables. 2 secretary, amanuensis. **pa*an** place for writing; desk. *kamar penulisan* study, writing room. **t·in·ulis** 1 inscribed. 2 destined. *Ḍèké tinulis dadi pemimpin.* He was destined to be a leader. **baṭik *** hand-worked batik. **djuru *** clerk; writer. **médja *** desk, writing table. **mesin *** typewriter. **ora weruh *** illiterate

tul-tis very close, almost on target (*shc from* TUTUL-TITIS). *Kari * meksa luput.* [The stone he threw] came close but it was still a miss.

tulung 1 help, assistance; to help. *ndjaluk ** to ask for help. **, *, anakku kèli.* Help! help! my child is drifting away! 2 please. *Kaṭoké ketjenḍaken, * didawakaké.* The trousers are too short; please lengthen them for me. ***-*** to call for help. *Aku krungu wong tulung².* I heard someone calling for help. ***-t·in·ulung** to help each other. *Wong mono kudu tulung-tinulung.* People should help one another. **te*** help; to help. *Wadjibé wong urip iku jèn ana, te* marang wong kang kemlaratan.* It is the duty of the Haves to help the Have-Nots. **ka*an** to be helped. *Gelis ke*an.* Help came immediately. **ñ/di*(i)** to help smn. *Aku tulungana.* Help me! *Botjah kuwi nangis sak-uwèn², kok ora ana sing nulungi.* The child has been crying for a long time but nobody attends to him! *** m̄·penṭung** to make a show of helping while actually hindering. *See also* PITULUNG

tulup blowgun. **ñ/di*(i)** to shoot pebbles *etc.* (at) with a blowgun. *Manuké di*i.* He blew pebbles at the bird. *kaja keṭèk di** dumbfounded and open-mouthed

tulus 1 genuine, sincere. *Solahé *.* He acts in a straightforward manner. *Ajuning rupamu ora * tekan batin, mung aju lahir baé.* Your beauty doesn't come from within–it's only skin deep. 2 unobstructed. *supaja *a tanduranė pari* so that the rice-planting can go forward. **ka*an** 1 sincerity, genuineness. 2 expeditious progress. **ñ/di*aké** to allow sth to go through unobstructed; to pave the way for, expedite

tum a banana-leaf wrapping. **nge/di*i** to wrap [food one is preparing for steaming] in a banana leaf

tum-, ṭum- *see also under* T, Ṭ- (*Introduction, 3.1.7*)

tuma *ng kr,* **itik** *or* **kiṭik** *ki* hair louse

tumâmâ to get struck. **ñ/di*kaké** to strike, hit. *See also* TAMA

tumambang *oj* [of sun] to rise

tuman to acquire a taste. *A bandjur *, bareng wis ngrasakaké legining woh mau.* After A tasted how sweet the fruit was, he kept wanting more. **di·te*** to be induced to like sth. **ñ*i** causing smn to acquire a taste. *Legining woh mau numani.* The sweet taste of that fruit grows on you.

tumang a supporting piece at the edge of a cooking pit. *See also* LAMBÉ

tumbak *ng,* **waos** *kr* 1 spear, lance. 2 land

measure: *ca.* $4\frac{1}{8}$ yards = 3.77 meters. ***an** 1 toy spear. 2 to spear each other. ***-*an** forbidden, taboo [of marriage between two males and their respective younger sisters]. **ñ/di*(i)** to stab smn with a spear. **pa·ñ*** 1 act of throwing a spear. 2 soldier who carries a spear. *** bérang** spear with a painted handle. *** bradja** five-headed spear. *** lilit(u)wi** spear with barber-pole stripes painted on the handle. *** tambuh** pretending not to see *or* understand. *** tjutjuk·an** tattletale

tumbal 1 a sacrificial animal symbolically representing human victims (of flood, *etc.*) killed to forestall such a life-destroying calamity. 2 ritual ceremony held to nullify the bad portent (indicated numerologically) of a forthcoming marriage. **ñ/di*i** 1 to sacrifice [a victim]. 2 to hold the above (2) ceremony for

tumbar (*or* **ke***) coriander. *** djinten** coriander

tumbas to buy (*kr for* TUKU)

tumbeng a small piece of wood inserted into the hole of a gamelan instrument to narrow it and regulate the tone. **ñ/di*** to insert such a piece into [an instrument]

tumbu a covered woven-bamboo basket. *kaja* *** olèh tutup** having a congenial spouse

tumbuk 1 to collide head-on. 2 to coincide [with], be the same [as]. 3 traditional ceremony held to celebrate smn's eight-year (*windu*) birthday, *i.e.* at the end of this 8th, 16th, 24th, 32d, and 64th years. ***an** *sms* * 1, 2, 3 *above. Aku rak wis pinter nunggang pit, masa bisaa *an!* I'm good at riding a bike–as if I'd run into anyone! *Mulangé *an karo anggoné aku mulang.* The class he teaches is the one I'll be teaching too. **ke*** to get bumped into. **ñ/di*** to collide with, knock against

tumeg fed up, sated

tumekèng to reach, get to (*contracted from* T·UM·EKA ING). *Wis * lampus.* He has reached the end of his life.

tumenggi(ng) to curl upward at the ends

ṭumil small amount. **sa*** a little bit

tumingal to see, watch; to have seen, to know of (*kr for* TUMON). *See also* TINGAL

tumis *var of* TOMIS

tumon *ng,* **tumingal** *kr* 1 to see, watch. *Wis suwé ora *.* I haven't seen you for a long time. *sing ** audience, spectators. 2 *ng kr* to have seen, to know of. *Apa *!* How could it be! *Sapa sing * ana sapi manak kutjing?* Who ever heard of a cow giving birth to a kitten! **ñ/di*i** to see, watch. *See also* TON

tumpa ***-*** one on top of the other. **ñ*-ñ*** forming a pile, all heaped up. *O kebangeten temen ta, kesusahan teka numpa² mengkéné.* I can't bear it–sorrows piling up this way.

tumpak 1 to ride (on) (*root form: kr for* TUNGGANG). 2 *oj* Saturday

tumpal 1 border design on the vertical edge of a sarong. 2 *oj* according to smn else's will. **numpal kèli** to travel around accompanying smn, with no destination of one's own

tumpang ***an** a ride. *Aku éntuk *an kantjaku.* I got a lift from a friend. **ka*an** to have sth on top of it. *anglo ka*an wadjan tjilik isi lilin* a brazier with a little pan of wax on it. **ñ*** 1 to be on *or* at the top. *Sikilé numpang médja.* He has his foot on the table. 2 to top smn, get in the last word. 3 to get a ride (from). *Nèk sekolah Ali numpang guruné.* Ali rides to school with his teacher. *olèh numpang* to get a lift. **numpang karang/karas/m̃·pangan** to stay with smn; to board at smn's house. **numpang rembug** to offer advice. **numpang ñ·susup** to take room and board in smn's house. **ñ/di*aké** to put sth on (top of). *Bukuné tumpangna médja.* Put the book on the table. *Buku²ku dak tumpang²aké.* I piled my books on top of each other. **ñ/di*i** 1 to be on (top of). *Bantalé adja nganti numpangi sibajèk.* Don't let the pillow rest on the baby. 2 to put sth on (top of), to add sth (to). *Sawisé di*i kapas, bandjur diperban.* He covered it with cotton and then bandaged it. *Guruné numpangi, "Lan sentosa."* "And it's strong, too," added the teacher. 3 to get board and lodging (from). *Embahku di*i (mangan) mahasiswa loro.* My grandparents have two students as boarders. 4 to get a ride (from). *Aku mau di*i Ali.* I gave Ali a ride ('I had Ali get a ride from me'). **pa·ñ*** passenger, rider. **t·um·umpang** 1 (resting) on. *Bukuné temumpang ing médja.* The book is on (top of) the table. 2 [of rice paddies] lying at a higher level (than). *Sawahé tumumpang sawahku.* His paddy is higher than mine. *** paruk** *rg var of* * SO *below.* *** sari** 1 roof part on a traditional Javanese house. 2 [a piece of land which is] planted with two different kinds of vegetation. * **so** *or* * **suh** piled up every which way. * **tinḍih** one on top of the other. *Bukuné ditumpuk * tinḍih nèng nḍuwur médja.* The books are stacked on the table.

tumpeng array of food for a ritual meal (*sla-met·an*): a cone of rice surrounded by the other dishes. **ñ*** 1 cone-shaped. 2 (*psv* **di***) to prepare the above meal

tumper 1 a burning stick removed from the fire. 2 an ember. **ñ*(-ñ*)** (to act) reckless, headlong, out of control. *numper² mung-suh sing matikel-tikel tjatjahé* to clash with an enemy force many times larger. *Wadya-balané numper pamupuhé.* The army fought savagely. *Keboné numper² pangamuké.* The kerbau ran amuck. * **tj·in·awet·an** ille-gitimate child

tumpes done away with. *Saomah * babar pi-san.* The entire family was wiped out. *Wa-dya akèh sing *.* Many of the soldiers were killed. **ñ/di*** to exterminate. **pa·ñ*** (act of) doing away with. *Penumpesan gerom-bolan mau bakalé mangan wektu akèh.* It will take a long time to wipe out the terror-ists. * **tapis** utterly wiped out, altogether destroyed

tumplak (*or* * **blak**) (having) spilled *or* poured out all over the place, *e.g.* rice from a tipped-over basket; secrets poured into an-other's ear. **ñ/di*** to spill/pour [things] by inverting the container. **(mantu) * pundji·ǹ** the final wedding for which parents are re-sponsible, *i.e.* the wedding of their youngest daughter

tumplek (blek) *rg var of* TUMPLAK BLAK

tumpuk in a pile; in large quantities. *Buku²-né wis *.* The books have been stacked up. *Ḍèwèké nganggo klambi * loro.* He's wear-ing two layers of clothing. ***an** heaped up. **an buku* piles of books. **an ḍuwit* loads of money. ***-*** *or* **te*an** piled high. *kata-ta *-** arranged in layers. **ma*-*** forming many piles. *Kabetjikanmu wis ma*-*.* You have heaped kindness on us. **ñ*-ñ*** form-ing many piles; in large quantities. *Ḍuwité numpuk².* He's rolling in money. **ñ/di*(i)** 1 to pile things up; to accumulate things. *Numpuka buku.* Stack the books. *numpuk banḍa* to amass wealth. 2 to hand in [an assignment]. *Garapané di*.* He turned in his homework. **t·um·umpuk** piled up. * **timbun** in piles; in large quantities. *Ba-rangé tumpuk-timbun.* There are loads of things there. * **unḍung** in a pile; in abund-ance. *Perkututé wis * unḍung.* He has lots of turtledoves. *Bungahku saja * unḍung.* We grew happier and happier.

tumrap 1 (*or* ***é**) of, regarding, applied to, about. *Pegawéan iki kangélan * wong sidji.* This work is too hard for one person. *ge-gremetan kang gawé kapitunan * manungsa* germs that are harmful to human beings. *Pijé penemumu *é perkara mau?* What's your opinion of the matter? *Tumrapé aku swarané melas asih.* To me, it was a piteous sound. *Klambi biru kuwi * banget kanggo ḍèké.* That blue blouse is very becoming to her. 2 placed, located, set up. *Désa mau * ing satengahing alas.* The village is located in the middle of the jungle. *See also* TRAP

tumruntun lined up. *Wong² sing antri lenga * dawa.* The people were standing in a long line to buy kerosene.

ṭumuk ***-*** [of walking gait] unsteady, slow and labored. *Saka sepuhé jèn tindak *-*.* He's so old that he walks very slowly. **ṭumak-*** 1 *sms* *-*. 2 unable to see well (because of *e.g.* poor light, defective vision). *See also* KEṬUMUK

tumus to spring from, grow out of. *sumbang-sinumbang sing * saka katresnan* mutual giv-ing which comes from love. **ñ/di*i** to lead to, result in. *Temahané numusi anané owah²-an kabinèt.* In the end, it led to a cabinet shake-up.

tumut to accompany, [do] with (*kr for* M·ÈLU). **ñ/dipun*aken** to have smn accom-pany *or* live with smn (*kr for* NG/DI·ÈLU·K̂AKÉ)

tuna (tuni *sbst? kr*) a loss, deficiency; to lose. *Karepé mono ja golèk baṭi, nanging malah *.* He hoped for a profit, but instead he took a loss. *gawé *né masjarakat* detrimental to society. **ke*** to suffer a loss. **ñ/di*kaké** to sell at a loss. **ñ/di*ni** to cause loss to. *Nunani lijan iku ora apik.* It's not right to make others suffer a loss. * **dungkap** inade-quacies, shortcomings. * **(ing) budi** stupid, short on brains. * **(ing) sastra** illiterate. * **ing we·wéka** careless. * **karja** unemployed. * **nétra** blind; the blind. * **satak baṭi sanak** to lose in worldly goods but gain a friend. * **susila** prostitution. *wanita * susila* a pros-titute. *See also* PITUNA

tunangan 1 fiancé(e). 2 to get engaged

tunḍa 1 one after the other; passing along from one to another. *rapat * kaping telu* the third meeting in close sequence. 2 *gram* doubled form. *n a relay system for transporting things. **ñ/di*** to arrange things in sequence. *Pos² mau dianggo nunḍa djaran sing nglakokaké kréta pos.* These outposts [along the way] are for keeping horses in readiness for the mail carts.

tundjang ***an** bonus; charitable donation to help smn in specific need. **an anak* bonus given to an employee whose wife has just had a child. **an Hari Raya* or **an Lebaran* Lebaran-day bonus. **an kematian* death benefit paid to an employee's widow. **ke*** to get knocked against *or* run over. *Ḍèké mati ke* montor.* He was run over by a car and killed. **ñ/di*** **1** to knock against, run into. **2** to provide financial support for

tundjel **ke*** to get pushed from behind. **ñ/di*** to push smn from behind

tundjem **ñ*** thrusting down(ward) strongly. *Montor maburé kobong tiba nundjem.* The burning plane plummeted downward. **ñ/di*aké** to thrust *or* implant sth deeply into. **t·um·undjem** *sms* Ñ* *above*

tundjuk **ñ/di*** to appoint, name

tundjung **1** lotus blossom. **2** copper spearhead. **ñ/di*** to color *or* dye sth violet, *i.e.* the color of the lotus blossom. *** tuwuh ing séla** an impossible thing

tundon ***é** actually, in fact

tunḍuk *rg* to bow the head; *fig* to be under smn's thumb. *Ḍèké * karo kekarepané bodjoné.* He always bows to his wife's wishes. **ñ*** [of head] bowed, to bow. **ñ/di*aké** to bow [the head]

tunḍun banana stalk with bunches of fruit growing on either side. *geḍang sa** a stalk of bananas. ***an** the bunches on the stalk

tunḍung **ñ/di*** to send smn off. *Lo, mangké ta kok ndjur kaja di*.* Leaving so soon? (to a departing guest). *Baturé di* sebab njolong.* She dismissed the servant for stealing.

ṭung *rpr* gamelan *gongs, or* gamelan music in general. **ṭang-*** *rpr* repeated gamelan sounds. **nge/di*aké** to hold [*esp.* the hand] up *or* out toward smn. *Tangané di*aké ndjaluk roti.* He held out his hand for a cookie. *Beḍilé di*aké marang aku.* The rifle was pointed at me. *See also* AṬUNG

tunggak stump. ***an** remaining portion. *Aku mentas ngrampungaké *an gawéjan wingi.* I've just finished up yesterday's work. **an pembajaran* amount remaining to be paid. **ke*** to trip over a stump. **ñ*** **1** resembling a stump. **2** (*psv* **di***) to delay a payment that is due. *Jèn nunggak mbajar bisa diḍenḍa.* If you're in arrears, you might get fined. *Tagihanku di*.* He hasn't paid me what he owes me. **3** to fail to be promoted to a higher class. **nunggak basa** to deliver only part of a message one was to pass along. **nunggak bodjo** to marry the former spouse of an older sibling. **nunggak semi** having the same name *or* title as one of one's forebears, *usu.* father or uncle. *Djenengé mas Broto nunggak semi éjangé.* Broto is named after his grandfather. *** djarak mradjak, * djati mati** the low-born rise and the high-born fall

tunggal *ng,* **tunggil** *kr* **1** joined in/at/by the same *x*. *wong sing * saomah* members of the same household. *kantjané sing * désa* people from the same village. ** bapak lija ibu* having the same father but a different mother. *Ḍèwèké mèlu lungguh * samédja.* She sat at the same table with him. **2** companion, partner. ** kantja sapagawéjan* colleague. **3** similar, comparable. *Isih ana *é?* Is there anything more to add? **te*an** to join, combine with. *te*an karo wong main* hanging around with gamblers. **ñ*** the same, joined *or* grouped together. *Surasané nunggal kaja kang ing lajang lijané.* The letter said the same thing as the other letter. *isih nunggal sasi* during the same month [as the foregoing]. *sobat nunggal sa perdjuwangan* comrades in arms. *nunggal gawé* to work in the same place. *tembung nunggal-misah* synonyms. *Ukara loro mau nunggal misah.* The two sentences mean the same thing. *nunggal rasa/turu* to sleep together. **ñ/di*aké** to join, put together. *Kéwan sepirang-pirang mau di*aké ing kanḍang mau.* All kinds of animals were put in the same cage. **sa*** one (*kr for* SIDJI: *see* SATUNGGAL). *** adjang** co-worker, colleague. *** banju** having received the same education; belonging to the same mystic school. *** kokoh·an** co-worker, colleague. *** rasa** tasting alike; having the same spiritual beliefs. *See also* PANUNGGAL

tunggang *ng,* **tumpak** *kr,* **titih** *ki* **(te)*an** means of transportation; that which is ridden. *Titihané pak tjilik pit.* My uncle gets around on a bicycle. *Kowé mau mréné nganggo *an apa?* What did you come here on? *Akèh te*an sing ptg sliwer.* All kinds of vehicles kept whizzing past. **ne·ñ*** to ride, get a ride. *Kowé mau mréné nenung-*

gang apa mlaku? Did you ride here or walk? **n̈/di*aké** to have/let smn ride. *Aku diundang sedulurku nang Djakarta di*aké sepur.* A Djakarta relative invited me for a visit and arranged my train transportation. **n̈/di*(i)** to ride (on); to take [a vehicle]. *Ibu nitih an̥dong tindak pasar.* Mother went to the marketplace in a carriage. **n̈/di*i** to perch *or* sit on (top of). *Adja nunggangi tumpukan kursi kuwi n̥dak tiba.* Don't sit on that pile of chairs–you'll fall. *** djalak** the broad back of a farm animal

tunggil in/at the same *x*; similar (*kr for* TUNGGAL). **sa*** one (*sbst? kr for* SATUNGGAL)

tunggu *ng*, **tengga** *kr* 1 to wait (for). ** bis* to wait for a bus. *Anggonku * luwih saka sak djam.* I waited over an hour. 2 to keep watch over, look after. *Aku tak * omah.* I'll [stay home and] look after the house. ***n̂** act of waiting/watching. *kamar tunggon* waiting room. **n̈/di*k̂aké** to look after (on smn's behalf). *Omahku ditunggokaké mbakjuku.* My sister took care of my house for me [while I was away]. **n̈/di*(n̂i)** 1 to wait (for). *Aku mau nunggu nganti rong djam.* I waited for two hours. *D̥èké tak * nganti rong djam ora teka²*. I waited for him for two hours but he never showed up. 2 to watch over, look after sth. *Liweté ditunggoni.* She kept watch of the rice as it cooked. *Bajiné sing nunggu sapa?* Who took care of the baby? *Bingkilé olèhé ndandani pit ditunggoni sing duwé nganti rampung.* The owner watched while they repaired his bicycle. **pa*n̂** act of waiting *or* watching

tungguk (**tjaos** *kr? ka?*) to serve [smn of high status] as guard. ***an** 1 act of serving smn as guard. 2 place where smn serves. **n̈/di*i** to guard smn('s place); to take one's turn at serving as guard

tunggul 1 banner, flag. *Kjai * Wulung* a celebrated flag owned by the Sultan of Jogjakarta. 2 tree stump. 3 (*or* **te***) what is most important. *barisan te** the first army unit. *Sirah iku te*ing awak.* The head is the most important part of the body. *See also* PANUNGGUL

tunggulang *inf var of* TANGGULANG

tungka **ke*** [an activity] is interrupted *or* overlapped by [another]. *Durung olèh wangsulan, ke* tekané Ali.* Before he got an answer, Ali came along [and diverted his attention]. *Aku kudu sinau nanging terus ke* ndelok TV.* I was supposed to be studying, but I was distracted by the TV.

tungkak heel. *adu ** heels together. ***an** heel portion of footwear. **an kaos sikil* the heel of a sock. **ke*** 1 blocked by smn's heels, *e.g.* when walking behind him. 2 to receive an unexpected visit when about to leave. **n̈/di*** to stamp *or* kick with the heel(s). **nungkak krama** to scoff at the rules of etiquette. *See also* KAK-KONG

tungkas message, instruction (*opt kr for* WELING)

t̥ungkruk to sit with the knees drawn up to the chest

tungku brick fireplace with a grill for cooking things over a wood fire

tungkul **ke*** absorbed, engrossed. **n̈*** 1 to bow the head. 2 (*psv* **di***) to distract, absorb smn's attention. 3 (*psv* **di***) to surrender to. *Ratuné nungkul mungsuh.* The king yielded to the enemy. **nungkul aris** to surrender without a struggle. **n̈/di*aké** to bow the head to; *fig* to cause smn to surrender *or* bow down to one. **pa·n̈*** tribute exacted by a king from his subjects. **t·um·ungkul** to bow the head

Tunglé first day of the six-day week

tungtung *var of* TUNTUNG

t̥ungul *rpr* sth appearing suddenly. **n̈*** to loom up, come into view. *See also* PENT̥UNGUL

tuni *sbst? kr for* TUNA

tuntak to spill out (*kr for* SUNTAK). **n̈*** to vomit (*kr for* M̈·WUTAH)

tuntas 1 with all the water wrung out of it; *fig* having run dry of ideas. 2 [of voices, sounds] to carry well. **n̈/di*aké** to cause to be/run dry

tuntek̄ *var of* TUNTAK

tunten and then (*root form: kr for* TULI)

t̥unt̥eng *intsfr* black. *ireng ** pitch black

tuntjeb **n̈/di*aké** to stick *or* embed sth [in, into]. *Wajangé di*aké nang debog.* The puppets are [held erect by being] stuck into the banana log.

tuntum healed, all well. **n̈/di*aké** to heal, cure

tuntun ***an** 1 instruction. *Wulangané diterangaké ing *an tjekakan.* He explained the lesson in a brief lecture. 2 placenta (*ki for* ARI², EMBING²). 3 umbilical cord; navel (*ki for* PUSER, WUDEL). **n̈/di*** to lead, guide, instruct. **pa·n̈*** 1 leader. 2 guidance. *buku panuntun* manual, guide

tuntung 1 tip, point. **ing irung* tip of the nose. 2 what is pointed *or* aimed at; in the direction of. **ing ati* one's goal, what one aims to achieve. **legi* on the sweet(-tasting) side. **ñ*** to point toward *or* in the direction of

tuntut banana blossom. ***an** to demand, claim. *Para guru paḍa mogok djalaran *ané ora dilulusaké.* The teachers struck because their demands were not met. **a*** [of banana trees] to come into blossom. **ñ/di*** 1 to demand, claim. 2 to prosecute. *nuntut sing matèni* to bring the murderer to justice. **pa·ñ*** prosecutor

ṭunuk **ṭunak-*** unable to see well, *esp.* because of poor light

tupiksa **ñ/di*** 1 to examine, investigate. *Nupiksa Jasa* a government research enterprise. 2 to read. *para nupiksa* (our) readers

tupriksa *var of* TUPIKSA

tur 1 also, in addition. *Sugih * betjik atiné.* He's rich, and kind too. 2 although, even though. *Tur wis dikanḍani lho, kok meksa lunga.* He insists on going, even though we told him not to. *** manèh** and furthermore

ṭur 1 *rpr* a drop of water dripping. 2 *rpr* a downward flow. **nge/di*aké** to pour sth from a spout. *ngeṭurakė banju* to pour water. **nge/di*i** to pour onto sth through a spout. *ngeṭuri tanduran* to water plants, *e.g.* with a watering can

tura *see* ASMARA

turâgâ *var of* TURANGGA

turah *ng,* **tirah** *kr* left over, remaining. ***an** (that which is) left over. *Jèn ana *an ḍuwit, ditjèlèngi.* Whenever he had money left over, he'd put it in the bank. **ñ/di*i** to consume less of sth in order to leave some for others. **sa*é** all that is left of sth. *Sa*é didum marang botjah² tjilik.* Everything that was left over was divided among the children.

turânggâ horse (*oj; ki for* DJARAN). **ka*n** 1 interpretation of the character of a woman, or a horse, from the physical characteristics. 2 animal nature. *Ḍèké ngreti marang ka*ning djago.* He understands roosters.

turas 1 urine (*ki for* UJUH). 2 to urinate (*ki for* NG·UJUH). **ñ/di*i** to urinate on sth (*ki for* NG·UJUH·I). **pa*an** a urinal. ***ing satrija** descendant of a nobleman

turé·né it is said (*md for* DJARÉ). ** adjeng késah.* I hear you're leaving.

turi 1 a certain flowering tree whose roots supply nitrogen to soil. 2 *turi* blossom. ** putih* white *turi* blossom(s) (eaten as a vegetable). ** bang* bitter-tasting red *turi* blossom(s) (used in folk medicines)

turis traveler. *narik ** to attract tourists

turisme tourism; act of going on tours

Turki Turkey. *wong ** Turk(s)

turna and furthermore

turné (to make) a tour of inspection

turnèh *inf var of* TUR MANÈH: *see under* TUR

turu *ng,* **tilem** *kr,* **saré** *ki* 1 to sleep. **, *, wis djam sewelas.* Go to sleep; it's 11 o'clock. *Durung suwé olèhé turu, tangi gragapan.* He hadn't been asleep long when he awoke with a start. 2 to go to bed. *Ḍèké mulih *.* He went home and went to bed. *mapan ** to go to bed. 3 (*or *-**) to go to sleep. *Aku mapan * manèh nanging nganti suwé ora bisa² *.* I went back to bed but I couldn't get to sleep for a long time. **(te)*n̂** to lie down; to lie around, relax. **ke*n̂** to drop off to sleep accidentally, to doze. **ñ/di·te*** to lull smn to sleep. *nenuru anaké* to put one's child to sleep. **ñ/di*k̂aké** to put smn to bed; to lay smn down. *nurokaké baji nang paturon* to lay the baby on the bed. *Aḍimu turokna kana.* Put your little brother to bed. **ñ/di*n̂i** 1 to sleep in/on. *nuroni tempat-tiḍur* to sleep in a bed. 2 to sleep (in the same bed) with. *dituroni sing lanang* to sleep with one's wife ('to be slept with by one's husband'). **pa*n̂** place for sleeping; bed, bedroom. *nata paturoné* to make one's bed. **sa·pa*n̂** (to sleep) in the same bed. *** ajam²** to sleep fitfully. *** angler** to sleep soundly. *** awan** (to take) a nap. *** kaḍar** to sleep out in the open. *** kasur di·kebut·i** to have an already comfortable life made even more pleasant. *** les** (to go) sound asleep. *** ke·pati** (to go) sound asleep

turuk *cr* female genitals

turun[a] 1 (**teḍak** *ki*) to descend genealogically. 2 descendant. *Ḍèwèké isih * prijaji.* He comes from an aristocratic family. *Kowé wis diwetja bakal mengku tanah Djawa sa-*-*mu.* It is predicted that you and your descendants will rule over Java. ***é wong ahli laku** descendant of a holy hermit. ***an** descent, ancestry. *Ḍèwèké iki isih *an ratu.* He is of royal descent. *wong Indonesia * Tionghoa* a Chinese-Indonesian. ***-t·um·urun** from one generation to the next. *Turun-tumurun keluarga X manggon ing kéné.* The X family has lived here for generations. **ñ*** inherited; hereditary. *lelara nurun* a hereditary illness. **ñ/di*aké** 1 to cause sth to descend. *Pemerintah njoba nurunaké rega gula.* The government tried to lower the price of sugar. 2 to transmit to one's descendants. *Kepinterané bapaké di*aké nang anak²é.* The father's intelligence has come down to his children. 3 to procreate [offspring]. *Putraning ratu sing sidji nurunaké Paṇḍawa lima, sidjiné nurunaké Kurawa satus.* The five Pandawas descended from one of the princes, the one hundred Kurawas from the other. *Babonku nurunaké djago adon.* My hen produced a fighting cock. **ñ/di*i** 1 to transmit through hereditary. 2 to copulate with [another animal]. **t·um·urun (teḍak** *ki*) to descend. *Dalané temurun.* The road goes down. *Para djawata tumurun nang Artja Pada.* The deities descended to earth. *Wong² saben dina ngarep-arep tumuruning udan.* Day after day the people looked for rain.

turun^b *ng,* **teḍak** *kr* ***an** a copy, duplicate. *Turunan idjazah kanggo nglamar gawéan kudu rangkep loro.* Copies of diplomas should be submitted in duplicate with job applications. **ñ/di*aké** to have smn copy; to have sth copied. **ñ/di*(i)** to copy, duplicate. *A nurun tjaṭetané B.* A copied B's notes. *Surat iki turunen kanggo arsip.* Copy this letter for the files.

turus 1 a cutting from which a new plant is raised. 2 a fish trap. ***an** raised from a cutting. *Ana sing *an, ana sing ḍeḍeran.* Some of them were raised from cuttings, some from seed. **ñ/di*** to grow [a plant] from a cutting

turut 1 along. * *pinggiré dalan* along the roadside. 2 *n* at a time. *Koperé gawanen * sidji.* Carry the suitcases one by one. ***an** a reading lesson in Arabic. *Olèhmu ngadji wis tekan *an pira?* How far are you in your Koran-reading lessons? **ka*an** to materialize. *Ke*an kang diarep-arep.* He got what he wanted. *Sapandjaluké bisa ke*an.* All of his requests were complied with. **ñ/di*** to follow, act according to, obey. *Turuten gambar² iki.* Do as shown in these pictures. **ñ*an** obedient, compliant. **ñ/di*i** to comply with. *Turutana pandjaluké.* Do as he asks. *Ḍèké mung nuruti sèntimèn.* He always reacts emotionally. * **usuk** [of voices, sounds] clear and carrying. * **wulu** as numerous as one's hairs. *Utangku turut wulu.* I'm up to my ears in debt. *See also* PITURUT

turwèlu *var of* TRUWÈLU

tus 1 hundred (*shf of* ATUS). *dji ** one per hundred. 2 pure, unadulterated. 3 *excl of reproof.* ***(-*)an** *shf of* ATUS·AN. **nge/di*(aké)** to dry sth. **pa*an** drain(pipe)

ṭus 1 *rpr* bursting open, *e.g.* a grape when bitten into. 2 *rg* almost! (*expression used in games when an object almost reaches its target, e.g. a marble landing close to the circle*)

tu:stèl a still camera

tusuk (*or* * **konḍé**) a decorative hairpin for ladies' hairdos. *See also* SUK

tut **nge/di*(aké)** (**n/di·ḍèrèk·aké** *ka*) to follow *or* accompany as a retainer. **t·in·ut** *ltry* to be followed. *Pituruté tinut déning sakèhing manungsa.* Most people follow his advice. *See also* ANUT, KATUT, NUT, TUT-BURI

ṭu:t 1 *rpr* a toot. 2 *rpr* the ejection of flatus

tutas *var of* TUNTAS

tut-buri *ng,* **tut-wingking** *kr* to follow. *Pak guru mlaku madju, botjah² *.* The teacher led the way and the children followed. **nge/di*** to follow smn. * **n·daja·ni** to lead from behind (Javanese principle of guided freedom). *See also* BURI, TUT

tuter car horn. **ñ/di*** to honk (at)

tutu *ng,* **gentang** *kr* ***ñ** hulled by pounding. *beras tuton* hand-husked rice. *suket tuton* a grass that grows among rice plants. **ñ/di*(ñi)** to pound [rice] to remove the hulls. *Pariné di* ana ing lesung, bèn dadi beras.* She hulled the rice in a wooden bowl.

tutug *ng,* **dumugi** *kr* 1 (up) to, as far as. *Tjritaku * seméné ḍisik.* I'll stop my story at this point. *Olèhé matja nembé * katja rong puluh.* He's read to page 20. 2 finished, over. *Olèhku nonton wajang mau bengi nganti *.* I watched the whole shadow play last night. *Apa * olèhmu ndeleng kapal?* Have you finished looking over the whole ship? ***é** (**sambet·ipun** *kr*) the continuation of [a serial story *etc.*]. **ka*an** (**ka·dugi·ñ** *kr*) achieved, fulfilled. *Pepénginanipun tansah kedugèn.* All of his wishes were fulfilled. **ñ*** (**ñj·sambet** *opt kr*) 1 to the end *or* utmost. *Saiki turua ḍisik sing nutug.* Get as much sleep as you can now. *Olèhmu nonton apa nganti nutug?* Did you watch right to the end? 2 (*psv* **di***;

ñj/dipun·sambet *opt kr*) to keep on; to resume. *Awohé bisa nutug nganti wité tuwa.* The tree gives fruit throughout its life. *Tjritané di* ana djilid loro.* The story is continued in Volume Two. **ñ/di*aké** to take sth up where it left off. *ngGoné njambut-gawé di*aké.* He resumed his work [after an interruption]. *Wis tutugna olèhmu pada mempeng njambut gawé.* Keep up the good work! *Tjrita iki arep di*aké minggu ngarep.* This story will be continued next week. **ñ/di*i** to comply with the wishes (of). *Apa kang dikepéngini tansah di*i.* She always gets whatever she wants.

tutuh *ng,* **tetah** *kr* ***an** one who gets blamed. **ke*** to get the blame when things go wrong. **ñ/di*** to blame; to reprimand. **ñ/di*(i)** to cut off/down. *Pang²é di*i bèn kétok padang.* He cut off the branches to let in more light.

tutuk mouth (*ki for* TJANGKEM)

ṭuṭuk 1 object used for hitting. *Golèkna * kono kuwi.* Get me something to hammer with. 2 (*or* *-*) to hit again and again. ** paku* to hammer a nail. **ñ/di*aké** to knock an implement [against sth]. *Olèhmu nutukaké palu kurang seru.* Your hammer blows aren't hard enough. **ñ/di*(i)** 1 to knock, rap. *Pak Tani nutuk endasé Kantjil.* The farmer whacked Mouse-Deer on the head. *Sawisé di*i, kulit mau nuli dipé.* The leather is pounded, then dried in the sun. 2 to play [a percussion instrument]. *gamelan sing di** percussion instrument

tuṭul spot(ted), speck(led). *Awakku metu *-*é ireng.* I broke out in black spots. *dluwang * mangsi* blotting paper. **ñ/di*** to jab (at), thrust. *Adja nganti nutul lambé awit malamé panas.* Don't touch [the wax dispenser] to your lips—the wax is hot. **nutul kétjap** *or* **nutul petis** to shoot at close range. **ñ/di*aké** to jab sth [into, at]. *Pèné di*aké mangsi.* He stabbed the pen into the ink.

ṭuṭul *rg var of* TOṬOL

tutup 1 a cover, means of closing. ** ḍahar* screen *or* net for covering food. 2 closed. *Kantor² paḍa *.* The offices are closed. *djas ** Javanese-style button-up jacket. 3 the close [of]. *dina *ing sekolahan* the last day of school. 4 to close, cover. *Angger ana bledèg muni * kuping.* At every thunderclap he covered his ears. ***an** 1 closed, covered. *djas *an* button-up jacket. *Omahé *.* The house is closed up. *lajang *an* a sealed letter. 2 object used as a cover *or* closing. *Godongé kanggo *an.* He covered it with the leaf. **ka*an** covered, closed. *ke*an ing saldju* covered with snow. **ñ/di*aké** 1 to close sth; to close for smn. 2 to use as a cover. *Godongé di*aké wadah.* He covered the box with the banana leaf. **ñ/di*(i)** 1 to close, cover. *Bukumu *en.* Close your book. *Wadahé di*.* He covered the container. *nutupi mripat* to cover the eyes. 2 to keep (en)closed *or* under cover. *Ḍèké di* merga korupsi.* He was jailed for corruption. **pa·ñ*** means of covering *or* closing. *Minangka panutup aku ngaturaké sugeng rawuh.* In closing, allow me to welcome you. **t·um·utup** covered, closed. *Pantjiné tumutup rapet.* The pan is tightly covered. *** kéjong** a certain weave for bamboo wall coverings. *** sadji** food cover of woven bamboo *or* wire

tutur 1 (**sandjang** *or* **tjrijos** *opt? kr*; **ḍawuh** *or* **ngendika** *or* **paring priksa** *ki*; **atur priksa** *or* **tjaos priksa** *ka*) advice; to say (to), tell. *Tutura keprijé penemumu.* Tell me what you think. *Adja tutur² lo.* Don't tell anyone! 2 to pick up, find by accident. *Adja tutur² ing dalan.* Don't pick up things in the street. **ñ/di*aké** (*social variants as for 1 above*) to tell smn; to tell (about). *Tuturna aku baé.* Just tell me about it. *kaanan kaja kang ko*aké mau* a situation like the one you told me about. **ñ/di*i** 1 (*social variants as for 1 above*) to tell, advise. *Anakmu nakal, tuturana.* Your child is naughty; speak to him. *Aku di*i pak guru dikon basa karo kowé sarta bapak.* The teacher said I should speak Krama to you and Dad. 2 to pick [things] up. *Akèh kéré paḍa nuturi tegesan.* Many beggars pick up cigarette butts (on the street). *Ajo ḍuwité di*i.* Come on, take the money. *See also* PITUTUR

tutus cord made of bamboo strands. **ñ/di*** to tie sth with such cord. *** kadjang** long, irregular stitching. *Dludjurané * kadjang.* She basted with long stitches.

tutut tame, submissive. *gadjah ** a tame elephant. **ka*an** 1 to come across [sth one is tracking down] in an unexpected place. 2 to have [one's illness] overcome. *Larané wis nemen, tak kira wis ora ke*an manèh.* His illness is so serious I don't think it can be cured. **ñ*** to obey, to follow advice. **ñ/di·te*** to tame, make submissive. *nenutut gadjah* to tame an elephant. **ñ/di*aké** to

tame, make submissive *or* obedient. ñ/**di∗i**
1 to follow, chase, (try to) catch up with.
nututi tjopèt to chase a pickpocket. *Sing
njupir muḍun, sing nunggang nututi muḍun.*
The driver got out and then the passengers
got out. *Saiki kudu nututi kalahé.* Now
they'll have to come from behind to win.
Ora wetara suwé motoré bisa tak ∗i. Pretty
soon I overtook his car. *Anggoné balapan
mlaju si A ke∗an si B.* B passed A in the
foot race. **2** to try to recover [losses]. *Bareng daganggané sing ilang di∗i tekan lija kuṭa.* He went to another city in an effort to
track down his lost merchandise. **nututi
lajang·an peḍot** to make a futile effort. *Menawa kowé isih arep golèk tjangkirmu sing
ilang prasasat nututi lajangan peḍot.* You're
wasting time looking for your lost cup. **nututi balang wis tiba** to lock the barn door
after the horse has been stolen

tut-wuri *var of* TUT-BURI
tuw- *see also under* TU- (*Introduction,
2.9.7*)
tuwa *ng*, **sepuh** *kr* **1** old; mature. *A duwé
anak loro, sing ∗ djenengé Slamet.* A has
two sons; the older one is called Slamet. *setengah ∗* middle-aged. **2** ripe, ready to eat.
Pelemé wis ∗. The mangoes are ripe. *Wédangé wis ∗.* The water is boiling, *i.e.* ready
to make drinks. **3** [of colors] dark. *idjo ∗*
dark green. *∗-∗* getting along in years.
te∗ an elder, guardian; chairman. **te∗nen**
having age spots on the skin. **ke∗n** excessively old/ripe/dark. ñ/**di∗kaké** to darken
[colors]; to burnish [gold]. **ñ∗ni** **1** to act elderly *or* mature. **2** (*psv* **di∗ni**) to act in the
capacity of guardian *or* elder to smn. *Sapa
sing nuwani perkumpulan iki?* Who's the
sponsor for this group? *∗* **nom** young and
old. *∗-nom·é* one's age. *Tuwa anomé sepira?* How old is he? *∗* **pikun** absent-
minded in one's old age. **wong ∗** **1** old person, elder. **2** parent(s). *See also* KAMITUWA,
PINITUWA

tuwak **1** a prop, a support. **2** an intoxicating liquor made from fermented coconut juice. ñ/**di∗** to prop sth up, support
sth
tuwan *var sp of* TUAN
tuwas **pa∗** *or* **pi∗** payment *or* compensation for one's time and trouble. *Mengkéna-
mengkéné iki apa ija bakal olèh pituwas.*
After all this trouble, I wonder if you'll get
anything for it! **tiwas-∗** in vain, for nothing. *See also* TIWAS
tuwèk old (*cr var of* TUWA). *pak ∗* old man.
mbok ∗ old woman. *∗* **ngèkèk** very old
ṭuwel **ṭuwal-∗** [of a child's cute hands] with
appealing motions. *Botjah iku lagi ṭuwal-∗
dolanan tali.* The child's hands look very
cute as he plays with a piece of string. **ka∗an**
rotation of the hands at the wrist (a classical dance movement). ñ/**di∗aké** to move *or*
rotate [the hands, with appealing motions]
ṭuweng **ṭuwang-∗** to keep twisting. ñ/**di∗aké**
to twist *or* contort [the body]. *See also*
KEṬUWENG
tuwi to visit (*kr for* TILIK)
tuwin and (*opt kr for* LAN, SAHA)
ṭuwi:t *rpr* the whistle of *e.g.* a locomotive
or boat
tuwu (*or* **te∗**) male nocturnal cuckoo (*var
of* (TE)TUHU)
tuwuh **1** outgrowth, sprout; *fig* descendant.
2 to come into existence, grow. *∗***an** ceremonial decoration for weddings symbolizing prosperity and fertility. **te∗an** plants,
growing things. ñ/**di∗aké** to grow, raise;
to give rise to. *nuwuhaké tresna* to arouse
love. ñ/**di∗i** to plant [an area]. *nuwuhi lemah nganggo kembang* to put flowers in the
soil to grow
tuwuk full; sated (*kr for* WAREG)
t.v. (*prn* **tivi**) *see* TÉLÉVISI
tw- *see under* TU(W)- (*Introduction, 2.9.7*)
tyang *ltry var of* TIJANG
tyas *oj* feelings, mood, emotions

U

u (*prn* **ü**) *alphabetic letter*

-u- *inf intensifying infix: inserted after a consonant, usu. the first, or before initial vowel. ir·u·eng* intensely black. *s·u·aja gedु·u·é* more and more enormous. *b·u·anget* or *bang·u·et* or *b·u·ang·u·et* very, extremely. *m·u·entas* just a *brief* moment ago. *dāw·u·â* very very long. *u·akèh* extremely many *or* much

uap *var sp of* UWAB

ubâjâ *ng,* **ubanggi** *kr* 1 reciprocal promise/commitment. 2 legal notification. **∗n** to promise reciprocally. *Wis paḍa ∗n mati urip dilakoni bebarengan.* They promised each other to stay together through thick and thin. **ma·ng∗** *ltry var of* NG∗. **ng/di∗kaké** to promise sth. *Bapaké ng∗kaké sepéḍah marang anaké.* The boy's father promised him a bicycle. **ng/di∗(ni)** to promise (to smn). *Aku ora kélingan jèn tau ng∗ mengkono.* I don't remember ever making such a promise. *Aku di∗ni bapak sepéḍah anjar.* Dad promised me a new bike. **∗ ng·adu** subpoena. **∗ ḍenḍa** notification of warning of a fine. **∗ ébra** legal notification of lapse of claim

ubak **ng/di∗** to stir up, rile

ubal **∗-∗an** rope made by twisting strands together. **ng/di∗** to twist [strands] into rope

ubanggi promise, commitment (*kr for* UBAJA)

ubârampé, ubârampi things needed for a special purpose. *beras sa∗né* rice and all the other things they needed. *Popok mono sawidjining ∗ baji kang baku.* Diapers are basic equipment for babies. *pasinaon bab filem lan ∗né* training in film-making and everything connected with it. *∗né negara kuwi ana lima.* There are five essential branches of government.

ubed wrapped, swathed. *setagèn ∗ papat* a sash wound around four times. **∗-∗** 1 to wear *or* put on [a wrapped clothing item]. *Ḍèké ∗-∗ katju.* He's wearing a kerchief around his neck. 2 (*or* **ubad-∗**) to stretch one's income. *pinter ubad-∗* skillful at making ends meet. **∗-∗an** to wear *or* put on [a wrapped clothing item]. *Sirahé ∗-∗an sarung.* He wound a sarong around his head. **m∗** *or* **mubad-m∗** evasive, devious. **ng/di∗aké** 1 to wrap sth around. *Sampur dipun ∗aken mangadjeng.* She twisted her sash around to the front. *Taliné di∗-∗aké ing paṭok.* The rope is wound around and around the stake. 2 to use [money] efficiently. *Gadjihé seṭiṭik, nanging merga pinter olèhé ng∗aké tjukup.* His salary is small, but he scrapes through by making every penny count. **ngubedaké ḍuwit** to invest money for profit. **ng/di∗-∗** to wrap sth around. *kursi sing di∗-∗ buntal goḍong* a chair festooned with garlands of leaves. *Sirahé isih di∗-∗ katju.* He has a kerchief around his head.

ubek̄ 1 inharmonious. *Tansah ∗ waé.* There is constant friction. 2 noisy. *Adja ∗ nang kono.* Don't make so much racket there. **ubak-∗** to keep moving around in the same general area. *Wis ana sepuluh tahun aku ubak-∗ manggon ana kuṭa Jogjakarta.* I've lived here and there in Jogjakarta for the past ten years. **∗-∗an** to mill around

ubel **∗-∗** head scarf, neck cloth. **ng/di∗-∗i** to wind [such a cloth] around. *Guluné di∗-∗ katju.* He wore a scarf around his neck.

ubeng **∗an** 1 rotation, time around. *Aku arep mlaju sa∗an.* I'll run one lap. 2 an evasive locution. **ubang-∗** 1 to move erratically. *Ḍèké ubang-∗ njingkiri aku.* He zigged and zagged to elude me. 2 evasive, not to the point. *Omonganmu ubang-∗ ora genah.* What you say is devious, I can't follow it. **∗-∗an** 1 to cross *or* miss each other, *e.g.* letters in the mail. 2 merry-go-round.

m✶ to spin, whirl; to go around. *m✶ seser*
to rotate rapidly. *Kitirané m✶.* The propeller is spinning. *Peṇḍapané digeḍègi m✶.* The
veranda has bamboo walls all around it.
m✶-m✶ *or* mubang-m✶ *or* m✶-m·inger 1 to
turn this way and that. *Turuné m✶-minger.*
He tossed and turned in his sleep. *patang
dina kanggo mubeng² ana Sala* four days
for sightseeing in Solo. *Sepuré jèn munggah
ménggak-ménggok, mubang-mubeng.* When
a train ascends a mountain, it twists and
turns back and forth, back and forth. 2 to
speak evasively, not come to the point.
ng/di✶aké to make/have sth go around.
ng✶aké kitiran to spin a propeller. *Aku
ndjaluk di✶-✶aké kuṭa.* I asked him to show
me around the city. ng/di✶i to surround,
encircle. *Omahé di✶i latar.* The house has a
yard around it. *Wong² paḍa ng✶i tjanḍi.*
The sightseers went all around the temple.
sa✶é around. *Sa✶é alun² dipasangi genḍéra
werna².* Flags were hung all around the
square. ✶ djantra cycle, pattern of behavior *or* events. ✶ inger conditions. *ubeng-
ingering djaman* what's going on in the
world

uber ✶-✶an 1 to chase smn. 2 to chase
each other. ng/di✶ to chase, hunt down

ubin *var of* OBIN

ubjar sparkling lights. m✶ to sparkle, glitter.
ng/di✶aké to cause to sparkle/glitter

ubjek intense. *Olèhé rembugan ✶.* They discussed it hotly.

ubjung ubjang-✶ *pl* to move about aimlessly. ng/di✶i to collaborate with. *Wis genah
A kang luput, malah di✶i, diréwangi.* Clearly A was at fault, yet others joined and supported him.

ublak ✶an beaten, stirred. *enḍog ✶an* beat-
en egg. ng/di✶ to stir rapidly, to beat

ublek̄ *var of* UBLAK

ublik *var of* TJUBLIK

ublug two-section rice-steaming kettle, with
the rice placed on a perforated plate above
boiling water (introduced during the Japanese occupation). ng/di✶ to steam [rice]
in this utensil

ubluk *var of* UBLAK

ubral *rg var of* OBRAL

ubreg noise, racket. *mBok adja ✶ waé.* Be
quiet! ng/di✶ to besiege with questions.
A ng✶ B bab kedadéjan wingi. A asked B all
about what happened yesterday.

ubres ng/di✶ to search (for). *Kamaré di✶*

Ali ora ana. He looked in Ali's room but
Ali wasn't there. *Dak ✶ ing patamanan.* I
searched for it in the park.

ubub ✶an a bellows. ng/di✶i to cause to
flare up. *Geniné di✶i nganggo ✶an.* He set
the flames leaping with a bellows. *Adja di✶i
lho, munḍak nesu manèh.* Don't stir him
up or he'll get mad again.

ubug ✶-✶ *rpr* the roar of wind *or* flames

ubung ✶an relation(ship). ✶an internasion-
al international relations. *✶ané karo Dasijun* his relationship with Dasijun. ng/di✶aké
to connect, bring into communication. *Aku
ng✶aké A karo B.* I put A in contact with B.
ng/di✶-✶aké to do one's best to connect
[things]. *Dèké ngubung-ubungaké impèné
karo kedadéjan mau.* He kept trying to connect his dream up with what had happened.
ng/di✶i to communicate with. *Aku di✶i
Slamet.* Slamet got in touch with me.
pa✶an 1 communication(s). 2 connecting
transportation

udag ng/di✶(-✶) to chase, run after

udak ng/di✶ to stir with a round-and-round
movement (rather than up and down: *cf.*
AḌUK). ng/di✶-✶ to get food *etc.* on(to) sth
where it doesn't belong. *Adja ng✶-✶ djangan.*
Don't get soup on it!

udâkârâ *ng,* udâkawis *kr* approximately.
nganti ✶ rong taun for about two years.
ng/di✶ to take a guess at. pa·ng✶ a guess,
an estimate

udâkawis *kr for* UDAKARA

udal (*or* ✶an) action of bubbling forth. *✶ing
banju saka tuk* the bubbling up of water
from a spring. m✶ to give water copiously

uḍal ng/di✶-✶ to open and spread around
the contents of; *fig* to reveal and spread [a
secret]. *ng✶-✶ koper* to unpack a suitcase.
A ng✶-✶ wadiné B. A blabbed B's secret.

udan *ng,* djawah *kr* rain; to rain. *mangsa ✶*
rainy season. *djas ✶* raincoat. *✶é wis terang.*
It's stopped raining. *✶ awu* a rain of ash
(from a volcano). *✶ angin* wind-and-rain
storm. *✶ panah* a rain of arrows. *✶ salah
mangsa* unseasonable rain. ✶-✶(an) (dje·
djawah *kr*) to run around naked in the rain
[children playing]. k✶an (*prn* kodanan *ng*)
to get rained on. *Dèké kodanan bandjur
ngéjub ing guwa.* He got caught in the rain
and took shelter in a cave. ng/di✶aké to fall
or pour on from above. *Para widadari ng✶-
aké kembang.* The nymphs showered down
blossoms. ng/di✶-✶aké to put sth out in the

rain. *ng∗-∗aké klasa reged* to put out a dirty mat to get washed in the rain. **ng/di∗i** to rain [objects] onto. *di∗i mimis* caught in a rain of bullets. *Ḍèké di∗i pitakonan werna²*. She bombarded him with questions. *Kantja²né ng∗i hadiah akèh banget.* Her friends showered her with gifts. ∗ **baja pépé** to rain while the sun is shining. ∗ **barat** rain mixed with high wind; *fig* out of the blue. *Ora ana ∗ ora ana barat, udjug² kok nesu!* All of a sudden you're mad for no reason at all! ∗ **keṭèk (adus)** to rain while the sun is shining. ∗ **klambi** light rain that dampens one's clothing. ∗ **matjan ḍéḍé** to rain while the sun is shining. ∗ **saldju** snow; to snow. ∗ **s(in)emèni** *or* ∗ **suwèni** rain approaching from afar with a roaring sound. ∗ **tekèk** *or* ∗ **wéwé** to rain while the sun is shining. ∗ **woh** hail; to hail

uḍang *rg var of* URANG

udani to know, be aware. **ng/di∗ni** to know *or* understand *or* be aware of sth

uḍar *ng kr,* **lukar** *ki* loose, loosened. *Talènané ∗.* The knot is loose. **ng/di∗i** to loosen, unbind. *ng∗i buntelan* to untie a bundle

udârâ *oj* sky; (up in) the air

udârâgâ multicolored

udâraos *kr for* UDARASA

udârâsâ *ng,* **udâraos** *kr* a guess, an opinion. **ng/di∗** to guess, form an opinion, think, suppose. **pa·ng∗** act of guessing *etc.*

uḍeg ∗-∗ sixth-generation ancestor *or* descendant

uḍek̄ *var of* UḌAK. **uḍak-∗** *or* **muḍak-m∗** to remain in the same general area. *Uḍak-∗ ana kono waé.* He's always hanging around there. *Saking djuḍeké mung muḍak-m∗ nang kantoré.* He was so perturbed he wouldn't leave the office.

udel *var of* UṬEL, WUDEL

uḍeng wrapped headdress (*kr for* IKET)

uḍèt 1 small freshwater eel (young of the WELUT). 2 *var of* OḌÈT

uḍet sash worn with a batik wraparound

udi **ng/di∗** to exert oneself, strive. *tansah ng∗ unḍaking kapinterané* constantly trying to increase one's skill. *Di∗ bisané klakon.* They made an effort to bring it about. **pa·ng∗** exertion, effort. *pang∗né nganti mataun-taun* many years' effort

udijânâ *oj* park, public garden

udik ∗-∗ *var of* UWIK²

uḍik upstream part of a river. ∗-∗ 1 alms. *maringi ∗-∗* to give alms. 2 tiny wigglers in river water. **m∗** to move upstream against the current. **ng/di∗aké** to navigate [a boat] upstream

uḍis **ng∗-∗** [of tiny insects] to creep, crawl

udja ∗**n-∗nan** 1 one who is treated permissively. 2 course of action one is determined to take. **ng/di∗** 1 to give in to. *ng∗ hawanepsu* to yield to one's passions. *Botjah tjilik di∗ ibuné.* The child's mother lets him do anything he pleases.

udjar 1 what smn says *or* advises. *Ḍèké ora krungu ∗é guru.* He didn't hear what the teacher said. *Aku turut sa∗mu.* I'll do anything you say. 2 (**punagi** *kr?*) a pledge to do sth if one's hopes *or* wishes are granted. **ng/di∗-∗(i)** to jaw (at), speak abusively (to)

udjeg **ng/di∗-∗** to keep after smn. *ng∗-∗ ndjaluk mangan* to keep asking for something to eat. *A ng∗-∗ B supaja mbajar utangé.* A kept hounding B to pay his debt.

udji ∗**an** test, examination. **ng/di∗** to test. *A ng∗ B.* A gave B an exam. *ng∗ katresnané* to test smn's love. *ng∗ emas* to assay gold

udjiwat **ng∗** to look invitingly out of the corners of the eyes. **ng/di∗i** to look at sth as above

udjub honoree of a ritual ceremony. **ng/di∗aké** to announce the name of [an honored one] at a ceremony. *ng∗aké slametan* to announce the name of the person in whose honor (*or* commemoration) a feast is given

udjud form, shape (*var of* WUDJUD). **ma∗** to take (the) shape (of). *Sarana pudjian, tjanḍi mau ma∗ sadjroning sawengi.* Through prayer, the temple took shape in a single night. **ng/di∗aké, ng/di∗i** *var of* M̈/DI·WUDJUD·AKÉ, M̈/DI·WUDJUD·I

udjug ∗-∗ suddenly, unexpectedly

udjung 1 peninsula. 2 kissing of the knees of a respected older relative (esteem-showing act performed on certain special occasions). 3 *oj* tip of a pointed weapon. ∗**an** 1 a mock duel with rattan stalks. 2 leaf (*rg kr for* GOḌONG). **ng/di∗i** to pay one's respects to smn as above (2). *ng∗i wong tuwané* to kiss the knees of one's parent(s)

udjur lengthwise dimension. ∗**an** a share of one's profits. *Sardi menang, aku diwènèhi ∗an limang gélo.* Sardi won and gave me five rupiahs out of his winnings. ∗-∗**an** 1 alongside each other lengthwise. *Botjah² jèn turu ∗-∗an.* The children sleep side by side. 2 to share each other's profits. **m∗** 1 in a lengthwise position; *fig* lucky. *Olèhé* *turu m∗ apa malang?* Do they sleep lengthwise or crosswise? 2 to horn in on smn's profits. *Jèn menang aku m∗.* If you win, share with me. **mudjur ngalor** to lie with the head toward the north (the position in which Javanese are buried); *fig* dead. **ng/di∗aké** to put (lengthwise) in a certain direction *or* position. *Menḍem wong di∗aké ngalor.* People are buried with the head to the north. *Jèn di∗aké ngétan, barangé bisa mlebu omah.* If we turn this thing eastward we'll be able to get it in the house. **ng/di∗i** to share one's profits with smn. *Aku di∗i limang gélo.* He gave me five rupiahs of his winnings. *See also* ALANG[b], M·ALANG[b]

udjus **udjas-∗** 1 unmannerly. 2 slipshod

udjwâlâ *oj* 1 beam, ray. 2 facial expression. **ng∗** 1 surrounded by a halo. 2 radiant, beaming

udrâsâ *see* MANTJA

udreg to quarrel. **∗-∗an** to quarrel with each other

uḍu betting stakes; money contributed to a gambling pool. **∗n̂** accompanied by gambling. *main kertu uḍon* to play cards for money. **ng/di∗n̂i** to place a bet, make a contribution. **∗ anḍil** 1 to contribute one's share. *Kabèh wis paḍa uḍu-anḍil.* Everybody has ante'd up. 2 contribution of sth significant, *e.g.* in a field of knowledge. **∗ tjangkem** to participate in the eating without bearing one's share of the cost

udubil(l)ah(i) (*or* **ng∗** *or* **ang∗**) 1 *excl of surprise or anger.* 2 surprising, astounding, amazing. *Wah, tjatjahé ∗!* There are so *many* of them!

udud (**ses** *opt? kr*) sth to smoke; to smoke. *kamar ∗* smoking room. *Jèn wong Éropah ∗é srutu utawa sigarèt.* Westerners smoke cigars and cigarettes. **ng/di∗(i)** to smoke sth. *ng∗i rokok* to smoke cigarettes regularly

uduk *var of* WUDUK. *See also* SEGA

udun *var of* WUDUN

uḍun *root form: var of* ḌUN. **∗an** ceremonial placing of a baby on the ground for the first time: *see also* ME·ḌUN, TEḌAK

udur a noisy and disruptive quarrel. **∗an** action of working a rice paddy cooperatively (*see also* KUDUR). **∗-∗an** to quarrel with each other. **ng/di∗aké** to quarrel about. *Kaja ngono waé kok di∗aké.* Why argue about a little thing like that?

udyânâ *var of* UDIJANA

uga *ng,* **ugi** *kr* 1 also, too; [not] either. *Ḍèké sugih, ∗ bagus.* He's rich, and handsome too. *Ora bisa madju, mundur ∗ ora bisa.* He couldn't go forward and he couldn't back up either. *Ḍèwèké arep nonton, mengkono ∗ kantjané.* He wanted to watch and so did his friend. *Ḍèwèké ora dojan nanas, semono ∗ aku.* He doesn't like pineapple and neither do I. 2 just at [a certain time]. *dina iku ∗* that very day. (*sa*)*iki ∗* right now, this very minute. **sa∗** provided, on condition that. *Aku ja gelem mèlu sa∗ kok traktir.* I'll go [eat] with you if you treat me.

ugah *rg var of* WEGAH

ugal **∗-∗an** to engage in wayward *or* disgraceful behavior

ugeg to move *or* rock back and forth making an effort; *fig* to waver between alternatives. *Matjan mau lagi ∗-∗ arep obah.* The [trapped] tiger struggled to move. **ng/di∗-∗** to move sth back and forth as above. *Pakuné di∗-∗ arep ditjopot.* He wiggled the nail back and forth to pull it out.

ugel **∗-∗** wrist

ugem **ng/di∗** to predict by astrological calculation. **ng/di∗i** to rely on, stand by, be true to. *Wong loro mau paḍa ng∗i aturé ḍéwé²*. Both of them stuck to their stories.

uger 1 rules, regulations. 2 testimony in a civil case. 3 pillar, supporting post. 4 if, provided; whenever, every time (*kr for* ANGGER?). **∗an** pertaining to court testimony. *lajang ∗an* summons, subpoena. **∗-∗** pillar, support. **∗-∗ lawang** a two-boy sibling combination. **ng/di∗** to tie sth to [a post, stake]. **ng/di∗i** 1 to regulate. 2 to take testimony in court. **pa∗an** regulation(s). *Jèn tanpa pa∗an negara bisa rusak.* Without regulation, a nation will fall apart. **sa∗** if, provided; in case. **∗ gugat** testimony of an accuser. **∗ wangsul·an** testimony of a defendant

uget **∗-∗** 1 tiny water worms. 2 mosquito larvae

ugi also, too (*kr for* UGA)

ugil **ugal-∗** to wriggle, squirm. **ng/di·ugal-∗-aké** to move sth this way and that, *e.g.* in an effort to free it

ugreg **ugrag-∗** poorly fitting. **ng/di·ugrag-∗** to move sth this way and that, *e.g.* in an effort to get it into the proper position, *or* in an ill-directed effort to move sth

ugung *rg var of* DURUNG. **∗an** overindulged, spoiled. *botjah ∗an* a spoiled child. **k∗** (*prn*

kogung) to get spoiled *or* overindulged. **ng/di*** to flatter, fawn on

uh *excl of distaste, disgust.* *, *obaté pahit.* Ugh, the medicine is bitter.

uja **ng*-*** to treat smn with scorn *or* contempt (*var of* ÑG-KUJA²)

ujab 1 disturbed, ill at ease. 2 itchy from hair lice. **m* (ati·né)** feeling ill at ease *or* disquieted. **ng/di*** to pull [another woman's hair, in anger]. **ng/di*i** to mix. *Bumbu gudangan kaé ujabana.* Mix the seasonings for the salad.

ujah *ng,* **sarem** *kr* salt. ***-*an** 1 salted. *iwak *-*an* salt fish. 2 *ng kr* a certain leaf used medicinally. **ng/di*aké** *ng kr* to sic [a dog] on smn. *Ḍèké ngingu asu galak kanggo ng*aké wong ala.* He keeps a fierce watchdog to drive off thieves. **ng/di*i** to salt sth. **ngujahi segara** to carry coals to Newcastle. *** amper** fine-grained salt. *** asem** salt and tamarind, for seasoning fish *or* for use as a compress. *Iki djenengé rak lélé marani ujah asem.* This is just asking for trouble! **ng/di*-asem·i** *or* **ng/di*i-asem** 1 to season with salt and tamarind. 2 to praise, *esp.* one's own children *or* belongings; to flatter, fawn on. *** gorèng** spiced fried shredded young coconut meat. *** lembut** fine-grained salt. *** suku** salt in briquets. *** tamper** fine-grained salt. *** tjarat** coarse salt. *** wuku** salt in briquets. *See also* GEBJAH

ujang uneasy, ill at ease. **ng/di*(aké)** to sell [rice]

ujeg complicated and active. ***-*an** to crowd each other. *Wong² sing nunggang paḍa *-*an nang bis.* The passengers were jammed onto the bus. **m*** characterized by complicated activity. *tjrita ḍétèktip sing m** an action-packed, complicated detective story. *rasukan asekar biru m** a blouse patterned with scattered blue flowers. **ng/di*(-*)** 1 to stir (up), agitate. 2 to massage with circular motions

ujel ***-*an** to crowd together, push against each other. **ng/di*-*** 1 to stroke, pat, rub with circular motions. 2 to pick on, be mean to

ujeng *var of* UNJENG

uju ***-*** *oj* pupil, disciple. ***n̂-*n̂** gamelan melody. **mang*-*** (*oj*) *sms* *-*. **ng*-*** to play gamelan melodies

ujug ***-*** unsteady. *Lakuné ujag-*.* He staggered along.

ujuh urine (**toja** *or* **sené** *kr,* **turas** *ki*). **k*an** to get urinated on. **ng*** to urinate. **ng/di*i** to urinate on(to). **pa*an** chamber pot. *See also* KEPOJUH, PUJUH

ujuk ***-*an** to gather around, form a crowd

ujun **ng/di*-*** 1 to engulf sth in a crowd. 2 to protect, safeguard. **sa*** a clump of sugarcane stalks growing from the same plant; *fig* a group of people with a common goal

ujung ***-*** *or* **ujang-*** to carry around *or* back and forth. *Aku jèn pinḍah omah kuwi wegah olèhé ujang-*.* What I hate about moving is lugging things. **ng/di*-*** *or* **ng/di·ujang-*** to carry sth around *or* back and forth. *Ali ng*-* barang²é merga wedi jèn ilang.* Ali carts his luggage around with him for fear of losing it.

ujup ***-*** a folk medicine used by nursing mothers. **ng/di*** to drink the above. **ng/di*aké** 1 to have smn drink the above. 2 to drink from a bowl *or* soup plate

ukanten *sbst kr for* UKARA

ukârâ sentence. *** *iki kramakna.* Put this sentence into Krama.

ukeb *rg var of* UNGKEB. **ng/di*i** to cover sth tightly

ukèh *inf var of* AKÈH

ukel 1 (in the shape of) a coil. 2 counting unit for thread, yarn, fiber. *lawé sa** a skein of thread. 3 ladies' hair style (*ki for* GELUNG). ***-*** *or* **ukal-*** to keep coiling *or* curling. **ng/di*** 1 to shape sth into a coil. 2 to pull a fistful of [smn's hair, in a wajang-style fight]. *** majang** a coil-shaped gesture in the classical dance. *** pakis** 1 a certain variation of the *gelung* hair style. 2 a coil-shaped gesture in the classical dance. 3 repeated coil shapes used as a batik design

uker powdered ochre used as a coloring substance

ukih *intensified form of* AKÈH

ukir ***an** 1 (*or* ***-*an**) carved design. 2 (**djedjer·an** *kr? ki?*) kris handle, *usu.* with decorative carving. **ng/di*** to carve decoratively

uku *var of* WUKU. ***n̂** a silver fifty-cent coin of colonial times. *** mas** gold coin the size of the above (*ukon*), used as an ornament

ukub 1 scented by burning incense. 2 *rg var of* UNGKEB. **ng/di*** to scent sth

ukum 1 law, rule(s). *nglanggar ** to break the law. *manut *é* according to the regulations. *ngèlmu ** jurisprudence. 2 punishment; sentence. **an mati* death penalty.

*wong *an* prisoner; one undergoing punishment. **ng/di*** to inflict a penalty. *Ali di* guru.* The teacher punished Ali. *Di* ḍenḍa Rp 250.* He was fined 250 rupiahs. **pa*an** punishment, sentence. *paukuman kundjara* a jail sentence. **pa·(ng)*an** place *or* equipment for inflicting punishment. *** adat** customary law (as contrasted with codified law). *** badan** corporal punishment. *** ḍenḍa** (penalty in the form of) a fine. *** gantung** death penalty by hanging. *** kisas** death penalty by beheading. *** pati** death penalty, death sentence. *** ullah** divine retribution

ukung *rpr* the cooing of a turtledove

ukur ***an** 1 unit of measurement. *Mèter kuwi *an dawa.* A meter is a measure of length. 2 standard, criterion. *Jèn ngakon uwong kudu nganggo *an.* When you ask someone to do something, you have to take into account his capacity for handling it. **ng/di*** to measure. *ngukur dawané* to measure the length. **sa*** what one would expect. *Menawa Slamet ora munggah ja wis sa* sebab ḍèwèké kesèd.* If Slamet doesn't pass nobody should be surprised—he's so lazy.

ula *ng,* **sawer** *kr* snake. ***-*** backbone, spinal column. ***-* dawa** an increasingly complicated situation. **ng*** snakelike. *** banju** water snake. *** deles** a certain black snake. *** djangan** a non-poisonous snake. *** gaḍung** a certain green snake. *** ng·langi** with back-and-forth motions. *brengos * nglangi* a thick wavy moustache. *Lakuné kaja ula nglangi.* She walks with a swaying gait. **ng*-ng·langi** moving from side to side. *Lakuné pit isih ngula-nglangi.* The bicycle is wobbling. *** naga** dragon, serpent. *** m̃·paran·i gitik** characteristically in the wrong place at the wrong time; always getting into trouble. *** tjabé** a certain small harmless snake

ulad flaring up. **m*-m*** to burn hugely. *geni mulad²* a great blazing fire

ulah 1 way of conducting oneself *or* handling sth. *prigel * gegaman* skilled in the use of weapons. ** kriḍa* handling of things, participation in activities; **-kriḍaning djagat* (*ltry*) world events. ** karosan* exertion of physical strength. ** negara* or ** pradja* statesmanship; *wong * negara* statesman. ** raga* athletics, sports. ** raga aèr* water sports. ** sastra* literature, letters. ** semu* assumed facial expression. 2 to cook (*var of* OLAH). **ng/di*** to handle sth. *Sawisé kabar mau di* nuli ditjétak.* The news was printed soon after it was analyzed.

ulam meat; fish (*kr for* IWAK)

ulâmâ (*or* **ng***) 1 member(s) of the Islamic priesthood. 2 true dedicated Moslem

ulami *sbst kr for* ULAMA

ulang ***an** 1 test, examination. **an umum* final exams. 2 drifting, wandering. *wong *an* rootless person, wanderer. **an tjumbon* servant who frequently deserts his posts. ***-*** to drift jobless, in search of work *or* living off others. **ng/di*** to repeat, do over. *Piḍatoné di* bola-bali.* He kept rehearsing his speech. *** tahun** birthday anniversary. *** ules** to go from place to place trying to find work

ulap ***-*** *oj, wj* to look into the distance shading the eyes with the hand (as a dramatic gesture). **ng/di*-*** *oj, wj* to look at sth in this way. **ng/di*i** to wipe off/away. *ng*i eluhé* to wipe away one's tears

ular ***-*** 1 words of wisdom offered at the beginning of a new venture, *e.g.* marriage. 2 sewing thread. **ng/di*-*i** 1 to advise smn as above. 2 to sew, mend

ulas ***an** comment. **an warta* news commentary. ***-*** 1 external appearance; facial expression. 2 (to say) for the sake of politeness. *"Wah kok ndadak répot² djeng," *-*é Siti.* "Don't put yourself to so much trouble," protested Siti.

ulat (*or* ***an**; **pa·surja·n** *ki*) facial expression. ** sumèh* a friendly, smiling expression. *nginebi ** to have an unwelcoming expression. *Sanadjan kowengani lawang nanging ko inebi ulat.* You open your door to him but not your heart. **m*** 1 to see, observe. 2 to look, appear, seem. 3 on the alert. **ng/di*(-*)aké** *or* **ng/di*(-*)i** to supervise. *ng*i baji* to baby-sit. *Déwan Perwakilan Rakjat iku kewadjibané ng*aké tindakané Pemerintah.* The duty of Parliament is to keep watch over the conduct of the government. **ngulati ala** to cast a disagreeable look at smn. **p*an** (*prn* **polatan** *or* **pulatan**) facial expression. *** m·aḍep ati karep** to want, covet

uleg ***an** ground-up seasonings. ***-*** mortar and pestle used in the kitchen for grinding seasonings. **ng/di*** to grind [spices *etc.*]

ulek̄ ***an** *or* **m*** vortex; *fig* deep down. *wanita kang manisé *an* a girl who is sweet to the very core. *rasa susah *an ing atiné* a profound sadness. **ng/di*-*** to keep handling *or* fussing with; *fig* to keep picking on smn. *Sedina kok ming ng*-* pit waé.* He's spent the whole day tinkering with his bicycle.

ulem (**atur** *ka*) ***an** 1 invited guest. 2 invitation. *kertu *an* a written invitation. ***-*(an)** an invitation to a social event. **ng/di*** to invite smn

uleng 1 inner roof of horizontally placed boards. 2 to hit each other. *gelut ** to have a fist fight. ***-* tjampur-bawur** bunch of mixed flowers for a religious offering. **ulang-*** inseparable. *A karo B pidjer ulang-* nang endi waé.* A and B are together everywhere. ***-*an** 1 to keep hitting each other. 2 to linger, permeate. *Ambuné *-*an.* The odor is pervasive. *Manisé mulek *-*an.* Her sweetness permeates all her actions. 3 to gather, flock together. *Manuk akèh paḍa *-*an.* A flock of birds gathered. **ng/di*** 1 to hit smn during a fight. 2 to embrace

uler 1 caterpillar. 2 counting unit for bananas. *geḍang rong ** two bananas. ***(-*)en** eaten away by caterpillars. **ng*** resembling a caterpillar. *Olèhé njambut-gawé ng*.* He works at a snail's pace. **nguler kilan** [of horses] to gallop. **nguler kambang** drifting with the current, not exerting oneself, taking it easy. *Njambut gawéné nguler kambang.* He works at a very leisurely pace. *nguler kambang satitahé* slow but sure. **nguler kèkèt** [of moustaches] thick and caterpillar-shaped. **ng/di*i** to steal a little at a time. *** djeḍung** a variety of caterpillar. *** kagèt** an S-shaped hook for hanging a lamp. *** kambang** leech. *** kèkèt** measuring worm, inchworm. *** ketèp** a variety of caterpillar

ules 1 the color of sth. *Bunglon molah-malih *é.* Chameleons keep changing color. *batik sing *é ptg tjlonèh* varicolored batik. *Sawah² *é idjo kuning.* The rice paddies were yellowish-green. 2 protective cloth; winding sheet. **ng/di*i** to cover *or* wrap with a cloth. *ng*i bantal* to put a case on a pillow. *** bantal** pillowcase

ulèt *var of* OLÈT

ulet 1 good at, skilled. *Ḍèwèké nèk golèk ḍuwit *.* He's a whiz at making money. 2 tough, hard to break *or* pierce; *fig* not easily discouraged. **ulat-*** 1 to struggle together, wrestle. 2 to talk circuitously. *Olèhé mangsuli ulat-*.* He gave an evasive answer. ***-*an** intertwined, tangled. **ng/di*** to intermix by kneading *or* churning. *ng* djladrèn* to knead dough. **ng/di*aké** to toughen sth. **ng/di*i** to mix into. *Banjuné di*i enḍut.* Mud had been churned into the water.

uli **ula-*** inseparable. *Sak sedulur ula-*.* They're as close as if they were related. **ng/di*-*** *or* **ng/di*ǹi** 1 to mix, blend. *Banjuné diulèni nganggo lenga.* He mixed oil into the water. 2 to pinch between thumb and finger

ulig counting unit for certain round-shaped foods. *sa*...* one [egg roll *etc.*]. ***-*an** (that which is) superior *or* in tip-top condition. *djago *-*an* an A-1 fighting cock. **ng/di*(-*)** 1 to massage, rub the hand over. 2 to whip [*e.g.* a fighting cock] into tip-top shape

ulih *ng,* **antuk** *kr* act of returning home *or* to one's place of origin. *Ulihé ora pati wengi.* He didn't get home very late. ***-*** 1 token of gratitude in return for a donation. 2 offering given to a faith healer in return for his services. ***-*an** to become reconciled [with a divorced spouse]. **ng/di*aké** 1 to return smn to his home *or* place of origin. 2 to return [a borrowed item]. *Iki lho ḍuwit sing daksilih kaé dak *aké.* Here's the money I owe you. **ng/di*-*aké** to keep urging smn to go back; to keep threatening to take smn back. **ng/di*i** to return to [what one has left]. *Ḍèwèké ng*i bodjoné sing wis dipegat.* He went back to his divorced wife. **ng/di*-*i** to bring home gifts (*var of* NG/DI-OLÈH-OLÈH-I). **sa*é** since one's return; as soon as one got back. *See also* MULIH, PULIH

ulik 1 to pick, pry (*root form: var of* UṬIK). 2 to pick lice from each other's hair (*ki for* PÉTAN)

uling a certain large eel. **ng*** to roll, pitch, swing. *Prauné ng*.* The boat pitched and tossed.

ulir bolt; small screw. ***an** 1 screwed on. 2 operated by a rotating knob, valve, *etc.* ***-*an** having threads. *paku *-*an* screw, threaded nail. **ng/di*** to turn [a screw, valve, *etc.*]. *** budi** brain power; **ng* budi** to use one's brains, find a way

ullah God (*var of* ALLAH *in certain fixed expressions*)

ulu 1 *oj* head. 2 leader, head. ***n̂** speaking *or* singing voice. *tekèk mati uloné* doomed by one's own words. ***-* (banju)** village official in charge of irrigation. *mantri* *-* irrigation supervisor. *ñ-*ñ head position [of smn who is lying down: *see also* DAGA·N]. *sawah ulon²* rice paddy that is easily accessible to irrigation during the dry season. **k*** (*prn* **kolu** *or* **kulu**) 1 to get swallowed. *Isiné semangka kolu.* He accidentally swallowed the watermelon seeds. 2 palatable. *Rasané sega mau ora kolu krungu tembung èlèk lagi mangan.* The ugly words I heard while I was eating took away my appetite. 3 willing to do wrong. *Ḍèké kolu didjak wong èlèk kaé.* She did as the bad man wanted. *Kolu matèni kéwan sing ora salah.* He killed an animal that hadn't harmed anyone. **ng/di*(ñi)** to swallow. **ngulu ambek·an** to hold one's breath. **ngulu idu** 1 to swallow (saliva). *Sawisé ng* idu, nuli nerusaké omongé.* He swallowed and went on talking. 2 to have the mouth watering. * **ati** heart. * **balang** commander, military head. * **bekti** *oj* gift to a powerful one. * **guntung** *oj* pupil, disciple

uluh *var of* WULUH

uluk *-* 1 to send up a salvo (of gunfire, fireworks). 2 a message from the king to the premier. 3 *ltry* an issue to be discussed. **m*** 1 to ascend. *muluk ing awang²* to go up in the air. 2 (*or* **m*-m***) high-flown; [of an objective] unrealistically high, unattainable. **ng/di*aké** 1 to make/let fly. *Lajanganku tak *né saiki ja.* I'm going to fly my kite now. 2 to salute smn with a salvo. **ng/di*-*i** to send word ahead, send a message to. * **salam** Islamic welcome/greeting; **ng*i salam** to greet *or* welcome smn in Islamic fashion

ulun *oj* 1 I, me; my. 2 servant, retainer. **mang*** to serve, be a subject of

ulung (*or* *-*) hawk, eagle (*var of* WOLUNG). ***-*an** to exchange, give to each other. *Pengantèn lanang wadon *-*an sega kuning.* The bride and groom exchanged [ceremonial] yellow rice. **m*** to get an unexpected gift. *ati mulung* to be in a generous mood. **ng/di*aké** 1 to give, hand over to. *Rokok di*aké.* Nardi handed him a cigarette. 2 to yield, submit. *Nasibé di*aké marang Kang Kuwasa.* He left his fate in the hands of God. **di*aké enḍas·é di·gonḍèl·i buntut·é** given grudgingly *or* half-heartedly. **ng/di*i** to give, hand over. *Nardi ng*i rokok Sunarko.* Nardi handed Sunarko a cigarette.

ulupis *var of* HOLOPIS

ulur 1 to extend, get let out (*e.g.* rope). 2 *var of* LUR, OLOR. ***an** act of letting out [rope *etc.*]. *-* 1 belly band for a horse. 2 ornamental waist-length necklace. 3 *rg* windstorm. **ng/di*-*** to play for time. *taktik ng*-* wektu* delaying tactics. **ng/di*-(aké)** 1 to let out [rope *etc.*]; to stretch [sth elastic]. 2 to refer [a lawsuit] to a higher court. **ng/di*i** 1 *sms* NG/DI*(AKÉ) 1. 2 to feed. *Sing ng*i wong tuwané anaké mbarep.* The oldest son provides food for his parents.

-um- *infix inserted after initial consonant.* 1 *activates the root meaning.* *l·um·aku* to walk. *l·um·ebu ing omah* to go in the house. *Guruné g·um·uju.* The teacher laughed. *pulo kang k·um·ambang* a floating island. *Kukusé k·em·elun.* The smoke billowed up. 2 (having been) X'ed. *pakarjan kang wis t·um·indak* work that has been done. *désa d·um·unung sapinggiring segara* a village located (placed) beside the sea. *t·em·èmplèk ing témbok* stuck to the wall. *Bareng titihan wis tj·em·awis...* When his horse had been made ready... 3 (to produce) the sound *or* effect represented by the root meaning. *Krungu swara dj·um·egur, g·um·luḍug.* They heard a thundering splashing sound. *Intené g·em·ebjar.* The diamond sparkled. 4 to behave in the manner of the root; considered (*or* considering oneself) as having the characteristic of the root. *g·um·eḍé* conceited, boastful. *s·um·anak* friendly. 5 just at the ideal stage (for) [the root meaning]. *Kolang-kaling iku jèn wajahé d·em·egan diunḍuhi.* This coconut meat is just right for eating now. 6 (*in second member of doubled root*) to [do] repeatedly. *turun-t·um·urun* to descend from generation to generation. *tangkar-t·em·angkar* to keep multiplying/flourishing/reproducing. *See also listings under individual entries; see also under* GUM-, KUM- *for* B-, P-, *and* W-*initial roots having -um- infix*

umah *rg var of* OMAH

uman to receive [what others receive]. *Ora * panduman apa².* He didn't get a portion at all. *Merga telat, ora * papan.* He was so late he didn't get a seat. **k*an** to be given [what others are given]. *Sanadyan ora k*an ja meneng baé.* Even though he didn't get any, he never spoke up. **ng/di*-*** to speak harshly to *or* about smn. **ng/di*i** to give out, dole out. *Aku ora di*i sega.* I wasn't given my portion of rice. *Ora ng*-*i sing enom.* He didn't give anything at all to the young people. **pa·ng*-*** a tongue-lashing

umat 1 the man in the street; the common people. 2 the community of true Moslems, in Java and throughout the world

umbah ***-* 1** to wash; to launder. *banju *-** water to be used for laundry. 2 having a menstrual period. *See also* KUMBAH

umbar ***an** (on the) loose. *asu *an* a stray dog. ***-*an** to do as one pleases, indulge oneself. **ng/di*** to let loose, leave unattended. *Pitiké *en.* Let the chicken loose. *Jèn pilek adja bandjur di* kesuwèn.* If you have a cold, don't let it go too long. *Anaké di* sakarepé ḍéwé.* He lets his son do anything he pleases. **ng* hawa** to indulge one's passions. **ng* kuntja** to loosen *or* spread one's batik wraparound to facilitate walking. **ng* suku** to go where the feet take one. **ng* swara** to boast, brag. **ng* tangan** to pick pockets

umbel *ng kr,* **gaḍing** *ki* (having) mucous, *esp.* in the nose

umbjung **ng/di*i** to accompany

umbleg *see* SADJEG

umblug **ng*** foamy, frothy. **ng/di*aké** to brag about sth, show sth off

umbruk 1 heap, pile. 2 a bet placed in the 'kitty.' ***(-*)an** *or* ***-*** *or* **m*** *or* **ng*(-*)** heaped, piled. *Ṭukulané *-*.* The plants lay in piles. *Sesukeré ng*.* The dung was heaped up. *dibuwang ng*-** thrown into the discard pile. **ng/di*aké** to heap [things] up. **sa*-*** in piles. *Ḍèké mulih saka pasar nggawa blandjan sa*-*.* She came home from the marketplace carrying heaps of purchases.

umbul ***-*** banners. **k*** (*prn* **kombul** *or* **kumbul**) 1 to get carried up in the air. 2 famous, well known. **m*** to ascend. *Baloné m* ing awang².* The balloon rose up in the air. *Balé ditépang m*.* He kicked the ball high. *m*ing rokèt* a rocket launching. **ng/di*aké** to raise, cause to ascend. *ng*aké balon* to launch a balloon. *Mretjoné di*-aké supaja mbleḍos.* He tossed the firecracker so it would go off in midair.

umbut 1 young rattan plant. 2 palm pith

umed ***-*** *or* **umad-*** to mouthe words; to mumble, mutter. **ng/di*-*aké** to move [the mouth] shaping words as if speaking

umek ***-*** [of people jabbering] loud, noisy; [of water] gurgling

umel **ng/di*-*i** to scold, grumble at

umès *var of* UMES

umes soggy, damp

umet ***-*an** to rotate, spin. **k*** (*prn* **komet**) bewildered, muddled. **m*** (**pujeng** *kr*) dizzy, groggy. **ng*aké** causing dizziness, headache, bewilderment. **ng/di*-*aké** to set sth rotating

umi:k ***-*** *or* **umak-*** to form soundless words. *Lambéné umak-*.* His lips mouthed words. *Ḍukun ngobong menjan karo umak-*.* The witch doctor burned incense and muttered. **ng*-*** *or* **ng·umak-*** to move [the lips] as above

umi:l *var of* UMIK

umjang *var of* OMJANG

umjung loud, boisterous

ummat *var sp of* UMAT

umob boiling vigorously. *lenga ** boiling oil. **ng*** to bring to a boil. **ng/di*aké** to cause to boil, bring to a boil

umok [of rivers] at flood level

umor 1 to feel nauseated. 2 *oj* (along) with; mixed. **ng*-*i** nauseating

umos porous. *genṭong ** an earthenware pitcher that water seeps out of

umpak 1 stone block used as the base of a pillar. 2 flattery, praise, flowery language. ***an** easily swayed by flattery. ***-*** 1 flattery. 2 transitional melody played between stanzas *or* repetitions of a song. **ng/di*** to praise, flatter, fawn on. **ng/di*i** to furnish [pillars] with stone bases. **pa·ng*** use of flowery language. *tembung pangumpak* sweet persuasive words. *** deder·ing tjuriga** kris part between handle and blade

umpal raft made of banana-tree wood. ***-*an** sth floating. **m*-m*** *or* **ng*-*** churning, turbulent. *Banjuné umob mumpal².* The water was boiling vigorously. *alun mumpal²* turbulent waves

umpan bait (*lit, fig*)

umpeg ***-*** short and fat

umpel ***-*an** sticking close to each other. *Sing nunggang bis okèh banget nganti *-*an.* The bus was jammed with passengers. **m*** to adhere to; to stick together. **ng*** to stay in the same place, stick around

umpeng narrow water channel

umpet ***an** 1 to hide, take cover. 2 hide-and-seek. **m*** to hide, conceal oneself. **ng/di*aké** to hide sth

um-pim-pah an informal method by which more than two people settle something:

played like UM-PING-SUT (*below*), except that with the count of *pah* all bring down a flat hand, either palm down *or* palm up: matching palms, the odd man is out, and the process is repeated until all but two have been eliminated

um-ping-su:t an informal method by which two people settle something: each raises his fist and brings it down in midair three times, counting *um, ping, sut:* with the syllable *sut,* each extends either a thumb (elephant), index finger (human being), or little finger (ant)–elephant wins over human being, human being wins over ant, ant wins over elephant

umpling 1 small kerosene lamp. 2 cone-shaped salty rice cake wrapped in coconut leaf. 3 tube-shaped opium container

umpluk suds, foam, froth. **m*** frothy, sudsy. **ng/di*aké** to make suds from/with. *ng*aké sabun* to swish soap around making suds

umplung cuspidor, spittoon

umpruk *var of* UMBRUK, UMPLUK

umpuk ***-*an** (to heap) in a pile. *Bukuné *-*an nang médja.* The books are piled up on his desk. **ng/di*-*** to pile. *ng*-* peṭi nang guḍang* to stack crates in a warehouse

umreg noisy, bustling, crowded

umuk to boast about oneself *or* one's possessions. ***-*an** to brag to each other, engage in one-upmanship. **ng/di*aké** *or* **ng/di*i** to boast about sth

umum 1 common. *kawruh ** common knowledge. *Tembung Éropah * ing Indonesia.* European words are commonplace in Indonesia. 2 public. *ing papan ** in a public place. *penemuning ** public opinion. *ḍokter ** general practitioner. 3 the public, the people. ***é** usually, commonly. **ng*** *ltry var of **. **ng/di*aké 1 (n/di·ḍawuh·aké** *ki*) to make public. *Guruné ng*aké bidjiné.* The teacher announced the marks. *Kuṭa mau wis di*aké ketularan koléra.* The city has been declared in a state of cholera epidemic. 2 to popularize. **pa·ng*an** public announcement, proclamation

umun ***-*** *intsfr* early. *ésuk *-** bright and early; before sunrise

umung *var of* UMJUNG

umur *ng kr,* **juswa** *ki* 1 (years of) age. **mu pira?* How old are you? **é kurang luwih enem taun.* He's about six. 2 time span; life span. *Pandjang juswanipun.* He had a long life. *Sapar *é 29 dina.* There are 29 days in (the month of) Sapar. 3 old, aged. ***-*an** 1 approximate age. **-*ané wis setengah tuwa.* She was roughly middle-aged. 2 comparative age. **-*ané si A karo si B tuwa si A.* A is older than B. **sa*ing djagung** (for) a very short time [*corn comes to maturity in about* $3^1/_2$ *months*]. **wis *** of age; to have become an adult. **durung *** under age

un *var of* HUN

unandika **ng*** to say *or* talk to oneself, to think out loud. **pa·ng*** what smn says to himself

unang *var of* ONANG

unar *var of* ONAR

unḍa **ng/di*(-*)** 1 to have/let fly. 2 to flourish [a weapon]. **pa·ng*n** string by which a bird *or* kite is flown. *** usuk** nearly the same

unḍag *inf var of* UNḌAGI

unḍagi 1 carpenter, woodworker. 2 skilled. *Bab njungging ḍèké wis *.* He's good at painting puppets.

unḍak *ng,* **inḍak** *kr* a rise, an increase. **ing blandja* a pay raise. ***an** 1 a supplement, an increase. *Aku éntuk *an gadjih satus rupiah.* I got a 100-rupiah raise. 2 *oj* horse, mount. ***-*an 1** stairs, stairway. *munggah *-*an* to go upstairs. 2 road edge, shoulder. **ka*an 1** to be surpassed. *Ḍèwèké tansah mbudidaja adja nganti ka*an kepinterané.* He always does his best so that nobody will outdo him. 2 to get overcharged. *Aku ka*an limang sèn.* I paid five cents too much. **m* 1** to increase, become greater. *Gawéanku m* terus.* My work load keeps increasing. *m* apik* (*utawa èlèk*) to get better (or worse). 2 to rise in rank. *m* saka klas sidji* to get promoted from first grade. **ng/di*aké** 1 to raise sth. *Pangkatku di*ké.* I got a promotion. *ng*aké pametuné pertanian* to increase agricultural production. *ng*aké kawruh* to add to one's knowledge. *ng*aké rega* to raise prices. 2 to exaggerate. **ng/di*i** to increase sth. *Aku di*i pangkatku.* I got a promotion. *Geḍé gambaré karo wudjudé, di*i saṭékruk.* The description exceeds the fact: it's been exaggerated.

unḍâmânâ **ng/di*** to give smn a tongue-lashing

undang *ng kr,* **timbal** *ki,* **atur** *ka* ***-* 1** to keep calling (to). *Adja *-* aku waé, aku wis krungu.* Don't keep calling me–I heard.

2 to invite. ***-*an** what smn is called. *Djenengé Basuki, *-*ané Tjuk.* His name is Basuki, but he's called Tjuk. **k*an** (*prn* **kondangan** *ng*) to attend a ritual feast (for a marriage, circumcision, *etc.*) at smn's invitation. **ng/di*(i)** to call (to). *Apa wis ng* ḍokter?* Have you sent for the doctor? *Undangen mréné.* Call him over here. *ngundangi djeneng* to call the roll. *Ng*-*i bodjoné.* He kept calling to his wife. **ng* kaum** 1 to ask a *kaum*'s advice on Islamic matters, *or* call a *kaum* to deliver a prayer at a ceremony. 2 to give up on sth one cannot get the answer to. *Wis suwé kok ora kok batang*[2] *tjangkrimané, ng* kaum apa pije?* All this time you've been guessing wrong on that conundrum—why don't you give up?

unḍang (*or* ***-***) regulation, law. *nglanggar *-** to break the law *or* the rules. *rantjangan ** proposed legislation. ***-* Ḍasar** (*abbr:* **U.U.D.**) the Indonesian Constitution. **ng/di*aké** to order, proclaim. *Pamaréntah ng*aké angger*[2] *sing nglarang ukuman mati.* The government has issued a decree forbidding capital punishment. *Partai mau di*aké dadi partai larangan.* The political party in question has been outlawed. **ng/di*i** to issue official information *or* orders to. *Rakjat wis di*i jèn reganing pangan bakal munḍak.* The public has been advised that food prices are going up.

unḍat **ng/di*-*** to rake up past mistakes, engage in recriminations

under ***(-*)an** heart, core, center. **ng/di*i** to encircle. *ng*i titik* to make a circle around a dot

unḍer **ng*** to remain in the same place. *Adja ming ng* nang ndjeron omah waé.* Don't just hang around the house! **ng/di*i** to stay around for a purpose. *Ng*i apa ta?* What are you hanging around for?

unḍi **unḍa-*** almost the same. *Umuré A unḍa-* karo umuré B.* A is just about the same age as B. **ng/di*** to decide by lot. *Di* sapa sing menang.* The winner was decided by drawing lots.

undjal (*or* **ng***) to let out [the breath]. *Undjal ambekan, djebul ora apa*[2]. He let out his breath—nothing had gone wrong after all. *Ḍèké * napas djero.* She sighed deeply. **ng*-*** [of babies] to kick the legs

undjel ***-*an** crowded with jostling people. **ng*-*** to jostle, elbow, shove

undjuk 1 what smn says (to an exalted person) [*ka: ltry, court style*]. *weling ** a message sent (to an exalted person) by word of mouth. 2 to drink (*root form: ki for* OMBÉ). ***-*** *ka* gift to an exalted person. **k*** (*prn* **kondjuk** *or* **kundjuk**) *ka* to give, submit (to an exalted person). *Serat kondjuk ing ngarsanipun Rama.* My dear Father (*salutation of a letter*). **m*** 1 *ka* to say. *Patihé m* ing Sang Nata, aturé...* The official said to the King... *m* sendika* to accept a command and be ready and willing to carry it out. 2 to move to a higher position. *Turuné m*.* He hitched himself higher up on the pillow as he slept. **ng/di*aké** 1 *ka* to submit, present. 2 to raise, elevate. *Olèhmu nggénḍong baji kuwi mbok di*aké.* Carry the baby a little higher up on your back. **ng*(-*)i uninga** *ka* to inform, notify

undjung ***an** leaf (*kr for* GOḌONG?). **m*-m*** heaped up, forming piles. **ng/di*(-*)aké** to pile [things] up

unḍuh ***an** 1 thing picked. *Geḍang iki apa *ané ḍéwé?* Did you pick this banana yourself? 2 second wedding celebration, held at the groom's home. ***-*an** act of picking. *Pelem iki gampang *-*ané.* These mangoes are easy to pick. **ng/di*-*** *or* **ng/di·unḍah-*** to pick repeatedly; to harvest many things. *Bareng tanduran wis dadi, saiki kari ngunḍah-* waé.* Now that the plants have ripened, all we have to do is pick the fruit. **ng/di*aké** to pick for smn. **ng/di*(i)** to pick [fruits *etc.*]; *fig* to reap [results]. *ng* tawon* to get honey from a beehive. *ng* wohing penggawéané* to harvest the fruits of one's labor. **ng* lajang·an** to disentangle a stuck kite. **ng* mantu** to have *or* acquire a son- *or* daughter-in-law. **ng* (pengantèn)** to convey the bride and groom to the groom's home for a second wedding celebration. *Kapan olèhé di*?* When are the newlyweds to be taken to the groom's home? **pa·ng*** act *or* way of picking *or* harvesting. *nggampangaké pengunḍuhé woh* to facilitate picking the fruit

unḍuk **k*an** (a place that is) hidden from view. *Botjahé umpetan ing k*an.* The child hid in a concealed place. *Tengeré k*an alang*[2]. The marker is covered over with shrubs. **m*-m*** to keep low and under cover. *Wong loro mau mlaju munḍuk*[2] *ing pamrih adja nganti konangan lijan.* The two men crouched as they ran so as not to be seen. *Munḍuk^2 njeḍaki aku.* He approached me bowing deeply. **ng/di∗(-∗)i** to approach under cover, sneak up on

unḍung **m∗-m∗** to exist in abundance. *Barangé munḍung^2.* He has a great many possessions. **ng/di∗-∗** to amass in abundance. *Beras sepirang-pirang di∗-∗ nang pelabuhan.* Great quantities of rice were piled up at the harbor.

undur (**lèngsèr** *ki?*) backward motion; withdrawal. *adju-∗ing politik* political progress and regression. **∗-∗** 1 a certain insect that walks backwards. 2 a tool for drilling/boring. **k∗an** to get backed into. *Aku mau mèh waé k∗an truk.* A truck nearly backed into me. **k∗an pa·laras·an** to leave without saying goodbye. **séda k∗an** *ki* to die in childbirth. **m∗** to withdraw, retreat, back away, move backwards. **ng/di∗** 1 to postpone. *Pemilihan umum tansah di∗-∗ waé.* They kept postponing the general election. *ng∗-∗ wektu* to employ delaying tactics. 2 to demote; to discharge. **ng/di∗aké** 1 to cause to go backward. *Djamé di∗aké.* He set his watch back. *Mungsuhé di∗aké.* They turned back the enemy. 2 to postpone sth. **ng/di∗-∗aké** to take [things] back. *Piringé di∗-∗aké kana, bandjur diasah pisan.* Clear the table and wash the dishes. **ng/di∗i** to back into *or* away from. *Mungsuhé di∗i.* They retreated from the enemy. *Motoré ng∗i asuné nganti mati.* The car backed into the dog and killed it. **ng∗i tuwa** to grow old

uneg **∗-∗en** *or* **m∗-m∗** queasy, nauseated. **ng/di∗-∗i** to cause a feeling of nausea. **pa·ng∗-∗** 1 sth one yearns to have. 2 feelings of ill will. *Panguneg-unegku menjang kowé tak tjritakké nang kowé bèn kowé ngerti.* I'll tell you what I have against you so that you'll understand.

unem spice container

uneng *var of* ONENG

ungak **∗-∗** to crane the neck in an effort to see; *fig* to consider the situation. **ng/di∗** to look at with craned neck. **ng/di∗-∗i** to keep craning the neck in search of sth

ungal *var of* UNGEL. **m∗** 1 protruding (*esp.* of the chest). *ḍaḍa m∗* with chest out. *watu sing m∗* a protruding rock. 2 to turn up the flame in an oil lamp. **ng/di∗aké** 1 to thrust forward [the chest]. 2 to brighten [an oil lamp]

ungas **k∗** (*prn* **kongas**) fragrant; *fig* illustrious at the moment, currently in the limelight. *filem stèr^2 sing ora pati kongas* obscure film stars. **ng/di∗-∗** to take whiffs of. **ng/di∗aké** to show sth off

ungel sound, noise; what smn/sth says (*kr for* UNI[a])

unggah *ng,* **inggah** *kr* a rise. *∗ing pangkat* a rise in rank, a promotion. **∗an** act of ascending. **∗-∗an** 1 means of ascent. *∗-∗ané ana papat.* There are four staircases. 2 promotion time at the end of a school year. 3 act of getting on top. *Djarané angèl ∗-∗ané.* The horse is hard to mount. *Jèn wis ngetjulaké rembug, angèl ∗-∗ané.* When he argues, it's hard to get the better of him. **m∗** 1 to rise, ascend. *Ajo paḍa m∗ saka wétan kana sa∗an.* Let's go up the east side this time [for a change]. *Banju ing kali kuwi m∗ nganti pirang^2 mèter.* The water rose many meters. *Rega panganan saiki wis m∗ ping pinḍo.* Food prices have doubled. *Dalané m∗ muḍun.* The road goes up and down. 2 to rise in rank. *Ḍèwèké ora m∗.* He didn't get promoted. **m∗ hadji/kadji** 1 to have made the pilgrimage to Mecca. 2 to profess one's faith. **m∗ papah·an** to marry the older sister of one's divorced *or* deceased wife. **ng/di∗aké** 1 to elevate sth. *A ng∗aké pangkaté B.* A gave B a promotion in rank. *Gambaré unggahna seṭiṭik.* Hang the picture a little higher. *ng∗aké padjeg lan reregan* to increase taxes and prices. 2 to put into storage. *Pariné sing wis garing wis di∗aké lumbung kabèh?* Is the dried rice all stored in the barn? **ng/di∗i** 1 to climb (on). *ng∗i gunung* to climb a mountain. 2 to top, exceed. *Aku ora bisa ng∗i rembugmu.* I can't top your argument. *Ana sing ng∗i pangan-jangku.* Someone else bid higher than I did. 3 (*or* **ng/di∗-∗i**) [of girls] to propose marriage to [a man]

unggar **ng/di∗(aké)** to release, unfold, give vent to. *ng∗aké karep* to do as one pleases

ungguh **unggah-∗** manners, etiquette. **unggah-∗ing basa** the social styles of Javanese speech used according to the social relationships among the speakers (*see Introduction, 5*). **ng/di·unggah-∗aké** to have smn behave properly. *Bapaké ngunggah-∗aké anaké.* The father told his son to mind his manners. **∗ tatakrama** manners, etiquette

unggul superior, outstanding. **∗an** contestant favored to win. **∗-∗an** to compete for supremacy. **ka∗an** supremacy, eminence.

m∗ superior, outstanding. **ng/di∗(-∗)aké** 1 to raise, elevate. 2 to consider superior *or* exalted. **ng/di∗i** to defeat, overcome

unggun campfire

ungik **ungak-∗** to hesitate, waver

ungkab **m∗** gaping open. **ng/di∗i** 1 to uncover, open. 2 to show sth off

ungkal whetstone, grindstone. **ng∗** 1 resembling a whetstone. *ngungkal gerang* (*ltry*) lantern-jawed. 2 (*psv* **di∗**) to sharpen [a blade] on a whetstone

ungkang *var of* ONGKANG

ungkat **ng/di∗-∗** to dwell on disagreeable past experiences

ungkeb **∗-∗** to lie face down. **ng/di∗** to cook *or* store [foods] in covered containers

ungkeg **ungkag-∗** a back-and-forth motion in the same spot. *Ḍèwèké ungkag-∗ ndudut paku.* He's trying to work the nail out. **ng/di∗-∗** *or* **ng/di·ungkag-∗** to keep moving sth back and forth to dislodge it. *ngungkag-∗ montor sing ora bisa madju* to rock a stuck car. *See also* UNGKREG

ungker 1 butterfly cocoon. 2 spool of thread

ungkih **k∗** (*prn* **kongkih**) to falter under pressure. **ng/di∗** 1 to push sth aside. 2 to move toward sth

ungkil **ng/di∗** to pry (out, up, open). *ng∗ ban* to remove a tire from a wheel. *ng∗ paku gedé seka témbok* to pry a large nail from the wall. *ng∗ peṭi nganggo linggis* to pry open a crate with a crowbar

ungkir **m∗** to deny, disavow. *m∗ djandji* to go back on a promise. *Maling mau m∗ menawa njolong pit.* The thief denied stealing the bicycle. **ng/di∗i** to refuse to acknowledge sth. *ng∗i djandji* to fail to keep a promise

ungkrah **ng/di∗-∗** to disarrange, put into disorder

ungkred **m∗** to shrink. **ng/di∗** to shrink *or* decrease sth; *fig* to cheat by giving short weight

ungkreg **ungkrag-∗** to move with difficulty in a tight spot. *Lawangé ketjiliken, ḍèké ungkrag-∗ ora bisa metu.* The door was so narrow he couldn't squeeze through. *Lakuning bis mung ungkrag-∗ waé.* The bus crawled along at a snail's pace. **ng/di·ungkrag-∗** to move sth back and forth. *Aku ngungkrag-∗ latji sing angèl dibukak kuwi.* I tried to work open the tight drawer. *See also* UNGKEG

ungkul exceeding. *Kekuwatanmu luwih ∗ tinimbang aku.* You're stronger than I am. **k∗an** (*prn* **kongkulan** *or* **kungkulan**) exceeded *or* surpassed by. *Ḍuwuré k∗an aḍiné.* His younger brother is taller than he is. **ng/di∗aké** to exceed, surpass. **ng/di∗i** to exceed, surpass. *Ajuné ora ana sing ng∗i.* No one is as beautiful as she is. *Larané atiku ng∗i lara tatuku iki.* The pain in my heart overshadowed the pain of my wound.

ungkung odds-on favorite, front runner

ungkur **∗-∗an** back-to-back. *Omah loro mau ∗-∗an.* The two houses are back to back. **ng/di∗aké** *or* **ng/di∗i** to turn one's back on; to have sth at one's back *or* behind one. *Ḍèké tansah ng∗i anaké.* He gave his son the cold shoulder. *Negara mau ngarepaké segara, ng∗aké gunung.* The country has the sea in front of it and mountains behind it. **sa∗é** after smn's departure *or* (*fig*) death. *Sa∗mu omahku dadi sepi.* Our house was lonely after you left. *See also* PUNGKUR

ungseb **k∗** (*prn* **kongseb**) to fall face down. **ng/di∗-∗aké** to press one's face to the ground

ungsed **ng/di∗** to move (in some direction). *di∗ memburi* to be moved back(ward). *Ng∗ siṭik, aku péngin linggih.* Inch over, I want to sit down.

ungsel *var of* USEL

ungser **ng/di∗aké** to spin *or* twirl sth

ungsi **∗ǹ** (that which is) used for refuge. *omah ungsèn* a home for refugees. **ng∗** 1 to flee. *ng∗ urip* (*pangan*) or *ng∗ golèk panguripan* to run for one's life. 2 to go away to [do]. *ng∗ manggon* to live smw else. *ng∗ njambut-gawé* to go smw else to work. *ng∗ mangan* to eat out. **ng/di∗k̀aké** to remove smn from [a threatened area]. *mBakju aḍi diungsèkaké ing omahé A.* He sent his brothers and sisters to A's home for safety. **ng/di∗ǹi** to flee to. *Aku ngungsèni désa.* I escaped to the village. **pa·ng∗** a refugee. **pa·ng∗ǹ** a place of refuge. *désa pengungsèn* a village where people take refuge

ungsil *var of* USIL

ungsir *var of* USIR

ungsum *var of* USUM

ungup **∗-∗** to peek, peep. *∗-∗ seka tjenḍéla* to peek out the window. **m∗** to show a little, begin to appear. *Kuntjupé kembang wis mungup²*. The flower buds are beginning to come out. *Djam 5:30 srengéngéné* *wis m∗ seka wétan.* By 5:30 the sun had begun to rise in the east. **m∗-m∗** to peek, peep. **ng/di∗aké** to show sth a little. *Tikus mau ng∗aké sirahé seka bolongan.* The mouse poked its head out of the hole.

uni[a] *ng,* **ungel** *kr* 1 sound, noise. *∗né gamelan* the sound of gamelan music. 2 what smn/sth says. *∗né djam sewelas.* [The clock] says 11:00. *∗né pije?* What does it say? What did he say? What kind of noise did it make? *Tekèk mau ∗né tekèk, tekèk.* The green lizard goes *tekèk, tekèk. Ḍèké ora manut marang ∗ning unḍang².* He doesn't pay any attention to what the regulations say. *kakéhan ∗* to talk too much. *ora duwé ∗* to never complain. **∗ǹ-∗ǹ 1** a saying. *Ana unèn²: wektu iku ḍuwit.* There's a saying that time is money. 2 what smn *or* sth says. *Gambar iḍup mau unèn²é basa Inggris.* The film captions were in English. **m∗** to say; to emit sounds. *Ing batin m∗...* He said to himself... *Ukara iki m∗ keprijé?* What does this sentence say? *Pringé paḍa m∗: geriiit².* The bamboo trees went creak-creak. *Gamelané wis m∗.* The gamelan music has begun. *m∗ sakenjoh-kenjohé* to blurt things out unthinkingly. **m∗-m∗ 1** to complain. 2 (**duka** *ki*) to speak angrily. **muna-m∗ (mungal-m·ungel** *kr*) to say over and over. *Saking senengé pidjer muna-muni.* He was so pleased he couldn't stop talking about it. **ng/di∗k̀aké** 1 to cause sth to produce sound. *ngunèk-aké goprak* to rattle a noisemaker for scaring off birds. *ngunèkaké suling* to play a pipe. *ngunèkaké beḍil* to fire a gun. 2 to say *or* read aloud. *Aku ngunèkaké lajang.* I read the letter out loud. **ng/di∗k̀-∗k̀aké** to complain loudly about. *Jèn renḍet seṭiṭik waé bandjur diunèk-unèkaké.* If she was just a little bit slow, she got yelled at. **ng/di∗ǹ(-∗ǹ)i** to speak harshly to. *Nèk djarané mogok diunèn-unèni.* When the horse fell exhausted, he yelled at it abusively. **sa∗-∗né 1** whatever one says. *Sauni-uniku salah.* Everything I say is wrong. 2 whatever one feels like babbling. *Baji kuwi mung m∗ sa∗-∗né waé.* Babies "talk" by making random noises.

uni[b] 1 (*or* **∗-∗** *or* **ng∗[-∗]**) former times. 2 (*or* **∗-bengi**) yesterday. *See also* WINGI

uni:k̄ unique

uning *var of* UNINGA

uninga 1 to know, understand (*ki for* NGERTI). 2 to see; to know (*ki for* WERUH). *(ng)atur(i) ∗* to tell, inform. **ka∗n** *ki, ltry* it is known. *Ka∗n bilih bulan punika umuripun majuta-juta tahun.* The moon is known to be millions of years old. **ka∗na** look here! let me tell you...! (*ki for* WERUH·A). **ng/di∗kaké** to make known. *Wis di∗kaké jèn bakal ana udan geḍé.* We've been informed that there's a big storm on the way. **ng/di∗ni** to know sth. *ng∗ni marang* to know of. *Perlu ng∗ni isiné buku iki.* You should know what's in this book.

univèrsitas university. *∗ Indonesia* the University of Indonesia (in Djakarta). *∗ Gadjah Mada* Gadjah Mada University (in Jogjakarta)

unja *oj* sound, noise

unjal **∗-∗an** fidgety, unable to sit still

unjar *rg* bundle, bunch [of plants]. **ng/di∗i** to bind [plants] in bundles

unjeng **∗-∗(an)** *ng kr,* **panengeran** *ki* **1** crown of the head. 2 the point on the crown of the head from which the hair growth radiates outward in all directions. **3** mark on an animal's hair similar to 2 above. **m∗** to spin, rotate

unjer **m∗** to spin, rotate. **ng∗-∗** to keep recurring in the same spot. *Rématikku kumat, krasa ng∗-∗ nang geger.* My rheumatism is bothering me—I keep having stabbing pains in the back. **ng/di∗-∗aké** to encircle. *Taliné di∗-∗aké nang wit.* He wound the rope around and around the tree.

unjet **ng/di∗-∗** to crush, squeeze

unjik the loser, the last one. **∗an** to come in last, to get the booby prize

unjug **∗-∗** *or* **unjag-∗** (to walk) in a brash and inconsiderate way. **m∗-m∗** *or* **munjag-m∗** to barge in, to sneak in unannounced. *Kena apa kowé munjuk² réné?* What the hell are you doing here?

unsur element. *∗ kimiawi* chemical element

unta camel. *manuk ∗* ostrich

untab outpouring of people. *∗ing wong ptg bilulung.* There was pandemonium as the people dispersed. **∗-∗an 1** to walk in single file. 2 [to be *or* do] almost the same, almost simultaneous(ly). *Tekané A ∗-∗an karo B.* A got here right after B. *Barang A karo B ∗-∗an.* Items A and B are very similar. **m∗** to pour out. *M∗ nepsuné.* He lost his temper. **ng/di∗aké 1** to see off *or* escort [a departing person]. *Ḍèké dak ∗aké tekan latar.* I went as far as the yard with him.

*Ḍèké ng*aké obahing bétjak kang wiwit alon² mlaku.* He stayed until her pedicab moved off slowly. 2 *ltry* to kill

untal **k*** to get swallowed. *Widjiné k**. He accidentally swallowed the seed. **ng/di*(i)** 1 to swallow whole. *ng* pil* to take a pill. 2 *cr* to eat

untar pimple, boil (*ki for* WUDUN)

untârâ *ng,* **untawis** *kr* 1 between, among (*var of* ANTARA). 2 *oj* north. 3 *oj* left (as contrasted with right). **ng/di*ni** to indicate, show. *Padésan wiwit obah, ng*ni jèn wis bangun ésuk.* The village came to life, a sign that day was breaking. **sa*** some (amount *or* interval of) time. *Wis sa* durung bisa merlokké sowan para tuwa.* I haven't managed to visit my parents for quite a while. *Aku kesel banget, arep turu sa* baé.* I'm very tired–I'm going to take a nap for a while. *Bapak rawuh djam pitu, let sa* terus ḍahar.* Father arrived home at seven, and after a while he ate dinner. *** segara** *ltry* abroad, over the seas

untawis *kr for* UNTARA

untek̄ ***-*an** *or* **m*** [of insects in a swarm] forming a bunch. *Tawoné *-*an ana susuhé.* The bees are crammed together in the hive.

untel ***-*an** forming an untidy heap. **m*** to stay close. *Olèhé turu m**. They slept close together. *Ḍèwèké m* ana ngomah.* He sticks close to home. **ng/di*-*** to rumple, crumple [*esp.* clothing]

unṭel **ng/di*-*** to wind sth carelessly *or* casually. *Ḍèwèké ng*-* rambuté.* She wound her hair in an erratic way (rather than in the traditional smooth bun).

unṭer 1 a creeping-vine batik pattern. 2 *var of* UNḌER. **ng/di*i** to apply the above pattern to batik

unṭet **ng/di*** to withhold. *Ḍèké ng* ḍuwit blandjan.* She kept out money from the household accounts. *ng* bab² sing ora njenengaké* to hold back the unpleasant facts

until bunch, bundle. **ng/di*i** to tie [*esp.* plants] into bundles

unting measure for harvested plants: the number that can be held in a bunch in the two hands with fingertips touching. ***an** (tied) in such bunches. **ng/di*i** to bundle [plants] in handful-sized bunches

untir **ng/di*** to hold sth firmly and twist it. *See also* PUNTIR

untjal long narrow sash worn as part of a classical dancer's costume. ***-*an** to toss back and forth. *A lan B *-*an bal.* A and B played catch. **ng/di*aké** *or* **ng/di*i** to toss

untjar a spray [of water]; a beam [of light]. **m*** [of water] to spray; [of light] to shine

untjeg piercing tool, awl. **ng/di*(i)** to make hole(s) with such an implement. ** iku nggo ng*i.* An awl is for making holes.

untjit ***-*an** to chase each other. **ng/di*-*** to chase sth/smn

untjlang **ng/di*(aké)** 1 to toss, flip. 2 to transfer smn against his will

untjlug ***-*an** unexpectedly, without forewarning. *Si A *-*an teka mréné.* A dropped in unexpectedly. **ng*** to walk with quick short steps and downcast eyes

untjlung *var of* UNTJLUG

untjrat **m*** to spurt up/out. **ng/di*i** to spurt onto

untjrit ***-*en** thin and sickly

untjul **m*** to emerge, come to the fore. *m* dadi negara geḍé* to emerge as a great nation. **ng/di*aké** to cause to emerge, bring to the fore

untjung small peacock (young of the MERAK)

untjuwé, untjuwi *var of* HUNTJUWÉ

untu 1 **(wadja** *or* **waos** *ki*) tooth. *aksara ** dental consonant (*T, D, N, S*). 2 cog, serration. 3 rung of a ladder. ***n̂** (that which is) tooth-shaped. *djagung saunton* a kernel of corn. ***n̂-*n̂** series of cogs *or* teeth. *roḍané geḍé nganggo unton²* the large toothed wheel. **ng*** resembling a tooth *or* cog. **ng/di*n̂-*n̂i** to equip with gears *or* cogs. *** palsu** false teeth. *** sopak·an** fake teeth. *** tengah** incisor, front tooth. *** walang** object in the shape of grasshopper teeth. *dondoman * walang* zigzag stitching. **ng*-walang** 1 resembling grasshopper teeth. 2 (*psv* **di*-walang)** to mesh [metal parts] with gears *or* cogs; to plant [things] in a zigzag row. *** m̀·widji timun** small, white, even teeth

unṭuk mound of earth. ***(-*)an** mound(s). **an pasir* a heap of sand. **m*́** 1 mound-shaped. 2 (*or* **m*-m***) foamy, frothy. **ng*** mound-shaped. **ng*(-*)** 1 (*psv* **di*[-*])** to heap sth into a mound. 2 boastful; to boast, brag. *** semut** anthill. *** tjatjing** 1 raised worm trail. 2 a type of pastry made from long thin strips of dough. *See also* PUNṬUK

untul young sugar-palm leaves

unṭul 1 sycophant, toady. 2 a non-fighting contestant (*usu.* a cricket *or gemak* bird) whose function is to goad the others to fight. 3 small two-wheeled carriage for transporting small freight. **ng*** 1 to be a hanger-on. 2 to follow along after smn, *e.g.* a child walking behind his mother. **ng/di*i** to use [a cricket, bird] to goad contestants (as above)

untung 1 lucky; by good luck. 2 profit, gain. ***-*an** to take a chance, risk one's luck. **ka*an** profit, gain. **ng/di*aké** *or* **ng/di*i** to be of benefit to. *Aturan iki ng*i wong akèh.* This regulation helps a great many people.

untup **m*-m*** slightly visible. *Ḍuwité katon muntup² ana ing sak.* A little of his money shows from his pocket. **ng/di*aké** to let [a little of sth] show; to let out a hint of what one is thinking

untut **ng/di*i** to eat sth by tipping the head back and dropping bits of the food into the mouth

unu *rg* **ng/di*** to regulate the flow of [irrigation water]

unuk (*or* ***-***) (to walk) hunched over with age

unur *rg* termite nest made of soil humped up on the ground

unus 1 a shape for kris blades. 2 *ltry* facial expression. **ng/di*** to draw [a weapon] from its sheath. *ng* peḍang* to draw a sword

upa 1 cooked rice grain. 2 *compounding element: see main entries below.* **ng/di*** to glue sth with cooked rice grains. **ng/di*-*** to feed smn mouthful by mouthful

upâbogâ **ng*** to earn one's daily bread, make a living. **pa·ng*** work by which one earns his living. *See also* BOGA

upâdamel to take charge (*root form: kr for* UPAGAWÉ)

upâdânâ *ltry* gift. *See also* DANA

upadi *oj* trick, ruse, scheme

upâdjiwâ livelihood, means of support. **ng*** to earn one's living. **pa·ng*** livelihood. *golèk pang** to earn one's living. *See also* DJIWA

upados trick, scheme (*kr for* UPAJA)

upâgawé *ng,* **upâdamel** *kr* **ng/di*** to take charge, attend to things. *See also* GAWÉ

upâjâ *ng,* **upados** *kr* trick, scheme. **ng/di*-(ni)** 1 to try to find a way to do sth. *Ajo di*ni bisané klakon.* Let's figure out how we can make it come true. 2 to seek. *Sang Prabu ḍawuh ng* usada.* The king ordered that a search be made for a remedy.

upâkârâ (**upâkawis** *ltry? kr*) 1 precious ornaments. 2 a good deed. **ng/di*** 1 to take care of, look after. *djuru ng** caretaker; chaperone; nurse. 2 to prepare a body for burial. **pa·ng*** 1 act of taking care of. *pang*né mripat* the care of the eyes. 2 act of preparing a body for burial

upâkarjâ *ltry var of* UPAKARA

upâkawis *ltry? kr for* UPAKARA

upâmâ *ng,* **upami** *kr* 1 such as, for example. *Jèn dimunasika, * dibeḍil, gadjah iku bandjur ngamuk.* If disturbed, for example shot at, elephants go on the rampage. 2 supposing; in case. ** kowé mréné pijé?* What about you coming here? 3 if. ** kowé dingonokaké apa seneng?* Would you like it if someone did that to you? 4 *ltry* like, as. *agalak medèni tur * djago wis otot* wild and scary like a brawny fighting cock. ***né** 1 (*or* ***né waé**) to take an example; let's suppose. *negara sing ana segara weḍiné kuwi *né negara Arab* countries having deserts—Arabia, for instance. 2 if [it were true]. *Upamané temenana...* Even if it were really true... **ng/di*kaké** to liken. *Ajuné kena di*kaké kaja widadari.* Her beauty is like an angel's. **sa*** if [it were true]. *Aku bisa tuku mobil sa* sugih.* If I were rich, I would buy a car. **tanpa *** beyond compare, unequaled

upami *kr for* UPAMA

upârenggâ *ltry* decorations, ornamentation. **ng/di*** to decorate. **pa·ng*** act of decorating. *Pang*né dipasrahaké aku.* The decorating has been assigned to me. *See also* RENGGA

upas 1 uniformed worker; employee. ** pos* mailman. ** kantor pos* post-office worker. ** tebu* guard who polices sugar-cane fields. ** kantor* office employee who cleans, opens up in the morning, locks up at night. ** (ka)-wedanan/(ka)bupatèn/lsp.* errand-runner for a *wedana/bupati/etc.* 2 poison; poisonous. **ng/di*i** to poison smn

upâsâkâ *ltry* novice *or* apprentice Buddhist priest

upâsâmâ *var of* UPASANTA

upâsantâ *ltry* patient and helpful

upat ***-*** a whip attached to a handle

upâtâ *var of* SUPATA

upâtjârâ 1 a formal court ceremony with speeches. 2 objects of state, carried along in all ceremonial processions. 3 the retinue of a dignitary during a ceremonial procession. 4 authority delegated to smn by a high official. ***n-*nan** to conduct a ceremony with much fanfare. *Kok ndadak upatjaran²an barang, mbok tjliménan waé.* Why all the pomp and circumstance?–why not just do things informally? **ng/di*** to beseech, supplicate. **ng/di*ni** to receive *or* greet smn formally. *** ka·prabu·n̂** royal objects of state

upet long narrow strip cut from a coconut-blossom sheath, used for igniting *e.g.* cigarettes, firecrackers

upeti tribute to those in authority (in olden times)

upih leaf sheath from the *djambé* tree, used for wrapping

upil 1 dried nose mucous. *uṭik² ** to pick the nose. 2 soot that collects on the wick of an oil lamp. **ng/di*(i)** 1 to smear mucous on(to). 2 to pick off [bits, kernels] from

upit ***-*** to wiggle, wag. *Buntuté *-*.* It wagged its tail.

upjek̄ (*or* ***-*an**) to make a racket

uplik small kerosene lamp consisting of a wick in a container of oil. **ng*** 1 [of the mouth] small. 2 resting in a precarious position

upret **ng/di*-*** to chase, pursue

uput ***-* (djeput)** very early in the morning. *Olèhé mangkat ésuk *-*.* He set out bright and early.

ura to spread out, move apart. ***-*** to sing for one's own pleasure; to sing non-classical songs. ***n-*n** song(s) sung for pleasure. **ng/di*-*** to keep separate/apart. **ng/di*k-*kaké** *or* **ng/di*n-*ni** to sing to/for smn

urab a miscellaneous mixture. *djangan ** a mixture of vegetables. ***-*an** to bawl smn out profanely. **ng/di*** to mix [a variety of things]. *** sari** a mixture of various kinds of flowers

urag *wong* ***an** wanderer, homeless one. **ng*** [of animals, plants] to grow old and die. *mati ng** to die of old age. **ng/di*aké** to keep [a plant, a pet] until it dies a natural death

urak smn's turn (at). *Sapa sing katiban * adus ḍisik?* Whose turn is it for first bath? (*wong*) ***an** boor, unmannerly person. **ng/di*** to drive away. *Manuké di*-*.* They shooed away the birds. *Ali tau monḍok nèng omah iki, ning terus di*.* Ali used to take room and board here, but he was asked to leave. **pa·ng*an** open area of the palace at Jogjakarta or Surakarta which serves as the servants' recreation and relaxation area as well as for palace news announcements

urang shrimp. *krupuk ** shrimp chips. *supit ** shrimp claw (*see also* SUPIT). ***-*an** a certain bird. ***-*ing mata** inner corners of the eyes. *** aju** a certain style earring. *** garing** dried salt shrimp. *** ontjèk·an** shelled shrimp. *** teles** fresh shrimp. *** watang** a certain large shrimp

urat 1 blood vessel. 2 muscle. 3 female genitals. 4 flesh, tissue. 5 leaf vein. **a*** *or* **ng*** female genitals. *** getih** blood vessel. *** sarap** nerve. *ḍokter ahli *-sarap* nerve specialist

urdah *var of* HURDAH

uré *var of* ORÉ

urek̄ ***an** the result of picking *or* crossing out (as NG*-* below). *Tatuné *an kruma iku wudjud elèng.* The pock marks from picking these spots are little holes. **ng/di*-*** *or* **ng/di*i** 1 to pick a hole in sth. *ng*i lemah* to hack a hole in soil. 2 to scribble; to cross out

urèn black mynah bird

ureng ***-*** maggot that infests mangoes. **m*** 1 annoyed, bothered. 2 [of fire] to glow. **ng*** to smoulder. **ng*(i)** infected. *Tatuné wis ng*.* His wound has festered.

urèt grub, larva

urik to cheat, to [do] unfairly. *Jèn main kertu ḍèké mesṭi *.* He always cheats at cards. *Ḍèké * olèhé ngiris roti, ora diparo bener.* He didn't cut the cake fairly–it wasn't in two equal halves. ***-*** scribbly, scrawly. **ng/di*i** to cheat smn in a game

uring **m*(-m*)** furious, expressing fury with loud talk and gestures. *Saja muring².* He got madder and madder. *Ing batin muring².* He raged inwardly. **ng/di*-*** to yell at smn in anger. *Ḍèwèké muring², sing di*-* aku!* He was furious, and he took it out on me!

urip *ng,* **gesang** *kr* 1 (**sugeng** *ki*) life; to live, be alive. *Punapa éjang taksih sugeng?* Is your grandfather still living? *mati sadjroning ** death in the midst of life. ** ing kéné njenengaké.* Life here is very enjoyable. *ragil ** youngest living member of a family. *bebrajaning ** society, the community. 2 (**sugeng** *ki*) to live, reside. ** ing kuṭa* to live in the city. 3 soul, spirit, inner life. *Teṭukulan dudu manungsa, ora duwé* *. Plants are not human–they have no souls. 4 to function, be in operation. *Radioné isih* *. The radio is on. *Geniné apa wis* *? Is the fire burning yet? 5 active, full of life. *tontonan* * lively entertainment. *banju* * whirlpool. *weḍi* * quicksand. ***an** to live *or* grow easily. *Suket*[2] *kuwi *an.* Grass springs up anywhere. *-* *ng kr* a dish prepared from *lélé* fish. ***-*an** barely alive. *Bajaré mung seṭiṭik, dadi *é ja mung *-*an.* His salary is so small he barely ekes out a living. *menḍem *-*an* to bury alive. **ka*an** life, existence. *ka*an betjik* the good life. **ng(a)*** *var of * after vowels or nasal sounds.* **ng/di*-*** (**ng/dipun·ge·gesang** *var kr*) to nurture. *Taneman mau di*-*.* He cared for the plant tenderly. *Pamaréntah wis karsa ng*-* kagunan baṭik.* The government wishes to encourage the art of batik-making. **ng/di*aké** 1 to restore the life *or* health of. 2 to enliven, make lively. 3 to make function. *ng*aké lampu* to turn on a light. *ng*aké mesin* to start up an engine. *ng*aké wajang* to manipulate a puppet. **ng/di*i** 1 to provide (the essentials of) life to/for. *ng*i lan njanḍangi anaké* to feed and clothe one's children. 2 to save smn's life. *A ng*i B.* A rescued B. 3 to restore to health *or* life. *Kéwané di*i ḍokter.* The veterinarian cured the animal. **pa·ng*an** a living, a livelihood. *Pang*ané jaiku adol beras.* He sells rice for a living.

urit ***an** 1 rice seedling. 2 embryo. **ng/di*(i)** to set out [rice seedlings] in the paddy

urmat (to show) respect; a salute, to salute. *awèh * marang* to show respect for; to salute. **ka*an** honor, respect, esteem. *kélangan ka*an* to lose face; [of girls] to lose one's virginity. **ng/di*i** to honor, pay homage to. **pa·ng*an** respect, esteem. *See also* KURMAT

urub flash, flare, flame. **é lampu gas iku semu idjo.* A gas lamp burns with a greenish flame. **ing nesuné* the flaring up of his temper. ***-*** kindling material. **k*** (*prn* **korub**) to get kindled/ignited. **m*** to burn, flare up. *Ana lampu èlèktris sing m*.* There was an electric light burning. *bahan*[2] *sing gampang m*é* materials which ignite easily. **m* ati·né** to get angry, flare up. **m* mubjar** reflecting light. *klambi m* mubjar* a dress which glitters/sparkles. **ng/di*aké** 1 to ignite, cause to burn. 2 to stir up [a fire] to make it burn brightly

urug (*or* ***-***) earth used for leveling *or* filling. ***an** earth used for filling *or* covering. *lemah *an anjaran* fresh fill. **k*an** to get buried *or* covered with earth *or* filled in by accident. **ng/di*(i)** to fill in, cover with earth. *Blumbangé di*.* They filled in the pool. *Lemahé ambles ng*i omah.* The landslide buried houses. **ng*i luwang·an** to rob Peter to pay Paul

uruh dirty foam in river *or* ditch water. ***-*(an)** dirty matter floating on the surface of water, *esp.* after rainfall. **m*** *or* **ng*** foamy, frothy, sudsy

urun to make a contribution. *A * Rp. limang èwu.* A gave 5,000 rupiahs. ** rembug* or ** uḍu* to contribute to a discussion. ***an** 1 amount contributed. 2 to contribute to a joint project. *Botjah*[2] *paḍa *an tuku bal.* The boys all chipped in to buy a ball. **ng/di*aké** to contribute sth. *ng*aké ḍuwit marang Taman Siswa* to give money to the Taman Siswa. **ng/di*i** to contribute to. *ng*i sekolahan Taman Siswa* to give to the Taman Siswa school. *** lanang/wadon** to offer one's son/daughter to prospective parents-in-law

urung 1 pillow case. 2 drum frame over which skins are stretched. 3 bamboo pipe for smoking opium. 4 *rg var of* DURUNG. ***-*** underground waterway, vein of water. **ng/di*-*** to escort smn by walking on either side of him

urup ***-*(an)** (the practice of) barter. **ng/di*aké** to swap. *A ng*aké sarungé karo djariké B.* A swapped his sarong for B's wraparound. **ng/di*i** to swap for [sth else]. *Sarungku di*i djarik.* I swapped my sarong for a wraparound.

urus ***an** affair, matter. *Dudu *anmu.* None of your business. **ané pulisi* a police matter. **an rumah-tangga* household affairs. **ora *an karo** not on speaking terms with. ***-*** (to take) a laxative. **ke*** to get dealt with. *Sekolahé anak*[2]*é ora keurus.* His children's schooling was neglected. **m*** to have diarrhea. **ng/di*(i)** to handle, take care of. *ng* bab administrasi umum* to handle public administrative matters. *Ḍèké ora ng* kuwarasané.* He didn't take care of his health. *Apa wis rampung anggoné paḍa ng* kartjis?* Have they finished seeing about their tickets?

*Bareng di**, *ḍèké ora salah.* After it was looked into, he was acquitted. *Saben dinané kantor pos iku ng***i lajang pirang*2. The post office handles countless letters every day. **ng*(i) dawa** to concern oneself with sth long and involved. **ng/di*-*i** to administer [a laxative]. *ng*-*i kastroli* to dose oneself with castor oil. **pa·ng*** manager. *pengurusé hotèl* the hotel manager. **ora *** ill-mannered

urut 1 along; alongside (of). ** pinggiring kali* along the riverbank. 2 in sequence. *angka ** consecutive numbers. ** sidji* one after the other, one by one. *tjrita ** a serial story. **é dawa.* The waiting line is long. ***an** in sequence; (as) a series. *Olèhé nata buku ora *an.* The books were not arranged in consecutive order. **an sepisan warnané abang, sing ping pinḍo biru.* The first series is red, the second blue. ***-*an** in sequence, serial(ly). *gambar *-*an* a series of pictures. **-*an miturut pangkat* lined up in order of rank. **ng/di*** 1 to go through *or* trace in sequence. *Djenengé di* saka nḍuwur mengisor.* He went over the list of names from top to bottom. 2 to massage sprained *or* displaced bones. **ng/di*aké** to have a massage from a faith healer. **sa*é** along(side of). *sa*ing dalan sepur* along the railroad tracks. *** katjang** 1 single file. 2 alternating. *Anakku lanang wédok lalang wédok, kaja urut katjang.* My children alternate: boy, girl, boy, girl.

usâdâ *oj* 1 medicine, remedy. 2 relating to health

usadi *var of* USADA

usah *inf var of* SUSAH[b]

usâhâ effort; to make an effort. *Embuh lulus embuh ora, ning pokoké aku wis * sabisa-bisaku.* Maybe I'll pass and maybe I won't, but I've done my best. **pa·ng*(n)** businessman; employer. **per*n** a business undertaking

usalli a prayer expressing one's sincere intention and faith. *matja ** to utter such a prayer as one begins worship

usap (*or* ***-***) sth used for wiping. ***-*** to wipe, rub. **ng/di*aké** to rub sth onto. *Lenga klentik di-usap*2*aké ing sirahé.* She worked coconut oil into her scalp. **ng/di*i** to wipe sth. *Kringeté di*i nganggo katju.* He mopped his brow with a handkerchief. *** tangan** handkerchief

usar sth spread as a coating. **ng/di*** to coat (with), to spread thinly. *di* putih resik* newly whitewashed. **ng/di*-*aké** to coat [sth] with. *Limé di-usar*2*aké ing dluwang.* He spread the glue on some paper. **ng/di*i** to coat sth [with]. *Tjiṭakan di-usar*2*i mertéga.* She buttered the cookie molds.

usé *var of* HUSÉ

usèk act of scrubbing a floor with a stone. *watu ** floor-scrubbing stone. **ng/di*** to scrub [a floor] with a stone *or* with a coconut-leaf-rib brush

usek̄ (*or* ***-*** *or* **usak̄-***) to move restlessly. *Jèn lingguh sing anteng, adja * waé.* Sit still —don't squirm. *Aku ora isa turu, ming usak-* waé.* I couldn't get to sleep, I just tossed and turned. **ng/di*-*aké** *or* **ng/di·usak-*aké** to rub *or* scrape sth back and forth. *Gegeré diusak-*aké nang témbok.* He rubbed his [itching] back against the wall.

usel **ng/di*-*** to cuddle up to. **ng/di*-*aké** 1 to press sth [against smn]. *Kutjing mau ng*-*aké sirahé nang sikilku.* The cat rubbed its head against my leg. 2 to create a job for smn. *Anaké kepeksa di*-*aké gawéan nang kantoré bapakné ḍéwé.* They had to make a place for him in his father's office.

useng 1 *intsfr* black. *ireng *-** jet black. 2 *var of* OSÈNG

user **ng/di*-*aké** to rub sth [into], massage with. *Obaté di*-*aké weteng.* She rubbed the ointment on his stomach.

usil restless, fidgety (rather than composed and quiet, as proper). **ng/di*-*** to touch *or* handle *or* move things constantly in a nervous, fidgety way

usir **ng/di*** to drive away, chase off

usreg restless, fidgety. ***-*an** *pl* restless. **ng*aké** fidgeting, squirming

usuk 1 vertical beam(s) on the lower part of a traditional-style roof. *milang ** or *ndeleng ** to lie on one's back loafing. 2 ribs, rib bones. **ng/di*i** to put on *or* repair [a beam as above]

usul 1 (to make) a suggestion, a proposal. 2 (*or* **asal-***) origin. **ng/di*aké** to suggest *or* propose sth to smn. *Ḍèké ng*aké supaja dianakaké sajembara.* He suggested holding a contest. **ng/di*i** to make a suggestion, offer a proposal

usul-udin Islamic faith. *Fakultas ** Faculty of (Islamic) Theology. *Kitab ** book of Islamic teachings

usum season [for...]; proper time. **é*

wong turu the time (of day) when people nap. ∗ *pelem* the mango season. ∗*é tandur* (rice) planting time. *jèn* ∗ *lelara* in times when illness is going around. ∗ *udan, adja lali pajung.* It's the rainy season–don't forget your umbrella. ∗-∗**an** to happen according to season. *Lumrahé woh-wohan iku* ∗-∗*an, ora setaun terus²an.* Most fruits are seasonal–they aren't available all year round. ∗ **panas** hot (dry) season; summer. ∗ **rontog** the season during which leaves fall; autumn. ∗ **saldju** snowy season, winter

usung ∗**an** equipment for carrying sth heavy. ∗*an wong tatu* a stretcher for the wounded man. ∗-∗ to lug things from one place to another. **ng/di**∗**(i)** to transport [sth heavy] jointly. *Wong² ng*∗ *lemari.* They carried the cupboard together. *Uwuh ing dalan mau di*∗*i ing tukang uwuh nganggo grobag.* The trash men carted off the street rubbish in oxcarts. **pa·ng**∗ act of transporting (as above). **pa·ng**∗**an** equipment for carrying sth heavy. ∗-∗ **lumbung 1** to carry other people's belongings in helping them move. 2 to carry out [a project] by soliciting money

usus 1 intestine(s). 2 feature, characteristic. ∗-∗ sash, cummerbund. ∗-∗ **karèt** a toy rubber snake. **ng**∗ resembling intestines. **ng**∗ **pitik** tangled, snarled. ∗ **buntu** appendix; (*or* **lara** ∗ **buntu**) appendicitis. ∗ **embing²** umbilical cord of an unborn baby. ∗ **geḍé** large intestine. ∗ **nom** *or* ∗ **tjilik** small intestine. ∗ **tuwa** large intestine

usut **ng/di**∗ to investigate. **pa·ng**∗**an** investigator

ut oh-oh! (*excl of surprise, dismay*)

utah to spill (out) (*var of* WUTAH). ∗-∗**an** vomitus. **k**∗ to get spilled. *Pantjiné tiba, mak sok djanganė kutah.* The pan fell and out poured the soup!

utak the brain

utâmâ *ng,* **utami** *kr* 1 good, virtuous. 2 important; prominent. *Iki luwih* ∗ *banget.* This is much better. This is far more important. ∗**né** it is advisable. ∗*né kowé nerusna olèhmu sekolah.* You ought to continue your studies. **ka**∗**n** virtue. *Dana-drijah kuwi sawidjining kautaman.* Generosity is a virtue. **ng/di**∗**kaké** to consider of greatest importance. *ng*∗*kaké tèhnik* to give priority to technology

utami *kr for* UTAMA

utang *ng,* **sambut** *kr* 1 (**sambut·an** *kr*) a debt. ∗*é arang wulu kutjing.* He's up to his ears in debt. 2 (**sambut·an** *kr*) credit. *Olèhmu tuku barang kuwi kentjèng apa* ∗*?* Did you pay cash for that, or buy it on credit? 3 (**ñj·sambut** *kr*) in debt. *Aku* ∗ *satus rupiah nang ḍèké.* I owe him 100 rupiahs. ∗**an** 1 a loan. 2 to borrow habitually. ∗-∗ (**ñj·sambut²** *kr*) 1 to borrow here and there. *Uripé* ∗-∗. He lives on credit. 2 to borrow repeatedly. ∗-∗**an** to borrow from each other; indebted to each other. **ng/di**∗ to incur a debt. *Anggoné tuku ng*∗. He bought it on credit. **ng/di**∗**aké** 1 to give sth as a loan. *ng*∗*aké ḍuwit* to lend money. 2 to sell sth on credit. *ng*∗*aké sanḍang-pangan* to sell food and clothing on credit. **ng/di**∗**i** to lend to. *Aku di*∗*i sèket rupiah.* He lent me 50 rupiahs. ∗ **apiutang** (**sambut-s·in·ambut** *kr*) to keep borrowing and lending. *perdjandjian utang piutang* reciprocal loan agreement. ∗ **budi** to owe a favor *or* a kindness. *Utang budi ja males budi.* A kind act should be repaid with a kind act. ∗ **kapi-potang** *sms* ∗ APIUTANG *above.* ∗ **lara ñj·saur lara** to repay in kind; an eye for an eye. ∗ **njawa** to owe one's life. ∗ **piutang** *sms* ∗ APIUTANG *above.* ∗ **ulang** to live by getting things, or sponging, from others. ∗ **urip** to owe one's life. *See also* PIUTANG, POTANG

utârâ *var of* UNTARA 2, 3 (**utawis** *kr*). **ng/di**∗**kaké** to explain, express, tell. *Ḍèké teka arep ng*∗*kaké bab perfileman.* He's come to tell about film-making.

utâwâ *ng,* **utawi** *kr* 1 or. *panggonané turu* ∗ *ngaso* a place to sleep or rest. 2 and (*joining parallel forms*). *Brambang* ∗ *bawang biasané sok diedol ombjokan.* Onions and garlic are usually sold in bunches. ∗ **lija²·né** and the like, and such things; or whatever...

utawi *kr for* UTAWA

utawis *kr for* UTARA*; var of* UNTAWIS

uṭeg busy, occupied (with). *Botjah²* ∗ *paḍa ngétung.* The children are busy doing arithmetic. **ng/di**∗-∗ to work busily at. *Ḍèké ng*∗-∗ *sekrup ora bisa tjopot².* He worked and worked at the bolt but he couldn't get it loose.

utek 1 brain. ∗ *sapi* cow's brain (as food). 2 brains; intelligence. ∗*é mati.* He doesn't use his brains. ∗*mu ana ngendi?* Use your head! *kegeḍèn endas kurang* ∗ too big a head with too little brain in it

uṭek̄ ∗-∗ *or* **uṭak**-∗ *or* **m**∗ *or* **ng**∗ to linger, dawdle, hang around. *Pikiranku * waé.* My thoughts kept straying. *Adja pidjer ng* nang omah waé.* Don't keep hanging around the house! **ng/di*-*** *or* **ng/di·uṭak-*** to keep touching with the fingers, to handle sth; to stir, mix (with fingers *or* implement). *** kliwer** to loiter. ** kliwer ing ḍapur* to hang around the kitchen

uṭel ***-*** short in stature. **ng*-*** too short to handle easily (*e.g.* an implement)

uter **ng/di*** 1 to shape into a round form. 2 to ball roots for transplanting

uṭi to busy oneself. *mBok adja * waé, lèrèn kéné.* Stop doing things and take a break!

uṭik ***-*** *or* **uṭak-*** to keep picking at. **-* upil* to pick one's nose. **ng/di*** to pick *or* pry with a long thin object. *Weḍi sing mlebu ana ing djam di* nganggo tjuṭik untu.* He flicked the sand out of his watch with a toothpick. **ng/di*-*** *or* **ng/di·uṭak-*** to keep picking at sth. *Karangan sing wis kok tik kuwi adja kok *-* manèh.* Don't make any more changes in that article now that you've typed it. *Aḍimu mbok adja kok *-* ta.* Quit picking on your little sister. *Soalé diuṭak-* nganti sak djam, ananging meksa ora bisa digarap.* He kept at the problem for an hour and still couldn't solve it. *Mesiné diuṭak-* nganti mlaku* (*rusak*). He tinkered with the machine until it worked (broke). **ng*-*** to arouse a dangerous adversary. *Adja ng*-* matjan turu.* Let sleeping dogs lie. **pa·ng*-*** 1 act of picking at sth. 2 a knife with a curved blade

util ***an** 1 act of picking pockets. 2 loot from picked pockets. **ng/di*** to pick pockets; to steal. *tukang ng** pickpocket. **ng/di*aké** to steal on smn's behalf. **ng/di*(i)** to steal from, pick smn's pocket. *Dodolanku adja nganti di*i wong.* Don't let anyone steal what I bought you. *See also* KUTIL

uṭil stingy, close-fisted

utjal *var of* OTJAL

utjap what smn says; to say. **é, Matur nuwun.* He said thank you. *tuwuhing ** source of discussion. ***an** 1 pronunciation. 2 utterance. **an mengkono ora patut.* Such talk is not proper. ***-*an** 1 topic of conversation *or* gossip. 2 proverb, saying. **k*** (*prn* **kotjap**) to be said *or* talked about. *Bab mau wis ora kotjap manèh.* It isn't mentioned any more. **k*a** it is told (that); now, it happened that... *Kotjapa nalika aku ésuké menjang sekolahan...* (It happened that) when I went to school the next morning... **ng*** to say, express, speak. *Ḍèké ora ng* apa²*. She didn't say anything. *Ḍèké ora bisa ng**. She couldn't speak. *ng** to express thanks. *ng* ala* to curse. **ng/di*aké** to give voice to. *Pitakonan mau ora tau di*aké.* The question was never uttered. *ng*aké djandji* to make a promise. *tetembungan sing di*aké wong Amérika* expressions used by Americans. **ng/di*-*aké** 1 to say, to pronounce, to utter. *Kowé sing ng*-*aké, aku sing nulis.* You say them and I'll write them down. 2 to cause to speak. *ng*-*aké wajang* to do a puppet's speaking for it (while manipulating it in a shadow play). **ng/di*-*i** to reprove, scold. **p*an** (*prn* **potjapan**) 1 speech. *potjapan² lan tembang²é ki ḍalang* the puppet-master's speeches and songs. 2 conversation. *dadi potjapan* to be(come) a topic of conversation, be talked about everywhere. 3 saying, expression. *Ana potjapané, adiguna adigang adigung.* There's a saying to the effect that one should not overrate one's strength, wisdom, and superiority. **pa·ng*** what smn says; act of saying *or* speaking. *Pang*é banter lan nesu.* He spoke loudly and angrily. *See also* KUMUTJAP, POTJAPAN

utjek̄ ***-*** to rub. **-* mripat* to rub the eyes. **ng/di*(-*)** 1 to rub one thing against another. 2 to criticize, pick on

utjel **ng/di*-*** to massage with the fingers

utjeng 1 a freshwater fish. 2 blossom of the *mlindjo* plant, eaten as a vegetable. 3 village official in charge of distributing irrigation water. 4 head of a certain village subsection (*ḍukuh*). ***-*** 1 lamp wick. 2 fuse

utji ***-*** a skin disease characterized by pustules

utjik **ng/di*-*** to nag, keep after, hound

utjul 1 loose, astray; to get loose. *Ḍèké * saka blenggu.* He slipped out of the handcuffs. 2 (**lukar** *ki*) to remove [clothing]. *tanpa * penganggo* without getting undressed. ** klambiné* to take off one's shirt. **ng/di*aké** to let sth go loose. *Aku utjulna.* Let me go! **ng/di*i** 1 to unfasten, free. *Paḍa ng*i tali²né balon.* The untied the ropes that held the balloon to earth. 2 (**ng/di·lukar·i** *ki*) to remove [clothing]. *Penganggomu kuwi utjulna kabèh.* Take off all your clothes.

utjut **ng/di*** to harvest [rice plants]

utri 1 a Javanese dessert made from

steamed cassava and sugar. 2 a variety of rice plant

utuh *var of* WUTUH

uṭuk ***-*** 1 small wooden box. 2 piggy bank. 3 (*prn* **uṭu:k**) *intsfr* early. *ésuk *-** first thing in the morning. **ng/di*-*** to treat with care

uṭun **ng/di*-*** to spoil, overindulge [a child]

utus to have smn do sth (*root form: ki for* KONGKON)

uṭut potential. *Ana *é.* He has good possibilities. Good things are expected of him. ** menang* bound to win. **ng/di*** 1 to peek slowly at [sth, *e.g.* a newly dealt playing card]. *Aku ng* rapotku saka seṭiṭik.* [Fearing the worst,] I peeked at my report card little by little. 2 to pick (*i.e.* steal) smn else's rice plants

uw- *see also under* W-; *see also Introduction, 2.9.5*)

uwa 1 parent's older sibling; person in the parents' age group. (*bu*) * aunt. (*pak*) * uncle. 2 counting unit for rice plants roughly equivalent to 1 *amet.* ***-*** a certain large black monkey. **ng/di*kaké** to treat *or* consider smn as one's aunt/uncle

uwab steam, water vapor. *daja ** steam power. *sepur ** steam engine. **ng*** to boil off, evaporate. *Banjuné ng*.* The water boiled away. *Banjuné segara ng*, ujahé kari.* The sea water evaporated, leaving the salt behind. **ng/di*aké** to cause to evaporate. *ng*aké banju* to let water evaporate

uwah *var of* OWAH

uwak *var of* UWA 1

uwal to be *or* break free/loose. **ng/di*aké** to release from bonds. *Tjentjanganė weḍus di*ké.* He untied the goat's tether.

uwan [of hair] gray. ***en** gray-haired

uwar **ng/di*-*aké** to tell, reveal, disclose

uwat labor pains. ***-*** things used as props *or* supports. **ng/di*-*aké** to exert oneself fully; to tighten one's hold on, hang onto (*var of* N̈G/DI·KUWAT-KUWAT·AKÉ). **sa(k) *** all of a sudden

uwed 1 string, *esp.* that used for spinning a top. 2 to work hard for one's daily bread. **ng/di*-*** to pat, caress. **ng/di*i** to wind string around [a top] preparatory to spinning it

uwèg 1 *rpr* a duck's quack. 2 *rg var of* WÈNÈH

uwek̄ **ng/di*-*** to press and rub. *Ḍèwèké ng*-* korèngé merga gatel.* He's rubbing his wounded place hard to make it stop itching.

uwel 1 fetal membrane. 2 stingy, tight-fisted. ***-*** crumpled. *kertas *-** crumpled-up paper. ***-*an** crowded. *Sepuré kebak banget, penumpangé nganti *-*an.* The train was so crowded the passengers were jammed in tight. **m*** to crowd, fill. *Wong sepirang-pirang m* ing kamar kono.* A large crowd jammed the room. **ng/di*-*** 1 to wad *or* crumple sth into a ball. 2 to embrace. *See also* KUWEL

uwèn **sa*-*** *or* **sa*-ijèn** for a considerable length of time. *Ḍèwèké ngentèni sa*-* ning kantjané ora teka²*. He waited for a long time, but his friend never showed up. *See also* SUWÉ

uweng **ng*-*** to buzz, hum. *Anginé ng*-*.* The wind made a sing-song noise.

uwer 1 a small piece of rolled leaf used for enlarging a pierced earring hole. 2 *rg* ring-shaped carving on a kris handle. **ng/di*i** to enlarge an earring piercing with a rolled leaf

uwi the large, round, edible turnip-like root of a certain climbing plant

uwik ***-*** itchy feeling around the anus caused by *kermi* worms. **uwak-*** to move the fingers busily *or* nervously. **ng/di*-*** *or* **ng/di·uwak-*** to pick (at) with the fingers; to move the fingers busily. *Adja ng*-* korèng.* Don't scratch at your cut.

uwil **uwal-*** busy *or* nervous movements of the fingers. **ng/di*** 1 to scrape, scratch. 2 to clean oneself after urinating *or* defecating. 3 to tear (up), shred. **ng/di*-*** to tear *or* shred again and again. *Rotiné di*-*.* He broke the break up into little pieces. **ng/di·uwal-*** to move the fingers busily *or* restlessly (at sth)

uwir ***-*an** sth that has been shredded *or* torn apart. **ng/di*-*** to tear (apart), shred. *Ibu ng*-* daging nganggo tangan.* Mother is tearing the meat into strips with her hands.

uwos uncooked rice (*kr for* BERAS)

uwuh ***-*** *or* **ng*(-*)** to call (out). **pa·ng*** 1 act of calling out. 2 (*or* **tembung pa·ng***) *gram* exclamation

uwung ***-*** 1 empty space. 2 the space right under the roof of a building. *See also* AWANG

uwur ***-*** jellyfish

uwus statement, expression, phrase. **ng/di*-*** to scold, berate

V

v (*prn* **fé**) *alphabetic letter*

vak 1 vocational skill. *sekolah* * a vocational school. 2 subject of study. * *matématik iku angèl.* Mathematics is a difficult subject.

vanḍel *var of* PANḌEL

véspa (*prn* **fèspā**) motor scooter (*originally a brand name*)

vètsin *var sp of* FÈTSIN

viol violin

vla custard. * *susu* milk custard. *saos* * custard sauce

vocaliā vocal music

voltase voltage, electrical power

vonis *var of* PONIS

vulpèn fountain pen

W

w (*prn* **wé**) *alphabetic letter. See also under* UW-*: Introduction, 2.9.5*

-w- *intensifying infix: var of* -U-

wa 1 *inf var of* UWA 1; *see also* SIWAK. 2 *var of* WUWA. 3 oh my! wow! *See also* INALILAHI

wa'alaikum salam *var of* WANGALAIKUM SALAM

wâdâ [of body parts] defective, misshapen. ***nan** a cruel *or* teasing nickname. ***n-*nan** to call each other insulting nicknames. **m̃/di*(ni)** to criticize smn by calling his attention to his physical faults. **m̃/di*ni** to call smn by a cruel *or* teasing nickname (*e.g. Si Tjatjing,* applied to a very thin person)

waḍag visible, corporeal (as contrasted with nonmaterial, spiritual)

waḍah 1 container. **é apa?* What has it got in it? What shall I put in it? * *sega* rice bowl. * *awu* ashtray. *gendul* * *banju ngombé* a bottle of drinking water. *tas* * *buku* book bag. *Roti sa*é ditjolong.* The cake was stolen along with the cake box. 2 receptacle for catching things (fruits, rain water) as they fall. **ñ/di*aké** to put sth [into]. *Maduné di*aké ing gendul.* They put the honey into bottles. **m̃/di*i** to put sth [into a container; where it belongs]. *Kapur mau di*i ana ḍus tjilik.* She put the chalk in a little box. *Waḍahana ing * awu.* Put it in the ashtray.

wadal sacrificial animal; *fig* one whose interests are sacrificed to smn's selfish purpose. **m̃/di*aké** to use as a sacrifice. *Samidjan madalaké enḍas kebo kuwi kanggo omah sing lagi digawé.* Samidjan buried the kerbau head as a good-luck sacrifice for the home he is building.

wadânâ 1 face; mouth (*ltry; ki for* RAI). *pada* * outward characteristics; look, appearance. 2 head of a government administrative district. *asistèn* * assistant district head (*see also* TJAMAT). **ka*n** 1 official residence of a district head. 2 the occupant of the above residence, *i.e.* the district head. 3 district administered by the above official. *prijaji sa'ka*n* officials from throughout the district. **ṁ/di*ni** to act as head of [a district]

waḍang *rg* **ṁ/di*** to eat rice; to eat a meal. **ṁ*an** always hungry. **sega *** last night's rice served for breakfast

waḍas a variety of limestone

wadé 1 batik goods as merchandise. *dikempit kaja *, didjudju kaja manuk* pampered, looked after solicitously. 2 *rg var of* SADÉ. **ka*an, ku*an** place in the market where batik goods are sold

waḍèh to give away secrets

wader a river fish. *** bang** goldfish

wadi *ng,* **wados** *kr* 1 a secret. *mbukak ** to reveal a secret. *nutupi ** to keep a secret. 2 secret vulnerable spot, Achilles heel. **we*** *ltry var of **. **ṁ*ṅi** mysterious, secretive. *Tindak-tanduké **. He acts furtive. **w·in·adi** (**w·in·ados** *kr*) occult, esoteric

wâdjâ 1 (**waos** *kr*) steel, iron. 2 tooth (*ki for* UNTU). ***n** *ng kr* frying pan

wadjang ***an** sexual intercourse. **ṁ/di*i** to have sexual intercourse with

wadjar plain, without embellishment *or* artifice

wadji *oj* horse

wadjib 1 obligation, duty. *Sembahjang sedina ping lima iku * kanggoné wong Islam.* Worship five times daily is a Moslem duty. ** sekolah* compulsory education. *Sing * ngetokaké aturan anjar bab padjek.* The authorities have issued a new tax regulation. 2 fee paid to a religious official who prays for one. **di*i** to be given a responsibility. *Ḍèké di*i nglumpukaké ḍuwit iuran.* He was assigned to collect the dues. **k(e)*an, ku*an** duty, obligation. *Kamardikan iku nggawa ku*an lan tanggung-djawab.* Freedom entails certain duties and responsibilities. **ṁ/di*aké** to make sth compulsory. *Pamaréntah madjibaké saben botjah sekolah.* The government requires that every child go to school.

wadjik 1 a sweet cake made of glutinous rice. 2 diamonds (playing-card suit). 3 *oj* horse. ***an** diamond-shaped. *** kleṭik** a stiff coconut-sugar pudding

wadon female (*var of* WÉDOK). **pa*an** *ng* (**pawèstri·ṅ** *kr,* **baḍong** *ki*) female genitals

waḍong wing-like part of a classical dancer's costume

wados secret (*kr for* WADI)

wadu 1 *oj* soldier(s), troops. 2 royal relative. *** adji** king's servant(s). *** wandawa** royal relative(s)

waḍu *var of* WAḌUH

waḍuh *excl of astonishment.* ** geḍéné!* Wow, look how big it is!

waḍuk 1 stomach (digestive organ). 2 stomach, belly (*cr equivalent of* WETENG). 3 water reservoir. *** beruk** a big eater

wadul a tattletale; to tattle (to). *Mentas disrengeni guruné, *!* The teacher bawled him out for being a tattletale. *Njilih dolanan ora diwènèhi, *!* I want your toy and you won't give it to me–I'm going to tell on you! *Warna * bapakné jèn mentas baé ditaboki kakangné.* Warno told his father that his brother had hit him. **we*** 1 to tattle habitually. 2 what smn says *or* tells. *We*é digugu.* People trust what he says. **ṁ/di·(we)*i** to tattle to smn. *Kok guruné nganti ngerti, sapa sing memaduli?* The teacher knows about it–who told him? **ṁ/di*aké** to tattle (on); to tell/tattle sth. *A madulaké B.* A told on B. *Wis di*aké marang bapak durung, jèn Warna metjahaké gelas?* Did you tell Dad that Warna broke the glass? **pi*** what smn says *or* tells. *See also* ADUL

wadung 1 axe, hatchet. 2 jack (playing card). **ṁ/di*** to cut wood with a *wadung*

wadya (*or* *** bala**) soldier(s), fighting force. *Sang Nata sa*né* the King accompanied by his troops. *See also* BALA

waé *inf var of* BAÉ[a]

wafat deceased

wagal a certain fish

Wagé fourth day of the five-day week

waged *sbst var of* SAGED

wagon railway car (passenger *or* freight)

wagu 1 ungainly, poorly proportioned. 2 unpleasing, lacking tastefulness

wah heavens! my! wow! ** énaké!* How delicious they were! ** sirahku kepjor²*. Oh–I feel faint.

wahânâ *oj* 1 vehicle, conveyance. 2 interpretation, meaning. **ṁ/di*ni** to symbolize. *Jèn ana prahara ajah ngéné iki mahanani jèn wong² bakal akèh redjekiné.* When a storm comes at a time like this, it's a sign of impending good fortune for many people. *See also* WAJANG[a]

wahdat person who leads a celibate life
wahing *ng kr,* **sigra** *ki* a sneeze; to sneeze. *obat* * medicine to make one stop sneezing
wahja external form. **ke*** expressed, externalized. **ṅ/di*kaké** to explain, express. **w·in·ahja** expressed outwardly
wahju heaven-sent fortune. *ketiban* * to be the recipient of a heavenly boon. **ke*ṅ, ku*ṅ** to receive manna from heaven
wahni *oj* fire
waing *var of* WAHING
wajah *ng,* **wantji** *kr* 1 time (period); the right time [for]. * *ésuk/bengi* in the morning/evening. *ing * ngaso* during rest period. *Wis *é turu.* It's time to go to bed. * *ngéné* at a time like this. * *(sa)ḍawuh* time (*ca.* 9 A.M.) when wives bring food to the men who have been working in the fields since dawn. 2 grandchild (*ki for* PUTU). **sa*-*** at any time, whenever
wajang[a] *ng,* **ringgit** *kr* 1 traditional Javanese drama depicting tales based on Indian epic literature and Javanese mythology. 2 puppet used for the above in shadow plays; *fig* one manipulated by smn. *Mung saderma dadi *.* Man is a puppet in God's hands. ***an** 1 shadow-play performance. *Umumé *an iku suwéné saka djam wolu bengi tekan djam lima ésuk.* Shadow plays generally last from 8 P.M. till 5 A.M. 2 *sms* WE*AN *below.* **we*** *ng kr* shadow ghost of a deceased person. **we*an** *ng kr* 1 shadow; reflection. *wedi ing *ané ḍéwé* constantly afraid of doing sth wrong. 2 landmark. *we*an désa* a village landmark. **ke*an, ku*an** *ng kr* in the shade of, overshadowed by. **ṅ*** to put on a wajang performance. **ṅ/di*aké** to perform sth as a wajang show. **ma*** wajang performance. **pa*an** place where a wajang drama is performed (*see also* P(A)·RINGGIT·AN). * **bèbèr** drama narrated as paper-scroll pictures are shown. * **bokong·an** puppet with a large billowing rear part. * **Djawa** leather-puppet dramas about the national hero Diponegoro. * **dupara** drama depicting events of Surakarta history. * **geḍog/geḍong** drama depicting adventures of the mythological hero Prince Pandji. * **golèk** 1 three-dimensional wooden puppet. 2 plays of the Ménak cycle, depicting Moslem epic figures, performed with these puppets. * **kiwa** a mark on the left side of the shadow-play screen symbolizing the bad people. * **kliṭik** *or* * **krutjil** play cycle about the Madjapahit period, depicted by flat wooden puppets. * **kulit** the chief form of shadow play, performed with leather puppets depicting plays of the Pendawa cycle; also, the puppets used for such performances. * **madya** play cycle depicting tales from East Javanese kingdoms. * **Ménak** Islamic Ménak cycle plays, performed by *wajang golèk* puppets. * **Pantja Sila** shadow plays in which the five Pendawas are presented symbolically as the Five Principles (*Pantja Sila*). * **potè(h)i** Chinese hand-puppet play. * **purwa** four cycles of mythological plays of which the Pandawa cycle is most important (*see* * KULIT *above*). * **suluh** shadow plays dramatizing events of Indonesia's recent revolutionary struggle. * **tengen** a mark on the right side of the shadow-play screen symbolizing the good forces. * **ṭengul** plays performed by *wajang golèk* puppets (*above*). * **ṭiṭi** Chinese hand-puppet play. * **wahana** shadow play depicting events of the 1920's. * **wlulang** *sms* * KULIT *above.* * **wong** plays performed as dance-drama by human beings
wajang[b] 1 back *or* neck meat of a kerbau (slivered and fried as snacks). 2 horse's neck muscles. 3 a certain palm-tree blossom. **ṅ*i** turbulent; in turmoil; in one's death throes
wajang-wujung in turmoil, turbulent. ***an** acting wild *or* frenzied. *Nalika ana gunung ndjeblug wong² paḍa *an.* When the volcano erupted, there was mass panic.
waju old, stale, having sat around too long. **(ke)*ṅ, (ku)*ṅ** having been kept too long. *Adja mangan barang wajon.* Don't eat stale things. *Krupuké kewajon.* The chips ought to be thrown out. **ṅ/di*ƙaké** to keep sth (around). *Legèn sing wis digoḍog kena diwajokaké sawetara dina.* Coconut sap that has been boiled can be kept for several days. **ora *** to not do any harm. *Njimpen buku ora *.* It doesn't hurt to have books on hand.
wajuh 1 a co-wife in a polygamous marriage. 2 to have *or* take an additional wife. *Ḍèké durung *.* He hasn't taken a second wife yet. *Ḍèké * papat.* He has four wives. **di*** to be joined by a co-wife when the husband takes another spouse. **ṅ*** to take another husband *or* wife. *Wong lanang iku jèn majuh gelem, jèn di* ora gelem.* Men are willing to have more than one wife, but they

don't want their wives to have more than one husband.

wajungjang [of animal coats] spotted. *asu ** a spotted dog

wajungjung *wj* **m̃/di*** to bind, tie up, handcuff

wak 1 parent's younger sibling (*shf of* SIWAK; *inf var of* WA 1). 2 *oj* body. * *mami* (*ltry*) I, me. ***né** *inf/rg var of* 1 *above*

wakaf *var of* WAKAP

wakap property, *esp.* a building or piece of productive land, donated as a non-profit-making religious foundation. **m̃/di*aké** to give [land *etc.*] as a *wakap*

waked *var of* WATES

wakes *var of* WATES

wakil (*abbr*: **wk.**) 1 representative. * *rakjat* a representative of the people. 2 substitute, deputy. * *présidèn* vice-president. **é njonjahku* a memento of my wife('s presence). 3 temporary, acting (as). **m̃/di*aké** to deputize, assign as representative, designate as a substitute. **m̃/di*i** to represent, substitute for, act for. **pa*an** *or* **per*an** representation; delegation, representative. *pa*an Indonesia ing negara² mantja* Indonesian (diplomatic) delegations in foreign countries

wakul rice-serving basket. ***an** 1 (placed) in a serving basket. *Segané *an apa piringan?* Is the rice in a serving basket or in a dish? 2 by the basket(ful). *Pelemé dolen *an waé.* Sell the mangoes by basketfuls. *See also* TJEMPAKA

wal- *see also under* L-, WL- (*Introduction, 2.9.3, 2.9.4*)

wâlâ 1 stem from which a bunch of coconuts grows. 2 *oj* child. 3 *oj* troops. 4 (*or* ***n**) gift given to the head of a village. ***-* kuwat·a** give me strength! (*appeal to God*)

walah **ku*an** *or* **ku*en** overwhelmed, unable to keep up *or* ahead. *Aku ku*en momong ḍèké, nakal banget.* I can't control him, he's so bad. *Ḍèké ke*an olèhé ngladèni panggawéan semono akèhé.* He can't handle that much extra work. * **tobat** *excl of dismay over sth beyond one's control*

walahualam *var of* WALLAHUALAM

walak ***-*** to depend on, be/go according to. **-* senengané ḍéwé.* It depends upon individual preference.

Walândâ *var of* WLANDA

Walandi *var of* WLANDI

walang locust, grasshopper, or similar insect with jointed legs. *mata* ***en** eyes bugging out. ***-*** worried, anxious; to worry about. **sa*-*** (in) small bits. *diedjur sa*-** crushed to pieces. * **ataga** all crawling creatures. * **ati(ǹ)** given to anxiety and worry; **m̃*-ati·ǹi** to worry about; to cause anxiety. * **drija** worried, anxious, restless, uneasy. * **gambuh** a variety of locust in which the female is larger than the male; **m̃*-gambuh·i** [a married couple] with the wife bigger than the husband. * **kaḍak** 1 stork. 2 blinkers worn by a horse; **m̃*-kaḍak** in a boastful *or* defiant attitude with hands on hips. * **kadung** praying mantis. * **kajun** 1 a variety of grasshopper. 2 worried, anxious. * **kapti** *or* * **karep** anxious, apprehensive; to worry (about). * **kerèk** praying mantis; **m̃*-kerèk** resembling a praying mantis; standing in a defiant attitude with hands on hips. * **ngataga** *sms* * ATAGA *above.* * **sangit** flying mite resembling a ladybug: characterized by a disagreeable burnt-food odor. *lonḍo² walang sangit nggénḍong kebo* a wolf in sheep's clothing. * **slisik** (so much as) the sound of a locust. *Ora ana * slisik.* It's dead quiet. * **taga** *sms* * ATAGA *above*

walat heaven-sent retribution. *Geḍé *é jèn wani karo wong tuwa.* You'll suffer grave consequences if you defy your parents. **di*i** to be the victim of divine retribution. **ku*, ke*** to receive one's retribution. *Wah aku ku*!* This is what I get! **m̃*i** causing retribution if offended against. *Manèni sedulur tuwa iku ora betjik, bisa malati.* Better not talk back to your older brother—something awful might happen to you.

Waldjiro (*shc from* SAWAL SIDJI LORO) name of a technique for calculating the date on which Lebaran will fall in any given year

waled 1 silt, sediment. 2 an accumulation, *e.g.* of back pay. **(ku)*an**, **(ke)*an** a silt deposit; *fig* an accumulation. **m̃*** to receive an accumulation. *Aku maled telung sasi.* I got three months' back pay.

walèh 1 to tell the truth. 2 tired (of), fed up (with). ***-* apa** 1 be frank! tell the truth! 2 the fact is...; to tell the truth... **m̃*aké** dull, tiresome. *Roti iku bisa malèhaké jèn dipangan saben dina.* Bread can get pretty uninteresting if you eat it every day.

waler 1 that which is forbidden *or* taboo. 2 fish viscera. ***an** *or* **we*** *sms* * 1. **m̃/di*i**

to set limits on, proscribe. *Sanadjan ḍèké wis maleri bab enggoné paḍa sesrawungan nanging meksa ditradjang.* He laid down rules about social conduct, but they were violated.

wales 1 retribution, revenge. 2 response; reaction; return. *Apa njata kabetjikan kuwi mesṭi *é ala?* Is good invariably repaid with evil? ***an** 1 a reply. 2 an unpleasant return. *Apa pendjalukmu tak turuti, djebul aku kena *anmu.* I did as you asked but got only ingratitude from you in return. 3 fishing rod. ***-*an** reciprocal; to reciprocate. **-*an lajang* to exchange letters. **-*an nggetak* to yell at each other. ***-w·in·ales** to avenge one another by turns. *Nganti turun ping pitu wales-winales.* The vengeance continued for seven generations. **we*** revenge, retribution. **ṁ/di*** 1 to repay. *Kéwan ija bisa males kabetjikan.* An animal, too, can return a kindness. *Mengko sida tak * temenan kowé.* I'll get back at you! 2 to [do] in retaliation. *ngantem di** to hit and get hit back. *males ukum* to retaliate. 3 to respond. *Saiki suraté durung tak *.* I haven't answered his letter yet. **ṁ/di*aké** to avenge smn. *Mengko tak *aké!* I'll get back at him for you! **ṁ/di*i** to respond (react, reply) to; to return sth. *malesi surat* to answer a letter. *Aku uga malesi mèsem.* I smiled back. **pa·ṁ*** what one gives back. *Semono ta pamalesmu marang kabèh kebetjikanku.* So *that's* your response to all my kindness! **pi*** return, revenge, retribution. *Kebetjikanmu muga² éntuk pi* ing tembé buri.* I hope all your kindness will be repaid in the future. *Muga² Gusti Allah paring pi* tindaké sing ambek sija.* May God send him retribution for his cruelty.

wali 1 guardian of the bride at a wedding ceremony. 2 disciple who spread Islam in Java. 3 *ltry var of* BALI. **ka*an/ku*an** *or* **ka*ṅ/ku*ṅ** pertaining to the disciples as Moslem missionaries. **ṁ/di*ṅi** to act as guardian to [a bride]. **ma*-*** again and again. *** hakim/kakim** male relative *or* religious official who represents the bride in working out the marriage arrangement with the groom. *** koṭa/kuṭa** city mayor

walih to change one's appearance/shape (*rg var of* MALIH)

walik on the contrary, the other way around, on the opposite side. *Umurku lagi mèh limalas, * kowé mung sepuluh taun.* I'm almost fifteen, but you're only ten. ***an** 1 (turned) the other way around. *Aksarané katulis *ané.* The letters were written upside down. 2 the opposite. **ané kiwa iku tengen.* The opposite of left is right. *pari *an* rice planted as a second crop during the dry season. ***é** the other side, *i.e.* the reverse. **wolak-*** 1 on both sides. *Mori iki wis dibaṭik wolak-*.* The batik design has been worked on both sides of this fabric. 2 the other way around. *Buku mau owah sawetara bab alang-udjuré, apadéné wolak-*é.* The book has been moved slightly, and it's upside down. **ke*, ku*** (turned) the other way around. *Klambimu ke*.* Your shirt is on backwards. *or* Your shirt is inside out. *Sepéḍa kena dak rèm ku* kéblaté.* I managed to brake the bike to a stop but it turned completely around. **ṁ/di·wolak-*** 1 to turn this way and that. *Bandjir enḍut panas sing molak-malik mili mangidul manèh.* The twisting flow of lava turned southward again. 2 [of things in a series] to go through the same motions, follow each other in a pattern. *Ombaké molak-malik, prauné gondjing.* The waves kept lapping and the boat rocked. *Bukuné diwolak-* meksa ora ketemu ḍuwité.* He leafed through the pages of the book but he couldn't find the money [that he had placed there]. **ṁ/di*aké** to reverse sth for smn. *Aku malikaké klambiné Siti.* I helped Siti turn her dress right side out. **ṁ/di*(i)** 1 to turn sth the other way around *or* in a different direction. *Waliken.* Turn it over. Turn it the other way around. *mlaku malik* to stand on one's head. *Geḍangé di*i nganggo sérok.* Turn the [frying] bananas with a pancake turner. *Petjuté di* dianggo nggebugi djarané.* He turned the whip around and beat the horse with the handle. *malik gunem* to twist smn's words, distort smn's meaning. 2 to change one's form magically. 3 to go back on one's word; to shift one's loyalty. **malik bumi** to turn traitor. **malik klambi** 1 to turn one's shirt inside out. 2 to turn traitor. **malik tingal** to go back on one's word; to shift one's loyalty. *** dadah 1** to massage a new mother's muscles back to normal. 2 to not want to become pregnant again. ***(an) dami·(ṅ)** to plant a second crop of rice during the dry season. *** gerèh 1** (worn) inside out, *esp.* so that the faded side will be on the inside. *Djariké*

** gerèh, mula kétok anjar.* She's wearing the wraparound inside out so it looks new. 2 to change off. *Jèn matja terus²an mboseni, kudu * gerèh karo nulis.* If it bores you to keep reading, change off with writing. *See also* ALIK, BALIK, SUWALIK

walikat shoulder blade(s)

walikukun a certain tree

walimah traditional wedding party and feasting, held after the formal ceremonies

walja *oj* *ltry var of* WALI

wallahualam who knows! (only) God knows!

waloh *var of* WALUH

walon *rg var of* WALUN

waluh pumpkin

waluja *ltry* healthy, well; having recovered *or* survived. ** sedjati* as good as new. **m̄/di*kaké** to restore sth to its original state. *malujakaké tjakrik baṭik klasik* to return to the classic batik designs. *Ibuné gawé bantjakan kanggo mulajakaké putrané sing mentas lara banget.* The mother held a ceremony to promote her child's complete recovery from his recent serious illness.

walulang *var of* LULANG

walun receiving blanket (flannel piece placed under *or* around a baby while attending to him)

walur a tuberous plant with edible roots

wal-wel *see* WEL

wal-wèlan *var of* WÈL-WÈLAN *under* WÈL

wal-wil *inf var of* DJOWAL-DJAWIL *under* DJAWIL

wânâ forest; uncultivated land (*kr for* ALAS *and wj compounding element: see main entries below*). *adegan * (wj)* forest scene

wânâdésa *ltry* forest territory

wanadri *ltry* terrain characterized by forests and mountains

wanantârâ *ltry* terrain characterized by forests with open country between; forest country in general

wanârâ *oj* monkey

wanari *oj* female monkey

wânâwâsâ 1 thick, dark forest. 2 forest dweller

wândâ 1 aspect, physical appearance, face. *a* susah* having a sad look. **né kenja kang gampangan.* She looks like a girl who would be open to a proposition. 2 nature, character. ** gègèr* hot-tempered. 3 syllable; word. *tembung sa** a monosyllabic word. 4 *wj* emotion *or* mood of a character (as represented by different forms of the same puppet figure of important characters). **m̄* swara** *gram* semivowel. *aksara manda swara* Javanese-script character denoting *WA, JA*

wandâwâ relatives, kinsmen. *See also* KULAWANDA(WA)

wandé 1 small shop (*kr for* WARUNG). 2 to fail to materialize (*kr for* WURUNG)

wandu 1 an unfeminine woman. 2 an asexual person

wanèh *var of* WENÈH

wang 1 jaw; jawbone. 2 money. 3 former monetary unit: *ca.* 8½ cents. *setali tiga ** six of one and half a dozen of the other. *sangang ** 75 cents. *** kuntji** down payment on rental *or* purchase price of a home. *** m̄·palang** well formed square jaws

wangalaikum salam *reply to the Islamic greeting* ASSALAMUALAIKUM

wangan irrigation ditch in a rice paddy

wangen (*or* ***an** *or* **we***) time limit. *tanpa *an* without limit of time. **m̄/di*(i)** to set a time limit (on, for). *Wis di*i telung menit.* They've given him three minutes.

wangi 1 fragrant. ** gandané.* It(s odor) is fragrant. *lenga ** perfume. 2 name. ***n̄** that which is fragrant. **we*** 1 sth fragrant; a fragrant odor. 2 *ltry var of **

wangkal 1 obstinate, self-willed. 2 an action contrary to smn's wishes *or* orders. **m̄/di*i** to defy. *Slamet mangkali kanḍané Bedjo.* Slamet disregarded what Bedjo said.

wangkang Chinese junk (boat)

wangké *oj* corpse

wangkil a trowel-like tool for weeding. **m̄*** to weed with a *wangkil.* **m̄/di*i** to remove the weeds from sth with the above implement. *Suketé di*i.* He dug the weeds out of the grass.

wangking 1 slim-waisted. 2 to wear sth at the back of the belt (*root form: ki for* SENGKELIT). ***an** kris (*ki, kr? for* KERIS)

wangkis **m̄/di*** to attach leather drum heads to [a drum]

wangkong the (paired) buttocks

wangkot (*or* **m̄*i**) stubborn, headstrong

wanglu *oj* ankle bone

wângsâ 1 relatives, kinsmen, family. 2 descendant. 3 people, race, nation

wangsal a fishing creel. ***an** a form of word manipulation used in verse and song: oblique reference to a word by using it as the first or (*usu.*) last syllable of a later word in the context. **m̈/di*aké** *or* **m̈/di*i** to manipulate [words] as above. *mangsalaké tembung* to express sth obliquely in a word. *Olèhé nembang nganggo di*i.* He sang using *wangsalan*'s.

wangsit guidance sent supernaturally, *e.g.* in a dream; through a seer. **we*an** a number of such messages. **m̈/di*(i)** to transmit guidance supernaturally

wangsul to return (*kr for* BALI). ***an** an answer. **we*** gift to a departing guest (*kr for* ANGSUL²). **m̈/di*i** to reply. *Wangsulana.* Answer!

wangun 1 design, shape. **é bunder.* It's round. 2 appearance, aspect. 3 suitable [to], in keeping [with]. *Tandangé * karo geḍéning pawakané.* He moves ponderously, in keeping with the largeness of his body. *Suarané ora * karo rupané.* Her voice doesn't go with her face. **é* it looks as if. *Asu iki édan, *é.* This dog is mad, from the looks of him. *Kok meneng waé *é susah.* She doesn't speak–something must be weighing on her. **(we)*an** 1 shape, form, figure. 2 building, structure. *Didegi *an anjar.* They put up a new building. **m̈/di*** to make sth in the shape of. **mangun tapabrata** to lead the ascetic life of a holy man

wanguntur *oj* throne

wangur *var of* WENGUR. **ke*an, ku*an** to get revealed in one's true form. *Saiki ku*an lan kabukak topèngé.* Now he has been found out and his mask has been torn away. **m̈/di*i** to reveal sth that has been kept concealed

wangwang hesitant, uncertain. **ke*** to be seen; to appear, look; to keep reappearing in the mind's eye. **m̈/di*** to stare at, watch fixedly

wangwung empty (*shf of* AWANG-UWUNG)

wani *ng,* **wantun** *kr* 1 bold, daring, willing to risk sth. *Arep mlebu ora *.* She wanted to go in, but she didn't dare. *Ḍèké durung pinter nunggang pit kok * nunggang.* He's not very good at riding a bike but he goes right ahead and rides one. *Jèn pantjèn satrija, * nglabuhi negara.* If you're truly noble, you're willing to die for your country. 2 defiant, arrogant. ** karo wong tuwané* to defy one's parents. 3 to desire [a woman] sexually. ***ǹ** daring in nature. ***-*** to [do] in defiance (of discretion, regulations, *etc.*). *Durung olèh idin, wis *-* negor wit djati.* They hadn't been given permission but they went ahead and cut down the teak trees anyway. **wona-*** (**wontanwantun** *kr*) to keep denying that one is afraid. **ku*(an)** *or* **ke*nen** foolhardy. **m̈/di·we*** to encourage, egg on. *memani wong supaja gelem diedu* to goad smn to fight. **m̈/di*k̀-*k̀aké** to steel oneself (to). *Kantjil suwé² diwanèk-wanèkaké njeḍaki menjang wong²an mau.* Mouse-Deer finally got up the nerve to go closer to the dummy. **m̈/di*ǹi** 1 to accept [a challenge]. 2 to act impudent *or* defiant toward. *** angas** *or* *** èrès** to put up a bold front. *** ing getih** bold, daring. *** tjur²an banju kenḍi** to be willing to swear (to). *See also* KUMAWANI

wanita female; woman. *mahasiswa ** female university student. *memanisé ** the sweet ways of woman. **ka*n** concerning *or* of interest to women

wanodya *oj* female

wantah pure; with nothing added. *banju ** plain water. *tembung krija * (gram)* an unaffixed verb. ***an** 1 pure; with nothing added. *Mas pat likur karat iku mas *an.* Twenty-four-carat gold is solid gold. 2 origin(al form); *gram* root, stem. **we*an** altogether. *Pemerintahan mau kudu diretul we*an.* The government must be completely refurbished. **m̈/di*aké** to tell in full. **sa*é** in full, as a whole, as in the original. *meḍaraké sa*é apa sing diwatja* to give a full account of sth one has read. **ora *** underhanded. *Usulku iki sarana ora * ditolak mentah.* This proposal of mine was rejected behind my back.

wantak *var of* MANTAK

wantârâ *var of* WETARA

wantawis *var of* WETAWIS

wantèh *var of* WÈNTÈH

wantèk 1 fast [of colors, *i.e.* not subject to fading *or* running]. 2 durable, long-wearing

wanter 1 brave, steadfast, determined. ** ing tékad* firmly determined. 2 fast (*var of* BANTER). **ka*an** courage, bravery, determination

wanti *ng,* **wantos** *kr* ***-*** time after time. *Wis *-* olèhé nggarap, nanging meksa durung bener.* He's done it over and over but it still isn't right. **m̈/di*-*** 1 to [do] again and again. *Olèhé nggarap manti².* He's done it over many times. 2 to keep telling *or* advising smn. *Wis tak *-* adja lali tuku mbako.* I kept telling him not to forget to buy the tobacco. *Di*-* embokné kudu* *sing weruh tata.* His mother told him again and again to mind his manners. **ma*-*** *var acv for* M̈*-M̈* *above.* **pa·m̈*-*** act of telling again and again. *Pamulangé mau nganggo pamanti-wanti marang para muridé kabèh.* They drill it into the students.

wantilan stake to which an elephant is tethered. *gadjah marani ** to submit voluntarily to risk

wantjah ***an** a shortening, contraction. *Tembung wondéné *ané wonten déné.* The word *wondéné* is shortened from *wonten déné.* **m̈/di*** to shorten, contract. **m̈/di*(i)** to criticize, find fault with. **m̈/di*i** to defy, challenge. *See also* PANTJAH

wantjak *oj* grasshopper, locust. **m̈*** to catch grasshoppers/locusts

wantji 1 (the right) time (for) (*kr for* WAJAH). 2 time, season (*kr for* MANGSA?)

wantos repeatedly; to tell, advise (*root form: kr for* WANTI)

wantu **ma*-*** repeatedly. *Olèhé njuwun ma*-*.* They made repeated requests. **banju *** water in which rice has been boiled. **watak *** character. *watak * sing betjik* good character. *kang baku ana ing watak*né wongé ḍéwé*[2] that which is basic to each person's nature

wantun bold; defiant (*kr for* WANI)

wanudya *oj* female

wanuh to know, be acquainted (with). *Aku * karo A.* I'm acquainted with A. *Aku durung *.* I don't know him. *Ora ana kang * tepung.* Nobody knows him. **(we)*an** acquaintance(ship). *mbandjuraké *an* to keep up an acquaintance. **we*an** to become acquainted with. **ka*an** an acquaintance. *ke*an djenengé Darma* a friend called Darma. **m̈*** to have become accustomed to. *Botjah kuwi manuh ngrokok.* That boy has the cigarette-smoking habit. **m̈/di·we*** to habituate smn (to). *memanuh Ali ngombé susu* to get Ali used to drinking milk. **m̈/di*aké** 1 to introduce, make acquainted with. 2 to accustom *or* habituate smn to. *Aku manuhaké Ali tangi ésuk.* I got Ali used to getting up early. **m̈/di*i** to be acquainted with. *sawidjining ḍokter kang wis tak *i* a doctor I know. *** **wani karo** to make advances to, to (try to) seduce

waon (*or* ***an**) to criticize habitually. **m̈/di*i** to criticize, find fault with. *See also* SENḌU·N̂

waos 1 spear; land measure (*kr for* TUMBAK). 2 tooth (*ki for* UNTU). 3 steel, iron (*kr for* WADJA). 4 to read (*root form: kr for* WATJA)

war- *see also under* R, WR- (*Introduction, 2.9.3, 2.9.4*)

wârâ 1 to say, speak. *Mung * baé.* It's just empty talk. 2 (*ltry*) *title used before girls' names.* ***-*** 1 announcement; advertisement. 2 to keep saying/telling. 3 *rg* about, approximately. **m̈/di*k-*kaké** to tell sth around. *Kanḍaku kuwi diwarakwarakaké marang sapa*[2]. He told everybody what I said. *** **ka·wuri** *ltry* widow

waradin *var of* RADIN

warah ***-*an** to teach each other. **we*** teaching(s). *we* Buḍa* Buddhist doctrine. *we*é wong tuwané* what his parents had taught him. **m̈/di*i** 1 to teach; to advise. *Aku marahi Ali basa Inggris.* I taught Ali English. *Jèn diwarahi ḍèwèké ora tau ngrungokké.* He never listens to the advice we give him. 2 to cause (to happen). *Sing marahi muni kuwi apané?* Which part makes the noise? *Kopi marahi betah melèk.* Coffee keeps you awake. *marahi salah tampa* to cause misunderstanding. 3 (*or* **sing m̈*i**) the reason is; because. *Rungoné wis suda akèh lho saiki, sing marai wis tuwa.* He's hard of hearing now, he's so old. **w·in·arah** to be given instruction. **w·in·arah·an** to teach each other

warak rhinoceros

warang (*or* ***an**) arsenic. **m̈*** to clean [a kris] with arsenic. **m̈/di*(i)** 1 to clean [a kris] with arsenic. 2 to poison smn with arsenic

waranggânâ 1 female singer who performs major vocal roles with a gamelan ensemble. ** swara mas* a golden-voiced lady singer. 2 angel

waras *ng,* **saras** *kr* 1 (**ḍangan** *or* **senggang** *ki*) healthy, well; recovered. *wong* (*sing*) ** a healthy person. *ora ** (*euph*) mentally ill. 2 [of land] untilled. *lemah ** fallow land. **ku*an, ke*an** good health. *seger ku*an* to look and/or feel healthy. *Ngrokok kuwi mbebajani kanggo ku*an.* Cigarette smoking is detrimental to the health. **m̈/di*aké** to cure, heal. *marasaké lelara* to cure a disease. *** **wiris** (**saras-siris** *kr*) hale and hearty. *Ḍèwèké waras-wiris, seger buger.* He's in the pink of condition.

warastra penis (*ki for* PELI?)

warâtâ *var of* RATA
wârâ-wiri *see* WIRI
wardi *var of* WERDI
wareg *ng,* **tuwuk** *kr* full; sated. *Wetengku wis* *. My stomach's full. *Wis * olèhé nonton.* They were fed up with watching the show. **ku*en, ke*en** excessively full. *Ali ngombé banju nganti ku*en.* Ali drank too much water. **ṁ/di*aké** *or* **ṁ/di*i** to cause fullness *or* satiety. *Panganan kuwi maregi.* That food is filling. *Olèhé mangan di*aké.* Eat your fill! **sa*é** one's fill. *Mangana sa*mu.* Eat all you can hold. *Ali bisa ndeleng bal-balan sa*é.* Ali was able to watch soccer matches to his heart's content.
warembol bun, roll
warèng 1 fifth-generation ancestor *or* descendant. *embah* * great-great-great-grandparent. 2 crossbreed between a chicken and a bantam rooster
wareng *see* BANṬÈNG
warga 1 family, relatives. 2 (member) of the same group. *para * padjeg* the taxpayers. ** negara* citizen. *See also* KULAWARGA
wargi *var of* WARGA
wari water (*oj*). **wora-*** hibiscus
warid *var of* WIRID
warih *var of* WARI
waring a fine-mesh material used *esp.* for fish nets
waris heir. *pati* * without heirs. ***an (tilar·an** *kr?,* **pusâkâ** *ki?*) inheritance, bequest. *olèh *an* to receive (as) a bequest, to inherit. *Angsalipun warisan saking leluhur.* It was handed down to him through the generations. **ṁ/di*aké** to bequeath. *Bapak arep marisaké dalem iki nèng aku.* Father will leave this house to me. **ṁ/di*(i)** to inherit. *Anak sing tuwa ḍéwé kuwi maris banḍané bapaké.* The oldest son inherits the father's possessions.
warna *ng,* **warni** *kr* 1 sort, variety. *Tandurané djeruk akèh *né.* There are many kinds of citrus plants. *Persèné * ḍuwit.* The tip was in the form of money. 2 color. **né kuning.* It's yellow. *Bakalé awarna biru.* The material is blue. ***-*** (of) various kinds; various kinds of things *or* ways. *piranti tjukur *-** all kinds of barbering equipment. *Panganggoné *-*.* They wore all kinds of clothing. *Didongèngi *-*.* He told them all kinds of stories. *wong² adol *-** people selling all sorts of things. *Wit²an iku pentjaré *-*.* Trees are propagated in a variety of ways. **(we)*n** various colors *or* kinds. *Asalé uwong kuwi bisa didelok saka wewarnané klambiné.* We can usually tell the social origin of a person from the way he dresses. **ṁ/di*kaké** *or* **ṁ/di*ni** to apply color to. *mernani gambar nganggo pulas* to color a picture with crayons. **ma*-*** (of) all kinds *or* colors. *kaanan mawarna-warna* a variety of circumstances. *Suket² kuwi ma*-* banget.* There's a tremendous variety of grasses. **sa*** (of) the same kind *or* color. **sa*né** all kinds of. *sawernaning barang dagangan* a variety of merchandise. *See also* MANÉKA, MANTJA
warni *kr for* WARNA
warok (*or* ***an**) 1 one who likes to lord it over others. 2 a quarrelsome person
warsa *oj* year. *kadalu* * to lapse, expire. *sa** one year. *** mintuna** Javanese year beginning on a Thursday (*significant in chronogrammatic reckoning*)
warsi *var of* WARSA
warsiki a variety of flower
warsita *var of* WASITA
warta *ng,* **wartos** *kr* news. *Apa *né ing dalan?* How was your trip? *djuru* * reporter. **ka*** *ltry* famous, renowned. **ka*n** *ltry* news. **ṁ/di*kaké** to give news (of). *Ḍèké wis diwartakaké mati, dumadakan teka waras wiris.* He was rumored to be dead, but he suddenly showed up alive and well. **ṁ/di*ni** to give news to. *Di*ni jèn bapaké wis séda.* They told him his father had died. **pa*** news. *Priksanen apa njata pa* mau.* Find out if the report is true.
wartawan journalist, correspondent. **ka*an** concerning the press; journalism. *** mantja (negara)** foreign correspondent. *See also* WARTA
warti *ltry var of* WARTA
wartos news (*kr for* WARTI)
waru a certain hibiscus tree, the fibers of whose bark (*agel*) are used for making rope and sacking material. *** lengis** a certain slender hibiscus whose trunk is used for lances. **si *** *the second of a pair of hypothetical people: see also* ḌAḌAP. *See also* KEMBANG
warung *ng,* **wandé** *kr* a shop, *usu.* built of wood or bamboo, where refreshments are dispensed *or* merchandise is displayed and sold, and often serving also as the owner's living quarters. ***an (wandé·an** *kr*) place where the above type of shop is located.

m̈∗ to operate the above type of establishment

was (*or* ∗-∗) apprehensive, on the lookout. **ngu/di∗aké** to watch, keep an eye on (*var of* NG/DI·AWAS·AKÉ). **ngu∗-∗i** nerve-wracking

wasalam *var sp of* WASSALAM

wasânâ final; end (*var of* WUSANA). *dwi* ∗ (*gram*) doubling of the final syllable (*e.g. tjeka*[*k*]*kak*). ∗ **walang wisma suku asta** to leave sth to smn else's judgment *or* discretion

wasésa 1 authority (*ltry var of* WISÉSA). *Botjah mau mung gumantung ana ∗né wong tuwa.* The child is completely under his parents' authority. 2 *gram* predicate. *djedjer lan* ∗ subject and predicate. **ka∗** under the sway of. *Atiné ka∗ déning hardaning kuwanèn.* He was ruled by his feelings of boldness. m̈/**di∗** 1 to exercise authority over. 2 to punish, discipline

wasi holy hermit, wise man living a solitary ascetic life

wasijat 1 last will and testament. 2 inheritance; heritage. 3 *wj* object given to smn to increase his powers. m̈/**di∗i** to bequeath sth to smn

wasir *var of* BAWASIR

wasis superbly competent. *Slamet* ∗ *tjara Inggris.* Slamet has a fine command of English. **w·in·asis** having superb competence. *Brataséna kang winasis* Brataséna the Superb. *See also* KUMAWASIS

wasit referee, arbiter

wasita counsel, guidance. **ka∗** to be given counsel. *wong sing ka∗ ing wangsit* one who receives supernatural guidance

waskiṭa *oj* 1 having intelligence and reasoning power for which one is held in high esteem. 2 able to predict the future by extrasensory perception. **ka∗n** intelligence and reasoning powers

waskom *var of* BASKOM

wasoh *var of* WASUH, WISUH

waspa tear(s) (*oj; ki for* LUH?)

waspâdâ watchful, on the alert. *Di∗ anggoné mapag mungsuh.* Keep on the alert when you go to face the enemy. **ka∗n** watchfulness, alertness. m̈/**di∗kaké** to look at intently. *Tjoba delengen lan waspadakna.* Take a good look at it.

waspaos *sbst kr for* WASPADA

wassalam *closing phrase of a letter: lit, 'and I greet you in return'*

wasserij (*prn* **waseré**) a laundry *or*

dry-cleaning establishment. *setoom* ∗ steam press

wasta *kr* **a∗** 1 named, called. 2 considered. *Tijang wau a∗ kainan.* These people are looked down on. **ka∗nan** called; known as; thought of as (*kr for* K(A)·ARAN·AN). m̈/**dipun∗ni** to call, name; to regard, consider; to accuse (*kr for* NG/DI·ARAN·I)

wastra *oj* 1 clothing. 2 batik wraparound skirt

wastu *see* TAUN

wasuh *rg var of* WISUH. m̈∗ 1 to menstruate. 2 (*psv* **di∗**) to wash. *masuh mori mawa sabun* to wash cotton fabric with soap. **pa·m̈∗an** washboard

waṭahṭiṭah *var of* WAṬAṬIṬAH

watak 1 nature, character(istic). *∗é sosial.* He's generous. ∗ *gemi* thrifty, economical. *Sing taksawang mung* ∗ *lan kapinteran.* The only thing I notice is a person's character and intellect. *ora* ∗ not in keeping, not in character. *ora* ∗ *guru* not the way a teacher ought to be. 2 *var of* MANTAK. ∗é ordinarily; characteristically. *Menungsa iku* ∗é *ngono.* That's the way people are. **we∗an** character(istic). *We∗an sing kaja mengkono kuwi ora apik.* Such a characteristic is undesirable. **a∗** characterized by. *Panḍu iku a∗ satrija lan sujud.* Boy Scouts are upstanding and compassionate. ∗ **wantu** character. *kawruh bab ∗-wantu* knowledge about character(-reading)

watang 1 bamboo spear used in a spear-throwing contest. 2 handle of a certain knife used for cutting trees. 3 bamboo clothes-drying pole. ∗**an** 1 the sport of jousting. 2 a handle. 3 opium-smoking pipe (*ki for* BEDUD·AN?). m̈/**di∗** to stab with a spear. **matang bubuk·en** to withdraw an accusation for lack of evidence. **matang tuna n̈·tumbak luput** 1 to accuse falsely. 2 to fail habitually to achieve one's goal

watârâ *var of* WETARA

waṭaṭiṭah *excl of surprise*

watawis *var of* WETAWIS

watek̄ 1 character, nature (*var of* WATAK). 2 tongue of a plow (the part hitched to the ox yoke)

wates 1 boundary; limit. ∗ *désa* village boundary. ∗ *kesabarané* the limits of his patience. *ngluwihi* ∗ to exceed the limit(s). *Kabèh² mau kudu ana aturan lan ∗é.* All of these things are subject to restrictions. 2 up to, as far as. *Tjlana mau diketok kira² tekan* *ing * ḍengkul.* She cut off the trousers at the knees. *Banju ing blumbang ḍuwuré * ḍaḍa.* The pond is chest-deep. ***an 1** boundary marker. 2 deadline. 3 *rg var of* SEMANGKA. **m̃/di*i** to set limits; to place a boundary. *matesi bunderan* to mark a circle [*e.g.* for playing marbles]. *Tindak ngono jèn ora di*i bisa mbebajani masarakat.* If such actions are not restricted, they can endanger society. *Aku arep matesi kamar tamu lan kamar ḍahar nganggo slintru.* I'm going to curtain off the living room from the dining room. *See also* TAPEL-WATES

watir *ng,* **watos** *kr* fearful (*shf of* KUWATIR, KUWATOS). **m̃*i** inspiring fear; constituting a danger. *Olèhé njetiri montor isih matiri.* He drives dangerously. *Obat iki matiri kanggo botjah tjilik.* This medicine is harmful to children.

wâtjâ *ng,* **waos** *kr* ***n(an) (waos·an** *kr***)** reading matter. *buku watjan* a reader, reading book. ***n-*n (waos²an** *kr***)** to sit around reading. **we*n(an)** *sms* *N(AN) *above.* **m̃/di*-*** *or* **m̃/di·wotja-* (m̃/dipun·waos-waos** *kr***)** to do some reading. *mBok motja-matja kéné tinimbang turu.* You might do a little reading instead of just sleeping. **m̃/di*kaké** to read to/for smn. **m̃/di*(ni)** 1 to read. 2 to recite, chant, sing. **pa·m̃*** act *or* way of reading. *Pamatjané ora kemba².* He kept right on reading.

watjak *var of* WANTJAK

watjânâ *ltry* word, expression, speech. **pra*** preface, introduction

watjutjal leather (*kr for* (WA)LULANG; *var of* TJUTJAL)

waton 1 to [do] randomly *or* for no compelling reason. ** ngomong* to talk aimlessly. *Anggoné nandur pari ora ming * waé ning perlu diladjur.* They don't plant rice just any old way–they set it in rows. *Barang mau ora migunani, * kepéngin ija dituku.* It wasn't a useful item, he just bought it because he felt like it. 2 reason, sense, logic. *Gunemané tanpa *.* He talks gobbledygook. *Iku *ku nari djeng X dadi bodjoku.* That's why I asked Miss X to marry me. 3 if, provided. ** kowé bajar ḍéwé, kena waé mèlu.* As long as you pay your own way, of course you can come along. 4 side *or* edge of a bamboo bed. **(a)we*** criterion, reason, logic. *Apa we* sing dianggo nemtokaké sapa sing salah?* What criteria will be applied for determining the guilty one? *Olèhé madoni awe* nalar kang bener.* His argument was based on sound logic. **m̃*** logical, factual. *Olèhé paḍa rembugan maton.* They discussed the matter rationally. **m̃/di*i** to set up a basis *or* criterion for. *** k·laku·n̂** in one's own time, at one's own pace. *See also* ADAT

watos fearful (*kr for* WATIR)

watu *ng,* **séla** *kr* stone, rock. ***nen** (to have *or* get) kidney stones. **m̃*** 1 hard, rock-like. 2 (*or* **di***) to place stones on; to smooth with a stone. *matu dalan* to put stones on a path. **pa*n̂** a piece of stone-filled land. *** api** flint for striking fire. *** beras** light porous rock. *** bobot** stone used as a counterweight. *** brani** magnet. *** g·um·antung** stalactite. *** gunḍul** boulder. *** item** hard black rock. *** kambang** pumice. *** karang** coral. *** karang·en** an itchy scalp condition. *** kumalasa** smooth flat rock. *** las** manganese. *** lintang 1** a certain variety of limestone. 2 a certain variety of gypsum. *** pasir** sandstone. *** petjah·an** rubble; broken-up stone. *** sumbul** sharp stones. *** tjenḍani** marble

waṭuh *var of* WAḌUH

watuk *ng kr,* **tjekoh** *ki* a cough; to cough. ***an** subject to frequent coughs. **m̃/di*aké** *or* **m̃/di*i** to make smn cough

watun **m̃/di*** to clear [land] of weeds

wau the (aforesaid); just now (*kr for* MAU)

waung *rg var of* BAUNG

wauta *see* SÈBET

wâwâ a certain large black monkey. **ka*** carried, borne. **m̃/di*** to carry. *gegremetan mawa wisa* poisonous insects. *See also* MAWA

wawah spacious. **m̃/di*i** to make room for sth

wawal crowbar. ***an** a dispute. **m̃/di*i** to argue with smn

wawan together with. ** gunem* to carry on a conversation *or* discussion [with]. ** padu* to carry on an argument [with]. ** sabda* to have a talk [with]. ** tjara(n)* an interview. *A nganakaké * tjara karo B.* A interviewed B.

wawang *oj* **m̃/di*** to watch intently. **pa·m̃*** idea, thought. *Ḍèké tansah duwé pamawang djero.* He always has deep thoughts.

wawar long tail hairs. *asu ** wild dog. *wulu ** long body hair. **m̃/di*i** to pick [coconut] from the shell and slice it. **sa*** one slice of coconut

wawas *****an** view(point). *Présiḍèn maringi *an bab pembangunan.* The President gave his views on economic development. *Kepri-jé *ané?* What did he think about it? **ṁ/di*** to watch intently. **ṁ/di*aké** to look *or* stare at. **pa·ṁ*** 1 view(point). *manut pamawasku* in my opinion. 2 one who expresses an opinion *or* offers advice. *See also* AWAS

wawi *var of* AWI

wawoh *rg var of* WAWUH

wawrat 1 weight; importance (*kr for* BOBOT). 2 pregnant (*kr for* Ṁ·WETENG). *****an** to go to the bathroom (*kr for* NG·ISING). *Tamunipun sampun *an.* The guests have washed up.

Wawu seventh year in the *windu* cycle

wawuh 1 to know, be acquainted with. 2 to be friends again, be reconciled. **ṁ/di*aké** 1 to introduce [people to each other]. 2 to reconcile, restore friendship between [estranged people]

W.C. (*prn* **wésé**) lavatory, toilet

wé 1 *excl expressing surprise.* 2 *oj* sun. 3 *oj* water. 4 *inf var of* BAÉ[a]. ***** **l(h)a** *excl of surprise. Wé lha ora dinjana kok teka.* Well well, I didn't expect you, but here you are! ***** **rekta kang ṁ·wuru·ṅi** *ltry* wine

we- *see also under* WA- (*Introduction, 2.9.2*)

wéda, wéḍa *oj* 1 the Veda. 2 wisdom contained in the Veda

weḍak powder. ***** *pupur* face powder. *****an** to powder one's face. **ṁ/di*i** to apply powder to. *Rainé di*i lamat*[2]. She put a thin layer of powder on her face.

wedal 1 emergence; product (*kr for* WETU). 2 *inf var of* WEKDAL

wédang 1 (**bentèr·an** *kr?*) boiling water for making hot drinks. 2 (**bentèr·an** *kr?*) hot tea. *disuguh ** to be served tea. *****an** to chat over a cup of tea. *****en** blistered from contact with scalding water *or* some irritating substance; [of lightning-struck vegetation] scorched and dried. **ṁ*** 1 to drink tea. 2 (*psv* **di***) to immerse in hot water. **ṁ*i** 1 to serve tea to. 2 accustomed to having a hot drink. 3 (*psv* **di*i**) to pour boiling water on sth. ***** **antah** plain boiling /boiled water. ***** **badjigur** a drink made of coconut milk, water, coconut sugar, and slices of coconut. ***** **bubuk** hot coffee. ***** **kopi** hot coffee. ***** **putih** boiling water (for hot drinks). *See also* DANG, WÉ

weḍar (*or* *****an**) expression, explanation. **ané bab iku tjeṭa banget.* His explanation of it was very clear. **ṁ/di*** to express, explain. *meḍar sabda* to make a speech; [of kings] to say, speak. *meḍar gagasan* to tell what one has in mind. **ṁ/di*aké** to explain *or* express (to/for smn). *Sang Buḍa meḍaraké piwulangé.* Buddha expounded his teachings. *Pegawai padjek meḍaraké peraturan padjek anjar.* A tax official explained the new tax regulations. **pa·ṁ*** act *or* way of explaining/expressing

Wédâtâmâ one of two classic works on Javanese philosophy (*see also* WULANG RÈH)

wedel *ng,* **tjeleb** *kr* indigo dye used in batik-making. *****an** dyed indigo. **ṁ/di*** to dye with *wedel.* **ṁ/di*aké** to apply indigo dye to [the unwaxed portions of fabric]

wèdi *see* SUDARA

wedi *ng,* **adjrih** *or* **djirih** *kr* 1 fear; afraid. ***** *karo* afraid of. *Adja *.* Don't be scared. *Ḍèwèké * jèn konangan.* He's afraid he'll get caught. *Suwé*[2] *ilang *né.* He gradually got over his fear. 2 awe, respect. *Kabèh wong ing désa iku paḍa * asih lan tresna marang ḍèwèké.* Everyone in the village regards him with reverence and love. *****ṅ** 1 timid. 2 (*or* *****ṅ·*ṅan** *or* **we*ṅ**) *ng kr* an animated scarecrow operated by strings from a covered platform in a rice paddy. **ke*ṅ** excessively afraid *or* awed. **ṁ·(we)*** a ghost; anything that frightens. *Sing diarani memedi iku klambi ana ing méméan.* The "ghost" was a shirt hanging out to dry! **memedi sawah** *or* **memedèn** rice-paddy scarecrow. **ṁ/di*kaké** to frighten. *Sing medèkaké dudu bantering banju ning djeroné.* What scares me is not the swift current but the depth of the water. **ṁ/di·(we)*ṅi** frightening; to frighten. *Rupané medèni banget.* It's very scary-looking. *Ḍèké diwedèni tikus.* He was frightened by a mouse. **ṁ/di*ṅ-*ṅi** 1 to throw a scare into smn. 2 to threaten. ***** **asih** (to feel) awe and reverence (toward). ***** **rai wani silit** afraid to come out and fight but brave enough to talk behind smn's back

weḍi sand. *segara ** desert. *****ṅ** sandy. *lemah weḍèn* sandy soil. **di*** *or* **ka*** covered *or* filled with sand. *ka* alus* covered with fine sand. **ṁ*** sand-like, crumbly; [of the texture of ripe *salak* fruit] pleasantly crumbly (*see also* GÉJOL). **pa*ṅ** sandy. ***** **kèngser** sand bank. ***** **krosok** coarse, sticky sand. ***** **urip** quicksand

wedidang 1 calf of the leg. 2 Achilles tendon
weḍit a variety of snake
wedjag *var of* WEDRUG
wedjah folk medicine drunk by nursing mothers to ensure adequate lactation
wedjak **ṁ/di*** to wring (out), squeeze
wedjânâ *var of* MEDJANA
wedjang (*or* ***an**) lengthy address delivered by an esteemed and respectfully heeded individual. **ṁ/di*** to deliver an address (as above). *Ḍèké lagi medjang anaké bab pigunané sekolah.* He's telling his son at some length of the advantages of schooling.
wedjani fee paid to a medicine man (*ḍukun*). **ṁ/di*** to make a payment to [a medicine man]
wedjar *var of* WEḌAR
wedjek̄ *var of* WEDJAK
wédok *ng,* **èstri** *kr,* **putri** *ki* female. *botjah ** girl. *anak ** daughter. *kantja ** my wife. *(pe)ngantèn ** bride. *sing ** wife. *Sing * djenengé Sri.* His wife's name is Sri. *wong ** woman. ***an** *ng kr* 1 female animal used for breeding purposes. 2 fond of women. 3 nut, female screw. **ku*an (pawèstrèn** *kr,* **baḍong** *ki*) female reproductive organs. **ṁ*(i)** fond of women. **ṁ*i** [of women] feminine; [of men] effeminate. **pa*an** *sms* KU*AN *above.* **wong * a·bau lawé·jan** woman with a dimple on her shoulder (a mark indicating that her husband will not live long). **wong * iku swarga nunut nraka katut** a woman's fortunes depend on those of her husband
weḍon a certain kind of ghost that resembles a corpse wrapped in a shroud. *banju ** (*rg*) water with which a corpse has been washed
wedos *sbst kr for* WEDI
wedrug path worn smooth by many feet
weḍung *ng kr,* **pa·siku·ṅ** *ki* a cleaver-like knife
weḍus *ng,* **ménda** *kr* goat; sheep. ** bisa ngembèk.* Goats baa. *daging ** lamb, mutton. ***an** 1 celebration at which mutton is served. 2 a certain herb *or* weed. *** bérok** large goat with a beard. *** Djawa** *or* *** gèmbèl** ordinary Javanese goat. *** gibas** thick-coated Australian sheep. *** kenḍit** sheep with a white stripe around its middle. *** di·umbar ing pa·katjang·an** one who gets the opportunity to enjoy sth highly desirable
wedya *oj* fear; awe, respect
wegah averse (to). *Ora * munggah gunung.* They don't hesitate to climb mountains. ***an** 1 averse to work, lazy. 2 easily revolted. **ṁ*aké** *or* **ṁ*i** causing aversion. *Omongané megahaké.* He talks obnoxiously. *Rak ja megah²aké ta?* It's disgusting, isn't it!
wegang *see* TATAH
wegig 1 intelligent; skilled. 2 crude, rough, rude. *denawa ** (*wj*) a crude giant
wèh[a] *ng,* **suka** *kr* ***-*** (**nje·ṅj·suka·ni** *kr*) to give [things]. **ngu/di*aké, nge/di*aké** to give sth. *nguwèhaké lajang* to hand over a letter. *Barang² di-wèh²aké marang tangga teparoné.* They showered the neighbors with gifts. **ngu/di*i, nge/di*i** 1 to give to. *Aku di*i panggonan lungguh.* I was given a seat. 2 to set up. *Sapinggiring dalan di*i tjagak² gendéra.* Flagpoles were placed along the streets. **pa*** gift; gifts brought to those back home. **w·in·èh** *ltry* to be given sth. *See also* AWÈH, WÈNÈH, WÈWÈH
wèh[b] *excl expressing fear or distaste. Nèk weruh wong nggawa beḍil, * entèk atiku.* It scares me to death to see someone carrying a gun. ** eneg kula!* Ugh, I'm sick of it.
wéja careless. *Jèn nganti *...* If you don't watch your step...
wèk 1 belonging to, the possession of (*shf of* DUWÈK). *Panahé *é ḍéwé.* It was his own arrow. 2 (*prn* **wèk̄**) *rpr* ripping. *Sarungku ketjanṭol pang: mak *, rekètèk, brèk.* My sarong caught on a branch and tore. 3 (*prn* **wèk̄**) *rpr* a duck's quack
wéka (*or* **we***) watchfulness. *Adja nganti kurang we*.* Don't be careless! *sepi ** or *tinggal ing ** or *tuna ing ** to let down one's guard, fail to stay alert. **ṁ/di*ni** to take precautions (against)
weka 1 tea stains in a teapot *or* teakettle. 2 a bad habit, an addiction. **ṁ*** 1 tea-stained. 2 addicted to a bad habit
wekan womb
wekas 1 the end, the last. 2 (to make) a request; (to give) a piece of advice, a message. **ku, kowé adja sok njatur lijan.* I tell you, you must never gossip. *Ḍèké * jèn mengko soré ora bisa teka.* He asked me to tell you he can't come tonight. 3 what smn is told *or* asked to do. ***an** 1 what smn is told *or* asked to do. *Apa *anku wis kok tuku?* Did you buy what I asked you to? 2 in/at the end; finally. *Sing teka *an, ora éntuk*

kursi. Those who came last didn't get seats. *wandané *an* the final syllable. **an ḍèké ngaku jèn njolong djamku.* At last he admitted that he had stolen my watch. **we*** *ltry var* or *pl form of* *. **ka*** to get sent on an errand. *Ḍèké ka* tuku susu nanging lali.* He was sent to get some milk but he forgot. **m̈/di*aké** to convey smn's request. *Apa unḍangan iki wis di*aké tanga²?* Have you taken the invitation to the neighbors? **m̈/di*(i)** to ask *or* instruct smn (to). *Aku di*(i) Ali supaja tuku rokok.* Ali asked me to get him some cigarettes. **pa·m̈*** 1 message; parting words. 2 youngest in the family

wekdal time (*kr for* WEKTU)

wekel diligent, industrious, serious

wèker alarm clock

weki **(ka)*n̈** uncertain, at a loss. *Sanget kewekèn ing galih.* He didn't know what to do. **m̈/di*n̈i** to frustrate *or* thwart [smn's wish, request]

wèks wax, polish. **nge/di*** to wax sth

wektja *var of* WETJA

wektu *ng*, **wekdal** *kr* 1 time (period). ** iki* (at) this time. ** semana* at that (remotely past) time. ** kapan* when? ** udan* rainy period. ** ésuk (awan, lsp.)* morning (noontime, *etc.*). 2 Moslem praying time. ** subuh* morning prayer time (*ca.* 5 A.M.). ** asar* afternoon praying time (*ca.* 4 P.M.). *nglakoni limang ** to be a true loyal Moslem, *i.e.* to pray five times a day as required

wèl ***-*an** 1 to shiver, tremble, shake. 2 to have the jitters, to fidget. *Adja *-*an waé.* Stop wiggling. *Olèhé mangsuli *-*an.* He answered nervously.

wel **wal-*** *rpr* eating quickly, hungrily, and with enjoyment. *Olèhé mangan wal-wel.* He ate with gusto.

wel- *see also under* L-, WL- (*Introduction, 2.9.3, 2.9.4*)

wéla ***-*** clear, distinct. *tjeṭa *-** very clear(ly visible, understandable). *kélingan *-** to remember distinctly. *Saka kadohan wis kétok *-*.* It can be seen clearly from a distance.

welad a thin, sharp piece of bamboo used for cutting. **m̈/di*** to cut with the above

welah 1 oar. ** iku kanggo nglakokaké prau.* Oars are for propelling a boat. 2 a slender bamboo plant (*kr for* WULUH). ***an** act of rowing. *Welahané alon banget.* He rowed slowly. **m̈/di*i** to propel [a boat] with oars. *tukang melahi* or **pa·m̈*** oarsman, rower

welak (*or* **we***) divine retribution in the form of a large-scale natural disaster

Welândâ *var of* WLANDA

welang a black-and-white-striped poisonous snake

welas[a] pity, sympathy; sympathetic, sorry for. *Ḍèké * marang botjah² kang wis tanpa ibu mau.* Her heart went out to the motherless children. *Wong tani ora duwé * seṭiṭik²a marang urèt mau.* Farmers have no mercy on these grubs. *Sang Prabu *, maling diparingi pangapura.* The King relented and pardoned the thief. ***an** sympathetic. *Wataké *an.* She has a compassionate nature. **ka*an** sympathy, pity. *Njuwun sih ka*an.* I plead for your mercy. **me·m̈*** 1 inspiring pity. *Wong wuta iku pantjèn memelas banget.* Blind people are indeed to be pitied. 2 having pity. *Aku melas marang wong wuta.* I feel sorry for blind people. **m̈/di*i** to feel sorry for. *Ḍèwèké mlepah² karebèn di*i.* He pretended to be badly off so that people would take pity on him. *Jèn kowé melasi aku bukuku balèkna.* If you have any pity for me, please return my book! **pi*** pity, compassion. *** asih** compassion; compassionate; **ka*-asih** *ltry* inspiring pity; **m̈*-asih** *sms* ME·M̈* *above. See also* KAMIWELASEN

welas[b] -teen (*var used with* SE- 'one' *and the kr numbers: see also* LAS 3). *sa*, se** eleven ('one-teen'). *kalih ** twelve. *tiga *, kawan *, gangsal ** thirteen, fourteen, fifteen. ***an** 1 (in) the teens. *Umuré lagi *an.* He's in his teens. 2 the eleventh item–thrown in free with a purchase of ten. *Pak, endi *ané?* Where's my free one? **m̈/di*i** to throw in an item free when ten are purchased. *Olèhku tuku rambutan mau *an: tuku rong puluh, di*i loro.* I got some *rambutan* fruits thrown in free: I bought twenty and they gave me two extras. **sedjinah *** eleven for the price of ten

weleg **m̈/di*** to give guidance in moral and ethical matters

welèh misfortune (interpreted as) occurring in retribution for one's wrong acts. **ku*, ke*** to have one's wrongdoing discovered and censured. *Adja sok ngina wong munḍak ka*.* Don't treat others with contempt, or something bad will happen to *you.* **m̈/di*aké** to bring smn's wrongdoing home to him. *A di∗aké anggoné ngapusi B.* A was reproached for having cheated B. **pa·ṁ∗** words of reproach for one's wrongdoing. **pi∗** retribution for misconduct

welèri a common variety of locust

weling *ng kr,* **tungkas** *ki* 1 an instruction; a message. *Welingku, jèn kowé ngingu, opènana tenan lo.* I tell you, if you keep pets, you must care for them well. 2 *ng kr* a certain small snake. **∗an** a message, an instruction; an errand (to be) done. *∗anmu uwis tak kanḍakaké marang Slamet.* I gave Slamet your message. *Enja, ∗anmu tjutjur.* Here's the cookie you asked for. **ṁ/di∗aké** 1 to convey [an instruction, a message]. 2 to send for. *Ibu melingaké Kuntjung.* Mother said Kuntjung is to come home. **ṁ/di∗(i)** to give an instruction, to ask smn to do an errand. *Aku di∗ tuku mbako.* He asked me to get him some tobacco. *meling panggonan* to make a reservation. **pa∗** *or* **pi∗** a message, an instruction. *Ngéling-élinga atur pi∗ku iki.* Keep in mind what I am telling you!

welit 1 a clump of tall, coarse wild grass held with a bamboo strip. 2 a thatched roof made with the above clumps. **ṁ/di∗** to make [a roof] with the above

wéloh *var of* WALUH

welon having split apart

welu 1 pale. 2 without energy, lackadaisical. 3 obstinate. **ma∗** *oj* pale

welur *rg var of* SELUR

welut eel. **ṁ∗** to catch eels, work as an eeler. *kaja ∗* **di·lenga·ni** evasive; undependable. **enggon ∗ di·dol·i uḍèt** to boast of one's achievements to others with similar or greater achievements

wenah *var of* BENAH

wenang (*or* **we∗**) (to have) authority, privilege. *Pamaréntah mènèhi wewenang paḍa marang sakabèhing wong.* The government gives equal privileges to all people. *we∗ sawah* the right of usufruct in a rice paddy. *Krama ∗* optional Krama (*Introduction, 5.6*). **ka∗** to have authority; to have the privilege *or* right. *Kowé ora ka∗ ngirim lajang iki tanpa tèkenku.* You are not authorized to send this letter without my signature. **ka∗an** to take an advantage, benefit oneself. **ṁ/di∗aké** to give authority to; to grant a privilege to. *Saben wong di∗aké setijar supaja bisa sugih lan seneng uripé.* Every individual is guaranteed the right to pursue prosperity and happiness. **sa∗-∗** overbearing, having no regard for others' rights. *Ḍèwèké digugat prakara olèhé sa∗-∗ marang duwèké lijan.* He was hated for his high-handed disregard for other people's property. **w·in·enang** *ltry* to have authority; to have the right *or* privilege

wéndra an edible sea fish

wendra unit of ten million. *sa∗* 10,000,000. *rong ∗* 20,000,000. **∗n** numbering in the tens of millions

wènèh *ng,* **suka** *kr* **∗an** that which is given. *Ali² iki barang ∗an.* This ring was given to me. **ṁ/di∗aké** *or* **ngu/di∗aké** *or* **nge/di∗aké** 1 to give sth. *Pelemé di∗aké B.* He gave the mangoes to B. 2 to put sth smw. *Buku mau kok ∗aké ana ing endi?* Where did you put that book? **ṁ/di∗i** *or* **ngu/di∗i** *or* **nge/di∗i** 1 to give to [a social equal]. *mènèhi pitulungan* to give help. 2 to put sth smw. *Sapa sing mènèhi gula kopiku?* Who put sugar in my coffee? **ṁ/di∗-∗i** *or* **ṁ/di·wonah-∗i** (**ñj/dipun·suka²ni** *kr*) 1 to give repeatedly. *monah-mènèhi tangga* to keep giving things to the neighbors. 2 (*or* **ṁ/di·we∗i**) to bring gifts to those back home. **sa∗(-∗)** whatever one gives. *Ḍuwit pira waé sa∗é ija ditampa.* Any donation is accepted. *See also social variants* ATUR[a], PARING, SAOS, TEḌA, TJAOS, UNDJUK; *see also* WÈH[a]

wenèh **sa∗** some, certain [ones]. *Sa∗ ana sing ora ngandel.* Some of them don't believe it. **sa∗ing...** some *x*'s. *sa∗ing baktéri²* certain bacteria. *Ana sa∗ing uwong sing isih ngandel marang gugon-tuhon.* There are people who still believe in superstitions. **sa∗-∗** all, every/any one. *Sa∗-∗ing titah bakal musna.* All living things will perish.

weng **∗-∗** *rpr* humming, *e.g.* wind *or* things blown about by wind; smn humming a tune

wenga **∗n** act of opening; *fig* open-handed, generous. **we∗n** awareness; enrichment of the spirit. **ṁ∗** open; to come open. *Koriné menga.* The door opened *or* was open. *wanda menga* (*gram*) an open syllable (*see also* SIGEG *and Introduction, 2.2*). **menga s·um·eblak** wide open. **ṁ/di∗kaké** to open sth. *mengakaké lawang* to open a door. **ṁ/di∗ni** 1 to keep opening; to keep open. 2 to open to/for. *Ḍajoh iku sanadjan kok ∗ni lawang nanging kok inebi ulat, iku paḍa baé karo ora kok temoni.* Even though you open your door to a guest, if you "close" your face [with an unwelcoming expression] it's the same as not receiving him.

wengi *ng*, **dalu** *kr* evening, night. *Ora nganti * aku wis turu.* I went to bed before nightfall. *ing wajah tengah ** in the middle of the night. *jèn ** at night. *tengah ** midnight. ** iki* this evening, tonight. ***né** the evening/night of the same (aforementioned) day. **né ḍèké teka.* He got there that evening. ***-*** 1 in the middle of the night. 2 (once) when it was night. ***ǹ-*ǹan** (*rg:* ***-*nan**) rather late at night. *Jèn numpak motor mabur wengèn²an, ongkosé luwih murah.* It's cheaper to fly at night. **ke*ǹ** late at night. *Tekané ing kuṭa kewengèn, toko² wis tutup kabèh.* When he reached town, it was very late; all the stores were closed. **sa*** one night; throughout the night. *Sa* ora nglilir.* He didn't wake up all night long. *Aku nginep kono ana sedina se*.* We stayed there one day and one night. *See also* BENGI

wengis stern, fierce-looking

wengkang **m̀/di*** to bend sth apart, separate sth forcibly. **m̀/di*-*** to move sth forcibly this way and that

wengkelan calf of the leg (*ki for* KÉMPOL, KÉNTOL)

wengkelang hard feces

wengku frame, edge, border. **we*ñ** people *or* area under smn's authority. *Wong kang dadi wewengkoné kabèh pada sumujud.* All the people under his authority loved him. **m̀/di*(ñi)** 1 to surround *or* enclose (with). *di* gunung ḍuwur²* hemmed in by high mountains. *mengkoni gambar* to frame a picture. 2 to have authority over. *Sapa sing mengkoni ḍaérah mau?* Whose sovereignty is that territory under? **pa·m̀*** forgiveness, pardon. *Jèn ana tjèwèté baé, adja kurang ing pamengku.* If anything is wrong with it, I hope you'll forgive us. *ngegungna pamengku* (*ltry*) tolerant, forgiving in nature

wengur disagreeable odor, *e.g.* of a snake. *Ambuné * arus.* It reeked of blood.

wèngwèng *see* SALAH

wening clear, pure, free from evil (*ltry var of* BENING). **m̀/di*aké** 1 to make clear *or* pure. 2 to focus one's attention. *Atiné ora bisa di*aké ana watjané.* He couldn't concentrate on his reading.

weninga *var of* WUNINGA

wenjed **m̀/di*** to crush, squeeze, bruise

wentah *var of* MENTAH

wentâlâ (*or* ***n**) *var of* MENTALA 2

wentar **ke*** famous, well known

wentârâ *var of* WETARA

wentawis *var of* WETAWIS

wèntèh (*or* **we*an**) clear, distinct, not blurred

wènten *rg var of* WONTEN

wènter a substance used for dyeing fabric. ***an** dyed with the above. **m̀/di*** to dye with the above

wentis thigh (*ki for* PUPU)

wèr *rpr* a whizzing sound. *Swaraning montor kang liwat mung kadingkala mak wèèèr.* There was only the occasional swishing sound of a car going past.

wer *rpr* a swift upward action. *Wadungé diangkat, *, ditibakaké, djros.* He raised the axe and brought it down [on the log]. **war-*** *describing whizzing motions. Pirang² montor war-wer ana dalan geḍé.* Cars kept swishing past on the highway.

wer- *see also under* R-, WR- (*Introduction, 2.9.3, 2.9.4*)

werak sap of the sugar-palm tree

werat *rg var of* AWRAT

werdi meaning conveyed. ***ǹ** [of animals] fecund. **m̀/di*ǹi** to give the meaning of, explicate. *merdèni tembung* to explain the meaning of a word

wereg *var of* BEREG

wereng insect pest that infests rice crops

wergul a marten-like animal (*var of* REGUL)

weri troublemaker. ** désa* village troublemakers, *i.e.* thieves

werit 1 inhabited by spirits. *Wit geḍé kuwi * banget.* That big tree is haunted. 2 [of philosophical lore] mystic, esoteric. 3 harshly authoritative. 4 lying in wait for prey

werna *inf var of* WARNA

werni *inf var of* WARNI

werta *inf var of* WARTA

wertos *inf var of* WARTOS

weru a certain variety of tree

weruh 1 (**sumerep** *kr*, **priksa** *or* **uninga** *ki*) to see. *Sapa² sing * ija seneng.* Everyone who sees it likes it. 2 (**sumerep** *kr*, **priksa** *or* **uninga** *ki*) to know. *Sapa * sebabé?* Who knows why? **é keprijé?* How do you know? *awèh ** to tell, inform. ***a** (**m̀·priksa·a** *or* **ka·uninga·na** *ki*) 1 look here! let me tell you...! *Weruha, aku iki* *pokrul, kudu olèh pituwas mriksa perkara iki.* See here, I'm a lawyer—I'm entitled to a fee for handling this case. 2 (as) if one had known *or* seen. *Atiku ketir² kaja mèlu weruh²a.* My heart pounded as though I had been there to see it. *-* 1 come to find out... *Aku wis ngelih banget, *-* segané wis entèk.* I was very hungry, but it turned out that the rice was all gone. 2 all of a sudden. *Weruh² ana ula metu saka krandjang.* Suddenly a snake emerged from the basket. **ka** (*usu.* **kawruh**) knowledge (*see also* KAWRUH). **ka*an** to be seen, caught (at), found out. *Olèhé njolong ke*an.* He was caught in the act of stealing. *Bareng ḍuwité diétung, ke*an jèn kurang satus rupiah.* When he counted the money, he discovered that 100 rupiahs was missing. **m̈/di*aké** to tell, inform. *Sapa sing meruhaké dunungé kètju mau?* Who disclosed where the bandits were hiding out? **m̈/di*i** 1 to know about. *Sing koweruhi tjritakna kabèh.* Tell everything you know about it. 2 to see. *Tudjuné ana sing meruhi omah kobong.* Fortunately someone saw the house burning. **sa*é** all that one knows; as far as one knows. *Sa*mu baé tjritakna!* Tell everything you know about it! *Sa*ku ḍèwèké durung mangkat.* So far as I know, he hasn't left yet. ***** **banju** to have begun to menstruate. ***** **ing** *or* ***** **marang** to know about, realize. ***** **paḍang hawa** to get born. *See also* KAWRUH

werut [of skin, wood, *etc.*] coarse-grained

wèsel *var of* WISEL

wesi *ng,* **tosan** *kr* iron. *tukang* ***** blacksmith. *tangan* ***** powerful hands. **m̈*** resembling iron. ***adji** 1 a revered kris. 2 a poisoned weapon. ***** **bang** *ng kr* red-hot iron. *** barut** metal band for reinforcing a crate. *** brani** magnet. *** gligi·m̈** iron bar. *** mléla** shiny black iron. *** tuwa** scrap iron

wèsmister *see* DJAM

westa *inf var of* WASTA

wèsṭi *oj* obstacle, danger

wèt ngu/di*-*, nge/di*-* to use sparingly. *Mesin mau kudu di-uwèt².* You mustn't overuse the machine. *Berasé di-ewèt².* They used the rice thriftily. **ngu/di*aké, nge/di*aké** to make sth last a long time; to preserve, conserve. *See also* AWÈT

wetah intact (*kr for* WUTUH)

wétan east. *ing prenah *é tanah Éropa* located east of Europe. *Asia Sisih Kidul* *****

Southeast Asia. ***an** pertaining to the Orient. *Bangsa *an umumé seneng sega.* Most Orientals like rice. ***-*an** the eastern part. **sa*(é)** to the east of. *ing sa* kuṭa wetara rong kilomèter* a couple of kilometers east of the city. *ing sa*é omahku* east of my house. *See also* ÉTAN, PANGÉTAN

wetârâ *ng,* **wetawis** *kr* 1 interval (of space, time). *ora* ***** *suwé* after a little while, pretty soon. *Wis* ***** *seminggu.* It's been a week now. 2 for *or* after (an interval of). 3 about, approximately. ***** *umur limang taun* about five years old. *médja* ***** *karo tengah kaki ḍuwuré* a table about a foot and a half high. *Suwéné* ***** *sak djaman.* It takes about an hour. **m̈/di*** 1 to make sth somewhat [*adjective*]. *Olèhé mangan di* akèh.* Make him eat a lot! 2 to make into several. *metara papan* to make several places [*e.g.* for people to sit]. **sa*** 1 an interval of time. *Meneng sak* *****. She didn't say anything for a while. 2 several, some (number *or* amount of). *sa* organisasi kontra-révolusionèr* several counter-revolutionary organizations. *Ana sa* kang kètjèr ing djogan.* Some of it was scattered on the floor. *** let** (*or* let *****) for *or* after (an interval of). *Let* ***** *limang menit, ḍèké teka.* He showed up five minutes later. *ing kiwa lan tengening omah let* ***** *telung mèter* for a space of three meters on either side of the house. *See also* DUGA

wetawis *kr for* WETARA

weteng stomach, belly (paḍaran *ki*). *lara* ***** (to have) a stomach ache. ***an** 1 (wawrat·an *ki*) pregnancy. 2 (kanḍut·an *ki*) unborn baby, foetus. 3 broad part of a chopping-knife blade. **m̈*** (wawrat *kr,* m·bobot *or* ng·kanḍut *ki*) 1 pregnant. *wong meteng* pregnant woman. 2 ready to give forth its appropriate product. **meteng mapak** [of growing rice plants] to have come into ear and be of uniform height. **m̈*aké** (m̈·wawrat·aken *kr,* m·bobot·aké *or* ng·kanḍut·aké *ki*) pregnant with, carrying [a child]. **m̈*i** *cr* to get smn pregnant

wétikna *var of* WITIKNA

wetja prediction, prophecy. **we*n** fact(s) imparted in a prophesy. **m̈/di*** to predict, foresee. **m̈/di*kaké** to reveal [occult matters]. **pa·m̈*** prediction. *pametja marang apa sing bakal klakon* prediction of things to come

wetu *ng,* **wedal** *kr* emergence; product. *wowohan *né padésan* fruits which are the products of rural areas. **né rembulan* moonrise. *Alus *ning tembung.* The words came out smoothly. *ora ana *né* [of land] barren, unproductive. ***n̂** 1 (**wijos·an** *kr*) birthday reckoned by combining the five-day and seven-day weekday names, *e.g.* Senèn Legi. 2 a product of, having emerged from. *barang² weton ing Indonesia* things produced in Indonesia. *weton sekolahan menengah* a high-school graduate. *kalawarti weton ing Balai Pustaka* a magazine put out by the Government Printing Office. ***n̂an** 1 (**wijos·an** *kr*) connected with a birthday. *slametan wetonan* birthday celebration. 2 (**wedal·an** *kr*) exported. *barang² wetonan lija negara* imported goods (*i.e.* goods exported from other countries). **di*k̂aké** to be brought *or* put out (*see also* NGETOKAKÉ *under* TU[b]). *Bukuné wetokna.* Get out your books. *Momotané kréta diwetokaké ing dalan sepur.* The cart was unloaded at the railroad. *Bajiné diwetokaké sarana opérasi.* The baby was delivered by caesarian section. **ka*** to emerge spontaneously. *Sok ke* tembungé mengkéné.* She often spoke as follows. **m̂*** to emerge *etc.* (*see* METU). **m̂/di*n̂i** 1 to bring forth. *Bodjoné wis nglahiraké djabang baji metoni wadon.* His wife had just given birth to a baby girl. 2 to go along *or* by way of [a route]. *Dalan iki sadjaké durung tau diwetoni wong.* This path had apparently never been traveled. 3 to hold a birthday celebration in smn's honor. *Anaké suk dina Senèn iki diwetoni.* They're celebrating their son's birthday this coming Monday. **pa*** 1 product, yield. 2 income. *See also* METU, TU[b]

wetuh *rg var of* WUTUH

wew- *see also under* W- (*Introduction, 3.1.3*)

wewah to increase, add to (*kr for* WUWUH)

wéwé malevolent female spirit

weweg large, compact, and muscular (as contrasted with flabby). *Blegeré *.* He's well built.

wèwèh (*or* **a***; **nje·n̂j·suka·ni** *kr*) to give repeatedly. *Ḍèwèké seneng awèwèh.* He's always giving things away. ***an** a gift; gifts brought by one returning home. **m̂/di*aké** (**n̂j/dipun·suka·kaken** *kr*) to give sth away. *mèwèhaké klambi sing lawas* to give away old clothes. **m̂/di*i** (**n̂j/dipun·(se)·suka·ni** *kr*) 1 to give repeatedly, give many things. 2 to bring gifts to those back home. **pa*** a gift; gifts brought to those back home. *See also* WÈH[a], WÈNÈH

wèwèng direction

wi *var of* AWI, UWI

wibâwâ (*or* **ka*n**) influence *or* authority held by a respected person *or* group

wibi *oj* mother

widâdâ *oj* safe and sound

widâdârâ male counterpart of a WIDADARI

widâdari angel, nymph. **m̂*n̂i** 1 the eve of a wedding. *lenggahan midadarèni* to sit up through the night before one's wedding: traditional practice for brides. 2 (*psv* **di*n̂i**) to hold a certain ceremony for [a bride, on her wedding eve]

widadi, widadya *var of* WIDADA

widagd(y)a *oj* intelligent; skilled

widajat heaven-sent help

widak ***an** sixty by sixty, sixty at a time. **sa*, se*, su*** sixty. *wong suwidak* sixty people. *sasi Djuni taun se* dji* in June of '61. *su* taun kepungkur* sixty years ago

widârâ a certain thorny tree; also, its (edible) fruits. ***n** a dish made of rice *or* cassava flour. *** gepak** house with verandas on all sides. *** putih, * upas** common varieties of the above fruit

widâsantun *rg kr for* WIDASARI

widâsari a certain tree; also, its blossom

wiḍé 1 fishnet, fish trap. 2 bamboo shutters. **m̂/di*** to catch fish with the above equipment (1)

wiḍeng a certain freshwater crab. **ke*an** bewildered, confused

widi 1 true, correct, accurate. 2 permission (*see also* IDI). 3 regulation, provision, rule. **di*(n̂i)** to receive God's blessing. **m̂/di*** to choose [sth appropriate]. *Kanggo tjalon pulisi di* nom²an sing geḍé ḍuwur.* For police candidates, they select tall, sturdy young men. **m̂/di*k̂aké** to double-check a count (for smn). *Widèkna.* Count it again! **m̂/di*n̂i** 1 to count sth again. *Ḍuwité diwidèni.* He double-checked the money. 2 to grant permission

wiḍig coconut-leaf mat for spreading *or* drying things on

widigd(y)a *var of* WIDAGD(Y)A

widja *oj* 1 seed. 2 child

widjâjâ 1 victory. 2 mystical power (in animistic belief). *** kusuma** a certain flower that blooms (between November and February or during the rainy season) only once, at night

widjang 1 distinct, with the elements properly sorted out; [of speech] clearly enunciated. *Aku ngrungokaké kanṭi* *. I made sure I had everything straight as I listened. *Kudu wani tumindak* *. You have to make every act count for something. 2 shoulders; [of shoulders] straight, well aligned. *-* *sms* * 1. **m̈/di*(-*)** to keep distinct. *Aku arep midjang² baktéri endi sing maédahi lan mbebajani.* I'm going to keep the useful bacteria separate from the harmful ones.

widji 1 seed. 2 descendant. *kepeḍotan* * broken lineage. *nandur* * *kèli* to guard descendants of worthy people against harm *or* against a curse placed upon their lineage. 3 gateway *or* opening in a fence *or* wall. ***ǹ** sesame seed (*see also* SAMBEL). **m̈*** resembling a seed. *untu midji timun* small, white, even teeth. **m̈/di*k̀aké** to breed descendants. *Wong apik iku biasané diwidjèkaké wong apik.* Worthwhile people usually come from worthwhile families. **m̈/di*ǹi** 1 to sow seeds in. *Sawahé wis diwidjèni.* The rice paddy has been sown. 2 to put sesame seeds in sth. 3 to have [descendants]. *Pak Ali midjèni ulama² ing désa iku.* Mr. Ali was the progenitor of religious scholars in the village. **pa*ǹan** a plot sown with rice seeds. *See also* SAWIDJI

widjik to clean the hands *or* feet (*ki for* WISUH; *root form, ki for* KOBOK). **(pa)*an** 1 [water] for washing the hands *or* feet. 2 a basin of water for washing

widjil 1 seed; descendant. **ing andana warih* descendant of a nobleman. 3 a classical verse form. 4 *oj* emergence (*modern equivalent:* WETU). **ka*an** birth; origin. **m̈*** 1 to sing/chant the above verse form. 2 to emerge *etc.* (*oj; modern equivalent,* METU)

widjung a variety of large wild boar

wido [of roosters] having greenish back feathers

wiḍungan animal foetus

widuri 1 a certain seacoast plant whose fluffy casings are borne on the wind. 2 a diamond-like jewel

widyâdârâ *var of* WIDADARA

widyâdari *var of* WIDADARI

widyastuti *oj* blessings, good wishes

wigar 1 to lose its force *or* effectiveness. 2 *oj* happy, glad

wigati *ng,* **wigatos** *kr* 1 important, serious. *ngrungokaké kanṭi* * to listen seriously. *prekara* * *kang kudu di-éling²* an important matter that must be kept in mind. 2 meaning, contents. *Apa *né lajang kuwi?* What does the letter say? **ka*ǹ** interest, concern. *Apa sing kok kanḍakaké tansah dadi kawigatènku.* What you say is always of interest to me. **m̈/di*k̀aké** to consider important, take an interest in. *migatèkaké kaanané keluwargané* to take an interest in smn's family. *See also* GATI

wigatos *kr for* WIGATI

wigih *-* *or* **wigah-*** to [do] hesitantly because of a social *or* moral restraint. *Olèhé mlaku *-* sebab para sepuh lenggah ing ngisor.* He hesitated to walk there because there were elderly people sitting on the floor.

wignja 1 *oj* skilled, well versed (in). 2 (*or* ***n**) Javanese-script diacritic accompanying a consonant character to denote syllable-final *ah*. **ka*n** skill, wisdom

wihang *var of* WIJANG 2

wihanten *kr for* WIHARA

wihârâ *ng,* **wihanten** *kr* place where holy men meditate and live ascetic lives

wijâgâ *var of* NIJAGA

wijagah through sheer determination and will power. *Jèn ora* * *ngrampungké gawéjan mau adja mbok teruské.* If you simply can't get the work done, don't go on with it. **m̈*** characterized by determination *or* effort of will. *Njambut-gawé kuwi kudu sing mijagah.* Work should be done with determination and will.

wijah usual, ordinary. ***é** usually. *See also* SAWIJAH

wijak **m̈/di*(i)** 1 to open sth out/apart (*var of* M̈/DI-PIJAK-(I)). 2 to discover, reveal. *mijak wadi* to disclose a secret

wijandjânâ *gram* phonetic stop sound (*P, T, Ṭ, TJ, K; B, D, Ḍ, DJ, G*)

wijang 1 *rg* to go, leave. * *endi?* Where are you going? 2 *ltry* unwilling, reluctant. *Adja* * *ing gawé.* Don't shy away from work.

wijar large, spacious (*kr for* AMBA)

wijârâ *var of* WIHARA

wijat *var of* AWIJAT

wijâtâ instruction, teachings. **m̈*ni** convincing; (*psv* **di*ni**) to convince. *Heh, heh, kowé kuwi kaja mijatan-mijatanana.* Well! you act as though you're pretty well convinced. **pa*n** educational institution. *pa*n luhur* university

wijoga *oj* deeply upset. **ka*n** a deep emotional upset

wijos 1 seed (*rg kr for* WIDJI). 2 gate(way) (*kr for* RÉGOL). 3 different (*rg kr for* SÉDJÉ). ***an** 1 birthday (*ki for* WETU·Ñ). 2 pertaining to birthdays (*ki for* WETU·ÑAN). ***é** *introductory word in a letter.* **m̃*** 1 to be born (*ki for* LAIR). 2 to pass (*ki for* LIWAT). 3 to go, leave (*ki for* LUNGA). 4 to come (*ki for* TEKA). 5 to go/come out (*ki for* M̃·WETU). **m̃/di*** to give birth to (*ki for* NG/DI·LAIR·AKÉ)

wikan *oj* to know. ***a** I don't know (*sbst kr for* EMBUH). **nga*i** to know, understand. *Ḍèwèké ngawikani prakara mau.* He knows about the problem.

wikrâmâ *var of* PIKRAMA

wiku ascetic learned man

wil 1 *wj* young ogre (child of a BUTA). 2 *inf var of* DJAWIL

wilâdâ a certain plant

wiladah bathing ritual performed forty days after giving birth

wilah 1 long, thin stick. * *pantjing* fishing rod. * *kaju* wooden pole. 2 [of cocks' combs] high and serrated (rather than small: *see* SUMPET). *djènggèr* * a high cock's-comb. 3 kris blade. 4 arrangement *or* layout of gamelan instruments for a performance. ***an** *sms* * 1, 3, 4. **m̃/di*** to steal a kris from the wearer

wilajah region. *-* *sing hawané panas* places where the climate is warm

wilang *ng,* **witjal** *kr* ***an** number. *tembung *an* number, numeral; quantity word. **an pepangkatan* ordinal number. **an petjahan* fraction. **an tjamboran* number having more than one digit. **an gegolongan* "group" number, *e.g. puluh* -ty. *tanpa *an* countless, innumerable. *éwon tanpa *an* countless thousands. **ka*** 1 to be counted. 2 to be regarded (as). *kuṭa sing wis ke* geḍé* a city which is considered large. **m̃*** 1 to count, enumerate. 2 to classify, categorize. **milang kori** to go to every house; *fig* to travel widely. **milang usuk** to lie around doing nothing. **m̃/di*aké** to classify, differentiate. *Ḍèwèké ora bisa milangaké endi sing bener lan endi sing salah.* He can't tell which is right and which is wrong. **pa·m̃*** act *or* way of counting; an enumeration. *Pamilangé salah, tjoba diétung sepisan manèh.* The calculation is wrong; try it again.

wilanten *var of* WLANTEN

wilâsâ *oj* sympathy, pity. **ka*n** compassion

wilet 1 snarled; complicated. 2 expert at speaking. 3 [of music] sweet, melodious. 4 [of gamelan music] interval between notes. **ka*** carried away by persuasive words. **m̃*** devious, rambling. *Miled ngendikané nganggo bebasan lan senépa.* His talk rambled on and on, full of proverbs and figures of speech. **ma*an** (in a) tangled *or* snarled (condition). *Lunging gaḍung manglung mawiletan.* The yam vines hung down in a tangle.

wilis 1 green; dark green; shiny green. 2 *rg var of* WILANG. *katjang* * green bean(s). *laler* * a certain green fly. *nglaler* * resembling this green fly; to behave badly. *manuk* * green bird with edible flesh (*see also* IDJO·AN). *paṭola* * or *tjinḍé* * green silk material. ***an** sedan chair *or* palanquin for distinguished persons. **tanpa *** innumerable, countless

wiludjeng well; safe and sound (*kr for* SLAMET)

wilwa possessed of an evil spirit

wimba *oj* 1 statue, likeness. 2 emergence (*modern equivalent:* WETU). **m̃*** 1 to emerge. 2 (*psv* **di***) to resemble. *Swarané mimba gluḍuk.* His voice is like thunder. ***ning lèk** the time of the new moon

wimbuh *oj* supplement (*see also* IMBUH)

win- *see also under* W- (*Introduction, 3.1.7*)

winarangkârâ *ltry* to be incarcerated (*form of* WRANGKA)

windu 1 a period (recurring in cycles of four) consisting of eight 210-day years (*taun Djawa*), each with its own name (*Alip, Éhé, Djimawai, Djé, Dal, Bé, Wawu, Djimakir*). 2 edge *or* lip of a well. ***ñ** 1 by the *windu,* according to *or* counting by *windu*'s. 2 many *windu*'s; *windu* after *windu.* 3 *windu*-birthday celebration (*see* M̃*Ñ *below*). **ka*** [of a time limit] to expire. *Wektuné mèh ke*.* The time has almost run out. **m̃*** 1 to recall, reminisce. *Jèn mindu barang sing betjik waé.* Just think back on the good things. 2 (*psv* **di***) to put sth on the edge of [a well]. **m̃/di*ñi** 1 to celebrate one's *windu* birthday (on the last day of each *windu* of one's life). 2 to furnish [a well] with a lip. **pa·m̃*ñ** lathe for shaping wood. *** adi** the first *windu* in the cycle of four: characterized by events of supreme greatness and significance. *** kunṭara** the second *windu:* characterized by creative activities. * **sengara** the third *windu:* characterized by natural disasters. * **santjaja** the fourth *windu:* characterized by cooperation and friendship

winga **ma*-*** *ltry* enraged, flushed with anger. *Dukané ma*-*.* or *Djadja bang ma*-*.* He was in a towering rage. *Rainé abang ma*-*.* His face burned with fury.

wingi yesterday. *ḍèk ** yesterday. ***ṅan·é** the day before yesterday. ***né** day before yesterday. ***-*** formerly, in the old days. * **soré** 1 yesterday evening. 2 new at. *guru * soré* a new (inexperienced) teacher. *botjah * soré* young and inexperienced. * **uni** in the past; former times. *Tentrem manèh kaja *-uni.* Things were calm again, as they had been before.

wingit *var of* WINGIT

wingka 1 shard of earthenware *or* roofing tile. 2 a cookie made of sticky-rice flour. **m̈*** hard like a tile fragment

wingking back, rear; later on; last [time] (*kr for* BURI)

wingkis ***an** gums (*ki for* GUSI). **m̈/di*** 1 to roll up [the sleeves: *lit, fig*]. *Ḍèwèké mingkis lengananè klambi.* He got ready to pitch in and work. 2 to fold the plait at the front of a batik wraparound (*see* WIRU)

wingko * **Babat** specialty cookies from the town of Babat

winibiting eye drops made from a folk-medicine recipe

winih 1 seed *or* cutting for starting a plant; *fig* root, cause. 2 heredity. *duwé * sing ora apik* to come of bad lineage. 3 animal used for breeding purposes. **m̈/di*i** to sow [earth] with seeds. **pa*an** seed bed

winong a variety of tree

winongwong *ltry* protected, watched over

wira *oj* 1 man. 2 manly, courageous. *prakosa wirèng* (= *wira ing*) *juda* strong and courageous in battle. *See also* PERWIRA

wiradat wish; intention. **m̈/di*i** to find a means of implementing a wish *or* intention. *Slamet miradati anggoné arep mbangun omah kanṭi adol sawah.* Slamet financed the building of his house by selling his rice paddy.

wirâgâ 1 physical body. 2 to behave in a deliberately appealing *or* provocative way. **né pantjèn ngresepaké.* She has a very attractive physical appearance. *or* She acts that way to attract others. **ka*n** behavior which one adopts deliberately, *e.g.* as an impersonation; in depicting a character in a dance-drama. **m̈*** to put on attractive *or* appealing ways. *Siti pinter miraga.* Siti knows how to act provocative. **m̈/di*kaké** to adopt [certain characteristics of behavior]. **pa·m̈*** bodily movements employed when behaving as above

wirâmâ *ltry var of* IRAMA

wiranḍungan *oj* slow, hesitant

wirang embarrassment, loss of face, mortification. *Utang * njaur *.* If you cause others to lose face, they will do the same to you. **ku*an, ke*an** 1 embarrassment. 2 to be embarrassed (by). *Sapa sing adi² ing tembé temtu ke*an.* Pride goes before a fall. **me·m̈*** *or* **m̈*aké** 1 embarrassing, causing embarrassment. 2 (*psv* **di·we*** *or* **di*aké**) to embarrass *or* mortify smn

wiraos *kr for* WIRASA

wirâsâ *ng,* **wiraos** *kr* context; meaning conveyed *e.g.* in a letter, gesture, action. **m̈*** 1 delicious-tasting. 2 (*psv* **di***) to search out the meaning of. *See also* RASA

wirasat *var of* PIRASAT

wirèng 1 (*or* ***an**) *wj* a dance representing a duel. 2 *contracted form of* WIRA ING

wiri **wira-*** *or* **wara-*** to move back and forth. *mabur wira-** to fly back and forth. *wira-* wong* traffic, flow of people. *wira-* ndjupuk banju* to keep going back for more water

wirid teachings, guidance. **m̈/di*** to teach, instruct, give guidance

wiring *var of* IRING. * **galih** [of fighting cocks] having red feathers and black legs. * **kuning** [of fighting cocks] having yellow legs. *djago * kuning* yellow-legged

wiris *see* WARAS

wirja *ltry* brave, courageous. **ka*n** courage, bravery

wirjawan *ltry* brave one. **ka*** courage (*see also* KAWIRJAWAN)

wirog a variety of large rat

wirong *var of* MIRONG

wiru corn-leaf cigarette wrapper (*sbst? kr for* KLOBOT). ***n̂** lengthwise accordion plaits formed in a batik wraparound (at the time the wearer puts it on) by finger-pressing the folds and clipping them in place. *wiron éngkol* plait (as above) folded with a rippling edge. **m̈/di*(n̂i)** to form plaits (in) [a wraparound] as above

wiruh *var of* WERUH

wirung ***an** *var of* IRUNG·AN

wis *ng*, **sampun** *kr* 1 to have [done, become]. *Kowé apa * adus?* Have you had your bath? *Udané apa * terang²?* Has it stopped raining? *Saiki * wengi.* It's night now. *Omahmu anjar apa * rampung?* Is your new house finished yet? *Wis suwé aku ora tilik.* I haven't been to see him for a long time. *Kakangku * gedé.* My brother is grown up. *Bareng * olèh telung dina...* When three days had gone by... *Segané * dadi.* The rice is done. *Kuwi * lumrah.* It's the usual thing now. ** kebandjur.* It's too late now. *Tjèlènganku * kebak.* My piggy bank is full. *Rak * ngerti ta, kowé?* You understand now, don't you? 2 to have begun [do]ing. *Jèn * sinau ora éling wektu.* Once he gets to studying, he's not aware of time. 3 over, finished; all right (now); that's enough. *Sikilku diresiki, jèn * diwènèhi tamba.* He cleaned my leg; then he put some medicine on it. *Wis, turu menèh.* OK, back to bed. *Wis, menenga waé ta.* That's enough out of you now. *Wis ta, endang salina!* Come *on,* hurry up and change clothes! *Olèhé matja buku * sewengi ḍeng, meksa durung *.* He read all night and he still hasn't finished the book. 4 yes (*in answer to questions containing* WIS *or* DURUNG). *Apa * adus?—*.* Have you had your bath?—Yes. *Durung mangan ḍèkè?—Wis.* Has he eaten yet?—Yes, he's eaten. ***a** even though sth has [done, been]. **a mangan, mangan manèh rak ora apa².* You have just eaten, but it's all right if you have more. ***an** 1 remaining, left over. *Rotiné tak pangan *an.* I ate the rest of the cake. *mBok dirampungné *àn.* Please finish up your work. 2 aftermath; conclusion. **an gawé* the end of the day's work; the time (*ca.* 11 A.M.) when the morning work in the fields is finished. *Wisan gawéné djam pira?* What time do you get out of work? *(w)ajah wisan gawé* rush hour after work. ***é** an end (to sth). *Perangé tanpa ana *é.* The war goes on and on. ***-*** completed, in the past. *Tudjuné dikon manḍek, oraa rak ora uwis².* Luckily we told him to stop: otherwise he would have gone on and on. *sing *-** what is over and done with. **ngu/di*i, nge/di*i** *ng kr* to finish sth. *Wis peteng, ndang diuwisi gawéané.* It's dark—hurry and finish the work. **sa*é** after; afterwards. *Sa*é sarapan, tata² arep sekolah.* After breakfast they got ready for school. *** arep** about to, on the verge of. *Sadjaké * arep udan.* It looks as if it's about to rain. *** dudu** to no longer [be sth]. *Ḍèwèké * dudu mahasiswa.* He isn't a student any more. *** ja** goodbye! so long! so much for that! *** kaja** just like. *Aku nganggep kowé * kaja sedulurku ḍéwé.* I think of you just as my own brother. *** mèh** on the point of. ** mèh setaun lawasé.* It's lasted for nearly a year now. ** mèh tekan.* They'll be here any minute. *** ora** to no longer [do]. ** adoh, * ora kétok.* It's so far off now you can't see it any longer. *** tau** to have (ever) [done, been]. *Bijèn * tau ditjakot asu édan.* He was once bitten by a mad dog. *Apa kowé * tau ndeleng pasar-malem?* Have you ever been to a fair?

wisa poison, venom. **m̃/di*ni** to poison. *Kutjingé mati di*ni ula.* The cat died of snake poisoning.

wisâjâ means *or* equipment, *esp.* for snaring fish. **m̃/di*** to catch *or* trap fish. *para djuru misaja* fishermen

wisâtâ trip, journey. *darma ** travel for the purpose of study *or* for pleasure (*esp.* a picnic). **m̃*** to travel, take a trip. *See also* PARIWISATA

wisatawan tourist

wisel 1 postal money order. 2 railroad siding; switch. **m̃/di*aké** to transmit [money] by postal money order. *See also* SALAH

wisésa 1 authority, control. *Hyang Maha ** God. *Botjah iku mung gumantung ana *né wong tuwa.* Children are controlled by their parents. 2 *gram* affix. *rimbag * -na* addition of the suffix *-an* to a root (*termed -na by the Javanese*). **ka*** under the control of. *ka* déning raga* a slave to one's physical self. **m̃/di*(ni)** to exercise authority over. *Di* ngajahi pegawéjané.* He was compelled to do the job. **pa·m̃*n** control, authority. *See also* PURBA-WISÉSA

wisik knowledge *or* words of advice imparted by supernatural beings *or* by seers. ***an** 1 *sms* *. 2 night wind. **m̃/di*** to impart knowledge to

wiski whiskey

wisma *oj* house. *** juju mangga borong** it's up to you; suit yourself

Wisnu Vishnu

wisoh *rg var of* WISUH

wistârâ *oj* story, narration, tale. **ka*** 1 expressed, told. *tjrita kang ka* ing lajang* *kabar* the story given in the newspaper. *Penggalih duka iku ora ka**. He didn't express his annoyance. 2 well known. *ka* kawanènané ing prang* known for his bravery in battle. **m̄/di*kaké** to tell, narrate

wisuda, wisuḍa 1 pure, clean. 2 high in social status. *kantor ** personnel office. *dina ** graduation day. ***n** act of appointing *or* installing. *upatjara *n* inauguration ceremony. **m̄/di*** to appoint smn to *or* inaugurate smn in [a position]. *misuḍa awaké ḍéwé dadi kaisar* to set oneself up as emperor. **pa·m̄*n** appointment; installation; promotion. *tumrap ing kala pamisuḍanipun pangkat Bupati* at the time of his installation as Regent. *See also* KULAWISUDA

wisuh *ng kr,* **widjik** *ki* to wash one's hands *or* feet. ***an** water *or* basin for washing the hands/feet. **m̄/di*i** to wash smn's hands/feet

wisuna 1 slander; false accusation. 2 (source of) difficulty. **ning djedjoḍoan* a source of trouble in marriage. *Ḍèwèké kena * ngarah patiné sikantja mau.* He's in serious trouble for trying to kill his friend.

wit 1 tree. 2 plant. ** pari* rice plant. 3 because; cause, root. **ing tresna saka kulina.* Love rises from proximity. ***-*an** 1 trees; heavily wooded area, place where plants grow luxuriantly. 2 imitation tree. *dolanan *-*an sing gawé saka plastik* a plastic toy tree. ***na** *or* ***né** *inf var of* WITIKNA. **né ḍèké ora ngresula, ḍuwité akèh.* No wonder he didn't complain–he had plenty of money. **sa*** one tree(ful) *or* plant(ful). *lombok sauwit* one pepper plant. *keṭèk sa** a treeful of monkeys; all the monkeys in the tree

witèkné *var of* WITIKNA

witikna because, in view of the fact that. *Djamé kepeksa tak edol, * aku ora duwé ḍuwit.* I had to sell the watch–I had no money.

witikné *var of* WITIKNA

witir *see* SALAT

witjaksânâ endowed with wisdom. *penggeḍé sing ** a wise leader

witjal number; to count (*root form: kr for* WILANG)

witjanten 1 talk, discussion (*kr for* TJATUR). 2 to say, speak (*kr for* TJLAṬU). 3 speech, conversation, way of talking (*kr for* WITJARA). ***an** to talk, converse (*kr for* (KE)·KANḌA·N)

witjara *ng,* **witjanten** *kr* 1 speech; conversation. *ahli ** expert speaker/conversationalist. *djuru ** announcer. 2 to speak in a deliberately attractive *or* provocative way. **m̄*** 1 *sms ** 2. 2 (**ngendika** *ki*) to speak. 3 (*psv* **di***) to discuss

wiwâhâ *ltry* 1 wedding. *Ardjuna ** (*wj*) the Wedding of Ardjuna. 2 wedding feast. **m̄/di*** 1 to marry (*i.e.* perform the marriage ceremony for) smn. 2 to celebrate [an event] with a feast

wiwal separating, coming apart. ** nalaré* unbalanced, crazy. **m̄/di*** to divorce [one's husband]. **pa·m̄*** money (to be) given to a wife who is divorcing her husband

wiwârâ *oj* hole, opening. *Tjangkemé mangap kaja *ning guwa.* His mouth gaped like the opening of a cave.

wiwéka watchfulness (*var of* WÉKA)

wiwir **m̄/di*** to extend *or* spread sth sideways

wiwit the beginning; beginning with; to begin. ** bijèn* for a long time; a long time ago *or* before. ** kapan* since when? ** mau* for some time now, for quite a while, all this time. ** mula* to begin with... (*opening line of a narrative*). ** sekawit* from the very beginning. ** 1913* (ever) since 1913. ** tjilik* since one's childhood, since [smn] was a child. *ḍèk * perang* at the beginning of the war. *Wiwit mlaku alon²*. He began to walk slowly. *Keṭopraké main * (saka) djam sanga tekan djam rolas bengi.* The show runs from 9 P.M. till midnight. *Moḍal kerdja kanggo pawitan *é mung Rp. sa juta.* The initial capital amounted to only a million rupiahs. ***(-*)an** (at) the beginning; the first (part); the origin. *saka minggu *an nganti pungkasan* from the first week to the last. *Wiwitané enḍog, bandjur dadi embug²an.* At the beginning it's an egg; later on it becomes a cocoon. *kaja ḍèk *an* the way it was at first. **m̄/di*i** to begin sth. *miwiti nggarap* to begin working. *Jèn nrowong gunung, olèhé miwiti saka kiwa-tengen.* When they tunnel through a mountain, they start from both ends at once. *See also* AWIT, KAWIT, SAKAWIT

wja *oj* don't!

wjandjânâ consonant sound *or* letter

wk. *see* WAKIL

wl. *see* WULAN

wl- *see also under* L- (*Introduction, 2.9.4*)

wlâkâ *var of* BLAKA

Wlândâ *ng,* **Wlandi** *kr* 1 Holland, the Netherlands. 2 a Netherlander. 3 a European; a Westerner. * *Amérika* an American. * *Inggris* an Englishman. **M̈/di*kaké** 1 to (have smn) become a Dutch citizen. 2 to translate into Dutch. **M̈*ni** to imitate Dutch (European, Western) people *or* ways. * **Ḍiḍong** Dutchman; Caucasian person. *See also* KUMALANDA

Wlandi *kr for* WLANDA

wlanten white, clean, pure. **m̈/di*** to whiten, purify, cleanse. **pa·m̈*** one who cleanses

wluku a plow. **m̈/di*** to plow. **m̈/di*k̂aké** 1 to plow for smn. 2 to have smn plow; to have sth plowed. **pa·m̈*** a plow

wlulang *var of* LULANG

wlungsung **m̈/di*** to provide smn with a change of clothing. **m̈*i** 1 to shed the old skin and grow a new one. *Ulané mlungsungi.* The snake changed its skin. 2 (*psv* **di***) to change one's attitude toward sth, to have a change of heart

wo well! why!

wod 1 *oj* root. **ing ati* beloved one. 2 *gram* monosyllabic root base. 3 (to extract) the square root. ***-*an** (various kinds of) roots

wogan a variety of caterpillar

woh fruit. *ngunḍuh * sawo* to pick *sawo* fruits. *ngunḍuh *ing panggawéné* to reap the fruits of one's labors. ***an** guava. ***-*an** various kinds of fruit. **a*** to bear fruit. *Wit krambilku lagi awoh sidji isih degan.* Our coconut tree has one young coconut on it. **pa*an** container for betel-chewing materials

wok 1 a shallow depression in the ground. 2 growth of (human) hair *or* (birds') feathers on the throat area. 3 hanging roots, of *e.g.* a banyan tree. ***an** 1 *sms* * 1. 2 (*or* ***-*an**) rotten decayed. *enḍog *an* a rotten egg

wok-keṭekur *rpr* the cooing of a dove

wol 1 wool. 2 *rpr* a large pinch of a fat person's flesh. 3 short, dwarfish

wolu eight. **las* eighteen. **likur* twenty-eight. *djam setengah ** 7:30. *Umuré pitung taun, * mlaku.* She's seven going on eight. ***n̂** *or* ***nan** by eights, eight at a time. *Rombongané wolunan.* There are eight in each group. **we*** (group *or* unit of) eight. *Wong we* lunga kabèh.* All eight of the people left. ***-*** by eights. *Barisé *-*.* They marched in ranks of eight. **ka*** 1 (*or* [ka]ping *) eight times; times eight; (for) the eighth time; eighth in a series. *Lotèng sap ka* mung mligi kanggo kamar ḍahar.* The eighth floor [of the hotel] is exclusively dining rooms. 2 the eighth month of the Javanese year (4 February–1 March). * **tengah** 7½. *See also* -AN (*suffix*) 8, 15, 16; -É[c] (*suffix*) 9; NG- (*prefix*) 6, 7; PRA-; WOLUNG

wolung 1 hawk; eagle. 2 eight (*as modifier: see also* WOLU). * *atus* (*èwu, juta*) eight hundred (thousand, million). * *djam* eight hours. *See also* NG- (*prefix*) 6, 7

wondéné now, and (while) (*kr for* ANADÉNÉ)

wondéning *var of* WONDÉNÉ

wondènten *md for* ANADÉNÉ

wong[a] *ng,* **tijang** *kr* 1 (**prijantun** *ki*) person; adult; man(kind); someone, a person. * *loro* two people. *Disenengi *.* He's popular. *Ora tau sija² marang *.* He's never mean to anyone. *Ḍèké seneng mitulungi *-*.* He likes to help people. *Saben * kena mlebu.* Anyone can go in. **-* lan botjah²* adults and children. *Iki *é sapa?* Whose group does this man belong in? *Tikus iku satruné *.* Rats are man's enemy. *dadi ** to be *or* become someone, *i.e.* a person of consequence. 2 one who. * *dodol ḍawet* a molasses seller. * *turu adja diganggu.* Don't disturb sleeping people. *Ana * sowan.* There's a visitor here. 3 physical characteristics of a person. **é pijé?–Lemu nganggo katja.* What's he like?–He's fat and wears glasses. ***-*an** 1 dummy, fake human being. *Sawah² dipasangi *-*an.* They set up scarecrows in the fields. 2 (**te·tijang·an** *kr*) personal characteristics. *Wong²ané kaja ngapa?* What sort of person is he? **ngu*** (*ng*) *var of* WONG, *esp. after vowel. diguju ngu** to get laughed at. *Ḍèké wis tau didol ngu*, mula saiki sapa² ditjurigani.* Somebody gypped him once, and now he's suspicious of everyone. **ngu*i** *ng* 1 to become an adult. 2 (*psv* **di*i**) to do, accomplish. *Gawéané diuwongi ḍéwé.* He did the job by himself. **sa*a** anybody at all, everybody. *Sak *a bisa nglakoni ngono.* Anyone can do that. * **aju** (*ltry*) *term of endearment for a female loved one.* * **ala** immoral person, *esp.* a thief. * **(pa·ng·)alas·an** woodsman, jungle inhabitant; boor. * **arum** *sms* * AJU *above.* * **bagus** (*ltry*) *term of endearment for a male loved one.* * **bumi** a native. **dudu *** extraordinary. * **geḍé** physically large person; important *or* high-ranking person. * **kuning** *term of endearment for one's female fair-skinned sweetheart.* * **lanang** man, adult male; husband. * **lija** 1 somebody else. 2 a non-relative. * **nakal** prostitute. * **ora duwé** poor person. * **pradja** one who lives at court; government official. * **tjilik** the little man, (one of) the common people. * **ṅ·tonton** spectator, member of the audience. * **tuwa** 1 old person. 2 parent(s). 3 person with respected powers of healing. * **urip** living people; human life. ** urip kok rekasa ngéné.* What hard lives we lead! * **wadon** *or* * **wédok** woman, adult female; wife

wong[b] *ng,* **tijang** *kr excl* 1 why! (*expressing deprecation*). ** wis gedé kok nangis.* A big boy like you, crying! 2 *word of explanation or justification. Mesti waé ditresnani, * betjik kelakuané.* No wonder they loved him; he was always kind. *Adja kéné, djero, * kowé ora bisa nglangi.* Not here!—it's deep, and you can't swim. 3 *requesting verification. Botjah² * wis mangan, konen turu.* The kids have eaten, haven't they?—send them to bed! *See also* LA WONG *under* LA

wonga *-* the space between the breasts

wongwa *oj* burning charcoal

wongwang *var of* WUNGWANG

wonten there is/are; to be, exist; in, on, at (*kr for* ANA[a]). **nga/dipun*aken** *or* **nga/dipun*i** to create, establish, bring about (*kr for* NG/DI·ANA·KAKÉ, NG/DI·ANA·NI)

wor combined/together with. *Berasé * wedi.* The rice has sand in it. *Ḍèké mangan * wong akèh.* He ate with a lot of other people. *adjur * kisma* (*wj*) dust, nothingness. **ngu/di*** to mix [things]. *Wong lanang² di* karo wong wédok².* The men were put in with the women. **ngu/di*aké** to put sth in with [sth else]. *Kutjingé adja di*ké asu.* Don't put the cat where the dog is! *ngu*aké beras karo djagung* to put rice in with the corn. **ngu/di*i** to mix sth [into sth else]. *Olèhé ngu*i pasir kakèhen.* You put too much sand in it. *Tambanana lirang di*i lenga klentik.* Dose him with sulfur and coconut oil. *See also* AWOR, MOR, WOWOR

worsuh helter-skelter, random, disorganized. *Olèhé tjrita ora pati tjeta, tur *.* His story wasn't clear, it was all scrambled. *Gawéané werna², nanging ora *.* There were all kinds of tasks, but they were well organized.

wortel carrot

wos 1 essence, contents. **ing lajangé* what the letter said. 2 raw rice (*kr for* BERAS). *See also* SARI

wosé extracted kernel *or* seed. ***ǹ** extracted. *kopi wosèn* coffee beans. *katjang wosèn* shelled nuts

wot 1 makeshift bridge of *e.g.* wood, bamboo, rope. ***-*an** to walk across a log *etc.* as a game. **ngu/di*, nge/di*** 1 to cross a makeshift bridge. 2 to move across a high narrow place (*e.g.* tightrope) by walking above it *or* hanging from it. * **gantung** small suspension bridge. * **ogal-agil** rickety bridge; *fig* the difficult straight-and-narrow path to heaven

wowog **ke*en, ku*en** distressed by the size *or* quantity of sth (*e.g.* having eaten too much). *Slamet ku*en weruh penggawéjan semono akèhé.* Slamet was staggered by the sight of so much work to be done.

wowohan *var of* WOH²AN

wowor ***an** ingredient. *Roti kuwi *ané apa?* What are the ingredients of bread? **ka*an** mixed with/into. *Berasé ka*an wedi.* There was sand in the rice. **ṁ/di*(i)** to mix sth into; to mix in. *Rotiné di*i djagung.* The bread has corn mixed into it. *mowor sambu* fifth columnist, spy who works from within. *See also* AWOR, WOR

wr- *see also under* R- (*Introduction, 2.9.4*)

wragad expense, cost (*var of* RAGAD). **ṁ/di*i** to pay the expenses of

wrâhâ *rg* wild boar

wrângkâ 1 *ltry* prison. 2 grand vizier. 3 (**sarung·an** *kr*) kris sheath (*see also* RANGKA). ***n** grand vizier. **we* dalem** grand vizier. **ṁ/di*** to incarcerate smn. **ṁ/di*ni** 1 to serve [a king] as grand vizier. 2 to provide [a kris] with a sheath. **pa*n** *ltry* incarceration in prison. * **dalem** grand vizier

wrasan to experience. *Kowé durung tau * pijé rekasané golèk duwit.* You don't know from experience how hard it is to earn a living. *Kowé apa wis * masakané?* Have you tasted her cooking?

wrat 1 heavy; important (*kr for* BOT). 2 to hold; to load (*root form: kr for* MOT)

wre- *see also under* WER- (*Introduction, 2.9.6*)

wreda, wreḍa *oj* old. * **Krama** a variety of the Krama speech style (*See Introduction, 5.5*)

wrena *var of* RENA 1
wresah a plant
wruh *oj* to know; to see. ***anamu** look here! let me tell you...! **ka*** knowledge (*see also* KAWRUH)
wuda *ng kr,* **lukar** *ki* naked. *botjah isih ** a very young child; *fig* an innocent/inexperienced child. **ka*n** bared, made naked. **m̀/di*ni** to undress smn
wuḍar *var of* UḌAR
wudel *ng kr,* **tuntun·an** *ki* navel. **ora duwé *** 1 stupid, brainless. 2 tireless. *Ajo lèrèn, kok kaja ora duwé *.* Let's take a break–you work too hard!
wudjud 1 shape, form, appearance. *Aku lali *é.* I forget what it looked like. **é idjo enom.* It was light green. 2 to be (in the form of). *Kéwan mau * laler.* The insect is a fly. *tanduran sing * térong, lombok, katjang* eggplant, pepper, and peanut plants. **we*an** of various shapes. *sakabèhing we*-an ing ngalam-donja iki* every single thing that exists in this world. **a*** to take (the) shape (of). *Kasugihané wong tani a* pari utawa radjakaja.* A farmer's wealth is in the form of rice or cattle. *retjané watu a* gadjah* a stone statue of an elephant. **m̀/di*aké** 1 to comprise, make up. *Tembung telu mau mudjudaké ukara.* These three words make a sentence. 2 to cause to materialize. *mudjudaké sing didjaluk* to bring about what he had asked for. 3 to depict. *Nalagarèng di*aké ala tanpa rupa.* Nalagarèng is depicted as being physically ugly. **m̀/di*i** 1 to comprise, make up. 2 to undergo, endure. *Bareng mati dak *i.* I am willing to die with him. *See also* UDJUD
wudlu to wash the face and hands ritually before praying. **m̀/di*n̂i** to bathe smn ritually in preparation for sth, *esp.* a bride (for her wedding); a corpse (for burial)
wudu *var of* WUDLU
wuḍu *var of* UḌU
wuduk fat(ty), rich (*oj*). *sega ** rice boiled in coconut milk
wudun *ng kr,* **untar** *ki* pimple, boil. ***en** to have a pimple/boil. *** brama** 1 boil, carbuncle. 2 lamprey. *** semat** a small painful abscess
wuh waste material, refuse. *krandjang ** wastebasket, trash container. ** iku dadi susuhing lelara werna²*. Garbage provides a breeding ground for all kinds of diseases. **pa*an** a square hole in the ground for the disposal of water material. *djugangan pa*-an* garbage pit
wujung 1 *oj* anger; angry. 2 *oj* sad(ness). 3 infatuated. ***an** war. *botjah *an* child born in war time. *See also* WAJANG-WUJUNG
wuk little girl (*adr, term of endearment: shf of* BAWUK). ***-*an** rotten, decayed. *enḍog *-*an* rotten egg
wukir *oj* mountain. *Indonesia iku negara pasir awukir.* Indonesia is a country of seacoasts and mountains.
wuk-keṭekur *var of* WOK-KEṬEKUR
wuku 1 one of thirty 7-day periods, each with its own name, which make up a 210-day Javanese year (*taun Djawa, taun Saka*). 2 seed; grain. *asem sa** tamarind grain/seed. 3 section of a bamboo *or* rattan stalk. **pa*n̂** astrological reckoning by *wuku*'s. *pawukoné wong among tani* a farmers' almanac. *Pawukon Mawa Gambar* Illustrated *Wuku*-Reckoning Chart
wukuh *rg var of* WUKU
wulan 1 (*abbr*: **wl.**) month (*kr for* SASI). 2 moon (*rg var of* (RE)MBULAN; *rg kr for* (RE)MBULAN). 3 date (*rg kr for* TANGGAL). ***an** 1 monthly; by the month (*kr for* SASI·Ǹ). 2 menstruation (*kr for* KÈL). *See also* TRIWULAN
wulang (**wutjal** *sbst? kr*) instruction, teachings. *Aku ndjaluk * kowé wis lali aldjabarku kabèh.* Please help me with my algebra–I've completely forgotten it. **(we)*an** that which is taught. **an iki kudu diapalaké.* This lesson is to be learned by heart. **m̀/di*aké** to teach [a subject]. *mulangaké ilmu bumi marang murid²* to teach geography to the pupils. **m̀/di*(i)** (**ng/di·asta·[ni]** *ki*) to teach. *mulang étung* to teach arithmetic. *Saben soré botjah² di*i ngadji.* Every evening the young people are taught to read the Koran. **pa·m̀*** 1 act *or* way of teaching. *Pamulangé gampang ditampa.* His teaching is easy to understand. 2 (*or* **pa·m̀*an**) school, place of learning. **pi*** instruction. *pi*é Gandhi* Gandhi's teachings. *** Rèh** one of two classic works on Javanese philosophy (*see also* WÉDATAMA). *** sarak** ill-mannered. *** wuruk** teachings
wulat **m̀/di*** to scrutinize, examine minutely
wulet *var of* ULET. *** kulit·é** invulnerable to weapons. *** umur·é** long-lived; immortal
wuli ear [of rice, corn]. ***ǹ** 1 in (the form

of) ears. 2 ears collectively. *Wulèné disisil.* The ears were pecked by the birds.

wulu 1 fur, feathers; body hair. 2 diacritic in the Javanese script which changes vowel *A* to *I*. 3 *var of* WUDLU. ***n̂** marked with the above diacritic. **pa·m̈*** hairy. *** dirga** a lengthening mark in Javanese orthography. *** kalong** *or* *** langseb** fine hair on the forehead and neck; upper-lip hair on women. *** sétan** a single hair on the skin. *** wawar** long body hair. *** pa·m̈·wetu** *or* *** wetu-(ning bumi)** agricultural product. *See also* WULU-TJUMBU

wuluh 1 a certain tart fruit. 2 gun barrel. 3 **(welah** *kr***)** a slender bamboo plant. 4 (*or* ***an**) iron pipe used as a lamp chimney. **m̈/di*** to clean [a kris] by rubbing it with the above fruit (1)

wulung 1 blue-black. *iket ** a blue-black wrapped headdress worn by *kyai*'s and *kaum*'s. *pring ** blue-black bamboo. 2 hawk (*var of* WOLUNG). **m̈/di*** to dye [fabric] blue-black

wulu-tjumbu 1 *wj, mythology* clown-servant. * *Madukara* the four clown-servants of the Pendawas: Semar and his sons Pétruk, Garèng, and Bugong. 2 friend *or* companion of unequal social status, *e.g.* a servant's child who grows up with the master's child

wungkal *var of* UNGKAL

wungkuk bent, crooked, deformed, hunchbacked

wungkul 1 whole, not yet cut *or* broken open; *fig* plain, simple, naive, unsophisticated. 2 [of hoofs] whole, not split (as contrasted with BELAH). *Djaran iku atratjak *.* Horses have unsplit hooves. ***an** (in) whole (condition)

wungkus wrapper, *esp.* of banana leaves. ***an** 1 a packet wrapped with banana leaf. 2 (food) cooked in a leaf wrapping. **m̈/di*-aké** 1 to wrap in banana leaves for smn. 2 to have smn wrap *or* have sth wrapped with banana leaves. **m̈/di*(i)** to wrap. *dipun * kalijan ron pisang* wrapped in banana leaves. **pa·m̈*** act of wrapping, *esp.* with leaves

wunglé albino

wungli a variety of tree

wungu 1 purple, violet, lavender. 2 to awaken smn (*root form: ki for* GUGAH). 3 to wake up (*root form: ki for* LÈK). 4 to get up (*ki for* TANGI). ***n̂** 1 to keep oneself awake at night (*ki for* LÈK²AN). 2 having a sharp sense of hearing (*ki for* TENGÈN). **m̈/di*** to make sth purple. **m̈/di*-k̂aké** to have sth colored *or* dyed purple

wungwang a hollow bamboo section

wungwung *var of* WUWUNG

wuni a certain tree; also, the tart fruits that grow in clusters on this tree

wuninga to know, understand (*ki for* UNING(A)). **ka*n** it is known (that...). *Ka*n bilih bulan punika umuripun majuta-juta taun.* The moon is known to be millions of years old. **ka*na** know! be advised! now look here!

wuntah *var of* WUTAH

wuntu *var of* BUNTU. *See also* TAUN

wunut a variety of tree

wur 1 the fragrant root of a certain plant (*klembak*), powdered and used for flavoring cigarette tobacco. 2 flight (*rg var of* BUR). ***-*** jellyfish (*var of* UWUR²). **ngu/di*(-*)-aké, nge/di*(-*)aké** to scatter/sprinkle sth. *Weḍiné di-uwur²aké ing djobin.* He scattered the sand on the tiled floor. **ngu/di*-(-*)i, nge/di*(-*)i** to scatter/sprinkle sth onto. *Di-wur²i bawang brambang gorèng.* She sprinkled it with fried onion and garlic. *See also* AWUR, WUWUR

wuragil *var of* RAGIL

wurahan (*or* **a*** *or* **ma***) noisy, loud. *surak ** to cheer lustily

wurda, wurḍa hundred-billion unit. *sa** 100,000,000,000. *rong ** 200,000,000,-000. *Kaṭahipun kirang langkung sa*.* There are about a hundred billion of them.

wuri *oj* 1 back, rear. 2 later on, in the future. *ing *-** in the future; ultimately, in the end. **ka*** 1 last, past. 2 left behind. *wara ka** widow

wurik [of hens] speckled

wurjan *oj* **ka*** to appear, be seen. *Ana satrija nembé ka*.* A nobleman appeared. *sawangan sing asri ka** a beautiful sight to behold

wursih higher on one side than the other (*shc from* ḌUWUR, SISIH)

wursita *wj* story, narration. *Wiwitané kang * djinawis...* The story begins... **ka*** it is told (that...)

wurtjita *var of* WURSITA

wuru intoxicated; drugged (*ki for* M·ENDEM). *** getih** out for blood; intoxicated with the heat of the battle

wuruh foam, suds. **m̈*** to foam up, become sudsy

wuruk advice, words of wisdom, teachings. ***an** that which is taught. *Iki *ané sapa?* Who taught you this? **ṁ/di*(i)** to teach, instruct

Wurukung *var of* WARUKUNG

wurung *ng,* **sandé** *or* **wandé** *kr* to fail to materialize. * *ora sida.* It was called off. *Arep kanḍa apa²* (2), *nanging *.* He was about to say something, but he changed his mind. **ku** *djedjoḍoan* the calling off of my marriage. ***an** a plan not carried out. *Botjah kaé *anku.* That's the girl I was to have married. **ṁ/di·(we)*(aké)** to prevent sth from happening; to foil, thwart. *Tekané Slamet ing kono murungaké nijat ala sing arep dileksanakaké déning wong mau.* Slamet's showing up there prevented the man from carrying out his bad intentions. **ṁ*an** easily angered. **pa·ṁ*** 1 a factor that prevents sth from happening. 2 cancellation of a projected activity. *pamurunging lakon* what makes the story fail; what makes the trip impossible. **ora *** inevitable. *Anak sing rèwèl mesṭi gampang muringé, ora * si botjah gẹnti didukani ibuné.* A fussy child loses his temper easily, and so he is bound to be scolded by his mother. *Nèkeré ndadak di-enḍil² olèhé mènèhké, ora * ja diwènèhké kabèh.* He reluctantly gave up his marbles one by one until finally he had let them all go. *** bahan** *or* *** dandan·an** *or* *** wong** to come to nothing; to fail to accomplish the objective. *Jèn dudu kowé sing tumindak, sida * dandanan.* If you hadn't stepped in, the whole thing would have come to nothing. ** wong ané, ngono baé ora bisa!* What a failure you are—you can't even do *that!* *Olèhé sinau tenanan ning * bahan.* He studied hard but he failed anyway.

wus *var of* WIS

wusânâ (in the) end, (at the) conclusion. *tanpa ** endless. *Ora ana *né.* There's no end to it. ** mung seméné aturku.* This concludes my report. *Goḍongé dadi kuning * garing.* The leaves turned yellow and finally dried up. ***né** *or* **ka*n** finally, in the end. *Ka*n ora sida lunga sebab udan.* After all that, he couldn't go because it rained.

wusdéné *ng,* **wusdènten** *kr* moreover, furthermore, and what is more

wusdènten *kr for* WUSDÉNÉ

wusu 1 a bow-shaped tool for cleaning kapok fibers. 2 hump *or* hunch on the back. **ṁ/di*ni** to clean [kapok fibers] with the above tool

wut 1 oops! oh-oh! 2 *rpr* a swish

wuta blind (*kr? ki? for* PITJAK). *wong ** a blind person. **ṁ*** 1 to go blind. 2 to act as though one were blind. *** sastra** illiterate. *** (pa·ṅ·)tingal(é)** blind; *fig* blind to what one does not wish to see

wutah to spill out. *Banjuné * kabèh.* The water all spilled. ***-*an (luntak·an** *kr, ki***)** vomitus. **ṁ*** 1 to pour out. *Gunung geniné sok mutah geni lan kukus.* The volcano often emits fire and smoke. 2 (**ṅ·tuntak** *kr,* **luntak** *kr? ki?*) to vomit. 3 [of colors] to run. **lara mutah ng·ising** cholera. **ṁ/di*aké** 1 to spill sth (out). *Kanggo apa mutahaké eluh?* What are you crying for? 2 (**ṅ/dipun·tuntak·aken** *kr,* **ng/di·luntak·aké** *ki*) to vomit sth. *Permènè diluntakaké.* He got sick on the candy. **ṁ/di*i** 1 to spill onto. *Wédangé mutahi sikilku.* The hot tea spilled on my foot. 2 to spit on. 3 (**ṅ/dipun·tuntak·i** *kr,* **ng/di·luntak·i** *ki*) to vomit sth. *** ati** generous. *** getih** one's native land. *kanggo kaperiuaning tanah * getihé* for the sake of one's fatherland

wutjal teachings (*sbst? kr for* WULANG)

wutuh *ng,* **wetah** *kr* intact. *Bali *, lo.* Please return it in good condition. *Enḍogé goḍogan mau isih *.* The boiled egg wasn't broken. *Wong * kuwi wong sing ora tjatjad.* A normal person is one who hasn't got anything wrong with him. *ḍuwit ** money that has not been changed into smaller denominations. *tjatjah ** integer. ***an** in an unbroken condition; whole. *Manis djangan sing *an setengah dridji.* A whole stick of cinnamon is half the size of your finger. *Dipun kumbah wetahan ngantos resik.* Wash it all over until it is clean. *woh sing *ané dawa* an oval-shaped fruit. ***-*an** completely, throughout. *Dipun bekta ḍateng sumur, dipun gujang wetah²an.* He took it to the well and washed it thoroughly. **ṁ/di·we*** to make *or* keep sth intact. *Pariné diwe*.* They didn't use any of the rice. *Memutuh kabudajan kita iku kuwadjiban kita kabèh.* It is our task to keep our culture free of foreign influences. **ṁ/di*aké** to make *or* leave intact. *Pitiké adja di-keṭok², di*aké waé.* Don't cut up the chicken; leave it whole. *** ajam** intact; unscathed

wutun *var of* JUTUN
wuwa measuring unit for rice plants: $^1/_2$ *amet,* or *ca.* 77 kilograms = 169 lbs.
wuwu 1 hawk; eagle. 2 a certain type of bamboo *or* wicker fish trap. * **rawa** a variety of hawk
wuwuh *ng,* **wewah** *kr* to increase; to add (to). * *apik* to get nicer. *Saja * senengé bal-balan.* He likes soccer more and more all the time. *Sapa sing durung *?* Who hasn't chipped in yet? ***an** an additional amount; a contribution. ***-* 1** to keep increasing. *Berasé *-*.* The amount of rice keeps increasing. *Dukané pak guru *-*.* The teacher got madder and madder at him. 2 furthermore; especially. **-* didukani pak guru.* On top of that, the teacher bawled him out. **ka*an** in addition. *Dudu wong sing tjukup, ke*an anaké ḍéwé akèh.* He's not a rich man, and on top of that he has many children of his own. **m̄/di*(i)** to increase sth; to add to. *ḍuwit kanggo muwuhi tuku beras* money to buy more rice. *Buku mau wis diowahi lan di*i Mas X.* This book has been revised and enlarged by X. *Olèhé ngenjang kok tetep waé ora gelem muwuhi.* It's his final bid; he won't go up a penny. *Ḍuwitmu jèn kurang tak *ané.* If you haven't got enough money, I'll give you some more. *Wis di*i sepuluh, meksa isih kurang.* I've given him ten more and it's still not enough.
wuwung (*or* ***an**) rooftop, house peak. *Omahé rong *.* The house has two roofed sections. *Akèh wong sing mènèk ing *an.* Many people climbed to rooftops [to escape the flood]. **m̄/di*** to cover [a roof peak] with semicircular tiles
wuwur **m̄/di*(-*)aké** to scatter/sprinkle sth. *Brambang gorèng di*aké ing bakmi.* She sprinkled fried onions on the noodles. **m̄/di*(-*)i** to scatter *or* sprinkle sth onto. *Djobiné di*i weḍi.* He sprinkled sand on the floor. *See also* WUR
wuwus to say; to speak. **m̄/di*** to tell; to say to

X-Y-Z

x (*prn* **iks**) *alphabetic letter*
y (*prn* **èi**) *alphabetic letter. See also under* J (*var sp of* Y)
z (*prn* **ȿèt**) *alphabetic letter. See also under* D, DJ, S (*Introduction, 2.6*)
zalf *var of* SALEP
zamzam *var of* DJANDJAM
zas-zis *rpr* air blowing through a narrow slit